000003

McDougal Littell

life

The
AMERICANS
Annotated Teacher's Edition

liberty

pursuit *of*
happiness

Authors

from left to right: Gerald A. Danzer, Professor or History and Director of the M.A. Program for Teachers of History at the University of Illinois at Chicago; J. Jorge Klor de Alva, Class of 1940 Professor of Comparative Ethnic Studies and Anthropology at Princeton University; Nancy Woloch, history teacher at Barnard College; Louis E. Wilson, Associate Professor and Chair of the Afro-American and African Studies Department at Smith College.

Acknowledgments
page 41: Excerpt from "The Fall of Tenochtitlan," from *The Broken Spears* by Miguel Leon-Portilla. Copyright © 1962, 1990 by Beacon Press. Expanded and updated edition © 1992 by Miguel Leon-Portilla. Reproduced by permission of Beacon Press, Boston.
Page 804: Excerpt from the song "Little Boxes," words and music by Malvina Reynolds. Copyright © 1962 by Schroder Music Company (ASCAP), renewed 1990. Used by permission of Schroder Music Company. All rights reserved.

ISBN 0-395-85183-1
Printed in the United States of America.
1 2 3 4 5 6 7 8 9–DWO–02 01 00 99 98 97

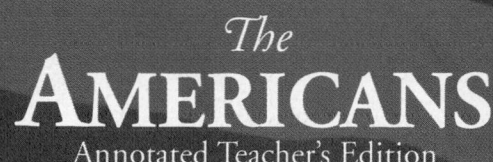

The
AMERICANS
Annotated Teacher's Edition

Table of Contents

Program Overview

The Americans is a highly integrated program that provides teachers with a practical and motivational approach to teaching U.S. history and to helping students think critically and reflectively. (For more information on each element, see pages T6–T18.)

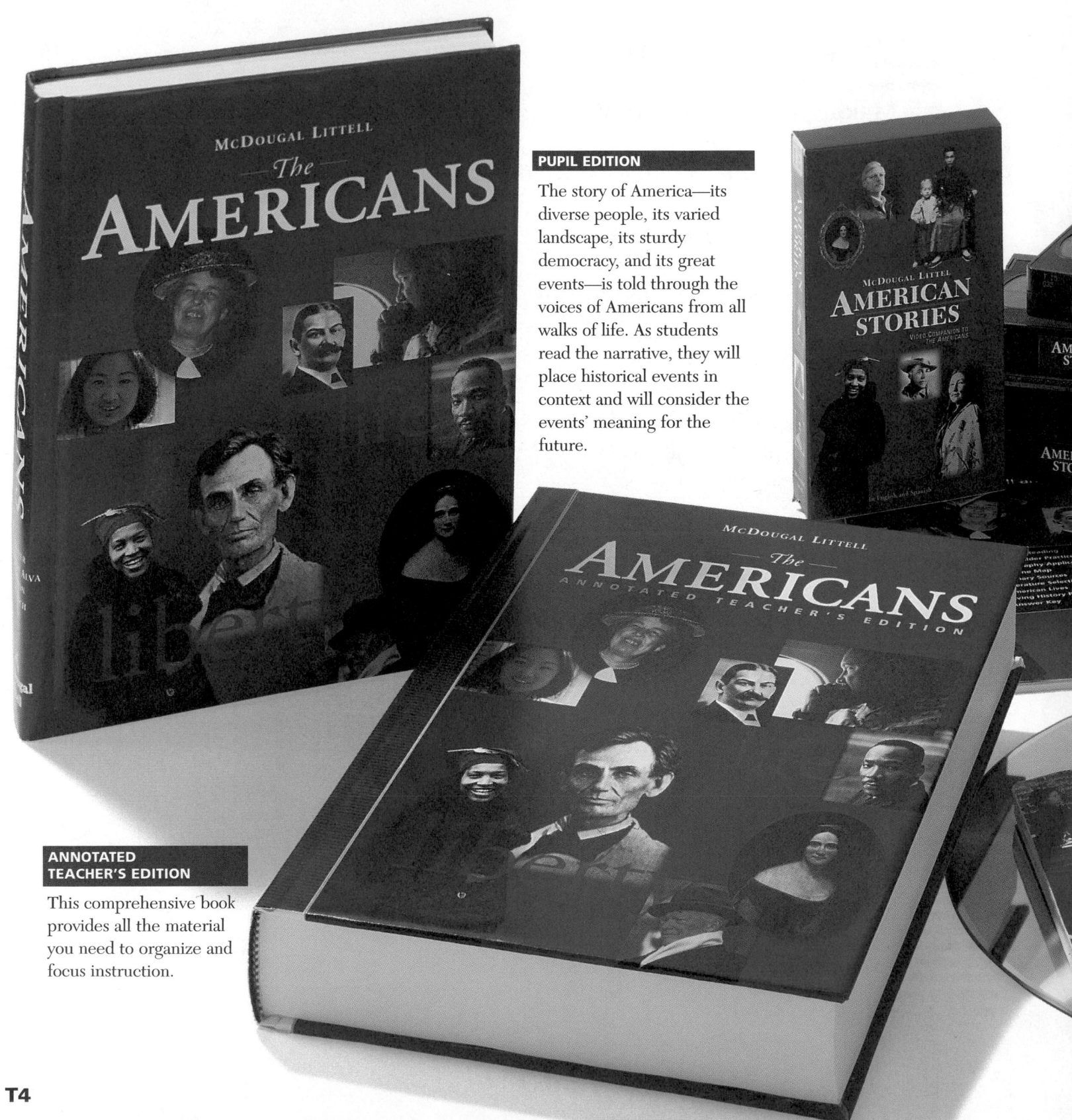

PUPIL EDITION

The story of America—its diverse people, its varied landscape, its sturdy democracy, and its great events—is told through the voices of Americans from all walks of life. As students read the narrative, they will place historical events in context and will consider the events' meaning for the future.

ANNOTATED TEACHER'S EDITION

This comprehensive book provides all the material you need to organize and focus instruction.

Documentary videos integrated with the text, five separate CD-ROM options, audiotapes, a videodisc portfolio, and extensive Internet resources provide a full range of technology enrichment options.

Extensive teacher's resource materials include everything teachers need in one easy-to-use package: in-depth resources organized by unit, a comprehensive guide to block scheduling, a complete assessment package, and more.

Making History Human

Stories, as every teacher knows, can capture students' imaginations, hold their attention, and teach important concepts all at once. When students experience historical events through the eyes of individuals, the events take on new meaning. Students therefore begin to make personal connections to the past.

The Americans, as its name suggests, focuses on the human face of history. When students dig into the events and see the people clearly, history for them will be more real, more accessible, and more exciting.

PERSONAL VOICES

Woven into the text are quotations from people who were involved in historical events. All Personal Voices are primary sources—authentic documents resonating with the passions and sharp personal observations of people who lived through the historical periods discussed.

A PERSONAL VOICE

Here we are, tremendously exhilarated, and there's a sea of dead. . . . [The platoon leader] was much moved. . . . He said, "Joe, lets make a resolution with these Russians here and also the ones on the bank: this would be an important day in the lives of the two countries." . . . It was a solemn moment. There were tears in the eyes of most of us. . . . We embraced. We swore never to forget.

JOSEPH POLOWSKY, quoted in *The Good War*

ONE AMERICAN'S STORY

Every major section of a chapter begins with the true story of an American who was touched by events discussed in the section. The American may have been a key decision-maker or simply an ordinary person caught up in historic events. Several subjects of One American's Story features are also the subjects of documentary videos that extend and enrich the text.

AMERICAN STORIES VIDEOS

Fifteen videos skillfully integrate the lives of individuals with historical events described in the text. These short documentary films introduce individuals who lived and struggled through some of the most vivid times in American history.

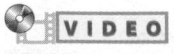

VIDEO

JUMP AT THE SUN: Zora Neale Hurston and the Harlem Renaissance

DAILY LIFE
1950–1960

The Emergence of the Teenager

DAILY LIFE

How did people live during various time periods? What was important to them? What were the lives of young people like? The Daily Life features show how people worked and played, while providing some thought-provoking facts about their lives.

KEY PLAYERS

Great men and women in positions of power or influence have often played key roles in American history. They are featured in short biographies that allow students to see them as individuals in both triumph and adversity.

KEY PLAYERS

HARRY S. TRUMAN
1884–1972

Young Harry S. Truman, the son of a Missouri livestock trader and his wife, did not seem destined for greatness. When he graduated from high school in 1901, he drifted from job to job—drugstore clerk, newspaper mailroom clerk, time-keeper, bank clerk, bookkeeper, farmer, World War I soldier. After the war, he invested in a men's clothing store; but the business failed, and he spent the next 15 years paying off business debts.

Discouraged by his business failure, Truman sought a career in politics. As a politician, his blunt and outspoken style won loyal friends and bitter enemies. As president, his decisiveness and willing-ness to accept responsibility for his decisions ("The Buck Stops Here" read a sign on his desk) earned him respect that has grown in the decades following his presidency.

JOSEPH STALIN
1879–1953

As a young revolutionary, Iosif Vissarionovich Dzhugashvili took the name Stalin, which means "man of steel."

His father was a failed shoemaker and an alcoholic. His mother helped support the family as a washerwoman. Following her wishes, Stalin entered a seminary, but he was eventually expelled for revolutionary activism.

Stalin is credited with turning the Soviet Union into a world power, but at a terrible cost to its citizens. He ruled with terror and brutality and saw "enemies" everywhere, even among friends and supporters. He subdued the population with the use of secret police and labor camps, and he is believed to have been responsible for the murder of millions of people in the Soviet Union.

Making History Relevant

Educators know that history comes alive when students are actively involved in their own learning. As students make connections between the past and the present, as they think about how historical events have influenced their lives, and as they imagine how lives might have been affected if events had happened differently, they discover that history is our nation's common memory. It binds us together in the present and helps us understand how to meet the challenges of the future.

ON THE WORLD STAGE

ON THE WORLD STAGE
While focusing on the history of the United States, the text never loses sight of the rest of the world. These short features help students relate events in the United States to international events.

WAR ON THE EASTERN FRONT

The Russian army surprised the Germans by mobilizing so rapidly in the early months of the war. Russian troops advanced quickly into German territory. The Germans turned the Russians back, however, at the Battle of Tannenberg in August 1914.

Throughout 1915, the Russians suffered successive defeats and continued to fall back into their own territory. By the end of 1915 they had suffered about 2.5 million casualties. Beyond the casualties, the war also caused massive bread shortages within Russia.

Demanding bread and peace, revolutionaries ousted the czar in March 1917 and established a provisional government led by Alexander Kerensky, who refused to pull Russia out of the war. In November, the Bolsheviks, led by V. I. Lenin and Leon Trotsky, overthrew the Kerensky government, set up a Communist state, and sought peace with the Central Powers.

HISTORICAL SPOTLIGHT

HISTORICAL SPOTLIGHT
Shining a spotlight on special persons or events can make history come alive for students as they gain information that extends and enriches the main text.

PAUL ROBESON

Paul Robeson was an all-American football player and Phi Beta Kappa member at Rutgers University. After earning a law degree in 1923, he entered on a distinguished international career as a singer and actor. (He is shown here playing Othello.) He was a vocal civil rights activist and a supporter of left-wing union activities, and he was sympathetic to the Soviet culture and political philosophy. In 1950, when he refused to sign an affidavit indicating whether he had ever been a member of the Communist Party, the State Department revoked his passport for seven years. During that time, he was unable to perform abroad and was blacklisted at home. His income fell from $150,000 to $3,000 a year.

TRACING THEMES
Paying attention to themes in the history classroom can help students understand that the forces guiding their lives also governed the lives of previous generations. By looking at broad themes over time, students can begin to make connections between the past and the present.

LIVING HISTORY
Every chapter begins with a project that actively involves students in their own learning as they explore an aspect of the period that interests them. At the end of the chapter, they finish the project and add it to their American history portfolios.

LIVING HISTORY

PLANNING A FIFTIES PARTY

Plan a 1950s party for your classmates and friends. To recreate the time as authentically as possible, use the information in the chapter and additional research or interviews to learn the following about fifties teenagers:

- how they dressed
- what they did for entertainment
- what music they listened to
- what they liked to eat

📁 **PORTFOLIO PROJECT** Create an invitation that tells guests what to wear and what they can expect to hear, see, taste, and do at the party. Keep a copy of the invitation in a folder. At the end of the chapter, you will write a radio advertisement for your party and add it to your American history portfolio.

NOW & THEN

SPIES

Spying is still an active business in both the United States and Russia. In February 1994, Aldrich Ames was arrested for spying. Ames was a "mole" within the CIA who turned over to the Russians the names of all the important U.S. spies at work in Russia, causing ten CIA agents to be executed and others to be imprisoned. Ames was convicted and sentenced to life in prison.

NOW & THEN
When students see connections between the past and the present, history becomes more real, more accessible, and more exciting to them. These features connect events discussed in the text with situations and events of today.

Making History Thought-Provoking

Developing an ability to think critically and reflectively is an important goal of social studies instruction because with this ability students become citizens who can make informed and responsible decisions. Because critical thinking is hard work, students need not only to know how to do it but to be given models and materials that help them become motivated and active thinkers. *The Americans* incorporates a variety of materials that help students develop the thinking skills that are crucial to successful learning.

POINT/COUNTERPOINT
In this feature, students encounter opposing viewpoints on historical controversies. The viewpoints are expressed in the words of primary sources, such as editorials; in the words of people involved in the controversies; and in the words of historians. Being open-minded enough to explore several sides of crucial issues is important training for thoughtful decision-making.

DIFFICULT DECISIONS IN HISTORY
The history of the United States is filled with difficult decisions—decisions that have often had long-term and far-reaching effects. Reflecting on these decisions and their results is an effective way for students to study the process of decision-making and to examine their own thinking patterns.

Difficult Decisions
IN HISTORY

TO PROHIBIT ALCOHOL OR NOT?

The question of whether to outlaw alcohol divided Americans. Many reformers and religious groups thought drinking was sinful, unhealthy, and devastating to families. They believed the government should protect the public's health and morals by making alcohol illegal.

Other Americans, including liberals, conservatives, intellectuals, and immigrant groups, did not believe alcohol consumption was sinful or dangerous in moderation. They believed that consuming alcohol was a personal, not a government, decision and resisted any group's trying to tell them how to live.

1. Examine the pros and cons of each position. Which do you agree with? What other factors, if any, do you think would influence your position?

2. If you were a legislator being asked to vote for the 18th Amendment, what would you say? Explain.

3. What issues might the experiment of prohibition relate to today? Should the government attempt to change people's moral behavior?

For more information about Prohibition and its repeal, click on *Social Studies* at http://www.mcdougallittell.com

The Persian Gulf War, 1990–1991

TURKEY

SYRIA
LEBANON
Beirut ⊙ ⊙ Damascus

Mediterranean Sea

Haifa ✳
Tel Aviv ✳ ⊙ Amman
Jerusalem ✳

ISRAEL
JORDAN

Baghdad ⊙

IRAN

IRAQ

Aug. 2, 1990
Iraq invades
Kuwait

Basra ⊙
KUWAIT

Jan. 16, 1991
Air attacks
begin against
Iraq

Feb. 23, 1991
Coalition launches
ground war

⊙ Kuwait City
Khafji ✳

• Tabuk

Hafar al Batin •

King Khalid •
Military City

Jubail ⊙

Al Manamah ⊙
QATAR

✳ Major missile target

↤ UN coalition forces

↤ Iraqi forces

⇠ US/UN naval forces

SAUDI ARABIA

Dhahran ✳

BAHRAIN   Doha ⊙   25°

⊙ Riyadh

EGYPT

0   200 Miles
0   400 Kilometers   N

Persian Gulf

35°

50°

GEOGRAPHY SKILLBUILDER
REGION *What did the UN coalition probably hope to achieve by moving forces into southern Iraq?* **MOVEMENT** *How did the movements of coalition ground forces show that the intention of the coalition in the Gulf War was primarily defensive, not offensive?*

VISUALS
The Americans presents information and builds critical-thinking skills through state-of-the-art maps and graphs throughout the text. Layers of visual information, accompanied by thought-provoking questions, encourage students to explore relationships, make predictions, and compare outcomes as they interpret these powerful visuals.

top. Women served along with men in the military during the Gulf War. bottom. Massive oil fires started by the Iraqis burned in Kuwait.

THINK THROUGH HISTORY
These questions in the margins of the text help students think critically about historical events. By using these questions, teachers can encourage and reward thinking in their classrooms.

> **THINK THROUGH HISTORY**
> **C.** *Clarifying*
> *What issues led to conflict in the Middle East?*

ASSESSMENTS
Section and chapter assessments explicitly draw on various critical-thinking strategies to help students focus on concept formation—on the crucial process of practicing to become proficient thinkers.

ANOTHER PERSPECTIVE
These short features expose students to different perspectives on historical events. By looking at events from a perspective other than the one given in the main text, students can develop their skills of analysis and reflection.

ANOTHER PERSPECTIVE

DENMARK'S RESISTANCE

In 1942, the Nazis began pressuring occupied Denmark to enforce the Nuremberg Laws against its Jews. The Danes resisted fiercely. Denmark's aged king, Christian X, is reported to have said,

> The Jews are part of the Danish nation. We have no Jewish problem. . . . If the Jews are forced to . . . wear the yellow star, I and my whole family shall wear it as a badge of honor.

Not only the royal family but thousands of Danes from all walks of life did just that.

Teacher's Resource Materials

From block scheduling to teaching students acquiring English, teachers are structuring their history lessons to make them work in today's classrooms.

The Americans provides a full range of options to help you teach our shared heritage in ways that meet the common, and even the uncommon, needs of your students.

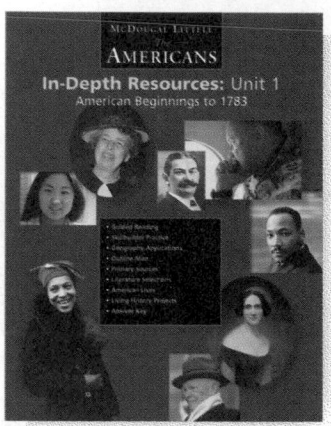

IN-DEPTH RESOURCES

One book for each unit, organized by chapter, includes the following complete set of options for reinforcement, practice, enrichment, and extension:

- **Guided Reading** worksheets develop essential reading skills.

- **Skillbuilder Practice** worksheets supplement the 12-page Skillbuilder Handbook in the pupil edition.

- **Geography Application** worksheets provide practice in geography skills.

- **Primary Source** materials feature political cartoons, facsimile pages, historical documents, diary entries, letters, and much more.

- **Literature Selection** pages let your students experience history through relevant works of literature.

- **American Lives** pages provide additional short biographies to augment those in each chapter.

- **Living History Project** worksheets help students organize and complete their Living History projects.

- **Standards for Evaluation** charts provide rubrics for assessing students' Living History projects.

PLANNING FOR BLOCK SCHEDULES

Includes teaching models, a pacing guide, sample lesson plans, and strategies for active learning.

TELESCOPING THE TIMES: CHAPTER SUMMARIES

Helps you address differences in reading speed, losses of time due to block scheduling, and the need to reteach.

ACCESS FOR STUDENTS ACQUIRING ENGLISH: SPANISH TRANSLATIONS

Provides strategies for teaching ESL students and Spanish translations of Chapter Summaries; of Guided Reading, Skillbuilder Practice, and Geography Application worksheets; and of outline maps.

WRITING FOR SOCIAL STUDIES

Support for writing history research papers, historical narratives, essays, interviews, oral histories, book reviews, and short reports.

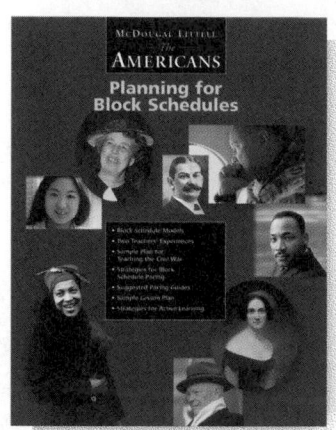

HISTORY FROM VISUALS: TRANSPARENCY PACKS

Enliven lessons with three volumes of transparencies:

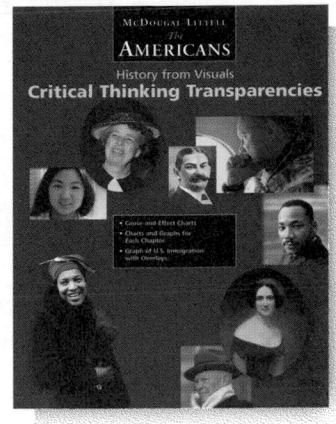

HUMANITIES
Political cartoons, fine art, photographs, and other artworks.

CRITICAL THINKING
Charts, graphs, and infographics, plus a cause-and-effect chart for each chapter.

GEOGRAPHY
Thirty-four new maps, plus a map of U.S. growth with overlays.

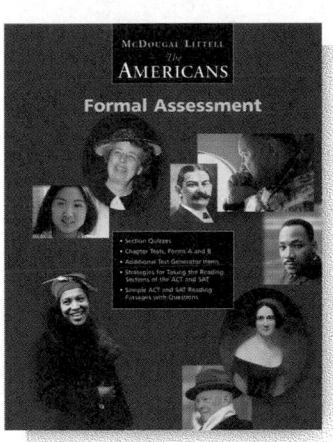

FORMAL ASSESSMENT
Section Quizzes
Chapter Tests, Forms A and B
Additional Test Questions
ACT/SAT Test Practice

ALTERNATIVE ASSESSMENT
Provides explanations and forms for a variety of assessment options, including cooperative learning, group discussion, role-playing, oral presentation, peer assessment, self-assessment, and portfolio assessment.

TEST GENERATOR
Includes all questions in the Section Quizzes and Chapter Tests, forms A and B—plus ten new test items for each chapter, leveled for basic and advanced students.

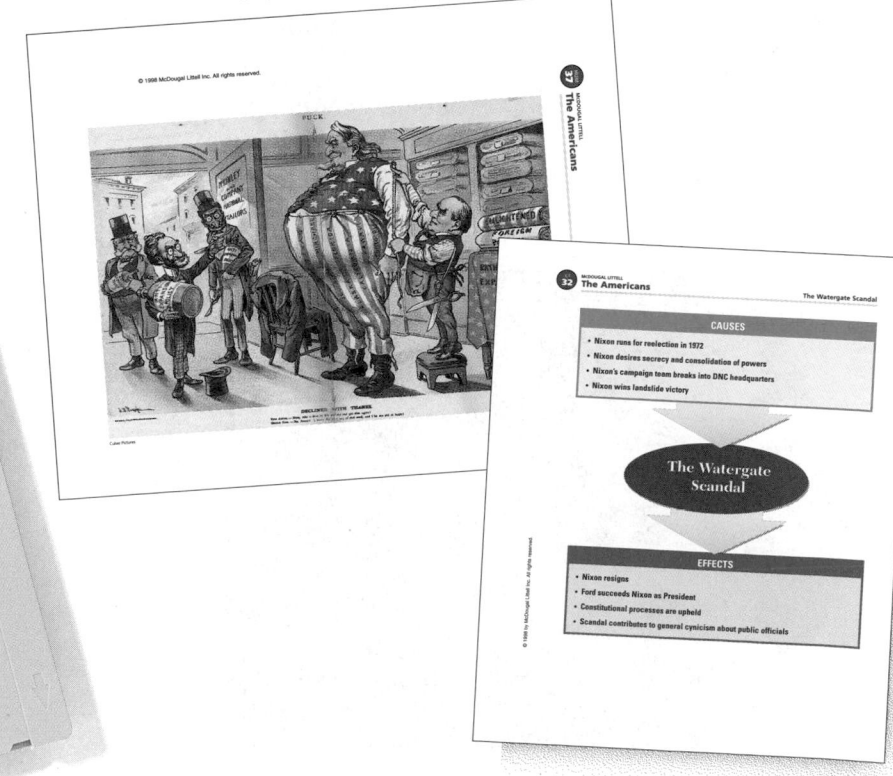

American Stories Video Series

American Stories is a powerful new video series integrated with the text of *The Americans*. Fifteen fascinating documentaries, each 8–10 minutes long, help you to introduce various sections of the text.

In addition, an invaluable Teacher's Resource Book helps you to fully exploit the power of the videos with everything from teaching tips to lesson-extending information and activities.

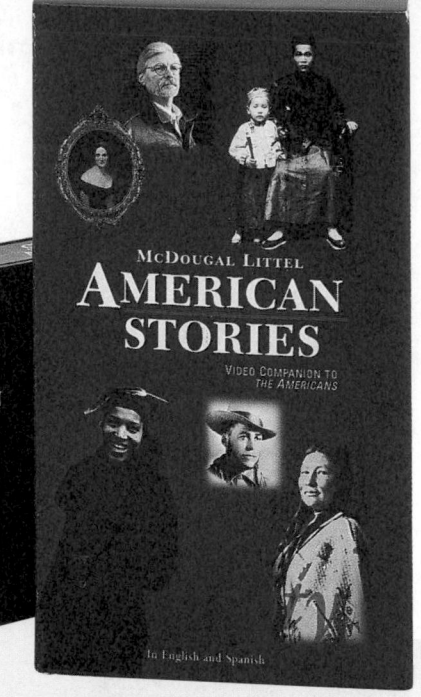

VIDEOCASSETTES
Volume 1: Videos 1–3
Volume 2: Videos 4–6
Volume 3: Videos 7–9
Volume 4: Videos 10–12
Volume 5: Videos 13–15

Video 1
PATRIOT FATHER, LOYALIST SON: The Divided House of Benjamin and William Franklin

Video 2
RECRUITED BY LEWIS AND CLARK: Patrick Gass Chronicles the Journey West

Video 3
WAR OUTSIDE MY WINDOW: Mary Chesnut's Diary of the Civil War

Video 4
TEACHER OF A FREED PEOPLE: Robert Fitzgerald and Reconstruction

Video 5
A WALK IN TWO WORLDS: The Education of Zitkala-Ša, a Sioux

Video 6
FROM CHINA TO CHINATOWN: Fong See's American Dream

Video 7
A CHILD ON STRIKE: The Testimony of Camella Teoli, Mill Girl

Video 8
JUMP AT THE SUN: Zora Neale Hurston and the Harlem Renaissance

Video 9
BROKE BUT NOT BROKEN: Ann Marie Low Remembers the Dust Bowl

Video 10
A SONG FOR HIS PEOPLE: Pedro J. González and the Fight for Mexican-American Rights

Video 11
ESCAPING THE FINAL SOLUTION: Kurt Klein and Gerda Weissmann Klein Remember the Holocaust

Video 12
THE COLD WAR COMES HOME: Hollywood Blacklists the Kahn Family

Video 13
JUSTICE IN MONTGOMERY: Jo Ann Gibson Robinson and the Bus Boycott

Video 14
MATTERS OF CONSCIENCE: Stephan Gubar and the Vietnam War

Video 15
POISONED PLAYGROUND: Lois Gibbs and the Crisis at Love Canal

VIDEODISCS
Disc 1: Videos 1–5
Disc 2: Videos 6–10
Disc 3: Videos 11–15

AMERICAN PORTFOLIO: A VIDEODISC FOR U.S. HISTORY Enhance any lesson with more than 1,500 still images, more than 70 maps (many of them animated), and approximately 25 minutes of historical film footage.

CD-ROM Resources

The Americans: Electronic Library of Primary Sources

Support, enrich, and extend each chapter of the text with a compendium of carefully selected primary sources. Discover a wealth of documents that have shaped American history, along with personal accounts drawn from letters, diaries, and oral histories.

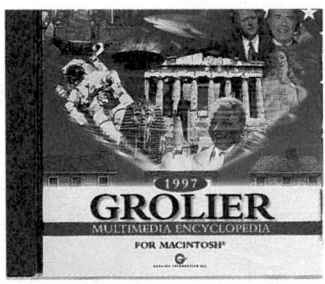

GROLIER'S MULTIMEDIA ENCYCLOPEDIA

This multimedia encyclopedia includes over 50,000 entries and 1,200 maps. Articles, historical time lines, and hyperlinks to World Wide Web sites are easily accessed, offering students multiple avenues to research topics of interest.

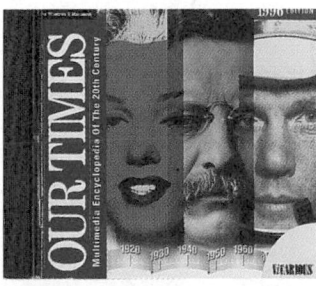

OUR TIMES MULTIMEDIA ENCYCLOPEDIA OF THE 20TH CENTURY

Students can find out what was happening, and who was who, in a multimedia exploration of the 20th century. Compelling video and audio tours, narrated by James Earl Jones, summarize key cultural, scientific, and political events. More information is available as students browse 52,000 articles and 2,500 charts, maps, and graphs. The content of *Our Times* is hyperlinked to *The Columbia Encyclopedia*, Fifth Edition.

FATEFUL LIGHTNING: A NARRATIVE HISTORY OF THE CIVIL WAR

A comprehensive narrative is enhanced with animated maps that detail campaigns and battles of the Civil War. In addition, reenactment video, contemporary photographs of Civil War battle sites, and music of the era help bring the sights and sounds of the Civil War to life.

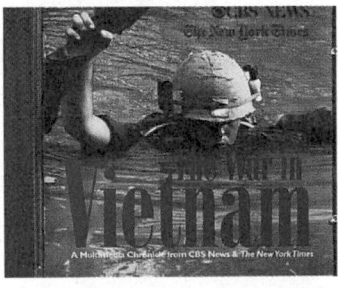

THE WAR IN VIETNAM

Over 1,000 articles from the *New York Times* and 40 minutes of video from CBS News are cross-indexed and arranged along time lines to provide students an opportunity to see, hear, and read about the Vietnam War as it was actually reported. Additional enhancements include interactive maps and special databases, such as a searchable list of names on the Vietnam Veterans Memorial in Washington, D.C.

Immigrants and Urbanization

Chapter Planning Guide

As you write your lessons to meet the special needs of today's classroom, you can depend on unparalleled support in the teacher's edition of *The Americans.*

Support begins with the convenient two-page planning guide found at the beginning of every chapter. From key ideas to technology connections, the guide features invaluable information and options to help you devise an effective course of instruction.

....

KEY IDEAS

A chronological, section-by-section summary of the key ideas in the chapter. The column of key ideas builds to a unifying theme for the whole chapter.

		TEACHING SUPPORT	**ASSESSMENT**
SECTION 1 **The New Immigrants** pp. 438–443	**Key Ideas** *New immigrants from southern and eastern Europe, Asia, the Caribbean, and Mexico face culture shock and prejudice—as well as the opportunity for a better life—in the United States.*	*In-Depth Resources: Unit 4* • Guided Reading, p. 37 • Skillbuilder Practice: Interpreting Graphs, p. 41 • Primary Source: Artifacts from Ellis Island, p. 46 • Literature: from *Call It Sleep* by Henry Roth, p. 50 **COOPERATIVE ACTIVITY** • Writing Letters or Poems About Immigrant Experiences, p. 441 (TE)	*Section 1 Assessment*, p. 443 (PE) *Self-Assessment*, p. 443 (TE) *Formal Assessment* • Section Quiz, p. 185 *Alternative Assessment Book* • Standards for Evaluating a Cooperative Activity
SECTION 2 **The Problems of Urbanization** pp. 446–451	*The rapid growth of cities creates many problems: how to provide adequate housing, transportation, water, and sanitation and how to fight fire and crime. The search for solutions begins.*	*In-Depth Resources: Unit 4* • Guided Reading, p. 38 • Geography Application, p. 42 • Outline Map, p. 44 • Primary Sources: from *How the Other Half Lives* by Jacob Riis, p. 47; from *Twenty Years at Hull-House* by Jane Addams, p. 48 • American Lives: Jane Addams, p. 53 **COOPERATIVE ACTIVITY** • Researching Natural Catastrophes, p. 449 (TE)	*Section 2 Assessment*, p. 451 (PE) *Self-Assessment*, p. 451 (TE) *Formal Assessment* • Section Quiz, p. 186 *Alternative Assessment Book* • Standards for Evaluating a Cooperative Activity
SECTION 3 **The Emergence of the Political Machine** pp. 452–454	*The political machine emerges as cities attempt to deal with the problems of rapid urbanization.*	*In-Depth Resources: Unit 4* • Guided Reading, p. 39 • Primary Source: from *The Shame of the Cities* by Lincoln Steffens, p. 49 • American Lives: Boss Tweed, p. 54 **COOPERATIVE ACTIVITY** • Creating Political Cartoons, p. 453 (TE)	*Section 3 Assessment*, p. 454 (PE) *Self-Assessment*, p. 454 (TE) *Formal Assessment* • Section Quiz, p. 187 *Alternative Assessment Book* • Standards for Evaluating a Cooperative Activity
SECTION 4 **Politics in the Gilded Age** pp. 455–457	*Local and national political corruption during the Gilded Age leads to a call for reform.*	*In-Depth Resources: Unit 4* • Guided Reading, p. 40	*Section 4 Assessment*, p. 457 (PE) *Self-Assessment*, p. 457 (TE) *Formal Assessment* • Section Quiz, p. 188
CHAPTER RESOURCES 436A	**Chapter Overview** *The population rises as immigrants supply a willing workforce for urban industrialization and a political base for many urban politicians. Abuses in local and national government prompt calls for reform.*	*In-Depth Resources: Unit 4* • Living History Project: Worksheet, p. 55; Standards, p. 56 *Telescoping the Times* • Chapter Summary, pp. 29–30 *Planning for Block Schedules*	*Chapter Assessment*, pp. 458–459 (PE) *Alternative Assessment*, p. 459 (PE) *Formal Assessment* • Chapter Test, forms A and B, pp. 189–194 *Test Generator* *Alternative Assessment Book* See explanation and forms for different kinds of alternative assessments including portfolio assessment.

TEACHING SUPPORT

For each section there is a bulleted listing of valuable ancillary support available, as well as references to related cooperative activities.

ASSESSMENT

Locates pages on which assessment, self-assessment, evaluation guidelines, quizzes, and tests are available for the section or chapter.

Geography Transparencies
- G15, Where Foreign Born Lived, 1900

 Electronic Library of Primary Sources
- Chinese Exclusion Act of 1882
- "Twelve Hundred More" by Anon
- from *The Days of Our Years* by Israel Kasovitch

AMERICAN STORIES VIDEO SERIES
"From China to Chinatown"
INTERNET RESOURCES
- See *McDougal Littell Learning On-Line* for links to information about Ellis Island and Angel Island.

 Humanities Transparencies
- H15, *Cliff Dwellers*

Critical Thinking Transparencies
- CT15, Urban Growth
- CT49, From Country to City: 1870–1920

Electronic Library of Primary Sources
- "The Modern City" by Jane Addams

Our Times
- San Francisco earthquake and fire
INTERNET RESOURCES
- See *McDougal Littell Learning On-Line* for links to information about Jane Addams and the San Franciso earthquake.

Grolier Multimedia Encyclopedia
- Thomas Nast and a history of editorial and political cartoons
INTERNET RESOURCES
- See *McDougal Littell Learning On-Line* for links to information about Thomas Nast.

INTERNET RESOURCES
- See *McDougal Littell Learning On-Line* for links to information about Chester A. Arthur and Benjamin Harrison.

 American Portfolio: A Videodisc for U.S. History, user's guide, pp. 146–155, 157
INTERNET RESOURCES
Learning On-Line: Social Studies
http://www.mcdougallittell.com

Block Scheduling (90 MINUTES)

Day 1

Section 1, pp. 438–443

 AMERICAN STORIES VIDEO SERIES
- "From China to Chinatown"

Section 2, pp. 446–451

Section Assessments, pp. 443, 451

Day 2

Section 3, pp. 452–454

Section 4, pp. 455–457

Section Assessments, pp. 454, 457

Chapter Assessment, pp. 458–459

| YEARLY PACING **Chapter 15 Total:** 2 days **Yearly Total:** 85 days |

See *Planning for Block Schedules* for special activities and pacing strategies.

Customizing for Special Populations

Students Acquiring English

Access for Students Acquiring English
- Guided Reading for Sections 1–4 (Spanish), pp. 148–151
- Chapter Summary (Spanish), pp. 146–147
- Skillbuilder Practice: Interpreting Graphs (Spanish), p. 152
- Geography Application: Industry and Urban Growth (Spanish), p. 153

 AMERICAN STORIES VIDEO SERIES
- "From China to Chinatown" (Spanish Track)
INTERNET RESOURCES
- See *McDougal Littell Learning On-Line* The Diverse Classroom.

Less Proficient Readers

In-Depth Resources: Unit 4
- Guided Reading for Sections 1–4, pp. 37–40
- Skillbuilder: Interpreting Graphs, p. 41
- Geography Application: Industry and Urban Growth, p. 42
- Outline Map: The Urbanization of America, p. 44

Telescoping the Times
- Chapter Summary, pp. 29–30

See additional strategies at point of use in the Teacher's Edition.

Gifted and Talented Students

In-Depth Resources: Unit 4
- Primary Sources: Artifacts from Ellis Island, p. 46; from *How the Other Half Lives* by Jacob Riis, p. 47; from *Twenty Years at Hull-House* by Jane Addams, p. 48; from *The Shame of the Cities* by Lincoln Steffens, p. 49
- American Lives: Jane Addams, p. 53; Boss Tweed, p. 54

See additional strategies at point of use in the Teacher's Edition.

Connections to Literature READINGS FOR STUDENTS

In-Depth Resources: Unit 4
- *Call It Sleep* by Henry Roth, p. 50

Enrichment Reading
- Dreiser, Theodore
  Sister Carrie.
  New York: Bantam, 1993
  Dreiser transforms the conventional "fallen woman" story into a study of the persistent idealism and the grasping and seductive materialism of the American culture.

- Yezierska, Anzia
  Bread Givers.
  New York: Persea Books, 1975
  This touching tale tells the story of Jewish immigrants trying to find their way in America and the conflict between a father of the old world and a daughter of the new world.

McDougal Littell *Literature Connections*

- Yoshiko Uchida, *Picture Bride* (with related readings) This novel follows the experiences of a Japanese woman who comes to America in 1917 to marry a man she has never met. The story ends in a Japanese internment camp in Utah in 1943.

McDougal Littell *The Language of Literature*
American Literature

- Américo Paredes, *The Legend of Gregorio Cortez*, p. 556
- Hisaye Yamamoto, *Seventeen Syllables*, p. 628
- Anzia Yezierska, *America and I*, p. 703
- Bernard A. Weisberger, from *A Nation of Immigrants*, p. 713
- Gish Jen, *In the American Society*, p. 717

Teacher's Edition **436B**

BLOCK SCHEDULING

A pacing guide for block scheduling.

CUSTOMIZING FOR SPECIAL POPULATIONS

Suggested resources for teaching students acquiring English, less proficient readers, and gifted and talented students. From worksheets and chapter summaries in Spanish to additional primary-source material, these suggestions offer practical help for basic classroom needs.

CONNECTIONS TO LITERATURE

Literature Connections from McDougal Littell are stand-alone books with related readings that offer in-depth literary supplements. A SourceBook provides student support materials for each selection.

TECHNOLOGY

Lists connections to technology resources available for each section, from CD-ROMs to Internet resources.

ENRICHMENT READING

Lists additional suggested literature options.

THE LANGUAGE OF LITERATURE

Connections to McDougal Littell's American literature text, *The Language of Literature*, can help in planning American studies courses

Lesson Support

The Americans teacher's edition supports instruction with everything from fascinating tidbits to practical graphic organizers. Side columns focus on core instruction, with optional ideas and teaching strategies being featured at the bottom of the pages.

GRAPHIC ORGANIZERS

Convey key information in a clear and convincing way to help students grasp concepts.

REFERENCES TO RESOURCE MATERIALS

Identify where to find additional support for teaching the section.

OBJECTIVE
③ INSTRUCT

Building the Great Society

▶ *Starting with the Student*
Have students use a chart like the one below to organize what they learn about the Great Society programs. Students should list each program and describe its purpose.

Program	Purpose

▶ *Discussing Key Ideas*
• Johnson presents his legislative program, which he calls the Great Society.
• Great Society programs bring about change in education, Social Security, housing, and immigration.
• The Great Society also seeks to protect the environment and consumers.

IN-DEPTH RESOURCES: UNIT 8
American Lives: Rachel Carson, p. 15

 CRITICAL THINKING TRANSPARENCIES
CT28, The Great Society

NOW & THEN
Medicare on the Line
Critical Thinking: Evaluating Ask students whether they think cutbacks should be made in Medicare. Is Medicare an entitlement? Should other federal programs be cut to help balance the budget? Or is Medicare in its present state too expensive to maintain?

NOW & THEN
MEDICARE ON THE LINE
When President Johnson signed the Medicare bill in 1965, only half of the nation's elderly had health insurance. Today, thanks largely to Medicare, most do. However, most experts agree that the country cannot afford to sustain Medicare in its present form for much longer, especially if the nation hopes to balance the federal budget.

Three trends are fueling these concerns: (1) people are living longer, (2) health care continues to become more advanced and more expensive, and (3) the large baby boomer generation is moving toward retirement age. Medicare costs are increasing 10 percent a year. In 1995, federal spending on Medicare was about $160 billion; in 2002, without changes in the program, it could top $345 billion.

Both Democrats and Republicans in Washington agree that cuts have to be made, but experience has shown that the issue is a political hot potato. Many people consider Medicare an "entitlement" that they expect to receive when they retire. Although most Americans want a balanced budget, a recent survey revealed that only 16 percent favored large cutbacks in Medicare to achieve it.

Building the Great Society

In May of 1964, Johnson had summed up his grand vision for America in a phrase: the **Great Society**. In a speech at the University of Michigan, the president declared that "the Great Society demands an end to poverty and racial injustice." But, he told the enthusiastic crowd, that was "just the beginning." Johnson envisioned a legislative program that would create not only a higher living standard and equal opportunity but also promote a richer quality of life.

A PERSONAL VOICE
The Great Society is a place where every child can find knowledge to enrich his mind and to enlarge his talents. It is a place where leisure is a welcome chance to build and reflect, not a feared cause of boredom and restlessness. It is a place where the city of man serves not only the needs of the body and the demands of commerce but the desire for beauty and the hunger for community. It is a place where man can renew contact with nature. It is a place which honors creation for its own sake and for what it adds to the understanding of the race. It is a place where men are more concerned with the quality of their goals than the quantity of their goods.

LYNDON JOHNSON, "The Great Society," May 22, 1964

LBJ set lofty goals for his nation and for himself. Like his idol FDR, he wanted to change America. He also knew that he had to act quickly to capitalize on his new mandate. During the years 1965 and 1966, the Johnson administration introduced a flurry of bills to Congress. By the time Johnson left the White House in 1969, Congress had passed 206 of his measures. For most of them, the president personally led the battle to get them passed.

LANDMARK LEGISLATION Johnson considered education "the key which can unlock the door to the Great Society." The Elementary and Secondary Education Act of 1965 provided more than $1 billion in federal aid to help public and parochial schools purchase textbooks and new library materials. This was the first major federal aid package for education in the nation's history.

LBJ and Congress brought about the first major change in Social Security since its adoption in 1935 by establishing Medicare and Medicaid. **Medicare** provides hospital insurance and low-cost medical insurance for almost every American age 65 or older. **Medicaid** extended health insurance to welfare recipients.

Congress also appropriated money to build some 240,000 units of low-rent public housing and help low- and moderate-income families pay for better private housing. It established a new federal department, the Department of Housing and Urban Development (HUD). As secretary of the new department, Johnson appointed Robert Weaver, the first African-American cabinet member in American history.

The Great Society also brought profound changes to the nation's immigration laws. The Immigration Act of 1924 and the National Origins Act of 1929 had established immigration quotas that discriminated strongly against people from outside Western Europe. The **Immigration Act of 1965** replaced the national origins system with an annual quota of 170,000 immigrants from the Eastern Hemisphere and 120,000 from the Western Hemisphere. Within this overall quota, no more than 20,000 persons from any one nation could enter the United States each year. Close relatives of American residents were exempt from the quotas. This act opened the door for many non-European immigrants to settle in the United States.

THINK THROUGH HISTORY
D. Comparing How are Medicare and Medicaid similar?
D. Answer Both provide government-sponsored health insurance.
E. Answer It replaced the national origins system, which discriminated against people from outside Western Europe.
THINK THROUGH HISTORY
E. Recognizing Effects How did the Immigration Act of 1965 change the nation's immigration system?

846 Chapter 28

TEACHING OPTIONS

Exploring Themes

Immigration and Migration Discuss the Immigration Act of 1965. Ask students how the legislation affected immigration to the United States. *Possible Response: It allowed the influx of people from Asia, Latin America, and other non-European regions.* In what ways was the act consistent with the ideals and goals of the Great Society? *Possible Response: It offered the opportunity of a better life to people in need.* How does the act's provisions continue to affect the United States today? *Possible Response: People allowed into the country under the act have greatly influenced mainstream American culture and lifestyle.*

846 Chapter 28

Making Connections Across the Curriculum

Government Discuss the creation of the Department of Housing and Urban Development. Ask students why the new federal department was created. *To address the problems of the nation's cities.* Why was the department considered necessary by the mid-1960s? *Possible Response: Explosive urban growth in the 1950s had resulted in many urban problems, including overcrowding and inadequate housing.* Then ask students to discuss any recently formed federal departments or programs, such as the war on drugs, created to address current problems.

MAKING CONNECTIONS (THEMATIC AND CROSS-CURRICULAR)

Provides insightful observations and meaningful examples showing how a particular topic relates to key themes and other areas of study.

Great Society Programs, 1964–1967

Poverty

1964 **Tax Reduction Act** cut corporate and individual taxes to stimulate growth.

1964 **Economic Opportunity Act** created Job Corps, VISTA, Project Head Start, and other programs to fight "war on poverty."

1965 **Medical Care Act** established Medicare and Medicaid programs.

1965 **Appalachian Regional Development Act** targeted aid for highways, health centers, and resource development in that economically depressed area.

Cities

1965 **Omnibus Housing Act** provided money for low-income housing.

1965 **Department of Housing and Urban Development** was formed to administer federal housing programs.

1966 **Demonstration Cities and Metropolitan Development Act** funded slum rebuilding, mass transit, and other improvements for selected " model cities."

Education

1965 **Elementary and Secondary Education Act** directed money to schools for textbooks, library materials, and special education.

1965 **Higher Education Act** funded scholarships and low-interest loans for college students.

1965 **National Endowments for the Arts and the Humanities** was created to financially assist painters, musicians, actors, and others in arts.

1967 **Corporation for Public Broadcasting** was formed to fund educational TV and radio broadcasting.

Discrimination

1964 **Civil Rights Act** outlawed discrimination in public accommodations, housing, and jobs; increased federal power to prosecute civil rights abuses.

1964 **Twenty-fourth Amendment** abolished the poll tax in federal elections.

1965 **Voting Rights Act** ended the practice of requiring voters to pass literacy tests and permitted the federal government to monitor voter registration.

1965 **Immigration Act** ended national-origins quotas established in 1924.

Environment

1965 **Wilderness Preservation Act** set aside over 9 million acres for national forest lands.

1965 **Water Quality Act** required states to clean up their rivers.

1965 **Clean Air Act Amendment** directed the federal government to establish emission standards for new motor vehicles.

1967 **Air Quality Act** set federal air pollution guidelines and extended federal enforcement power.

Consumer Advocacy

1966 **Truth in Packaging Act** set standards for labeling consumer products.

1966 **National Traffic and Motor Vehicle Safety Act** set federal safety standards for the auto and tire industries.

1966 **Highway Safety Act** required states to set up highway safety programs.

1967 **Department of Transportation** was created to deal with national air, rail, and highway transportation.

Skillbuilder Answer The programs were wide-ranging, which reflected an expanding role for the federal government in addressing certain areas of American society.

The Great Society addressed more than economic and social ills—it also embraced, among other things, protecting the environment and consumers. In 1962, *Silent Spring*, a book by Rachel Carson, had called attention to a hidden danger: the effects of pesticides on the environment. Carson's book and the following public outcry resulted in the Water Quality Act of 1965, which required states to clean up rivers. "Today we begin to be masters of our environment," declared Johnson as he signed the bill into law. He also ordered the federal government to search out the worst chemical polluters. "There is no excuse . . . for chemical companies and oil refineries using our major rivers as pipelines for toxic wastes." Such words and actions helped trigger the environmental movement in the United States. (See Chapter 32.)

Hand in hand with environmental protection arose a new concern for consumer protection. Consumer advocates convinced Congress to pass major safety laws, including a truth-in-packaging law that set standards for labeling consumer goods. Ralph Nader, a young lawyer, wrote a book, *Unsafe at Any Speed*, that sharply criticized the U.S. automobile industry for ignoring safety

SKILLBUILDER
INTERPRETING CHARTS
What did the Great Society programs indicate about the federal government's changing role?

Ralph Nader

HISTORY FROM VISUALS

Great Society Programs, 1964–1967

Reading the Chart Point out that the chart organizes the Great Society programs in distinct categories. Then ask students in which year the greatest number of programs were passed. *1965.* How is this fact connected to the results of the 1964 election? *Johnson hurried through a flurry of bills soon after the election to take advantage of his mandate.*

Extension Ask students what the scope of the Great Society programs suggests about the Johnson administration. *Possible Responses: The administration was ambitious, compassionate, liberal.* Why did the number of programs drop off after 1967? *Possible Response: Because Johnson began to focus his energies on the Vietnam War.*

MORE ABOUT . . .
Ralph Nader

In 1965, *Life* magazine named Ralph Nader one of "the 100 greatest Americans." Editors of the magazine described Nader as "the champion we never knew we needed against an enemy we never suspected was there." The enemy was consumer fraud, and Ralph Nader, a young lawyer from Connecticut, took aim at the "designed-in dangers" of the automobile. Inspired by Nader's example, legions of like-minded people called "Nader's Raiders" helped usher in a new era of consumer advocacy.

IN-DEPTH RESOURCES: UNIT 8
Primary Source: *Unsafe at Any Speed*, p. 10

HISTORY FROM VISUALS

Provides a variety of notes, learning strategies, and extension activities to help students make the most of charts, graphs, political cartoons, and key historical photographs.

MORE ABOUT...

Provides terrific nuggets of information that supplement the text.

ANSWERS

Answers to Think Through History and Skillbuilder questions are conveniently placed on the page in the Teacher's Edition.

TEACHING OPTION

Cooperative Activity: Outlining Provisions for a Great Society Program

Task: Groups of four to five students will select a category and outline provisions for a Great Society-inspired program that addresses a problem today.

Purpose: To get a sense of the scope and purpose of the Great Society programs.

Activity: Students should get together in groups and discuss some of the major problems that face society today. Encourage students to use the categories and bills listed in the chart on page 847 to spark ideas. Students

should then agree on a problem they would like to address and write an outline describing the problem and a proposed solution. The outline should detail the roles of the individuals and groups involved in the solution.

📁 **Building a Portfolio:** Students who add their outlines to their portfolios should attach a note explaining the extent to which the government should involve itself in the issue.

ALTERNATIVE ASSESSMENT BOOK
Standards for Evaluating a Cooperative Activity

Standards for Evaluation
Outlines should . . .

• address an important problem in society
• describe the roles of the people involved in effecting a solution
• be consistent with the vision of the Great Society programs

Teacher's Edition **847**

COOPERATIVE ACTIVITIES

Suggest some great ways for students to work together and enhance their interest in and understanding of history.

Reading and Learning History from Textbooks

DONNA M. OGLE
Professor, Reading and Language
National-Louis University

Active, engaged readers make the best learners. Researchers have found that successful readers connect text information with what they already know. These readers build associations among ideas, create visual images of what they are reading, and continually refine their interpretations as they gather more information.

Encouraging active, engaged reading is difficult for teachers when they find that many students have learned to ignore their textbooks. This is often due to texts that are too difficult conceptually and are too dense in information. It is possible, however, for teachers and students to find texts that meet their needs.

SUPPORTING READERS

Often we see students who don't have a foundation of information and experience on which to build. If there are not strong connections, experiences, or foundations, then the amount of support and elaboration provided by the text and teacher are critical. That support and elaboration can be provided in a variety of ways.

Personal Connections For some students, personal stories and human connections can bring a subject such as history alive. Taking a personal point of view and thinking as if they were living the experiences can deepen students' learning. Studies on these techniques have generally shown significant increases in learning. *The Americans* uses personal stories throughout to support student learning.

A PERSONAL VOICE
Here we are, tremendously exhilarated, and there's a sea of dead. . . . [The platoon leader] was much moved. . . . He said, "Joe, lets make a resolution with these Russians here and also the ones on the bank: this would be an important day in the lives of the two countries." . . . It was a solemn moment. There were tears in the eyes of most of us. . . . We embraced. We swore never to forget.

JOSEPH POLOWSKY, quoted in *The Good War*

Visual Information Visual information is a resource that many readers rely on heavily when reading unfamiliar material. When text content is unfamiliar, the visual materials accompanying the text can provide strong support for the creation of meaning, especially in expository material. Pictures create a visual context and make abstractions of time and space more real; photos and artifacts create a grounding for new ideas; maps and other spatial features, such as charts, help readers asso-

ciate and compare ideas. The more opportunity there is to learn through our visual sense, the more avenues for thinking are stimulated and supported.

Learning Styles We know that readers have different styles of constructing meaning—some rely heavily on verbal input and discussion, some need visual supports, and some need to make notes and drawings or create graphic organizers as they learn. For still others, creating opportunities to challenge ideas and make comparisons engages their minds. The richer the thinking that is encouraged, the more likely students are to learn. Posing problems, comparing and contrasting ideas, and presenting different points of view on issues stimulates deeper engagement and leads to more learning than does a simple exposition of factual information. The Point/Counterpoint feature does just that.

POINT ▷ **COUNTERPOINT**

"The United States must occasionally intervene militarily in regional conflicts."

"The United States should not intervene militarily in regional conflicts."

Students Learning English Second-language learners, in particular, need to have information and ideas presented to them in multiple ways. Since many of these students are unfamiliar with the concepts and events of American history, being able to "see" history helps them make it real to themselves. Attending to illustrations of all kinds is essential for these students. The more ways the same information and ideas are presented, the more likely they are to be able to construct an adequate understanding of what they are studying.

In addition, the greater variety of materials second-language learners can read on the same topic, the more deeply they will understand the language and concepts. Seeing the same concepts presented by different authors in different types of writing (first-person accounts, newspapers, official documents) and from different points of view helps these students build a better understanding of new ideas and terminology. Then, having opportunities to discuss ideas and share interpretations can solidify their growing understanding.

EVOLVING FORMS OF READING

Today's students need to be able to read in ways earlier generations did not.

Nonlinear Materials Today, students must

- gather ideas from multiple sources: resource books, magazines, computerized databases, CD-ROMs, the Internet
- know how to evaluate these sources and make decisions about their content
- find their way through nonlinear materials, such as by deciding which area of a computer screen contains the information they want
- make decisions about what level of knowledge and elaboration they need

Graphic Layouts Today's readers must deal with informational materials that come in formats such as

- multiple columns of text with many pictures, graphs, and maps
- single-column texts with with large marginal areas used for problems, illustrations, highlighted information, and thought-provoking ideas
- combinations of layouts

THE TEACHER'S ROLE

Are our students prepared with strategies for reading and learning in the 21st century? Are they able to shift from one form of text presentation to another easily? Do they know how to construct meaning from multiple sources?

Strategies for Teachers You can help your students become active, engaged, and confident readers. Here are some strategies you might try:

- Observe your students and ask them how they read.
- Do a "think aloud" as students begin to read a text. Ask them to tell you where they look on the page; when they look at the charts, maps, and pictures; and when they read the headings and titles.
- Introduce the text layout and features, and discuss students' options for reading.
- Show students that all material on a page does not have to be read in order.
- Have students experiment with reading the graphics first before reading the text on a page.
- Demonstrate how headings and subheadings can help readers find specific information.
- Use graphic organizers and reading guides to help students gain confidence.

Reading and discussing different types of written material and material expressing different points of view will help students learn to look deeply into and think critically about what they read. Help them learn to enjoy the search for information and ideas!

The Western Front, 1914–1917

GEOGRAPHY SKILLBUILDER **LOCATION** *Where did the Western front extend from northwest to southeast?* **MOVEMENT** *About how many miles separated the city of Paris from German forces at the point of their closest approach?*

A PERSONAL VOICE
[We] found the side streets blocked with their carts. Into these they had thrown mattresses, or bundles of grain, and heaped upon them were families of three generations. Old men in blue smocks, white-haired and bent, old women in caps, the daughters dressed in their one best frock and hat, and clasping in their hands all that was left to them, all that they could stuff into a pillow-case or flour-sack. . . . Heart-broken, weary, hungry, they passed in an unending caravan.
RICHARD HARDING DAVIS, quoted in *Hooray for Peace, Hurrah for War*

Unable to save Belgium, the British and French retreated to the Marne River in France, where they managed to stop the German advance in September 1914. By the spring of 1915, two lines of deep, rat-infested trenches zigzagged across northern and eastern France. German soldiers occupied one line, Allied soldiers the other line. Between them lay **"no man's land"**—a barren expanse of mud pockmarked with shell craters and filled with barbed wire entanglements. Every once in a while, the soldiers would climb out of their trenches and try to overrun enemy lines, while machine guns blazed and poison gas filled the air.

The slaughter was unbelievable. For example, during the Battle of the Somme—which began on July 1, 1916, and lasted until mid-November—the British lost 60,000 men the first day alone. Final casualties totaled about 1.2 million—650,000 Germans, 420,000 British, and nearly 200,000 French. Yet only seven miles of ground changed hands. This bloody **trench warfare,** in

Soldiers climb out of a trench and charge an enemy position.

Trench Warfare

Information presented in multiple ways.

Single column text with space for questions and captions in the margins.

Block Schedules

"Some of my favorite active-learning strategies, such as role-playing and simulations, work even better with the block."

Debra Brown, teacher, Houston, Texas

"While I was not an ardent fan of block scheduling during the planning stage, I quickly became a convert after working under a block schedule for a few months."

Marsee Perkins, teacher, Orlando, Florida

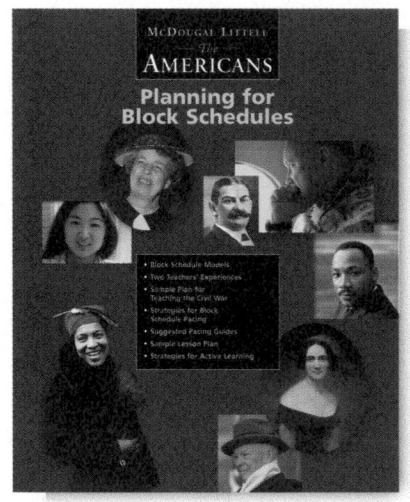

What is block scheduling, this new way of organizing the school day? What benefits does it offer teachers and students? For Debra Brown and Marsee Perkins, the block schedule has some clear advantages. You can find out about various types of block schedules and get the advice of these two experienced teachers by examining *Planning for Block Schedules*, found in the teacher resource materials for *The Americans*.

In contrast to the traditional school day of six to eight single class periods, block schedules have fewer classes, each lasting anywhere from 85 to 100 minutes. The longer classes provide teachers with convenient periods of teaching time and students with fewer subjects on which to concentrate. Block schedules can take a variety of forms: *Planning for Block Schedules* shows several of the most common of these.

Sample Alternate-Day (A/B) Schedule

Period	Length in Minutes	Monday	Tuesday	Wednesday	Thursday	Friday	Monday
BLOCK ONE	112	Class A	Class D	Class A	Class D	Class A	Class D
passing	8						
BLOCK TWO	112	Class B	Class E	Class B	Class E	Class B	Class E
passing							
lunch							
passing							

Sample Semester Plan (4/4) Schedule

Period	Length in Minutes	First Semester	Second Semester
BLOCK ONE	90	Class A	Class E
passing	8		
BLOCK TWO	90	Class B	Class F
passing	8		
lunch	50		

Block schedules offer teachers opportunities for using a variety of active-learning strategies. *Planning for Block Schedules* provides explanations of and suggestions for implementing a variety of collaborative and cooperative activities that work well in block-schedule classrooms.

As you plan your own classes, you will find helpful sample lesson plans and blank forms in *Planning for Block Schedules*.

Internet Resources

McDougal Littell's Web site, **McDougal Littell Learning On-Line,** offers you an opportunity to become part of a nationwide community of teachers and students using *The Americans.* With a user-friendly format, *McDougal Littell Learning On-Line* helps you meet the challenges of teaching in today's diverse classroom by providing access to a wide range of resources related to the chapters of the textbook.

Our *Social Studies* content area page gathers some of the best links on the Internet—screened by our editors—to help you extend lessons, expand your research, and boost your own creativity.

Educator's Digest Browse through article abstracts in our collection of social studies reference materials.

Professional Development Calendar Consult this on-line calendar for the latest information on upcoming events and conferences related to social studies education.

Frequently Asked Questions Find answers to common history- and program-related questions—and submit your own.

Monthly Special Feature Author profiles, web-site guests, and other special events are all a part of this monthly feature.

TEACHER TO TEACHER

Communicate and collaborate on-line with teachers across the country—teachers who share your own challenges and rewards.

TEACHER LINKS LIBRARY

Need more information on anything from colonial life to the Clinton presidency? Explore hundreds of annotated links to sites dealing with specific topics discussed in *The Americans.*

 For more information about a topic, click on *Social Studies* at http://www.mcdougallittell.com

http://www.mcdougallittell.com

Pacing Guide

The following pacing guide shows how the chapters in *The Americans* can be adapted to fit your specific course needs. The guide is based on 170 days of instruction during the school year. For **block schedules**, see *Planning for Block Schedules* in the teacher's resource materials.

	U.S. History Survey	Civil War to Present	20th Century	Beginnings to 1920
UNIT 1 AMERICAN BEGINNINGS TO 1783				
Chapter 1 Beginnings to 1506 Three Worlds Meet	(days)	(days)	(days)	(days)
1. Peopling the Americas	2	1	1	3
2. Native American Societies Around 1492	1	.5	.5	2
3. West African Societies Around 1492	1	.5	.5	2
4. European Societies Around 1492	1	1	.5	2
5. Transatlantic Encounters	1	.5	.5	2
Chapter 2 1492–1690 The American Colonies Emerge				
1. Spain's Empire in the Americas	2	1	1	3
2. An English Settlement at Jamestown	1	.5	.5	2
3. Puritan New England	2	1	1	2
4. Settlement of the Middle Colonies	1	.5	.5	2
Chapter 3 1651–1765 The Colonies Come of Age				
1. England and Its Colonies	1	1	1	2
2. The Agricultural South	2	.5	.5	2
3. The Commercial North	2	.5	.5	2
4. The French and Indian War	1	.5	.5	2
Chapter 4 1765–1783 The War for Independence				
1. The Stirrings of Rebellion	2	1	1	2
2. Ideas Help Start a Revolution	1	.5	.5	2
The Declaration of Independence	1	.5	.5	2
3. Struggling Toward Saratoga	2	.5	.5	2
4. Winning the War	2	1	1	3
Total Days for Unit	**26**	**12.5**	**12**	**39**
UNIT 2 1781–1850 A NEW NATION				
Chapter 5 1781–1788 Shaping a New Nation				
1. Experimenting with Confederation	2	1	1	3
2. Drafting the Constitution	2	.5	.5	2
3. Ratifying the Constitution	2	.5	.5	2
The Living Constitution	2	1	1	2
Chapter 6 1789–1816 Launching the New Nation				
1. Washington Heads the New Government	1	1	1	2
2. Foreign Affairs Trouble the Nation	1	.5	.5	2
3. Jefferson Alters the Nation's Course	1	.5	.5	2
4. The War of 1812 Erupts	1	.5	.5	2

For **block schedules**, see *Planning for Block Schedules* in the teacher's resource materials.

	U.S. History Survey	Civil War to Present	20th Century	Beginnings to 1920
Chapter 7 1817–1840 Balancing Nationalism and Sectionalism				
1. Regional Economies Create Differences	1	1	.5	2
2. Nationalism at Center Stage	1	.5	.5	2
3. The Age of Jackson	1	.5	.5	2
4. Jackson, States' Rights, and the National Bank	1	1	.5	2
Chapter 8 1820–1850 Reforming American Society				
1. Religion Sparks Reform	1	.5	.5	2
2. Slavery and Abolition	1	1	1	3
3. Women and Reform	1	.5	.5	2
4. The Changing Workplace	1	.5	.5	2
Total Days for Unit	**20**	**11**	**10**	**34**
UNIT 3 1825–1877 AN ERA OF GROWTH AND DISUNION				
Chapter 9 1825–1850 Expanding Markets and Moving West				
1. The Market Revolution	1	1	1	2
2. Manifest Destiny	1	1	1	2
3. Expansion in Texas	1	.5	.5	2
4. The War with Mexico	1	.5	.5	2
Chapter 10 1850–1861 The Union in Peril				
1. The Divisive Politics of Slavery	1	1	.5	2
2. Protest, Resistance, and Violence	1	1	1	2
3. The Birth of the Republican Party	1	.5	.5	2
4. Slavery and Secession	1	1	1	3
Chapter 11 1861–1865 The Civil War				
1. The Civil War Begins	2	1	1	2
2. The Politics of War	1	2	1	2
3. Life During Wartime	1	2	1	2
4. The North Takes Charge	2	2	1	3
5. The Legacy of the War	2	2	1	2
Chapter 12 1865–1877 Reconstruction and Its Effects				
1. The Politics of Reconstruction	1	1	.5	2
2. Reconstructing Society	2	2	1	3
3. The Collapse of Reconstruction	1	2	.5	2
Total Days for Unit	**20**	**20.5**	**13**	**35**
UNIT 4 1876–1917 MIGRATION AND INDUSTRIALIZATION CHANGE SOCIETY				
Chapter 13 1876–1900 Changes on the Western Frontier				
1. Native American Culture in Crisis	1	2	1	3
2. The Growth of the Cattle Industry	1	1	.5	2
3. Settling on the Great Plains	1	1	.5	2
4. Farmers and the Populist Movement	1	1	.5	2

For block schedules, see *Planning for Block Schedules* in the teacher's resources materials.

	U.S. History Survey	Civil War to Present	20th Century	Beginnings to 1920
Chapter 14 1876–1900 The Industrial Age				
1. The Expansion of Industry	1	1	.5	2
2. The Age of the Railroads	1	1	.5	2
3. Big Business Emerges	1	1	.5	2
4. Workers of the Nation Unite	1	2	1	3
Chapter 15 1876–1914 Immigrants and Urbanization				
1. The New Immigrants	1	2	2	2
2. The Problems of Urbanization	1	1	2	2
3. The Emergence of the Political Machine	1	1	1	2
4. Politics in the Gilded Age	1	1	1	2
Chapter 16 1877–1917 Life at the Turn of the Century				
1. Science and Urban Life	1	1	1	2
2. Education and Culture	1	2	2	2
3. Segregation and Discrimination	1	1	2	2
4. Dawn of Mass Culture	1	1	1	2
Total Days for Unit	**16**	**20**	**17**	**34**
UNIT 5 1890–1920 MODERN AMERICA EMERGES				
Chapter 17 1890–1920 The Progressive Era				
1. The Origins of Progressivism	2	2	2	3
2. Women in Public Life	1	1	1	2
3. Teddy Roosevelt's Square Deal	1	2	2	2
4. Progressivism Under Taft	1	1	1	2
5. Wilson's New Freedom	1	1	1	2
Chapter 18 1890–1920 America Claims an Empire				
1. Imperialism and America	1	1	1	2
2. The Spanish-American-Cuban War	1	1	1	2
3. Acquiring New Lands	1	2	2	2
4. America as a World Power	1	1	1	2
Chapter 19 1914–1920 The First World War				
1. World War I Begins	2	2	2	3
2. American Power Tips the Balance	1	2	2	2
3. The War at Home	2	2	2	2
4. Wilson Fights for Peace	1	1	1	2
Total Days for Unit	**16**	**19**	**19**	**28**
UNIT 6 1920–1940 THE TWENTIES AND THE GREAT DEPRESSION				
Chapter 20 1920–1929 Politics of the Roaring Twenties				
1. Americans Struggle with Postwar Issues	2	2	2	
2. "Normalcy" and Isolationism	1	1	1	
3. The Business of America	1	2	2	

For **block schedules**, see *Planning for Block Schedules* in the teacher's resource materials.

	U.S. History Survey	Civil War to Present	20th Century	Beginnings to 1920
Chapter 21 1920–1929 The Roaring Life of the 1920s				
1. Changing Ways of Life	1	2	2	
2. The Twenties Woman	1	1	1	
3. Education and Popular Culture	1	1	1	
4. The Harlem Renaissance	1	1	2	
Chapter 22 1929–1933 The Great Depression Begins				
1. The Nation's Sick Economy	2	2	2	
2. Hardship and Suffering During the Depression	1	2	2	
3. Hoover Struggles with the Depression	1	1	1	
Chapter 23 1933–1940 The New Deal				
1. A New Deal Fights the Depression	2	2	2	
2. The Second New Deal Takes Hold	1	1	1	
3. The New Deal Affects Many Groups	1	2	2	
4. Society and Culture	1	1	1	
5. The Impact of the New Deal	1	1	1	
Total Days for Unit	**18**	**22**	**23**	
UNIT 7 1931–1960 WORLD WAR II AND ITS AFTERMATH				
Chapter 24 1931–1941 World War Looms				
1. Dictators Threaten World Peace	1	1	2	
2. War in Europe	2	2	2	
3. The Holocaust	2	2	2	
4. America Moves Toward War	1	2	2	
Chapter 25 1941–1945 The United States in World War II				
1. Mobilization on the Home Front	2	2	2	
2. The War for Europe and North Africa	2	3	3	
3. The War in the Pacific	2	2	2	
4. The Impact of the War	2	2	2	
Chapter 26 1945–1960 Cold War Conflicts				
1. Origins of the Cold War	2	2	2	
2. The Cold War Heats Up	2	2	2	
3. The Cold War at Home	1	2	2	
4. Two Nations Live on the Edge	1	1	2	
Chapter 27 1946–1959 The Postwar Boom				
1. Postwar America	1	2	2	
2. The American Dream in the Fifties	1	1	2	
3. Popular Culture	1	1	1	
4. The Other America	1	1	1	
Total Days for Unit	**24**	**28**	**31**	

For **block schedules**, see *Planning for Block Schedules* in the teacher's resource materials.

	U.S. History Survey	Civil War to Present	20th Century	Beginnings to 1920
UNIT 8 1954–1975 LIVING WITH GREAT TURMOIL				
Chapter 28 1960–1968 The New Frontier and the Great Society				
1. Kennedy and the Cold War	2	2	2	
2. The New Frontier	1	2	2	
3. The Great Society	1	1	2	
Chapter 29 1954–1970 Civil Rights				
1. Taking On Segregation	2	2	2	
2. The Triumphs of a Crusade	1	2	2	
3. Challenges and Changes in the Movement	1	1	2	
Chapter 30 1954–1975 The Vietnam War Years				
1. Moving Toward Conflict	1	1	1	
2. U.S. Involvement and Escalation	1	1	1	
3. A Nation Divided	1	1	2	
4. 1968: A Tumultuous Year	1	2	2	
5. The End of the War and Its Legacy	2	2	2	
Chapter 31 1960–1975 An Era of Social Change				
1. Latinos and Native Americans Seek Equality	2	2	2	
2. Women Fight for Equality	1	2	2	
3. Culture and Counterculture	1	1	2	
Total Days for Unit	**18**	**22**	**26**	
UNIT 9 1968–1996 NEARING THE CENTURY MARK				
Chapter 32 1968–1980 An Age of Limits				
1. The Nixon Administration	1	1	2	
2. Watergate: Nixon's Downfall	1	1	1	
3. The Ford and Carter Years	1	2	2	
4. Environmental Activism	1	1	1	
Chapter 33 1980–1992 The Conservative Tide				
1. A Conservative Movement Emerges	1	1	1	
2. Conservative Policies Under Reagan and Bush	1	1	1	
3. American Society in a Conservative Age	1	1	2	
4. Changes in America's Foreign Policy	1	2	2	
Chapter 34 1992–1996 The United States in Today's World				
1. The Clinton Presidency	1	1	2	
2. The New Global Economy	1	1	2	
3. Technology and Modern Life	1	1	1	
4. The Changing Face of America	1	2	2	
Total Days for Unit	**12**	**15**	**19**	

McDOUGAL LITTELL

life

The
AMERICANS

liberty

pursuit *of*
happiness

"The Genius of America lies in its capacity to forge a single nation from peoples of remarkably diverse racial, religious, and ethnic origins. . . . The American identity will never be fixed and final: it will always be in the making."

Arthur M. Schlesinger

ELEANOR ROOSEVELT, *page 665*
Humanitarian, author, First Lady

NORMAN SCHWARZKOPF, *page 1000*
U.S. general during Persian Gulf War

LUIS MUÑOZ RIVERA, *page 535*
Advocate for Puerto Rican independence

MAYA LIN, *page 912*
Designer of the Vietnam Memorial

DR. MARTIN LUTHER KING, JR.
page 862
Civil rights leader

ABRAHAM LINCOLN, *page 299*
Sixteenth President of the United States

MARY CHESNUT, *page 323*
Author of personal account of the Civil War

ZORA NEALE HURSTON, *page 630*
Author during the Harlem Renaissance

DWIGHT D. EISENHOWER, *page 744*
U.S. general and thirty-fourth President of the United States

BENJAMIN FRANKLIN, *page 99*
Author, printer, scientist, diplomat

JOHN F. KENNEDY, *page 830*
Thirty-fifth President of the United States

ZITKALA-ŠA, *page 380*
Native American author

SUSAN B. ANTHONY, *page 504*
Leader of woman suffrage
movement

CESAR CHAVEZ, *page 922*
Founder of the United Farm Workers union

— *The* —
AMERICANS

Gerald A. Danzer

J. Jorge Klor de Alva

Louis E. Wilson

Nancy Woloch

McDougal Littell
A HOUGHTON MIFFLIN COMPANY
Evanston, Illinois • Boston • Dallas

Authors

Gerald A. Danzer, Ph.D.

Gerald A. Danzer is Professor of History and Director of the M.A. Program for Teachers of History at the University of Illinois at Chicago. He served from 1992 to 1994 as Chair of the Council for Effective Teaching and Learning at UIC and was Director of the Chicago Neighborhood History Project. Dr. Danzer's area of specialization is historical geography, in which he has written *Discovering the Past Through Maps and Views* and numerous other publications. Before entering university teaching, Dr. Danzer taught high school history in the Chicago area. Dr. Danzer received his Ph.D. in history from Northwestern University.

J. Jorge Klor de Alva, J.D. and Ph.D.

J. Jorge Klor de Alva is Class of 1940 Professor of Comparative Ethnic Studies and Anthropology at the University of California at Berkeley and former Professor of Anthropology at Princeton University. Dr. Klor de Alva's interests include interethnic relations, historical ethnography, and educational reform. His publications include *The Aztec Image of Self and Society* and *Interethnic Images: Discourse and Practice in the New World, 1492–1992*, as well as more than ten other books and more than seventy scholarly articles. Dr. Klor de Alva earned his J.D. from the University of California at Berkeley and his Ph.D. in history/anthropology from the University of California at Santa Cruz.

Louis E. Wilson, Ph.D.

Louis E. Wilson is Associate Professor and Chair of the Afro-American and African Studies Department at Smith College. Previously Dr. Wilson was on the faculty at the University of Colorado, Boulder, and was a senior Fulbright Scholar at the University of Ghana, Legon. Dr. Wilson is the author of *The Krobo People of Ghana to 1892: A Political, Social, and Economic History* and *Genealogical and Militia Data on Blacks, Indians, and Mustees from Military American Revolutionary War Records*. Dr. Wilson is currently writing a book entitled *Forgotten Patriots: African Americans and Native Americans in the American Revolution from Rhode Island*. In 1991, Dr. Wilson received The Blackwell Fellowship and Prize as Outstanding Black New England Scholar. Dr. Wilson received his Ph.D. in history from the University of California at Los Angeles.

Nancy Woloch, Ph.D.

Nancy Woloch teaches history at Barnard College, where she has been on the faculty since 1988. Dr. Woloch's scholarly interest has been the history of women in the United States, and in this area she has published *Women and the American Experience* and *Early American Women: A Documentary History, 1600–1900*. She is also the author of *Muller v. Oregon* and the co-author of *The American Century*. Dr. Woloch was the recipient of a National Endowment for the Humanities Fellowship for Younger Humanists. She received her Ph.D. in history and American studies from Indiana University.

Acknowledgments begin on page 1136.

ISBN 0-395-85182-3

Printed in the United States of America.

1 2 3 4 5 6 7 8 9–DWO–02 01 00 99 98 97

Consultants and Reviewers

Senior Consultant

Winthrop D. Jordan
Professor of History and
   Afro-American Studies
University of Mississippi
Oxford, Mississippi

Constitution Consultant

Melvin Dubnick
Professor of Political Science
Rutgers University, Trenton
Trenton, New Jersey

Contributing Writer

Miriam Greenblatt
Educational Writer and Consultant
Highland Park, Illinois

Multicultural Advisory Board

The multicultural advisors reviewed the manuscript for appropriate historical content.

Pat A. Brown
Director of the Indianapolis
   Public Schools Office of African
   Centered Multicultural Education
Indianapolis Public Schools
Indianapolis, Indiana

Curtis L. Walker
Executive Officer, Office of
   Equity and Compliance
Pittsburgh Public Schools
Pittsburgh, Pennsylvania

Ogle B. Duff
Associate Professor of English
University of Pittsburgh
Pittsburgh, Pennsylvania

Mary Ellen Maddox
Black Education Commission
   Director
Los Angeles Unified School District
Los Angeles, California

Jon Reyhner
Associate Professor and Coordinator
   of the Bilingual Multicultural
   Education Program
Northern Arizona University
Flagstaff, Arizona

Ruben Zepeda
Compliance Advisor
Language Acquisition and Curriculum
   Development
Los Angeles, California

Content Consultants

The content consultants reviewed the manuscript for historical depth and accuracy and for clarity of presentation.

Catherine Clinton
Fellow of the W.E.B. Du Bois Institute
Harvard University
Cambridge, Massachusetts

Theodore Karaminski
Professor of History
Loyola University
Chicago, Illinois

Joseph Kett
Professor of History
University of Virginia
Charlottesville, Virginia

Jack Rakove
Professor of History
Stanford University
Stanford, California

Harvard Sitkoff
Professor of History
University of New Hampshire
Durham, New Hampshire

Teacher Review Panels

The following educators provided ongoing review during the development of prototypes, the table of contents, and key components of the program.

Florida Teacher Panel

David Debs
Mandarin High School
Jacksonville, Florida

Ronald Eckstein
Hudson High School
Hudson, Florida

Glenn Hallick
Vanguard High School
Ocala, Florida

Lou Morrison
Lake Weir High School
Ocala, Florida

Brenda Sims Palmer
Lehigh High School
Lehigh Acres, Florida

Marsee Perkins
Maynard Evans High School
Orlando, Florida

Kent Rettig
Pensacola High School
Pensacola, Florida

Jim Sutton
Edgewater High School
Orlando, Florida

Sharman Feliciani
Land O'Lakes High School
Land O'Lakes, Florida

Mary Kenney
Astronaut High School
Titusville, Florida

Flossie Gautier
Bay High School
Panama City, Florida

Illinois Teacher Panel

Rosemary Albright
Conant High School
Hoffman Estates, Illinois

Jeff Anhut
Wheaton Warrenville South High School
Wheaton, Illinois

James Crider
Downers Grove South High School
Downers Grove, Illinois

John Devine
Elgin High School
Elgin, Illinois

George Dyche
West Aurora High School
Aurora, Illinois

Diane Ring
St. Charles High School
St. Charles, Illinois

Jim Rosenberg
Crystal Lake South High School
Crystal Lake, Illinois

Pam Zimmerman
Stevenson High School
Lincolnshire, Illinois

v

Reviewers (continued)

Texas Teacher Panel

Patricia Brison
Bellaire High School
Bellaire, Texas

Debra Brown
Eisenhower High School
Houston, Texas

Gwen Cash
Clear Creek High School
League City, Texas

Kyle Howard
Cooper High School
Lubbock, Texas

Melody Kenney
Turner High School
Carrollton, Texas

James Lee
Lamar High School
Arlington, Texas

Janie Maldonado
Lanier High School
Austin, Texas

LeAnna Morse
Memorial High School
McAllen, Texas

Gloria Remijio
Del Valle High School
El Paso, Texas

Alice White
Bryan Adams High School
Dallas, Texas

Manuscript Reviewers

The following educators reviewed the prototype chapter and the manuscript for the entire book.

Arman Afshani
North Tonawanda High School
North Tonawanda, New York

Debra Brown
Eisenhower High School
Houston, Texas

Dianne Bumgarner
Ashbrook High School
Mt. Holly, North Carolina

Maurice Bush
South Point High School
Crouse, North Carolina

Bruce Campbell
Bemidji High School
Bemidji, Minnesota

James Crider
Downers Grove South
  High School
Downers Grove, Illinois

Gary Gregus
Shakopee High School
Shakopee, Minnesota

Patti Harrold
Edmond Memorial
  High School
Edmond, Oklahoma

Terry Holt
South Rowan High School
China Grove, North Carolina

Al Juengling
Lane Technical High School
Chicago, Illinois

James Lee
Arlington High School
Arlington, Texas

Brenda Sims Palmer
Lehigh Senior High School
Fort Myers, Florida

David Pasternak
Edison Technical High School
Rochester, New York

Dean Pedersen
North Fayette High School
West Union, Iowa

Kent Rettig
Pensacola High School
Pensacola, Florida

Diane Ring
St. Charles High School
St. Charles, Illinois

Susan Roe
C. E. Jordan High School
Durham, North Carolina

Tom Sewell
Inglemoor High School
Bothell, Washington

Wayne Sylvester
Pentucket High School
Westbury, Massachusetts

Bill Von Vihl
Conifer High School
Conifer, Colorado

Nancy Williams
Jersey Village High School
Houston, Texas

Student Board

The following students reviewed prototype materials for the textbook.

John Afordakos
Chantilly High School
Fairfax County, Virginia

Marisha Cook
Rockford East High School
Rockford, Illinois

Matthew Cornejo
New Bedford High School
New Bedford, Massachusetts

Kevin Dodd
Lanier High School
Austin, Texas

Melissa Dugan
Mount Lebanon High School
Mount Lebanon, Pennsylvania

Denise Ford
Douglas Byrd Sr. High School
Cumberland County,
  North Carolina

Rebecca Freeman
Foshay Learning Center
Los Angeles, California

Tonya Gieseking
Broad Ripple High School
Indianapolis, Indiana

Yolande Godfrey
Ocean Township High School
Ocean Township, New Jersey

Norma Jaquez
Odessa High School
Ector County, Texas

Mary McCarthy
Penfield High School
Penfield, New York

Dan McKinley
Bulkeley High School
Hartford, Connecticut

Ms. Kris Miller
Midland High School
Cabell County, West Virginia

Brandi Nichols
Meadowdale High School
Dayton, Ohio

Michael Pancherz
Clear Lake High School
Houston, Texas

Elizabeth Porter
Burnsville High School
Burnsville, Minnesota

Edwin Reyes
Miami Palmetto High School
Dade County, Florida

Misty Sisk
Jackson High School
Jacksonville, Florida

Christopher Sizemore
Community High School
Ann Arbor, Michigan

Jennifer Vasquez
Gilbert High School
Gilbert, Arizona

Everett Wheeler-Bell
East High School
Denver, Colorado

LuKisha Williams
Mackenzie High School
Detroit, Michigan

vii

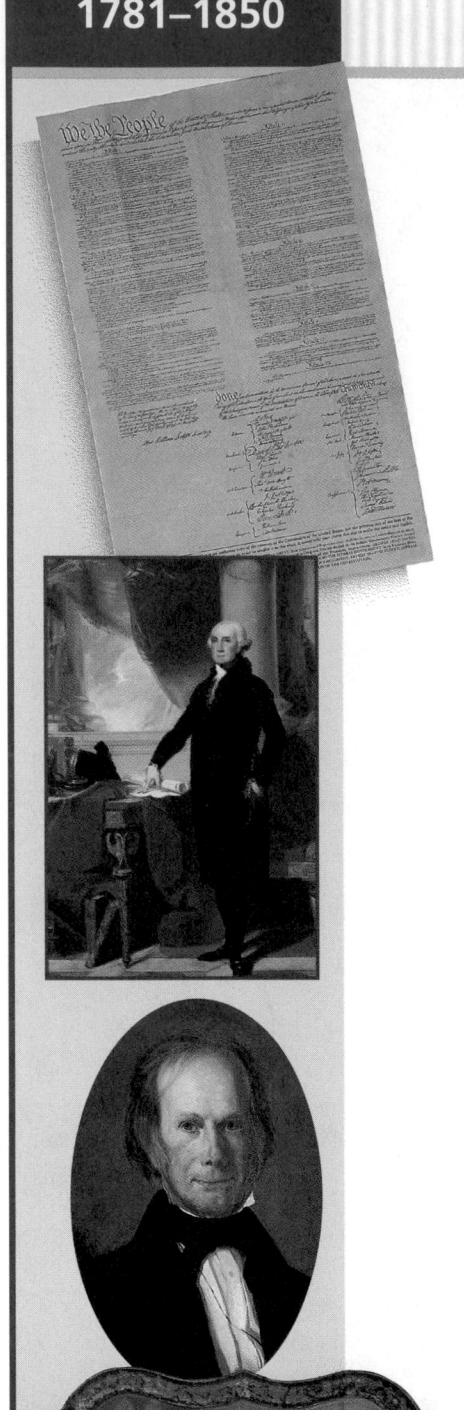

A New Nation

viii

An Era of Growth and Disunion

Unit 3
1825–1877

ix

Unit 4
1876–1917

Migration and Industrialization Change Society

Modern America Emerges

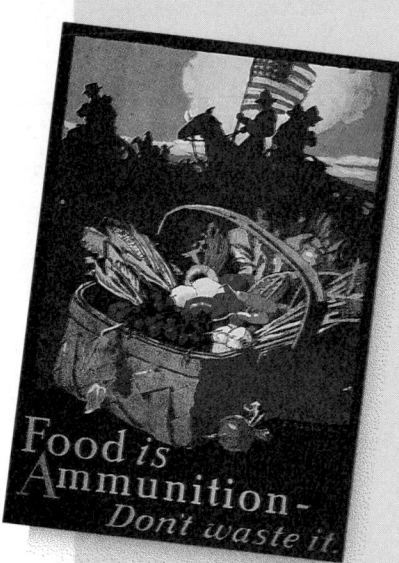

The Twenties and the Great Depression

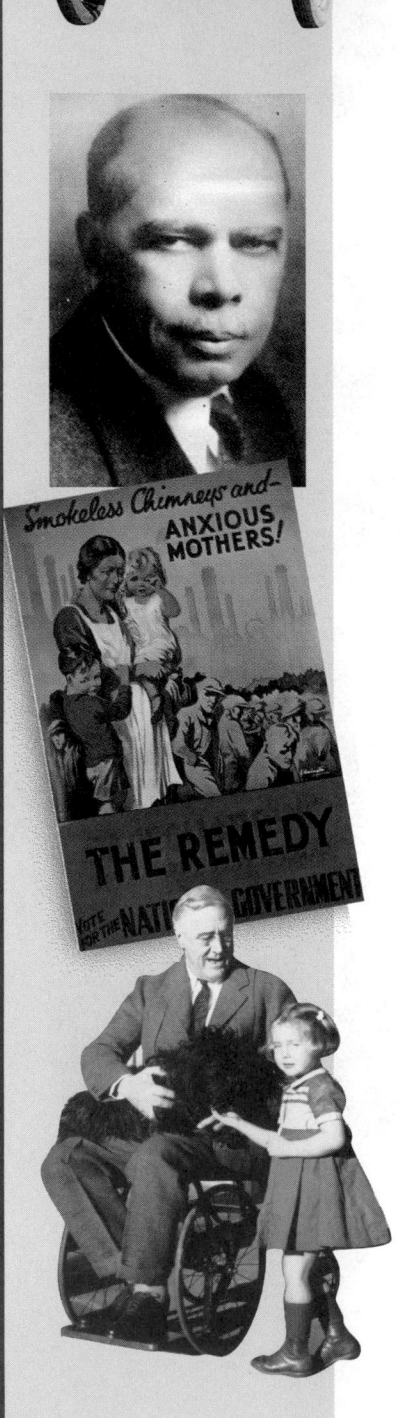

xii

World War II and Its Aftermath

xiii

Unit 8
1954–1975

Living with Great Turmoil

xiv

Nearing the Century Mark

REFERENCE SECTION

Contents   1034

Skillbuilder Handbook

The Skillbuilder Handbook is at the back of the book on pages 1035–1058. Refer to it when you need help in answering Think Through History questions, doing the activities entitled Interact with History, or answering questions in Section Assessments and Chapter Assessments. The handbook will also help you answer questions about maps, charts, and graphs.

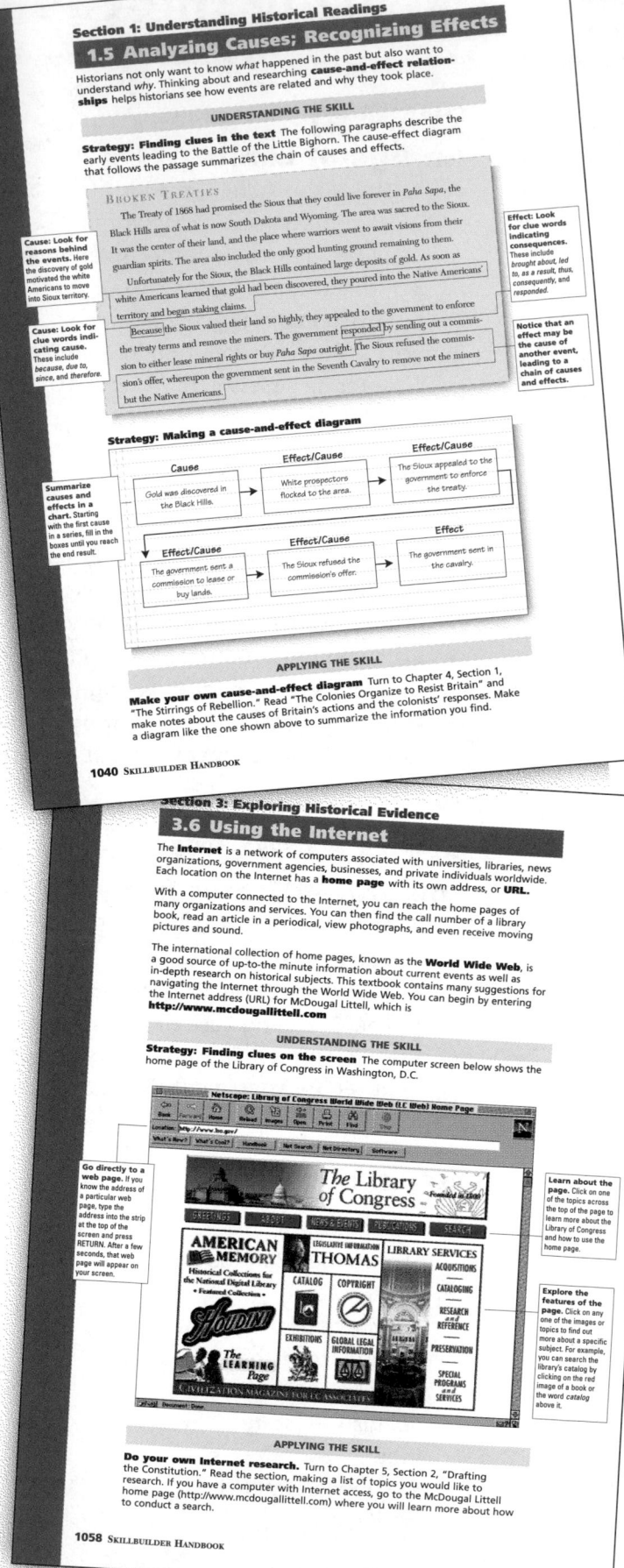

American Stories Video Series

 American Stories *is a powerful video series integrated with the text of The Americans. Fifteen fascinating documentaries, each 8 to 10 minutes long, help introduce various sections of the text.*

BENJAMIN FRANKLIN

ZITKALA-ŠA

ZORA NEALE HURSTON

TONY KAHN

LOIS GIBBS

xvii

Special Features

* represents topics with Internet links

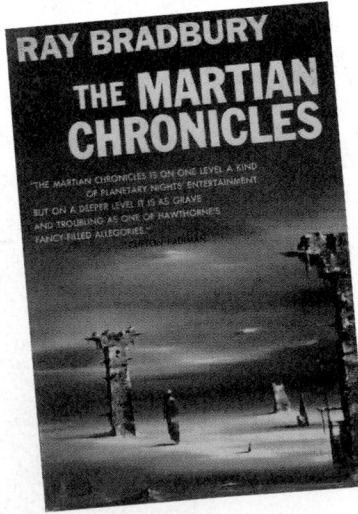

NOW & THEN

KEY PLAYERS

* represents topics with Internet links

Special Features

 * represents topics with Internet links

HISTORICAL SPOTLIGHT

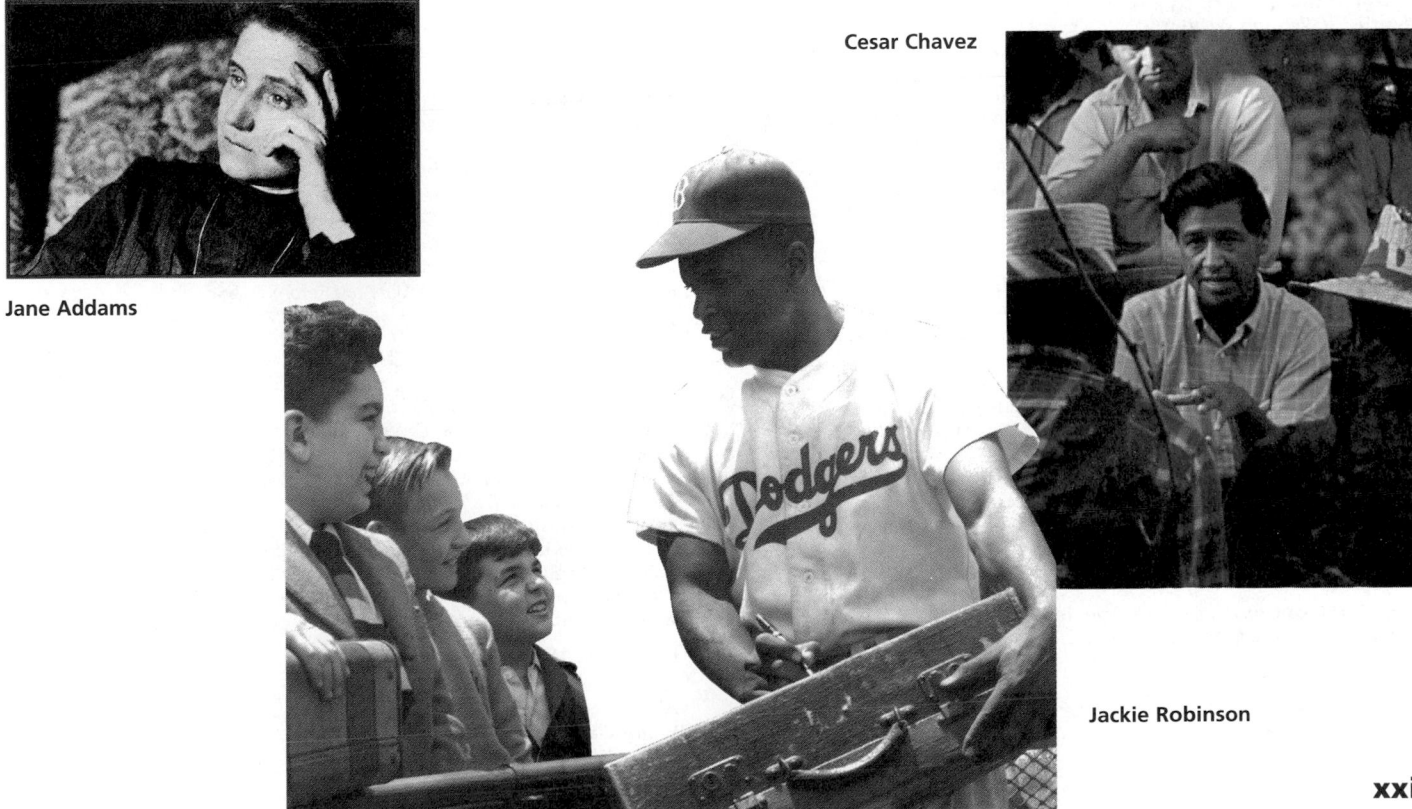

Jane Addams

Cesar Chavez

Jackie Robinson

xxi

Primary Sources and Personal Voices

A PERSONAL VOICE
"Women . . . [took] equally active part with men in the whole antislavery struggle."
ELIZABETH CADY STANTON, in *Elizabeth Cady Stanton*

xxii

Primary Sources and Personal Voices

A PERSONAL VOICE

"Last weekend was the worst dust storm we ever had."

ANN MARIE LOW, *Dust Bowl Diary*

A PERSONAL VOICE

"Seeing how badly they treated Mexicans back in the days of my youth, I could have started a rebellion. But now [1984] there could be a cultural understanding so that . . . we might understand eath other."

PEDRO J. GONZALEZ, in *The Los Angeles Times,* December 9, 1984

A PERSONAL VOICE
"Today. . . [m]y faith in the Constitution is whole."

BARBARA JORDAN, in *Notable Black American Women*

A PERSONAL VOICE
"It is not just those of us who have reached the top who are fighting this daily battle."

GERALDINE FERRARO, in *Vital Speeches of the Day*

Historical and Political Maps

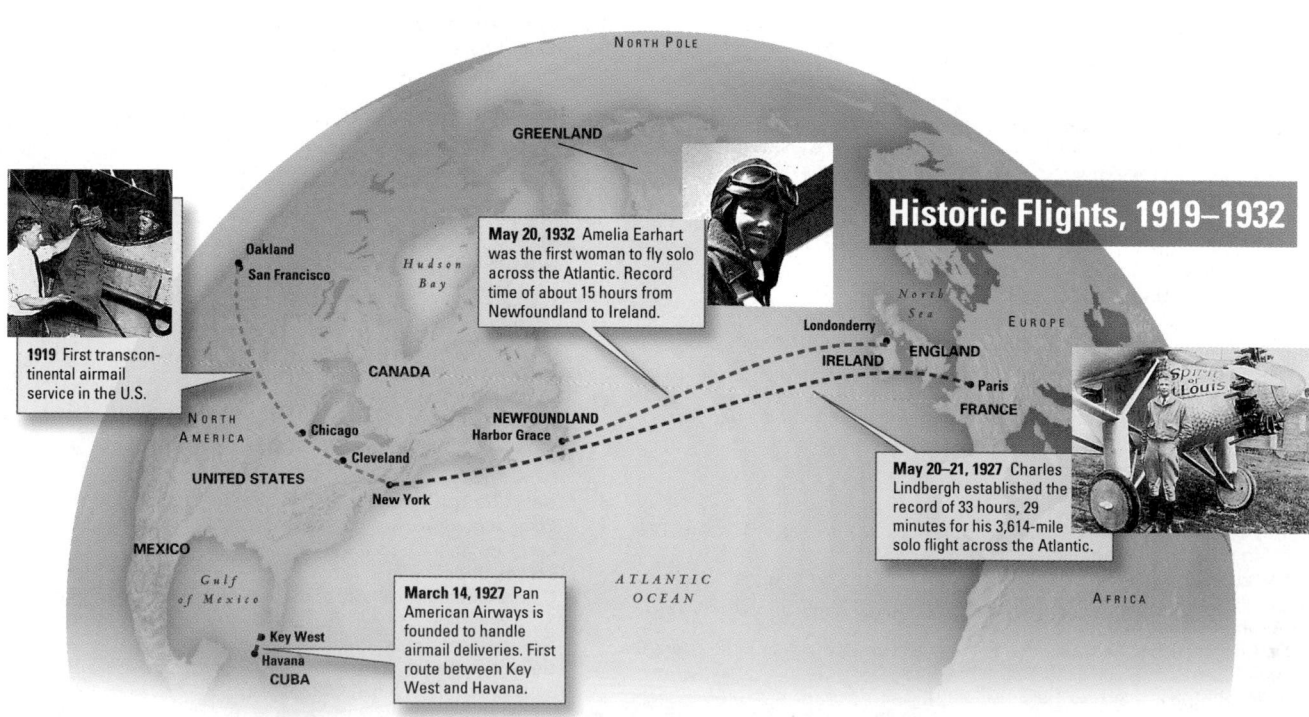

Historic Flights, 1919–1932

May 20, 1932 Amelia Earhart was the first woman to fly solo across the Atlantic. Record time of about 15 hours from Newfoundland to Ireland.

1919 First transcontinental airmail service in the U.S.

May 20–21, 1927 Charles Lindbergh established the record of 33 hours, 29 minutes for his 3,614-mile solo flight across the Atlantic.

March 14, 1927 Pan American Airways is founded to handle airmail deliveries. First route between Key West and Havana.

The Underground Railroad, 1850–1860

Free states
Slave states
Areas with slave population of 50% or more in 1860
Routes of the Underground Railroad

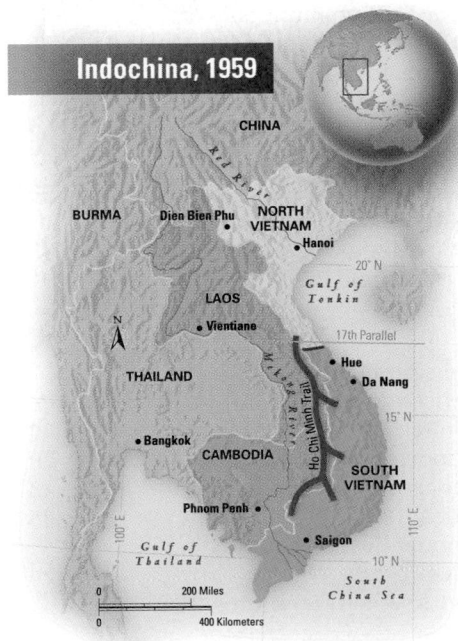

Indochina, 1959

Charts, Graphs, Infographics, Tables, and Time Lines

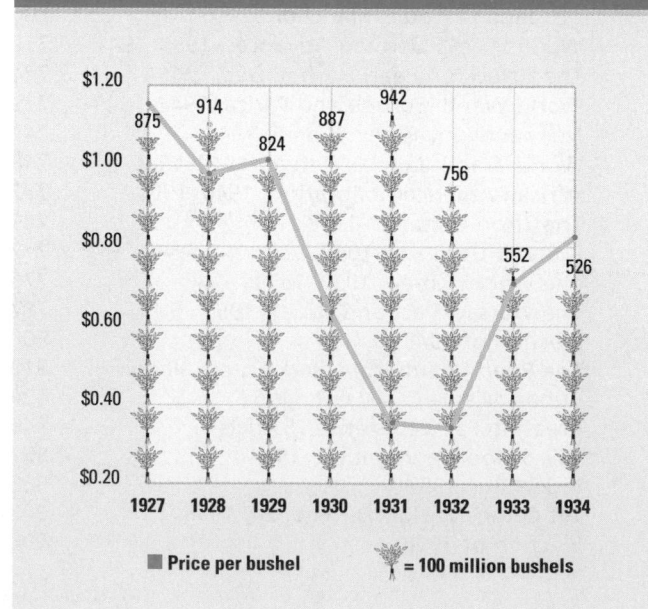

Wheat Production and Wheat Prices

875 914 824 887 942 756 552 526

$1.20 $1.00 $0.80 $0.60 $0.40 $0.20

1927 1928 1929 1930 1931 1932 1933 1934

■ Price per bushel   = 100 million bushels

Inventions That Tamed the Prairie

INVENTION	BARBED WIRE	STEEL PLOW	REAPER	STEEL WINDMILL
Invention's solution ③	Prevents animals from trampling crops	Makes planting more efficient	Saves crops by speeding up harvesting	Brings up underground water for irrigation
Farming Condition ②	No timber for fences	Difficult and time-consuming planting	Crop damage and death	Crop dehydration
Prairie Problem ①	Treeless landscape	Hard-packed soil	Sudden frost, hailstorms	Unpredictable rainfall

To help introduce The Americans, *high school students around the country were asked to talk about the United States. They talked about what it means to be an American today, what the American dream means to them, and what changes await America in the 21st century. In addition, the young women talked about what challenges they see for American women. Here are some of their thought-provoking responses. As you read them, think about what your responses would be to the issues and themes they raise.*

TUAN MINH TRUONG, FLORIDA

"As an American, I enjoy many wonderful rights, which my parents and siblings could not enjoy in Vietnam. Being American means having the chance for a better future.

I think America's greatest challenge is to eliminate unemployment. Though unemployment is a big problem, we can only tackle it by opening up many opportunities for everyone."

AMY GRASS, COLORADO

"My American dream is that nobody living in America is homeless or poor. Everyone should have a home and a good job to support themselves and their families.

The most important challenge facing women in the 21st century is equal opportunity. Although women's position in society has greatly improved, it is still not perfect. I think women will have great opportunities making discoveries with technology and working beside others as equals."

EFRIAM CORTEZ KNIGHT, FLORIDA

"Being an American means being in a position of global leadership. America continually sets the precedents that the entire world follows.

The greatest challenge facing America is exploring space. We will face this challenge through our everchanging, advancing technologies. In the 21st century, Americans will be living on space stations orbiting Earth. I intend to obtain my Ph.D. in physics at Florida State University and then will proceed to work for NASA."

NELLY DELEON, NEW JERSEY

"Being an American means to me opportunity. My parents immigrated from Guatemala more than 14 years ago to give us a chance to become successful. My American dream is to graduate from a top college and become a leader.

I believe America's greatest challenge is racism. One way to face this challenge is for television to stop showing stereotyped characters."

NATALIE MELISSA STEEN
NORTH CAROLINA

"I think the 21st century will bring better health and increasing jobs in America. This is because of the fast growing technology today in the medical field and in computers. Perhaps the technology of the 21st century will even bring a cure for AIDS and other diseases.

Even though women have been struggling for equality in America for hundreds of years, I think that struggle will continue well into the 21st century. In coming years there will be more women doctors, lawyers, and maybe even a woman President of the United States!"

CLAY HOWARD, ILLINOIS

"I feel that the American dream has two parts. The first is material—for example, owning a house and your own car. These are important to people because they indicate self-sufficiency and accomplishment. The other part involves improvement. People almost always want to be better off financially and content with what they've done with their lives. On top of that, people always want better lives for their children.

The idea that America is a lighthouse for the rest of the world makes me tremendously proud. The ideas framed in the Declaration of Independence are the principles that make America great."

YOLANDA WILSON
NORTH CAROLINA

"My American dream is to have a successful walk through life. Like my ancestors, I want to be a success. I don't think the task will be easy or simple but at the end, I hope to find happiness.

I think America's greatest challenge is the drugs and crime. I believe if the people of America make laws harder and educate children about drugs and their damage, we can start solving the drug and crime problem."

JASON HRCEK, COLORADO

"My American dream is to have peaceful relations within our country as well as a healthier economy. I feel that this country has been built on having a united culture of different people who have shared a common dream.

I think that life in the 21st century will change for the better. I feel that many more Americans will realize what effect they can have if they would unite to better the nation. A change for the better can only occur if many Americans stand together."

Themes of United States History

The students whose responses you just read touched on several themes, including the promise of technology, the rights enjoyed by Americans, and the roles of women in the 21st century. As you study U.S. history, you will encounter these and other themes again and again. The Americans *focuses on nine themes, described on these pages. What do you think are the important issues raised by each theme?*

The American Dream

You live in a nation founded on dreams of freedom, opportunity, prosperity, and progress. The most enduring of these visions is the American dream—the belief held by most Americans that if they work hard, and play by the rules, then they and their children will be better off. But just what does "better off before" mean? More money in the bank? A cleaner environment? That is something you and your generation will have to decide as you dream your own dreams.

NOW THEN What American dreams do you observe people today pursuing?

Science and Technology

Americans have always had a deep respect for the power of science and technology to improve life. In the past two centuries, new inventions, new technologies, and scientific breakthroughs have transformed the United States—and continue to appear at a dizzying pace. Which ones will change your life? You can be sure that some will, and in ways that no one can yet predict.

NOW THEN How do you think science and technology will change American life in the 21st century?

Economic Opportunity

America has always been a land of economic opportunity. Blessed with fertile land and abundant resources, this has been a country where anyone who has worked hard has had a chance to prosper. Indeed, American history is full of heartening "rags-to-riches" success stories. Just as inspiring are the heroic struggles of women and minorities who fought long and hard to improve their economic prospects. As your generation enters the workforce, you and your friends will have the opportunity to write your own success stories.

NOW THEN What do you think are the most exciting economic opportunities for Americans today?

Women in America

Half of all Americans are women. But only recently have their contributions and concerns found their way into history books. American women have helped shape the social and political history of every era. In their private roles as wives and mothers, they have strengthened families and raised America's children. In their more public roles as workers, reformers, and crusaders for equal rights, they have attacked the nation's worst social ills and challenged barriers to women's full participation in American life. Look around you and you will see how much women have accomplished in their fight for equality.

NOW THEN What do you think is the most important goal for American women today?

Cultural Diversity

E Pluribus Unum—Out of Many, One. Pick up a quarter or a dollar bill and you'll find this Latin motto on the Great Seal of the United States. From first settlement, this has been a land of many peoples, cultures, and faiths. This mixing of ethnic, racial, and religious groups has produced a rich and uniquely American culture. It has also led to competition and conflict. Today, the United States is more diverse than ever. The nation's motto still remains, *E Pluribus Unum*.

NOW THEN How do you think America today is enriched by its diversity?

Immigration and Migration

Restlessness seems to be part of the national character of Americans. This country was first settled by and has remained a magnet for immigrants. One out of every eleven people living in the United States today was born in another country. Moreover, every year one out of every six Americans moves to a new address.

NOW THEN Why do you think people continue to have the dream of immigrating to the United States?

Constitutional Concerns

The United States Constitution consists of the basic principles on which the government of the United States was established in 1789. Since then, these principles have been tested and stretched and argued about endlessly. Some 10,000 amendments have been proposed to the Constitution in efforts to improve it. Remarkably, only 27 have been adopted. Constitutional amendments continue to be proposed, so stay tuned. The work of constitution making is far from over!

NOW THEN If you could add one amendment to the Constitution, what would it be? Why?

Expanding Democracy

When Americans first began their experiment with democracy, only white men with property could vote or hold office. Over the past two centuries, women, African Americans, and other groups have fought for and won the right to vote and to participate in government. Today the challenge facing American democracy is getting people to exercise the right to vote. In 1996, only 49 percent of eligible voters cast ballots in the presidential election.

NOW THEN What do you think can be done to bring more Americans into the democratic process?

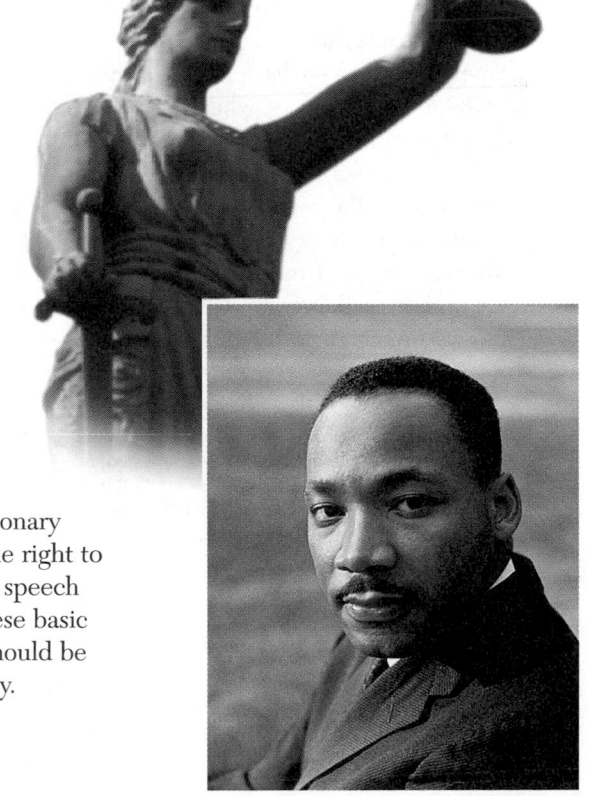

Civil Rights

The American system of government is based on a simple but revolutionary idea: Every citizen has certain rights and liberties. Among them are the right to participate in government and to exercise such liberties as freedom of speech and worship. The most important duty of government is to protect these basic civil rights. Deciding who should have what rights, how these rights should be exercised, and how to protect a person's civil rights is anything but easy. Defining and protecting our civil rights is not likely to get any easier.

NOW THEN What issue of civil rights do you think is most critical in the United States today?

xxxiii

Themes of Geography

History shapes people, and people shape history. Just as surely, the land—where it lies and what it looks like—shapes the people, and the people in turn shape the land. This shaping process is the subject matter of geography. Paying attention to the following themes of geography can help you recognize when geographic forces are at work in the story of the United States.

These themes can also help you understand how you and people you know have been affected by your geographic surroundings.

Location

Location is fundamental. Geographers speak of absolute location—the latitude and longitude of an area—and of relative location—where an area is in relation to another area.

In absolute terms, the city of San Francisco lies at 37.8° north latitude and 122.5° west longitude. This information allows you to pinpoint San Francisco on a map. In relative terms, San Francisco lies at the western edge of the huge landmass of North America and looks out across the vast Pacific Ocean. This information helps explain San Francisco's history as an area where people and ideas have come together.

NOW THEN Locate your city or town on both a political and a physical map. How has location influenced the history of your city or town?

Place

Place, in geography, refers to what an area looks like, in both physical and human terms. The physical setting of an area—its landforms, soil, climate, and resources—are aspects of place. So are the numbers and cultures of the people who inhabit an area.

San Francisco's site at the tip of a hilly peninsula provides a natural harbor that has made the city an important international port. It is connected to the American River—where gold was discovered in 1848—by other rivers, which made it a boom town in the mid-1800s. Its position along a major fault line has subjected it to periodic earthquakes, the most disastrous in 1906.

During its history, San Francisco has attracted people from within North America as well as from Europe, Asia, and various Pacific islands, making it one of the most diverse cities in the United States.

NOW THEN What is unique about the place where you live and the people who live there? What past events contributed to its uniqueness?

San Francisco Bay Area

San Rafael

Berkeley

Sausalito
Alcatraz

37° 50' N

Golden Gate Bridge

Oakland

PACIFIC OCEAN

San Francisco

San Francisco-Oakland Bay Bridge

N
0   6 Miles

0   12 Kilometers

South San Francisco

San Francisco Bay

122° 35' W

San Mateo

Belmont

Metropolitan areas

City of San Francisco

xxxiv

Region

Geographers use the idea of region as a way of summarizing the characteristics that different places have in common. Regions can be small or large, and a place can belong to more than one region.

As a part of the Pacific Coast region of the United States, San Francisco shares with cities like Seattle, Washington, and Portland, Oregon, a mild, rainy climate and an economic interest in international shipping. As a part of California, San Francisco shares concerns about the economic and environmental health of the state as a whole.

NOW THEN To what region or regions does your area belong? How have the characteristics and concerns of your region changed over the last generation?

Movement

One place or region can influence another even when the distance between them is great. Geographers seek evidence of this influence in the movement of people, raw materials, manufactured goods, and even ideas. Over time, patterns of movement can provide clues to an area's past or hints about its future.

San Francisco has been the site of many important movements of people and cultures. It has been a port of entry for immigrants, many of them Asian. It also lies along the path that Spanish missionaries trod in their quest to convert California's native peoples. The movements of these and other groups into San Francisco have helped to make the area what it is today.

NOW THEN When and by what groups was your area settled? What trends in movement can you see today that may shape the future of your area?

Human/Environment Interaction

Wherever people live, especially in large numbers, they affect the environment in the way they modify—and add to—their natural surroundings. They build shelters to defend against extremes of climate. They clear trees to create farmland. They turn the earth inside out to extract its resources.

People in the San Francisco Bay area have built bridges in order to move more easily from one point to another. And, over time, people have modified the bay itself, reducing its area by about one-third as they filled in tidelands for development.

NOW THEN How have people in your area modified their surroundings? What consequences might these modifications have for your area in the future?

xxxv

How to Use This Book

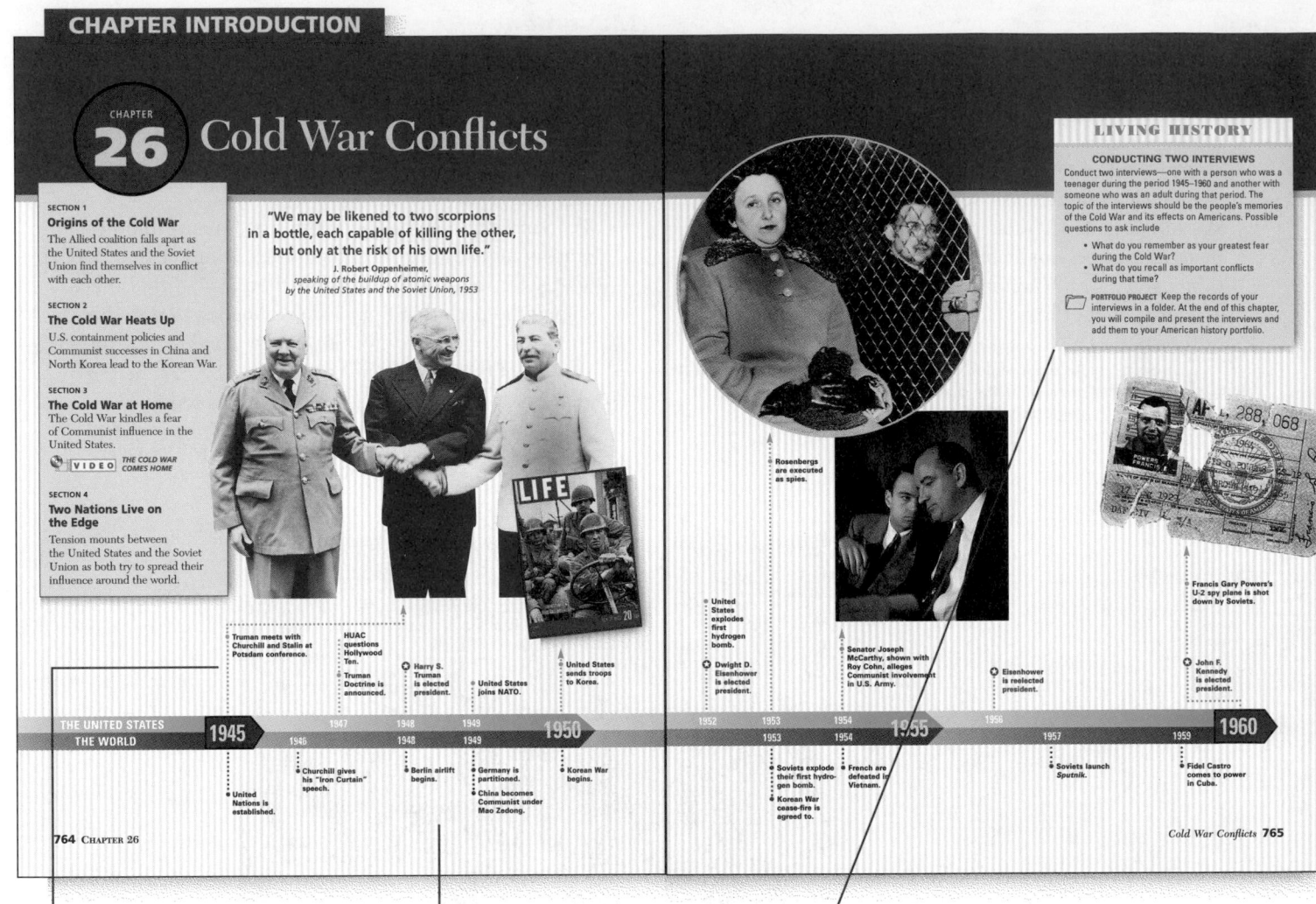

CHAPTER 26 Cold War Conflicts

SECTION 1
Origins of the Cold War
The Allied coalition falls apart as the United States and the Soviet Union find themselves in conflict with each other.

SECTION 2
The Cold War Heats Up
U.S. containment policies and Communist successes in China and North Korea lead to the Korean War.

SECTION 3
The Cold War at Home
The Cold War kindles a fear of Communist influence in the United States.

VIDEO THE COLD WAR COMES HOME

SECTION 4
Two Nations Live on the Edge
Tension mounts between the United States and the Soviet Union as both try to spread their influence around the world.

"We may be likened to two scorpions in a bottle, each capable of killing the other, but only at the risk of his own life."

J. Robert Oppenheimer, *speaking of the buildup of atomic weapons by the United States and the Soviet Union, 1953*

LIVING HISTORY

CONDUCTING TWO INTERVIEWS
Conduct two interviews—one with a person who was a teenager during the period 1945–1960 and another with someone who was an adult during that period. The topic of the interviews should be the people's memories of the Cold War and its effects on Americans. Possible questions to ask include
• What do you remember as your greatest fear during the Cold War?
• What do you recall as important conflicts during that time?

PORTFOLIO PROJECT Keep the records of your interviews in a folder. At the end of this chapter, you will compile and present the interviews and add them to your American history portfolio.

Timeline

THE UNITED STATES / THE WORLD

United States events:
- Truman meets with Churchill and Stalin at Potsdam conference.
- HUAC questions Hollywood Ten.
- Truman Doctrine is announced.
- Harry S. Truman is elected president.
- United States joins NATO.
- United States sends troops to Korea.
- United States explodes first hydrogen bomb.
- Dwight D. Eisenhower is elected president.
- Senator Joseph McCarthy, shown with Roy Cohn, alleges Communist involvement in U.S. Army.
- Eisenhower is reelected president.
- Rosenbergs are executed as spies.
- Francis Gary Powers's U-2 spy plane is shot down by Soviets.
- John F. Kennedy is elected president.

1945 — 1946 — 1947 — 1948 — 1949 — 1950 — 1952 — 1953 — 1954 — 1955 — 1956 — 1957 — 1959 — 1960

World events:
- United Nations is established.
- Churchill gives his "Iron Curtain" speech.
- Berlin airlift begins.
- Germany is partitioned.
- China becomes Communist under Mao Zedong.
- Korean War begins.
- Soviets explode their first hydrogen bomb.
- Korean War cease-fire is agreed to.
- French are defeated in Vietnam.
- Soviets launch *Sputnik*.
- Fidel Castro comes to power in Cuba.

764 CHAPTER 26

Cold War Conflicts **765**

TIME LINE Every chapter begins with an illustrated time line of the major events in the chapter. The time line is brought to life by images of people who made history during the period.

WORLD EVENTS In addition to events in the United States, the time line includes world events.

LIVING HISTORY Every chapter begins with Living History, a project in which you explore an aspect of the period that interests you. At the end of the chapter, you will finish your project and add it to your American history portfolio.

STATE-OF-THE-ART MAPS
The text features numerous maps, developed with state-of-the-art computer technology. Geography Skillbuilder questions help you draw conclusions about the relationship between geography and history.

The Skillbuilder Handbook at the back of the book helps you improve your map-reading skills.

GEOGRAPHY STRAND

Postwar Germany, 1949

- Non-Communist countries
- Communist countries
- West Germany
- East Germany

GEOGRAPHY SKILLBUILDER
LOCATION *In which part of Germany was Berlin located?*
PLACE *What effects might the division of Berlin have had on its citizens?*

xxxvi

ONE AMERICAN'S STORY Each section begins with an authentic story about a person who played a key role in or was affected by the events that will be discussed in the section.

A PERSONAL VOICE Throughout the text are many quotations and comments by people about historical events. All Personal Voices are primary sources—authentic documents from the historical period.

AMERICAN STORIES VIDEOS Integrated into the text are 15 videos, which form a series entitled *American Stories*. These 15 fascinating documentaries skillfully integrate the lives of individuals with historical events described in the textbook. The videos are available from McDougal Littell for use with *The Americans*.

THINK THROUGH HISTORY Questions in the margin help you think about historical events. The Skillbuilder Handbook helps you answer the questions.

---

❸ The Cold War at Home

TERMS & NAMES
• HUAC
• Hollywood Ten
• blacklist
• Alger Hiss
• Ethel and Julius Rosenberg
• Senator Joseph McCarthy
• McCarthyism

LEARN ABOUT the Hollywood Ten, two famous spy cases, and Senator Joseph McCarthy
TO UNDERSTAND how and why fear of communism swept the nation.

TERMS & NAMES
The key people, events, and places in the section are listed.

ONE AMERICAN'S STORY

Tony Kahn made the neighbors uncomfortable because they thought his father, Gordon Kahn, was a Communist. In 1947, Gordon Kahn had been a successful screenwriter for almost 20 years. However, when a congressional committee began to investigate Communists in Hollywood, Kahn was blacklisted—named as too dangerous to hire. Later, in 1951, he was scheduled to testify before the committee himself.

To save himself, Kahn simply had to name others as Communists, but he refused. Rather than face the congressional committee, he fled to Mexico. Not only was Kahn's career ruined, but his wife and sons suffered from his being blacklisted for the next 25 years! Tony Kahn remembers how the Cold War hurt him and his family.

A PERSONAL VOICE
The first time I was called a Communist, I was four years old. . . . I'll never forget the look in our neighbors' eyes when I walked by. I thought it was hate. I was too young to realize it was fear.
TONY KAHN, from *The Cold War Comes Home*

The members of the Kahn family were among thousands of victims of the anti-Communist hysteria that gripped this country in the late 1940s and early 1950s. At first, only those in potentially influential positions were accused of being "Reds," or Communists. However, by the end of the period that some historians call the Great Fear, no one was safe from false charges.

▶ VIDEO *THE COLD WAR COMES HOME:*
Hollywood Blacklists the Kahn Family

Tony Kahn

Fear of Communist Influence

In the early years of the Cold War, many Americans believed that there was good reason to be concerned about the security of the United States. The Soviet domination of Eastern Europe and the Communist takeover of China shocked the American public, fueling a fear that communism would spread around the world.

In addition, several factors contributed to a growing suspicion of Communist influence within the United States. At the height of World War II, about 80,000 Americans claimed membership in the Communist Party; some people feared that these Communists' first loyalty was to the Soviet Union. In 1945, federal officials discovered that two State Department workers and one naval intelligence officer had stolen classified documents and passed them to a pro-Communist magazine. In the same year, a clerk at the Soviet embassy in Ottawa, Canada, defected to the West, bringing documents showing that a spy had been giving the Soviet Union secret information about the atomic bomb.

As such incidents came to light, strongly anti-Communist Republicans began to accuse the Truman administration of being soft on communism. [...] that his critics were making too much of what one [...] munist bugaboo," but he recognized the need to

THINK THROUGH HISTORY
A. Analyzing Causes What were causes of the fear of communism in the U.S.?

Cold War Conflicts **779**

Causes and Effects of McCarthyism

CAUSES	EFFECTS
• Soviets successfully establish Communist regimes in Eastern Europe after World War II. • Soviets develop the atomic bomb more quickly than expected. • Korean War ends in a stalemate. • Republicans gain politically by accusing Truman and Democrats of being soft on communism.	• Millions of Americans are forced to take loyalty oaths and undergo loyalty investigations. • Activism by labor unions goes into decline. • Many people are hesitant to speak out on public issues for fear they will be accused of having Communist leanings. • Anticommunism continues to drive U.S. foreign policy.

SKILLBUILDER **INTERPRETING CHARTS** How did world events help lead to McCarthyism? How did McCarthyism affect the behavior of individual Americans?

I CAN'T DO THIS TO ME!

SKILLBUILDER
INTERPRETING POLITICAL CARTOONS
What does this cartoon suggest about McCarthy's downfall?

Senate investigation. McCarthy's bullying of witnesses alienated the audience and cost him public support. The Senate condemned him for improper conduct that tended "to bring the Senate into disrepute." Three years later McCarthy died a broken man, suffering from the effects of alcoholism.

OTHER ANTI-COMMUNISTS Others besides Joseph McCarthy made it their mission to root communism out of American society. By 1953, 39 states had passed laws making it illegal to advocate the violent overthrow of the government, even though such laws clearly violated the constitutional right of free speech. Across the nation, cities and towns passed similar laws.

At times, the fear of communism seemed to have no limits. In Indiana, professional wrestlers had to take a loyalty oath. In experiments run by newspapers, pedestrians on the street refused to sign petitions that quoted the Declaration of Independence because they were afraid the ideas were Communist. The government investigated union leaders, librarians, newspaper reporters, and scientists. It seemed that no profession was safe from the Red hunt. The FBI even interviewed a Washington, D.C., bootblack 70 times before deciding he could shine shoes in the Pentagon.

During this era many Americans tried so hard to root out communism that they were sometimes willing to compromise their own freedom. But even those measures did not stop the escalation of the Cold War.

SKILLBUILDER: INTERPRETING CHARTS
Numerous charts, graphs, and tables present information and ideas in a highly visual format. Every chart, graph, and table has a Skillbuilder question for thinking and discussion. The Skillbuilder Handbook helps you interpret graphs, charts, and tables.

SKILLBUILDER: INTERPRETING POLITICAL CARTOONS Throughout American history, cartoonists have used humor to make serious points. The text has numerous political cartoons, each one with a Skillbuilder question. The Skillbuilder Handbook helps you interpret political cartoons.

SECTION ASSESSMENT Four questions at the end of every section will help you study and understand the events in that section.

• **Question 1** reviews the Terms & Names.
• **Question 2** is a summarizing question, accompanied by a diagram to help you organize events.
• **Questions 3 and 4** ask you to interpret, make decisions, evaluate, and form opinions about the events in the section.

Section ❸ Assessment

1. TERMS & NAMES
Identify:
• HUAC
• Hollywood Ten
• blacklist
• Alger Hiss
• Ethel and Julius Rosenberg
• Senator Joseph McCarthy
• McCarthyism

2. SUMMARIZING Recreate the web below on your paper and fill in events that illustrate the main idea in the center.

Anti-Communist fear gripped the country.

3. MAKING DECISIONS If you had lived in this period and been accused of being a Communist, what would you have done?

THINK ABOUT
• the Hollywood Ten, who refused to answer questions
• the Rosenbergs, who pleaded the Fifth Amendment
• those who informed on others to save themselves

4. ROLE-PLAYING HISTORY Get together with three classmates, with each group member playing one of the following roles: Harry Truman, a member of HUAC, Judge Irving Kaufman, and Joseph McCarthy. As the person you have chosen, explain your motivation for opposing communism.

784 CHAPTER 26

xxxvii

How to Use This Book

CHAPTER ASSESSMENT

Every Chapter Assessment has three parts:
- Reviewing the Chapter
- Thinking Critically
- Alternative Assessment

REVIEWING THE CHAPTER This column has ten questions about the Terms & Names and ten questions about the main ideas of the chapter.

THINKING CRITICALLY This column has five or six thought-provoking questions about the most important events in the chapter. There is always a graphic organizer—a diagram in which you demonstrate your knowledge in a visual way.

ALTERNATIVE ASSESSMENT This column allows you to demonstrate your understanding of the chapter through projects and research.
- There is always a research project, with the option of using a CD-ROM.
- Fifteen of the alternative assessment projects are linked to *American Stories* videos, available with *The Americans*.
- Many of the projects involve cooperative learning, in which you work in teams.

Chapter 26 Assessment

REVIEWING THE CHAPTER

TERMS & NAMES For each term below, write a sentence explaining its significance in the 1950s and the Cold War. For each name below, explain the person's role in Cold War events.

1. containment
2. NATO
3. Mao Zedong
4. Korean War
5. McCarthyism
6. John Foster Dulles
7. brinkmanship
8. CIA
9. Nikita Khrushchev
10. U-2 incident

MAIN IDEAS

SECTION 1 (pages 766–772)

Origins of the Cold War

11. What were the goals of U.S. foreign policy during the Cold War?
12. Explain the Truman Doctrine and describe how Americans reacted to it.
13. What was the purpose of the NATO alliance?

SECTION 2 (pages 773–778)

The Cold War Heats Up

14. What global events helped to bring about U.S. involvement in Korea?
15. What issue of military strategy led to a disagreement between General Douglas MacArthur and President Truman, eventually costing MacArthur his job?
16. What goals did the United States achieve by fighting in Korea? What goals did it fail to achieve?

SECTION 3 (pages 779–784)

The Cold War at Home

17. What actions of Joseph McCarthy worsened the national hysteria about communism?
18. How did the spy case of the Rosenbergs feed anti-Communist sentiment in America?

SECTION 4 (pages 785–789)

Two Nations Live on the Edge

19. By what means did the U.S. government, including the CIA, fight the Cold War around the world?
20. What technological developments during the 1950s contributed to an arms race that would last for more than 30 years?

792 CHAPTER 26

THINKING CRITICALLY

1. **CONTAINMENT** Create a cause-and-effect diagram, similar to the one shown, for each of these events: (a) the United States' adoption of a policy of containment and (b) the beginning of the nuclear arms race between the United States and the Soviet Union.

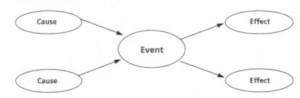

2. **CONSTITUTIONAL CONFLICT** What government actions in response to widespread anti-Communist sentiment do you think conflicted with the individual freedoms guaranteed in the Bill of Rights? Which of these actions were justified?

3. **COLD WAR CONFLICTS** Reread the quotation from J. Robert Oppenheimer on page 764. Do you agree with his assessment of the U.S.-Soviet conflict during the Cold War? Explain your opinion.

4. **GEOGRAPHY OF THE SOVIET UNION** Look carefully at the map on page 769. How did the absence of a natural barrier on the western border of the Soviet Union affect post–World War II Soviet foreign policy? Explain your answer.

5. **AMERICAN STUDIES: SCIENCE FICTION** Which of the quoted science fiction works do you think best exemplifies the concerns of the Cold War? Explain your answer.

6. **ANALYZING PRIMARY SOURCES** Read the following excerpt from a memorandum President Truman wrote in 1953, explaining his refusal to use the atomic bomb during the Korean War. Then answer the questions below.

> In 1945 I had ordered the A Bomb dropped on Japan at two places devoted almost exclusively to war production. We were at war. We were trying to end it in order to save the lives of our soldiers and sailors. . . . We stopped the war and saved thousands of casualties on both sides.
> In Korea we were fighting a police action with sixteen allied nations to support the World Organization which had set up the Republic of Korea. We had held the Chinese after defeating the North Koreans and whipping the Russian Air Force.
> I just could not make the order for a Third World War. I know I was *right*.
> **PRESIDENT TRUMAN**, from *Off the Record: The Private Papers of Harry S. Truman*

How does Truman make the difference between using the atomic bomb against Japan and using it against China? Do you agree or disagree with Truman's reasons? Why?

ALTERNATIVE ASSESSMENT

1. **REPORTING WORLD NEWS**
What was happening around the world while the United States was concentrating on the Cold War?

Prepare a script and a plan for visuals for a television news segment that summarizes one international news event that happened during the 1950s.

CD-ROM To identify and research the international event that interests you, use the CD-ROM *Our Times* and other resources.

- Use a storyboard format to plan your visuals—sketches of people and events you would show, perhaps graphs or maps—and figure out what the narrator will say as each picture is shown.
- In your script, narrate the highlights of the event and analyze its effect on U.S. foreign-policy decisions.

2. **LEARNING FROM MEDIA**
VIDEO View the McDougal Littell video for Chapter 26, *The Cold War Comes Home*. Discuss the following questions with a small group of classmates and then do the cooperative learning activity.

- How was Gordon Kahn caught up in events beyond his control?
- What alternatives did Gordon Kahn have? Do you think he chose the right path? Explain your opinion.
- From whose point of view is the story told? How does that viewpoint affect your opinion of the events?
- Gordon Kahn is portrayed as a victim in the video. How could he have been portrayed differently?
- Cooperative Learning With your group, create a report card to evaluate the video. Decide what criteria you will use to evaluate it, and come up with a grade for each criterion. Share and defend your final report card.

3. **PORTFOLIO PROJECT**
Use the Living History activity to expand your portfolio.

LIVING HISTORY

PRESENTING YOUR INTERVIEWS
Write and present to your class your two interviews with people who have memories of the Cold War era.

- Review the interviews. Has your study of the Cold War suggested any other questions that you would like to ask? If so, try to contact your interviewees again to ask the questions.
- Make a written transcript of each complete interview.
- Decide what you will present from each interview. If you omit some parts, use ellipses (. . .) to mark your omissions.
- Write an introduction for each interview. The introduction should include the interviewee's name and a description of what he or she was doing during the Cold War era.

Save your interviews, along with the tapes and transcripts you used in preparing them, in your American history portfolio.

Cold War Conflicts 793

Bridge to Chapter 27

Review Chapter 26

ORIGINS OF THE COLD WAR After World War II ended, the differing global economic and political goals of the United States and the Soviet Union resulted in a nonmilitary conflict known as the Cold War. The United States provided aid to European nations through the Marshall Plan and joined the defensive alliance known as the North Atlantic Treaty Organization (NATO).

THE COLD WAR HEATS UP In China the Communists defeated the Nationalists in 1949. Starting in 1950, the United States and other UN countries fought a war in Korea to keep South Korea from being overrun by North Korean Communists. The fighting ended in 1953, with Korea still divided into two countries.

THE COLD WAR AT HOME Anti-Communist sentiment gripped the United States in the late 1940s and the 1950s, causing the government to investigate the loyalty of millions of its employees. Alger Hiss was sent to prison, and Ethel and Julius Rosenberg were executed as Communist spies. Senator Joseph McCarthy accused hundreds of people of being Communists, and his unfounded accusations ruined many lives.

TWO NATIONS LIVE ON THE EDGE Throughout the 1950s people lived in fear of nuclear destruction as the United States and the Soviet Union engaged in a nuclear arms race. The Soviet leader Nikita Khrushchev sent tanks to crush a reform movement in Hungary in 1956. The Eisenhower Doctrine warned that the United States would defend the Middle East against Communist aggression. The launching of the first Sputnik satellite in 1957 spurred a space race between the two superpowers, and the United States sent U-2 spy planes into Soviet airspace. In May 1960, the Soviets shot down a U-2 plane and convicted the pilot, Francis Gary Powers, of espionage.

Preview Chapter 27
Although the Cold War had an enormous impact on domestic affairs in the 1950s, many Americans experienced the decade as a time of prosperity rather than a time of anti-Communist fear. Popular culture celebrated the growing middle class and its suburban lifestyle, although many minorities and poor people were excluded from economic gains. You will learn about these significant developments in the next chapter.

ANALYZING PRIMARY SOURCES
The final Thinking Critically question asks you to analyze either a primary source—such as a speech or a letter—or a political cartoon.

PORTFOLIO PROJECT / LIVING HISTORY Do you remember the Living History project that you started at the beginning of the chapter? Now you will finish that project and add it to your American history portfolio.

BRIDGE TO THE NEXT CHAPTER This special review-and-preview feature thoughtfully summarizes the main ideas in the chapter and gives a sneak preview of the next chapter. The Bridge helps you connect events in U.S. history.

xxxviii

Television: Making the News

Since the 1950s, television not only has become a major vehicle for reporting the news but has increasingly helped to create it. In fact, TV networks themselves made news at the Republican National Convention in August 1996. The networks chose to limit their coverage because they thought that fuller coverage would merely constitute an extended advertisement for the party, which had already chosen its candidates. The shift away from news to "infotainment" that the networks were protesting is a sign of the fierce competition among a bewildering variety of network and cable alternatives. This "media muddle" promises to blur even further the already indistinct line between reporting the news and making it.

Robert Dole and Jack Kemp accept the presidential and vice-presidential nominations at the 1996 Republican National Convention.

NOW & THEN

This special feature updates a historical topic or issue by relating it to an event that is making news today.

Some Now & Then features are longer, like this one about television and the news. Other Now & Then features provide briefer—but equally relevant—connections between past and present.

Now & Then and other features in the book include suggestions for using the Internet.

DAILY LIFE

This two-page feature gives you a close look at everyday life, such as education, work, leisure, and family, in different eras. There is a special focus on teenagers and their connection to family and community.

1954
The power of television not only to report the news but actually to make it became apparent in 1954. In that year the Communist-hunting senator Joseph McCarthy, in U.S. Senate hearings that were televised live, accused the U.S. Army of coddling Communists. As many as 20 million Americans watched the combative senator bully witnesses and slander people who had no chance to defend themselves. McCarthy's televised antics had finally thrust him into the villain's role.

1967
By 1967, with a television set in virtually every household in America, nightly news broadcasts had become established as a powerful influence on public opinion. For example, American support for the Vietnam War plummeted as millions of viewers saw Vietnamese civilians mutilated by U.S. bombs and chemical sprays. When Walter Cronkite, a CBS newscaster, announced in 1968 the likelihood that "a bloody experience of Vietnam" would end in a stalemate, President Lyndon Johnson admitted, "If I've lost Walter, then it's over."

1974
The Watergate scandal that toppled Richard Nixon's presidency in 1974 played to a rapt TV audience. During the Senate hearings in 1973, the televised testimony of John Dean, the president's counsel, had convinced two out of three Americans that the president had committed a crime by planning or covering up the Watergate break-in. The House Judiciary Committee delayed its final deliberations on Nixon's impeachment until prime TV time, allowing the maximum number of people to watch.

INTERACT WITH HISTORY

1. **DRAWING CONCLUSIONS** In each example shown, how did television influence the outcome of events?

   SEE SKILLBUILDER HANDBOOK, PAGE 1050.

2. **TRACKING THE MEDIA** Watch an evening news show for three or four evenings. How does it cover its lead stories? With interviews? With videotapes? Read newspaper reports of the same events and compare them with the TV coverage. Which is more comprehensive?

   For more about television broadcast news, click on *Social Studies* at http://www.mcdougallittell.com

DATA FILE This column in every Daily Life feature contains fascinating facts and statistics about the historical era discussed in the chapter.

DAILY LIFE
1950 — 1960

The Emergence of the Teenager

Life after World War II brought changes in the family. For the first time, the teenage years were recognized as an important and unique developmental stage between childhood and adulthood. The booming postwar economy made it possible for teenagers to stay in school instead of working to help support their families and allowed their parents to give them generous allowances. American business, particularly the music and movie industries, rushed to court this new consumer group.

Ads, like this one for the soft drink Seven-Up, used clever slogans about the latest trends to influence teens' decisions about which products to buy.

Slumber party? Gee that's dandy!
Look your sharpest everyone!
Snappy PJ's come in handy
"Fresh up" parties sure are fun!

① THE TEEN MOVIE SCENE
Teenagers with money in their pockets often found themselves at the movies. Hollywood responded by producing films especially for them, like *The Blackboard Jungle*. This film tells the story of the confrontation between an idealistic young teacher and a gang of delinquents.

② TEENS AS CONSUMERS
Pimple creams and lipsticks were just a few of the products aimed at teenagers with money to spend. Teens even dreamed of buying their own cars. This 1953 Corvette was simply "the rage."

③ ROCKING TO A NEW BEAT
Teenagers seeking an identity found it in rock 'n' roll, a fresh form of music that delighted teenagers and enraged their parents. Elvis Presley *right*, the King of Rock 'n' Roll, helped create the new sound by blending country, gospel, and the African-American rhythm and blues sung by performers such as B. B. King *below*. The songs' insistent beat underscored themes of alienation and unhappiness in love.

"Fresh up" with Seven-Up!
THE ALL-FAMILY DRINK!
You like it ...it likes you!

DATA FILE

U.S. School Enrollments, 1950—1990

■ Elementary ■ High School ■ College

Source: Statistical Abstract of the United States 1994

Teenagers and Employment, 1950—1990

■ males 16-19 years ■ females 16-19 years

Source: Statistical Abstract of the United States 1995

Teenage Tidbits
- A *Life* magazine survey showed that, during the decade, 1950s teenagers spent $20 million on lipstick alone.
- In 1956, a total of 42,000 drive-in movie theaters—heavily frequented by teenagers—took in one-quarter of the year's total box-office receipts.
- College enrollments more than doubled between 1946 and 1960.
- Teen income in 1956—$7 billion
- Combined teen income in 1956—$7 billion
- Weekly credit payment for record player—$1.00

INTERACT WITH HISTORY

1. **DRAWING CONCLUSIONS** What were the causes of the emergence of the teenage market in the 1950s? To answer, review the entire feature, including the Data File.

   SEE SKILLBUILDER HANDBOOK, PAGE 1040.

2. **ANALYZING MOVIES TODAY** What types of movies do American movie studios make for the teenage market today? How do these movies differ from those made in the 1950s?

   For more about youth in the fifties, click on *Social Studies* at http://www.mcdougallittell.com

818 CHAPTER 27

The Postwar Boom 819

INTERACT WITH HISTORY Every special feature concludes with questions and ideas for exploring the topic in greater depth. There are frequently suggestions for exploring the topic through the Internet. The McDougal Littell website address on the World Wide Web is provided. The Skillbuilder Handbook helps you answer the questions.

xxxix

American Beginnings to 1783

Giovanni da Verrazano Discovering the Bay of New York in 1524

Lithograph done in 1868 by an unknown American artist.

Art Note
Lithographs became a common way to create art for the mass market in the 19th century. Popular subjects were views of cities and towns, portrayals of everyday life, and imagined historical scenes such as this.

▶ *Previewing the Unit*
Unit 1 covers a grand sweep of history—from the arrival of the first Americans after the last Ice Age through settlement by diverse colonists and up to the gaining of independence. Complex societies of Native Americans come into contact with peoples from Europe and Africa, resulting in a cultural mingling filled with tension and adaptation. British colonies develop, expand, and mature. Eventually the colonists' differences with Great Britain impel them toward independence.

UNIT 1

"Pleasant it looked, this newly created world."

from a WINNEBAGO POEM

CHAPTER 1
BEGINNINGS TO 1506
Three Worlds Meet

CHAPTER 2
1492–1690
The American Colonies Emerge

CHAPTER 3
1651–1765
The Colonies Come of Age

CHAPTER 4
1765–1783
The War for Independence

American Beginnings to 1783

① The water
New York offered a fine natural harbor that the Europeans could use as a locus for exploration and settlement. It and other points of first contact between Native Americans and Europeans provided the locales for the first attempts to reconcile differing views of the land.

② The ship
Giovanni da Verrazano (1480?–1527) was an Italian explorer who sailed along the coast of North America for France and entered New York Bay. Today the Verrazano-Narrows Bridge spans the strait that divides the upper and lower sections of that bay. Connecting Staten Island to Long Island, it is the longest suspension bridge in the United States.

③ The light
The artist uses light to reinforce the Eurocentric view of the painting. The dawn, associated with the European ship, sheds its light on the continent. White settlers and their descendants viewed their role as one of civilizing the New World.

Discussing the Quotation

The Winnebago poet celebrated the land. Another writer, expressing a view common to many European settlers, saw more than a beautiful land—he saw something to be owned:

"Let us . . . go to the place that God will show us to possess in peace and plenty, a land more like the Garden of Eden, which the Lord planted, than any part else of all the earth."

William Symonds, Puritan minister

FOR DISCUSSION:
- What attitudes toward the land do the poet and the minister share?
- What attitudes are different?
- How might such attitudes affect future relations between Native Americans and colonists?

Discussing the Art

This 19th-century lithograph, with its lush landscape and noble people waiting on the brink of discovery, presents a romantic vision of the past and a romanticized view of discovery.

FOR DISCUSSION:
- Why did the artist portray this scene from the Native Americans' point of view?
- Who is on the ship?
- Why have they come?
- How does the image relate to the quotation?

4 The people
Native Americans are shown in a romantic way. Shaved heads and decorative feathers were typical images of the "exotic" cultures of native peoples—even though these features were not typical of many groups. The artist seems to be perpetuating the stereotype of "noble savages."

5 The drama
The expressions and gestures of the onlookers heighten the drama of the scene. The central figure —perhaps a chief—and the woman to his right seem to show surprise. With his outstretched hand facing down, the standing man seems to deny the sight.

6 The land
The artist borrows from the romantic view of nature championed by the Hudson River school of the mid–1800s. These painters emphasized the grandeur and beauty of nature in the wild. Note the lush greenery, the jutting rock, and the refreshing stream.

PLANNING GUIDE
Three Worlds Meet

	Key Ideas	**TEACHING SUPPORT**	**ASSESSMENT**
SECTION 1 Peopling the Americas *pp. 4–7*	As early as 40,000 years ago, ancient peoples first settle in the Americas.	*In-Depth Resources: Unit 1* • Guided Reading, p. 1 • Primary Source: Hopewell Artifact, p. 9 • American Lives: The Anasazi, p. 16 **COOPERATIVE ACTIVITIES** • Investigating Early American Cultures, p. 6 (TE)	*Section 1 Assessment,* p. 7 (PE) *Self-Assessment,* p. 7 (TE) *Formal Assessment* • Section Quiz, p. 5 *Alternative Assessment Book* • Standards for Evaluating a Cooperative Activity
SECTION 2 Native American Societies Around 1492 *pp. 8–13*	North America in the 1400s is populated by hundreds of diverse groups with well-established trading and cultural patterns.	*In-Depth Resources: Unit 1* • Guided Reading, p. 2 • Skillbuilder Practice: Interpreting Maps, p. 6 • Primary Source: *from* The Iroquois Constitution, p. 10 **COOPERATIVE ACTIVITY** • Mapping Native American Cultures, p. 9 (TE) • Preparing a Time Capsule, p. 12 (TE)	*Section 2 Assessment,* p. 13 (PE) *Self-Assessment,* p. 13 (TE) *Formal Assessment* • Section Quiz, p. 6 *Alternative Assessment Book* • Standards for Evaluating a Cooperative Activity
SECTION 3 West African Societies Around 1492 *pp. 14–19*	West Africa in the 1400s is home to a variety of peoples who interacted with the wider world through trade.	*In-Depth Resources: Unit 1* • Guided Reading, p. 3 **COOPERATIVE ACTIVITIES** • Planning an Itinerary, p. 15 (TE) • Post Cards from West Africa, p. 18 (TE)	*Section 3 Assessment,* p. 19 (PE) *Self-Assessment,* p. 19 (TE) *Formal Assessment* • Section Quiz, p. 7 *Alternative Assessment Book* • Standards for Evaluating a Cooperative Activity
SECTION 4 European Societies Around 1492 *pp. 20–26*	Changes that occur in Western European societies spur the Age of Exploration in the 1400s.	*In-Depth Resources: Unit 1* • Guided Reading, p. 4 • Geography Application: The Earth's Wind Systems, p. 7 • American Lives: Queen Isabella, p. 17 **COOPERATIVE ACTIVITY** • Advertising a Joint-Stock Company, p. 24 (TE)	*Section 4 Assessment,* p. 26 (PE) *Self-Assessment,* p. 26 (TE) *Formal Assessment* • Section Quiz, p. 8 *Alternative Assessment Book* • Standards for Evaluating a Cooperative Activity
SECTION 5 Transatlantic Encounters *pp. 27–33*	Columbus's voyage in 1492 sets events in motion that permanently change Africa, Europe, the Americas, and the rest of the world.	*In-Depth Resources: Unit 1* • Guided Reading, p. 5 • Primary Source: from *The Journal of Christopher Columbus,* p. 11 • Literature: from *The Memoirs of Christopher Columbus* by Stephen Marlowe **COOPERATIVE ACTIVITY** • Writing a News Story, p. 28 (TE) • Designing Storybooks, p. 29 (TE)	*Section 5 Assessment,* p. 33 (PE) *Self-Assessment,* p. 33 (TE) *Formal Assessment* • Section Quiz, p. 9 *Alternative Assessment Book* • Standards for Evaluating a Cooperative Activity
CHAPTER RESOURCES	**Chapter Overview** Native Americans create complex societies spread throughout the continents. Peoples in Europe and Africa develop their own cultures, which they will eventually contribute to American society.	*In-Depth Resources: Unit 1* • Living History Project: Worksheet, p. 18; Standards, p. 19 *Telescoping the Times* • Chapter Summary, pp. 1–2 *Planning for Block Schedules*	*Chapter Assessment,* pp. 34–35 (PE) *Alternative Assessment,* p. 35 (PE) *Formal Assessment* • Chapter Test, forms A and B, pp. 10–15 Test Generator *Alternative Assessment Book* See explanation and forms for different kinds of alternative assessments including portfolio assessment.

INTERNET RESOURCES
• See *McDougal Littell Learning On-Line* for links to information about Toltec Mounds, the Maya and the Anasazi.

Humanities Transparencies
• H2, Ritual Cache Figure

Electronic Library of Primary Sources
• from the *Memoirs of Melchior Diaz*

INTERNET RESOURCES
• See *McDougal Littell Learning On-Line* for links to information about the Pueblo and the Iroquois.

Grolier Multimedia Encyclopedia
• Islamic Art and Architecture

Electronic Library of Primary Sources
• On the Beginnings of the Portuguese-African Slave Trade by Gomes Eannes de Azurara

INTERNET RESOURCES
• See *McDougal Littell Learning On-Line* for links to information about West Africa

Geography Transparencies
• G1, Voyages: 1271–1850

Critical Thinking Transparencies
• CT35, Inventions: 1190–1492

Grolier Multimedia Encyclopedia
• Queen Isabella I

INTERNET RESOURCES
• See *McDougal Littell Learning On-Line* for links to information about the Reformation

Humanities Transparencies
• H1, Manuscript of North America

Critical Thinking Transparencies
• CT1, Exploration of the Americas

Electronic Library of Primary Sources
• from *La Reacion* by Alvar Nunez Cabeza de Vaca

INTERNET RESOURCES
• See Interact with History p. 32 (PE) for an activity that includes the Internet as an enrichment option.

American Portfolio: A Videodisc for U.S. History, user's guide, pp. 1–10, 12, 14, 16

INTERNET RESOURCES
Learning On-Line: Social Studies
http://www.mcdougallittell.com

Block Scheduling (90 MINUTES)

Day 1
Section 1, pp. 4–7
Section Assessment, p. 7

Day 2
Section 2, pp. 8–13
Section 3, pp. 14–19
Section Assessments, pp. 13, 19

Day 3
Section 4, pp. 20–26
Section 5, pp. 27–33
Chapter Assessment, pp. 34–35

YEARLY PACING *Chapter 1 Total:* 3 days *Yearly Total:* 85 days

See *Planning for Block Schedules* for special activities and pacing strategies.

Customizing for Special Populations

Students Acquiring English

Access for Students Acquiring English
• Guided Reading for Sections 1–5 (Spanish), pp. 9–13
• Chapter Summary (Spanish), pp. 7–8
• Skillbuilder Practice: Interpreting Maps, (Spanish), p. 14
• Geography Application: The Earth's Wind Systems, (Spanish), p. 15

INTERNET RESOURCES
• See *McDougal Littell Learning On-Line* The Diverse Classroom.

Less Proficient Readers

In-Depth Resources: Unit 1
• Guided Reading for Sections 1–5, pp. 1–5
• Skillbuilder: Interpreting Maps, p. 6
• Geography Application: The Earth's Wind Systems, p. 7

Telescoping the Times
• Chapter Summary, pp. 1–2

See additional strategies at point of use in the Teacher's Edition.

Gifted and Talented Students

In-Depth Resources: Unit 1
• Primary Source: Hopewell Artifact, p. 9; *from the Iroquois Constitution,* p. 10; from *The Journal of Christopher Columbus,* p. 11
• American Lives: The Anasazi, p. 16; Queen Isabella, p. 17

See additional strategies at point of use in the Teacher's Edition.

Connections to Literature READINGS FOR STUDENTS

In-Depth Resources: Unit 1
• from *The Memoirs of Christopher Columbus: A Novel* p. 13

Enrichment Reading
• Dorris, Michael.
The Crown of Columbus.
New York: HarperCollins, 1991.
In this novel an anthropologist finds a lost diary of Columbus and embarks on a quest for the truth about the great explorer.

• Visenor, Gerlad.
The Heirs of Columbus.
Hanover, N.H.: Unitersity Press of New England, 1991.
This novel interweaves history, science, and fantasy as Native American heirs of Christopher Columbus try to claim a misrepresented heritage.

McDougal Littell *Literature Connections*

• Chinua Achebe,
Things Fall Apart (*with related readings*) *Contact with outside forces brings deep changes to a traditional community.*

McDougal Littell *The Language of Literature*
American Literature

• William Bradford,
from Of Plymouth Plantation, p. 88

• Alicia Crane Williams,
Women and Children First: The Mayflower Pilgrims, p. 96

• Olaudah Equiano,
from The Interesting Narrative of the Life of Olaudah Equiano, p. 101

America's Beginnings to 1506

▶ *Starting with the Student*
Call on students to define the word *immigrant*. Then challenge the class to a one-minute brainstorming session in which they name all the immigrant groups that settled in what is today the United States. Ask students which of these groups they think arrived first. Use this exercise as an opportunity to introduce the term "First Americans" and to discuss one of the key American history themes of this book—cultural diversity.

PREVIEWING THE CHAPTER
• Point out that the settlement of the Americas is an ongoing story, with people continuing to arrive even today.
• Refer students to the time line, pointing out the enormous range of time that will be covered in the first chapter.

MORE ABOUT . . .
Edward Countryman
A resident of Dallas, Texas, Edward Countryman is a professor of history at Southern Methodist University. He is the author of *The Americans: A Collision of Histories,* from which the opening quote is taken.

CHAPTER
1

Three Worlds Meet

SECTION 1
Peopling the Americas
As early as 40,000 years ago, ancient peoples first settle in the Americas.

SECTION 2
Native American Societies Around 1492
North America in the 1400s is populated by hundreds of diverse groups with well-established trading and cultural patterns.

SECTION 3
West African Societies Around 1492
West Africa in the 1400s is home to a variety of peoples who interacted with the wider world through trade.

SECTION 4
European Societies Around 1492
Changes that occur in Western European societies spur the Age of Exploration in the 1400s.

SECTION 5
Transatlantic Encounters
Columbus's voyage in 1492 sets events in motion that permanently change Africa, Europe, the Americas, and the rest of the world.

> "Three separate histories collided in the Western Hemisphere half a millennium ago, and American history began."
>
> Edward Countryman

Adena culture begins building large earthen mounds, such as the Great Serpent Mound, in what is now southern Ohio.

Olmec society, which created this colossal head of stone, forms in what is now southern Mexico.

THE AMERICAS
THE WORLD

1200 B.C.

800 B.C.

1000 B.C.   753 B.C.

● **Israel becomes a kingdom.**   ● **Rome is founded.**

38,000 B.C.   12,000 B.C.   3500 B.C.

● **Asian peoples begin to migrate to America across the Beringia land bridge.**

● **The land bridge disappears, ending the migration from Asia.**

● **Corn is raised as a domesticated crop in central Mexico.**

2 CHAPTER 1

THEMES IN CHAPTER 1

Immigration and Migration	*Cultural Diversity*		*Science and Technology*
Everyone in the United States has ancestors who originally came from somewhere else. All eras in U.S. history have been shaped by the movement of peoples across America in search of opportunity. See Teacher's Edition notes, pp. 5 and 30.	For thousands of years, the cultures of Europe, sub-Saharan Africa, and America developed independently and, for the most part, in isolation. Within each region, differences in environmental and historical experience generated enormous cultural diversity. Long before contact with Europe, diverse Native American societies were	in contact with one another through trade. An extensive network of forest trails and river roads brought distant peoples into contact. Eventually, European exploration led to the meeting of many diverse cultures in America. See Teacher's Edition notes, pp. 10 and 17.	New war technology, including gunpowder and the cannon, gave European monarchs the tools to forge powerful nations. New maritime technology—navigational tools and the caravel—propelled these nations to sea. See Teacher's Edition note, p. 25.

LIVING HISTORY

RESEARCHING A CULTURE

This chapter introduces a few of the many groups of people whose cultures had an impact on America. Choose one group to learn more about—a Native American society, a West African society, or a European society. Collect materials for a visual presentation of the location and culture of that people through a map and examples of artwork or artifacts of the population. Write captions to point out what you have learned about the people from what they have left behind. Then, in a report, draw conclusions about the group's culture and technological knowledge.

📁 **PORTFOLIO PROJECT** Keep your visuals and report in a folder. At the end of the chapter you will present your report and display your visuals as part of your American history portfolio.

Montezuma becomes ruler of the Aztec Empire, whose powerful warriors include the elite eagle knights represented by this life-sized ceramic figure.

Hopewell culture, which created this mica bird claw, flourishes in the Midwest.

League of the Iroquois is formed.

Christopher Columbus first reaches America.

People first settle the Hawaiian Islands.

Viking Leif Ericson reaches what is now Newfoundland.

200 300   1000

A.D. 100   622   1096   1506

1400   1440   1453   1494 1500

The prophet Muhammad founds Islam.

The Crusades begin.

Columbus dies in Spain.

Portuguese begin West African slave trade.

Johannes Gutenberg develops printing press.

Treaty of Tordesillas defines Portuguese and Spanish claims in the Western Hemisphere.

Three Worlds Meet **3**

ALTERNATIVE ASSESSMENT
LIVING HISTORY

RESEARCHING A CULTURE

Some strategies for narrowing and focusing this activity may include the following:

- Students may wish to choose a group that represents their own ancestry.
- Those choosing a Native American group to research may want to find a group from their local area. Students should remember that there are hundreds of Native American groups from which to choose.
- Students may consider the availability of visual materials as they choose a group to research.
- To generate ideas, students might use a cluster diagram that looks like this:

IN-DEPTH RESOURCES: UNIT 1 See worksheet and standards for evaluation, pp. 18, 19.

RECOMMENDED RESOURCES

Books for the Teacher

Davidson, Basil. *The Lost Cities of Africa.* Boston: Little, 1987.

Jennings, Francis. *The Founders of America.* New York: Norton, 1993. Native Americans.

Tuchman, Barbara. *A Distant Mirror.* New York: Knopf, 1978. Riveting account of medieval Europe.

Books for the Student

Champagne, Duane. *Native Americans.* Detroit: Visible Ink, 1994. Many tribes.

The First Americans. Alexandria, Va.: Time-Life, 1992.

Fuentes, Carlos. *The Buried Mirror.* Boston: Houghton, 1992. Illustrated essay on Spain's influence in the New World.

Videos

500 Nations. Warner Home Video, 1995. An 8-part documentary series on the Indians of North America. Also available in CD-ROM.

Great Explorers. National Geographic, 1978. Filmstrip. Columbus, Magellan, Drake, Cook.

Maya. Invision Communications, 1993. History of the Maya.

Software

Columbus: Day by Day. CD-ROM. Educational Software Institute, 800-955-5570.

History and Culture of Africa. CD-ROM. Educational Software Institute, 800-955-5570.

Imperialism. CD-ROM. Educational Software Institute, 800-955-5570.

The Native Americans. CD-ROM. Philips Media Software, 800-883-3767.

Teacher's Edition 3

OBJECTIVES

① To explain how ancient peoples arrived in America and settled there.

② To describe the diverse cultures that developed in North and South America.

SKILLBUILDER

• Understanding geography: region, place, p. 7

CRITICAL THINKING

• Synthesizing, p. 5
• Recognizing effects, p. 5
• Summarizing, pp. 6, 7
• Applying, p. 7
• Evaluating, p. 7

FOCUS & MOTIVATE

▶ **Starting with the Student**
Help students consider the "push-pull" factors involved in migration by asking these questions.

• What are some of the geographic features of the area in which students live?

• Suppose students moved to another state. What motivations might they have for migrating?

• For what reasons do people migrate from one region to another?

OBJECTIVE
① **INSTRUCT**

Ancient Peoples Come to the Americas

▶ **Discussing Key Ideas**
• Exactly when and how the first peoples came to America is not known.

• Hunters may have crossed a land bridge 40,000 years ago.

• Cultures changed with the introduction of agriculture.

IN-DEPTH RESOURCES: UNIT 1
Guided Reading, p. 1

ACCESS FOR STUDENTS ACQUIRING ENGLISH
Guided Reading (Spanish), p. 9

TERMS & NAMES
• Olmec
• Maya
• Aztec
• Inca
• Hohokam
• Anasazi
• Adena
• Hopewell
• Mississippian

① Peopling the Americas

LEARN ABOUT the ancient peoples who first settled in the Americas
TO UNDERSTAND how diverse cultures developed as people adapted their ways of life to the varied landscape of the Americas.

ONE AMERICAN'S STORY

Thomas Canby took a trip 40,000 years into the past. Canby, a writer with *National Geographic* magazine, spent a year with archaeologists as they searched ancient burial sites around the Western Hemisphere to learn more about the earliest Americans and their world. The fragile skeletons and artifacts uncovered by the archaeologists painted for Canby a stunning picture of that time.

A PERSONAL VOICE
What a wild world it was! To see it properly, we must board a time machine and travel back into the Ice Age. The northern half of North America has vanished, buried beneath ice sheets two miles thick. Stretching south to Kentucky, they buckle earth's crust with their weight. . . . Animals grow oversize. . . . Elephant-eating jaguars stand as tall as lions, beavers grow as big as bears, South American sloths as tall as giraffes. With arctic cold pushing so far southward, walrus bask on Virginia beaches, and musk-oxen graze from Maryland to California.

THOMAS CANBY, "The Search for the First Americans," *National Geographic,* September 1979

Thomas Canby

Through the work of archaeologists, and the words of writers such as Canby, this world comes alive, and Americans today are able to see what it might have been like to live among the first Americans. In this chapter, you will learn about three complex societies that intersected in North America in the late 1400s: the European, the West African, and the Native American. There are several reasons to begin an American history book this way.

First, the United States is a nation of immigrants, and this pattern of immigration has been present since the very dawn of American history. Second, in the last twenty years, historians have placed much greater emphasis on the interaction of European, West African, and Native American cultures in shaping the culture of the United States. Finally, studying how European, West African, and Native Americans came into contact starting in the 1400s helps to understand some of the challenges that face the United States today.

It is with the ancient peoples of the Americas that the story of America truly begins.

Ancient Peoples Come to the Americas

No one knows for sure when the first Americans arrived, but it may have been as long as 40,000 years ago. Whenever they came, it was at a time when the glaciers of the last Ice Age had locked up huge amounts of the earth's water, lowering sea levels and creating a land bridge between Asia and Alaska across what is now the Bering Strait. Ancient trailblazers trekked across the frozen strip called Beringia into North America, where they hunted for food. Much later, their descendants developed agriculture, which allowed them to settle the land.

HUNTING AND GATHERING It is not known whether these ancient explorers used the Arctic land corridor as their sole route into the Americas. Experts suspect that most came by foot, but some groups may have edged down the Pacific coast in boats fashioned from the bones and hides of animals—boats that are much like the kayaks used by modern-day Inuit.

What appears more certain, from the discovery of chiseled spearheads and charred bones at ancient sites, is that the earliest Americans lived as big-game

Hunters roaming over 10,000 years ago in what is now southern Arizona used this large spear point to kill a woolly mammoth.

4 CHAPTER 1

---

hunters. Their most challenging and rewarding prey was the woolly mammoth. Weighing more than a ton, this animal provided food, clothing, and bones for making shelters and tools.

As the Ice Age ended, around 12,000 to 10,000 years ago, this hunting way of life also ended. Temperatures warmed, glaciers melted, and sea levels once again rose. Travel to the Americas by foot ceased as the ancient land bridge disappeared below the Bering Sea.

At different times in different places, people gradually switched to hunting smaller game and gathering what the earth offered. They fashioned baskets to collect nuts, wild rice, chokecherries, gooseberries, and currants. They invented snares—and later, bows and arrows—to hunt small game such as jackrabbits and deer. They wove nets to fish the streams and lakes.

While many ancient groups established settlements in North America, others continued south into present-day Mexico and South America. Wherever they roamed—from the parched deserts of what is now Arizona to the steamy jungles of Central America—the first Americans carved out unique ways of life that were adapted to the variety of environments they inhabited.

THE DEVELOPMENT OF AGRICULTURE Between 10,000 and 5,000 years ago, a revolution quietly took place in what is now central Mexico. There, people of the Americas began to raise plants as food. Some archaeologists believe that maize (corn) was the first plant that ancient Americans domesticated, or adapted and raised for human use. Other plants followed—gourds, pumpkins, peppers, beans, and more. Eventually, the techniques of agriculture spread throughout the Americas as people in each region began to produce their food from the land.

The rise of agriculture brought tremendous changes to the Americas. Agriculture made it possible for people to remain in one place. It also enabled them to accumulate and store surplus food. As their surplus increased, people had the time to develop skills and more complex ideas about the world. From this agricultural base rose larger, more stable societies and increasingly complex cultures.

Complex Societies Flourish in the Americas

Around 3,000 years ago, the first Americans began to form larger communities and build flourishing civilizations. A closer look at the more prominent of these societies in both North and South America offers a glimpse of the diversity and complexity of the early American world.

Today, Alaska and Siberia are separated by the Bering Strait, a strip of sea only 56 miles wide. During the last Ice Age, glaciers moved south from the North Pole, which drew water from the Bering Sea and exposed more land. This formed the Beringia land bridge, over which the earliest Americans probably migrated from Asia.

ASIA

Beringia Land Bridge

NORTH AMERICA

Siberia

Alaska

(Bering Strait)

A. Answer They first lived as big-game hunters, then gradually shifted to hunting and gathering.

THINK THROUGH HISTORY
A. Synthesizing What were the means of survival of the earliest peoples of the Americas?

B. Answer Made it possible for people to stay in one place, accumulate and store food, and build larger, more stable societies and complex cultures.

THINK THROUGH HISTORY
B. Recognizing Effects What were the effects of agriculture on the hunting and gathering peoples of the Americas?

HISTORY FROM VISUALS
Beringia Land Bridge

Reading the Map Have students identify the direction of migration. Ask them to name the continents connected by the Beringia Land Bridge.

Extension Turn to the world map on p. 1060 in this book. What body of water covers the land bridge today? How far apart are the closest tips of Alaska and Siberia?

OBJECTIVE
② INSTRUCT

Complex Societies Flourish in the Americas

▶ **Starting with the Student** As students read about the many different cultures in the Americas, have them create a chart to fill in as they read this chapter. Their charts should list each cultural group and its special characteristics.

Culture	Descriptions

▶ **Discussing Key Ideas**
• The first empires of the Americas developed in what is now southern Mexico.
• The cultural achievements in the Americas rivaled those of ancient cultures elsewhere in the world.

TEACHING OPTIONS

Exploring Themes

Immigration and Migration Discuss with students the meaning of the words *immigration* and *migration*. *(Immigration is the act of moving to a region of which one is not a native. Migration is the act of moving from one area or region to another.)* Discuss the "push-pull" factors that have always compelled people to immigrate and migrate. *These factors include the need for food, the need for adventure, the wish to escape from or be united with family members, and the need for economic and employment opportunities. While many immigrants sought religious and political freedom, others suffered the complete loss of freedom through enslavement.*

Teaching Less Proficient Readers

Clarifying Ideas Before reading Section 1, pages 4–7, have less proficient readers apply the five steps of the SQ3R study method:

1. **Survey** Skim paragraphs and topic headings and look over the two maps and the time lines.
2. **Question** Jot down any questions about the early peoples of the Americas and how they lived.
3. **Read** Read pages 4–7, looking for answers to the questions.
4. **Recite** Discuss and record the answers found.
5. **Review** Review the information, checking for answers to any questions that remain.

EMPIRES OF MIDDLE AND SOUTH AMERICA Archaeologists believe the first empire of the Americas emerged as early as 1200 B.C. in what is now southern Mexico. There the **Olmec** peoples created a thriving civilization in the humid rain forest along the coast of the Gulf of Mexico. Other civilizations influenced by the Olmec appeared in the wake of their mysterious collapse around 400 B.C. They included the **Maya,** who built a dynamic culture in Guatemala and the Yucatan Peninsula between A.D. 250 and 900, and the ancestors of the Mexica peoples, known today as the **Aztec,** who swept into the Valley of Mexico in the 1200s.

The mainland of South America had its accomplished societies as well. The most prominent of these empire builders were the **Inca,** who around A.D. 1400 rose from the ruins of earlier societies to create a glittering empire that stretched nearly 2,500 miles along the mountainous western coast of South America.

All of these empires boasted achievements that rivaled ancient cultures elsewhere in the world. All possessed great skills at mining and working precious metals, such as gold and silver. All built great cities or ceremonial centers with huge palaces, temple-topped pyramids, and central plazas. To record their histories, some of the later groups invented some form of glyphic writing— using symbols or images to express words or ideas.

HISTORICAL SPOTLIGHT

THE "OTHER" PYRAMIDS

The stone pyramids of Egypt, which were used as elaborate tombs for Egyptian kings more than 4,000 years ago, are some of today's most recognizable structures. However, they were not the only pyramids to tower over the ancient world.

On the American side of the Atlantic, the Maya built giant flat-topped pyramids whose front stairs led to a rooftop temple, where a Mayan priest performed religious ceremonies.

Farther north, in what is now the town of Cahokia, Illinois, the Mississippian peoples sculpted more than 100 massive earthen mounds, which served as tombs, temples, and foundations for elaborate homes. The largest of these mounds is Monk's Mound, which is 100 feet high and covers about 16 acres at its base—three acres more than the largest pyramid in Egypt.

ANCIENT DESERT FARMERS As early as 3,000 years ago, several North American groups, including the **Hohokam** and **Anasazi,** introduced into the arid deserts of the present-day Southwest such domesticated crops as corn, beans, and squash. By 300 B.C. to A.D. 1300, each group had grown large enough to carve out its own civilization. The Hohokam settled in the valleys of the Salt and Gila rivers in central Arizona, while the Anasazi took to the mesa tops, cliff sides, and canyon bottoms of the Four Corners region—an area where the present-day states of Utah, Colorado, Arizona, and New Mexico meet.

MOUND BUILDERS To the east of the Mississippi River, in a far-flung region extending from the Great Lakes to the Gulf of Mexico, another series of complex societies developed—the **Adena,** the **Hopewell,** and the **Mississippian.** Originating around 800 B.C. and continuing one after the other into the 1500s, these societies excelled at trade and at building massive earthen structures. Some Adena and Hopewell structures consisted of huge burial mounds filled with finely crafted copper ornaments and stone pipes. Other mounds were shaped like animals, but these effigies, or likenesses, can only be seen clearly from the air. The Mississippians, the last and most complex of the Mound Builder societies, constructed gigantic pyramids.

While peoples such as the Mississippian and Aztec still flourished at the time Christopher Columbus first reached American shores in 1492, others had long since disappeared or given way to new societies. Despite their fate, these early peoples were the ancestors of the many and diverse Native American groups that inhabited North America on the eve of its encounter with the European world.

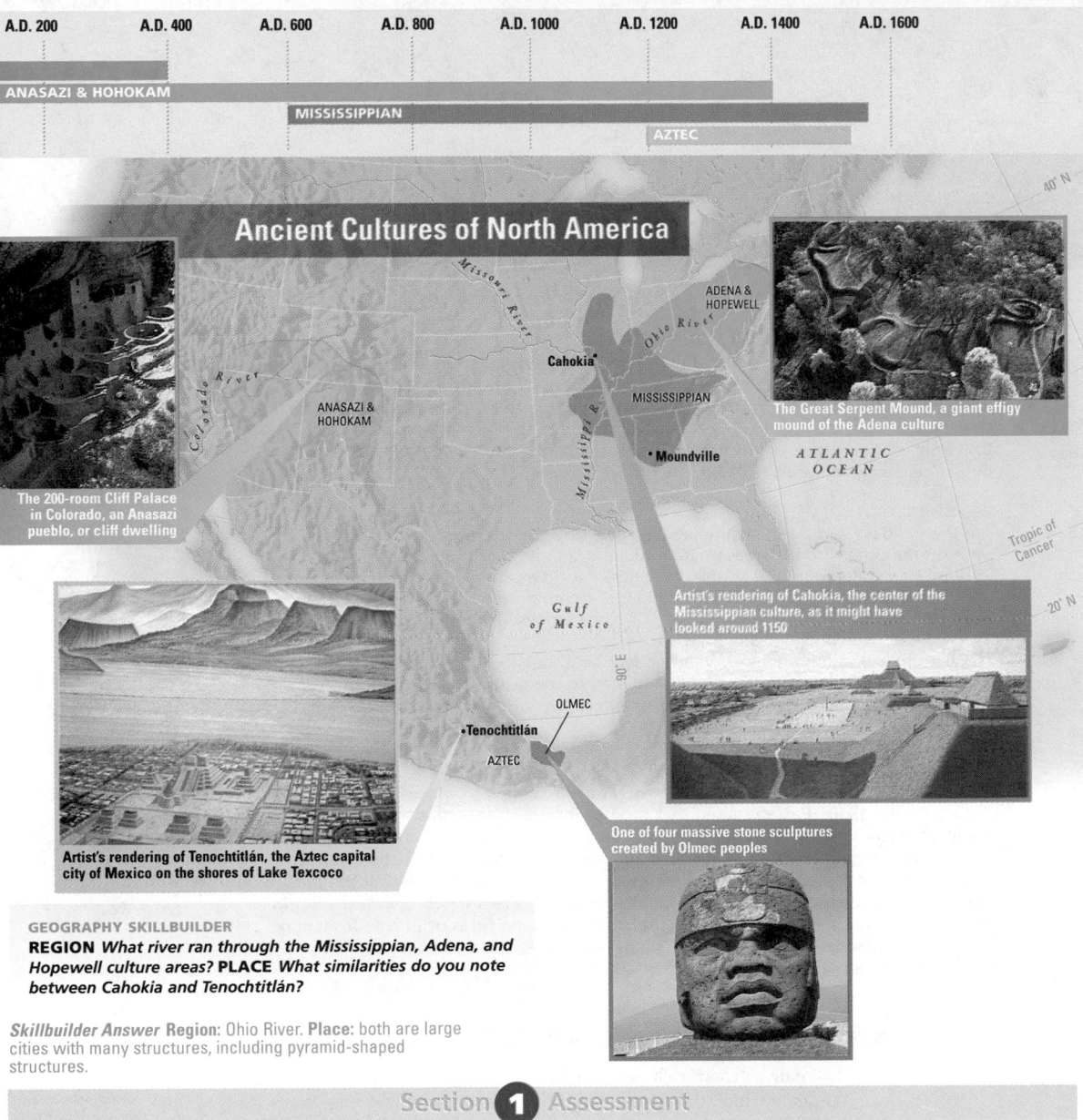

A.D. 200   A.D. 400   A.D. 600   A.D. 800   A.D. 1000   A.D. 1200   A.D. 1400   A.D. 1600

ANASAZI & HOHOKAM

MISSISSIPPIAN

AZTEC

Ancient Cultures of North America

Missouri River

ADENA & HOPEWELL

Ohio River

Cahokia

MISSISSIPPIAN

The Great Serpent Mound, a giant effigy mound of the Adena culture

Colorado River

ANASAZI & HOHOKAM

Mississippi R.

Moundville

ATLANTIC OCEAN

40° N

The 200-room Cliff Palace in Colorado, an Anasazi pueblo, or cliff dwelling

Gulf of Mexico

Tropic of Cancer

20° N

Artist's rendering of Cahokia, the center of the Mississippian culture, as it might have looked around 1150

90° E

OLMEC

Tenochtitlán

AZTEC

Artist's rendering of Tenochtitlán, the Aztec capital city of Mexico on the shores of Lake Texcoco

One of four massive stone sculptures created by Olmec peoples

GEOGRAPHY SKILLBUILDER
REGION *What river ran through the Mississippian, Adena, and Hopewell culture areas?* **PLACE** *What similarities do you note between Cahokia and Tenochtitlán?*

Skillbuilder Answer **Region:** Ohio River. **Place:** both are large cities with many structures, including pyramid-shaped structures.

Section 1 Assessment

1. TERMS & NAMES

Identify:
• Olmec
• Maya
• Aztec
• Inca
• Hohokam
• Anasazi
• Adena
• Hopewell
• Mississippian

2. SUMMARIZING In a chart like the one below, list the early civilizations of the Americas. Include the approximate dates they existed and their locations. Explain how one of the civilizations adapted to the characteristics of its location.

Civilization	Dates	Location

3. EVALUATING Which of the ancient empires that flourished in the Americas do you think was most advanced? Support your choice with details from the text.

THINK ABOUT
• ways in which the culture adapted to its environment
• the achievements of the culture
• the qualities of advanced civilizations today

4. APPLYING Evaluate the technology of the ancient cultures of the Americas. Which single accomplishment do you find most remarkable and why?

THINK ABOUT
• South American groups
• desert peoples
• Mississippian and Mayan peoples

Three Worlds Meet **7**

ANSWERS

1. TERMS AND NAMES

Olmec, p. 6

Maya, p. 6

Aztec, p. 6

Inca, p. 6

Hohokam, p. 6

Anasazi, p. 6

Adena, p. 6

Hopewell, p. 6

Mississippian, p. 6

2. SUMMARIZING

Possible Responses: Olmec: 1200 B.C. to 400 B.C., southern Mexico; Maya: A.D. 250 to 900, Guatemala and Yucatan Peninsula; Aztec: A.D. 1200s to 1500s, Valley of Mexico; Inca: emerged A.D. 1400, western coast of South America; Anasazi and Hohokam: A.D. 100 to A.D. 1400, Southwest; Adena and Hopewell: 800 B.C. to A.D. 400, east of Mississippi River; Mississippian: A.D. 600 to 1500s, east of Mississippi River.

3. EVALUATING

Possible Responses: The Inca empire, because it was a vast, glittering, organized empire; the Adena society, because it built structures with delicate copper ornaments and stone pipes; the Mississippian, because of its elaborate architectural mounds.

4. APPLYING

Possible Responses: The mining and metalworking of South American and Mexican civilizations—they crafted artifacts from gold and silver; the agricultural achievements of the desert people—they domesticated crops such as corn, beans, and squash in arid land; the giant pyramids of the Mound Builders—they built elaborate mounds that rivaled the famous pyramids of Egypt in structure and scale.

OBJECTIVES

1. To explain how the environment of North America provided for diverse societies.

2. To identify some of the practices and beliefs that Native American groups in North America had in common.

SKILLBUILDERS

• Understanding geography: region, p. 11
• Interpreting charts, p. 12

CRITICAL THINKING

• Contrasting, pp. 9, 10
• Recognizing effects, p. 11
• Comparing, p. 13
• Summarizing, p. 13
• Synthesizing, p. 13
• Clarifying, p. 13

FOCUS & MOTIVATE

▶ **Starting with the Student**
• Point out the size and diversity of the United States today. Brainstorm with students some of the practices and beliefs that hold the country together as a people and a nation.

MORE ABOUT . . .
Essie Parrish

Born in 1902, Essie Parrish learned her love of tradition from her grandmother and other elders. "I used to like to be around the old people," she recalled. "They used to talk of the old ways."

Parrish, who served as spiritual leader of the Kashaya Pomo from 1943 until her death in 1979, worked with anthropologists to ensure that these ways would be recorded. She participated in more than two dozen films and helped compile a Kashaya dictionary and a collection of tribal songs and legends. By the time Parrish died, the Kashaya Pomo numbered less than 100.

② Native American Societies Around 1492

TERMS & NAMES
• Kashaya Pomo
• Kwakiutl
• Pueblo
• Iroquois
• kinship
• division of labor

LEARN ABOUT Native American societies, trade, and culture
TO UNDERSTAND the diversity of Native American peoples and how they interacted with one another.

ONE AMERICAN'S STORY

Essie Parrish awakened the past with her words. As a storyteller and medicine woman for the Kashaya Pomo, a Native American tribe, Parrish kept alive a time when her people flourished in their homeland along the Sonoma coast of northern California. One day in 1958, she invited Robert Oswalt, an anthropologist at the University of California, to join her on a journey back to the 1540s. As Parrish began her story, the years fell away.

> **A PERSONAL VOICE**
> In the old days, before the white people came up here, there was a boat sailing on the ocean from the south. Because before that . . . [the Kashaya Pomo] had never seen a boat, they said, "Our world must be coming to an end. Couldn't we do something? This big bird floating on the ocean is from somewhere, probably from up high. . . ." [T]hey promised Our Father [a feast] saying that destruction was upon them.
> When they had done so, they watched [the ship] sail way up north and disappear. They were saying nothing had happened to them—the big bird person had sailed northward without doing anything—because of the promise of a feast. . . . So they held a feast and a big dance.
> **ESSIE PARRISH,** quoted in *Kashaya Texts*

The event so shocked the Kashaya Pomo that it became a fixed part of their oral history. By the 1950s, Parrish feared that this history might be lost as the Kashaya Pomo declined in number.

However, the history of the Kashaya Pomo, and of North America's other native peoples, did not disappear. The work of researchers like Parrish and Oswalt has produced a broad picture of the Native American world before it collided with the world of European explorers and settlers. Their picture shows the faces of people from hundreds of cultures, speaking words from many languages, and describing traditions that each generation has handed down to the next.

Dressed for a ceremony, spiritual leader Essie Parrish wears a feathered headdress and holds two bead-covered staffs.

Native Americans Live in Diverse Societies

The native groups that peopled North America were as diverse as the environments in which they lived. From the cool ocean air of the West Coast, to the scorching deserts of the Southwest, to the lush forests of the Eastern Woodlands, the North American continent provided for many different ways of life. A sampling of these regions hints at the rich flavor of the societies that populated the Native American world some 500 years ago.

CALIFORNIA Not one land, but many lands—that's how the **Kashaya Pomo** and other native peoples of what is now California saw the region in which they lived. The rugged topography was made up of dozens of valleys and plateaus. Diverse environments included a long coastline, a lush northwestern rain forest, and a parched southern desert with palm-shaded springs.

The peoples of California adapted their lives to fit these amazingly diverse physical settings. The Kashaya Pomo, who lived in marshlands along the central coast, hunted waterfowl with slingshots and nets. To the north of them, the

8 CHAPTER 1

SECTION 2 RESOURCES

PRINT RESOURCES

IN-DEPTH RESOURCES: UNIT 1
Guided Reading, p. 2
Skillbuilder Practice: Interpreting Maps, p. 6
Primary Source: *from* The Iroquois Constitution, p. 10

ACCESS FOR STUDENTS ACQUIRING ENGLISH
Guided Reading (Spanish), p. 10
Skillbuilder Practice: Interpreting Maps (Spanish), p. 14

FORMAL ASSESSMENT
Section Quiz, p. 6

ALTERNATIVE ASSESSMENT BOOK
See forms for supporting and scoring alternative activities.

TECHNOLOGY RESOURCES

HUMANITIES TRANSPARENCIES
H2, Ritual Cache Figure

CD-ROM Electronic Library of Primary Sources

VIDEO *American Portfolio: A Videodisc for U.S. History*
user's guide, pp. 1–10

INTERNET McDougal Littell Learning On-Line
http://www.mcdougallittell.com

Making Connections Across the Curriculum

Composition In "The Gettysburg Address" Lincoln relies heavily on two rhetorical devices: *antithesis*, or contrast, and *tricolon*, the division of a concept into three rhythmical units.
Here are some examples:

• Antithesis—"The brave men, *living* and *dead*, who struggled here, have consecrated it, far above our poor power to add or detract.

• Tricolon—"*government of the people, by the people, for the people . . .*"

Have students find other examples of these rhetorical devices.

Making Connections Across Time

From Orations to Sound Bites In Lincoln's time public figures typically delivered two-hour, not two-minute, speeches. Speechmaking was then considered a highly valued form of communication. Political rallies, national holidays, and civic events were occasions for local orators to show off their speaking skills. Today's audiences generally admire brevity. They prefer "sound bite" politics—an expression stemming from the short 10-second excerpts that TV news editors "bite" out of a lengthy speech or other broadcast event. Current political leaders tailor their remarks to adapt to this TV format.

Confederate ordnance (ammunition) put it differently, commenting that "the Confederacy totters to its destruction."

the Gettysburg Address

In November 1863, four months after Vicksburg and Gettysburg, the government held a ceremony to dedicate a new national cemetery on the Gettysburg battlefield. The authorities invited Edward Everett, a noted orator, to deliver the main speech at the dedication. When Lincoln accepted a belated invitation to attend, the authorities invited him to add "a few appropriate remarks."

After Everett gave a flowery two-hour oration, Lincoln spoke for a little more than two minutes. According to historian Garry Wills, Lincoln's **Gettysburg Address** "remade America." Before the speech, people said, "The United States *are*." Afterwards, they said, "The United States *is*." In other words, Lincoln's words helped the country to realize that it was not just a collection of individual states; it was a single nation.

THE GETTYSBURG ADDRESS

Fourscore and seven years ago our fathers brought forth on this continent a new nation, conceived in Liberty and dedicated to the proposition that all men are created equal. Now we are engaged in a great civil war, testing whether that nation, or any nation so conceived and so dedicated, can long endure. We are met on a great battlefield of that war. We have come to dedicate a portion of that field, as a final resting-place for those who here gave their lives that that nation might live. It is altogether fitting and proper that we should do this.

But, in a larger sense, we can not dedicate—we can not consecrate—we can not hallow—this ground. The brave men, living and dead, who struggled here, have consecrated it, far above our poor power to add or detract. The world will little note, nor long remember, what we say here, but it can never forget what they did here. It is for us the living, rather, to be dedicated here to the unfinished work which they who fought here have thus far so nobly advanced. It is rather for us to be here dedicated to the great task remaining before us—that from these honored dead we take increased devotion to that cause for which they gave the last full measure of devotion—that we here highly resolve that these dead shall not have died in vain—that this nation, under God, shall have a new birth of freedom—and that government of the people, by the people, for the people, shall not perish from the earth.

ABRAHAM LINCOLN, *The Gettysburg Address*, November 19, 1863

ANOTHER PERSPECTIVE

ON LINCOLN'S SPEECH

At the time of the Gettysburg Address, many dismissed it as a poor speech. Lincoln himself was displeased with his performance. "That speech won't scour," he said afterward. "It's a flat failure."

A writer for the London *Times* also criticized the speech. "The ceremony was rendered ludicrous by . . . the sallies of that poor President Lincoln." However, Edward Everett, the other speaker, recognized the speech's greatness. Writing to Lincoln, he said, "I should be glad if I could flatter myself that I came as near to the central idea of the occasion, in two hours, as you did in two minutes."

---

③ INSTRUCT
OBJECTIVE

The Gettysburg Address

▶ **Discussing Key Ideas**
• Lincoln delivers a brief speech to commemorate the soldiers killed at the Battle of Gettysburg.
• Lincoln's Gettysburg Address clarifies the North's reasons for fighting the war and underscores his faith in democratic values.

ANOTHER PERSPECTIVE

Have students identify the qualities of Lincoln's speech that Edward Everett most admired. Ask them if Everett would have agreed with this quotation from Shakespeare's play *Hamlet:* "Brevity is the soul of wit."

Extension Ask students to discuss why capturing Vicksburg was so difficult. Possible Responses: The city is set on a high bluff overlooking the river; Union troops had to travel far south by water through bayous.

the North's military strategy of dividing the Confederacy along the Mississippi River.

GEOGRAPHY SKILLBUILDER

MOVEMENT How many days did it take Union forces to reach Vicksburg after the victory at Jackson?

LOCATION Which river lies just to the east of Vicksburg?

Skillbuilder Answers
Movement: five days
Location: the Big Black

April 30 Grant's army crosses unopposed Mississippi.

Port Gibson

Confederate positions
Union victory
Railroad

N   10 Miles   20 Kilometers

THINK THROUGH HISTORY
A. Contrasting
What were the different environments of California that led to its diverse Native American population?

A. Answer Long coastline, rain forests, deserts, marshlands, rocky foothills, and mountains.

Yurok and Hupa searched the forests for acorns and set up fish traps in gushing mountain streams.

NORTHWEST COAST Just as California's natural plenty supported a relatively dense population, so too did the vast natural resources of the Northwest Coast. Here, teeming waterways and dense forests supplied ample food—fish, game, berries—and wood for housing, boats, and tools to sustain large communities year-round. Ever present was the sea. On a coastline that stretched from what is now southern Alaska to Oregon, peoples such as the **Kwakiutl,** Nootka, and Haida collected shellfish from the beaches and hunted the ocean for whales, sea otters, and seals.

A Kwakiutl artisan created this painted wooden animal mask to be worn in a religious ceremony.

Of all the sea creatures that filled their world, none meant more to the Northwest Coast peoples than the salmon. At various times in the warm-weather months, salmon clogged the coastal inlets as they swam up rivers to spawn, or lay eggs. Entire villages emptied as men, women, and children harvested thousands of pounds of fish. With deft strokes of a knife, they sliced the catch into thin strips and hung the red meat on racks to dry.

Peoples such as the Kwakiutl celebrated their abundance by decorating their craftwork with magnificent totems, symbols of the ancestral spirits that guided each family. They displayed these symbols representing animals or humans on masks, headgear, and the bows of boats. Kwakiutl families also portrayed their heritage on huge totem poles set in front of their cedar-plank houses. A family's totems announced its status. A complex totem pole designed by a master carver indicated wealth.

As a further display of status, leading Kwakiutl families organized potlatches, elaborately staged ceremonies in which they gave away large quantities of their possessions. A family's reputation depended upon the size of its potlatch—that is, on how much wealth it gave away. The family might spend up to 12 years planning the event. However, the Kwakiutl believed that accounts balanced out over time, since the host of one potlatch would be a guest at many future ones.

SOUTHWEST In the dry Southwest, the **Pueblo** and Pima tribes, descendants of the Hohokam and Anasazi, lived in a harsher environment than peoples of either California or the Northwest Coast. By 1300, the Pueblo, and a related tribe, the Hopi, had moved away from the cliff houses of their Anasazi ancestors. The Pueblo built new settlements near waterways such as the Rio Grande and its tributaries. However, the Hopi and the Acoma, who continued to live near the cliffs, collected rainwater in rock cisterns and carefully parceled it out to fields and kitchens.

Throughout the region, people drew upon their ancient heritage. They lived in multi-story houses made of adobe. They coaxed crops of corn, beans, melons, and squash from the sun-parched but fertile soil. In the manner of their ancestors, they built underground kivas, or ceremonial chambers, where the Pueblo men held religious ceremonies and councils.

The lyrics to the songs they sang may have resembled the ones recalled by a Hopi chief named Lolomai at the start of the 1900s. "This is the song of the men from my kiva," Lolomai explained. "It tells how in my

The Mogollon culture of New Mexico placed bowls such as these in graves to accompany the dead. These offerings were ritually "killed" at burial to release their spirits, which accounts for the large hole in the center of this bowl.

NOW & THEN

WHO OWNS THE PAST?

The silent bones of the distant past have stirred a present-day controversy. In November of 1990, Congress passed the Native American Graves Protection and Repatriation Act to regulate the excavation of Native American burial sites. A provision of the Act requires the return of skeletal remains and other artifacts to Native Americans who can prove they are culturally connected with the material.

This provision has sparked a debate. Some archaeologists claim that tribal remains should be dug up and made part of the nation's heritage. Native American groups contend the artifacts belong to their heritage and should stay either buried or with them. Other archaeologists have sided with Native Americans, saying that ancestral remains belong with their descendants and not in a museum.

OBJECTIVE
① INSTRUCT

Native Americans Live in Diverse Societies

▶ **Discussing Key Ideas**
• Native Americans adapt to and live in diverse physical settings.
• Bountiful natural environments support denser populations than areas with harsher environments.
• Native Americans alter natural environments as they develop hunting and agricultural techniques.

IN-DEPTH RESOURCES: UNIT 1
Guided Reading, p. 2

ACCESS FOR STUDENTS ACQUIRING ENGLISH
Guided Reading (Spanish), p.10

NOW & THEN
Who Owns the Past?
***Critical Thinking:
Analyzing an Issue*** Call on students to state the central issue in the debate over preserving Native American artifacts and skeletal remains. What are the two points of view on this issue? Ask students to suggest arguments in support of each point of view. Compare these arguments to identify the main areas of agreement and disagreement. What, if any, compromises can students suggest?

ELECTRONIC LIBRARY OF PRIMARY SOURCES
from the *Memoirs of Mechor Diaz*

TEACHING OPTION

Cooperative Activity: Mapping Native American Cultures

Task: Groups of students will research the four Native American culture regions and create displays for each region.

Purpose: To help students understand how Native Americans created societies to fit the environments in which they lived.

Activity: Divide the class into four groups and assign one of the regions to each group. Have students research the cultural areas and write reports and develop visual displays for them. Make sure that groups research the geographi-

cal environments of the regions and relate how the different environments produced different kinds of cultural groups. Also have students include pictures of native arts and artifacts, myths, poems, or other materials that would help bring another dimension to their reports.

📁 **Building a Portfolio:** Students should write a note indicating their contribution to the report before adding it to their portfolio.

ALTERNATIVE ASSESSMENT BOOK
Standards for Evaluating a Cooperative Activity

Standards for Evaluation
Reports should . . .

• clearly describe the environment
• show how the environment and the cultures are related
• include specific examples, such as pictures or poems

Point out to students that the figure next to the poem is a Kachina. A Kachina can be one of three things: a spirit that the Hopis believe in, a masked dancer impersonating a Kachina, or a carved likeness—a Kachina doll. Most Pueblo peoples have Kachinas, but the Hopis have the largest number—more than 250, each with its own story and purpose.

Native Americans Share Cultural Patterns

▶ *Starting with the Student*
- Have students cite examples of how trade or contact with other regions in the United States has touched their community. For example, what regional foods can they order at restaurants? What foods or products are "imported" from other states?

▶ *Discussing Key Ideas*
- Trade links Native American peoples and promotes the sharing of ideas and customs.
- Native Americans base their identity on a strong attachment to the land, which can be neither traded nor sold.
- Spiritual beliefs and social structures guide Native American life, from birth to death.

IN-DEPTH RESOURCES: UNIT 1
Primary Source: *from* The Iroquois Constitution, p. 10

---

kiva the chief and his men are praying to make the corn grow the next year for all the people."

A PERSONAL VOICE
Thus we, thus we
The night along,
With happy hearts
Wish well one another.

In the chief's kiva
They, the fathers . . .
Plant the double ear—
Plant the perfect corn-ear.
So the fields shall shine
With tassels white of perfect corn-ears.

Hither to them, hither come,
Rain that stands and cloud that rushes!

LOLOMAI, quoted in *The Indians' Book*

This Kachina doll represented the corn spirit in Hopi religious ceremonies.

EASTERN WOODLANDS The rugged mountains and deserts of the Southwest contrasted sharply with the woodlands east of the Mississippi River. Here, hardwood forests stretched from the Great Lakes and the St. Lawrence River in the north to the Gulf of Mexico in the south. Beneath the leafy canopy of the Northeast, peoples of the **Iroquois** nation hunted game animals, such as wild turkeys, deer, and bear, that hid in the tangled undergrowth. Nuts, berries, and tree fruit ripened in the summer and fall. Fish filled the region's many lakes and rivers year-round.

The tribes that lived in the Eastern Woodlands shared much in common. They built villages in forest clearings and blended agriculture with hunting and gathering. They traveled by foot over well-known trails or by canoe over inland waterways. Because of the vast supply of trees, most groups developed woodworking tools, such as stone axes, to craft everything from snowshoes to canoes.

This elegant wooden bowl, fashioned as a double-headed turtle, was made by a Niantic artisan in the area of what is now Connecticut. Everyday objects such as this were common trade items among New England groups.

The peoples of the Eastern Woodlands also differed from one another in many ways. They spoke numerous languages, practiced a variety of customs, and lived in different environments. In the Northeast, where winters could be long and harsh, people relied heavily on wild animals for clothing and food. In the warmer Southeast, groups lived mainly off the land, growing such crops as corn, squash, and beans.

THINK THROUGH HISTORY
B. *Contrasting* In what ways did food production differ among the Native American societies?
B. Answer Groups that lived along the sea coasts were able to rely on the ocean for their food; those living in the Southwest had to rely mostly on crops; groups in the Eastern Woodlands could gather food, including wild game, crops, and fish from many sources.

Native Americans Share Cultural Patterns

Although no two Native American societies were alike, they did share certain broad patterns. Common throughout many of the cultures were patterns of trade, views of land use, and certain religious beliefs and social values.

TRADING NETWORKS Trade was one of the biggest factors in making Native American peoples familiar with one another's ways. As tribes established permanent settlements, many of these settlements became known to their neighbors for specific products or skills. The Nootka of the Northwest Coast mastered whaling. The Ojibwa of the upper Great Lakes collected wild rice. The Taos of the Southwest made a golden-hued pottery. These items, and many more, were traded both locally and long distance.

While people sometimes bartered for goods to meet their basic needs, many wanted exotic objects to dazzle their eyes, heal their bodies, or satisfy a craving for some rich or foreign food. In the Eastern Woodlands, Algonquian merchants went from village to village offering hard-to-find items such as colored feathers, pieces of copper, powdered pigments, and medicinal plants. On the Nass River in British Columbia, the Tsimshian set up "grease camps" to

10 CHAPTER 1

TEACHING OPTIONS

Making Connections Across the Curriculum

Music Request a volunteer to read aloud the song lyrics recalled by Lolomai. Then read this quote by the chronicler who recorded Lolomai's words: "Hopi music is born of the environment." What aspect of the environment does this song reflect? *The parched desert, in which rain was perceived as a blessing.* Assign interested students to compose another corn-planting song. Suggest that students use the image of butterflies, a symbol of pollination among the Hopi.

Exploring Themes

Cultural Diversity Explore the link between cultural diversity and trade by pointing out the great distances that Native Americans traveled to obtain the goods and products of other peoples. Ask: How did trade familiarize culturally distinct Native Americans with one another? Have students skim through the remaining sections of the chapter. What other culturally distinct peoples were brought together as a result of trade? Based on section heads and art, what word do students think best describes the outcome of most of these contacts: *cooperation* or *conflict*?

North America in the 1400s

KWAKIUTL
NOOTKA
CREE
BLACKFOOT
CHIPPEWA
NEZ PERCÉ
OTTAWA ALGONQUIAN
CHINOOK
ARIKARA OJIBWA
MANDAN
CROW *Great Lakes*
SAUK HURON IROQUOIS
DAKOTA
(Sioux)
POTAWATOMI
WAMPANOAG
PEQUOT
NARRAGANSETT
SHOSHONE
CHEYENNE IOWA MIAMI DELAWARE
KATO
POMO ARAPAHO PAWNEE SUSQUEHANNA
(Kashaya)
PACIFIC KANSAS POWHATAN
OCEAN PAIUTE NAVAJO KIOWA
SHAWNEE TUSCARORA
CHUMASH HOPI ZUNI APACHE OSAGE
PIMA PUEBLO CHEROKEE
TAOS *ATLANTIC* 30° N
COMANCHE CHICKASAW *OCEAN*
CHOCTAW
APACHE CREEK
SEMINOLE

Native American Cultures
- Subarctic
- Northwest Coast
- California
- Plateau
- Plains
- Eastern Woodlands
- Southeastern
- Southwest
- Great Basin
- Mesoamerican
- Caribbean
- — Major trade routes

HUICHOL
Gulf
of Mexico Tropic of Cancer
TAINO 20° N
Caribbean Sea
0   500 Miles
0   1000 Kilometers AZTEC MAYA
HUICHOL

Skillbuilder
Answer
Wampanoag,
Pequot,
Narragansett,
Delaware,
Powhatan,
Susquehanna,
Iroquois,
Algonquian,
Ottawa, Huron,
Shawnee, Miami,
Potawatomi,
Sauk, Ojibwa,
Chippewa

C. Answer It
allowed the
different groups
to interact with
one another and
enabled them to
exchange foods
and goods.
THINK THROUGH HISTORY
C. Recognizing
Effects In what
ways did trade link
Native Americans?

swap oil boiled from the rotting bodies of tiny candlefish. The oil could be smelled ten miles downwind, but the Haida and Tlingit prized the grease as an ingredient for sauce and gravy. To get it, they gave the Tsimshian copper, blankets, canoes, and more.

Traveling merchants and trading centers could be found all over North America, especially at points where two cultures came together. On the western edge of the Midwest plains, where the nomadic tribes of the plains roamed in search of food, the Taos slipped through a pass in the Sangre de Cristo Mountains to set up trade fairs. They exchanged their pottery, crops, and cotton blankets for eagle feathers, buffalo hides, or shells from the Gulf Coast. Along the Columbia River in the Northwest, the Chinook set up a thriving marketplace where peoples from east and west of the Rocky Mountains spread out trade goods from their local environments.

Not all business involved face-to-face exchanges. Traders received and passed along items from far-off places they had never even seen. Through the use of intermediaries, goods could travel hundreds and sometimes thousands of miles from their original source. So extensive was the network of forest trails and river roads that an English sailor named David Ingram claimed in 1568 to have walked along Native American trade routes all the way from Mexico to the Atlantic Coast.

LAND USE Native Americans traded many things, but land was not one of them. They looked upon the land as the source of life, not as a commodity to be sold or bartered. "We cannot sell the lives of men and animals," said one Blackfoot chief in the 1800s, "therefore we

HISTORICAL SPOTLIGHT

CROP PROTECTORS

The Native Americans did not have the luxury of modern-day pesticides to keep hungry insects from devouring their crops. So they enlisted the help of some birds.

The peoples of the Southeast Woodlands had discovered that purple martins, which loved eating insects, also enjoyed living in the tribes' birdhouses made from dried fruit skins. The farmers staked the birdhouses around their corn crops, and the small, aggressive birds did the rest. Aside from dining on large numbers of insects, they also fought off crows and blackbirds, two of the biggest corn-eaters in the forest.

Three Worlds Meet **11**

The Power of Dreams

Native Americans throughout the Americas believed that spirits spoke to them in dreams and visions. One widespread vision preserved in the oral histories of Native Americans across the continents involved the coming of light-skinned strangers. A few, such as the Aztec, believed the strangers were gods. Many others saw them as destroyers. Recalled one Wintu woman at the turn of the century, "My grandpa, before white people came, had a dream. . . . My grandpa say: 'White Rabbit'—he mean white people—'gonta devour our grass, our seed, our living. We won't have nothing.'"

HUMANITIES TRANSPARENCIES
H2, Ritual Cache Figure

HISTORY FROM VISUALS

Native American Village Life

Reading the Diagram Ask students to notice that the drawing is a primary source, an eyewitness or firsthand account of history, because it was drawn by a colonist who observed the Secotan. The numbers and key have been added to help students gain an understanding of Secotan village life.

Extension Have students work in pairs to find evidence in the drawing that shows how Native Americans lived off the land, using the natural resources to provide for their daily needs. Do students think that the drawing supports the information in the text? Why or why not?

cannot sell this land." This view of the earth would lead to many clashes with the arriving Europeans, who believed that land could be bought and sold.

Native Americans altered the land as little as possible, disturbing it for only the most important activities such as food gathering or farming. A woman shaman, or priestess, from the Wintu of California expressed this age-old respect for the land as she spoke to anthropologist Dorothy Lee.

A PERSONAL VOICE

When we dig roots, we make little holes. When we build houses, we make little holes. . . . We shake down acorns and pine nuts. We don't chop down the trees. We use only dead wood [for fires]. . . . But the white people plow up the ground, pull down the trees, [and the] tree says, "Don't. I am sore. Don't hurt me."

WINTU WOMAN, quoted in *Freedom and Culture*

RELIGIOUS BELIEFS Nearly all Native Americans thought of the natural world as filled with spiritual presences. Past generations remained alive for them as guides in the present. All objects—both living and non-living—possessed a voice that might be heard if one listened closely. "I hear what the ground says," remarked Young Chief of the Cayuses in 1858. "The ground says, 'It is the Great Spirit that placed me here.' The Great Spirit tells me to take care of the Indians."

In this spiritually rich world, some cultures had one Supreme Being. Young Chief used the name "Great Spirit." Other groups used names such as "Great Mystery," "the Creative Power," or "the Creator." In general, Native Americans believed the spirits gave them rituals and customs to guide their lives. If humans followed these practices, they lived in peace and prosperity. If they did not, they lived in sorrow and poverty.

Native American Village Life

John White, one of the first English colonists to arrive in North America, made several drawings of Native American life in the Chesapeake region in 1585. This engraving was copied from White's original drawing by Theodor de Bry and published in 1590. The image shows the village life of the Secotan people, who lived near Roanoke Island, North Carolina.

1 Agriculture
A Secotan guards the ripened corn crop to keep away hungry birds and animals. A tobacco field appears to the left of this field, and other corn fields and a pumpkin patch appear below it.

2 Hunting
Warriors hunt for deer.

3 The Home
Huts, whose sides can be rolled up for ventilation, are woven from thick plant stems.

4 Social Life
Villagers prepare for a community feast. The fire for this feast appears up the path in the heart of the village.

5 Religion
Residents dance around a circle of idols in a religious ceremony. Across the main path lies a prayer circle with fire.

Cooperative Activity: Preparing a Time Capsule

Task: To prepare a time capsule, students will select items that they think best represent Native American culture on the eve of contact with Europe.

Purpose: To help students appreciate the diverse accomplishments of Native Americans.

Activity: Explain to students that the purpose of a time capsule is to preserve representative articles of a current civilization for a future age. Tell students to imagine they are members of one of the Native American groups that they

encountered in Sections 1 and 2. Assign them to select four items for a time capsule to be opened in the year 2000. Have students present their choices in the form of a poster. For a general class discussion, each student can prepare one of the items for presentation.

ALTERNATIVE ASSESSMENT BOOK
Standards for Evaluating a Cooperative Activity

SOCIAL ORGANIZATION Bonds of **kinship,** or strong ties among family members, ensured the continuation of tribal customs and rituals. Elders instructed the young in the ways of the people. In exchange, the young honored the elders and also paid respect to their departed ancestors.

The tasks assigned to men and women varied with the society. Among the Iroquois and Hopi, for example, women owned the household items, and families traced their descent from mother to grandmother to great-grandmother, and so on. In other Native American cultures, men owned the family possessions and traced their ancestry through their father's kin.

The **division of labor**—the assignment of different tasks by gender, age, or status—formed the basis for government and economic distribution. Each age and each gender had jobs to perform and decisions to make, and each level of society had its specific functions. Among the Kwakiutl, for example, rank extended from slaves (usually rivals captured in wars or raids) to commoners to nobility. Slaves performed the most menial jobs, while nobles made sure that Kwakiutl law was obeyed, including the requirement that the wealthy hold potlatches.

The basic unit of organization among all Native American groups was the family, defined broadly by most groups to include aunts, uncles, cousins, and other relatives. Some tribes went further and organized the families into clans, or groups of families descended from a common ancestor. Among the Iroquois, for example, members of a clan often lived together in huge bark-covered longhouses. Each extended family had its own hearth and cooking fire. All families, however, participated in decision making for the community.

Not all Native American groups lived together for long periods of time. In environments where people hunted and gathered, groups broke into smaller bands for more efficient hunting. On the plains, for example, families searched the grasslands for buffalo. In the dry Great Basin between the Sierra Nevada and the Rockies, they followed seasonal food sources, such as birds that migrated to spring wetlands. In each location, the group reassembled only to celebrate important occasions.

In the late 1400s, on the eve of the encounter with the Europeans, the rhythms of Native American family life were well-established. All phases of a person's life—birth, marriage, and death—were guided by traditions that often went back thousands of years. On the other side of the Atlantic, in West Africa, customs equally as old guided another group of diverse peoples. In 1492, the societies of West Africa, which would be greatly affected by European contact with the Americas, consisted of unique cultures, each one with a long and rich history.

D. Answer
Families were a vital part of all Native American cultures, but while some families were very large and included extended members, others were small and more nomadic.

THINK THROUGH HISTORY

D. *Comparing* What similarities and differences existed among Native American family structures?

NOW & THEN

SCHEMITZUN

The sights and sounds of the Native American world come alive each fall for several days in the small Connecticut town of Mashantucket. Here, to the pounding of drums, performers and visitors from nearly 500 Native American tribes meet under a massive tent for Schemitzun, the "World Championship of Powwow." *Powwow* is a native word meaning a conference, or gathering.

Traditionally a dance to celebrate the corn harvest, Schemitzun has survived to become an occasion for Native Americans from all around the country to meet, share their art and culture, and celebrate their heritage.

Section 2 Assessment

1. TERMS & NAMES

Identify:
- Kashaya Pomo
- Kwakiutl
- Pueblo
- Iroquois
- kinship
- division of labor

2. SUMMARIZING Recreate the tree diagram below on your paper. Fill it in with an example of how a Native American society adapted to the environment of each region shown.

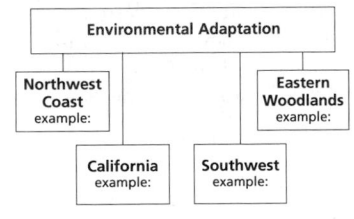

Environmental Adaptation

Northwest Coast example: / Eastern Woodlands example: / California example: / Southwest example:

3. SYNTHESIZING In your opinion, were the many Native American groups more diverse than they were similar? Cite specific examples to explain your answer.

THINK ABOUT
- adaptation to physical settings
- the role of tradition
- the variety of goods and languages encountered in trading

4. CLARIFYING What three words would you use to describe the Native American societies that flourished 500 years ago? Use evidence from the text to support your choice of words.

THINK ABOUT
- the natural resources in their regions
- their tools and artwork
- their rituals, customs, and traditions

Three Worlds Meet **13**

ANSWERS

1. TERMS & NAMES

Kashaya Pomo, p. 8

Kwakiutl, p. 9

Pueblo, p. 9

Iroquois, p. 10

kinship, p. 13

division of labor, p. 13

2. SUMMARIZING

Possible Responses: **California:** The Kashaya Pomo adapted to marshlands—snared waterfowl. **Northwest Coast:** The Kwakiutl adapted to coast and ocean—collected shellfish; hunted whales and seals. **Southwest:** The Acoma adapted to cliffs—used rock cisterns to collect rainwater. **Eastern Woodlands:** The Iroquois adapted to woodlands—hunted wild game.

3. SYNTHESIZING

Possible Responses: Students answering *more diverse* might cite the wide variety of dwellings, items crafted and traded, diet and crops, artwork, ways of hunting, religious beliefs, and languages. Students answering *similar* might say that all societies adapted well to their environment; all preserved strong family ties; all held strong beliefs in spirits; all shared the goal of living in harmony with nature.

4. CLARIFYING

Possible Responses: Ingenious or *versatile,* because of how well they used their natural environments; *creative* or *innovative,* because their artwork was so varied, well crafted, and well designed; *family-centered,* because they valued their living and ancestral family members; *spiritual,* because they believed so strongly in the spirit world; *community-minded,* because they worked together so well.

OBJECTIVES

① To explain how the arrival of Europeans in West Africa altered well-established trading patterns.

② To summarize the diverse accomplishments of the kingdoms of Songhai, Benin, and Kongo.

③ To describe life in West Africa and the role slavery played in these societies.

SKILLBUILDER

• Understanding geography: location, human-environment interaction, p. 15

CRITICAL THINKING

• Recognizing effects, p.16
• Comparing, pp. 17, 19
• Synthesizing, p. 19
• Summarizing, p. 19
• Analyzing, p. 19

FOCUS & MOTIVATE

▶ **Starting with the Student**
• Tell students that during the civil rights movement, some African Americans wore T-shirts with the slogan "Africa is a continent, not a nation."
• Ask students to explain what this slogan means. *That there is a tendency to generalize about Africa rather than see it as a continent made up of more than 50 nations and hundreds of ethnic groups.*

OBJECTIVE
① **INSTRUCT**

West Africa and the Wider World

▶ **Discussing Key Ideas**
• For thousands of years, life in West Africa is shaped by three distinct climate zones—the desert, the savanna, and the rain forest.
• Trade brings goods, ideas, and a major religion—Islam—to West Africa.

(continued on next page)

❸ West African Societies Around 1492

TERMS & NAMES
• savanna
• Islam
• plantation
• Songhai
• Benin
• Kongo
• lineage

LEARN ABOUT trade, societies, and culture in West Africa
TO UNDERSTAND the diversity of West African peoples and how they interacted with one another and the rest of the world.

ONE AFRICAN'S STORY

Leo Africanus was a boy of about 14 when he laid eyes on the renowned city of Timbuktu in the West African empire of Songhai. A Muslim born in Spain and raised in North Africa, Leo Africanus visited the city with his uncle, who was sent by a North African sultan on a diplomatic mission to the emperor of Songhai, Askia Muhammad. At the time they made their journey, in 1513, Songhai was as large as any kingdom in Africa—and among the largest in the world—and the emperor held enormous wealth and power.

Young but well educated, Leo Africanus was greatly impressed by the bustling prosperity of Timbuktu and its lively intellectual climate. He later recorded his impressions of the city in a book.

A PERSONAL VOICE

Here are many shops . . . of merchants, and especially as such as weave linen and cotton cloth. And hither do the Barbary [North African] merchants bring cloth of Europe. . . . Here are great store of doctors, judges, priests, and other learned men, that are bountifully maintained at the king's cost and charges, and hither are brought divers manuscripts or written books out of Barbary, which are sold for more money than any other merchandise.

LEO AFRICANUS, *The History and Description of Africa Done into English by John Pory*

These ancient boards from Africa contain sayings from the Qur'an, the holy scripture of Islam. They were used for teaching.

The written accounts of Leo Africanus provide a glimpse into the world of West Africa in the 1400s, a region that was home to a variety of peoples with long-established, sophisticated societies. From this region of Africa, and particularly from the coastal areas of West and West-Central Africa, would come most of the enslaved peoples brought to the Americas. These people would have a tremendous impact on American history and culture.

West Africa and the Wider World

The region of West Africa has three distinct climate zones, which have shaped the ways of life there for thousands of years. In the south, tropical rain forests blanket the Atlantic coast and extend deep across central Africa. Within these dense forests, numerous diverse peoples lived in societies ranging from simple village communities to wealthy kingdoms. Between the forests and the vast, desolate Sahara to the north lies a broad swath of open **savanna,** a dry grassland dotted with trees and bushes. The great Niger River connects the areas, sweeping in a broad arc across the savanna and desert, through the forest, and into the sea. As the source of water and a pathway for trade, the Niger's waters nourished the cultures and cities, such as Timbuktu, that arose in the savanna.

Although geographically separated from Europe and Asia, West Africa by the 1400s had long been connected to the wider world through trade. For centuries, expanding trade had brought into the region new goods, new ideas, and new beliefs, including those of the Islamic religion. Then, in the mid-1400s, the degree of interaction with the world increased with the arrival of European traders on the West African coast.

SECTION 3 RESOURCES

PRINT RESOURCES

IN-DEPTH RESOURCES: UNIT 1
Guided Reading, p. 3

ACCESS FOR STUDENTS ACQUIRING ENGLISH
Guided Reading (Spanish), p. 11

FORMAL ASSESSMENT
Section Quiz, p. 7

ALTERNATIVE ASSESSMENT BOOK
See forms for supporting and scoring alternative activities.

TECHNOLOGY RESOURCES

CD-ROM *Grolier Multimedia Encyclopedia*
Electronic Library of Primary Sources

INTERNET McDougal Littell Learning On-Line
http://www.mcdougallittell.com

THE SAHARA HIGHWAY The Timbuktu that Leo Africanus described was the hub of a well-established trading network that connected nearly all of West Africa to the coastal ports of North Africa, and through these ports to markets in Europe and Asia. For Leo Africanus and his uncle to reach Timbuktu, they traveled trade routes across the Sahara that had been used for centuries. Along these routes, desert caravans carried goods from Mediterranean cities and salt from Saharan mines to exchange for gold, ivory, kola nuts, dyed cotton cloth, and slaves from the forest kingdoms to the south. At the crossroads of this trade, cities such as Timbuktu, Gao, and Jenne became busy commercial centers. The empires that controlled these trade routes and cities grew wealthy and powerful.

Traders from North Africa brought more than goods across the Sahara—they also brought their Islamic faith, which gained increasing influence over savanna cultures. **Islam,** founded in Arabia in 622 by the prophet Muhammad, spread quickly across the Middle East and North Africa. By the 1200s, Islam had become the court religion of the large savanna empire of Mali, and it was later embraced by the rulers of Songhai, including Askia Muhammad. Despite its official status, however, Islam did not yet have much influence over the daily lives and worship practices of most West Africans in the late 1400s.

THE PORTUGUESE ARRIVE The peoples of West Africa and Europe knew little of each other before the 1400s. This began to change as Portuguese mariners established trading contacts along the West African coast starting in the 1440s. These contacts, which began in the trade for gold but soon shifted to human cargo, would have an enormous impact on the interaction between West Africa and the Americas.

HISTORICAL SPOTLIGHT

ISLAM
The prophet Muhammad (about A.D. 570–632) worked as a merchant in Mecca, a trading city on the Arabian peninsula. When he was about 40, he believed the angel Gabriel appeared to him and told him to preach a new religion to the Arabs. This religion became known as Islam, which in Arabic means "surrender to Allah." (*Allah* is the Arabic word for God.) The followers of Islam are called Muslims, "those who submit to God's will."

The words that Muhammad received from God were recorded by his followers in the Qur'an, the holy book of Islam. The Qur'an teaches that "there is no God but Allah, and Muhammad is His Prophet." (Islam, like Judaism and Christianity, is monotheistic, or based on the belief in one god.) The Qur'an also sets forth certain duties for righteous Muslims that include a series of daily prayers, an obligation to charity, and a pilgrimage to the holy city of Mecca.

(continued from page 14)
- Trade with the Portuguese opens new markets for African slaves.

IN-DEPTH RESOURCES: UNIT 1
Guided Reading, p. 3

ACCESS FOR STUDENTS ACQUIRING ENGLISH
Guided Reading (Spanish), p. 11

HISTORICAL SPOTLIGHT
Islam

Critical Thinking: Making Comparisons Ask students to begin a chart comparing three of the world's monotheistic religions: Christianity, Islam, and Buddhism. Suggest that they use the following headings to organize their research: Name of Supreme Being, Holy Book, Distinguishing Duties or Beliefs, Key Prophets or Founders, Approximate Age.

 GROLIER MULTIMEDIA ENCYCLOPEDIA Islamic Art and Architecture

HISTORY FROM VISUALS
West Africa in the 1400s

Reading the Map Point out the map key. Ask students to identify the main environmental regions in West Africa. *Desert, savanna, and rain forest.* Which kingdoms lay within the rain forest and the savanna? *Rain forest: Benin and Kongo; savanna: Songhai.*

Extension On the contemporary map of the world, on pp. 1060–1061, have students find the names of the present-day nations that now exist where these three ancient kingdoms once did. *Congo: Kongo; Nigeria: Benin; Mali: Songhai*

GEOGRAPHY SKILLBUILDER
LOCATION *Where did most of the trade routes intersect?*
HUMAN-ENVIRONMENT INTERACTION *What obstacles must traders have faced on these routes?*

West Africa in the 1400s

PORTUGAL
Lisbon
EUROPE
40° N
10° W
20° E
ASIA
Algiers
Tunis
MOROCCO
Tripoli
30° N
Marrakech
Mediterranean Sea
Alexandria
Cairo
TUAT
AFRICA
Sabha
Tropic of Cancer
In Salah
Ghat
EGYPT
Taghaza
SAHARA
Red Sea
20° W
Walata
Gao
KANEM-BORNU
SONGHAI
Timbuktu
Jenne
HAUSA STATES
Bobo Dioulasso
Kano
N
IFE
Kano
Kong
AKAN
Oyo
BENIN
ETHIOPIA
ATLANTIC OCEAN
0   500 Miles
0   1000 Kilometers
Gulf of Guinea
Equator
São Tomé Príncipe
Mbanza KONGO
Luanda
10° S
Niger River
Benue River

□ Desert
□ Savanna
■ Rain forest
■ Nile River Valley
— Major trade routes
-- Boundary of West African kingdoms at greatest extent

Skillbuilder Answer
Location: In Salah. **Human-Environment Interaction:** *Possible Answers:* harsh desert environment, dense forests, long distances.

Three Worlds Meet **15**

 Cooperative Learning Activity: Planning an Itinerary

Task: Students will plan an itinerary for a merchant traveling from Tripoli to Timbuktu in about the year 1500.

Purpose: To help students understand the economic exchanges that fueled the growth of West African empires.

Activity: Assign groups of students to plan a North African trading expedition to Timbuktu. Students should determine a route map, trade items carried to Timbuktu, trade items sought in Timbuktu, number of camels, estimated travel time, etc. (Helpful tip: Arabian camels can carry up to 100 pounds in weight. They travel about 4 miles per hour and can cover up to 47 miles a day.)

📁 ***Building a Portfolio:*** Students who add the itineraries to their portfolios should attach notes pointing out aspects of the material they think are especially strong.

ALTERNATIVE ASSESSMENT BOOK
Standards for Evaluating a Cooperative Activity

Standards for Evaluation
Itineraries should . . .

- reflect routes and distances shown on map
- include exchanges mentioned in the text, such as those made at Saharan salt mines
- use concrete details and lists of trade items

In 1324, Mansa Musa, the Muslim leader of Mali, took a pilgrimage to Mecca that left Europeans awestruck. Statistics from witnesses in Cairo, Egypt, dazzled listeners: the king's caravan consisted of 600,000 people, including 500 slaves—each armed with a six-pound gold staff—and 80 camels —each loaded with bags of gold dust weighing up to 100 pounds apiece.

The event literally put Mali on the maps of Europe. In 1377 a Spanish mapmaker drew a wall at the northern edge of the Sahara Desert. On the other side sat the Mali king luring Arab traders across the sands with a huge gold nugget.

 ELECTRONIC LIBRARY OF PRIMARY SOURCES On the Beginnings of the Portuguese-African Slave Trade by Gomes Eannes de Azurara

---

OBJECTIVE
② INSTRUCT

Three African Kingdoms

▶ *Discussing Key Ideas*
- Europeans are startled by the sophistication and power of West African kingdoms when they first encounter them.
- The central governments of these kingdoms oversee empires based upon trade and tribute.
- West African culture revolves around family and religion.

By the 1470s, Portuguese traders had established an outpost on the West African coast near the large Akan goldfields, the source of much West African gold. Other trading outposts soon followed, from which the Portuguese gained not only gold but pepper, ivory, and other goods. In return, they traded copper, brass, and fine cloth.

In the 1480s the Portuguese claimed two uninhabited islands off the African coast, Príncipe and São Tomé. Discovering that the soil and climate were perfect for growing sugar cane, they established large sugar plantations there. **Plantations** are farms on which a single crop, usually one that requires much human labor, is grown on a large scale. To work these plantations, the Portuguese began importing slaves from the West African mainland.

These early contacts with Portuguese traders would have two significant consequences for West Africa and the Americas. First, direct trade between the Portuguese and the coastal peoples of West Africa bypassed the trade routes across the Sahara and pulled the coastal region closer to Europe. Second, the Portuguese began the West African slave trade. At first this trade was limited to a small number of West Africans purchased from village chiefs, usually captives from rival groups. The Portuguese sent these enslaved West Africans to work on Portuguese plantations. However, the success of the Portuguese slave plantations created a model that eventually would be duplicated on a much vaster scale in the Americas—including the British North American colonies.

Three African Kingdoms

In the late 1400s, western Africa was a land of thriving trade, diverse cultures, and many rich and well-ordered states. Three powerful kingdoms that flourished at this time were Songhai, Benin, and Kongo.

SONGHAI From about 600 to 1600, a succession of empires—first Ghana, then Mali, and finally Songhai—gained power and wealth by controlling the trans-Sahara trade. The rulers of these empires grew enormously rich by taxing the goods that passed through their realms. In 1067 an Arab geographer in Spain named Al Bakri described the duties (import and export taxes) levied in Ghana.

> **A PERSONAL VOICE**
> For every donkey loaded with salt that enters the country, the king takes a duty of one golden *dinar* [about 1/8 ounce of gold], and two *dinars* from every one that leaves. From a load of copper the duty due to the king is five *mithquals* [also about 1/8 ounce of gold], and a load of merchandise ten *mithquals*. . . . The [gold] nuggets found in all the mines . . . are reserved for the king, only gold dust being left for the people.
> **AL BAKRI**, as quoted in *Africa in the Days of Exploration*

THINK THROUGH HISTORY
A. Recognizing Effects In what ways did interaction with the Portuguese affect West Africa?

A. Answer Trade brought new goods, bypassed Sahara, brought coastal region closer to Europe; new era of slave trade began.

A desert caravan reaches the fabled city of Timbuktu.

TEACHING OPTION

Making Connections Across the Curriculum

Art The bronze workers of Benin mastered the "lost wax" method of casting—a technique once used by ancient Egyptians. Works were so beautiful that Europeans tried to attribute them to non-Africans, including wanderers from the lost continent of Atlantis. To produce the works, artists followed these steps.

- Fashion a figure in clay and pour melted wax over it.
- Carve fine details in the dried wax.

- Cover the image with mud and set it in the sun to dry.
- Heat the dried figure until the wax melts.
- Pour molten bronze—a mixture of copper and zinc—into the resulting mold.
- Chip off the mud to reveal the work of art.

With such wealth, the rulers who controlled the north-south trade routes could gather large armies and conquer new territory. They could also build cities, administer laws, and support the arts and education. So it was with two great rulers of the **Songhai** empire, which in the mid-1400s gained control of the trade from Mali. The first king, Sunni Ali, pushed the borders of Songhai to limits greater than those of any previous West African empire. His military prowess became legendary—in his entire reign, from 1464–1492, he never lost a single battle.

The second great ruler, Askia Muhammad, was a master organizer, a devout Muslim, and a lover of learning. He organized Songhai into administrative districts and appointed officials to govern, collect taxes, and regulate trade, agriculture, and fishing. Under his rule, Timbuktu regained its reputation as an important education center as it drew scholars from all over the Islamic world.

BENIN At its height in the 1500s, Songhai's reach extended across much of West Africa. However, it did not control the forest kingdoms. Songhai's horse-mounted soldiers might thunder across the savanna, but they could not penetrate the belt of dense rain forest along the southern coast. Protected by the forest, peoples such as the Akan, Ibo, Edo, Bini, Ifi, Oyo, and Yoruba lived in kingdoms that thrived in the 1400s and 1500s.

Although the forests provided protection from conquest, they opened for trade. Traders carried goods or paddled them along the Niger River out of the forests to the savanna. The brisk trade with Songhai and North Africa, and later with Portugal, helped the forest kingdoms grow in size. In the 1400s one of these kingdoms, **Benin,** dominated a large region around the Niger Delta. Leading the expansion was a powerful oba (ruler) named Ewuare. Stories that have been passed down to today recall Ewuare's triumphs in the mid-1400s.

An unknown Yoruba artist in the kingdom of Ife produced this bronze head of a king in the 1100s. The highly developed bronze artistry of Ife was handed down to the kingdom of Benin, which arose later in the same area.

A PERSONAL VOICE
He fought against and captured 201 towns and villages. . . . He took their rulers captive and he caused the people to pay tribute to him. He made good roads in Benin City. . . . In fact the town rose to importance and gained the name of city during his reign. It was he who had the innermost and greatest of the walls and ditches made around the city, and he also made powerful charms and had them buried at each of the nine gateways of the city so as to ward against any evil.

CHIEF JACOB EGHAREVBA, from *A Short History of Benin*

Within this great walled city, the oba headed a highly organized system of government, in which appointed chiefs governed over districts. Through other appointed officials, he controlled all trade in the kingdom and managed the development of industries such as goldsmithing and brass-smithing. He also exchanged ambassadors with Portugal as early as the late 1400s. Under the sponsorship of Ewuare and his successors, metalworkers produced stunning and sophisticated works of art, particularly in the form of bronze sculptures and plaques.

KONGO Within another stretch of rain forest, about a thousand miles south of West Africa in West Central Africa, the powerful kingdom of Kongo arose on the lower Zaire (Congo) River. In the late 1400s, **Kongo** consisted of a series of small kingdoms organized under a single leader called the Manikongo. The Manikongo, who could be either a man or a woman, lived in a home state in what is today the northern part of Angola. The Manikongo held kingdoms together by a system of royal marriages, taxes, and, when necessary, war and

THINK THROUGH HISTORY
B. Comparing *How was the government in Benin similar to that of Askia Muhammad?*

B. Answer Both were highly organized and used appointed officials to administer districts and control economic activity.

Three Worlds Meet **17**

Askia meant "thief" or "usurper," which is what staunch followers of Sunni Ali called Mohammed Abou Bekr Et-Toui when he seized the throne from Sunni Ali's son and hand-picked successor in 1493. Abou Bekr mocked his critics by renaming himself Askia Mohammed.

More than 50 years old, the new ruler soon returned to school. Leaving the empire in charge of his ablest generals, Askia traveled to Egypt to study the art of government and systems of weights and measures. He used this knowledge to reorganize the empire.

By the end of Askia's life, Arab scholars had given him a new name. Instead of calling him Mohammed the Usurper, they called him Askia the Great.

West African Culture

▶ *Discussing Key Ideas*
• Most West Africans live in villages, where life centers around the extended family.
• A complex system of religious beliefs, as well as a division of labor, guides interactions among people.
• Although West Africans practice slavery, it is neither based upon race nor usually perpetuated from one generation to the next.

MORE ABOUT . . .
West African Society

In West Africa, the task of preserving a people's history was the role of the griots—a class of professional storytellers. Traditionally assigned to important families or rulers, griots spent years learning all the important facts about a people and memorizing them. In addition, they served as advisors, masters of ceremony, and official spokespersons.

The first enslaved Africans to arrive in the Americas carried this tradition of storytelling with them and used it as a way to keep alive their connections with the ancestral homeland.

tribute. By the 1470s, the Manikongo oversaw an empire estimated at over 4 million people.

The Bakongo, the people of the Kongo, knew how to mine, smelt, and work iron ore into well-wrought tools and weapons. They had also turned the weaving of palm leaf threads into a fine art and produced with the threads fabric that looked to Europeans like velvet. The Portuguese sailors who first reached Kongo in 1483 were impressed by similarities between the Kongo and their own world. Its system of government—a collection of provinces centralized under one strong king—resembled that of most European nations at the time.

West African Culture

The world of most West Africans in the late 1400s was a local one. Even within kingdoms or states, most people lived in small villages, where life revolved around family, the community, and tradition. Their ways varied greatly, but they followed some common patterns. These patterns would influence the future interactions of African peoples with Europeans and shape the experience of enslaved Africans in the Americas.

FAMILY AND GOVERNMENT Bonds of kinship—ties among people of the same **lineage,** or line of common descent—formed the basis of most aspects of life in rural West Africa. Some societies, such as the Akan, were matrilineal—that is, people traced their lineage through their mother's family. These lineage ties determined not only loyalties but also inheritances and whom people could marry. Societies such as the Ibo also encouraged people to find a mate outside of their lineage groups. These family patterns had the effect of creating a complex web of family alliances.

Within a family, age carried rank. The oldest living descendant of the group's common ancestor exercised control over family members and also represented them in councils of the larger groups to which a family might belong, such as a kingdom. These larger groups shared a common language, a common past, and often, a common territory. One leader or chief might speak for the group as a whole. But this person rarely spoke without consulting a council of elders made up of the heads of individual extended families.

RELIGION Religion was important in all aspects of African life. Political leaders from chiefs to kings claimed authority on the basis of religion. For example, the ruler of the Ife kingdom claimed to descend from the first person placed on earth by the "God of the Sky." Religious rituals were also central to the everyday activities of farmers, hunters, and fishers.

Nature, as West Africans knew it, was filled with spirits. People saw spiritual forces in both living and non-living objects. They also gave great significance to the voices of departed ancestors who spoke to the elders in dreams. Although West African peoples might consult, through prayer and ritual, with a variety of ancestral spirits and lesser gods, most believed in a single Creator. The Bakongo, for example, believed in *Nzambi ampungu,* the Creator of all things, and so had little trouble seeing why Christians or Muslims believed in a supreme God. However, the Bakongo and other traditional

For centuries many peoples of Central Africa have created guardian figures called *bwiti,* to protect the remains of their deceased ancestors. This *bwiti* of wood covered with brass strips was produced by the Hongwe of Gabon in the early 1900s.

Cooperative Activity: Post Cards from West Africa

Task: Students will design post cards that capture some distinctive feature of one of the representative West African kingdoms.

Purpose: To illustrate in pictures and words the accomplishments of a West African society.

Activity: Assign groups of three or four students to create post cards that Arab or Portuguese travelers might have sent from Timbuktu, Benin City, or the ManiKongo's court.

The front of the post card should show a scene or object from the place visited. The back of the post card should include a brief message describing the sights. Have students "touring" different sites exchange post cards.

📁 **Building a Portfolio:** Students who add the post cards to their portfolios should attach a note describing their contributions to the work.

ALTERNATIVE ASSESSMENT BOOK
Standards for Evaluating a Cooperative Activity

Standards for Evaluation
Post cards should . . .

• have drawings that reflect written descriptions or art in the text
• express reasonable reactions from the travelers to specific sights and events of a particular society

cultures could not understand why Christian and Muslim conquerors insisted that West Africans give up worshipping spirits, the unseen presences that they believed carried out the Creator's work. Out of this difference grew many cultural conflicts.

LIVELIHOOD Throughout West Africa, people supported themselves by age-old methods of farming, herding, hunting, and fishing and also by mining and trading. Almost all groups believed in collective ownership of land. Individuals might farm the land, but it returned to the family or village when not in use.

Clearing and cultivating the dense tropical forest demanded hard work from the men, women, and older children in the village. Families or groups in West African villages specialized in certain crops or products. These became items for trade, often at central markets in the village. Villagers traded the products of rain forest farms, such as plantains, bananas, peanuts, and yams, as well as fish or game. They also bartered for products crafted by artisans, including dyed fabrics and ceremonial ivory carvings.

People on the dry savanna depended on rivers, such as the Niger, to nourish their crops of wheat and other grains and water their livestock. On the western coast, along the Senegal and Gambia rivers, farmers converted tangled mangrove swamps into rice fields. This grain—and the skills for growing it—would accompany West Africans to the Americas.

USE OF SLAVE LABOR To get the day's labor done, West African peoples divided tasks by age and by status in society. At the lowest rung in some societies were slaves. However, in Africa, people were not born into slavery nor did slavery necessarily mean a lifetime of servitude. In Africa, slaves could escape their bondage in a number of ways. Sometimes they were adopted into or they married into the family they served. Others escaped into the familiar African countryside. However, conditions were different for Africans in the Americas. There, a new type of slavery emerged that continued from generation to generation and was based on race.

While slavery came to dominate the interaction between Africans and Europeans, it was not of utmost importance to the Portuguese sailors who first explored the African coast. At this time, in the late 1400s, a variety of political, social, and economic changes in Europe spurred rulers and adventurers to push outward into unexplored reaches of the ocean.

C. Answer
Most people were rural, social networks based on kinship and lineage were complex, extended family was important, people generally believed in a single creator and numerous spiritual forces, groups believed in collective land ownership, farming was difficult.

THINK THROUGH HISTORY
C. *Synthesizing* *Describe West African culture.*

NOW & THEN

KENTE CLOTH

Today people of African descent all over the world value the multicolored fabric known as kente cloth as a symbol of Africa. For African Americans who choose to wear kente cloth or display it in their homes, the fabric serves as a tangible link to West African cultures from which their ancestors came.

Artisans of the Asante (Ashanti) people of modern Ghana have woven kente cloth for centuries. Working at looms, they produce long strips of cloth of complex designs and varying colors. These strips are then sewn together into a brilliant fabric that sparkles with reds, greens, blues, golds, and whatever other hues the weavers chose as dyes.

Section ③ Assessment

1. TERMS & NAMES

Identify:
- savanna
- Islam
- plantation
- Songhai
- Benin
- Kongo
- lineage

2. SUMMARIZING Copy the main topics shown on the outline below and fill it in with factual details related to each topic.

    I. West Africa's Climate Zones

    II. West Africa's Major Geographical Features

    III. Three West African Kingdoms and Their Climate Zones

Write a main idea for each topic.

3. ANALYZING What factors do you think contributed to the thriving trade system that flourished in West Africa? Use evidence from the text to support your response.

THINK ABOUT
- geographic location and features
- the kinds of goods exchanged
- the societies that emerged in West Africa

4. COMPARING What similarities can you find between West African kingdoms around 1492 and America today?

THINK ABOUT
- the power of leaders
- social and commercial organization
- intellectual and artistic activity

Three Worlds Meet **19**

ANSWERS

1. TERMS & NAMES

savanna, p. 14

Islam, p. 15

plantation, p. 16

Songhai, p. 17

Benin, p. 17

Kongo, p. 17

lineage, p. 18

2. SUMMARIZING

I. Climate zones—desert, tropical rain forests, and savanna.
II. Geographical Features—Sahara Desert; Atlantic coastline; Niger River.
III. Kingdoms—Songhai (savanna); Benin (rain forest); Kongo (rain forest).

3. ANALYZING

Possible Responses: The Niger River was a pathway for trade, linking the rain forests to the savanna; coastal areas were easily accessible to Portuguese traders; a high demand existed for West African goods, which later included slaves; sophisticated societies existed with leaders who capably directed economic activity, such as trade.

4. COMPARING

Possible Responses: A system of importing and exporting goods; extensive foreign trade; major centers of commerce that became big cities and enjoyed great wealth; powerful and well-ordered states; an organized system of government; a system of taxation; large armies; cities and laws; money for arts and education; exchange of ambassadors; production of sophisticated works of art.

NOW & THEN
Kente Cloth

***Critical Thinking:
Analyzing a Quote*** Read aloud this quote by one African-American youth: "A lot of us are getting back to our culture, such as dressing in African materials. This gives us self-esteem and identity." Ask students to summarize the connection between African fabrics and African-American pride. Then assign the feature. Explore why kente cloth is especially valued by African Americans.

ASSESS & RETEACH

Section 3 Assessment
Suggest that students put the explanation of each term or name on a flash card. Have them hold each card up and challenge classmates to guess the person, place, word, or event.

Self-Assessment
Have students make a list of questions they had about Africa before reading this section. Then ask them to list the answers provided by this section.

Section Quiz

FORMAL ASSESSMENT
Section Quiz, p. 7

Reteach
Use the map of West African kingdoms and trade routes to help review the main ideas of the section.

CLOSE

The arrival of Europeans on the coast of Africa altered established patterns of life in Africa and began its long-term involvement with western Europe.

Teacher's Edition **19**

OBJECTIVES

1 To describe the life of medieval Europeans.

2 To identify the forces that weakened the power of the Roman Catholic Church.

3 To summarize the changes that helped expand the European world view.

4 To explain how trade, travel, and technology combined to lead Europeans to sea.

SKILLBUILDERS

• Understanding geography: movement, location, p. 23
• Interpreting charts, pp. 24, 26

CRITICAL THINKING

• Summarizing, pp. 21, 26
• Recognizing effects, p. 22
• Synthesizing, p. 25
• Analyzing motives, p. 26
• Analyzing, p. 26
• Drawing conclusions, p. 26

FOCUS & MOTIVATE

▶ *Starting with the Student*
• To discuss the value of exploration, determine by a show of hands whether students would support an increase in taxes to pay for a costly U.S. mission into deep space—the area beyond our solar system.
• Have students share reasons they would support or oppose the tax.

MORE ABOUT . . .
Prince Henry the Navigator

Prince Henry may have been nicknamed the Navigator, but he rarely went exploring himself; instead, he planned and financed explorations. His own biggest adventure came at age 19, when he and his two brothers, hoping to prove themselves worthy of knighthood, led an armada and captured Ceuta, a Muslim stronghold on the African coast opposite Gibraltar.

TERMS & NAMES
• Prince Henry
• hierarchy
• nuclear family
• Crusades
• Reformation
• joint-stock company

4 European Societies Around 1492

LEARN ABOUT the changes emerging in western European societies
TO UNDERSTAND how these changes spurred the Age of Exploration.

ONE EUROPEAN'S STORY

Prince Henry of Portugal, often called "Henry the Navigator," refused to let superstition interfere with his quest to discover what lands existed along the western coast of Africa. Beginning in the 1420s, he dispatched expedition after expedition down the African coast, but for a decade none ventured farther than the cliffs of Cape Bojador on the continent's northern Atlantic coast. His able mariners were halted there by fear—a fear fueled by legends that nothing good lay beyond this point. Finally, in 1434, a Portuguese ship rounded the cape and launched the age of European exploration.

Many factors sparked Prince Henry's interest in promoting overseas discovery—including finding new wealth. However, according to the Prince's biographer, Gomes Eanes de Zurara, his driving motivation was the need to know.

> **A PERSONAL VOICE**
> The noble spirit of this Prince . . . was ever urging him both to begin and to carry out very great deeds. For which reason . . . he had also a wish to know the land that lay beyond the isles of Canary and that Cape called Bojador, for that up to his time, neither by writings, nor by the memory of man, was known with any certainty the nature of the land beyond that Cape. . . . it seemed to him that if he or some other lord did not endeavor to gain that knowledge, no mariners or merchants would ever dare to attempt it. . . .
> **GOMES EANES DE ZURARA,** *The Chronicle of the Discovery and Conquest of Guinea*

Prince Henry's curiosity was typical of the "noble spirit" of the Renaissance, a period when Europeans began to challenge old assumptions about the world. In the 1300s and 1400s, changes in European society, politics, and the economy led to a renewed interest in trade and learning. These interests drove bold seafarers, ambitious rulers, and risk-taking merchants to seek opportunities beyond Europe's borders. The result was the exciting era of European expansion.

Prince Henry the Navigator

The European Social Order

In the late 1400s, the changes that led the Portuguese to venture out to sea were well underway. However, they affected different parts of western Europe—a patchwork of many peoples, languages, and political units—at different times. For the majority of Europeans, change came slowly. Most Europeans, like most Native Americans and most Africans, lived in small villages, bound to the land and to rhythms of life that had been in place for centuries.

THE SOCIAL HIERARCHY European societies were hierarchical—arranged by order of rank or class. Monarchs and nobles, the land-owning elite, held most of the wealth and power at the top of the **hierarchy.** At the bottom labored the peasants, who constituted the large majority of the people. A system of loyalties and responsibilities bound the two groups together. The nobility offered their peasants land and protection. In return, the peasants supplied nobles with livestock or crops—and sometimes with service in time of war.

SECTION 4 RESOURCES

 PRINT RESOURCES

IN-DEPTH RESOURCES: UNIT 1
Guided Reading, p. 4
Geography Application: The Earth's Wind Systems, p. 7
American Lives: Queen Isabella, p. 17

ACCESS FOR STUDENTS ACQUIRING ENGLISH
Guided Reading (Spanish), p. 12
Geography Application: The Earth's Wind Systems (Spanish), p. 15

FORMAL ASSESSMENT
Section Quiz, p. 8

ALTERNATIVE ASSESSMENT BOOK
See forms for supporting and scoring alternative activities.

 TECHNOLOGY RESOURCES

GEOGRAPHY TRANSPARENCIES
G1, Voyages of Discovery and Exploration: 1271–1850

CRITICAL THINKING TRANSPARENCIES
CT35, Inventions: 1190–1492

CD-ROM *Grolier Multimedia Encyclopedia*

VIDEO *American Portfolio: A Videodisc for U.S. History*
user's guide, p. 12

INTERNET McDougal Littell Learning On-Line
http://www.mcdougallittell.com

Within the social structure, few individuals moved beyond the position they were born into. Europeans generally accepted this fact and viewed their lot as part of a larger order ordained by God and reflected in the natural world. Writing in the late 1500s, William Shakespeare expressed the value of this natural order in one of his plays.

A PERSONAL VOICE
The heavens themselves, the planets, and this center [earth]
Observe degree, priority, and place . . .
Take but degree away, untune that string,
And hark! what discord follows. . . .

WILLIAM SHAKESPEARE, from *Troilus and Cressida*

A group that did experience mobility was the growing number of artisans and merchants, the people who crafted and sold goods for money. Although this group was relatively small in the 1400s, the profit they earned from trade would eventually make them a valuable source of tax revenue to monarchs seeking to finance costly overseas exploration and expansion.

THE FAMILY IN SOCIETY While Europeans recognized and respected kinship ties, the extended family did not play as important a role for them as it did in Native American and African societies at this time. Instead, life centered around the **nuclear family,** the household made up of a mother and father and their children. As in other societies, gender determined the division of labor. Among peasant families, for example, men generally did most of the field labor and herded livestock. Women did help in the fields, but they also handled child care and household tasks, such as preparing and preserving the family's food.

Men dominated all areas of life in Europe. The husband ruled the household, and when he died, any property generally went to a male heir, usually the eldest son. Men also held political power and authority in the Roman Catholic Church. Despite the custom, women throughout society found ways to exert their influence. However, most Europeans believed that outright female authority contradicted God's natural order, and even powerful women, such as Queen Elizabeth I of England, carefully courted the male-dominated upper classes.

A. Answer Men dominated all areas of life, including family, political power, and church hierarchy.

THINK THROUGH HISTORY
A. Summarizing Describe the relationship between men and women in European society.

Peasants tend to their fields in the month of June, outside the walls of a lavish castle. This illustration comes from *Très riches heures*, a prayer book made for a French nobleman. The book portrays scenes from daily life throughout the year.

Christianity Shapes the European Outlook

The Roman Catholic Church was the dominant institution in western Europe. The leader of the church—the pope—and his bishops had great political as well as spiritual authority. In the spiritual realm, church leaders determined most matters of faith. It was the role of parish priests to convey the accepted interpretation of God's word to the people. Their message encouraged people to endure the drudgery and suffering of life on earth with the promise of eternal life in heaven for those who believed. Bishops and priests also administered important rituals called the sacraments—such as baptism and communion—that assured salvation.

Hand in hand with the belief in salvation was the call to convert people of other faiths. The Bible encouraged Christians, "Go into all the world and preach the word to all creation. Whoever believes and is baptized will be saved,

Three Worlds Meet **21**

OBJECTIVE
① **INSTRUCT**

The European Social Order

▶*Discussing Key Ideas*
• Europeans live in a world that includes nobility, artisans, merchants, and peasants.
• Daily life centers around the nuclear family, composed of a husband, a wife, and their children.
• Although exceptional women wield influence, medieval life is dominated by men.

IN-DEPTH RESOURCES: UNIT 1
Guided Reading, p.4
ACCESS FOR STUDENTS ACQUIRING ENGLISH
Guided Reading (Spanish), p. 12

OBJECTIVE
② **INSTRUCT**

Christianity Shapes the European Outlook

▶*Discussing Key Ideas*
• The Roman Catholic Church is a major influence on the culture of western Europe.
• The Crusades, although begun as a holy war, serve to open the rest of the world to Europe.
• The Reformation divides Christian Europe and launches centuries of religious turmoil.

TEACHING OPTIONS

Making Connections Across the Curriculum

Literature Point out to students that literature can be an important primary source for a historical period. Literature can reflect the thinking, beliefs, and values of people at a particular time. Have students name some of the novels or short stories that they think reflect our times. *(Their suggestions might include the works of J. D. Salinger or Toni Morrison.)* Then refer them to the quotation from Shakespeare's play *Troilus and Cressida.* Ask: How do the lines illustrate the medieval hierarchy? What does Shakespeare suggest will happen if that order is challenged? Refer students to the adjacent illustration. What views did the artist share with Shakespeare?

Making Connections Across Cultures

Comparing Life in Europe and America Assign pairs of students to compare the above picture of medieval life with the diagram of a Secotan village on page 12. What similarities and differences can students spot? Emphasize, in particular, that both societies lived in small agricultural communities that depended upon the communal efforts of their members. As an extension, request volunteers to turn the picture of a medieval village into a diagram modeled after the one on page 12.

Teacher's Edition **21**

"King Isabella"

**Critical Thinking:
Summarizing** Ask students
to write an obituary summarizing Queen Isabella's
accomplishments. Encourage them to analyze the role
she played in the colonization of America. As a variation, students might present
the obituary in the form of a
poem entitled "A Woman's
Place."

 *GROLIER MULTIMEDIA
ENCYCLOPEDIA* Queen
Isabella I

OBJECTIVE
③ INSTRUCT

Changes Come to Europe

▶ *Discussing Key Ideas*
- After disastrous famines
  and the Black Death,
  Europe enters a period of
  great change.
- The growth of commerce
  and an expanding population fuel the rise of cities.
- Monarchs consolidate their
  power and forge national
  identities.
- A spirit of confidence and
  inquiry replaces the uncertainty of the past.

KEY PLAYER

**"KING ISABELLA"
1451–1504**
Queen Isabella, who played a
central role in European exploration
by sponsoring Christopher
Columbus's voyages to the
Americas, made her mark on the
Old World as well. As co-ruler of
Spain, Isabella actively participated
in her country's religious and
military matters.

In championing Spain's
Catholicism, the queen often fought
openly with the pope to make sure
that her candidates were appointed
to positions in the Spanish church.
In addition, Isabella had tasted
battle far more than most rulers,
either male or female. The queen
rode among her troops in full armor,
personally commanding them in
Ferdinand's absence. Whenever
Isabella appeared astride atop a
horse, her troops shouted: "Castile,
Castile, for our King Isabella!"

but whoever does not believe will be condemned." This missionary call
spurred Europe to reach out beyond its borders first to defend, and
then to spread, the faith.

CRUSADING CHRISTIANITY The emergence of Islam in the world in
the 600s was to cause European Christians centuries of worry. Within
100 years after the birth of Islam, Muslim armies had taken control of
a huge region stretching from the banks of the Indus River to the
sands of Morocco, and they were knocking on Europe's door. By 732,
Muslims had conquered most of the Iberian Peninsula, where Spain
and Portugal sit.

To regain this territory, Spanish Christians waged a campaign
called the *reconquista*, or reconquest. By 1492, the force of the combined kingdoms of Queen Isabella of Castile and King Ferdinand of
Aragon, who married in 1469, finally drove the Muslims from the
peninsula, ending more than seven centuries of religious warfare
there. A united Spain stood ready to make its presence felt on the
world scene and to spread Christianity around the globe.

Meanwhile, Christian armies from all over western Europe
responded to the church's call to force the Muslims out of the Holy
Land around Jerusalem. From 1096 to 1270, Europeans launched a
series of military expeditions to the Middle East under the banner of
the Christian cross. In the end, these bloody **Crusades** failed to "rescue" the Holy Land, but the urge to turn back the Muslim challenge
remained strong.

The Crusades had two consequences that would help push
European society toward exploration and expansion. First, they
sparked an increase in trade, as Europeans brought back with them a
new taste for products from Asia. Second, the Crusades weakened the
power of European nobles, many of whose lives or fortunes were lost
in the wars. Monarchs eventually took advantage of the nobles' weakened ranks to consolidate their own power. Later, to increase their
wealth and power, monarchs sponsored exploration to new lands.

DECLINE IN CHURCH AUTHORITY The Crusades had a third long-term consequence: the decline of the power of the pope. The ultimate
failure of these campaigns helped reduce the prestige of the papacy
(the office of the pope), which had led the quest. Power struggles in the 1300s
and 1400s between the church and European kings further reduced papal
authority and tipped the balance of power to the monarchies.

Differences over church authority, as well as corrupt practices among the
clergy, made many in the church eager for reforms. In the early 1500s, the
desire for change led to a movement called the **Reformation,** which divided
Christianity in western Europe into Catholicism and Protestantism. This split
would deepen the rivalries between European nations during the period of
American colonization one hundred years later and send newly formed
Protestant sects to seek religious freedom across the Atlantic.

B. Answer
The Crusades
helped increase
the power of
monarchs (who
would go on to
sponsor
exploration) and
sparked
increased trade;
the Reformation
further propelled
the era of
American
colonization and
settlement.

THINK THROUGH HISTORY
**B. Recognizing
Effects** How did
*religious changes
in Europe help
spur exploration
of new lands?*

Changes Come to Europe

Problems in the church were but one concern for Europeans in the 1400s. As
the century began, European societies were slowly recovering from a series of
disasters in the 1300s. From 1314 to 1316, catastrophe struck in the form of
heavy rain and disease. Crops rotted in flooded fields, while anthrax, a cattle disease, wiped out whole herds. Thousands of peasants died of starvation. Then,
beginning in the 1340s, an epidemic of plagues known as the Black Death swept

---

TEACHING OPTIONS

Teaching Less Proficient Readers

Cause-and-Effect Chart Make sure students understand the
meaning of cause and effect. (See the Skillbuilder Lesson on
page 1040.) Then use the graphic organizer to help students
identify the causes and effects of the Crusades and the
Reformation.

Teaching Gifted and Talented Students

Researching the Crusades Have interested students
research the Crusades and compose reports and displays to
present to the rest of the class. Several recent books that you
might suggest are *The Oxford Illustrated History of the
Crusades,* 1995, published by Oxford University Press;
*Dungeon, Fire, and Sword: The Knights Templar in the
Crusades* by John J. Robinson, 1991, published by M. Evans &
Co.; *Holy War: The Crusades and Their Impact on Today's
World* by Karen Armstrong, 1991, published by Doubleday.
Suggest that students work together to decide who will focus
on which topic, such as Christianity and Islam, knighthood, or
trade, during this period.

through the continent. The plague ultimately caused the deaths of some 20 million people, or as much as a fourth of Europe's population. While the plagues terrorized Europe, long wars also raged on the continent, including the Hundred Years' War between England and France.

However, amid this turmoil, modern Europe began to take shape. As it rebounded from the Black Death, Europe experienced vigorous growth and change. The expansion of Europe resulted from several processes that blossomed in the 1400s, including the growth of commerce, population growth and the rise of towns, the rise of nations, and emergence of the Renaissance spirit. At the dawn of the Age of Exploration, these forces pushed Europeans to look to other lands.

THE GROWTH OF COMMERCE The Crusades had opened up Asian trade routes and whetted the European appetite for the luxuries of lands to the east—silk and porcelain from China, tea from India, rugs from Persia, and more. Europeans especially valued spices from Asia such as cinnamon, cloves, nutmeg, and pepper. In those days European farmers slaughtered most of their pigs and cattle in late autumn and, in the absence of refrigeration, preserved the meat by packing it between layers of salt. Spices helped disguise the spoiled and salty taste of the meat.

Merchants in Italian city-states such as Venice and Florence were the first to profit from trade with Asia. They traded with the Muslim merchants who controlled the flow of goods through much of the Middle East. The goods exchanged in this trade included tin from Cornwall, pearls from Ceylon, cop-

Skillbuilder Answer
Movement: By sea from Antioch to Venice, and on to Vienna, or over land through Constantinople.
Location: All were ports with access to the Mediterranean Sea.

GEOGRAPHY SKILLBUILDER
MOVEMENT *Over what routes might goods have traveled from Asia to the city of Vienna?* **LOCATION** *How were Venice, Genoa, and Lisbon well situated for trade?*

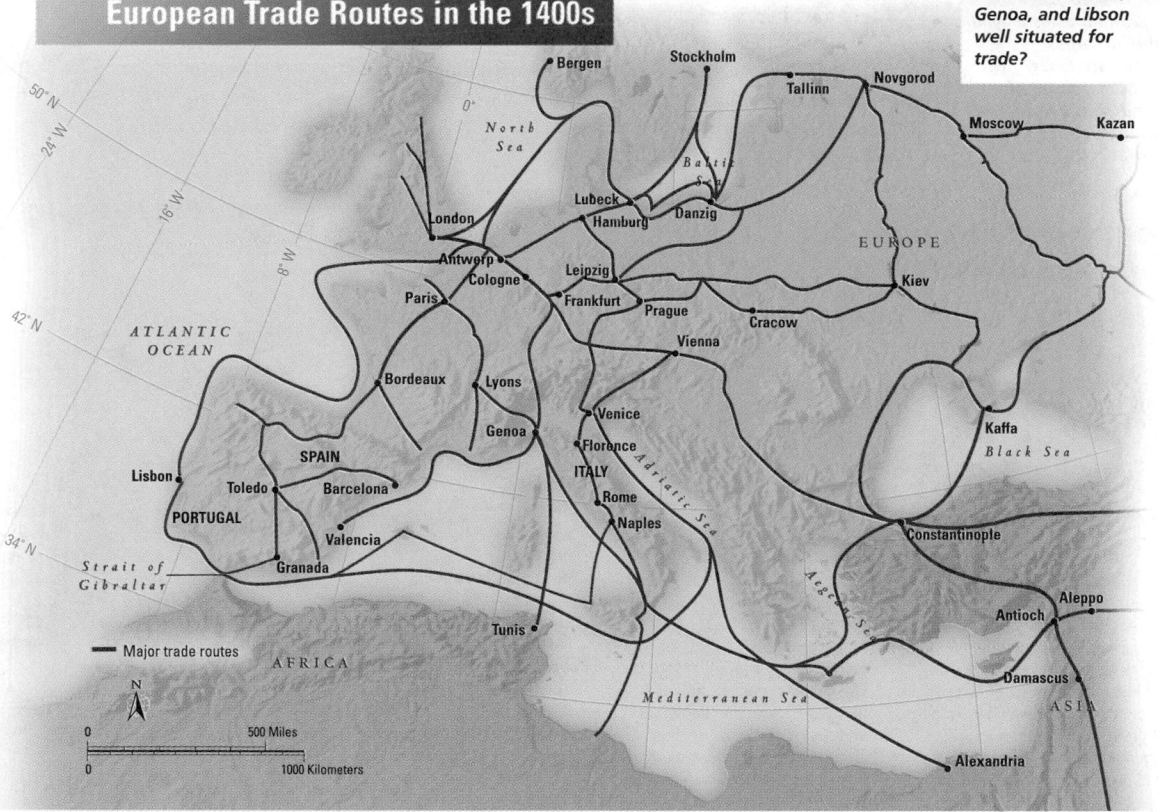

European Trade Routes in the 1400s

Major trade routes

Three Worlds Meet **23**

MORE ABOUT . . .
The Black Death
The Black Death came to Europe's door in 1347 aboard a ship that dropped anchor in the harbor of Messina, Sicily. Its deck was littered with dead and near-dead sailors, their bodies covered with boils and black blotches from internal bleeding.

This disease, also known as the bubonic plague, was spread by fleas carried by rats or by drinking contaminated water. It spread with such speed and deadly force that one chronicler in Siena, Italy, lamented, "Nobody wept no matter what his loss because almost everybody expected death. . . . And people said and believed, 'This is the end of the world.'"

HISTORY FROM VISUALS
European Trade Routes in the 1400s
Reading the Map Have students use their pencil erasers to trace the route a ship would take to get from Lisbon to Constantinople. Ask: How did Italy's location help explain why its merchants commanded much of Europe's trade in 1492?

Extension Have students predict the European nations most likely to benefit from new markets in the Americas. *Those on the west coast, including England, France, Spain, and Portugal.*

TEACHING OPTIONS

Making Connections Across Time

The Spread of Contagious Diseases Today Share information in the "More About" feature with students. Explain that pandemics, or epidemic diseases over a wide region, go hand in hand with the expansion of trade and travel. Mention that some present-day nations, such as the developing nations of eastern Africa, often require foreign visitors to present immunization cards to prove vaccination against contagious diseases. A heated debate has developed in the United States over whether the nation should institute "disease checks" at its borders. What do students think?

Making Connections Across the Curriculum

Economics Discuss the link between profit and individual enterprise—the cornerstone of a capitalist economy. Then use these questions to explore how the desire for profit helped fuel the commercial expansion of Europe: How did merchants hope to earn a profit? *By selling goods for more than they paid for them.* How did bankers hope to earn a profit? *By charging interest on credit and loans.* How might merchants and bankers use these profits to earn more profits? *By investing them in new ventures.*

The first European reference to gunpowder appeared in a 1268 description of Chinese firecrackers by Roger Bacon: "We find the . . . noise exceeding the roar of strong thunder, . . . and a flash brighter than the most brilliant lightning." But neither the noise nor the light warded off Europeans, who eagerly took to the Chinese invention, adding improvements of their own.

Gunpowder proved so successful in blowing apart castle walls that Europeans tried to figure out how they might use it to blow apart ships. By the time Columbus sailed for America, shipbuilders had figured out a way. They added a gun deck, with gun ports pierced in the hull—an innovation that introduced a whole new dimension to naval warfare.

HISTORY FROM VISUALS
Changes in Europe in the 1400s

Reading the Diagram Point out the "before and after" illustrations on the diagram. Ask students to state in words the change depicted in each set of illustrations.

Extension Challenge students to extend concepts in the diagram by adding illustrations and captions for other changes, such as "Use of Firearms" and "New Methods of Navigation."

CRITICAL THINKING TRANSPARENCIES
CT35, Inventions: 1190–1492

---

per from Poland, saffron from India, lead from Sardinia, and dried apricots from Persia.

Two modern business institutions also emerged in Italy at this time: international banking houses and corporations. International banks could transfer money and credit among business operations in different cities. Corporations emerged at this time as **joint-stock companies,** which permitted numerous investors to pool their wealth. The development of joint-stock companies was particularly important because they would finance many of the colonial expeditions to the Americas.

POPULATION GROWTH During the 1400s, Europe's population grew rapidly, and by the end of the century the population had rebounded from the devastation of the Black Death. This increase, in turn, stimulated a rise in prosperity, the expansion of commerce, and the growth of towns. Trade opportunities increased, which led to interest in exploring new markets, discovering new products, and opening new trade routes. Population pressures would also lead Europeans to settle in the Americas once colonies had been established.

THE RISE OF NATIONS The Crusades weakened the nobles and strengthened monarchs. This provided western European monarchs with the opportunity to seize more direct control over their lands. Ambitious kings and queens extended their reach by collecting new taxes, raising professional armies, and forming stronger central governments. Among the new allies of the monarchs were merchants, who willingly spent a portion of their new-found wealth on taxes in exchange for the protection or expansion of trade. By the late 1400s, four major nations were taking shape in western Europe: Portugal, Spain, France, and England.

Monarchs increased their power by investing some of the tax revenues in new weapons, which they used to limit the power of the independent nobles. Beginning in the 1300s, large forces armed with longbows overpowered knights in armor, and cannon fire crumbled their castle walls. These new weapons, along with hand-held firearms that were developed in the 1400s, would also outmatch the weapons of the Africans and Native Americans.

Skillbuilder Answer
Press: *Possible Answer:* The printing press quickly put the Renaissance ideas on paper and made them available to a great number of people. **Commerce:** *Possible Answer:* As commerce grew in Europe, merchants looked for new markets and sources of goods.

SKILLBUILDER
INTERPRETING CHARTS
What role do you think the printing press played in the growth of Renaissance ideas? How might the growth of commerce in Europe have spurred overseas exploration?

Changes in Europe in the 1400s

The Growth of Commerce
With the growth of trade, the hub of economic activity began to shift away from the feudal manor and toward towns. Merchants expanded their businesses by reinvesting profits, borrowing from banks, or forming joint-stock companies. This activity laid the foundation for a new economic system—capitalism— based on investment and profit.

Population Growth
A population boom made land scarcer and more valuable. Prosperous landowners had more money to spend on goods, fueling economic growth and increased trade that benefited merchants. At the same time, higher rents and less open land forced more peasants to look for work in towns and cities.

The Rise of Nations
Strong monarchs began consolidating power, weakening the feudal system and building new national identities. To manage the new countries, these monarchs needed money and the support of the middle class. This led to more political power for townspeople, who paid taxes and served the crown.

The Renaissance Spirit
A revival of learning and curiosity about the world led to a new way of thinking. It encouraged people to value education, the arts and sciences, and individual achievement and glory. This attitude spread rapidly after the development of the printing press.

24 CHAPTER 1

Cooperative Learning Activity: Advertising a Joint-Stock Company

Task: Students will create an advertisement luring investors to buy shares in a joint-stock company.

Purpose: To show how joint-stock companies spurred trade and colonization by reducing financial risks.

Activity: Assign students to design advertisements for investors in the Dutch East Indies Company—a joint-stock company set up to

establish trading posts along the coast of Africa and on islands off India. The goal is to wrest part of the trade in spices and tea away from Italian merchants and from the Portuguese who have already carved footholds in the area.

Building a Portfolio: Suggest that students add a letter to their portfolio that begins, "This poster demonstrates knowledge of. . . ."

ALTERNATIVE ASSESSMENT BOOK
Standards for Evaluating a Cooperative Activity

Standards for Evaluation
Advertisements should . . .

• make clear the financial incentives offered by a joint-stock company
• state how investments will be used
• demonstrate a knowledge of persuasive techniques

Finally, in one person—the king or queen of a unified nation—existed the power and the means to finance overseas exploration. The monarchs had a powerful motive to encourage the search for new land and trading routes: money to maintain a standing army and a large bureaucracy. By the mid-1400s, Europe's gold and silver mines were running low. So, the monarchs of Portugal, Spain, France, and England began looking overseas for wealth.

THE RENAISSANCE SPIRIT "Thank God it has been permitted to us to be born in this new age, so full of hope and promise," exclaimed Matteo Palmieri, a scholar in 15th-century Italy. Palmieri's optimism captured the enthusiastic spirit of the Renaissance, a term meaning the "rebirth." Started in Italy, a region stimulated by commercial contact with Asia and Africa, the Renaissance soon spread to the rest of Europe. European scholars rediscovered the texts of ancient philosophers, mathematicians, geographers, and scientists. They also investigated the works of Arab scholars carried home from the Crusades.

The spread of the Renaissance was greatly propelled by Johannes Gutenberg's invention of the printing press around 1440. This development made books easier and cheaper to produce, which allowed larger numbers of people to own and read books. The first book to be mass-produced was Gutenberg's edition of the Bible. Other works soon followed, and among the most popular items were travel stories such as those told by Marco Polo. In 1477, just over 20 years after the first Bible had been printed, Polo's book became a bestseller.

The Renaissance encouraged people to regard themselves as individuals, to have confidence in what they might achieve, and to look forward to the fame their achievements might bring. This attitude prompted many to seek glory through adventure, discovery, and conquest.

C. Answer The rise of nations, population growth and the rise of towns, rise of commerce, the Renaissance spirit.

THINK THROUGH HISTORY
C. Synthesizing What changes were occurring in European society in the 1400s?

Europe Enters a New Age of Expansion

The European interest in overseas expansion probably began in the 1200s with the journey of Marco Polo to China. In his journal, the Venetian merchant praised the wares of Asia: precious stones, pearls, silks, and objects of gold and silver. Europeans knew about such items from the Crusades. But with the publication of Polo's vivid—and sometimes exaggerated—account, the lands that produced these items came alive in their minds. The appearance of the first printed version in 1477 caused renewed interest in the east. If Europeans could not force out the Muslims who controlled the trade routes to Asia, they would find some way to get around them.

Polo, like other European merchants, traveled to Asia by overland routes. Merchants who traveled these routes faced a long and dangerous journey. Each local ruler taxed the goods that passed through his realm. At any time, the goods or the profits might fall into the hands of bandits. The expense and peril involved in such routes led Europeans to seek alternative routes. European merchants and explorers reexamined the maps drawn by ancient geographers, such as Ptolemy, an Egyptian who lived in the second century, and listened to the reports of travelers who had journeyed through Asia and Africa.

In the 1400s, Europeans used the work of Ptolemy and Arab and Jewish scholars to revive the art of cartography, or mapmaking. Although imperfect, the maps inspired Europeans to start exploring alternative water routes to Asia.

SAILING TECHNOLOGY Europeans, however, needed more than maps to guide them into uncharted waters. Out on the open seas, winds easily blew ships off

ON THE WORLD STAGE

CHINESE EXPLORATION

By the time Portuguese ships crept cautiously down the west coast of Africa, the Chinese already had sailed well beyond their shores. By 1414, the Chinese explorer Zheng He had led a fleet of ships—the largest of which stretched 440 feet in length—throughout the Indian Ocean. He and his crew reached ports in Indochina, Indonesia, and southwest India, and they would eventually reach the east coast of Africa.

Zheng He sailed for neither wealth nor fame. Instead, the Chinese emperor Yongle had sent Zheng He to track down a rival rumored to be building an invasion fleet somewhere in the west. Yongle had also hoped to display any unusual objects that Zheng He might bring back from his journeys.

A Chinese mariner's compass. The Chinese are thought to have invented the first magnetic compass.

OBJECTIVE
④ **INSTRUCT**

Europe Enters a New Age of Expansion

▶ *Starting with the Student*
• Ask students if any of them know how to use a compass. If so, have them describe how it works. If not, supply a compass for a demonstration.

▶ *Discussing Key Ideas*
• The travels of Marco Polo spur European interest in Asia.
• In an effort to find sea routes to Asia, Europeans study the works of ancient geographers and Arab and Jewish scholars.
• The Portuguese take the lead in using state-of-the-art navigation techniques to sail around the tip of Africa.

📽 *GEOGRAPHY TRANSPARENCIES*
G1, Voyages of Discovery and Exploration: 1271–1850

ON THE WORLD STAGE
Chinese Exploration

Critical Thinking: Making Comparisons Have students create a chart comparing the Chinese and Portuguese voyages to Africa. Headings might include Key Explorers, Direction of Travel, Lands Explored, Motives for Exploration, Impact on Africa.

Extension The feature suggests that Zheng He brought back "curiosities" from eastern Africa. Ask students what they think he might have chosen.

TEACHING OPTIONS

Exploring Themes

Science and Technology Point out that technological advances often bring about great social changes, both positive and negative. Then have students, individually or in groups, find technological advances mentioned in this section—the use of gunpowder, the invention of the printing press, the use of new navigational instruments, and the design of the caravel. Have students make a chart in which they assess the changes that each of these inventions brought to Europe. As a final question, ask: How did these inventions help push Europe into an age of expansion?

Making Connections Across Time

From Printing Press to Computer Explore how the printing press created a "knowledge revolution" in the 1400s and 1500s. Do students think the computer has created a comparable knowledge explosion today? Challenge students familiar with the Internet to go to McDougal Littell Learning On-Line to explore some of today's access to information. Students should click on Social Studies and then find *The Americans*, Chapter 1. As students explore the many resources related to our understanding of history in the Americas, ask what they most enjoy about the experience. What concerns them?

 http://mcdougallittell.com

Teacher's Edition 25

Reading the Diagram Be sure students know the meaning of words such as *lateen, sternpost, rudder, draft,* and *hold* as they read the diagram.

Extension Have students write a short essay or poem explaining how the caravel proved the old adage "Bigger is not always better."

IN-DEPTH RESOURCES: UNIT 1
Geography Application: The Earth's Wind Systems, p. 7

ASSESS & RETEACH

Section 4 Assessment

Have students work together to answer the questions. Tell them to note the location of the answers in the text.

Self-Assessment

Suggest that students conduct a one-minute freewriting exercise in which they record everything they learned in this section. At the end, have them evaluate whether these were the most important points in the section.

Section Quiz

FORMAL ASSESSMENT
Section Quiz, p. 8

Reteach

Have students tell you which of the section assessment questions they found to be the most difficult. Hold a class discussion to go over the answers.

CLOSE

Commercial expansion led to competition among nations and made monarchs more willing to finance overseas ventures. Christopher Columbus took advantage of these rivalries to win support for a voyage that changed the course of world history.

The Caravel

The caravel, the ship used by most early Portuguese and Spanish explorers, had many advantages over earlier vessels. It was lighter, swifter, and more maneuverable than other ships.

1 The triangular lateen sails, an innovation borrowed from Muslim sailors, allowed the caravel to sail efficiently against the wind. Rigged with lateens, the ship could tack (sail on a zigzag course) more directly into the wind than could a square-rigged ship.

2 The sternpost rudder made the caravel highly maneuverable.

3 The shallow draft made the ship ideal for exploration close to shore.

4 The large hold was capable of carrying the considerable cargo needed for long voyages.

SKILLBUILDER
INTERPRETING CHARTS
How did the triangular sail differ from those before? How was this a major advantage?

Skillbuilder Answer
Sails: The triangular sail allowed the ship to tack, or zigzag, and thus sail into the wind. **Advantage:** *Possible Answer:* It gave the Caravel the advantage of sailing in almost any direction, as opposed to having wind direction determine where the ship could go.

course. With only the sun, moon, and stars to guide them, few sailors willingly ventured beyond the sight of land. To overcome their fears, European ship captains in the 1400s experimented with the compass and the astrolabe, navigating tools that helped sailors plot direction at sea. They also took advantage of innovations in sailing ships that allowed them to sail against the wind.

PORTUGAL TAKES THE LEAD The leader in developing and employing these innovations was Portugal, led by Prince Henry the Navigator. Himself only an armchair navigator, he earned his nickname by establishing a state-of-the-art sailing school to train mariners and by sponsoring the earliest voyages.

For almost 40 years, Prince Henry sent his captains sailing south along the west coast of Africa. Portuguese explorations continued after Prince Henry died. Bartolomeu Dias rounded the southern tip of Africa in 1488. Vasco da Gama reached India ten years later. Now Portuguese traders could sail directly to Eastern Asia via the Indian Ocean. As a result, their costs fell and their profits rose.

For six decades, the Portuguese stood alone in their search for a sea route to Asia. Then, while cartographers redrew their maps to show the route around Africa, an Italian sea captain named Christopher Columbus traveled from nation to nation with his own collection of maps and figures. Columbus believed there was an even shorter route to Asia—one that headed west across the Atlantic.

When he asked for financing, Portugal's King John turned him down flatly, but a more willing audience awaited Columbus in Spain. There an advisor to Queen Isabella pointed out to her majesty that support of the proposed venture would cost less than a week's entertainment of a foreign official. It was a cheap price to show up her Portuguese neighbors, thought Isabella. So, she summoned Columbus to appear before the Spanish court.

THINK THROUGH HISTORY
D. *Analyzing Motives* What was Portugal's main motive in exploring the African coast?

D. Answer To increase their trading profits by finding a water route directly to Eastern Asia.

Section 4 Assessment

1. TERMS & NAMES

Identify:
• Prince Henry
• hierarchy
• nuclear family
• Crusades
• Reformation
• joint-stock companies

2. SUMMARIZING Recreate the web below on your paper. Fill it in with events and forces that illustrate the changes in western Europe that spurred the Age of Exploration.

3. ANALYZING Which event of the late-15th and early-16th-century western Europe do you think had the most far-reaching impact? Explain and support your answer.

THINK ABOUT
• the importance of religion
• the role of adventurers and explorers
• the rise in prosperity

4. DRAWING CONCLUSIONS Why do you think other European nations lagged behind Portugal in joining the race for overseas exploration? Support your reasons with details from the text.

THINK ABOUT
• the geography of Portugal
• the power of monarchs in the 1400s
• the economic and political situation of European nations during this time

26 CHAPTER 1

ANSWERS

1. TERMS & NAMES

Prince Henry, p. 20

hierarchy, p. 20

nuclear family, p. 21

Crusades, p. 22

Reformation, p. 22

joint-stock company, p. 24

2. SUMMARIZING

Possible Responses: **Political:** rise of centralized states; declining papal authority. **Economic:** growth of commerce; emergence of joint-stock companies. **Social:** renewed missionary calling; population growth. **Technological:** improvements in mapmaking, in sailing ships, and in navigating instruments; invention of printing press. **Cultural:** Renaissance spirit of adventure and curiosity; interest in travel stories.

3. ANALYZING

Possible Responses: The *reconquista,* because it set the stage for future Spanish conquest to spread Christianity around the globe; the Reformation, because it caused many people to seek religious freedom in America; the invention of the printing press, because it spread ideas; advances in cartography and sailing, because they promoted trade and the urge to discover and conquer other lands.

4. DRAWING CONCLUSIONS

Possible Responses: Portugal was along the Atlantic Ocean and physically connected only to Spain. Though the power of European monarchs was growing, they may not as yet have had the funds to finance overseas exploration. Other European nations did not yet have trained mariners, innovative sailing ships, or a leader such as Prince Henry. France and England were still embroiled in the Hundred Years' War.

5 Transatlantic Encounters

TERMS & NAMES
- Christopher Columbus
- Taino
- colonization
- Treaty of Tordesillas
- Columbian Exchange

LEARN ABOUT Columbus's transatlantic voyages and early interaction with Native Americans
TO UNDERSTAND how these encounters permanently changed Africa, Europe, the Americas, and the world.

ONE EUROPEAN'S STORY

In January 1492, the Genoese sailor **Christopher Columbus** stood before the Spanish court with what was at the time an unthinkable plan: he would find a route to Asia by sailing west across the Atlantic Ocean. While Queen Isabella was intrigued by Columbus's idea, her advisors were less enthusiastic. In the end, she dismissed the 41-year-old captain.

As a dejected Columbus plotted his next move, influential people in the Spanish court spoke on his behalf. Priests talked of the chance to spread Christianity. Financiers listed the names of merchants eager to invest in overseas trade.

The arguments won the crown's support. After more than a decade of appealing to royal courts throughout Europe, Columbus finally had found a monarch to finance his voyage. On August 3, 1492, he embarked on a journey destined to change the course of world history. A seeker of fame and fortune, he began his journal by restating the deal he had struck with Spain.

> **A PERSONAL VOICE**
> [B]ased on the information that I had given Your Highnesses about the land of India and about a Prince who is called the Great Khan [of China], which in our language means "King of Kings," Your Highnesses decided to send me . . . to the regions of India, to see . . . the peoples and the lands, and to learn of . . . the measures that could be taken for their conversion to our Holy Faith. . . . Your Highnesses . . . ordered that I shall go to the east, but not by land as is customary. I was to go by way of the west, whence until today we do not know with certainty that anyone has gone. . . .
> **CHRISTOPHER COLUMBUS,** *The Log of Christopher Columbus*

Christopher Columbus

Columbus did not find a route to Asia. Instead, he stepped onto an island in the Caribbean Sea and set in motion a process that brought together the American, European, and African worlds. These worlds would clash as they created new societies.

Columbus Crosses the Atlantic

Nobody paid much attention as the *Niña*, *Pinta*, and *Santa Maria* slid out of a Spanish port in the predawn hours of August 3, 1492. Although they were setting out into the unknown, their crews included no soldiers, priests, or ambassadors—only sailors and cabin boys with a taste for the sea. In a matter of months, however, Columbus's fleet would make history as it reached the sandy shores of what was to Europeans an astonishing new world.

FIRST ENCOUNTERS At about 2 A.M. on October 12, 1492, the long-awaited cry came. Juan Rodriguez Bermejo, a lookout aboard the *Pinta*, caught sight of two white sand dunes sparkling in the moonlight. In between lay a mass of dark rocks. "Tierra! Tierra!" he shouted. "Land! Land!"

At dawn Columbus went ashore. His eyes fastened on a group of people who called themselves the **Taino,** or "noble ones." In this glance, two worlds collided. As Columbus stepped ashore, he planted, along with flowing Spanish banners, the first seeds of conquest. In words the Taino did not understand, he renamed their island San Salvador, or "Holy Savior," and claimed it for Spain.

Three Worlds Meet **27**

SECTION 5 RESOURCES

PRINT RESOURCES

IN-DEPTH RESOURCES: UNIT 1
Guided Reading, p. 5
Primary Source: from *The Journal of Christopher Columbus*, p. 11
Literature: from *The Memoirs of Christopher Columbus: A Novel*, p. 13

ACCESS FOR STUDENTS ACQUIRING ENGLISH
Guided Reading (Spanish), p. 13

FORMAL ASSESSMENT
Section Quiz, p. 9

ALTERNATIVE ASSESSMENT BOOK
See forms for supporting and scoring alternative activities.

TECHNOLOGY RESOURCES

HUMANITIES TRANSPARENCIES
H1, Manuscript map of North America from Florida to Chesapeake Bay

CRITICAL THINKING TRANSPARENCIES
CT1, Exploration of the Americas

CD-ROM Electronic Library of Primary Sources

VIDEO *American Portfolio: A Videodisc for U.S. History* user's guide, pp. 12., 14, 16

INTERNET McDougal Littell Learning On-Line
http://www.mcdougallittell.com

Section 5 Overview

OBJECTIVES

1. To identify motives behind Spanish exploration and colonization of the Caribbean.
2. To evaluate the effects of contact upon Native Americans.
3. To assess the impact of the Atlantic slave trade upon Africa and the Americas.
4. To understand that the Columbian Exchange was a milestone in world history.
5. To discuss how the massive movement of people to the Americas produced a new society.

SKILLBUILDERS

- Understanding geography: human-environment interaction, p. 31
- Interpreting charts, p. 33

CRITICAL THINKING

- Summarizing, pp. 28, 33
- Recognizing effects, p. 29
- Analyzing causes, p. 30
- Analyzing issues, p. 31
- Generalizing, p. 33
- Analyzing effects, p. 33

FOCUS & MOTIVATE

▶ *Starting with the Student*
- Ask students to imagine how it would feel to venture into the unknown, where there are no accounts from someone who has gone before, no maps, and no assurance of ever coming back.
- Point out that Columbus did exactly that.

OBJECTIVE
1 **INSTRUCT**

Columbus Crosses the Atlantic

▶ *Discussing Key Ideas*
- Two worlds collide when Columbus and the Taino meet.

(continued on next page)

Teacher's Edition 27

(continued from page 27)

- Columbus's activities in the Caribbean foreshadow the objectives behind Spanish colonization.

IN-DEPTH RESOURCES: UNIT 1
Guided Reading, p. 5
Primary Source: from *The Journal of Christopher Columbus*, p. 11

ACCESS FOR STUDENTS ACQUIRING ENGLISH
Guided Reading (Spanish), p. 13

MORE ABOUT . . .
Christopher Columbus

Even death did not stop Columbus's journeys across the Atlantic. After he died in 1506, his remains rested for several decades in Valladolid, Spain. But it was decided that his body should rest on the other side of the Atlantic.

With great ceremony, he was laid to rest in Santo Domingo, the capital of Hispaniola. When Spain ceded the island to France, officials moved his remains to Cuba. When the United States seized Cuba from Spain, the remains—or alleged remains—were returned to Spain.

 ELECTRONIC LIBRARY OF PRIMARY SOURCES
from A Letter to the Treasurer of Spain *by Christopher Columbus*

HISTORICAL SPOTLIGHT
The Vikings

Critical Thinking: Formulating Historical Questions Ask students to make a list of everything that they know about the Vikings. Then have them make a list of questions they have about them. Suggest that they do library or Internet research to answer at least one of their questions about the Vikings.

HISTORICAL SPOTLIGHT

THE VIKINGS
The first Europeans to reach North America were probably Vikings. About 985, the Norwegian Viking Eric the Red crossed the Atlantic in an open boat and set up two colonies on Greenland. Some fifteen years later, his son, Leif, voyaged farther to a place he called Vinland the Good because of its abundant grapes. Historians now believe that present-day Newfoundland is Leif Ericson's Vinland. In 1963, archaeologists discovered a half-burned timbered house of Norse design there that dates to about the year 1000.

According to Norwegian sagas, or tales of great deeds, another Norwegian expedition followed Leif Ericson and stayed in Newfoundland for three years. Then the Skraelings, as the saga calls the native peoples, drove away the colonists, and the Vikings never returned.

On the first day of their encounter, the generosity of the Taino startled Columbus. "They are friendly and well-dispositioned people who bear no arms," he wrote in his log. "They traded and gave everything they had with good will." But after only two days, Columbus offered an assessment in his journal that had dark overtones for the future. In an entry addressed to Isabella and Ferdinand, he wrote:

> **A PERSONAL VOICE**
> [I]t would be unnecessary to build . . . [a fort here] because these people are so simple in deeds of arms. . . . If Your Highnesses order either to bring all of them to Castile or to hold them as captivos [slaves] on their own island it could easily be done, because with about fifty men, you could control and subjugate them, making them do whatever you want.
>
> **CHRISTOPHER COLUMBUS,** quoted in *Columbus the Great Adventurer*

GOLD, LAND, AND RELIGION On his second day in the Americas, Columbus expressed one of the main reasons he had embarked on his journey. "I have been very attentive," he wrote, "and have tried very hard to find out if there is any gold here." When he did not find gold on San Salvador, he left to look elsewhere. Columbus spent a total of 96 days exploring four coral islands in the present-day Bahamas and the coastlines of two larger Caribbean islands, known today as Cuba and Hispaniola. All along the way, he claimed lands and bestowed names. "It was my wish to bypass no island without taking possession," wrote the captain. Nor did he wish to neglect his promise to assert Christian domination. "In every place I have entered, islands or lands, I have always planted a cross," he noted on November 16. Several weeks later, he predicted, "Your Highnesses will order a city . . . built in these regions [for] these countries will be easily converted."

SPANISH FOOTHOLDS In early January 1493, Columbus began the trip back to Spain. Convinced that he had landed on islands off Asia known to Europeans as the Indies, Columbus called the people he met *los indios.* The term translated into "Indian," a word mistakenly applied to all the diverse peoples of the Americas.

The reports Columbus relayed of his journey thrilled the Spanish monarchs, who funded three more voyages. On his return to the Americas in September 1493, Columbus was no longer an explorer, but an empire builder. He commanded a fleet of some 17 ships and several hundred soldiers armed with cannons, crossbows, and swords. He also oversaw five priests and more than 1,000 colonists ready to settle the land. Among the colonists were *hidalgos,* or members of the minor nobility, mostly those who could not inherit land in Spain because of an elder brother's claim. Like Columbus, they came to the Americas to win fame and fortune.

These soldiers, priests, and colonists, and the many others that followed, would take first the Caribbean and then much of the Americas away from the Native Americans. Their arrival on Hispaniola, the island presently shared by Haiti and the Dominican Republic, signaled the start of a cultural clash that would continue for the next five centuries.

The Impact on Native Americans

The Taino who greeted Columbus in 1492 could not have known what would soon follow. The Europeans would bring with them colonization. While the Taino

A. Answer He searched for gold and began to assert Christianity among the Native Americans, two activities that will be the guiding motives behind Spain's colonization attempts in the Americas.

THINK THROUGH HISTORY
A. Summarizing *What were the main activities that Columbus undertook after arriving in the Americas?*

Cooperative Activity: Writing a News Story

Task: Students will write a news story on Columbus's return to Spain in 1493.

Purpose: To illustrate the effect of Columbus's voyage upon the era in which he lived.

Activity: Assign groups of students to write news stories based on the classic questions: *who? what? when? where? why?* and *how?* Students should try to imagine the scene when Columbus arrived and to describe in detail how various people looked and acted.

Have students use the library and the Internet to research what items Columbus brought back to Spain from the Americas. Students should include in their stories descriptions of the items and the reactions of the Spanish court.

📁 *Building a Portfolio:* Encourage students to attach rough and revised drafts to the final story.

ALTERNATIVE ASSESSMENT BOOK
Standards for Evaluating a Cooperative Activity

Standards for Evaluation
News stories should . . .

- answer the questions *who, what, where, when, why, how*
- be written from the perspective of 1493
- follow the style of a news article, with a dateline, by-line, and headline

resisted their attempts at control, there was little they could do against the diseases that also accompanied the new settlers.

METHODS OF COLONIZATION By the time Columbus had set sail for Hispaniola, Europeans had already developed a pattern for **colonization**—the establishment of outlying settlements that are controlled by the parent country. During the Crusades, Italians from Venice had taken over Arab sugar farms in what is now Lebanon. By the late 1400s, the Portuguese had established plantation colonies on islands off the coast of West Africa, and Spain had conquered the Canary Islands.

From this experience, Europeans learned the value of the plantation system to produce popular crops such as sugar. They also realized the economic benefits of using forced labor. Finally, they learned to use European weapons to dominate a people with less sophisticated weapons. These tactics would be used in full against the peoples that the Europeans called Indians.

RESISTANCE AND CONQUEST The natives of the Caribbean, however, did not succumb to Columbus and the Spaniards without fighting. In November of 1493, Columbus attempted to conquer the present-day island of St. Croix. Instead of surrendering, the inhabitants defended themselves by firing rounds of poisoned arrows. The Spaniards won easily, but the struggle proved that Native Americans would not yield in the easy conquest predicted by Columbus.

Efforts to control the Taino who inhabited Hispaniola were even more difficult. After several rebellions, the Taino submitted to Columbus for several years but revolted again in 1495. The Spanish response was swift and strong. They tracked down the rebels with the cry "*¡Tómalos!*" ("Get them!") A later settler, the missionary Bartolomé de Las Casas criticized the Spaniards' brutal response to the natives.

> **A PERSONAL VOICE**
> This tactic begun here . . . [will soon] spread throughout these Indies and will end when there is no more land nor people to subjugate and destroy in this part of the world.
> **BARTOLOME DE LAS CASAS,** quoted in *Columbus*

DISEASE RAVAGES THE NATIVE AMERICANS The diseases Europeans unknowingly brought with them devastated the Native Americans. Measles, mumps, chicken pox, and typhus were just some of the diseases that traveled to the Americas with the European settlers. Native Americans, who had not developed any natural immunity to these diseases, died by the thousands. According to one estimate, nearly one-third of Hispaniola's estimated 300,000 inhabitants died during Columbus's time there. By 1508, fewer than 100,000 survivors lived on the island. Sixty years later, only two villages were left.

These illnesses would soon spread to the rest of the Americas. More surely than any army, disease conquered region after region.

A medicine man ministers to an Aztec with smallpox, a deadly disease brought to the Americas by Europeans.

B. Answer The world collapsed, as many were forced to work for the Europeans, and much of their population was depleted by disease brought by Europeans.

THINK THROUGH HISTORY
B. Recognizing Effects What impact did Columbus's arrival have upon the inhabitants of the Caribbean?

Three Worlds Meet **29**

The Impact on Native Americans

▶ *Discussing Key Ideas*
- The Europeans create a system of forced labor among Native Americans.
- The introduction of European diseases decimates Native American populations.

MORE ABOUT . . .
Native American Resistance

Cuban history records an account of a Native American from Hispaniola named Hatuey who fiercely resisted the Spanish. Captured while seeking to organize Native Americans in Cuba, Hatuey faced death at the stake.

A friar promised him paradise if he converted to Christianity. Hatuey asked if there were any Spaniards in paradise. The friar replied that only the good ones were. Hatuey gave the following response:

"The best are good for nothing, and I will not go where there is a chance of meeting one of them."

Cooperative Activity: Designing Storyboards

Task: Students will create storyboards showing Spanish colonization of Hispaniola from the Native American perspective.

Purpose: To illustrate the effects of the arrival of the Spaniards on such peoples as the Taino.

Activity: Have groups of students create storyboards that present a visual history of the Spanish conquest of the Taino. Suggest that students use the art on this page as a model. A helpful tip might be to tell students to think of storyboards as frames in a filmstrip or a comic book.

📁 **Building a Portfolio:** Before adding the storyboards to portfolios, students might script a story line, or a broad statement of the theme.

ALTERNATIVE ASSESSMENT BOOK
Standards for Evaluating a Cooperative Activity

Standards for Evaluation
Storyboards should . . .

- depict key events from the arrival of Columbus on Hispaniola to the coming of the first enslaved Africans
- show an understanding of the effects of colonization upon the Taino

The Impact on Africans

▶ **Starting with the Student**
For an account of the emotional effects of the slave trade, you might request volunteers to research and read aloud an appropriate extract from the story of Olaudah Equiano. Suggest that they look for a copy of *The Classic Slave Narratives,* introduced and edited by Henry Louis Gates, Jr.

▶ **Discussing Key Ideas**
• The high death toll among Native Americans leads Spaniards to turn to enslaved Africans for labor.
• The demand for slaves in the Americas drains West African cultures of many of their most fit members.
• At least 12 million Africans crossed to the Americas from the 1500s to the 1800s as part of the slave trade.

The Impact on Europeans

▶ **Discussing Key Ideas**
• Columbus's voyages transform life on four continents, including Europe.
• Competition over colonies ignites national rivalries, drawing Europeans into wars that take on a global dimension.
• The Columbian Exchange brings about a massive transfer of plants and animals among the continents.

The Impact on Africans

By 1502, a small number of Africans were working in the copper mines on Hispaniola. Columbus's voyages, which linked the two worlds of America and Europe, had touched yet a third world. With the decline of the native work force due mainly to disease, the European settlers of the Americas turned to Africa for slaves. In the years to come, European slave ships would haul hundreds of thousands of Africans across the Atlantic to toil in the Americas.

A NEW SLAVE LABOR FORCE The use of Native Americans as slaves was a controversial issue with the Spaniards. The native peoples proved difficult to enslave, and by the 1500s, many of them were succumbing to disease. Furthermore, the Spanish monarchy increasingly opposed using Native Americans as slaves. Las Casas also became a strong proponent of protecting their freedom. Unfortunately, he and other Spaniards saw the use of Africans as a possible solution to the colonies' labor shortage. Advised Las Casas, "The labor of one . . . [Negro] . . . [is] more valuable than that of four Indians; every effort should be made to bring many . . . [Negroes] from Guinea."

As more natives died, the demand for Africans grew. The price of enslaved Africans rose, and more Europeans jumped into the African slave trade. By 1515, the first shipment of sugar produced in the Americas by African slaves arrived in Spain. Just 23 years after Columbus first set foot in the Americas, African slavery was on its way to becoming an essential part of the European-American economic system.

AFRICAN LOSSES The Atlantic slave trade would devastate many African societies, particularly in West Africa. Starting in the 1500s, African cultures lost many of their fittest members—their young and able—to a trade that valued strength and endurance. Although controversy exists over the exact numbers, one estimate holds that perhaps 250,000 enslaved Africans landed in the Americas during the 1500s alone. Another 200,000 would arrive between 1601 and 1621. And before the slave trade ended in the 1800s, it would drain Africa of at least 12 million people.

The Impact on Europeans

Columbus's voyages had profound effects on Europe as well. Major shifts in power occurred, as nations competed for the opportunities presented by overseas colonization. Merchants and monarchs saw a chance to increase their wealth and influence. Ordinary people by the thousands saw a chance to live in a new world, free of the hierarchy that bound them both economically and socially. Within a century, thousands of Europeans would begin to cross the Atlantic in what became one of the biggest voluntary migrations in world history.

NATIONAL RIVALRIES Not surprisingly, overseas expansion inflamed national rivalries on the European continent. Portugal, the pioneer of navigation and exploration, deeply resented Spain's sudden conquests.

C. Answer The resistant nature of the Native Americans made them difficult to control; much of the native population was dying from disease; the Spanish crown had grown very much opposed to the use of Native Americans as slaves.

THINK THROUGH HISTORY
C. *Analyzing Causes* What factors led to the use of African slaves in the early Spanish colonies?

The Columbian Exchange

NORTH AMERICA

Avocado
Corn
Sweet Potato
Quinine
Peppers
Pineapple
Squash
Turkey
Pumpkin

SOUTH AMERICA

TEACHING OPTION

Exploring Themes

Immigration and Migration With the arrival of the first enslaved Africans in the Americas, the stage was set for the variety of peoples—Native American, European, and African—that would create the diverse nations of this hemisphere. Even today, with thousands of immigrants flooding into the United States from Asia and Latin America, the makeup of the U.S. population still reflects the deep impact of contact. Share with students this data from the 1990 census.

Ancestry Groups of Americans	
Group	Millions
1. German	58
2. Irish	39
3. English	33
4. African	24
5. Italian	15
6. Mexican	12
7. French	10
8. Polish	9
9. Native American	9
10. Dutch	6

In 1493, Pope Alexander VI, a Spaniard, stepped in to avoid war between the two nations by identifying different regions of exploration for each country. In the **Treaty of Tordesillas,** signed in 1494, Spain and Portugal agreed to divide the Western Hemisphere between them. Lands to the west of an imaginary vertical line drawn in the Atlantic, including most of the Americas, belonged to Spain. Lands to the east of this line, including Brazil, belonged to Portugal.

THINK THROUGH HISTORY
D. *Analyzing Issues* Why might Spain and Portugal have been willing to go to war over the issue of overseas exploration?

D. Answer Both countries had taken the lead, and soon became competitors in exploration and colonization, and both countries knew of the possibilities for wealth and power that came from establishing dominance in this area.

The plan proved to be impossible to enforce. Its one long-lasting effect was to give Portugal a colony—Brazil—in what was largely a Spanish South America. Otherwise, the agreement had no effect on the English, Dutch, or French, all of whom began colonizing the Americas during the late 1500s and early 1600s.

THE COLUMBIAN EXCHANGE The voyages of Columbus and those after him led to the discovery of new plants and animals to Europeans, Africans, and the inhabitants of the Americas. Ships took items from the Americas back to Europe and to Africa, and introduced Western Hemisphere items into the Eastern Hemisphere. This global transfer of living things, called the **Columbian Exchange,** began with Columbus's first voyage and still continues today.

Foods from the Americas enriched diets around the world. Corn and potatoes from the Americas became staples of European and African diets. Manioc, or cassava, a starchy root that is ground into flour (it is the source of tapioca), became a basic source of nutrition in parts of Africa. Europeans, Africans, and Asians also quickly absorbed such foods from the Americas as squash, pumpkins, tomatoes, chilies, peanuts, and cocoa into their diets.

Traffic across the Atlantic did not flow in just one direction, however. Europeans introduced various livestock animals into the Americas, including horses, cattle, and pigs. Foods from Africa (including some that originated in Asia) migrated west with the slave ships—black-eyed peas, bananas, plantains

Skillbuilder Answer
Human-Environment Interaction: *Possible Answer:* It has given the people of each hemisphere new foods and sources of nutrition.

GEOGRAPHY SKILLBUILDER
HUMAN-ENVIRONMENT INTERACTION
How do you think the Columbian Exchange has enriched each hemisphere?

HISTORY FROM VISUALS
The Columbian Exchange
Reading the Map Point out the number of continents involved in the exchange. *Four.* Ask students why this back-and-forth flow of goods has been called an "ecological revolution."

Extension Have students expand the map and add other items involved in the exchange. A source of information is *The Seeds of Change,* a book sponsored by the Smithsonian Institution on the 500th anniversary of Columbus's arrival in the Americas.

MORE ABOUT . . .
The Columbian Exchange
Nobody is sure when or how products from the Americas reached China. Today, however, American staples play an important role in feeding China's huge population. To appreciate the impact of the Columbian Exchange upon Chinese diets, consider these statistics from the 1980s.

• China's potato harvests were double North America's and were one-quarter as large as those of Europe, the world's leading potato producer.
• China's corn harvests were equal to those of Europe and 28 percent as large as those in the United States, the world's leading corn producer.
• China raised 80 percent of the world's sweet potatoes, leaving other regions far, far behind.

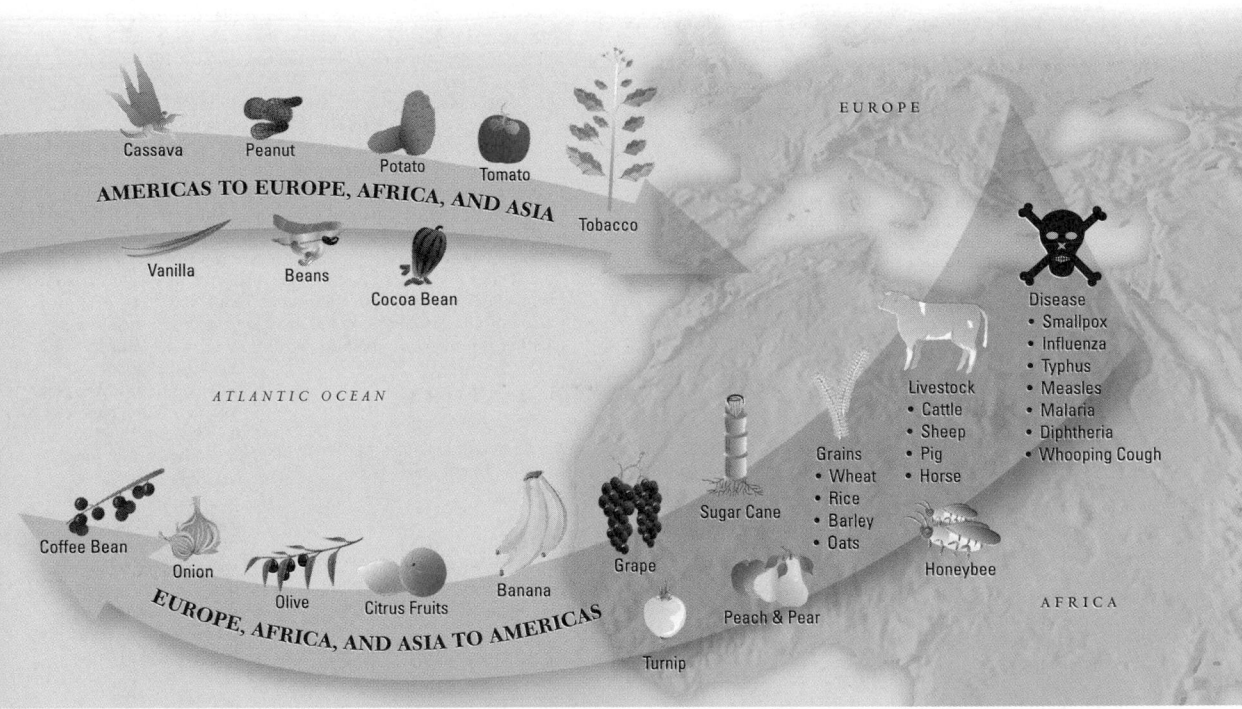

AMERICAS TO EUROPE, AFRICA, AND ASIA

Cassava · Peanut · Potato · Tomato · Tobacco · Vanilla · Beans · Cocoa Bean

ATLANTIC OCEAN

EUROPE

Coffee Bean · Onion · Olive · Citrus Fruits · Banana · Grape · Sugar Cane · Grains • Wheat • Rice • Barley • Oats · Peach & Pear · Turnip · Honeybee

EUROPE, AFRICA, AND ASIA TO AMERICAS

Livestock • Cattle • Sheep • Pig • Horse

Disease • Smallpox • Influenza • Typhus • Measles • Malaria • Diphtheria • Whooping Cough

AFRICA

Cooperative Learning Activity: Mapping Corn Production

Task: Students will research global corn production and show the results on a map.

Purpose: To show the impact of the Columbian Exchange.

Activity: Assign students to research corn production by nation, with each group focusing on a different nation. Tell them this information can be found in almanacs such as *The Information Please Almanac* or *The World Almanac.* Have them record their findings on an outline map of the world.

Recommend that they develop a key to show categories of production. (Helpful tip: Amounts are recorded in thousands of metric tons and range from less than 100 to over 200,000.) Students should also think of an appropriate title for their map, such as "Corn: The Native American Gift to the World."

ALTERNATIVE ASSESSMENT BOOK
Standards for Evaluating a Cooperative Activity

▶ **Starting with the Student**

• You might open discussion of this topic by asking students this question: What is an American?.

• Suggest that students read pp. xxx–xxxi, in the front of this book, on what it means to be an American.

▶ **Discussing Key Ideas**

• Nobody in 1492 could predict the momentous significance of Columbus's arrival in the Americas.

• Following in Columbus's wake, people came from all parts of the world.

• Together they produced the diverse society that forms the United States.

 CRITICAL THINKING TRANSPARENCIES
CT1, Exploration of the Americas

 ELECTRONIC LIBRARY OF PRIMARY SOURCES from *La Relacion* by Álvar Núñez Cabeza de Vaca

**POINT-
COUNTERPOINT**
Columbus's Legacy

▶ **Starting with the Student**

• Ask students to think about heroes of their own whom, at some point, they heard unfavorably criticized. How did it make them feel?

▶ **Discussing Key Ideas**

• Some historians believe that Columbus was a ruthless man of violence who did more harm than good.

• Some historians believe that in spite of the violence and deception brought about by Columbus, the results of his efforts are clearly on the side of progress.

(a type of banana), eggplant, and yams. In addition, Europeans brought their technology, including wheeled vehicles, guns, and iron tools to other parts of the world.

A New Society Is Born

Christopher Columbus lived on Hispaniola until 1500. That year, Ferdinand and Isabella, dissatisfied with the explorer's inability to maintain order on the island, requested that he leave. After further travels throughout the Caribbean, Columbus reluctantly returned to Spain in 1504, where he died two years later. The daring sea captain went to his grave disappointed that he had not reached China.

Neither Columbus nor anyone else could have foreseen the long chain of events that his voyages set in motion. In time, settlers from England would transplant their cultures to colonies in North America. From within these colonies would emerge a new society—and a new nation—based on ideas of representative government and religious tolerance.

The story of the United States of America thus begins with a meeting of peoples and cultures that radically transformed the North American, African, and European worlds. The upheaval threw unfamiliar peoples and customs together on a grand scale. The Europeans would impose their ways on North America, but never completely. Their need to borrow from the peoples they sought to

POINT ▶ **COUNTERPOINT**

"The legacy of Columbus is primarily one of 'genocide, cruelty, and slavery.'"

Should Columbus be hailed by Americans as a hero? Many don't see it that way. Speaking to the experience of Native Americans, for example, the activist Suzan Shown Harjo insists that "this half millennium of land grabs and one-cent treaty sales has been no bargain." The historian Hans Konig concurs that Columbus's legacy should be deplored rather than celebrated: "The year 1492 opened an era of genocide, cruelty, and slavery on a larger scale than had ever been seen before."

While acknowledging that progress involves both benefits and losses, critics such as the historian Howard Zinn argue that the actions of the European conquistadors and settlers were unnecessarily cruel and plainly immoral. As Zinn asks, "If there are necessary sacrifices to be made for human progress, is it not essential to hold to the principle that those to be sacrificed must make the decision themselves?"

Moreover, Zinn asks, "What did the people of Spain get out of all that death and brutality visited on the Indians of the Americas?" Konig provides an answer: "All the gold and silver stolen and shipped to Spain did not make the Spanish people richer. . . . They ended up [with] . . . a deadly inflation, a starving population, the rich richer, the poor poorer, and a ruined peasant class."

"Columbus's achievements were historic and heroic."

Historians who appreciate Columbus acknowledge the destruction that followed but argue that change and conflict were inevitable. They maintain that Columbus was a man of his time and therefore accepted the values of the age in which he lived.

However, despite the violence he unleashed, his fateful voyages produced many long-term benefits—including making possible the creation of a new democratic society. As the journalist Paul Gray notes, "Columbus's journey was the first step in a long process that eventually produced the United States of America, a daring experiment in democracy that in turn became a symbol and a haven of individual liberty for people throughout the world."

Other historians suggest that respect is due Columbus for the sheer dimension of the change he caused. "The Columbian discovery was of greater magnitude than any other discovery or invention in human history, . . . both because of the . . . development of the New World and because of the numerous other discoveries that have stemmed from it," asserts the historian Paolo Emilio Taviani. "Notwithstanding errors, egoism, and unheard-of violence, the discovery was an essential . . . factor in ushering in the modern age."

 INTERACT WITH HISTORY

1. **COMPARING** How does each side view the tradeoff between the "human progress" and the "unheard-of violence" resulting from Columbus's voyages? Which side do you agree with? Why?

 SEE SKILLBUILDER HANDBOOK, PAGE 1041.

2. **WRITING A MONOLOGUE** Do research to find out more about the Tainos and Columbus. Use your material to write a monologue from the point of view of either (1) the Taino or (2) Columbus or a member of his expeditions.

INTERNET For more about Columbus, click on *Social Studies* at
http://www.mcdougallittell.com

---

1. Comparing

Possible Responses: *The first view does not seem to allow for any recognition of "human progress" in the legacy of Columbus. The second view seems to give much more respect, viewing the legacy of Columbus as inevitable to human progress. Students will vary in their opinions about where Columbus really stands, some seeing him as the one who introduced unspeakable violence and deception into the Americas, others seeing him as a hero of unprecedented bravery who set off for what might have been the edge of the earth, opening the gates to "a daring experiment in democracy."*

2. Writing a Monologue

Have students research the Taino and other native peoples at the library or on the Internet. The subject listing in the Dewey decimal system is Indians of North America, which should help to get them started. Review with students the elements of a monologue. Remind them that in a monologue, which is like a one-sided conversation, the person speaking is not expecting a response from anyone. That person is simply revealing his or her thoughts and feelings. An effective monologue can be very dramatic and powerful.

dominate proved too strong. Furthermore, the Native Americans and Africans resisted giving up their cultural identities. The new nation that emerged would bear the touch of these three worlds, as well as others, in a distinctly multicultural society. Throughout the history of the United States, this multiculturalism would be one of its greatest challenges and also one of its greatest assets.

Skillbuilder Answer
Shift: The shift led to a dramatic decline in the Native American population. **Decline:** Europeans' diseases as well as their efforts to conquer Native Americans led to this great decline.

HISTORY FROM VISUALS
Atlantic Population Shift, 1492 to the Early 1800s

Reading the Map and Graph Point out the different kinds of information that are recorded on the arrows and in the bar graph. What is the dramatic story recorded in the bar graph?

Extension Ask students to check a reference such as *Information Please Almanac* for current immigration statistics. From what countries did most immigrants come in the past five years?

HUMANITIES TRANSPARENCIES
H1, Manuscript map of North America from Florida to Chesapeake Bay

Atlantic Population Shift, 1492 to the Early 1800s

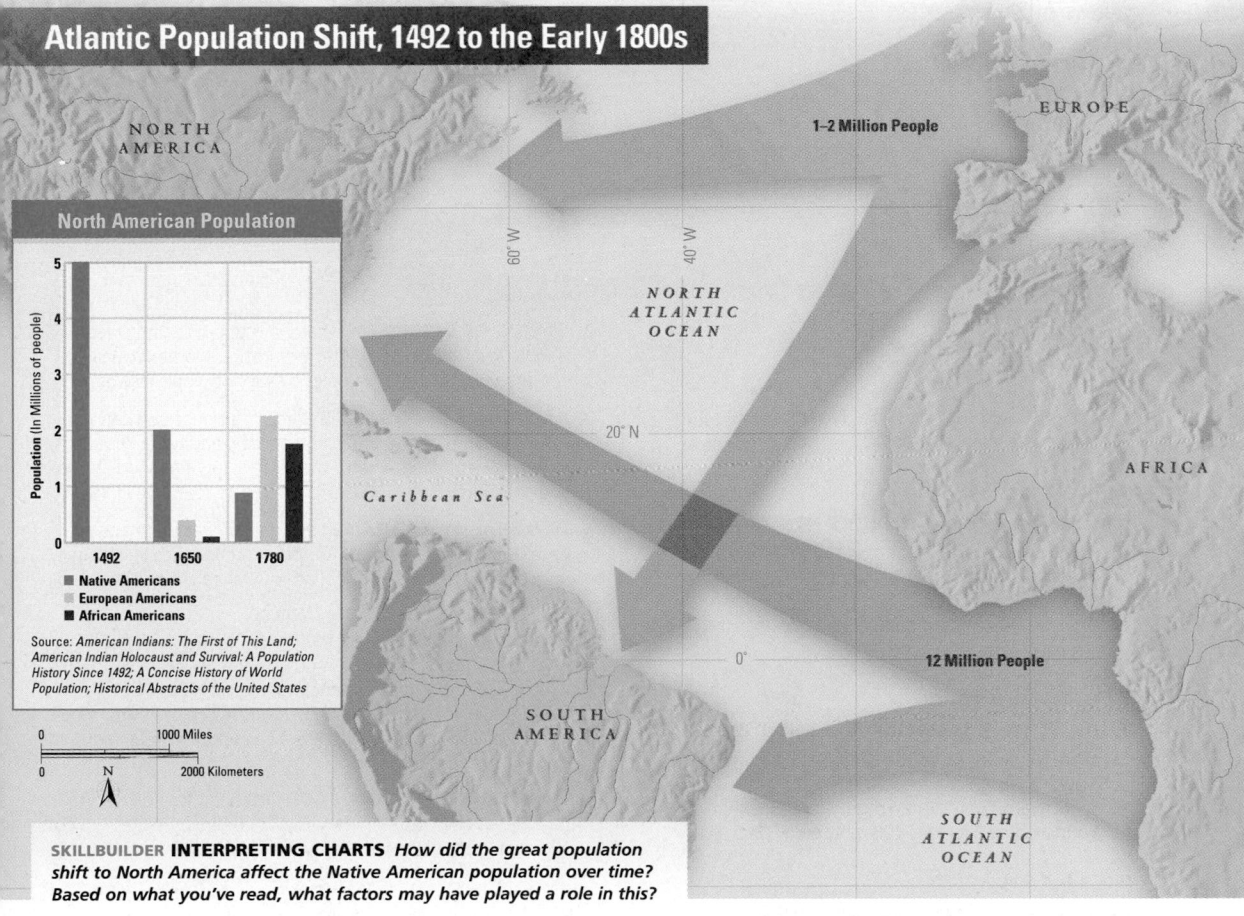

North American Population

Population (In Millions of people)

1492 1650 1780

■ Native Americans
■ European Americans
■ African Americans

Source: *American Indians: The First of This Land; American Indian Holocaust and Survival: A Population History Since 1492; A Concise History of World Population; Historical Abstracts of the United States*

1–2 Million People

EUROPE

NORTH AMERICA

60° W   40° W

NORTH ATLANTIC OCEAN

20° N

Caribbean Sea

0°

AFRICA

12 Million People

SOUTH AMERICA

SOUTH ATLANTIC OCEAN

0   1000 Miles
0   2000 Kilometers

SKILLBUILDER INTERPRETING CHARTS *How did the great population shift to North America affect the Native American population over time? Based on what you've read, what factors may have played a role in this?*

Section 5 Assessment

1. TERMS & NAMES

Identify:
• Christopher Columbus
• Taino
• colonization
• Treaty of Tordesillas
• Columbian Exchange

2. SUMMARIZING Create a time line of the major events of Columbus's voyages and interactions with Native Americans. Use the dates already plotted on the time line below as a guide.

1492   1495   1504

1493   1500

How did the Americas change during his lifetime as a result of his voyages?

3. GENERALIZING A stereotype is an oversimplified opinion or image. What stereotypes do you think Columbus and his soldiers might have formed about Native Americans, and Native Americans might have formed about Spaniards? Why?

THINK ABOUT
• Columbus's journal entries
• Columbus and his soldiers' methods of colonization
• Native Americans' attempts to resist conquest

4. ANALYZING EFFECTS What do you think were three of the most important long-term consequences of Columbus's encounters in the Americas?

THINK ABOUT
• conquering and claiming land
• forced labor of Native Americans and Africans
• the impact on Africa, Europe, and the Americas

Three Worlds Meet **33**

ASSESS & RETEACH

Section 5 Assessment
Suggest that students write down important points that they want to include in each answer before beginning to write.

Self-Assessment
Ask students what they now know about Columbus that surprises them? Why?

Section Quiz

FORMAL ASSESSMENT
Section Quiz, p. 9

Reteach
Use the map on pages 30–31 (the Columbian Exchange) to review the main ideas of the section.

CLOSE

The voyages of Columbus turned the world upside down. People who had developed independently of each other for thousands of years suddenly met in a series of dramatic and painful encounters. The struggle to live together and the culture that resulted introduces a key theme in our nation's story.

ANSWERS

1. TERMS & NAMES
Christopher Columbus, p. 27
Taino, p. 27
colonization, p. 29
Treaty of Tordesillas, p. 31
Columbian Exchange, p. 31

2. SUMMARIZING
Possible Responses: **1492:** Columbus's first voyage to the Americas. **1493:** Columbus's return trip to the Americas; Columbus's conquest of St. Croix despite resistance by its Native Americans. **1495:** Rebellion of Taino of Hispaniola against Spanish. **1500:** Columbus asked to leave Hispaniola because of his inability to maintain order. **1504:** Columbus returns to Spain.

3. GENERALIZING
Possible Responses: Columbus's stereotypes of Native Americans: gentle, weak-willed, and uncivilized; spiritually and physically inferior; rebellious and difficult to control. Native American stereotypes of Spaniards: brutal, violent, and cruel; intolerant and disrespectful; greedy and exploitive.

4. ANALYZING EFFECTS
Possible Responses: The entrenched pattern of violating human rights in the process of conquering new lands; the African slave trade and its tragic outcomes; the emergence of various nations in North and South America; the permanent altering of global environments and societies as a result of the Columbian Exchange; the multicultural character of the United States.

TERMS & NAMES
1. Maya, p. 6
2. Hohokam, p. 6
3. Kwakiutl, p. 9
4. kinship, p. 13
5. Islam, p. 15
6. lineage, p. 18
7. Prince Henry, p. 20
8. Reformation, p. 22
9. Christopher Columbus, p. 27
10. colonization, p. 29

MAIN IDEAS
Answers will vary.

11. During the last Ice Age, perhaps 40,000 years ago, the earliest people trekked across a land bridge between Asia and Alaska. Some may have traveled down the Pacific coast in boats resembling kayaks.

12. The Inca developed skills for mining and working precious metals; the Anasazi built homes in Southwest canyon walls.

13. The Kwakiutl constructed totem poles that portrayed their heritage; the Hopi and others sang songs and used rituals taken from their ancestors.

14. Trading networks; viewing the land as the source of life; the extended family as the central unit of social organization.

15. Goods from Mediterranean cities and salt from Saharan mines were exchanged for gold, ivory, kola nuts, dyed cotton cloth, and slaves. North African traders also brought their Islamic faith.

16. Songhai, Benin, and Kongo.

17. Weakened power of European nobles; increased interest in trade; decline of papal authority.

18. Bartolomeu Dias rounded the southern tip of Africa in 1488; Vasco da Gama reached India in 1498.

19. Establishing plantation colonies; reaping the economic benefits of forced labor; using European weapons and coercive tactics.

20. Columbus never attained his goal of reaching China.

Chapter 1 Assessment

REVIEWING THE CHAPTER

TERMS & NAMES For each term, person or group named below, explain the historical significance of the following.

1. Maya	6. lineage
2. Hohokam	7. Prince Henry
3. Kwakiutl	8. Reformation
4. kinship	9. Christopher Columbus
5. Islam	10. colonization

MAIN IDEAS

SECTION 1 (pages 4–7)
Peopling the Americas
11. What theories explain when and how the first people arrived in the Americas?
12. Give two examples of how ancient societies demonstrated their resourcefulness in adapting to their physical environments.

SECTION 2 (pages 8–13)
Native American Societies Around 1492
13. Provide two examples of how Native American societies drew upon or honored their cultural heritage.
14. Describe three broad cultural patterns that the diverse Native American societies shared.

SECTION 3 (pages 14–19)
West African Societies Around 1492
15. What exchanges of goods and ideas occurred as a result of trade routes across the Sahara?
16. What were three West African kingdoms that flourished in the late 1400s and early 1500s?

SECTION 4 (pages 20–26)
European Societies Around 1492
17. What three effects did the Crusades have on European society in the 1400s?
18. What were the most significant Portuguese explorations?

SECTION 5 (pages 27–33)
Transatlantic Encounters
19. What methods of colonization, based on earlier models, did Spain use in conquering the native peoples in the Americas?
20. What unfulfilled goal left Columbus disappointed at the end of his life?

THINKING CRITICALLY

1. **FAMILY SYSTEMS** Create a Venn diagram like the one shown to indicate differences and similarities between Native American and West African family systems.

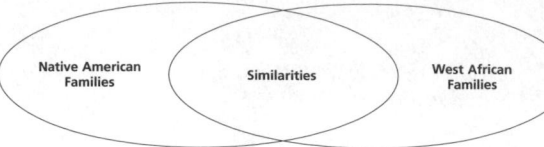

FAMILY SYSTEMS

Native American Families — Similarities — West African Families

2. **STATUS OF WOMEN** In what ways do you think Queen Isabella was like and different from other women in 15th-century Europe? Cite examples to support your answer.

3. **AMERICA'S BEGINNINGS** Reread the quote by Edward Countryman on page 2. Do you agree or disagree with his comment regarding when American history began? Support your opinion.

4. **GEOGRAPHY OF TRADE** Look carefully at the maps on pages 15 and 23. How are Timbuktu and Venice similar in regard to trade? Based on what you've read, what impact did trade have on these cities?

5. **HYPOTHESIZING** Review the Point-Counterpoint feature on page 32. Imagine that Columbus could not make his voyage to America. Do you think America would likely have been colonized in the same way if Portuguese explorers were the first Europeans to land in America? Support your opinion with evidence from the chapter.

6. **ANALYZING PRIMARY SOURCES** Read the following passage by the contemporary Native American writer N. Scott Momaday. Then answer the questions that follow.

> "The earth is our mother. The sky is our father." This concept of nature. . . is at the center of the Native American world view. . . . The Native American's attitudes toward this landscape have been formulated over a long period of time, a span that reaches back to the end of the Ice Age. . . . [T]he Indian has assumed a deep ethical regard for the earth and the sky, a reverence for the natural world. . . . It is this ancient ethic of the Native American that must shape our efforts to preserve the earth and the life upon and within it.
>
> **N. SCOTT MOMADAY,** "A First American Views His Land," *National Geographic*

What does Momaday think that other Americans can learn from Native Americans? Why do you suppose he feels the need to give this warning? Support your response.

THINKING CRITICALLY

1. FAMILY SYSTEMS
Possible Responses: Native American Families: Iroquois clan members lived together in longhouses; Iroquois and Hopi women owned household items. West African Families: Lineage determined inheritance and marriage partners; Ibo people encouraged finding a mate outside lineage group. Similarities: Matrilineal and patrilineal kinship systems; elders' high status within family; extended families or clans.

2. STATUS OF WOMEN
Possible Responses: Similarities include demonstrating her subordinate status by deferring to her husband: she took an active military role only in her husband's absence. Differences include defying the conventional role of women: fighting openly with the pope; feeling at ease wielding power and authority; dressing in armor and acting as a military commander in her husband's absence.

3. AMERICA'S BEGINNINGS
Possible Responses: Students agreeing might say that American history grew from its cross-cultural beginnings, which occurred because of Columbus's mistake over 500 years ago. Students disagreeing might say that America was not America then; true American history began when the country was established; others might say that American history began more than 500 years ago, because Native Americans and their customs were on the continent long before that.

ALTERNATIVE ASSESSMENT

1. RECORDING HISTORY

How does point of view affect how history is recorded?

Relate an event described by Cabeza de Vaca in his *La Relación* from the viewpoint of a Native American, or rewrite another early explorer's journal entry from the viewpoint of a different ethnic group.

 Use *Electronic Library of Primary Sources* or your library resources to read excerpts from *La Relación* or other early explorers' journals.

- After reading, list the assumptions and conclusions drawn by the writer about the ethnic group he encountered.
- Envision the encounter between groups from the point of view of another group (such as Native Americans). Write a journal entry describing the physical appearance and behavior from that point of view.
- Share your "journal entries" with others. Read to see how realistic one another's entries are.

2. COMPARING SOCIETIES

Cooperative Learning In a small group, create a poster or chart that compares an ancient society with contemporary American society. Present both similarities and differences. To help you plan, consider the following points in your comparison:

- social structures
- political organizations
- housing
- cultural and technological achievements
- religious beliefs and rituals

Group members should work together to verbally and visually present their comparisons.

3. PORTFOLIO PROJECT

 Use the Living History activity to expand your portfolio.

LIVING HISTORY

PRESENTING A CULTURE

You have collected materials for a visual presentation on a particular Native American, West African, or European society. Now prepare the final presentation.

Give a trial presentation in front of a friend. Then assess the presentation together as you consider the following questions:
- Does it show many different aspects of the society?
- Are the conclusions logical?
- Are the visuals exciting?

 Display your visuals and present your report to the class. Save your visuals and report in your American history portfolio.

Review Chapter 1

THE EARLIEST AMERICANS During the last Ice Age, nomadic bands of hunters trekked across a land bridge linking Asia to Alaska. Future generations migrated throughout the Americas. The development of agriculture prompted the creation of larger, more complex societies, which began flourishing in these regions about 3000 years ago.

NATIVE AMERICANS In the 1400s, diverse native groups lived in a wide range of environments—the West Coast, the Northwest Coast, the Southwest, and the Eastern Woodlands. These societies interacted with one another through trade and generally shared certain broad cultural patterns—customs and rituals, regard for nature and the land, spiritual beliefs, and strong family ties.

WEST AFRICANS In the 1400s, many different societies, ranging from simple village communities to wealthy kingdoms, existed in West Africa. In the mid-1400s, West Africa's interaction with the wider world changed with the arrival of Portuguese explorers.

WESTERN EUROPEAN EXPLORATION In the late 1400s, political, economic, social, cultural, and technological changes spurred Europeans to explore the African coast and cross the Atlantic Ocean. The Portuguese took the lead in the search for a sea route to Asia. Then, in 1492, Spain financed Christopher Columbus's voyage across the Atlantic Ocean to find a shorter route to Asia. Instead, he landed on a Caribbean island. This first encounter led to a convergence of cultures that radically transformed the North American, African, and European worlds.

Preview Chapter 2

As Europeans started to settle North America from 1492 to 1700, conflict prevailed in the interactions among European, African, and Native American cultures. After Columbus, the Spaniards continued to explore the Americas while imposing harsh colonial rule on the native peoples they conquered. In the 1600s, English settlers began claiming land and establishing colonies along the Atlantic coast of North America. You will learn about these and other significant developments in the next chapter.

Three Worlds Meet **35**

---

1. RECORDING HISTORY
Standards for Evaluation
An effective journal entry should meet the following criteria:
- Provides the viewpoint of another ethnic group.
- Includes appropriate details.
- Offers personal observations.

2. COMPARING SOCIETIES
Standards for Evaluation
A comparison chart should meet the following criteria:
- Is organized by similarities and differences.
- Lists points of similarity and dissimilarity.
- Expresses all comparisons clearly.
- Provides specific examples from the text.

3. PORTFOLIO PROJECT
LIVING HISTORY
Standards for Evaluation
A presentation should meet the following criteria:
- Presents many different aspects of a society.
- Shows good organization.
- Draws logical, relevant conclusions.
- Includes clear, coherent visuals.

IN-DEPTH RESOURCES: UNIT 1
See the form for scoring this activity on page 19.

THINKING CRITICALLY

4. GEOGRAPHY OF TRADE
Possible Responses: They're both at the hub of a major trade network. Both cities became busy commercial centers, and the empires that controlled them grew wealthy and powerful.

5. HYPOTHESIZING
Possible Responses: Students answering yes might say that Portugal and Spain did not differ in significant ways in their approach to colonization, religion, slavery, conquest; so the outcome would probably have been the same. Students answering no might cite Portuguese knowledge of

navigation; Portugal probably would not have "accidentally" found America and therefore might have viewed its people differently.

6. ANALYZING PRIMARY SOURCES
Possible Responses: A reverence for the earth; a realization of the need for conservation; an urgency to preserve the earth and its life because it's morally right to do that; a realization of how long the Native Americans were on this continent and how they did not harm the environment during all those years. Perhaps he

gives this warning because Americans need to respect the earth, and to reverse pollution in order to save the earth for future generations.

PLANNING GUIDE
The American Colonies Emerge

	Key Ideas	TEACHING SUPPORT	ASSESSMENT
SECTION 1 Spain's Empire in the Americas *pp. 38–43*	The Spanish gain the first foothold in the Americas, as they conquer much of Mexico and what is now the southern part of the United States.	**In-Depth Resources: Unit 1** • Guided Reading, p. 20 • Skillbuilder Practice: Developing Historical Perspective, p. 24 • Outline Map: Spain Explores North America, p. 27 • American Lives: Malinche, p. 36 **COOPERATIVE ACTIVITIES** • Writing About Popé's Rebellion, p. 42 (TE)	*Section 1 Assessment*, p. 43 (PE) *Self-Assessment*, p. 43 (TE) *Formal Assessment* • Section Quiz, p. 18 *Alternative Assessment Book* • Standards for Evaluating a Cooperative Activity
SECTION 2 An English Settlement at Jamestown *pp. 44–49*	English settlers endure early years of hardship to establish England's first permanent colony in North America.	**In-Depth Resources: Unit 1** • Guided Reading, p. 21 • Geography Application: The Jamestown Fort, History Reclaimed, p. 25 • Primary Sources: from *The Travels and Works of Captain John Smith*, p. 29; Tobacco Labels, p. 30	*Section 2 Assessment*, p. 49 (PE) *Self-Assessment*, p. 49 (TE) *Formal Assessment* • Section Quiz, p. 19
SECTION 3 Puritan New England *pp. 52–57*	English Puritans settle New England with the hope of establishing a model society based on their religious views.	**In-Depth Resources: Unit 1** • Guided Reading, p. 22 • Primary Sources: from The Mayflower Compact, p. 31; from John Winthrop's Journal, p. 32 • American Lives: John Winthrop, p. 37 • Literature: Poems by Anne Bradstreet, p. 33 **COOPERATIVE ACTIVITIES** • Investigating Puritan Life, p. 54 (TE)	*Section 3 Assessment*, p. 57 (PE) *Self-Assessment*, p. 57 (TE) *Formal Assessment* • Section Quiz, p. 20 *Alternative Assessment Book* • Standards for Evaluating a Cooperative Activity
SECTION 4 Settlement of the Middle Colonies *pp. 58–61*	Different groups settle what will become the English middle colonies, establishing in the early years a region of marked diversity, tolerance, and peaceful relations with Native Americans.	**In-Depth Resources: Unit 1** • Guided Reading, p. 23 • Literature: from *World's End* by T. Coraghessan Boyle, p. 35 **COOPERATIVE ACTIVITY** • Mapping Colonial Economic Activities, p. 60 (TE)	*Section 4 Assessment*, p. 61 (PE) *Self-Assessment*, p. 61 (TE) *Formal Assessment* • Section Quiz, p. 21 *Alternative Assessment Book* • Standards for Evaluating a Cooperative Activity
CHAPTER RESOURCES	**Chapter Overview** As the Spanish build an empire in the southern United States, other European nations plant colonies in North America. The English come to dominate the Atlantic Coast.	**In-Depth Resources: Unit 1** • Living History Project: Worksheet, p. 38; Standards, p. 39 *Telescoping the Times* • Chapter Summary, pp. 3–4 *Planning for Block Schedules*	*Chapter Assessment*, pp. 62–63 (PE) *Alternative Assessment*, p. 63 (PE) *Formal Assessment* • Chapter Test, forms A and B, pp. 22–27 Test Generator *Alternative Assessment Book* See explanation and forms for different kinds of alternative assessments including portfolio assessment.

Humanities Transparencies
• H3, Cortes receiving necklace from Aztecs

Grolier Multimedia Encyclopedia
• Spanish Armada

INTERNET RESOURCES
• See *McDougal Littell Learning On-Line* for links to information about Central American history and Florida and the Conquistadores.

Electronic Library of Primary Sources
• *from* the First Charter of Virginia by King James I
• *from The General History of Virginia* by John Smith

INTERNET RESOURCES
• See Interact with History p. 51 (PE) for activities that include the Internet as an enrichment option.

Critical Thinking Transparencies
• CT2, Puritan Migration

Electronic Library of Primary Sources
• from *The Journey of the Ship May-Flower* by Thomas Jones; from *The Book of the General Laws* by the Inhabitants of New Plimouth; from a captivity narrative by Quinton Stockwell

INTERNET RESOURCES
• See *McDougal Littell Learning On-Line* for links to information about Anne Hutchinson and Massachusetts Bay Colony.

Geography Transparencies
• G2, European Colonies Around 1600
• G35, Original Thirteen Colonies

Grolier Multimedia Encyclopedia
• George Fox, founder of the Society of Friends

INTERNET RESOURCES
• See *McDougal Littell Learning On-Line* for links to information about William Penn and the Quakers.

American Portfolio: A Videodisc for U.S. History, user's guide, pp. 13–26

INTERNET RESOURCES
Learning On-Line: Social Studies
http://www.mcdougallittell.com

Block Scheduling (90 MINUTES)

Day 1	Day 2	Day 3
Section 1, pp. 38–43	Section 3, pp. 52–57	Review Sections 1–4
Section 2, pp. 44–49	Section 4, pp. 58–61	Geography Spotlight: The Jamestown Settlement, pp. 50–51
Section Assessments, pp. 43, 49	Section Assessments, pp. 57, 61	Chapter Assessment, pp. 62–63

YEARLY PACING *Chapter 2 Total:* 3 days *Yearly Total:* 85 days

See *Planning for Block Schedules* for special activities and pacing strategies.

Customizing for Special Populations

Students Acquiring English

Access for Students Acquiring English
• Guided Reading for Sections 1–4 (Spanish), pp. 18–21
• Chapter Summary (Spanish), pp. 17–18
• Skillbuilder Practice: Developing Historical Perspective, p. 23
• Geography Application: The Jamestown Fort, p. 24
• Outline Map: Spain Explores North America, p. 24

INTERNET RESOURCES
• See *McDougal Littell Learning On-Line* The Diverse Classroom.

Less Proficient Readers

In-Depth Resources: Unit 1
• Guided Reading for Sections 1–4, pp. 20–23
• Skillbuilder: Developing Historical Perspective, p. 24
• Geography Application: The Jamestown Fort, History Reclaimed, p. 25
• Outline Map: Spain Explores North America, p. 27

Telescoping the Times
• Chapter Summary, pp. 3–4

See additional strategies at point of use in the Teacher's Edition.

Gifted and Talented Students

In-Depth Resources: Unit 1
• Primary Sources: from *The Travels and Works of Captain John Smith,* p. 29; Tobacco Labels, p. 30; *from* The Mayflower Compact, p. 31; from John Winthrop's Journal, p. 32
• American Lives: Malinche, p. 36; John Winthrop, p. 37

See additional strategies at point of use in the Teacher's Edition.

Connections to Literature READINGS FOR STUDENTS

In-Depth Resources: Unit 1
• *Poems* by Anne Bradstreet, p. 33
• *from* World's End by T. Coraghessan Boyle, p. 35

McDougal Littell *Literature Connections*

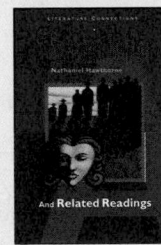

• **Nathaniel Hawthorne,** *The Scarlet Letter* (with related readings) In this novel, set in Puritan America, sin, shame, and intolerance dominate the lives of the characters.

McDougal Littell *The Language of Literature*
   American Literature
• Álvar Núñez Cabeza de Vaca, from *La Relación,* p. 80
• William Bradford, from *Of Plymouth Plantation,* p. 88
• Alicia Crane Williams, *Women and Children First: The Mayflower Pilgrims,* p. 96

OVERVIEW

The American Colonies Emerge

▶ *Starting with the Student*
- In the context of the 50 states, would students describe their state as an old or a new state? Why?
- In terms of European settlement, which four states do students think have the oldest histories?
- What factors account for the early settlement of what are now Florida and New Mexico?

PREVIEWING THE CHAPTER
- Have students use the art and time line to list the peoples who lived in North America by 1690.
- What evidence shows that the coming together of these peoples sometimes resulted in conflict?
- What entries on the time line show that unrest in Europe contributed to settlement of North America?

MORE ABOUT . . .
Amerigo Vespucci

Born in Italy in 1454, Vespucci is believed to have visited the mainland of South America about five years after Columbus's voyage across the Atlantic. Vespucci wrote that he had found a "new world," a land that was not part of Asia. Later, a German map maker who thought that Vespucci had been the first European explorer to arrive there named the land America.

The American Colonies Emerge

SECTION 1
Spain's Empire in the Americas

The Spanish gain the first foothold in the Americas, as they conquer much of Mexico and what is now the southern part of the United States.

SECTION 2
An English Settlement at Jamestown

English settlers endure early years of hardship to establish England's first permanent colony in North America.

SECTION 3
Puritan New England

English Puritans settle New England with the hope of establishing a model society based on their religious views.

SECTION 4
Settlement of the Middle Colonies

Different groups settle what will become the English middle colonies, establishing in the early years a region of marked diversity, tolerance, and peaceful relations with Native Americans.

"I have found a continent more densely populated and abounding in animals than our Europe, Asia, and Africa. We may rightly call this continent the New World."

Amerigo Vespucci

Hernando Cortés conquers the Aztec Empire.

Spanish settlers establish St. Augustine in Florida.

THE UNITED STATES
THE WORLD

1492

1521   1565   1590
1526   1557   1588

Mughal Empire begins in India.

Portugal establishes trading post at Macao, in China.

England defeats the Spanish Armada.

THEMES IN CHAPTER 2

Immigration and Migration

Settlers from Spain and then from England moved into the Americas to establish colonies. Native Americans resisted encroachments, but Europeans triumphed. The physical landscape changed as settlers built permanent settlements.

See Teacher's Edition notes, pp. 48, 56.

Cultural Diversity

Driven to North America by diverse motives and from diverse countries, settlers carved out equally diverse colonies. From these colonies sprang Spanish New Mexico, English Virginia, Puritan New England, Dutch New York.

See Teacher's Edition notes, pp. 41, 59.

Expanding Democracy

English settlers who traveled to the Americas carried their political traditions and ideals with them, including the belief in self-government. Dissenters such as Roger Williams and Anne Hutchinson and dreamers such as William Penn dared to introduce freedoms unheard of in Europe, such as religious tolerance and expanded suffrage. Once planted, these traditions would inspire individuals and groups to struggle for yet greater rights and liberties in the centuries ahead.

See Teacher's Edition note, p. 55.

LIVING HISTORY

WRITING A COLONIZATION TALE

Many books have been written about people who start new colonies—in outer space, on imaginary desert islands, and in real history. Write your own colonization tale of the present day or past history. It can be a short story or a comic book.

The story or comic book should relate some of the experiences you had. As you tell the tale, be sure to explain the reasons you left, who and what you took with you, where you went, how you got there, and the problems you faced both on the journey and at arrival.

PORTFOLIO PROJECT Save your tale in a folder for your American history portfolio. You will revise and share your work at the end of the chapter.

WRITING A COLONIZATION TALE

Discuss ways to go about writing the tale:

- Brainstorm possible topics for colonization tales. Ask students to mention stories they think would be good models.
- Discuss possible approaches for developing the tales. Would a short story work, or would a comic book be better?
- Discuss the importance of using descriptive details to create a vivid picture of their colony.
- Discuss the importance of telling a story that includes a beginning, a middle, and an end.

Project Planning Guide

Step 1	Students choose the topic for their colonization tale.
Step 2	Students brainstorm details.
Step 3	Students write a draft of their tale.
Step 4	Students revise and edit their tale and prepare a final copy.

IN-DEPTH RESOURCES: UNIT 1
See worksheet and standards for evaluation, pp. 38, 39.

Timeline events:

- John Smith and other English settlers establish Jamestown.
- Anne Hutchinson is banished from New England.
- Spanish settlers establish Santa Fe.
- Ship carrying African laborers arrives at Jamestown.
- The Puritans led by John Winthrop found the Massachusetts Bay Colony.
- King Philip's War begins.
- The Pilgrims land at Plymouth.
- Virginia becomes a royal colony.
- England takes New Amsterdam from the Dutch.
- Bacon's Rebellion erupts.
- William Penn receives charter for Pennsylvania.

Timeline: 1607 1610 1619 1620 1624 1630 1638 **1640** 1664 1675 1676 1681 **1690**
1591   1629   1644 1649   1660

- The Songhai Empire falls to Moroccan invaders.
- Charles I of England dismisses Parliament.
- Manchus establish Qing dynasty in China.
- Charles I is beheaded; Puritan leader Oliver Cromwell assumes power in England.
- The English monarchy is restored.

The American Colonies Emerge **37**

RECOMMENDED RESOURCES

Books for the Teacher

Bennett, Jr., Lerone. *Before the Mayflower: A History of Black America.* New York: Penguin, 1984.

Miller, John C. *Life in Colonial America.* New York: Dell, 1966.

Quinn, Arthur. *A New World.* New York: Berkley, 1994.

Weber, David J. *The Spanish Frontier in North America.* New Haven: Yale UP, 1992.

Books for the Student

Schouweiler, Tom. *The Lost Colony of Roanoke.* San Diego: Greenhaven, 1991.

Scott, John Anthony. *The British Colonies in North America, 1607–1750.* New York: Facts on File, 1992.

Simmons, Marc. *Coronado's Land: Daily Life in Colonial New Mexico.* Albuquerque: U New Mexico, 1991.

Videos

Cavaliers and Craftsmen. Atlas Video, 1993. Colonial Williamsburg and Jamestown.

Life in a California Mission. AIMS Media, 800-367-2467. Mission daily life.

The Marriage of Pocohontas. Dir. Emma De'ath. Ambrose Video, 1995.

Where America Began. Finley-Holiday Film Corp., 1988. Colonial Williamsburg.

Software

Colonization. CD-ROM. MicroProse, 1995.

Colonization. Diskette. Tom Snyder Productions/Software, 80 Coolidge Hill, Watertown, MA, 02172-2817.

Seven Cities of Gold. Electronic Arts, 800-245-4525.

Pilgrim Quest II. CD-ROM. Decision Development Corp., 800-835-4332.

OBJECTIVES

(1) To describe the pattern of conquest that the Spanish used to subdue Native American peoples.

(2) To summarize the goals of the Spanish explorers and settlers who pushed into what is now the United States.

(3) To summarize reasons Native Americans in the northern borderlands resisted the Spanish.

SKILLBUILDER

• Understanding geography: movement, place, p. 39

CRITICAL THINKING

• Analyzing causes, pp. 40, 43
• Analyzing motives, p. 41
• Contrasting, p. 42
• Summarizing, p. 43
• Forming an opinion, p. 43
• Generalizing, p. 43

FOCUS & MOTIVATE

▶ *Starting with the Student*
• Ask students what they recall about the early European settlements in the Americas. How did the Europeans treat the native peoples and resources they found there?
• Ask students to speculate about what they think might happen when the technology to travel to and settle on other planets is available.

OBJECTIVE
(1) INSTRUCT

The Spanish Claim a New Empire

▶ *Discussing Key Ideas*
• Cortés subdues the Aztec, aided by Spanish firearms, diseases, and native allies.
• The Spaniards live among native peoples, imposing their own culture upon them.

(continued on next page)

1 Spain's Empire in the Americas

TERMS & NAMES

• conquistador
• Hernando Cortés
• *mestizo*
• *encomienda*
• Juan Ponce de León
• *congregación*
• New Mexico
• Popé

LEARN ABOUT the Spanish conquests of Central and North America
TO UNDERSTAND what new and lasting ways of life the Spanish settlers brought to the Americas.

ONE AMERICAN'S STORY

In 1519, the native world near Tabasco in southeastern Mexico changed forever. That year, Hernando Cortés stepped onto the American mainland and marched inward, looking to claim new lands for Spain. The peoples of the Tabasco resisted the invaders but were no match for the Spaniards' rifles and cannons.

In surrendering, the natives handed over to the Spaniards 20 women, one of whom came to be called Doña Marina, or Malinche. Malinche, sold into slavery as a child, aligned herself with the Spanish. She quickly mastered the Spanish language and acted as a translator and guide for Cortés as he fought and negotiated his way through Mexico. Malinche also proved to be a brave and daring warrior. Bernal Díaz del Castillo, one of Cortés's foot soldiers, noted her courage.

A PERSONAL VOICE

Doña Marina who, although a native woman, possessed such manly valor that, although she had heard every day how the Indians were going to kill us and eat our flesh with chili, and had seen us surrounded in the late battles, and knew that all of us were wounded or sick, yet never allowed us to see any sign of fear in her, . . . only . . . courage.

BERNAL DÍAZ DEL CASTILLO, quoted in *Notable Latin American Women*

Malinche *(center)* translates for the Spaniards and the Aztec.

Malinche played a key role in the early stages of an event that would transform the Americas forever: the Spanish conquests. In their quest for land and wealth, Cortés and other Spanish explorers carved out colonies in Mexico, South America, and regions that would become part of the United States. As the first European settlers in the Americas, the Spanish greatly enriched their empire and left a mark on the cultures of North and South America that still exists today.

The Spanish Claim a New Empire

This mask, created by Aztec masons, is a mosaic of turquoise stones with the teeth and eyes made of shell.

In the wake of Columbus's voyages, Spanish explorers took to the seas to claim new colonies for Spain. Lured by the prospect of vast lands filled with gold and silver, these explorers, known as **conquistadores** (conquerors), pushed first into the Caribbean region—the islands and coast of Central and South America. Then they swept through Mexico and south to the tip of South America. Along the way, the conquistadores—with the help of superior weapons, native allies, and the spread of disease—destroyed native communities. The conquest produced the riches that made Spain the wealthiest, most powerful nation on earth in the 1500s.

CORTÉS SUBDUES THE AZTEC Soon after landing in Mexico, **Hernando Cortés** learned of a vast and wealthy empire in the region's interior. As the conquistador and his force of 600 men, 17 horses, numerous dogs, and 10 cannons trudged inland, he learned more about the powerful Mexica, or Aztec, empire. The Aztec, members of the diverse Nahua peoples of central Mexico, dominated the region. Cortés, a gifted diplomat as well as military leader, convinced those Nahua

38 CHAPTER 2

SECTION 1 RESOURCES

European Exploration of the Americas, 1492–1682

Explorers' Routes
- → Spanish
- → French
- → English

Labels on map:
GREENLAND
Arctic Circle
ICELAND
Hudson 1610
Hudson 1609
Hudson Bay
Cabot 1497
ENGLAND
Cartier 1534-35
EUROPE
FRANCE
NORTH AMERICA
Marquette 1673
LaSalle 1682
PORTUGAL
SPAIN
Coronado 1540-42
De Soto 1539-42
ATLANTIC OCEAN
AZORES
Santa Fe
40° N
PACIFIC OCEAN
Cabrillo 1542-43
Ponce de León 1512-13
CANARY ISLANDS
MADEIRA
Verrazzano 1524
Tropic of Cancer
Cabeza de Vaca 1535-36
Gulf of Mexico
St. Augustine
Columbus 1492
Cortés 1519
CUBA
HISPANIOLA
Veracruz
Santo Domingo
Columbus 1493-95
AFRICA
Caribbean Sea
Columbus 1502-03
120° W
Tenochtitlán (Mexico City)
Balboa 1510-13
Columbus 1498
Equator
Pizarro 1530-33
SOUTH AMERICA
Vespucci 1499

80° N

(continued from page 38)

- High death rates among Native Americans lead Spain to use enslaved Africans for labor.
- Wealth from the Americas turns Spain into the most powerful nation in Europe.

IN-DEPTH RESOURCES: UNIT 1
Guided Reading, p. 20
American Lives: Malinche, p. 36

ACCESS FOR STUDENTS ACQUIRING ENGLISH
Guided Reading (Spanish) , p. 19

HUMANITIES TRANSPARENCIES
H3, Cortés Receiving Necklace

HISTORY FROM VISUALS

European Exploration of the Americas, 1492–1682

Reading the Map Explain that the arrows show more than the routes followed by each explorer. They also connect European nations with the lands they later sought to claim. Which explorer laid the basis for Spanish claims to California? *Cabrillo.* Which explorer laid the basis for French claims to Canada? *Cartier.*

Extension Divide the class into small groups and have each group research and write a brief biography of an explorer whose travels are shown on the map. Have an individual from each team report their findings to the class.

IN-DEPTH RESOURCES: UNIT 1
Outline Map: Spain Explores North America, p. 27

GEOGRAPHY SKILLBUILDER
MOVEMENT *How many voyages to the Americas did Columbus make?* **PLACE** *What years did England and France sail to the Americas, and which regions did they explore?*

Skillbuilder Answer
Movement: Four. **Location:** The English sailed to the Americas in 1497, 1609, and 1610. They explored the east coast of the present-day United States and upper Canada. The French sailed in 1524, 1534-5, 1673, and 1682. They explored parts of Canada, as well as the midwestern and southern United States.

---

who had long resented the spread of Aztec power to join his ranks. After marching for weeks through 200 miles of difficult mountain passes, Cortés and his legions finally looked on the magnificent Aztec capital of Tenochtitlán. With nearly 140,000 residents, the city was one of the largest urban centers in the world at that time.

The Spaniards marveled at Tenochtitlán, with its towering temples and elaborate engineering works—including a system that brought fresh water into the city. "We were amazed," Bernal Díaz said of his first glimpse of Tenochtitlán. "Some of our soldiers even asked whether the things we saw were not a dream." While the Aztec city astonished the Spaniards, the capital's glittering gold stock seemed to hypnotize them. "They picked up the gold and fingered it like monkeys," one Nahua witness recalled. "They hungered like pigs for that gold."

The Aztec emperor, Montezuma, convinced at first that Cortés was an armor-clad god, agreed to give the Spanish explorer a share of the empire's existing gold supply. The conquistador was not satisfied. Cortés, who admitted that he and his comrades had "a disease of the heart that only gold can cure," eventually forced the Aztec to mine more gold and silver. In the spring of 1520, the Aztec rebelled against the Spaniards' intrusion. Regarding Montezuma as a traitor, the Aztec are believed to have stoned their ruler to death before driving out Cortés's forces.

While they had successfully repelled the Spanish invaders, the natives found they could do little to stop the much stronger invisible warrior that marched alongside the Europeans—disease. By the time Cortés launched a

---

TEACHING OPTIONS

Teaching Less Proficient Readers

Taking Notes Distribute three-by-five-inch index cards to students. Have them turn each subhead under "The Spanish Claim a New Empire" into a question; for example, How did Cortés subdue the Aztecs? Instruct students to write each question on the front of one of the index cards. Tell students to answer the question by taking notes on the back of each card as they read. Repeat this process with the rest of the section. Students can exchange their "flash cards" to quiz each other or to review for the section quiz.

Making Connections Across the Curriculum

Writing Students' English teachers might use the dramatic events about the arrival of the Spaniards at Tenochtitlán for a writing assignment, such as a monologue or a soliloquy, that one of the following people might have delivered: Doña Marina, Cortés, or Montezuma. As students prepare to write their assignments, suggest that they think about what was happening, about the thoughts and feelings that the person might be experiencing, and how these would color their perceptions of the events.

A Native American depiction of Aztec archers battling Cortés's troops.

KEY PLAYER

HERNANDO CORTÉS
1485–1547

Cortés made himself the enemy of thousands of Native Americans, but the daring conquistador had few friends among Spaniards either. Spanish authorities on Cuba, where Cortés owned land, accused the conquistador of murdering his wife, Catalina Juárez. "There were ugly accusations, but none proved," wrote Juárez's biographer.

In addition, the Cuban governor, Diego Velázquez, who resented Cortés's arrogance, relieved him of the command of a gold-seeking expedition to the mainland. Cortés left Cuba anyway. As he fought his way through Mexico, Cortés had to battle not only the Native Americans, but also the Spanish forces that Velázquez sent to arrest him.

counterattack in 1521, the Spanish and their native allies overran an Aztec force that was greatly reduced by smallpox and measles. After several months of fighting, the invaders sacked and burned Tenochtitlán, and the Aztec surrendered. While flames still flickered in the shattered capital, Cortés laid plans for the colony of New Spain, whose capital he called Mexico City. Within three years, Spanish churches and homes rose from the foundations of old native temples and palaces.

SPANISH PATTERN OF CONQUEST In building their new American empire, the Spaniards drew from techniques used during the *reconquista* of Spain over the Muslims. When conquering the Muslims, the Spanish lived among them and imposed upon them their Spanish culture.

Because the Spanish settlers to the Americas, known as *peninsulares*, were mostly men, marriage between the Spanish settlers and native women was common. These marriages created a large **mestizo**—or mixed Spanish and Native American—population. Their descendants live today in Mexico, other Latin American countries, and the United States. At the site of the Aztec surrender in modern-day Mexico City, a plaque commemorates the birth of this new people. The inscription reads, in part, "It was neither a triumph nor a defeat: it was the painful birth of the mestizo nation that is Mexico today."

Although the Spanish conquerors lived among and intermarried with the native people, they also oppressed them. In their effort to exploit the land for its precious resources, the Spanish forced the native workers to labor within a system known as **encomienda.** Under this system—which the Spaniards employed in the Caribbean as well as on the American mainland—natives farmed, ranched, or mined for Spanish landlords, who had received the rights to their labor from Spanish authorities. The holders of *encomiendas* promised the Spanish rulers to act fairly and respect the workers, but many of them abused their charges and worked many laborers to death, especially inside dangerous mines.

The harsh pattern of labor that emerged under the *encomienda* system caused priests such as Antonio de Montesinos to demand its end. As early as 1511, he delivered a fiery sermon in which he attacked the use of the native population for slave labor.

A PERSONAL VOICE
Tell me, by what right or justice do you hold these Indians in such a cruel and horrible servitude? . . . Why do you keep them so oppressed and exhausted, without giving them enough to eat or curing them of the sicknesses they incur from the excessive labor you give them? . . . Are you not bound to love them as you love yourselves? Don't you understand this? Don't you feel this?
FRAY ANTONIO DE MONTESINOS, as quoted in *Reflections, Writing for Columbus*

As more and more natives died from disease, the *encomienda* system grew more brutal. Spanish overseers expected the same amount of work from fewer laborers and forced the natives to work longer and harder. In 1542, the Spanish monarchy, which had tried to encourage fair treatment of native subjects, abolished the *encomienda* system. To meet their intense labor needs, the Spaniards instead turned to other labor systems and began to use African slaves.

SPAIN ENTERS A GOLDEN AGE As the gold and silver from Spanish conquests flowed across the Atlantic, Spain fulfilled a boast made in a 1495 ballad. "O King Don Fernando and Doña Isabel," said the song, "With you the golden years begin." For Spain, the 1500s truly were golden. Spanish explorers blazed sea routes that spanned the globe, and they also plunged deeper into the Americas. Between 1522 and 1528, various lieutenants of Cortés conquered other native peoples, including many of the Maya in Yucatan and Guatemala. In 1532, dreams of gold-filled continents stirred anew when Francisco Pizarro, with the help of guns and disease, plundered the fabulously wealthy Inca Empire on the western slope of South America.

For much of the 16th century, other European nations struggled to match Spain's power. During this time, the Spanish built a wide-reaching overseas empire, which included New Spain (Mexico and parts of Guatemala), as well as other lands in Central and South America and the Caribbean. While other European nations barely imagined American colonies of their own, the Spanish built immense cathedrals and a university in Mexico City.

The Conquistadores Push North

Dreams of new conquests, coupled with fears that European nations might invade their American empire from the north, prompted Spain to back a series of expeditions into what would become the southeastern and southwestern United States. Finding little gold or silver there, Spain established in this region of North America a string of far-flung outposts to protect its empire in Mexico and to spread its culture and religion to the Native Americans.

EXPLORING FLORIDA In 1513, **Juan Ponce de León,** a Spanish soldier who had conquered Puerto Rico five years earlier, set out to investigate the stories of a vast land north of the Caribbean. On Easter Sunday—a day the Spaniards called *Pascua Florida*, or "Feast of Flowers"—Ponce de León spied a tree-covered beach. In honor of the holiday, he named the land *La Florida*. For almost five decades, the Spaniards probed *La Florida* and the surrounding areas for gold, battling the local residents, disease, and starvation. In 1562, fed up with the lack of economic success, Spain abandoned further exploration of Florida.

Within months of Spain's departure, a band of French settlers arrived near present-day Jacksonville. Accompanying the settlers were French pirates, or buccaneers, who quickly took interest in Spain's treasure-filled ships sailing from the Gulf of Mexico. Consequently, Spain reversed its decision to abandon Florida and ordered one of its fiercest warriors, Pedro Menendez de Aviles, to drive the French out of the area.

Menendez not only drove out the French, but in 1565 he established a lonely outpost, which he called St. Augustine, on the Florida coast. Perched on the edge of the Spanish empire, the fort suffered attacks by various European nations trying to wedge their way into the Caribbean in quest of their own colonies. However, the Spanish settlement survived to become the oldest European-founded city in the present-day United States.

SETTLING THE SOUTHWEST The first Spanish expeditions into what is now the southwestern United States began in the decade following Pizarro's triumph in South America. In 1540, Francisco Vásquez de Coronado led the most ambitious venture, as he roamed throughout much of present-day Arizona, New Mexico, Texas, Oklahoma, and Kansas in search of another wealthy empire to conquer. After wandering for two years, the only precious metal he carried home was his own battered gold-plated armor.

The Spaniards who followed in Coronado's wake came to the Southwest largely to search for veins of silver ore or to spread the Catholic religion. While

THINK THROUGH HISTORY
B. *Analyzing Motives* What prompted Spain's renewed interest in conquering Florida?

B. Answer With France's settlement in Florida, European nations were in striking distance of Spain's new empire and its riches.

> "*Think, then, what must be the effect on me and mine, of the sight of you and your people, . . . entering with such speed and fury into my country, . . . as to strike terror into our hearts.*"

NATIVE AMERICAN CHIEF,
TO SPANISH EXPLORER HERNANDO DE SOTO

MORE ABOUT . . .
St. Augustine
St. Augustine owes its existence, in large part, to pirates. The trouble started with a Spanish cargo of treasure. Intercepted by a French corsair, the cargo landed in the court of French king Francis I, opening a new trade—pirating from the Spanish.

After pirates repeatedly set fire to St. Augustine, the Spanish ordered construction of a fort called Castillo de San Marcos. Built in 1672 from huge blocks of coquina, a rock made from fused seashells, the fort served as an active Spanish outpost well into the 1700s. Today it stands as one of the oldest major national landmarks in the United States.

OBJECTIVE
② **INSTRUCT**

The Conquistadores Push North

▶ *Discussing Key Ideas*
- Dreams of new conquests and competition from other European nations leads Spain northward.
- Finding little gold in the northern borderlands, the Spaniards focus instead on the conversion of the Native Americans.

TEACHING OPTIONS

Making Connections Across the Curriculum

Literature To develop an understanding of the Aztec people at the time of their defeat, read these lines by an Aztec poet:

Weep, my people:
know that with these disasters
we have lost the Mexican nation.
The water has turned bitter,
our food is bitter!
These are the acts of the Giver of Life.

Ask students to describe the poet's feelings. What title would students suggest for the poem? As an extension activity, have students write another stanza.

Exploring Themes

Cultural Diversity The Spanish search for more golden empires to conquer led the conquistadores northward into what is now the United States. The missionaries and settlers who followed in their footsteps established a chain of scattered outposts that would eventually reach from Florida through the Southwest and into California. The addition of these lands to the United States centuries later would increase the diversity of an already diverse nation.

Teacher's Edition **41**

The wood carving on this page is known as a santo, or saint. The artisans, or santeros, who craft them continue a tradition rooted in colonial New Mexico. The art form began about 200 years ago when artisans along the New Mexican frontier carved figures out of pieces of cottonwood and painted them bright colors. Most sat on church altars or in the homes of wealthy patrons.

MORE ABOUT . . .
Everyday Life in New Mexico

While the Spanish sought to impose their culture on the Native Americans, some of the native ways were adopted by the Spanish. In the early 1600s many settlers along the frontier exchanged their Spanish fabrics for *gamuza* —the softly tanned deer or antelope hide called chamois in English and worn by the Native Americans, including fringed leather jackets and buckskin boots.

OBJECTIVE
③ INSTRUCT

Resistance to the Spanish

▶ *Discussing Key Ideas*
• Spanish priests in New Mexico try to transform Native American cultures.
• Brutal suppression of native religious practices leads the Pueblo to rebel.
• Challenges from other European nations force Spain to slow colonization in northern borderlands.

the conquistadores came to the Americas in search of wealth, the Spanish priests who accompanied them came in search of converts. As the native population dwindled from disease, Spanish priests moved the surviving natives into large communities called *congregaciónes,* where they sought to convert Native Americans to the Catholic faith.

Finding little gold but many souls in the lands north of New Spain, the Spanish monarchy assigned mostly priests to explore and colonize lands in the future United States. In its Royal Orders of New Discoveries of 1573, Spain outlined the duties of these spiritual conquistadores. When converting the Native Americans, priests were ordered to provide them with "the many . . . essentials of life—bread, silk, linen, horses, cattle, tools, and weapons, and all the rest that Spain has had."

Spain also instructed its priests to teach Native Americans "the trades and skills with which they might live richly." Franciscan friars, priests dedicated to the teachings of St. Francis of Assisi, took up this task. To win new converts, the brown-robed priests learned the native languages and offered spiritual as well as political protection to the newly baptized.

In the winter of 1609–1610, Pedro de Peralta, governor of Spain's northern holdings, called **New Mexico,** led settlers to a tributary of the upper Rio Grande. Together they built a capital called Santa Fe, or "Holy Faith." In the next two decades, a string of Christian missions arose among the Pueblos in the area. The hooves of pack mules wore down a 1,500-mile trail known as *el Camino Real,* or "the Royal Road," as they carried goods back and forth between Santa Fe and Mexico City.

Spain, however, had little interest in the trade goods that trickled in from the borderlands—cattle hides, piñon nuts, and the wool-and-cotton blankets woven by Pueblo artisans. Instead, the Spanish rulers saw the scattered missions, forts, and small ranches that dotted the lands of New Mexico as headquarters for advancing the Catholic religion. They also viewed them as buffers against advances by other European countries into New Spain.

This depiction of the Virgin Mary and the infant Jesus from the early 1900s reflects the intermingling of Spanish and Indian cultures in New Mexico.

Resistance to the Spanish

The Catholic missionaries who settled north of Mexico not only tried to Christianize the peoples they encountered but also attempted to impose Spanish culture on them. The native inhabitants of New Mexico resisted and eventually rebelled against the Spaniards' attempts to transform their lives and beliefs.

Because Coronado's forces had burned and plundered many Indian villages, many Native Americans retaliated by killing the Spanish friars who remained behind.

42 CHAPTER 2

THINK THROUGH HISTORY
C. *Contrasting* How did Spain's colony in New Mexico differ from its colonies in New Spain?

C. Answer New Mexico was less rich in gold and silver; "spiritual conquistadores" were more concerned with spreading the Catholic religion among the native peoples than with procuring wealth from the land.

 Cooperative Activity: Writing About Popé's Rebellion

Task: Students will create a short story.

Purpose: To understand causes and effects of Popé's Rebellion.

Activity: Have groups of students recount the story of Popé's Rebellion. Each group will write only one part of the story based on the following four parts.

1. Arrival of the Spanish: *Popé could hardly believe his eyes! Rumbling toward his village was a strange group of people.*

2. Forced Conversion of the Pueblo: *"You must give up your religion," said the Spanish.*

3. Planning the Rebellion: *"We must plan carefully to defeat the terrible Spaniards."*

4. The Rebellion and Its Outcome: *Popé burned with hatred as the battle begun.*

📁 **Building a Portfolio** Students might title their stories and add them to their portfolios.

ALTERNATIVE ASSESSMENT BOOK
Standards for Evaluating a Cooperative Activity

Standards for Evaluation Stories should . . .

• show clear understanding of the rebellion
• focus on their particular part of the story
• use language that helps re-create the situation

CONFLICT IN NEW MEXICO While Spanish priests converted scores of Native Americans in New Mexico, tension marked the relationship between the priests and their new converts. As they sought to transform the Native Americans' cultures, Spanish priests and soldiers smashed and burned objects held sacred by local communities and suppressed many of their ceremonial dances and rituals.

During the 1670s, priests and soldiers around Santa Fe began forcing Native Americans to help support the missions by paying a tribute, an offering of either goods or services. The tribute was usually a bushel of maize or a deer hide, but the Spanish also forced Native Americans to work for them and sometimes abused them physically. Native Americans who practiced their native religion or refused to pay tribute were beaten.

POPÉ'S REBELLION One unfortunate Native American who felt the sting of a Spanish whip was the Pueblo religious leader, **Popé**. The priests punished Popé for his worship practices, which they interpreted as witchcraft. The whipping left the Pueblo leader scarred with hatred and ready for rebellion. In 1680, he led a well-organized uprising against the Spanish that involved some 17,000 warriors from villages all over New Mexico. The triumphant fighters destroyed Catholic churches, executed priests, and drove the Spaniards back into New Spain. "The heathen," one Spanish officer wrote about the uprising, "have concealed a mortal hatred for our holy faith and enmity for the Spanish nation." For the next 14 years—until the Spanish regained control of the area—the southwest region of the future United States once again belonged to its original inhabitants.

By this time, however, the rulers of Spain had far greater concerns. Nearly 80 years before Popé ran the Spanish out of New Mexico, England had defeated the Spanish Armada, ending Spain's naval dominance in the Atlantic and had begun forging colonies of its own along the eastern shore of North America.

While the Spanish heritage still lives in the peoples and cultures of the Southwest and Southeast, the English—who migrated to their colonies in vastly superior numbers—eventually dominated the land. However, they faced many challenges. England's first colony in the Americas, a community established in 1607 along the marshy shores of Virginia, struggled many decades to survive.

D. Answer
Spanish attempts to destroy their culture and repressive measures, which included forcing natives to pay a tribute and harsh punishment.

THINK THROUGH HISTORY
D. Analyzing Causes Why did the Native Americans of New Mexico revolt against the Spanish settlers?

ON THE WORLD STAGE

THE DEFEAT OF THE SPANISH ARMADA

The year 1588 signaled the beginning of the end of Spanish dominance over Europe and the Americas. That year, the Spanish Armada—the naval fleet assembled to invade England—went down to defeat.

After a series of English raids on his treasure ships, King Philip II of Spain dispatched in the summer of 1588 about 130 ships carrying nearly 19,000 soldiers into the English Channel. England, however, was ready. English war ships outmaneuvered the Spanish vessels and bombarded the Armada with their heavier long-range cannons.

Aiding the English cannons were powerful storms that destroyed much of the Armada. Its defeat dealt a blow to Spain's military power and opened the way for the rest of Europe to venture into the Americas.

ON THE WORLD STAGE
The Defeat of the Spanish Armada
Critical Thinking:
Analyzing Point out that the English ships that challenged the Spanish Armada were faster, easier to maneuver, and were able to shoot their cannons from greater distances. Discuss how these technological factors could have helped the English to defeat the huge numbers of Spanish ships and sailors.

GROLIER MULTIMEDIA ENCYCLOPEDIA
Spanish Armada

ASSESS & RETEACH

Section 1 Assessment
Ask students to work in pairs to answer the questions. As they write their answers, have them note passages that support their answers.

Self-Assessment
Have students explore their own understanding of the clash between the Spanish and American cultures by making a list of the Spanish expectations and the Native American responses.

Section Quiz

FORMAL ASSESSMENT BOOK
Section Quiz, p. 18

Reteach
Use the map on page 39 to help review the main ideas of the section.

Section 1 Assessment

1. TERMS & NAMES

Identify:
- conquistador
- Hernando Cortés
- mestizo
- *encomienda*
- Juan Ponce de León
- *congregación*
- New Mexico
- Popé

2. SUMMARIZING Recreate the web below on your paper and fill in the events related to the main idea in the center.

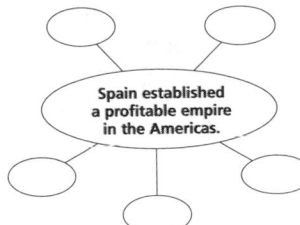

Spain established a profitable empire in the Americas.

3. FORMING AN OPINION Do you agree or disagree with the statement that the Spanish conquest of the Aztec, which led to the creation of Mexico, "was neither a triumph nor a defeat"? Support your opinion with references to the text.

THINK ABOUT
- the actions of the conquistadores
- the effects of disease on the native peoples
- the *encomienda* system
- the mestizo population in Mexico today

4. GENERALIZING State three main ideas about Spanish exploration and settlement north of Mexico, and their interaction with Native Americans there.

THINK ABOUT
- the explorations of Ponce de León and Coronado
- the establishment of St. Augustine and Santa Fe
- the activities of Spanish friars
- Native American acts of resistance

The American Colonies Emerge **43**

ANSWERS

1. TERMS AND NAMES

conquistador, p. 38
Hernando Cortés, p. 38
mestizo, p. 40
encomienda, p. 40
Juan Ponce de León, p. 41
congregación, p. 42
New Mexico, p. 42
Popé, p. 43

2. SUMMARIZING

Possible Responses: Cortés conquered the Aztec; Spain took gold and silver from Mexico; Spaniards established the *encomienda* system; many natives died from disease; Spanish established settlements from Mexico north to Florida and New Mexico.

3. FORMING AN OPINION

Possible Responses: Students who agree might point to the large mestizo population in Mexico—reflecting mixed Spanish and native heritage; those disagreeing might argue that the native peoples were conquered by force, depleted by disease, and subjugated under a harsh labor system, and therefore had little choice but to submit to Spanish influence.

4. GENERALIZING

Possible Responses: Early Spanish explorers failed to find much gold or silver north of Mexico, so settlement was limited to far-flung missions and defensive outposts; Spanish missionaries provided Native Americans with material goods, education, and protection, but sometimes abused them and suppressed their culture; some Native Americans converted to Christianity, but others resisted violently.

CLOSE

Little more than 60 years after the arrival of Cortés in Mexico, Spain had carved out a huge empire in the Americas. Its wealth and power made Spain the envy of Europe and inspired other monarchs to back expansion overseas. One of the biggest challenges to Spain would come from England, a nation with a large restless and landless population.

Teacher's Edition **43**

OBJECTIVES

1 To identify the obstacles facing the first English settlers in North America.

2 To contrast the English and Spanish patterns of conquest.

3 To describe the economic and social inequities that triggered Bacon's Rebellion.

CRITICAL THINKING

• Analyzing causes, p. 45
• Contrasting, p. 48
• Analyzing motives, p. 48
• Summarizing, p. 49
• Analyzing, p. 49
• Recognizing effects, p. 49

FOCUS & MOTIVATE

▶ *Starting with the Student*
• Have students brainstorm the qualities that an explorer, such as an astronaut, should possess.
• Which, if any, of these qualities do students think would make an effective leader? Which, if any, would be liabilities?

OBJECTIVE
1 INSTRUCT

An English Foothold in North America

▶ *Discussing Key Ideas*
• English investors fund Jamestown.
• Disease, the search for gold, and conflict with Native Americans threaten the colony.
• Production of tobacco saves Jamestown.
• A shortage of labor leads Virginia to turn to indentured servants and, later, enslaved Africans.

IN-DEPTH RESOURCES: UNIT 1
Guided Reading, p. 21
Primary Source: from *The Travels and Works of Captain John Smith*, p. 29

ACCESS FOR STUDENTS ACQUIRING ENGLISH Guided Reading, (Spanish), p. 20

---

2 An English Settlement at Jamestown

TERMS & NAMES
• John Smith
• Jamestown
• Powhatan
• headright system
• indentured servant
• royal colony
• Nathaniel Bacon

LEARN ABOUT the reasons for the English settlement at Jamestown
TO UNDERSTAND how this settlement endured an uncertain start and conflict with Native Americans.

ONE AMERICAN'S STORY

John Smith craved adventure. Smith's father had urged him to be a merchant, but the restless Englishman wanted to be only one thing: a soldier. In 1600, at age 20, Smith trekked across Europe and helped Hungary fight a war against the Turks. For his heroic battle efforts, the Hungarians offered a knighthood to Smith, who inscribed his coat of arms with the phrase *Vincere est vivere*—"to conquer is to live."

The daring and often arrogant adventurer returned to England in 1604, where his thirst for new challenges led him to gaze across the Atlantic. In 1606, he approached the members of the Virginia Company, a group of merchants charged with planting an English colony in North America. He entertained them with stories of his exploits and offered his services as a colonist. Smith later recalled the opportunities that he saw open to him and others of a less noble background.

> ### A PERSONAL VOICE
> What man who is poor or who has only his merit to advance his fortunes can desire more contentment than to walk over and plant the land he has obtained by risking his life? . . . Here nature and liberty . . . [give] us freely that which we lack or have to pay dearly for in England. . . . What pleasure can be greater than to grow tired from . . . planting vines, fruits, or vegetables? . . .
>
> **JOHN SMITH,** *The General History of Virginia*

Smith would need all of his cunning and strength to steer the English colony through what turned out to be a disastrous beginning. With the help of Smith's leadership and, later, the production of the profitable crop of tobacco, England's small settlement in North America survived. The colony grew, and even as its settlers battled with Native Americans and with one another, they established a claim on the land that would become the United States.

John Smith was a self-proclaimed soldier-of-fortune, a sea captain, and a poet.

An English Foothold in North America

This poster reflects an attempt to attract settlers to the early Virginia colony.

England's first significant attempt to carve out a colony of its own in North America (after an earlier failed attempt at Roanoke) nearly collapsed, as disease and starvation threatened the new settlement. However, through the determination of its colonists and the development of a marketable crop, England's first permanent settlement in North America took shape.

THE BUSINESS OF COLONIZATION The rulers of England—unlike the Spanish—decided not to fund the risky venture of colonizing the Americas. Instead, King James I in 1606 granted a charter, or official permit, to two joint-stock companies, the Virginia companies of London and Plymouth. Numerous investors had pooled their wealth in order to finance the trip to North America. The Virginia Company of Plymouth soon disbanded, leaving only the Virginia Company of London, later simply called the Virginia Company.

The Virginia Company had lured financial supporters with the chance of reaping wealth in the form of gold or silver for a relatively small investment. England was to get something from the expedition, too. The King's charter guaranteed that the English monarch would receive one-fifth of all gold and silver found by the colonists.

SECTION 2 RESOURCES

PRINT RESOURCES

IN-DEPTH RESOURCES: UNIT 1
Guided Reading, p. 21
Geography Application: The Jamestown Fort, p. 25
Primary Sources: from *The Travels and Works of Captain John Smith*, p. 29; Tobacco Labels, p. 30

ACCESS FOR STUDENTS ACQUIRING ENGLISH
Guided Reading (Spanish), p. 20
Geography Application: The Jamestown Fort (Spanish), p. 24

FORMAL ASSESSMENT
Section Quiz, p. 19

ALTERNATIVE ASSESSMENT BOOK
See forms for supporting and scoring alternative activities.

TECHNOLOGY RESOURCES

CD-ROM Electronic Library of Primary Sources

VIDEO *American Portfolio: A Videodisc for U.S. History* user's guide, pp. 17–20

INTERNET McDougal Littell Learning On-Line
http://www.mcdougallittell.com

In April of 1607, nearly four months after the Virginia Company's three ships—and nearly 150 passengers and crew members—had pushed out of an English harbor, the North American shore rose on the horizon. Reaching the coast of Virginia, the vessels slipped into a broad coastal river and sailed inland until they reached a small peninsula. There, the colonists climbed off their ships and claimed the land as theirs. They named the settlement **Jamestown** and the river the James, in honor of their king.

A DISASTROUS START John Smith sensed trouble from the beginning. Nearly all of the settlers seemed to be consumed by one thought—the discovery of gold. Because the investors in the colony demanded a quick return on their investment, the colonists directed much of their energy toward searching the land for riches. As Smith later put it, "There was no talk, no hope, no work, but dig gold, wash gold, refine gold, load gold." Smith warned of disaster, but few listened to the arrogant captain, who had made few friends on the voyage over.

Disease from infected river water struck first. Hunger soon followed. The colonists, many of whom were unaccustomed to a life of labor, had refused to clear fields, plant crops, or even gather shellfish from the river's edge. After several months, one settler described the terrifying predicament.

A PERSONAL VOICE
Thus we lived for the space of five months in this miserable distress . . . our men night and day groaning in every corner of the fort, most pitiful to hear. If there were any conscience in men, it would make their hearts to bleed to hear the pitiful murmurings and outcries of our sick men for relief, every night and day for the space of six weeks: some departing out of the World, many times three or four in a night; in the morning their bodies trailed out of their cabins like dogs, to be buried.
JAMESTOWN COLONIST, quoted in *A New World*

By the winter of 1607 only 38 colonists remained alive. Standing among them was John Smith, who took control of the settlement. "You see that power now rests wholly with me," he announced. "You must now obey this law, . . . *he that will not work shall not eat.*" Smith held the colony together by forcing the colonists to farm. He also received food and support from the nearby **Powhatan** peoples, who had watched warily as the English established their settlement. Smith, a seasoned soldier, knew the Powhatan easily could wipe out the settlement. So he flattered and negotiated his way into winning an uneasy friendship with the group's leader, Chief Powhatan.

Just as Jamestown began to look like a real village, tragedy struck. A stray spark ignited a gunpowder bag Smith was wearing and set him on fire. Badly burned, Smith headed back to England, leaving Jamestown to fend for itself.

In the spring of 1609, the Virginia Company dispatched another 600 colonists, including women and children, to Jamestown. The newcomers arrived to find a settlement of disorganized colonists who were being threatened by angry Powhatan. Fearing the growing English presence, the Powhatan killed much of the colonists' livestock and harassed those settlers who attempted to hunt or farm. By the winter of 1609, conditions in Jamestown had deteriorated to the point of famine. In what became known as the "starving time," colonists ate roots, rats, snakes, and even boiled shoe leather. Of the hundreds of settlers who began the winter, only about 60 survived to see the relief ship that arrived in the spring.

A. Answer Disease, the unwillingness of many colonists to work, and the hostile actions by the Powhatan.

THINK THROUGH HISTORY
A. *Analyzing Causes* Why was the early settlement at Jamestown a near disaster?

THE MYSTERY OF ROANOKE
England's first attempt to plant a colony in North America ended under a shroud of mystery. In 1585, an English navigator named Sir Walter Raleigh (pictured above with his son) led a small group of colonists to modern-day Roanoke Island on what are now called the Outer Banks of North Carolina. The first colonists soon abandoned the settlement and returned to England.

In 1587, Raleigh sent a second group of colonists, led by John White, to reestablish the Roanoke settlement. White sailed back to England for more supplies but did not return until 1590.

Upon his arrival, White discovered that the colonists had vanished. All that remained at the village were some rusted debris and the word "CROATOAN" (a Native American tribe) carved into a tree. Historians believe that the lost colonists may have starved to death or either joined with or were attacked by local Native American tribes.

The American Colonies Emerge **45**

MORE ABOUT . . .
Tobacco

The following statistics from the *Virginia Statistical Abstract* show Virginia's rank among leading tobacco-growing states today. Ask students to rank these states in order of production. Ask, Where does Virginia fall? How about North Carolina?

Tobacco Production in 1996 (in thousands of pounds)	
Florida	18,469
Georgia	103,500
Kentucky	448,630
Maryland	12,000
North Carolina	600,700
South Carolina	115,000
Tennessee	116,500
Virginia	100,099
West Virginia	3,700
U.S. Total	1,580,549

NOW & THEN
Tobacco and North Carolina's Economy

▶ **Starting with the Student**
Ask students to think about the economy of the region in which they live.

• Is the economy dependent on one main source or is there a variety of sources?
• How could a one-source economy pose problems for a region?

▶ **Discussing Key Ideas**
• Tobacco has been a major crop in North Carolina and has accounted for a substantial portion of that state's economy.
• Health concerns related to tobacco have been raised ever since it was introduced in England.
• Today, North Carolina has diversified its economy to make up for the decrease in smoking in the last 30 years.

IN-DEPTH RESOURCES: UNIT 1
Primary Source: *from* Tobacco Labels, p. 30

SAVED BY "BROWN GOLD" The newcomers saw no reason to stay. They packed up the surviving colonists and abandoned the ill-fated settlement. This might have been the end of Jamestown if the crew of a second English ship sailing into the James River had not convinced the fleeing colonists to turn around. Under the watchful eye of new leaders, who did not hesitate to flog or even hang colonists found neglecting their work, Jamestown again grew. However, equally important in the colony's revival was the development of a highly profitable crop: tobacco.

Europeans had become aware of tobacco soon after Columbus's first return from the West Indies. In 1612, the Jamestown colonist John Rolfe experimented with tobacco seeds from South America and a harsh strain of the weed that local Native Americans had grown for years. Rolfe's cross-breeding resulted in a high-quality tobacco strain for which the citizens of England soon clamored. The demand for tobacco provided the colonists with the commodity they needed to build the colony. By the late 1620s, colonists exported more than 1.5 million pounds of "brown gold" to England each year.

THE SEARCH FOR A SUPPLY OF LABOR In order to grow tobacco, the Virginia Company needed a key ingredient that was missing from the colony—field laborers. In an effort to lure settlers to Jamestown, the Virginia Company introduced the **headright system** in 1618. Under this system, each new arrival received 50 acres of land and another 50 acres for each family member who migrated. Immigration to the colony jumped.

Most of those who arrived in Virginia, however, came not under the headright system, but as **indentured servants.** In exchange for passage to North America, and food and shelter upon arrival, an indentured servant agreed to a limited term of servitude—usually four to seven years. Indentured servants were usually from the lower classes of English society and therefore had little to lose by leaving for a new world.

NOW & THEN

Tobacco and North Carolina's Economy

Some people call it a dangerous drug. Others call it a legitimate crop. Though opinions vary, one thing is certain: tobacco has long been a key element of the Southern economy. As one North Carolina farmer told the *New York Times* in 1996, "Tobacco has been here since the 1600s and will continue to be."

Today, North Carolina is the nation's top tobacco-producing state. Farm sales of tobacco pump $1 billion into the state's economy every year. Manufacturing of tobacco products adds another $11 billion.

In recent years, however, tobacco revenues have shrunk as a percentage of the state's cash farm income, from 46% of the total in 1964 to 15% in 1996. North Carolina is weaning itself from tobacco and developing a more diversified economy. A major reason is the declining consumption of tobacco in the United States, caused by public concern over the link between tobacco and deadly diseases such as cancer.

The focal point of North Carolina's diversified economy is the Research Triangle, so called for the cluster of major universities in Raleigh, Durham, and Chapel Hill. These universities cooperate in research and development in many areas, including technology and health care. New industries are fueling North Carolina's growth, but agriculture and traditional industries such as tobacco, textiles, and furniture remain very important.

North Carolina Today

Winston-Salem
food products
furniture
machinery
tobacco products

Asheville
the arts
furniture
lumber and paper

Charlotte
banking
chemicals
computers
printing
telecommunications
textiles

Greensboro
heavy equipment
telecommunications
finance

Raleigh, Durham, and Chapel Hill
computers
instruments
medicines
research
telecommunications
textiles

Map legend:
- General farming
- Cotton
- Cotton and general farming
- Tobacco and general farming
- Special crops and general farming

Map labels: Winston-Salem, Greensboro, Durham, Chapel Hill, Raleigh, Asheville, Charlotte

---

INTERACT WITH HISTORY

1. Summarizing

Possible Responses: *In the early years, tobacco played a major role in North Carolina's economy. Over the next several hundred years, tobacco continued to be a major crop and North Carolina ranked first in the country in tobacco production. In recent years, with concern about how tobacco use contributes to health problems, it does not provide the percentage of profits that it once did, although North Carolina is still the major tobacco producer in the nation.*

2. Researching

You may wish to give students a form to help them organize their analysis of industry in their area. A form might contain the following items:

Industries	Product	Number of Employees	Years in Community

THE FIRST AFRICAN LABORERS Another group of laborers—Africans—first arrived in Virginia aboard a Dutch merchant ship in 1619. Records suggest that the Jamestown colonists treated the group of about 20 Africans as indentured servants. After a few years, most of the Africans received land and freedom. Meanwhile, other Africans continued to arrive in the colony in small numbers, but it would be several decades before the English colonists in North America began the systematic use of Africans as slave labor.

One reason for this was economics. In Virginia, where tobacco served as currency in the early 1600s, an indentured servant could be purchased for 1,000 pounds of tobacco, while a slave might cost double or triple that amount. However, by the late 1600s, a decline in the indentured servant population coupled with an increase in the colonies' overall wealth spurred the colonists to begin importing slaves in huge numbers. From that time, most arrivals to North America came aboard wretched slave ships, not as indentured servants but as slaves to be sold.

Clashes with Native Americans

As the English settlers expanded their settlement, their uneasy relations with the Native Americans worsened. The colonists' desire for more land—to accommodate their growing numbers as well as their demand for more crop space—led to warfare with the original inhabitants of Virginia.

THE ENGLISH PATTERN OF CONQUEST As has been explained, the Spanish settlers intermarried frequently with the native population of Mexico, Central America, and South America, creating a large population of mestizos. The English, on the other hand, followed a pattern of driving away the peoples they defeated. This pattern showed itself in England's conquest of Ireland during the

The first Africans to arrive in Virginia came as the result of a deal with a Dutch ship captain who traded them for food. The Africans had Spanish-sounding names—Pedro, Angelo, Antoney, and Isabella—so the colonists suspected the Dutch had stolen them from a Spanish slave ship. The Spaniards often baptized and renamed enslaved Africans.

OBJECTIVE
2 INSTRUCT

Clashes with Native Americans

▶ *Starting with the Student*
- Ask students if they know of any conflicts in their area between groups who must share resources such as tax dollars or the use of buildings.
- Ask students to discuss what happens when large groups or nations argue over territory or shared resources

▶ *Discussing Key Ideas*
- Unlike the Spaniards, the English live separately from the Native Americans.
- The English seek to push Native Americans from their land.
- Turmoil in Virginia leads James I to declare it a royal colony.

North Carolina in the Colonial Era

- General farming
- Tobacco
- Rice and indigo

Questions about smoking and health arose with the first shipments of tobacco to London from the Jamestown colony. King James I, worried about the health effects of smoking, opposed the cultivation of tobacco, which he called a "stinking weed." Nevertheless, the income from tobacco exports was too great to ignore, and by the 1620s the tobacco trade was booming. Virginia settlers began migrating to what is now North Carolina in the 1620s in search of new lands for raising tobacco.

A Virginia planter oversees slaves packing tobacco leaves for shipment to England (18th-century engraving).

INTERACT WITH HISTORY

1. **SUMMARIZING** What role has tobacco played in the North Carolina economy, and how is that changing?

 SEE SKILLBUILDER HANDBOOK, PAGE 1037.

2. **RESEARCHING** Find out more about the industries in your area. What do they produce? How long have they been in your community? How many persons do they employ? Make a chart or another kind of graphic organizer to present your information.

TEACHING OPTIONS

Making Global Connections

The West Indies and the Chesapeake For a time the Spanish held a monopoly on tobacco, cultivating the sweet-tasting variety native to the West Indies and selling it at a high price in Europe. When Virginians began to cultivate tobacco on the low-lying alluvial plains around the Chesapeake Bay, they sold their more plentiful crops at lower prices than the Spaniards did. As a result, the Spanish turned their West Indian tobacco plantations into sugar plantations—producing a product that would eventually lure New England merchants to the Caribbean.

Making Connections Across Time

Indentured Labor Indentured servitude still exists in parts of the developing world. In India and Pakistan, for example, poverty-stricken parents will bond their children to shops where they receive food and clothes in exchange for their labor. Adults sometimes bond themselves, too, so that they can pay off old debts or gain the use of land. Ask interested students to investigate efforts to end this practice by such groups as Free the Children, a Canadian organization founded by teenager Craig Kielburger.

In 1644, at nearly 100 years of age, Opechancanough organized one last futile assault. So infirm that he had to be carried on a stretcher, the chief still led a two-year struggle that left more than 500 settlers dead. Upon capturing the chief, Governor Berkeley sentenced him to a Jamestown prison, where a soldier resentful of the Powhatan uprising shot him in the back of the head.

Economic Differences Split Virginia

▶ **Starting with the Student**
- Challenge students to brainstorm adjectives that they associate with the word *rebellion*.
- Ask them what these adjectives tell them about the general goal or purpose of a *rebellion*.
- Explore when, if ever, students think a rebellion is justified.

▶ **Discussing Key Ideas**
- Indentured servants have almost no rights.
- Former indentured servants live in poverty along the frontier.
- A rebellion erupts when planters refuse to back frontier settlers in clashes with Native Americans.
- The rebellion exposes class differences.

C. Smith taketh the King of Pamavnkee prisoner - 1608.

John Smith takes the Powhatan chief, Opechancanough, prisoner.

1500s and 1600s. England's Laws of Conquest declared, in part, "Every Irishman shall be forbidden to wear English apparel or weapons upon pain of death." The same laws also banned marriages between the English and Irish.

The English brought this pattern of colonization with them to North America. Viewing the Native Americans as being "like the wild Irish," the English settlers had no desire to live among or intermarry with the Native Americans they defeated. Their conquest over the native peoples was total and complete—which is one reason a large mestizo population never developed in the United States.

THE SETTLERS BATTLE NATIVE AMERICANS
As the English settlers recovered in the years following the starving time, they never forgot the Powhatan's hostility during that deadly winter. In retaliation, the leaders of Jamestown demanded tributes of corn and labor from the local native peoples. Soldiers pressed these demands by setting Powhatan villages on fire and kidnapping hostages, especially children. One of the kidnapped children, Chief Powhatan's daughter, Pocahontas, married John Rolfe in 1614. This lay the groundwork for a half-hearted peace. However, the peace would not last, as colonists continued to move further into Native American territory and seize more land to grow tobacco.

By 1622, English settlers had worn out the patience of Chief Opechancanough, Chief Powhatan's brother and successor. In a well-planned attack, Powhatan raiding parties struck at colonial villages up and down the James River, and killed more than 340 colonists. The attack forced the Virginia Company to send in more troops and supplies, leaving it nearly bankrupt. In 1624, James I, disgusted by the turmoil in Virginia, revoked the company's charter and made Virginia a **royal colony**—one under direct control of the king. England sent more troops and settlers to strengthen the colony and to conquer the Powhatan. By 1644, nearly 10,000 English men and women lived in Virginia, while the Powhatan population continued to fall.

Economic Differences Split Virginia

The English colonists who migrated to North America in increasing numbers battled not only Native Americans but sometimes each other. By the 1670s, one-quarter of the free white men in Virginia were former indentured servants who, while they had completed their servitude, had little money to buy land. Because they did not own land, these former indentured servants could not vote and enjoyed almost no rights in colonial society.

These poor colonists lived mainly on the western outskirts of Virginia, where they constantly fought with Native Americans for land. In 1675, a bloody clash between Virginia's frontier settlers and local natives revealed an underlying tension between the colony's poor whites and its wealthy landowners and sparked a pitched battle between the two classes.

B. Answer The Spanish generally absorbed the peoples they conquered and lived among them, while the English sought to live separately from the peoples they defeated.

THINK THROUGH HISTORY
B. Contrasting How did the English pattern of conquest differ from that of the Spanish?

THINK THROUGH HISTORY
C. Analyzing Motives Why did the colonists continue to move onto Native American land?
C. Answer To accommodate the growing population and create more farm space.

Exploring Themes

Immigration and Migration The English settlers who moved into Virginia had no interest in living among the Native Americans. Instead they wanted to drive them off the land. The practice of pushing Native Americans ever westward continued well into the 1800s, when the United States government finally confined remaining native peoples to reservations.

Teaching Gifted and Talented Students

Conducting a Mock Trial Have students imagine that Nathaniel Bacon had not died—that Governor Berkeley had captured him instead. Ask students to create a mock trial in which the governor charges Bacon with treason. Remind students that Bacon had the right to a jury trial, but members of the jury would have been drawn from the same land-owning class that exercised the franchise. Encourage students to do outside research to ensure historical authenticity.

Nathaniel Bacon

BACON'S REBELLION In June of 1675, a dispute between the Doeg tribe and a Virginia frontier farmer grew into a bloodbath. A group of frontier settlers who were pursuing Doeg warriors murdered fourteen friendly Susquehannock and then executed five chiefs during a peace conference. Fighting soon broke out between Native Americans and frontier colonists, who pleaded to Virginia's governor, William Berkeley, for militia support. The governor, acting on behalf of the "planters"—Virginia's wealthy plantation farmers—refused to finance a war for the colony's poor frontier settlers.

Berkeley's refusal did not sit well with a twenty-nine-year-old planter named **Nathaniel Bacon.** Bacon, a tall, dark-haired, hot-tempered son of a wealthy Englishman, detested Native Americans. He called them "wolves" who preyed upon "our harmless and innocent lambs." In 1676, Bacon broke from his old friend Berkeley and raised an army to fight Native Americans on the Virginia frontier.

Governor Berkeley quickly declared Bacon's army—one-third of which was made up of landless settlers and debtors—illegal. Hearing this news, Bacon marched on Jamestown in September of 1676 to confront colonial leaders about a number of grievances, including the frontier colonists' lack of representation in the House of Burgesses—Virginia's colonial legislature. The march turned violent. The rebels set fire to the town, as Berkeley and numerous planters fled by ship. However, Bacon had little time to enjoy his victory. He died of illness a month after storming Jamestown. Upon Bacon's death, Berkeley returned to Jamestown and easily subdued the leaderless rebels.

D. Answer The colonial system offered them few rights in society and little protection from Native Americans.

THINK THROUGH HISTORY
D. Summarizing Why were the frontier settlers discontented with the colonial system?

Although Bacon's Rebellion failed, it exposed the growing power of the colony's former indentured servants. Virginia's "rabble," as many planters called the frontier settlers, resented being taxed and governed without their consent—a complaint that both wealthy and poor colonists would voice against Great Britain 100 years later in 1776.

However, at the time, Bacon's Rebellion spurred the planter class to cling more tightly to power. Meanwhile, farther to the north, another group of English colonists, who had journeyed to North America, for religious reasons, were plotting their own course into the future.

The American Colonies Emerge **49**

Section ② Assessment

1. TERMS & NAMES

Identify:
• John Smith
• Jamestown
• Powhatan
• headright system
• indentured servant
• royal colony
• Nathaniel Bacon

2. SUMMARIZING Create a time line of the major developments in the colonization of Virginia, using a form such as the one below.

Which event do you think was the most critical turning point? Why?

3. ANALYZING In your judgment, what were the benefits and drawbacks of using indentured servants for labor in Virginia? Support your judgment with references to the text.

THINK ABOUT
• the labor demands of growing tobacco
• the characteristics and cost of indentured servants
• the causes and consequences of Bacon's Rebellion

4. RECOGNIZING EFFECTS The success of tobacco farming in Virginia had wide-ranging effects. Describe its impact on each of these groups: the Jamestown colonists, indentured servants, the Powhatan, the planters.

THINK ABOUT
• the early history of the Jamestown settlement
• the headright system and indentured servitude
• Powhatan attacks on colonial villages
• Bacon's Rebellion

ANSWERS

1. TERMS AND NAMES

John Smith, p. 44
Jamestown, p. 45
Powhatan, p. 45
headright system, p. 46
indentured servant, p. 46
royal colony, p. 48
Nathaniel Bacon, p. 49

2. SUMMARIZING

1607 Jamestown founded; 1609 Starving time began; 1612 John Rolfe developed new strain of tobacco; 1618 Headright system introduced; 1619 First Africans arrived in Virginia; House of Burgesses first met; 1622 Chief Opechancanough led raids on settlers; 1624 James I made Virginia a royal colony; 1675 Fighting erupts between settlers and Native Americans on frontier; 1676 Bacon's Rebellion erupts.

3. ANALYZING

Possible Responses: Benefits: indentured servants were available, willing, and economical labor, and for many years they helped meet colony's labor needs; Drawbacks: term of service relatively short; since they earned little or no money during service, former servants were unable to buy land, remained poor, and had few rights.

4. RECOGNIZING EFFECTS

Possible Responses: Jamestown colonists—tobacco revived a failing colony; indentured servants—tobacco provided opportunity for work and new life, though limited long-term prospects; Powhatan—tobacco required much land, and its success led to colonial expansion, which Powhatan attacks did not deter; planters—gained most of tobacco wealth.

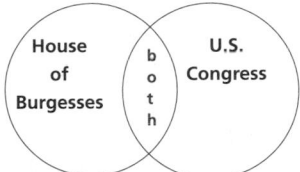
Teacher's Edition   49

OBJECTIVES

1 To show how geography played a role in determining locations of settlements.

2 To identify the criteria settlers tried to meet in establishing Jamestown.

FOCUS & MOTIVATE

▶ **Starting with the Student**
Tell students to imagine that they are part of a group of people moving to another part of the world.

- What specific criteria would you set for choosing a new locale?
- How might these change if the area to which you were moving was a wilderness with few inhabitants?

 ELECTRONIC LIBRARY OF PRIMARY SOURCES
from *The General History of Virginia* by John Smith

MORE ABOUT . . .
Malaria

Malaria is caused by a parasite that lives in *Anopheles* mosquitoes and is transmitted to a human host by the mosquito's bite. The mosquito's role in spreading the disease was scientifically proved only in the late 19th century by a French physician, Charles Louis Alphonse Laveran. Laveran's work on tropical diseases won him the 1907 Nobel Prize for medicine.

The Jamestown Settlement

Every time people choose a new place to settle, they consider two aspects of its geographic location: the site and the situation. *Site* refers to the physical characteristics of a particular spot: the landforms, the quality of the soil, and the type of vegetation. *Situation*, on the other hand, concerns the relationship between the site and its surrounding area. How close is it to the sea? to other settlements? to resources? to avenues of transportation like roads or harbors?

The first settlers of Jamestown were mainly concerned about defense. The English feared attack from two groups: (1) rival power Spain, whose powerful navy could attack by sea, and (2) Native Americans, who could attack by land. The colonists also needed an area that would support their settlement with fresh water and fertile soil.

As the leaders of the Jamestown expedition explored the Chesapeake Bay and its rivers, they argued about where to erect a fort and plant their settlement. No one place seemed to meet all the criteria. The place they chose was well situated for defense. The land was flat and nearly surrounded by water. In other ways, however, the site was disastrous. Much of the land was marshy, and there were swarms of mosquitoes. At that time no one knew that mosquitoes carried deadly malaria.

Pottery jug found on the site of the Jamestown fort.

SETTLEMENT CRITERIA When the Virginia Company sent the Jamestown expedition, it gave specific instructions regarding the location. The four major criteria are shown in these maps. Three of the four criteria concern defense. The settlements were actually attacked twice by Native Americans—in 1622 and 1644—but a much feared invasion by the Spanish never occurred.

The fourth criteria—a healthful and fertile place—addressed its suitability for living. While fertile, the island proved to be unhealthful.

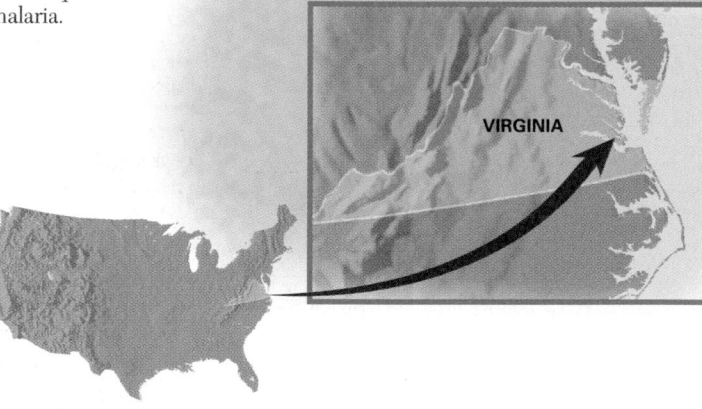

CRITERION 1 A location upstream on a major river flowing from the northwest.

JAMESTOWN ISLAND

James River

CRITERION 2 A location where the river narrowed so that musket fire could reach enemy ships from both banks.

VIRGINIA

RECOMMENDED RESOURCES

Books

Bridenbaugh, Carl. *Jamestown, 1544–1699.* New York: Oxford UP, 1980. A brief, respected history.

Deetz, James. *In Small Things Forgotten.* Garden City, NY: Anchor, 1996. Objects from everyday colonial life.

Noël Hume, Ivor. *Martin's Hundred.* New York: Dell, 1982. Lost James River colony.

Smith, John. *Captain John Smith's History of Virginia.* Indianapolis: Bobbs-Merrill, 1979. Selections from Smith's work, first published in 1624.

Videos

Cavaliers and Craftsmen: Colonial Williamsburg & Jamestown. Atlas Video, 1986. Reenacts everyday life, with background period music.

Colonial America: The Beginnings. CRM Films. Focuses on the settling of America and early colonial life.

Search for a Century. Colonial Williamsburg Foundation, 1980. Documents the dig for the early Virginia colony lost in 1618 at Martin's Hundred.

Where America Began. Finley-Holiday Film Corp., 1988. Tours the restorations at Jamestown, Williamsburg, and Yorktown, Virginia.

Software

ColonyQuest. Decision Development Corp., distributed by ESI. A simulation placing students in Jamestown in about 1610, where as settlement leaders they must establish a tobacco plantation, hire workers, and face many other challenges.

CRITERION 4 A healthful and fertile place.

0 ____ 1 Mile
0 ____ 2 Kilometers

N

SITE AND SITUATION The map below shows the situation of Jamestown on the James River, and the map to the right gives a detailed view of the site the colonists selected—a marshy island in the James River.

Back River Marsh

James Fort Site

Pitch and Tar Swamp

JAMESTOWN ISLAND

James River

Chesapeake Bay

ATLANTIC OCEAN

CRITERION 3 No Native American settlement between Jamestown and the sea.

0 ____ 10 Miles
0 ____ 20 Kilometers

The Jamestown colonists chose the highest point on the island—just 14 feet above sea level—on which to erect their fort. The site of this original fort, which burned down a year after it was built, remained a mystery for centuries. In 1996, archaeologists announced that they had unearthed the actual James Fort.

The map above shows the location of the three-sided fort along the probable shoreline of the island (erosion has altered the island's shape over the years).

INTERACT WITH HISTORY

1. **EVALUATING DECISIONS** Consider the four criteria the Virginia Company gave the colonists for the location of Jamestown. Given what happened in Jamestown, how well do you think the colonists did in choosing their site?

   SEE SKILLBUILDER HANDBOOK, PAGE 1048.

2. **RESEARCHING THE JAMESTOWN REDISCOVERY** The unearthing of the original James Fort has led to the discovery of artifacts, skeletons, and other archaeological evidence of Jamestown's past. Some of the findings may cast a new light on the early history of the settlement—and also on the quality of the location the settlers chose. Do research to find out more about the James Fort archaeological dig and its connection to the geography of Jamestown. Present your findings to the class.

   INTERNET For more about Jamestown, click on *Social Studies* at http://www.mcdougallittell.com

The American Colonies Emerge **51**

INSTRUCT

▶*Discussing Key Ideas*
• Defense was a key concern in choosing the site of the Jamestown colony.
• Because of their concern for defense and ignorance about malaria-carrying mosquitoes, the settlers chose a marshy area that proved unhealthful.

HISTORY FROM VISUALS
Reading the Images
Study the maps and the four points specifying an ideal location.

• To what "sea" does point 3 refer? *Atlantic Ocean*
• Why do you think the criteria stressed a river location near the sea? *Possible Responses: Easier to find and supply; easier to escape; good for trade; water was chief means of transport.*

MORE ABOUT . . .
The James Fort Discovery

"We are at ground zero, the genesis of America," observed William Kelso, leader of the team that unearthed the James Fort artifacts in 1996. The man whose skeleton they found, and who may have bled to death from the musket ball embedded in his leg, may have been George Kendall, possibly put to death as a suspected spy for Spain.

IN-DEPTH RESOURCES: UNIT 1
Geography Application: The Jamestown Fort, p. 25

INTERACT WITH HISTORY

1. Evaluating Decisions

Possible Answers: *In meeting three of the four criteria, the colonists did well, considering the unknown nature of the terrain. Because they failed to choose a healthful site, the colonists did poorly, since the high death rate almost nullified the positive effects of the other criteria. The colonists were still vulnerable to attack as well as disease. The colonists were still placed in a precarious position because the Virginia Company cared mainly about profits and neglected the colonists' welfare.*

2. Researching the Jamestown Rediscovery

Standards for Evaluation
Information should . . .

• be presented orally, in writing, or in a graphic display, such as a poster
• include details obtained through up-to-date sources such as periodicals, the Internet, and/or the Jamestown restoration itself or another appropriate organization
• focus on any new details that the findings provide about the suitability of the Jamestown site and the early history of the settlement

Teacher's Edition **51**

OBJECTIVES

1 To identify the motives that led Puritans to New England.

2 To summarize the principles of government established by the dissenters who fled to Rhode Island.

3 To explain the reasons the Pequot and the Wampanoag took stands against the colonists.

SKILLBUILDER

• Understanding geography: place, p. 56

CRITICAL THINKING

• Analyzing motives, p. 53
• Analyzing issues, p. 55
• Comparing, p. 56
• Recognizing effects, p. 57
• Summarizing, p. 57
• Drawing conclusions, p. 57
• Interpreting, p. 57

FOCUS & MOTIVATE

▶ **Starting with the Student**
• If students were to create an ideal community, what features would it have?
• In this ideal community, how would students handle dissenters, or people who objected to the pattern of living?

OBJECTIVE

1 INSTRUCT

Puritans Create a "New England"

▶ **Discussing Key Ideas**
• Puritan settlers come to America to practice their religious beliefs freely.
• They seek to build a model society.
• A close relationship exists between church and state.
• Families provide the basis of Puritan society.

IN-DEPTH RESOURCES: UNIT 1
Guided Reading, p. 22

ACCESS FOR STUDENTS ACQUIRING ENGLISH
Guided Reading (Spanish), p. 21

3 Puritan New England

TERMS & NAMES
• John Winthrop
• Puritan
• Separatist
• Massachusetts Bay Colony
• Roger Williams
• Anne Hutchinson
• Pequot War
• Metacom
• King Philip's War

LEARN ABOUT the reasons English Puritans came to North America
TO UNDERSTAND the characteristics of the Massachusetts Bay Colony and how the colonists interacted with Native Americans.

ONE AMERICAN'S STORY

Anne Dudley loved to wander the rich English estates of Tattershall Castle, where her father, Thomas Dudley, managed the property and household of the Earl of Lincoln. She especially enjoyed the Earl's library. In an age when few women had an extensive education, Anne had the benefit of a private tutor who encouraged her to read the Earl's many books.

In 1628, at age 16, Anne married Simon Bradstreet, one of a group of Puritans who frequently visited the Earl to discuss their ideas about reforming the Church of England. These ideas were unpopular with the English monarchy and church leaders, who persecuted the Puritans for their views. Eager to practice their beliefs without interference, Simon, Anne, and her parents joined other Puritans who hoped to create a "holy" community in New England. There Anne Dudley Bradstreet became America's first English-speaking poet, and her poems would provide posterity with a glimpse of Puritan life and values.

Like other early settlers, Anne was disappointed with her first sight of the shoddy houses and muddy streets of New England's villages. "But," she wrote, "after I was convinced it was the way of God, I submitted to it." She and thousands of other Puritans set out to impose their vision of divine order on their communities and on the "wilderness" surrounding it. However, the Puritans' growing numbers and determined views threatened the way of life of Native Americans and would lead to violent clashes between the two groups.

This picture of Anne Bradstreet is a detail from a window in St. Botolph's Church, Lincolnshire, England.

Puritans Create a "New England"

Puritans cherished their Bibles, passing them down as family treasures from one generation to the next. This Bible belonged to Governor William Bradford of the Plymouth Colony.

It was March of 1630 when Anne Bradstreet and her family boarded the *Arbella*. The flagship of the Puritan expedition to America, the ship carried many prominent passengers, including **John Winthrop**, a lawyer who would be the first governor of the Massachusetts Bay Colony. At this time, the English settlement at Jamestown was still struggling to survive. Unlike the profit-minded colonists at Jamestown, however, the Puritans emigrated to build a model new society—what Governor Winthrop called a "City upon a Hill."

PURITANS AND PILGRIMS King Henry VIII (1491–1547) had brought the Reformation to England in the 1530s when he broke with Roman Catholicism to form a separate church, the Church of England. Although the church was free of Catholic control, the **Puritans** felt that it had kept too much of the Catholic ritual and tradition. They wanted to purify it by eliminating all traces of Catholicism.

Puritans embraced the idea of a "priesthood of all believers," in which every worshipper should experience God directly through faith, prayer, and study of the Bible—rather than through services and rituals conducted by church priests. Accordingly, Puritans placed great importance on the Bible, and all men and women had to know how to read so they could consult the Bible themselves. Puritans held ministers in respect, but they objected to the authority of Anglican (Church of England) bishops. Rather, Puritans believed that individual church congregations should hold the power to hire—and fire—their ministers.

SECTION 3 RESOURCES

PRINT RESOURCES

IN-DEPTH RESOURCES: UNIT 1
Guided Reading, p. 22
Primary Sources: *from* The Mayflower Compact, p. 31
from John Winthrop's Journal, p. 32
Literature: Poems by Anne Bradstreet, p. 33
American Lives: John Winthrop, p. 37

ACCESS FOR STUDENTS ACQUIRING ENGLISH
Guided Reading (Spanish), p. 21

FORMAL ASSESSMENT
Section Quiz, p. 20

ALTERNATIVE ASSESSMENT BOOK
See forms for supporting and scoring alternative activities.

TECHNOLOGY RESOURCES

CRITICAL THINKING TRANSPARENCIES
CT2, Puritan Migration

CD-ROM Electronic Library of Primary Sources

VIDEO *American Portfolio: A Videodisc for U.S. History*
user's guide, pp. 18–20

INTERNET McDougal Littell Learning On-Line
http://www.mcdougallittell.com

Some Puritans felt they should remain in the Church of England and reform it from within. Other Puritans did not think that was possible, so they formed independent congregations with their own ministers. The **Separatists,** as they were called, met in secret because James I was determined to punish those who did not follow the Anglican form of worship. One congregation of Separatists, known today as the Pilgrims, fled from England to Holland and eventually migrated to America. There, in 1620, this small group of families founded the Plymouth Colony, the second permanent English colony in North America.

THE MASSACHUSETTS BAY COMPANY Meanwhile, other Puritans turned their thoughts toward New England in the 1620s. They were not Separatists, but they were discouraged about Anglican reform. Furthermore, they felt the burden of increasing religious persecution, political repression, and dismal economic conditions. Many Puritans were convinced that England was doomed. "I am . . . persuaded God will bring some heavy affliction upon this land," wrote John Winthrop to his wife in 1629. But, he added confidently, "[the Lord would] provide a shelter and a hiding place for us." Winthrop and others thought this refuge would be in America.

In 1629, Winthrop and some of his well-connected friends obtained a royal charter for a joint-stock enterprise, the Massachusetts Bay Company. The charter included a land grant and provisions for a government but failed to say where the company's headquarters would be. Winthrop and his friends took advantage of this omission and boldly transferred both the charter and the company's headquarters to New England. This strategy meant that when the Puritans migrated, they took with them the authority for an independent government.

The migration that began in 1630 was greater in size and more thorough in planning than all previous expeditions to North America. During that year, 17 ships (including the *Arbella)* carried about 1,000 English men, women, and children—Puritan and non-Puritan—to the **Massachusetts Bay Colony.** Aboard these vessels were ample provisions and many skilled artisans, including one of the best shipwrights in England. The Puritans carried no exotic cash crops, no cumbersome mining equipment—just the tools and supplies to establish good English farms and villages.

The planning paid off. There was no starving time in the Massachusetts Bay Colony. The colony's success quickly encouraged a steady flow of people from across the Atlantic—about 20,000 English souls between 1630 and 1640 in a movement called the Great Migration. The port town of Boston soon became the colony's thriving capital. Settlers established other towns nearby and eventually incorporated the Plymouth Colony into the Massachusetts Bay Colony.

"CITY UPON A HILL" The Puritans believed they had a special covenant, or agreement, with God. To fulfill their part, the Puritans were to create a moral society that would serve as a beacon for others to follow. God would reward them with peace and prosperity. In a sermon delivered aboard the *Arbella,* Winthrop expressed the sense of mission that bound the Puritans together.

> **A PERSONAL VOICE**
> We must be knit together in this work; . . . we must uphold [each other] . . . in all meekness, gentleness, patience and liberality [generosity]. We must delight in each other, make others' conditions our own, rejoice together, mourn together, labor and suffer together. . . .
> So shall we keep the unity of the spirit, in the bond of peace. . . . Ten of us will be able to resist a thousand of our enemies. For we must consider that we [in New England] shall be as a City upon a Hill, the eyes of all people are on us.
>
> **JOHN WINTHROP,** "A Model of Christian Charity"

THINK THROUGH HISTORY
A. *Analyzing Motives* Why did the Puritans leave England?

A. Answer Some Pilgrims left to break with the church and escape persecution; other Puritans left to escape political and religious persecution and avoid political, social, and economic turmoil.

HISTORICAL SPOTLIGHT

THE MAYFLOWER COMPACT

Although the Pilgrims aimed for Virginia, their ship, the *Mayflower,* strayed far off course to Cape Cod. The Pilgrims knew that New England lay too far north for their colonial charter to be valid. They were also afraid that non-Pilgrim passengers would challenge their authority. Before departing the ship, the Pilgrim men signed a compact, or agreement, in which they created a civil government and pledged loyalty to the king.

The Mayflower Compact stated that the purpose of their government in America would be to frame "just and equal laws . . . for the general good of the colony." Laws approved by the majority would be binding on Pilgrims and non-Pilgrims alike. The document became an important landmark in the development of the American system of democratic government.

HISTORICAL SPOTLIGHT
The Mayflower Compact

Read aloud the "supremacy clause" of the Constitution (Article VI, Section 2).

This Constitution . . . . shall be the supreme law of the land; and the judges in every state shall be bound thereby, anything in the constitution or laws of the state to the contrary notwithstanding.

Discuss with students the similarities between this provision and the Mayflower Compact. Point out the faith the English colonists placed in written constitutions—i.e., the rule of law.

IN-DEPTH RESOURCE: UNIT 1
Primary Source: *from* The Mayflower Compact, p. 31

 ELECTRONIC LIBRARY OF PRIMARY SOURCES
from *The Journal of the Ship Mayflower,* by Thomas Jones

MORE ABOUT . . .
John Winthrop

John Winthrop studied at Trinity College in the University of Cambridge. While there, he became a Puritan. He grew increasingly troubled by the problems faced by Puritans in England. Winthrop tasted the wrath of royalists when his beliefs cost him a lucrative job as an attorney in the royal courts.

IN-DEPTH RESOURCE: UNIT 1
Primary Source: *from* John Winthrop's Journal, p. 32
American Lives, John Winthrop, p. 37

TEACHING OPTIONS

Making Connections Across the Curriculum

Language Arts Write these three terms on the chalkboard: *purify, puritan, puritanical.* Ask students to brainstorm the words or images that come to mind for each of these words. Construct class definitions for the three words, and compare/contrast them with their dictionary definitions. In terms of history, how were the terms *purify* and *puritan* related? What traits of the Puritans might have inspired the term *puritanical?* As an extension, discuss whether students think the Puritans have been unfairly stereotyped over time.

Making Connections Across Time

Thanksgiving Americans link Thanksgiving to a 1621 feast held by the Pilgrims. Despite all the traditions, very little is known about the event except a brief description provided in a letter by Edward Winslow. Said Winslow: "Our harvest being gotten in, our governor sent four men on fowling, that we might, after a special manner, rejoice together after we had gathered the fruit of our labors. . . . At which time, . . . many Indians coming amongst us, . . . [including} Massasoit, with some 90 men, whom for three days we entertained and feasted, and they went and killed five deer, which they . . . bestowed on our governor."

Teacher's Edition 53

MORE ABOUT . . .
Puritan Families

Even by the standards of the times, the Puritans lived extraordinarily long lives, with 20 percent of the men living to age 80.

Reasons for the long life spans may have included a cool climate to slow the spread of disease, pure drinking water, and less-crowded conditions than were found in Europe. Whatever the cause, the historian John Murrin claimed that New Englanders "invented" grandparents. For one of the first times in history, large numbers of people lived to see their children grow up and have children of their own.

 CRITICAL THINKING TRANSPARENCIES
CT2, Puritan Migration

 ELECTRONIC LIBRARY OF PRIMARY SOURCES
from *The Book of the General Laws* by the Inhabitants of New Plimouth

MORE ABOUT . . .
Puritan Women

Puritan emphasis on reading the Bible encouraged a higher rate of literacy among Puritan women in New England than women in England or among women elsewhere in the colonies. As late as the 1750s, only one out of three women in England could sign her name. In the colonies as a whole, less than half of all women could read in the 17th century and even fewer could write. Most Puritan women, however, learned to read and write at home. They were expected, though, to keep their writings private.

This 17th-century oil painting depicts the New England lawyer and merchant John Freake. His ornate lace collar reflects the pride that many Puritans took in their appearance.

Winthrop envisioned his city upon a hill as a "holy commonwealth"—a community whose members worked together toward common goals and lived according to Christian principles. This vision, however, did not stem from a belief in either social equality or political democracy. Explained Winthrop in his shipboard sermon, God had decreed that "some must be rich, some poor, some high and eminent in power and dignity, others mean [common] and in subjugation."

Although Puritans made no effort to create a democracy, political power was spread more broadly than in England. Soon after founding the colony, the Massachusetts Bay Company extended the right to vote to include not only stockholders but all adult male members of the Puritan church. Their numbers accounted for an estimated 40 percent of the colony's men, a large electorate by the standards of Europe in the 1630s. These "freemen," as they were called, voted annually for members of a lawmaking body called the General Court, which in turn chose the governor.

CHURCH AND STATE As this system of self-government evolved, so did the close relationship between the government and the Puritan church. Puritan ministers possessed no formal political authority, nor could they hold office. However, since only formal members of the Puritan church held political rights, the Puritan view dominated Massachusetts society. Taxes supported the Puritan church, and laws required church attendance.

Puritan officials insisted that they, as God's "elect," had a duty to carry out the will of God. Puritan laws criminalized such sins as drunkenness, swearing, theft, and idleness. "No person . . . should spend his time idly or unprofitably," decreed the General Court in 1633, "under pain of such punishment as the court shall think meet [appropriate] to inflict."

Why did the Puritans include idleness in their catalog of sins? They believed that God "called" people to their work. Whatever the vocation one was called to, God required men and women to work long and hard at it. This "Puritan work ethic" helped contribute to the rapid growth and success of the New England colonies.

IMPORTANCE OF THE FAMILY Unlike settlers in Virginia, Puritans generally crossed the Atlantic as families rather than as single men or women. "Without family care," declared one minister, "the labor of Magistrates and Ministers . . . is likely to be in great measure unsuccessful." Within the family, authority rested with the father. Husbands and wives shared child-rearing responsibilities, but wives were expected to defer to their husbands in matters of importance.

Puritans kept a watchful eye on the actions of husbands, wives, and children, and the community stepped in when necessary. If parents failed to nip disobedience in the bud, they might find their children placed in more "God-fearing" homes. If a husband and wife quarreled too much, a court might intervene as a form of marriage counseling. If they still bickered, one or both might end up in the stocks or the pillory.

54 CHAPTER 2

 TEACHING OPTION

Cooperative Activity: Investigating Puritan Life

Task: Students will investigate the Puritans in colonial Massachusetts and create a visual display of their research.

Purpose: To understand the customs and traditions, family life and community life, of the Puritans in Massachusetts.

Activity: Divide the class into small groups to research and create displays of various aspects of Puritan life. Have students begin their research before they go to the library by identifying topics and dividing them among the groups. Topics might include food, clothing, religious practices, social customs, laws and traditions, work and income, education, and entertainment. Then students can research their topics, collecting facts, figures, and images that help depict and explain life in a Puritan community. Ask them to create visual displays that include drawings, sketches, maps, charts, color photocopies, and diagrams, as well as written descriptions of their findings and present them to the class.

ALTERNATIVE ASSESSMENT BOOK
Standards for Evaluating a Cooperative Activity

Despite the stern moral sensibility, Puritans knew joy. "I prize thy love more than whole mines of gold," wrote Anne Bradstreet in a poem to her husband. And in a poem to her children, she exclaimed, "Long did I keep you soft and warm." However, Puritans generally kept such displays of affection private.

Dissent in the Puritan Community

The Puritans came to America not to foster freedom of religion but to follow their own form of worship, and they were intolerant of people who had other religious beliefs. Puritan leaders felt particularly threatened by two dissenters, Roger Williams and Anne Hutchinson, whom they feared challenged the social order upon which the colony was founded.

THE FOUNDING OF PROVIDENCE "Forced religion stinks in the nostrils of God," declared **Roger Williams** in a sermon to his Salem congregation. Williams, an extreme Separatist, expressed two controversial views. First, he declared that the English settlers had no rightful claim to the land unless they purchased it from Native Americans. He called the royal charter that granted the lands a "National Sinne" and demanded that it be revised to reflect Native American claims. Second, Williams declared that government officials had no business punishing settlers for their religious beliefs. He felt every person should be free to worship according to his or her conscience.

To the Puritan leaders of Massachusetts, the first idea was absurd, and the second was heresy—it violated the religious beliefs of the Puritans. The outraged General Court ordered Williams to be arrested and returned to England. Before this order was carried out, Williams fled Massachusetts. In January 1636, he headed southward to the headwaters of Narragansett Bay. There he negotiated with the local Narragansett tribe for land to set up a new colony, which he called Providence. In Providence, later the capital of Rhode Island, Williams guaranteed separation of church and state and religious freedom.

THE BANISHMENT OF ANNE HUTCHINSON Puritan leaders soon banished another dissenter, **Anne Hutchinson.** To strict Puritans, she posed an even greater threat than Williams. In Bible readings at her home, Hutchinson taught that "the Holy Spirit illumines [enlightens] the heart of every true believer." In other words, worshippers needed neither the church nor its ministers to interpret the Bible for them.

Such ideas, in the opinion of Puritan leaders, made Hutchinson "a woman not fit for our society." At a public trial, they charged her with violating the laws of the family, church, and state. Said John Winthrop, who as governor, served as both judge and prosecutor, "You have rather bine [been] a Husband than a Wife, and a Preacher than a Hearer, and a Magistrate than a Subject." Hutchinson, however, refused to recant her opinions.

Puritan leaders banished Hutchinson from the colony in 1638. Along with a band of followers, she and her family trudged to Rhode Island. After the death of her husband in 1642, Hutchinson moved with her younger children to New Netherland, where the Dutch also practiced religious toleration. The following year, she died in a war fought between the Dutch and Native Americans.

Native Americans Resist Colonial Expansion

While Williams and his followers were settling Rhode Island, thousands of other white settlers fanned out to western Massachusetts and to new colonies in New Hampshire and Connecticut. From the beginning, Native Americans had helped the colonists, providing them land, giving them agricultural advice, and engaging them in trade—trade that helped many Puritan merchants prosper.

THINK THROUGH HISTORY
B. Analyzing Issues What two principles did Providence guarantee that Massachusetts Bay did not?
B. Answer Separation of church and state and religious toleration.

"The Holy Spirit illuminates the heart of every true believer."

ANNE HUTCHINSON

This statue of Anne Hutchinson stands in Boston, Massachusetts. Ironically, she was banished from Massachusetts for leading religious discussions.

The American Colonies Emerge **55**

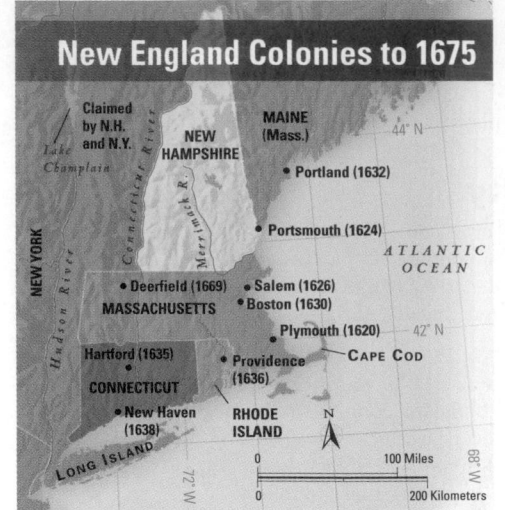

New England Colonies to 1675

Claimed by N.H. and N.Y.

Lake Champlain

MAINE (Mass.)

NEW HAMPSHIRE

44° N

• Portland (1632)

NEW YORK

• Portsmouth (1624)

ATLANTIC OCEAN

• Deerfield (1669) • Salem (1626)
MASSACHUSETTS • Boston (1630)

• Plymouth (1620) 42° N

Hartford (1635) • Providence (1636) CAPE COD

CONNECTICUT

• New Haven (1638) RHODE ISLAND

LONG ISLAND

N

0   100 Miles
0   200 Kilometers

GEOGRAPHY SKILLBUILDER

PLACE *What was the earliest major European settlement in the New England colonies?*

PLACE *What characteristics did Boston have that made it a good place for a settlement?*

However, as Native Americans saw their own people killed by European diseases and their lands claimed, they recognized that the rapid spread of the settlers meant an end to their way of life. This conflict of cultures and interests led to some of the most intense fighting between settlers and Native Americans in the early English colonies.

DISPUTES OVER LAND AND RELIGION Disputes between the Puritans and Native Americans arose over two issues—land and religion. For every acre a colonial farmer needed to support life, a Native American needed twenty for hunting, fishing, and agriculture. To Native Americans, no one owned the land—it was there for everyone to use. Native Americans saw land treaties with Europeans more as agreements in which they received gifts—blankets, guns, iron tools, or whatever—to share the land for a limited time. Europeans, however, saw the treaties as a one-time deal in which Native Americans permanently sold their land to new owners.

Similar misunderstandings existed over religion. Puritans considered Native Americans heathens— people without a faith. At first, Puritans tried earnestly to convert them, which many Native Americans resisted. Over time, as hostility between the two groups grew, many Puritans tended to view the Native Americans as agents of the devil who presented a constant threat to their godly society. Rather than convert the Native Americans, the New England colonists set out to remove or destroy native societies. For their part, Native Americans developed a similarly hard view toward the white invaders.

THE PEQUOT WAR The first major conflict arose in Connecticut in 1637, when the Pequot nation decided to take a stand against the colonists. The colonists formed an alliance with the Narragansett, old enemies of the Pequot. The result of the **Pequot War** was the near destruction of the Pequot nation. The end came in May 1637, when about 90 English colonists and hundreds of their Native American allies surrounded a Pequot fort on the Mystic River. After setting the fort on fire, the colonists shot Pequot men, women, and children as they tried to escape or surrender. The murder was so awful that the Narragansett pleaded, "This is evil, this is evil, too furious, too many killed." The colonists ignored them, until all but 5 out of about 400 people in the fort had died.

That day, the survivors, including the Narragansett, witnessed a kind of warfare different and more brutal than any they had ever known. The massacre led a Narragansett leader named Miantonomo to warn other tribes of the English. In a speech to the Montauk of Long Island, he declared,

This British engraving shows the Pequot Fort near Stonington, Connecticut. The fort was destroyed in 1637.

The figure of the Indians fort or Palizado in NEW ENGLAND And the maner of the destroying It by Captayne Vnderhill And Captayne Mason

---

TEACHING OPTIONS

Exploring Themes

Immigration and Migration When the Puritans moved into New England, they introduced new ideas of land use that conflicted with those held by Native Americans. They cut down trees and farmed tracts of land which were owned by individual families. When New Englanders defeated the Native Americans who lived in the region, they also set in motion forces that would reshape the region's landscape. The densely forested woodlands would soon be sacrificed for well-defined villages and towns.

Making Connections Across Time

Pequot Land Rights In 1973, Elizabeth George Plouffe, the last Pequot occupying a tiny reservation, died. When Connecticut moved to convert the land into a park, Plouffe's grandson, Richard "Skip" Hayward, honored a promise to "hold onto the land." After a series of court suits, Hayward and the Pequot who joined him won a $900,000 settlement. The Pequot invested the money in a giant casino complex and used the profits to revitalize their culture. Since the 1970s, the number of Pequot have grown from about 50 to more than 250.

A PERSONAL VOICE

You know our fathers had plenty of deer and skins, our plains were full of deer, as also our woods, and of turkeys, and our coves full of fish and fowl. But these English have gotten our land, they with scythes cut down the grass, and with axes fell the trees; their cows and horses eat the grass, and their hogs spoil our clam banks, and we shall all be starved. . . .

For so are we all Indians as the English are, and say brother one to another; so must we be one as they are, otherwise we shall be all gone shortly.

MIANTONOMO, quoted in *Changes in the Land*

KING PHILIP'S WAR There was no further major warfare between Puritans and Native Americans for almost forty years. However, great tension continued to exist. The colonial population had swelled to more than 50,000. Deprived of their land and livelihood, many Native Americans had to toil for the English to earn a living. They also had to obey Puritan laws such as no hunting or fishing on Sunday, the Sabbath day. Wampanoag chief **Metacom,** whom the English called King Philip, bristled under these restrictions. In a last-ditch effort to wipe out the invaders, he organized his tribe and several others into an alliance.

The eruption of **King Philip's War** in the spring of 1675 startled the Puritans with its intensity. Using hit-and-run tactics, Native Americans attacked and burned outlying settlements throughout New England. Within months they were striking the outskirts of Boston. The alarmed and angered colonists responded by killing as many Native Americans as they could, even some from friendly tribes. For over a year, the two sides waged a war of mutual brutality and destruction. Finally, food shortages, disease, and heavy casualties wore down the Native Americans' resistance, and they gradually surrendered or fled.

The English paid a high price for their victory. Native Americans had attacked 52 colonial villages, destroying 16. About one-tenth of the colonial men of military age in New England were killed. Thus, a higher proportion of the total population died in King Philip's War than in either the American Revolution or the bloody Civil War of the 1860s.

Wampanoag casualties included Metacom, the victim of a bullet fired by a Native American ally of the English. The Puritans had previously captured his wife and son and sold them into slavery in the West Indies. To commemorate their victory, the Puritans exhibited Metacom's head at Plymouth for 20 years. With his defeat, Native American power in southeastern New England was gone forever.

D. Answer
Immediate: high casualties among colonists, end of Native American power in southeastern New England; students might suggest that long-term effects are the continual encroachment of Native American land by colonial societies.

THINK THROUGH HISTORY

D. Recognizing Effects
What were the immediate effects of King Philip's War? What long-term effects would you predict?

KEY PLAYER

METACOM
(?–1676)

As a youth, Metacom watched his father, Massasoit, befriend the Puritans and offer them land, advice, and protection from other tribes. As a sign of friendship, the Puritans gave Massasoit's sons English names. Metacom received the name Philip, after Philip of Macedon, the father of Alexander the Great.

However, English names did not make English subjects. In 1662, after the death of his father and older brother, 24-year-old Metacom became chief of the Wampanoag. Whereas his father had kept peace with the English, Metacom found it increasingly difficult to live on their terms, as he saw white settlers take more and more land and subject his people to much humiliation.

Metacom bided his time for 13 years, while he secretly forged an alliance among northeastern tribes. The breaking point came in 1675, when Puritan authorities executed three Wampanoag for the murder of a tribal informer. In retaliation, Metacom and his allies attacked colonial villages, and King Philip's War began.

Critical Thinking: Evaluating Decisions
Ask students to evaluate Metacom's decisions in his relations with the English settlers, first biding his time, and then after 13 years forging a secret alliance that eventually led to war. *Some students will suggest that he was justified, having been pushed to the breaking point; others will suggest that he should have made earlier attempts to reach a compromise with the English.*

ASSESS & RETEACH

Section 3 Assessment
Divide questions among groups of students, and have them present their answers orally.

Self-Assessment
Ask students to evaluate Puritan attitudes toward dissent by creating a pro-and-con chart that weighs the benefits and drawbacks of social conformity.

Section Quiz

FORMAL ASSESSMENT BOOK
Section Quiz, p. 20

Reteach
Use the map, "New England Colonies to 1675," to help review the main ideas of the section.

CLOSE

The Puritans came to North America to build a model community based on religious conformity. The well-ordered society that emerged in Massachusetts contrasted sharply with the diverse collection of peoples that came to form what are now New York and Pennsylvania.

Section 3 Assessment

1. TERMS & NAMES

Identify:
- John Winthrop
- Puritan
- Separatist
- Massachusetts Bay Colony
- Roger Williams
- Anne Hutchinson
- Pequot War
- Metacom
- King Philip's War

2. SUMMARIZING Identify the effects of each of the causes listed in the chart below.

Cause	Effect
Persecution of Puritans in England	
Puritan belief in hard work	
Roger Williams's dissenting beliefs	
Rapid colonial expansion in New England	
Defeat of King Philip	

3. DRAWING CONCLUSIONS
Why do you think Puritan leaders viewed Anne Hutchinson as a threat to their society? Use evidence from the text to support your answer.

THINK ABOUT
- Puritan beliefs
- characteristics of Puritan society
- Hutchinson's teachings

4. INTERPRETING Imagine you have been called upon to negotiate between the New England colonists and Native Americans. What would you tell each side about the other to help them overcome their misunderstandings?

THINK ABOUT
- the views of the colonists and Native Americans on land and religion
- the Pequot War and King Philip's War

The American Colonies Emerge **57**

ANSWERS

1. TERMS AND NAMES

John Winthrop, p. 52
Puritan, p. 52
Separatist, p. 53
Massachusetts Bay Colony, p. 53
Roger Williams, p. 55
Anne Hutchinson, p. 55
Pequot War, p. 56
Metacom, p. 57
King Philip's War, p. 57

2. SUMMARIZING

Entries may include the following:
(Cause: Persecution of Puritans in England.) Effect: Puritan migration to New England.
(Cause: Puritan belief in hard work.) Effect: Rapid growth and success of Massachusetts Bay.
(Cause: Williams's dissenting beliefs.) Effect: Founding of new colony based on his principles.
(Cause: Rapid colonial expansion in New England.) Effect: Conflict with Native Americans,

including Pequot War and King Philip's War.
(Cause: Defeat of King Philip.) Effect: End of Native American power in southeastern New England.

3. DRAWING CONCLUSIONS

Possible Responses: Puritans believed that their way of worship was the only way, that their leaders carried out the will of God, and that society needed to be tightly knit and maintain strict

control over behavior; Puritan leaders may have felt especially threatened by Hutchinson's views since she was a woman, and the church and society were male dominated.

4. INTERPRETING

Answers will vary but should reflect an understanding of the impact of colonial growth on Native Americans, the nature of disputes over land and religion, and the impact of the wars for both sides.

❹ Settlement of the Middle Colonies

LEARN ABOUT the settlement of New Netherland and Pennsylvania
TO UNDERSTAND how these settlements developed into thriving, diverse, and peaceful colonies.

OBJECTIVES

① To describe the pattern of life in New Netherland.

② To explain reasons for the social and religious diversity of Pennsylvania.

SKILLBUILDERS

• Understanding geography: region, p. 59
• Interpreting charts, p. 61

CRITICAL THINKING

• Summarizing, pp. 59, 61
• Comparing, p. 59
• Contrasting, p. 60
• Evaluating decisions, p. 61
• Drawing conclusions, p. 61

ONE AMERICAN'S STORY

William Penn had frustrated his father, Admiral Sir William Penn. After a rebellious youth, the younger Penn had gone on to study law and seemed to settle into the uncontroversial life of an English gentleman. However, in 1667, at age 22, he committed himself to the Society of Friends, or Quakers, a Protestant sect whose religious and social beliefs were radical for the time. The Quakers were persecuted extensively in England, and Penn himself was jailed several times for expressing his views. His father died in 1670, brokenhearted.

Ironically, his late father would play a key role in helping William Penn realize his dream—establishing a haven for Quakers in America. King Charles II had owed Penn's father money, which Penn asked to be repaid with American land. Charles agreed, and in 1681 he gave Penn a charter for Pennsylvania. Penn had big plans for his colony—a government run on Quaker principles of equality, cooperation, and religious toleration. However, he did not reveal the true nature of his plans before receiving the charter. As Penn confided to a friend,

> **A PERSONAL VOICE**
> For matters of liberty and privilege, I propose that which is extraordinary, and to leave myself and successors no power for doing mischief, that the will of one man may not hinder the good of a whole country; but to publish those things now and here, as matters stand, would not be wise. . . .
> **WILLIAM PENN,** quoted in *A New World*

This chalk drawing shows William Penn at about the age of 50.

While Penn only partially realized his "extraordinary" plans, the tolerant Quaker principles on which he established his colony attracted many settlers of different faiths. His respectful and peaceful relations with Native Americans also stood in sharp contrast to both the Virginia and Massachusetts colonies. As a thriving, multiethnic society, early Pennsylvania also followed the lead of its neighbors to the northeast, New York and New Jersey, whose course was set by their first colonists, the Dutch.

FOCUS & MOTIVATE

▶ *Starting with the Student*
• Ask students if they have known anyone who believed so strongly in something that he or she would defy family and society to pursue his or her beliefs.
• What risks does the person take and what are the possible benefits?

OBJECTIVE
① **INSTRUCT**

The Dutch Found New Netherland

▶ *Discussing Key Ideas*
• The Dutch establish New Netherland to expand their fur trade.
• New Netherland opens its doors to a wide variety of people.
• England takes over New Netherland to remove the "Dutch wedge" separating its colonies.

Dutch settlers in the New Netherlands trade pelts with Native Americans.

The Dutch Found New Netherland

While English Puritans were establishing colonies in New England, the Dutch were founding one to the south. As early as 1609, Henry Hudson—an Englishman employed by the Dutch—sailed up the river that now bears his name. The Dutch soon established a fur trade with the Iroquois and built trading posts on the Hudson River at Fort Orange (now Albany) and on Manhattan Island, at the mouth of the river.

In 1621, the Dutch government granted the newly formed Dutch West India Company permission to colonize **New Netherland** and expand the thriving fur trade. New Amsterdam (now New York City), founded in 1625, became the capital of the colony. By the 1630s, the Dutch had built a number of enormous estates along both sides of the Hudson River. In 1655, they extended their claims by taking over New Sweden, a tiny colony of Swedish and Finnish settlers that had established a rival fur trade along the Delaware River.

SECTION 4 RESOURCES

PRINT RESOURCES

IN-DEPTH RESOURCES: UNIT 1
Guided Reading, p. 23
Literature: from *World's End* by T. Coraghessan Boyle, p. 35

ACCESS FOR STUDENTS ACQUIRING ENGLISH
Guided Reading (Spanish), p. 22

FORMAL ASSESSMENT
Section Quiz, p. 21

ALTERNATIVE ASSESSMENT BOOK
See forms for supporting and scoring alternative activities.

TECHNOLOGY RESOURCES

GEOGRAPHY TRANSPARENCIES
G2, European Colonies Around 1600
G35, Original Thirteen Colonies

CD-ROM *Grolier Multimedia Encyclopedia*

VIDEO *American Portfolio: A Videodisc for U.S. History* user's guide, pp. 20–26

INTERNET McDougal Littell Learning On-Line
http://www.mcdougallittell.com

IN-DEPTH RESOURCES: UNIT 1
Guided Reading, p. 23

ACCESS FOR STUDENTS ACQUIRING ENGLISH
Guided Reading (Spanish), p. 22

GEOGRAPHY TRANSPARENCIES
G2, European Colonies Around 1600

A DIVERSE COLONY Although the Dutch company profited from its fur trade, it was slow to attract Dutch colonists. To encourage settlers to come and stay, the colony opened its doors to a variety of people. Gradually, more Dutch as well as Germans, French, Scandinavians, and other Europeans settled the area. The colony also included many Africans, free as well as enslaved. By the 1660s, in fact, one-fifth of New Netherland's population was of African ancestry. The colony's population was so ethnically diverse that one visitor called it a great "confusion of tongues." The Dutch reputation for religious tolerance also drew people of many faiths, including Protestants, Catholics, Muslims, and Jews.

These settlers generally enjoyed friendlier relations with the Native Americans than did the English colonists in New England and Virginia. The Dutch were less interested in conquering the Native Americans than in trading with them for furs. The first Dutch traders had the good sense not to anger the powerful and well-organized Iroquois, who controlled a large territory between Dutch traders to the south and French traders to the north. However, the Dutch did engage in fighting with various Native American groups over land claims and trade rivalries.

ENGLISH TAKEOVER To the English, New Netherland had become a "Dutch wedge" separating its northern and southern colonies. In 1664, King Charles II granted his brother James, the Duke of York (who later became James II), permission to drive out the Dutch. When the duke's fleet arrived in New Amsterdam's harbor, Peter Stuyvesant, the autocratic and unpopular Dutch governor, raised a call to arms, which the townspeople largely ignored. Severely outmanned, Stuyvesant surrendered to the English without firing a shot. The Duke of York, the new **proprietor,** or owner, of the colony, renamed it New York. The duke later gave a portion of this land to two of his friends, naming the territory New Jersey for the British island of Jersey.

The Quakers Settle Pennsylvania

The acquisition of New Netherland was but one step in England's quest to extend its American empire after 1660. That year the English monarchy was restored after a period of civil war and Puritan rule. The new king, Charles II, owed debts—both financial and political—to his prominent supporters, including a sum of 16,000 pounds to William Penn's father. As payment for this debt, Charles gave the younger Penn a large property that the king insisted be called Pennsylvania, or "Penn's Woods," after Penn's father. Following this, in 1682, Penn acquired more land from the Duke of York, the three counties that became Delaware.

PENN'S "HOLY EXPERIMENT" William Penn well knew that England in the late 1660s was no place for Quakers. The **Quakers** believed that God's "inner light" burned inside everyone. They held services without formal ministers, allowing any person to speak as the spirit moved him or her. They dressed plainly, refused to defer to persons of rank, and embraced pacifism by opposing war and refusing to serve in the military. For their radical views, they were scorned and harassed by Anglicans and Puritans alike.

THINK THROUGH HISTORY
A. Summarizing What were the important characteristics of New Netherland society?
A. Answer Ethnically diverse, religiously tolerant, generally good relations with Native Americans.

B. Possible Answer Both groups believed in direct, personal experience of God, rather than through rituals conducted by priests; however, Puritan churches had ministers, while Quakers did not.
THINK THROUGH HISTORY
B. Comparing How do these Quaker beliefs compare with Puritan beliefs?

Middle Colonies to 1700

(map)

New Netherland (ceded to England in 1664)

English colonies

Lake Huron, L. Ontario, Lake Erie, Hudson R., Susquehanna R., Delaware R., Appalachian Mountains

Ft. Orange (Albany)
NEW YORK
New Amsterdam (New York)
PENNSYLVANIA
NEW JERSEY
Philadelphia
Ft. Christina (Wilmington) DELAWARE

0   100 Miles
0   200 Kilometers

ATLANTIC OCEAN

GEOGRAPHY SKILLBUILDER
REGION What major river formed part of the border separating New Netherland from the English middle colonies?

Skillbuilder Answer The Delaware River.

ON THE WORLD STAGE

THE ENGLISH CIVIL WAR AND RESTORATION

From 1642 to 1649, England was torn apart by a great civil war between loyalists to the King and those who were loyal to Parliament, many of whom were Puritans. The armies of Parliament were victorious, and Charles I was executed in 1649. For a decade, England became a commonwealth, or republic, headed first by Oliver Cromwell, a Puritan, and then by his son Richard.

However, the English grew weary of the rather grim and sober Puritan rule, and in 1660 the monarchy was restored under Charles II. Following the Restoration, new colonies took shape, including New York and Pennsylvania. In 1663, Charles awarded a group of key supporters the land between Virginia and Spanish Florida, which became North and South Carolina. The addition of these colonies, as well as Maryland, which had been chartered in 1634, and Georgia, later chartered in 1732, brought the number of England's colonies to 13.

The American Colonies Emerge **59**

HISTORY FROM VISUALS
Middle Colonies to 1700
Reading the Map
Have students examine the map key. Ask, How does this key help you to understand why the English called New Netherland "the Dutch wedge"? *It is in the shape of a wedge between New England and other English colonies.*

OBJECTIVE
② **INSTRUCT**

The Quakers Settle Pennsylvania

▶ *Discussing Key Ideas*
• William Penn founds Pennsylvania on Quaker principles of tolerance.
• His respect of Native American land rights promotes peace.
• Penn recruits settlers from all over Europe.

ON THE WORLD STAGE
The English Civil War and Restoration
Read this explanation of the English Civil War by a Puritan.

"The question in dispute between the King's party and us was whether the King should govern as a god by will . . . ; or whether the people should be governed by laws made by themselves and live under a Government derived from their own consent."

Ask, What was the main issue in the war? *How the people should be governed.*

TEACHING OPTIONS

Exploring Themes

Cultural Diversity To attract settlers, the Dutch of New Netherland opened their colony to people of all backgrounds, including free Africans. William Penn followed the Dutch example in Pennsylvania. From these actions resulted colonies of extraordinary diversity and vitality.

Making Connections Across Cultures

Dutch Words The cultural exchanges that occurred among the peoples of colonial America can be illustrated by the number of Dutch words that have slipped into English usage. According to New York's New Netherland Project, a sampling includes: *cookie, snack, skating, duffel, knapsack, stove, dollar, caboodle, hodgepodge, pinkie, yacht, cruiser,* and more. Ask students to find other words from other cultures that have become part of American English.

MORE ABOUT . . .
Philadelphia

MORE ABOUT . . .
Philadelphia

William Penn worked with the surveyor Thomas Holme to systematically plan the layout of Philadelphia. It consisted of a 22-by-8 block grid. Penn set aside the central block for the "capital square" and four other blocks for public use. From 1683 to 1799, Philadelphia served as the capital of Pennsylvania. Its location along the Delaware River helped to turn it into a cosmopolitan city as diverse as New York. By 1730, about 10,000 people lived in Philadelphia, including a migrant from Boston named Benjamin Franklin.

GROLIER MULTIMEDIA ENCYCLOPEDIA
George Fox, Founder of the Society of Friends

MORE ABOUT . . .
The Delaware

The Delaware called themselves Lenape or Leni-Lenape, meaning "true men." Europeans renamed the Lenape of Pennsylvania the Delaware because they lived along the Delaware River and its tributaries. In reality, the Delaware formed part of a large group of peoples that extended into the colony of New Netherland.

The westward push of settlers forced the Delaware across the Appalachians and eventually across the Mississippi River.

By 1990, the Delaware numbered about 9,300, with most living on reservations or in towns in Oklahoma and in Ontario, Canada.

More than any other colonial founder, Penn wanted to establish a good and fair society in keeping with Quaker ideals. He saw his colony as a "holy experiment" in living, a place without a land-owning aristocracy. To achieve this goal, Penn guaranteed every adult male settler 50 acres of land and the right to vote. His plan for government called for a representative assembly and freedom of religion. As a lasting symbol of his Quaker beliefs, Penn also helped plan a capital he called the "City of Brotherly Love," or Philadelphia.

Penn's constitution also provided for a separate assembly for the three southern counties along the Delaware Bay. Delaware thereby gained a somewhat separate existence. However, it continued to have the same governor as Pennsylvania.

NATIVE AMERICAN RELATIONS Like most Quakers, Penn believed that people approached in friendship would respond in friendship—sooner or later. So even before setting foot in North America, Penn arranged to have a letter read to the Delaware, the tribe that inhabited his settlement area. Aware that the Delaware had already been ravaged by European diseases and war, Penn wrote,

A *19th-century painting* (*above*) portrays the signing of a peace treaty in 1682 between William Penn and the Delaware Indians—an event some historians believe never took place. A Quaker silver collar (*top*) offered to local Native Americans as a token of peace.

A PERSONAL VOICE
Now I would have you well observe, that I am very sensible of the unkindness and injustices that has been too much exercised towards you by the people of these parts of the world, who have sought . . . to make great advantages by you, . . . sometimes to the shedding of blood. . . . But I am not such a man. . . . I have great love and regard toward you, and I desire to win and gain your love and friendship by a kind, just, and peaceable life. . . .
WILLIAM PENN, quoted in *A New World*

Like Roger Williams before him, Penn believed that the land belonged to the Delaware and other Native Americans, and he saw to it that they were paid for it. To be sure that his colonists treated the Native peoples fairly, he regulated trade with them and provided for a court comprised of both colonists and Native Americans to settle any differences. The Native Americans respected Penn, and for more than 50 years the Pennsylvania colony had no major conflicts with Native Americans who lived in the colony.

A THRIVING COLONY Penn faced the same challenge as the Dutch West India Company. As proprietor, he needed to attract settlers—farmers, builders, and traders—to create a profitable colony. After opening the colony to Quakers, he vigorously recruited immigrants from around western Europe. Glowing advertisements for the colony were printed in German, Dutch, and French. In time, settlers came in numbers, including thousands of Germans who brought with them craft skills and farming techniques that helped the colony to thrive.

Penn himself spent only about four years in Pennsylvania. And despite the colony's success, he never profited financially as proprietor and died in poverty in 1718. Meanwhile, his idealistic vision had faded but not failed. His own Quakers were a minority in a colony thickly populated by people from all over western Europe. Slavery was introduced, and, in fact, many prominent Quakers in Pennsylvania owned slaves. However, the principles of equality, cooperation, and religious tolerance on which he founded his vision would eventually become fundamental values of the new American nation.

C. Possible Answer Penn desired to gain respect and friendship and paid Native Americans for land; Puritans generally viewed Native Americans as heathens controlled by the forces of evil and eventually set out to remove or destroy them.

THINK THROUGH HISTORY
C. Contrasting How did Penn's actions toward the Native Americans differ from those of the Puritans?

Cooperative Activity: Mapping Colonial Economic Activities

Task: Students will create a pictorial map showing the economic activities of the 13 English colonies.

Purpose: To illustrate the economic diversity of the colonies.

Activity: Request volunteers to draw a wall-size outline map of the 13 colonies. Tell them to show only the political boundaries on the map. (They might use an opaque projector to copy the map on page 61 onto poster paper.) Then assign groups of students one or more of the colonies, and have

them think of various symbols to show the ways in which people earned a living in these colonies at this time. For extra credit, have students devise symbols that illustrate the main economic activities in French and Spanish possessions.

Note: If you have any students with a strong interest in cartography, refer them to *Pictorial Maps,* by Nigel Holmes (NY: Watson-Guptill Publications, 1991) as a reference.

ALTERNATIVE ASSESSMENT BOOK
Standards for Evaluating a Cooperative Learning Activity

The Thirteen Colonies to the Mid-1700s

Legend:
- British possessions
- New England Colonies
- Middle Colonies
- Southern Colonies
- French possessions
- Spanish possessions

Colony	Founded	Economic activities
Massachusetts	Plymouth 1620 Mass. Bay 1630	shipbuilding, shipping, fishing, lumber, rum, meat products
New Hampshire	1623	ship masts, lumber, fishing, trade
Connecticut	1636	shipping, livestock, foodstuffs
Rhode Island	1636	rum, iron foundries, shipbuilding, snuff, livestock
New York	1625	furs, wheat, glass, shoes, livestock, shipping, shipbuilding, rum, beer, snuff

Colony	Founded	Economic activities
Delaware	1638	trade, foodstuffs
New Jersey	1664	trade, foodstuffs, copper
Pennsylvania	1681	flour, foodstuffs, paper, iron, wheat, flax, shipbuilding

Colony	Founded	Economic activities
Virginia	1607	tobacco, wheat, cattle, iron
Maryland	1632	tobacco, wheat, snuff
North Carolina	1663	naval supplies, tobacco, furs
South Carolina	1663	rice, indigo, silk
Georgia	1732	indigo, rice, naval supplies, lumber

SKILLBUILDER INTERPRETING CHARTS
How did the New England and Middle colonies' economies differ in general from the South's economy? What may have accounted for this difference?

Skillbuilder Answer Activities The New England and middle colonies' main economic activities were shipbuilding and trade, while the South's economy was based largely on agriculture. Differences: One reason for the differences may have been the climate. The South's warm, stable climate was more conducive to agriculture.

Section 4 Assessment

1. TERMS & NAMES

Identify:
- William Penn
- New Netherland
- proprietor
- Quaker

2. SUMMARIZING Compare the colonies of New Netherland and Pennsylvania using a Venn diagram such as the one below.

New Netherland only

Both

Pennsylvania only

Write a paragraph comparing and contrasting the two colonies.

3. EVALUATING DECISIONS Both New Netherland and Pennsylvania encouraged settlers to come from all over western Europe. Do you think this was a good decision for these colonies? Why or why not?

THINK ABOUT
- the reasons each colony was founded
- the need for each colony to attract settlers
- growth and changes in the two colonies

4. DRAWING CONCLUSIONS How did Penn succeed in achieving his goals for Pennsylvania and how did he fail? Explain.

THINK ABOUT
- Penn's "holy experiment"
- Penn's actions towards Native Americans
- changes in Pennsylvania after its founding

ANSWERS

1. TERMS AND NAMES
William Penn, p. 58
New Netherland, p. 58
proprietor, p. 59
Quaker, p. 59

2. SUMMARIZING
Possible Responses: New Netherland only: founded by the Dutch; built on fur trade.
Both: attracted colonists from many ethnic groups; practiced religious toleration; became a proprietary colony; established good relations with Native Americans.
Pennsylvania only: shaped by Quaker ideals; avoided a land-owning aristocracy.

3. EVALUATING DECISIONS
Possible Responses: Yes—both colonies grew and prospered, and they both practiced religious toleration; *No*—Dutch unable to hold New Netherland, and Quakers—on whose principles the "holy experiment" was founded—soon became a minority.

4. DRAWING CONCLUSIONS
Possible Responses:
Pennsylvania established freedom of religion and a representative assembly, practiced religious tolerance, maintained peace for 50 years, and thrived; but Quakers became a minority, slavery was introduced, and Penn did not profit financially.

HISTORY FROM VISUALS
The Thirteen Colonies in the Mid-1700s
Reading the Map
Tell students that this map provides many different types of information. Have them identify some of these categories: *physical topography east of the Mississippi, political boundaries of the colonies, economic activities of the colonies, European holdings west of the Mississippi River, etc.*

 GEOGRAPHY TRANSPARENCIES
G35, Original Thirteen Colonies

ASSESS & RETEACH

Section 4 Assessment
If students were writing questions for the Section Assessment, which would they include? How do their choices compare with those of the editors?

Self-Assessment
Have students create a before-and-after chart showing what they knew about the early histories of New York and Pennsylvania prior to reading Section 4 and what they learned as a result of their reading.

Section Quiz

FORMAL ASSESSMENT BOOK
Section Quiz, p. 21

Reteach
Use the map on the last page of this section to help review the main ideas of the section.

CLOSE

By the late 1600s, three distinct regions had emerged in British North America. Yet despite their diversity, the 13 colonies shared certain basic beliefs, such as the belief in self-government, that would hold them together as a people and a nation.

TERMS & NAMES
1. conquistador, p. 38
2. mestizo, p. 40
3. Popé, p. 43
4. John Smith, p. 44
5. indentured servant, p. 46
6. John Winthrop, p. 52
7. Anne Hutchinson, p. 55
8. Metacom, p. 57
9. proprietor, p. 59
10. Quaker, p. 59

MAIN IDEAS
Answers will vary.

11. High rate of intermarriage created large mestizo population; some Native Americans became Roman Catholics.

12. They often fought back, notably against Cortés and in Popé's Rebellion.

13. He developed a high-quality strain of tobacco that became the key to Virginia's economic development.

14. Colonists desired more land for their growing population and for raising crops.

15. Frontier settlers were angry at the powerful planters for their refusal to order attacks on Native Americans.

16. They left England because of religious persecution, only church members had political power, great concern for public morality, and people viewed their society as a "City upon a Hill."

17. Both argued for greater individual religious freedom. Williams escaped before being arrested, while Hutchinson was put on trial and cast out of Massachusetts Bay.

18. Settlers demanded more land; the two groups had differing ideas about the land and religion.

19. The Dutch welcomed settlers from many countries, including people of many religious faiths.

20. Every adult male received land and the right to vote, there was a representative assembly and freedom of religion, the capital was called the "City of Brotherly Love," and Native Americans were treated fairly.

62   Chapter 2

Chapter 2 Assessment

REVIEWING THE CHAPTER

TERMS & NAMES For each term below, write a sentence explaining its connection to the emergence of the American colonies. For each person below, explain his or her role in these colonies.

1. conquistador
2. mestizo
3. Popé
4. John Smith
5. indentured servant
6. John Winthrop
7. Anne Hutchinson
8. Metacom
9. proprietor
10. Quaker

MAIN IDEAS

SECTION 1 *(pages 38–43)*

Spain's Empire in the Americas
11. How did Mexican culture develop out of both Spanish and Native American elements?
12. How did Native Americans react to Spanish efforts to establish colonies?

SECTION 2 *(pages 44–49)*

An English Settlement at Jamestown
13. Explain how John Rolfe transformed the Virginia colony.
14. What conditions caused tension and warfare between settlers and Native Americans in Virginia?
15. What caused Bacon's Rebellion?

SECTION 3 *(pages 52–57)*

Puritan New England
16. Describe the role of religion in the lives of Puritans living in the Massachusetts Bay Colony.
17. How were the experiences of Roger Williams and Anne Hutchinson similar and different?
18. What caused conflicts between New England colonists and Native Americans?

SECTION 4 *(pages 58–61)*

Settlement of the Middle Colonies
19. Why did New Netherland develop a reputation for diversity?
20. How did Pennsylvania reflect William Penn's Quaker ideals?

THINKING CRITICALLY

1. **COLONISTS AND NATIVE AMERICANS** Using a chart like the one below, summarize the way settlers and Native Americans interacted in each of the following regions.

Region	Interaction
New Mexico	→
Virginia	→
New England	→
Pennsylvania	→

2. **GLOBAL INTERACTIONS** John Winthrop dreamed that New England would be "as a City upon a Hill" in which "the eyes of all people are on us." Do you think the United States is a place that people around the world look up to? Should it be? Explain your answer.

3. **A NEW WORLD** Reread the quote on page 36 by Amerigo Vespucci, who explored the coast of South America in 1501. What impressed him about this land? Why do you think he called it "the New World"?

4. **GEOGRAPHY OF JAMESTOWN** Historian Samuel Eliot Morrison has written that the Jamestown colonists made the "usual mistake of first-comers in America by settling on a low, swampy island." What qualities of such a location might have enticed the colonists to settle there?

5. **ANALYZING PRIMARY SOURCES** In 1630, the Puritan minister John Cotton delivered a sermon to John Winthrop and his followers as they embarked on their voyage to America. In it, Cotton tried to reassure the future colonists that they could legitimately claim a new land. He compared the Puritans' mission to that of God's "chosen people"—the Hebrew people whom, according to the Bible, God had led to Israel "that they may dwell in a place of their own."

> God makes room for a people . . . when He makes a country, though not altogether void of inhabitants, yet void in that place where they reside. Where there is a vacant place, there is liberty for Christians to come and inhabit, though they neither buy it nor ask their leaves. . . . So that it is free from that common grant for any to take possession of vacant countries. Indeed, no nation is to drive out another without special commission from Heaven, such as the Israelites had, unless the natives do unjustly wrong them, and will not recompense the wrongs done in a peaceable [way]. And then they may right themselves by lawful war and subdue the country unto themselves.
>
> **JOHN COTTON,** *The Divine Right to Occupy the Land*

How does Cotton justify the right of Puritans to settle in America? Would a Native American have shared Cotton's view that the Puritans are free to settle in a "vacant place"? How might the ideas in the passage have been used to justify the actions of the Puritans toward Native Americans?

THINKING CRITICALLY

1. COLONISTS AND NATIVE AMERICANS
Students may include the following entries:
Region: New Mexico
Interaction: settlers tried to impose Catholic faith and Spanish culture on Native Americans but met strong resistance
Region: Virginia
Interaction: settlers conquered Native Americans and seized their land
Region: New England

Interaction: some settlers tried to convert Native Americans to Christianity, but many wanted to remove or destroy native societies; Native Americans helped colonists early on but later mounted organized resistance
Region: Pennsylvania
Interaction: Quakers respected Native American rights and negotiated treaties for land

2. GLOBAL INTERACTIONS
Students may argue that people in other lands admire the wealth, stable government, and civil liberties in the United States. Others may point out that foreigners do not look up to the poverty, violence, and racism they see in the United States.

ALTERNATIVE ASSESSMENT

1. ROLE-PLAYING A TRIAL How did lawyers defend their clients against some of the colonists' very strict laws?

Using legal documents from colonial days, find out the legal punishments for infractions of certain laws in specific colonies, such as boys running away in Massachusetts. Role-play a trial for your class.

 CD-ROM Use the CD-ROM *Electronic Library of Primary Sources* and other reference materials to research a specific law and punishment in 17th-century America.

- **Cooperative Learning** With a group of students, plan to act out a trial. Each student should play a different part, including judge, defendant, prosecuting attorney, defending lawyer, and witnesses. Ahead of time, each person should know the law and plan his or her arguments carefully.

- Act out the trial in front of the rest of the class, who will act as the jury. Let the jury decide the verdict and the punishment as if they were colonists. Then, have a class discussion about the value of the law and its punishment.

2. PRESENTING A TV TALK SHOW Create an imaginary television talk show about this topic: What makes a colony successful? Guests should include early colonists in North America such as Hernando Cortés, John Smith, Anne Hutchinson, William Penn, or other people mentioned in this chapter. Prepare a script detailing the questions that the host will ask and possible responses for each guest.

3. PORTFOLIO PROJECT

 Use the Living History activity to expand your portfolio.

LIVING HISTORY

REVISING YOUR COLONIZATION TALE
You have written your present-day colonization tale. Now think about how you might revise it.

- Consider the experiences of actual colonists and natives. What details from these could you adapt to enrich your tale?
- Ask a friend to read the tale and comment on content and organization. Make changes as appropriate.

After you have revised your tale, add a title page and cover. Then share your tale with the class or combine it with others to create a classroom anthology of colonization tales. Add your work to your American history portfolio.

Review Chapter 2

THE SPANISH IN NORTH AMERICA Within a century of Columbus's first trip across the Atlantic, gold and silver from the Americas made Spain the richest country in the world. The Spanish conquered the native peoples and forced labor from them, but they also frequently intermarried with the natives. The Spanish also attempted to impose Spanish culture and the Catholic religion on native peoples, but many natives resisted.

JAMESTOWN AND VIRGINIA Like the Spanish, the English saw opportunity for great wealth in North America. However, the first permanent English settlement in North America, Jamestown, began with disaster. After disease, famine, and conflicts with Native Americans almost caused the colony to fail, a tobacco economy saved it. Continuing tensions between colonists and Native Americans and between rich and poor colonists erupted in Bacon's Rebellion (1676).

MASSACHUSETTS AND NEW ENGLAND In Massachusetts, religious motives spurred the Puritans to flee England for North America. The government and Puritan church attempted to maintain tight control over behavior in the community. Puritan leaders banished Roger Williams and Anne Hutchinson, both of whom challenged Puritan authority and teachings. The spread of colonial settlements led to clashes with Native Americans, whom the colonists defeated in the Pequot War (1637) and King Philip's War (1675).

THE MIDDLE COLONIES Compared to colonists in New England and Virginia, those in New Netherland (later New York and New Jersey) and Pennsylvania had friendly relations with Native Americans. In addition, these two colonies attracted diverse populations of people from various parts of Europe and of various religious faiths.

Preview Chapter 3

As England's American colonies developed, so did tension between the colonies and England over trade and politics. And as the colonies grew, regional differences increased. The Southern colonies relied upon plantation agriculture and, increasingly, slavery. The Northern and middle colonies developed industry, small farms, and trade. The colonies united with Great Britain to drive the French out of North America. You will learn about these significant developments in the next chapter.

The American Colonies Emerge **63**

1. ROLE-PLAYING A TRIAL
Standards for Evaluation
An effective trial should meet the following criteria:

- Demonstrates knowledge of the law and crime that is being prosecuted.
- Follows proper courtroom procedure.
- Presents thoughtful, logical arguments.
- Shows an understanding of the colonial period and its laws and customs.

2. PRESENTING A TV TALK SHOW
Standards for Evaluation
A script should meet the following criteria:

- Introduces a wide range of historical characters.
- Presents an interesting and stimulating range of questions and answers.
- Is organized in a thoughtful manner.
- Is carefully researched and engagingly written.

3. PORTFOLIO
LIVING HISTORY
Standards for Evaluation
A tale should meet the following criteria:

- Focuses on an interesting aspect of the past or the present.
- Includes a variety of detail that enriches the story.
- Has a plot that shows what it's like to be a colonist.
- Gives a clear sense of time and place.
- Is thoughtfully organized with a beginning, middle, and end.

IN-DEPTH RESOURCES: UNIT 1
See the form for scoring this activity on page 39.

THINKING CRITICALLY

3. A NEW WORLD
He was impressed by the number and variety of animal life. New World: *Possible Response:* Because it was new to Europeans; because it was a continent unto itself and not part of Asia.

4. GEOGRAPHY OF JAMESTOWN
Possible Response: Location seemed to meet some of criteria set forth by founders —*e.g.,* on a major river, upstream where river narrowed, defensible; low open area

might have appealed because it would have been easier to reach, build on, haul supplies to, clear, and so forth, than a higher wooded area.

5. ANALYZING PRIMARY SOURCES
Possible Response: Cotton argues that by "making room" in a sparsely populated land, God indicates approval of establishing a new community, and that Christians have a right to take possession of land on which no people actually live; a Native

American might disagree with the idea that America is "vacant" and therefore open for others to "take possession of," though he or she might not necessarily disagree with the idea that outsiders could settle in and share the land; the passage may have helped justify the colonists' attempts to remove or destroy native societies.

PLANNING GUIDE
The Colonies Come of Age

		TEACHING SUPPORT	ASSESSMENT	
SECTION 1 **England and Its Colonies** *pp. 66–70*	**Key Ideas** *England and its North American colonies prosper under a beneficial trade relationship, but tensions emerge as the colonies push for more political and economic freedom.*	*In-Depth Resources: Unit 1* • Guided Reading, p. 40 **COOPERATIVE ACTIVITIES** • Timelines of America's English Rulers, p. 69 (TE)	*Section 1 Assessment*, p. 70 (PE) *Self-Assessment*, p. 70 (TE) *Formal Assessment* • Section Quiz, p. 30 *Alternative Assessment Book* • Standards for Evaluating a Cooperative Activity	
SECTION 2 **The Agricultural South** *pp. 71–76*	*The Southern colonies develop a labor-intensive plantation economy, which leads to a mostly rural society and the growth of slavery.*	*In-Depth Resources: Unit 1* • Guided Reading, p. 41 • Skillbuilder Practice: Visual Sources, p. 44 • Geography Application: The Triangular Trade, p. 45 • Primary Source: from *History of the Dividing Line*, p. 47 • American Lives: Olaudah Equiano, p. 54 **COOPERATIVE ACTIVITY** • Words from African Languages, p. 75 (TE)	*Section 2 Assessment*, p. 76 (PE) *Self-Assessment*, p. 76 (TE) *Formal Assessment* • Section Quiz, p. 31 *Alternative Assessment Book* • Standards for Evaluating a Cooperative Activity	
SECTION 3 **The Commercial North** *pp. 77–82*	*The Northern colonies develop an economy fueled by commerce and trade, which leads to a diverse and urban society. There, important religious and intellectual changes occur that affect all the colonies.*	*In-Depth Resources: Unit 1* • Guided Reading, p. 42 • Primary Sources: from Salem Witch Trials, p. 48; from *Autobiography of Ben Franklin*, p. 49; from *New England Primer*, p. 50 • American Lives: J. Edwards, p. 55 • Literature: from *The Crucible* by Arthur Miller, p. 51 **COOPERATIVE ACTIVITIES** • Debating Theories About Salem, p. 80 (TE)	*Section 3 Assessment*, p. 82 (PE) *Self-Assessment*, p. 82 (TE) *Formal Assessment* • Section Quiz, p. 32 *Alternative Assessment Book* • Standards for Evaluating a Cooperative Activity	
SECTION 4 **The French and Indian War** *pp. 83–87*	*The British and their colonists defeat the French in North America, enlarging Great Britain's New World empire and causing new British-colonial friction.*	*In-Depth Resources: Unit 1* • Guided Reading, p. 43 **COOPERATIVE ACTIVITY** • Annotated Maps, p. 85 (TE)	*Section 4 Assessment*, p. 87 (PE) *Self-Assessment*, p. 87 (TE) *Formal Assessment* • Section Quiz, p. 33 *Alternative Assessment Book* • Standards for Evaluating a Cooperative Activity	
CHAPTER RESOURCES	**Chapter Overview** *As British colonies in North America grow, their economies and societies develop sectional differences. After the British push the French out of the region, relations between the colonists and the British become more tense.*	*In-Depth Resources: Unit 1* • Living History Project: Worksheet, p. 56; Standards, p. 57 *Telescoping the Times* • Chapter Summary, pp. 5–6 *Planning for Block Schedules*	*Chapter Assessment*, pp. 90–91 (PE) *Alternative Assessment*, p. 91 (PE) *Formal Assessment* • Chapter Test, forms A and B, pp. 34–39 Test Generator *Alternative Assessment Book* See explanation and forms for different kinds of alternative assessments including portfolio assessment.	

Electronic Library of Primary Sources
• *from "A Short Discourse on the Present State of the Colonies" by William Keith*

INTERNET RESOURCES
• See *McDougal Littell Learning On-Line* for links to information about the colonies and the Glorious Revolution.

 Critical Thinking Transparencies
• CT37, Africans in the Colonies

 Electronic Library of Primary Sources
• *from The Interesting Narrative of the Life of Olaudah Equiano*

INTERNET RESOURCES
• See *McDougal Littell Learning On-Line* for links to information about the middle passage and the slave trade.

 Humanities Transparencies
• H4, A Woman's Work

Geography Transparencies
• G3, Colonial Economies: product map

 Grolier Multimedia Encyclopedia
• Salem Witch trials

Electronic Library of Primary Sources
• *from Sinners in the Hands of an Angry God* by Jonathan Edwards

INTERNET RESOURCES
• See *McDougal Littell Learning On-Line* for links to information about the Salem witch trials.

Critical Thinking Transparencies
• CT3, French and Indian War

INTERNET RESOURCES
• See Interact with History p. 89 (PE) for an activity that includes the Internet as an enrichment option.

 American Portfolio: A Videodisc for U.S. History, user's guide, pp. 23–28, 32

INTERNET RESOURCES
Learning On-Line: Social Studies
http://www.mcdougallittell.com

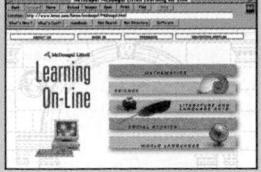

Block Scheduling (90 MINUTES)

Day 1
Section 1, pp. 66–70
Section 2, pp. 71–76
Section Assessments, pp. 70, 76

Day 2
Section 3, pp. 77–82
Section 4, pp. 83–87

Day 3
Review Sections 1–4
Daily Life: Colonial Courtship, pp. 88–89
Chapter Assessment, pp. 90–91

YEARLY PACING *Chapter 3 Total:* 3 days *Yearly Total:* 85 days

See *Planning for Block Schedules* for special activities and pacing strategies.

Customizing for Special Populations

Students Acquiring English

Access for Students Acquiring English
• Guided Reading for Sections 1–4 (Spanish), pp. 30–33
• Chapter Summary (Spanish), pp. 28–29
• Skillbuilder Practice: Visual Sources (Spanish), p. 34
• Geography Application: The Triangular Trade, p. 35

INTERNET RESOURCES
• See *McDougal Littell Learning On-Line* The Diverse Classroom.

Less Proficient Readers

In-Depth Resources: Unit 1
• Guided Reading for Sections 1–4, pp. 40–43
• Skillbuilder: Visual Sources, p. 44
• Geography Application: The Triangular Trade, p. 45

Telescoping the Times
• Chapter Summary, pp. 5–6

See additional strategies at point of use in the Teacher's Edition.

Gifted and Talented Students

In-Depth Resources: Unit 1
• Primary Sources: from *History of the Dividing Line* by William Byrd, p. 47; The Salem Witch Trials, p. 48; from *The Autobiography* by Benjamin Franklin, p. 49; from *The New England Primer*, p. 50
• American Lives: Olauda Equiano, p. 54; Jonathan Edwards, p. 55

See additional strategies at point of use in the Teacher's Edition.

Connections to Literature READINGS FOR STUDENTS

In-Depth Resources: Unit 1
• from *The Crucible* by Arthur Miller, p. 51

Enrichment Reading
• Charles Johnson.
Middle Passage.
New York: Antheneum, 1990.
A slave ship voyages from New Orleans to Africa and back in 1830.

• Jessamyn West.
Massacre at Fall Creek.
New York: Harcourt, 1975.
In the early 1800s, five men are charged with murdering several Native Americans. This novel follows their trials.

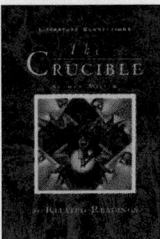

• Arthur Miller, *The Crucible* (with related readings) In this play, a witch hunt in Puritan New England has overtones of McCarthyism.

McDougal Littell *Language of Literature* American Literature
• from *The Interesting Life of Olaudah Equiano*, p. 101
• Anne Bradstreet, "To My Dear and Loving Husband" and "Upon the Burning of Our House, July 10, 1666," p. 149
• Salem Court, The Examination of Sarah Good, p. 154
• Jonathan Edwards, *from* "Sinners in the Hands of an Angry God," p. 160
• Stephen Vincent Benét, "We Aren't Superstitious," p. 168

The Colonies Come of Age

▶ **Starting with the Student**
Ask students what they know about colonial America.

- What sorts of people lived in the 13 colonies?
- What was their attitude toward England?
- How was life different in the South and the North?

PREVIEWING THE CHAPTER

- Have students examine the time line and illustrations.
- Ask students to skim the chapter, focusing on art, headings, and objectives.
- Take students' suggestions of subjects they expect the chapter to cover.

MORE ABOUT . . .
Michel Guillaume Jean de Crèvecoeur

Born in France in 1735, Crèvecoeur moved to Canada to fight in the French and Indian War. Later he became a farmer in New York, where he married and had a family. With the outbreak of the Revolution, Crèvecoeur, whose wife was from a Loyalist family, found himself in a political position in which he was persecuted by both sides. He captured this experience and many others describing daily life in America in his very popular *Letters from an American Farmer*.

CHAPTER
3

The Colonies Come of Age

SECTION 1
England and Its Colonies

England and its North American colonies prosper under a beneficial trade relationship, but tensions emerge as the colonies push for more political and economic freedom.

SECTION 2
The Agricultural South

The Southern colonies develop a labor-intensive plantation economy, which leads to a mostly rural society and the growth of slavery.

SECTION 3
The Commercial North

The Northern colonies develop an economy fueled by commerce and trade, which leads to a diverse and urban society. There, important religious and intellectual changes occur that affect all the colonies.

SECTION 4
The French and Indian War

The British and their colonists defeat the French in North America, enlarging Great Britain's New World empire and causing new British-colonial friction.

"Here individuals of all nations are melted into a new race . . . whose labors and posterity will one day cause great change in the world."

Michel Guillaume Jean de Crèvecoeur

James II creates the Dominion of New England.

Scots-Irish and German immigrants begin to arrive.

The College of William and Mary is chartered in Williamsburg, Virginia.

● English Parliament passes Navigation Acts.

● First Indian reservations created in Virginia.

French explorer LaSalle claims Louisiana for France.

THE UNITED STATES								
THE WORLD	**1651**	1653		1682	1686	1689	1693	**1700**
		1652		1683	1687 1688			

● Dutch settlers establish Cape Town in South Africa.

Manchus of China conquer island of Formosa (Taiwan).

● Isaac Newton publishes his theories of motion and gravitation.

● William and Mary take power in Britain's Glorious Revolution.

THEMES IN CHAPTER 3

Economic Opportunity	*Science and Technology*	*Cultural Diversity*	*Women in America*
Despite advances, the principles of mercantilism inhibited colonial growth and prosperity. Under these principles, a colony existed solely to benefit the parent country by supplying raw materials and buying goods.	The Enlightenment spread from Europe to the Americas, bringing with it an optimistic belief in reason and science that prompted many discoveries and inventions. In general, the Enlightenment brought an openness to new ideas.	An influx of European immigrants, especially in the North, and of African slaves, especially in the South, made the thirteen colonies a cultural mosaic.	Females in colonial America had few rights of their own. In some cases, religion as well as law served to keep women under their husbands' rule. Among the Quakers, however, a belief in the divine spirit of all led to more equality for females.
See Teacher's Edition note, p. 67.	See Teacher's Edition note, p. 81.	Most of French settlers in Acadia were driven out by the English and came to settle in Louisiana.	See Teacher's Edition note, p. 72.
		See Teacher's Edition note, p. 78.	

RESEARCHING A REGION

This chapter describes changing ways of life in the colonies and regional differences between the Northern and Southern colonies. Regional differences still exist in the United States today. Choose a region of the United States that you find interesting. Research aspects of politics, economics, or culture that developed in or are unique to that place.

📁 **PORTFOLIO PROJECT** As you gather research, keep it in a folder for your American history portfolio. At the end of the chapter, you will present your research in a visual display.

- **Olaudah Equiano arrives as slave in West Indies.**
- **Number of Africans in North America exceeds 230,000.**

- **British triumph in Battle of Quebec marks turning point in French and Indian War.**
- **Treaty of Paris ends French and Indian War.**

- **Benjamin Franklin publishes** *Poor Richard's Almanack.*
- **Zenger trial establishes freedom of the press.**
- **South Carolina slaves rise up in Stono Rebellion.**
- **Great Awakening begins.**
- **French and Indian War begins.**
- **Parliament passes Sugar Act.**

| 1732 | 1734 | 1739 | **1740** | | 1754 | 1756 | 1759 | 1763 | 1764 | **1765** |

| 1707 | 1717 | | 1739 | | | | | 1763 | |

- **The Act of Union unites England and Wales with Scotland to form Great Britain.**
- **Spain creates Viceroyalty of New Granada in the northern part of South America.**
- **In Japan, 84,000 farmers protest heavy taxation.**
- **Treaty of Paris recognizes British control over much of India.**
- **British captain James Cook reaches Australia.**

The Colonies Come of Age **65**

ALTERNATIVE ASSESSMENT
LIVING HISTORY

RESEARCH A REGION
Discuss ways of gathering research for the display:

- Discuss how to break the larger topics of students' research into smaller topics to investigate.
- Suggest that students write to the chamber of commerce and the department of travel and tourism of cities and states in the region that they are investigating, requesting recent information and brochures.
- Suggest ways to present research visually, including photographs, color copies, sketches, maps, charts, graphs, and other ways that come to mind.

Project Planning Guide

Step 1	Students choose a region in the United States.
Step 2	Students research topics, keeping separate files for each.
Step 3	Students include a variety of visual details,
Step 4	Students compile their research and arrange their presentation.

IN-DEPTH RESOURCES: UNIT 1
See worksheet and standards for evaluating, pp. 56, 57.

RECOMMENDED RESOURCES

Books for the Teacher

Hofstadter, Richard. *America at 1750.* New York: Vintage, 1973. Colonial society.

Jensen, Joan M. *Loosening the Bonds.* New Haven: Yale, 1986. Lives of farm women in the Middle Colonies.

Miller, Perry. *Errand into the Wilderness.* Cambridge, Mass.: Harvard, 1964. Essays on colonial America.

Books for the Student

Foner, Eric, ed. *Nat Turner.* Englewood Cliffs, NJ: Prentice-Hall, 1971. Turner in his own and contemporaries' words.

Hawke, David Freeman. *Everyday Life in Early America.* New York: Harper, 1988. Everything from how settlers cleared land to race relations.

Videos

Colonial Economy. CRM Films, 800-421-0833. Analyzes colonial economy.

Los colonos ingleses. Films for the Humanities & Sciences, 800-257-3767. English colonies–narrated in Spanish.

Northwest Passage. Dir. King Vidor. MGM/UA, 1940. Hollywood tale set in French and Indian War.

Benjamin Franklin: Citizen-Sage of a New Age. American Lifestyle Series. Laserdisc. AIMS Media, 1980.

Software

Fortress of Louisbourg. CD-ROM. Available from Educational Software Institute, 800-955-5570.

TERMS & NAMES
- mercantilism
- balance of trade
- Parliament
- Navigation Acts
- Dominion of New England
- Sir Edmund Andros
- Glorious Revolution
- salutary neglect

❶ England and Its Colonies

LEARN ABOUT mercantilism, the Navigation Acts, and the Glorious Revolution
TO UNDERSTAND the changing economic and political relationships between England and its North American colonies.

OBJECTIVES

① To explain the economic relationship between England and its American colonies.

② To describe how tensions arose between England and the colonies.

③ To summarize how salutary neglect of the colonies after 1688 planted the seeds of self-government.

SKILLBUILDER
- Interpreting Charts, p. 70

CRITICAL THINKING
- Clarifying, p. 66
- Recognizing effects, p. 67
- Analyzing causes, p. 68
- Synthesizing, p. 70
- Summarizing, p. 70
- Interpreting, p. 70
- Forming an opinion, p. 70

FOCUS & MOTIVATE

▶ *Starting with the Student*
- What financial responsibilities do parents and children have for each other?
- Could a similar relationship exist between a parent nation and its colonies? Should it? Explain your answers.

OBJECTIVE

① INSTRUCT

England and Its Colonies Prosper

▶ *Starting with the Student*
- Have students recall things that they have traded over the years.
- In each case, how did the trade benefit both sides? Did one person benefit more than the other? Why or why not?

▶ *Discussing Key Ideas*
- In the economic system of mercantilism, a nation's wealth comes in part from selling more goods than it buys.

(continued on the next page)

ONE AMERICAN'S STORY

In 1739, 17-year-old Eliza Lucas's father left their home in South Carolina to help Great Britain fight the Spanish in the West Indies. With him gone and her mother ill, Eliza became the manager of the family's three rice plantations. Though she wrote to a friend that the work "requires more business and fatigue of other sorts than you can imagine," she ran the plantations well. Among her successes were experiments growing indigo, a plant whose leaves produced a deep blue dye that was highly prized for clothing in Europe. Eliza hoped that her South Carolina-grown indigo would add not only to her family's fortune but to that of the British empire.

> **A PERSONAL VOICE**
> We please ourselves with the prospect of exporting in a few years a good quantity from hence, and supplying our mother country [Great Britain] with a manufacture for which she has so great a demand, and which she is now supplied with from the French colonies, and many thousand pounds per annum [year] thereby lost to the nation, when she might as well be supplied here, if the matter were applied to in earnest.
> **ELIZA LUCAS PINCKNEY**, quoted in *South Carolina: A Documentary Profile of the Palmetto State*

As English settlers like the Lucases forged new societies in North America, they were ever mindful of the home country across the Atlantic. From Massachusetts to Georgia, the new colonies existed primarily for the benefit of England. The colonies exported to England a rich variety of raw materials, such as lumber and furs, and in return they imported the manufactured goods that England produced. This economic relationship benefited both England and its colonies, and their economies flourished. By the middle of the 1600s, however, this relationship was showing signs of strain as the colonists began to push for more economic and political freedom.

Indigo was plentiful in colonial times. Today it grows in only a few places in the United States.

England and Its Colonies Prosper

Eliza Lucas was one of many colonists who benefited from the system of trade between the colonies and the home country. In truth, though, the purpose of the system was mainly to enrich the English empire. Beginning in the 16th century, the nations of Europe competed for wealth and power through a new economic system called **mercantilism,** in which colonies played a critical role.

MERCANTILISM According to the theory of mercantilism, a nation could increase its wealth and power in two ways: by obtaining as much gold and silver as possible, and by establishing a favorable **balance of trade,** in which it sold more goods than it bought. A nation's ultimate goal under mercantilism was to become self-sufficient so that it did not have to depend on other countries for goods.

The key to this process was the establishment of colonies. Under mercantilism, colonies provided products, especially raw materials, that could not be found in the home country. For example, England, with its scarcity of forests, could now go to the thick woods of New England instead of purchasing from Scandinavia the towering pine trees needed to build its naval vessels. In addition to playing the role of supplier, the colonies under mercantilism also provided a market for the home country to sell the goods it produced.

The silver Spanish piece of eight *(below left)* and the gold British guinea *(below right)*, were coins used by colonial merchants.

A. Answer Under mercantilism, the colonies existed primarily to benefit the parent country by supplying it with materials it did not have and acting as a market for goods that the parent country did produce.

THINK THROUGH HISTORY
A. Clarifying Under mercantilism, what was the relationship between a home country and its colonies?

66

SECTION 1 RESOURCES

📁 **PRINT RESOURCES**

IN-DEPTH RESOURCES: UNIT 1
Guided Reading, p. 40

ACCESS FOR STUDENTS ACQUIRING ENGLISH
Guided Reading (Spanish), p. 30

FORMAL ASSESSMENT
Section Quiz, p. 30

ALTERNATIVE ASSESSMENT BOOK
See forms for supporting and scoring alternative activities.

💿 **TECHNOLOGY RESOURCES**

CD-ROM Electronic Library of Primary Sources

INTERNET McDougal Littell Learning On-Line
http://www.mcdougallittell.com

THE NAVIGATION ACTS By the mid-1600s, the American colonies were fulfilling their mercantilist role, at least partially. The colonists exported to England large amounts of raw materials and staples—lumber, furs, fish, grain, and tobacco. In addition, the men and women of the colonies were good customers for manufactured English goods such as wooden furniture, iron utensils, books, and china.

However, not all the products the colonists produced for export ended up on English docks. Some of the colonists' sturdy lumber and strong tobacco made its way into the harbors of Spain, France, and Holland. With the nations of Europe clamoring for their goods, many colonial merchants could not resist the potential for further wealth.

England viewed these actions as an economic threat. According to mercantilist theory, any wealth flowing from the colonies to another nation came at the expense of the home country. As a result, beginning in 1651, England's **Parliament,** the country's legislative body, moved to tighten control of colonial trade by passing a series of measures known as the Acts of Trade and Navigation. These **Navigation Acts,** as they were called, ordered the following:

1. No country could trade with the colonies unless the goods were shipped in either colonial or English ships.
2. All vessels had to be manned by crews that were at least three-quarters English or colonial.
3. The colonies could export certain products, including tobacco and sugar—and later rice, molasses, and furs—only to England.
4. Almost all goods traded between the colonies and Europe first had to be unloaded at an English port. This gave jobs to English dockworkers and money to the English treasury in the form of import taxes on the goods.

The system created by the Navigation Acts obviously benefited England. It proved to be good for most colonists as well. By restricting trade to English or colonial ships, the acts spurred a boom in the colonial shipbuilding industry. Also, because England now wanted as many materials as possible from the colonies, the English helped support the development of numerous colonial industries.

Tensions Emerge

The Navigation Acts, however, did not sit well with everyone. A number of colonial merchants resented the trade restrictions, and many continued to smuggle, or trade illegally, goods to and from other countries. For years England did little to stop these violations. Finally, in 1684, King Charles II acted, punishing the colonists that he believed most resisted English authority: the leaders and merchants of Massachusetts.

B. Answer The Acts benefited both, as they gave England more control over its colonial trade and spurred the growth of numerous colonial industries.

THINK THROUGH HISTORY
B. *Recognizing Effects* What effects did the Navigation Acts have on both Britain and its colonies?

Trade between England and her colonies benefited many colonial merchants. This painting depicts the wealthy New England trader Moses Marcy.

The Colonies Come of Age **67**

(continued from page 66)
• The Navigation Acts control trade to and from the colonies to benefit England.
• Though the colonies are seen mostly as a means to benefit the home country, the colonists often benefit as well.

IN-DEPTH RESOURCES: UNIT 1
Guided Reading, p. 40

ACCESS FOR STUDENTS ACQUIRING ENGLISH Guided Reading (Spanish), p. 30

HISTORY FROM VISUALS
New England Trader
Reading the Art Ask students what words they would use to describe the man in the painting. *Possible Responses: Wealthy, comfortable, satisfied, leisurely.*

Extension Ask what the scene implies about colonial expansion or mercantilism. *Highly beneficial; brought prosperity.*

OBJECTIVE
(2) **INSTRUCT**

Tensions Emerge

▶ *Discussing Key Ideas*
• Charles II and his successor James II crack down on Massachusetts, greatest violator of the Navigation Acts.
• After England's Glorious Revolution of 1688, the Massachusetts charter is restored.

TEACHING OPTIONS

Exploring Themes

Economic Opportunity Stress that mercantilism held back colonial growth and prosperity. The Scottish economist Adam Smith, father of modern economics, attacked mercantilism in his landmark work, *The Wealth of Nations* (1776), arguing that full production and free markets would benefit all parties.

Ask students to evaluate the mercantile ideal of having a favorable balance of trade with one's colonies. *Possible Responses: Makes home nation rich; makes home nation self-sufficient in terms of raw materials; curtails colonial buying power and thus home nation revenues; feeds colonial resentment and rebellion.*

Making Connections Across the Curriculum

Economics Clarify that the balance of trade is the result of money made and spent on imports and exports. Encourage students to discuss arguments that still persist about whether trade should be regulated by government or not. *Benefits of free trade include lower consumer prices, higher-wage export jobs, and overseas economic stability that may help curb wars, terrorism, etc. Drawbacks include job losses in some industries, possible loss of manufacturing base, and loss of revenue to foreign creditors.*

A CRACKDOWN IN MASSACHUSETTS Charles certainly had evidence to support his view. The Puritan leaders of Massachusetts had long professed their hostility to the crown's authority. For instance, in the years immediately following the passage of the Navigation Acts, the colony's leaders suggested that their corporate charter did not require them to obey the Acts or any other laws passed by Parliament. By 1678, their stance had not changed: "the lawes of England," stated a Massachusetts government report, "doe not reach America."

In 1684, after failing to persuade Massachusetts to follow English laws regulating everything from trade to religious toleration, England revoked the colony's corporate charter. Massachusetts, the "Puritan utopia," was suddenly a royal colony, under strict control of the crown.

THE DOMINION OF NEW ENGLAND James II, King Charles's brother, succeeded him in 1685 and immediately aggravated the situation. Seeking to make the colonial governments more obedient, he consolidated the northern colonies, disbanded their local assemblies, and placed them under a single ruler in Boston. Within two years, the land from southern Maine to New Jersey was united into one vast colony, the **Dominion of New England.**

James picked an old ally, **Sir Edmund Andros,** to rule the Dominion. Andros, a veteran military officer from an aristocratic English family, made his hard-line attitude toward the colonists clear: "You have no more privileges left you, than not to be sold for slaves." Within weeks of arriving in Boston, Andros managed to make thousands of enemies. He angered Puritans by questioning the lawfulness of their religion. He made it clear that the Navigation Acts would be enforced and smugglers prosecuted vigorously. Furthermore, he outlawed local assemblies and levied taxes without any input from local leaders.

Andros's actions outraged the Northern colonists. In 1687, the colonists of Massachusetts sent their most prominent minister, Increase Mather, to London to try to get their old charter restored and Andros recalled. However, before Mather could put his diplomatic skills to work, a bloodless revolution in England changed the entire political picture.

THE GLORIOUS REVOLUTION While James's actions had made him few friends in the colonies, his religious leanings made him even less popular back home. A Roman Catholic who ruled with little respect for Parliament, James had little idea how much his subjects valued their Protestantism and their parliamentary rights. When James fathered a son in 1688, England suddenly faced the possibility of a dynasty of Roman Catholic monarchs.

To head off that possibility, Parliament that year invited James's Protestant daughter, Mary, and her husband, William of Orange, to jointly rule the country. William and his army sailed from Holland and took the throne without a single shot being fired, as James fled to France. In the aftermath of these events, which became known as the **Glorious Revolution,** Parliament passed a series of laws establishing its power over the Crown.

Upon learning of the events in England, the colonists of Massachusetts staged a bloodless rebellion of their own, arresting Andros and his royal councilors. Andros tried to escape Boston dressed as a woman but was captured after someone noticed the army boots he was wearing. Parliament rapidly restored to their original status the colonies that had been absorbed by the Dominion of New England. In restoring Massachusetts's charter, however, the English

ON THE WORLD STAGE

SCOTLAND

IRELAND (under British rule) ENGLAND

WALES

ENGLAND BECOMES GREAT BRITAIN

During the period covered in this chapter, England completed the process of unifying its island. This process started when England joined with Wales in 1536. However, nearly 200 more battle-filled years passed before the English unified the island by incorporating Scotland to the north. Since around 1100, the Scots, descendants of a Celtic tribe that had migrated from Ireland, had continually resisted English attempts at control.

Weary from constant warfare, the two countries signed the Act of Union in 1707, which joined them under the United Kingdom of Great Britain. The Scots dissolved their parliament and sent members to the British Parliament. Tensions continued throughout that century, however, as the Scots revolted on several occasions. Today the United Kingdom of Great Britain and Northern Ireland includes England, Scotland, Wales, and Northern Ireland.

English Rulers' Colonial Policies

CHARLES II (1660–1685)
Angered by Massachusetts's refusal to obey English law, he revoked the colony's charter in 1684 and brought it directly under England's control.

JAMES II (1685–1688)
He consolidated the New England colonies into the Dominion of New England in 1685 and enlisted Sir Edmund Andros to rule the region.

WILLIAM AND MARY (1688–1702)
They overthrew James II in the Glorious Revolution of 1688 and helped establish the supremacy of Parliament, which dissolved the Dominion of New England and restored the colonies' charters.

government made several changes. The new charter, granted in 1691, called for the king to appoint the governor of Massachusetts and required more religious toleration and non-Puritan representation in the colonial assembly. The Puritans would no longer be able to persecute such groups as the Quakers and members of the Church of England.

England Loosens the Reins

In the years after 1688, England turned much of its attention away from the colonies and toward France, with whom England was competing for control of Europe. The home country still expected the colonies to perform their duties of exporting raw materials and importing manufactured goods, but as long as they did so, Parliament saw little reason to spend large amounts of money and soldiers to aggressively enforce its colonial laws.

SALUTARY NEGLECT Ironically, England ushered in its new policy with an attempt, on paper at least, to increase its control over the colonies. In the years immediately following the Glorious Revolution, Parliament strengthened the Navigation Acts in two ways. First, it moved smuggling trials from usually sympathetic colonial courts (which often found colonial smugglers innocent) to admiralty courts over which Crown-appointed English judges presided. Second, it created the Board of Trade, an advisory board with broad powers to monitor colonial trade.

While England appeared to tighten its colonial grip, in reality it loosened its hold. English officials only lightly enforced the new measures, as they settled into an overall colonial policy that became known as **salutary neglect.** Salutary—beneficial—neglect meant that England relaxed its enforcement of most regulations in return for continued economic loyalty by the colonies. So long as raw materials continued flowing into the homeland and the colonists continued to buy English-produced goods, Parliament did not think it necessary to supervise the colonies closely.

THE SEEDS OF SELF-GOVERNMENT This policy of neglect had an important effect on politics as well as economics in the American colonies. In nearly every colony, a governor appointed by the Crown served as the highest authority. The governor

A form of self-government that arose in New England was the town meeting, in which eligible citizens voted on local laws. Town meetings were typically held in the community meetinghouse, which also accommodated church services and other public gatherings. This drawing depicts a meetinghouse built at Plymouth, Massachusetts, in 1683.

The Colonies Come of Age **69**

70 Chapter 3

presided over a political structure that included an advisory council, usually appointed by the governor, and a local assembly, elected by eligible colonists (land-owning white males). The governor wielded a wide range of powers. He had the authority to call and disband the assembly as well as appoint and dismiss judges. The governor also oversaw all aspects of colonial trade.

However, just as with England's economic policies, its colonial governors were stronger in print than in practice. For example, the colonial assembly initiated and passed laws, as well as raised money through taxes. The governor could veto any law but did so at the risk of going hungry—because the colonial assembly, not London, paid the governor's salary. Using this power of the purse liberally, the colonists influenced the governor in a variety of ways, from the approval of laws to the appointment of judges.

Under Great Britain's less-than-watchful eye, the colonies were developing a taste for self-government that would ultimately create the conditions for rebellion down the road. Nehemiah Grew, a British mercantilist, voiced one of the few early concerns about the colonies' growing self-determination. He warned his fellow countrymen in 1707.

A PERSONAL VOICE

The time may come . . . when the colonies may become populous and with the increase of arts and sciences strong and politic, forgetting their relation to the mother countries, will then confederate and consider nothing further than the means to support their ambition of standing on their own legs.

NEHEMIAH GREW, quoted in *The Colonial Period of American History*

However, the policy of salutary neglect that characterized British and colonial relations throughout the first half of the 1700s worked in large part because of the colonists' loyalty to the crown. The men and women of the colonies still considered themselves subjects of Great Britain, eager to benefit the empire as well as themselves. Aside from a desire for more economic and political breathing room, the colonies shared little in common with one another that would unite them against England. In particular, the Northern and Southern colonies were developing distinct societies, based on sharply contrasting economic systems.

Colonial Government

England's North American colonies were a mixture of royal, proprietary, and corporate colonies. Whatever their form of charter, however, most colonies were similar in the structure of their government.

BRITISH CROWN

ROYAL GOVERNOR
• appointed by the Crown
• oversaw colonial trade
• had final approval on laws
• could dismiss colonial assembly

COUNCIL
• appointed by governor
• advisory board to governor
• acted as highest court in each colony

COLONIAL ASSEMBLY
• made laws
• had authority to tax
• paid governor's salary
• elected by eligible colonists

SKILLBUILDER
INTERPRETING CHARTS
In what ways did the royal governor and colonial assembly share power?

Section 1 Assessment

1. TERMS & NAMES

Identify:
• mercantilism
• balance of trade
• Parliament
• Navigation Acts
• Dominion of New England
• Sir Edmund Andros
• Glorious Revolution
• salutary neglect

2. SUMMARIZING Create a problem-solution chart similar to the one below. Fill it in with steps that England took to solve its economic and political problems with the colonists.

> **Problem:**
> Keeping the colonies under England's economic and political control

> **England's Solutions:**
> 1. 1651—
> 2. 1686—
> 3. After 1688—

3. INTERPRETING In 1707 the British mercantilist Nehemiah Grew forecast that the colonies, "forgetting their relation to their mother countries, will then confederate and consider nothing further than the means to support their ambition of standing on their own legs." Explain why the British did not want this to happen.

THINK ABOUT
• the goals of mercantilism
• what might happen to Great Britain's economy if Grew's prediction came true

4. FORMING AN OPINION Britain passed legislation and established policies to control the American colonies but was inconsistent in its enforcement of those policies. Do you think this approach to governing the colonies was effective or ineffective? Why?

THINK ABOUT
• the Navigation Acts
• the policy of salutary neglect
• the positive and negative outcomes of aggressively enforcing policies

70 CHAPTER 3

2 The Agricultural South

TERMS & NAMES
- cash crop
- triangular trade
- middle passage
- Stono Rebellion

LEARN ABOUT how the South became a labor-intensive, agricultural society
TO UNDERSTAND the growth of slavery in the Southern colonies.

ONE AMERICAN'S STORY

In the fall of 1773, Philip Vickers Fithian left his home in Princeton, New Jersey, for an unfamiliar world. Fithian, a theology student, had agreed to tutor the children of Robert Carter III and his wife at their Virginia manor house, known as "Nomini Hall." The magnificent brick mansion, which anchored their 13,500-acre plantation, sat on a hill overlooking the Potomac and Nomini rivers.

Surrounding it were more than 30 smaller houses, most of them living quarters for servants and slaves. Fithian, who kept a journal of his one-year stay there, recalled an evening walk along the property.

> **A PERSONAL VOICE**
> We stroll'd down the Pasture quite to the River, admiring the Pleasantness of the evening, & the delightsome Prospect of the River, Hills, Huts on the Summits, low Bottoms, Trees of various Kinds, and Sizes, Cattle & Sheep feeding some near us, & others at a great distance on the green sides of the Hills . . . I love to walk on these high Hills . . . where I can have a long View of many Miles & see on the Summits of the Hills Clusters of Savin Trees, through these often a little Farm-House, or Quarter for Negroes.
> **PHILIP VICKERS FITHIAN,** *Journal & Letters of Philip Vickers Fithian*

The Carter plantation was just one of the many large properties that dominated the landscape of the Southern colonies by the mid 1600s. These large farms played a dominant role in the South's economy, which came to rely heavily on agriculture. The development of this plantation economy led to a largely rural society, in which African slaves played an unwilling yet important role.

The Shirley plantation house in Virginia is representative of many old Southern mansions. Built in 1723, it was the birthplace of the mother of the Civil War general Robert E. Lee.

A Plantation Economy Arises

Since the early days of Jamestown, when the planting of tobacco helped save the settlement, the Southern colonists had staked their livelihood on the fertile soil that stretched from the Chesapeake region to Georgia. Robert Carter, like his father and grandfather before him, specialized in raising a single **cash crop**—one grown primarily for sale rather than for the farmer's own use. In Maryland, Virginia, and North Carolina, planters grew the broad green leaves of tobacco. Planters in South Carolina and Georgia harvested rice and later indigo as cash crops.

Throughout the South, plantations developed instead of towns. These large farms sprang up along the rivers that snaked through the region, so that planters could ship their goods directly to the northern colonies and Europe without the need for city dock facilities. Farmers also had no need for city warehouses, since they stored their goods on the plantation. Finally, because plantation owners produced much of what they needed on their property, they saw little reason for shops, bakeries, and markets. There were a number of cities in the South, including Charles Town (later Charleston), South Carolina—one of the most thriving port cities in the British empire. On the whole, however, the South developed largely as a rural and self-sufficient society.

The Colonies Come of Age **71**

Section 2 Overview

OBJECTIVES

(1) To trace the development of a plantation economy in the American South.

(2) To explain the way of life in the Southern colonies.

(3) To describe the slave trade and the role of slavery in the plantation economy.

(4) To describe life for colonial slaves.

CRITICAL THINKING

- Identifying problems, p. 73
- Analyzing causes, p. 73
- Synthesizing, p. 75
- Summarizing, p. 76
- Drawing conclusions, p. 76
- Analyzing issues, p. 76

FOCUS & MOTIVATE

▶ **Starting with the Student**
- How would you live if you were very wealthy?
- Is it possible to live such a life without relying on the hard work of other, poorer people? Explain your answer.

OBJECTIVE
(1) INSTRUCT

A Plantation Economy Arises

▶ **Discussing Key Ideas**
- The fertile soil of the South nurtures an agricultural economy in which growing cash crops makes some planters rich.
- The economy is dominated by large, virtually self-sufficient plantations.

IN-DEPTH RESOURCES: UNIT 1
Guided Reading, p. 41

ACCESS FOR STUDENTS ACQUIRING ENGLISH Guided Reading (Spanish), p. 31

SECTION 2 RESOURCES

PRINT RESOURCES

IN-DEPTH RESOURCES: UNIT 1
Guided Reading, p. 41
Skillbuilder Practice: Visual Sources, p. 44
Geography Application: The Triangular Trade, p. 45
Primary Source: from *History of the Dividing Line* by William Byrd, p. 47
American Lives: Olaudah Equiano, p. 54

ACCESS FOR STUDENTS ACQUIRING ENGLISH
Guided Reading (Spanish), p. 31
Skillbuilder Practice: Visual Sources (Spanish), p. 34
Geography Application: The Triangular Trade (Spanish), p. 35

FORMAL ASSESSMENT
Section Quiz, p. 31

ALTERNATIVE ASSESSMENT BOOK
See forms for supporting and scoring alternative activities.

TECHNOLOGY RESOURCES

CRITICAL THINKING TRANSPARENCIES
- CT37, Africans in the Colonies

CD-ROM Electronic Library of Primary Sources

VIDEO *American Portfolio: A Videodisc for U.S. History* user's guide, pp. 23, 24

INTERNET McDougal Littell Learning On-Line
http://www.mcdougallittell.com

Teacher's Edition **71**

A Southern Plantation

Reading the Art The paint-ing shows the hierarchy on the plantation, with the big house at the top and center, the smaller houses "sup-porting" the big house, and the docks and boat at the bottom on the river.
Extension Ask what activi-ties the scene suggests were important to plantation society. *Possible Responses: Agriculture, shipping.*

Many Southern tobacco planta-tions were like small towns unto themselves, with outbuildings that might house car-penters, black-smiths, or even a school for the owner's children. The ideal location was on a major waterway so that the owner could easily load his tobacco for ship-ment to London and other desti-nations.

OBJECTIVE
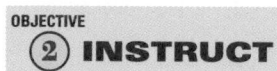

Life in Southern Society

As they read, have students list the different social groups in the Southern colonies and the vital details about each group.

Group	Details
Planters	
Small Farmers	
Women	
Indentured Servants	
Slaves	

▶ *Discussing Key Ideas*
• The plantation economy brings prosperity to a few large landowners, but for most, life is a constant struggle.
• Women and indentured servants have virtually no rights in the South.

IN-DEPTH RESOURCES: UNIT 1
Primary Source: from *History of the Dividing Line* by William Byrd, p. 47

Colonial copper skillets such as this had long handles that let the homemaker remove the skillet from the fire without burning herself.

Life in Southern Society

As the Southern colonies grew, they became home to diverse groups, as well as to many prosperous farmers and traders. However, life in the South—as else-where in the colonies—proved difficult for women and indentured servants.

A DIVERSE AND PROSPEROUS PEOPLE During the 1700s, large numbers of European immigrants traveled to North America in search of a new start. The influx of immigrants helped create a diverse population in both the Northern and Southern colonies. In the South, thousands of Germans settled throughout Maryland, Virginia, and as far south as South Carolina. There they raised grain, livestock, and tobacco. A wave of Scots and Scots-Irish also settled in the South, residing mainly along the fertile hills of western North Carolina.

While small farmers formed the majority of the Southern population, the planters—owners of large profitable plantations—controlled much of the South's economy. They also controlled its political and social institutions. The activities at the Carter mansion described by Philip Fithian reflected the luxury of planter life. Fithian recalled attending numerous balls, banquets, dance recitals, and parties that continued for several days.

By the mid-1700s, however, life was good for many other Southern colonists, particularly those in the Chesapeake region. Due to a large growth in the entire colonies' export trade, colonial standards of living rose dramatically in the years from 1700 to 1770. Colonists in the Chesapeake, where tobacco prices had rebounded after tumbling during the late 1600s, saw the greatest economic boom. From 1713 to 1774 tobacco exports there tripled, and many Chesapeake farmers and merchants prospered.

THE ROLE OF WOMEN Women in Southern society—and Northern society as well—shared a common trait: second-class citizenship. Women had few legal or social rights: they could not vote, preach, or own property.

Throughout the day, the average Southern woman worked over a hot fire baking bread or boiling meat. In between cooking tasks, she stepped outside to milk the cows, slaughter pigs for ham and bacon, and tend the garden. Back inside, she sewed, washed clothes, and cleaned. Women of the

---

TEACHING OPTIONS

Exploring Themes

Women in America Note that until recent times females were second-class citizens with few rights of their own. Believed to be ill equipped for "serious" academic subjects, even daughters of wealthy Southern planters were usually taught only the basics of reading, writing, and arithmetic and otherwise educated in the social graces or in domestic tasks, such as canning and preserving food, sewing, and embroidery.

Ask students whether they think that gender prejudice still affects education, requesting that they cite examples.

Teaching Gifted and Talented Students

Comparing and Contrasting Ask students to research the lives of wealthy landowners in Britain and compare and con-trast them with the lives of plantation owners in the Southern colonies. Students' final reports might take the form of a fic-tional correspondence between a planter and an English aris-tocrat or a short piece of historical fiction in which the son or daughter of a wealthy Southern planter goes to England to be educated. Encourage students to speculate on how the English aristocracy would treat their American counterparts.

planter class escaped most of these tasks, as servants handled the household chores. Upper-class women, however, bowed to their husbands. An excerpt from Virginia plantation owner William Byrd's diary hints at Lucia Pat Byrd's subservient position: "My wife and I had another scold about mending my shoes," Byrd wrote, "but it was soon over by her submission."

A. Answer Women, despite their class status, were regarded as second-class citizens beholden to men in almost every way. Indentured servants, even if they survived their harsh years of labor, often were relegated to the outskirts of society.

THINK THROUGH HISTORY
A. Identifying Problems What difficulties did women and indentured servants face in Southern society?

INDENTURED SERVANTS Occupying an even lower rung than women on Southern society's ladder were indentured servants. Many of these young, mostly white men had traded a life of prison or poverty in Europe for limited servitude in North America. They had virtually no rights while in bondage. Those who lived through their harsh years of labor—and many did not—saw their lives improve only slightly as they struggled to survive on the western outskirts of the Southern colonies.

While historians estimate that indentured servants made up a significant portion of the colonial population in the 1600s—between one-half and two-thirds of all white male immigrants after 1630—their numbers declined toward the end of the century. With continuing reports of hardship in the New World, many laborers in Europe decided to stay home. Faced with a depleted labor force and a growing agricultural economy, the Southern colonists turned to another group to meet their labor needs: slaves.

Slavery Becomes Entrenched

The English colonists did not intend to make African slavery an institution. They gradually turned to the use of African slaves after efforts to meet their labor needs with enslaved Native Americans and indentured servants failed. Nonetheless, during the 1600s and 1700s, plantation owners and other colonists would subject hundreds of thousands of Africans to a life of intense labor and cruelty in North America.

B. Answer Since slaves worked for life, they were cost-effective. They also were used to the Southern climate, and the colonists believed the Africans to be naturally inferior and thus could reconcile subjugating them to a life of bondage.

THINK THROUGH HISTORY
B. Analyzing Causes What were the main reasons that the English colonists turned to African slaves to fill their depleted labor force?

THE EVOLUTION OF SLAVERY In the early days of the colonies, the English, like their Spanish counterparts, had forced Native Americans to work for them. However, the English settlers found it increasingly difficult to enslave Native Americans. Aside from being reluctant to learn English labor techniques, Native Americans could easily escape because they had far better knowledge of the fields and forests than did the colonists.

As the indentured servant population fell, the English colonists turned to African slaves as an attractive alternative. The main reason was economics. Although slaves cost more than indentured servants, a slave worked for life and thus brought a much larger return for the investment. In addition, most white colonists saw the Africans' dark skin as a sign of inferiority and had few reservations about subjecting them to a life of servitude. By 1690, nearly 13,000 slaves toiled in the Southern colonies. By 1750, the number of slaves in the South had increased to almost 200,000.

THE EUROPEAN SLAVE TRADE Before the English colonists of North America began importing African slaves, Africans had been laboring as slaves for years in the English colonies of the West Indies. During the late 1600s, English planters in Jamaica and Barbados imported tens of thousands of African slaves to work the large and prosperous sugar plantations. By 1690, the African population on Barbados was about 60,000—three times that of the white population.

During the 17th century, Africans had become part of a transatlantic trading network described, somewhat inaccurately, as the **triangular trade**. This term referred to the process by which merchants carried rum and other goods

ON THE WORLD STAGE

SERFDOM THROUGHOUT THE WORLD

Indentured servants were just one of several peasant groups throughout the world forced to toil in the fields during the 17th century. Eastern Europe and Asia depended on the system of serfdom, in which serfs—peasant laborers beholden to a landlord—lived and worked on a master's land.

While economic conditions in the 1300s and after prompted the countries of Western Europe to abandon the practice of serfdom, this change did not come to Eastern Europe and Asia until much later. Peasants in Russia continued to work exclusively for landlords until 1861, when Alexander II's Edict of Emancipation granted the country's serfs their personal freedom and an allotment of land. In China, land-bound peasants worked for landowners until 1949, when the People's Republic of China freed all serfs.

ON THE WORLD STAGE
Serfdom Throughout the World
Critical Thinking: Comparing and Contrasting Note that serfs were bound for life, as were their offspring. Then ask whether serfs were more like the indentured servants or slaves of North America. *Possible Responses:* Indentured servants, because they had ethnic background similar to that of masters; slaves, because they were bound in perpetuity.

OBJECTIVE
③ INSTRUCT

Slavery Becomes Entrenched

▶*Discussing Key Ideas*
• Because black Africans were thought better able to endure the harsh physical demands of plantation labor in hot climates, African slavery becomes institutionalized.
• Slaves come to America on the so-called "middle passage," the middle part of the trans-Atlantic route known as the triangular trade.
• The crossing is harsh, with nearly 20 percent perishing on slave ships.

IN-DEPTH RESOURCES: UNIT 1
Geography Application: the Triangular Trade, p. 45

TEACHING OPTIONS

Making Connections Across the Curriculum

Biology Explain that specific populations may develop immunities to diseases to which they are often exposed. Such immunity can occur when those who contract severe cases of the disease die and those with total or partial resistance survive and pass on their resistance genetically. Native Americans, for example, died in great numbers because they had no resistance to the diseases brought over by Europeans. Black Africans' ability to fight off malaria is a genetically transmitted trait that also makes them prone to the often fatal disease of sickle-cell anemia. Students might research and report on other genetically transmitted diseases and immunities.

Making Connections Across the Curriculum

Literature Point out that the writings of William Byrd (1674–1744), quoted at the top of the page, are often read in the study of American literature. Owner of the great plantation of Westover on Virginia's James River (where he founded the city of Richmond on his own lands), Byrd had a library of over four thousand books, reputedly the largest of that time in the English colonies. Educated in England, he later spent time there as a colonial agent and was a member of the Royal Society (of scientists and philosophers). His extensive diaries are noted for their charming style and keen eye for detail.

MORE ABOUT . . .
Olaudah Equiano

Also known as Gustavus Vassa, Equiano was enslaved and sold in the West Indies in about 1762. Eventually freed, he became an active abolitionist in England and helped lead the way for the establishment of Freetown, Sierra Leone, as an African sanctuary for freed slaves. In 1789 Equiano published *The Interesting Narrative of the Life of Olaudah Equiano, or Gustavus Vassa, the African.* The book was a best seller, which Equiano later followed with his *Miscellaneous Verses.*

 ELECTRONIC LIBRARY OF PRIMARY SOURCES
from *The Interesting Narrative of the Life of Olaudah Equiano*

IN-DEPTH RESOURCES: UNIT 1
American Lives: Olaudah Equiano, p. 54

HISTORY FROM VISUALS
Slave Ship

Reading the Art Ask students what words they would use to describe the scene depicted. *Possible Responses: Crowded, unsanitary, dark, communal.* Ask students what the diagram of the slave ship suggests about the slave traders' attitude toward their passengers.

Extension Have students discuss the degree of accuracy in the scene, based on the information in the text. *Some students may feel that the scene presents a somewhat idealized view by showing two slaves conversing, another relaxing in the foreground, and so on.*

from New England to Africa; there they exchanged their merchandise for slaves, whom they transported to the West Indies and sold for sugar and molasses; these goods they then shipped to New England to be distilled into rum. The "triangular" trade, in fact, encompassed a network of trade routes criss-crossing the Northern and Southern colonies, the West Indies, England, Europe, and Africa. The network carried an array of traded goods, from furs and fruit to tar and tobacco, as well as African people.

THE MIDDLE PASSAGE The voyage that brought Africans to the West Indies and later to North America was known as the **middle passage**, because it was considered the middle leg of the transatlantic trade triangle. Sickening cruelty characterized this journey. In the bustling ports along West Africa, European traders branded Africans with red-hot irons for identification purposes and packed them into the dark holds of large ships. On board a slave ship, Africans fell victim to whippings and beatings from merchants as well as diseases that swept through the vessel. The smell of blood, sweat, and excrement filled the hold, as the African passengers lived in their own vomit and waste. One African, Olaudah Equiano, recalled the inhumane conditions on his trip from West Africa to the West Indies at age 11 in 1756.

A PERSONAL VOICE
The closeness of the place, and the heat of the climate, added to the number in the ship, which was so crowded that each had scarcely room to turn himself, almost suffocated us. This produced copious perspirations, so that the air soon became unfit for respiration from a variety of loathsome smells, and brought on a sickness amongst the slaves, of which many died.

OLAUDAH EQUIANO, *The Interesting Narrative of the Life of Olaudah Equiano*

Whether they died from disease or from cruel treatment by merchants, or whether they committed suicide, as many did by plunging into the ocean,

Olaudah Equiano

A British naval officer painted the above scene of the deck of the slave ship *Albanez* in 1846. It portrays conditions that were found on many slave ships. The diagram at the right shows how slave traders often placed as many slaves as possible on their ships.

74 CHAPTER 3

TEACHING OPTION

Skillbuilder Mini-Lesson: Interpreting Visual Sources

Explaining the Skill Visual sources such as these images of slave ships can reveal much about the times in which they were created. The artist's choice of details, the mood created with color and light, and the purpose of the piece, either known or guessed, all give the observer information for an interpretation.

Applying the Skill: Interpreting Visual Sources Have students examine the images of slave ships on this page and note who created them. Then ask these questions:

1. What conditions would you expect on board the ship in the diagram? *Cramped; hot; painful.*

2. What mood does the painting convey? *Blue suggests a calm, cool environment. Sunlight gives a sense of well being.*

3. What seem to be the artists' attitudes toward their subjects? *Students may say that neither artist views Africans as worthy of respect. The artist of the diagram views the captives simply as cargo. The painter seems to think, or wants others to think, that conditions on board were humane.*

IN-DEPTH RESOURCES: UNIT 1
Skillbuilder Practice: Visual Sources, p. 44

74 Chapter 3

nearly 20 percent of the Africans aboard each slave ship perished during the brutal trip to the New World.

SLAVERY IN THE SOUTH Africans who survived their ocean voyage entered an extremely difficult life of bondage in North America. Most slaves—probably 80 to 90 percent—worked in the fields. On large plantations, a white slave owner directed their labor. On smaller farms, slaves often worked alongside their owner.

The other 10 to 20 percent of slaves worked in the house of their owner or as artisans. Domestic slaves cooked, cleaned, and raised the master's children. While owners did not subject their domestic slaves to the rigors of field labor, they treated them with equal cruelty, doling out such punishments as whippings and beatings. Other slaves developed skills as artisans—carpenters, blacksmiths, and bricklayers. Owners often rented these slaves out to work on other plantations.

Whatever their task, slaves led a grueling existence. Full-time work began around age 12 and continued until death. John Ferdinand Smyth, an English traveler, described a typical slave workday.

> **A PERSONAL VOICE**
> He (the slave) is called up in the morning at daybreak, and is seldom allowed time enough to swallow three mouthfuls of hominy, or hoecake, but is driven out immediately to the field to hard labor, at which he continues, without intermission, until noon . . . About noon is the time he eats his dinner, and he is seldom allowed an hour for that purpose . . . They then return to severe labor, which continues in the field until dusk in the evening.
>
> **JOHN FERDINAND SMYTH,** quoted in *Planters and Pioneers*

Slave owners whipped and beat those slaves they thought were disobedient or disrespectful. In Virginia, the courts did not consider slave owners guilty of murder for killing their slaves during punishment.

Africans Cope in Their New World

The Africans who stepped off the slave ships into North America came from a variety of different cultures and spoke different languages. Forced to labor in a strange new land, these diverse peoples bonded together for support and fought against their plight in different ways.

CULTURE AND FAMILY In the midst of the horrors of slavery, Africans developed a way of life based strongly on their cultural heritage. Slaves wove baskets and molded pottery as they had done in their homeland. They kept alive their musical traditions and retold the stories of their ancestors. Because slave merchants tore apart many African families, slaves created new families among the people with whom they lived. If a master sold a parent to another plantation, other slaves stepped in to raise the children left behind.

The African influence remained particularly strong among the slaves of South Carolina and Georgia. By the mid 1700s, planters in these colonies had imported large numbers of Africans with rice-growing expertise to help develop rice as the colonies' main cash crop. Because many of these slaves came from the same region in West Africa, they remained in tightly knit families.

One of the most important rituals Africans kept alive in North America was their dance. From Maryland to Georgia, slaves continued to practice what became known in the colonies as the ring shout, a circular dance linked to the African burial ceremony. While variations of the dance brought to North America differed throughout the regions in West and Central Africa, the dance paid tribute to the group's ancestors and gods and usually involved loud chants and quick, circular steps. Despite the white colonists' efforts to eradicate it, the ritual endured.

C. Answer Slaves practiced as much of their cultural heritage as they could, and they resisted their "owners" in various ways.

THINK THROUGH HISTORY
C. *Synthesizing* How did slaves maintain their culture?

This gourd fiddle *(top)* and drum *(above),* both made by slaves, reflect ways in which enslaved African-Americans continued their African traditions.

The Colonies Come of Age **75**

NOW & THEN
Gullah

Critical Thinking: Interpreting Write on the chalkboard the following sentence: *'Twix' me na una 'e duh badmout 'em fuh trut, enti?* Have a volunteer (preferably someone only marginally familiar with black dialect) say the sentence aloud and then try to "translate" it into standard English. *Between me and you, he truly insulted him, didn't he?* Explain that the sentence is in Gullah, and note that the expression "to badmouth" has become part of American slang.

OBJECTIVE
④ INSTRUCT

Africans Cope in Their New World

▶ *Starting with the Student*
• How would you feel if, through no fault of your own, you had to live your life in a highly restricted environment?
• Do you think you could eventually adapt to such a life? Why or why not?

▶ *Discussing Key Ideas*
• Drawn together by a common plight, slaves from a variety of African cultures maintain their traditions.
• Sometimes they resist their plight, as in the Stono Rebellion of 1739.

🏛 **CRITICAL THINKING TRANSPARENCIES**
CT37, Africans in the Colonies

TEACHING OPTION

 Cooperative Activity: Words from African Languages

Purpose: To help students recognize the contributions of African languages to the English language.

Activity: Ask students to work in small groups and use a dictionary or a book about the history of English language to find words from African languages that have entered the English language. (In addition to *goober, juke,* and *voodoo,* other additions include words for foods, such as *gumbo* and *okra,* and words for musical instruments, such as *banjo* and *marimba.* Additional words include *chimpanzee, mamba, limbo* (the dance), *tango* and *mambo* (through Spanish), and possibly the slang *hip* or *hep.)*

Ask students to keep a list of their words and their definitions as well as their country of origin. Have students create a display of their work, including pictures, photographs, or objects that help define or identify the words of African origin. Have students present their displays to the class, and answer any questions that their classmates might have.

ALTERNATIVE ASSESSMENT BOOK
Standards for Evaluating a Cooperative Activity

Teacher's Edition 75

Reading the Artifact Point out how the poster was created with details about the slave that were supplied by his owner.

Extension Ask students to discuss what they can learn, both about the slave and his owner, from reading this poster.

ASSESS & RETEACH

Section 2 Assessment
Students might work in pairs to respond to the questions.

Self-Assessment
To assess what they have learned in this section, have students write their own questions, exchange them with a partner, and answer their partner's questions. Partners can then review the section together to find or clarify information for their incorrect answers.

Section Quiz
FORMAL ASSESSMENT
Section Quiz, p. 31

Reteach
Use the illustrations in this section to help review the main ideas.

CLOSE

The plantation economy made some Southerners very rich, but it also made the South increasingly dependent on slavery.

RESISTANCE AND REVOLT Slaves also resisted their position of subservience. Throughout the colonies, planters reported slaves faking illness, breaking tools, and staging work slowdowns. One master noted the difficulty in forcing African slaves to accept their lot, commenting that if a slave "must be broke, either from Obstinacy, or which I am more apt to suppose, from Greatness of Soul, [it] will require . . . hard Discipline. . . . You would really be surpriz'd at their Perseverance . . . they often die before they can be conquer'd."

Some slaves pushed their resistance to open revolt. One such uprising, the **Stono Rebellion,** began on a September Sunday in 1739. That morning, about 20 slaves gathered at the Stono River just south of Charleston. Wielding guns and other weapons, they killed several planter families and marched south, beating drums and loudly inviting other slaves to join them in their plan to flee to Spanish-held Florida.

By late Sunday afternoon, a white militia had surrounded the group of escaping slaves. The two sides clashed, and many slaves died in the fighting. Those captured were executed. Despite the rebellion's failure, it sent a chill through many Southern colonists and led to the tightening of harsh slave laws already in place. However, slave rebellions continued into the 1800s.

Despite the severe punishment that escape attempts brought, a number of slaves tried to run away. The runaway notices published in the various newspapers throughout Virginia would show that from 1736 to 1801, 1,680 enslaved men and women in that state took to flight. Many who succeeded in running away from their masters found refuge with Native American tribes, and marriage between runaway slaves and Native Americans was common.

As the Southern colonies grew, they became ever more dependent on the use of African slavery. This was not the case in the Northern colonies, where slaves existed in far fewer numbers, due mainly to an economy driven by commerce rather than agriculture. This economic distinction spurred the North to develop in ways that differed greatly from the South.

"For in every human breast God has implanted a principle, which we call love of freedom."

PHILLIS WHEATLEY, AFRICAN-AMERICAN POET, 1774

$150 REWARD

RANAWAY from the subscriber, the night of the 2d instant, a negro ma who calls himself *Henry May,* about years old, 5 feet 6 or 8 inches high, ordinary color, rather chunky built, bu head, and has it divided mostly on side, and keeps it very nicely comb has been raised in the house, and is a rate dining-room servant, and was tavern in Louisville for 18 month expect he is now in Louisville tryin make his escape to a free state, (in all probability to Cincinnati, Ohio.) haps he may try to get employment on a steamboat. He is a good coo is handy in any capacity as a house servant. Had on when he left. cassinett coatee, and dark striped cassinett pantaloons, new—he had clothing. I will give $50 reward if taken in Louisvill; 100 dollars if one hundred miles from Louisville in this State, and 150 dollars if tak of this State, and delivered to me, or secured in any jail so that I can g again. WILLIAM BURK
Bardstown, Ky., September 3d, 1838.

Slave owners went to great lengths to capture runaway slaves, as this poster attests.

Section ❷ Assessment

1. TERMS & NAMES
Identify:
• cash crop
• triangular trade
• middle passage
• Stono Rebellion

2. SUMMARIZING Recreate the chart with five tiers shown below to depict the social order of Southern society. Fill in the tiers with brief descriptions of the different classes or divisions of people, ranging from most powerful at the top to least powerful at the bottom.

1.	planters
2.	
3.	
4.	
5.	

3. DRAWING CONCLUSIONS In what ways do you think the development of the Southern economy and society might have been imbalanced? Support your answer with examples.

THINK ABOUT
• the basis of the South's economy
• the types of crops grown
• the distribution of power in Southern society

4. ANALYZING ISSUES In what ways was slavery a brutal system? Consider the whole of the slave experience, and support your statement with examples from the text.

76 CHAPTER 3

ANSWERS

1. TERMS AND NAMES
cash crop, p. 71

triangular trade, p. 73

middle passage, p. 74

Stono Rebellion, p. 76

2. SUMMARIZING
Possible Responses: Classes of people from top tier to bottom tier follow:

Planters (or plantation owners)—controlled the South's economy, as well as its political and social structure; Small Farmers—made up majority of Southern population; Women—had limited legal, political, and social rights; Indentured Servants—had virtually no rights while in bondage; African Slaves—formed economic base of plantation system.

3. DRAWING CONCLUSIONS
Possible Responses: Examples of Southern economic imbalance: The South was almost exclusively a rural society based on an agricultural economy; most planters specialized in raising a single cash crop, rather than a variety of crops. Social imbalance: the economy primarily benefited only an elite class of planters; a select group of powerful planters were on top and a large group of powerless slaves were on the bottom.

4. ANALYZING ISSUES
Possible Responses: Free people were enslaved on the basis of race alone and were treated as merchandise; neither slaves nor their children could free themselves from the system; slaves were transported and lived under inhumane conditions; work was long and grueling; families were often torn apart; slaves' lives were completely controlled.

❸ The Commercial North

LEARN ABOUT economic changes in the Northern colonies and intellectual and religious changes in all the colonies
TO UNDERSTAND the beginnings of economic, political, and social differences with England.

ONE AMERICAN'S STORY

John Adams grew up on a Massachusetts farm. Although he loved the woods and meadows of his rural home, he decided to become an educated professional, not a farmer. He went to Harvard for four years and later studied the law under the guidance of an older lawyer. Even after Adams began his legal practice, he continued to educate himself by reading books on law. However, he found such studying hard to do in Boston, the bustling port city where his work often took him. In 1759 he wrote,

A PERSONAL VOICE
Who can study in Boston Streets? I am unable to observe the various objects that I meet, with sufficient precision. My Eyes are so diverted with Chimney Sweeps, Carriers of Wood, Merchants, Ladies, Priests, Carts, Horses, Oxen, Coaches, Market men and Women, Soldiers, Sailors, and my Ears with the Rattle Gabble of them all that I cant think long enough in the Street upon any one Thing to start and pursue a Thought.

JOHN ADAMS, *The Diary and Autobiography of John Adams*

Adams's experience illustrates several of the changes happening in the New England and Middle colonies during the 18th century. The growth of thriving commercial cities with diverse economic opportunities gradually made the North radically different from the agricultural South. In addition, interest in education was on the rise, partially due to intellectual and religious movements. These movements brought about social changes that contributed to the colonies' eventual break with England.

John Adams

Industry Grows in the North

The theory of mercantilism held that colonies existed to help the home country amass wealth. However, the American colonies found their own economy prospering more. From 1650 to 1750, the colonies' economy grew twice as fast as Great Britain's economy did. Much of this growth occurred in the New England and Middle colonies.

A DIVERSIFIED ECONOMY Unlike the South, the New England and Middle colonies typically produced several cash crops per farm instead of a single one such as rice or tobacco. Cold winters and rocky soil limited New Englanders to small farms not suited to such crops. In more fertile areas, such as New York and Pennsylvania, farmers raised a diversity of crops and animals, including wheat, corn, cattle, and hogs. They produced so much that they sold their surplus food to the West Indies, where raising sugar cane produced such tremendous profits that planters did not want to waste land growing food for the slaves who worked their fields.

A diverse commercial economy also developed in the New England and Middle colonies. Grinding wheat, harvesting fish, and sawing lumber became thriving industries. Colonists also manufactured impressive numbers of ships

The Colonies Come of Age **77**

Section 3 Overview

OBJECTIVES
① To trace the development of a varied and thriving economy in the North.
② To explain the diverse society of the North and the tensions that led to witchcraft trials in Salem.
③ To summarize the influence of the Enlightenment and the Great Awakening.

SKILLBUILDER
- Interpreting charts, p. 78

CRITICAL THINKING
- Synthesizing, p. 78
- Recognizing effects, pp. 79, 81, 82
- Analyzing causes, p. 80
- Summarizing, p. 82
- Analyzing, p. 82
- Applying, p. 82

FOCUS & MOTIVATE

▶ **Starting with the Student**
- What do you like and/or dislike about city life?
- How does the largest city near you influence life in your community?

OBJECTIVE
① **INSTRUCT**

Industry Grows in the North

▶ **Discussing Key Ideas**
- The Northern colonies have a diversified economy that by the mid-18th century is thriving.
- Ports grow into bustling cities, introducing problems as well as benefits.

IN-DEPTH RESOURCES: UNIT 1
Guided Reading, p. 42

ACCESS FOR STUDENTS ACQUIRING ENGLISH Guided Reading (Spanish), p. 32

 GEOGRAPHY TRANSPARENCIES
G3, Colonial Economies

SECTION 3 RESOURCES

 PRINT RESOURCES

IN-DEPTH RESOURCES: UNIT 1
Guided Reading, p. 42
Primary Sources: *from* The Salem Witch Trials, p. 48
from The Autobiography of Benjamin Franklin, p. 49
from The New England Primer, p. 50
Literature: from *The Crucible* by Arthur Miller, p. 51
American Lives: Jonathan Edwards, p. 55

ACCESS FOR STUDENTS ACQUIRING ENGLISH
Guided Reading (Spanish), p. 32

FORMAL ASSESSMENT
Section Quiz, p. 32

ALTERNATIVE ASSESSMENT BOOK
See forms for supporting and scoring alternative activities.

TECHNOLOGY RESOURCES

HUMANITIES TRANSPARENCIES
H4, A Woman's Work

GEOGRAPHY TRANSPARENCIES
G3, Colonial Economies

CD-ROM *Grolier Multimedia Encyclopedia*
Electronic Library of Primary Sources

VIDEO *American Portfolio: A Videodisc for U.S. History*
user's guide, pp. 23, 25

INTERNET McDougal Littell Learning On-Line
http://www.mcdougallittell.com

Northern Society Is Diverse

▶ *Starting with the Student*
• How would input from many different people change a class or school project?
• How may input from people of different cultural backgrounds change life in a city or region?

▶ *Discussing Key Ideas*
• An influx of European immigrants helps make Northern society diverse.
• Slavery exists in the North, although the North is not as dependent on slavery as the South.
• Most Northern women have few legal rights.
• Social and economic tensions contribute to the infamous Salem witchcraft trials of the 1690s.

HISTORY FROM VISUALS
Colonial Diversity—1700 and 1755

Reading the Graph Ask who was the second-largest colonial ethnic group both in 1700 and in 1755. *Africans.*

Extension Ask from what part of Europe the immigrants to the 13 colonies appear to have come. *Northern; western.*

 ELECTRONIC LIBRARY OF PRIMARY SOURCES
from *How Our Cities Looked* by Lord Adam Gordon

Philadelphia in 1720 was already a bustling colonial port. Ocean-going ships could reach the city by sailing up the Delaware River.

Skillbuilder Answer
Germans, Scots-Irish, and Irish

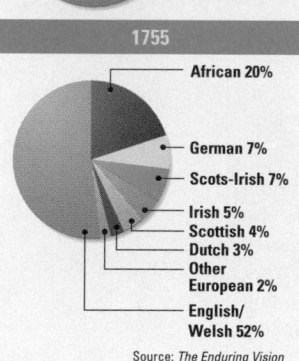

Colonial Diversity

1700

- African 11%
- Dutch 4%
- Scottish 3%
- Other European 2%
- English/Welsh 80%

1755

- African 20%
- German 7%
- Scots-Irish 7%
- Irish 5%
- Scottish 4%
- Dutch 3%
- Other European 2%
- English/Welsh 52%

Source: *The Enduring Vision*

SKILLBUILDER
INTERPRETING CHARTS
What new ethnic groups had settled in the American colonies by 1755?

and quantities of iron. By the 1770s, the colonists had built one-third of all British ships and were producing more iron than England did. While at times the North's economy dipped, many colonists prospered. In particular, the number of merchants grew. By the mid-1700s, merchants were one of the most powerful groups in the North.

URBAN LIFE The expansion in trade caused port cities to grow. Only one major port, Charles Town, existed in the South. In contrast, the North boasted Boston, New York, and Philadelphia. In fact, Philadelphia eventually became the second largest port (after London) in the British empire and was quite sophisticated by standards of the 1700s: it had police patrols, paved streets, and whale-oil lamps to light the sidewalks.

City streets grew ever more crowded—some people hurrying about on foot, others on horseback, and others herding livestock to a butcher. The high concentration of people caused problems not found in rural areas. Firewood and clean water were scarce. Fire and diseases spread rapidly because of the closely spaced buildings, and garbage and human excrement were difficult to dispose of.

Cities also faced the problem of poverty. Some of the poor were immigrants too weakened by the grueling ocean voyage to work. Others were laborers hurt by economic downturns; still others were widows and orphans. In 1752, Boston minister Charles Chauncey fretted over "the Swarms of Children, of both Sexes, that are continually strolling and playing about the Streets of our Metropolis, clothed in Rags, and brought up in Idleness and Ignorance."

Northern Society Is Diverse

Northern society was composed of diverse groups that sometimes had conflicting interests. Groups whose interests clashed with those of the people in power included immigrants, African Americans, and women.

INFLUX OF IMMIGRANTS Even more so than the South, the Northern colonies attracted a variety of immigrants. During the 18th century, about 585,000 Europeans migrated to America. Before 1700, most immigrants came as indentured servants from England, but by 1755 more than a third of European immigrants were coming from other countries. Dr. Alexander Hamilton, a physician, commented on the variety of the people he observed in a Philadelphia tavern one night in 1744: "There were Scots, English, Dutch, Germans, and Irish; there were Roman Catholics, Church men [Anglicans], Presbyterians, Quakers, Newlightmen, Methodists, Seventh day men, Moravians, Anabaptists and one Jew."

THINK THROUGH HISTORY
A. Synthesizing
In what ways was the Northern economy diverse?

A. Answer
Northern farms produced a great diversity of foodstuffs; the North had many cities, with a wide variety of industries and occupations.

TEACHING OPTIONS

Exploring Themes

Cultural Diversity Stress that the influx of European immigrants, especially in the North, and of African slaves, especially in the South, brought cultural diversity to the colonies. Clarify that European immigrants were not confined to the North; for example, many of the Scots-Irish, instead of settling in western Pennsylvania, headed further south into Appalachia; and quite a few Scots fleeing the Jacobite rebellions settled in North Carolina. Point out that some French and Spanish immigrants also came to North America around this time but usually settled in French and Spanish colonies elsewhere on the continent.

Making Connections Across Time

Urban Light and Blight Have students compare and contrast the benefits and drawbacks of city life in colonial times with those of urban life today. They might list the colonial benefits and drawbacks mentioned or implied here—bustling commerce, cultural diversity, fuel shortages, problems with the water supply, poor sanitation, and so on—and then consider whether these same qualities manifest themselves in cities today. What generalizations, if any, do students feel they can make about urban life?

The Germans and the Scots-Irish were the largest non-English European immigrant groups. Germans began arriving in Pennsylvania in the 1680s. Most were fleeing economic devastation that was the legacy of a long war earlier in the century. However, some German religious sects, such as the Mennonites, came to Pennsylvania because of William Penn's policy of religious freedom and because they shared the Quakers' opposition to war.

The Scots-Irish—descendants of Scottish Protestants who had colonized northern Ireland in the 1500s and early 1600s—entered mostly through Philadelphia. They commonly came as families, rather than as single males. Many established farms in frontier areas such as western Pennsylvania, where they often clashed with Native Americans.

Other ethnic groups included the Dutch in New York, Scandinavians in Delaware, and Jews in such cities as Newport and Philadelphia. The different groups did not always get along well. Benjamin Franklin, echoing the sentiments of many English colonists, made the following complaint in 1751:

A PERSONAL VOICE

Why should the [Germans] be suffered to swarm into our Settlements, and, by herding together, establish their Language and Manners to the Exclusion of ours? Why should Pennsylvania, founded by the English, become a Colony of *Aliens,* who will shortly be so numerous as to Germanize us instead of our Anglifying them?

BENJAMIN FRANKLIN, "Observations Concerning the Increase of Mankind"

THINK THROUGH HISTORY
B. Recognizing Effects
What were the negative and positive effects of the growing ethnic diversity in the colonies?

B. Answer One negative effect was conflict and distrust between the different groups. One positive effect was that the wide variety of peoples created an eclectic and diverse society.

The English colonists were not the only ones to view other groups with suspicion. A German clergyman urged the young people of his community not to marry Scots-Irish, charging they were "lazy, dissipated [immoral], and poor." However, in spite of this distrust, immigrants from many countries lived side by side, thus furthering the evolution of a truly diverse American society.

SLAVERY IN THE NORTH Because raising wheat and corn did not require as much labor as tobacco and rice, Northerners had less incentive to turn to slavery than did Southerners. However, slavery did exist in New England and was extensive throughout the Middle colonies, as were racial prejudices against blacks—free or enslaved.

While still considered property, most slaves in New England enjoyed greater legal standing than slaves elsewhere in the colonies. They could sue and be sued, and they had the right of appeal to the highest colonial courts. Unlike slaves in the plantation colonies—who could testify only against each other—New England slaves also could offer testimony against white persons in cases not involving Africans.

As in the South, however, slaves in the North led harsh lives and were considered less than human beings. Laws forbade them to gather together or to carry weapons, and there were no laws to protect them from cruel treatment. Reacting to the harsh conditions, slaves sometimes rebelled. A slave uprising occurred in 1712 in New York, leading to the execution of 21 slaves. In 1741, a series of suspicious fires and robberies led New Yorkers to fear another uprising. They decided to make an example of the suspected ringleaders, burning 14 slaves alive and hanging 18—even though the main witness to the alleged conspiracy was a known liar.

WOMEN IN NORTHERN SOCIETY As in the South, women in the North had extensive work responsibilities but few legal rights. Most people in the colonies still lived on farms, and farm women faced unceasing labor: weaving cloth; sewing clothes; tending the garden and livestock; baking and pre-

QUAKER WOMEN

Because Quakers believed that the divine spirit lives in every human being, they rejected a church structure that gave one group special privileges at the expense of another. One of the most extraordinary applications of their belief in equality was the role they allowed women. In contrast to Puritans and other Protestants, Quakers allowed women to speak out in church meetings (as in the painting below) and to participate in making important church decisions.

MORE ABOUT . . .
The Pennsylvania Dutch

The Quaker William Penn invited many other persecuted religious sects to his colony, including the Amish, Schwenkenfelders, Dunkards, Moravians, and Mennonites. Most of these groups came from the Rhineland region of what is now Germany, but English speakers called them *Pennsylvania Dutch,* in part because of confusion with *Deutsch,* the German word for German.

MORE ABOUT . . .
Slavery in the North

Because the North had fewer slaves and its economy was less dependent on them, laws governing slaveholding did not evolve to the degree that they did in the South. Thus, while slavery in the North could be as brutal as in the South, it was less widespread. In those areas in the North where male slaves could hire themselves out for wages, it was not unknown for a slave to earn enough cash to purchase his own and his family's freedom.

HISTORICAL SPOTLIGHT
Quaker Women

Have students research Quaker life, focusing on women in particular, and compare and contrast Quaker women's lives with those of women today.

ELECTRONIC LIBRARY OF PRIMARY SOURCES
A Letter Regarding Relations with the Indians by Samuel Sewall

HUMANITIES TRANSPARENCIES
H4, A Woman's Work

TEACHING OPTIONS

Teaching Less Proficient Readers

Formal and Archaic Language Pair less proficient readers with other students to help them decipher the somewhat formal and archaic language (i. e., "Why should the [Germans] be suffered to swarm into our Settlements . . .") in the remarks by John Adams, Benjamin Franklin, and Jonathan Edwards that appear in this section, pp. 77–82. Ask students to work together, using a dictionary if necessary, to create more modern versions of the remarks. You might point out that the Hamilton cited here (p. 78) is not the Alexander Hamilton who won fame during and just after the Revolution.

Making Connections Across Time

Resenting Newcomers Encourage students to discuss more recent examples of attitudes similar to those expressed in the quotation from Benjamin Franklin. Point out that Franklin himself was a generally open-minded individual (an early critic of slavery, for example) who at one time even printed a German-language newspaper. Then have students think about and discuss ways to recognize and diffuse cultural conflicts.

The Witchcraft Trials

The Salem trials came at the end of a violent era of religious factionalism and zealotry. What some call ".the witchcraft mania" already had a long history in Europe, with 500,000 people, mainly women, being burned or hanged as witches during the Renaissance.

 GROLIER MULTIMEDIA ENCYCLOPEDIA
Salem Witch Trials

IN-DEPTH RESOURCES: UNIT 1
Primary Sources: *from* The Salem Witch Trials, p. 48

NOW & THEN
Salem Memorial

Invite students to discuss examples in recent decades of hearings that some have called witch-hunts, such as the Army-McCarthy hearings. Ask what people mean by a political witch-hunt.
Possible Responses: Charges false or unfair; accusers really out to get someone whose views differ.

The Colonists Consider New Ideas

▶ *Discussing Key Ideas*
* The Enlightenment stresses the use of reason and the scientific method.
* The Great Awakening stirs people to rededicate themselves to God.
* Though the movements have opposing world views, both stress individualism and the questioning of authority.

---

serving food; and making such necessities as soap and candles. Whether she lived on a farm or in town, a colonial wife had virtually no legal rights. She could not vote, enter into contracts, buy or sell property, or keep her own wages if she worked outside the home. Only single women and widows could run their own businesses. If a husband died, his widow often moved to a city, hoping to support her family by working as a nurse, teacher, laundress, seamstress, or servant. If she was lucky enough to have a little money, she might open a shop, inn, or boardinghouse.

In New England, religion as well as law served to keep women under their husbands' rule. Puritan clergymen emphasized that wives were to submit to their husbands, saying, "Wives are part of the House and Family, and ought to be under a Husband's Government: they should Obey their own Husbands."

WITCHCRAFT TRIALS IN SALEM The strict limitations on women's roles, as well as the tensions produced by uneven economic growth, and the strained relations with the Native Americans, and misdirected religious zeal, contributed to one of the most bizarre episodes in American history. In April 1692, several Salem girls accused an African slave woman, Tituba, of practicing witchcraft, or strange magic. In this Puritan New England town, where the constant fear of Native American attacks prompted a preoccupation with violence and death, the girls received a great deal of attention for their accusations. When the girls went on to accuse others of witchcraft, the episode snowballed.

Those who were unjustly accused tried to save themselves by naming other "witches." Hysteria gripped the town as more and more people made false accusations. The resulting trials led to the convictions and executions of several innocent people.

The accusations fell into two significant patterns that highlighted class and social and religious values in conflict. First, Salem had recently undergone economic growth that benefited the town's residents unequally. Many of the accusers lived in the poorer half of town and brought charges against those who lived in the more prosperous area. Second, a high proportion of victims were women who might be considered too independent—either because they stood to inherit property or because they had violated such Puritan standards of behavior as attending church regularly.

The accusations continued until the girls dared to charge such prominent citizens as the governor's wife. Finally realizing that they had been hearing false evidence, the court officials closed the court. The witchcraft hysteria ended—but not before 19 persons had been hanged and another person killed by being crushed to death. In addition, four "witches" died in jail, and about 150 spent time in prison.

SALEM MEMORIAL

The 20 people executed for witchcraft in Salem were denied Christian funerals and thrown into mass graves. In 1992, 300 years later, the city of Salem tried to make amends by erecting a memorial in their honor. The memorial is a rectangular park, enclosed by a rough stone wall. Sticking out from the wall are 20 stone slab benches, each inscribed with one of the victim's names and date of death. Planted in the park are six black locust trees, the species from which the victims were supposedly hanged. In addition, the victims' own statements of innocence are inscribed into the stone threshold to the park.

THINK THROUGH HISTORY
C. Analyzing Causes *What conflicts lay behind the Salem witch hunts in 1692?*

C. Answer A preoccupation with violence and death brought on by fear of Native American attacks, as well as the class, social, and religious tensions that existed in the town.

The Colonists Consider New Ideas

The Salem trials of 1692 caused many people to question the existence of witchcraft. During the 1700s, individuals began to make other changes in the way they viewed the world. Both an intellectual movement—the Enlightenment—and a religious movement—the Great Awakening—led to these changes in thinking throughout the 13 colonies.

THE ENLIGHTENMENT During the Renaissance, philosophers in Europe began to stress the use of reason and the scientific method to obtain knowledge. Scientists began looking beyond religious beliefs and traditional assumptions for answers about how the world worked. In doing so, they increasingly relied on careful observation and reasoning to discover the natural laws and principles governing the world and human behavior. Led by Nicolaus Copernicus, Galileo Galilei, and Sir Isaac Newton, people soon determined that the earth revolved around the sun and not vice versa. They also concluded that the world is gov-

---

 Cooperative Activity: Debating Theories About Salem

Task: Students will research different explanations about the Salem witchcraft episode and then discuss them in position papers and an informal debate.

Purpose: To help students recognize that there may be multiple explanations for historic events.

Activity: In researching the Salem episode, different students should focus on the different explanations sometimes offered—economic

and social jealousies, political change in Massachusetts, fear of Native Americans, medical hysteria, a history of religious fanaticism, a fungus in the rye grain. They should then argue for one particular explanation as the main cause of the episode.

📁 **Building a Portfolio:** Students might place their position papers in their portfolios.

ALTERNATIVE ASSESSMENT BOOK
Standards for Evaluating a Cooperative Activity

Standards for Evaluation
Position papers and debate arguments should . . .

* include a clear statement of the person's position
* use quotations, statistics, and other factual details to support that statement
* be clear and well organized

erned not by chance or miracles, but by fixed mathematical laws. These ideas about nature prevailed in the 1700s in a movement called the **Enlightment.**

Enlightenment ideas traveled from Europe to the colonies. One outstanding Enlightenment figure in the colonies was **Benjamin Franklin.** Franklin eagerly took to the notion of obtaining truth through experimentation and reason. For example, his most famous experiment—flying a kite in a thunderstorm—demonstrated that lightning is a form of electrical power, not a mysterious act of God. Franklin's experiments resulted in several practical inventions, including lightning rods, bifocal glasses, and a stove that heated rooms more efficiently than did earlier models.

Enlightenment ideas spread quickly through the colonies in numerous books and pamphlets. While only one-third of males in England could read, in many colonies, more than 50 percent of white males were literate. Literacy was particularly high in New England because the Puritans had long supported public education to make sure that everyone could read the Bible.

The Enlightenment also had a profound effect on political thought in the colonies. Colonial statesmen such as Thomas Jefferson would use reason to conclude that individuals have natural rights, which governments must respect. Enlightenment principles eventually would lead many colonists to question the authority of the British monarchy.

THE GREAT AWAKENING While the Enlightenment prompted many to explore new scientific theories, other colonists wanted to revive the doctrines of their Puritan ancestors. By the early 1700s, the Puritan church had lost influence. The new Massachusetts charter of 1691 forced Puritans to allow freedom of worship and banned the practice of permitting only Puritan church members to vote.

Furthermore, as Puritan merchants prospered, they developed a taste for fine houses, stylish clothes, and good food and wine. Their interest in maintaining the strict Puritan code declined. Material comfort was accompanied in the early 1700s by a decline in church membership. Many people seemed to be doing so well in this world that they paid little attention to the next.

Jonathan Edwards, of Northampton, Massachusetts, was one member of the clergy who sought to revive the intensity and dedication of the original Puritan vision. Edwards preached that church attendance was not enough for salvation; people must feel their sinfulness and feel God's love for them. In his

THINK THROUGH HISTORY
D. Recognizing Effects What effect did the Enlightenment have on political thought in the colonies?

D. Answer Colonists used reason to conclude that individuals have natural rights, which governments must respect; colonists began questioning the authority of British monarchy.

KEY PLAYERS

BENJAMIN FRANKLIN
1706–1790
A true student of the Enlightenment, Benjamin Franklin thought he could use human reason and an orderly method to make himself perfect. In his autobiography, he records how he decided on a list of 13 virtues he thought he should have. Then, every night, he reviewed whether his behavior lived up to those standards and recorded his faults in a notebook.

According to Franklin, he took great pleasure in seeing his character improve. Originally, he concentrated on only 12 virtues until a Quaker friend told him he was too proud. Franklin promptly added a 13th virtue to the list—the virtue of humility, which he never achieved.

JONATHAN EDWARDS
1703–1758
Descended from a long line of Puritan ministers, Jonathan Edwards denied that humans had the power to perfect themselves. He believed that "however you may have reformed your life in many things," all were sinners who were destined for hell unless they had a "great change of heart."

Edwards was a brilliant thinker who entered Yale College when he was only 13. His preaching was one of the driving forces of the Great Awakening. Ironically, when the religious revival died down, Edwards's own congregation rejected him for being too strict about doctrine. Edwards moved to Stockbridge, Massachusetts, in 1751, where he lived his remaining years as missionary to a Native American settlement.

MORE ABOUT . . .
The Enlightenment
A major idea from the Elightenment was that a social contract existed between a government and those it governed. This meant that those who were governed gave their consent to be governed in return for certain benefits. They also had the right to change a government that did not meet its side of the contract. This idea was made widespread by English philosopher John Locke, whose work was read by Virginia's Thomas Jefferson, a noted Enlightenment thinker and chief author of the Declaration of Independence.

KEY PLAYERS
Franklin and Edwards
Critical Thinking: Compare and Contrast
Have students compare and contrast Franklin's and Edwards's ideas, particularly the two men's views of the individual and of destiny. A Venn diagram may be helpful in making this comparison.

Franklin's Ideas

Shared Ideas

Edwards's Ideas

IN-DEPTH RESOURCES: UNIT 1
Primary Sources: from *The Autobiography of Benjamin Franklin,* p. 49; from *The New England Primer,* p. 50

The Colonies Come of Age **81**

TEACHING OPTIONS

Exploring Themes

Science and Technology Stress that the Enlightenment that spread from Europe to the Americas brought with it an optimistic belief in science and reason that prompted a general spirit of inquiry and invention as well as an openness to new ideas. Point out that electricity was still a new and mysterious idea when Franklin conducted his famed experiments, which duplicated and expanded the work being done in France and England at the time. Franklin himself coined or popularized several of the terms used in the study of electricity—*conductor, battery, positive,* and *negative,* for example.

Making Connections Across the Curriculum

Literature Note that both Franklin's autobiography and Edwards's sermon are American literary landmarks. The autobiography is viewed as a pioneering expression of the recurring American theme of self-reliance; the sermon is noted for its powerful, poetic style.

Have students identify and evaluate the central metaphor in the passage from Edwards's sermon cited in A Personal Voice on page 82. Central metaphor: *God holding a person over Hell compared to a person holding a spider or another "loathsome insect" over the fire. Evaluations will vary.*

Teacher's Edition **81**

George Whitefield

Whitefield's tremendous success as a preacher can be attributed in part to his acting ability. In his sermons he would first play the role of God and then switch to the role of the devil. "What a spell he casts over an audience," said Jonathan Edwards's wife, "by proclaiming the simplest of truths of the Bible. I have seen upwards of a thousand people hang on his words with breathless silence, broken only by an occasional half-suppressed sob."

 ELECTRONIC LIBRARY OF PRIMARY SOURCES

from *Sinners in the Hands of an Angry God* by Jonathan Edwards

---

ASSESS & RETEACH

Section 3 Assessment

Have students work in small groups to discuss the questions and assess one another's responses.

Self-Assessment

Have students create a two-column chart on which they compare their own responses (column 1) with the portions of the text that best answer each question (column 2).

Section Quiz

FORMAL ASSESSMENT
Section Quiz, p. 32

Reteach

Use the circle graphs on page 78 and the other features to help review the main ideas of this section.

CLOSE

The North had a more diverse economy and population than the South. Both the Enlightenment and the Great Awakening fostered individualism and prompted colonists to question authority.

The Anglican minister George Whitefield was a major force behind the Great Awakening. Arriving in the North American colonies from England in the mid 1740s, Whitefield preached dramatic sermons that brought many listeners to tears.

most famous sermon, given in 1741, Edwards vividly described God's mercy toward sinners:

> **A PERSONAL VOICE**
> The God that holds you over the pit of Hell, much as one holds a spider or other loathsome insect over the fire, abhors [hates] you, and is dreadfully provoked; his wrath toward you burns like fire; he looks upon you as worthy of nothing, but to be cast into the fire . . . and yet 'tis nothing but his hand that holds you from falling into the fire every moment.
> **JONATHAN EDWARDS**, from "Sinners in the Hands of an Angry God"

Other preachers traveled from village to village, stirring people to rededicate themselves to God. For example, George Whitefield, an English minister, acted out his sermons. These traveling preachers attracted thousands, making it necessary for revival meetings to be held outdoors. The resulting religious revival, known as the **Great Awakening,** lasted throughout the 1730s and 1740s.

The Great Awakening brought many colonists, as well as Native Americans and African Americans, into organized Christian churches for the first time. As the movement gained momentum, it also challenged the authority of established churches. Some colonists abandoned their old Puritan or Anglican congregation, refusing even to pay the taxes that supported the community's established church. At the same time, independent denominations such as Baptist and Methodist gained new members. The Great Awakening also led to an increased interest in higher education, as several Protestant denominations founded colleges such as Princeton, Brown, Columbia, and Dartmouth to train ministers for their rapidly growing churches.

While the Great Awakening and the Enlightenment emphasized opposing ideas—emotionalism versus reason—they shared a similar result. Both caused people to question traditional authority. Moreover, both stressed the importance of the individual—the Enlightenment by emphasizing human reason and the Great Awakening by de-emphasizing the role of church authority.

These movements were two of the many factors that eventually led the colonists to question Britain's authority over their lives. This gradual separation between Britain and the colonies was further hastened by another significant event, a North American war between Great Britain and France in which the colonists fought on Britain's side.

E. Answer It made Christianity more diverse ethnically and racially, and it strengthened new denominations and weakened old ones.

THINK THROUGH HISTORY
E. Recognizing Effects What effects did the Great Awakening have on organized religion in the colonies?

Section ③ Assessment

1. TERMS & NAMES

Identify:
• Enlightenment
• Benjamin Franklin
• Jonathan Edwards
• Great Awakening

2. SUMMARIZING Recreate the tree diagram below on your paper and fill it in with historical examples that illustrate the main idea in the top box.

The Diversity of Northern Colonies		
Economy	Population	Religious Groups
examples	examples	examples

Name the advantages and disadvantages this kind of society might have.

3. ANALYZING How do you think a person who believed in the ideas of the Enlightenment might have assessed the Salem witchcraft trials? Support your response with reasons.

THINK ABOUT
• the kinds of evidence presented at the trials
• the hysteria that gripped the town
• Enlightenment ideas of careful observation and reasoning

4. APPLYING What positive and negative trends do you think emerged in the northern colonies during the 1700s that still affect the United States today? Support your responses with details from the text.

THINK ABOUT
• the rise of cities
• the influx of immigrants
• the status of women and African Americans
• the results of the Enlightenment and the Great Awakening

82 CHAPTER 3

ANSWERS

1. TERMS AND NAMES

Enlightenment, p. 80

Benjamin Franklin, p. 81

Jonathan Edwards, p. 81

Great Awakening, p. 82

2. SUMMARIZING

Possible Responses:
Economy—several cash crops; fisheries, mills, manufacturing.

Population—English, Germans, Scots-Irish, and other immigrant groups; African slaves.

Religious Groups: Anglicans, Roman Catholics, Quakers, Methodists, other Protestant denominations, Jews.

3. ANALYZING

Possible Responses: The Salem witchcraft trials reveal what can happen when superstition and emotions rather than reason dominate people's perceptions and thinking. In reaching their verdicts, court officials allowed intense emotions to cloud the issues, did not separate fact from opinion, and believed accusations that were not supported by evidence.

4. APPLYING

Possible Responses: Positive trends might include immigration as beneficial; the value of education, the spirit of scientific inquiry, belief in individual rights that government must respect, religious diversity. Negative trends might include urban problems, such as poverty and overcrowding; racial, ethnic, and gender bias; mistrust of immigrants; violence against minorities.

The French and Indian War

TERMS & NAMES
• George Washington
• French and Indian War
• William Pitt
• Pontiac
• Proclamation of 1763
• George Grenville
• Sugar Act

LEARN ABOUT the British victory over France in North America
TO UNDERSTAND the growing tensions between Great Britain and its colonies.

Section 4 Overview

OBJECTIVES

1 To summarize the French-British colonial rivalry.

2 To summarize the French and Indian War.

3 To explain the war's effects on the relationship between Britain and its colonies.

ONE AMERICAN'S STORY

Joseph Nichols and other Massachusetts men joined British soldiers in fighting the French near the Hudson River in 1758. Yet even though the colonists and British had banded together against a common enemy, the two groups held conflicting ideas about authority. On October 31, 1758, Nichols recorded the following dispute.

> **A PERSONAL VOICE**
> About sunrise, the chief officer of the fort came to our regiment and ordered all our men up to the falls to meet the wagons and teams. Our men seemed to be loath to go before they eat. Those that refused to turn out, he drove out, and some he struck with his staff, which caused a great uproar among us. Our people in general declare in case we are so used tomorrow, blows shall end the dispute.
>
> **JOSEPH NICHOLS,** quoted in *A People's Army*

This "uproar" demonstrates that although the British and their colonists shared certain goals—such as driving the French from North America—they differed in their views about proper authority and individual freedom. During the war between Great Britain and France for a North American empire, these conflicting viewpoints triggered divisions between Great Britain and its colonies that would never heal.

In the French and Indian War, the colonists and the British fought side by side for seven years. In this scene, British General Edward Braddock meets his defeat and death on his march to Fort Duquesne in July of 1755.

SKILLBUILDERS

• Understanding geography: region, p. 85
• Interpreting charts, p. 87

CRITICAL THINKING

• Contrasting, p. 84
• Recognizing effects, p. 86
• Analyzing causes, p. 87
• Summarizing, p. 87
• Making decisions, p. 87
• Hypothesizing, p. 87

FOCUS & MOTIVATE

▶ *Starting with the Student*
• Have you ever experienced that your friendship with one person caused a rift with another?
• Could a similar situation occur between nations? Explain your answer.

Rivals for an Empire

Why did the British and their colonists want to force France out of North America? In the 1750s, France was Great Britain's biggest rival in the struggle to build a world empire, and one major area of contention between them was the rich Ohio River valley just west of Pennsylvania and Virginia. The colonists wanted Great Britain to prevail in the region because they were eager to expand the colonies westward from the increasingly crowded Atlantic seaboard.

FRANCE'S NORTH AMERICAN EMPIRE The conflict between the French and British colonies began long before the 1750s. From the start, New France, the French colony in North America, was quite different from the British colonies. France had begun its North American empire in 1534 when Jacques Cartier explored the St. Lawrence River. In 1608, explorer Samuel Champlain founded Quebec City, the first permanent French settlement in North America.

After establishing Quebec, the French penetrated the heart of the North American continent. French priest Jacques Marquette and trader Louis Joliet explored the Great Lakes and the upper Mississippi River. Sieur Robert Cavelier de La Salle explored the lower Mississippi in 1682 and claimed the entire river valley for France, naming it Louisiana in honor of the French king, Louis XIV.

The Colonies Come of Age **83**

OBJECTIVE

1 INSTRUCT

Rivals for an Empire

As students read, they may find it helpful to create a chart of French explorers and their explorations.

▶ *Discussing Key Ideas*
• France's colonial claims in Canada and America are based on the efforts of several explorers.
• Rivalries smolder between the French and English colonies.
• The French focus less on settlement and more on economic exploitation.

IN-DEPTH RESOURCES: UNIT 1
Guided Reading, p. 43

ACCESS FOR STUDENTS ACQUIRING ENGLISH
Guided Reading (Spanish), p. 33

SECTION 4 RESOURCES

PRINT RESOURCES

IN-DEPTH RESOURCES: UNIT 1
Guided Reading, p. 43

ACCESS FOR STUDENTS ACQUIRING ENGLISH
Guided Reading (Spanish), p. 33

FORMAL ASSESSMENT
Section Quiz, p. 33

ALTERNATIVE ASSESSMENT BOOK
See forms for supporting and scoring alternative activities.

TECHNOLOGY RESOURCES

CRITICAL THINKING TRANSPARENCIES
CT3, French and Indian War

VIDEO *American Portfolio: A Videodisc for U.S. History*
user's guide, pp. 27, 28, 32

INTERNET McDougal Littell Learning On-Line
http://www.mcdougallittell.com

Britain Defeats an Old Enemy

▶ **Discussing Key Ideas**

• The French and Indian War is a British-French war for control of America.

• Early British losses in the war lessen colonial respect for the British army.

• Britain gains control of Canada and most of North America east of the Mississippi.

• The Proclamation of 1763, forbidding settlers west of the Appalachians, stirs colonial resentment.

 CRITICAL THINKING TRANSPARENCIES
CT3, French and Indian War

MORE ABOUT . . .
The Fur Trade

Fashionable top hats made from beaver skins were extremely popular in Europe beginning in the late 16th century. Because of this demand for beaver, the fur trade proved enormously successful for all involved until the fur supply began to decrease and silk hats replaced beaver hats as the fashion in Europe.

HISTORICAL SPOTLIGHT
Washington's Resignation

Critical Thinking:
Speculating Have students speculate about why Washington's commission was reduced. *Possible Responses: He had surrendered; to reduce growing military costs; British contempt for colonial military.*

French explorer
Jacques Cartier

However, by 1760 the European population of New France had grown to only about 80,000 (compared to more than a million in the British colonies). A large number of French colonists had no desire to build towns or raise families; these included young single men who engaged in the fur trade and Catholic priests who wanted to convert Native Americans.

The French were not so much interested in occupying the territories they claimed as in exploiting them economically. By the late 1500s, one of the big fashion trends in Europe was hats made of beaver skin. Beavers were almost extinct in Europe but were plentiful in North America, leading to a thriving trade in furs. Hurons, Ottawas, Ojibwas, and other Native Americans did most of the trapping and then traded the furs to the French for such items as guns, hatchets, blankets, mirrors, and beads.

Because they needed Native Americans as economic partners, the French developed good relations with them. Out of the French-Native American trade relations developed several military alliances. As early as 1609, for example, the Hurons and other Native American bands used Champlain's help to defeat one of their traditional enemies, the Mohawk Iroquois.

Britain Defeats an Old Enemy

As the French empire in North America expanded, it collided with the growing British empire. Before the conflict in which Joseph Nichols took part, France and Great Britain had already fought three separate and indecisive wars in the previous half-century. Each of these wars began in Europe but spread to their colonies around the world, including battles in North America. In 1754, after six relatively peaceful years, the French-British conflict reignited. In that year, the French built Fort Duquesne at the place where the Allegheny and Monongahela rivers join to form the Ohio. But the Virginia government had granted 200,000 acres of land in the Ohio country to a group of wealthy planters, so the Virginia governor sent a group of militiamen to order the French to leave.

The small band, led by an ambitious 22-year-old named **George Washington,** established an outpost about 60 miles from Fort Duquesne called Fort Necessity. After Washington's militia attacked a small detachment of French soldiers and took some prisoners, the French swiftly counterattacked. In the battle that followed in July 1754, the French inflicted such heavy losses on the outnumbered Virginians that Washington was forced to surrender. Although neither side realized it, this small battle at Fort Necessity was the opening of the **French and Indian War,** the fourth war between Great Britain and France for control of North America.

EARLY FRENCH VICTORIES A year after his defeat, Washington again headed west from Virginia, this time as an aide to British general Edward Braddock, whose mission was to drive the French out of the Ohio Valley.

Braddock's first task was to relaunch an attack on Fort Duquesne, located where Pittsburgh now stands. As Braddock and nearly 1,500 soldiers neared the fort, French soldiers and their Native American allies ambushed them. The British soldiers—accustomed to enemies who marched in straight rows rather than fighting from behind trees—turned and fled.

The cowardice of the supposedly invincible British army surprised Washington, who himself showed incredible courage. As he tried to rally the troops, two horses were shot from under him and four bullets

---

HISTORICAL SPOTLIGHT

WASHINGTON'S RESIGNATION

George Washington's military career nearly ended shortly after it started. In 1754, as the British prepared to wage war on France in North America, Washington eagerly awaited a position with the regular British army.

In reassembling his army to become part of a British regiment, the commander of the Virginia militia offered Washington the rank of captain—a demotion from his position as colonel. Washington angrily rejected the offer as well as a late proposal that he retain the rank of colonel but have the authority and pay of a captain. "If you think me capable of holding a commission that has neither rank nor emolument [pay] annexed to it," Washington declared to a friend before resigning, "you must entertain a very contemptible opinion of my weakness, and believe me more empty than the commission itself."

The young Virginian's patriotism, however, was too strong. He swallowed his pride and relaunched his military career as a volunteer aide to General Braddock in the spring of 1755.

TRACING MAIN IDEAS
A. *Contrasting*
How was the French empire in North America unlike the British empire?

A. Answer France focused on the fur trade rather than on settlement and sent out Roman Catholic missionaries, who tried to convert Native Americans more than the English Protestants did.

Making Connections Across Cultures

French Americans Note that beginning in the 16th century small groups of Huguenots, or French Protestants, came to the New World to escape religious persecution. After the English acquired Acadia (Nova Scotia and nearby areas, including New Brunswick and part of Quebec and Maine), many French settlers fled or were deported from the region. Those who resettled in the French territory of Louisiana became known as Cajuns, a corruption of *Acadians,* while French settlers who came directly to Louisiana were called Creoles. When the U.S. purchased Louisiana in 1803, these French Americans too became part of the American mosaic.

Teaching Gifted and Talented Students

Tracing Changing Developments Interested students might work with a partner to research and report on the complexity of French-British relations in Canada from about 1700. Final reports might take the form of two annotated fictional family trees, one for a family of French background and another for a family of British background, in which family members across the centuries make remarks about the current British-French situation. Encourage volunteers to give oral readings of their final efforts.

pierced his coat—although he escaped unharmed. He wrote to his mother that "the Virginia troops showed a good deal of bravery, and were near all killed . . . [but the British soldiers] broke and ran as sheep pursued by dogs and it was impossible to rally them." Many other colonists besides Washington began to question the ability of the British army, which suffered defeat after defeat during 1755 and 1756.

PITT AND THE IROQUOIS TURN THE TIDE   Angered by French victories, Britain's King George II selected new leaders to run his government in 1757. One of these was **William Pitt,** an energetic, self-confident young politician. "I know," he boasted, "that I can save this country and no one else can." Borrowing money heavily, Pitt planned to assemble the largest, best-equipped army ever seen in North America—nearly 50,000 soldiers.

Under Pitt, the reinvigorated British army finally began winning battles, which prompted the powerful Iroquois to agree to support them. This agreement gave Britain some Native American allies to balance those of France.

In September 1759, the war took a dramatic and decisive turn on the Plains of Abraham just outside Quebec. Under the cover of night, British troops under General James Wolfe approached Quebec by scaling the high cliffs that protected the city. Catching the French and their commander, the Marquis de Montcalm, by surprise, they fought and won a short but deadly battle. The British triumph at Quebec gave them victory in the war.

The war officially ended in 1763 with the Treaty of Paris. Great Britain claimed Canada and virtually all of North America east of the Mississippi River. This included Florida, which Britain took over from Spain, an ally of France. The treaty permitted Spain to keep possession of lands west of the Mississippi and the city of New Orleans that it had gained from France in 1762. France kept control of only a few small islands near Newfoundland and in the West Indies. The other losers in the war were Native Americans, who found the victorious British harder to bargain with than the French had been.

GEOGRAPHY SKILLBUILDER
Although the British gained a huge territory, they attempted to limit colonial settlement with the Proclamation Line of 1763.
REGION *What happened to France's possessions between 1754 and 1763?*

European Claims in North America, 1754–1763

In 1754

- British territory
- French territory
- Spanish territory
- Disputed territory

Quebec

Hudson Bay

Great Lakes

St. Lawrence River

Mississippi River

ATLANTIC OCEAN

FLORIDA

New Orleans

SANTO DOMINGO

Gulf of Mexico   Tropic of Cancer

CUBA

JAMAICA

Caribbean Sea

0   500 Miles
0   1,000 Kilometers

After 1763

Québec

Hudson Bay

Great Lakes

Proclamation Line of 1763

St. Lawrence River

Mississippi River

ATLANTIC OCEAN

New Orleans

SANTO DOMINGO

Gulf of Mexico   Tropic of Cancer

CUBA

JAMAICA

PACIFIC OCEAN

VICTORY BRINGS NEW PROBLEMS Ownership of the Ohio River valley brought Great Britain trouble. In particular, Native Americans resented the growing number of British settlers crossing the Appalachian Mountains and feared the settlers would soon drive away the game they depended on for survival. In the spring of 1763, the Ottawa leader **Pontiac** recognized that the French loss was a loss for Native Americans.

> **A PERSONAL VOICE**
> When I go to see the English commander and say to him that some of our comrades are dead, instead of bewailing their death, as our French brothers do, he laughs at me and at you. If I ask for anything for our sick, he refuses with the reply that he has no use for us. For all this you can well see that they are seeking our ruin. Therefore, my brothers, we must all swear their destruction and wait no longer.
>
> **PONTIAC,** quoted in *Red and White*

Many soldiers kept the powder for their muskets in cow horns, on which they often carved their name and decorations.

Led by Pontiac, Native Americans captured eight British forts in the Ohio Valley and laid siege to two others. In angry response, British officers deliberately presented smallpox-infected blankets to two Delaware chiefs during peace negotiations, and the virus spread rapidly among the Native Americans. Weakened by disease and tired of fighting, most Native American groups negotiated treaties with the British by the end of 1765.

To avoid further costly conflicts with Native Americans, the British government banned all settlement west of the Appalachian Mountains. This ban, called the **Proclamation of 1763,** established a Proclamation Line along the Appalachians, which the colonists could not cross. (See the map on page 85.) The ban angered colonists, who were eager to expand westward. Ironically, the ban actually undermined British authority. The British could not enforce the Proclamation of 1763 any more effectively than they could enforce the Navigation Acts, and colonists continued to move onto Native American lands.

The Colonies and Britain Grow Apart

Because the Proclamation of 1763 sought to halt expansion, it convinced the colonists that the British government did not care about their needs. A second result of the French and Indian War—Britain's financial crisis—brought about new laws that reinforced the colonists' opinion even more.

PROBLEMS RESULTING FROM THE WAR After the war, the British government stationed 10,000 troops in its newly acquired territories to keep the Native Americans and former French subjects under control. Although the British government saw this army as protection for the colonies, the colonists themselves did not see it that way. They viewed the troops as a standing army that might turn against them if they exercised too much liberty.

Maintaining the troops in North America added an annual expense of 400,000 pounds to an already strained British budget. Britain had borrowed so much money during the war that it nearly doubled its national debt, from 72 million pounds to more than 132 million. Hoping to lower the debt, King George III, who had succeeded his grandfather in 1760, chose a financial expert, **George Grenville,** to serve as prime minister in 1763.

GRENVILLE ANGERS COLONISTS By the time Grenville took over, tensions between Britain and one colony, Massachusetts, were on the rise. During the French and Indian War, the British had cracked down on colonial smuggling to ensure that merchants were not doing business in any French-held territories. In 1760, the royal governor of Massachusetts authorized the use of the writs of assistance, a general search warrant that allowed British customs officials to search any colonial ship or building they believed to be holding smuggled

"They that give up essential liberty to obtain a little temporary safety deserve neither liberty nor safety."

BENJAMIN FRANKLIN

---

goods. Because many merchants worked out of their residences, the writs enabled British officials to enter and search colonial homes whether there was evidence of smuggling or not. The merchants of Boston were outraged.

Grenville's actions, however, soon angered merchants throughout the colonies. The new prime minister noticed that the American customs service, which collected duties, or taxes on imports, collected only 2,000 pounds a year and was losing money. Grenville concluded that the colonists were smuggling goods into the country without paying duties. In 1764 he decided to enact a law known as the **Sugar Act.**

The Sugar Act did three things. It halved the duty on foreign-made molasses (in the hopes that colonists would pay a lower tax rather than risk arrest by smuggling). It placed duties on certain imports that had not been taxed before. Most important, it strengthened the enforcement of the law by establishing a new court, called a vice-admiralty court, in Halifax, Nova Scotia. Prosecutors could charge accused smugglers there, where a single judge, rather than a jury of sympathetic colonists, would decide the case. Admiralty judges received 5 percent of any cargo the courts confiscated from convicted smugglers, so they had a strong motive for finding accused persons guilty.

Colonial merchants complained that the Sugar Act would reduce their profits, and many charged that the British government was violating their rights. Merchants and traders claimed that Parliament had no right to tax the colonists because the colonists had elected no representatives to the body. The new regulations, however, had little effect on colonists outside the world of merchants and traders. Many colonists grumbled but did not seriously protest the new measures.

THINK THROUGH HISTORY
C. Analyzing Causes What were the economic causes of tension between the colonists and Britain?

C. Answer Sugar Act duties, which reduced colonial merchants' profits; crackdown on smuggling

TWO VIEWS COLLIDE By the end of 1764, the colonies and Great Britain were disagreeing more and more about how the colonies should be taxed and governed. During the French and Indian War, colonists lost much of their respect for the British army. They learned it was not invincible and that British officers treated their soldiers "little better than slaves," as one colonist put it. After the war, colonists fumed as Britain installed a standing army on their frontier and passed measures that violated long-standing rights of British citizens. While most colonists still considered themselves loyal subjects of the king, they grew increasingly dissatisfied with the way Parliament governed them. These feelings of dissatisfaction soon would swell into outright rebellion.

Tension Between Britain and the Colonies

CAUSE	EFFECT
British station troops along the colonies' western borders to control Native Americans.	Colonists view the troops as a threat to their own activities and desire for liberty.
Britain establishes Proclamation Line to contain colonial expansion westward.	Proclamation Line angers colonists, who ignore the boundary and continue moving westward.
British Parliament imposes greater taxes on the colonists to help pay for the massive war debt.	Many colonial merchants protest the increased duties as taxation without representation.

SKILLBUILDER
INTERPRETING CHARTS
What three actions of the British offended the colonists?

Section 4 Assessment

1. TERMS & NAMES

Identify:
• George Washington
• French and Indian War
• William Pitt
• Pontiac
• Proclamation of 1763
• George Grenville
• Sugar Act

2. SUMMARIZING Create a time line of the major events relating to the French and Indian War and its aftermath. Use the dates already plotted on the time line below as a guide.

How long was the war? Why do you think it lasted so long?

3. MAKING DECISIONS If you were an eastern Native American living during the French and Indian War, would you form a military alliance with France or Great Britain? Support your choice with reasons.

THINK ABOUT
• Native Americans' past relations with France and Britain
• goals of France versus Britain in North America
• what Native Americans might gain or lose depending on who wins the war

4. HYPOTHESIZING What if the outcome of the war had been different and France had won? How might this have affected the 13 colonies?

THINK ABOUT
• the actual outcome of the Peace of Paris
• France's patterns of colonization
• France's relations with Native Americans

The Colonies Come of Age **87**

ANSWERS

1. TERMS AND NAMES
George Washington, p. 84
French and Indian War, p. 84
William Pitt, p. 85
Pontiac, p. 86
Proclamation of 1763, p. 86
George Grenville, p. 86
Sugar Act, p. 87

2. SUMMARIZING
Possible Responses:
1754—Outbreak of French and Indian War
1759—British triumph at Quebec
1763—End of French and Indian War with the Treaty of Paris; colonists' expansion halted with the Proclamation of 1763; Britain's postwar financial crisis; appointment of George Grenville as prime minister
1764—Passage of the Sugar Act

3. MAKING DECISIONS
Possible Responses: Alliance with France: Past relationships between Native Americans and the French were friendly; economic partners in the fur trade and military alliances in the past; French rarely seized land for agricultural settlements. Alliance with Britain: Native Americans impressed because the British were winning battles; by aligning with the winner, Native Americans might avoid Britain's retaliation for their support of France.

4. HYPOTHESIZING
Possible Responses: The colonies might have retained more of their forests and wildlife because French colonists tended not to establish agricultural settlements; the U.S. today might be less densely populated; Native Americans might have had higher status within American society and played a larger role in shaping the history and culture of the nation; French might have become the national language.

OBJECTIVES

1. To compare and contrast the courtship customs of different colonial groups.

2. To summarize marriage statistics among different colonial groups.

FOCUS & MOTIVATE

▶ **Starting with the Student**
Have students imagine that they are reporting current-day American social customs to foreign readers.

- What would you say about the age at which typical Americans begin dating? About the age at which they marry?
- What specific courtship or dating customs would you mention?

MORE ABOUT . . .
The Puritans

In contrast to Church of England teachings, the Puritans felt marriage should be a civil contract, claiming that nowhere in the Bible was it tied to the ministry. Performed by Governor Bradford, the first Pilgrim marriage was between recent widow Susanna Fuller White and widower Edward Winslow, who went on to become the colony's governor and in that capacity performed marriages himself.

DAILY LIFE
1651–1765

Colonial Courtship

The concept of dating among teenagers was nonexistent in colonial times. Young people were considered either children or adults, and as important as marriage was in the colonies, sweethearts were older than you might suspect. The practices of courtship and marriage varied among the different communities, as you will see in the examples below.

FRONTIER OR BACKCOUNTRY PEOPLE
Andrew Jackson, depicted with his wife in the painting above, "stole" his wife (she was willing) from her first husband. Jackson was following a custom of the backcountry people, who lived along the western edge of the colonies. These colonists, mostly Scots-Irish, based their marriages on the old custom of "abduction"—stealing the bride—often with her consent. Even regular marriages began with the groom and his friends coming to "steal" the bride. Much drinking and dancing accompanied these wild and hilarious weddings.

PURITANS For Puritans, marriage was a civil contract, not a religious or sacred union. Although adults strictly supervised a couple's courting, parents allowed two unusual practices. One was the use of a courting stick, a long tube into which the couple could whisper while the family was in another room. The other was the practice of "bundling": a young man spent the night in the same bed as his sweetheart, with a large bundling board (shown below) between them.
Before marrying, the couple had to allow for Puritan leaders to voice any objections to the marriage at the meeting house. Passing that, the couple would marry in a very simple civil ceremony and share a quiet dinner.

RECOMMENDED RESOURCES

Books

Emrich, Duncan. *The Folklore of Weddings and Marriage.* New York: American Heritage, 1970. An illustrated study of marriage and the marriage ceremony.

Lemay, J. A. Leo. *Robert Bolling Woos Anne Miller.* Charlottesville: UP of Virginia, 1990. Love and courtship in colonial Virginia in 1760.

Longfellow, Henry W. "The Courtship of Miles Standish" in *Evangeline and Selected Tales and Poems.* New York: New American Library, 1964. A Romantic-era narrative poem about a famous colonial-era courtship.

Rothman, Ellen K. *Hands and Hearts.* New York: Basic, 1984. A history of courtship in America.

Videos

Colonial America, 1500–1600. Master Vision, 1982. Colonial customs and traditions.

The Colonial Way of Life. CRM Films. Diverse American colonists create a unified culture.

The Marriage of Pocahontas. Dir. Emma De'ath. Ambrose Video, 1995. A look at a famous marriage and its historical effects.

THE SOUTH Many African slaves married in a "jumping the broomstick" ceremony, in which the bride and groom jumped over a broomstick to seal their union. Although there is disagreement, among African-American scholars, some suggest that the above painting depicts a slave wedding on a South Carolina plantation in the late 1700s.

QUAKERS Quaker couples intent on marrying needed the consent not only of the parents but also of the whole Quaker community. Quakers who wanted to marry had to go through a 16-step courtship phase before they could wed. Quaker women, however, were known to reject men at the last minute.

VIRGINIA In Virginia, marriage was a sacred union. Since the marriage often involved a union of properties, and love was not necessary, parents were heavily involved in the negotiations. In this illustration from a dance manual *(left)*, a young upper-class couple work to improve their social graces by practicing an elaborate dance step.

DATA FILE

Average Age at Marriage in Colonial Times

GROUP	MALES	FEMALES
Puritan	26	23
Virginians	26	19
Quakers		
in Delaware	31	29
in Penn. & N.J.	26	22
Philadelphians	26	23
Frontier People	21	19
Modern Americans	25	24

Who Married in Colonial Times?

PURITANS:

- 98% of males and 94% of females married
- Grooms were usually a few years older than brides
- Only one bachelor in original Puritan community; spinsters called "thornbacks"
- Discouraged marriages between first cousins

VIRGINIANS:

- 25% of males never married; most females married
- Grooms nearly 10 years older than brides
- Allowed first-cousin marriages

QUAKERS:

- 16% of women single at age 50
- forbade first-cousin marriages

FRONTIER PEOPLE:

- Almost all women and most men married
- Ages of bride and groom about the same
- Youngest group to marry

Who Could Divorce in Colonial Times?

Puritans:	Yes
Virginians:	No
Quakers:	No

Source: David Hackett Fischer, Albions Seed

INTERACT WITH HISTORY

1. **COMPARING** What was a common characteristic of courtship among Puritans, Quakers, and Virginians?

    SEE SKILLBUILDER HANDBOOK, PAGE 1041.

2. **COMPARING COURTSHIP NOW AND THEN** Research modern courtship practices by interviewing your parents or relatives. Write a brief paper comparing and contrasting modern-day and colonial courtship practices.

   For more about colonial daily life, click on *Social Studies* at http://www.mcdougallittell.com

The Colonies Come of Age **89**

REVIEWING THE CHAPTER

TERMS & NAMES
1. mercantilism, p. 66
2. Navigation Acts, p. 67
3. Glorious Revolution, p. 68
4. triangular trade, p. 73
5. middle passage, p. 74
6. Benjamin Franklin, p. 81
7. Great Awakening, p. 82
8. George Washington, p. 84
9. French and Indian War, p. 84
10. Proclamation of 1763, p. 86

MAIN IDEAS
Answers will vary.

11. To become economically self-sufficient by accumulating gold and silver; establishing a balance of trade; and founding colonies.

12. To impose greater authority over the northern colonies. When James II lost the throne, the colonists' rebellion led to its collapse.

13. The South was primarily rural. Plantations sprang up along rivers, so that planters could ship goods without the need of city dock facilities. Families produced most goods on the plantations.

14. Considered inferior to men, women had limited legal, political, and social rights. Most Southern women did household work and farm chores.

15. Nonviolent: faking illness, working slowly, running away. Violent: open slave revolts.

16. Agricultural Economy—producing several cash crops per farm. Commercial Economy—several thriving industries; trade mainstay of seaport cities' economy.

17. Franklin's experiments and inventions, Jefferson's view of individuals' natural rights, and the colonists' questioning of authority.

18. The French—they became economic partners and sometimes military allies of Native Americans.

19. William Pitt helped strengthen the British army and prompted the Iroquois to support them.

20. Halved the duty on foreign-made molasses, placed duties on other imports; established a vice-admiralty court to prosecute smugglers.

REVIEWING THE CHAPTER

TERMS & NAMES For each item below, write a sentence explaining its connection to colonial America from 1651 to 1764. For each person below, explain his role during this era.

1. mercantilism	6. Benjamin Franklin
2. Navigation Acts	7. Great Awakening
3. Glorious Revolution	8. George Washington
4. triangular trade	9. French and Indian War
5. middle passage	10. Proclamation of 1763

MAIN IDEAS

SECTION 1 (pages 66–70)

England and Its Colonies

11. What was a nation's ultimate goal under mercantilism and how did Great Britain strive to achieve this goal?
12. Why was the Dominion of New England formed and what caused its collapse?

SECTION 2 (pages 71–76)

The Agricultural South

13. Why did plantations develop instead of towns in most parts of the South?
14. What were the status and ways of life of women in the Southern colonies?
15. Cite examples of both nonviolent and violent resistance to slavery in the South.

SECTION 3 (pages 77–82)

The Commercial North

16. Briefly describe the diverse agricultural and commercial economy that developed in New England and the Middle colonies.
17. How were the philosophical ideas of the Enlightenment expressed in the American colonies?

SECTION 4 (pages 83–87)

The French and Indian War

18. Which of the following groups—the English, the French, or the Spanish—had developed the best relations with Native Americans? Why?
19. Briefly explain why Great Britain won the French and Indian war.
20. What were the provisions of the Sugar Act? Why did it anger many colonial merchants?

THINKING CRITICALLY

1. **RELATIONSHIP BETWEEN ENGLAND AND COLONIES** Create a chart like the one below on your paper. For each of the listed events, describe the effects on the political and economic relationship between Great Britain and its colonies.

Event	Effect on relationship with colonies
Navigation Acts	
salutary neglect	
French and Indian War	
Proclamation of 1763	
Sugar Act	

2. **POLITICAL THOUGHT** In what ways did Benjamin Franklin demonstrate the ideas of the Enlightenment? Give reasons to support your answer.

3. **MELTING POT** Reread the quote by de Crèvecoeur on page 64. What might the quote mean to Americans today?

4. **GEOGRAPHY OF THE COLONIES** Look carefully at the map on page 85. Why might the British government have chosen the Appalachian mountain range to be the line drawn by the Proclamation of 1763? What purpose did the mountain range serve?

5. **COLONIAL COURTSHIP** Based on the descriptions of colonial courtship in various communities, why do you think highly structured practices of courtship and marriage were common during this time? Think about the individual's relationship to the community and the cultural values of the time.

6. **ANALYZING PRIMARY SOURCES** During the 1700s, there was an influx of European immigrants to the northern colonies. Read the following excerpt from Gottlieb Mittelberger's memoir *Journey to Pennsylvania in the Year 1750,* in which he reflects on his painful experiences as a German immigrant.

> Work and labor in this new and wild land are very hard and manifold. . . . Besides, there is . . . an arduous journey lasting half a year, during which he has to suffer, more than with the hardest work. . . . [I]f he has [no money], he must work his debt off as a slave and poor serf. Therefore, let everyone stay in his own country and support himself and his family honestly. Besides I say that those who suffer themselves to be persuaded and enticed away by the man-thieves are very foolish if they believe that roasted pigeons will fly into their mouths in America or Pennsylvania without their working for them.
>
> **GOTTLIEB MITTELBERGER,** *Journey to Pennsylvania in the Year 1750*

How does Mittelberger characterize the ordeal of newcomers to America? If you were thinking of immigrating to America in the 1700s, would Mittelberger's warning about the impending hardships influence your decision? Why or why not?

THINKING CRITICALLY

1. RELATIONSHIP BETWEEN ENGLAND AND COLONIES
Possible Responses: Navigation Acts: economic boom; political resentment; **salutary neglect:** both economies prosper; colonists learn to govern themselves; **French and Indian War:** won vast new territories for Great Britain, caused Britain a financial crisis, settlers lost confidence in British army; **Proclamation of 1763:** angers colonists, can't be enforced, causes more financial strains; **Sugar Act:** colonial anger over taxes, increasing disagreements.

2. POLITICAL THOUGHT
Possible Responses: Franklin's belief that he could use human reason and an orderly method to perfect himself might also be used in trying to create a flawless government. His optimism about self-improvement could justify reforms that correct the imperfections of a society and government. His beliefs could support progressive policies.

3. MELTING POT
Possible Responses: Some might say that in relation to the whole world, Americans are a separate and "new" race with optimism and attitudes far different from other countries; others will object to the "melting pot" idea and think that while many "races" are represented, each has maintained its own identity, and that America is more a "salad bowl" of a variety of peoples living together.

ALTERNATIVE ASSESSMENT

1. COMMEMORATIVE SPEECH

By 1765, all the colonies except Pennsylvania and Georgia were at least 100 years old. What were some of the achievements that colonists had secured by this time? What were some of the costs of colonial growth?

Write a short (3–4 minute) speech commemorating the 100th anniversary of the founding of a colony.

 Use the CD-ROM *Electronic Library of Primary Sources* and other resources to review significant political, economic, and social developments.

- Write your speech based on your research, taking into account both hardships and triumphs. What were the key turning points? What lessons are important to remember? And, on the eve of the 100th anniversary, what challenges or difficulties are you prepared to forecast?

- Conclude your speech by reflecting back to the charter establishing the colony. Has the history of the past 100 years supported or strayed from the original colonists' intentions?

- Share your speech with your classmates.

2. CONTRASTING COLONIES

During the period from 1650 to 1750, slavery became predominant in some American colonies but not in others. What geographic, social, and economic conditions caused this to happen?

Cooperative Learning Work with a small group to create a chart that contrasts differences between a colony that relied on large numbers of African-American slaves (for example, Virginia, Georgia, South Carolina), with a colony that did not have large numbers of slaves (for example, Massachusetts, Pennsylvania, or Rhode Island). Include such factors as geographic location, economic activity, kinds of work done by slaves and non-slaves, and religious beliefs.Compare your chart with those of groups that have selected different colonies to contrast.

3. PORTFOLIO PROJECT

 Use the Living History activity to expand your portfolio.

LIVING HISTORY

PRESENTING YOUR RESEARCH

You have researched a region or locale of the United States for its original or unique characteristics. Now create a visual presentation of your findings in the form of a poster, slide show, or museum exhibit. For each characteristic you tell about, be sure to explain its origin, why it developed in this place, and whether it has spread elsewhere.

Have another student review your presentation and suggest improvements. After you put the finishing touches on it, share it with the class and include it in your American history portfolio.

Review Chapter 3

RELATIONS WITH ENGLAND Under mercantilism, the American colonies were valuable economically to England, and the colonies prospered as well. By the mid-1600s, this relationship was coming apart as colonists pushed for more economic and political freedom. Parliament tried to curb this threat by passing the Navigation Acts. After the Glorious Revolution of 1688, England exercised a policy of salutary neglect by relaxing its enforcement of trade laws.

SOUTHERN AND NORTHERN COLONIES The Southern colonies developed a booming plantation economy. The South was a sharply divided society in which a small number of wealthy landowners exploited indentured servants and later African slaves. African slaves' strong cultural identity and resistance to their subservient position helped them deal with their plight.

The Northern colonies developed primarily a commercial economy with diverse industries and seaport cities. Diverse ideas and beliefs also emerged. The Enlightenment, an intellectual movement, and the Great Awakening, a religious movement, emphasized two opposing ideas—reason and emotionalism—that affected all 13 colonies. Both movements caused people to question traditional authority.

THE FRENCH AND INDIAN WAR In 1754, France and Great Britain clashed over frontier claims in the French and Indian War. Britain gained the upper hand after a decisive battle at Quebec. The war officially ended in 1763 with Great Britain controlling Canada and almost all of North America east of the Mississippi River. The British victory created new disputes with Native Americans and colonists over land, and Britain's steps to recover from its financial crisis led to further hostile relations with the colonists.

Preview Chapter 4

Following the French and Indian War, Great Britain's policies to raise more revenue and tighten its control over the American colonies provoked their resistance, which eventually escalated into the American Revolution. The colonists declared their independence and waged war against the British in New England, the middle states, and the South. Foreign allies contributed to the American victory. You will learn about these and other significant developments in the next chapter.

The Colonies Come of Age **91**

THINKING CRITICALLY

4. GEOGRAPHY OF THE COLONIES
Possible Responses: The purpose of the line was to prevent colonists from going farther west into Native American lands; a mountain range like the Appalachians presents a natural barrier that could serve as a "wall"; the whereabouts of any other line would be confusing.

5. COLONIAL COURTSHIP
Possible Responses: Conformity was important; individual freedom and choice were not yet a priority; parents' authority over their children and respect toward elders were cultural values; relations between men and women affect the welfare of the entire community.

6. ANALYZING PRIMARY SOURCES
Possible Responses: Mittelberger describes the physical discomforts of the transatlantic journey, the arduous labor of the indentured servant, and the disillusionment about life in America. Some students might heed Mittelberger's warning, citing that the adjustments they would face would be too overwhelming. Other students might disregard his warning, citing their ability to persevere the hardships mentioned and their belief that they have paved the way for a better life for future generations.

		TEACHING SUPPORT	**ASSESSMENT**

Key Ideas

SECTION 1 The Stirrings of Rebellion *pp. 94–98*	*The colonies unite in their resistance to Britain, as soldiers in Massachusetts fire the "shot heard 'round the world."*	***In-Depth Resources: Unit 1*** • Guided Reading, p. 58 • Primary Source: The Boston Tea Party, p. 65 • Literature: from *April Morning* by Howard Fast, p. 69 **COOPERATIVE ACTIVITIES** • Letters from Committees of Correspondence, p. 96 (TE)	***Section 1 Assessment,*** p. 98 (PE) ***Self-Assessment,*** p. 98 (TE) ***Formal Assessment*** • Section Quiz, p. 42 ***Alternative Assessment Book*** • Standards for Evaluating a Cooperative Activity
SECTION 2 Ideas Help Start a Revolution *pp. 99–106*	*Ideas about freedom and self-determination spur the colonies to declare independence.*	***In-Depth Resources: Unit 1*** • Guided Reading, p. 59 • Primary Source: Political Cartoon, p. 67 • American Lives: Mercy Otis Warren, p. 72 **COOPERATIVE ACTIVITY** • Creating a Political Pamphlet, p. 100 (TE) • Paraphrasing the Declaration, p. 105 (TE)	***Section 2 Assessment,*** p. 103 (PE) ***Self-Assessment,*** p. 103 (TE) ***Formal Assessment*** • Section Quiz, p. 43 ***Alternative Assessment Book*** • Standards for Evaluating a Cooperative Activity
SECTION 3 Struggling Toward Saratoga *pp. 107–111*	*The colonists overcome early losses and eventually score a major victory at Saratoga.*	***In-Depth Resources: Unit 1*** • Guided Reading, p. 60 • Primary Source: *from* Valley Forge Diary, p. 68 • American Lives: Haym Salomon, p. 73 **COOPERATIVE ACTIVITIES** • Reporting on the Revolution, p. 108 (TE)	***Section 3 Assessment,*** p. 111 (PE) ***Self-Assessment,*** p. 111 (TE) ***Formal Assessment*** • Section Quiz, p. 44 ***Alternative Assessment Book*** • Standards for Evaluating a Cooperative Activity
SECTION 4 Winning the War *pp. 112–117*	*The colonists enlist the help of European allies, defeat the mighty British army, and establish a new nation.*	***In-Depth Resources: Unit 1*** • Guided Reading, p. 61 • Skillbuilder Practice: Analyzing Causes, Recognizing Effects, p. 62 • Geography Application: The Seige of Yorktown, p. 63 **COOPERATIVE ACTIVITY** • Broadside Ballad of the Revolution, p. 114 (TE)	***Section 4 Assessment,*** p. 117 (PE) ***Self-Assessment,*** p. 117 (TE) ***Formal Assessment*** • Section Quiz, p. 45 ***Alternative Assessment Book*** • Standards for Evaluating a Cooperative Activity

Chapter Overview

CHAPTER RESOURCES	*The colonists' clashes with the British government lead them to declare independence. With French aid, they overcome early setbacks to win their freedom from Great Britain.*	***In-Depth Resources: Unit 1*** • Living History Project: Worksheet, p. 74; Standards, p. 75 ***Telescoping the Times*** • Chapter Summary, pp. 7–8 ***Planning for Block Schedules***	***Chapter Assessment,*** pp. 120–121 (PE) ***Alternative Assessment,*** p. 121 (PE) ***Formal Assessment*** • Chapter Test, forms A and B, pp. 46–51 **Test Generator** ***Alternative Assessment Book*** See explanation and forms for different kinds of alternative assessments including portfolio assessment.

Electronic Library of Primary Sources
- *from* "Resolutions for American Duties" from British Parliamentary Debates
- "The Mother Country," a popular song by Benjamin Franklin
- *from* "An Account of a Late Military Massacre" by Paul Revere
- "Resolutions" by the Association of the Sons of Liberty

INTERNET RESOURCES
- See *McDougal Littell Learning On-Line* for links to information about the Boston Tea Party and colonial life.

 Humanities Transparencies
- H5, *Bunker Hill* by Howard Pyle
- H31, Political Cartoon on the Battle of Bunker Hill by Matthew Darly

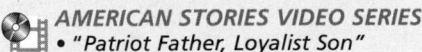 *Electronic Library of Primary Sources*
- *from Common Sense* by Paine

AMERICAN STORIES VIDEO SERIES
- "*Patriot Father, Loyalist Son*"

INTERNET RESOURCES
- See *McDougal Littell Learning On-Line* for links to information about the Declaration of Independence.

 Grolier Multimedia Encyclopedia
- George Washington

INTERNET RESOURCES
- See *McDougal Littell Learning On-Line* for links to information about Valley Forge.

 Humanities Transparencies
- H32, "Mrs. General Washington"
- H6, Signing of the Treaty of Paris, 1783

Geography Transparencies
- G4, North America, 1783

Critical Thinking Transparencies
- CT4, War for Independence

INTERNET RESOURCES
- See *McDougal Littell Learning On-Line* for links to information about Benedict Arnold and Lafayette

 American Portfolio: A Videodisc for U.S. History, user's guide, pp. 28–31, 33–36, 38

INTERNET RESOURCES
Learning On-Line: Social Studies
http://www.mcdougallittell.com

Block Scheduling (90 MINUTES)

Day 1	Day 2	Day 3
Section 1, pp. 94–98	**Section 2,** pp. 99–106	**Section 3,** pp. 107–111
Section Assessment, p. 98	**Section Assessment,** p. 103	**Section 4,** pp. 112–117
	AMERICAN STORIES VIDEO SERIES	**Section Assessments,** pp. 111, 117
	• "*Patriot Father, Loyalist Son*"	**Declaration of Independence,** pp. 104–106
		Chapter Assessment, pp. 120–121

YEARLY PACING *Chapter 4 Total:* 3 days *Yearly Total:* 85 days

See *Planning for Block Schedules* for special activities and pacing strategies.

Customizing for Special Populations

Students Acquiring English

Access for Students Acquiring English
- Guided Reading for Sections 1–4 (Spanish), pp. 39–42
- Chapter Summary (Spanish), pp. 37–38
- Skillbuilder Practice: Analyzing Causes, Recognizing Effects (Spanish), p. 43
- Geography Application: The Seige of Yorktown (Spanish), p. 44

 AMERICAN STORIES VIDEO SERIES
- "*Patriot Father, Loyalist Son*" (Spanish Tract)

INTERNET RESOURCES
- See *McDougal Littell Learning On-Line* The Diverse Classroom.

Less Proficient Readers

In-Depth Resources: Unit 1
- Guided Reading for Sections 1–4, pp. 58–61
- Skillbuilder: Analyzing Causes, Recognizing Effects, p. 62
- Geography Application: The Seige of Yorktown, p. 63

Telescoping the Times
- Chapter Summary, pp. 7–8

See additional strategies at point of use in the Teacher's Edition.

Gifted and Talented Students

In-Depth Resources: Unit 1
- Primary Source: The Boston Tea Party, p. 65; Political Cartoon, p. 67; *from* Valley Forge Diary, p. 68
- American Lives: ; Mercy Otis Warren, p. 72; Haym Salomon, p. 73

See additional strategies at point of use in the Teacher's Edition.

Connections to Literature READINGS FOR STUDENTS

In-Depth Resources: Unit 1
- **from** *April Morning* **by Howard Fast,** p. 69

Enrichment Reading
- **Roberts, Kenneth.** *Oliver Wiswell.* New York: Doubleday, 1940. *This historically accurate story of the American Revolution is told from the viewpoint of a Tory.*

- **Edwards, Sherman,** *1776: A Musical Play.* New York: Penguin, 1987. *This lively musical play is about Jefferson and Adams and the Declaration of Independence.*

McDougal Littell *The Language of Literature* American Literature
- **Dave Barry, "The Boston Tea Party,"** p. 211
- **Phillis Wheatley, "Letter to the Rev. Samson Occom,"** p. 216
- **Abigail Adams, "Letter to John Adams,"** p. 216
- **Benjamin Franklin,** *from* **Poor Richard's Almanack,"** p. 226
- **Red Jacket, Lecture to a Missionary,** p. 229

The War for Independence

The War for Independence

▶ **Starting with the Student**
Ask students to tell what they already know about the American Revolution: the events leading up to it, its memorable battles, its heroes, and its results. Then discuss the opening quotation. Ask students,

- What makes the quotation so powerful?
- What insights about the Revolution does it convey?

PREVIEWING THE CHAPTER

Have students skim the chapter, reading headings and the Terms & Names to the right of section titles. Ask them to list the terms and names in three columns—familiar, partly familiar, and unfamiliar—and then to focus, as they read the chapter, on the terms and names in their second and third columns.

MORE ABOUT . . .
Patrick Henry

A lawyer noted for fine oratory, Patrick Henry was elected to the Virginia House of Burgesses in 1764, served as a delegate to the First Continental Congress, and was Virginia's governor during the Revolution. A member of his state's convention to ratify the Constitution, he is widely credited with getting the Bill of Rights included.

SECTION 1
The Stirrings of Rebellion

The colonies unite in their resistance to Britain, as soldiers in Massachusetts fire the "shot heard 'round the world."

SECTION 2
Ideas Help Start a Revolution

Ideas about freedom and self-determination spur the colonies to declare independence.

VIDEO *PATRIOT FATHER, LOYALIST SON*

THE DECLARATION OF INDEPENDENCE

SECTION 3
Struggling Toward Saratoga

The colonists overcome early losses and eventually score a major victory at Saratoga.

SECTION 4
Winning the War

The colonists enlist the help of European allies, defeat the mighty British army, and establish a new nation.

"... give me liberty, or give me death!"

Patrick Henry

Colonial women organize spinning bees to protest British taxes on textiles.

● British Parliament passes the Stamp Act.

Colonists stage the Boston Tea Party.

THE UNITED STATES
THE WORLD

1765   1767   1773

                    1769   1770

● Chinese forces invade Burma.

● Scotland's James Watt makes a steam engine capable of running other machines.

● Tukolor Kingdom arises in the former Songhai region of West Africa.

THEMES IN CHAPTER 4

Economic Opportunity

Economic factors were a major cause of the Revolution. Britain's policies squelched the colonies' economic development and expansion into new territories, and taxes imposed without the consent of the colonists outraged them.

See Teacher's Edition note, p. 95.

Expanding Democracy

Written by Thomas Jefferson and adopted by the Continental Congress on July 4, 1776, the Declaration of Independence (along with the Constitution) forms the foundation on which America's democratic values rest. Among Jefferson's democratic ideas are these: (1) all human beings are entitled to the "inalienable" rights of "life, liberty, and the pursuit of happiness"; and (2) a government and those it governs are part of a contract in which the government receives its power from the governed, who are entitled to change the government if it threatens these rights.

See Teacher's Edition note, p. 101.

Women in America

During the Revolution, women managed farms and businesses while the men were off fighting. Women also supported the Patriot cause by making ammunition and other supplies and by helping to feed and house soldiers in their area.

See Teacher's Edition note, p. 110.

CONDUCTING A SURVEY

Select short excerpts from the Declaration of Independence. Then, without identifying the source, read the passages aloud to individuals to get their response. (You may make minor changes in rewording for clarity.) Ask your listeners if they agree or disagree with the ideas expressed and why. Write down their remarks and organize the results of your survey in a visual display.

Consider using a graphic device or poster such as the following as you organize your results:

- a graph
- a chart
- a poster with quotes

📁 **PORTFOLIO PROJECT** Keep your written results and your visual display in the folder for your American history portfolio. At the end of the chapter, you will share your results with classmates.

CONDUCTING A SURVEY

Discuss with students ways of going about conducting the survey:

- Read through the Declaration of Independence, noting passages that catch your interest.
- Select a few thought-provoking passages, and copy each onto a note card.
- Attach a sheet of paper to each card so that you can record the responses of people you survey.
- Choose a variety of people to survey, including men and women and boys and girls of different ages and from different groups.
- Select a way to display your findings—such as a chart, a graph, or a poster.

Project Planning Guide

Step 1	Students select passages for survey.
Step 2	Students decide whom to interview.
Step 3	Students conduct interviews and record their findings.
Step 4	Students compile their findings in a visual display.

IN-DEPTH RESOURCES: UNIT 1
See worksheet and standards for evaluation, pp. 74–75.

Washington crosses the Delaware.

Thomas Paine publishes *Common Sense*.

Colonists declare independence.

Fighting erupts at Lexington and Concord.

Second Continental Congress convenes.

Joseph Brant leads raids against Americans during the war.

Parliament passes Intolerable Acts.

First Continental Congress convenes.

Colonists and British wage the Battle of Bunker Hill.

Colonists' victory at Saratoga marks a turning point in the war.

France enters the Revolutionary War.

The British surrender at Yorktown.

Colonists and British sign Treaty of Paris, ending war.

1774   1775   1776   1777   1778   1781   **1783**

1776   1778   1779   1782

Reign of Louis XVI begins in France.

Adam Smith's *Wealth of Nations* is published.

French and Dutch help rebellious colonists.

Spain declares war on Britain.

French occupy Senegal.

Spain puts down a colonial rebellion in Peru.

The War for Independence **93**

RECOMMENDED RESOURCES

Books for the Teacher

Boorstin, Daniel J. *The Lost World of Thomas Jefferson*. New York: Holt, 1948. A famous study of Jeffersonian thinking.

Draper, Theodore. *A Struggle for Power*. New York: Times, 1996. Thorough study of the British and the colonists.

Leckie, Robert. *George Washington's War*. New York: HarperCollins, 1992. Readable narrative history.

Silverman, Kenneth. *A Cultural History of the American Revolution*. New York: Crowell, 1976.

Books for the Student

Bailyn, Bernard. *Faces of Revolution*. New York: Vintage, 1992. Profiles of a wide variety of subjects.

Evans, Elizabeth. *Weathering the Storm*. New York: Scribner's, 1975. Revolutionary-era journal entries by women.

Hibbert, Christopher. *Redcoats and Rebels: The American Revolution Through British Eyes*. New York: Norton, 1990.

Videos

The American Revolution. History Channel home video. Six-tape documentary.

Nace una nación. Films for the Humanities & Sciences, 800-257-3767. The Revolution in Spanish.

Paul Revere: Messenger of Liberty. AIMS Media, 1980.

Software

The American Revolution. CD-ROM. Queue, 1994.

Revolution '76. 3 Diskettes. Britannica Software, 1989.

Teacher's Edition   **93**

OBJECTIVES

1. To summarize colonial resistance to British attempts at taxation.

2. To trace the mounting tension in Massachusetts.

3. To describe how fighting broke out in Concord.

CRITICAL THINKING

• Summarizing, p. 95
• Forming opinions, pp. 96, 98
• Analyzing motives, p. 98
• Synthesizing, p. 98
• Hypothesizing, p. 98

FOCUS & MOTIVATE

▶ *Starting with the Student*
Ask students these questions:

• How do small quarrels between people mushroom into larger fights?
• Might the same thing happen between nations, or between a parent nation and its colony? Explain.

MORE ABOUT . . .
Crispus Attucks

Catapulted to fame at his death, Crispus Attucks had lived an otherwise obscure life. He was most likely African American, and historians often identify him as a runaway slave named Crispus who was known to have escaped his Framingham, Massachusetts, owner in 1750 and who probably spent most of the next 20 years aboard New England whaling ships. After his death, his body was carried to Boston's Faneuil Hall, where it lay in state for three days. In 1888, Boston erected a monument to Attucks and the others who died in what came to be called the Boston Massacre.

---

1 The Stirrings of Rebellion

TERMS & NAMES
• Stamp Act
• Samuel Adams
• Townshend Acts
• Boston Massacre
• committee of correspondence
• Boston Tea Party
• King George III
• Intolerable Acts
• martial law

LEARN ABOUT the growing conflict between Great Britain and the American colonies
TO UNDERSTAND the American Revolution and how it began.

ONE AMERICAN'S STORY

Crispus Attucks, a sailor of African and Native American ancestry, was leading an angry group of laborers from Dock Square in Boston to the customshouse the night of March 5, 1770. British soldiers, stationed in the tension-filled city to keep the peace, had clashed with colonists that afternoon. By evening another enraged crowd gathered and marched to the customshouse on snowy King Street. At first, the crowd heckled the British sentry on guard, calling him a "lobsterback" to mock his red uniform. Then more soldiers arrived, and the mob began hurling stones and snowballs at them. At that moment, Crispus Attucks and his followers arrived.

A PERSONAL VOICE
This Attucks . . . appears to have undertaken to be the hero of the night; and to lead this army with banners . . . up to King street with their clubs . . . this man with his party cried, do not be afraid of them. . . . He had hardiness enough to fall in upon them, and with one hand took hold of a bayonet, and with the other knocked the man down.

JOHN ADAMS, quoted in *The Black Presence in the Era of the American Revolution*

Attucks's action ignited the troops. Ignoring orders not to shoot civilians, one soldier and then several others fired on the crowd. Five people were killed; three were wounded. Crispus Attucks was, according to a newspaper account, the first to die.

Relations between Britain and the colonists had been strained for years. But now the tensions had boiled over. No one knew it that clear, cold night, but Crispus Attucks would become one of the first colonists to die in an all-out war for freedom.

Crispus Attucks

The Colonies Organize to Resist Britain

In order to finance debts from the French and Indian War, as well as from European wars, Parliament had turned hungry eyes on the colonies' resources. British leaders saw nothing tyrannical in their plans for new colonial rules and taxes. Their actions, however, set the stage for conflict.

THE STAMP ACT The seeds of increased tension were sown in March 1765 when Parliament, persuaded by Prime Minister George Grenville, passed the **Stamp Act**. It was the first tax that affected colonists directly because it was levied on goods and services. Previous taxes, such as those levied by the Sugar Act, had been indirect, involving duties on imports.

The Stamp Act required colonists to purchase special stamped paper for every legal document, license, newspaper, pamphlet, and almanac, and imposed special "stamp duties" on packages of playing cards and dice. The tax reached into every colonial pocket—rich and poor. Colonists who disobeyed the law were to be tried in the vice-admiralty courts, where no juries were present and convictions were probable.

With the passage of the Stamp Act, the colonists lost respect for the king's officeholders in America. They also realized that British interests were not identical to their own. The growing unrest and resentment of laborers in the cities created a situation that was ripe for protest. As the grievances of the colonists exploded, colonial political leaders would mobilize the working class to action.

SECTION 1 RESOURCES

PRINT RESOURCES

IN-DEPTH RESOURCES: UNIT 1
Guided Reading, p. 58
Primary Source: The Boston Tea Party, p. 65
Literature: from *April Morning* by Howard Fast, p. 69

ACCESS FOR STUDENTS ACQUIRING ENGLISH
Guided Reading (Spanish), p. 39

FORMAL ASSESSMENT
Section Quiz, p. 42

ALTERNATIVE ASSESSMENT BOOK
See forms for supporting and scoring alternative activities.

TECHNOLOGY RESOURCES

CD-ROM Electronic Library of Primary Sources

VIDEO *American Portfolio: A Videodisc for U.S. History*
user's guide, pp. 28, 29, 31

INTERNET McDougal Littell Learning On-Line
http://www.mcdougallittell.com

STAMP ACT PROTESTS When word of the Stamp Act reached the colonies in May of 1765, the colonists united in their defiance. Boston shopkeepers, artisans, and laborers organized a secret resistance group called the Sons of Liberty. One of its founders was Harvard-educated **Samuel Adams,** who, although unsuccessful in business and deeply in debt, proved himself to be a powerful and influential political activist.

By the end of the summer, the Sons of Liberty members were demonstrating and protesting throughout the colonies. They harassed customs workers, stamp agents, and sometimes royal governors. Facing mob threats and demonstrations, stamp agents all over the colonies resigned. The Stamp Act was to become effective on November 1, 1765, but colonial protest prevented any stamps from being sold.

During 1765 and early 1766, the individual colonial assemblies confronted the Stamp Act measure. Virginia's lower house adopted several resolutions put forth by a 29-year-old lawyer named Patrick Henry. These resolutions stated that Virginians could be taxed only by the Virginia assembly—that is, only by their own representatives. Other assemblies passed similar resolutions.

The colonial assemblies also made a strong collective protest. In October 1765, delegates from nine colonies met in New York City. This Stamp Act Congress issued a Declaration of Rights and Grievances, which stated that Parliament lacked the power to impose taxes on the colonies because the colonists were not represented in Parliament. More than 10 years earlier, the colonies had rejected Benjamin Franklin's Albany Plan of Union, which called for a joint colonial council to address defense issues. Now, for the first time, the separate colonies began to act as one.

Colonial merchants added their weight to the resistance. In October 1765, about 200 New York traders agreed to a nonimportation policy—a boycott of British goods—until the Stamp Act was repealed. Merchants in Boston and Philadelphia soon followed suit. This boycott was a serious action because under Britain's policy of mercantilism, the home country was economically dependent on purchases of its goods by the colonies. The colonists reasoned that since the American colonies bought a substantial portion (about 40 percent) of Britain's manufactured goods, British merchants would force Parliament to repeal the Stamp Act.

The widespread boycott worked. In March 1766, Parliament repealed the Stamp Act; but on the same day, to make its power clear, Parliament issued the Declaratory Act. This act asserted Parliament's full right to make laws "to bind the colonies and people of America . . . in all cases whatsoever."

THE TOWNSHEND ACTS Within a year after Parliament repealed the Stamp Act, a young, newly appointed minister named Charles Townshend impetuously decided on a new method of gaining revenue from the American colonies. His proposed revenue laws, passed by Parliament in 1767, became known as the **Townshend Acts.** Unlike the Stamp Act, which was a direct tax, these were indirect taxes, or duties levied on imports—glass, lead, paint, and paper—as they came into the colonies from Britain. The acts also imposed a three-penny tax on tea, the most popular drink in the colonies.

The colonists reacted with rage and well-organized resistance. Educated Americans spoke out against the Townshend Acts, protesting "taxation without representation." Boston's Samuel Adams called for another boycott of British goods, and American women of every rank in society became involved in the protest. Writer Mercy Otis Warren of Massachusetts urged women to lay their British "female ornaments aside," foregoing "feathers, furs, rich sattins and . . . capes." Wealthy women stopped buying British luxuries and joined other women in spinning bees—public displays of spinning and weaving of colonial-

The colonists' view of the stamp tax is clear in the skull and crossbones emblem that warns of the effects of the Stamp Act.

THINK THROUGH HISTORY
A. Summarizing
How did the colonists respond to the Stamp Act?

A. Answer
Colonists harassed stamp agents, adopted resolutions denouncing the Stamp Act, and boycotted British goods.

NOW & THEN

TAXES
Anger among taxpayers is not a thing of the past. On June 4, 1996, Wisconsin voters threw Republican state senator George Petak out of office. The reason: Petak had promised voters he wouldn't vote to raise sales taxes to fund a new stadium for the Milwaukee Brewers baseball team, but at the last minute he changed his mind and voted for the tax. Voters were so angry they forced a recall election and voted Petak out of office.

OBJECTIVE
1 INSTRUCT

The Colonies Organize to Resist Britain

▶**Discussing Key Ideas**
• The Stamp Act of 1765, the first direct tax on colonists, provokes such widespread protest that Parliament repeals it.
• Not long afterward, Britain imposes the Townshend Acts, indirect taxes on imports, which also meet with widespread resistance.

IN-DEPTH RESOURCES: UNIT 1
Guided Reading, p. 58

ACCESS FOR STUDENTS ACQUIRING ENGLISH
Guided Reading (Spanish), p.39

ELECTRONIC LIBRARY OF PRIMARY SOURCES
from "Resolutions for American Duties" from the British Parliament; "The Mother Country" by Benjamin Franklin

NOW & THEN
Taxes

Ask students how the Wisconsin voters' political status was different from that of colonial Americans. *The voters were able to vote their senator out of office; the colonists had no vote on taxation.*

TEACHING OPTIONS

Exploring Themes

Economic Opportunity Underscore the strong role economic factors played in causing the Revolution. Remind students that Britain not only imposed new taxes but also followed policies that squelched the colonies' economic development and their expansion into the newly acquired territories. Stress that the taxes especially outraged colonists because they had no representation in the taxing body, the British Parliament. Be sure students understand the difference between a direct tax—similar to a sales tax today—and an indirect tax, or duty paid by a shipper or importer that is passed along to consumers via a price increase.

Teaching Less Proficient Readers

Guided Reading Suggest that students focus their reading by turning each heading and subheading into a question and then reading the material below it to find the answer. For example, the main section heading on page 94 could be turned into this question:

How did the colonies organize to resist Britain?

The subheadings in this section could be turned into these questions: What was the Stamp Act? Who protested the Stamp Act, and how did they protest? What were the Townshend Acts?

Teacher's Edition **95**

A close associate of Samuel Adams, John Hancock also represented Massachusetts at the Continental Congress. Hancock was its president when members signed the Declaration of Independence; that is why his signature came first and was the largest.

OBJECTIVE
② INSTRUCT

Tension Mounts in Massachusetts

▶ **Starting with the Student**
Students might make a tree diagram showing the chain of events that led to the start of the Revolution.

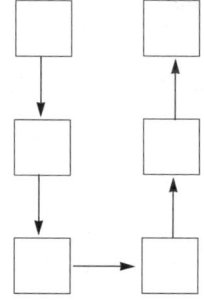

▶ **Discussing Key Ideas**
• Colonial resistance and British countermeasures lead to the Boston Massacre of 1770 and the Boston Tea Party of 1773.
• George III gets Parliament to punish Boston by passing laws that colonists call the Intolerable Acts.
• In 1774, the First Continental Congress meets in Philadelphia to draw up a declaration of colonial rights.

 ELECTRONIC LIBRARY OF PRIMARY SOURCES
from "An Account of a Late Military Massacre" by Paul Revere

---

made cloth designed to show colonists' determination to boycott British-made cloth. Housewives also boycotted British tea and exchanged recipes for tea made from birch bark and sage.

Conflict intensified in June 1768. British agents in Boston seized the *Liberty*, a ship belonging to local merchant John Hancock. The customs inspector claimed that Hancock had smuggled in a shipment of wine from Madeira and had failed to pay the customs taxes. The seizure triggered riots against customs agents. In response, the British stationed 4,000 troops in Boston to curb the violence—one soldier for every four citizens. This show of force led the colonists one step closer to revolution.

Tension Mounts in Massachusetts

The presence of British soldiers in Boston's streets charged the air with hostility. The city soon erupted in bloody clashes between British soldiers and colonists and later in a daring tea protest, all of which pushed the colonists and Britain closer to war.

THE BOSTON MASSACRE One sore point was the competition for jobs between colonists and poorly paid soldiers who looked for extra work in local shipyards during off-duty hours. On the cold afternoon of March 5, 1770, a fistfight broke out over jobs. That evening a mob gathered in front of the customshouse and taunted the guards. When Crispus Attucks and other dockhands appeared on the scene, an armed clash erupted, leaving Attucks and four others dead in the snow. Instantly, Samuel Adams and other agitators labeled this confrontation the **Boston Massacre,** thus presenting it as a British attack on defenseless citizens. Propaganda about the "massacre," including an engraving of the incident by colonist Paul Revere (shown below), inflamed Massachusetts colonists as nothing had before.

Despite strong feelings on both sides, the political atmosphere relaxed somewhat during the next three years. Lord Frederick North, the new minister, realized that the Townshend Acts were costing more to enforce than they would ever bring in: in their first year, the taxes raised only 295 pounds, while the cost of sending British troops to Boston was 170,000 pounds. North convinced Parliament to repeal the Townshend Acts, except for the tax on tea.

Tensions rose again in 1772 after a group of Rhode Island colonists attacked a British customs schooner that patrolled the coast for smugglers. The colonists boarded the vessel, which had accidentally run aground near Providence, and burned it to the waterline. In response, King George named a special commission to seek out the suspects and bring them to England for trial.

The plan to haul Americans to England for trial ignited widespread alarm. The assemblies of

THINK THROUGH HISTORY
B. Forming Opinions Do you think the colonists' reaction to the seizing of the *Liberty* was justified?
B. Answer
Possible responses: Yes, England's policy of taxing goods that the colonies traded with other countries was unjust; no, customs agents were simply doing their duty by searching ships they believed to be involved in smuggling.

Paul Revere's engraving of the Boston Massacre appeared in the *Boston Gazette* and was sold as a poster.

British Actions and Colonial Reactions, 1765–1775

1765 STAMP ACT		1767 TOWNSHEND ACTS		1770 BOSTON MASSACRE	
British Action	**Colonial Reaction**	**British Action**	**Colonial Reaction**	**British Action**	**Colonial Reaction**
Britain passes the Stamp Act, a tax law requiring colonists to purchase special stamped paper for printed items.	Colonists harass stamp distributors, boycott British goods, and prepare a Declaration of Rights and Grievances.	Britain taxes certain colonial imports and stations troops at major colonial ports to protect customs officers.	Colonists protest "taxation without representation" and organize new boycott of imported goods.	British troops stationed in Boston are taunted by an angry mob. The troops fire into the crowd, killing five men.	Colonial agitators label the conflict a "massacre" and publish a dramatic engraving depicting the violence.

96 CHAPTER 4

Cooperative Activity: Letters from Committees of Correspondence

Task: Groups of students will pretend to be committees of correspondence, writing letters committee members might have written in 1774.

Purpose: To understand the colonists' reactions to British actions.

Activity: Each group should pretend to live in different colonies and should address its letter to different groups in colonial society.

Students might supplement historical details from their texts with information that they research in library books or other references.

 Building a Portfolio: Remind students to choose their strongest work for their portfolio. If they feel that this assignment qualifies, they should place a copy of it in their portfolio.

ALTERNATIVE ASSESSMENT BOOK
Standards for Evaluating a Cooperative Activity

Standards for Evaluation
Letters should . . .

• report on events occurring around 1774 in the writer's area
• include the writer's feelings
• indicate the rebellious political climate and possibly suggest a course of action

Massachusetts and Virginia set up **committees of correspondence** to communicate with other colonies about this and other threats to American liberties. By 1774, such committees formed a buzzing communication network linking leaders in nearly all the colonies.

THE BOSTON TEA PARTY Early in 1773, Lord North faced a new problem. The East India Company, which held an official monopoly on tea imports, had been hit hard by the colonial boycotts. With its warehouses bulging with 17 million tons of tea, the company was nearing bankruptcy. To save it, North devised the Tea Act, which granted the company the right to sell tea to the colonies free of the taxes that colonial tea sellers had to pay. This action cut colonial merchants out of the tea trade, because the East India Company could sell their tea directly to consumers for less. North hoped the American colonists would simply buy the cheaper tea; instead, they protested violently.

On the moonlit evening of December 16, 1773, a large group of Boston rebels disguised themselves as Native American Mohawks and proceeded to take action against three British tea ships anchored in the harbor. John Andrews, an onlooker, wrote a letter on December 18, 1773, describing what happened.

> **A PERSONAL VOICE**
> They muster'd . . . to the number of about two hundred, and proceeded . . . to Griffin's wharf, where [the three ships] lay, each with 114 chests of the ill fated article . . . and before nine o'clock in the evening, every chest from on board the three vessels was knock'd to pieces and flung over the sides.
> They say the actors were Indians from Narragansett. Whether they were or not . . . they appear'd as such, being cloath'd in Blankets with the heads muffled, and copper color'd countenances, being each arm'd with a hatchet or axe. . . .
>
> **JOHN ANDREWS,** quoted in *1776: Journals of American Independence*

In this incident, later known as the **Boston Tea Party,** the "Indians" dumped 15,000 pounds of the East India Company's tea into the waters of Boston harbor.

A View of the Town of Concord, painted by an unknown artist, shows British troops drilling on the village green before the fighting began.

THE INTOLERABLE ACTS King George III was infuriated by this organized destruction of British property, and he pressed Parliament to act. In 1774, Parliament responded by passing a series of measures that colonists called the **Intolerable Acts.** One law shut down Boston harbor because the colonists had refused to pay for the damaged tea. Another, the Quartering Act, authorized British commanders to house soldiers in private homes and vacant buildings. In addition to these measures, General Thomas Gage, commander in chief of British forces in North America, was appointed the new governor of Massachusetts. To keep the peace, he placed Boston under **martial law,** or rule imposed by military forces.

King George hoped to isolate Massachusetts by singling it out for special punishment, but his actions only strengthened the colonies' unity. The committees of correspondence quickly moved into

This bottle contains tea that colonists threw into Boston harbor during the Boston Tea Party.

1773 TEA ACT		1774 INTOLERABLE ACTS		1775 LEXINGTON AND CONCORD	
British Action	**Colonial Reaction**	**British Action**	**Colonial Reaction**	**British Action**	**Colonial Reaction**
Britain gives the East India Company special concessions in the colonial tea business and shuts out colonial tea merchants.	Colonists in Boston rebel, dumping 15,000 pounds of East India Company tea into Boston harbor.	King George tightens control over Massachusetts and places Boston under martial law.	Colonial leaders form the First Continental Congress and draw up a declaration of colonial rights.	General Gage orders troops to march to Concord, Massachusetts, and seize colonial weapons.	Minutemen intercept the British and engage in battle—first at Lexington, and then at Concord.

The War for Independence **97**

Fighting Erupts at Lexington and Concord

▶ *Discussing Key Ideas*

• Warned that approaching British troops will attempt to seize their stockpiled weapons, civilian soldiers—minutemen—make their stand on April 19, 1775, in Concord.

• The shots fired prove to be the opening shots of the American Revolution.

MORE ABOUT . . .
Paul Revere

A talented Boston silversmith, Paul Revere engraved several political cartoons like the one on page 96 and even learned to make gunpowder for the war effort. He participated in the Boston Tea Party and won fame as a messenger.

ASSESS & RETEACH

Section 1 Assessment

Have pairs of students evaluate each other's responses before finalizing them.

Self-Assessment

Have students create and respond to a series of questions in order to show what they learned in the section and what they still want to find out. Students can review the section to find some of the information.

Section Quiz

FORMAL ASSESSMENT
Section Quiz, p. 42

Reteach

Use the Guided Reading Worksheet for Section 1 to help in reviewing the main ideas of this section.

IN-DEPTH RESOURCES: UNIT 1
Guided Reading, p. 58

CLOSE

British taxation and crackdowns on tax resistance promoted colonial unity. The escalating tensions led to armed rebellion.

98   Chapter 4

---

action and assembled the First Continental Congress. In September 1774, 56 delegates met in Philadelphia and drew up a declaration of colonial rights. They defended the colonies' right to run their own affairs. They supported the protests in Massachusetts and stated that if the British used force against the colonies, the colonies should fight back. They also agreed to reconvene in May 1775 if their demands weren't met.

Fighting Erupts at Lexington and Concord

After the First Continental Congress, colonists in many eastern New England towns stepped up military preparations. Minutemen, or civilian soldiers, quietly stockpiled firearms and gunpowder. General Gage soon learned about these activities. In the spring of 1775, he ordered troops to march from Boston to nearby Concord, Massachusetts, and seize illegal weapons.

Colonists in Boston were watching, and on the night of April 18, 1775, Paul Revere, William Dawes, and Samuel Prescott rode out to spread word that 700 British troops were headed for Concord. The darkened countryside rang with church bells and gunshots—prearranged signals, sent from town to town, that the British were coming.

The king's troops reached Lexington, Massachusetts, five miles short of Concord, on the cold, windy dawn of April 19. As they neared the town, they saw 70 minutemen drawn up in lines on the village green. The British commander ordered the minutemen to leave, and the colonists began to move out without laying down their muskets. Then someone fired, and the British soldiers sent a volley of shots into the departing militia. Eight minutemen were killed and nine more were wounded, but only one British soldier was injured. The Battle of Lexington lasted only 15 minutes.

The British marched on to Concord, where they found an empty arsenal. The next day, British soldiers lined up to march back to Boston, but the march quickly became a slaughter. Between 3,000 and 4,000 minutemen had assembled overnight, and they now fired on the marching troops from behind stone walls and trees. British soldiers fell by the dozen. Only the arrival of reinforcements from Boston saved them from complete disaster.

Bloodied and humiliated, the remaining British soldiers made their way back to Boston that night. They were probably too tired to notice that the surrounding hills were dotted with campfires over which salt pork and johnnycakes were cooking. Colonists had become enemies of Britain and now held Boston and its encampment of British troops under siege.

The "brown Bess" musket was a popular gun during the early days of the war. Although it was highly inaccurate from a distance, it could be reloaded quickly and was deadly at close range.

Section ① Assessment

1. TERMS & NAMES

Identify:
• Stamp Act
• Samuel Adams
• Townshend Acts
• Boston Massacre
• committee of correspondence
• Boston Tea Party
• King George III
• Intolerable Acts
• martial law

98 CHAPTER 4

2. SYNTHESIZING Create a cluster diagram like the one shown and fill it in with events that demonstrate the conflict between Great Britain and the American colonies.

Conflict grows

Choose one event to further explain in a paragraph.

3. HYPOTHESIZING What opinion might a British soldier have had about the Boston Massacre? Explain and support your response.

THINK ABOUT
• the start of the conflict on March 5, 1770
• the behavior of Crispus Attucks and other colonists
• the use of the event as propaganda

4. FORMING AN OPINION Explain whether you think the British government acted wisely in its dealings with the colonies between 1765 and 1775. Support your explanation with examples from the text.

THINK ABOUT
• the reasons for British actions
• the reactions of colonists
• the results of British actions

ANSWERS

1. TERMS & NAMES

Stamp Act, p. 94
Samuel Adams, p. 95
Townshend Acts, p. 95
Boston Massacre, p. 96
committee of correspondence, p. 97
Boston Tea Party, p. 97
King George III, p. 97
Intolerable Acts, p. 97
martial law, p. 97

2. SYNTHESIZING

Possible Responses: forming of Sons of Liberty; protesting of Stamp Act; seizure of the *Liberty*, Boston Massacre; Boston Tea Party; closing of Boston harbor; Quartering Act; placing of Boston under martial law; stockpiling of arms; stationing of British troops at Concord; Battle of Lexington; colonists' retaliation at Concord.

3. HYPOTHESIZING

Possible Responses: Soldiers may have felt vulnerable, surrounded by a hostile crowd; they may have been physically provoked; they probably resented the term "Boston Massacre" because, although some deaths occurred, there was no massacre; they may have felt that they were unfairly taunted.

4. FORMING AN OPINION

Possible Responses: Some may argue that Parliament only clamped down when colonists became too rebellious. Others may say that taxing tea to save the East India Company was politically naive; that Parliament should have avoided confrontational tactics such as the Intolerable Acts.

② Ideas Help Start a Revolution

LEARN ABOUT debates in the Continental Congress and increasing tensions in the colonies in 1775–1776

TO UNDERSTAND why Americans declared independence in spite of their divided loyalties.

TERMS & NAMES
- Second Continental Congress
- Olive Branch Petition
- *Common Sense*
- Thomas Jefferson
- Declaration of Independence
- Patriot
- Loyalist

ONE AMERICAN'S STORY

Benjamin Franklin, the famous American writer, scientist, statesman, and diplomat, represented the colonies in London throughout the growing feud with Britain. As resistance in the colonies turned to bloodshed, however, Franklin fled London in 1775 and sailed home to Philadelphia.

But one thing nagged him: his son William sided with the Crown. William Franklin, the royal governor of New Jersey, had an English wife, was stubbornly loyal to King George, and opposed the rebellious atmosphere in the colonies. William regularly wrote letters to the British authorities in which he reported on the conflict in the colonies. In a letter written on August 2, 1775 to Lord Dartmouth, William stated his position and that of others who resisted revolutionary views.

William Franklin

A PERSONAL VOICE
There is indeed a dread in the minds of many here that some of the leaders of the people are aiming to establish a republic. Rather than submit . . . we have thousands who will risk the loss of their lives in defense of the old Constitution. [They] are ready to declare themselves whenever they see a chance of its being of any avail.

WILLIAM FRANKLIN, quoted in *A Little Revenge: Benjamin Franklin and His Son*

Because of William's stand on colonial issues, communication between him and his father virtually ceased. The break between Benjamin Franklin and his son mirrored the chasm that now divided American from American, and the colonies from Britain. The notion of fighting Britain frightened and horrified some colonists even as it inspired others. But, in the end, a set of ideas spurred the colonists to declare independence from their home country.

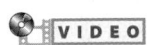 **VIDEO** *PATRIOT FATHER, LOYALIST SON:*
The Divided House of Benjamin and William Franklin

The Colonies Hover Between Peace and War

In May of 1775, colonial leaders convened a second Continental Congress in Philadelphia to debate their next move. Beyond their meeting hall, however, events continued moving quickly, as minutemen and British soldiers clashed in a bloody battle outside Boston and an increasingly furious King George readied his country for war.

THE SECOND CONTINENTAL CONGRESS The loyalties that divided colonists sparked endless debates at the **Second Continental Congress.** Some delegates were militant radicals ready to fight for independence. Others, more moderate, argued for peaceful reconciliation with Great Britain. John Adams of Massachusetts suggested a sweeping, radical plan—that each colony set up its own government and that the Congress declare the colonies independent. Furthermore, he argued, the Congress should consider the militiamen besieging Boston to be the Continental Army and name a general to lead them.

The War for Independence **99**

SECTION 2 RESOURCES

 PRINT RESOURCES

IN-DEPTH RESOURCES: UNIT 1
Guided Reading, p. 59
Primary Source: Political Cartoon, p. 67
American Lives: Mercy Otis Warren, p. 72

ACCESS FOR STUDENTS ACQUIRING ENGLISH
Guided Reading (Spanish), p. 40

FORMAL ASSESSMENT
Section Quiz, p. 43

ALTERNATIVE ASSESSMENT BOOK
See forms for supporting and scoring alternative activities.

TECHNOLOGY RESOURCES

HUMANITIES TRANSPARENCIES
H5, *Battle of Bunker Hill* by Howard Pyle
H31, Political Cartoon on the Battle of Bunker Hill by Matthew Darly

CD-ROM Electronic Library of Primary Sources

VIDEO *American Stories* video series
American Portfolio: A Videodisc for U.S. History
user's guide, pp. 29, 30, 33, 34

INTERNET McDougal Littell Learning On-Line
http://www.mcdougallittell.com

Section 2 Overview

OBJECTIVES
1. To examine efforts made to avoid bloodshed as the colonies hovered between peace and war.
2. To summarize the philosophical and political background of the Declaration of Independence.
3. To contrast the attitudes of Loyalists and Patriots.

CRITICAL THINKING
- Analyzing Causes, p. 101
- Summarizing, pp. 102, 103
- Analyzing Motives, p. 103
- Hypothesizing, p. 103
- Interpreting, p. 103

FOCUS & MOTIVATE

▶ *Starting with the Student*
- Watch the video "Patriot Father, Loyalist Son," which tells about the deep political divisions between Benjamin Franklin, committed Patriot, and his only son, who remained loyal to Britain.
- Use the *Video Resource Book* for activities, primary sources, and answers to your students' questions about the Franklins.

 AMERICAN STORIES VIDEO SERIES
"Patriot Father, Loyalist Son"
Videocassette: Volume 1

Videodisc: Disc 1, Side A, Chapter 2

OBJECTIVE
① **INSTRUCT**

The Colonies Hover Between Peace and War

▶ *Discussing Key Ideas*
- As delegates to the Second Continental Congress, held in Philadelphia, argue over independence, events overtake them.

(continued on next page)

Teacher's Edition **99**

(continued from p. 99)

- In June 1775, British troops outside Boston engage the colonial militia in the Battle of Bunker Hill.
- The Continental Congress offers peace with the Olive Branch Petition, which George III rejects.

IN-DEPTH RESOURCES: UNIT 1
Guided Reading, p. 59

ACCESS FOR STUDENTS ACQUIRING ENGLISH
Guided Reading (Spanish), p. 40

HUMANITIES TRANSPARENCIES:
H5, *Battle of Bunker Hill*
H31, *Political Cartoon on Bunker Hill*

MORE ABOUT . . .
John Dickinson

Called the "penman of the Revolution," John Dickinson won fame for his newspaper series *Letters from a Farmer in Pennsylvania,* which presented his powerful arguments against the Townshend Acts. As a Pennsylvania delegate to the Continental Congress, he refused to sign the Declaration of Independence, still hoping for reconciliation with Britain. He nevertheless fought valiantly in the Patriot militia and later represented Delaware at the Constitutional Convention.

This painting shows "Bunker's Hill" before the battle, as shells from Boston set nearby Charlestown ablaze. At the battle, the British demonstrated a maneuver they used throughout the war. They massed together, were visible for miles, and failed to take advantage of ground cover.

Moderate John Dickinson of Pennsylvania strongly disagreed with Adams's call for revolt. In private, he confronted Adams.

PERSONAL VOICE
What is the reason, Mr. Adams, that you New England men oppose our measures of reconciliation? . . . If you don't concur with us in our pacific system, I and a number of us will break off from you in New England, and we will carry on the opposition by ourselves in our own way.

JOHN DICKINSON, quoted in *Patriots: The Men Who Started the American Revolution*

The debates raged on into June, but one stubborn fact remained: colonial militiamen were still encamped around Boston. The Congress agreed to recognize them as the Continental Army and appointed as its commander a 43-year-old veteran of the French and Indian War, George Washington. The Congress, acting like an independent government, also authorized the printing of paper money to pay the troops and organized a committee to deal with foreign nations. These actions came just in time.

THE BATTLE OF BUNKER HILL Cooped up in Boston, British General Thomas Gage decided to strike at militiamen who had dug in on Breed's Hill, north of the city and near Bunker Hill. On the steamy summer morning of June 17, 1775, Gage sent out 2,400 redcoats, British soldiers so named for the scarlet jackets they wore. The British, sweating in wool uniforms and heavy packs, began marching up Breed's Hill in their customary broad lines. The colonists held their fire until the last minute, then began to mow down the advancing redcoats. The surviving British troops made a second attack, and then a third. The third assault succeeded, but only because the militiamen ran low on ammunition.

By the time the smoke cleared, the colonists had lost 311 men, while the British had suffered over 1,000 casualties. The misnamed Battle of Bunker Hill would prove to be the deadliest battle of the war.

THE OLIVE BRANCH PETITION By July, the Second Continental Congress was readying the colonies for war though still hoping for peace. Most of the delegates, like most colonists, felt deep loyalty to George III and blamed the bloodshed on the king's ministers. On July 8, 1775, the Congress sent the king the so-called **Olive Branch Petition,** urging a return to "the former harmony" between Britain and the colonies.

King George flatly rejected the petition. Furthermore, he issued a proclamation stating that the colonies were in rebellion and urged Parliament to order a naval blockade of the American coast.

Proclamatic

Cooperative Activity: Creating a Political Pamphlet

Task: Small groups of students will create political pamphlets promoting the Loyalist or Patriot cause.

Purpose: To understand the colonists' feelings about the war.

Activity: Each group should work together to produce a folded pamphlet designed to persuade colonists to accept the Loyalist or Patriot position. Tell students to imagine that

the pamphlet will be printed and circulated soon after a particular episode or event—the Battle of Bunker Hill, for example, or the signing of the Declaration of Independence.

Building a Portfolio: Students who choose to place a pamphlet in their portfolio should attach a note to it pointing out their contributions.

ALTERNATIVE ASSESSMENT BOOK
Standards for Evaluating a Cooperative Activity

Standards for Evaluation
Pamphlets should . . .

- express a Loyalist or Patriot view
- use persuasive language
- reflect events of the day
- end with some kind of call to action
- include an eye-catching front page, possibly with hand-drawn illustrations

The Patriots Declare Independence

Although most colonists found fault with the British army and British office-holders, they had maintained feelings of loyalty to the king and were uncertain about the idea of independence. Many colonists wanted to return to a state of peaceful coexistence with Britain. However, in the months following the Olive Branch Petition, colonial public opinion began to shift. The colonists were influenced by the powerful words of an angry citizen and later by the lofty ideas of a thin document.

COMMON SENSE In *Common Sense,* an anonymous 47-page essay published in pamphlet form, the colonist Thomas Paine attacked King George and the monarchy. Paine, a recent immigrant, argued that responsibility for British tyranny lay with "the royal brute of Britain." Paine explained that his own revolt against the king began with Lexington and Concord.

> **A PERSONAL VOICE**
> No man was a warmer wisher for a reconciliation than myself, before the fatal nineteenth of April, 1775, but the moment the event of that day was made known, I rejected the hardened, sullen-tempered Pharaoh of England forever . . . the wretch, that with the pretended title of Father of His People can unfeelingly hear of their slaughter, and composedly sleep with their blood upon his soul.
>
> **THOMAS PAINE,** *Common Sense*

Thomas Paine helped to overcome any last doubts about separating from Britain with his pamphlet *Common Sense.*

A. Answer The Massachusetts militia asked Congress to take over the army; bloodshed at Breed's Hill; King George rejected the Olive Branch Petition and declared the colonies in revolt.

THINK THROUGH HISTORY
A. Analyzing Causes
What events led the Continental Congress to urge each colony to form an independent government?

Paine declared that the time had come for colonists to proclaim an independent republic. He argued that independence, which was the American "destiny," would allow America to trade freely with other nations for guns and ammunition and win foreign aid from British enemies. Finally, Paine stated, independence would give American colonists the chance to create a better society—one free from tyranny with equal social and economic opportunities for all.

Common Sense was widely read (some 150,000 copies were sold) and widely applauded. In April 1776, George Washington wrote, "I find *Common Sense* is working a powerful change in the minds of many men."

DECLARING INDEPENDENCE In May 1776, events pushed the wavering Continental Congress toward a decision. North Carolina had declared itself independent, and a majority of Virginians told their delegates that they favored independence. At last, the Congress urged each colony to form its own government. On June 7, Virginia delegate Richard Henry Lee moved that "these United Colonies are, and of a right ought to be, free and independent States."

While talks on this fateful motion were underway, the Congress appointed a committee to prepare a formal declaration explaining the reasons for the colonies' actions. Virginia lawyer **Thomas Jefferson,** known for his broad knowledge and skillfully crafted prose, was chosen to express the committee's points.

Jefferson's masterful **Declaration of Independence** drew on the concepts of English philosopher John Locke, who was part of the intellectual movement known as the Enlightenment. Enlightenment thinkers stressed reason and logic, and they believed that humans could progress and develop a better society.

Locke maintained that people enjoy "natural rights" to life, liberty, and property. Furthermore, he contended, people willingly come together in a social contract—an agreement in which the people consent to choose and obey a government so long as it safeguards their natural rights. If the government becomes tyrannical, Locke maintained, people have the right and the duty to resist it.

These documents are laws that were issued by the Second Continental Congress, which served as the government of the United States during the Revolutionary War.

PROCLAMATION.
WHEREAS, in just Punishment of

 BY THE UNITED
CONGRESS ASSE

PROPOSITION

OBJECTIVE
② INSTRUCT

The Patriots Declare Independence

▶ ***Starting with the Student***
Ask students whether they have ever had to make a direct statement of what they believed were their rights in a particular situation. Then ask them how they went about doing this and what the response was.

▶ ***Discussing Key Ideas***
• Thomas Paine's *Common Sense* makes a persuasive case for independence.
• Thomas Jefferson's Declaration of Independence, adopted by the Continental Congress on July 4, 1776, expresses the argument in more philosophical terms.

MORE ABOUT . . .
Thomas Paine

Thomas Paine came to Philadelphia in 1774 on the advice of Ben Franklin, whom Paine had met in London. Two years later, Paine published *Common Sense,* donating most of his profits to the Revolutionary cause. He later returned to England, where his defense of the French Revolution, *The Rights of Man,* prompted an indictment for treason. Fleeing to France, he was caught up in the Reign of Terror and imprisoned there. While in prison, he published *The Age of Reason,* an attack on organized religion that won him many enemies.

ELECTRONIC LIBRARY OF PRIMARY SOURCES:
from *Common Sense* by Thomas Paine

TEACHING OPTIONS

Making Connections Across the Curriculum

Literature In addition to *Common Sense,* Paine is famous for his series of pamphlets *The Crisis.* The first of these appeared in December 1776, when the dispirited American troops had just retreated across New Jersey. Paine's patriotic message, beginning "These are the times that try men's souls," proved so stirring that General Washington ordered the pamphlet read to all his troops. Paine continued the series until 1783; he also served as aide-de-camp to General Nathanael Greene.

Encourage students to discuss patriotic songs, speeches, or other literature that they find especially inspiring.

Exploring Themes

Expanding Democracy Point out that the Declaration of Independence (along with the Constitution) forms the foundation on which America's democratic values rest. The concept of natural, or inalienable, rights contrasts with the aristocratic idea that some people have qualities bestowed by lineage or breeding, and thus are entitled to more privileges. The idea of a government holding power by consent of the governed is often called the social contract, which contrasts with the idea of the divine right of kings, or God-given right of monarchs to rule.

Loyalists

Charles Inglis A clergyman of the Church of England, Charles Inglis was loyal to the king and argued against independence: "By reconciliation with Britain, [an end] would be put to the present calamitous war by which many lives have been lost, and so many more must be lost if it continues."

Joseph Brant Mohawk chief Joseph Brant was loyal to the British and told a gathering of Iroquois: "If we did nothing for the British . . . there will be no peace for us. Our throats will be cut by the Red Coat man or by America . . . . We should go and join the father [England] . . . this is the only way for us."

Thomas Robinson A prominent Delaware politician and storekeeper, Thomas Robinson refused the call to stop selling British tea. He soon sided with Great Britain and called the Second Continental Congress an "unconstitutional body of men." Members of the Congress in turn labeled him an "enemy to his country."

MORE ABOUT . . .
"Our Lives, Our Fortunes, and Our Sacred Honor"
The closing pledge in the Declaration of Independence was not idle rhetoric; those signing the document did indeed place themselves in great jeopardy. Just 30 years earlier, the English had killed or driven from their homeland many Highland Scots who had been involved in the second Jacobite rebellion. In 1776, the Catholics in Ireland, because of widespread Catholic support for James II in 1689, were still living under harsh penal laws that severely restricted their freedom.

DIFFICULT DECISIONS IN HISTORY
Reconciliation or Independence?
After students answer the questions, have volunteers choose sides and stage a discussion in which they promote their side of the argument.

OBJECTIVE

③ **INSTRUCT**

Americans Choose Sides

▶ *Discussing Key Ideas*
• Americans become either Loyalists, who oppose independence, or Patriots, who favor it.
• Within ethnic and religious groups, and even within families, loyalties are often divided.

IN-DEPTH RESOURCES: UNIT 1
Primary Source: Pro-British political cartoon, p. 67

Difficult Decisions
IN HISTORY

RECONCILIATION OR INDEPENDENCE?
Many American colonists in 1775 were not convinced that independence from Britain was a good idea. They felt deep loyalty to the king and were accustomed to British rule and the order that it had created.

Many others believed in Thomas Paine's ideas and wanted to be rid of tyranny as well as be free to pursue their own economic gains and political ideals.

1. Consider the points of view of different groups of colonists, including slaves, in 1775. What factors do you think would have most strongly influenced each group's preference for independence or reconciliation? Explain your answer.

2. Imagine that the delegates at the Second Continental Congress had voted for reconciliation. What events do you think would have followed—both in the short run and the long run? Give reasons to support your answer.

Jefferson referred to people's natural rights as inalienable rights—ones that can never be taken away. Jefferson described these rights as "life, liberty, and the pursuit of happiness." In keeping with Locke's ideas, Jefferson then declared that governments "derive their powers from the consent of the governed"—that is, from the people. This consent gave the people the right "to alter or to abolish" any government that threatened their inalienable rights and to install a government that would uphold these principles. On the basis of this reasoning, the American colonies declared their independence from Britain, listing in the Declaration the numerous ways in which the British king had taken away the "inalienable rights" of the Americans.

The Declaration states flatly that "all men are created equal." When this phrase was written, it expressed the common belief that free citizens were political equals. It did not claim that all people had the same ability or ought to be of equal wealth. It was not meant to embrace women, Native Americans, and African American slaves—a large number of Americans. However, Jefferson's words presented ideals that would later help these groups challenge traditional attitudes.

In his first draft, Jefferson included an eloquent attack on the cruelty and injustice of the slave trade. However, South Carolina and Georgia, the two colonies most dependent on slavery, objected. In order to gain the votes of those two states, Jefferson dropped the offending passage.

On July 2, 1776, the delegates voted unanimously that the American colonies were free, and on July 4, 1776, they adopted the Declaration of Independence. While delegates created a formal copy of the Declaration, the document was read to a crowd in front of the Philadelphia State House—now called Independence Hall. A rush of pride and anxiety ran through the **Patriots**—the supporters of independence—when they heard the closing vow: "We mutually pledge to each other our Lives, our Fortunes, and our Sacred Honor."

Americans Choose Sides

Americans now faced a difficult, bitter choice: revolution or loyalty to the crown. This issue divided communities, friends, and even families all over the colonies.

LOYALISTS AND PATRIOTS The exact number of **Loyalists**—those who opposed independence and remained loyal to the crown—is unknown. Many with Loyalist sympathies changed sides as the war progressed.

THINK THROUGH HISTORY
B. *Summarizing* What reasons did Jefferson give to justify revolt by the colonies?
B. Answer When a government fails to protect people's inalienable rights, these people have a right to rebel and form a government that will protect their rights.

Making Connections Across Time

Independence Day Note that Independence Day was first celebrated in Philadelphia on July 4, 1777, the one-year anniversary of the adoption of the Declaration of Independence. Flag Day, June 14, commemorates the Continental Congress's 1777 adoption of the Stars and Stripes as the U.S. flag; it is a legal holiday only in Pennsylvania.

Ask students if they feel that present-day celebrations of these holidays show sufficient appreciation of the events they commemorate. Should Flag Day be a legal holiday in all 50 states? Have students explain their answers.

Teaching Gifted and Talented Students

Oral Presentation Have students choose one of the Loyalists or Patriots portrayed at the top of pages 102–103 and do research to find out more about him or her. Students should pool their information in an oral presentation that includes readings of the quotations in their textbooks as well as other statements by or about the historical figures they research.

IN-DEPTH RESOURCES: UNIT 1
American Lives: Mercy Otis Warren, p. 72

Patriots

Nathanael Greene A pacifist Quaker, Nathanael Greene nonetheless chose to fight against the British. "I am determined to defend my rights and maintain my freedom or sell my life in the attempt."

James Armistead The state of Virginia paid tribute to devoted revolutionary James Armistead, who as a slave had been permitted to enlist under General Lafayette: "At the peril of his life [Armistead] found means to frequent the British camp, and thereby faithfully executed important commissions entrusted to him by the marquis."

Mercy Otis Warren Patriot Mercy Otis Warren wrote, "I see the inhabitants of our plundered cities quitting the elegancies of life, possessing nothing but their freedom, I behold faction & discord tearing up an Island we once held dear and a mighty Empire long the dread of distant nations, tott'ring to the very foundation."

HISTORY FROM VISUALS
Colonists Choose Sides
Reading the Art Have a student clarify what Armistead apparently did. *Spied in the British camp.*

Extension Encourage students to name other Loyalists and Patriots besides those shown on pages 102–103. *Possible Additions: William Franklin, Loyalist; Ben Franklin and Thomas Jefferson, Patriots.*

Some Loyalists felt a special tie to the king because they had served as judges, councilors, or governors. Most Loyalists, however, were ordinary people of modest means. They included some people who lived far from the cities and knew little of the events that turned other colonists into revolutionaries. Other people remained loyal because they thought that the British were going to win the war and they wanted to avoid being punished as rebels. Still others were Loyalists because they thought that the crown would protect their rights more effectively than the new colonial governments would.

THINK THROUGH HISTORY
C. Analyzing Motives How did the thinking of Loyalists differ from that of Patriots?

C. Answer Loyalists maintained respect for the king and preferred British rule; Patriots agreed with Paine and wanted to be free of tyrannical rules imposed by Britain.

Patriots drew their numbers from people who saw economic opportunity in an independent America. The patriot cause embraced farmers, artisans, merchants, landowners, and elected officials. German colonists in Pennsylvania, Maryland, and Virginia also joined the fight for independence. As a group, the Patriots made up a little less than half of the colonial population.

TAKING SIDES The conflict presented dilemmas for other groups as well. The Quakers generally supported the Patriots but did not fight, because they did not believe in war. Many African Americans fought on the side of the Patriots, while others joined the Loyalists since the British promised freedom to slaves who would fight for the crown. Most Native Americans supported the British because they viewed colonial settlers as a bigger threat to their lands.

Now the colonies were plunged into two wars—a war for independence and a civil war in which Americans found themselves on opposing sides. The price of choosing sides could be high. In declaring their independence, the Patriots had invited war with the mightiest empire on earth.

ASSESS & RETEACH

Section 2 Assessment Students might work in pairs to respond to the questions.

Self-Assessment To assess what they have learned, students might write their own questions, exchange them with a partner, and try to answer their partner's questions.

Section Quiz
FORMAL ASSESSMENT Section Quiz, p. 43

Reteach Use the video "Patriot Father, Loyalist Son" to review the deep personal struggle many colonists had over breaking with Britain.

 AMERICAN STORIES VIDEO SERIES "Patriot Father, Loyalist Son"

CLOSE

Swept up in escalating violence and spurred by inspiring political rhetoric, the colonies declared their independence and began a revolution that divided colonial loyalties.

Section 2 Assessment

1. TERMS & NAMES
Identify:
• Second Continental Congress
• Olive Branch Petition
• *Common Sense*
• Thomas Jefferson
• Declaration of Independence
• Patriot
• Loyalist

2. SUMMARIZING Recreate the cluster diagram below on your paper. Fill it in with details presenting causes, ideas, and results related to the Declaration of Independence.

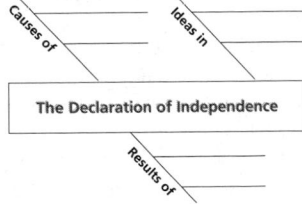

Causes of / Ideas in / The Declaration of Independence / Results of

3. HYPOTHESIZING Imagine that King George had accepted the Olive Branch Petition and tried a diplomatic resolution with the Congress. Do you think colonists would still have pressed for independence?

THINK ABOUT
• the attitudes of the king and Parliament toward the colonies
• the impact of fighting at Lexington, Concord, and Breed's Hill
• the writings of Thomas Paine

4. INTERPRETING Why do you think that when Jefferson borrowed Locke's ideas, he changed the rights of men from "life, liberty, and the pursuit of property" to "life, liberty, and the pursuit of happiness"?

THINK ABOUT
• Jefferson's reputation as a lawyer and scholar
• the politically charged climate of rebellion and loyalty
• the socioeconomic groups living in America

The War for Independence **103**

ANSWERS

1. TERMS & NAMES
Second Continental Congress, p. 99
Olive Branch Petition, p. 100
Common Sense, p. 101
Thomas Jefferson, p. 101
Declaration of Independence, p. 101
Patriot, p. 102
Loyalist, p. 102

2. SUMMARIZING
Possible Responses: **Causes of:** Second Continental Congress met; King George rejected Olive Branch Petition; Thomas Paine published *Common Sense.* **Ideas in:** colonies independent; government based on a social contract; inalienable rights of Americans. **Results of:** colonies became independent; colonists forced to choose revolution or loyalty.

3. HYPOTHESIZING
Possible Responses: Students answering yes might cite British efforts to keep the colonists subservient; colonists' memories of recent battles; Thomas Paine's persuasive arguments for independence. Students answering no might say that most Americans were loyal to the king and did not want independence.

4. INTERPRETING
Possible Responses: He felt that "pursuit of happiness" had universal appeal and that no one could argue against it; as a lawyer, he knew the emotional power of words; perhaps he felt that the wording might sway some Loyalists; he knew that many Americans didn't own property, and he wanted to include them.

The Declaration of Independence

The text printed here shows the spelling and punctuation of the handwritten original. Selected words and phrases are explained below, to help students understand some of the 18th-century language and to help clarify meaning.

unalienable Rights rights that cannot be taken away

light and transient causes unimportant reasons

shewn shown

usurpations *unjust seizures of power*

Despotism *rule by a tyrant with absolute power*

let facts be submitted to a candid world The colonists can no longer suffer the abuses of their government and thus must change it. What follows is a list of charges against King George III.

He *King George III*

inestimable priceless

Th Jefferson

John Adams

Chs. Livingston

Beny. Franklin

Roger Sherman

In Congress, July 4, 1776.

A Declaration by the Representatives of the United States of America, in General Congress assembled.

When in the Course of human events, it becomes necessary for one people to dissolve the political bands which have connected them with another, and to assume among the powers of the earth, the separate and equal station to which the Laws of Nature and of Nature's God entitle them, a decent respect to the opinions of mankind requires that they should declare the causes which impel them to the separation.

We hold these truths to be self-evident, that all men are created equal, that they are endowed by their Creator with certain <u>unalienable Rights</u>, that among these are Life, Liberty and the pursuit of Happiness; that, to secure these rights, Governments are instituted among Men, deriving their just powers from the consent of the governed; that whenever any Form of Government becomes destructive of these ends, it is the Right of the People to alter or to abolish it, and to institute new Government, laying its foundation on such principles and organizing its powers in such form, as to them shall seem most likely to effect their Safety and Happiness. Prudence, indeed, will dictate that Governments long established should not be changed for <u>light and transient causes</u>; and accordingly all experience hath <u>shewn</u> that mankind are more disposed to suffer, while evils are sufferable, than to right themselves by abolishing the forms to which they are accustomed. But when a long train of abuses and <u>usurpations</u>, pursuing invariably the same Object, evinces a design to reduce them under absolute <u>Despotism</u>, it is their right, it is their duty, to throw off such Government, and to provide new Guards for their future security.

Such has been the patient sufferance of these Colonies; and such is now the necessity which constrains them to alter their former Systems of Government. The history of the present King of Great Britain is a history of repeated injuries and usurpations, all having in direct object the establishment of an absolute Tyranny over these States. To prove this, <u>let facts be submitted to a candid world</u>.

<u>He</u> has refused his Assent to Laws, the most wholesome and necessary for the public good.

He has forbidden his Governors to pass Laws of immediate and pressing importance, unless suspended in their operation till his assent should be obtained; and, when so suspended, he has utterly neglected to attend to them.

He has refused to pass other Laws for the accommodation of large districts of people, unless those people would relinquish the right of Representation in the Legislature, a right <u>inestimable</u> to them, and formidable to tyrants only.

He has called together legislative bodies at places unusual, uncomfortable, and distant from the depository of their public Records, for the sole purpose of fatiguing them into compliance with his measures.

He has dissolved Representative Houses repeatedly, for opposing with manly firmness his invasions on the rights of the people.

He has refused for a long time, after such dissolutions, to cause others to be elected; whereby the Legislative powers, incapable of Annihilation, have returned to the people at large for their exercise; the State remaining in the mean time exposed to all the dangers of invasions from without, and convulsions within.

He has endeavoured to prevent the population of these States; for that purpose obstructing the Laws for Naturalization of Foreigners; refusing to pass others to encourage

104 Chapter 4

their migration hither, and raising the conditions of new Appropriations of Lands.

He has obstructed the Administration of Justice, by refusing his Assent to Laws for establishing Judiciary powers.

He has made Judges dependent on his Will alone, for the tenure of their offices, and the amount and payment of their salaries.

He has erected a multitude of New Offices, and sent hither swarms of Officers to harass our people and eat out their substance.

He has kept among us, in times of peace, Standing Armies, without the Consent of our legislatures.

He has affected to render the Military independent of and superior to the Civil power.

He has combined with others to subject us to a jurisdiction foreign to our constitution and unacknowledged by our laws; giving his Assent to their Acts of pretended Legislation:

For quartering large bodies of armed troops among us;

For protecting them, by a mock Trial, from punishment for any Murders which they should commit on the Inhabitants of these States;

For cutting off our Trade with all parts of the world;

For imposing Taxes on us without our Consent;

For depriving us, in many cases, of the benefits of Trial by Jury;

For transporting us beyond Seas to be tried for pretended offenses;

For abolishing the free System of English Laws in a neighboring Province, establishing therein an Arbitrary government, and enlarging its Boundaries so as to render it at once an example and fit instrument for introducing the same absolute rule into these Colonies;

For taking away our Charters, abolishing our most valuable laws, and altering fundamentally the Forms of our Governments;

For suspending our own Legislatures, and declaring themselves invested with power to legislate for us in all cases whatsoever.

He has abdicated Government here, by declaring us out of his Protection and waging War against us.

He has plundered our seas, ravaged our Coasts, burnt our towns, and destroyed the lives of our people.

He is at this time transporting large Armies of foreign Mercenaries to compleat the works of death, desolation, and tyranny, already begun with circumstances of Cruelty & perfidy scarcely paralleled in the most barbarous ages, and totally unworthy the Head of a civilized nation.

He has constrained our fellow Citizens, taken Captive on the high Seas, to bear Arms against their Country, to become the executioners of their friends and Brethren, or to fall themselves by their Hands.

He has excited domestic insurrections amongst us, and has endeavoured to bring on the inhabitants of our frontiers the merciless Indian Savages, whose known rule of warfare is an undistinguished destruction of all ages, sexes and conditions.

The War for Independence **105**

eat out their substance drain the resources of the colonies by forcing them to support more government officials

quartering furnishing with housing

foreign Mercenaries professional soldiers hired to serve in a foreign army

domestic insurrections rebellions at home

This engraving shows Thomas Jefferson's design for the Great Seal of the United States.

In every stage of these Oppressions We have Petitioned for Redress in the most humble terms; Our repeated Petitions have been answered only by repeated injury. A Prince, whose character is thus marked by every act which may define a Tyrant, is unfit to be the ruler of a free people.

Nor have We been wanting in attentions to our British brethren. We have warned them from time to time of attempts by their legislature to extend an unwarrantable jurisdiction over us. We have reminded them of the circumstances of our emigration and settlement here. We have appealed to their native justice and magnanimity, and we have conjured them by the ties of our common kindred, to disavow these usurpations, which would inevitably interrupt our connections and correspondence. They too have been deaf to the voice of justice and of consanguinity. We must, therefore, acquiesce in the necessity, which denounces our Separation, and hold them, as we hold the rest of mankind, Enemies in War, in Peace Friends.

We, therefore, the Representatives of the United States of America, in General Congress, Assembled, appealing to the Supreme Judge of the world for the rectitude of our intentions, do, in the name, and by the Authority of the good People of these Colonies solemnly publish and declare, That these United Colonies are, and of Right ought to be, Free and Independent States; that they are Absolved from all Allegiance to the British Crown, and that all political connection between them and the State of Great Britain is, and ought to be, totally dissolved; and that as Free and Independent States, they have full Power to levy War, conclude Peace, contract Alliances, establish Commerce, and do all other Acts and Things which Independent States may of right do.

And for the support of this Declaration, with a firm reliance on the protection of divine Providence, we mutually pledge to each other our Lives, our Fortunes, and our sacred Honor.

[Signed by]

John Hancock [President of the Continental Congress]

[GEORGIA]	[SOUTH CAROLINA]	[PENNSYLVANIA]	[NEW JERSEY]
Button Gwinnett	Edward Rutledge	Robert Morris	Richard Stockton
Lyman Hall	Thomas Heyward, Jr.	Benjamin Rush	John Witherspoon
George Walton	Thomas Lynch, Jr.	Benjamin Franklin	Francis Hopkinson
	Arthur Middleton	John Morton	John Hart
[RHODE ISLAND]		George Clymer	Abraham Clark
Stephen Hopkins	[MARYLAND]	James Smith	
William Ellery	Samuel Chase	George Taylor	[NEW HAMPSHIRE]
	William Paca	James Wilson	Josiah Bartlett
[CONNECTICUT]	Thomas Stone	George Ross	William Whipple
Roger Sherman	Charles Carroll		Matthew Thornton
Samuel Huntington		[DELAWARE]	
William Williams	[VIRGINIA]	Caesar Rodney	[MASSACHUSETTS]
Oliver Wolcott	George Wythe	George Read	Samuel Adams
	Richard Henry Lee	Thomas McKean	John Adams
[NORTH CAROLINA]	Thomas Jefferson		Robert Treat Paine
William Hooper	Benjamin Harrison	[NEW YORK]	Elbridge Gerry
Joseph Hewes	Thomas Nelson, Jr.	William Floyd	
John Penn	Francis Lightfoot Lee	Philip Livingston	
	Carter Braxton	Francis Lewis	
		Lewis Morris	

IN CONGRESS, JULY 4, 1776.

The unanimous Declaration of the thirteen united States of America.

TEACHING OPTION

Making Connections Across Cultures

Slavery In his rough draft of the Declaration, Thomas Jefferson included a strongly worded attack on the institution of slavery. The passage was dropped to gain the votes of South Carolina and Georgia—both slave-owning states.

Jefferson wrote: "He [King George] has waged cruel war against human nature itself, violating it's most sacred rights of life and liberty in the persons of a distant people who never offended him, captivating and carrying them into slavery in another hemisphere, or to incur miserable death in their transportation thither. This piratical warfare, the opprobrium of infidels powers, is the warfare of the Christian king of Great Britain." Jefferson also characterizes the slave trade as "execrable commerce" and an "assemblage of horrors."

Have students discuss the possible impact on U.S. history this passage might have had if it had been included in the Declaration.

❸ Struggling Toward Saratoga

TERMS & NAMES
• Trenton
• Saratoga
• Valley Forge
• inflation
• profiteering

LEARN ABOUT the early battles of the American Revolution, waged with civilian help,
TO UNDERSTAND how events led to a major defeat of the British at Saratoga.

ONE AMERICAN'S STORY

Albigense Waldo worked as a surgeon at Valley Forge outside Philadelphia, which served as the site of the Continental Army's camp during the winter of 1777–1778. The months there were brutal. The colonists had just handed the British a major defeat at Saratoga, but there was no end to the war in sight. British troops occupied Philadelphia, and as they found quarters inside warm homes, the underclothed and underfed Patriots huddled in makeshift huts in the freezing snow-covered woods. Waldo, who wrote of his stay at Valley Forge, reported on what was a common sight at the camp.

A PERSONAL VOICE
Here comes a bowl of beef soup full of dead leaves and dirt. There comes a soldier. His bare feet are seen through his worn-out shoes—his legs nearly naked from the tattered remains of an only pair of stockings—his Breeches [trousers] are not sufficient to cover his nakedness—his Shirt hanging in Strings—his hair disheveled—his face meager.

ALBIGENSE WALDO, quoted in *Valley Forge, the Making of an Army*

General Washington's troops march to Valley Forge.

After the colonists had declared independence, few people thought the rebellion would last very long. A divided colonial population of about two and a half million people faced a nation of 10 million that was backed by a worldwide empire. In the early years of the war, American defeat seemed certain. The ordeal at Valley Forge marked a low point for General Washington's troops, but even as it occurred, the Americans' hopes of winning began to improve.

The War Moves to the Middle States

The colonists suffered an initial loss to the British in the battle for New York, which along with the other Middle States served as the Revolutionary War's early battleground. "These are the times that try men's souls," Thomas Paine lamented after the Continental Army's early defeat.

DEFEAT IN NEW YORK The British retreated from Boston in March 1776, moving the theater of war to the Middle States. As part of a grand plan to stop the rebellion by isolating New England, the British decided to seize New York City. Two brothers, General William Howe and Admiral Richard Howe, sailed into New York harbor in the summer of 1776 with the largest British expeditionary force ever assembled—32,000 soldiers, including thousands of German mercenaries, or soldiers who fight solely for money. The Americans called these troops Hessians, because many of them came from the German region of Hesse.

General Howe was not intent on a destructive confrontation in New York. He preferred to intimidate the ragtag colonial army into surrender, humiliate General Washington, and put an end to the uprising. The Howe brothers even carried instructions to discuss peace terms and to offer amnesty, or pardon, to any patriot who would surrender and pledge his allegiance to King George.

Washington rallied 23,000 men to New York's defense. But he was vastly outnumbered, and most of his troops were untrained recruits with poor equipment.

> *"These are the times that try men's souls."*
>
> **THOMAS PAINE**

The War for Independence **107**

SECTION 3 RESOURCES

 PRINT RESOURCES

IN-DEPTH RESOURCES: UNIT 1
Guided Reading, p. 60
Primary Source: *from Valley Forge Diary*, p. 68
American Lives: Haym Salomon, p. 73

ACCESS FOR STUDENTS ACQUIRING ENGLISH
Guided Reading (Spanish), p. 41

FORMAL ASSESSMENT
Section Quiz, p. 44

ALTERNATIVE ASSESSMENT BOOK
See forms for supporting and scoring alternative activities.

 TECHNOLOGY RESOURCES

GEOGRAPHY TRANSPARENCIES
G4, North America, 1783

CD-ROM *Grolier Multimedia Encyclopedia*

VIDEO *American Portfolio: A Videodisc for U.S. History*
user's guide, pp. 34, 38

INTERNET McDougal Littell Learning On-Line
http://www.mcdougallittell.com

Section 3 Overview

OBJECTIVES
① To trace the progress of the war through the turning point at Saratoga and the winter at Valley Forge.
② To examine the colonial economy and civilian life during the Revolution.

SKILLBUILDER
• Understanding geography: location, place, p. 109

CRITICAL THINKING
• Analyzing effects, p. 108
• Identifying problems, pp. 110, 111
• Summarizing, p. 111
• Hypothesizing, p. 111
• Evaluating, p. 111

FOCUS & MOTIVATE

▶ **Starting with the Student**
• Ask students to describe a sports event or contest in which a seemingly weaker person defeated a stronger one.
• Ask them how a seemingly weaker army might defeat a stronger one in a military situation.

OBJECTIVE
① **INSTRUCT**

The War Moves to the Middle States

Students might create a time line to organize the events described in this section.

event	event	event
date	date	date

▶ **Discussing Key Ideas**
• After being driven from New York City, the Continental Army under George Washington wins the Battle of Trenton but suffers major defeats the following year in Pennsylvania.

(continued on next page)

(continued from p. 107)

- The American victory at Saratoga in October 1777 is a turning point in the Revolution, prompting France's entry on the American side.
- With French aid not expected for months, the Continental Army spends a brutal winter in Valley Forge, Pennsylvania.

IN-DEPTH RESOURCES: UNIT 1
Guided Reading, p. 00

ACCESS FOR STUDENTS ACQUIRING ENGLISH
Guided Reading (Spanish), p. 00

MORE ABOUT . . .
The Opposing Armies

The Continental Army was officially formed by the Continental Congress in June 1775 from the standing militias that all colonies except Pennsylvania possessed. The Congress also voted to raise ten new companies of riflemen and put George Washington in charge of the entire army. The British hired German mercenaries, most of them Hessians (from Hesse-Kassel in what is now central Germany), to supplement their forces.

KEY PLAYER
George Washington

Critical Thinking:
Analyzing Effects Ask students how the British at Trenton might have felt about Washington. *Possible Response: They might have considered him sneaky and perhaps dishonorable to attack the day after Christmas.*

 GROLIER MULTIMEDIA ENCYCLOPEDIA
George Washington

KEY PLAYER

GEORGE WASHINGTON
1732–1799

During the Revolutionary War, Commander in Chief George Washington became a national hero. An imposing man, Washington stood six feet two inches tall. He was broad-shouldered, calm, and dignified, and he was an expert horseman. But it was Washington's character that won hearts and, ultimately, the war.

Time and again, Washington roused dispirited men into a fighting force. At Princeton, he galloped on his white horse into the line of fire, shouting and encouraging his men. At Valley Forge, he bore the same cold and privation as every suffering soldier. Time and again, Washington's tactics saved his smaller, weaker force to fight another day. By the end of the war, the entire nation idolized General Washington, and adoring soldiers crowded near him just to touch his boots when he rode by.

The battle for New York ended in late August with heavy losses and an American retreat. Michael Graham, a Continental Army volunteer, described the chaotic withdrawal on August 27, 1776.

A PERSONAL VOICE
It is impossible for me to describe the confusion and horror of the scene that ensued: the artillery flying . . . over the horses' backs, our men running in almost every direction, . . . and the enemy huzzahing when they took prisoners. . . . At the time, I could not account for how it was that our troops were so completely surrounded but have since understood there was another road across the ridge several miles above Flatbush that was left unoccupied by our troops. Here the British passed and got betwixt them and Brooklyn unobserved. This accounts for the disaster of that day.
MICHAEL GRAHAM, quoted in *The Revolution Remembered: Eyewitness Accounts of the War for Independence*

By late fall, the British had pushed Washington's army across the Delaware River into Pennsylvania. Fewer than 8,000 men remained under Washington's command. The rest had deserted or had been killed or captured.

THE BATTLE OF TRENTON Washington desperately wanted some sort of victory to inspire his men. Their enlistment terms would end on December 31, and Washington knew he needed a victory to keep them from going home.

Washington resolved to risk everything on one bold stroke set for Christmas night 1776. In the face of a fierce storm, he led 2,400 men across the ice-choked Delaware River in small rowboats.

By 8 A.M. the next morning, the men had marched nine miles through sleet and snow to the objective—**Trenton,** New Jersey, held by a garrison of Hessians. Lulled into confidence by the storm, most of the Hessians had drunk too much rum the night before and were still sleeping it off. In a surprise attack, the Americans killed 30 of the enemy and took 918 captives and six Hessian cannons.

The victory was so stunning that many of Washington's soldiers promptly re-enlisted. Those who returned were cheered on by another astonishing victory six days later against 1,200 British stationed at Princeton. With these successes to buoy the men, Washington marched the army into winter camp near Morristown, in northern New Jersey.

THE FIGHT FOR PHILADELPHIA As the muddy fields dried out in the spring of 1777, the British, anticipating victory, looked forward to the year's campaign. General Howe had a plan to seize the American capital at Philadelphia. His troops left New York by sea, sailed up the Chesapeake Bay, and landed near the capital in late August. The Continental Congress fled the city while Washington's troops tried to block the redcoats at nearby Brandywine Creek. The Americans lost the pitched battle, and the pleasure-loving General Howe settled in to enjoy the hospitality of Philadelphia's grateful Loyalists.

Later, Washington launched a strike on the British encampment at nearby Germantown. Early on, things went well for the Americans, but patches of dense fog and smoke created so much confusion that at one point Americans fired on one another. Once again, Howe won.

VICTORY AT SARATOGA In the meantime, one of Howe's fellow British generals was marching straight into the jaws of disaster. General "Gentlemen Johnny" Burgoyne had

---

A. Answer These victories restored the soldiers' confidence after numerous losses and motivated many men to re-enlist and continue fighting in the war.

THINK THROUGH HISTORY
A. Analyzing Effects Why were the victories at Trenton and Princeton so important to the Continental Army?

Military Strengths and Weaknesses
UNITED STATES

Strengths:
- Familiarity of home ground
- Leadership of George Washington and other officers
- Inspiring cause—independence

Weaknesses:
- Most soldiers untrained and undisciplined
- Shortage of food and ammunition
- Inferior navy
- No central government to enforce wartime policies

TEACHING OPTION

Cooperative Activity: Reporting on the Revolution

Task: Groups of students will create front pages of newspaper issues reporting on different Revolutionary battles.

Purpose: To understand the military, psychological, and historical effects of different Revolutionary battles.

Activity: Each group should decide how often its paper comes out (daily, weekly) and who the audience is (Loyalists, Patriots, or both, or perhaps people overseas). Students should choose

one battle and, if necessary, do further research to cover it completely. The front page might include straight news, interviews, background pieces, and human-interest features (about soldiers or civilians affected by war, for example). Different students might serve as researchers, writers, editors, and layout designers.

 Building a Portfolio: Remind students to choose their strongest work for their portfolio.

ALTERNATIVE ASSESSMENT BOOK
Standards for Evaluating a Cooperative Activity

Standards for Evaluation
Front pages should . . .

- include headlines and the newspaper's name
- present facts accurately, telling who, what, where, when, and, when appropriate, how and why
- contain several types of articles—straight news, interviews, and so on
- be geared to a particular audience

a complex scheme and persuaded the London high command to let him follow through with it. According to Burgoyne's plan, he would lead an army down a route of lakes from Canada to Albany, where he would meet Howe's troops as they arrived from New York City. The two generals would then join forces to isolate New England from the rest of the colonies.

However, Burgoyne first had to travel through forested wilderness. He had 4,000 redcoats, 3,000 mercenaries, and 1,000 Mohawks under his command. His army had to move 30 wagons containing 138 pieces of artillery and his extra personal items, such as fine clothes, champagne, and other luxuries. The farther south Burgoyne's forces traveled into the dense woods, the more resistance they encountered.

Beyond Lake Champlain, New York, swamps and gullies, as well as thick underbrush, bogged down the army. Food supplies ran low. At the same time, militiamen and soldiers from the Continental Army gathered from all over New York and New England. Every time the two sides clashed—as at Bennington, Vermont—Burgoyne lost several hundred men. Even worse, Burgoyne didn't realize that Howe was preoccupied with conquering and occupying Philadelphia and wasn't coming to meet him.

Massed American troops finally surrounded Burgoyne at **Saratoga,** where he surrendered his battered army to General Horatio Gates on October 17, 1777. The surrender at Saratoga dramatically changed Britain's war strategy. From that time on, the British were reluctant to send troops into the countryside. Instead, they generally kept their men along the coast, no more than 50 miles away from the big guns and supply bases of the British fleet.

A TURNING POINT Saratoga was important psychologically as well as militarily. Americans now had proof that they could defeat the British regulars, even though American forces were still outnumbered. At the same time, British confidence took a heavy blow. The full impact of Saratoga was felt when the news reached Paris and London.

The American victory aroused the interest of the French, who saw an opportunity to avenge their defeat at the hands of the British in the French and Indian War. Since early 1776, the French had secretly sent weapons and ammunition to the Patriots. The Saratoga victory, however, bolstered French trust in the American army to the extent that France agreed to support the Revolution openly. The French recognized American independence and signed an alliance, a treaty of cooperation, with the Americans in February 1778. According to the terms, France agreed not to make peace with Britain unless Britain recognized American independence.

WINTER AT VALLEY FORGE While this hopeful turn of events took place in Paris,

GREAT BRITAIN

Strengths:
• Strong, well-trained army and navy
• Strong central government with available funds
• Support of colonial Loyalists and Native Americans

Weaknesses:
• Large distance separating Britain from battlefield
• Troops unfamiliar with terrain
• Weak military leaders

The War for Independence **109**

Map

Revolutionary War, 1775–1778

Gen. Montgomery — Quebec, 1775
MAINE (Mass.)
Montreal
CANADA (British)
St. Lawrence River
Lake Champlain
Gen. Arnold
Fort Ticonderoga, 1775, 1777
NEW HAMPSHIRE
Saratoga, 1777
Lexington, 1775
Concord, 1775
Bunker Hill, 1775
Albany
Gen. Gates
Boston
Lake Ontario
MASS.
NEW YORK
RHODE ISLAND
CONNECTICUT
Lake Erie
Gen. Washington
New York — Gen. Howe
PENNSYLVANIA
Long Island, 1776
Trenton, 1776
NEW JERSEY
Valley Forge
Philadelphia
Brandywine, 1777
APPALACHIAN MOUNTAINS
MARYLAND
DELAWARE
ATLANTIC OCEAN
VIRGINIA
75° W
38° N
N

← American campaign
← British campaign
★ American victory
★ British victory

0   200 Miles
0   400 Kilometers

GEOGRAPHY SKILLBUILDER
LOCATION *From which city did General Burgoyne march his troops to Saratoga?*
PLACE *What characteristics did many of the battle sites have in common? Why do you think this was so?*

Skillbuilder Answer
Location: Montreal.
Place: Sites— they were near either the Atlantic Ocean or a river. Reason— *Possible Response:* rivers and oceans, which provided troops with transportation, were strategically important to both sides.

Margin notes (left)

Skillbuilder Answer
Colonists: *Possible Responses:* familiarity of home ground, strong leadership, and the inspiring cause of independence. **British:** *Possible Responses:* unfamiliarity with the terrain, weak military leadership, and the large distance between Britain and the battlefield. **Familiarity:** *Possible responses:* they would be able to hide and flee more easily from the British and engage more efficiently in hit and run warfare.

SKILLBUILDER INTERPRETING CHARTS *What do you think was the key strength for the colonists? the key weakness for Britain? How might familiarity of their home ground help the colonists?*

Right column (Teacher's Edition notes)

HISTORY FROM VISUALS
Revolutionary War, 1775–1778
Reading the Map Have students trace the American campaign with their pencil erasers as they study the map.

Extension Have students name the site at which Burgoyne's troops scored a victory on the way to Saratoga. *Fort Ticonderoga.*

MORE ABOUT . . .
"Gentleman Johnny" Burgoyne
Handsome, charming, hard-drinking, hard-gambling—Burgoyne more than earned his nickname by living up to the stereotype of the 18th-century English gentleman. Yet, for all his flaws, Burgoyne showed far more concern for his troops than did the typical British commanding officer, and he was idolized by his men as "the soldier's friend."

HISTORY FROM VISUALS
Military Strengths and Weaknesses
Reading the Chart Ask students what they would add to the British weaknesses. *Possible Response: Use of mercenaries, who had no real stake in the outcome.*

Extension Ask students what additional shortages they think the American troops may have faced. *Possible Responses: Low pay, received at irregular intervals; lack of uniforms and boots.*

IN-DEPTH RESOURCES: UNIT 1
Primary Source: Valley Forge Diary, p. 68

TEACHING OPTIONS

Teaching Less Proficient Readers

Learning Visually Visual learners may find it easier to absorb information about Revolutionary battles if they map the details out themselves. Encourage students to expand on the maps in this and the next section of their text, creating a single map with all the important battle sites. You may want to give students copies of Geography Transparency 4 to help them create their own maps. Each visual learner might work with a more verbal partner who supplies appropriate details from the text and/or from additional research about the Revolution.

 GEOGRAPHY TRANSPARENCIES
G4, North America, 1783

Making Connections Across Time

Revolutionary Battlefields The site of the Battle of Saratoga is now a historical park tourists can drive through, stopping at various exhibits along the way. In fact, most of the other battlesites mentioned here and elsewhere in the chapter have commemorative monuments, parks, or museums that people can visit today. Have students choose different Revolutionary sites to describe to classmates in oral reports or special exhibits. Students might include personal accounts or photos as well as information from tourist brochures, travel books, Internet sites, local historical societies, and/or organizations such as the Sons of the Revolution.

Colonial Life During the Revolution

▶ **Starting with the Student**
Ask students these questions:

- How does financial hardship affect people's behavior and attitudes?
- How might the effects of financial hardship be different during a time of war than during peacetime?

▶ **Discussing Key Ideas**

- Inflation and shortages spell economic hardship for colonists; eventually, financiers organize the government's finances.
- Women contribute to the war effort by helping to arm, clothe, and feed the army, and even by fighting.

ECONOMIC BACKGROUND
"Not Worth a Continental"

Ask students what effect the inflated currency may have had on Patriot morale, and why. *Negative effect: The bad economic situation could have angered people and sapped their support of the Patriot cause; Positive effect: The Patriots may have had an incentive to win quickly—to end the economic hardship.*

IN-DEPTH RESOURCES: UNIT 1
American Lives: Haym Salomon, p. 73

This U.S. Continental currency twenty-dollar banknote was issued in 1778.

ECONOMIC BACKGROUND

"NOT WORTH A CONTINENTAL"

When Congress began printing the paper money called Continentals, it had no gold or silver to back up the currency; it simply promised that the money would be good when the war was won. But Americans had their doubts about a victory—and about the worth of the Continentals. Furthermore, everyday goods were in short supply due to the British blockade and the heavy demands for staples by the army.

Consequently, prices for goods rose. Congress responded to the rising prices by printing more money but quickly learned that having too much money in circulation lowers its value. The value of Continental currency dropped so much that people use the phrase "not worth a Continental" to refer to anything worthless.

Washington and his Continental Army were fighting to stay alive at winter camp in **Valley Forge,** Pennsylvania, a wooded hillside 20 miles west of Philadelphia. Unfortunately, Congress had little money for supplies for the troops. Even worse, once the French alliance was established, Congress was so optimistic about victory that it paid little attention to Washington's desperate pleas for supplies. The result was devastating.

Throughout the winter, 10,000 soldiers braved wind, snow, and ice with tattered clothes, few blankets, and little food. They built makeshift wood and clay huts 14 by 16 feet, each housing 12 men. They slept on straw and lived on fire cakes—a flour and water mixture baked over open fires. More than 2,000 soldiers died, yet the survivors didn't desert. They often joked to keep their spirits up. Their endurance and suffering filled Washington's letters to the Congress and his friends.

A PERSONAL VOICE
It may be said that no history . . . can furnish an instance of an Army's suffering uncommon hardships as ours have done. . . . To see men without Clothes to cover their nakedness, without Blankets to lay on, without Shoes, by which their Marches might be traced by the blood of their feet, and almost as often without Provision as with; marching through frost and snow, and at Christmas taking up their Winter Quarters within a day's march of the Enemy, without a Hut to cover them until they could be built and submitting to it without a murmur, is a mark of patience and obedience which in my opinion can scarcely be paralleled.

GEORGE WASHINGTON, quoted in *Ordeal at Valley Forge*

It would take months for French aid to arrive. In the meantime, the British controlled New York and parts of New England and wintered comfortably in Philadelphia while the meager army of Patriots struggled to survive.

Colonial Life During the Revolution

The Revolutionary War touched the life of every American, not just the men on the battlefield and the leaders struggling to pilot America through the storm. The war upset the economy and forced people into new ways of living and thinking.

FINANCING THE WAR One huge problem that the Continental Congress faced was paying the troops. When the Congress ran out of hard currency—silver and gold—it borrowed money by selling bonds to American investors and foreign governments, especially France. It also printed paper money called Continentals, the same name given to Revolutionary soldiers. As Congress printed more and more money, its value plunged, causing rising prices, or **inflation.** In New York during one three-month period, the cost of sugar and beef doubled in price. The cost of sewing pins tripled.

The Congress also struggled against many odds to equip the beleaguered army. With few munitions factories and with the British navy blockading the coast, the Americans had to smuggle arms and ammunition from Europe. To make matters worse, corrupt government officials engaged in **profiteering,** selling scarce goods for a profit. Moreover, some merchants hoarded goods, while others sold shoddy goods to make a quick return, leaving some soldiers with spoiled meat, cheap shoes, and defective weapons.

In 1781, the Congress appointed a rich Philadelphia merchant named Robert Morris as superintendent of finance. His associate was Haym Salomon, a Jewish political refugee from Poland.

Morris and Salomon begged and borrowed on their personal credit. They raised funds from Philadelphia's Quakers and Jews. In time, they organized the

B. Answer Colonists faced inflation— the rise in the price of goods—as well as profiteering, the selling of scarce goods for a profit.

THINK THROUGH HISTORY
B. Identifying Problems
What economic problems did the Americans face in financing the war?

TEACHING OPTIONS

Making Connections Across Cultures

Jews in Early America Most of the first Jews in America were Sephardic (Southern European) Jews whose ancestors had fled to Holland from Spain and Portugal to escape the Inquisition. They settled first in New Amsterdam (later New York) and then in other colonies. Traditionally merchants, not farmers (in medieval times, farming was often forbidden to Europe's Jews), they remained mostly in port cities. Haym Salomon, a Polish Jew, was a later arrival, coming to New York in 1772. Arrested by the British for spying, he escaped to Philadelphia, where he aided the Patriot cause.

Exploring Themes

Women in America Women played an important role in the Revolution managing farms and businesses while the men were off fighting. Women also supported the Patriot cause by making ammunition, clothing, and other supplies for the troops and by helping to feed and house soldiers in their area. Those women who traveled with their soldier husbands usually remained in the army camps, doing cooking, washing, and sewing; attending to wounds and illnesses when necessary; and occasionally taking up arms themselves.

government's finances and set up a supply system for the army. On September 8, 1781, a Continental major wrote in his diary, "This day will be famous in the Annals of History for being the first on which the Troops of the United States received one Month's Pay in Specie [coin]."

CIVILIANS AT WAR The demands of war also affected civilians. When men marched off to fight, many wives stepped into their husbands' shoes, managing farms, shops, and businesses as well as households and families. Women joined the war effort too. Many made ammunition from their household silver. Benjamin Franklin's daughter, Sarah Franklin Bache, organized the women of Philadelphia to help the troops, as a French visitor recalled in December 1780.

> **A PERSONAL VOICE**
> She conducted us into a room filled with needlework, recently finished by the ladies of Philadelphia. This work consisted neither of embroidered . . . waist-coats, nor of gold and silver brocade—but of shirts for the soldiers of Pennsylvania. The ladies had bought the linen from their own private purses, and had gladly cut out and stitched the shirts themselves. On each shirt was the name of the married or unmarried lady who made it, and there were 2,200 shirts in all.
>
> **MARQUIS DE CHASTELLUX,** quoted in *Travels in North America*

Hundreds of women followed their husbands to the battlefield, where they washed, mended, and cooked for the troops. A few women risked their lives in combat. At Fort Washington, New York, Margaret Corbin replaced a gunner who was shot and then was shot herself. Mary Ludwig Hays (known as Molly Pitcher) took her husband's place at a cannon when he was wounded at the Battle of Monmouth.

These self-reliant women sparked a slight shift in attitudes. Traditional society viewed women as subordinate to their husbands, but during the war, women tasted new freedoms and felt a growing sense of self-confidence. While the Revolution did not win major freedoms for American women, it did shape a new ideal for them—to rear the next generation to be Patriots.

The war opened some doors for African Americans. Thousands of slaves escaped to freedom in the chaos of war. Some fled to the cities, where they passed as free people, or to the frontier, where they sometimes joined Native American tribes. About 5,000 African Americans served in the Continental Army, where their courage, loyalty, and talent impressed white Americans. Native Americans, however, remained on the fringes of the Revolution. Some fought for the British but most preferred to remain independent and true to their own cultures.

Molly Pitcher was the heroine of the battle of Monmouth, New Jersey, which was fought in 1778. For her heroism, Washington made her a sergeant.

C. Answer They had to cope with rising prices, devalued money, and shortages of goods; women had to take on new responsibilities; African Americans continued to face the issue of freedom.

THINK THROUGH HISTORY
C. Identifying Problems
What were the problems faced by civilians during the war?

Section 3 Assessment

1. TERMS & NAMES
Identify:
• Trenton
• Saratoga
• Valley Forge
• inflation
• profiteering

2. SUMMARIZING On a chart like the one below, list each early battle of the American Revolution and its outcome.

Battle	Outcome

Explain which battle had the largest impact on the American forces and why.

3. HYPOTHESIZING Imagine that Burgoyne and the British had captured Saratoga in 1777. How might the course of the war have changed?

THINK ABOUT
• the military strength of the British
• the fighting skills of the Americans
• French support of the colonists

4. EVALUATING If you were a woman civilian during the beginning of the American Revolution, what problem caused by the war do you think would affect you the most?

THINK ABOUT
• inflation and the scarcity of goods
• the absence of the men
• the demands of the war effort

The War for Independence **111**

ANSWERS

1. TERMS & NAMES

Trenton, p. 108

Saratoga, p. 109

Valley Forge, p. 110

inflation, p. 110

profiteering, p. 110

2. SUMMARIZING

Possible Responses: New York—British force Continental Army to retreat; Trenton— colonial victory prompts re-enlistments; Philadelphia— British victory forces Congress to flee; Saratoga—colonial win leads to alliance with France.

3. HYPOTHESIZING

Possible Responses: Since most Americans were not trained soldiers, they might not have been able to stop the British from moving inland; as more British troops moved into the country-side, they might have learned to cope with America's rough terrain and might have won the war; fearing an American defeat, the French may have been discouraged from providing further help to the colonists.

4. EVALUATING

Possible Responses: the problem of trying to keep a large family fed, safe, and healthy with so little food and so few other provisions; the excessive workload created by having to make so many items, to manage houses and workplaces or farms, and to send supplies to troops.

MORE ABOUT . . .
Molly Pitcher
Mary Hays earned her nickname "Molly Pitcher" by bringing water to her husband's artillery station to quench the thirst of the soldiers during the Battle of Monmouth, New Jersey, fought on a hot June day in 1778. As a young girl, she had been a servant in Carlisle, Pennsylvania, where she met and married a local barber, William Hays, who enlisted as a gunner in 1775. With her soldier husband, she spent the winter of 1777 and 1778 at Valley Forge. After the Revolution, the state of Pennsylvania awarded her an annual pension of $40 in recognition of her services to the Patriot cause.

ASSESS & RETEACH

Section 3 Assessment
You might have a student volunteer lead a class discussion of the questions and answers.

Self-Assessment
Have students make a two-column chart about the Revolutionary struggle leading up to the victory at Saratoga. In the left column, they should list what they knew before reading, and in the right column, what they learned in this section.

Section Quiz

FORMAL ASSESSMENT
Section Quiz, p. 44

Reteach
Use the maps and other graphic aids to help in reviewing the main points of the section.

CLOSE

Early in the war, the colonists faced economic and physical hardship. The Patriot's victory at Saratoga was a turning point in the war.

① To describe the contributions of European allies.

② To trace the Revolution in the Southern colonies.

③ To summarize the British surrender at Yorktown.

④ To recognize the symbolic value of the Revolution.

SKILLBUILDER

• Understanding geography: place, movement, p. 114

CRITICAL THINKING

• Analyzing issues, pp. 113, 116
• Summarizing, pp. 115, 117
• Forming opinions, p. 117
• Analyzing causes, p. 117
• Evaluating, p. 117

FOCUS & MOTIVATE

▶ **Starting with the Student**
Ask students these questions:
• What does the American Revolution mean to them?
• What do students think it has meant to oppressed peoples the world over?

OBJECTIVE
① INSTRUCT

European Allies Shift the Balance

▶ **Discussing Key Ideas**
• Experienced European soldiers such as Friedrich von Steuben help mold the Continental Army.
• European idealists such as Lafayette also contribute to the American cause.

IN-DEPTH RESOURCES: UNIT 1
Guided Reading, p. 61

ACCESS FOR STUDENTS ACQUIRING ENGLISH
Guided Reading (Spanish), p. 42

TERMS & NAMES
• Friedrich von Steuben
• Marquis de Lafayette
• Charles Cornwallis
• Yorktown
• Treaty of Paris
• egalitarianism

④ Winning the War

LEARN ABOUT the Southern campaign of the Revolutionary War and the colonists' maneuvers to reverse British advances
TO UNDERSTAND how the Americans won the war.

ONE AMERICAN'S STORY

Colonel William Fontaine of the Virginia militia stood with the American and French armies lining a road near Yorktown, Virginia, on the afternoon of October 19, 1781. The French were dressed in bright coats and white trousers, and their white-and-gold silk flags floated on the autumn air. The American troops, standing proudly behind their generals, wore rough hunting shirts and faded Continental uniforms. Colonel Fontaine later described the feelings of these victorious soldiers as they watched the British lay down their arms.

> **A PERSONAL VOICE**
> I had the happiness to see that British army which so lately spread dismay and desolation through all our country, march forth on the [19th] at 3 o'clock through our whole army, drawn up in two lines about 20 yards distance and return disrobed of all their terrors. . . . You could not have heard a whisper or seen the least motion throughout our whole line, but every countenance was erect and expressed a serene cheerfulness.
> **COLONEL WILLIAM FONTAINE,** quoted in *The Yorktown Campaign and the Surrender of Cornwallis, 1781*

This famous painting by John Trumball of the British surrender at Yorktown is historically inaccurate. Neither Washington nor British general Cornwallis was present at the ceremony.

The American Revolution had finally ended, and the Americans had won—a fact that astonished the world. Several years before, in the depths of the Valley Forge winter, few would have thought such an event possible.

European Allies Shift the Balance

In February 1778, in the midst of the frozen winter at Valley Forge, American troops began an amazing transformation. **Friedrich von Steuben,** a Prussian captain and talented drillmaster, volunteered his services to Washington at Valley Forge and went to work "to make regular soldiers out of country bumpkins." Von Steuben taught the colonial soldiers to stand at attention, execute field maneuvers, fire and reload quickly, and wield bayonets. With the help of such European military leaders, the raw Continental Army was becoming an effective fighting force.

"The moment I knew she [America] was fighting for freedom, I burnt with the desire of bleeding for her."

MARQUIS DE LAFAYETTE

LAFAYETTE AND THE FRENCH Other foreign military men, such as the **Marquis de Lafayette,** also arrived to offer their help. A brave, idealistic 20-year-old French aristocrat, Lafayette cared passionately about the American cause and wrote to the president of the Continental Congress, "The moment I heard of America I lov'd her. . . . The moment I knew she was fighting for freedom, I burnt with the desire of bleeding for her." The young Lafayette joined Washington's staff and bore the misery of Valley Forge, lobbied for French reinforcements in France in 1779, and led a command in Virginia in the last years of the war.

Since France needed time to organize forces and send them to America, the French alliance did not immediately improve conditions for the Continental Army. As a result, the years following Valley Forge were tough, often discouraging ones for the struggling Americans.

SECTION 4 RESOURCES

 PRINT RESOURCES

IN-DEPTH RESOURCES: UNIT 1
Guided Reading, p. 61
Skillbuilder Practice: Analyzing Causes; Recognizing Effects, p. 62
Geography Application: The Seige of Yorktown, p. 63

ACCESS FOR STUDENTS ACQUIRING ENGLISH
Guided Reading (Spanish), p. 42
Skillbuilder Practice: Analyzing Causes; Recognizing Effects (Spanish), p. 43
Geography Application: The Seige of Yorktown (Spanish), p. 44

FORMAL ASSESSMENT
Section Quiz, p. 45

ALTERNATIVE ASSESSMENT BOOK
See forms for supporting and scoring alternative activities.

TECHNOLOGY RESOURCES

HUMANITIES TRANSPARENCIES
H32, "Mrs. General Washington Bestowing Thirteen Stripes on Britannia"
H6, Signing of the Treaty of Paris, 1783

GEOGRAPHY TRANSPARENCIES
G4, North America: 1783

CRITICAL THINKING TRANSPARENCIES
CT4, War for Independence

CD-ROM *Grolier Multimedia Encyclopedia*

VIDEO *American Portfolio: A Videodisc for U.S. History* user's guide, pp. 35, 36

INTERNET McDougal Littell Learning On-Line http://www.mcdougallittell.com

The British Move South

After their devastating defeat at Saratoga, the British changed their military strategy; in the summer of 1778 they began to shift their operations to the South. There, they could seize port cities and use them to launch attacks on the French, who were striking at British ships in the West Indies. The British also hoped to rally Loyalists in the South, reclaim their former colonies in the region, and then slowly fight their way back north.

EARLY BRITISH SUCCESS IN THE SOUTH At the end of 1778, a British expedition easily took Savannah, Georgia, and by the spring of 1779, a royal governor once again commanded Georgia. In 1780, General Henry Clinton, who had replaced Howe in New York, and the ambitious general **Charles Cornwallis** sailed south with 8,500 men. In their greatest victory of the war, the British captured Charles Town, South Carolina, in May 1780 and marched 5,500 American soldiers off as prisoners of war. Clinton then left for New York, leaving Cornwallis to command the British forces in the South and to conquer South and North Carolina.

For most of 1780, Cornwallis succeeded. As the redcoats advanced, they were supported by thousands of African Americans who had escaped from Patriot slave owners to join the British and win their freedom. In August, Cornwallis's army smashed American forces at Camden, South Carolina, and within three months the British had established forts across the state. However, when Cornwallis and his forces advanced into North Carolina, Patriot bands attacked them and cut British communication lines. The continuous harassment forced Cornwallis and his men to retreat to South Carolina.

BRITISH REVERSES IN 1781 Washington ordered Nathanael Greene, his ablest general, to march south and harass Cornwallis as he retreated. Greene divided his force into two groups, sending 600 soldiers under the command of General Daniel Morgan to South Carolina. Cornwallis in turn sent Lieutenant Colonel Banastre Tarleton and his troops to pursue Morgan's soldiers.

Morgan and his men led the British on a grueling chase through rough countryside. When the forces met in January 1781 at Cowpens, South Carolina, the British expected the outnumbered Americans to flee; but the Continental Army fought back, forcing the redcoats to surrender.

Angered by the defeat at Cowpens, Cornwallis attacked Greene two months later at Guilford Court House, North Carolina. Cornwallis won the battle,

Daniel Morgan's colonial forces defeated a crack British regiment under General Tarleton at the battle of Cowpens. More than 200 British soldiers were killed or wounded, and 600 were taken prisoner. This painting, *The Battle of Coupens* by William Ranney, shows that the Americans included both white and African-American soldiers.

113

ON THE WORLD STAGE

ALLIANCES AGAINST BRITAIN

During the 18th century, the major European nations were intense rivals who competed for colonies and power. France, hoping to break up Britain's empire and protect French holdings in the West Indies, allied itself with the American colonies. The French feared that if Britain regained the colonies, it might seize French colonies in the West Indies in order to pay for the war.

The French alliance with the Americans was decisive in that it transformed the American War for Independence into a full-scale European conflict. In 1779, Spain joined the war as an ally of France and allowed the American navy to use the Spanish port of New Orleans as a base for the war at sea. In 1780, the Netherlands also declared war on Britain. By then Britain faced an international fight with no allies of its own.

Reading the Map After students have read the section on the Yorktown surrender, ask them what the blue arrow in the Atlantic Ocean represents on the map. *The French naval force blocking the entrance to Chesapeake Bay.*

Extension Ask students what conclusions they might draw, based on the map, about the Spanish strategy. *Possible Response: Spain took advantage of the British forces' being occupied elsewhere to make inroads along the Gulf of Mexico.*

MORE ABOUT . . .
Nathanael Greene

A devout Quaker, Nathanael Greene turned from the pacifism of his religion and embraced the Patriot cause. He was elected commander of the Rhode Island forces in 1775 and fought in Boston and New York City and at Trenton, Brandywine, and Germantown before succeeding Horatio Gates as commander of the Southern army. A clever strategist, Greene weakened a British force of superior numbers and eventually drove the British back to Charleston. After the Revolution, South Carolina and Georgia rewarded his efforts with land and money.

Revolutionary War, 1778–1781

American/French campaign
British campaign
American/French victory
British victory
Spanish victory
Thirteen Colonies
Other British territory

GEOGRAPHY SKILLBUILDER
PLACE *Where were most of the later Revolutionary battles fought?*
MOVEMENT *Why might General Cornwallis's retreat to Yorktown have left him at a military disadvantage?*

Although most of the important battles of the war took place along the Atlantic coast, fighting also took place elsewhere. On the western frontier, the American general George Rogers Clark captured Ft. Kaskaskia and Ft. Vincennes from the British. The Spanish, who entered the war on the American side in 1779, captured several British outposts in the southwest.

Skillbuilder Answer
Place: the South.
Movement: Possible response: Yorktown bordered the ocean, leaving Cornwallis more vulnerable to being surrounded on land.

but the victory cost him nearly a fourth of his troops—93 were killed, 413 were wounded, and 26 were missing.

Greene had weakened the British, but he worried about the fight for the South. On April 3, 1781, he wrote a letter to Lafayette, asking for help.

A PERSONAL VOICE
[I] wish you to March your force Southward by Alexandria & Fredricksburg to Richmond. . . . It is impossible for the Southern States with all the exertions they can make under the many disadvantages they labour to save themselves. Subsistence is very difficult to be got and therefore it is necessary that the best of troops should be employed. . . . Every exertion should be made for the salvation of the Southern States for on them depend the liberty of the Northern.

NATHANAEL GREENE, from *The Papers of General Nathanael Greene, Volume VIII*

After the exhausting battle in the Carolinas, Cornwallis chose to move the fight to Virginia. First he tried to capture the divisions led by Lafayette and von Steuben. When that failed, Cornwallis made a fateful mistake: he led his army of 7,200 onto the peninsula between the James and York rivers and camped at **Yorktown,** a few miles from the original English settlement of Jamestown. Cornwallis planned to fortify Yorktown, take Virginia, and then move north to join Clinton's forces.

TEACHING OPTION

Cooperative Activity: Broadside Ballad of the Revolution

Task: Small groups of students will work together to compose a broadside ballad celebrating a famous event of the Revolution.

Purpose: To understand people's feelings toward Revolutionary heroes and events.

Activity: Explain that a broadside ballad was a song—printed on a broadside, a large sheet of paper—that usually celebrated a dramatic event such as a battle, a crime, or a disaster. A primitive attempt at mass communication, the

broadside was distributed like a newspaper. Many ballads printed on broadsides eventually passed into oral tradition. Have groups set their broadside ballads to familiar tunes or to melodies composed by more musically gifted students.

Building a Portfolio: Students placing a ballad in their portfolio should attach a note describing their contribution to the work.

ALTERNATIVE ASSESSMENT BOOK
Standards for Evaluating a Cooperative Activity

Standards for Evaluation
Ballads should . . .

• celebrate a particular event of the Revolution
• express Loyalist or Patriot sympathies
• be based on facts, but may stretch a point for dramatic effect

The British Surrender at Yorktown

A combination of good luck and well-timed decisions now favored the American cause. In 1780, a French army of 6,000 landed in Newport, Rhode Island, after the British left the city to focus on the South. The French had stationed one fleet there and were operating another in the West Indies. At this crucial moment, the Marquis de Lafayette suggested that the American and French armies join forces with the two French fleets to attack Cornwallis at Yorktown.

VICTORY AT YORKTOWN Following Lafayette's plan, the Americans and the French closed in on Cornwallis. A French naval force defeated a British fleet and then blocked the entrance to the Chesapeake Bay, thereby obstructing British sea routes to the bay. Meanwhile, 17,000 French and American troops surrounded the British on the Yorktown peninsula and bombarded them day and night. The siege of Yorktown lasted about a month. On October 17, 1781, with his troops outnumbered by more than two to one and exhausted from constant shelling, Cornwallis finally raised the white flag of surrender.

On October 19, a triumphant Washington, the French generals, and their troops assembled to accept the British surrender. At the last minute, Cornwallis pleaded illness and sent General Charles O'Hara in his place. After O'Hara handed over his sword, the British troops laid down their arms. The world was amazed that the Americans had defeated the mighty British empire. In his diary Captain Johann Ewald, a German officer, tried to explain this astonishing turn of events.

> **A PERSONAL VOICE**
> With what soldiers in the world could one do what was done by these men, who go about nearly naked and in the greatest privation? Deny the best-disciplined soldiers of Europe what is due them and they will run away in droves, and the general will soon be alone. But from this one can perceive what an enthusiasm—which these poor fellows call "Liberty"—can do!
>
> **CAPTAIN JOHANN EWALD,** *Diary of the American War*

SEEKING PEACE Peace talks began in Paris in 1782. Representatives of four nations—the United States, Great Britain, France, and Spain—joined the negotiations, and each nation looked out for its own interests. Britain hoped to avoid giving America full independence. France supported American independence but feared America's becoming a major power. Spain was interested in acquiring the land between the Appalachian Mountains and the Mississippi River.

Many observers expected the savvy European diplomats to outwit the Americans at the bargaining table. But the Continental Congress chose an able team of negotiators—John Adams, Benjamin Franklin, and John Jay of New York. Together the three demanded that Britain recognize American independence before any other negotiations began. Once Britain agreed to full independence, the talks officially opened.

In September 1783, the delegates signed the **Treaty of Paris,** which confirmed U.S. independence and set the boundaries of the new nation. The United States now stretched from the Atlantic Ocean to the Mississippi River and from Canada to the Florida border.

Some provisions of the treaty promised future trouble. The British made no attempt to protect the land interests of their Native American allies, and the treaty did not specify when the British would evacuate their American forts. On the other side, the Americans agreed that British creditors could collect debts owed them by Americans

B. Answer The protection of lands belonging to Native Americans who aligned with the British, and a timetable for British evacuation of their American forts.

THINK THROUGH HISTORY
B. Summarizing What issues did the Treaty of Paris leave unresolved?

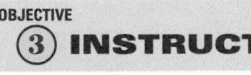

HISTORICAL SPOTLIGHT

BENEDICT ARNOLD

In the early years of the Revolution, Benedict Arnold, a popular Patriot soldier and leader, helped defend New England and then served as the American commandant of Philadelphia. In the later years of the war, however, he married a wealthy woman with British sympathies. Over time, Arnold accumulated debts to support his wife, and she convinced him to pin his hopes on the British.

Despite Arnold's suspicious connections, Washington gave him an assignment he requested—command of West Point, a strategic fort on the Hudson River, north of New York City. Arnold had secretly decided to turn traitor and hand West Point over to the British, but the Americans discovered the plot at the last minute. Arnold escaped to the British and ultimately died in Britain, scorned by both sides as a traitor.

The Continental Congress officially adopted a flag with 13 stripes and 13 stars in 1777.

The War Becomes a Symbol of Liberty

▶ *Discussing Key Ideas*
- For many people throughout the world, the Revolution becomes a symbol of liberty.
- Postwar egalitarianism emphasizes ability, effort, and virtue over wealth or breeding in defining a man's worth.
- Revolutionary ideals add fuel to the antislavery movement.
- The Revolution does not give women new rights, nor does it stop the displacement of Native Americans.

DIFFICULT DECISIONS IN HISTORY

What Should a Loyalist Do?

Conduct a survey, after students have answered the questions, to find out where they think most Loyalists would have chosen to live.

Difficult Decisions
IN HISTORY

WHAT SHOULD A LOYALIST DO?

After the war, Loyalists who stayed in America were viewed as traitors; they risked harassment for having chosen to support the losing side. The many who had lost their land during the war or would later have their land taken by state governments were forced to start over from scratch.

Loyalists who chose to leave faced other problems. Many set out for Canada—particularly Nova Scotia—only to find the climate harsh and depressing. Former slaves who went to Canada found the white Loyalists hostile; most of them eventually resettled in Sierra Leone, West Africa. Loyalists who went to England were treated as second-class citizens and encountered such a high cost of living that they soon found themselves in debt.

1. Imagine the pros and cons of each alternative. If you had been a Loyalist living in America at the end of the war, where would you have chosen to live? Why?
2. What should the new American government have done with the Loyalists? Should they have been treated as traitors or accepted into the new society? Explain and support your opinion.

and promised to allow Loyalists to sue in state courts for recovery of their losses. The state governments, however, later failed to honor this agreement.

While treaty negotiations were in progress, 34,000 British troops and thousands of Loyalists packed their belongings and left the United States. The last British troops boarded their ships and sailed from New York Harbor in November, 1783. A few days later, George Washington marched into a cheering New York City and bade farewell to his officers.

The War Becomes a Symbol of Liberty

With the signing of the Treaty of Paris, all European nations recognized the United States of America. Former British subjects now possessed a new identity as free Americans, loyal to a new ideal. The American Revolution would inspire the world as both a democratic revolution and a war for independence.

THE IMPACT ON AMERICAN SOCIETY Revolutionary ideals set a new course for American society. During the war, class distinctions between rich and poor had begun to blur as the wealthy wore homespun clothing and as military leaders showed respect for all of their men. Changes like these stimulated a rise of **egalitarianism**—a belief in the equality of all people—which fostered a new attitude: the idea that ability, effort, and virtue, not wealth or family, defined one's worth.

The egalitarianism of the 1780s, however, applied only to white males. Most African Americans were still enslaved, and even those who were free usually faced discrimination and poverty. Still, the idea of human equality as asserted in the Declaration of Independence had great significance for African Americans, since it spurred the growth of opposition to slavery. In the North, political leaders like James Otis, Thomas Paine, and Benjamin Rush, as well as Quaker reformers such as John Woolman, realized the injustice of slavery and campaigned against it. Also, free African Americans worked with white reformers to protest the continuation of slavery. By 1804, many New England and Middle states had taken steps to outlaw slavery.

The Southern states, where slavery was more entrenched, did not outlaw the practice, but most made it easier for slave owners to free their slaves. Planters in the Upper South debated the morality of slavery, and some, including George Washington, freed their slaves. In Maryland and Virginia, the number of free blacks increased from about 4,000 in 1775 to over 20,000 following the war. The slavery debate generally did not reach the Deep South, although some Southerners did have grave misgivings about it.

The postwar egalitarianism also did not bring any new political rights to women. A few states made it possible for women to divorce, but common law still dictated that married women's property belonged to their husbands. Women had shown, though, that they were capable of serving their nation as more than just wives and mothers. In so doing, they created a foundation for future changes in their status—both in the family and in society.

For Native Americans, the Revolution brought uncertainty. During both the French and Indian War and the Revolution, many Native American communities had either been destroyed or displaced, and the Native American population east of the Mississippi had declined by about 50 percent. Postwar developments further threatened Native American interests, as settlers seeking equal economic opportunity began to move onto tribal lands left unprotected by the Treaty of Paris.

C. Answer The war fostered the idea that ability, effort, and virtue—not family or wealth—defined one's worth. This egalitarianism, however, applied only to white men.

THINK THROUGH HISTORY
C. *Analyzing Issues* Why did the belief in equality rise after the American Revolution? What were the exceptions to this egalitarianism?

TEACHING OPTIONS

Making Connections Across Time

Events as Symbols Ask students what events in more recent times have symbolic value for people around the world. Encourage students to consider not only military and political events but also events or advances in other areas—for example, a landmark in space exploration or the opening of the Olympic games.

Making Connections Across the Curriculum

Humanities Note that the Congress's choice of a quotation from Virgil as a motto for the reverse side of the Great Seal was in keeping with the influence of classicism, or neoclassicism, in which Western artists and thinkers glorified and emulated the achievements of ancient Greece and Rome. This influence was especially important in the new United States, where the leaders often saw themselves as heirs to the democracy of ancient Athens and the republican government of ancient Rome. Other examples of this classicism were the use of the Latin motto *E pluribus unum* on the Great Seal; domed buildings such as the Capitol in Washington, D.C.; and the linking of the new nation with a goddess called Columbia.

HISTORY FROM VISUALS

Thirteen Colonies Primary Source Map

Reading the Map Ask students what they find unusual about this early map. *Possible Responses: The states have different borders than they have today; the country seems squashed, with west to east elongated compared to north and south.*

Have students do some research in encyclopedias and atlases to find other maps of the original 13 states to compare with the one on this page.

 GEOGRAPHY TRANSPARENCIES

G4, North America: 1783

D. Possible responses: Important challenges could include: how would the government unify the colonies; how would the government remain answerable to the people; how would all aspects of society have a say in the government.

THINK THROUGH HISTORY

D. Forming Opinions *In your opinion, what was the single biggest challenge facing the new country?*

In the closing days of the Revolution, the Continental Congress had chosen a quotation from the works of the Roman poet Virgil as a motto for the reverse side of the Great Seal of the United States. The motto, *Novus Ordo Seclorum,* means "a new order of the ages." Establishing a government and resolving internal problems in that new order would be a tremendous challenge for citizens of the newborn United States.

THE CHALLENGE OF CREATING A GOVERNMENT In adopting the Declaration of Independence, Americans had rejected the British system of government, in which kings and nobles held power. In its place, they set out to build a stable republic, a government of the people. Creating this republic forced Americans to address complex questions: Who should participate in government? How should the government answer to the people? How could a government be set up so that opposing groups of citizens would all have a voice?

This 1784 map was one of the first produced to show the boundaries of the new nation. Although it was called "A New and Correct Map of the United States of North America," it contained much inaccurate information, such as incorrect placement of rivers. These inaccuracies show that Americans still had much to discover about the geography of their vast country.

ASSESS & RETEACH

Section 4 Assessment

Have students work in small groups to discuss the questions and review one another's responses.

Self-Assessment

Have students create a two-column chart in which they compare their own responses to each question (column 1) with the portions of the text that best answer each question (column 2).

Section Quiz

FORMAL ASSESSMENT
Section Quiz, p. 45

Reteach

Use the Think Through History questions to help in reviewing this section.

 CRITICAL THINKING TRANSPARENCIES

CT4, War for Independence

Section 4 Assessment

1. TERMS & NAMES

Identify:
• Friedrich von Steuben
• Marquis de Lafayette
• Charles Cornwallis
• Yorktown
• Treaty of Paris
• egalitarianism

2. SUMMARIZING Choose five significant battles, events, or developments described in this section. For each, write a newspaper headline that summarizes its significance.

Then, choose one of the headlines and write the first paragraph of the article.

3. ANALYZING CAUSES Do you think the colonists could have won independence without aid from foreigners? Explain.

THINK ABOUT
• the military needs of the Americans and strengths of the French
• the outcomes at Cowpens and Guilford Court House
• the Americans' belief in their fight for independence

4. EVALUATING What were the effects of the Revolutionary War on the American colonists?

THINK ABOUT
• political effects
• economic effects
• social effects

The War for Independence **117**

ANSWERS

1. TERMS & NAMES

Friedrich von Steuben, p. 112

Marquis de Lafayette, p. 112

Charles Cornwallis, p. 113

Yorktown, p. 114

Treaty of Paris, p. 115

egalitarianism, p. 116

2. SUMMARIZING

Possible Responses: Von Steuben, Lafayette Lead Europeans in Aiding Rebels; Colonists Conquer Britain at Yorktown; Successful Treaty Negotiations Include Seeds of Trouble; Leaders of Revolution Claim Slavery Violates Human Equality; Native Americans Uncertain About Future with New Nation.

3. ANALYZING CAUSES

Possible Responses: **No** The colonists needed the French fleet to block sea routes and the French troops in order to win the battle at Yorktown; the poorly trained American troops needed Von Steuben's expert training. **Yes** The sheer determination of the American Patriots would have carried them to victory; American troops were weakening the British and winning in the Carolinas; once isolated at Yorktown, the British might still have been defeated.

4. EVALUATING

Possible Responses: Politically, the colonists gained a great deal of stature, as they became leaders of a large, independent country. Economically, the war forced many colonists to confront inflation and profiteering. Socially, the war sparked a growing sense of egalitarianism among the colonists.

CLOSE

With the aid of France and other nations, the American Patriots managed to defeat one of the world's most powerful nations in a war that became a symbol of liberty for centuries to come.

OBJECTIVES

1. To explain women's contributions to the American Revolution.

2. To summarize the struggle for political power by American women over the centuries.

Women and Political Power

They have always been there, from the earliest days up to the present moment—the women of America: mothers, sisters, daughters, wives. Throughout the history of the United States, women have played whatever roles they felt were necessary to build and to better this country. They also worked and fought to expand their own political power, a power that throughout American history has been largely been denied them.

FOCUS & MOTIVATE

▶ **Starting with the Student**
Have students consider their own definitions of the term "women's rights." Ask them,

• Which aspects of the definition relate to political power?

• In their opinion, what is the state of women's rights in America today?

MORE ABOUT . . .
Women in Political Power

Note that in addition to holding more elected offices than ever before, American women in the late 20th century have broken the "glass ceiling" in appointed political offices. In the 1980s, President Reagan appointed the first woman to the Supreme Court, Sandra Day O'Connor. A decade later, President Clinton appointed Janet Reno to be the first woman attorney general of the United States. On Clinton's reelection in 1996, he appointed the first woman, Madeleine K. Albright (who had been serving as UN ambassador), to the top Cabinet position of secretary of state.

1770s
PROTEST AGAINST BRITAIN

In the tense years leading up to the American Revolution, women found ways to participate in the protest movement against the British. Colonial women boycotted tea and British-made clothing. In the painting to the right, depicting Sarah Morris Mifflin and her husband Thomas, Sarah Mifflin spins her own thread rather than use British thread.

1828
SENECA FALLS

As America grew, women became acutely aware of their unequal status in society, particularly their lack of suffrage, or the right to vote. In 1848, two women—Elizabeth Cady Stanton and Lucretia Mott—launched the first woman suffrage movement in the United States at the Seneca Falls Convention in Seneca Falls, N.Y. During the convention, the participants crafted the Declaration of Sentiments, shown at the right bearing Stanton's picture. The Declaration demanded greater rights for women, including the right to vote.

A WOMAN'S DECLARATION

Elizabeth Cady Stanton.

1920
THE RIGHT TO VOTE

More than a half-century after organizing for the right to vote, women finally won their struggle. In 1920, the United States adopted the Nineteenth Amendment, which granted women the right to vote. Pictured to the right is one of the many suffrage demonstrations of the early 1900s that helped garner public support for the amendment.

118 CHAPTER 4

RECOMMENDED RESOURCES

Books

Gurko, Miriam. *The Ladies of Seneca Falls.* New York: Schocken, 1976. America's woman suffrage movement.

Hoffert, Sylvia D. *When Hens Crow.* Bloomington: Indiana UP, 1995. Women's rights in pre-Civil War America.

Schneir, Miriam, ed. *Feminism: The Essential Historical*

Writings. New York: Random, 1972. Includes the Seneca Falls declaration, Sojourner Truth's speeches, Virginia Woolf's writings, and much more.

Videos

One Woman, One Vote. PBS Video, 1995. TV documentary about the woman suffrage movement.

Sojourner Truth: Ain't I a Woman? Coronet/MTI, 1989. Focuses on Truth's famous speech.

Women in American Life. National Women's History Project, 1988. From the Civil War to the late 1970s.

Software

Women in America. CD-ROM. Woodbridge, CT: Research Publications, 1994.

TimeLiner 4.0. Tom Snyder Productions. Software for making time lines, available with a *Women in History Data Disk* containing 17 sample time lines that cover prominent women as well as the women's movement.

1972–1982
THE EQUAL RIGHTS AMENDMENT MOVEMENT

During the mid-1900s, as more women entered the workforce, many women recognized their continuing unequal status, including the lack of equal pay for equal work. By passing an Equal Rights Amendment, some women hoped to obtain the same social and economic rights as men. Although millions supported the amendment, many men and women feared the measure would prompt unwanted change. The ERA ultimately failed to be ratified for the Constitution.

ERA YES

1996
WOMEN IN CONGRESS

In spite of the failure of the ERA, many women have achieved strong positions for themselves—politically as well as socially and economically. Pictured above are several of the 58 women members of the 104th U.S. Congress.

VOTES FOR US — WHEN — WE ARE WOMEN

INTERACT WITH HISTORY

1. **SYNTHESIZING** How did women's political status change from 1770 to 1996?

   SEE SKILLBUILDER HANDBOOK, PAGE 1051.

2. **RESEARCHING AND REPORTING** Think of a woman in your community who played an important role, either in the past or in the present. What kinds of things did this woman do? What kind of support did she receive in the community? What kind of problems did she run into?

The War for Independence **119**

Chapter 4 Assessment

TERMS & NAMES

1. Stamp Act, p. 94
2. Boston Massacre, p. 96
3. committee of correspondence, p. 97
4. Olive Branch Petition, p. 100
5. *Common Sense,* p. 101
6. Thomas Jefferson, p. 101
7. Saratoga, p. 109
8. Valley Forge, p. 110
9. Marquis de Lafayette, p. 112
10. Yorktown, p. 114

MAIN IDEAS

11. They distributed propaganda, harassed British officials, boycotted British goods, and rioted against custom agents.

12. Colonists opposed the tax on tea and the efforts by the British to cut colonial merchants out of the tea trade. The event angered the British and united colonists. After the event, Parliament passed the Intolerable Acts.

13. Eight colonists were killed at Lexington; dozens of British soldiers died in the fighting at Concord and on the march back to Boston.

14. He meant that free white males were political equals, not that all Americans had equal opportunity.

15. Many remained deeply loyal to the king and the British order; some worked for the British; some were politically unaware; some expected the rebels to lose.

16. The colonists won the battle—a victory Washington needed, in part to encourage soldiers to re-enlist.

17. The plan to isolate New England.

18. Civilians lent money to the government, made ammunition and clothing, and took over the civilian roles of those who became soldiers.

19. France provided military, diplomatic, and economic support for the colonists.

20. It had to form a government, handle problems resulting from provisions in the peace treaty, and live up to its ideals.

REVIEWING THE CHAPTER

TERMS & NAMES For each term below, write a sentence explaining its connection to the American Revolution. For each person below, explain his role in the event.

1. Stamp Act
2. Boston Massacre
3. committee of correspondence
4. Olive Branch Petition
5. *Common Sense*
6. Thomas Jefferson
7. Saratoga
8. Valley Forge
9. Marquis de Lafayette
10. Yorktown

MAIN IDEAS

SECTION 1 (pages 94–98)

The Stirrings of Rebellion

11. What methods did colonists use to protest actions by Parliament between 1765 and 1775?
12. Describe the causes and the results of the Boston Tea Party.
13. What were the results of fighting at Lexington and Concord?

SECTION 2 (pages 99–106)

Ideas Help Start a Revolution

14. What did Jefferson mean, and not mean, by the phrase "all men are created equal"?
15. Why did many colonists not support independence?

SECTION 3 (pages 107–111)

Struggling Toward Saratoga

16. Why was the Battle of Trenton significant?
17. What British military plan did the colonial victory at Saratoga ruin?
18. Explain how civilians supported the war effort in the colonies.

SECTION 4 (pages 112–117)

Winning the War

19. How did France help the colonies during the American Revolution?
20. Describe three significant challenges facing the United States when the American Revolution ended.

THINKING CRITICALLY

1. **THE PATH TO INDEPENDENCE** Create a dual-path chart showing how the colonies became independent. On one path, list four or more military events, such as battles and changes in command. On the other, list four or more political events, including protests, publication of documents, and legal actions.

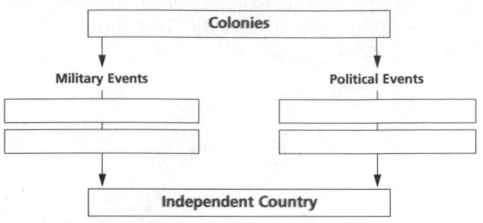

2. **SUPPORTING REVOLT** Review France's role in helping the colonies rebel against Great Britain. Under what conditions, if any, do you think the United States should help other countries win or maintain their independence today? Explain your opinion.

3. **THE FIGHT FOR LIBERTY** Reread the quote by Patrick Henry on page 92. How do his words reflect the feelings behind the American Revolution? Support your ideas.

4. **DEMOCRATIC VALUES** Paraphrase the first two sentences of the Declaration of Independence, simplifying and modernizing the language.

5. **GEOGRAPHY OF THE REVOLUTIONARY WAR** Look at the maps on pages 109 and 114. How did the region in which the war was fought change from 1775 to 1781?

6. **ANALYZING PRIMARY SOURCES** Read the following excerpt from an essay by two historians on how scholars have interpreted the American Revolution. Then answer the questions that follow.

> The American Revolution is, perhaps, the single most significant event in this country's history. . . . But scholars disagree about using the term "revolutionary" to describe how new or different these developments were. Some historians argue that the Revolution was solely a colonial rebellion aimed at achieving only the limited goal of independence from Britain. Colonial society, they say, was a democratic society and there was a consensus among Americans about keeping things as they were once the break with Britain had been accomplished. Others claim that the Revolution was accompanied by a violent social upheaval—a class conflict—as the radical lower classes sought to gain a greater degree of democracy in what had been a basically undemocratic society in the colonial era. The question is, then, was the Revolution revolutionary, or was it not?
> **GERALD N. GROB and GEORGE ATHAN BILLIAS,**
> *Interpretations of American History*

What is the basic disagreement between historians discussed in this passage? Which side do you agree with and why?

THINKING CRITICALLY

1. THE PATH TO INDEPENDENCE

Possible Responses: Military path—Concord; Continental Army formed; Bunker Hill; Saratoga; open support from France; Yorktown. Political path—Stamp Act Congress; committees of correspondence; Continental Congress; Declaration of Independence; recognition by France; Treaty of Paris.

2. SUPPORTING REVOLT

Possible Responses: Some students may say that the United States should support movements against tyrannical governments, should only support new countries when national security would be threatened if it did not support them, or should get involved in other countries' battles only when human rights are overwhelmingly ignored and civilians are murdered. Others may say that the United States should not be involved in the internal affairs of other countries at all.

3. THE FIGHT FOR LIBERTY

Possible Responses: Life under British rule was not free and therefore not worth living; revolution was the only solution, even if death resulted; there was no turning back from the need to revolt against oppression.

ALTERNATIVE ASSESSMENT

1. CREATING A POLITICAL PAMPHLET In the years leading up to the American Revolution, how did political rhetoric influence and inspire the colonists?

Write a political pamphlet that takes a stand on a controversial issue from the 1760s or 1770s.

CD-ROM Use the CD-ROM *Electronic Library of Primary Sources* and other resources to research the sources of conflict between England and the colonists from 1760 to 1775.

- Choose a political issue or act that sparked protest from the colonists, and write a political pamphlet that either defends Parliament and the king or urges colonial resistance. Use Thomas Paine's *Common Sense* as a model.

Clearly state your points and persuade your readers with reasons and examples. Revise and edit your writing and turn it into pamphlet form, adding visuals if you wish. Share your pamphlet with classmates.

2. LEARNING FROM MEDIA

VIDEO View the McDougal Littell Video for Chapter 4, *Patriot Father, Loyalist Son.* Discuss the following questions in small groups.

- What was William's stance on the Stamp Act?
- How did William and Ben differ in their view of the Boston Tea Party?
- What did William fear the worsening relationship between the colonies and Britain would lead to? What was his solution?
- What happened to William as a result of his Loyalist stance?

3. PORTFOLIO PROJECT

Use the Living History activity to expand your portfolio.

LIVING HISTORY

PRESENTING SURVEY RESULTS

Review and assess the results of your survey. Ask yourself the following questions.
- Did I select excerpts that provoked interesting responses?
- Did I question enough individuals?
- Did I create an interesting and informative visual?

Share your survey with your classmates by reading some responses and displaying your visual. Look for patterns among the class's responses. Are they surprising or predictable? As a class, discuss the reactions. After the discussion, add your survey to your American history portfolio.

R eview Chapter 4

REBELLION BREWS Beginning in 1765, Parliament attempted to collect more tax revenue from the colonies to help repay Great Britain's debts from the French and Indian War. Colonists responded to both the Stamp Act and Townshend Act with waves of protest. They angrily complained that they were being taxed by a Parliament in which they had no representatives. Conflict centered in Boston, where five colonists died in the Boston Massacre in 1770, and Patriots destroyed 15,000 pounds of tea during the Boston Tea Party in 1773.

REVOLUTION BEGINS The battles at Concord and Lexington in April 1775, and at Bunker Hill two months later, turned the conflict between the colonies and Great Britain into an open war. These battles, along with the writings of Thomas Paine, spurred increasing support for independence. On July 4, 1776, the Second Continental Congress adopted the Declaration of Independence, formally breaking the ties between the colonies and Great Britain.

WAR AND VICTORY During the first years of the war, the most significant battle was the Americans' victory at Saratoga, New York, in October 1777. After this victory, France agreed to use its military power to openly support the revolution against its rival Great Britain. On the homefront, American women supported the war effort by taking over the roles of men who left to become soldiers and by making ammunition, clothes, and other items. Even with the backing of the French and of many civilians, the Continental Army suffered from lack of supplies, particularly during the winter of 1778 at Valley Forge. The decisive battle of the war occurred at Yorktown, where American and French forces combined to conquer the British on October 17, 1781. The peace treaty, signed in 1783, recognized the independence of the United States.

P review Chapter 5

Among the first challenges facing the new United States was to establish an effective system of government. The existing national government, under the Articles of Confederation, was soon replaced by a new and stronger one, operating under the Constitution that still is in force today. You will learn about these significant developments in the next chapter.

The War for Independence **121**

1. CREATING A POLITICAL PAMPHLET
Standards for Evaluation
An effective political pamphlet will meet the following criteria:

- Focuses on one political act or issue from the 1760s or 1770s that caused conflict between the colonists and England.
- Takes a clear stand on one side or the other.
- States arguments clearly and persuades effectively.
- Is presented in a clear and attractive manner.

2. LEARNING FROM MEDIA
Answers to the questions:

- William strongly opposed the act and used his powers as governor to fight it.
- William thought that the colonists had gone too far and had made an illegal attack on property. Ben thought the colonists were justified because Britain was attempting to unconstitutionally tax the colonists.
- He feared it would lead to war. He believed that to avoid war, the colonies must remain loyal to Britain, that to act otherwise was treason.
- The Continental Congress interrogated him and placed him in jail until the war's end. Afterward, William fled America to live in England.

3. PORTFOLIO PROJECT
LIVING HISTORY
Standards for Evaluation
A survey will meet the following criteria:

- Contains a thought-provoking selection of quotes from the Declaration of Independence.
- Contains responses from a wide variety of people.
- Is organized with responses clearly following the quotes to which they correspond.
- Is displayed in a way that is clear as well as visually attractive.

IN-DEPTH RESOURCES: UNIT 1
See the form for scoring this activity on page 75.

THINKING CRITICALLY

4. DEMOCRATIC VALUES
Possible Responses: When the people of a colony must break away from a ruling country and become a separate country, which is natural and right for them to do, they must give their reasons for doing so. We believe that all men are created equal and that they have rights that cannot be taken away. These rights are to life, to freedom, and to the right to live as they wish. Government, which gets its power from the people, exists to protect the people.

If a colony wants to separate from its mother country, it is justified in seeking independence as its own nation; out of respect for the people of the ruling country, it should provide them with reasons.

5. GEOGRAPHY OF THE REVOLUTIONARY WAR
Possible Responses: Early battles were focused in the North; the conflict spread to include the South and territory to the west.

6. ANALYZING PRIMARY SOURCES
Possible Responses: Historians disagree over whether the Revolution was only a military and political upheaval or also a social upheaval. Students answering political/military might say that its main goal was freedom from British rule and that social revolution was secondary. Students answering social as well as political/military might say that its success depended on the support of common folk, who in turn thought they'd gain financial and political power if the Revolution succeeded.

Teacher's Edition **121**

HISTORY AND ART

Washington Addressing the Constitutional Convention

Detail of oil painting by Junius Brutus Stearns (1856).

Art Note
Stearns (1810–1885) was a Vermont-born painter of portraits, scenes of everyday life, and recreated history. This painting is one of a series of five he painted of Washington. These paintings were the basis of a series of lithographs sold to a general public eager for patriotic scenes.

▶ **Previewing the Unit**
Unit 2 details the effort to write and ratify a new plan for government, the U.S. Constitution, and the struggles of the new nation with internal political divisions and challenges from abroad. As the nation expands to the west at the expense of Native Americans, disagreements over slavery drive a growing wedge between North and South. Meanwhile, reformers work to better American society, and African Americans and women push for equality.

UNIT
2

"*The true foundation of republican government is the equal right of every citizen.*"
THOMAS JEFFERSON

CHAPTER 5
1781–1788
Shaping a New Nation

THE LIVING CONSTITUTION

CHAPTER 6
1789–1816
Launching the New Nation

CHAPTER 7
1817–1840
Balancing Nationalism and Sectionalism

CHAPTER 8
1820–1850
Reforming American Society

1781–1850
A New Nation

❶ Other figures
This illustration is a detail of Stearns's painting. His original portrays many other delegates, including two who played important roles at the Constitutional Convention: Benjamin Franklin and James Madison.

❷ Alexander Hamilton
Hamilton was a strong advocate of the need to replace the Articles of Confederation. He is opposite George Washington, which suggests the close working relationship the two enjoyed during the Revolution and Washington's presidency. The sheaf of papers in his hand suggests his Federalist writings urging ratification of the Constitution.

❸ The people
Stearns studied abroad for a time. Like other 19th-century American artists, he used European techniques in attempting to create an American art. The poses of most figures suggest those in da Vinci's *The Last Supper*, though the expressions are less dramatic.

Discussing the Quotation

Jefferson says that equality is universal. But as many Americans have known, that was not true in 1787: "When the Constitution . . . was completed, . . . I was not included in that 'We the People.' . . . But through . . . amendment, interpretation, and court decision, I finally have been included." Barbara Jordan, African American member of Congress

FOR DISCUSSION:
- What does Jefferson mean by "equal rights"?
- Why does Jordan say she was "not included" in the Constitution?
- How did the Constitution itself make it possible for equal rights to become available to more people?

Discussing the Art

Stearns makes Washington the main figure in four ways. His natural height (over six feet) is enhanced by placing him on a dais. His presence alone seems to balance the majority of the figures on the left side of the painting. Finally, the papers he holds are presumably the Constitution itself.

FOR DISCUSSION:
- Why was Washington a good subject for patriotic painting at a time of rising sectional tensions?
- How does the image show the inequality that Jordan describes in her quotation?

4 The people
Some delegates are talking, but most are intent on listening to Washington. Though he is off to one side, he is clearly the focal point of the painting.

5 Abraham Baldwin
Abraham Baldwin of Georgia helped draft the Great Compromise of the Constitution. The compromise created two houses of Congress to settle the dispute between small states and large states over state representation in the national legislature.

6 George Washington
Washington played a vital role at the convention, more in his presence alone than in his actions as presiding officer. Many delegates were concerned about the power of the new federal government. Confidence in Washington's judgment and the assumption that he would be the first president helped ease much of this concern.

		TEACHING SUPPORT	ASSESSMENT
SECTION 1 **Experimenting with Confederation** *pp. 126–129*	**Key Ideas** *The United States adopts the Articles of Confederation as the basis of its government, but the Articles prove too weak to handle the new nation's problems.*	*In-Depth Resources: Unit 2* • Guided Reading, p. 1 **COOPERATIVE ACTIVITIES** • Letters to the Editor, p. 128 (TE)	*Section 1 Assessment,* p. 129 (PE) *Self-Assessment,* p. 129 (TE) *Formal Assessment* • Section Quiz, p. 54 *Alternative Assessment Book* • Standards for Evaluating a Cooperative Activity
SECTION 2 **Drafting the Constitution** *pp. 132–136*	*The delegates to the Philadelphia convention in 1787 decide to throw out the Articles of Confederation and to create a new constitution.*	*In-Depth Resources: Unit 2* • Guided Reading, p. 2 • Skillbuilder Practice: Analyzing Issues, p. 4 • Primary Source: *from The U.S. Constitution, First Draft,* p. 7 • Literature: *from Legacy* by James A. Michner, p. 11 **COOPERATIVE ACTIVITY** • Debating the Issues, p. 134 (TE)	*Section 2 Assessment,* p. 136 (PE) *Self-Assessment,* p. 136 (TE) *Formal Assessment* • Section Quiz, p. 55 *Alternative Assessment Book* • Standards for Evaluating a Cooperative Activity
SECTION 3 **Ratifying the Constitution** *pp. 137–141*	*Federalists and Antifederalists debate the Constitution. Federalists promise to add a bill of rights and finally swing the needed votes to ratify.*	*In-Depth Resources: Unit 2* • Guided Reading, p. 3 • Geography Application: The Constitution Becomes a Reality, p. 5 • Primary Sources: *from The Federalist No. 2,* p. 8; Patrick Henry's Antifederalist Speech, p. 9; Political Cartoon, p. 10 • American Lives: Patrick Henry, p. 14; John Jay, p. 15 **COOPERATIVE ACTIVITIES** • Creating a Media Ad, p. 138 (TE)	*Section 3 Assessment,* p. 141 (PE) *Self-Assessment,* p. 141 (TE) *Formal Assessment* • Section Quiz, p. 56 *Alternative Assessment Book* • Standards for Evaluating a Cooperative Activity
The Living Constitution *pp. 144–169*	*The full text of the Constitution including explanatory notes and critical thinking questions.*	*In-Depth Resources: Unit 2* • Guided Reading, pp. 18, 19, 20, 21 • Skillbuilder Practice: Clarifying, p. 22 • Geography Application: The Electoral College, p. 23 • American Lives: James Madison, Thurgood Marshall, pp. 25, 26 **COOPERATIVE ACTIVITIES** • Proposing Laws, p. 148 (TE) • Reviewing the Constitution, p. 165 (TE)	*Living Constitution* *Formal Assessment* • Section Quiz, pp. 65, 66, 67, 68 *Alternative Assessment Book* • Standards for Evaluating a Cooperative Activity
CHAPTER RESOURCES	**Chapter Overview** *The new nation under federalism is unstable, leaders set up a convention to settle issues but end up with creating a new governmental structure.*	*In-Depth Resources: Unit 2* • Living History Project: Worksheet, pp. 16, 27; Standards, pp. 17, 28 *Telescoping the Times* • Chapter Summary, pp. 9–10 *Planning for Block Schedules*	*Chapter Assessment,* pp. 142–143, 168–169 (PE) *Alternative Assessment,* pp. 143, 169 (PE) *Formal Assessment* • Chapter Test, forms A and B, pp. 57–62, 69–74 Test Generator *Alternative Assessment Book* See explanation and forms for different kinds of alternative assessment including portfolio assessment.

Geography Transparencies
• G5, Land Ceded by States: 1782–1802

INTERNET RESOURCES
• See *McDougal Littell Learning On-Line* for links to information about the Articles of Confederation and 18th century America.

Critical Thinking Transparencies
• CT5, Constitutional Convention

Electronic Library of Primary Sources
• from Notes Taken During the Debate on the Slave Trade by James Madison

INTERNET RESOURCES
• See *McDougal Littell Learning On-Line* for links to information about the Constitutional Convention and James Madison.

Electronic Library of Primary Sources
• from "The Federalist #51," by Publius; *On the Constitution* by Benjamin Franklin; from "On the Federal Government" by Trench Coxe; from "The Federal Constitution Is Wisely Formed," by Anonymous

INTERNET RESOURCES
• See Interact with History, p. 139 (PE) for an activity that includes the Internet as an enrichment option.

INTERNET RESOURCES
• See Interact with History, p. 167 (PE) for an activity that includes the Internet as an enrichment option.

American Portfolio: A Videodisc for U.S. History, user's guide, pp. 39, 40, 41, 45

INTERNET RESOURCES
Learning On-Line: Social Studies
http://www.mcdougallittell.com

Block Scheduling (90 MINUTES)

Day 1
Section 1, pp. 126–129
Section 2, pp. 132–136
Section Assessments pp. 129, 130

Day 2
Section 3, pp. 137–141
Chapter Assessment, pp. 142–143

Day 3
The Constitution, pp. 146–157

Day 4
The Constitution, pp. 158–167
Assessment, pp. 168–169

YEARLY PACING *Chapter 5 and Constitution Total:* 4 days *Yearly Total:* 85 days

See *Planning for Block Schedules* for special activities and pacing strategies.

Customizing for Special Populations

Students Acquiring English

Access for Students Acquiring English
• Guided Reading for Sections 1–3 (Spanish), pp. 48–50; Constitution, pp. 54–57
• Chapter Summary (Spanish), pp. 46–47
• Skillbuilder Practice: Analyzing Issues (Spanish), p. 51; Clarifying (Spanish), p. 58
• Geography Application: The Constitution Becomes a Reality (Spanish), pp. 52–53; The Electoral College (Spanish), pp. 59–60

INTERNET RESOURCES
• See *McDougal Littell Learning On-Line* The Diverse Classroom.

Less Proficient Readers

In-Depth Resources: Unit 2
• Guided Reading for Sections 1–3, pp. 1–3
• Guided Reading for the Constitution, pp. 18–21
• Skillbuilder Practice: Analyzing Issues, p. 4; Clarifying, p. 22
• Geography Application: The Constitution Becomes a Reality, p. 5; The Electoral College, p. 23

Telescoping the Times
• Chapter Summary, pp. 9–10

See additional strategies at point of use in the Teacher's Edition.

Gifted and Talented Students

In-Depth Resources: Unit 2
• Primary Sources: from the U.S. Constitution, First Draft, p. 7; from *The Federalist* No. 2, p. 8; Patrick Henry's Antifederalist Speech, p. 9; political cartoon, p. 10
• American Lives: Patrick Henry, p. 14; John Jay, p. 15; James Madison, p. 25; Thurgood Marshall, p. 26

See additional strategies at point of use in the Teacher's Edition.

Connections to Literature READINGS FOR STUDENTS

In-Depth Resources: Unit 2
• from *Legacy* by James A. Michner, p. 11

Enrichment Reading
• Collier, James Lincoln. *The Winter Hero.* New York: Simon and Schuster, 1978. *In this novel, a young boy becomes involved in Shays's Rebellion in western Massachusetts as the young nation struggles to shape its laws.*

• Anderson, Joan. *1787: A Novel.* New York: Harcourt, 1987. *An aide to James Madison during the 1787 Constitutional Convention experiences that historic summer.*

• Irving, Washington. *Rip Van Winkle & The Legend of Sleepy Hollow.* Tarrytown, New York: Sleepy Hollow Press, 1980. *These much loved ghost stories are set in colonial America.*

McDougal Littell *The Language of Literature* American Literature

• Patrick Henry, "Speech in the Virginia Convention," p. 206

• Michel-Guillaume Jean de Crèvecoeur, "What Is an American?" p. 223

Shaping a New Nation

> **▶ Starting with the Student**
> Ask students to pretend that they are going to start a new after-school service club—one that raises money to help local charities. Discuss the issues that would need to be resolved:
>
> • How will the club be organized?
> • Who will coordinate fundraisers?
> • Who will handle money?

PREVIEWING THE CHAPTER

• Read the section titles and descriptions, noting the three-step process of shaping a new nation.

• Compare the opening quotation to another from James Madison: "If men were angels, no government would be necessary. If angels were to govern men, neither external nor internal controls on government would be necessary." How do these quotes sum up Madison's attitudes toward humankind and toward government?

SECTION 1

Experimenting with Confederation

The United States adopts the Articles of Confederation as the basis of its government, but the Articles prove too weak to handle the new nation's problems.

SECTION 2

Drafting the Constitution

The delegates to the Philadelphia convention in 1787 decide to throw out the Articles of Confederation and to create a new constitution.

SECTION 3

Ratifying the Constitution

Federalists and Antifederalists debate the Constitution. Federalists promise to add a bill of rights and finally swing the needed votes to ratify.

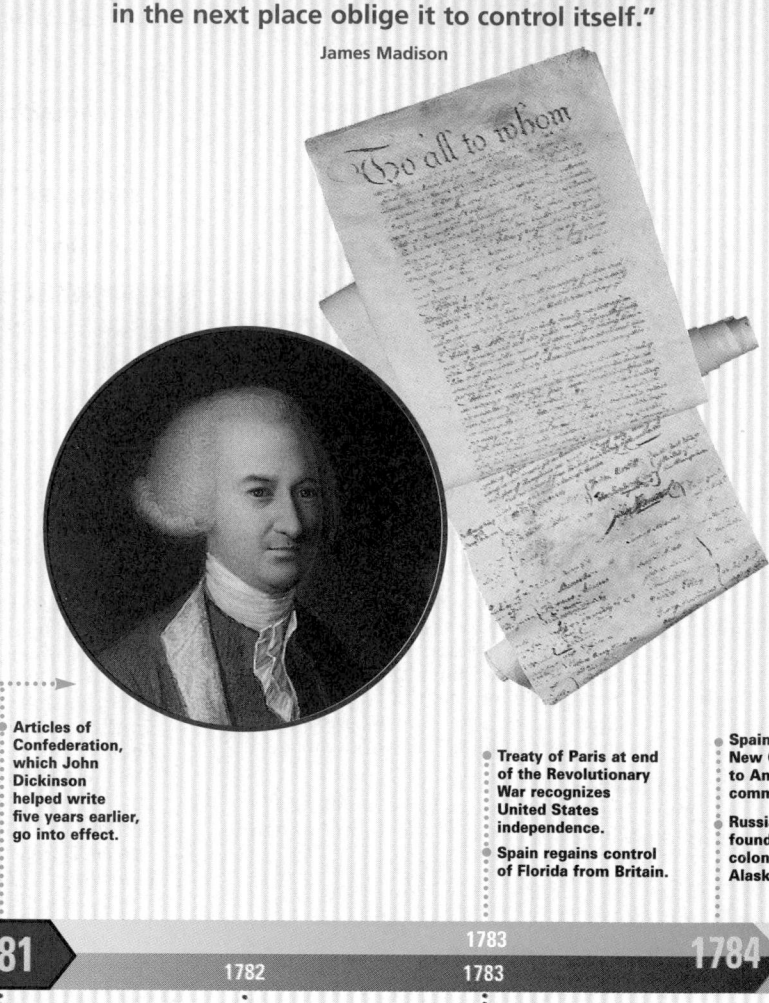

"In framing a government which is to be administered by men over men, the great difficulty lies in this: you must first enable the government to control the governed; and in the next place oblige it to control itself."

James Madison

● Articles of Confederation, which John Dickinson helped write five years earlier, go into effect.

● Treaty of Paris at end of the Revolutionary War recognizes United States independence.

● Spain regains control of Florida from Britain.

● Spain cl
New Orl
to Amer
commer

● Russian
found fi
colony i
Alaska.

| THE UNITED STATES | **1781** | | **1783** | **1784** |
| THE WORLD | | **1782** | **1783** | |

● Joseph II allows religious toleration in Austria.

● Rama I founds new dynasty in Siam, with Bangkok as the capital.

● Russia annexes the Crimean Peninsula.

● Ludwig van Beethoven's first works are printed.

124 CHAPTER 5

THEMES IN CHAPTER 5

Civil Rights

State constitutions guaranteed citizens' rights without maintaining equality. Until the Constitution was amended in 1870 and 1920, states continued to grant voting rights on the basis of race and gender.

See Teacher's Edition note, p. 127.

Constitutional Concerns

One of the greatest problems faced by the new confederation was unequal representation of citizens within states, which led to rebellion against unfair taxation. These rebellions a few years earlier had been considered a justifiable response to Britain's tyranny. In the new nation, however,

the challenge to political authority signaled the need for a strong central government.

The United States as we now know it was created in an atmosphere of conflict and compromise. Federalist demands for a strong central government overpowered Antifederalist objections. Yet,

the Antifederalist insistence on the protection of individual rights via a bill of rights created a government in which the needs of the nation were balanced with the rights of the individual.

See Teacher's Edition notes, pp. 133 and 140.

LIVING HISTORY

CREATING A CONSTITUTION

Create a constitution by supposing that you are a delegate to a constitutional convention. Work with a small group of people to create a constitution for your class or school. Be sure your constitution answers such questions as the following:

• How will laws be passed?
• How will laws be enforced?
• How can laws be changed?

📁 **PORTFOLIO PROJECT** As you work out compromises for your new government, save your notes in a folder. You will present your constitution and add it to your American history portfolio.

Encourage students to imagine that they are creating a new school from the ground up. They will decide how it will be organized and run. Students should begin by determining the primary goals of their school and how those goals can best be met. Students should address the following issues:

• Who will run the school?
• Who will decide what will be taught?
• How will students be evaluated?
• What ground rules for student and staff behavior will there be?
• How will the guilt or innocence of someone accused of breaking rules be determined?

Students should add to this list as they plan a new school.

IN-DEPTH RESOURCES: UNIT 2
See worksheet and standards for evaluation, pp. 16, 17.

Timeline

• **Daniel Shays leads a rebellion of farmers in Massachusetts.**

• **Treaty of Hopewell concerning Native American lands is signed.**
• **New York state outlaws slavery.**

• **Annapolis Convention is held.**
• **Council of Virginia guarantees religious freedom.**

• **Northwest Ordinance is passed.**
• **First Federalist Papers are published by Hamilton, Madison, and Jay.**

• **James Madison helps write the Constitution at Independence Hall (above). The Constitution is ratified.**

| 1785 | 1786 | 1787 | **1788** |

| 1785 | 1786 | 1787 | |

• **A British preacher, Edmund Cartwright, invents the first power loom.**
• **Jean-Pierre Blanchard and John Jeffries cross the English Channel in a balloon.**

• **Uranium is discovered.**
• **Lord Cornwallis becomes Governor General of India.**

• **Sierra Leone in Africa is made a haven for freed American slaves**
• **Turkey declares war on Russia.**

• **Austria declares war on Turkey.**
• **Bread riots erupt in France.**

Shaping a New Nation **125**

RECOMMENDED RESOURCES

Books for the Teacher

The Federalist Papers. New York: Bantam, 1987.

Madison, James. *Notes of Debates in the Federal Convention of 1787.* New York: Norton, 1987.

Morris, Richard B. *Witness at the Creation.* Holt, 1985.

Books for the Student

Armstrong, Virginia Irving. *I Have Spoken: History Through the Voices of the Indians.* Chicago: Sage, 1971.

Rutland, Robert. *James Madison and the Search for Nationhood.* Washington, DC: Library of Congress, 1981. Illustrated sketch of Madison's life and work; full of letters.

Videos

Background of the Constitution. Sound filmstrip. Filmfax Productions, 1986

Bill of Rights in Action. Encyclopaedia Britannica, 800-554-9862. Connection of Bill of Rights to current issues.

Creating a Stronger Union. RMI Media, 800-745-5480. Ratification of Constitution.

Launching the New Government. Coronet, 800-621-2131. Story of Confederation Congress.

The Problems of Confederation. RMI Media, 800-745-5480.

Software

U.S. History: Government, Part 1. CD-ROM Educational Software Institute, 800-955-5570.

OBJECTIVES

1 To explain differing ideas of republicanism.

2 To identify three basic issues the Continental Congress debated in drafting the Articles of Confederation.

3 To describe the political and economic problems faced by the Confederation.

SKILLBUILDER
• Interpreting charts, p. 129

CRITICAL THINKING
• Comparing, pp. 126, 128
• Analyzing causes, p. 127
• Synthesizing, p. 129
• Sequencing history, p. 129
• Analyzing, p. 129
• Evaluating an opinion, p. 129

FOCUS & MOTIVATE

▶ *Starting with the Student*
• What would happen to a football team if every player concentrated on setting individual records rather than winning games?
• What would happen to the national government if each state pursued its own interests rather than those of the nation as a whole?

OBJECTIVE
1 **INSTRUCT**

Americans Debate Republicanism

▶ *Discussing Key Ideas*
• Differing ideas of republicanism influence state constitutions.
• State constitutions reflect fear of centralized authority.
• All states guarantee specific rights for citizens, but they differ widely in granting voting rights.

IN-DEPTH RESOURCES: UNIT 2
Guided Reading, p. 1

ACCESS FOR STUDENTS ACQUIRING ENGLISH
Guided Reading (Spanish), p. 48

---

1 **Experimenting with Confederation**

TERMS & NAMES
• republic
• republicanism
• Articles of Confederation
• confederation
• Land Ordinance of 1785
• Northwest Ordinance of 1787

LEARN ABOUT conflicting interpretations of the role of national government
TO UNDERSTAND why the Articles of Confederation proved too weak to handle the nation's problems.

ONE AMERICAN'S STORY

John Dickinson understood, perhaps better than other delegates to the Continental Congress, the value of compromise. In 1776 Dickinson led the opposition to American independence and refused to sign the Declaration of Independence. Yet, eight days after the Declaration was adopted, Dickinson presented Congress with the first draft of the plan for setting up a workable government for the new states. When the Pennsylvania assembly failed to reelect him to Congress, he joined the Delaware militia to fight for the independence he had once opposed. In 1779 Dickinson returned to Congress as a delegate from Delaware. At that time he explained the principles that guided his decisions.

A PERSONAL VOICE
Two rules I have laid down for myself throughout this contest . . . first, on all occasions where I am called upon, as a trustee for my countrymen, to deliberate on questions important to their happiness, disdaining all personal advantages to be derived from a suppression of my real sentiments . . . openly to avow [declare] them; and, secondly, . . . whenever the public resolutions are taken, to regard them though opposite to my opinion, as sacred . . . and to join in supporting them as earnestly as if my voice had been given for them.

JOHN DICKINSON, quoted in *The Life and Times of John Dickinson, 1732–1808*

Dickinson's two rules became guiding principles for the leaders who faced the formidable task of starting a new nation.

Americans Debate Republicanism

John Dickinson

John Dickinson later recalled that when he was chosen to draft the proposal for a new government, "there was no question concerning forms of Government . . . We knew that the people of this country must unite themselves under some form of Government and that this could be no other than the republican form." However, the task of creating a new government posed a great challenge. Fighting the Revolutionary War gave the states a common goal, but they remained reluctant to unite under a strong central government.

BASIS FOR A REPUBLIC Americans believed that a democracy, government directly by the people, placed power in the hands of the uneducated masses. Therefore, they favored a **republic**—a government in which citizens rule through their elected representatives—which placed power in the hands of capable leaders. **Republicanism,** the idea that governments should be based on the consent of the people, meant different things to different Americans.

Some believed that a republic must be based on virtue. The new government could only succeed, they argued, if people placed the good of the nation above their personal interests.

Other Americans believed that a republic would benefit from self-interest. They asserted that if a government allowed independent citizens to pursue their own economic and political interests, the whole nation would benefit.

A. Answer One view held that people should put national interests above their own interests. The other held that the nation benefited from people pursuing their own interests. Both promoted the good of the nation.

THINK THROUGH HISTORY
A. Comparing How were the two views of republicanism different? How were they alike?

126 CHAPTER 5

SECTION 1 RESOURCES

PRINT RESOURCES

IN-DEPTH RESOURCES: UNIT 2
Guided Reading, p. 1

ACCESS FOR STUDENTS ACQUIRING ENGLISH
Guided Reading (Spanish), p. 48

FORMAL ASSESSMENT
Section Quiz, p. 54

ALTERNATIVE ASSESSMENT BOOK
See forms for supporting and scoring alternative activities.

TECHNOLOGY RESOURCES

GEOGRAPHY TRANSPARENCIES
G5, Land Ceded by States: 1782–1802

VIDEO *American Portfolio: A Videodisc for U.S. History*
user's guide, p. 39

INTERNET McDougal Littell Learning On-Line
http://www.mcdougallittell.com

As the states created their own constitutions, they wrestled with how to put into practice the ideals of republicanism. In trying to do so, the state constitutions shared certain similarities. They limited the powers of government leaders. They guaranteed specific rights for citizens, including freedom of speech, religion, and the press. In general, they emphasized liberty over equality and reflected a fear of centralized authority rather than the need for effective central government.

At the same time, state constitutions differed widely in granting the right to vote. Some states, like Pennsylvania, granted voting rights to all white males. Other states, like Maryland, continued to make property ownership a requirement for voting.

Despite the rise of a new feminine ideal—as reflected in the concept of republican motherhood—women did not have the right to vote in most of the states. However, New Jersey gave voting rights to all free property owners, neglecting to specify males. Consequently, some New Jersey women gained the right to vote—at least until 1807, when this right was revoked.

The Continental Congress Debates

While the states developed their individual constitutions, the Continental Congress tried to draft one for the states as a whole. That was very difficult to do because there was so much disagreement over what the role of the Congress should be. The delegates had to answer three basic questions.

REPRESENTATION BY POPULATION OR BY STATE? The states had come together as independent political units. Although the states were equal to one another, they were unequal in land size, wealth, and population. These differences posed a serious dilemma. Should delegates to a national congress represent people or states? Should each state elect the same number of representatives regardless of its population? Or should states with large populations have more representatives than states with small populations?

For the time being, the members of the Continental Congress looked on themselves as representing independent states. As a result, they made the decision that each state would have one vote regardless of population.

SUPREME POWER: CAN IT BE DIVIDED? Until this time most people assumed that a government could not share supreme power. That is, either a government had supreme power or it did not. If it did not, it could not function.

However, the Congress proposed a new type of government in a set of laws called the **Articles of Confederation**—one in which two levels of government shared fundamental powers. State governments were supreme in some matters, while the national government was supreme in other matters. The delegates called this new form of government a **confederation,** or alliance.

The Articles of Confederation gave the new national government power to declare war, make peace, and sign treaties. It could borrow money, set standards for coins and for weights and measures, establish a postal service, and deal with Native American peoples. The Articles, however, created no separate executive department to enforce the acts of Congress and no national court system to decide the meaning of laws.

HISTORICAL SPOTLIGHT

REPUBLICAN MOTHERHOOD

An important issue in the early years of the nation was the role that women should play in the republic. As a result of social and economic changes before and during the Revolutionary War, women took more active roles. They were especially involved in preparing the next generation of patriots by instilling republican values in their children. The image on this historical silk embroidery represents this aspect of republican motherhood. An example was Eliza Pinckney of South Carolina, who influenced her two sons, Charles Cotesworth Pinckney and Thomas Pinckney, to become distinguished political leaders of the republic. As she later declared, "No pleasure can equal that which a mother feels when she knows her children have acted their part well through life."

Shaping a New Nation **127**

Role-Playing Ask students to write a response to the Kaskaskia chief's requests from the viewpoint of a government leader in 1793.

OBJECTIVE
③ INSTRUCT

The Confederation Encounters Problems

▶ **Starting with the Student**
Have students analyze the problems of the Confederation by identifying the causes and effects of each. Synthesize students' work in a classroom chart like this:

Problem	Cause	Effect

▶ **Discussing Key Ideas**
• Equal representation among the states leads to crisis in national unity.
• Debtors and creditors debate the merits of paper money and high taxes.
• War debt and national disunity create chaos in foreign relations.

ANOTHER PERSPECTIVE

John Baptist de Coigne, a Kaskaskia chief, was among a group of Indians from the Northwest Territory who met with leaders of the U.S. government in 1793. He expressed the Native American view of the westward expansion of white settlers during the previous ten years:

Order your people to be just. They are always trying to get our lands. They come on our lands, they hunt on them; kill our game and kill us. Keep them on one side of the line, and us on the other. Listen, my father, to what we say, and protect the nations of the Wabash and the Mississippi in their lands.

Under the Articles of Confederation there was a "want of concert in matters where common interest requires it."

JAMES MADISON

WESTERN LANDS: WHO GETS THEM? By 1779, twelve states had agreed to accept the new government, but conflict over western lands delayed final approval for two more years. Some states, by their original charters, had claims to lands west of the Appalachian Mountains. Maryland, which had no such claims, refused to approve the Articles until all states turned over their western lands to the United States. It feared that states with land claims would expand and overpower smaller states. Beginning in 1781, the landed states gave up their western claims and with Maryland's approval, the Articles of Confederation went into effect in March 1781.

The Confederation Congress then faced the question of how to govern the public lands west of the Appalachians. The territory north of the Ohio River offered rich land for settlers. Congress passed the **Land Ordinance of 1785,** which established a plan for surveying the land, as is shown in the Geography Spotlight on pages 130–131. In the **Northwest Ordinance of 1787,** Congress provided a procedure for dividing the land into no less than three nor more than five territories. The Northwest Ordinance also set requirements for the admission of new states, which, however, seemed to overlook Native American land claims. There were three basic requirements or stages for becoming a state:

• First, Congress would appoint a territorial governor and judges.
• Second, when a territory had 5,000 voting residents, the settlers could write a temporary constitution and elect their own government.
• Third, when the total population of a territory reached 60,000, the settlers could write a state constitution, which had to be approved by Congress before it granted statehood.

The Northwest Ordinance established a clear, orderly process by which new territories in the West would become states.

The Confederation Encounters Problems

The Land Ordinance of 1785 and the Northwest Ordinance of 1787 became the Confederation's greatest achievements. These laws established a blueprint for future growth of the nation. In dealing with more immediate issues, the Confederation encountered overwhelming problems.

POLITICAL AND ECONOMIC PROBLEMS The most serious problem was that the country under the Confederation lacked national unity. Each state functioned independently by pursuing its own interests rather than those of the nation as a whole. In addition, the Confederation didn't recognize the differences in population among the states. Each state, regardless of its population, had only one vote in Congress. Thus, the political power of Georgia, with a population of 25,000 in 1770, was equal to that of Massachusetts, with a population of 270,000. Furthermore, the Articles could not be amended without the consent of all the states. Therefore, changes in government were difficult to achieve.

Currency, such as this example from early Connecticut, was issued by the colonies and states.

128 CHAPTER 5

C. Answer The Land Ordinance of 1785 established a plan for surveying the land, whereas the Northwest Ordinance of 1787 provided for dividing the land into three to five territories and established the requirements for the admission of new states.

THINK THROUGH HISTORY
C. Comparing *What was the difference between the Land Ordinance of 1785 and the Northwest Ordinance of 1787?*

Cooperative Activity: Letters to the Editor

Task: Students will write letters to the editor, expressing the viewpoint of a citizen regarding problems of the Confederation.

Purpose: To understand how weaknesses of the Confederation affected citizens.

Activity: Assign groups of three to five students to investigate problems the Confederation encountered. Then have group members assume the roles of a farmer, a mer-

chant, or another citizen and write a letter to the editor of a newspaper stating how these problems affect them.

📁 **Building a Portfolio:** If students feel their letter qualifies as an example of their best work, they should place it in their portfolio.

ALTERNATIVE ASSESSMENT BOOK
Standards for Evaluating a Cooperative Activity

Standards for Evaluation
Letters should . . .

• state the problem from the viewpoint of a citizen
• relate the problem to a weakness of government
• suggest a change in government that would solve the problem
• use appropriate style for a letter to the editor

The most serious economic problem was the huge debt that the Confederation Congress amassed during the Revolutionary War. The war had cost the nation $160 million—a huge amount of money in those days. The Continental Congress had borrowed from foreign countries and had printed its own paper money. After the war, Continental currency became worthless, giving rise to the expression "not worth a Continental." Lacking the power to tax, Congress requested the states' approval to impose a tariff, or tax on imported goods. It planned to use the revenue to repay foreign loans. One state, Rhode Island, rejected the proposed tax, so it was not adopted. The Confederation Congress also had no control over interstate or foreign trade.

BORROWERS VERSUS LENDERS Another problem caused by the debt from the Revolution was the struggle between creditors (lenders of money) and debtors (borrowers of money). After the war, wealthy people who had lent money to the states favored high taxes so that the states would be able to pay them back. However, high taxes sent many farmers into debt and creditors often sued farmers in court. If a creditor won a case, the government seized the farmer's land and animals and sold them at auction.

Debtors and creditors also disagreed over the usefulness of paper money. Debtors wanted to increase the supply of money to lessen its value and enable them to pay off their debts with cheap currency. Creditors, in contrast, wanted to keep the supply of money low so that it would keep its full value. Both groups had much to lose.

FOREIGN-RELATIONS PROBLEMS The lack of support by states for national concerns gave Congress foreign-relations problems. First, since the United States could not repay its debts to British merchants and would not compensate loyalists for property losses, Britain refused to evacuate its military forts on the Great Lakes. Furthermore, Spain's presence on the borders of the United States posed another threat to westward expansion. In 1784 Spain closed the Mississippi River to American navigation. This deprived western farmers of a means of shipping their crops to eastern markets through New Orleans. Though Northerners were willing to give up navigation rights on the Mississippi in exchange for more profitable trade concessions, Westerners and Southerners insisted on access to the Mississippi. Thus, negotiations with Spain failed.

The problems Congress encountered in dealing with foreign nations pointed to basic weaknesses of the Confederation government. Americans' fear of giving the national government too much power had resulted in a government that lacked sufficient power to deal with the nation's problems. The forthcoming Constitutional Convention would change all of this.

D. Answer A lack of national unity.

THINK THROUGH HISTORY
D. Synthesizing
What was the fundamental cause of the nation's problems under the Articles of Confederation?

Weaknesses of the Articles of Confederation

- Congress could not enact and collect taxes.
- Congress could not regulate interstate or foreign trade.
- Each state had only one vote in Congress, regardless of population.
- Nine out of 13 states needed to agree to pass any law.
- The Articles could be amended only if all states approved.
- There was no executive branch to enforce laws of Congress.
- There was no national court system to settle congressional law disputes.
- There were 13 separate states that lacked national unity.

SKILLBUILDER
INTERPRETING CHARTS
How many states were needed to approve changes in the Articles of Confederation? Why did these weaknesses lead to an ineffective government?

Skillbuilder Answer All states *Possible response:* Without the ability to collect taxes or to regulate interstate or foreign trade and with no executive branch or national court system, the government was weak. It was also weak because each state had only one vote, it took nine of the 13 states to pass any law, and it took all 13 states to amend the Articles of Confederation.

Reading the Chart
Remind students that the different colors in the chart do not indicate different categories. The colors are there to make the chart easier to read.

Extension Have students identify at least one consequence of each weakness of the Articles of Confederation listed in the table.

ASSESS & RETEACH

Section 1 Assessment
Assign the questions as homework or as a classroom activity.

Self-Assessment
Students can reflect on their understanding of the section by using a list to show what caused the weaknesses of the Articles of Confederation.

Section Quiz

FORMAL ASSESSMENT
Section Quiz, p. 54

Reteach
Have students work in small groups to review the Think Through History questions in Section 1. As a class, discuss answers and clarify understandings.

CLOSE

The Articles of Confederation passed laws that provided for the future growth of the United States. However, serious weaknesses resulting from Americans' fear of centralized authority limited the Confederation's ability to deal with the political and economic problems that the new nation faced.

Section 1 Assessment

1. TERMS & NAMES
Identify:
- republic
- republicanism
- Articles of Confederation
- confederation
- Land Ordinance of 1785
- Northwest Ordinance of 1787

2. SEQUENCING HISTORY
Create a time line like the one below, showing at least five important events of the first ten years of the new nation.

| event one | | event three |
| event two | | event four |

What was the most important event, and why do you think so?

3. ANALYZING How did the states' desire for a weak central government reflect their fears and uncertainties about government in general?

THINK ABOUT
- why the Revolutionary War was fought
- the colonies' individual identities
- fear of loss of power

4. EVALUATING AN OPINION
Do you agree or disagree with the idea that a republic was a better form of government for the new nation than a democracy? Explain your opinion.

THINK ABOUT
- the difference between a republic and a democracy
- who would have participated in a democracy
- who chose the republic over the democracy

Shaping a New Nation **129**

ANSWERS

1. TERMS & NAMES
republic, p. 126
republicanism, p. 126
Articles of Confederation, p. 127
confederation, p. 127
Land Ordinance of 1785, p. 128
Northwest Ordinance of 1787, p. 128

2. SEQUENCING HISTORY
Possible Responses:
1776 Declaration of Independence
1777 Congress adopts the Articles of Confederation
1779 12 states, all but Maryland, accept new government
1781 Maryland approves the Articles of Confederation and they go into effect
1785 The Land Ordinance of 1785
1787 The Northwest Ordinance of 1787

3. ANALYZING
Possible Responses: The states didn't want another strong central power like that of Great Britain. Individual state governments did not want to lose their powers.

4. EVALUATING AN OPINION
Possible Responses: Students who agree may say that a republic could elect the best educated and informed leaders to represent the citizens, and that having everyone participate in a democracy might lead to problems. Students who disagree may say that in a democracy, it might be good for all the citizens to participate in its government, and that many of the common citizens might not want the more educated and wealthier members of the society to be the new leaders.

The Land Ordinance of 1785

When states ceded, or gave up, their western lands to the United States, the new nation became "land rich" even though it was "money poor." Government leaders searched for a way to use the land to fund such causes as public education.

The fastest and easiest way to raise money would be to sell huge parcels of thousands of acres at a time. However, then only rich people would be able to purchase land. The Land Ordinance of 1785 came down on the side of small landowners by making the parcels affordable.

The Land Ordinance established a plan for dividing the land. The government would first survey the land, dividing it into townships of 36 square miles, as shown on the map below. Then each township would be divided into 36 sections of one square mile; each was equal to about 640 acres. An individual or a family could purchase a section and divide it into farms or smaller units. A typical farm of the period was often equal to one-quarter section, or 160 acres. The minimum price per acre was one dollar.

The map on the next page was probably drawn by Rufus Putnam. It shows how a township, now in Meigs County, Ohio, was divided in 1787 into parcels of full square-mile sections and smaller, more affordable plots. The names of the original buyers are written on the full sections.

Government leaders hoped the buyers would occupy their lands, develop farms, and establish democratic communities. In this way American settlements would spread across the western territories in an orderly way. Government surveyors repeated the process thousands of times as Americans transformed the continent with their frontier geometry.

In 1787, the Congress further provided for the orderly development of the Northwest Territory by passing the Northwest Ordinance. The ordinance established how states would be created out of the territory.

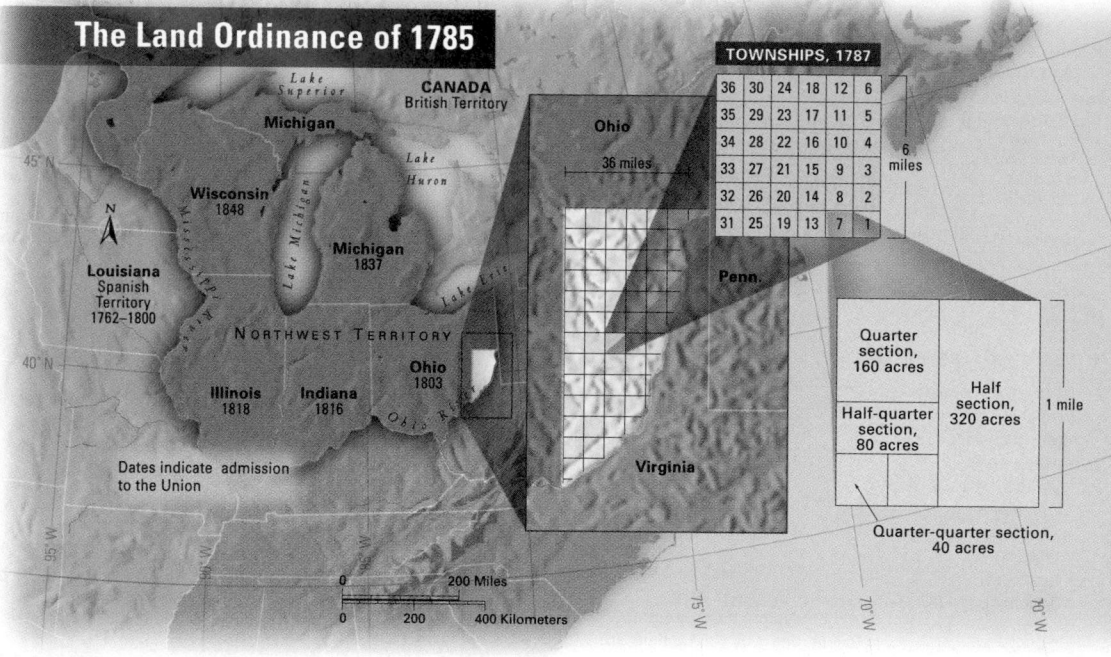

The Land Ordinance of 1785

Lake Superior

CANADA
British Territory

Michigan

Lake Huron

Wisconsin
1848

Lake Michigan

Michigan
1837

Louisiana
Spanish
Territory
1762–1800

NORTHWEST TERRITORY

Lake Erie

Illinois
1818

Indiana
1816

Ohio
1803

Ohio River

Dates indicate admission to the Union

0   200 Miles
0   200   400 Kilometers

TOWNSHIPS, 1787

36	30	24	18	12	6
35	29	23	17	11	5
34	28	22	16	10	4
33	27	21	15	9	3
32	26	20	14	8	2
31	25	19	13	7	1

Ohio

36 miles

6 miles

Penn.

Virginia

Quarter section, 160 acres

Half section, 320 acres

Half-quarter section, 80 acres

1 mile

Quarter-quarter section, 40 acres

RECOMMENDED RESOURCES

Books

Eckert, Allan W. *Gateway to Empire.* Boston: Little, 1983. A history of the Old Northwest.

Hunter, Lloyd A. *Pathways to the Old Northwest.* Indianapolis: Indiana Historical Society, 1988. A study of the Northwest Ordinance.

Onuf, Peter S. *Statehood and Union: A History of the Northwest Ordinance.* Bloomington: Indiana UP, 1987.

Williams, Frederick D. *The Northwest Ordinance.* Michigan State UP, 1989. A collection of essays.

Videos

Settling the Old Northwest. Encyclopaedia Britannica. A dynamic account of the conflicts between Native Americans and early settlers.

U.S. Expansion: The Northwest Territory. Coronet/MTI, 1989. A history of the Old Northwest from Native American days to the growth of Chicago in the late 19th century.

Westward Movement I: Settlers of the Old Northwest Territory. Encyclopaedia Britannica. A study of settlement in the post-Revolutionary era.

A TOWNSHIP

TOWNSHIP N.° VII RANGE N.° XIV   SCALE of forty chains to one inch

A **RELIGION** To encourage the growth of religion within the township, the surveyors set aside a full section of land. Most of the land within the section was sold to provide funds for a church and a minister's salary. This practice was dropped after a few years because of concern about the separation of church and state.

B **EDUCATION** The ordinance encouraged public education by setting aside section 16 of every township for school buildings. Local people used the money raised by the sale of land within this section to build a school and hire a teacher. This section was centrally located so that students could reach it without traveling too far.

C **REVENUE** Congress reserved two or three sections of each township for sale at a later date. Congress planned to sell the sections then at a tidy profit. The government soon abandoned this practice because of criticism that it should not be involved in land speculation.

D **WATER** Rivers and streams were very important to early settlers. They used them for transportation. Of most interest, however, was a meandering stream, which indicated flat bottomland that was highly prized for its fertility.

E **SMALL PARCELS** The land company divided the interior of the township into smaller parcels for sale to individuals.

▶ **Starting with the Student**
• Have students find out more about land settlement in their own area. Into what sort of lots or tracts was the land originally divided?

▶ **Discussing Key Ideas**
• The Land Ordinance of 1785 encourages small landowners to settle in the Northwest Territories.
• The Northwest Ordinance of 1787 establishes the process by which the territories would enter the union as states.
• The two ordinances set a pattern for the nation's future westward expansion.

HISTORY FROM VISUALS
Reading the Images Have students study and compare the different maps and insets.
• In what sense was the area in question the "Northwest"? *It was the northwesternmost land possessed by the new nation at this time.*
• What bodies of water essentially defined the boundaries of the Old Northwest? *The Great Lakes, the Ohio River, and the Mississippi River.*

INTERACT WITH HISTORY

1. **SYNTHESIZING** How did the Land Ordinance of 1785 provide for the orderly development of the Northwest Territory? How did it make land affordable?

   SEE SKILLBUILDER HANDBOOK, PAGE 1051.

2. **CHOOSING A TOWNSHIP SECTION** Use the information in this feature to answer the questions.

   • If you had lived in 1787 and wanted to purchase a full section of land in the township shown on this page, which one would you select? Would you want to be near water? Would you want to be near the center of the township? Would it be important to you to be close to a school? Explain your choice.

   • List advantages that your section seems to offer.

Shaping a New Nation **131**

INTERACT WITH HISTORY

1. Synthesizing	2. Choosing a Township Section
Possible Response: It surveyed the land and established a plan for parceling it out. Instead of dividing the land into huge parcels that only the rich could afford, it allowed families or individuals to purchase smaller parcels and to subdivide them further if necessary.	**Possible Responses:** Among the advantages students may consider important are fertile soil; reasonably flat, passable terrain; distance from Native Americans; and proximity to a church, to a school, to one or more streams, to friends or loved ones also settling in the area, and/or to the more built-up "civilization" in Pennsylvania and Virginia in the east. Students should choose a parcel that has the maximum number of the advantages that they consider important.

TERMS & NAMES
- Shays's Rebellion
- James Madison
- Roger Sherman
- Great Compromise
- Three-Fifths Compromise
- legislative branch
- executive branch
- judicial branch
- checks and balances
- electoral college

Section 2 Overview

OBJECTIVES

(1) To identify events that led nationalist leaders to call for a convention to strengthen the government.

(2) To summarize the key conflicts at the Constitutional Convention and explain how they were resolved through compromise.

(3) To describe the form of government established by the Constitution.

SKILLBUILDERS
- Interpreting charts, pp. 134, 135

CRITICAL THINKING
- Analyzing causes, p. 133
- Evaluating decisions, p. 133
- Analyzing issues, p. 134
- Analyzing motives, p. 134
- Contrasting, p. 136
- Forming opinions, p. 136
- Summarizing, p. 136
- Analyzing, p. 136
- Evaluating an opinion, p. 136

FOCUS & MOTIVATE

▶ **Starting with the Student**
Ask students to think about disputes they have had that were successfully resolved by compromise.

- What steps did they take to reach the compromise?
- What did they give up or change their mind about in order to reach a peaceful solution?

MORE ABOUT . . .
Daniel Shays

Although the farmers' revolt of 1787 bears his name, Daniel Shays was only one of several leaders of the rebellion. Shays held political office at Pelham, Massachusetts, and he became sympathetic to the farmers' plight. When the state militia scattered the rebels at Springfield, Shays escaped to Vermont. The government placed a death penalty on his head but later pardoned him.

---

② Drafting the Constitution

LEARN ABOUT debates and compromises at the Constitutional Convention
TO UNDERSTAND how early leaders created a totally new form of government.

ONE AMERICAN'S STORY

Daniel Shays was angry. A veteran of the Revolutionary War battles at Bunker Hill and Saratoga, he had returned to his farm in western Massachusetts. Because of the heavy debt that he carried, however, he faced debtors' prison. After risking his life in the Revolutionary War, he was now on the brink of failure. The problem for Shays was that he was the victim of too much taxation and too little paper money with which to pay his taxes.

Like Shays, many farmers in Massachusetts had reached the breaking point in 1786. People in the coastal towns, where merchants had sold goods to farmers on credit, had pushed through a state tax that fell heavily on farmers in the western part of the state. The farmers petitioned the assembly for relief—but their pleas fell on deaf ears. The assembly included only a few representatives from western Massachusetts.

All through the summer and fall of 1786, farmers kept demanding the courts be closed so they would not lose their farms to creditors. Their discontent boiled over into mob action in January of 1787 when Daniel Shays led a motley army of 1,200 farmers in forcing the courts to close. Shays's army then marched through the snow toward the arsenal at Springfield.

State officials hurriedly called out the militia to head off the army of farmers. Four of the rebels were killed and the rest were scattered. Clearly, though, if farmers were rebelling, there was something seriously wrong with the new government.

Shays's Rebellion not only resulted in the death of four rebels, but also greatly disturbed some of the nation's leaders.

Nationalists Strengthen the Government

Shays's Rebellion, as the farmers' protest came to be called, caused panic and dismay throughout the nation. Every state had debt-ridden farmers. Would rebellion spread from Massachusetts elsewhere? Not only was private property in danger, but so was the new nation's reputation. As George Washington himself exclaimed, "What a triumph for our enemies . . . to find we are incapable of governing ourselves."

It was clearly time to talk about a stronger national government. Since the states had placed such severe limits on the government to prevent abuse of power, the government was unable to solve many of the nation's problems.

CALL FOR CONVENTION One of the nation's biggest problems was trade between the states, which led to quarrels over taxes on one another's goods and disagreements over navigation rights. George Washington wrote.

> **A PERSONAL VOICE**
> The consequences of . . . [an] inefficient government are too obvious to be dwelt upon. Thirteen sovereignties pulling against each other, and all tugging at the federal head, will soon bring ruin upon the whole. . . . Let us have [government] by which our lives, liberty, and property will be secured or let us know the worst at once.
> **GEORGE WASHINGTON**

132 CHAPTER 5

SECTION 2 RESOURCES

 PRINT RESOURCES

IN-DEPTH RESOURCES: UNIT 2
Guided Reading, p. 2
Skillbuilder Practice: Analyzing Issues, p. 4
Primary Source: *from* The U.S. Constitution, First Draft, p. 7
Literature: from *Legacy* by James A. Michener, p. 11

ACCESS FOR STUDENTS ACQUIRING ENGLISH
Guided Reading (Spanish), p. 49
Skillbuilder Practice: Analyzing Issues (Spanish), p. 51

FORMAL ASSESSMENT
Section Quiz, p. 55

ALTERNATIVE ASSESSMENT BOOK
See forms for supporting and scoring alternative activities.

TECHNOLOGY RESOURCES

CRITICAL THINKING TRANSPARENCIES
CT5, Constitutional Convention

CD-ROM Electronic Library of Primary Sources

VIDEO *American Portfolio: A Videodisc for U.S. History*
user's guide, p. 40

INTERNET McDougal Littell Learning On-Line
http://www.mcdougallittell.com

A. Answer They may have feared other uprisings. Shays's Rebellion showed the weakness of the national government in dealing with economic problems.

THINK THROUGH HISTORY
A. Analyzing Causes Why do you think news of Shays's Rebellion made states decide to participate in the Philadelphia convention?

In September 1786, nationalist leaders such as James Madison and Alexander Hamilton called a meeting of delegates from all the states to discuss problems of interstate trade. Only five states sent representatives to the convention, held in Annapolis, Maryland. However, those present decided to call for another meeting of all the states the following year in Philadelphia to deal with trade and other national problems.

At about the same time that the call went out, the disturbing news of Shays's Rebellion in Massachusetts spread throughout the states. The incident convinced twelve states to send delegates to the Philadelphia convention called by Congress in 1787.

HIGHLIGHTS OF THE CONVENTION
In May of 1787, appointed delegates from all the states except Rhode Island gathered at the State House in Philadelphia in the same room in which the Declaration of Independence had been signed eleven years earlier. In spite of the sweltering heat, the windows were tightly closed to ensure secrecy by preventing outsiders from hearing the discussions.

Most of the 55 delegates were lawyers, merchants, or planters. Many were wealthy, well-educated men in their thirties or forties. They included some of the most outstanding leaders of the time—Benjamin Franklin, Alexander Hamilton, and George Washington, to name a few. Thomas Jefferson, who was ambassador to France, could not attend. Washington was elected presiding officer unanimously.

KEY PLAYERS

JAMES MADISON
1751–1836
The oldest of 12 children, **James Madison** grew up in Virginia. He was a sickly child who suffered all his life from physical ailments. Because of a weak speaking voice, he decided not to become a minister and thus entered politics.

Madison's Virginia Plan resulted from extensive research that he had done on political systems before the meeting. He asked Edmund Randolph, a fellow delegate from Virginia, to present the plan because his own voice was too weak to be heard throughout the assembly.

Besides providing brilliant political leadership, Madison kept a record of the debates that took place at the convention. Because of his plan and his leadership, Madison is known as the Father of the Constitution.

ROGER SHERMAN
1721–1793
Born in Massachusetts, **Roger Sherman** was an awkward man. He spoke with a New England dialect that some people found laughable. As a young man, he became a successful merchant. He also studied law and became so active in politics that he had to quit his business.

Sherman served on the committee to draft the Declaration of Independence. When he returned to Philadelphia for the Constitutional Convention in 1787, he was 66 years old. He introduced a plan—later called the Great Compromise—that resolved the issue of state representation in the national legislature. Roger Sherman was the only man to sign the Declaration of Independence, the Articles of Confederation, and the Constitution.

B. Answer Some students might say the government under the Articles had too many problems to be fixed by revisions. Other students might say by creating a new government the delegates violated what they were authorized to do.

Conflict Leads to Compromise

Most of the delegates recognized the need to strengthen the central government. Within the first five days of the meeting, they gave up the idea of fixing the Articles of Confederation and decided to form a whole new government.

THINK THROUGH HISTORY
B. Evaluating Decisions Do you think the delegates made a wise choice in deciding to replace the Articles of Confederation rather than revise them? Why or why not?

DEBATING THE CENTRAL ISSUES The first big conflict involved the rights of the states. The delegates feared giving too much power to a central government, yet their experience under the Articles of Confederation had taught them the consequences of an inefficient national government.

The second conflict involved protecting the rights of a population made up of people from many different walks of life. The delegates realized the need to prevent one group—wealthy landowners or merchants—from dominating another group—small farmers or workers. The delegates needed to protect the rights of both minorities and the majority.

Shaping a New Nation **133**

OBJECTIVE
① INSTRUCT

Nationalists Strengthen the Government

▶*Discussing Key Ideas*
• Shays's Rebellion underscores the consequences of a weak national government.
• Delegates from 12 states meet to deal with national problems.

IN-DEPTH RESOURCES: UNIT 2
Guided Reading, p. 2

ACCESS FOR STUDENTS ACQUIRING ENGLISH
Guided Reading (Spanish), p. 49

KEY PLAYERS
Madison and Sherman
Critical Thinking: Analyzing Motives
• What limitations did each of these men have to overcome? *Possible Responses: Madison was sickly, with a weak speaking voice. Sherman spoke in a New England dialect and was awkward.*

OBJECTIVE
② INSTRUCT

Conflict Leads to Compromise

▶*Discussing Key Ideas*
• Delegates at the convention seek to increase the strength of the national government while preserving states' rights.
• Delegates puzzle over balancing the interests of a variety of societal groups.
• Roger Sherman's Great Compromise leads to the Three-Fifths Compromise.

TEACHING OPTIONS

Exploring Themes

Constitutional Concerns Discuss the forms of protest Massachusetts farmers used in seeking relief from their economic problems.

• How was Shays's Rebellion like the American Revolution? *Possible Response: Students may point out that the farmers' actions reflected the values stated in the Declaration of Independence.*
• Why did the farmers' revolt cause fear and disapproval among Americans? *Possible Response: It emphasized the weakness of government.*

Teaching Gifted and Talented Students

Analyzing a Primary Source Document Log on to the McDougal Littell web page and explore the Internet resources for Chapter 5 of *The Americans*. First, use the address listed below to access Learning On-Line, the McDougal Littell home page, then click on Social Studies and then find *The Americans*. For Chapter 5, you will find a treasure trove of resources about the Constitutional Convention. After exploring, choose one resource to examine in depth. Write a description and review of the material you chose and share your findings with the class.

 http://www.mcdougallittell.com

The convention faced two fundamental questions:
• How could it strengthen the national government while preserving the rights of the states?
• How could it balance conflicting interests of different groups within society?

BIG STATES VERSUS SMALL STATES One big issue the delegates faced was giving fair representation to both large and small states. Madison's Virginia Plan proposed a bicameral, or two-house, legislature, with membership based on each state's population. The voters would elect members of the lower house, who would then elect members of the upper house. Both houses would vote for the country's president and judges.

Delegates from the small states vigorously objected to the Virginia Plan because it gave more power to states with large populations. The Virginia Plan would give the four largest states a majority in both houses of Congress. Small states supported William Paterson's New Jersey Plan, which proposed a single-house congress in which each state had an equal vote. The New Jersey Plan would give control of Congress to the seven smallest states if they had voted together—even though these states included only 25 percent of the nation's population.

Proponents of the plans became deadlocked, and the debate dragged on through the hot and humid summer days. At times the tempers of the delegates seemed even hotter than the weather. Finally, Roger Sherman suggested the **Great Compromise,** which offered a two-house Congress to satisfy both small and big states. Each state would have equal representation in the Senate, or upper house. The size of the population of each state would determine its representation in the House of Representatives, or lower house. Voters of each state would choose members of the House. The state legislatures would choose members of the Senate.

Sherman's plan satisfied those who favored government by the people because it allowed voters to participate directly in choosing representatives. It also satisfied those who defended states' rights because it preserved the power of state legislatures.

SLAVERY-RELATED ISSUES The Great Compromise settled one major issue but led to conflict over another. Representation based on population raised the question of whether slaves should be counted as people. Southern delegates, whose states had large numbers of slaves, wanted slaves included in the population count that determined the number of representatives in the House. Northern delegates, whose states had few slaves, argued against counting slaves as part of the population. Not counting them would give the northern states more representatives than the southern states in the House of Representatives. The **Three-Fifths Compromise** called for three-fifths of a state's slaves to be counted as population.

The Three-Fifths Compromise settled the political issue, but it did not address the economic issue of slavery. The Southern states wanted to resume the importing of slaves, which had stopped during the Revolutionary War. They worried that if Congress were given power to regulate foreign trade, it might do away with the slave trade. To resolve this issue, the convention gave Congress the power to regulate trade but prevented it from interfering with the slave

Key Conflicts in the Constitutional Convention

CENTRAL GOVERNMENT vs. STRONG STATES	
• Authority derives from the people.	• Authority comes from the states.
• In a new plan of government, the central government should be stronger than the states.	• Under a modified Articles of Confederation, the states should remain stronger than the central government.

LARGE STATES vs. SMALL STATES	
• Congress should be composed of two houses.	• Congress of one house should be preserved.
• Number of delegates to both houses of Congress should be assigned according to population.	• Each state should have one vote.

NORTH vs. SOUTH	
• Slaves should not be counted when deciding the number of congressional delegates.	• Slaves should be counted when determining congressional representation.
• Slaves should be counted when levying taxes.	• Slaves should not be counted when levying taxes.

SKILLBUILDER
INTERPRETING CHARTS *Why do you think the Southern states wanted slaves counted for determining the number of representatives in the House of Representatives?*
Skillbuilder Answer Representation: Possible answer: Including slaves would increase the South's official population and number of representatives.

C. Answer Big states: favored representation based on population. *Small states:* favored equal representation for each state.

THINK THROUGH HISTORY
C. Analyzing Issues How would you characterize the conflict between big states and small states?

D. Answer Possible answer: Slave trade had been stopped during the war. Some people in the North were opposed to slavery, which a national government with much power could probably stop or regulate.

THINK THROUGH HISTORY
D. Analyzing Motives Why do you think the Southern states feared that Congress might do away with the slave trade?

134 CHAPTER 5

---

trade for at least twenty years. Thus, 1808 would be the earliest that the slave trade could be outlawed. Although the proposal passed, not all the delegates agreed with it. James Madison predicted, "Twenty years will produce all the mischief that can be apprehended from the liberty to import slaves. So long a term will be more dishonorable to the National character than to say nothing about it in the Constitution."

Creating a New Government

After the delegates reached agreement on the difficult questions of slavery and representation, they dealt with other issues somewhat more easily. They divided power between the states and the national government, and they separated the national government's power into three branches. Thus, they created an entirely new government.

DIVISION OF POWERS   The new system of government was a form of federalism that divided power between the national government and the state governments. The powers granted to the national government by the Constitution are known as delegated powers, or enumerated powers. These include such powers as control of foreign affairs, providing national defense, regulating trade between the states, and coining money. Powers not specifically granted to the national government but kept by the states are called reserved powers. These include powers such as providing for and supervising education, establishing marriage laws, and regulating trade within a state.

Some powers were shared by both the national and the state governments. Both levels of government share such important powers as the right to tax, to borrow money, and to pay debts. They also share the powers to establish courts.

SEPARATION OF POWERS   The delegates protected the rights of the states, but they also granted some powers exclusively to the national government. At the same time, they limited the authority of the national government. First, they created three branches of government—a **legislative branch** to make laws, an **executive**

Skillbuilder Answer No elected officials: the judicial branch. No checks and balances: Possible answer: Each branch might try to expand its powers, possibly leading to turmoil and a form of autocratic government, such as a dictatorship, by the winning branch.

SKILLBUILDER
INTERPRETING CHARTS
Which branch of the federal government has no elected officials? What do you think might happen if the federal government operated without checks and balances?

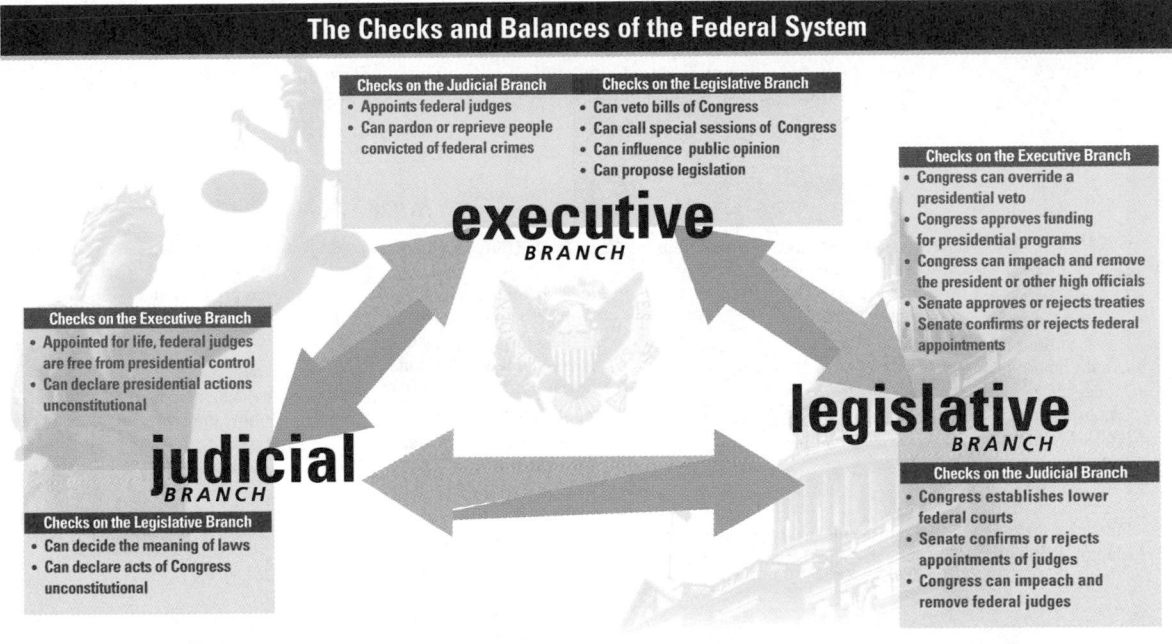

The Checks and Balances of the Federal System

Checks on the Judicial Branch
- Appoints federal judges
- Can pardon or reprieve people convicted of federal crimes

Checks on the Legislative Branch
- Can veto bills of Congress
- Can call special sessions of Congress
- Can influence public opinion
- Can propose legislation

executive
BRANCH

Checks on the Executive Branch
- Appointed for life, federal judges are free from presidential control
- Can declare presidential actions unconstitutional

judicial
BRANCH

Checks on the Legislative Branch
- Can decide the meaning of laws
- Can declare acts of Congress unconstitutional

Checks on the Executive Branch
- Congress can override a presidential veto
- Congress approves funding for presidential programs
- Congress can impeach and remove the president or other high officials
- Senate approves or rejects treaties
- Senate confirms or rejects federal appointments

legislative
BRANCH

Checks on the Judicial Branch
- Congress establishes lower federal courts
- Senate confirms or rejects appointments of judges
- Congress can impeach and remove federal judges

Shaping a New Nation **135**

OBJECTIVE
③ **INSTRUCT**

Creating a New Government

▶ *Discussing Key Ideas*
- Delegates at the Constitutional Convention distribute power between the states and the national government.
- The three branches of government—judicial, executive, and legislative—are created, along with corresponding checks and balances of power.

IN-DEPTH RESOURCES: UNIT 2
Primary Source: *from* The U.S. Constitution, First Draft, p. 7

HISTORY FROM VISUALS
The Checks and Balances of the Federal System
Reading the Infograph
Suggest to students that they read the graph by pairing branches. For example, they can read how the judicial branch checks the executive and how the executive branch checks the judicial. In this way they get a better sense of how each branch balances the power of the others.

Extension How does the system of checks and balances strengthen the government rather than weaken its power? *Possible Response: The system preserves the power of government by ensuring that no branch becomes powerful enough to diminish the power of another branch.*

TEACHING OPTION

Skillbuilder Mini-Lesson: Analyzing Motives

Explaining the Skill Analyzing an issue involves finding and describing different parts of the issue. To analyze the issue of drug abuse students might identify what the central problems are, who is involved, and what solutions might be possible.

Applying the Skill: The Division of Powers Have students read the paragraphs on the division of powers and answer the following questions to begin analyzing the issue of who should have power and how it should be divided.

1. What is the central problem related to this issue? *How to strengthen the power of the national government while preserving the rights of the states.*

2. What solution was found to this issue? *Give the central government powers dealing with other countries and between states. Give states power over local concerns and activities within the state.*

3. How successful does the solution seem? *Many students will say that it is successful, because the country still operates under the original system.*

IN-DEPTH RESOURCES: UNIT 2
Skillbuilder Practice: Analyzing Issues, p. 4

NOW & THEN
Line-Item Veto
Critical Thinking: Clarifying
- How might the line-item veto increase the power of the executive branch?
- How can the system of checks and balances ensure that the executive branch does not become too powerful?

MORE ABOUT . . .
The Electoral College
In most states, committees of each party choose candidates for presidential electors. It is the electors whom voters select when voting for president. Ballots generally list the names of the presidential candidates rather than the names of the electors. For this reason, many voters do not realize that they are voting for electors rather than voting directly for the president.

ASSESS & RETEACH

Section 2 Assessment
Have students complete the Section 2 Assessment in class or as homework.

Self-Assessment
Ask students to summarize the three key conflicts in the Constitutional Convention. Students should compare their summaries with those of a partner.

Section Quiz
FORMAL ASSESSMENT
Section Quiz, p. 55

Reteach
Use the charts and graphs in this section to focus understanding on complex issues.

CLOSE

The Confederation's inability to deal with the nation's problems convinced nationalists to call for a convention to strengthen the government. Delegates soon decided to replace rather than revise the Articles of Confederation. Through debate and compromise, they created a new form of government.

136 Chapter 5

---

branch to carry out laws, and a **judicial branch** to hear cases. Separation of powers among the legislative, executive, and judicial branches of government clearly distributed political authority.

Then the delegates established a system of **checks and balances** to prevent any one branch from dominating the other two. The president had considerable power, but the Senate had to approve some of the president's decisions, such as treaties and appointments. The president could veto acts of Congress, but Congress could override the veto by a two-thirds vote. The Supreme Court later assumed the power to interpret the Constitution, but the president appointed the justices, and Congress could bring them to trial for abuses of power. Look at the chart on page 135. It shows other aspects of the checks and balances system.

The procedure the delegates established for electing the president reflected their fear of placing too much power in the hands of the people. Instead of choosing the president directly, each state would choose a number of electors equal to the number of senators and representatives the state had in Congress. This group of electors chosen by the states, known as the **electoral college,** would then cast ballots for the presidential candidates.

CHANGING THE CONSTITUTION After four months of debate and compromise, the delegates succeeded in creating a Constitution that was a living document. In other words, by making the Constitution flexible, the delegates enabled it to pass the test of time. They provided a means of changing the Constitution through the amendment process. See the chart on page 156.

George Washington adjourned the convention on September 17, 1787. Of the forty-one delegates who attended that session, only three had enough concerns about the document that they refused to sign it. Although one delegate had gone home ill, another delegate signed for him. Even George Washington was somewhat uncertain about the future of the new plan of government. He remarked to a fellow delegate when the convention adjourned: "I do not expect the Constitution to last for more than twenty years." The convention's work was over, but the new government could not become a reality until the voters agreed. So the Constitution of the United States of America was sent to the Congress, which submitted it to the states for approval.

NOW & THEN

LINE-ITEM VETO
On January 1, 1997, the line-item veto became law. It provides the president with the power to reject parts of appropriations bills—those that designate public funds for special purposes such as a new public building—without rejecting an entire bill.

Those in favor of the law say it will reduce excessive spending. Those opposed to it argue that it shifts the balance of power between the legislative and executive branches by giving the president authority over spending issues. They also point out that the Constitution requires the president to approve or disapprove of bills in their entirety. The line-item veto faces challenges in court to determine whether it is constitutional.

E. Answer Division of powers: divided power between the states and the national government; separation of powers: separated powers among the legislative, executive, and judicial branches of national government

THINK THROUGH HISTORY
E. Contrasting How did division of powers differ from separation of powers?

F. Answer After more than 200 years, it is still the fundamental document for the structure of the nation's federal government.

THINK THROUGH HISTORY
F. Forming Opinions How has the Constitution passed the test of time?

Section 2 Assessment

1. TERMS & NAMES
Identify:
- Shays's Rebellion
- James Madison
- Roger Sherman
- Great Compromise
- Three-Fifths Compromise
- legislative branch
- executive branch
- judicial branch
- checks and balances
- electoral college

2. SUMMARIZING Recreate the web below on your paper and fill it in with specific issues that were debated.

Issues debated at the Constitutional Convention

Choose one issue and explain how the delegates resolved that issue.

3. ANALYZING In what ways did the new system of government fulfill the nation's need for a stronger central government and at the same time allay its fear of a government with too much power?

THINK ABOUT
- the division of powers
- the separation of powers
- the system of checks and balances

4. EVALUATING AN OPINION Do you agree or disagree with the creation of a system of checks and balances? Explain your answer.

THINK ABOUT
- the main task of each branch
- how the branches function
- the efficiency of governmental operations

136 Chapter 5

ANSWERS

1. TERMS & NAMES
Shays's Rebellion, p. 132
James Madison, p. 133
Roger Sherman, p. 133
Great Compromise, p. 134
Three-Fifths Compromise, p. 134
legislative branch, p. 135
executive branch, p. 135
judicial branch, p. 136
checks and balances, p. 136
electoral college, p. 136

2. SUMMARIZING
Entries on the web may include the following:
Problem of regulating interstate trade
Central government has no power to tax
Worthless money
Central government has no power in foreign affairs
States working against each other
Shays's Rebellion

3. ANALYZING
Students may point out that the Constitution clearly gave certain powers to the national government, and it reserved certain powers for the states. The three branches of the national government—the executive, the legislative, and the judicial—were designed with a system of checks and balances so that no one branch could dominate the other two.

4. EVALUATING AN OPINION
Possible Responses: Students who agree may say that the checks and balances are a good way of keeping the branches from becoming too powerful. Students who disagree may say that the checks and balances sometimes create dissension between one branch and another, resulting in prolonged debates and the failure to make timely and well-supported decisions.

3 Ratifying the Constitution

LEARN ABOUT arguments for and against ratification
TO UNDERSTAND how the Constitution became the law of the land.

TERMS & NAMES
- ratification
- Federalist
- Antifederalist
- *Federalist Papers*
- Bill of Rights

Section 3 Overview

OBJECTIVES

1. To contrast Federalist and Antifederalist arguments over ratification of the Constitution.

2. To explain how and why the Bill of Rights was added to the Constitution.

CRITICAL THINKING

- Analyzing issues, pp. 139, 140
- Comparing and contrasting, p. 139
- Applying, p. 141
- Summarizing, p. 141
- Evaluating, p. 141
- Analyzing, p. 141

ONE AMERICAN'S STORY

John Jay enjoyed retelling an incident that took place at King's College in New York City in 1764, a few weeks before the end of his senior year. Jay was present when some of his classmates got out of hand and broke a dining table in the college hall. The president of King's College questioned the students, but each denied knowing who was responsible. Jay also denied breaking the table, but when the president asked if he knew who was guilty, Jay replied, "I do not choose to tell you, sir."

Infuriated, the president had the students appear before a faculty committee. Jay came prepared with a copy of the college rules. He defended himself by pointing out that the rules did not require one student to inform on another. The faculty disagreed with Jay's interpretation of the rules and suspended him.

Years later, Jay's commitment to principle and spirit of unity would serve him well when he argued for ratification of the newly written Constitution. He warned how other nations would view the United States if it did not unify itself.

> ### A PERSONAL VOICE
> What a poor pitiful figure will America make in their eyes! How liable would she become not only to their contempt, but to their outrage; and how soon would dear-bought experience proclaim that when a people or family so divide, it never fails to be against themselves.
>
> **JOHN JAY,** Federalist Number IV

Whether Jay was defending himself or his country's Constitution, he relied on strong principles and a commitment to unity. His arguments played a key role in ratifying the Constitution.

John Jay

Federalists and Antifederalists

The delegates to the Philadelphia convention, including John Jay, had spent four months drafting the Constitution. The debates over **ratification**—official approval by the people of the United States—took more than twice that long. Newspapers printed the full text of the new Constitution. Many Americans were shocked by the radical changes it proposed. They had expected the convention to merely amend the Articles of Confederation. Supporters and opponents battled over controversies that threatened to shatter the framers' hope of uniting the states. Some of the delegates to the Constitutional Convention must have wondered if all their hard work in writing the Constitution had been in vain.

CONTROVERSIES OVER THE CONSTITUTION The framers set up a procedure for ratification that called for each state to hold a special convention. The voters would elect the delegates to the convention, who would then vote to accept or reject the Constitution. Ratification required approval by at least nine states. This system largely bypassed the state legislatures, whose members were likely to oppose the Constitution, since it reduced the power of the states. It also gave the framers an opportunity to campaign for delegates in their states who would support ratification.

Shaping a New Nation **137**

FOCUS & MOTIVATE

▶ ***Starting with the Student***
Ask students to suppose they have spent a great deal of time writing a composition for one of their classes. It is exactly the way they think it should be, but the teacher will not accept it without some additions.

- Would students make the changes? Why or why not?

OBJECTIVE

1 **INSTRUCT**

Federalists and Antifederalists

▶ *Discussing Key Ideas*
- Federalists try to persuade the states to ratify the Constitution.
- Antifederalists argue against the Constitution because it lacks a bill of rights.

IN-DEPTH RESOURCES: UNIT 2
Guided Reading, p. 3
Primary Source: Patrick Henry's Antifederalist Speech, p. 9
American Lives: John Jay, p. 14

ACCESS FOR STUDENTS ACQUIRING ENGLISH
Guided Reading (Spanish), p. 50

SECTION 3 RESOURCES

PRINT RESOURCES

IN-DEPTH RESOURCES: UNIT 2
Guided Reading, p. 3
Geography Application: The Constitution Becomes a Reality, p. 5
Primary Sources: from *The Federalist* No. 2, p. 8; Patrick Henry's Antifederalist Speech, p. 9; Political Cartoon, p. 10
American Lives: John Jay, p. 14; Patrick Henry, p. 15

ACCESS FOR STUDENTS ACQUIRING ENGLISH
Guided Reading (Spanish), p. 50
Geography Application: The Constitution Becomes a Reality (Spanish), p. 52

FORMAL ASSESSMENT
Section Quiz, p. 56

ALTERNATIVE ASSESSMENT BOOK
See forms for supporting and scoring alternative activities.

TECHNOLOGY RESOURCES

CD-ROM Electronic Library of Primary Sources

VIDEO *American Portfolio: A Videodisc for U.S. History* user's guide, pp. 40, 41, 45

INTERNET McDougal Littell Learning On-Line
http://www.mcdougallittell.com

The authorship of the *Federalist Papers* remained secret until 1804, when it was revealed by Alexander Hamilton. Hamilton was facing the duel that would cost him his life. He wrote a brief note crediting the authors of the *Federalist Papers,* but was somewhat inaccurate in stating which essays each author had written. Historians attribute 51 of the essays to Hamilton, 29 to Madison, and the remaining five to Jay.

IN-DEPTH RESOURCES: UNIT 2
Primary Sources: from *The Federalist* No. 2, p. 8; Political Cartoon, p. 10
American Lives: Patrick Henry, p. 15

 ELECTRONIC LIBRARY OF PRIMARY SOURCES from "The Federalist #51," by Publius

NOW & THEN
South Africa Creates a Bill of Rights

Starting with the Student
▶ • What do students remember about the system of apartheid?
• Why might a country with a history of institutionalized racism need an extremely detailed bill of rights?

Discussing Key Ideas
▶ • Before 1994, the South African government operates on the principle of apartheid, or "apartness."
• In 1996, South African lawmakers ratify a constitution guaranteeing equal rights to blacks and whites.
• A very detailed and comprehensive bill of rights is created to counteract any lingering effects of institutionalized racism.

"You are not to inquire how your trade may be increased, nor how you are to become a great and powerful people, but how your liberties can be secured."
PATRICK HENRY

"They . . . divided the powers, that each [branch of the legislature] might be a check upon the other . . . and I presume that every reasonable man will agree to it."
ALEXANDER HAMILTON

138 CHAPTER 5

Supporters of the Constitution called themselves **Federalists,** a name referring to a balance of power between the states and the national government. Their opponents became known as **Antifederalists** because they opposed having such a strong central government and thus were against the Constitution.

The Federalists insisted that the division of powers and the system of checks and balances would protect Americans from the tyranny of centralized authority. Antifederalists countered with a long list of possible abuses of power by a strong central government. These included a fear that the government would serve the interests of the privileged minority and ignore the rights of the majority. Antifederalists also raised doubts that a single government could manage the affairs of a large country. Their leading argument, however, centered on the Constitution's lack of protection for individual rights.

THE OPPOSING FORCES Leading Federalists included framers of the Constitution such as George Washington and James Madison. They used their experience and powers of persuasion to win support for the document they had drafted. They received heavy support from urban centers, where merchants, skilled workers, and laborers saw the benefit of a national government that could control trade. Small states and those with weak economies also favored a strong central government that could protect their interests.

Leading Antifederalists included revolutionary heroes and political leaders such as Patrick Henry, Samuel Adams, and Richard Henry Lee. They received support from rural areas, where people saw little benefit in a strong government that might add to their tax burden. Large states and those with strong economies, such as New York, which had had greater freedom under the Articles of Confederation, at first leaned against the Constitution.

Both sides waged a war of words in the public debate over ratification. The **Federalist Papers,** a series of eighty-five essays defending the Constitution, appeared in New York newspapers between October 1787 and April 1788. They were published over the signature "Publius," but they were written by Federalist leaders Alexander Hamilton, James Madison, and John Jay. The *Federalist Papers* provided an analysis and an explanation of the Constitution that remain important today, such as the separation of powers and the division of powers. *Letters from the Federal Farmer,*

NOW & THEN

South Africa Creates a Bill of Rights

On May 8, 1996, South African lawmakers leaped to their feet and danced in the aisles of South Africa's Parliament. They had just passed a landmark constitution guaranteeing equal rights for blacks and whites in the new South Africa. Included in this constitution is a bill of rights modeled in part on the United States Bill of Rights, though with significant differences.

The South African bill of rights, like the Bill of Rights in the United States Constitution, grew out of a history of

South Africa's President Nelson Mandela, *center,* with two of his deputy presidents, celebrates the approval of the new constitution by the constitutional assembly in Parliament at Cape Town, South Africa, on May 8, 1996. The deputy on the left is Thabo Mbeki, and the deputy on the right is F. W. de Klerk, a former president of South Africa.

TEACHING OPTION

Cooperative Activity: Creating a Media Ad

Task: Groups of students will prepare a script for a media ad presenting Federalist or Antifederalist views.

Purpose: To examine arguments over ratification of the Constitution.

Activity: Students should consider how Federalists or Antifederalists might use television or radio to promote ideas, and then choose a particular medium and message.

Groups should prepare a script for a 30-second ad promoting a particular viewpoint. Students should include ideas for accompanying sound and/or pictures.

📁 **Building a Portfolio:** Students should identify their contributions to the script on the copy they place in their portfolios.

ALTERNATIVE ASSESSMENT BOOK
Standards for Evaluating a Cooperative Activity

Standards for Evaluation
Media ads should . . .

• accurately depict the viewpoint of Federalists or Antifederalists
• state reasons supporting the viewpoint
• include persuasive language
• be appropriate for the chosen medium

written by Richard Henry Lee, was the most widely read Antifederalist publication. Lee listed the rights the Antifederalists believed should be protected, such as freedom of the press and of religion, guarantees against unreasonable searches of people and their homes, and the right to a trial by jury.

THINK THROUGH HISTORY
A. *Analyzing Issues What were the Antifederalists' major arguments against the Constitution?*

Both sides had strong arguments, but most newspapers favored the Federalist cause. Besides, no Antifederalist could match the influence of such leaders as George Washington and Benjamin Franklin. Despite these Federalist advantages, the Constitution's lack of a **Bill of Rights**—a formal summary of citizens' rights and freedoms—was a strong Antifederalist argument.

oppression and tyranny. For most of the twentieth century, South Africa's white minority government denied basic rights to blacks and other people of color. This system of racial discrimination, known as apartheid, finally came crashing down in 1994 with the election of a coalition government under Nelson Mandela. Soon after, the new government began the long process of creating a new constitution and bill of rights.

From the start, South African lawmakers made the writing of the constitution a public event. They invited ideas and opinions, which led to a vigorous public debate. In contrast, the United States Constitution was written in private by a small group of men.

In addition, the South African bill of rights is a much broader and more detailed document than the U.S. Bill of Rights. For example, two pages are devoted to the rights of arrested, detained, and accused persons. One page is devoted to the rights of children. The document forbids discrimination of all kinds and protects the rights of minorities. It also guarantees every citizen the right to freedom of travel within the country, which was often denied blacks under apartheid. In addition, the bill of rights guarantees a range of social and economic rights—including the right to adequate housing, food, water, education, and health care—which were often denied blacks under apartheid. Nevertheless, the cost of providing these basics will make it difficult for the government to deliver on these promises.

Nelson Mandela, the first black president of South Africa, greets a crowd celebrating the new constitution. Mandela, who had been imprisoned in 1962 for fighting for rights for black South Africans, was released from prison in 1990. He became South Africa's president after receiving 62 percent of the vote in the 1994 election.

|||| INTERACT WITH HISTORY ||||

1. **COMPARING AND CONTRASTING** What makes South Africa's bill of rights similar to the U.S. Bill of Rights? How is it different?

    SEE SKILLBUILDER HANDBOOK, PAGE 1041.

2. **RESEARCHING SOUTH AFRICA** Using library resources, find out more about the South African constitution and bill of rights. Also re-search conditions in South Africa that led to the writing of a new constitution. With a partner, prepare a short oral report on your findings and present it to the class.

    For more about South Africa, click on *Social Studies* at http://www.mcdougallittell.com

MORE ABOUT . . .
Nelson Mandela
Nelson Mandela was born in Umtata, a village in the Transkei territory of South Africa where his father was a tribal chief. In 1944, working as a lawyer, Mandela joined the African National Congress, or ANC. This group was opposed to the policy of apartheid. Mandela gained national fame in the 1950s for leading protests against the government. In 1962, Mandela was arrested and convicted of sabotage and conspiracy and sentenced to life imprisonment. Many South African groups refused to negotiate with the government until Mandela was released. Finally, after almost 30 years in prison, Mandela was released in 1990. Just four years later, Mandela became South Africa's first black president.

MORE ABOUT . . .
The South African Constitution
The following is an excerpt from the Preamble: We, the people of South Africa, / Recognise the injustices of our past; / Honour those who suffered for justice and freedom in our land; / Respect those who have worked to build and develop our country; and / Believe that South Africa belongs to all who live in it, united in our diversity. . . .

INTERACT WITH HISTORY

1. *Comparing and Contrasting*

Possible Responses: *The two bills of rights are similar in that they were both inspired by the experiences of an oppressive and tyrannical regime. The two bills are different in that the South African government made the writing of the constitution a national event, inviting opinions and vigorous public debate. The United States Constitution was written in private by a small group of men. Also, the South African bill of rights is more detailed and comprehensive than the United States Bill of Rights.*

2. *Researching South Africa*

Review with students how to find and use resources other than encyclopedias. You may want to review how to use periodical indexes, the card catalog or electronic filing system used by your library, particular search engines on the Internet, and Internet newsgroups. You may also want to give students a few pointers for public speaking. For example: speak slowly, clearly, and loud enough for the whole class to hear you; do not read your report to the class, outline your talk on note cards so that you can speak naturally; if eye contact with the audience is too difficult, look at the tops of people's heads.

The Bill of Rights Leads to Ratification

▶ **Starting with the Student**

• What rights as a U.S. citizen do students exercise on a regular basis?

• What rights are exercised when students:
Buy a newspaper?
Attend a religious service?
Attend a political rally?

▶ **Discussing Key Ideas**

• Antifederalists' demand a bill of rights so that citizens are protected from the potential tyranny of a strong national government.

• For two years, Federalists and Antifederalists at the state level debate over ratifying the Constitution.

• In 1789, the new Constitution is ratified by the minimum number of states; two years later, the Bill of Rights is ratified.

IN-DEPTH RESOURCES, UNIT 2
Geography Application: The Constitution Becomes a Reality, p. 5

 ELECTRONIC LIBRARY OF PRIMARY SOURCES

On the Constitution by Benjamin Franklin; *from* "On the Federal Government" by Tench Coxe; *from* "The Federal Constitution is Wisely Formed" by Anonymous

MORE ABOUT . . .
Richard Henry Lee

Antifederalist leader Richard Henry Lee was a member of a prominent Virginia family. He and his brother Francis Lightfoot Lee both signed the Declaration of Independence. The Lee brothers were ancestors of Confederate General Robert E. Lee.

All state constitutions guaranteed individual rights, and seven of them included a bill of rights. However, the proposed U.S. Constitution contained no guarantee that the government would protect the rights of the people or of the states. Even some supporters of the Constitution, such as Thomas Jefferson, viewed its lack of a bill of rights as a serious drawback to ratification:

A PERSONAL VOICE
I like much the general idea of framing a government, which should go on of itself, peaceably, without needing continual recurrence to the State legislatures. . . . I will now tell you what I do not like. First, the omission of a bill of rights. . . . Let me add, that a bill of rights is what the people are entitled to against every government on earth, general or particular; and what no just government should refuse.

THOMAS JEFFERSON, letter to James Madison from Paris, December 20, 1787

WHY PEOPLE DEMANDED A BILL OF RIGHTS   The Antifederalists' demand for a bill of rights stemmed from their fear of a strong central government. The states, with their guarantees of individual liberties, served as protectors of the people. Antifederalists argued that since the Constitution weakened the states, the people needed a national bill of rights to protect them. They wanted written guarantees that the people would have freedom of speech, of the press, and of religion. They demanded assurance of the right to trial by jury and the right to bear arms.

Federalists insisted that the Constitution granted only limited powers to the national government so that it could not violate the rights of the states or of the people. They also pointed out that the Constitution gave the people the power to protect their rights through the election of trustworthy leaders. In the end, though, the Federalists yielded to people's overwhelming desire and promised to add a Bill of Rights if the states would ratify the Constitution.

RATIFICATION OF THE CONSTITUTION Delaware led the country in ratifying the Constitution, by unanimous vote, in December 1787. In June 1788, New Hampshire fulfilled the requirement for ratification by becoming the ninth state to approve the Constitution. Nevertheless, Virginia and New York had not voted, and the new government needed these very large and influential states.

Powerful adversaries squared off in Virginia. Patrick Henry, Richard Henry Lee, and James Monroe led the opposition. Richard Henry Lee, a prominent political figure of his time, claimed that those in favor of the Constitution were voluntarily placing themselves under the power of an absolute ruler:

A PERSONAL VOICE
'Tis really astonishing that the same people, who have just emerged from a long and cruel war in defense of liberty, should now agree to fix an elective despotism [absolute power] upon themselves and their posterity.

RICHARD HENRY LEE

James Madison, Edmund Randolph, and George Washington campaigned for ratification in Virginia. Although few could compete with Patrick Henry's spellbinding speeches, it was Madison's logical arguments and Washington's

A parade in New York in 1788 celebrates the new Constitution and features the "Ship of State" float. It has Alexander Hamilton's name on it to emphasize the key role he played in launching the new government.

THINK THROUGH HISTORY
B. *Analyzing Issues* What were the arguments made by Antifederalists and Federalists over adding a Bill of Rights to the Constitution?

B. Answer
Antifederalists: The Constitution created a powerful national government, making a bill of rights necessary to protect the people.
Federalists: The Constitution gave only limited powers to the national government and so it could not violate the rights of states or people.

TEACHING OPTIONS

Exploring Themes

Constitutional Concerns Identify groups of Americans who were excluded from protection under the Bill of Rights in 1791. Discuss why those groups were excluded. What rights were denied them? Emphasize that governments reflect the ideas and values of the time. The civil rights movement and the women's movement brought about the inclusion and equal protection under law of excluded groups. By organizing, petitioning the government, and raising public awareness, excluded groups gained access to those rights previously withheld from them.

Making Connections Across Cultures

Native Americans One of the world's oldest democracies is that of the Iroquois Confederacy. It has been suggested that Benjamin Franklin, once a colonial Indian commissioner, had been inspired by the Iroquois when he wrote the Articles of Confederation in 1777. Find out more about how the Iroquois Confederacy was structured and run. Write a one-to-two page paper comparing and contrasting the Iroquois Confederacy with the United States Government of 1788. Use reference works such as *500 Nations: An Illustrated History of North American Indians* by Alvin M. Josephy, Jr.

influence that brought Federalist victory. Virginia approved the Constitution by a narrow margin of 89 to 79 on June 25, 1788.

The struggle for New York pitted John Jay and Alexander Hamilton against a strong Antifederalist majority. Jay and Hamilton launched an effective public campaign through the *Federalist Papers.* News of ratification by New Hampshire and Virginia strengthened the Federalists' cause. On July 26, 1788, New York ratified by a vote of 30 to 27. Although Rhode Island did not accept the Constitution until 1790, the new government became a reality in 1789.

ADOPTION OF A BILL OF RIGHTS In several states, ratification had hinged on the Federalists' pledge to add a Bill of Rights. James Madison undertook responsibility for carrying out that pledge. He studied the 80 amendments the state ratifying conventions had suggested. From these, he produced a list for Congress to consider. In September 1789, Congress submitted 12 amendments to the state legislatures for ratification. By December 1791, the required three-fourths of the states had ratified ten of the amendments, which became known as the Bill of Rights.

The first eight amendments spell out the personal liberties the states had requested. The First Amendment guarantees citizens' rights to freedom of religion, speech, the press, and political activity. The Second and Third amendments protect citizens from the threat of standing armies. According to these amendments, the government cannot deny citizens the right to bear arms as members of a militia of citizen-soldiers, nor can the government house troops in private homes in peacetime. The Fourth Amendment prevents the search of citizens' homes without proper warrants. The Fifth through the Eighth amendments guarantee fair treatment for individuals accused of crimes. The Ninth Amendment makes it clear that people's rights are not restricted to just those specifically mentioned in the Constitution. Finally, the Tenth Amendment clarifies that the people and the states have all the powers the Constitution does not specifically give to the national government or deny to the states.

The protection of rights and freedoms did not apply to all Americans at the time the Bill of Rights was adopted. Native Americans and slaves were excluded. Women were not mentioned in the Constitution. A growing number of free blacks did not receive adequate protection from the Constitution. Although many states permitted free blacks the right to vote, the Bill of Rights offered them no protection against discrimination and hostility from whites. The expansion of democracy came from later amendments. The flexibility of the United States Constitution made it a model for governments around the world.

*C. Answer
Possible
response:* It showed that the Constitution could be changed to meet the fundamental rights and protection of the people.

THINK THROUGH HISTORY
C. Applying *How did the adoption of the Bill of Rights show the flexibility of the Constitution?*

Section 3 Assessment

1. TERMS & NAMES

Identify
• ratification
• Federalist
• Antifederalist
• *Federalist Papers*
• Bill of Rights

2. SUMMARIZING Summarize the rights and freedoms that are guaranteed by the Bill of Rights, using a chart such as the one shown below.

Amendment	Brief Summary
1.	
2.	
3.	
4.	
5.	

Which rights are still sources of controversy today?

3. EVALUATING Do you think the Federalists or the Antifederalists had the more valid arguments? Support your opinion with examples from the text.

THINK ABOUT
• who each group represented
• their experience with the Articles of Confederation
• their experience with Great Britain

4. ANALYZING The states ratified the Constitution only after the Bill of Rights was added. In your opinion, what is the most important value of the Bill of Rights?

THINK ABOUT
• powers of the national government and of the states
• why people demanded a bill of rights
• the rights it guarantees

Shaping a New Nation **141**

MORE ABOUT . . .
The Bill of Rights

In 1941, President Franklin D. Roosevelt proclaimed December 15 as Bill of Rights Day. This day of national observance commemorates the date on which the Bill of Rights became part of the Constitution in 1791.

ASSESS & RETEACH

Section 3 Assessment

Divide students into groups and assign one of the assessment questions to each group. After groups have answered the questions, form new groups consisting of one member of each original group. Have students share the answers to the questions.

Self-Assessment

Have each student review the answers derived from the group sharing sessions.

Section Quiz

FORMAL ASSESSMENT
Section Quiz, p. 56

Reteach

Have students work in groups to outline the section. Instruct them to use the boldfaced headings as main ideas. Then have them fill in the supporting details from the text.

CLOSE

Debates over ratification of the Constitution centered around lack of protection for individual rights. By pledging to add a bill of rights, Federalists succeeded in gaining ratification. The same Constitution remains in effect today. The first ten amendments, ratified in 1791, became the Bill of Rights. Later amendments have expanded democracy to include all Americans.

REVIEWING THE CHAPTER

TERMS & NAMES
1. republic, p. 126
2. confederation, p. 127
3. Northwest Ordinance of 1787, p. 128
4. Shays's Rebellion, p. 132
5. James Madison, p. 133
6. Roger Sherman, p. 133
7. Great Compromise, p. 134
8. Federalist, p. 138
9. Antifederalist, p. 138
10. Bill of Rights, p. 139

MAIN IDEAS
11. A democracy might give individuals too much power.

12. They had just fought a Revolutionary War to free themselves from the strong central government of Great Britain.

13. A huge debt from the Revolutionary War, no power to tax, no control over interstate or foreign trade, and no power to deal with foreign relations.

14. The weakness of the government, the huge debt, the inability to levy taxes, Shays's Rebellion, and problems with foreign nations.

15. Big and little states compromised; the Three-Fifths Compromise settled the issue of counting slaves.

16. Southern states feared if Congress were given the power to regulate foreign trade, it might not allow slave trade.

17. The executive, the legislative, and the judicial branches prevent any one branch from dominating the others.

18. **For:** It created a strong central government but reserved powers for the states and created a system of checks and balances for the central government. **Against:** Strong central government might increase taxes; citizens' rights/freedoms not protected enough.

19. Series of essays that analyzed the Constitution and explained why ratifying it would be beneficial.

20. Believed the states and the individual rights of citizens were sufficiently protected.

REVIEWING THE CHAPTER

TERMS & NAMES For each term below, write a sentence explaining its connection to the period surrounding the Articles of Confederation and the Constitution. For each person below, explain his or her role concerning the Articles of Confederation or the Constitution.

1. republic
2. confederation
3. Northwest Ordinance of 1787
4. Shays's Rebellion
5. James Madison
6. Roger Sherman
7. Great Compromise
8. Federalist
9. Antifederalist
10. Bill of Rights

MAIN IDEAS

SECTION 1 (pages 126–129)

Experimenting with Confederation
11. Why did the new states prefer a republic rather than a democracy for their government?
12. Why did the states fear a strong central government?
13. In what ways was the confederation too weak to handle the nation's problems?

SECTION 2 pages (132–136)

Drafting the Constitution
14. What issues and events led to the Constitutional Convention?
15. In what ways did compromise play a critical role in the drafting of the Constitution?
16. Why was the slave trade an issue at the Constitutional Convention?
17. Briefly explain the separation of powers established by the Constitution.

SECTION 3 pages (137–141)

Ratifying the Constitution
18. What were the arguments for and against ratifying the Constitution?
19. What were the *Federalist Papers* and what effect did they have on ratification?
20. Why did the states ratify the Constitution once a Bill of Rights was promised?

THINKING CRITICALLY

1. **FEDERALISTS AND ANTIFEDERALISTS** Create a chart in which you list the beliefs and goals of the Federalists and the Antifederalists.

Federalists	Antifederalists

2. **CONSTITUTIONAL PRINCIPLES** James Madison was a brilliant political leader who kept a record of the debates at the Constitutional Convention. He also wrote in favor of ratifying the Constitution. See his quote on page 124. Do you agree or disagree with Madison's statement about government control? Explain your position.

3. **COMPROMISE** Which compromise during the Constitutional Convention was the more important in your view, the Great Compromise or the Three-Fifths Compromise? Explain your choice.

4. **GEOGRAPHY OF THE LAND ORDINANCE OF 1785** In what ways was the land of the Northwest Territory distributed in a democratic way?

5. **ANALYZING PRIMARY SOURCES** Read the following observation that Benjamin Franklin made about the chair in which George Washington sat during the Constitutional Convention.

> Whilst the last members were signing it, Doctr. Franklin looking towards the President's chair, at the back of which a rising sun happened to be painted, observed to a few members near him, that painters had found it difficult to distinguish in their art a rising from a setting sun. I have, said he, often and often in the course of the session . . . looked at that [sun] behind the President without being able to tell whether it was rising or setting: But now at length I have the happiness to know that it is a rising, and not a setting sun.
>
> **JAMES MADISON,** *The Records of the Federal Convention of 1787*

What is Franklin referring to when he talks about a rising and a setting sun? What does Franklin's comparison tell you about the confidence members of the Convention had about the success of the Constitution?

THINKING CRITICALLY

1. FEDERALISTS AND ANTIFEDERALISTS
Possible Responses: **Federalists:** in favor of Constitution; wanted a stronger central government; saw benefits for business and trade with regulation of interstate commerce; **Antifederalists:** opposed to the Constitution; did not want a strong central government; did not want to have taxes raised

2. CONSTITUTIONAL PRINCIPLES
Possible Responses: Students who agree with Madison might mention that government control of those governed is necessary to avoid chaos and control of itself is necessary to avoid a form of authoritarian power such as a dictatorship. Students who disagree with Madison might mention that a strong government is one that wants to keep everything under control and that functions efficiently.

3. COMPROMISE
Possible Responses: Students who choose the Great Compromise might mention that it was absolutely essential to reach a compromise between the large states and the small states or an effective new government could not be created. Students who choose the Three-Fifths Compromise might point out how critical it was to reach an agreement on the issue of slaves or a government consisting of the Southern states and the Northern states could never be formed.

ALTERNATIVE ASSESSMENT

1. DEBATING ISSUES

How did the delegates to the Constitutional Convention in Philadelphia in 1787 achieve compromise in drafting the U.S. Constitution?

 CD-ROM Use the CD-ROM *Electronic Library of Primary Sources* and other resources to investigate an issue under debate in the Constitutional Convention.

- Choose an issue of disagreement. Read the section of the Constitution that contains the final compromise as well as documents that show the various sides of the issue before a compromise was reached.
- Work in pairs. Each partner should draft a three-minute speech defending one side of the issue.
- Present your debate to the class, giving a short rebuttal after the other point of view has been given. Have the class evaluate the two sides of the argument before reminding your classmates how the issue was resolved.

Add your debate speeches to your American history portfolio.

2. WRITING AN EDITORIAL

Use encyclopedias, history textbooks, and other sources to research the Constitutional Convention of 1787 in Philadelphia. Focus on the fact that the Convention sessions were held in secrecy. Be sure to consider the following points:

- Why the sessions were held in secrecy
- How George Washington, president of the convention, looked upon the secrecy
- Who was opposed to the secrecy

Pretend you are a newspaper editor in Philadelphia in 1787. Using the information from your research, write an editorial in favor of, or opposed to, the secrecy in which the meetings of the Constitutional Convention were held.

3. PORTFOLIO PROJECT

Use the Living History activity to expand your portfolio.

LIVING HISTORY

REVISING YOUR CONSTITUTION

You and your group have drafted a new constitution for your class or school. As a group, revise your constitution, asking yourself the following questions.

- Do you need to add, delete, or change anything?
- Is a bill of rights needed?

Then present your constitution to your class. Compare your constitution to those presented by other groups, noting its strengths and weaknesses. Finally, put a copy of your constitution and your evaluation in your American history portfolio.

Bridge to the Constitution

Review Chapter 5

CREATING A NEW GOVERNMENT Although the Revolutionary War provided a common goal for the emerging nation, deciding how to govern that new nation involved much disagreement. The states believed that they should be ruled by a republic—but a republic with limited power.

PROBLEMS UNDER THE ARTICLES OF CONFEDERATION It took the states until 1781 to adopt the Articles of Confederation, partly because they could not decide how to deal with the territories west of the Appalachian Mountains. The Northwest Ordinance provided for new territories to be granted statehood when they had a large enough population.

The new republic encountered many problems during this early period. It was unable to pay its huge war debt, and it had problems with Britain and Spain.

CONSTITUTIONAL CONVENTION In 1786–1787 Shays's Rebellion in western Massachusetts caused widespread alarm. It prompted states to send delegates to the Constitutional Convention, which planned to revise the Articles of Confederation. However, the Convention decided to create an entirely new Constitution. It agreed to a two-house legislature, which satisfied the desires of both the large states and the small states. Through the Three-Fifths Compromise, the Convention settled the issue of counting slaves for representation by agreeing that three-fifths of all slaves would be counted as part of the population. The Constitution made a division of powers between the federal government and the states and also created a system of checks and balances within the central government.

RATIFYING THE CONSTITUTION Ratification of the Constitution required that at least nine of the thirteen states approve it. Supporters of the Constitution were called Federalists; those in opposition were called Antifederalists. The one major objection to the Constitution was that it did not include a Bill of Rights.

Preview the Constitution

The delegates to the Constitutional Convention did an outstanding job with a difficult task. The Constitution they created overcame many problems the nation had had under the Articles of Confederation. You will learn about the Constitution next and then in Chapter 6 about the new government that it created.

Shaping a New Nation **143**

---

1. DEBATING ISSUES
Standards for Evaluation
A position speech should meet the following criteria:

- Clearly and concisely states a position.
- Rebuttal is logical and effective and addresses specific points in the opposing argument.
- Displays thorough knowledge of the subject.

2. WRITING AN EDITORIAL
Standards for Evaluation
An editorial should meet the following criteria:

- Clearly and concisely makes a logical argument.
- Uses strong details to support the argument.
- Displays thorough research of the subject by the use of specific examples.

3. PORTFOLIO PROJECT
LIVING HISTORY
Standards for Evaluation
A constitution should meet the following criteria:

- Creates a clear and well-ordered structure for the school.
- Specifies rules for students and staff to follow.
- Supports the goals of government envisioned by students.
- Contains clear explanations of rules and procedures.

IN-DEPTH RESOURCES: UNIT 2
See the form for scoring this activity on page 17.

THINKING CRITICALLY

4. GEOGRAPHY OF THE LAND ORDINANCE OF 1785

Possible Responses: The land of the Northwest Territory was distributed in a democratic way to the Americans who wanted to settle there because it was divided into parcels of different sizes so that even those with relatively little money could afford to purchase land.

5. ANALYZING PRIMARY SOURCES

Possible Responses: Students might say Franklin is referring to the new nation. They will probably say that after a long summer of debating the issues, the delegates must have felt relieved that they had come up with a plan that they thought most could live with.

The Living
Constitution

The Living Constitution

Starting with the Student
Ask students what they
know about the
Constitution. Then, discuss
the opening quotation.

• What comparisons does
  Wilson draw?
• What do students think
  these comparisons reveal
  about the purpose of the
  Constitution?

PREVIEWING THE CONSTITUTION

• Go over the five purposes
  of the Constitution.
• Point out the Constitutional
  Insights throughout the
  text. These side notes
  address key questions
  about the historical
  document.
• Have students answer the
  Think Through the
  Constitution questions as
  they read to check their
  understanding of impor-
  tant issues.

MORE ABOUT . . .
Woodrow Wilson

Wilson (1856–1924) believed
that the U.S. government,
like the Constitution, was
designed to endure. In his
first inaugural address,
Wilson stated, "We have
built up . . . a great system
of government, which has
stood through a long age as
in many respects a model
for those who seek to set liberty upon foundations that
will endure against fortu-
itous change, against storm
and accident."

> "The Constitution was not made to fit us like a straightjacket. In its elasticity lies its chief greatness."
>
> **President Woodrow Wilson**

The official purpose of the delegates who met in Philadelphia in 1787 was to change the Articles of Confederation. They soon made a fateful decision, however, to ignore the Articles and to write an entirely new constitution.

Purposes of the Constitution

The delegates who met in Philadelphia in 1787 the—"Framers"—had to fulfill five purposes to create an effective constitution.

1. Establish Legitimacy

First, the Framers had to establish the new government's legitimacy—its right to rule. Every government must do so.

Legitimacy for the Framers of the United States Constitution had to be based on a compact or contract among those who are to be ruled. This is why the Constitution starts with the words: "We the people of the United States . . . do ordain and establish this Constitution."

2. Create Appropriate Structures

The second purpose for the Framers was to create appropriate structures for the new government. The Framers were committed to the principles of representative democracy. They also believed any new government must include an important role for state governments and ensure that the states retained some legitimacy to rule within their borders.

To achieve their goals, the Framers created the Congress, the presidency, and the judiciary to share the powers of the national government. They also created a system of division of powers between the national government and the state governments.

144 UNIT 2

The American Dream	*Immigration and Migration*	*Civil Rights*	*Women in America*
The Constitution incorporates the vision 18th-century Americans had for their new nation and provides the flexibility to adapt to a changing society. It remains as vital today as it was 200 years ago. See Teacher's Edition note, p. 147.	The United States is often called a nation of immigrants. Through naturalization, hundreds of thousands of immigrants become U.S. citizens each year. The Constitution gives Congress the power to establish a uniform rule of naturalization. See Teacher's Edition note, p. 150.	The Fourteenth Amendment guarantees equal protection of the law for all citizens. Subsequent civil rights legislation provides for equal opportunity as well. The broadening of equality through affirmative action policies led to conflict. See Teacher's Edition note, p. 161.	Ratification of the Nineteenth Amendment was the culmination of years of struggle by women's movements in the United States. Beginning in 1878, a woman suffrage amendment was introduced annually in Congress for 40 years. See Teacher's Edition note, p. 163.

3. Describe and Distribute Power

Having created such an elaborate set of structures, the Framers had as their third purpose the description and distribution of governmental powers among those structures. The powers of the national government, which are those of Congress, are listed in Article 1, Section 8, of the Constitution. Many of the executive powers belonging to the president, are listed in Article 2, Sections 2 and 3. The courts are given judicial powers in Article 3. The words of Article 4 imply that the states retain authority over many public matters.

4. Limit Government Powers

The fourth purpose of the Framers was to limit the powers of the structures they created. Limits on the national government's powers are found in Article 1, Section 9. Some of the limits on the powers of state governments are found in Article 1, Section 10. There the states Framers enumerate things that are delegated to the national government and so cannot be done by the states.

5. Allow for Change

The Framers' fifth purpose was to include some means for changing the Constitution. Here they faced a dilemma: they wanted to make certain that the government endured by changing with the times, but they did not want to expose the basic rules of government to so many changes that the system would be unstable. So in Article 5 they created a difficult but not impossible means for amending the Constitution.

How well did the Framers fulfill their five purposes? The Constitution has been an effective framework for governing the United States for more than 200 years. As you read this government "contract," ask yourself how each provision reflects the Framers' success in fulfilling their five major purposes.

LIVING HISTORY

RESEARCHING A CONSTITUTIONAL QUESTION

As you study the Constitution, think about a constitutional question that interests you. Here are some possible questions.

- How much, if at all, can the federal government or a state government restrict the sale of firearms?
- Under what conditions does the president have the power to order American troops into battle without congressional approval?
- Under what conditions may a police officer conduct a search of the inside of an automobile?

Once you have chosen a constitutional question, research that question in articles and books on the Constitution. Also check the indexes of well-known newspapers such as the *New York Times* for articles that are relevant.

📁 **PORTFOLIO PROJECT** Save your research in a folder for your American history portfolio. After studying the Constitution, you will write an opinion essay on the constitutional question you chose.

The Constitution, which appears on pages 146–165, is printed on a blue background, while the explanatory notes next to an article, section, or clause are printed on white. Each article is divided into sections, and sections are subdivided into clauses. Headings have been added, and the spelling and punctuation modernized for easier reading. Portions of the Constitution no longer in use have been crossed out. The Constitutional Insight questions and answers will help you understand significant issues related to the Constitution.

RECOMMENDED RESOURCES

Books for the Teacher

Garraty, John, ed. *Quarrels That Have Shaped the Constitution.* New York: Harper, 1988. Landmark cases.

Lyons, Owen, and others. *Exiled in the Land of the Free.* Santa Fe, N.M.: Clear Light, 1992. Argues that Native American political organization influenced the Constitution.

St. John, Jeffrey. *Forge of Union, Anvil of Liberty.* Ottawa, Ill.: Jameson, 1992. Story of Bill of Rights and first election.

Books for the Student

Ketcham, Ralph, ed. *The Anti-Federalist Papers and the Constitutional Convention Debates.* New York: Mentor, 1986. Leading tracts against the Constitution.

Morris, Richard B. *Witnesses at the Creation.* New York: Holt, 1985. Lives of Madison, Hamilton, and Jay.

Videos

The Congress. Direct Cinema, 800-525-0000. History of the institution.

The Constitution in the Information Age. Sweet Pea Communications, 800-235-4922. Relevance of Constitution today.

Skokie: Rights or Wrong? New Day Films, 22 Riverview Drive, Wayne, NJ 07470. Debate over a free speech issue today.

Software

How a Bill Becomes a Law. Diskette. Word Associates, 3226 Robincrest Drive, Northbrook, IL 60062.

U.S. Constitution Tutor. Diskette. Educational Software Institute, 800-955-5570.

U.S. History: Government, Part 1. CD-ROM. Educational Software Institute, 800-955-5570.

1 To explain the purpose for establishing the Constitution.

2 To identify powers of the legislature

SKILLBUILDER
• Interpreting charts, p. 148

FOCUS & MOTIVATE

▶ **Starting with the Student**
• What do students prize most about living in a democracy?

OBJECTIVE
1 INSTRUCT

THE PREAMBLE
▶ **Discussing Key Ideas**
• The Constitution reflects the most treasured goals of the American people.

OBJECTIVE
2 INSTRUCT

ARTICLE 1. THE LEGISLATURE
▶ **Discussing Key Ideas**
• The legislature is directly responsible to the people.
• Qualifications and terms of office differ for senators and representatives.
• The enumerated powers are the powers of Congress.
• The Constitution limits the power of Congress.

IN-DEPTH RESOURCES: UNIT 2
Guided Reading, p. 18
American Lives: James Madison, p. 25

ACCESS FOR STUDENTS ACQUIRING ENGLISH
Guided Reading (Spanish), p. 54

THINK THROUGH THE CONSTITUTION
Possible Responses:
A. Yes—Citizens vote directly for congressional representatives and write them letters voicing views and concerns. No—The effectiveness of the president's leadership and decision-making most affects citizens.
B. Yes—keeps representatives more accountable to their constituents. No—limits representatives' time to carry out their agendas.

146 **The Living Constitution**

PREAMBLE

Why does the Preamble say, "We the people of the United States . . . ordain and establish" the new government? The Articles of Confederation was an agreement among the states. But the Framers of the Constitution wanted to be sure its legitimacy came from the American people, not from the states, which might decide to withdraw their support at any time. This is a basic principle of the Constitution.

ARTICLE 1

Constitutional Insight **Section 1** *Why does the first article of the Constitution focus on Congress rather than on the presidency or the courts?* The Framers were intent on stressing the central role of the legislative branch in the new government, because it is that branch that represents the people most closely and is directly responsible to them. This is why Section 8 of this article lists the major powers of the national government as legislative powers.

A. THINK THROUGH THE CONSTITUTION *Do you think Congress is still the branch of the federal government that is most directly responsible to the people? Why or why not?*

Constitutional Insight **Section 2.1** *Why are members of the House of Representatives elected every two years?* The House of Representatives was designed to be a truly representative body, with members who reflect the concerns and sentiments of their constituents as closely as possible. The Framers achieved this timely representation by regarding two years as reasonable time for members of the House of Representatives to serve for a term.

B. THINK THROUGH THE CONSTITUTION *Do you think electing members of the House of Representatives every two years is a good idea? Why or why not?*

The original manuscript of the Constitution is now kept in the National Archives in Washington, D.C.

146 UNIT 2

The Constitution

Preamble. *Purpose of the Constitution*

We the people of the United States, in order to form a more perfect Union, establish justice, insure domestic tranquility, provide for the common defense, promote the general welfare, and secure the blessings of liberty to ourselves and our posterity, do ordain and establish this Constitution for the United States of America.

Article 1 *The Legislature*

SECTION 1. CONGRESS All legislative powers herein granted shall be vested in a Congress of the United States, which shall consist of a Senate and House of Representatives.

SECTION 2. THE HOUSE OF REPRESENTATIVES

1. Elections The House of Representatives shall be composed of members chosen every second year by the people of the several states, and the electors in each state shall have the qualifications requisite for electors of the most numerous branch of the state legislature.

2. Qualifications No person shall be a Representative who shall not have attained to the age of twenty-five years, and been seven years a citizen of the United States, and who shall not, when elected, be an inhabitant of that state in which he shall be chosen.

3. Number of Representatives Representatives and direct taxes shall be apportioned among the several states which may be included within this Union, according to their respective numbers, ~~which shall be determined by adding to the whole number of free persons, including those bound to service for a term of years, and excluding Indians not taxed, three fifths of all other Persons.~~ The actual Enumeration shall be made within three years after the first meeting of the Congress of the United States, and within every subsequent term of ten years, in such manner as they shall by law direct. The number of Representatives shall not exceed one for every thirty thousand, but each state shall have at least one Representative; ~~and until such enumeration shall be made, the state of New Hampshire shall be entitled to choose three, Massachusetts eight, Rhode Island and Providence Plantations one, Connecticut five, New York six, New Jersey four, Pennsylvania eight, Delaware one, Maryland six, Virginia ten, North Carolina five, South Carolina five, and Georgia three.~~

POSITION	MINIMUM AGE	RESIDENCY	CITIZENSHIP
Requirements for Holding Federal Office			
Representative	25	state in which elected	7 years
Senator	30	state in which elected	9 years
President	35	14 years in the United States	natural-born
Supreme Court Justice	none	none	none

📁 **PRINT RESOURCES**

4. Vacancies When vacancies happen in the representation from any state, the executive authority thereof shall issue writs of election to fill such vacancies.

5. Officers and Impeachment The House of Representatives shall choose their Speaker and other officers; and shall have the sole power of impeachment.

SECTION 3. THE SENATE

1. Numbers The Senate of the United States shall be composed of two Senators from each state, chosen by the legislature thereof, for six years; and each Senator shall have one vote.

2. Classifying Terms Immediately after they shall be assembled in consequence of the first election, they shall be divided as equally as may be into three classes. The seats of the Senators of the first class shall be vacated at the expiration of the second year, of the second class at the expiration of the fourth year, and of the third class at the expiration of the sixth year, so that one third may be chosen every second year; and if vacancies happen by resignation, or otherwise, during the recess of the legislature of any state, the executive thereof may make temporary appointments until the next meeting of the legislature, which shall then fill such vacancies.

3. Qualifications No person shall be a Senator who shall not have attained to the age of thirty years, and been nine years a citizen of the United States, and who shall not, when elected, be an inhabitant of that state for which he shall be chosen.

4. Role of Vice-President The Vice-President of the United States shall be President of the Senate, but shall have no vote, unless they be equally divided.

5. Officers The Senate shall choose their other officers, and also a President pro tempore, in the absence of the Vice-President, or when he shall exercise the office of President of the United States.

6. Impeachment Trials The Senate shall have the sole power to try all impeachments. When sitting for that purpose, they shall be on oath or affirmation. When the President of the United States is tried, the Chief Justice shall preside: and no person shall be convicted without the concurrence of two-thirds of the members present.

7. Punishment for Impeachment Judgment in cases of impeachment shall not extend further than to removal from office, and disqualification to hold and enjoy any office of honor, trust or profit under the United States; but the party convicted shall nevertheless be liable and subject to indictment, trial, judgment and punishment, according to law.

SECTION 4. CONGRESSIONAL ELECTIONS

1. Regulations The times, places and manner of holding elections for Senators and Representatives, shall be prescribed in each state by the legislature thereof; but the Congress may at any time by law make or alter such regulations, except as to the places of choosing Senators.

2. Sessions The Congress shall assemble at least once in every year, and such meeting shall be on the first Monday in December, unless they shall by law appoint a different day.

Constitutional Insight **Section 3.1** *Why are members of the Senate elected every six years?* The Framers believed that too much democracy might lead to instability. So they decided senators should have a six-year term and be elected by the state legislatures rather than directly by the people. The 17th Amendment, as you will see later, changed part of this. The Framers also staggered the terms of the senators so that only one-third of them are replaced at any one time. This stabilizes the Senate still further.

C. THINK THROUGH THE CONSTITUTION *Do you think it is important for the Senate today to have more stability than the House of Representatives has? If so, why?*

Constitutional Insight **Sections 3.6 and 3.7** *Have high-level public officials ever been impeached?* Impeachment is a formal accusation of criminal behavior or serious misbehavior that the House of Representatives can bring against a public official (such as the president, a member of the president's cabinet, or a judge). Once accused by the House, the official must stand trial before the Senate, which can find him or her guilty or not guilty. Only one president, Andrew Johnson, was ever impeached, but the Senate failed to find him guilty by one vote.

D. THINK THROUGH THE CONSTITUTION *Do you think a president should be impeached if he or she is connected to a crime? Should a president be put on trial for a crime while he or she is still in office? Explain.*

The Living Constitution **147**

How a Bill in Congress Becomes a Law

1 A bill is introduced in the House or Senate and referred to a standing committee for consideration.

2 A bill may be reported out of committee with or without changes—or it may be shelved.

3 Either house of Congress debates the bill and may make revisions. If passed, the bill is sent to the other house.

4 If the House and Senate pass different versions of a bill, both versions go to a conference committee to work out the differences.

5 The conference committee submits a single version of the bill to the House and the Senate.

6 If both houses accept the compromise version, the bill is sent to the president for signature.

7 If the president signs the bill, it becomes law.

8 If the president vetoes the bill, the House and Senate may override the veto by a two-thirds majority of the members present in each house, and then the bill becomes law.

SKILLBUILDER INTERPRETING CHARTS *How is the constitutional principle of checks and balances reflected in the process of how a bill becomes a law?*

Skillbuilder Answer Possible Answer: *Both* the House and Senate must pass a common version of a bill, which the president may accept or reject (veto). If the president rejects it, it still will become a law with a two-thirds vote in each house. So, the House and Senate can check each other *and* the president, while the president can check the Congress.

Constitutional Insight **Section 5.2** *What kinds of rules does Congress make for itself?* The Constitution gives each body control over most of its rules of procedure and membership. Rules are important, for they help shape the kind of laws and policies that pass each body. Senate rules allow a filibuster, whereby a senator holds the floor as long as he or she likes in order to block consideration of a bill the senator dislikes. In recent years, a "cloture" rule has been used to end debate if 60 or more members vote to do so.

In contrast, the House of Representatives has rules to limit debate. A rules committee has the primary task of determining how long a bill on the floor of the House may be discussed, and whether any amendments can be offered to the bill. In recent years, the power of the Rules Committee has been limited, but being able to shape the rules remains a powerful tool of members of Congress.

E. THINK THROUGH THE CONSTITUTION *Why do you think the position of chairman of the Rules Committee is a powerful one?*

148 UNIT 2

SECTION 5. RULES AND PROCEDURES

1. Quorum Each house shall be the judge of the elections, returns and qualifications of its own members, and a majority of each shall constitute a quorum to do business; but a smaller number may adjourn from day to day, and may be authorized to compel the attendance of absent members, in such manner, and under such penalties as each house may provide.

2. Rules and Conduct Each house may determine the rules of its proceedings, punish its members for disorderly behavior, and, with the concurrence of two-thirds, expel a member.

3. Congressional Records Each house shall keep a journal of its proceedings, and from time to time publish the same, excepting such parts as may in their judgment require secrecy; and the yeas and nays of the members of either house on any question shall, at the desire of one-fifth of those present, be entered on the journal.

4. Adjournment Neither house, during the session of Congress, shall, without the consent of the other, adjourn for more than three days, nor to any other place than that in which the two houses shall be sitting.

148 **The Living Constitution**

SECTION 6. PAYMENT AND PRIVILEGES

1. Salary The Senators and Representatives shall receive a compensation for their services, to be ascertained by law, and paid out of the treasury of the United States. They shall in all cases, except treason, felony and breach of the peace, be privileged from arrest during their attendance at the session of their respective houses, and in going to and returning from the same; and for any speech or debate in either house, they shall not be questioned in any other place.

2. Restrictions No Senator or Representative shall, during the time for which he was elected, be appointed to any civil office under the authority of the United States, which shall have been created, or the emoluments whereof shall have been increased during such time; and no person holding any office under the United States, shall be a member of either house during his continuance in office.

SECTION 7. HOW A BILL BECOMES A LAW

1. Tax Bills All bills for raising revenue shall originate in the House of Representatives; but the Senate may propose or concur with amendments as on other Bills.

2. Law-Making Process Every bill which shall have passed the House of Representatives and the Senate, shall, before it become a law, be presented to the President of the United States; if he approves he shall sign it, but if not he shall return it, with his objections to that house in which it shall have originated, who shall enter the objections at large on their journal, and proceed to reconsider it. If after such reconsideration two-thirds of that house shall agree to pass the bill, it shall be sent, together with the objections, to the other house, by which it shall likewise be reconsidered, and if approved by two-thirds of that house, it shall become a law. But in all such cases the votes of both houses shall be determined by yeas and nays, and the names of the persons voting for and against the bill shall be entered on the journal of each house respectively. If any bill shall not be returned by the President within ten days (Sundays excepted) after it shall have been presented to him, the same shall be a law, in like manner as if he had signed it, unless the Congress by their adjournment prevent its return, in which case it shall not be a law.

3. Role of the President Every order, resolution, or vote to which the concurrence of the Senate and House of Representatives may be necessary (except on a question of adjournment) shall be presented to the President of the United States; and before the same shall take effect, shall be approved by him, or being disapproved by him, shall be repassed by two-thirds of the Senate and House of Representatives, according to the rules and limitations prescribed in the case of a bill.

"It's awful the way they're trying to influence Congress. Why don't they serve cocktails and make campaign contributions like we do?"

SKILLBUILDER INTERPRETING POLITICAL CARTOONS
What point do you think the cartoonist is making about influencing Congress?
Skillbuilder Answer The cartoonist is suggesting that Congress can be influenced in various ways.

Constitutional Insight **Section 7.2** *How often do presidents use the veto, and how often is that action overridden?* The use of the veto, which is the refusal to approve a bill, depends on many factors, especially the political conditions of the time. Some presidents—for example, John Adams and Thomas Jefferson—never used the veto power of the presidency. Others used it hundreds of times. Usually, Congress is unable to produce the votes (those of two-thirds of the members present in each house) needed to override presidential vetoes. The following chart gives selected numbers of presidential vetoes.

F. THINK THROUGH THE CONSTITUTION *Do you think it should be easier for Congress to override the president's veto? Why or why not?*

Presidential Vetoes		
PRESIDENT	**VETOES**	**VETOES OVERRIDDEN**
Andrew Johnson 1865–1869	29	15
Franklin D. Roosevelt 1933–1945	635	9
George Bush 1989–1993	46	1

The Living Constitution **149**

The Images on Money

The faces on various denominations of paper money compose a gallery of famous political leaders in American history. On the back are notable symbols, scenes, or architecture.

Amount	Front	Back
$1	George Washington	Great Seal
$2	Thomas Jefferson	Signing of the Declaration of Independence
$5	Abraham Lincoln	Lincoln Memorial
$10	Alexander Hamilton	U.S. Treasury
$20	Andrew Jackson	White House
$50	Ulysses S. Grant	U.S. Capitol
$100	Benjamin Franklin	Independence Hall

THINK THROUGH THE CONSTITUTION
Possible Response:
G. The clause provides the necessary flexibility for the federal government, which has expanded over time, to carry out its functions by implied powers.

Constitutional Insight **Section 8** *Just how powerful is the national government?* In the Constitution, the powers of the national government are the powers given to Congress in Section 8 of Article 1. The first 17 clauses of Section 8, which are specific, are often called the national government's enumerated powers. They confer on Congress a host of powers dealing with issues ranging from taxation and the national debt to calling out the armed forces of the various states to governing the nation's capital district (Washington, D.C.).

The 18th and final clause is different. It gives Congress the power to do what is "necessary and proper" to carry out the previous list of powers. Thus, the enumerated powers of Congress "to lay and collect taxes," "to borrow money," "to regulate commerce," and "to coin money" imply the power to create a bank in order to execute these enumerated powers. Early in the country's history, this "elastic clause," as it has been called, was used by Congress to establish the controversial Bank of the United States in 1791 and the Second Bank of the United States in 1816.

G. THINK THROUGH THE CONSTITUTION *Why do you think the elastic clause is still important today?*

Section 8.6 Because of much counterfeiting of the U.S. $100 bill, especially in Asia, a new design was created in 1996. It includes an enlarged portrait of Benjamin Franklin, a security thread running beneath the longer serial number, a microprinted word on the number 1 of 100, color-shifting ink, and a watermark to the right of Franklin's portrait. These all make the bill more difficult to counterfeit than it previously was.

SECTION 8. POWERS GRANTED TO CONGRESS

1. Taxation   The Congress shall have power to lay and collect taxes, duties, imposts and excises, to pay the debts and provide for the common defense and general welfare of the United States; but all duties, imposts and excises shall be uniform throughout the United States;

2. Credit   To borrow money on the credit of the United States;

3. Commerce   To regulate commerce with foreign nations, and among the several states, and with the Indian tribes;

4. Naturalization, Bankruptcy   To establish a uniform rule of naturalization, and uniform laws on the subject of bankruptcies throughout the United States;

5. Money   To coin money, regulate the value thereof, and of foreign coin, and fix the standard of weights and measures;

6. Counterfeiting   To provide for the punishment of counterfeiting the securities and current coin of the United States;

7. Post Office   To establish post offices and post roads;

8. Patents, Copyrights   To promote the progress of science and useful arts, by securing for limited times to authors and inventors the exclusive right to their respective writings and discoveries;

9. Federal Courts   To constitute tribunals inferior to the Supreme Court;

10. International Law   To define and punish piracies and felonies committed on the high seas, and offenses against the law of nations;

11. War   To declare war, grant letters of marque and reprisal, and make rules concerning captures on land and water;

12. Armed Forces   To raise and support armies, but no appropriation of money to that use shall be for a longer term than two years;

13. Navy   To provide and maintain a navy;

14. Regulation for Armed Forces   To make rules for the government and regulation of the land and naval forces;

15. Militia   To provide for calling forth the militia to execute the laws of the Union, suppress insurrections and repel invasions;

16. Regulations for Militia   To provide for organizing, arming, and disciplining, the militia, and for governing such part of them as may be employed in the service of the United States, reserving to the states respectively, the appointment of the officers, and the authority of training the militia according to the discipline prescribed by Congress;

17. District of Columbia   To exercise exclusive legislation in all cases whatsoever, over such District (not exceeding ten miles square) as may, by cession of particular states, and the acceptance of Congress, become the seat of the government of the United States, and to exercise like authority over all places purchased by the consent of the legislature of the state in which the same shall be, for the erection of forts, magazines, arsenals, dockyards, and other needful buildings—and

18. Elastic Clause   To make all laws which shall be necessary and proper for carrying into execution the foregoing powers, and all other powers vested by this Constitution in the government of the United States, or in any department or officer thereof.

Exploring Themes

Immigration and Migration   Legal immigrants may become naturalized citizens of the United States by following a procedure established by Congress. Applicants must be at least 18 years old and must have resided permanently in the United States for a minimum of the previous five years. They must prove that they are of good moral character and that they are loyal to American principles of government. Applicants must pass an examination that tests their knowledge of U.S. history and government. A final hearing takes place in a court, where the applicant takes a loyalty oath in front of a judge.

Making Connections Across the Curriculum

Literature   In Mark Twain's novel *A Connecticut Yankee in King Arthur's Court,* an inventive 19th-century mechanic discovers he has journeyed in time to 6th-century Camelot. Twain's ingenuity was not limited to creating colorful characters. He too dabbled as an inventor and, through a power granted to Congress in Section 8.8, was issued patents for the following contrivances:

- 1871—suspenders
- 1873—"Mark Twain's Self-Pasting Scrapbook"
- 1885—an educational game designed to enhance players' memory of key dates in history

SECTION 9. POWERS DENIED CONGRESS

1. Slave Trade   ~~The migration or importation of such persons as any of the states now existing shall think proper to admit, shall not be prohibited by the Congress prior to the year one thousand eight hundred and eight, but a tax or duty may be imposed on such importation, not exceeding ten dollars for each person.~~

2. Habeas Corpus   The privilege of the writ of habeas corpus shall not be suspended, unless when in cases of rebellion or invasion the public safety may require it.

3. Illegal Punishment   No bill of attainder or ex post facto Law shall be passed.

4. Direct Taxes   No capitation, ~~or other direct,~~ tax shall be laid, unless in proportion to the census or enumeration herein before directed to be taken.

5. Export Taxes   No tax or duty shall be laid on articles exported from any state.

6. No Favorites   No preference shall be given by any regulation of commerce or revenue to the ports of one state over those of another: nor shall vessels bound to, or from, one state, be obliged to enter, clear, or pay duties in another.

7. Public Money   No money shall be drawn from the treasury, but in consequence of appropriations made by law; and a regular statement and account of receipts and expenditures of all public money shall be published from time to time.

8. Titles of Nobility   No title of nobility shall be granted by the United States: and no person holding any office of profit or trust under them, shall, without the consent of the Congress, accept of any present, emolument, office, or title, of any kind whatsoever, from any king, prince, or foreign state.

SECTION 10. POWERS DENIED THE STATES

1. Restrictions   No state shall enter into any treaty, alliance, or confederation; grant letters of marque and reprisal; coin money; emit bills of credit; make anything but gold and silver coin a tender in payment of debts; pass any bill of attainder, ex post facto law, or law impairing the obligation of contracts; or grant any title of nobility.

2. Import and Export Taxes   No state shall, without the consent of the Congress, lay any imposts or duties on imports or exports, except what may be absolutely necessary for executing it's inspection laws: and the net produce of all duties and imposts, laid by any state on imports or exports, shall be for the use of the treasury of the United States; and all such laws shall be subject to the revision and control of the Congress.

3. Peacetime and War Restraints   No state shall, without the consent of Congress, lay any duty of tonnage, keep troops, or ships of war in time of peace, enter into any agreement or compact with another state, or with a foreign power, or engage in war, unless actually invaded, or in such imminent danger as will not admit of delay.

MODERN-DAY PIRATES
(SECTION 8.10)

Pirates no longer sail the high seas—today they are more likely to be surfing the Internet. Software piracy, or the illegal duplication and sale of software, cost the American software industry in 1995 an estimated $500 million. Most of this loss was due to pirated software products that were illegally duplicated in China. As a result of software piracy, legitimate software producers lose markets in China and in much of the Third World, where the pirated goods are sold. For example, it is estimated that 99 percent of all software sold in Indonesia is pirated.

In 1995, Congress threatened the Chinese government with $2 billion in punitive tariffs if it didn't crack down on piracy. China threatened to retaliate with its own set of equally harsh trade sanctions. However, the two countries narrowly averted a trade war just hours before tariffs would have been imposed, when the Chinese government agreed to shut down 15 factories producing pirated CD-ROMs and software.

Constitutional Insight   **Section 9**   *Why didn't the Framers include a bill of rights in the original Constitution?* Actually, they did. Article 1, Section 9, contains limits on the powers of Congress, just as the first ten amendments (which we call the Bill of Rights) do. While some of the provisions focused on such issues as slavery and taxation, there are three explicit prohibitions dealing with citizen rights:

- **Writ of *habeas corpus*.** Section 9, Clause 2, says that, except in time of rebellion or invasion, Congress cannot suspend people's right to a writ of *habeas corpus.* This means that people cannot be held in prison or jail without being formally charged with a crime.

- **Bill of attainder.** Section 9, Clause 3, prohibits the passage of any law that convicts or punishes a person directly and without the benefit of a trial. Any legislative law that would punish someone without recourse to a court of law is called a "bill of attainder."

- ***Ex post facto* law.** The same clause prohibits *ex post facto* laws. Such a law would make illegal an act that was legal when it was performed.

The fact that these particular rights were protected by the original document issued by the Framers reflects both the Framers' experiences during the Revolution and their fear of excessive government power.

H. THINK THROUGH THE CONSTITUTION   *Why are American citizens today so intent on having protections against government actions?*

The Living Constitution   **151**

Critical Thinking: Drawing Conclusions Which clauses of Article I, Section 8, grant Congress the power to deal with software piracy? *3, 8.* Why do you think China agreed to the demands of Congress? *Possible Responses: To avert a trade war; to avoid a tense economic relationship.*

MORE ABOUT . . .
Habeas Corpus
During the Civil War, President Lincoln suspended the writ of habeas corpus to suppress disloyalty and dissent. Consequently, over 13,000 suspected Confederate sympathizers in the Union were arrested without trial, although most were soon released. Initially, Jefferson Davis, president of the Confederacy, condemned Lincoln for dragging "upright men and innocent women . . . to distant dungeons." By 1862, Davis had made an about-face on this issue; that year he too suspended habeas corpus.

FORMAL ASSESSMENT
Quiz: Preamble and Article 1, p. 65

THINK THROUGH THE CONSTITUTION
Possible Response:
H. Today's Americans still prize personal freedom and fear government's potential to abuse power.

TEACHING OPTION

Making Global Connections

Titles of Nobility   Though the U.S. Constitution bars public officials from assuming titles of nobility, this has not been the practice in many other countries around the world. Here are some examples:

Royal Title	Status	Country of Origin
Czar/Czarina	ruler	Russia (until 1917)
Emir	native ruler	parts of Asia and Africa
Pharaoh	ruler	ancient Egypt
Rajah	prince	India
Shah	ruler	Iran (until 1979)
Sultan	ruler	Muslim states

Article 2

OBJECTIVE

 To explain the powers and duties of the president.

FOCUS & MOTIVATE

▶ **Starting with the Student**
• What traits do students think a president needs to lead the country? Why?

OBJECTIVE

① **INSTRUCT**

ARTICLE 2. THE EXECUTIVE

▶ **Discussing Key Ideas**
• The Constitution empowers the president to carry out the nation's laws.

IN-DEPTH RESOURCES: UNIT 2
Guided Reading, p. 19

ACCESS FOR STUDENTS ACQUIRING ENGLISH
Guided Reading (Spanish), p. 55

MORE ABOUT . . .
The Electoral College

In 1824, Andrew Jackson received the largest number of popular votes but did not have an electoral majority. The House of Representatives chose John Quincy Adams to be president.

IN-DEPTH RESOURCES: UNIT 2
Geography Application: The Electoral College, p. 23.

THINK THROUGH THE CONSTITUTION
Possible Responses:
I. To make sure laws are faithfully executed.
J. To ensure smooth and orderly transfer of leadership.

ARTICLE 2

Constitutional Insight **Section 1.1** *What exactly is "executive power"?* We know the president has it, but nowhere is it explicitly defined. It is most often defined as the power to carry out the laws of the land, but of course no one person can handle such a chore alone. A more appropriate definition is found in Section 3 of this Article, which empowers the president to "take care that the laws be faithfully executed. . . . "In this sense, the president isn't merely an administrator, but rather the chief administrator.

I. THINK THROUGH THE CONSTITUTION *Why is it important to have an executive who is the chief administrator?*

Constitutional Insight **Section 1.6** *What happens when the vice-president succeeds a dead or incapacitated president?* Section 1.6 instructs that the vice-president shall assume the duties of the presidential office. But until the Twenty-fifth Amendment was added to the Constitution in 1967, there was no explicit statement in the document that said the vice-president is to become president. That tradition owes its origin to John Tyler, the tenth president of the United States, who in 1841 succeeded William Henry Harrison—the first president to die in office. Tyler decided to take the oath of office and assume the title of president of the United States. Congress voted to go along with his decision, and the practice was repeated after Lincoln was assassinated. It would take another century for the written provisions of the Constitution to catch up with the practice.

J. THINK THROUGH THE CONSTITUTION *Why is it important to know the order of succession if and when the president dies?*

Article 2. *The Executive*

SECTION 1. THE PRESIDENCY

1. Terms of Office The executive power shall be vested in a President of the United States of America. He shall hold his office during the term of four years, and, together with the Vice-President, chosen for the same term, be elected, as follows:

2. Electoral College Each state shall appoint, in such manner as the Legislature thereof may direct, a number of electors, equal to the whole number of Senators and Representatives to which the State may be entitled in the Congress; but no Senator or Representative, or person holding an office of trust or profit under the United States, shall be appointed an elector.

3. Former Method of Electing President The electors shall meet in their respective states, and vote by ballot for two persons, of whom one at least shall not be an inhabitant of the same state with themselves. And they shall make a list of all the persons voted for, and of the number of votes for each; which list they shall sign and certify, and transmit sealed to the seat of the government of the United States, directed to the President of the Senate. The President of the Senate shall, in the presence of the Senate and House of Representatives, open all the certificates, and the votes shall then be counted. The person having the greatest number of votes shall be the President, if such number be a majority of the whole number of electors appointed; and if there be more than one who have such majority, and have an equal number of votes, then the House of Representatives shall immediately choose by ballot one of them for President; and if no person have a majority, then from the five highest on the list the said House shall in like manner choose the President. But in choosing the President, the votes shall be taken by States, the representation from each state having one vote; a quorum for this purpose shall consist of a member or members from two-thirds of the states, and a majority of all the states shall be necessary to a choice. In every case, after the choice of the President, the person having the greatest number of votes of the electors shall be the Vice-President. But if there should remain two or more who have equal votes, the Senate shall choose from them by ballot the Vice-President.

4. Election Day The Congress may determine the time of choosing the electors, and the day on which they shall give their votes, which day shall be the same throughout the United States.

5. Qualifications No person except a natural-born citizen, or a citizen of the United States at the time of the adoption of this Constitution, shall be eligible to the office of President; neither shall any person be eligible to that office who shall not have attained to the age of thirty-five years, and been fourteen years a resident within the United States.

6. Succession In case of the removal of the President from office, or of his death, resignation, or inability to discharge the powers and duties of the said office, the same shall devolve on the Vice-President, and the Congress may by law provide for the case of removal, death,

---

TEACHING OPTION

Making Connections Across the Curriculum

U.S. Government The Presidential Succession Act, passed in 1886 and amended as necessary, determines who would assume the duties of president if the president and vice-president should die or become disabled. The order of succession for the next ten leaders follows:

1. Speaker of the House of Representatives
2. President pro tempore of the Senate
3. Secretary of state
4. Secretary of the treasury
5. Secretary of defense
6. Attorney general
7. Secretary of the interior
8. Secretary of agriculture
9. Secretary of commerce
10. Secretary of labor

What if the person designated to succeed does not meet the qualifications for president stated in the Constitution? *The presidency would pass to the next eligible member who fulfills those qualifications.*

resignation or inability, both of the President and Vice-President, declaring what officer shall then act as President, and such officer shall act accordingly, until the disability be removed, or a President shall be elected.

7. Salary The President shall, at stated times, receive for his services, a compensation, which shall neither be increased nor diminished during the period for which he shall have been elected, and he shall not receive within that period any other emolument from the United States, or any of them.

8. Oath of Office Before he enter on the execution of his office, he shall take the following oath or affirmation:—"I do solemnly swear (or affirm) that I will faithfully execute the office of President of the United States, and will to the best of my ability, preserve, protect and defend the Constitution of the United States."

SECTION 2. POWERS OF THE PRESIDENT

1. Military Powers The President shall be commander in chief of the Army and Navy of the United States, and of the militia of the several states, when called into the actual service of the United States; he may require the opinion, in writing, of the principal officer in each of the executive departments, upon any subject relating to the duties of their respective offices, and he shall have power to grant reprieves and pardons for offenses against the United States, except in cases of impeachment.

2. Treaties, Appointments He shall have power, by and with the advice and consent of the Senate, to make treaties, provided two-thirds of the Senators present concur; and he shall nominate, and by and with the advice and consent of the Senate, shall appoint ambassadors, other public ministers and consuls, judges of the Supreme Court, and all other officers of the United States, whose appointments are not herein otherwise provided for, and which shall be established by law; but the Congress may by law vest the appointment of such inferior officers, as they think proper, in the President alone, in the courts of law, or in the heads of departments.

3. Vacancies The President shall have power to fill up all vacancies that may happen during the recess of the Senate, by granting commissions which shall expire at the end of their next session.

SECTION 3. PRESIDENTIAL DUTIES
He shall from time to time give to the Congress information of the state of the Union, and recommend to their consideration such measures as he shall judge necessary and expedient; he may, on extraordinary occasions, convene both houses, or either of them, and in case of disagreement between them, with respect to the time of adjournment, he may adjourn them to such time as he shall think proper; he shall receive ambassadors and other public ministers; he shall take care that the laws be faithfully executed, and shall commission all the officers of the United States.

Constitutional Insight **Section 2.1** *Just how much authority does the president have as "commander in chief" of the armed forces?* While Congress has the power to declare war and to support and maintain an army and navy, only the president has the power to give orders to American military forces. There have been several instances in U.S. history when presidents have used that authority in spite of congressional wishes.

The president involved the armed forces of the United States in the Korean War from 1950 to 1953 without Congress declaring war. Likewise, American presidents involved hundreds of thousands of American troops in the Vietnam War.

K. THINK THROUGH THE CONSTITUTION *Why is it important that the commander in chief of the armed forces of the United States be the president (a civilian) rather than a military general?*

NOW & THEN

THE WAR POWERS RESOLUTION (SECTION 2.1)

How much power the president has to make war has long been a subject of debate. In 1964, President Lyndon B. Johnson persuaded the Senate to pass the Gulf of Tonkin Resolution, which virtually gave Johnson a free hand in conducting the Vietnam War.

Due to fallout from the Vietnam War, in 1973 Congress enacted the War Powers Resolution, making the president more accountable to Congress for any military actions he or she might take. Every president since Richard Nixon has called the act unconstitutional. Nevertheless, within 48 hours after sending troops into an international crisis, presidents have sent a report to Congress that included the information required by the War Powers Resolution.

In the Persian Gulf War in 1990–1991, President George Bush sent American troops into Kuwait without congressional action. Subsequently, Congress passed a joint resolution authorizing the use of American military forces in the Persian Gulf War.

In 1993, President Bill Clinton sent additional American forces into Somalia, where our country already had troops. He notified Congress of this action within the required 48 hours. As of 1996 the constitutionality of the War Powers Resolution had not been challenged or determined.

Constitutional Insight **Section 3** *Is it necessary for the president to deliver a State of the Union address before a joint session of Congress at the start of each legislative year?* The Constitution only requires that the president report to Congress on the state of the Union from time to time, and nowhere does it call for an annual address. That tradition started in 1913, with President Woodrow Wilson who wanted to influence Congress to take action without delay on some legislation that he thought was important. Unlike most presidents since John Adams, President Wilson delivered his State of the Union addresses in person.

L. THINK THROUGH THE CONSTITUTION *How does the president use the State of the Union address today?*

The Living Constitution **153**

NOW & THEN
The War Powers Resolution

Critical Thinking: Drawing Conclusions How does the War Powers Resolution balance the power of the executive and legislative branches of government? Students might create a chart with the following headings to illustrate their answer.

Executive Power	Legislative Power

MORE ABOUT . . .
Executive Title

The proper form of address for the chief executive is "Mr. President" (or "Madam President"). George Washington chose this title, in spite of suggestions that he should assume a more noble one. For example, John Adams thought Washington should be called "His Highness, the President of the United States of America, and Protector of their Liberties."

THINK THROUGH THE CONSTITUTION
Possible Responses:
K. To make military decisions from a broader perspective; to safeguard the nation from becoming a military dictatorship.
L. To inform Congress of key domestic and foreign policies that the administration will address; to recommend legislative measures.

TEACHING OPTIONS

Making Connections Across the Curriculum

Music "Hail to the Chief who in triumph advances!" This line from Sir Walter Scott's narrative poem *The Lady of the Lake* became the inspiration for James Sanderson's song "Hail to the Chief." It made its debut as music paying homage to the nation's chief executive in 1821 at James Monroe's second-term inauguration ceremony. This song had become a tribute to the president by 1845, when James Polk assumed office. Today bands typically play the instrumental arrangement of "Hail to the Chief." You may wish to have students listen to the song on the following sound recording: United States Marine Band, *The President's Own*, Washington S. Marine Corps, 1983.

Teaching Less Proficient Readers

Organizing Information To help students keep track of the president's powers, put this organizational tree on the chalkboard and help them fill in the missing examples.

Teacher's Edition **153**

Article 3

Although Andrew Johnson (the only president to be impeached) was impeached by an overwhelming vote of the House of Representatives in 1868, at his trial before the Senate he was found not guilty by just one vote.

ARTICLE 3

Constitutional Insight **Section 2.1** *What is judicial review? Is it the same as judicial power?* Actually, they are not the same. Judicial power is the authority to hear cases involving disputes over the law or the behavior of people. Judicial review, in contrast, is an action the courts can take by passing judgment on the constitutionality of a law or government action that is being disputed. Interestingly, nowhere does the Constitution mention judicial review. There are places where it is implied (for example, in the supremacy clause of Article 6), but the only explicit description of authority for the courts is the reference to judicial power in Section 1 of Article 3.

M. THINK THROUGH THE CONSTITUTION *Why is judicial review, although not mentioned in the Constitution, an important action of the Supreme Court?*

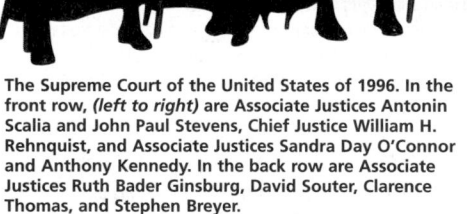

The Supreme Court of the United States of 1996. In the front row, *(left to right)* are Associate Justices Antonin Scalia and John Paul Stevens, Chief Justice William H. Rehnquist, and Associate Justices Sandra Day O'Connor and Anthony Kennedy. In the back row are Associate Justices Ruth Bader Ginsburg, David Souter, Clarence Thomas, and Stephen Breyer.

154 UNIT 2

SECTION 4. IMPEACHMENT The President, Vice-President and all civil officers of the United States, shall be removed from office on impeachment for, and conviction of, treason, bribery, or other high crimes and misdemeanors.

Article 3. *The Judiciary*

SECTION 1. FEDERAL COURTS AND JUDGES The judicial power of the United States, shall be vested in one Supreme Court, and in such inferior courts as the Congress may from time to time ordain and establish. The judges, both of the Supreme and inferior courts, shall hold their offices during good behavior, and shall, at stated times, receive for their services, a compensation, which shall not be diminished during their continuance in office.

SECTION 2. THE COURT'S AUTHORITY

1. General Authority The judicial power shall extend to all cases, in law and equity, arising under this Constitution, the laws of the United States, and treaties made, or which shall be made, under their authority;—to all cases affecting ambassadors, other public ministers and consuls;—to all cases of admiralty and maritime jurisdiction;—to controversies to which the United States shall be a party;—to controversies between two or more states;—between a state and citizens of another state;—between citizens of different states;—between citizens of the same state claiming lands under grants of different states, and between a state, or the citizens thereof, and foreign states, citizens or subjects.

2. General Authority In all cases affecting ambassadors, other public ministers and consuls, and those in which a state shall be party, the Supreme Court shall have original jurisdiction. In all the other cases before mentioned, the Supreme Court shall have appellate jurisdiction, both as to law and fact, with such exceptions, and under such regulations as the Congress shall make.

3. Trial by Jury The trial of all crimes, except in cases of impeachment, shall be by jury; and such trial shall be held in the state where the said crimes shall have been committed; but when not committed within any state, the trial shall be at such place or places as the Congress may by law have directed.

SECTION 3. TREASON

1. Definition Treason against the United States, shall consist only in levying war against them, or in adhering to their enemies, giving them aid and comfort. No person shall be convicted of treason unless on the testimony of two witnesses to the same overt act, or on confession in open court.

2. Punishment The Congress shall have power to declare the punishment of treason, but no attainder of treason shall work corruption of blood, or forfeiture except during the life of the person attainted.

Article 4. *Relations Among States*

SECTION 1. STATE ACTS AND RECORDS   Full faith and credit shall be given in each state to the public acts, records, and judicial proceedings of every other state. And the Congress may by general laws prescribe the manner in which such acts, records and proceedings shall be proved, and the effect thereof.

SECTION 2. RIGHTS OF CITIZENS
1. Citizenship   The citizens of each state shall be entitled to all privileges and immunities of citizens in the several states.

2. Extradition   A person charged in any state with treason, felony, or other crime, who shall flee from justice, and be found in another state, shall on demand of the executive authority of the state from which he fled, be delivered up, to be removed to the state having jurisdiction of the crime.

3. Fugitive Slaves   No person held to service or labor in one state, under the laws thereof, escaping into another, shall, in consequence of any law or regulation therein, be discharged from such service or labor, but shall be delivered up on claim of the party to whom such service or labor may be due.

SECTION 3. NEW STATES
1. Admission   New states may be admitted by the Congress into this Union; but no new state shall be formed or erected within the jurisdiction of any other state; nor any state be formed by the junction of two or more states, or parts of states, without the consent of the legislatures of the states concerned as well as of the Congress.

2. Congressional Authority   The Congress shall have power to dispose of and make all needful rules and regulations respecting the territory or other property belonging to the United States; and nothing in this Constitution shall be so construed as to prejudice any claims of the United States, or of any particular state.

SECTION 4. GUARANTEES TO THE STATES   The United States shall guarantee to every state in this Union a republican form of government, and shall protect each of them against invasion; and on application of the legislature, or of the executive (when the legislature cannot be convened) against domestic violence.

ARTICLE 4

Constitutional Insight **Section 2.1** *Why do college students attending public universities outside their state of residence have to pay higher tuition fees?* The Supreme Court has interpreted the "privileges and immunities" clause to allow higher tuition fees (and fees for hunting permits, etc.) for nonresidents when a state can give a "substantial reason" for the difference. Since state colleges and universities receive some financial support from the state's taxpayers, the difference is regarded as justified in most states. If a student establishes residency in the state, he or she can pay in-state tuition after one year.

N. THINK THROUGH THE CONSTITUTION *Do you think it is fair that a nonresident must pay higher tuition at a state college than must a resident of that state? Explain.*

Constitutional Insight **Section 3.1** *Should there be a West Virginia?* The Constitution states that "no new state shall be formed or erected within the jurisdiction of any other state" without the permission of the legislatures of the states involved and of the Congress. Vermont, Kentucky, Tennessee, and Maine were created from territory taken from existing states, with the approval of the sitting legislatures. West Virginia, however, is a different story. During the Civil War, the residents of the westernmost counties of Virginia were angry with the decision of their state to secede from the Union. They petitioned Congress to have their counties declared a distinct state. Congress agreed, and so the state of West Virginia was created. After the Civil War, the legislature of Virginia gave its formal approval, perhaps because it was in no position to dispute the matter.

O. THINK THROUGH THE CONSTITUTION *Suppose a section of Texas should decide to become a new state today. Could it do this? Why or why not?*

The Living Constitution **155**

OBJECTIVE

(1) To describe how the states are interdependent and subject to the federal government.

FOCUS & MOTIVATE

▶ ***Starting with the Student***
• What would happen if criminals could escape punishment by fleeing to another state?

OBJECTIVE
(1) **INSTRUCT**

ARTICLE 4. RELATIONS AMONG STATES
▶ ***Discussing Key Ideas***
• States must respect one another's laws, records, and court rulings.
• U.S. citizens have equal rights in all states.
• Congress has authority over the states.

IN-DEPTH RESOURCES: UNIT 2
Guided Reading, p. 20

ACCESS FOR STUDENTS ACQUIRING ENGLISH
Guided Reading (Spanish), p. 56

THINK THROUGH THE CONSTITUTION
Possible Responses:
N. Yes—Higher tuition fees for nonresidents are fair because state tax dollars, which residents have to pay, help support state colleges. No—Based on Section 2.1, all U.S. citizens should be entitled to attend any state college nationwide without penalty of higher tuition fees.
O. Yes, if Congress and the legislature of Texas gave their approval.

Making Connections Across the Curriculum

Geography   Floods, drought, hurricanes, earthquakes, tornadoes—all of these natural disasters can be classified as examples of "domestic violence." As ordained in Article 4, Section 4, the federal government guarantees that it will protect the states in the event of such disasters. The Federal Civil Defense Act of 1950 permits the president to declare a national disaster following these kinds of emergencies and to pave the way for supplying federal funds and aid to victims.

Have students research the natural disasters that are most likely to occur in their region of the country. For example, students who live along the San Andreas Fault in California might investigate earthquakes, while students who live in the Plains states might explore tornadoes. Encourage students to create visual aids, such as maps, diagrams, or cause-and-effect charts, to illustrate their findings.

Articles 5 and 6

OBJECTIVES

① To cite ways of proposing and ratifying amendments.

② To explain the authority of federal law.

SKILLBUILDER

• Interpreting charts, p. 156

FOCUS & MOTIVATE

▶ **Starting with the Student**
• Do students think rules at home and school should be flexible? Why or why not?
• Baseball teams must bow to umpires' rulings. How does this situation compare to states' compliance with federal laws?

OBJECTIVE ① INSTRUCT

ARTICLE 5. AMENDING THE CONSTITUTION
▶ **Discussing Key Ideas**
• The Constitution establishes guidelines for proposing and ratifying amendments.

OBJECTIVE ② INSTRUCT

ARTICLE 6. SUPREMACY OF THE NATIONAL GOVERNMENT
▶ **Discussing Key Ideas**
• States yield to national law.

THINK THROUGH THE CONSTITUTION
Possible Response:
P. National disunity might result if U.S. citizens were subject to conflicting laws.

SKILLBUILDER INTERPRETING CHARTS *Why does it take more votes to ratify an amendment than to propose one?*
Skillbuilder Answer The Framers of the Constitution wanted to make it more difficult to ratify amendments than to propose them so that ideas could be considered but not too easily accepted.

ARTICLE 6

Constitutional Insight **Section 2** *Just how "supreme" is the "law of the land"?* The federal Constitution and all federal laws and treaties are the highest law of the land. All state constitutions and laws and all local laws rank below national law and cannot be enforced if they contradict national law. For example, if the United States enters into a treaty with Great Britain protecting migratory Canadian geese, the states must change their laws to fit the provisions of that agreement. That was the decision of the Supreme Court in the case of *Missouri* v. *Holland* (1920). The state of Missouri argued that the national government could not interfere with its power to regulate hunting within its borders, but the Supreme Court concluded that the treaty was a valid exercise of national power and therefore took priority over state and local laws. The states had to adjust their rules and regulations accordingly.

P. THINK THROUGH THE CONSTITUTION *What would happen if the national law were not supreme?*

156 UNIT 2

Amending the Constitution

PROPOSAL STAGE	RATIFICATION STAGE
• Two-thirds vote of members present in both houses of Congress (33 amendments proposed)	• Three-fourths of state legislatures (25 amendments ratified)
or	or
• National convention convened by Congress at request of two-thirds of state legislatures (no amendments proposed)	• Constitutional conventions in three-fourths of the states (one amendment, the 21st ratified)

Article 5. *Amending the Constitution*

The Congress, whenever two-thirds of both houses shall deem it necessary, shall propose amendments to this Constitution, or, on the application of the legislatures of two-thirds of the several states, shall call a convention for proposing amendments, which, in either case, shall be valid to all intents and purposes, as part of this Constitution, when ratified by the legislatures of three-fourths of the several states, or by conventions in three-fourths thereof, as the one or the other mode of ratification may be proposed by the Congress; provided ~~that no amendment which may be made prior to the year one thousand eight hundred and eight shall in any manner affect the first and fourth clauses in the ninth section of the first article;~~ and that no state, without its consent, shall be deprived of its equal suffrage in the Senate.

Article 6. *Supremacy of the National Government*

SECTION 1. VALID DEBTS All debts contracted and engagements entered into, before the adoption of this Constitution, shall be as valid against the United States under this Constitution, as under the Confederation.

SECTION 2. SUPREME LAW This Constitution, and the laws of the United States which shall be made in pursuance thereof; and all treaties made, or which shall be made, under the authority of the United States, shall be the supreme law of the land; and the judges in every state shall be bound thereby, anything in the constitution or laws of any state to the contrary notwithstanding.

SECTION 3. LOYALTY TO CONSTITUTION The Senators and Representatives before mentioned, and the members of the several state legislatures, and all executive and judicial officers, both of the United States and of the several states, shall be bound by oath or affirmation, to support this Constitution; but no religious test shall ever be required as a qualification to any office or public trust under the United States.

TEACHING OPTION

Cooperative Activity: Proposing and Ratifying Amendments

Task: Student groups will attempt to propose an amendment by two-thirds majority of the group and ratify the amendment by three-fourths majority of the class.

Purpose: To gain understanding of the amendment process.

Activity: Divide students into groups of six. Each group will propose an amendment by a two-thirds majority of its members. Each group will then present its amendment to the class for ratification. A three-fourths majority

vote is required. Conclude with a class discussion of the following questions:

• Which was more difficult to achieve—a two-thirds majority to propose the amendment or a three-fourths majority to ratify it?
• Do you think the procedure for amending the Constitution provides enough flexibility for the document to change with the times? Why or why not?

ALTERNATIVE ASSESSMENT BOOK
Standards for Evaluating a Cooperative Activity

Article 7. *Ratification*

The ratification of the conventions of nine states, shall be sufficient for the establishment of this Constitution between the states so ratifying the same.

Done in convention by the unanimous consent of the states present the seventeenth day of September in the year of our Lord one thousand seven hundred and eighty-seven and of the independence of the United States of America the twelfth. In witness whereof we have hereunto subscribed our names,

George Washington—President and deputy from Virginia

NEW HAMPSHIRE: *John Langdon, Nicholas Gilman*

MASSACHUSETTS: *Nathaniel Gorham, Rufus King*

CONNECTICUT: *William Samuel Johnson, Roger Sherman*

NEW YORK: *Alexander Hamilton*

NEW JERSEY: *William Livingston, David Brearly, William Paterson, Jonathan Dayton*

PENNSYLVANIA: *Benjamin Franklin, Thomas Mifflin, Robert Morris, George Clymer, Thomas FitzSimons, Jared Ingersoll, James Wilson, Gouverneur Morris*

DELAWARE: *George Read, Gunning Bedford Jr., John Dickinson, Richard Bassett, Jacob Broom*

MARYLAND: *James McHenry, Dan of St Thomas Jenifer, Daniel Carroll*

VIRGINIA: *John Blair, James Madison Jr.*

NORTH CAROLINA: *William Blount, Richard Dobbs Spaight, Hugh Williamson*

SOUTH CAROLINA: *John Rutledge, Charles Cotesworth Pinckney, Charles Pinckney, Pierce Butler*

GEORGIA: *William Few, Abraham Baldwin*

The cartoonist celebrated the ratification of the Constitution by New York as the 11th state. This left only North Carolina and Rhode Island to complete all 13 pillars of the federal structure.

The Living Constitution **157**

ARTICLE 7

Constitutional Insight **Why was ratification by only 9 states sufficient to enact the Constitution?** In taking such a momentous step as replacing one constitution (the Articles of Confederation) with another, the Framers might have been expected to require the agreement of all 13 states. But the Framers were political realists. They knew that they would have a difficult time winning approval of the proposed constitution from all 13 states. But they also knew they had a good chance of getting 9 or 10 of the states "on board" and that the rest would follow. Their strategy worked, but just barely. While they had the approval of 8 states by June 1788, 2 of the most important states—Virginia and New York—had not yet decided to ratify. Without the approval of either of these influential states, the new government would have a difficult time surviving. Finally, by the end of July, both had given their blessing to the new constitution, but not without intense debate. And then there was the last holdout—Rhode Island. Not only did Rhode Island refuse to send delegates to the Constitutional Convention in 1787, but it turned down ratification several times before finally giving its approval under a cloud of economic and even military threats from neighboring states. Rhode Island entered the Union reluctantly on May 29, 1791.

Q. THINK THROUGH THE CONSTITUTION *Do you think all 50 states would ratify the Constitution today? Why or why not?*

OBJECTIVE

(1) To explain how the Constitution was ratified.

FOCUS & MOTIVATE

▶ *Starting with the Student*
- Ask students belonging to school clubs if all members approve of their clubs' rules.

OBJECTIVE
(1) **INSTRUCT**

ARTICLE 7. RATIFICATION

▶ *Discussing Key Ideas*
- Ratification requires approval by nine states.

HISTORY FROM VISUALS
Political Cartoon

Reading the Cartoon Ask students to describe the pillars representing North Carolina and Rhode Island. *North Carolina's pillar is toppling, and Rhode Island's is cracking.*

Extension Point out that the 13 pillars are arranged in the order (from left to right) that these states ratified the Constitution.

FORMAL ASSESSMENT
Quiz: Articles 4–7, p. 68

THINK THROUGH THE CONSTITUTION
Possible Responses:
Q. Yes—All states would recognize the Constitution's value and flexibility. No—Unresolved differences over states' sovereignty and rights might emerge.

TEACHING OPTION

Making Connections Across Time

Durability and Flexibility of the Constitution Have students compare the following views of the Constitution. What does each of the quotes say about the document's durability and flexibility?

- "A Constitution is framed for ages to come, and is designed to approach immortality as nearly as human institutions can approach it. . . . The people made the Constitution, and the people can unmake it. It is the creature of their own will, and lives only by their will."
John Marshall, *Cohens* v. *Virginia*, 1821

- "When the Constitution was first framed, I predicted that it would last fifty years. I was mistaken. . . . But I was mistaken only in point of time. The crash will come, but not so quick as I thought."
Aaron Burr, 1835

- "Amendments to the Constitution ought to not be too frequently made; . . . [if] continually tinkered with it would lose all its prestige and dignity, and the old instrument would be lost sight of altogether in a short time."
President Andrew Johnson, 1866

OBJECTIVE

1. To identify basic freedoms guaranteed by the first ten amendments.

FOCUS & MOTIVATE

▶ **Starting with the Student**
  • Ask students to name their rights as U.S. citizens. Then have them create a chart comparing the rights they cited with the Bill of Rights.

OBJECTIVE
1 INSTRUCT

THE BILL OF RIGHTS
▶ **Discussing Key Ideas**
  • The Bill of Rights protects individuals by limiting the power of the national government.

IN-DEPTH RESOURCES: UNIT 2
Guided Reading, p. 21

ACCESS FOR STUDENTS ACQUIRING ENGLISH
Guided Reading (Spanish), p. 57

THINK THROUGH THE CONSTITUTION
Possible Responses:
A. Sometimes one person's freedom of speech infringes on another's personal freedom.
B. Reasons include valuing guns for hunting, target practice, and self-defense; honoring the constitutional right to bear arms; prizing personal freedom in a democracy.
C. Most oppose invasion of privacy and want protection against police brutality.
D. The verdict of the first trial would have no enduring validity.

BILL OF RIGHTS

Constitutional Insight **AMENDMENT 1** *Do Americans have an absolute right to free speech?* The right to free speech is not without limits. In the case of *Schenck* v. *the United States* (1919), Justice Oliver Wendell Holmes wrote that this right does "not protect a man in falsely shouting fire in a theatre and causing panic." Thus, there are some forms of speech that are unprotected by the First Amendment. This allows Congress to make laws regarding the expression of some forms of speech.

A. THINK THROUGH THE CONSTITUTION *Why is there controversy over freedom of speech today?*

Constitutional Insight **AMENDMENT 2** *Do you have a constitutional right to own and possess guns?* In light of government efforts at gun control, this has become a very visible political issue as well as a constitutional question. For most legal scholars, it was answered in 1875 when the Supreme Court held that the Second Amendment only protects the right of states to maintain and equip a militia. As long as Congress does not interfere with that state function when it regulates the ownership and possession of guns, then it can impose gun control, as it did in the passage of the Brady Bill in 1995. Also, since the Second Amendment applies to the federal government, state and local governments can place limitations on weapons. A number of governments have laws that do not allow the carrying of concealed weapons, that require the registration of guns, and so forth.

B. THINK THROUGH THE CONSTITUTION *Why do you think that a great number of American citizens believe the right to own guns is very important?*

Constitutional Insight **AMENDMENT 4** *Can the police search your car without a court-issued search warrant when they stop you for speeding?* The answer, according to Supreme Court decisions, depends on whether they have good reasons—called "probable cause"—for doing so. If a state trooper notices bloody clothing on the back seat of a vehicle she stops for a traffic violation, there might be probable cause for her to insist on searching the vehicle. There is probably not sufficient reason for a search if the trooper is merely suspicious of the driver because of the way he is acting. In such cases, the trooper may make a casual request, such as "Do you mind if I look inside your vehicle?" If the answer is no, then according to the Court, the driver has waived his or her constitutional right against unreasonable searches.

C. THINK THROUGH THE CONSTITUTION *Why do you think the right against unreasonable searches and seizures is highly important to most people?*

Constitutional Insight **AMENDMENT 5** *Can you be tried twice for the same offense?* The prohibition against "double jeopardy" protects you against having the same charge twice brought against you for the same offense, but you can be retried on different charges related to that offense.

D. THINK THROUGH THE CONSTITUTION *What do you think could happen if a person could be tried twice for the same offense?*

158 UNIT 2

Bill of Rights: Amendments 1–10
Passed by Congress September 25, 1789. Ratified December 15, 1791.

AMENDMENT 1. RELIGIOUS AND POLITICAL FREEDOM (1791) Congress shall make no law respecting an establishment of religion, or prohibiting the free exercise thereof; or abridging the freedom of speech, or of the press; or the right of the people peaceably to assemble, and to petition the Government for a redress of grievances.

AMENDMENT 2. RIGHT TO BEAR ARMS (1791) A well-regulated militia, being necessary to the security of a free state, the right of the people to keep and bear arms, shall not be infringed.

AMENDMENT 3. QUARTERING TROOPS (1791) No soldier shall, in time of peace be quartered in any house, without the consent of the owner, nor in time of war, but in a manner to be prescribed by law.

AMENDMENT 4. SEARCH AND SEIZURE (1791) The right of the people to be secure in their persons, houses, papers, and effects, against unreasonable searches and seizures, shall not be violated, and no warrants shall issue, but upon probable cause, supported by oath or affirmation, and particularly describing the place to be searched, and the persons or things to be seized.

AMENDMENT 5. RIGHTS OF ACCUSED PERSONS (1791) No person shall be held to answer for a capital, or otherwise infamous crime, unless on a presentment or indictment of a Grand Jury, except in cases arising in the land or naval forces, or in the militia, when in actual service in time of war or public danger; nor shall any person be subject for the same offense to be twice put in jeopardy of life or limb; nor shall be compelled in any criminal case to be a witness against himself, nor be deprived of life, liberty, or property, without due process of law; nor shall private property be taken for public use, without just compensation.

TEACHING OPTION

Skillbuilder Mini-Lesson: Clarifying

Explaining the Skill Clarifying, or confirming one's understanding of what someone else has said, is a basic skill in communicating and in studying any subject. Clarifying readings from primary sources such as the Constitution should first involve defining unfamiliar words and working through complicated sentence structures to restate the ideas in simpler language.

Applying the Skill Understanding the Constitution Ask students to read the first amendment on this page, then answer the following questions:

1. What does *respecting* mean? *"about, in relation to"*
2. What word does *thereof* refer to? *"religion"*
3. What does *abridging* mean? *"to curtail or diminish"*
4. What is a redress of grievances? *"righting a wrong"*
5. What rights are covered in this amendment? (*Freedom of religion; freedom of speech and the press; and freedom to hold meetings and to ask the government to solve problems or make up for wrongdoings.*)

IN-DEPTH RESOURCES: UNIT 2
Skillbuilder Practice: Clarifying, p. 22

AMENDMENT 6. RIGHT TO A SPEEDY, PUBLIC TRIAL (1791) In all criminal prosecutions, the accused shall enjoy the right to a speedy and public trial, by an impartial jury of the State and district wherein the crime shall have been committed, which district shall have been previously ascertained by law, and to be informed of the nature and cause of the accusation; to be confronted with the witnesses against him; to have compulsory process for obtaining witnesses in his favor, and to have the assistance of counsel for his defense.

AMENDMENT 7. TRIAL BY JURY IN CIVIL CASES (1791) In suits at common law, where the value in controversy shall exceed twenty dollars, the right of a trial by jury shall be preserved, and no fact tried by a jury, shall be otherwise reexamined in any court of the United States, than according to the rules of the common law.

AMENDMENT 8. LIMITS OF FINES AND PUNISHMENTS (1791) Excessive bail shall not be required, nor excessive fines imposed, nor cruel and unusual punishments inflicted.

These people are holding a candlelight vigil to protest capital punishment (the death penalty) as cruel and unusual, an issue the Supreme Court has addressed in relation to the Eighth Amendment.

AMENDMENT 9. RIGHTS OF PEOPLE (1791) The enumeration in the Constitution, of certain rights, shall not be construed to deny or disparage others retained by the people.

AMENDMENT 10. POWERS OF STATES AND PEOPLE (1791) The powers not delegated to the United States by the Constitution, nor prohibited by it to the States, are reserved to the States respectively, or to the people.

Constitutional Insight **AMENDMENT 6** *What are the Miranda rights?* The term comes from the Supreme Court's decision in *Miranda* v. *Arizona* (1966), in which the justices established the basic rules that police must follow when questioning a suspect. If suspected, you must be told that you have a right to remain silent and that anything you say "can and will" be used against you. You also need to be informed that you have a right to an attorney and that the attorney may be present during questioning.

E. THINK THROUGH THE CONSTITUTION *How do the Miranda rights protect you?*

Constitutional Insight **AMENDMENT 8** *Is the death penalty "cruel and unusual punishment"?* This question was tackled by the Supreme Court in *Furman* v. *Georgia* (1972), a case in which a majority of the justices declared capital punishment unconstitutional. At least two of the justices in the majority felt that the death penalty was inherently cruel and unusual and thus in violation of the Eighth Amendment. Three other members of the Court felt the death penalty was unconstitutional because it was not applied consistently with regard to a person's race, gender, and other factors. In the case of *Gregg* v. *Georgia* (1976), the Court declared that punishment by death does not inherently violate the Eighth Amendment. Today a majority of states, and the federal government, sanction some forms of capital punishment in their legal codes.

F. THINK THROUGH THE CONSTITUTION *Do you think the death penalty is cruel and unusual punishment? Explain your position.*

Constitutional Insight **AMENDMENT 9** *Do you have a right to privacy?* Until 1965, no such right had ever been explicitly stated by the courts. That year, in the case of *Griswold* v. *Connecticut*, the Court said there is an implied right of American citizens to make certain personal choices without interference from the government; this case concerned the right to use birth control. Years later, in *Roe* v. *Wade* (1973), the same logic was used to declare unconstitutional a Texas law restricting a woman's right to an abortion in the first stages of pregnancy. Since that decision, both the right to privacy and abortion rights have become the center of major political controversies.

G. THINK THROUGH THE CONSTITUTION *How do you define the right to privacy?*

The Living Constitution **159**

Amendments 11–27

OBJECTIVE

1 To summarize Constitutional Amendments 11–27.

FOCUS & MOTIVATE

▶ *Starting with the Student*

- Ask students to think about how parents change the standards for their children's behavior as time passes.
- Why do parents drop some old rules and create new ones?

OBJECTIVE

1 INSTRUCT

▶ *Discussing Key Ideas*

- Amendments 11–27 reflect ways the Constitution has developed to meet the changing needs of society and historical trends.
- Amendments 15, 19, and 26 give voting rights to specific groups.

THINK THROUGH THE CONSTITUTION
Possible Responses:
A. Reflected the growing role of political parties in nominating presidential and vice-presidential candidates; ensured that the president and vice-president belong to the same party.

Constitutional Insight **AMENDMENT 12** *Why did the election of 1800 result in the Twelfth Amendment?* The election ended in a tie vote between the Republican running mates, Thomas Jefferson and Aaron Burr, and it therefore had to be decided by the House of Representatives. Finally, Alexander Hamilton decided that his political enemy Jefferson would make a better president than Burr, and the election was decided in Jefferson's favor on the House's 36th ballot. Almost immediately Hamilton and others designed an amendment that established that the presidential electors would vote for both a presidential and vice-presidential candidate. This amendment prevents a repeat of the problem in the 1800 election.

A. THINK THROUGH THE CONSTITUTION *Why is the Twelfth Amendment important?*

Amendments 11–27

AMENDMENT 11. LAWSUITS AGAINST STATES (1798) Passed by Congress March 4, 1794. Ratified February 7, 1795. Proclaimed 1798. Note: Article 3, Section 2, of the Constitution was modified by Amendment 11.

The Judicial power of the United States shall not be construed to extend to any suit in law or equity, commenced or prosecuted against one of the United States by citizens of another state, or by citizens or subjects of any foreign state.

AMENDMENT 12. ELECTION OF EXECUTIVES (1804) Passed by Congress December 9, 1803. Ratified June 15, 1804.

Note: A portion of Article 2, Section 1, of the Constitution was superseded by the 12th Amendment.

The electors shall meet in their respective states and vote by ballot for President and Vice-President, one of whom, at least, shall not be an inhabitant of the same state with themselves; they shall name in their ballots the person voted for as President, and in distinct ballots the person voted for as Vice-President, and they shall make distinct lists of all persons voted for as President, and of all persons voted for as Vice-President, and of the number of votes for each, which lists they shall sign and certify, and transmit sealed to the seat of the government of the United States, directed to the President of the Senate;—the President of the Senate shall, in the presence of the Senate and House of Representatives, open all the certificates and the votes shall then be counted;—the person having the greatest number of votes for President, shall be the President, if such number be a majority of the whole number of electors appointed; and if no person have such majority, then from the persons having the highest numbers not exceeding three on the list of those voted for as President, the House of Representatives shall choose immediately, by ballot, the President. But in choosing the President, the votes shall be taken by states, the representation from each state having one vote; a quorum for this purpose shall consist of a member or members from two-thirds of the states, and a majority of all the states shall be necessary to a choice. And if the House of Representatives shall not choose a President whenever the right of choice shall devolve upon them, ~~before the fourth day of March next following~~, then the Vice-President shall act as President, as in the case of the death or other constitutional disability of the President. The person having the greatest number of votes as Vice-President, shall be the Vice-President, if such number be a majority of the whole number of Electors appointed, and if no person have a majority, then from the two highest numbers on the list, the Senate shall choose the Vice-President; a quorum for the purpose shall consist of two-thirds of the whole number of Senators, and a majority of the whole number shall be necessary to a choice. But no person constitutionally ineligible to the office of President shall be eligible to that of Vice-President of the United States.

AMENDMENT 13. SLAVERY ABOLISHED (1865) Passed by Congress January 31, 1865. Ratified December 6, 1865.

Note: A portion of Article 4, Section 2, of the Constitution was superseded by the 13th Amendment.

Teaching Less Proficient Readers

Summarizing Main Ideas Pair less proficient readers with more proficient readers to summarize the key points of Amendments 11–27. Have student pairs follow these steps.

1. **Skim** pages 160–165 together, noting the boldfaced titles of the amendments and sections.
2. **Closely read** each amendment, one at a time, along with any accompanying Constitutional Insight.
3. **Rewrite** the title of each amendment as a main-idea sentence that highlights the most important concept.

To help students get started, you may wish to write some examples on the chalkboard as models:

Amendment 12: Presidential electors will cast votes for president and vice-president on separate ballots.

Amendment 13: Slavery must end in the United States and its territories.

Amendment 14: All native-born and naturalized Americans are granted citizenship and will enjoy the privileges of equal protection under the law.

Section 1 Neither slavery nor involuntary servitude, except as a punishment for crime whereof the party shall have been duly convicted, shall exist within the United States, or any place subject to their jurisdiction.

Section 2 Congress shall have power to enforce this article by appropriate legislation.

AMENDMENT 14. CIVIL RIGHTS (1868) Passed by Congress June 13, 1866. Ratified July 9, 1868.

Note: Article 1, Section 2, of the Constitution was modified by section 2 of the 14th Amendment.

Section 1 All persons born or naturalized in the United States, and subject to the jurisdiction thereof, are citizens of the United States and of the state wherein they reside. No state shall make or enforce any law which shall abridge the privileges or immunities of citizens of the United States; nor shall any state deprive any person of life, liberty, or property, without due process of law; nor deny to any person within its jurisdiction the equal protection of the laws.

Section 2 Representatives shall be apportioned among the several states according to their respective numbers, counting the whole number of persons in each state, ~~excluding Indians not taxed~~. But when the right to vote at any election for the choice of electors for President and Vice-President of the United States, Representatives in Congress, the Executive and Judicial officers of a State, or the members of the Legislature thereof, is denied to any of the male inhabitants of such State, being twenty-one years of age, and citizens of the United States, or in any way abridged, except for participation in rebellion, or other crime, the basis of representation therein shall be reduced in the proportion which the number of such male citizens shall bear to the whole number of male citizens twenty-one years of age in such state.

Section 3 No person shall be a Senator or Representative in Congress, or elector of President and Vice-President, or hold any office, civil or military, under the United States, or under any state, who, having previously taken an oath, as a member of Congress, or as an officer of the United States, or as a member of any state legislature, or as an executive or judicial officer of any state, to support the Constitution of the United States, shall have engaged in insurrection or rebellion against the same, or given aid or comfort to the enemies thereof. But Congress may by a vote of two-thirds of each house, remove such disability.

Section 4 The validity of the public debt of the United States, authorized by law, including debts incurred for payment of pensions and bounties for services in suppressing insurrection or rebellion, shall not be questioned. But neither the United States nor any state shall assume or pay any debt or obligation incurred in aid of insurrection or rebellion against the United States, or any claim for the loss or emancipation of any slave; but all such debts, obligations and claims shall be held illegal and void.

Section 5 The Congress shall have power to enforce, by appropriate legislation, the provisions of this article.

Constitutional Insight **AMENDMENT 14,**

Section 1 *Which personal status takes priority: that of U.S. citizen or of state citizen?* The Fourteenth Amendment firmly notes that Americans are citizens of both the nation and the states but that no state could "abridge the privileges or immunities" of U.S. citizens, deprive them "of life, liberty, or property, without due process of law," or deny them "equal protection of the laws."

What does it mean to have "equal protection of the laws"? The laws of the national government and those of the states apply in the same way to all citizens. The Supreme Court has declared that not only does the due-process clause of the Fifth Amendment apply to the states as well as to the national government, but other parts of the Bill of Rights, such as that protecting freedom of speech, also apply. The civil rights movement received a boost from the Supreme Court's decision in *Brown* v. *Board of Education of Topeka, Kansas* (1954), which declared that the legal segregation of schools and, by implication, other public services and facilities was unconstitutional. The Court reasoned that "separate facilities are inherently unequal."

B. THINK THROUGH THE CONSTITUTION *Do you agree or disagree with the Supreme Court's decision that separate facilities are unequal? Explain your position.*

The lawyers who successfully argued against segregation in the *Brown* v. *Board of Education* case in 1954 are *(left to right)* George E.C. Hayes, Thurgood Marshall, and James M. Nabrit.

The Living Constitution **161**

MORE ABOUT . . .
*Thurgood Marshall
(1908–1993)*

Reacting to the *Brown* v. *Board of Education* ruling, Thurgood Marshall (pictured on this page) declared, "I was so happy, I was numb." The outcome of the case—Marshall's most stunning victory up to that time—heralded his brilliant legal career to come. In 1967, he became the first African American to serve as a Supreme Court justice. He dedicated his life to championing civil rights and battling racial injustice.

IN-DEPTH RESOURCES: UNIT 2
American Lives: Thurgood Marshall, p. 26.

THINK THROUGH THE CONSTITUTION
Possible Responses:
B. Agree—if separate facilities vary widely in quality and are vehicles for fostering discrimination. Disagree—if separate facilities are uniform in quality.

Making Connections Across Cultures

Korematsu v. United States After the Japanese attack on Pearl Harbor in 1941, the U.S. government moved 120,000 Japanese Americans to internment camps. Two-thirds of these people were native-born U.S. citizens. Because of their Japanese heritage, the government claimed they were a security risk. In *Korematsu* v. *United States* (1944), the Supreme Court upheld internment as a justifiable wartime measure. In 1988, however, Congress made a public apology and paid $20,000 to each person who had been sent to a government camp. Ask students which parts of the Constitution apply to this case? *(Possible Responses: Article 1, Section 9; Amendments 5, 14.)*

Exploring Themes

Civil Rights In the 1960s, the government began promoting affirmative action to help many African Americans, women, and other minorities gain education and jobs. Affirmative-action programs involve making special efforts to hire or enroll groups that have suffered from discrimination in the past. In the late 1970s, though, some people began to criticize these programs as "reverse discrimination" that set hiring or enrollment quotas depriving whites of opportunities. The fate of affirmative action is yet to be decided. Ask students how affirmative action might have made up for past violations of civil rights.

A pay-as-you-go tax plan began in 1913. It provided for employers to withhold tax from employees' paychecks and send the money directly to the Internal Revenue Service. On April 15 of each year, taxpayers file a tax return stating how much taxable income they received the previous year. If the amount withheld is less than they are required to pay according to a tax rate schedule, they must pay additional taxes. If it is more than they are required to pay, they receive a refund.

THINK THROUGH THE CONSTITUTION
Possible Responses:

C. Reasons include unawareness of candidates and issues; voter apathy.

D. Yes— provides revenue to support federal government and its programs. No—provides federal government with the incentive to overspend at the taxpayers' expense; can be imposed unfairly.

E. The senators are more directly responsible to voters.

F. Yes—to help ensure that citizens adhere to the same high standards of ethical behavior. No—to avoid possible invasion of privacy.

Constitutional Insight **AMENDMENT 15** *Can you be denied the right to vote?* The Fifteenth Amendment prohibits the United States or any state from keeping citizens from voting because of race or color or because they were once slaves. However, a person convicted of a crime can be denied the right to vote, as can someone found to be mentally incompetent.

C. THINK THROUGH THE CONSTITUTION *Why do you think so many people do not exercise the right to vote?*

Constitutional Insight **AMENDMENT 16** *How has the ability of Congress to impose taxes been amended?* The Sixteenth Amendment imposes a federal income tax and in so doing changes Article 1, Section 2, Clause 3, and Section 9, Clause 4, by stating that Congress has the power to place an income tax, which is a direct tax, on people without apportioning such a tax among the states according to their population.

D. THINK THROUGH THE CONSTITUTION *Do you think Congress should have the power to place an income tax on the people of the nation? Explain your answer.*

Constitutional Insight **AMENDMENT 17** *How has the way senators are elected been changed?* The Seventeenth Amendment changes Article I, Section 3, Clause 2, by stating that senators shall be elected by the people of each state instead of by the state legislatures.

E. THINK THROUGH THE CONSTITUTION *Why is the direct election of senators by the people of each state important?*

Constitutional Insight **AMENDMENT 18** *Besides its being the only amendment to be repealed, what is so distinct about the Prohibition amendment?* It is the only amendment thus far that deals directly with a public policy issue. The failure of Prohibition is often cited by opponents of more recent constitutional amendments that sought to legislate morality, such as by restricting abortion. They point to it as an example of the inability of amendments to change people's behavior.

F. THINK THROUGH THE CONSTITUTION *Do you think Congress should try to legislate morality? Why or why not?*

Federal agents prepare to smash containers of illegal whiskey.

162 UNIT 2

AMENDMENT 15. RIGHT TO VOTE (1870) Passed by Congress February 26, 1869. Ratified February 3, 1870.

Section 1 The right of citizens of the United States to vote shall not be denied or abridged by the United States or by any state on account of race, color, or previous condition of servitude.

Section 2 The Congress shall have power to enforce this article by appropriate legislation.

AMENDMENT 16. INCOME TAX (1913) Passed by Congress July 12, 1909. Ratified February 3, 1913.
Note: Article 1, Section 9, of the Constitution was modified by the 16th Amendment.

The Congress shall have power to lay and collect taxes on incomes, from whatever source derived, without apportionment among the several states, and without regard to any census or enumeration.

AMENDMENT 17. DIRECT ELECTION OF SENATORS (1913) Passed by Congress May 13, 1912. Ratified April 8, 1913.
Note: Article 1, Section 3, of the Constitution was modified by the 17th Amendment.

Clause 1 The Senate of the United States shall be composed of two Senators from each state, elected by the people thereof, for six years; and each Senator shall have one vote. The electors in each state shall have the qualifications requisite for electors of the most numerous branch of the state legislatures.

Clause 2 When vacancies happen in the representation of any State in the Senate, the executive authority of such state shall issue writs of election to fill such vacancies: Provided, that the legislature of any state may empower the executive thereof to make temporary appointments until the people fill the vacancies by election as the legislature may direct.

Clause 3 This amendment shall not be so construed as to affect the election or term of any Senator chosen before it becomes valid as part of the Constitution.

AMENDMENT 18. PROHIBITION (1919) Passed by Congress December 18, 1917. Ratified January 16, 1919. Repealed by Amendment 21.

Section 1 After one year from the ratification of this article the manufacture, sale, or transportation of intoxicating liquors within, the importation thereof into, or the exportation thereof from the United States and all territory subject to the jurisdiction thereof for beverage purposes is hereby prohibited.

Section 2 The Congress and the several states shall have concurrent power to enforce this article by appropriate legislation.

Section 3 This article shall be inoperative unless it shall have been ratified as an amendment to the Constitution by the legislatures of the several states, as provided in the Constitution, within seven years from the date of the submission hereof to the states by the Congress.

TEACHING OPTION

Making Connections Across the Curriculum

Film In 1927, moviegoers flocked to see *Underworld,* featuring Chicago mobsters who reaped huge profits as bootleggers—providers of illegal liquor. This film set the stage for a series of gangster films to follow. They portrayed the lawlessness and rise of organized crime stemming from the rampant violation of the Eighteenth Amendment. In real life, hoodlums like Al Capone controlled large-scale bootlegging operations. On the silver screen, characters modeled after Al Capone and his thugs masterminded crime waves and struggled to outsmart

federal agents. Among the most popular films were *Little Caesar* (1930), *The Public Enemy* (1931), and *Scarface* (1932).

Though actual bootleggers became extinct with the repeal of Prohibition in 1933, fictional bootleggers still played leading roles in gangster films until the end of the decade. The movie *The Roaring Twenties,* released in 1939, was one of the last films to glamorize the era of speakeasies and "bathtub gin."

AMENDMENT 19. WOMAN'S SUFFRAGE (1920) Passed by Congress June 4, 1919. Ratified August 18, 1920.

Section 1 The right of citizens of the United States to vote shall not be denied or abridged by the United States or by any state on account of sex.

Section 2 Congress shall have power to enforce this article by appropriate legislation.

AMENDMENT 20. "LAME DUCK" SESSIONS (1933) Passed by Congress March 2, 1932. Ratified January 23, 1933.

Note: Article 1, Section 4, of the Constitution was modified by Section 2 of this Amendment. In addition, a portion of the 12th Amendment was superseded by Section 3.

Section 1 The terms of the President and Vice-President shall end at noon on the 20th day of January, and the terms of Senators and Representatives at noon on the 3rd day of January, of the year in which such terms would have ended if this article had not been ratified; and the terms of their successors shall then begin.

Section 2 The Congress shall assemble at least once in every year, and such meeting shall begin at noon on the 3rd day of January, unless they shall by law appoint a different day.

Section 3 If, at the time fixed for the beginning of the term of the President, the President elect shall have died, the Vice-President elect shall become President. If a President shall not have been chosen before the time fixed for the beginning of his term, or if the President elect shall have failed to qualify, then the Vice-President elect shall act as President until a President shall have qualified; and the Congress may by law provide for the case wherein neither a President elect nor a Vice-President elect shall have qualified, declaring who shall then act as President, or the manner in which one who is to act shall be selected, and such person shall act accordingly until a President or Vice-President shall have qualified.

Section 4 The Congress may by law provide for the case of the death of any of the persons from whom the House of Representatives may choose a President whenever the right of choice shall have devolved upon them, and for the case of the death of any of the persons from whom the Senate may choose a Vice-President whenever the right of choice shall have devolved upon them.

Section 5 Sections 1 and 2 shall take effect on the 15th day of October following the ratification of this article.

Section 6 This article shall be inoperative unless it shall have been ratified as an amendment to the Constitution by the legislatures of three-fourths of the several states within seven years from the date of its submission.

AMENDMENT 21. REPEAL OF PROHIBITION (1933) Passed by Congress February 20, 1933. Ratified December 5, 1933.

Section 1 The eighteenth article of amendment to the Constitution of the United States is hereby repealed.

Section 2 The transportation or importation into any State, Territory, or Possession of the United States for delivery or use therein of intoxicating liquors, in violation of the laws thereof, is hereby prohibited.

Constitutional Insight **AMENDMENT 19** *When did women first get the right to vote in the United States?* Women had the right to vote in the state of New Jersey between 1776 and 1807, because in establishing voting qualifications the state constitution did not use the term *men*. In 1807, a new state constitution limited the franchise to men. In 1920, the Nineteenth Amendment prohibited the United States or any state from denying women the right to vote.

G. THINK THROUGH THE CONSTITUTION *How does the right of women to vote affect politics today?*

Constitutional Insight **AMENDMENT 20** *Why is the Twentieth Amendment usually called the lame duck amendment?* A lame duck is a person who continues to hold office after his or her replacement has been elected. Such a person is called a lame duck because he or she no longer has any strong political influence. The Twentieth Amendment lessens the time between the election of a new president and vice-president in November and the assumption of these offices, which it sets at January 20th instead of March 4th. It lessens the time new members of Congress must wait to take their seats from 13 months to about 2 months. They are now seated on the January 3rd following the November election. As a result, the lame duck period is now quite short.

H. THINK THROUGH THE CONSTITUTION *Why did the Framers build in a longer lame duck period?*

On January 20, 1937, President Roosevelt took the oath of office for his second term. This was the first time the inauguration took place on January 20, thanks to the Twentieth Amendment.

Constitutional Insight **AMENDMENT 21** *What is unique about the Twenty-first Amendment?* Besides being the only one that explicitly repeals another amendment, the 21st is the first, and thus far the only one, to be ratified by the state convention method outlined in Article 5. Congress, probably fearing that state legislatures would not deal swiftly with the issue of repeal, chose to have each state call a special convention to consider the amendment. The strategy worked well, for the elected delegates to the convention represented public opinion on the issue and ratified the amendment without delay.

I. THINK THROUGH THE CONSTITUTION *Why is it necessary to pass another amendment to revoke or remove an existing amendment?*

The Living Constitution **163**

Critical Thinking: Forming Opinions The issue of restricting the term of office for senators and representatives still sparks debate. Those who serve for several terms often bring with them a wealth of legislative experience and contribute to the stability of Congress. Do you think forcing experienced leaders to leave Congress because of term limits would disrupt this stability? Why or why not?

THINK THROUGH THE CONSTITUTION
Possible Responses:

J. Agree—curbs presidential powers; limits one-party control of White House; avoids possibility of dictatorial rule. Disagree—extended terms desirable during crises such as war; disrupts agenda of an effective president.

K. Yes—Washington, D.C., residents would have essentially the same privileges as the citizens of the nation's 50 states. No—The capital's size and population are not comparable to those of the other 50 states.

L. Since poll taxes can no longer be used to keep African Americans from voting, more African-American candidates have won elections.

Constitutional Insight **AMENDMENT 22** *Why are presidents subject to a two-term limit?* The Twenty-second Amendment legislates the tradition of a two-term limit started by George Washington and broken by Franklin Roosevelt (elected to four terms).

J. THINK THROUGH THE CONSTITUTION *Do you agree or disagree that the president of the United States should be held to no more than two terms? Explain your answer.*

NOW & THEN

CONGRESSIONAL TERM LIMITS (AMENDMENT 22)

In the early 1990s there was a national movement to establish congressional term limits. However, in 1995, the Supreme Court struck down all state laws limiting congressional terms, stating they were unconstitutional because they did not deal with age, residency, or citizenship.

As a result of the Supreme Court decision, Congress would need to pass a constitutional amendment to establish congressional term limits. In 1951 Congress did pass an amendment—the Twenty-second—to limit a president to two terms.

Constitutional Insight **AMENDMENT 23** *Why were residents of the District of Columbia without a vote in presidential elections?* First, the city was merely an idea at the time the Constitution was written. Second, no one expected the district to include many residents. Third, the Framers designed the electoral college on a state framework. By 1961, however, the fact that nearly 750,000 Americans living in the nation's capital could not vote in presidential elections was an embarrassment. The Twenty-third Amendment gives Washington, D.C., residents the right to vote in presidential elections by assigning them electoral votes.

K. THINK THROUGH THE CONSTITUTION *Do you think the District of Columbia should be made a separate state?*

Constitutional Insight **AMENDMENT 24** *Why was the poll tax an issue important enough to require an amendment?* The poll tax was used in some places to prevent African-American voters—at least the many who were too poor to pay the tax—from participating in elections. As the civil rights movement gained momentum, the abuse of the poll tax became a major issue, but the national government found it difficult to change the situation because the constitutional provisions in Article 1, Section 4, leave the qualifications of voters in the hands of the states. The Twenty-fourth Amendment changed this by prohibiting the United States or any state from including payment of any tax as a requirement for voting.

L. THINK THROUGH THE CONSTITUTION *What impact do you think the Twenty-fourth Amendment has had on elections?*

Section 3 This article shall be inoperative unless it shall have been ratified as an amendment to the Constitution by conventions in the several states, as provided in the Constitution, within seven years from the date of the submission hereof to the states by the Congress.

AMENDMENT 22. LIMIT ON PRESIDENTIAL TERMS (1951)
Passed by Congress March 24, 1947. Ratified February 27, 1951.

Section 1 No person shall be elected to the office of the President more than twice, and no person who has held the office of President, or acted as President, for more than two years of a term to which some other person was elected President shall be elected to the office of the President more than once. But this Article shall not apply to any person holding the office of President when this Article was proposed by the Congress, and shall not prevent any person who may be holding the office of President, or acting as President, during the term within which this Article becomes operative from holding the office of President or acting as President during the remainder of such term.

Section 2 This article shall be inoperative unless it shall have been ratified as an amendment to the Constitution by the legislatures of three-fourths of the several states within seven years from the date of its submission to the states by the Congress.

AMENDMENT 23. VOTING IN DISTRICT OF COLUMBIA (1961)
Passed by Congress June 16, 1960. Ratified March 29, 1961.

Section 1 The District constituting the seat of Government of the United States shall appoint in such manner as Congress may direct: A number of electors of President and Vice-President equal to the whole number of Senators and Representatives in Congress to which the District would be entitled if it were a State, but in no event more than the least populous State; they shall be in addition to those appointed by the States, but they shall be considered, for the purposes of the election of President and Vice-President, to be electors appointed by a State; and they shall meet in the District and perform such duties as provided by the twelfth article of amendment.

Section 2 The Congress shall have power to enforce this article by appropriate legislation.

AMENDMENT 24. ABOLITION OF POLL TAXES (1964) Passed by Congress August 27, 1962. Ratified January 23, 1964.

Section 1 The right of citizens of the United States to vote in any primary or other election for President or Vice-President, for electors for President or Vice-President, or for Senator or Representative in Congress, shall not be denied or abridged by the United States or any State by reason of failure to pay any poll tax or other tax.

Section 2 The Congress shall have power to enforce this article by appropriate legislation.

AMENDMENT 25. PRESIDENTIAL DISABILITY, SUCCESSION (1967)
Passed by Congress July 6, 1965. Ratified February 10, 1967.

Note: Article 2, Section 1, of the Constitution was affected by the 25th Amendment.

Section 1. In case of the removal of the President from office or of his death or resignation, the Vice-President shall become President.

TEACHING OPTION

Cooperative Activity: Preparing Voting Requirements

Task: Student groups will discuss voting requirements they would like to see enacted for the next election.

Purpose: To gain insight into the decision-making process for establishing voting rights.

Activity: Divide students into groups of six. Each group will address the following questions:

- Should the age of eligibility for voting be amended in any way?

- Who do you think should be eligible to vote? Whose voting rights should be denied?
- Do you think that people who vote should be able to read and write?
- Should an elementary school diploma be a voting requirement? What about a high school diploma?
- Should military or community service be a requirement?

Groups should discuss their voting requirements with the class.

ALTERNATIVE ASSESSMENT BOOK
Standards for Evaluating a Cooperative Activity

Section 2 Whenever there is a vacancy in the office of the Vice-President, the President shall nominate a Vice-President who shall take office upon confirmation by a majority vote of both houses of Congress.

Section 3 Whenever the President transmits to the President pro tempore of the Senate and the Speaker of the House of Representatives his written declaration that he is unable to discharge the powers and duties of his office, and until he transmits to them a written declaration to the contrary, such powers and duties shall be discharged by the Vice-President as Acting President.

Section 4 Whenever the Vice-President and a majority of either the principal officers of the executive departments or of such other body as Congress may by law provide, transmit to the President pro tempore of the Senate and the Speaker of the House of Representatives their written declaration that the President is unable to discharge the powers and duties of his office, the Vice-President shall immediately assume the powers and duties of the office as Acting President. Thereafter, when the President transmits to the President pro tempore of the Senate and the Speaker of the House of Representatives his written declaration that no inability exists, he shall resume the powers and duties of his office unless the Vice-President and a majority of either the principal officers of the executive department or of such other body as Congress may by law provide, transmit within four days to the President pro tempore of the Senate and the Speaker of the House of Representatives their written declaration that the President is unable to discharge the powers and duties of his office. Thereupon Congress shall decide the issue, assembling within forty-eight hours for that purpose if not in session. If the Congress, within twenty-one days after receipt of the latter written declaration, or, if Congress is not in session, within twenty-one days after Congress is required to assemble, determines by two-thirds vote of both houses that the President is unable to discharge the powers and duties of his office, the Vice-President shall continue to discharge the same as Acting President; otherwise, the President shall resume the powers and duties of his office.

AMENDMENT 26. 18-YEAR-OLD VOTE (1971) Passed by Congress March 23, 1971. Ratified July 1, 1971.

Note: Amendment 14, Section 2, of the Constitution was modified by Section 1 of the 26th Amendment.

Section 1 The right of citizens of the United States, who are eighteen years of age or older, to vote shall not be denied or abridged by the United States or by any State on account of age.

Section 2 The Congress shall have power to enforce this article by appropriate legislation.

AMENDMENT 27. CONGRESSIONAL PAY (1992) Passed by Congress September 25, 1789. Ratified May 7, 1992.
'No law, varying the compensation for the services of the Senators and Representatives, shall take effect, until an election of representatives shall have intervened.

President Richard M. Nixon *(above)* signs the Twenty-sixth Amendment to the Constitution, adopted in 1971. A teenager *(right)* exercises her right to vote.

Constitutional Insight **AMENDMENT 26** *Why was the Twenty-sixth Amendment passed?* Granting 18-year-olds the right to vote became an issue in the 1960s, during the Vietnam War, when people questioned the justice of requiring 18-year-old men to submit to the military draft but refusing them the right to vote. In 1970, Congress passed a Voting Rights Act giving 18-year-olds the right to vote in elections. When the constitutionality of this act was challenged, the Supreme Court decided that states had to honor the 18-year-old vote for congressional and presidential elections but could retain higher age requirements for state and local elections. To avoid confusion at the polls, the Twenty-sixth Amendment was passed by both chambers of Congress on March 23, 1971, and ratified by July 1, 1971. It guarantees 18-year-olds the right to vote in national and state elections.

M. THINK THROUGH THE CONSTITUTION *Do you think 18-year-olds should have the right to vote? Why or why not?*

Constitutional Insight **AMENDMENT 27** *How long did it take to ratify this amendment?* Although the Twenty-seventh Amendment was originally one of the 12 amendments proposed in 1789 as part of what became the Bill of Rights, it was not ratified until 1992. This amendment, which deals with congressional compensation, allows the members of Congress to vote for an increase in their pay but prohibits the increase from taking effect until after an election.

N. THINK THROUGH THE CONSTITUTION *Do you think members of Congress should be able to vote for a pay increase? Explain your answer.*

The Living Constitution **165**

MORE ABOUT . . .
Amendment 25

In 1973 Vice-President Spiro Agnew resigned from office. Under the provisions of the Twenty-fifth Amendment, Congress approved President Nixon's appointment of Gerald Ford to fill the vacancy. When Nixon resigned a year later, Ford became president. President Ford then named Nelson Rockefeller as vice-president. Congress approved Rockefeller's appointment. That was the only time in history when neither the president nor the vice-president had been elected to office.

FORMAL ASSESSMENT
Quiz: The Amendments, p. 68

THINK THROUGH THE CONSTITUTION
Possible Responses:

M. Yes—capable of learning about candidates and issues; mature enough to make informed decisions; old enough for military service. No—capable of following military orders but not mature enough to make sound, independent decisions.

N. Yes—If members abused this privilege, they could be voted out of office. No—As public servants, they should not be granted this privilege.

TEACHING OPTION

Cooperative Activity: Reviewing the Constitution

Task: To review the Constitution.

Purpose: To gain a deeper understanding of the Constitution.

Activity: Assign groups of four students two articles or sections of the document to summarize and explain in contemporary language. You may vary the number of articles or sections assigned depending on their length, as well as the size of your class. All groups will present their summaries and, in effect, teach one another the whole document.

Suggest that students create bulleted lists of key points as a study aid. Here is an example:

Article 2. The Executive

Section 2. Powers of the President

• Acts as commander in chief of the armed forces
• Makes treaties (with the consent of Congress)
• Appoints ambassadors
• Meets with heads of state
• Appoints Supreme Court justices

ALTERNATIVE ASSESSMENT BOOK
Standards for Evaluating a Cooperative Activity

Teacher's Edition **165**

FOCUS & MOTIVATE

▶ **Starting with the Student**
Lead students in a discussion of the significance of voting.

- Why do students think so many people, especially between the ages of 18 and 21, fail to vote?
- How might people's attitudes toward voting change if the privilege were suddenly denied?

MORE ABOUT . . .
The Voting Rights Act of 1965

A landmark of the civil rights movement, the Voting Rights Act of 1965 had several important provisions. One did away with devices like literacy tests used in many Southern states to prevent African Americans from voting. Another gave the United States attorney general authority to enroll voters in areas where groups such as African Americans were clearly not voting in reasonable numbers.

Voting Rights

When the American colonists declared their independence from Great Britain in 1776, the state constitutions that were drafted established not only the governing bodies of the states but also the voting rights of the people. These voting rights were maintained by the central government of the Articles of Confederation.

When the delegates met in Philadelphia in 1787, they decided to create a new government instead of revising the Articles of Confederation. In Article 1, Section 4 of the Constitution, they prescribed the legislation of voting rights as a function of state legislatures, with the provision that Congress could "at any time by law make or alter such regulations."

1789
MALE PROPERTY OWNERS

In the early years of the United States, property qualifications for male voters, which had long existed, were relaxed in some states (Pennsylvania, Delaware, North Carolina, Georgia, and Vermont) to include any male taxpayer. Most state constitutions also required that a voting male be at least 21 years of age.

Those who qualified to vote were generally white, although some states allowed free African Americans to vote (New Jersey did until 1807, as did New York until 1821, Rhode Island until 1822, and Pennsylvania until 1837). Slaves could not vote in any state.

Women could not vote, except in New Jersey until 1807. Native Americans could vote in no states. The 1789 painting at right is of Daniel Boardman, a white male property owner. What about the painting suggests that he was a qualified voter?

1870
AFRICAN-AMERICAN MALES

The Fifteenth Amendment to the United States Constitution attempted to guarantee African-American males the right to vote by stating that the right of U.S. citizens "to vote shall not be denied or abridged [curtailed] by the United States or by any state on account of race, color, or previous condition of servitude." The picture above shows African-American males voting in a state election in 1867. African-American males, however, were often kept from voting through the use of poll taxes, which were finally abolished by the Twenty-fourth Amendment in 1964, and literacy tests, which were suspended by the Voting Rights Act of 1965.

166 Unit 2

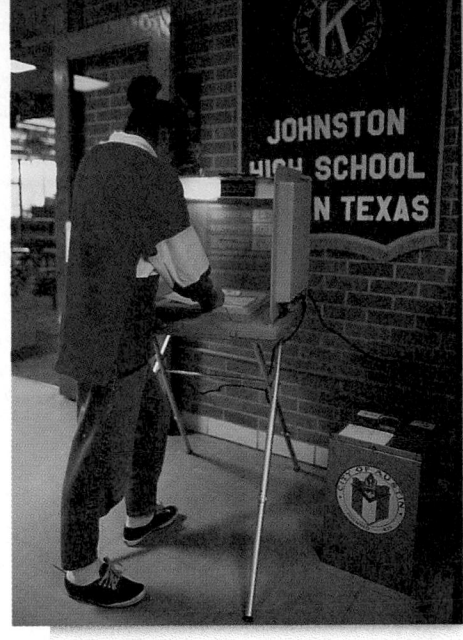

1971
EIGHTEEN-YEAR-OLD VOTE

The Twenty-sixth Amendment, ratified in 1971, granted the right to vote to citizens of the United States "eighteen years of age or older." Voting rights for young people had become an issue in the 1960s, during the Vietnam War. Many people questioned drafting 18-year-olds to fight but refusing them the right to vote. The picture at left shows a young person exercising her new right to vote.

I WISH MA COULD VOTE

1920
WOMAN SUFFRAGE

In 1920, the Nineteenth Amendment, granting voting rights to women, was finally ratified. Women's fight to gain voting and other rights had been going on ever since colonial times. Abigail Adams, in a letter in 1776, reminded her husband that in writing a new code of laws he and his colleagues should "remember the ladies." Elizabeth Cady Stanton, Susan B. Anthony, and many other women, such as those shown marching in a woman suffrage parade in 1919, worked tirelessly for women's voting rights.

Four years after ratification of the Nineteenth Amendment, in 1924, citizenship—including the right to vote—was extended to Native Americans.

INTERACT WITH HISTORY

1. **DRAWING CONCLUSIONS** What does the information on these pages demonstrate about voting rights in the United States? How did the Constitution help bring about the changes?

 SEE SKILLBUILDER HANDBOOK, PAGE 1050.

2. **ANALYZING DATA** Research voter turnout statistics from the 1800s and compare them to contemporary statistics.

   For more about voting news, click on *Social Studies* at http://www.mcdougallittell.com

The Living Constitution **167**

INSTRUCT

▶ *Starting with the Student*
- Have students research and report on the motor-voter law passed in the early 1990s.
- Ask students to find out more about voting and voting restrictions in their state. How far in advance need a person register in order to vote in the next election? Can a person register by mail? What must a person do if he or she moves within the state? What rules govern voting in party primaries?

▶ *Discussing Key Ideas*
- American voting rights gradually expand over the years.
- The Fifteenth, Nineteenth, and Twenty-sixth Amendments to the Constitution expand the vote to African-American males, women, and Americans between 18 and 21, respectively.

HISTORY FROM VISUALS
Reading the Images

Have students examine the art on these pages.

- What words do you think of when you examine each picture?
- Why do you think the women marching for suffrage held that particular sign? *Possible Responses: To appeal to men's love for or loyalty to their mothers; to stress a valuable role of women in society.*

INTERACT WITH HISTORY

1. *Drawing Conclusions*	2. *Analyzing Data*
Possible Answers: Voting rights in the United States gradually expanded over time. Various groups (women, African Americans, 18-year-olds) often had to struggle to achieve the right to vote. The initial clause concerning who could vote was expanded by constitutional amendments.	Strategies for researching voter turnout statistics can include: • Check the library for histories of presidential elections. These books often include extensive discussions of voter turnout. • Infotrak, a computer database of thousands of magazines, permits a key word search and will supply many references under "voter turnout." • The *Congressional Quarterly* weekly reports are a good source of current information. • The *Readers' Guide to Periodical Literature* is a basic source for magazine articles.

REVIEWING THE CONSTITUTION

MAIN IDEAS
Answers will vary

1. House members are elected from congressional districts and Senate members from each state. The legislature makes laws.

2. The number of representatives is based on population, while each state has two senators only.

3. Any four powers: to tax, borrow money, regulate commerce, coin money, establish post offices, create federal courts, declare war, raise armed forces, make laws.

4. Congress: to suspend *habeas corpus,* illegally punish people, levy direct taxes, levy export taxes on goods from any state, show preference among states, take money illegally from the treasury, confer titles of nobility.

   States: all powers listed in Article 1, Section 10, for example, to enter treaties on their own, coin money, illegally imprison people, lay import/export taxes, engage in war on their own.

5. To carry out the laws made by Congress.

6. The Electoral College, by vote of the states' electors.

7. If convicted upon impeachment.

8. The president nominates them; the Senate approves.

9. Those appealed from lower courts; not to hear a case means the lower court ruling stands with no further appeal.

10. It exemplifies cooperation among the states.

11. Three-fourths of the states, or 38 states.

12. To protect citizens' rights and to get the Constitution ratified.

13. No, there are limits; you cannot yell, "Fire!" in a crowded theater and incite a riot.

14. They were worried by Eisenhower's illness and Kennedy's assassination.

15. The Twenty-seventh Amendment; prevents Congress's use of taxpayers' money for members' own gain.

168   **The Living Constitution**

REVIEWING THE CONSTITUTION

MAIN IDEAS

Article 1. The Legislature

1. Why does the legislative branch of the government represent the people most directly? What is the principal job of this branch?
2. Why are there more members of the House of Representatives than of the Senate?
3. Name four powers Congress has.
4. What powers are denied to Congress? to the states?

Article 2. The Executive

5. What is the main function of the executive branch?
6. Who officially elects the president of the United States? Explain.
7. How can the president lose his or her job before election time?

Article 3. The Judiciary

8. How are Supreme Court justices appointed?
9. What kinds of cases go before the Supreme Court? Why is the Court's decision whether to hear a case important?

Article 4. Relations Among States

10. Extradition is the bringing of a criminal back into the state in which he or she committed the crime. How is this an example of relations among states?

Article 5. Amending the Constitution

11. How many states must ratify an amendment for it to become law? Why do you think it takes this many?

The Amendments

12. Why was the Bill of Rights added to the Constitution almost immediately after its ratification?
13. Does the First Amendment allow complete freedom of speech—the right to say anything you want at any time, anywhere? Explain your answer.
14. Why did Congress add an amendment that spells out exactly how presidential succession should be handled?
15. What is the newest amendment? What protection does that amendment give to the American people?

168

THINKING CRITICALLY

1. **FEDERAL POWER** How does the Constitution reflect the fear of too strong a central government?

2. **CONSTITUTIONAL POWERS** The powers of the federal government are divided among the three branches. Create a chart that shows how the Constitution Framers used checks and balances to ensure that no one branch of the government could become much stronger than the others.

Executive	Legislative	Judicial

3. **PASSAGE OF BILLS** Because of the process by which bills become laws, what problems may occur when the president and a majority of Congress are from different political parties?

4. **RIGHT OF APPEAL** Many people today object to the fact that convicted criminals "clog up the courts" with their many appeals to have new trials. What gives criminals the right to appeal? Do you think their appeals should be limited? Explain your opinion.

5. **AMENDMENTS** Why did the Framers make it so difficult to amend the Constitution? Do you agree or disagree with their philosophy? Explain.

6. **SPEEDY TRIAL** The Bill of Rights guarantees a defendant a speedy, public trial. What motivated the Framers to include this right? Do you think it is being observed today? Explain.

7. **VOTING RIGHTS** Amendments 15, 19, and 26 give voting rights to specific groups. Why was it necessary for Congress to spell out these groups' rights in amendments?

8. **ELASTICITY OF THE CONSTITUTION** Reread President Wilson's quote on page 144. Do you agree or disagree? Provide information to support your position.

THINKING CRITICALLY

1. FEDERAL POWER
Possible Responses: Students might point out that the Constitution divides powers among three branches; provides checks by each branch on the others; states in the Preamble that the people are the source of power.

2. CONSTITUTIONAL POWERS
Executive: may veto legislation; appoints Supreme Court justices and other federal judges; may grant reprieves and pardons; may call special sessions of Congress.
Legislative: makes the laws; may override presidential vetoes; may impeach and try the president, cabinet officers, and federal judges; controls money; establishes lower courts; the Senate approves treaties and presidential appointments.
Judicial: decides the meaning of laws; may declare acts of Congress or executive acts unconstitutional; free from presidential control because justices are appointed for life.

3. PASSAGE OF BILLS
President may veto bills; Congress may override veto; a stalemate could occur.

4. RIGHT OF APPEAL
Article 3, Section 2, gives the right to appeal. ***Possible Responses:*** Some students might say appeals should be limited to keep from overloading the courts. Others might say that appeals should be every person's right.

5. AMENDMENTS
They didn't want the swaying opinions of the times to prompt changes in the law of the land without a great deal of thought.
Possible Responses: Making it difficult to amend the Constitution makes sure that it doesn't get changed too often. But some may say that the process is so difficult that some good changes never get made.

9. ANALYZING PRIMARY SOURCES Read the following excerpt from The Federalist #51 by James Madison. This was one of a series of essays written to urge passage of the Constitution during the ratification process. After you read, answer the questions that follow.

> Ambition must be made to counteract ambition. The interest of the man must be connected with the constitutional rights of the place. It may be a reflection on human nature that such devices should be necessary to control the abuses of government. But what is government itself but the greatest of all reflections on human nature? If men were angels, no government would be necessary. . . . In framing a government which is to be administered by men over men, the great difficulty lies in this: You must first enable the government to control the governed; and in the next place, oblige it to control itself. A dependence on the people is, no doubt, the primary control on the government; but experience has taught mankind the necessity of auxiliary precautions.

a. Based on this passage, how do you think Madison judges human nature? Do you agree with his view? Explain your answer.

b. How does the Constitution enable the government to control the governed? How does the Constitution provide for the government to control itself?

10. INTERPRETING POLITICAL CARTOONS What do you think the cartoonist is suggesting about FDR's third term?

ALTERNATIVE ASSESSMENT

1. RESEARCHING SUPREME COURT CONTROVERSIES
The Supreme Court has often been a source of controversy. Become an expert on one controversy surrounding the Court—either a controversy related to a ruling or one related to members of the Court itself.

Present a complete explanation of the controversy to your classmates, showing both sides and the results.

 CD-ROM Use the CD-Rom *Our Times,* focusing on parts such as "The Right to Remain Silent," "Death Sentence for Jim Crow," "Scottsboro Boys," "Anita Hill Hearings," or "The Battle for Baby M." Or you may use newspaper and magazine articles to research your controversy.

- List the facts on each side of the controversy. Clarify the controversy as objectively as you can. Summarize the results. Finally, add your own opinion and reasons for it.

- Present your explanation to the class. Make sure to present the facts first, then your opinion.

2. RESEARCHING THE COSTS OF ELECTIONS
How much money was spent in the last presidential election by each candidate? How much was spent by the current senators and representatives from your state? Use magazines, newspapers, or the Internet to help you find this information. Some candidates may have home pages on the Internet. Look them up if you can. How are candidates using the Internet? Present your discoveries to the class.

3. DEBATING AN AMENDMENT
Cooperative Learning Think about controversial issues of today, such as gun control, the death penalty, and the rights of the accused. Choose a pertinent amendment to support, eliminate, or change in light of these issues. With three like-minded classmates, form a team to debate your issue against a group who disagrees. Research and plan your arguments carefully. Then hold a debate in front of your class. Allow the class to choose the winner.

4. PORTFOLIO PROJECT
 Use the Living History activity to expand your portfolio.

LIVING HISTORY

WRITING ABOUT A CONSTITUTIONAL QUESTION
Write an essay on the constitutional issue that you have researched. State your opinion about the issue and then support that opinion with reasons based on your research. Edit and polish your essay and then have a classmate read it and suggest improvements. Finally, read your essay aloud or post it on a bulletin board for others to read. Afterward, put it in your American history portfolio.

The Living Constitution **169**

THINKING CRITICALLY

6. SPEEDY TRIAL
They wanted to protect citizens from illegal imprisonment. *Possible Responses:* Some students might claim that it is observed today in principle, but that the process of honoring a defendant's rights does slow down legal procedures. Other students might point out that all the legal protections of the rights of an accused today really make it impossible for a person to have a speedy trial.

7. VOTING RIGHTS
Original voters were white, male property owners. Each group enfranchised since then fought for its rights.

8. ELASTICITY OF THE CONSTITUTION
Possible Responses: Many students will agree, citing the Supreme Court's ability to interpret and Congress's ability to amend the document. Those who disagree might say that it's too hard to change the Constitution.

9. ANALYZING PRIMARY SOURCES
a. Madison feels that humans are imperfect, will take advantage when possible, and need to be controlled. *Possible Responses:* Some students might agree that human beings are imperfect and need to be controlled, especially those who hold governing positions. Other students might suggest that human beings are imperfect and governing officials must have authority to maintain law and order.

b. The Constitution gives the federal government power over the states and citizens to make and enforce laws; it provides for the government to control itself through the system of checks and balances among the branches.

10. INTERPRETING POLITICAL CARTOONS
That Roosevelt very much wants a third term.

		TEACHING SUPPORT	**ASSESSMENT**

	Key Ideas		
SECTION 1 Washington Heads the New Government *pp. 172–176*	*George Washington is the overwhelming choice to be the first president. Washington and other national leaders successfully shape the new government.*	**In-Depth Resources: Unit 2** • Guided Reading, p. 29 • Skillbuilder Practice: Contrasting, p. 33 • American Lives: Alexander Hamilton, p. 43 **COOPERATIVE ACTIVITIES** • Debating Hamilton's and Jefferson's Views, p. 173 (TE)	***Section 1 Assessment,*** *p. 176 (PE)* ***Self-Assessment,*** *p. 176 (TE)* ***Formal Assessment*** • Section Quiz, p. 77 ***Alternative Assessment Book*** • Standards for Evaluating a Cooperative Activity
SECTION 2 Foreign Affairs Trouble the Nation *pp. 177–181*	*The young nation faces conflict with European powers outside its borders and with Native Americans within its borders.*	**In-Depth Resources: Unit 2** • Guided Reading, p. 30 **COOPERATIVE ACTIVITY** • Writing a Treaty, p. 179 (TE)	***Section 2 Assessment,*** *p. 181 (PE)* ***Self-Assessment,*** *p. 181 (TE)* ***Formal Assessment*** • Section Quiz, p. 78 ***Alternative Assessment Book*** • Standards for Evaluating a Cooperative Activity
SECTION 3 Jefferson Alters the Nation's Course *pp. 184–188*	*Thomas Jefferson is elected the third president. His administration makes the Louisiana Purchase, which more than doubles the size of the United States.*	**In-Depth Resources: Unit 2** • Guided Reading, p. 31 • Geography Application: The Louisiana Purchase, p. 34 • Primary Sources: Presidential Campaign Song, p. 36; *from* The Journal of Lewis and Clark, p. 37; Botanical Drawings, p. 38 **COOPERATIVE ACTIVITIES** • Taking Part in an Expedition, p. 187 (TE)	***Section 3 Assessment,*** *p. 188 (PE)* ***Self-Assessment,*** *p. 188 (TE)* ***Formal Assessment*** • Section Quiz, p. 79 ***Alternative Assessment Book*** • Standards for Evaluating a Cooperative Activity
SECTION 4 The War of 1812 Erupts *pp. 189–191*	*Tensions build between the United States and Great Britain, resulting in the War of 1812. The British partially burn the White House and Capitol.*	**In-Depth Resources: Unit 2** • Guided Reading, p. 32 • Primary Source: Dolley Madison's Letter to Her Sister, p. 39 • American Lives: Tecumseh, p. 44	***Section 4 Assessment,*** *p. 191 (PE)* ***Self-Assessment,*** *p. 191 (TE)* ***Formal Assessment*** • Section Quiz, p. 80
CHAPTER RESOURCES	**Chapter Overview** *As the new government takes hold, the United States sees the growth of political parties. A land purchase doubles the nation's size and another war with Britain confirms American independence.*	**In-Depth Resources: Unit 2** • Living History Project: Worksheet, p. 45 • Living History Project: Standards, p. 46 ***Telescoping the Times*** • Chapter Summary, pp. 11–12 ***Planning for Block Schedules***	***Chapter Assessment,*** *pp. 194–195 (PE)* ***Alternative Assessment,*** *p. 195 (PE)* ***Formal Assessment*** • Chapter Test, forms A and B, pp. 81–86 **Test Generator** ***Alternative Assessment Book*** See explanation and forms for different kinds of alternative assessments including portfolio assessment.

Humanities Transparencies
• H7, "The Republican Court"

 Grolier Multimedia Encyclopedia
• Thomas Jefferson, Alexander Hamilton

Electronic Library of Primary Sources
• "Proclamation Regarding the Whiskey Rebellion" by George Washington

INTERNET RESOURCES
• See McDougal Littell Learning On-Line for links to information about George Washington and Thomas Jefferson

 Grolier Multimedia Encyclopedia
• Second Amendment

Electronic Library of Primary Sources
• *from* the Inaugural Address of 1797 by John Adams

INTERNET RESOURCES
• See McDougal Littell Learning On-Line for links to information about Gouverneur Morris and John Adams

 AMERICAN STORIES VIDEO SERIES
• "Recruited by Lewis and Clark"

 Geography Transparencies
• G6, The Wilderness Road

 Electronic Library of Primary Sources
• *from* the Louisiana Purchase
• *from* A Letter of Instruction to Meriwether Lewis by Thomas Jefferson

INTERNET RESOURCES
• See McDougal Littell Learning On-Line for links to information about Lewis and Clark and Aaron Burr

 Critical Thinking Transparencies
• CT6, The War of 1812

INTERNET RESOURCES
• See McDougal Littell Learning On-Line for links to information about Tecumseh, Andrew Jackson, and William Henry Harrison

 American Portfolio: A Videodisc for U.S. History, user's guide, pp. 40–45, 50

INTERNET RESOURCES:
Learning On-Line: Social Studies
http://www.mcdougallittell.com

Block Scheduling (90 MINUTES)

Day 1
Section 1, pp. 172–176
Section 2, pp. 177–181
Section Assessments pp. 176, 181

 AMERICAN STORIES VIDEO SERIES
• "Recruited by Lewis and Clark"

Day 2
Section 3, pp. 184–188
Section 4, pp. 189–191
Section Assessments, pp. 188, 191
Chapter Assessment, pp. 194–195

YEARLY PACING *Chapter 6 Total:* 2 days *Yearly Total:* 85 days

See *Planning for Block Schedules* for special activities and pacing strategies.

Customizing for Special Populations

Students Acquiring English

Access for Students Acquiring English
• Guided Reading for Sections 1–4 (Spanish), pp. 63–66
• Chapter Summary (Spanish), pp. 61–62
• Skillbuilder Practice: Contrasting (Spanish) p. 67
• Geography Application: The Louisiana Purchase (Spanish), p. 68–69

 AMERICAN STORIES VIDEO SERIES
• "Recruited by Lewis and Clark" (Spanish track)

INTERNET RESOURCES
• See *McDougal Littell Learning On-Line* The Diverse Classroom.

Less Proficient Readers

In-Depth Resources: Unit 2
• Guided Reading for Sections 1–4, pp. 29–32
• Skillbuilder: Contrasting, p. 33
• Geography Application: The Louisiana Purchase, p. 34

Telescoping the Times
• Chapter Summary, pp. 11–12

See additional strategies at point of use in the Teacher's Edition.

Gifted and Talented Students

In-Depth Resources: Unit 2
• Primary Sources: Presidential Campaign Song, p. 36; *from* The Journal of Lewis and Clark, p. 37; Botanical Drawings, p. 38; Dolly Madison's Letter to Her Sister, p. 39
• American Lives: Alexander Hamilton, p. 43; Tecumseh, p. 44

See additional strategies at point of use in the Teacher's Edition.

Connections to Literature READINGS FOR STUDENTS

In-Depth Resources: Unit 2
• from *Burr* by Gore Vidal, p. 40

Enrichment Reading
• O'Dell, Scott.
Streams to the River, River to the Sea.
Boston: Houghton Mifflin, 1986
Sacajawea, the Native American woman who accompanied Lewis and Clark as an interpreter and guide, narrates this lively fictional account of their journey.
• Thom, James Alexander
From Sea to Shining Sea
New York: Ballantine Books, 1984
America's westward expansion is the focus of this powerful novel. The story concerns the American revolution, a journey west through untamed wilderness, the Lewis and Clark expedition, and the excitement of building a nation from sea to shining sea.

• Nevin, David
1812: A Novel.
New York: Forge, 1996.
This well-researched novel brings to life the people and battles of the early 1800s.

Launching the New Nation

▶ **Starting with the Student**
Ask students what they already know about the nation's early years. Who were the first U.S. presidents? What challenges did they face?

PREVIEWING THE CHAPTER

- Review with students the section titles and summaries. Note the video in Section 3.
- Ask students to think about why the first few decades of a country's history might be important in shaping its future.
- Have students, in small groups, create a list of issues they think a new government would need to address. Students should then read the chapter to determine if and how the items on their lists are handled.

MORE ABOUT . . .
Benjamin Franklin

In a letter to Franklin written in 1789, George Washington summarized the statesman's many qualities: "If to be venerated for benevolence [generosity], if to be admired for talents, if to be esteemed for patriotism, if to be beloved for philanthropy [charity], can gratify the human mind, you must have the pleasing consolation to know that you have not lived in vain."

CHAPTER
6

Launching the New Nation

SECTION 1
Washington Heads the New Government

George Washington is the overwhelming choice to be the first president. Washington and other national leaders successfully shape the new government.

SECTION 2
Foreign Affairs Trouble the Nation

The young nation faces conflict with European powers outside its borders and with Native Americans within its borders.

SECTION 3
Jefferson Alters the Nation's Course

Thomas Jefferson is elected the third president. His administration makes the Louisiana Purchase, which more than doubles the size of the United States.

 VIDEO *Recruited by Lewis and Clark*

SECTION 4
The War of 1812 Erupts

Tensions build between the United States and Great Britain, resulting in the War of 1812. The British partially burn the White House and Capitol.

"Our constitution is in actual operation; everything appears to promise that it will last; but in this world nothing is certain but death and taxes."

Benjamin Franklin

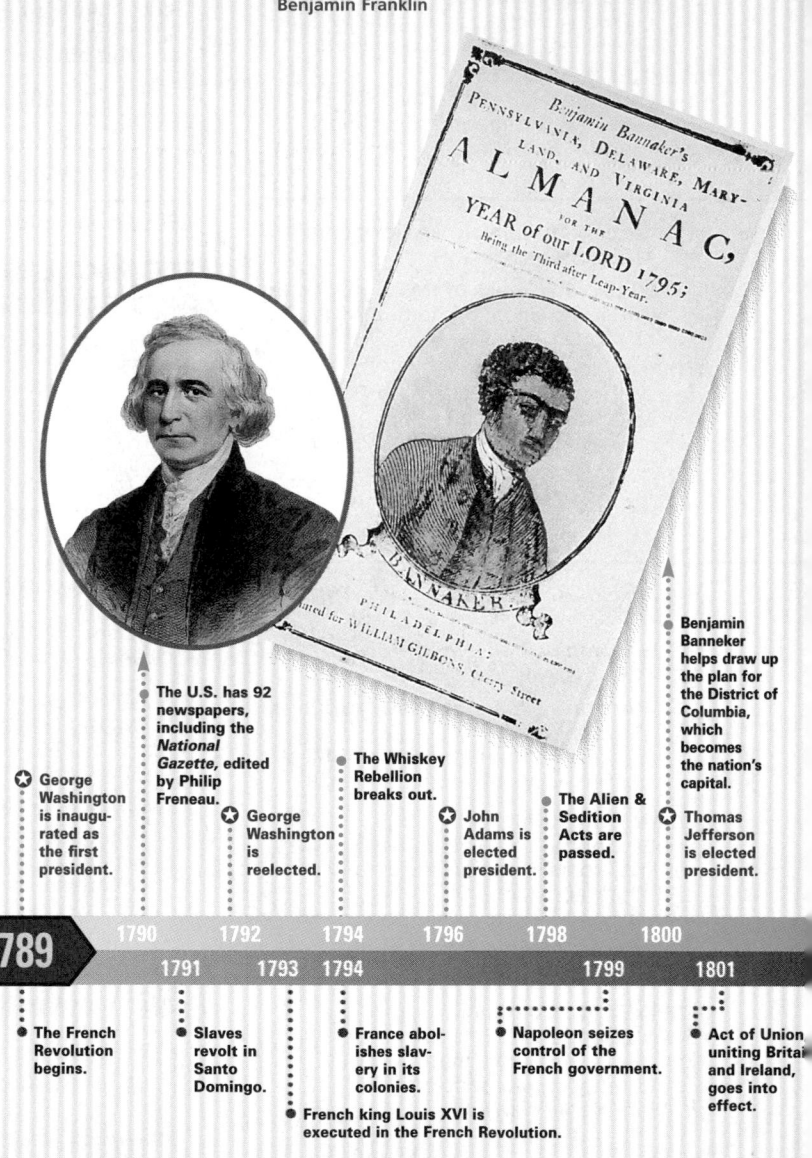

- ✪ **George Washington** is inaugurated as the first president.
- The U.S. has 92 newspapers, including the *National Gazette*, edited by Philip Freneau.
- ✪ **George Washington** is reelected.
- The Whiskey Rebellion breaks out.
- ✪ **John Adams** is elected president.
- The Alien & Sedition Acts are passed.
- Benjamin Banneker helps draw up the plan for the District of Columbia, which becomes the nation's capital.
- ✪ **Thomas Jefferson** is elected president.

THE UNITED STATES
THE WORLD

1789 1790 1792 1794 1796 1798 1800
1791 1793 1794 1799 1801

- The French Revolution begins.
- Slaves revolt in Santo Domingo.
- France abolishes slavery in its colonies.
- French king Louis XVI is executed in the French Revolution.
- Napoleon seizes control of the French government.
- Act of Union uniting Britain and Ireland, goes into effect.

THEMES IN CHAPTER 6

Economic Opportunity

In the 1700s and early 1800s, the U.S. economy was largely based on agricultural products. The government used these products to begin developing a profitable trade with Europe.

See Teacher's Edition note, p. 174.

Immigration and Migration

Soon after the new government was launched, the United States began extending its borders. Many courageous people were willing to brave hardships and dangers to pioneer the country's westward expansion.

See Teacher's Edition note, p. 178.

Constitutional Concerns

The new government's leaders often differed in their interpretation of the Constitution. *Marbury* v. *Madison* affirmed the Supreme Court's right to review Congressional acts and practices and to declare them unconstitutional.

Another Constitutional Concern involves war powers.

Although the president dominates foreign policy, only Congress has the power to declare war. President Madison needed Congress to declare war and to appropriate the money to fight it.

See Teacher's Edition notes, pp. 186 and 190.

PREPARING A TELEVISION NEWS BROADCAST

The Lewis and Clark expedition explored much of the North American continent that had been acquired by the United States in the Louisiana Purchase. The expedition provided useful information about the West—its topography and animal life, as well as about the Native Americans who lived in the territory explored by the expedition.

As you read about the Louisiana Purchase and the Lewis and Clark expedition, compile a list of information that you can use to write a script for a television news broadcast about the expedition. Make a list of what visual images you will use to illustrate your report.

📁 **PORTFOLIO PROJECT** Keep your lists in a folder for your American history portfolio. At the end of the chapter, you will use your lists to create a television news broadcast about the expedition.

- The Lewis and Clark expedition begins.
- Aaron Burr kills Alexander Hamilton in a duel.
- The War of 1812 includes many sea battles between the fleets of Britain and the United States.
- The Battle of New Orleans is fought.
- France and the U.S. agree to the Louisiana Purchase.
- ✪ Thomas Jefferson is reelected.
- ✪ James Madison is elected president.
- ✪ James Madison is reelected.
- The Treaty of Ghent ends the War of 1812.
- ✪ James Monroe is elected president.

1803 | 1804 | 1808 | 1812 | 1814 | 1815 | **1816**
1804 | 1806 1807 | 1810 | | 1815

- Haiti declares independence from France.
- Britain outlaws the slave trade.
- The Mexican War of Independence begins.
- Napoleon is defeated at Waterloo.
- The British occupy the Cape of Good Hope in South Africa.

Launching the New Nation **171**

PREPARING A TELEVISION NEWS BROADCAST

Discuss methods for creating a television report:

- Ask students to think about television reports they have seen on shows such as *60 Minutes, 48 Hours,* and *Nightline.*
- Discuss the elements of a successful television news report, such as vivid images, clear and concise commentary, and personal points of view.
- Ask students to consider how they might use quotations and primary documents in their reports. See especially the primary sources for this chapter in the **In-Depth Resources: Unit 2.**
- Suggest that students use a chart like the one below to organize their ideas.

News Report Ideas	
Script Information	Ideas for Images

IN-DEPTH RESOURCES: UNIT 2
See worksheet and standards for evaluation, pp. 45, 46.

RECOMMENDED RESOURCES

Books for the Teacher

Sugden, John. *Tecumseh's Last Stand.* Norman: U of Oklahoma P, 1985. Readable story.

Taylor, Alan. *William Cooper's Town.* New York: Knopf, 1995. Life on the frontier in Cooperstown, New York.

Books for the Student

Ambrose, Stephen E. *Undaunted Courage.* New York: Simon, 1996.

Life of Meriwether Lewis, with full account of trip.

Koch, Adrienne, and William Peden, eds. *The Life and Selected Writings of Thomas Jefferson.* New York: Random, 1993. Includes some of his political thinking.

Videos

The Building of the Capitol. Republic Pictures Home Video,

800-826-2295. Creating Washington, D.C.

Chalmette. National Audiovisual Center, 301-703-1858. Story of Battle of New Orleans.

George Washington: The Man Who Wouldn't Be King. PBS Home Video, 800-424-7963.

Views of a Vanishing Frontier. PBS Home Video, 800-424-7963. Documentary about expedition following route of Lewis and Clark.

Software

The French Revolution (World History Series). CD-ROM. Educational Software Institute, 800-955-5570.

Lewis & Clark: American Journals. Diskette. Educational Software Institute, 800-955-5570.

OBJECTIVES

1. To explain how the United States confronted the difficult task of forming a new government.

2. To show how the political ideas of Hamilton and Jefferson differed.

3. To describe how political differences evolved into a two-party system.

SKILLBUILDER

• Interpreting charts, p. 174

CRITICAL THINKING

• Drawing conclusions, p. 173
• Analyzing issues, pp. 174, 176
• Contrasting, pp. 174, 175
• Summarizing, p. 176
• Evaluating, p. 176
• Analyzing, p. 176

FOCUS & MOTIVATE

▶ **Starting with the Student**
• Ask students what the structure is of their school's student government.
• Ask them how it represents the views and concerns of all students.

OBJECTIVE

① **INSTRUCT**

The New Government Takes Shape

▶ **Discussing Key Ideas**
• The Judiciary Act of 1789 establishes the details of a federal court system.
• Washington chooses trusted leaders to advise him on foreign affairs, military matters, and finances.

IN-DEPTH RESOURCES: UNIT 2
Guided Reading, p. 29

ACCESS FOR STUDENTS ACQUIRING ENGLISH
Guided Reading (Spanish), p. 63

172 Chapter 6

---

① **Washington Heads the New Government**

TERMS & NAMES
• Judiciary Act of 1789
• Alexander Hamilton
• cabinet
• national bank
• Republican
• two-party system
• protective tariff
• excise tax

LEARN ABOUT the first steps taken by the Washington administration
TO UNDERSTAND how key decisions set precedents for the nation's future.

ONE AMERICAN'S STORY

George Washington had no desire to be president after the Constitutional Convention. His dream was to settle down to a quiet life at his Virginia estate, Mount Vernon. The American people had other ideas, though. They wanted a strong national leader of great authority as their first president. As the hero of the Revolution, Washington was the unanimous choice in the first presidential ballot. When the news reached him on April 16, 1789, Washington reluctantly accepted the call to duty. Two days later he set out for New York City to take the oath of office.

George
Washington

A PERSONAL VOICE

About ten o'clock I bade adieu [farewell] to Mount Vernon, to private life, and to domestic felicity [happiness]; and with a mind oppressed with more anxious and painful sensations than I have words to express, set out for New York . . . with the best dispositions [intentions] to render service to my country in obedience to its call, but with less hope of answering its expectations.

GEORGE WASHINGTON, *The Diaries of George Washington*

When Washington took office as the first president of the United States under the Constitution, he and Congress faced a daunting task—to create an entirely new government. The momentous decisions that these early leaders made have resounded through American history.

The New Government Takes Shape

"We are in a wilderness without a single footstep to guide us."

JAMES MADISON

Washington took charge of a political system that was a bold experiment. Never before had a nation tried to base a government on the ideals of republican rule and individual rights, ideals that stemmed from the theories of Enlightenment thinkers such as the English philosopher John Locke. These ideals were noble—but no one knew if a government based on the will of the people could really work.

Although the Constitution provided a strong foundation, it was not a detailed blueprint for governing. To create a working government, Washington and Congress had to make many practical decisions—such as how to raise revenues and provide for defense—with no precedent, or prior example, for American leaders to follow. Perhaps James Madison put it best: "We are in a wilderness without a single footstep to guide us."

JUDICIARY ACT OF 1789 One of the first tasks Washington and Congress tackled was the creation of a judicial system. The Constitution had authorized Congress to set up a federal court system, headed by a Supreme Court, but it failed to spell out the details. How many additional courts should there be? What would happen if federal court decisions conflicted with state laws?

The **Judiciary Act of 1789** answered these critical questions, creating a judicial structure that has remained essentially intact. This law provided for a Supreme Court consisting of a Chief Justice and five associate justices. It also set up three federal circuit courts and thirteen federal district courts throughout the country. (The numbers of justices and courts increased over time.) Section 25 of

172 CHAPTER 6

SECTION 1 RESOURCES

 PRINT RESOURCES

IN-DEPTH RESOURCES: UNIT 2
Guided Reading, p. 29
Skillbuilder Practice: Contrasting, p. 33
American Lives: Alexander Hamilton, p. 43

ACCESS FOR STUDENTS ACQUIRING ENGLISH
Guided Reading (Spanish), p. 63
Skillbuilder Practice: Contrasting (Spanish), p. 67

FORMAL ASSESSMENT
Section Quiz, p. 77

ALTERNATIVE ASSESSMENT BOOK
See forms for supporting and scoring alternative activities.

TECHNOLOGY RESOURCES

HUMANITIES TRANSPARENCIES
H7, "The Republican Court"

CD-ROM *Grolier Multimedia Encyclopedia*
Electronic Library of Primary Sources

VIDEO *American Portfolio: A Videodisc for U.S. History*
user's guide, p. 40

INTERNET McDougal Littell Learning On-Line
http://www.mcdougallittell.com

THINK THROUGH HISTORY
A. Drawing Conclusions
Why did federal law have to be "the supreme Law of the Land" in the new nation?
A. Answer If states could pass laws that contradicted federal law, the authority of the federal government might be undermined and jeopardize the stability of the Union.

the Judiciary Act, one of the most important provisions of the law, allowed state court decisions to be appealed to a federal court when constitutional issues were raised. This section guaranteed that federal laws remained "the supreme Law of the Land," as stated in Article 6 of the Constitution.

WASHINGTON SHAPES EXECUTIVE BRANCH At the same time that Congress shaped the judiciary, Washington faced the task of building an executive branch to help him make policies and carry out the laws passed by Congress. In 1789, when Washington took office, the executive branch of government consisted of only two officials, the president and the vice-president. To help these leaders govern, Congress created three executive departments: the Department of State, to deal with foreign affairs; the Department of War, to handle military matters; and the Department of the Treasury, to manage finances.

To head these departments, Washington chose capable leaders he knew and trusted. He picked Thomas Jefferson as secretary of state, **Alexander Hamilton** as secretary of the treasury, and Henry Knox, who had served as Washington's general of artillery during the Revolution, as secretary of war. Finally, he chose Edmund Randolph as attorney general, the chief lawyer of the federal government. These department heads soon became the president's chief advisers, or **cabinet**. Over time, meetings between the president and his cabinet became a regular feature of the executive branch.

KEY PLAYERS

ALEXANDER HAMILTON
1755–1804

Born into poverty in the British West Indies, Alexander Hamilton was orphaned at age 11 and went to work as a shipping clerk. He later made his way to New York, where he attended King's College (now Columbia University). He joined the army during the Revolution and became an aide to General Washington. Intensely ambitious, Hamilton quickly moved up in society. Although in his humble origins Hamilton was the opposite of Jefferson, he had little faith in the common citizen and sided with the interests of upper-class Americans. Hamilton said of Jefferson's beloved common people: "Your people, sir, is a great beast!"

THOMAS JEFFERSON
1743–1826

The writer of the Declaration of Independence, Thomas Jefferson began his political career at age 26, when he was elected to Virginia's colonial legislature. In 1779, he was elected governor of Virginia, and in 1785 he was appointed minister to France. He served as secretary of state from 1789 to 1793. A Southern planter, Jefferson was also an accomplished scholar, the architect of Monticello (his Virginia house), an inventor (of, among other things, a machine that made copies of letters), and the founder of the University of Virginia in 1819. Despite his elite background and his ownership of slaves, he was a strong ally of the small farmer and average citizen.

Hamilton and Jefferson Debate

Washington appointed both Hamilton and Jefferson to executive posts not only because they were brilliant thinkers, but also because they had very different political ideas. By having both men in his cabinet, Washington ensured a range of opinion in his administration. However, the differences between the two also caused bitter disagreements, many of which centered on Hamilton's plan for the economy.

HAMILTON AND JEFFERSON IN CONFLICT Political divisions in the new nation were great. No two men embodied these differences more than Hamilton and Jefferson. Hamilton believed in a strong central government led by a prosperous, educated elite of upper-class citizens. Jefferson distrusted a strong central government and the rich. He favored strong state and local governments rooted in popular participation. Hamilton believed that commerce and industry were the keys to a strong nation. Jefferson favored a society of farmer-citizens.

Launching the New Nation **173**

KEY PLAYERS
Jefferson and Hamilton
Critical Thinking:
Compare and Contrast
Ask students to create a chart comparing the lives of Jefferson and Hamilton. *Possible Headings: Family, Early Life, Beliefs, Political Career.*

IN-DEPTH RESOURCES: UNIT 2
American Lives: Alexander Hamilton p. 43

GROLIER MULTIMEDIA ENCYCLOPEDIA
Thomas Jefferson, Alexander Hamilton

MORE ABOUT . . .
Washington's Appointments
Washington found that it wasn't so simple to fill the Cabinet and make other appointments. Friends and relatives both felt they had a claim to the positions —his nephew even asking for the post of federal district attorney for Virginia. The president turned him down, however, for he was determined to appoint only the best and most experienced men he could find.

OBJECTIVE
② **INSTRUCT**

Hamilton and Jefferson Debate

▶ *Discussing Key Ideas*
• Hamilton and Jefferson disagree on the role of government and on economic issues.
• Hamilton proposes creating a national bank.
• In order to gain favor from Southerners for his ideas, Hamilton suggests that the capital be moved to the District of Columbia.

Cooperative Activity: Debating Hamilton's and Jefferson's Views

Task: Student groups will debate the role of the federal government from Hamilton's and Jefferson's perspectives.

Purpose: To help students understand a fundamental disagreement about government that still divides people today.

Activity: Divide groups of eight to ten students into two teams. Have one team debate in support of Hamilton's views, such as the need for a strong national government, a loose interpretation of the Constitution, and an economy based on shipping and manufacturing. Have the other team debate in support of Jefferson's views, such as the need for a limited

national government, a strict interpretation of the Constitution, and an economy based on farming. Students should focus on issues contemporary to Hamilton and Jefferson, such as methods of repayment of war debt, the institution of a national bank, and whether power should rest with the states or at the national level. Within the groups, each student should research one part of the argument, then collaborate with the others to prepare for the debate.

ALTERNATIVE ASSESSMENT BOOK
Standards for Evaluating a Cooperative Activity

Contrasting Views of the Federal Government

Reading the Chart Point out to students that viewpoints are paired horizontally in the chart. You might also encourage students to explain what is meant by a "loose" and a "strict" interpretation of the Constitution.

Extension Ask students to identify modern issues that divide Americans due to the differences between "loose" and "strict" interpretations of the Constitution. *Possible Responses: The controversies over gun control and the right to bear arms, or over freedom of speech and book banning.*

HAMILTON	JEFFERSON
• Concentrating power in federal government	• Sharing power with state and local governments
• Fear of mob rule	• Fear of absolute power or ruler
• Strong national government	• Limited national government
• Republic of a wise elite	• Democracy of virtuous farmers and tradespeople
• Loose interpretation of the Constitution	• Strict interpretation of the Constitution
• National bank constitutional (loose interpretation)	• National bank unconstitutional (strict interpretation)
• Economy based on shipping and manufacturing	• Economy based on farming
• Payment of national and state debts (favoring creditors)	• Payment of only the national debt (favoring debtors)
• Supporters: merchants, manufacturers, landowners, investors, lawyers, clergy	• Supporters: the "plain people" (farmers, tradespeople)

SKILLBUILDER INTERPRETING CHARTS *Whose view of the federal government was a wealthy person more likely to favor? Why? How do you think Jefferson differed from Hamilton in his view of people and human nature?*

Skillbuilder Answer
Wealthy: Hamilton's. Because Hamilton's view favored a national bank, shipping and manufacturing, and payment of debts. **Human nature:** *Possible answers:* Jefferson had greater faith in people's ability to govern themselves. His view reflected a more positive view of human nature.

MORE ABOUT . . .
The National Debt

Hamilton's decision to have the federal government assume state debts incurred during the Revolution created a national debt that has never been fully paid off. Throughout American history, wars have been largely responsible for increasing the debt. Before World War I (1914–1918), for example, the national debt was only about $1 billion. After the war, the debt rose to about $25 billion. Other wars before the 1980s each raised the debt sharply; however, by 1980 other factors played a larger role in increasing the debt. By 1991, the national debt was about $3.6 trillion.

Overall, Hamilton's vision of America was that of a country much like Great Britain, with a strong central government, commerce, and industry. In general, Hamilton's views found more support in the North, particularly New England, whereas Jefferson's views won endorsement in the South and the West.

HAMILTON'S ECONOMIC PLAN As secretary of the treasury, Hamilton's job was to set in order the nation's finances and to put the nation's economy on a firm footing. To do this, he proposed a plan to manage the country's debts and a plan to establish a national banking system.

The public debt of the United States in 1790 (most of it incurred during the Revolution) was many millions of dollars, according to Hamilton's calculations in his *Report on Public Credit*. The national government was responsible for about two-thirds of this debt, and individual states were responsible for the rest. The new nation owed some of the debt to foreign governments and some to private citizens, including soldiers who had received bonds—certificates that promised payment plus interest—for their service during the war.

Hamilton proposed to pay off the foreign debt and to issue new bonds to cover the old ones. He also proposed that the federal government assume the debts of the states, a suggestion that made many people in the South furious because some Southern states had already paid off most of their debts. Southerners resented assumption of state debts because they thought that they would be taxed to help pay the debts incurred by the Northern states. Although this would increase the federal debt, Hamilton reasoned that assuming state debts would give creditors—the people who originally loaned the money—an incentive to support the new federal government. If the government failed, these creditors would never get their money back.

PLAN FOR A NATIONAL BANK This line of reasoning also motivated Hamilton's proposal for a **national bank** that would be funded by both the federal government and wealthy private investors. This bank would issue paper money and handle tax receipts and other government funds. By drawing wealthy investors into the venture, Hamilton hoped to tie them to the country's welfare.

Hamilton's proposals aroused a storm of controversy. Opponents of a national bank, including James Madison, claimed that the bank would forge an unhealthy alliance between the government and wealthy business interests. Madison also argued that since the Constitution made no provision for a national bank, Congress had no right to authorize it. This argument began the debate between those who favored a loose (or broad) interpretation of the

THINK THROUGH HISTORY
B. Contrasting How did Jefferson's and Hamilton's views of government differ?
B. Answer Jefferson emphasized the rights of states and average citizens. Hamilton emphasized the rights of the national government and ruling elite.

THINK THROUGH HISTORY
C. Analyzing Issues Why did the new nation need to pay off its debts?
C. Answer Demonstrating that the new government was financially responsible would make it more credible in the eyes of creditors, including foreign governments, and bolster the government's reputation.

174 CHAPTER 6

Exploring Themes

Economic Opportunity Discuss how the U.S. economy has changed over the past 200 years. Early on, the U.S. economy relied on agriculture, a system favored by Jefferson. After the Industrial Revolution in the 1800s, the economy relied more on manufacturing, a system favored by Hamilton.

Ask students how Jefferson and Hamilton might view the state of the economy today. *Possible Responses: Jefferson would be saddened by the decline of family-owned farms and of working-class wages. Hamilton would approve of the growth of industry but be shocked at the huge national debt.*

Teaching Less Proficient Readers

Activating Prior Knowledge Before students begin reading pages 174 and 175, initiate a brief discussion about debts and banks. Ask the following questions:

• What institution can people turn to when they don't have enough money to pay for something?
• How do banks make a profit?
• What happens when people have trouble paying off their debts to a bank?

Have students keep the answers to these questions in mind as they read about Hamilton's economic plans.

Constitution and those who favored a strict (or narrow) interpretation, a vital debate that has continued throughout U.S. history. In the end, however, Hamilton convinced Washington and a majority in Congress to accept his views, and the federal government established the Bank of the United States.

THE DISTRICT OF COLUMBIA To win support for his debt plan from Southern states, Hamilton offered a suggestion: What if the nation's capital were moved from New York City to a new city in the South, on the banks of the Potomac River? The South had always been concerned about domination by the more urban North, so this idea pleased Southerners, particularly Virginians such as Madison and Jefferson, who believed that a Southern site for the capital would make the government more responsive to their interests. With this incentive, Virginians agreed to back the debt plan. In 1790, the debt bill passed Congress, along with authorization for the construction of a new national capital in the District of Columbia.

Pierre L'Enfant, a French engineer, drew up plans for the new capital. L'Enfant was later fired by George Washington for being obstinate. He was replaced by Andrew Ellicott, who redrew L'Enfant's plan, but kept much of the grand vision. An African-American surveyor, Benjamin Banneker, assisted Ellicott with the surveying work. They made their plan on a grand scale, incorporating boulevards, traffic circles, and monuments reminiscent of European capitals. (See American Studies on page 192.) By 1800, the capital had been moved to its new site on the Potomac, between Maryland and Virginia.

The First Political Parties

President Washington tried to remain above the arguments between Hamilton and Jefferson and to encourage them to work together despite their basic differences. These differences were so great however, that the two men continued to clash over government policy; their conflict divided the cabinet and fueled the growing division in national politics.

FEDERALISTS AND REPUBLICANS The split in Washington's cabinet helped give rise to the country's first political parties. The two parties formed around one of the key issues in American history—the power and size of the federal government in relation to state and local governments. Those who shared Hamilton's vision of a strong central government called themselves Federalists. Those who supported Jefferson's vision of strong state governments called themselves **Republicans.** No relation to today's Republican Party, Jefferson's Republicans—later called Democratic Republicans—were in fact the ancestors of today's Democratic Party. Republicans believed in a limited central government, an agrarian economy, strong state governments, and a democratic system based on broader popular participation.

These parties originated as political clubs or groups, which met to discuss issues and spread their opinions. For the 1792 election, the Republicans did not field a candidate to oppose Washington, whose own views clearly leaned toward the Federalist side. However, the very existence of political parties worried many leaders, including Washington, who saw

D. Answer
Federalists believed in a strong central government, while Republicans believed in a limited central government.

THINK THROUGH HISTORY
D. Contrasting
How did the Federalists and Republicans differ from each other?

NOW & THEN

WASHINGTON, D.C.
There is a movement today to make the District of Columbia a state. A majority of voters in Washington, D.C., have supported statehood. A constitutional convention met and drew up a state constitution, which was approved by the District's voters. Washington's voters have also approved a new state name—*New Columbia.* The proposed constitution has been sent to the U.S. Congress but no vote on the issue has yet been taken.

In the past, residents of the District had only limited rights to participate in government. In 1973 an act of Congress established the District's present system of local government. This includes a mayor and city council elected by the people. The federal government, however, has final authority in all governmental matters in the District.

President Washington *(right)* meets with his first cabinet *(from left to right)* Henry Knox, secretary of war; Thomas Jefferson, secretary of state; Edmund Randolph *(with back turned)*, attorney general; and Alexander Hamilton, secretary of treasury.

Launching the New Nation **175**

---

parties as a danger to national unity. At the close of his presidency, Washington criticized what he called "the spirit of party."

A PERSONAL VOICE
It serves always to distract the public councils and enfeeble the public administration. It agitates the community with ill-founded jealousies and false alarms; kindles the animosity of one part against another; foments [incites] occasionally riot and insurrection. It opens the door to foreign influence and corruption....

GEORGE WASHINGTON, *Farewell Address, 1796*

Despite criticism, the two parties had continued to develop. The **two-party system**—initially Federalists and Republicans—was well established by the time Washington left office.

THE WHISKEY REBELLION During Washington's second term, an incident occurred that reflected the tension between federal and regional interests. Previously, Congress had passed a **protective tariff,** an import tax on goods produced in Europe. This tax brought in a great deal of revenue, but Secretary Hamilton wanted more. So he pushed through an **excise tax** (sales tax) to be levied on whiskey.

Most whiskey producers were small frontier farmers. Their major crop was corn. Corn was too bulky to carry across the Appalachian Mountains and sell in the settled areas along the Atlantic. Therefore, the farmers distilled the corn into whiskey, which could be more easily sent to market on the backs of mules.

Since whiskey was the main source of cash for these frontier farmers, Hamilton knew that the excise tax would make them furious. So it did. In 1794, farmers in western Pennsylvania refused to pay the tax. They beat up federal marshals in Pittsburgh, and they even threatened to secede from the Union.

Hamilton looked upon the Whiskey Rebellion as an opportunity for the federal government to show that it could enforce the law along the Western frontier. Accordingly, some 15,000 militiamen were called up. Accompanied by Washington part of the way and by Hamilton all the way, the federal troops hiked over the Alleghenies and scattered the rebels without the loss of a single life.

A group of rebels in the Whiskey Rebellion tar and feather a tax collector.

The Whiskey Rebellion was a milestone in the consolidation of federal power in domestic affairs. At the same time, the new government was also facing critical problems and challenges in foreign affairs—particularly in its relations with Europe and with Native American peoples west of the Appalachians.

E. Answer In the Whiskey Rebellion, the national government showed that it was capable of acting in a unified and effective way without help from the states, a lesson that would come in handy in dealing with foreign powers.

THINK THROUGH HISTORY
E. Analyzing Issues Why was the Whiskey Rebellion important for the federal government?

Section 1 Assessment

1. TERMS & NAMES
Identify:
• Judiciary Act of 1789
• Alexander Hamilton
• cabinet
• national bank
• Republican
• two-party system
• protective tariff
• excise tax

2. SUMMARIZING In a chart, list the leaders, beliefs, and goals of the country's first political parties.

Federalists	Republicans

If you had lived in that time, which party would you have favored?

3. EVALUATING How would you judge President Washington's decision to put two such opposed thinkers as Hamilton and Jefferson in his cabinet?

THINK ABOUT
• both men's merits
• their philosophies
• the conflicts that developed

4. ANALYZING Would you have supported Hamilton's economic plan? Explain why or why not.

THINK ABOUT
• the money problems the nation faced
• other problems the nation faced

176 Chapter 6

ANSWERS

TERMS & NAMES
• neutrality
• Edmond Genêt
• Thomas Pinckney
• Little Turtle
• John Jay
• sectionalism
• XYZ Affair
• Alien and Sedition Acts
• nullification

② Foreign Affairs Trouble the Nation

LEARN ABOUT key international issues in the late 18th century
TO UNDERSTAND how the United States developed its foreign policy.

Section 2 Overview

OBJECTIVES

① To summarize developing foreign policy with France, Great Britain, and Spain.

② To explain how the United States dealt with Native Americans and with British interests west of the Appalachians.

③ To identify some of the deep divisions between Federalists and Republicans.

SKILLBUILDERS

• Understanding geography: location, human-environment interaction, p. 179
• Interpreting charts, p. 181

CRITICAL THINKING

• Analyzing motives, p. 178
• Recognizing effects, p. 178, 180
• Summarizing, p. 181
• Hypothesizing, p. 181
• Evaluating, p. 181
• Analyzing, p. 181

ONE AMERICAN'S STORY

Gouverneur Morris, the man responsible for the final draft of the Constitution, witnessed one of the great events of history—the French Revolution. He arrived in Paris in early 1789. On July 14, a mob stormed the Bastille, the infamous French prison, releasing the prisoners and killing the prison governor. Not long afterward, Morris got a close look at revolutionary violence. Walking on a Paris street, he came upon a mob parading the dismembered body of a royal official:

A PERSONAL VOICE

The Head and Body of Mr. de Foulon are introduced in Triumph. The Head on a Pike, the Body dragged naked on the Earth. Afterwards this horrible Exhibition is carried thro the different Streets. His crime [was] to have accepted a Place in the Ministry. This mutilated form of an old Man of seventy five is shewn to Bertier, his Son in Law, the Intend't. [another official] of Paris, and afterwards he also is put to Death and cut to Pieces, the Populace carrying about the mangled Fragments with a Savage Joy.

GOUVERNEUR MORRIS, quoted from his journal

At first Morris sympathized with the French revolutionaries and their calls for "liberty, equality, fraternity." Then, as the violence escalated, Morris turned against the French Revolution. The young nation, too, took different views of the events underway in France as it debated whether or not to support the French Revolution.

French revolutionaries storm the Bastille in Paris, France, on July 14, 1789.

U.S. Response to Events in Europe

Most Americans initially supported the French Revolution because, like the American Revolution, it was inspired by the ideal of republican rule. Heartened by the American struggle against royal tyranny, the French set out to create a government based on the will of the people. The alliance between France and the United States, created by the Treaty of 1778, served as an additional bond between the two nations. The official attitude of the United States toward the French Revolution was one of the most important foreign policy questions that the young nation faced.

REACTIONS TO FRENCH REVOLUTION Despite the bonds between the nations, Americans soon became divided over the Revolution. In early 1793, a radical group called the Jacobins seized power in France. They beheaded the French king, Louis XVI, and launched the Reign of Terror against their opponents, sending moderate reformers and royalists alike to the guillotine. These events led many Americans to question their support of the Revolution.

In an excess of revolutionary zeal, the Jacobins also declared war on other monarchies, including Great Britain. Because of their alliance with the United States, the French expected American help. The American reaction tended to

Launching the New Nation **177**

SECTION 2 RESOURCES

📁 **PRINT RESOURCES**

IN-DEPTH RESOURCES: UNIT 2
Guided Reading, p. 30

ACCESS FOR STUDENTS ACQUIRING ENGLISH
Guided Reading (Spanish), p. 64

FORMAL ASSESSMENT
Section Quiz, p. 78

ALTERNATIVE ASSESSMENT BOOK
See forms for supporting and scoring alternative activities.

💿 **TECHNOLOGY RESOURCES**

CD-ROM *Grolier Multimedia Encyclopedia*
Electronic Library of Primary Sources

VIDEO *American Portfolio: A Videodisc for U.S. History*
user's guide, pp. 41, 43, 45

INTERNET McDougal Littell Learning On-Line
http://www.mcdougallittell.com

FOCUS & MOTIVATE

▶ **Starting with the Student**
• How do students handle disputes with their friends? How do they handle disputes with their enemies?
• How do they think the U.S. government should handle disputes with other countries today?

OBJECTIVE
① **INSTRUCT**

U.S. Response to Events in Europe

▶ **Discussing Key Ideas**
• The American people are divided over whether or not to support the French Revolution.
• The United States secures the rights from Spain to claim land west of the Appalachians.

IN-DEPTH RESOURCES: UNIT 2
Guided Reading, p. 30

ACCESS FOR STUDENTS ACQUIRING ENGLISH
Guided Reading (Spanish), p. 64

② INSTRUCT

Native Americans Resist White Settlers

▶ **Starting with the Student**
Have students create a cause-and-effect chart like the one below to show the effects stemming from Native Americans' rejection of the Treaty of Paris.

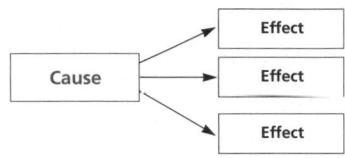

▶ **Discussing Key Ideas**
• Through battle, the United States obtains lands in Ohio from Native Americans.
• Britain signs the Jay Treaty, which gives the United States control of western territories.

split along party lines. Republicans, such as Jefferson and Madison, wanted to honor the 1778 treaty and support France. Federalists, such as Hamilton, wanted to back the British. President Washington took a middle position. On April 22, 1793, he issued a declaration of **neutrality,** a statement that the United States would support neither side in the conflict. Hamilton and Jefferson came to agree, recognizing that war was not in the new nation's interest.

Earlier in April, the French had sent a young diplomat, **Edmond Genêt,** to win American support. Instead of following diplomatic procedure and presenting his credentials to the Washington administration, Genêt began to recruit Americans for the war effort against Great Britain.

This violation of American neutrality and diplomatic protocol outraged Washington, who demanded that the French recall Genêt. By then, however, Genêt's political backers had fallen from power in Paris. Fearing for his life, the young envoy remained in the United States and became a U.S. citizen. Although Jefferson protested against Genêt's actions, Federalists called Jefferson a radical because he supported France. Frustrated by these attacks and by his ongoing feud with Hamilton, Jefferson resigned from the cabinet in 1793.

TREATY WITH SPAIN While the Washington administration tried to steer a middle course between Britain and France, it also pursued negotiations with Spain. The United States wanted to secure land claims west of the Appalachian Mountains and to gain shipping rights on the Mississippi River. To do this, it needed to come to an agreement with Spain, which still held Florida and the Louisiana Territory. This territory extended northward from Louisiana and included a vast area of land west of the Mississippi River. Spain was worried about possible joint British-American action against the Louisiana Territory. Sensing that Spain might be willing to strike a deal, U.S. Ambassador **Thomas Pinckney** pushed for a treaty.

Pinckney's Treaty of 1795 won virtually every point with Spain that the Americans desired. Spain gave up all claims to land east of the Mississippi and recognized the 31st parallel as the northern boundary of Florida. Spain also agreed to open the Mississippi River to American traffic and allow American traders to use the port at New Orleans. This treaty was important because it helped pave the way for expansion west of the Appalachians.

THINK THROUGH HISTORY
A. *Analyzing Motives* Why did the U.S. want to maintain neutrality?
A. Answer There was a general agreement that war was not in the new nation's interest.

THINK THROUGH HISTORY
B. *Recognizing Effects* Why did the United States want access to the Mississippi River?
B. Answer Travel and trade were difficult on the frontier, and the Mississippi offered the easiest means of transport for frontier farmers and merchants.

Native Americans Resist White Settlers

Pioneers had been moving west of the Appalachians since before the Revolution. After the war, pioneers in even greater numbers migrated west in pursuit of fertile and abundant land. They assumed that the 1783 Treaty of Paris, in which Great Britain had ceded land rights west of the Appalachians, gave them free rein to settle the area.

But the British still maintained forts in the Northwest Territory—an area that included Ohio, Indiana, Illinois, Michigan, and Wisconsin—in direct violation of the treaty. In addition to this continued British presence, the settlers met fierce resistance from the original inhabitants.

FIGHTS IN THE NORTHWEST Native Americans in the Northwest Territory never accepted the provisions of the Treaty of Paris. They continued to claim their tribal lands and demanded direct negotiations with the United States. They also took heart from the presence of British troops, who encouraged their resistance. When white settlers moved into their territory, the Native Americans often attacked them.

To gain control over the area of what is now Ohio, the federal government sent an army led by General Josiah Harmar. In 1790, Harmar's troops clashed with a confederacy of Native American groups led by a Miami chieftain named

"We have beaten the enemy twice under different commanders."

LITTLE TURTLE

Exploring Themes

Immigration and Migration Discuss the reasons for the westward migration. Explain that many settlers sought rich farmland and greater opportunities in the West. They were willing to endure hardships and fight Native Americans to achieve their goals.

Ask students where Americans tend to migrate today, and why they move to these places. *Possible Responses: The West, the Southwest, the Southeast; the weather and economy in these places appeal to many people.*

Making Connections Across Cultures

The Native American Perspective Remind students that the Native Americans had been the sole inhabitants of the West for hundreds of years. The westward expansion eventually destroyed their way of life. Recently, Native American groups have worked to regain ancestral works of art and skeletal remains from museums and collectors. (For more information, see Now & Then, "Who Owns the Past," in Chapter 1, p. 9.)

Ask students why Native Americans might be doing this. *Possible Response: Native Americans want their culture and traditions to be respected.*

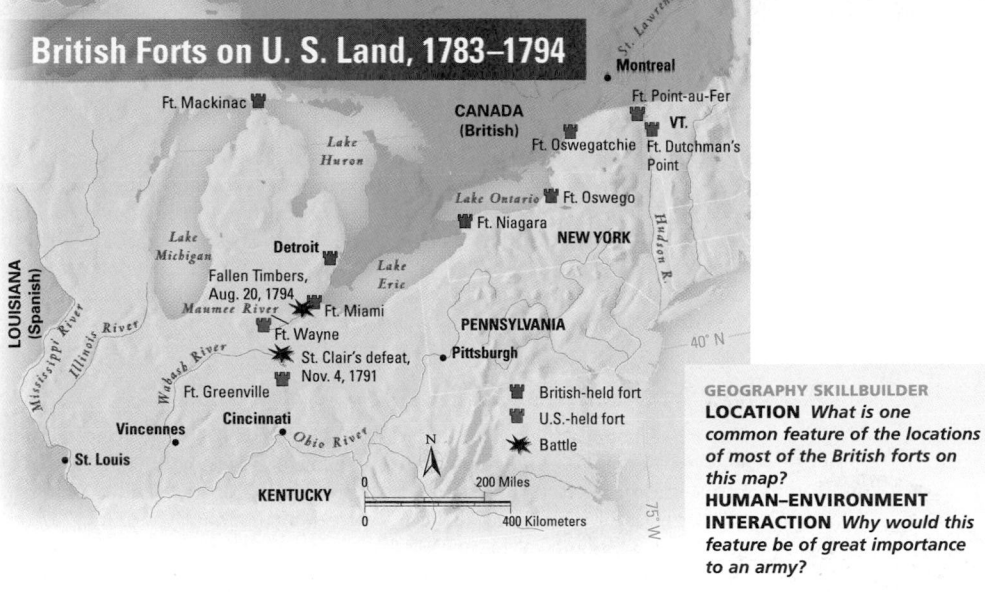

British Forts on U. S. Land, 1783–1794

Ft. Mackinac
CANADA (British)
Ft. Point-au-Fer
Ft. Oswegatchie
VT.
Ft. Dutchman's Point
Lake Huron
Lake Ontario
Ft. Oswego
Ft. Niagara
NEW YORK
Lake Michigan
Detroit
Lake Erie
Fallen Timbers, Aug. 20, 1794
Maumee River
Ft. Miami
Ft. Wayne
LOUISIANA (Spanish)
Illinois River
Mississippi River
Wabash River
St. Clair's defeat, Nov. 4, 1791
Ft. Greenville
PENNSYLVANIA
Pittsburgh
40° N
Vincennes
Cincinnati
Ohio River
St. Louis
N
KENTUCKY
0   200 Miles
0   400 Kilometers
75° W

■ British-held fort
■ U.S.-held fort
✦ Battle

GEOGRAPHY SKILLBUILDER
LOCATION *What is one common feature of the locations of most of the British forts on this map?*
HUMAN–ENVIRONMENT INTERACTION *Why would this feature be of great importance to an army?*

Little Turtle. The Native Americans won that battle. The following year, the Miami Confederacy inflicted an even worse defeat on a federal army led by General Arthur St. Clair.

BATTLE OF FALLEN TIMBERS Finally, in 1792, Washington appointed General Anthony Wayne to lead federal troops against the Native Americans. Known as "Mad Anthony" for his reckless courage, Wayne spent an entire year drilling his men. Greatly impressed, Little Turtle said of Wayne

A PERSONAL VOICE
We have beaten the enemy twice under different commanders. . . . The Americans are now led by a chief who never sleeps. . . . We have never been able to surprise him. . . . It would be prudent to listen to his offers of peace.
LITTLE TURTLE, Miami chieftain, in a speech to his allies

The other chiefs did not agree with Little Turtle and replaced him with a less able leader. On August 20, 1794, Wayne defeated the Miami Confederacy at the Battle of Fallen Timbers, near present-day Toledo, Ohio. After the battle, Wayne's army marched defiantly past the British Fort Miami, only two miles away, and then built an American post nearby.

This victory ended Native American resistance in Ohio. The following year, the Miami Confederacy signed the Treaty of Greenville, agreeing to give up most of the land in Ohio in exchange for an annual payment of $10,000. This settlement continued a pattern in which Native Americans received much less for their land than it was worth from settlers and the government. Meanwhile, in the Northwest Territory, new sources of conflict were developing between Britain and the United States.

JAY'S TREATY At the time of the Battle of Fallen Timbers, **John Jay** was in London to negotiate a treaty with Britain. One of the disputed issues was which nation would control territories west of the Appalachian Mountains. When news of Wayne's victory at Fallen Timbers arrived, the British agreed to evacuate their posts in the Northwest Territory because they did not wish to fight both the United States and Napoleon's France, with whom they were in conflict, at the same time.

Skillbuilder Answer
Location: They are located on or near water (on lakes or rivers). **Human-Environment Interaction:** A lake or river allows an army to move soldiers to and from a fort quickly, making it easier to respond effectively to enemy attacks.

The Miami war chief Little Turtle negotiates with General Anthony Wayne.

Launching the New Nation **179**

Reading the Map Though present-day political boundaries are not shown, students can use rivers to find the southern boundaries of Ohio and Indiana and the western boundary of Illinois. Encourage students to use the rivers and cities shown to help them understand geographical relationships between battle and fort sites.

Extension Ask students why most of the forts were located along bodies of water. *Possible Responses: For commerce, defense, and transportation.*

MORE ABOUT . . .
The Battle of Fallen Timbers

Although well-trained, General Wayne's troops were greatly outnumbered. Nearly 2,000 Shawnee, Ottawa, and Chippewa planned to attack Wayne's men. But Wayne had devised a plan of his own. He sent an advance party to draw the Native American warriors out of hiding. The warriors chased the American soldiers, who led them to Wayne's troops. Forced out in the open to fight a conventional battle, the Native Americans were surrounded on all sides. The battle was over within 40 minutes.

TEACHING OPTION

Cooperative Activity: Writing a Treaty

Task: Student groups will draft a treaty that deals fairly with the Native Americans in the dispute over land in Ohio.

Purpose: To help students understand that the Native Americans were frequently cheated in their dealings with settlers and the U.S. government.

Activity: Divide groups of eight to ten students into two teams. Have one team represent the interests of General Wayne and the United States. Have the other team represent the interests of Little Turtle and the Native American

people. Students should draw up a treaty that makes fair concessions to both sides. For example, the United States might allow the Native Americans to continue using the land, and the Native Americans might agree to leave the settlers in peace.

📁 **Building a Portfolio:** Students adding the treaty to their portfolios should include a note pointing out their own contribution to the treaty.

ALTERNATIVE ASSESSMENT BOOK
Standards for Evaluating a Cooperative Activity

Standards for Evaluation
Treaties should . . .

• use neutral language to address the positions of both parties equally
• include specific provisions for the use of the land
• include provisions for enforcing the treaty

Teacher's Edition **179**

Adams Provokes Criticism

▶ **Starting with the Student**
- As citizens, do students have the right to criticize the government?
- Do they think there should be any limits to what they can say?

▶ **Discussing Key Ideas**
- Tensions mount between the United States and France, but Adams avoids war.
- The Alien and Sedition Acts divide Federalists and Republicans.

MORE ABOUT . . .
John Adams

Unlike Washington, John Adams did not achieve great popularity during his political career. Because he was frequently blunt and impatient, people perceived him as a cold man. However, those who knew Adams well, loved him. Even Jefferson, his political opponent, wrote to a friend that Adams was "so amiable, that I pronounce you will love him if ever you become acquainted with him." Relations between the two men became strained after about 1790. However, after Adams and Jefferson retired from public life, they renewed their friendship. Remarkably, both men died on July 4, 1826. Adams's last words were "Thomas Jefferson still survives."

 ELECTRONIC LIBRARY OF PRIMARY SOURCES from the Inaugural Address of 1797 by John Adams

---

Although Jay's Treaty, signed on November 19, 1794, was a diplomatic victory, the treaty provoked outrage at home. For one thing, it allowed the British to continue their fur trade on the American side of the U.S.-Canadian border. This angered Western settlers.

Another point was even more controversial. Jay had gone to London to negotiate neutral shipping rights for American vessels trading in the Caribbean. Because the United States had not taken sides in the British-French conflict, Americans believed that their ships had the right to free passage. The British, however, had seized a number of these ships, confiscating their crews and cargo. Jay's Treaty did not resolve this problem, and Americans were furious. Nevertheless, the treaty managed to pass the Senate.

Adams Provokes Criticism

Portrait of a young John Adams by Joseph Badger (1708-1765).

The bitter political fight over Jay's Treaty, along with the growing division between Federalists and Republicans, convinced Washington not to seek a third term in office. In his Farewell Address, he urged the United States to "steer clear of permanent alliances" with other nations. Then, in 1797, he retired to his home at Mount Vernon.

In the presidential election of 1796, Americans faced a new situation: a contest between opposing parties. The Federalists nominated Vice-President John Adams for president and Thomas Pinckney for vice-president. The Republicans chose Thomas Jefferson, with Aaron Burr as his running mate.

In the election, Adams received 71 electoral votes, while Jefferson received 68. Because the Constitution stated that the runner-up should become vice-president, the country found itself with a Federalist president and a Republican vice-president. What had seemed sensible when the Constitution was written had become a problem because of the unexpected rise of political parties.

The election also underscored the growing danger of **sectionalism**—placing the interests of one region over those of the nation as a whole. Almost all the electors from the Southern states voted for Jefferson, while all the electors from the Northern states voted for Adams.

ADAMS TRIES TO AVOID WAR Soon after taking office, President Adams faced his first crisis: a looming war with France. The French government, which regarded the Jay Treaty as a violation of the French-American alliance, refused to receive the new American ambassador and began to seize American ships bound for Britain. Adams sent a three-man team to Paris to negotiate a solution.

This team, which included future Chief Justice John Marshall, planned to meet with the French foreign minister, Talleyrand. Instead, the French sent three low-level officials, whom Adams called "X, Y, and Z" in his report to Congress. The French officials demanded a $250,000 bribe as payment for seeing Talleyrand. News of this insult, which became known as the **XYZ Affair,** provoked a wave of anti-French feeling at home. "Millions for defense, but not one cent for tribute" became the slogan of the day. In 1798, Congress created a navy department and authorized American ships to seize French vessels. For the next two years, an undeclared naval war raged between France and the United States.

The Federalists called for a full-scale war against France, but Adams refused to take that step. Through diplomacy, the two countries eventually smoothed over their differences. Adams damaged his standing among the Federalists, but he kept the United States out of war.

THE ALIEN AND SEDITION ACTS Although Republicans cheered Adams for avoiding war with France, they criticized him mercilessly on many other issues. Tensions between Federalists and Republicans rose to a fever pitch. Adams regarded Republican ideas as dangerous to the welfare of the nation. He and other Federalists accused the Republicans of favoring foreign powers.

180 CHAPTER 6

THINK THROUGH HISTORY
C. Recognizing Effects *How did events in the Northwest Territory affect U.S. relations with Britain?*

C. Answer Wayne's defeat of Native American forces helped to bring about the signing of Jay's Treaty. The British, worried also about a U.S.-French alliance, began to remove their forts and acknowledge U.S. land rights in the area.

TEACHING OPTIONS

Making Connections Across the Curriculum

Literature Many government leaders charged that the Alien and Sedition Acts violated freedom of speech and freedom of press. Likewise, many people today believe that banning books and other published material is unconstitutional. Throughout U.S. history, some people have tried to censor books they judge to be obscene or objectionable in some way. Discuss with students whether banning or censoring books (or song lyrics or material on the Internet) should be practiced.

Teaching Less Proficient Readers

Making Connections Students may have difficulty understanding the XYZ Affair and the Alien and Sedition Acts. Helping them to connect to the emotion in these dramatic events may aid in comprehension. Ask these questions:
- How might Chief Justice Marshall have felt when he was asked to pay to see the French foreign minister? *Possible Response: Marshall was insulted and angry.*
- Why might a new government react to criticism more harshly than a well-established government? *Possible Response: A new government may not be sure of its authority and would be more likely to become frightened or defensive.*

Many immigrants were active in the Republican party. Some of the most vocal critics of the Adams administration were foreign-born. They included French and British radicals as well as recent Irish immigrants who lashed out at anyone who was even faintly pro-British, including the Federalist Adams.

To counter what they saw as a growing threat against the government, the Federalists pushed through Congress in 1798 four measures that became known as the **Alien and Sedition Acts.** Three of these measures, the Alien Acts, raised the residence requirement for American citizenship from 5 years to 14 years and allowed the president to deport or jail any alien considered undesirable.

The fourth measure, the Sedition Act, set fines and jail terms for anyone expressing opinions considered damaging to the government. Under the terms of this act, the federal government prosecuted and jailed a number of Republican editors, publishers, and politicians. Outraged Republicans called the laws a violation of freedom of speech guaranteed by the First Amendment.

VIRGINIA AND KENTUCKY RESOLUTIONS The two main Republican leaders, Jefferson and James Madison, decided to organize opposition to the Alien and Sedition Acts by appealing to the states. Madison drew up a set of resolutions that were adopted by the Virginia legislature, while Jefferson wrote resolutions that were approved in Kentucky. The Kentucky Resolutions in particular asserted the principle of **nullification**—that states had the right to nullify, or consider void, any act of Congress that they deemed unconstitutional. Virginia and Kentucky viewed the Alien and Sedition Acts as unconstitutional because they violated the First Amendment and deprived citizens of their rights.

The resolutions also called for other states to adopt similar declarations. No other state did so, however, and the issue died out by the next presidential election. Nevertheless, the resolutions showed that the balance of power between the states and the federal government remained a controversial issue. In fact, the election of 1800 between Federalist John Adams and Republican Thomas Jefferson would center on this critical debate.

Federal and State Conflicts

Alien and Sedition Acts	Virginia and Kentucky Resolutions
• The President is authorized to deport or imprison any alien considered "dangerous to the peace and safety of the United States." • Fines and a prison sentence could be imposed on anyone trying to hinder the operation of the government or expressing "false, scandalous, and malicious statements" against the government.	• Virginia and Kentucky claimed the right to declare null and void the Alien and Sedition Acts because they violated the Bill of Rights. • Virginia and Kentucky claimed the right to declare null and void federal laws going beyond powers granted by the Constitution to the central government.

Section 2 Assessment

1. TERMS & NAMES

Identify:
• neutrality
• Edmond Genêt
• Thomas Pinckney
• Little Turtle
• John Jay
• sectionalism
• XYZ Affair
• Alien and Sedition Acts
• nullification

2. SUMMARIZING List some of the disputes mentioned in this section. Indicate the dispute and each side's arguments.

DISPUTE	
One side	Other side

Then choose one dispute and defend one side's arguments.

3. EVALUATING Do you agree with the Republicans that the Alien and Sedition Acts were a violation of the First Amendment? Were they necessary? Support your opinion.

THINK ABOUT
• the intent of the First Amendment
• what was happening in Europe
• what was happening in America

4. ANALYZING Should the United States have officially supported the French revolutionaries against the British? Support your opinion with examples from the text.

THINK ABOUT
• Federalist and Republican attitudes toward France and Great Britain
• the Reign of Terror
• U.S. gratitude to France for its support against Britain

Launching the New Nation **181**

A N S W E R S

1. TERMS & NAMES

neutrality, p. 178

Edmond Genêt, p. 178

Thomas Pinckney, p. 178

Little Turtle, p. 179

John Jay, p. 179

sectionalism, p. 180

XYZ Affair, p. 180

Alien and Sedition Acts, p. 181

nullification, p. 181

2. SUMMARIZING

French Revolution:
1. historic ties, struggle against tyranny. 2. Reign of Terror, against another war with England.
Jay's Treaty:
1. continued British fur trade, British seizure of American ships. 2. British leave posts in Northwest Territory.
War with France:
1. France seizes American ships. 2. Adams refuses war, finds diplomatic solution.

3. EVALUATING

Those who agree with the Federalists will say that the country needed to control the vocal members of the Republican Party from stirring up discontent and seeming to threaten the stability of the young government. Those who agree with the Republicans will see these measures as a violation of freedom of speech—specifically, a citizen's right to criticize the policies of the Federalist administration of John Adams.

4. ANALYZING

Students who think the U.S. should have supported the French Revolution might say that the Americans owed the French a favor because of France's support during the American Revolution. They might also mention the Treaty of 1778. Those who think the U.S. should not have supported the Revolution should mention the beheading of the king and the Reign of Terror, as well as the Edmond Genêt incident.

Teacher's Edition   **181**

OBJECTIVES

(1) To describe details of upper-class American daily life in the new nation.

(2) To explain why portraits are limited to portraying wealthy people.

FOCUS & MOTIVATE

▶ *Starting with the Student*
Have students share their definitions of the term "couch potato."

• What activities occupy most of the students' indoor leisure time?

• Considering what was and was not yet invented, how do they think people spent their indoor leisure time 200 years ago?

MORE ABOUT . . .
Taking Tea

Although the East India Company had promoted tea drinking in England since the 17th century, the practice of having an "afternoon tea," or light meal with tea, began in Holland. The Dutch brought the custom to their colony of New Amsterdam (later New York), from where it spread to other American colonies. In Britain "afternoon tea" did not become entrenched until about 1840, when the Duchess of Bedford made it fashionable.

DAILY LIFE
1789-1816

Life of the Upper Crust

Before photography, having your portrait painted was the only way to have your likeness reproduced for posterity—and only the rich could afford it. That is why the colonial paintings feature the upper crust, not ordinary people. While aristocrats in the new nation tried to distance themselves from the rest of society, they had a difficult time convincing everyone else that they were better than most Yankees.

❸ **ENGLISH TEA SET** The porcelain tea set on the table shows this family's wealth and aristocratic manner. Once the Revolution ended, tea drinking became an established social ritual, and owning the latest and best tea sets was a sign of wealth.

❷ **THE "HEAD" AND THE QUEEN'S NIGHTCAP** Queen Marie Antoinette of France made the "head" the "in" hairstyle for the rich and famous. It meant that the woman wore a huge wad of stuffing on her head, with her hair drawn over it, including ribbons and curls. The hair was glued into place over the stuffing with flour paste. Then the "head" was powdered white. Older women wore a large ruffled cap called a "Queen's Nightcap" to cover their hair between visits to the hairdresser. It was not worn to bed.

❶ **MEDIAN AGE** The median age of Americans in about 1800 was 16. The median means that almost half of all Americans were under 16 and half were 16 or older. In 1993, the median age of Americans was 33.

The Samuels Family by Johann Eckstein. Ellen Kelleran Gardner Fund, Courtesy, Museum of Fine Arts, Boston

182 CHAPTER 6

RECOMMENDED RESOURCES

Books

Bushman, Richard L. *The Refinement of America.* New York: Knopf, 1992. Customs in postrevolutionary America.

Davidson, Marshall B. *The American Heritage History of American Antiques from the Revolution to the Civil War.* New York: American Heritage, 1968.

Schlesinger, Arthur M. *The Birth of the Nation.* Boston: Houghton, 1981. A reissue of his 1968 book.

Simmons, Amelia. *American Cookery.* Bedford, MA: Applewood, 1996. One of America's earliest cookbooks, first published in 1796.

Smith, Barbara Clark. *After the Revolution.* Washington: National Museum of American History, 1985. A Smithsonian history of everyday American life in the late 18th century.

Wolf, Stephanie Grauman. *As Various as Their Land.* New York: Harper, 1993. An examination of 18th-century Americans from all walks of life.

Videos

Life in America 1800. AIMS. A portrait of the daily life of a rural New England family in the early 19th century; part of AIMS's Had You Lived Then series.

Virginia Plantations. Paradise Productions, dist. Atlas Video, 1986. An examination of wealthy plantation life.

4 PORTRAITS To have his or her portrait painted, the subject might have to sit six hours at a time for as many as 15 sittings. The most famous portrait painter in the new nation was John Singleton Copley, who was so busy that he required patrons to make appointments months in advance for sittings. This portrait by Copley is of a merchant named Thomas Hancock.

5 WIGS AND BREECHES Men commonly wore wigs until about 1800; some even styled their own hair to look like wigs. Boys over age six in wealthy families often wore wigs, too, but their clothing was different from their father's. Boys wore longer pants in two-piece suits and sported a collarless round neck covered with a white ruffled shirt collar. Dad wore tight knee breeches with stockings; later the breeches were longer. The buckled shoes worn by Mr. Samuels here show that he was probably a Federalist, as the Republicans usually wore shoes with laces.

Federalist   Republican

6 PERSONAL HYGIENE Most people did not take baths because they thought the practice was unhealthy. Elizabeth Drinker, a Quaker lady, wrote in her diary that she tried the shower her husband installed in the backyard and she "bore it better than I expected, not having been wet all over at once, for 28 years past."

DATA FILE

Household Size

In the 1790s, a household of 12 persons was not nearly as unusual as it is today. The chart below shows how the number of persons in a household has changed since 1790.

Number of households (in percent) vs Person/Persons (1, 2, 3, 4, 5, 6, 7 or more)

■ 1790   ■ 1990

Source: *Statistical Abstract of the United States 1995; Historical Statistics of the United States Colonial Times to 1970*

Food

Early American meals were not very tasty.

- Lack of refrigeration, few spices, and cooking over an open fire often left meats tough and tasteless.
- Early Americans ate great amounts of animal fat.
- Green vegetables were considered "animal fodder," not for humans; but when eaten, they were overcooked.
- Fresh fruit spoiled quickly and could cause cholera if washed in polluted water.
- In an age of no refrigeration, milk turned sour in two hours in the summer.
- Poor people in cities ate saltpork with bread and molasses.
- People ate as much as they could afford to eat.
- Because of their poor nutrition, many Americans were pale, sickly, and lacked energy.

INTERACT WITH HISTORY

1. **DRAWING CONCLUSIONS** What details on this page show that the upper crust valued formality?

 SEE SKILLBUILDER HANDBOOK, PAGE 1050.

2. **CREATING A PORTRAIT** Suppose a portrait of a family were painted today. What details would be different? Draw, paint, or create a collage from magazine pictures to replace the family portrait on these pages with an updated one. Give written details about the elements in your collage.

Launching the New Nation **183**

OBJECTIVES

① To identify some of the significant changes brought about during the early years of Jefferson's presidency.

② To provide examples of the Federalists' declining power.

③ To summarize the importance of the Louisiana Purchase and the Lewis and Clark expedition.

CRITICAL THINKING

- Drawing conclusions, pp. 185, 188
- Summarizing, pp. 186, 188
- Hypothesizing, p. 187
- Evaluating, p. 188
- Analyzing, p. 188

FOCUS & MOTIVATE

▶ **Starting with the Student**
Watch the video "Recruited by Lewis and Clark" to learn about Patrick Gass and the people and places encountered by the most dangerous and ambitious expedition the United States had ever undertaken.

- Using the *Video Resource Book* as a guide, hold a class discussion. Focus on other events in the colonies occurring at the same time as the Lewis and Clark expedition, and engage in extension activities using key primary sources.

AMERICAN STORIES VIDEO SERIES
"Recruited by Lewis and Clark"
Videocassette: Volume 1

Videodisc: Disc 1, Side A, Chapter 3

MORE ABOUT . . .
Patrick Gass

On October 11, 1804, Gass writes: "We waited for an answer from the Indians. About 12 o'clock, they came, and brought some corn, beans and squashes, which they presented to us. The chief said he was glad to see us."

TERMS & NAMES
- Aaron Burr
- Judiciary Act of 1801
- midnight judge
- John Marshall
- *Marbury* vs. *Madison*
- judicial review
- Louisiana Purchase
- Meriwether Lewis
- William Clark
- Sacajawea

❸ Jefferson Alters the Nation's Course

LEARN ABOUT key decisions made by the Jefferson administration
TO UNDERSTAND how the country was expanding and changing.

ONE AMERICAN'S STORY

Patrick Gass lived to see many remarkable events in the birth and growth of the nation. Born on June 12, 1771, before the Revolution, he died nearly a century later, on April 2, 1870. During that time, the country grew from the original 13 colonies to 38 states. Gass played a part in that expansion as a participant in one of the most famous frontier explorations of all time: the Lewis and Clark expedition. Setting out in 1804, this expedition traveled overland from St. Louis, Missouri, to the Pacific Ocean. Along the way, Gass kept a journal, in which he took notes on the people and places he saw and the dramatic events he witnessed. The following passage from his journal entry of May 14, 1805, re-creates one of those events:

A PERSONAL VOICE
This forenoon we passed a large creek on the North side and a small river on the South. About 4 in the afternoon we passed another small river on the South side near the mouth of which some of the men discovered a large brown bear, and six of them went out to kill it. They fired at it; but having only wounded it, it made battle and was near seizing some of them, but they all fortunately escaped, and at length succeeded in dispatching it. These bears are very bold and ferocious; and very large and powerful. The natives say they have killed a number of their brave men.

PATRICK GASS, from *A Journal of the Voyages and Travels of a Corps of Discovery*

This engraving of a sketch from Patrick Gass's journal shows a member of the expedition treed by an oddly drawn grizzly bear.

By charting unexplored territory, the Lewis and Clark expedition helped lay the foundations for Western expansion. It was one of the great achievements of the Jefferson presidency.

 VIDEO *RECRUITED BY LEWIS AND CLARK: Patrick Gass Chronicles the Journey West*

Jefferson Wins Presidential Election of 1800

The presidential political campaign of 1800 was a hard-fought struggle between Thomas Jefferson, a Republican, and his Federalist opponent, President John Adams. Each party hurled wild charges at the other. To Republicans, Adams was a tool of the rich who wanted to turn the executive branch into a British-style monarchy. To Federalists, Jefferson was a dangerous supporter of revolutionary France and an atheist bent on destroying organized religion. The bitterness of the conflict was probably inevitable. The government was only 12 years old. Americans were not accustomed to the peaceful transfer of power from one political group to another. Nevertheless, both sides limited their fighting to votes, not guns.

In the balloting, Jefferson defeated Adams by eight electoral votes. However, since Jefferson's running mate, **Aaron Burr,** received the same number of votes in the Electoral College as Jefferson, the House of Representatives was called upon to choose between the two highest vote getters. For six feverish days, the House took one ballot after another—35 ballots in all. Finally, Alexander Hamilton intervened. Although he opposed Jefferson's policies, he feared Burr even more. Hamilton persuaded enough Federalists to cast blank votes to give Jefferson a majority of two votes. Burr then became vice-presi-

---

 PRINT RESOURCES

IN-DEPTH RESOURCES: UNIT 2
Guided Reading, p. 31
Geography Application: The Louisiana Purchase, p. 34
Primary Source: Presidential Campaign Song, p. 36; *from* The Journal of Lewis and Clark, p. 37; Botanical Drawings, p. 38
Literature: from *Burr* by Gore Vidal, p. 40

ACCESS FOR STUDENTS ACQUIRING ENGLISH
Guided Reading (Spanish), p. 65
Geography Application: The Louisiana Purchase (Spanish), p. 68

FORMAL ASSESSMENT
Section Quiz, p. 79

ALTERNATIVE ASSESSMENT BOOK
See forms for supporting and scoring alterntative activities.

 TECHNOLOGY RESOURCES

GEOGRAPHY TRANSPARENCIES
G6, The Wilderness Road

CD-ROM Electronic Library of Primary Sources

VIDEO *American Stories* video series: "Recruited by Lewis and Clark"; *American Portfolio: A Videodisc for U.S. History* user's guide, pp. 44, 45, 50

INTERNET McDougal Littell Learning On-Line
http://www.mcdougallittell.com

dent. Although Hamilton opposed Jefferson's philosophy of government, he regarded Jefferson as much more qualified for the presidency than Burr.

The deadlock revealed a flaw in the electoral process as spelled out in the Constitution. As a result, Congress passed the Twelfth Amendment, which called for electors to cast separate ballots for president and vice-president. This system is still in effect today.

PEACEFUL TRANSFER OF POWER Despite the bitter feelings provoked by the 1800 election, Jefferson's inauguration took place without incident. This peaceful transfer of power from one party to another showed the world that the American Republic could withstand political change.

In his inaugural address, Jefferson extended the hand of peace to his opponents. "Every difference of opinion is not a difference of principle," he said. "We are all Republicans; we are all Federalists." Nevertheless, Jefferson planned to wage a "peaceful revolution" to restore the republican ideals of 1776 against the strong-government policies of Federalism.

SIMPLIFYING THE PRESIDENCY Jefferson believed that a simple government best suited the needs of a republic. In a symbolic gesture, he walked to his own inauguration rather than ride in a carriage. As president, he took off his powdered wig and sometimes wore work clothes and frayed slippers when receiving visitors. This informality contrasted with the formality of the Washington and Adams administrations.

In accord with his belief in decentralized power, Jefferson also tried to reduce the size of government and cut costs wherever possible. He reduced the size of the army, halted a planned expansion of the navy, and lowered expenses for government social functions. He also rolled back Hamilton's economic program by eliminating all internal taxes and reducing the influence of the Bank of the United States. Jefferson strongly favored free trade, rather than government-controlled trade and tariffs. He believed free trade would benefit the United States because of a shortage of raw materials and food in Europe that could be supplied by Americans.

SOUTHERN DOMINANCE OF POLITICS Jefferson was the first president to take office in the new federal capital, Washington, D.C. Though in appearance the city was a primitive place of dirt roads and few buildings, its location between Virginia and Maryland reflected the growing importance of the South in national politics. In fact, Jefferson and the two presidents who followed him—James Madison and James Monroe—all were from Virginia.

This pattern of Southern dominance underscored the declining influence of both New England and the Federalists in national political life. The decline of the Federalists was hastened by Jefferson's political moderation. Also, many Federalists refused to participate in political campaigns because they did not want to appeal to the common people for support. Furthermore, national expansion worked against the Federalists because settlers in the new states tended to vote for the Republicans, who represented farmers' interests.

The Federalists Lose Power

As president, Jefferson took steps to reduce the role of the Federalist Party in government. Under Washington and Adams, Federalists had filled the vast majority of government positions. Jefferson reversed this pattern by replacing some Federalist officials with Republican ones. By 1803, the government bureaucracy was more evenly balanced between Republicans and Federalists.

JOHN MARSHALL AND THE SUPREME COURT Federalists continued to exert great influence in the judicial branch, however. Just prior to leaving office,

HISTORICAL SPOTLIGHT

PEACEFUL TRANSFER OF POWER vs. ARMED REBELLION

Gabriel Prosser, an African-American slave in Virginia, demanded the rights promised all Americans under a republic. Denied any political voice, Prosser felt he had no other option than to fight for those rights; thus, he attempted to lead an armed rebellion.

On August 30, 1800, he assembled a thousand slaves from nearby plantations for a planned attack on Richmond (the state capital), with the intention of making Virginia a state for African Americans. The attack was thwarted by the Virginia militia and Prosser was captured and hanged, but other slave revolts would soon follow.

"We are all Republicans; we are all Federalists."

THOMAS JEFFERSON

In 1806, Burr's dreams of personal glory led him to carry out a plan that led to his arrest and trial for treason. No one really knows what Burr planned, but he seems to have envisioned creating his own empire stretching from the Ohio River to Mexico. "The gods invite us to glory and fortune," Burr wrote to his co-conspirator, General James Wilkinson. "It remains to be seen whether we deserve the boon." Apparently they did not. Wilkinson informed Jefferson of the conspiracy while Burr was on his way to New Orleans.

OBJECTIVE
③ INSTRUCT

The United States Expands West

▶ *Starting with the Student*
Have students make a time line of events leading up to the Louisiana Purchase and the Lewis and Clark expedition.

1762   1803

      1800   1804

▶ *Discussing Key Ideas*
• France sells the Louisiana Territory to the United States.
• Jefferson sends an expedition led by Lewis and Clark to explore the new territory.

ELECTRONIC LIBRARY OF PRIMARY SOURCES
from the Louisiana Purchase Treaty

IN-DEPTH RESOURCES: UNIT 2
Geography Application: The Louisiana Purchase, p. 34

President Adams had pushed a law through Congress, the **Judiciary Act of 1801,** that increased the number of federal judges by sixteen. In an attempt to control the political direction of future federal judicial decisions, Adams promptly filled most of these positions with Federalists. These judges were called **midnight judges** because Adams signed their appointments late on the last day of his administration. Adams also appointed **John Marshall,** a staunch Federalist, as Chief Justice of the Supreme Court. Marshall would serve on the Court for more than 30 years, handing down decisions that would strengthen the power of the Supreme Court and the federal government.

Adams's packing of the courts with Federalists angered Jefferson and the Republicans. Since the documents authorizing some of the appointments were signed but not delivered by the time Adams left office, Jefferson argued that these appointments were invalid.

MARBURY V. MADISON This argument led to one of the most important Supreme Court decisions of all time: *Marbury v. Madison* (1803). William Marbury, a Federalist, was one of Adams's last-minute judicial appointments, but he never received his official papers. When he demanded that James Madison, the Republican secretary of state, deliver the papers, Madison refused. In a famous ruling, Federalist Chief Justice John Marshall said that Congress's Judiciary Act of 1789, which would have forced Madison to hand over the papers, was unconstitutional because the Constitution contained no provision for the Supreme Court to issue such orders as the act required.

This decision was in part a victory for the Republicans, since the Federalist Marbury never got his commission. However, the decision made a key Federalist point by affirming the principle of **judicial review**—the ability of the Supreme Court to declare an act of Congress unconstitutional. Later, this principle became a cornerstone of American law and government.

HAMILTON DUELS WITH BURR Despite the decline of Federalism during the Jefferson years, Alexander Hamilton remained a powerful influence. It was Hamilton who, in 1800, had convinced key Federalist legislators to back Jefferson rather than Burr. Then, in 1804, Hamilton backed Burr's opponent in the race for governor of New York and in the process described Burr as "a dangerous man, and one who ought not to be trusted with the reins of government." Burr responded by challenging Hamilton to a duel. Though Hamilton despised dueling, he accepted, because his sense of honor compelled him to prove his courage. In the duel, Burr shot and killed Hamilton, who deliberately fired in the air. The nation had lost a great political thinker, and the Federalists had lost a great leader.

The United States Expands West

During Jefferson's presidency, Americans continued their westward migration across the Appalachians. Between 1800 and 1810, the population of Ohio grew from 45,000 to 231,000, with similar growth rates in Kentucky, Tennessee, and adjoining territories. Although pioneer life was hard, the pioneers kept coming. One traveler made these observations about settlers along the Ohio River in 1802.

> **A PERSONAL VOICE**
> The houses that they inhabit are built upon the borders of the river, . . . whence they enjoy the most delightful prospects [views]; still, their mode of building does not correspond with the beauties of the spot, being nothing but miserable log houses, without windows, and so small that two beds occupy the greatest part of them.
>
> **F. A. MICHAUX,** from *Travels to the West of the Allegheny Mountains*

Most of the settlers who arrived in Ohio, Kentucky, and Tennessee came through the Cumberland Gap, a natural passage through the Appalachians near

186 Chapter 6

THINK THROUGH HISTORY
B. Summarizing
What is judicial review, and why is it important?

B. Answer This is the principle that the Supreme Court has the right to review acts of Congress to see if they are constitutional. The Supreme Court checks the power of Congress.

Exploring Themes

Constitutional Concerns Discuss why judicial review became an important cornerstone of American law and government. Why is it important to have a provision that allows for checks on legislative acts? Why does that power reside with the Supreme Court? *Possible Response: It is important to review acts to ensure they do not violate rights set down in* the Constitution. The power resides with the Supreme Court because this branch of the federal government is impartial.

Ask students to name some acts or practices that have been deemed unconstitutional by the Supreme Court. *Possible Response: Segregation.*

THINK THROUGH HISTORY
C. Hypothesizing
What do you think were motives for people to migrate west of the Appalachians?

C. Answer To build a new life; to find a less-settled place to live; to own land and property; to realize a dream of independence.

where Kentucky, Tennessee, and Virginia meet. A generation earlier, in 1775, Daniel Boone, one of America's great frontier guides, had led the clearing of a road from Virginia, through the Cumberland Gap, to what is now Louisville, Kentucky. When it was finished, the Wilderness Road, almost 300 miles long, became one of the major routes for westward migration.

THE LOUISIANA PURCHASE Soon Jefferson had the opportunity to extend American territory. In 1800, Napoleon Bonaparte of France persuaded Spain to return the Louisiana Territory it had received in 1762. The French ruler intended to use the territory as a breadbasket for the French West Indies. When news of the secret transfer leaked out, Americans reacted with alarm. Jefferson feared that a strong French presence in the midcontinent would force the United States into an alliance with Britain.

The Lewis and Clark Expedition, 1804–1806

Meriwether Lewis and William Clark led an expedition to explore the new territory acquired by the United States in the Louisiana Purchase. The map shows the route of their expedition and includes brief summaries (drawn from their published journals) of typical events that occurred on specific dates during the trip. Also shown are various artifacts from the trip.

December 8, 1805–March 23, 1806. Winter camp at Ft. Clatsop. Lack of provisions forces departure. Wind high.

April 25–26, 1805 High winds and cold enough for water to freeze on oars. Lewis searches by land for Yellowstone R. Rejoins Clark at the junction of Missouri and Yellowstone.

April 7, 1805 Party of 32, including Clark's black servant York, French-Canadian trader Charbonneau, his wife Sacajawea, and their son, depart at 5 P.M. to continue journey. High northwest wind but otherwise fair weather.

November 3, 1804 Hard wind from northwest. Begin to set up winter camp.
December 17, 1804 Coldest weather yet—45 degrees below zero—sentinels have to be changed every half hour.

Fort Clatsop ⑥

⑦

Traveler's Rest

⑦

Three Forks

July 3, 1806 Party breaks up. Lewis takes direct route to falls of the Missouri. Clark takes route to Jefferson and Yellowstone rivers.
August 11, 1806 Mistaken for an elk, Lewis accidentally shot in thigh by member of party. In pain, he rejoins Clark's party the next day.

⑤ ④ ■ Fort Mandan ③

CANADA (British)

August 20, 1804 Sergeant Floyd dies, only fatality of expedition, and is buried.

①

②

May 14, 1804 Depart camp near St. Louis about 4 P.M. Heavy rain.

St. Louis

LOUISIANA PURCHASE (1803)

⑧

September 23, 1806 Reach St. Louis at 12 noon. Lewis's shortcut saved 579 miles. Total mileage 7,689.

Lewis & Clark's compass

NEW SPAIN

0   500 Miles
0   1000 Kilometers

N

→ Journey west, 1804–1805
→ Journey home, 1806
---- Lewis's route
--- Clark's route
■ Fort

● New Orleans

187

MORE ABOUT . . .
Daniel Boone

In 1778, Boone was captured by the Shawnee. They forced him to run between two rows of warriors while they beat him. By running in a zigzag pattern, he escaped serious injury. He lowered his head and knocked the last warrior down. Boone had many adventures in the wilderness, but the frontier still drew him. In 1799, he left his home in Kentucky to go west yet again. When asked why, Boone replied, "Too many people! Too crowded! Too crowded! I want more elbow-room."

HISTORY FROM VISUALS
The Lewis and Clark Expedition, 1804–1806

Reading the Map Point out that the summaries are listed from 1 to 10 and should be read in a counter-clockwise direction. The arrows point to the locations where the events took place. You might display a physical map of the region to give students an idea of the terrain the exploration party covered.

Extension Ask students to write a journal entry based on one of the summaries shown on the map.

ELECTRONIC LIBRARY OF PRIMARY SOURCES *from* A Letter of Instruction to Meriwether Lewis by Thomas Jefferson; *from* A List of Requirements by Meriwether Lewis

IN-DEPTH RESOURCES: UNIT 2
Primary Sources: from The Journals of Lewis and Clark, p. 37; Botanical Drawings, p. 38

TEACHING OPTION

Cooperative Activity: Taking Part in an Expedition

Task: Have groups of four to five students explore an area with which they are unfamiliar—a park, neighborhood, zoo, public recreation area—and write a report on what they find there.

Purpose: To help students understand what is involved in organizing and carrying out an exploratory expedition.

Activity: Students should prepare for their expedition by making a list of the equipment they will need. During the expedition, students should take notes on the area's terrain and cli-

mate and the people they encounter there. They should also make judgments about the area. Do they recommend that others visit it? Why or why not?

Building a Portfolio: If students consider that this report represents some of their best work, they may want to place the report in their portfolio.

ALTERNATIVE ASSESSMENT BOOK
Standards for Evaluating a Cooperative Activity

Standards for Evaluation
Reports should

• provide a detailed account of the area's geography, climate, and population

• include students' assessment of the area as a good or bad place to visit

Teacher's Edition   187

Ask students to consider what knowledge Sacajawea would have had about the area of the country being explored that could have helped the expedition. *Possible Response: Her knowledge of food sources, local topography, and dominant weather patterns.*

ASSESS & RETEACH

Section 3 Assessment

Have students work with a partner to answer the questions.

Self-Assessment

To explore their understanding of Section 3, ask students to make a two-column chart. In the first column, they should jot down what they knew previously about the events covered in the section. In the second column, they should list what they have learned.

Section Quiz

FORMAL ASSESSMENT
Section Quiz, p. 79

Reteach

Use the section quiz to help review the main ideas of the section.

CLOSE

The Louisiana Purchase greatly expanded the boundaries of the United States. The territory provided land and opportunity for many courageous Americans. Westward expansion would fire people's imagination and ambition for many more years to come.

188 Chapter 6

Jefferson decided to see whether he could resolve the problem by buying New Orleans and western Florida from the French. He sent James Monroe to join American ambassador Robert Livingston in Paris. Before Monroe arrived, however, Napoleon had abandoned his vision of an empire in America. France's most important island colony was Haiti, then known as Saint Domingue. In the 1790s, under the leadership of Toussaint L'Ouverture, the black slaves in Haiti had revolted, and they eventually took over the government. When Napoleon failed to reconquer the colony, he saw no reason to keep Louisiana. In 1803, he offered to sell the entire Louisiana Territory to the United States.

With no time to consult their government, Monroe and Livingston went ahead and closed the deal for $15 million. Jefferson, though, was not certain that the purchase was constitutional. As a strict constructionist, he doubted whether the Constitution gave the government the power to acquire new territory. At the same time, he realized that the vast new lands could form the "empire of liberty" that was his vision for the nation. After a delay, he submitted the treaty finalizing the purchase, and the Senate ratified it.

With the **Louisiana Purchase,** the United States doubled in size. In general, the Louisiana Purchase was considered to cover the land drained by the western tributaries of the Mississippi River. Jefferson, who wanted to simplify and decentralize the government, had expanded the power of the presidency and the central government.

LEWIS AND CLARK Jefferson was eager to explore the new territory. In 1803, he appointed **Meriwether Lewis** to lead an expedition from St. Louis to the Pacific coast. Lewis chose **William Clark** as his second-in-command. Jefferson instructed Lewis and Clark to carry out scientific studies along the way and to document the native cultures they found. They kept detailed journals of their expedition. The previous page shows the route of their journey, as well as summaries of typical events on the trip. Starting off with some 50 soldiers and woodsmen, the expedition later took on a Native American woman, **Sacajawea,** who served as interpreter and guide.

The Lewis and Clark expedition took two years and four months and was a great success. It brought back invaluable information about the West and showed that cross-country travel was possible. It also opened the way for settlement of the West and strengthened American claims to the Oregon Territory on the northwest coast. The Louisiana Purchase and the Lewis and Clark expedition contributed to the success of Jefferson's first term in office, but trouble with Britain loomed on the horizon.

HISTORICAL SPOTLIGHT

SACAJAWEA

Sacajawea, a member of the Shoshone nation, was a key member of the Lewis and Clark expedition. A young woman, perhaps 16, at the start of the journey, she helped the party forage for food and understand the ways of the native peoples they met. She also had her young baby with her, which helped convince Native American tribes that the expedition was a peaceful one.

D. Answer It more than doubled the size of the nation. Also, since the Constitution did not clearly authorize the president to buy territory, it represented an increase in presidential power.

THINK THROUGH HISTORY
D. Drawing Conclusions *Why was the Louisiana Purchase important?*

Section 3 Assessment

1. TERMS & NAMES

Identify:
• Aaron Burr
• Judiciary Act of 1801
• midnight judge
• John Marshall
• *Marbury* vs. *Madison*
• judicial review
• Louisiana Purchase
• Meriwether Lewis
• William Clark
• Sacajawea

2. SUMMARIZING Make a chart showing the differences between Jefferson's presidency and Washington's.

WASHINGTON	JEFFERSON

Which seems more like today's presidency?

3. EVALUATING Why were the Louisiana Purchase and the Lewis and Clark expedition important to the expansion of the United States?

THINK ABOUT
• the timing of these events
• the long-term effects

4. ANALYZING Why was *Marbury* v. *Madison* such an important case both in the early days of the country and for its future?

THINK ABOUT
• what was being argued
• Judge Marshall's decision
• its effects on the future

188 CHAPTER 6

ANSWERS

1. TERMS & NAMES

Aaron Burr, p. 184

Judiciary Act of 1801, p. 186

midnight judge, p. 186

John Marshall, p. 186

Marbury vs. *Madison,* p. 186

judicial review, p. 186

Louisiana Purchase, p. 188

Meriwether Lewis, p. 188

William Clark, p. 188

Sacajawea, p. 188

2. SUMMARIZING

Answers should include

WASHINGTON	JEFFERSON
formal manner	informal manner
formal clothes	informal clothes
carriage to inauguration	walked to inauguration
bigger government	reduced size of government
larger military	reduced size of military
higher taxes	reduced taxes

3. EVALUATING

The population was growing and people were ready to move west and settle new lands. With the Purchase, the country received a great deal of land, and with the expedition, it gained valuable information about the new territory.

4. ANALYZING

The case was significant because it affirmed the principle of judicial review—that the Supreme Court could declare a law unconstitutional and thus be an effective check on the legislative branch. In this case the unconstitutional law was the Judiciary Act of 1789. From this point on, the principle of judicial review has played an important role in American government, by testing laws whose constitutionality has been questioned.

④ The War of 1812 Erupts

TERMS & NAMES
- blockade
- impressment
- embargo
- war hawk
- William Henry Harrison
- Tecumseh
- Andrew Jackson
- Treaty of Ghent
- armistice

LEARN ABOUT the growing conflict between the United States and Britain
TO UNDERSTAND how events led to the War of 1812.

Section 4 Overview

OBJECTIVES
1 To explain the events that led to the War of 1812.
2 To summarize the course of the war.

SKILLBUILDERS
- Understanding geography: location, human-environment interaction, p. 190
- Interpreting charts, p. 191

CRITICAL THINKING
- Analyzing causes, p. 190
- Clarifying, p. 190
- Summarizing, p. 191
- Evaluating, p. 191
- Analyzing, p. 191

ONE AMERICAN'S STORY

During the War of 1812, Samuel Wilson became a symbol for the nation. The owner of a meat-packing business in Troy, New York, he began supplying barrels of salted meat to the army, stamping the barrels with the initials "U.S.," for United States. One of Wilson's employees joked that the letters stood for "Uncle Sam," Wilson's nickname. Soon army recruits were calling themselves "Uncle Sam's soldiers." One of Wilson's great-nephews, Lucius Wilson, spoke about his famous relative in 1917.

A PERSONAL VOICE
He was the old original Uncle Sam that gave the name to the United States. . . . [He] engaged in many enterprises, employed many hands [workers], had extensive acquaintance, was jolly, genial, generous, and known and called "Uncle Sam" by everyone.

LUCIUS E. WILSON, quoted in *Uncle Sam: The Man and the Legend*

The story took on the features of a legend. Uncle Sam came to symbolize American values of honesty and hard work. The war during which the phrase caught on was just around the corner for the United States.

This cartoon by Thomas Nast shows an aggressive Uncle Sam confronting the cartoonist in the Blue Room of the White House. Nast's portraits of Uncle Sam helped to shape the figure in the public imagination.

The War Hawks Demand War

Jefferson's popularity soared after the Louisiana Purchase, and he won reelection in 1804. During his second term, renewed fighting between Britain and France threatened American shipping. In 1806, Napoleon decided to exclude British goods from Europe. In turn, Great Britain decided that the best way of attacking Napoleon's Europe was to **blockade** it, or seal up its ports and prevent ships from entering or leaving. By 1807, Britain had seized more than 1,000 American ships and confiscated their cargoes, and France had seized about half that number.

GRIEVANCES AGAINST BRITAIN Although both France and Britain engaged in these acts of aggression, Americans focused their anger on the British. One reason was the policy of **impressment,** the British practice of seizing Americans at sea and "impressing," or drafting, them into the British navy. Another reason was the *Chesapeake* incident. In June 1807, the commander of a British warship demanded the right to board and search the U.S. naval frigate *Chesapeake* for British deserters. When the U.S. captain refused, the British opened fire, killing three Americans and wounding 18.

Jefferson convinced Congress to declare an **embargo,** a ban on exporting products to other countries. He believed that the Embargo Act of 1807 would hurt Britain and the other European powers and force them to honor American neutrality. Unfortunately, the embargo stifled American business, and Congress eventually lifted the order in 1809.

Launching the New Nation **189**

FOCUS & MOTIVATE

▶ *Starting with the Student*
- Ask students to think about recent conflicts they have had with other people. How have they solved them?
- Ask them how two countries might resolve differences instead of going to war.

OBJECTIVE
1 **INSTRUCT**

The War Hawks Demand War

▶ *Discussing Key Ideas*
- Britain seizes American ships and sailors and opens fire on the *Chesapeake*.
- American troops battle Native Americans for possession of the Indiana Territory.

IN-DEPTH RESOURCES: UNIT 2
Guided Reading, p. 32

ACCESS FOR STUDENTS ACQUIRING ENGLISH
Guided Reading (Spanish), p. 66

SECTION 4 RESOURCES

PRINT RESOURCES

IN-DEPTH RESOURCES: UNIT 2
Guided Reading, p. 32
Primary Source: Dolley Madison's Letter to Her Sister, p. 39
American Lives: Tecumseh, p. 44

ACCESS FOR STUDENTS ACQUIRING ENGLISH
Guided Reading (Spanish), p. 66

FORMAL ASSESSMENT
Section Quiz, p. 80

ALTERNATIVE ASSESSMENT BOOK
See forms for supporting and scoring alternative activities.

TECHNOLOGY RESOURCES

CRITICAL THINKING TRANSPARENCIES
CT6, The War of 1812

VIDEO *American Portfolio: A Videodisc for U.S. History*
user's guide, pp. 44, 48, 49, 51

INTERNET McDougal Littell Learning On-Line
http://www.mcdougallittell.com

Teacher's Edition **189**

The War Brings Mixed Results

▶ **Starting with the Student**
Have students create a chart like the one below, listing the positive and negative results of the War of 1812.

War of 1812: Results	
Positive	Negative

▶ **Discussing Key Ideas**
• The United States declares war against Britain, but the U.S. military is ill-prepared.
• After suffering losses on both sides, the United States and Great Britain sign a peace treaty.

HISTORY FROM VISUALS
The War of 1812

Reading the Map Ask students to make a chronological list of the dates and places in the text boxes. Ask them how many years the map information covers. *Answer: A bit more than three years.*

Extension Ask students to research the burning of the White House in 1814. Ask them what famous story is associated with that event. *Answer: The story of Dolly Madison rescuing the portrait of George Washington.*

 CRITICAL THINKING TRANSPARENCIES
CT6, The War of 1812

IN-DEPTH RESOURCES: UNIT 2
Primary Source: Dolley Madison's Letter to Her Sister, p. 39
American Lives: Tecumseh, p. 44

"The Great Spirit gave this great land to his red children."

TECUMSEH

GRIEVANCES AGAINST NATIVE AMERICANS Anger against Britain did not vanish, however. A group of young Congressmen from the South and the West, known as the **war hawks,** continued to beat the drums of war. The leaders of this group were John C. Calhoun of South Carolina and Henry Clay of Kentucky, the Speaker of the House of Representatives.

One issue that inflamed the war hawks was the presence of Native Americans in the Indiana Territory, an area in which they wanted to expand white settlement. Trouble began in 1809 when General **William Henry Harrison,** the governor of the Indiana Territory, invited several Native American chiefs to Fort Wayne, Indiana, and persuaded them to sign away 3 million acres of tribal land to the U.S. government.

A confederacy of Native Americans, led by the Shawnee chief **Tecumseh,** began organizing to fight for their homeland against intruding white settlers. In 1811, while Tecumseh was absent, his brother led the Shawnee in an attack on Harrison and his troops but was defeated. Harrison's victory at the Battle of Tippecanoe made him a national hero. When the war hawks discovered that the Native American confederacy was using arms from British Canada, they again called for war. Their rallying cry was "On to Canada!"

The War Brings Mixed Results

GEOGRAPHY SKILLBUILDER
LOCATION *Why do you think there were a number of battles on the Great Lakes?* **HUMAN-ENVIRONMENT INTER-ACTION** *Why do you think the British blockaded the coast from Boston to Virginia?*

In the election of 1808, another Virginia Republican—James Madison—coasted to victory against a weak Federalist opponent, Charles C. Pinckney. By the spring of 1812, President Madison had decided to go to war against Britain. Madison believed that Britain was trying to strangle American trade and cripple the American economy. Congress approved the war declaration in early June.

THINK THROUGH HISTORY
A. Analyzing Causes Why did the war hawks object to the presence of Native Americans in the Indiana Territory?
A. Answer The war hawks wanted Native American lands, and they thought that certain tribes were siding with the British.

B. Answer Madison believed Britain was trying to strangle American trade and cripple the economy.
THINK THROUGH HISTORY
B. Clarifying Why did Madison decide to declare war?

The War of 1812

Lake Champlain, Sept. 11, 1814
U.S. gains control of lake, and British retreat to Canada.

Fort Mackinac, July 17, 1812

CANADA (British)

Montreal

York (Toronto), April 27, 1813

Boston

Fort George / Fort Niagara

Thames, Oct. 5, 1813
Death of Tecumseh leads to collapse of Native American support for British.

Fort Erie, August 2–September 21, 1814

New York

Detroit

Tippecanoe, Nov. 7, 1811
With British support, Native Americans try to stop U.S. westward expansion, resulting in Harrison's victory.

Fort Dearborn, August 15, 1812

ATLANTIC OCEAN

Delaware Bay

Ohio R.

Chesapeake Bay

U.S. forces, 1812–1813
British forces, 1814
U.S. victory
British victory
Native American victory
Fort

Put-in-Bay, Sept. 10, 1813
U.S. naval forces under Oliver Hazard Perry gain control of Lake Erie.

Baltimore, Sept. 12–14, 1814
British fail to capture city and withdraw from Chesapeake Bay in October.

Washington, D.C., Aug. 24–25, 1814
British burn Capitol, White House, and other important buildings.

France, April 1814
Overthrow of Emperor Napoleon allows British to concentrate on war against U.S.

New Orleans, Jan. 8, 1815
After defeating Native Americans in Mississippi Territory, Andrew Jackson moves to defend this city. Battle fought two weeks after peace treaty was signed at Ghent, December 24, 1814.

Horseshoe Bend, March 27, 1814

Fort Mims, August 30, 1813

FLORIDA (Spanish)

Pensacola

0   200 Miles
0   400 Kilometers

Making Connections Across Cultures

African Americans in Jackson's Army General Andrew Jackson issued a call to "Free Colored Inhabitants" of Louisiana in an attempt to recruit troops to resist British forces. His urgent call read: "To every noble-hearted, generous freeman of color, volunteering to serve during the present contest with Great Britain . . . will be paid the same bounty in money and lands, now received by the white soldiers. . . ." He went further and said, "You will not, by being associated with white men in the same corps, be exposed to improper comparisons or unjust sarcasm." A number of freemen did respond to his appeal.

Exploring Themes

Constitutional Concerns Although President Madison decided to go to war against Great Britain in 1812, under the Constitution only Congress can declare war. As commander in chief of the armed services, the president dominates foreign policy, but Congress controls the purse. Even if presidents did have the power to declare war, they need money to fund the war effort. The money must be gotten from Congress. Some presidents have fought undeclared wars to avoid Congressional debates, but funding is always a problem.

FAILURE IN CANADA Declaring war was one thing—but fighting it was another. Republican funding cuts had left the American military ill-prepared for war. As a result, the first attempts to invade Canada were disastrous.

The next year things went better. A fleet under the command of Oliver Hazard Perry defeated a British fleet on Lake Erie, and American soldiers retook Detroit and won several battles. Tecumseh was killed at the Battle of the Thames, and with his death, the confederacy collapsed. However, the superior numbers of the British navy began to tell—by the end of 1813, most American ships were bottled up in port.

BRITISH BURN THE WHITE HOUSE By 1814, the British were raiding and burning towns all along the Atlantic coast. The redcoats brushed aside some hastily assembled American troops and entered Washington, D.C., on August 24. Madison and other federal officials had to flee from their own capital. The British burned the Capitol, the White House, and other public buildings.

In the meantime, General **Andrew Jackson** of Tennessee gathered troops to protect New Orleans. On January 8, 1815, Jackson's troops met a superior British force at the Battle of New Orleans. The 5,400 Americans lay lodged behind walls of cotton bales, awaiting the 8,000 redcoats. The British commander ordered a direct assault. Hundreds of British troops died, while just a handful of Americans lost their lives.

Ironically, British and American diplomats had already signed a peace agreement, but news of the pact had not reached Jackson in time. The **Treaty of Ghent,** signed on Christmas Eve 1814, declared an **armistice,** or end to the fighting. Although it did not address the issues of impressment or neutral shipping rights, Americans were eager for peace and welcomed the treaty.

Within a few years, the United States and Great Britain were able to reach agreement on many of the issues left open at Ghent. In 1815, a commercial treaty reopened trade between the two countries. In 1817, the Rush-Bagot agreement limited the number of warships on the Great Lakes. In 1818, a British-American commission set the northern boundary of the Louisiana Territory at the 49th parallel as far west as the Rocky Mountains. The two nations then agreed to a ten-year joint occupation of the Oregon Territory. The War of 1812 confirmed American independence and strengthened nationalism.

The War of 1812 brought to a close the critical first 23 years of the United States under the Constitution. As the chart on this page shows, the young nation could boast of many truly remarkable achievements during this period. Yet the most remarkable achievements may well have been the most difficult—the peaceful unification of different regions to form a single nation, and the beginning of a national identity.

**Achievements of the United
States, 1789–1812**

- **President Washington and other national leaders created an effective executive and judicial branch of government.**
- **The Federalist and Republican political parties expressed their political differences through democratic means.**
- **The federal government took effective action to govern domestic affairs.**
- **The Louisiana Purchase more than doubled the area of the United States.**
- **The United States established itself on the world stage.**

Section 4 Assessment

1. TERMS & NAMES

Identify:
- blockade
- impressment
- embargo
- war hawk
- William Henry Harrison
- Tecumseh
- Andrew Jackson
- Treaty of Ghent
- armistice

2. SUMMARIZING In the web below, show the reasons why the war hawks wanted war with Great Britain.

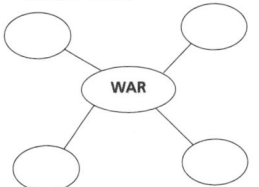

3. EVALUATING What was the most important achievement of the U.S. in this period?
THINK ABOUT
- relations between the U.S. and Britain
- the results of the war

4. ANALYZING What do you think was the most important reason for American success at the Battle of New Orleans?
THINK ABOUT
- the size of the forces
- the location of the battle
- the strategies

Launching the New Nation **191**

ANSWERS

1. TERMS & NAMES

blockade, p. 189

impressment, p. 189

embargo, p. 189

war hawk, p. 190

William Henry Harrison, p. 190

Tecumseh, p. 190

Andrew Jackson, p. 191

Treaty of Ghent, p. 191

armistice, p. 191

2. SUMMARIZING

Answers should include
- Britain seized American ships.
- Britain seized American citizens at sea and drafted them into the British navy.
- the *Chesapeake* incident.
- British Canadians supplied arms to Native Americans.

3. EVALUATING

Answers will vary but might include that the War of 1812 confirmed American independence and nationalism; in this period the U.S. took its place on the world stage.

4. ANALYZING

Some students will credit Jackson's establishing a strong defensive position behind walls of cotton bales. Others may cite the British commander's mistake in ordering a direct assault.

Teacher's Edition **191**

American Studies

OBJECTIVES

① To recognize the influence of the neoclassical movement in the United States.

② To describe how neoclassicism affected the design and architecture of the nation's new capital.

FOCUS & MOTIVATE

▶ ***Starting with the Student***
Ask students to think about buildings near where they live or other places they have visited.

- Which buildings show neoclassical influences?
- What are some specific elements in the buildings that suggest neoclassical design?

MORE ABOUT . . .
Early Washington, D.C.

Pierre L'Enfant soon lost his job, and for years his design for the new capital was largely a dream on paper. Thomas Jefferson did, however, convince President Washington to hold competitions for the design of the Capitol and of the President's House, as the White House was originally called. Designed by Irish-born architect James Hoban, the President's House was the first public building started, but only one wing was done when First Lady Abigail Adams moved in. The rest of the city was largely woods and mosquito-infested swampland—"romantic," as Mrs. Adams described it, "but a wild wilderness at present."

Neoclassical Style in Federal Architecture

The neoclassical movement, in which artists and thinkers imitated the styles and attitudes of ancient Greece and Rome, was nowhere more popular than in the newly independent United States. The Americans thought of themselves as heirs to the democracy of the ancient Greek city-state of Athens and the glory of the Roman republic. The very names they chose for the new American government—words like *senator, president, congress,* and *constitution,* for example—had their origins in ancient times. Similarly, early American architects drew on ancient models, trying to capture the balance, logic, and order that they associated with classical Greek and Roman styles.

Thomas Jefferson, one of the founding fathers, popularized classical models with the buildings he himself designed —such as the University of Virginia Library, whose domed rotunda (or circular area under the dome) and portico (or pillared porch) echo those of the Pantheon, a Roman temple that Jefferson saw as a symbol of classical wisdom and virtue. A similar design was used for the Jefferson Memorial, the monument to the great Virginian built over a century later in Washington, D.C.

WASHINGTON D.C.

THE CREATION OF WASHINGTON, D.C. As a former surveyor, President George Washington took great interest in the design of the new capital that would later be named for him. He discussed his ideas with the French engineer Pierre L'Enfant, who also took advice from Thomas Jefferson, himself a talented architect. L'Enfant's final design, created by a six-person team that included Benjamin Banneker, mapped out a city of neoclassical elegance. The executive and legislative branches of government were to be housed in separate areas connected by spacious tree-lined boulevards reflecting the freedom of the new republic.

192 Chapter 6

RECOMMENDED RESOURCES

Books
Garrett, Wendell. *Classic America: The Federal Style & Beyond.* New York: Rizzoli, 1992. Neoclassical architecture and interior design in America.

Price, Robert L., ed. *The Washington Post Guide to Washington.* New York:

McGraw, 1989. A comprehensive guide.

McLaughlin, Jack. *Jefferson and Monticello.* New York: Knopf, 1988. Jefferson's career as an architect.

Seale, William. *The President's House.* Washington: White House Historical Assoc., 1986.

Videos

America's Monumental Story. Video Vacation, 1991. A historic tour of Washington and its landmarks.

The Building of the Capitol. Republic Pictures, 1986.

Thomas Jefferson's Monticello. AIMS. Actor E. G. Marshall tours Jefferson's home.

Washington, D.C. Encyclopædia Britannica, 1984. A profile of the city built on the Potomac.

Washington Monuments. Atlas Video, 1987. An overview of the city and its landmarks.

THE WHITE HOUSE The White House has been the residence and office of every president except George Washington. Begun in 1792, it was first occupied by President John Adams and his wife Abigail.

THE SUPREME COURT The white marble exterior of the Supreme Court Building, which stands east of the Capitol, resembles a Greek temple.

COLUMNS AND CAPITALS A column consists of a shaft (the pillar) and a capital (the top). The U.S. Capitol building uses an American variation on the classical capitals of ancient Greece and Rome. Ears of corn, a typical American crop, serve as an emblem for the American republic.

PENNSYLVANIA AVENUE

LINCOLN MEMORIAL

The White House

NATIONAL GALLERY OF ART

THE MALL

Capitol Building

Supreme Court

WASHINGTON MONUMENT

LIBRARY OF CONGRESS

JEFFERSON MEMORIAL

Potomac River

Potomac River

EAST FRONT OF THE CAPITOL OF THE UNITED STATES
On rising ground at the center of L'Enfant's plan was the nation's chief legislative building, the Capitol—designed by William Thornton and named after the Capitoline hill in ancient Rome. With its dome and impressive Corinthian pillars, the Capitol was indeed reminiscent of an ancient Greek or Roman temple. Thomas Jefferson once called it "the first temple dedicated to the sovereignty of the people."

INTERACT WITH HISTORY

1. **ANALYZING ASSUMPTIONS**
Comment on the significance of the Capitol's location in the original plans for Washington, D.C. Why do you think the President's House, as the White House was then called, was not placed at the center of the city?

SEE SKILLBUILDER HANDBOOK, PAGE 1047.

2. **PREPARING A REPORT** Report on the extent to which the architectural styles of ancient Greece and Rome have influenced the public buildings in your own state.

Launching the New Nation **193**

TERMS & NAMES

1. Alexander Hamilton, p. 173
2. cabinet, p. 173
3. neutrality, p. 178
4. Alien and Sedition Acts, p. 181
5. John Marshall, p. 186
6. Louisiana Purchase, p. 188
7. Lewis and Clark, p. 188
8. embargo, p. 189
9. Tecumseh, p. 190
10. Andrew Jackson, p. 191

MAIN IDEAS
Answers will vary.

11. Creating a judicial system, appointing a cabinet, establishinf a national bank, and moving the capital to Washington, D.C.

12. Washington knew that he would receive a range of opinions on various issues.

13. It tested the strength of the new federal government, which broke up rebel action with military force.

14. **The French Revolution:** U.S. remained neutral; **Negotiations with Britain for control of land west of the Appalachians:** Britain evacuated the Northwest Territory, but did not give U.S. shipping rights in the Carribean; **The XYZ Affair:** provoked a wave of anti-French hostility and an undeclared naval war

15. Declared neutrality, used diplomacy

16. Took Native American land at will, attacked Native Americans, negotiated land treaties with Native American groups but underpaid them

17. Simplifying the presidency, a peaceful power transfer, *Marbury* v. *Madison* decision, Louisiana Purchase, Lewis and Clark expedition begun

18. Thousands of pioneers moved west; the nation became much larger.

19. British Canadian support of Native Americans, seizure of American ships, British impressment of American sailors, the *Chesapeake* incident

20. An armistice with Great Britain

REVIEWING THE CHAPTER

TERMS & NAMES For each term below, write a sentence explaining its connection to the early days of the new government. For each person below, explain his role in launching the new government.

1. Alexander Hamilton
2. cabinet
3. neutrality
4. Alien and Sedition Acts
5. John Marshall
6. Louisiana Purchase
7. Lewis and Clark
8. embargo
9. Tecumseh
10. Andrew Jackson

MAIN IDEAS

SECTION 1 *(pages 172–176)*

Washington Heads the New Government

11. What were the first steps taken by the Washington administration in building a new government?
12. Why did President Washington allow both Thomas Jefferson and Alexander Hamilton to be among his closest advisers?
13. Why was the Whiskey Rebellion a significant event in the early days of the new government?

SECTION 2 *(pages 177–181)*

Foreign Affairs Trouble the Nation

14. What were three major international issues at this time and how did the United States respond to them?
15. How did the United States manage to stay out of war during this period?
16. How did the expanding nation deal with the Native Americans?

SECTION 3 *(pages 184–188)*

Jefferson Alters the Nation's Course

17. What were some of the accomplishments of Jefferson's first administration?
18. How did the Louisiana Purchase change the United States?

SECTION 4 *(pages 189–191)*

The War of 1812 Erupts

19. What events led to the War of 1812?
20. What did the Treaty of Ghent accomplish?

THINKING CRITICALLY

1. **FEDERALISTS AND REPUBLICANS** Create a chart listing some of the more important differences in beliefs and goals between Federalists and Republicans. Whose ideas do you think made more sense? Explain your choice.

Federalists	Republicans

2. **TESTING THE CONSTITUTION** Reread the quote by Benjamin Franklin at the beginning of the chapter. What does his statement tell you about his attitude toward the Constitution?

3. **DAILY LIFE** What might have been some of the advantages and disadvantages of daily life in this period? Imagine that through time travel you are transported back to 1800. Write two paragraphs describing what you like and dislike about the age.

4. **GEOGRAPHY OF THE LEWIS AND CLARK EXPEDITION** What would you say is the most important accomplishment of the Lewis and Clark expedition?

5. **ANALYZING PRIMARY SOURCES** Study the American political cartoon below portraying the XYZ Affair. France is the monster with five heads demanding money, with the American diplomats answering, "Cease bawling, monster! We will not give you sixpence!" Why are the characters depicted in this way? What other details in the cartoon show the negative attitude of the cartoonist toward his subject?

THINKING CRITICALLY

1. FEDERALISTS AND REPUBLICANS
Possible Responses: **Federalists:** wanted a strong central government; wanted a republic of wise elite; favored a strong national banking system; had strong support in the North; favored commercial interests
Republicans: favored strong state governments; favored a society of farmer-citizens; against a national bank; had strong support in South and West; favored agrarian interests

2. TESTING THE CONSTITUTION
Possible Responses: Franklin seems to hope that the Constitution will last, but he knows that few things in life are certain except death and the need governments have for money.
Franklin's attitude seems to be that although the Constitution is functioning and will probably last, there is no guarantee of its continuing survival.

3. DAILY LIFE
Possible Responses: Some students may say they would like the excitement of crafting a new nation. Others may note the discomfort and slowness of travel and the difficulties of communication.

ALTERNATIVE ASSESSMENT

1. DESCRIBING HISTORY

How did the inaugural addresses of the first presidents help to define the new nation?

Write an eyewitness account of a presidential inaugural address between 1789 and 1816.

 Use the CD-ROM *Electronic Library of Primary Sources* and other resources to review the inaugural addresses of Washington, Adams, Jefferson, or Madison.

- Assume a specific point of view as the spectator: where you are from, what kind of work you do, and so forth.
- From that point of view, describe the address as an eyewitness. Describe your reaction to the speech.

2. LEARNING FROM MEDIA

VIDEO View the McDougal Littell Video for Chapter 6, *Recruited by Lewis and Clark.*
Discuss the following questions in groups.

- What were some facts that the Corps of Discovery, including Patrick Gass, learned about the territory they explored?
- What role did Sacajawea play on the expedition? How did her presence contribute to the Corps of Discovery?
- What different Native American tribes and peoples did the expedition encounter?
- How might his participation in the Lewis and Clark expedition have changed Patrick Gass?

3. PORTFOLIO PROJECT

Use the Living History activity to expand your portfolio.

LIVING HISTORY

PREPARING A TELEVISION NEWS BROADCAST

Write and present to the class your television news broadcast about the Lewis and Clark expedition.

- After reading about the Lewis and Clark expedition, are there certain questions, issues, or events that you need more information about? If so, consult encyclopedia articles and books for more information.
- Write a script for your broadcast, in which you touch upon the major points of the expedition.
- Choose images to illustrate your newscast. What images do you want to show to illustrate your words?
- Write an introduction and a conclusion in which you present an overview and then a summary of the Corps of Discovery.
- Be prepared to present your television news broadcast, along with your lists of important information and visual images. Add your script and images to your American history portfolio.

Review Chapter 6

THE NEW GOVERNMENT George Washington proved to be a wise and strong leader of the new nation. With the Constitution as a foundation, Washington and the new Congress went to work creating and shaping a government that could deal effectively with the everyday problems. Political parties were born at this time. Alexander Hamilton's economic plan proposed to deal with the country's debts and set up a national banking system.

TROUBLESOME FOREIGN AFFAIRS Although issues with France divided Americans, the Republicans and Jefferson usually supported the French, while the Federalists and Hamilton supported Britain. President Washington managed to keep the nation out of war by taking a position of neutrality. Adams's presidency brought the passage of the Alien and Sedition Acts. The nation continued to expand its borders.

JEFFERSON'S PRESIDENCY Jefferson introduced a simpler, more American style to the presidency, and the nation moved further away from the influence and style of the British. He also cut the costs of running the federal government. Jefferson more than doubled the size of the country through the Louisiana Purchase from France in 1803. He sent Lewis and Clark on an expedition to the west.

THE WAR OF 1812 America found it impossible to maintain its position of neutrality in the war between France and Britain. Impressment of American sailors by the British infuriated the country. Jefferson tried to halt the British hostility with an embargo, but this action only hurt American business. In 1812, during Madison's presidency, America went to war with Britain. America struggled in battle against British troops and eventually won. Andrew Jackson proved to be a victorious military leader at New Orleans.

Preview Chapter 7

After the war, the country continued to grow and develop, but different regions found themselves heading in different directions. At the same time, white settlers were moving farther and farther west. The nation was beginning to find itself divided on a number of issues including economics, slavery, Native American lands, and women's rights.

Launching the New Nation **195**

THINKING CRITICALLY

4. GEOGRAPHY/THE LEWIS AND CLARK EXPEDITION

Possible Responses: Responses should include one of the following: mapping new territory, collecting samples of new animal and plant life, or gaining information about Native Americans.

5. ANALYZING PRIMARY SOURCES

Possible Responses: France is depicted as a monster with a dagger in its hand, because French agents attempted to extort huge sums of money from American diplomats. Other negative details include the guillotine, showing a victim and a tattered woman, as well as the "Civic Feast" in the foreground at which the participants are eating frogs.

---

1. DESCRIBING HISTORY
Standards for Evaluation
An eyewitness account should meet the following criteria:

- Shows how a presidential inaugural address presages the direction of the country under that president.
- Displays knowledge of the original text of the inaugural address; refers to specific passages in the account.
- Creates strong eyewitness persona, using historically accurate details.

2. LEARNING FROM MEDIA
Answers to the questions:

- They found that overland travel to the Pacific Coast was possible but that a continuous water route was improbable. The Corps gathered information about plants and animals, as well as about Native Americans.
- Sacajawea played a key role as an interpreter and guide. At a crucial point in the journey, Sacajawea led the men through mountains to her tribe, the Shoshones, who furnished horses for the expedition.
- The Missouris, Sioux, Mandans, Shoshones, Assiniboins, and Clatsops were just a few of the tribes the Corps encountered.
- *Possible Responses:* Students may conclude that participating in this historic expedition brought Gass a degree of confidence and fame. Because Gass did not settle down until he was sixty years old, one might conclude that the journey made him restless.

3. PORTFOLIO
LIVING HISTORY
Standards for Evaluation
A news broadcast should meet the following criteria:

- Presents a colorful description of the major points of the expedition.
- Includes appropriate images.
- Makes logical connections between text and images.
- Shows good organization.
- Includes a clear, coherent script.
- Includes an effective introduction and conclusion.

IN-DEPTH RESOURCES: UNIT 2
See the form for scoring this activity on page 46.

CHAPTER 7

PLANNING GUIDE
Balancing Nationalism and Sectionalism

	Key Ideas	TEACHING SUPPORT	ASSESSMENT	
SECTION 1 Regional Economies Create Differences *pp. 198–203*	Henry Clay seeks to unify the country—even as various sections of the nation develop different economic systems.	*In-Depth Resources: Unit 2* • Guided Reading, p. 47 • American Lives: Henry Clay, p. 63 **COOPERATIVE ACTIVITIES** • Debating the Merits of Progress, p. 200 (TE)	*Section 1 Assessment,* p. 203 (PE) *Self-Assessment,* p. 203 (TE) *Formal Assessment* • Section Quiz, p. 89 *Alternative Assessment Book* • Standards for Evaluating a Cooperative Activity	
SECTION 2 Nationalism at Center Stage *pp. 204–208*	Nationalism exerts a strong influence through the nation's courts, foreign affairs, and westward expansion.	*In-Depth Resources: Unit 2* • Guided Reading, p. 48 • Skillbuilder Practice: Synthesizing, p. 51 • American Lives: James Beckwourth, p. 64 **COOPERATIVE ACTIVITY** • A Skit About Pioneer Life, p. 207 (TE)	*Section 2 Assessment,* p. 208 (PE) *Self-Assessment,* p. 208 (TE) *Formal Assessment* • Section Quiz, p. 90 *Alternative Assessment Book* • Standards for Evaluating a Cooperative Activity	
SECTION 3 The Age of Jackson *pp. 209–213*	Andrew Jackson's policies give voice to common people but violate Native American rights.	*In-Depth Resources: Unit 2* • Guided Reading, p. 49 • Geography Application: Jackson Finally Becomes President, p. 52 • Outline Map: The Indian Removal Act of 1830, p. 54 • Primary Sources: Political Cartoon, p. 56; *from* the Cherokee Nation's Appeal to the American People, p. 57 • Literature: from *The President's Lady* by Irving Stone, p. 60	*Section 3 Assessment,* p. 213 (PE) *Self-Assessment,* p. 213 (TE) *Formal Assessment* • Section Quiz, p. 91	
SECTION 4 Jackson, States' Rights, and the National Bank *pp. 214–219*	Andrew Jackson deals with two issues—states' rights and the Bank of the United States—that have a long-lasting impact on the American nation.	*In-Depth Resources: Unit 2* • Guided Reading, p. 50 • Primary Source: *from* the Hayne-Webster Debates, p. 58 **COOPERATIVE ACTIVITY** • Discussing States' Rights, p. 216 (TE)	*Section 4 Assessment,* p. 219 (PE) *Self-Assessment,* p. 219 (TE) *Formal Assessment* • Section Quiz, p. 92 *Alternative Assessment Book* • Standards for Evaluating a Cooperative Activity	
CHAPTER RESOURCES	**Chapter Overview** American leaders devise a far-sighted policy of improvements as North, South, and West develop distinct economies, but the sections gradually grow to guard their sectional interests.	*In-Depth Resources: Unit 2* • Living History Project, Worksheet, p. 65; Standards, p. 66 *Telescoping the Times* • Chapter Summary, pp. 13–14 *Planning for Block Schedules*	*Chapter Assessment,* pp. 220–221 (PE) *Alternative Assessment,* p. 221 (PE) *Formal Assessment* • Chapter Test, forms A and B, p. 10–15 **Test Generator** *Alternative Assessment Book* See explanation and forms for different kinds of alternative assessment including portfolio assessment	

Critical Thinking Transparencies
• CT7, Industrial Revolution

Electronic Library of Primary Sources
• *from* the First Inaugural Address of 1817 by James Monroe
• *from A Narrative of the Life and Adventures of Charles Ball A Black Man*

INTERNET RESOURCES
• See *McDougal Littell Learning On-Line* for links to information about the Erie Canal, Eli Whitney, and Henry Clay

INTERNET RESOURCES
• See *McDougal Littell Learning On-Line* for links to information about The Monroe Doctrine and John Quincy Adams

Geography Transparencies
• G7, Population Density: 1790–1830

Electronic Library of Primary Sources
• *from* a Message to Congress on the Indian Policy by Andrew Jackson

INTERNET RESOURCES
• See *McDougal Littell Learning On-Line* for links to information about the Trail of Tears and Andrew Jackson

Humanities Transparencies
• H33, President Andrew Jackson destroying the Bank of the United States: Lithograph Cartoon, 1828

Electronic Library of Primary Sources
• *from* an Address to the People of the United States by John C. Calhoun
• *from* a Proclamation to the People of the United States by Andrew Jackson

INTERNET RESOURCES
• See *McDougal Littell Learning On-Line* for links to information about Martin Van Buren and William Henry Harrison

American Portfolio: A Videodisc for U.S. History, user's guide, pp. 53–55, 64–67

INTERNET RESOURCES:
Learning On-Line: Social Studies
http://www.mcdougallittell.com

Block Scheduling (90 MINUTES)

Day 1
Section 1, pp. 198–203
Section 2, pp. 204–208
Section Assessments pp. 203, 213

Day 2
Section 3, pp. 209–213
Section 4, pp. 214–219
Chapter Assessment, pp. 220–221

YEARLY PACING *Chapter 7 Total:* 2 days *Yearly Total:* 85 days

See *Planning for Block Schedules* for special activities and pacing strategies.

Customizing for Special Populations

Students Acquiring English

Access for Students Acquiring English
• Guided Reading for Sections 1–4 (Spanish), pp. 72–75
• Chapter Summary (Spanish), pp. 70–71
• Skillbuilder Practice: Synthesizing (Spanish), p. 76
• Geography Application: Jackson Finally Becomes President (Spanish), p. 77
• Outline Map: The Indian Removal Act of 1830 (Spanish), p. 79

INTERNET RESOURCES
• See *McDougal Littell Learning On-Line* The Diverse Classroom.

Less Proficient Readers

In-Depth Resources: Unit 2
• Guided Reading for Sections 1–4, pp. 47–50
• Skillbuilder: Synthesizing, p. 51
• Geography Application: Jackson Finally Becomes President, p. 52
• Outline Map: The Indian Removal Act of 1830, p. 54

Telescoping the Times
• Chapter Summary, pp. 13–14

See additional strategies at point of use in the Teacher's Edition.

Gifted and Talented Students

In-Depth Resources: Unit 2
• Primary Sources: Political Cartoon, p. 56; *from* The Cherokee Nation's Appeal to the American People, p. 57; *from* The Hayne-Webster Debates, p. 58
• American Lives: Henry Clay, p. 63; James Beckwourth, p. 64

See additional strategies at point of use in the Teacher's Edition.

Connections to Literature READINGS FOR STUDENTS

In-Depth Resources: Unit 2
• *from The President's Lady* by Irving Stone, p. 60

Enrichment Reading
• Kingsolver, Barbara.
Pigs in Heaven.
New York: Harper & Row, 1994.
In this modern novel, a Native American child is the center of a complex situation involving family and heritage.

• Benét, Stephen Vincent.
The Devil and Daniel Webster.
New York: Henry Holt, 1995.
The great orator and politician Daniel Webster does vigorous battle with the devil in this classic tale.

Balancing Nationalism and Sectionalism

▶ *Starting with the Student*
Ask students to discuss what nationalism and sectionalism mean. Then discuss the opening quotation.

- What difference does Calhoun draw between a "Nation" and a "Union"?
- What does he suggest about the power of states?
- Is Calhoun a nationalist or a sectionalist?

PREVIEWING THE CHAPTER

Ask students to consider what it means to be part of a region. Do students more readily identify themselves as U.S. citizens or, for example, Midwesterners or Southerners? Would they be more likely to support a presidential candidate from their region? Would they be more likely to support programs benefiting their region than those benefiting the entire country? Students should think about these allegiances as they read this chapter.

CHAPTER
7

Balancing Nationalism and Sectionalism

SECTION 1

Regional Economies Create Differences

Henry Clay seeks to unify the country—even as various sections of the nation develop different economic systems.

SECTION 2

Nationalism at Center Stage

Nationalism exerts a strong influence through the nation's courts, foreign affairs, and westward expansion.

SECTION 3

The Age of Jackson

Andrew Jackson's policies give voice to common people but violate Native American rights.

SECTION 4

Jackson, States' Rights, and the National Bank

Andrew Jackson deals with two issues—states' rights and the Bank of the United States—that have a long-lasting impact on the American nation.

> "I never use the word 'Nation' in speaking of the United States. We are not a Nation, but a Union, a confederacy of equal and sovereign States."
>
> John C. Calhoun

The Missouri Compromise is agreed to.

U.S. acquires Florida from Spain.

James Monroe is reelected president.

Construction begins on the Erie Canal.

Jim Beckwourth travels west with a fur-trading expedition.

THE UNITED STATES
THE WORLD

1817 — 1819 — 1820 — 1821 — 1822 — **1823**

1819

Simón Bolívar defeats the Spanish and becomes president of Colombia.

Napoleon dies in exile.

Brazil becomes independent from Portugal.

Mexico becomes a republic.

Liberia is founded by freed U.S. slaves on west coast of Africa.

THEMES IN CHAPTER 2

Science and Technology

In the early 1800s, the efficient machines and processes of the Industrial Revolution began to transform industry and society, particularly in New England. Thousands of people left rural areas to find jobs in the new manufacturing centers.

See Teacher's Edition note, p. 199.

Constitutional Concerns

The supremacy of the Constitution and of federal laws was a source of great debate in the years before the Civil War. Chief Justice John Marshall, a strong federalist, thwarted the states' rights designs of a Democratic and Democratic Republican government. In 1828, Calhoun maintained that individual states had the right to interpret laws and acts to determine their constitutionality. The debate underscored the nation's regional and economic divisions.

See Teacher's Edition notes, pp. 205 and 215.

Expanding Democracy

After Congress passed the Indian Removal Act of 1830, the Cherokee Nation fought for just treatment through the U.S. legal system. In spite of their efforts, however, the Cherokee were eventually forced from their homes.

See Teacher's Edition note, p. 211.

CREATING A POLITICAL ADVERTISEMENT

Discuss ways of planning the political campaign poster:

- Choose a politician widely photographed in the media.
- Research the politician's strengths and weaknesses.
- Decide whether you want to create an ad for or against the politician.
- Determine which qualities of the politician you will stress.
- Find photos that reflect those qualities.
- Create a pithy slogan that sums up your message.

To help students organize their information, suggest that they make a web diagram like the one below.

IN-DEPTH RESOURCES: UNIT 2
See worksheet and standards for evaluation, pp. 65, 66.

LIVING HISTORY

CREATING A POLITICAL ADVERTISEMENT

As you will read, Andrew Jackson was the first presidential candidate to really develop a political "image" as a campaign strategy. He was followed by Martin Van Buren and William Henry Harrison. This image-making is a large part of politics today—as you will see when you watch political advertisements on television and notice how the candidate is portrayed.

- Study pictures and words that help create a candidate's image.
- Then pick a political candidate from today and create your own political advertisement, in the form of a poster, for that candidate.
- Aim for a particular look or impression you want the public to get—positive or negative.
- Choose pictures and words that help convey that image.

PORTFOLIO PROJECT Keep your poster in your folder for your American history portfolio. At the end of the chapter you will compare your poster with others.

- ★ John Quincy Adams is elected president.
- ● John Adams and Thomas Jefferson die on July 4.
- ● Indian Removal Act is passed.
- ★ Andrew Jackson is elected president.
- ★ Andrew Jackson is reelected president.
- ★ Martin Van Buren is elected president.
- ● The Cherokee travel the Trail of Tears to the Indian Territory.
- ★ William Henry Harrison is elected president.
- ★ John Tyler succeeds Harrison as president.

1824	1826	1828	1830	1832	**1833**	1836	1838		**1840**
1825			1830		1835	1837		1839	

- ● Decembrist revolt in Russia is defeated.
- ● France invades Algeria.
- ● Parliament passes an act outlawing employment of children under nine years of age.
- ● Victoria becomes Queen of England.
- ● The Opium War breaks out in China.
- ● The Zulu nation in Africa clashes with Boer settlers.

Balancing Nationalism and Sectionalism **197**

RECOMMENDED RESOURCES

Books for the Teacher

Ehle, John. *Trail of Tears.* New York: Anchor, 1988. Cherokee removal vividly told.

Pessen, Edward. *Jacksonian America.* Urbana: U of Illinois P, 1985. Overview.

Books for the Student

Peterson, Merrill D. *The Great Triumvirate.* New York: Oxford UP, 1987. Lives of Webster, Clay, and Calhoun.

Sterling, Dorothy, ed. *We Are Your Sisters.* New York: Norton, 1984. Personal stories of African-American women before, during, and after Civil War.

Videos

The Autobiography of Miss Jane Pittman. Dir. John Korty. BroadwayVideo, 1974. Dramatization of former slave remembering her life.

Canals and Steamboats. Agency for Instructional Technology, 800-457-4509. Internal improvements.

Civilized Tribes. Cinema Guild, 212-246-5522. Story of the southeastern tribes.

Software

Andrew Jackson: A Man for the People. New Video Group, 1995.

The Industrial Revolution in America. CD-ROM. Educational Software Institute, 800-955-5570.

U.S. History: Jacksonian Democracy. CD-ROM. Educational Software Institute, 800-955-5570.

OBJECTIVES

(1) To describe the effects of the Industrial Revolution on the United States.

(2) To explain how two different agricultural systems developed in the North and South.

(3) To summarize the American System, a plan devised to unite the country.

SKILLBUILDERS

- Interpreting graphics, p. 200
- Interpreting graphs, p. 201
- Understanding geography: human-environment interaction, p. 202

CRITICAL THINKING

- Recognizing effects, pp. 199, 203
- Summarizing, pp. 199, 202, 203
- Comparing, p. 201
- Analyzing effects, p. 203
- Synthesizing, p. 203

FOCUS & MOTIVATE

▶ *Starting with the Student*
- What handmade goods do students use today?
- What computer technology do students use on a daily basis? Consider whether the computer revolution is having as much of an effect on modern life as the Industrial Revolution had on life in the 18th and 19th centuries.

MORE ABOUT . . .
Eli Whitney

In 1792, Whitney went to Georgia to study law. While there, he lived in the house of a woman named Catherine Greene. To help pay for his upkeep, Whitney fixed things around the woman's home. His mechanical skill impressed her. One night, a guest in Mrs. Greene's home complained that he could not grow cotton profitably because of the time it took to clean it. Mrs. Greene said, "Mr. Whitney can make a machine to clean it." By April 1793, he had.

① Regional Economies Create Differences

TERMS & NAMES
- Eli Whitney
- interchangeable parts
- mass production
- Industrial Revolution
- Henry Clay
- American System
- Tariff of 1816
- National Road
- Erie Canal

LEARN ABOUT the different economic systems that developed in various sections of the nation
TO UNDERSTAND why and how Henry Clay sought to unify the country.

ONE AMERICAN'S STORY

In 1798 inventor **Eli Whitney** acquired a contract with the U.S. government to manufacture 10,000 muskets in just two years. He had never made a musket. Moreover, at the time, arms factories could produce only about 250 muskets a year because each musket was made individually, and each part had to be handmade to fit each weapon.

In 1801, his muskets overdue, he showed up in Washington, D.C., with various musket parts in different crates. In a dramatic presentation in front of President John Adams and his cabinet, he demonstrated the interchangeability of these parts by putting together a musket from pieces chosen at random from each box.

How had he done this? For the Cabinet demonstration, he used a process of hand forging, hand filing, and "fitting soft"—fitting parts together loosely. Nonetheless, Whitney and others were developing machine tools with which unskilled workers could turn out uniform parts.

A PERSONAL VOICE
One of my primary objects is to form the tools so the tools themselves shall fashion the work and give to every part its just proportion—which when once accomplished will give expedition, uniformity, and exactness to the whole. . . .
In short, the tools which I contemplate are similar to an engraving on copper plate from which may be taken a great number of impressions exactly alike.

ELI WHITNEY, quoted in *Eli Whitney and the Birth of American Technology*

Eli Whitney

Whitney's initial efforts failed because of a lack of start-up money and precision machine tools. Eventually, however, Whitney and others perfected this practice, which they used early in the next century. This advance speeded up the manufacture of goods and improved their reliability. Inventions and ideas such as these caused dramatic changes in the way Americans labored in the coming century. These changes would affect different regions of the young nation in different ways.

Another Revolution Affects America

During the 19th century, new approaches to manufacturing, such as Whitney's **interchangeable parts** for muskets, took industry out of American households and artisans' workshops and put it, instead, in large semi-mechanized factories. The factory system (using power-driven machinery and laborers assigned to different tasks) made **mass production** possible—the production of goods in large quantities. This development eliminated costly craftsmen who created one object from start to finish. Consequently, factory manufacturing became the cheapest way to produce goods—and eventually the most profitable. These changes in manufacturing brought about an **Industrial Revolution**—a massive change in social and economic organization resulting from the replacement of hand tools by machines and the development of large-scale industrial production.

GREAT BRITAIN STARTS A REVOLUTION This industrial revolution actually first began in Great Britain. It was in Britain, during the 18th century, that inventors first came up with ways to generate power using swiftly flowing streams and burning bountiful supplies of coal. Inventors then developed power-driven machinery and ways to use this machinery to quickly mass-produce goods such as textiles.

SECTION 1 RESOURCES

 PRINT RESOURCES

IN-DEPTH RESOURCES: UNIT 2
Guided Reading, p. 47
American Lives: Henry Clay, p. 63

ACCESS FOR STUDENTS ACQUIRING ENGLISH
Guided Reading (Spanish), p. 72

FORMAL ASSESSMENT
Section Quiz, p. 89

ALTERNATIVE ASSESSMENT BOOK
See forms for supporting and scoring alternative activities.

 TECHNOLOGY RESOURCES

CRITICAL THINKING TRANSPARENCIES
CT7, Industrial Revolution

CD-ROM Electronic Library of Primary Sources

VIDEO *American Portfolio: A Videodisc for U.S. History*
user's guide, pp. 53, 54, 55

INTERNET McDougal Littell Learning On-Line
http://www.mcdougallittell.com

Since advances in diet, medicine, and sanitation enabled people to live longer, the country soon had more people than it had jobs—making labor, another important resource, abundantly available and cheap. British merchants built the first factories, and when these factories prospered, their owners had the money to build more factories, invent more labor-saving machines, and industrialize the nation.

THE INDUSTRIAL REVOLUTION IN THE UNITED STATES Many of the same resources that enabled the British to mechanize industries and develop profitable large-scale factory operations were also plentiful in the United States: rushing rivers, rich deposits of coal and iron ore, and a steady stream of unskilled immigrants eager to find work. However, the primary source of income in America after the War of Independence was international trade, not manufacturing.

Events such as President Thomas Jefferson's Embargo Act of 1807 and the War of 1812 turned the attention of Americans away from international trade and toward the development of domestic industries. Jefferson's embargo, which prohibited Americans from shipping goods to Europe, brought to a standstill the once-thriving foreign trade and shipping businesses. In fact, by the time President Madison lifted the embargo in 1810, many shipping centers—especially those in New England—had shut down, which left the many people who relied on them to search for other sources of income.

Then, just as these seaports recovered, the United States went to war against Britain in the War of 1812, which resulted in naval blockades along much of the coastline. With ships unable to get in or out of U.S. harbors, foreign trade again came to a halt. Americans had to invest their capital in ventures other than international trade and shipping. The most obvious alternative was to develop industries at home for manufacturing goods that could no longer be imported.

NEW ENGLAND INDUSTRIALIZES Probably nowhere else in the nation was the push to invest in industry as great as it was in New England. Its citizens had depended upon shipping and foreign trade for income. Agriculture was not highly profitable. Consequently, New Englanders were more ready than most Americans to embrace new forms of manufacturing—and prime among these were mechanized textile mills.

In 1793, a British immigrant named Samuel Slater had established in Pawtucket, Rhode Island, the first successful mechanized textile factory in America. In Britain he had memorized the plans for a complete textile mill. Then he built the cotton-spinning machines he had operated in a British textile factory. Others imitated his operation. However, Slater's factory and those modeled after it still only mass-produced one part of finished cloth: thread.

Then, in 1813, three Bostonians revolutionized the American textile industry by mechanizing all the stages in the manufacture of cloth. Using plans for an English mill, Francis Cabot Lowell, Nathan Appleton, and Patrick Tracy Jackson built a weaving factory in Waltham, Massachusetts, and outfitted it with power machinery. By 1822 Appleton and Jackson had profited so much from their factory that they decided to build a larger operation in Lowell, Massachusetts, a town named for their deceased partner, Francis Lowell. The changes that their operation triggered in Lowell exemplify those that occurred throughout New England at this time. By the late 1820s, quiet little Lowell had become a booming manufacturing center. Thousands of people—mostly young women who came to Lowell because their families' farms were declining—journeyed there in search of work.

Samuel Slater's cotton mill drew its power from the Blackstone River in Pawtucket, Rhode Island.

A. Answer Shipping and foreign trade came to a standstill, causing people who worked in those businesses to seek other kinds of work and invest in other businesses.

THINK THROUGH HISTORY
A. *Recognizing Effects* What effects did the Embargo Act of 1807 and the War of 1812 have on Americans involved in shipping and foreign trade?

THINK THROUGH HISTORY
B. *Summarizing* Why did manufacturing develop in New England?

B. Answer Many people depended on shipping and foreign trade for income and so they welcomed new forms of manufacturing.

OBJECTIVE
① INSTRUCT

Another Revolution Affects America

▶ *Discussing Key Ideas*
• New inventions and manufacturing methods result in an Industrial Revolution.
• The United States begins developing industries.
• New England embraces new forms of mechanized manufacturing.

IN-DEPTH RESOURCES: UNIT 2
Guided Reading, p. 47

ACCESS FOR STUDENTS ACQUIRING ENGLISH
Guided Reading (Spanish), p. 72

MORE ABOUT . . .
Samuel Slater
Slater worked for six years in an English textile mill. In 1789, after he had learned the workings of the cotton-spinning machine, he decided to come to the United States. However, Slater was forced to leave England in disguise. Because Great Britain led the world in the production of textiles, the government forbade any person who knew how to design and operate spinning machines to leave the country. Once Slater had established his own mill in Pawtucket, he hired children aged 7 to 14 to operate the equipment. By the time he died, Slater owned mills throughout New England.

 CRITICAL THINKING TRANSPARENCIES
CT7, Industrial Revolution

TEACHING OPTIONS

Exploring Themes

Science and Technology Discuss how the new manufacturing methods transformed not only industry but also society. Ask students what effect the new emphasis on industry had on cities in New England. How did the creation of these new industries affect rural areas? How did it affect families? *Possible Responses: Industrial cities thrived, while many rural areas declined. Many traditional families broke up when sons and daughters left their parents' farms to find work in the factories.*

Making Connections Across the Curriculum

Economics Ask students how the Industrial Revolution affected the U.S. economy. *Possible Response: It heralded the beginning of the shift from an agriculturally based economy to one based on industry.*

Why did mining become a more important industry during this time? *Possible Response: Because coal and iron ore were needed to develop the new industries.*

Two Agricultural Systems Develop

▶ *Discussing Key Ideas*
- Northern agriculture and manufacturing support each other without slavery.
- In the South, farmers use slave labor on huge cotton plantations.

NOW & THEN
Agricultural Technology and Population Movement

Critical Thinking:
Evaluating Ask students what life must be like for the children of migrant workers. What kind of education do you think they receive? What kind of future can many of them look forward to? *Possible Response: The children probably receive a haphazard education and are likely to become migrant workers themselves.*

HISTORY FROM VISUALS
The Cotton Gin

Reading the Chart Have students calculate how many pounds of cotton per day ten workers could clean before and after the invention of the cotton gin. *Response: Before—10 pounds; after—500 pounds*

Extension Ask students how the cotton gin made life both easier and more difficult for workers. *Possible Response: It made cotton cleaning easier, but it also encouraged slavery and put more pressure on workers to produce.*

Two Agricultural Systems Develop

Northeasterners, prompted by changing economic conditions, invested their capital in factories and manufacturing operations. Southerners, on the other hand, reaped huge profits from cotton by the mid-1790s. As a result, the North and South continued to develop two distinct economies. They also developed very different agricultural systems.

AGRICULTURE IN THE NORTH Farmers moving into the Old Northwest—the area north of the Ohio River encompassing the states of Ohio, Indiana, Illinois, Wisconsin, and Michigan—usually established small farms on which they continued to grow virtually all that they needed and very rarely sold their produce to distant markets. One traveler to the area shortly after the War of 1812 described a typical pioneer in this territory.

A PERSONAL VOICE
With his axe on his shoulder, his family and stock in a light wagon, he plunges into forests, which have never heard the woodman's stroke, clears a space sufficient for his dwelling, and first year's consumption, and gradually converts the lonely wilderness into a flourishing farm.

FRANCIS HALL, quoted in *American Vistas: 1607–1877*

As cities grew, however, farming began to change. These farmers discovered that they could raise one or two crops or types of livestock (such as corn and cattle), sell what they produced at city markets, and then purchase with cash whatever else they needed from stores—increasingly, items manufactured in Northern factories. As a result, a market economy began to develop in which agriculture and manufacturing each supported the growth of the other—and neither depended upon slave labor.

Economic arguments were not the only reasons given to rationalize slavery, but they were important. Lacking an economic justification for the enslavement of African Americans, some Northerners began to voice their religious and political opposition to slavery. Consequently, by 1804 all the states that then existed north of Delaware had enacted laws to abolish slavery or provide for its gradual end.

COTTON BECOMES KING IN THE SOUTH Eli Whitney's invention of a cotton gin (short for "cotton engine") in 1793 had helped to set the South on a different course of development from the North. Whitney's gin made it possible for

NOW & THEN

AGRICULTURAL TECHNOLOGY AND POPULATION MOVEMENT
The development of agricultural technology over the years has resulted in large population movements. Today, increased production on huge farms and a dwindling number of workers on small farms has meant that, according to some estimates, as many as a million migrant workers move seasonally following the harvest.

In the past, it was the cotton gin that led to a mass movement of planters and slaves into Alabama, Mississippi, and Louisiana. A century later (in the 1930s), mechanical cotton pickers replaced huge communities of share-croppers. Consequently, technology fostered population movement once again, and many African Americans moved from the rural South to Southern and Northern cities.

Skillbuilder Answer Process: A machine could remove the seeds more quickly and less expensively than could a person.

SKILLBUILDER INTERPRETING GRAPHICS *Why was this new process more efficient than removing seeds by hand?*

The Cotton Gin

BEFORE COTTON GIN
1 worker cleans 1 lb. of cotton/day

AFTER COTTON GIN
1 worker cleans 50 lbs. of cotton/day

❶ A hand crank turns a series of rollers.

❷ A roller, with tight rows of wire teeth, removes seeds from the cotton fiber.

❸ The teeth pass through a slotted metal grate, pushing the cotton fiber through but not the seeds, which are too large to pass.

❹ The cotton seeds fall into a hopper.

❺ A second roller with brushes removes the cleaned cotton from the roller.

❻ A clearer compartment catches the cleaned cotton.

TEACHING OPTION

Cooperative Activity: Debating the Merits of Progress

Task: Student groups will role-play citizens in the 1800s and debate whether to oppose or support the construction of a local textile mill.

Purpose: To study effects of the Industrial Revolution.

Activity: Students should research how the Industrial Revolution changed the lives of the working and middle classes. Half the students in each group will oppose the mill opening,

and the other students will support it. Students should use specific examples of living and working conditions before and during the Industrial Revolution to defend their positions. Students taking each position will work together to develop well-reasoned arguments to explain their views.

ALTERNATIVE ASSESSMENT BOOK
Standards for Evaluating a Cooperative Activity

Southern farmers to grow short-staple (or short-fiber) cotton for a profit. Long-staple (long-fiber) cotton grew well in the coastal areas of South Carolina and Georgia, but short-staple cotton was the only cotton that would grow well in the interior regions. Since cotton was in great demand in Britain—and, increasingly, in the North—an efficient machine for cleaning the seeds from short-staple cotton was a major breakthrough. Anyone who could supply the textile mills of Britain and New England with cleaned cotton could profit tremendously.

Armed with Whitney's gin, or one of the many improved versions of the gin devised by later inventors, poor, nonslaveholding farmers eagerly charged into the area between the Appalachians and the Mississippi south of the Ohio to grab land and begin cultivating this cash-producing crop. Wealthier planters followed, bought up huge areas of land, and then put an enormous slave labor force to work cultivating it. By 1820, this plantation system of farming transformed Louisiana, Mississippi, and Alabama into a booming Cotton Kingdom. In this way, the cotton gin accelerated the expansion of slavery.

SLAVERY BECOMES ENTRENCHED Because plantation farming involved the use of a large labor force, and slaves could provide that workforce more profitably than paid workers, rich and powerful plantation owners wanted slavery to remain legal in the South. Although slave importation had declined during the American Revolution, by the 1820s the demand for slaves began to grow. Increases in cotton production and increases in the number of slaves owned paralleled each other. From 1790 to 1810, cotton production surged from 3,000 bales a year to 178,000 bales, while the number of slaves in the South leapt from 700,000 to 1,200,000. By 1808 slave traders had brought 250,000 additional Africans to the United States—as many as had been brought to mainland American colonies between 1619 and 1776.

Not all Southern blacks were slaves, of course. Some communities of free blacks had gained their freedom through various means by the 1800s. In the South, some slaves managed to buy their freedom with wages they earned by hiring themselves out to other whites after they'd finished their daily work for their owners. Others ran away, were freed in legal wills, or were granted their freedom after long years of service.

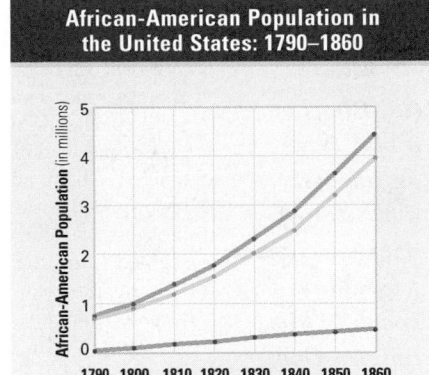

African-American Population in the United States: 1790–1860

■ Total ■ Slave ■ Free

Source: U.S. Department of Commerce, U.S. Bureau of the Census, *Negro Population: 1790–1915.*

C. Answer Small farms developed in the North, while large plantations developed in the South.

THINK THROUGH HISTORY
C. *Comparing* How were the agricultural systems of the North and South different?

Clay Proposes the American System

As the North and South developed different economies, the creation of a plan to unify the nation became increasingly important. In 1815, President Madison presented such a plan to Congress. He hoped his agenda would both unite the different regions of the country and create a strong, stable economy that would make the nation self-sufficient. His plan included three major points:

- establishing a protective tariff;
- resurrecting the national bank (established during Washington's administration under Hamilton's guidance, and then much reduced in influence under Jefferson);
- sponsoring the development of transportation systems as well as as other internal improvements.

The plan held promise. Recognizing this, even former critics of the president—**Henry Clay** and John C. Calhoun—rallied behind it. House Speaker Henry Clay began to promote it as the **American System.**

Balancing Nationalism and Sectionalism **201**

"He [Clay] is a bad man, an imposter, a creator of wicked schemes. I wouldn't speak to him, but, by God, I love him."

JOHN C. CALHOUN

As Clay explained it, the American System would unite the nation's economic interests. An increasingly industrial North would produce the manufactured goods that farmers in the South and West would buy. Meanwhile, a predominantly agricultural South and West would raise most of the grain, meat, and cotton needed in the North. A nationally accepted currency and improved transportation network would facilitate this exchange of goods. With each part of the country sustaining the other, Americans would finally be economically independent of Britain and other European nations.

TARIFFS AND THE NATIONAL BANK Why were the tariffs on imports proposed by Madison and promoted by Clay necessary? Ever since the end of the War of 1812, British merchants had flooded the United States with iron, textiles, and other merchandise they had stockpiled during the war, and they priced these goods far below the cost of American-made merchandise. Consequently, few Americans bought the more expensive American-made products. Something needed to be done to enable these American-made items to compete with their lower-priced foreign competitors. Since placing a tariff on imports would increase the cost of foreign goods and thereby eliminate their price advantage, that seemed to be the best solution. To aid American industries, President James Madison proposed the **Tariff of 1816.** Moreover, tariff revenues would help pay for internal improvements such as roads, canals, and lighthouses.

Most Northeasterners welcomed protective tariffs with relief. However, people in the South and West, whose livelihoods did not depend on manufacturing, were not as eager to tax European imports. They resented any government intervention that would make previously inexpensive goods more expensive. Nevertheless, Clay, who was from the West (Kentucky), and Calhoun, a southerner and congressman (from South Carolina), managed to sway the members of Congress from their regions to approve the Tariff of 1816 in the national interest.

THINK THROUGH HISTORY
D. *Summarizing* What was the intention of the American System?
D. Answer The American System united the nation's economic interests by having the North produce manufactured goods that farmers in the South and West would buy, while the South and West would raise the grain, livestock, and cotton needed in the North.

Major Roads and Canals, 1840

Road
Canal

0 — 200 Miles
0 — 400 Kilometers

Skillbuilder Answer
Human-Environment Interaction: Roads cover more of the country.
Region: the northeast.

GEOGRAPHY SKILLBUILDER
HUMAN-ENVIRONMENT INTERACTION *Judging from the map, were roads or canals a more powerful factor in unifying the United States in the first half of the 1800s?* **REGION** *Which region had the heaviest concentration of roads and canals?*

TEACHING OPTIONS

Attitudes toward the proposed Second Bank of the United States (BUS) weren't as divided by region, since a national bank would benefit the people of all regions. At the time, regional banks issued their own currency, and often banks and businesses in a region honored only the currency issued there. This regional system made it difficult for people in one part of the country to do business with those in another. The Second Bank would make available a currency guaranteed to be accepted nationwide. In 1816, Congress voted to charter the Second Bank of the United States for a 20-year period.

ERIE CANAL AND OTHER INTERNAL IMPROVEMENTS For people in different regions to do business with one another and for the economy to grow, people had to communicate, travel, and transport goods more cheaply and easily. Building roads and canals, however, cost money, and the funding of this construction was a major issue.

In the end, the states funded the improvements to their own transportation systems. To solve the problem of financing, many states built turnpikes, which paid for themselves through the collection of tolls paid by users who, literally, turned a pike (or spiked pole) to continue their journey along the road. The federal government experimented with building highways when it began constructing the **National Road** in 1811. By 1838 it extended from Cumberland, Maryland, to Vandalia, Illinois.

One of the most impressive projects was a canal: the **Erie Canal.** This 363-mile long "Big Ditch," as it was called at the time, was begun in 1817 and by 1825 had linked the Hudson River to Lake Erie—or, in effect, the Atlantic Ocean to the Great Lakes. Other states became eager to build their own canals when they saw the financial benefits that New York state reaped from the Erie Canal. Just 12 years after it had opened, canal tolls had completely paid for its construction. New York City had become the dominant port in the country. In their rush to make similar profits, other states built over 3,000 miles of canals by 1837.

Even before workers completed the Erie Canal, however, people were pleased with the way the country was developing. In 1816, they elected James Monroe of Virginia as president. Soon after his inauguration in 1817, Monroe took a goodwill tour of New England, during which he received a warm welcome in Boston. The idea of a Republican from Virginia being welcomed in this northern Federalist stronghold impressed the nation. The Boston *Columbian Centinel* declared that Americans had entered an "Era of Good Feelings."

E. Answer It connected the Atlantic Ocean to the Great Lakes; it helped the economy of New York state; it made New York City the dominant port; it inspired the building of other canals.

**THINK THROUGH HISTORY
E. Recognizing Effects** What were some of the effects of the building of the Erie Canal?

NOW & THEN

FREIGHT TRANSPORTATION
Freight in the United States is today carried by many means of transportation as the following graph shows.

Domestic Airlines 0.4%
Water 15.0%
Oil Pipelines 18.4%
Railroads 38.1%
Truck 28.1%

In the 1820s and 1830s, canals were the main means of freight transportation. After 1850, the railroads took the lead in freight transportation. The construction of the interstate highway system beginning in the 1950s produced 41,000 miles of highways and made trucks an important means of freight transportation.

Source: *Statistical Abstract of the United States, 1995. The United States Waterways and Ports: A Chronology,* Vol. 1, 1541–1871.

Section 1 Assessment

1. TERMS & NAMES

Identify:
- Eli Whitney
- interchangeable parts
- mass production
- Industrial Revolution
- Henry Clay
- American System
- Tariff of 1816
- National Road
- Erie Canal

2. SUMMARIZING In a chart, write newspaper headlines that tell the significance of each date.

Dates	Headlines
1793	
1801	
1815	
1825	
1838	

Write the first paragraph of the story that follows one of the headlines.

3. ANALYZING EFFECTS What shifts in population involving the United States might be attributed to advances in technology and changes in regional economies during America's Industrial Revolution? Support your answer with examples from the text.

THINK ABOUT
- the industrialization of New England
- agricultural changes in the South
- improvements in internal transportation systems

4. SYNTHESIZING How was the American System expected to unite the nation's economic interests?

THINK ABOUT
- the industrial North
- the agricultural South and West
- currency and transportation

Balancing Nationalism and Sectionalism **203**

ANSWERS

1. TERMS & NAMES

Eli Whitney, p. 198

interchangeable parts, p. 198

mass production, p. 198

Industrial Revolution, p. 198

Henry Clay, p. 201

American System, p. 201

Tariff of 1816, p. 202

National Road, p. 203

Erie Canal, p. 203

2. SUMMARIZING

Possible Responses:
1793—Eli Whitney Invents the Cotton Gin; Samuel Slater Opens Textile Factory Run by Machines
1801—Eli Whitney Demonstrates Interchangeable Parts
1815—Madison Presents the "American System" to Congress
1825—Erie Canal Completed; Atlantic Ocean Linked to Great Lakes
1838—National Road Connects Maryland to Illinois

3. ANALYZING EFFECTS

Possible Responses: Textile machinery—farm workers to factories; cotton gin—more cotton plantations—large numbers of African slaves; Erie Canal—more people to urban areas.

4. SYNTHESIZING

Possible Responses: The industrial North would produce manufactured goods that the South and West would buy. The agricultural South and West would raise grain, livestock, and cotton needed in the North. A national currency and improved transportation would aid in the exchange of goods.

OBJECTIVES

(1) To show how the federal government asserted its jurisdiction over state governments.

(2) To explain that foreign affairs were guided by national self-interest.

(3) To summarize the issues that divided the country as the United States expanded its borders.

SKILLBUILDERS

- Understanding geography: place, region, p. 206
- Understanding geography: region, p. 208

CRITICAL THINKING

- Summarizing, pp. 205, 208
- Synthesizing, pp. 207, 208
- Hypothesizing, p. 208
- Forming opinions, p. 208

FOCUS & MOTIVATE

▶ **Starting with the Student**
Ask students to think about how members of a group make decisions.

- Who should have the final authority?
- How is the relationship between the group and its members like that between the federal and state governments?

OBJECTIVE
(1) INSTRUCT

The Supreme Court Boosts National Power

▶ **Starting with the Student**
Encourage students to organize what they learn in this section about the Supreme Court rulings in a chart like this:

(continued on next page)

---

2 Nationalism at Center Stage

TERMS & NAMES
- John Quincy Adams
- nationalism
- Monroe Doctrine
- Jim Beckwourth
- Missouri Compromise

LEARN ABOUT the growth of nationalism in the United States
TO UNDERSTAND how it affected Supreme Court decisions, federal government policy decisions, and westward expansion in the early 1800s.

ONE AMERICAN'S STORY

Robert Fulton built a boat propelled by a steam engine. In 1807 his *Clermont* made a 150-mile trip up the Hudson River from New York City to Albany in 32 hours. This successful demonstration marked the beginning of the steamboat era. Another one of Fulton's boats, the *Paragon,* the third steamboat to operate on the Hudson, was so luxurious that it had a paneled dining room and bedrooms. Fulton said of the *Paragon* that it was a "whole floating town . . . . [it] beats everything on the globe. . . ." Fulton posted regulations on his opulent steamboats.

A PERSONAL VOICE
As the steamboat has been fitted up in an elegant style, order is necessary to keep it so; gentlemen will therefore please to observe cleanliness, and a reasonable attention not to injure the furniture; for this purpose no one must sit on a table under the penalty of half a dollar each time, and every breakage of tables, chairs, sofas, or windows, tearing of curtains, or injury of any kind must be paid for before leaving the boat.

ROBERT FULTON, quoted in *Steamboats Come True: American Inventors in Action*

This advertisement for the Hudson River Steamboat Line was issued on May 23, 1826.

Steamboats carried freight as well as passengers, and this new method of transportation spread quickly to the Ohio and Mississippi rivers. Over the next twenty years hundreds of steamboats plied the Western rivers flowing into the Mississippi, and they sailed on some Eastern rivers as well. The steamboat was one of a number of factors that helped to unite the economic life of the North and the South, and contributed to the growing national spirit.

The Supreme Court Boosts National Power

In 1808, Robert Fulton and Robert Livingston received a charter from the New York legislature that gave them the exclusive right to run steamboats on rivers in that state. They profited from this state charter, which granted them a monopoly (exclusive legal control of a commercial activity), by charging steamboat operators for licenses to operate on various stretches of river.

One of these operators was Aaron Ogden. Licensed by Fulton and Livingston (under the laws of New York state) to run his steamship line between New York and New Jersey, Ogden believed that he was the only operator legally entitled to run a steamboat service on this stretch of the Hudson. Then Thomas Gibbons began to run a similar service in the same area, claiming that he was entitled to do so according to federal law. Ogden believed that Gibbons violated his exclusive right by competing for business, so he took Gibbons to court to stop him. However, in 1824, the Supreme Court ruled that interstate commerce could be regulated only by the federal government. In other words, Ogden's "exclusive" right granted by New York was not legal since the route crossed state lines. Gibbons was also entitled to run a steamship line between the two states.

More important, by clarifying that Congress had authority over interstate commerce, the *Gibbons* v. *Ogden* decision helped to ensure that the federal

---

SECTION 2 RESOURCES

 PRINT RESOURCES

IN-DEPTH RESOURCES: UNIT 2
Guided Reading, p. 48
Skillbuilder Practice: Synthesizing, p. 51
American Lives: James Beckwourth, p. 64

ACCESS FOR STUDENTS ACQUIRING ENGLISH
Guided Reading (Spanish), p. 73
Skillbuilder Practice: Synthesizing (Spanish), p. 76

FORMAL ASSESSMENT
Section Quiz, p. 90

ALTERNATIVE ASSESSMENT BOOK
See forms for supporting and scoring alternative activities.

TECHNOLOGY RESOURCES

VIDEO *American Portfolio: A Videodisc for U.S. History* user's guide, p. 64

INTERNET McDougal Littell Learning On-Line
http://www.mcdougallittell.com

government has the power to regulate just about everything that crosses state lines. In modern life, that authority means everything from air traffic to television and radio waves to interstate cellular communications. In addition, this decision led to future rulings favoring competition over monopolies. In this way, nationalism exerted a strong influence on the legal system.

STRENGTHENING GOVERNMENT ECONOMIC CONTROL *Gibbons* v. *Ogden* wasn't the first case in which Chief Justice John Marshall guided the Supreme Court to a ruling that strengthened the federal government's control over the economy. In *McCulloch* v. *Maryland* (1819), the Court's ruling also supported the national government over the state governments.

Maryland had levied a heavy tax on the local branch of the Bank of the United States, hoping to tax it out of existence. Marshall declared that if such situations were allowed, states would in effect be overturning laws passed by Congress. The Chief Justice denied the right of Maryland to tax the Bank, stating that "the power to tax is the power to destroy." He declared the Bank of the United States constitutional.

A. Answer In a series of decisions, the Supreme Court strengthened federal economic power and limited state powers.

THINK THROUGH HISTORY
A. Summarizing *In what ways did the Supreme Court boost federal power?*

LIMITING STATE POWERS Under Chief Justice Marshall, the Supreme Court made several rulings that blocked state interference in business and commerce—even when this meant overturning state law. In *Fletcher* v. *Peck* (1810), for example, the Court nullified a Georgia law that had violated individuals' constitutional right to enter into contracts. In the *Dartmouth College* v. *Woodward* (1819) decision, the Court declared that the state of New Hampshire could not revise the original charter it had granted to the college's trustees in colonial times because a charter was a contract, and the Constitution did not permit states to interfere with contracts.

Nationalism Shapes Foreign Policy

While John Marshall guided the Supreme Court to decisions that increased the power of the federal government, Secretary of State **John Quincy Adams** established foreign policy guided by a belief in **nationalism.** Adams believed that national interests and national unity should be placed ahead of regional concerns and that foreign affairs should be guided by national self-interest.

TERRITORY AND BOUNDARIES High on Adams's list of national interests was the security of the nation and expansion of its territory. To further these interests, Adams worked out a treaty with Great Britain to reduce the Great Lakes fleets of both countries to only a few military vessels. The Rush-Bagot Treaty (1817) eventually led the United States and Canada to completely demilitarize their common border. Adams also arranged the Convention of 1818, which fixed the U.S. border at the 49th parallel up to the Rocky Mountains. Finally, he reached a compromise with Britain to jointly occupy the Oregon Territory, the territory west of the Rockies, for ten years.

There remained one outstanding piece of business. Most Americans assumed that Spanish Florida would eventually become part of the United States, and American settlers began to move in on their own. Then, in 1819, Adams convinced Don Luis de Onís, Spanish minister to the United States, that Spain would do well to give up Florida before impatient Americans simply seized it. Too weak to police its New World territories, Spain ceded Florida to

 John Marshall, Chief Justice of the United States (about 1832), by William James Hubard.

(continued from p. 204)

Case	Ruling
Gibbons v. Ogden	
McCulloch v. Maryland	
Fletcher v. Peck	
Dartmouth College v. Woodward	

▶ *Discussing Key Ideas*
- The Supreme Court's rulings strengthen the federal government's control over the economy.
- The Supreme Court rules that state laws can be overturned when they violate the Constitution.

IN-DEPTH RESOURCES: UNIT 2
Guided Reading, p. 48

ACCESS FOR STUDENTS ACQUIRING ENGLISH
Guided Reading (Spanish), p. 73

OBJECTIVE
② **INSTRUCT**

Nationalism Shapes Foreign Policy

▶ *Discussing Key Ideas*
- The United States works out agreements with Great Britain and Spain that help ensure its security and expand its borders.
- The Monroe Doctrine supports the independent nations of the Western Hemisphere against European interference.

Teaching Less Proficient Readers

Clarifying Ideas Have pairs of students work together to clarify the main ideas in this section. Encourage partners to follow these steps:

1. Read pages 204 and 205 of the text together.

2. Make a list of the Supreme Court decisions discussed on the pages.

3. Write down any questions you have about the decisions.

4. Finally, discuss the decisions and work with your partner to answer all of your questions.

Exploring Themes

Constitutional Concerns Remind students that Marshall was Chief Justice while the United States was governed by Democratic-Republicans and Democrats. Most of these leaders believed in states' rights. However, Marshall was a Federalist. He believed in a strong central government.

Ask students why Marshall's beliefs and not those of the presidents influenced the Supreme Court's decisions. *Possible Response: The Supreme Court is independent of Congress and the president.*

Boundary Settlements of the United States, 1803–1819

Reading the Map Have students note that the arrow pointing toward Florida represents boundary pressure from Spain and Portugal, and that the arrow pointing toward Alaska represents the boundary pressure from Russia.

Extension Ask students to list some of the reasons the United States wanted to expand its boundaries to the West. *Possible Responses: To increase its resources; to facilitate trade with Asia; to increase its power.*

MORE ABOUT . . .
The Monroe Doctrine

Great Britain proposed joining in an alliance with the United States and issuing a joint warning against the European aggressors. Monroe and former presidents Jefferson and Madison favored the idea. Jefferson said that with Great Britain "on our side, we need not fear the whole world." But Secretary of State Adams warned against forming such an alliance. He did not want the United States to seem like "a cockboat [rowboat] in the wake of the British man-of-war." Besides, he reasoned, the British would protect the nation's interests whether they formed an alliance with the United States or not. Monroe decided to take Adams's advice and created a strictly American policy.

Boundary Settlements of the United States, 1803–1819

Convention of 1818 with Great Britain

Adams-Onís Treaty of 1819

Oregon Country

Boundary pressure from foreign powers

CANADA

Great Lakes

Adams-Onís Treaty Line, 1819 (with Spain)

PACIFIC OCEAN

ATLANTIC OCEAN

MEXICO (Spanish)

Gulf of Mexico

500 Miles

1000 Kilometers

GEOGRAPHY SKILLBUILDER PLACE
What country lies north of the territory ceded to the U.S. in the Convention of 1818 with Great Britain? **REGION**
What body of water lies due south of the eastern lands gained by the U.S. in the Adams-Onis Treaty?

Skillbuilder Answer
Place: Canada. **Region:** Gulf of Mexico.

the United States in the Adams-Onís Treaty and disavowed any claims it had to the Oregon Territory.

THE MONROE DOCTRINE When Napoleon invaded Portugal and Spain in 1807, the two countries did not have the money or manpower to fight Napoleon and keep control of their overseas territories at the same time. But when Napoleon was defeated in 1815, Portugal and Spain wanted to reclaim their former colonies in Latin America.

Meanwhile, the Russians, who had been in Alaska since 1784, were establishing trading posts in what is now California. In 1821 the Tsar of Russia claimed that Alaska's southern boundary was the 51st parallel, north of Vancouver, Canada. He forbade all foreign vessels from using the coast north of this line.

With Spain and Portugal trying to move back into their old colonial areas, and with Russia pushing in from the northwest, the United States knew it had to do something. Many Americans were interested in acquiring northern Mexico and the Spanish colony of Cuba. Moreover, the Russian action posed a threat to American trade with China, which brought huge profits.

Accordingly, in his 1823 message to Congress, President Monroe warned all European powers not to interfere with affairs in the Western Hemisphere. They should not attempt to create new colonies, he said, or try to overthrow the newly independent republics in the hemisphere. The United States would consider such action "dangerous to our peace and safety." At the same time, the United States would not involve itself in European affairs or interfere with

---

Skillbuilder Minilesson: Synthesizing

Explaining the Skill Synthesizing involves combining information from a number of sources to come up with a new, more complete understanding of a subject. Students might first think about ideas or facts they have just learned and then put those new ideas in the context of information they already have. Last, they should work to develop new understandings or ideas about the information.

Applying the Skill: Think Through History Question In order to answer the question at the top of page 207, students will need to first identify the national interests covered on

earlier pages of the textbook. The national interests include:

1. The desire to expand U.S. territory by acquiring northern Mexico, Florida, and Cuba.
2. Continued trade with China, which was very profitable for Americans.
3. National security.

The next step is to examine the foreign policies in the light of these interests.

IN-DEPTH RESOURCES: UNIT 2
Skillbuilder Practice: Synthesizing, p. 51

existing colonies in the Western Hemisphere. These principles became known as the **Monroe Doctrine.**

Because the United States lacked the armed forces to support the doctrine, European nations ignored Monroe's speech. However, the Monroe Doctrine represented an important step onto the world stage by the assertive young nation.

Nationalism Pushes America West

While various presidents established policies that expanded U.S. territory, American settlers pushed into the Northwest Territory (present-day Ohio, Indiana, Illinois, Wisconsin, and Michigan), felling forests in some regions and turning lush prairies into farms and waterfronts into city centers in other regions.

EXPANSION TO THE WEST While some settlers went west to escape debts or even the law, most pushed westward in search of economic gain—for land was not only plentiful and fertile but cheap. One Illinois settler, Elias Pym Fordham, in his *Personal Narrative of Travels . . . ,* shed some light on the financial gains that may have tempted so many British immigrants to this area: "If he is a plain working farmer, £500 will make him more independent than an English gentleman with £1,000 per annum." Fordham also revealed some of the social gains available out West. He wrote, "No white man or woman will bear being called a servant. . . . Hirelings must be spoken to with Civility and cheerfulness." That type of equality didn't exist in the East.

One could also change occupations more easily on the frontier, as a Swedish immigrant observed.

> **A PERSONAL VOICE**
> The speed with which people here change their life calling and the slight preparation generally needed to leave one calling for another are really surprising. . . . A man who today is a mason may tomorrow be a doctor, the next day a cobbler, and still another day a sailor, druggist, waiter, or school master.
> **GUSTAF UNONIOUS,** quoted in *American Vistas: 1607–1877*

The Northwest Ordinance of 1787 had laid out a system for a territory to obtain statehood as soon as its population reached about 60,000. At that point, the people of a territory could petition the Union for admission, draft a state constitution, elect representatives, and become part of the United States, once Congress approved.

THE MISSOURI COMPROMISE In 1819, however, when settlers in Missouri requested admission into the Union, conflict arose. In Missouri, the new spirit of nationalism was challenged by an issue that had previously confronted the framers of the Constitution. That issue was slavery.

Until 1818, the United States had consisted of ten free and ten slave states. With the admission of Illinois as the 11th free state in 1818, Southerners expected that Missouri would become the 11th slave state—to maintain the balance between free states and slave states in Congress. When New York Congressman James Tallmadge amended the Missouri statehood bill to require Missouri to gradually free its slaves, a bill which passed the House, Southerners perceived this as a threat to their power and blocked the bill's passage in the Senate. As arguments raged on, Alabama was then admitted to the Union as a slave state. With 11 free to 11 slave states, Missouri's status became crucial to maintaining the delicate balance between slave and free states—a balance that was critical if the nation was to avoid collapse into sectionalism.

HISTORICAL SPOTLIGHT

JIM BECKWOURTH 1798–1867?

James Pierson Beckwourth was the toughest kind of pioneer, a mountain man. The son of a white man and an African-American woman, he ventured westward with a fur-trading expedition in 1823 and found the place that would become his home for nearly the next quarter century—the Rocky Mountains. He greatly impressed the Crow, who gave him the name "Bloody Arm" because of his skill as a fighter.

Beckwourth served from 1837 until 1850 as an Army scout and trading-post operator. In 1850, he discovered a passage in the Sierra Nevada range that led to California's Sacramento Valley and decided to settle down near the pass and become a rancher. "In the spring of 1852 I established myself in Beckwourth Valley, and finally found myself transformed into a hotel-keeper and chief of a trading-post. "

The Missouri Compromise, 1820–1821

Reading the Map Ask students how the Missouri Compromise promoted sectionalism. *Response: It revealed how the issue of slavery clearly divided the country into the North and the South.*

Extension How was the Missouri Compromise a victory for the South? How was it a victory for the North? *Possible Response: The South gained Missouri but yielded a vast block of territory to the North.*

ANOTHER PERSPECTIVE

Slavery and the Union

Critical Thinking:
Analyzing Ask students why Jefferson's words were prophetic. *Response: The slavery issue would lead to the Civil War.*

ASSESS & RETEACH

Section 2 Assessment

Have pairs of students take turns quizzing each other on the questions.

Self-Assessment

To determine their understanding of the section, ask students to define *nationalism* and to provide two specific examples of nationalism discussed in the section.

Section Quiz

FORMAL ASSESSMENT
Section Quiz, p. 90

Reteach

Have students outline difficult sections, using the heads and subheads as a framework.

CLOSE

Nationalism influenced Supreme Court decisions, foreign policy, and westward expansion in the early 1800s. Meanwhile, growing sectionalism threatened to divide the union.

The Missouri Compromise, 1820–1821

- Free states and territories
- Closed to slavery by Missouri Compromise
- Slave states and territories
- Open to slavery by Missouri Compromise

Skillbuilder Answer
Region: Missouri and Kentucky. **Region:** Arkansas Territory and Florida Territory

GEOGRAPHY SKILLBUILDER
REGION *What two slave states bordered the free state of Illinois?*
REGION *In what two territories besides the slave states was slavery permitted?*

C. Answer Congress agreed to admit Maine to the Union as a free state; slavery would not be permitted in any other part of the Louisiana Purchase territory north of 36°30′—with the exception of Missouri; Missouri was admitted to the Union as a slave state. The Missouri Compromise was important because it temporarily settled the problem of slavery in federal territories.

THINK THROUGH HISTORY
C. Synthesizing *What agreements did Congress reach that are regarded collectively as the Missouri Compromise. Why were they important at the time?*

ANOTHER PERSPECTIVE

SLAVERY AND THE UNION
Former President Thomas Jefferson feared for the Union's future in the light of the Missouri Compromise. His words would prove prophetic.

"[T]his momentous question, like a firebell in the night, awakened and filled me with terror. I considered it at once as the knell of the Union. It is hushed, indeed, for the moment. But this is a reprieve only, not a final sentence."

THOMAS JEFFERSON, from a letter to John Holmes, April 22, 1820

The slaveholding states claimed that Northerners were trying to end slavery. Northerners accused Southerners of plotting to extend the institution into new territories. Hostilities became so intense that at times people on both sides even mentioned civil war and the end of the Union. Indeed, the issues that came to light during these debates foreshadowed the war to come. "[W]e have the wolf by the ears," wrote the aging Thomas Jefferson of this crisis, "and we can neither safely hold him, nor safely let him go."

Under the leadership of Henry Clay, however, Congress managed to avert such a crisis with a series of agreements collectively called the **Missouri Compromise.** Maine was admitted as a free state and Missouri as a slave state, thus preserving the sectional balance in the Senate. The rest of the Louisiana Territory was split into two spheres of interest, one for the slaveholders and one for free settlers. The dividing line was set at 36° 30′ north latitude. South of the line, slavery was legal. North of the line—except for Missouri—slavery was banned.

President Monroe signed the Missouri Compromise in 1820. For a generation, the problem of slavery in federal territories seemed settled.

Section 2 Assessment

1. TERMS & NAMES
Identify:
- John Quincy Adams
- nationalism
- Monroe Doctrine
- Jim Beckwourth
- Missouri Compromise

2. SUMMARIZING Recreate the organizational tree diagram below on your paper, and fill it in with historical examples that illustrate the main idea in the top box.

```
        Influence of Nationalism
        |         |          |
   Nation's    Foreign    Westward
   courts      affairs    expansion
      |           |          |
   example    example    example
```

3. HYPOTHESIZING Speculate on the short- and long-term goals that President Monroe might have had in mind when he formulated the Monroe Doctrine in 1823. Support your answer with reasons.

THINK ABOUT
- European nations' presence in the Western Hemisphere during this time
- the influence of nationalism on foreign policy
- the nation's westward expansion

4. FORMING OPINIONS Based on the Missouri Compromise and the controversy that preceded it, do you think the new spirit of nationalism in the United States was strong or fragile? Support your opinion with reasons.

THINK ABOUT
- the definition of nationalism
- the issues debated in Congress about slavery
- the series of agreements comprising the Missouri Compromise

208 CHAPTER 7

ANSWERS

1. TERMS & NAMES
John Quincy Adams, p. 205
nationalism, p. 205
Monroe Doctrine, p. 207
Jim Beckwourth, p. 207
Missouri Compromise, p. 208

2. SUMMARIZING
Possible Responses: Nation's Courts—*Gibbons* v. *Ogden* decision allows federal government to regulate interstate commerce. Foreign Affairs—Rush-Bagot Treaty: United States and Canada demilitarize their common border; the Monroe Doctrine warns European powers to end colonization and intervention in Western Hemisphere. Westward Expansion—Government policies expand U.S. territory westward; American settlers push into the Northwest.

3. HYPOTHESIZING
Possible Responses: To protect American trade; to diminish the power of Spain, Portugal, France, and Russia in the Western Hemisphere; to provide for national security; to encourage continuing U.S. territorial expansion in the Western Hemisphere.

4. FORMING OPINIONS
Students answering "strong" might argue that loyalty to the Union prevailed over sectional differences; Northerners and Southerners opted to maintain national unity by balancing political power and regional concerns. Students answering "fragile" might emphasize that the Missouri Compromise temporarily settled the problem of slavery in federal territories, but the issue of slavery and its divisiveness was not resolved.

3 The Age of Jackson

TERMS & NAMES
- Andrew Jackson
- Democratic Republican Party
- spoils system
- Sequoya
- Indian Removal Act
- Trail of Tears

LEARN ABOUT Andrew Jackson's rise to power and his political views
TO UNDERSTAND why his administration instituted policies that gave voice to common people but violated the rights of Native Americans.

The portrait of Thomas Jefferson *(above left)* was painted when he was 78 by the artist Thomas Sully. The portrait of John Adams was begun in 1798 by Gilbert Stuart and finished after 1828 by Jane Stuart.

ONE AMERICAN'S STORY

During an extended conversation that Thomas Jefferson and John Adams had in 1776, recorded by John Adams, Adams tried to convince Jefferson to draft the Declaration of Independence.

A PERSONAL VOICE
"You should do it!"
"What can be your reasons?"
"Reason first—You are a Virginian, and a Virginian ought to appear at the head of this business. Reason second—I am obnoxious, suspected, and unpopular. You are very much otherwise. Reason third—You can write ten times better than I can."
"Well," said Jefferson, "if you are decided, I will do as well as I can."

JOHN ADAMS, quoted in *John Adams: A Biography in His Own Words*

Thus began a friendship that would last, off and on, for over 50 years. Then, on July 4, 1826, 50 years to the day since the delegates had approved the Declaration of Independence Jefferson had drafted, both men died. "Thomas Jefferson survives," were Adams's last words but, a few hours earlier and many miles away, Jefferson had already died.

Their deaths represented the passing of the era of the leaders who founded the nation. Now the presidency moved on to another generation, first to John Quincy Adams and then to Andrew Jackson. Jackson would be the dominating figure of this era—so much so that it was to be called the Age of Jackson.

Expanding Democracy Changes Politics

When John Adams died, his son, John Quincy Adams, was in the second year of his single term as president. John Quincy Adams, who had succeeded James Monroe as President, was not effective as the nation's chief executive. The principal reason was Andrew Jackson, his chief political opponent.

TENSION BETWEEN ADAMS AND JACKSON   Trouble for Adams began with his election in 1824. **Andrew Jackson** had actually won the most popular votes but lacked the majority of electoral votes required to take office. The House of Representatives then had to decide the outcome since no candidate received a majority of the votes in the Electoral College. Because of his power in the House, Henry Clay could swing the election either way. Jackson's supporters urged Clay to support their candidate because he had the largest popular vote.

Clay, however, disliked Jackson personally and mistrusted his lack of political experience. "I cannot believe," Clay commented, "that killing twenty-five hundred Englishmen at New Orleans qualifies [him] for the various difficult and complicated duties of [the presidency]." Adams, on the other hand, agreed with Clay's American System. The two men held a private talk, and Adams was elected President by a majority of the states represented in the House.

Jacksonians, or followers of Jackson, accused Adams of stealing the presidency. Then, because Adams appointed Clay secretary of state, Jacksonians

Balancing Nationalism and Sectionalism **209**

Section 3 Overview

OBJECTIVES

1. To describe the expansion of suffrage and Jackson's appeal to the common citizen.
2. To explain the spoils system as practiced by Jackson.
3. To summarize the effects of the Indian Removal Act of 1830.

SKILLBUILDER
- Understanding geography: place, movement, p. 213

CRITICAL THINKING
- Clarifying, p. 211
- Analyzing issues, p. 211
- Summarizing, p. 213
- Making decisions, p. 213
- Interpreting, p. 213

FOCUS & MOTIVATE

▶ *Starting with the Student*
- Ask students their opinion on voting. Do they think it is a privilege or a pointless gesture? Do they plan to exercise their right to vote when they are 18?
- Do they think a government has the right to displace the native peoples of the countries it conquers? Why or why not?

OBJECTIVE
1 **INSTRUCT**

Expanding Democracy Changes Politics

▶ *Discussing Key Ideas*
- Jackson creates problems for Adams's presidency.

(continued on next page)

SECTION 3 RESOURCES

PRINT RESOURCES

IN-DEPTH RESOURCES: UNIT 2
Guided Reading, p. 49
Geography Application: Jackson Finally Becomes President, p. 52
Outline Map: The Indian Removal Act of 1830, p. 54
Primary Source: Political Cartoon, p. 56; *from* the Cherokee Nation's Appeal to the American People, p. 57
Literature: from *The President's Lady* by Irving Stone, p. 60

ACCESS FOR STUDENTS ACQUIRING ENGLISH
Guided Reading (Spanish), p. 74
Geography Application: Jackson Finally Becomes President Spanish, p. 77

FORMAL ASSESSMENT
Section Quiz, p. 91

ALTERNATIVE ASSESSMENT BOOK
See forms for supporting and scoring alternative activities.

TECHNOLOGY RESOURCES

GEOGRAPHY TRANSPARENCIES
G7, Population Density: 1790 and 1830

CD-ROM Electronic Library of Primary Sources

VIDEO *American Portfolio: A Videodisc for U.S. History* user's guide, pp. 64, 65, 66, 67

INTERNET McDougal Littell Learning On-Line
http://www.mcdougallittell.com

Teacher's Edition   **209**

(continued from page 209)

- The easing of property requirements for voting greatly enlarges the electorate.

IN-DEPTH RESOURCES: UNIT 2
Guided Reading, p. 49

ACCESS FOR STUDENTS ACQUIRING ENGLISH
Guided Reading (Spanish), p. 74

OBJECTIVE
② INSTRUCT

Jackson's New Presidential Style

▶ *Discussing Key Ideas*
- Jackson appeals to the common citizen.
- Expanded suffrage helps Jackson win the 1828 election.
- Jackson's spoils system rewards loyal supporters.

IN-DEPTH RESOURCES: UNIT 2
Geography Application: Jackson Finally Becomes President, p. 52

DIFFICULT DECISIONS IN HISTORY
Voting Restrictions
Critical Thinking:
Analyzing Tell students that many Americans in the Age of Jackson believed the United States should be governed by a small aristocratic group of educated and public-spirited landowners. Ask students where these ideas might have originated. *Possible Response: Many people probably adapted this idea from their mother country, Great Britain, or from another country ruled by a monarchy or divided by a class system.*

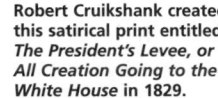

Difficult Decisions IN HISTORY

VOTING RESTRICTIONS

In 1821, New York legislator Nathan Sanford argued that the old requirements that restricted voting rights to property holders should change. At the time, only those white males who owned property could vote. Those who agreed with this restriction argued that the vested interest of property owners in the stability of the government made them more responsible. Those who disagreed with property restrictions argued that those who did not own property were also affected by the laws and so should be able to vote.

Sanford believed that all taxpayers should have the right to vote, and not just those paying property taxes. He proposed that if one was a citizen and had lived within the state for six months, one should be entitled to vote.

1. Examine the issues Sanford raised about who should vote. What other issues would you have brought up in the debate?
2. If you had been a New York legislator taking part in this debate in 1821, would you have revised voting restrictions or not? Explain your reasons.

Robert Cruikshank created this satirical print entitled *The President's Levee, or All Creation Going to the White House* in 1829.

210 CHAPTER 7

claimed Adams had struck a corrupt bargain. The Jacksonians withdrew from the Republican Party to form the **Democratic Republican Party** (forerunner of today's Democratic Party).

Over the next four years, Jacksonians did whatever they could to sabotage Adams's policies. Aware that many voters distrusted the national bank and disliked tariffs, Jacksonians opposed both.

DEMOCRACY AND CITIZENSHIP During Adams's presidency, most states had eased voting requirements a citizen had to fulfill to be able to vote, thereby enlarging the voting population. Fewer states had property qualifications for voting, which also meant that many more individuals could vote. White males in most states now voted directly for the members of the Electoral College rather than through their legislators. In the election of 1824, approximately 350,000 white males voted for the presidency. In 1828, over three times that number voted, and their votes helped Andrew Jackson.

However, certain groups still lacked political power. Free blacks and women did not enjoy the freedoms and privileges of white males.

Jackson's New Presidential Style

The expansion of voting rights meant that a candidate for president had to be able to speak to the concerns and hopes of common people. Andrew Jackson had this common touch to an extraordinary degree.

JACKSON'S APPEAL TO THE COMMON CITIZEN During the 1828 election campaign, Jackson characterized Adams as an intellectual elitist and, by contrast, portrayed himself as a man of humble origins— even though he was actually a wealthy plantation owner. Jackson won the election by a landslide. He was so popular that record numbers of people came to Washington to see "Old Hickory" inaugurated. Mrs. Samuel Harrison Smith described the scene.

A PERSONAL VOICE
The President, after having been *literally* nearly pressed to death and almost suffocated and torn to pieces by the people in their eagerness to shake hands with Old Hickory [Jackson], had retreated through the back way, or south front, and had escaped to his lodgings at Gadsby's. Cut glass and china to the amount of several thousand dollars had been broken in the struggle to get the refreshments. Punch and other articles had been carried out in tubs and buckets, but had it been in hogsheads [casks] it would have been insufficient; ice creams and cake and lemonade for 20,000 people, for it is said that number were there, though I think the estimate exaggerated. Ladies fainted, men were seen with bloody noses, and such a scene of confusion took place as is impossible to describe; those who got in could not get out by the door again but had to scramble out of windows.

MRS. SAMUEL HARRISON SMITH, from a letter dated March 1829

JACKSON'S SPOILS SYSTEM If Jackson knew how to inspire loyalty and enthusiasm during a campaign, he also knew how to use the powers of the presidency upon gaining office. He announced that in order to give common people a chance to participate in government, his appointees to federal jobs would serve a maximum of four-year terms. Unless there was a regular turnover of personnel, he

---

TEACHING OPTIONS

Making Connections Across the Curriculum

U.S. Government Today, almost all adults over the age of 18 can vote in national and local elections, with the exception of a few groups of people, including those convicted of serious crimes. Discuss with students whether denying some convicted criminals the right to vote is constitutional. *Possible Responses: Some students may say that once the crime is committed, the criminal forfeits all rights of citizenship; others may feel that after serving their prison terms the criminals should regain the right to vote.*

Making Connections Across Time

Electoral College The electoral college method of electing the president of the United States has always been controversial. Research another close presidential race in which the effectiveness of the Electoral College has been questioned, such as Kennedy vs. Nixon or Harrison vs. Cleveland. In a brief one- to two-page paper, explain the results of the election and why people used those results to find fault with the Electoral College.

210 Chapter 7

declared, officeholders would become inefficient and corrupt.

This policy of "rotation in office" enabled Jackson to give away huge numbers of jobs to friends and political allies. He fired nearly 10 percent of federal government employees, most of them holdovers from the Adams administration, and he gave their jobs to loyal Jacksonians. Jackson's friends also became his primary advisors, dubbed his "kitchen cabinet" because they supposedly slipped into the White House through the kitchen. Jackson's administration essentially practiced the **spoils system** of government, from an old saying that in war "to the victor belong the spoils of the enemy." In the spoils system, incoming political parties throw out former appointees and replace them with their own friends.

The Removal of Native Americans

Since the 1600s, the attitude of white settlers toward the Native Americans had fluctuated. Sometimes many whites seemed to favor the displacement and dispossession of all Native Americans. At other times dedicated individuals tried to convert Native Americans to Christianity, turn them into farmers, and absorb them into the white culture.

Since the end of the War of 1812, some Southeastern tribes had begun to adopt the European culture of their white neighbors. These tribes—the Cherokee, Choctaw, Seminole, Creek, and Chickasaw—were called the Five Civilized Tribes. The Cherokee, for example, had created a formal government with a legislature consisting of two houses, just as the United States had; a court system; and, by 1827, a constitution modeled after the U.S. Constitution. Using an alphabet devised by Cherokee George Guess (**Sequoya**), the tribe also published its own bilingual newspaper. However, these "civilized tribes" still occupied large areas of valuable land in Georgia, North and South Carolina, Alabama, Mississippi, and Tennessee—and planters and miners wanted that land.

INDIAN REMOVAL ACT OF 1830 Jackson thought that assimilation could not work. Another possibility—allowing Native Americans to live in their own areas—would have required too many troops to keep the areas free of white settlers who wanted tribal lands. Jackson believed the only solution was to move the Native Americans from their lands to areas farther west.

Congress passed the **Indian Removal Act** in 1830. Under this law, the federal government provided funds to negotiate treaties that would force the Native Americans to move west. About ninety treaties were signed. For Jackson, the removal policy was "not only liberal, but generous," because it would enable Native Americans to maintain their way of life.

THE TRAIL OF TEARS Jackson began using his newly won authority immediately. In 1830, he pressured the Chocktaw to sign a treaty that required them to move from Mississippi. In 1831, he ordered U.S. troops to forcibly remove the Sauk and Fox from their lands in Illinois and Missouri. In 1832, he forced the Chickasaw to leave their lands in Alabama and Mississippi.

Meanwhile, the Cherokee Nation tried to win just treatment through the U.S. legal system. Chief Justice John Marshall refused to rule on the first case the Cherokee brought against Georgia, though, because in his view the Cherokee Nation had no federal standing; it was neither a foreign nation nor a state but, rather, a "domestic dependent nation." Undaunted, the Cherokee

---

teamed up with Samuel Austin Worcester, a missionary who had been jailed for teaching Indians without a state license—they knew the Court would have to recognize a citizen's right to be heard.

The Court ruled on *Worcester* v. *Georgia* in 1832. The Cherokee finally won all the rights that were their due. The Court recognized the Cherokee Nation as a distinct political community whose people Georgia was not entitled to regulate by law and whose lands Georgia was not entitled to invade. Jackson refused to abide by the Supreme Court decision, saying: "John Marshall has made his decision; now let him enforce it."

Cherokee leader John Ross still tried to fight the state in the courts, but other Cherokee began to promote relocation. In 1835, federal agents declared the minority who favored relocation the true representatives of the Cherokee Nation and promptly had them sign the Treaty of New Echota. This treaty gave the last eight million acres of Cherokee land to the federal government in exchange for approximately $5 million and land in Oklahoma. The signing of this treaty marked the beginning of the Cherokee exodus. However, when by 1838 nearly 20,000 Cherokee still remained in the East, President Martin Van Buren (Jackson's successor) ordered their forced removal.

U.S. Army troops under the command of General Winfield Scott rounded up the Cherokee and drove them into camps to await the journey. A Baptist missionary who was a witness to the forced evacuation of the Cherokee sent dispatches describing the scene to the *Baptist Missionary Magazine*.

POINT
COUNTERPOINT
The Indian Removal Act

▶ **Starting with the Student**
• Ask students how they might feel if their family was forced to move to another neighborhood.
• Would they protest a law that took away property they believe rightfully belongs to them?

▶ **Discussing Key Ideas**
• Both critics and supporters of the Indian Removal Act present compelling arguments defending their positions.
• Critics reject President Jackson's claim that removal offers Native Americans needed protection from white settlers.
• Jackson asserts that the Indian Removal Act defuses the conflicts between state and federal governments over the issue of Native Americans.

IN-DEPTH RESOURCES: UNIT 2
Primary Source: *from* the Cherokee Nation's Appeal to the American People, p. 57

 ELECTRONIC LIBRARY OF PRIMARY SOURCES *from* a Message to Congress on the Indian Policy by Andrew Jackson

POINT ▶ COUNTERPOINT

"The Indian Removal Act of 1830 was a terrible injustice."

John Marshall, Chief Justice of the Supreme Court, believed that the Cherokee had "an unquestionable right" to their territory "until title should be extinguished by voluntary cession to the United States."

In their protest against the Indian Removal Act, the Cherokee people referred to past treaties with the federal government and stated, "We have a perfect and original right to remain without interruption and molestation." Congressman Edward Everett of Massachusetts described Indian removal as "inflicting the pains of banishment from their native land on seventy or eighty thousand human beings." Rejecting claims that the removal was necessary to protect the Indians against white settlers, Everett demanded, "What other power has the Executive over a treaty or law, but to enforce it?"

In their 1832 protest against the Act, the Creek pointedly asked, "Can [our white brethren] exempt us from intrusion in our promised borders, if they are incompetent to our protection where we are?"

"The Indian Removal Act of 1830 was unfortunate but necessary."

Blame for the displacement of Native Americans was sometimes placed on the states or on the law which, it was argued, all people must obey. As Secretary of War John Eaton explained to the Creek of Alabama: "It is not your Great Father who does this; but the laws of the Country, which he and every one of his people is bound to regard."

President Andrew Jackson contended that the Indian Removal Act would put an end to "all possible danger of collision between the authorities of the General and State Governments on account of the Indians."

Jackson also claimed that the Indian Removal Act would protect Native Americans against further encroachment. He found support for his point of view from Secretary of War Lewis Cass, who defended "the progress of civilization and improvement." Cass wished "that the aboriginal population had accommodated themselves to the inevitable change of their condition," but asserted that "such a wish is vain."

INTERACT WITH HISTORY

1. **ANALYZING ISSUES** On what central issue regarding the Indian Removal Act did Jackson and Native American tribes disagree? Explain your opinion of the Act.

 SEE SKILLBUILDER HANDBOOK, PAGE 1046

2. **WRITING A PROPOSAL** Research the history of one of the Eastern tribes and write a proposal different from the Indian Removal Act that might have served the tribe better.

INTERACT WITH HISTORY

1. Analyzing Issues

Possible Responses *A key point of disagreement was the issue of whether the Indian Removal Act would truly protect Native Americans against hostile confrontations with white settlers. President Andrew Jackson contended that the Act would safeguard Native Americans from white encroachment. The Creek, however, questioned the credibility of Jackson's rationale: "Can [our white brethren] exempt us from intrusion in our promised borders, if they are incompetent to our protection where we are?"*

2. Writing a Proposal

Suggest that students use a flow chart like the one below to help them develop and organize their proposals.

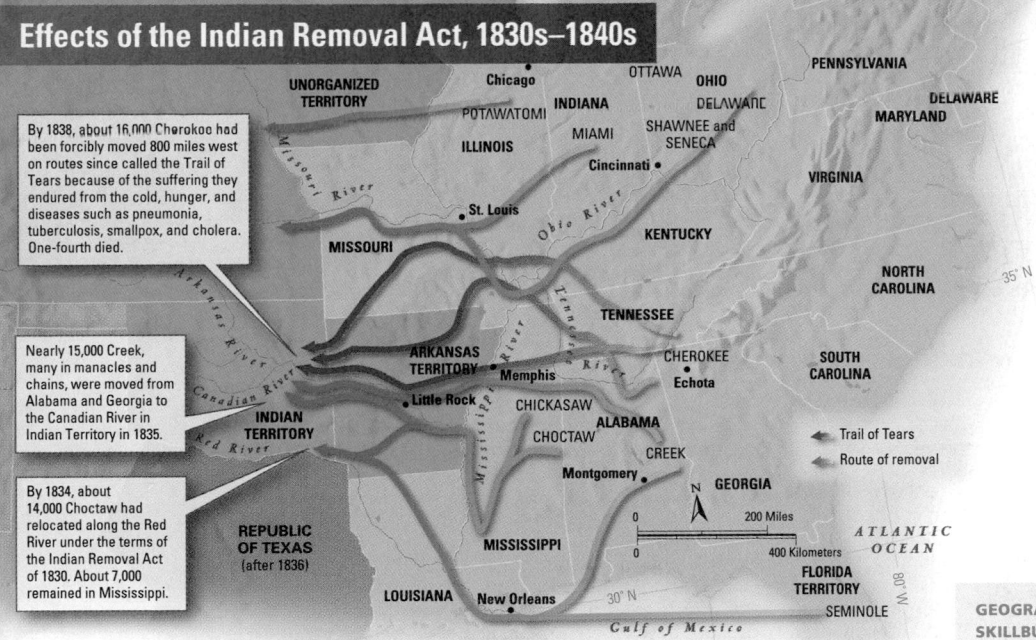

Effects of the Indian Removal Act, 1830s–1840s

By 1838, about 16,000 Cherokee had been forcibly moved 800 miles west on routes since called the Trail of Tears because of the suffering they endured from the cold, hunger, and diseases such as pneumonia, tuberculosis, smallpox, and cholera. One-fourth died.

Nearly 15,000 Creek, many in manacles and chains, were moved from Alabama and Georgia to the Canadian River in Indian Territory in 1835.

By 1834, about 14,000 Choctaw had relocated along the Red River under the terms of the Indian Removal Act of 1830. About 7,000 remained in Mississippi.

Trail of Tears
Route of removal

A PERSONAL VOICE

The Cherokees are nearly all prisoners. They have been dragged from their houses, and encamped at the forts and military posts, all over the nation. In Georgia, especially, multitudes were allowed no time to take anything with them, except the clothes they had on. Well-furnished houses were left a prey to plunderers, who, like hungry wolves, follow in the train of the captors. These wretches rifle the houses, and strip the helpless, unoffending owners of all they have on earth. Females, who have habituated to comforts and comparative affluence, are driven on foot before the bayonets of brutal men.

EVAN JONES, quoted in *The Trail of Tears*

Beginning in October and November of 1838, the Cherokee were sent off in groups of about one thousand each on the long journey. The 800-mile trip was made partly by steamboat and railroad but mostly on foot. As the winter came on, more and more of the Cherokee died en route. Along the way, government officials stole the Cherokees' money, while outlaws made off with their livestock. The Cherokee buried more than a quarter of their people along the **Trail of Tears.** When they reached their final destination, they ended up on land far inferior to that which they had been forced to leave.

Section ③ Assessment

1. **TERMS & NAMES**
   Identify:
   • Andrew Jackson
   • Democratic Republican Party
   • spoils system
   • Sequoya
   • Indian Removal Act
   • Trail of Tears

2. **SUMMARIZING** Create a time line in which you list key events relating to Jackson's political career. Write the events above or below the dates.

   1824   1830
   1828   1832

   Now make a time line for key events in the political career of a current politician.

3. **MAKING DECISIONS** If you were a U.S. citizen voting in the 1828 presidential election, would you cast your ballot for John Quincy Adams or Andrew Jackson? Support your choice.

   THINK ABOUT
   • each candidate's background and political experience
   • each candidate's views of the national bank and tariffs
   • where you live—the South, West, or New England

4. **INTERPRETING** In your opinion, what factors set the stage for the Indian Removal Act of 1830 and the Trail of Tears? Support your answer.

   THINK ABOUT
   • the attitude of white settlers toward Native Americans
   • Jackson's justification of the Indian Removal Act
   • why Jackson was able to defy the Supreme Court's ruling in *Worcester v. Georgia*

Balancing Nationalism and Sectionalism **213**

ANSWERS

1. TERMS & NAMES
Andrew Jackson, p. 209
Democratic Republican Party, p. 210
spoils system, p. 211
Sequoya, p. 211
Indian Removal Act, p. 211
Trail of Tears, p. 213

2. SUMMARIZING
Possible Responses:
1824—Jackson loses presidential election to John Quincy Adams.
1828—Jackson wins presidential election.
1830—Jackson pushes Congress to pass Indian Removal Act.
1832—Jackson refuses to enforce Supreme Court ruling on *Worcester v. Georgia.*

3. MAKING DECISIONS
Possible Responses: Students who live in New England might vote for Adams because he represents their economic interests; students who live in the South or West might vote for Jackson because of his appeal to the common citizen.

4. INTERPRETING
Possible Responses: Racial prejudice, differences in lifestyle, desire for the Indian lands, white settlers' belief in their rights to the land.

OBJECTIVES

① To explain why the protective tariff laws raised the issue of states' rights.

② To summarize how Jackson destroyed the Bank of the United States.

③ To identify some of the results of Jackson's economic policies.

SKILLBUILDER

• Interpreting political cartoons, p. 217

CRITICAL THINKING

• Summarizing, pp. 215, 218, 219
• Synthesizing, p. 216
• Contrasting, p. 216
• Analyzing motives, p. 217
• Analyzing causes, p. 218
• Generalizing, p. 219
• Analyzing, p. 219

FOCUS & MOTIVATE

▶ **Starting with the Student**
Have students imagine that some people in the class strongly disagree with the majority opinion.

• Would they dismiss those objections?
• Would they allow the ones who disagree to withdraw from the group?
• Would they try to reach a compromise?

MORE ABOUT . . .
Daniel Webster

After Hayne's first speech of the debates, Congressman Edward Everett asked Webster whether he had taken notes. Webster held up a small piece of paper. "I have it all," he said, "that is his speech." The following day, Webster's speech completely countered Hayne's argument. A member of the House told Webster, "Mr. Webster, I think you had better die now, and rest your fame on that speech." Overhearing the remark, Hayne said, "You ought not to die: a man who can make such speeches as that ought never to die."

TERMS & NAMES
• Daniel Webster
• John C. Calhoun
• Tariff of Abominations
• Bank of the United States (BUS)
• Whig
• Martin Van Buren
• Panic of 1837
• William Henry Harrison
• John Tyler

④ Jackson, States' Rights, and the National Bank

LEARN ABOUT Jackson's policies on states' rights and economic issues
TO UNDERSTAND why there were growing divisions and economic problems that threatened the spirit of nationalism.

ONE AMERICAN'S STORY

On January 26, 1830, **Daniel Webster** rose in the Senate and delivered one of the great speeches of American history. Parts of this speech have been memorized by thousands of schoolchildren over the years and have helped shape their view of the Union.

A PERSONAL VOICE

When my eyes shall be turned to behold for the last time the sun in heaven, may I not see him shining on the broken and dishonored fragments of a once glorious Union. . . . Let their last feeble and lingering glance rather behold the gorgeous ensign of the republic . . . bearing for its motto, no such miserable interrogatory as "What is all this worth?" nor those other words of delusion and folly, "Liberty first and Union afterwards"; but everywhere, spread all over in characters of living light . . . that other sentiment, dear to every true American heart—Liberty *and* Union, now and forever, one and inseparable!

DANIEL WEBSTER, from a speech delivered in the Senate on January 26, 1830

A phrase that Webster dismissed as folly—"Liberty first and Union afterwards" —was spoken by John C. Calhoun, one of Webster's great opponents in the struggle between states' rights and federal authority. The question of how much power the federal government should have and how much power the states should have came to a head over the issue of tariffs.

Daniel Webster

A Tariff Raises the States' Rights Issue

When the War of 1812 ended, British manufacturers wanted to destroy their American competitors by flooding the U.S. market with inexpensive goods. In response, Congress in 1816 passed a tariff to protect the infant American industries. The tariff was increased in 1824 and again in 1828.

THE NULLIFICATION THEORY Jackson's vice-president, **John C. Calhoun** of South Carolina, called it a **Tariff of Abominations**, a "disgusting and loathsome" tariff. As an agricultural region dependent on cotton, the South had to compete in the world market. Yet the high tariff on manufactured goods reduced British exports to the United States and, because of this, Britain bought less cotton. With the decline in British goods, the South was now forced to buy the more expensive Northern manufactured goods. From the South's point of view, the North was getting rich at the expense of the South. One observer remarked that when Southerners "see the flourishing villages of New England they cry, 'We pay for all this.'"

Calhoun was in a peculiar and dangerous position. He had long been known as a nationalist spokesman, and he had supported the protective tariff of 1816. He was on his way to a career as a national statesman and had served under both Adams and Jackson as vice-president. The situation in his home state, however, had made him change his views. South Carolina's economy failed to recover fully from an economic depression. Cotton prices remained low because planters and their slaves were moving to more fertile lands in Alabama and in the lower Mississippi River Valley, which produced much more cotton. Some South

---

SECTION 4 RESOURCES

PRINT RESOURCES

IN-DEPTH RESOURCES: UNIT 2
Guided Reading, p. 50
Primary Source: *from* the Hayne-Webster Debates, p. 58

ACCESS FOR STUDENTS ACQUIRING ENGLISH
Guided Reading (Spanish), p. 75

FORMAL ASSESSMENT
Section Quiz, p. 92

ALTERNATIVE ASSESSMENT BOOK
See forms for supporting and scoring alternative activities.

TECHNOLOGY RESOURCES

HUMANITIES TRANSPARENCIES
H33, President Andrew Jackson destroying the Bank of the United States: Lithograph cartoon, 1828

CRITICAL THINKING TRANSPARENCIES
CT7, The Industrial Revolution

CD-ROM Electronic Library of Primary Sources

VIDEO *American Portfolio: A Videodisc for U.S. History* user's guide, pp. 65, 66, 67

INTERNET McDougal Littell Learning On-Line
http://www.mcdougallittell.com

Carolina politicians began to wonder if Calhoun really cared about the needs of his state. He soon showed them that he did.

Calhoun devised a nullification theory, which basically questioned the legality of applying some federal laws in sovereign states. Calhoun's argument was that the United States Constitution was based on a compact among the sovereign states. If the Constitution had been established by 13 sovereign states, he reasoned, then they must still be sovereign, and each had the right to determine whether an act of Congress was constitutional. If it was not, then each state had the right to declare the offending law nullified, or illegal, within its borders. If the states did not have this right, Calhoun argued, then a majority in the federal government might trample on the rights of a minority. In 1828 Calhoun wrote down his theory in a document entitled "The South Carolina Exposition," but he did not sign his name to it. Nor did he say what he privately felt. Calhoun believed that if the federal government refused to permit a state to nullify a federal law, the state had the right to withdraw from the Union. (See Tracing Themes on states' rights, page 306.)

THINK THROUGH HISTORY
A. Summarizing *What was Calhoun's nullification theory?*

A. Answer Calhoun argued that since the U.S. Constitution was based on a compact among sovereign states, then the states must still be sovereign and had the right to determine whether an act of Congress was unconstitutional and, if it was, to declare it illegal within its borders.

KEY PLAYERS

JOHN C. CALHOUN
1782–1850

John Caldwell Calhoun entered national politics in 1811 with his election to the House of Representatives, where he was labeled a War Hawk for his support of the War of 1812. Then, in 1817, President Monroe asked him to become his Secretary of War. In this capacity, he improved the army's organization.

In 1824, this brilliant, ambitious, and handsome man with dark, flashing eyes won by a landslide the office of vice-president—a position he held under John Quincy Adams. In 1828, he won the vice-presidency again, this time as the running mate of Adams's opponent, Andrew Jackson.

A hard and humorless man, Calhoun took a tough position on slavery, arguing that it was not only necessary but even good: "There never has yet existed a wealthy and civilized society in which one portion of the community did not . . . live on the labor of the other."

DANIEL WEBSTER
1782–1852

In New England he was known as the "godlike Daniel." New Hampshire native Daniel Webster, famous for his eloquent speeches on behalf of a strong national government, actually began his career in the opposite camp—in favor of states' rights. After moving to Boston, Massachusetts, in 1816, however, his views on states' rights changed. New England was becoming a booming textile manufacturing center, and manufacturers needed a strong national government to protect their interests.

Webster was best known for his skill as an orator. As a congressman and, later, a senator, he captivated Congress with his speeches. However, Webster always had his eye on the presidency. Thus, it was his great disappointment that he failed to win this office despite several attempts to do so. At the end of his life he said, "I have given my life to law and politics. Law is uncertain and politics is utterly vain."

HAYNE AND WEBSTER DEBATE STATES' RIGHTS The tariff question (and the underlying states' rights issue) was discussed in one of the great debates in American history. For more than a week in January 1830, visitors to the Senate listened to Senator Robert Hayne of South Carolina debate Senator Daniel Webster of Massachusetts. Hayne delivered a pointed condemnation of the tariff.

A PERSONAL VOICE
The measures of the federal government . . . will soon involve the whole South in irretrievable ruin. But even this evil, great as it is, is not the chief ground of our complaints. It is the principle involved in the contest—a principle, which substituting the discretion of Congress for the limitations of the constitution, brings the States and the people to the feet of the federal government, and leaves them nothing they can call their own.

SENATOR ROBERT HAYNE from a speech to Congress, January 21, 1830

On January 26 Webster replied to Hayne's argument, saying that he could not conceive of a "middle course, between submission to the laws, when regularly pronounced constitutional, on the one hand, and open resistance, which is revolution, or rebellion, on the other."

Balancing Nationalism and Sectionalism **215**

OBJECTIVE
① INSTRUCT

A Tariff Raises the States' Rights Issue

▶ **Starting with the Student**
Have students make a chart like the one below to show the impact of the tariff laws and the nullification theory.

Tariff Laws	Impact:

Nullification Theory	Impact:

▶ **Discussing Key Ideas**
- Calhoun opposes the tariff laws and questions the legality of some federal laws.
- The tariff question and the states' rights issue spur the Webster-Haynes debates.
- South Carolina threatens to withdraw from the Union.

IN-DEPTH RESOURCES: UNIT 2
Guided Reading, p. 50
Primary Source: *from* the Hayne-Webster Debates, p. 58

ACCESS FOR STUDENTS ACQUIRING ENGLISH
Guided Reading (Spanish), p. 75

KEY PLAYERS
Calhoun and Webster
Critical Thinking:
Analyzing Ask students to explain how the two men's beliefs were influenced by regional economics. *Possible Response: Calhoun, a Southerner, opposed tariffs and supported slavery, both of which were considered necessary to the South's economy. Webster realized that the North's economy thrived under a strong national government.*

He then identified the key question: was the Union the creation of state legislatures or of the people? If it was the creation of state legislatures, Webster conceded that they should be entitled to control the Union—if they could agree how to do so. He believed, however, that the Union was "made for the people; made by the people; and answerable to the people."

Once the debates ended, the people wanted to hear President Jackson's position. He kept them waiting until the spring. Then, on April 13, at a public dinner, he clarified his position in a toast: "Our Union: it must be preserved." (For the record, he agreed to have it reported as, "Our Federal Union: it must and shall be preserved.") Calhoun replied with a toast of his own: "The Union, next to our liberty, the most dear; may we all remember that it can only be preserved by respecting the rights of the States and distributing equally the benefit and burden of the Union." The two men would not work together again.

SOUTH CAROLINA REBELS Two years later, in 1832, the issue of states' rights was finally put to a test when Congress passed a tariff law that South Carolina legislators still found unacceptable. They responded by declaring the tariffs of 1828 and 1832 "unauthorized by the Constitution" and "null, void, and no law"—and then they threatened to secede, or withdraw, from the Union, if customs officials tried to collect duties.

Jackson was furious. He took South Carolina's action as a challenge to him personally as well as to the nation as a whole. Although himself a Southerner and a slaveholder, he believed that South Carolina's action in declaring a federal law null and void flouted the will of the people as expressed in the U.S. Constitution. He declared South Carolina's actions treasonous and threatened to hang Calhoun and march federal troops into South Carolina to enforce the tariff. To make good on his threats, Jackson next urged Congress to pass the Force Bill, which it did in 1833. This bill allowed the federal government to use the army and navy against South Carolina if state authorities resisted paying proper duties.

A bloody confrontation seemed inevitable until Henry Clay stepped in and forged a compromise in 1833 between all the parties concerned. The Great Compromiser proposed a tariff bill that would gradually lower duties over a ten-year period. For now, the crisis between states' rights and federal authority was controlled, but the issue would continue to cause conflict in the 1840s and 1850s and would be a major cause of the Civil War.

"Disunion by armed force is treason."

ANDREW JACKSON

Jackson Attacks the National Bank

Although Andrew Jackson never did go to war against South Carolina, he did wage a war—a very personal war—on the **Bank of the United States (BUS),** located in Philadelphia. In fact, during the same year he dealt with the South Carolina crisis, 1832, he made his first attack on the bank by vetoing the bill to recharter it.

JACKSON OPPOSES THE BANK The Second Bank's 20-year charter was not due to expire until 1836, but Henry Clay and Daniel Webster wanted to introduce the renewal earlier to make it a campaign issue. They thought that Jackson might veto a new charter and, in so doing, lose some of his support. They underestimated, however, both the public's dislike of the BUS and Jackson's political skill.

Early in his career Jackson had lost money in financial speculations, and that experience made him deeply suspicious of banks. He believed that the national bank's conservative credit policies had helped to bring about the financial Panic of 1819. In Jackson's eyes, the national bank symbolized Eastern wealth and power. He regarded the national bank as an agent of the wealthy,

---

whose members cared nothing for Jackson's common people. Because of the bank's financial strength and influence on the economy, Jackson saw it as a threat to American democracy. He thought it might bribe officials and even try to buy elections with the intent of controlling the government and changing its character.

Jackson and his allies made certain that the general public came to think of the BUS as a privileged institution that served to "make the rich richer and the potent more powerful," as Senator Thomas Hart Benton of Missouri, a Jackson supporter, described it. Jacksonians did have some powerful facts to support their opinions. Since all federal tax revenues were deposited in the BUS rather than state or private banks, the Second Bank did have an unfair advantage over other banks. Furthermore, since BUS stockholders, not average American taxpayers, earned the interest from these deposits, a privileged few were making money that should have benefited all the taxpayers. In addition, the bank's president, Nicholas Biddle, often extended loans to congressmen at much lower rates of interest than the bank gave to the average citizen.

PET BANKS In 1832, Jackson told Martin Van Buren (who would become his next vice-president) that the bank was a "monster" that corrupted "our statesmen" and wanted "to destroy our republican institution." "The bank, Mr. Van Buren, is trying to kill me, but *I will kill it.*" After his reelection in 1832, he tried to kill the BUS before its charter ran out in 1836 by pressuring the secretary of the treasury to withdraw all government deposits from the bank's branches and place them in certain state banks—called "pet banks" because of their loyalty to the Democratic Party. When the secretary refused to carry out Jackson's orders, the president fired him and then appointed a new secretary who undermined the national bank by placing all new deposits in pet banks.

In an attempt to save the BUS, Nicholas Biddle decided to have the bank call in—or demand repayment of—loans to individuals and privately owned businesses. He also refused to make new loans. He claimed that he was forced to do this because the bank was not being rechartered; he hoped that this news would cause a frustrated public to demand the passage of a new bank charter.

This practice did succeed in forcing many merchants and manufacturers into bankruptcy, and these businessmen did, in turn, descend on Washington, D.C., to plead with Jackson for help. Jackson firmly told them they were talking to the wrong man. "Go to Nicholas Biddle," he said.

Pressure from financial leaders finally forced Biddle to adopt a more generous loan policy. However, the entire chain of events had by this time cost Biddle much of his backing, even with the Eastern business community. In 1836, when its charter expired, the Second Bank of the United States became just another Philadelphia bank. Five years later, it had to close its doors.

CONSEQUENCES OF JACKSON'S POLICIES While the owners of Jackson's pet banks—state banks loyal to Jackson in which federal funds were held—voiced joy at this turn of events, New York bankers were even more delighted. They picked up the pieces of the Philadelphia BUS, and established New York as the new financial capital of the United States.

Jackson's tactics and policies, however, had angered many people, including some members of his own Democratic Party. Believing that Jackson had

BORN TO COMMAND.

OF VETO MEMORY.

HAD I BEEN CONSULTED.

KING ANDREW THE FIRST.

In this cartoon, Andrew Jackson (portrayed as a king) tramples on the Constitution.

SKILLBUILDER
INTERPRETING POLITICAL CARTOONS
What does this cartoon suggest about Andrew Jackson's attitude toward the constitutional limits on the powers of the presidency?
Skillbuilder Answer The cartoon suggests that Jackson acts like a tyrant, trampling on the laws of the land.

Balancing Nationalism and Sectionalism **217**

Successors Deal with Jackson's Legacy

▶ **Discussing Key Ideas**

• As president, Martin Van Buren confronts the consequences of Jackson's economic policies, which result in bank closings, bankrupt businesses, and widespread unemployment.

• Van Buren loses the election of 1840 to Whig Party candidate William Henry Harrison.

• When Harrison dies after one month in office, John Tyler, who opposes the Whig program for economic recovery, becomes president.

ON THE WORLD STAGE
The International Panic of 1837

Critical Thinking: Cause and Effect Ask students to create a cause-and-effect chart. Students should list some of the events that led to the panic and identify some effects of the panic. *Possible Responses: Causes —European nations' troubled economies, British and U.S. loans recalled; Effects —plummeting value of goods, unemployment, poverty.*

---

acted more like a king than a president, his foes dubbed him "King Andrew the First." Then, in 1834, the discontented—including Henry Clay and Daniel Webster—channeled their frustrations into action; they formed a new political party called the **Whig** Party. Their choice of names summed up their beliefs, for the Whigs were a group in Britain that tried to limit royal power, and *Whig* had come to mean anyone opposed to an excessively powerful chief executive.

Successors Deal with Jackson's Legacy

When Jackson announced that he would not run for a third term, the Democrats chose Vice-President **Martin Van Buren** as their candidate. The newly formed Whig Party, which in 1836 was not able to agree on a single candidate, ran three regional candidates against him. With Jackson's support Van Buren won the election easily.

MARTIN VAN BUREN Along with the presidency, however, Van Buren inherited the dire consequences of Jackson's bank war and money policies. When Jackson had his secretary of the treasury deposit all new federal funds into pet banks rather than the BUS, many of these were wildcat banks. These were banks that printed bank notes wildly in excess of the gold and silver they had on deposit. Such wildcat banks were doomed to fail when many people attempted to redeem their currency for gold or silver.

Since the notes printed by wildcat banks were nearly worthless, the federal government was left holding the bag when people used them to purchase land from the government. Jackson realized what was happening and issued the Specie Circular, which made only gold and silver, called specie, acceptable payment for public land. This order, which went into effect on August 15, 1836, sent people rushing to banks to trade paper currency for gold and silver and, in turn, many banks, which had limited specie, suspended the redemption of bank notes for gold and silver.

By May 1837, New York banks stopped accepting all paper currency. Other banks soon did the same. In the **Panic of 1837,** bank closings and the collapse of the credit system cost many people their savings, bankrupted hundreds of businesses, and put more than a third of the population out of work.

Van Buren tried to help by reducing federal spending, but that caused already declining prices to drop further. Then he tried to set up an independent treasury that would use only gold and silver coin. In 1840, Congress established this treasury, but the demand for gold and silver it created worsened matters.

HARRISON AND TYLER That same year, the Democratic Party candidate Van Buren ran for reelection against Whig Party candidate **William Henry Harrison**—but this time the Whigs had an advantage. They used the campaign strategy that had won Jackson his elections; they portrayed Harrison, the old war hero, as a man of the people and Van Buren as a pampered, privileged aristocrat. Actually, Van Buren was more of a common man; he was the son of a tavern owner and never earned much money. Harrison, on the other hand, came from a wealthy family and lived in a 16-room mansion.

The editor of a Democratic newspaper, intending to insult the Whig candidate, declared that if Harrison were given an annual pension of $2,000 and a barrel of hard cider (an alcoholic beverage), the old man would be content to live in a log cabin. This played into Whig hands; a log cabin and hard cider became campaign symbols of Harrison as a man of the people.

ON THE WORLD STAGE

THE INTERNATIONAL PANIC OF 1837

Although the financial crisis that came to be known as the Panic of 1837 was in part caused by Jackson's policies toward the Bank of the United States, these were not the only causes. The U.S. economy was affected by the economies of other nations.

During the 1830s, for example, British investment in the United States boomed as British banks made huge loans to U.S. banks. Then, when hard times came to European nations, they recalled their loans to Britain, which forced the British banks to recall their loans to American banks.

However, since U.S. banks had already lent this money, they, in turn, had to ask their customers to repay their loans. This forced many people to sell their goods, which caused the prices of goods to plummet.

THINK THROUGH HISTORY
E. Summarizing Why was the Whig party formed?
E. Answer The Whig Party was formed in opposition to Andrew Jackson's policies; it was made up of people opposed to a too powerful president.

THINK THROUGH HISTORY
F. Analyzing Causes How did Jackson's actions hurt the nation's economy?
F. Answer Jackson had funds deposited in pet banks— many of which turned out to be wildcat banks— and issued the Specie Circular, which set off a rush on banks and contributed to the Panic of 1837.

TEACHING OPTIONS

Making Connections Across Time

The Great Depression Like the Panic of 1837, the Great Depression in the 1930s resulted in bank closings, unemployment, and human suffering. To aid recovery, the U.S. government assumed greater control over banks and the stock market. To support new programs, the government also changed how it spent money. Instead of spending as much as it collected, the government began spending more.

What was the probable result of this policy? *Possible Response: It greatly increased the national debt.*

Making Connections Across the Curriculum

Economics Remind students that the Panic of 1837 forced many people to sell their goods at the same time. As a result, the prices of these goods fell. Point out that this sequence of events illustrates the law of supply and demand. This law states that prices fall when the supply of goods increases.

Ask students what happens to prices when the supply of goods decreases. *Prices rise.*

Harrison won and began his term with confidence. He immediately took steps to enact the Whig program to revitalize the economy, which was still in a severe depression. Then, just a month after his inauguration, he died of pneumonia.

John Tyler, Harrison's vice-president and successor, was a strong-minded Virginian who opposed many parts of the Whig program for economic recovery. The Whigs had put Tyler on the ballot to pick up Southern votes; they never thought he would play much of a role in government. During the next four years, however, they would come to see his inclusion on the ticket as a grave mistake—and thus to refer to President Tyler as "His Accidency."

A LEGACY OF TWO PARTIES Just as in the 1790s, when people divided politically into Jeffersonian Republicans and Hamiltonian Federalists, so did people in the 1830s divide into two distinct parties, each with loyal followers. They identified themselves either as Jacksonian Democrats (which developed from the Democratic-Republicans, an offshoot of Jefferson's Republican party) or as Whigs. These parties held center stage until the 1850s.

This almanac cover promoted the candidacy of William Henry Harrison for president.

The style of politics, however, had drastically changed since the 1790s. The new politicians appealed more to passion than to reason. They courted popularity in a way that John Quincy Adams and his predecessors never would have done. Political speeches became a form of mass entertainment, involving far more Americans in the political process. The average citizen became more politically aware and had more political involvement than ever before.

G. Answer
Appeal to passion rather than reason; courted popularity; speeches become mass entertainment; average citizen more involved.

THINK THROUGH HISTORY
G. Summarizing In what ways did Jackson influence the political process?

Section 4 Assessment

1. TERMS & NAMES
Identify:
• Daniel Webster
• John C. Calhoun
• Tariff of Abominations
• Bank of the United States (BUS)
• Whig
• Martin Van Buren
• Panic of 1837
• William Henry Harrison
• John Tyler

2. SUMMARIZING In a two-column chart, list the key issues that Jackson confronted. Then list the important legacies he left to the nation.

Jackson's Presidency

Issues	Legacies

Explain how one of these legacies has continued to today.

3. GENERALIZING In what ways do you think the tariff crises of 1828 and 1832 might be considered important milestones in American history before the Civil War? Use evidence from the text to support your response.

THINK ABOUT
• Calhoun's nullification theory
• the Hayne-Webster debates
• why Jackson pushed Congress to pass the Force Bill

4. ANALYZING How do you think Jackson might have countered the Whig Party's accusation that he was acting like a king? Support your answer with reasons.

THINK ABOUT
• his policies and political appeal
• the image of himself that Jackson projected to his supporters

ANSWERS

1. TERMS & NAMES
Daniel Webster, p. 214
John C. Calhoun, p. 214
Tariff of Abominations, p. 214
Bank of the United States, p. 216
Whig, p. 218
Martin Van Buren, p. 218
Panic of 1837, p. 218
William Henry Harrison, p. 218
John Tyler, p. 219

2. SUMMARIZING
Possible Responses:
Issues—states' rights versus federal power over the Tariff of 1832; Jackson versus the bank over its threat to American democracy.

Legacies—another version of the two-party system; presidential elections as popularity contests; average citizen's broader political awareness.

3. GENERALIZING
Possible Responses: South Carolina's nullification of the tariffs of 1828 and 1832 resulted in a clash between the federal government and South Carolina that might have escalated into a military conflict. The issue of states' rights was brought forward and would eventually be a major cause of the Civil War. Discussions and debates over the tariff produced important interpretations of the Constitution on the issues of states' rights.

4. ANALYZING
Possible Responses: Jackson believed he served the best interests of the common people, unlike the Whigs, who were agents of the aristocracy. Jackson might also contend that he used, not abused, the power of his office to preserve the democratic principles of the Constitution.

REVIEWING THE CHAPTER

TERMS & NAMES

1. Eli Whitney, p. 198
2. Industrial Revolution, p. 198
3. John Quincy Adams, p. 205
4. nationalism, p. 205
5. Missouri Compromise, p. 208
6. Andrew Jackson, p. 209
7. Trail of Tears, p. 213
8. spoils system, p. 211
9. Bank of the United States, p. 216
10. Whig, p. 218

MAIN IDEAS

11. Development of interchangeable parts, division of labor and power-driven machinery, mass production of goods.

12. Northeast favored the tariff; South and West opposed it.

13. Laid groundwork for the government's authority to regulate interstate transportation and communication systems; led to future rulings favoring competition over monopolies.

14. National interests and national unity more important than regional concerns; national self-interest should shape foreign policy.

15. Missouri's admission as a free state or a slave state would upset the existing sectional balance.

16. Easing of voting requirements increased number of voters. Over three times as many white males voted in 1828 as in 1824, and they elected Andrew Jackson.

17. Exterminating the Native Americans, assimilating them into white culture, allowing them to live in their own areas, or moving them to lands farther west.

18. Declared South Carolina's actions treasonous, threatened to hang Calhoun, and secured congressional approval to use the military to enforce the tariff.

19. He mistrusted the bank, regarding it as insensitive to the needs of common people and believing its financial strength and power threatened American democracy.

20. The Whigs used image making to manipulate voters' perceptions of the presidential candidates.

REVIEWING THE CHAPTER

TERMS & NAMES For each item below, write a sentence explaining its historical significance during the first half of the 19th century. For each person below, explain his role in political or economic events of this period.

1. Eli Whitney
2. Industrial Revolution
3. John Quincy Adams
4. nationalism
5. Missouri Compromise
6. Andrew Jackson
7. Trail of Tears
8. spoils system
9. Bank of the United States (BUS)
10. Whig

MAIN IDEAS

SECTION 1 *(pages 198–203)*

Regional Economies Create Differences

11. What were the key changes in technology, work procedures, and methods of organizing manufacturing that spurred the Industrial Revolution?

12. How did people in the Northeast, the South, and the West react to the Tariff of 1816?

SECTION 2 *(pages 204–208)*

Nationalism at Center Stage

13. Cite two ways in which the *Gibbons v. Ogden* decision set the stage for future Supreme court rulings.

14. Explain the belief that guided the foreign policy of Secretary of State John Quincy Adams.

15. Why did Missouri's request for admission into the Union heighten the sectional rivalry between the North and the South?

SECTION 3 *(pages 209–213)*

The Age of Jackson

16. What changes occurred in the voting population and in voting patterns between the presidential elections of 1824 and 1828?

17. What four alternatives did Jackson have in shaping a policy to tackle the problem of Native Americans?

SECTION 4 *(pages 214–219)*

Jackson, States' Rights, and the National Bank

18. What aggressive measures was Jackson willing to take in retaliation for South Carolina's threat to secede in 1832?

19. Why did Jackson oppose the Bank of the United States?

20. How did the Whig Party's tactics to win the 1840 presidential election mirror Jackson's earlier campaign strategies?

THINKING CRITICALLY

1. **COMPROMISE VERSUS CONFRONTATION** Create a continuum similar to the one below, labeled with *compromise* at one end and *confrontation* at the other. Mark where you think Andrew Jackson, Henry Clay, and John C. Calhoun would fall on the continuum. Support your ratings with historical events in which these men played a critical role.

compromise   confrontation

2. **NATIONAL CHARACTER** Westward expansion helped shape the personal identity of Americans in the early 1800s. What values and traits characterized many Western settlers of this era? Think about Jim Beckwourth's life (profiled in the Historical Spotlight in Section 2) and the rise of the common man during the Jackson era.

3. **DEFINING A NATION** Reread the quote by John C. Calhoun on page 196. How do you think his choice of words reflects issues of the time? Explain your opinion.

4. **GEOGRAPHY OF THE CANAL NETWORKS** Look carefully at the roads and canals map on page 202. How would you explain the concentration of canals in the North?

5. **INDIAN REMOVAL ACT** Based on arguments presented by the critics and supporters of the Indian Removal Act of 1830, do you think it was possible for Jackson and Native Americans to bridge their differences on this issue? Why or why not?

6. **ANALYZING PRIMARY SOURCES** Read the following excerpt from Andrew Jackson's message on vetoing the renewal of the Second Bank's charter in 1832. Then answer the questions below.

> Every man is equally entitled to protection by law; but when the laws undertake to add to these natural and just advantages artificial distinctions, to grant . . . exclusive privileges, to make the rich richer and the potent more powerful, the humble members of society—the farmers, mechanics, and laborers—who have neither the time nor the means of securing like favors to themselves, have a right to complain of the injustice of their Government. There are no necessary evils in government. Its evils exist only in its abuses. If it would confine itself to equal protection, and, as Heaven does its rains, shower its favors alike on the high and the low, the rich and the poor, it would be an unqualified blessing. In the act [to recharter the bank] before me there seems to be a wide and unnecessary departure from these just principles.
>
> **ANDREW JACKSON,** *A Compilation of the Messages and Papers of the Presidents, 1789–1902*

How does Jackson seem to justify his veto of renewing the bank's charter? Based on this excerpt, what do you think is Jackson's vision of government's role in a democracy?

THINKING CRITICALLY

1. COMPROMISE VERSUS CONFRONTATION

Possible Responses: Jackson—Near the confrontation end. Examples include his collision with Calhoun and South Carolina during the tariff crisis of 1832; his veto of the bank's recharter and the campaign he waged to destroy the bank; his open defiance of the Supreme Court's ruling on Cherokee's land rights in Georgia.
Calhoun—Near the confrontation end. Examples include Calhoun's combative role in the tariff crisis of 1832, in which South Carolina threatened to secede.

Could be seen as more conciliatory earlier in his political career because he supported the Tariff of 1816.
Clay—Near the compromise end. Examples include his leadership role in Congress when he helped draft the Missouri Compromise and avert a sectional crisis; during the tariff crisis he helped the nation avoid an armed clash when he forged a compromise in 1833 to gradually lower duties over a 10-year span. Could be seen as confrontational when he joined with Daniel Webster to form the Whig Party.

2. NATIONAL CHARACTER

Possible Responses: Belief in social equality, social mobility, and individual freedom; expanded job opportunities and social roles; greater confidence in the democratic process because of increased suffrage and the admission of new states to the union; optimism; resourcefulness and versatility; rugged individualism.

3. DEFINING A NATION

Possible Responses: Calhoun implies that the states are not united under one government; use of the word *sovereign*

ALTERNATIVE ASSESSMENT

1. PATENTING AN INVENTION

How did technological developments of the early 19th century change the way Americans lived, worked, or traveled?

Prepare a patent application for a technological development in early-19th-century America. Describe the purpose of the development and what changes it will cause.

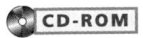 **CD-ROM** Use *Grolier's Multimedia Encyclopedia* and other resources to choose a technological development and apply to patent it. Possible inventions include the cotton gin, the steam engine and the spinning mule.

- Include a picture of what you are applying to patent and refer to it in your application. (Draw one yourself or download or copy one from your reference materials.)

- In your application, describe how the invention works, what it produces or accomplishes, what kind of labor it requires, its effects on environmental conditions, and its effects on how people live or work.

2. RESEARCHING EARLY INDUSTRIALIZATION

 In his book *The Machine in the Garden,* Leo Marx makes the following observations about American industrialization in the early 1800s:

By 1829 . . . a profitable factory system was firmly established in New England; new roads and canals and cities were transforming the landscape; on rivers and in ocean harbors the steamboat was proving the superiority of mechanized transport. . . . And it was the miraculous machinery of the age, beyond all else, which made it obvious that things were getting better all the time.

Using library resources and the Internet, research a technological innovation from the early 1800s and its impact on the nation's progress. For Internet research, click on **Social Studies** at http://www.mcdougallittell.com and write an essay presenting your findings. Add your essay to your American history portfolio.

3. PORTFOLIO PROJECT

 Use the Living History activity to expand your portfolio.

LIVING HISTORY

PRESENTING YOUR POLITICAL ADVERTISEMENT

You have created a poster that gives a certain image to your political candidate.

- Share your poster with others and compare and contrast the images various class members created for their candidates.

- Choose the most negative, the most positive, and the most effective from the poster images.

- In a class discussion, decide what makes an effective political advertisement and what kind of image would be considered positive to today's public.

- Finally, add your poster to your American history portfolio.

Bridge to Chapter 8

Review Chapter 7

REGIONAL ECONOMIES AND NATIONALISM

Technological innovations in agriculture, manufacturing, and transportation dramatically transformed American life. These beginnings of the Industrial Revolution in America affected the method of producing goods and cultivating crops, stimulated economic growth, and altered trade patterns. Distinctive regional economies evolved.

Henry Clay promoted the American System to unite the country's economic interests and to create a more self-sufficient and stable economy. Congress then voted for a new tariff, a new national bank, and internal improvements. This legislation reflected the growing sentiment of nationalism. John Marshall guided the Supreme Court to decisions that boosted federal power. Secretary of State John Quincy Adams established foreign policies that helped ensure national security and expand U.S. territory. President Monroe formulated the Monroe Doctrine. The Missouri Compromise of 1820 temporarily defused a sectional conflict over slavery.

JACKSON'S PRESIDENCY AND LEGACY Expanded suffrage contributed to Andrew Jackson's landslide victory in the 1828 presidential election. Jackson instituted polices that gave people a greater voice in the government. He carried out policies to force Native Americans to move from their homelands. South Carolina nullified a new federal tariff and threatened to secede from the Union in 1832. Jackson pushed Congress to pass the Force Bill, allowing the federal government to take military action against South Carolina to enforce the tariff. Declaring war on the national bank, Jackson vetoed its recharting. President Van Buren inherited the dire consequences of Jackson's bank war and financial policies—an economic depression that helped put William Henry Harrison in office.

Preview Chapter 8

The spirit of democracy during Jackson's administration helped set the stage for reform as groups rallied to correct problems caused by social, political, economic, and technological changes of the early 1800s. Religious revival and the emergence of early industry sparked reform movements. The abolition of slavery and the fight for women's rights were among the crusades waged during this time. You will learn about these and other developments in the next chapter.

Balancing Nationalism and Sectionalism **221**

1. PATENTING AN INVENTION

Standards for Evaluation

A patent application should meet the following criteria:

- Identifies one invention and provides a detailed description of its workings and the labor required to operate it.
- Describes how this invention will affect society, paying special attention to living and working conditions of the people associated with it.
- Displays thorough research of the invention, using at least three different sources.
- Provides an illustration of the invention.

2. RESEARCHING EARLY INDUSTRIALIZATION

Standards for Evaluation

An essay should meet the following criteria:

- Focuses on a particular invention and describes its innovative characteristics in detail.
- Provides concrete examples of how that invention affected society.
- Displays thorough research— at least two sources should be from the Internet.
- Makes logical connections in a clear and concise manner.

3. PORTFOLIO PROJECT
LIVING HISTORY

Standards for Evaluation

A poster should meet the following criteria:

- Presents a clear and coherent message.
- Utilizes images to communicate information about the politician.
- Includes a brief, catchy slogan that promotes or discredits the candidate.
- Shows consistency.

IN-DEPTH RESOURCES: UNIT 7
See the form for scoring this activity on page 66.

THINKING CRITICALLY

implies that the states have final, permanent authority and focuses attention on the issue of states' rights versus the power of the federal government; the words *Union* and *confederacy* foreshadow the divisiveness and civil war to come.

4. GEOGRAPHY OF THE CANAL NETWORKS

Possible Responses: The North needed to link the Great Lakes to major rivers and to the Atlantic Ocean; the North has more cities and industry than the South, which is mostly rural.

5. INDIAN REMOVAL ACT

Possible Responses: Some students might say that if judicial and legislative branches had enforced their views on Native Americans' right to the land, a compromise might have been reached. Others might say that both Jackson and Native Americans were too entrenched in beliefs about land rights to compromise. Also, Jackson's prejudice about the "savage habits" of Native Americans and his goal to "strengthen the southwestern frontier" probably made compromise impossible.

6. ANALYZING PRIMARY SOURCES

Possible Responses: Jackson underscores his commitment to the 19th century democratic principles of equal rights and equal opportunity of all white male Americans and government by popular consent. He views the bank as a government agent of the aristocracy, not the common people. Government, according to Jackson, should be responsive to the rights and concerns of all citizens, who are active participants in the democratic process.

		TEACHING SUPPORT	ASSESSMENT
SECTION 1 Religion Sparks Reform *pp. 224–228*	**Key Ideas** Changes in the political and economic arenas contribute to the Second Great Awakening, a renewal of religious sentiment that brings about a host of social reform movements.	**In-Depth Resources: Unit 2** • Guided Reading, p. 67 • Primary Source: *from* Dorothea Dix's Pleas on Behalf of the Mentally Ill, p. 74 **COOPERATIVE ACTIVITIES** • Survey on Education Reform, p. 227 (TE)	**Section 1 Assessment**, p. 228 (PE) **Self-Assessment**, p. 228 (TE) **Formal Assessment** • Section Quiz, p. 101 **Alternative Assessment Book** • Standards for Evaluating a Cooperative Activity
SECTION 2 Slavery and Abolition *pp. 229–234*	Slavery becomes an explosive issue, as more Americans join reformers working for abolition.	**In-Depth Resources: Unit 2** • Guided Reading, p. 68 • Primary Sources: Propaganda Images, p. 75; *from* Appeal to the Christian Women of the South, p. 76 • American Lives: Frederick Douglass, p. 81 **COOPERATIVE ACTIVITY** • Daily Lives in Contrast, p. 232 (TE)	**Section 2 Assessment**, p. 234 (PE) **Self-Assessment**, p. 234 (TE) **Formal Assessment** • Section Quiz, p. 102 **Alternative Assessment Book** • Standards for Evaluating a Cooperative Activity
SECTION 3 Women and Reform *pp. 235–239*	Women reformers expand their efforts from reform movements such as abolition and temperance to work for women's rights.	**In-Depth Resources: Unit 2** • Guided Reading, p. 69 • Skillbuilder Practice: Identifying Problems, p. 71 • Primary Source: *from* The Seneca Falls Declaration of Sentiments, p. 77 • American Lives: Elizabeth Cady Stanton, p. 87 **COOPERATIVE ACTIVITIES** • Interviewing Women Reformers, p. 237 (TE)	**Section 3 Assessment**, p. 239 (PE) **Self-Assessment**, p. 239 (TE) **Formal Assessment** • Section Quiz, p. 103 **Alternative Assessment Book** • Standards for Evaluating a Cooperative Activity
SECTION 4 The Changing Workplace *pp. 240–245*	A growing industrial workforce faces problems arising from changes in manufacturing and the creation of the factory system.	**In-Depth Resources: Unit 2** • Guided Reading, p. 70 • Geography Application: The Dramatic Rise of Immigration, p. 72 **COOPERATIVE ACTIVITY** • Writing a List of Demands, p. 243	**Section 4 Assessment**, p. 245 (PE) **Self-Assessment**, p. 245 (TE) **Formal Assessment** • Section Quiz, p. 104 **Alternative Assessment Book** • Standards for Evaluating a Cooperative Activity
CHAPTER RESOURCES	**Chapter Overview** A religious revival sweeps the United States. In its wake, many people press for reforms including the end of slavery, the granting of equal rights to women, and increased rights for workers.	**In-Depth Resources: Unit 2** • Living History Project: Worksheet, p. 83; Standards, p. 84 **Telescoping the Times** • Chapter Summary, pp. 15–16 **Planning for Block Schedules**	**Chapter Assessment**, pp. 000–000 (PE) **Alternative Assessment**, p. 000 (PE) **Formal Assessment** • Chapter Test, forms A and B, p. 105–110 **Test Generator** **Alternative Assessment Book** See explanation and forms for different kinds of alternative assessments including portfolio assessment.

Humanities Transparencies
• H8, "Religions Camp Meeting" by J. Maze Burbank

Critical Thinking Transparencies
• CT42, Increasing School Enrollment: 1840–1860

INTERNET RESOURCES
• See *McDougal Littell Learning On-Line* for links to information about de Tocqueville, Thoreau, and Hawthorne.

Geography Transparencies
• G8, Distribution of Slaves, 1790 and 1860

Electronic Library of Primary Sources
• from *The Anti-Slavery Movement* by Frederick Douglass
• from *Declaration of Sentiments* by the American Anti-Slavery Society
• from *Incidents* by Harriet Jacobs

INTERNET RESOURCES
• See *McDougal Littell Learning On-Line* for links to information about Frederick Douglass.

Grolier Multimedia Encyclopedia
• Lucretia Mott

Electronic Library of Primary Sources
• *Disappointment is the Lot of Women* by Lucy Stone

INTERNET RESOURCES
• See *McDougal Littell Learning On-Line* for links to information about Sojourner Truth and Elizabeth Cady Stanton.

Critical Thinking Transparencies
• CT8, Reform Movement Summary

Electronic Library of Primary Sources
• from "Pleasures of Factory Life" by Sarah Bagley

INTERNET RESOURCES
• See Interact with History p. 247 (PE) for an activity that includes the Internet as an enrichment option.

American Portfolio: A Videodisc for U.S. History, user's guide, pp. 53, 54, 69–78

INTERNET RESOURCES
Learning On-Line: Social Studies
http://www.mcdougallittell.com

Block Scheduling (90 MINUTES)

Day 1
Section 1, pp. 224–228
Section 2, pp. 229–234
Section Assessments pp. 228, 234

Day 2
Section 3, pp. 235–239
Section 4, pp. 240–245
Section Assessments, pp. 239, 245
Daily Life: Working at Mid-Century, pp. 246–247
Chapter Assessment, pp. 248–249

> **YEARLY PACING** *Chapter 8 Total:* 2 days *Yearly Total:* 85 days

See *Planning for Block Schedules* for special activities and pacing strategies.

Customizing for Special Populations

Students Acquiring English

Access for Students Acquiring English
• Guided Reading for Sections 1–4 (Spanish), pp. 83–86
• Chapter Summary (Spanish), pp. 81–82
• Skillbuilder Practice: Identifying Problems (Spanish), p. 87
• Geography Application: The Dramatic Rise of Immigration (Spanish), p. 88

INTERNET RESOURCES
• See *McDougal Littell Learning On-Line* The Diverse Classroom.

Less Proficient Readers

In-Depth Resources: Unit 2
• Guided Reading for Sections 1–4, pp. 67–70
• Skillbuilder: Identifying Problems, p. 71
• Geography Application: The Dramatic Rise of Immigration, p. 72

Telescoping the Times
• Chapter Summary, pp. 15–16

See additional strategies at point of use in the Teacher's Edition.

Gifted and Talented Students

In-Depth Resources: Unit 2
• Primary Sources: *from* Dorothea Dix's Plea on Behalf of the Mentally Ill, p. 74; Propaganda Images, p. 75; *from* Appeal to the Christian Women of the South, p. 76; *from* The Seneca Falls Declaration of Sentiments, p. 77
• American Lives: Frederick Douglass, p. 81; Elizabeth Cady Stanton, p. 82

See additional strategies at point of use in the Teacher's Edition.

Connections to Literature READINGS FOR STUDENTS

In-Depth Resources: Unit 2
• from *The Confessions of Nat Turner* by William Styron
p. 78

McDougal Littell *The Language of Literature*
American Literature

• Henry Wadsworth Longfellow, "A Psalm of Life"
p. 272
• Washington Irving, "The Devil and Tom Walker"
p. 276
• Ralph Waldo Emerson, *from* "Self-Reliance"
p. 291
• Margaret Fuller, *from* "Memoirs"
p. 294

• Henry David Thoreau, *from* Walden
p. 297
• Delbert L. Earisman, Thoreau, a Hippie in History
p. 308
• Walt Whitman, *Selected Poems*
p. 312

McDougal Littell *Literature Connections*

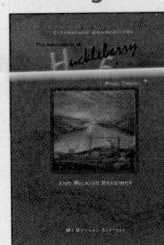

• Mark Twain, *The Adventures of Huckleberry Finn (with related readings)* Through a remarkable river journey with two unforgettable characters, Twain captures the essence of America in the early 19th century.

Reforming American Society

▶ *Starting with the Student*
Ask students what they already know about abolition and other reform movements in the 19th century. Who were some of the leaders of these movements? What reforms did they call for?

PREVIEWING THE CHAPTER
Ask students to study the time line and pick out one or two items about which they have questions.

MORE ABOUT . . .
Ralph Waldo Emerson
Throughout much of his life, Ralph Waldo Emerson (1803–1882) experienced poverty, sickness, and deep sorrow. Until the age of 30, he suffered from a lung disease and bouts of temporary blindness. He also endured the deaths of his wife and son. Nonetheless, Emerson developed a philosophy based on optimism and individualism. He believed that people can find the truth within themselves. In his essay "Self-Reliance," Emerson wrote: "What I must do, is all that concerns me, not what the people think."

CHAPTER
8

Reforming American Society

SECTION 1
Religion Sparks Reform
Changes in the political and economic arenas contribute to the Second Great Awakening, a renewal of religious sentiment that brings about a host of social reform movements.

SECTION 2
Slavery and Abolition
Slavery becomes an explosive issue, as more Americans join reformers working for abolition.

SECTION 3
Women and Reform
Women reformers expand their efforts from reform movements such as abolition and temperance to work for women's rights.

SECTION 4
The Changing Workplace
A growing industrial workforce faces problems arising from changes in manufacturing and the creation of the factory system.

"What is a man born for but to be a Reformer, a Re-maker of what man has made; a renouncer of lies; a restorer of truth and good . . . ?"

Ralph Waldo Emerson, 1841

- **Lowell textile mills open.**

Sojourner Truth is freed from slavery.

- Nat Turner leads slave rebellion.

- William Lloyd Garrison publishes *The Liberator.*

- French historian Alexis de Tocqueville tours the United States.

| THE UNITED STATES | **1820** | 1822 | 1827 | **1830** |
| THE WORLD | | 1821 | 1825 | |

- Napoleon dies.
- Decembrist revolt in Russia occurs.
- George IV rules Great Britain.

222 CHAPTER 8

THEMES IN CHAPTER 2

Cultural Diversity	*Expanding Democracy*	*Women in America*	*Science and Technology*
In the early 1800s, African Americans began forming their own churches, which became important cultural and social centers in their communities, as well as an important forum for the fight against slavery. See Teacher's Edition note, p. 225.	The growing pains of the new nation are evident, as the notion of the United States as a democracy is challenged by abolitionists using both violent and nonviolent means to fight slavery. See Teacher's Edition note, p. 230.	As female abolitionists fought for the rights of the disenfranchised, they realized that they too had no rights and began supporting other reforms that benefited women. See Teacher's Edition note, p. 238.	By the 1830s, new manufacturing techniques had revolutionized industry and transformed society in New England. However, not everyone benefited from these changes. See Teacher's Edition note, p. 242

LIVING HISTORY

REFORMING THROUGH VISUALS

The reformers in this chapter fight against injustices in society by speaking, writing, and taking action. Use the following steps to help you explore an injustice today.

- Document what you feel is an injustice in your community or in society through pictures—either photographs, cutouts from magazines, or printouts from the Internet.
- Compile a pictorial essay that shows different aspects of the injustice you are publicizing.

📁 PORTFOLIO PROJECT Save your pictorial essay in a folder for your American history portfolio. You will revise and share your work at the end of the chapter.

REFORMING THROUGH VISUALS

Help students identify a topic for this activity by giving them the following steps:

- Brainstorm with friends about injustices you notice in your community.
- Look through newspapers and magazines to find stories about problems in your community and state.
- Look for a manageable topic about which visuals are available.

Sources for Visuals
Suggest the following sources for gathering the visuals:

- Local newspapers and community fliers
- Newsmagazines such as *Time* and *Newsweek*
- General magazines such as *National Geographic*
- Libraries for books of pictorial essays
- The Internet for images from newspapers and art museums
- Your own photographs

IN-DEPTH RESOURCES: UNIT 2
See worksheet and standards for evaluation, pp. 83, 84.

Timeline

- First strike occurs in Lowell textile mills.
- National Trades' Union is formed.
- Grimké sisters lecture on the evils of slavery.
- Frederick Douglass flees to Massachusetts.
- Henry David Thoreau lives at Walden Pond.
- Utopian community is established at Brook Farm.
- Dorothea Dix campaigns for public hospitals for the mentally ill.
- Seneca Falls women's rights convention is held.

1834   1837   1838   **1840**   1841   1845   1848   **1850**
1833   1839   1845   1848

- Britain abolishes slavery in the empire.
- French and British develop first photographs.
- World's Anti-Slavery Convention is held in Europe.
- Irish potato famine kills over a million people.
- *Communist Manifesto* is published.

Reforming American Society **223**

RECOMMENDED RESOURCES

Books for the Teacher

Brooks, Van Wyck. *The Flowering of New England.* Boston: Houghton, 1981. Originally published in 1936, this book describes the intellectual currents in New England.

Buckmaster, Henrietta. *Let My People Go.* Columbia: U of South Carolina, 1992. Story of the Underground Railroad.

Walters, Ronald G. *American Reformers 1815–1860.* New York:

Hill, 1978. Covers all major reform movements.

Books for the Student

Douglass, Frederick. *A Narrative of the Life of Frederick Douglass.* New York: Macmillan, 1962. From his childhood to his escape.

Griffith, Elisabeth. *In Her Own Right.* New York: Oxford UP, 1992. Life of Elizabeth Cady Stanton.

Videos

The Abolitionists. 1987. Agency for Instructional Technology, 800-457-4509. Brief account of work of Garrison, Douglass.

Frederick Douglass. Dir. William Greaves. Mike Craven Productions, 1996. Life of abolitionist.

A History of Slavery in America. Schlessinger Video Productions, 1994, 800-843-3620.

The Life of Sojourner Truth: "Ain't I a Woman?" Videodisc. Available from Educational Software Institute, 800-955-5570.

Software

Her Heritage. CD-ROM. Pilgrim New Media, 1994. Educational Software Institute, 800-955-5570.

Social Reform Movements. CD-ROM. Educational Software Institute, 800-955-5570.

1 Religion Sparks Reform

TERMS & NAMES
• Charles G. Finney
• Second Great Awakening
• revival
• Ralph Waldo Emerson
• transcendentalism
• Henry David Thoreau
• Dorothea Dix
• utopian community

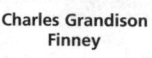

LEARN ABOUT the Second Great Awakening and other spiritual reform movements
TO UNDERSTAND how religion shaped the social and political reform movements of the period.

ONE AMERICAN'S STORY

When **Charles Grandison Finney** preached, his listeners shrieked, moaned, and fainted. The most famous preacher of the era, Finney inspired emotional religious conversions, or renewals of religious faith, using a speaking style that was as much high drama as religious urging. Converted at the age of 29, Finney traveled by horseback to deliver his message to frenzied audiences eager to be converted. During his preaching, Finney seated the most likely converts on a special "anxious bench," where he could fasten his eyes upon them. Finney knew the depth of the conversion experience.

A PERSONAL VOICE

I know this is all algebra to those who have never felt it . . . But to those who have experienced the agony of wrestling, prevailing prayer, for the conversion of a soul, you may depend on it, that soul . . . appears as dear as a child is to the mother who brought it forth with pain.

CHARLES G. FINNEY, *Lectures on Revivals*

Charles Grandison Finney

The convert's duty was to spread the word about personal salvation to others. This religious activism was part of an overall reform movement that started in the 1830s. These reforms included women's rights, school reform, and abolition, the movement to outlaw slavery. All of these movements emerged as responses to rapid changes in American society such as early industrial growth, westward migration, and increasing immigration. Another source of these reform movements was the broad religious movement that swept the United States after 1800 known as the **Second Great Awakening.**

The Second Great Awakening

Finney and his contemporaries were participants in the Second Great Awakening. These preachers rejected the 18th-century Calvinistic belief that God determined one's salvation or damnation—whether a person went to heaven or hell. Instead, they emphasized individual responsibility for seeking salvation and insisted that people could improve themselves and society.

Religious ideas current in the early 19th century promoted the power of the individual and emphasized individualism and responsibility, similar to the emphasis of Jacksonian democracy on the power of the common citizen. Christian churches split over these ideas, as various denominations competed to proclaim the message of a democratic God, one who extends the possibility of salvation to all people. The forum for their message was the revival meeting, where some preachers could draw audiences of 25,000 or more at outdoor camp meetings.

REVIVALISM These emotional meetings were called **revivals,** religious gatherings designed to awaken religious faith through impassioned preaching. A revival meeting might begin on a Thursday and continue until the following

Tuesday. During the day the participants studied the Bible and examined their souls. In the evening they heard emotional preaching that could make them cry out, burst into tears, or tremble with fear.

Revivalism swept across the United States in the early 19th century. On the frontier, people sat on planks laid across tree stumps and listened by the light of bonfires. Peter Cartwright, a traveling Methodist preacher, recalled one such meeting: "The power of God fell on the assembly, and there was an awful shaking among the dry bones. Several fell to the floor and cried for mercy."

Some of the most intense revivals took place in a part of western New York known as the burned-over district because of the religious fires that frequently burned there. Charles Finney fanned these flames, conducting his most successful revivals in Rochester, New York, in 1830–1831. The Rochester revivals earned Finney the reputation of "the father of modern revivalism."

Revivalism had a strong impact on the American public. According to one estimate, in 1800 just one in 15 Americans belonged to a church, but by 1850 one in 6 was a member. Yet, revivalism was not to everyone's liking.

THE UNITARIAN MOVEMENT Criticizing the revivals for their public emotionalism, another growing religious group, the Unitarian movement, nevertheless shared with revivalism a faith in the individual. Instead of appealing to the emotions, Unitarians emphasized reason and appeals to conscience as the paths to perfection.

In New England, the Unitarians quickly attracted a wealthy and educated following. In place of the dramatic conversions produced by the revivals, the Unitarians believed conversion was a gradual process rather than the result of a single, brilliant moment in a revival. William Ellery Channing, a prominent Unitarian leader, asserted that the purpose of Christianity was "the perfection of human nature, the elevation of men into nobler beings." Unitarians, like revivalists, held the conviction that individual and social reform were both possible and important.

THE AFRICAN–AMERICAN CHURCH The urge to reform was growing among African Americans, too. As revivals spread through the South, many slaveholders feared that enslaved African Americans might use the message of individual salvation to attack slavery. Slaves in the rural South—though they were segregated in pews of their own—worshiped in the same churches, heard the same sermons, and sang the same hymns as did the slave owners. Enslaved African Americans, however, interpreted the Christian message as a promise of freedom for their people.

In the East, many free African Americans worshiped in separate black churches, like Richard Allen's Bethel African Church in Philadelphia. While enslaved, Allen had experienced a religious conversion. He went on to purchase his freedom and establish the Bethel African Church, which by 1816 would

This early-19th-century tray depicts the African-American preacher Lemuel Haynes preaching to the parishioners in his Vermont Congregational Church.

Reforming American Society **225**

become the African Methodist Episcopal Church. From his pulpit, Allen inspired his congregation to strengthen its faith as well as fight against slavery.

A PERSONAL VOICE

Our only design is to secure to ourselves, our rights and privileges to regulate our affairs temporal and spiritual, the same as if we were white people, and to guard against any oppression which might possibly arise from the improper prejudices or administration of any individual having the exercise of Discipline over us.

RICHARD ALLEN, quoted in *Segregated Sabbaths*

Membership in the African Methodist Episcopal Church grew rapidly, in part because it offered more than simply a place to worship. The church became a political, cultural, and social center for African Americans, providing schools and other services that whites denied free blacks.

Eventually the African-American church developed a political voice and organized the first black national convention, held in Philadelphia in September 1830. Richard Allen convened the meeting, in which participants agreed to explore the possible settlement of free African Americans and fugitive slaves in Canada. Allen's convention was the first of what would become an annual convention of free blacks in the North. The African-American church gave its members a deep inner faith, a strong sense of community—and the spiritual support to oppose slavery.

Transcendentalism

Many reform-minded individuals sought an alternative to traditional religion but, like the Unitarians, found revivalism too public a forum for religious expression. Some of those people were drawn to ideas articulated by New England writer and philosopher **Ralph Waldo Emerson.**

An admirer of William Ellery Channing, Emerson had fallen into a religious crisis after the death of his young wife in 1831. Grief-stricken, Emerson traveled to England, where he met William Wordsworth and Thomas Carlyle, writers who embodied romanticism, a style of art, literature, and thought that stressed that people should develop unique and emotional forms of expression. Building on these romantic ideals, Emerson eventually developed a belief in **transcendentalism,** a philosophical and literary movement that emphasized living a simple life and celebrated the truth found in nature and in personal emotion and imagination, rather than in any organized system of belief.

Exalting the dignity of the individual, the transcendentalists fought for humanitarian reforms such as the abolition of slavery and improved conditions in prisons. They also contributed to an artistic revolution, spawning a literary movement that stressed American ideals of optimism, freedom, and self-reliance.

Emerson's friend **Henry David Thoreau** put the idea of self-reliance into practice. Abandoning community life, he built himself a cabin on the shore of Walden Pond near Concord, Massachusetts, where he lived alone for two years. In *Walden* (1854), Thoreau advised readers to follow their inner voices.

"Trust thyself."

RALPH WALDO
EMERSON

A PERSONAL VOICE
I learned this, at least, by my experiment: that if one advances confidently in the direction of his dreams, and endeavors to live the life which he has imagined, he will meet with a success unexpected in common hours . . . If you have built castles in the air, your work need not be lost; that is where they should be. Now put the foundations under them.

HENRY DAVID THOREAU, *Walden*

Thoreau and Emerson clearly expressed the idea, at the root of most reforms, that human nature could be remade.

School and Prison Reform

By the mid-19th century, thousands of Americans from a variety of philosophical positions had joined together to fight one or more of the social ills that troubled the young nation. Some social reformers focused their attention on schools and other institutions.

IMPROVING EDUCATION Before the 1850s, no uniform educational policy existed in the United States. School conditions varied across regions and school attendance was not compulsory. Classrooms were not divided by grade, throwing younger and older pupils together. Few children continued in school beyond the age of 10.

In the 1830s, Americans increasingly began to demand tax-supported public schools. For example, in 1834 Pennsylvania established a tax-supported public school system. Although the system was optional, a storm of opposition erupted from well-to-do taxpayers who saw no reason to support schools that their children, enrolled in private schools, would not attend. Opposition also came from some German immigrants who feared their children would forget the German language and culture. Within three years, however, about 42 percent of children who were of elementary-school age in Pennsylvania attended public school.

Other states soon followed Pennsylvania's example. By the 1850s every state had provided for a system of public elementary schools. In states farther west and in Southern states, however, it took years before the schools were established statewide. As a result, in 1860 only 15 percent of children in those areas attended school.

One remarkable leader in the public school reform movement was Horace Mann of Massachusetts. After a childhood spent at work rather than in school, Mann declared, "If we do not prepare children to become good citizens . . . if we do not enrich their minds with knowledge, then our republic must go down to destruction, as others have gone before it." In 1837 he became the first secretary of the Massachusetts board of education. In the 11 years he served, Mann doubled the money that the state spent on schools, instituted curriculum reforms, and established teacher training programs.

REFORMING ASYLUMS AND PRISONS Like Horace Mann, **Dorothea Dix** was compelled by personal experience to join the movement for social reform. On visiting a Massachusetts house of correction, Dix was horrified to discover that jails often housed mentally ill people. Almost everywhere, Dix observed them "chained, naked, beaten with rods, and lashed into obedience." In 1842 she sent a report of her findings to the Massachusetts legislature, which passed

HISTORICAL SPOTLIGHT

McGUFFEY'S READERS
If you had attended school during the mid- to late 1800s, you probably would have used a McGuffey's reader. William H. McGuffey, a teacher and preacher from Ohio, first published his popular grade-school reading books in the 1830s. The readers, which had sold millions of copies by 1870, taught reading, writing, and arithmetic, as well as the democratic cultural values of hard work, honesty, and love of country. They contained little moral lessons to live by, such as "Idleness is the nest in which mischief lays its eggs."

Reforming American Society **227**

Americans Form Utopian Communities

▶ *Discussing Key Ideas*
• The utopian communities reflect the idealism of the reform movement.

HISTORICAL SPOTLIGHT
Hawthorne at Brook Farm
Critical Thinking: Contrasting Ask students to contrast the romantic writer's notion of nature with Hawthorne's experience at Brook Farm. *Possible Response: The Romantics found inspiration for their writing in nature, while Hawthorne's farmwork kept him from his writing.*

ASSESS & RETEACH

Section 1 Assessment
Go over the section assessment questions in class as a review.

Self-Assessment
Ask students to discuss what surprised them about the social reforms of the 1830s. What insights about social reform did they gain from this section?

Section Quiz

FORMAL ASSESSMENT
Section Quiz, p. 101

Reteach
Use question 3 on the Section 1 Assessment to help you review the main ideas of the section.

CLOSE

During the early 1800s, religious and philosophical movements that emphasized the power of the individual swept the United States. By the mid-1800s, many people involved in these movements began to fight for social reform. They would soon become active in other reform movements, especially abolition.

228 Chapter 8

---

a law aimed at improving conditions. Between 1845 and 1852, Dix persuaded nine Southern states to set up public hospitals for the mentally ill.

Criminals in prison also benefited from the efforts of reformers. French writer Alexis de Tocqueville visited the United States in 1831 to observe its penitentiary system. Observing prisoners who were physically punished or isolated for extended periods, Tocqueville concluded that "while society in the United States gives the example of the most extended liberty, the prisons of the same country offer the spectacle of the most complete despotism [rigid and severe control]." Reformers quickly took up the cause. Prison reformers—and Dorothea Dix in her efforts on behalf of the mentally ill—emphasized the idea of rehabilitation, treatment that might restore the sick or imprisoned person to a useful position in society. There was, as revivalists suggested, hope for everyone.

Americans Form Utopian Communities

Some of the optimism that found expression in religious and social reform also spurred the establishment of **utopian communities,** experimental groups who lived together and tried to create a "utopia," or perfect place. These communities varied in their philosophies and living arrangements but shared common goals such as self-sufficiency. One of the best-known utopian communities was established in New Harmony, Indiana. Another was Brook Farm, located near Boston.

In 1841 transcendentalist George Ripley established Brook Farm to "prepare a society of liberal, intelligent and cultivated persons, whose relations with each other would permit a more wholesome and simple life than can be led amidst the pressure of our competitive institutions." Brook Farm was planned for 24 people who would share the ownership and the work. At first, few people lived full-time at Brook Farm; most of the members held other jobs.

A fire destroyed the main building at Brook Farm in 1845, and the commune closed four years later. Actually, none of the utopian communities was very successful. Brook Farm and other communities failed primarily because their members could not agree on philosophies and operating methods.

The failure of the utopian communities did not lessen the zeal of the religious reformers. Many became active in other reform movements. In fact, the growing movement to abolish slavery was drawing heated debate from Northerners and Southerners alike.

HISTORICAL SPOTLIGHT

HAWTHORNE AT BROOK FARM
New England writer Nathaniel Hawthorne spent about eight months at Brook Farm in 1841. He hoped to find solitude in which to write, but instead spent close to ten hours a day working in the barns and fields. He was forced to conclude that life there was "unnatural and unsuitable" for him.

Ten years after he left Brook Farm, Hawthorne, now considered an established author, wrote *The Blithedale Romance* (1852). A fictional account of communal life based on Brook Farm, the book suggests that striving for perfection may yield unexpected results.

D. Answer The transcendentalists believed in being close to nature and in living a simple life. At Brook Farm, people could live more simply and try to be self-sufficient.

THINK THROUGH HISTORY
D. Synthesizing
Why might the idea of utopian communities appeal to the transcendentalists?

Section ❶ Assessment

1. TERMS & NAMES
Identify:
• Charles G. Finney
• Second Great Awakening
• revival
• Ralph Waldo Emerson
• transcendentalism
• Henry David Thoreau
• Dorothea Dix
• utopian community

2. SUMMARIZING In a web similar to the one below, fill in events and ideas that relate to the Second Great Awakening.

Create a poster advertising a revival in the 1830s.

3. SYNTHESIZING Consider the philosophical and religious ideas expressed during the Second Great Awakening. What were the key values and beliefs that guided 19th-century reformers' actions?

THINK ABOUT
• concepts of individualism and individual salvation
• attitudes toward social responsibility
• the viewpoints of Finney, Channing, and Emerson

4. RECOGNIZING EFFECTS How do you think the 19th-century reform movements might have influenced reform movements today?

THINK ABOUT
• 19th-century reforms in schools, prisons, and asylums
• who is responsible for reform
• the social problems that are addressed today

228 CHAPTER 8

ANSWERS

1. TERMS & NAMES
Charles G. Finney, p. 224
Second Great Awakening, p. 224
revival, p. 224
Ralph Waldo Emerson, p. 226
transcendentalism, p. 226
Henry David Thoreau, p. 227
Dorothea Dix, p. 227
utopian communities, p. 228

2. SUMMARIZING
Students' webs may include revivals, the Unitarian movement, Charles Finney, the African Methodist Episcopal Church, Ralph Waldo Emerson, school and prison reform, and transcendentalism.

3. SYNTHESIZING
Possible Responses: Most students may note that the reformers shared a strong belief in the power of the individual to improve himself or herself, and in individual responsibility for improving society as well.

4. RECOGNIZING EFFECTS
Possible Responses: Students may say that educational reform continues today. Others may be aware of current trends in prison reform or in treatment of the mentally ill. Still others may argue that the abolition movement, for example, eventually grew into a broader civil rights movement in the 20th century.

2 Slavery and Abolition

TERMS & NAMES
- abolition
- William Lloyd Garrison
- emancipation
- David Walker
- Frederick Douglass
- Nat Turner
- antebellum
- gag rule

LEARN ABOUT the abolition movement, the lives of African Americans, and debates over slavery
TO UNDERSTAND the growing rift between the North and the South.

ONE AMERICAN'S STORY

James Forten's great-grandfather had been brought from Africa to the American colonies in chains, but James was born free. In 1781, the 15-year-old James went to sea to fight for American independence. Captured by the British and offered passage to England, the patriotic youth refused, saying, "I am here a prisoner for the liberties of my country; I never, NEVER, shall prove a traitor to her interests."

By the 1830s Forten had become a wealthy sailmaker, with a fortune rumored to exceed $100,000. A leader of Philadelphia's free black community, Forten took an active role in a variety of political causes. Though some people argued that free blacks should return to Africa, Forten disagreed and responded with sarcasm.

James Forten

A PERSONAL VOICE
Here I have dwelt until I am nearly sixty years of age, and have brought up and educated a family. . . . Yet some ingenious gentlemen have recently discovered that I am still an African; that a continent three thousand miles, and more, from the place where I was born, is my native country. And I am advised to go home. . . . Perhaps if I should only be set on the shore of that distant land, I should recognize all I might see there, and run at once to the old hut where my forefathers lived a hundred years ago.

JAMES FORTEN, quoted in *Forging Freedom: The Formation of Philadelphia's Black Community 1720–1840*

Forten's unwavering belief that he was an American not only led him to oppose colonization—the effort to resettle free blacks in Africa—but also pushed him fervently to oppose slavery.

Abolitionists Speak Out

By the 1820s more than 100 antislavery societies were advocating that black Americans be resettled in Africa. In 1817, the American Colonization Society had been founded to encourage black emigration. These early antislavery societies generally were based on the belief that African Americans were an inferior race that could not coexist with white society. Most free blacks, on the contrary, considered America their home, and only about 1,400 blacks emigrated to Africa between 1820 and 1830. As one black pastor from New York angrily proclaimed in the 1820s, "We are *natives* of this country. We only ask that we be treated as well as *foreigners.*"

African Americans increasingly were joined by whites in openly criticizing slavery. Much of the white support for **abolition,** the movement to outlaw slavery, came from preachers like Charles G. Finney, who termed slavery "a great national sin." The most radical white abolitionist was a young editor named William Lloyd Garrison.

WILLIAM LLOYD GARRISON Active in religious reform movements in Massachusetts, **William Lloyd Garrison** began a publishing career in 1828 as editor of an antislavery paper. Three years later he established his own paper, *The Liberator,* to deliver an uncompromising message: immediate **emancipation,**

Reforming American Society **229**

Section 2 Overview

OBJECTIVES

1. To identify some of the key black and white abolitionists.
2. To describe the experience of slaves in rural and urban areas.
3. To summarize the proslavery debate in the South.

SKILLBUILDER
- Interpreting charts, p. 231

CRITICAL THINKING
- Synthesizing, p. 230
- Contrasting, p. 231
- Summarizing, pp. 233, 234
- Recognizing effects, p. 233
- Forming opinions, p. 234
- Comparing and contrasting, p. 234

FOCUS & MOTIVATE

▶ *Starting with the Student*
Ask students to think about a time when they stood up for something they believed.

- Was the position unpopular? How were they treated by those who opposed them? Did they persuade anyone to agree with them?
- How do they think the abolitionists were treated by those who supported slavery?

OBJECTIVE
1 **INSTRUCT**

Abolitionists Speak Out

▶ *Discussing Key Ideas*
- White abolitionist William Lloyd Garrison alienates many whites with his radical views.
- Most free blacks are denied the opportunity to rise above the limitations imposed by white society.

(continued on next page)

SECTION 2 RESOURCES

PRINT RESOURCES

IN-DEPTH RESOURCES: UNIT 2
Guided Reading, p. 68
Primary Sources: Propaganda Images, p. 75; *from* Appeal to the Christian Women of the South, p. 76
Literature: from *The Confessions of Nat Turner* by William Styron, p.78
American Lives: Frederick Douglass, p. 81

ACCESS FOR STUDENTS ACQUIRING ENGLISH
Guided Reading (Spanish), p. 84

FORMAL ASSESSMENT
Section Quiz, p. 102

ALTERNATIVE ASSESSMENT BOOK
See forms for supporting and scoring alternative activities.

TECHNOLOGY RESOURCES

GEOGRAPHY TRANSPARENCIES
G8, Distribution of Slaves, 1790 and 1860

CD-ROM Electronic Library of Primary Sources

VIDEO *American Portfolio: A Videodisc for U.S. History* user's guide, pp. 72–73, 75–78

INTERNET McDougal Littell Learning On-Line
http://www.mcdougallittell.com

(continued from page 229)

- Escaped slave Frederick Douglass becomes an eloquent voice in the antislavery movement.

IN-DEPTH RESOURCES: UNIT 2
Guided Reading, p. 68

ACCESS FOR STUDENTS ACQUIRING ENGLISH
Guided Reading (Spanish), p. 84

MORE ABOUT . . .
Frederick Douglass

When Douglass arrived in New England, he discovered that prejudice prevented him from finding suitable work. He was forced to do odd jobs for three years. "There was no work too hard—none too dirty," he stated. Douglass found a new profession in 1841 when he became a lecturer in the antislavery movement. He lent his voice to the cause of racial equality for the next 50 years. He also became an active participant in the struggle. In the early 1840s, for example, Douglass protested segregated seating on trains by sitting in cars reserved for whites. Once, when he refused to leave the car, a group of white men tried to force him out of his seat. When Douglass resisted, the men pulled the railroad seat out of the floor of the car— with Douglass hanging on to the seat.

IN-DEPTH RESOURCES, UNIT 2
American Lives: Frederick Douglass, p. 81

 ELECTRONIC LIBRARY OF PRIMARY SOURCES
from *The Anti-Slavery Movement* by Fredrick Douglass
from *Declaration of Sentiments* by the American Anti-Slavery Society
The Question of Negro Slavery by William J. Grayson

"I consider it settled that the black and white people of America ought to share common destiny."

FREDERICK DOUGLASS, 1851

230 CHAPTER 8

the freeing of slaves, with no payment to slaveholders. With his steel-rimmed glasses, the prematurely bald Garrison appeared to be an unlikely rebel, but his words thundered boldly.

> **A PERSONAL VOICE**
> I am aware that many object to the severity of my language, but is there not cause for severity? I *will be* as harsh as truth, and as uncompromising as justice. On this subject [immediate emancipation], I do not wish to think or speak or write with moderation. . . . I am in earnest—I will not equivocate—I will not excuse—I will not retreat a single inch—AND I WILL BE HEARD.
> **WILLIAM LLOYD GARRISON,** *The Liberator*

Before Garrison's call for the immediate emancipation of slaves, support for that position had been limited. Beginning in the 1830s, however, white abolitionists began to respond to Garrison's words. Garrison founded the New England Anti-Slavery Society in 1832 and then helped found the national American Anti-Slavery Society the following year. He enjoyed widespread black support; three out of four early subscribers to *The Liberator* were African Americans. Whites who opposed abolition, however, hated Garrison. In 1835 a Boston mob dragged him through town at the end of a rope.

Even whites who supported the cause of abolition opposed Garrison when he attacked churches and the government for failing to condemn slavery. Garrison alienated whites even more when he associated with David Walker, whom some whites viewed as a radical—or extreme in his views.

FREE BLACKS   **David Walker,** a free black North Carolinian who had moved to Boston, urged blacks to rise up and take their freedom by force. In his *Appeal to the Colored Citizens of the World,* published in 1829, Walker advised African Americans to fight for freedom rather than to wait for slave owners to end slavery. He wrote, "The man who would not fight . . . ought to be kept with all his children or family, in slavery or in chains to be butchered by his cruel enemies."

The majority of free blacks expressed less extreme views than Walker but still formed scores of antislavery societies by the end of the 1820s. In 1850, most of the nation's 434,000 free blacks worked as day laborers for white employers in the South, but some held jobs as artisans, craftsmen, or seamstresses. In the North, free blacks faced a segregated society and job discrimination that opened only the lowest-paying jobs to them. Recalling his youth in Providence, Rhode Island, in the 1830s, William J. Brown wrote, "To drive carriages, carry a market basket after the boss, and brush his boots, or saw wood and run errands was as high as a colored man could rise." Frederick Douglass, however, rose above the limitations that white society had imposed.

FREDERICK DOUGLASS   Born into slavery in 1817, **Frederick Douglass** had been taught to read and write by the wife of one of his owners. Her husband ordered her to stop teaching Douglass, however, because reading "would forever unfit him to be a slave." When Douglass realized that knowledge could be his "pathway from slavery to freedom," he studied harder.

By 1838, Douglass held a skilled job as a ship caulker in Baltimore. He plied his trade

THINK THROUGH HISTORY
A. Synthesizing
What was radical at the time about Garrison's and Walker's ideas on abolition?

A. Answer
Garrison criticized churches and the government; Walker advocated armed black revolt.

TEACHING OPTIONS

Exploring Themes

Expanding Democracy   Discuss the different ways both white and black abolitionists fought against slavery. Note that some abolitionists favored force, while others used nonviolent methods.

Ask students which method was probably more effective. *Possible Responses: Violent methods might have been more effective in bringing antislavery to the public's attention; nonviolent methods might have been more likely to win people's sympathy and support.*

Teaching Gifted and Talented Students

Writing an Article for The Liberator   Ask students to use the library or other resources to find excerpts from *The Liberator.* Then have them write an article for the paper. The article should:

- address an injustice going on in the world today
- call for some action to be taken
- maintain the tone and style of Garrison's antislavery paper

Encourage students to compile their articles in an "anti-injustice" paper that the rest of the class can read.

well and earned the highest wages in the yard, but Douglass's slave owner took his pay each week. After a disagreement with his owner, Douglass decided to escape. Borrowing the identity of a free black sailor and carrying official papers, Douglass stepped onto a train. When he reached New York, he tasted freedom for the first time.

Douglass became an eager reader of *The Liberator*, which, he said, "sent a thrill of joy through my soul, such as I had never felt before." When Garrison heard him speak of his experiences, he was so impressed he sponsored Douglass as a lecturer for the American Anti-Slavery Society.

A superb speaker, Douglass thrilled huge audiences. "I appear before the immense assembly this evening as a thief and a robber," he would say. "I stole this head, these limbs, this body from my master, and ran off with them." Hoping that abolition could be achieved without violence, Douglass broke with Garrison in 1847 and began his own antislavery newspaper. He named it *The North Star*, after the star that guided runaway slaves to freedom. For every escapee like Douglass, however, thousands more continued to be enslaved.

Life Under Slavery

As Americans debated the issue of slavery with increased vigor after 1830, slaves continued to live under the system. In fact, the population of slaves in America had nearly doubled in the years between 1810 and 1830, growing from 1.1 million to roughly 2 million.

The institution of slavery had changed substantially since the 18th century. In those days, most slaves were male, had recently arrived from the Caribbean or Africa, and spoke one of several non-English languages. Most of these slaves worked on small farms alongside people with whom they could not easily communicate. By 1830, however, the numbers of male and female slaves had become more equal. The majority had been born in America and spoke enough English to be able to communicate with other slaves. The rise of the plantation in the late 18th century brought further change to slaves' lives.

RURAL SLAVERY Most slaves lived and worked on large plantations in groups of ten or more. Men, women, and even children toiled from dawn to dusk in the fields. The whip of the overseer or slave driver frequently reminded them to hurry.

Southern Slave Plantations

Southern plantations varied widely in terms of wealth and prosperity, as these photographs show.

AFRICAN AMERICANS IN THE SOUTH

Slaves in groups of 10–99 (61%)
Free African Americans (6%)
Slaves in groups of 100 or more (8%)
Slaves in groups of 1–9 (25%)

Sources: 1860 figures from *Eighth Census of the United States*; Lewis C. Gray, *History of Agriculture in the Southern United States*

SKILLBUILDER
INTERPRETING CHARTS Based on the pie chart, what was the smallest group of African Americans living in the South in 1860? Who do you think owned smaller groups of slaves (groups of one to nine)?

Reforming American Society **231**

Reading the Photograph
Ask students how they can
tell that the photograph was
probably taken on a
Southern plantation. *Their
clothing, the presence of a
slave as a nurse, the
expense of photographs at
the time.*

Extension Have students
use a web like the one
below to compare the lives
of rural and urban slaves.
Students should identify the
features that characterized
both types of slavery.

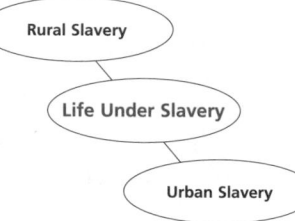

MORE ABOUT . . .
Rural Slavery

Often slaves on farms with
fewer than 15 slaves
received the most humane
treatment because they
worked alongside their
slaveowners. Former slave
Annette Milledge said, "My
marster was jus' like a father
to me. . . . I might say I was
free myself in slavery times,
my people treat me so
good." On the other hand,
Easter Jones, who was also
owned by a small slave-
owning family, had different
recollections. According to
an interviewer who spoke to
the woman years after her
slavery, Jones said, "[T]here
was nothing but hard work
and cruel treatment."

Solomon Northup, who was born free and later enslaved, recalled the never
ending labor.

A PERSONAL VOICE
The hands are required to be in the cotton field as soon as it is light in the
morning, and, with the exception of ten or fifteen minutes, which is given
them at noon to swallow their allowance of cold bacon, they are not permitted
to be a moment idle until it is too dark to see, and when the moon is full, they
often times labor till the middle of the night. They do not dare to stop even at
dinner time, nor return to the quarters, however late it be, until the order to
halt is given by the driver.

SOLOMON NORTHUP, *Twelve Years a Slave*

Planters' children—
like Charlotte Helen
Middleton, shown with
her nurse Lydia in 1857—
often were tended by
slaves who had been
forced to give up
their own
children.

In the few hours spent not working, slaves shared small, cramped slave
quarters, furnished only with rough wooden chairs and tables. Glassless windows exposed them to the elements year round, while chimneys made of sticks
and dry mud made cooking fires a constant fire hazard. By contrast, the slave owner's family enjoyed the "big house," which
might have been a large mansion with the finest furnishings or a less impressive home that still was grand compared to the slave quarters.

Some slaves living on plantations became
house slaves and worked as servants in the big
house. These servants, who worked as cooks,
butlers, or maids, were under the constant
scrutiny of the slave owners. One woman
recalled preferring field work to house work
because "we could talk and do anything we
wanted to, just so we picked the cotton."

Though by 1850 most slaves lived on
plantations or large farms that employed ten
or more slaves, many lived on small farms,
laboring beside their owners. Others lived and
worked in the cities.

URBAN SLAVERY By the 1830s the promise
of cotton wealth had lured many Southern
whites into farming, thus creating a shortage of
white laborers for such industries as mining and
lumber. As a result, there was a constant demand
for slaves as workers in mills and on ships. Slaves who
had had an opportunity to develop specialized skills on
plantations were equally in demand in Southern cities. For
example, African Americans filled most skilled occupations such
as blacksmithing or carpentry, resulting in a large class of skilled black laborers in Charleston and Savannah. In fact, enslaved African Americans in the
South could often hire themselves out as skilled artisans more easily than
free blacks in the North, where racial discrimination forced them into the
least-skilled jobs.

Many slave women and children worked the same jobs as men in
Southern textile mills, factories, mines, and lumberyards. Slave owners "hired
out" their slaves to factory owners. In return, the slave owners collected the
pay of their slaves without having to supervise their activities. Thus, urban
slaves spent more time beyond the watchful eye of their slave owners.
Frederick Douglass remarked on differences between rural and urban slavery, noting that "a city slave is almost a freeman, compared with a slave on the
plantation. He is much better fed and clothed, and enjoys privileges
altogether unknown to the slave on the plantation." Douglass also noted that

232 CHAPTER 8

Cooperative Activity: Daily Lives in Contrast

Task: Groups of students will research the daily lives of plantation owners and slaves in the 1830s and present a "A Day in
the Life of . . ." report.

Purpose: To help students understand the underlying attitudes and needs of these two important groups.

Activity: Assign some groups to focus on plantation owners
and some groups to focus on slaves. Using library resources
and the Internet, students will search for information and visuals to make their presentations effective. Some groups may
wish to create posters that divide a day into various segments; others may use photographs of restored plantations
and of artifacts from the period to enhance their "A Day in the
Life of . . ." presentations.

ALTERNATIVE ASSESSMENT BOOK
Standards for Evaluating a Cooperative Activity

THINK THROUGH HISTORY
C. Summarizing
Briefly describe the
work experiences
of Southern slaves.

C. Answer Most
worked on
plantations, either
in the fields or
indoors as
domestic
servants. Others
worked on farms
or as artisans or
unskilled laborers
in cities.

"a vestige of decency" in the cities limited the acts of "atrocious cruelty" to slaves that were common on plantations.

Still, whether in cities or on farms, slaves never lost sight of their goal of freedom. For some, it was time to take action.

NAT TURNER'S REBELLION In August 1831, **Nat Turner,** a plantation slave in Virginia's Southampton County, organized a bloody rebellion that left many dead and strengthened the resolve of Southern whites to defend slavery and control their slaves.

Six years earlier, Turner had fled his owner's plantation after a severe beating. Instead of fleeing northward as his father had done, however, the devout Turner returned to preach to other African Americans. While in the Virginia woods, he experienced a vision that he interpreted as a call to "lead and organize his fellow slaves in a struggle for freedom."

Six months after a partial eclipse of the sun convinced him that the time was ripe, Turner's anger over slavery finally boiled over. Gathering more than 50 followers as he moved from plantation to plantation, Turner's band attacked four plantations and slaughtered about 70 white inhabitants. By the fifth attack, an alarm alerted whites, who captured and executed 16 members of Turner's band. Though Turner himself hid out for several weeks, eventually he was captured, tried, and hanged. In the retaliation that followed, whites killed more than 200 blacks, most of whom had never heard of Nat Turner.

HISTORICAL SPOTLIGHT

SLAVE REVOLTS

Nothing disproved the slave owners' myth that slaves were happy more than the periodic slave revolts that erupted. At the time, Nat Turner's 1831 rebellion was merely the most recent example of slave desperation.

In 1811, more than 300 slaves rebelled in Louisiana and marched on New Orleans with spikes and axes before a well-trained militia with firearms stopped them. Gabriel Prosser hatched a plot to take over Richmond in 1800, and Denmark Vesey led a conspiracy to control Charleston in 1822. Both of these conspiracies were thwarted by the authorities before larger rebellions occurred.

Slave Owners Oppose Abolition

The Turner rebellion frightened and outraged slaveholders. In some states, people argued that the only way to prevent slave revolts was through emancipation. Others, however, chose to tighten restrictions on all African Americans to prevent them from plotting insurrections.

VIRGINIA DEBATE Virginia governor John Floyd confided in his diary his wish for a "law . . . gradually abolishing slavery in this State." By January 1832 the state legislature was hotly debating that very prospect, and the capital's newspaper published the discussions. "Nothing else could have prompted [the discussions]," reported the Richmond *Enquirer,* "but the bloody massacre in the month of August."

The debate over the future of slavery in Virginia had been initiated by non-slaveholding whites who lived in western Virginia. Thomas Jefferson's grandson, along with other whites who advocated gradual abolition, argued that slavery injured the state and endangered whites. Their motion for abolition lost by a 73 to 58 vote, primarily because the state legislature was balanced toward eastern slaveholders rather than non-slaveholders in the western part of the state. That loss finally closed the debate on slavery in the **antebellum**—pre-Civil War—South.

THINK THROUGH HISTORY
D. Recognizing
Effects How did
Turner's revolt
harden Southern
white attitudes
about privileges for
blacks?

D. Answer The
rebellion was
bloody and
frightened slave
owners. Many
Southern whites
believed that the
only way to
prevent such
revolts was to
eliminate what
fews privileges
slaves enjoyed.

REGULATING AFRICAN AMERICANS In addition to forcing the Virginia debate, whites' fear of future slave revolts had another important effect. Some, if not most, slave owners believed that education and privilege inspired revolt. Thus, many slave owners pushed their state legislatures to further tighten controls on African Americans. These controls became known as slave codes.

In 1833, for example, Alabama forbade free and enslaved blacks from preaching the gospel unless "respectable" slaveholders were present. The next year Georgia followed suit. In 1835 North Carolina became the last Southern state to deny the vote to free blacks. In some states, free blacks lost the right to own guns, purchase alcohol, assemble in public, and testify in court. Slaves

HISTORICAL SPOTLIGHT
Slave Revolts

Critical Thinking: Drawing Conclusions Ask students to speculate about what probably happened to the slaves involved in the revolts once they were caught. *Possible Response: They were probably killed.* Why were these slaves willing to sacrifice their lives? *Possible Responses: They felt that life wasn't worth living as a slave; they hoped to secure freedom for future generations of African Americans.*

OBJECTIVE
③ **INSTRUCT**

Slave Owners Oppose Abolition

▶ *Discussing Key Ideas*
• In Virginia, a proposal to abolish slavery is defeated, thus ending the debate on the issue in the pre-Civil War South.
• Fearing more slave revolts, many Southern states impose harsh regulations on both free and enslaved blacks.
• Southern slave owners defend the practice of slavery, while Southern congressmen use the gag rule to prevent debate on the issue.

IN-DEPTH RESOURCES, UNIT 2
Primary Sources: Propaganda Images, p. 75; *from* Appeal to the Christian Women of the South, p. 76

Making Connections Across the Curriculum

Literature Give students the excerpt from William Styron's Pulitzer Prize-winning novel *The Confessions of Nat Turner.*

Although it is based on the transcript of testimony given by Nat Turner, Styron calls his novel a "meditation on history" rather than a factual account of the rebellion. He says that "in writing *The Confessions of Nat Turner* I at no time pretended that my narrative was an exact transcription of historical events; had perfect accuracy been my aim I would have written a work of history rather than a novel."

In the novel, Nat Turner tells about the first assault on a sleeping white family: "I heaved myself silently over the sill into the

dark hallway, into the very bosom of the cavernous snoring noise that muffled the sound of my feet as they struck the creaking floor. I was all aslime with sweat beneath my shirt, my mouth had the dry bitter taste of a walnut shell. It's not I who's doing this, I thought abruptly, it is someone else." After students read the excerpt, ask them if they think making Turner's story into a novel is justified. What could be the benefits of writing about these events as a story?

IN-DEPTH RESOURCES: UNIT 2
Literature Selection: from *The Confessions of Nat Turner* by William Styron, p. 78

Jamaica was the site of
many violent slave rebellions
and free black insurrections.
Research the history of these
and write a two-page sum-
mary of your findings.

ASSESS & RETEACH

Section 2 Assessment

Have students work individually to answer the ques-
tions, then have them check
their answers with a partner.

Self-Assessment

Ask students to review what
they wrote for item 3 on the
section assessment and discuss their response with a
partner. How did the discussion affect their opinions?

Section Quiz

FORMAL ASSESSMENT
Section Quiz, p. 102

Reteach

Reread the section on "Life
Under Slavery" and discuss
how the information chal-
lenged students' percep-
tions of slavery in the
United States in the early to
mid-19th century.

CLOSE

By the 1830s, both whites
and blacks had formed antislavery societies. Some of
these abolitionists advo-
cated violence, while others
wanted to use peaceful
means, to end slavery. In
spite of the abolitionists'
efforts, however, the number of slaves continued to
rise in the South. The issue
caused heated debates
between the North and the
South. It was clear that the
issue was creating deep
divisions in the nation.

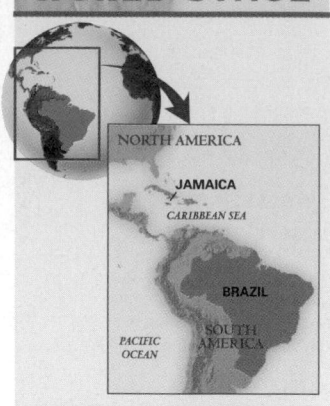

ON THE WORLD STAGE

SLAVERY IN THE AMERICAS

Slaves formed a smaller percentage
of the total population in the
American South than in the
Caribbean and in Brazil. African
slaves formed almost 80 percent of
the population of Jamaica, a colony
of Great Britain. Because so many
slaves in that country died,
plantation owners demanded a
constant renewal of their supply of
slaves from Africa, thus maintaining
the Atlantic slave trade. A growing
British antislavery movement
resulted in the end of slavery in the
British empire in 1834.

Brazil also had a large
proportion of slaves. During the
1800s slaves made up more than
half the colonial population of Brazil
and worked primarily on large
coffee plantations. Slavery was
finally abolished in Brazil in 1888.

---

could no longer own private property, learn to read and write, or work
independently as carpenters or blacksmiths in some Southern cities.

To further control the actions of slaves, some whites formed vigilance
committees, bands of armed men who rode through the countryside intimidating slaves and discouraging them from attempts at escape or rebellion.
Frederick Douglass had said that "no man can put a chain about the ankle of
his fellow man without at last finding the other end fastened about his own
neck." Though some white Southerners were feeling the weight of that chain,
others denied it existed.

PROSLAVERY ARGUMENTS   Some proslavery advocates used the Bible
to defend slavery, citing passages that counseled servants to obey their
masters. Slavery, Southern slave owners argued, actually benefited blacks
by fostering Christian civilization among enslaved peoples. Southern white
Christian churches gradually shifted their positions on slavery during this
period. While some ministers had attacked slavery in the early 1800s, by
the 1830s most agreed that slavery and Christianity could coexist.

Slave owners also invented the myth of the happy slave, a beloved
member of the plantation family. To this image they contrasted that of the
Northern wage slave, a wage-earning immigrant or free black, who worked
for pennies in dark and airless factories. George Fitzhugh, a Virginia slave
owner, argued that whereas Northern mill owners fired their workers
when they became too old or sick to work, Southerners cared for their
slaves for a lifetime.

Despite these rationalizations in favor of slavery, abolitionists continued
their campaign for emancipation. One maneuver was to swamp Congress
with petitions to end slavery in the District of Columbia. Southern congressmen countered in 1836 by securing the adoption of a **gag rule,** a rule limiting or preventing debate on an issue. The gag rule prevented discussion in
Congress of abolitionist petitions, which meant that citizens submitting petitions had been deprived of their right to have them heard. Former president
John Quincy Adams, a representative from Massachusetts, fought against the
gag rule, even as the focus of the argument at times shifted from abolishing
slavery to the constitutional right to petition Congress. The gag rule eventually was repealed in 1845.

Nevertheless, opposition to the existence of slavery steadfastly refused
to disappear. As abolitionists' efforts intensified during the 1850s, some
turned to violence. The more clear-sighted began to sound the alarm: this
turmoil over slavery would lead to a divided nation.

THINK THROUGH HISTORY
E. *Summarizing*
*What arguments
did Southern
proslavery whites
employ to defend
slavery?*

E. Answer That
slavery was
condoned in the
Bible, that it
civilized both
whites and
blacks, that
slaves were
happy, and that
Northern "wage
slaves" were
worse off than
Southern slaves.

Section 2 Assessment

1. TERMS & NAMES
Identify:
• abolition
• William Lloyd
Garrison
• emancipation
• David Walker
• Frederick
Douglass
• Nat Turner
• antebellum
• gag rule

2. SUMMARIZING In a two-
column chart, list the major
antislavery and proslavery actions
that occurred from 1820 to 1850.

Antislavery Actions	Proslavery Actions

3. FORMING OPINIONS Which
do you think was a more effective
strategy—violence or non-
violence—for achieving the abolitionists' goal of eliminating
slavery? Why?

THINK ABOUT
• Garrison's and Walker's remarks
• Frederick Douglass's views
• abolitionists' petitions to
Congress
• Southerners' reactions to Nat
Turner's rebellion

**4. COMPARING AND
CONTRASTING** Analyze the
similarities and differences
between the situations of free
blacks in the North and slaves in
the South. Use details from this
section to support your analysis.

THINK ABOUT
• the experiences of African-
American workers in the North
• the conditions of rural and urban
slaves
• slave owners' perceptions of the
Northern "wage slave"

234 CHAPTER 8

ANSWERS

1. TERMS & NAMES

abolition, p. 229

William Lloyd Garrison, p. 229

emancipation, p. 229

David Walker, p. 230

Frederick Douglass, p. 230

Nat Turner, p. 233

antebellum, p. 233

gag rule, p. 234

2. SUMMARIZING

Students' lists for antislavery
actions might include publication of *The Liberator* and *Appeal
to the Colored Citizens of the
World,* formation of antislavery
societies, and Nat Turner's
rebellion. Students' lists for
proslavery actions might include
the defeat of the Virginia motion
for abolition, tighter slave regulations, the growth of vigilance
committees, and the 1836 gag
rule.

3. FORMING OPINIONS

Possible Responses: Some students may indicate that violence
was a more effective strategy
because it forced the nation to
pay more attention to the issue
of slavery. Others, however, may
point out that antislavery violence tended to elicit equally
strong reactions from slaveholders, who responded with violence of their own.

4. COMPARING AND CONTRASTING

Possible Response: Blacks in
the North were forced into the
lowest paid, least desirable jobs.
Slaves in the South might labor
in cotton fields or work in the
homes of their owners. Some
Southern slaves had skilled jobs
in factories, but their wages
went to their owners.

③ Women and Reform

TERMS & NAMES
- Elizabeth Cady Stanton
- Lucretia Mott
- cult of domesticity
- Sarah and Angelina Grimké
- temperance movement
- Seneca Falls convention
- Sojourner Truth

LEARN ABOUT traditional women's roles and reform activities
TO UNDERSTAND the early development of the women's rights movement.

ONE AMERICAN'S STORY

Elizabeth Cady Stanton timed her marriage in 1840 so that she and her new husband could travel together to London. She later explained, "Mr. Stanton was going to Europe as a delegate to the World's Anti-Slavery Convention, and we did not wish the ocean to roll between us." Like her husband, she ardently supported abolition.

Stanton also believed that women deserved the same rights as men. In fact, she had even persuaded the minister to omit the word "obey" from her vow in the marriage ceremony because she felt no need to "obey one with whom I supposed I was entering into an equal relation." At the antislavery convention, Stanton and the other women delegates received an unpleasant surprise.

A PERSONAL VOICE

Delegates from all the antislavery societies of civilized nations were invited, yet, when they arrived, those representing associations of women were rejected. Though women were members of the American National Anti-Slavery Society, accustomed to speak and vote in all its conventions, and to take equally active part with men in the whole antislavery struggle, and were there as delegates from associations of men and women, as well as those distinctively of their own sex, yet all alike were rejected because they were women.

ELIZABETH CADY STANTON, quoted in *Elizabeth Cady Stanton*

For the rest of the convention, Stanton had to sit and listen from a curtained gallery. She soon found a friend in the 47-year-old Quaker abolitionist **Lucretia Mott**. Stanton and Mott vowed "to hold a convention as soon as we returned home, and form a society to advocate the rights of women." It would take the friends eight years to fulfill their resolution.

Elizabeth Cady Stanton

Women's Roles in the Mid-1800s

In the early 19th century, women like Stanton and Mott faced limited options. Prevailing customs, later called the **cult of domesticity,** demanded that women restrict their activities after marriage to the home and family. Housework and child care were considered the only proper activities for married women, and they were denied full participation in the larger community.

By 1850, however, roughly one in five white women had worked for wages for a few years before they were married. If a woman remained single, she might find work as a servant, seamstress, or teacher. About one in ten single white women worked outside the home, earning about half the pay men received to do the same job.

Women could neither vote nor sit on juries in the early 1800s even if they were taxpayers. Typically, when a woman married, her property and any money she earned became her husband's. In many instances, married women lacked guardianship rights over their children.

THINK THROUGH HISTORY
A. Identifying Problems What were the main problems faced by women in the mid-1800s?

Reforming American Society **235**

SECTION 3 RESOURCES

PRINT RESOURCES

IN-DEPTH RESOURCES: UNIT 2
Guided Reading, p. 69
Skillbuilder Practice: Identify Problems, p. 71
Primary Source: *from* The Seneca Falls Declaration of Sentiments, p. 77
American Lives: Elizabeth Cady Stanton, p. 82

ACCESS FOR STUDENTS ACQUIRING ENGLISH
Guided Reading (Spanish), p. 85
Skillbuilder Practice: Identifying Problems (Spanish), p. 87

FORMAL ASSESSMENT
Section Quiz, p. 103

ALTERNATIVE ASSESSMENT BOOK
See forms for supporting and scoring alternative activities.

TECHNOLOGY RESOURCES

CD-ROM *Grolier Multimedia Encyclopedia*
Electronic Library of Primary Sources

VIDEO *American Portfolio: A Videodisc for U.S. History*
user's guide, pp. 71–72

INTERNET McDougal Littell Learning On-Line
http://www.mcdougallittell.com

Section 3 Overview

OBJECTIVES

① To explain why women's opportunities were limited in the mid-1850s.

② To identify the reform movements women participated in.

③ To describe the progress of the expanding women's rights movement.

SKILLBUILDER

- Interpreting tables, p. 238

CRITICAL THINKING

- Identifying problems, p. 235
- Summarizing, pp. 236, 237, 239
- Contrasting, p. 239
- Analyzing issues, p. 239
- Evaluating, p. 239

FOCUS & MOTIVATE

▶ *Starting with the Student*
- Ask students if they consider themselves feminists or do they think women should play a more traditional role in society?
- What, if any, limits do they think should be imposed on women in the workplace or in some other sphere?

OBJECTIVE
① INSTRUCT

Women's Roles in the Mid-1800s

▶ *Discussing Key Ideas*
- In the early 19th century, the cult of domesticity narrowly restricts women's activities.
- Women receive unequal wages on the job and unequal treatment under the law.

IN-DEPTH RESOURCES: UNIT 2
Guided Reading, p. 69

ACCESS FOR STUDENTS ACQUIRING ENGLISH
Guided Reading (Spanish), p. 85

Women Mobilize for Reform

▶ **Discussing Key Ideas**

• Although most men oppose their efforts, many women actively take part in the abolitionist cause.

• The suffering of wives at the hands of drunken husbands prompts many women to support temperance reform.

• Women work to improve their educational opportunities and health care.

IN-DEPTH RESOURCES, UNIT 2
American Lives: Elizabeth Cady Stanton, p. 82

 ELECTRONIC LIBRARY OF PRIMARY SOURCES
Disappointment Is the Lot of Women by Lucy Stone

KEY PLAYER
Lucretia Mott

Critical Thinking: Contrasting Ask students to contrast Lucretia Mott with the early-19th-century's image of the ideal woman. How does Mott's personality conflict with that of women who embody the cult of domesticity? How do her activities contrast with those of more traditional women? *Possible Responses: Mott is strong-willed and active rather than passive. She voices her opinions and takes part in the world outside her own home.*

 GROLIER MULTIMEDIA ENCYCLOPEDIA
Lucretia Mott

Women Mobilize for Reform

Despite such limits, women actively participated in all the important reform movements of the 19th century. Like their fathers, husbands, and brothers, many middle-class white women had been inspired by the optimistic message of the Second Great Awakening to improve society. From abolition to health reform, women joined the battle. Men who disapproved of women reformers like Stanton and Lucretia Mott shut them out of meetings, and occasionally even pelted them with rotten eggs. Eventually women reformers responded by expanding their reform efforts to seek equal rights for themselves.

WOMEN ABOLITIONISTS **Sarah** and **Angelina Grimké**, the daughters of a South Carolina slaveholder, spoke eloquently for abolition. In 1836 Angelina Grimké published an *Appeal to Christian Women of the South*, in which she called upon women to "overthrow this horrible system of oppression and cruelty." Women abolitionists also raised money, distributed literature, and collected signatures for petitions to Congress.

Some men supported women's efforts. William Lloyd Garrison, for example, voluntarily joined the women who had been denied participation in the World's Anti-Slavery Convention in 1840. Garrison said, "After battling so many long years for the liberties of African slaves, I can take no part in a convention that strikes down the most sacred rights of all women." Many men, however, denounced the female abolitionists. The Massachusetts clergy criticized the Grimké sisters for assuming "the place and tone of man as public reformer."

Opposition only served to make women reformers more determined. The abolitionist cause became a powerful spur to other reform causes, as well as to the women's rights movement. In the 1840s, Lucy Stone, who retained her own name when she married, became the first female abolitionist speaker to give lectures solely devoted to the problem of women's rights.

WORKING FOR TEMPERANCE Another spur to the development of the women's rights movement was the **temperance movement,** the effort to prohibit the drinking of alcohol. Speaking at a temperance meeting in Albany, New York, in 1852, Mary C. Vaughan attested to the evils of alcohol.

THINK THROUGH HISTORY
B. Summarizing
In what ways were women excluded from the abolitionist movement?

B. Answer
Women were sometimes shut out of meetings and occasionally even pelted with eggs.

> **A PERSONAL VOICE**
> There is no reform in which woman can act better or more appropriately than temperance. I know not how she can resist or turn aside from the duty of acting in this; its effects fall so crushingly upon her . . . she has so often seen its slow, insidious, but not the less surely fatal advances, gaining upon its victim. . . . Oh! the misery, the utter, hopeless misery of the drunkard's wife!
>
> **MARY C. VAUGHAN,** quoted in *Women's America*

Mary C. Vaughan encouraged other women to support temperance reform. "We are learning," she said, "that our part in the drama of life is something beside inactive suffering and passive endurance."

In the early 19th century alcoholic drink flowed freely in America. Rum, gin, whiskey, beer, wine, and hard cider helped Americans wash down the salted meat and fish that dominated their diet. Until the development of anesthetics—drugs to deaden feeling during surgery—in the 1840s, doctors dosed their patients with whiskey or brandy before operating. Politicians even bought votes with free drinks.

Many Americans, however, recognized drunkenness as a serious problem. Lyman Beecher, a prominent Connecticut minister, had begun lecturing against all use of liquor in 1825. A year later, the American Temperance Society was

KEY PLAYER

LUCRETIA MOTT
1793–1880

History has it that Lucretia Mott was so talkative as a child that her mother called her Long Tongue. As an adult, she used her considerable public speaking skills to campaign against slavery.

Mott became interested in women's rights when she learned that her salary as a teacher would be roughly half of what a man might receive. She was a prominent figure at the Seneca Falls convention, at which she delivered the opening and closing addresses. Mott and her husband later acted on their abolitionist principles by taking in runaway slaves escaping on the Underground Railroad.

Skillbuilder Mini-Lesson: Identifying Problems

Explaining the Skill Identifying problems in history means finding and summarizing the difficulties faced by a group of people at a certain time. Being able to point to and explain a problem can lead to a thorough understanding of a situation. In reading history, students will find that some problems may be stated directly, while others might be implied by the ways people act. For example, gang violence in a community probably indicates that problems exist in the economic opportunities, housing conditions, family structure, or other areas of community life.

Applying the Skill: Women and Reform Help students identify some of the problems women worked to reform in the early 1800s. *Slavery; lack of equality for women; drunkenness.*

Next ask whether the problems were stated directly in the text or were implied by people's actions. *Most are stated directly. Some people's treatment of women reformers suggests that traditional views of women's roles were restrictive.*

IN-DEPTH RESOURCES: UNIT 2
Skillbuilder Practice: Identifying Problems, p. 71

founded. Within a few years, more than a thousand local temperance societies dotted the country, holding rallies, producing pamphlets, and bringing about a decline in the consumption of alcohol that would continue into the 1860s.

EDUCATION FOR WOMEN Work for abolition and temperance accompanied gains in education for women. Until the 1820s, American girls had few educational opportunities beyond elementary school. As Sarah Grimké complained in *Letter on the Equality of the Sexes and the Condition of Women* (1838), a woman who knew "chemistry enough to keep the pot boiling, and geography enough to know the location of the different rooms in her house" was considered learned enough. Grimké believed that increased education for women was a better alternative.

Sarah *(top)* and Angelina Grimké *(bottom)* were Southern women who ran their own school and spoke out against the horrors of slavery.

> **A PERSONAL VOICE**
> I spent the early part of my life among the butterflies of the fashion world. . . . I must say, their education is miserably deficient. . . . Men may reject what I say because it wounds their pride but I believe they will find that woman as their equal is unquestionably more valuable than woman as their inferior both as a moral and intellectual being.
>
> **SARAH GRIMKÉ**, *Letter on the Equality of the Sexes and the Condition of Women*

In 1821, Emma Willard opened one of the nation's first academically oriented schools for girls in Troy, New York. In addition to classes in domestic sciences, the Troy Female Seminary offered classes in math, history, geography, languages, art, music, writing, and literature. The Troy Female Seminary became the model for a new type of women's school. Despite tremendous ridicule—people mocked that "they will be educating cows next"—Willard's school prospered.

In 1837 Mary Lyon surmounted heated resistance to found another important institution of higher learning for women, Mount Holyoke Female Seminary (later Mount Holyoke College) in South Hadley, Massachusetts. In the same year Ohio's Oberlin College admitted four women to its degree program, thus becoming the nation's first coeducational college.

Black women enjoyed even fewer educational opportunities than their white counterparts. In 1831 Prudence Crandall, a white Quaker, opened a school for girls in Canterbury, Connecticut. One of her students was an African-American girl named Sarah Harris. The townspeople protested so vigorously against desegregated education that Crandall decided in 1833 to have only African-American students. This aroused even more opposition, and in 1834, Crandall was forced to close the school and leave town. Only after the Civil War would the severely limited educational opportunities for black women finally, though slowly, begin to expand.

THINK THROUGH HISTORY
C. Summarizing
What gains did women make in education in the 1820s and 1830s? Did these gains extend to African-American women?

. Answer White women found increasing opportunities for higher, and more academic, education. These gains did not extend to African-American women.

WOMEN AND HEALTH REFORM In the mid-19th century, educated women also began to work for health reform. Elizabeth Blackwell, who in 1849 became the first woman to graduate from medical college, later opened the New York Infirmary for Women and Children. In the 1850s, Catharine Beecher, Lyman Beecher's daughter and a respected educator in her own right, undertook a national survey of women's health. To her dismay, Beecher found three sick women for every healthy one. It was no wonder: women rarely bathed or exercised, and they wore fashionable clothing that included corsets so restrictive that breathing sometimes was difficult.

Reforming American Society **237**

Changes in Women's Lives, 1820–1850

Reading the Table Ask students what percentage of women were in the labor force in the 1850s. *10%.* How many children on average were born to white women in that decade? *Five.* How might these two figures be related? *Possible Response: As white women spent more time outside the home, they spent less time having children.*

Extension Ask students how the decline in birthrate might have affected women's health in the 1850s. *Possible Response: The decline probably improved their health because many women at that time died during childbirth.*

Women's Rights Movement Emerges

▶ *Discussing Key Ideas*

• Women and men gather to discuss women's rights at the Seneca Falls convention.

• Participants at the convention agree on all issues except women's right to vote.

• Sojourner Truth articulates the rights of African-American women.

IN-DEPTH RESOURCES, UNIT 2
Primary Source: *from* The Seneca Falls Declaration of Sentiments, p. 77

SKILLBUILDER
INTERPRETING TABLES
Which decade saw the steepest decline in the white birthrate? How might growing industries affect the number of women in the labor force?
Skillbuilder Answers
Decade: *1840–1850.*
Industries: *Possible answer:* Machinery reduced the need for physical strength and opened up job opportunities for women. Women's acceptance of lower wages made them attractive to employers.

Changes in Women's Lives in the U.S., 1820–1850

CHANGES	1820	1830	1840	1850
Percentage of women in labor force	6	6	8	10
Average number of children per white woman	7	7	6	5
White birthrate per 1000 population	53	51	48	43

Source: Nancy Woloch, *Women and the American Experience*

Amelia Bloomer, publisher of a temperance newspaper, came up with a solution for one of these health problems. Bloomer wrote about (and often wore herself) a costume of loose-fitting pants tied at the ankles and covered by a short skirt. Readers besieged her with requests for the sewing pattern. Most women who sewed the "bloomers," however, seldom dared venture outdoors in them, as many men were outraged that women would presume to wear pants.

Women's Rights Movement Emerges

The reform movements of the mid-19th century fed the growth of the women's movement by providing women with increased opportunities to act outside the home. Margaret Fuller, for example, began her public career as a teacher in a school organized by Bronson Alcott, a transcendentalist reformer who was also the father of Louisa May Alcott. Fuller was also a gifted essayist whose writings on American and European literature won international acclaim. Her literary talent and friendship with Emerson landed her a job as the editor of the transcendentalist journal, *The Dial.* In 1845, Fuller published *Woman in the Nineteenth Century*, a work that demanded equality and fulfillment for women. In it she argued that a woman need "not as a woman to act or rule but . . . as a soul to live free and unimpeded."

This colorized woodcut portrays the Seneca Falls convention, which was held in the local Methodist church. The nation's press ridiculed the convention and its "Declaration of Sentiments."

Meanwhile, Elizabeth Cady Stanton and Lucretia Mott, having been ardent abolitionists, decided to act on their resolution to hold a women's rights convention. In 1848, they convened the **Seneca Falls convention,** named for the town in New York in which it was held. Stanton and Mott spent a day composing an agenda and a detailed statement of grievances. Stanton carefully modeled this "Declaration of Sentiments" on the Declaration of Independence. The second paragraph began with a revision of very familiar words: "We hold these truths to be self-evident: that all men and women are created equal. . . ." Some of the resolutions in the declaration spoke to the circumstances with which women reformers had struggled.

A PERSONAL VOICE
Resolved, That all laws which prevent woman from occupying such a station in society as her conscience shall dictate, or which place her in a position inferior to that of man, are contrary to the great precept of nature, and therefore of no force or authority.
Resolved, That woman is man's equal—was intended to be so by the Creator, and the highest good of the race demands that she should be recognized as such.

Declaration of Sentiments, Seneca Falls convention, 1848

238 CHAPTER 8

TEACHING OPTIONS

Exploring Themes

Women in America Discuss the reforms women fought for in the mid-1800s. Encourage students to compare the position of women during this period to that of slaves. Then ask students why fighting for abolition and other reforms inspired women to begin fighting for their own rights. *Possible Response: While fighting for the rights of slaves, many women recognized that their own human rights had been denied.*

Making Connections Across Time

The Women's Movement in the 1960s Tell students that in the 1960s, a new wave of women's movements emerged. Women formed organizations and demonstrated, demanding equal pay and job opportunities, childcare, and other social programs. Ask students how the social climate of the period contributed to the reawakened interest in women's rights. *Possible Response: The 1960s was another period of great social change, marked by the civil rights movement and student protests.*

THINK THROUGH HISTORY
D. Contrasting
How did the Seneca Falls convention differ from the World's Anti-Slavery Convention held in 1840?

D. Answer
Women planned and ran the Seneca Falls convention, while they were not allowed to participate in the World's Anti-Slavery Convention.

More than 300 women and men gathered at the Wesleyan Methodist Church for the convention. The participants approved all parts of the declaration unanimously—including several resolutions to encourage women to participate in all public issues on an equal basis with men—except one. The one exception, which still passed by a narrow majority, was the resolution calling for women "to secure to themselves their sacred right to the elective franchise," the right to vote. The right of suffrage remained a controversial aim. Opponents of women's suffrage believed women should not vote because they were too dependent—on husbands and fathers for economic and legal protection—to exercise the right freely. Others simply thought suffrage was an extreme solution to a nonexistent problem. As Lucy Stone's sister wrote in 1846, "I can't vote, but what care I for that, I would not if I could."

While women reformers made significant contributions to improving social conditions in the mid-19th century, life was not perfect. After all, slavery became more entrenched than it had been—and conditions for slaves worsened. In fact, African-American women found it difficult to gain recognition of their problems and reform efforts. One such woman was Isabella Baumfree, a slave for the first 30 years of her life, who took the name **Sojourner Truth** when she decided to sojourn (travel) throughout the country arguing for abolition. At a women's rights convention in 1851, the tall, muscular black woman refuted the arguments that because she was a woman she was weak, or because she was black, she was not feminine. The reformer who chaired the convention recorded remarks long attributed to Truth.

With her dignified bearing and powerful voice, Sojourner Truth made audiences snap to attention. Truth fought for women's rights, abolition, prison reform, and temperance.

A PERSONAL VOICE
Look at me! Look at my arm! I have ploughed, and planted, and gathered into barns, and no man could head me. And ain't I a woman? I could work as much and eat as much as a man—when I could get it—and bear the lash as well! And ain't I a woman? I have borne thirteen children, and seen most all sold off to slavery, and when I cried out with a mother's grief, none but Jesus heard! And ain't I a woman?

SOJOURNER TRUTH, quoted in *Narrative of Sojourner Truth*

As Truth proved, hard work was a central fact of life for most women. In the mid-19th century, this continued to be the case as women entered the emerging industrial workplace. Once there, they found new problems that called for reform.

Section 3 Assessment

1. TERMS & NAMES

Identify:
- Elizabeth Cady Stanton
- Lucretia Mott
- cult of domesticity
- Sarah and Angelina Grimké
- temperance movement
- Seneca Falls convention
- Sojourner Truth

2. SUMMARIZING In a diagram similar to the one shown, fill in historical events, ideas, or people that relate to the main idea.

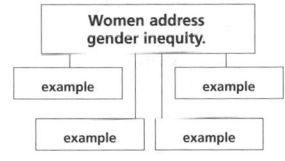

Women address gender inequity.
- example
- example
- example
- example

Write a paragraph about the method you think was most effective.

3. ANALYZING ISSUES The Seneca Falls "Declaration of Sentiments" asserted that "woman is man's equal." In what ways would that change the status women held at that time? Cite facts to support your answer.

THINK ABOUT
- women's social, economic, and legal status in the early and mid-1800s
- married women's domestic roles
- single women's career opportunities and wages

4. EVALUATING On a scale of 1 to 5, rank women's participation in the following social reforms from most important to least important: education, health, temperance, abolition, women's rights. Justify your rankings with details from the text.

THINK ABOUT
- the problems that each social reform was directed toward
- which reforms seem the most crucial, and why

Reforming American Society **239**

MORE ABOUT . . .
Sojourner Truth

With her deep, thunderous voice and dignified manner, Sojourner Truth was a powerful speaker. Few people knew she was illiterate. For 40 years, she traveled and spoke out against injustice. A man making fun of her once said, "I don't care any more for your talk than I do for the bite of a flea." Truth laughed and replied, "Maybe not, but the Lord willing, just like the flea, I'll keep you scratching."

ASSESS & RETEACH

Section 3 Assessment
Have pairs of students work on the questions and share their answers with another pair of students.

Self-Assessment
To document what students have learned, have them make a list of the insights they have gained into the changing status of women in the mid-1800s.

Section Quiz

FORMAL ASSESSMENT
Section Quiz, p. 103

Reteach
Skim the section, noting the major women reformers and their causes. Ask students to create a list to help them keep track of this information.

CLOSE

By the mid-1800s, women reformers active in the anti-slavery movement began to be concerned about their own rights. They fought for temperance, educational and health reforms, and even the right to vote. Rejecting the cult of domesticity, more and more women entered the industrial workplace. The problems they found there would demand new reforms.

ANSWERS

1. TERMS & NAMES
Elizabeth Cady Stanton, p. 235
Lucretia Mott, p. 235
cult of domesticity, p. 235
Sarah and Angelina Grimké, p. 236
temperance movement, p. 236
Seneca Falls convention, p. 238
Sojourner Truth, p. 239

2. SUMMARIZING
Students' examples might be drawn from the following: the cult of domesticity, Stanton, Mott, the Grimké sisters, Troy Female Seminary, Elizabeth Blackwell, Amelia Bloomer, Margaret Fuller, Seneca Falls convention.

3. ANALYZING ISSUES
Possible Responses: Women on an equal status with men would change their subservient role. It would give them rights to property and to their children, and it even implied the right to equal wages for the same jobs.

4. EVALUATING
Possible Responses: Students will choose various rankings, but they should note that women were deeply involved in the issues of abolition and temperance and less heavily involved in issues of women's rights.

OBJECTIVES

① To show how new manufacturing techniques shifted the production of goods from home to factory.

② To describe the conditions female employees endured in factories.

③ To summarize the attempts of factory workers to organize unions.

SKILLBUILDER

- Understanding geography: region, location, p. 241

CRITICAL THINKING

- Analyzing causes, p. 243
- Evaluating decisions, p. 243
- Recognizing effects, pp. 241, 244, 245
- Analyzing issues, p. 245
- Forming opinions, p. 245

FOCUS & MOTIVATE

▶ **Starting with the Student**
Ask students to think about working conditions and about job protests they know about.

- Were job complaints or strikes successful? Why or why not?
- Do they think workers have the right to demand better conditions?

MORE ABOUT . . .
Susan Miller

When Susan Miller's alcoholic father died, the Millers could not pay off the mortgage on their farm. Susan asked the landlord to allow her family to remain while she worked to pay off the debt. The landlord objected to her working at the Lowell factory: "I do not think it is right for a young girl like you, to put yourself in the way of all sorts of temptation." But Susan was determined. A year after she had paid off the mortgage, she went back to the farm—now her brother's property—where she lived as a guest.

---

❹ The Changing Workplace

TERMS & NAMES
- putting-out system
- master
- journeyman
- apprentice
- strike
- National Trades' Union

LEARN ABOUT changes in manufacturing and factories
TO UNDERSTAND the problems faced by the emerging industrial workforce.

ONE AMERICAN'S STORY

In 1841 a brief biography appeared in the *Lowell Offering,* the first journal written by and for female mill workers. A young girl who toiled in the mill—now identifiable only by the initials F.G.A.—wrote under the name Susan Miller about her decision to save her family's farm by working in the Lowell, Massachusetts, textile (cloth) mills. Acknowledging the danger of the unfamiliar machinery, the determined girl nevertheless insisted, "If I am careful, I need not fear any injury."

At first, Susan found the factory work "dispiriting," but eventually she came to accept it and to take comfort in the company of the other girls who worked and lived with her in Lowell. Most of all, Susan felt proud of the wages she sent home.

A PERSONAL VOICE
Every morning the bells pealed forth the same clangor, and every night brought the same feeling of fatigue. But Susan felt, as all factory girls feel, that she could bear it for a while. There are few who look upon factory labor as a pursuit for life. It is but a temporary vocation; and most of the girls resolve to quit the Mill when some favorite design is accomplished. Money is their object—not for itself, but for what it can perform; and paydays are the landmarks which cheer all hearts, by assuring them of their progress to the wished-for goal.

F.G.A., quoted in *Lowell Offering*, 1841

The *Lowell Offering* was published from 1841 to 1845.

Just a few decades earlier, work outside the home might not have been an option for girls like "Susan." At the same time that women's roles began to expand, changes occurred in the way goods were manufactured. The movement of thousands of women from farms to factory work after 1820 signaled an important historical development for many working men and women: the movement of production from the home to the factory.

Industry Changes Work

Before "Susan" and other girls began to abandon quiet farms for New England's noisy textile mills, women had spun and sewed most of their family's clothing from raw fibers. In fact, in the early 19th century Americans produced in their own homes almost all of the manufactured items their families needed. Moving production from the home to the factory split families, created new communities, and transformed traditional relationships between employers and employees. The textile industry pioneered the new manufacturing techniques that would alter work disciplines, the rules and behavior required of workers, for most Americans.

RURAL MANUFACTURING Until the second decade of the 19th century, only the first step in the manufacture of clothing—the spinning of cotton into thread—had been successfully mechanized in America. People then finished the work in what was called the **putting-out system,** a system of production in

---

SECTION 4 RESOURCES

 PRINT RESOURCES

IN-DEPTH RESOURCES: UNIT 2
Guided Reading, p. 70
Geography Application: The Dramatic Rise of Immigration, p. 72

ACCESS FOR STUDENTS ACQUIRING ENGLISH
Guided Reading (Spanish), p. 86
Geography Application: The Dramatic Rise of Immigration (Spanish), p. 88

FORMAL ASSESSMENT
Section Quiz, p. 104

ALTERNATIVE ASSESSMENT BOOK
See forms for supporting and scoring alternative activities.

 TECHNOLOGY RESOURCES

CRITICAL THINKING TRANSPARENCIES
CT8, Reform Movement Summary

CD-ROM Electronic Library of Primary Sources

VIDEO *American Portfolio: A Videodisc for U.S. History* user's guide, pp. 53–54

INTERNET McDougal Littell Learning On-Line
http://www.mcdougallittell.com

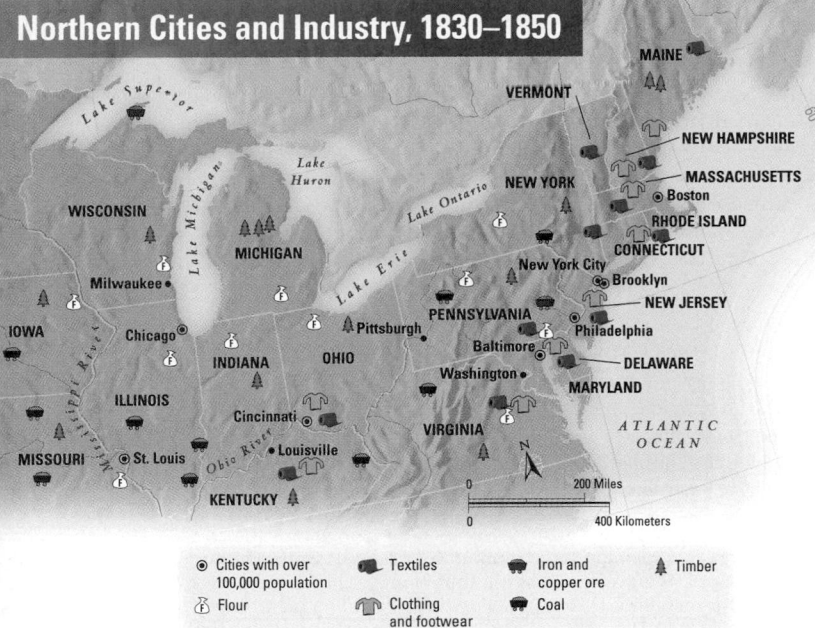

Northern Cities and Industry, 1830–1850

NORTHERN CITIES, 1830–1850

- Cincinnati, Ohio
- Philadelphia, Pennsylvania
- New York, New York

Source: U.S. Bureau of the Census, Seventh Census

Map Legend:
- Cities with over 100,000 population
- Flour
- Textiles
- Clothing and footwear
- Iron and copper ore
- Coal
- Timber

OBJECTIVE
① INSTRUCT

Industry Changes Work

► **Discussing Key Ideas**
- Mechanization allows many industries to carry out the manufacturing process in factories.
- Unskilled workers leave their farms to labor in the factories.

IN-DEPTH RESOURCES: UNIT 2
Guided Reading, p. 70

ACCESS FOR STUDENTS ACQUIRING ENGLISH
Guided Reading (Spanish), p. 86

HISTORY FROM VISUALS
Northern Cities and Industry, 1830–1850

Reading the Map
Encourage students to look carefully at the many levels of information in this map and graph. What manufactured goods are associated with most of the largest cities? *Textiles and clothing.*

Extension Point out that, as the map shows, there were few factories in the South. Then ask students what part the South played in the growth of manufacturing. *Possible Response: The South grew cotton on large plantations for use in the textile and clothing factories.*

---

which manufacturers provided the materials for goods to be produced in the home. Though women did most of this work, men and children sometimes helped too. The participants in this cottage industry brought the finished articles to the manufacturer, who paid them by the piece and gave them new materials for the next batch of work.

When Patrick Tracy Jackson, Nathan Appleton, and Francis Cabot Lowell opened their Waltham and Lowell, Massachusetts, weaving factories (see Chapter 7, page 199), their power looms replaced the putting-out system. Mechanizing the entire process and housing all the tools in the same place slashed the production time, as well as the cost, of textile manufacture. By the 1830s, the company Lowell and his partners had formed—the Boston Manufacturing Company—owned eight factories with over 6,000 employees, at an investment of over $6 million.

EARLY FACTORIES Textiles led the way, but other areas of manufacture also shifted from homes to factories. In the early 19th century, skilled artisans had typically produced items that a family could not make for itself—furniture and tools, for example. Like participants in the putting-out system, the artisans usually worked in shops attached to their own homes. The most experienced, called **masters,** might be assisted by **journeymen,** skilled workers employed by masters, and by **apprentices,** young workers learning their craft. Master artisans and their assistants traditionally crafted their products by hand until the 1820s, when manufacturers began using production processes that depended on the use of interchangeable parts.

The rapid spread of factory production revolutionized industry in the next two decades. The cost of making and repairing household items dramatically dropped. In addition, new machines allowed unskilled workers to perform tasks that once had taken the effort of trained artisans. To do this work, though, the unskilled workers needed to move from their rural homes to factory towns such as Lowell. There they shifted from farm work to boring and repetitive factory work and to the tight restrictions imposed by factory managers. Nowhere were these restrictions more rigid than in the factory town of Lowell, Massachusetts.

A. Answer
Factory production reduced the cost of making and repairing goods. It allowed unskilled laborers to handle tasks that had required skilled workers.

THINK THROUGH HISTORY
A. Recognizing Effects How did factory production change American manufacturing?

GEOGRAPHY SKILLBUILDER
REGION *In areas where the textile industry was strong, what other industry was also prominent?*
LOCATION *How did the location of New York City, Philadelphia, and Cincinnati encourage their growth as industrial towns?*

Skillbuilder Answer
Region: Footwear and clothing. **Location:** The three cities are located on or near rivers. The rivers were natural highways for shipping goods, provided waterpower to operate machinery, and allowed for quick disposal of waste.

Reforming American Society **241**

TEACHING OPTIONS

Making Connections Across the Curriculum

Economics Discuss how the new mechanization processes affected the cost of making household items. Explain that a company's profit is the amount of money it earns from the sale of its products after all the production expenses have been paid. Then ask students what effect mechanization must have had on factory profits. *It often increased them, especially when the cost of maintaining machines was less than the cost of the wages of the workers that the machines replaced.*

Teaching Less Proficient Readers

Analyzing Effects Have students create a chart on a piece of paper with the heading Effects. As students read pages 20 to 22, ask them to list any effects of the new manufacturing techniques they can identify. Remind students that an effect is an event that is brought about by another event or fact. When they have finished reading the section, have students exchange their lists with a partner and compare information.

Farm Girl to Factory Worker

▶ *Discussing Key Ideas*
- Mill owners seek young female employees because they can control the girls' behavior and pay them less than men.
- Factory work involves long hours, unhealthy conditions, and hard work.
- Strikes for higher wages at Lowell fail.

Have students create a chart like the one below to compare the life of a farm girl with that of a factory worker. Students should compare such factors as hours worked, conditions, wages, lodging, and tasks performed.

Factors	Farm Girl	Factory Worker
Hours		
Conditions		
Wages		
Lodging		
Tasks		

NOW & THEN
Telecommuting

Critical Thinking: Predicting Point out that telecommuting allows employees to live almost anywhere. Then ask students to predict what an increase in the number of telecommuters might have on the growth of cities in the future. *Possible Response: The increase might reduce the population of cities and large commercial centers as people move to other, less congested areas.*

Farm Girl to Factory Worker

Under the strict control of female supervisors, a workforce consisting almost entirely of unmarried farm girls clustered in Lowell and the other mill towns that soon dotted New England. At their boarding houses, the "mill girls" lived under strict curfews. The supervisors closely monitored the girls' behavior and church attendance. Despite this scrutiny, however, many mill girls enjoyed the companionship of their co-workers. Most mill girls also liked earning money. By 1828 women made up nine-tenths of the workforce in the New England mills—and four out of five of the women were not yet 30 years old.

THE LOWELL MILL Mill owners sought female employees because they could pay women wages lower than those of men who did similar jobs. To the girls in the mills, though, textile work offered better pay than their only alternatives: teaching, sewing, and domestic work. In an 1846 letter to her father in New Hampshire, 16-year-old Mary Paul expressed her satisfaction with her situation at Lowell.

A PERSONAL VOICE
I am at work in a spinning room tending four sides of warp which is one girl's work. The overseer tells me that he never had a girl get along better than I do. . . . I have a very good boarding place, have enough to eat. . . . The girls are all kind and obliging. . . . I think that the factory is the best place for me and if any girl wants employment, I advise them to come to Lowell.

MARY PAUL, quoted in *Women and the American Experience*

Like Mary Paul, who eventually left factory work to become a housewife, most female workers stayed at Lowell for only a few years. Harriet Hanson Robinson, a mill girl who married and became involved in the abolition and women's rights movements, applauded the mill girls' influence in carrying "new fashions, new books, new ideas" back to their homes.

CONDITIONS AT LOWELL The workday at Lowell began at 5 A.M., Mary Paul wrote her father, with a bell ringing "for the folks to get up. At seven they are called to the mill. At half past twelve we have dinner, are called back again at one and stay until half past seven."

NOW & THEN

TELECOMMUTING
Telecommuting, the practice of working at home with modem-linked computers rather than in office buildings, has mushroomed in the United States in the 1990s.

In the mid-19th century, an increasing number of American workers worked in factories rather than in homes and on farms. At the end of the 20th century, however, many Americans were establishing electronic work centers at home. These telecommuters use new technologies—such as cellular phones, laptop computers, and fax machines—to perform jobs that formerly needed to be done in offices. Employers win more productive workers, while telecommuters win flexible working hours and reduced commuting time.

One research firm predicts that in the early 21st century, as many as 14 million employees in fields as diverse as architecture, writing, and radiology will telecommute.

This depiction of Lowell, Massachusetts, in 1834 shows the factories along the river banks.

TEACHING OPTION

Exploring Themes

Science and Technology Discuss the economic and social changes brought about by the new technology used in the factories. Ask students whether they think the new manufacturing techniques ultimately improved the quality of people's lives in the mid-19th century or created more problems. Then ask them to compare these positive and negative effects with those resulting from the new technologies—computers, fax machines, robotics—in today's society.

Possible Response: *The new technology in the mid-19th century created many new jobs for unskilled workers, but the work was tedious and the conditions in the factories were unhealthful. The new technology in the late-20th century eliminated many jobs for unskilled workers but made life easier for many people.*

These hours probably didn't seem unduly long to farm girls, but heat, darkness, and poor ventilation in the factories contributed to discomfort and illness. Overseers would nail windows shut to seal in the humidity they thought prevented the threads from breaking, so that in the summer the weaving rooms felt like ovens. In the winter, pungent smoke from whale-oil lamps blended with the cotton dust to make breathing difficult.

Mill conditions deteriorated further in the 1830s. Managers forced workers to increase their pace. Between 1836 and 1850, Lowell owners tripled the number of spindles and looms but hired only 50 percent more workers to operate them. In the mid-1840s one mill manager said, "I regard my workpeople just as I regard my machinery. So long as they can do my work for what I choose to pay them, I keep them, getting out of them all I can."

Factory rules tightened too. After gulping a noon meal, workers now had to rush back to the weaving rooms to avoid fines for lateness. In 1834, when the Lowell mills announced a 15 percent wage cut, 800 mill girls organized a **strike,** a work stoppage in order to force an employer to respond to demands.

STRIKES AT LOWELL Under the heading "UNION IS POWER," the Lowell strikers of 1834 issued a proclamation declaring that they would not return to work "unless our wages are continued to us as they have been." For its part, the company threatened to recruit local women to fill the strikers' jobs. Criticized by the Lowell press and clergy, most of the strikers agreed to return to work at reduced wages. The mill owners fired the strike leaders.

In 1836, Lowell mill workers struck again, this time over an increase in their board charges that was equivalent to a 12.5 percent pay cut. Twice as many women participated as had two years earlier. Only 11 at the time of the strike, Harriet Hanson Robinson later recalled the protest.

> **A PERSONAL VOICE**
> As I looked back at the long line that followed me, I was more proud than I have ever been since at any success I may have achieved, and more proud than I shall ever be again until my own beloved State gives to its women citizens the right of suffrage [voting].
>
> **HARRIET HANSON ROBINSON,** quoted in *Women's America*

As in 1834, however, the company prevailed. After firing the strike leaders and dismissing Harriet Hanson Robinson's widowed mother, a boarding-house supervisor, the managers watched as most of the strikers returned to their spindles and looms.

The Lowell workers did not give up their fight for better working conditions after these setbacks. Indeed, in the 1840s, the mill girls took their concerns to the political arena. In 1844, Sarah Bagley founded the Lowell Female Labor Reform Association to petition the Massachusetts state legislature, which had established a committee to consider legislation for a ten-hour work day. The proposed legislation failed, but the Lowell Association was able to help defeat a local legislator who opposed the bill.

Mid-19th century "mill girls" often worked 12-hour days, six days a week—but for many, it was their first chance to earn money. These Massachusetts mill workers are holding shuttles, which were used during weaving.

> "*I regard my workpeople just as I regard my machinery.*"
>
> **TEXTILE MILL MANAGER, 1840s**

B. Answer Managers made workers work faster and gave them less free time. Rules became more rigid.

THINK THROUGH HISTORY
B. Analyzing Causes What factors contributed to the worsening conditions workers endured at Lowell beginning in the 1830s?

C. Answer Students may say the decision was a good one because it made the workers' grievances known. Others may say it was not a good decision because it did not bring about change.

THINK THROUGH HISTORY
C. Evaluating Decisions Based on the results, do you think the decision to strike at Lowell was a good one?

MORE ABOUT . . .
Factory Life
By the late 1820s, conditions in the boarding houses where the factory workers lived had begun to worsen. Six or eight women shared a crowded room, often squeezing three in one bed. After working 13 or more hours a day, the women were often fed only bread and gravy for supper. In 1828, mill women in Dover, New Hampshire, went on strike—the first organized by mill women on their own. The community was shocked as several hundred young women paraded down the street, carrying banners and shooting off gunpowder. Like other early strikes, however, this one was soon over, the leaders dismissed and blacklisted.

 ELECTRONIC LIBRARY OF PRIMARY SOURCES
from "Pleasures of Factory Life" by Sarah Bagley

Reforming American Society **243**

Workers Seek Better Conditions

▶ **Discussing Key Ideas**
• Workers in the 1830s and 1840s organize dozens of strikes.
• Some Irish immigrants are willing to work for low wages, while others join unions and organize strikes.
• The National Trades' Union wins the right to strike by appealing to the Massachusetts supreme court.

MORE ABOUT . . .
Irish Immigration

More than half of the Irish immigrants who fled to the United States were women, many of whom became maids or textile workers. By the 1840s, in fact, Irish women were replacing American women in the Lowell mills. The poorer Irish men often dug canals and cellars or served white families. To secure this work, the Irish competed directly with poor free blacks. Irish men who could secure skilled labor competed with native-born white workers. As a result, according to one immigrant, there was "no love for [the Irish worker]—no protection of life—[he] can be shot down, run through, kicked, cuffed, spat upon. . . ."

IN-DEPTH RESOURCES: UNIT 2
Geography Application: The Dramatic Rise of Immigration, p. 72

Workers Seek Better Conditions

Female textile workers were not the only laborers seeking better wages and working conditions. As conditions for all workers deteriorated during the 1830s, skilled artisans, who had originally formed unions to preserve their own interests, began to ally themselves with unskilled laborers. When Philadelphia coal workers struck for a 10-hour day in 1835, for example, carpenters, cigar makers, shoemakers, leatherworkers, and other artisans joined them in what became the first general strike in the United States.

Although only 1 or 2 percent of workers in the United States were organized, the 1830s and 1840s saw dozens of strikes—many for higher wages, but some for a shorter workday. Employers won most of these strikes because they could easily replace unskilled workers with strikebreakers who would toil long hours for low wages. Many of these strikebreakers were immigrants who had just escaped even worse poverty in Europe.

IMMIGRATION INCREASES European immigration rose dramatically in the United States between 1830 and 1860. In the decade 1845–1854 alone nearly 3 million immigrants were added to a population that had numbered only about 20 million. While some emigrated from England, Scandinavia, Switzerland, and Holland, most of the immigrants were German or Irish.

Most immigrants avoided the South because slavery limited their economic opportunity and Southerners were generally hostile to European, particularly Catholic, immigrants. The German immigrants clustered in the upper Mississippi Valley and in the Ohio Valley, primarily in Illinois, Ohio, Wisconsin, and Missouri. Most German immigrants had been farmers in Europe, but some became professionals, artisans, and shopkeepers in the United States.

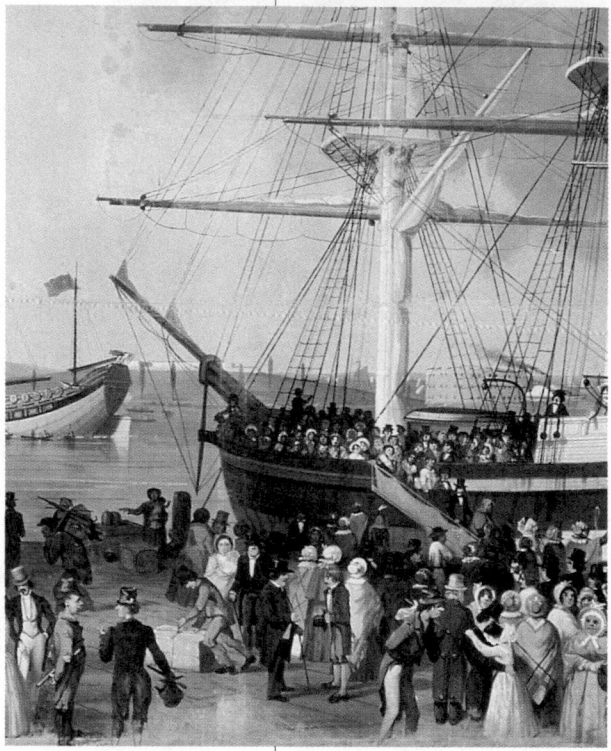

The swelling numbers of immigrants arriving at New York harbor in the mid-19th century made common scenes like this one painted by Samuel Waugh in 1847.

Irish immigrants congregated in the large cities of the East, where they performed whatever work they could find. Nearly a million Irish immigrants had settled in America between 1815 and 1844. Between 1845 and 1854 Irish immigration soared after a blight destroyed the peasants' staple crop, potatoes, which led to a famine in Ireland. The Great Potato Famine killed as many as 1 million of the Irish people and drove about 1.3 million more to new homes in America.

Irish immigrants faced bitter prejudice, both because they were Roman Catholic and because they were poor. Frightened by allegations of a Catholic conspiracy to take over the country, Protestant mobs in New York, Philadelphia, and Boston rampaged through Irish neighborhoods. Native-born artisans, whose wages had fallen because of competition from unskilled laborers and factory production, considered Irish immigrants the most unfair competition of all. Their willingness to work for low wages under terrible conditions made the desperate Irish easy prey for employers who sought to break strikes with cheap labor.

Other Irish immigrants, however, soon began to view unions as an opportunity to advance their prospects. In fact, Irish dockworkers organized New York City's most famous strike of the 1840s. When Irish women tailors organized the

D. Answer
Immigrants were willing to work for lower wages and in terrible conditions, so employers could hire them as strikebreakers. Other workers saw them as competition.

THINK THROUGH HISTORY
D. Recognizing Effects *How did the influx of new immigrants from Germany and Ireland affect circumstances in the workplace?*

TEACHING OPTIONS

Making Connections Across Cultures

Irish Americans The Irish had been coming to America since the colonial era. They fought in the revolution and their labor was important to building the canals, roads, and railroads of the new nation. As they overcame the bitter prejudice against their Catholicism and their poverty, the Irish produced the architect Louis Sullivan, the novelist Henry James, and the philosopher William James. Descendants of Irish immigrants have given this country many of its leaders, including President John F. Kennedy and industrialist Henry Ford as well as many of its police officers, politicians, jurists, and entertainers.

Making Connections Across Time

Recent Immigration Trends Point out that most of the immigrants in the 19th century came from Europe. Tell students that since 1965, a new wave of immigrants has settled in the United States. Many of the immigrants came from Mexico, Cuba, Haiti, and Vietnam. Ask students why these immigrants might have wanted to leave their homelands. *Possible Responses: Poverty, unemployment, war.* Encourage students to compare these reasons with those of the immigrants in the mid-19th century.

Ladies Industrial Association in New York City in 1845, their leader, Elizabeth Gray, denounced "tyrant employers." Though employers retained great power through the 1840s, unions did manage to win a few victories.

NATIONAL TRADES' UNION   In their earliest attempts to organize, journeymen formed trade unions specific to each trade. For example, journeymen shoemakers organized one of the nation's earliest strikes in 1806. During the 1830s, the trade unions in different towns began to join together to establish unions for such trades as carpentry, shoemaking, weaving, printing, and comb making. By means of these unions, the workers sought to standardize wages and conditions throughout each industry.

This "hammer and hand" symbol appeared in *The Union* and was part of an appeal that called workers to a mass protest against "tyrant" managers.

Journeymen's organizations from several industries united in 1834 to form the **National Trades' Union,** which represented a variety of occupations. The national trade-union movement faced fierce opposition from bankers and owners, who threatened the unions by forming associations of their own. In addition, workers' efforts to organize were at first hampered by court decisions declaring strikes illegal.

In 1842, however, the Massachusetts Supreme Court supported workers' right to strike in the case of *Commonwealth v. Hunt.* In this case, Chief Justice Lemuel Shaw declared that Boston's journeymen bootmakers could act "in such a manner as best to subserve their own interests." A prominent American court finally had upheld the rights of labor. Although by 1860, barely 5,000 workers were members of what would now be called labor unions, far larger numbers of workers, 20,000 or more, participated in strikes for improved working conditions and wages.

Reform in the workplace came in response to changes in the fledgling industrial system in the United States. Indeed, the religious and social reform movements in the nation in the mid-19th century went hand in hand with economic changes that set in place the foundation for the modern American economy. While some Americans poured their efforts into reforming society, others sought new opportunities for economic growth and expansion. As the nation adjusted to the newly emerging market economy, migration west became a popular option.

E. Answer The movement was important because it united workers from a variety of occupations into one labor organization.

THINK THROUGH HISTORY
E. *Recognizing Effects* Why was the national trade-union movement important?

Section ④ Assessment

1. TERMS & NAMES

Identify:
• putting-out system
• master
• journeyman
• apprentice
• strike
• National Trades' Union

2. RECOGNIZING EFFECTS
Create a chart similar to the one shown and complete it by filling in relevant events.

Worsening conditions in factories

Workers' responses:
1.
2.

Add your own ideas about dealing with factory conditions to the list of workers' responses.

3. ANALYZING ISSUES Do you think the positive effects of mechanizing the manufacturing process outweighed the negative effects? Why or why not?

THINK ABOUT
• changes in job opportunities for artisans, women, and unskilled male laborers
• changes in employer-employee relationships
• working conditions in factories
• the cost of manufactured goods

4. FORMING OPINIONS If you were working in a factory during the mid-1800s, would you be a striker or a strikebreaker? Support your choice with reasons.

THINK ABOUT
• how your decision would be affected by whether you were a native-born American or an immigrant
• how your decision would be affected by whether you were an artisan or an unskilled laborer
• the outcome of most strikes during the 1830s and 1840s

Reforming American Society **245**

ANSWERS

1. TERMS & NAMES

putting-out system, p. 240

master, p. 241

journeyman, p. 241

apprentice, p. 241

strike, p. 243

National Trades' Union, p. 245

2. RECOGNIZING EFFECTS

Possible Responses: Students' lists should include the 1834 and 1836 strikes at Lowell, the 1835 coal workers' strike in Philadelphia, the formation of the Ladies Industrial Association in 1845, and the formation of the National Trades' Union in 1834.

3. ANALYZING ISSUES

Possible Responses: Some students may refer to the reduced cost of manufactured items and to expanding opportunities for women and unskilled male laborers. Other students may mention the breaking up of families and communities when people left home to work in factories.

4. FORMING OPINIONS

Possible Responses: Those supporting strikes would probably be native-born Americans working in skilled trades. Strikebreakers might have been unskilled recent immigrants desperate for any kind of work.

Teacher's Edition **245**

OBJECTIVES

1 To describe working conditions in mid-19th-century America.

2 To compare and contrast the lot of mill workers, field slaves, and farmers of the day.

FOCUS & MOTIVATE

▶ **Starting with the Student**
Ask students who have part-time jobs to describe the working conditions at their jobs.

• How do working conditions today compare to conditions during the mid-19th century?

• What changes in their working conditions would they propose to their bosses?

MORE ABOUT . . .
The Industrial Revolution

When the small arms industry at the end of the 18th century pioneered the use of standard parts needed for mass production, that in turn expanded textile, metal, tool, and other industries. By 1860, manufacturing accounted for over a third of all U.S. production. Workers in industrialized nations enjoyed higher living standards than ever before, especially when they began to fight for shorter hours, higher wages, and better factory conditions.

Working at Mid-Century

In the years before the Civil War, most workers labored from dawn to dusk, six days a week, without benefits. While many Northerners criticized the South for exploiting slave labor, Southerners criticized the industrial wage system, mostly in the North, for exploiting free workers. Both North and South used children—cheap labor—for full workdays. While 10-year-old slave children worked in the fields like adults, one Northern mill employed 100 children ages 4–10. Look for similarities and differences in the lives of the workers discussed here and consider how work life has changed from then to now.

Courtesy George Eastman House

MILL WORKERS Approximately 80 percent of textile mill workers were young women between the ages of 15 and 30. The girls' day began with a bell for a quick breakfast in the boarding house, followed by a march to the factory, where they tended the spinning machines all day. They put up with heavy dust, the roar of machines, hot humid air into which water was sprayed to prevent threads from breaking, and windows nailed shut to keep in humidity.

When competitive pressure was on the owners, the girls had to speed up their work and endure lower wages. Children made $1 a week; older girls made $3 a week; men $6.

LENGTH OF DAY: 12 hours
TYPE OF LABOR: operating machines
PAYMENT: $1 to $6 a week

246 CHAPTER 8

TIME TABLE OF THE LOWELL MILLS,
Arranged to make the working time throughout the year average 11 hours per day.
TO TAKE EFFECT SEPTEMBER 21st, 1853.
The Standard time being that of the meridian of Lowell, as shown by the Regulator Clock of AMOS SANBORN, Post Office Corner, Central Street.

From March 20th to September 19th, inclusive.
COMMENCE WORK, at 6.30 A. M. LEAVE OFF WORK, at 6.30 P. M., except on Saturday Evenings. BREAKFAST at 6 A. M. DINNER, at 12 M. Commence Work, after dinner, 12.45 P. M.

From September 20th to March 19th, inclusive.
COMMENCE WORK at 7.00 A. M. LEAVE OFF WORK, at 7.00 P. M., except on Saturday Evenings. BREAKFAST at 6.30 A. M. DINNER, at 12.30 P.M. Commence Work, after dinner, 1.15 P. M.

BELLS.
From March 20th to September 19th, inclusive.
Morning Bells. / Dinner Bells. / Evening Bells.
First bell, ... 4.30 A. M. Ring out, ... 12.00 M. Ring out, ... 6.30 P. M.
Second, 5.30 A. M.; Third, 6.20. Ring in, ... 12.35 P. M. Except on Saturday Evenings.

From September 20th to March 19th, inclusive.
Morning Bells. / Dinner Bells. / Evening Bells.
First bell, ... 5.00 A. M. Ring out, ... 12.30 P. M. Ring out at. . . . . 7.00 P. M.
Second, 6.00 A. M.; Third, 6.50. Ring in, ... 1.05 P. M. Except on Saturday Evenings.

SATURDAY EVENING BELLS.
During APRIL, MAY, JUNE, JULY, and AUGUST, Ring Out, at 6.00 P. M.
The remaining Saturday Evenings in the year, ring out as follows:

SEPTEMBER.
First Saturday, ring out 6.00 P. M.
Second " " 5.45 "
Third " " 5.30 "
Fourth " " 5.20 "

OCTOBER.
First Saturday, ring out 5.05 P. M.
Second " " 4.55 "
Third " " 4.45 "

NOVEMBER.
Third Saturday ring out 4.00 P. M.
Fourth " " 3.55 "

DECEMBER.
First Saturday, ring out 3.50 P. M.
Second " " 3.55 "
Third " " 3.55 "

JANUARY.
Third Saturday, ring out 4.25 P. M.
Fourth " " 4.35 "

FEBRUARY.
First Saturday, ring out 4.45 P. M.
Second " " 4.55 "
Third " " 5.00 "

RECOMMENDED RESOURCES

Books

Danhof, Clarence H. *Change in Agriculture.* Cambridge: Harvard UP, 1969. American agricultural innovations from 1820 to 1870.

Davis, Rebecca Harding. *Life in the Iron Mills.* Old Westbury, NY: Feminist, 1972. An *Uncle Tom's Cabin* for factory workers, first published in 1861.

Laurie, Bruce. *Artisans into Workers.* New York: Hill, 1989. The history of labor in 19th-century America.

Mellon, James, ed. *Bullwhip Days.* New York: Weidenfeld, 1988. African Americans recall slavery.

Robinson, Harriet H. *Loom and Spindle.* Kailua, HI: Press Pacifica, 1976. Autobiography of a textile worker.

Zimiles, Martha. *Early American Mills.* New York: Potter, 1973. Early factories in New England.

Videos

Black People in the Slave South, 1850. Encyclopaedia Britannica.

The Industrial Revolution: Beginnings in the United States. Encyclopaedia Britannica.

The Plantation South. Encyclopaedia Britannica. The Southern plantation system.

Software

The Industrial Revolution in America. Queue. The rise of industry before and after the Civil War.

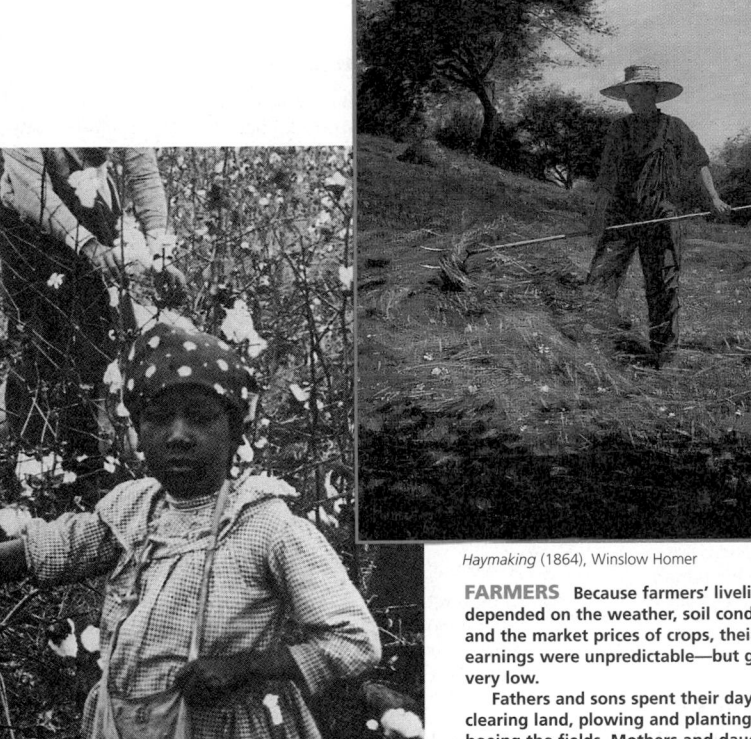

Annual Cost of Maintaining a Field Slave

A typical Southern plantation owner in 1848–1860 would spend the following to take care of a field slave for one year.

Taxes $0.80
Medical Care $1.75
Food/Clothing $8.50
Supervision $10.00

TOTAL $21.05 Source: *Slavery and the Southern Economy,* Harold D. Woodman, editor

Workers in the Mid-19th-Century

Average monthly earnings from 1830 to 1850 for a few common occupations:

JOB	YEAR	MONTHLY EARNINGS
Artisan	1830	$ 45
Laborer	1830	$ 26
Teacher, male	1840	$ 15
Teacher, female	1840	$ 7
Northern farmhand	1850	$ 13
Southern farmhand	1850	$ 9

Source: *Historical Statistics of the United States*

Workers in the 1990s

Average monthly salaries for each profession.

JOB	MONTHLY SALARY
Teacher—elementary	$ 2,758
Teacher—high school	$ 2,900
Construction worker	$ 2,399
Service worker	$ 1,518

Source: *Employment and Statistics,* June 1996, U.S. Department of Labor; *Statistical Abstract of the United States, 1994*

Haymaking (1864), Winslow Homer

FARMERS Because farmers' livelihoods depended on the weather, soil conditions, and the market prices of crops, their earnings were unpredictable—but generally very low.

Fathers and sons spent their days clearing land, plowing and planting, and hoeing the fields. Mothers and daughters raised vegetable gardens for family consumption, helped harvest fields, cared for livestock, made clothing, and cared for the family.

LENGTH OF DAY: dawn until after dark
TYPE OF LABOR: planting, tending crops, caring for livestock
PAYMENT: dependent on crop prices

FIELD SLAVES The field slave's day during harvest began with a bell an hour before dawn, a quick breakfast, and then a march to the fields. Men, women, and children spent the entire day picking cotton, bundling it, and coming back after dark carrying bales of cotton to the gin house. They then made their own suppers and ate quickly before falling asleep on wooden planks.

None of the other antebellum workers had such harsh and often brutal discipline imposed on them as slaves did. For most, the master's whip was the constant threat for lagging in their work.

LENGTH OF DAY: pre-dawn until after dark
TYPE OF LABOR: picking and bundling cotton
PAYMENT: substandard food and shelter

INTERACT WITH HISTORY

1. **DRAWING CONCLUSIONS** What attitudes about women and children do you see reflected in work patterns during the mid-19th century?

SEE SKILLBUILDER HANDBOOK, PAGE 1050.

2. **RESEARCHING CHILDREN'S RIGHTS** Report on labor laws and societal changes that protected children's rights and prevented child labor in factories.

For more about child labor, click on *Social Studies* at http://www.mcdougallittell.com

---

▶ **Starting with the Student**
- Ask students to imagine that they lived in mid-19th-century America. What job would they have chosen and why?
- Have students comment on any surprising information in the data file. You might point out that while a teacher's salary was low, the job often came with free living quarters adjoining the schoolhouse.

▶ **Discussing Key Ideas**
- Mid-19th-century labor conditions were far harsher than they are today.
- Women usually received lower wages than men.
- Child labor and slave labor were exploited.

HISTORY FROM VISUALS

Reading the Images

Study the pictures and the graphics in the data file.

- Of the three types of work shown, which earned the most and enjoyed the best conditions? *mill worker*
- Why do you think women were paid less than men? *Possible Responses: Supposedly not supporting families; to leave more for men supporting families; sexist prejudice; more timid about demanding raises; in jobs requiring physical strength, often less productive; in jobs requiring education, generally had less of it.*

---

1. Drawing Conclusions

Possible Responses: Work patterns reflected a sexist attitude toward women and a low opinion of both women and children. Attitudes included a willingness to exploit both and a willingness to treat lower-class women and children badly even while coddling upper-class women and children.

2. Researching Children's Rights

Standards for Evaluation
Reports should . . .

- trace abuses of child labor and the laws designed to correct them
- provide accurate factual information
- support general statements with examples and other details
- enhance the presentation of statistics and other information by using visual aids such as graphs and charts if possible

Chapter 8 Assessment

TERMS & NAMES

1. Second Great Awakening, p. 224
2. revival, p. 224
3. Ralph Waldo Emerson, p. 226
4. abolition, p. 229
5. William Lloyd Garrison, p. 229
6. Frederick Douglass, p. 230
7. Elizabeth Cady Stanton, p. 235
8. temperance movement, p. 236
9. strike, p. 243
10. National Trades' Union, p. 245

MAIN IDEAS
Answers will vary.

11. Belief in the individual's ability to improve himself or herself and society, and in a democratic God who would offer salvation to all.

12. Living a simple life and seeking truth in nature and in personal emotion and imagination.

13. Dix fought for better conditions in prisons and asylums and helped to pioneer the concept of rehabilitation in the treatment of criminals and the mentally ill.

14. **Garrison:** immediate emancipation of all slaves; **Walker:** violent resistance to slavery; **Douglass:** nonviolent resolution to the issue of slavery.

15. **Rural slaves:** worked long hours in the fields, endured physical punishment; **Urban slaves:** skilled artisans, wages taken; **All:** poor living and working conditions.

16. Tighter controls, vigilante committees to intimidate slaves, prohibited slaves from learning to read or write.

17. Women's activities restricted after marriage to the home and family, had few legal protections, and could not vote.

18. To gain support for a women's rights movement and to vote on a set of resolutions declaring women's equality with men.

19. Long hours at low pay in hot, humid factories, under the strict supervision of managers.

20. Represented workers from several industries and occupations, a more unified organization than separate trade unions specific to each trade.

REVIEWING THE CHAPTER

TERMS & NAMES For each term below, write a sentence explaining its significance during the mid-19th-century era of reform. For each person below, explain his or her role in the reform movements.

1. Second Great Awakening
2. revival
3. Ralph Waldo Emerson
4. abolition
5. William Lloyd Garrison
6. Frederick Douglass
7. Elizabeth Cady Stanton
8. temperance movement
9. strike
10. National Trades' Union

MAIN IDEAS

SECTION 1 *(pages 224–228)*

Religion Sparks Reform

11. What new religious ideas set the stage for the reform movements of the mid-19th century?
12. Briefly explain the concept of transcendentalism.
13. How did Dorothea Dix contribute to the reform movement?

SECTION 2 *(pages 229–234)*

Slavery and Abolition

14. Summarize the key abolitionist beliefs of William Lloyd Garrison, David Walker, and Frederick Douglass.
15. Describe the conditions of rural and urban slavery.
16. What steps did white Southerners take to suppress slave revolts?

SECTION 3 *(pages 235–239)*

Women and Reform

17. What conditions for women later became known as the cult of domesticity?
18. What was the purpose of the Seneca Falls convention?

SECTION 4 *(pages 240–245)*

The Changing Workplace

19. Briefly describe young women's working conditions in the Lowell mills.
20. Why was the formation of the National Trades' Union important?

THINKING CRITICALLY

1. **REFORM MOVEMENTS** Use a diagram similar to the one shown below to give details about the various reform movements that grew out of mid-19th-century religious reform.

2. **CHANGES FOR WOMEN** In what ways did the reform movements affect the lives of women, both white and black, free and enslaved? Use details from the chapter to support your answer.

3. **ADDRESSING INJUSTICE** If you were a 19th-century reformer, which cause would you most actively support, and how would you go about swaying public opinion? Explain your responses using examples from the chapter.

4. **GEOGRAPHY OF GROWING INDUSTRY** Look carefully at the map on page 241. Based on the pattern of industries represented on the map, what conclusions can you come to about the kinds of industries that were the first to expand toward the West?

5. **ANTEBELLUM WORKING CONDITIONS** Based on the descriptions of workers' lives in the mid-1800s, what similarities and differences can you see among workers in different industries? Support your answer with references to the text.

6. **ANALYZING PRIMARY SOURCES** Read the following excerpt from Ralph Waldo Emerson's essay "Man, the Reformer," published in 1841. Then answer the questions below.

> What is a man born for but to be a Reformer, a Remaker of what man has made; a renouncer of lies; a restorer of truth and good. . . . The power, which is at once spring and regulator in all efforts of reform, is faith in Man, the conviction that there is infinite worthiness in him which will appear at the call of worth, and that all particular reforms are the removing of some impediment. . . . I see at once how paltry is all this generation of unbelievers, and what a house of cards their institutions are, and I see what one brave man, what one great thought might effect.
>
> **RALPH WALDO EMERSON,** *"Man, the Reformer"*

How does Emerson characterize reformers' beliefs and goals? Do you think he presents an accurate profile? Support your opinion with historical examples of reformers.

THINKING CRITICALLY

1. REFORM MOVEMENTS
Possible Responses: Abolition: Leaders: Garrison, Walker, Douglass; Actions: publication of *The Liberator,* publication of Walker's *Appeal,* Nat Turner rebellion; Temperance: Leader: Lyman Beecher; Actions: formation of American Temperance Society; Women's Rights: Leaders: Stanton, Mott; Actions: Seneca Falls convention; Educational Reform: Leaders: Horace Mann, Grimké sisters, Emma Willard; Actions: tax-supported public schools

instituted, teacher training programs developed, Troy Female Seminary opened.

2. CHANGES FOR WOMEN
Possible Responses: Students may indicate that reform movements gave middle-class white women an opportunity to participate in public life, ultimately leading increased numbers to enter the workplace. Women's efforts on behalf of abolition eventually led to a women's rights movement. For enslaved women, the abolition movement was their best hope

for freedom. Former slaves like Sojourner Truth became powerful speakers on behalf of abolition, finding an avenue into the public sphere that had been denied to all women just a decade before.

3. ADDRESSING INJUSTICE
Answers will vary. Students should give cogent reasons for the cause they choose and refer to specific details from the text in identifying their methods.

ALTERNATIVE ASSESSMENT

1. ABOLITION RALLY

What means did the abolitionists use to try to convince the public that slavery should be abolished?

Cooperative Learning Plan and stage a political rally to protest the existence of slavery. Divide up the following tasks among members of your group.

CD-ROM Use the CD-ROM *Grolier's Multimedia Encyclopedia* and additional resources to research the ideas and key players of the abolition movement, focusing on the years 1820 to 1850.

- Prepare a short speech promoting abolition, referring in your speech to key events, people, or ideas that have helped shape your beliefs.
- Create a poster or banner using images and words to clearly communicate your support of the abolition movement.

2. COMMUNITY PLANNING

If you were a 19th-century reformer, what kind of utopian community would you form? Groups should present oral reports that describe their plans for their utopian communities. Include specific references to information in the chapter as well as visual aids.

Cooperative Learning Meet in small groups to design your perfect society. To help you plan, discuss the following questions with group members:

- How are the values or beliefs of people in the community similar to or different from beliefs shared by 19th-century utopian communities?
- What laws or guidelines should you establish that might promote a spirit of harmony?
- Which reform movements from the chapter would your community support?
- How will your community survive financially? How do people in the community earn a living?

3. PORTFOLIO PROJECT

Use the Living History activity to expand your portfolio.

LIVING HISTORY

PRESENTING YOUR VISUALS

After you have compiled a visual portrayal of an injustice in your world, have a classmate review it and answer the following questions:

- Does the essay summarize the problem clearly?
- How could the conclusion be stronger?

When you have revised the essay based on your classmate's suggestions, prepare it to send to a newspaper or a politician to try to get some action taken. Then display the essay in the classroom before adding it to your American history portfolio.

Bridge to Chapter 9

Review Chapter 8

AN ERA OF REFORM As Americans entered the mid-19th century, new religious theories sparked a broad range of reform movements. Revivalism, Unitarianism, and transcendentalism all prized the potential for individual and social reform. The revivalists relied on emotional appeals to preach this message, while Unitarians emphasized rational appeals to conscience. Transcendentalists, whose leaders included Ralph Waldo Emerson, valued freedom and self-reliance. Along with other reformers, they fought for improvements in education and prisons and for abolition—the movement to outlaw slavery.

THE RISE OF ABOLITION Americans disagreed about the issue of slavery. In 1831, William Lloyd Garrison, a radical white abolitionist, demanded the immediate emancipation of slaves. That same year the Virginia slave Nat Turner led a violent revolt. Frederick Douglass, an escaped slave who became an abolitionist, hoped abolition could be achieved nonviolently. Slave owners, though, opposed abolition and pressured lawmakers to tighten regulations on slaves and free blacks. While some women defended slavery, many worked for abolition, which heightened their awareness of their own limited economic and legal rights.

REFORMS FOR WOMEN AND WORKERS Besides their involvement in other social reforms, including temperance, women reformers like Elizabeth Cady Stanton began to tackle the issue of gender inequity. As women's roles expanded, the method of manufacturing goods also changed. Thousands of women moved from farms to work in factories, particularly New England textile mills. Mill girls and artisans addressed the problems of poor working conditions and decreasing wages in the strike wave of the mid-1830s. The spirit of reform spread to the workplace as workers organized strikes and trade unions to gain higher wages and better working conditions.

Preview Chapter 9

Rapid social, technological, and economic changes revolutionized American life. Expansion to Texas and the West led to conflicts, as Americans waged war on Mexico to gain territory in the Southwest. Tensions mounted over slavery in newly acquired or conquered lands. You will learn about these and other significant developments in the next chapter.

Reforming American Society **249**

---

1. ABOLITION RALLY
Standards for Evaluation
A plan for an abolition rally should meet the following criteria:

- Shows evidence of specific knowledge of the abolition movement including key events, people, and ideas.
- The speech contains limited and focused ideas with concrete references to specific events.
- The poster or banner uses appropriate and appealing visuals.

2. COMMUNITY PLANNING
Standards for Evaluation
A plan for a utopian community should meet the following criteria:

- Addresses the key aspects of communities: laws, economics, values, social organization.
- Provides specific details to support each part of the plan.
- Provides solutions for such problems as the power of leaders and the division of property.

3. PORTFOLIO PROJECT
LIVING HISTORY
Standards for Evaluation
A pictorial essay should meet the following criteria:

- Focuses on a single injustice.
- Contains a strong message about and thorough coverage of the injustice.
- Includes forceful images that support the message.

IN-DEPTH RESOURCES: UNIT 2
See the form for scoring this activity on page 84.

THINKING CRITICALLY

4. GEOGRAPHY OF GROWING INDUSTRY
Possible Responses: The mining, timber, and flour industries have expanded into Iowa and Missouri on this map, but the textile and clothing industries have expanded only as far west as Louisville, Kentucky. Most students may conclude from this that the first industries to expand into new territories are often those that harvest natural resources—in this case, iron and copper ore, coal, and wheat.

5. ANTEBELLUM WORKING CONDITIONS
Possible Responses: Similarities: long hours, poor living and working conditions. Differences: field slaves had very harsh lives, urban slaves had skilled jobs, free workers could keep their wages.

6. ANALYZING PRIMARY SOURCES
Possible Responses: Emerson suggests that all reform is positive and good, because it is brought about by humans, in whom he has a deep faith. He sees reformers as working for the "truth and good" in society. Students might refer to the positive changes brought about during the mid-19th-century reform era, and to the contributions made by specific reformers. Students who do not share Emerson's attitude toward reform might suggest that reform is a lengthy, not always successful, process, and that some reformers were motivated by their own selfish interests rather than the public good. They may also suggest that one person alone cannot accomplish much.

HISTORY AND ART

Soldiers in the trenches of Petersburg, Virginia

Photograph by unknown artist (1865).

Art Note

Beginning with a photograph taken at Fort Sumter three days after its capture by the South, about 2,000 photographers took about one million pictures of the Civil War. Many were portraits, but some showed soldiers in the field or the death and devastation after battle. Most photographers worked for businesses that sold prints of their images. Some photographers were hired by the armies and governments of North and South.

▶ *Previewing the Unit*

Unit 3 opens with a description of how the United States expands to the Pacific Ocean. While the nation grows, so does conflict between North and South. The Southern states decide to leave the Union to preserve their way of life. The North wins a long, bloody civil war. In its aftermath, African Americans briefly are granted full civil rights—until the federal government stops preventing discrimination.

UNIT 3

"Government of the people, by the people, for the people, shall not perish from the earth."

ABRAHAM LINCOLN

CHAPTER 9
1825–1850
Expanding Markets and Moving West

CHAPTER 10
1850–1861
The Union in Peril

CHAPTER 11
1861–1865
The Civil War

CHAPTER 12
1865–1877
Reconstruction and Its Effects

250 UNIT 3

1825–1877
An Era of Growth and Disunion

1 Petersburg campaign
Confederate troops endured a 10-month siege starting in June 1864 to hold Petersburg, Virginia, a vital railroad center. Casualties, illness, lack of supplies, and desertions whittled their army down. Union troops finally captured the rail lines on April 2, 1865; one week later Lee surrendered to Grant.

2 Blurred image
Photography in this period required fairly long exposure time for the film . Subjects had to remain still for at least several seconds and often much longer; if they moved, they created a blurred image, as here. This explains why there are almost no photographs of Civil War soldiers in combat.

3 Volunteers
Most of the soldiers on both sides volunteered. They joined units that were organized by state. They were amateur soldiers from all walks of life who received little training before going into battle.

251

Discussing the Quotation

Lincoln's words are taken from the Gettysburg Address. He delivered the speech at the dedication of a cemetery for soldiers killed in the war.

FOR DISCUSSION:
- How do Lincoln's words connect the cause of the North with the principles of the American Revolution?
- How do his words give meaning to the sacrifice of those who were killed?
- Could the soldiers in this photograph be considered as part of an army of, by, and for the people?

Discussing the Image

Exhibitions of civil war photographs were one way of informing people about the war. After one such exhibition, an observer said, "Mr. Brady [the photographer] has brought home the terrible earnestness of war."

FOR DISCUSSION:
- Why did photographs like these have such an impact on people?
- What other ways might Americans at home have of getting news from the front during the war?

4 Trench warfare
For much of the war, soldiers built extensive earthworks like these trenches. Troops attacking entrenched armies often suffered heavy casualties. Diseases spread quickly among soliders in trenches.

5 Supplies
The photo reveals the superior resources of the North. The soldiers all wear complete uniforms. Some have capes, and some have large packs. Southern troops lacked clothing, food, and ammunition throughout the war. By Petersburg, near the war's end, their shortages were severe.

6 The landscape
Four years of war left many areas—especially in the South—devastated. The area around these Union soldiers is largely bare of trees, which were cut down to make fortifications, buildings, and campfires or were destroyed by fire.

	Key Ideas	TEACHING SUPPORT	ASSESSMENT
SECTION 1 The Market Revolution *pp. 254–259*	Technological changes create greater economic interdependence and more economic diversity among the regions of the nation.	***In-Depth Resources: Unit 3*** • Guided Reading, p. 1 • Primary Source: Advertisement, p. 8 👥 **COOPERATIVE ACTIVITY** • Researching the Electronics Revolution, p. 256 (TE)	***Section 1 Assessment,*** p. 259 (PE) ***Self-Assessment,*** p. 259 (TE) ***Formal Assessment*** • Section Quiz, p. 113 ***Alternative Assessment Book*** • Standards for Evaluating a Cooperative Activity
SECTION 2 Manifest Destiny *pp. 260–265*	Increasing numbers of people move west and use the idea of Manifest Destiny to justify settling the land.	***In-Depth Resources: Unit 3*** • Guided Reading, p. 2 • Skillbuilder Practice: Analyzing Assumptions, p. 5 • Primary Sources: Black Hawk's Farewell Speech, p. 9; On the Oregon Trail, p. 10 👥 **COOPERATIVE ACTIVITY** • Interviewing Settlers, p. 263 (TE)	***Section 2 Assessment,*** p. 265 (PE) ***Self-Assessment,*** p. 265 (TE) ***Formal Assessment*** • Section Quiz, p. 114 ***Alternative Assessment Book*** • Standards for Evaluating a Cooperative Activity
SECTION 3 Expansion in Texas *pp. 268–272*	American settlers flock to Texas when Mexico offers land grants, but conflict develops over religion and other cultural differences, including slavery.	***In-Depth Resources: Unit 3*** • Guided Reading, p. 3 • American Lives: Lorenza de Zavala, p. 15 👥 **COOPERATIVE ACTIVITY** • Creating a Pictorial Essay of the Alamo, p. 271 (TE)	***Section 3 Assessment,*** p. 272 (PE) ***Self-Assessment,*** p. 272 (TE) ***Formal Assessment*** • Section Quiz, p. 115 ***Alternative Assessment Book*** • Standards for Evaluating a Cooperative Activity
SECTION 4 The War with Mexico *pp. 273–277*	Tension over the U.S. annexation of Texas leads to war with Mexico and results in huge territorial gains for the United States.	***In-Depth Resources: Unit 3*** • Guided Reading, p. 4 • Geography Application: Mexico Cedes Land to the United States, p. 6 • Primary Source: President Polk's Speech, p. 9 • American Lives: Robert E. Lee, p. 16 👥 **COOPERATIVE ACTIVITY** • Creating a Newspaper About the Gold Rush, p. 276 (TE)	***Section 4 Assessment,*** p. 277 (PE) ***Self-Assessment,*** p. 277 (TE) ***Formal Assessment*** • Section Quiz, p. 116 ***Alternative Assessment Book*** • Standards for Evaluating a Cooperative Activity
CHAPTER RESOURCES	**Chapter Overview** The economy of the United States grows, and so does the nation's territory, as settlers move west. Texas is annexed from Mexico, and vast lands in the west are obtained by war.	***In-Depth Resources: Unit 3*** • Living History Project: Worksheet, p. 17; Standards, p. 18 ***Telescoping the Times*** • Chapter Summary, pp. 17–18 ***Planning for Block Schedules***	***Chapter Assessment,*** pp. 278–279 (PE) ***Alternative Assessment,*** p. 279 (PE) ***Formal Assessment*** • Chapter Test, forms A and B, pp. 117–121 💻 **Test Generator** ***Alternative Assessment Book*** See explanation and forms for different kinds of alternative assessments including portfolio assessment.

Geography Transparencies
• G9, American Cities: 1820, 1860

Grolier Multimedia Encyclopedia
• Charles Goodyear; Samuel Morse

INTERNET RESOURCES
• See Interact with History, p. 257 (PE) for an activity that includes the Internet as an enrichment option.

Electronic Library of Primary Sources
• from *The Discovery of the Oregon Trail* by Robert Stuart

INTERNET RESOURCES
• See Interact with History, p. 267 (PE) for an activity that includes the Internet as an enrichment option.

Grolier Multimedia Encyclopedia
• Stephen F. Austin, Texas Revolution

Electronic Library of Primary Sources
• "Alamo Massacre" by Andrea Castañón Villanueva

INTERNET RESOURCES
• See *McDougal Littell Learning On-Line* for such topics as the Alamo and Sam Houston.

Humanities Transparencies
• H9, *General Winfield Scott*

Critical Thinking Transparencies
• CT9, Westward Movement
• CT43, Growth of U.S. Population and Area: 1790–1850

Electronic Library of Primary Sources
• from The Treaty of Guadalupe Hidalgo; from *The Golden Frontier*

INTERNET RESOURCES
• See *McDougal Littell Learning On-Line* for such topics as the California gold rush.

American Portfolio: A Videodisc for U.S. History, user's guide, pp. 60–61, 79–85

INTERNET RESOURCES
Learning On-Line: Social Studies
http://www.mcdougallittell.com

Block Scheduling (90 MINUTES)

Day 1

Section 1, pp. 254–259

Section 2, pp. 260–265

Section Assessments, pp. 259, 265

Geography Spotlight: Mapping the Oregon Trail, pp. 266–267

Day 2

Section 3, pp. 268–272

Section 4, pp. 273–277

Review Sections 1–4

Chapter Assessment, pp. 278–279

YEARLY PACING *Chapter 9 Total:* 2 days *Yearly Total:* 85 days

See *Planning for Block Schedules* for special activities and pacing strategies.

Customizing for Special Populations

Students Acquiring English

Access for Students Acquiring English
• Guided Reading for Sections 1–4 (Spanish), pp. 92–95
• Chapter Summary (Spanish), pp. 90–91
• Skillbuilder Practice: Analyzing Assumptions (Spanish), p. 96
• Geography Application: Mexico Cedes Land to the United States, p. 97

INTERNET RESOURCES
• See *McDougal Littell Learning On-Line* The Diverse Classroom.

Less Proficient Readers

In-Depth Resources: Unit 3
• Guided Reading for Sections 1–4, pp. 1–4
• Skillbuilder: Analyzing Assumptions, p. 5
• Geography Application: Mexico Cedes Land to the United States, p. 6

Telescoping the Times
• Chapter Summary, pp. 17–18

See additional strategies at point of use in the Teacher's Edition.

Gifted and Talented Students

In-Depth Resources: Unit 3
• Primary Sources: Advertisement, p. 8; Black Hawk's Farewell Speech, p. 9; On the Oregon Trail, p. 10; *from* President James Polk's Speech, p. 11
• American Lives: Lorenza de Zavala, p. 15; Robert E. Lee, p. 16

See additional strategies at point of use in the Teacher's Edition.

Connections to Literature READINGS FOR STUDENTS

In-Depth Resources: Unit 3
• from *Roughing It* by Mark Twain, p. 12

Enrichment Reading
• Harte, Bret
"The Outcasts of Poker Flat," from *The Outcasts of Poker Flat and other Selected Stories.*
New York: American House, 1982.
In this story of the west, characters with limited provisions in an overnight camp in the mountains face a snowstorm.

• Marius, Richard
Bound for the Promised Land.
Nashville, Tenn.: Rutledge Hill Press, 1993.
As he searches for his father who disappeared during the California gold rush, a young man crosses the country with a collection of naive adventurers and scoundrels.

• Michener, James
Texas.
New York: Ballantine, 1987.
Spanning four and a half centuries, this saga of Texas begins in the early 1500s. Paths of the characters and their descendants cross and recross as the narrative develops.

Expanding Markets and Moving West

▶ *Starting with the Student*
Ask students what they know about the technological advances and westward expansion of the mid–19th century. Then discuss the opening quotation. Ask the following:

• What did people expect to gain by settling in this "new and happy land"?
• Why did the West attract the American people?

PREVIEWING THE CHAPTER
• Go over the time line and images in class. Ask students to identify the events and people they want to learn more about.
• Ask students to jot down questions that they hope will be answered in the chapter.

MORE ABOUT . . .
Ignatius Donnelly
Ignatius Donnelly (1831–1901) was a reformer and politician who helped form the Populist Party. The Populist Party advocated changes that would support the common people, especially laborers and farmers, many of whom migrated west. Born in Philadelphia, Donnelly took his own advice about moving west and in 1857 settled in Minnesota.

CHAPTER
9

Expanding Markets and Moving West

SECTION 1
The Market Revolution
Technological changes create greater economic interdependence and more economic diversity among the regions of the nation.

SECTION 2
Manifest Destiny
Increasing numbers of people move west and use the idea of Manifest Destiny to justify settling the land.

SECTION 3
Expansion in Texas
American settlers flock to Texas when Mexico offers land grants, but conflict develops over religion and other cultural differences, including slavery.

SECTION 4
The War with Mexico
Tension over the U.S. annexation of Texas leads to war with Mexico and results in huge territorial gains for the United States.

"Why should we weep to sail in search of fortune? Cheer for the West, the new and happy land."

Ignatius Donnelly

Chief Black Hawk, as portrayed by Charles Bird King (1833), leads Sauk in rebellion against the United States.

● The Erie Canal connects the East to the regions west of the Appalachians.

✪ Andrew Jackson is elected president.

● Joseph Smith establishes the Mormon church.

✪ Andrew Jackson is reelected.

THE UNITED STATES					
1825		**1828**	**1830**	**1832**	
THE WORLD	1826	1828		1831	1833

● Russia declares war on Persia.

● Uruguay becomes an independent republic.

● Belgium separates from the Netherlands.

● Great Britain passes first child labor law.

252 CHAPTER 9

THEMES IN CHAPTER 9

Economic Opportunity	*Cultural Diversity*	*Immigration and Migration*	*Constitutional Concerns*
The accelerating pace of the U.S. economy spurred investment in new industries. Many businessmen prospered during the market revolution, but their laborers didn't always share in the profits. See Teacher's Edition note, p. 255.	Most Native Americans, when forced from their traditional lands by U.S. westward expansion, tried to retain their cultural traditions. To preserve their heritage, some Native Americans fought to keep white settlers away from their homes. See Teacher's Edition note, p. 262.	The people who migrated west braved long journeys and rough living conditions to pursue the promise of new land. During the 1820s, the Mexican government offered enormous land grants that lured many American settlers to Texas. See Teacher's Edition note, p. 269.	To acquire new territory, President Polk wanted to go to war against Mexico in 1846. However, as stipulated in the Constitution, he first had to convince Congress to declare war. See Teacher's Edition note, p. 274.

LIVING HISTORY

ADVERTISING A NEW INVENTION

During the mid-19th century, inventions and improvements changed the way Americans lived and worked. Choose one of the inventions or technological improvements mentioned in the chapter and create an advertisement that would make it attractive to people of the era. Use these guidelines to help you prepare your ad:

- Identify the audience that your advertisement would target.
- Think about the qualities of the invention or improvement that you want to emphasize.
- Come up with a catchy slogan to reach your audience.

📁 **PORTFOLIO PROJECT** Sketch a simple version of your advertisement to save in a folder for your American history portfolio. You will revise and share your work at the end of this chapter.

ADVERTISING A NEW INVENTION

Offer students these suggestions for generating ideas for their ads:

- Consider why popular, modern ads are successful.
- Then consider how these ads reach their audience. Do the ads use language and images that appeal to a certain group?

Project Planning Guide

Step 1	Students study both contemporary and 19th-century ads for ideas.
Step 2	Students choose a focus for their ad.
Step 3	Students decide what feature of the invention or improvement they want to emphasize.
Step 4	Students use humor, slogans, and graphics to reach their audience.
Step 5	Students place the ad in their folder.

IN-DEPTH RESOURCES: UNIT 3
See worksheet and standards for evaluation, pp. 17, 18.

Sam Houston *(above)* is elected president of the Republic of Texas.

Brigham Young and the Mormons found Salt Lake City.

John Deere invents the steel plow.

Samuel F. B. Morse sends first long-distance telegraph message.

California gold rush begins.

Treaty of Guadalupe Hidalgo ends the U.S. war with Mexico.

Charles Goodyear invents vulcanized rubber.

John Tyler becomes president when President Harrison dies.

Martin Van Buren is elected president.

James K. Polk is elected president.

Zachary Taylor is elected president.

1836 1837 1839 1840 1841 1844 1847 1848 1850
1835 1837 1842 1847 1848

Ferdinand I becomes emperor of Austria.

Constitutional revolts occur in Lower and Upper Canada.

Treaty of Nanjing resolves Opium War between Britain and China.

Liberia becomes a republic.

Marx and Engels issue the *Communist Manifesto*.

Expanding Markets and Moving West **253**

RECOMMENDED RESOURCES

Books for the Teacher

de Voto, Bernard. *Year of Decision: 1846.* Boston: Little, 1943. Westward expansion.

Eisenhower, John S. D. *So Far from God.* New York: Random, 1978. Narrative of Mexican War.

Goetzmann, William H. *Exploration and Empire.* New York: Norton, 1978. Explorers.

Books for the Student

Schlissel, Lillian, ed. *Women's Diaries of the Westward Journey.* New York: Schoken, 1992. Women pioneers' experiences in their own words.

Smith, George Winston, and Charles Judah, eds. *Chronicles of the Gringos.* Albuquerque: U of New Mexico Press, 1968. U.S. soldiers' accounts of the Mexican War.

Videos

Adelante Mujeres 1992. Women Make Movies, 212-925-0606. Story of Mexican-American women from Spanish conquest to today.

The Alamo. A&E Home Video, 1966. Two-tape documentary.

The Donner Party. PBS Home Video, 1992. Story of ill-fated wagon train.

Software

500 Nations. CD-ROM. Microsoft, 800-555-4512.

The Oregon Trail. CD-ROM. MECC, 1993. 6160 Summit Drive North, Minneapolis, MN 55430-4003.

The Santa Fe Trail. Diskette. Educational Activities, 800-645-3739.

OBJECTIVES

1 To describe how industrialization and capitalism shaped the U.S. economy.

2 To identify the inventions that enhanced people's lives and helped fuel the country's economic growth.

3 To explain how improved transportation and communication helped link America's regions and made them interdependent.

CRITICAL THINKING

• Recognizing effects, pp. 255, 258
• Contrasting, p. 257
• Analyzing causes, p. 258
• Drawing conclusions, p. 259
• Summarizing, p. 259
• Comparing, p. 259

FOCUS & MOTIVATE

▶ *Starting with the Student*
• Ask students what inventions and technologies have made their lives more enjoyable.
• Have them discuss how these technologies might have helped the economy.

MORE ABOUT . . .
The Erie Canal

In 1815, the profession of civil engineering was unknown in the United States. The construction of the Erie Canal was largely supervised by three men—James Geddes, Benjamin Wright, and Canvass White—who had little engineering training and experience. White, for example, traveled to England and walked along 2,000 miles of towpaths in order to learn about canal construction. As the president of the American Society of Civil Engineering observed in 1882, "Few men have ever accomplished so much with so little means."

---

❶ The Market Revolution

TERMS & NAMES
• specialization
• market revolution
• capitalism
• entrepreneur
• Samuel F. B. Morse
• telegraph
• John Deere
• Cyrus McCormick

LEARN ABOUT innovations in transportation, communication, and manufacturing during the early 19th century
TO UNDERSTAND how markets for products grew rapidly throughout the United States.

ONE AMERICAN'S STORY

At sunrise on July 4, 1817, a cannon blast from the United States arsenal in Rome, New York, announced the groundbreaking for the Erie Canal. With visiting dignitaries and local residents in attendance, many leaning on shovels to symbolize the digging of the canal, Samuel Young opened the groundbreaking ceremony.

A PERSONAL VOICE
We have assembled here to commence the excavation of the Erie Canal. This work when accomplished will connect our western inland seas with the Atlantic Ocean. . . . By this great highway, unborn millions will easily transport their surplus productions to the shores of the Atlantic, procure their supplies, and hold a useful and profitable intercourse with all the maritime nations of the earth. . . . Let us proceed then to the work, animated by the prospect of its speedy accomplishment, and cheered with the anticipated benedictions of a grateful posterity.

SAMUEL YOUNG, quoted in *Erie Water West*

Boats often formed traffic jams while waiting to pass through the locks on the Erie Canal, shown in this 1838 engraving of Lockport, New York.

Although the engineers on the canal project had more eagerness than experience, they successfully supervised a work force that built 83 locks to raise and lower barges. When it was completed, the canal stretched 363 miles from Albany, New York, to Lake Erie.

On November 4, 1825, a fleet of boats traveled to the gala opening celebration in New York City and fulfilled Young's predictions. The lead boat, the *Seneca Chief*, carried whitefish from Lake Erie and flour and butter from Michigan, Ohio, and Buffalo, New York, to the people of New York City. At the celebration, New York's governor, De Witt Clinton, poured a keg of water from Lake Erie into the Atlantic Ocean as the crowd cheered the "Wedding of the Waters."

As Young implied, the freight of the *Seneca Chief* symbolized the economic importance of the canal. The canal ushered in a new era, in which technology and improved transportation sent new products to markets across the United States.

U.S. Markets Expand

In the early 19th century, rural American workers had produced their own goods or traded with neighbors to supply almost all of their needs. Farm families grew crops and raised animals for food and made their own clothing, candles, and soap. At local markets, family members sold wood, eggs, or butter for cash, which they used to purchase the coffee, tea, sugar, and horseshoes they couldn't produce themselves.

By mid-century, however, the United States had become more industrialized, especially in the Northeast, where the rise of textile mills and the factory system changed the lives of both workers and consumers. Now, workers spent their earnings on goods produced by other workers. Farmers began to shift from self-sufficiency—raising a wide variety of food for their own families—to **specialization,** raising one or two crops that they could sell at home or abroad.

SECTION 1 RESOURCES

PRINT RESOURCES

IN-DEPTH RESOURCES: UNIT 3
Guided Reading, p. 1
Primary Source: Advertisement, p. 8

ACCESS FOR STUDENTS ACQUIRING ENGLISH
Guided Reading (Spanish), p. 92

FORMAL ASSESSMENT
Section Quiz, p. 113

ALTERNATIVE ASSESSMENT BOOK
See forms for supporting and scoring alternate activities.

TECHNOLOGY RESOURCES

GEOGRAPHY TRANSPARENCIES
G9, American Cities: 1820, 1860

CD-ROM *Grolier Multimedia Encyclopedia*

VIDEO *American Portfolio: A Videodisc for U.S. History*
user's guide, pp. 60, 61, 85

INTERNET McDougal Littell Learning On-Line
http://www.mcdougallittell.com

These developments brought about a **market revolution,** in which people bought and sold goods rather than making them for themselves. The market revolution led to a striking change in the U.S. economy and in the daily lives of Americans. Over a few decades, goods and services multiplied while incomes rose. In fact, in the decade of the 1840s, the national economy grew more than it had in the first 40 years of the century.

THE ENTREPRENEURIAL SPIRIT The quickening pace of U.S. economic growth depended on **capitalism,** the economic system in which private businesses and individuals control the means of production—such as factories, machines, and land—and use them to earn profits. For example, in 1813, Francis Cabot Lowell and his fellow Boston merchants had put up $400,000 to form the Boston Manufacturing Company, which produced textiles. Other businessmen supplied their own funds to create capital—the money, property, machines, and factories that fueled America's expanding economy.

These businessmen, called **entrepreneurs** from a French word that means "to undertake," invested their own money in new industries. In doing this, entrepreneurs risked losing their investment if a venture failed, but they also stood to earn huge profits if they succeeded. Alexander Mackay, a Scottish journalist who lived in Canada and traveled in the United States, applauded the entrepreneurs' competitive spirit.

> **A PERSONAL VOICE**
> America is a country in which great fortunes have yet to be made. . . . All cannot be made wealthy, but all have a chance of securing a prize. This stimulates to the race, and hence the eagerness of the competition.
> **ALEXANDER MACKAY,** quoted in *The Western World*

IMPACT ON HOUSEHOLD ECONOMY While entrepreneurial activity boosted America's industrial output, American agriculture continued to flourish. Workers in industrial cities needed food, which they could not produce on their own. To meet this demand for food, American farmers began to use mechanized farm equipment produced in factories. Farmers, therefore, produced important goods for the American industrial machine and became important consumers of manufactured items.

Manufactured items grew less expensive as technological advances lowered prices. For example, a clock that had cost $50 to craft by hand in 1800 could be turned out by machine for half a dollar by mid-century. Falling prices meant that many American workers, on farms as well as in cities, became consumers and purchased new products not only for work, but for comfort as well.

Inventions and Improvements

New inventions and technologies, many developed or perfected in the United States, contributed immensely to changes in American life. While some inventions simply made life more enjoyable, others fueled the economic revolution of mid-century and transformed manufacturing, transportation, and communication.

SHOES AND SEWING MACHINES Inventor-entrepreneurs began to develop goods to make life more comfortable for more people. For example, Charles

A. Answer The cost of consumer goods dropped so more workers could become consumers.

THINK THROUGH HISTORY
A. Recognizing Effects Describe the impact of the market revolution on potential consumers.

Singer's foot-treadle sewing machine was patented in 1851 and soon dominated the industry.

(continued from page 255)

▶ **Discussing Key Ideas**
- Vulcanized rubber and the sewing machine bring improvements to private life and to industry.
- The telegraph is a boon to business communication and to transportation.
- Farmers and manufacturers use new waterways and railroads to ship their goods.

KEY PLAYER
Samuel F. B. Morse
Critical Thinking:
Analyzing Ask students to speculate on the impact the telegraph had on the press's reporting of the news. *Possible Response: The telegraph could have been used to transmit news as soon as it happened to any newspaper connected to a telegraphic system.* Ask them what machines today have replaced the telegraph. *Possible Responses: telephones, computers, communications satellites.*
Ask students to find the Morse code in an encyclopedia and to create a brief message using the system of dots and dashes. Then have students form pairs and translate their partner's message.

GROLIER MULTIMEDIA ENCYCLOPEDIA
Samuel Morse

KEY PLAYER

SAMUEL F. B. MORSE
1791–1872

While Samuel Morse was a student at Yale University, he learned about the new science of electricity and constructed batteries in a chemistry class. More interested in art than science, however, Morse embarked on a distinguished career in painting. Realizing that he would never support himself as an artist, Morse continued his scientific work.

By the end of 1837, Morse and an associate named Leonard Gale had built an electromagnetic telegraph. Morse's first model could send messages 10 miles on a wire that wound continuously around his workroom.

Congress granted Morse $30,000 in 1843 to build a test line between Baltimore and Washington, D.C. The successful transmission of his coded message won the inventor international fame.

Goodyear developed vulcanized rubber in 1839. Unlike untreated India rubber, the new product didn't freeze in cold weather or melt in hot weather. Although people first used vulcanized rubber to protect their boots and shoes from snow and mud, the product eventually became indispensable for automobile tires.

A natural place for the growth of industrialization was in producing clothing, a process greatly aided by the invention of the sewing machine. Patented by Elias Howe in 1846, the sewing machine found its first use in shoe factories. Homemakers appreciated I. M. Singer's addition of the foot treadle, which drastically reduced the time it took to sew garments. More importantly, the treadle sewing machine led to the factory production of clothing. When clothing prices tumbled by more than 75 percent, increasing numbers of working people could afford to buy clothes at a store.

INSTANT COMMUNICATION As new transportation links carried goods and people across vast spaces, new communication links began to put people into instant contact with one another. Improving on a device developed by Joseph Henry, **Samuel F. B. Morse,** a New England artist, created the **telegraph** in 1837. In 1844, Morse tapped out in code the words "What hath God wrought?" The message sped from Washington, D.C., over a metal wire. In less than a second, Morse's words had reached Baltimore, Maryland, prompting an immediate reply. Morse's successful long-distance transmission fulfilled the predictions that Benjamin French, an assistant clerk of the House of Representatives, had made: "[The telegraph] is one of the greatest inventions of the age, and will eventually be laid down all over the Union."

Businessmen used the new communication device to transmit orders and relay up-to-date information on prices and sales. The new railroads employed the telegraph to keep trains moving regularly and to warn engineers of safety hazards. By 1853, 23,000 miles of telegraph wire crossed the country.

THE TRANSPORTATION REVOLUTION Better and faster transportation became essential to the expansion of agriculture and industry. Farmers and manufacturers alike sought more direct ways to ship their goods to market. In 1807, Pennsylvanian Robert Fulton had ushered in the steamboat era when his boat, the *Clermont,* made the 150-mile trip up the Hudson River from New York City to Albany in 32 hours—very fast for the era. Ships that had previously only been able to drift southward down the Mississippi with the current could now turn around to make the return trip because they were powered by steam engines. By 1830, 200 steamboats traveled the nation's western rivers that flowed into the Mississippi and slashed freight rates as well as voyage times.

NOW THEN

From Telegraph to Internet

What do the telegraph and the Internet have in common? They are both tools for instant communication. While the telegraph relied on a network of wires that spanned the country, the Internet—an international network of smaller computer networks—allows any computer user to communicate instantly with any other computer user in the world.

1837
Samuel Morse invents the telegraph, the first instant electronic communicator. Morse taps on a key to send bursts of electricity down a wire to the receiver, where an operator "translates" the coded bursts into understandable language—within seconds after they are sent.

256 CHAPTER 9

TEACHING OPTION

Cooperative Activity: Researching the Electronics Revolution

Task: Small groups of students will research and write reports on modern forms of electronic communication.

Purpose: To explore the impact of inventions on today's society.

Activity: Each student in the group will prepare a report on one form of modern electronic communication: computer, fax machine, e-mail, or the Internet, for example. If possible, students should use computers and the

Internet to conduct their research. They might also illustrate their reports with computer graphics. Group members should then get together to discuss their findings and compile their reports.

📁 **Building a Portfolio:** Students who add the report to their portfolio should attach a note indicating their own contribution.

ALTERNATIVE ASSESSMENT BOOK
Standards for Evaluating a Cooperative Activity

Standards for Evaluation
Reports should . . .

- be well documented with facts
- use specific details to support statements
- be clear and well organized
- include graphics that illustrate students' findings

256 **Chapter 9**

Water transport was particularly important in moving raw materials such as lead and copper, and heavy machinery. Where waterways didn't exist, Americans excavated them. In 1816, America had dug a mere 100 miles of canals. A quarter of a century later, the country boasted more than 3,300 miles of canals.

The Erie Canal was the nation's first major canal, and it was used heavily. Shipping charges fell to about a tenth of the cost of sending goods over land. Before the first shovel broke ground on the Erie Canal in 1817, for example, freight charges between Buffalo, New York, and New York City averaged 19 cents a ton per mile. By 1830, costs had fallen to less than two cents a ton per mile.

The canal's success led to dozens of other canal projects. Farmers in Ohio no longer depended on Mississippi passage to New Orleans. They could now ship their grain via canal and river to New York City, the nation's major port.

1953

Improvements in electronic communication lead to the development of one of the first computers, at the University of Pennsylvania. The government soon begins using computers for scientific and intelligence work. However, during the Cold War, fear of nuclear war leads to the search for a communication system safe from bombing and not dependent on a central authority.

1876

Alexander Graham Bell invents the telephone, which relies on a steady stream of electricity, rather than electrical bursts, to transmit sounds. Advances in the telephone have made it possible today to pick up a phone and talk to someone halfway around the world or even in space!

1964

Scientists come up with the idea of a decentralized computer network that sends messages in small packets from one computer station to another. The Pentagon develops several supercomputer centers that can transfer data from individual computers to other computers on high-speed transmission lines. However, this first and very successful network is soon overworked and outdated. As more universities and individuals join the network, they refine the system and form the complex of networks called the Internet.

1997

Today, on the Internet, through e-mail (electronic mail) or on-line conversation, any two people can have instant dialogue. The Internet is growing incredibly fast, partly because of the relatively reasonable cost of belonging to a network and using its services. The Internet has become the modern tool for instant global communication not only of words, but images, too. And it is just as amazing now as the telegraph was in its time.

INTERACT WITH HISTORY

1. **CONTRASTING** Based on what you have read, what advantages does the Internet have over the telegraph?

   SEE SKILLBUILDER HANDBOOK, PAGE 1041.

2. **EXPLORING THE INTERNET** On a computer, access the Internet and try to find information about the origin and use of this modern-day communication phenomenon.

    For more about using the Internet, click on *Social Studies* at http://www.mcdougallittell.com

Expanding Markets and Moving West **257**

NOW & THEN
From Telegraph to Internet

▶ ***Starting with the Student***

Have students think about futuristic inventions for communicating that have been featured in science fiction movies or stories. Ask the following:

• What are these devices and how do they work?

• If these devices actually existed, how would they revolutionize people's lives?

▶ ***Discussing Key Ideas***

• The telegraph, the telephone, and the Internet all represent amazing breakthroughs in communication.

• Advances in computer technology pave the way for more sophisticated electronic communication systems.

• The Internet provides instant global communication.

INTERACT WITH HISTORY

1. Contrasting

Possible Responses: *Advantages of the Internet include the efficiency of transmission; more direct communication, either by e-mail or on-line conversations; messages not coded, greater potential to broaden its application; more affordable for people to purchase.*

2. Exploring the Internet

Have students use the following steps to explore the Internet:

1. Go to Learning on Line, McDougal Littell's web site.
2. Choose Social Studies.
3. Choose Teachers' Lounge.
4. Choose Teacher-Links Library.
5. Choose *The Americans,* Chapter 9.

To help guide students in their research, encourage them to generate a list of questions about the history and use of the Internet.

New Markets Link Regions

▶ *Starting with the Student*
- Ask students what industries thrive in their region of the United States.
- Ask them what kinds of products are in short supply.

▶ *Discussing Key Ideas*
- The Northeast becomes the country's center of commerce, producing manufactured goods affordable for most Americans.
- Two efficient, inexpensive inventions—the steel plow and the mechanical reaper—help farmers cultivate land and harvest crops in the Midwest.
- The South remains agricultural, relying on crops such as cotton, tobacco, and rice.

 GEOGRAPHY TRANSPARENCIES
G9, American Cities, 1820, 1860

ON THE WORLD STAGE
Britain's Cotton Imports
Critical Thinking: Interpreting
Ask students to explain the significance of the statement, "Cotton is King." *Possible Responses: Cotton reigns as the most significant source of income in the South's economy; cotton dominates life in the South; cotton's sphere of influence extends to Great Britain, where cotton directly or indirectly provides jobs; cotton exerts intimidating power over the British.*

The canals also opened the heartland of America to world markets by binding the Northeast to the Midwest.

EMERGENCE OF RAILROADS The heyday of the canals lasted only until the 1860s, though, due to the rapid emergence of railroads. Although shipping by rail cost significantly more in the 1840s than did shipping by canal, railroads offered the important advantage of speed. In addition, they could operate in the winter, and they brought goods to people who did not live near waterways. By the 1840s, steam engines pulled freight at ten miles an hour—more than four times faster than canal boats traveled. Passengers found such speeds exciting also, although early train travel was far from comfortable, as Samuel Breck, a Philadelphia merchant, complained.

A PERSONAL VOICE
If one could stop when one wanted, and if one were not locked up in a box with 50 or 60 tobacco-chewers; and the engine and fire did not burn holes in one's clothes . . . and the smell of the smoke, of the oil, and of the chimney did not poison one . . . and [one] were not in danger of being blown sky-high or knocked off the rails—it would be the perfection of travelling.
SAMUEL BRECK, quoted in *American Railroads*

Eventually, railroads grew to be both safe and reliable, and the cost of rail freight gradually came down. By 1850, almost 10,000 miles of track had been laid, and by 1859, railroads carried 2 billion tons of freight a year.

New Markets Link Regions

By the 1840s, improved transportation and communication made America's regions interdependent. Steamboats went up as well as down the Mississippi, linking North to South. The Erie Canal, railroads, and telegraph wires now linked the East and the West. Arteries like the National Road, funded by Congress in 1816, had also opened up western travel. By 1818, the road extended from Cumberland, Maryland, west to Wheeling, Virginia; by 1852, it reached as far west as Vandalia, Illinois.

ON THE WORLD STAGE
BRITAIN'S COTTON IMPORTS
By 1836, the American South, the world's leading producer of cotton, was also the leading supplier of cotton to Great Britain. In all, Great Britain imported three-quarters of its cotton from the South, and sent back manufactured goods in return. Cotton directly or indirectly provided work for one in five people in Britain, then the world's leading industrial power.

For its part, Britain relied so heavily on Southern cotton that cotton growers incorrectly assumed that the British would actively support the South during the Civil War. "No power on earth dares to make war upon it," a South Carolina senator boldly declared in 1858, "Cotton is King."

The growing links between America's regions contributed to the development of regional specialties. The East manufactured textiles and machinery. The West's grain and livestock fed hungry factory workers in eastern cities and in Europe. The South exported its cotton to England as well as to New England.

NORTHEAST SHIPPING AND MANUFACTURING Heavy investment in canals and railroads transformed the Northeast into the center of American commerce. Following the opening of the Erie Canal in 1825, New York City became the central link between American agriculture and European markets. In fact, more cotton was exported through New York than through any other American city.

The most striking development of the era, however, was the rise in manufacturing. Although most Americans still lived in rural areas and only 14 percent of workers had manufacturing jobs, these workers produced more and better goods at lower prices than had ever been produced before. Many of these goods became affordable for ordinary Americans, and improvements in transportation allowed people to purchase items from distant places. Some products, like farm equipment, helped make people more productive, too.

MIDWEST FARMING As the Northeast began to industrialize, many people moved to farm the fertile soil of the Midwest. First, however, they had to work very hard to make the land arable, or fit to cultivate.

THINK THROUGH HISTORY
B. Recognizing Effects How did new products, communication methods, and modes of transportation help the U.S. economy to grow?

B. Answer New products led to growing numbers of consumers. New methods of communication and transportation made the operation of business more efficient and profitable.

THINK THROUGH HISTORY
C. Analyzing Causes How did the transportation revolution bind U.S. regions to one another and to the rest of the world?

C. Answer Canals, railroads, and improved roads reduced the price of shipping goods from one region to another, and moved products from the country's interior to international ports like New York City.

TEACHING OPTIONS

Making Connections Across Time

Transporting Freight Today Tell students that trains are still used more than any other means of transportation to convey freight in the United States. Trucks carry the second largest amount. Ships are also used, because they provide the least expensive means of sending freight. Air transport is used only infrequently because of the high costs involved. Ask students to do some research and to create a chart to compare the advantages and disadvantages of these forms of freight transportation today.

Making Connections Across the Curriculum

Literature Nineteenth-century American writers Walt Whitman, Emily Dickinson, and Henry David Thoreau all found railroads and locomotives fascinating. Ask students to read the following literary examples:
- "To a Locomotive in Winter" by Walt Whitman (poem)
- "I Like to See It Lap for Miles" by Emily Dickinson (poem)
- "Sounds" from *Walden* by Henry David Thoreau (prose)

Invite students to compare and contrast each writer's portrayal of the locomotive.

Many wooded areas had to be cleared before fields could be planted. Two ingenious inventions allowed farmers to develop the fertile farmland more efficiently and cheaply, and made farming more profitable. In 1837, a blacksmith named **John Deere** invented the steel plow, which enabled farmers to replace their oxen with faster horses. By the late 1850s, Deere's factory in Moline, Illinois, was selling 13,000 plows each year.

Once harvest time arrived, **Cyrus McCormick's** invention, the mechanical reaper, permitted one farmer to do the work of five hired hands. The reaper was packed in parts and shipped to the farmer, along with a handbook of directions for assembling and operating the machine.

Armed with plows and reapers, ambitious farmers could shift from subsistence farming to growing cash crops, such as wheat and corn. The same trains and canals that brought them plows and reapers from distant factories would then carry their crops to markets in the East and in Europe.

SOUTHERN AGRICULTURE While the Northeast embraced commerce and industry, most of the South remained agricultural and relied on such crops as cotton, tobacco, and rice. Southerners who had seen the North's "filthy, overcrowded, licentious factories" looked with disfavor on industrialization. Even if wealthy Southerners wanted to build factories, they usually lacked the capital to do so because they had invested so much in land and the slaves required to plant and harvest these crops.

Though the transportation and communication revolutions were less advanced in the South, these improvements helped keep Americans from every region in touch with one another. Furthermore, they changed the economic relationships between the regions, creating new markets where there had been none. Meanwhile, these changes encouraged Southerners as well as Northerners to seek land and wealth in the seemingly limitless West.

THINK THROUGH HISTORY
D. *Drawing*
Conclusions Why
were the reaper
and the steel plow
important?

D. Answer They
made farming
more efficient
and more
profitable.

"OUR FIELD IS THE WORLD."

McCormick Harvesting Machine Co., Chicago.
ESTABLISHED 1831.

The unusual shape of the McCormick reaper—which first appeared in 1851 at the Crystal Palace Exhibition in London—earned it a description in the London *Times* as "a cross between a flying machine, a wheelbarrow, and an Astly chariot."

Section **1** Assessment

1. TERMS & NAMES

Identify:
• specialization
• market revolution
• capitalism
• entrepreneur
• Samuel F. B. Morse
• telegraph
• John Deere
• Cyrus McCormick

2. SUMMARIZING Create a time line like the one below, on which you label and date the important innovations in transportation, communication, and manufacturing during the early 19th century.

1825   1850

Write a paragraph explaining which innovation was most important, and why.

3. COMPARING Describe the economies of the different regions of the United States in the mid-1800s. Use details from the section to support your answer.

4. DRAWING CONCLUSIONS During the 1830s and 1840s, transportation and communication linked the country more than ever before. How did these advances affect ordinary Americans?

THINK ABOUT
• the new kinds of transportation
• changes in communications

Expanding Markets and Moving West **259**

ANSWERS

1. TERMS & NAMES

specialization, p. 254

market revolution, p. 255

capitalism, p. 255

entrepreneur, p. 255

Samuel F. B. Morse, p. 256

telegraph, p. 256

John Deere, p. 259

Cyrus McCormick, p. 259

2. SUMMARIZING

Possible Answers: 1825—Erie Canal opens; 1837—Deere invents steel plow; 1839—Goodyear develops vulcanized rubber; 1844—Morse sends first telegraph message; 1846—Howe patents sewing machine.

3. COMPARING

Possible Answers: North—urban, industrial; South—agrarian, dependent on slave labor; Midwest—agricultural, important in supplying food to the East and to Europe.

4. DRAWING CONCLUSIONS

Possible Answers: Most students may indicate that new means of transportation brought ordinary Americans new goods to purchase and that the telegraph made instant communication possible between Americans in different parts of the country.

MORE ABOUT . . .
Southern Plantation
Owners
Planter-aristocrats provided much of the political and social leadership in the South. Their money purchased large mansions, fine furniture, and private education for their children. The rich planters lived like semifeudal lords, even occasionally staging jousting tournaments on their plantations.

IN-DEPTH RESOURCES: UNIT 3
Primary Source: Advertisement for McCormick's reaper, p. 8

ASSESS & RETEACH

Section 1 Assessment

Have pairs of students evaluate each other's responses before finalizing them.

Self-Assessment

To document what students have learned, have them make a list of the insights they have gained regarding the impact of technological changes on the American economy and on American society.

Section Quiz

FORMAL ASSESSMENT
Section Quiz, p. 113

Reteach

Use the time lines students created for item 2 on the Section Assessment to review key innovations of the early 19th century.

CLOSE

In the mid-1800s, industrialization helped expand markets throughout the United States. New developments in communication and transportation spurred the growth of agriculture and industry and linked the nation's regions. These developments also prompted many Americans to seek even greater opportunities in the West.

OBJECTIVES

(1) To summarize the reasons American settlers headed west during the mid-1800s.

(2) To describe the impact of westward expansion on Native Americans.

(3) To identify the westward trails and some of the people who used them.

SKILLBUILDERS

- Interpreting charts, p. 261
- Understanding geography; region, movement, p. 263

CRITICAL THINKING

- Clarifying, p. 261
- Analyzing causes, p. 261
- Recognizing effects, p. 262
- Analyzing motives, p. 265
- Forming opinions, p. 265
- Summarizing, p. 265
- Evaluating, p. 265
- Analyzing issues, p. 265

FOCUS & MOTIVATE

▶ **Starting with the Student**
Ask students to think about a time when they moved to a new community, changed schools, or experienced some other major change in their lives.

- Ask them whether they felt the change gave them an opportunity to make a fresh start.

OBJECTIVE
(1) **INSTRUCT**

The Frontier Lures Settlers

▶ **Discussing Key Ideas**
- Many Americans feel that westward expansion is the country's manifest destiny.
- Most Americans settle in the West for practical reasons—to claim land and to seek new markets.

IN-DEPTH RESOURCES: UNIT 3
Guided Reading, p. 2

ACCESS FOR STUDENTS ACQUIRING ENGLISH
Guided Reading (Spanish), p. 93

❷ Manifest Destiny

TERMS & NAMES
- manifest destiny
- Santa Fe Trail
- Oregon Trail
- Mormons
- Joseph Smith
- Brigham Young
- Fifty-Four Forty or Fight

LEARN ABOUT the lure of the West and the idea of manifest destiny
TO UNDERSTAND why Americans moved West in growing numbers.

ONE AMERICAN'S STORY

Amelia Stewart and Joel Knight met and married in Boston in 1834. Within a few years, the Knights moved to Iowa, where they settled for 16 years. In 1853, they gathered their seven children, packed their household belongings into a covered wagon, and headed west again.

Amelia Knight's diary of her family's five-month journey to Oregon began with a brief note, "Started From Home." She went on to describe the varied scenery, "the beautiful Boise River, with her green timber," which delighted the family, as well as the "months of travel on the dry, dusty sage plains, with nothing to relieve the eye." She told of camping by hot springs where she could brew tea without starting a fire, of cows dying along the road, and of the rich wild currants that provided a family feast. Knight wrote her last entry when she and her family reached their destination, Oregon.

A PERSONAL VOICE

[M]y eighth child was born. After this we picked up and ferried across the Columbia River, utilizing skiff, canoes and flatboat to get across, taking three days to complete. Here husband traded two yoke of oxen for a half section of land with one-half acre planted to potatoes and a small log cabin and lean-to with no windows. This is the journey's end.

AMELIA STEWART KNIGHT, quoted in *Covered Wagon Women*

Amelia Stewart Knight

Knight's situation was by no means unique; probably one in five women who made the trek was pregnant. Her condition, however, did nothing to lighten her workload, as every woman and even young children shouldered important responsibilities on the trail.

The Frontier Lures Settlers

The West drew increasing numbers of American settlers during the mid-19th century despite the hardships of the journey and the difficult living conditions at the journey's end. Many Americans assumed that the United States would extend its dominion to the Pacific Ocean and create a vast republic that would spread the blessings of democracy and civilization across the continent.

AMERICAN MISSION   Thomas Jefferson had dreamed that the United States would become an "empire of liberty" by expanding across the continent "with room enough for our descendants to the hundredth and thousandth generation." Toward that end, Jefferson's Louisiana Purchase in 1803 had doubled the young nation's size.

For a quarter century after the War of 1812, Americans explored this huge territory in limited numbers. Then, in the 1840s, expansion fever gripped the country. Americans began to believe that their movement westward and southward was destined and ordained by God.

John L. O'Sullivan, editor of the *United States Magazine and Democratic Review*, described the annexation of Texas in 1845 as "the fulfillment of our manifest destiny to overspread the continent allotted by Providence for the free

SECTION 2 RESOURCES

PRINT RESOURCES

IN-DEPTH RESOURCES: UNIT 3
Guided Reading, p. 2
Skillbuilder Practice: Analyzing Assumptions, p. 5
Primary Sources: Black Hawk's Farewell Speech, p. 9; On the Oregon Trail, p. 10
Literature: *Roughing It* by Mark Twain, p.12

ACCESS FOR STUDENTS ACQUIRING ENGLISH
Guided Reading (Spanish), p. 93
Skillbuilder Practice: Analyzing Assumptions (Spanish), p. 96

FORMAL ASSESSMENT
Section Quiz, p. 114

ALTERNATIVE ASSESSMENT BOOK
See forms for supporting and scoring alternative activities.

TECHNOLOGY RESOURCES

CD-ROM Electronic Library of Primary Sources

VIDEO *American Portfolio: A Videodisc for U.S. History* user's guide, pp. 60, 61, 85

INTERNET McDougal Littell Learning On-Line
http://www.mcdougallittell.com

THINK THROUGH HISTORY
A. Clarifying
Explain the concept of manifest destiny.

A. Answer The term refers to the belief that U.S. expansion into the West was inevitable.

B. Answer Manifest destiny; desire for land; expansion of markets and trade opportunities; economic problems in the East.

THINK THROUGH HISTORY
B. Analyzing Causes What were some of the causes of U.S. westward expansion?

development of our yearly multiplying millions." Americans immediately seized on the phrase **"manifest destiny"** to express their belief that the United States' destiny was to expand to the Pacific Ocean and into Mexican territory. They also believed that this destiny was manifest, or obvious and inevitable.

ATTITUDES TOWARD THE FRONTIER Manifest destiny, O'Sullivan proclaimed, meant that American settlers should possess the "whole of the continent" that God "has given us for the development of the great experiment of liberty and . . . self-government." Most Americans, however, also had practical reasons for moving west.

The abundance of land in the West was the greatest attraction. Whether for farming or speculation, land ownership was an important step toward prosperity. As the number of western settlers climbed, merchants and manufacturers followed, seeking new markets for their goods.

While Americans had always traded with Europe, the transportation revolution increased opportunities for trade with Asia as well. Several harbors in the Oregon Territory would help expand trade with China and Japan and also serve as naval stations for a Pacific fleet.

Many Americans endured the rigors of the westward trek because of personal economic problems in the East. The Panic of 1837, for example, had disastrous consequences and convinced many Americans, native-born as well as immigrant, that they would be better off attempting a fresh start in the West.

Settlers and Native Americans

As American settlers moved west in rapidly growing numbers, they inevitably had an impact on Native American communities. Most Native Americans tried to maintain their cultural traditions, even if forced to move from traditional lands. Some tried to assimilate into—or become part of—the advancing white culture. Still others, although relatively few in number, fought to keep whites away from their homes.

THE BLACK HAWK WAR In the early 1830s, white settlers in western Illinois and eastern Iowa placed great pressure on the Native American people there to move west of the Mississippi River. Representatives from several Native American tribes visited Chief Black Hawk of the Sauk tribe. One representative told of a prophet who had a vision of future events involving Black Hawk.

A PERSONAL VOICE
He said that the Big Black Bird Hawk was the man to lead the [Native American] nations and win back the old homes of the people; that when the fight began . . . the warriors would be without number; that back would come the buffalo . . . that had disappeared; and that in a little while the white man would be driven to the eastern ocean and across to the farther shore from whence he came.

TRIBAL ELDER, quoted in *Native American Testimony*

The story of that vision convinced Black Hawk to lead a rebellion against the United States. Known as the Black Hawk War, the four-month rebellion started in Illinois and spread to the Wisconsin Territory. It ended in June 1832, when Illinois militia members slaughtered 200 Sauk and Fox people. As a result, the Sauk and Fox tribes were forcibly removed to areas west of the Mississippi.

This engraving portrays the defeat of the Sauk under Black Hawk by a U.S. force led by General Henry Atkinson in 1832.

HISTORY FROM VISUALS
Why They Went West
Reading the Chart Ask students to speculate on which groups of people would have benefited economically from westward expansion, based on the list of reasons. *Possible Responses: Southern planters, Northern merchants, small farmers, immigrants.*

Extension Have small groups of students discuss which motives—economic or idealistic—had a greater influence on people's decision to move west.

OBJECTIVE
② INSTRUCT

Settlers and Native Americans

▶ *Discussing Key Ideas*
• Some Native Americans resist westward expansion by white settlers.
• Some settlers and Native Americans coexist, with neither side dominating the other.
• The Fort Laramie treaty gives land to various groups of Native Americans in exchange for their cooperation during westward expansion.

IN-DEPTH RESOURCES: UNIT 3
Primary Source: Black Hawk's Farewell Speech, p. 9

Expanding Markets and Moving West **261**

Teacher's Edition **261**

The Oglala Sioux

Critical Thinking:
Analyzing Ask students why the establishment of a privately financed health clinic is especially significant for the Oglala Sioux. *Possible Response: For many years, the Oglala Sioux were plagued with health problems such as alcoholism and high rates of infant and adult mortality.*

OBJECTIVE
③ **INSTRUCT**

Trails West

▶ *Discussing Key Ideas*
- American traders travel the Santa Fe Trail to New Mexico.
- Missionaries and pioneers seeking land endure months of hardship on the Oregon Trail.
- The Mormons go west to flee from persecution.
- The United States obtains from Britain all rights to the Oregon Territory.

NOW ● THEN

THE OGLALA SIOUX

Today, about 20,000 Oglala Sioux live on the Pine Ridge reservation in South Dakota. Signs of new growth dot the landscape. Opposite the tribal offices stand a new gas station and store, and a privately financed health clinic.

It wasn't long ago, however, that living conditions for the Oglala Sioux were poor. For many years, unemployment hovered over 50 percent, while rates of suicide, alcoholism, infant mortality, and deaths from influenza and pneumonia far exceeded national averages.

Tourism is partly responsible for bringing improved conditions to the Oglala Sioux. Because Pine Ridge boasts some of the most beautiful territory in the northern plains, the growing tourist industry has become the largest source of revenue.

Charging Eagle, (1996) Tom Lindfors.

RELATIONS ON THE MIDDLE GROUND The middle ground, according to historian Richard White, was a place that neither the Native Americans nor the settlers dominated. As long as settlers needed Native Americans as trading partners and guides in unfamiliar territory, relations between settlers and Native Americans could be beneficial, if not pleasant. Amelia Knight described such an encounter on the middle ground.

A PERSONAL VOICE
Traveled 13 miles, over very bad roads, without water. After looking in vain for water, we were about to give up as it was near night, when husband came across a company of friendly Cayuse Indians about to camp, who showed him where to find water . . . we bought a few potatoes from an Indian, which will be a treat for our supper.

AMELIA STEWART KNIGHT, quoted in *Covered Wagon Women*

As settlers pushed west, the middle ground moved westward with them. By the 1840s, the middle ground was well west of the Mississippi, because the Indian Removal act of 1830 and other Indian removal treaties had pushed Native Americans off their lands to make room for the settlers.

FORT LARAMIE TREATY As settlers moved west, small numbers of displaced Native Americans occasionally attacked them. The U.S. government responded to the settlers' fears of attack by calling a conference near what is now Laramie, Wyoming. The Cheyenne, Arapaho, Sioux, Crow, and other tribes joined U.S. representatives in swearing "to maintain good faith and friendship in all their mutual intercourse, and to make an effective and lasting peace." The 1851 Treaty of Fort Laramie provided various Native American groups with control of the central plains, a 400-mile-wide swath of flat land east of the Rocky Mountains that stretched roughly from the Arkansas River north to Canada. The Native Americans promised not to attack settlers and agreed to allow the construction of government forts and roads. In exchange, the government pledged to honor the agreed-upon boundaries and to make annual payments.

Still the settlers flowed westward, trampling Native American hunting lands and slaughtering buffalo and elk, while the U.S. government repeatedly violated its side of the treaty. Subsequent treaties demanded that Native Americans abandon their lands and move to reservations.

THINK THROUGH HISTORY
C. *Recognizing Effects* What were the effects of the U.S. government policies toward Native Americans at this time?

C. Answer The U.S. government at first agreed to boundaries that protected Native American territories, but later broke these agreements and moved Native Americans to different lands.

Trails West

While the continued movement of U.S. settlers into the West had disastrous effects on the Native American communities there, the journey was perilous for traders and settlers as well. Nevertheless, thousands made the trek, using a series of old Native American trails and new routes. Some went in search of trade opportunities while others went for religious reasons, to serve as missionaries or to flee from persecution.

THE SANTA FE TRAIL One of the busiest and most famous avenues of trade was the **Santa Fe Trail,** which led 780 miles from Independence, Missouri, to Santa Fe, New Mexico.

On the Santa Fe Trail each spring between 1821 and 1848, American traders loaded their covered wagons with cloth, knives, and guns, and set off toward Santa Fe. For about the first 150 miles—to Council Grove, Kansas—traders traveled individually. After that, fearing attacks by Kiowa and Comanche, among other tribes, traders banded into organized groups of up to 100 wagons. First the traders elected a captain, who then selected four lieutenants. Each lieutenant

---

TEACHING OPTIONS

Teaching Less Proficient Readers

Clarifying Ideas Some students may have trouble understanding the impact the white settlers had on Native Americans. Have these students work together in pairs and follow these steps:

1. Together, read pages 261 and 262.
2. List as many reactions of Native Americans to white settlers as you can.
3. Write down any questions you have about these reactions.
4. Work together to find the answers in the text.

Exploring Themes

Cultural Diversity Explain that most Native Americans tried to maintain their culture even after they were pushed out of their homes. Ask students why Native Americans struggled to retain their traditions. *Possible Response: Because their traditions helped unify them and gave them an identity.* Ask them how Native Americans' desire to retain their culture conflicted with the concept of manifest destiny. *Possible Response: Supporters of manifest destiny believed that U.S. expansion was destined and ordained by God. White settlers wanted Native Americans to give up their own religions and culture and to accept white religion and culture.*

Trails West, 1860

BLACKFOOT

Missouri River

45° N

125° W

Portland

YAKIMA

NEZ PERCÉ

CROW

SIOUX

CASCADE RANGE

40° N

Ft. Hall

CHEYENNE

PAWNEE

Council Bluffs

Nauvoo

35° N

Sacramento

Salt Lake City

San Francisco

PACIFIC OCEAN

SIERRA NEVADA

UTE

St. Louis

Independence

NAVAJO

Cimmaron Cutoff

Santa Fe

CHEROKEE
CREEK
SEMINOLE
CHOCTAW
CHICKASAW

Ft. Smith

120° W

Los Angeles

30° N

El Paso

Mississippi River

Legend:
— Oregon Trail
••• California Trail
- - Santa Fe Trail
ooo Old Spanish Trail
— — Mormon Trail
═══ Butterfield Overland Mail

N

0   200 Miles
0   400 Kilometers

GEOGRAPHY SKILLBUILDER

REGION
Approximately how long was the trail from St. Louis to El Paso?
MOVEMENT *At a wagon train speed of 15 miles a day, about how long would that trip take?*

Skillbuilder Answer
Region: About 1,100 miles.
Movement: Roughly 74 days.

was placed at the head of one column of wagons. As these wagon trains rumbled their way slowly across the plains, scouts rode along the column to check for danger. At night the traders formed the wagons into squares with their wheels interlocked, forming a corral for horses, mules, and oxen.

Cooperation, though, came to an abrupt end when Santa Fe came into view. Traders immediately charged off on their own as each tried to be the first to enter the Mexican province of New Mexico. After a few days of trading and resting, they loaded their wagons with silver, gold, and furs, restocked their pack animals, and headed back to Missouri. These traders established the first visible American presence in New Mexico and in the Mexican province of Arizona.

THE OREGON TRAIL In 1836, Marcus and Narcissa Whitman, Methodist missionaries, made their way into the Oregon Territory to set up mission schools to convert and educate Native Americans. By driving their wagon as far as Fort Boise (near present-day Boise, Idaho), they proved that wagons could travel on the **Oregon Trail,** which started in Independence, Missouri, and ended in Portland, Oregon. Their letters east praising the fertile soil and abundant rainfall attracted hundreds of other Americans to the Oregon Trail. The route from Independence, Missouri, to Portland, Oregon, traced some of the same paths that Lewis and Clark had followed several decades earlier.

Following the Whitmans' lead, some of the Oregon pioneers bought wooden-wheeled wagons called prairie schooners, covered with sailcloth and pulled by oxen. Most of the pioneers walked, however, pushing handcarts loaded with a few precious possessions. They packed dried pork, beans, and corn to sustain them, along with one or two iron pots for cooking. The trip took months, even if all went well. Lucy Deady, who traveled the Oregon Trail in 1846 at the age of 11, described the thunderstorms that caused everything to be "soaked with the driving rains" and made the oxen stampede. She also recalled crossing a desert for

HISTORY FROM VISUALS
Trails West, 1860

Reading the Map Point out the topographic features on the map. Ask students to discuss what effect the terrain along the trails would have had on the settlers' progress. *Possible Response: Most of the trails took the settlers over rugged mountain ranges and across rivers. Crossing such terrain probably slowed travel time considerably.*

Extension Ask students to determine which trail is the longest. *The Butterfield Overland Mail route is approximately 1,800 miles.*

MORE ABOUT . . .
The Westward Settlers

After Lodisa Frizzell began her journey westward, she wrote in her diary: "Who is there that does not recollect their first night when started on a long journey, the well-known voices of our friends still ring in our ears." Many of the diaries of women who traveled west describe missed friendships. Men, on the other hand, seemed less preoccupied with losing old friends. As one man wrote in his diary about his wife, "She thought much of home—friends—prospects —& present condition. I tried to have her get above these things."

 ELECTRONIC LIBRARY OF PRIMARY SOURCES
The Discovery of the Oregon Trail by Robert Stuart

IN-DEPTH RESOURCES: UNIT 3
Primary Source: On the Oregon Trail, p. 10

TEACHING OPTION

 Cooperative Activity: Interviewing Settlers

Task: One student will interview four or five others who role-play settlers on the westward trails.

Purpose: To explore life on the westward trails in depth.

Activity: Each group decides who will be the interviewer and who will role-play the settlers. The interviewer should pose as a reporter of the time who wants to convey the true flavor of life on the trails to a newspaper audience. The interviewer should prepare a list of ques-

tions, asking settlers why they are heading west, what they have experienced on the trail, and what they hope for the future. Have students tape their interviews. Play each audiotape in class.

📁 **Building a Portfolio:** Students who add their audiotape to their portfolio should include a note detailing their role in the interviews.

ALTERNATIVE ASSESSMENT BOOK
Standards for Evaluating a Cooperative Activity

Standards for Evaluation
Audiotapes should . . .

• detail specific experiences on the trails
• contain information explaining why Mormon settlers decided to go West
• convey the hopes and fears of the settlers

The Mormons' Desert Settlement

Deseret, a word meaning "honey bee," in the *Book of Mormon,* referred to the hard work and industry needed to make their Salt Lake settlement a success. In the late 1840s, Mormons indeed worked hard irrigating the desert near the Great Salt Lake and making the land productive. Their efforts were threatened, however, in 1848 by swarms of grasshoppers that invaded the land where they had planted their crops. Fortunately, sea gulls from the Great Salt Lake ate the grasshoppers, saving the crops from destruction. The Mormons considered this event a miracle. The sea gull eventually became Utah's state bird, and the grasshopper that had invaded became known as the Mormon cricket. Although the Mormons' application for admission to the Union as the State of Deseret was denied, Utah's nickname is the Beehive State.

> *"Eastward I go only by force, but westward I go free."*
>
> HENRY DAVID THOREAU

two days and one night: "There was no water at all, so we filled every keg and dish . . . so the cattle should have water as well as ourselves." Fever, diarrhea, and cholera plagued people, some of whom were buried along the side of the trail.

Caravans provided protection against possible attack by Native Americans. They also helped combat the loneliness of the difficult journey, as Catherine Haun, who migrated from Iowa, explained.

A PERSONAL VOICE

Womenfolk visited from wagon to wagon or congenial friends spent an hour walking, ever westward, and talking over our home life back in 'the states'; telling of the loved ones left behind; voicing our hopes for the future . . . and even whispering a little friendly gossip of emigrant life.

CATHERINE HAUN, quoted in *Frontier Women*

By 1844, about 5,000 Americans had arrived in Oregon and were farming in its green and fertile Willamette Valley.

THE MORMON MIGRATION One group that migrated westward along the Oregon Trail wanted to escape persecution. These people were the **Mormons,** a religious community that would play a major role in the settling of the West.

Mormon history began in upstate New York in 1827, when **Joseph Smith** announced that he had received a special message from God in a book "written upon golden plates" buried in a hillside. Placing America at the center of Christian history, Smith's translation of the Book of Mormon attracted an eager following. Smith and five associates established the Mormon church—or Church of Jesus Christ of Latter Day Saints—in Fayette, New York, in 1830.

Plagued by persecution and seeking to convert Native Americans, Smith and a growing band of followers determined to move west. They settled in Commerce, Illinois, which he renamed Nauvoo in 1839. Within five years, the community on the Mississippi River reached 20,000 members. A hostile public reacted violently to Smith's view of himself as a prophet and his revelation that male members of the church could engage in polygamy, the practice of having more than one wife. When Smith's angry Nauvoo neighbors printed denunciations of polygamy, Smith was jailed for destroying their printing press. In 1844, an anti-Mormon mob broke into the jail, hauled out Smith and his brother, and murdered them.

After Smith's death, a new leader named **Brigham Young** urged the Mormons to move farther west. Thousands of believers walked north to Nebraska, across Wyoming to the Rockies, and then southwest. In 1847, the Mormons stopped at the edge of the lonely desert near the Great Salt Lake, just beyond the mountains of what was then Mexico. Realizing that the land's isolation would protect the

This photograph of the interior of a covered wagon reveals why pioneers often were forced to lighten their loads by leaving treasured possessions along the trail.

In this painting by William Henry Jackson, Mormon wagons wait to ferry across the Missouri River at Council Bluffs, Iowa, in 1846.

TEACHING OPTIONS

Making Connections Across Time

The Mormons Today Explain that today the Mormon church still thrives in Utah, and that Mormons make up about 70 percent of Utah's population. Although the church outlawed polygamy in 1890, Mormons still follow many of Joseph Smith's and Brigham Young's teachings and practices, including a deep commitment to Mormons' welfare. The church today maintains an extensive educational system that includes Brigham Young University in Provo, Utah. Mormons also promote the arts and music. The Mormon Tabernacle Choir in Salt Lake City is famous throughout the world for its concert tours.

Teaching Gifted and Talented Students

Writing a Journal on the Trail Invite interested students to find out more about Mormons' westward migration and to write a journal as a Mormon pioneer. Suggest that students follow the steps in this flow chart:

Examine primary sources for accounts of settlers' experiences.	→	Write journal entries from the point of view of a Mormon pioneer.	→
Include details that bring the experiences to life.		Share the journal with the class.	

THINK THROUGH HISTORY
D. *Analyzing Motives* Why did the Mormons move farther west in their search for a home?

D. Answer The Mormons were fleeing from religious persecution.

Mormons from attack, Young boldly declared, "This is the place."

The Mormons awarded plots of land to each family according to its size but established common ownership of two critical resources—water and timberland. Soon they had coaxed settlements and farms from the bleak landscape by irrigating their fields. Salt Lake City blossomed out of the land the Mormons called Deseret.

RESOLVING TERRITORIAL DISPUTES The migration of large numbers of American settlers brought to a head disputes with other countries over control of some Western lands, particularly Oregon. For years, rival nations—including Britain, France, Russia, Spain, and the United States—had claimed this rich territory. By the early 19th century, France, Spain, and Russia had abandoned their claims, leaving only Britain and the United States to dispute the Oregon Territory.

The Oregon Territory was only one point of contention between the United States and Britain. In the early 1840s, Great Britain still claimed areas near the Canadian border in parts of what are now Maine and Minnesota. To avoid war, Britain and the United States agreed to split the disputed territories in half. The Webster-Ashburton Treaty of 1842 settled these territorial disputes in the East and the Midwest, but the two nations merely continued the "joint occupation" of the Oregon Territory that the two countries had first established in 1818.

In 1844, Democrat James K. Polk's presidential platform called for annexation of the entire Oregon Territory. In his inaugural speech, the new president declared, "Our title to the whole of the Territory of Oregon is clear and unquestionable, and already are our people preparing to perfect that title by occupying it with their wives and children."

E. Answer Polk believed in manifest destiny. He campaigned for annexation of the Oregon territory, and claimed the U.S. had an "unquestionable" right to it.

THINK THROUGH HISTORY
E. *Forming Opinions* Do you think President Polk supported manifest destiny? Explain.

Reflecting widespread support for the president's views, newspapers adopted the slogan **"Fifty-Four Forty or Fight."** This slogan referred to the latitude 54°40', the northern limit of the disputed Oregon Territory. By the mid-1840s, however, formerly popular beaver hats had gone out of style and the fur trade subsequently declined. As a result, Britain's interest in the territory along the Columbia River waned. On the American side, President Polk's advisors deemed the land north of the forty-ninth parallel of latitude unsuited for agriculture. Consequently, the two countries peaceably agreed in 1846 to extend the mainland boundary along that parallel westward from the Rocky Mountains to Puget Sound, establishing the current boundary between the United States and Canada.

Unfortunately, establishing the boundary in the Southwest with Mexico would not be so easy.

HISTORICAL SPOTLIGHT

LIFE ON THE OREGON TRAIL

Settlers making their way west faced epidemic diseases, such as cholera. No treatment existed and the victim often died within 24 hours. With no time for elaborate funerals, it was not uncommon for a wagon train to leave the sick person by the side of the road. Sometimes the sufferer was left with a "watcher," whose job was to dig the soon-to-be-needed grave—often while the victim watched. Historians suspect that occasionally, due to the haste of the watcher to catch up with the wagon train, the victim probably was buried while still alive.

Life on the trail wasn't all bad, though. The lack of firewood on large parts of the Oregon Trail forced the pioneers to use buffalo dung for cooking fuel—but it also served another purpose. Children threw buffalo "chips" for fun, inventing what may have been the ancestor of the 20th-century Frisbee.

HISTORICAL SPOTLIGHT
Life on the Oregon Trail
Critical Thinking: Drawing Conclusions Ask students what conclusions they can draw, based on these descriptions, about the lives of adults and children who traveled the westward trails. *Possible Response: The adults must have experienced anguish when having to leave behind a dying companion or loved one; even though the journey was hard, the children retained their playfulness.*

ASSESS & RETEACH

Section 2 Assessment
Have pairs of students evaluate each other's supporting evidence for questions 3 and 4.

Self-Assessment
Have students create a two-column chart to help them explore how their understanding developed from reading Section 2. In the first column, students should list what they knew about westward expansion before they read the section. In the second column, they should jot down what they learned.

Section Quiz

FORMAL ASSESSMENT
Section Quiz, p. 114

Reteach
Review the map on page 263 to reinforce students' learning about the various trails west and the groups of people who used them.

Section 2 Assessment

1. TERMS & NAMES

Identify:
- manifest destiny
- Santa Fe Trail
- Oregon Trail
- Mormons
- Joseph Smith
- Brigham Young
- Fifty-Four Forty or Fight

2. SUMMARIZING Use a diagram like this one to compare the motives of settlers on the Oregon, Santa Fe, and Mormon trails.

Which do you think was the most common motive? Explain.

3. EVALUATING What were the benefits and drawbacks of the belief in manifest destiny? Use specific references to the section to support your response.

THINK ABOUT
- the various reasons for the move westward
- the settlers' point of view
- the impact on Native Americans
- the impact on the nation as a whole

4. ANALYZING ISSUES Do you think the same attitudes exist today that created the concept of manifest destiny? Explain.

THINK ABOUT
- issues and events that resulted in a belief in manifest destiny
- effects of this belief on U.S. residents, including Native Americans

Expanding Markets and Moving West **265**

ANSWERS

1. TERMS & NAMES

manifest destiny, p. 261

Santa Fe Trail, p. 262

Oregon Trail, p. 263

Mormons, p. 264

Joseph Smith, p. 264

Brigham Young, p. 264

Fifty-Four Forty or Fight, p. 265

2. SUMMARIZING

Settlers on all three trails sought new economic opportunities and new land. Mormons also sought freedom from religious persecution. Some settlers on the Oregon and Santa Fe trails were attracted by new markets for goods and services. Some travelers were interested in expanding trade with China and Japan; missionaries wanted to convert Native Americans.

3. EVALUATING

Possible Responses: Students may identify the wide range of new opportunities for people as a benefit of the belief in manifest destiny. They may also point out that westward expansion would result in a nation that stretched across the continent and that had vast resources. Most students will recognize that the treatment of Native Americans constitutes a drawback of the belief in manifest destiny.

4. ANALYZING ISSUES

Possible Responses: Some students will say that Americans still feel that it is their destiny to spread the concepts of liberty and self-government. Other students may indicate that Americans now have a more global perspective and are not interested in expansion of physical boundaries but in expansion of trading opportunities.

CLOSE

The West drew increasing numbers of settlers in the mid–19th century. They endured a long, arduous journey on westward trails to claim new land and markets. Belief in manifest destiny pushed the country to expand its borders and obtain the Oregon Territory.

Geography Spotlight

FOCUS & MOTIVATE

▶ **Starting with the Student**
Ask students to imagine traveling to a place they never visited before. Ask the following:

• Why would a map be useful?

• What troubles would a person encounter who was creating the first accurate map of the area?

MORE ABOUT . . .
The Oregon Trail

About 2,000 miles long, the Oregon Trail was the longest-used overland route to the West. Fur traders and missionaries used the trail years before Frémont's mapping expedition. In 1843, a year after Frémont's first expedition, the missionaries Marcus and Narcissa Whitman led 1,000 settlers along the trail. All told, about 12,000 pioneers traversed the trail to Oregon, their wagon wheels cutting so deep that the tracks are still visible today along some parts of the trail. After railroads made wagon trains obsolete, the trail was used to drive cattle and sheep east to market.

Mapping the Oregon Trail

In 1841, Congress appropriated $30,000 for a survey of the Oregon Trail and named John C. Frémont to head the expedition. Frémont earned his nickname "the Pathfinder" by leading four major expeditions, including artists, scientists, and cartographers—among them the German-born cartographer Charles Preuss—to explore the American West between 1842 and 1848. When Frémont submitted the report of his first expedition, from mid-June to mid-October 1842, Congress immediately ordered the printing of 10,000 copies that were widely distributed.

The "Map of the Road from Missouri to Oregon," drawn by Preuss, appeared in seven sheets. Though settlers first used this route in 1836, it was not until 1846 that Preuss published his map to guide them. The trickle of settlers westward would soon become a flood. Maps like the Preuss map shown here became essential to the economic development of the West.

5 THE WHITMAN MISSION
The explorers came upon the Whitmans' missionary station. They found thriving families living primarily on potatoes of a "remarkably good quality."

THE OREGON TRAIL The long, narrow map at right is called a "strip" map, a map that shows a thin strip of the earth's surface—in this case, the last stretch of the trail before reaching Fort Wallah-Wallah.

6 THE NEZ PERCE PRAIRIE
Chief Looking Glass (here, in 1871) and the Nez Perce had "harmless" interactions with Frémont and his expedition.

RECOMMENDED RESOURCES

Books

Egan, Ferol. *Frémont, Explorer for a Restless Nation.* Garden City, NY: Doubleday, 1977. A biography of Frémont.

Ghent, William James. *The Road to Oregon.* London: Longmans, 1929. A noted chronicle of the Oregon Trail.

Guthrie, A. B. *The Way West.* Boston: Houghton, 1949. A

Pulitzer Prize–winning novel about the Oregon Trail.

Parkman, Francis. *The Oregon Trail.* New York: Viking, 1989. Reprint of the famous 1849 chronicle of Parkman's 1,700-mile journey from Missouri to Wyoming and back.

Videos

As the Wind Rocks the Cradle. APL Educational Video, 1991. A pioneer woman describes her experiences on the trail west.

The Real West. Filmic Archives. The Oregon Trail and the people of the American West, narrated by Gary Cooper.

Settling the Oregon Territory. Encyclopaedia Britannica. How a belief in manifest destiny brought settlers to Oregon.

The West. PBS Video, 1996. Ken Burns's nine-part look at the American West includes Episode 2, "Empire upon the Trails."

Software

Oregon Trail I and II. MECC, 1993. Award-winning simulation of a covered-wagon journey from Missouri to Oregon.

Wagon Train 1848. MECC. Puts users in the shoes of pioneers traveling the Oregon Trail.

1 FT. BOISE OUTPOST Emigrants reached Ft. Boise in mid-September, with 400 miles of terrain still to cover. Though salmon were plentiful in summer, Frémont noted that in the winter Native Americans often were forced to eat "every creeping thing, however loathsome and repulsive," to stay alive.

October 10-11, 1843

Latitude 44'

Fort Boisée

Snake River or Lewis Fork of the Columbia

Owyhee River

Longitude 117°

October 11-12

October 12-13

October 14-15

SNAKE INDIANS

October 15-16

Burnt River

October 16-17

Longitude 118°

45°

2 MAP NOTATION Preuss recorded dates, rivers, distances, temperatures, and other geographical features as the expedition progressed along the trail.

3 RECORDING NATURAL RESOURCES On October 13, Frémont traveled through a desolate valley of the Columbia River to a region of "arable mountains," where he observed "nutritious grasses" and good soil that would support future flocks and herds.

4 CROSSING THE MOUNTAINS Pioneers on the trail cut paths through the Blue Mountains, a wooded range that Frémont believed had been formed by "violent and extensive igneous [volcanic] action."

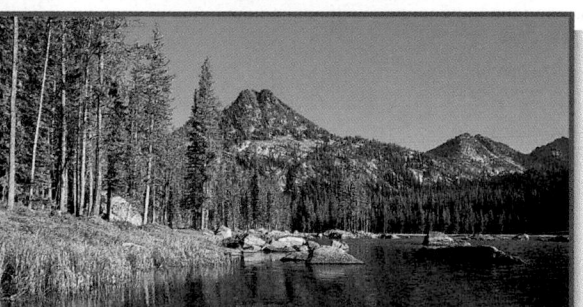

INTERACT WITH HISTORY

1. **INTERPRETING MAPS** Use the map to identify natural obstacles that settlers faced on the Oregon Trail.

    SEE SKILLBUILDER HANDBOOK, PAGE 1054.

2. **RESEARCHING WESTERN TRAILS** Do research to find out more about early mapping efforts for other western trails. Then choose one of the trails and sketch an enlarged map of one section. Label features such as rivers and mountains, and provide notes highlighting areas of particular interest

    INTERNET For more about the Oregon Trail, click on *Social Studies* at http://www.mcdougallittell.com

Expanding Markets and Moving West **267**

OBJECTIVES

1 To explain why Mexico encouraged American settlement of Texas.

2 To describe the struggle between Mexico and the Anglo settlers over Texas.

SKILLBUILDER

• Understanding geography: place, region, p. 270

CRITICAL THINKING

• Recognizing effects, p. 268
• Analyzing motives, p. 269
• Contrasting, pp. 270, 272
• Comparing, pp. 271, 272
• Analyzing, p. 272
• Synthesizing, p. 272

FOCUS & MOTIVATE

▶ **Starting with the Student**
• Ask students who they think has the greater claim to a piece of land—the absentee owner or the person who takes care of it.
• How do they think these two should resolve their differences over land rights?

OBJECTIVE
1 INSTRUCT

Americans Settle in the Southwest

▶ **Discussing Key Ideas**
• Friction grows between Native American and Mexican inhabitants of Texas.
• Mexico encourages American settlement in Texas to protect the territory against Native American attacks and to stimulate trade with the United States.
• Stephen F. Austin uses Mexico's land grants to establish a colony of American farmers in Texas.

IN-DEPTH RESOURCES: UNIT 3
Guided Reading, p. 3
ACCESS FOR STUDENTS ACQUIRING ENGLISH
Guided Reading (Spanish), p. 94

TERMS & NAMES
• Stephen F. Austin
• land grant
• Antonio López de Santa Anna
• Texas Revolution
• Alamo
• Sam Houston
• Republic of Texas
• annex

3 Expansion in Texas

LEARN ABOUT the issues involved in American settlement in Texas
TO UNDERSTAND why America and Mexico came into conflict over Texas.

ONE AMERICAN'S STORY

In 1821, **Stephen F. Austin** led the first of several groups of American settlers to a fertile area "as good in every respect as man could wish for, land first rate, plenty of timber, fine water— beautifully rolling" along the Brazos River. Drawn by the promise of inexpensive land and economic opportunity, Austin established a colony of American settlers in *Tejas,* or Texas, then the northernmost province of the Mexican state of Coahuila. However, Austin's plans didn't work out as well as he had hoped; 12 years later, he found himself in a Mexican prison and his new homeland in an uproar. After his release, Austin spoke about the impending crisis between Texas and Mexico.

A PERSONAL VOICE
Texas needs peace, and a local government; its inhabitants are farmers, and they need a calm and quiet life. . . . (But) my efforts to serve Texas involved me in the labyrinth of Mexican politics. I was arrested, and have suffered a long persecution and imprisonment. . . . I fully hoped to have found Texas at peace and in tranquillity, but regret to find it in commotion; all disorganized, all in anarchy, and threatened with immediate hostilities. . . . Can this state of things exist without precipitating the country into a war? I think it cannot.

STEPHEN F. AUSTIN, quoted in *Lone Star: A History of Texas and Texans*

Austin's warning proved to be well-founded. The conflict between Texas and Mexico would soon escalate into a bloody struggle.

Americans Settle in the Southwest

During three long centuries of Spanish rule, only a few thousand Mexican settlers had migrated to the vast landscape of what is now Texas. Despite the region's rich natural resources and a climate conducive to agriculture, a number of problems scared off many Mexican settlers. One was the growing friction between Native American and Mexican inhabitants of the area.

HISPANIC AND NATIVE AMERICAN POPULATIONS   Since the earliest Spanish settlements, the Native American and Mexican populations in the Southwest had come into close contact. Before Mexico won its independence in 1821, Spain's system of Roman Catholic missions in California, New Mexico, and Texas was staffed with Franciscan priests who tried to convert Native Americans to Catholicism and to settle them on mission lands. To protect the missions, Spanish soldiers manned nearby *presidios,* or forts.

The mission system declined during the 1820s and 1830s, after Mexico had won independence. After wresting the missions from Spanish control, the Mexican government offered the surrounding lands to government officials and ranchers. While some Native Americans were forced to remain as unpaid laborers, many others fled the missions, returning to their nomadic ways. When

268 CHAPTER 9

A. Answer After 1921, Mexico gave away their lands and tried to capture Native Americans for forced labor. Native American groups retaliated with violence.

THINK THROUGH HISTORY
A. Recognizing Effects How did relations between the Mexicans and Native Americans in the Southwest change after 1821?

SECTION 3 RESOURCES

PRINT RESOURCES

IN-DEPTH RESOURCES: UNIT 3
Guided Reading, p. 3
American Lives: Lorenzo de Zavala, p. 15

ACCESS FOR STUDENTS ACQUIRING ENGLISH
Guided Reading (Spanish), p. 94

FORMAL ASSESSMENT
Section Quiz, p. 115

ALTERNATIVE ASSESSMENT BOOK
See forms for supporting and scoring alternative activities.

TECHNOLOGY RESOURCES

CD-ROM *Grolier Multimedia Encyclopedia*
Electronic Library of Primary Sources

VIDEO *American Portfolio: A Videodisc for U.S. History*
user's guide, pp. 79–81, 85

INTERNET McDougal Littell Learning On-Line
http://www.mcdougallittell.com

Mexicans captured Native Americans for forced labor, groups of hostile Comanche and Apache retaliated by sweeping through Texas, terrorizing Mexican settlements, and stealing livestock that supported many of the American settlers and Mexican settlers, or *Tejanos*.

THE IMPACT OF MEXICAN INDEPENDENCE Trade opportunities between Mexico's northern provinces and the United States multiplied. *Tejano* livestock, mostly longhorn cattle, provided tallow, hides, and other commercial goods to trade in Santa Fe, New Mexico, north and west of Texas.

Newly free, Mexico sought to improve its economy. Toward that end, the country eased trade restrictions and made trade between Mexico's northern provinces and the United States more attractive than trade between northern Mexico and other sections of Mexico. Gradually, the ties loosened between Mexico and the northern provinces, which included present-day New Mexico, California, Texas, Arizona, Nevada, and Utah.

Mexico was beginning to discover what Spain had previously learned: owning a vast territory did not necessarily mean controlling it. Mexico City—the seat of a Mexican government that often seemed indifferent to the problems of settlers in Texas—lay far from the northern provinces. Native American groups, such as the Apache and the Comanche, continued to threaten the thinly scattered Mexican settlements in New Mexico and Texas. Consequently, the new Mexican government began to look for ways to strengthen ties between Mexico City and the northern provinces.

THINK THROUGH HISTORY
B. Analyzing Motives What did Mexico hope to gain from American settlement in Texas?

B. Answer Mexico hoped to protect against raids by Native Americans and horse thieves, and to bring American manufactured goods into Mexico.

MEXICO INVITES U.S. SETTLERS To prevent border violations by horse thieves and to protect the territory from Native American attacks, the Mexican government encouraged American farmers to settle in Texas. The Mexican government also hoped that these farmers would purchase farm implements from the United States, which would increase the flow of manufactured goods into Mexico.

In 1821, and again in 1823 and 1824, Mexico offered enormous **land grants** to agents, who were called *empresarios*. The *empresarios*, in turn, attracted American settlers, who eagerly bought land for twelve and a half cents an acre in return for a pledge to obey Mexican laws and observe the official religion of Roman Catholicism.

Many Americans rushed at the chance. The same restless determination that produced new inventions and manufactured goods fed the American urge to remove any barrier to settlement of the West, whether those barriers were human or natural. The population of Anglo, or English-speaking, settlers from Europe and the United States soon surpassed the population of *Tejanos* who lived in Texas. Until the 1830s, these transplanted Americans were content to live as naturalized Mexican citizens.

AUSTIN IN TEXAS The most successful *empresario,* Stephen F. Austin, established a colony in Texas between the Brazos and Colorado rivers, where "no drunkard, no gambler, no profane swearer, and no idler" would be allowed. By 1825, Austin had issued 297 land grants to the group that later became known as Texas's Old Three Hundred. Each family received 177 extraordinarily inexpensive acres of farmland, 15,000 acres for stock grazing, and a 10-year exemption from paying taxes. "I am convinced," Austin said, "that I could take on fifteen hundred families as easily as three hundred if permitted to do so."

Land had a low price, but life proved difficult at the outset, especially for American-born women. In 1825, an *empresario* named Green DeWitt established a colony on the lower Lavaca River, where he was visited by a

TEX-MEX CULTURE
Ever since Mexico first invited Anglo settlers to Texas in the 1820s, the Anglo and Mexican cultures of Texas have shaped one another, especially in terms of music, food, and language.

For example, *Tejano* music reflects roots in Mexican mariachi as well as American country and western music and is now a $100 million industry. As for food, salsa now outsells ketchup in the United States and you can hear ads for *"un* Quarter Pounder *con queso"* (a Quarter Pounder with cheese) on Spanish-language radio.

As Enrique Madrid, who lives in the border area between Texas and Mexico, says, "We have two very powerful cultures coming to terms with each other every day on the banks of [the Rio Grande] and creating a new culture."

NOW & THEN
Tex-Mex Culture
Critical Thinking: Generalizing Discuss the cultural interactions between Mexicans and Texans today. Ask students to form a generalization explaining what typically happens when any two cultural groups live close to each other. *Possible response: They adopt aspects of each other's culture.*

Have student pairs create a concept web like the one below as they brainstorm elements that define a culture.

GROLIER MULTIMEDIA ENCYCLOPEDIA
Stephen F. Austin, Texas Revolution

TEACHING OPTIONS

Teaching Less Proficient Readers

To help students understand the impact of Mexican independence, have them create a cause-and-effect chart like the one below and fill in the missing information.

Exploring Themes

Immigration and Migration Discuss the migration of Americans to Texas. Ask students why the settlers wanted to move to Texas. *Possible Response: They were attracted by the abundant, low-priced land.* Ask them how they think the settlers' eagerness to settle in Texas reflected the idea of manifest destiny. *Possible Response: The settlers may have felt that Texas was destined to become a part of the United States.*

Texas Fights for Independence

▶ **Discussing Key Ideas**
• Anglo settlers in Texas rebel against Santa Anna's oppressive government and declare their independence from Mexico.
• In 1845, Texas becomes the 28th state in the Union.

IN-DEPTH RESOURCES: UNIT 3
American Lives: Lorenzo de Zavala, p. 15

HISTORY FROM VISUALS
War for Texas Independence, 1835–1836

Reading the Map Point out that the star-shaped symbols on the map are color-coded to represent either Texan victories or Mexican victories. Have students make a two-column chart showing the Texans' win-loss record, based on information in the map.
Responses: Texan wins—San Antonio and San Jacinto; Texan losses—Alamo, Goliad, and Refugio.

Extension Ask students what the names of the Texan cities suggest about both Mexican and American influence on the region.
Possible Response: Some of the cities are Spanish names; others are English. One city—Washington-on-the-Brazos—reflects the influence of both cultures.

Kentucky blacksmith named Noah Smithwick. Smithwick later recalled life in Texas.

"Gone to Texas."

SIGNS ON ABANDONED HOMES

A PERSONAL VOICE
Men talked hopefully of the future; children reveled in the novelty of the present; but the women—ah, there was where the situation bore the heaviest. . . . There was no house to keep in order; the meager fare was so simple as to require little time for its preparation. There was no poultry, no dairy, no garden, no books . . . no schools, no churches—nothing to break the dull monotony of their lives, save an occasional wrangle among the children and dogs.
NOAH SMITHWICK, quoted in *Texas: An Album of History*

At Stephen F. Austin's capital in San Felipe, Smithwick found a more established town with "weddings and other social gatherings." He stayed briefly with a family in a simple home but later learned that "in the course of time the pole cabin gave place to a handsome brick house and that the rude furnishings were replaced by the best the country boasted."

Confident that Texas eventually would yield great wealth, Americans increasingly discussed extending the U.S. boundaries to the river they called the Rio Grande (known in Mexico as the Rio Bravo). President John Quincy Adams had previously offered to buy Texas for $1 million; President Andrew Jackson later upped the bid to $5 million. Mexico not only refused to sell Texas, but also began to have second thoughts about its hospitality to Anglo immigrants.

Skillbuilder Answer
Place: The Red River.
Region: *Possible Answer:* Both the Republic of Texas and Mexico claimed a large stretch of territory west of the Republic of Texas.

Texas Fights for Independence

As Texas's Anglo population surged, tensions erupted with Mexico over cultural differences, including slavery. The overwhelmingly Protestant Anglo settlers spoke English instead of Spanish. Furthermore, many of the settlers were Southern cotton or sugar farmers, who had brought slaves with them to Texas. Mexico, which had abolished slavery in 1829, insisted in vain that the Texans free their slaves.

In 1830, Mexico sealed its borders against any further immigration from the United States and slapped a heavy tax on the importation of American goods. Mexican troops rode into Texas to enforce Mexican law. Mexico, however, lacked sufficient troops to police its borders well. Despite immigration restrictions, the Anglo population of Texas doubled between 1830 and 1834. In 1834, Austin won a repeal of Mexico's 1830 prohibition of immigration. By 1835, more than 1,000 Americans streamed into Texas each month, scrawling the initials "G.T.T." on their doors to indicate that they had "Gone to Texas." A year later, Texas's population included only 4,000 *Tejanos*, but about 30,000 Native Americans, 30,000 Anglos, and 5,000 African Americans.

Meanwhile, Mexican politics had become increasingly unstable. Austin noted, "The political character of this country seems to partake of its geological features—all is volcanic." Austin had traveled to Mexico City late in 1833 to present petitions for

GEOGRAPHY SKILLBUILDER
PLACE *What geographical feature marked the northern border of the Republic of Texas?*
REGION *After 1836, what does the map show as a major disagreement still remaining between Texas and Mexico?*

THINK THROUGH HISTORY
C. *Contrasting* List some of the cultural conflicts caused by the influx of white settlers into Texas.

C. Answer The white settlers were Protestants, spoke English, and brought slaves, which defied Mexican law.

War for Texas Independence, 1835–1836

Land disputed by Texas and Mexico

UNITED STATES

Red River

Brazos River · Sabine River · Trinity River · Colorado River

REPUBLIC OF TEXAS · Nacogdoches

Alamo, Mar. 6, 1836 · Waterloo (Austin) · Washington-on-the-Brazos
San Antonio, Dec. 10, 1835 · Houston · San Jacinto, Apr. 21, 1836

Rio Grande

Santa Anna

Goliad, Mar. 20, 1836 · Matagorda · Galveston

Nueces River

Refugio, Mar. 14, 1836

0 200 Miles
0 400 Kilometers

• Laredo · Corpus Christi · Gulf of Mexico

→ Texan forces
→ Mexican forces
✷ Texan victory
✷ Mexican victory

MEXICO · Matamoros

TEACHING OPTIONS

Making Connections Across Time

Immigration Restrictions Today Point out that in the early 1830s, Mexico wanted to police its borders to keep American immigrants out of Texas. Tell students that today American officials patrol the borders to keep illegal Mexican immigrants out of the United States. Ask students to compare the reasons the Americans migrated to Mexico with the reasons compelling Mexicans to enter the United States today. *Possible Response: Many of the Americans sought farmland in Texas, while many of the Mexicans today seek greater economic opportunities in the United States.*

Making Connections Across Cultures

Shifting National Identity When Stephen F. Austin entered Texas in 1821, he said, "I bid an everlasting farewell to my native country, determined to fulfill rigidly all the duties and obligations of a Mexican citizen." Austin sincerely tried to "Mexicanize" himself. He learned Spanish and signed his name as "Don Estévan F. Austin." However, he became disillusioned with the Mexican government after his unjust imprisonment in Mexico. Weak and pale and plagued by a nagging cough, Austin reluctantly called for war.

greater self-government for Texas to Mexican president **Antonio López de Santa Anna.** While Austin was there, Santa Anna, convinced that Mexico would not be able to handle democracy, suspended the 1824 Mexican constitution and had Austin arrested and imprisoned for inciting revolution. After Santa Anna suspended local powers in Texas and other Mexican states, several rebellions erupted, including what would eventually come to be known as the **Texas Revolution.**

Henry Arthur McArdle conveys the brutality of the fighting in *Dawn at the Alamo*, painted between 1876 and 1883.

"REMEMBER THE ALAMO!" Austin had argued with Santa Anna for self-government for Texas, but without success. When he returned to Texas in 1835, he was convinced that war was its "only recourse." Determined to force Texas to obey laws he had established, Santa Anna marched toward San Antonio at the head of a 4,000-man army. At the same time Austin and his followers issued a call for Texans to arm themselves.

In San Antonio the commander of the Anglo troops, Lieutenant Colonel William Travis, moved his men into the **Alamo,** a Franciscan mission and fort. Travis believed that maintaining control of the Alamo would prevent Santa Anna's movement further north. Among Travis's troops were the famous frontiersmen Jim Bowie, who had designed the razor-sharp knife that still bears his name, and Davy Crockett, who sported a distinctive round fox cap with a long tail hanging down his back.

From February 23 until March 6, 1836, Santa Anna and his men attacked the rebels holed up in the Alamo. In a February 24 letter, Commander Travis addressed "the People of Texas and all Americans in the World." He wrote, "Our flag still waves proudly from the walls—*I shall never surrender or retreat.*"

The 12-day siege finally ended when Mexican troops succeeded in scaling the Alamo's walls. All 187 U.S. defenders and hundreds of Mexicans died—estimates suggest as many as 1,500. Only a few women and children were spared, including Mrs. Susanna Dickenson, the wife of Travis's artillery commander. Carried out of the compound wounded, she noticed "Colonel Crockett lying dead. . . . I even remember seeing his peculiar cap by his side."

Even as the battle for the Alamo raged, Texans declared their independence from Mexico on March 2, 1836. Believing that Mexico had deprived them of their fundamental rights, the Texas rebels likened themselves to the American colonists who had chafed under British rule 60 years earlier. On March 16, they ratified a constitution based on that of the United States. David G. Burnet became president of Texas's temporary government and Lorenzo de Zavala, a Mexican-American foe of Santa Anna, became vice-president.

THE LONE STAR REPUBLIC Later in March, Santa Anna's troops executed 445 rebels at Goliad. The Alamo and Goliad battles proved costly for Santa Anna, however, for the Texas rebels had been whipped into a fury. Six weeks after the defeat at the Alamo, the rebels' commander-in-chief, **Sam Houston,** and 900 men quietly surprised a group of Mexicans near the San Jacinto River.

With shouts of "Remember the Alamo!" the Texans killed 630 of Santa Anna's soldiers in 15 minutes and captured Santa Anna, who allegedly attempted to escape by dressing in a private's uniform. The victorious Texans set Santa Anna free after he signed the Treaty of Velasco, which granted independence to Texas.

Expanding Markets and Moving West **271**

KEY PLAYERS

SANTA ANNA
1795–1876

Antonio López de Santa Anna reportedly once said, "If I were God, I would wish to be more." Santa Anna began his career fighting for Spain in the war over Mexican independence. Later, he switched sides to fight for Mexico.

Declaring himself the "Napoleon of the West," Santa Anna took control of the government shortly after Mexico won independence in 1821. He spent the next 35 years alternately serving as president, leading troops into battle, and living in exile. Santa Anna served as president of Mexico five times. Repeatedly ousted from office, he was viewed as unprincipled, extravagant, and inept at governing.

SAM HOUSTON
1793–1863

Sam Houston ran away from home in Tennessee at about 15 and lived for three years with the Cherokee. He later fought in the U.S. army, studied law, was elected to Congress, and became governor of Tennessee.

In his memoirs Houston told of listening in vain for the signal guns indicating that the Alamo still stood. "I listened with an acuteness of sense which no man can understand whose hearing has not been sharpened by the teachings of the dwellers of the forest."

The Republic of Texas chose Houston to be its first president. When Texas became a state, he was elected to the U.S. Senate.

The Mexican government later refused to acknowledge the forced treaty and still hoped to regain Texas, or at least keep it independent of the United States. However, France and Great Britain both recognized Texas's new status. In July 1836, Sam Houston was elected president of the **Republic of Texas.** The new nation, commonly called the Lone Star Republic, established an army and a navy and proudly flew its white and red silk flag with the lone azure star.

TEXAS JOINS THE UNION Most Texans hoped that the United States would **annex,** or incorporate, their republic, but U.S. opinion divided along sectional lines. Southerners sought to extend slavery, which already had been established in Texas. Northerners feared that the annexation of more slave territory would tip the uneasy balance in the Senate in favor of slave states—and prompt war with Mexico.

In 1838, Texas's president, Sam Houston, invited the United States to annex Texas. John Quincy Adams, who as president of the United States had earlier supported purchasing Texas, now was instrumental in preventing the House of Representatives from voting on annexation. Houston repeated his offer in 1842 but again was rejected, this time by President John Tyler's Secretary of State Daniel Webster, who shared Adams's antislavery views. The 1844 U.S. presidential election featured a debate on westward expansion, and the winner, James K. Polk, a slaveholder, firmly favored the annexation of Texas "at the earliest practicable period."

On December 29, 1845, Texas became the 28th state in the Union. A furious Mexican government recalled its ambassador from Washington. Events were moving quickly toward war.

E. Answer The North did not want to admit a slave state, which would tip the balance of power between free and slave states. The South wished to annex Texas and extend slavery, which already existed in Texas.

THINK THROUGH HISTORY
E. Contrasting Explain the differences between the Northern and Southern positions on the annexation of Texas.

Section 3 Assessment

1. TERMS & NAMES

Identify:
- Stephen F. Austin
- land grant
- Antonio López de Santa Anna
- Texas Revolution
- Alamo
- Sam Houston
- Republic of Texas
- annex

2. ANALYZING Use a diagram similar to this one to analyze the relationship between Mexican authorities and Americans settling in Texas.

	Mexico	Settlers
Goals		
Actions		
Outcomes		

What other actions might Mexico or the settlers have taken to avoid conflict?

3. COMPARING Compare and contrast Santa Anna and Stephen Austin as leaders. Use details from the section to explain your answer.

THINK ABOUT
- Santa Anna's role as president of Mexico
- Santa Anna's qualities as a military leader
- Austin's settlement in Texas
- Austin's abilities as a negotiator

4. SYNTHESIZING Which group or country gained the most from the entry of Texas into the United States? Who lost the most? Support your opinion with specific references to the section.

ANSWERS

1. TERMS & NAMES

Stephen F. Austin, p. 268

land grant, p. 269

Antonio López de Santa Anna, p. 271

Texas Revolution, p. 271

Alamo, p. 271

Sam Houston, p. 271

Republic of Texas, p. 272

annex, p. 272

2. ANALYZING

Mexico's goals: To protect northern provinces; to bring in U.S. goods. **Settlers' goals:** To use land grants to set up homesteads. **Actions:** Mexico offers land grants, closes borders, and institutes patrols. **Actions:** Settlers ignore Mexican rules by bringing in slaves. Settlers ignore border restrictions and try to negotiate with Mexico. **Outcomes for Mexico:** Refuses purchase offers; loses Texas to the United States. **Outcomes for settlers:** Win independence; form the Republic of Texas.

3. COMPARING

Possible Answers: Students should note that Santa Anna was ambitious, restless, and sometimes reckless. They may point out that Austin was a successful land agent and was strict about the kinds of behavior tolerated in his settlements.

4. SYNTHESIZING

Possible Answer: Most students will say that the United States gained the most from the annexation of Texas, which added a huge portion of land to the country. Some students may indicate that Mexico lost the most because of the loss of its land, while others may suggest that Native Americans lost the most. Students should use details from the section to support their positions.

④ The War with Mexico

TERMS & NAMES
• James K. Polk
• Zachary Taylor
• Stephen Kearny
• Bear Flag Republic
• Winfield Scott
• Treaty of Guadalupe Hidalgo
• Gadsden Purchase
• forty-niners
• gold rush

LEARN ABOUT the American war with Mexico
TO UNDERSTAND how the United States pursued its goal of expanding across the continent.

ONE AMERICAN'S STORY

Robert E. Lee was born in Virginia in 1807 to a family related to George Washington. He graduated from the new U.S. Military Academy at West Point in 1829. After decades of distinguished service, Lee eventually would resign his commission in the U.S. Army to lead the Confederate Army in the Civil War. In 1846, however, the war with Mexico provided the 40-year-old captain with his first combat experience. Among the soldiers whom Lee directed in battle was his younger brother, Sidney Smith Lee. The elder Lee wrote about the battle.

A PERSONAL VOICE

No matter where I turned, my eyes reverted to [my brother], and I stood by his gun whenever I was not wanted elsewhere. Oh, I felt awfully, and am at a loss what I should have done had he been cut down before me. I thank God that he was saved. . . . [The service from the American battery] was terrific, and the shells thrown from our battery were constant and regular discharges, so beautiful in their flight and so destructive in their fall. It was awful! My heart bled for the inhabitants. The soldiers I did not care so much for, but it was terrible to think of the women and children.

ROBERT E. LEE, in a letter cited in *R. E. Lee* by Douglas Southall Freeman

William Edward West painted Robert E. Lee in the dress uniform of a U.S. Army lieutenant of engineers.

In a letter to his son a month later, Robert E. Lee repeated his disgust at the ugliness of war, saying, "You have no idea what a horrible sight a field of battle is." In recoiling at the ugliness of the war with Mexico, Lee hardly stood alone. From the start, Americans hotly debated whether the United States should pursue the war.

Polk Urges War

Hostilities between the United States and Mexico, which had flared during the Texas Revolution in 1836, reignited over the American annexation of Texas in 1845. The two countries might have solved these issues peaceably if not for the continuing instability of the Mexican government and the stubbornness of the U.S. president, **James K. Polk.**

Polk now believed that war with Mexico would bring not only Texas, but also New Mexico and California, into the Union. The president supported Texas's claims in disputes with Mexico over the Texas-Mexico border. While Texas insisted that its southern border extended to the Rio Grande, Mexico maintained that Texas's border stopped at the Nueces River, 100 miles northeast of the Rio Grande.

SLIDELL'S REJECTION   Meanwhile, the Mexican political situation was confusing and unpredictable. In 1844, Santa Anna had been ousted by General José Herrera. In November 1845, "Polk the Purposeful" sent a Spanish-speaking emissary, John Slidell, to Mexico to offer $25 million to buy Texas, California, and New Mexico. When Slidell arrived in Mexico City, Herrera refused to receive him. Hoping for Mexican aggression that would unify Americans behind

Expanding Markets and Moving West **273**

Section 4 Overview

OBJECTIVES

① To summarize the conflicting attitudes on waging war with Mexico.

② To describe key battles that helped the United States win the war with Mexico.

③ To identify U.S. territories gained from Mexico.

SKILLBUILDER

• Understanding geography: location, region, p. 275

CRITICAL THINKING

• Recognizing effects, pp. 274, 277
• Analyzing causes, p. 274
• Summarizing, p. 276
• Analyzing motives, p. 277
• Evaluating, p. 277
• Forming opinions, p. 277

FOCUS & MOTIVATE

▶ **Starting with the Student**
• Ask students what reasons, if any, they think justify war.
• Ask them whether acquiring more land is a justifiable reason for war.

OBJECTIVE
① **INSTRUCT**

Polk Urges War

▶ **Discussing Key Ideas**
• Polk blockades the Rio Grande after Mexico rejects his offer to buy territory.
• The Mexican War sparks controversy between the North and the South over the slavery issue.

IN-DEPTH RESOURCES: UNIT 3
Guided Reading, p. 4
American Lives, Robert E. Lee, p. 16

ACCESS FOR STUDENTS ACQUIRING ENGLISH
Guided Reading (Spanish), p. 95

SECTION 4 RESOURCES

 PRINT RESOURCES

IN-DEPTH RESOURCES: UNIT 3
Guided Reading, p. 4
Geography Application: Mexico Cedes Land to the United States, p. 6
Primary Source: President Polk's Speech, p. 11
American Lives: Robert E. Lee, p. 16

ACCESS FOR STUDENTS ACQUIRING ENGLISH
Guided Reading (Spanish), p. 95

FORMAL ASSESSMENT
Section Quiz, p. 116

ALTERNATIVE ASSESSMENT BOOK
See forms for supporting and scoring alternative activities.

 TECHNOLOGY RESOURCES

HUMANITIES TRANSPARENCIES
H9, *General Winfield Scott*

CRITICAL THINKING TRANSPARENCIES
CT8, Westward Movement
CT43, Growth of U.S. Population and Area: 1790–1850

CD-ROM Electronic Library of Primary Sources

VIDEO *American Portfolio: A Videodisc for U.S. History* user's guide, pp.81–85

INTERNET McDougal Littell Learning On-Line
http://www.mcdougallittell.com

Teacher's Edition   **273**

The War Begins

▶ **Starting with the Student**
Have students make a time line like the one below to chronicle U.S. military victories during the war with Mexico.

1846   1847

▶ **Discussing Key Ideas**
- Claiming that Mexico struck the first blow, the United States declares war against Mexico.
- U.S. forces quickly gain control of New Mexico and California.
- The United States invades Mexico and wins many significant battles.

IN-DEPTH RESOURCES: UNIT 3
Primary Source: President Polk's Speech, p. 11

MORE ABOUT . . .
Zachary Taylor

Taylor's victories during the war with Mexico made him a popular hero in the United States. Recruiting posters declared, "Here's to Old Zach! Glorious Times! Roast Beef, Ice Cream, and Three Months' Advance!" Taylor's exploits even inspired dances, such as the "Rough and Ready Polka" and the "General Taylor Quick Step."

---

a war, Polk then issued orders for General **Zachary Taylor** to march to the Rio Grande and blockade the river. Mexicans viewed this action as a violation of their territorial rights. Though many Americans shared Polk's goals for expansion, public opinion divided over resorting to military action. Slavery would soon emerge as the key issue complicating this debate.

SECTIONAL ATTITUDES TOWARD WAR   At first, Southern Whigs denounced the Democratic president's attitude toward war. Even John C. Calhoun, who had earlier plotted to annex Texas as a slave state, opposed the seizure of so much land from Mexico. However, many Southerners saw Texas as an opportunity to extend slavery and increase Southern power in Congress. Furthermore, the Wilmot Proviso, a proposed amendment to a military appropriations bill of 1846, prohibited slavery in lands that might be gained from Mexico. This attack on slavery solidified Southern support for war by transforming the debate on war into a debate on slavery.

Many Northerners opposed war. A Whig representative from Illinois, Abraham Lincoln, questioned the war's justification. Antislavery Whigs and abolitionists saw the war as a plot to expand slavery and ensure Southern domination of the Union. In a resolution adopted by the Massachusetts legislature, Charles Sumner proclaimed that "the lives of Mexicans are sacrificed in this cause; and a domestic question, which should be reserved for bloodless debate in our own country, is transferred to fields of battle in a foreign land."

The War Begins

> *"The lives of Mexicans are sacrificed in this cause."*
>
> CHARLES SUMNER,
> SENATOR FROM
> MASSACHUSETTS

With General Taylor positioned at the Rio Grande in 1845, John C. Frémont led an American military exploration party across the mountains into California's Salinas Valley, another violation of Mexico's territorial rights. The Mexican government had had enough.

Mexico responded to Taylor's invasion of the territory it claimed by sending troops across the Rio Grande. In a skirmish at Matamoros, Mexican soldiers killed 11 American soldiers. Polk immediately sent a war message to Congress, declaring that by shedding "American blood upon American soil," Mexico itself had started the war. Representative Abraham Lincoln questioned the truthfulness of the president's message, asking "whether our citizens, whose blood was shed, as in his message declared, were or were not, at that time, armed officers and soldiers, sent into that settlement by the military order of the President." Lincoln introduced the "Spot Resolution," asking Polk to certify the spot where the skirmish had occurred. Truthful or not, Polk's message swayed Congress, which voted overwhelmingly in favor of war, despite significant dissent across the country.

KEARNY MARCHES WEST   In 1846, as part of his plan to seize New Mexico and California, Polk ordered General **Stephen Kearny** to march from Fort Leavenworth, Kansas, across the desert to Santa Fe, New Mexico. Kearny earned the nickname "the Long Marcher" as he and his men crossed 800 miles of barren ground on their way to Santa Fe. They were met there by a New Mexican contingent that included upper-class Mexicans who wanted to join the United States. New Mexico fell to the United States without a shot.

After dispatching some of his troops south to Mexico, the Long Marcher led the rest on another long trek, this time to southern California.

THE BEAR FLAG REPUBLIC   By the beginning of the 19th century, Spanish settlers had established more than 20 missions along the California coast. After independence, the Mexican government took over these missions, just as it had done in Texas. By the late 1830s, about 7,000 Mexican settlers had migrated to California to set up cattle ranches, where they pressed Native Americans into

---

THINK THROUGH HISTORY
A. Recognizing Effects How did the issue of slavery affect the debate over the war with Mexico?

A. Answer Northerners opposed war, seeing it as a way to extend slavery to Texas. Many Southerners favored war for the same reason.

THINK THROUGH HISTORY
B. Analyzing Causes How did President Polk provoke Mexico to attack U.S. forces?

B. Answer Polk purposely ordered American soldiers to invade territory that Mexico claimed as its own; when Mexico attacked, Polk quickly claimed that Mexico had started the war.

Exploring Themes

Constitutional Concerns   Discuss Polk's message to Congress, which convinced members to vote in favor of declaring war against Mexico. Point out that Polk needed to sway the Congress because according to the Constitution, only Congress can declare war. Ask students why the Constitution did not give this authority to the president. *Possible Response: Because it would give the president too much power.* Then ask how some presidents have sidestepped this constitutional provision. *Possible Response: By waging undeclared wars.*

Making Connections Across Time

The Gulf of Tonkin Incident   Explain that in 1964, President Lyndon Johnson announced that North Vietnamese torpedo boats had attacked two U.S. destroyers in the Gulf of Tonkin, off North Vietnam's coast. Despite much confusion surrounding the details, the incident prompted Johnson to launch bombing raids on North Vietnam and to ask Congress to take "all necessary means to repel any armed attack against the forces of the United States and to prevent further aggression." Have students compare Johnson's maneuver with Polk's effort to instigate war. *Possible Response: Both claimed the enemy was the aggressor.*

The War with Mexico, 1846–1847

- ☐ Acquired by U.S. in Texas annexation of 1845
- ▨ Acquired by U.S. in Treaty of Guadalupe Hidalgo, 1848
- ▨ Acquired by U.S. in Gadsden Purchase, 1853
- ✦ Battle site
- ➡ U.S. forces
- ➡ Mexican forces

0   300 Miles
0   600 Kilometers

GEOGRAPHY SKILLBUILDER
LOCATION *From which locations in Texas did U.S. forces come to Buena Vista?*
REGION *Which territory was added to the United States in 1853? Why was that addition so significant?*

The United States, 1830

The United States, 1853

service as workers. By the mid-1840s, about 700 Americans also made their homes in California.

Polk's offer to buy California in 1845 aroused the indignation of the Mexican government. A group of American settlers, led by Frémont, seized the town of Sonoma in June 1846. Hoisting a flag that featured a grizzly bear, the rebels proudly declared their independence from Mexico and proclaimed the nation of the **Bear Flag Republic.** Kearny arrived from New Mexico and joined forces with Frémont and an American naval expedition led by Commodore John D. Sloat. The Mexican troops quickly gave way, leaving U.S. forces in control of California.

THE WAR IN MEXICO For American troops in Mexico, one military victory followed another. Though Mexican soldiers gallantly defended their own soil, their army labored under poor leadership. In contrast, U.S. soldiers served under capable officers like Captain Robert E. Lee and Captain Ulysses S. Grant, both West Point graduates.

The American invasion of Mexico lasted about a year and featured a pair of colorful generals, Zachary Taylor and **Winfield Scott.** Affectionately nicknamed "Old Rough and Ready" because he sported a casual straw hat and plain brown coat, Taylor attacked and captured Monterrey in September 1846, but allowed the Mexican garrison to escape.

Meanwhile, Polk hatched a bizarre scheme with Santa Anna, who had been living in exile in Cuba since August 1845. If Polk would help him sneak back to Mexico, Santa Anna promised, he would end the war and mediate the border dispute in Polk's favor. Polk agreed, but Santa Anna returned to Mexico, resumed the presidency, and took command of the army. In February 1847, he ordered an attack on Taylor's forces at Buena Vista. Though the Mexican army boasted superior numbers, its

Skillbuilder Answer
Location: San Antonio, Corpus Christi. **Region:** Gadsden Purchase; it was significant because it completed the present-day borders of the United States (except for Alaska and Hawaii).

LOS NIÑOS HEROES

Though most Americans know little about the war with Mexico, Mexicans view the war as a crucial event in their history.

On September 14, 1847, General Winfield Scott captured Mexico City after the hard-fought Battle of Chapultepec, the site of the Mexican military academy. There, six young cadets leaped from Chapultepec Castle, to commit suicide rather than surrender to the U.S. Army. A monument that honors *Los Niños Heroes* (the boy heroes) inspires pilgrimages every September 13 to commemorate the battle.

Expanding Markets and Moving West **275**

America Claims the Spoils of War

▶ *Discussing Key Ideas*
- The terms of the Treaty of Guadalupe Hidalgo enlarge U.S. territory by about one-third.
- Zachary Taylor wins the 1848 presidential election.
- The discovery of gold in California sparks gold fever and the rapid growth of San Francisco.

IN-DEPTH RESOURCES: UNIT 3
Geography Application: Mexico Cedes Land to the United States, p. 6

 ELECTRONIC LIBRARY OF PRIMARY SOURCES
from the Treaty of Guadalupe Hidalgo

 CRITICAL THINKING TRANSPARENCIES
CT43, Growth of U.S. Population and Area: 1790–1850

NOW & THEN
Blue Jeans: The Hot Commodity

Critical Thinking: Evaluating Ask students how Levi Strauss's decision to make pants for the miners reflected the entrepreneurial spirit. *Possible Responses: Using his own capital, Strauss took a chance on creating a new industry; he saw a possible demand and manufactured the goods to meet it.*

---

soldiers suffered from exhaustion. Taylor's more rested troops pushed Santa Anna into Mexico's interior.

Scott's forces took advantage of Santa Anna's disrupted strategy and captured Veracruz in March. The regal General Scott always wore a full-dress blue uniform with a yellow sash, which won him the nickname "Old Fuss and Feathers." Scott supervised an amphibious landing at Veracruz, in which an army of 10,000 men landed on an island off Veracruz in 200 ships and ferried 67 boats in less than 5 hours, an extraordinary military feat at the time. Scott's troops then set off for Mexico City, which they captured on September 14, 1847. Covering 260 miles, Scott's army had lost not a single battle.

America Claims the Spoils of War

For Mexico, the war in which it lost 50,000 men and nearly half its land marked an ugly milestone in its relations with the United States. America's victory came at the cost of about 13,000 men. Of these, nearly 2,000 died in battle or from wounds and more than 11,000 perished from diseases, such as yellow fever. However, the magnitude of the land gained by the United States was astounding. It enlarged U.S. territory by approximately one-third.

THE TREATY OF GUADALUPE HIDALGO On February 2, 1848, the United States and Mexico signed the **Treaty of Guadalupe Hidalgo.** Mexico agreed to the Rio Grande border for Texas and ceded the New Mexico and California territories to the United States. The United States agreed to pay $15 million for the Mexican cession, which included present-day California, Nevada, New Mexico, Utah, most of Arizona, and parts of Colorado and Wyoming. The treaty guaranteed Mexicans freedom of religion, protection of property, bilingual elections, and open borders.

Five years later, in 1853, President Franklin Pierce would authorize his emissary James Gadsden to pay Mexico an additional $10 million for another piece of territory south of the Gila River. Along with the settlement of Oregon and the Treaty of Guadalupe Hidalgo, the **Gadsden Purchase** established the current borders of the lower 48 states.

TAYLOR'S ELECTION IN 1848 Suffering from poor health, Polk declined to run for reelection in 1848. The Democrats nominated the colorless Lewis Cass and remained silent about the extension of slavery into America's vast new holdings. A small group of antislavery Democrats nominated Martin Van Buren to lead the Free-Soil Party, which supported a congressional prohibition on the extension of slavery into the territories. Van Buren captured 10 percent of the popular vote and no electoral votes. The Whig nominee, war hero Zachary Taylor, narrowly won the election. Taylor's victory, however, was soon overshadowed by a glittering discovery in one of America's new territories.

THE CALIFORNIA GOLD RUSH In January 1848, James Marshall, an American carpenter working on John Sutter's property in the California Sierra Nevadas, discovered gold at Sutter's Mill. Word of the chance discovery traveled with lightning speed.

Soon after the news reached San Francisco, the whole town hustled to the Sacramento Valley to pan for gold. Lacking staff and readers, San Francisco's newspaper, the *Californian*, suspended publication. An editorial in the final issue, dated May 29, complained that the whole country "resounds with the sordid cry of gold, GOLD, GOLD! while the field is left half-plowed, the house half-built, and everything neglected but the manufacture of shovels and pickaxes."

On June 6, 1848, Monterey's Mayor Walter Colton sent a scout to

NOW & THEN

BLUE JEANS: THE HOT COMMODITY

Though gold miners in 1848 counted on striking it rich, some of the largest fortunes went to those who clothed the miners. Levi Strauss, founder of Levi Strauss and Company, the San Francisco blue jeans manufacturer, originally intended to sell canvas tents to the California miners. However, he soon found that the canvas could be made into sturdy pants with rivets on the seams and pockets for the miners' tools.

What began as an article of clothing designed to meet a simple need today is woven into the fabric of American culture and the global economy. Having cashed in on the California gold rush, in the late 1900s Levi Strauss and Company is panning for blue jeans "gold" in India, where the market for blue jeans is estimated at $130 million. Blue jeans, the universal souvenir, are carried in countless suitcases to countries all over the world.

THINK THROUGH HISTORY
C. Summarizing
Explain the importance of the Treaty of Guadalupe Hidalgo and the Gadsden Purchase.

C. Answer
Together with the settlement of the Oregon question, the Treaty of Guadalupe Hidalgo and the Gadsden Purchase settled the boundaries of mainland United States.

TEACHING OPTION

 Cooperative Activity: Creating a Newspaper About the Gold Rush

Task: Groups of four or five students will put together a newspaper about the discovery of gold in California.

Purpose: To explore the causes and effects of the California gold rush.

Activity: Group members should divide the tasks. Some students might write background articles on the discovery; others might do features on the miners. Students should also include editorials and advertisements relevant

to the period (for example, ads for Levi Strauss's blue jeans). Pictures, photos, and other graphics should illustrate the articles and ads. If possible, students should design and print the newspaper using a desktop publishing program.

📁 **Building a Portfolio:** Students who wish to add their newspaper to their portfolio should include a note summarizing their contributions to the project.

Standards for Evaluation
Newspapers should . . .

- include stories that answer the journalist's five W's—who, what, where, when, why
- convey the excitement of gold fever
- include graphics that illustrate the stories and ads

ALTERNATIVE ASSESSMENT BOOK
Standards for Evaluating a Cooperative Activity

report on what was happening. When the scout returned on June 14, the mayor described the scene that had taken place in the middle of the town's main street.

A PERSONAL VOICE
The blacksmith dropped his hammer, the carpenter his plane, the mason his trowel, the farmer his sickle, the baker his loaf, and the tapster [bartender] his bottle. All were off for the mines, some on horses, some on carts, and some on crutches, and one went in a litter. . . . I have only a community of women left, and a gang of prisoners, with here and there a soldier who will give his captain the slip at first chance. I don't blame the fellow a whit; seven dollars a month, while others [prospectors] are making two or three hundred a day!

WALTER COLTON, quoted in *California: A Bicentennial History*

The crowded buildings and the forest of masts in this 1850 photograph of San Francisco (*above right*) contrast sharply with, *above left,* Victor Prevost's 1847 painting, *View of San Francisco* (formerly Yorba Buena).

As gold fever traveled eastward, overland migration to California skyrocketed from 400 in 1848 to 44,000 in 1850. The rest of the world soon caught the fever, as the so-called **forty-niners** made their way in 1849 to the California **gold rush** from Asia, South America, and Europe.

Because of its location as a supply center, San Francisco became "a pandemonium of a city," according to one traveler. Indeed, the city's population exploded from 1,000 in 1848 to 35,000 in 1850. Ferrying people and supplies, ships clogged San Francisco's harbor with a forest of masts.

By 1849, California's population exceeded 100,000, including Mexicans, free African-American miners, and slaves. A constitutional convention in 1849 drew up a state constitution that outlawed slavery. California's application for statehood provoked fiery protest in Congress and became just one more sore point between irate Northerners and Southerners, each intent on winning the sectional argument over slavery.

Section 4 Assessment

1. TERMS & NAMES
Identify
- James K. Polk
- Zachary Taylor
- Stephen Kearny
- Bear Flag Republic
- Winfield Scott
- Treaty of Guadalupe Hidalgo
- Gadsden Purchase
- forty-niners
- gold rush

2. RECOGNIZING EFFECTS
Draw a chart showing how the boundaries of the U.S. mainland were formed.

Effect: | Present-day U.S. borders

Causes: [ ] [ ] [ ]

3. EVALUATING How would you evaluate President Polk's attitude and behavior toward Mexico? Use specific references to the chapter to support your response.

THINK ABOUT
- Polk's position on expansion
- his actions once in office
- his relationship with Santa Anna

4. FORMING OPINIONS Would you have supported the controversial war with Mexico? Why or why not? Explain your answer, including details from the chapter.

THINK ABOUT
- the positions of the North and the South on the war
- the different viewpoints of the United States and Mexico

Expanding Markets and Moving West **277**

REVIEWING THE CHAPTER

TERMS & NAMES

1. market revolution, p. 255
2. capitalism, p. 255
3. Samuel F. B. Morse, p. 256
4. manifest destiny, p. 261
5. Oregon Trail, p. 263
6. Brigham Young, p. 264
7. Alamo, p. 271
8. Sam Houston, p. 271
9. Treaty of Guadalupe Hidalgo, p. 276
10. forty-niners, p. 277

MAIN IDEAS
Answers will vary.

11. The canal allowed goods and raw materials to move more quickly and at a lower cost between the two regions.

12. Inventions—sewing machine, vulcanized rubber, telegraph. Technological advancements—canals, steam power.

13. Transportation systems made the Northeast a manufacturing and commercial center. The steel plow and reaper made the Midwest an agricultural giant. Steam engines allowed the South to ship agricultural products north.

14. People were eager to settle the western land. They believed it was a destiny ordained by God.

15. The desire to farm, to buy land for speculation, to develop new markets, to convert Native Americans, to escape economic problems, and to escape religious persecution.

16. Vast amounts of land were made available for very little money.

17. Thousands of Americans went to Texas, and the two groups clashed over culture, language, religion, and slavery.

18. A large Mexican army killed all 187 defenders of the Alamo. As many as 1,500 Mexicans also died. Fury over the defeat at the Alamo spurred Texans to defeat Mexico.

19. President Polk sent troops into disputed territory to form a blockade, and Mexico attacked.

20. The United States gained Texas, California, and other western land from Mexico; it also settled disputes with Britain over Oregon and the northern boundaries of the country.

REVIEWING THE CHAPTER

TERMS & NAMES For each term below, write a sentence explaining its significance for the economic and physical expansion of the United States in the mid-19th century. For each person below, explain his role in events leading to this expansion.

1. market revolution
2. capitalism
3. Samuel F. B. Morse
4. manifest destiny
5. Oregon Trail
6. Brigham Young
7. Alamo
8. Sam Houston
9. Treaty of Guadalupe Hidalgo
10. forty-niners

MAIN IDEAS

SECTION 1 (pages 254–259)

The Market Revolution

11. In what ways did the Erie Canal connect the western territories and the Northeast?
12. What inventions and technological advancements changed lives as part of the market revolution?
13. How did the inventions and innovations of the mid-19th century encourage various regions to specialize in certain industries?

SECTION 2 (pages 260–265)

Manifest Destiny

14. Why was the concept of manifest destiny such an appealing one to America in the 1840s?
15. Describe the factors that drew settlers west during the first half of the 19th century.

SECTION 3 (pages 268–272)

Expansion in Texas

16. What made Americans want to settle in Texas?
17. What were the causes of the war between Americans and Mexicans over Texas?
18. Describe the battle of the Alamo and explain why it is an important symbol in U.S. history.

SECTION 4 (pages 273–277)

The War with Mexico

19. What developments caused the United States to go to war with Mexico?
20. How did the United States pursue its goal of expanding across the continent during the 1840s?

THINKING CRITICALLY

1. **AMERICAN GOALS** What were America's goals and ideals during this period of expansion and economic change? Draw a chart in which you list goals from the period, how they were achieved, and in what ways their effects were positive or negative.

Goal	How Achieved	Positive/Negative Effects

2. **AMERICANS IN TEXAS** Why did Americans rebel against Mexican rule when they settled in Texas? Explain your answer.

3. **IDEAL OF THE WEST** Reread the quote by Ignatius Donnelly on page 252. Do you agree with his description of the West as a "new and happy land"? Support your opinion with concrete references to the chapter.

4. **GEOGRAPHY OF THE OREGON TRAIL** Review the map on pages 266–267. In what ways would this map have been helpful to settlers following the Oregon Trail to a new home? Explain your answer.

5. **NEW COMMUNICATIONS** What was the impact of the new methods of communication during this period? Use details from the text to support your response.

6. **ANALYZING PRIMARY SOURCES** Anna Howard Shaw was 12 years old in 1859 when she, her three sisters, younger brother, and mother became homesteaders in northern Michigan. She later described her experiences.

> We all had an idea that we were going to a farm, and we expected some resemblance at least to the prosperous farms we had seen in New England. What we found awaiting us were the four walls and the roof of a good-sized loghouse, standing in a small cleared strip of wilderness, its doors and windows represented by square holes, its floor also a thing of the future, its whole effect achingly forlorn and desolate. . . . I shall never forget the look my mother turned upon the place. . . . Our little world had crumbled under our feet. Never before had we seen our mother give way to despair.
>
> **ANNA HOWARD SHAW,** quoted in *American Women*

How does Shaw describe the expectations and reality of homesteading? What hardships and burdens do you think Shaw and her family had to face?

THINKING CRITICALLY

1. AMERICAN GOALS
Possible Answers: Goals: finding new markets; increasing personal economic opportunities; expanding the borders of the country. How achieved: by increasing westward expansion and trade; by inventing new machines; by going to war to acquire new land. Positive effects: expanded U.S. borders; made the United States more technologically advanced; settled the West. Negative effects: displaced Native Americans; expanded slavery; lost lives in warfare.

2. AMERICANS IN TEXAS
Possible Response: Most students may suggest that the settlers who moved to Texas were filled with the same spirit of independence that led American colonists to rebel against Britain. They might further note that the people who were the most independent and courageous were often those who left established homes and took the risk of settling in new lands, and that such people did not want to follow other people's rules.

3. IDEAL OF THE WEST
Possible Responses: Some students may agree that the West was full of promise, while others may state that exploring the West brought with it numerous and violent conflicts with Native Americans as well as hardships for pioneers and questions about slavery.

ALTERNATIVE ASSESSMENT

1. MAPPING EFFECTS OF EXPANSION

- During the 1830s and 1840s, the U.S. government expanded its control over territories in the West. What effect did changing borders and new territories have on different population groups?
- **Cooperative Learning** Working with a small group, draw two maps of the United States, one showing its territorial boundaries as of 1830, the other showing its territorial boundaries as of 1850.

 Use the CD-ROM *Electronic Library of Primary Sources* and other resources to identify the following on each map:

1. the location of Native American tribes
2. the U.S.-Mexican border
3. the location of slave states and territories
4. the routes of the major trails that settlers followed

- Prepare an oral presentation in which you compare these maps, analyzing the differences. Give political, economic, and historical reasons why the maps show differences.

2. EXPLORING PRIMARY SOURCES

Today's information about western settlement comes from primary sources like diaries or journals. Find other diary or journal passages about settling the West, using the library or the Internet. How are the experiences revealed similar to or different from those described in this chapter? Use one of the following formats to address this question:

- Write an essay comparing the experiences revealed in the new passages with those from the chapter.
- Choose one passage and develop a brief dramatic monologue that reveals the writers' experiences.

3. PORTFOLIO PROJECT

Use the Living History activity to expand your portfolio.

LIVING HISTORY

REVISING YOUR ADVERTISEMENT

After you have developed your advertisement for a 19th-century invention or technological improvement, ask a friend to look at it and answer the following questions:

- How well does the ad address its audience?
- Does the ad provide enough information on the way the product or improvement functions?

When you have made changes based on your friend's comments, share your advertisement with the class. Then add it to your American history portfolio.

Review Chapter 9

AMERICA'S CHANGING ECONOMY During the early part of the 19th century, America's economy responded to innovations in the areas of manufacturing, transportation, communication, and agriculture. The invention of the telegraph, along with the growth of canals and railroads, connected regions and people. The introduction of new farm implements transformed the Midwest into the breadbasket for the nation. People began to specialize, selling what they grew or produced and receiving cash in return. The market revolution brought about the development of specialized regional economies.

WESTWARD EXPANSION Many Americans believed in manifest destiny, the idea that it was America's calling to expand to the Pacific Ocean. Settlers headed west on the Santa Fe and Oregon trails in search of new farmland and new markets. The Mormons moved west to escape religious persecution. Native Americans lost their homelands to U.S. settlers.

CONFLICT IN TEXAS After Mexico won independence, its northern provinces began trading with the United States. The Mexican government offered Texas land grants to U.S. settlers. Cultural conflict developed and although Mexico restricted immigration, Americans continued to pour in. Tension gave way to fighting, and Americans declared Texas an independent republic in 1836. Texas became the 28th state in 1845.

WAR WITH MEXICO President Polk provoked war by sending troops into Mexican territory. California and New Mexico gave in to American demands quite easily, and American troops captured Mexico City. The Mexican government gave up about a third of its land in exchange for $15 million. In 1848, a gold rush in California brought thousands of people from all over the world. California applied for admission to the Union as a free state.

Preview Chapter 10

The United States faced controversy over which of the new states being admitted to the Union would be slave states and which would be free. The country found itself dangerously close to a war erupting from within. You will read about these and other significant developments in Chapter 10.

Expanding Markets and Moving West **279**

ALTERNATIVE ASSESSMENT

1. MAPPING EFFECTS OF EXPANSION
Standards for Evaluation
A map should meet the following criteria:

- Displays historically accurate representations of U.S. territory as of 1830 and 1850.
- Reflects careful research, with information drawn from a variety of sources.
- Contains clear, complete map keys, including color codes and symbols for locations and routes highlighted on the maps.

2. EXPLORING PRIMARY SOURCES
Standards for Evaluation
COMPARISON ESSAY
An essay should meet the following criteria:

- Cites at least three similarities or differences in various firsthand accounts of western settlement.
- Uses specific examples to support points of comparison.
- Follows a consistent and orderly plan of organization.

MONOLOGUE
A monologue should meet the following criteria:

- Uses language that reflects how the character would talk.
- Contains authentic details about western settlement.

3. PORTFOLIO PROJECT
LIVING HISTORY
Standards for Evaluation
An advertisement should meet the following criteria:

- Focuses on the target audience of mid–19th–century consumers.
- Contains details to help the target audience make informed purchasing decisions about the product.
- Includes a clever slogan that captures the audience's attention.
- Uses persuasive language effectively.

IN-DEPTH RESOURCES: UNIT 3
See the form for scoring this activity on page 18.

THINKING CRITICALLY

4. GEOGRAPHY OF THE OREGON TRAIL
Most students should indicate that the map contains valuable information about the terrain and shows the location of bodies of water and forts.

5. NEW COMMUNICATIONS
Possible Responses: New methods of communication made the conduct of business more efficient by allowing speedy transmission of orders and other information. The telegraph linked regions in a network of instant communication.

6. ANALYZING PRIMARY SOURCES
Possible Responses: They expected an established farm with comfortable living quarters; the reality was an incomplete dwelling in the middle of desolate wilderness. They would have had to conquer their despair, finish building their home, grow food, find water, protect themselves from wild animals, and try to survive.

PLANNING GUIDE
The Union in Peril

		TEACHING SUPPORT	ASSESSMENT
SECTION 1 The Divisive Politics of Slavery *pp. 282–287*	**Key Ideas** *The issue of slavery continues to dominate U.S. politics in the early 1850s, despite the Compromise of 1850.*	***In-Depth Resources: Unit 3*** • Guided Reading, p. 19 • Geography Application: Slave Populations in the United States, p. 24 • American Lives: John C. Calhoun, p. 33 **COOPERATIVE ACTIVITY** • Planning a Debate, p. 285 (TE)	*Section 1 Assessment,* p. 287 (PE) *Self-Assessment,* p. 287 (TE) ***Formal Assessment*** • Section Quiz, p. 125 ***Alternative Assessment Book*** • Standards for Evaluating a Cooperative Activity
SECTION 2 Protest, Resistance, and Violence *pp. 288–294*	*Proslavery and antislavery factions disagree over the treatment of fugitive slaves and the spread of slavery to the territories.*	***In-Depth Resources: Unit 3*** • Guided Reading, p. 20 • Skillbuilder Practice: Analyzing Causes, p. 23 • Primary Source: The Underground Railroad, p. 26 • American Lives: Harriet Tubman, p. 34 **COOPERATIVE ACTIVITIES** • Experiencing the Underground Railroad, p. 289 (TE) • Responding to *Uncle Tom's Cabin,* p. 290 (TE)	*Section 2 Assessment,* p. 294 (PE) *Self-Assessment,* p. 294 (TE) ***Formal Assessment*** • Section Quiz, p. 126 ***Alternative Assessment Book*** • Standards for Evaluating a Cooperative Activity
SECTION 3 The Birth of the Republican Party *pp. 295–298*	*Many factors—including an increase in immigration and the collapse of the Whig Party—lead to a political split over the issue of slavery.*	***In-Depth Resources: Unit 3*** • Guided Reading, p. 21	*Section 3 Assessment,* p. 298 (PE) *Self-Assessment,* p. 298 (TE) ***Formal Assessment*** • Section Quiz, p. 127
SECTION 4 Slavery and Secession *pp. 299–305*	*A series of controversial events heighten the sectional conflict and bring the nation to the brink of war under President Buchanan's weak leadership.*	***In-Depth Resources: Unit 3*** • Guided Reading, p. 22 • Primary Sources: *from* The Lincoln-Douglas Debates, p. 27; John Brown's Last Speech, p. 28 **COOPERATIVE ACTIVITY** • Writing a Newspaper Account, p. 301 (TE)	*Section 4 Assessment,* p. 305 (PE) *Self-Assessment,* p. 305 (TE) ***Formal Assessment*** • Section Quiz, p. 128 ***Alternative Assessment Book*** • Standards for Evaluating a Cooperative Activity
CHAPTER RESOURCES	**Chapter Overview** *The growing conflict over slavery divides North and South. When compromise fails, division results: after the election of 1860, Southern states secede from the Union.*	***In-Depth Resources: Unit 3*** • Living History Project: Worksheet, p. 35; Standards, p. 36 ***Telescoping the Times*** • Chapter Summary, pp. 19–20 ***Planning for Block Schedules***	*Chapter Assessment,* pp. 308–309 (PE) *Alternative Assessment,* p. 309 (PE) ***Formal Assessment*** • Chapter Test, forms A and B, pp. 129–134 **Test Generator** ***Alternative Assessment Book*** See explanation and forms for different kinds of alternative assessments including portfolio assessment.

Critical Thinking Transparencies
• CT10, Compromise of 1850
• CT44, Population Growth: 1820–1860

Grolier Multimedia Encyclopedia
• Stephen Douglas

INTERNET RESOURCES
• See *McDougal Littell Learning On-Line* for links to information about Henry Clay and the Compromise of 1850.

Humanities Transparencies
• H10, *No. 10 Harriet Tubman series* by Jacob Lawrence

Electronic Library of Primary Sources
• from The Fugitive Slave Act; from "The Function of Conscience" by Theodore Parker; "The Story of Eliza Harris" by Levi Coffin; "On Slavery" by Harriet Tubman

INTERNET RESOURCES
• See *McDougal Littell Learning On-Line* for links to information about the underground railroad.

INTERNET RESOURCES
• See *McDougal Littell Learning On-Line* for links to information about political parties.

Geography Transparencies
• G10, Presidential Elections: 1856, 1860

Critical Thinking Transparencies
• CT10, Compromise of 1850

Electronic Library of Primary Sources
• from the Inaugural Address of Jefferson Davis, 1861

INTERNET RESOURCES
• See *McDougal Littell Learning On-Line* for links to information about Abraham Lincoln.

American Portfolio: A Videodisc for U.S. History, user's guide, pp. 87–93

INTERNET RESOURCES
Learning On-Line: Social Studies
http://www.mcdougallittell.com

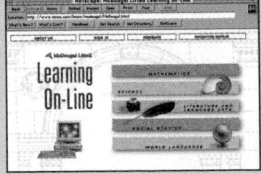

Block Scheduling (90 MINUTES)

Day 1
Section 1, pp. 282–287
Section 2, pp. 288–294
Section Assessments, pp. 287, 294

Day 2
Section 3, pp. 295–298
Section 4, pp. 299–305
Section Assessments, p. 298, 305
Tracing Themes: Constitutional Concerns—States Rights, pp. 306–307
Chapter Assessment, pp. 308–309

YEARLY PACING *Chapter 10 Total:* 2 days *Yearly Total:* 85 days

See *Planning for Block Schedules* for special activities and pacing strategies.

Customizing for Special Populations

Students Acquiring English

Access for Students Acquiring English
• Guided Reading for Sections 1–4 (Spanish), pp. 101–104
• Chapter Summary (Spanish), pp. 99–100
• Skillbuilder Practice: Analyzing Causes (Spanish), p. 105
• Geography Application: Slave Populations in the United States (Spanish), p. 106

INTERNET RESOURCES
• See *McDougal Littell Learning On-Line* The Diverse Classroom.

Less Proficient Readers

In-Depth Resources: Unit 3
• Guided Reading for Sections 1–4, pp. 19–22
• Skillbuilder: Analyzing Causes p. 23
• Geography Application: Slave Populations in the United States, p. 24

Telescoping the Times
• Chapter Summary, pp. 19–20

See additional strategies at point of use in the Teacher's Edition.

Gifted and Talented Students

In-Depth Resources: Unit 3
• Primary Sources: The Underground Railroad, p. 26; from The Lincoln-Douglas Debates, p. 27; John Brown's Last Speech, p. 28;
• American Lives: John C. Calhoun, p. 33; Harriet Tubman, p. 34

See additional strategies at point of use in the Teacher's Edition.

Connections to Literature READINGS FOR STUDENTS

In-Depth Resources: Unit 3
• from *Uncle Tom's Cabin* by Harriet Beecher Stowe, p. 30

Enrichment Reading
• Vidal, Gore
Lincoln.
New York: Ballantine, 1985
This novel reveals the political and personal struggles of President Lincoln as he guides the nation through the Civil War while confronting his own personal and family tragedies.

• Jacobs, Harriet
Incidents in the Life of a Slave Girl.
Cambridge Mass.: Harvard University Press, 1987.
This is one of the few existing slave narratives authored by a woman. In this powerful story, Jacobs describes her ultimately successful struggle for freedom.

McDougal Littell *The Language of Literature*
American Literature

• Frederick Douglass, from *Narrative of the Life of Frederick Douglass, and American Slave,* p. 446
• Frances Ellen Watkins Harper "Free Labor," p. 458

The Union in Peril

▶ **Starting with the Student**
Have students read the Lincoln quotation. Then ask them the following questions:

- In Lincoln's view, which is more important, abolishing slavery or having a unified country?
- Do you think American society today would be better or worse if the Union had peaceably broken up into two nations?

PREVIEWING THE CHAPTER
- Go over the titles and brief descriptions of the sections.
- Ask students: Why do you think this chapter features the efforts of two women rather than two men?
- Have students look at the time line and point out events and pictures that intrigue them.
- Have students take a few moments to write questions that they expect to be answered in the chapter.

CHAPTER

10 The Union in Peril

SECTION 1

The Divisive Politics of Slavery

The issue of slavery continues to dominate U.S. politics in the early 1850s, despite the Compromise of 1850.

SECTION 2

Protest, Resistance, and Violence

Proslavery and antislavery factions disagree over the treatment of fugitive slaves and the spread of slavery to the territories.

SECTION 3

The Birth of the Republican Party

Many factors—including an increase in immigration and the collapse of the Whig Party—lead to a political split over the issue of slavery.

SECTION 4

Slavery and Secession

A series of controversial events heighten the sectional conflict and bring the nation to the brink of war under President Buchanan's weak leadership.

> "Can we as a nation continue together *permanently—forever*—half slave and half free?"
>
> Abraham Lincoln, 1855

Harriet Tubman becomes a conductor on the Underground Railroad.

Harriet Beecher Stowe publishes *Uncle Tom's Cabin*.

Congress passes Compromise of 1850.

The nation mourns the deaths of Henry Clay and Daniel Webster.

The Republican Party forms.

California enters the Union.

⊙ Franklin Pierce is elected president.

Congress approves the Kansas-Nebraska Act.

| THE UNITED STATES | **1850** | | 1852 | | 185 |
| THE WORLD | | 1851 | 1852 | 1853 | 185 |

Taiping rebellion in China begins.

South African Republic is established.

Crimean War begins.

Charles Dickens's *Hard Times* is published.

THEMES IN CHAPTER 10

Immigration and Migration

Most of the people migrating to the United States hoped to start a new life. Most had not anticipated the amount of hard work necessary to get by in their new home, and few were aware that their American Dream could be thwarted by those who had come before.

See Teacher's Edition notes, pp. 284, 296.

Between 1840 and 1860, millions of European immigrants poured into the United States, most from Ireland and Germany. All brought their own talents and experience, all making their own unique contribution to the emerging nation.

Women in America

Although the era of the 1840s and 1850s saw a few women, including Harriet Tubman and Harriet Beecher Stowe, attain prominence, many women led harsh lives, struggling to eke out an existence for themselves and their families.

See Teacher's Edition note, p. 291.

Constitutional Concerns

By the 1840s, the issue of slavery was to consume a major part of the work of the federal legislature. Issues included the status of slaves as property and the rights of states to choose or reject slavery and to secede.

See Teacher's Edition note, p. 304.

LIVING HISTORY

SURVEYING SECTIONALISM TODAY

Many of the events in this chapter deal with problems caused by sectional differences between the North and the South. Take an informal survey in which you ask people to identify ways in which various sections of the country differ today. Some questions to ask might include:

- What differences in speech, lifestyle, and customs can you think of?
- What images come to mind when you think of different parts of the country?
- What TV, newspaper, or magazine slogans or ads seem to you to be aimed at specific regions?

📁 **PORTFOLIO PROJECT** Save the results of your survey in a folder for your American history portfolio. You will share the results of your survey at the end of the chapter.

Chief Justice Roger Taney, *left,* announces decision in case involving Dred Scott, *above.*

A POLITICAL RACE

SURVEYING SECTIONALISM TODAY

Discuss ways of going about conducting the survey:

- Try to find people who have lived in different parts of the country.
- Ask them to identify the parts of the country in which they lived.
- Compile some biographical data about the interviewees to help your audience understand the survey.
- Prepare a list of questions in advance.
- Ask for anecdotes that may help to explain sectional differences.
- With the permission of the interviewee, use a tape recorder during the interview and take notes.

Project Planning Guide

Step 1	Students choose the people they are going to interview.
Step 2	Students prepare survey questions.
Step 3	Students conduct their surveys.
Step 4	Students collect their survey tapes and other relevant information in their folders.

IN-DEPTH RESOURCES: UNIT 3
See worksheet and standards for evaluation, pp. 35, 36.

Timeline

- **James Buchanan is elected president.** (1856)
- **John Brown attacks the arsenal at Harpers Ferry, Virginia.** (1859)
- ★ **Abraham Lincoln is elected president.** (1860)
- **The Confederacy forms.** (1861)

1855 — 1856 — 1857 — 1859 — 1860 — 1861

- **British engineer Henry Bessemer develops process to produce steel.** (1856)
- **Mexico institutes a new constitution.** (1857)
- **Sepoy Rebellion in India begins.**
- **Charles Darwin's *Origin of Species* is published.** (1859)

The Union in Peril **281**

RECOMMENDED RESOURCES

Books for the Teacher

Foner, Eric. *Free Soil, Free Labor, Free Men.* New York: Oxford UP, 1970. Early years of Republican Party.

Quarles, Benjamin. *Allies for Freedom.* New York: Oxford UP, 1974. African Americans and John Brown.

Stampp, Kenneth. *America in 1857.* New York: Oxford UP, 1990. Sectional conflict as Buchanan takes office.

Books for the Student

Angle, Paul M. *The Complete Lincoln-Douglas Debates.* Chicago: U of Chicago, 1991. Introduction discusses issues.

Bode, Carl. *Midcentury America.* Carbondale: Southern Illinois UP, 1972. A look at society in 1850.

Botkin, B. A., ed. *Lay My Burden Down.* New York: Dell, 1973. Remembrances of slavery collected by Federal Writers' Project.

Videos

Andrew Johnson. 1983. Social Studies School Service, 800-421-4246. Johnson's antislavery stance in antebellum Tennessee.

Cotton as King and Curse. U.S.A. Information Service, 1985. Cotton's impact on South.

Daniel Webster. 1983. Social Studies School Service, 800-421-4246. Compromise of 1850 debate.

Roots of Resistance. PBS Home Video, 1989. 800-424-7963. Story of Underground Railroad.

A Woman Called Moses. Dir. Paul Wendkos. Xenon Home Video, 1978. Life of Tubman.

Software

African American History: Slavery to Civil Rights. CD-ROM. Queue, 1995. Educational Software Institute, 800-955-5570.

OBJECTIVES

1 To describe the growing differences between the North and the South in their economy and way of life.

2 To explain why the Wilmot Proviso failed to pass and the issue of California statehood became so important.

3 To show how the efforts of Clay, Webster, and Douglas produced the Compromise of 1850 and a temporary halt to talk of secession.

SKILLBUILDERS
- Interpreting tables, p. 283
- Interpreting charts, p. 286

CRITICAL THINKING
- Summarizing, pp. 283, 287
- Analyzing motives, p. 284
- Recognizing effects, pp. 284, 287
- Hypothesizing, p. 287
- Evaluating, p. 287

FOCUS & MOTIVATE

▶ **Starting with the Student**
- How can differences among students affect the climate of a school?
- What kinds of differences could lead to problems of unity within a country?

OBJECTIVE

1 INSTRUCT

Differences Between North and South

▶ **Discussing Key Ideas**
- By 1850 the growth of railroads, factories, and immigration creates an industrial North.
- The South has an agricultural economy, based mainly on cotton, that depends on slave labor.

IN-DEPTH RESOURCES: UNIT 3
Guided Reading, p. 19

ACCESS FOR STUDENTS ACQUIRING ENGLISH
Guided Reading (Spanish), p. 101

TERMS & NAMES
- Wilmot Proviso
- secession
- Compromise of 1850
- popular sovereignty
- Stephen A. Douglas
- Millard Fillmore

1 The Divisive Politics of Slavery

LEARN ABOUT the controversy over slavery in the territories
TO UNDERSTAND why the Compromise of 1850 was adopted.

ONE AMERICAN'S STORY

Senator John C. Calhoun was a sick man, so sick that he had missed four months of debate over whether California should enter the Union as a free state. On March 4, 1850, wrapped in flannels, he tottered onto the Senate floor. Explaining that he was too ill to deliver a speech that he had prepared, Calhoun asked Senator James M. Mason of Virginia to deliver it for him.

> **A PERSONAL VOICE**
> I have, Senators, believed from the first that the agitation of the subject of slavery would, if not prevented by some timely and effective measure, end in disunion. . . . The agitation has been permitted to proceed . . . until it has reached a period when it can no longer be disguised or denied that the Union is in danger. You have thus had forced upon you the greatest and the gravest question that can ever come under your consideration: How can the Union be preserved?
>
> **JOHN C. CALHOUN,** quoted in *The Compromise of 1850,* edited by Edwin C. Rozwenc

Senator Calhoun called on the North to give the South "justice, simple justice." He demanded that slavery be allowed throughout the territories won in the war with Mexico. If it was not, he declared, the South would secede, or withdraw, from the Union.

Senator William H. Seward of New York disagreed, saying that "there is a higher law than the Constitution." Seward believed that freedom came from God. The North would not rest, he implied, until slavery had been abolished everywhere. Once again, the issue of slavery had brought about a political crisis, deepening the gulf between the North and the South.

John C. Calhoun

Differences Between North and South

Senator Calhoun argued that although the North and the South had been politically equal when the Constitution was adopted, the "perfect equilibrium" between the two sections no longer existed. At any rate, the two sections certainly had developed different ways of life by the 1850s.

INDUSTRY AND IMMIGRATION IN THE NORTH The North was industrializing rapidly as factories turned out ever-increasing amounts of products, from textiles and sewing machines to farm equipment and guns. Railroad tracks—with more than 20,000 miles of track laid during the 1850s—were reaching across the section. They carried wheat, iron ore, and other raw materials eastward and manufactured goods and settlers westward. Small towns like Chicago matured into cities almost overnight, due to the sheer volume of goods and people arriving by railroad. Telegraph wires being strung along the railroad tracks tied the North together, providing a network of instant communication.

Immigrants fleeing from famine and poverty in Europe—mostly from Ireland and Germany—entered the industrial workplace in growing numbers. Many immigrants became factory workers, while others moved westward to try their luck

---

SECTION 1 RESOURCES

PRINT RESOURCES

IN-DEPTH RESOURCES: UNIT 3
Guided Reading, p. 19
Geography Application: Slave Populations in the United States, p. 24
American Lives: John C. Calhoun, p. 33

ACCESS FOR STUDENTS ACQUIRING ENGLISH
Guided Reading (Spanish), p. 101
Geography Application: Slave Populations in the United States (Spanish), p. 106

FORMAL ASSESSMENT
Section Quiz, p. 125

ALTERNATIVE ASSESSMENT BOOK
See forms for supporting and scoring alternative activities.

TECHNOLOGY RESOURCES

CRITICAL THINKING TRANSPARENCIES
CT10, Compromise of 1850
CT44, Population Growth: 1820–1860

CD-ROM *Grolier Multimedia Encyclopedia*

VIDEO *American Portfolio: A Videodisc for U.S. History* user's guide, pp. 87, 88

INTERNET McDougal Littell Learning On-Line
http://www.mcdougallittell.com

as farmers and miners. In any case, they soon became voters—with a strong opposition to slavery. In their eyes, slaves represented unfair labor competition because they could perform work that otherwise would be done by free workers.

For example, in Boston in 1850, nearly half of all Irish immigrants worked in unskilled jobs. These people often competed with African Americans for jobs. They feared the expansion of slavery for two reasons. First, it might bring slave labor into direct competition with free labor, or people who work for wages. Second, it threatened to reduce the status of white workers who could not successfully compete with slaves. Opposition to the expansion of slavery, however, did not mean that immigrant workers were sympathetic with the plight of black slaves. In 1850 in New York City, Irish immigrants marched to the polls shouting that African Americans should "go back to Africa, where they belong."

AGRICULTURE AND SLAVERY IN THE SOUTH Unlike the North, the South remained a predominantly rural society, consisting mostly of plantations and small farms. The Southern economy relied on agriculture, especially on cotton production—which had become the staple crop of the South since Eli Whitney's invention of the cotton gin in 1793. In fact, though one-third of the nation's population lived in the South in 1850, the South produced only 10 percent of the nation's manufactured goods. At the same time that Northern railroad lines were expanding, Southerners were slower to take advantage of technological advances in transportation, mostly using rivers to transport goods. In addition, the population of the South grew much more slowly than that of the North. Few immigrants settled in the South, because African Americans, whether enslaved or free, filled most of the available jobs for artisans, mechanics, and laborers.

The conflict over slavery, however, rattled Southern society. Those few immigrants who did settle in the South presented significant opposition to slavery. For example, German Americans in Texas and Baltimore openly opposed slavery. German newspapers in these areas published editorials in favor of universal voting rights and freedom for African Americans. Furthermore, while blacks dreamed of an end to slavery, many whites feared that any restriction of slavery would lead to a social and economic revolution. Calhoun believed that such a revolution would condemn blacks as well as whites "to the greatest calamity, and the [South] to poverty, desolation, and wretchedness."

African Americans in Southern Populations, 1860

% IN TOTAL POPULATION

State	%
Tennessee	25%
Arkansas	26%
Texas	30%
Virginia	34%
North Carolina	36%
Georgia	44%
Florida	45%
Alabama	45%
Louisiana	49%
Mississippi	55%
South Carolina	59%

Source: U.S. Census 1860.

SKILLBUILDER
INTERPRETING TABLES
In which Southern states were African Americans in the majority? How might a large population of freed slaves affect politics in the South?

Skillbuilder Answer
States: Mississippi and South Carolina. **Politics:** *Possible Answer:* Large numbers of blacks, as slaves or citizens, would severely threaten the political control of whites in the South.

Slavery in the Territories

On August 8, 1846, David Wilmot, a Democratic congressman from Pennsylvania, heightened tensions between the two sections. Wilmot added an amendment to a military appropriations bill that proposed that "neither slavery nor involuntary servitude shall ever exist" in any territory the United States might acquire as a result of the war with Mexico. In practical terms, the **Wilmot Proviso** meant that California, as well as the territories of Utah and New Mexico, would be closed to slavery forever.

THE WILMOT PROVISO Northerners gradually came to support the Wilmot Proviso. Although most Northerners were not abolitionists, they were already angry over the refusal of Southern congressmen to vote for internal improvements, such as building canals and roads. They also feared that adding slave territory

The Union in Peril **283**

The Senate Debates

▶ *Discussing Key Ideas*
- The issue of slavery in the new territories causes the South to threaten secession from the Union.
- Henry Clay's Compromise of 1850 seeks to appease both sides by admitting California as a free state, proposing a stronger fugitive slave law, and allowing Utah and New Mexico to decide about slavery for themselves.
- Although the Senate rejects Clay's compromise as a package, Stephen Douglas breaks the bill into parts; as a result, the Compromise of 1850 becomes law.

MORE ABOUT . . .
Calhoun, Clay, and Webster

Calhoun, Clay, and Webster were known collectively as the Great Triumvirate, dominating American politics between 1800 and 1850. They were excellent orators, serving in the Senate and other public offices: Calhoun as secretary of war and vice-president; Clay as speaker of the House; and Webster as a congressman and secretary of state. Each had presidential ambitions, but all failed to achieve their goal. The Compromise of 1850 proved to be the last hurrah for all three.

"I tell you, the prospect ahead is dark, cloudy, thick, and gloomy."

ALEXANDER H. STEPHENS

would give slave states more members in Congress and deny economic opportunity to free workers. Beginning with Ohio and Michigan, nearly all of the Northern states passed resolutions endorsing the Wilmot Proviso.

Southerners opposed the Proviso, which some believed raised complex constitutional issues. Slaves were property, Southerners claimed, and property was protected by the Constitution. Laws like the Wilmot Proviso would undermine such constitutional protections.

In addition, Southerners argued that the territories belonged to all of the states in common and that Congress had no right to limit the spread of slavery there. Many Southerners feared that if the Wilmot Proviso became law, the inevitable addition of new free states to the Union would swing the balance of power permanently toward the North. Southern governors and legislatures denounced the Proviso, and the Richmond, Virginia, *Enquirer* gravely proclaimed that "the days of this glorious Union" were numbered because of the action of "the madmen of the North." The House of Representatives approved the Proviso, but the Senate rejected it. The Proviso then was attached to a different bill, and was once again passed by the House but rejected by the Senate. Congressman Alexander H. Stephens of Georgia issued a dire prediction.

A PERSONAL VOICE
The North is going to stick the Wilmot amendment to every appropriation and then all the South will vote against any measure thus clogged. Finally a tremendous struggle will take place and perhaps [President] Polk in starting one war may find half a dozen on his hands. I tell you, the prospect ahead is dark, cloudy, thick and gloomy.

ALEXANDER H. STEPHENS, quoted in *The Coming of the Civil War*

STATEHOOD FOR CALIFORNIA The next flare in the political fire came from California. As a result of the gold rush, California had grown so quickly in population that it skipped the territorial phase of becoming a state. From September to November 1849, the Californians held a constitutional convention, during which they adopted a state constitution, elected a governor and a legislature, and applied for admission to the Union.

California's new constitution forbade slavery, a fact that alarmed and angered many Southerners. They had assumed that, because most of California lay south of the Missouri Compromise line of 36°30', it would be open to slavery. They had hoped that the compromise struck in 1820 would apply to new territories, including California, which would have become a slave state.

President Zachary Taylor, although himself a slaveholder, supported California's admission as a free state because he believed that its climate and terrain were not suited to slavery. More importantly, he felt that the South could counter abolitionism most effectively by leaving the slavery issue up to individual territories rather than Congress. However, Taylor soon found that feelings in the South were more passionate than he had expected. Southerners saw the move to block slavery in the territories as an attack on the Southern way of life—and began to question whether the South should remain in the Union.

The Senate Debates

The 31st Congress opened in December 1849 in an atmosphere of distrust and bitterness. The question of statehood for California topped the agenda. Of equal concern was the border dispute in which the slave state of Texas claimed the eastern half of the New Mexico territory, where the issue of slavery had not yet been settled. In the meantime, hotheads from both the North and the South added fuel to the sectional fire. Northerners demanded the abolition of slavery in the District of Columbia, while Southerners accused the North of failing to

THINK THROUGH HISTORY
B. Analyzing Motives Explain why Northerners favored the Wilmot Proviso and Southerners did not.

B. Answer Northerners wanted to prevent the extension of slavery into the territories, because it might cause more slave states to enter the Union. Southerners did not want Congress deciding the issue of slavery.

THINK THROUGH HISTORY
C. Recognizing Effects Why did California's application for statehood cause an uproar?

C. Answer Although California's voters opposed slavery, most of the state lay south of the Missouri Compromise line and therefore legally should have been open to slavery.

TEACHING OPTIONS

Exploring Themes

Immigration and Migration The period of large-scale immigration in the 1840s and 1850s introduced new faces onto the American scene. The Gold Rush and the building of railroads brought people from Asia, and cheap land brought farmers from western Europe. The newcomers brought vitality and a willingness to work. Providing a steady source of labor, they enriched a nation moving into a new industrial era.

Making Connections Across Time

California Then and Now Ask students to look at a topographical map of California (see Atlas, p. 1064). Then have them discuss the following questions:

1. Was President Taylor correct in his belief that the climate and the terrain were not suited to agriculture?

2. Does California have a large agricultural base today? *Yes.* If so, what group of people do most of the work in the California fields? *Migrant workers.*

3. In what way is the labor of these workers comparable to the work of slaves in 1850? *Intense physical labor, little pay, meager living conditions, little hope for a better life.*

enforce the Fugitive Slave Act of 1793. As passions mounted, threats of Southern **secession,** the formal withdrawal of a state from the Union, became more frequent. Could anything be done to prevent the United States from becoming two nations instead of one?

CLAY'S COMPROMISE Once again, Henry Clay worked night and day to shape a compromise that both the North and the South could accept. Though ill, he visited his old rival Daniel Webster on January 21, 1850, and obtained Webster's support. Eight days later, Clay rose unsteadily to his feet to present to the Senate a series of resolutions later called the **Compromise of 1850,** which he hoped would settle "all questions in controversy between the free and slave states, growing out of the subject of Slavery."

TERMS OF THE COMPROMISE Clay's compromise, summarized on the chart shown on page 286, contained provisions to appease Northerners as well as Southerners. To please the North, the compromise provided that California be admitted to the Union as a free state. To please the South, the compromise proposed a new and more effective fugitive slave law.

Other provisions of the compromise had elements that appealed to both sections. For example, Northerners were happy with a provision that allowed residents of the territories of New Mexico and Utah **popular sovereignty,** the right of residents of a territory to vote for or against slavery. That provision appealed to Southerners as well. Also, as part of the compromise, the federal government would pay Texas $10 million to surrender its claim on New Mexico. This provision satisfied Northerners, because, in effect, it limited slavery in Texas to its current borders. For Southerners, the money would help to defray Texas's expenses and debts from the war with Mexico.

On February 5 Clay defended his resolutions and begged both the North

Clay Proposes the Compromise, 1850

1. Daniel Webster was a strong supporter of Clay's compromise bill. He left the Senate, however, before Stephen Douglas could engineer the passage of all of the bill's provisions.

2. Henry Clay offered his compromise to the Senate in March 1850. In his efforts to save the Union, Clay earned for himself the name the Great Compromiser.

3. John C. Calhoun remained opposed to the compromise. He died barely a month after Clay proposed it.

The Union in Peril **285**

The Compromise of 1850

Reading the Chart Ask students to look at the goals of both Calhoun and Webster on the chart. Then ask them to list the key terms of the compromise. Using both the text and the chart, put an *S* (South) or an *N* (North) next to each term to show which side benefited from it.

The Compromise of 1850		
CALHOUN'S GOAL	**TERMS OF THE COMPROMISE**	**WEBSTER'S GOAL**
Calhoun believed strongly in states' rights over federal power and held the interests of the slaveholding South as his highest priority. He had long believed that "the agitation of the subject of slavery would . . . end in disunion." He blamed the sectional crisis on Northern abolitionists and argued that the South had "no concession or surrender to make" on the issue of slavery.	• California admitted as a free state • Utah and New Mexico territories decide about slavery • Slavery not abolished in the District of Columbia without consent of its residents and the state of Maryland, and then only if owners are paid for their losses • The trading of enslaved persons (but not slavery) banned in the District of Columbia • Stricter fugitive slave law	Webster had argued with Northern Whigs that slavery should not be extended into the territories. Upon hearing Calhoun's threat of secession, he took to the Senate floor and endorsed Clay's compromise "for the preservation of the Union . . . a great, popular, constitutional government, guarded by legislation, by law, by judicature, and developed by the whole affections of the people."

MORE ABOUT . . .
Millard Fillmore

Millard Fillmore never received a regular education because, as a boy, he had to work at odd jobs in order to earn a living. However, he read law in his spare time and continued reading extensively after he became a lawyer. When he took office as president in 1850 and discovered that the White House did not contain a single book, he persuaded Congress to allocate money for a library. The amount? Two hundred fifty dollars.

MORE ABOUT . . .
John C. Calhoun

When Calhoun died, admirers carried his coffin in a triumphal procession from Washington, D.C., to Charleston, South Carolina, where he was buried beneath a marble tombstone in St. Philip's courtyard. But as a soldier said in 1865, Calhoun's real monument turned out to be "Southern society torn up by the roots, and servants become masters."

IN-DEPTH RESOURCES: UNIT 3
American Lives: John C. Calhoun, p. 33

SKILLBUILDER
INTERPRETING CHARTS *How did Calhoun and Webster disagree over states' rights? How did the compromise try to satisfy both sides?*
Skillbuilder Answer
States' rights: Calhoun believed maintaining states' rights was more important than the preservation of the Union; Webster believed saving the Union was more important than states' rights. **Slavery:** The compromise had provisions to satisfy each side. For the North, it admitted California as a free state. For the South, it set up a stricter fugitive slave law.

and the South to consider them thoughtfully. The alternative was disunion—and, in Clay's opinion, quite possibly war.

A PERSONAL VOICE
And such a war as it would be, following the dissolution of the Union! Sir, we may search the pages of history, and none so ferocious, so bloody, so implacable, so exterminating . . . would rage with such violence. . . . I implore gentlemen, I adjure them, whether from the South or the North . . . to pause at the edge of the precipice, before the fearful and dangerous leap be taken into the yawning abyss below.
HENRY CLAY, quoted in *Voices from the Civil War*

CALHOUN AND WEBSTER RESPOND Clay's speech marked the start of one of the greatest political debates in U.S. history. Within a month, Calhoun presented the Southern case for slavery in the territories. He was followed three days later by Daniel Webster, who began his eloquent appeal for national unity by saying, "I wish to speak today, not as a Massachusetts man, nor as a [N]orthern man, but as an American. . . . 'Hear me for my cause.'" He urged Northerners to satisfy the South by passing a stricter fugitive slave law, and he warned Southern firebrands about the danger of secession.

A PERSONAL VOICE
I hear with distress, and anguish the word "secession," especially when it falls from the lips of those who are eminently patriotic. . . . Secession! Peaceable secession! Sir, your eyes and mine are never destined to see that miracle. . . . There can be no such thing as a peaceable secession. . . . Is the great Constitution under which we live . . . to be thawed and melted away by secession, as the snows on the mountain melt under the influence of a vernal sun—disappear almost unobserved and run off? No, sir! No, sir! I will not state what might produce the disruption of the Union; but, sir, I see it as plainly as I see the sun in heaven. What that disruption must produce . . . [would be] such a war as I will not describe.
DANIEL WEBSTER, Seventh of March speech, quoted in *The American Spirit*

Webster's speech became one of the most famous in the history of the Senate. The packed Senate chamber was stunned to see long-time foes Clay and Webster finally—for the first and last time—on the same side.

THE COMPROMISE IS ADOPTED Despite the efforts of Clay and Webster, the Senate rejected the proposed compromise in July. Tired, ill, and discouraged,

286 CHAPTER 10

TEACHING OPTIONS

Making Connections Across the Curriculum

Literature The period of the 1850s not only produced books about slavery and abolition but in addition, events of the time became the basis for many novels and short stories written almost a century later. One author who based much of his work on American historical figures was Stephen Vincent Benét. Two of his best-known works relevant to the period are the short story "The Devil and Daniel Webster" and the epic poem, *John Brown's Body,* which won the Pulitzer Prize for poetry in 1929.

Teaching Gifted and Talented Students

The Devil and Daniel Webster Two activities that might be used for talented students relate to Stephen Vincent Benét's short story "The Devil and Daniel Webster."

1. Ask students to read "The Devil and Daniel Webster." Then ask them to make a list of the qualities of the character of Daniel Webster in the story and compare them with the qualities of the real-life Daniel Webster in the textbook.

2. Students may want to write a short story of their own, using one of the personalities in this section as a character in their work.

Clay withdrew from the fight and left Washington. In the final months, Senator **Stephen A. Douglas** of Illinois picked up the pro-compromise reins.

A resourceful politician, Douglas developed a shrewd plan. Clay had presented his compromise as an omnibus bill, meaning that all of its resolutions were to be voted on as a package. Douglas wisely realized that the compromise was doomed to failure if it was offered this way, because every member of Congress opposed at least one of its provisions. To avoid another defeat, Douglas unbundled the package of resolutions and reintroduced them one at a time, hoping to obtain a majority vote for each measure individually. Thus, any individual congressman could vote for the provisions that he liked and vote against, or abstain from voting on, those that he disliked. It appeared as though Douglas had found the key to passing the entire compromise.

The unexpected death of President Taylor aided Douglas's efforts. After standing in the broiling sun, listening to an Independence Day oration, the President gulped down a large quantity of cherries and iced milk, and promptly fell ill with gastroenteritis. His doctors blistered and bled him and pumped him full of opium and quinine. Despite their efforts, Taylor died on July 9. His successor, **Millard Fillmore,** quickly made it clear that he supported the compromise.

In the meantime, the South had retreated from its extreme position. Calhoun's death from tuberculosis had removed one obstacle to compromise. Congressman Stephens and other Southern leaders came out in favor of Clay's individual proposals as being the best the South could secure without radical action. At last, in September, after eight months of effort, the Compromise of 1850 was voted into law.

The new President embraced the compromise as the "final settlement" of the question of slavery and sectional differences. For the moment, the crisis over slavery in the territories had passed. However, the relief was short-lived. Even as crowds in Washington celebrated the passage of the compromise, the next crisis loomed ominously on the horizon—enforcement of the new fugitive slave law.

D. Answer The compromise passed because each resolution had enough support from either the North or the South to pass when voted on separately.

THINK THROUGH HISTORY
D. Recognizing Effects What was the result of Douglas's unbundling of Clay's resolutions?

KEY PLAYER

STEPHEN A. DOUGLAS 1813–1861

Stephen A. Douglas's political cleverness, oratorical skill, and personal drive earned him the nickname the Little Giant—a reference to the fact that he stood only 5'4" tall.

Douglas's political skill engineered the passage of the Compromise of 1850 when all of the efforts of senatorial warriors, such as Clay, had failed. Douglas later became the well-known opponent of Abraham Lincoln in both a senatorial and a presidential election. Like Lincoln, he was self-educated. Douglas started studying law while still in his teens.

After becoming a judge, Douglas served two terms in the House of Representatives and then was elected to the Senate. However, he never achieved his ultimate political goal: the presidency.

Section 1 Assessment

1. TERMS & NAMES

Identify:
• Wilmot Proviso
• secession
• Compromise of 1850
• popular sovereignty
• Stephen A. Douglas
• Millard Fillmore

2. SUMMARIZING Create a chart similar to this one. Complete it by indicating each region's position on the issue or how each region was affected by the trend.

Trend or Issue	North	South
1.		
2.		
3.		
4.		
5.		

Choose one issue and propose a compromise to settle it.

3. HYPOTHESIZING Review issues and events in this section that reflect the growing conflict between the North and the South. Do you think there are any points at which a different action or leader might have resolved the conflict? Support your opinion with references from this section.

THINK ABOUT
• issues raised by the Wilmot Proviso, California's statehood, and the Compromise of 1850
• reasons for Northerners' anger with the South
• constitutional issues raised by Southerners
• political impact of adding new free states

4. EVALUATING Do you think the North or the South won more significant concessions in the Compromise of 1850? Explain your answer.

THINK ABOUT
• issues that were most sensitive in 1850
• issues that had the greatest long-range impact
• issues that might be solved by other compromises
• issues that would affect the territories

The Union in Peril **287**

ANSWERS

1. TERMS & NAMES

Wilmot Proviso, p. 283

secession, p. 285

Compromise of 1850, p. 285

popular sovereignty, p. 285

Stephen A. Douglas, p. 287

Millard Fillmore, p. 287

2. SUMMARIZING

Possible Answer: North— extensive industry and railroads, high immigration, supported internal improvements, supported Wilmot Proviso, opposed slavery in California. South—little industry and few railroads, little immigration, opposed internal improvements, opposed Wilmot Proviso, supported slavery in California.

3. HYPOTHESIZING

Possible Response: Some students may suggest that a president stronger than Taylor or congressional leaders less opinionated than Calhoun might have been able to bring the North and the South to compromise earlier. Others may think that no one could have headed off the conflict, because of the complete division over slavery.

4. EVALUATING

Possible Response: Students might argue that the compromise favored the North, because the measures on California, New Mexico, and Utah could strengthen future antislavery interests in Congress. Students who believe the South benefited most might note that by strengthening the Fugitive Slave Act, the compromise reinforced the legal basis of slavery.

OBJECTIVES

① To explain the Fugitive Slave Act and how abolitionists and the Underground Railroad succeeded in defying this law.

② To show how Douglas's desire for a northern route for a transcontinental railroad helped destroy the Missouri Compromise and the Compromise of 1850.

③ To give examples of the violence created by the race between Northerners and Southerners to gain control of Kansas.

SKILLBUILDERS

• Understanding geography: location, p. 290
• Understanding geography: place, region, p. 293

CRITICAL THINKING

• Recognizing effects, pp. 289, 294
• Summarizing, pp. 289, 294
• Contrasting, p. 291
• Analyzing issues, p. 292
• Analyzing causes, p. 293
• Synthesizing, p. 294

FOCUS & MOTIVATE

▶ **Starting with the Student**
Tell students to imagine that they are slaves escaping to the North. Ask students what they are risking.

MORE ABOUT . . .
Charlotte Forten

Charlotte Forten was the first black teacher to take part in an experiment conducted during the Civil War on the Sea Islands off the South Carolina coast. After Union forces captured the islands in the fall of 1861, Lincoln decided to send teachers there to educate the former slaves. Fifty-three white teachers took up their duties in the spring of 1862. Forten arrived six months later, in time to observe a regiment of black freedmen receive news of the Emancipation Proclamation.

TERMS & NAMES
• Fugitive Slave Act
• personal liberty laws
• Underground Railroad
• Harriet Tubman
• Harriet Beecher Stowe
• *Uncle Tom's Cabin*
• Kansas-Nebraska Act
• John Brown
• Bleeding Kansas

② Protest, Resistance, and Violence

LEARN ABOUT the Fugitive Slave Act and the Kansas-Nebraska Act
TO UNDERSTAND how the controversy over slavery became increasingly violent.

ONE AMERICAN'S STORY

On June 2, 1854, some 50,000 people lined the streets of Boston. Flags flew at half-mast, and black cloths covered many of the city's storefronts. A black coffin bearing the words "The Funeral of Liberty" dangled from a window to protest the returning of Anthony Burns to slavery. Federal soldiers, with bayonets ready for action, marched toward the harbor. In the center of the troops strode a lone African American named Anthony Burns. The soldiers were taking the fugitive back to slavery in Virginia. Charlotte Forten, a free African American whose grandfather had fought in the Revolutionary War, wrote about the day in her journal.

A PERSONAL VOICE
Today Massachusetts has again been disgraced. . . . With what scorn must that government be regarded, which cowardly assembles thousands of soldiers to satisfy the demands of slaveholders; to deprive of his freedom a man, created in God's own image, whose sole offense is the color of his skin! . . . A cloud seems hanging over me, over all our persecuted race, which nothing can dispel.

CHARLOTTE FORTEN, quoted in *The Underground Railroad*, by Charles L. Blockson

Charlotte Forten's grandfather was the Philadelphia abolitionist James Forten.

Anthony Burns's return to slavery followed passage of the Fugitive Slave Act. Passed as part of the Compromise of 1850, this law brought the evils of slavery home to more Northerners, who began to realize that slavery could exist only if they allowed it to. As a result, antislavery sentiment in the North soared. "We went to bed one night old-fashioned, conservative, compromise Union Whigs," wrote textile manufacturer Amos A. Lawrence, "and waked up stark mad Abolitionists."

Fugitive Slaves and the Underground Railroad

Many people were surprised at the harsh terms of the **Fugitive Slave Act.** Under the law, alleged fugitives were not entitled to a trial by jury, despite the Sixth Amendment provision calling for a jury trial where the value in question exceeded $20. Nor could fugitives testify on their own behalf. A statement by a slaveowner, with a description of the escapee, was all that was required to have a slave returned. Frederick Douglass bitterly summarized the situation.

A PERSONAL VOICE
The colored men's rights are less than those of a jackass. No man can take away a jackass without submitting the matter to twelve men in any part of this country. A black man may be carried away without any reference to a jury. It is only necessary to claim him, and that some villain should swear to his identity. There is more protection there for a horse, for a donkey, or anything, rather than a colored man.

FREDERICK DOUGLASS, quoted in *Voices from the Civil War*

In addition, federal commissioners charged with enforcing the law were to receive a $10 fee if they returned an alleged fugitive, but only $5 if they freed him or her, an obvious incentive to return people to slavery. Finally, anyone convicted of helping an alleged fugitive was liable for a fine of $1,000, imprisonment for six months, or both.

SECTION 2 RESOURCES

 PRINT RESOURCES

IN-DEPTH RESOURCES: UNIT 3
Guided Reading, p. 20
Skillbuilder Practice: Analyzing Causes, p. 23
Primary Source: The Underground Railroad, p. 26
Literature: from *Uncle Tom's Cabin* by Harriet Beecher Stowe, p. 30
American Lives: Harriet Tubman, p. 34

ACCESS FOR STUDENTS ACQUIRING ENGLISH
Guided Reading (Spanish), p. 102
Skillbuilder Practice: Analyzing Causes (Spanish), p. 105

FORMAL ASSESSMENT
Section Quiz, p. 126

ALTERNATIVE ASSESSMENT BOOK
See forms for supporting and scoring alternative activities.

TECHNOLOGY RESOURCES

HUMANITIES TRANSPARENCIES
H10, *No. 10 Harriet Tubman series* by Jacob Lawrence

CD-ROM Electronic Library of Primary Sources

VIDEO *American Portfolio: A Videodisc for U.S. History*
user's guide, pp. 88–90

INTERNET McDougal Littell Learning On-Line
http://www.mcdougallittell.com

ENFORCING THE LAW Infuriated by the Fugitive Slave Act, some Northerners resisted it by organizing vigilance committees to send endangered African Americans to safety in Canada. Others resorted to violence to rescue fugitive slaves. For example, in 1854, angry Bostonians broke into a courthouse and killed a guard during an unsuccessful attempt to rescue the fugitive Anthony Burns. Nine Northern states passed **personal liberty laws** forbidding the imprisonment of runaway slaves. Personal liberty laws also guaranteed that fugitive slaves would have jury trials. Moreover, Northern lawyers dragged these trials out—sometimes for three or four years—in order to increase slave catchers' expenses. Southern slaveowners were appalled at Northern resistance to fugitive slave laws, prompting one Harvard law student from Georgia to tell his mother, "Do not be surprised if when I return home you find me a confirmed disunionist."

THINK THROUGH HISTORY
A. *Recognizing Effects* What effect did the Fugitive Slave Act have on abolitionist feelings in the North?

A. Answer It created a great deal of resentment and resulted in some people turning to violence.

HARRIET TUBMAN AND THE UNDERGROUND RAILROAD For slaves, escaping from slavery was indeed a dangerous process. It meant traveling on foot at night without any sense of distance or direction, except for the North Star and other natural signs. It meant avoiding patrols of armed men on horseback and struggling through forests and across rivers. Often it meant going without food for days at a time. Harry Grimes, a slave who ran away from North Carolina, described the difficulties of escaping to the North.

> **A PERSONAL VOICE**
> In the woods I lived on nothing. . . . I stayed in the hollow of a big poplar tree for seven months. . . . I suffered mighty bad with the cold and for something to eat. One time a snake come to the tree . . . and I took my axe and chopped him in two. It was a poplar leaf moccasin, the poisonest kind of snake we have. While in the woods all my thoughts was how to get away to a free country.
>
> **HARRY GRIMES,** quoted in *The Underground Railroad*, by Charles L. Blockson

Once fugitives like Harry Grimes reached the North, many elected to remain there and take their chances in avoiding slave catchers. Other fugitives, however, continued their journey all the way to Canada to be completely out of reach of their owners.

As time went on, free African Americans and white abolitionists developed a secret network of people who would hide fugitive slaves at great risk to themselves. This system of escape routes became known as the **Underground Railroad.** These "conductors" hid fugitives in secret tunnels and false cupboards, provided them with food and clothing, and escorted or directed them to the next "station" in disguise.

THINK THROUGH HISTORY
B. *Summarizing* How did the Underground Railroad operate?

B. Answer "Conductors" would hide fugitive slaves and help them work their way North from one "station" to the next.

One of the most famous conductors was **Harriet Tubman,** born a slave in Maryland in 1820 or 1821. As a young girl, she suffered a severe head injury when a plantation overseer hit her with a lead weight. The blow damaged her brain, causing her to lose consciousness several times a day. To compensate for her disability, Tubman increased her strength until she became strong enough to perform tasks that most men could not do. In 1849, after Tubman's owner died, she determined to make a break for freedom and succeeded in reaching Philadelphia.

Shortly after passage of the Fugitive Slave Act, Tubman resolved to become a conductor on the Underground Railroad. In all, she made 19 trips back to the South and is said to have helped 300 slaves—including her own parents—flee to freedom. Southern authorities put a price of $40,000 on her head, but

"There's two things I got a right to and these are Death and Liberty. One or the other I mean to have."

HARRIET TUBMAN

Harriet Tubman was called "Moses" by those she helped escape on the Underground Railroad. In her later years, Tubman opened a home for elderly African Americans.

289

HISTORY FROM VISUALS

The Underground Railroad, 1850–1860

Reading the Map Point out that the arrows show the movement of people from the South to the North. Ask students to notice the multiple routes and their lengths and to imagine the numbers of people required to make the operation work.

Extension Ask students to discuss the importance of the waterways in the slaves' journeys north. *The use of rivers, canals, and lakes was a way of avoiding capture; the ports served as entryways to the North and Canada.*

IN-DEPTH RESOURCES: UNIT 3
Primary Source: The Underground Railroad, p. 26
American Lives: Harriet Tubman, p. 34

 ELECTRONIC LIBRARY OF PRIMARY SOURCES
"On Slavery" by Harriet Tubman

HISTORY FROM VISUALS

Handbill

Reading a Handbill Have students examine the handbill, then ask: Which people in Boston is this handbill addressing? *African American freemen and fugitives, abolitionists, people running the Underground Railroad.*

Extension Ask students to create a similar handbill as it might have appeared in the South.

 ELECTRONIC LIBRARY OF PRIMARY SOURCES
from The Fugitive Slave Act
from "The Function of Conscience" by Theodore Parker

The Underground Railroad, 1850–1860

Free states
Slave states
Areas with slave population of 50% or more in 1860
Routes of the Underground Railroad

With about 30,000 fugitive slaves in the North by 1850, abolitionists used posters and handbills like this one made in Boston in 1851 to warn fugitives of the danger of slave catchers.

GEOGRAPHY SKILLBUILDER
LOCATION *Name three cities that were destinations on the Underground Railroad.*
LOCATION *Why do you think these cities were destinations?*

Skillbuilder Answer
Location: *Possible Answers: Chicago, Detroit, Montreal, Erie (Penn.), Sandusky (Ohio).*
Location: These cities were all far away from the South. Also, their size allowed fugitives more opportunities for hiding.

neither Tubman nor the slaves she helped were ever captured. Later, she became an ardent speaker for abolition. Meanwhile, another abolitionist voice spoke out in a book that brought slavery into the homes of a great many Americans.

UNCLE TOM'S CABIN In 1852, **Harriet Beecher Stowe** published **Uncle Tom's Cabin.** The book stirred strong reactions from Northerners and Southerners alike. The novel immediately became a best seller. Three thousand copies sold on the first day, one hundred thousand in less than three months, and more than a million by the middle of 1853. In addition, dozens of traveling theatrical companies performed dramatized versions all across the country, sometimes with real bloodhounds on stage.

Although many of its characters were stereotypes and its scenes unbelievable, *Uncle Tom's Cabin* delivered the message that slavery was not just a political contest, but also a great moral struggle. The novel's plot was melodramatic. Readers tensed with excitement as the slave Eliza fled across the frozen Ohio River, clutching her infant son in her arms. They rejoiced when kindly Augustine St. Clare purchased Uncle Tom, an old man who had been a slave all his life, after Uncle Tom rescued St. Clare's daughter, Little Eva, from drowning. They wept when Simon Legree, a wicked Northern slaveowner who moved to the South, bought Uncle Tom after St. Clare died, and had him whipped to death.

290 CHAPTER 10

TEACHING OPTION

Cooperative Activity: Responding to Uncle Tom's Cabin

Task: Pairs of students will write letters to the editor either criticizing or praising *Uncle Tom's Cabin.*

Purpose: To help students examine the impact of the book on people at that time.

Activity: Have students read selections from *Uncle Tom's Cabin.* After analyzing the novel, students should write letters criticizing or praising the book for its literary style, accu-

racy, or characters; or they might condemn or praise it for its impact on people at the time.

Building a Portfolio: Students adding the letter to their portfolios should attach notes describing the process of writing the letter.

ALTERNATIVE ASSESSMENT BOOK
Standards for Evaluating a Cooperative Activity

IN-DEPTH RESOURCES: UNIT 3
Literature: from *Uncle Tom's Cabin* by Harriet Beecher Stowe, p. 30

Standards for Evaluation
Letters should . . .

• state a clear point of view
• support ideas with specific examples from the novel
• demonstrate an understanding of attitudes of the time
• use appropriate letter form and style

In quick response, Northern abolitionists increased their protests against the Fugitive Slave Act, while Southerners criticized the book as an attack on the South as a whole. Several Southern writers wrote novels that attempted to show that *Uncle Tom's Cabin* was based on lies. Even the most successful of those novels, however, was unable to dispel the conviction that slavery was evil (even when it involved basically good people) and that it damaged families, white as well as black. The furor over *Uncle Tom's Cabin* had barely begun to settle when a new controversy over slavery drew heated debate.

Tension in Kansas and Nebraska

Abolitionist feelings in the North further intensified when the issue of slavery in the territories—supposedly settled by the Compromise of 1850—surfaced once again. Ironically, Senator Stephen Douglas, who had helped to steer the compromise to victory, was the person most responsible for resurrecting the issue.

DOUGLAS AND POPULAR SOVEREIGNTY As early as 1844, Douglas was pushing to organize the Nebraska Territory. In 1854, he developed a proposal to divide the area into two territories, Nebraska and Kansas. His motives were complicated. On one hand, Douglas was pushing for the construction of a railroad between Chicago—his hometown, where he also owned real estate—and San Francisco. To do so, he had to make a deal with Southerners, who wanted the railroad to start in Memphis or New Orleans.

In addition, Douglas was anxious to organize these territories because he believed that most of the nation's people wished to see the western lands incorporated into the Union. Along with many other Democrats, Douglas believed that continued expansion would unify his party and the nation. He also believed that popular sovereignty—that is, the right of residents of a given territory to vote on slavery for themselves—provided the most fair and democratic way to organize the new state governments. But what Douglas failed to realize was how strongly opposed to slavery Northerners had become.

The Compromise of 1850 had provided for popular sovereignty in New Mexico and Utah. To Douglas, popular sovereignty seemed like an excellent way to decide whether slavery would be allowed in the Nebraska Territory. The only difficulty was that, unlike New Mexico and Utah, the Nebraska Territory lay north of the Missouri Compromise line of 36°30' and therefore was legally closed to slavery. Douglas assumed, though, that the territory of Nebraska would enter the Union as two states—one free and one slave and maintain the balance in the Senate between North and South.

Actually, Douglas was convinced that slavery could not exist on the open prairies, since none of the crops relying on slave labor could be grown there. However, to win Southern support for his railroad route, Douglas decided to support repeal of the Missouri Compromise—which now would make slavery legal north of the 36°30' line—though he predicted it would cause "a storm" in Congress. His prediction was right.

THE KANSAS–NEBRASKA ACT On January 23, 1854, Douglas introduced a bill in Congress to divide the Nebraska Territory into Nebraska in the north and Kansas in the south. If passed, it would repeal the Missouri Compromise and establish popular sovereignty for both territories. As Douglas expected,

KEY PLAYER

HARRIET BEECHER STOWE
1811–1896

Harriet Beecher Stowe was born in Connecticut into a prominent reform family. Her father was Presbyterian minister and temperance advocate Lyman Beecher. Her brother, Henry, was a clergyman and abolitionist, and her sister, Catherine, was a noted educator.

Stowe moved with her family to Cincinnati, where the issue of slavery—once rather remote—became painfully familiar. She never forgot standing on the banks of the Ohio River, watching boats fill with slaves from Kentucky to be shipped to slave markets. Her hatred of slavery grew until she resolved to express herself in writing, and *Uncle Tom's Cabin* resulted. The novel made such an impact that when Abraham Lincoln met Stowe a decade later, during the Civil War, he said, "So this is the little lady who made the big war."

The Union in Peril **291**

Reading the Map Point out
that the three maps on
pages 292–293 should be
studied both individually
and as a group. Have stu-
dents note the changing
political balance over the
years and ask them to note
the reasons for the changes.

Extension What major
changes took place in the
West between 1820 and
1850? *California became a
free state, the Southwest territories were opened to slavery, the Northwest territories
were closed to slavery.*

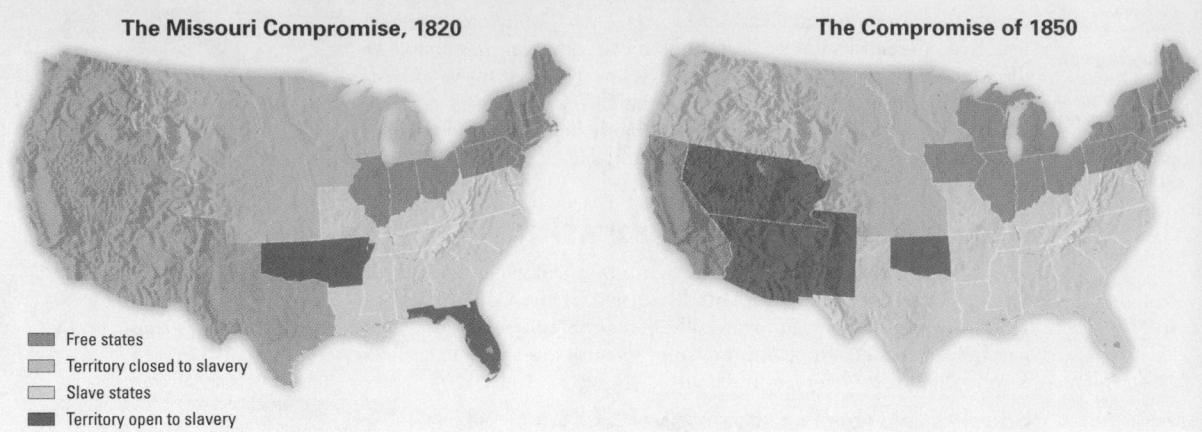

Free and Slave States and Territories, 1820–1854

The Missouri Compromise, 1820

The Compromise of 1850

- ■ Free states
- ■ Territory closed to slavery
- ■ Slave states
- ■ Territory open to slavery

"Bleeding Kansas"

▶ *Starting with the Student*
Discuss the differences
between a civil war and a
revolutionary war.

- How would each affect a
  country?
- Can students think of a
  recent example of civil
  war?

▶ *Discussing Key Ideas*
- The North and the South
  vie for control of Kansas,
  and the clash of proslavery
  and antislavery forces eventually leads to violence.
- Fanaticism on both sides,
  including John Brown's
  Pottawatomie Massacre,
  results in tragedy and death
  in "Bleeding Kansas."
- Charles Sumner is attacked
  and beaten by Preston
  Brooks in the Senate, as
  the controversy surrounding Kansas is debated by
  the lawmakers.

congressional debate over the bill was bitter. Some Northern congressmen, including Senator Charles Sumner of Massachusetts, saw the bill as part of a plot to turn the territories into slave states. Southerners strongly defended the proposed legislation, with nearly 90 percent of Southern congressmen voting for it. The bitterness spilled over into the general population, which deluged Congress with petitions both for and against the bill.

In the North, Douglas found himself burned in effigy—crude images of him that were set afire—for betraying the Missouri Compromise. Yet he did not waver. He believed strongly that popular sovereignty was the democratic way to resolve the slavery issue.

> **A PERSONAL VOICE**
> If the people of Kansas want a slaveholding state, let them have it, and if they want a free state they have a right to it, and it is not for the people of Illinois, or Missouri, or New York, or Kentucky, to complain, whatever the decision of the people of Kansas may be.
>
> **STEPHEN A. DOUGLAS,** quoted in *The Civil War,* by Geoffrey C. Ward

With the help of President Franklin Pierce, a Democrat elected in 1852, Douglas steered his proposal through the Senate. The bill passed in the House and the **Kansas-Nebraska Act** became law in 1854 after months of struggle. All eyes turned westward, as the fate of the new territories hung in the balance.

"Bleeding Kansas"

The race for the possession of Kansas was on. New York Senator William Seward threw down the gauntlet. "Come on, then, gentlemen of the Slave States. . . . We will engage in competition for the virgin soil of Kansas and God give the victory to the side that is stronger in numbers as it is in right."

From both the North and the South, men poured into the Kansas territory. Some were simply Missouri farmers in search of new land. Most were sent by emigrant aid societies, formed specifically to oppose slavery in the territories by supplying rifles, animals, seed, and farm equipment to antislavery migrants.

By March 1855 Kansas had enough settlers to hold an election for a territorial legislature. However, thousands of "border ruffians" from the slave
state of Missouri, led by Senator David Atchison, crossed into Kansas with

THINK THROUGH HISTORY
D. *Analyzing
Issues* Explain
why popular
sovereignty was so
controversial.

D. Answer It was
controversial
because it meant
a repeal of the
Missouri
Compromise and
that any new
territory or state
was open to
slavery.

TEACHING OPTION

Making Connections Across Cultures

Riots The violent outbreaks in Kansas can be characterized as riots. Since the beginning of history, riots have occurred throughout the world. Social scientists generally classify riots into two groups: instrumental riots and expressive riots.

Instrumental riots happen when groups use violence to protest specific issues. Sometimes the violence is an attempt to change policies or to improve specific conditions. The situation in Kansas involved a wild mix of protests over the actions of the proslavery and antislavery groups, inflamed passions over the issue of slavery, and instances of misunderstanding

and misinformation.

Expressive riots occur when people in a minority group use violence to protest their conditions, such as poor housing, few job opportunities, inferior schools, and police brutality.

Ask students to consider the kinds of violence they read about or witness today. They should think about their own neighbor-hoods as well as places around the world such as the Middle East, Bosnia, and South Africa. What parallels can they draw with the eruptions in Kansas in the 1850s? What do they think are the long-term effects of violence?

The Kansas-Nebraska Act of 1854

GEOGRAPHY SKILLBUILDER
PLACE *How did the number of slave states change between 1820 and 1854?* **PLACE** *How did the status of California change, as shown on the maps?* **REGION** *How did the Kansas-Nebraska Act affect the amount of land that was open to slavery?*

Skillbuilder Answer **Place:** Slave states increased by three. **Place:** *Possible Answer:* In 1820 that region was a territory open to slavery; as a result of the Compromise of 1850, it entered the Union as a free state. **Region:** *Possible Answer:* The Act increased the land that was open to slavery.

MORE ABOUT . . .
Border Ruffians
Violence was nothing new for the "border ruffians." Fifteen years before the struggle over Kansas, these ruffians had persecuted and burned the Mormons out of Missouri. When Senator David Atchison wrote to Jefferson Davis about his plans for Kansas, he said: "We will be compelled to shoot, burn & hang, but the thing will soon be over. We intend to 'Mormonize' the Abolitionists."

KEY PLAYERS
John Brown
Critical Thinking: Evaluating Ask students if they would have supported or opposed John Brown's actions, had they lived in the 1850s. Do they think that John Brown's actions helped or hindered the abolitionist cause? Discuss reasons for their responses.

---

their revolvers cocked and voted illegally. They won a fraudulent majority for the proslavery candidates, who set up a government at Lecompton and promptly issued a series of proslavery acts. Furious over events in Lecompton, abolitionists organized a rival government in Topeka in the late summer of 1855.

"THE SACK OF LAWRENCE" It wasn't long before violence surfaced in the struggle for Kansas. Antislavery settlers had founded a town named Lawrence. A proslavery grand jury condemned Lawrence's inhabitants as traitors and called on the local sheriff to arrest them. On May 21, 1856, a proslavery posse of 800 armed men swept into Lawrence to carry out the grand jury's will. With wild yells the posse burned down the antislavery headquarters, destroyed two newspapers' printing presses, and looted many houses and stores. Abolitionist newspapers dubbed the event "the sack of Lawrence."

"THE POTTAWATOMIE MASSACRE" The uproar from Lawrence soon reached **John Brown,** an antislavery fanatic who believed that God had called on him "to break the jaws of the wicked" slaveowners. Brown had the mistaken impression that a proslavery posse in Lawrence had killed five men. He was set on revenge. Later that month, he and his followers, including his own sons, pulled five men from their beds in the proslavery settlement of Pottawatomie Creek, hacked off their hands, and stabbed them with broadswords.

The massacre triggered dozens of incidents throughout Kansas. Some 200 people were killed. John Brown fled Kansas but left behind men and women who lived with rifles by their sides. People began calling the territory **Bleeding Kansas,** as it had become a violent battlefield in a civil war.

VIOLENCE IN THE SENATE Violence was not restricted to Kansas, however. On May 19, Senator Charles Sumner delivered an impassioned speech in the Senate, entitled "The Crime Against Kansas." For two days he verbally attacked his colleagues for their support of slavery. Sumner was particularly abusive toward the aged senator Andrew P. Butler of South Carolina, sneering at him for his proslavery beliefs and making fun of his impaired speech.

E. Answer Because the Kansas-Nebraska Act opened the territory to slavery, and both proslavery and antislavery forces battled for control of the territorial government.

THINK THROUGH HISTORY
E. Analyzing Causes Why did Kansas become a center of controversy over the issue of slavery?

KEY PLAYER

JOHN BROWN
1800–1859

Most people who knew the abolitionist John Brown believed him to be mentally unbalanced—it was generally said that insanity ran in his family. An unsuccessful businessman, Brown tried a variety of ventures from farming to land speculation, but he failed every time. Brown began to hate slavery when he saw a white man beating a young slave with a shovel. He devoted the last 21 years of his life to fighting for abolition.

Brown became a powerful symbol of the issue of slavery in both the North and the South. But his fevered drive to put an end to slavery ended with his execution in 1859.

The Union in Peril **293**

TEACHING OPTION

Skillbuilder Mini-Lesson: Analyzing Causes

Explaining the Skill In history, causes are typically connected to geographical, economic, or social forces, or to political or governmental actions. Causes might also be related to the feelings or ambitions of a group or an individual. For example, economic considerations and desire for a better life were behind the movement of many settlers to the West.

Applying the Skill: Think Through History Question To answer the Think Through History question on this page, students will need to identify the events, actions, and emotions that caused different groups to compete for control of the Kansas territory. Ask students these questions:

1. What laws or government actions prompted competition for Kansas? *The Kansas-Nebraska Act.*

2. Why did this law pose a problem? *It allowed voters in a territory to decide for themselves whether to allow slavery.*

3. What emotions were involved? *Sectional loyalties were inflamed. Both antislavery and proslavery states wanted Kansas to side with them.*

IN-DEPTH RESOURCES: UNIT 3
Skillbuilder Practice: Analyzing Causes, p. 23

Southern Chivalry

Reading a Cartoon Ask students to label the two most important characters in this cartoon. What side did each character represent? Ask for opinions on the meaning of the caption.

Extension Have students review the main events of this section and then create a cartoon based on one of the most important personalities or events. They should include a caption and the approximate date that the cartoon might have appeared.

ASSESS & RETEACH

Section 2 Assessment

Have students work in pairs or small groups to help each other answer the questions.

Self-Assessment

To demonstrate their understanding of the growing tensions over slavery, ask students to write statements summarizing the positions of people on both sides of the issue.

Section Quiz

FORMAL ASSESSMENT
Section Quiz, p. 126

Reteach

Use the maps on pages 292-293 to help review the main ideas of the section.

CLOSE

The compromises that had been tried from the time of the Wilmot Proviso until the Kansas-Nebraska Act could not satisfy either the North or the South. The tensions that resulted led to new political alliances as well as to violence.

On May 22 Butler's nephew, Congressman Preston S. Brooks, walked into the Senate chamber and over to Sumner's desk. "I have read your speech twice over, carefully," Brooks said softly. "It is a libel on South Carolina and Mr. Butler, who is a relative of mine." With that, he lifted up his cane and struck Sumner on the head five or six times before the cane broke. Sumner suffered shock and apparent brain damage and did not return to his Senate seat for more than three years.

Southerners applauded Brooks and showered him with new canes, including one from the city of Charleston, South Carolina, inscribed with the words, "Hit him again!" Northerners condemned the incident as yet another example of Southern brutality and antagonism toward free speech. Northerners and Southerners, it appeared, had met an impasse.

The widening gulf between the North and the South had far-reaching implications for party politics as well. As the two sections grew further apart, the old national parties were torn apart and new political parties emerged, including a party for antislavery Northerners.

THINK THROUGH HISTORY
F. Summarizing Describe Northern and Southern reactions to the incident between Brooks and Sumner.

F. Answer The South saw Brooks as a hero who defended the honor of his family and state. The North saw the incident as an act of brutality.

The original caption of this 1856 cartoon gives the Northern view of Preston Brook's beating of Charles Sumner.

SOUTHERN CHIVALRY — ARGUMENT versus CLUB'S.

Section ❷ Assessment

1. TERMS & NAMES

Identify:
• Fugitive Slave Act
• personal liberty laws
• Underground Railroad
• Harriet Tubman
• Harriet Beecher Stowe
• *Uncle Tom's Cabin*
• Kansas-Nebraska Act
• John Brown
• Bleeding Kansas

2. SUMMARIZING Create a time line highlighting the major events in the growing conflict between the North and the South. Use a form similar to the one below.

```
[event one]        [event three]
        [event two]        [event four]
```

Select one event and explain in a paragraph how it was representative of North–South conflict.

3. RECOGNIZING EFFECTS Explain how *Uncle Tom's Cabin* affected the abolitionist cause. Use details from the section to support your answer.

4. SYNTHESIZING Explain the concept of popular sovereignty and describe Northern and Southern reactions to it as a way of making decisions about slavery in the territories. Use evidence from the text to support your answer.

294 CHAPTER 10

ANSWERS

1. TERMS & NAMES

Fugitive Slave Act, p. 288

personal liberty laws, p. 289

Underground Railroad, p. 289

Harriet Tubman, p. 289

Harriet Beecher Stowe, p. 290

Uncle Tom's Cabin, p. 290

Kansas-Nebraska Act, p. 292

John Brown, p. 293

Bleeding Kansas, p. 293

2. SUMMARIZING

1849 Harriet Tubman escapes slavery and reaches Philadelphia.
1850 Congress passes Fugitive Slave Act.
1852 Harriet Beecher Stowe publishes *Uncle Tom's Cabin.*
1854 Congress passes the Kansas-Nebraska Act.
1855 Two governments are established in Kansas.
1856 The sack of Lawrence and the Pottawatomie massacre occur.

3. RECOGNIZING EFFECTS

Possible Answer: The book caused abolitionists to increase their protests against the Fugitive Slave Act. It also reinforced the idea that slavery was evil.

4. SYNTHESIZING

Possible Answer: Popular sovereignty let inhabitants vote to determine whether slavery would be allowed in a territory. The North feared more slave states joining the Union; the South feared the addition of more free states. Both the North and the South wanted to avoid a shift in the congressional balance of power between slave and free states.

The Birth of the Republican Party

TERMS & NAMES
• Horace Greeley
• Franklin Pierce
• nativism
• Know-Nothing Party
• Free-Soil Party
• Republican Party
• John C. Frémont
• James Buchanan

LEARN ABOUT the impact of slavery, immigration, and sectionalism on U.S. politics
TO UNDERSTAND why new political parties emerged in the mid-19th century.

ONE AMERICAN'S STORY

As editor of the *New York Tribune*, which he founded in 1841, **Horace Greeley** always spoke his mind. A staunch abolitionist, Greeley consistently argued in his columns against popular sovereignty and in favor of violent resistance to slave catchers.

In the early 1850s, Greeley became frustrated with the Whig Party's shifting position on slavery. In March 1855, he issued a call to political arms for "the friends of freedom" to "be girding up their loins for future contests" and join a new antislavery political party, the Republican Party.

A PERSONAL VOICE
[The Republicans have] the heart, the conscience and the understanding of the people with them. . . . All that is noble, all that is true, all that is pure, all that is manly, and estimable in human character, goes to swell the power of the anti-slavery party of the North. That party is no longer the faction, the handful of men it once was. . . . It now embraces every Northern man who does not want to see the government converted into a huge engine for the spread of slavery over the whole continent, every man who is and was opposed to . . . the passage of the Kansas-Nebraska bill.

HORACE GREELEY, quoted in *The Coming of the Civil War*

Greeley no doubt exaggerated the virtues of the Republicans, but his appeal accurately reflected the changing national political scene. With the pressure of abolitionism and continuing tension over slavery, many Americans needed a national political voice. That voice was to be the Republican Party.

Horace Greeley

New Political Parties Emerge

By the end of 1856, the nation's political landscape had a very different appearance than it had exhibited in 1848. The Whig Party had split over the issue of slavery and had lost support in both the North and the South. The Democratic Party, which had survived numerous crises in its history, was still alive, though scarred. The new Republican Party moved within striking distance of the presidency.

SLAVERY DIVIDES WHIGS The Whig Party—founded in 1834 as a reaction against President Andrew Jackson—had long been divided into Northern "conscience" (antislavery) Whigs and Southern "cotton" (proslavery) Whigs. In 1850, the two factions took opposing positions on the Fugitive Slave Act.

The division widened in 1852 when the Whigs nominated General Winfield Scott, a hero of the war with Mexico, for the presidency. Because Scott owed his nomination to Northern Whigs who opposed the Fugitive Slave Act, he gave only lukewarm support to the Compromise of 1850. Southern Whigs, however, had supported the compromise in order to portray themselves as both proslavery and pro-Union. As a result of Scott's position, the Whig vote in the South fell from 50 percent in 1848, to 35 percent in 1852, handing the election to the Democratic candidate, **Franklin Pierce.** In 1854 the Kansas-Nebraska Act

The Union in Peril **295**

SECTION 3 RESOURCES

 PRINT RESOURCES

IN-DEPTH RESOURCES: UNIT 3
Guided Reading, p. 21

ACCESS FOR STUDENTS ACQUIRING ENGLISH
Guided Reading (Spanish), p. 103

FORMAL ASSESSMENT
Section Quiz, p. 127

ALTERNATIVE ASSESSMENT BOOK
See forms for supporting and scorng alternative activities.

 TECHNOLOGY RESOURCES

VIDEO *American Portfolio: A Videodisc for U.S. History*
user's guide, pp. 88, 89

INTERNET McDougal Littell Learning On-Line
http://www.mcdougallittell.com

Section 3 Overview

OBJECTIVES

1 To identify the political parties that emerged as the North and the South forged new alliances.

2 To summarize the reasons that led voters to align with a particular party and to explain why Buchanan won the election of 1856.

CRITICAL THINKING

• Recognizing effects, pp. 296, 298
• Analyzing motives, p. 297
• Summarizing, p. 298
• Contrasting, p. 298
• Synthesizing, p. 298

FOCUS & MOTIVATE

▶ *Starting with the Student*
When it comes to presidential elections today, most people would agree the United States has a two-party system. What advantages or disadvantages would result if we had three or more parties in a presidential race?

OBJECTIVE
1 INSTRUCT

New Political Parties Emerge

▶ *Discussing Key Ideas*
• With the nation divided over issues ranging from slavery to immigration to sectionalism, numerous political parties emerge.
• Slavery divides and eventually destroys the Whig Party; anti-immigrant and anti-Catholic sentiment generate the Know-Nothing Party.

IN-DEPTH RESOURCES: UNIT 3
Guided Reading, p. 21

ACCESS FOR STUDENTS ACQUIRING ENGLISH
Guided Reading (Spanish), p. 103

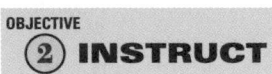

MORE ABOUT . . .
Franklin Pierce

Pierce was only a lukewarm supporter of the Union during the Civil War. He criticized Lincoln's administration unmercifully, calling it "cruel, arbitrary, and oppressive." He believed that the Emancipation Proclamation was unconstitutional and supported McClellan in the 1864 election. As a result, Pierce became so unpopular in his state of New Hampshire that the citizens of the capital, Concord, refused to erect a statue in his honor until 50 years after his death in 1869.

OBJECTIVE
② INSTRUCT

Antislavery Parties Form

▶ *Starting with the Student*
Ask students to think about starting a new political party.

• What steps are necessary to be put on the ballot?
• How does a new party go about attracting followers?

▶ *Discussing Key Ideas*
• The Republican Party evolves out of two earlier political parties, the Liberty Party and the Free-Soil Party.
• The Republican Party attracts a broad spectrum of voters.
• The party is finally united by opposition to slavery and violence in "Bleeding Kansas."

The campaign banner for the Know-Nothing Party *(above)* reflects its members' fear and resentment of immigrants. The term "native Americans" as used in the banner refers to all citizens born in the United States. The Free-Soilers' banner *(opposite page)* features John C. Frémont and calls for an end to the spread of "slave power" in the nation.

completed the demise of the Whigs, who once again took opposing positions on the issue. Unable to agree on a national platform, the Southern faction splintered as its members looked for a proslavery, pro-Union party to join, while Whigs in the North sought a political alternative of their own.

NATIVISM One alternative that appeared was the American Party. The American Party had its roots in a secret organization known as the Order of the Star-Spangled Banner, which had been founded in 1849. Members of this society, frightened by the huge increase in immigration to the country, expressed a belief in **nativism,** the favoring of native-born people over immigrants.

Primarily middle-class Protestants, nativists were dismayed not only at the total number of new immigrants, but also at the number of Catholics among them. Anti-Catholic bias—the fear of "Papal Power"—often rested on a fear that Catholicism threatened democracy. Because the religion held the Pope as its ultimate authority, nativists feared that Catholics would be influenced by the Pope on issues involving the United States. To nativists, the Catholic immigrants who had flooded into the country during the 1830s and 1840s could form a conspiracy to overthrow democracy.

Members of the Order of the Star-Spangled Banner used secret handshakes and passwords, and were instructed to answer questions about their activities by saying, "I know nothing." When nativists formed the American Party in 1854, it soon became known as the **Know-Nothing Party.**

Nativists supported a longer naturalization period for immigrants, thus delaying the time when these new residents would be able to vote. While the Democratic Party courted immigrant voters, nativists opposed them and voted for Know-Nothing candidates. The Know-Nothing Party did surprisingly well at the polls in 1854, even capturing the governorship of Massachusetts. However, like the Whig Party, the Know-Nothings split over the issue of slavery in the territories. Southern Know-Nothings, including the former Whigs who had joined their ranks, looked for another alternative to the Democrats. Meanwhile, Northern Know-Nothings began to edge toward the Republican Party.

THINK THROUGH HISTORY
A. Recognizing Effects What effect did the Kansas-Nebraska Act have on the Whig Party?
A. Answer The Kansas-Nebraska Act split the party and destroyed it, with both Southern Whigs and Northern Whigs joining other parties.

Antislavery Parties Form

Two forerunners of the Republican Party had emerged during the 1840s. In 1844 the tiny abolitionist Liberty Party—formed for the purpose of pursuing the cause of abolition by passing new laws—received only a small percentage of votes in the presidential election. However, the Liberty Party won enough votes to throw the election to Democratic candidate James K. Polk instead of Whig candidate Henry Clay.

In 1848 the **Free-Soil Party,** which opposed the extension of slavery into the territories, chose former Democratic President Martin Van Buren as its candidate. Although the Free-Soil Party failed to win any electoral votes in 1848, it received ten percent of the popular vote, sending a clear message: even if some Northerners did not favor abolition, they definitely opposed the extension of slavery to the territories.

Exploring Themes

Immigration and Migration Native-born Americans' fears of immigrants can be better understood by looking at the huge influx of Europeans during this time. Immigration to the United States soared between the 1840s and the 1860s. During the decade beginning in 1845, 3 million immigrants arrived from Europe. The largest immigrant group during this period was the Irish, followed closely by the Germans. In addition, people arrived from Scandinavia, Great Britain, Holland, and Switzerland. Almost 2 million Irish departed for America when the Great Potato Famine struck their own land, beginning in 1845.

Although some of the immigrants from Europe came seeking religious or political asylum, most came with the desire to create new and more successful lives for themselves. Although they came filled with hope, many soon faced the reality of their new life. A few found tremendous financial success, but most found a life of hard labor and low pay. Worse, they met with the resentment of native-born Americans who saw the new immigrants—especially the Irish, who would work for almost no money—as a threat to their own security.

Interested students may want to research their own immigrant roots and write a report on their findings.

THE FREE-SOILERS' VOICE Northern opposition to slavery in the territories was not necessarily based on positive feelings toward African Americans. It was not unusual for Northerners to be free-soilers without being abolitionists. Unlike abolitionists, a number of Northern free-soilers supported racist laws prohibiting settlement by blacks in their communities and denying them the right to vote.

What free-soilers primarily objected to was slavery's competition with free white workers, or a wage-based labor force, upon which the North depended. For instance, free-soiler Abraham Lincoln believed that "the man who labored for another last year, this year labors for himself, and next year . . . will hire others to labor for him." The extension of slavery directly threatened the free labor system.

THINK THROUGH HISTORY
B. Analyzing Motives Why did most free-soilers object to slavery?

B. Answer Most free-soilers objected to slavery because they believed that white workers could not get jobs in competition with slaves.

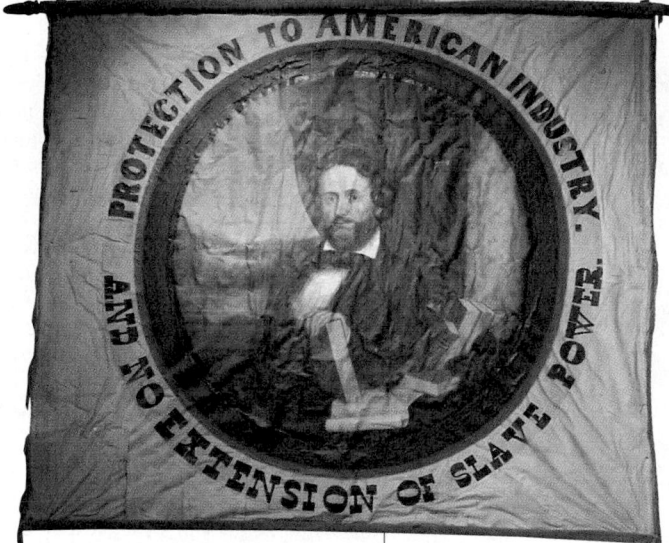

Free-soilers detected a dangerous pattern in such events as the passage of the Fugitive Slave Act and the repeal of the Missouri Compromise. They were convinced that a conspiracy existed on the part of the "diabolical Slave Power" to spread slavery throughout the United States. Something or someone, according to the free-soilers, had to prevent this spread.

REPUBLICAN PARTY On February 28, 1854, opponents of slavery in the territories met at a schoolhouse in Ripon, Wisconsin, where they recommended the formation of a new political party. Similar meetings were held in several Northern states, and on July 6 the new **Republican Party** was formally organized in Jackson, Michigan.

The Republican Party was united in opposing the Kansas-Nebraska Act and keeping slavery out of the territories. Otherwise, though, it embraced a wide range of opinions. As the party grew, it took in free-soilers, antislavery Whigs and Democrats, and nativists, mostly from the North. The conservative faction hoped to resurrect the Missouri Compromise. At the opposite extreme were some radical abolitionists.

The party also attracted such groups as temperance supporters who wanted to prohibit the sale of liquor, small farmers who wanted land grants in the West, and commercial farmers and manufacturers who needed more internal improvements if they were to prosper. The Republican Party's ability to draw support from such diverse groups provided the strength for it to win a political tug-of-war with the other parties.

The primary competition for the Republican Party was the Know-Nothing Party, which was very well organized at the state level. Both parties targeted the same groups of voters. By 1855 the Republicans had set up party organizations in about half of the Northern states, but they lacked a national organization. What they needed was some new development that would refocus people's attention and concern on the slavery issue. Then, in quick succession, came the fraudulent territorial election in Kansas in March 1855, the sack of Lawrence, the Pottawatomie massacre, and the caning of Sumner in 1856. Between "Bleeding Kansas" and "Bleeding Sumner," the Republicans had the issues they needed to challenge the Democrats for the presidency in 1856.

"Free Trade, Free Labor, Free Speech, and Free Men"

FREE-SOILERS'
CAMPAIGN SLOGAN, 1844

MORE ABOUT . . .
John C. Frémont
Frémont was 43 in 1856 when he was chosen by the Republicans as their presidential candidate, making him the youngest presidential nominee thus far. He was definitely a "glamour boy" candidate, not only because of his fabled explorations of Oregon and California but also because of his marriage to 16-year-old Jessie Benton, daughter of Senator Thomas Hart Benton of Missouri. It was Jessie who wrote most of Frémont's *Report of the Exploring Expedition to . . . Oregon and North California,* which opened the country's eyes to the wealth of California and the feeble control held there by Mexico.

The Union in Peril **297**

Teaching Less Proficient Readers

Organizing Data This section deals with a large amount of data—names and dates—which sometimes discourages the less proficient reader. Pair these students with more proficient ones. Have pairs make a chart listing the names of each party, including important dates arranged chronologically, as well as the important political positions each party took. This chart should cover pages 295 through 297. Use the model at right as a graphic organizer. When complete, it should enable the less proficient reader to use the data in understanding the material. Students can use the chart later to review the section.

Political Parties Arising in the United States, 1844–1856

Name	Date	Political positions	Results
Liberty	1844	Tried to pass pro-abolitionist laws	Threw election to Polk
Know-Nothing			
Republican			
Free Soil			

*The Impending Crisis
of the South*

Ask students to imagine
themselves as book publishers in the 1850s. Given a
choice, would they publish
Uncle Tom's Cabin or *The
Impending Crisis of the
South*? Give three reasons
to support the choice.

MORE ABOUT . . .

*The 1856 Republican
Convention*

The first national Republican
convention adopted a rule
stating that a presidential
nomination required only a
majority vote of the delegates. Democratic Party
rules, on the other hand,
called for a two-thirds
majority. This difference
between the two parties
continued well into the 20th
century.

ASSESS & RETEACH

Section Assessment

Assign pairs of students to
help each other answer the
questions.

Self-Assessment

Ask students to write a short
paragraph summarizing the
main concepts of this section.

Section Quiz

FORMAL ASSESSMENT
Section Quiz, p. 127

Reteach

To help review the main
ideas of the section, have
students make a chart listing
the different political parties
formed during this period.

CLOSE

By the election of 1856, the
Know-Nothings and the
Whigs had declined as
forces in American politics.
James Buchanan, a Demo-
crat, won the election, but
the Republican Party was on
the rise.

**HISTORICAL
SPOTLIGHT**

**THE IMPENDING CRISIS
OF THE SOUTH**

Published in 1857, Hinton Rowan
Helper's *The Impending Crisis of the
South* portrayed poor, white
Southern workers as the chief
victims of slavery. Helper, a
nonslaveholding North Carolinian,
argued that abolishing slavery would
improve economic conditions for the
section's white residents. When the
Republican Party—including *New
York Tribune* editor Horace
Greeley—began to distribute the
book, Southern commitment to the
Union further weakened.

THE ELECTION OF 1856   The Republicans chose as their candidate
free-soiler **John C. Frémont,** the famed "pathfinder" who had
mapped the Oregon Trail and led U.S. troops into California during
the war with Mexico. The Know-Nothings split their allegiance, with
Northerners endorsing Frémont and Southerners selecting former
Whig President Millard Fillmore as their candidate despite his relatively undistinguished political career. For all practical purposes, the
Whigs had disappeared from the political arena.

The Democrats nominated **James Buchanan** of Pennsylvania.
Although he was a Northerner, most of his Washington friends were
Southerners. Furthermore, as ambassador to Great Britain, he had
been out of the country during the disputes over the Kansas-Nebraska
Act in 1854. Thus, he was "Kansasless"—he had antagonized neither
the North nor the South. Buchanan was the only truly national candidate. To balance support between the North and South, the Democrats
chose John C. Breckinridge of Kentucky as Buchanan's running mate.

If Frémont had won, the South might well have seceded then and
there. Judge P. J. Scruggs of Mississippi put it bluntly.

A PERSONAL VOICE
The election of Frémont would present, at once, to the people of the South,
the question whether they would tamely crouch at the feet of their despoilers,
or . . . openly defy their enemies, and assert their independence. In my judgment, anything short of immediate, prompt, and unhesitating secession, would
be an act of servility that would seal our doom for all time to come.

P. J. SCRUGGS, quoted in *The Coming of the Civil War*

Buchanan, however, carried the day. Although he received only 45 percent
of the popular vote, he won the entire South except for Maryland. Frémont,
who carried 11 of the 16 free states, came in a strong second with 33 percent,
while Fillmore unable to crack Buchanan's hold on the South, brought up the
rear with 22 percent.

The meaning was clear. First, the Democrats could win the presidency with
a national candidate who could compete in the North without alienating
Southerners. Second, the Know-Nothings, like the Whigs, were in decline
nationally. Third, the Republicans were a political force in the North.

The 1856 presidential campaign had been hard-fought. However, the dissension that characterized party politics in the 1850s was only a pale preview of
the turmoil that would divide the nation before the end of the decade.

C. Answer
Because it
established the
party as an
alternative to the
Whigs and
Democrats, and
showed that the
Republicans
would be
powerful
contenders in the
future.

THINK THROUGH HISTORY
C. *Recognizing
Effects Why was
the election of 1856
so important to the
growth of the
Republican Party?*

Section ③ Assessment

1. TERMS & NAMES

Identify:
• Horace Greeley
• Franklin Pierce
• nativism
• Know-Nothing
  Party
• Free-Soil Party
• Republican Party
• John C. Frémont
• James Buchanan

2. SUMMARIZING Show how
various events led to the growth
of the Republican Party in the
1850s. Use a chart similar to the
one below.

Growth of
Republican
Party

Which event was most important
in the rise of the Republican
Party?

3. CONTRASTING How did the
attitudes toward slavery held by
abolitionists, free-soilers, and
Know-Nothings differ? Explain
your answer.

THINK ABOUT
• the ultimate goal of
  abolitionists
• the reason free-soilers
  objected to slavery
• what caused the split in the
  Know-Nothing Party

4. SYNTHESIZING Imagine that
you are living in a small town in
Illinois in 1855. Write a flyer
attracting people to a meeting of
the new Republican Party in
Illinois.

THINK ABOUT
• issues that concern voters
• reasons that people might
  want to leave their current
  political parties
• signs that the Republican Party
  will be successful

298 CHAPTER 10

ANSWERS

1. TERMS & NAMES

Horace Greeley, p. 295

Franklin Pierce, p. 295

nativism, p. 296

Know-Nothing Party, p. 296

Free-Soil Party, p. 296

Republican Party, p. 297

John C. Frémont, p. 298

James Buchanan, p. 298

2. SUMMARIZING

Whig Party divides over slavery.
Know-Nothing Party divides
over slavery. **Free-Soil Party**
opposes slavery in the territories. **Temperance advocates**
support Republicans. **Small
farmers** want land grants in the
West. **Commercial farmers** and
manufacturers want internal
improvements. **Bleeding Kansas**
angers opponents of slavery.
Caning of Sumner angers
Northerners.

3. CONTRASTING

Possible Answer: Abolitionists
opposed slavery on moral
grounds, wanted it abolished
where it already existed, and
opposed its extension into the
territories. Free-soilers opposed
slavery because slavery reduced
the number of jobs available to
whites, not because of moral
principles. Know-Nothings were
divided over the issue of slavery,
with Southerners generally supporting it and Northerners
opposing it.

4. SYNTHESIZING

Student flyers should oppose
slavery in the territories. They
might also mention the weakness of existing parties and the
support of influential people
such as Horace Greeley.

4 Slavery and Secession

TERMS & NAMES
- Abraham Lincoln
- Dred Scott
- Roger B. Taney
- Freeport Doctrine
- Harpers Ferry
- Confederate States of America
- Jefferson Davis

LEARN ABOUT the increasingly divisive effects of slavery on national politics in the late 1850s
TO UNDERSTAND why the South seceded.

ONE AMERICAN'S STORY

On June 16, 1858, the Republican Party of Illinois nominated its state chairman, **Abraham Lincoln**, to run for the U.S. Senate against Democratic incumbent Stephen A. Douglas. That night Lincoln launched his campaign with a ringing address to the convention.

A PERSONAL VOICE

"A house divided against itself cannot stand." I believe this government cannot endure, permanently half *slave* and half *free*. I do not expect the Union to be *dissolved*—I do not expect the house to *fall*—but I do expect it will cease to be divided. It will become *all* one thing or *all* the other. Either the *opponents* of slavery will arrest the further spread of it . . . or its *advocates* will push it forward, till it shall become alike lawful in *all* the States, *old* as well as *new, North* as well as *South*.
ABRAHAM LINCOLN, in an 1858 speech

Lincoln was correct in that the United States could not survive for long with such a deep gulf between the North and the South—but was he right that the Union would not dissolve?

The next two years would determine the accuracy of that prediction. At the moment, with a weak President in James Buchanan and new legal questions over slavery, many people in the United States viewed the future with apprehension. Some suspected that events to come would lead like a trail of powder to a final explosion.

This photograph shows the younger Lincoln in about 1858, before the Civil War took its toll.

Slavery Dominates Politics

For the strongest of leaders, the passions inspired by the issue of slavery were difficult to control. For President Buchanan, an indecisive man and a poor politician, slavery-related controversies plagued his administration. The first one arose just two days after he took office on March 4, 1857.

DRED SCOTT V. SANFORD **Dred Scott** was a slave whose owner took him from the slave state of Missouri to free territory in Illinois and Wisconsin and back to Missouri. Scott sued his owner for his freedom on the grounds that living in a free state—Illinois—and a free territory—Wisconsin—had made him a free man. The Missouri court ruled in favor of Scott's new owner, John F. A. Sanford, and the case was appealed to the U.S. Supreme Court.

The Supreme Court faced two basic legal questions. First, was Scott a citizen of the United States? If not, then he could not sue in federal court, and the case would have to be thrown out. Second, did residence in a free territory make Scott a free man, even though he had returned to a slave state?

The *Dred Scott* decision was handed down on March 6, 1857. Chief Justice **Roger B. Taney** wrote the Supreme Court's opinion. A Southerner, Taney had owned slaves but freed them and even purchased the freedom of others. According to Taney's interpretation of the Constitution, however, Dred Scott

The Union in Peril **299**

Section 4 Overview

OBJECTIVES

1. To summarize the impact of the *Dred Scott* decision and the Lecompton constitution on the issue of slavery.

2. To explain why Douglas believed slavery would fade away and Lincoln believed abolishing it required free-soil legislation.

3. To list the events that led to Lincoln's election and the establishment of the Confederate States of America.

CRITICAL THINKING

- Recognizing effects, pp. 300, 303, 304
- Analyzing motives, p. 300
- Comparing, p. 301
- Summarizing, p. 305
- Forming opinions, p. 305
- Analyzing issues, p. 305

FOCUS & MOTIVATE

▶ *Starting with the Student*
- What qualities do people look for in a candidate for president?
- What part does physical appearance play in the success of a candidate?

OBJECTIVE
1 **INSTRUCT**

Slavery Dominates Politics

▶ *Discussing Key Ideas*
- The Supreme Court's pro-slavery decision in the *Dred Scott* case further inflames the North.
- Stephen Douglas becomes a Northern hero when he succeeds in having the Lecompton constitution overturned through a referendum.

IN-DEPTH RESOURCES: UNIT 3
Guided Reading, p. 22

ACCESS FOR STUDENTS ACQUIRING ENGLISH
Guided Reading (Spanish), p. 104

SECTION 4 RESOURCES

 PRINT RESOURCES

IN-DEPTH RESOURCES: UNIT 3
Guided Reading, p. 22
Primary Sources: *from* The Lincoln-Douglas Debates, p. 27;
John Brown's Last Speech, p. 28

ACCESS FOR STUDENTS ACQUIRING ENGLISH
Guided Reading (Spanish), p. 104

FORMAL ASSESSMENT
Section Quiz, p. 128

ALTERNATIVE ASSESSMENT BOOK
See forms for supporting and scoring alternative activities.

 TECHNOLOGY RESOURCES

GEOGRAPHY TRANSPARENCIES
G10, Presidential Elections: 1856, 1860

CRITICAL THINKING TRANSPARENCIES
CT10, Compromise of 1850

CD-ROM Electronic Library of Primary Sources

VIDEO *American Portfolio: A Videodisc for U.S. History*
user's guide, pp. 90–93

INTERNET McDougal Littell Learning On-Line
http://www.mcdougallittell.com

Dred Scott's lawsuit
dragged on for years and
set off even more
controversy over slavery.

lacked any legal standing to sue in federal court because he was not,
and never could be, a citizen. African Americans were "a subordinate
and inferior class of beings," the decision read, with "no rights which
the white man was bound to respect." Two justices had strongly disagreed, pointing out that several colonies and states had allowed
African Americans to vote. A majority of the Court, however, con-
curred that Scott lacked the legal standing to sue in federal court.

Moreover, the Court ruled that being in free territory did not
make a slave free. The Fifth Amendment protected property, and
for territories to exclude slavery, the Court argued, would be to
deprive slaveowners of their property. In effect, the Court had
declared the Missouri Compromise unconstitutional. This was the
first time since *Marbury* v. *Madison* (1803) that the Court ruled an
act of Congress unconstitutional.

Sectional passions exploded immediately. Many Northerners
showered a torrent of abuse upon the Supreme Court, in part
because a majority of its justices were Southerners. Warnings about
the slave states' influence on the national government spread.
Southern slaveholders, on the other hand, were jubilant. In their interpretation,
the *Dred Scott* decision not only permitted the extension of slavery but actually
guaranteed it. The issue of slavery in the territories held center stage, and once
again, events in Kansas inflamed the issue.

THE LECOMPTON CONSTITUTION In the fall of 1857, the proslavery government at Lecompton, Kansas, developed a constitution and applied for admission to the Union. Free-soilers—who by this time outnumbered proslavery
settlers in Kansas by nearly ten to one—rejected the proposed constitution
because it protected the rights of slaveholders already living in Kansas. The legislature called for a referendum in which the people could vote on the proslavery constitution. They voted against it.

At this point President Buchanan made a poor decision: he
endorsed the proslavery Lecompton constitution. He owed his presidency to Southern support and believed that since Kansas contained
only about 200 slaves, the free-soilers were overreacting.

Buchanan's endorsement provoked the wrath of fellow Democrat
Stephen A. Douglas, who did not care "whether [slavery] is voted
down or voted up." What he cared about was popular sovereignty.
Backed by an antislavery coalition of Republicans and Northern
Democrats, Douglas persuaded Congress to authorize another refer-
endum on the constitution. In the summer of 1858, voters rejected the
constitution once again. Northerners hailed Douglas as a hero,
Southerners scorned him as a traitor, and the two wings of the
Democratic Party moved still farther apart over the issue of slavery.

Lincoln-Douglas Debates

That summer witnessed the start of one of Illinois's greatest political
contests: the 1858 race for the U.S. Senate between Democratic
incumbent Douglas and Republican challenger Abraham Lincoln. To
many outsiders it must have seemed like an uneven match. Douglas
was a two-term senator with an outstanding record and a large campaign chest. Who was Lincoln?

A self-educated man with a dry wit, Lincoln was known locally as a successful lawyer and politician. Elected to one term in Congress in 1846 as a Whig, he
broke with his party after the passage of the Kansas-Nebraska Act in 1854 and
became a Republican two years later.

As the senatorial campaign progressed, the Republican Party decided that Lincoln needed to counteract the "Little Giant's" well-known name and extensive financial resources. As a result, Lincoln challenged Douglas to a series of seven open-air debates to be held throughout Illinois on the issue of slavery in the territories. Douglas accepted the challenge, and the stage was set for some of the most celebrated debates in U.S. history.

At the debates, Lincoln made a striking contrast to his opponent, over whom he towered. He seemed even taller because of his stove pipe hat. While Douglas was stocky and energetic, Lincoln was thin and gangling. While Douglas dressed smartly, Lincoln's clothes were usually plain and rumpled. Nonetheless, those who knew "Honest Abe" both respected and trusted him.

POSITIONS AND ARGUMENTS Lincoln and Douglas had very different speaking styles. Douglas exuded self-confidence, pacing back and forth on the stage and dramatically using his fists to pound home his points. Lincoln, on the other hand, solemnly delivered his comments, using direct and plain language.

The two men's positions were simple and consistent. Douglas believed deeply in popular sovereignty, allowing the residents of a territory to vote for or against slavery in that territory. Although he did not think that slavery was immoral, he did believe that it was a backward labor system unsuitable to the prairie agriculture of Kansas and Nebraska. The people, Douglas figured, understood this and would vote Kansas and Nebraska free.

However, Lincoln, like many free-soilers, believed that slavery was immoral—a labor system based on greed, in which one person owned another purely for the sake of wealth and power. Lincoln did not expect individuals to give up slavery any sooner than he expected them to give up greed, unless Congress passed free-soil legislation.

The crucial difference between the two was that Douglas believed that popular sovereignty would allow slavery to pass away on its own, while Lincoln doubted that slavery would cease to spread without legislation outlawing slavery in the territories. Neither man wanted slavery in the territories, but they disagreed on how to keep it out.

In the course of the debates, each candidate tried to distort the views of the other. Lincoln tried to make Douglas look like a defender of slavery and of the *Dred Scott* decision. Neither charge was true. In turn, Douglas accused Lincoln of being an abolitionist and an advocate of racial equality. Lincoln responded by saying, "I am not, nor ever have been, in favor of bringing about in any way the social and political equality of the white and black races." He did, however, insist that slavery was a moral, social, and political wrong that should not be allowed to spread.

In their second debate, held at Freeport, Lincoln asked his opponent a crucial question. Could the settlers of a territory vote to exclude slavery before the territory became a state? Everyone knew that the Dred Scott decision said no—that territories could not exclude slavery. Popular sovereignty, Lincoln implied, was thus an empty phrase.

THE FREEPORT DOCTRINE The senator's response became known as the **Freeport Doctrine.** Douglas contended, "Slavery cannot exist a day or an hour anywhere, unless it is supported by local police regulations."

The Lincoln-Douglas debates created quite a spectacle, partly due to the 6'4" Lincoln's one-foot height advantage over Douglas.

MORE ABOUT . . .
The Lincoln–Douglas Debates
At the time of the Lincoln-Douglas debates, newspapers seldom reported political events objectively because the papers depended on political organizations for their survival. Affiliating with a political party guaranteed a newspaper a certain number of subscribers, as well as legal and political advertising. In exchange, the paper was expected to print the party line. Partisan reporting appeared not only on the editorial pages, but on the news pages as well. As a result, people reading the "text" of the Lincoln-Douglas debates were not reading exact transcriptions of what the two men said.

Granted, newspapers reporting the debates utilized the new technique of verbatim reporting by trained stenographers. But after the stenographers sent in their notes, partisan editors took over. They eliminated ungrammatical sentences, divided run-on sentences, and remedied other problems, but only for whichever candidate their paper supported. Thus, the best way for a Chicagoan in 1858 to learn what Lincoln actually said was to read the pro-Democratic *Times,* while Douglas's actual words were most accurately presented in the *Republican Press* and *Tribune* (known today as the *Chicago Tribune*).

IN-DEPTH RESOURCES: UNIT 3
Primary Source: *from* The Lincoln Douglas Debates, p. 27

ECONOMIC BACKGROUND
The Panic of 1857

Have students create a cause and effect chart, showing the steps that led from the initial employee's embezzlement of company funds in 1857 to the business failures in 1859.

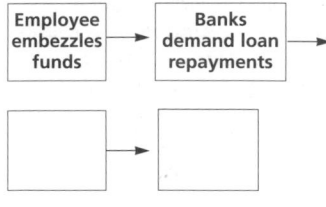

OBJECTIVE
③ **INSTRUCT**

Passions Erupt

▶ **Discussing Key Ideas**
• John Brown's raid on Harpers Ferry once again focuses the nation's attention on the issue of slavery.
• The execution of John Brown further divides the country, arousing strong feelings on both sides.

MORE ABOUT . . .
John Brown's Raid

The members of John Brown's raiding party at Harpers Ferry included five African Americans. Dangerfield Newby, who was killed in the raid, had been born a slave. So had Shields Green, who was captured and hanged. The three remaining blacks had been born free. Osborn Perry Anderson escaped after the raid and later fought in the Civil War, Lewis Sheridan Leary died in the attack, and John A. Copeland, Jr., was captured and hanged.

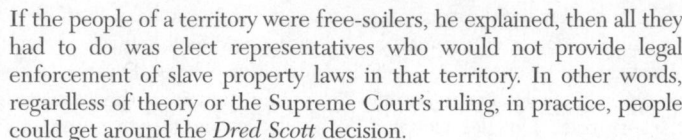

THE PANIC OF 1857

The Buchanan administration became widely unpopular not only because of the President's handling of the slavery issue but also because of the economic depression during his tenure.

The Panic of 1857 began on August 24 when the New York branch of an Ohio insurance company went bankrupt because an employee embezzled its funds. As news spread by telegraph, depositors rushed to recover their money. To pay them, the banks demanded immediate repayment of loans from businesses. Unable to both repay and finance daily operations, many crippled businesses closed down, and hundreds of thousands of men and women lost their jobs.

In the last four months of the year, nearly 5,000 businesses collapsed, and another 8,000 had failed by 1859.

In *John Brown Going to His Hanging* (1942), the African-American artist Horrace Pippin captures the starkness of the scene.

If the people of a territory were free-soilers, he explained, then all they had to do was elect representatives who would not provide legal enforcement of slave property laws in that territory. In other words, regardless of theory or the Supreme Court's ruling, in practice, people could get around the *Dred Scott* decision.

Douglas won the Senate seat, but his response had worsened the split between the Northern and Southern wings of the Democratic Party. As for Lincoln, his attacks on the "vast moral evil" of slavery drew national attention, and some Republicans began thinking of him as an excellent candidate for the presidency in 1860.

Passions Erupt

If 1858 was a year of talk, then 1859 turned out to be a year of action. Most Americans probably would have welcomed a respite from the issue of slavery and the economic troubles caused by the Panic of 1857. Instead, "God's angry man," John Brown, reemerged on the scene and ended all hopes of a compromise over slavery between the North and the South.

HARPERS FERRY While politicians debated the slavery issue, John Brown was studying the slave uprisings in ancient Rome and on the French island of Haiti. He believed that the time was ripe for similar uprisings in the United States. Brown secretly obtained financial backing from several prominent Boston abolitionists. On the night of October 16, 1859, he led a band of 21 men, black and white, into **Harpers Ferry,** Virginia (now West Virginia). His aim was to seize the federal arsenal there, distribute the captured arms to slaves in the area, and start a general slave uprising.

No such uprising occurred, though. Instead, local troops killed eight of Brown's men. Then a detachment of U.S. Marines, commanded by Colonel Robert E. Lee, raced to Harpers Ferry, stormed the engine house where Brown and his men had barricaded themselves, killed two more of the raiders, and captured Brown. Brown was turned over to Virginia to be tried for treason.

Historians have long argued about Brown's true motive for the raid. That he hated slavery with all his heart, there is no doubt. However, if he had really wanted to start a slave uprising, why did he fail to tell slaves in the area about his plans beforehand? Why didn't he provide his men with enough food to last for even one day? No one knows for sure. In any case, Brown certainly hoped that his actions would arouse Northern fury and start a war for abolition.

JOHN BROWN'S HANGING On December 2, 1859, Brown was hanged for treason in the presence of federal troops and a crowd of curious observers. Public reaction was immediate and intense in both sections of the country. Although Lincoln and Douglas condemned Brown as a murderer, many other Northerners expressed admiration for him or his cause. The raid itself

TEACHING OPTION

Cooperative Activity: Researching John Brown's Raids

Tasks: Teams of four will research background material in this chapter and other sources in order to write a short report explaining John Brown's motives for his actions both at the Pottawatomie massacre and Harpers Ferry.

Purpose: To explore Brown's motives.

Activity: After researching the events, group members should meet to decide their position

on Brown's motives and to choose the data that best support their position. The team should write a short report explaining what they believe were the motives behind John Brown's actions.

📁 **Building a Portfolio:** Students who feel the report is a good example of their work should add it to their portfolios.

ALTERNATIVE ASSESSMENT BOOK
Standards for Evaluating a Cooperative Activity

Standards for Evaluation
Reports should . . .

• show evidence of careful research using a variety of sources
• use specific details to support statements
• be clear and well organized

may have been the work of a madman, they acknowledged, but Brown's motive was "sublime." Bells tolled at the news of his execution, guns fired salutes, and huge crowds gathered to hear fiery speakers denounce the South. Some Northerners began to call Brown a martyr for the sacred cause of freedom.

The response was equally extreme in the South, where outraged mobs assaulted whites who were suspected of holding antislavery views. Harpers Ferry terrified Southern whites, who were convinced the North was plotting slave uprisings everywhere. Even long-time supporters of the Union called for secession. As one former Unionist explained, "I am willing to take the chances of . . . disunion, sooner than submit any longer to Northern insolence and Northern outrage."

Lincoln Is Elected President

Despite the tide of hostility that now flowed between North and South, the Republican Party eagerly awaited its presidential convention in May 1860. When the convention began, almost everyone believed that the party's candidate would be Senator William H. Seward of New York. However, events took a dramatic turn.

THE REPUBLICAN CONVENTION The convention took place in Chicago, which had quickly transformed itself into a convention city with more than 50 hotels and an 18,000-square-foot wooden meeting center named the Wigwam. Republicans flooded into the frontier city in such crowds that, despite the preparations, many ended up sleeping on pool tables in the hotels.

The convention opened to a surging crowd of delegates, newsmen, and spectators. The 4,500-person delegate floor overflowed within minutes. To gain seating in the galleries—which were meant for gentlemen who had come with ladies—determined men even offered schoolgirls a quarter for their company. The first day of the convention passed in forming committees, listening to prayers, and gossiping about politics. As events came to a close, campaign managers for the candidates retreated to their headquarters and began bargaining for delegates' votes, often late into the night.

Seward appeared to have everything needed to be a successful candidate for President: the credentials of having led antislavery forces in Congress, the financial support of New York state political organizations—and a desire to be the center of attention. In fact, Seward himself had little doubt that he would be nominated. Well before the actual voting took place, Seward drafted his senatorial resignation speech, which he planned to deliver when his nomination became official.

However, Seward's well-known name and reputation may have worked against him. It was probably Lincoln's relatively unknown name that won him the nomination. Unlike Seward, he had not had much chance to offend his fellow Republicans. The delegates rejected Seward and his talk of an "irrepressible conflict" between the North and the South. On the third ballot, they nominated Lincoln, who seemed to them to be more moderate in his views. Although Lincoln pledged to halt the further spread of slavery "as with a chain of steel," he also tried to reassure the South that a Republican administration would not "directly, or indirectly, interfere with their slaves or with them about their slaves." His reassurances fell on deaf ears. In Southern eyes, he was a "black Republican," whose election would be "the greatest evil that has ever befallen this country."

The Union in Peril **303**

Reading the Graphics
Have students note that the numbers on the map indicate the number of electoral votes for each state.

Extension Discuss how the election might have had different results if the Democratic Party had not split.

Southern Secession

▶ **Discussing Key Ideas**
• South Carolina leads the way as seven slave states secede from the Union.
• The secessionist states form the Confederacy and elect Jefferson Davis as their president.
• President Buchanan declares secession illegal, and eight slave states remain part of the Union.

ELECTRONIC LIBRARY OF PRIMARY SOURCES
from the Inaugural Address of Jefferson Davis, 1861

MORE ABOUT . . .
"Dixie's Land"
"Dixie's Land," or "Dixie," was written in 1859 by an Ohio man named Daniel Decatur Emmett. The song was an immediate hit in both the North and the South. It was played not only at Jefferson Davis's inauguration but at Lincoln's inauguration as well, although with different words. The song later became the unofficial anthem of the Confederacy.

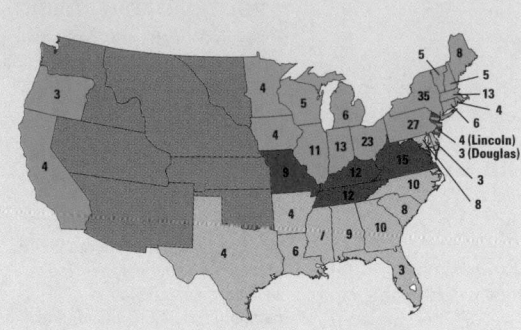

Election of 1860

ELECTORAL AND POPULAR VOTES

Party	Candidate	Electoral votes	Popular vote
■ Republican	Abraham Lincoln	180	1,865,593
■ Southern Democratic	J. C. Breckinridge	72	848,356
■ Constitutional Union	John Bell	39	592,906
■ Northern Democratic	Stephen Douglas	12	1,382,713

THE ELECTION OF 1860 As the campaign developed, three major candidates vied for office, in addition to Lincoln. The Democratic Party finally split over the issue of slavery. Northern Democrats rallied behind Douglas and his doctrine of popular sovereignty. Southern Democrats, who supported the *Dred Scott* decision, lined up behind Vice-President John C. Breckinridge of Kentucky. Former Know-Nothings and Whigs from the South, along with some moderate Northerners, organized the Constitutional Union Party, which ignored the issue of slavery altogether. They nominated John Bell of Tennessee as their candidate.

When the votes were counted, Lincoln emerged as the winner. Like Buchanan in the previous election, he received less than half the popular vote—fewer than 1.9 million to a combined total of more than 2.8 million for all of his opponents. In fact, although Lincoln defeated his combined opponents in the electoral vote by 180 to 123, he received no electoral votes from the South. Unlike Buchanan, Lincoln had sectional rather than national support, carrying every free state but not even appearing on the ballot in most of the slave states due to Southern hostility toward him. The outlook for the Union was grim.

Southern Secession

"*The time for compromise has now passed.*"

JEFFERSON DAVIS

Lincoln's victory convinced Southerners—who had viewed the struggle over slavery partly as a conflict between the states' right of self-determination and federal government control—that they had lost their political voice in the national government. Fearful that Northern antislavery Republicans would submit the South to what Edmund Ruffin of Virginia called "the most complete subjection and political bondage," some Southern states decided to act. South Carolina led the way, seceding from the Union on December 20, 1860. Four days later, the news reached Northern-born William Tecumseh Sherman, superintendent of the Louisiana State Seminary of Learning and Military Academy (now Louisiana State University). In utter dismay, Sherman poured out his fears for the South.

A PERSONAL VOICE
This country will be drenched in blood. . . . [T]he people of the North . . . are not going to let the country be destroyed without a mighty effort to save it. . . . Besides, where are your men and appliances of war to contend against them? . . . You are rushing into war with one of the most powerful, ingeniously mechanical and determined people on earth—right at your doors. . . . Only in spirit and determination are you prepared for war. In all else you are totally unprepared.
WILLIAM TECUMSEH SHERMAN, quoted in *None Died in Vain*

Even Sherman underestimated the depth and intensity of the South's commitment to its cause: the continuance of the slave labor system and the preservation of states' rights. For many Southern planters, the cry of "States' rights!" had come to mean complete independence of Southern states from federal government control. Most white Southerners also feared that an end to their entire

E. Answer
Lincoln's election convinced the South that Northerners intended to attack slavery everywhere and that it was time to secede.

THINK THROUGH HISTORY
E. Recognizing Effects How did Lincoln's election affect the South?

TEACHING OPTIONS

Making Connections Across the Curriculum

Music Play the song "Dixie" for the class and ask why they think the song had such an important role in the history of the Civil War. *Both the original lyrics and the tune reminded Southerners of the good life that existed before the war. The melody itself was upbeat and adopted by the North.* Discuss how at a time when the piano was relatively unknown and opera and symphonic music were rarely played, local bands became important for both political and social activities, although a variety of small instruments such as fiddles and banjos also contributed to the music of the era.

Exploring Themes

Constitutional Concerns With the secession of South Carolina from the Union, the Constitution faced one of its greatest challenges yet: Did a state have the right to secede from the Union? And when Mississippi, Alabama, Florida, Georgia, Louisiana, and Texas followed, forming the Confederacy, drafting their own constitution, and electing their own president, what was the Union then to do? After the initial confusion, strong feelings began to surface, and still more states seceded, agreeing with the rest of the Confederacy that their rights as states had been totally disregarded by the North.

way of life was at hand. Many were desperate for one last chance to preserve this way of life and saw secession as the only way. Mississippi followed South Carolina's lead and seceded on January 9, 1861. Florida seceded the next day. Within a few weeks, Alabama, Georgia, Louisiana, and Texas had also seceded.

THE SHAPING OF THE CONFEDERACY On February 4, 1861, delegates from the secessionist states met in Montgomery, Alabama, where they formed the **Confederate States of America,** or Confederacy. The Confederate constitution closely resembled that of the United States, but with a few notable differences. The most important point of the Confederate constitution was that it "protected and recognized" slavery in new territories. The constitution also stressed that each state in the Confederacy was to be "sovereign and independent," a provision that during the next four years would hamper efforts to unify the South.

On February 9, delegates to the Confederate constitutional convention unanimously elected Senator **Jefferson Davis** of Mississippi as president and former congressman Alexander Stephens of Georgia as vice-president. Davis had made his position on the crisis clear, noting that to present a show of strength to the North, the South should "offer no doubtful or divided front." At his inauguration in Montgomery, Davis declared to a cheering crowd, "The time for compromise has now passed." His listeners responded by singing "Farewell to the Star-Spangled Banner" and "Dixie."

THE CALM BEFORE THE STORM As the nation awaited Lincoln's inauguration in March, its citizens were confused. What would happen now? Seven slave states had seceded and formed a new nation. Eight slave states remained within the Union. Would they secede also?

In the White House, President Buchanan seemed equally uncertain about the future. He announced that secession was illegal, but that it also would be illegal for him to do anything about it. In effect, he tied his own hands. Even if he had not been so timid, though, there was not much that he could have done.

One problem was that Washington was very much a Southern city. There were secessionists in Congress and in all of the departments of the federal government, as well as in the President's Cabinet. Consequently, mass resignations took place. To some people it seemed as if the federal government were melting away.

The North had heard threats of secession so often that when it finally happened, no one was shocked. But one key question remained in everyone's minds: would the North allow the South to leave the Union in peace—or war?

HISTORICAL SPOTLIGHT

SECESSION AND THE BORDER STATES

Four slave states—Maryland, Kentucky, Missouri, and Delaware—were undecided about secession. Lincoln believed that these states would be essential to the success of the Union if war broke out. They had large populations, numerous factories, and access to the Ohio River, which would be needed to move troops and supplies. Moreover, Maryland nearly surrounded Washington, D.C., the seat of government.

Lincoln faced a choice: free the slaves and make abolitionists happy, or ignore slavery for the moment to keep from alienating the border states. He chose the latter, but that did not prevent violent conflicts between secessionists and Unionists in Maryland, Kentucky, and Missouri. With the intervention of the militia, and some political maneuvering in those states' legislatures, Lincoln kept the four border states in the Union.

Section 4 Assessment

1. TERMS & NAMES

Identify:
- Abraham Lincoln
- Dred Scott
- Roger B. Taney
- Freeport Doctrine
- Harpers Ferry
- Confederate States of America
- Jefferson Davis

2. SUMMARIZING List six major events described in this section and explain how each one sharpened the North-South conflict. Use a diagram like the one below.

Event	Result
1.	→
2.	→
3.	→

3. FORMING OPINIONS If you had been voting in the presidential election of 1860, for whom would you have voted? Explain your reasoning by using specific references to the chapter.

THINK ABOUT
- each candidate's views on slavery and other issues
- each candidate's experience and personality
- each candidate's ability to keep the country united

4. ANALYZING ISSUES Do you think Lincoln made the right decision in choosing not to free the slaves immediately once the Confederacy had been formed?

THINK ABOUT
- the number of states that had already seceded
- the importance of the border states
- possible reactions if he had freed the slaves

The Union in Peril **305**

States' Rights

The power struggle between states and the federal government has caused controversy since the country's beginning. At its worst, the conflict resulted in the Civil War. Even in the 1990s, however, state and federal governments have squared off on several issues.

- In 1996, the Supreme Court declared illegal congressional district maps in Texas and North Carolina that were drawn to maximize minority representation.

- In 1994, Florida sued the federal government to reimburse the state $1.5 billion for providing social services like education and health care for illegal immigrants. A federal judge dismissed the case.

Constitutional conflicts between states' rights and federal jurisdiction are pictured here. As you read, see how each issue was resolved.

1787
CONSTITUTIONAL CONVENTION

ISSUE: The Constitution tried to resolve the original debate over states' rights versus federal authority.

At the Constitutional Convention in Philadelphia, George Washington supported the Federalists, who upheld a strong national government after the Articles of Confederation failed. The prominent Federalists included James Madison and Ben Franklin. The Antifederalists, such as Patrick Henry and Richard Henry Lee, preferred that most of the power remain with the states. The convention compromised—the Constitution reserves certain powers for the states, delegates other powers to the federal government, divides some powers between state and federal governments, and tries to balance the differing needs of the states through two houses of Congress.

1832
NULLIFICATION

ISSUE: The state of South Carolina moved to nullify, or declare void, a tariff set by Congress.

In this cartoon, President Andrew Jackson is playing a game called bragg. One of his opponents, Vice-President John C. Calhoun, is hiding two cards, "Nullification" and "Anti-Tariff," behind him. Jackson is doing poorly in this game, but he eventually won the real nullification dispute. When Congress passed high tariffs on imports in 1832, politicians from South Carolina, led by Calhoun, tried to nullify the tariff law, or declare it void. Jackson threatened to enforce the law with federal troops. Congress reduced the tariff to avoid a confrontation, and Calhoun resigned his vice-presidency.

306

RECOMMENDED RESOURCES

Books

Ellis, Richard E. *The Union at Risk.* New York: Oxford UP, 1987. An exploration of Jacksonian democracy, states' rights, and the nullification crisis.

Mason, Alpheus Thomas, ed. *The States' Rights Debate.* New York: Oxford UP, 1972, rev. ed. A collection of views on antifederalism and the Constitution.

Wilkinson, J. Harvie. *From Brown to Bakke.* New York: Oxford UP, 1979. An account of 20th-century Supreme Court decisions regarding school integration.

Videos

The Civil War: Union at Risk. Encyclopaedia Britannica, 1989. A look at constitutional issues and the war.

Federalism. MTI Film & Video, 1986. Focuses on federal vs. state and local government powers. Part of *The Constitution: That Delicate Balance,* an award-winning documentary series.

Hamilton and Jefferson on Democracy. Encyclopaedia Britannica, 1982. Part of the *Bill of Rights in Action* series.

Software

U.S. Government: The First 200 Years. Clearvue, dist. ESI. Various political issues.

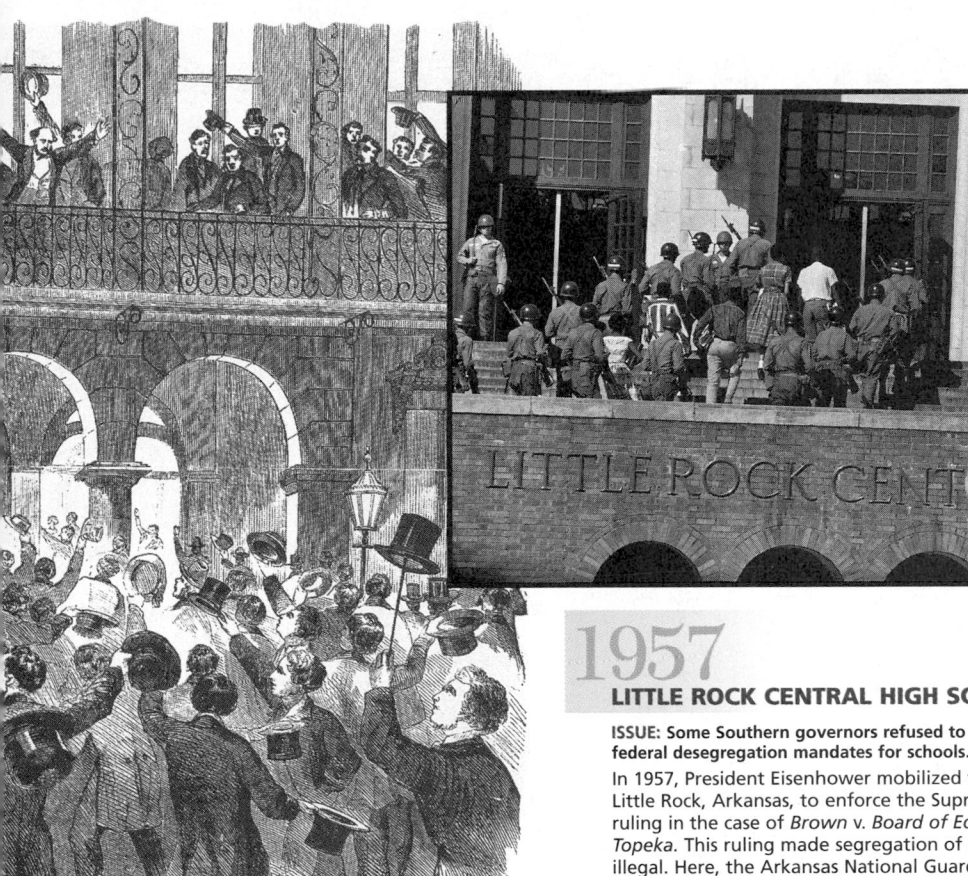

1957
LITTLE ROCK CENTRAL HIGH SCHOOL

ISSUE: Some Southern governors refused to obey federal desegregation mandates for schools.

In 1957, President Eisenhower mobilized federal troops in Little Rock, Arkansas, to enforce the Supreme Court's 1954 ruling in the case of *Brown* v. *Board of Education of Topeka.* This ruling made segregation of public schools illegal. Here, the Arkansas National Guard escorted nine African-American students into Little Rock Central High School against the wishes of Governor Orval Faubus, who had tried to prevent the students from entering the school. After this incident, Faubus closed the high schools in Little Rock in 1958 and 1959, thereby avoiding desegregation.

1860
SOUTH CAROLINA'S SECESSION

ISSUE: The conflict over a state's right to secede, or withdraw, from the Union led to the Civil War.

In December 1860, Southern secessionists cheered "secession" enthusiastically in front of the Mills House *(above)*, a hotel in Charleston, South Carolina. South Carolina seceded after the election of Abraham Lincoln, whom the South perceived as anti-states' rights and antislavery. Lincoln took the position that states did not have the right to secede from the Union, and in 1861, he sent troops to reinforce Fort Sumter in Charleston. South Carolinians fired on the fort because they felt they had to defend their newly proclaimed independence. The Union's victory in the Civil War ended the most serious challenge to federal authority: states did not have the right to secede from the Union.

INTERACT WITH HISTORY

1. **SYNTHESIZING** For each incident pictured, create a chart that tells who was on each side of the issue, summarizes each position, and explains how the issue was resolved.

   SEE SKILLBUILDER HANDBOOK, PAGE 1051.

2. **RESEARCHING STATES' RIGHTS TODAY**
   Research one of the controversies in the bulleted list in the opening paragraph or another states' rights controversy. Decide which side you support. Write a paragraph explaining your position on the issue.

The Union in Peril **307**

TERMS & NAMES
1. secession, p. 285
2. popular sovereignty, p. 285
3. Compromise of 1850, p. 285
4. Stephen A. Douglas, p. 287
5. Fugitive Slave Act, p. 288
6. Harriet Tubman, p. 289
7. Harriet Beecher Stowe, p. 290
8. Kansas-Nebraska Act, p. 292
9. John Brown, p. 293
10. Dred Scott, p. 299

MAIN IDEAS
11. North: had more industry, more railroads, more telegraphs, more immigrants; South: had agricultural economy, based on slavery.

12. Because Southerners controlled the Senate.

13. It allowed California to be admitted as a free state and Utah and New Mexico to decide about slavery, and it prevented the abolition of slavery within the District of Columbia without the consent of its residents. It included a tougher fugitive slave law and a provision for the federal government to pay Texas $10 million to surrender its claims on New Mexico.

14. Stowe's book had wide impact; Tubman reached fewer people through her speeches but still had strong influence.

15. Nebraska Territory divided into Nebraska in the north and Kansas in the south; established popular sovereignty in each territory; resulted in a bitter debate in Congress and a bloody fight in Kansas.

16. Because of its opposition to slavery in the territories; the Whigs and Know-Nothings split over slavery.

17. Democrat James Buchanan won; the Know-Nothing and Whig parties declined.

18. The Supreme Court ruled that slaves were property—slaveowners could take property with them into the territories.

19. Both opposed slavery in the territories. Lincoln thought the federal government should ban it; Douglas relied on popular sovereignty.

20. Southerners believed Lincoln would seek to further reduce the states' power and increase the federal government's power.

REVIEWING THE CHAPTER

TERMS & NAMES For each term below, write a sentence explaining its connection to the growing conflict between the North and the South in the 1850s. For each person below, explain his or her role in this conflict.

1. secession
2. popular sovereignty
3. Compromise of 1850
4. Stephen A. Douglas
5. Fugitive Slave Act
6. Harriet Tubman
7. Harriet Beecher Stowe
8. Kansas-Nebraska Act
9. John Brown
10. Dred Scott

MAIN IDEAS

SECTION 1 (pages 282–287)

The Divisive Politics of Slavery

11. Describe the economic differences between the North and the South in the 1850s.
12. Explain why the Wilmot Proviso failed to pass in the Senate.
13. What were the major terms of the Compromise of 1850?

SECTION 2 (pages 288–294)

Protest, Resistance, and Violence

14. Compare the impact of Harriet Tubman and Harriet Beecher Stowe on antislavery attitudes in the North.
15. What were the basic provisions and results of the Kansas-Nebraska Act?

SECTION 3 (pages 295–298)

The Birth of the Republican Party

16. Why did the Republican Party grow as the Whig and Know-Nothing parties declined in the 1850s?
17. Summarize the results of the election of 1856.

SECTION 4 (pages 299–305)

Slavery and Secession

18. How did the *Dred Scott* decision affect slavery in the territories?
19. Compare and contrast Abraham Lincoln's and Stephen A. Douglas's views about slavery in the territories.
20. Why was the South so upset by Lincoln's election?

THINKING CRITICALLY

1. **COMPARING ATTITUDES TOWARD SLAVERY** Make a scale of attitudes on slavery like the one below. Place the names of five people from this chapter on the scale. Write a summary explaining why you placed each name where you did.

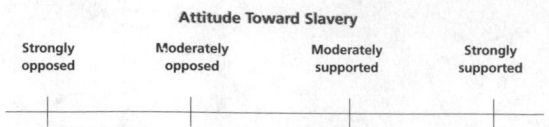

Attitude Toward Slavery

| Strongly opposed | Moderately opposed | Moderately supported | Strongly supported |

2. **EVALUATING HISTORICAL FIGURES** John Brown, Harriet Tubman, Harriet Beecher Stowe, and Stephen Douglas all opposed slavery. Explain whether you consider any of these people to be heroes. Defend your viewpoint with references from the chapter.

3. **GEOGRAPHY OF THE UNDERGROUND RAILROAD** Review the map on page 290. Think about the terrain and bodies of water that escaping slaves would have faced. In what ways might these physical features have helped or hindered a fugitive's progress?

4. **PRESERVING THE UNION** Reread the quote by Abraham Lincoln on page 280. How might Stephen Douglas and John Brown have answered Lincoln's question? Use details from the chapter to support your response.

5. **EXAMINING STATES' RIGHTS** The secession of Southern states from the Union reflected the long-standing conflict over federal versus state powers. Do you agree with Lincoln and the federal government that the states did not have the right to secede from the Union? Support your opinion with specific references to the chapter and the feature on states' rights.

6. **ANALYZING PRIMARY SOURCES** Three weeks after Lincoln was elected, Northerner George Templeton Strong described in his diary the reaction to threats of secession:

> I think . . . that the Republican leaders are frightened and ready to concede everything, to restore the Missouri Compromise line and satisfy the fugitive slave remedies of the South. A movement that way has certainly begun. But it may be too soon for the North and too late for the South. . . . How will it be received in Massachusetts and western New York? Will Republicans feel that they have been sold by their leaders, and recalcitrate [harden] into more intense anti-Southern feeling? I think they will and that many Republicans will enroll themselves as Abolitionists.
>
> **GEORGE TEMPLETON STRONG,** *The Diary of George Templeton Strong*

Why does Strong think the Republican leaders will give in? What does he think will happen if they do?

---

1. COMPARING ATTITUDES TOWARD SLAVERY
Possible Answers: **Strongly opposed:** William Seward, David Wilmot, Anthony Burns, Charlotte Forten, Frederick Douglass, Harriet Tubman, Harriet Beecher Stowe, John Brown, Dred Scott, Abraham Lincoln. **Moderately opposed:** Henry Clay, Daniel Webster, Millard Fillmore, Stephen Douglas, John Frémont. **Moderately supported:** Zachary Taylor, James Buchanan, Roger B. Taney, John Breckinridge. **Strongly supported:** John Calhoun, Alexander Stephens, Preston Brooks, Jefferson Davis.

2. EVALUATING HISTORICAL FIGURES
Student responses should reflect understanding of the strengths and weaknesses of each individual and an awareness of their contributions to the movement for abolition.

3. GEOGRAPHY OF THE UNDERGROUND RAILROAD
Possible Answers: The major physical features that escaping slaves would have faced include the Appalachian Mountains, the Mississippi River, and such rivers as the Ohio and the Missouri. Students should indicate that rivers provided a quick avenue of escape but also were under the careful scrutiny of antislavery forces. The mountains provided caves and forests in which escaping slaves could hide, but parts of the mountains were rugged and difficult to cross.

ALTERNATIVE ASSESSMENT

1. CREATING A PUBLIC SERVICE ANNOUNCEMENT

What is the right balance of power between states and the federal government? Create a public service announcement on a conflict involving states' rights.

CD-ROM Use the CD-ROM *Electronic Library of Primary Sources* and other resources to research a historical or contemporary conflict involving states' rights. For some suggestions, see Tracing Themes: Constitutional Concerns, pages 306–307.

- After you have selected a conflict, decide where you stand on this issue. Plan a short commercial to support your position.
- Clearly state your points and persuade your readers with reasons and examples. Prepare a storyboard or visual presentation and share your commercial with classmates.

2. ROLE–PLAYING THE COMPROMISE OF 1850

Cooperative Learning Working in a group, prepare a play about the debate over the Compromise of 1850. Research the main characters, including Calhoun, Clay, Webster, and Douglas. Look for details in their speech and mannerisms that make them distinctive historical figures. Use the following guidelines to prepare your play.

- Write a script for the play that includes lively, dramatic dialogue about the relevant issues.
- Assign a role to each member of your group and rehearse the play together several times.
- Find a few simple, appropriate props to use.

Present the play and ask students how historically accurate—and how convincing—they found your portrayal of events.

3. PORTFOLIO PROJECT

📁 Use the Living History activity to expand your portfolio.

LIVING HISTORY

PRESENTING YOUR SURVEY

Prepare a presentation of the results of your survey. You might write a report, create a graph or a poster, or draw a map that shows differences between sections. Then share your presentation with a small group and ask for comments on the following points.

- Survey questions: Were they well-chosen?
- Conclusions: Does the survey clearly identify sectional differences?
- Are the survey results well-presented?

After you have made any necessary changes in the survey's presentation, post it in your classroom before adding it to your American history portfolio.

Bridge to Chapter 11

Review Chapter 10

SECTIONAL DIFFERENCES By 1850, Northern society and Southern society differed greatly. The North was more industrial and attracted more immigrants than the South did. Most importantly, the South relied on slavery and the North opposed it.

Congress tried to reconcile the two sections in the Compromise of 1850. Under this compromise, shaped by Henry Clay and pushed through Congress by Stephen Douglas, Congress admitted California as a free state, but passed a stricter fugitive slave law.

GROWING ABOLITION The 1850 Fugitive Slave Act pleased Southerners, but it outraged Northerners. Northerners often refused to return escaped slaves, many of whom had fled via the Underground Railroad with the help of conductors, such as Harriet Tubman. In 1852, Harriet Beecher Stowe's antislavery novel, *Uncle Tom's Cabin*, further divided the North and the South. The growing conflict between supporters and opponents of slavery turned the territory of Kansas into a battleground after the passage of the Kansas-Nebraska Act in 1854.

NEW POLITICAL ALLIANCES As slavery increasingly dominated politics, it divided the existing political parties. Both the Whigs and the anti-immigrant, anti-Catholic Know-Nothings split into Northern and Southern factions. Southerners looked for a political alternative, while many Northerners joined the newly organized Republican Party.

TO THE BRINK OF WAR The gap between the North and the South widened after the *Dred Scott* decision, which effectively opened all territories to slavery. The debate over slavery in the territories became a crucial issue in Illinois, where Lincoln and Douglas each wanted to be senator. Douglas was elected to the Senate, but Lincoln became a national Republican leader and was elected president in 1860. Within months after his election, seven Southern states seceded from the Union.

Preview Chapter 11

With the secession of the Southern states, the North and the South went to war. The resulting conflict, known as the Civil War, lasted four long, bloody years. You will learn about these significant developments in the next chapter.

The Union in Peril **309**

ALTERNATIVE ASSESSMENT

1. CREATING A PUBLIC SERVICE ANNOUNCEMENT
Standards for Evaluation
An effective public service announcement should meet the following criteria:

- Opens with a clear statement defining the issue.
- States the speaker's position.
- Uses well-researched, well-documented evidence to support the position.
- Anticipates and answers possible challenges.

2. ROLE-PLAYING THE COMPROMISE OF 1850
Standards for Evaluation
A play script should meet the following criteria:

- Dramatizes the key conflicts surrounding the debate over the Compromise of 1850.
- Divides the action into scenes.
- Uses realistic dialogue that reveals the viewpoints of the historical figures portrayed.
- Contains stage directions that authentically show the historical figures' gestures and speaking styles.

3. PORTFOLIO PROJECT
LIVING HISTORY
Standards for Evaluation
A survey should meet the following criteria:

- Includes a statement explaining the purpose and methods.
- Contains clearly worded questions that elicit a broad range of responses.
- Interprets the significance of respondents' answers in a concluding summary.

IN-DEPTH RESOURCES: UNIT 3
See the form for scoring this activity on page 36.

THINKING CRITICALLY

4. PRESERVING THE UNION
Possible Responses: Most students may suggest that Douglas would respond in a moderate way, perhaps even indicating that the country could continue half slave and half free, while John Brown would probably exclaim that such a situation could not continue.

5. EXAMINING STATES' RIGHTS
Possible Responses: Answers will vary. Both sides should argue their position using specific textual references from this chapter or earlier chapters.

6. ANALYZING PRIMARY SOURCES
Possible Responses: Students should explain that Strong thinks the Republican leaders will give in and attempt to conciliate the South because they are frightened at the prospect of secession. If the Republicans do give in, Strong suggests, many members of the party may become more intensely anti-Southern and more inclined to be abolitionists.

CHAPTER 11

PLANNING GUIDE
The Civil War

	Key Ideas	**TEACHING SUPPORT**	**ASSESSMENT**
SECTION 1 The Civil War Begins *pp. 312–317*	*The secession of Southern states causes the North and the South to take up arms.*	*In-Depth Resources: Unit 3* • Guided Reading, p. 37 • Skillbuilder Practice: p. 41 • Geography Application: Resources of the North and South, p. 43 • Outline Map: p. 45 • American Lives: David Farragut, p. 54 **COOPERATIVE ACTIVITY** • Researching the Battle of Bull Run, p. 314 (TE)	*Section 1 Assessment,* p. 317 (PE) *Self-Assessment,* p. 317 (TE) *Formal Assessment* • Section Quiz, p. 137 *Alternative Assessment Book* • Standards for Evaluating a Cooperative Activity
SECTION 2 The Politics of War *pp. 318–322*	*President Lincoln issues the Emancipation Proclamation and makes slavery the focus of the war.*	*In-Depth Resources: Unit 3* • Guided Reading, p. 38 • Primary Sources: The Emancipation Proclamation, p. 47; Recruiting Poster, p. 48 **COOPERATIVE ACTIVITY** • The Emancipation Proclamation: Tracing Its Origins, p. 319 (TE)	*Section 2 Assessment,* p. 322 (PE) *Self-Assessment,* p. 322 (TE) *Formal Assessment* • Section Quiz, p. 138 *Alternative Assessment Book* • Standards for Evaluating a Cooperative Activity
SECTION 3 Life During Wartime *pp. 323–328*	*The war creates social and economic changes as people struggle with the loss of family members, property destruction, and the impending end of slavery.*	*In-Depth Resources: Unit 3* • Guided Reading, p. 39 • Primary Source: from *Mary Chesnut's Civil War,* p. 49 • American Lives: Clara Barton, p. 55 **COOPERATIVE ACTIVITY** • Role-playing Soldiers and Citizens, p. 326 (TE)	*Section 3 Assessment,* p. 328 (PE) *Self-Assessment,* p. 328 (TE) *Formal Assessment* • Section Quiz, p. 139 *Alternative Assessment Book* • Standards for Evaluating a Cooperative Activity
SECTION 4 The North Takes Charge *pp. 329–337*	*After a Union victory in the bloody battle at Gettysburg, a weary Robert E. Lee surrenders to U. S. Grant at Appomattox.*	*In-Depth Resources: Unit 3* • Guided Reading, p. 40 • Primary Source: On the Burning of Columbia, South Carolina, p. 50 **COOPERATIVE ACTIVITY** • News Accounts of a City Under Siege, p. 332 (TE)	*Section 4 Assessment,* p. 337 (PE) *Self-Assessment,* p. 337 (TE) *Formal Assessment* • Section Quiz, p. 140 *Alternative Assessment Book* • Standards for Evaluating a Cooperative Activity
SECTION 5 The Legacy of the War *pp. 340–345*	*The Civil War settles long-standing disputes over states' rights and slavery.*	*In-Depth Resources: Unit 3* • Guided Reading, p. 41 • Literature: Poems by Walt Whitman, p. 51 **COOPERATIVE ACTIVITY** • Researching the Technology of Warfare, p. 343 (TE)	*Section 5 Assessment,* p. 345 (PE) *Self-Assessment,* p. 345 (TE) *Formal Assessment* • Section Quiz, p. 141 *Alternative Assessment Book* • Standards for Evaluating a Cooperative Activity
CHAPTER RESOURCES	**Chapter Overview** *For four bloody years, North and South struggle in the Civil War as the North tries to restore the Union and to end slavery. Finally, Northern advantages in population, industry, and resources ensure victory.*	*In-Depth Resources: Unit 3* • Living History Project: Worksheet, p. 56; Standards, p. 57 *Telescoping the Times* • Chapter Summary, pp. 21–22 *Planning for Block Schedules*	*Chapter Assessment,* pp. 346–347 (PE) *Alternative Assessment,* p. 347 (PE) *Formal Assessment* • Chapter Test, forms A and B, pp. 142–147 **Test Generator** *Alternative Assessment Book* See explanation and forms for different kinds of alternative assessments including portfolio assessment.

Geography Transparencies
• G11, Union and Confederacy: 1861
• G37, Slavery and the Civil War

 Electronic Library of Primary Sources
• Letters to His Family by Robert E. Lee
• *Fateful Lightning*
• Civil War Maps

INTERNET RESOURCES
• See *McDougal Littell Learning On-Line* for links to information about the Civil War.

INTERNET RESOURCES
• See *McDougal Littell Learning On-Line* for links to information about the Emancipation Proclamation.

 Electronic Library of Primary Sources
• from *Letters to Eliza from a Union Soldier* by George Fowle
• from *Diary of a Confederate Soldier* by John S. Jackman

 AMERICAN STORIES VIDEO SERIES
• "War Outside My Window"

INTERNET RESOURCES
• See *McDougal Littell Learning On-Line* for links to information about Vicksburg and the Gettysburg address.

 Humanities Transparencies
•H11, *Abraham Lincoln Riding into Richmond, Virginia*

 Grolier Multimedia Encyclopedia
•Lincoln's Inaugural Address

INTERNET RESOURCES
• See Interact with History p. 339 (PE) for an activity that includes the Internet as an enrichment option.

 Critical Thinking Transparencies
•CT11, Civil War
•CT45, North vs. South

INTERNET RESOURCES
• See *McDougal Littell Learning On-Line* for links to information about Ford's Theater and Frederick Douglass.

 American Portfolio: A Videodisc for U.S. History, user's guide, pp. 96–113, 115–116

INTERNET RESOURCES
Learning On-Line: Social Studies
http://www.mcdougallittell.com

Block Scheduling (90 MINUTES)

Day 1
Section 1, pp. 312–317
Section Assessment, p. 317

Day 2
Section 2, pp. 318–322
Section 3, pp. 323–328
 AMERICAN STUDIES VIDEO SERIES
"War Outside My Window"
Section Assessments, pp. 322, 328

Day 3
Section 4, pp. 329–337
Section Assessment, p. 337

Day 4
Section 5, pp. 340–345
Section Assessment, p. 345
Chapter Assessment, pp. 346–347

YEARLY PACING *Chapter 11 Total:* 4 days *Yearly Total:* 85 days

See *Planning for Block Schedules* for special activities and pacing strategies.

Customizing for Special Populations

Students Acquiring English

Access for Students Acquiring English
• Guided Reading for Sections 1–5 (Spanish), pp. 110–114
• Chapter Summary (Spanish), pp. 108–109
• Skillbuilder Practice: Following Chronological Order (Spanish), p. 115
• Geography Application: Resources of the North and South (Spanish), p. 116

AMERICAN STORIES VIDEO SERIES
"War Outside my Window" (Spanish track)

INTERNET RESOURCES
• See *McDougal Littell Learning On-Line* The Diverse Classroom.

Less Proficient Readers

In-Depth Resources: Unit 3
• Guided Reading for Sections 1–5, pp. 37–41
• Skillbuilder: Following Chronological Order, p. 41
• Geography Application: Resources of the North and South, p. 43
• Outline Map: The States Choose Sides, p. 45

Telescoping the Times
• Chapter Summary, pp. 21–22

See additional strategies at point of use in the Teacher's Edition.

Gifted and Talented Students

In-Depth Resources: Unit 3
• Primary Sources: The Emancipation Proclamation, p. 47; Recruiting Poster, p. 48; from *Mary Chesnut's Civil War,* p. 49; On the Burning of Columbia, South Carolina, p. 50
• American Lives: David Farragut, p. 54; Clara Barton, p. 56

See additional strategies at point of use in the Teacher's Edition.

Connections to Literature READINGS FOR STUDENTS

In-Depth Resources: Unit 3
• Poems by Walt Whitman, p. 51

Enrichment Reading
• Crane, Stephen
The Red Badge of Courage.
New York: Pocket Books, 1994
This classic novel of the Civil War tells of a young soldier's battle experiences.

• Benét, Stephan Vincent
John Brown's Body.
New York: Holt, 1990.
This classic narrative poem won the Pulitzer Prize in 1929. Benét attempts to give a complete picture of the Civil War as seen through the eyes of several characters.

McDougal Littell *Literature Connections*
• Margaret Walker,
Jubilee (with related readings) This Civil War novel tells of a mixed-race woman who was reared on a southern plantation. Filled with knowledge of the times and the people, this stunning tale is told with devastating truth.

McDougal Littell *The Language of Literature*
American Literature
• James Russell Lowell,
Stanzas on Freedom, p. 458
• Ambrose Bierce,
"An Occurrence at Owl Creek Bridge," p. 464
• Lewis Beach,
"The Clod," p. 477

OVERVIEW

The Civil War

▶ *Starting with the Student*
Ask students what they know about the Civil War. Why did Americans choose sides and fight one another? Then discuss the opening quotation.

- What is Lee's vision of events to follow?
- What do you think he considers to be "our national sins"?

PREVIEWING THE CHAPTER

- Ask students to look at the photos and art throughout the chapter, and point out the key historical figures or dramatic scenes pictured.
- Have students examine the time line to acquaint them with the order in which events of the war unfolded.
- Have students brainstorm a list of topics they expect the chapter to cover.

MORE ABOUT . . .
Robert E. Lee

Award-winning author and Civil War historian Bruce Catton views General Robert E. Lee as a throwback to medieval times: "Lee was tidewater Virginia, and in his background were family, culture, and tradition . . . the age of chivalry transplanted to a New World which was making its own legends and its own myths. He embodied a way of life that had come down through the age of knighthood and the English country squire."

310 Chapter 11

CHAPTER
11

The Civil War

SECTION 1
The Civil War Begins
The secession of Southern states causes the North and the South to take up arms.

SECTION 2
The Politics of War
President Lincoln issues the Emancipation Proclamation and makes slavery the focus of the war.

SECTION 3
Life During Wartime
The war creates social and economic changes as people struggle with the loss of family members, property destruction, and the impending end of slavery.

 VIDEO *War Outside My Window*

SECTION 4
The North Takes Charge
After a Union victory in the bloody battle at Gettysburg, a weary Robert E. Lee surrenders to U. S. Grant at Appomattox.

SECTION 5
The Legacy of the War
The Civil War settles long-standing disputes over states' rights and slavery.

"Whatever may be the result of the contest I foresee that the country will have to pass through a terrible ordeal . . . for our national sins."

General Robert E. Lee

Fort Sumter is taken by Confederates.

Virginia, Arkansas, Tennessee, and North Carolina secede.

General McClellan is appointed commander of the main Union army.

The *Monitor* and the *Merrimack* conduct the first battle of ironclad ships.

Union general U.S. Grant captures Ft. Henry and Ft. Donelson in Tennessee.

Union avoids defeat at Shiloh.

Jefferson Davis is elected president of the Confederacy.

Union loses at Bull Run.

THE UNITED STATES

THE WORLD

1861

April   July   Nov.   Feb. March April

Feb. Mar.

Victor Emmanuel II's Kingdom of Italy is inaugurated.

Serfs in Russia are emancipated by Alexander II.

310 Chapter 11

THEMES IN CHAPTER 11

Constitutional Concerns	*Economic Opportunity*	*Science and Technology*
Among the major constitutional concerns that emerged during the Civil War were states' rights and the president's wartime powers. The secession of Virginia and three more states at the outbreak of the war further stretched the constitutional interpretation that states could dissolve their compact with the government and leave the Union. To end slavery, President Lincoln used his constitutional war powers as commander in chief by issuing the Emancipation Proclamation. See Teacher's Edition notes, pp. 313, 320.	Northern industries furnishing wartime products such as clothing and weapons experienced an economic spurt. This industrial growth helped many manufacturers, especially those with government contracts, accumulate great wealth during the Civil War. See Teacher's Edition note, p. 325.	The Civil War is considered one of the first modern wars because of the many advances in technology applied to combat. For example, technological improvements in rifles and bullets not only made killing more efficient but also changed the strategies for conducting war. See Teacher's Edition note, p. 342.

LIVING HISTORY

CREATING A CIVIL WAR GAME

Create a board game that will help you keep track of people and events from the Civil War. You might use a map of the United States as a game board. Consider these suggestions.

- Keep track of dates, locations, and key people as you read.
- Add to your game board the cities where important battles were fought.
- Identify who or what your game pieces will be.
- Develop a strategy for moving game pieces around the board.

📁 **PORTFOLIO PROJECT** Save your game in a folder for your American history portfolio. You will play the game and make additions or changes at the end of the chapter.

CREATING A CIVIL WAR GAME

Discuss suggestions for designing the game.

- Think about video games that simulate combat experiences. Some of the rules or situations in these games might be adapted to a Civil War game.
- Examine the maps in this chapter and in other sources that might be useful models for game boards.
- Consider using game pieces that represent important military leaders profiled in this chapter.
- Read the instructions for other board games to help organize your own set of instructions.
- Devise a point system or some other method for players to keep score.

Project Planning Guide

Step 1	Students design their game boards.
Step 2	Students decide who the game pieces will represent.
Step 3	Students prepare a set of game instructions.
Step 4	Students save their games in their folders.

IN-DEPTH RESOURCES: UNIT 3
See worksheet and standards for evaluation, pp. 56, 57.

Lincoln gives Grant control of all Union armies.

Stonewall Jackson is accidentally shot and killed after the Confederate win at Chancellorsville.

Petersburg and Richmond fall to the Union. Lee surrenders to Grant at Appomattox.

The Confederates win the Second Battle of Bull Run.

Draft riots erupt in New York. Union wins at Gettysburg and Vicksburg.

Lincoln is assassinated.

Antietam results in huge casualties. Lincoln issues the Emancipation Proclamation.

The Emancipation Proclamation takes effect.

Union troops control much of the western theater of the war.

Abraham Lincoln is reelected.

Andrew Johnson becomes president.

Aug. Sept. / Sept.	**1863**	Jan.	May / June	July	Nov.	March / June July	Nov.	**1865**

Otto von Bismarck is named minister-president of Prussia.

Shir 'Ali Khan becomes amir of Afghanistan.

Maximilian of Austria becomes the new emperor of Mexico.

Taiping Rebellion in China ends with the fall of Nanking.

The Civil War **311**

RECOMMENDED RESOURCES

Books for the Teacher

McPherson, James M. *Battle Cry of Freedom.* New York: Oxford, 1988. Definitive one-volume history of the war.

Foote, Shelby. *The Civil War.* 3 vols. New York: Random House, 1958–1974. Highly readable history of the war.

Wills, Garry. *Lincoln at Gettysburg.* New York: Simon, 1992. The impact of the Gettysburg Address on America's democratic ideals.

Books for the Student

Redkey, Edwin, ed. *A Grand Army of Black Men.* New York: Cambridge, 1992. African-American soldiers' letters.

Smith, George Winston, and Charles Judah, eds. *Life in the North During the Civil War.* Albuquerque: U of New Mexico Press, 1966. Letters, speeches, diaries, and newspaper articles detailing the home front.

Videos

The Civil War. Prod. Ken Burns. PBS. 1989. A compelling documentary in six parts.

Friendly Persuasion. Dir. William Wyler. Lorimar, 1956. Drama of Quakers during Civil War.

Glory. Dir. Edward Zwick. RCA/Columbia, 1989. Drama of African-American regiment in the Civil War. This film has an R rating and should be reviewed by the teacher before presentation.

With Malice Toward None: Lincoln's Second Inaugural. Videodisc. Coronet, 800-621-2131.

Software

American Heritage History of the Civil War. CD-ROM. Simon & Schuster Interactive, 800-223-2348.

The Civil War. CD-ROM. Compton's New Media, 1992.

OBJECTIVES

① To explain how the Civil War began.

② To explain Northerners' and Confederates' short-sightedness about the outcome of the war.

③ To profile the Northern generals and their initial campaigns in the west.

④ To explain Northern and Southern military strategies to capture their enemy's' capital.

SKILLBUILDERS

• Interpreting graphs, p. 313
• Understanding geography: region, place, p. 315

CRITICAL THINKING

• Analyzing causes, p. 313
• Contrasting, pp. 314, 316
• Summarizing, pp. 316, 317
• Evaluating decisions, p. 317
• Hypothesizing, p. 317
• Drawing conclusions, p. 317

FOCUS & MOTIVATE

▶ **Starting with the Student** Have students think of crisis situations in which someone had to make a tough decision.

OBJECTIVE
① **INSTRUCT**

Confederates Fire on Fort Sumter

▶ **Discussing Key Ideas**
• The Confederacy challenges Lincoln shortly after his inauguration.
• In 1861, Confederate forces' shelling of Fort Sumter ignites the Civil War.
• Virginia's secession spells a terrible loss to the Union.

IN-DEPTH RESOURCES: UNIT 3
Guided Reading, p. 37

ACCESS FOR STUDENTS ACQUIRING ENGLISH
Guided Reading (Spanish), p. 110

---

① # The Civil War Begins

LEARN ABOUT the military strategies and actions of the first two years of the Civil War
TO UNDERSTAND how the war became a more prolonged, deadly conflict than anyone had predicted.

TERMS & NAMES
• Fort Sumter
• Anaconda plan
• Bull Run
• Stonewall Jackson
• George McClellan
• Ulysses S. Grant
• Shiloh
• David G. Farragut
• Robert E. Lee
• Antietam

ONE AMERICAN'S STORY

On April 18, 1861, the federal supply ship *Baltic* dropped anchor off the coast of New Jersey. Aboard was Major Robert Anderson, a 35-year army veteran on his way from Charleston, South Carolina, to New York City. That day, Anderson wrote a report to the secretary of war, describing his most recent command.

A PERSONAL VOICE
Having defended Fort Sumter for thirty-four hours, until the quarters were entirely burned, the main gates destroyed by fire, . . . the magazine surrounded by flames, . . . four barrels and three cartridges of powder only being available, and no provisions but pork remaining, I accepted terms of evacuation . . . and marched out of the fort . . . with colors flying and drums beating . . . and saluting my flag with fifty guns.

ROBERT ANDERSON, quoted in *Fifty Basic Civil War Documents*

Major Robert Anderson observes the firing at Fort Sumter.

The flag that Major Anderson saluted was the Stars and Stripes. After it came down, the Confederates raised their own flag, the Stars and Bars. The confederate attack on Fort Sumter signaled the start of the Civil War.

Confederates Fire on Fort Sumter

With seven of the southernmost states already seceded from the Union, the Confederate states lost no time in taking a strong stance. As soon as the Confederacy was formed on February 4, 1861, Confederate soldiers began taking over federal installations in their states—courthouses, post offices, and especially forts. By the time of Abraham Lincoln's inauguration on March 4, only four Southern forts remained in Union hands. The most important was **Fort Sumter,** on an island in Charleston harbor.

The day after his inauguration, the new president received an urgent dispatch from the fort's commander, Major Anderson. The Confederacy was demanding that he surrender or face an attack, and his supplies of food and ammunition would last six weeks at the most.

The news presented Lincoln with a dilemma. If he ordered the navy to shoot its way into Charleston harbor and reinforce Fort Sumter, he would be responsible for starting hostilities between the North and the South, which might prompt the slave states still in the Union to secede. On the other hand, if he ordered the fort evacuated, he would be treating the Confederacy as a legitimate nation with the right to evict foreigners from its territory. Such an action would anger the Republican Party, weaken his administration, and endanger the Union by encouraging foreign governments to recognize the Confederacy. The nation waited to see what he would do.

SECTION 1 RESOURCES

PRINT RESOURCES

IN-DEPTH RESOURCES: UNIT 3
Guided Reading, p. 37
Skillbuilder Practice: Following Chronological Order, p. 41
Geography Application: Resources of the North and South, p. 43
Outline Map: The States Choose Sides, p. 45
American Lives: David Farragut, p. 54

ACCESS FOR STUDENTS ACQUIRING ENGLISH
Guided Reading (Spanish), p. 110
Skillbuilder Practice: Following Chronological Order (Spanish), p. 115
Geography Application: Resources of the North and South (Spanish), p. 116
Outline Map: The States Choose Sides (Spanish), p. 118

FORMAL ASSESSMENT
Section Quiz, p. 137

ALTERNATIVE ASSESSMENT BOOK
See forms for supporting and scoring alternative activities.

TECHNOLOGY RESOURCES

GEOGRAPHY TRANSPARENCIES
G11, Union and Confederacy: 1861
G37, Slavery and the Civil War

CD-ROM Electronic Library of Primary Sources
Fateful Lightning

VIDEO *American Portfolio: A Videodisc for U.S. History*
user's guide, pp. 96–98, 100, 109, 111

INTERNET McDougal Littell Learning On-Line
http://www.mcdougallittell.com

FIRST SHOTS Once again, as he had during his debates with Stephen Douglas, Lincoln executed a clever political maneuver. He would not abandon Fort Sumter, but neither would he reinforce it. He would merely send in "food for hungry men."

Now it was Jefferson Davis who faced a dilemma. If he did nothing, he would damage the image of the Confederacy as a sovereign, independent nation. Some Confederate states might even decide to rejoin the Union. On the other hand, if he ordered an attack on Fort Sumter, he would turn peaceful secession into war.

Davis chose war. At 4:30 A.M. on April 12, Confederate batteries began thundering away to the cheers of Charleston's citizens, who acted as though they were watching a fireworks display. The South Carolinians bombarded the fort with more than 4,000 rounds before Anderson surrendered. The deadly struggle between North and South was under way.

VIRGINIA SECEDES News of Fort Sumter's fall united the North. When Lincoln called for 75,000 volunteers to serve for three months, the response was overwhelming. In Iowa, 20 times the state's quota rushed to enlist. Indiana offered twice the number of regiments that had been requested. And so it went throughout the Northern states.

Lincoln's call for troops provoked a very different reaction in the states of the upper South. On April 17, Virginia, unwilling to fight against other Southern states, seceded—a terrible loss to the Union. Virginia was the most heavily populated state in the South, the most industrialized (with a crucial iron works and navy yard), and perhaps the most prestigious, as it was the birthplace of seven presidents. In May, Arkansas, North Carolina, and Tennessee followed Virginia, bringing the number of Confederate states to eleven. However, the western counties of Virginia were antislavery, so they seceded from Virginia and were admitted into the Union as West Virginia in 1863. The four remaining slave states—Maryland, Delaware, Kentucky, and Missouri—remained in the Union,

THINK THROUGH HISTORY
A. *Analyzing Causes* Why did Jefferson Davis declare war?
A. Answer He was afraid that some Southern states might rejoin the Union.

Skillbuilder Answer **Industry:** The North. **Outcome:** Based on the data, it appears that the North might win an easy victory.

> "The die was cast; war was declared . . . and we were all afraid it would be over and we [would] not be in the fight."
>
> **SAM WATKINS,** CONFEDERATE SOLDIER

SKILLBUILDER
INTERPRETING GRAPHS
Based on the graphs, which side had the advantage in terms of industrial production? What does the data suggest about the future outcome of the war?

MORE ABOUT . . .
Fort Sumter
There were no casualties during the actual battle for Fort Sumter. However, during the fifty-gun salute to Old Glory, the wind blew a burning ember onto a stack of cartridges, which exploded, wounding five Union soldiers and killing one.

HISTORY FROM VISUALS
Northern and Southern Strengths, 1860
Reading the Chart Point out that labels alongside the vertical axes of the three bar graphs explain the numbers shown—the population in millions.

Extension Have students refer to the data on the bar graphs to approximate the ratio of eligible recruits to the total population for both the North and the South. *Response: North—1 to 5; South—1 to 10.*

IN-DEPTH RESOURCES: UNIT 3
Geography Application: Resources of the North and South, p. 43

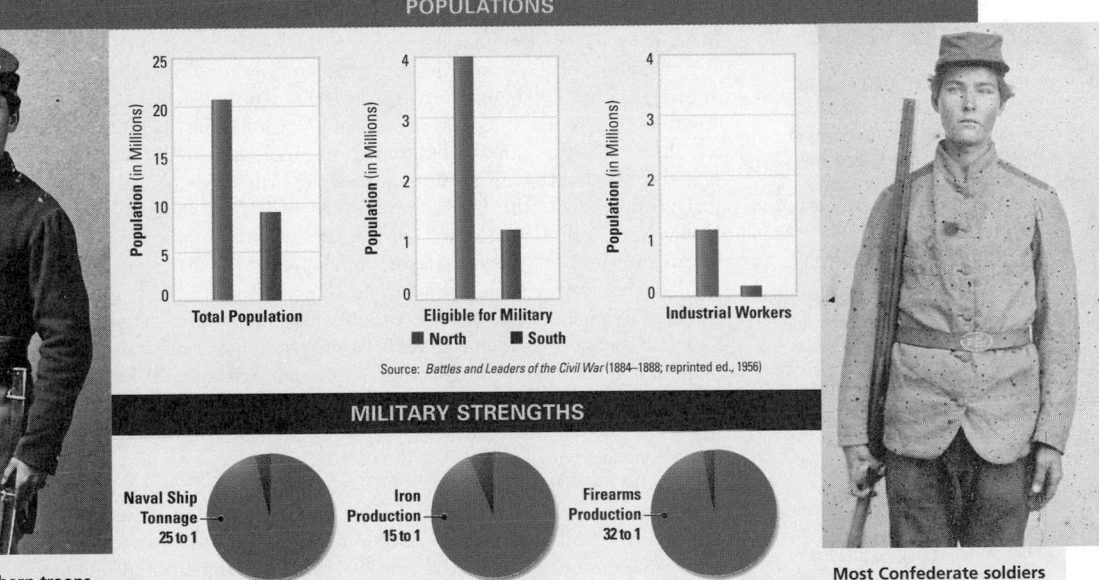

Northern and Southern Strengths, 1860

POPULATIONS

Population (in Millions): Total Population; Eligible for Military; Industrial Workers
■ North ■ South

Source: *Battles and Leaders of the Civil War* (1884–1888; reprinted ed., 1956)

MILITARY STRENGTHS

Naval Ship Tonnage 25 to 1 — Iron Production 15 to 1 — Firearms Production 32 to 1

■ North ■ South

Source: *Times Atlas of World History.* Time Books, London, 1978

Most Northern troops saw the war as a struggle to preserve the Union.

Most Confederate soldiers fought to protect the South against Northern aggression.

The Civil War **313**

TEACHING OPTIONS

Making Global Connections

The Breakup of the Soviet Union The United States is not the only country where parts of a nation withdrew from the rest of the country. In 1990 the Soviet Union under Mikhail S. Gorbachev tried to create a more democratic society. Sensing the weakness of the new regime, a series of non-Russian republics, once considered part of the Soviet Union, began to secede from the Union. Lithuania, the first to secede, declared its independence on February 9, 1991. Others followed.

Exploring Themes

Constitutional Concerns Clashing constitutional interpretations on the issue of states' rights versus national supremacy reached a dramatic climax in the Civil War. The outbreak of the war spurred four more states—Virginia, Arkansas, North Carolina, and Tennessee—to secede from the Union and join the seven states that had formed the Confederate States of America. Echoing John C. Calhoun's view of states' rights, the constitution of the Confederacy begins, "We, the People of the Confederate States, each state acting in its sovereign independent character . . . "

Americans Expect a Short War

► **Starting with the Student**
- Sportscasters and fans sometimes mistakenly predict that one team will win an easy victory over its opponent. Have students cite examples.
- Why are forecasts about the outcome of sporting events sometimes wrong?

► **Discussing Key Ideas**
- The North's strategy is to blockade Southern ports, split the South along the Mississippi River, and capture Richmond.
- The South's main strategy is to fend off invasion.
- The South wins the first battle of the war at Bull Run.

HISTORICAL SPOTLIGHT
Picnic at Bull Run

Critical Thinking:
Analyzing What factors do you think contributed to both soldiers' and civilians' false perceptions about the war? *Possible Responses:* Naiveté about the horrors of warfare; romantic notions about soldiers' combat experiences; idealistic views about heroism and bravery; self-righteousness about their reasons for fighting; underestimation of the enemy's resolve.

---

although secessionist feeling was strong enough that many of the citizens in those states fought for the Confederacy.

Americans Expect a Short War

Northerners and Confederates alike expected a short, glorious war. Soldiers left for the front with bands playing and crowds cheering. Both sides felt that right was on their side, and both were convinced that their opponents were boastful bluffers who would collapse after a few whiffs of gunpowder.

UNION AND CONFEDERATE STRATEGIES In reality the two sides were unevenly matched. The Union enjoyed enormous advantages in resources over the South—more manpower, more factories, greater food production, and a more extensive railroad system. In addition, Lincoln proved to be a decisive yet patient leader, skillful at balancing political factions.

The Confederacy likewise enjoyed some advantages, notably "King Cotton" (and the profits it earned on the world market), first-rate generals, a strong military tradition, and soldiers who were highly motivated because they were defending their homeland. However, its civilian leadership was poor, and several Southern governors were so obstinate in their assertion of states' rights that they refused to cooperate with Jefferson Davis and his Confederate administration.

Both sides adopted military strategies suited to their objectives and resources. The Union, which had to conquer the South to win, devised a three-part plan: (1) the Union navy would blockade Southern ports, so they could neither export cotton nor import much-needed manufactured goods, (2) Union riverboats and armies would move down the Mississippi River and split the Confederacy in two, and (3) Union armies would capture the Confederate capital at Richmond, Virginia.

Northern newspapers dubbed the strategy the **Anaconda plan,** after a snake that suffocates its victims in its coils. Because the Confederacy's goal was its own survival as a nation, its strategy was mostly defensive. However, Southern leaders encouraged their generals to attack—and even to invade the North—if the opportunity arose.

BULL RUN The first bloodshed occurred about three months after Fort Sumter fell. Lincoln ordered an army of about 30,000 inexperienced Union soldiers to move toward the Confederate capital at Richmond, Virginia, only 100 miles from Washington, D.C. On July 21, the troops that left Washington came upon an equally inexperienced Confederate army encamped near the little creek of **Bull Run,** just 25 miles from the Union capital. Lincoln commanded General Irwin McDowell to attack the Confederates, noting "You are green, it is true, but they are green also; you are all green alike."

The battle was a seesaw affair. In the morning the Union army gained the upper hand, but the Confederates held firm, inspired by General Thomas J. Jackson. "There is Jackson standing like a stone wall!" another general shouted, originating the nickname **Stonewall Jackson.** In the afternoon more Confederate reinforcements arrived and turned the tide of battle into the first victory for the South. The routed Union troops began a panicky retreat to the capital.

Fortunately for the Union, the Confederates were too exhausted and disorganized to follow up their victory with an attack on Washington. Still, Confederate morale soared. Bull Run "has secured our independence," declared a Georgia secessionist, and many Southern soldiers, confident that the war was over, left the army and went home.

HISTORICAL SPOTLIGHT

PICNIC AT BULL RUN

Before the First Battle of Bull Run, the inexperienced soldiers weren't the only ones who expected the war to "be a picnic." The civilian population was similarly naive about the realities of battle. In Washington, ladies and gentlemen put on their best clothes and mounted their carriages and horses. Carrying baskets of food and iced champagne, they rode out to observe the first encounter of the war.

The battle did not turn out to be the enjoyable entertainment viewers expected. When the Confederates forced the Union troops to retreat, the Federals' progress was held up by the carriages of the panicking civilians. After that disaster, no one in the North predicted that the war would be over with just one skirmish.

THINK THROUGH HISTORY
B. *Contrasting* Contrast the strengths of the North and the South.

B. Answer The North had more resources such as manpower, factories, and railroad lines. The South had cotton profits, good generals, and the motivation of defending its homeland.

Cooperative Activity: Researching the Battle of Bull Run

Task: Student groups will research the first Battle of Bull Run from the perspective of four different people and perform role-plays.

Purpose: To explore an event from multiple points of view.

Activity: Assign teams of four, and have each member chose one of the following roles—a Northern soldier, a Southern soldier, a civilian spectator, and a newspaper reporter. Students should then examine books about the Battle of

Bull Run and relevant primary sources. Have students write descriptions based on their research and read them aloud. Classmates should guess whose point of view is represented in each description.

📁 **Building a Portfolio:** Students adding their descriptions to their portfolios should attach a note pointing out their own contributions.

ALTERNATIVE ASSESSMENT BOOK
Standards for Evaluating a Cooperative Activity

Standards for Evaluation
Descriptions should . . .

- present vivid details about the location of the battle and the people
- include battle movements
- give sufficient information to reveal the fictional narrator of each piece

Civil War, 1861–1863

ILLINOIS · INDIANA · OHIO · New York · PENNSYLVANIA · Philadelphia · NEW JERSEY

MARYLAND · DEL. · Washington · Charleston · KENTUCKY · Perryville, Oct. 8, 1862 · Richmond · VIRGINIA · AREA OF INSET

MISSOURI · Ft. Henry, Feb. 6, 1862 and · Ft. Donelson, Feb. 16, 1862 · Nashville, Feb. 6, 1862 · NORTH CAROLINA

TENNESSEE · Chattanooga · ARKANSAS · Memphis · Shiloh, Apr. 7, 1862 · Atlanta · SOUTH CAROLINA · Ft. Sumter, Apr. 12–13, 1861

MISSISSIPPI · ALABAMA · GEORGIA · Montgomery · Savannah

LOUISIANA · Vicksburg, July 4, 1863 · Mobile · ATLANTIC OCEAN

Port Hudson, July 8, 1863 · Pensacola · TEXAS · New Orleans, Apr. 26, 1862 · FLORIDA

0 200 Miles · 0 400 Kilometers · Gulf of Mexico · Union Blockade · Union Blockade

Inset (Virginia area):

PENNSYLVANIA · Gettysburg, July 1–3, 1863 · NEW JERSEY

Antietam, Sept.17, 1862 · MARYLAND · DELAWARE · Washington

Winchester, May 25, 1862 · First Battle of Bull Run, July 21, 1861 · Second Battle of Bull Run, Aug. 30, 1862

BEAUREGARD 1861 · Chancellorsville, May 4, 1863 · Fredericksburg, Dec. 13, 1862 · Richmond

Seven Days' Battle, June 25–July 1, 1862 · VIRGINIA · Chesapeake Bay · James River · Rappahannock River · McCLELLAN 1862

Legend:
- United States
- Confederate States
- Occupied by Union 1863
- Occupied by Confederacy 1863
- Union forces
- Confederate forces
- Union victory
- Confederate victory
- Union blockade

GEOGRAPHY SKILLBUILDER
REGION *In which region of the country did Northern forces have the most success?*
PLACE *In which states did Confederate troops attempt invasions of the North?*

Skillbuilder Answers
Region: The West. Place: Kentucky, Pennsylvania, and Maryland.

Union Armies in the West

Lincoln responded to the defeat at Bull Run by calling for the enlistment of 500,000 men to serve for three years instead of three months. Three days later, he called for an additional 500,000 men. He also appointed General **George McClellan** to lead this new Union army, encamped near Washington. While McClellan drilled his men—soon to be known as the Army of the Potomac—the Union forces in the west began the fight for control of the Mississippi.

FORTS HENRY AND DONELSON In February 1862 a Union army invaded western Tennessee. At its head was General **Ulysses S. Grant,** a rumpled West Point graduate who had failed at everything he had tried in civilian life—whether as a farmer, bill collector, real estate agent, or store clerk. He was, however, a brave, tough, and decisive military commander.

In just 11 days, assisted by four ironclad gunboats, Grant's forces captured two Confederate forts that held strategic positions on important rivers, Fort Henry on the Tennessee River and Fort Donelson on the Cumberland River. In the latter victory, when the Southern commander sought terms for surrender, Grant informed him that "no terms except unconditional and immediate surrender can be accepted." The Confederates surrendered and, from then on, people said that Grant's initials stood for "Unconditional Surrender" Grant.

SHILOH One month after the victories at Fort Henry and Fort Donelson, in late March 1862, Grant gathered his troops near a small Tennessee church named **Shiloh,** which was close to the Mississippi border. Grant failed to entrench his men or to set out adequate guards and patrols. On April 6 thousands of yelling Confederate soldiers rushed out of the woods and attacked the surprised Union forces. Many Union troops were shot while making coffee; some died while they were still lying in their blankets.

By nightfall, Union forces were on the edge of disaster. Grant then demonstrated his determination. He reorganized his troops, ordered up reinforcements, and counterattacked at dawn the following day. By mid-afternoon of April 7, the Confederate forces had retreated.

The Civil War **315**

TEACHING OPTIONS

Making Connections Across Time

Military Strategies Strategies of warfare had changed considerably from the Revolutionary War to the Civil War. The British had marched in formation across a battlefield, but Washington had learned how to use Native American tactics, such as the ambush, to win the war. The Battle of Shiloh taught Grant the importance of digging trenches so that soldiers could hide in them. In future battles, he would fortify the encampment and send out scouts to explore the region and enemy sites. The lessons of trench warfare learned during the Civil War served well until World War I, when new technology, such as tanks and airplanes, again changed the way wars were fought.

Making Connections Across the Curriculum

Sports The military language of combat has made its way to the gridiron. For example, when one team is blocking and one team is tackling, the opposing football players are said to be "in the trenches." Other football expressions borrowed from warfare follow:

- offensive and defensive formations
- flanks
- throw a bomb
- blitz

Ask students to draw parallels between the actions on a battlefield and the actions on a football field.

Admiral David Farragut, shown here in a photograph by Mathew Brady, won a strategic victory for the Union in taking the port city of New Orleans.

The Battle of Shiloh taught both sides a strategic lesson. Generals now recognized the importance of sending out scouts, digging trenches, and building fortifications. Shiloh also demonstrated what a bloody slaughter the war was becoming, as nearly one-fourth of the 100,000 men who fought there were killed, wounded, or captured.

Although the battle seemed to be a draw, it had a long-range impact on the war. The Confederate failure to hold on to its Ohio-Kentucky frontier showed that at least part of the Union's three-way strategy, the drive to take the Mississippi and split the Confederacy, might succeed.

FARRAGUT ON THE LOWER MISSISSIPPI As Grant pushed toward the Mississippi River, a Union fleet of about 40 ships approached the river's mouth in Louisiana. Its commander was sixty-year-old **David G. Farragut;** its assignment, to seize New Orleans, the Confederacy's largest city and busiest port.

On April 24, Farragut ran his fleet past two Confederate forts in spite of booming enemy guns and fire rafts heaped with burning pitch. Five days later, the U.S. flag flew over New Orleans. During the next two months, Farragut took control of much of the lower Mississippi, including the towns of Baton Rouge and Natchez.

Between Grant and Farragut, the Union had nearly achieved its goal of cutting the Confederacy in two. Only Port Hudson, Louisiana, and Vicksburg, Mississippi, perched high on a bluff above the river, still stood in the way.

The War for the Capitals

As the campaign in the west progressed and the Union navy tightened its blockade of Southern ports, the third part of the North's three-part strategy—the plan to capture the Confederate capital at Richmond—faltered. One of the problems was General McClellan.

Although he was an excellent administrator and popular with his troops, McClellan was incredibly cautious. After five full months of training an army of 150,000 men, he insisted that he could not move against Richmond until he had 270,000 men. He complained that there were only two bridges across the Potomac, not enough for an orderly retreat should the Confederates repulse the Federals. Northern newspapers began to mock his daily bulletins of "All quiet on the Potomac," and even the patient Lincoln commented that he would like to "borrow McClellan's army if the general himself was not going to use it."

"ON TO RICHMOND" After dawdling all winter, McClellan finally got under way in the spring of 1862. He transported the Army of the Potomac down the Potomac to Chesapeake Bay. The army landed on the peninsula between the York and James rivers in Virginia and began moving slowly toward the Confederate capital, where it met a Confederate army commanded by **Robert E. Lee.**

Lee was very different from McClellan—modest rather than vain, and willing to go beyond military textbooks in his tactics. He had opposed secession and even freed his slaves. However, after Fort Sumter fell, he declined an offer to head the Union army and cast his lot with his beloved state of Virginia.

Determined to save Richmond, Lee moved against McClellan in a series of battles known collectively as the Seven Days' Battles, fought from June 25 to July 1, 1862. Although the Confederates had fewer soldiers and suffered higher casualties, Lee's determination and unorthodox tactics so unnerved McClellan that he backed away from Richmond and down the peninsula to the sea.

ANTIETAM Now it was Lee's turn to move against the enemy's capital. On August 29 and 30, his troops won a resounding victory at the Second Battle of Bull Run. A few days later, they crossed the Potomac into the Union state of Maryland. Mary Bedinger Mitchell, who lived in a Potomac River town, described the starving Confederate troops.

> **A PERSONAL VOICE**
> All day they crowded to the doors of our houses, with always the same drawling complaint: "I've been a-marchin' and a-fightin' for six weeks stiddy, and I ain't had n-a-r-thin' to eat 'cept green apples an' green cawn, an' I wish youd please to gimme a bite to eat." . . . That they could march or fight at all seemed incredible.
>
> **MARY BEDINGER MITCHELL,** quoted in *Battle Cry of Freedom*

At this point McClellan had a tremendous stroke of luck. A Union corporal, exploring a meadow where the Confederates had camped, found a copy of Lee's army orders wrapped around a bunch of cigars! The plan revealed that Lee's and Stonewall Jackson's armies were separated for the moment.

THINK THROUGH HISTORY
E. Evaluating Decisions Do you think Lincoln's decision to fire McClellan was a good one? Why or why not?

For once McClellan acted quickly and ordered his men forward after Lee. The two armies fought on September 17 near a sluggish creek called the **Antietam.** It proved to be the bloodiest single-day battle in American history. Casualties totaled more than 26,000, nearly double the number suffered in the War of 1812 and the war with Mexico combined. But instead of pursuing the battered Confederate army and possibly ending the war, however, McClellan, cautious as always, did nothing. Though the battle itself was a standoff, the South, which had lost a quarter of its men, retreated the next day across the Potomac into Virginia.

On November 7, 1862, Lincoln fired McClellan. This solved one problem by getting rid of the general whom Lincoln characterized as having "the slows." However, the president faced the problems of smoothing over diplomatic conflicts with Britain and answering the demands of abolitionists.

Lincoln and McClellan confer on the battlefield at Antietam, Maryland, in this 1862 photograph by Alexander Gardner.

Section 1 Assessment

1. TERMS & NAMES

Identify:
- Fort Sumter
- Anaconda plan
- Bull Run
- Stonewall Jackson
- George McClellan
- Ulysses S. Grant
- Shiloh
- David G. Farragut
- Robert E. Lee
- Antietam

2. SUMMARIZING For each month listed below, create a newspaper headline summarizing a key Civil War battle that occurred. Write your headlines in a chart like the one shown.

1861	
month	headline
• April	
• July	

1862	
month	headline
• February	
• April	
• September	

3. HYPOTHESIZING What if Virginia had not seceded from the Union in 1861? Speculate on how this might have affected the course of the war. Support your answer with examples.

THINK ABOUT
- Virginia's influence on other Southern states
- Virginia's location and its human and material resources
- how the North's military strategy might have been different

4. DRAWING CONCLUSIONS What do you think were General McClellan's major tactical errors? Support your response with details from the text.

THINK ABOUT
- the North's and South's military strategies
- the outcome of the Seven Days' Battles and the Second Battle of Bull Run
- events at the battle of Antietam

The Civil War **317**

ANSWERS

1. TERMS & NAMES

Fort Sumter, p. 312

Anaconda plan, p. 314

Bull Run, p. 314

Stonewall Jackson, p. 314

George McClellan, p. 315

Ulysses S. Grant, p. 315

Shiloh, p. 315

David G. Farragut, p. 316

Robert E. Lee, p. 316

Antietam, p. 317

2. SUMMARIZING

Headlines will vary slightly but should point to these events: 1861: April: Confederates Shell Fort Sumter—War; July: Confederate Triumph at Bull Run; 1862: February: Grant's Forces Capture Fort Henry and Fort Donelson; April: Grant Beats Back Attack at Shiloh—Farragut Seizes New Orleans; September: McClellan Falters After Victory at Antietam

3. HYPOTHESIZING

Possible Response: Arkansas, North Carolina, and Tennessee may have decided not to secede from the Union. West Virginia would not have become a new Union state. The Anaconda plan would have been modified. The Union may have won an early victory because of Virginia's large population, along with its iron works and naval yard. Robert E. Lee, whose home state was Virginia, might have headed the Union army.

4. DRAWING CONCLUSIONS

Possible Response: Since McClellan's men were prepared, he should have made an offensive move sooner than the spring of 1862; since McClellan's troops outnumbered Lee's, he should not have backed down at Richmond; he should have planned to attack Lee's men— who were weakened and hungry—after their retreat from Antietam.

OBJECTIVES

1. To explain why Britain remained neutral.

2. To explain Lincoln's motives for issuing the Emancipation Proclamation and the document's effects.

3. To identify the political dilemmas facing the North and South.

CRITICAL THINKING

- Analyzing causes, p. 319
- Summarizing, pp. 320, 322
- Forming opinions, p. 322
- Analyzing issues, p. 322

FOCUS & MOTIVATE

▶ **Starting with the Student**
Ask students to imagine that someone has two friends who are angry at each other. Should that person get involved in the argument?

- What actions can a nation take when it has to deal with two other nations that are at war with each other?

MORE ABOUT . . .
William Yancey

Yancey began his political career as a Jacksonian Democrat, but after marrying into a wealthy planter family, he adopted upper-class attitudes. He was a spell-binding orator with a melodious voice and expressive hands. After his failed trip to Europe, he was elected to the Confederate Senate but served only one year. He died in office in 1863.

---

② The Politics of War

TERMS & NAMES
- Emancipation Proclamation
- habeas corpus
- Copperhead
- conscription
- bounty

LEARN ABOUT the political issues that arose during the Civil War
TO UNDERSTAND how divided Americans were over the course and purpose of the war.

William Yancey

ONE AMERICAN'S STORY

William Yancey of Alabama, one of the die-hard Southerners known as Fire-Eaters, urged secession as early as 1851. After secession occurred, Yancey believed, as did many Southerners, that Great Britain was so economically dependent on Southern cotton that it would have to formally recognize the Confederacy as an independent nation.

Shortly after the war began, Yancey and two other Confederate diplomats traveled to London to ask for such recognition. Although the British Secretary of State for Foreign Affairs met with them twice, he would not commit his nation to recognizing the Confederacy. In May 1861, Britain announced its neutrality. Insulted, Yancey returned home and told his fellow Southerners not to hope for British aid.

A PERSONAL VOICE
You have no friends in Europe. . . . The sentiment of Europe is anti-slavery, and that portion of public opinion which forms, and is represented by the government of Great Britain is abolition. They will never recognize our independence until our conquering sword hangs dripping over the prostrate heads of the North. . . . It is an error to say that "Cotton is King." It is not. It is a great and influential factor in commerce, but not its dictator.

WILLIAM YANCEY, quoted in *The Civil War: A Narrative*

In spite of Yancey's words, many Southerners continued to hope that economic necessity would force Britain to come to their aid. Meanwhile, abolitionists waged a public opinion war against slavery, not only in Europe, but in the North. President Lincoln was forced to juggle several political issues, including pressure to emancipate the slaves.

Britain Remains Neutral

A number of economic factors made Britain no longer dependent on Southern cotton. Not only had Britain accumulated a huge cotton inventory just before the outbreak of war, it also found new sources of cotton in Egypt and India. Moreover, when Britain's wheat crop failed, Northern wheat and corn replaced cotton as an essential import. As one magazine put it, "Old King Cotton's dead and buried." Britain decided that neutrality was the best policy—at least for a while.

THE *TRENT* INCIDENT In the fall of 1861, an incident occurred to test that neutrality. The Confederate government sent two diplomats, James Mason and John Slidell, to Britain in a second attempt to gain British recognition of the Confederacy. The two men traveled aboard a British merchantman, the *Trent*. Captain Charles Wilkes of the American warship *San Jacinto* stopped the *Trent* and arrested the two men. The British threatened war against the Union and dispatched 8,000 troops to Canada. Aware of the need to fight just "one war at a time," Lincoln decided to free the two prisoners, publicly claiming that Wilkes had acted without orders. Britain was as relieved as the United States was to find a peaceful way out of the crisis.

THE *ALABAMA* CLAIMS Although Britain did not recognize the Confederacy, it did sell the South ships with which to fight the Union blockade. One, the

---

SECTION 2 RESOURCES

 ### PRINT RESOURCES

IN-DEPTH RESOURCES: UNIT 3
Guided Reading, p. 38
Primary Sources: The Emancipation Proclamation, p. 47; Recruiting Poster, p. 48

ACCESS FOR STUDENTS ACQUIRING ENGLISH
Guided Reading (Spanish), p. 111

FORMAL ASSESSMENT
Section Quiz, p. 138

ALTERNATIVE ASSESSMENT BOOK
See forms for supporting and scoring alternative activities.

TECHNOLOGY RESOURCES

VIDEO *American Portfolio: A Videodisc for U.S. History* user's guide, pp. 99, 108, 115–116

INTERNET McDougal Littell Learning On-Line
http://www.mcdougallittell.com

Alabama, sank or captured 64 American merchant vessels before it was sunk. When the war was over, the United States presented Britain with a bill for over $19 million in damages—which Britain ignored. The two nations eventually agreed to arbitrate the dispute and in 1872 an international tribunal awarded the United States $15.5 million.

Proclaiming Emancipation

As the South struggled in vain to gain foreign recognition, abolitionist feeling grew in the North. Some Northerners believed that just winning the war would not be enough if the issue of slavery was not permanently settled. Representative George Julian of Indiana declared that "the mere suppression of the rebellion will be an empty mockery of our suffering and sacrifices, if slavery shall be spared to canker the heart of the nation anew, and repeat its diabolical deeds."

LINCOLN'S VIEW OF SLAVERY Although Lincoln disliked slavery, he did not believe that the federal government had the power to abolish it where it already existed. When Horace Greeley urged him in 1862 to transform the war into an abolitionist crusade, Lincoln replied that his goal was to save the Union.

A PERSONAL VOICE
My paramount object in this struggle *is* to save the Union, and is *not* either to save or destroy Slavery. If I could save the Union without freeing *any* slave, I would do it; and if I could save it by freeing *all* the slaves, I would do it; and if I could do it by freeing some and leaving others alone, I would also do that. . . . I have here stated my purpose according to my view of *official* duty, and I intend no modification of my oft-expressed *personal* wish that all men, everywhere, could be free.
ABRAHAM LINCOLN, quoted in *Fifty Basic Civil War Documents*

As the war progressed, however, Lincoln did find a way to use his constitutional war powers to end slavery. The Confederacy used the labor of slaves to build fortifications and grow food. Lincoln's powers as commander in chief allowed him to order his troops to seize enemy resources. Therefore, he decided that, just as he could order the Union army to take Confederate supplies, he could also authorize the army to emancipate slaves.

A strategic benefit of emancipation was that it would discourage Britain from supporting the Confederacy because British abolitionists opposed helping a slaveholding nation. Emancipation was not just a moral issue; it became a weapon of war.

KEY PLAYERS

ABRAHAM LINCOLN
1809–1865
People question why Lincoln believed so passionately in the Union. A possible answer lies in his life story. He was born into poverty, the son of illiterate parents. Lincoln once said that in his boyhood there was "absolutely nothing to excite ambition for education," yet he hungered for knowledge.

He educated himself and, after working as rail splitter, flatboatman, storekeeper, and surveyor, he taught himself to be a lawyer. This led to careers in law and politics—and eventually to the White House. In Europe at that time, people were more or less fixed in the station into which they had been born. In the United States—founded on the belief that all men were created equal—Lincoln was free to achieve whatever he could. Small wonder that he fought to preserve the democracy he described as "the last best hope of earth."

JEFFERSON DAVIS
1808–1889
Davis, who was named after Thomas Jefferson, was born in Kentucky but grew up in Mississippi. After graduating from West Point, he alternated army service with life as a planter. He served in the U.S. Senate from 1847 to 1851 and again from 1857 to 1861, resigning when Mississippi seceded.

His election as president of the Confederacy dismayed him. As his wife Varina wrote, "I thought his genius was military, but as a party manager he would not succeed. He did not know the arts of the politician and would not practice them if understood, and he did know those of war." Varina was right. Davis fought frequently with other Confederate leaders and was blamed for the refusal of many Southern states to put the Confederacy's welfare above their own.

The Civil War **319**

British Reaction

Critical Thinking:
Analyzing Motives Ask students to discuss why British workers would praise Lincoln and his proclamation. *Possible Response: Many workers were sympathetic to the plight of slaves because they too were exploited laborers.*

MORE ABOUT . . .
Reactions to the Proclamation

In 1963, Martin Luther King, Jr., expressed his admiration for the Emancipation Proclamation in his speech, "I Have a Dream," delivered on the steps of the Lincoln Memorial. "Five score years ago, a great American, in whose symbolic shadow we stand, signed the Emancipation Proclamation. This momentous decree came as a great beacon light of hope to millions of Negro slaves who have been seared in the flames of withering injustice. It came as a joyous daybreak to end the long night of captivity."

IN-DEPTH RESOURCES: UNIT 3
Primary Source: The Emancipation Proclamation, p. 47

ON THE WORLD STAGE

BRITISH REACTION

Conservative newspapers in Britain criticized the fact that the Emancipation Proclamation ended slavery in areas where Lincoln had no control but not in areas where he did. Most Britons, however, agreed with the Proclamation. In Manchester, for example, 6,000 workers resolved that "the erasure of that foul blot upon civilization and Christianity—chattel slavery—during your Presidency will cause the name of Abraham Lincoln to be honored and revered by posterity." The overwhelming thrust of public opinion virtually guaranteed that the British government would not recognize the Confederate government.

EMANCIPATION PROCLAMATION On January 1, 1863, Lincoln issued his **Emancipation Proclamation.** The following portion captured national attention.

> All persons held as slaves within any state, or designated part of a state, the people whereof shall then be in rebellion against the United States, shall be then, thenceforth, and forever free. . . . And upon this act, sincerely believed to be an act of justice, warranted by the Constitution upon military necessity, I invoke the considerate judgment of mankind and the gracious favor of almighty God.

The Proclamation did not free any slaves immediately because it applied only to areas behind Confederate lines, outside Union control. Since the Proclamation was a military action aimed at the states in rebellion, it did not apply to Southern territory already occupied by Union troops nor to the slave states that had not seceded. Nevertheless, the Proclamation had immense symbolic importance. As Union general Régis de Trobriand put it: "We . . . were now the missionaries of a great work of redemption, the armed liberators of millions. . . . The war was ennobled; the object was higher."

REACTIONS TO THE PROCLAMATION For many, the Proclamation gave the war a high moral purpose by turning the struggle into a fight to free the slaves. In Washington, D.C., the Reverend Henry M. Turner, a free-born African American, watched the capital's inhabitants receive the news of emancipation.

A PERSONAL VOICE
Men squealed, women fainted, dogs barked, white and colored people shook hands, songs were sung, and by this time cannons began to fire at the navy yard. . . . Great processions of colored and white men marched to and fro and passed in front of the White House. . . . The President came to the window . . . and thousands told him, if he would come out of that palace, they would hug him to death. . . . It was indeed a time of times, and nothing like it will ever be seen again in this life.

HENRY M. TURNER, quoted in *Voices from the Civil War*

Free blacks also welcomed the section of the Proclamation that allowed them to enlist in the Union army. Even though many had volunteered at the beginning of the war, the regular army had refused to take them. Now they could help put an end to slavery.

However, the Emancipation Proclamation did not please everyone in the North. The Democrats claimed that it would only prolong the war by antagonizing the South. Many Union soldiers accepted it grudgingly, saying they had no love for abolitionists or African Americans, but they would support emancipation if that was what it took to reunify the nation.

Confederates reacted to the Proclamation with fury. Jefferson Davis called it the "most execrable [hateful] measure recorded in the history of guilty man." As Northern Democrats had predicted, the Proclamation made the Confederacy more determined than ever to fight to preserve its way of life.

After the Emancipation Proclamation, compromise was no longer possible. The Confederacy knew that if it lost, its slave-holding society would perish, and the Union knew that it could win only by completely defeating the Confederacy. From January 1863 on, it was a war to the death.

Lincoln presents the Emancipation Proclamation to his cabinet, 1862.

THINK THROUGH HISTORY
B. *Summarizing* In what way was the Emancipation Proclamation a part of Lincoln's military strategy?

B. Answer It allowed free blacks to enlist in the Union army, helped persuade Britain not to support the South, and added moral inspiration to the cause of the North.

TEACHING OPTIONS

Exploring Themes

Constitutional Concerns Though the slavery issue was one of the root causes of the Civil War, most Northerners and Southerners were unwilling to admit it. Lincoln held that the federal government had no power over slavery in the slave states and insisted that his main goal was preservation of the Union. Gradually, however, the more radical members of Congress began to pass laws intended to free the slaves. Lincoln did not think such laws were constitutional and refused to enforce them.

By the end of 1862, Lincoln recognized the need to take action. He used his war powers as commander in chief to authorize the Union army to free the slaves just as he authorized Union soldiers to seize Confederate supplies. The culmination of these measures was the Emancipation Proclamation of January 1, 1863.

Both Sides Face Political Problems

Neither side in the Civil War was completely unified. The North harbored thousands of Confederate sympathizers, while the South had thousands of Union sympathizers. Such divided loyalties created two problems: How should the respective governments handle their critics? How could they ensure a steady supply of fighting men for their armies?

DEALING WITH DISSENT Lincoln dealt forcefully with disloyalty and dissent. For example, when a Baltimore crowd attacked a Union regiment on its way to Washington a week after Fort Sumter, Lincoln sent federal troops to Maryland. He also suspended in that state the writ of **habeas corpus,** a court order that requires authorities to bring a person held in jail before the court to determine why he or she is being jailed. As a result, more than 13,000 suspected Confederate sympathizers in the Union were arrested and held without trial, although most were soon released. The President also seized telegraph offices to make sure no one used the wires for subversion. When Supreme Court Justice Roger Taney declared that Lincoln had gone beyond his constitutional powers, the president ignored his ruling.

Among those arrested were **Copperhead** politicians, Northern Democrats who advocated peace with the South. (A copperhead is an easily concealed poisonous snake.) The most notable Copperhead was Ohio congressman Clement Vallandigham, who was tried by a military court for urging Union soldiers to desert and for advocating an armistice. When even some Republicans objected to having a military court try a civilian for making speeches, Lincoln commuted Vallandigham's sentence from imprisonment to banishment to the South.

Jefferson Davis at first denounced Lincoln for suspending habeas corpus and dragging "upright men and innocent women . . . to distant dungeons." However, he soon confronted the same difficulty as Lincoln: how to balance winning a war with preserving civil liberties. When civilian Union sympathizers in eastern Tennessee burned a vital railroad bridge, Davis ordered them "executed on the spot by hanging." He, too, suspended habeas corpus in 1862.

Just as Davis ultimately followed Lincoln's example, so have other presidents. Lincoln's action in dramatically expanding presidential powers to meet the crises of wartime set a precedent in U.S. history. Since then, some presidents have cited war or "national security" as a reason to expand the powers of the executive branch of government.

CONSCRIPTION Although both armies originally relied on volunteers, heavy casualties and widespread desertions led to **conscription,** a draft that would force certain members of the population to serve in the army. The Confederacy passed a draft law in 1862—the first in American history—and the Union followed suit in 1863. Both laws ran into trouble.

The Confederate law drafted all able-bodied white men between the ages of 18 and 35. (In 1864 the limits changed to 17 and 50.) However, the law allowed wealthy draftees to hire substitutes to serve in their places, and it exempted planters who owned 20 or more slaves. Poor Confederates howled that it was a "rich man's war and poor man's fight." In addition, the governors of North Carolina and Georgia decided to ignore the law on the grounds that it "strikes down the sovereignty of the States." In spite of these exemptions and protests, almost 80 percent of eligible men served in the Confederate army.

The Union law drafted men between 20 and 45 for three years, although it, too, allowed draftees to hire substitutes. It provided for commutation, or paying a $300 fee to avoid conscription altogether. In addition, many Northern states offered volunteers cash payments called **bounties,** which led to "bounty

The Civil War **321**

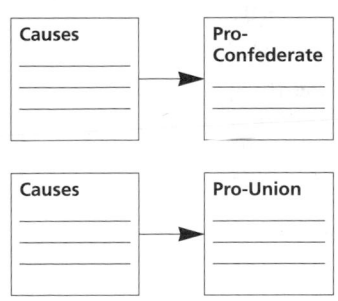

ANOTHER PERSPECTIVE

THE CHEROKEE AND THE WAR
Another nation divided by the Civil War was the Cherokee Nation, located in the Indian Territory that eventually became part of Oklahoma. Both the North and the South wanted the Cherokee on their side because Indian Territory was an excellent grain and livestock producing area. For their part, the Cherokee felt drawn to both sides—to the Union because federal treaties guaranteed Cherokee political and property rights, and to the Confederacy because many Cherokee owned slaves.

After an attempt at neutrality, the Cherokee signed a treaty with the South in October 1861. However, the alliance did not last. Efforts by the pro-Confederate leader Stand Watie to govern the Cherokee Nation failed, and federal troops invaded Indian Territory. Many Cherokee deserted from the Confederate army and went into hiding or fled to Kansas, where they joined the Union army. In February 1863 the Cherokee Nation revoked the Confederate treaty.

Violence erupted in New York City in July 1863 as thousands of rioters resisted the draft.

jumping." Men would enlist, take their bounties, desert the army, assume a different name, and rejoin the army somewhere else to collect another bounty. In the end, only 46,000 draftees actually went into the army, while 87,000 paid the $300 commutation fee and 118,000 provided substitutes. Ninety-two percent of the approximately 2 million soldiers who served in the Union army volunteered.

DRAFT RIOTS Northern resentment over the draft led to several riots. The worst one occurred in New York City and was sparked by opposition, mostly among Irish immigrants, to Republican war policies such as emancipation. The city was a tinderbox waiting to explode. Poor people were crowded into slums, crime and disease were rampant, and poverty was ever-present. When officials began to draw names for the draft, angry men gathered all over the city to complain. They thought it unfair that poor white workers should have to fight a war to free slaves who (they believed) would then swarm north and take all the jobs.

For four days, July 13–16, mobs of men and women, about two-thirds of them Irish, rampaged through the city. First they wrecked draft offices, the offices of Republican newspapers, and the homes of antislavery leaders. Then they attacked well-dressed men on the street (who looked as though they could pay the $300 commutation fee) and especially African Americans. The rioters lynched 11 African Americans and smashed the homes of hundreds. They even burned a black orphanage. By the time federal troops ended the riot, more than 100 persons lay dead.

Draft riots were not the only dramatic development away from the battlefield. During the war, sweeping changes occurred in the economy of both sides as well as in the roles played by African Americans and women.

C. Answer Low wages and high unemployment, fear of job competition from African Americans, miserable living conditions, and the economic unfairness of the draft law.

THINK THROUGH HISTORY
C. Analyzing Causes What factors played a part in the 1863 riot in New York City?

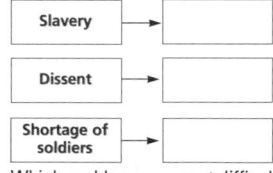

Section 2 Assessment

1. TERMS & NAMES

Identify:
• Emancipation Proclamation
• habeas corpus
• Copperhead
• conscription
• bounty

2. SUMMARIZING Create a diagram similar to this one. Fill it in with the political measures that Lincoln took to solve the problems his administration faced.

Slavery	→	
Dissent	→	
Shortage of soldiers	→	

Which problem was most difficult to handle, and why?

3. FORMING OPINIONS Do you think that Lincoln's measures to deal with disloyalty and dissent represented an abuse of power? Why or why not?

THINK ABOUT
• conditions of wartime versus peacetime
• Lincoln's primary goal
• Supreme Court Justice Roger Taney's view of Lincoln's powers

4. ANALYZING ISSUES Why do you think the Emancipation Proclamation might be considered a turning point of the Civil War? Support your answer with references to the section.

THINK ABOUT
• how the Emancipation Proclamation redefined the purpose of the war
• the Proclamation as a political maneuver
• the Proclamation's effect on military actions

322 CHAPTER 11

LEARN ABOUT the wartime experiences of civilians, soldiers, and African Americans
TO UNDERSTAND the social and economic changes created by the Civil War.

ONE AMERICAN'S STORY

Mary Chesnut was the daughter of a South Carolina governor and the wife of a U.S. senator who resigned his office to serve in the Confederate government. During the war, she recorded her observations and thoughts in a diary, which she kept under lock and key. Because of her prominent social position, she witnessed many key events of the time, including the formation of the Confederate government and the attack on Fort Sumter. Chesnut's diary describes not only these important events but also the details of daily life in the South—marriages and flirtations, hospital work, and dinner parties.

Toward the end of the war, Chesnut's social standing could not protect her from hardship. In 1864, she wrote about the economic effects of the war.

A PERSONAL VOICE.
September 19th . . . My pink silk dress I have sold for six hundred dollars, to be paid in installments, two hundred a month for three months. And I sell my eggs and butter from home for two hundred dollars a month. Does it not sound well—four hundred dollars a month, regularly? In what? "In Confederate money." Hélas! [Alas!]

MARY CHESNUT, quoted in *Mary Chesnut's Civil War*

Rampant inflation, or a sharp increase in the cost of living, had made Confederate money almost worthless, so that $400 was worth only a dollar or two in prewar currency. Inflation was just one of the ways the war affected the lives of people on both sides. In addition to affecting the economy, the war had a profound impact on the roles and actions of all Americans—civilians as well as soldiers, African Americans as well as whites.

 VIDEO *WAR OUTSIDE MY WINDOW*
Mary Chesnut's Diary of the Civil War

Mary Boykin Chesnut, whose portrait was painted in 1856 by Samuel Osgood, kept a detailed account of life during the Civil War.

African Americans Fight for Freedom

African Americans played an important role in the struggle to end slavery. Some served as soldiers, while others took action away from the battlefield.

AFRICAN–AMERICAN SOLDIERS When the Civil War started, it was a white man's war. Neither the Union nor the Confederacy accepted African Americans as soldiers.

In 1862, Congress passed a law allowing African Americans to serve in the military. It was only after the Emancipation Proclamation, however, that large-scale enlistment occurred. Although African Americans made up only 1 percent of the North's population, by war's end nearly 10 percent of the Union army was African American. The majority consisted of former slaves from Maryland, Pennsylvania, and Virginia and other parts of the Confederacy. African-American soldiers participated in about 500 skirmishes and battles.

The Civil War **323**

OBJECTIVES

1 To explain African Americans' role in the struggle to end slavery.

2 To explain the decline of the Southern economy and the expansion of the Northern economy.

3 To describe the terrible conditions that Union and Confederate soldiers endured.

CRITICAL THINKING

• Summarizing, pp. 324, 328
• Analyzing causes, pp. 325, 326, 327
• Comparing and contrasting, p. 328
• Synthesizing, p. 328

FOCUS & MOTIVATE

▶ **Starting with the Student** Watch the video "War Outside My Window" to find out Mary Chesnut's firsthand impressions of the Civil War.

• Using the *Teacher's Resource Book* as a guide, hold a class discussion about Chesnut's vivid portrayal of the Civil War era.

 AMERICAN STORIES VIDEO SERIES
"War Outside My Window"
Videocassette: Volume 1

Videodisc: Disc 1, Side A, Chapter 4.

IN-DEPTH RESOURCES: UNIT 3
Primary Source: from *Mary Chesnut's Civil War*, p. 49

SECTION 3 RESOURCES

 PRINT RESOURCES

IN-DEPTH RESOURCES: UNIT 3
Guided Reading, p. 39
Primary Source: from *Mary Chesnut's Civil War*, p. 49
American Lives: Clara Barton, p. 55

ACCESS FOR STUDENTS ACQUIRING ENGLISH
Guided Reading (Spanish), p. 112

FORMAL ASSESSMENT
Section Quiz, p. 139

ALTERNATIVE ASSESSMENT BOOK
See forms for supporting and scoring alternative activities

 TECHNOLOGY RESOURCES

CD-ROM Electronic Library of Primary Sources

VIDEO *American Stories* video series.
American Portfolio: A Videodisc for U.S. History
user's guide, pp. 97, 100–101, 106–107

INTERNET McDougal Littell Learning On-Line
http://www.mcdougallittell.com

OBJECTIVE
1 **INSTRUCT**

African Americans Fight for Freedom

▶ **Discussing Key Ideas**
• By 1862 African Americans are accepted as Union soldiers but still face discrimination.

(continued on the next page)

(continued from page 323)

- As the North pushes into the Confederacy, slaves begin resisting and sabotaging the plantation economy.

IN-DEPTH RESOURCES: UNIT 3
Guided Reading, p.39

ACCESS FOR STUDENTS ACQUIRING ENGLISH
Guided Reading (Spanish), p. 112

HISTORICAL SPOTLIGHT
Glory for the 54th Massachusetts
Critical Thinking: Generalizing Ask students to list adjectives that characterize the conduct of the African-American 54th Massachusetts Infantry. *Possible Responses: Courageous, loyal, gallant, fearless, daring, resolute.*

MORE ABOUT . . .
"Contrabands"
In May 1861, three slaves working for the Confederate army escaped and fled to the camp of Union general Benjamin Butler in Virginia. The next day the slaves' owner entered the camp under a flag of truce and insisted that Butler return his property under the terms of the Fugitive Slave Law. Butler replied that since Virginia was a seceded state, the Fugitive Slave Law did not apply. The escaped slaves were "contrabands of war," and he had the right to confiscate enemy property. From then on, slaves who crossed into Union lines were called contrabands.

African Americans, like those of Battery A of the 2nd United States Colored Artillery (shown here at gun drill), made up 10 percent of Union forces.

HISTORICAL SPOTLIGHT

GLORY FOR THE 54TH MASSACHUSETTS
In July 1863, the all-African-American 54th Massachusetts Infantry, including two sons of Frederick Douglass, led an assault on Fort Wagner, near Charleston harbor. The attack failed and more than 40 percent of the soldiers were killed (although Douglass's sons survived). Among the survivors was Sergeant William Carney, the first African American to win a Congressional Medal of Honor. Among the dead was the white commander, Colonel Robert G. Shaw.

As the New York *Tribune* pointed out, "If this Massachusetts 54th had faltered when its trial came, 200,000 troops for whom it was a pioneer would never have been put into the field. . . . It did not falter." Shaw's father declared that his son lay "with his brave, devoted followers who fell dead over him and around him. . . . What a bodyguard he has!"

Although accepted as soldiers, African Americans suffered discrimination. They served in separate regiments commanded by white officers. No African American was allowed to rise above the rank of captain. White privates earned $13 a month, plus a $3.50 clothing allowance. Black privates earned only $10 a month, with no clothing allowance. Blacks protested, and several regiments served without pay for months rather than accept the lesser amount. Congress finally equalized the pay of white and African-American soldiers in 1864.

The mortality rate for African-American soldiers was higher than that for white soldiers, primarily because many African Americans were assigned to labor duty in the germ-ridden garrisons, where they were likely to catch typhoid, pneumonia, malaria, or some other deadly disease. Then, too, the Confederacy would not treat captured African-American soldiers as prisoners of war. Many were executed on the spot, and those who were not killed were returned to slavery. A particularly gruesome massacre occurred at **Fort Pillow,** Tennessee, in 1864. Confederate troops under General Nathan Bedford Forrest butchered more than 200 African-American prisoners and some whites, shooting the prisoners as they begged for their lives.

Even though most Southerners opposed the idea of African-American soldiers, the Confederacy did consider drafting slaves and free blacks in 1863 and again in 1864. One Louisiana planter argued that since slaves "*caused* the fight," they should share in the burden of battle. To which Georgia general Howell Cobb answered that "if slaves will make good soldiers our whole theory of slavery is wrong." Nevertheless, the South did arm some slaves in the spring of 1865 as the war drew to a close and the Confederate army was desperate for men.

SLAVE RESISTANCE IN THE CONFEDERACY As Union forces pushed deeper into Confederate territory, thousands of slaves fled from their owners and sought freedom behind the lines of the Union army. Though most slaves remained on plantations, their conditions of work changed. With only women and boys to oversee their work, some slaves performed their tasks poorly or not at all. Sometimes they sabotaged the plantations by breaking plows, destroying fences, and neglecting to feed and water the livestock. When Southern plantation owners fled before approaching Union troops, many slaves often refused to be dragged along. They just stayed where they were so they could welcome the Yankees, who had the power to liberate them.

For whites who remained on farms and plantations in the South, slave resistance compounded the difficulty of waiting for new information from the front and coping with changes brought about by the war. Occasional violent incidents between slaves and whites contributed to the generalized feeling of fear. When Mary Chesnut's cousin was murdered by two of her most trusted slaves, Chesnut wrote that "the murder has clearly driven us all wild."

THINK THROUGH HISTORY
A. Summarizing *How did African Americans contribute to the struggle to end slavery?*

A. Answer By fighting for the North, by running away from slavery, and by sabotaging plantations in the South.

Making Connections Across Cultures

Soldiers' Songs Civil War soldiers composed countless lyrics that reflected their combat experiences and reasons for fighting. Captain Lindley Miller, the author of "The Marching Song of the First Arkansas Regiment," claimed that it was "a good song to fight with." Two verses of lyrics follow:

Oh, we're the bully soldiers of the "First of Arkansas,"
We are fighting for the Union, we are fighting for the law,
We can a hit a Rebel further than a white man ever saw,
As we go marching on.

*Glory, glory hallelujah,
Glory, glory hallelujah,
Glory, glory hallelujah,
As we go marching on.*

See, there above the center, where the flag is waving bright,
We are going out of slavery; we're bound for freedom's light;
We mean to show Jeff Davis how the Africans can fight,
As we go marching on!

Chorus

Fearful of a general slave uprising, Southerners tightened slave patrols and spread rumors about how Union soldiers abused runaways. No general uprising occurred, but slave resistance gradually weakened the plantation system. By 1864 even many Confederates realized that slavery was doomed.

The War Affects Regional Economies

The decline of the plantation system was not the only economic effect that the Civil War caused. Other effects included inflation and a new type of federal tax. In general, the war expanded the North's economy while shattering that of the South.

SOUTHERN SHORTAGES The Confederacy soon faced a food shortage due to three factors: the drain of manpower into the army, the Union occupation of food-growing areas, and the loss of slaves to work in the fields. Meat became a once-a-week luxury at best, and even such staples as rice and corn were in short supply. Food prices skyrocketed. In 1861 the average family spent $6.65 a month on food. By mid-1863, it was spending $68 a month—if it could find any food to buy. The situation grew so desperate that in 1863 hundreds of women and children—and some men—stormed bakeries and rioted for bread. Mrs. Roger A. Pryor remembered talking to an 18-year-old member of a mob in Richmond on April 2, 1863.

> **A PERSONAL VOICE**
> As she raised her hand to remove her sunbonnet, her loose calico sleeve slipped up, and revealed a mere skeleton of an arm. She perceived my expression as I looked at it, and hastily pulled down her sleeve with a short laugh. "This is all that's left of me!" she said. "It seems real funny, don't it? . . . We are going to the bakeries and each of us will take a loaf of bread. That is little enough for the government to give us after it has taken all our men."
>
> **MRS. ROGER A. PRYOR,** quoted in *Battle Cry of Freedom*

The mob broke up only when President Jefferson Davis climbed up on a cart, threw them all the money he had, and ordered them to disperse or be shot. The next day, the Confederate government distributed some of its stocks of rice.

The Union blockade of Southern ports created shortages of other items, too, including salt, sugar, coffee, nails, needles, and medicines. One result was that many Confederates smuggled cotton into the North in exchange for gold, food, and other goods. Deploring this trade with the enemy, one Confederate general raged that cotton had made "more damn rascals on both sides than anything else."

THINK THROUGH HISTORY
B. *Analyzing Causes* What caused food shortages in the South?

B Answer Union blockade and occupation; loss of manpower in terms of slaves and soldiers.

NORTHERN ECONOMIC GROWTH Overall, the war's effect on the economy of the North was much more positive. Although a few industries, such as cotton textiles, declined, most boomed. The army's need for uniforms, shoes, guns, and other supplies supported woolen mills, steel foundries, coal mines, and many other industries. Because the draft reduced the available workforce, western wheat farmers bought reapers and other labor-saving machines, which benefited the companies that manufactured those machines.

The economic boom had a dark side, though. Wages did not keep up with prices, and many people's standard of living declined. When white male workers went out on strike, employers hired free blacks, immigrants, women, and boys to replace them for lower pay.

Food was scarce in the South during the Civil War. Here, women clamor for their families' shares of milk.

The Civil War **325**

ECONOMIC
BACKGROUND
Money and Taxes

Critical Thinking:
Analyzing Causes and Effects
• What repercussions might have occurred as a result of the South's taking 10 percent of a farmer's surplus crops? *Possible Response: Anger and a growing loss of confidence because food was in short supply and worth more than paper money.*
• Why didn't the North use a similar means of raising money? *Possible Responses: The North was not as dependent on crops, was making money on manufactured goods, and preferred to use the income tax to get revenue.*

Women of the Women's Central Association of Relief record shipments to the field in their office in New York.

OBJECTIVE
③ **INSTRUCT**

Soldiers Suffer on Both Sides

▶ *Discussing Key Ideas*
• Soldiers withstand deplorable conditions.
• Prisoners of war suffer inhumane treatment.
• The U.S. Sanitary Commission improves healthcare for Union soldiers.
• The work of Clara Barton and other nurses helps lower soldiers' death rates.

ELECTRONIC LIBRARY OF PRIMARY SOURCES
from *Letters to Eliza from a Union Soldier* by George Fowle
from *Diary of a Confederate Soldier* by John S. Jackman

ECONOMIC
BACKGROUND

MONEY AND TAXES

To raise revenue, both the Union and the Confederacy issued paper money. The Union passed a law declaring that its currency was legal tender, so everyone had to accept it. The law succeeded because the public maintained confidence in the Northern economy.

The Confederacy did not declare its currency legal tender, so each state had its own currency. As a result, the public lost faith in Confederate currency, its value plummeted, and prices soared. The Confederacy's war inflation rate was 9,000 percent; prices were 90 times higher at the end of the war than at the beginning. The Union inflation rate was 80 percent.

The two governments also differed in their tax policies. The Confederacy raised revenue by taking one-tenth of a farmer's surplus crops. The Union passed an income tax, collecting 3 percent of incomes between $600 and $10,000 a year and 5 percent of incomes above $10,000.

Northern women—who like many Southern women, replaced men in factories and on farms—also obtained government jobs for the first time. They worked mostly as clerks, copying ledgers and letters by hand. Although they earned less than men, they remained as a regular part of the Washington workforce after the war.

Because of the booming economy and rising prices, many businesses in the North made immense profits. This was especially true of those with government contracts, mostly because such contractors often cheated. They supplied uniforms and blankets made of "shoddy"—fibers reclaimed from rags—that came apart in the rain. They passed off spoiled meat as fresh and demanded twice the usual price for guns. This corruption spilled over into the general society. The New York *Herald* commented on the changes in the American character: "The individual who makes the most money—no matter how—and spends the most—no matter for what—is considered the greatest man. . . . The world has seen its iron age, its silver age, its golden age, and its brazen age. This is the age of shoddy."

As the Northern economy grew, Congress decided to help pay for the war by tapping its citizens' wealth. In 1863 the U.S. government collected the nation's first **income tax,** a tax that takes a specified percentage of the income that an individual earns. This tax ended in 1872. In 1894, when Congress passed another income tax law, the Supreme Court declared it unconstitutional.

Soldiers Suffer on Both Sides

Both Union and Confederate soldiers had marched off to war thinking it would prove to be a glorious affair. They were soon disillusioned, not just by heavy battlefield casualties but also by such unhealthy things as filthy surroundings, a limited diet, and inadequate medical care. In the 1860s, the technology of killing had far outrun the technology of health care.

LIVES ON THE LINES Most soldiers, except when fighting or marching, lived amid heaps of rubbish, spoiled food scraps, and open pits containing human excrement. Garbage disposal in army camps was almost unheard of, and few soldiers bothered to use latrines. Most soldiers had little regard for personal cleanliness. Although army regulations called for washing hands and faces every day and taking a complete bath once a week, many soldiers failed to do so. The soldiers also failed to wash their clothing for weeks at a time. As a result, body lice, dysentery, and diarrhea were common.

THINK THROUGH HISTORY
C. Analyzing Causes Why was the war less damaging to the economy of the North than to that of the South?

C. Answer Military demand spurred the more industrial Northern economy; a manpower shortage and Union occupation crippled the South's agriculture-based economy.

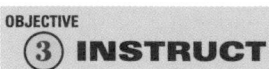
Cooperative Activity: Role-playing Soldiers and Citizens

Task: Pairs of students will role-play a soldier and his close relative and write letters to each other from these two characters' viewpoints.

Purpose: To help students gain a personal perspective of soldiers' and civilians' ordeals during the Civil War.

Activity: Each partner will assume the identity of either a soldier or a family member. Pairs will refer to the text and explore primary

sources for content ideas. Partners will then write and exchange two sets of letters describing their daily lives and commenting on the progress of the war.

📁 **Building a Portfolio:** Remind students to choose their strongest work for their portfolios. If they feel their assignment qualifies, they should place their letters in their portfolios.

ALTERNATIVE ASSESSMENT BOOK
Standards for Evaluating a Cooperative Activity

Standards for Evaluation
Letters should . . .

• be modeled on primary sources from the Civil War
• use specific details about the setting, the events, and the feelings of the participants in the war
• imitate the diction and tone of actual letters

Army food rations were far from appealing. Union troops subsisted on beans, bacon, pickled beef, and hardtack—square biscuits that were supposedly hard enough to stop a bullet. As one Yankee wrote:

> The soldiers' fare is very rough,
> The bread is hard, the beef is tough;
> If they can stand it, it will be,
> Through love of God, a mystery.

Confederate troops fared equally poorly. Their most common food was "cush," a stew of small cubes of beef and crumbled cornbread mixed with bacon grease. Fresh vegetables were hardly ever available. Both sides loved coffee, but Southern soldiers had to make do with substitutes brewed from peanuts, potatoes, dried apples, or corn. Yankees and Rebels alike often ran short of utensils in which to cook food and tableware with which to eat it.

PRISONS If conditions in the army camps were bad, those in war prisons were atrocious. The worst Confederate camp, at **Andersonville,** Georgia, jammed 33,000 men into an area of 26 acres, or about 34 square feet per man. The prisoners had no shelter from the broiling sun or chilling rain except what they made themselves by scratching holes in the dirt and rigging a covering of blankets and sticks. They drank from the same stream that served as their sewer. Twenty-nine percent of Andersonville's prisoners died. Part of the blame rested with the camp's commander, Henry Wirz (whom the North eventually executed as a war criminal). The South's lack of food and tent canvas also contributed to the appalling conditions. In addition, the prisons were overcrowded because the North had halted prisoner exchanges when the South refused to return African-American soldiers who had been captured in battle.

Prison camps in the North—such as those at Elmira, New York, and at Camp Douglas, Illinois—were only slightly better. Northern prisons provided about five times as much space per man, barracks for sleeping, and adequate amounts of food. However, thousands of Confederates, unaccustomed to cold winters and with little or no heat, contracted pneumonia and died. Hundreds of others suffered from dysentery and malnutrition, from which some did not recover. Historians estimate that 15 percent of Yankees in Southern prisons died, while 12 percent of Confederate prisoners died in Northern prisons.

D. Answer Poor sanitation, malnutrition, and exposure caused disease and starvation.

THINK THROUGH HISTORY
D. Analyzing Causes *Why did so many prisoners of war die?*

Wounded Union troops recuperate after battle near makeshift field hospitals.

WORKING TO IMPROVE CONDITIONS Soon after Fort Sumter fell, a group of Northern women and doctors convinced the federal government to set up the United States Sanitary Commission. Its task was twofold: to improve the hygienic conditions of army camps and to recruit and train nurses. The "Sanitary" proved a great success. It sent out agents to teach soldiers such things as how to avoid polluting their water supply. It developed hospital trains and hospital ships to transport wounded men from the battlefield.

Women volunteers held "sanitary fairs" to raise money for medicines and bandages, and some 3,000 women served as army nurses. At the age of 60, Dorothea Dix became the nation's first superintendent of women nurses. To discourage any nurses who were simply looking for romance, Dix insisted that applicants be over 30 and "very plain-looking." About two-thirds of Union nurses were men.

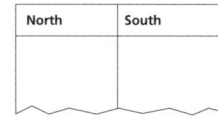
NOW & THEN

BATTLEFIELD MEDICINE
In the Vietnam War (1954–1973) about one in every 400 wounded Americans died. In the Civil War, about one out of six died.

Medical knowledge was extremely limited in the mid-19th century. Doctors knew nothing about bacteria and how they infect the body, so they never sterilized their instruments. Antibiotics were unknown, so the only way to stop gangrene was by amputation. Anesthetics such as chloroform and ether were often in short supply.

Although both the Union and the Confederacy had a special ambulance corps to evacuate the wounded to field hospitals, many wounded died before the horse-drawn carts could get them there.

CLARA BARTON One dedicated Union nurse was **Clara Barton,** who began the war as a clerk in the U.S. Patent Office, the first woman to hold the position. Barton quickly dedicated herself to caring for the sick and wounded, often at the front lines of battle. As a war nurse, she collected and distributed supplies and dug bullets out of soldiers' bodies with her penknife. Barton was particularly good at anticipating troop movements and sometimes arrived at the battlefield with bandages and other supplies before the battle had even begun. After her courage and steadfastness under fire at Antietam, a surgeon described her as the "angel of the battlefield."

As a result of the Sanitary's work and the tireless efforts of people like Clara Barton, the death rate among Union wounded, although terrible by 20th-century standards, showed considerable improvement over previous wars.

The Confederacy did not have a sanitary commission, but thousands of Southern women volunteered for nursing duty. Sally Tompkins, for example, performed so heroically in her hospital duties that she eventually was commissioned as a captain, and Belle Boyd acted as both a nurse and a Confederate spy. Boyd was rumored to have once braved the heat of battle to carry information to Stonewall Jackson himself.

The nation as a whole benefited because women devoted so much time and energy to nursing. A series of battles in the Mississippi Valley and in the East soon sent casualties flooding into Northern and Southern hospitals alike.

Union nurses like Clara Barton, above, and Louisa May Alcott themselves faced the hazards of disease in field hospitals.

Section 3 Assessment

1. TERMS & NAMES
Identify:
• Fort Pillow
• income tax
• Andersonville
• Clara Barton

2. SUMMARIZING In a two-column chart, list the economic changes that occurred in the North and South as a result of the Civil War.

Economic Changes

North	South

Explain how these changes affected each section.

3. COMPARING AND CONTRASTING What effects did the Civil War have on women and African Americans?

THINK ABOUT
• new opportunities in both the North and the South
• discriminatory practices that persisted for both groups

4. SYNTHESIZING Imagine you were one of the Northern women and doctors who convinced the government to establish the Sanitary Commission. What reasons would you have offered to justify this commission? Use details from the text to support your response.

THINK ABOUT
• the health dangers soldiers faced
• the twofold task of the Sanitary Commission

328 CHAPTER 11

ANSWERS

The North Takes Charge

TERMS & NAMES
• Gettysburg
• Chancellorsville
• Vicksburg
• Gettysburg Address
• William Tecumseh Sherman
• Appomattox

LEARN ABOUT the battles and political events of the final two years of the war
TO UNDERSTAND why the Union won the Civil War.

ONE AMERICAN'S STORY

Shortly after three o'clock in the afternoon of July 3, 1863, from behind a stone wall on a ridge south of the little town of Gettysburg, Pennsylvania, Union troops watched thousands of Confederate soldiers advance across an open field. They came steadily, at a pace of about 100 yards a minute. They came silently, neither firing their guns nor giving the usual rebel yell, waiting to do so until they reached the Northerners. Union officer Frank Aretas Haskell described the scene.

A PERSONAL VOICE
More than half a mile their front extends . . . man touching man, rank pressing rank. . . . The red flags wave, their horsemen gallop up and down, the arms of [thirteen] thousand men, barrel and bayonet, gleam in the sun, a sloping forest of flashing steel. Right on they move, as with one soul, in perfect order without impediment of ditch, or wall, or stream, over ridge and slope, through orchard and meadow, and cornfield, magnificent, grim, irresistible.

FRANK ARETAS HASKELL, quoted in *The Civil War* by Geoffrey C. Ward

An hour later, dead and wounded Confederates littered the ground by the thousands. Murderous crossfire from massed Union guns had cut down more than half of the Confederate force. Pickett's charge (named later for its commander, General George E. Pickett) may have been dramatic, but tactically it was out-of-date. Because of the North's heavy weaponry, it had become suicide for unprotected troops to assault a strongly fortified position.

Armies Clash at Gettysburg

Pickett's charge was part of a three-day battle at **Gettysburg,** which many historians consider the turning point of the Civil War. The battle of Gettysburg crippled the South so badly that General Lee would never again invade a Northern state.

PRELUDE TO GETTYSBURG The year 1863 actually had begun well for the South. On December 13 of the preceding year, Lee's army had inflicted a bloody defeat on the Army of the Potomac at Fredericksburg, Virginia, when Union troops under General Ambrose Burnside tried unsuccessfully to storm the Confederate stronghold on the hills of Marye's Heights.

Then, during the first four days of May, the South defeated the North again at **Chancellorsville,** Virginia. Lee outmaneuvered Union general Joseph Hooker (who had replaced Burnside) and forced the Union army to retreat. The North's only consolation after Chancellorsville came as the result of an accident. As General Stonewall Jackson returned from a patrol on May 2, Confederate guards mistook him for a Yankee and shot him in the left arm. A surgeon amputated his arm the following day. When Lee heard the news, he exclaimed, "He has lost his left arm but I have lost my right." For Lee, the true loss was still to

Confederate general George Pickett led a massive infantry attack called Pickett's charge against Union troops at Gettysburg.

The Civil War **329**

OBJECTIVES
1. To describe the battle at Gettysburg and its outcome.
2. To describe Grant's siege of Vicksburg.
3. To summarize key points of the Gettysburg Address.
4. To trace the final events of the war, leading to the surrender at Appomattox.

SKILLBUILDERS
• Understanding geography: movement, pp. 330, 333, 335.
• Understanding geography: location, pp. 330, 333

CRITICAL THINKING
• Analyzing motives, pp. 330, 336
• Recognizing effects, pp. 331, 332, 334
• Summarizing, pp. 333, 337
• Analyzing issues, p. 337
• Evaluating, p. 337

FOCUS & MOTIVATE

▶ *Starting with the Student*
Have students describe incidents reported on the TV news of innocent civilians killed during military conflicts in foreign countries. Ask for students' reactions to these events.

OBJECTIVE
1 **INSTRUCT**

Armies Clash at Gettysburg

▶ *Discussing Key Ideas*
• Lee decides to press north and invade Pennsylvania.
• On the first day of battle at Gettysburg, both armies attempt to position themselves on high ground.
• On the second day, the Union lines hold firm.
• By the close of the third day, both sides have endured staggering losses and Lee's army retreats.

IN-DEPTH RESOURCES: UNIT 3
Guided Reading, p. 40

ACCESS FOR STUDENTS ACQUIRING ENGLISH
Guided Reading (Spanish), p. 113.

Battle of Gettysburg, July 1863

Reading the Map Review the color coding on the map key representing Union and Confederate positions for each day of the battle. Have students reread the portions of the text corresponding to the military maneuvers that occurred on July 1–3 to help them visualize how these map symbols illustrate the daily progression of the battle.

Extension Ask students to figure out the approximate length of the battle area in miles from north to south. *Response: About 4 miles.*

MORE ABOUT . . .
The Rebel Yell

The distinctive rebel yell—a high-pitched combination of a shout and a yelp—was initially heard at the First Battle of Bull Run, when General Stonewall Jackson urged his men to "yell like furies!" After the war's end, a Union veteran described the yell as follows: "There is nothing like it this side of the infernal region. The peculiar corkscrew sensation that it sends down your backbone under these circumstances can never be told. You have to feel it, and if you say you did not feel it, and heard the yell, you have *never* been there."

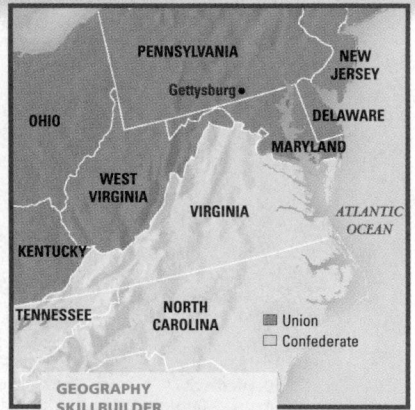

Battle of Gettysburg, July 1863

	July 1	July 2	July 3
Union positions			
Confederate positions			

- ········· Roads
- ╫╫╫╫╫ Railroad
- ➔ Confederate assaults

GEOGRAPHY SKILLBUILDER
MOVEMENT *Which side clearly took the offensive in the battle of Gettysburg?* **LOCATION** *Based on the information in the top map, indicate what factor may have made it easier for reinforcements to enter the Gettysburg area.*

Skillbuilder Answer
Movement: The Confederates took the offensive. **Location:** *Possible Answer:* Roads from many directions converge in the Gettysburg area.

330 CHAPTER 11

come; Jackson caught pneumonia and died May 10.

Despite Jackson's tragic death, Lee decided to press his military advantage and invade the North. He needed supplies, he hoped that an invasion would force Lincoln to pull troops away from Vicksburg, and he thought that a major Confederate victory on Northern soil might tip the political balance of power in the Union to the pro-Southern Copperheads. Accordingly, he crossed the Potomac into Maryland and then pushed on into Pennsylvania.

GETTYSBURG Near the sleepy town of Gettysburg, Pennsylvania, the most decisive battle of the war was fought. To the casual observer, the town seemed like an unlikely spot for a bloody battle—and indeed, no one planned to fight there.

The Battle of Gettysburg began in part because of shoes—or rather, because of a lack of shoes. Confederate soldiers led by A. P. Hill, many of them barefoot, heard there was a supply of footwear in Gettysburg and went to find it, and also to meet up with forces under General Lee. When Hill's troops marched towards Gettysburg, they encountered something other than shoes and Lee. They ran into a couple of brigades of Union cavalry under the command of John Buford, an experienced officer from Illinois, that had arrived one day earlier.

Buford noted that several roads converged on the town and that it was surrounded with hills and ridges. He ordered his men to take defensive positions on the high ground. When Hill's troops marched towards the town from the west, Buford's men were waiting. The shooting attracted more troops and each side sent for reinforcements. By July 2, 90,000 Yankees took the field against 75,000 Confederates.

The Northern armies, now placed under the command of General George Meade, had taken strong defensive positions north and west of Gettysburg but began to fall back under a furious rebel assault. The Confederates succeeded in dislodging these Union troops and took control of the town. As Lee rode along the lines, however, he knew that the battle would not be won unless the Northerners were also forced to yield their positions on Cemetery Ridge, the high ground south of Gettysburg.

THE SECOND DAY On July 2, Lee ordered General James Longstreet to attack Cemetery Ridge, which was held by Union troops. At about 4:00 P.M., Longstreet's troops advanced from Seminary Ridge, where they were positioned in a peach orchard and wheat field that stood between them and most of the Union army on Cemetery Ridge.

The yelling Rebels pushed through Union troops, who had mistakenly left their positions on Little Round Top, a hill that overlooked much of the southern portion of the battlefield. For a time, nothing stood between the rebel soldiers and Little Round Top but a Union signal corps. A brigade of Alabamans attacked Little Round Top. If they had taken the hill and placed artillery upon it, they could have decimated the left flank of the Union lines.

THINK THROUGH HISTORY
A. *Analyzing Motives* What did Lee hope to gain by invading the North?
A. Answer Lee hoped to win a Confederate victory and build Southern support in the North.

TEACHING OPTION

Teaching Less Proficient Readers

Tracking Sequence To help less proficient readers trace the sequence of military actions during the Battle of Gettysburg, put the following set of three flow charts on the board. Then have students fill in the boxes with key events arranged in chronological order.

July 1 Hill's troops run into Union cavalry. → Event → Event → Event

July 2 Lee orders attack of Cemetery Ridge. → Event → Event → Event

July 3 Union forces retake some previous rebel gains. → Event → Event → Event

As the Alabamans approached the hill, however, the Union leaders learned of the exposed hill and sent a brigade to defend it. Union colonel Joshua L. Chamberlain, who had been a language professor before the war, led his Maine troops to meet the rebel attack. The "fighting professor" succeeded in repulsing repeated Confederate attacks, but his men were running out of ammunition and more than a third of the brigade had succumbed to the battle.

While the Rebels organized for yet another assault, Chamberlain ordered his men to fix bayonets and charge at the Confederates in the valley. The Rebels, exhausted by the uphill fighting and the 25-mile march of the previous day, were shocked by the Union assault and surrendered in droves. Chamberlain and his men succeeded in saving the Union lines from certain rebel artillery attacks from Little Round Top. Although the Union troops had been forced to concede some territory, their lines withheld the withering Confederate onslaught of July 2.

THE THIRD DAY   Lee was optimistic, however, that his army had substantially weakened the Northern forces. With one more day of determined attack, he felt he could break the Union defenses. On the morning of July 3, fighting resumed on the north end of the line where, after seven hours, Union forces managed to retake some of the rebel gains from the day before. However, this was just a prelude to the decisive engagement.

In the early afternoon, Lee ordered an artillery barrage on the middle of the Union lines. For two hours, the two armies fired at one another in a vicious exchange that could be heard in Pittsburgh. Thinking the Union artillery had been silenced by the rebel guns, Longstreet ordered his men, including those under the command of General Pickett, to attack the center of the Union lines. Deliberately, they marched across the farmland between their position and the Union high ground. Suddenly, Northern artillery renewed its barrage. Some of the Confederates had nearly reached the Union lines when Yankee infantry fired on them as well. The Union volleys crippled the attackers. Devastated, the Confederates staggered back to their lines. The Northerners had succeeded in holding the high ground south of Gettysburg.

Confederate generals, knowing how badly their forces were hurt, desperately rallied their troops against a Union counterattack that was certain to follow. General Meade, however, never ordered that attack. He did not know how weakened Lee's army was and still feared General James E. B. (Jeb) Stuart's cavalry was loose somewhere behind his lines.

Jeb Stuart's cavalry had missed most of the first two days of fighting, and Lee planned to make the most of them on the third day. Lee sent them circling around the right flank of Meade's forces, hoping they would surprise the Union troops from the rear and meet Longstreet's men in the middle. Stuart's campaign stalled, however, when his men clashed with Union forces under Robert Gregg three miles away.

Unaware that Gregg had stopped Stuart, Meade contented himself with the knowledge that he had turned away a ferocious assault by the victor of Chancellorsville. After the battle, Lee gave up any hopes of invading the North and led his army in a long, painful retreat back to Virginia through a pelting rain.

The three-day battle produced staggering losses. Total casualties were more than 30 percent. Union losses included 23,000

"It's all my fault, my fault."

GEN. ROBERT E. LEE
ON THE FAILURE OF
PICKETT'S CHARGE

This engraving of the Battle of Gettysburg reveals the strategic role that land features can play in determining the outcome of a battle.

Grant Wins at Vicksburg

▶ **Starting with the Student**
Have students cite emergency situations, such as natural disasters, in which people might be forced to evacuate their homes. How do disaster victims cope with the disruption and the constant threat of danger?

▶ **Discussing Key Ideas**
• Grant's troops stage a six-week siege of Vicksburg.
• Grant's victory leads to the splitting of the Confederacy along the Mississippi River.

MORE ABOUT . . .
The Siege of Vicksburg

A few of the hillside caves where civilians hid during the siege were surprisingly homelike. Some of the dugout rooms contained rugs, beds, and chairs. Despite these minor luxuries, most of the makeshift cave dwellers in Vicksburg suffered extreme discomfort. One women remarked, "It was living like plant roots." Another recollected, "We were in hourly dread of snakes. The vines and thickets were full of them."

men killed or wounded; for the Confederacy, 28,000 were killed or wounded. Fly-infested corpses lay everywhere—in the open fields, behind fences, in bushes, streams, and crevices of rock. The stiffened, swollen bodies of dead horses added to the horror. The stench was unbearable.

Despite the devastation on the field, however, Northerners were enthusiastic about the victory. Some had never seen such excitement in the capital. The Army of the Potomac proved its mettle in breaking "the charm of Robert Lee's invincibility." Lee was so depressed after the defeat that he offered his resignation to Jefferson Davis, but Davis refused it. Lee would continue to lead his men brilliantly in the next two years of the war, but neither he nor the Confederacy would ever recover from the loss at Gettysburg—or the surrender of Vicksburg, which occurred the very next day.

THINK THROUGH HISTORY
C. Recognizing Effects Why was the battle of Gettysburg a disaster for the South?

C. Answer It cost a huge number of casualties and put the South on the defensive.

Grant Wins at Vicksburg

While the Army of the Potomac was destroying Confederate hopes in the hilly terrain of central Pennsylvania, Union general Ulysses S. Grant continued his campaign to gain control of the Mississippi River. **Vicksburg** was one of only two Confederate holdouts preventing the Union from taking complete control of the Mississippi, an important waterway for transporting goods. Vicksburg itself was particularly important because it rested on bluffs above the river from which guns could control all water traffic. In the winter of 1862–1863, Grant tried several schemes to reach Vicksburg and take it from the Confederates. Nothing seemed to work—until the spring of 1863.

VICKSBURG UNDER SIEGE In order to weaken Confederate defenses that protected Vicksburg, Grant sent Benjamin Grierson, a former music teacher from Illinois, to lead his cavalry brigade east through the heart of Mississippi. Grierson succeeded in destroying rail lines and distracting Confederate forces from Union infantry working its way toward Vicksburg. Grant was able to land his troops south of Vicksburg late on April 30 and immediately send his men in search of Confederate troops in Mississippi. In 18 days, Union forces whipped several rebel units and sacked Jackson, the capital of the state.

Civilians in Vicksburg dug caves into the hillsides, where they endured a six-week siege by Union troops.

Their confidence growing with every victory, Grant and his troops rushed to Vicksburg, hoping to take the city while the rebels were reeling from their losses. Grant ordered two frontal assaults on the city, neither of which was successful. So, in the last week of May 1863, Grant settled in for a siege. He set up a steady barrage of artillery, shelling the city from both the river and the land for several hours a day and forcing its residents into caves that they dug out of the yellow clay hillsides.

Food supplies ran so low that people ate dogs and mules. A few hardy souls ate fried rats, which they claimed had a flavor "fully equal to that of squirrels." At last some of the starving Confederate soldiers defending Vicksburg sent their commander a petition saying, "If you can't feed us, you had better surrender."

On July 3, 1863, the same day as Pickett's charge, the Confederate commander of Vicksburg asked Grant for terms of surrender. The city fell on July 4. Five days later Port Hudson, Louisiana, the last Confederate holdout on the Mississippi, also fell—and the Confederacy was cut in two. As Lincoln put it, "The Father of Waters again goes unvexed to the sea." In Richmond, the chief of

---

Cooperative Activity: News Accounts of a City Under Siege

Task: Students role-play a team of reporters covering the siege of Vicksburg and write news articles.

Purpose: To heighten students' awareness of civilians' ordeals during wartime.

Activity: Have groups of three to four students research the siege of Vicksburg's impact on civilians. Assuming the identity of a war correspondent, each group member should

choose an angle of the siege to cover. Examples include the extreme psychological stress, the food shortages, and the people's plummeting morale. Group members should review one another's drafts and suggest revisions.

📁 **Building a Portfolio:** Students who think their news accounts represent their strongest work should place them in their portfolios.

ALTERNATIVE ASSESSMENT BOOK
Standards for Evaluating a Cooperative Activity

Standards for Evaluation
News accounts should . . .

• show evidence of research beyond the text
• include vivid details, anecdotes, and factual information
• create a sense of immediacy

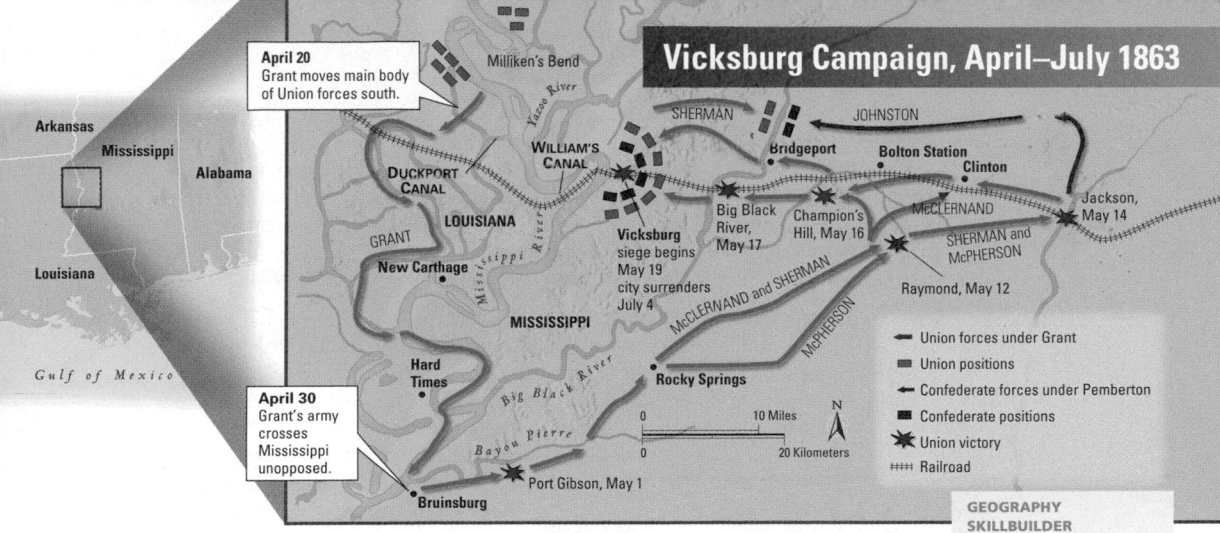

Vicksburg Campaign, April–July 1863

April 20
Grant moves main body of Union forces south.

April 30
Grant's army crosses Mississippi unopposed.

Union forces under Grant
Union positions
Confederate forces under Pemberton
Confederate positions
Union victory
Railroad

0 10 Miles
0 20 Kilometers

Confederate ordnance (ammunition) put it differently, commenting that "the Confederacy totters to its destruction."

The Gettysburg Address

In November 1863, four months after Vicksburg and Gettysburg, the government held a ceremony to dedicate a new national cemetery on the Gettysburg battlefield. The authorities invited Edward Everett, a noted orator, to deliver the main speech at the dedication. When Lincoln accepted a belated invitation to attend, the authorities invited him to add "a few appropriate remarks."

After Everett gave a flowery two-hour oration, Lincoln spoke for a little more than two minutes. According to historian Garry Wills, Lincoln's **Gettysburg Address** "remade America." Before the speech, people said, "The United States *are*." Afterwards, they said, "The United States *is*." In other words, Lincoln's words helped the country to realize that it was not just a collection of individual states; it was a single nation.

GEOGRAPHY SKILLBUILDER
MOVEMENT *How many days did it take Union forces to reach Vicksburg after the victory at Jackson?*
LOCATION *Which river lies just to the east of Vicksburg?*

Skillbuilder Answers
Movement: Five days.
Location: The Big Black River.

THE GETTYSBURG ADDRESS
Fourscore and seven years ago our fathers brought forth on this continent a new nation, conceived in Liberty and dedicated to the proposition that all men are created equal. Now we are engaged in a great civil war, testing whether that nation, or any nation so conceived and so dedicated, can long endure. We are met on a great battlefield of that war. We have come to dedicate a portion of that field, as a final resting-place for those who here gave their lives that that nation might live. It is altogether fitting and proper that we should do this.

But, in a larger sense, we can not dedicate—we can not consecrate—we can not hallow—this ground. The brave men, living and dead, who struggled here, have consecrated it, far above our poor power to add or detract. The world will little note, nor long remember, what we say here, but it can never forget what they did here. It is for us the living, rather, to be dedicated here to the unfinished work which they who fought here have thus far so nobly advanced. It is rather for us to be here dedicated to the great task remaining before us—that from these honored dead we take increased devotion to that cause for which they gave the last full measure of devotion—that we here highly resolve that these dead shall not have died in vain—that this nation, under God, shall have a new birth of freedom—and that government of the people, by the people, for the people, shall not perish from the earth.

ABRAHAM LINCOLN, *The Gettysburg Address*, November 19, 1863

D. Answer That it was one nation rather than just a collection of states, that it was worth dying for, and that it should not be destroyed.

THINK THROUGH HISTORY
D. Summarizing *What beliefs about the United States did Lincoln express in the Gettysburg Address?*

ANOTHER PERSPECTIVE

ON LINCOLN'S SPEECH
At the time of the Gettysburg Address, many dismissed it as a poor speech. Lincoln himself was displeased with his performance. "That speech won't scour," he said afterward. "It's a flat failure."

A writer for the London *Times* also criticized the speech. "The ceremony was rendered ludicrous by . . . the sallies of that poor President Lincoln."

However, Edward Everett, the other speaker, recognized the speech's greatness. Writing to Lincoln, he said, "I should be glad if I could flatter myself that I came as near to the central idea of the occasion, in two hours, as you did in two minutes."

The Civil War **333**

TEACHING OPTIONS

Making Connections Across the Curriculum

Composition In "The Gettysburg Address" Lincoln relies heavily on two rhetorical devices: *antithesis*, or contrast, and *tricolon*, the division of a concept into three rhythmical units. Here are some examples:

• Antithesis—"The brave men, *living* and *dead*, who struggled here, have consecrated it, far above our poor power to *add* or *detract*.
• Tricolon—"government *of the people, by the people, for the people* . . ."

Have students find other examples of these rhetorical devices.

Making Connections Across Time

From Orations to Sound Bites In Lincoln's time public figures typically delivered two-hour, not two-minute, speeches. Speechmaking was then considered a highly valued form of communication. Political rallies, national holidays, and civic events were occasions for local orators to show off their speaking skills. Today's audiences generally admire brevity. They prefer "sound bite" politics—an expression stemming from the short 10-second excerpts that TV news editors "bite" out of a lengthy speech or other broadcast event. Current political leaders tailor their remarks to adapt to this TV format.

The Confederacy Wears Down

▶ **Starting with the Student**
• Factors such as a string of losses, players' injuries, and low attendance at games can damage the morale of a sports team. Ask students what factors they think might contribute to declining morale of troops at war.

▶ **Discussing Key Ideas**
• The desertion of Confederate soldiers and the growth of peace movements reflect the South's deteriorating morale.
• Grant appoints Sherman commander of the Military Division of the Mississippi.
• Grant's attack on Lee's forces in Virginia results in heavy casualties.
• Sherman's march through the South causes widespread destruction.
• The fall of Atlanta contributes to Lincoln's reelection in 1864.
• Lee's surrender to Grant at Appomattox in 1865 marks the end of the Civil War.

KEY PLAYERS
Grant and Lee

Critical Thinking: Compare and Contrast Have students create a two-column chart comparing Grant and Lee. *Possible Headings: Background, Military Career, Leadership Style, Character Traits.*

The Confederacy Wears Down

The twin defeats at Gettysburg and Vicksburg cost the South much of its limited manpower. The Confederacy was already low on food, shoes, uniforms, guns, and ammunition. No longer able to attack, it could hope only to hang on long enough to destroy Northern morale and work toward an armistice. That plan proved increasingly unlikely, partially because Southern newspapers, state legislatures, and individuals began to call openly for peace, and partially because Lincoln finally found not just one but two generals who would fight.

MORALE IN THE CONFEDERACY As the war progressed, morale on the Confederacy's home front deteriorated. Farmers resented the tax that took part of their crops, especially since the property of rich planters—slaves—escaped taxation entirely. Many soldiers deserted after receiving pleading letters from home about the lack of food and the shortage of labor to work the farms. In every Southern state except South Carolina, there were soldiers who decided to fight for the Union army. For example, 2,400 Floridians served in the Union army, and volunteers from Virginia made up the Loudon Rangers.

In the meantime, members of the Confederate Congress squabbled among themselves. Some even resorted to physical attack with everything from fists and inkstands to revolvers and Bowie knives. In South Carolina, the governor was upset when troops from his state were placed under the command of officers from another state. Such discord made it impossible for Jefferson Davis to govern effectively.

In mid-1863, people who wanted peace held more than 100 open meetings in North Carolina. A similar peace movement sprang up in Georgia in early 1864. Although the movements failed, by mid-1864, Assistant Secretary of War John Campbell was forced to acknowledge that active opposition to the war "in the mountain districts of North Carolina, South Carolina, Georgia, and Alabama menaces the existence of the Confederacy as fatally as . . . the armies of the United States."

GRANT APPOINTS SHERMAN In March 1864, President Lincoln appointed Ulysses S. Grant, the hero of the battle at Vicksburg, commander of all Union armies. Grant in turn appointed **William Tecumseh Sherman** as commander of the

THINK THROUGH HISTORY
E. Recognizing Effects How did discontent among members of the Confederate Congress affect the war?

E. Answer Such discontent kept Jefferson Davis from governing effectively, which weakened the Confederate war strategy.

KEY PLAYERS

ULYSSES S. GRANT
1822–1885

U. S. Grant took a long time to discover himself—just about as long as it took the rest of the world to figure out who he was. Born Hiram Ulysses Grant, he allowed a clerk at West Point to record his name incorrectly as Ulysses Simpson Grant. Thereafter, he went by the name U.S. Grant.

Grant once said of himself, "A military life held no charms for me." Yet, a military man was what he was destined to be. He fought in the war with Mexico—even though he termed it "wicked"— because he believed his duty was to serve his country. His next post was on the Pacific, where Grant grew so lonely for his family that he resigned.

When the Civil War broke out, the Illinois governor made Grant a colonel of volunteers because the federal government didn't want him! However, once Grant began fighting in Tennessee, Lincoln was quick to recognize his special strength. When newspapers demanded Grant's dismissal after Shiloh, Lincoln replied firmly, "I can't spare this man. He *fights.*"

ROBERT E. LEE
1807–1870

Lee was an aristocrat, related to some of Virginia's leading families. In fact, his father, Light-Horse Harry Lee, had been one of George Washington's best generals, and his wife was the granddaughter of Martha Washington. His sense of family honor may have contributed to his allegiance to his state. As a man who never owned a slave and who freed those that his wife inherited, Lee fought for the Confederacy only because of his loyalty to his beloved Virginia. "I did only what my duty demanded. I could have taken no other course without dishonor," he said.

As a general, Robert E. Lee was tactically brilliant, but he seldom challenged Confederate civilian leaders about their failure to provide his army with adequate food, clothing, or weapons. On the other hand, his soldiers almost worshiped him because he never abused them and always insisted on sharing their hardships. To his men, he was "Uncle Robert," just as in the North, the Union troops called Grant "Uncle Sam."

Making Connections Across Time

1960s Peace Movement In the 1960s, the increasing unpopularity of the Vietnam War also spurred an antiwar movement. Broadway staged antiwar musicals, and folk singers and rock stars composed antiwar lyrics. College students nationwide participated in sit-ins, strikes, and marches. Backers of the peace movement came from a wide range of backgrounds. Many people who opposed U.S. military involvement in Vietnam believed that the United States was unjustifiably intervening in a civil war, not unlike the nation's own Civil War fought a century earlier.

As the Vietnam War progressed, President Johnson's administration was concerned with how the growing protest movement sharply divided the American public into supporters and opponents. Cyrus Vance, who was a member of Johnson's informal advisory group eventually known as the Wise Men, remarked later, "We were weighing not only what was happening in Vietnam, but the social and political effects in the United States, the impact on the U.S. economy, the attitudes of other nations. The divisiveness in the country was growing with such acuteness that it was threatening to tear the United States apart."

Civil War, 1863–1865

New York
PENNSYLVANIA
NEW JERSEY
ILLINOIS
INDIANA OHIO
Philadelphia
DELAWARE
Washington, D.C.
MARYLAND
Richmond
Charleston
MISSOURI
KENTUCKY
AREA OF INSET
Nashville,
Dec. 16, 1864 ★ TENNESSEE
Raleigh,
Apr. 13, 1865
NORTH CAROLINA
Chattanooga–Lookout
Mountain, Nov. 25, 1863 ★ Wilmington,
Chickamauga, Sept. 20, 1863 Feb. 22, 1865
Memphis
ARKANSAS
Atlanta, Sept. 2, 1864 SOUTH
CAROLINA
ALABAMA
MISSISSIPPI Montgomery
Savannah, Dec. 22,
1864
GEORGIA
LOUISIANA
ATLANTIC
OCEAN
Mobile
TEXAS
Pensacola
Mobile Bay,
Aug. 5, 1864 FLORIDA
New Orleans

Gulf
of Mexico

0   200 Miles
0   400 Kilometers

Union Blockade
Union Blockade

Inset map
MARYLAND
Washington, D.C.
Wilderness,
May 6, 1864
VIRGINIA
Spotsylvania,
May 12, 1864
Richmond
Appomattox
Courthouse,
Apr. 9, 1865–
Lee surrenders
to Grant
Cold Harbor,
June, 1864
Petersburg,
June 1864– April 1865

United States
Confederate States
Occupied by
Union 1865
Union forces
Confederate forces
★ Union victory
★ Confederate victory
▲▲▲ Union blockade

GEOGRAPHY SKILLBUILDER
MOVEMENT *What route did General Sherman and his troops follow from Chattanooga?* **MOVEMENT** *From what battle did Grant and Lee go to Appomattox?*

Skillbuilder Answers
Movement: They went to Atlanta; then Savannah, Georgia; and then north to Raleigh, North Carolina.
Movement: Petersburg.

Military Division of the Mississippi. These two appointments would change the course of the war.

Old friends and comrades in arms, both men believed in total war. They shared the conviction that not only was it necessary to fight the South's armies and government, but it was essential to fight its civilian population as well. They reasoned that, first, civilians produced the weapons, grew the food, and transported the goods on which the armies relied. Second, the strength of the people's will kept the war going. If the Union destroyed that will to fight, the Confederacy would collapse.

GRANT AND LEE IN VIRGINIA Grant's overall strategy was to grind up Lee's army in Virginia while Sherman raided Georgia. Grant's basic tactic was to attack and then attack again. Even if his casualties ran twice as high as those of Lee—and they did—the North could afford it. The South could not.

Starting in May 1864, Grant threw his troops into battle after battle, the first in a wooded area known as the Wilderness near Fredericksburg, Virginia. The fighting was brutal, made even more so by fire spreading through the thick trees. The string of battles continued at Spotsylvania, Cold Harbor (where Grant lost 7,000 men in one hour), and finally Petersburg, which would remain under Union attack from June 1864, nearly to the war's end.

During the period from May 4 to June 18, 1864, Grant lost 65,000 men—which the North could replace—to Lee's 35,000 men—which the South could not replace. Democrats and Northern newspapers called Grant a butcher. Future Supreme Court justice Oliver Wendell Holmes, then a Union lieutenant, commented in a letter about how "immense the butcher's bill has been." However, Grant kept going because he had promised Lincoln, "Whatever happens, there will be no turning back."

SHERMAN'S MARCH In the meantime, Sherman moved south toward the transportation center of Atlanta. After he occupied it on September 2, 1864, a Confederate army tried to circle around him and cut his railroad supply lines. Instead of waiting for the

"Atlanta is ours."

WILLIAM TECUMSEH SHERMAN

HISTORY FROM VISUALS
Civil War, 1863–1865
Reading the Map Emphasize the close distance between Washington, D.C., and Richmond, Virginia, as shown on the inset. Also point out the parallel movements of Union and Confederate forces in the vicinity of the capitals during the final two years of the Civil War.

Extension Ask students to describe the path of Sherman's march. *Response: Southeast through Georgia to the Atlantic coast.*

MORE ABOUT . . .
Sherman on War
Before burning Atlanta, Sherman ordered its citizens evacuated. The mayor of Atlanta wrote a letter of protest, to which Sherman replied that war is inherently cruel and cannot be changed into something humane. "The only way the people of Atlanta can hope once more to live in peace and quiet at home, is to stop the war, which can only be done by admitting that it began in error and is perpetuated in pride. We don't want . . . your lands, or any thing you have, but we do want and will have a just obedience to the laws of the United States."

IN-DEPTH RESOURCES: UNIT 3
Primary Sources: On the Burning of Columbia, South Carolina, p. 50

 ELECTRONIC LIBRARY OF PRIMARY SOURCES
from a Letter to General Hood by General Sherman
from a Letter to General Sherman by General Hood

TEACHING OPTIONS

Making Connections Across Time

Military Tactics Civil War historian Bruce Catton offered these observations on total war: "In the Civil War it was all or nothing. . . . Once a little blood had been shed, there was no halfway point at which the two sides could get together and compromise. . . . If you are fighting a total war, the enemy's army is not your own target. What you are really shooting for is the ability to carry on the fight. This means you will hit wherever you can with any weapon that comes into your hand." The Civil War set the stage for the way the two world wars in the twentieth century would be waged: Both military and civilian populations participated.

Making Connections Across the Curriculum

Journalism The telegraph, invented in 1844, had its greatest effect on news reporting during the Civil War. Journalists covering battle sites, such as Fredericksburg, Spotsylvania, and Petersburg, relayed their accounts by telegraph. Because technical difficulties sometimes occurred while transmitting their stories, journalists tried to report the outcome of the battle first and then describe the events more concisely. This approach to newswriting was the forerunner of the form called the *inverted pyramid,* in which the lead sentence summarizes the most important point of the story.

MORE ABOUT . . .

The 1864 Election Campaign

Mudslinging in presidential campaigns is nothing new. In 1864, McClellan's partisans hurled such epithets at Lincoln as "filthy storyteller, despot, liar, robber, swindler, buffoon, and Ignoramus Abe." Even more vicious was the accusation that the President had laughed and joked during a visit to Antietam shortly after the bloody battle there. A close Lincoln supporter urged him to issue a denial. Lincoln, however, told his supporter to "let the thing alone" and added: "If I have not established character enough to give the lie to this charge, I can only say that I am mistaken in my own estimate of myself. In politics, every man must skin his own skunk. These fellows are welcome to the hide of this one. Its body has already given forth its unsavory odor."

GROLIER MULTIMEDIA ENCYCLOPEDIA
Lincoln's Inaugural Addresses

Columbia, South Carolina, experienced some of the war's worst destruction, as this 1865 photograph shows.

Confederate army to attack, Sherman decided to take the offensive. He would abandon his supply lines and march southeast through Georgia to the sea, creating a wide path of destruction and living off the land as he went. He would make Southerners "so sick of war that generations would pass away before they would again appeal to it." In mid-November he burned most of Atlanta and set out toward the coast. A Georgia girl named Eliza Frances Andrews described the result.

A PERSONAL VOICE
About three miles from Sparta we struck the "burnt country." . . . The fields were trampled down and the road was lined with carcasses of horses, hogs, and cattle that the invaders, unable either to consume or to carry away with them, had wantonly shot down, to starve out the people and prevent them from making their crops. . . . The dwellings that were standing all showed signs of pillage . . . while here and there lone chimney stacks, "Sherman's sentinels," told of homes laid in ashes.

ELIZA FRANCES ANDREWS, quoted in *Voices from the Civil War*

After reaching the ocean and taking Savannah just before Christmas, Sherman's troops turned north to help Grant "wipe out Lee." Following behind them now were about 25,000 former slaves eager for freedom. As the army marched through South Carolina in 1865, it inflicted even more destruction than it had in Georgia. As an Ohio private explained, "Here is where treason *began* and, by God, here is where it shall end!" The army burned almost every house in its path. In contrast, when Sherman's forces entered North Carolina, which had been the last state to secede, they stopped destroying private homes and—anticipating that the end of the war was near—instead began handing out food and other supplies to people they encountered.

THE ELECTION OF 1864 Despite the war, politics in the Union went on as usual. As the 1864 presidential election approached, Lincoln faced heavy opposition from two directions, the Democrats and factions within his own party. Many Democrats, dismayed at the war's length, its high casualty rates, and recent Union losses, joined pro-Southern Copperheads to nominate George McClellan on a platform of an immediate armistice. Still resentful over having been fired by Lincoln, McClellan was delighted to run.

Lincoln's other opponents, the radical Republicans, were harsher in their proposals on how to readmit the Confederate states to the Union at war's end. They formed a third political party and nominated John C. Frémont as their candidate. To attract Democrats, Lincoln's supporters dropped the Republican name, retitled themselves the National Union Party, and chose Andrew Johnson, a pro-Union Democrat from Tennessee, as Lincoln's running mate.

Lincoln was pessimistic about his chances. "I am going to be beaten," he said in August, "and unless some great change takes place, *badly* beaten." However, some great change did take place. On August 5, Admiral David Farragut entered Mobile Bay in Alabama and closed this major Southern port. On September 2, Sherman telegraphed, "Atlanta is ours." By month's end, Frémont withdrew from the presidential race. On October 18, 1864, General Philip Sheridan finally

THINK THROUGH HISTORY
F. Analyzing Motives What were Sherman's objectives in marching his troops from Atlanta to Savannah?

F. Answer Sherman wanted to show Georgia's civilians the destructive nature of war and thus destroy the will of Confederate civilians to continue the war.

TEACHING OPTION

Teaching Gifted and Talented Students

Researching the Election of 1864 Ask students to investigate the election of 1864. Students should identify the candidates, the political parties they represented, the events that influenced the election, and the final outcome. The research should include the final figures of the popular and electoral vote:

• Abraham Lincoln—212 electoral votes; 2,206,938 popular votes.

• George McClellan—21 electoral votes; 1,803,787 popular votes.

Encourage students to use charts and graphs to report their findings. For example, they may wish to create bar graphs showing the number of electoral and popular votes each candidate received and circle graphs to show the percentages of electoral and popular votes.

chased the Confederates out of Shenandoah Valley in northern Virginia. The victories buoyed the North, and with the help of absentee ballots cast by Union soldiers, Lincoln won a second term with 54 percent of the popular vote.

THE SURRENDER AT APPOMATTOX   By late March 1865, it was clear that the end of the Confederacy was near. Grant and Sheridan were approaching Richmond from the west, while Sherman was approaching from the south. On April 2—in response to news that Lee and his troops had been overcome by Grant's forces at Petersburg—President Davis and his government abandoned their capital, setting it afire to keep the Yankees from taking it. Union troops entered Richmond the following day and immediately went to work fighting fires. Despite their efforts to extinguish the flames, fire destroyed some 900 buildings and damaged hundreds more.

On April 9, 1865, at a farmhouse near **Appomattox** Courthouse, Lee and Grant met to arrange a Confederate surrender. The terms were generous. Lincoln did not want to impose harsh terms on the Confederates, so Grant paroled Lee's soldiers and sent them home with their personal possessions, horses, and three days worth of rations. Officers were permitted to keep their sidearms. Within a month all remaining Confederate resistance collapsed.

After four long years, the Civil War was over—but what were its human and economic costs? How did it change the lives of those who took part in it?

G. Answer He wanted to bring the South back into the Union as smoothly as possible.

THINK THROUGH HISTORY
G. Analyzing Motives Why do you think Lincoln didn't want to punish the Confederacy?

Thomas Lovell's *Surrender at Appomattox* is a modern rendering of Lee's surrender to Grant in McLean's farmhouse. This is Lovell's version of the scene—no photographs of the event exist.

Section 4 Assessment

1. TERMS & NAMES

Identify:
- Gettysburg
- Chancellorsville
- Vicksburg
- Gettysburg Address
- William Tecumseh Sherman
- Appomattox

2. SUMMARIZING Create a time line of the major battles and political events relating to the final two-and-a-half years of the Civil War. Use the dates already plotted on the time line below as a guide.

```
|---------|---------|---------|
  May      March     April
  1863     1864      1865
```

Choose one event that was the turning point and explain why.

3. ANALYZING ISSUES Grant and Sherman presented a logical rationale for using the strategy of total war. Do you think the end—defeating the Confederacy—justified the means—causing harm to civilians? Explain.

THINK ABOUT
- their reasons for targeting the civilian population
- Sherman's quoted remarks about his march to Georgia
- Eliza Frances Andrews's observations about Sherman's march

4. EVALUATING Do you think that a general's win-loss record on the battlefield is the best gauge of measuring his greatness as a military leader? Why or why not?

THINK ABOUT
- Grant's campaign in Virginia, Sherman's march to Atlanta, and Lee's surrender
- Democrats' and Northern newspapers' criticism of Grant
- the criteria you would use to evaluate a military leader

The Civil War **337**

ANSWERS

1. TERMS & NAMES

Gettysburg, p. 329

Chancellorsville, p. 329

Vicksburg, p. 332

Gettysburg Address, p. 333

William Tecumseh Sherman, p. 334

Appomattox, p. 337

2. SUMMARIZING

Possible Responses: May (1863)—South defeats North at Chancellorsville. July (1863)—North defeats South at Gettysburg and Vicksburg. November (1863)—Lincoln delivers Gettysburg Address. March (1864)—Lincoln appoints Grant commander of Union armies. September (1864)—Sherman takes Atlanta. April (1865)—Lee surrenders at Appomattox. Students' choices of turning points will vary.

3. ANALYZING ISSUES

Possible Responses: Students who think that the end does justify the means might say that winning the war and abolishing slavery is worth the cost of civilian lives. Students who think that the end does not justify the means might cite that the killing of defenseless citizens in any war is immoral.

4. EVALUATING

Possible Responses: Yes—It is the best gauge because it objectively measures a general's success or failure as a military commander. No—Other criteria such as character and skills as a military strategist are equally important measures of a general's military greatness. Students should support their opinions with details from the text.

ASSESS & RETEACH

Section Assessment

Assign pairs of students to help each other answer the questions.

Self-Assessment

Have students reread the events plotted on the time lines they created for Item 2. Ask them to identify the events they find hard to understand and why.

Section Quiz

FORMAL ASSESSMENT
Section Quiz, p. 140

Reteach

Use the Guided Reading Worksheet for Section 4 to help review the main ideas of the section.

IN-DEPTH RESOURCES: UNIT 3
Guided Reading, p. 40

CLOSE

The Civil War ended with the surrender at Appomattox in April 1865. The task of reflecting on the horrible toll of the war and healing the nation loomed ahead.

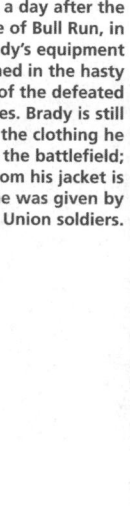

Civil War Photography

Civil War Photography

OBJECTIVES

(1) To describe photography in the Civil War era.

(2) To explain the role that Mathew Brady and other early photographers played in chronicling the war.

Photography was still in its infancy at the time of the Civil War. A complex process, it required lengthy preparation before a shot was taken, and the photograph was developed afterward on the site. Nevertheless, America's first news photographers were able to capture the fighting for the home audience with a shocking reality never before achieved.

The best known of these early photographers was Mathew Brady, who had already won fame with portraits of the rich and famous taken by him or his staff at his studios in New York City and Washington, D.C. During the war, Brady traveled with the Union army and recorded with grim accuracy the battle-torn landscapes and weary participants of this tragic episode of American history.

BRADY ON SITE This photo of Brady was taken on July 22, 1861, a day after the First Battle of Bull Run, in which Brady's equipment was smashed in the hasty retreat of the defeated Union forces. Brady is still dressed in the clothing he wore on the battlefield; protruding from his jacket is the sword he was given by Union soldiers.

FOCUS & MOTIVATE

Starting with the Student

Ask students why they consider photographs or homemade videos important.

- What sorts of events inspire pictures, and what role do they later play in people's lives?
- Might news photos or videos play a similar role in the history of a nation? Explain.

MORE ABOUT . . .
Mathew Brady

Brady learned the basics of photography from Samuel F. B. Morse of telegraph fame and opened his first studio in New York City in 1844. Soon he began to photograph the celebrities of his day, taking pictures of such well-known figures as politician Daniel Webster and writer Edgar Allan Poe. His efforts to photograph the Civil War led to financial ruin when the U.S. government at first failed to recompense him as he had anticipated. Brady also suffered from financial woes because his best photographers invariably left his employ when he refused to credit their efforts.

EQUIPMENT Early cameras like this one were clumsy to carry and required a stand or tripod. At first, photographers produced shiny images on copper plates, called daguerreotypes after their French inventor, Louis Daguerre. By the 1860s, however, Brady and other photographers were using the collodion process, which captured a negative image used to produce multiple prints.

338 CHAPTER 11

RECOMMENDED RESOURCES

Books

Catton, Bruce. *The American Heritage Picture History of the Civil War.* New York: American Heritage, 1960. A 2-volume pictorial history.

Meredith, Roy. *Mathew Brady's Portrait of an Era.* New York: Norton, 1982. Brady's photos of mid-19th-century life.

Neely, Mark E., et al. *The Confederate Image: Prints of a Lost Cause.* Chapel Hill: U of North Carolina P, 1987. Images from the Confederate point of view.

Ward, Geoffrey C. *The Civil War: An Illustrated History.* New York: Knopf, 1990. The companion volume to the Ken Burns/PBS miniseries, featuring many Brady photos.

Videos

The Civil War. Ambrose Video Publishing, 1991. Documentary narrated by news anchor Tom Brokaw.

Civil War Journal. Guidance Associates. A 6-video collection showing the human side of war.

Civil War Journal. 1993, 1994. Two sets of videocassettes narrated by anchor Danny Glover.

Software

The Illustrated Civil War. IT Makers. Historic illustrations and text.

PORTABLE DARKROOM Since early photographs required lengthy preparation and immediate development, Brady and his assistants had to travel with their own darkroom wagons, like the one shown here. The wagons became known as Brady's "What's It Wagons" because, when soldiers saw one for the first time, someone always asked, "What's it?"

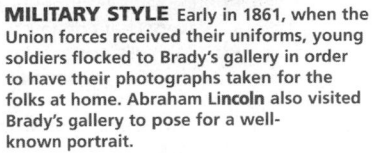

MILITARY STYLE Early in 1861, when the Union forces received their uniforms, young soldiers flocked to Brady's gallery in order to have their photographs taken for the folks at home. Abraham Lincoln also visited Brady's gallery to pose for a well-known portrait.

FAMILY CAMP It was not uncommon for soldiers to bring their entire families to camp, as this scene of the 31st Pennsylvania Regiment reveals. Some officers even brought along servants. Such privileges grew scarcer as the war progressed.

INTERACT WITH HISTORY

1. **RECOGNIZING EFFECTS** What effects do you think the development of photography, with its realistic images, had on American public opinion during the Civil War? Why?

    SEE SKILLBUILDER HANDBOOK, PAGE 1040.

2. **CREATING A PHOTO GALLERY** Create your own photographic gallery of an event of local or national importance. You might take your own photographs, or you might clip and display photos from newspapers, magazines, and other sources. In either case, be sure to include a brief caption describing each shot and explaining its significance.

   INTERNET For more about the Civil War, click on *Social Studies* at http://www.mcdougallittell.com

The Civil War **339**

❺ The Legacy of the War

LEARN ABOUT the economic, political, military, and social consequences of the Civil War
TO UNDERSTAND why historians consider the Civil War a crucial turning point in U.S. history.

ONE AMERICAN'S STORY

Garland White, a former slave from Virginia, was one of the Yankee soldiers who marched into Richmond after it fell. White, chaplain of the 28th United States Colored troops, was returning to the state where he had once served in bondage. As the soldiers marched along the city streets, thousands of African Americans cheered. A large crowd of soldiers and civilians gathered in the neighborhood where the slave market had been. Garland White remembered the scene.

A PERSONAL VOICE
I marched at the head of the column, and soon I found myself called upon by the officers and men of my regiment to make a speech, with which, of course, I readily complied. A vast multitude assembled on Broad Street, and I was aroused amid the shouts of 10,000 voices, and proclaimed for the first time in that city freedom to all [humankind].

GARLAND H. WHITE, quoted in *Been in the Storm So Long*

In a nearby building, several African Americans remained behind bars because a slave trader named Robert Lumpkin had not been able to sell them before Richmond's fall. Hearing White's announcement, these slaves began to chant "Slavery chain done broke at last!" The soldiers opened their cells and set them free. Chaplain White began to cry with joy and was unable to continue speaking. Several hours later, he had an even greater reason to rejoice. He found his mother, after a separation of some 20 years.

Freedom for slaves was not the only legacy of the Civil War. The struggle transformed the nation's economy, its government, the conduct of warfare, and the future careers of many of its participants.

Union troops in the South sometimes came upon slave markets like this one in Atlanta.

The War Changes the Nation

In 1869 Professor George Ticknor of Harvard commented that since the Civil War, "It does not seem to me as if I were living in the country in which I was born." The Civil War caused tremendous political, economic, technological, and social change in the United States. It also exacted a high price in the cost of human life.

POLITICAL CHANGES The United States underwent great political change because of the Civil War. Decades before the war began, Southern states had used the threat of secession when federal policies angered them. After the war, the federal government assumed supreme national authority and no state ever threatened secession again. As a political theory, the states' rights issue did not go away; it simply led in a different direction than secession. Late 20th century arguments about states' rights versus federal control focus on such issues as whether the state or national government should determine how to use local resources.

THINK THROUGH HISTORY
A. Recognizing Effects How did the power of the federal government increase during the war?

A. Answer The government passed laws that gave it more control over U.S. citizens, including an income tax and conscription.

In addition to ending the threat of secession, the war greatly increased the federal government's power. Before the Civil War, the federal government had little impact on most people's daily lives. Most citizens dealt only with their local governments. During the war, however, the federal government passed laws that gave it much more control over individual citizens. The government reached into people's pockets by taxing private incomes, required everyone to accept its new paper currency (even those who had previously contracted to be repaid in coins), and tore reluctant men from their families to fight in the war. After the war, U.S. citizens could no longer assume that the national government in Washington was too far away to bother with them.

ECONOMIC CHANGES The Civil War had a profound impact on the nation's economy. Between 1861 and 1865, the federal government did much to help business, in part through subsidizing construction of a national railroad system. The government also passed the National Bank Act of 1863, which set up a system of federally chartered banks, the first such banks since the Second Bank of the United States had expired in 1836. The act also set requirements for loans and provided for banks to be inspected. These measures helped to make the banking system safer for investors.

The effect of the war on American industry was mixed. While some industries experienced a decline in production, others flourished. For example, the cotton textile industry showed a 74 percent decline in production, while war-related industries like firearms, woolens, and wagon building grew right from the start of the war. Production levels for some industries, including iron and coal mining, dropped early in the war, but eventually caught up and even surpassed expected levels of growth by the war's end.

Furthermore, the government's purchase of massive amounts of wartime supplies had opened up all sorts of opportunities for entrepreneurs. Many government suppliers grew rich and thus had money to invest in new businesses after the war was over. The economy of the Northern states boomed. By war's end, the North had produced more coal, iron, merchant ships, and other products than the entire country had in 1860.

The war devastated the South economically. It not only marked the end of slavery as a labor system, but it also wrecked most of the region's industry, wiped out 40 percent of the livestock, destroyed much of the South's farm machinery and railroads, and left thousands of acres of uncultivated farmland in weeds.

B. Answer The gap widened because the North's economy grew as a result of the war, while the South's economy was nearly destroyed due to the end of slavery and the damage to the region's industry.

THINK THROUGH HISTORY
B. Analyzing Issues How did the war widen the economic gap between the North and the South?

The economic gap between North and South had widened drastically. Before the war, Southern states held 30 percent of the national wealth; in 1870 they held only 12 percent. In 1860, Southerners earned about 70 percent of the Northern average; in

Though both Union and Confederate soldiers were lucky to escape the war with their lives, thousands—like this young amputee—faced an uncertain future.

The Costs of the Civil War

CASUALTIES

Bar graph: Casualties (in thousands), vertical axis labeled 0, 100, 200, 300, 400, 500, 600, 700, 800.
- Civil War (Union and Confederacy)
- All Other U.S. Wars

■ Union
■ Confederacy

ECONOMIC COSTS

- Federal loans and taxes to finance the war totaled $2.6 billion.
- Taxes brought in another $667 million.
- Federal debt on June 30, 1865 rose to $2.7 billion.
- Confederate debt ran over $700 million.
- Union inflation reached 182% in 1864 and 179% in 1865.
- Confederate inflation rose to 9,000% by the end of the war.

Sources: *The World Book Encyclopedia; Historical Statistics of the United States: Colonial times to 1970; The United States Civil War Center*

SKILLBUILDER INTERPRETING GRAPHS *Based on the bar graph, how did the combined Union and Confederate losses compare with those of other wars? Why was inflation worse in the Confederacy than in the Union?*

The Civil War **341**

HISTORICAL SPOTLIGHT

THE *MONITOR* AND THE *MERRIMACK*

A Union ship, the *Merrimack,* had sunk off the coast of Virginia. The Confederates recovered the ship and renamed it the *Virginia,* though the Union continued to use the ship's original name.

In the fall of 1861, Confederate secretary of the navy Stephen R. Mallory put engineers to work bolting iron plates onto the steam frigate. When Union secretary of the navy Gideon Welles heard about it, he asked naval engineer John Ericsson for help. Ericsson designed and built a ship, the *Monitor,* that resembled a "gigantic cheese box" on "an immense shingle," with two guns mounted on a revolving turret.

On March 8, 1862, the *Merrimack/Virginia* single-handedly attacked three wooden Union warships, sinking the first, burning the second, and driving the third aground.

On March 9, the *Monitor* arrived, and the two ironclads hammered away at each other until the *Merrimack* backed off. Although the fight was a draw, naval warfare was never the same again. The era of wooden fighting ships was over.

1870, they earned less than 40 percent. This economic disparity between the regions would not diminish until the 20th century.

COSTS OF THE WAR The human costs of the Civil War were staggering. They affected almost every American family.

Approximately 360,000 Union soldiers and 260,000 Confederates died, nearly as many as in all other American wars combined. Another 275,000 Federals and 260,000 Rebels were wounded. For years, armless and legless veterans were a common sight on the nation's streets and roads. One soldier was killed or wounded for every four slaves who became free. In addition, the war occupied the lives of some 3,000,000 men—nearly 10 percent of the nation's population of 31,000,000—for four long years. It disrupted their education, their careers, and their families.

The Civil War's economic costs were likewise staggering. Historians estimate that the Union and the Confederate governments combined spent about $20 billion during the four years of war, or five times what the government had spent in the previous 80 years! The costs did not stop when the war ended. Twenty years later, interest payments on the war debt plus veterans' pensions still accounted for almost two-thirds of the federal budget.

A REVOLUTION IN WARFARE The Civil War was one of the first modern wars. During the war, advances in technology made the machinery of warfare important for victory. The two deadliest technological improvements were the rifle and the minie ball. Rifles were more accurate than old-fashioned muskets, because grooves inside the barrel forced the bullet to spin at a great speed, which made it fly straighter and farther. In addition, by the end of the war, both sides were using long-range breech-loading rifles, which means the guns were loaded near the end of the barrel, not the muzzle. Soldiers could load these rifles much more quickly and therefore fire more rounds during battle. The minie ball was a soft lead bullet that was more destructive than earlier bullets and contributed to a higher casualty rate.

Because of the changes in technology, military strategy had to change. As Pickett's charge demonstrated in 1863, massed assaults on fortified positions were no longer effective. The accuracy of the long-range rifles made the old-fashioned cavalry charge obsolete. Horses became nearly useless except to carry supplies.

The *Monitor* and the *Merrimack,* depicted in this 1891 painting by J. G. Tanner, fought the first battle of ironclad ships on March 9, 1862.

342

At the top of the page:

The new rifle proved to be an effective and deadly weapon.

C. Answer More accurate weapons ended reliance on unprotected infantry charges and started the use of trench warfare. Ironclad ships made wooden navies obsolete.

THINK THROUGH HISTORY
C. Recognizing Effects How did technology affect military strategy during the Civil War?

At Petersburg the next summer, the two sides engaged in trench warfare, living in trenches for ten months, lobbing shells at each other, and hoping for a break in the enemy lines or perhaps even a surrender. The new rifle plus the new bullet killed far more people than older weapons, giving entrenched defenders a great advantage in mass infantry attacks. Trench warfare would be used again in World War I, early in the 20th century. Grant and Sherman's tactic of total war also foreshadowed the military strategies of the 20th century, in which two world wars inflicted massive suffering on civilians.

Two other modern weapons used in the Civil War were hand grenades and land mines. Another technological improvement was the ironclad ship, which could splinter wooden ships, withstand cannon fire, and resist burning. Grant used four ironclad ships when he captured Forts Henry and Donelson. On March 9, 1862, every navy in the world became obsolete after the North's ironclad **Monitor** traded broadsides with the South's ironclad **Merrimack.** Although the battle ended in a draw, it signaled the end of wooden warships.

The War Changes Lives

The war not only revolutionized weaponry and military tactics, but it changed individual lives. Perhaps the biggest change came for African Americans.

NEW BIRTH OF FREEDOM The Emancipation Proclamation, which Lincoln had issued under his war powers, freed only those slaves who lived in the rebelling states. The government had to decide what to do about the border states, where slavery still existed.

The president believed that the only solution was a constitutional amendment abolishing slavery. The Republican-controlled Senate approved an amendment in the summer of 1864, but the House, with its large Democratic membership, did not. After Lincoln's reelection, the amendment was reintroduced in the House in January of 1865. This time the administration convinced a few Democrats to vote in favor of the amendment with promises of government jobs after they left office. The amendment passed with two votes to spare. Spectators—many of them African Americans who were now allowed to sit in the congressional galleries—burst into cheers, while Republicans on the floor shouted in triumph.

By year's end 27 states, including eight from the South, had ratified the **Thirteenth Amendment.** The U.S. Constitution now stated that "Neither slavery nor involuntary servitude, except as a punishment for crime whereof the party shall have been duly convicted, shall exist within the United States."

LEADERS RETURN TO CIVILIAN LIFE After the war ended, military leaders in both the North and the South had to find new directions for their lives.

George McClellan retired to Europe for three years. He liked Europe, he explained, because no one there told lies about him. He then came back to the United States and, after serving as chief engineer in New York City's Department of Docks, won the 1878 election for governor of New Jersey. He died in 1885.

Former slaves, like the four-generation family shown here, celebrated the passage of the Thirteenth Amendment, which abolished slavery.

The Civil War **343**

OBJECTIVE
2 INSTRUCT

The War Changes Lives

▶ **Starting with the Student**
- Ask students what they know about the kinds of problems war veterans face when they return to civilian life.
- Have them discuss why this transition is often so difficult.

▶ **Discussing Key Ideas**
- The Thirteenth Amendment abolishes slavery.
- Civil War veterans adapt to civilian life.
- Lincoln is assassinated in 1865.

MORE ABOUT . . .
Confederates in Exile
Following the Civil War, some 10,000 political and military leaders of the Confederacy left the United States for foreign lands. The largest group—about 4,000—fled to Brazil. The second largest group settled in Mexico. British Honduras (now known as Belize) provided a haven for some 200 former Confederate soldiers, who developed splendid plantations there. About three-quarters of the Confederates who went into exile returned to the United States after President Andrew Johnson's Christmas pardons in 1868. About 2,500, however, never came back.

TEACHING OPTION
Cooperative Activity: Researching the Technology of Warfare

Task: Student pairs will research a technological or strategic innovation used during the Civil War. They will then collaborate on writing a description of the innovation.

Purpose: To help students analyze the way a technological device operates and its historical application.

Activity: Have partners use the library and Internet resources to find information and drawings or photographs of the strategic innovation. Students with artistic ability may wish

to include a cutaway drawing with labeled parts to accompany the written description. Student pairs should present a brief presentation explaining how the innovation works.

📁 **Building a Portfolio:** If students think this assignment represents a superior effort, they should place their descriptions in their portfolio.

ALTERNATIVE ASSESSMENT BOOK
Standards for Evaluating a Cooperative Activity

Standards for Evaluation
Descriptions of innovations should . . .

- show evidence of careful research based on both print and visual sources
- explain the parts and operating principles of the innovation

Teacher's Edition **343**

William Tecumseh Sherman remained in the army and spent most of his time fighting Native Americans in the West. He resisted all attempts to draw him into politics. When Republicans tried to convince him to run for the presidency in 1884, he replied, "If nominated I will not run; if elected I will not serve." He died in 1891.

After fleeing Richmond, Jefferson Davis was captured the following month in Georgia. The Union army locked him in an underground prison cell in Fort Monroe. Davis was too proud to ask for amnesty, and the Union held him for two years without bringing him to trial. Released on bond in 1867, he spent the rest of his life living off charity and writing his memoirs. He never renounced his belief in the Confederate cause and died in 1889.

Robert E. Lee lost Arlington, the plantation that his wife had inherited. The quartermaster general of the Union had turned Lee's front lawn into a cemetery for the Union dead so that no one would ever live in the house again. After the war, Lee became president of Washington College in Virginia, now known as Washington and Lee University. Although he swore renewed allegiance to the United States, Congress refused to restore his citizenship. Still, Lee never spoke bitterly of Northerners or the Union. He died in 1870.

CIVILIANS FOLLOW NEW PATHS   Many veterans returned to their small towns and farms after the war. Others, as Grant noted, "found they were not satisfied with the farm, the store, or the workshop of the villages, but wanted larger fields." Many moved to the burgeoning cities in search of opportunity or went west to build the transcontinental railroad or to mine for gold.

Others tried to turn their wartime experience to good. The horrors that Union nurse Clara Barton witnessed during the war inspired her to spend her life helping others. In 1870, Barton went to Europe to rest and recuperate from her work during the war. In Switzerland, she became involved in the activities of the International Committee of the Red Cross during the Franco-Prussian War. Returning to the United States in 1873, Barton campaigned for an American branch of the organization, and in 1881 the American Red Cross was established. Barton led the Red Cross for 23 years and broadened its purpose to provide relief to civilians as well as soldiers in times of natural disaster or war.

Another Civil War nurse was the poet Walt Whitman. After his younger brother was wounded at Fredericksburg, he volunteered for service in a Washington hospital, where he cared for Union and Confederate soldiers alike. He wrote two books of poetry about the war, including poems about Abraham Lincoln, "When Lilacs Last in the Dooryard Bloom'd" and "O Captain! My Captain!"

THINK THROUGH HISTORY
D. Summarizing *What were some of the effects the war had on individuals?*

D. Answer African Americans gained their freedom, many soldiers tired of the rural life they had before the war, and many leaders had to find new careers.

THE ASSASSINATION OF LINCOLN   Whatever plans Lincoln had to reunify the nation after the war, he never got to implement them. On April 14, 1865, five days after Lee surrendered to Grant at Appomattox, Lincoln and his wife went to Ford's Theatre in Washington to see a British comedy, *Our American Cousin*. As the play drew to its close, a man silently opened the unguarded doors to the presidential box. He crept up behind Lincoln, raised a pistol, and fired, hitting the president in the back of his head.

The assassin, **John Wilkes Booth**—a 26-year-old actor and Southern sympathizer—then waved a knife in the air and leaped down to the stage. In doing so, he caught his spur on one of the flags draped across the front of the box. Booth landed hard on his left leg and broke it. He rose and said something that the audience had trouble understanding. Some thought it was the state motto of Virginia, "*Sic semper tyrannis*"—in English "Thus be it ever to tyrants." Others thought he said, "The South is avenged!" Then he limped offstage into the wings.

Despite his broken leg, Booth managed to escape. Twelve days later, Union cavalry trapped him in a Virginia tobacco shed, set the building on fire, and, when Booth still refused to surrender, shot him and then dragged him out.

"I have begun to deem myself a coward and to despise my own existence."
JOHN WILKES BOOTH, ON NOT HAVING JOINED THE CONFEDERATE ARMY

John Wilkes Booth

TEACHING OPTIONS

Making Connections Across Time

Assassinations   Lincoln was the first of four presidents to fall prey to an assassin's bullet. In 1881, a mentally disturbed office seeker shot President James Garfield while entering a railroad station in Washington, D.C. In 1901, an anarchist at the Pan-American Exposition in Buffalo, New York, shot President William McKinley soon after his reelection. In 1963, a sniper killed John Kennedy, who was riding in a motorcade in Dallas, Texas. Andrew Jackson, Franklin Roosevelt, Harry Truman, Gerald Ford, and Ronald Reagan were all targets of failed assassination attempts.

Making Connections Across the Curriculum

Literature   Walt Whitman describes Lincoln's funeral train in the poem "When Lilacs Last in the Dooryard Bloom'd":

Coffin that passes through lanes and streets,
Through day and night with the great cloud darkening the land,
With the pomp of the inloop'd flags with the cities draped in black,
With the show of the States themselves as of crape-veil'd women standing,
With processions long and winding and the flambeaus of the night,
With the countless torches lit, with the silent sea of faces . . .

Booth is said to have died whispering, "Tell my mother I died for my country. I did what I thought was best."

After Lincoln was shot, he remained unconscious throughout the night. He died at 7:22 A.M. the following morning, April 15. It was the first time a president of the United States had been assassinated. Secretary of the Navy Gideon Welles recorded people's reactions in his diary.

Lincoln's body lay in state in Springfield, Illinois *(above, left)*. The last known photograph of the president was taken by Alexander Gardner on April 10, 1865—four days before Lincoln was assassinated *(above, right)*.

A PERSONAL VOICE
It was a dark and gloomy morning, and rain set in. . . . On the Avenue in front of the White House were several hundred colored people, mostly women and children, weeping and wailing their loss. This crowd did not appear to diminish through the whole of that cold, wet day; they seemed not to know what was to be their fate since their great benefactor was dead, and their hopeless grief affected me more than almost anything else, though strong and brave men wept when I met them.
GIDEON WELLES, quoted in *Voices from the Civil War*

The funeral train that carried Lincoln's body from Washington to his hometown of Springfield, Illinois, took 14 days for its journey. Approximately 7 million Americans, or almost one-third of the entire Union population, turned out to publicly mourn their martyred leader.

The Civil War had ended. Slavery and secession were no more. Now the country faced two different problems: how to restore the Southern states to the Union and how to integrate approximately 4 million newly free African Americans into national life.

Section 5 Assessment

1. TERMS & NAMES

Identify:
• *Monitor*
• *Merrimack*
• Thirteenth Amendment
• John Wilkes Booth

2. SUMMARIZING Copy the multiple-effects chart below on your paper and fill it in with consequences of the Civil War.

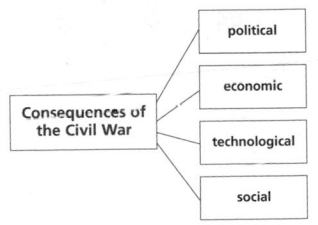

Consequences of the Civil War → political / economic / technological / social

3. ANALYZING ISSUES What political and social issues from the Civil War era do you think are still issues today? Use details from the text to support your answer.

THINK ABOUT
• the Thirteenth Amendment
• the changing role of the federal government during and after the Civil War
• the new weapons used to fight the war

4. HYPOTHESIZING Imagine that you are a member of a group of Southern leaders who must rebuild the South after the war. What would you recommend that the government do to help the South?

THINK ABOUT
• the economic devastation of the South
• the human costs of the war
• the numbers of newly freed slaves

The Civil War **345**

ANSWERS

1. TERMS & NAMES

Monitor, p. 343

Merrimack, p. 343

Thirteenth Amendment, p. 343

John Wilkes Booth, p. 344

2. SUMMARIZING

Possible Responses: **Political**—Freed enslaved people; ended secession threat; increased federal government's power. **Economic**—Strengthened banking system; stimulated economic growth of the North and contributed to economic decline of the South; created sizable war debt. **Technological**—Heightened importance of weaponry in warfare, led to new military strategies, such as trench warfare. **Social**—Disrupted families because of the staggering loss of lives; many disabled veterans.

3. ANALYZING ISSUES

Possible Responses: Race relations; states' rights versus federal control; individual rights versus federal control; the federal deficit; the impact of technology in waging war.

4. HYPOTHESIZING

Possible Responses: Special funding or a farm act to help the South rebuild its farms and acquire new equipment; a livestock program to help farmers replace animals; training programs for unskilled newly freed slaves; programs for severely injured veterans; a special tax on Northern businesses (which had boomed because of the war) to benefit the rebuilding of Southern businesses.

REVIEWING THE CHAPTER

TERMS & NAMES

1. Ulysses S. Grant, p. 315
2. Robert E. Lee, p. 316
3. Emancipation Proclamation, p. 320
4. conscription, p. 321
5. income tax, p. 326
6. Andersonville, p. 327
7. Gettysburg Address, p. 333
8. Appomattox, p. 337
9. Thirteenth Amendment, p. 343
10. John Wilkes Booth, p. 344

MAIN IDEAS

11. North—Blockade Southern ports; split the Confederacy; capture Richmond. South — Ward off Union invasion.

12. North—More manpower, factories, and railroads; stronger leadership. South—Cotton, first-rate generals, motivated armies.

13. Free-born African Americans rejoiced and many joined the Union army. Democrats made the Proclamation a campaign issue. Many Union soldiers voiced lukewarm support. The Confederacy condemned it.

14. Citing war or national security to expand the powers of the executive branch.

15. To protest discriminatory wages, many African-American soldiers served without pay for several months. Some slaves sabotaged Southern plantations. Southern bread riots broke out in 1863. Many white male workers went on labor strikes.

16. Fort Pillow—Confederate troops butchered African-American prisoners and some whites. Andersonville—Union prisoners of war endured atrocious conditions.

17. Farmers' resentment toward unfair tax policies; mass desertion of Confederate soldiers; peace movements.

18. Civilians produced weapons, grew food, and transported wartime goods.

19. The federal government subsidized building of a national railroad, strengthened the banking system, and contracted for wartime supplies with entrepreneurs.

20. Breech-loading rifles, minie balls, hand grenades, etc.

346 Chapter 11

REVIEWING THE CHAPTER

For each item below, write a sentence explaining its connection to the Civil War. For each person named below, explain his role in Civil War events.

TERMS & NAMES

1. Ulysses S. Grant
2. Robert E. Lee
3. Emancipation Proclamation
4. conscription
5. income tax
6. Andersonville
7. Gettysburg Address
8. Appomattox
9. Thirteenth Amendment
10. John Wilkes Booth

MAIN IDEAS

SECTION 1 *(pages 312–317)*

The Civil War Begins

11. What were the military strategies of the North and South at the onset of the Civil War?
12. What advantages did the North have over the South? What advantages did the South have over the North?

SECTION 2 *(pages 318–322)*

The Politics of War

13. How did each of these groups—slaves, free-born African Americans, Democrats, Union soldiers, and the Confederacy—react to the Emancipation Proclamation?
14. What precedent in governing the nation did Lincoln set for future wartime presidents?

SECTION 3 *(pages 323–328)*

Life During Wartime

15. What acts of protest or resistance occurred in both the North and South because of economic and social changes during the war?
16. Briefly describe the war crimes committed against prisoners at Fort Pillow and Andersonville.

SECTION 4 *(pages 329–337)*

The North Takes Charge

17. Cite events that illustrate the South's deteriorating morale after defeats at Gettysburg and Vicksburg.
18. What was Grant and Sherman's rationale for using the strategy of total war?

SECTION 5 *(pages 340–345)*

The Legacy of the War

19. How did the Civil War provide the economic foundation for the United States to become an industrial giant?
20. Give examples of new military machinery and technological improvements in weapons used during the Civil War.

346 CHAPTER 11

THINKING CRITICALLY

1. **FEDERAL POWER** Create a continuum similar to the one below, labeled with *less federal control* at one end and *more federal control* at the other. Mark where the Union and Confederacy would fall on the continuum, based on Abraham Lincoln's and Jefferson Davis's policies during the Civil War. Support your ratings with reasons and historical events from the text.

less federal control   more federal control

2. **CIVIL WAR FIRSTS** On a scale of 1 to 5, rank the following ground-breaking events related to the Civil War era from most historically significant to least historically significant. Give reasons to support your rankings.

   • first contested national election in wartime
   • first draft law passed
   • one of the first modern wars
   • first time women employed in government jobs
   • first time U.S. government collected income tax

3. **THE NATION'S ORDEAL** Reread the quote by Robert E. Lee on page 310. What views do you think his words reflect? Explain your opinion.

4. **GEOGRAPHY OF BATTLE** Compare the two maps on page 315 and page 335. What do they tell you about the progress of the Civil War from 1861–1865? What do they show about the geography of the land where many battles were fought? Explain your answer.

5. **PHOTOGRAPHY IN THE CIVIL WAR** In what ways do you think early cameras might be compared to the television set as a medium for bringing history and the realities of war into the American public's living rooms?

6. **ANALYZING PRIMARY SOURCES** In his diary entry "Death of President Lincoln" from *Specimen Days,* Walt Whitman makes the following observation about Lincoln's assassination.

   > April 16, '65.—I find in my notes of the time, this passage on Abraham Lincoln: He leaves for America's history and biography, so far, not only its most dramatic reminiscence—he leaves, in my opinion, the greatest, best, most characteristic, artistic, moral personality. . . . By many has this Union been help'd; but if one name, one man, must be pick'd out, he, most of all, is the conservator of it, to the future. He was assassinated—but the Union is not assassinated . . . Death does its work, obliterates a hundred, a thousand—President, general, captain, private—but the Nation is immortal.
   >
   > **WALT WHITMAN,** *Specimen Days*

   Do you agree or disagree with the way Whitman characterizes Lincoln's character and his legacy? Why?

THINKING CRITICALLY

1. FEDERAL POWER

Possible Responses: Most students will place the Confederacy toward the left side of the continuum and the Union toward the right side. Though many Southern governors adhered to their conviction of states' rights, students should address some of the measures that Jefferson Davis took to exert more federal control—suspending habeas corpus, passing a draft law, and taxing farmers. Students should also cite measures that show how the federal government expanded under Lincoln—for example, draft laws, the federal income tax, and the National Bank Act.

2. CIVIL WAR FIRSTS

Rankings will vary widely, but should be well supported with reasons.

3. THE NATION'S ORDEAL

Possible Responses: Lee might be implying that slavery was wrong. Also, since he says "national sins," he might be implying that both sides—the Confederacy and the Union—were guilty of wrong. He might be referring to Northerners who supported slavery as also being in the wrong; or to the whole idea of secession and the bloodshed that followed as wrong. Perhaps he viewed the whole war as a necessary punishment for the national wrong of slavery.

ALTERNATIVE ASSESSMENT

1. REPORTING ABOUT THE CIVIL WAR

How were battles of the Civil War fought? Who were the leaders? the soldiers? What were war conditions like?

- Acting as a reporter for an international newspaper, write an eyewitness account of a battle in the American Civil War.

CD-ROM Use the CD-ROM *Fateful Lightning* and other reference materials to research the events of a specific battle, including information on key players and details about the setting.

- Think about the information you would share with a foreign audience living in the days before radio, television, or film. Include details about people, places, and events, as well as relevant historical background to enhance your account.

- Conclude your report with a prediction of which side will win and how America might change as a result of the war.

2. LEARNING FROM MEDIA

VIDEO View the McDougal Littell video for Chapter 11, *War Outside My Window*. Discuss the following questions in small groups; then do the cooperative learning activity.

- What is your overall impression of Mary Chesnut?
- How would you describe her attitude toward the North?
- What, if anything, surprised you about the diary entries?
- What similarities and differences might you find between Mary Chesnut's diary and the diary of an upper-class woman living in the North during the war?
- **Cooperative Learning** As a group, create additional diary entries that Mary Chesnut might have written. Make sure that the entries are in keeping with her personality, values, and writing style. Share your final product with the rest of the class.

3. PORTFOLIO PROJECT

 Use the Living History activity to expand your portfolio.

LIVING HISTORY

PLAYING YOUR CIVIL WAR GAME

After you have finished creating your board game, play the game with other students. Ask them to answer the following questions:

- Is the game fun?
- How could the game be more challenging?
- Does it reflect military strategies, key geographical areas, and important figures of the Civil War?

When you have made changes based on the students' suggestions, let other classmates play the game. Then add it to your American history portfolio.

Review Chapter 11

BEGINNING OF THE CIVIL WAR In 1861, Confederate forces fired on Fort Sumter, igniting a war between the states. Both sides adopted military strategies suited to their objectives and resources. The Union devised a three-pronged strategy—blockade Southern ports, divide the Confederacy along the Mississippi River, and capture Richmond. The South's defensive strategy hinged on warding off Union invasion. Heavy casualties in the West shattered both sides' illusions that the war would end swiftly.

POLITICAL, SOCIAL, AND ECONOMIC ISSUES The Union government used diplomacy to maintain Britain's neutrality. In 1863, Lincoln issued the Emancipation Proclamation, which framed the war as a crusade to end slavery. Lincoln expanded his powers to suppress dissent—a problem also found in the Confederacy. Faced with military shortages, both sides enacted draft laws. In 1862, the Union Congress passed a law allowing African Americans to serve in the military. The war also opened new job opportunities for women while expanding the North's economy and damaging the South's.

DECISIVE BATTLES AND THE AFTERMATH In 1863, heavy casualties at Gettysburg crippled Confederate forces, while the fall of Vicksburg to Union troops split the Confederacy in two. In 1864, Union forces launched offensives that also targeted civilians. Grant hammered Lee's troops in Virginia while Sherman raided Georgia. The Civil War ended with Lee's surrender at Appomattox in April 1865. The war not only freed the slaves, but also transformed the nation's economy, its government, the conduct and technology of warfare, and the future careers of many of its participants. Lincoln was assassinated before he could implement his plans to shape the nation's future.

Preview Chapter 12

Power struggles within the federal government erupted after Lincoln's assassination. Under his successor, President Andrew Johnson, the nation began to tackle the problems of Reconstruction (1865–1877): how to restore Southern states to the Union, guarantee freedom for the former slaves, and rebuild a devastated society. You will learn about these and other developments in the next chapter.

The Civil War **347**

ALTERNATIVE ASSESSMENT

1. REPORTING ABOUT THE CIVIL WAR

Standards for Evaluation
A strong eyewitness account should meet the following criteria:

- Focuses on one specific battle from the Civil War.
- Shows evidence of research from a variety of sources.
- Includes descriptive details, personal observations, and facts.
- Creates a sense of immediacy.

2. LEARNING FROM THE MEDIA

Answers to the questions:

Answers will vary. Possible answers follow:

- Intelligent, feisty, articulate sensitive, insightful.
- Critical and disdainful.
- Mary Chesnut's insights into the politics of war; her access to Jefferson Davis; her account of the outrageous prices of staple items during the war.
- Similarities—Observations of the war's hardships; commentaries on personal grief and worries. Differences—Opposing views on reasons for fighting; contrasting experiences with money shortages.

3. PORTFOLIO PROJECT

LIVING HISTORY
An effective board game should meet the following criteria:

- Shows thoughtful planning.
- Includes clear, easy-to-follow directions.
- Reflects an understanding of Civil War history.
- Shows clear, coherent organization of Civil War information.

IN-DEPTH RESOURCES: UNIT 3
See the form for scoring this activity on page 57.

THINKING CRITICALLY

4. GEOGRAPHY OF BATTLE

Possible Responses: Maps show that the Union occupied many more states between 1863 and 1865. The end of the war—final battles and surrender at Appomattox—took place very near the site of the Seven Days' Battle in the early days of the war. Geography shows that many battles were fought in hilly regions where the terrain must have been rugged and fighting difficult, especially if enemy troops were in the hills above.

5. PHOTOGRAPHY IN THE CIVIL WAR

Possible Responses: Both the early camera and the television set have satisfied Americans' desire for a visual portrayal of news events; both conveyed images about war to a broad audience.

6. ANALYZING PRIMARY SOURCES

Possible Responses: Students who agree with Whitman's assessment might say that Lincoln is deserving of such high praise because he helped abolish slavery and save the Union. Students who disagree may say that Whitman is overrating Lincoln's moral character, citing that the Emancipation Proclamation might be considered an act of military necessity, rather than morality, and that Lincoln condoned Grant's strategy of waging total war.

CHAPTER 12

Reconstruction and Its Effects

	Key Ideas	**TEACHING SUPPORT**	**ASSESSMENT**	
SECTION 1 The Politics of Reconstruction *pp. 350–355*	*Presidents Lincoln and Johnson face congressional opposition to their Reconstruction plans. Congress wins control, and Radical Reconstruction begins.*	*In-Depth Resources: Unit 3* • Guided Reading, p. 58 • American Lives: Thaddeus Stevens, p. 71 • Literature: from *Jubilee* by Margaret Walker, p. 68 **COOPERATIVE ACTIVITY** • Debating President Johnson's Impeachment, p. 354 (TE)	*Section 1 Assessment,* p. 355 (PE) *Self-Assessment,* p. 355 (TE) *Formal Assessment* • Section Quiz, p. 150 *Alternative Assessment Book* • Standards for Evaluating a Cooperative Activity	
SECTION 2 Reconstructing Society *pp. 356–365*	*The South must rebuild its ravaged economy in the aftermath of war. African Americans begin to exercise freedoms denied to them during their enslavement.*	*In-Depth Resources: Unit 3* • Guided Reading, p. 59 • Geography Application: The Economic Effects of the Civil War, p. 62 • Primary Sources: Frederick Douglass on Voting Rights, p. 64; from *Proud Shoes* by Pauli Murray, p. 65 • American Lives: Hiram Revels, p. 72 **COOPERATIVE ACTIVITY** • Writing a Dialogue, p. 362 (TE)	*Section 2 Assessment,* p. 365 (PE) *Self-Assessment,* p. 365 (TE) *Formal Assessment* • Section Quiz, p. 151 *Alternative Assessment Book* • Standards for Evaluating a Cooperative Activity	
SECTION 3 The Collapse of Reconstruction *pp. 366–373*	*Continued opposition to Radical Reconstruction in the South and economic problems in the North bring the Reconstruction process to an end.*	*In-Depth Resources: Unit 3* • Guided Reading, p. 60 • Skillbuilder Practice: Evaluating Decisions, p. 61 • Primary Sources: from An Inquiry on the Condition of the South, p. 66; Political Cartoon, p. 67 **COOPERATIVE ACTIVITY** • Staging a Presidential Debate, p. 368 (TE)	*Section 3 Assessment,* p. 373 (PE) *Self-Assessment,* p. 373 (TE) *Formal Assessment* • Section Quiz, p. 152 *Alternative Assessment Book* • Standards for Evaluating a Cooperative Activity	
CHAPTER RESOURCES	**Chapter Overview** *As Congress enacts a policy of punishing the South for the Civil War, African Americans struggle to establish new lives. Eventually, the North tires of Reconstruction, and Southern whites regain control over the states.*	*In-Depth Resources: Unit 3* • Living History Project: Worksheet, p. 73; Standards, p. 74 *Telescoping the Times* • Chapter Summary, pp. 23–24 *Planning for Block Schedules*	*Chapter Assessment,* pp. 374–375 (PE) *Alternative Assessment,* p. 375 (PE) *Formal Assessment* • Chapter Test, forms A and B, pp. 153–158 *Test Generator* *Alternative Assessment Book* See explanation and forms for different kinds of alternative assessments including portfolio assessment.	

Humanities Transparencies
• H12, *The Fifteenth Amendment*
• H34, *A. Johnson, Tailor*

Electronic Library of Primary Sources
• *from* the Black Codes of Mississippi of 1865
• *from* the Civil Rights Act of 1866

INTERNET RESOURCES
• See *McDougal Littell Learning On-Line* for links to information about Reconstruction and Andrew Johnson.

Geography Transparencies
• G12, The Barrow Plantation

Electronic Library of Primary Sources
• *from* an Interview with a Former Slave by Annie Ruth Davis
• *from* an Address on Reconstruction by Thaddeus Stevens

AMERICAN STORIES VIDEO SERIES
• "Teacher of a Freed People"

INTERNET RESOURCES
• See *McDougal Littell Learning On-Line* for links to information about Hiram Rhoades.

Critical Thinking Transparencies
• CT12, Reconstruction

Grolier Multimedia Encyclopedia
• excerpt from *The Personal Memoirs of U.S. Grant*
• Horace Greeley and the Penny Press

INTERNET RESOURCES
• See *McDougal Littell Learning On-Line* for links to information about Ulysses S. Grant and the Ku Klux Klan.

American Portfolio: A Videodisc for U.S. History, user's guide, pp. 115–120

INTERNET RESOURCES
Learning On-Line: Social Studies
http://www.mcdougallittell.com

Block Scheduling (90 MINUTES)

Day 1
Section 1, pp. 350–355
Section 2, pp. 356–365

 AMERICAN STORIES VIDEO SERIES
• "Teacher of a Freed People"
Section Assessments, pp. 355, 365

Day 2
Section 3, pp. 366–373
Section Assessment, p. 373
Chapter Assessment, pp. 374–375

YEARLY PACING *Chapter 12 Total:* 2 days *Yearly Total:* 85 days

See *Planning for Block Schedules* for special activities and pacing strategies.

Customizing for Special Populations

Students Acquiring English

Access for Students Acquiring English
• Guided Reading for Sections 1–4 (Spanish), pp. 122–124
• Chapter Summary (Spanish), pp. 120–121
• Skillbuilder Practice: Evaluating Decisions (Spanish), p. 125
• Geography Application: The Economic Effects of the Civil War (Spanish), p. 126

 AMERICAN STORIES VIDEO SERIES
• "Teacher of a Freed People"

INTERNET RESOURCES
• See *McDougal Littell Learning On-Line* The Diverse Classroom.

Less Proficient Readers

In-Depth Resources: Unit 3
• Guided Reading for Sections 1–3, pp. 58–60
• Skillbuilder: Evaluating Decisions, p. 61
• Geography Application: The Economic Effects of the Civil War, p. 62

Telescoping the Times
• Chapter Summary, pp. 23–24

See additional strategies at point of use in the Teacher's Edition.

Gifted and Talented Students

In-Depth Resources: Unit 3
• Primary Sources: Frederick Douglass on Voting Rights, p. 64; from *Proud Shoes* by Pauli Murray, p. 65; *from* An Inquiry on the Condition of the South, p. 66; Political Cartoon, p. 67
• American Lives: Thaddeus Stevens, p. 71; Hiram Revels, p. 72

See additional strategies at point of use in the Teacher's Edition.

Connections to Literature READINGS FOR STUDENTS

In-Depth Resources: Unit 3
• from *Jubilee* by Margaret Walker, p. 68

Enrichment Reading
• Mitchell, Margaret
Gone with the Wind.
New York: Simon & Schuster, 1936
This great Civil War saga follows the characters through the war and Reconstruction. It was made into a spellbinding movie.

• Morrison, Toni
Beloved.
New York: Knopf, 1987
Winner of the Pulitzer Prize in 1988, this novel tells the powerfully moving story of remarkable events in the life and spirit of an ex-slave.

McDougal Littell *Literature Connections*

• Ernest Gaines,
The Autobiography of Miss Jane Pittman
(with related readings) *In this novel a black woman who has lived 110 years tells her memorable story as both a slave and as a witness to the civil rights movement of the 1960s.*

Reconstruction and Its Effects

CHAPTER

12

Reconstruction and Its Effects

▶ **Starting with the Student**
Ask students what the word *reconstruction* means to them. Then discuss the opening quotation.

- Who were the four million that Garrison was talking about?
- What does his opposition of auction-block and ballot-box refer to?

PREVIEWING THE CHAPTER

- Have students read the titles and brief descriptions of the sections. Explain that the video in Section 2 focuses on Robert Fitzgerald, an African American who taught in a Freedman's school.
- Discuss events on the time line that particularly puzzle or interest students.

MORE ABOUT . . .
William Lloyd Garrison
William Lloyd Garrison (1805–1879) was one of the country's leading abolitionists. He published *The Liberator* from 1831 until slavery was abolished in 1865. At that point, he proposed disbanding the American Anti-Slavery Society. However, his proposal was defeated after an impassioned speech by Frederick Douglass, who insisted, "Slavery is not abolished until the black man has the ballot."

SECTION 1
The Politics of Reconstruction

Presidents Lincoln and Johnson face congressional opposition to their Reconstruction plans. Congress wins control, and Radical Reconstruction begins.

SECTION 2
Reconstructing Society

The South must rebuild its ravaged economy in the aftermath of war. African Americans begin to exercise freedoms denied to them during their enslavement.

 VIDEO *TEACHER OF A FREED PEOPLE*

SECTION 3
The Collapse of Reconstruction

Continued opposition to Radical Reconstruction in the South and economic problems in the North bring the Reconstruction process to an end.

"Nothing in all history [equaled] this wonderful, quiet, sudden transformation of four millions of human beings from . . . the auction-block to the ballot-box."

William Lloyd Garrison

- Carpetbaggers take part in Reconstruction.

- After the Civil War, many Southerners return to war-ravaged homes.
- Thirteenth Amendment is ratified.
- ✪ Andrew Johnson becomes president when President Lincoln is assassinated.

- President Johnson campaigns for moderate Reconstruction policies.

- United States buys Alaska from Russia for $7.2 million.
- Former Confederate states are divided into military districts.

- President Johnson is impeached.
- Fourteenth Amendment is ratified.
- ✪ Ulysses S. Grant is elected president.

THE UNITED STATES **1865** 1866 1867 1868
THE WORLD 1866 1867 1869

- Austro-Prussian War ends.

- Emperor Maximilian is executed in Mexico.

- Mohandas K. Gandhi is born in India.

348 CHAPTER 12

THEMES IN CHAPTER 12

Constitutional Concerns	*Civil Rights*	*Expanding Democracy*	*Cultural Diversity*
Shifts in political power brought the executive, legislative, and judicial branches of government into conflict. Fundamental rights, such as the right to vote or to own land, came under scrutiny. See Teacher's Edition notes, pp. 351, 363.	The Fourteenth Amendment failed to reinforce civil rights actions when the Supreme Court severely limited its range. However, the amendment did become the constitutional anchor for recent civil rights legislation. See Teacher's Edition note, p. 353.	Among the freedoms black men and women embraced when slavery was abolished was the freedom to make their own decisions. This included choices about family life and the kind of work they did. Women resisted laboring in the fields. See Teacher's Edition note, p. 360.	Cultural diversity, one of this country's greatest strengths, provoked ugly incidents of racial prejudice. Lust for political and economic power led the Ku Klux Klan to commit terrorist and murderous acts that shamed the nation. See Teacher's Edition, p. 367.

LIVING HISTORY

RESEARCHING A BIOGRAPHY

Research the life of someone who lived through the Reconstruction period. This person could be an African American, a scalawag, a carpetbagger, a planter, a farmer, or a businessperson. To get ideas, look through books on Reconstruction. Include details of

- the person's early life
- the person's experiences during Reconstruction
- the effects of those experiences on his or her later life

Add photos, quotations from diaries, or anecdotes to make your biography more interesting.

📁 **PORTFOLIO PROJECT** Save your materials in a folder. At the end of the chapter, you will write a biography of the person for your American history portfolio.

TILDEN.   **HAYES.**

OF THE TWO EVILS
CHOOSE THE LEAST.

Frederick Douglass is flanked by two African-American senators, Blanche K. Bruce and Hiram Revels.

Horace Greeley shown in caricature runs for president as a Liberal Republican.

Hayes-Tilden presidential election results in deadlock.

Grant administration's attempt to annex Dominican Republic fails.

Federal troops withdraw from the South, ending Reconstruction.

Fifteenth Amendment is ratified.

United States and Great Britain sign Treaty of Washington.

Financial panic results in economic depression.

Specie Resumption Act is passed.

Rutherford B. Hayes is inaugurated president.

870	1871	1872	1873	1875	1876	**1877**
			1873		1876	

Unification of Italy is completed.

Portugal colonizes Angola in southwest Africa.

Korea becomes independent nation.

Reconstruction and Its Effects **349**

RESEARCHING A BIOGRAPHY

Discuss ways of doing research for the biography:

- Who would students like to know more about—someone of their age, sex, and cultural background, or someone very different? Have them look for a subject who lived before, during, and after Reconstruction.
- Is sufficient information about their subject available? Have students select someone who is well-known and about whom adequate data exist.
- Ask students to collect quotes and anecdotes that show how their subject reacted to events and what other people thought about the person.

Project Planning Guide

Step 1	Students choose the person they will write about.
Step 2	Students do preliminary research.
Step 3	Students collect information, quotes, anecdotes, and pictures about their subject.
Step 4	Students organize their information in a folder before writing the biography.

IN-DEPTH RESOURCES: UNIT 3
See worksheet and standards for evaluation, pp. 73, 74.

RECOMMENDED RESOURCES

Books for the Teacher

Benedict, Michael Les. *The Impeachment of Andrew Johnson.* New York: Norton, 1973.

Franklin, John Hope. *Reconstruction After the Civil War,* 2nd ed. Chicago: U of Chicago P, 1994. By a distinguished African-American historian.

Trelease, Allen W. *White Terror.* Baton Rouge: Louisiana State UP,

1971. Chronicle of the Ku Klux Klan.

Books for the Student

Foner, Eric. *A Short History of Reconstruction.* New York: Oxford UP, 1991. Brief but thorough and readable overview.

Sterling, Dorothy, ed. *The Trouble They Seen.* New York: Da Capo Press, 1994. African Americans remember Reconstruction.

Videos

The Background of the Reconstruction Period. Phoenix/BFA, Films and Video, 1986.

1861 to 1877. CRM Films, 800-421-0833. About African-American civil rights.

Reconstructing the South. Dir. Paul Bosner. PBS Video, 1987. RMI Media, 800-745-5480.

Software

African American History: Slavery to Civil Rights. Queue, 1995. Educational Software Institute, 800-955-5570.

U.S. History: Reconstruction. Educational Software Institute, 800-955-5570.

① To summarize President Lincoln's Reconstruction policies.

② To identify differences between presidential and congressional Reconstruction policies.

③ To summarize reasons for President Johnson's impeachment.

④ To plot steps taken by Congress to protect rights of former slaves.

SKILLBUILDERS

• Understanding geography: place, p. 354
• Interpreting charts, p. 355

CRITICAL THINKING

• Clarifying, p. 351
• Contrasting, p. 352
• Recognizing causes, p. 353
• Summarizing, pp. 353, 355
• Recognizing effects, pp. 354, 355
• Hypothesizing, p. 355
• Making decisions, p. 355

FOCUS & MOTIVATE

▶ **Starting with the Student**
If two people disagree and neither individual is willing to compromise, how might the issue be decided?

OBJECTIVE
① **INSTRUCT**

Presidential Reconstruction— Phase One

▶ **Discussing Key Ideas**
• The president and some members of Congress differ on how to handle Reconstruction.
• Lincoln favors a lenient policy toward the Confederate states.
• Radical Republicans oppose Lincoln's plan.

IN-DEPTH RESOURCES: UNIT 3
Guided Reading, p. 58

ACCESS FOR STUDENTS ACQUIRING ENGLISH
Guided Reading (Spanish), p. 122

---

❶ The Politics of Reconstruction

LEARN ABOUT presidential and congressional Reconstruction policies from 1865 to 1870
TO UNDERSTAND how political leaders set out to rebuild the nation after the Civil War.

TERMS & NAMES
• Andrew Johnson
• Reconstruction
• Radical Republican
• Thaddeus Stevens
• Wade-Davis Bill
• Freedmen's Bureau
• black codes
• Fourteenth Amendment
• Fifteenth Amendment

ONE AMERICAN'S STORY

Andrew Johnson, who succeeded Abraham Lincoln as president, was born to a poor North Carolina family and lost his father when he was three. Unable to attend school, he taught himself to read and later learned from his wife how to write. When Johnson was 14, he became a tailor's apprentice. After two years he ran away, eventually settling in Tennessee, where he set up his own tailor's shop. He also entered politics and won several important offices, including those of congressman, governor, and U.S. senator.

After secession, Johnson was the only senator from a Confederate state to remain loyal to the Union. Even though he had once owned slaves, by 1863 he supported abolition. He hated the wealthy, slave-owning planters of the South, whom he held responsible for dragging poor whites into the war. Early in 1865, he endorsed harsh punishment for the rebellion's leaders.

A PERSONAL VOICE
The time has arrived when the American people should understand what crime is, and that it should be punished, and its penalties enforced and inflicted.... Treason must be made odious... traitors must be punished and impoverished... their social power must be destroyed. I say, as to the leaders, punishment. I say leniency, conciliation, and amnesty to the thousands whom they have misled and deceived.
ANDREW JOHNSON, quoted in *Reconstruction: The Ending of the Civil War*

President Andrew Johnson

On becoming president, Johnson faced not only the issue of whether to punish or pardon former Confederates but also a larger problem: how to bring the defeated Confederate states back into the Union.

Presidential Reconstruction—Phase One

Reconstruction, the time period following the Civil War, lasted from 1865 to 1877. In its broadest sense, this was the period during which the U.S. began to rebuild after the Civil War. The term also refers to the process the federal government used to readmit the defeated Confederate states to the Union. Complicating the process was the fact that Abraham Lincoln, Andrew Johnson, and the members of Congress all had different ideas about how Reconstruction should be handled. Lincoln's and Johnson's plans, together referred to as presidential Reconstruction, were the first to be implemented.

LINCOLN'S TEN-PERCENT PLAN Although Lincoln did not live to carry out his plan, before his death he made it clear that he favored a lenient Reconstruction policy. Even in the midst of war, he had considered how to treat Confederate states if the Union should win. In reality, Lincoln believed, the Confederate states had never left the Union, because secession was constitutionally impossible. He contended that it was individuals, not states, who had rebelled and that the Constitution gave the president the power to pardon individuals.

350 CHAPTER 12

SECTION 1 RESOURCES

PRINT RESOURCES

IN-DEPTH RESOURCES: UNIT 3
Guided Reading, p. 58
Literature: *from Jubilee* by Margaret Walker, p.68
American Lives: Thaddeus Stevens, p. 71

ACCESS FOR STUDENTS ACQUIRING ENGLISH
Guided Reading (Spanish), p. 122

FORMAL ASSESSMENT
Section Quiz, p. 150

ALTERNATIVE ASSESSMENT BOOK
See forms for supporting and scoring alternative activities.

TECHNOLOGY RESOURCES

HUMANITIES TRANSPARENCIES
H12, *The Fifteenth Amendment*
H34, A. Johnson, Tailor

CD-ROM Electronic Library of Primary Sources

VIDEO *American Portfolio: A Videodisc for U.S. History*
user's guide, pp. 115–120

INTERNET McDougal Littell Learning On-Line
http://www.mcdougallittell.com

In December 1863, Lincoln announced his Proclamation of Amnesty and Reconstruction, also known as the Ten-Percent Plan. Under this plan, the government would pardon all Confederates—except high-ranking Confederate officials and those accused of crimes against prisoners of war—who would swear allegiance to the Union and promise to obey its laws. As soon as ten percent of those on the 1860 voting lists took this oath of allegiance, a Confederate state could form a new state government and send representatives and senators to Congress.

Lincoln intended his Ten-Percent Plan to make the South's return as quick and easy as possible. On March 4, 1865, in his second inaugural address, Lincoln described his hope for a reunited nation.

"Let us strive on to finish the work we are in."

ABRAHAM LINCOLN

A PERSONAL VOICE
With malice toward none, with charity for all . . . let us strive on to finish the work we are in, to bind up the nation's wounds, to care for him who shall have borne the battle and for his widow and orphan, to do all which may achieve and cherish a just and lasting peace among ourselves and with all nations.

ABRAHAM LINCOLN, second inaugural address

Under Lincoln's terms, four states—Arkansas, Louisiana, Tennessee, and Virginia—moved toward readmission to the Union. However, Lincoln's moderate Reconstruction plan angered a minority of Republicans in Congress, known as **Radical Republicans.** The Radicals had led the way in supporting abolition and the war, and they now proposed laws to ensure African-American rights. Led by Senator Charles Sumner of Massachusetts and Representative **Thaddeus Stevens** of Pennsylvania, the Radicals wanted to destroy the political power of former slaveholders. Most of all, they wanted African Americans to be given full citizenship and the right to vote. In 1865, the idea of African-American suffrage was truly radical; no other country that had abolished slavery had given former slaves the vote.

RADICAL REACTION In July 1864, the Radicals responded to the Ten-Percent Plan by passing the **Wade-Davis Bill,** which proposed that Congress, not the president, be responsible for Reconstruction. It also declared that for a state government to be formed, a majority—not just ten percent—of those eligible to vote in 1860 would have to take a solemn oath to support the Constitution.

Lincoln used a pocket veto to kill the bill after Congress adjourned. The Radicals responded hotly, calling Lincoln's pocket veto an outrage and asserting that Congress had supreme authority. They warned Lincoln to confine himself to executive duties and to leave Reconstruction to Congress. Thus, the stage was set for a presidential-congressional confrontation on the issue of Reconstruction.

Presidential Reconstruction—Phase Two

John Wilkes Booth's assassination of Lincoln in April 1865 left Lincoln's successor, the former Democrat Andrew Johnson, to deal with the Reconstruction controversy. A staunch Unionist and an enemy of wealthy Southern planters, Johnson had often expressed his intent to deal harshly with Confederate leaders. Most white Southerners therefore considered Johnson a traitor to his region, while Radicals believed that he was one of them. Both were wrong.

JOHNSON CONTINUES LINCOLN'S POLICIES In May 1865, with Congress in recess, Johnson announced his own plan to reconstruct the seven remaining Confederate states. He declared that each of these states—Alabama, Florida, Georgia, Mississippi, North Carolina, South Carolina, and Texas—could be

Reconstruction and Its Effects **351**

THINK THROUGH HISTORY
A. *Clarifying* What was President Lincoln's planned approach to Reconstruction?

A. Answer He wanted to make the South's return as quick and easy as possible.

HISTORICAL SPOTLIGHT

THE POCKET VETO
According to the Constitution, a president has ten days to either sign or veto a bill passed by Congress. If the president does neither, the bill will automatically become law. When a bill is passed less than ten days before the end of a congressional session, however, the president can prevent its becoming law by simply ignoring, or "pocketing," it. This so-called pocket veto effectively kills the bill. During his presidency, Lincoln used two regular vetoes and five pocket vetoes.

KEY PLAYER

THADDEUS STEVENS
1792–1868
The Radical Republican leader Thaddeus Stevens had a commanding physical presence—piercing eyes, a thin-lipped mouth, and a tall, thin body. In spite of a deformed foot, he was an expert horseman and swimmer. He was also famous for his quick wit and sarcasm. One colleague called him "a rude jouster in political and personal warfare."

Before being elected to Congress, he had practiced law in Pennsylvania, where he defended runaway slaves. Stevens hated slavery and in time came to hate white Southerners as well. He declared, "I look upon every man who would permit slavery . . . as a traitor to liberty and disloyal to God."

After Stevens died, at his own request he was buried in an integrated cemetery, because he wanted to show in death "the principles which I advocated throughout a long life: equality of man before his Creator."

readmitted to the Union if it would meet several conditions. Each state would have to declare its secession illegal, swear allegiance to the Union, and ratify the Thirteenth Amendment, which abolished slavery.

To the dismay of Thaddeus Stevens and the Radicals, Johnson's plan differed little from Lincoln's. The major difference was that Johnson tried to break the planters' power by excluding high-ranking Confederates and wealthy Southern landowners from taking the oath needed for voting privileges. The Radicals were especially upset that Johnson's plan, like Lincoln's, failed to address the needs of former slaves in three areas: land, voting rights, and protection under the law.

If Johnson's policies angered Radicals, they relieved most white Southerners. Johnson's support of states' rights instead of a strong central government reassured Southern states that they could do as they wished about African-American voting rights. In addition, even though Johnson had promised to punish traitors, he pardoned more than 13,000 former Confederates because he believed that "white men alone must manage the South" and thought that former slaves should not gain the right to vote.

The remaining ex-Confederate states quickly agreed to Johnson's terms. Within a few months, these states—except Texas—held conventions to draw up new state constitutions, set up new state governments, and elect representatives to Congress. However, some Southern states did not fully comply with the conditions for returning to the Union. For example, Mississippi did not ratify the Thirteenth Amendment.

Despite such instances of noncompliance, in December 1865, the newly elected Southern legislators arrived in Washington to take their seats. Fifty-eight of them had previously sat in the Congress of the Confederacy, six had served in the Confederate cabinet, and four had fought against the United States as Confederate generals. Johnson pardoned them all—a gesture that infuriated the Radicals.

PRESIDENTIAL RECONSTRUCTION COMES TO A STANDSTILL
When the 39th Congress convened in December 1865, the Radical Republican legislators, led by Thaddeus Stevens, disputed Johnson's claim that Reconstruction was complete. Many of them believed that the Southern states were not much different from what they had been before the war. As a result, Congress refused to admit the Southern legislators newly elected under Johnson's Reconstruction plan.

At the same time, moderate Republicans pushed for new laws to remedy weaknesses they saw in Johnson's plan. In February 1866, Congress voted to continue and enlarge the **Freedmen's Bureau.** The bureau, established by Lincoln in the last month of the war, assisted former slaves and poor whites in the South by distributing clothing and food and by setting up more than 40 hospitals, 4,000 primary schools, 61 industrial institutes, and 74 teacher-training establishments.

CIVIL RIGHTS ACT OF 1866 A month later, Congress passed the Civil Rights Act of 1866, which gave African Americans citizenship and forbade states from passing discriminatory laws—**black codes**—that severely restricted African Americans' lives. Mississippi and South Carolina had first enacted black codes in 1865, and other Southern states had rapidly followed suit.

Black codes had the effect of restoring many of the restrictions of slavery by prohibiting blacks from carrying weapons, serving on juries, testifying against whites, marrying whites, starting their own businesses, and traveling without permits. In some states, African Americans could not rent or lease farmland. Even worse, in many areas resentful whites used violence to keep

---

THINK THROUGH HISTORY
C. Recognizing Causes How did black codes help bring about the passage of the Civil Rights Act of 1866?

C. Answer They convinced Congress that African Americans needed federal laws to protect them.

blacks from improving their position in society. To many members of Congress, the passage of black codes indicated that the South had not given up the idea of keeping African Americans in bondage.

Johnson shocked everyone when he vetoed both the Freedmen's Bureau bill and the Civil Rights Act. Congress, Johnson contended, had gone far beyond "anything contemplated by the authors of the Constitution." These vetoes proved to be the opening shots in a battle between the president and Congress. By rejecting the two bills, Johnson alienated the moderate Republicans who were trying to improve his Reconstruction plan. He also angered the Radicals by appearing to support Southerners who denied African Americans their full rights. Johnson had not been in office a year when presidential Reconstruction ground to a halt.

Congressional Reconstruction

Angered by Johnson's actions, radical and moderate Republican factions decided to work together to shift the control of the Reconstruction process from the executive branch to the legislature, beginning a period of "congressional Reconstruction."

MODERATES AND RADICALS JOIN FORCES In mid-1866, moderate Republicans joined with Radicals to override the president's vetoes of the Civil Rights and Freedmen's Bureau bills. The Civil Rights Act of 1866 became the first major legislation ever enacted over a presidential veto. In addition, Congress drafted the **Fourteenth Amendment,** which provided a constitutional basis for the Civil Rights Act.

The Fourteenth Amendment made "all persons born or naturalized in the United States" citizens of the country. All were entitled to equal protection of the law, and no state could deprive any person of life, liberty, or property without due process of law. The amendment did not specifically give African Americans the vote, but it did specify that if any state prevented a portion of its male citizens from voting, that state would lose a percentage of its congressional seats equal to the percentage of citizens kept from the polls. Another provision barred most Confederate leaders from holding federal or state offices unless they were permitted to do so by a two-thirds majority vote of Congress.

THINK THROUGH HISTORY
D. Summarizing What were the main benefits that the Fourteenth Amendment offered African Americans?

D. Answer It made them citizens, promised them due process of law, and tried to discourage states from denying them suffrage.

Congress adopted the Fourteenth Amendment and sent it to the states for approval. If the Southern states had voted to ratify it, most Northern legislators and their constituents would have been satisfied to accept them back into the Union. President Johnson, however, believed that the amendment treated former Confederate leaders too harshly and that it was wrong to force states to accept an amendment that their legislators had no part in drafting. Therefore, he advised the Southern states to reject the amendment. All but Tennessee did reject it, and the amendment was not ratified until 1868.

1866 CONGRESSIONAL ELECTIONS The question of who should control Reconstruction became one of the central issues in the bitter 1866 congressional elections. Johnson went on a long speaking tour, urging voters to elect representatives who agreed with his Reconstruction policy. But his train trip from Washington to St. Louis and Chicago and back, which he called the "swing around the circle," was a disaster. Johnson offended many voters with his rough language and undignified behavior. His audiences responded by jeering at him and cheering General Grant, who had accompanied Johnson on his tour.

In addition, race riots in Memphis, Tennessee, and New Orleans, Louisiana, caused the deaths of at least 80

During his 1866 speaking tour, President Johnson frequently was met by hostile crowds who rejected his Reconstruction policies.

353

---

*Southern Military
Districts, 1867*

Reading the Map What
states were under the command of General Philip
Sheridan? *Texas and
Louisiana.*

Extension Discuss with students why Tennessee was
not part of a military district.
*It had already ratified the
Fourteenth Amendment by
the time the Reconstruction
Act of 1867 was passed, and
was readmitted to the Union
on that basis.*

HISTORICAL SPOTLIGHT

*The Impeachment of
President Johnson*

**Critical Thinking:
Analyzing Causes** The
House impeached Johnson
primarily because he fired
Secretary of War Edward
Stanton. What do you think
were additional causes for
the House's action? *Possible
Answer: Radicals felt he was
not enforcing the Recon-
struction Act.*

HUMANITIES
TRANSPARENCIES
H34, A. Johnson, Tailor

MORE ABOUT . . .

Presidential Succession

Following President
Lincoln's assassination and
Johnson's assumption of
the presidency, the office of
vice-president was left
vacant. If the Senate had
convicted Johnson, he
would have been succeeded
by the president pro
tempore of the Senate—
Benjamin Wade, the Radical
Republican coauthor of the
Wade-Davis Bill.

Southern Military Districts, 1867

VIRGINIA
1870

NORTH
CAROLINA
1868

TENNESSEE
(not part of a military district)
1866

SOUTH
CAROLINA
1868

ARKANSAS
1868

GEORGIA
1870

MISSISSIPPI
1870

ALABAMA
1868

*ATLANTIC
OCEAN*

TEXAS
1870

LOUISIANA
1868

FLORIDA
1868

*Gulf
of Mexico*

Military District and Commander
- ☐ General John Schofield
- ☐ General Daniel Sickles
- ☐ General John Pope
- ☐ General Edward Ord
- ☐ General Philip Sheridan

1870 Date state readmitted
to union

0 — 200 Miles
0 — 400 Kilometers

GEOGRAPHY SKILLBUILDER PLACE *Which former Confederate state
was not included in any military district?* **HUMAN-ENVIRONMENT
INTERACTION** *When was Tennessee readmitted to the Union?*

**Skillbuilder
Answers Place:**
Tennessee **Human-
Environment
Interaction:** 1866

HISTORICAL SPOTLIGHT

THE IMPEACHMENT OF PRESIDENT JOHNSON

The House of Representatives has
the sole power to impeach federal
officials, who are then tried in the
Senate. On February 24, 1868, the
House impeached President
Johnson, primarily on charges that
he violated the Tenure of Office Act.
Johnson's lawyers disputed these
charges by pointing out that
President Lincoln, not Johnson, had
appointed Secretary Stanton, so the
act did not apply.

On the day the final vote was
taken at the trial, tension mounted
in the jammed Senate galleries.
Would the Radicals get the two-
thirds vote needed for conviction?
People in the Senate chamber held
their breath as one by one the
senators gave their verdicts. When
the last senator declared "Not
guilty," the vote was 35 to 19, one
short of the two-thirds majority
needed to convict the president.

African Americans. Such violence
convinced Northern voters that the
federal government must step in to
protect former slaves. In the 1866
elections, moderate and radical
Republicans won a landslide victory
over Democrats. The Republicans
gained a two-thirds majority in
Congress, ensuring them the numbers they needed to override presidential vetoes. By March 1867, the
40th Congress was ready to move
ahead with its Reconstruction policy.

RECONSTRUCTION ACT OF 1867
Radicals and moderates joined in
passing the Reconstruction Act of
1867, which did not recognize state
governments formed under the
Lincoln and Johnson plans—except
for that of Tennessee, which had
ratified the Fourteenth Amendment
and had been readmitted to the
Union. The bill divided the other
ten former Confederate states into five military districts, each headed by a
Union general, as shown in the map on this page. The voters in the districts—
all African-American men, plus those white men who were not disqualified by
the Fourteenth Amendment—would elect delegates to the conventions that
would be called for the purpose of writing new state constitutions. The
bill also required these new constitutions to grant African-American
men the vote and required states to ratify the Fourteenth
Amendment. Once a state had met these terms, Congress would allow
it to reenter the Union.

Johnson vetoed the Reconstruction bill, because, he said, it was
"in palpable conflict with the plainest provisions of the Constitution."
Congress promptly overrode the veto.

JOHNSON IMPEACHED Radical leaders next turned their energies to
getting rid of the antagonistic president. The Radicals felt that Johnson
was not carrying out his constitutional obligation to enforce the
Reconstruction Act. For instance, he removed military officers who
helped African Americans. Because the Radicals thought Johnson was
blocking Reconstruction, they looked for grounds on which to impeach
him—that is, to formally charge him with misconduct in office.

In March 1867, Congress had passed the Tenure of Office Act,
which stated that the president could not remove cabinet officers "during the term of the president by whom they may have been appointed"
without the consent of two-thirds of the Senate. One purpose of this act
was to protect Secretary of War Edward Stanton, an ally of the
Radicals, whose support Congress needed to support Reconstruction.

Johnson, along with many others, was certain that the act was
unconstitutional because it made the executive branch answerable to
the legislature. Still, the act had to be tested in court. Johnson fired
Secretary of War Stanton to force just such a test. His action provided
the Radicals with the opportunity they needed to initiate impeachment
proceedings. The House brought 11 charges of impeachment against Johnson,
9 of which were based on his violation of the Tenure of Office Act.

**THINK THROUGH HISTORY
E. Recognizing
Effects** How did
the election of 1866
affect Republicans'
ability to carry
out their Recon-
struction plan?
E. Answer The
election gave
them a majority
large enough to
pass laws and to
override vetoes.

TEACHING OPTION

Cooperative Activity: Debating President Johnson's Impeachment

Task: Student groups will debate the
impeachment of President Johnson.

Purpose: To understand the issues that led to
the impeachment of the president by the
House and to the Senate's decision not to convict him.

Activity: Groups of three to four students will
choose lots to determine which position they
will uphold—for or against the president's con-

viction. They will then debate the issue in front
of the rest of the class, who will act as the
Senate and will vote on the impeachment on
the basis of the arguments presented by the
two sides.

ALTERNATIVE ASSESSMENT BOOK
Standards for Evaluating a Cooperative Activity

Standards for Evaluation
Presentations should . . .

- show evidence of sound
  research using multiple
  sources
- exhibit good oral pre-
  sentation skills
- use specific details in an
  effort to persuade the
  audience

Major Reconstruction Legislation

LEGISLATION	PROVISIONS
Freedmen's Bureau Acts (1865–66)	Offered assistance, such as medical aid and education, to freed slaves and war refugees
Civil Rights Act of 1866	Granted citizenship and equal protection under the law to African Americans
Reconstruction Act of 1867	Abolished governments formed in the former Confederate states Divided those states into five military districts Set up requirements for readmission into the Union
Enforcement Act of 1870	Protected the voting rights of African Americans and gave the federal government power to enforce the Fifteenth Amendment
Civil Rights Act of 1875	Outlawed racial segregation in public services Assured the right of African Americans to serve as jurors

Johnson's trial before the Senate began in March 1868 and lasted 11 weeks. Until the final day, no one knew what the outcome would be. In the end, despite many members' strong feelings against Johnson, the Senate did not find the president guilty.

U. S. GRANT ELECTED The Democrats knew that they could not win the 1868 presidential election with Johnson, so they nominated the wartime governor of New York, Horatio Seymour. Seymour's Republican opponent was the Civil War hero Ulysses S. Grant. In November, Grant won the presidency by the impressive margin of 214 to 80 in the electoral college. The popular vote, however, was less decisive. Out of almost 6 million ballots cast, Grant received a majority of only 310,000 votes. About 500,000 Southern African Americans had voted, most of them for Grant. The importance of the African-American vote to the Republican Party was obvious.

F. Answer The African-American vote provided a margin of victory for Grant, the Republican candidate.

THINK THROUGH HISTORY
F. Recognizing Effects What role did African Americans play in Grant's election?.

After the election, the Radicals feared that pro-Confederate Southern whites might try to place limits on black suffrage. Therefore, the Radicals introduced the **Fifteenth Amendment,** which states that no one can be kept from voting because of "race, color, or previous condition of servitude." Most Northern states at this time barred African Americans from voting, so these states would be also affected by the Fifteenth Amendment.

The Fifteenth Amendment, which was ratified by the states in 1870, was an important victory for the Radicals. Such political achievements were not, however, the only changes taking place in the Reconstruction period. The period was also a time of profound social and economic changes in the South—changes that would affect the region for many years to come.

SKILLBUILDER
INTERPRETING CHARTS
What was the primary focus of the major Reconstruction legislation?
Skillbuilder Answer
Reestablishing the union and providing for the needs and rights of the freed slaves.

Section 1 Assessment

1. **TERMS & NAMES**
   Identify:
   • Andrew Johnson
   • Reconstruction
   • Radical Republican
   • Thaddeus Stevens
   • Wade-Davis Bill
   • Freedmen's Bureau
   • black codes
   • Fourteenth Amendment
   • Fifteenth Amendment

2. **SUMMARIZING** Recreate the web diagram below on your paper and fill it in with events, plans, or legislation that represent attempts at Reconstruction.

   Reconstruction attempts

   In a paragraph, explain the outcome of one of these attempts at Reconstruction.

3. **HYPOTHESIZING** Describe how Reconstruction might have been different if Abraham Lincoln had lived.

   THINK ABOUT
   • Lincoln's plan for Reconstruction
   • Lincoln's relationship with Radical Republicans
   • Lincoln's ability to negotiate

4. **MAKING DECISIONS** Do you think the Radical Republicans were justified in impeaching President Johnson? Why or why not?

   THINK ABOUT
   • the controversy over Reconstruction policies
   • the meaning of the Tenure of Office Act
   • Johnson's vetoes

Reconstruction and Its Effects **355**

ANSWERS

1. TERMS & NAMES
Andrew Johnson, p. 350
Reconstruction, p. 350
Radical Republican, p. 351
Thaddeus Stevens, p. 351
Wade-Davis Bill, p. 351
Freedmen's Bureau, p. 352
black codes, p. 352
Fourteenth Amendment, p. 353
Fifteenth Amendment, p. 355

2. SUMMARIZING
Possible Responses: Abraham Lincoln's Ten-Percent Plan; Wade-Davis Bill; attempts to continue and enlarge Freedmen's Bureau; Civil Rights Act of 1866; Fourteenth Amendment; Reconstruction Act of 1867; impeachment of Johnson; Fifteenth Amendment. Paragraph should explain how the attempt was a failure or a success.

3. HYPOTHESIZING
Possible Responses: Some students might think that nothing would have been different: Lincoln might have battled and lost against congressional Republicans just as Johnson did. Others might argue that Lincoln had more popular support than did Johnson, and could have negotiated with Congress more effectively.

4. MAKING DECISIONS
Possible Responses: Students might argue that Johnson should have been removed for his Reconstruction policies and lack of cooperation with Congress. Others might argue that since the Tenure of Office Act was unconstitutional, impeachment was wrong; also, his removal might have weakened the presidency.

HISTORY FROM VISUALS
Major Reconstruction Legislation
Reading the Chart Which of the legislation listed dealt with civil rights of former slaves? *The Civil Rights Acts of 1866 and 1875 and the Enforcement Act of 1870.*

Extension Have students write two or three sentences explaining why, in their opinion, the Enforcement Act of 1870 was necessary.

ASSESS & RETEACH

Section 1 Assessment
Assign pairs of students to help each other answer the questions.

Self-Assessment
Have students create a two-column chart to trace their growing knowledge about Reconstruction. In the first column, they should list what they knew about Reconstruction before reading the section. In the second column, they should list what they discovered.

Section Quiz

FORMAL ASSESSMENT
Section Quiz, p. 150

Reteach
Use the Guided Reading Worksheet for Section 1 to help review the main ideas of the section.

IN-DEPTH RESOURCES: UNIT 3
Guided Reading, p. 58

CLOSE

The Fourteenth and Fifteenth Amendments and the civil rights bills that helped enforce them were important political victories for Radical Republicans and former slaves. However, social and economic changes were also taking place in the South.

 HUMANITIES TRANSPARENCIES
H12, *The Fifteenth Amendment*

Teacher's Edition **355**

TERMS & NAMES
• scalawag
• carpetbagger
• Hiram Revels
• sharecropping
• tenant farming

2 Reconstructing Society

LEARN ABOUT the political, social, and economic changes that took place in the South following the Civil War
TO UNDERSTAND the roles that various groups played in the rebuilding of Southern society.

Section 2 Overview

OBJECTIVES

1. To summarize economic problems in the South.
2. To identify differences among members of Republican Party in the South.
3. To describe attitudes of white Southerners.
4. To list efforts of former slaves to improve their lives.

SKILLBUILDERS

• Interpreting political cartoons, p. 358
• Interpreting charts, p. 364

CRITICAL THINKING

• Identifying problems, p. 357
• Comparing, p. 358
• Analyzing motives, p. 359
• Summarizing, pp. 362, 365
• Analyzing issues, p. 363
• Analyzing causes, p. 365
• Generalizing, p. 365
• Interpreting, p. 365

FOCUS & MOTIVATE

▶ **Starting with the Student**
Watch the video "Teacher of a Freed People: Robert Fitzgerald and Reconstruction" to find out how Reconstruction affected one African American.

AMERICAN STORIES VIDEO SERIES
"Teacher of a Freed People"

Video cassette: Volume 2

Videodisc: Disc 1, Side B, Chapter 2

OBJECTIVE

① **INSTRUCT**

Conditions in the Postwar South

▶ **Discussing Key Ideas**
• The South suffers devastating economic losses.
• Per capita wealth of whites falls dramatically.

(continued on next page)

356   **Chapter 12**

ONE AMERICAN'S STORY

Robert G. Fitzgerald was born a free African American in Delaware in 1840. During the Civil War, he served in both the U.S. Army and the U.S. Navy. In 1866, the Freedmen's Bureau sent Fitzgerald to teach in a small Virginia town, where he held classes six hours a day, five days a week, as well as night school two evenings a week. His students were former slaves of all ages who were hungry to learn reading, writing, spelling, arithmetic, and geography. Since textbooks were scarce, Fitzgerald often had to teach from the *Farmer's Almanac* and the Bible. A year after his arrival, Fitzgerald looked back on what he had accomplished.

A Freedmen's school similar to the one where Robert Fitzgerald taught

A PERSONAL VOICE
I came to Virginia one year ago on the 22nd of this month. Erected a school, organized and named the Freedman's Chapel School. Now (June 29th) have about 60 who have been for several months engaged in the study of arithmetic, writing, etc. etc. This morning sent in my report accompanied with compositions from about 12 of my advanced writers instructed from the Alphabet up to their [present] condition, their progress has been surprisingly rapid.
ROBERT G. FITZGERALD, quoted in *Proud Shoes*

Fitzgerald spent 14 months in Virginia and then went to North Carolina, where he lived until his death in 1919. He was one of many who labored diligently against the ignorance and poverty that slavery had forced upon most African Americans. The need to help former slaves, however, was just one of many issues the nation confronted during Reconstruction. In addition, Southerners had to adapt to political, social, and economic changes that no one could have predicted just ten years before.

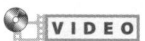

VIDEO *TEACHER OF A FREED PEOPLE*
Robert Fitzgerald and Reconstruction

Conditions in the Postwar South

Southern families like this one lost their homes and most of their possessions because of economic problems after the Civil War.

Under the congressional Reconstruction program, state constitutional conventions met and Southern voters elected new, Republican-dominated governments. By 1868, the former Confederate states of Alabama, Arkansas, Florida, Louisiana, North Carolina, and South Carolina had reentered the Union (joining Tennessee, which had re-entered earlier). The remaining four ex-Confederate states completed the process by 1870. However, even after all the states were back in the Union, the Republicans did not end the process of Reconstruction because they wanted to make economic changes in the South.

PHYSICAL AND ECONOMIC CONDITIONS Because the Civil War was fought mostly on Southern soil, many of the new Southern state governments faced the challenge of physically rebuilding a battle-scarred region. The Union general William T. Sherman estimated that his troops alone had destroyed about $100 million worth of Confederate property in Georgia and South Carolina. A visitor to Charleston, South

Carolina, described "vacant houses . . . rotting wharves . . . deserted warehouses . . . miles of grass-grown streets." Charred buildings, twisted railroad tracks, demolished bridges, neglected roads, and abandoned farms had to be restored or replaced.

The economic effects of the war on the South were devastating. Southern planters returned home to find that the value of their property had plummeted. Those who had invested in Confederate bonds had little hope of recovering their investments. Throughout the South, farmers who owned small plots of land fell into debt because property values had declined. Many small farms were ruined or were in disrepair. As a result of these factors, wealth throughout the South fell dramatically. In one county of Alabama, for example, the wealth per capita among whites dropped from $18,000 in 1860 to about $3,000 in 1870.

Not only were many of the South's economic resources destroyed, but the region's population was devastated. More than one-fifth of the adult white men of the Confederacy died in the war. Many of those who did return from battle were maimed for life. Tens of thousands of Southern African-American men also died, either fighting for the Union or working in Confederate labor camps. In addition, the women and children who had stayed at home often suffered from malnutrition and illness.

PUBLIC WORKS PROGRAMS The Republican governments began public works programs to repair the physical damage and to provide social services. They built roads, bridges, and railroads and established orphanages and institutions for the care of the mentally ill and disabled. They also created the first public school systems that most Southern states had ever had. To carry out these ambitious projects, state governments grew larger and spent more money than before the war.

Economic problems made the tasks of rebuilding the South and extending the role of state governments difficult. Few financial resources were available, since fighting the war had depleted the South's assets and Northern capitalists were reluctant to invest in the region. To raise money, most Southern state governments increased poll taxes and imposed property, sales, and luxury taxes. Between 1860 and 1870, taxes in the South almost tripled. The deepening financial crisis that developed in the South after the Civil War drained existing resources and slowed the region's recovery from the struggle.

Politics in the Postwar South

Another difficulty facing the new Republican governments was that the three groups making up the Republican Party in the South—scalawags, carpetbaggers, and African Americans—often had conflicting goals.

SCALAWAGS AND CARPETBAGGERS Although the terms *scalawag* and *carpetbagger* were negative labels imposed by the Republicans' Democratic opponents, historians still use the terms when referring to the two groups.

Scalawags were white Southerners who joined the Republican Party. Some scalawags wanted the South to industrialize as quickly as possible and believed that this could best be done under a Republican government. Others had supported the Union in the war. The majority were small farmers who

A. Answer
Repairing physical damage, meeting social needs such as education, raising money.

THINK THROUGH HISTORY
A. Identifying Problems What were the main postwar problems that Reconstruction governments in the South had to solve?

Clearing battlefields of human remains was just one of many tasks facing Reconstruction governments.

ANOTHER PERSPECTIVE

NORTH CAROLINA REPUBLICANS

Even though many white Southern Republicans were more interested in their own economic benefit than in African-American civil rights, there were exceptions. One North Carolina Republican declared,

I am willing to give them [whites and blacks] all an equal start in the race. I am for 'Liberty, Union, and political equality.'

Reconstruction and Its Effects **357**

(continued from page 356)
- The region's population is drastically reduced and weakened.
- Taxes are raised to fund public works and social services.

IN-DEPTH RESOURCES: UNIT 3
Guided Reading, p. 59
Primary Source: from *Proud Shoes* by Pauli Murray, p. 65

ACCESS FOR STUDENTS ACQUIRING ENGLISH
Guided Reading (Spanish), p. 123

OBJECTIVE
② INSTRUCT

Politics in the Postwar South

▶ *Starting with the Student*
Ask students what feelings they might expect African Americans and white Southerners to have after the Civil War and how their feelings might affect their political actions.

▶ *Discussing Key Ideas*
- Southern Republicans—scalawags, carpetbaggers, and African Americans—have very different aims.
- African Americans undergo a fundamental change in status.
- White Southerners must deal with defeat.

ANOTHER PERSPECTIVE
North Carolina Republicans

Critical Thinking: Summarizing Have students paraphrase the North Carolina statement in their own words. Ask them to try to convey the tension between individual economic interests and a sense of fair play.

TEACHING OPTIONS

Making Connections Across Time

Reconstruction and the Marshall Plan Discuss with students the aftermath of the Civil War. Ask students who had the responsibility of building up the South again, the federal government or the individual Southern states. Then ask students what they know about the Marshall Plan, which provided U.S. aid to Europe following World War II. Tell them that George Marshall said his aid program was "directed not against any country or doctrine but against hunger, poverty, desperation, and chaos." Ask how this plan was similar to efforts to aid the defeated South.

Making Connections Across the Curriculum

Writing Have students write a description of a Southern homestead as seen by a Southerner—man or woman, black or white—returning there after the war. The description may take the form of a letter to a friend, a scene in a short story, or a passage in a history book. Students may wish to base the description on photographs in this chapter or in other books in their school library. Remind them to consider who they are writing the description for, and to use words and phrases that evoke all the senses.

Reading the Cartoon Have
students identify specific
details used by the cartoonist to convey his view that
the carpetbagger is greedy.
*Possible Responses: The
large sack full of goods that
he carries; the clenching of
his fists; the tight grip he
has on his bag; his pinched
facial expression.*

Extension Horace Greeley
described carpetbaggers as
having "both arms around
the Negroes and their hands
in their rear pockets, seeing
if they can't pick a dollar out
of them." Have students
draw a cartoon expressing
this or another point of view
on carpetbaggers.

MORE ABOUT . . .

Thomas Nast

Thomas Nast (1840–1902)
greatly influenced all political cartoonists who suc-
ceeded him. He created
symbols that are still used
today, including the
Democratic donkey, the
Republican elephant, and
Santa Claus. His work
appeared in the magazine
Harper's Weekly. The drawings that Nast created during the Civil War are
credited with generating
public support for the Union
cause.

**SKILLBUILDER
INTERPRETING
POLITICAL CARTOONS**
*This cartoon from a
Southern Democratic
newspaper depicts Carl
Schurz, a liberal
Republican who
advocated legal equality
for African Americans.
What does the portrayal
suggest about
carpetbaggers?*

Skillbuilder Answer
That they are greedy
Northerners who intend
to plunder the South.

"We are not
prepared for
this suffrage.
But we can
learn."

**WILLIAM BEVERLY
NASH**

wanted to improve their economic position and did not want the
former wealthy planters to regain power. There were, however,
some scalawags who hoped to gain political office with the help
of African-American voters and then enrich themselves as much
as they could. Southern Democrats unfairly pointed to these
unscrupulous individuals as representative of all white
Southern Republicans.

Carpetbaggers were Northerners who moved to the
South after the war. This negative name came from the belief
that they arrived with so few belongings that they carried
everything in a small traveling bag made of carpeting. Like
the scalawags, carpetbaggers had mixed motives. Some were
Freedmen's Bureau agents, teachers, and ministers who felt
a moral duty to help former slaves. Others were Union soldiers who wanted to buy land or businesspeople who hoped to
start new industries. Still others were adventurers who exploited the South's
postwar turmoil for their own profit.

AFRICAN-AMERICAN VOTERS The third and largest group of Southern
Republicans—African Americans—gained voting rights as a result of the
Fifteenth Amendment. During Reconstruction, African-American men registered to vote for the first time; eight out of ten of them supported the
Republican Party. Although many former slaves could neither read nor
write and were politically inexperienced, they were eager to exercise their
voting rights.

A PERSONAL VOICE
We are not prepared for this suffrage. But we can learn. Give a man tools and
let him commence to use them and in time he will learn a trade. So it is with
voting. We may not understand it at the start, but in time we shall learn to do
our duty.
WILLIAM BEVERLY NASH, quoted in *The Trouble They Seen: Black People Tell the Story of Reconstruction*

In many areas, almost 90 percent of the qualified African-American voters
voted. Early in 1868, a Northerner in Alabama observed that "in defiance of
fatigue, hardship, hunger, and threats of employers," African Americans
flocked to the polls.

POLITICAL DIFFERENCES The differences among the goals of scalawags, carpetbaggers, and African Americans led to a lack of unity in the Republican
Party. In particular, few scalawags shared the Republican commitment to civil
rights and suffrage for African Americans. Over time, many of them returned
to the Democratic Party.

In addition, some Republican governors began to appoint white
Democrats to office in an attempt to persuade more white voters to vote
Republican. This policy backfired—it convinced very few white Democrats to
change parties, and it made blacks feel that they had been betrayed.

The new status of African Americans required fundamental changes in the
attitudes of most Southern whites. Some whites supported the Republicans
during Reconstruction and thought that the end of slavery would ultimately
benefit the South. In addition, some Southern farmers and merchants thought
that investment by Northerners would help the South recover from the war.

Many white Southerners, though, refused to accept blacks' new status and
resisted the idea of equal rights. A Freedmen's Bureau agent noted that some
"Southern whites are quite indignant if they are not treated with the same deference as they were accustomed to" under the system of slavery.

Moreover, white Southerners had to adjust to defeat and to the day-to-day
involvement of Northerners in their lives. Eva B. Jones, the wife of a former

THINK THROUGH HISTORY
B. Comparing
*What were some
similarities in
the goals of
scalawags and
carpetbaggers?
carpetbaggers and
African
Americans?*

B. Answer Some
carpetbaggers
and scalawags
shared the goal
of making a
profit. African
Americans
and some
carpetbaggers
shared the goal
of improving
African-American
lives.

Teaching Gifted and Talented Students

Creating a Voting Handbook Ask students to reread the
quote by William Beverly Nash on this page and to consider
what a man living in the South during Reconstruction needed
to learn about voting. Have the students outline a pamphlet
that might have been distributed to freedmen who were voting for the first time. How might the pamphlet meet the needs
of freed slaves who were only barely literate? Have students
include suggestions for nonverbal additions to the pamphlet.

IN-DEPTH RESOURCES: UNIT 3
Primary Source: Frederick Douglass on Voting Rights, p. 64

Making Connections Across the Curriculum

U.S. Government Discuss with students the incredible
turnout of African-American voters when they first received
the right to vote. Ask students if they know the percent of registered voters who voted during recent community, state, or
national elections. Interested students might volunteer to
research the latest records available to them. If possible, have
them look for voting records broken down by ethnic groups.

Confederate officer, understood how difficult that adjustment was for many. In a letter to her mother-in-law, she expressed emotions that were typical of those felt by many ex-Confederates.

A PERSONAL VOICE

We have seen hope after hope fall blighted and withering about us, until our country is no more—merely a heap of ruins and ashes. A joyless future of probable ignomiy, poverty, and want is all that spreads before us. . . . You see, it is with no resigned spirit that *I* yield to the iron yoke our conqueror forges for his fallen and powerless foe. The degradation of a whole country and a proud people is indeed a mighty, an all-enveloping sorrow.

EVA B. JONES, quoted in *The Children of Pride: A True Story of Georgia and the Civil War*

Not all white Southerners were willing to remain in the devastated region. Several thousand planters emigrated to Europe, Mexico, and Brazil after the war.

Former Slaves Improve Their Lives

During this period of turmoil in the South, African Americans saw Reconstruction as a chance to build better lives for themselves. Before emancipation, slaves had been forbidden to travel without permission, to marry legally, to attend school, and to live and work as they chose. After the war, the 4 million former slaves gained the opportunity to make everyday decisions and to take control of their lives.

NEW-WON FREEDOMS At first, many former slaves were cautious about testing the limits of their freedom. One freedman explained, "We was afraid to move. Just like . . . turtles after emancipation. Just stick our heads out to see how the land lay." As the reality of freedom slowly sank in, however, freed African Americans faced many decisions. What were they to do? They had no land, no jobs, no tools, no money, and few skills besides those of farming. How would they feed and clothe themselves? How and where would they live?

One of the first decisions that former slaves had to make was whether to remain where they were. During slavery, white planters had forbidden them to travel without a pass and had enforced that rule by patrolling the roads. During Reconstruction, African Americans took advantage of their new freedom to go where they wanted. One former slave from Texas explained the passion for traveling: "They seemed to want to get closer to freedom, so they'd know what it was like— like it was a place or a city."

The majority of freed African Americans who moved, however, were not just testing their freedom. Thousands were eager to leave plantations that they associated with the oppression of the slave system and move to Southern towns and cities where they could find jobs. Between 1865 and 1870, the African-American population of the ten largest Southern cities doubled.

REUNIFICATION OF FAMILIES Another major reason for former slaves to travel was their desire to track down family members. Slavery had split many African-American families apart; spouses sometimes lived on different plantations and children were separated

Many former slaves bought charts like this one to keep track of their family histories.

Reconstruction and Its Effects **359**

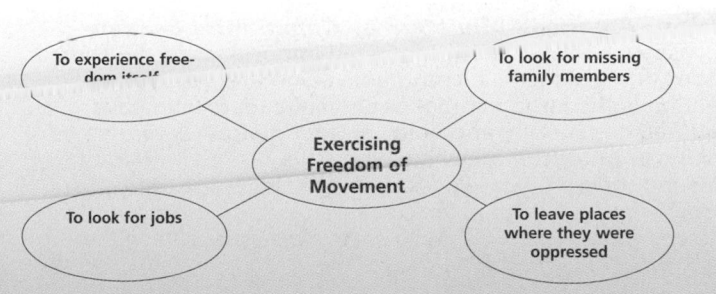

Changing Family Roles

Evolving family roles among freed men and women were a result of many factors. Former slaves were now able to decide which family members would work and what work they would do. Because few men could make a living as sharecroppers or tenant farmers, however, many black women and children continued to work. Most children attended school, though, and only worked after classes.

MORE ABOUT . . .
African-American Colleges

The nation's first colleges for African Americans opened during Reconstruction. Fisk University in Nashville, Tennessee, was established as a liberal arts college in 1866. Howard University, named for Gen. Oliver O. Howard, head of the Freedmen's Bureau, opened in 1867 in Washington, D.C. It offered courses in law, medicine, education, and pharmacy. Hampton Institute in Hampton, Virginia, emphasized industrial arts. It was founded in 1868. Between 1878 and 1912 it received federal aid for educating Native Americans as well.

from their parents. During Reconstruction, many freed African Americans traveled in search of their loved ones. In 1865, for example, one man walked 600 miles from Georgia to North Carolina, looking for his wife and children. The Freedmen's Bureau worked to reunite families, and African-American newspapers printed poignant "Information Wanted" notices about missing relatives. Tragically, in many cases the lost family members were never found.

When husbands and wives were reunited, they took advantage of the new laws that allowed them to marry legally. For the first time, they were able to raise their children without the fear that someone would sell them. In the security of marriage, many former slaves adopted traditional family roles. Husbands took on the role of primary providers, and wives stopped working in the fields so that they could tend to their children and houses as they had seen white women do.

EDUCATION Because slaves had been punished if they tried to learn how to read and write, more than 90 percent of the freed African Americans over the age of 20 were illiterate in 1870. During Reconstruction, however, freed people of all ages—grandparents, parents, children—sought an education.

With the assistance of the Freedmen's Bureau, African-American churches, Northern charitable organizations, and state governments, African Americans organized their own schools, colleges, and universities, such as Hampton Institute in Hampton, Virginia. They raised money to buy land, to build schools, and to pay teachers' salaries. By 1870, African Americans had spent more than $1 million on education. Initially, most teachers in black schools were Northern whites, about half of whom were women. However, educated African Americans like Robert G. Fitzgerald also became teachers, and by 1869, black teachers outnumbered whites in these schools.

Some white Southerners, outraged by the idea of educated African Americans, responded violently. For example, the former slave Washington Eager was murdered because, as his brother explained, he had become "too big a man . . . he [could] write and read and put it down himself."

Despite the threat of violence, freed people were determined to learn. By 1877, more than 600,000 African Americans were enrolled in elementary schools.

CHURCHES AND VOLUNTEER GROUPS
During slavery, many plantation slaves had attended white churches and camp meetings with their owners. Resenting the preachers who urged them to obey their masters, the slaves had also held their own "praise meetings," religious gatherings that featured singing, shouting, and preaching by self-taught slave preachers.

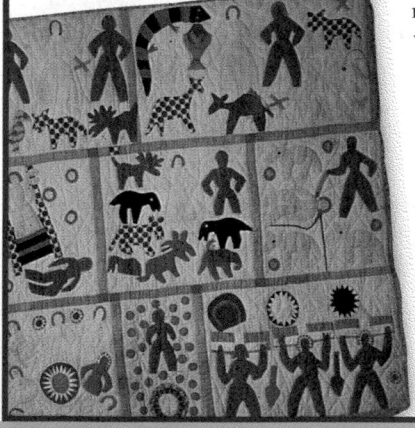
This quilt, made by an African-American woman named Harriet Powers in the 1880s, illustrates how former slaves found ways to proclaim their beliefs—in this case, biblical stories—both publicly and artistically.

From Sharecropper to Shareholder

In the several generations since emanci... many African-American families have m... long, difficult journey from sharecroppe... business owner. For many, education w... key. Higher education, like other oppor... has been slower to come to blacks than... whites. Some African Americans have g... ahead by opening businesses, such as gr... stores, which don't require them to have... college degree. Higher education is usu... needed for further advancement, howev...

1875
Sharecropping was one of the few choices open to former slaves, as well as to poor whites, following the Civil War. As sharecroppers, people could farm land on the plantation for themselves, but they had to turn over much of the profit to the landowner. This system gave them little chance of getting ahead.

Making Connections Across Time

African-American Ministers as Community Leaders
Discuss with students the continued importance of the church in the African-American community. One example you might mention is the large number of church leaders who have assumed community and political leadership. Ask for names of African-American ministers who have played important roles in modern times. *Possible Response: Students may suggest Martin Luther King, Jr., or Jesse Jackson. Some students may mention Malcolm X, who served a similar role in the Black Muslim community.*

Exploring Themes

Expanding Democracy Discuss with students the fact that enslaved men and women had little to say about whom they would live with, how they would raise their children, or the kind of work they would do—basic economic and social decisions that should be ensured to people living in democracies. Exercising their freedom of choice was surely one of the reasons newly liberated black women resisted working in the fields——to make sure that the decision rested with them and their families—not with the plantation owner.

After the war many African Americans founded their own churches, which were usually Baptist or Methodist, and held services similar to the earlier praise meetings. Because churches were the principal institution that African Americans fully controlled, African-American ministers emerged as influential community leaders. They often played an important role in the broader political life of the country as well.

Besides organizing their own schools and churches, freed African Americans formed thousands of volunteer organizations. They established their own fire companies, debating clubs, mutual-aid societies, drama groups, trade associations, and political organizations. These groups not only fostered African-American independence but also provided financial and emotional support for their members. In

1990
In the 1990s, the number of African-American–owned businesses is increasing nearly twice as fast as the number of majority-owned businesses, and not simply because blacks are a growing portion of the population. Education has played a major role.

1996
His grandfather was a sharecropper; his father, a mail clerk. Now Vernon Jordan is an influential corporate director, attorney, and adviser to President Clinton. Not only did he realize the value of education in achieving his own goals, but he served as director of the Voter Education Project and as executive director of the United Negro College Fund to help other African Americans achieve their goals. Jordan headed President Clinton's transition team in 1992 and also serves as director of the Ford Foundation and of 11 of America's largest corporations.

Recent Trends for African Americans

AFRICAN-AMERICAN EDUCATION

1970
1993

0   20   40   60   80   100
Percentage Receiving Education Level

■ College
■ High School

NEW BLACK-OWNED BUSINESSES

1987
1992   +46%
   +26%

0   .5   1   1.5   2
Millions of Businesses

■ New Black-Owned Businesses
■ Total New Businesses

Source: *The U.S. Census Bureau*

INTERACT WITH HISTORY

1. **DRAWING CONCLUSIONS** How does the number of new African-American-owned businesses compare with the number of new businesses overall for the period shown? What conclusions can you draw from this information and from success stories like Vernon Jordan's?

   SEE SKILLBUILDER HANDBOOK, PAGE 1050.

2. **GATHERING DATA** Interview someone you know who has started a small business. Ask the person what he or she needed in order to get started. Ask about experience, education, money, and business partners. Present a short report to the class. Together create a class chart summarizing what you have learned about the effects of various factors on success in business.

Reconstruction and Its Effects **361**

addition, these volunteer organizations offered African Americans opportunities to develop their leadership skills.

BLACK RECONSTRUCTION After the war, African Americans took an active role in the political process. Not only did they vote, but they organized black conventions to demand equal rights and protection under the law. They also joined influential political groups, such as the Union League. Some served as delegates to the state constitutional conventions held between 1867 and 1869.

The period from 1865 to 1877 is sometimes called Black Reconstruction because of African-American involvement in politics. For the first time, African Americans held office in local, state, and federal government. At first, most African Americans in politics were freeborn. By 1867, however, former slaves were playing an increasing role in political organizations and were winning a greater number of offices. Many of these black officeholders were ministers or teachers who had been educated in the North.

Nevertheless, even though there were more black voters than white voters in the South, African-American officeholders remained in the minority. Only South Carolina had a black majority in the state legislature. No Southern state elected an African-American governor. Moreover, out of 125 Southerners elected to the U.S. Congress during congressional Reconstruction, only 16 were African Americans. Among these was **Hiram Revels,** the first African-American senator.

LAWS AGAINST SEGREGATION By the end of 1866, most of the Republican Southern state governments had repealed the black codes. African-American legislators took social equality a step further by proposing bills to desegregate public transportation. In 1871, Texas passed a law prohibiting railroads from making distinctions between groups of passengers, and several other states followed suit. However, many antisegregation laws were not enforced. State orphanages, for example, usually had separate facilities for white and black children.

African Americans themselves were often more interested in black community than in total integration. By establishing separate African-American institutions—such as schools, churches, and social organizations—they were able to promote African-American leadership and escape the interference of the whites who had so long dominated their lives.

KEY PLAYER

HIRAM REVELS
1827–1901
Hiram Revels of Mississippi, pictured above on the far left, was born of free parents in Fayetteville, North Carolina. Because he could not obtain an education in the South, he attended Knox College in Illinois. As an African Methodist Episcopal minister, he recruited African Americans to fight for the Union during the Civil War and also served as an army chaplain.

In 1865, Revels settled in Mississippi, where he helped organize African-American churches and schools. He served on the Natchez city council and then was elected to Mississippi's state senate in 1869. In 1870, Revels became the first African American elected to the U.S. Senate. Ironically, he held the seat that had once belonged to Jefferson Davis, the former president of the Confederacy.

THINK THROUGH HISTORY
D. Summarizing
How did freed African Americans try to improve their lives?
D. Answer They searched for missing family members, sought an education, formed churches and volunteer groups, and demanded political power.

Changes in the Southern Economy

When asked to explain the idea of freedom, Garrison Frazier, a former slave turned Baptist minister, said that it consisted in "placing us where we could reap the fruit of our own labor." To accomplish this, Frazier said, freed African Americans needed "to have land, and turn it and till it." Most former slaves strongly desired to own property. Few, however, had enough money to buy land, and those who did have cash were frequently frustrated by whites' refusal to sell property to them.

40 ACRES AND A MULE In January 1865, during the Civil War, General Sherman had promised the freed slaves who followed his army 40 acres per family and the use of army mules. Soon afterward, about 40,000 freed persons settled on 400,000 acres in coastal Georgia and South Carolina. Some of this land had been abandoned by its owners, and the government seized the rest from planters who had supported the Confederacy. The freed African

Americans farmed their plots until August 1865, when President Johnson ordered that the original landowners be allowed to reclaim their land and evict the former slaves.

Many freed African Americans asserted that they deserved part of the planters' land. An Alabama black convention declared, "The property which they hold was nearly all earned by the sweat of *our* brows." Some Radical Republicans agreed. Thaddeus Stevens called for the government to confiscate the plantations of 70,000 or so "chief rebels" and to redistribute part of the land to former slaves. However, his plan failed because many Republicans considered private property a basic American right that must not be violated. As a result, Congress either rejected land-reform proposals or passed weak legislation. An example was the 1866 Southern Homestead Act. Although it set aside 44 million acres in the South for freed blacks and loyal whites, the land was swampy and unsuitable for farming. Furthermore, few homesteaders had the resources—seed, tools, plows, and horses—to farm successfully.

RESTORATION OF PLANTATIONS Although African Americans and poor whites wanted to own small farms, the planter class wanted to restore the plantation system, in which many acres were devoted to a single profitable cash crop, such as cotton. Some wealthy Northern merchants and owners of textile mills encouraged the planters in their efforts to reestablish plantations and resume widespread cotton production.

Planters claimed that to make the plantation system work, they needed to have almost complete control over their laborers. When the planters had owned slaves, they had forced young and old and men and women to work in the fields for extremely long hours. Now the planters feared that they might not be able to make a profit, since they had to pay their laborers wages and could no longer force African Americans to put in such brutally long workdays. In addition, many former slaveholders deeply resented having to negotiate for the services of former slaves.

Planters also faced a labor shortage, caused by a number of factors. The high death toll of the war had reduced the number of able-bodied workers. Many African-American women and children refused to work in the fields after they were freed. Laborers sometimes left plantations to seek better working conditions at other plantations. Finally, many freed persons felt that raising cotton under the direction of white overseers was too much like slavery. As an alternative, some worked in mills or on railroad construction crews.

Field hands display the day's peanut harvest.

(continued from page 362)

Discussing Key Ideas
• Freed slaves hunger for land.
• Planters need a labor force to restore their plantations.
• Both groups dislike the wage-labor system and look to sharecropping and tenant farming as alternatives.
• Falling cotton prices lead to some economic diversification.

IN-DEPTH RESOURCES: UNIT 3
Geography Application: The Economic Effects of the Civil War, p. 62

 ELECTRONIC LIBRARY OF PRIMARY SOURCES
from an Address on Reconstruction by Thaddeus Stevens

MORE ABOUT . . .
40 Acres and a Mule
Large numbers of freed slaves followed Sherman's army on its march to the sea. He ordered coastal land to be set aside for freed slaves as a way of relieving himself of this problem. He later claimed that he intended the occupation of the land by the former slaves to be only temporary. The freed African Americans, however, were reluctant to give up the land once they had settled on it.

 GEOGRAPHY TRANSPARENCIES
G12, The Barrow Plantation, 1860, 1881

THINK THROUGH HISTORY
E. Analyzing Issues *Thaddeus Stevens believed that giving land to former slaves was more important than giving them the vote. Do you agree or disagree? Why?*

E. Answer Agree—because freed persons needed their own land in order to gain economic independence; Disagree—because the right to vote gave freed men the power to change society's laws.

TEACHING OPTION

Exploring Themes

Constitutional Concerns Have students read together the Fifth Amendment on page 158. Then have them focus on this excerpt: "No person shall be . . . deprived of life, liberty, or property, without due process of law; nor shall private property be taken for public use, without just compensation."

Have students discuss the issue of each person's right to private property. Ask students to explain why the government did not simply take away land from large plantation owners and give it to former slaves. *Possible Response: It would be a*
violation of the Fifth Amendment because the government would be confiscating private property.

Ask students what the government might have done to protect the right to private property for both plantation owners and freedmen. *Possible Responses: President Johnson could have kept General Sherman's promise of "40 acres and a mule" for former slaves; since as slaves they had been deprived of their right to own land, freedmen should have been compensated by the government.*

The Sharecropper Cycle of Poverty

Reading the Diagram

When and where in the diagram does the cycle of sharecropping begin? *Possible Responses: When the landowner gives the sharecropper land and seed, at the top of the chart.*

Extension Have students create a similar diagram for tenant farming. Ask them to begin their cycle with a sharecropper who has saved enough money to purchase tools and a horse or mule, and rent some land.
Possible items in cycle: Purchases tools and mule; rents land; buys seed; buys food and clothing, some on credit; plants crop; harvests crop; sells crop; pays rent and debts; saves a little if possible.

CRITICAL THINKING TRANSPARENCIES

CT46, Agricultural Production in the South: 1850–1900

The Sharecropper Cycle of Poverty

The cycle begins here.

Sharecropper is given land and seed by landowner.

The plots are small, so crop yields are low.

Buys food and clothing on credit.

Same crop year after year eventually depletes the soil.

Plants crop

Sharecropper is at the mercy of the market.

Harvests crop and gives landowner his share.

Sells remaining crop at market.

Crooked landowners charge unfair fines.

Pays off account with merchants.

If he has any leftover cash

Sharecropper becomes tenant farmer and a new cycle begins.

Sharecroppers were supposed to have a chance to climb the economic ladder, but by the time they had shared their crops and paid their debts, they rarely had any money left. A sharecropper frequently became tied to one plantation, having no choice but to work until his debts were paid.

INTERPRETING CHARTS

How did the sharecropping system make it hard for small farmers to improve their standard of living?

Skillbuilder Answer The system was rigged so they had little or no money left at the end of the year.

Others tried to support themselves through subsistence farming—growing just enough food for their own families. To stop this trend, white planters were determined to keep the former slaves from getting land that they could use to support themselves.

SHARECROPPING AND TENANT FARMING Without their own land, freed African Americans could not grow crops to sell or to use to feed their families. Therefore, economic necessity forced many former slaves to sign labor contracts with planters. In exchange for wages, housing, and food, freedmen worked in the fields. Although the Freedmen's Bureau promoted this wage-labor system, it did not satisfy either freedmen or planters. On the one hand, freedmen thought that the wages were too low and that white employers had too much control over them. On the other hand, planters often lacked sufficient cash to pay workers. These conditions led planters and laborers to experiment with two alternative arrangements: sharecropping and tenant farming.

In the system of **sharecropping,** landowners divided their land and gave each worker—either freed African American or poor white—a few acres, along with seed and tools. When crops were harvested, each worker gave a share of his crop, usually half, to the landowner. This share paid the owner back and ended the arrangement until it was renewed the following year. The chart on this page shows the sharecropping system in detail.

In theory, "croppers" who saved a little and bought their own tools could drive a better bargain with landowners. Those who bought their own horses or mules might even become tenants and rent land for cash in a system known as **tenant farming.** Eventually they might move up the economic ladder to become outright owners of their farms.

The arrangement seldom worked that way in practice, however. Most tenant farmers bought their supplies on credit. Merchants charged high prices in return for a claim on a share of the farmer's future crops. Consequently, farmers did not harvest enough crops to pay for both past debts and future supplies. The end result was that very few farmers saved enough cash to buy their farms.

COTTON NO LONGER KING Another economic change turned Southern agriculture upside down: cotton was no longer king. During the war, demand

---

Making Connections Across the Curriculum

Economics Ask students to compare the sharecropper cycle of poverty shown on this page with the diagram they created showing the cycle of tenant farming. Students should recognize that the cycle for tenant farmers differed little from that for sharecroppers. The major distinction was that tenant farmers owned their own tools and theoretically were in a position to negotiate a better bargain with their landlord. However, the vagaries of the market meant that many tenant farmers bought tools on credit and ended up in the same cycle of poverty as sharecroppers.

Making Connections Across Time

Cotton Production Today Ask students if they know who produces the world's cotton today. Some students may be surprised to learn that the United States produces 20 percent of the world's cotton, second only to China, which produces 25 percent. Within the United States, Texas produces the most—over 1 million short tons. Three states—Texas, California, and Mississippi—together produce more than 50 percent of the nation's annual crop of cotton.

for Southern cotton had begun to drop as other countries increased their cotton production. As a result, prices plummeted after the war. In 1869, the price of cotton was 16.5 cents per pound. By the late 1870s, the price had fallen to about 8 cents per pound. Instead of diversifying —or varying—their crops, Southern planters tried to make up for the lower prices by growing more cotton—which only drove down prices even further, creating a vicious cycle.

Agricultural problems did lead to attempts to diversify the economy of the South. Textile mills sprang up, and a new industry—tobacco-product manufacturing—took hold. Diversification helped raise the average wage in the South, though it was still much lower than that of Northern workers.

At the end of the Civil War, most of the state banks in the South were saddled with Confederate debts. In the following years, falling cotton prices and mounting planters' debts caused many banks to fail. The only credit that Southerners in rural areas could get was that offered by local merchants. Despite efforts to improve the Southern economy, the devastating economic impact of the Civil War rippled through Southern life into the 20th century.

Many whites, frustrated by their loss of political power and by the South's economic stagnation, took out their anger on African Americans. In the late 1860s and early 1870s, certain white groups embarked on a campaign to terrorize African Americans into giving up their political rights and their efforts at economic improvement.

Successful Southern industries included an ironworks in Birmingham and plants that manufactured new tobacco products.

Section 2 Assessment

1. TERMS & NAMES

Identify:
• scalawag
• carpetbagger
• Hiram Revels
• sharecropping
• tenant farming

2. SUMMARIZING List five problems facing the South after the Civil War, and at least one attempted solution for each one. Use a table such as this one.

Problem	Attempted Solution

3. GENERALIZING How did the Civil War weaken the Southern economy? Give examples to support your viewpoint.

THINK ABOUT
• the devastation of the war
• economic conditions
• changes in agriculture

4. INTERPRETING Which accomplishment of African Americans during Reconstruction do you consider most significant? Explain your choice.

THINK ABOUT
• the development of a free African-American community
• the lingering effects of slavery
• opportunities for leadership

Reconstruction and Its Effects **365**

ANSWERS

1. TERMS & NAMES

scalawag, p. 357

carpetbagger, p. 358

Hiram Revels, p. 362

sharecropping, p. 364

tenant farming, p. 364

2. SUMMARIZING

Possible Responses: Physical devastation/ public works programs; Former slaves separated from their families/search for family members; Lack of education/how schools established; Lack of land/Southern Homestead Act; Labor shortage/sharecropping or tenant farming.

3. GENERALIZING

Possible Responses: Destruction of bridges and roads; devastation of population; devaluation of property; increased personal and government debts; falling cotton prices; lack of land for freedmen; increased taxes.

4. INTERPRETING

Possible Responses: Founding of churches, because African Americans controlled them and their ministers emerged as leaders; establishing schools, because they provided the first opportunity for many African Americans to learn to read and write; involvement in politics, because political power was a means of attaining equal rights.

(1) To summarize violent actions by opponents of Reconstruction.

(2) To Identify reasons for the shift of political power from the Southern Republicans to the Southern Democrats.

(3) To describe the effect of the Supreme Court's decisions on Reconstruction.

(4) To identify reasons for the collapse of congressional Reconstruction.

(5) To list achievements and failures of Reconstruction.

SKILLBUILDERS

• Interpreting political cartoons, pp. 368, 370

CRITICAL THINKING

• Analyzing motives, pp. 367, 370
• Analyzing effects, p. 368
• Clarifying, p. 369
• Analyzing Issues, p. 371
• Recognizing effects, p. 373
• Sequencing history, p. 373
• Analyzing, p. 373
• Evaluating, p. 373

FOCUS & MOTIVATE

▶ *Starting with the Student*
• How do students react when they have a good idea but don't have the money or power to implement it?
• How would they deal with opponents who had the money or power they lacked?

MORE ABOUT . . .
Henry McNeal Turner

Turner, like many supporters of Reconstruction, was bitterly disappointed when it failed. In response, he left politics and devoted himself to the ministry. Turner continued to be an outspoken advocate of African-American emigration to Africa. When in 1878 an African-American-run steamship left Charleston for Africa carrying 200 emigrating blacks, Turner gave the journey his benediction.

366 **Chapter 12**

---

③ The Collapse of Reconstruction

TERMS & NAMES
• Ku Klux Klan
• Panic of 1873
• redemption
• Rutherford B. Hayes
• Samuel J. Tilden
• home rule

LEARN ABOUT the political, economic, and social problems that plagued the nation from 1873 to 1877
TO UNDERSTAND why Reconstruction ultimately collapsed.

Henry M. Turner

ONE AMERICAN'S STORY

Henry McNeal Turner was born a free African American in South Carolina in 1834. He became a minister of the African Methodist Episcopal Church and served as a chaplain for black troops in the Civil War.

After the war, Turner worked briefly for the Freedmen's Bureau and later became a delegate to Georgia's constitutional convention and was elected to the state's first Reconstruction legislature.

In 1868, white Georgia legislators, who were in the majority in both houses, expelled 27 black members of the state senate and house of representatives. The new state constitution gave African Americans the right to vote, they argued, but not to hold office. Outraged by this expulsion, Turner addressed the Georgia House of Representatives.

A PERSONAL VOICE
Whose Legislature is this? Is it a white man's Legislature or is it a black man's . . . ? It is said that Congress never gave us the right to hold office. I want to know . . . if the Reconstruction measures did not base their action on the ground that no distinction should be made on account of race, color or previous condition! . . . We have built up your country. We have worked in your fields, and garnered your harvests, for two hundred and fifty years! Do we ask you for compensation . . . ? We are willing to let the dead past bury its dead; but we ask you now for our rights.
HENRY M. TURNER, quoted in *The Trouble They Seen: Black People Tell the Story of Reconstruction*

Turner and his colleagues petitioned the U.S. Congress and were eventually reinstated in office. But by the time Congress acted, more than a year later, their terms were almost at an end. Turner was deeply embittered by this experience. He also continued to speak out about racial injustice. By the end of the 19th century, he had become a leading proponent of African-American emigration to Africa.

Unfortunately, Henry Turner was far from being the only African American to suffer injustice during Reconstruction.

Opposition to Reconstruction

Most white Southerners swallowed whatever resentment they felt over African-American suffrage and participation in government. Some whites expressed their feelings by refusing to register to vote. However, a minority took more direct action, like the Georgia legislators who expelled Henry Turner and his colleagues from the state legislature. In addition, some bitter Southern whites used violence to intimidate African Americans and keep them from participating in politics.

KU KLUX KLAN During the period of congressional Reconstruction, some white Southerners formed vigilante groups, which whipped, tortured, and murdered former slaves in an attempt to restore white supremacy. The most notorious and widespread of these groups was the **Ku Klux Klan.**

Founded by six Confederate veterans, the Ku Klux Klan began as a social club in Tennessee in 1866. As membership in the group spread rapidly through

---

SECTION 3 RESOURCES

PRINT RESOURCES

IN-DEPTH RESOURCES: UNIT 3
Guided Reading, p. 60
Skillbuilder Practice: Evaluating Decisions, p. 61
Primary Sources: An Inquiry on the Condition of the South, p. 66; Political Cartoon, p. 67

ACCESS FOR STUDENTS ACQUIRING ENGLISH
Guided Reading (Spanish), p. 124
Skillbuilder Practice: Evaluating Decisions (Spanish), p. 125

FORMAL ASSESSMENT
Section Quiz, p. 152

ALTERNATIVE ASSESSMENT BOOK
See forms for supporting and scoring alternative activities.

TECHNOLOGY RESOURCES

CRITICAL THINKING TRANSPARENCIES
CT12, Reconstruction

CD-ROM *Grolier Multimedia Encyclopedia*

VIDEO *American Portfolio: A Videodisc for U.S. History* user's guide, pp. 115–120

INTERNET McDougal Littell Learning On-Line
http://www.mcdougallittell.com

THINK THROUGH HISTORY
A. Analyzing
Motives
What were the
goals of the KKK?

A. Answer To
destroy the
Republican Party,
oust the
Reconstruction
governments,
help planters
control African-
American
laborers, and
prevent African
Americans from
exercising their
political rights.

the South, Democratic politicians and former Confederate officers took control of many of the new chapters and turned them into violent terrorist organizations. By 1868, the Klan existed in every Southern state. Its goals were to destroy the Republican Party, to throw out the Reconstruction governments, to aid the planter class in controlling African-American laborers, and to prevent African Americans from exercising their political rights.

To achieve these goals, the Klan resorted to burning cabins and churches and murdering innocent people. Between 1868 and 1871, the Klan and other secret groups killed several thousand men, women, and children. Some of the victims were white Republicans, such as the North Carolina state senator John Stephens, who answered warnings that his life was in danger by saying that some 3,000 African-American voters had supported him "at the risk of persecution and starvation" and that he would not abandon them. The Klan assassinated Stephens in 1870.

The Klan also attacked other Southern whites who tried to help African Americans. Teachers, landowners who rented to African Americans, and merchants who bought African Americans' cotton crops frequently suffered Klan violence.

ANTI-BLACK VIOLENCE The vast majority of Klan victims were African Americans, however. Abram Colby, who organized a branch of Georgia's Equal Rights Association and later served as a Republican member of the Georgia legislature, testified before Congress about Klan atrocities.

A PERSONAL VOICE
[The Klan] broke my door open, took me out of bed, took me to the woods and whipped me three hours or more and left me for dead. They said to me, "Do you think you will ever vote another damned radical ticket?" . . . I supposed they would kill me anyhow. I said, "If there was an election tomorrow, I would vote the radical ticket." They set in and whipped me a thousand licks more, with sticks and straps that had buckles on the ends of them.

ABRAM COLBY, from *Testimony Taken by the Joint Select Committee to Inquire into the Condition of Affairs in the Late Insurrectionary States*

As the violence increased, more whites turned against the Klan. One Klan leader, the former Confederate general Nathan Bedford Forrest, even tried to get the organization to disband. However, enough whites remained silent about the outrages for the terrorism to continue.

While the Klan operated in secret, some Southern Democrats openly used violence to intimidate Republicans. Before the 1875 state election in Mississippi, Democrats rioted, disrupted rallies, attacked Republican leaders, and murdered prominent African Americans. Their terrorist campaign frightened the African-American majority away from the polls, and white Democratic candidates swept the election. In the 1876 elections, Democrats in Florida, South Carolina, and Louisiana adopted similar tactics to prevent African Americans from voting.

ECONOMIC PRESSURE The Klan and other secret groups tried to prevent African Americans from making economic, as well as political, progress. For example, Klansmen frequently killed livestock belonging to former slaves. They attacked African Americans who owned their own land to force them to labor for white landowners. Finally, the Klan often whipped African Americans who complained about their employers or who worked in occupations other than agriculture.

Although the Ku Klux Klan disguised themselves, the results of their terrorism were unmistakable.

"The Klan . . . whipped me three hours or more and left me for dead."

ABRAM COLBY

Reconstruction and Its Effects **367**

OBJECTIVE
① INSTRUCT

Opposition to Reconstruction

▶ *Starting with the Student*
Discuss with students the emotional climate in the South. Have them create a cluster diagram showing events that led to tension.

Tension in the South

▶ *Discussing Key Ideas*
• The Ku Klux Klan unleashes terrorism against African Americans.
• Reconstruction opponents exert economic pressure.
• Congressional legislation curtails Klan violence but weakens the Republican Party in the South.

IN-DEPTH RESOURCES: UNIT 3
Guided Reading, p. 60

ACCESS FOR STUDENTS ACQUIRING ENGLISH
Guided Reading (Spanish), p. 124

MORE ABOUT . . .
Resistance to the Ku Klux Klan

In areas where the Ku Klux Klan was most active, legal resistance proved to be ineffective. In Meridian, Mississippi, an 1871 court hearing of three African Americans charged with "incendiary speeches" was interrupted by gunshots. The Republican judge and two of the defendants were killed, and in the rioting that followed 30 African Americans were murdered.

IN-DEPTH RESOURCES: UNIT 3
Primary Source: An Inquiry on the Condition of the South, p. 66

TEACHING OPTIONS

Exploring Themes

Cultural Diversity Discuss with students the devastating effect that racial prejudice has had on American society. Many of the Ku Klux Klan's goals were political and economic, such as legislative control and a cheap, reliable labor force. However, their illegal, murderous actions were directed at one racial group—blacks—and their white supporters. Ask students what other groups have also suffered from racial persecution in this country's history. *Possible Responses: Students may identify the treatment of Native Americans or immigrant minorities.* Discuss what steps have been and can be taken to help Americans live with—and learn from— cultural diversity.

Making Connections Across the Curriculum

Writing Freed slaves were bitterly disappointed that white leaders were not more vocal in their opposition to the Klan. "One short letter (from a prominent former North Carolina governor) could put down all these outrages," one black legislator insisted. Have students write a short letter from the point of view of a white Southern leader condemning the terrorist acts of the Klan. Remind the students that their audience will be Klan members who have participated in violence or who have supported it. Ask students to construct persuasive arguments that would be convincing to such an audience.

Teacher's Edition   367

Scandals and Money Crises Hurt Republicans

▶ **Starting with the Student**
Ask students to think about how people react today when they hear of violent or terrorist actions occurring in another country or in another part of this country. How do those reactions compare with reactions of Northerners to murderous acts of the Ku Klux Klan?

▶ **Discussing Key Ideas**
• Scandals weaken the Republican Party.
• Reformers within the party join Democrats in backing Horace Greeley, who loses the election to Grant.
• Bank and business failures cause the Panic of 1873 and an economic depression.
• The nation debates the gold standard.

 GROLIER MULTIMEDIA ENCYCLOPEDIA
excerpt from *The Personal Memoirs of U. S. Grant*

HISTORY FROM VISUALS
Interpreting Political Cartoons

Reading the Cartoon What political scandals can students identify from the packets lying outside the barrel? *Possible Responses: Secretary of War Belknap's acceptance of bribes; the Whiskey Ring bribery scandal.*

Extension Have students write a paragraph explaining the cartoon to someone unfamiliar with the history, such as a younger child or a foreign pen pal.

More frequently, white Southerners used nonviolent economic pressure to exert control over African Americans. In fact, economic necessity forced most former slaves to work for whites as wage laborers or sharecroppers. Some white Southern employers and merchants refused to hire or do business with African Americans who voted Republican. Officials knew because they watched people vote. The fear of economic reprisals kept many former slaves from voting for Republican candidates or from going to the polls at all.

LEGISLATIVE RESPONSE To curtail Klan violence and Democratic intimidation, Congress passed a series of Enforcement Acts in 1870 and 1871. One act provided for the federal supervision of elections in Southern states. Another act gave the president the power to use federal troops in areas where the Klan was active.

By this time, several groups—the federal government, African Americans, and many white Southerners—opposed the Klan's activities. Because of this opposition the Klan's activities decreased, but individual acts of violence against blacks and white Republicans continued.

SHIFTS IN POLITICAL POWER Although Congress seemed to shore up Republican power with the Enforcement Acts, it soon passed legislation that severely weakened the power of the Republican Party in the South. Many white Southerners complained that their most experienced leaders had been barred from public service.

To remedy this situation, in May 1872, Congress passed the Amnesty Act. This act returned the right to vote and the right to hold federal and state offices to about 160,000 former Confederates—who would almost certainly vote Democratic. Only about 500 of the highest-ranking Confederate leaders did not regain their political rights under this act. In the same year Congress allowed the Freedmen's Bureau to expire, believing that it had fulfilled its purpose. As a result of these actions, Southern Democrats had an opportunity to shift the balance of political power in their favor.

B. Answer It restored political rights to 160,000 former Confederates, who were almost all Democrats.

THINK THROUGH HISTORY
B. *Analyzing Effects* How did the Amnesty Act strengthen Democratic power?

Scandals and Money Crises Hurt Republicans

U. S. GRANT: "I HOPE I GET TO THE BOTTOM SOON."

SKILLBUILDER
INTERPRETING POLITICAL CARTOONS
What does this cartoon imply about President Grant's ability to deal with corruption in his administration?

As Republicans struggled to maintain their hold on Reconstruction governments in the South, widespread political corruption in the federal government weakened their party. During the early 1870s, scandals plagued the Grant administration. These scandals diverted public attention in the North away from conditions in the South.

FRAUD AND BRIBERY President Grant, who was elected for a second term in 1872, was considered an honest man and was never found guilty of any wrongdoing. However, he had had no political experience before becoming president and found it difficult to believe that others might use him for their own political advantage. When making political appointments, he often selected friends and acquaintances rather than people of proven ability. Too frequently, Grant's appointees turned out to be dishonest.

Beginning in 1872, a series of long-simmering scandals associated with Grant's administration boiled over. First, the *New York Sun* exposed the Crédit Mobilier affair, in which a construction company had skimmed off outrageously large profits from a government railroad contract. This scandal involved several leading Republicans, including Grant's first vice-president, Schuyler Colfax.

Next came the exposure of the so-called Whiskey Ring, in which internal revenue collectors and other officials accepted bribes from whiskey distillers who wanted to avoid paying taxes on their product—a conspiracy that defrauded the federal government of millions of dollars in revenue. One of the

Skillbuilder Answer That Grant was in over his head when dealing with corrupt appointees.

 Cooperative Activity: Staging a Presidential Debate

Task: Students will stage a debate between the two presidential candidates in the 1870 election—incumbent president Grant and Horace Greeley.

Purpose: To enable students to explore in depth political issues and the differences between the two candidates.

Activity: Students should form two teams—one supporting President Grant and the other supporting Horace Greeley. The teams should choose one member to represent the candidate. The others will serve as advisors during their candidate's presentation and as questioners of the opposing candidate.

Suggest that students follow these steps:

• Research their candidate's position on important issues of the time.
• Identify the opposing candidate's positions, including major strengths and weaknesses.
• Prepare a list of questions for the debate. These will serve both as points on which teams can examine the opposing candidate and as a way of structuring their own candidate's position.

ALTERNATIVE ASSESSMENT BOOK
Standards for Evaluating a Cooperative Activity

238 persons indicted in this scandal was Grant's private secretary, General Orville E. Babcock. Grant refused to believe that such a close associate was guilty and helped him escape conviction.

Finally, in 1876, an investigation revealed that Secretary of War William W. Belknap had accepted bribes from merchants who wanted to keep their profitable trading concessions in Indian territory. The House of Representatives impeached Belknap, who promptly resigned. The public also learned that the secretary of the navy had taken bribes from shipbuilders and the secretary of the interior had had shady dealings with land speculators. As the evidence of widespread dishonesty mounted, many grew disgusted with the blatant corruption in the Grant administration.

REPUBLICAN UNITY SHATTERED Reformers within the Republican party went on the attack against this graft and corruption. A group of Missouri Republicans, angered by the corruption, called for honest, efficient government. They banded together to form the Liberal Republican Party in 1872.

As the 1872 presidential election approached, the Liberal Republicans held a separate convention to nominate a candidate. They chose Horace Greeley, the editor of the *New York Tribune* and a vocal pre–Civil War abolitionist, as their nominee. He had supported some Radical Republican actions—abolition and the Fourteenth and Fifteenth Amendments. However, he had broken with Radicals by calling for universal amnesty for Confederates and for an end to military rule in the South. Claiming that Reconstruction governments had achieved their purpose, he wanted former slaves to fend for themselves.

Believing that it would take a united effort to oust Grant, the Democrats also nominated Greeley—even though he had once called them "murderers . . . drunkards, cowards, liars, thieves." Nevertheless, Greeley lost the 1872 presidential election to Grant by a wide margin. "I was the worst beaten man that ever ran for that high office," Greeley said, "and I have been assailed so bitterly that I hardly know whether I was running for President or the penitentiary." Physically exhausted by his rigorous campaign, Greeley died a few weeks after the election—before the electoral college made his defeat official.

Although the Liberal Republicans did not succeed in winning the White House, they did weaken the Radicals' hold over the Republican Party. The breakdown of Republican unity made it even harder for the Radicals to continue to impose their Reconstruction plan on the South.

PANIC OF 1873 As if political scandals were not enough for the country to deal with, a depression hit the nation in 1873. The economy had been expanding since the end of the Civil War, so that investors became convinced that business profits would continue to increase indefinitely. Eager to take advantage of new business opportunities in the South, Northern and Southern investors borrowed enormous amounts of money and built new facilities as quickly as possible.

Unfortunately, many of those who invested in these new businesses took on more debt than they could afford. A Philadelphia banker named Jay Cooke invested heavily in railroads. Not enough investors bought shares in Cooke's railroad lines to cover his

THINK THROUGH HISTORY
C. *Clarifying*
How widespread was the corruption in the Grant administration?

C. Answer It involved his first vice-president, his personal secretary, and three members of his cabinet.

ON THE WORLD STAGE

THE DOMINICAN REPUBLIC

Although the United States focused largely on domestic problems during Reconstruction, the nation did have one significant dealing with a foreign power. In 1870, President Grant attempted to annex the Dominican Republic, one of two nations on the Caribbean island of Hispaniola (the other being Haiti).

This action aroused a storm of controversy. The plan's supporters believed that annexation would increase Caribbean trade and spread "the blessings of our free institutions." Opponents pointed out that the Dominican Republic was caught up in a civil war and felt that the United States should avoid involvement in the conflict. The Senate rejected the annexation treaty.

Small businesses, banks, and the stock market collapsed during the Panic of 1873, and people rushed to salvage their savings.

ON THE WORLD STAGE
The Dominican Republic
Critical Thinking: Analyzing Issues Ask students to research the turbulent history of the Dominican Republic and its capital, Santo Domingo. What relationship has the United States had to this country? *U.S. involvement has ranged from sending troops to quell civil disturbances to dominating and controlling the economy. Many Dominicans have emigrated to the United States.*

MORE ABOUT . . .
Horace Greeley
Greeley (1811–1872) was known for the phrase "Go West, young man," which he popularized in the *New York Tribune.* This pioneering spirit also led to inconsistencies in his beliefs and actions. Though he was a leader in the antislavery movement, at one time he also favored peaceable secession. He signed the bail bond of Jefferson Davis, president of the Confederacy, and most of his campaign speeches criticized Reconstruction and called for local self-government.

GROLIER MULTIMEDIA ENCYCLOPEDIA
Horace Greeley and the Penny Press

TEACHING OPTION

Making Global Connections

A New Nationalism The attempt to annex the Dominican Republic was in part an expression of a new spirit of nationalistic expansionism that swept the country after the Civil War. It was not the only attempt to expand the territory of the United States during this period, however. Earlier, during the Johnson administration, Secretary of State William Henry Seward had successfully negotiated the purchase of Alaska from Russia. Seward had also attempted to purchase the Danish West Indies, but was unsuccessful.

Some supporters of expansionism saw the proposed annexation of the Dominican Republic as the opening move in a strategy that might eventually include Canada, Mexico, and the whole of the Caribbean in the American republic. They talked about demonstrating the virtues of democracy and hoped that the freeing of slaves in the United States might speed the abolition of slavery in Cuba and Puerto Rico.

Reading the Cartoon What specific aspects of the cartoon convey the feeling of panic? *Possible Answer: The outlandish size, unnatural proportions, and frightening features of the figure.*

Extension Have students write a one-paragraph description of the cartoon that explains the caption.

Judicial and Popular Support Fades

Ask students to create flow charts following the legislative and judicial histories of the Fourteenth and Fifteenth Amendments. As students read this section, have them fill in relevant Supreme Court decisions. The chart might look like this:

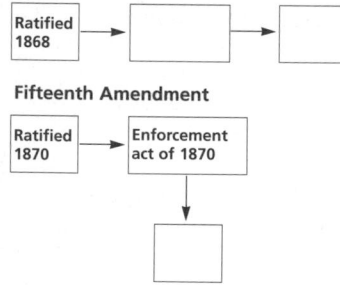

Fourteenth Amendment

Ratified 1868 → ☐ → ☐

Fifteenth Amendment

Ratified 1870 → Enforcement act of 1870 → ☐

▶ **Discussing Key Ideas**
• Supreme Court decisions undermine the Fourteenth and Fifteenth Amendments.
• Northerners begin to withdraw support for Reconstruction.

---

ballooning construction costs, and he could not pay his debts. In September 1873, Cooke's banking firm, the nation's largest, went bankrupt, setting off a series of financial failures known as the **Panic of 1873.** Smaller banks closed, and the stock market temporarily collapsed. Within a year, 89 railroads went broke. By 1875, more than 18,000 companies had folded. In the five-year depression triggered by the panic, 3 million workers lost their jobs.

CURRENCY DISPUTE An economic depression—a period of high unemployment and reduced business activity—followed the Panic of 1873. The depression also fueled a dispute over currency, a dispute that had its roots in the Civil War. During the war, the federal government had begun to issue greenbacks, paper money that was not backed by equal value in gold. When the war ended, many financial experts advocated withdrawing the greenbacks and returning the nation completely to a currency backed by gold. This action would have reduced the number of dollars in circulation.

In contrast, Southern and Western farmers and manufacturers who were in debt wanted the government to issue even more greenbacks. They believed that "easy money"—a large money supply—would help them pay off their debts. Instead, the government reduced the number of greenbacks in circulation.

In 1875, Congress passed the Specie Resumption Act, which promised to put the country back on the gold standard. This act sparked further debate over monetary policies. As the economy improved in 1879, the controversy died down. However, the passionate debate over the money question in the 1870s was one of many factors that drew the attention of voters and politicians away from Reconstruction.

PANIC SWEEPS THROUGH WALL STREET.

SKILLBUILDER INTERPRETING POLITICAL CARTOONS Why are people deserting the financial institutions of Wall Street as the Panic of 1873 sweeps away the results of overborrowing?

Skillbuilder Answer Because they've lost their savings.

D. Answer They believed that they could pay their debts more easily if there was a lot of money in circulation.

THINK THROUGH HISTORY D. Analyzing Motives Why did people who were in debt want greenbacks to stay in circulation?

Judicial and Popular Support Fades

In 1874, a Southern Democratic senator wrote, *"Radicalism* is dissolving—going to pieces." Indeed, political scandals, economic problems, and the restoration of political rights to former Confederate Democrats seriously weakened the Radical Republicans. In addition, the Supreme Court began to undo some of the social and political changes that the Radicals had made.

SUPREME COURT DECISIONS AGAINST Although Congress had passed important laws to protect the political and civil rights of African Americans, the Supreme Court began to take away those same protections. During the 1870s, the Court issued a series of decisions that undermined both the Fourteenth and Fifteenth Amendments.

In the *Slaughterhouse* cases of 1873, for example, the Court decided that the Fourteenth Amendment protected only the rights people had by virtue of their citizenship in the United States, such as the right of interstate travel and the right to federal protection when traveling on the high seas and abroad. The Court contended that most of Americans' basic civil rights were obtained through their citizenship in a state and that the amendment did not protect those rights.

Another setback for Reconstruction was *U.S.* v. *Cruikshank* in 1876, in which the Court ruled that the Fourteenth Amendment did not give the federal government the right to punish individual whites who oppressed blacks. The same year, in *U.S.* v. *Reese,* the Court ruled in favor of officials who had barred African Americans from voting, stating that the Fifteenth Amendment did not "confer the right of suffrage on anyone" but merely listed grounds on which states could not deny suffrage. By the late 1870s, the Supreme Court's restrictive rulings had narrowed the scope of these amendments so much that the federal government no longer had much power to protect the rights of

---

Skillbuilder Mini-Lesson: Evaluating Decisions

Explaining the Skill Historians look at decisions made in the past and evaluate them based, in part, on the short- and long-term consequences of those decisions. For example, students might at first be glad they accepted an after-school job because of the extra spending money it provides. However, that decision may not seem as good after their school performance slips from having less time to study.

Applying the Skill: Evaluating Supreme Court Decisions Have students review the description of the Supreme Court's ruling in *U.S.* v. *Reese* on this page.

1. What were the short-term effects of this decision? *Local officials could find loopholes in the laws to prevent freedmen from voting for reasons not stated in Amendment 15.*

2. What were the long-term effects? *Freed persons couldn't elect representatives who would help them gain equality, so they remained politically and economically oppressed.*

3. Was the decision in *U.S.* v. *Reese* a good one?

IN-DEPTH RESOURCES: UNIT 3
Skillbuilder Practice: Evaluating Decisions, p. 61

African Americans. These decisions would have a long-lasting negative impact on African Americans' efforts to gain equality.

NORTHERN SUPPORT FADES   As the Supreme Court rejected Reconstruction policies in the 1870s, Northern voters grew indifferent to events in the South. Weary of the "Negro question" and "sick of carpet-bag government," many Northern voters shifted their attention to such national concerns as the Panic of 1873 and the corruption in Grant's administration. In addition, a desire for reconciliation between the regions spread through the North. Although political violence continued in the South and African Americans were denied civil and political rights, the tide of public opinion in the North began to turn against Reconstruction policies.

As both judicial and public support decreased, Republicans began to back away from their commitment to Reconstruction. The impassioned Radicals who had led the fight for congressional Reconstruction, Charles Sumner and Thaddeus Stevens, were dead. Business interests diverted the attention of both moderates and Radicals, and scalawags and carpetbaggers deserted the Republican Party. Moreover, Republicans gradually came to realize that government could not impose the moral and social changes needed for former slaves to make progress in the South. As a result, Republicans slowly retreated from the policies of Reconstruction.

Democrats "Redeem" the South

As the Republicans' hold on the South loosened, Southern Democrats began to regain control of the region. Between 1869 and 1875, Democrats recaptured the state governments of Alabama, Arkansas, Georgia, Mississippi, North Carolina, Tennessee, Texas, and Virginia. As a result of **redemption**—as the Democrats called their return to power in the South—and a political deal made during the national election of 1876, congressional Reconstruction came to an end.

ELECTION OF 1876   In 1876, the Republicans decided not to run the scandal-plagued Grant for a third term. Instead, they chose the stodgy governor of Ohio, **Rutherford B. Hayes.** Smelling victory, the Democrats put up one of their ablest leaders, Governor **Samuel J. Tilden** of New York. Tilden had helped clean up the graft that had flourished in New York City under the corrupt Tweed Ring.

As most people expected, Tilden carried the popular vote. However, he fell one short of the number of electoral votes needed to win, and 20 electoral votes were disputed. Congress appointed a commission to deal with the problem. The commission, which had a Republican majority, gave the election to the Republican, Hayes, even though he had received a minority of the popular vote.

How did a man who had lost the popular election become president? In the oldest tradition of politics, party leaders made a deal. Although Republicans controlled the electoral commission, Democrats controlled the House of Representatives, which had to approve the election results. Southern Democrats made it known that they were willing to accept Hayes if they could get something in return.

HISTORICAL SPOTLIGHT

THE ELECTORAL COLLEGE AND THE 1876 ELECTION

The nation was in such turmoil over the disputed election of 1876 that people talked of another civil war. Of the 20 contested electoral votes, 19 came from Florida, South Carolina, and Louisiana. Republican officials in those states threw out election returns from counties where violence kept Republican voters from the polls. The Democrats refused to accept the altered returns, and each party sent its own set of results to Washington, D.C.

Democrats screamed that the Republicans had stolen the election; their Republican opponents charged that Tilden had tried to win through violent intimidation. Fortunately for the country, the warlike slogans proved to be political rhetoric. After a joint session of Congress met to witness the counting of the electoral votes (as illustrated below), which did not settle the dispute, the parties struck a deal. The Compromise of 1877 kept the peace and satisfied many.

▶ **Starting with the Student**
Based on what they learned in this chapter, have students vote on whether they think Reconstruction was a success or a failure.

▶ **Discussing Key Ideas**
• Reconstruction governments cannot guarantee the rights of former slaves.
• Former slaves experience ongoing poverty and discrimination.
• For a time, African Americans become involved at all levels of government.
• They establish families, schools, and churches, and achieve some independence in Southern society.

CRITICAL THINKING TRANSPARENCIES
CT12, Reconstruction

MORE ABOUT . . .
Hayes's Cabinet

Hayes kept his part of the bargain that put him in office. The Southern conservative that he appointed to his cabinet was David M. Key, a Democratic senator from Tennessee. Key was given the post of Postmaster General.

MORE ABOUT . . .
Home Rule

Home rule summed up what all the Southern states wanted. Legislation under home rule pushed the South back toward slavery. South Carolina and Florida, for example, expanded the convict labor system until it resembled involuntary servitude.

POINT ▶ COUNTERPOINT

"Reconstruction was a failure."

Reconstruction governments were charged with the responsibility of securing hard-won rights guaranteed to former slaves by constitutional amendments, but they failed to make these guarantees stick.

• State Republican parties could not keep together black-white voter coalitions that would enable them to stay in power and continue political reform.

• Radical Republican governments were unable to enact land reform or to provide former slaves with the economic resources needed to break the "cycle of poverty." African Americans who continued to work the land wound up as sharecroppers or tenant farmers rather than as landowners.

• Racial bias was a national, not a regional, problem. After the Panic of 1873, Northerners were more concerned with economic problems than with the problems of former slaves.

At the end of Reconstruction, former slaves found themselves once again in a subordinate position in society. The historian Eric Foner concludes, "Whether measured by the dreams inspired by emancipation or by the more limited goal of securing blacks' rights as citizens. . . . Reconstruction can only be judged a failure."

"Reconstruction was a success."

Reconstruction was an attempt to create a social and political revolution despite economic collapse and the opposition of a large portion of the white South. Under these conditions its accomplishments were extraordinary.

• African Americans only a few years removed from slavery participated at all levels of government.

• State governments had some success in solving social problems; for example, they funded public school systems open to all citizens.

• African Americans established institutions that had been denied them during slavery: schools, churches, and families.

• The breakup of the plantation system led to some redistribution of land, from which African Americans benefited.

W. E. B. Du Bois summarized the achievements of the period this way: "It was Negro loyalty and the Negro vote alone that restored the South to the Union; established the new democracy, both for white and black."

Despite their loss of ground during the period that followed Reconstruction, African Americans were successful in carving out a measure of independence within Southern society.

INTERACT WITH HISTORY

1. **COMPARING** What are the two major arguments made by each side over whether Reconstruction was a success? Which perspective do you agree with, and why?

SEE SKILLBUILDER HANDBOOK, PAGE 1041.

2. **RESEARCHING RECONSTRUCTION'S LEGACY** One historian has referred to Reconstruction as "America's Unfinished Revolution." Is the United States still dealing with issues left over from that period? Use newspaper stories, magazine articles, or other sources of information to back your arguments. Make a short presentation in class.

The price they demanded was, first of all, the withdrawal of federal troops from Louisiana and South Carolina—two of the three Southern states that Republicans still governed. Second, the Democrats wanted federal money to build a railroad from Texas to the West Coast and to improve Southern rivers, harbors, and bridges. Third, they wanted Hayes to appoint a conservative Southerner to the cabinet. In the Compromise of 1877, Republican leaders agreed to these demands, and Hayes was peacefully inaugurated. The acceptance of this compromise meant the end of Reconstruction in the South.

HOME RULE IN THE SOUTH After the 1876 election, Republicans and Democrats disputed the results in Louisiana's and South Carolina's elections, and both states ended up with two rival state governments! When Hayes later removed the federal troops in those states, the Democrats took over.

Florida also had questionable election returns, but the state supreme court ruled in favor of the Democrats. As a result, Republicans no longer controlled the government of any Southern state.

Under **home rule**—the ability to run state governments without federal intervention—so-called Redeemers made sweeping changes. They passed laws that restricted the rights of freed slaves, wiped out social programs, slashed taxes, and dismantled public school systems.

INTERACT WITH HISTORY

1. Comparing

Possible Responses: *Those saying that Reconstruction was a failure argue that former slaves were not much better off at the end of Reconstruction: they were still in a subordinate position; they had lost many rights that had been guaranteed through constitutional amendments; racial bias continued.*

Those saying that Reconstruction was a success argue that African Americans were able to become more independent in Southern society: they participated in government; they established schools and churches; they owned some land.

2. Researching Reconstruction's Legacy

You may wish to give students the following suggestions to help them find sources and organize information for their reports:

• Begin research in the library. Ask the librarian where to find specialized reference books on the topic.
• Check the *Readers' Guide to Periodical Literature* or Infotrak, a computer database of periodicals, for articles on the topic.
• Search for specialized books such as Eric Foner's *America's Reconstruction: People and Politics After the Civil War.*
• Check the Internet for sites dealing with the Civil War and Reconstruction.

LEGACY OF RECONSTRUCTION During congressional Reconstruction, African Americans had striven to achieve equality, and many Radical Republicans had tried to assist them in reaching their goal. However, Reconstruction ended without much real progress in the battle against discrimination. Charles Harris, an African-American Union Army veteran and former Alabama legislator, expressed his frustration in an 1877 letter.

> *"We obey laws; others make them."*
>
> **CHARLES HARRIS**

A PERSONAL VOICE
We obey laws; others make them. We support state educational institutions, whose doors are virtually closed against us. We support asylums and hospitals, and our sick, deaf, dumb, or blind are met at the doors by . . . unjust discriminations. . . . From these and many other oppressions . . . our people long to be *free*.

CHARLES HARRIS, from American Colonization Society Papers in the *Congressional Record*

Although Radical Republicans wanted to help the former slaves, many historians believe that they made several serious mistakes. First, they assumed that extending citizenship, suffrage, and other civil rights to freed persons would enable them to protect themselves through participation in government, especially in lawmaking. However, Congress did not adequately protect those rights, and the Supreme Court undermined them. Second, the Radicals balked at giving land to former slaves so that they could become economically independent of the landowning planter class. Finally, the Radicals did not fully realize how much deep-seated racism in society would weaken the social and educational changes that Congress had tried to make.

But Congressional Reconstruction was not a complete failure. The Thirteenth Amendment permanently abolished slavery in all of the states. Furthermore, Radical Republicans did succeed in passing the Fourteenth and Fifteenth Amendments, and although the Supreme Court narrowed the interpretation of the amendments during the 1870s, they remained part of the Constitution. In the 20th century, the amendments provided the necessary constitutional foundation for important civil rights legislation.

In addition, for many years after the end of Reconstruction, the African-American community proudly looked back on the period as a time when they voted, held political office, and made important achievements. African Americans had founded many black colleges and volunteer organizations, and the percentage of literate African Americans had gradually increased. In contrast, after 1877, when Democrats regained control of the South, most white Americans put the memory of Reconstruction behind them. They turned their attention to other matters, such as expansion into the western frontier.

Although President Hayes united the North and the South, his presidency marked the end of newly won political and civil rights for former slaves.

Sidebar (left margin)

F. Answer Negatives—Democrats overthrew Radical reforms and curtailed African-American civil rights; many African Americans and poor whites were trapped in a cycle of poverty due to sharecropping; Positives—African Americans founded churches, schools, and volunteer organizations; they also displayed political and social leadership that inspired their descendants.

THINK THROUGH HISTORY
F. Recognizing Effects What were some negative and positive results of Reconstruction?

Sidebar (right margin)

ASSESS & RETEACH

Section 3 Assessment
Have students answer question 1 by themselves. Then have them work with a partner to answer questions 2, 3, and 4.

Self-Assessment
Have students select two answers they feel they could improve. Ask them to rewrite the answers to make them more complete and coherent.

Section Quiz
FORMAL ASSESSMENT
Section Quiz, p. 152

Reteach
Review the arguments in the Point Counterpoint feature on page 372 to help consolidate students' understanding of Reconstruction's legacy.

CLOSE

Political scandals and economic difficulties split the Republican Party and divert Northerners' attention from the problems of the South. Lack of judicial support for Reconstruction legislation leads to a resumption of home rule and a curtailing of rights for former slaves.

Section 3 Assessment

1. TERMS & NAMES
Identify:
• Ku Klux Klan
• Panic of 1873
• redemption
• Rutherford B. Hayes
• Samuel J. Tilden
• home rule

2. SEQUENCING HISTORY
Create a time line of the major events contributing to the end of Reconstruction, using a form such as the one below.

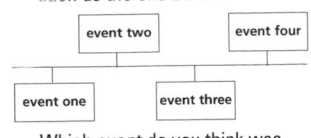

Which event do you think was most significant and why?

3. ANALYZING Do you think the Republican Party would have remained strong in the South if Congress had not passed the Amnesty Act? Explain and support your opinion.

THINK ABOUT
• the Republican commitment to Reconstruction
• the goals of the Ku Klux Klan
• the political and economic crises facing the nation

4. EVALUATING Do you think the political deal to settle the election of 1876 was an appropriate solution? Explain why or why not.

THINK ABOUT
• the causes of the conflict over the election
• other possible solutions to the controversy
• the impact of the settlement

Reconstruction and Its Effects **373**

ANSWERS

1. TERMS & NAMES
Ku Klux Klan, p. 366
Panic of 1873, p. 370
redemption, p. 371
Rutherford B. Hayes, p. 371
Samuel J. Tilden, p. 371
home rule, p. 372

2. SEQUENCING HISTORY
Possible Responses: 1866 Ku Klux Klan founded; 1870–1871 Enforcement Acts passed; 1872 Amnesty Act passed; 1872 Crédit Mobilier; 1873 Panic; 1873 Supreme Court issued *Slaughterhouse* rulings; 1876 Hayes elected president. Students should support their choice of a significant event with its immediate and long-range impact.

3. ANALYZING
Possible Responses: **Yes**—Republican Reconstruction successes were a sign of growing Republican political strength despite interference from the Klan and Congress's Enforcement Acts. **No**—Intimidation by the Klan and by Democrats, and the Grant administration scandals had weakened Republican political power.

4. EVALUATING
Possible Responses:
Appropriate—The deal showed how a democracy can settle conflict with compromise.
Inappropriate—The deal was a sign of corruption, not democracy, because it did not acknowledge the popular vote. It also ended federal efforts to help African Americans in the South.

REVIEWING THE CHAPTER

TERMS & NAMES
1. Andrew Johnson, p. 350
2. Radical Republican, p. 351
3. Freedmen's Bureau, p. 352
4. Fourteenth Amendment, p. 353
5. Fifteenth Amendment, p. 355
6. carpetbagger, p. 358
7. Hiram Revels, p. 362
8. sharecropping, p. 364
9. Ku Klux Klan, p. 366
10. Rutherford B. Hayes, p. 371

REVIEWING MAIN IDEAS
11. Johnson wanted to break the planters' power by denying voting privileges to high-ranking Confederates and wealthy landowners.

12. Congress passed it; Johnson vetoed it; moderates joined with Radicals in Congress to override the veto.

13. They thought he was obstructing Reconstruction efforts.

14. The vote of 500,000 African Americans, who helped the Republican U. S. Grant win.

15. Former slaves, white Southerners called scalawags, and people known as carpetbaggers who had traveled to the South after the Civil War.

16. They traveled to find family members and jobs; organized schools, colleges, universities, churches, and volunteer organizations; and participated in politics.

17. They paid freedmen low wages and trapped them in the sharecropping and tenant-farming cycle of poverty.

18. Some regained power through terror, others by the compromise over the election of 1876.

19. Political scandals such as Crédit Mobilier and the Whiskey Ring; the Panic of 1873; economic depression and currency disputes.

20. Even though Hayes lost the popular vote, he won the election by agreeing to end Reconstruction in the South.

Chapter 12 Assessment

REVIEWING THE CHAPTER

TERMS & NAMES For each term below, write a sentence explaining its connection to Reconstruction. For each person below, explain his or her role in events of the period.

1. Andrew Johnson	6. carpetbagger
2. Radical Republican	7. Hiram Revels
3. Freedmen's Bureau	8. sharecropping
4. Fourteenth Amendment	9. Ku Klux Klan
5. Fifteenth Amendment	10. Rutherford B. Hayes

MAIN IDEAS

SECTION 1 (pages 350–355)

The Politics of Reconstruction
11. How did Andrew Johnson's plan to reconstruct the Confederate states differ from Lincoln's?
12. How did the Civil Rights Act of 1866 become law?
13. Why did the Radicals want to impeach Andrew Johnson?
14. What factor played a significant role in the 1868 presidential election?

SECTION 2 (pages 356–365)

Reconstructing Society
15. What three groups made up the Republican party in the South during Reconstruction?
16. In what ways did emancipated slaves exercise their freedom?
17. How did white landowners in the South reassert their economic power in the decade following the Civil War?

SECTION 3 (pages 366–373)

The Collapse of Reconstruction
18. How did Southern whites regain political power during Reconstruction?
19. What economic and political developments weakened the Republican party during Grant's second term?
20. What significance did the victory by Rutherford B. Hayes in the 1876 presidential race have for Reconstruction?

THINKING CRITICALLY

1. **NATIONAL ELECTIONS** Recreate the chart shown below on your paper. Then list the results and significance of the national elections of 1866, 1868, 1870, 1872, and 1876.

Year	Results	Significance

2. **CIVIL RIGHTS** What might Americans today learn from the civil rights experiences of African Americans during Reconstruction?

3. **AUCTION BLOCK TO BALLOT BOX** Reread the quote by William Lloyd Garrison on page 348. Do you agree that Reconstruction transformed the lives of African Americans? Explain your opinion.

4. **RECONSTRUCTING RECONSTRUCTION** How do you think Reconstruction could have been made more effective in rebuilding the South and ensuring the rights of the freed slaves?

5. **ECONOMIC OPPORTUNITY** Do you think the changes in the South during Reconstruction benefited Southerners? Support your opinion.

6. **ANALYZING PRIMARY SOURCES** Toby, a slave in South Carolina, was held in servitude by his former master even after receiving his freedom. After four years, Toby escaped and headed for Texas with Govie, who became his wife. This is how he described their lives.

> I don't know as I 'spected nothing from freedom, but they turned us out like a bunch of stray dogs, no homes, no clothing, no nothing, not 'nough food to last us one meal. After we settles on that place, I never seed man or women 'cept Govie, for six years, cause it was a long ways to anywhere. All we had to farm with was sharp sticks. We'd stick holes and plant corn, and when it come up we'd punch up the dirt round it. We didn't plant cotton, 'cause we wouldn't eat that. I made bows and arrows to kill wild game with, and we never went to a store for nothing. We made our clothes out of animal skins.
>
> **TOBY,** quoted in *The Black Americans: A History in Their Own Words*

Summarize the problems Toby faced on becoming free. In your opinion, what might the federal government have done to help former slaves economically?

THINKING CRITICALLY

1. NATIONAL ELECTIONS
Possible Responses: 1866—Republicans win large majority—Congress able to override presidential vetoes; 1868—Grant wins with small margin in the popular vote—shows importance of African-American votes; 1870—first African American elected to the U.S. Senate—demonstrates ability of African Americans to win elections; 1872—Grant reelected president—Republican unity shattered by Liberal Republicans; 1876—Hayes wins presidential election—end of Reconstruction in the South.

2. CIVIL RIGHTS
Possible Responses: The federal government needs to help people protect their rights; we have to be ever vigilant so that civil rights laws or amendments do not become diminished by newer laws; reliance on the government can fail because of bias, corruption, or lack of leadership.

3. AUCTION BLOCK TO BALLOT BOX
Possible Responses: Students who agree may focus on the end of slavery and the guarantee of citizenship. Those who disagree may emphasize that by 1876, ongoing discrimination and poverty had prevented African Americans from transforming their lives.

ALTERNATIVE ASSESSMENT

1. CREATING A RECONSTRUCTION DIARY

The many new laws passed during the period of Reconstruction had widespread effects on all Southerners.

Write a diary entry describing life in the Reconstruction South from the point of view of one of the following: a freed slave, a Freedmen's Bureau worker, or a Democratic member of a Southern state legislature.

CD-ROM Use the CD-ROM *Electronic Library of Primary Sources* and other resources to research the economy, society, and laws of the Reconstruction South.

- Decide the point of view from which you will write. In your diary entry, tell your opinion of the laws and social and economic conditions, and describe their impact on your daily life.
- Share your diary entry with your classmates and discuss the different points of view that are reflected in your diaries.

2. LEARNING FROM MEDIA

VIDEO View the video for Chapter 12, *Teacher of a Freed People*. Discuss the following questions in small groups.

- What was Robert Fitzgerald's experience in the Civil War?
- Which experiences in Fitzgerald's life helped foster his passion for learning and teaching?
- Why were many Southern whites so resistant to the policies of Reconstruction?
- What measures did whites use to thwart blacks' progress toward full citizenship?
- How did Fitzgerald respond to the difficulties he faced?
- What legacy did Robert Fitzgerald leave his children?
- How have you benefited from your ancestors' struggles? How do you plan to carry on their legacy?

3. PORTFOLIO PROJECT

Use the Living History activity to expand your portfolio.

LIVING HISTORY

WRITING YOUR BIOGRAPHY

Use the materials you have collected about a Reconstruction figure to write a biography of that person. Show how
- experiences during early life and Reconstruction affected the person
- the person expressed his or her political beliefs

Give your first draft to another student to read. Make changes based on the feedback you get. Add your biography to your American history portfolio.

Bridge to Chapter 13

Review Chapter 12

THE POLITICS OF RECONSTRUCTION Americans disagreed over how to reconstruct the country following the devastation of the Civil War. Presidents Abraham Lincoln and Andrew Johnson proposed lenient policies toward the Confederate states. However, Thaddeus Stevens and other Radical Republicans in Congress argued that the federal government needed to protect former slaves. After moderate and Radical Republicans won a landslide in the 1866 elections, Congress took control of Reconstruction, passing the Reconstruction Act of 1867. The fierce battle between the executive and the legislature resulted in the impeachment, but not the removal from office, of Andrew Johnson.

REBUILDING THE SOUTH The weakness of Johnson and other Democrats allowed the Republicans to dominate Reconstruction. Republican Ulysses S. Grant was elected president in 1868, and Southern Republicans—a mixture of former slaves, scalawags, and carpetbaggers—quickly took control of state governments. Sweeping social changes occurred as former slaves gained mobility and the right to attend school and organize churches for the first time, and began building a new African-American culture.

WHITE SOUTHERNERS REACT Many white Southerners resisted Republican control and opposed African-American freedom. Planters made it difficult for former slaves and poor whites to escape poverty through a system of sharecropping. Democrats overthrew Republican governments in the South, and groups such as the Ku Klux Klan attempted to prevent African Americans from attending schools, voting, or becoming prosperous. As Southerners joined the Democratic ranks, political scandals and the Panic of 1873 weakened the Republicans. Finally, Rutherford B. Hayes won the election of 1876 through a compromise in which Republicans agreed to halt Reconstruction.

Preview Chapter 13

During and after Reconstruction, Americans continued expanding westward. This expansion caused destruction of the buffalo and crises for Native Americans, the growth of a new cattle industry and society on the Great Plains, and a reform movement known as populism. You will learn about these significant developments in the next chapter.

Reconstruction and Its Effects **375**

---

1. CREATING A RECONSTRUCTION DIARY
A diary entry should meet the following criteria:

- Identifies and maintains a consistent point of view.
- Provides realistic details and examples.
- Clearly describes social and economic conditions.
- Uses well-researched evidence to support statements in the diary.

2. LEARNING FROM MEDIA
Answers to the questions:

- He was a Union soldier who fought at the Battle of Petersburg, Virginia, in 1864.
- Fitzgerald's schooling at Lincoln University inspired him to become a teacher in the Freedman's Bureau.
- Many Southern whites believed that "a black man had no rights which a white man was bound to respect."
- Some whites used intimidation and violence.
- Fitzgerald raised a family and continued to teach.
- His example of perseverance, pride, and courage.
- Answers should include specific details about ancestors' struggles and students' own responses.

3. PORTFOLIO PROJECT
LIVING HISTORY
Standards for Evaluation
A biography should meet the following criteria:

- Clearly identifies and describes the person.
- Explains what makes the person a significant Reconstruction figure.
- Uses specific examples to show how Reconstruction influenced the person.
- Uses quotations and anecdotes whenever possible to illustrate the person's life.
- Supports statements with evidence from a variety of sources.

IN-DEPTH RESOURCES: UNIT 3
See the form for scoring this activity on page 74.

THINKING CRITICALLY

4. RECONSTRUCTING RECONSTRUCTION
Possible Responses: The Supreme Court and legislators could have more actively upheld legislation ensuring the civil rights of freed slaves; officials could have fought violence against African Americans; Northerners could have invested in the South and helped give the struggling economy a basis on which to build.

5. ECONOMIC OPPORTUNITY
Possible Responses: Certain aspects of Reconstruction were harmful, such as the formation of terrorist groups like the Klan, and political divisiveness and deals, as in the election of 1876. However, building schools and diversifying the economy were helpful. Although African Americans made many gains, the bias against them was so strong that it was hard for them to progress financially or politically.

6. ANALYZING PRIMARY SOURCES
Possible Responses: The government could have provided former slaves with fertile farmland, money, or tools. The government could have passed a law making planters give either money or land to freedmen for their past work. However, such efforts to redistribute land might have simply angered whites even more and caused more terrorism.

Migration and Industrialization Change Society

HISTORY AND ART

The intersection of Orchard and Hester Streets in New York's Lower East Side

Oil over a photograph by unknown artist (1905).

Art Note
By the turn of the century, lithographs and woodcuts had largely been replaced by photographs as the most-used medium for prints aimed at the mass market. Though color film had not yet been developed, photo studios could still provide color images. Skilled workers hand-tinted the photographs.

▶ *Previewing the Unit*
Unit 4 describes how the United States transforms itself from a mostly rural, agricultural society to an urban, industrial one. Farmers, miners, and ranchers settle all regions of the West, costing Native Americans their land. Large businesses begin to dominate the economy. Providing much of the labor for these huge new concerns are millions of immigrants who stream to the major cities of the North and East. New manufacturing and selling techniques begin to create mass consumer markets for goods and services.

UNIT

4

"People are the common denominator of progress."

JOHN KENNETH GALBRAITH

CHAPTER 13
1876–1900
Changes on the Western Frontier

CHAPTER 14
1876–1900
The Industrial Age

CHAPTER 15
1876–1914
Immigrants and Urbanization

CHAPTER 16
1877–1917
Life at the Turn of the Century

376 UNIT 4

1876–1914
Migration and Industrialization Change Society

❶ Lower East Side
New York's Lower East Side became home to hundreds of thousands of immigrants, especially those from southern and eastern Europe around the turn of the century. The population density was estimated at 500 to 1,000 people per acre—among the highest in the world.

❷ Street peddlers
About a quarter of the immigrants who settled in New York—and high proportions in other cities as well—worked as street peddlers. Licenses were cheap, as were the goods they sold. Selling gave immigrants a chance to interact with others who spoke their language.

❸ Horse-drawn carts
In 1905, when this photo was taken, horse-drawn carts were still the main means of transportation. Electric-powered elevated railways or subways provided mass transit. The automobile had only just started to become available.

Discussing the Quotation

In the nearly 40 years from 1876 to 1914, millions of immigrants came to the United States. This great influx of people was a key element in what Galbraith calls "progress."

FOR DISCUSSION:
- Why did people come?
- How did they contribute to the economy?
- How did their arrival shape American society?
- What was the "common denominator" for the residents of the Lower East Side, who had immigrated from so many different countries?

Discussing the Image

Photographs can document more accurately than a painting the appearance and atmosphere of a time and place. The people and objects captured on film tell us much about how people once lived.

FOR DISCUSSION:
- What goods are being sold in stores and by peddlers? What does this say about New York in 1905?
- What kinds of people are pictured and what are they doing?
- How are the people dressed, and how does that compare with today?

4 Tenements

The Lower East Side was full of tenements—apartment buildings that often had one family per room. Reformers passed laws that limited buildings in size to leave some open space; limited the number of people in a unit; required that all rooms have access to fresh air; and required running water and toilet facilities. Still, the buildings were crowded. Many families used their units not only to live but also to work. One building on Orchard Street today is home to the Lower East Side Tenement Museum.

5 Street signs

The city in 1905 was poised between its past and its future. Signs marking streets, paved streets, and manhole covers (lower right) show some features that we would recognize today. But note the absence of traffic signs, traffic lights, and streetlights.

	Key Ideas	**TEACHING SUPPORT**	**ASSESSMENT**
SECTION 1 Native American Culture in Crisis *pp. 380–387*	*Pursuit of economic opportunity leads settlers to push westward, forcing confrontation with established Native American cultures.*	**In-Depth Resources: Unit 4** • Guided Reading, p. 1 • Bulleted text, p. 00 • Skillbuilder Practice: Hypothesizing, p. 5 • Primary Source: The Battle of Little Bighorn, p. 8 • American Lives: Chief Joseph, p. 15 👥 **COOPERATIVE ACTIVITIES** • Cross-Cultural Debate, p. 382 (TE) • Composing Boarding School Journals, p. 386 (TE)	*Section 1 Assessment*, p. 387 (PE) *Self-Assessment*, p. 387 (TE) *Formal Assessment* • Section Quiz, p. 161 *Alternative Assessment Book* • Standards for Evaluating a Cooperative Activity
SECTION 2 The Growth of the Cattle Industry *pp. 388–393*	*The cattle industry thrives as the culture of the Great Plains Indians declines, and a new worker—the cowboy—appears on the scene.*	**In-Depth Resources: Unit 4** • Guided Reading, p. 2 👥 **COOPERATIVE ACTIVITY** • Researching Cowboy Music, p. 392 (TE)	*Section 2 Assessment*, p. 393 (PE) *Self-Assessment*, p. 393 (TE) *Formal Assessment* • Section Quiz, p. 162 *Alternative Assessment Book* • Standards for Evaluating a Cooperative Activity
SECTION 3 Settling on the Great Plains *pp. 396–400*	*The promise of cheap, fertile land draws thousands of settlers westward to seek their fortunes as farmers.*	**In-Depth Resources: Unit 4** • Guided Reading, p. 3 • Geography Application: The Regions of the West, p. 6 • Primary Sources: Railroad Poster, p. 9; Letter from a Woman Homesteader, p. 10 • Literature: from *My Ántonia* by Willa Cather, p. 12 👥 **COOPERATIVE ACTIVITY** • Advertising Agricultural Inventions, p. 399 (TE)	*Section 3 Assessment*, p. 400 (PE) *Self-Assessment*, p. 400 (TE) *Formal Assessment* • Section Quiz, p. 163 *Alternative Assessment Book* • Standards for Evaluating a Cooperative Activity
SECTION 4 Farmers and the Populist Movement *pp. 401–405*	*Farmers band together to address their economic problems, giving rise to the Populist movement.*	**In-Depth Resources: Unit 4** • Guided Reading, p. 4 • Primary Source: *from* William Jennings Bryan's "Cross of Gold" Speech, p. 11 • American Lives: Mary Elizabeth Lease, p. 16 👥 **COOPERATIVE ACTIVITY** • Researching Populist Reforms, p. 403 (TE)	*Section 4 Assessment*, p. 405 (PE) *Self-Assessment*, p. 405 (TE) *Formal Assessment* • Section Quiz, p. 164 *Alternative Assessment Book* • Standards for Evaluating a Cooperative Activity
CHAPTER RESOURCES	**Chapter Overview** *In the late 1800s, growing numbers of white settlers move to the West, and Native Americans lose their lands. Railroads cross the nation, and both the cattle kingdom and Populism rise and fall.*	**In-Depth Resources: Unit 4** • Living History Project: Worksheet, p. 17; Standards, p. 18 **Telescoping the Times** • Chapter Summary, pp. 25–26 **Planning for Block Schedules**	*Chapter Assessment,* pp. 406–407 (PE) *Alternative Assessment,* p. 407 (PE) *Formal Assessment* • Chapter Test, forms A and B, pp. 165–170 💻 **Test Generator** *Alternative Assessment Book* See explanation and forms for different kinds of alternative assessments including portfolio assessment.

Humanities Transparencies
• H13, *Sierra Nevada Mountains*

Geography Transparencies
• G13, *Railroad Land Grants: 1871*

Grolier Multimedia Encyclopedia
• Indian Wars

AMERICAN STORIES VIDEO SERIES
• "A Walk in Two Worlds"

INTERNET RESOURCES
• See *McDougal Littell Learning On-Line* for links to information about Chief Sitting Bull and the Battle of Little Big Horn.

Grolier Multimedia Encyclopedia
• Cattle Raising

Electronic Library of Primary Sources
• from *The Log of a Cowboy*

INTERNET RESOURCES
• See Interact with History p. 395 (PE) for an activity that includes the Internet as an enrichment option.

Critical Thinking Transparencies
• CT13, Transcontinental Railroad
• CT47, Population Changes in the West, 1850–1900

Electronic Library of Primary Sources
• from *Letters of a Woman Homesteader*

INTERNET RESOURCES
• See *McDougal Littell Learning On-Line* for links to information about sod houses and homesteading.

Grolier Multimedia Encyclopedia
• from a speech on free silver by William Jennings Bryan
• overview of the Populist Party

INTERNET RESOURCES
• See *McDougal Littell Learning On-Line* for links to information about William McKinley.

American Portfolio: A Videodisc for U.S. History, user's guide pp. 121–129, 132–133, 135–139, 157, 160

INTERNET RESOURCES
Learning On-Line: Social Studies
http://www.mcdougallittell.com

Block Scheduling (90 MINUTES)

Day 1
Section 1, pp. 380–387

 AMERICAN STORIES VIDEO SERIES
• "A Walk in Two Worlds"

Section 2, pp. 388–393
Section Assessments, pp. 387, 393

Day 2
Section 3, pp. 396–400
Section 4, pp. 401–405
Section Assessments, pp. 400, 405
Chapter Assessment, pp. 406–407

YEARLY PACING *Chapter 13 Total:* 2 days *Yearly Total:* 85 days

See *Planning for Block Schedules* for special activities and pacing strategies.

Customizing for Special Populations

Students Acquiring English

Access for Students Acquiring English
• Guided Reading for Sections 1–4 (Spanish), pp. 130–133
• Chapter Summary (Spanish), pp. 128–129
• Skillbuilder Practice: Hypothesizing (Spanish), p. 134
• Geography Application: The Regions of the West (Spanish), p. 135

 AMERICAN STORIES VIDEO SERIES
• "A Walk in Two Worlds"

INTERNET RESOURCES
• See *McDougal Littell Learning On-Line* The Diverse Classroom.

Less Proficient Readers

In-Depth Resources: Unit 4
• Guided Reading for Sections 1–4, pp. 1–4
• Skillbuilder: Hypothesizing, p. 5
• Geography Application: The Regions of the West, p. 6

Telescoping the Times
• Chapter Summary, pp. 25–26

See additional strategies at point of use in the Teacher's Edition.

Gifted and Talented Students

In-Depth Resources: Unit 4
• Primary Sources: The Battle of Little Bighorn, p. 8; Railroad Poster, p. 9; Letter from a Woman Homesteader, p. 10; *from* William Jennings Bryan's "Cross of Gold" Speech, p. 11
• American Lives: Chief Joseph, p. 15; Mary Elizabeth Lease, p. 16

See additional strategies at point of use in the Teacher's Edition.

Connections to Literature READINGS FOR STUDENTS

In-Depth Resources: Unit 0
• from *My Ántonia* by Willa Cather, p. 12

Enrichment Reading
• Rolvaag, Ole Edvart
Giants in the Earth.
New York: HarperCollins, 1991
This heroic tale focuses on Norwegian settlers in the plains of South Dakota. This has been called one of the "most powerful novels that has been written about pioneer life in America."

• Cather, Willa
O Pioneers!
New York: Penguin, 1994
O Pioneers! is the story of Alexandra Bergson, the daughter of Swedish immigrants whose devotion to the land sustains her against the hardships and suffering of prairie life.

McDougal Littell *Language of Literature*

• White Thunder, Black Elk, *Judge Roy Bean*, p 511
• Black Elk, told through John G. Neihardt, *High Horse's Courting,* from *Black Elk Speaks,* p 521
• Chief Joseph, *I Will Fight No More Forever,* p 527
• Elinore Pruitt Stewart, from *Letters of a Woman Homesteader,* p 551

McDougal Littell *Literature Connections*

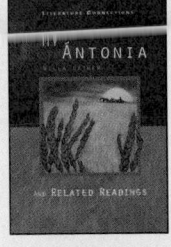

• Willa Cather, *My Ántonia*
In this novel about a woman of the Nebraska prairie, Willa Cather writes with passion and truth about the land and characters she remembered from her childhood.

Changes on the Western Frontier

▶ **Starting with the Student**
Ask students what the word *frontier* means to them. Have them look up the word in a dictionary, then have them answer the following questions:

- What images come to mind when you think of the Western frontier?
- Where did the frontier begin? Where did it end?
- Are there any frontiers left in this country today? If so, what are they? If not, why not?

PREVIEWING THE CHAPTER
- Go over the titles and brief descriptions of the sections.
- Have students gather in small groups and discuss their ideas about the Old West.
- Ask students to write down the questions they expect to find answered in this chapter.

MORE ABOUT . . .
Chief Joseph

Chief Joseph (1840?–1904) was joint leader of a Nez Perce band. He agreed to have his people leave their homeland in the Wallowa Valley in Oregon. After warriors killed some settlers, the band was pursued for more than 1,700 miles. Chief Joseph surrendered and later died without being allowed to return to his homeland.

CHAPTER
13
Changes on the Western Frontier

SECTION 1
Native American Culture in Crisis
Pursuit of economic opportunity leads settlers to push westward, forcing confrontation with established Native American cultures.

 VIDEO *A WALK IN TWO WORLDS*

SECTION 2
The Growth of the Cattle Industry
The cattle industry thrives as the culture of the Great Plains Indians declines, and a new worker—the cowboy— appears on the scene.

SECTION 3
Settling on the Great Plains
The promise of cheap, fertile land draws thousands of settlers westward to seek their fortunes as farmers.

SECTION 4
Farmers and the Populist Movement
Farmers band together to address their economic problems, giving rise to the Populist movement.

378 Chapter 13

"My people have always been the friends of white men. Why are you in such a hurry?"

Chief Joseph of the Nez Perce to U.S. Army general O. O. Howard, 1877

Passengers aboard railroad cars shoot buffalo for sport.

- Red Cloud, chief of the Oglala Sioux, states his people's case in Washington, D.C.

- George A. Custer and his troops are killed at Little Bighorn.

- The long cattle drive enjoys its heyday.

- Thomas A. Edison invents the light bulb.

| THE UNITED STATES | **1870** | 1871 | 1872 | 1876 | 1879 | **1880** |
| THE WORLD | | | 1872 | | | |

- Impressionism becomes an influential art form in France.

- Secret ballot is adopted in Great Britain.

THEMES IN CHAPTER 13

The American Dream	*Cultural Diversity*	*Economic Opportunity*	*Women in America*
The dreams of Native Americans and those of white settlers and immigrants conflicted, and violent confrontations often resulted. See Teacher's Edition note, p. 383.	Cowboys were a melting pot of diverse cultures—whites, African Americans, Mexicans, and Native Americans. These diverse groups lived and worked together harmoniously, despite cultural clashes in the society at large. See Teacher's Edition note, p. 391.	A major lure of the frontier was economic opportunity. The government contributed to economic development by financing the building of railroads and making land available to settlers at little or no cost. Economic opportunity was influenced by currency issues and economic panic. See Teacher's Edition notes, pp. 390 and 402.	Pioneer women played a crucial role on the frontier. Despite isolation and loneliness, they worked on the land and provided food, clothing, emotional support, and even medical care for their families. See Teacher's Edition note, p. 398.

LIVING HISTORY

COMPILING A WESTERN TRAVEL GUIDE

Write a travel guide for Western travelers in the 1870s based on what you learn in this chapter and on additional research. First decide who your readers are—settlers, cowboys, miners, or farmers. Then write your guide in parts, such as the following:

- what to bring (e.g., 400 lbs. of flour per person)
- how to get there (e.g., what transportation and route to take and where to stop along the way)
- how to avoid dangers (e.g., snakes, swollen rivers, lightning, and bandits)
- add visual material, such as maps, to your guide to make it more useful

📁 **PORTFOLIO PROJECT** Keep the guide in a folder for your American history portfolio. You will revise and present your guide at the end of the chapter.

Wearing shirts like this Arapaho one, Native Americans follow the Paiute prophet Wovoka in performing the Ghost Dance, in the hope of reclaiming their lands.

William Jennings Bryan runs for president in support of free silver.

Buffalo Bill tours the world with his Wild West Show.

The worst blizzard in American history causes a great "die-up" of cattle on the plains.

Collapse of railroads triggers Depression of 1893.

1881 1885 1887 1889 **1890** 1893 1896 **1900**
                                    1894 1899

French occupy Tunisia.

Gottlieb Daimler invents the internal combustion engine.

Berlin Conference partitions Africa among European nations.

Sino-Japanese War is fought.

Boer War in South Africa begins.

Changes on the Western Frontier **379**

COMPILING A WESTERN TRAVEL GUIDE

Help students plan their travel guides by making the following suggestions:

- Make a list of questions your readers would want answered before setting out on a trip west.
- Decide what section of the West you will cover in your guide.
- Consider the sections you will include. For each section, list the main ideas you will cover and where to find the information.
- Decide how to illustrate your guide. You can either photocopy maps and pictures from source material or draw your own.

Travel Guide Decision Tree

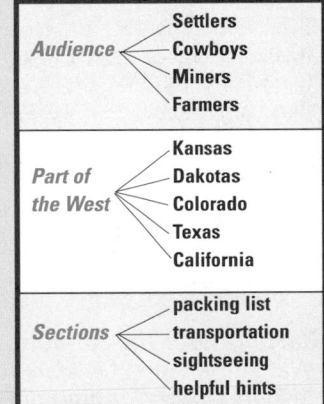

Audience	Settlers
	Cowboys
	Miners
	Farmers

Part of the West	Kansas
	Dakotas
	Colorado
	Texas
	California

Sections	packing list
	transportation
	sightseeing
	helpful hints

IN-DEPTH RESOURCES, UNIT 4
See worksheet and standards for evaluation, pp. 17, 18.

RECOMMENDED RESOURCES

Books for the Teacher

Brown, Dee. *Bury My Heart at Wounded Knee.* New York: Bantam, 1970. A Native American view of the West.

Josephy, Alvin M., Jr. *The Indian Heritage of America.* Boston: Houghton, 1991.

Ward, Geoffrey C. *The West: An Illustrated History.* New York: Little, 1996.

Books for the Student

Freeman, Russell. *Cowboys of the Wild West.* New York: Scholastic, 1985.

Jeffrey, Julie. *Frontier Women.* New York: Hill and Wang, 1979.

Stratton, Joanne L. *Pioneer Women.* New York: Simon, 1981.

Videos

How the West Was Lost (3 tapes), *How the West Was Lost II* (4 tapes). Discovery Channel Home Video.

The West. 9-part series. Produced by Stephen Ives and Ken Burns. Time-Life Video, 1996.

Software

500 Nations. CD-ROM. Microsoft, 800-555-4512.

The Wild West. CD-ROM. Educational Software Institute, 800-955-5570.

OBJECTIVES

(1) To describe the culture of Native Americans living on the Great Plains.

(2) To contrast the cultures of Native Americans and white settlers and to explain why white settlers moved west.

(3) To identify restrictions imposed by the government on Native Americans and to describe the consequences.

(4) To summarize the continuing conflict between Native Americans and settlers moving west.

(5) To identify the government's policy of assimilation.

(6) To summarize the causes and effects of the Battle of Wounded Knee.

SKILLBUILDERS

- Understanding geography: location, movement, p. 383
- Interpreting charts, p. 386

CRITICAL THINKING

- Summarizing, pp. 381, 387
- Analyzing causes, pp. 382, 384
- Clarifying, p. 383
- Recognizing effects, pp. 386, 387
- Evaluating, p. 387

FOCUS & MOTIVATE

▶ **Starting with the Student**
- Watch the video "A Walk in Two Worlds" to find out how a young Native American's life was affected by white settlement of the Western frontier.
- Using the *Teacher's Resource Book* as a guide, discuss with students experiences they may have had as minorities in another culture—in a new country, a new town, or even a new school. How was their experience similar to or different from that of Zitkala-Ša?

AMERICAN STORIES VIDEO SERIES

"A Walk in Two Worlds"
Videocassette: Volume 2

Videodisc: Disc 1, Side B, Chapter 3

1 Native American Culture in Crisis

TERMS & NAMES
- Great Plains
- Homestead Act
- exoduster
- Sand Creek Massacre
- Sitting Bull
- George A. Custer
- assimilation
- Dawes Act
- Ghost Dance
- Battle of Wounded Knee

LEARN ABOUT the Native Americans' and settlers' ways of life
TO UNDERSTAND the conflicts that occurred during settlement of the Western frontier.

ONE AMERICAN'S STORY

Zitkala-Ša was born into a Sioux tribe in 1876. As she grew up on the Great Plains, she learned the ways of her people and explored the world around her, which seemed alive with spirits. "I grew sober with awe and was alert to hear a long-drawn-out whistle rise from the roots of [the plum tree] . . . this strange whistle of departed spirits." When she was eight years old, she had a chance to go to a Quaker missionary school in Indiana. Though her mother warned her of the "white men's lies," Zitkala-Ša was eager to see "the wonderful Eastern land." She was not prepared, however, for the loss of dignity and identity she experienced, which was symbolized by the cutting of her hair.

A PERSONAL VOICE

I cried aloud, shaking my head all the while until I felt the cold blades of the scissors against my neck, and heard them gnaw off one of my thick braids. Then I lost my spirit. Since the day I was taken from my mother I had suffered extreme indignities. . . . And now my long hair was shingled like a coward's! In my anguish I moaned for my mother, but no one came to comfort me. . . . Now I was only one of many little animals driven by a herder.

ZITKALA-ŠA, quoted in *Impressions of an Indian Childhood*

Zitkala-Ša experienced firsthand the clash of two very different cultures that occurred as ever-growing numbers of white settlers moved onto the Great Plains, where Native Americans had lived for thousands of years. In the resulting struggle, the Native American way of life was changed forever.

 VIDEO *A WALK IN TWO WORLDS*
The Education of Zitkala-Ša, a Sioux

Zitkala-Ša (Gertrude Simmons Bonnin)

The Culture of the Plains Indians

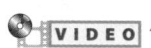

Like most Native Americans in the West, Zitkala-Ša knew very little about the world east of the Mississippi River. Most Easterners knew equally little about the West, picturing a vast desert occupied by savage tribes. That view was quite inaccurate. In fact, two distinct and highly developed Native American ways of life existed on the **Great Plains,** the grassland extending through the west-central portion of the United States (see map on page 383).

On the eastern side, near the lower Missouri River, tribes such as the Osage and Iowa planted crops and lived in small villages. Farther west, in what is now Nebraska and South Dakota, nomadic tribes such as the Sioux and Cheyenne gathered wild foods and hunted buffalo.

This Yankton Sioux coup stick was intricately carved.

THE IMPORTANCE OF THE HORSE AND THE BUFFALO After the Spanish brought horses to New Mexico in 1598, the Native American way of life began to change. As the native peoples acquired horses—and then guns—they were able to travel farther and hunt more efficiently. By the 1700s, almost all the tribes on the Great Plains had abandoned their farming villages to roam the plains and hunt buffalo.

380

SECTION 1 RESOURCES

 PRINT RESOURCES

IN-DEPTH RESOURCES: UNIT 4
Guided Reading, p. 1
Skillbuilder Practice: Hypothesizing, p. 5
Primary Source: The Battle of Little Bighorn, p. 8
American Lives: Chief Joseph, p. 15

ACCESS FOR STUDENTS ACQUIRING ENGLISH
Guided Reading (Spanish), p. 130
Skillbuilder Practice: Hypothesizing (Spanish), p. 134

FORMAL ASSESSMENT
Section Quiz, p. 161

ALTERNATIVE ASSESSMENT BOOK
See forms for supporting and scoring alternative activities.

TECHNOLOGY RESOURCES

HUMANITIES TRANSPARENCIES
H13, Sierra Nevada Mountains

GEOGRAPHY TRANSPARENCIES
G13, Railroad Land Grants: 1871

CD-ROM *Grolier Multimedia Encyclopedia*
Electronic Library of Primary Sources

VIDEO *American Stories* video series: "A Walk in Two Worlds"; *American Portfolio: A Videodisc for U.S. History* user's guide, pp. 121–124, 126, 128, 132–133

INTERNET McDougal Littell Learning On-Line
http://www.mcdougallittell.com

This increased mobility often led to war when hunters in one tribe trespassed on other tribes' hunting grounds. For the young men of a tribe, taking part in war parties and raids was a way to win prestige. But a Plains warrior gained more honor by "counting coup," or touching a live enemy and escaping unharmed, than by killing. Moreover, it was not unusual for warring tribes to call a truce so they could trade goods, share news, or enjoy harvest festivals.

While the horse gave Native Americans increased mobility, the buffalo provided many of their basic needs. Native Americans made tepees from buffalo hides and also used the skins for clothing, shoes, and blankets. Buffalo meat was dried into jerky or mixed with berries and fat to make a staple food called pemmican. Buffalo sinews were used to make thread and bowstrings; buffalo bones and horns, to make tools and toys. The buffalo, like the horse, had become central to life on the plains.

FAMILY LIFE Native Americans on the plains usually lived in small extended family groups with ties to other bands that spoke the same language. The men went on hunting or raiding parties to obtain food and supplies and shared what they had obtained with the group. The women helped butcher the game and prepared the hides that the men brought back to the camp.

Despite their communal way of life, however, the people of the plains valued individualism. Young men trained to become hunters and warriors; young women sometimes chose their own husbands. The Plains tribes believed that powerful spirits controlled the events in the natural world, and men or women who demonstrated particular sensitivity to the spirits became medicine men, or shamans.

Children learned proper behavior and the culture of the tribe through stories and myths, games, and good examples. No individual was allowed to dominate the group; the leaders of a tribe ruled by counsel rather than by force. Land was held in common for the use of the whole tribe.

Settlers Push Westward

The culture of the white settlers differed in many ways from that of the Native Americans on the plains. Unlike Native Americans, who believed that land could not be owned, the settlers defined a better life and prosperity in terms of personal property. Owning land and a house, making a mining claim, or starting a business would give them a stake in the country. Prospectors, settlers, and ranchers alike argued that the Native Americans had forfeited their rights to the land because they hadn't settled down to "improve" it. Concluding that the plains were "unsettled," settlers streamed westward to claim the land.

Changes on the Western Frontier **381**

THINK THROUGH HISTORY
A. Summarizing
How did the horse and the buffalo influence Native American life on the Great Plains?

A. Answer The horse gave them increased mobility, extending their hunting territory and promoting clashes with other tribes. They hunted the buffalo, using it for food, clothing, shelter, and tools.

A Sioux encampment near the South Dakota-Nebraska border presents a peaceful scene, but a portrait of a Sioux man and woman shows their defiance.

OBJECTIVE
① INSTRUCT

The Culture of the Plains Indians

▶ **Discussing Key Ideas**
• The horse and the buffalo are central to the nomadic life of the Plains Indians.
• Plains Indians live communally in small groups that value individualism. Ask students to begin a chart of the culture of the Plains Indians, which they will add to as they progress through the chapter.

	Plains Indians
Settled/ Nomadic	
Food	
Housing	

IN-DEPTH RESOURCES: UNIT 4
Guided Reading, p. 1

ACCESS FOR STUDENTS ACQUIRING ENGLISH
Guided Reading (Spanish), p. 130

OBJECTIVE
② INSTRUCT

Settlers Push Westward

Starting with the Student
▶ Have students contrast the culture of the white settlers with that of the Plains Indians by adding a column to their charts.

	Plains Indians	White Settlers
Settled/Nomadic		
Food		

▶ **Discussing Key Ideas**
• White settlers move westward to claim land, to farm, or to mine for gold.
• The Homestead Act of 1862 offers free land to settlers.

TEACHING OPTIONS

Teaching Less Proficient Readers

Main Ideas and Supporting Details Have students work in pairs to identify the main ideas of the section and the details that support them. Suggest they follow these steps:

1. Read pages 380–382 of the text together.
2. Individually list the main ideas (e.g., the importance of the buffalo) and details that support the main ideas (e.g., the uses of the buffalo).
3. Compare lists and agree on one statement of main ideas and supporting details.

Making Connections Across Cultures

Other Frontier Experiences The United States is only one of many countries—Canada, Brazil, Australia, Russia, and South Africa, for example—that were shaped by frontier experiences. Here is a comparison of the American and South African experiences. "The North American and southern African frontiers . . . were products of the same general process: the expansion of Europe and of capitalism. . . . Frontier zones successively closed and came under white control and new zones opened up, as whites moved westward in North America and north and east in southern Africa."

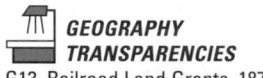
THE LURE OF SILVER AND GOLD The prospect of striking it rich was one powerful attraction of the West. The gold fever that had flared in California in 1849 never really died out, and the discovery of gold in Colorado in 1858 drew tens of thousands of miners to the region.

The glitter of gold must have blinded prospective miners to other concerns because mining camps and tiny frontier towns were filthy, ramshackle quarters. Rows of tents and shacks with dirt "streets" and wooden sidewalks had replaced unspoiled streams and picturesque landscapes. Fortune seekers of every description—including Irish, German, Swedish, Polish, Chinese, and African-American men—crowded the camps and boomtowns. A few hardy, business-minded women tried their luck, too, working as laundresses, freight haulers, or even miners. Cities such as Virginia City, Nevada, and Helena, Montana, originated as mining camps on Native American land.

FARMING THE GREAT PLAINS Another powerful attraction of the West was the land itself. In 1862, Congress passed the **Homestead Act,** offering 160 acres of land free to anyone who would live on and cultivate it for five years. From 1862 to 1900, between 400,000 and 600,000 families took advantage of the government's offer. They came from the South and from New England, eager to exchange their worn-out fields for more fertile land farther west. Some German and Scandinavian farmers unable to earn a living in their native lands were lured to America by public relations campaigns sponsored by the railroad companies. Several thousand settlers were **exodusters**—African Americans who moved from the post-Reconstruction South to Kansas in a great exodus. Free land alone was not enough to lure farmers onto the Great Plains, however. They also needed a reliable way to get there and to ship their crops to growing urban markets.

Many settlers traveled west in prairie schooners, sturdy descendants of the Conestoga wagon. The white canvas tops made the wagons look like ships sailing across the open plains.

In 1862, Congress passed the Pacific Railroad Act, which granted huge amounts of money and land to the Union Pacific and Central Pacific Railroads. The Central Pacific began laying track at Sacramento in 1863. The Union Pacific began near Omaha in 1865. Both companies hired thousands of immigrants, many Chinese among them, to build bridges, dig tunnels, and lay track.

Before the railroads came west, hardy travelers rode west on horseback or in wagon trains that were cold in winter, hot in summer, and vulnerable to attack by Native Americans and outlaws. Until completion of a transcontinental route in 1869, long-distance travel was dangerous, uncomfortable, and slow. After 1869, however, people could ride from coast to coast in ten days or less. Still, the railroads were not for everyone. A "bargain" fare from Omaha to Sacramento cost about $40—more than a month's pay for the average person. Yet the trains were relatively luxurious. All of them had indoor toilets, and most of the cars were heated. For $75, travelers could ride on padded seats. For another $4 per night, they could reserve a place in a Pullman Palace Car, complete with beds. Instead of heading west at the rate of 15 miles a day in a covered wagon, aspiring settlers could speed along at 50 miles an hour.

B. Answer
Government acts and railroad lines made it easier to travel west, where white settlers could take advantage of mining and farming opportunities.

THINK THROUGH HISTORY
B. *Analyzing Causes* Why did white settlers suddenly flood the Great Plains?

The Government Restricts Native Americans

While allowing more settlers to move westward, the railroads also influenced the government's policy toward the Native Americans who lived on the plains. In 1834, the federal government had passed an act that designated the entire Great Plains as one enormous reservation, or land set aside for Native American tribes. In response to the increasing stream of settlers in the 1850s, however, the government changed its policy. In order to open up more land for white settlers, it began signing treaties that created definite boundaries for each tribe.

Shrinking Native American Lands, 1894, and Battle Sites, 1860s–1890s

(continued from page 382)

1819

1894

1996

BLACKFOOT
NEZ PERCE
SHASTA
CHEYENNE
Little Bighorn 1876
SIOUX
SHOSHONE
ARAPAHO SHOSHONE
SIOUX
Fetterman Massacre, 1866
Wounded Knee, 1890
UTE
NAVAJO
UTE
Sand Creek Massacre, 1864
HOPI
GREAT PLAINS
PAWNEE
APACHE
ARAPAHO CHEYENNE
APACHE COMANCHE KIOWA
Rocky Mountains
40° N
35° N
30° N
PACIFIC OCEAN
120° W
115° W
100° Meridian
Mississippi River
Gulf of Mexico

☐ Great Plains
☐ Indian reservation
✳ Battle site

0   500 Miles
0   1000 Kilometers

▶Discussing Key Ideas

• The government sets aside land for Native Americans but later reverses its policy and limits the land occupied by individual tribes.
• Native Americans fight to retain their traditional hunting grounds.
• The government forces the Sioux to sign the Treaty of 1868, which restricts them to a reservation.

HISTORY FROM VISUALS

Shrinking Native American Lands, 1894, and Battle Sites, 1860s

Reading the Map Make sure students understand that the small maps indicate changes in the buffalo population over time and that the large map is a blowout—or more detailed version—of the central small map.

Extension Have students work in pairs to find out how the land of a particular reservation shown on the map is used today.

THINK THROUGH HISTORY
C. Clarifying
What was the government's policy toward Native American land?

C. Answer The government wanted to restrict all Native Americans to designated land.

Most Native Americans did not agree to sign treaties with the government, though, and many of the "chiefs" who did sign did not represent their tribes. Many tribes, including the Cheyenne and the Sioux, continued to hunt on their traditional lands, clashing with settlers and miners—with tragic results.

MASSACRE AT SAND CREEK   One of the most tragic events occurred in 1864. The Cheyenne, who had been forced into a barren area of the Colorado Territory known as the Sand Creek Reserve, began raiding nearby trails and settlements for food and supplies. Colorado governor John Evans ordered the militia to attack the raiders but urged the Cheyenne who did not want to fight to report to Fort Lyon, near the reserve, where they would be safe from harm. Most of the Cheyenne moved back to Sand Creek for the winter, flying both the American flag and a white flag as a sign of their peaceful intentions.

General S. R. Curtis, U.S. army commander in the West, sent a telegram to militia colonel John Chivington that read, "I want no peace till the Indians suffer more." In response, Chivington and his troops descended on the 500 Cheyenne camped at Sand Creek at dawn on November 29, 1864. Chivington had his own reasons to want revenge on Native Americans, because they had killed his family. Without warning, Chivington and his men attacked the sleeping village. The exhausted warriors and terrified women and children never had a chance to defend themselves. Chivington's soldiers killed about 200 inhabitants, mostly women and children, and mutilated the bodies. After the **Sand Creek Massacre,** as this battle came to be called, Chivington was treated as a hero in his hometown, Denver.

DEATH ON THE BOZEMAN TRAIL   Another tribe, the Sioux, were angered by white settlement along the Bozeman Trail, which the government had opened

GEOGRAPHY SKILLBUILDER
LOCATION
Which battles took place on Native American land?
MOVEMENT
About what percentage of Native American lands had the government taken over by 1894? About what percentage had Native Americans recovered by 1996?

Skillbuilder Answers
Location: Little Bighorn, Wounded Knee;
Movement: 1874—about 90%; 1996—none.

Changes on the Western Frontier **383**

Making Connections Across the Curriculum

Geography Have students consult an atlas to determine the quality of the land set aside for Native Americans by 1895. They should consider if the land was agricultural, if it contained mining resources, or if it was barren and nonproductive. Ask students what conclusions they draw from their research. *Possible Response: The most desirable land was given or sold to white settlers or to mining companies. Much of the land that Native Americans received was poor for farming and contained few natural resources.*

Exploring Themes

The American Dream Discuss the dreams Native Americans might have had for their life in the United States. Ask students to consider how the dreams of white settlers and immigrants conflicted with those of the Native Americans. *Possible Answer: Both groups wanted to use Western land and its resources.* Discuss provisions that might have been made to enable both groups to realize their dreams. *Possible Answer: Lands might have been set aside for the Native Americans and the resources (including the buffalo) left untouched so the people could pursue their way of life.*

Teacher's Edition **383**

KEY PLAYER
Sitting Bull

Ask students to describe the attributes suggested by the name Sitting Bull. How might those character traits be useful to a warrior, a tribal leader, and a representative of his people? *Possible Answer: The strength, deter-mination, and even stub-bornness suggested by Sitting Bull's name might enable him to be a stalwart supporter of his people's cause.*

OBJECTIVE
④ **INSTRUCT**

Bloody Battles Continue

▶ *Discussing Key Ideas*
- Conflict escalates as settle-ment continues and Native Americans resist restriction to reservations.
- The Black Hills—sacred Sioux territory—become a contested area as the gov-ernment tries to secure its gold resources.
- Custer's defeat shocks white Americans and leads to increased army raids and the defeat of the Sioux.

💿 **GROLIER MULTIMEDIA ENCYCLOPEDIA**
Indian wars

MORE ABOUT . . .
Gall

Gall was a leader of the Hunkpapa Sioux. Remembering the U.S. Army bullets that wiped out his family, Gall fought at the battle of Little Bighorn armed only with a hatchet.

KEY PLAYER

SITTING BULL
1831–1890

As a child, Sitting Bull was known as Hunkesni, or Slow; he earned the name Tatanka Yotanka (Sitting Bull) after a fight with the Crow Indians, a traditional enemy of the Sioux.

Sitting Bull led his people by the strength of his character and purpose. He was a warrior, counselor, and medicine man, and he was determined that the whites leave Sioux territory. His most famous fight was at the Little Bighorn River. About his opponent, George Armstrong Custer, he said, "They tell me I murdered Custer. It is a lie. . . . He was a fool and rode to his death."

After Sitting Bull's surrender to the federal government in 1881, his dislike of whites did not change, although he loved to shake hands, learned to sign his name, and took drawing lessons from a German artist. He was killed by Native American police at Standing Rock Reservation on December 15, 1890.

---

during the Civil War. This major transportation route ran directly through the Black Hills of South Dakota, sacred land the Sioux called *Paha Sapa*. Their chief, Red Cloud (Mahpiua Luta), appealed to the government to help stop the settlement, but soldiers continued to build forts on the trail. When talking proved futile, Sioux, Arapaho, and Cheyenne warriors began a guerrilla war, sending small bands on surprise raids to harass the troops. On December 21, 1866, Crazy Horse and several other warriors lured Captain William J. Fetterman and his company of soldiers into an ambush at Lodge Trail Ridge. The warriors surrounded the soldiers and killed them all. Native Americans called this fight the Battle of the Hundred Slain. Whites called it the Fetterman Massacre.

Skirmishes followed for about a year, until the government agreed to close the Bozeman Trail. In return, the Sioux signed the historic Treaty of 1868, in which they agreed to live on a reservation along the Missouri River. The terms of this treaty resembled those of treaties concluded the previous year. In these treaties, the southern Kiowa, Comanche, Cheyenne, and Arapaho promised to live on large reserva-tions in return for protection and supplies from the U.S. government.

Conflicts between the whites and Native Americans continued despite these treaties. Several factors contributed to the ongoing hostilities. Promised supplies often arrived late and were of poor quality and insufficient quantity. In addition, the Treaty of 1868 had been forced on the Sioux. **Sitting Bull** (Tatanka Yotanka), a medicine man and leader of the Hunkpapa Sioux, had never signed it. Although the Oglala and Brulé Sioux had signed the treaty, they expected to be able to continue using their traditional hunting grounds and to come and go on the reservation as they pleased.

Bloody Battles Continue

The Treaty of 1868 provided only a temporary halt to warfare. The conflict between the two cultures continued as settlers moved west-ward across the plains and Native American tribes resisted the restrictions of the reservations. A Sioux warrior explained why.

> **A PERSONAL VOICE**
> [We] have been taught to hunt and live on the game. You tell us that we must learn to farm, live in one house, and take on your ways. Suppose the people living beyond the great sea should come and tell you that you must stop farming, and kill your cattle, and take your houses and lands, what would you do? Would you not fight them?
> **GALL, A HUNKPAPA SIOUX,** quoted in *Bury My Heart at Wounded Knee*

RAIDS BY THE KIOWA AND COMANCHE In late 1868, war broke out yet again, this time on the southern plains, as Kiowa and Comanche refused to move to the reservation in the Texas panhandle. They began a raiding spree that continued for six years and finally led to the Red River War of 1874–75. The U.S. Army responded to the Native Americans' guerrilla warfare by herding the friendly tribes-people onto reservations and opening fire on all others. General Philip Sheridan, a Union Army veteran, gave orders to "destroy their villages and ponies, to kill and hang all warriors, and to bring back all women and children."

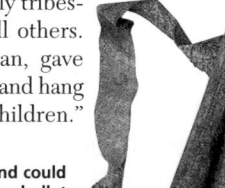

The Sioux war bow, *right*, was accurate up to 100 yards and could shoot arrows more rapidly than a single-shot rifle could fire bullets.

384 CHAPTER 13

D. Answer It had been forced on some of the Sioux, and Native Americans were not given adequate protection or supplies.

THINK THROUGH HISTORY
D. *Analyzing Causes* Why was the Treaty of 1868 ineffective?

With these tactics, the army crushed the resistance on the southern plains.

GOLD RUSH Within four years of the Treaty of 1868, while battles raged, miners began flooding into the Black Hills to search for gold. The Sioux, Cheyenne, and Arapaho protested—to no avail. By 1874, the rumor of gold had grown so strong that the army sent **George Armstrong Custer,** Civil War hero and colonel in the Seventh Cavalry, to investigate and send back a report.

When Custer reported that the Black Hills had gold "from the grass roots down," a gold rush was on. Red Cloud and Spotted Tail, another Sioux chief, appealed again to government officials in Washington, who responded with an offer to purchase the land. When the Sioux refused to sell their sacred ground, the stage was set for the last battles of the Plains wars.

CUSTER'S LAST STAND In early June 1876, the Sioux and Cheyenne held a Sun Dance in which Sitting Bull had a vision of soldiers and some Native Americans falling from their horses. He interpreted the vision as a sign that victory would come for his people. Soon after, a successful battle with the Seventh Cavalry at Rosebud Creek in south central Montana prepared the tribes for the military's next move. When Lieutenant Colonel Custer and his batallion reached the Little Bighorn River, the Native Americans were ready for them.

On June 25, Custer rode out in search of glory. He expected to pit his disciplined regiment against 1,500 warriors. Custer's plan had several flaws, however. First, despite warnings from Indian scouts, he underestimated the number of Native American warriors. Between 2,000 and 3,000 awaited his attack. Second, his men and horses were exhausted. Third, he split up his regiment and attacked with barely 200 men. Led by Crazy Horse, the warriors—in warpaint and bonnets and with raised spears or rifles—outflanked and overpowered Custer's troops. Within 20 minutes, Custer and all of his men were dead.

The American people were shocked and angered at Custer's defeat. Many criticized him for his bad judgment, but the nation as a whole demanded revenge. The army continued to raid Native American camps and to slaughter the buffalo. By late 1876, the Sioux were beaten. Sitting Bull and a few followers took refuge in Canada, where they remained until 1881.

The Government Supports Assimilation

Eventually, to prevent his people's starvation, even the proud Sitting Bull was forced to surrender. Later, in 1885, he became an attraction in William F. "Buffalo Bill" Cody's Wild West Show.

The Native Americans still had supporters in the United States, however, and debate over the treatment of Native Americans continued. Well-known writer Helen Hunt Jackson, for example, exposed the government's many broken promises in her 1881 book *A Century of Dishonor*: "It makes little difference . . . where one opens the record of the history of the Indians; every page and every year has its dark stain."

Sometimes, the "friends" of the Native Americans were not much more helpful than their enemies. Many sympathizers were supporters of **assimilation,** in which Native Americans were expected to give up their beliefs and way of life and become part of the white culture. Although the Native Americans had lost much land and their means of independent living, they did not want to lose their culture as well.

FAILURE OF THE DAWES ACT In 1887, in an effort to make assimilation the official government policy, Congress passed the **Dawes Act.** The aim was to "Americanize" the Native Americans by cultivating in them the desire to own property and to farm. The Dawes Act broke up the reservations and distributed some of the reservation land—160 acres for farming or 320 acres for grazing—

Changes on the Western Frontier **385**

The Winchester '76 rifle, which was widely used by government troops, had a large loading slot, and could fire 16 bullets without reloading.

"*Stripped of the beautiful romance with which we have so long been willing to envelop him . . . the Indian forfeits his claim to the [name] 'noble red man.'*"

GEORGE A. CUSTER

E. Answer Death of Custer and all his men, demand for revenge by American people, continued raids on Native American camps.

THINK THROUGH HISTORY
E. Recognizing Effects
What were the results of Custer's last stand?

MORE ABOUT . . .
George Armstrong Custer
Lt. Col. Custer (1839–1876) went to the West after a distinguished career in the Civil War. Although he was last in his class at West Point, he became, at age 23, the youngest general in the Union Army. (He was later demoted.) Native Americans called him Yellow Hair, because he wore his blond hair in long ringlets.

IN-DEPTH RESOURCES: UNIT 4
Primary Source: The Battle of Little Bighorn, p. 8

OBJECTIVE
⑤ INSTRUCT

The Government Supports Assimilation

▶**Discussing Key Ideas**
• Some Americans propose that Native Americans be assimilated into the dominant white culture.
• The Dawes Act is an attempt to provide Native American families with individual plots of former reservation land, but much of the best land is sold to speculators.
• Native American children are taken away from their families and educated in boarding schools in the "white man's ways."
• Buffalo hunters, tourists, and fur traders destroy the very basis of the Great Plains culture—the buffalo.

TEACHING OPTION

Skillbuilder Mini-Lesson: Hypothesizing

Explaining the Skill Historians develop hypotheses, or possible explanations, about events to better understand why the events happened, what the consequences were or might be, and why the events are significant. Then they test their hypotheses against historical evidence to check their validity.

Applying the Skill: The Dawes Act Have students read about assimilation and the Dawes Act at the bottom of this page and write a hypothesis about why these efforts failed. *Some students might say the Native American and white cultures were too different and it was a misguided plan to begin with. Others might suggest that Native Americans didn't*

receive the money or the fertile land promised them. Then have students read page 386 through "Educating the Native Americans" and see if the facts prove or disprove their hypothesis. *Possible Answers: In many cases, Native Americans received neither the land nor the money from its sale; the good land was taken by whites; educators tried to wipe out Native American culture, making "Americanized" young people unable to fit in either culture.* Suggest that students revise their hypotheses if evidence proved their original ones wrong.

IN-DEPTH RESOURCES: UNIT 4
Skillbuilder Practice: Hypothesizing, p. 5

Teacher's Edition **385**

to each adult head of a Native American family. The government would sell the remainder of the reservation to settlers, and the resulting income would be used by Native Americans for farm implements. But the Native Americans received nothing from the sale of these lands. By 1934, whites had taken over 65 percent of the territory that had been set aside for Native Americans. Speculators, who bought land to sell at a profit, grabbed most of the best land. Much of the land that remained was useless for farming.

EDUCATING THE NATIVE AMERICANS While the Dawes Act addressed the physical assimilation of Native Americans, education addressed their minds and spirits. Off-reservation boarding schools, like the one attended by Zitkala-Ša, flourished. Among the reformers was Richard H. Pratt, who founded the Carlisle boarding school in Pennsylvania to "kill the Indian and save the man." The Carlisle school and others like it taught Native American children that their traditional ways were backward and superstitious. The teachers promoted the values of white civilization and then returned the "educated" children to the reservations, where the skills they had learned were useless. What resulted was a generation of Native American young people caught in a tragic conflict between the culture of their parents and that of their teachers. They didn't fit in on the reservations, yet they faced discrimination when they tried to live in the white world.

THE DESTRUCTION OF THE BUFFALO Perhaps the most significant blow to tribal life on the plains was the destruction of the buffalo. Railroad companies like the Kansas Pacific hired buffalo hunters to accompany the workers and supply them with meat as they laid track westward, often in violation of treaties. Working for the railroads, hunter William F. Cody killed nearly 4,300 bison in eight months, earning the nickname "Buffalo Bill." Trappers, who had already destroyed beaver and other wildlife, now turned to the buffalo as a source of income. "Wherever the Whites are established," a Sioux chief bitterly observed, "the buffalo is gone, and the red hunters must die of hunger."

Tourists and fur traders also shot buffalo for sport from speeding railroad trains. General Sheridan noted with approval that buffalo hunters were destroying the Plains Indians' main source of food, clothing, shelter, and fuel. In 1800, approximately 15 million buffalo roamed the plains; by 1886, fewer than 600 remained. In 1900, the United States sheltered, in Yellowstone National Park, a single wild herd of buffalo.

The Legend of the Buffalo

1800 15,000,000

1865 1,000

1996 200,000

The buffalo provided the Plains Indians with more than just a high-protein food source.

THE SKULL of the buffalo was considered sacred and was used in many Native American rituals.

THE HIDE was by far the most precious part of the buffalo. Native American clothing, tepees, and even arrow shields were made from buffalo hide.

THE BONES of the buffalo were made into hide scrapers, tool handles, sled runners, and hoe blades The hoofs were ground up and used as glue.

THE HORNS were carved into bowls and spoons.

The Battle of Wounded Knee

Although some people tried to improve the lives of Native Americans, the Sioux continued to suffer reduced rations, increased restrictions, and the loss of their cattle to disease. In desperation, they turned to Wovoka, a Paiute prophet who had had a vision in which Native American lands would be restored, the buffalo would return, and the whites would disappear. Wovoka promised that if the Sioux performed a ritual called the **Ghost Dance,** this vision would be realized.

The Ghost Dance movement spread rapidly among the 25,000 Sioux on the Dakota reservation. Its popularity alarmed military leaders and the local reservation agent, who decided to arrest Sitting Bull. On a drizzly December morning in 1890, 39 Indian policemen were sent to arrest him. As two of the policemen pulled Sitting Bull out of his cabin, Sitting Bull's bodyguard, Catch-the-Bear, shot one of them. The falling policeman aimed at Sitting Bull, fired, and killed him. A free-for-all resulted.

As the shots rang out, Sitting Bull's horse abruptly sat down and began performing the tricks it had learned in the Wild West Show with Buffalo Bill. For a moment, at least, it seemed to observers that the horse was performing the outlawed Ghost Dance.

The army wasn't satisfied with the death of Sitting Bull. On December 29, 1890, the Seventh Cavalry—Custer's old division that had been defeated at Little Bighorn—rounded up 340 starving and freezing Sioux at Wounded Knee Creek in South Dakota. The soldiers demanded that the Native Americans give up all their weapons. One Native American resisted this order and fired his rifle. The soldiers fired back with deadly cannons.

Within minutes, the Seventh Cavalry slaughtered 300 unarmed Native Americans, including several children. The soldiers left the corpses to freeze on the ground. This action, the **Battle of Wounded Knee,** brought the Indian wars—and an entire era—to a bitter end.

G. Answer
Spread of the Ghost Dance movement, killing of Sitting Bull.

THINK THROUGH HISTORY
G. Analyzing Causes
What events led to the Battle of Wounded Knee?

A PERSONAL VOICE
I did not know then how much was ended. When I look back now from this high hill of my old age, I can still see the butchered women and children lying heaped and scattered all along the crooked gulch as plain as when I saw them with eyes still young. And I can see that something else died there in the bloody mud, and was buried in the blizzard. A people's dream died there. It was a beautiful dream.

BLACK ELK, quoted in *Black Elk Speaks*

HOMECOMING

"I never thought I'd see the day," said Earl (Taz) Conner, a direct descendant of the best known of the Nez Perce, Chief Joseph. Forced off their tribal lands in Wallowa County, Oregon, in 1877, the Nez Perce in the United States, now numbering 4,000, are returning almost 120 years later.

When hard times hit during the 1990s, Wallowa community leaders saw a chance to bring money to the area by taking advantage of people's growing interest in Native Americans. They obtained a grant and asked for contributions to develop a Nez Perce cultural center, which they hope will be a big tourist draw. In the words of Soy Redthunder, another tribe member, "The whites may look at it as an economic plus, but we look at it as a homecoming."

Section 1 Assessment

1. TERMS & NAMES
Identify:
- Great Plains
- Homestead Act
- exoduster
- Sand Creek Massacre
- Sitting Bull
- George A. Custer
- assimilation
- Dawes Act
- Ghost Dance
- Battle of Wounded Knee

2. SUMMARIZING Fill in supporting details about the culture of the Plains Indians.

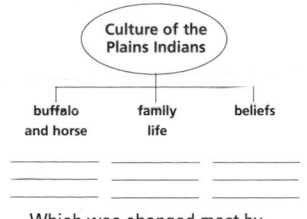

Which was changed most by white settlement?

3. RECOGNIZING EFFECTS This chapter says that the destruction of the buffalo was "perhaps the most significant blow to tribal life." Explain why you agree or disagree with this statement.

THINK ABOUT
- how Native Americans used the buffalo
- how Native Americans viewed ownership of land

4. EVALUATING Why do you think the assimilation policy of the Dawes Act failed? Support your opinion with information from the text.

THINK ABOUT
- the experience of Native Americans such as Zitkala-Ša
- the attitudes of many white leaders toward Native Americans
- the merits of owning property
- the importance of people's cultural heritage

Changes on the Western Frontier **387**

ANSWERS

OBJECTIVES

1 To trace the development of the cattle industry.

2 To describe both the myth and the reality of the American cowboy.

3 To explain the end of cattle ranching on the open plains.

SKILLBUILDER

- Understanding geography: region, place, p. 390

CRITICAL THINKING

- Summarizing, pp. 389, 393
- Analyzing causes, p. 390
- Contrasting, p. 391
- Forming opinions, p. 392
- Synthesizing, p. 393
- Comparing and contrasting, p. 393

FOCUS & MOTIVATE

▶ **Starting with the Student**
Have students answer the following questions and save their answers to reexamine after reading the section.

- What are students' images of cowboys?
- How have movies and novels influenced those images?
- How true do students think those images are to the reality of life on the open range?

MORE ABOUT . . .
The Texas Longhorn
Texas longhorn cattle were bred from Spanish and British stock. They had large ears and long legs. Their most prominent feature, though, was their horns, which could reach 6 feet from tip to tip. They got moisture by eating the prickly pear cactus and could go for days without water. Longhorns were nervous and easily spooked, and stampedes were not uncommon.

❷ The Growth of the Cattle Industry

LEARN ABOUT the cowboy's life and work
TO UNDERSTAND the difference between the myth and the reality of the cowboy.

A group of cowboys take a well-earned rest before heading back out on the trail.

ONE AMERICAN'S STORY

Cowboy G. D. Burrows remembered his life on the trails as one of "going hungry, getting wet and cold, riding sore-backed horses, going to sleep on herd and losing cattle, getting 'cussed' by the boss [and] scouting for 'gray-backs' (body lice)." Yet Burrows claimed that his memory of the discomforts faded whenever he delivered a herd and rode into town.

He would put on new high-heeled boots and striped pants and sit through performance after performance of local entertainment. After a few days, having gone broke, he would borrow money and head back to the ranch for the winter.

> ### A PERSONAL VOICE
> I would put in the fall and winter telling about the big things I had seen up North. The next spring I would have the same old trip, the same old things would happen in the same old way, and with the same old wind-up. I put in 18 or 20 years on the trail, and all I had in the final outcome was the high-heeled boots, the striped pants, and about $4.80 worth of other clothes.
>
> **G. D. BURROWS,** quoted in *The Trail Drivers of Texas*

By taking over Native American lands and eliminating the buffalo, whites opened up a vast stretch of western land that would soon be transformed by a new way of life—cattle ranching—and a new American hero—the cowboy. Over a century after his heyday, this independent, but often overworked and lonely, figure still captures the American imagination.

The Cattle Industry Becomes Big Business

As the great herds of buffalo disappeared, horses and cattle flourished on the plains. Before long, cattle were plentiful and ranching had become big business from Texas to Kansas.

THE FIRST COWBOYS Horses and cattle had been introduced to the New World by Spanish explorers. Among the small, quick horses brought to Mexico in 1519 by Hernando Cortés was the piebald pinto, which added a variety of color to the endless plains. The **longhorn** cattle brought by the Spaniards, first to the West Indies and then to Mexico, were sturdy, long-horned, short-tempered breeds that were accustomed to the dry grasslands of Andalusia, in southern Spain. The Spanish settlers used the horses as work animals and the cattle for food.

The Spanish herds thrived on the grassy Mexican plains, with some ranches eventually including as many as 150,000 head of cattle. To help them with these herds, the Spaniards employed their native Aztec prisoners as vaqueros, or cowboys. At first, most of the vaqueros worked on foot. But as the herds grew, the vaqueros learned to use horses to manage the cattle. These first cowboys quickly became expert riders skilled in the use of *la reata*, or "the lariat," which they used to rope and control the herds.

388 CHAPTER 13

SECTION 2 RESOURCES

 PRINT RESOURCES

IN-DEPTH RESOURCES: UNIT 4
Guided Reading, p. 2

ACCESS FOR STUDENTS ACQUIRING ENGLISH
Guided Reading (Spanish), p. 131

FORMAL ASSESSMENT
Section Quiz, p. 162

ALTERNATIVE ASSESSMENT BOOK
See forms for supporting and scoring alternative activities.

 TECHNOLOGY RESOURCES

CD-ROM *Grolier Multimedia Encyclopedia*
Electronic Library of Primary Sources

VIDEO *American Portfolio: A Videodisc for U.S. History*
user's guide, pp. 125, 127, 128

INTERNET McDougal Littell Learning On-Line
http://www.mcdougallittell.com

When silver was discovered in northern Mexico, the Spanish ranchers and their vaqueros herded their cattle north to provide food for the miners. In 1598, some of the ranchers drove their herds into what is now New Mexico, where they taught the Pueblo Indians how to ride and rope.

About a hundred years later, other Spaniards crossed the Rio Grande and settled in Texas, on the southern Great Plains. Over the years, thousands of cows and many horses escaped or strayed on the open range and bred with the wild herds. These herds flourished in the United States as they had in Mexico.

THE INFLUENCE OF MEXICAN CULTURE As American as the cowboy seems today, his way of life stemmed directly from that of those first Spanish ranchers in Mexico. The American settlers had never managed large herds on an open range, and they learned from their Mexican neighbors how to round up, rope, brand, and care for the animals. Even the animals themselves, the Texas longhorns that came to symbolize the West, were descendants of Spanish cattle.

The American cowboy's clothes, food, and vocabulary were also heavily influenced by his Mexican forerunner. The Mexican vaquero was the first to wear spurs, which he attached with straps to his bare feet and used to control his horse. His *chaparreras*, or leather overalls, became known as chaps. He ate *charqui*, or "jerky," dried strips of meat. The Spanish *caballo bronco*, or "rough horse" that ran wild, became known as a bronco or bronc. The strays the vaquero called *mesteños*, or "homeless ones," were the same mustangs the American cowboy tamed and prized. The Mexican *rancho* became the model for the American ranch. Finally, the English words *corral* and *rodeo* were borrowed directly from Spanish. In habit, as in the pronunciation of the word itself, the Mexican vaquero was the true forerunner of the American buckaroo.

The American cowboy, of course, added his own signature to his adopted way of life. Cowboy boots were designed with pointed toes to fit inside stirrups and with high heels to keep the feet from sliding through. Chaps were padded with wool or fur to offer protection against the cold northern climate. The bandanna became such an all-purpose necessity that it was once proposed as the official flag of the open range. This cowboy trademark served as a sun screen, tourniquet, dust mask, washcloth, strainer for muddy water, face covering for dead cowboys, noose for hanging horse thieves, and blindfold for skittish horses. Then there was the six-shooter—the gun that could fire six shots without reloading and that came to symbolize not only the cowboy but the entire Old West.

THE IMPORTANCE OF THE RAILROADS Despite the plentiful herds of cattle in Texas and throughout the West, cowboys were not in great demand until the railroads reached the Great Plains.

Before the Civil War, ranchers for the most part didn't stray far from their homesteads with their cattle. They sold some hides and animal fat, or tallow, to Western markets along the coast of the Gulf of Mexico but generally just watched their herds increase. There were, of course, some exceptions. During

A. Answer
Mexicans taught American cowboys how to rope and ride. They greatly influenced cowboys' language, clothes, and activities.

THINK THROUGH HISTORY
A. Summarizing *What does the American cowboy tradition owe to the Mexican vaquero?*

The cowboy's days, like the line of longhorns he herded seemed to stretch endlessly. William Henry David Koerner depicts this boredom in his painting *And So, Unemotionally, There Begun One of the Wildest and Strangest Journeys Ever Made in Any Land.*

The Cattle Industry Becomes Big Business

▶ *Discussing Key Ideas*
- Spanish explorers introduce horses and cattle into the Southwest.
- Many aspects of cowboy culture—food, clothing, vocabulary—are borrowed from Spanish ranchers in Mexico.
- The growth of the railroads provides a market for the booming cattle industry.

IN-DEPTH RESOURCES: UNIT 4
Guided Reading, p. 2

ACCESS FOR STUDENTS ACQUIRING ENGLISH
Guided Reading (Spanish), p. 131

MORE ABOUT . . .
The Cowboy Hat

A cowboy could tell a lot about another cowboy by looking at his hat. If the hat had a wide brim and a high crown, the wearer was from the Southwest, where he needed extra protection from the sun. If the hat had a narrow brim and a low crown, the hat's owner was probably from the northern plains, where it was very windy. A hat did more than cover a cowboy's head, though. It served as a pillow, a bucket to carry water, a fan to start a fire, and a paddle to slap a steer and control a stampede.

Teaching Less Proficient Readers

Using Graphic Organizers Pair less proficient readers with proficient readers, and Spanish-speaking students with non-Spanish speakers. Ask a Latino student to pronounce the Spanish words in the text, and then pronounce the English equivalent yourself, emphasizing the similarity in sound. Then have students read pages 388 and 389 together and keep in mind how each item was used. Ask them to create a table such as the one shown on the right, listing the Spanish name, the English name, and the use of each item.

Spanish term	English term	Use
chaparreras	chaps	to protect riders' legs when riding through the brush
charqui	jerky	"fast food" for the trail
—	pointed boots	to fit through stirrups

HISTORY FROM VISUALS

Cattle Trails and the Railroads, 1870s–1890s

Reading the Map Have students locate the beginnings of the cattle trails and follow the arrows to their termination at railroad junctions.

Extension Have students work in pairs to plot three possible routes from ranch to meatpacking center. Ask them to use the map scale to measure the distances the cattle traveled on foot and by train.

MORE ABOUT . . .

Joseph McCoy

This entrepreneur was a real showman, and may have been the source of the term "the real McCoy." To advertise Abilene as a shipping center, he hired cowboys to capture large buffalo, one of which weighed over 2,300 pounds. He sent three of these buffalo by train to Chicago, exhibiting them at every stop along the way. This promotion was so successful that cattle buyers thronged to Abilene before the hotel was ready, and McCoy had to house them in several large tents.

Range hands use sticks to prod longhorns into railcars. This work earned them the nickname "cowpokes."

GEOGRAPHY SKILLBUILDER
REGION *At what cities did the cattle trails and the railroads intersect to form cattle-shipping centers?*
PLACE *Which cities were served by the most railroads?*

Skillbuilder Answer
Region: Abilene, Kansas; Ellsworth, Kansas; Sedalia, Missouri; Kansas City, Missouri; Oglala, Nebraska; Cheyenne, Wyoming.
Place: Cheyenne, Wyoming and Albuquerque, New Mexico.

the California gold rush in 1849, some hearty cattlemen on horseback braved a long trek, or drive, through Apache country and across the desert to collect $25 to $125 a head for their cattle. Others suffered through quicksand and hazardous swamps to reach the market in New Orleans. In 1854, two ranchers even drove their cattle 700 miles to Muncie, Indiana, where they loaded them on stock cars bound for New York City. When the cattle were unloaded in New York, the stampede that followed caused a panic on Third Avenue. Parts of the country were obviously not ready for mass transportation of animals.

CITY DWELLERS DEMAND MORE BEEF After the Civil War, however, the demand for beef skyrocketed. There was a large market for beef in cities, where the population continued to grow. At the Chicago Union Stock Yards, which opened on Christmas Day, 1865, Texas cattlemen heard rumors that their longhorns would be worth $40 a head. By spring 1866, the railroads had reached Sedalia, Missouri. From the railhead at Sedalia, ranchers could ship their cattle to Chicago and markets throughout the East. Unfortunately, they found that the route to Sedalia was riddled with obstacles: hostile weather, such as thunderstorms; rough land, such as rain-swollen rivers; and farmers who did not want cattle trampling their crops and spreading disease. In 1866, angry farmers blockaded cattle in Baxter Springs, Kansas, and prevented them from reaching Sedalia. As a result, some herds had to be sold at cut-rate prices and others died of starvation.

The next year, the cattlemen found a more convenient route, thanks to cattle dealer Joseph McCoy of Springfield, Illinois. McCoy approached several Western towns with plans to create a shipping yard where the trails and rail lines came together. St. Louis, Missouri, turned down McCoy's plan, but the tiny Kansas town of Abilene agreed enthusiastically.

McCoy purchased grassy land around Abilene and built pens to hold the cattle for shipping. He also built a three-story hotel downtown. He helped survey the Chisholm Trail—the major cattle route from San Antonio, Texas, through

B. Answer Expanded rail lines and increased demand for beef after the Civil War

THINK THROUGH HISTORY
B. Analyzing Causes What developments led to the rapid growth of the cattle industry?

390 CHAPTER 13

TEACHING OPTIONS

Exploring Themes

Economic Development The railroads directly influenced major meatpacking centers such as Chicago and Omaha, as well as shipping centers such as Abilene and Sedalia. This economic development occurred at the expense of Native Americans, however. Ask students about the government's attitude towards the railroads, the ranchers, and the Native Americans. *Students might say that the government was sympathetic to ranchers and meat producers because they benefited the economy. These sympathies emerged in the government's repressive policy toward Native Americans.*

Making Global Connections

Ranching in Argentina Horses and cattle introduced from Spain into Mexico and then north into the American West also spread south and found a natural home on the pampas, or grassy plains, of Argentina. A cowboy culture similar to the one of the American West developed there and spread rapidly. Argentina continues to be one of the world's largest exporters of beef and other cattle products.

Oklahoma to Kansas. Thirty-five thousand head of cattle were shipped out of the yard in Abilene during its first year in operation. Business more than doubled to 75,000 the following year. Soon ranchers began hiring cowboys to drive their cattle to Abilene. Within a few years, the Chisholm Trail was worn wide and deep. An American legend was born.

The Truth About Cowboys

The meeting of the Chisholm Trail and the railroad in Abilene ushered in the heyday of the cowboy. As many as 55,000 worked the plains between 1866 and 1885. Although novels, folklore, and picture postcards depicted the cowboy as Anglo-American, about 25 percent of cowboys were African American and about 12 percent Mexican. The highly romanticized American cowboy of myth rode the open range, fighting and shooting villains. Meanwhile, the real-life cowboy was doing real work.

THE COWBOY'S LIFE A cowboy generally worked 10 to 14 hours a day on a ranch and 18 or more on the trail, alert at all times for dangers that might harm or upset the herds. The average cowboy was a wiry young man of 24, bowlegged from a life in the saddle. Some cowboys were as young as 15; most were broken down by the time they were 40. A cowboy owned his saddle, but his trail horse belonged to his boss. He was an expert rider and roper. If he did carry a gun, he probably never shot anyone. A cowboy knew how to calm cattle and head off stampedes, but he probably never headed off—or even saw—a holdup. Prairie fires and lightning worried him more than Indians, and he was more likely to die from a riding accident or pneumonia than from ambush by outlaws.

The ordinary cowboy worked hard all summer for cattlemen who often banned drinking, gambling, and cursing. When winter came, he lived off his savings or rambled from ranch to ranch doing odd jobs for a meal and a bed. Legendary figures like **James Butler "Wild Bill" Hickok** and **Martha Jane Cannary (Calamity Jane),** although serving as models for the Western hero, never dealt with cows. Their fame had more to do with stories in popular dime novels than with real cowboy life.

Hickok served as a scout and a spy during the Civil War and, later, as a marshal in Abilene, Kansas. He was a violent man who was shot and killed while holding a pair of aces and a pair of eights in a poker game, a hand still known as the "dead man's hand." Calamity Jane was an expert markswoman who dressed like a man. She spread exaggerated stories about herself, and some historians believe she actually may have been a scout for Colonel George Custer. Wild Bill and Calamity Jane had also been entertainers—Hickok on the stage in a play called *Scouts of the Prairie* and Calamity Jane in Wild West shows. Although the shows drew large audiences, they bore little resemblance to the real life of the West.

ROUNDUP The cowboy's season began with a spring roundup, in which he and other hands from the ranch rode the open range and chased all the longhorns they could find into a large corral. They kept the herd penned there for several days, until the cattle were so hungry that they preferred grazing to running away. Then the cowboys sorted through the herd, claiming the cattle that were marked with the brand of their ranch and calves that still needed to be branded. Branding cattle required both brute force and riding and roping skill. A cowboy first had to separate the calf from its protective mother, rope it, and then drop it to the ground. Then he held the struggling animal while searing the ranch's emblem into its hide with a hot branding iron.

"I was at all times along with the men when there was excitement or adventure to be had.... When I joined Custer I donned the uniform of a soldier."

MARTHA JANE CANNARY (CALAMITY JANE)

C. Answer The cowboy's life was hard, boring, and unromantic, unlike the romanticized myth of exciting gunfights and adventure.

THINK THROUGH HISTORY
C. Contrasting How did the cowboy's life differ from the myth about it?

Changes on the Western Frontier **391**

Reading the Chart Have students examine the sequence of images and determine how long the cowboy's day might be. *When he had night duty, a cowboy might put in a 20-hour day.*

Extension Have students consult an almanac to determine about how many hours a cowboy was in his saddle, from dawn to dusk, if the long drive took place in the early summer.

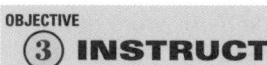

OBJECTIVE
③ INSTRUCT

The End of the Cattle Frontier

▶ **Starting with the Student**
Ask students what events might cause major physical changes on the earth or social changes in people's ways of life. *Students might mention factors such as severe weather, diseases, migration and immigration, depletion of natural resources, and technological inventions.*

▶ **Discussing Key Ideas**
• Overgrazing combined with a series of natural disasters brings an end to the cattle frontier.
• The invention of barbed wire transforms the open plains into fenced-in ranches and farms.

A Cowboy's Day on the Long Drive

No self-respecting cowboy ever went far on foot. He lived his life in the saddle, protected from sun and rain by his hat, chaps, bandanna, and boots. On his saddle he carried a lariat, a bedroll, and anything else he might need at a moment's notice.

4:12 A.M. A cowboy slept outdoors in all kinds of weather. The chuck wagon was the meeting place for the trail crew every workday before dawn.

11:18 A.M. One of the tasks the cowboy liked least was crossing rivers. Cattle were often swept away in the swift current.

THE LONG DRIVE After the herd was gathered and branded, the trail boss chose a crew for the **long drive** to Abilene or other shipping yards. This overland transport of the animals often lasted about three months. A typical drive included one cowboy for every 250 to 300 head of cattle; a cook who drove the chuck wagon, set up camp, and fixed the meals; and a wrangler who cared for the extra horses. The trail boss earned $100 or more a month for supervising the drive and negotiating with settlers and Indians. The cook's monthly salary was between $35 and $50. Although the wrangler usually earned less than a dollar a day, he had few expenses and his wages equaled what he could earn at other jobs.

During the long drive, the cowboy was in the saddle from dawn to dusk. He drank coffee and ate beans, bacon, bread, and, if he was lucky, dried fruit. He slept on the ground and bathed in rivers. He risked death every day of the drive, especially at river crossings, where cattle often hesitated and were swept away. Because lightning was a constant danger, cowboys piled their spurs, buckles, and other metal objects at the edge of their camp to avoid attracting lightning bolts. Thunder, or even a sneeze, could cause a stampede of runaway cattle.

PERSONAL VOICE
We went back to look for him, and we found him among the prairie dog holes, beside his horse. The horse's ribs [were] scraped bare of hide, and all the rest of horse and man was mashed into the ground as flat as a pancake. The only thing you could recognize was the handle of his six-shooter. We tried to think the lightning hit him, and that was what we wrote his folks down in Henrietta, Texas. But we couldn't really believe it ourselves. I'm afraid it wasn't the lightning. I'm afraid his horse stepped into one of them holes and they both went down before the stampede.

TEDDY BLUE ABBOTT, quoted in *The American West*

After three months or more of long days on the trail, the cowboy would hear a train whistle or glimpse some chimney smoke. He would break into cheers and song, deliver the cattle, and celebrate in town. After a bath and a shave, a good meal and a card game or two, he would head back to the ranch to collect his pay.

The End of the Cattle Frontier

Almost as quickly as cattle herds had multiplied and ranching had become big business, the cattle frontier met its end. Overgrazing of the land, extended bad weather, and the invention of barbed wire were largely responsible.

NATURAL DISASTERS The promise of great profits to be had on the plains drew increasing numbers of ranchers. Herds of cattle crowded the plains and destroyed the grass. Sheepherders also invaded in great numbers, sparking range wars with cattlemen, who complained that "everything in front of a sheep is eaten and everything behind is killed." Then, in 1883, drought struck the

D. Answer
Students might respond that the romanticized cowboy's independence, strength, and style are traits Americans admire.

THINK THROUGH HISTORY
D. *Forming Opinions* Why do you think the romantic myth of the American cowboy has proved to be so enduring?

TEACHING OPTION

Cooperative Activity: Researching Cowboy Music

Task: Small groups of students will research cowboy music and select one song for analysis. They will write a report and prepare it for presentation to the class.

Purpose: To explore the importance of music and its message about the cowboy's life.

Activity: Students should research how cowboys used music as entertainment and as a means of communication. They should select one song and should prepare a written report

and presentation that includes the song (tape-recorded, sung, or read) and an analysis of how it reflects cowboy life.

📁 **Building a Portfolio:** Students who add their reports to their portfolios should attach a note indicating their own contribution to the report and perhaps commenting on the reaction of the class.

📂 **ALTERNATIVE ASSESSMENT BOOK**
Standards for Evaluating a Cooperative Activity

Standards for Evaluation
Reports should

• demonstrate evidence of research
• include specific details about the song to support the analysis
• show good organization

2:34 P.M. Capturing strays was part of the job. The cowboy had to master the "art of the lariat," or roping and handling the cattle.

7:19 P.M. The cowboy's greatest fear was a stampede. Controlling a runaway herd tested all his skills.

1:00 A.M. Some cowboys didn't sleep much. Each night a few men patrolled the herd for rustlers, and they often sang songs to calm the cattle.

HISTORICAL SPOTLIGHT
The Wild West Show
Critical Thinking: Recognizing Stereotypes
Discuss with students how the Wild West show might have helped perpetuate the myths about cowboys and Native Americans.

Great Plains. Water holes and streams dried up. Prairie fires blazed, and at least one desperate rancher fought a fire with blood from slaughtered longhorns. Another drought three years later turned the overgrazed land to rock-hard desert. Temperatures soared to 115 degrees, leading Texans to claim that their potatoes were coming up cooked and ready to eat.

The dry, blazing heat was followed by the worst blizzard in American history. On January 28, 1887, temperatures fell to 68 degrees below zero and winds reached 60 miles an hour. For three days and nights, snow fell at the rate of an inch an hour. Hundred-foot ravines filled with snow and trapped cattlemen and their herds. Ranchers lost from 40 to 90 percent of their livestock. Granville Stuart, the cattleman who had introduced longhorns into Montana, vowed in despair, "I never wanted to own again an animal that I couldn't feed or shelter."

BARBED WIRE After the "die-up" of 1887, as it was called, most ranchers turned to smaller herds of high-grade stock that would yield more meat per animal. Unlike the hardy, free-grazing longhorns, however, high-grade cattle needed care and feeding throughout the year. Ranchers bought or rented large tracts of land so they could raise hay for their herds. To keep the cattle from straying or trampling the crops, ranchers fenced the land with barbed wire, which had been invented by an Illinois farmer, Joseph Glidden, to keep dogs out of his wife's garden. It was cheap and easy to use, and it caught on fast. In his first year in business, 1874, Glidden had sold 10,000 pounds of barbed wire. In 1878, he sold almost 27 million pounds.

This simple invention of twisted wire became a major factor in transforming the open plains into a series of fenced-in ranches and farms. The era of the wide-open West was over.

E. Answer
Drought, a blizzard, and the invention of barbed wire

THINK THROUGH HISTORY
E. Synthesizing
What events led to the end of the cattle frontier?

HISTORICAL SPOTLIGHT

THE WILD WEST SHOW
In 1889, William F. Cody toured the country with a show called Buffalo Bill's Wild West. The show featured trick riding and roping exhibitions, and it thrilled audiences with mock battles between cowboys and Indians. A command performance of the show was even given for Queen Victoria in London on June 26, 1892. In her journal, she said,

> There were Cow Boys, Red Indians, Mexicans, Argentinos taking part, and then a wonderful riding display by Cossacks, accompanied by curious singing, and a war dance by the Indians. The whole was a very pretty wild sight.

Wild Bill Hickok, Annie Oakley, Calamity Jane, and even Sitting Bull toured the country in Wild West shows. Their performances helped bring the West off the plains and into American myth.

ASSESS & RETEACH

Section 2 Assessment
Assign pairs of students to ask each other the questions and find supporting evidence in the text.

Self-Assessment
Have students look back at the questions they answered about cowboys at the beginning of the section. Ask them to note new information they learned from their reading and discuss how their ideas have changed.

Section Quiz

FORMAL ASSESSMENT
Section Quiz, p. 162

Reteach
Use the map on page 390 and the visual at the top of pages 392 and 393 to help students review the main ideas about the cattle industry and cowboys.

Section 2 Assessment

1. TERMS & NAMES

Identify:
- longhorn
- James Butler "Wild Bill" Hickok
- Martha Jane Cannary (Calamity Jane)
- long drive

2. SUMMARIZING In a diagram similar to the one below, identify the reasons for the rise and the decline of the cattle frontier.

```
                    Cattle Frontier
        rise                        decline
```

How might the decline of the cattle frontier have been prevented?

3. COMPARING AND CONTRASTING How were cowboys in the United States similar to and different from Mexican vaqueros?

THINK ABOUT
- their reasons for working
- the skills required
- the equipment they used
- their ethnic backgrounds

4. SYNTHESIZING Write a monologue in which someone in this section, such as a typical cowboy, discusses life on the cattle frontier. Prepare to present the monologue to your class.

THINK ABOUT
- how the person knows about the cattle frontier
- the person's attitude to the frontier
- how the person expresses his or her attitude

CLOSE

Overgrazing, a series of natural disasters, and the fencing of the open range brought an end to the domination of cattle ranching in the West. The land became available for farming, but farmers faced hardships of their own.

Changes on the Western Frontier **393**

ANSWERS

1. TERMS & NAMES

longhorn, p. 388

James Butler "Wild Bill" Hickok, p. 391

Martha Jane Cannary (Calamity Jane), p. 391

long drive, p. 392

2. SUMMARIZING

Rise of the Cattle Frontier:
Mexican culture
railroads
growth of Eastern cities

Decline of the Cattle Frontier:
overgrazing
natural disasters
invention of barbed wire

3. COMPARING AND CONTRASTING

Vaqueros were sometimes prisoners, while cowboys were usually hired workers. Both used similar skills—horse riding, roping, and handling cattle—and similar equipment, such as chaps, spurs, and lariats. Most vaqueros were Mexicans, while about two-thirds of cowboys were Anglo Americans, another quarter were African Americans.

4. SYNTHESIZING

In the monologue, students should present the unromanticized reality of the cattle frontier.

OBJECTIVES

1 To summarize the role of gold in luring people to the American West.

2 To describe people's experiences in their often fruitless efforts to find gold.

FOCUS & MOTIVATE

▶ *Starting with the Student*
- Students might be interested to know that the phrase *strike it rich* originated during the American gold rush of 1849. The term was later generalized to include other sources of quick wealth.
- Discuss natural resources other than gold that figure in modern American dreams of striking it rich. *Students might mention oil and precious stones, such as diamonds.*

MORE ABOUT . . .
Placer Mining

The word *placer* (pronounced plăs'ər) comes not from the English word *place,* but from the Spanish word *placer,* which means "sandbar," one of the places that placer deposits are found. Placer deposits are created when gold-bearing rock is eroded and the particles are washed downstream. Because gold is heavier than other minerals, it is deposited more quickly, often in places like sandbars, where the current of the stream slows down.

Mining: Some Struck It Rich— Most Struck Out

GOLD! Between the Civil War and the turn of the century, this precious metal was discovered in scattered sites from the Black Hills of Dakota and Cripple Creek, Colorado, to Nome, Alaska. The dream of riches lured hundreds of thousands of hopeful prospectors into territories that were previously inhabited only by Native Americans. The fortune seekers came from all walks of life: grizzled veterans from the gold rush of 1849, young men seeking adventure, middle-class professionals, and even some families.

A FAMILY AFFAIR
This early placer, or surface, mine at Cripple Creek attracted many women and children. It grew out of the vision of a young rancher, Bob Womack. He had found gold particles there washed down from another location and was convinced that the Cripple Creek area was literally a gold mine.
But because Womack was unreliable and generally disliked, the community ignored him. When a German count struck gold there, however, business boomed. Womack died penniless—but the mines produced a $400 million bonanza.

SLUICES AND ROCKERS
In 1898, prospectors like this mother and son in Fairbanks, Alaska, found sluicing to be more efficient than panning, since it could extract gold from soil. They would shovel soil into a sluice—a trough through which water flowed—and the water would carry off lightweight materials. The gold sank to the bottom, where it was caught in wooden ridges called cleats. A rocker, shown at the left of the picture, was a portable sluice that combined the mobility of panning with the efficiency of sluicing.

RECOMMENDED RESOURCES

Books
London, Jack. *Novels and Stories.* New York: Viking, 1982. *The Call of the Wild, White Fang,* "Klondike," "To Build a Fire," and other tales of the North.

Marks, Paula Mitchell. *Precious Dust.* New York: William Morrow, 1994. Mining and prospecting in the gold rush.

Seelye, John, ed. *Stories of the Old West.* New York: Penguin, 1994. Tales of mining and cattle ranches.

Time-Life Books. *The Miners.* New York: Time-Life Books, 1976. Illustrated history of mining in the West.

Twain, Mark. *Roughing It.* Berkeley: U of California P, 1996. Twain's witty 1872 account of his experiences in

the mining camps and towns of the West after the Civil War.

Ward, Geoffrey. *The West: An Illustrated History.* Boston: Little, 1996. Companion volume to the 1996 PBS series.

Videos

Had You Lived Then: Life in a Gold Mining Camp. AIMS.

The Way West. PBS Video, 1994. A 6-hour miniseries from the California Gold Rush to the Battle of Wounded Knee.

The West. Time-Life Video, 1996. A look at the American West.

Software

America Goes West. Queue. Mountain men, placer gold, ranch life, and other aspects of the American West.

Yukon Trail. MECC. Students venture back to the Klondike Gold Rush of 1896.

IN THE BOWELS OF THE EARTH

Although surface gold could be extracted by panning and sluicing, most gold was located in veins in underground rock. Mining these deposits involved digging tunnels along the vein of gold and breaking up tons of ore—hard and dangerous work. Tunnels often collapsed, and miners who weren't killed were trapped in utter darkness for days.

Heat was a problem, too. As miners descended into the earth, the temperature inside the mine soared. At a depth of 3,000 feet, the water that invariably flooded the bottom of a mine could be 160° F. One miner who fell into such water up to his hips lost all the skin from his legs and eventually died.

Cave-ins and hot water weren't the only dangers that miners faced. The pressure in the underground rock sometimes became so intense that it caused deadly explosions. There were freak accidents, too. In one mine, a dog that attempted to jump over an open shaft missed and fell 300 feet. It landed on two miners and killed them.

PANNING FOR GOLD

At the start of a gold rush, prospectors usually looked for easily available gold—particles eroded from rocks and washed downstream. Panning for it was easy—even children could do it. They scooped up mud and water from streambeds in a flat pan and swirled it. The circular motion of the water caused the sand to wash over the side and the remaining minerals to form layers according to weight. Gold, which is heavier than most minerals, sank to the bottom.

DATA FILE

Boom to Bust

This old signpost from Gleeson, Nevada, illustrates how a gold rush town that mushroomed overnight died just as quickly when the gold ran out.

Long Odds

These statistics for the Klondike gold rush, from 1896 to 1899, show the incredible odds against striking it rich.

100,000 people set out for the Klondike.

40,000 make it.

20,000 stake claims.

4,000 prospectors find gold.

200 become rich.

Deadly Digging

An estimated 7,500 people died while digging for gold and silver during the Western gold rushes—more people than died in all the Indian wars.

Ongoing Gold Rush

In 1996, entrepreneurs advertised a map on the Internet showing likely places for prospecting. They claimed, "In the winter of 1995, abnormally high levels of snow blanketed the California Sierra-Nevada Mountains. The runoff of snow melt will provide unprecedented opportunities for the discovery of newly deposited GOLD!!!"

INTERACT WITH HISTORY

1. **DRAWING CONCLUSIONS** What characteristics did gold miners seem to have in common? Use the information about the Klondike in the Data File to calculate the odds of striking it rich.

   SEE SKILLBUILDER HANDBOOK, PAGE 1050.

2. **RESEARCHING GHOST TOWNS** Research the history of a ghost town from boom to bust. Present a short report on life in the town, and its attempts to survive beyond the gold rush.

    For more about gold mining, click on *Social Studies* at http://www.mcdougallittell.com

INSTRUCT

▶ *Discussing Key Ideas*

- In the second half of the 19th century, the possibility of finding gold draws many people to the American West.
- Few succeed in this dangerous pursuit of wealth.

HISTORY FROM VISUALS

▶ *Reading the Images*

- Ask students what they think life would be like in the Cripple Creek placer mining camp. What aspects of the photograph suggest this to them?
- Have any students been inside a mine? What was the experience like? Do they think they would be able to tolerate the dangers, heat, poor air, and close quarters in the bowels of the earth?
- Bring in a pan such as the one shown at the bottom of page 395. Fill it with sand and water and give students a chance to try panning.

MORE ABOUT . . .
Mining Hazards

In very deep mines, the pressure within the rock built to such levels that the rock itself sometimes exploded, killing miners with flying debris. Miners were also notoriously careless with the copper blasting caps they used to set off dynamite. When children found the caps, their attempts to explore the inside could set off an explosion. In some mining camps, an average of one boy a week lost fingers in such mishaps.

INTERACT WITH HISTORY

1. Drawing Conclusions

Possible Answers: *Optimism, persistence, ambition, independence, physical strength, endurance, greed, and, possibly, foolishness.*

The odds of striking it rich if one set off for the Klondike were 200 in 100,000, or 1 in 500. The odds if one made it to the Klondike were 200 in 40,000, or 1 in 200.

2. Researching Ghost Towns

Standards for Evaluation
Reports should

- focus on a single ghost town
- trace the town's experiences from boom to bust and beyond in chronological order
- explain how the discovery of gold established or expanded the town
- discuss the town's attempts to survive beyond the gold rush
- provide accurate details based on research

OBJECTIVES

(1) To explain the rapid settlement of the Great Plains after they were opened for homesteading.

(2) To describe how early settlers met the challenges of surviving on the plains and transformed them into profitable farm land.

SKILLBUILDER

• Interpreting charts, p. 399

CRITICAL THINKING

• Synthesizing, p. 397
• Analyzing effects, p. 397
• Summarizing, pp. 398, 400
• Clarifying, p. 399
• Recognizing effects, p. 400
• Generalizing, p. 400
• Evaluating, p. 400

FOCUS & MOTIVATE

▶ *Starting with the Student*
• Ask the class to think about the students who set the trends in the school and what qualities they have in common.
• Which of these qualities do they think were shared by pioneers on the Great Plains?

OBJECTIVE
(1) INSTRUCT

Settlers Flock Westward to Farm

▶ *Discussing Key Ideas*
• Transcontinental railroads open up the West for settlement.
• The government encourages settlement by offering free land.

(continued on next page)

TERMS & NAMES
• homesteader
• soddy
• Morrill Land Grant Acts
• bonanza farm

❸ Settling on the Great Plains

LEARN ABOUT the life of farmers on the Great Plains
TO UNDERSTAND how the settlers endured hardships and transformed the land.

ONE AMERICAN'S STORY

When Esther Clark Hill was a girl on the Kansas prairie, her father often left the family to go on hunting or trading expeditions. His trips left Esther's mother, Allena Clark, alone on the farm with her children, crops, and sheep. One spring, when the sheep got stuck on the wrong side of the river, Esther watched her mother drive the family wagon back and forth through the rising water until all the sheep were safe.

Esther also remembered her mother holding on to the reins of a runaway mule team, "her black hair tumbling out of its pins and over her shoulders, her face set and white, while one small girl clung with chattering teeth to the sides of the wagon." The men in the settlement spoke admiringly about "Leny's nerve," but Esther thought that daily life itself presented a greater challenge than either of those crises.

Plains settlers, like this one depicted in Harvey Dunn's painting *Pioneer Woman,* had to be strong and self-reliant. They also had to have a clear vision of the future for their families on the prairie.

> **A PERSONAL VOICE**
> I think, as much courage as it took to hang onto the reins that day, it took more to live twenty-four hours at a time, month in and out, on the lonely and lovely prairie, without giving up to the loneliness.
> **ESTHER CLARK HILL,** quoted in *Pioneer Women*

As the railroads penetrated the frontier and the days of the free-ranging cowboy ended, hundreds of thousands of families migrated west, lured by vast tracts of cheap, fertile land. In their effort to establish a new life, they endured extreme hardships and loneliness.

Settlers Flock Westward to Farm

It took 263 years—from the first settlement at Jamestown until 1870—to turn 400 million acres of forests and prairies into flourishing farms. Changing the second 400 million acres took only 30 years, from 1870 to 1900. Federal land policy and the completion of the transcontinental railroads made this rapid settlement possible.

RAILROADS OPEN THE WEST From 1850 to 1871, the federal government made huge land grants to the railroads—170 million acres, worth half a billion dollars—for laying track in the West. In one grant, both the Union Pacific and the Central Pacific received 10 square miles of public land for every mile of track laid in a state and 20 square miles of land for every mile of track laid in a territory.

In 1867, the two companies began a race to lay track. The Central Pacific moved eastward from Sacramento and the Union Pacific moved westward from Omaha. They hired Civil War veterans, Irish and Chinese immigrants, African Americans, and Mexican Americans to do the grueling labor. During the winter

SECTION 3 RESOURCES

PRINT RESOURCES

IN-DEPTH RESOURCES: UNIT 4
Guided Reading, p. 3
Geography Application: The Regions of the West, p. 6
Primary Sources: Railroad Poster, p. 9; Letter from a Woman Homesteader, p. 10
Literature: from *My Ántonia* by Willa Cather, p. 12

ACCESS FOR STUDENTS ACQUIRING ENGLISH
Guided Reading (Spanish), p. 132
Geography Application: The Regions of the West (Spanish), p. 135

FORMAL ASSESSMENT
Section Quiz, p. 163

ALTERNATIVE ASSESSMENT BOOK
See forms for supporting and scoring alternative activities.

TECHNOLOGY RESOURCES

CRITICAL THINKING TRANSPARENCIES
CT13, Transcontinental Railroad
CT47, Population Changes in the West, 1850–1900

CD-ROM Electronic Library of Primary Sources

VIDEO *American Portfolio: A Videodisc for U.S. History*
user's guide, pp. 126–129, 135–139

INTERNET McDougal Littell Learning On-Line
http://www.mcdougallittell.com

of 1868, workers for the Union Pacific cut their way through the solid rock of the mountains, laying up to eight miles of track a day. Both companies reached Utah by the spring of 1869 and met at Promontory on May 10. They marked the completion of the first transcontinental track with a ceremony and a golden spike. Only 15 years later, the country boasted four transcontinental railroads, and the East and West coasts were linked.

The railroad companies sold some of their land to farmers for two to ten dollars an acre. Some companies sent agents to Europe to recruit buyers. Due to wars, overpopulation, and lack of economic opportunity, many Europeans came to the American West. By 1880, 44 percent of the settlers in Nebraska and more than 70 percent of those in Minnesota and Wisconsin were immigrants.

THINK THROUGH HISTORY
A. Synthesizing How did the railroads help open the West?

A. Answer They made it possible for people to travel quickly and also recruited settlers.

GOVERNMENT SUPPORT FOR SETTLEMENT By 1900, more than 400,000 families had taken advantage of the Homestead Act of 1862, which offered 160 acres of land free to anyone who would cultivate it for five years. Despite the massive response by **homesteaders**, or settlers on this free land, the legislation didn't always work exactly as the federal government had planned. For example, private speculators and railroad and state government agents used the law for their own gain. Cattlemen fenced and claimed open lands, while miners and woodcutters claimed national resources. Railroad companies held land to sell later instead of building promised extensions of their lines. Only about 10 percent of the land was actually settled by the families for whom it was intended. In addition, not all plots of land were of equal value. Although 160 acres could provide a decent living in the fertile soil of Iowa or Minnesota, settlers on drier Western land required larger plots to make farming worthwhile.

B. Answer By making land available cheaply through various land grants

THINK THROUGH HISTORY
B. Analyzing Effects In what ways did governmental policies encourage settlement of the West?

Because settlement of the West became a goal for the government, it strengthened the Homestead Act and passed additional legislation to encourage settlers. Thousands of African Americans responded to Kansas governor John P. St. John's offer to settle in his state. In 1889, a major land giveaway in what is now Oklahoma attracted thousands of people. In less than 24 hours, land-hungry settlers claimed 2 million acres in a massive land rush. Some of them took possession of the land before the government officially declared it open. Because these settlers claimed land sooner than they were supposed to, Oklahoma came to be known as the Sooner State. Although speculators and businesses continued to buy land intended for individual families, the land-grant acts did continue to draw people westward.

Ho for Kansas!

Brethren, Friends, & Fellow Citizens:
I feel thankful to inform you that the
REAL ESTATE
AND
Homestead Association,
Will Leave Here the

15th of April, 1878,

In pursuit of Homes in the Southwestern Lands of America, at Transportation Rates, cheaper than ever was known before.
For full information inquire of
Benj. Singleton, better known as old Pap,
NO. 5 NORTH FRONT STREET.
Beware of Speculators and Adventurers, as it is a dangerous thing to fall in their hands.
Nashville, Tenn., March 18, 1878.

Posters like the one shown above drew hundreds of thousands of settlers to the West. Among the settlers were thousands of exodusters—freed slaves who left the South to seek land and better lives.

397

(continued from page 396)

• Thousands of settlers respond, including African Americans and European immigrants.
• In response to the rapid disappearance of open land, the government sets aside some public land to preserve the wilderness.

IN-DEPTH RESOURCES: UNIT 4
Guided Reading, p. 3

ACCESS FOR STUDENTS ACQUIRING ENGLISH
Guided Reading (Spanish), p. 132

MORE ABOUT . . .
Building the Railroads

On the Central Pacific line, over 90 percent of the labor force, about 12,000, were Chinese. They labored under extremely difficult conditions—including avalanches and 40-foot snowdrifts—for as little as $35 a month. White workers often received $40 to $60 a month—plus board and lodging.

IN-DEPTH RESOURCES: UNIT 4
Primary Source: Railroad poster, p. 9

 CRITICAL THINKING TRANSPARENCIES
CT13, Transcontinental Railroad

HISTORY FROM VISUALS
Reading the Photo Ask students what they can tell about the people in the photograph. Have them think about
• the way they are dressed
• their posture and expressions
• the setting

CRITICAL THINKING TRANSPARENCIES
CT47, Population Changes in the West, 1850–1900

TEACHING OPTION

Teaching Less Proficient Readers

Previewing and Visualizing Preview the text on page 397, "Government Support for Settlement," before asking students to read it. Point out that the Homestead Act of 1862 didn't work out exactly as the government had hoped and only 10 percent of the land was actually homesteaded. The rest was swallowed up by speculators, cattlemen, miners, lumber companies, and railroads. To remedy this situation, the government passed additional legislation regulating the provision of land. After students read the text, have them organize the information in a concept web such as that shown on the right.

THE CLOSING OF THE FRONTIER As settlers gobbled up Western land, the government decided to take action to protect and preserve the wilderness. In 1870, General Henry D. Washburn, who was surveying land near the Yellowstone River in northwestern Wyoming for the Northern Pacific Railroad, was overwhelmed by the area's geysers and bubbling springs, "objects new in experience . . . and possessing unlimited grandeur and beauty."

Instead of claiming the area for the railroad, he asked Congress to help protect it from settlement. In 1872, the federal government set aside land to create Yellowstone National Park. Seven years later, the Department of the Interior forced railroads to give up their claim to Western land holdings that were equal to the area of New York, New Jersey, Pennsylvania, Delaware, Maryland, and Virginia combined. Still, a great deal of public land had been claimed. By 1880, individuals had bought more than 19 million acres of government-owned land.

The Western frontier was fast disappearing, although it continued to influence, and even define, the American spirit. In an 1893 essay entitled "The Significance of the Frontier in American History," historian Frederick Jackson Turner declared that the frontier had ceased to exist.

A PERSONAL VOICE
The existence of an area of free land, its continuous recession, and the advance of American settlement westward, explain American development. . . . Now, four centuries from the discovery of America, at the end of a hundred years of life under the Constitution, the frontier has gone and with its going has closed the first period of American history.
FREDERICK JACKSON TURNER, "The Significance of the Frontier in American History"

Turner's argument was very influential during the late 19th century. It was incorrect in two ways, however. Much uninhabited land still remained. Turner also ignored Native Americans, African Americans, and Latinos. But he did express how important the idea of the frontier was to Americans.

C. Answer That it had ceased to exist
THINK THROUGH HISTORY
C. Summarizing What was Turner's view of the American frontier in 1893?

Settlers Meet the Challenges of the Plains

The settlers who had been drawn to the frontier faced extreme hardships—droughts, floods, fires, blizzards, locust plagues, and occasional raids by outlaws and Native Americans. Probably two-thirds of the settlers stayed, however. The number of people living west of the Mississippi River exploded from 1 percent of the nation's population in 1850 to almost 30 percent by the turn of the century.

A pioneer family stands in front of their soddy near Coburg, Nebraska, in 1887.

DUGOUTS AND SODDIES Settlers had to provide shelter for themselves before they could even begin to prepare their land for farming. Since trees were scarce on the Western plains, most settlers built their homes from the land itself. Many pioneers dug their homes into the sides of ravines or small hills. A stovepipe jutting from the roof was often the only clear sign of such a dugout home.

Those who moved to the broad, flat plains often made freestanding houses by stacking blocks of prairie turf. Like a dugout, a sod home, or **soddy,** was warm in winter, cool in summer, and was an island of color when wildflowers bloomed on its roof. Soddies were small, however, and offered little light or air. They were havens for snakes, insects, and other pests. Although they were fireproof, they leaked continuously when it rained.

WOMEN'S WORK Rain was the least of the worries that the families who inhabited these makeshift houses had to contend with. Virtually alone on the flat, endless prairie, they had to be almost superhumanly self-sufficient. Women were especially burdened. They did much of the work of feeding and clothing their families. They often worked beside the men in the fields, plowing the land and planting and harvesting the predominant crop, wheat. They raised cows, hogs, sheep, chickens—and children. They milked the cows, skimmed cream, churned butter, and made cheese. They sheared the sheep, carded wool, and sewed or knit clothes for their families. They hauled water from wells that they helped to dig, made soap and candles from tallow, did laundry by hand, and ironed clothes with a heavy flatiron. They milled the grain, baked bread, and cooked meals over an open fire. At harvest time, they canned fruits and vegetables and made sausages and jam. They doctored their families—and often other people—for everything from cradle cap to snakebites. "With a razor as a lance and a pair of embroidery scissors," a pioneer woman "once removed three fingers from the crushed hand of a railroad brakeman." They also sponsored schools and churches in an effort to provide for the future.

THINK THROUGH HISTORY
D. Clarifying
How were women central to the homesteading process?
D. Answer
Women helped work the land and handled a multitude of household chores, including raising children.

TECHNICAL AND EDUCATIONAL SUPPORT FOR FARMERS Establishing a homestead was challenging work. Once that was accomplished, however, farming the prairie year in and year out became an ongoing and sometimes overwhelming task. The thick prairie sod broke wooden plows, and reaping wheat by hand with a scythe was slow, backbreaking work. In 1837, John Deere had invented a steel plow that could slice through heavy soil. And in 1847, Cyrus McCormick had begun to mass produce and aggressively market a mowing and reaping machine he had developed in 1834. A mass market for these devices didn't fully develop, however, until the last quarter of the century with the migration of farmers onto the plains.

New and improved devices quickly followed, such as the spring-tooth harrow to prepare the soil (1869), the grain drill to plant the seed, and barbed wire to fence the land (1874). The first successful harvester, the cord binder, was patented in 1878. Then came a reaper that could cut and thresh wheat in one pass. By 1890, more than 900 manufacturers of farm equipment had sprung up. In 1830, it had taken about 183 minutes to produce a bushel of grain; by 1900, with the use of these machines, it took only 10 minutes. These inventions made more grain available and meant more money for farmers.

The federal government supported farmers by financing agricultural education. The **Morrill Land Grant Acts** of 1862 and 1890 gave federal land to the states to help finance agricultural colleges, and the Hatch Act of 1887

Skillbuilder Answer
Problem: crop dehydration. **Invention:** answers will vary.

SKILLBUILDER
INTERPRETING CHARTS *What farming problem did the steel windmill solve? Which invention do you think had the greatest impact on Western agriculture? Why?*

HISTORY FROM VISUALS
Inventions That Tamed the Prairie

Reading the Chart Make sure students understand that they should read the chart from the bottom to the top—that each prairie problem led to a difficult farming condition, which, in turn, was solved by a particular invention.

Extension Have students research the types of agricultural technology used today, such as computer-controlled operations, fertilizers, and insecticides.

MORE ABOUT . . .
John Deere

In 1837, John Deere (1804–1886), a blacksmith, invented the steel plow. He used an old circular steel saw as the basis of his plow. As the plow turned, the heavy, sticky prairie soil fell away cleanly from the blade. Deere initially used hard steel manufactured in England, but then had Pittsburgh steelmakers create a similar steel. This invention was so popular that he was producing 10,000 plows a year by 1857.

Inventions That Tamed the Prairie

INVENTION	BARBED WIRE	STEEL PLOW	REAPER	STEEL WINDMILL
Invention's solution ❸	Prevents animals from trampling crops	Makes planting more efficient	Saves crops by speeding up harvesting	Brings up underground water for irrigation
Farming Condition ❷	No timber for fences	Difficult and time-consuming planting	Crop damage and death	Crop dehydration
Prairie Problem ❶	Treeless landscape	Hard-packed soil	Sudden frost, hailstorms	Unpredictable rainfall

TEACHING OPTION

👥 *Cooperative Activity: Advertising Agricultural Inventions*

Task: Student groups will write advertisements for one of the agricultural inventions pictured on this page.

Purpose: To help students understand the importance of the inventions in cultivating the plains.

Activity: Assign groups of three or four students to plan, write, and illustrate advertising posters or leaflets for barbed wire, the steel plow, the reaper, or the steel windmill. The advertisements should be directed at new settlers. Students may wish to include the history of the invention and a diagram showing how it is used.

📁 **Building a Portfolio:** Students who add their advertisements to their portfolios should attach a note indicating their contribution to the advertisement.

ALTERNATIVE ASSESSMENT BOOK
Standards for Evaluating a Cooperative Activity

Standards for Evaluation
Advertisements should

• indicate knowledge of the importance and use of the invention
• show awareness of the audience for whom they are intended
• demonstrate creativity and effectiveness

established agricultural experiment stations to communicate new developments in agriculture to farmers in every state. The work of agricultural researchers began to pay off when they developed grains for arid soil and techniques for dry farming, which helped the lands to retain moisture. These innovations enabled the dry eastern plains to flourish and become "the breadbasket of the nation."

FARMERS IN DEBT But elaborate machinery was expensive, and farmers often had to borrow money to buy it. When prices for wheat were high, farmers usually could repay their loans. When wheat prices fell, however, farmers needed to raise more crops to make ends meet. This situation gave rise to a new type of farming in the late 1870s. Railroad companies and investors such as George Cass and Oliver Dalrymple created massive **bonanza farms,** enormous single-crop spreads of 10,000 acres or more. The Cass-Cheney-Dalrymple farm near Fargo, North Dakota, for example, covered 24 square miles. By 1900, even the average farmer had nearly 150 acres under

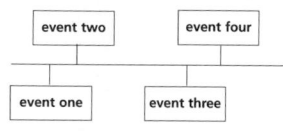

Bonanza farms like this one required the labor of hundreds of men and horses. They brought in big money for their owners when times were good and overwhelming debts when drought struck in the late 1880s.

cultivation. Some farmers mortgaged their land to buy more property, and as farms grew bigger, so did farmers' debts. Between 1885 and 1890 much of the plains experienced drought, and the large, single-crop operations couldn't compete with smaller farmers, who could be more flexible in the crops they grew. The bonanza farms slowly folded, and by 1896 Dalrymple, the "bonanza king," was bankrupt.

Farmers also felt pressure from the rising cost of shipping grain. Railroads charged Western farmers a higher fee than they did farmers in the East. Also, the railroads sometimes charged more for short hauls, for which there was no competing transportation, than for long hauls. The railroads claimed that they were merely doing business, but farmers resented being taken advantage of. "No other system of taxation has borne as heavily on the people as those extortions and inequalities of railroad charges," said Henry Demarest Lloyd in an article in the March 1881 edition of the *Atlantic Monthly.*

Many farmers found themselves growing as much grain as they could grow, on as much land as they could acquire, for the doubtful privilege of going further into debt. But they were not defeated by these conditions. Instead, these challenging conditions drew farmers together in a common cause.

Section 3 Assessment

1. TERMS & NAMES

Identify:
• homesteader
• soddy
• Morrill Land Grant Acts
• bonanza farm

2. SEQUENCING HISTORY

Create a time line of at least four events that shaped the settling of the Great Plains.

| event two | | event four |
| event one | | event three |

Write a paragraph speculating on how history would be different if one of these events hadn't happened.

3. GENERALIZING Review the changes in technology that influenced the life of settlers on the Great Plains in the late 1800s. Explain how you think settlement of the plains would have been different without these inventions.

THINK ABOUT
• the tasks done by the settlers
• tools and methods previously used
• the inventions that became widely used in the late 1800s

4. EVALUATING How successful were governmental efforts to promote settlement of the Great Plains? Give examples to support your answer.

THINK ABOUT
• the growth in population on the Great Plains
• the role of railroads in the economy
• the results of the Homestead Act

400 CHAPTER 13

TERMS & NAMES
- Oliver Kelley
- Grange
- Populism
- bimetallism
- William McKinley
- William Jennings Bryan
- "Cross of Gold" speech

LEARN ABOUT pressures that made farming increasingly unprofitable
TO UNDERSTAND the rise and fall of the Populist movement.

ONE AMERICAN'S STORY

Mary Elizabeth Lease—the daughter of Irish immigrants—had always had an independent streak. As a young adult in the early 1870s, Mary left her family home in Pennsylvania to become a schoolteacher on the Kansas plains. After she met and married Charles Lease and they moved to a farm, she joined the growing Farmers' Alliance. She soon began speaking on issues of concern to farmers. Lease joked that her tongue was "loose at both ends and hung on a swivel," but her golden voice and deep blue eyes hypnotized her listeners.

> ### A PERSONAL VOICE
> What you farmers need to do is to raise less corn and more *Hell!* We want the accursed foreclosure system wiped out. . . . We will stand by our homes and stay by our firesides by force if necessary, and we will not pay our debts to the loan-shark companies until the Government pays its debts to us.
> **MARY ELIZABETH LEASE,** quoted in "The Populist Uprising"

Although farmers had endured great hardships in helping to transform the plains from the "Great American Desert" into the "breadbasket of the nation," every year they reaped less and less of the bounty they had sowed with their sweat.

Mary Elizabeth Lease

Farmers Unite to Address Common Problems

In the late 1800s, many farmers were trapped in a vicious economic cycle. The prices for crops were falling, and farmers often mortgaged their farms so they could buy more land and produce more crops in an attempt to break even. Good farming land was becoming scarce, though, and the banks took over the mortgages of increasing numbers of farmers who couldn't make payments on their loans. Moreover, the railroads also took advantage of farmers by charging them excessive prices for shipping and storage.

THE DEMAND FOR CHEAPER MONEY The troubles of the farmers were part of a larger economic problem that was affecting the entire nation. The period after the Civil War was marked by deflation, which meant that the amount of money in circulation decreased and the value of every dollar therefore increased. As a result, the cost of goods and services fell. This was good news for consumers because their dollars bought more products. It was bad news for farmers, however, because they received less money for their crops. They also had to repay loans on their property with dollars that were worth more than the ones they had borrowed. In effect, they lost money at every turn.

The farmers thought the only solution to their problem was to force prices up by increasing the money supply. During a period of inflation—the opposite of deflation—the value of each dollar falls because there are more dollars in circulation. The result is what is called "cheap money." When money is cheap, the prices of goods and services tend to rise.

When the Civil War ended, the farmers tried to persuade the government to increase the money supply by printing more greenbacks—the paper currency issued during the war. When the government refused, the farmers demanded

A. Answer It would increase prices for their products.

THINK THROUGH HISTORY
A. Analyzing Motives Why did farmers think that an increased money supply would help solve their economic problems?

Changes on the Western Frontier **401**

Section 4 Overview

OBJECTIVES

(1) To identify the problems farmers faced and their cooperative efforts to solve them.

(2) To explain the rise and fall of the Populist Party.

SKILLBUILDERS

- Interpreting political cartoons, p. 402
- Interpreting charts, p. 404

CRITICAL THINKING

- Analyzing motives, p. 401
- Analyzing causes, pp. 402, 403, 405
- Recognizing effects, p. 402
- Analyzing issues, p. 404
- Applying, p. 405
- Forming an opinion, p. 405

FOCUS & MOTIVATE

▶ *Starting with the Student* Have students read the biography of Mary Elizabeth Lease and discuss how she might have come to be such a vocal promoter of the farmers' cause.

IN-DEPTH RESOURCES: UNIT 4
American Lives: Mary Elizabeth Lease, p. 16

OBJECTIVE
(1) **INSTRUCT**

Farmers Unite to Address Common Problems

▶ *Starting with the Student* Discuss the problems farmers faced. Ask students to create a flow chart describing the development of those problems. Their charts might look like this:

Crop prices fall. → Farmers mortgage farms to buy more land.

↓

Banks take over mortgages and farmers lose land.

(continued on next page)

Teacher's Edition **401**

(continued from page 401)

► **Discussing Key Ideas**
  • Farmers go into debt because of deflation and high shipping costs and demand monetary reform.
  • Farmers form organizations to address their common problems.

IN-DEPTH RESOURCES: UNIT 4
Guided Reading, p. 4

ACCESS FOR STUDENTS ACQUIRING ENGLISH
Guided Reading (Spanish), p. 133

HISTORY FROM VISUALS
Political Cartoons

Reading the Cartoon Make sure students understand that the people who form the railroad ties are businessmen and bankers who supported the railroad interests.

Extension Have students write a title or a caption for the cartoon.

HISTORICAL SPOTLIGHT
The Colored Farmers' National Alliance

Critical Thinking: Analyzing Discuss why landowners and suppliers were more hostile to black farmers than to white farmers.

OBJECTIVE
② **INSTRUCT**

The Rise and Fall of Populism

► **Discussing Key Ideas**
  • The Populist Party provides a political power base for the farmers' alliances.

(continued on next page)

SKILLBUILDER
INTERPRETING POLITICAL CARTOONS How does this cartoon illustrate the plight of the farmers?

Skillbuilder Answer
They're at the mercy of the railroads and their warnings are being ignored by businessmen and industrialists.

HISTORICAL SPOTLIGHT

THE COLORED FARMERS' NATIONAL ALLIANCE

A white Baptist missionary, R. M. Humphrey, organized the Colored Farmers' National Alliance in 1886 in Houston, Texas. By 1891, the organization claimed a membership of more than a million, though the more likely figure was about a fourth of that. Like their counterparts in the white alliances, members of the local Colored Farmers' alliances promoted cooperative buying and selling. Unlike white organizations, however, the black alliances had to work mostly in secret to avoid racially motivated violence at the hands of angry landowners and suppliers.

unlimited coinage of silver. That tactic also failed. With the passage of the Bland-Allison Act in 1878, from $2 million to $4 million was added to the silver supply each month, but that amount wasn't enough to produce the cheaper money the farmers wanted.

PROBLEMS WITH THE RAILROADS Meanwhile, farmers paid outrageously high prices to transport grain. It sometimes cost as much to ship a bushel of grain as they received for it. Because of the lack of competition among the railroads, it might cost them more to ship grain from the Dakotas to Minneapolis than from Chicago to England by boat. What's more, railroads made secret agreements with middlemen—grain brokers and merchants—that allowed the railroads to control grain storage prices and to influence the market price of crops.

Farmers who were short of cash mortgaged their crops or their farms for credit with which to buy seed and supplies. Suppliers charged high rates of interest and sometimes even charged more for items bought on credit than they did for cash purchases. Farmers got caught in a cycle of credit that meant longer hours and more debt every year. Clearly, it was time for reform.

THE FARMERS' ALLIANCE But to push effectively for reforms, farmers needed to organize. In 1867, a farmer named **Oliver Kelley** started the Patrons of Husbandry, an organization for farmers popularly known as the **Grange.** Its original purpose was to provide a social outlet and an educational forum for isolated farm families. By the 1870s, however, Grange members spent most of their time and energy fighting the railroads. The Grange's battle plan included teaching its members how to organize, to set up farmers' cooperatives, and to sponsor state legislation to regulate railroads.

The Grange gave rise to other organizations, such as Farmers' Alliances. These organizations included teachers, preachers, newspaper writers and editors, and others who sympathized with farmers. Alliances sent lecturers from town to town throughout the 1880s to educate people about lower interest rates on loans, government control over railroads and banks, an increase in the money supply, and high tariffs to protect farmers from foreign grain markets. Spellbinding speakers such as Mary Elizabeth Lease helped get the message across.

Membership grew to more than 4 million men and women—mostly in the South and the West. The Southern Alliance, which included white Southern farmers, was the largest. Approximately 250,000 African Americans in 16 states belonged to the Colored Farmers' National Alliance. Some alliance members even promoted cooperation between black and white alliances. But most members feared being branded as supporters of racial mingling and accepted the separation of the organizations.

The Rise and Fall of Populism

Leaders of the alliance movement realized that to make far-reaching changes, they would need to build a base of political power. **Populism**—the movement of the people—was born with the founding of the Populist, or People's, Party, in 1891.

B. Answer
Deflation, high railroad rates, cycle of mortgage and debt.

THINK THROUGH HISTORY
B. *Analyzing Causes* What were some of the causes of farmer's economic problems?

C. Answer These organizations provided farmers with ways to organize and to respond to social and political problems.

THINK THROUGH HISTORY
C. *Recognizing Effects* How did the Grange and the Farmers' Alliances pave the way for the Populist Party?

402 CHAPTER 13

TEACHING OPTIONS

Making Connections Across Cultures

Ask students to consider the positive and negative aspects of organizations with restricted membership based on race, gender, politics, or religion. *Students may reply that such organizations give minority groups representation and power. Such restricted organizations might not have adequate membership to be effective politically, however. Often, several such special-interest groups join to help one another achieve their goals.*

Exploring Themes

Economic Opportunity Discuss the concept of "cheap money" and its meaning for the economy by pointing out two factors that determine the value of money—how long it takes to earn it and how much it can buy. Then discuss the relation between the time to earn a dollar, how "cheap" it is, and its buying power. *Answer: The less time it takes to earn a dollar, the "cheaper" it is and the less buying power it has.*

THE POPULIST PARTY On July 4, 1892, in the spirit underlying the founding of the nation, a Populist Party convention in Omaha, Nebraska, demanded reforms to lift the burden of debt from farmers and other workers and to give the people a greater voice in their government.

The financial reforms they proposed included an increase in the money supply, which would produce a rise in prices received for goods and services; a graduated income tax, which would tax high incomes more heavily than low incomes; and a federal loan program. The proposed governmental reforms included election of U.S. senators by popular vote, single terms for the president and the vice-president, and a secret ballot to end vote fraud. Finally, to represent labor as well as farming interests, the Populists called for an eight-hour workday and restrictions on immigration.

Most Americans considered these reforms to be radical at the time they were proposed. Yet the proposed changes were so attractive to struggling farmers and desperate laborers that in 1892 the Populist presidential candidate won more than a million votes—almost 10 percent of the total vote. In the West, the People's Party elected five senators, three governors, and about 1,500 state legislators. While the Populists lacked the power of the two major parties, they clearly had become a force in the political life of the country. Their programs eventually became the platform of the Democratic Party and kept alive the concept that the government is responsible for reforming social injustices.

THE PANIC OF 1893 Then, in 1893, political issues were forced aside by economic concerns. During the 1880s, the economy had grown too fast. Farmers and businesspeople had overextended themselves with debts and loans. Railroad construction had expanded faster than markets. In February 1893, the Philadelphia and Reading Railroad went bankrupt. The Erie Railroad failed in July, followed by the Northern Pacific, the Union Pacific, and the Santa Fe. Related industries, such as iron and steel, were the first to be affected. A general business collapse was not far behind. The stock market collapsed and banks stopped giving loans. The government's gold reserves fell as people panicked and traded paper money for gold. The price of silver also dropped dramatically, causing silver mines to close. By the fall, more than 8,000 businesses, 156 railroads, and 400 banks had failed. By the end of the year, more than 15,000 businesses had folded.

Investments declined, and consumer purchases, wages, and prices also fell. Panic deepened into depression as 1 million people lost their jobs. By December 1894, a fifth of the workforce was unemployed. In New York City alone, some 20,000 people were not only jobless but homeless as well. In Detroit, the mayor turned vacant lots over to the poor so they could grow food. Some farm families, like the Orcutts of Kansas, suffered from both agricultural problems and unemployment. Mrs. Susan Orcutt expressed the experience of many Americans.

D. Answer
Overexpansion of key industries, especially the railroads, and a shrinking federal gold reserve.

THINK THROUGH HISTORY
D. Analyzing Causes What caused the Panic of 1893?

> **A PERSONAL VOICE**
> I take my Pen In hand to let you know that we are Starving to death It is Pretty hard to do without any thing to Eat hear in this God for saken country we would have had Plenty to Eat if the hail hadent cut our rye down and ruined our corn and Potatoes. . . . My Husband went a way to find work and came home last night and told me that we would have to Starve he has bin in ten countys and did not Get no work.
>
> **SUSAN ORCUTT,** quoted in *Making America*

FREE SILVER The Populist Party had done well in the elections of 1892 and 1894, and economic conditions had not improved as the 1896 presidential campaign approached. Populists watched as the two major parties became deeply divided

ECONOMIC BACKGROUND

BOOM OR BUST?

The cycle of prosperity and depression—boom and bust—that the U.S. economy went through during the 19th century was not peculiar to this country or to that century. All industrialized societies experience this cycle.

A boom occurs during industrial expansion when it seems that business profits will continue to expand as well. As production increases, so does the demand for raw materials, machinery, and labor. Prices and wages rise—and, consequently, business profits decrease.

As profits decrease, companies slow their expansion. The need for raw materials, machinery, and labor decreases correspondingly. With a decline in production and an increase in unemployment, people give up looking for work. Production decreases even more, and the unemployment lines grow longer. If the situation continues, a panic or a depression sets in.

(continued from page 402)

- The Populist Party proposes financial and governmental reforms.
- Farmers suffer increasingly as a general business collapse deepens into an economic depression.
- The metal backing paper currency becomes a major issue in the 1896 presidential campaign.
- The Populist Party and Democrats both back William Jennings Bryan, who favors a bimetal policy.
- Bryan is defeated and the Populist Party collapses.

GROLIER MULTIMEDIA ENCYCLOPEDIA
overview of the Populist Party

ECONOMIC BACKGROUND
Boom or Bust?

Ask students to diagram the boom and bust cycle. Their diagram might look like this:

Wages rise → Prices rise → Demand falls → Profits decrease → Business activity falls → Incomes fall → Prices fall → Demand increases → Companies begin to recover → Production increases → Wages rise

---

TEACHING OPTION

Cooperative Activity: Researching Populist Reforms

Task: Small groups of students research and write a report on the outcome of the reforms promoted by the Populist Party.

Purpose: To help students understand the Populist platform and recognize that minor political parties can have far-reaching effects.

Activity: Student groups will use history texts, encyclopedias, or the Internet to research one of the platform planks of the Populist Party mentioned on page 403. They should determine if the reform has subse-

quently been enacted, if the issue is still being debated, or if it has now been forgotten. Finally, they will write a report on the issue to be shared with the class.

📁 **Building a Portfolio:** Students who decide to add reports to their portfolios should attach a note describing their contribution to the report and indicating their personal stand on the reform issue.

ALTERNATIVE ASSESSMENT BOOK
Standards for Evaluating a Cooperative Activity

Standards for Evaluation
Reports should . . .

- clearly state the reform proposed by the Populists
- show evidence of appropriate research
- explain the outcome of the issue and give supporting details

U.S. Currency

The U.S. monetary system was established by the Coinage Act of 1792. It was a bimetallic system in which both gold and silver were used as legal tender. The government began issuing paper currency during the Revolutionary War, but it printed so much that the money became almost worthless. It was not until the 1860s that the government again issued paper money, "greenbacks," that could not be exchanged for gold or silver. Paper currency is no longer backed by any metal.

KEY PLAYER
William Jennings Bryan
Critical Thinking:
Synthesizing Ask students to consider the paradox of Bryan's fame as an orator while many of the causes he supported did not succeed.

 GROLIER MULTIMEDIA ENCYCLOPEDIA
from a speech on free silver by William Jennings Bryan

HISTORY FROM VISUALS
Gold Bugs and Silverites
Reading the Chart Suggest to students that they first read the chart vertically to understand how the Gold Bug and Silverite positions may lead respectively to deflation and inflation. Then have them read it horizontally to compare characteristics of the two positions.

Extension Ask students to consider categories they might add to the chart.

KEY PLAYER

WILLIAM JENNINGS BRYAN
1860–1925

William Jennings Bryan might be considered a patron saint of lost causes, largely because he let beliefs, not politics, guide his actions. He resigned his position as secretary of state (1913–1915) under Woodrow Wilson, for example, to protest the president's movement away from neutrality regarding the war in Europe. Near the end of his life, he appeared as the chief witness for the state of Tennessee in the famous Scopes "monkey trial," contesting the teaching of evolution in public schools. He is perhaps best characterized by a quote from his own "Cross of Gold" speech: "The humblest citizen of all the land, when clad in the armor of a righteous cause, is stronger than all the hosts of Error."

---

in a struggle between different regions and economic interests. The businessmen and bankers of the industrialized Northeast were Republicans, and the farmers and laborers of the agrarian South and West were Democrats.

The central issue of the campaign was the metal that would be the basis of the nation's monetary system. On one side were the "free silverites," who favored **bimetallism,** a policy in which the government would give people either gold or silver in exchange for paper currency or checks. On the other side were the "gold bugs," who favored the gold standard, or dollars backed solely with gold.

The backing of currency was such an important campaign issue because people regarded paper money as worthless if it could not be turned in for gold or silver. Because silver was more plentiful than gold, backing currency with both metals, as the free silverites advocated, would make more currency (with less value per dollar) available—cheap money. Supporters of bimetallism hoped that this measure would stimulate the stagnant economy. Adoption of the gold standard would provide a more stable, but expensive, currency.

BRYAN AND THE "CROSS OF GOLD" Stepping into the debate, the People's Party called for bimetallism and free coinage of silver. Yet, their strategy was undecided: Should they join forces with sympathetic candidates in the major parties and risk losing their political identity, or should they maintain their own party and risk losing the election?

As the 1896 campaign progressed, the Republican Party stated its firm commitment to the gold standard and nominated **William McKinley,** a conservative Ohioan, for president. After a serious debate, the Democratic Party came out in favor of a combined gold and silver standard, including unlimited coinage of silver. While the party was trying to settle on a candidate at the Democratic convention, **William Jennings Bryan,** a former member of Congress from Nebraska and the editor of the Omaha *World-Herald,* delivered an impassioned address to the assembled delegates. An excerpt of what has become known as the **"Cross of Gold" speech** follows.

E. Answer Because people thought that paper currency had value only if it could be turned in for precious metals such as gold or silver.

THINK THROUGH HISTORY
E. Analyzing Issues Why was the metal that backed paper currency such an important issue in the 1896 presidential campaign?

Skillbuilder Answer
Farmers: They would get more money for their crops. **City Dwellers:** Probably gold bugs, because many were bankers and businessmen who would benefit from stable money.

SKILLBUILDER INTERPRETING CHARTS *How would farmers benefit from inflation? Do you think city dwellers would be gold bugs or silverites? Why?*

Gold Bugs and Silverites

	GOLD BUGS	SILVERITES
Who They Were	bankers and businessmen	farmers and laborers
What They Wanted	gold standard "tight money" (less money in circulation)	bimetallism "cheap money" (more money in circulation)
Why	loans would be repaid in stable money	products would be sold at higher prices
Effects	**DEFLATION** • prices fall • value of money increases • fewer people have money	**INFLATION** • prices rise • value of money decreases • more people have money

---

Making Connections Across the Curriculum

Oral Communication Have students recite the selection from William Jennings Bryan's "Cross of Gold" speech on page 405. Students may make other selections from the expanded speech in the primary sources. Encourage students to use oratorical techniques such as eye contact, gestures, pauses, and stress. Have students speculate why Bryan's oratory was considered so powerful.

IN-DEPTH RESOURCES: UNIT 4
Primary Source: *from* "The 'Cross of Gold' Speech" by William Jennings Bryan, p. 11

Making Connections Across Time

Third Parties Ask students what they know about third parties in national politics today. Are they effective? If so, in what way? *Students might mention Ross Perot's Reform Party, the Green Party, or the Libertarian Party. Their answers may include a range of opinions, from a lack of effectiveness, to exerting an effective influence on the major parties by concentrating on a few issues and by siphoning off votes.*

You come to us and tell us that the great cities are in favor of the gold standard; we reply that the great cities rest upon our broad and fertile prairies. Burn down your cities and leave our farms, and your cities will spring up again as if by magic; but destroy our farms and the grass will grow in the streets of every city in the country. . . . Having behind us the producing masses of this nation and the world, supported by the commercial interests, the laboring interests, and the toilers everywhere, we will answer their demand for a gold standard by saying to them: You shall not press down upon the brow of labor this crown of thorns, you shall not crucify mankind upon a cross of gold.

WILLIAM JENNINGS BRYAN, Democratic Convention speech, Chicago, July 8, 1896

A cartoon about William Jennings Bryan's "Cross of Gold" speech

Bryan's speech won him a full hour of wild applause—and the Democratic nomination. Still, the People's Party was hesitant to accept him as its candidate, since the Democratic Party had nominated for vice-president a wealthy banker from Maine named Arthur Sewall—who showed no sympathy for the farmers. Yet the Populists feared splitting the anti-McKinley vote between Bryan and a third candidate. After much debate, the People's Party nominated Bryan for president and Populist Thomas E. Watson of Georgia, an important figure in the Southern alliance movement, for vice-president. In this way, the Populists hoped both to retain their party identity and platform and to back a presidential candidate who could win.

THE END OF POPULISM Even with the support of the Populists, however, Bryan faced a difficult campaign. His free-silver stand had led gold bug Democrats to nominate their own candidate. It also weakened his support in cities, where consumers feared inflation because it would make goods more expensive. In addition, Bryan's meager funds could not match the millions backing McKinley.

Bryan attempted to make up for his lack of funds by spreading himself widely. He campaigned in 27 states, covering 18,000 miles and sometimes made as many as 20 speeches a day. McKinley, on the other hand, campaigned from the front porch of his home in Canton, Ohio, while thousands of well-known people toured the country speaking on his behalf.

When the returns were in, McKinley had approximately 7 million votes and Bryan about 6.5 million. As expected, McKinley carried the East, while Bryan carried the South and the farm vote of the Middle West. The voters of the industrial Middle West and the voters of the growing middle class, with their fear of inflation, brought McKinley into office.

With McKinley's election, Populism collapsed, burying the hopes of the farmers. The movement left two powerful legacies, however: a message that the downtrodden could organize and have political impact, and an agenda for reforms, many of which would be enacted in the 20th century.

F. Answer It collapsed because it did not appeal to urban laborers and because it became overly focused on the issue of free silver.

THINK THROUGH HISTORY
F. Analyzing Causes Why did the Populist movement collapse?

Section 4 Assessment

1. TERMS & NAMES

Identify:
- Oliver Kelley
- Grange
- Populism
- bimetallism
- William McKinley
- William Jennings Bryan
- "Cross of Gold" speech

2. ANALYZING CAUSES AND EFFECTS Identify the causes for the rise of the Populist Party and the effects the party had.

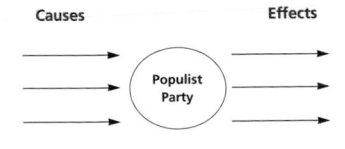

Causes   Effects

Populist Party

Which effect has the most influence today?

3. APPLYING Rank the following four factors in order of the impact you think they had on bringing an end to the Populist Party:
- support for free silver
- lack of wealthy backers
- advocating a greater voice in government
- third-party status

4. FORMING AN OPINION Who do you think was most to blame for the Panic of 1893: (1) farmers and businesspeople, (2) railroads and banks, or (3) government? Support your answer with information from the text.

THINK ABOUT
- the actions of each group prior to the Panic of 1893
- the causes of the panic
- the business cycle

Changes on the Western Frontier **405**

ANSWERS

1. TERMS & NAMES

Oliver Kelley, p. 402

Grange, p. 402

Populism, p. 402

bimetallism, p. 404

William McKinley, p. 404

William Jennings Bryan, p. 404

"Cross of Gold" speech, p. 404

2. ANALYZING CAUSES AND EFFECTS

Causes:
Falling prices for crops
Inability to repay loans
High railroad rates
Effects:
New ideas that later became law
Political forum for addressing special interests
Message of hope to downtrodden

3. APPLYING

Rankings will vary but should be supported with examples from the text.

4. FORMING AN OPINION

Answers will vary but should include support from the text.
Possible Reasons:
Farmers and businesspeople—because they overextended themselves.
Railroads and banks—because they expanded so rapidly.
Government—because it did not regulate borrowing or take measures to rescue the economy.

Chapter **13** Assessment

TERMS & NAMES
1. Homestead Act, p. 382
2. Sitting Bull, p. 384
3. George A. Custer, p. 385
4. assimilation, p. 385
5. James B. (Wild Bill) Hickok, p. 391
6. Martha Jane Cannary (Calamity Jane), p. 391
7. Morrill Land Grant Acts, p. 399
8. Populism, p. 402
9. William McKinley, p. 404
10. William Jennings Bryan, p. 404

MAIN IDEAS
11. Native Americans—hunters and gatherers; settlers—farmers. Native Americans—communal property; settlers—individual property. Native Americans—migratory; settlers—settled.

12. The Native Americans' successful fight for the closing of the Bozeman Trail was followed by the breaking of the treaty by the U.S. government.

13. It was a failure.

14. With the growth of cities, the market for beef increased. The development of railways provided a link between the cattle frontier and the cities.

15. Over one-third were non-white—mostly African American or Mexican.

16. While cowboy myths focused on excitement and on the dangers of confrontations with Native Americans or outlaws, cowboys actually led a hard, often boring life.

17. The Homestead Act and the Morrill Land Grant Acts.

18. They were self-reliant and strong, building houses in the sides of hills or out of sod and working long, hard hours.

19. High railroad rates, crop failures, and the inability to repay loans.

20. They hoped that backing the dollar with both gold and silver and increasing the coinage of silver by putting more money in circulation would raise prices and allow farmers to get out of debt.

REVIEWING THE CHAPTER

TERMS & NAMES For each term below, write a sentence explaining its connection to the late 1800s and changes on the Great Plains. For each person below, explain how he or she influenced life on the Great Plains.

1. Homestead Act
2. Sitting Bull
3. George A. Custer
4. assimilation
5. James B. (Wild Bill) Hickok
6. Martha Jane Cannary (Calamity Jane)
7. Morrill Land Grant Acts
8. Populism
9. William McKinley
10. William Jennings Bryan

MAIN IDEAS

SECTION 1 (pages 380–387)

Native American Culture in Crisis
11. Identify three significant differences between the culture of the Native Americans and that of the white settlers on the Great Plains.
12. How did the conflict over the Bozeman Trail symbolize the difficulties Native Americans faced?
13. How effective was the Dawes Act in promoting assimilation of Native Americans into white culture?

SECTION 2 (pages 388–393)

The Growth of the Cattle Industry
14. Why did the cattle industry become a big business in the late 1800s?
15. How did cowboy culture reflect the ethnic diversity of the United States?
16. How did the real life of cowboys differ from the myths about them?

SECTION 3 (pages 396–400)

Settling on the Great Plains
17. What measures did the government take to support settlement of the frontier?
18. How did settlers overcome the challenges of living on the Great Plains?

SECTION 4 (pages 401–405)

Farmers and the Populist Movement
19. What economic problems confronted American farmers in the 1890s?
20. According to farmers and other supporters of free silver, how would bimetallism help the economy?

THINKING CRITICALLY

1. **BREADBASKET FOR THE NATION** Create a cause-and-effect diagram identifying the reasons that agricultural output from the Great Plains increased during the late 1800s.

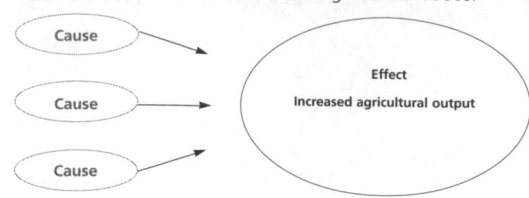

2. **WESTWARD HO** In the quote on page 378, Chief Joseph said, "My people have always been the friends of white men. Why are you in such a hurry?" Why do you think white people were in such a hurry to settle the West and had so little regard for the Native Americans who inhabited the land? Give evidence to support your position.

3. **GO FOR THE GOLD** Imagine you are a miner in Colorado in 1887. Tell about events in your daily life that would encourage or discourage a friend living in New York City who is considering joining you.

4. **GEOGRAPHY AND SETTLEMENT** Look back at the map on page 390. Near what geographical feature were most cities located? How do you think the railroads changed this pattern of settlement?

5. **COWBOY STEREOTYPES** Explain why you think the myth of the cowboy had such a powerful hold on the American imagination, even though it was an inaccurate portrayal of real life.

6. **ANALYZING PRIMARY SOURCES** Read the following excerpt from a speech by Red Cloud in 1870 during a visit to Washington, D.C. Then answer the question below.

> The Great Father [the President] may be good and kind but I can't see it. . . .[He] has sent his people out there and left me nothing but an island. Our nation is melting away like the snow on the sides of the hills where the sun is warm, while your people are like the blades of grass in the spring when the summer is coming.
>
> **RED CLOUD,** quoted in *Bury My Heart at Wounded Knee*

How does Red Cloud compare the Native Americans and the settlers? Explain whether you agree or disagree with his assessment of the Great Father.

THINKING CRITICALLY

1. BREADBASKET FOR THE NATION
Possible Answers: **Causes:** Increased land in production, resulting from various government programs to encourage settlement.
Population growth.
New technology, including the steel plow, the McCormick mowing and reaping machine, barbed wire, the spring-tooth harrow, the grain drill, and the cord binder.
New methods and crops, such as grains suitable for dry soil and techniques for dry farming.

2. WESTWARD HO
Answers will vary, but students might mention greed, the pioneering spirit, and the belief that Native Americans were savages.

3. GO FOR THE GOLD
Lists should include details about the miner's daily life, such as the tedium of panning and sluicing for gold, the discomfort of the mining towns, the hazards of the mines, the hard work, and the difficulty of finding large amounts of gold.

ALTERNATIVE ASSESSMENT

1. ANALYZING IMAGES OF THE WEST

Images of the American West have helped shape popular ideas, and even some myths, about this region. What messages are conveyed in historical or contemporary images of the West? How do these images support or contradict what you have learned about the history of the West?

Write an analysis essay by selecting and analyzing four images of the West.

CD-ROM Use the CD-ROM *Grolier's Multimedia Encyclopedia* and other resources to find images of the West. You can use historical or contemporary images or both.

- Choose four distinct images that show a variety of people, places, or activities. Write an analysis of these images for their historic and emotional content.

- Consider the following in your analysis: Who created the images? When and why were they made? What information or message does each convey about the geography or history of the West? In what ways does this information support or contradict your knowledge about the West?

2. LEARNING FROM MEDIA

VIDEO View the video for Chapter 13, *A Walk in Two Worlds*. Discuss the following questions in small groups.

- What options did Native Americans have as white settlers threatened their life on the plains?

- How might the American government have acted differently toward the Native Americans?

- How did Zitkala-Ša react to life in the boarding school?

- In what ways did Zitkala-Ša benefit from her education?

- What lessons about clashes of cultures did you learn from Zitkala-Ša's experiences walking in two worlds?

- How might people make interactions with other cultures a positive, rather than a negative, experience?

3. PORTFOLIO PROJECT

Use the Living History activity to expand your portfolio.

LIVING HISTORY

REVISING YOUR TRAVEL GUIDE

After you have written the parts of your travel guide, ask a friend to read it and answer the following questions:

- Is the guide helpful for your intended reader?
- What illustrations, maps, charts, or other visual materials would make the guide more interesting?

Make changes based on your friend's suggestions and add a cover to your book. Then share your guidebook or display it in your classroom before adding it to your American history portfolio.

R eview Chapter 13

NATIVE AMERICANS Between the 1850s and 1890, settlers flocked to the West in search of gold or land. In the process, they nearly destroyed the traditional culture of Native Americans living on the Great Plains. Competition for land often led to bloody conflicts, including the Sand Creek Massacre (1864), Custer's Last Stand (1876), and the Battle of Wounded Knee (1890).

THE CATTLE INDUSTRY As the settlers took over the Native American lands, they developed a thriving cattle industry. Learning skills and borrowing terminology from Mexicans, cowboys herded cattle and shipped them by railroad to growing cities in the East. The cowboy became one of America's most romantic figures. By the 1880s, however, droughts, blizzards, and the introduction of barbed wire ended the cattle frontier.

SETTLING ON THE GREAT PLAINS The government actively promoted the settlement of the Great Plains by subsidizing the construction of railways, providing free land, and sponsoring agricultural research. Settlers on the Great Plains often lived in dugouts or soddies, and they struggled to survive inclement weather and isolation. By the 1880s, many farmers suffered from growing debts and rising railroad rates.

THE POPULIST MOVEMENT In an attempt to deal with their economic troubles, farmers organized to demand changes. The Grange and various Farmer's Alliances became active in politics. Building on farmers' discontent, the Populist movement grew rapidly, particularly after the Panic of 1893. In 1896, the Populist Party nominated noted orator William Jennings Bryan for president. With Bryan's loss to conservative William McKinley, though, the Populist Party lost its momentum.

P review Chapter 14

The changes that led to the decline of the frontier were just the beginning of widespread economic and social developments that ushered in a whole new way of life at the end of the 19th century. The availability of natural resources, new inventions, and a receptive market combined to fuel an industrial boom. Large businesses grew larger, and workers united to demand higher pay, shorter hours, and safer working conditions. You will learn about these significant developments in the next chapter.

Changes on the Western Frontier **407**

1. ANALYZING IMAGES OF THE WEST

Standards for Evaluation

An analysis of images of the West should meet the following criteria:

- Clearly describes the images.
- Indicates the historical significance of each artist's choice of material and way of presenting it.
- Compares the messages of the images and draws a conclusion about the meaning of the West.

2. LEARNING FROM MEDIA

Answers to the questions:

- They could have either fought to retain their lands or accepted their loss.
- The government might have upheld Native Americans' claims to Western lands and restricted settlement by farmers and prospectors.
- She resisted the loss of her native identity.
- She gained the skills necessary to function in the white world and to fight for the cause of her people.
- Cultural values cannot be imposed on people without their consent.
- People could respect those with different values and ways and embrace interaction as a way to expand their own understanding.

3. PORTFOLIO PROJECT

LIVING HISTORY

Standards for Evaluation

A travel guide should meet the following criteria:

- Shows awareness of the needs and knowledge of the target audience.
- Presents appropriate and detailed information in an organized format.
- Includes lively visual materials that engage readers' interest and enhance the usefulness of the guide.

IN-DEPTH RESOURCES: UNIT 4

See the form for scoring this activity on page 18.

THINKING CRITICALLY

4. GEOGRAPHY AND SETTLEMENT

Rivers. *Possible Answer:* Railroads converted rivers from pathways into barriers to cross. Cities such as Abilene, Kansas, grew because of their position on the railroad rather than on a river. The shift from river to rails gave people greater flexibility in establishing trade routes, businesses, and cities.

5. COWBOY STEREOTYPES

The romance of the independent, hardworking man pitting himself against the elements has a powerful attraction for people of all times whose lives are boring and dependent on others.

6. ANALYZING PRIMARY SOURCES

Red Cloud's nation is disappearing like melting snow; the settlers are intruding like growing grass. Some students may agree that the president deserved blame, citing the ill treatment Native Americans received. Others may argue that the president was less at fault for abuses to the Native Americans than were the settlers and the military.

The Industrial Age

	Key Ideas	**TEACHING SUPPORT**	**ASSESSMENT**
SECTION 1 The Expansion of Industry *pp. 410–413*	*Industry booms as natural resources, creative ideas, and growing markets fuel technological development.*	**In-Depth Resources: Unit 4** • Guided Reading, p. 19 • Geography Application: The Changing Labor Force, p. 24 • Primary Source: The Birth of the Telephone, p. 26 **COOPERATIVE ACTIVITY** • Tracking the Growth of Steel, p. 411 (TE)	*Section 1 Assessment,* p. 413 (PE) *Self-Assessment,* p. 413 (TE) *Formal Assessment* • Section Quiz, p. 173 *Alternative Assessment Book* • Standards for Evaluating a Cooperative Activity
SECTION 2 The Age of the Railroads *pp. 416–420*	*The growth and consolidation of the railroads benefit the nation but lead to corruption and regulation.*	**In-Depth Resources: Unit 4** • Guided Reading, p. 20 • Literature: *from "The Bride Comes to Yellow Sky"* by Stephen Crane, p. 30 **COOPERATIVE ACTIVITY** • Debating Company Towns, p. 419 (TE)	*Section 2 Assessment,* p. 420 (PE) *Self-Assessment,* p. 420 (TE) *Formal Assessment* • Section Quiz, p. 174 *Alternative Assessment Book* • Standards for Evaluating a Cooperative Activity
SECTION 3 Big Business Emerges *pp. 421–425*	*The expansion of industry in the North results in the growth of big business and the development of a new social philosophy.*	**In-Depth Resources: Unit 4** • Guided Reading, p. 21 • Skillbuilder Practice: Forming Opinions, p. 23 • Primary Sources: *from "Wealth and Its Uses"* by Andrew Carnegie, p. 27; *from History of the Standard Oil Company,* p. 28 • American Lives: Andrew Carnegie, p. 35	*Section 3 Assessment,* p. 425 (PE) *Self-Assessment,* p. 425 (TE) *Formal Assessment* • Section Quiz, p. 175 *Alternative Assessment Book* • Standards for Evaluating a Cooperative Activity
SECTION 4 Workers of the Nation Unite *pp. 426–433*	*Laborers form unions to better their working conditions and pay. Despite some success, they eventually lose ground against government-supported business interests.*	**In-Depth Resources: Unit 4** • Guided Reading, p. 22 • Primary Source: Labor Poster, p. 29 • American Lives: Mary Harris "Mother" Jones, p. 34 **COOPERATIVE ACTIVITY** • Reporting on Union Goals, p. 431 (TE)	*Section 4 Assessment,* p. 433 (PE) *Self-Assessment,* p. 433 (TE) *Formal Assessment* • Section Quiz, p. 176 *Alternative Assessment Book* • Standards for Evaluating a Cooperative Activity
CHAPTER RESOURCES	**Chapter Overview** *Technological innovations and the growth of the railroad industry help fuel an industrial boom. Some business leaders follow corrupt practices, and workers, suffering harsh working conditions, try to organize.*	**In-Depth Resources: Unit 4** • Living History Project: Worksheet, p. 35; Standards, p. 36 **Telescoping the Times** • Chapter Summary, pp. 27–28 **Planning for Block Schedules**	*Chapter Assessment,* pp. 434–435 (PE) *Alternative Assessment,* p. 435 (PE) *Formal Assessment* • Chapter Test, forms A and B, pp. 177–182 **Test Generator** *Alternative Assessment Book* See explanation and forms for different kinds of alternative assessments including portfolio assessment.

Geography Transparencies
• G14, Mining and Industry

Critical Thinking Transparencies
• CT14, Industrial Growth

Grolier Multimedia Encyclopedia
• Edison and Bell

 Electronic Library of Primary Sources
• How Women Are Treated by the Pullman Company by Jennie Curtiss

INTERNET RESOURCES
• See Interact with History p. 415 (PE) for an activity that includes the Internet as an enrichment option.

 Critical Thinking Transparencies
• CT48, Horizontal Consolidation and Vertical Integration

 Grolier Multimedia Encyclopedia
• The Growth of Railroads

INTERNET RESOURCES
• See *McDougal Littell Learning On-Line* for links to information about George Pullman and railroads.

 Humanities Transparencies
• H35, "The Bosses of the Senate": American antitrust cartoon, 1889, by Joseph Keppler

 Electronic Library of Primary Sources
• "The Two Acre Lot" by Horatio Alger

Our Times
• Freedom and Free Enterprise

INTERNET RESOURCES
• See *McDougal Littell Learning On-Line* for links to information about Andrew Carnegie.

 Humanities Transparencies
• H14, *The Gun Foundry* by John Furguson Weir

 Electronic Library of Primary Sources
• from "141 Die in Factory Fire"
• On the Goals of Trade Unions by Samuel Gompers

INTERNET RESOURCES
• See *McDougal Littell Learning On-Line* for links to information about the Pullman strike.

 American Portfolio: A Videodisc for U.S. History, user's guide, pp. 135–139, 141–142, 148, 160, 166

INTERNET RESOURCES
Learning On-Line: Social Studies
http://www.mcdougallittell.com

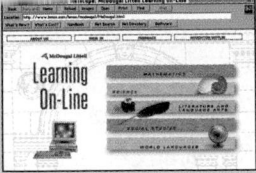

Block Scheduling (90 MINUTES)

Day 1

Section 1, pp. 410–413
Geography Spotlight: Industry Changes the Environment, pp. 414–415
Section 2, pp. 416–420
Section Assessments, pp. 413, 420

Day 2

Section 3, pp. 421–425
Section 4, pp. 426–433
Section Assessments, pp. 425, 433
Chapter Assessment, pp. 434–435

YEARLY PACING *Chapter 14 Total:* 2 days *Yearly Total:* 85 days

See *Planning for Block Schedules* for special activities and pacing strategies.

Customizing for Special Populations

Students Acquiring English

Access for Students Acquiring English
• Guided Reading for Sections 1–4 (Spanish), pp. 139–142
• Chapter Summary (Spanish), pp. 137–138
• Skillbuilder Practice: Forming Opinions (Spanish), p. 143
• Geography Application: The Changing Labor Force (Spanish), p. 144

INTERNET RESOURCES
• See *McDougal Littell Learning On-Line* The Diverse Classroom.

Less Proficient Readers

In-Depth Resources: Unit 4
• Guided Reading for Sections 1–4, pp. 19–22
• Skillbuilder: Forming Opinions, p. 23
• Geography Application: The Changing Labor Force, p. 24

Telescoping the Times
• Chapter Summary, pp. 27–28

See additional strategies at point of use in the Teacher's Edition.

Gifted and Talented Students

In-Depth Resources: Unit 4
• Primary Sources: The Birth of the Telephone, p. 26; from "Wealth and Its Uses" by Andrew Carnegie, p. 27; from *History of the Standard Oil Company,* p. 28; Labor Poster, p. 29
• American Lives: Andrew Carnegie, p. 33; Mary Harris "Mother" Jones, p. 34

See additional strategies at point of use in the Teacher's Edition.

Connections to Literature READINGS FOR STUDENTS

In-Depth Resources: Unit 4
• *from* "The Bride Comes to Yellow Sky" by Stephen Crane, p. 30

Enrichment Reading
• **Brown, Dee**
Hear That Lonesome Whistle Blow.
New York: Simon and Schuster, 1994
By the end of the 19th century the Iron Horse has conquered the West—railroads linked the two coasts of the United States. In Hear That Lonesome Whistle Blow, *Dee Brown tells the story of this extraordinary undertaking.*

• **Goble Paul**
Death of the Iron Horse.
New York: Aladdin Books, 1993
A group of Cheyenne braves derail and raid a freight train in 1867 as an act of defiance against the white man's encroachment on their land.

McDougal Littell *The Language of Literature*
American Literature

• **Mark Twain,**
from The Autobiography of Mark Twain, p. 531

• **Jones, Mary Harris "Mother"**
The Autobiography of Mother Jones.
Chicago: Kerr, 1990
This self-portrait by the feisty union activist is a fascinating account of one woman's activism.

• **Leyendecker, Liston**
Palace Car Prince.
Nivot, Colo.: University Press of Colorado, 1992
The flamboyant story of George Pullman is told in this detailed biography.

The Industrial Age

▶ *Starting with the Student*
Ask students what images the phrase "The Industrial Age" brings to mind. Who do they think the key players in the chapter might be? Then discuss the opening quotation.

- How would they paraphrase the quotation from "Mother" Jones?
- Based on the image that accompanies the quotation and on the time line, what do they think the people fought for during the industrial age?

PREVIEWING THE CHAPTER

- Have students examine the entries and images on the time line. What issues seem to characterize the era?
- What questions would they like to have answered by the chapter?

MORE ABOUT . . .
"Mother" Jones

Mary Harris "Mother" Jones (1830–1930) worked tirelessly during most of her long life to win decent working conditions and adequate pay for laborers. She particularly supported miners and railroad workers.

The Industrial Age

SECTION 1

The Expansion of Industry

Industry booms as natural resources, creative ideas, and growing markets fuel technological development.

SECTION 2

The Age of the Railroads

The growth and consolidation of the railroads benefit the nation but lead to corruption and regulation.

SECTION 3

Big Business Emerges

The expansion of industry in the North results in the growth of big business and the development of a new social philosophy.

SECTION 4

Workers of the Nation Unite

Laborers form unions to better their working conditions and pay. Despite some success, they eventually lose ground against government-supported business interests.

"The militant, not the meek, shall inherit the earth."

Mary Harris "Mother" Jones

"Mother" Jones supports the Great Railroad Strike of 1877.

Munn v. *Illinois* establishes government regulation of railroads.

Crédit Mobilier scandal is exposed.

Alexander Graham Bell invents the telephone.

Thomas A. Edison invents the light bulb.

John D. Rockefell Standard Company controls 9 of U.S. re business.

| THE UNITED STATES | 1870 | 1872 | 1876 | 1877 | 1879 | 1880 |
| THE WORLD | | 1872 | | | | |

Franco-Prussian War is fought.

Japan introduces universal military service.

Diamonds are discovered in South Africa.

408 CHAPTER 14

THEMES IN CHAPTER 14

Science and Technology

The rapid expansion of the railroads from coast to coast and the development of new inventions and improved technologies ushered in a new age for America and Americans. All aspects of life—where people lived, how they worked, what they ate, and how they spent their leisure time—were changed forever.

See Teacher's Edition note, p. 418.

The American Dream

Newcomers to this country and settlers who crowded the frontier hopefully pursued the American dream of opportunity to create a good life for themselves and their families. For some, however—men, women, and children who toiled long hours for low pay—the dream remained out of reach.

See Teacher's Edition notes, pp. 422 and 427.

Women in America

Industrialization enabled women to enter the labor force in great numbers. They played a significant role in the labor movement and worked tirelessly to improve working conditions for themselves and their children. They wanted recognition for their contributions, however, and "Equal pay for equal work" became their rallying cry.

See Teacher's Edition note, p. 432.

Haymarket riot turns public sentiment against unions.

Interstate Commerce Act is passed.

Railroad time goes into effect across the country.

Unions fight back in Great Railroad Strike.

Congress passes the Sherman Antitrust Act.

President Cleveland sends federal troops to Illinois to end the Pullman strike.

1883 **1886** **1887** **1890** **1894** **1900**

881 **1883** **1885** **1896**

Germany becomes first nation to provide national health insurance.

Adult males gain the vote in Great Britain.

Colonization of sub-Saharan Africa reaches its peak.

First modern Olympic Games are held in Athens, Greece.

France institutes freedom of the press.

Indian National Congress is established.

The Industrial Age **409**

RECOMMENDED RESOURCES

Books for the Teacher

Dulles, Foster Rhea. *Labor in America: A History.* New York: Harlan Davidson, 1993.

Foner, Philip Sheldon. *Women and the American Labor Movement.* New York: Free Press, 1979.

Josephson, Matthew. *The Robber Barons.* San Diego: Harcourt, 1995.

Books for the Student

Alger, Horatio, Jr. *Struggling Upward and Other Works.* New York: Crown, 1945.

Brown, Dee. *The Year of the Century.* New York: Scribner's, 1966.

Carnegie, Andrew. *Autobiography of Andrew Carnegie.* Boston: Houghton, 1986.

Videos

American History: The Game of Monopoly. MasterVision, 969 Park Avenue South, New York, NY 10020.

Labor's Struggle. RMI Media, 800-745-5480.

Andrew Carnegie: The Original Man of Steel. Videodisc. American Lifestyle Series. Educational Software Institute, 800-955-5570.

Software

The Industrial Revolution in America. CD-ROM. Educational Software Institute, 800-955-5570.

OBJECTIVES

1 To explain how the abundance of natural resources, new recovery and refining methods, and new uses for them led to intensive industrialization.

2 To identify inventions that changed the way people lived and worked.

SKILLBUILDER

• Understanding geography: human-environment interaction, location, p. 411

CRITICAL THINKING

• Analyzing causes, pp. 411, 413
• Recognizing effects, pp. 412, 413
• Clarifying, p. 413
• Summarizing, p. 413
• Drawing conclusions, p. 413

FOCUS & MOTIVATE

▶ *Starting with the Student*
• Ask students to imagine living without electricity, the light bulb, or the telephone. How would their daily activities be affected?
• How eager do they think people would have been to acquire these conveniences when they became available?

MORE ABOUT . . .
Mark Twain

Mark Twain (1835–1910) was an enthusiastic traveler. He made many trips to the East and West coasts of the United States, to Hawaii, to Europe, and he even circled the globe. Yet, at least in his books, he seemed to resist change. His most popular books, *Adventures of Tom Sawyer* and *The Adventures of Huckleberry Finn,* took place before the Civil War. In *A Connecticut Yankee in King Arthur's Court,* he ridiculed the boorish ways of modern society.

---

1 The Expansion of Industry

TERMS & NAMES
• Edwin L. Drake
• Bessemer process
• Thomas Alva Edison
• Christopher Sholes
• Alexander Graham Bell

LEARN ABOUT new technological processes and inventions
TO UNDERSTAND the developments that fueled industrialization.

ONE AMERICAN'S STORY

Born and raised in Missouri, Samuel Clemens spent so much of his life on the Mississippi River that it might well have flowed in his veins. Even his pen name—Mark Twain—came from riverboat jargon meaning "two fathoms (12 feet) deep" and signifying safe waters. From his vantage point as a Mississippi River pilot, he saw the United States transform itself from a sleepy, rural nation with ports at small towns along the river to an industrial power.

> **A PERSONAL VOICE**
> Natchez, like her near and far river neighbors, has railways now—and is adding to them—pushing them hither and thither into all rich outlying regions. . . . The changes in the Mississippi River are great and strange, yet were to be expected; but I was not expecting to live to see Natchez and these other river towns become manufacturing strongholds and railway centers.
> **MARK TWAIN,** *Life on the Mississippi*

The industrial development and technological change that began shortly after the Civil War overwhelmed Mark Twain and other Americans. The vitality of the time was contagious, however, and possibilities seemed unlimited. The land was rich in valuable resources, labor was plentiful, and inventors were bursting with creative ideas.

Samuel Clemens (Mark Twain) relaxes on a riverboat.

Natural Resources Fuel Industrialization

Immediately after the Civil War, the United States was still a mostly rural nation. By the 1920s—a mere 60 years later—it had become the leading industrial power in the world. This immense technological boom was due to three major factors: a wealth of natural resources, an explosion of inventions, and a growing urban population that provided markets for new products.

BLACK GOLD Though eastern Native American tribes made fuel and medicine from crude oil long before Europeans arrived on the continent, early American settlers had little use for it. In 1840, however, Canadian geologist Abraham Gesner realized that kerosene could be used to light lamps and discovered how to distill it from oil or coal. The industrialization of America was underway.

Before the Civil War, people had skimmed oil from creeks, where it had seeped to the earth's surface. It wasn't until 1859, when retired railroad conductor **Edwin L. Drake** successfully used a steam engine to drill for oil near Titusville, Pennsylvania, that removing it from beneath the earth's surface became practical. This technological breakthrough touched off an oil boom that spread to Kentucky, Ohio, Illinois, and Indiana. Petroleum-refining industries grew up in Cleveland and Pittsburgh as entrepreneurs rushed to transform the oil into precious kerosene. Gasoline, a byproduct of the refining process, originally was thrown away. When the automobile was invented in the 1890s, gasoline became the most important form of black gold.

SECTION 1 RESOURCES

PRINT RESOURCES

IN-DEPTH RESOURCES: UNIT 4
Guided Reading, p. 19
Geography Application: The Changing Labor Force, p. 24
Primary Source: The Birth of the Telephone, p. 26

ACCESS FOR STUDENTS ACQUIRING ENGLISH
Guided Reading (Spanish), p. 139
Geography Application: The Changing Labor Force (Spanish), p. 144

FORMAL ASSESSMENT
Section Quiz, p. 173

ALTERNATIVE ASSESSMENT BOOK
See forms for supporting and scoring alternative activities.

TECHNOLOGY RESOURCES

GEOGRAPHY TRANSPARENCIES
G14, Mining and Industry

CRITICAL THINKING TRANSPARENCIES
CT14, Industrial Growth

CD-ROM *Grolier Multimedia Encyclopedia*
Electronic Library of Primary Sources

VIDEO *American Portfolio: A Videodisc for U.S. History*
user's guide, pp. 137, 139, 142

INTERNET McDougal Littell Learning On-Line
http://www.mcdougallittell.com

Natural Resources and the Birth of a Steel Town, 1886–1906

Pittsburgh

○ Steel mills, 1886
● Steel mills, 1906

Major industrial city
Other cities
Coal mining
Iron ore mining
Oil
Steel mills

300 Miles
600 Kilometers

BESSEMER STEEL PROCESS   Fortunately, oil was not the only natural resource that was plentiful in the United States. The industrial age would not have been possible without abundant deposits of coal and iron which could be turned into steel. In 1887, prospectors discovered rich iron ore deposits more than 100 miles long and from one to three miles wide in and around the Mesabi Range of Minnesota. At the same time, coal production skyrocketed—from 33 million tons in 1870 to more than 250 million tons in 1900.

Iron is a strong metal, but it is heavy, breaks when compressed, and rusts when wet. It also generally contains other elements, such as carbon. Removing the carbon from iron produces a lighter, more flexible, rust-resistant metal—steel. The raw materials necessary to make steel were readily available; all that was needed was a cheap and efficient manufacturing process. The **Bessemer process,** developed independently by British manufacturer Henry Bessemer and American ironmaker William Kelly around 1850, soon came into widespread use. This technique involved injecting air into molten iron, which removed the carbon and sparked its fiery transformation into steel. By 1880, manufacturers used the new method to produce more than 90 percent of the nation's steel. In this age of rapid change and innovation, even the successful Bessemer process was bettered by 1886 and was eventually replaced by the open-hearth process. With this technique, manufacturers could produce quality steel from scrap metal as well as from raw materials.

NEW USES FOR STEEL   The railroads, with their thousands of miles of track, became the biggest customers for steel, but inventors soon found additional uses for it. Joseph Glidden's barbed wire and McCormick's and Deere's farm machines helped transform the plains into the food producer of the nation. Steel—in the form of the tin-plated steel can—even revolutionized the storage of food, which changed Americans' diets.

Steel changed the face of the country as well, as it made innovative construction possible. One of the most remarkable structures was the Brooklyn Bridge. Completed in 1883, it spanned 1,595 feet of the East River in New York City. Its

The Industrial Age **411**

Reading the Time Line Ask
students how much time
elapsed between the invention of the steam engine
used in trains and the internal combustion engine used
in cars. *170 years.* How
much time between the
combustion engine and the
airplane? *43 years.*

OBJECTIVE
② INSTRUCT

Inventions
Promote Change

▶ **Starting with the Student**
Discuss with students how
their lives would be made
more difficult without electricity. Have them make a
chart listing ways they use
electricity and nonelectrical
alternatives. The chart might
look like this:

Electricity

Use	Substitute
Pencil ener	Knife, or sharp-mechanical sharpener
Clothes clothesline	Outdoor dryer

▶ **Discussing Key Ideas**
• The harnessing of electricity transforms American
business.
• A profusion of inventions
promotes rapid change.
• New products affect people at home and at work.

IN-DEPTH RESOURCES: UNIT 4
Primary Source: The Birth of the
Telephone, p. 26

 *GROLIER MULTIMEDIA
ENCYCLOPEDIA*
Edison and Bell

The Technological Explosion

						Magnetic Compass
5000 B.C.	5000 B.C.	3500 B.C.	1000 B.C.	A.D. 1000	A.D. 1100	1200
	Plow	Wheel	Sundial			

steel cables were suspended from towers higher than any man-made structure
except the pyramids of Egypt. Like those ancient marvels, the completed bridge
was called a "wonder of the world." Nonetheless, many people were skeptical
about its structural soundness. P. T. Barnum—the flamboyant showman—helped
dispel their doubts when he drove a herd of elephants across the bridge.

Two years later, setting the stage for a new era of expansion upward as well
as outward, William Le Baron Jenney designed the first skyscraper with a steel
frame—the Home Insurance Building in Chicago. Before Jenney had his
pioneering idea, the weight of buildings was supported entirely by their walls.
This meant that the taller the building, the thicker the walls had to be, so the
height was limited. With a steel frame to support the building, however,
architects could build as high as they wanted. As structures soared into the
air, not even the sky seemed to limit what Americans could achieve.

Inventions Promote Change

By capitalizing on natural resources and their own ingenuity, inventors and
their inventions changed more than the physical shape of life. They affected the
very way people lived and worked.

THE POWER OF ELECTRICITY In 1876, **Thomas Alva Edison** became a
pioneer on the new industrial frontier when he established the world's first
research laboratory in Menlo Park, New Jersey. Edison perfected the incandescent
light bulb there and followed up his invention with an entire system for producing
and distributing electrical power. Inventor George Westinghouse added
innovations that made electricity safer and less expensive. Edison's company
organized power plants across the country, while Westinghouse encouraged
scientists to create applications for the new source of energy.

The harnessing of electricity completely changed the nature of business in America. By 1890, electric power ran numerous machines ranging
from fans to printing presses. This inexpensive, convenient source of
energy soon became available in homes and spurred the invention of
increasing numbers of appliances. Electric streetcars made travel
cheap and efficient and also promoted the outward growth of cities.

More important, electricity allowed manufacturers to locate their
plants wherever they wanted—not just near sources of power. This
enabled industry to grow as never before. Huge operations, such as
meatpackers Armour and Swift, and efficient processes that they used,
became the models for new consumer industries.

INSPIRED INVENTIONS Edison's incandescent light bulb, patented in
1880, was only one of several revolutionary developments.
Another upheaval in the workplace took
place after **Christopher Sholes**
invented the typewriter in 1867, and
James Densmore improved and sold
it in 1873. Next to the light bulb, however, perhaps the most dramatic
invention was the telephone, unveiled
by **Alexander Graham Bell** and
Thomas Watson in 1876. Although
coast-to-coast phone service did not

Most great ideas
went through
painstaking
development.
Shown below
are the first light
bulb and patent
drawings of it
and the tele-
phone—just two
of more than
51,000 patents
issued between
1876 and 1880.

THINK THROUGH HISTORY
B. *Recognizing
Effects* How did
electricity change
American life?

B. Answer It
changed the
nature of
business, made
the invention of
new appliances
possible, and
helped cities and
industries grow.

TEACHING OPTION

Teaching Less Proficient Readers

Using a Chart Pair less proficient readers with more able
ones. After students read pages 412 and 413, have each pair
create a chronological chart listing the date and the inventor
for each invention mentioned. Completed invention charts
might look like this:

Date	Inventor	Invention
1851	Isaac Merritt Singer	Continuous-stitch sewing machine
1868	Christopher Sholes	Typewriter
1873	James Densmore	Improved typewriter
1876	Alexander Graham Bell and Thomas Watson	Telephone
1880	Thomas Alva Edison	Incandescent light bulb

Timeline:

Cannon	Movable-Type Press	Steam Engine	Cotton Gin	
1300 1350	1440	1690	1793	1910

1826 31 37 46 60 67 73 76 77 79 95 1903

- Reaper
- Telegraph
- Sewing Machine
- Internal Combustion Engine
- Dynamite
- Typewriter
- Light Bulb
- Phonograph
- Telephone
- Electric Motor
- Radio
- Motion Pictures
- X-Ray Machine
- Airplane
- Photography

THINK THROUGH HISTORY
C. *Analyzing Causes What caused the explosion of inventions in the late 19th century?*

C. Answer Development of natural resources and a growing, receptive market.

begin until 1915 and was slow and expensive, this invention laid the groundwork for a worldwide communications network.

NEW PRODUCTS AND LIFESTYLES The country's expanding urban population provided a potential market for new inventions and products. What people may not have foreseen, however, is how much their everyday lives would change as a result of the innovations of the industrial age.

Inventions such as the typewriter and the telephone particularly affected office work and opened up new jobs for women. While women made up less than 5 percent of all office workers in 1870, by 1910 they accounted for nearly 40 percent of the clerical work force. Most of these approximately 500,000 working women were single, white, native-born, and between 15 and 24.

New inventions also had a tremendous impact on jobs that traditionally had been done at home, and on factory work. Whereas most women had previously hand-sewn their families' clothes, for example, the invention of the sewing machine created a demand for professional garment workers. These laborers—men, women, and children—worked long hours, often under unhealthy conditions. Although machinery freed other factory workers from back-breaking labor, many, realizing that they were easily replaceable, felt a loss of self-worth and pride.

D. Answer They created new jobs and made factory work easier, but contributed to a loss of workers' self-esteem.

THINK THROUGH HISTORY
D. *Clarifying How did new inventions affect the nation's workers?*

While some workers lost power in the workplace as a result of industrialization, they gained it back as consumers in the marketplace. New industries arose to advertise and promote consumer goods. Companies like American Tobacco, for example, offered trading cards, premiums, and prizes with their products. The consumer had become an important new force in American business.

With all its positive and negative effects, industrialization contributed to an improved standard of living overall. By 1890, new inventions had lowered the average work week by ten hours. Goods such as phonographs, bicycles, and cameras provided new opportunities for recreation. Industries, from the smallest to the largest and most powerful, would never be the same.

HISTORICAL SPOTLIGHT

ILLUMINATING THE LIGHT BULB

Shortly after moving into a long wooden shed at Menlo Park, Edison and his associates set to work to develop the perfect incandescent bulb. Arc lamps already lit some city streets and shops, but these lamps used an electric current passing between two sticks of carbon, and they were glaring and inefficient.

Edison and his team hoped to create a long-lasting lamp with a soft, steady glow, and they began searching for a filament that would burn slowly and stay lit. Edison tried wires, sticks, blades of grass, and even hairs from his assistants' beards. Finally, a piece of carbonized bamboo from Japan did the trick. The Edison company used bamboo filaments until 1911, when they began using tungsten filaments, which are still in use today.

Section 1 Assessment

1. TERMS & NAMES

Identify:
- Edwin L. Drake
- Bessemer process
- Thomas Alva Edison
- Christopher Sholes
- Alexander Graham Bell

2. SUMMARIZING List several technological breakthroughs and explain their impact on society.

Technological Breakthrough	Impact

Write a paragraph that explains the impact of one of these breakthroughs.

3. DRAWING CONCLUSIONS Do you think that consumers gained power as industry expanded in the late 19th century? Why or why not?

THINK ABOUT
- how consumers can influence manufacturers
- efforts 19th-century businesses made to win customers

4. RECOGNIZING EFFECTS Which invention or development described in this section had the greatest impact on society? Give reasons to justify your choice.

THINK ABOUT
- the applications of inventions
- the impact of inventions on people's daily lives
- the effect of inventions on the workplace

The Industrial Age **413**

ANSWERS

1. TERMS & NAMES

Edwin L. Drake, p. 410

Bessemer process, p. 411

Thomas Alva Edison, p. 412

Christopher Sholes, p. 412

Alexander Graham Bell, p. 412

2. SUMMARIZING

Possible Answers:
oil drill—initiated oil boom
Bessemer steel process—made steel production cheaper and more efficient
barbed wire and farm machines—increased farmers' output
light bulb—made artificial light widely available
telephone—revolutionized communications

3. DRAWING CONCLUSIONS

Possible Responses: Agree—Availability of products and increase in promotional gimmicks. Disagree—Lower incomes and increasing dependence on manufactured (rather than home-made) products.

4. RECOGNIZING EFFECTS

Possible Responses: Some students will cite electricity as the invention with the greatest impact because it changed the nature of business, of travel, and of home and social life. Others will cite the telephone and the Bessemer steel process for similar reasons.

HISTORICAL SPOTLIGHT
Illuminating the Light Bulb
Critical Thinking: Clarifying Share with students Thomas Edison's definition of genius: "1 percent inspiration and 99 percent perspiration." Ask them to discuss how his search for the perfect lamp filament illustrates this definition.

IN-DEPTH RESOURCES: UNIT 4
Geography Application: The Changing Labor Force, p. 24

 ELECTRONIC LIBRARY OF PRIMARY SOURCES
How Women Are Treated by the Pullman Company

ASSESS & RETEACH

Section 1 Assessment
Have students create questions on the material in the chapter, then separate into teams and test each other in a game-show format.

Self-Assessment.
Have students mark the questions on the Section 1 Assessment that they could not answer. Ask them to find the answers in the text.

Section Quiz

FORMAL ASSESSMENT
Section Quiz, p. 173

Reteach
Use the chart in Critical Thinking Transparency 14 to review the causes and effects of industrial growth.

CRITICAL THINKING TRANSPARENCIES
CT14, Industrial Growth

CLOSE

An industrial explosion created a demand for shipping routes for both raw materials and finished products and increased the demand for rail networks. Technological advances in the production of steel made rapid expansion of the railroads possible.

Teacher's Edition **413**

Industry Changes the Environment

By the mid-1870s, industrialization was well on the way to changing almost every aspect of American life. Cleveland, Ohio, located on the shores of Lake Erie and not far from raw materials, was an industrial city waiting to be born. What no one could predict at the time was the dark side of its rapid development and technological progress.

❶ FROM HAYSTACKS TO SMOKESTACKS
In 1874, parts of Cleveland were still rural, with farms like this one dotting the landscape. But the smokestacks of the Standard Oil Refinery in the distance indicate that industrialization had already begun.

❷ REFINING THE LANDSCAPE Industries like the Standard Oil Refinery in Cleveland in 1889 soon became a source of prosperity for both the state and the entire country. The pollution they belched into the atmosphere, however, was the beginning of an ongoing problem—how to balance industrial production and environmental destruction.

WEST PART OF THE **14ᵗʰ Ward** OF **CLEVELAND**
Scale 400 Feet to an Inch.

RECOMMENDED RESOURCES

Books

Burns, Noel M. *Erie: The Lake That Survived.* Totowa, NJ: Rowman & Allanheld, 1985. How cleanup efforts helped Lake Erie recover from pollution.

Miggins, Edward M., and Thomas F. Campbell. *The Birth of Modern Cleveland.* Cranbury, NJ: Associated UP, 1988. A history of the city from 1865 to 1930.

Schuyler, David. *The New Urban Landscape.* Baltimore: Johns Hopkins UP, 1986. Environmental aspects of the growth of American cities in the 19th century.

Tarbell, Ida M. *The History of the Standard Oil Company.* Mattituck, NY: Amereon, 1993.

Videos

Great Lakes, Fragile Seas. National Geographic and WQED, 1991. Past pollution and present efforts to correct it.

The Rise of the American City. Encyclopaedia Britannica. The growth of cities and consequent problems they face.

U.S. Cities. Encyclopaedia Britannica. Focus on industrial development.

Software

Balance of the Planet. CD-ROM. Broderbund. Students must find ways to sustain industry but protect the environment.

Planetary Manager. National Geographic. Impact of fossil fuels, solid-waste management, and water pollution.

Pollution Patrol. Entrex. The city of Misery is plagued by pollution.

3 LIFE IN THE BIG CITY Although the serenity and slow pace of preindustrial life were becoming a thing of the past, urban growth improved people's daily lives in many ways. Factories were built near transportation centers, and working-class housing sprang up for the laborers. Rail lines carried the lifeblood of the city, and electric streetcars made urban travel faster and more pleasant than ever before.

4 A RIVER OF FIRE Industrial pollution would affect not only the air people breathed but also the water they drank. Refineries and steel mills discharged so much oil into the Cuyahoga River that major fires broke out on the water in 1936, 1952, and 1969. This 1952 blaze destroyed three tugboats, three buildings, and the ship repair yards. In the decade following the 1969 fire, changes in the way industrial plants operated and creation of wastewater treatment plants helped restore the quality of the water.

INTERACT WITH HISTORY

1. **ANALYZING ISSUES** What impact did Cleveland's industrial development have on its environment?

 SEE SKILLBUILDER HANDBOOK, PAGE 1046.

2. **RESEARCHING AN URBAN ENVIRONMENT** Use library resources or the Internet to learn the steps Cleveland has taken in recent years to improve its environment. Report your findings to the class.

 For more about Cleveland, click on *Social Studies* at http://www.mcdougallittel.com

The Industrial Age **415**

OBJECTIVES

1. To identify the role of the railroads in unifying the country.

2. To list positive and negative effects of railroads on the nation's economy.

3. To summarize reasons for, and outcomes of, the demand for railroad reform.

SKILLBUILDERS

- Understanding geography: location, place, p. 418
- Interpreting political cartoons, p. 420

CRITICAL THINKING

- Analyzing issues, p. 417
- Recognizing effects, p. 418
- Analyzing motives, p. 419
- Summarizing, pp. 419, 420
- Clarifying, p. 420
- Analyzing causes, p. 420
- Making decisions, p. 420
- Synthesizing, p. 420

FOCUS & MOTIVATE

▶ *Starting with the Student*

- What name might students give the present age? *Possible Response: "The Age of the Car" or "The Age of the Computer."* In formulating their answers, have them consider the technology that exerts the most influence on all aspects of American life.
- Do they think the railroads may have played a similar role in American life in the late 19th century? Why or why not?

MORE ABOUT . . .
Pullman, Illinois

George Pullman kept costs in his company town low by standardizing the design of the houses and by prefabricating the materials in Pullman shops. The town of Pullman became a part of Chicago in 1889.

② The Age of the Railroads

TERMS & NAMES
- transcontinental railroad
- George M. Pullman
- Crédit Mobilier
- *Munn* v. *Illinois*
- Interstate Commerce Act

LEARN ABOUT the growth and consolidation of the railroads
TO UNDERSTAND their influence on the expansion of industry.

The town of Pullman was carefully laid out and strictly controlled.

ONE AMERICAN'S STORY

In October 1884, economist Richard Ely visited the town of Pullman, Illinois, just south of Chicago, to write about it for *Harper's* magazine. At first, Ely was impressed with the atmosphere of order, planning, and well-being in the town George M. Pullman had designed for the employees of his railroad-car factory. After talking at length with a dissatisfied company officer, Walter E. Burrows, Ely concluded that the town of Pullman had a fatal flaw: it restricted its residents. Pullman employees were compelled to obey rules in which they had no say. Ely concluded that "the idea of Pullman is un-American."

A PERSONAL VOICE
It is benevolent, well-wishing feudalism [a repressive medieval social system], which desires the happiness of the people, but in such a way as shall please the authorities. . . . If free American institutions are to be preserved, we want no race reared as underlings. . . . [The town should include] cooperative features [that would] awaken in the residents an interest and pride in Pullman.

RICHARD T. ELY, "Pullman: A Social Study"

As the railroads grew, their influence extended to every facet of American life, including, as in the town of Pullman, the personal lives of its citizens. They determined the time standard of the country and influenced the growth of towns and communities. The unchecked power of railroad companies led to widespread abuses, however, which spurred citizens to demand and win federal regulation of the industry.

Railroads Span Time and Space

Chinese laborers did dangerous work blasting through the Sierra Nevada to lay track for the Central Pacific Railroad.

Railroads had captured the imagination of Americans ever since the 1830s, when Horatio Allen imported the first steam locomotive from Britain. The iron horse could cross vast distances and terrains that exhausted horses and excluded riverboats. Rails made local transit reliable and westward expansion possible for business as well as for people. Realizing how important railroads were to the settlement of the West and the development of the country, the government made huge land grants and loans to the railroad companies.

A NATIONAL NETWORK By 1856, the railroads extended west to the Mississippi River, and three years later, they crossed the Missouri. A decade later, crowds across the United States cheered as the Central Pacific and Union Pacific Railroads met at Promontory, Utah, on May 10, 1869. A golden spike marked the linking of the nation by the first **transcontinental railroad.** Other transcontinental lines followed, and regional lines multiplied as well. At the start of the Civil War, the nation had about 30,000 miles of track. By 1890, that figure was nearly seven times higher.

ROMANCE AND REALITY The railroads lent romance to long-distance travel by bringing the dreams of unsettled land, adventure, and a fresh start within the

SECTION 2 RESOURCES

PRINT RESOURCES

IN-DEPTH RESOURCES: UNIT 4
Guided Reading, p. 20
Literature: *from* "The Bride Comes to Yellow Sky" by Stephen Crane

ACCESS FOR STUDENTS ACQUIRING ENGLISH
Guided Reading (Spanish), p. 140

FORMAL ASSESSMENT
Section Quiz, p. 174

ALTERNATIVE ASSESSMENT BOOK
See forms for supporting and scoring alternative activities.

TECHNOLOGY RESOURCES

CRITICAL THINKING TRANSPARENCIES
CT48, Horizontal Consolidation and Vertical Integration

CD-ROM *Grolier Multimedia Encyclopedia*

VIDEO *American Portfolio: A Videodisc for U.S. History* user's guide, pp. 135–137

INTERNET McDougal Littell Learning On-Line
http://www.mcdougallittell.com

grasp of many Americans. This romance was made possible, however, only at the expense of the railroad workers, whose lives were stark and harsh. The Central Pacific Railroad employed thousands of Chinese immigrants, and the Union Pacific hired Irish immigrants and desperate, out-of-work Civil War veterans to lay track across treacherous terrain. Accidents, pneumonia, and other diseases maimed and killed thousands of men each year. In 1888, when the first railroad statistics were published, the casualties totaled more than 2,000 employees killed and 20,000 injured.

All railroad workers—whether surveyors, tracklayers, or engineers, firemen, and brakemen—faced difficult conditions and numerous hazards for very little pay. As an employee of the Baltimore and Ohio Railroad complained, "We eat our hard bread and tainted meat two days old on sooty cars up the road, and when we come home, find our children gnawing on bones and our wives complaining that they cannot even buy hominy and molasses for food."

Although the railroads paid all their employees poorly, Asians and African Americans usually earned less than whites. The average pay for whites working an eight-hour day was $40 to $60 a month plus free meals. Chinese immigrants hired by the Central Pacific performed similar tasks from dawn to dusk for about $35 a month—and they had to supply their own food. The immigrants' working conditions were particularly miserable as well. In 1866, for example, the railroad hired them to dig a tunnel through a granite mountain. For five months of that year, the Chinese lived and worked in camps surrounded by 40 feet of snow. Hundreds of the men were buried in avalanches or later found frozen, still clutching their shovels or picks.

RAILROAD TIME In spite of these difficult working conditions, the railroad laborers helped to transform the country from a collection of individual localities into a united nation. Though linked in space, each community still operated on its own time, with noon when the sun was overhead. The time in Boston, for example, was almost 12 minutes later than the time in New York. Illinois had 27 different local times and Wisconsin, 38. Travelers riding from Maine to California had to reset their watches at least 20 times.

To remedy this problem, in 1870, Professor C. F. Dowd proposed that the earth's surface should be divided into 24 time zones, one for each hour of the day. The zones would begin at Greenwich, England, which is at 0° longitude. He suggested that the United States institute four zones: Eastern, Central, Mountain, and Pacific. The railroad companies endorsed Dowd's plan enthusiastically, and many towns followed suit.

Finally, on November 18, 1883, railroad crews and towns across the country synchronized their watches. In 1884, an international conference set worldwide

HISTORICAL SPOTLIGHT

RAILROAD LORE

As the railroads expanded, they left a lasting mark on American culture as well as on its economy. People hung pictures of famous trains on their walls and adopted railroad phrases such as "working up a full head of steam" and "getting sidetracked."

The songs that railroad laborers sang as they worked, such as "I've Been Working on the Railroad" and "The Wabash Cannonball," soon gained widespread popularity. Tall tales, anecdotes, and romantic lore about hoboes who rode the rails spread faster than the lines themselves.

Even the railroad companies got into the game. The Erie railroad printed so many anecdotes, verses, and jokes on its timetables that passengers began calling it the "Erie Joke Book."

Railroad workers in Armstrong, Kansas, show off their "iron horses" like prize thoroughbreds in a stable.

Reading the Map Have students study the distribution of railroads throughout the country and the land forms associated with various regions. What connections can they draw? *Possible Answer: The greatest concentration of railroads is in the relatively flat Midwest.*

Extension Have students trace possible railroad routes from Boston to Sacramento, from Cleveland to Los Angeles, or from Seattle to Omaha.

OBJECTIVE
② INSTRUCT

Opportunities and Opportunists

▶ **Discussing Key Ideas**
- The growth of railroad lines promotes trade and interdependence among cities and leads to the development of new markets.
- Communities of workers spring up, including company-managed, planned towns.
- Some corrupt industrialists make huge profits at the expense of workers and stockholders.

ANOTHER PERSPECTIVE
On the Wrong Track

Ask students why people might resist change. Have them write a paragraph objecting to a modern development, such as supersonic air travel, e-mail, or cellular telephones.

Major Railroad Lines, 1870–1890

Time Zones
- Eastern
- Central
- Mountain
- Pacific

···· Railroads by 1870
···· Railroads by 1890

GEOGRAPHY SKILLBUILDER
LOCATION *What factor contributed to the rapid growth of Chicago, Minneapolis, and Denver during the 1870s and 1880s?*
PLACE *Which state was served by the fewest major railroads?*

Skillbuilder Answer
Location: Their location as rail hubs **Place:** Nevada

ANOTHER PERSPECTIVE

ON THE WRONG TRACK
While the railroads captured the imagination of most 19th-century Americans, there were those who didn't get on the bandwagon. For example, the writer Herman Melville raged against the smoke-belching iron horse and the waves of change it set in motion the way his character Captain Ahab raged against the white whale and the sea in *Moby Dick.* "Hark! here comes that old dragon again—that gigantic gadfly . . . snort! puff! scream! Great improvements of the age," Melville fumed. "Who wants to travel so fast? My grandfather did not, and he was no fool."

time zones that incorporated railroad time, although the U.S. Congress didn't officially adopt railroad time as the standard for the nation until 1918.

A PERSONAL VOICE
The sun will be requested to rise and set by railroad time. . . . People will have to marry by railroad time and die by railroad time. Ministers will be required to preach by railroad time, banks will open and close by railroad time; in fact, the Railroad Convention has taken charge of the time business, and the people may as well set about adjusting their affairs in accordance with its decree.
EDITORIAL IN THE *INDIANAPOLIS SENTINEL*, November 1883

As strong a unifying force as the railroads were, however, they also opened the way for abuses that led to social and economic unrest.

Opportunities and Opportunists

The growth of the railroads influenced not only Americans' concepts of time and space but also the industries and businesses in which Americans worked. Iron, coal, steel, lumber, and glass industries grew rapidly as they tried to keep pace with the railroads' demand for raw materials and parts. The rapid spread of railroad lines also fostered the growth of towns, helped establish new markets and offered rich opportunities for both visionaries and profiteers.

NEW TOWNS AND MARKETS By linking previously isolated cities, towns, and settlements, the railroads promoted trade and interdependence. As part of a nationwide network of suppliers and markets, individual towns began to specialize in particular products. Chicago soon became known for its stockyards and Minneapolis for its grain industries, and these cities prospered by selling mass quantities of their products to the entire country. New towns and communities also grew

THINK THROUGH HISTORY
B. *Recognizing Effects* How might the development of industry been affected if the railroads had not existed?

B. Answer Industry would have developed more slowly and most businesses probably would have been smaller and more local.

Making Connections Across Time

Railroads Today Ask students the reasons for and the effects of current cutbacks in railroad service. *Railroads can't accommodate the fast pace of modern life, and they have lost passengers to both airlines and high-speed interstate buses. Also, tracks have not been properly maintained, leading to slowdowns and accidents. The railroads now serve mainly as middlemen—piggy-back freight haulers that transport containers loaded directly from ships to connecting points where they are unloaded, connected to cabs, and trucked the rest of their journey by road.*

Exploring Themes

Science and Technology The new technology that contributed to the rapid growth of the railroads and, in turn, benefitted from them had negative as well as positive effects on society. Ask students to consider the effects on different groups of people, such as farmers, ranchers, Native Americans, settlers, and business owners. Based on these negative effects, what lessons can be learned from the rapid growth of the railroads? *Possible Answer: New technology brings not only opportunity but breeds opportunists, individuals who seize the opportunity to profit at the expense of others.*

up along the railroad lines. Cities as diverse as Abilene, Kansas; Flagstaff, Arizona; Denver, Colorado; and Seattle, Washington, all owed their prosperity, if not their very existence, to the railroads.

PULLMAN The railroads helped cities not only grow up, but branch out as well. In 1880, for example, **George M. Pullman** built a factory for manufacturing sleepers and other railroad cars on the prairie miles from the center of Chicago. Since increasing demand for the Pullman Company's cars required a large and steady workforce, he built a town nearby for his employees. In 1881, the first resident moved in.

Pullman's idea of a company town for his employees was inspired in part by New England textile manufacturers, who had traditionally provided housing for their workers. Pullman was a model town, providing clean, well-constructed brick houses and apartment buildings with at least one window in every room—a luxury for city dwellers. In addition, the town offered its residents medical and legal offices, shops, a church, a library, a theater, and an athletic field.

As Richard Ely observed, however, the town of Pullman remained firmly under company control. For example, residents were not allowed to loiter on their front steps or to drink alcohol. Pullman hoped that his tightly controlled environment would ensure a stable workforce. The widespread dissatisfaction of employees like Walter Burrows proved Pullman wrong, however. The situation worsened and led to a violent strike in 1893.

CRÉDIT MOBILIER The desire for control and profit that led Pullman to create his company town—and that enraged many of his employees —was common among industrialists. Some railroad magnates, or powerful and influential industrialists, carried it even further into self-serving corruption. In one of the most infamous schemes, in 1868, stockholders in the Union Pacific Railroad formed a construction company called **Crédit Mobilier** that enabled them to skim off railroad money for themselves. They gave this company a contract to lay track at two to three times the actual cost—and pocketed the profits. To prevent government meddling, they donated shares of stock to about 20 representatives in Congress.

A congressional investigation of the company, spurred by reports in the *New York Sun*, eventually found that the officers of the Union Pacific had pocketed up to $23 million in stocks, bonds, and cash. Testimony implicated such well-known and respected federal officials as Vice-President Schuyler Colfax, House Speaker James G. Blaine, and Congressman James Garfield, who later became president. Although these public figures made off with their profits scot-free, the reputation of the Grant administration and the Republican Party was tarnished.

The Grange and the Railroads

The corruption in the railroads further enraged the people who relied on this means of transport for their living. Farmers were especially affected, and the Grangers began demanding governmental control over the railroads.

RAILROAD ABUSES Farmers were angry with railroad companies for a host of reasons. They were upset by misuse of government land grants, which the railroads sold to other businesses rather than to settlers to promote westward expansion, as the government intended. The railroads also entered into formal agreements to fix prices and keep farmers in their debt. In addition, they charged different customers different rates, often demanding more for a short haul—for which there was no alternative carrier—than they did for a long haul.

C. Answer Employees resented having their personal lives controlled by their employer.

THINK THROUGH HISTORY
C. Analyzing Motives Why did the residents of the Pullman company town resent the company?

D. Answer By charging too much for railroad construction, keeping the extra money for themselves, and paying off government officials.

THINK THROUGH HISTORY
D. Summarizing How did railroad owners use the Crédit Mobilier company to make huge, undeserved profits?

Pullman cars brought luxury to the rails, as shown in this advertisement from about 1890.

The Grange and the Railroads

▶ ***Starting with the Student***
Remind students what they learned in Chapter 13 about the problems farmers had with the railroads. List some of those complaints on the board: *high prices to ship goods to market; railroads' attempts to control prices for the sale and storage of grain.*

▶ ***Discussing Key Ideas***
• Farmers resent abuses inflicted on them by the railroads.
• The Grangers take political action against the railroads.
• Controversy arises over regulation of the railroads.
• The Supreme Court rules that railroads are involved in interstate commerce and should be federally regulated.
• The financial breakdown of many railroads triggers a national economic collapse.
• Railroads begin consolidating—a trend that other businesses follow.

The Industrial Age **419**

Cooperative Activity: Debating Company Towns

Task: Students will debate the pros and cons of towns owned and operated by companies for their workers and will write evaluations of the debate.

Purpose: To understand how individual points of view on a historical issue can differ widely.

Activity: Small groups of students will choose lots to determine their position on the issue. Groups will then research their position, considering why companies built the towns, why workers chose to live there, advantages and disadvantages to both the company and

the workers, and alternatives for both parties. Groups should take turns debating one another, with the rest of the class evaluating the outcome of the debate.

📁 ***Building a Portfolio*** Students who add their materials to their portfolios should indicate their contribution to the debate and include an evaluation of their group's performance.

ALTERNATIVE ASSESSMENT BOOK
Standards for Evaluating a Cooperative Activity

Standards for Evaluation
Evaluations should . . .

• identify sound research and logical presentation
• analyze oral skills and use of persuasive techniques
• include specific details to support arguments

Teacher's Edition **419**

Reading the Cartoon
What do the strings that are attached to the trains suggest about how these tycoons controlled the railroads?

Extension Have students write a caption for the cartoon that helps the reader understand it.

ASSESS & RETEACH

Section 2 Assessment

Have students work in small groups to answer the questions. Have them indicate the portion of the text that best substantiates each answer.

Self-Assessment

Have students write one or two sentences about the most surprising thing they learned in this section.

Section Quiz

FORMAL ASSESSMENT
Section Quiz, p. 174

Reteach

Have a small group of students volunteer to present a summary of the main ideas of the section to the class.

CLOSE

The growth of the railroads affected every facet of American life. Their eventual consolidation inaugurated the age of big business.

GRANGER LAWS In response to these abuses by the railroads, the Grangers took political action. They sponsored state and local political candidates, elected legislators, and pressed for laws to protect their interests. In 1871, as a result of their pressure, Illinois authorized a commission "to establish maximum freight and passenger rates and prohibit discrimination." In the wake of this success, Grangers throughout the West convinced state legislators to pass similar laws.

The Grangers also set up a fund to help citizens sue for violations of these Granger laws. The railroads fought back, challenging the constitutionality of the regulatory laws. In 1877, however, in the case of **Munn v. Illinois,** the Supreme Court upheld the Granger laws by a vote of seven to two. The states thus won the right to regulate the railroads for the benefit of farmers and consumers. The Grangers also helped establish an important principle—the federal government's right to regulate private industry to serve the public interest.

INTERSTATE COMMERCE ACT The Grangers' triumph was short-lived, however. In 1886, the Supreme Court ruled that a state could not set rates on interstate commerce—railroad traffic that either came from or was going to another state. In response to public outrage, Congress passed the **Interstate Commerce Act** in 1887. This act reestablished the right of the federal government to supervise railroad activities and established a five-member Interstate Commerce Commission (ICC) for that purpose. The ICC had difficulty regulating railroad rates because of a long legal process and resistance from the railroads. The final blow to the Commission came in 1897, when the Supreme Court ruled that it could not set maximum railroad rates. Not until 1906, when President Theodore Roosevelt began his campaign for railroad regulation, did the ICC gain the power it needed to be effective.

THE PANIC OF 1893 Despite the inability of the ICC to regulate the railroads, corporate abuses, mismanagement, overbuilding, and intense competition pushed many railroads to the brink of bankruptcy. Because the railroads were so crucial to the nation's economy, their financial problems played a major role in a nationwide economic collapse. The Panic of 1893 was the worst depression the nation had seen: 500 banks and 15,000 businesses failed, and 3 million people lost their jobs. By the middle of 1894, a quarter of the nation's railroads had been taken over by banks. Large firms such as J. P. Morgan & Company and entrepreneurs such as Cornelius Vanderbilt and his son William seized many of the railroads. As the 20th century dawned, seven powerful companies held sway over two-thirds of the nation's railroad tracks.

Businesses of all kinds soon followed the path of consolidation that the railroads had blazed. The age of big business had begun.

**SKILLBUILDER
INTERPRETING POLITICAL CARTOONS** *What does this railroad giant, formed by William Vanderbilt (top), Cyrus W. Field (bottom left), and Jay Gould (bottom right), imply about the railroad trusts?*

Skillbuilder Answer They exerted total control over the nation's railroad system.

E. Answer The farmers took united political action and pressed legislators to enact laws to protect them.

**THINK THROUGH HISTORY
E. Clarifying**
How did the Grangers, who were largely poor farmers, do battle with the giant railroad companies?

F. Answer Corporate abuses and mismanagement, overbuilding, and intense competition.

**THINK THROUGH HISTORY
F. Analyzing Causes** What were the causes of the Panic of 1893?

Section 2 Assessment

1. **TERMS & NAMES**
   Identify:
   • transcontinental railroad
   • George M. Pullman
   • Crédit Mobilier
   • *Munn v. Illinois*
   • Interstate Commerce Act

2. **SUMMARIZING** Recreate the web below on your paper and fill in effects of the rapid growth of railroads.

   Rapid growth of railroads

3. **MAKING DECISIONS** Do you think the government and private citizens could have done more to curb the corruption and power of the railroads? Give examples to support your opinion.

   THINK ABOUT
   • the reasons that the railroads had power
   • the rights of railroad customers and workers
   • the scope of government regulations

4. **SYNTHESIZING** Do you agree or disagree with Herman Melville's opinion of the railroads as expressed in "Another Perspective"? Why or why not?

   THINK ABOUT
   • effects of the railroads on business and industry
   • effects of the railroads on daily life
   • aspects of life before the railroads

420 CHAPTER 14

ANSWERS

1. TERMS & NAMES

transcontinental railroad, p. 416

George M. Pullman, p. 419

Crédit Mobilier, p. 419

Munn v. *Illinois*, p. 420

Interstate Commerce Act, p. 420

2. SUMMARIZING

Possible Responses:
Governmental regulation of private industry; growth of towns and cities; creation of nationwide market; greed and corruption; consolidation of railroads,

3. MAKING DECISIONS

Possible Responses:
Yes—Consumer boycotts, greater government regulation, and prosecution of corrupt officials.
No—*Munn* v. *Illinois* broke new ground in government's regulation of industry; enacting additional regulation would take a long time.

4. SYNTHESIZING

Possible Responses:
Some students will say that Melville's opposition to change was stubborn and old fashioned. Others may agree that the noise and social changes brought by the railroads were unpleasant.

③ Big Business Emerges

TERMS & NAMES
• Andrew Carnegie
• vertical integration
• horizontal consolidation
• Social Darwinism
• monopoly
• holding company
• John D. Rockefeller
• trust
• Sherman Antitrust Act

LEARN ABOUT Social Darwinism and the rise of industry
TO UNDERSTAND the government's attempt to regulate big business.

ONE AMERICAN'S STORY

Born in Scotland to penniless parents, **Andrew Carnegie** came to this country in 1848, at age 13. He worked 12 hours a day, six days a week in a cotton mill. Several years later, he became a messenger for a telegraph service and worked his way up to become a skilled telegrapher and head of the messenger service. Impressed by the boy's energy, Thomas A. Scott, the local superintendent of the Pennsylvania Railroad, hired him as a private secretary. He was glad he did.

One evening when Scott was out, Carnegie singlehandedly relayed messages that unsnarled a tangle of freight and passenger trains. Scott repaid him by giving him a chance to buy stock in a promising company. Since Carnegie had no money saved, his mother mortgaged the family home to make the purchase possible. Soon Carnegie received his first dividend, or share of the profits.

> ### A PERSONAL VOICE
> One morning a white envelope was lying upon my desk, addressed in a big John Hancock hand to "Andrew Carnegie, Esquire." . . . All it contained was a check for ten dollars upon the Gold Exchange Bank of New York. I shall remember that check as long as I live. . . . It gave me the first penny of revenue from capital—something I had not worked for with the sweat of my brow. "Eureka!" I cried, "Here's the goose that lays the golden eggs."
>
> **ANDREW CARNEGIE,** *Autobiography of Andrew Carnegie*

Andrew Carnegie was one of the first industrial moguls to make his own fortune. His rise from rags to riches, along with his passion for giving his fortune away to charities and other noble causes, made him a model of the American success story.

Andrew Carnegie

Carnegie's Innovations

Carnegie was so inspired by his first investment experience that he continued buying stock in new companies and inventing new business practices. By 1865, he had earned so much money in dividends that he was able to leave his job at the Pennsylvania Railroad. He entered the steel business in 1873, shortly after touring a British steel mill and witnessing the awesome spectacle of the Bessemer process in operation. By 1899, the Carnegie Company manufactured more steel than all the factories in Great Britain.

MANAGEMENT TECHNIQUES Carnegie's success was due in part to management practices that he initiated and that soon became widespread. First, he continually searched for ways to make better products more cheaply. He incorporated new techniques and machinery in his plants and hired chemists and metallurgists to improve the quality of his steel. Detailed accounting systems enabled him to track the precise cost of each process and every item. Second, he attracted talented people to his operations. He hired top-notch assistants, offered them stock in the company, and encouraged competition among them to increase production and cut costs.

A. Answer
Efficient production methods, quality control, cost tracking, and commitment and competition among competent workers.

THINK THROUGH HISTORY
A. Summarizing
What were Andrew Carnegie's management techniques?

The Industrial Age **421**

SECTION 3 RESOURCES

PRINT RESOURCES

IN-DEPTH RESOURCES: UNIT 4
Guided Reading, p. 21
Skillbuilder Practice: Forming Opinions, p. 23
Primary Sources: *from* "Wealth and Its Uses" by Andrew Carnegie, p. 27; from *History of the Standard Oil Company,* p. 28
American Lives: Andrew Carnegie, p. 33

ACCESS FOR STUDENTS ACQUIRING ENGLISH
Guided Reading (Spanish), p. 141
Skillbuilder Practice: Forming Opinions (Spanish), p. 143

FORMAL ASSESSMENT
Section Quiz, p. 175

ALTERNATIVE ASSESSMENT BOOK
See forms for supporting and scoring alternative activities.

TECHNOLOGY RESOURCES

HUMANITIES TRANSPARENCIES
H35, "The Bosses of the Senate": American antitrust cartoon, 1889, by Joesph Keppler

CD-ROM Our Times
Electronic Library of Primary Sources

VIDEO *American Portfolio: A Videodisc for U.S. History* user's guide, p. 138

INTERNET McDougal Littell Learning On-Line
http://www.mcdougallittell.com

Section 3 Overview

OBJECTIVES

① To identify management and business strategies that contributed to the success of business tycoons such as Andrew Carnegie.

② To explain Social Darwinism and its effects on society.

③ To cite methods used by ruthless businessmen to eliminate free competition.

④ To describe the reasons for the slow industrialization of the south.

SKILLBUILDER

• Interpreting political cartoons, p. 424

CRITICAL THINKING

• Summarizing, pp. 421, 423, 425
• Synthesizing, pp. 422, 425
• Recognizing effects, p. 422
• Forming opinions, p. 424
• Evaluating, p. 425
• Analyzing, p. 425

FOCUS & MOTIVATE

▶ *Starting with the Student*
Ask students whether they think a poor person could become a billionaire in today's world. What qualities do they think such a person would need?

OBJECTIVE
① **INSTRUCT**

Carnegie's Innovations

▶ *Discussing Key Ideas*
• Andrew Carnegie uses new management techniques to improve the quality and cut the cost of producing steel.
• New business strategies enable Carnegie to control the steel industry.

IN-DEPTH RESOURCES: UNIT 4
Guided Reading, p. 21
American Lives: Andrew Carnegie, p. 33

ACCESS FOR STUDENTS ACQUIRING ENGLISH
Guided Reading (Spanish), p. 141

BUSINESS STRATEGIES In addition to improving his own manufacturing operation, Carnegie attempted to control the entire steel industry as much as possible. He did this mainly by a process known as **vertical integration,** in which he bought out all his suppliers—coal and iron mines, ore freighters, and railroad lines. Controlling the raw materials, transportation systems, and every stage of the manufacturing process gave him total power over the quality and cost of his product.

Carnegie also attempted to buy out competing steel producers in a process known as **horizontal consolidation.** In this process, companies producing similar products merge. Having gained control over both his suppliers and his competition, Carnegie almost monopolized the steel industry. By the time he sold his business in 1901, the Carnegie Company was producing 80 percent of the nation's steel.

Social Darwinism and Business

Carnegie explained his extraordinary success by pointing to his hard work, shrewd investments, and innovative business practices. Late 19th-century social philosophers, on the other hand, thought that Carnegie's achievement could be explained by a new theory—Social Darwinism.

PRINCIPLES OF SOCIAL DARWINISM The philosophy of **Social Darwinism** grew out of English biologist Charles Darwin's theory of biological evolution, which was published in the *Origin of Species* in 1859. Darwin had observed not only that individuals of a particular species differ, but also that some individuals flourish and pass their traits along to the next generation, while others do not. He explained this as a process of natural selection, which he claimed weeds out weaker individuals and enables the strongest to survive.

Darwin's biological theories captured the interest of economists, who used his ideas to justify laissez faire (a French term meaning "allow to do"). In practice, laissez faire translated into an absence of regulation in the marketplace. In his 1862 book *First Principles,* British philosopher Herbert Spencer spelled out the principles of Social Darwinism—that free competition in the economy, like natural selection in the biological arena, would ensure survival of the fittest. An economics professor at Yale University, William Graham Sumner, went even farther in saying that success and failure in business were actually governed by natural law and that no one—particularly the government—had the right to intervene.

Herbert Spencer

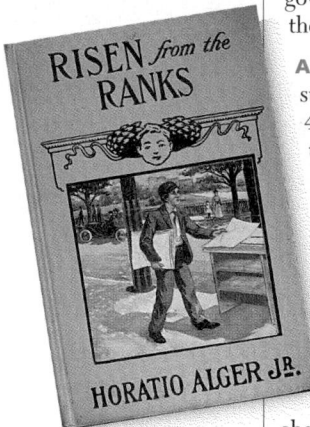

Horatio Alger's books promoted the possibility of rags-to-riches success for anyone willing to work hard.

422 CHAPTER 14

A NEW DEFINITION OF SUCCESS In providing support for the survival and success of the most capable, Social Darwinism naturally made sense to the 4,000 millionaires who had emerged since the Civil War. However, because the theory supported the notion of individual responsibility and blame, it also appealed to the Protestant work ethic of many Americans. Social Darwinism supported the belief that riches were simply a sign of God's favor and that the poor must be lazy or inferior people who deserved their lot in life.

Popular literature reinforced the emerging cult of the individual. Horatio Alger was one of the most successful writers of the time, and readers gobbled up his inspirational stories. His 135 dime novels, which sold millions of copies each, often featured an orphan or street urchin who rose to good fortune through model behavior. Though Alger's characters were often extraordinarily lucky, their virtue made them deserve their good fortune. While Alger's stories supported the work ethic, they implied that there was no shame in humble or lowly beginnings. Instead, they focused on the opportunities that awaited those who were upright, energetic, and smart, and popularized the goal of "pulling yourself up by your own bootstraps."

Fewer Control More

Although some economists and businessmen endorsed the "natural law" of competition in theory, they did not give themselves over to it wholeheartedly in practice. In fact, some entrepreneurs actually did everything they could do to control or eliminate the competition that threatened the growth of their business empires.

GROWTH AND CONSOLIDATION Many industrialists took the approach that "if you can't beat them, join them." That approach set the stage for the rise of an oligopoly—a market in which only a few sellers provided a particular product. An oligopoly was formed when businesses producing similar products joined together. This horizontal consolidation often took the form of a merger. Mergers usually occurred when one corporation bought out the stock of another. A firm that managed to buy out all its competitors could achieve a **monopoly,** or complete control over its industry's production, quality, wages paid, and prices charged.

One way to create a monopoly was to set up a **holding company,** a corporation that did nothing but buy out the stock of other companies. Headed by banker J. P. Morgan, United States Steel was one of the most successful holding companies. In 1901, when it bought the largest manufacturer, Carnegie Steel, for almost $500 million, it became the world's largest business organization.

Corporations such as the Standard Oil Company, established by **John D. Rockefeller,** took a different approach to mergers and joined with competing companies in a trust agreement. Participants in a **trust** turned their stock over to a group of trustees—people who ran the separate companies as one large corporation. In return, the companies received certificates that entitled them to dividends on profits earned by the trust. Trusts were not legal mergers, however. Rockefeller made the most of this legal gray area to gain total control of the oil industry in America.

ROCKEFELLER AND THE ROBBER BARONS Rockefeller's achievement was remarkable. In 1870, the Standard Oil Company of Ohio processed two or three percent of the country's crude oil. Within a decade it controlled 90 percent of the refining business. Rather than passing savings along to employees or consumers, however, he reaped large profits. He paid his employees extremely low wages and drove his competitors out of business by selling his oil at a lower price than it cost to produce it. Then, when he had control of the market, he hiked prices far above their original level to gain back his money. Rockefeller's agents also used their clout to win rebates on railroad shipping costs and kickbacks from the higher fees railroads charged to other firms.

Alarmed at the ruthless tactics of industrialists, critics began to call them robber barons, after the feudal lords who had owned estates in Europe during the Middle Ages. Men such as Rockefeller, Morgan, and Carnegie defended their wealth by pointing to the charities they sponsored and the philanthropy in which they engaged. Indeed, they often gave away fortunes that others could only dream about. Although Rockefeller held onto most of his wealth, he still gave away over $500 million, establishing the Rockefeller Foundation, providing $80 million to found the University of Chicago, and creating a medical institute that helped stamp out yellow fever.

Andrew Carnegie actually gave away less money than Rockefeller did—a mere $325 million—but he was a fiery evangelist for his self-styled "gospel of wealth." He believed that people should be allowed

THINK THROUGH HISTORY
D. Summarizing
What strategies enabled big business to eliminate competition?

D. Answer
Horizontal and vertical mergers, and the creation of monopolies, holding companies, and trusts.

The Industrial Age **423**

"WHAT A FUNNY LITTLE GOVERNMENT!"

SKILLBUILDER INTERPRETING POLITICAL CARTOONS *How does this cartoon depict the power of Rockefeller's Standard Oil empire?*

to make as much money as they could but then should pass it along to worthy causes. Carnegie's donations—90 percent of the wealth he accumulated during his lifetime—helped fund Carnegie Hall in New York City, the Carnegie Foundation, and 3,000 libraries across the nation. His fortune still supports the arts and learning today. "It will be a great mistake for the community to shoot the millionaires," he said, "for they are the bees that make the most honey, and contribute most to the hive even after they have gorged themselves full."

SHERMAN ANTITRUST ACT Despite Carnegie's defense of millionaires, the government took a stand against monopolies. Out of concern that expanding corporations would stifle free competition, in 1890 Congress passed the **Sherman Antitrust Act.** The act stated that any attempt to interfere with free trade among the states or internationally by forming a trust was illegal.

Enforcement of the Sherman act proved to be nearly impossible, however. Because the act didn't clearly define terms such as *trust*, prosecuting companies was not easy. In addition, if firms such as Standard Oil felt pressure from the

POINT ▶ COUNTERPOINT

POINT
"The tycoons of the late 19th century were ruthless robber barons."

Some historians and journalists charge that 19th-century industrialists built their great fortunes at the expense of competitors, customers, and workers. They point to the monopolies and combinations that guaranteed industrialists cheap labor and allowed them to set their own prices.

They also point out that the industrialists made hundreds of millions of dollars, while the average industrial worker earned $350 a year. The novelist Edward Bellamy noted that "the individual laborer, who had been relatively important to the small employer, was reduced to insignificance and powerlessness against the great corporation."

The manufacturer George Rice, who was forced out of business by the Standard Oil Company, struck out bitterly against that industrial giant. He declared that "there is no crime in the calendar—save possibly murder—of which it is not guilty or capable. It is the blue-ribbon enemy of everything moral."

The journalist Ida Tarbell agreed about the industrialists. "I never objected to their corporate form. I was willing that they should combine and grow as big and rich as they could, but by legitimate means. But they never played fair."

COUNTERPOINT
"The tycoons of the late 19th century were effective captains of industry."

Many prominent industrialists defended their wealth and achievements in both words and deeds. Some contributed generously to educational and cultural institutions, and they justified their techniques as good business practice. John D. Rockefeller, for example, declared, "I believe in the spirit of combination and cooperation when properly conducted. . . . It helps to reduce waste, and waste is a dissipation of power."

The historian Joseph Pusateri has since noted that Standard Oil "transformed an industry marked by chronic excess capacity, instability, and general aimlessness, into one of the cutting edges of an enormous American economic expansion."

Another historian, H. Wayne Morgan, went even further when he stated, "The stereotype of the Robber Baron is much overdrawn. It must be balanced with the fuller picture, showing the new technology he often brought to his industry, the wealth and resources he developed for the economy in general, [and] the social good he sometimes did with his money." The captain of industry, Morgan suggested, should be a model for every working person. Anyone, he implied, could become another Rockefeller or Carnegie.

INTERACT WITH HISTORY

1. **ANALYZING ISSUES** On which points do critics and admirers of the tycoons agree? With which side do you agree?

   SEE SKILLBUILDER HANDBOOK, PAGE 1046.

2. **WRITING A DIALOGUE** Research the point of view of industrialists and workers and write a dialogue between characters representing each point of view. For additional support for the arguments, use library resources.

424 CHAPTER 14

INTERACT WITH HISTORY

1. Analyzing Issues

Possible Answers:
- Industrialists made huge fortunes by applying effective business practices.
- Some students may say that the good the industrialists did with their money justified their business practices. Others may say that their exploitation of workers and the public was unjustified.

2. Writing a Dialogue

You may want to suggest that students use a pro-and-con chart to organize the two sides of the arguments for their dialogues. The framework of their charts may look like this:

Robber Barons or Captains of Industry?

	Pro	Con
Personal gain		
Effective business practices		
Model for working people		
Contribution to society		

government, they simply dissolved their trusts and reorganized into single corporations. The Supreme Court also refused to support the act and threw out seven of the eight cases the federal government brought against trusts. Eventually, the government stopped trying to enforce the Sherman Antitrust Act, and the consolidation of business continued.

Business Boom Bypasses the South

The industrialization that fueled this growth and controversy was concentrated in the North, where natural and urban resources were plentiful. The South, on the other hand, was still trying to recover from physical devastation caused by the Civil War. It lacked capital—money for investment—and had only a few cities, factors which all slowed economic growth.

ECONOMIC CAUSES Before the Civil War, several banks served the South, providing capital for some business and educational ventures. This situation changed after the war, however, when people with capital were unwilling to invest in what they considered to be a poor risk. Northern businesses already owned 90 percent of the stock in the most profitable Southern enterprise, the railroads, which kept Southerners in a stranglehold. The Southern economy remained basically agricultural, with farmers at the mercy of railroad rates. The few brave business entrepreneurs suffered not only from excessive transportation costs, but also from high tariffs on raw materials and manufactured goods that they needed to import. The post-Reconstruction South seemed to have no way to climb out of the pit of economic stagnation.

SOCIAL CAUSES In addition to economic obstacles to industrial growth, social factors were just as powerful. Southern businesses had to compete with well-established Northern companies not only for capital and markets, but also for skilled workers. One Southern businessman complained, "The shops north owe their success largely to the mechanics in their employ. . . . Down here anybody who can pull a monkey wrench and pound his machine with a hammer and cuss the builder for making such a machine is called a mechanic." Growth did take place rapidly, though, in Southern industries such as forestry and mining, and in the tobacco, furniture, and textile industries. This local growth did change and improve the lives of millions of Americans.

Despite the South's delayed entry into the Industrial Age, though, Northern wage earners were not much better off than Southern laborers. This exploitation drew American workers together in a nationwide labor movement to demand their rights.

F. Answer Post-Civil-War devastation and Northern ownership of the railroads made it hard for the South to grow economically.
THINK THROUGH HISTORY
F. Synthesizing *How did economic factors limit industrialization in the South?*

Section 3 Assessment

1. TERMS & NAMES
Identify:
• Andrew Carnegie
• vertical integration
• horizontal consolidation
• Social Darwinism
• monopoly
• holding company
• John D. Rockefeller
• trust
• Sherman Antitrust Act

2. SUMMARIZING Compare the lives and beliefs of Andrew Carnegie and John D. Rockefeller using a Venn diagram.

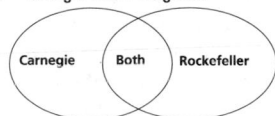
Carnegie   Both   Rockefeller

Write a paragraph defending or criticizing these tycoons' accomplishments.

3. EVALUATING Do you agree or disagree with the principles of Social Darwinism? Support your opinion.

THINK ABOUT
• why some people succeed and others don't
• the responsibility individuals have for each other in a society
• the role of government in its citizens' lives

4. ANALYZING If you were a business consultant at the end of the 19th century, what advice would you offer the people of the South to help them boost their economy?

THINK ABOUT
• differences between the North and the South
• the impact of industrialization on the North
• why the South experienced slow economic development

The Industrial Age **425**

ANSWERS

1. TERMS & NAMES

Andrew Carnegie, p. 421

vertical integration, p. 422

horizontal consolidation, p. 422

Social Darwinism, p. 422

monopoly, p. 423

holding company, p. 423

John D. Rockefeller, p. 423

trust, p. 423

Sherman Antitrust Act, p. 424

2. SUMMARIZING

Entries on the Venn diagram may include the following:
Carnegie: Born in Scotland; steel magnate; used vertical integration to expand; gave away 90 percent of his wealth.
Both: Leaders of business; extremely wealthy; philanthropists.
Rockefeller: Oil magnate; formed trusts; used ruthless tactics; paid low wages; kept most of his wealth.

3. EVALUATING

Possible Responses: **Agree**—In society, as in nature, the strongest or most powerful survive and succeed; **Disagree**—People should cooperate and take responsibility for others, which means sharing the fruits of their success with the less fortunate.

4. ANALYZING

Possible Responses: Southern investors could invest in northern enterprises, turning profits back to the South; Northerners could be asked to open branches of their businesses in the South; Southern businessmen could write proposals for new businesses and ask for loans from Northern banks; people might try to start cottage industries.

1 To describe the exploitation of workers, including women and children.

2 To summarize the emergence and growth of unions.

3 To identify the various types of unions.

4 To explain the violent reactions of industry and government to union strikes.

5 To identify the influence of women in the labor movement.

6 To describe the role of the government in opposing union activity.

SKILLBUILDER

• Interpreting charts, p. 430

CRITICAL THINKING

• Analyzing issues, p. 427
• Contrasting, p. 429
• Summarizing, pp. 430, 433
• Recognizing effects, p. 431
• Clarifying, p. 432
• Identifying causes, p. 433
• Evaluating, p. 433
• Hypothesizing, p. 433

FOCUS & MOTIVATE

▶ **Starting with the Student** Ask students how they would convince school officials to change a policy they didn't like.

OBJECTIVE
1 INSTRUCT

Workers Are Exploited

▶ **Starting with the Student** Discuss with students what they know about working conditions today. Ask them to record this information in a now-and-then chart, which they will complete as they read the section.

Working Conditions

	Now	Then
Day/week	5–5-1/2	6
Hours/day	7–8	12
Benefits	insurance vacation	

(continued on next page)

4 Workers of the Nation Unite

TERMS & NAMES
• Samuel Gompers
• American Federation of Labor (AFL)
• collective bargaining
• Eugene V. Debs
• socialism
• Industrial Workers of the World (IWW)
• scab
• Mary Harris "Mother" Jones

LEARN ABOUT the conditions that led workers to form unions
TO UNDERSTAND the struggles between labor and management.

ONE AMERICAN'S STORY

Seamstress Aurora Phelps had experienced first-hand the changes brought about by industrialization. Like other girls and women in her trade, Phelps saw new production methods reduce the job of a garment worker to a dull, repetitive, and unskilled task. Although these management techniques lowered costs for consumers and increased profits for business owners, they did nothing to improve working conditions for Phelps and other laborers in 1869.

A PERSONAL VOICE

When I was younger, girls learned full trades, now they do not—one stitches seams, another makes buttonholes, and another sews on the buttons. Once girls learned to do all these, and then they learned to cut garments and carried on business. . . . [Now] you can see them in those shops, seated in long rows, crowded together in a hot, close atmosphere, working at piecework, 30, 40, 60 or 100 girls crowded together, working at 20 and 25 cents a day.

AURORA PHELPS, quoted in *The Revolution* by Susan B. Anthony

Women do tedious piecework in a New York hat factory in about 1900.

Workers were tired of seeing their lives grow more difficult and less rewarding as businesses grew bigger and richer during the last half of the 19th century. They decided that they needed to band together to demand better pay and better conditions.

Workers Are Exploited

Industrial innovations angered Aurora Phelps because they diminished workers' skills and sense of accomplishment. The working conditions of the time also included long hours for low pay under substandard conditions.

LONG HOURS AND DANGER Seamstresses, like factory workers in most industries, worked 12 or more hours a day, six days a week. One of the largest employers, the steel mills, often demanded a seven-day work week. Employees were not entitled to vacation, sick leave, unemployment compensation, or reimbursement for injuries suffered on the job.

Yet injuries were commonplace. In 1882, an average of 675 laborers were killed in work-related accidents each week. In 1890, the fatality rate for railroad workers was one in 300. Many of these were brakemen, who had to balance on the icy roofs of speeding railroad cars. Hazardous working conditions abounded in other industries as well. Factories often were dirty, poorly ventilated, and poorly lit; workers had to perform repetitive, mind-dulling tasks hour after hour, often with dangerous or faulty equipment.

WOMEN AND CHILDREN Workers had little choice but to put up with those deplorable conditions in sweatshops. In addition, wages were so low that most families could not survive unless everyone held a job. Between 1890 and 1910,

---

SECTION 4 RESOURCES

PRINT RESOURCES

IN-DEPTH RESOURCES: UNIT 4
Guided Reading, p. 22
Primary Source: Labor Poster, p. 29
American Lives: Mary Harris "Mother" Jones, p. 34

ACCESS FOR STUDENTS ACQUIRING ENGLISH
Guided Reading (Spanish), p. 142

FORMAL ASSESSMENT
Section Quiz, p. 176

ALTERNATIVE ASSESSMENT BOOK
See forms for supporting and scoring alternative activities.

TECHNOLOGY RESOURCES

HUMANITIES TRANSPARENCIES
H14, *The Gun Foundry* by John Furguson Weir

CD-ROM Electronic Library of Primary Sources

VIDEO *American Portfolio: A Videodisc for U.S. History*
user's guide, pp. 141, 148, 160, 166

INTERNET McDougal Littell Learning On-Line
http://www.mcdougallittell.com

for example, the number of women working for wages doubled from 4 million to more than 8 million. Twenty percent of the boys and ten percent of the girls under age 15—some as young as five years old—also held full-time jobs. Many of these children worked from dawn to dusk, wasted by hunger and exhaustion that made them prone to crippling accidents. With little time or energy left for school, child laborers forfeited their futures to help their families make ends meet. Reformer Jacob Riis described conditions faced by the "sweaters" in these tenement workshops.

Many young girls sacrificed their youth and health in sweatshops such as this North Carolina cotton mill.

A PERSONAL VOICE

The bulk of the sweater's work is done in the tenements, which the law that regulates factory labor does not reach. . . . In [them] the child works unchallenged from the day he is old enough to pull a thread. There is no such thing as a dinner hour; men and women eat while they work, and the "day" is lengthened at both ends . . . far into the night.

JACOB RIIS, *How the Other Half Lives*

Most of the work available to women and children was tedious and required few skills; not surprisingly, these jobs paid the lowest wages—often as little as 27 cents for a child's 14-hour day. In 1899, for example, women earned an average of $269 a year, nearly half men's average pay of $498. The very next year Andrew Carnegie made $23 million—with no income tax.

Labor Unions Emerge

THINK THROUGH HISTORY
A. *Analyzing Issues* How did industrial working conditions contribute to the growth of the labor movement?
A. Answer Poor working conditions and low wages forced workers to organize into unions to demand fair treatment.

Laborers thought they at least deserved fair wages and decent working conditions. Business leaders were merging and consolidating their forces, so it seemed reasonable for workers to do the same. Laborers of all types—skilled and unskilled, female and male, black and white—joined together in unions to try to improve their lot.

NATIONAL LABOR UNION The concept of labor unions wasn't a new one. Skilled workers had had small local unions since the early 1800s. The first large-scale national organization of laborers, the National Labor Union (NLU), was formed in 1866 by an ironworker named William H. Sylvis. The NLU consisted of about 300 local unions from 13 states.

To make the union as representative and effective as possible, Sylvis urged local chapters to admit women and African Americans. Although carpenters and cabinetmakers agreed to open their locals to African Americans, other unions refused, leading to the creation of the Colored National Labor Union (CNLU). Nevertheless, NLU membership grew to 640,000; and in 1868, the NLU persuaded Congress to legalize an eight-hour day for government workers. The union gained enough momentum to form its own political party—the Labor Reform Party—and to run its own candidate in the 1872 presidential election.

KNIGHTS OF LABOR While NLU organizers concentrated mainly on linking existing local unions, Uriah Stephens focused his attention on individual workers, and, in 1868, organized the Noble Order of the Knights of Labor. Its motto was "An injury to one is the concern of all."

Membership in the Knights of Labor was officially open to all workers, regardless of race, gender, or degree of skill. Like the NLU, the Knights supported an eight-hour work day and advocated "equal pay for equal work" by men and women. They saw strikes, or refusals to work, as a last resort and instead advocated arbitration, or settlement of disagreements by an impartial person.

HISTORICAL SPOTLIGHT

AFRICAN AMERICANS IN THE LABOR MOVEMENT

In 1869, delegates at a national convention of African Americans were so angered by their exclusion from the NLU that they formed the Colored National Labor Union (CNLU). Led by Isaac Meyers *(above)*, a caulker from Baltimore, the CNLU vigorously avoided strikes and preached cooperation between management and labor. It was committed to political reform and staunchly supported the Republican Party.

The CNLU disbanded in the early 1870s, but many African-American laborers did find a home in the Knights of Labor, the first union to bring blacks into the growing white labor movement.

Despite the union activities of African Americans, management often used them as strikebreakers. Some white union members then retaliated with violence in black communities. Clearly, the unity of the working class had not been achieved.

The Industrial Age **427**

(continued from page 426)

▶ **Discussing Key Ideas**
• Laborers work long hours, often in unsafe conditions, with no benefits.
• Many women and children work at tedious jobs that require little skill and pay low wages to help their families survive.

IN-DEPTH RESOURCES: UNIT 4
Guided Reading, p. 22
Primary Source: Labor Poster, p. 29

ACCESS FOR STUDENTS ACQUIRING ENGLISH
Guided Reading (Spanish), p. 142

OBJECTIVE
② **INSTRUCT**

Labor Unions Emerge

▶ **Discussing Key Ideas**
• Several local unions merge into national organizations.
• Some unions exclude women and African Americans, leading African Americans to form unions of their own.
• Unions use different tactics—some favoring strikes and others, arbitration.

 ELECTRONIC LIBRARY OF PRIMARY SOURCES
On the Goals of Trade Unions by Samuel Gompers

HISTORICAL SPOTLIGHT
African Americans in the Labor Movement
Critical Thinking: Drawing Conclusions Why might the CNLU have preferred to negotiate rather than to strike? *Possible Response: Because its membership was small, strikes might not have been effective.*

TEACHING OPTIONS

Making Connections Across Time

Do Sweatshops Exist Today? Discuss with students whether or not sweatshops exist today. Ask under what conditions they would most likely be found. *Possible Answer: Sweatshops are illegal today, and public awareness and disdain run high. They are most likely to be found where legal regulations are difficult to enforce. Public outcry has also been raised against products made in foreign sweatshops and sold in this country.*

Exploring Themes

The American Dream The necessity of working in sweatshops destroyed many women's and children's dreams. This work not only destroyed their health, but children often dropped out of school or neglected their studies, which handicapped them the rest of their lives. In the assembly-line system that existed in many factories, woman learned only a limited skill, which prevented them from getting better jobs. Discuss how people might maintain their dreams in the face of such hardships.

Teacher's Edition **427**

Union Movements Diverge

▶ **Starting with the Student**
Ask students what attributes they associate with influential leaders. Discuss the importance of leadership in the effectiveness of an organization.

▶ **Discussing Key Ideas**
• Craft unions bring together workers who do similar jobs in different industries.
• Industrial unions include all workers in a specific industry.
• Labor activists share many concerns with socialists.
• Agricultural workers in the West and Southwest also organize into unions.

NOW & THEN
Underage and on the Job

▶ **Starting with the Student**
Ask students if any of them work after school or on weekends. What benefits have they gained from working? What, if any, negative effects has working had on their academic performance and social life?

▶ **Discussing Key Ideas**
• Many modern teenagers hold part-time jobs while going to school.
• In the late 19th and early 20th centuries, many children worked out of necessity.
• Public outcry against the horrendous effects of child labor led to a legal ban.
• Increasing numbers of children still work illegally.

Membership in the Knights of Labor grew slowly, until Terence V. Powderly, a mechanic from Scranton, Pennsylvania, became its head in 1881. Under Powderly's leadership, the Knights expanded from 28,000 members in 1880 to about 700,000 in 1886. Although the Knights of Labor declined rapidly after the failure of a series of strikes, other unions continued to organize.

Union Movements Diverge

As labor activism spread, it diversified, and factions within the union movement emerged. Two major types of unions made great gains under forceful leaders. The labor movement also received support from socialists and social reformers.

CRAFT UNIONISM AND SAMUEL GOMPERS One approach to the organization of labor was craft unionism, which included all skilled workers from many

NOW & THEN

Underage and on the Job

Is working a good thing? Many American teenagers seem to think so. Three out of four high school juniors and seniors work at least part-time, in the evenings and on weekends.

Most do so to earn spending money or to save for college. Typically, they work in low-wage service jobs—at fast-food restaurants or discount stores, for example. Some teenagers work long hours out of economic necessity. Some neglect their schoolwork in the process, but most manage to balance work with educating themselves for the future and enjoying their youth.

Today, part-time jobs teach young people valuable skills, such as discipline and self-reliance.

1885
In the late-19th and early-20th centuries, many urban teenagers and children went to work full-time out of necessity. Factory wages were so low that children often had to work to help support their families. Forced to take on adult responsibilities at an early age, child laborers barely experienced their youth. Going to school to prepare for a brighter future was a luxury these underage workers rarely enjoyed.

1889
The long hours and horrendous working conditions for children like these Pennsylvania coal miners eventually provoked a public backlash. Though it took many years and great effort, state legislatures finally passed laws banning or restricting child labor. In 1938, the federal government followed suit with the Fair Labor Standards Act. This law banned most employment for children and limited teenagers under 18 to jobs outside the manufacturing and construction industries.

INTERACT WITH HISTORY

1. Contrasting

Possible Answers: *Most teenagers who work today do so voluntarily to earn extra money for expenses or for college, not to support their families. They generally work part-time so they can pursue both their education and a social life. The Fair Labor Standards Act protects the abuse of child labor, although violations of the law are on the rise.*

2. Writing a Proposal

You may wish to suggest that students organize their proposals by following an outline such as this:

   I. Thesis statement—summary of ways that work can enhance schooling

  II. Most important enhancement—main idea and supporting details

 III. Next most important enhancement—main idea and supporting details

 IV. Least important enhancement—main idea and supporting details

  V. Summary—restatement of thesis

B. Answer Craft unionism included skilled workers from many different industries; industrial unionism included skilled and unskilled workers in a specific industry.

THINK THROUGH HISTORY
B. Contrasting
How did craft unionism and industrial unionism differ?

different industries. Under the leadership of leaders such as **Samuel Gompers,** the Cigar Makers' International Union joined with other trade and craft unions in 1886 to form the **American Federation of Labor (AFL).** With Gompers as its president, the AFL focused on **collective bargaining,** or group negotiations, to reach written agreements between workers and employers. Unlike the Knights of Labor, the AFL used strikes as a major tactic, rather than as a last resort, to achieve its aims. Successful strikes helped the AFL win higher wages and shorter work weeks for skilled workers. Between 1890 and 1915, the average weekly wages in unionized industries rose from $17.50 to $24, and the average work week fell from almost 54.5 to just under 49 hours.

INDUSTRIAL UNIONISM AND EUGENE DEBS   Some labor leaders felt that the strength of unions lay in reaching beyond skilled workers to include all laborers—skilled and unskilled—who worked in a specific industry. This concept captured the imagination of **Eugene V. Debs,** who made the first major attempt to form such an industrial union—the American Railway Union (ARU). Most of the new union's members were unskilled and semiskilled laborers, but skilled engineers and firemen joined too. In 1894, the new union won a strike for higher wages. Within two months, its membership climbed to 150,000, dwarfing the 90,000 enrolled in the four skilled railroad brotherhoods. Though the ARU, like the Knights of Labor, never recovered from the losses suffered in a major strike, it had its effect.

> **A PERSONAL VOICE**
> Brothers of the American Railway Union, even in defeat, our rewards are grand beyond expression. . . . The American Railway Union . . . espoused the cause of justice. It furrowed the land deeper with the plows of Truth and Courage than had fallen to the lot of any labor organization since time began, and the seeds of emancipation which it sowed . . . are germinating and a new era is destined to dawn upon labor.
>
> **EUGENE V. DEBS,** "Proclamation to American Railway Union," 1895

SOCIALISM AND THE IWW   Eugene Debs and some other labor activists eventually came to believe that the problems faced by workers were symptoms of an underlying problem with the American capitalist system. They believed that the principles on which the economy were based—private ownership of business and free competition—made the rich richer and the poor poorer. These activists turned to **socialism,** an economic and political system that features government control of business and property and equal distribution of wealth. Socialism had obvious appeal for the downtrodden workers, whom it would empower. But it threatened the wealthy, whose wealth it would confiscate.

Socialism, carried to its extreme form—communism, as advocated by the German philosopher Karl Marx—would result in the overthrow of the capitalist system. Most socialists in late 19th-century America drew back from this goal, however,

> *"Show me the country in which there are no strikes, and I will show you that country in which there is no liberty."*

SAMUEL GOMPERS

TERACT WITH HISTORY

NTRASTING How have times changed working teens? Support your answer.
SEE SKILLBUILDER HANDBOOK, PAGE 1041.

RITING A PROPOSAL With a group classmates, discuss the value of work erience for young people. How might rk be used to enhance, rather than limit, ure opportunities? Write a short proposal nmarizing your ideas.

1995
Despite legal restrictions, however, the illegal use of underage labor is on the rise. According to the Labor Department, between 1980 and 1992 the number of child-labor violations doubled to more than 19,000 a year. Many of these underage workers are immigrants working in the fields, in sweatshops, or in other makeshift factories, where wages are low and health and safety conditions are often appalling. Although most young people are better off than they were a century ago, for some of them, times haven't changed much.

MORE ABOUT . . .
Samuel Gompers
With the exception of 1895, Samuel Gompers (1850–1924) remained president of the AFL until his death. He became the first registered member of the Cigar Makers' International Union at age 14, and continued to work in cigar shops for 20 years, even after he became active in union activities.

MORE ABOUT . . .
The Union Label
The AFL was an early user of the union label, which was put on products to identify them as having been made in union shops. Union supporters were encouraged to look for the union label in products they bought.

The Industrial Age **429**

TEACHING OPTIONS

Making Connections Across Cultures

The European Roots of Socialism Socialism came into its own as a social, political, and economic system in the early 19th century in response to the problems brought about by the industrial revolution in western Europe. Although some European immigrants brought their socialist ideas to America with them, the movement never developed the following it had in Europe. Discuss with students why this might be the case. *Students might respond that the United States offered greater opportunities than Europe, even to the poor. They might say that the American dream of individual opportunity and incentive worked against socialist ideals.*

Making Connections Across Time

The Socialist Party in the United States Ask students what they know about the Socialist Party in the United States today. You might want to tell them that the most important leader of the Socialist Party after Eugene Debs's death was Norman Thomas. Thomas ran as a third-party candidate in every presidential election from 1928 to 1948. You might want to have students use the Internet to research Socialist Party candidates currently running for local, state, or national offices.

The Growth of Union Membership, 1878–1904

Reading the Graph Have students trace the lines showing the development of each union. Ask them when AFL membership and total union membership in the nation were essentially the same. *About 1897.*

Extension Have students research the membership of the AFL today. *13,200 as of 1993.* You might also ask them to identify other influential unions, such as the Teamsters Union.

MORE ABOUT . . .
The Sugar Beet and Farm Laborers' Union of Oxnard

When the Sugar Beet and Farm Laborers' Union of Oxnard applied to the AFL for a charter, Samuel Gompers informed the union secretary, a Mexican, that Chinese and Japanese workers must be excluded from membership. The farm laborers rejected Gompers's conditions.

OBJECTIVE
④ INSTRUCT

Strikes Turn Violent

▶ **Starting with the Student** Discuss with students the circumstances that can breed violence. *Possible Answer: When groups with conflicting goals clash, especially when one group feels powerless or fears the other.*

▶ **Discussing Key Ideas**
• Riots erupt as workers in various industries strike.

(continued on next page)

SKILLBUILDER
INTERPRETING CHARTS *Which strikes did not lead to a decline in union membership?*
Skillbuilder Answer The Wabash Railroad Strike and the Great Northern Strike.

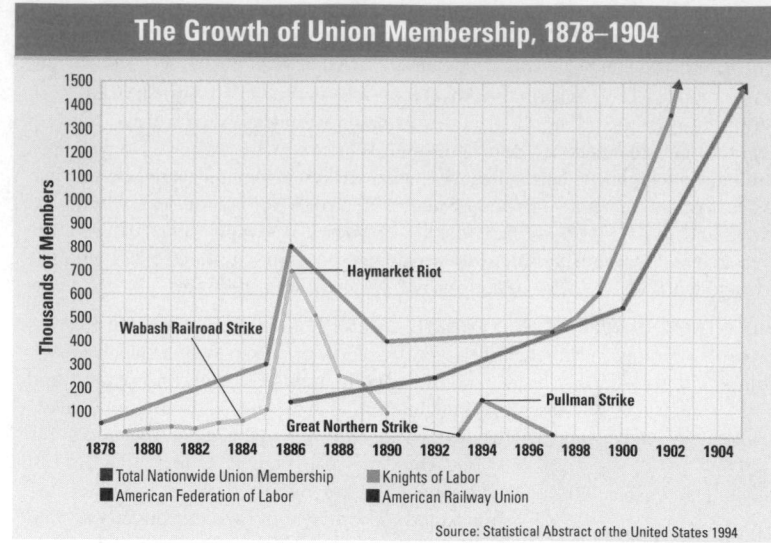

The Growth of Union Membership, 1878–1904

Source: Statistical Abstract of the United States 1994

and worked within the labor movement to achieve better conditions for workers. In 1905, a group of radical unionists and socialists in the West organized the **Industrial Workers of the World (IWW),** or the Wobblies. Headed by William "Big Bill" Haywood, the Wobblies included miners, lumberers, and cannery and dock workers. Unlike the ARU, the IWW welcomed women and African Americans, but membership never topped 150,000. Its only major strike victory took place in 1912. Yet the Wobblies, like the ARU, gave dignity and a sense of solidarity to unskilled workers barred from other groups.

OTHER LABOR ACTIVISM IN THE WEST Asian and Mexican agricultural workers in the West and Southwest also organized unions. In April 1903, about 1,000 Japanese and Mexican workers organized a successful strike in the sugar-beet fields of Ventura County, California. In the wake of their victory, they formed the Sugar Beet and Farm Laborers' Union of Oxnard. In Wyoming, the State Federation of Labor supported a union of Chinese and Japanese miners who sought the same wages and treatment as other union miners. These small, independent unions increased the overall strength of the labor movement and helped fuel the increasing tension between labor and management.

THINK THROUGH HISTORY
C. Summarizing *How did socialists work within the labor movement?*

C. Answer They joined unions, such as the IWW, to strike for fair treatment.

Strikes Turn Violent

As union members took action to reverse long hours and ongoing wage cuts, industry and government acted forcefully to put down the strikes, which they saw as a threat to the entire capitalist system.

THE GREAT STRIKE OF 1877 A turning point in labor history took place in July 1877. Workers for the Baltimore and Ohio Railroad (B&O) went on strike to protest their second wage cut in several months. This strike spread quickly to every railroad line east of the Mississippi and then to the Missouri Pacific and other western lines. For more than a week, most freight and even some passenger traffic covering over 50,000 miles stopped in its tracks. Riots erupted in Baltimore, Pittsburgh, Chicago, St. Louis, and San Francisco. Some industrialists feared a socialist revolution.

B&O president John Garret wired President Rutherford B. Hayes, urging him to stop the strikes because the strikers were impeding interstate commerce. Hayes agreed and ordered troops to clear the way. The strikers retreated, and by August 2, the trains were running again.

430 CHAPTER 14

TEACHING OPTIONS

Teaching Gifted and Talented Students

Joe Hill and the Wobblies Although it had relatively few members, the IWW spoke out loudly for the underdogs of the labor movement—women, ethnic minorities, and unskilled laborers. Interested students may wish to investigate the legacy of idealistic social activism left by the Wobblies. Suggest that they begin by researching the life of Joe Hill, who was immortalized in a ballad popular with labor groups.

Making Connections Across Time

Agricultural Activism Today Discuss with students union activities among agricultural workers today. You might want to mention Cesar Chavez, who founded the National Farm Workers Association in 1962, and ask what they know about the strategies he pioneered in the late 1960s. *Chavez appealed to consumers across the nation to boycott the sale of nonunion grapes. Later he used the same strategy to put pressure on nonunion lettuce growers.*

THE HAYMARKET AFFAIR Encouraged by this modest success, labor leaders continued to press for change. On the evening of May 4, 1886, 1,200 people gathered at Chicago's Haymarket Square to protest the killing of a striker by police at the International Harvester plant the day before. Rain began to fall at about 10 o'clock, and the crowd was already dispersing when police arrived. Then someone tossed a bomb into the police line. As the confrontation veered out of control, police fired into the crowd. Seven police officers and several workers died in the riot. No one ever learned who threw the bomb, but the three speakers and five other radicals were charged with inciting a riot. All eight men were convicted; four were hanged and one committed suicide in prison. As a result of the Haymarket violence, the public began to turn against the labor movement.

THINK THROUGH HISTORY
D. *Recognizing Effects* What was one major effect of the Haymarket Affair?
D. Answer Public hostility to the labor movement

THE HOMESTEAD STRIKE This violence against strikers and rising public anger did not stop workers from fighting against unfair treatment. The Carnegie Steel Company's Homestead plant in Pennsylvania, for example, was ripe for a strike. Writer Hamlin Garland described conditions at the plant.

> **A PERSONAL VOICE**
> The streets of the town were horrible; the buildings were poor; the sidewalks were sunken and full of holes. Everywhere groups of pale, lean men slouched in faded garments, grimy with the soot and grease of the mills. . . . The mill itself was hell: A roar of a hundred lions, a thunder as of cannons . . . jarring clang of falling iron, burst of fluttering flakes of fire, scream of terrible saws, shifting of mighty trucks with hiss of Steam!
>
> **HAMLIN GARLAND,** quoted in *McClure's* magazine

The steelworkers finally went on strike on July 6, 1892, after the company president, Henry Clay Frick, announced his plan to cut wages. Frick hired armed guards from the Pinkerton Detective Agency to protect the plant so he could hire **scabs,** or strikebreakers, to keep it operating. In a battle that left three detectives and six workers dead, the steelworkers ousted the Pinkertons and kept the plant closed until the Pennsylvania National Guard arrived on July 12. At that time, Frick reopened the plant. The strike continued until November, but by then the union had lost much of its support and gave in to the company. It would take 40 years for steelworkers to mobilize once again.

THE PULLMAN STRIKE Strikes continued in other industries, however. During the Panic of 1893 and the economic depression that followed, the Pullman Company laid off 3,000 of its 5,800 employees and cut the wages of the rest by 25 to 40 percent. But the company did not cut the cost of its employee housing, and after paying rent, most workers took home less than $6 a week. One man with a grim sense of humor framed a two-cent check.

After the depression lifted and business improved, the Pullman Company hired back 2,000 workers, but it failed to restore wages or decrease rents. Outraged and desperate, the workers called for a strike in the spring of 1894. Eugene Debs asked for arbitration, but Pullman refused to negotiate with the strikers; so the ARU began boycotting Pullman trains.

Striking Pullman workers lash out at armed deputies accompanying an engine out of the railyard in Blue Island, Illinois, in 1894.

431

(continued from page 430)

Discussing Key Ideas
• Management appeals to the government to stop striking railroad workers.
• Many companies retaliate against striking workers.

MORE ABOUT . . .
The Haymarket Affair
The three surviving men of the eight convicted of the Haymarket bombings were pardoned by the governor of Illinois, John Peter Altgeld. He justified the pardon because he believed that the accused had not received a fair trial. Altgeld was a staunch supporter of labor, and in 1894, he opposed President Grover Cleveland's decision to send federal troops into Pullman to stop striking railroad workers.

HUMANITIES TRANSPARENCIES
H14, *The Gun Foundry* by John Ferguson Weir

TEACHING OPTION

Cooperative Activity: Reporting on Union Goals

Task: Small groups of students will research the goals of a union and write a report indicating if and when those goals were met.

Purpose: To help students understand the causes and effects of union activity.

Activity: Each group of students should research the history of a particular union. Groups should identify the main goals established by the union and determine which goals

were met and when. They should write a report for presentation to the class accompanied by visual aids such as time lines or charts.

Building a Portfolio: Students who decide to add reports to their portfolios should attach a note indicating their contribution to the report.

ALTERNATIVE ASSESSMENT BOOK
Standards for Evaluating a Cooperative Activity

Standards for Evaluation
Reports should . . .

• show evidence of research from a variety of sources
• identify union goals and indicate whether they have been achieved
• include visuals

Women in the Labor Movement

▶ **Starting with the Student**
Ask students why they think many unions did not include women in their ranks, despite their prominence in the work force. *Possible Answer: Traditional prejudice against women, belief that their place was in the home, and the fact that they generally didn't work in skilled trades.*

▶ **Discussing Key Ideas**
• Women play significant roles in unions that admit them.
• Public exposure of dangerous and unhealthy working conditions for children leads to the passage of laws banning child labor.
• After the tragic Triangle Shirtwaist Factory fire, New York state passes strict fire codes and other reforms.

KEY PLAYERS
Eugene V. Debs

Critical Thinking: Synthesizing Have students write a paragraph describing the relationship between Debs's labor activism and his belief in socialism.

"Mother" Jones

Critical Thinking: Analyzing Motives Ask students to consider what might have driven Mary Harris to become the "Mother" of union activism. Have them support their opinion in a short paragraph.

IN-DEPTH RESOURCES: UNIT 4
American Lives: Mary Harris "Mother" Jones, p. 34

 ELECTRONIC LIBRARY OF PRIMARY SOURCES
from "141 Die in Factory Fire"

KEY PLAYERS

EUGENE V. DEBS 1855–1926

Eugene V. Debs realized his true calling while he was in prison following the Pullman strike in 1894. The failure of the strike and Debs's disillusionment with the conditions of workers under capitalism turned him into a fervent socialist. He became a spokesperson for the Socialist Party of America and was its candidate for president five times. In 1912, he won 900,000 votes—an amazing six percent of the totals. "I say now," Debs vowed, "that while there is a lower class, I am in it; while there is a criminal element, I am of it; while there is a soul in prison, I am not free."

"MOTHER" JONES 1830–1930

Mary Harris "Mother" Jones—born in Ireland and raised in Canada—became a leading figure in the American labor movement after her husband and children died of yellow fever in 1867. According to a reporter who followed "the mother of the laboring class" on her children's march in 1903, "She fights their battles with a Mother's Love"—and she continued fighting them until her death at age 100. Maternal as she was, Mother Jones was definitely not the kind of woman admired by John D. Rockefeller and other industrialists: "God almighty made women," she protested, "and the Rockefeller gang of thieves made ladies."

In the searing heat of the Triangle fire, the fire escape twisted away from the building, hurling panicked women to the brick courtyard nine floors below.

At Debs's urging, both the strike and the boycott remained peaceful—until Pullman hired strikebreakers. Violence broke out, and President Grover Cleveland sent in federal troops to end the strike. In the bitter aftermath, Debs was jailed, Pullman fired most of the strikers, and the railroads blacklisted many others, so they could never again get railroad jobs.

Women in the Labor Movement

Although women were barred from many unions, they were not silent onlookers to labor struggles. United behind powerful leaders, they raised their voices to demand better working conditions, equal pay for equal work, and an end to child labor.

MINES, MILLS, AND "MOTHER" JONES Perhaps the most prominent organizer in the women's labor movement was **Mary Harris "Mother" Jones.** Daughter of an Irish union activist, Jones supported the Great Strike of 1877 and later joined the United Mine Workers of America (UMW). She endured death threats and jail with the coal miners, who gave her the nickname "Mother" Jones.

Not one to stand aside while others took risks, Mother Jones often led the miners in strikes. She advised them to stay home and avoid violence and persuaded their wives instead to march to the mine entrances, where they banged pots and pans to scare the strikebreakers. She also led mill women in sympathy strikes and encouraged them to shame their strikebreaking husbands into joining unions. In 1903, to expose the cruelties of child labor, she led 80 mill children—many with hideous deformities and injuries—on a march to the home of President Theodore Roosevelt. Their crusade gained widespread publicity and influenced the passage of child labor laws.

PAULINE NEWMAN AND THE GARMENT WORKERS Other organizers also achieved significant gains for women laborers. In 1909, at age 16, Pauline Newman became the first female organizer of the International Ladies' Garment Workers' Union (ILGWU). A garment worker from the age of eight, Newman also joined the Women's Trade Union League (WTUL) and supported the "Uprising of the 20,000." This massive 1909 strike by the makers of tailored women's blouses, also known as shirtwaists, won labor agreements for some strikers but did nothing to change their deplorable working conditions.

The public could no longer ignore the deadly reality of those conditions after a fire broke out at the Triangle Shirtwaist Factory in New York City on March 25, 1911. The fire spread swiftly through the oil-soaked machines and piles of cloth, and engulfed the seventh, eighth, and ninth floors of the building. As the women tried to flee, they discovered that the company had locked all but one of the exit doors to prevent theft by the workers and to keep out union organizers.

THINK THROUGH HISTORY
E. Clarifying In what ways did strikes threaten industry?
E. Answer
Strikes challenged the power of employers to control conditions, wages, and their own profits.

TEACHING OPTIONS

Exploring Themes

Women in America Women played a crucial role in the labor movement. Point out that the Knights of Labor included as one of its goals "equal pay for equal work." Discuss with students whether this goal has been achieved. Make sure they are aware that activists are still fighting for passage of the Equal Rights Amendment, and that equal work still brings women less pay than it does men.

Making Connections Across the Curriculum

Mathematics Have students make a bar graph showing the relative annual earnings of men and women. Have them use these figures and research and add others, if desired:

1899: women $ 267; men $ 498
1904: women $ 289; men $ 540
1909: women $ 339; men $ 631

Graphs might look like this:

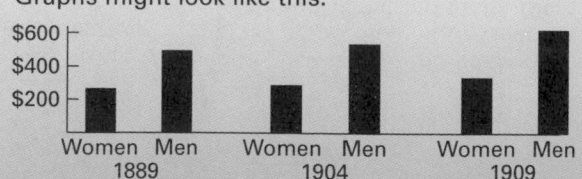

The unlocked door was blocked by fire. The factory had no sprinkler system, and the single fire escape collapsed almost immediately. Many of the 500 workers were trapped inside the building, and 146 died. Some were found huddled with their faces raised to a small window. Others jumped to their deaths on the sidewalk or were impaled on the spikes of a fence.

Public outrage flared in the aftermath of the fire, especially when a jury acquitted the factory owners of manslaughter. In response, the state of New York set up a task force to study factory working conditions. The task force finally convinced the New York legislature to establish strict fire codes, a 54-hour maximum work week for women and minors, a prohibition on Sunday work, and the abolition of child labor under the age of 14 years.

F. Answer They struck in support of mine, mill, and garment workers and won improved conditions for women and children.

THINK THROUGH HISTORY
F. Summarizing What tactics did women organizers use to achieve labor reforms?

Government Pressure on Unions

Despite these gains, union members faced growing opposition from industrialists, who enlisted the help of the federal government to put down strikers.

LEGAL ACTION AGAINST STRIKERS The more powerful the unions became, the more employers came to fear them. Management took steps to weaken labor's influence by refusing to recognize or negotiate with unions as representatives of the workers. Many employers forbade union meetings, fired union members, and forced new employees to sign "yellow-dog contracts," swearing that they would not join a union or take part in a strike.

Finally, industrial leaders, with the helpful rulings of the courts, turned the Sherman Antitrust Act against labor. All a company had to do was say that a strike, picket line, or boycott would hurt interstate trade, and the state or federal government would issue an injunction, or court order, prohibiting the labor action.

G. Answer Court decisions, such as support for the Sherman Antitrust Act, which made unions less effective; negative public opinion; and economic hardship and prejudice against many potential members.

THINK THROUGH HISTORY
G. Identifying Causes Why did labor unions start to decline in the 1890s?

ORGANIZING BECOMES MORE DIFFICULT These legal limitations made it more and more difficult for unions to be effective. In addition, although the public was generally sympathetic to workers, they became angry when strikes caused shortages of goods. Many feared disorder, chaos, and even socialist revolution. The unions were also losing members: in 1910, only 8.3 percent of industrial workers and 5 percent of the general working population belonged to unions. Ongoing prejudice against minorities and immigrants also kept many willing laborers from helping to form what WTUL activist Rose Schneiderman called "a strong working class movement" that would enable "the working people to save themselves."

Difficult Decisions
IN HISTORY

STRIKE! MANAGEMENT OR LABOR?
The decision to strike or not to strike was not—and is not—an easy one. Because many workers faced poor conditions for terribly low wages, they protested by withholding their most valuable resource—their labor. In the words of the leader of the Women's Trade Union League, Rose Schneiderman, "It is up to the working people to save themselves."

Management, on the other hand, felt that workers were under contract to provide their labor. In the eyes of employers, strikers not only violated that contract but kept companies from providing essential services. A newspaper editorial applauded President Cleveland's action in stopping the Pullman strike in 1894, "nominally for the expedition of the mails, but really for the preservation of society."

1. Think about the basic goals and values behind labor's and management's positions in the Pullman strike. Which side do you support?
2. If you were called in to arbitrate in this strike, how would you attempt to reach a settlement? Explain why you would use that approach.

For more about labor unions, click on *Social Studies* at http://www.mcdougallittell.com

OBJECTIVE
(6) INSTRUCT

Government Pressure on Unions

▶ *Discussing Key Ideas*

• Employers fear the power of unions, and ask the government for help.
• The courts use the Sherman Antitrust Act against labor.
• The public withdraws support from unions, whose membership declines.

DIFFICULT DECISIONS IN HISTORY
Strike! Management or Labor?

Critical Thinking: Identifying Problems
Have students make a chart listing the problems workers faced and the solutions other than strikes they might have tried.

ASSESS & RETEACH

Section 4 Assessment
Ask students to discuss questions 3 and 4 and answer them as a group.

Self-Assessment
Have students determine if incorrect answers were related to content or to critical thinking skills and review the appropriate material.

Section Quiz

FORMAL ASSESSMENT
Section Quiz, p. 176

Reteach
Draw a time line from 1876 to 1911 on the board and have students fill in major events in labor activism.

CLOSE

Low wages and poor working conditions compelled workers to form unions and to press for changes. Some reforms were achieved, but when industrialists joined forces with the federal government, the effectiveness of unions began to decline.

Teacher's Edition 433

Section **4** Assessment

1. **TERMS & NAMES**
Identify:
• Samuel Gompers
• American Federation of Labor (AFL)
• collective bargaining
• Eugene V. Debs
• socialism
• Industrial Workers of the World (IWW)
• scab
• "Mother" Jones

2. **SEQUENCING HISTORY**
Create a time line of major events in labor activism between 1876 and 1911.

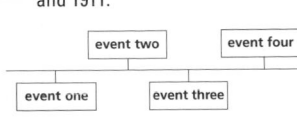

Write a news report describing the most important event you listed.

3. **EVALUATING** Do you think workers were wise to organize unions in the late 19th century? Why or why not?

THINK ABOUT
• working conditions in the late 19th century
• how unions presented their demands
• management efforts to oppose unions

4. **HYPOTHESIZING** If the government had supported unions instead of management in the late 19th century, how might the lives of workers have been different?

THINK ABOUT
• the strength of management
• the issues behind labor disputes
• the government's actions and power

The Industrial Age **433**

ANSWERS

1. TERMS AND NAMES

Samuel Gompers, p. 429
American Federation of Labor (AFL), p. 429
collective bargaining, p. 429
Eugene V. Debs, p. 429
socialism, p. 429
Industrial Workers of the World (IWW), p. 430
scab, p. 431
Mary Harris "Mother" Jones, p. 432

2. SEQUENCING HISTORY

Possible events:
1866 NLU organized
1868 KOL organized
1869 CNLU organized
1877 The Great Strike
1886 Haymarket Affair
1886 AFL organized
1892 Steelworkers go on strike
1894 The Pullman Strike
1905 IWW organized
1911 The Triangle Shirtwaist Factory fire

3. EVALUATING

Possible Responses: Some students will say that workers had to organize unions despite opposition because working conditions were so dreadful. Others will point out that union activity often resulted in worse conditions and loss of jobs and so was ultimately unwise.

4. HYPOTHESIZING

Possible Responses: Labor relations would have been more peaceful; unions would have grown; management might not have been able to fire union members; the Haymarket affair might not have happened; workers might have won higher pay and better working conditions; industries' profits might have been somewhat lower.

Chapter 14 Assessment

REVIEWING THE CHAPTER

TERMS & NAMES
1. Thomas Alva Edison, p. 412
2. Alexander Graham Bell, p. 412
3. George M. Pullman, p. 419
4. Interstate Commerce Act, p. 420
5. Social Darwinism, p. 422
6. Sherman Antitrust Act, p. 424
7. Samuel Gompers, p. 429
8. American Federation of Labor (AFL), p. 429
9. Eugene V. Debs, p. 429
10. Mary Harris "Mother" Jones, p. 432

REVIEWING MAIN IDEAS
11. Steel created demand for coal and iron ore; it was used extensively in the railroad, agriculture, food, and construction industries.

12. They opened up new jobs for women, drew people to the cities, and made jobs less technically demanding.

13. Railroads linked distant places, making them more interdependent, and they created a uniform time system for the country.

14. Railroads were very powerful and often corrupt.

15. The long legal process and resistance from the railroads hampered implementation of the Interstate Commerce Act.

16. They supported the cult of the individual and the work ethic.

17. They used ruthless tactics to amass great wealth.

18. The South had fewer natural and urban resources and less capital for investment.

19. Workers realized that they needed to unite to protect themselves and to improve their pay, shorten their hours, and improve their working conditions.

20. Government support of management; the use of violence and scabs to break strikes.

REVIEWING THE CHAPTER

TERMS & NAMES For each term below, write a sentence explaining its connection to the industrialization of the late 19th century. For each person below, explain his or her role in industrialization.

1. Thomas Alva Edison
2. Alexander Graham Bell
3. George M. Pullman
4. Interstate Commerce Act
5. Social Darwinism
6. Sherman Antitrust Act
7. Samuel Gompers
8. American Federation of Labor (AFL)
9. Eugene V. Debs
10. Mary Harris "Mother" Jones

MAIN IDEAS

SECTION 1 (pages 410–413)

The Expansion of Industry

11. How did the growth of the steel industry influence the development of other industries?
12. How did inventions and developments in the late 19th century change the way people worked?

SECTION 2 (pages 416–420)

The Age of the Railroads

13. How did railroads help unify the United States?
14. Why did people, particularly farmers, demand regulation of the railroads in the late 19th century?
15. Why were attempts at railroad regulation often unsuccessful?

SECTION 3 (pages 421–425)

Big Business Emerges

16. How did Horatio Alger's stories reflect the doctrines of Social Darwinism?
17. Why were business leaders such as John D. Rockefeller called robber barons?
18. Why did the South industrialize more slowly than the North did?

SECTION 4 (pages 426–433)

Workers of the Nation Unite

19. Why did workers form unions in the late 19th century?
20. What factors limited the success of unions?

THINKING CRITICALLY

1. **INDUSTRIALIZATION: PRO AND CON** What do you think were the overall costs and benefits of industrialization? Summarize your ideas in a chart such as the one below.

Industrialization

Costs	Benefits

2. **UNIONS TODAY** Consider the problems that workers faced in the late 19th century and those that workers face today. Based on what you know about unions, how important do you think they are for workers today? Give reasons to support your answer.

3. **INHERITING THE EARTH** Reread the quote by "Mother" Jones on page 408. Do you agree that people will be rewarded more if they fight for their rights than if they meekly accept their lot? Support your opinion with information from the text.

4. **GEOGRAPHY OF THE CITIES** Look at the map on page 418. How do you think the expansion of the railroads influenced the growth of cities in the Midwest and the West?

5. **INDUSTRY AND NATURE** How do you think the growth of industry affected people's connection to nature? Consider factors such as whether people became more or less dependent on natural resources and where they worked.

6. **ANALYZING PRIMARY SOURCES** After Rutherford B. Hayes left the presidency in 1881, he often expressed concern over the growing concentration of wealth in the country.

> No man, however benevolent, liberal, and wise, can use a large fortune so that it will do half as much good in the world as it would if it were divided into moderate sums and in the hands of workmen who had earned it by industry and frugality.
>
> **RUTHERFORD B. HAYES,** *March 19, 1886 entry, Diary and Letters of Rutherford Birchard Hayes*

Consider how men like Carnegie and Rockefeller got their wealth and how they used it. Do you agree with Rutherford B. Hayes's statement? Explain and support your opinion.

THINKING CRITICALLY

1. INDUSTRIALIZATION: PRO AND CON
Costs: Iincreased power of big business; corruption; labor-management conflicts; dangerous jobs; loss of pride in work; Social Darwinism.
Benefits: Better transportation; new methods of communication; less isolation for communities; opportunities for women; new concepts in buildings.

2. UNIONS TODAY
Some students may say that unions are not as important today because most workers have less-hazardous jobs; others may support the need for modern unions and emphasize the ongoing conflicts between workers and managers.

3. INHERITING THE EARTH
Those who agree may cite the positive results of social protest, such as safer working conditions, shorter work days, and no child labor; those who disagree may mention the death and injury that can result from militant protest.

ALTERNATIVE ASSESSMENT

1. REPORTING ABOUT UNIONS

How did workers stand up for their rights in the face of dangerous and exploitative working conditions in the new industrial economy of 1870 to 1890?

Acting as a reporter for a television news magazine, report on and explain a particular labor situation of the time.

 CD-ROM Use the CD-ROM *Grolier's Multimedia Encyclopedia* and other reference materials to research labor strikes and union organizing in this period.

- Research different types of unions and strikes from the period (the issues, and the responses of corporations and the government to striking workers).
- Choose one incident of labor unrest to report to your class in detail, comparing and contrasting it with other incidents. Give the audience background of the event, tell what happened, including the results, and add your own commentary about the situation.

2. RESEARCHING INDUSTRIALIZATION

Industrialization changed the way people worked and felt about their jobs in the late 19th century. Write a short report that explains how one particular industry, such as steelmaking or oil production, changed life in the United States.

Use library resources to do research about the industry you have chosen. Think about these questions.

- How did the industry affect Americans' daily lives?
- What were key innovations that made the industry flourish?
- What were the conditions like for workers in the industry?

When you have finished your research, write a short report that explains how the industry effected American life. Add your report to your American history portfolio.

3. PORTFOLIO PROJECT

📁 Use the Living History activity to expand your portfolio.

LIVING HISTORY

REVISING YOUR SCIENCE FICTION STORY

You have written a science fiction story about a society that did not undergo industrialization. Now ask one of your classmates to read the story and give you feedback that will help you improve it.

- Does the story have a conflict, and is the conflict resolved by the end?
- Does the story have a setting that is not industrialized?
- Does it make clear how the characters provided food and shelter?
- Does the story show the characters in social and cultural activities?

After you have revised your story, publish it as part of a class collection. Then add it to your American history portfolio.

Bridge to Chapter 15

Review Chapter 14

INVENTIONS AND INDUSTRIALIZATION In the late 19th century, the harnessing of abundant natural resources and an explosion of inventions radically changed industry and daily life in the United States. Drake's oil well, Bessemer's steel-making process, Edison's light bulb, and Bell's telephone were only some of these revolutionary developments. New industries flourished, creating new products and jobs for both men and women.

THE AGE OF THE RAILROADS Railroads, typical of these growing industries, provided great benefits, but at a high cost. While railroads linked towns and cities across the country, the workers who built them faced low pay and dangerous conditions. Corrupt management, demonstrated in the Crédit Mobilier scandal, abounded and angered the public. Demands by farmers for regulation resulted in the formation of the Interstate Commerce Commission but did not prevent railroads from becoming a powerful political and economic force.

THE POWER OF BUSINESS Like the railroads, other large corporations exerted increasing power in government and in society. Andrew Carnegie, John D. Rockefeller, and others accumulated tremendous personal fortunes, often using ruthless tactics. Many justified their actions by citing the doctrine of Social Darwinism—the wealthy deserved their success and the poor deserved their poverty.

LABOR RESPONDS Workers responded to the growing power of business by joining together in unions. Labor activists fought for better working conditions and adequate pay through strikes and protests. However, the government supported management in its attack on unions and weakened the power of labor.

Preview Chapter 15

Industrialization created new job opportunities, mostly in cities. To fill these jobs, migrants from rural parts of the United States and immigrants—primarily from southern and eastern Europe—flocked to urban areas. This rapid urban growth created ongoing challenges for cities. You will learn about these significant developments in the next chapter.

The Industrial Age **435**

---

1. REPORTING ABOUT UNIONS
Standards for Evaluation
An effective report should meet the following criteria:

- Provides adequate background information and a clear description of the labor situation.
- Compares and contrasts the situation with other labor incidents.
- Indicates the outcome of the event and offers a personal response to it.

2. RESEARCHING INDUSTRIALIZATION
A report on an industry should meet the following criteria:

- Describes the nature of the industry and its effect on people's daily lives.
- Explains technological innovations that helped the industry flourish.
- Indicates what working in the industry was like.

3. PORTFOLIO PROJECT
LIVING HISTORY
Standards for Evaluation
A science fiction story should meet the following criteria:

- Depicts a society in which the effects of industrialization do not play a part.
- Clearly describes the setting.
- Provides detailed information about people's daily lives.
- Introduces and resolves a conflict.

IN-DEPTH RESOURCES: UNIT 4
See the form for scoring this activity on page 36.

THINKING CRITICALLY

4. GEOGRAPHY OF THE CITIES
Railroads expanded urban areas at railroad hubs, enabled movement of goods into and out of central points, allowed people to relocate, and connected remote or inaccessible areas to the rest of the nation.

5. INDUSTRY AND NATURE
People became more dependent on resources such as iron ore and coal, moved off farms and into cities, but didn't consider the effects of pollution on the environment.

6. ANALYZING PRIMARY SOURCES
Students should support their opinions of Howe's statement with examples from the text.

	Key Ideas	**TEACHING SUPPORT**	**ASSESSMENT**	
SECTION 1 **The New Immigrants** *pp. 438–443*	*New immigrants from southern and eastern Europe, Asia, the Caribbean, and Mexico face culture shock and prejudice—as well as the opportunity for a better life—in the United States.*	**In-Depth Resources: Unit 4** • Guided Reading, p. 37 • Skillbuilder Practice: Interpreting Graphs, p. 41 • Primary Source: Artifacts from Ellis Island, p. 46 • Literature: from *Call It Sleep* by Henry Roth, p. 50 **COOPERATIVE ACTIVITY** • Writing Letters or Poems About Immigrant Experiences, p. 441 (TE)	*Section 1 Assessment,* p. 443 (PE) *Self-Assessment,* p. 443 (TE) *Formal Assessment* • Section Quiz, p. 185 *Alternative Assessment Book* • Standards for Evaluating a Cooperative Activity	
SECTION 2 **The Problems of Urbanization** *pp. 446–451*	*The rapid growth of cities creates many problems: how to provide adequate housing, transportation, water, and sanitation and how to fight fire and crime. The search for solutions begins.*	**In-Depth Resources: Unit 4** • Guided Reading, p. 38 • Geography Application, p. 42 • Outline Map, p. 44 • Primary Sources: from *How the Other Half Lives* by Jacob Riis, p. 47; from *Twenty Years at Hull-House* by Jane Addams, p. 48 • American Lives: Jane Addams, p. 53 **COOPERATIVE ACTIVITY** • Researching Natural Catastrophes, p. 449 (TE)	*Section 2 Assessment,* p. 451 (PE) *Self-Assessment,* p. 451 (TE) *Formal Assessment* • Section Quiz, p. 186 *Alternative Assessment Book* • Standards for Evaluating a Cooperative Activity	
SECTION 3 **The Emergence of the Political Machine** *pp. 452–454*	*The political machine emerges as cities attempt to deal with the problems of rapid urbanization.*	**In-Depth Resources: Unit 4** • Guided Reading, p. 39 • Primary Source: from *The Shame of the Cities* by Lincoln Steffens, p. 49 • American Lives: Boss Tweed, p. 54 **COOPERATIVE ACTIVITY** • Creating Political Cartoons, p. 453 (TE)	*Section 3 Assessment,* p. 454 (PE) *Self-Assessment,* p. 454 (TE) *Formal Assessment* • Section Quiz, p. 187 *Alternative Assessment Book* • Standards for Evaluating a Cooperative Activity	
SECTION 4 **Politics in the Gilded Age** *pp. 455–457*	*Local and national political corruption during the Gilded Age leads to a call for reform.*	**In-Depth Resources: Unit 4** • Guided Reading, p. 40	*Section 4 Assessment,* p. 457 (PE) *Self-Assessment,* p. 457 (TE) *Formal Assessment* • Section Quiz, p. 188	
CHAPTER RESOURCES	**Chapter Overview** *The population rises as immigrants supply a willing workforce for urban industrialization and a political base for many urban politicians. Abuses in local and national government prompt calls for reform.*	**In-Depth Resources: Unit 4** • Living History Project: Worksheet, p. 55; Standards, p. 56 **Telescoping the Times** • Chapter Summary, pp. 29–30 **Planning for Block Schedules**	*Chapter Assessment,* pp. 458–459 (PE) *Alternative Assessment,* p. 459 (PE) *Formal Assessment* • Chapter Test, forms A and B, pp. 189–194 **Test Generator** *Alternative Assessment Book* See explanation and forms for different kinds of alternative assessments including portfolio assessment.	

Geography Transparencies
• G15, Where Foreign Born Lived, 1900

 Electronic Library of Primary Sources
• Chinese Exclusion Act of 1882
• "Twelve Hundred More" by Anon
• from *The Days of Our Years* by Israel Kasovitch

 AMERICAN STORIES VIDEO SERIES
"From China to Chinatown"

INTERNET RESOURCES
• See *McDougal Littell Learning On-Line* for links to information about Ellis Island and Angel Island.

 Humanities Transparencies
• H15, *Cliff Dwellers*

Critical Thinking Transparencies
• CT15, Urban Growth
• CT49, From Country to City: 1870–1920

 Electronic Library of Primary Sources
• "The Modern City" by Jane Addams

Our Times
• San Francisco earthquake and fire

INTERNET RESOURCES
• See *McDougal Littell Learning On-Line* for links to information about Jane Addams and the San Franciso earthquake.

 Grolier Multimedia Encyclopedia
• Thomas Nast and a history of editorial and political cartoons

INTERNET RESOURCES
• See *McDougal Littell Learning On-Line* for links to information about Thomas Nast.

INTERNET RESOURCES
• See *McDougal Littell Learning On-Line* for links to information about Chester A. Arthur and Benjamin Harrison.

 American Portfolio: A Videodisc for U.S. History, user's guide, pp. 146–155, 157

INTERNET RESOURCES
Learning On-Line: Social Studies
http://www.mcdougallittell.com

Block Scheduling (90 MINUTES)

Day 1

Section 1, pp. 438–443

 AMERICAN STORIES VIDEO SERIES
• "From China to Chinatown"

Section 2, pp. 446–451

Section Assessments, pp. 443, 451

Day 2

Section 3, pp. 452–454

Section 4, pp. 455–457

Section Assessments, pp. 454, 457

Chapter Assessment, pp. 458–459

YEARLY PACING *Chapter 15 Total:* 2 days *Yearly Total:* 85 days

See *Planning for Block Schedules* for special activities and pacing strategies.

Customizing for Special Populations

Students Acquiring English

Access for Students Acquiring English
• Guided Reading for Sections 1–4 (Spanish), pp. 148–151
• Chapter Summary (Spanish), pp. 146–147
• Skillbuilder Practice: Interpreting Graphs (Spanish), p. 152
• Geography Application: Industry and Urban Growth (Spanish), p. 153

 AMERICAN STORIES VIDEO SERIES
• "From China to Chinatown" (Spanish Track)

INTERNET RESOURCES
• See *McDougal Littell Learning On-Line* The Diverse Classroom.

Less Proficient Readers

In-Depth Resources: Unit 4
• Guided Reading for Sections 1–4, pp. 37–40
• Skillbuilder: Interpreting Graphs, p. 41
• Geography Application: Industry and Urban Growth, p. 42
• Outline Map: The Urbanization of America, p. 44

Telescoping the Times
• Chapter Summary, pp. 29–30

See additional strategies at point of use in the Teacher's Edition.

Gifted and Talented Students

In-Depth Resources: Unit 4
• Primary Sources: Artifacts from Ellis Island, p. 46; from *How the Other Half Lives* by Jacob Riis, p. 47; from *Twenty Years at Hull-House* by Jane Addams, p. 48; from *The Shame of the Cities* by Lincoln Steffens, p. 49
• American Lives: Jane Addams, p. 53; Boss Tweed, p. 54

See additional strategies at point of use in the Teacher's Edition.

Connections to Literature READINGS FOR STUDENTS

In-Depth Resources: Unit 4
• *Call It Sleep* by Henry Roth, p. 50

Enrichment Reading
• Dreiser, Theodore
Sister Carrie.
New York: Bantam, 1993
Dreiser transforms the conventional "fallen woman" story into a study of the persistent idealism and the grasping and seductive materialism of the American culture.

• Yezierska, Anzia
Bread Givers.
New York: Persea Books, 1975
This touching tale tells the story of Jewish immigrants trying to find their way in America and the conflict between a father of the old world and a daughter of the new world.

McDougal Littell *Literature Connections*

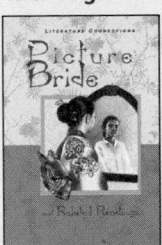

• Yoshiko Uchida, *Picture Bride* (with related readings) This novel follows the experiences of a Japanese woman who comes to America in 1917 to marry a man she has never met. The story ends in a Japanese internment camp in Utah in 1943.

McDougal Littell *The Language of Literature*
American Literature

• Américo Paredes. *The Legend of Gregorio Cortez,* p. 556
• Hisaye Yamamoto, *Seventeen Syllables,* p. 628
• Anzia Yezierska, *America and I,* p. 703
• Bernard A. Weisberger, from *A Nation of Immigrants,* p. 713
• Gish Jen, *In the American Society,* p. 717

Immigrants and Urbanization

▶ ***Starting with the Student***
Ask students why the topics "immigrants" and "urbanization" are linked together in the title. Then have them discuss the following questions:

• What does Horace Greeley's statement mean?
• What problems might new immigrants face?

PREVIEWING THE CHAPTER
• Go over the titles and brief descriptions of the sections, particularly noting the video in Section 1.
• Have students list, as they read the chapter, the reasons that immigrants left their native lands.
• Ask students to note a fact about immigrants that they can learn from the time line.

MORE ABOUT . . .
The Statue of Liberty

The Statue of Liberty was a gift from France commemorating that country's alliance with the United States during the American Revolution. The statue's pedestal is inscribed with a poem by Emma Lazarus that ends with the words: " 'Give me your tired, your poor, / Your huddled masses yearning to breathe free, / . . . I lift my lamp beside the golden door!' "

CHAPTER
15

Immigrants and Urbanization

SECTION 1
The New Immigrants
New immigrants from southern and eastern Europe, Asia, the Caribbean, and Mexico face culture shock and prejudice—as well as the opportunity for a better life—in the United States.

VIDEO *FROM CHINA TO CHINATOWN*

SECTION 2
The Problems of Urbanization
The rapid growth of cities creates many problems: how to provide adequate housing, transportation, water, and sanitation and how to fight fire and crime. The search for solutions begins.

SECTION 3
The Emergence of the Political Machine
The political machine emerges as cities attempt to deal with the problems of rapid urbanization.

SECTION 4
Politics in the Gilded Age
Local and national political corruption during the Gilded Age leads to a call for reform.

436 CHAPTER 15

"We cannot all live in the city, yet nearly all seem determined to do so."

Horace Greeley

Statue of Liberty is dedicated.

• Boss Tweed is indicted for fraud and extortion.

⭐ Rutherford B. Hayes becomes president.

⭐ James A. Garfield is elected president.

⭐ Chester A. Arthur succeeds to presidency after Garfield is assassinated.

⭐ Grover Cleveland is elected president.

THE UNITED STATES
THE WORLD

1870 1871 **1877** **1880** 1881 1884 18

1876 18

• Otto von Bismarck unifies the new German Empire.

• Porfirio Díaz seizes power in Mexico.

Gold is discovered in South Africa.

THEMES IN CHAPTER 15

Immigration and Migration

In the 1990s, immigration has once again become a major political issue in many parts of the country. Contemporary concerns include illegal immigration, the maintaining of U.S. borders, and legal protection and social benefits for immigrants.

436   Chapter 15

The settlers' quest for rich farmland, the California gold rush, the Homestead Act, the transcontinental railroad, and the Great Depression all contributed to migration within the United States. The nation remains highly mobile today.

See Teacher's Edition notes, pp. 440 and 442.

Cultural Diversity

Immigrants arrived with their own religious beliefs, language, and social customs. In the cities, many immigrants took advantage of the abundant opportunities to enrich their lives. They went to museums, theaters, and concerts.

See Teacher's Edition note, p. 448.

The American Dream

Free public education has long been a part of the American dream. Such public education enabled many immigrants to enter into their new world. In school, children learned about democracy and civic responsibility.

See Teacher's Edition note, p. 448.

LIVING HISTORY

LIVING HISTORY

TRACING THE GROWTH OF A TOWN

Write a biography of your town or neighborhood. Using what you've learned in this chapter about how cities grow and why people immigrate, discuss some of the following:

- the town's or neighborhood's founders
- major ethnic groups, including when they arrived and what they contributed to the area
- the problems created by growth and the way that the problems were solved
- what the future of the town/neighborhood might be
- include maps, photos, and newspaper stories about interesting local events

📁 **PORTFOLIO PROJECT** Keep these materials in a folder for your American history portfolio. You will present the biography to the class at the end of the chapter.

TRACING THE GROWTH OF A TOWN

Discuss the following ways of gathering information for a biography of a town or neighborhood:

- Use the local newspaper, library, or museum to find books, maps, and other information.
- Prepare questions and then interview older members of the community, tape-recording their comments.
- Get permission to visit schools, places of worship, the Chamber of Commerce, and other sites of interest.
- Check your own family's sources for photographs and memorabilia.

Project Planning Guide

Step 1	Students prepare a list of persons and places to visit.
Step 2	Students gather information from the persons and places they have listed in Step 1.
Step 3	Students organize the data they have collected.
Step 4	Students write a summary of the town's past and predict the town's future.

IN-DEPTH RESOURCES: UNIT 4
See worksheet and standards for evaluation on pp. 55, 56.

Timeline events:

- Immigration soars for Europeans, such as these Dutch children.
- Tenements abound in New York City.
- First electric subway is opened in Boston.
- Conspicuous spending by Mrs. Jay Gould and other wives of wealthy industrialists characterizes the Gilded Age.
- Benjamin Harrison is elected president.
- Grover Cleveland is elected president for a second term.
- William McKinley is elected president.
- Hawaii is annexed by United States.
- Wright Brothers make first successful airplane flight.

1890 — 1892 — 1896 — 1897 — 1898 — **1900** — 1903 — 1908 — **1914**
1895 — 1901 — 1911

- X-rays are discovered by Wilhelm Roentgen.
- Commonwealth of Australia is created.
- Manchu dynasty in China is overthrown.
- Panama Canal opens.

Immigrants and Urbanization **437**

RECOMMENDED RESOURCES

Books for the Teacher

Higham, John. *Strangers in the Land.* New York. Atheneum, 1965. Immigrants and nativists.

McCullough, David. *The Great Bridge.* New York: Simon, 1972. Building Brooklyn Bridge.

Takaki, Ronald. *A Different Mirror.* Boston: Little, 1993. Hispanic and Asian experience.

Books for the Student

Callow, Alexander B. *The Tweed Ring.* New York: Oxford UP, 1966. Story of the most notorious political machine.

Kessler-Harris, Alice. *Out to Work.* New York: Oxford UP, 1982. Women in the industrialized workplace.

Ratzel, Friedrich. *Sketches of Urban and Cultural Life in America.* New Brunswick, NJ:

Rutgers UP, 1988. German traveler describes American society.

Videos

The Brooklyn Bridge. Direct Cinema, 1982. Building the bridge.

The Great San Francisco Earthquake. PBS Home Video, 1988, 800-424-7963. Documentary.

Journey to America. PBS Home Video, 1988, 800-424-7963.

Journey to Freedom: The Immigrant Experience. Laserdisc.

Ragtime. Dir. Miloš Forman Ragtime/Sunley, 1981.

Educational Software Institute, 800-955-5570.

Software

Who Built America? CD-ROM. Voyager, 800-446-2001.

OBJECTIVES

1 To summarize the various parts of the world from which immigrants came to the "golden door."

2 To describe the journey immigrants endured and how they passed through the immigration stations.

3 To explain the kinds of discrimination immigrants faced and the actions taken by nativists.

SKILLBUILDER

• Understanding geography: movement, p. 439

CRITICAL THINKING

• Summarizing, pp. 439, 443
• Analyzing motives, p. 440
• Identifying problems, p. 441
• Clarifying, p. 442
• Analyzing causes, p. 443
• Forming opinions, p. 443
• Synthesizing, p. 443

FOCUS & MOTIVATE

▶ Starting with the Student
Have students watch the video "From China to Chinatown" to learn about American attitudes toward Chinese immigrants such as Fong See.

Using the Video Resource Book as a guide, hold a class discussion, explore the background of the See family (both in China and in the United States), and engage in extension activities using key primary sources.

AMERICAN STORIES VIDEO SERIES
"From China to Chinatown"

Videocassette: Volume 2

Videodisc: Disc 2, Side A, Chapter 2

1 The New Immigrants

TERMS & NAMES
• Ellis Island
• Angel Island
• culture shock
• melting pot
• Chinese Exclusion Act
• Gentlemen's Agreement

LEARN ABOUT why people emigrate and the challenges they face
TO UNDERSTAND the impact of immigration on the United States in the late 19th and early 20th centuries.

ONE AMERICAN'S STORY

In 1871, 14-year-old Fong See came from China to "Gold Mountain"—the United States—to search for his father and brothers, who had emigrated here. Fong See found his father in San Francisco and sent him back to China. Fong See stayed, worked at menial jobs, and saved enough money to buy a business. Despite widespread restrictions against the Chinese, he became a very successful and influential importer and was able to marry, move to Los Angeles, and sponsor many other Chinese who wanted to enter the United States. Fong See had achieved the American dream. However, his great-granddaughter Lisa See recalls, he was not satisfied.

A PERSONAL VOICE
He had been trying to achieve success ever since he had first set foot on the Gold Mountain. His dream was very "American." He wanted to make money, have influence, be respected, have a wife and children who loved him. In 1919, when he traveled to China, he could look at his life and say he had achieved his dream. But once in China he suddenly saw his life in a different context. In America, was he really rich? Could he live where he wanted? . . . Did *Americans* care what he thought? . . . The answers played in his head—no no no.
LISA SEE, *On Gold Mountain*

Fong See (*second from left*) and family, 1901.

Despite Fong See's success in America and his standing as a leader in the Chinese-American community, he could not, upon his death in 1957, be buried next to his Caucasian wife because California cemeteries were still segregated.

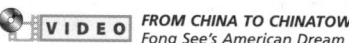 **FROM CHINA TO CHINATOWN**
Fong See's American Dream

Through the "Golden Door"

Millions of immigrants like Fong See entered the United States in the late 19th and early 20th centuries because they were lured by the promise of a better life. Some of these immigrants sought to escape difficult conditions—such as poverty, famine, land shortages, or religious or political persecution—in their native countries. Others, known as "birds of passage," intended to immigrate temporarily in order to make money and then return to their homelands.

IMMIGRANTS FROM EUROPE Between 1870 and 1920, approximately 20 million Europeans arrived in the United States. Before 1890, most immigrants came from countries in western and northern Europe, including Great Britain, Ireland, and Germany. Beginning in the 1890s, however, increasing numbers came from southern and eastern Europe, especially Italy, Austria-Hungary, and Russia. In 1905 alone, nearly a million people arrived from these countries through the "golden door" to the land of opportunity.

Many of these new immigrants left their homelands to escape religious persecution. Whole villages of Jews—businesspeople, intellectuals, workers, and farmers—were driven out of Russia by pogroms. These were organized anti-Semitic

438 CHAPTER 15

PRINT RESOURCES

IN-DEPTH RESOURCES: UNIT 4
Guided Reading, p. 37
Skillbuilder Practice: Interpreting Graphs, p. 41
Primary Source: Artifacts from Ellis Island, p. 46
Literature: from *Call It Sleep* by Henry Roth, p. 50

ACCESS FOR STUDENTS ACQUIRING ENGLISH
Guided Reading (Spanish), p. 148
Skillbuilder Practice: Interpreting Graphs (Spanish), p. 152

FORMAL ASSESSMENT
Section Quiz, p. 185

ALTERNATIVE ASSESSMENT BOOK
See forms for supporting and scoring alternative activities.

TECHNOLOGY RESOURCES

GEOGRAPHY TRANSPARENCIES
G15, Where Foreign Born Lived, 1900

CD-ROM Electronic Library of Primary Sources

VIDEO *American Stories* video series
American Portfolio: A Videodisc for U.S. History
user's guide, pp. 149–152

INTERNET McDougal Littell Learning On-Line
http://www.mcdougallittell.com

Where They Came From and Where They Settled, 1900

Scandinavia 11%
England 8%
Italy 5%
Russia 4%
Poland 3.5%
Mexico
China
Japan
Ireland 16%
Germany 26%
Other 25%

Settlement figures in hundreds of thousands

New York
480
425
199
165
135
66
42
7

Wisconsin
242

Illinois
332
129
114
64
64
28
23
61
30
23

Massachusetts
249
82
32
28
26

Pennsylvania
212
205
114
72
66
50

Ohio
204
55
44

California
72
44
40
35
10
8

Texas
72
48

Germany
Ireland
Scandinavia
England
Italy
Russia
Poland
Mexico
China
Japan

GEOGRAPHY SKILLBUILDER
MOVEMENT
Where did the greatest number of Italian immigrants settle? Which two states combined had about the same number of Irish immigrants as Illinois?

Skillbuilder Answer
Italians: New York.
Irish: Ohio and Wisconsin.

campaigns that led to the massacre of Jews during the early 1880s and early 1900s.

Other Europeans left because of rising population. Between 1800 and 1900, the population in Europe more than doubled to 432 million. This population explosion resulted in a lack of land available for farming. Farmers as well as laborers often found themselves competing for too few industrial jobs. Some emigrated to the United States, where jobs were supposedly plentiful.

Finally, there was a spirit of reform and revolt in Europe, especially after the political disturbances in France, Germany, Italy, and elsewhere in the late 1840s. Many young European men and women were still influenced by the spirit of these movements and sought to start independent lives in the United States.

IMMIGRANTS FROM CHINA AND JAPAN While waves of Europeans arrived on the shores of the East Coast, Chinese immigrants came to the West Coast in smaller numbers. Between 1851 and 1883, about 200,000 Chinese arrived. Many came to seek their fortunes after the discovery of gold in 1848 sparked the California gold rush. The Chinese helped build the nation's first transcontinental railroad as well as other railroads in the West. When the railroads were completed, they turned to farming, mining, and domestic service. Chinese immigration was sharply limited by a congressional act in 1882.

In 1884, the Japanese government allowed Hawaiian planters to recruit Japanese workers, and a Japanese emigration boom began. When the United States annexed Hawaii in 1898, Japanese emigration to the West Coast increased. As word of comparatively high American wages spread in Japan, the number of Japanese who entered the United States each year reached about 10,000. By 1920, more than 200,000 Japanese lived on the West Coast.

A. Answer
Mainly from eastern and southern Europe, Asia, and Mexico

IMMIGRANTS FROM THE WEST INDIES AND MEXICO Between 1880 and 1920, about 260,000 immigrants arrived in the eastern and southeastern United States from the West Indies. They came from Jamaica, Cuba, Puerto Rico, and other islands. Many West Indians left their homelands because jobs were scarce.

THINK THROUGH HISTORY
A. Summarizing
Where did the new immigrants come from?

The Mexican population in the United States also increased. Unlike the Europeans, Asians, and West Indians, however, some Mexicans became U.S. residents without even leaving home. As a result of the statehood of Texas in 1845 and the end of the Mexican War in 1848, the United States acquired vast

Immigrants and Urbanization **439**

OBJECTIVE
(1) INSTRUCT

Through the "Golden Door"

▶ *Discussing Key Ideas*
• Immigrants come from Europe, Japan, China, the West Indies, and Mexico.
• Some emigrate because of overpopulation, famine, or religious or political persecution.

IN-DEPTH RESOURCES: UNIT 4
Guided Reading, p. 37

ACCESS FOR STUDENTS ACQUIRING ENGLISH
Guided Reading (Spanish), p. 148

ELECTRONIC LIBRARY OF PRIMARY SOURCES
from *The Days of Our Years* by Israel Kosovitch

HISTORY FROM VISUALS
Where They Came From and Where They Settled, 1900

Reading the Map Show students that the map, bar graph, and pie chart present essentially the same information in different ways in order to make the material easier to understand. Tell them, for example, that green is used on the pie chart to represent the Irish and that it is used again on the bar graphs to show Irish immigrants.

Extension Ask students to use a world almanac to find the latest U.S. immigration figures. Then have them prepare a bar graph showing the percentage of immigrants from each continent.

IN-DEPTH RESOURCES: UNIT 4
Skillbuilder Practice: Interpreting Graphs, p. 41

GEOGRAPHY TRANSPARENCIES
G15, Where Foreign Born Lived, 1900

TEACHING OPTION

Skillbuilder Mini-Lesson: Interpreting Graphs

Explaining the Skill Graphs offer illustrations of statistics and often make numerical information and relationships easier to grasp. Visual features such as color and size as well as verbal labels and measurements on a graph all help clarify the information presented.

Applying the Skill: Where They Came From Have students study the graphs on this page, noting how the colors and the relative sizes of the bars and the pie-graph wedges communicate information. Then ask,

1. Which state has the most countries represented in its immigrant population? *New York.* The fewest? *Texas.*

2. Which states have Scandinavian populations? *Illinois, Wisconsin, New York, Massachusetts.*

3. What similarities and differences in foreign settlement do you see between the eastern states and California? *Both have sizable German and Irish populations. No significant Italian or Russian population in California, but that state has more Chinese and Japanese than the eastern states.*

IN-DEPTH RESOURCES: UNIT 4
Skillbuilder Practice: Interpreting Graphs, p. 41

Teacher's Edition **439**

Life in the New Land

▶ **Starting with the Student**
Ask students to describe the most difficult journey they have ever undertaken.

- Ask them how it compares with the kind of journey immigrants faced.
- Have students tell what hardships endured by immigrants were similar to hardships they faced on their journey.

▶ **Discussing Key Ideas**
- Immigrants endure a frightening and uncomfortable journey in crowded, unsanitary quarters.
- Immigrants on both coasts have to pass a physical exam, prove they are literate in a language, meet legal requirements, and have at least $25.
- The newcomers seek out people of their own native culture.

MORE ABOUT . . .
The Transatlantic Journey

Toward the end of the 1800s, the price for a steerage ticket across the Atlantic was only $15, considerably less than it had been at the start of the 1800s. Why the cheaper fare? Toward the end of the century, the United States was exporting to Europe bulky raw materials, such as cotton, timber, tobacco, and wheat. On the return trip, the ships carried less bulky luxury items, such as china, linens, and wines. That left plenty of room for passengers.

territories from Mexico. Many of the residents of these territories chose to become American citizens.

Other Mexicans immigrated to the United States to find work or to flee political turmoil. As a result of the 1902 National Reclamation Act (also known as the Newlands Act), which encouraged the irrigation of arid land, new farmland was created in many Western states, including Texas, Arizona, and California. This farmland drew Mexican farm workers northward to seek jobs. After 1910, political and social upheavals in Mexico prompted even more immigration. Nearly a million people—7 percent of the population of Mexico at the time—came to the United States over the next 20 years.

Life in the New Land

No matter what part of the globe immigrants came from, they faced many adjustments. Having left behind all that was familiar, they were plunged into an alien—and often unfriendly—culture.

A DIFFICULT JOURNEY By the 1870s, almost all immigrants traveled by steamship. The trip across the Atlantic Ocean from Europe took approximately one week, while the Pacific crossing from Asia took nearly three weeks. For many immigrants, the long sea journey was stormy, uncomfortable, and frightening.

Many immigrants traveled in steerage, or in the cargo holds below a ship's waterline. Rarely allowed on deck, immigrants spent most of the trip crowded together in the gloom, unable to exercise or catch a breath of fresh air. They often had to sleep in lice-infested bunks and share toilet facilities with many other passengers. Under these conditions, diseases spread quickly, and some immigrants died before they reached their destination. For those who survived, like Rosa Cavalleri from Italy, the first glimpse of America could be breathtaking.

> ### A PERSONAL VOICE
> *America! . . .* We were so near it seemed too much to believe. Everyone stood silent—like in prayer. . . . Then we were entering the harbor. The land came so near we could almost reach out and touch it. . . . Everyone was holding their breath. Me too. . . . Some boats had bands playing on their decks and all of them were tooting their horns to us and leaving white trails in the water behind them.
>
> **ROSA CAVALLERI**, quoted in *Rosa: The Life of an Italian Immigrant*

Many foreign governments issued passports to their citizens who were planning to emigrate. In this way they could control the number of trained professionals and young men of military age who left the country.

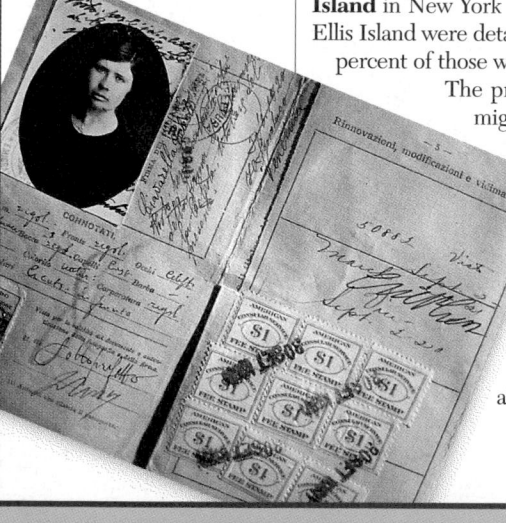

ELLIS ISLAND After initial moments of excitement, the immigrants faced loneliness, homesickness, and the anxiety of not knowing whether they would be admitted to the United States. They had to pass inspection at immigration stations, such as the one at Castle Garden in New York, which was later moved to **Ellis Island** in New York Harbor. About 20 percent of the immigrants who arrived at Ellis Island were detained for a day or more before being inspected. Only about 2 percent of those who reached Ellis Island had to return home, however.

The processing of immigrants on Ellis Island was an ordeal that might take five hours or more. First, they had to pass a physical examination by a doctor. If they were found to have a serious health problem or a contagious disease, such as tuberculosis, they were promptly sent home. Those who passed the medical exam then reported to a government inspector. The inspector checked documents and questioned immigrants to determine whether they met the legal requirements to enter the United States. The requirements included passing a literacy test in their native language, proving that they were able to work, and showing that they had at least $25. One

THINK THROUGH HISTORY
B. Analyzing Motives What do you think were the most important reasons for emigration?
B. Answer The desire to escape intolerable conditions such as land shortages, famine, and political or religious persecution; the prospect of jobs, cheap land, or higher wages.

TEACHING OPTIONS

Exploring Themes

Immigration and Migration A large influx of immigrants into the United States in recent years has created challenges for the nation much as the immigration of 1870–1920 did. In the 1990s, immigration has become a major political issue in many parts of the country. California, Texas, Florida, Illinois, New York, and New Jersey claim 70% of the nation's legal and illegal immigrants. Among the issues the nation must face are how to fund border patrols, how to deal with illegal immigrant workers, and what legal protection and social benefits should be provided to legal immigrants.

Making Connections Across Cultures

Cultural Heritage One of the fascinating exhibits at the Ellis Island Museum is a display of items immigrants brought with them from their countries of origin. Since passengers in steerage were allowed only a hundred pounds of goods, immigrants had to be very selective in what they took. Among the cherished items on display are musical instruments, pieces of lace finery, cobblers' tools, books, religious items, family pictures, and handmade quilts. Ask students why each of these objects would have been treasured by its owner.

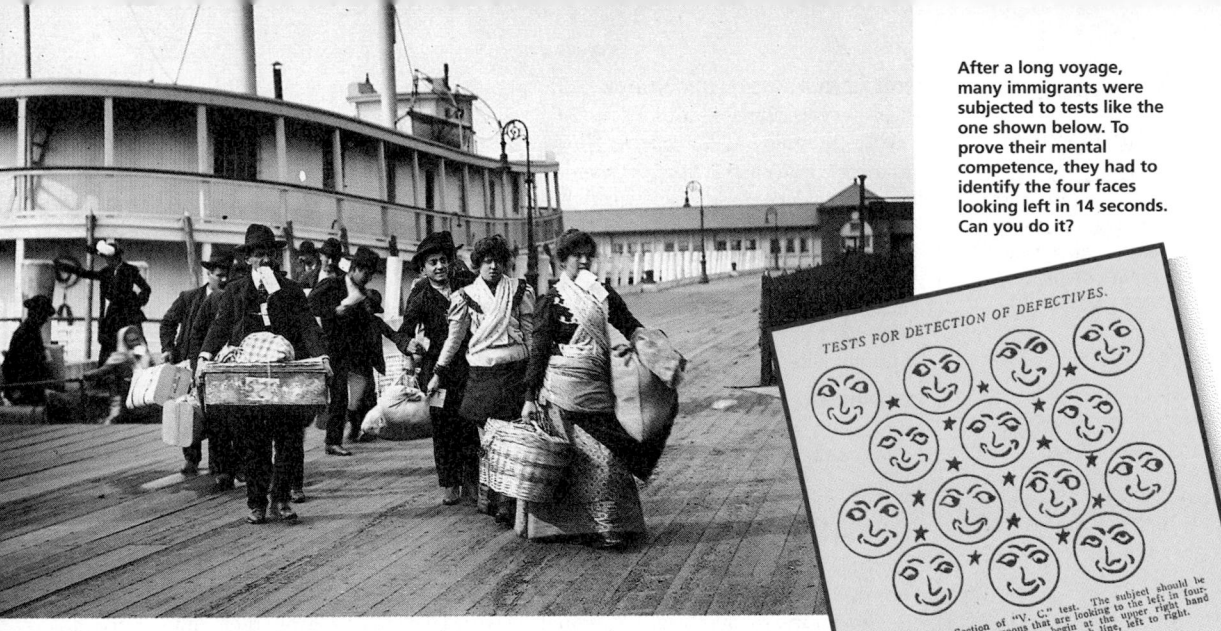

After a long voyage, many immigrants were subjected to tests like the one shown below. To prove their mental competence, they had to identify the four faces looking left in 14 seconds. Can you do it?

TESTS FOR DETECTION OF DEFECTIVES.

MORE ABOUT . . .
Ellis Island
The buildings on Ellis Island were restored in the 1980s, and the Ellis Island Immigration Museum opened in 1990. Have students compare Ellis Island in New York Harbor with Angel Island in San Francisco Bay by making a chart listing similarities and differences between the two places.

Place	Similarities	Differences
Ellis Island		
Angel Bay		

IN-DEPTH RESOURCES: UNIT 4
Primary Source: Artifacts from Ellis Island, p. 46

such inspector, Edward Ferro, an Italian immigrant himself, gave this glimpse of the process.

A PERSONAL VOICE

The language was a problem of course, but it was overcome by the use of interpreters. We had interpreters on the island who spoke practically every language.

It would happen sometimes that these interpreters—some of them—were really softhearted people and hated to see people being deported, and they would, at times, help the aliens by interpreting in such a manner as to benefit the alien and not the government.

EDWARD FERRO, quoted in *I Was Dreaming to Come to America*

From 1892 to 1943, Ellis Island was the chief immigration station in the United States. More than 16 million immigrants passed through its noisy, bustling facilities. During the peak immigration years from 1905 to 1907, as many as 11,000 immigrants a day hurried down the long staircase leading to the ferry that would take them to New York City and their new lives.

ANGEL ISLAND While European immigrants arriving on the East Coast passed through Ellis Island, Asians—primarily Chinese—arriving on the West Coast gained admission at **Angel Island** in San Francisco Bay. Between 1910 and 1940, about 50,000 Chinese immigrants entered the United States through Angel Island. In contrast to the procedure at Ellis Island, processing at Angel Island included harsh questioning and a long detention while government officials decided whether to admit or reject an immigrant.

C. Answer
Medical and government inspections and, on Angel Island, harsh inspections and detention

THINK THROUGH HISTORY
C. Identifying Problems *What difficulties did immigrants face in gaining admission to the United States?*

Angel Island consisted of filthy, ramshackle buildings in which Chinese immigrants were confined like prisoners. To protest these terrible conditions, some immigrants rioted in 1919. Others expressed their feelings by composing poems, which they wrote on the walls. Some of these poems express the difficulties of the journey, anger at being detained, and disappointment with their new home. One immigrant summarized it this way: "Everyone says travelling to North America is / a pleasure. / I suffered misery on the ship and sadness in / the wooden building. / After several interrogations, still I am not / done."

An Angel Island "wall poem" provides an intimate look at what Chinese immigrants experienced there.

Immigrants and Urbanization **441**

TEACHING OPTION
Cooperative Activity: Writing Letters or Poems About Immigrant Experiences

Task: Students will write letters or poems based on an imagined immigrant experience.

Purpose: To sensitize students to the difficulties faced by newcomers in a strange land.

Activity: Ask each group of three or four students to select a particular immigrant experience. The group should create a letter or poem expressing one immigrant's feelings, observations, and ways of dealing with the problems of being a newcomer. One student might be the recorder, a second the facilitator, another the timekeeper, and a fourth the presenter of the group's letter or poem.

📁 **Building a Portfolio:** Students adding a letter or poem to their portfolio should attach a note pointing out their own contribution to the work.

ALTERNATIVE ASSESSMENT BOOK
Standards for Evaluating a Cooperative Activity

Standards for Evaluation
Letters or poems should . . .

• reflect the background and feelings of the writer
• give adequate details about the setting and the events
• be written using appropriate form and style

Teacher's Edition **441**

One of the problems that immigrant parents faced was the generation gap that arose between themselves and their children. The parents seldom sounded like the teachers at school and did not look like the people whose pictures appeared in newspapers. The children, eager to move into the mainstream of American life, were often embarrassed by their parents. Furthermore, the children frequently stopped reciting their traditional prayers and speaking their parents' native tongue. This greatly saddened the parents, who wondered if the price of coming to the United States was too high.

Immigration Restrictions

▶ *Discussing Key Ideas*
• As increasing numbers of immigrants enter the country, anti-immigrant sentiment grows.
• Asians are discriminated against more than whites, and from 1882 until 1943 most Chinese immigration is banned.
• The Gentlemen's Agreement limits Japanese immigration.

💿 ***ELECTRONIC LIBRARY OF PRIMARY SOURCES*** *from the* Chinese Exclusion Act of 1882; "Twelve Hundred More" by Anonymous (a popular anti-Chinese song)

"There she lies, the great Melting Pot."

ISRAEL ZANGWILL,
BRITISH AUTHOR AND
COINER OF THE TERM
"MELTING POT"

Residents of San Francisco's Chinatown survey their adopted country from a doorway in Rag Alley.

EXPERIENCING CULTURE SHOCK Immigrants also had to deal with **culture shock**—confusion and anxiety resulting from immersion in a culture whose ways of thinking and acting they didn't understand. Some con men and thieves took advantage of the newcomers' bewilderment and stole their money and possessions. Most immigrants faced the ongoing nightmare of finding a place to live, getting a job, and dealing with the problems of daily life while trying to understand an alien language and customs.

Many immigrants reacted to culture shock by seeking out people who shared their cultural values, practiced their religion, and spoke their native language. Ethnic communities sprang up in areas that had large concentrations of immigrants.

COOPERATION FOR SURVIVAL The ethnic communities were life rafts for immigrants, who often clung to them fiercely. People pooled their money to build a neighborhood church or synagogue. They formed social clubs where young and old could meet to share experiences, offer mutual support, and enjoy one another's company. Groups of immigrants set up aid societies that furnished medical treatment for members and helped with medical costs. They founded orphanages and old people's homes and established cemeteries. They even published newspapers in their own languages.

Committed to their own cultures but also trying hard to grow into their new identities, many immigrants came to think of themselves as "hyphenated" Americans. As hard as they tried to fit in, these new Polish- and Italian- and Chinese-Americans felt increasing friction as they rubbed shoulders with people born and raised in the United States. Native-born people often disliked the immigrants' unfamiliar customs and languages and viewed them as a threat to the American way of life.

D. Answer They helped one another, forming ethnic enclaves, social clubs, and aid societies.

THINK THROUGH HISTORY
D. *Clarifying*
How did immigrants deal with the challenges they faced?

Immigration Restrictions

At the turn of the century, many native-born Americans thought of their country as a **melting pot,** a mixture of people of different cultures and races who blended together by abandoning their native languages and customs. Many new immigrants, however, refused to give up their cultural identities in order to merge into American society. As growing numbers of immigrants entered the country, strong anti-immigrant feelings emerged, and the government reacted by passing legislation that restricted immigration.

THE RISE OF NATIVISM One response to the growing numbers of immigrants in the United States was nativism, or overt favoritism toward native-born Americans. Nativist sentiments gave rise to anti-immigrant groups and led to a demand for immigration restrictions. Others did not mind immigrants who came from the "right" countries—identified by one observer as "British, German, and Scandinavian stock, historically free, energetic, progressive." However, many disliked immigrants from the "wrong" countries—"Slav, Latin, and Asiatic races, historically down-trodden . . . and stagnant."

Nativism gained support as suspicion and fear of foreigners grew. For example, many native-born Americans, the majority of whom were Protestants, feared the growing influence of Roman Catholics and Jews who were emigrating from Europe in increasing numbers. Nativist groups like the American Protective Association, founded in 1887, launched vicious anti-Catholic attacks, and many colleges, businesses, and social clubs refused to admit Jews.

Some Americans believed that Anglo-Saxons—the Germanic ancestors of the English—were superior to other ethnic groups, an idea widespread in the 19th century. Acting on that belief, the Immigration Restriction

---

Exploring Themes

Immigration and Migration Americans have been on the move since the founding of the nation. Many early settlers stayed along the coast, but others moved westward in search of rich farmland. Southerners moved west, to Kentucky and Tennessee, when their land began to erode. The California gold rush and the offer of free land through the Homestead Act of 1862 spurred more migration from east to west, as did the building of the transcontinental railroad. The Great Depression and drought of the 1930s put Americans on the move again.

Making Connections Across Time

Relations with Russia and Japan In mediating an end to the Russo-Japanese War in 1905, President Theodore Roosevelt was interested in restricting the power of two nations that had the potential to become great international powers. In the closing days of World War II, Japan was America's archenemy. Russia, although an ally in 1945, was soon to become America's nemesis in the Cold War. Today, Japan is one of America's most important trading partners, and Russia is struggling with change as it develops closer ties to the West.

League, a nativist group founded in Boston in 1894, campaigned to keep out "undesirable classes" from southern and eastern Europe. At the league's urging, Congress passed a bill in 1896 that required a literacy test for these new immigrants. Although President Cleveland vetoed the bill, it was a powerful statement of public sentiment.

ANTI-ASIAN SENTIMENT On the West Coast, prejudice against Asians was first directed at the Chinese. This sentiment was particularly strong because the Chinese, in addition to having a "strange" language and unfamiliar customs, looked markedly different from most native-born Americans. In the 1800s and early 1900s, most Chinese men wore their hair in a long braid, called a queue, and dressed in quilted cotton jackets, broad cotton pants, and wide-brimmed hats.

The depression of 1873 intensified anti-Chinese sentiment in California. Jobs were scarce, and native-born workers feared that work would go to Chinese immigrants, who would accept lower wages. Violent anti-Chinese riots erupted, and labor groups exerted political pressure on the government to restrict Asian immigration. Terence V. Powderly, the head of the Knights of Labor, spoke forcefully for general restrictions on the Chinese. The founder of the Workingmen's Party, Denis Kearney, headed the anti-Chinese movement in California. He made hundreds of speeches throughout the state, each ending with the message, "The Chinese must go!"

In 1882, Congress slammed the door on Chinese immigration for ten years by passing the **Chinese Exclusion Act.** This act banned entry to all Chinese except students, teachers, merchants, tourists, and government officials. In 1892, Congress extended the law for another ten years. In 1902, Chinese immigration was prohibited indefinitely; the law was not repealed until 1943.

THE GENTLEMEN'S AGREEMENT The same fears that led to anti-Chinese agitation spread to include the Japanese and other Asian people in the early 1900s. In 1906, the local board of education in San Francisco segregated all Chinese, Japanese, and Korean children and put them in special Asian schools. Anti-American riots erupted in Japan in response to this segregation, prompting President Theodore Roosevelt to intervene. He persuaded San Francisco authorities to withdraw the segregation order. In exchange, under the **Gentlemen's Agreement** of 1907–1908, Japan's government agreed to limit emigration to the United States.

Although doorways for immigrants had been all but closed to Asians on the West Coast, cities in the East and the Midwest teemed with European immigrants—and with urban opportunities and challenges.

THINK THROUGH HISTORY
E. Analyzing Causes Why do you think Asians received such harsh treatment in California?
E. Answer The differences in their appearance and languages provoked racial and cultural prejudice and fear; they provided competition in the job market.

ON THE WORLD STAGE

RUSSIA

MANCHURIA *Sea of Japan*

MONGOLIA

CHINA JAPAN

RUSSO–JAPANESE WAR
As the United States turned its back on Chinese immigrants at the end of the 19th century, a nationalistic group in China—the Boxers—was attempting to drive all foreigners from its country. In 1900, Russia occupied Manchuria, China's northern province, in order to intervene in the Boxer Rebellion. Four years later, when Russia had not retreated, the Japanese invaded the region, sparking the Russo-Japanese War. Japan won striking victories, but as its resources dwindled, it turned to President Theodore Roosevelt to mediate the conflict. Roosevelt agreed, reasoning that it was in America's interest to contain both Russia and Japan. Japan's show of power increased distrust of the island nation and increased the level of anti-Japanese feeling in the United States.

Section 1 Assessment

1. TERMS & NAMES
Identify:
- Ellis Island
- Angel Island
- culture shock
- melting pot
- Chinese Exclusion Act
- Gentlemen's Agreement

2. SUMMARIZING Create a diagram such as the one below. List two or more causes of each effect.

Causes	⟶	Effect
1. 2. 3.		Immigrants leave their home countries.
1. 2. 3.		Immigrants face hardships in the United States.
1. 2. 3.		Some nativists want to restrict immigration.

3. FORMING OPINIONS Which group of immigrants faced the greatest challenges settling in the United States? Why?

THINK ABOUT
- the difficulties of travel to the United States
- where the immigrants settled
- the opportunities open to each immigrant group

4. SYNTHESIZING What arguments can you make against nativism and anti-immigrant feeling?

THINK ABOUT
- the personal qualities of immigrants
- the reasons for anti-immigrant feeling
- the contributions of immigrants to the United States

Immigrants and Urbanization **443**

ON THE WORLD STAGE
Russo-Japanese War
Critical Thinking: Analyzing Issues Ask students to distinguish between mediating a foreign dispute and intervening in such a dispute. Have them suggest recent instances in which American presidents have mediated or intervened. *President Carter mediated the dispute between Israel and Egypt; President Clinton has intervened in Haiti and in Bosnia by sending in American soldiers.*

ASSESS & RETEACH

Section 1 Assessment
Have groups of students divide up the questions and work together to find the answers.

Self-Assessment
Have students develop an analogy between the controversy surrounding immigration in 1870–1920 and the controversy surrounding immigration today.

Section Quiz

FORMAL ASSESSMENT
Section Quiz, p. 185

Reteach
Show the video "From China to Chinatown" again and discuss the immigration issues raised in the film.

AMERICAN STORIES VIDEO SERIES "From China to Chinatown"

ANSWERS

1. TERMS & NAMES
Ellis Island, p. 440
Angel Island, p. 441
culture shock, p. 442
melting pot, p. 442
Chinese Exclusion Act, p. 443
Gentlemen's Agreement, p. 443

2. SUMMARIZING
Possible Responses:
Leaving home countries: Poverty; religious persecution; shortage of agricultural land; lack of industrial jobs; spirit of reform.
Facing hardships in U.S.: New, unfamiliar culture; harsh interrogation and detention; prejudice and discrimination; problems of urban life; culture shock.

Nativists wanting to restrict immigration: Growing immigration; suspicion and fear of differences; religious intolerance; racial prejudice; economic depression.

3. FORMING OPINIONS
Possible Response: Many students may say that the Chinese faced the most prejudice, because of their different appearance and customs, and because of the

fear that they would take jobs away from native-born workers.

4. SYNTHESIZING
Possible Responses: Immigrants were brave and willing to work hard; there is cultural value in being exposed to many customs and ways of life; nativists themselves were descendants of immigrants.

CLOSE

European immigrants, eager to find work and new opportunities, poured into the cities of the East and the Midwest. Anti-Asian sentiment led the United States to ban Chinese immigration and to limit Japanese immigration for almost 60 years.

What Is the American Dream?

What is the American dream? A 17th-century colonist's setting sail in search of religious freedom? An 18th-century revolutionary's fighting for political independence? A 19th-century African-American freedman's farming his own plot of land in Kansas? A 20th-century couple's buying their first home or car? It is all of these—and more. The American dream has as many faces as there are Americans. And it's still being dreamed.

European and Asian Immigrants Immigrants, hoping to escape religious persecution or to explore new economic opportunities, left their homelands by the thousands in pursuit of a chance for a better life.

OBJECTIVES

① To explore Americans' different definitions of the American dream.

② To recognize the role of the American dream in inspiring immigration to and migration within America.

FOCUS & MOTIVATE

▶ **Starting with the Student**
The phrase "the American dream" recurs in political discussions. Ask students what the term means to them. Then ask whether they think the meaning is the same for every generation.

MORE ABOUT . . .
The American Dream for African Americans

African-American leaders have often defined the American dream as one of equal rights and opportunities for all Americans. Martin Luther King, Jr., described it in his famous "I Have a Dream" speech, delivered at the Lincoln Memorial in Washington, D.C., in 1963. Two years earlier, at Lincoln University in Pennsylvania, King delivered a commencement address entitled "The American Dream," in which he told his audience: "America is essentially a dream, a dream as yet unfulfilled. It is a dream of a land where men of all races, of all nationalities and of all creeds can live together as brothers."

1890
CHANGING FRONTIERS

As immigrants flooded onto both coasts of the United States and white settlers pushed westward, many competing dreams collided.

1620
THE PILGRIMS

A group of people who wanted the freedom to practice their religion risked a treacherous voyage across the Atlantic to build a colony in an unknown land.

African Americans
After the Civil War, many emancipated African Americans in the South became share-croppers or tenant farmers. Others later moved north and west, looking for work and for opportunities for their children.

444 Chapter 15

RECOMMENDED RESOURCES

Books

Hearn, Charles R. *The American Dream in the Great Depression.* Westport, CT: Greenwood, 1977. How hard times affected the American dream.

Hochschild, Jennifer L. *Facing Up to the American Dream.* Princeton, NJ: Princeton UP, 1995. How race and class differences affect the American dream.

Terkel, Studs. *American Dreams, Lost and Found.* New York: Pantheon, 1980. Interviews with average Americans presenting their views of the American dream.

Videos

The American Dream Contest. Pyramid, 1989. Twelve winners in a contest in which Americans aged 9 to 17 created concepts for short films on the American dream.

The American Dream: Myth or Reality? Guidance Associates. The evolution of the American dream in 19th-century America.

The Promised Land. Discovery and BBC. The expectations and discoveries of African Americans who migrated from the rural South to urban Chicago in the 20th century; narrated by Morgan Freeman.

1950
LIFE IN THE SUBURBS

After World War II, many people believed that their troubles were behind them. The American dream blossomed in the form of a new home, a big car, and a nuclear family.

1990
THE RECURRING DREAM

As America moves toward the millennium, minorities and other Americans—like this Latino owner of a tortilla factory in Texas—continue to overcome obstacles and hardships to realize their dreams. In the words of President Bill Clinton, "The American Dream that we were all raised on is a simple but powerful one— if you work hard and play by the rules, you should be given a chance to go as far as your God-given abilities will take you."

Native Americans
The Native Americans had their dream—their traditional life lived on the Western plains. Until the coming of the white settlers, they thrived on the land, free to move about or to cultivate its bounty.

INTERACT WITH HISTORY

1. **ANALYZING ISSUES** Think about the competing dreams presented in 1890—Changing Frontiers. What factors might determine whether an individual's American dream is realized?

    SEE SKILLBUILDER HANDBOOK, PAGE 1046.

2. **LIVING THE DREAM** What is your American dream for the 21st century? How do you plan to fulfill it? What conflicts or obstacles might you have to overcome? Write down your thoughts and save them in a folder for your American history portfolio. Revisit and revise your dream periodically.

Immigrants and Urbanization **445**

OBJECTIVES

1 To describe the movement of immigrants to cities and the opportunities they found there.

2 To explain how cities dealt with problems related to housing, transportation, water supply, sanitation, and fire and police protection.

3 To describe some of the organizations and people who offered help to urban immigrants.

SKILLBUILDER

• Understanding geography: place, movement, p. 447

CRITICAL THINKING

• Analyzing motives, p. 447
• Contrasting, p. 447
• Identifying problems, p. 448
• Recognizing effects, pp. 449, 451
• Comparing, p. 450
• Analyzing causes, p. 451
• Summarizing, p. 451
• Evaluating, p. 451

FOCUS & MOTIVATE

▶ **Starting with the Student**
Ask students to suggest ways of helping a newly arrived foreign student adjust to school. Have them tell how the suggestions would help the newcomer to solve some of his or her problems.

MORE ABOUT . . .
Jacob Riis

Riis worked as a police reporter for the New York *Tribune* and, later, for the New York *Evening Sun.* He taught himself the new technique of using flashlight powder to take pictures indoors so that he could illustrate his newspaper articles with photographs. His book *How the Other Half Lives* was published in 1890. An immediate bestseller, it led to the rise of exposé journalism.

IN-DEPTH RESOURCES: UNIT 4
Primary Source: from *How the Other Half Lives* by Riis, p. 47

❷ The Problems of Urbanization

TERMS & NAMES
• urbanization
• row house
• dumbbell tenement
• Social Gospel movement
• settlement house
• Jane Addams

LEARN ABOUT the rapid growth of American cities in the late 1800s and early 1900s
TO UNDERSTAND the promise and problems of urbanization.

ONE AMERICAN'S STORY

In 1870, at age 21, Jacob Riis left his native Denmark and arrived penniless in the United States. Like many other immigrants, he experienced hunger, homelessness, and life in the slums. Riis overcame the challenges of living in a new country, however, and eventually became a journalist and a tireless reformer. He used his talents to expose the conditions in which he had grown up—the overcrowded, airless, filthy tenements that still housed New York City's poor.

> **A PERSONAL VOICE**
> Be a little careful, please. The hall is dark and you might stumble over the children pitching pennies back there. Not that it would hurt them; kicks and cuffs are their daily diet. They have little else. . . . Close? [Stuffy?] Yes! What would you have? All the fresh air that enters these stairs is from the hall-door that is forever slamming. . . . Here is a door. Listen! That short hacking cough, that tiny helpless wail— what do they mean? . . . The child is dying with measles. With half a chance it might have lived; but it had none. That dark bedroom killed it.
> **JACOB RIIS,** *How the Other Half Lives*

As many as 12 people slept in rooms such as this one in New York City, photographed by Jacob Riis about 1889. The rent was five cents per night.

Making a living in the late 19th and early 20th centuries was not easy. Natural and economic disasters had hit farmers hard, both in Europe and in the United States, and the promise of industrial jobs drew millions of people to American cities. The urban population exploded, jumping from 10 million to 54 million between 1870 and 1920. This rapid urban growth not only revitalized the cities but also created serious problems. As Jacob Riis observed firsthand, these problems had a powerful impact on the new urban poor.

Urban Opportunities

The lure that drew people to the cities was largely the same one that had attracted settlers to the West and immigrants to America—opportunity. In these bustling, industrialized centers, people saw a chance to work, escape poverty, and carve out a better life for themselves and their children. The technological boom in the 19th century not only revolutionized age-old occupations such as farming but also contributed to the growing industrial strength of the United States. New mills, factories, mines, and transportation systems needed millions of workers who lived close to the workplaces, most of which were located in the northeastern part of the United States. While many settlers pushed westward to start new lives on the frontier, thousands of other people were drawn to the Northeast and Midwest. The result was rapid **urbanization,** or growth of cities, in those regions.

IMMIGRANTS SETTLE IN CITIES   Most of the immigrants who streamed into the United States in the late 19th century became city dwellers because cities were the cheapest and most convenient places to live. Most Irish immigrants, for example, initially settled in Boston, New York City, and Philadelphia not far from the ports where they landed. Cities also offered unskilled laborers steady jobs in

---

PRINT RESOURCES

IN-DEPTH RESOURCES: UNIT 4
Guided Reading, p. 38
Geography Application: Industry and Urban Growth, p 42
Primary Sources: from *How the Other Half Lives* by Riis, p. 47;
  from *Twenty Years at Hull-House* by Addams, p. 48
American Lives: Jane Addams, p. 53

ACCESS FOR STUDENTS ACQUIRING ENGLISH
Guided Reading (Spanish), p. 149
Geography Application: Industry and Growth (Spanish), p. 153

FORMAL ASSESSMENT
Section Quiz, p. 186

ALTERNATIVE ASSESSMENT BOOK
See forms for supporting and scoring alternative activities.

TECHNOLOGY RESOURCES

HUMANITIES TRANSPARENCIES
H15, *Cliff Dwellers* by George Bellows, 1913

CRITICAL THINKING TRANSPARENCIES
CT15, Urban Growth
CT49, From Country to City: 1870–1920

CD-ROM *Our Times*
Electronic Library of Primary Sources

VIDEO *American Portfolio: A Videodisc for U.S. History*
user's guide, pp. 146–149

INTERNET McDougal Littell Learning On-Line
http://www.mcdougallittell.com

mills and factories and provided the social support of other immigrant families. By 1890, there were twice as many Irish residents in New York City as in Dublin, Ireland, and the world's largest Polish population was not in Warsaw, Poland, but in Chicago. By 1910, immigrant families made up more than half the total population of 18 major American cities.

Immigrants often clustered in ethnic neighborhoods with others from the same country—or even from the same province or village. Living among people who shared their background enabled the newcomers to speak their own language and practice their customs and religion while learning about their new home with the aid of those who had come before. The cities became vibrant, colorful collages of various ethnic groups—"an extraordinary crazy quilt," as Jacob Riis called the New York of 1890. Unfortunately, many native-born Americans felt threatened by these mushrooming ethnic communities and expressed their fear by becoming hostile. Overcrowding soon became a problem as well, one that was intensified by the migration of new urbanites from America's rural areas.

MIGRATION FROM COUNTRY TO CITY Farming technology improved rapidly in the second half of the 19th century, which was good news for some farmers but bad news for others. Inventions such as the McCormick reaper and the steel-bladed plow made farming more efficient but meant that fewer laborers were needed to work the land. As use of the new equipment spread across the country, farms merged, and many rural people could not find jobs in agriculture. They left their land and agricultural way of life and made their way to cities to find whatever jobs they could.

Many of the southern farmers who lost their jobs were African Americans. Other African Americans in the rural South also became aware of the opportunities in large cities. Between 1890 and 1910, about 200,000 African Americans moved north and west to cities such as Chicago and Detroit, as they tried to escape racial violence, economic hardship, and political oppression. Many found conditions in these cities only somewhat better than those they left behind. Because of racial prejudice and their inadequate education, they were often forced to take low-paying factory jobs or to work as domestic servants.

URBAN CULTURAL OPPORTUNITIES Although people moved to cities for economic reasons, cultural opportunities offered an additional attraction. In contrast to the relatively slow pace of life in both immigrants' native villages and American rural communities, life in the city was varied and exciting. Each city had a personality all its own. In New York City, you had an opportunity to see the first moving pictures. In Chicago, you could join your neighbors on an outing to the Columbian Exposition or to Buffalo Bill's Wild West Show. In

---

Ethnic Enclaves in New York City, 1910

Austrian
German
Irish
Italian
Russian
Scandinavian

Light tint indicates at least 20% of population.
Darker tint indicates 40% of population or more.

Non-residential

No group with more than 20% of population

Boundary between Brooklyn and Queens

BRONX

MANHATTAN

QUEENS

BROOKLYN

GEOGRAPHY SKILLBUILDER
PLACE *What general pattern of settlement do you notice in this map of ethnic neighborhoods in New York City in 1910?*
MOVEMENT *What was the largest ethnic group in Brooklyn? in Queens?*

Skillbuilder Answer
Place: Immigrants often settled with others of similar backgrounds.
Movement: Brooklyn— Russian; Queens— German.

Immigrants and Urbanization **447**

A. Answer For mutual support

THINK THROUGH HISTORY
A. Analyzing Motives Why did immigrants tend to group together in the cities?

B. Answer Both groups had to find jobs. African-American farmworkers faced the additional challenge of racial prejudice.

THINK THROUGH HISTORY
B. Contrasting How was the experience of moving to cities similar and different for African-American farmworkers and other farmworkers?

Urban Opportunities

▶*Discussing Key Ideas*
• Most new immigrants settle in cities because cities are the cheapest and most convenient places to live.
• New technology makes farming more efficient, resulting in the loss of jobs for some farmworkers, who move to cities.
• Cities offer diverse cultural opportunities.

IN-DEPTH RESOURCES: UNIT 4
Guided Reading, p. 38
Geography Application: Industry and Growth, p. 42

ACCESS FOR STUDENTS ACQUIRING ENGLISH
Guided Reading (Spanish), p. 149

CRITICAL THINKING TRANSPARENCIES
CT15, Urban Growth
CT49, From Country to City: 1870–1920

HISTORY FROM VISUALS
Ethnic Enclaves in New York City, 1910

Reading the Map Point out that each ethnic group is represented by two colors.

Extension Ask students to review the map and answer the following question:
• In what ways was the building of bridges an important improvement? *People and businesses had better access to areas away from the port; it was easier to commute to work and to visit family.*

TEACHING OPTIONS

Making Connections Across Time

Immigrants and the Economy Most immigrants coming into the United States today start by taking low-paying jobs as domestics, unskilled workers, or workers in the burgeoning service industries, such as fast-food restaurants, laundries, car washes, and dry cleaners. An immigrant's income may be subsidized by state or local funds until the immigrant becomes self-supporting. Such government welfare was not available for earlier immigrants, although charitable organizations, both religious and secular, offered assistance. Today's immigrants provide revenue to the government by paying sales and income taxes, neither of which existed in the 19th century.

Teaching Gifted and Talented Students

Making a Map of Your Town or City Ask students to do some research in the library and on the Internet to discover what ethnic groups have played an important role in the history of their community. Have them use the results of their research to make a map, similar to "Ethnic Enclaves in New York City, 1910," that shows what groups lived in their community, and where, at a specific time. They might use the year 1910, or they might show the ethnic makeup of their community at a later time.

Urban Problems

▶ **Starting with the Student**
Ask students to list reasons they might want to live in a city. Then ask them to make a list of problems related to urban living.

▶ **Discussing Key Ideas**
• As the urban population increases, cities struggle with many problems.
• Among the problems cities face are overcrowded, unsanitary housing; mass transportation needs; lack of a fresh water supply; and fires and crime.

🏛 **HUMANITIES TRANSPARENCIES**
H15, *Cliff Dwellers* by George Bellows, 1913

HISTORICAL SPOTLIGHT
Streetcar Suburbs

Critical Thinking: Cause and Effect Use the diagram in this feature to discuss with students how better transportation after 1880 improved the lives of the people living in urban and suburban settings.

MORE ABOUT . . .
Row-House Living

Living in a row house was comfortable. Each room had a brass fixture for gas jets or electric bulbs. The furnace fire glowed all night, so people did not wake up shivering with cold. A gas flame heated the water in the water tank and fueled the stove. And every house had a bathroom with running water and an indoor toilet.

Boston, you could travel to the ball field and watch the hometown Boston Nationals battle their way to a championship title. Cultural attractions such as these sometimes made up for the hardships that life in the city presented.

Urban Problems

As the urban population skyrocketed, city governments faced serious problems, such as how to provide adequate housing, transportation, water, and sanitation and how to deal effectively with fire and crime.

HOUSING When the industrial age began, housing options for working-class families in major cities were few and far from satisfactory. Families could buy a house on the outskirts of town, but they had to commute to work on often inadequate public transportation. They could also rent rooms in a boardinghouse in the central city, sharing kitchen and dining-room facilities with other families. As the urban population increased, however, new types of housing were designed that eliminated some disadvantages of each of those options. For example, **row houses**—attached single-family dwellings that shared side walls with other similar houses—packed many single-family residences on a single block.

After working-class families moved away from the central city, immigrants often took over their old housing, installing two or three families in a one-family residence. As Jacob Riis noted, these multifamily dwellings, called tenements, were overcrowded and unsanitary.

To improve such slum conditions, New York City passed a law in 1879 that set minimum standards for plumbing and ventilation in apartment buildings. To meet these standards, landlords began building **dumbbell tenements,** long, narrow, five- or six-story buildings that were shaped like barbells. The central part was indented on either side to allow for an air shaft and, thus, an outside window for each room.

Since garbage was picked up infrequently, people sometimes dumped it into the air shafts, where it attracted rats and vermin. To keep out the stench, residents nailed windows shut. Though established with good intent, dumbbell tenements soon became even worse places to live than the converted single-family residences.

TRANSPORTATION Getting around the city safely and efficiently was as much of a problem as finding a steady job and a decent place to live. Before industrialization, people went on foot or by horse-drawn vehicles. But innovations in mass transit enabled large numbers of workers to go to and from jobs more easily. Cable cars driven by moving underground cables were introduced in San Francisco in 1873. In 1888, the first practical electric streetcar line began operating in Richmond, Virginia. In addition, new modes of transportation were developed to take advantage of space available above and below street level. In Boston, for example, electric subways began running underneath the city's busy streets in 1897. By the early 20th century, mass-transit networks in many urban areas linked city neighborhoods to one another and outlying communities to the central business district and other focal points. As urban populations kept expanding, cities were hard-pressed to keep old transportation systems in good repair and to build new ones to meet the growing demand.

C. Answer
Overcrowding and unsanitary conditions

THINK THROUGH HISTORY
C. Identifying Problems What housing problems did urban working-class families face?

HISTORICAL SPOTLIGHT

STREETCAR SUBURBS
By the late 19th century, electric streetcars were carrying more than 2 billion passengers a year in cities throughout the United States. This new mode of transportation changed not only the way people traveled but also where they lived. As streetcar lines extended out from the heart of the city, people who were not wealthy were no longer limited to living within walking distance of the workplace. Modest single-family homes and multifamily dwellings sprang up in the urban outskirts served by these lines. These streetcar suburbs offered middle- and working-class families an attractive alternative to inner-city life.

| CITY CENTER | Pedestrian city 2 miles | 1880 Horse-drawn streetcar 3.5 miles | 1900 Electric streetcar 6 miles |

Exploring Themes

Cultural Diversity In 1900, the average annual income of American workers was about $500. Many workers who lived in cities, however, were able to enrich their drab existence by taking advantage of the many cultural activities that were offered. Places such as Hull House in Chicago and the Henry Street Settlement House in New York offered classes in art, music, and drama. Museums offered free days, and ethnic groups, such as the Yiddish theater in New York, provided reasonably priced entertainment in a particular group's native language.

Exploring Themes

The American Dream To many new immigrants, free public education was a miracle. One immigrant recalled her father had "brought his children to school as if it were an act of consecration." At schools, the children learned about democracy, voting, and civic responsibility. They also gained language proficiency and a background in American history. Many immigrant parents who worked during the day attended night school, where they, too, learned the English language, American history, and how democracy works.

WATER Cities also faced the problem of supplying fresh water that was safe to drink. Before industrialization, many people bought water for drinking and cooking from vendors on horse-drawn carts. As the urban population grew in the 1840s and 1850s, cities such as New York and Cleveland built public water-works to handle the increasing demand. As late as the 1860s, however, the residents of many cities had grossly inadequate water mains and piped water—or none at all. Even in large cities like New York, homes seldom had indoor plumbing, and residents had to collect water in a pail from a faucet on the street and heat it for bathing. The necessity of improving water quality to control diseases such as cholera and typhoid fever was obvious. To make city water safer, chlorination was introduced in 1893 and filtration in 1908. These innovations spread slowly, however. In the early 20th century, many city dwellers still had no access to safe water.

Sanitation problems in big cities were overwhelming. It was not unusual to see a dead horse in the street.

SANITATION As the cities grew, so did the challenge of keeping them clean. Most were teeming with unsanitary conditions. Horse manure piled up on the streets, sewage flowed through open gutters, and factories spewed foul smoke into the air. Without a dependable system of trash removal, people dumped their garbage into alleys and streets. Although private contractors called scavengers were hired to sweep the streets, collect garbage, and clean outhouses, they often did not do the jobs they were paid to do. Sewer lines and sanitation departments, which many cities instituted by 1900, helped somewhat in keeping cities clean, but the task of providing healthful urban living conditions was an ongoing challenge for urban leaders.

D. Answer Lack of fresh water and inadequate sanitation created health hazards.

THINK THROUGH HISTORY
D. Recognizing Effects How did conditions in cities affect people's health?

FIRE The limited water supply in many cities contributed to another menace: the spread of fires. Major fires occurred in almost every large American city during the 1870s and 1880s. In addition to lacking water to combat blazes once they started, most cities were packed with wooden dwellings, which were like kindling waiting to be ignited. The use of candles and kerosene heaters was also

Fire: Enemy of the City

THE GREAT CHICAGO FIRE OCTOBER 8, 1871	THE SAN FRANCISCO EARTHQUAKE APRIL 18, 1906
• The fire burned for 29 hours.	• The quake lasted 28 seconds; fires burned for 4 days.
• An estimated 300 people died.	• An estimated 478 people died.
• 100,000 were left homeless.	• 250,000 were left homeless.
• More than 3 square miles of the central city was destroyed.	• Fire swept through 5 square miles of the city.
• Property loss was estimated at $200 million.	• Property loss was estimated at $500 million.
• 17,500 buildings were destroyed.	• 28,000 buildings were destroyed.

The Great Chicago Fire

The Great Chicago Fire was preceded by a succession of small fires that broke out during the first week of October 1871. At that time, the city was particularly susceptible to fires because there had been almost no rain for three months. On the night of October 8, so the story goes, a wagon driver named Daniel "Peg Leg" Sullivan was drinking whiskey in the barn of his neighbor, Mrs. Catherine O'Leary, as he often did. That night, Sullivan apparently took one nip too many and dropped a kerosene lamp into a pile of hay. Mrs. O'Leary's barn caught fire—and the rest is history. The fire was so destructive that even Chicago's marble courthouse, which had just been built for $1 million and had been considered fireproof, collapsed in the blaze.

OBJECTIVE
③ INSTRUCT

Reformers Mobilize

▶ **Starting with the Student**
Ask students the following questions:

• If you could start an organization to help some group less fortunate than you, what kind of organization would it be?
• How would you go about setting up such an organization?

(continued on next page)

---

a fire hazard. In San Francisco, deadly fires often broke out in the aftermath of an earthquake. Jack London described the fires that broke out during the San Francisco earthquake of 1906.

A PERSONAL VOICE
On Wednesday morning at a quarter past five came the earthquake. A minute later the flames were leaping upward. In a dozen quarters south of Market Street, in the working-class ghetto, and in the factories, fires started. There was no opposing the flames. . . . The streets were humped into ridges and depressions . . . steel rails were twisted into perpendicular and horizontal angles. And the great water mains had burst. All the shrewd contrivances and safeguards of man had been thrown out of gear by thirty seconds twitching of the earthcrust.

JACK LONDON, *The Story of an Eyewitness*

At first, firefighters were generally volunteers and were not always available when their services were needed. Cincinnati, Ohio tackled this problem when it established the nation's first paid fire department in 1853. By 1900, most cities had full-time professional fire departments. Invention of the automatic fire sprinkler in 1874 and replacement of many wooden buildings with structures made of brick, stone, and concrete also made cities safer. Despite these various improvements, however, blazes still got out of control. John R. Chapin, an artist for *Harper's Weekly*, described the destruction done by the Great Chicago Fire of 1871: "[The blaze] was devouring the most stately and massive buildings as though they had been the cardboard playthings of a child. . . . One after another they dissolved, like snow on a mountain."

CRIME As the populations of cities increased, so did crime. Pickpockets and thieves flourished in urban crowds, while con men fooled non-English-speaking immigrants and naive country people with clever scams. Crime-ridden areas of certain cities, which were controlled by gangs of young toughs, became known as Murderers' Alleys or Robbers' Roosts. Although New York City organized the first full-time, salaried police force in 1844, it and most other city law enforcement units were too small to adequately protect residents from rising crime and violence.

E. Answer
Possible answers: Overcrowding; a lack of affordable housing, health issues, fire, crime, and prejudice toward new immigrants.

THINK THROUGH HISTORY
E. Comparing
Which of the problems facing late-19th-century city dwellers remain problems today?

Reformers Mobilize

As problems in cities mounted, some Americans worked to find solutions. Social reformers—mostly young, educated men and women from the middle class—established programs to aid the poor and to improve urban life.

Jane Addams helped children who might otherwise have turned to crime leave the streets and improve their lives.

TEACHING OPTIONS

Making Connections Across Time

Gangs Then and Now From the 1850s on, in such cities as Boston, New York, and Chicago, some young immigrants formed gangs for mutual protection and survival. From acts of petty crime, scams against new immigrants, and theft, gangs moved into politics, electioneering, and the stuffing of ballot boxes. Today, gangs still flourish in the major cities and even in suburbia. Some deal in petty crime, others in drug trafficking, big-time gambling, and counterfeiting.

Teaching Less Proficient Readers

Clarifying Ideas To help students clarify the problems in the cities in the late 1800s, copy this chart onto the chalkboard and have students fill it in.

Problems	Causes	Solutions
Housing		
Transportation		
Water		
Sanitation		
Fire		
Crime		

THE SOCIAL GOSPEL MOVEMENT Social welfare reformers targeted their efforts at relieving the poverty of immigrants and other city dwellers. An early reform program, the **Social Gospel movement,** preached salvation through service to the poor. Social Gospel ministers such as Walter Rauschenbush of New York City, and Washington Gladden of Columbus, Ohio, who called his teachings "Applied Christianity," inspired followers to erect churches in poor communities and persuaded some business leaders to treat workers more fairly.

THE SETTLEMENT-HOUSE MOVEMENT Inspired by the message of the Social Gospel movement, many 19th-century reformers responded to the call to help the urban poor. In the late 1800s, a few reformers established **settlement houses,** community centers in slum neighborhoods that provided assistance and friendship to local men, women, and children—especially immigrants. Many settlement workers lived at the houses so they could learn firsthand about some of the problems caused by urbanization and help create solutions.

Run largely by middle-class, college-educated women, settlement houses promoted education, culture, and social services. They provided classes in such subjects as English, health, crafts, drama, music, and painting, and offered college extension courses. They sponsored reading circles in which volunteers read books aloud to help educate the illiterate. Settlement houses also sent visiting nurses into the homes of the sick and provided whatever aid was needed to secure "support for deserted women, insurance for bewildered widows, damages for injured operators, furniture from the clutches of the installment store."

Early settlement houses in the United States, founded by Charles Stover and Stanton Coit, opened in New York City in 1886. **Jane Addams** and Ellen Gates Starr founded Chicago's Hull House in 1889, and Lillian D. Wald established New York's Henry Street Settlement House in 1895. In 1890, Janie Porter Barrett founded Locust Street Social Settlement in Hampton, Virginia, the first settlement house for African Americans. By 1910, about 400 settlement houses were operating in cities across the country.

The Social Gospel and settlement-house movements firmly established the need for social responsibility toward the urban poor and a means of addressing some of the ongoing problems of urbanization. A new type of political structure developed in an attempt to deal with these urban issues. But it soon created problems of its own.

F. Answer Both movements focused on social problems that the urban poor faced, such as isolation and exploitation. The Social Gospel promoted social consciousness and the settlement houses provided actual aid to the poor.

THINK THROUGH HISTORY
F. Analyzing Causes How did the Social Gospel and settlement-house movements help the urban poor meet the challenges of city life?

KEY PLAYER

JANE ADDAMS
1860–1935
Jane Addams was a community worker, a champion of organized labor, and a peace advocate. In all things, she believed that the best approach to problem solving was to "learn from life itself."

During a trip overseas, she visited England's Toynbee Hall, the first settlement house. She viewed the problems of urban life firsthand—and resolved to do something about them. She founded Hull House in Chicago, where she began working to solve neighborhood problems. In time her concerns expanded. She became an antiwar activist, a spokesperson for racial justice, and an advocate for quality-of-life issues, from infant mortality to better care for the aged. In 1931 she was a co-winner of the Nobel Peace Prize.

Until the end of her life, Addams insisted that she was just a "very simple person." But many who know what she accomplished consider her a source of continuing inspiration.

(continued from page 450)

▶ *Discussing Key Ideas*
• Reform-minded church leaders inspire the building of churches in poor neighborhoods and espouse efforts to help the indigent.
• Settlement houses are established in slum areas.

KEY PLAYER
Jane Addams

Critical Thinking: Drawing Conclusions After students have read the information about Jane Addams, have them discuss on what basis they think Addams qualified for the Nobel Peace Prize. *Possible Response: She was a peace advocate, an antiwar activist, and a fighter for racial justice.*

IN-DEPTH RESOURCES: UNIT 4
American Lives: Jane Addams, p. 53
Primary Source: from *Twenty Years at Hull-House* by Addams, p. 48.

 ELECTRONIC LIBRARY OF PRIMARY SOURCES
"The Modern City and the Municipal Franchise for Women" by Jane Addams

ASSESS & RETEACH

Section 2 Assessment
Have students answer the questions and then note the pages on which the answers can be found.

Self-Assessment
Ask students to choose one of the urban problems discussed in this section and write a one-paragraph solution to the problem.

Section Quiz

FORMAL ASSESSMENT
Section Quiz, p. 186

Reteach
Survey students to find out what part of this section was difficult for them. Use the graphic on page 447 as a discussion starter.

CLOSE

Rapid population growth revitalized the cities but also brought new problems.

Section 2 Assessment

1. TERMS & NAMES
Identify:
• urbanization
• row house
• dumbbell tenement
• Social Gospel movement
• settlement house
• Jane Addams

2. SUMMARIZING Recreate the spider map below on your paper. Write three urban problems on the vertical lines. Fill in details about attempts that were made to solve each problem.

SOLUTIONS TO URBAN PROBLEMS

3. RECOGNIZING EFFECTS What effects did the migration from rural areas to the cities in the late 19th century have on urban society?

THINK ABOUT
• the reasons people moved to cities
• the problems caused by rapid urban growth
• the impact of urban growth on rural areas

4. EVALUATING Do you think the Social Gospel reformers and those who started settlement houses had realistic goals? Why or why not?

THINK ABOUT
• the motives of the reformers
• the types of reforms they supported
• the impact of their reforms

ANSWERS

1. TERMS & NAMES

urbanization, p. 446

row house, p. 448

dumbbell tenement, p. 448

Social Gospel movement, p. 451

settlement house, p. 451

Jane Addams, p. 451

2. SUMMARIZING

Students should choose three problems to develop. inadequate housing—dumbbell tenements, row houses; inadequate transportation—new streetcar lines, subways; unsafe water—public waterworks, chlorination, filtration; poor sanitation—sewer lines, sanitation departments;

frequent fires—full-time fire departments, replacement of wooden buildings with brick, stone, and concrete ones; high crime—improved police protection.

3. RECOGNIZING EFFECTS

Possible Responses: Overcrowding; competition for jobs.

4. EVALUATING

While some students might criticize the reformers and their efforts as unrealistic, others might defend their accomplishments. Students' opinions should be supported with adequate reasons.

OBJECTIVES

① To explain the role of political machines and political bosses.

② To describe how politicians' greed and fraud cost taxpayers millions of dollars.

SKILLBUILDERS

• Interpreting cartoons, p. 454
• Interpreting charts, p. 454

CRITICAL THINKING

• Summarizing, pp. 453, 454
• Analyzing motives, p. 453
• Comparing, p. 454
• Generalizing, p. 454
• Analyzing causes, p. 454

FOCUS & MOTIVATE

▶ *Starting with the Student*
Ask students if they have ever given someone a gift with the intention of getting something in return. Then ask them if they believe that such a practice is common among politicians today.

MORE ABOUT . . .
George Washington Plunkitt

Plunkitt believed in giving people something in exchange for their votes. He furnished emergency lodging and clothing to families hit by fire. He found jobs for the unemployed. He put in a good word for youngsters who got into trouble with the police. He paid court fines for constituents who were picked up for being drunk. "The poor are the most grateful people in the world," he pointed out, "and, let me tell you, they have more friends in their neighborhoods than the rich have in theirs."

---

③ The Emergence of the Political Machine

TERMS & NAMES
• graft
• political machine
• kickback
• Tammany Hall
• Tweed Ring
• Thomas Nast

LEARN ABOUT the emergence of political machines in American cities in the 19th century
TO UNDERSTAND the role that politics played in shaping urban life.

ONE AMERICAN'S STORY

George Washington Plunkitt was born in 1842 to Irish immigrants in New York City. He quit school when he was 11 years old and went to work in a butcher's shop. Despite a lack of formal education, Plunkitt became a shrewd leader in Tammany Hall, New York City's Democratic political machine. He worked his way up the political ladder from precinct captain to ward boss to state senator. In the process, he became a millionaire, largely through **graft,** or illegal use of political influence for personal gain.

A PERSONAL VOICE
There's an honest graft, and I'm an example of how it works. . . . My party's in power in the city, and it's goin' to undertake a lot of public improvements. Well, I'm tipped off, say, that they're going to lay out a new park at a certain place. . . . I see my opportunity and I take it. I go to that place and I buy up all the land I can. . . . There's a rush to get my land, which nobody cared particular for before. . . . Ain't it perfectly honest to charge a good price and make a profit on my investment and foresight? Of course it is. Well, that's honest graft.

GEORGE WASHINGTON PLUNKITT, quoted in *The Bosses* by Ralph G. Martin

A corrupt 19th-century political boss robs the city treasury by easily cutting through the red tape that bogs the government down.

"Honest" or not, graft and corruption not only lined the pockets of political bosses like Plunkitt but also oiled the workings of the emerging urban political machines.

Political Machines Run the Cities

In the late 19th century, cities were in trouble. Rapid growth, inefficient government, and a climate of Social Darwinism opened the way for a new power structure, the political machine, and a new politician, the city boss.

THE POLITICAL MACHINE The **political machine** was an organized group that controlled the activities of a political party in a city and offered services to voters and businesses in exchange for political or financial support. In the decades after the Civil War, political machines seized control of local government in major cities such as Baltimore, New York, Philadelphia, Boston, and San Francisco.

The political machine was organized like a pyramid. At the pyramid's base were local precinct workers and captains, who worked to gain voters' support on a city block or in a neighborhood and who reported to a ward boss. At election time, a ward boss worked to secure the vote in all of the precincts in a ward—a city's electoral district. In return for their votes, people received city jobs, contracts, or political appointments. Ward bosses helped the poor and gained their votes by doing favors or providing services. As Martin Lomasney, elected ward boss of Boston's West End in 1885, explained, "There's got to be in every ward a guy that any bloke can go to . . . and get help—not justice and the law, but help."

At the top of the pyramid was the city boss. The boss controlled the activities of a political party throughout the city. Like a finely tuned machine,

452 CHAPTER 15

SECTION 3 RESOURCES

 PRINT RESOURCES

IN-DEPTH RESOURCES: UNIT 4
Guided Reading, p. 39
Primary Source: from *The Shame of the Cities* by Lincoln Steffens, p. 49
American Lives: Boss Tweed, p. 54

ACCESS FOR STUDENTS ACQUIRING ENGLISH
Guided Reading (Spanish), p. 150

FORMAL ASSESSMENT
Section Quiz, p. 187

ALTERNATIVE ASSESSMENT BOOK
See forms for supporting and scoring alternative activities.

TECHNOLOGY RESOURCES

CD-ROM *Grolier Multimedia Encyclopedia*

VIDEO *American Portfolio: A Videodisc for U.S. History* user's guide, p. 149

INTERNET McDougal Littell Learning On-Line
http://www.mcdougallittell.com

THINK THROUGH HISTORY
A. Summarizing
In what form was a political machine organized?

A. Answer Like a pyramid—precinct workers and captains formed the base. The city boss was at the top.

precinct captains, ward bosses, and the city boss worked together to elect their candidate and guarantee the success of the machine.

THE ROLE OF THE POLITICAL BOSS The city boss controlled thousands of municipal jobs, including those in the police, fire, and sanitation departments. Whether or not a boss officially served as mayor, he controlled business licenses and inspections and influenced the courts and other municipal agencies. Bosses like Roscoe Conkling in New York used their power to build parks, sewer systems, and waterworks and gave money to schools, hospitals, and orphanages. Bosses could also provide government support for new businesses, a service for which they were often paid extremely well.

It was not only money that gave city bosses the drive to deal with urban issues. By solving problems, bosses could reinforce voters' loyalty, win additional political support, and extend their influence.

IMMIGRANTS AND THE POLITICAL MACHINE Immigrants received sympathetic understanding from the political machines and in turn became loyal supporters. Many political bosses were first-generation or second-generation immigrants who had been raised in poverty. Few were educated beyond grammar school. They entered politics early and worked their way up from the bottom. They could speak to immigrants in their own language and understood the challenges that newcomers faced. The bosses not only understood the immigrants' problems but were able to provide solutions. The machines helped immigrants become naturalized, find a place to live, and get a job—the newcomers' most pressing needs. In return, the immigrants provided what the political bosses needed most—votes.

"Big Jim" Pendergast, an Irish-American saloonkeeper, worked his way up from precinct captain to Democratic city boss in Kansas City by aiding Italian, African-American, and Irish voters in his ward. By 1900, he controlled Missouri state politics as well, because he effectively gathered political support.

> **A PERSONAL VOICE**
> I've been called a boss. All there is to it is having friends, doing things for people, and then later on they'll do things for you. . . . You can't coerce people into doing things for you—you can't make them vote for you. I never coerced anybody in my life. Wherever you see a man bulldozing anybody he don't last long.
>
> **JAMES PENDERGAST,** quoted in *The Pendergast Machine*

> *"All there is to it is . . . doing things for people, and then later on they'll do things for you."*
>
> **JAMES PENDERGAST**

Municipal Graft and Scandal

Although the well-oiled political machines provided city dwellers with vital services, many political bosses fell victim to greed and corruption as their power and influence grew.

ELECTION FRAUD AND GRAFT Since the power of political machines and the loyalty of voters were not always enough to carry an election, some political machines turned to fraud. They padded the lists of eligible voters with the names of dogs, children, and people who had died. Then, under these names, they cast as many votes as were needed to win. In a Philadelphia election, for example, a precinct with 100 registered voters returned 252 votes.

Once a political machine got its candidates into office, it could take advantage of numerous opportunities for graft. For example, after hiring a person to work on a construction project for the city, a political machine could ask the worker to turn in a bill that was higher than the actual cost of materials or labor. The worker then "kicked back" a portion of the earnings to the machine. Taking these **kickbacks,** or illegal payments, for their services made many political machines—and individual politicians—very wealthy.

Immigrants and Urbanization **453**

OBJECTIVE
① INSTRUCT

Political Machines Run the Cities

▶ **Discussing Key Ideas**
- In major cities, political machines provide services to voters in exchange for political or financial support.
- Political bosses control thousands of municipal jobs and regulate business licenses and inspections.
- Many of the bosses are immigrants who have worked their way up through the political system.

IN-DEPTH RESOURCES: UNIT 4
Guided Reading, p. 39

ACCESS FOR STUDENTS ACQUIRING ENGLISH
Guided Reading (Spanish), p. 150

OBJECTIVE
② INSTRUCT

Municipal Graft and Scandal

▶ **Discussing Key Ideas**
- To maintain their power and to make money, some political machines turn to election fraud, bribery, and graft.
- The efforts of political cartoonist Thomas Nast help bring down Boss Tweed and Tammany Hall, New York City's powerful Democratic machine.

IN-DEPTH RESOURCES: UNIT 4
Primary Source: from *The Shame of the Cities* by Lincoln Steffens, p. 49

"THE TAMMANY TIGER LOOSE"

SKILLBUILDER INTERPRETING CARTOONS *Who watches in the stands as the Tammany Hall tiger destroys the principles of truth and justice the nation is based on?*
Skillbuilder Answer
Cartoon: The public

Skillbuilder Answer
Almost two

SKILLBUILDER INTERPRETING CHARTS *How many Alaskas could have been purchased with the funds used to build Tweed's City Hall?*

Other ways that political machines made money were by granting favors to businesses in return for cash and by accepting bribes to allow illegal activities, such as gambling, to flourish. Politicians were able to get away with shady dealings because the police rarely interfered. Until about 1890, police forces were hired and fired by political bosses. Eventually, however, most cities removed from the hands of political bosses the responsibility for hiring police and established more impartial hiring procedures.

THE TWEED RING SCANDAL William Marcy Tweed, one of the earliest and most powerful bosses, became head of **Tammany Hall,** New York City's powerful Democratic political machine, in 1863. Between 1869 and 1871, the **Tweed Ring,** a group of corrupt politicians led by Boss Tweed, pocketed as much as $200 million from the city in kickbacks and payoffs. One scheme involving extravagant graft was the construction of the New York County Courthouse, which cost taxpayers $11 million. The actual construction cost was $3 million; the rest of the money went into the pockets of Tweed and his followers.

The widespread, profound graft practiced by Tammany Hall under Boss Tweed's leadership gradually aroused public outrage. **Thomas Nast,** a political cartoonist, ridiculed Tweed in the *New York Times* and in *Harper's Weekly.* Nast's work particularly angered Tweed, who reportedly said, "I don't care what the papers write about me—my constituents can't read; but . . . they can see pictures!"

The Tweed Ring was finally broken in 1871. Tweed was indicted on 220 counts of fraud and extortion, and in 1873, he was sentenced to 12 years in jail. After serving two years of his sentence, Tweed escaped. He was later recaptured in Spain when Spanish officials identified him from a Thomas Nast cartoon. By that time, corruption had become an issue in national politics.

C. Answer Both amassed huge fortunes—not always legally—but also did some social good.

THINK THROUGH HISTORY
C. Comparing *How were politicians like Boss Tweed similar to industrial moguls like Carnegie and Rockefeller?*

Boss Tweed's World-Class Expenses

Construction of City Hall in New York (1861-1874)	$145 million
Funding for New York state schools (1870)	$88 million
Purchase of Alaska from Russia (1867)	$76 million

Expenditures in 1997 dollars

Source: University of Southern California and *The Ninth Census* (1870)

Section 3 Assessment

1. TERMS & NAMES

Identify:
- graft
- political machine
- kickback
- Tammany Hall
- Tweed Ring
- Thomas Nast

2. SUMMARIZING In a two-column chart, list at least three advantages and three disadvantages of political machines.

Advantages	Disadvantages

Write an editorial defending or condemning the political machines.

3. GENERALIZING Read the quotation from James Pendergast on page 453. Explain whether you agree or disagree that machine politicians did not coerce people.

THINK ABOUT
- the types of power exerted by political machines
- the consequences of failing to support the machine
- the ways citizens in a democracy can influence the government

4. ANALYZING CAUSES Why do you think corruption such as that practiced by the Tweed Ring was able to flourish in the late 19th century?

THINK ABOUT
- the trends in business during that era
- the problems faced by cities
- the way machine politicians won the support of voters

454 CHAPTER 15

ANSWERS

4 Politics in the Gilded Age

TERMS & NAMES
- patronage
- civil service
- Rutherford B. Hayes
- Stalwarts
- James A. Garfield
- Chester A. Arthur
- Pendleton Act
- Grover Cleveland
- Benjamin Harrison

LEARN ABOUT the national effects of political corruption in the late 19th century
TO UNDERSTAND why Americans wanted reform.

ONE AMERICAN'S STORY

Writer Mark Twain not only observed the transformation of 19th-century America by industrialization but also took advantage of the opportunities it offered. Twain invested in many projects, most of them—including a publishing company and an unworkable typesetting machine—resounding failures. Perhaps those experiences spurred him to collaborate with journalist and writer Charles Dudley Warner on a satirical novel about their time, *The Gilded Age.* That title has since come to represent the period from the 1870s to the 1890s, when the external glitter of wealth concealed a corrupt political core and reflected a growing gap between the very few rich and the many very poor.

A PERSONAL VOICE
In a state where there is no fever of speculation, no inflamed desire for sudden wealth, where the poor are all simple-minded and contented, and the rich are all honest and generous, where society is in a condition of primitive purity, and politics is the occupation of only the capable and the patriotic, there are necessarily no materials for such a history as we have constructed.
MARK TWAIN and CHARLES DUDLEY WARNER, *The Gilded Age*

Although the Gilded Age, like Twain and Warner's fictional era, was a time of unrestricted corruption, it was also a time of movement toward political reform.

Glaring inequalities—such as this luxurious apartment house rising behind a New York City shantytown in 1889—characterized the Gilded Age.

Civil Service Replaces Patronage

The desire for power and money that made local politics corrupt in the Industrial Age also infected national politics.

A. Answer By allowing people to be hired for government jobs on the basis of political beliefs, rather than competence, and by making possible opportunities for misuse of influence.

THINK THROUGH HISTORY
A. Recognizing Effects How did the spoils system contribute to government incompetence and fraud?

PATRONAGE AND THE SPOILS SYSTEM SPUR REFORM Since the beginning of the 19th century, presidents had complained about the problem of **patronage,** or giving government jobs to people who had helped a candidate get elected. The theory was that winning candidates deserved the spoils, or the benefits to be seized after a victory. This method of rewarding political supporters existed as far back as Andrew Jackson's presidency and was known as the spoils system.

People from cabinet members to workers who scrubbed the steps of the capitol owed their jobs to patronage. As might be expected, some government employees were not qualified for the positions they filled. Moreover, political appointees, whether qualified or not, sometimes used their positions for personal gain.

The spoils system not only led to incompetence and fraud but also interfered with the daily functioning of government. With each change of administration, thousands of positions had to be filled. Instead of addressing important national issues, politicians distributed government jobs.

Reformers began to press for a federal merit system to replace the spoils system. Under the merit system, jobs in **civil service**—government administration—would go to the most qualified persons, no matter what political views

Immigrants and Urbanization **455**

SECTION 4 RESOURCES

 PRINT RESOURCES

IN-DEPTH RESOURCES: UNIT 4
Guided Reading, p. 40

ACCESS FOR STUDENTS ACQUIRING ENGLISH
Guided Reading (Spanish), p. 151

FORMAL ASSESSMENT
Section Quiz, p. 188

ALTERNATIVE ASSESSMENT BOOK
See forms for supporting and scoring alternative activities.

 TECHNOLOGY RESOURCES

VIDEO *American Portfolio: A Videodisc for U.S. History* user's guide, pp. 153, 154, 155, 157

INTERNET McDougal Littell Learning On-Line
http://www.mcdougallittell.com

Section 4 Overview

OBJECTIVES

① To describe measures taken by Presidents Hayes, Garfield, and Arthur to reform the spoils system.

② To explain the positions taken by presidents Cleveland, Harrison, and McKinley on the tariff issue.

CRITICAL THINKING

- Recognizing effects, pp. 455, 456
- Analyzing motives, p. 456
- Analyzing causes, p. 457
- Summarizing, p. 457
- Hypothesizing, p. 457
- Forming an opinion, p. 457

FOCUS & MOTIVATE

▶ *Starting with the Student*
- Ask students to discuss how they would go about getting a job. Ask them whether or not they would get help from a friend or a friend's parent. Then have them discuss whether they think it is fair to use "connections."
- Remind students that the spoils system began in the early 19th century. Ask them why they think it lasted so long.

OBJECTIVE
① **INSTRUCT**

Civil Service Replaces Patronage

▶ *Discussing Key Ideas*
- Patronage results in incompetence and fraud in government.
- Hayes takes measures to reform civil service.
- Garfield wins the 1880 election but is assassinated the following year.
- With Arthur's civil service reform, Congress passes the Pendleton Act in 1883.

IN-DEPTH RESOURCES: UNIT 4
Guided Reading, p. 40

ACCESS FOR STUDENTS ACQUIRING ENGLISH
Guided Reading (Spanish), p. 151

Teacher's Edition **455**

The Presidency Takes Its Toll

"Nobody ever left the presidency with less regret ...than I do."

Rutherford B. Hayes (1877–1881)

"Assassination can be no more guarded against than death by lightning."

James A. Garfield (1881)

"There doesn't seem to be anything else for an ex-president to do but ...raise big pumpkins."

Chester A. Arthur (1881–1885)

they held or who recommended them. Civil servants would keep their jobs as long as their work was satisfactory.

HAYES LAUNCHES REFORM About a month after being declared the winner of the 1876 election, President **Rutherford B. Hayes** wrote in his diary, "Now for Civil-Service Reform." Hayes could not get legislative support for his ideas, so he used other means.

Hayes began by naming independents to his cabinet. One of these officials took the unheard-of step of firing clerks who had no work to do. Hayes also set up a commission to investigate the nation's customshouses, which were notoriously corrupt. On the basis of the commission's report, Hayes fired the two top officials of New York City's customshouse, where all of the more than 1,000 employees had spent most of their time working for the Republican Party. These firings enraged New York Republican senator and political boss Roscoe Conkling and his supporters, the Stalwarts.

GARFIELD CONTINUES REFORM Hayes decided not to run for reelection in 1880. At the Republican convention, a free-for-all broke out between the **Stalwarts,** who opposed changes in the spoils system—and reformers. The reformers themselves were split. One group, the Mugwumps, wanted civil-service reform while the other, the Half-Breeds, wanted reform but were loyal to the party. Since neither Stalwarts nor reformers could win a majority of delegates, the convention settled on an independent presidential candidate, Ohio congressman **James A. Garfield.**

Garfield had ties to reformers, however, so to balance the ticket, the Republicans nominated for vice-president one of Conkling's supporters, **Chester A. Arthur.** Arthur, in fact, was one of the two New York customshouse officials Hayes had fired. Despite Arthur's inclusion on the ticket, Garfield gave reform Republicans most of his patronage jobs once he was elected. The Stalwarts were furious.

On July 2, 1881, as President Garfield walked through the Washington, D.C., train station, two gunshots were fired, both wounding the president. His attacker, a mentally imbalanced lawyer named Charles Guiteau, whom Garfield had turned down for a job, shouted, "I did it and I will go to jail for it. I am a Stalwart and Arthur will be president." Garfield finally died from his wounds on September 19, killed, some say, not so much by the bullets as by his doctors' blundering. In any case, Guiteau was convicted of murder and was hanged.

ARTHUR TURNS REFORMER AND SUPPORTS CIVIL SERVICE
Despite his ties to Conkling and the Stalwarts, Chester Arthur turned reformer when he became president. His first message to Congress urged legislators to pass a civil service law.

The resulting **Pendleton Act** of 1883 authorized a bipartisan civil service commission to make appointments to federal jobs through the merit system—that is, on the basis of performance on an examination. By 1901, more than 40 percent of all federal jobs had been classified as civil service positions. Today, the merit system covers about 90 percent of all federal jobs.

The Pendleton Act had mixed consequences. On the one hand, increasing numbers of federal jobs were held by qualified people, and public administration became more honest and efficient. On the other hand, because officials no longer could pressure government employees for campaign contributions, politicians had to find other sources of funds. Since the most obvious source was wealthy business owners, the alliance between government and big business became stronger than ever.

456 CHAPTER 15

B. Answer Because they thought his antireform views would balance presidential candidate James A. Garfield's belief in civil-service reform

THINK THROUGH HISTORY
B. Analyzing Motives Why did the Republicans include Chester Arthur as their vice-presidential candidate in the 1880 elections?

C. Answer
Positive: More competent and honest federal workers; **Negative:** Closer ties between government and big business.

THINK THROUGH HISTORY
C. Recognizing Effects What were the positive and the negative effects of the Pendleton Act?

TEACHING OPTIONS

Making Connections Across the Curriculum

Economics In "A Personal Voice" on page 457, President Grover Cleveland confesses his ignorance of a basic economic concept, the tariff. A tariff is a tax imposed by a government on imported or exported goods. The issue of tariffs has been important throughout American history. Manufacturing interests have tended to support tariffs on imports because they keep the prices for imported goods high, so that it is cheaper for consumers to buy domestic goods. Consumers, on the other hand, have tended to oppose tariffs because they add to the cost of imported goods.

Teaching Less Proficient Readers

Use the chart below to help students summarize some advantages and disadvantages of high and low tariffs.

	High Tariffs	Low Tariffs
Advantages	protect domestic industry	Keep down the cost of goods
Disadvantages	cause prices to rise	discourage domestic industry

Efforts to Regulate Tariffs Fail

Political reformers also addressed another issue—the tariff. Most Americans agreed that tariffs were necessary to protect domestic industries from foreign competition. But they did cause prices to rise. The question was how high tariffs should be.

HARRISON AND HIGH TARIFFS—1; CLEVELAND—0 In 1884, the Democratic Party captured the presidency for the first time in 28 years with the election of **Grover Cleveland.** Carl Schurz, a former secretary of the interior, recalled a conversation he'd had with the newly elected president.

> **A PERSONAL VOICE**
> [Cleveland asked] what big question he ought to take up when he got into the White House. I told him . . . the tariff. The man bent forward and buried his face in his hands. . . . After two or three minutes he straightened up and . . . said to me, "I am ashamed to say it, but the truth is I know nothing about the tariff."
> **CARL SCHURZ,** quoted in *The Politicos*

Cleveland learned fast, though, and tried to lower tariff rates, but Congress refused to support him.

In 1888, Cleveland ran for reelection on a low-tariff platform against former Indiana Republican Senator **Benjamin Harrison,** the grandson of President William Henry Harrison. Harrison's campaign was financed by large contributions from companies that wanted tariffs even higher than they were. Although Cleveland won about 100,000 more popular votes than Harrison, Harrison took a majority of the electoral votes and the presidency. Once in office, he won passage of the McKinley Tariff Act of 1890, which raised tariffs to their highest level.

CLEVELAND TRIES AGAIN In 1892, Cleveland was elected again—the only president to serve two nonconsecutive terms. He supported a bill for lowering the McKinley Tariff but refused to sign it because it didn't lower tariffs enough. The Wilson-Gorman Tariff became law in 1894 without the president's signature. In 1897, William McKinley was inaugurated president and raised tariffs once again.

The attempt to reduce the tariff had failed, but the spirit of reform was not dead. New developments in areas ranging from technology and education to mass culture and social policy helped redefine American society as the United States moved into the 20th century.

D. Answer
Because of political pressure exerted by companies that benefited from the tariff

THINK THROUGH HISTORY
D. Analyzing Causes *Why do you think tariff reform failed?*

NOW & THEN

TARIFFS VERSUS NAFTA
Since 1789, when the United States first placed a tariff on certain foreign goods, the issue of tariffs has been hotly debated. In 1993, Congress passed the North American Free Trade Agreement (NAFTA). This agreement eliminated most trade barriers between the United States, Canada, and Mexico.

While critics believed that NAFTA would cost some American workers their jobs because companies would hire cheap Mexican labor, supporters argued that this agreement would create new jobs as Mexican markets opened up to American products. The results remain to be seen.

OBJECTIVE
②INSTRUCT

Efforts to Regulate Tariffs Fail

▶ *Discussing Key Ideas*
- Cleveland runs on a low-tariff platform and loses the presidency to Harrison, who raises tariffs.
- In his second term, Cleveland fails to lower tariffs.

NOW & THEN
Tariffs Versus NAFTA
Have students write an editorial about tariffs. Some topics that might be dealt with include jobs and the cost of goods.

ASSESS & RETEACH

Section 4 Assessment
Have students work individually to answer the questions; then have them share with the class the charts they drew up for item 2.

Self-Assessment
Ask students to review what they wrote for item 3. As they give their opinions about the Pendleton Act, ask students what new ideas they have.

Section Quiz

FORMAL ASSESSMENT
Section Quiz, p. 188

Reteach
Survey students to find out what material in the section was the most difficult for them. Then review that material with students.

Section 4 Assessment

1. TERMS & NAMES

Identify:
- patronage
- civil service
- Rutherford B. Hayes
- Stalwarts
- James A. Garfield
- Chester A. Arthur
- Pendleton Act
- Grover Cleveland
- Benjamin Harrison

2. SUMMARIZING In a chart similar to the one below, list three politicians mentioned in this section. Give the position of each and his stand on a major issue, such as civil service reform or lowering tariffs.

Leader	Position	Stand

Which one would you have voted for and why?

3. HYPOTHESIZING How do you think politics in the United States would have been different if the Pendleton Act had not been passed?

THINK ABOUT
- the act's impact on federal workers
- the act's impact on political fundraising
- conflicts within the Republican Party at the time

4. FORMING AN OPINION If you had been running for Congress in 1892, would you have supported a reduction in tariffs? Why or why not?

THINK ABOUT
- the needs of the voters in your state
- the economic impact of reducing tariffs
- the social consequences of a reduction in tariffs

Immigrants and Urbanization **457**

ANSWERS

1. TERMS & NAMES

patronage, p. 455
civil service, p. 455
Rutherford B. Hayes, p. 456
Stalwarts, p. 456
James A. Garfield, p. 456
Chester A. Arthur, p. 456
Pendleton Act, p. 456
Grover Cleveland, p. 457
Benjamin Harrison, p. 457

2. SUMMARIZING

Leader	Position	Stand
Rutherford B. Hayes	president ('77–'81)	for civil service reform
Roscoe Conkling	NY senator	against civil service reform
Chester A. Arthur	president ('81–'85)	supported Pendleton Act
Grover Cleveland	president ('85–'89, '93–'97)	supported lower tariffs
Benjamin Harrison	president ('89–'93)	supported higher tariffs

3. HYPOTHESIZING

Possible Response: Federal employment would have continued to be dominated by politics, politicians would have been less dependent on big business for campaign funds, and a key issue would have continued dividing the Republicans.

4. FORMING AN OPINION

Responses should reflect awareness that high tariffs might help businesses at the expense of consumers.

CLOSE

In the Gilded Age, political reformers began to replace the evils of patronage with a civil service system. They did not have the same success in reducing the high tariffs that protected American industry.

Teacher's Edition 457

Chapter 15 Assessment

REVIEWING THE CHAPTER

TERMS & NAMES
1. melting pot, p. 442
2. Gentlemen's Agreement, p. 443
3. urbanization, p. 446
4. Jane Addams, p. 451
5. graft, p. 452
6. political machine, p. 452
7. Thomas Nast, p. 454
8. patronage, p. 455
9. Chester A. Arthur, p. 456
10. Pendleton Act, p. 456

MAIN IDEAS
11. Poverty, famine, shortage of land, lack of jobs, religious or political persecution, and a spirit of rebellion and independence.

12. Culture shock, the negative effects of nativism, and the struggle to make a living.

13. Industrialization, new technology, and an influx of workers.

14. The need to provide adequate housing, transportation, water, and sanitation, and to fight fire and crime.

15. Efforts to help alleviate poverty of immigrants and other city dwellers; building churches in poor neighborhoods.

16. The growing need for city services and the large number of immigrants required a new power structure.

17. Tweed took the corruption practiced by many other city bosses to unprecedented heights.

18. Inefficiency, fraud, and incompetence.

19. Increased efficiency, decreased fraud, and closer ties between government and big business.

20. Cleveland wanted to reduce tariffs; Harrison wanted to keep them high.

REVIEWING THE CHAPTER

TERMS & NAMES For each term below, write a sentence explaining its connection to immigration and urbanization in the late 19th century. For each person below, explain his or her role in these developments.

1. melting pot
2. Gentlemen's Agreement
3. urbanization
4. Jane Addams
5. graft
6. political machine
7. Thomas Nast
8. patronage
9. Chester A. Arthur
10. Pendleton Act

MAIN IDEAS

SECTION 1 *(pages 438–443)*

The New Immigrants

11. What trends or events in other countries prompted people to move to the United States in the late 19th and early 20th centuries?
12. What difficulties did many of these new immigrants face?

SECTION 2 *(pages 446–451)*

The Problems of Urbanization

13. Why did cities in the United States grow rapidly in the decades following the Civil War?
14. What problems did this rapid growth pose for cities?
15. What solutions to urban problems did supporters of the Social Gospel propose?

SECTION 3 *(pages 452–454)*

The Emergence of the Political Machine

16. Why did machine politics become common in big cities in the late 19th century?
17. How was Boss Tweed alike and different from other big city bosses?

SECTION 4 *(pages 455–457)*

Politics in the Gilded Age

18. What government problems arose as a result of the spoils system?
19. What effects did the Pendleton Act have on the running of the federal government?
20. Summarize the views of Grover Cleveland and Benjamin Harrison on tariffs.

THINKING CRITICALLY

1. **RESULTS AND REACTIONS** Create a diagram similar to the one below showing one result of and one reaction against each of these trends: (a) the increase in immigration, (b) the increase in machine politics.

	Result	Reaction
Increased Immigration	→ —— → ——
Increased Machine Politics	→ —— → ——

2. **POLITICS TODAY** Compare the current system of politics with the political machines described in this chapter. Which system is more effective? Explain your opinion.

3. **URBAN URGE** In the opening quotation of this chapter on page 436, Horace Greeley indicated that everyone seemed to want to live in the city. Why do you think this was true at the end of the 19th century? Do you think it is still true today? Why or why not?

4. **GEOGRAPHY OF PEOPLE AND POLITICS** How do you think immigration and migration influenced the development of American political power structures in the late 19th century? Explain your answer.

5. **POWER OF THE PENCIL** Why do you think political cartoons such as Thomas Nast's had such an impact during the late 19th century?

6. **ANALYZING PRIMARY SOURCES** Read the following introduction by the journalist Lincoln Steffens to his collection of articles exposing horrible urban conditions and political corruption. Then answer the questions.

> Democracy with us may be impossible and corruption inevitable, but these articles, if they have proved nothing else, have demonstrated beyond doubt that we can stand the truth; that there is pride in the character of American citizenship; and that this pride may be a power in the land.
>
> LINCOLN STEFFENS, *The Shame of the Cities*

Do you agree with Steffens that democracy is impossible and corruption inevitable in American politics? How might the pride of American citizens become a powerful voice for a better American government and way of life?

THINKING CRITICALLY

1. RESULTS AND REACTIONS
Possible Answers:
Increase in immigration
    Result: growth of urban populations
    Reaction: growth of nativism
Increase in machine politics
    Result: widespread corruption
    Reaction: support for civil service reform

2. POLITICS TODAY
Students might note that politicians still give out patronage jobs and that governmental fraud and incompetence have not been eliminated. They should give solid reasons to support their opinion regarding which system is more effective.

3. URBAN URGE
At the end of the 19th century, cities offered jobs and other economic opportunities. Regarding the situation today, students might mention the current exodus from the cities or their ongoing status as centers of business and industry.

ALTERNATIVE ASSESSMENT

1. REPORTING ON THE CHINESE EXCLUSION ACT

In 1882, Congress passed the Chinese Exclusion Act, which closed the door to Chinese immigrants. No other ethnic group was discriminated against in this way. How might people have supported and opposed this act?

Assume you are a journalist covering a town meeting about the Chinese Exclusion Act. Write a report of the debate for the local newspaper.

 Use the CD-ROM *Electronic Library of Primary Sources* and other resources to review the provisions of the Chinese Exclusion Act and to research the history of Chinese immigrants.

- Think about the geographic, social, and economic makeup of your town. How might these factors influence people's opinions about Chinese immigrants? Try to present a variety of attitudes.

2. LEARNING FROM MEDIA

 View the video for Chapter 15, *From China to Chinatown.* Discuss the following questions in small groups.

- Why did Fong See first come to America?
- How did Fong See overcome the difficulties that faced Asian immigrants in America in the late 19th and early 20th centuries?
- What motivated him to return to China?
- What did Lisa See learn about living in a multicultural society from her great-grandfather's experience?
- How are immigrants treated in America today?
- What lessons does Fong See's story have for present-day Americans?

3. PORTFOLIO PROJECT

 Use the Living History exercise to expand your portfolio.

LIVING HISTORY

REVISING YOUR TOWN BIOGRAPHY

After completing the biography of your town or neighborhood, ask a friend or two to read it and to answer the following questions. If possible, choose one reader who is familiar with the town and one who is not.

- What interested you most about my biography?
- What would you like to know more about?
- Do you agree with my prediction about the future of my town? Why or why not?

Make changes based on your friends' suggestions, and finalize your biography for your American history portfolio. You also might consider making an oral presentation to your class or to an audience at the local library or community center.

Review Chapter 15

IMMIGRATION INCREASES In the late 19th and early 20th centuries, millions of people from Europe, China, Japan, the Caribbean, and Mexico fled poverty and persecution in their homelands and moved to the United States. Many immigrants endured nativism and culture shock in their new home in the hope of building a better life for themselves and their children.

CHALLENGES OF THE CITIES Most immigrants settled in cities, where they joined millions of newcomers from rural communities in the United States. While cities offered jobs in growing factories and mills, they were overcrowded, dirty, and unsafe. In response to urban problems, reformers such as Washington Gladden and Jane Addams worked to help the urban poor.

THE POLITICAL MACHINE As cities and their problems grew, a new power structure emerged—the political machine. Machines and their bosses often were notoriously corrupt and got rich from graft, kickbacks, and bribes. But they also provided jobs, legal assistance, and support that many poor people needed. Among the most famous machine politicians was New York's Boss Tweed, who was jailed in 1873.

NATIONAL POLITICS IN THE GILDED AGE In national politics, two main issues emerged—civil-service reform and the tariff. The passage of the Pendleton Act of 1883 marked a victory for those who wanted to reform the patronage system for hiring federal employees. In 1888, Democratic President Grover Cleveland, a supporter of low tariffs, was defeated by the high-tariff candidate, Republican Benjamin Harrison.

Preview Chapter 16

In addition to forces such as immigration, industrialization, and urbanization, developments in science and technology also helped reshape life in the United States in the late 19th century. These developments—from the skyscraper to the amusement park—affected many aspects of life in cities, from education and the role of women to leisure activities. Despite these advances, however, social problems such as racial segregation and discrimination continued to plague society. You will learn about these significant developments in the next chapter.

Immigrants and Urbanization **459**

1. REPORTING ON THE CHINESE EXCLUSION ACT
Standards for Evaluation

A report on the debate for the local newspaper should meet the following criteria:

- Presents several different views on the issue.
- Cites a number of provisions of the Chinese Exclusion Act.
- Describes the geographic, social, and economic make-up of the town.
- Shows the connection between people's opinions and their own interests.

2. LEARNING FROM MEDIA
Answers to the questions:

- Fong See came to America to search for his father.
- Fong See overcame difficulties by a combination of hard work and clever business tactics.
- Fong See returned to China to see his family and share with them the wealth he had earned in America.
- Lisa See learned from her great-grandfather's experience that hard work and perseverance are necessary when living in a multicultural society.
- Accept all reasonable responses.
- Accept all reasonable responses.

3. PORTFOLIO PROJECT
LIVING HISTORY
Standards for Evaluation

A biography should meet the following criteria:

- Includes information about the town's founders.
- Describes the town's major ethnic groups.
- Discusses the problems created by growth.
- Predicts the future of the town.
- Includes maps, photos, or other illustrations about local events.

IN-DEPTH RESOURCES: UNIT 4
See the form for scoring this activity on page 56.

THINKING CRITICALLY

4. GEOGRAPHY OF PEOPLE AND POLITICS

The growth of cities resulting from immigration and migration led to the need for vital services, and the political machines stepped in to provide them. Also, more representatives in Congress came from cities, which gave urban areas increased national influence.

5. POWER OF THE PENCIL

Students might mention that the cartoons could be understood even by people who couldn't read English or that the political bosses' corruption was so glaring that satirical cartoons were the perfect vehicle for fueling public outrage.

6. ANALYZING PRIMARY SOURCES

Students should give solid reasons to support their opinion regarding the possibility of democracy. They might suggest that pride in America might be translated into participation in government at many levels.

		TEACHING SUPPORT	**ASSESSMENT**

Key Ideas

SECTION 1
Science and Urban Life

pp. 462–466

Advances in science and technology address urban problems, including lack of space and inadequate systems of transportation and communication.

In-Depth Resources: Unit 4
• Guided Reading, p. 57
• Geography Application: New York's Central Park, p. 62
• Primary Sources: *from* Orville Wright's Diary, p. 64; Advertisement, p. 65

 COOPERATIVE ACTIVITY
• Planning Ideal Cities, p. 464 (TE)

Section 1 Assessment, p. 466 (PE)
Self-Assessment, p. 466 (TE)
Formal Assessment
• Section Quiz, p. 197
Alternative Assessment Book
• Standards for Evaluating a Cooperative Activity

SECTION 2
Education and Culture

pp. 467–472

The impulses of moral uplift and economic necessity spur changes in education, a rise in national literacy, and the promotion of high culture.

In-Depth Resources: Unit 4
• Guided Reading, p. 58
• Primary Source: *from* "The Talented Tenth" by W. E. B. Du Bois, p. 66
• American Lives: W. E. B. Du Bois, p. 71

 COOPERATIVE ACTIVITY
• Reforming Public Education, p. 468 (TE)

Section 2 Assessment, p. 472 (PE)
Self-Assessment, p. 472 (TE)
Formal Assessment
• Section Quiz, p. 198
Alternative Assessment Book
• Standards for Evaluating a Cooperative Activity

SECTION 3
Segregation and Discrimination

pp. 473–477

African Americans lead the fight against institutionalized racism in the form of voting restrictions and Jim Crow laws.

In-Depth Resources: Unit 4
• Guided Reading, p. 59
• Skillbuilder Practice: Primary Sources, p. 61
• Primary Source: *from* "Lynching and the Excuse for It" by Ida B. Wells, p. 67

 COOPERATIVE ACTIVITY
• Debating Discrimination, p. 476 (TE)

Section 3 Assessment, p. 477 (PE)
Self-Assessment, p. 477 (TE)
Formal Assessment
• Section Quiz, p. 199
Alternative Assessment Book
• Standards for Evaluating a Cooperative Activity

SECTION 4
Dawn of Mass Culture

pp. 478–485

Americans have more time for leisure activities and a modern mass culture emerges, especially through newspapers and retail advertising.

In-Depth Resources: Unit 4
• Guided Reading, p. 60
• Literature: from *Ragtime* by E. L. Doctorow
• American Lives: Lillian Gish, p. 72

COOPERATIVE ACTIVITY
• Writing Sports History, p. 480 (TE)
• Critiquing Historical Films, p. 482 (TE)

Section 4 Assessment, p. 485 (PE)
Self-Assessment, p. 485 (TE)
Formal Assessment
• Section Quiz, p. 200
Alternative Assessment Book
• Standards for Evaluating a Cooperative Activity

CHAPTER RESOURCES

Chapter Overview

As the twentieth century begins, American culture changes due to new technological advances, cultural forms, and mass media. Some Americans, though, protest discrimination that denies them rights.

In-Depth Resources: Unit 4
• Living History Project: Worksheet, p. 73; Standards, p. 74
Telescoping the Times
• Chapter Summary, pp. 31–32
Planning for Block Schedules

Chapter Assessment, pp. 488–489 (PE)
Alternative Assessment, p. 489 (PE)
Formal Assessment
• Chapter Test, forms A and B, pp. 201–206

 Test Generator
Alternative Assessment Book
See explanation and forms for different kinds of alternative assessments including portfolio assessment.

Geography Transparencies
- G16, Telephone Long Distance Lines: 1890–1917

 Electronic Library of Primary Sources
- from "Automobiles: The Other Side of the Shield" by Frederick Dwight
- From *A Visit to the World's Columbian Exposition* by Charles E. Bolton

INTERNET RESOURCES
- See *McDougal Littell Learning On-Line* for links to information about Louis Sullivan and Eastman Kodak.

 Critical Thinking Transparencies
- CT16, Expansion of Education
- CT50, School Enrollment: 1870–1920

 Grolier Multimedia Encyclopedia
- W. E. B. Du Bois
- Thomas Eakins

INTERNET RESOURCES
- See *McDougal Littell Learning On-Line* for links to information about W. E. B. Du Bois and Mark Twain.

 Grolier Multimedia Encyclopedia
- Jim Crow Laws

Electronic Library of Primary Sources
- from *The Autobiography of Ida B. Wells*

INTERNET RESOURCES
- See *McDougal Littell Learning On-Line* for links to information about Jim Crow laws, Ida B. Wells, and the Chinese Exclusion Act.

 Humanities Transparencies
- H16, *Washington Square North* by Ferdinand Lundgren

 Electronic Library of Primary Sources
- from "The Base-Ball Season" in Harper's Weekly
- from *The Movies, Mr. Griffith, and Me* by Lillian Gish

INTERNET RESOURCES
- See Interact with History P. 483 (PE) for an activity that includes the Internet as an enrichment option.

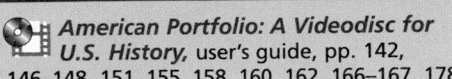 *American Portfolio: A Videodisc for U.S. History*, user's guide, pp. 142, 146–148, 151, 155, 158, 160, 162, 166–167, 178

INTERNET RESOURCES
Learning On-Line: Social Studies
http://www.mcdougallittell.com

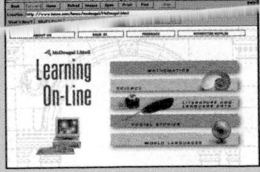

Block Scheduling (90 MINUTES)

Day 1
Section 1, pp. 462–466
Section 2, pp. 467–472
Section Assessments, pp. 466, 472

Day 2
Section 3, pp. 473–477
Section 4, pp. 478–485
Daily Life: New Ways to Play, pp. 486–487
Chapter Assessment, pp. 488–489

YEARLY PACING Chapter 16 Total: 2 days Yearly Total: 85 days

See *Planning for Block Schedules* for special activities and pacing strategies.

Customizing for Special Populations

Students Acquiring English

Access for Students Acquiring English
- Guided Reading for Sections 1–4 (Spanish), pp. 159–162
- Chapter Summary (Spanish), pp. 157–158
- Skillbuilder Practice: Primary Sources, p. 163
- Geography Application: New York's Central Park, p. 164–165

INTERNET RESOURCES
- See *McDougal Littell Learning On-Line* The Diverse Classroom.

Less Proficient Readers

In-Depth Resources: Unit 4
- Guided Reading for Sections 1–4, pp. 57–60
- Skillbuilder: Primary Sources, p. 61
- Geography Application: New York's Central Park, p. 62

Telescoping the Times
- Chapter Summary, pp. 31–32

See additional strategies at point of use in the Teacher's Edition.

Gifted and Talented Students

In-Depth Resources: Unit 4
- Primary Sources: *from* Orville Wright's Diary, p. 64; Camera Advertisement, p. 65; *from* "The Talented Tenth" by W. E. B. Du Bois, p. 66; *from* "Lynching and the Excuse for It" Ida B. Wells, p. 67

See additional strategies at point of use in the Teacher's Edition.

Connections to Literature READINGS FOR STUDENTS

In-Depth Resources: Unit 4
- from *Ragtime* by E. L. Doctorow

Enrichment Reading
- **Anderson, Sherwood**
  Winesburg Ohio.
  New York: Penguin, 1996
  In this modern classic, Anderson mixes his memories of his childhood in Clyde, Ohio, with his observations of life in turn-of-the-century Chicago. In the novel, the inhabitants of Winesburg confide their disappointed dreams and dashed hopes to a young reporter. This deeply honest portrait of life in small-town America was a shock to many readers at the time.

- **Erdrich, Louise**
  Tracks.
  New York: HarperCollins, 1989
  This novel, third in a cycle, tells the story of a group of Chippewa and their culture under siege in a white man's world.

- **Wilder, Thornton**
  Our Town.
  New York: Scholastic, 1990
  This Pulitzer Prize winning play explores universal themes of life, love, and death by going beneath the surface of everyday life in the small New England town of Grover's Corners, New Hampshire, at the turn of the century.

McDougal Littell *Literature Connections*
American Literature

- Carl Sandburg, "Chicago" p. 668
- Edgar Lee Masters, "Lucinda Matlock" p. 668
- Edwin Arlington Robinson, "Richard Cory" p. 675
- Paul Laurence Dunbar, "We Wear the Mask" p. 675

American Life at the Turn of the Century

▶ *Starting with the Student*
Ask students what they know about American life a hundred years ago. How did Americans work and play? What new inventions were changing people's ways of life? Then ask these questions:

• Do you agree with the quotation? Why or why not?
• If you applied the quotation to America today, what would you offer as the best or worst?

PREVIEWING THE CHAPTER

• Have students examine the time line and list the things that look familiar to them.
• Remind students that many aspects of the modern world in which they live emerged at this time in history.

MORE ABOUT . . .
James Weldon Johnson

The first African American to be accepted to the Florida bar, Johnson later served as a U.S. consul in Venezuela. He had a varied career in the arts, composing and performing for a song-and-dance act with his brother John, editing anthologies of African-American verse and spirituals, and penning fine prose and poetry of his own.

Life at the Turn of the Century

SECTION 1
Science and Urban Life

Advances in science and technology address urban problems, including lack of space and inadequate systems of transportation and communication.

SECTION 2
Education and Culture

The impulses of moral uplift and economic necessity spur changes in education, a rise in national literacy, and the promotion of high culture.

SECTION 3
Segregation and Discrimination

African Americans lead the fight against institutionalized racism in the form of voting restrictions and Jim Crow laws.

SECTION 4
Dawn of Mass Culture

Americans have more time for leisure activities and a modern mass culture emerges, especially through newspapers and retail advertising.

> "Every nation should be judged by the best it has been able to produce, not by the worst."
>
> James Weldon Johnson, 1871–1938

Ida B. Wells crusades against lynching.

Construction of the Brooklyn Bridge is completed.

Mark Twain publishes *The Adventures of Huckleberry Finn.*

James Naismith invents basketball.

F. W. Woolworth opens his "five-and-ten-cent" store.

| THE UNITED STATES | **1877** | 1879 | | 1883 | 1884 | | 1891 |
| THE WORLD | | 1878 | | 1882 | 1884 | 1889 | |

Bicycle touring club is founded in Europe.

Triple Alliance between Italy, Austria-Hungary, and Germany is formed.

A 14-nation conference on the division of Africa is held in Berlin.

Barnum & Bailey Circus opens in London.

460 CHAPTER 16

THEMES IN CHAPTER 16

Science and Technology	*Immigration and Migration*	*Civil Rights*	*Women in America*
Technology helped cities grow upward with skyscrapers and outward with better roads, bridges, subways, and streetcars to accommodate the influx of immigrants and rural migrants to the urban areas. See Teacher's Edition notes, p. 463.	Education was a vital tool for assimilating the millions of immigrants who came to America. Besides schools, employers, labor unions, and political organizations helped immigrants assimilate. See Teacher's Edition notes, p. 469.	Booker T. Washington and W. E. B. Du Bois struggled for African-American equality, although they differed on tactics. Washington stressed a gradual approach that would lead to economic independence. Du Bois demanded immediate assimilation. See Teacher's Edition notes, p. 474.	Women's lifestyles in the United States continued to evolve. Women expanded their educational and occupational opportunities. Some traditional restrictions on female behavior loosened, as seen in the changing clothing styles and leisure activities. See Teacher's Edition Notes, p. 479.

CATALOGING MASS CULTURE

The mass culture that emerged at the turn of the century was a product of advancements in technology and expanding educational and cultural opportunities. Create your own version of a mail-order catalog displaying objects, places, and events that contributed to the formation of American mass culture. Consider these guidelines:

- Keep notes as you read about changes in the American landscape.
- Think about people and events that caused change.

📁 **PORTFOLIO PROJECT** Keep your catalog in a folder. At the end of this chapter, you will add illustrations to the catalog and display it as part of your American history portfolio.

The Wright brothers successfully complete the first airplane flight at Kitty Hawk, North Carolina.

Ringling Bros. and Barnum & Bailey circuses merge.

W. E. B. Du Bois publishes *The Souls of Black Folk*.

Coney Island opens in New York.

McKinley is assassinated.

D. W. Griffith's epic film, *The Birth of a Nation*, is released.

⭐ **Theodore Roosevelt becomes president.**

⭐ **Theodore Roosevelt is elected president.**

⭐ **William H. Taft is elected president.**

⭐ **Woodrow Wilson is elected president.**

⭐ **Woodrow Wilson is reelected.**

William McKinley is reelected. ⭐

| 1895 | **1900** | 1901 | 1903 | 1904 | 1907 | 1908 | 1912 | 1915 | 1916 | **1917** |

| 4 | | | | 1904 | | 1910 | | 1914 | | |

The African nation of Uganda becomes a British protectorate.

German psychoanalyst Sigmund Freud publishes *The Interpretation of Dreams*.

Russo-Japanese War breaks out.

Japan annexes Korea.

World War I begins in Europe.

Life at the Turn of the Century **461**

CATALOGING MASS CULTURE

Show the class some catalogs from an art or natural history museum. Point out how they are organized. Then help students determine the items to include in their catalogs. They might follow these steps:

- Prepare a list of possible methods for illustrating the changes, events, and people. Consider creating original art, taking photographs, and copying photos from periodicals or books.
- Use a chart to help determine which events, people, and places are the most important and easily illustrate mass culture and social change. Then include them in the catalog.
- Do additional research if necessary to write the catalog descriptions of each item, event, or person included.

Important	Easy to Illustrate Effectively

IN-DEPTH RESOURCES: UNIT 4
See worksheet and standards for evaluation, pp. 73, 74.

RECOMMENDED RESOURCES

Books for the Teacher

Ayers, Edward L. *The Promise of the New South: Life after Reconstruction.* New York: Oxford UP, 1992.

Schlereth, Thomas J. *Victorian America: Transformations in Everyday Life, 1876–1915.* New York: Harper, 1991.

Books for the Student

Bryson, Bill. *Made in America.* New York: Morrow, 1994.

Du Bois, W. E. B. *The Souls of Black Folk.* New York: Signet, 1995.

McCullough, David. *The Great Bridge.* New York: Simon, 1972. A lively account of the building of the Brooklyn Bridge.

Videos

Baseball. Dir. Ken Burns. PBS Home Video, 1994. "Inning 1" discusses the origins of professional baseball.

Booker T. Washington's Tuskegee America. AIMS Media, 1987.

Coney Island. Direct Cinema, 800-525-0000.

Hollywood: A Celebration of the American Silent Film. Dir. David Gill and Kevin Brownlow. Image Entertainment, 1990.

Mr. Sears's Catalogue. PBS Home Video, 800-424-7963.

TERMS & NAMES
- Louis Sullivan
- Frederick Law Olmsted
- Central Park
- Daniel Burnham
- Orville and Wilbur Wright
- web-perfecting press
- Linotype machine
- George Eastman

① Science and Urban Life

LEARN ABOUT developments in architecture, transportation, and communication
TO UNDERSTAND how technological changes at the turn of the century affected American cities.

New Yorkers celebrated the opening of the Brooklyn Bridge with a huge fireworks display, but a herd of P. T. Barnum's circus elephants had to cross the bridge before people trusted its safety.

ONE AMERICAN'S STORY

The 1,595-foot-long Brooklyn Bridge, connecting Brooklyn to the island of Manhattan in New York City, was called the "eighth wonder of the world" when it opened in 1883. Workers took 14 years to build what was then the world's largest suspension bridge. Each day the laborers working on the foundation descended to work in a caisson, or watertight chamber, that lay deep beneath the East River.

Within the chamber, the warm air dripped with mist. E. F. Farrington, a mechanic who worked on the bridge, described the working conditions.

A PERSONAL VOICE

Inside the caisson everything wore an unreal, weird appearance. There was a confused sensation in the head, like "the rush of many waters." The pulse was at first accelerated, then sometimes fell below the normal rate. The voice sounded faint, unnatural, and it became a great effort to speak. What with the flaming lights, the deep shadows, the confusing noise of hammers, drills, and chains, the half-naked forms flitting about . . . one might, if of a poetic temperament, get a realizing sense of Dante's Inferno.

E. F. FARRINGTON, quoted in *The Great Bridge*

Although Farrington claimed that working beneath the water made conditions difficult, the bridge was a huge success. Within a year of its completion, the bridge carried 37,000 commuters daily. Four years later, trains across the bridge ran 24 hours a day and carried more than 30 million travelers each year. This section explores the impact of innovations, such as the Brooklyn Bridge, that laid the groundwork for modern American life.

Technology and City Life

Many people crossed the Brooklyn Bridge each day on their way to and from work. After all, it was the increasing number of industrial jobs more than any other factor that drew people to America's cities. By 1890, Chicago and Philadelphia claimed more than a million residents. By 1900, New York boasted a population of 3.5 million people.

Although in 1870, the populations of only 25 American cities had reached 50,000 people, 58 cities made that claim by 1890. Four out of ten Americans made their homes in cities by the turn of the century. As rural and immigrant people entered the cities, one enthusiastic city dweller hailed the "mighty streams of human beings that forever flow up and down the thoroughfares."

To accommodate these streams of people, cities needed to expand upward as well as outward. Technological advances, like the ones that contributed to the construction of the Brooklyn Bridge, soon began to address the urbanizing nation's needs for space, transportation, and communication. One remedy for the ever-shrinking space for new residents was to build upward.

SKYSCRAPERS Architects were able to design taller buildings than ever before because of two factors: the invention of elevators and the development of internal steel skeletons to bear the weight of buildings. In 1890, the architectural pioneer **Louis Sullivan** designed the ten-story Wainwright Building in St. Louis, which he called a "proud and soaring thing." The tall building's appearance was graceful because its steel framework supported both floors and walls. The unusual form of another skyscraper, the Flatiron Building, seemed perfect for its location at one of New York's busiest intersections. Daniel Burnham designed this slender 285-foot tower in 1902.

The skyscraper soon became America's greatest contribution to architecture, "a new thing under the sun" according to architect Frank Lloyd Wright, who studied under Sullivan. Skyscrapers solved the practical problem of how to make the best use of limited and expensive space. The buildings also served as towering symbols of a rich and optimistic society.

ELECTRIC TRANSIT As skyscrapers expanded upward, changes in transportation allowed cities to spread outward. Before the Civil War, horses had drawn the earliest streetcars over iron rails embedded in city streets. In some cities during the 1870s and 1880s, underground moving cables powered streetcar lines. Electricity, however, transformed urban transportation.

In 1888, Richmond, Virginia, became the first American city to electrify its urban transit. After Richmond installed streetcars driven by electric motors powered by an overhead wire, other cities installed electric streetcars. By the turn of the century, intricate networks of electric streetcar lines carried the residents of outlying neighborhoods to downtown department stores, offices, banks, and factories. In Kansas City in 1891, a journalist named William Allen White exclaimed that the city's streetcars were "marvels." The small "walking city," whose limits depended on how far people's legs could carry them, soon gave way to a sprawling metropolis crisscrossed with mass transit lines.

New railroad lines also fed the growth of suburbs, whose residents could now commute to downtown jobs. By 1890, 70,000 suburban commuters made the daily trip to Chicago. New York's northern suburbs alone supplied 100,000 commuters each day to the central business district.

Faced with congestion on their streets, a few large cities moved their streetcars above street level, creating elevated or "el" trains. Other cities like New York built subways by moving their rail lines underground. These streetcars, elevated trains, and subways enabled cities to annex suburban developments that mushroomed along the advancing transportation routes. Indeed, many suburbs wanted to be annexed by the larger city so that the train lines would reach them. Between 1860 and 1890, Boston grew from 5 square miles to 39 square miles. At the same time, Chicago expanded from 17 square miles to 178 square miles.

Steel-cable suspension bridges, of which the Brooklyn Bridge proved the most spectacular example, also brought a city's sections closer together. Sometimes these bridges even provided recreational opportunities. In his design for the Brooklyn Bridge, for example, designer John Augustus Roebling provided an elevated promenade whose "principal use will be to allow people of leisure, and old and young invalids, to promenade over the

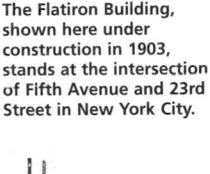

The Flatiron Building, shown here under construction in 1903, stands at the intersection of Fifth Avenue and 23rd Street in New York City.

MORE ABOUT . . .
Louis Sullivan
Often called the father of modern American architecture, Sullivan produced most of his finest work in partnership with Dankmar Adler, a skillful businessman and expert in acoustics. Their landmark works include the Auditorium Building in Chicago and the Wainwright Building in St. Louis.

HISTORY FROM VISUALS
The Flatiron Building
Reading the Art Ask what urban improvements are visible in this picture. *Possible Responses: A skyscraper with steel construction, streetcars, and sidewalks.*

Extension Ask why the Flatiron Building has a triangular shape. *Possible Responses: To make the best use of space between two streets that meet in a V; to win fame and tenants; to be different; to create exotic tapered-corner offices for higher rent.*

MORE ABOUT . . .
The Brooklyn Bridge
Like most of the workers who built the bridge, John Roebling immigrated to America, arriving from Prussia (Germany) in 1831. A few weeks after his bridge plans won approval, he died of tetanus, which he contracted when his toes were crushed by a boat docking near the bridge site. His son Washington supervised the actual construction but was eventually bedridden from repeated bouts of "caisson disease," or the bends.

TEACHING OPTIONS

Exploring Themes

Science and Technology Technology helped cities spread both upward and outward. New construction methods created ever-taller skyscrapers as well as better roads and bridges to connect the downtown with outlying areas. Streetcars, subways, and other new means of rapid transit also promoted urban sprawl. Faster ships brought increasing numbers of immigrants to America, most of whom settled first in their ports of entry. Improved agricultural technologies allowed more and more children of farm families to leave rural America for the economic opportunities of the cities.

Making Connections Across Time

Mass Transit Today Encourage students to discuss recent advances in public transportation as well as some of the problems that plague mass transit today. *Recent advances include monorails, magnetic and "bullet" (very fast) trains, and supersonic aircraft; problems include funding shortages, decaying infrastructure, overcrowding, crime, and graffiti.*

Critical Thinking: Comparing Ask students to discuss why nature and wildlife might be important to city life and to identify a city, town, or neighborhood that they feel displays aspects of Howard's plan.

MORE ABOUT . . .
Central Park

The call to preserve a piece of park land on the island of Manhattan was made as early as 1844 by poet and editor William Cullen Bryant and echoed by eminent landscape designer Andrew Jackson Downing. The campaign took twelve years, but in 1856 the city purchased most of the park's 840 acres with $5 million in state funds. The unappetizing land had a garbage dump, a bone-boiling works, and many shacks and squatters' farms.

> **IN-DEPTH RESOURCES: UNIT 4**
> Geography Application: New York's Central Park, p. 62

HISTORY FROM VISUALS
Daniel Burnham's Chicago Plan

Reading the Art Ask students to consider the patterns of the streets in Burnham's plan. Why would someone plan streets set on a grid bisected by diagonals? *The grid makes the city easy to navigate. Streets running into the city center help create a unified city.*

Extension Ask students what aspects of urban planning they can identify in their own (or the nearest) city or town.

ON THE WORLD STAGE

THE GARDEN CITY

Urban planning in the United States had European counterparts. For example, in *Tomorrow: A Peaceful Path to Social Reform* (1898), the British city planner Ebenezer Howard described a planned residential community called a garden city.

Howard set out to combine the benefits of urban life with easy access to nature. He designed a city plan based on concentric circles—with a town at the center and a wide circle of rural or agricultural land on the perimeter. The town center included a garden, concert hall, museum, theater, library, and hospital. The circle around the town center included a park, a shopping center, a conservatory, a residential area, and industry. Six wide avenues radiated out from the town center.

Howard's plan, first executed in 1903 at Letchworth, England, has served as a model for other planned towns well into the 20th century.

---

bridge on fine days, in order to enjoy the beautiful views and the pure air." This need for open spaces in the midst of crowded commercial cities inspired the emerging science of urban planning.

THE SCIENCE OF URBAN PLANNING Even before skyscrapers and advances in transportation began to make life in the cities more comfortable, city planners in several cities sought to restore a measure of serenity to the urban environment by designing parks and recreational areas. **Frederick Law Olmsted,** farmer, surveyor, and journalist, spearheaded the movement for planned urban parks.

In 1858, Olmsted teamed with English architect Calvert Vaux to draw up a plan for "Greensward," which became **Central Park** in New York. Olmsted envisioned the park as a rustic haven in the center of the busy city. The finished park boasted boating and tennis facilities, a zoo, and bicycle paths, all in a natural setting whose curved lines provided a pleasing contrast to the straight-line grid of New York's streets. Olmsted hoped that the park's beauty would soothe the city's inhabitants and let them enjoy a "natural" setting.

> **A PERSONAL VOICE**
> The main object and justification [of the park] is simply to produce a certain influence in the minds of people and through this to make life in the city healthier and happier. The character of this influence is a poetic one and it is to be produced by means of scenes, through observation of which the mind may be more or less lifted out of moods and habits into which it is, under the ordinary conditions of life in the city, likely to fall.
>
> **FREDERICK LAW OLMSTED,** quoted in *Frederick Law Olmsted's New York*

In the 1870s, Olmsted planned landscaping for Washington, D.C., and St. Louis. He also drew the initial designs for the Fenway, Boston's park system. Boston's Back Bay area, originally a 450-acre swamp, was drained and developed to include elegant streets and cultural attractions.

The Chicago Plan

464 CHAPTER 16

This map from Daniel Burnham's original plan of Chicago looks deceptively like an ordinary map today. But at the time, it was almost revolutionary in its vision, and it inspired city planners to draft plans for cities all over the country.

1 Chicago's Lakefront Urban planners attempted to preserve recreational space somewhere in each city. Burnham's greatest legacy to Chicago may have been his idea for a lakefront park system, complete with beaches, playing fields, and playgrounds.

2 Neighborhood Parks Though not all cities could claim a lakefront vista for recreation, most cities sprinkled neighborhood parks where their residents needed them. Urban planners provided for local parks—such as Lincoln Park in Chicago—so that "the sweet breath of plant life" would be available to everyone.

3 Harbors For cities on the Great Lakes, the shipping business depended on accessible harbors. Burnham saw the advantage of harbors for recreation and commercial purposes. He advocated moving the harbors away from the central business districts to free space for public use.

4 The City Center Burnham redesigned the street pattern to create a group of long streets that would converge on a grand plaza, a practice reflected in other American cities. Major thoroughfares that converged at a city's center helped create a unified city from a host of neighborhoods.

TEACHING OPTION

Cooperative Activity: Planning Ideal Cities

Task: Groups of students will create plans of ideal cities for today or for future decades.

Purpose: To understand the achievements of turn-of-the-century urban planners.

Activity: Groups of four or five students should brainstorm for imaginative ideas to solve specific urban problems, such as overcrowding, affordable housing, efficient transportation, economic development, and

recreation. Each student should focus on one topic, and then each group should incorporate these ideas into plans for an ideal city. Students' plans should include economic zones, roads, civic institutions, parks, schools, and housing units.

📁 **Building a Portfolio:** Students should polish their plans and save them for their portfolio.

Standards for Evaluation
Final plans should . . .

- demonstrate careful consideration of the services needed by urban residents
- clearly label business and industrial districts, parks, schools, and housing units
- be drawn to a reasonable scale

By contrast, Chicago, with its explosive growth from 30,000 people in 1850 to 300,000 in 1870, represented a nightmare of unregulated expansion. As Rudyard Kipling complained of the city, "Having seen it, I urgently desire never to see it again." Fortunately for the growing city, Chicago architect **Daniel Burnham** was intrigued by the prospect of remaking the city. Burnham worked by the motto, "Make no little plans. They have no magic to stir men's blood." He oversaw the transformation of a swampy area near Lake Michigan into a glistening White City for Chicago's 1893 Columbian Exposition. Majestic exhibition halls, statues, and a lagoon greeted 27 million visitors who came to the city.

Many urban planners saw in Burnham's White City glorious visions of future cities. Burnham, however, left Chicago an even more important legacy: an overall plan for the city, crowned by elegant parks strung along Lake Michigan. As a result, Chicago's lakefront today features curving banks of grass and sandy beaches instead of a jumbled mass of piers and warehouses.

THINK THROUGH HISTORY
B. Summarizing
List three major changes in cities near the turn of the century. What effect did each have?

"Make no little plans."

DANIEL BURNHAM

New Technologies Transform Communications

B. Answer Possible Answers: Skyscrapers conserved space by allowing cities to grow upward; new transportation systems and bridges drew neighborhoods closer together; urban planning put parks into cities.

While science and technology pushed American cities upward and outward, new developments in communications brought people closer together in time. In addition to a railroad network that now spanned the nation, advances in aviation, printing, and photography helped to speed the transmission of information.

AIRPLANES AND MAIL DELIVERY During the early 20th century, **Orville and Wilbur Wright,** two brothers who manufactured bicycles in Dayton, Ohio, experimented with new engines powerful enough to keep objects aloft that were "heavier-than-air." The Wright brothers began by building a glider. Eventually they built their own four-cylinder internal combustion engine, chose a propeller, and designed a biplane with a 40-foot wingspan. Their first successful flight—on December 17, 1903, at Kitty Hawk, North Carolina—covered 120 feet and lasted 12 seconds.

The public paid little attention to the Wright brothers' achievement. Only two newspapers in the country even bothered to print the story. The rest probably shared the "national suspicion that the sky was a place only for birds, angels, and fools." Within two years, however, the Wright brothers had increased their flights to 24 miles. By 1908, the pioneer aviators had attracted the interest of the U.S. government.

When the Wright brothers tested their airplane, Orville, the pilot, had to position himself on the lower wing next to the motor to steer the plane.

THINK THROUGH HISTORY
C. Clarifying
How did the use of mail planes bring people in different regions of the country closer together?

C. Answer Mail planes made it faster and easier for people in different regions to communicate.

Convinced of the great potential of flight, the government established the first transcontinental airmail service in 1920. At first, it took a day and a half for mail to travel between New York and San Francisco. Flights were suspended at night, and mail continued by train. By 1925, however, 61 of the 96 planes flying the mail could fly at night.

A REVOLUTION IN PRINTING Thanks to better public education, the literacy rate in the United States rose to nearly 90 percent. As Americans demonstrated an increased interest in reading, publishers turned out ever-increasing numbers of books, magazines, and newspapers to meet the demand. A series of technological advances in printing aided their efforts.

Less expensive paper and better printing presses helped lower the cost of printing. After chemists discovered that wood pulp could be used to make paper, American mills began to produce huge quantities of cheap paper. The new paper proved durable enough to withstand high-speed presses like the one invented by William Bullock. His electrically powered **web-perfecting press** printed on both sides of a continuous paper roll, rather than on just one side,

MORE ABOUT . . .
The Columbian Exposition
Celebrating the 400th anniversary of Columbus's landing in America, the 1893 World's Columbian Exposition was held in Chicago after cities across the nation competed to be the site. The White City sported the latest in electric lighting. President Grover Cleveland opened the fair by flicking a switch in Washington, D.C., to turn on the lights in Chicago.

ELECTRONIC LIBRARY OF PRIMARY SOURCES
from *A Visit to the World's Columbian Exposition* by Charles E. Bolton

OBJECTIVE
(2) **INSTRUCT**

New Technologies Transform Communications

▶**Discussing Key Ideas**
• Pioneered by the Wright brothers, airplanes revolutionize communications as well as transportation.
• Advances in paper and printing spur the publication of newspapers, books, and magazines, while better photography greatly enhances journalism.

IN-DEPTH RESOURCES: UNIT 4
Primary Source: *from* Orville Wright's Diary, p. 64

GEOGRAPHY TRANSPARENCIES
G16, Long Distance Telephone Lines, 1890–1917

TEACHING OPTIONS

Teaching Less Proficient Readers

Visual Learners Students who learn better visually than verbally may benefit from drawing a two-column chart that lists the technological developments that improved urban life at the turn of the century and their applications.

Technological Improvements	Uses
electricity	streetcars, elevated trains and subways
steel construction	suspension bridges, skyscrapers
internal combustion engines	automobiles, airplanes

Making Connections Across the Curriculum

Science Have interested students research and write a brief report on the Wright brothers' experiments with the principles of aerodynamics, such as lift and drag, that led to the invention of the airplane.

Students might give their final reports orally with accompanying illustrations, via computer with appropriate graphics, or in a special exhibit or bulletin-board display.

Teacher's Edition **465**

466 **Chapter 16**

KEY PLAYER

GEORGE EASTMAN
1854–1932

In 1877, a bank clerk named George Eastman took up photography as a hobby. For one day's outing he had to lug more than 100 pounds of equipment, including heavy glass plates. To lighten his load, Eastman replaced the glass plates with celluloid film that could be rolled onto a spool.

In 1888, Eastman sold his first roll-film camera. The purchase price of $25 included a 100-picture roll of film. After taking the pictures, the photographer would send the camera back to Eastman's Rochester, New York, factory. For $10, the pictures were developed and returned with the camera loaded with a brand-new roll of film.

Eastman called his new camera a Kodak, because the made-up name was short, memorable, and easy to pronounce. It came with simple operating instructions, popularized by the slogan "You press the button—We do the rest."

---

then cut, folded, and counted the pages as they came down the line. Faster production and lower costs made newspapers and magazines more affordable. People could now buy newspapers for a penny a copy, and the price of most magazines plunged from about 25 cents to a nickel.

New inventions also sped the tedious process of typesetting. The **Linotype machine,** which was invented by Ottmar Mergenthaler and first used by a newspaper in 1886, streamlined the process of setting type. Illustration also became easier in the 1880s, when the process of chemical engraving enabled printers to reproduce paintings and photographs cheaply and accurately. As a result, illustrations filled newspapers, magazines, and books and became even more commonplace as photography improved.

PHOTOGRAPHY FOR EVERYONE Before the 1880s, photography was a professional activity, difficult for the casual hobbyist. Because of the time required to take a picture and the weight of the equipment, a photographer could not shoot a moving object. In addition, photographers had to develop their shots immediately.

New techniques eliminated the need to develop pictures right away. **George Eastman** developed a paper-based film as an alternative to the heavy glass plates previously used. Now, instead of carrying their dark rooms around with them, photographers could send their film to a studio for processing. When professional photographers were slow to begin using the new film, Eastman decided to aim his product at the masses.

In 1888, Eastman invented his Kodak camera. Easily held and operated, the Kodak camera prompted millions of Americans to become amateur photographers. The camera also helped to create the field of photojournalism. Reporters could now photograph events as they occurred. When the Wright brothers first flew their simple airplane at Kitty Hawk, an amateur photographer captured the first successful flight on film.

Transformations in communication, transportation, and the use of space reshaped the American landscape toward the end of the 19th century. At the same time, developments in education changed the American lifestyle.

D. Answer New printing methods sped production and lowered costs for newspapers. New techniques in photography made it possible for reporters to photograph events as they happened.

THINK THROUGH HISTORY
D. Synthesizing
How did printing and photography change newspapers?

Section 1 Assessment

1. TERMS & NAMES
Identify:
- Louis Sullivan
- Frederick Law Olmsted
- Central Park
- Daniel Burnham
- Orville and Wilbur Wright
- web-perfecting press
- Linotype machine
- George Eastman

2. SUMMARIZING Create three diagrams like this one and label each with one of these types of urban changes: city design, transportation, and communication. Fill in examples for each category.

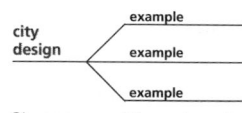

city design — example / example / example

Choose one of the categories and create a poster that shows changes that occurred.

3. FORMING OPINIONS Which development in science and technology described in this section had the greatest impact on American culture? Use details from the text to justify your choice.

THINK ABOUT
- short-term and long-term effects of each development
- how each development affected the attitudes and lives of people at the time

4. SYNTHESIZING If you had been an urban planner at the turn of the century, what new ideas would you have included in your plan for the ideal city?

THINK ABOUT
- Olmsted's plans for Central Park and the Fenway in Boston
- Burnham's ideas for Chicago
- the concept of the garden city

466 CHAPTER 16

ANSWERS

1. TERMS & NAMES
Louis Sullivan, p. 463
Frederick Law Olmsted, p. 464
Central Park, p. 464
Daniel Burnham, p. 465
Orville and Wilbur Wright, p. 465
web-perfecting press, p. 465
Linotype machine, p. 466
George Eastman, p. 466

2. SUMMARIZING
Student diagrams might include these:

City design: Suspension bridges; skyscrapers; urban planning; parks.

Urban transportation: Street cars; commuter trains; el trains; subways.

Communications: Web-perfecting press; Linotype machine; photography; airplanes.

3. FORMING OPINIONS
Possible Answer: Students should cite reasons, such as the long-term impact of air travel or the widespread influence of low-cost printing, to support their opinions.

4. SYNTHESIZING
Possible Response: Students' plans might mention additional recreational facilities or increased numbers of parks, or other personal preferences.

Education and Culture

LEARN ABOUT changes in education and the promotion of high culture
TO UNDERSTAND how these developments affected America's changing identity.

Section 2 Overview

OBJECTIVES

1. To trace the expansion of public education at the turn of the century.
2. To summarize the educational opportunities open for immigrants.
3. To describe the expansion of higher education.
4. To show how expanding education enhanced American culture.

SKILLBUILDER
- Interpreting Graphs, p. 468

CRITICAL THINKING
- Drawing Conclusions, p. 468
- Analyzing Causes, p. 469
- Recognizing Effects, p. 470
- Synthesizing, p. 471
- Summarizing, p. 472
- Developing Historical Perspective, p.472
- Hypothesizing, p. 472

ONE AMERICAN'S STORY

William Torrey Harris was an educational reformer who saw the public schools as a great instrument "to lift all classes of people into . . . civilized life." As superintendent of schools in St. Louis from 1868 to 1880 and U.S. commissioner of education from 1889 to 1906, Harris advised teachers to "lift" students by enforcing strict discipline. "The pupil," he preached, "must have his lessons ready at the appointed time, must rise at the tap of the bell, move to the line, return; in short, go through all the evolutions with equal precision." Such discipline, according to Harris, would properly prepare students for responsible citizenship.

> **A PERSONAL VOICE**
> We believe that a child can easily learn the lesson of willing obedience to lawful authority. We would therefore, place him upon the basis upon which he must stand when he leaves our care; under such circumstances alone we can predict that those whose school record is good will make useful citizens.
> **WILLIAM TORREY HARRIS**, quoted in *Public Schools and Moral Education*

Many other middle-class reformers agreed with Harris and viewed the public schools as training grounds for employment and citizenship. People believed that economic development depended on scientific and technological knowledge. As a result, they viewed education as a key to greater security and social status. Others saw the public schools as the best opportunity to assimilate the millions of immigrants entering American society. Most people also believed that education was necessary for a stable and prosperous democratic nation.

Compulsory school attendance laws, though slow to be enforced, expanded school enrollments and filled classrooms like this one at the turn of the century.

Expanding Public Education

Although most states had public school systems by the Civil War, many school-aged children still received no formal schooling at all. In the South, only North Carolina had a public school system by the 1860s. Throughout the nation, the majority of students who went to school left within four years, and few went to high school.

These facts alarmed educational reformers like Harris. Reformers argued that without a proper education, young Americans would not have the knowledge or skills to take part in civic affairs or get good jobs in an industrial society. In the 1870s, reformers worked to extend schooling to more children, to increase the number of years of mandatory school attendance, and to lengthen the school year.

SCHOOLS FOR CHILDREN Between 1865 and 1895, 31 states passed laws requiring 12 to 16 weeks a year of compulsory school attendance for children between the ages of eight and fourteen. By 1900, almost three-quarters of American children between those ages attended school, mostly in the cities. Students studied a curriculum that emphasized reading, writing, and arithmetic.

Life at the Turn of the Century **467**

 PRINT RESOURCES

IN-DEPTH RESOURCES: UNIT 4
Guided Reading, p. 58
Primary Source: *from* "The Talented Tenth" by W. E. B. DuBois, p. 66
American Lives: W. E .B. DuBois, p. 71

ACCESS FOR STUDENTS ACQUIRING ENGLISH
Guided Reading (Spanish), p. 160

FORMAL ASSESSMENT
Section Quiz, p. 198

ALTERNATIVE ASSESSMENT BOOK
See forms for supporting and scoring alternative activities.

TECHNOLOGY RESOURCES

CRITICAL THINKING TRANSPARENCIES
CT16, Expansion of Education
CT50, School Enrollment: 1870–1920

CD-ROM *Grolier Multimedia Encyclopedia*

VIDEO *American Portfolio: A Videodisc for U.S. History* user's guide, pp. 151, 158, 166, 167

INTERNET McDougal Littell Learning On-Line
http://www.mcdougallittell.com

FOCUS & MOTIVATE

▶ **Starting with the Student**
- Ask students to consider what kinds of futures their education is preparing them for.
- Ask them how an educational system might help a nation meet its social needs.

1. **INSTRUCT**

Expanding Public Education

▶ **Discussing Key Ideas**
- States try to improve and expand public education to produce good citizens and skilled workers.
- High schools emerge as industrial work demands more educated workers.
- Discriminatory educational policies deny most African Americans equal educational opportunities.

IN-DEPTH RESOURCES: UNIT 4
Guided Reading, p. 58

ACCESS FOR STUDENTS ACQUIRING ENGLISH
Guided Reading (Spanish), p. 160.

Reading the Graph Remind the students that each stick figure in the graph equals 2 million students. Therefore, the six stick figures in the top row (1870) equal 12 million students.

Extension Have students research the total school enrollment for the years given in the graph, or you might wish to give them the data and ask them to create an additional column for the graph.

Year	School Enrollment
1870	6,872,000
1880	9,868,000
1890	14,479,000
1900	16,885,000
1910	19,372,000
1920	23,278,000

Source: *Historical Statistics of the United States*, pp. 368–70.

CRITICAL THINKING TRANSPARENCIES

CT16, Expansion of Education
CT50, School Enrollment: 1870–1920

Expanding Education/Decreasing Illiteracy

YEAR	SCHOOL AGE POPULATION (5 TO 18 YEARS OF AGE)	ILLITERACY (% OF TOTAL POPULATION)
1870	12,000,000	20.0%
1880	15,065,767	17.0%
1890	18,543,201	13.0%
1900	21,404,322	10.7%
1910	24,360,888	7.7%
1920	27,728,788	6.0%

= 2,000,000 students

Source: *Statistical Abstract of the United States, 1921; Historical Statistics of the United States*

SKILLBUILDER
INTERPRETING GRAPHS *How much did the illiteracy rate drop from 1870 to 1920? Does the number of immigrants arriving during this period make the reduction in illiteracy more or less impressive? Why?*

Skillbuilder Answer
Rate: 14%.
Immigrants: *Possible Answer:* More impressive, because millions of immigrants could not read when they arrived in America.

However, the emphasis on rote memorization and the uneven quality of teachers drew criticism. Joseph Mayer Rice, a New York pediatrician, visited 36 cities and interviewed 1,200 teachers. He observed numerous problems, including teachers who focused more on their students' posture than their mastery of academic subjects. At many schools, strict rules and physical punishment made students miserable. One 13-year-old boy explained to a Chicago school inspector why he hid in a warehouse basement instead of going to school.

A PERSONAL VOICE
They hits ye if yer don't learn, and they hits ye if ye whisper, and they hits ye if ye have string in yer pocket, and they hits ye if yer seat squeaks, and they hits ye if ye don't stan' up in time, and they hits ye if yer late, and they hits ye if ye ferget the page.

ANONYMOUS, quoted in *The One Best System*

Despite such problems, children began attending school at a younger age. Kindergartens, which had been created outside the public school system to offer childcare for employed mothers, became increasingly popular. The number of kindergartens surged from 200 in 1880 to 3,000 in 1900, and public school systems began to add kindergartens to their programs.

Although the pattern in public education during this era was one of growth, opportunities differed sharply for white and black students. In 1880, about 62 percent of white school-age children attended school, compared to only 34 percent of African-American children. Not until the 1940s would public school education become available to the majority of black children living in the South.

THE GROWTH OF HIGH SCHOOLS In the new industrial age, people realized that the economy demanded advanced technical and managerial skills. Moreover, business leaders like Andrew Carnegie pointed out that keeping workers loyal to capitalism required society to "provide ladders upon which the aspiring can rise."

The number of public high schools jumped from 800 in 1878 to 5,500 in 1898. While fewer than 72,000 students had attended high school in 1870, more than a half million students attended by the turn of the century. The high school curriculum expanded to include courses in science, civics, home economics, history, and literature. In addition, new vocational courses helped prepare male graduates for industrial jobs in drafting, carpentry, and mechanics, and female graduates for work as secretaries and bookkeepers.

A. Answer Public schools multiplied and improved their curricula, and they granted many more children the opportunity to be educated for jobs and citizenship.

THINK THROUGH HISTORY
A. Drawing Conclusions *Explain why many people saw public school as a "ladder upon which the aspiring can rise."*

This boys' track meet is typical of high school athletics at the turn of the century.

TEACHING OPTION

Cooperative Activity: Reforming Public Education

Task: Groups of students will form a school reform committee and create a plan to reform public schools at the turn of the century.

Purpose: To understand the methods and goals of turn-of-the-century educational reformers.

Activity: Groups of five or six students will act as a school board at the turn of the cen-

tury. They are to devise a plan to reform their school district to address an influx of new immigrants, increasing school age populations, and new industrial jobs available in their area.

📁 **Building a Portfolio:** Students should save their reform plans and place them in their portfolio.

Standards for Evaluation
Reform plans should . . .

• address the cultural issues that might arise from a large immigrant population
• provide adequate school capacity for increased population
• devise a curriculum that creates skilled workers
• propose a reasonable funding plan

RACIAL DISCRIMINATION Although white enrollment in public high schools surged after 1880, African Americans for the most part were excluded from public secondary education. In 1890, fewer than 1 percent of black teenagers attended high school. Two out of three of these students went to private schools, which received no government financial support. By 1910, about 3 percent of African Americans between the ages of 15 and 19 attended high school, but most of these students still attended private schools.

Education for Immigrants

Unlike African Americans, immigrants were not locked out of schools. In fact, they were encouraged to go to school. Ten million European immigrants settled in the United States between 1860 and 1890. Many Jewish immigrants fled poverty and oppression in Eastern Europe to pursue economic and educational opportunities in America. Years after she became a citizen, Russian Jewish immigrant Mary Antin recalled the large numbers of non-English-speaking immigrant children. By the end of the school year, they could recite "patriotic verses in honor of George Washington and Abraham Lincoln, with a foreign accent, indeed, but with plenty of enthusiasm."

Most immigrants sent their children to America's free public schools where they quickly became "Americanized." Others were dismayed by the prospect. Some people resented the suppression of their native languages in favor of English.

Catholics were especially concerned because many public school systems had mandatory Bible readings from the King James (Protestant) version and refused to observe holidays in honor of Catholic saints. Instead of sending their children to such schools, Catholic communities often set up parochial schools to give their children a Catholic education.

Thousands of adult immigrants attended night school to learn English and to qualify for American citizenship. Employers, too, offered daytime programs to Americanize their workers. At his Model T plant in Highland Park, Michigan, Henry Ford established a "Sociology Department." It sent case workers into immigrants' homes because "men of many nations must be taught American ways, the English language, and the right way to live."

Ford's idea about the "right way to live" was not universally accepted, however. Labor activists often protested that Ford's educational goals were aimed at weakening the trade union movement by teaching workers not to confront management.

Expanding Higher Education

Although the number of students attending high school at the turn of the century increased, only a minority of Americans could claim a high school diploma. At the same time, an even smaller minority—only 2.3 percent—of America's young people attended colleges and universities.

With few exceptions, college students came from middle-class or wealthy families. College prepared well-to-do young men for successful careers in business or the professions. Between 1880 and 1900, more than 150 new colleges were founded. Between 1880 and 1920, college enrollments more than quadrupled. In addition, colleges instituted major changes in curricula and admission policies.

CHANGES IN UNIVERSITIES Through most of the 19th century, the traditional college curriculum concentrated on classical languages

B. Answer Public schools and adult classes taught English to all members of the family; Americanization also took place in the workplace.

THINK THROUGH HISTORY
B. Analyzing Causes What institutions encouraged European immigrants to become assimilated?

> *"I believe that the motion picture is destined to revolutionize our educational system."*
>
> THOMAS EDISON, 1922

NOW & THEN

TECHNOLOGY AND SCHOOLS

In 1922, Thomas Alva Edison wrote, "I believe that the motion picture is destined to revolutionize our educational system and that in a few years it will supplant . . . the use of textbooks." Today's high schools show that the brilliant inventor was mistaken.

Recently, some people have predicted that computers will replace traditional classrooms and texts. According to a 1995 survey, three-quarters of the nation's schools plan on installing at least two computers per classroom.

Computers allow video course-sharing, in which students from separate schools view the same classes. Students also use computers to access up-to-the-minute scientific data, such as weather information.

For many teens, though, the lure of using the computer to access the Internet is more social than educational. One small study revealed that only one-quarter of teens' e-mail messages related to schoolwork—most of their messages were social.

Life at the Turn of the Century **469**

TEACHING OPTIONS

Exploring Themes

Immigration and Migration Note that education was a vital tool for assimilating the millions of immigrants who came to America from 1880 to 1920. Not only did immigrant children attend school by day, but their parents often took adult education courses at night or went through Americanization programs at work. Immigrants were also indirectly assimilated on the job through the labor unions and political organizations that many of them joined. Encourage students to offer their own definitions of Americanization and to discuss its importance.

Teaching Less Proficient Readers

Guided Reading Suggest that students focus their reading by turning each heading and subheading into a question and then reading the material below it to find the answer. For example, the subheadings on pages 468 and 469 could be turned into these questions:

• Why did high schools grow?
• What group faced discrimination and in what ways?
• What education was provided for immigrants?
• How was higher education expanded?

HISTORICAL SPOTLIGHT
Women in College Life

Critical Thinking: Hypothesizing Even though the number of women attending college was climbing at the turn of the century, they still remained a minority on campus. You might ask students to consider how college administrators and professors addressed the presence of female students.

MORE ABOUT . . .
Stanford University

Railroad magnate Leland Stanford donated a Palo Alto farm to provide land for the new university. The sandstone buildings, designed by Frederick Law Olmsted, were styled to resemble the old Spanish missions of California.

MORE ABOUT . . .
W. E. B. Du Bois

Du Bois (often *DuBois;* pronounced *doo bois'*) attended Fisk University in Nashville before going to graduate school at Harvard. Although his doctorate was in history, he was really more of a sociologist who devoted his scholarship to fighting racism. Du Bois used statistical evidence to disprove racist myths that were used to support segregation. Among his early writings with this goal was *The Philadelphia Negro* (1899), the first case study of an African-American community.

IN-DEPTH RESOURCES: UNIT 4
Primary Source: *from "The Talented Tenth"* by W. E. B. DuBois, p. 66
American Lives: W. E. B. DuBois, p. 71

GROLIER MULTIMEDIA ENCYCLOPEDIA
from *The Souls of Black Folk* by W. E. B. Du Bois

HISTORICAL SPOTLIGHT

WOMEN IN COLLEGE LIFE

College life at the turn of the century saw important social changes.

From roughly 1870 to 1910, many sororities, or social organizations of women students, were started at colleges and universities across the country. Though organizations for male students—fraternities—had existed since the mid-19th century, it wasn't until decades later that enough women attended colleges to form similar organizations.

Sororities shared one goal with universities: promoting high academic achievement. Sororities also performed charitable work and provided social activities for their members. Today, about 540,000 women belong to sororities in the United States.

Medical students and their professors work in the operating theater of the Moorland-Spingarn Research Center at Howard University.

such as Greek and Latin, philosophy, theology, and mathematics. America's industrial development changed the nation's educational needs at the college level, as it had at the primary and secondary levels. By the turn of the century, a new institution, the research university, emerged to meet these modern needs. Research universities offered courses in modern languages, engineering, economics, the physical sciences, and the new disciplines of psychology and sociology. They also established professional schools in law and medicine.

Some research universities were founded by wealthy capitalists who wanted to ensure an ample supply of engineers and scientists. In Palo Alto, California, Leland Stanford and his wife, Jane Lathrop Stanford, donated $24 million to open Stanford University in 1885 in memory of their son. In 1891, the University of Chicago was founded with gifts totaling $34 million from John D. Rockefeller. By the end of his life, Rockefeller had given the university more than $80 million.

In addition to private colleges and universities (which required entrance exams), state universities in the Midwest and California began to admit high school graduates without a test, using the high school diploma as the entrance requirement.

Higher education also changed because of developments in medicine. During the Civil War, wounds killed only half as many soldiers as infections caused by doctors who, ignorant of the effects of germs, failed to wash their hands. After the war, American medical professionals who had been trained in Germany and France restructured American medical education to include basic hygiene, laboratory experience, and courses in biology, chemistry, and physics. By the turn of the century, medical education was set on a firm course. Professional programs in architecture, engineering, and law also benefited from reforms.

HIGHER EDUCATION FOR AFRICAN AMERICANS After the Civil War, thousands of freed African Americans pursued education, despite their exclusion from white colleges and universities. All-black schools soon opened to educate merchants, ministers, physicians, dentists, and teachers. With the help of the Freedmen's Bureau and Northern groups like the American Missionary Association, African Americans founded Howard, Atlanta, and Fisk universities and Hampton Institute, all of which opened between 1865 and 1868.

White and black charitable organizations that supported black colleges, however, could not financially support or educate a sufficient number of black college graduates to provide enough doctors, lawyers, and teachers to meet the needs of the segregated communities. By 1900, out of a population of 9.2 million African Americans, only 3,880 had graduated from colleges or professional schools. In 1910, 5 percent of the white population attended college, compared to less than one-third of 1 percent of the African-American community.

W. E. B. Du Bois became the first African American to receive a Ph.D. from Harvard in 1895. "The honor, I assure you," the aristocratic Du Bois said, "was Harvard's." Born to a middle-class family in Massachusetts, Du Bois believed blacks should seek a liberal arts education so

THINK THROUGH HISTORY
C. *Recognizing Effects* How did the Civil War affect medical education?

C. Answer Because of the number of deaths from infection during the war, reformers sought changes in medical schools to ensure a rigorous education for doctors.

TEACHING OPTIONS

Making Connections Across Time

Trends in Education At the turn of the century, public-school education typically consisted of eight years of grade school and four years of high school. Some educators believed that middle-grade students would learn and socialize better in a different format, and the junior high school was born. More recent trends include block scheduling, the increased use of video and computer technologies, and preschool training.

Encourage students to discuss new ideas in education, such as the voucher system, charter schools, and Americorps.

Making Connections Across Cultures

Campus Diversity Until the late 19th century, most American college students were wealthy white males. Throughout the 20th century, however, the number of women, minorities, and international students has climbed. These groups of people brought fresh perspectives to the intellectual and cultural aspects of campus life that have expanded the focus of scholarship and created new departments and programs (such as Afro-American Studies). Sometimes this diversity results in tensions, and campus groups have come into conflict over issues like speech codes (rules regulating potentially offensive language).

that the African-American community would have well-educated leaders. Toward this end, Du Bois proposed that a group of educated blacks, the most "talented tenth" of the African-American community, attempt to achieve immediate inclusion into mainstream American life. "We are Americans, not only by birth and by citizenship," Du Bois argued, "but by our political ideals. . . . And the greatest of those ideals is that ALL MEN ARE CREATED EQUAL."

Another prominent African American, **Booker T. Washington,** believed that racism would end once African Americans acquired useful labor skills and proved their economic value to society. Washington, who was born a slave in Virginia, graduated from Hampton Institute after his emancipation. In 1881, he opened his own school in Alabama, the Tuskegee Normal and Industrial Institute. Tuskegee aimed to enable its black graduates to teach and to do agricultural, domestic, or mechanical work. "No race," Washington said, "can prosper till it learns that there is as much dignity in tilling a field as in writing a poem."

Education Influences Culture

As increasing numbers of Americans attended school and learned to read, the cultural vistas of ordinary Americans expanded. Art galleries, libraries, books, and museums also brought new cultural opportunities to more people.

PROMOTING FINE ARTS   Public schools and colleges were only one source of education for Americans. By 1900, at least one art gallery graced every large city. Often, wealthy patrons established art galleries and museums to share the art treasures they had acquired for their palatial houses.

In the late 19th century, some American artists, including **Thomas Eakins,** began to embrace realism, an artistic school that aimed at portraying real life even in its grittier forms. Eakins filled his canvases with muscular rowers who looked especially lifelike because of his study of anatomy and experience in dissecting bodies at a medical school. In his drawing classes at the Pennsylvania Academy of Fine Arts, Eakins employed nude models, which led wealthy Philadelphians to call for his dismissal. The same wealthy patrons had already been offended by Eakins's realist approach to portrait painting.

The realist movement in American art is embodied by *The Champion Single Sculls (Max Schmitt in a Single Scull),* (1871) by Thomas Eakins.

Americans' preoccupation with the problems and prospects of their cities found expression in the works of artists such as Robert Henri in the early 20th century. Henri and his counterparts became known as the Ashcan school because of their portrayals of urban poverty and working-class people.

Both Eakins and the Ashcan school artists soon were challenged by the European development known as abstract art, a shocking non-representational form of modernist expression that most people found difficult to understand. When an exhibit of European modernists opened at the National Guard Armory in New York in 1913, half a million people eagerly viewed the works of Pablo Picasso, Henri Matisse, and others.

Life at the Turn of the Century **471**

OBJECTIVE
④ **INSTRUCT**

Education Influences Culture

▶ *Starting with the Student*
• Ask students to discuss what kinds of topics, issues, and activities (such as music, literature, film, or other hobbies) that education has helped them appreciate.

▶ *Discussing Key Ideas*
• The expansion of education broadens Americans' cultural horizons, with art galleries, libraries, and museums making culture available to more people.
• Many turn-of-the-century artists and writers embrace social realism, attempting to portray life as it is really lived.
• Increased literacy boosts sales of "dime novels" and other light fiction.

MORE ABOUT
Thomas Eakins

Except for four years in Europe, when he studied art in France and viewed the masterpieces of Spain, Eakins spent virtually his entire life in the city of his birth, Philadelphia. His pioneering efforts in realism at first met with scorn. *The Gross Clinic,* the realistic depiction of a surgery, now deemed his masterpiece, was rejected for display at the Centennial Exposition held in Philadelphia in 1876.

 GROLIER MULTIMEDIA ENCYCLOPEDIA
Thomas Eakins with an example of his work

TEACHING OPTIONS

Making Global Connections

Technology and Culture   Stress that improved communications and transportation made culture far more international, enabling successful Americans to travel overseas and more foreign art and artists to visit America. Mark Twain satirized foreign sights and ways through the supposedly naive American world traveler in *The Innocents Abroad,* a narrative based on his own experiences on a tour of Mediterranean Europe and the Holy Land. Painter Mary Cassatt and authors Henry James, Edith Wharton, and Stephen Crane are just a few of the many turn-of-the-century American artists and intellectuals who spent extensive time in Europe.

Making Connections Across the Curriculum

Art   Note that the Ashcan (often *Ash Can*) School got its name because its paintings portrayed urban life with gritty realism. Artists Robert Henri, Everett Shinn, John Sloan, Arthur B. Davies, Ernest Lawson, Maurice Prendergast, George Luks, and William Glackens opposed New York's conservative exhibit rules in 1907 and together displayed their work at a 1908 exhibit. They later became a part of the Ashcan School, of which Edward Hopper was also a member.

Have students examine and critique paintings by Ashcan School artists. Ask them what aspects of turn-of-the-century urban life the paintings portray.

Teacher's Edition   **471**

Clemens grew up in the Mississippi River town of Hannibal, Missouri, and took his pen name from a riverboat pilot's cry, "Mark twain!"—which meant the water was two fathoms deep, or safe for the boat to cross. Twain's satirical pen gave late 19th-century America its nickname, the Gilded Age, which was the title of a novel he coauthored with Charles Dudley Warner. A pioneer work of American realism, *The Adventures of Huckleberry Finn* is usually cited as Twain's masterpiece. "All modern American literature," Ernest Hemingway once said, "comes from one book by Mark Twain called *Huckleberry Finn.*"

ASSESS & RETEACH

Section 2 Assessment
Students might work in pairs to respond to the questions.

Self-Assessment
To assess what they have learned, students might write their own questions, exchange them with a partner, and try to answer their partner's questions.

Section Quiz

FORMAL ASSESSMENT
Section Quiz, p. 198

Reteach
Ask students to consider the three most important changes in education at the turn of the century and give the reasons they occurred.

CLOSE
Education, which expanded to train the work force and teach good American citizenship, also led to new cultural achievements.

In many cities, inhabitants could walk from the new art gallery to the new public library, sometimes called "the poor man's university." Recalling his boyhood yearning for books, wealthy industrialist Andrew Carnegie donated $60 million to build public libraries all over the country. The cities that built the libraries provided the land and levied taxes to buy books and pay librarians. By 1900, free circulating libraries in America numbered in the thousands.

POPULAR FICTION As literacy rates rose, intellectual leaders debated the role of literature in society. Some felt literature should uplift America's literary tastes, which tended toward crime tales and Western adventures. Editors at *The Nation, Atlantic Monthly,* and *North American Review* combed their publications to remove sexual or anti-Christian material, slang, and tragic endings.

Others wanted a more realistic portrayal of American life. Samuel Langhorne Clemens, the novelist and humorist better known as **Mark Twain,** inspired a host of other young authors when he declared his independence of "literature and all that bosh." Though some critics of the day felt Twain's work was little better than mild amusement, some of his books have become classics of American literature. *The Adventures of Huckleberry Finn,* for example, remains famous for its realistic rendering of American life along the Mississippi River.

Known as a regionalist for her realistic portrayals of the dialect and detail of New England village life, Sarah Orne Jewett's *The Country of the Pointed Firs* (1896) captured the simplicity of life in South Berwick, Maine. Other writers of the era—Theodore Dreiser, Stephen Crane, Jack London, and Willa Cather, for example—portrayed characters less polished than the upper-class men and women of Henry James's or Edith Wharton's novels.

Most people, however, preferred to read light fiction. Harlan F. Halsey churned out one popular novel after another and sometimes produced a book a day. Such books sold for a mere ten cents, hence their name, "dime novels." Dime novels typically told glorified adventure tales of the West and featured heroes like Edward Wheeler's Deadwood Dick. Wheeler published his first Deadwood Dick novel in 1877 and, in less than a decade, produced over 30 more.

The highly popular dime novels often featured adventure stories.

Although art galleries and libraries attempted to raise cultural standards, many Americans had scant interest in high culture—and others did not have access to it. African Americans, for example, were excluded from visiting museums and other white-controlled cultural institutions. They and other racial and ethnic groups struggled against this discrimination and enforced segregation in all parts of the country.

E. Answer
New printing technologies and America's growing literacy rate.

THINK THROUGH HISTORY
E. *Summarizing*
What factors contributed to the popularity of dime novels?

Section ❷ Assessment

1. TERMS & NAMES
Identify:
• W. E. B. Du Bois
• Booker T. Washington
• Thomas Eakins
• Mark Twain

2. SUMMARIZING List at least three developments in education at the turn of the century and their major results, using a diagram like the one shown.

Development	Result
1.	
2.	
3.	

Write a paragraph explaining which educational development you think was most important.

3. DEVELOPING HISTORICAL PERSPECTIVE Compare the impact of museums, libraries, and other cultural institutions in the early 20th century with their impact in today's society. Are these institutions more or less important today than they were then?

THINK ABOUT
• the audience museums and libraries reached then and now
• the role of museums and libraries in modern mass culture, then and now

4. HYPOTHESIZING How might the economy and culture of the United States have been different without the expansion of public schools?

THINK ABOUT
• the goals of public schools and whether those goals have been met
• why people supported expanding public education
• the impact of public schools on the development of private schools

---

ANSWERS

1. TERMS & NAMES
W. E. B. Du Bois, p. 470
Booker T. Washington, p. 471
Thomas Eakins, p. 471
Mark Twain, p. 472

2. SUMMARIZING
Students might include some of the following entries:
• Compulsory education laws: Literacy increased.
• Increase in number of kindergartens: Immigrants became "Americanized."
• Growth of high schools: College enrollments increased.
• Discrimination against African Americans: All-black colleges founded.

• New curriculums in colleges: Increased interest in high culture.

Students' paragraphs will vary but should include reasons for their choices.

3. DEVELOPING HISTORICAL PERSPECTIVE

Possible Answer: Students may note that in the early 20th century, cultural institutions promoted high culture, rather than the mass culture that was emerging. Today, museums and libraries are more integrated int the modern mass culture and reach larger audiences.

4. HYPOTHESIZING

Possible Answer: Without publi schools, economic growth, the adapting of immigrants to American life, and the growth o high culture might have slowed However, private schools might have developed more rapidly.

Segregation and Discrimination

TERMS & NAMES
- Ida B. Wells
- literacy test
- poll tax
- grandfather clause
- Jim Crow laws
- segregation
- *Plessy* v. *Ferguson*
- debt peonage

LEARN ABOUT racial tensions in the late 19th century
TO UNDERSTAND the persistence of racial discrimination in America.

ONE AMERICAN'S STORY

African Americans clutched at their dreams of equality in the years following Reconstruction. In both the South and the North, though, a system of segregation and discrimination prevented equal access to schools, jobs, and housing. **Ida B. Wells** refused to accept this system.

Born into slavery shortly before emancipation, Wells was raised in a well-respected and politically active African-American family. The death of her parents in a yellow fever epidemic rushed her into an adulthood that included caring for her younger siblings. In the early 1880s, she moved to Memphis to become an editor of a local paper.

Racial justice had been a persistent theme in Wells's reporting, but the events of 1892 turned that idea into a crusade. On March 9, three of Wells's friends were lynched. The men had opened a store called the People's Grocery that successfully competed with a nearby white-owned store. The competition escalated into violence and the three black proprietors were arrested. Later a white mob formed, grabbed the three men from the jail and killed them. Wells recognized lynching for what it was.

A PERSONAL VOICE
Thomas Moss, Calvin McDowell, and Lee Stewart had been lynched in Memphis . . . [where] no lynching had taken place before. . . . This is what opened my eyes to what lynching really was. An excuse to get rid of Negroes who were acquiring wealth and property and thus keep the race terrorized.

IDA B. WELLS, quoted in *Crusade for Justice*

Ida B. Wells

As Wells denounced the lynching, the local white press in Memphis called for her to be lynched. She decided she was no longer safe in Memphis and moved to the North, where she continued her fight against lynching by writing, lecturing, and organizing for civil rights.

The racial hostility Wells encountered in Memphis was common in late-19th-century America. All African Americans faced constant threats to their civil rights—as workers, as consumers, and as citizens—throughout the United States. Nor were African Americans the only group to experience oppression. Native Americans, Chinese immigrants, and Mexican residents also encountered bitter forms of discrimination in the American West.

African Americans Fight Legal Discrimination

As African Americans exercised their newly won political and social rights during Reconstruction, they faced hostile, and often violent, opposition from whites. After the federal government lifted military authority over the Southern states in 1877, white Southern Democrats reclaimed control over their state governments and quickly instituted laws to subject African Americans to second-class citizenship. African Americans eventually fell victim to laws restricting their civil rights but never stopped fighting for equality.

VOTING RESTRICTIONS For at least ten years after the end of Reconstruction in 1877, African Americans in the South continued to vote and occasionally to

Life at the Turn of the Century **473**

SECTION 3 RESOURCES

 PRINT RESOURCES

IN-DEPTH RESOURCES: UNIT 4
Guided Reading, p. 59
Skillbuilder Practice: Primary Sources, p. 61
Primary Source: *from* "Lynching and the Excuse for It" by Ida B. Wells, p. 67

ACCESS FOR STUDENTS ACQUIRING ENGLISH
Guided Reading (Spanish), p. 161
Skillbuilder Practice: Primary Sources (Spanish), p. 163

FORMAL ASSESSMENT
Section Quiz, p. 199

ALTERNATIVE ASSESSMENT BOOK
See forms for supporting and scoring alternative activities.

TECHNOLOGY RESOURCES

CD-ROM *Grolier Multimedia Encyclopedia*
Electronic Library of Primary Sources

VIDEO *American Portfolio: A Videodisc for U.S. History*
user's guide, pp. 151, 155, 169, 171

INTERNET McDougal Littell Learning On-Line
http://www.mcdougallittell.com

Section 3 Overview

OBJECTIVES

1 To trace the development of legal discrimination against African Americans in the South and their struggle against it.

2 To summarize turn-of-the-century race relations in the North as well as in the South.

3 To identify discrimination against Mexican Americans, Chinese Americans, and others in the American West.

SKILLBUILDER
- Interpreting Charts, p. 474

CRITICAL THINKING
- Summarizing, pp. 475, 477
- Identifying problems, p. 477
- Contrasting, p. 477

FOCUS & MOTIVATE

▶ *Starting with the Student*
- You might ask students whether they have ever been unfairly discriminated against.
- Ask them how such treatment affects both the victim and the perpetrator.

OBJECTIVE
1 INSTRUCT

African Americans Fight Legal Discrimination

Students might create a chart summarizing the types of laws that weakened African-American voting rights in the South.

Laws	Explanation
literacy tests	test of potential voter's reading skill, often made harder for blacks
polltax	annual tax required to be able to vote
grandfather clause	law to refranchise whites who lost the vote because of other voting restrictions

(continued on next page)

Teacher's Edition **473**

(continued from page 473)

▶ **Discussing Key Ideas**

- White Southerners institute voting restrictions and segregation laws, reducing African Americans to second-class citizenship.
- In *Plessy* v. *Ferguson* in 1896, the Supreme Court made "separate but equal" the law of the land. In practice, the separation was enforced, but the equality was not.

IN-DEPTH RESOURCES: UNIT 4
Guided Reading, pp. 59

ACCESS FOR STUDENTS ACQUIRING ENGLISH
Guided Reading (Spanish), p. 161

MORE ABOUT . . .
Jim Crow

Thomas Dartmouth ("Daddy") Rice was the father of American minstrel shows, musical entertainment in which blacks, or whites in blackface, poked fun at the singing and dancing of African-American slaves. Winning fame as a "Negro impersonator," Rice created the character of Jim Crow in an 1828 minstrel routine that conveyed the stereotype of the simple, happy-go-lucky black who loves to dance and sing for "de white folks." Minstrel shows became hugely popular by mid-century when companies like the Virginia Minstrels and Bryant's Minstrels went on tour and the most famous of all, the Christy Minstrels, performed Stephen Foster songs on Broadway in New York City.

 GROLIER MULTIMEDIA ENCYCLOPEDIA
Jim Crow Laws

SKILLBUILDER
INTERPRETING CHARTS
What do you think Justice Brown meant when he said the Constitution would not put people "on the same plane"? How did Justice Harlan oppose Brown's opinion?
Skillbuilder Answer
Possible Answer: Brown meant the laws would not make people equal. Harlan wrote a dissenting opinion and argued that it was wrong to have laws that distinguished people solely on the basis of race.

hold political office. By the end of the century, however, Southern states had adopted a broad system of legal policies of racial discrimination and devised methods to weaken African-American political power.

All Southern states imposed new voting restrictions. The Supreme Court generally refused to view such legislation as a violation of the Thirteenth, Fourteenth, and Fifteenth Amendments, and thus these new laws denied legal equality to African Americans. For example, some states required that prospective voters be literate. To enforce that requirement, voter registration officials administered a **literacy test.** Registrars often asked blacks more difficult questions than they asked whites, or gave them a test in a foreign language. The officials administering the test could pass or fail applicants as they wished.

Another requirement was the **poll tax,** an annual tax that had to be paid to gain access to the voting booth. Black as well as white sharecroppers, who usually lacked the cash to pay the tax, were frequently unable to vote.

To reinstate white voters who may have failed the literacy test or could not pay the poll tax, several Southern states added a **grandfather clause** to their constitutions. Louisiana was the first to do so in 1898. The clause stated that even if a man failed the literacy test or could not afford the poll tax, he was still entitled to vote if he, his father, or his grandfather had been eligible to vote before January 1, 1867. The date is important because before that time freed slaves did not have the right to vote. The grandfather clause therefore did not allow them to vote.

During the 1870s and 1880s, the Supreme Court failed to overturn these laws—even though the laws surrendered all federal protections for African Americans' civil rights. For example, in *United States* v. *Reese* in 1876, the Supreme Court argued that the Fifteenth Amendment did not automatically give the vote to anyone. It simply made it illegal to use a person's race as a reason for denying the right to vote. Since laws establishing poll taxes and literacy tests said nothing about race, the Supreme Court allowed them to stand.

JIM CROW LAWS   At the same time that African Americans lost voting rights, Southern state and local governments passed laws to separate white and black people in public and private facilities. These laws came to be known as **Jim Crow laws** after a minstrel show character who sang a comic song ending in the words "Jump, Jim Crow." By the early 20th century, the word **segregation** was used to describe this system of separating people on the basis of race. Racial segregation developed in schools, hospitals, parks, and transportation systems throughout the South.

PLESSY V. FERGUSON   Eventually a legal case reached the U.S. Supreme Court to test the constitutionality of segregation. Homer A. Plessy, classified as a black man in Louisiana because he was one-eighth African American, had been denied a seat in a railroad car reserved for white passengers. Plessy

Plessy v. Ferguson

DISSENTING OPINION	MAJORITY OPINION
Justice John Marshall Harlan	Justice Henry P. Brown
"The thin disguise of 'equal' accommodations for passengers in railroad coaches will not mislead anyone nor atone for the wrong this day done."	"If one race be inferior to the other socially, the Constitution of the United States cannot put them upon the same plane."

474 CHAPTER 16

Teaching Gifted and Talented Students

Legal Briefs   Encourage interested students to research the arguments and decisions in *Plessy* v. *Ferguson* or another famous Supreme Court case in the history of civil rights, such as the Dred Scott decision of 1857 or *Brown* v. *Board of Education of Topeka* (1954). Final reports may consist of written briefs or dramatizations in which small groups of students present each case to classmates.

Exploring Themes

Civil Rights   Note that W. E. B. Du Bois and Booker T. Washington were both pioneers in the struggle for African-American rights, although their approaches differed. Washington stressed a gradual approach through education and suggested that African Americans focus on developing skills that would lead to economic independence. Du Bois demanded more rapid change and insisted on an immediate end to segregation. Washington's approach was more acceptable to many progressive whites who argued for greater social equality but feared Du Bois's approach was too radical.

challenged the Louisiana law that required railroad companies to segregate white and black passengers. He contended that the law denied him his rights under Louisiana's constitution and took the issue to court. The railroad argued that the separate facilities for black people were just as good as the ones for whites.

The Supreme Court sided with the railroad. In 1896, in ***Plessy v. Ferguson,*** the Court ruled that separation of the races in public accommodations was legal and did not violate the Fourteenth Amendment. The decision established the doctrine of "separate but equal," which allowed states to maintain segregated facilities for blacks and whites so long as they provided equal service. The decision permitted legalized racial segregation for almost 60 years. Unfortunately for African Americans, the "separate" part of the law was enforced far more often than the "equal" part, and facilities labeled "colored" rapidly declined in quality.

Turn-of-the-Century Race Relations

African Americans faced not only formal discrimination but also informal rules and customs, called racial etiquette, that regulated relationships between whites and blacks. Usually, these customs belittled and humiliated African Americans, affirming their second-class status.

African Americans had to show deference to whites, including children, and endure humiliating treatment. For example, blacks and whites never shook hands, which would imply equality. Blacks had to yield the sidewalk to white pedestrians, and black men always had to remove their hats for whites.

Some moderate reformers like Booker T. Washington advocated gradual improvements for African Americans. Washington thought it was best to avoid demands for legal equality, which most whites staunchly opposed, and concentrate on creating economic opportunities. Washington earned support from whites because he tacitly accepted segregation while he suggested whites and blacks work together for social progress.

> **A PERSONAL VOICE**
> To those of the white race . . . I would repeat what I say to my own race, "Cast down your bucket where you are." . . . Cast down your bucket among these people who have, without strikes and labor wars, tilled your fields, cleared your forests, builded your railroads and cities, and brought forth treasures from the bowels of the earth, and helped make possible this magnificent representation of the progress of the South. . . . In all things that are purely social we can be as separate as the fingers, yet one as the hand in all things essential to mutual progress.
> **BOOKER T. WASHINGTON,** *Atlanta Exposition Address, 1895*

By helping to improve the economic skills of African Americans, Washington hoped to pave the way for long-term gains. People like Ida B. Wells and W. E. B. Du Bois, however, thought the problems of inequality were too urgent to ignore.

VIOLENCE African Americans who did not follow the racial etiquette could face severe punishment. Minor breaches might be overlooked, or met with a mild reprimand. Serious violations could provoke serious, and often violent, response. If the offended white person complained to the African American's employer, the employee could lose his or her job.

All too often, African Americans who were accused of violating the etiquette were lynched. Between 1885 and 1900, more than 2,500 African-American men

HISTORICAL SPOTLIGHT

WASHINGTON AND DU BOIS DEBATE

Booker T. Washington's Atlanta Exposition address won the applause of whites throughout the country. Arguing for a gradual approach to racial equality, Washington suggested that "it is at the bottom of life we must begin, and not at the top."

Ten years later, W. E. B. Du Bois denounced this view of gradual equality and belittled it as the "Atlanta Compromise." Demanding full social and economic equality for African Americans, Du Bois founded the Niagara Movement in 1905 and announced that "persistent manly agitation is the way to liberty."

In 1910 the Niagara Movement became the National Association for the Advancement of Colored People (NAACP) and Du Bois the editor of its journal, *The Crisis.* He wrote, "We refuse to surrender . . . leadership . . . to cowards and trucklers. We are men; we will be treated as men."

and women were shot, burned, or hanged without trial in the South. Lynching—an illegal execution, without a trial, carried out by a mob—peaked in the 1880s and 1890s but continued well into the 20th century.

Like the three friends of Ida B. Wells, blacks were often targeted for a lynching if they showed signs of becoming successful. They were also in danger if someone accused them of showing too little respect for whites, especially white women.

Crusaders like Ida B. Wells fought a nationwide struggle to remove impediments to racial equality. Although most African Americans lived in the segregated South, those in the North also faced discrimination in housing, education, and work.

DISCRIMINATION IN THE NORTH By 1900, a small but growing number of African Americans lived in Northern cities. Many African Americans, who believed legends of harmonious race relations in the North, migrated to Northern cities in search of better paying jobs and social equality. But upon their arrival, African Americans experienced racial discrimination similar to that in the South.

African Americans found themselves forced into segregated neighborhoods. Local residents and realtors prevented African Americans from moving into white neighborhoods. Blacks also faced discrimination in the workplace. Labor unions often denied them membership and employers hired them only as a last resort and fired them before white employees.

Sometimes the competition between African Americans and working class whites became violent, as in the New York City race riot of 1900. Violence erupted when Arthur J. Harris, a young black man, killed a white police officer he believed was mistreating Harris's wife. Word of the killing spread and whites demanded revenge. As one local reporter noted, "Men and women poured by the hundreds from the neighboring tenements" and attacked blacks wherever they found them. Northern blacks, however, were not alone in facing such discrimination. Nonwhites in the West also faced oppression.

Discrimination in the West

White Americans were not the only people to populate the West. Native Americans continued to live in the western territories claimed by the United States. Asian Americans traveled to the Pacific coast of North America in search of wealth and work. Mexicans continued to inhabit the American Southwest. African Americans were also present, especially in former slave areas such as Texas. Often these communities were culturally diverse as people of differing ethnic and racial groups worked and lived side by side. Still, racial tensions often made life uncomfortable for nonwhites.

MEXICAN WORKERS Mexicans in the Southwest often faced difficult conditions because of racial discrimination. In the 1880s and 1890s, the Southern Pacific and Santa Fe railroads hired more Mexicans than any other ethnic group to construct rail lines in Arizona, southern California, Nevada, and New Mexico. Railroad managers hired Mexicans not only because they were accustomed to the Southwest's hot, dry climate but also because they were forced to work for less money than other ethnic groups.

Mexican workers were also vital to the development of mining and agriculture in the Southwest. When the 1901 Newlands Reclamation Act provided government assistance for irrigation projects, many desert areas in the Southwest bloomed. Raising grapes, lettuce, citrus fruit, and cotton required manual labor, and Mexicans, who had worked so well for the railroads, provided a major source of agricultural labor.

These Mexican workers sometimes found themselves reduced to **debt peonage,** a system of involuntary servitude in which the laborer is forced to work off a debt. After slavery was abolished, some Mexicans, as well as African Americans in the territories of New Mexico and Arizona, were forced into debt peonage. Not until 1911 did the U.S. Supreme Court declare involuntary peonage to be a violation of the Thirteenth Amendment.

EXCLUDING THE CHINESE Between 1850 and 1880, the Chinese immigrant population in the United States grew from 7,520 to more than 100,000. The Chinese had come to the United States to work and formed a major part of the labor force in the West. Not only did they help build the transcontinental railroad but they were indispensible to important industries in California. Chinese immigrants made up more than half of all shoemakers, more than four-fifths of all cigar makers, and roughly one-third of all woolen mill operators.

With so many Chinese people working, a growing group of whites feared losing out in job competition with them. Consequently, Chinese people often found themselves pushed into segregated schools and neighborhoods. A strong anti-Chinese immigration movement developed, and not only in the West. Congress overwhelmingly passed the Chinese Exclusion Act in 1882. The act prohibited almost all further immigration of Chinese to the United States and suspended naturalization for those who were already present.

Anti-Chinese feeling was so strong that street riots against the Chinese were not uncommon.

While racial discrimination posed terrible legal and economic problems for nonwhites throughout the United States, that was not the whole story of turn-of-the-century America. Due to rapid industrialization and improvements that made daily life and work easier, more people, especially whites, found leisure time for new recreational activities and money to spend on a growing array of consumer products. Americans began to flock to the latest trends—and a mass culture was born.

MORE ABOUT . . .
The Chinese Exclusion Act of 1882
The Chinese Exclusion Act of 1882 emerged not simply as an example of American racism. The act was part of a broader social concern over class tensions in an industrial society. At first, the act only restricted the immigration of Chinese laborers for ten years, in order to protect the jobs of white workers and reduce the kinds of tensions that led to events like the Railroad Strike of 1877. Nevertheless, the act expanded to include "all persons of the Chinese race" in 1888. It was then extended another ten years in 1892 and made indefinite in 1902.

Section 3 Assessment

1. TERMS & NAMES

Identify:
• Ida B. Wells
• literacy test
• poll tax
• grandfather clause
• Jim Crow laws
• segregation
• *Plessy* v. *Ferguson*
• debt peonage

2. SUMMARIZING Use a cluster like this one to identify people, places, legal issues, and events related to discrimination at the turn of the century.

3. IDENTIFYING PROBLEMS Explain how segregation and discrimination affected the lives of African Americans at the turn of the century. Use details from the section to support your explanation.

4. CONTRASTING How did the challenges and opportunities for Mexicans in the United States differ from those for African Americans? Give examples to support your viewpoint.

THINK ABOUT
• the type of work each group did
• the wages paid each group
• the effects of government policies on each group

Life at the Turn of the Century **477**

ANSWERS

TERMS & NAMES
- vaudeville
- ragtime
- Joseph Pulitzer
- William Randolph Hears
- department store
- mail-order catalog
- rural free delivery

Section 4 Overview

OBJECTIVES

1 To give examples of turn-of-the-century popular sports and other leisure activities.

2 To describe turn-of-the-century trends in music and the performing arts.

3 To summarize the growing circulation of newspapers.

4 To describe turn-of-the-century innovations in marketing and advertising.

SKILLBUILDER

- Interpreting Political Cartoons, p. 483

CRITICAL THINKING

- Developing Historical Perspective, p. 479
- Analyzing Motives, p. 480
- Synthesizing, pp. 482, 485
- Summarizing, pp. 483, 485
- Analyzing Causes , p. 483
- Forming Opinions, p. 485

FOCUS & MOTIVATE

▶ **Starting with the Student**
- Ask students about their favorite leisure activities.
- Ask how some or all of these activities affect American life in general.

OBJECTIVE
1 INSTRUCT

American Leisure

▶ **Discussing Key Ideas**
- Playgrounds, playing fields, and amusement parks help provide vital outdoor activity to city dwellers.
- Bicycle riding and tennis become popular crazes that help liberate females from corsets and less tangible confinements.
- Sports like boxing and the evolving game of baseball draw crowds of spectators.

IN-DEPTH RESOURCES: UNIT 4
Guided Reading, pp. 60

ACCESS FOR STUDENTS ACQUIRING ENGLISH
Guided Reading (Spanish), p. 162

---

4 Dawn of Mass Culture

LEARN ABOUT transformations in leisure activities, shopping, and advertising
TO UNDERSTAND the emergence of modern mass culture.

The sprawling amusement park at Coney Island became a model for other urban amusement parks.

ONE AMERICAN'S STORY

At the foot of Brooklyn on a narrow sandbar just nine miles from busy Manhattan rose the most famous urban amusement park in the world: Coney Island. In 1886, its principal developer, George Tilyou, bragged, "If Paris is France, then Coney Island, between June and September, is the world." Indeed, tens of thousands of visitors mobbed Coney Island after work each evening and on Sundays and holidays. When Luna Park, Coney Island's amusement center, opened in May 1903, a reporter described the scene that greeted 45,000 people.

A PERSONAL VOICE
[Inside the park was] an enchanted, storybook land of trellises, columns, domes, minarets, lagoons, and lofty aerial flights. And everywhere was life—a pageant of happy people; and everywhere was color—a wide harmony of orange and white and gold. . . . It was a world removed—shut away from the sordid clatter and turmoil of the streets.

BRUCE BLEN, quoted in *Amusing the Million*

Couples at Coney Island cuddled in the Tunnel of Love, tested their luck at games of chance, and enjoyed exciting new rides. A schoolteacher who walked fully dressed into the ocean explained her unusual behavior by saying, "It has been a hard year at school, and when I saw the big crowd here, everyone with the brakes off, the spirit of the place got the better of me." Leisure opportunities like Coney Island offered Americans a few hours of escape from the hard workweek.

The end of the century saw the rise of a "mass culture" in the United States. New recreational activities, as well as the rise of a consumer culture and nation-wide advertising campaigns, blended regional differences. Middle-class Americans from all over the country shared experiences and identities.

American Leisure

"EIGHT HOURS FOR WORK, EIGHT HOURS FOR REST, AND EIGHT HOURS FOR WHAT WE WILL" declared a popular slogan for the carpenters' union in Worcester, Massachusetts, in 1889. Eight hours for "what we will" often meant leisure activities. As the century drew to a close, many urban Americans escaped the congested cities to enjoy new leisure activities such as amusement parks, bicycling, tennis, and spectator sports.

AMUSEMENT PARKS To meet the needs of city dwellers for recreational activities, Chicago, New York, and other cities began setting aside precious green space for the outdoor enjoyment of their residents. Many cities distributed small playgrounds and playing fields around the city so that most neighborhoods had park space for public recreation.

Some cities constructed amusement parks on their outskirts. Often built by trolley-car companies that sought more passengers, these parks boasted picnic

---

SECTION 4 RESOURCES

 PRINT RESOURCES

IN-DEPTH RESOURCES: UNIT 4
Guided Reading, p. 60
Literature: from *Ragtime* by E. L. Doctorow, p. 68
American Lives: Lillian Gish, p. 72

ACCESS FOR STUDENTS ACQUIRING ENGLISH
Guided Reading (Spanish), p. 162

FORMAL ASSESSMENT
Section Quiz, p. 200

ALTERNATIVE ASSESSMENT BOOK
See forms for supporting and scoring alternative activities.

 TECHNOLOGY RESOURCES

HUMANITIES TRANSPARENCIES
H16. Washington Square by Ferdinand Lundgren

CD-ROM Electronic Library of Primary Sources

VIDEO *American Portfolio: A Videodisc for U.S. History* user's guide, pp. 142, 146–147, 162

INTERNET McDougal Littell Learning On-Line
http://www.mcdougallittell.com

grounds and a variety of rides to amuse visitors. The first roller coaster drew daredevil customers to Coney Island in 1884, and the first Ferris wheel turned in Chicago at the World's Fair in 1893. Loop-the-Loop, another Coney Island roller coaster, took passengers on a terrifying upside-down ride. Writer Albert Bigelow Paine described the sensation.

A PERSONAL VOICE
A fierce upward rush of air, a wild grip at a loosening hat, and an instant later the shock. We were on the loop. We were shooting upward as a billow that breaks against the cliff; we were curling over as the wave curls backward; we were darting down to inevitable annihilation!

ALBERT BIGELOW PAINE, quoted in *Coney Island*

Clearly, many Americans were ready for new and innovative forms of entertainment—and a whole panorama of recreational activities soon became available.

BICYCLING AND OTHER CRAZES At the turn of the century, new pastimes such as bicycling entertained women as well as men. With their huge front wheels and solid rubber tires, the first American bicycles, manufactured by Colonel Albert A. Pope in the 1870s, challenged their brave riders. Because a bump might toss the cyclist over the handlebars, bicycling began as a males-only sport. The 1884 introduction of the "safety bicycle" with its smaller wheels and air-filled tires made the activity safer, and the Victor safety bicycle with a dropped frame and no crossbar appealed to women.

Abandoning their tight corsets, women bicyclists donned shirtwaists (tailored blouses) and "split" skirts in order to cycle more comfortably. This attire soon became popular for daily wear. The bicycle also freed women from the scrutiny of the ever-present chaperone. Suffragist Susan B. Anthony declared that, "I think [bicycling] has done more to emancipate women than anything else in the world. It gives women a freedom and self-reliance." Fifty thousand men and women had taken to cycles by 1888. Two years later 312 American firms turned out 10 million bikes.

Americans took up the sport of tennis as enthusiastically as they had taken up cycling. The modern version of this sport originated in England in 1873. A year later, the United States saw its first tennis match. Socialite Florence Harriman recalled how in the 1880s her father returned from England with one of New York's first tennis sets. At first, neighbors thought the elder Harriman had installed the nets to catch birds. Before tennis caught on with his neighbors, Harriman taught the game to his footman so the servant could participate as a fourth for doubles.

Hungry or thirsty after tennis or cycling? Turn-of-the-century enthusiasts turned to new snacks with recognizable brand names. They could munch on a

NOW & THEN

SKATES TO BLADES
The fastest growing sport in the country, in-line skating, captured 22 million enthusiasts by the end of 1994. The national craze for in-line skating echoes an earlier enthusiasm for roller skating, which New Yorker James Plimpton invented in 1863. By the 1880s, America boasted 3,000 hard maple rinks for roller skates.

Roller skates, or "quad" skates, glide on two wheels on each side of the skate. The modern in-line skates, invented by Minnesotan Scott Olson in 1979, feature wheels running in a straight line from front to back.

In-line skating attracts equal numbers of males and females from every economic bracket, ethnic group, geographic region, and age group, though the majority of skaters are under age 17. In New York's Central Park, a 6.2-mile paved loop attracts large crowds of skaters each day.

Bicycling could be done alone or in groups—though it was rare to find the whole group on one bicycle!

MORE ABOUT . . .
Turn-of-the-Century Health Foods

Several well-known foods were originally sold for dubious health purposes. John Harvey Kellogg spent years trying to create the cereal that eventually became corn flakes. In addition, Quaker Oats and Fleischmann's Yeast both claimed to curb nervousness and constipation.

MORE ABOUT . . .
Boxing

Like horse racing, boxing was enormously popular among 18th-century English gentlemen. Then fought without gloves, it was extremely brutal until boxer Jack Broughton introduced a set of rules in 1743. In the 1860s the Marquis of Queensberry sponsored new rules that, among other things, required boxers to wear gloves. Though American boxing star John L. Sullivan was a bare-knuckle champion, he began fighting under the Marquis of Queensberry rules when he found that many U.S. towns and cities would legalize boxing only if gloves were worn.

ELECTRONIC LIBRARY OF PRIMARY SOURCES
"The Baseball Season" in *Harper's Weekly*

Hershey chocolate bar, developed in 1894, and wash down the chocolate with a Coca-Cola® or a Pepsi-Cola®. An Atlanta pharmacist named John S. Pemberton formulated Coca-Cola as a cure for headache in 1886. He and his partner settled on the name to advertise that the ingredients included extracts from Peruvian coca leaves as well as African cola nuts. Ten years later, Calab D. Bradham of New Bern, North Carolina, introduced Coca-Cola's main competitor, Pepsi-Cola.

SPECTATOR SPORTS American men and women not only participated in sports such as tennis and cycling, but they also became avid fans of spectator sports. Though boxing and baseball had begun as popular informal activities, by the turn of the century they became profitable businesses. Fans who couldn't attend an important match jammed barber shops or hotel lobbies to listen to telegraphed transmissions of the contest's highlights.

When John L. Sullivan, the first great heavyweight boxer, captured his title in 1882, he fought most of his bouts with bare knuckles. The Great John L. traveled the country offering up to $10,000 to anyone who could survive four rounds in the ring with him. Finally, in 1892, James J. "Gentleman Jim" Corbett knocked him out in the 21st round. For his victory Corbett relied on fast footwork and diligent practice and followed the new Marquis of Queensberry rules for the sport.

In the first World Series, held in 1903, *above*, the Boston Pilgrims defeated the Pittsburgh Pirates on the Huntington Avenue baseball grounds in Boston. Johnny Evers *right*, was part of a famous Chicago Cubs infield.

BASEBALL New rules also transformed baseball into a professional sport. In 1845, a group of wealthy New Yorkers set down regulations that combined aspects of two children's games that English immigrants had brought to the United States. Fifty baseball clubs sprang up by 1850, and New York alone boasted 12 clubs in the mid-1860s.

In 1869, a professional team named the Cincinnati Red Stockings stormed the country. Other clubs soon took to the road, which led to the formation of the National League in 1876 and the American League in 1901. In the first World Series, held in 1903, the Boston Pilgrims beat the Pittsburgh Pirates. African-American baseball players, who were excluded from both leagues because of racial discrimination, formed their own clubs and two leagues—the Negro National League and the Negro American League.

Summer afternoon baseball games drew a wide variety of people to the bleachers and grandstands. More than 51,000 fans attended an 1887 championship series between St. Louis and Detroit. Novelist Mark Twain raved that baseball was "the very symbol . . . and visible expression of the drive and push and rush and struggle of the raging, tearing, booming nineteenth century." An 1886 article in *Harper's Weekly* noted that the new national pastime had "seized upon the American people, irrespective of age, sex, or other condition." By the 1890s, baseball resembled today's sport, with a published game schedule, official rules, and a standard-sized diamond.

B. Answer Sports offered one way to fill increased leisure time. Americans could participate directly in sports like bicycling or indirectly in spectator sports like baseball.

THINK THROUGH HISTORY
B. Analyzing Motives Why do you think sports were so popular with Americans at the end of the century?

480 CHAPTER 16

Going to the Show

Like sports, other forms of entertainment attracted audiences of working people with leisure time to fill. Two other advances fostered the new mass entertainment: improved railroad transportation and new media technology such as motion pictures. Enterprising companies now formed traveling groups of entertainers who brought live performances to cities and small towns around the country.

LIVE PERFORMANCES The companies that booked talent typically featured stars, popular performers who could attract large audiences and compensate for the less-talented supporting actors. Three popular female stars guaranteed a full house wherever they performed—the "divine" Sarah Bernhardt, a French actress; the actress Lillie Langtry of Great Britain; and the singer Jenny Lind, "the Swedish Nightingale."

Audiences could choose serious drama, exciting melodrama, or vaudeville shows. To many audiences, serious drama meant Shakespeare's tragedies, with the talented Edwin Booth playing the lead.

Melodramas, such as *Under the Gaslight*, featured improbable plots enacted by hapless heroes and heroines who inevitably evaded disaster at the last minute.

Vaudeville performances included song, dance, slapstick comedy, and sometimes even a chorus line of female performers. Promoters sought large audiences with varied backgrounds. Writing in *Scribner's Magazine* in October 1899, actor Edwin Milton Royle hailed vaudeville theater as "an American invention."

A PERSONAL VOICE
[Vaudeville] appeals to the businessman, tired and worn, who drops in for half an hour on his way home; to the person who has an hour or two before a train goes, or before a business appointment; to the woman who is wearied of shopping; to the children who love animals and acrobats; to the man with his sweetheart or sister, to the individual who wants to be diverted but doesn't want to think or feel; to the American of all grades and kinds who wants a great deal for his money.

EDWIN MILTON ROYLE, quoted in *Victorian America*

The biggest spectacle of all proved to be the annual visit of the circus, which its founders P. T. Barnum and Anthony Bailey touted as "The Greatest Show on Earth." Established in 1881, the Barnum & Bailey Circus arrived by railroad train and gathered trapeze artists, acrobats, lion tamers, clowns, elephants, and stallions under a big tent. There, the daring performers delighted audiences of adults and children alike.

Until the 1890s, African-American performers filled roles mainly in minstrel shows that featured exaggerated imitations of African-American music and dance and reinforced racist stereotypes of blacks. By the turn of the century, minstrel shows were largely replaced by more sophisticated musicals, and many black performers entered vaudeville shows.

RAGTIME At the same time, an exciting new form of music called **ragtime** began to draw hoards of listeners. A blending of African-American spirituals and European musical forms, ragtime had originated in the 1880s in the saloons of the South. The strains of ragtime music had impressed African-American

"It [the circus] was the embodiment of all that was skillful and beautiful in human action."

HAMLIN GARLAND

P. T. Barnum earned his reputation as a hustler. His traveling circus sideshows often claimed to feature two-headed animals or humans who were well over 100 years old.

pianist and composer Scott Joplin on his tours through black communities from New Orleans to Chicago. Joplin's first ragtime composition, "Maple Leaf Rag," made him famous in the first decade of the 20th century as a rage for ragtime seized the country. Ragtime became an important element in the development of American jazz.

THE SILVER SCREEN Early in the 20th century, live entertainment began to get competition from motion pictures. The first films, one-reel 10-minute sequences, consisted mostly of vaudeville skits or faked newsreels. Early audi-ences found plenty to marvel at in random scenes of galloping horses and run-away trains. In 1903, *The Great Train Robbery* increased the popularity of both Westerns and a plot among silver screen audiences.

Like the melodramas of the stage, popular serials featured a hero or heroine who narrowly averted one disaster after another. One popular serial, *The Perils of Pauline*, starred Pearl White in the title role. Pauline, a headstrong heiress seek-ing adventure, fought off Indians, fell off cliffs, and was tied to a railroad track in front of an oncoming train. To the relief of her amazed audience, though, her courageous boyfriend always saved her just in the nick of time.

D. W. Griffith's epic three-hour 1914 film, *The Birth of a Nation*, made movie history by pioneering bold new techniques such as close-ups, fade-outs, and blockbuster scenes. The story the film told, however, inflamed racial prej-udice by glorifying the Ku Klux Klan and portraying African Americans as a threat to white morality. The National Association for the Advancement of Colored People (NAACP), founded in 1909, organized protests against the film's racist portrayal of Reconstruction.

By 1914, the typical film consisted of a two-hour silent feature with a famous star such as Mary Pickford, Lillian Gish, or Charlie Chaplin. These beloved stars soon inspired more adoration than the stars of the theater had ever won. Movies' low admission price of just a nickel ensured their continuing popularity among all classes of people. Unlike live performances, movies could be shown all over the country at the same time and spread the current ideas and trends that contributed to the formation of a mass culture.

ELECTRONIC LIBRARY OF PRIMARY SOURCES
from *The Movies, Mr. Griffith, and Me*
by Lillian Gish

NOW & THEN

Going to the Movies

Perhaps the most popular form of entertainment for Americans in the 1990s continues to be the motion picture. While seven out of ten households own videocassette recorders (VCRs), modern theaters lure audiences by showing big-screen blockbuster films—highly advertised movies that often include popular stars and sophisticated special effects.

482 CHAPTER 16

1903
The first modern film—an eight-minute silent feature called *The Great Train Robbery*—debuts in five-cent theaters called nickelodeons. Entrepreneurs quickly see that by repeating films as often as 16 times a day, they can generate greater profits than with costly vaudeville and stage productions. By 1907, an estimated 3,000 nickelodeons dot the country.

1927
Films become more popular when sound is added to movies in 1927 and color soon afterward. Huge audiences fill larger and grander theaters with names like "Majestic," "Ritz," and "Palace." Movie palaces, like the one shown above, boast beautiful lobbies, promenades with exquisite artwork, and graceful staircases. Weekly movie attendance doubles from 40 million in 1922 to 80 million in 1930.

Mass Circulation Newspapers

Americans increasingly found coverage of their favorite new sports or shows in newspapers that looked for ways to captivate the masses of readers. Instead of headlines like "POLITICS IN ALBANY," newspapers began using sensational headlines. For example, to introduce its story about the horrors of the Johnstown, Pennsylvania, flood, in which more than 2,000 people lost their lives, one newspaper used the headline "THE VALLEY OF DEATH."

Newspapers also devised promotional stunts. In 1889, for example, the New York *World* sent reporter Nellie Bly around the world in imitation of a fictional character in Jules Verne's novel *Around the World in Eighty Days*. After reporting from exotic locales, Bly returned to her starting place in just over 72 days.

Joseph Pulitzer, a Hungarian immigrant who had bought the *World* in 1883, pioneered popular innovations, such as a large Sunday edition, comics, sports coverage, and women's news. Pulitzer's paper emphasized "sin, sex, and sensation" in an attempt to outdo his main competitor, **William Randolph Hearst,** who had purchased the New York *Morning Journal* in 1895. The wealthy Hearst, who already owned the San Francisco *Examiner*, sought to outdo Pulitzer by filling the *Journal* with exaggerated tales of personal scandals, cruelty, hypnotism, and even the imaginary conquest of Mars.

The escalation of their circulation war drove both papers to even more sensational news coverage. By 1898, the circulation of each paper had reached more than one million copies a day.

SKILLBUILDER
INTERPRETING POLITICAL CARTOONS
According to the cartoonist, where are Pulitzer and Hearst leading American journalism?

Skillbuilder Answer Possible Answer: Pulitzer and Hearst are leading journalism to its probable destruction.

D. Answer By printing lurid headlines, devising promotional stunts, making up news, and instituting Sunday editions, comics and coverage of sports and women's news.

THINK THROUGH HISTORY
D. *Summarizing How did the* World *and the* Journal *lure readers?*

New Ways to Sell Goods

Along with enjoying new leisure activities, Americans also changed the way they shopped. The combination of concentrated urban markets and vast quantities of reasonably priced manufactured goods encouraged city merchants to look for new sales methods. Americans at the turn of the century witnessed the opening of the shopping center, the development of department and chain stores, and the birth of modern advertising.

1950s
Movie attendance plummets from 60 million per week in 1950 to 40 million per week by 1960. The enormous popularity of television results in fewer people going to the movies but the new drive-in movie, which appeals to young suburban families and to teenagers with new driver's licenses, brings some of them back. The drive-in movie's popularity peaks in 1958, when the United States claims 4,000 of the outdoor theaters.

1990s
The popularity of videocassette recorders and of network and cable TV continues to threaten the movie industry. Nevertheless, developers anchor shopping malls with huge multiplex theaters showing many films at the same time. Between 1980 and 1991, the number of screens in the United States increases by 62 percent, but movie attendance remains flat, largely because VCRs and satellite dishes keep movies at Americans' fingertips.

INTERACT WITH HISTORY

1. **ANALYZING CAUSES**
Explain the factors that affected movie theater attendance since the emergence of motion pictures.

 SEE SKILLBUILDER HANDBOOK, PAGE 1040.

2. **COMPARING MEDIA**
Contrast the experiences of watching a movie on television with going to a movie in a theater. Consider factors such as cost, comfort, convenience, privacy, and enjoyment in analyzing the two experiences.

 For more about movies, click on *Social Studies* at http://www.mcdougallittell.com

Life at the Turn of the Century **483**

MORE ABOUT . . .
Marshall Field's

Marshall Field's became the
world's biggest department
store, serving as many as
250,000 customers a day by
1900. Helping Field in his
efforts was Harry Selfridge,
a Wisconsin native who
began working at Field's
as a stock boy in 1879.
Selfridge's innovations
included gift certificates,
annual sales, the bargain
basement, and the practice
of reminding customers
how many days were left for
Christmas shopping.

MORE ABOUT . . .
F. W. Woolworth

Frank Winfield Woolworth
opened his first "five-and-
ten" (or "five-and-dime")
variety stores in Utica,
New York, and Lancaster,
Pennsylvania, in 1879. The
Utica store failed, but the
Lancaster store was so successful that he opened 21
like it in the next decade. In
1909, he successfully
expanded into Great Britain
and Ireland.

URBAN SHOPPING As cities grew, their populations made promising targets for enterprising manufacturers and merchants. The nation's first shopping center opened in Cleveland, Ohio, in 1890. A glass-topped arcade contained four levels of jewelry, leather goods, and stationery shops. The arcade also provided band music on Sundays so that middle-class Cleveland residents could spend their Sunday afternoons strolling through the arcade and gazing at the inviting window displays.

The growth of cities led to specialization, with separate districts within the city housing financial services, hotels and entertainment, light manufacture, and trade. Financial districts in the largest cities contained banks, insurance companies, and the headquarters of large corporations. A nearby hotel and entertainment area provided services to the city's visitors. An adjoining district of light manufacturing might include clothing and printing factories. Nearby wholesale trade districts consisted of warehouses and wholesalers' offices.

Retail shopping districts formed in the middle of the city, where public transportation could easily bring shoppers from outlying areas. To anchor these retail shopping districts, ambitious merchants established something completely different, the modern department store.

THE DEPARTMENT STORE Marshall Field of Chicago pioneered the concept of the **department store.** At the beginning of his career, Field worked as a sales clerk in a dry goods store and discovered that paying close attention to each woman customer could increase sales considerably. In 1865, Marshall Field decided to open his own store based on the motto, "Give the lady what she wants." Field's store allowed women to take merchandise home on approval and return it if it didn't satisfy them. Marshall Field himself advised the head of his upholstery department never to forget that "we are the servants of the public."

Advertising directed at women appeared in such specialized publications as the *Chicago Magazine of Fashion*. A lavish, colorful two-page spread in the magazine's premiere issue featured Field's "Fashion Specials." Field's pioneered the bargain basement, which sold bargain goods that were "less expensive but reliable," and opened a restaurant where women shoppers might lunch at their leisure.

THE CHAIN STORE While department stores like Marshall Field's prided themselves on offering a variety of personal services, new chain stores—groups of stores under the same ownership—advertised the bargains they could offer by buying in quantity and limiting personal service. In the 1870s, F. W. Woolworth found that if he offered an item at a very low price, "the consumer would purchase it on the spur of the moment" because "it was only a nickel." Woolworth didn't raise the nickel or dime price of items at his "five-and-dime store" until 1932. By 1911, the chain boasted 596 stores and sold more than a million dollars in merchandise a week.

The popularity of the five-and-ten-cent store chain matched that of the chain grocery stores. The chains didn't carry the variety of items today's shoppers expect, but they employed modern sales methods, such as offering brand names, standardized packaging, and high-volume, low-cost sales.

TURN–OF–THE–CENTURY ADVERTISING An explosion in advertising also heralded modern consumerism. Expenditures for advertising were under $10 million a year in 1865 but increased tenfold to $95 million by 1900, partly because of improvements in printing pictures.

Though few American magazines carried advertising before the 1870s, by 1900 a host of magazines contained ads for new products.

Patent medicines grabbed the largest number of advertising lines. Next came soaps, followed by baking powders, cereals such as Cream of Wheat and Quaker Oats, the Eastman Kodak Company, and clothing makers. In addition to newspapers and magazines, advertisers used other ingenious methods to push products. Passengers riding the train between New York and Philadelphia in the 1870s might look up to see signs for Dr. Drake's Plantation Bitters on barns, houses, billboards, and even rocks.

MAIL–ORDER CATALOGS **Mail-order catalogs** from Montgomery Ward and Sears and Roebuck brought department store merchandise to farmers and residents of small towns. Taking advantage of printing improvements, Ward's catalog, launched in 1872, provided instructions in ten languages to help customers order products. Richard Sears, who started his company in 1886, brought out what he called a consumer's guide twice a year. Early catalogs came with a letter from Sears reassuring customers that the company received "hundreds of orders every day from young and old who never [before] sent away for goods." Customers needn't be afraid of making a mistake in their order. "Tell us what you want, in your own way," cajoled Sears, "written in any language, no matter whether good or poor writing, and your goods will be sent promptly to you." By 1910, about 10 million Americans shopped by mail each year.

RURAL FREE DELIVERY The United States Post Office boosted mail-order businesses in 1896 by starting a **rural free delivery** (RFD) system that brought packages directly to every home. Now the catalogs could advise consumers to "give the letter and money to the mail carrier and he will get the money order at the post office and mail it in the letter for you." In 1913, the initiation of parcel post made it possible to send a 50-pound package from Chicago to any location in the country.

At the turn of the century, Americans experienced tremendous changes—most of which were positive—in their lives. However, the nation's growing industrial sector created problems that some believed the federal government should address. The spirit of progressive reform brought about lasting changes in the role of government in Americans' lives.

THINK THROUGH HISTORY
E. Synthesizing
How did American methods of selling goods change at the turn of the century?

E. Answer New department stores allowed women to take merchandise home on approval and offered bargain goods; shoppers used rural free delivery to shop by mail.

NOW & THEN

CATALOGS TODAY

Though catalogs were quite a novelty when Sears and Montgomery Ward arrived on the scene, in 1996 more than 13 billion catalogs filled American mail boxes. That figure averages out to nearly two per household each week, and mail-order buying continues to increase. Catalog sales grew over 40 percent between 1991 and 1997, when they were expected to reach $71 billion.

What do today's consumers order? Clothing ranks first and home furnishings second.

Many current retailers use mail-order catalogs for advertising because they know that catalog customers will shop in their stores as well. In fact, 20 percent of women subsequently visit the store that sent them the catalog, thereby boosting its walk-in business.

NOW & THEN
Catalogs Today
Critical Thinking: Analyzing Causes Have students consider why catalog shopping has become so popular. *Possible Responses: More women are juggling work and family and have little time to shop in stores; more people living in rural areas because they can work or run a business from home are too far from the cities and suburbs where most stores are; crime has dissuaded some shoppers from visiting department stores and malls; catalog retailers have grown more sophisticated in offering the right goods to the right customers.*

ASSESS & RETEACH

Section 4 Assessment
Have students work in small groups to discuss the questions and review one another's responses.

Self-Assessment
Have students create a two-column chart on which they compare their own responses to the section assessment (column 1) with the portions of the text that best answer each question (column 2).

Section Quiz

FORMAL ASSESSMENT
Section Quiz, p. 200

Reteach
Use the Guided Reading Worksheet for Section 4 to help review the main ideas of this section.

IN-DEPTH RESOURCES: UNIT 4
Guided Reading, p. 60

Section 4 Assessment

1. TERMS & NAMES

Identify:
- vaudeville
- ragtime
- Joseph Pulitzer
- William Randolph Hearst
- department store
- mail-order catalog
- rural free delivery

2. SUMMARIZING Recreate the spider diagram below on your paper. Label the diagonals "Leisure" and "Shopping," and add examples to each.

Modern mass culture emerges.

3. SYNTHESIZING Write an advertisement for one of the leisure activities described in this section.

THINK ABOUT
- the audience you are trying to appeal to
- the image you want to create
- the place or publication in which your advertisement will appear

4. FORMING OPINIONS Do you think the publication of sensational stories in newspapers is justified? Why or why not?

THINK ABOUT
- the reasons Hearst and Pulitzer included those stories
- the effect that adding sensational stories had on the newspapers' circulation
- the purpose that you believe newspapers should serve

Life at the Turn of the Century **485**

ANSWERS

1. TERMS & NAMES

vaudeville, p. 481

ragtime, p. 481

Joseph Pulitzer, p. 483

William Randolph Hearst, p. 483

department store, p. 484

mail-order catalog, p. 485

rural free delivery, p. 485

2. SUMMARIZING

Students may include the following entries:

Leisure: Amusement parks; bicycling; tennis; boxing; baseball; theater: vaudeville; ragtime music; movies.

Shopping: Shopping centers; department stores; chain stores; advertising; mail-order catalogs.

3. SYNTHESIZING

Advertisements should use creativity to appeal to the growing number of middle-class consumers.

4. FORMING OPINIONS

Students may indicate that including sensational stories is justified, because the public can always choose not to purchase a newspaper with such stories. Some might argue that such stories are dishonest and have no place on the pages of a newspaper.

CLOSE

From movies to shopping to advertising, the turn of the century saw the birth of the American mass culture that has dominated 20th-century life.

OBJECTIVES

1. To explain how the shift to an urban, industrial economy spurred Americans to seek outdoor leisure activities.

2. To identify sites and activities that turn-of-the-century Americans enjoyed in their leisure time.

FOCUS & MOTIVATE

▶ **Starting with the Student**
Have students imagine that they have a dull job that keeps them indoors during the workweek.

• What kinds of places would they want to spend their leisure time?
• What kinds of leisure activities would they want to do?

MORE ABOUT . . .
The Bicycle Craze

Though bicycles developed gradually, it was not until the closing decades of the 19th century that they became popular. At the Centennial Exhibition in Philadelphia in 1876, a British firm displayed an "ordinary English bicycle" that caught the attention of manufacturer Albert A. Pope, who soon converted his Massachusetts air-pistol factory into a bicycle works. Within a decade, America had over 50,000 cyclists, with just about every big city sporting a bicycle club. By the turn-of-the-century bicycle manufacturing had grown into a $60 million business in America alone.

New Ways to Play

As Americans moved from rural areas to cities, they developed new urban lifestyles. Unlike agricultural work schedules that varied by the season (heavy during harvest and planting, light during winter), urban work schedules remained essentially the same throughout the year. As more and more people worked weekdays indoors, they desired to spend their weekend and evening leisure time outdoors.

In most cities in the mid-19th century, children had only the streets to play in. But as streets became more crowded with traffic and commerce, they became dangerous places for children. Jacob Riis proposed a series of parks for New York so that children and families could have a pleasant and safe place to play or relax. For most Americans—who could not afford expensive toys and fancy vacations—new urban parks, like New York's Central Park, provided safe spaces and affordable facilities for outdoor leisure.

CENTRAL PARK

Built between 1857 and 1876, Central Park covers 840 acres in the middle of Manhattan island in New York City. In 1857, the New York state legislature paid $5 million for the land, which was occupied by farms, livestock, and some open sewers.

The park's terrain was shaped by workers following a design by Frederick Law Olmsted and Calvert Vaux that included flat, grassy areas, rolling hills, woods, and ravines.

PATHWAYS Many parks now include paths for joggers or bicyclists. After the 1880s, when modern bicycles were developed, bicycling through the park became a popular activity for both men and women.

Many people enjoyed taking long walks through the park. Others took carriage rides or sat on benches and watched the passersby.

The Picnic Grounds
(1906–1907) John Sloan

486 CHAPTER 16

RECOMMENDED RESOURCES

Books

Hall, Lee. *Olmsted's America.* Boston: Little, 1995. The landscape designer's vision for urban America.

Kinkead, Eugene. *Central Park, 1857–1995.* New York: Norton, 1990. The birth, decline, and renewal of New York City's best-known park.

Nasaw, David. *Going Out.* New York: Basic, 1993. A history of American leisure and public amusements.

Rogers, Elizabeth Barlow. *Frederick Law Olmsted's New York.* New York: Praeger, 1972. A book published with the input of the Whitney Museum of American Art in New York City.

Videos

The Innocent Years. From America: A Look Back series. Social Studies, School Services, 800-421-4246.

New Beginnings (1895–1904). AIMS Media. Educational Software Institute, 800-955-5570. America at the turn of the century.

Olmsted and Central Park. Dir. Philip Gittelman. NVC Arts, 1983. Part of the home video collection of New York's Metropolitan Museum of Art.

Turn-of-the-Century America. Guidance Associates. An exploration of American society and everyday life.

2 **BOATING** Although most people did not have the money to own a boat, Central Park had a number of lakes and lagoons where people could rent one and go for a row.

Along the banks, one could see women holding parasols to protect themselves from the summer sun. Picnickers with wicker baskets search for a grassy place to spread a blanket.

ICE–SKATING Even in the middle of winter, people would find enjoyable outdoor activities. Frozen ponds and lakes provided perfect settings for people to ice-skate.

In the 1850s, Jackson Haines had designed and produced a skate with a steel blade to replace the wooden skates with iron blades—turning skating into a speedier, more graceful form of exercise popular with all social classes.

DATA FILE

Changes in the U.S. Work Week

YEAR	HOURS PER WEEK
1860	66
1890	60
1920	47

A LOOK AT THE FACTS:

A shorter work week meant many Americans had more time for leisure activities—and certainly took advantage of it.

- In 1890, an average of 60,000 fans attended professional baseball games daily.

- In 1893, a crowd of 50,000 attended the Princeton-Yale football game.

- *A Trip to Chinatown,* one of the popular new musical comedies, ran for an amazing 650 performances.

- In 1900, 3 million phonograph records of Broadway-produced musical comedies were sold.

- The love of the popular musicals contributed to the sale of $42 million of musical instruments in 1900.

- By 1900, almost 500 men's social clubs existed. Nine hundred college fraternity and sorority chapters recorded over 150,000 members.

Public Parks

Between 1902 and 1919, the number of public parks in the United States grew dramatically:

Source: Robert Lewis,"Well-Directed Play,"
Impressions of a Gilded Age, Marc Chenetier and Rob Kroes, eds., University of Amsterdam, 1983

INTERACT WITH HISTORY

1. **SYNTHESIZING** What summary statements about the culture and attitudes of this time period can you make? Is this a period of history that you would have liked to have witnessed? Why or why not?

   SEE SKILLBUILDER HANDBOOK, PAGE 1051.

2. **DESIGNING A MURAL** Work with a partner to design a mural for your classroom that expresses the nature of American life at the turn of the century. Use details above and from the chapter to help you capture the many changes that were taking place.

Life at the Turn of the Century **487**

REVIEWING THE CHAPTER

TERMS & NAMES
1. Louis Sullivan, p. 463
2. Orville and Wilbur Wright, p. 465
3. W. E. B. Du Bois, p. 470
4. Booker T. Washington, p. 471
5. Mark Twain, p. 472
6. Ida B. Wells, p. 473
7. Jim Crow laws, p. 474
8. *Plessy* v. *Ferguson*, p. 475
9. vaudeville, p. 481
10. rural free delivery, p. 485

MAIN IDEAS
11. Skyscrapers allowed for cities to grow upward, and electric trains allowed cities to expand outward.

12. Paper and printing became less expensive, photography became widespread, and airplanes came into use to deliver mail.

13. The number of schools and students in them increased, and new subjects were added.

14. They did not like how schools Americanized their children, particularly in matters of religion.

15. Both portrayed a more realistic, less genteel, world than did works by earlier painters and writers.

16. The Supreme Court upheld the constitutionality of segregation and state voting restrictions, and Congress passed the Chinese Exclusion Act.

17. They helped build the railroads and provided labor for the growing agricultural industry.

18. The growing number of people in cities escaped from the hard workweek with many of the same leisure activities. They also used more mass produced, widely advertised, brand-name goods.

19. *Possible Responses:* Visiting amusement parks, riding bicycles, watching sports, going to the circus or show, reading magazines and novels.

20. Shopping centers, department stores, chain stores, modern advertising, and mail-order catalogs developed in this period.

Chapter 16 Assessment

REVIEWING THE CHAPTER

TERMS & NAMES For each term below, write a sentence explaining its connection to American life at the turn of the 19th century. For each person below, explain his or her significance during this period.

1. Louis Sullivan
2. Orville and Wilbur Wright
3. W. E. B. Du Bois
4. Booker T. Washington
5. Mark Twain
6. Ida B. Wells
7. Jim Crow laws
8. *Plessy* v. *Ferguson*
9. vaudeville
10. rural free delivery

MAIN IDEAS

SECTION 1 (pages 462–466)

Science and Urban Life

11. How did new technology promote urban growth around the turn of the century?
12. In what ways did methods of communication improve in the late 19th and early 20th centuries?

SECTION 2 (pages 467–472)

Education and Culture

13. How did public schools change during the late 19th century?
14. Why did some immigrants oppose sending their children to public schools around the turn of the century?
15. How were the paintings of Thomas Eakins and the literature of Mark Twain similar?

SECTION 3 (pages 473–477)

Segregation and Discrimination

16. In what ways was racial discrimination supported by federal government actions and policies?
17. How did Mexicans help make the Southwest prosperous in the late 19th century?

SECTION 4 (pages 478–485)

Dawn of Mass Culture

18. Why did a mass culture develop in the United States in the late 19th century?
19. What leisure activities flourished at the turn of the century?
20. What innovations in retail methods changed how Americans shopped during this time period?

THINKING CRITICALLY

1. **CULTURAL CHANGE** Create a table similar to the one shown and list at least six major trends at the turn of the century and their major impact.

Trend	Impact
1.	
2.	
3.	
4.	
5.	
6.	

2. **THE AMERICAN PROMISE** Reread the quote by James Weldon Johnson on page 460. Based on your reading about the turn of the century, what would you identify as the "best" and "worst" aspects of that time period? Explain, using details from the chapter.

3. **MAKING CONNECTIONS** How did changes around the turn of the century link individuals and regions in the United States more closely together?

4. **EVALUATING DAILY LIFE** Considering the changes occurring around the turn of the century, do you think daily life for a typical American was getting better or worse?

5. **ANALYZING PRIMARY SOURCES** The historian Henry Steele Commager claimed that the decade of the 1890s was "the watershed of American history."

> On the one side lies an America predominantly agricultural; . . . an America still in the making, physically and socially; an America on the whole self-confident, self-contained, self-reliant, and conscious of its unique character and of a unique destiny. On the other side lies the modern America, predominantly urban and industrial; inextricably involved in world economy and politics; . . . experiencing profound changes in population, social institutions, economy, and technology; and trying to accommodate its traditional institutions and habits of thought to conditions new and in part alien.
>
> **HENRY STEELE COMMAGER,** quoted in *The American Mind*

Explain whether you agree with Commager that the 1890s marked a significant turning point in American history.

THINKING CRITICALLY

1. CULTURAL CHANGE
Possible student entries include the following trends and impacts:

Skyscrapers: Cities grew upward.

Improved printing: Cost of newspapers and magazines decreased.

Expansion of public education: Literacy increased.

Research universities: A modern curriculum developed.

Voting restrictions: Voting by African Americans declined.

Jim Crow laws: Segregation expanded in the South.

Increased leisure time: Spectator sports and other forms of entertainment became popular.

New ways to sell goods: Consumers had greater choices.

2. THE AMERICAN PROMISE
Possible Responses: Students may say that the best aspects include new technologies to deal with urban problems, expanded educational opportunities, and new leisure activities. The worst aspects of the era would include legalized segregation and discrimination, lynching, and Jim Crow laws.

ALTERNATIVE ASSESSMENT

1. CREATING AN ADVERTISEMENT

How did innovations in manufacturing and retailing affect people's lives between 1900 and 1915?

- Create a magazine or newspaper advertisement for one product of the era between 1900 and 1915.

CD-ROM Use the CD-Rom *Our Times* and other reference materials to research new inventions and products of this era. You might choose to investigate a new invention or trend in transportation, communication, or leisure activities.

- Think about the best way to entice your audience to buy your product.

- Find pictures or create your own images. Write the advertising copy, including the price and relevant information about the product. Create and polish your advertisement.

- Collect all the advertisements into one booklet to share with the class.

2. BRINGING HISTORY TO LIFE

Select a book, play, movie, or song that was popular at the turn of the century. For possible selections, look in literature anthologies, songbooks, and histories of popular culture. Then choose one of these avenues for sharing your selection with your classmates:

- Prepare an oral presentation about the selection you've chosen, in which you discuss its history and significance to the time period.

- Create a poster or other visual displaying the selection and providing annotations that highlight points of interest.

- **Cooperative Learning** With a partner, create a short theatrical presentation based upon the pieces you each selected. Discuss differences between the attitudes portrayed in the selections and those of people today.

3. PORTFOLIO PROJECT

Use the Living History activity to expand your portfolio.

LIVING HISTORY

PRESENTING YOUR CATALOG

After you have written your catalog entries, ask a friend to look through it and answer the following questions:

- Does the catalog accurately reflect the culture of the era?
- What other catalog entries should be added?

When you have made changes based on your friend's suggestions, add illustrations and display the catalog in your classroom. Then add your catalog to your American history portfolio.

Bridge to Chapter 17

Review Chapter 16

TECHNOLOGICAL ADVANCEMENTS Innovations in science and technology around the turn of the last century provided the foundation for modern American life. Skyscrapers, electric streetcars, and urban planning shaped rapidly growing American cities. The web-perfecting press, the Linotype machine, and the mail plane brought the country closer together through improved communication.

EXPANDING EDUCATION Public schools and the growing number of colleges provided the educated workforce that businesses needed. Immigrant populations entered schools and faced gradual "Americanization." As the population of educated people grew, so did the demand for literature, libraries, and art museums.

DISCRIMINATION IN AMERICA Few African Americans benefited from the expanding educational system. In education, voting rights, and other areas of life, discrimination and segregation became more firmly entrenched. In *Plessy* v. *Ferguson*, the Supreme Court supported Jim Crow laws that imposed rigid segregation throughout the South. Worse, the lynching of African Americans became commonplace. Mexicans in the Southwest and Chinese immigrants in the West also had to deal with prejudice.

MASS CULTURE EMERGES The growing urban population turned to new forms of recreation. Amusement parks, bicycle riding, tennis, boxing, baseball, vaudeville, ragtime music, and movies each attracted large followings. With the development of mass culture came high-circulation newspapers and new methods of selling goods. Shopping centers, department stores, chain stores, and modern advertising provided consumers with greater selection and lower prices than ever before.

Preview Chapter 17

Rapid changes in American life brought new problems—increased poverty, changing moral standards, and corruption in government. Reformers who initiated the progressive movement demanded more attention to social justice, moral values, and clean government. You will learn about these significant developments in the next chapter.

Life at the Turn of the Century **489**

---

1. CREATING AN ADVERTISEMENT

Standards for Evaluation

An effective advertisement should meet the following criteria:

- Clearly identifies the product in a memorable way.
- Gives the audience reasons to use the product, including information about its price and how it works.
- Uses attractive design features to gain and hold viewers' attention.

2. BRINGING HISTORY TO LIFE

Standards for Evaluation

An oral presentation should meet the following criteria:

- Clearly places the book, play, movie, or song in its proper historical context.
- Uses reviews from the era to support the significance of the piece to the time period.

A visual presentation should meet the following criteria:

- Uses clear and concise annotations.
- Accurately reflects the main point of the piece.
- Uses visual images that reflect the era that the piece came from.

A theatrical presentation should meet the following criteria:

- Incorporates both items chosen by the students.
- Focuses on one significant issue that emerged during the era.
- Gives historically accurate portrayals of turn-of-the-century people and issues.

3. PORTFOLIO PROJECT

LIVING HISTORY

Standards for Evaluation

An effective catalog should meet the following criteria:

- Is organized around categories or themes of mass culture.
- Provides a balanced representation of people and events from the era.
- Uses visuals that are both appropriate and appealing.
- Includes written captions that explain the visuals.

IN-DEPTH RESOURCES: UNIT 4
See the form for scoring this activity on page 74.

THINKING CRITICALLY

3. MAKING CONNECTIONS

Possible Response: Improvements in communication and transportation, expansion of education, and creation of mass culture all introduced the connections between people in various parts of the country.

4. EVALUATING DAILY LIFE

Some students might mention that greater choice of goods, greater educational opportunity, and new forms of recreation made life better for many people. Others might point out that life was not better for many minorities and that rapid economic change often disrupts the lives of many people.

5. ANALYZING PRIMARY SOURCES

Most students might say that this time period did mark a turning point in American history, noting the significant changes in technology, education, and leisure activities. Students should support their responses with references to the text.

Modern America Emerges

Parade of suffragists in New York City

Tinted photograph by unknown artist (1912).

Art Note
Photographs like this one became an increasingly important part of newspaper coverage in the early 1900s. New printing processes allowed papers to reproduce photos more clearly, and their use became increasingly popular.

▶ *Previewing the Unit*
Unit 5 describes how the modern United States begins taking shape in the first two decades of the 1900s. Americans embrace the progressive movement, which leads to greater government involvement in many aspects of life. Starting with the move to gain colonies overseas and ending with efforts to make peace after World War I, America also plays a greater role in world affairs than ever before.

UNIT 5

1890–1920
Modern America Emerges

"*Far better it is to dare mighty things, to win glorious triumphs, than to take rank with those poor spirits who neither enjoy much nor suffer much.*"

THEODORE ROOSEVELT

CHAPTER 17
1890–1920
The Progressive Era

CHAPTER 18
1890–1920
America Claims an Empire

CHAPTER 19
1914–1920
The First World War

490 UNIT 5

❶ Action photography
By the time this photograph was taken in 1912, technical improvements had enhanced the power of photography. This photo captures the women in the middle of their march. Some faces—like this woman's —are quite expressive.

❷ Parades
A New York group, the Equality League, held the first suffrage parade in 1910. The League was formed and led by Harriot Stanton Blatch, daughter of Elizabeth Cady Stanton. The parade became an annual spring event in New York and spread throughout the country.

❸ All walks of life
The suffragist parades included women from all walks of life— professional women, industrial workers, waitresses and maids, and mothers with children. Writing about a 1912 parade, a reporter said "all marched with an intensity of purpose that astonished the crowds that lined the street."

Discussing the Quotation

The Theodore Roosevelt quotation comes from a speech he gave in 1899, when he was governor of New York. Within two years, he became president and was in a position to "dare mighty things" himself.

FOR DISCUSSION:
- What do Roosevelt's words say about the attitudes of American leaders in the early 1900s?
- What changes to society might Americans in 1900 have wanted?
- How did the suffragists exemplify Roosevelt's desire to "dare mighty things"?

Discussing the Image

Woman suffrage seemed to many to be a radical departure for American society. To make their goal more acceptable, suffragists tried to show that they fit squarely within American tradition. The banner reads, "We demand equal representation for equal taxation."

FOR DISCUSSION:
- How does the slogan on the banner help the cause?
- How would parading with children help the cause of suffragists?

---

❹ Formality

The years leading up to World War I were a period marked by formality of dress. The parading women wear long skirts, and many wear hats and gloves.

❺ Wide streets

The suffragists' New York parades proceeded up Fifth Avenue, a major street in the city. By using one of the city's most important streets, they gave their parade greater visibility. The tactic would be adopted by leaders of other protest movements later in the century.

❻ Patriotic symbols

The suffragists helped promote their cause by using patriotic symbols. Many carried flags. Stars decorated the red sashes that many wore. This marcher sports a patriotic red, white, and-blue hat.

	Key Ideas	TEACHING SUPPORT	ASSESSMENT
SECTION 1 The Origins of Progressivism *pp. 494–500*	*Social and economic changes during the late 19th century create broad reform movements in American society.*	**In-Depth Resources: Unit 5** • Guided Reading, p. 1 • Skillbuilder Practice: Formulating Historical Questions, p. 6 • Primary Sources: Child Labor in the Coal Mines, p. 9; Declaration of the WCTU, p. 10 • American Lives: Robert LaFollette, p. 16 **COOPERATIVE ACTIVITY** • Learning about Muckrakers, p. 497 (TE)	*Section 1 Assessment*, p. 500 (PE) *Self-Assessment*, p. 500 (TE) ***Formal Assessment*** • Section Quiz, p. 209 ***Alternative Assessment Book*** • Standards for Evaluating a Cooperative Activity
SECTION 2 Women in Public Life *pp. 501–504*	*Many of the social and economic changes that give rise to progressivism lead women into public life as reformers and workers.*	**In-Depth Resources: Unit 5** • Guided Reading, p. 2 • Primary Sources: Poster, p. 11; *from* "The Status of Women" by Susan B. Anthony, p. 12 **COOPERATIVE ACTIVITY** • Creating Political Placards, p. 503 (TE)	*Section 2 Assessment*, p. 504 (PE) *Self-Assessment*, p. 504 (TE) ***Formal Assessment*** • Section Quiz, p. 210 ***Alternative Assessment Book*** • Standards for Evaluating a Cooperative Activity
SECTION 3 Teddy Roosevelt's Square Deal *pp. 505–511*	*Theodore Roosevelt pursues a reform agenda known as the Square Deal. His energetic style contributes to the emergence of the modern presidency.*	**In-Depth Resources: Unit 5** • Guided Reading, p. 3 • Literature: from *The Jungle* by Upton Sinclair, p. 13 **COOPERATIVE ACTIVITY** • Creating Political Cartoons, p. 507 (TE)	*Section 3 Assessment*, p. 511 (PE) *Self-Assessment*, p. 511 (TE) ***Formal Assessment*** • Section Quiz, p. 211 ***Alternative Assessment Book*** • Standards for Evaluating a Cooperative Activity
SECTION 4 Progressivism Under Taft *pp. 512–515*	*William H. Taft pursues a more cautious progressive program during his one term as president.*	**In-Depth Resources: Unit 5** • Guided Reading, p. 4 **COOPERATIVE ACTIVITY** • Reporting Election Results, p. 514 (TE)	*Section 4 Assessment*, p. 515 (PE) *Self-Assessment*, p. 515 (TE) ***Formal Assessment*** • Section Quiz, p. 212 ***Alternative Assessment Book*** • Standards for Evaluating a Cooperative Activity
SECTION 5 Wilson's New Freedom *pp. 516–521*	*Woodrow Wilson claims the presidency as a progressive leader and establishes a strong reform agenda.*	**In-Depth Resources: Unit 5** • Guided Reading, p. 5 • Geography Application: The Movement Toward Woman Suffrage, p. 7 • American Lives: Carrie Chapman Catt, p. 17 **COOPERATIVE ACTIVITY** • Writing Letters to the Editor, p. 519 (TE)	*Section 5 Assessment*, p. 521 (PE) *Self-Assessment*, p. 521 (TE) ***Formal Assessment*** • Section Quiz, p. 213 ***Alternative Assessment Book*** • Standards for Evaluating a Cooperative Activity
CHAPTER RESOURCES	**Chapter Overview** *In the first two decades of the 1900s, Americans embrace the Progressive movement and many of its reforms.*	**In-Depth Resources: Unit 5** • Living History Project: Worksheet, p. 18; Standards, p. 19 ***Telescoping the Times*** • Chapter Summary, pp. 33–34 ***Planning for Block Schedules***	***Chapter Assessment***, pp. 522–523 (PE) ***Alternative Assessment***, p. 523 (PE) ***Formal Assessment*** • Chapter Test, forms A and B, pp. 214–219 **Test Generator** ***Alternative Assessment Book*** See explanation and forms for different kinds of alternative assessments including portfolio assessment.

Geography Transparencies
• G17, Continental United States in 1900

Critical Thinking Transparencies
• CT51, Child Labor, 1890–1930

Electronic Library of Primary Sources
• On the Need for Child Labor Laws

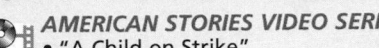
AMERICAN STORIES VIDEO SERIES
• "A Child on Strike"

INTERNET RESOURCES
• See *McDougal Littell Learning On-Line* for links to information about Hull House and Prohibition.

Electronic Library of Primary Sources
• from *The United States of America* v. *Susan B. Anthony*

INTERNET RESOURCES
• See *McDougal Littell Learning On-Line* for links to information about Susan B. Anthony and the suffrage movement.

Electronic Library of Primary Sources
• from "Whatever Is, Is Wrong" by E. W. Scripps

Our Times
• Upton Sinclair

INTERNET RESOURCES
• See *McDougal Littell Learning On-Line* for links to information about Theodore Roosevelt and W. E. B. Du Bois.

Humanities Transparencies
• H36, I Must Have Been Dozing

Grolier Multimedia Encyclopedia
• Conservation in the United States
• Bull Moose Party

INTERNET RESOURCES
• See *McDougal Littell Learning On-Line* for links to information about Gifford Pinchot and William H. Taft.

Critical Thinking Transparencies
• C17, Progressive Movement

Grolier Multimedia Encyclopedia
• from a speech on the rights of labor by William Taft
• multimedia map of women's suffrage

INTERNET RESOURCES
• See *McDougal Littell Learning On-Line* for links to information about Woodrow Wilson and Carrie Chapman Catt.

American Portfolio: A Videodisc for U.S. History, user's guide, pp. 155, 159, 165–175

INTERNET RESOURCES
Learning On-Line: Social Studies
http://www.mcdougallittell.com

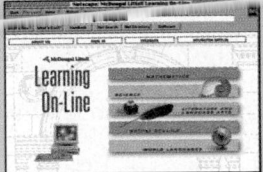

Block Scheduling (90 MINUTES)

Day 1
Section 1, pp. 494–500
 AMERICAN STORIES VIDEO SERIES
"A Child on Strike"
Section 2, pp. 501–504
Section Assessments, pp. 500, 504

Day 2
Section 3, pp. 505–511
Section 4, pp. 512–515
Section Assessments, pp. 511, 515

Day 3
Section 5, pp. 516–521
Section Assessment, pp. 521
Chapter Assessment, pp. 522–523

YEARLY PACING *Chapter 17 Total:* 3 days *Yearly Total:* 85 days

See *Planning for Block Schedules* for special activities and pacing strategies.

Customizing for Special Populations

Students Acquiring English

Access for Students Acquiring English
• Guided Reading for Sections 1–5 (Spanish), pp. 168–172
• Chapter Summary (Spanish), pp. 166–167
• Skillbuilder Practice: Formulating Historical Questions (Spanish), p. 143
• Geography Application: The Movement Toward Woman Suffrage (Spanish), p.174

 AMERICAN STORIES VIDEO SERIES
• "A Child On Strike" (Spanish track)

INTERNET RESOURCES
• See *McDougal Littell Learning On-Line* The Diverse Classroom.

Less Proficient Readers

In-Depth Resources: Unit 5
• Guided Reading for Sections 1–5, pp. 1–5
• Skillbuilder: Formulating Historical Opinions, p. 6
• Geography Application: The Movement Toward Woman Suffrage, p. 7

Telescoping the Times
• Chapter Summary, pp. 33–34

See additional strategies at point of use in the Teacher's Edition.

Gifted and Talented Students

In-Depth Resources: Unit 5
• Primary Sources: Child Labor in the Coal Mines, p. 9; Declaration of the WCTU, p. 10; Poster, p. 11; *from "The Status of Women"* by Susan B. Anthony
• American Lives: Robert LaFollette, p. 16; Carrie Chapman Catt, p. 17

See additional strategies at point of use in the Teacher's Edition.

Connections to Literature   READINGS FOR STUDENTS

In-Depth Resources: Unit 5
• from *The Jungle* by Upton Sinclair, p. 13

Enrichment Reading
Dos Passos, John
U.S.A.
New York: Penguin Books, 1996
The three separate novels of U.S.A. sharply satirize twentieth-century America in every region and at every social level. The characters, with their materialism and personal greed, reflect Dos Passos' belief that such behavior leads to moral decay and emptiness.

Pérez, N.A.
Breaker
Boston: Houghton, 1988
After his father's death, 14-year old Pat is forced to work in the coal mines in his Pennsylvania town. He becomes involved in the big mine workers strike of 1902.

Sandberg, Carl
Chicago Poems
New York: Dover, 1994
This is Sandberg's first book of poetry. The free-verse poems celebrate the voices of the people and are concerned with themes of injustice and fear of the effects of industrialization on humanity.

McDougal Littell *The Language of Literature*
American Literature

• **Charlotte Perkins Gilman,** "The Yellow Wallpaper," p. 605
• **Barbara Ehrenreich and Deirdre English,** from *Complaints and Disorders: The Sexual Politics of Sickness,* p. 619
• **Kate Chopin,** "The Story of an Hour," p. 623

The Progressive Era

▶ **Starting with the Student**
Ask students what the word *progressive* means to them. Then discuss the opening quotation.

• Ask the students what Wilson meant when he said democracy "releases the energies" of people.
• What does the "release of energy" suggest to students about what might happen during the progressive era?

PREVIEWING THE CHAPTER
• Ask students to read the brief section summaries.
• Point out that the video in Section 1 portrays the story of Camella Teoli, a child injured while working in a Massachusetts mill.

MORE ABOUT . . .
Woodrow Wilson

Woodrow Wilson (1856–1924) became president in 1912, when the progressive movement was well underway. Believing he had been elected with a mandate for continued social reform, Wilson asserted, "We stand in the presence of a revolution whereby America will insist upon recovering in practice those ideals which she has always professed."

492 **Chapter 17**

The Progressive Era

SECTION 1
The Origins of Progressivism
Social and economic changes during the late 19th century create broad reform movements in American society.

 VIDEO *A CHILD ON STRIKE*

SECTION 2
Women in Public Life
Many of the social and economic changes that give rise to progressivism lead women into public life as reformers and workers.

SECTION 3
Teddy Roosevelt's Square Deal
Theodore Roosevelt pursues a reform agenda known as the Square Deal. His energetic style contributes to the emergence of the modern presidency.

SECTION 4
Progressivism Under Taft
William H. Taft pursues a more cautious progressive program during his one term as president.

SECTION 5
Wilson's New Freedom
Woodrow Wilson claims the presidency as a progressive leader and establishes a strong reform agenda.

492 CHAPTER 17

"I believe in democracy because it releases the energies of every human being."
Woodrow Wilson

• Suffragists unite behind the National American Woman Suffrage Association (NAWSA).

• Congress passes Sherman Antitrust Act.

• Grover Cleveland ✪ is elected president for a second term.

• Illinois Factory Act prohibits child labor.

• Anti-Saloon League is founded.

• ✪ William McKinley is elected president.

✪ Theodore Roosevelt becomes president.

• McKinley is assassinated.

• ✪ William McKinley is reelected president.

THE UNITED STATES						
THE WORLD	**1890**	1892 1893	1895 1896		**1900**	1901
		1891	1895			

• Construction of the Trans-Siberian railroad across Russia begins.

• Italian Guglielmo Marconi invents radio telegraphy.

• The Commonwealth of Australia is created.

THEMES IN CHAPTER 17

Economic Opportunity

The progressive movement responded to a growing public demand for government involvement to curb big business and to deal with the nation's economic issues.

See Teacher's Edition note, p. 496.

Women in America

Women entered the work force in increasing numbers. Though usually paid less than their male counterparts, their increasing visibility in the public arena helped spur the movement toward woman suffrage.

During the progressive era, woman suffrage finally was achieved, brought about in part because of the increased role of women in public life due to the beginning of World War I. Ratification of the Nineteenth Amendment took place in 1920.

See Teacher's Edition notes, pp. 502, 518.

Constitutional Concerns

Theodore Roosevelt changed the role of the president, using the White House as a "bully pulpit" to influence public policy and expanding the responsibilities of the office. His actions shaped what would become known as the modern presidency.

See Teacher's Edition note, p. 506.

LIVING HISTORY

PLANNING A SUFFRAGE CAMPAIGN

Suppose woman suffragists—those who worked to win women the right to vote—had been able to use today's communications media to win support for their argument. Plan your own campaign for suffrage and consider the following:

- Use television, the Internet, and other modern devices to convince the public and the government to pass an amendment giving women the right to vote.

- Work with a partner or group to plan in detail your TV ads and other campaign strategies.

PORTFOLIO PROJECT Keep your ideas in a folder. At the end of the chapter, you will present your campaign to the class and add it to your American history portfolio.

- **Niagara Convention** promotes militant pursuit of African-American rights.

- **Membership in the Women's Christian Temperance Union** grows to 245,000.

- **National Association for the Advancement of Colored People (NAACP)** is founded.

- **Upton Sinclair** publishes *The Jungle*.

- **Sixteenth Amendment** creates federal income tax.

- **Payne-Aldrich Tariff** is passed.

- **Seventeenth Amendment** provides for direct election of senators.

- **Congress passes Eighteenth Amendment,** outlawing alcohol.

- **Congress passes Nineteenth Amendment,** which grants women the vote.

- **National Child Labor Committee** forms.

☆ **Theodore Roosevelt** is elected president.

William H. Taft ☆ is elected president.

☆ **Woodrow Wilson** is elected president.

Woodrow Wilson ☆ is reelected president.

- **U.S. enters World War I.**

| 1904 | 1905 | 1906 | 1908 | 1909 | **1910** | 1912 | 1913 | 1916 | 1917 | 1919 | **1920** |

1907

1914 · 1916

- **France and Japan** agree on "open door" policy toward China.

- **World War I** begins in Europe.

- **Mexican revolutionary "Pancho" Villa** raids Columbus, New Mexico.

- **Olympic Games** are held at Antwerp, Belgium.

The Progressive Era **493**

PLANNING A SUFFRAGE CAMPAIGN

Discuss these ideas for conducting the suffrage campaigns:

- Discuss the overall strategy for the campaign: What message about suffrage do students want to convey?
- Have groups sketch a diagram or write an outline that summarizes their campaign strategy.
- Have students develop effective slogans to use for their campaigns.

Project Planning Guide

Step 1	Student teams outline a strategy to achieve suffrage.
Step 2	Student groups assign members to handle various aspects of the campaign.
Step 3	Students complete the elements chosen as part of their campaign strategies.
Step 4	Students assemble the pieces of their campaign in their folders.

IN-DEPTH RESOURCES: UNIT 5
See worksheet and standards for evaluation, pp. 18, 19.

RECOMMENDED RESOURCES

Books for the Teacher

Schlereth, Thomas J. *Victorian America: Transformations in Everyday Life, 1876–1915.* New York: HarperCollins, 1991. A useful overview of the period.

Woloch, Nancy. *Women and the American Experience.* New York: Knopf, 1984. An introduction to the history of American women.

Books for the Student

Addams, Jane. *Twenty Years at Hull House.* Urbana: U of Illinois P, 1990. Addams's story of the settlement house.

Schneir, Miriam, ed. *Feminism: The Essential Historical Writings.* New York: Random House, 1972. A collection of primary-source materials.

Wilson, Dorothy Clarke. *Bright Eyes: The Story of Susette La Flesche, an Omaha Indian.* New York: McGraw, 1974. A readable account.

Videos

One Woman, One Vote. Prod. Ruth Pollak. PBS Home Video. 1995. Final drive for woman suffrage.

Theodore Roosevelt: Roughrider to Rushmore. Prod. Arthur Drooker. A&E Home Video, 1996. Bold life of an energetic president.

TR, the Story of Theodore Roosevelt. Prod. David Grubin. PBS Home Video, 1996. Four-hour biography.

Software

Her Heritage. CD-ROM. Pilgrim New Media, 1994. Biographical profiles of famous American women.

Social Reform Movements. CD-ROM. Educational Software Institute.

U.S. History: Government, Part 2. CD-ROM. Educational Software Institute.

OBJECTIVES

1 To explain the four goals of progressivism.

2 To summarize progressive efforts to clean up local government.

3 To identify progressive efforts to clean up state government, protect workers, and reform elections.

CRITICAL THINKING

- Summarizing, pp. 495, 496, 498, 500
- Contrasting, p. 497
- Recognizing effects, p. 499
- Synthesizing, p. 500
- Forming opinions, p. 500

FOCUS & MOTIVATE

▶ **Starting with the Student**
Watch the video "A Child on Strike" to learn how a young girl injured in a woolen mill is affected by progressivism.

- Using the *Teacher's Resource Book* as a guide, discuss Camella Teoli's experience in the mill. Use extension activities, including primary sources, to help students understand the use of child labor.

AMERICAN STORIES VIDEO SERIES
"A Child on Strike"

Videocassette: Volume 3

Videodisc: Disc 2, Side A, Chapter 3

MORE ABOUT . . .
Camella Teoli

Even First Lady Helen Taft attended the congressional hearings on child labor in which Teoli was one of 36 children to testify. Teoli continued to work for the Lawrence mills for over 40 years, marrying a fellow worker and retiring at the age of 63. Teoli is buried in Lawrence, where a walkway on the town common is named for her.

---

1 The Origins of Progressivism

TERMS & NAMES
- progressive movement
- Florence Kelley
- prohibition
- muckraker
- scientific management
- Robert M. La Follette
- initiative
- referendum
- recall
- Seventeenth Amendment

LEARN ABOUT political, economic, and moral roots of progressivism
TO UNDERSTAND how progressive reforms changed modern America.

ONE AMERICAN'S STORY

In 1900, three-year-old Camella Teoli and her family came from Italy to join Camella's father, who had immigrated earlier to work in the textile mills of Lawrence, Massachusetts. To help support the family, Teoli's wife and his older children all went to work in the mills. Camella began working at the Washington Woolen Mill when she was about 12 years old. On July 9, 1909, a machine used for twisting cotton into thread tore off part of the girl's scalp, sending her to the hospital for many weeks. A six-inch scar marked the injury for the rest of Camella's life.

In 1912, more than 20,000 Lawrence mill workers went on strike over wage cuts. The mill owners had responded to a Massachusetts law reducing hours for women and children by cutting all workers' salaries and increasing the work pace. The striking workers, who could barely get by on an average of about $9 per week, refused to accept less.

Prominent supporters of the strike arranged for a group of Washington Woolen Mill workers, including Camella Teoli, to testify before a congressional committee. Camella's shocking story soon made headlines across the United States. When asked why she went on strike, Camella answered simply, "Because I didn't get enough to eat at home." She explained to the committee how she had gone to work before reaching the legal age of 14.

Angry crowds confront the militia at the Lawrence mill workers' strike in 1912.

A PERSONAL VOICE
I used to go to school, and then a man came up to my house and asked my father why I didn't go to work, so my father says I don't know whether she is 13 or 14 years old. So, the man say you give me $4 and I will make the papers come from the old country [Italy] saying that you are 14. So my father gave him the $4, and in one month came the papers that I was 14. I went to work, and about two weeks later got hurt in my head.
CAMELLA TEOLI, at congressional hearings, March 1912

The Lawrence workers held out for nine weeks and won the sympathy of the nation as well as a ten percent pay raise. Stories like Camella's set off a national investigation of labor conditions. As reformer Mary Heaton Vorse said, "What we saw in Lawrence affected us so strongly that this moment in time in Lawrence changed life for us." Indeed, across the country, people organized to address the problems of industrialization.

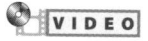 **A CHILD ON STRIKE**
The Testimony of Camella Teoli, Mill Girl

Four Goals of Progressivism

At the dawn of the new century, middle-class reformers addressed many of the problems that had contributed to the social upheavals of the 1890s. Journalists and writers exposed the unsafe conditions that factory workers, including women and children, often faced. Intellectuals questioned the dominant role of large corporations in American society. Political reformers struggled to make government more responsive to the people. Together, these reform efforts formed the **progressive movement,** which aimed to return control of the government to the people, restore economic opportunities, and correct injustices in American life.

SECTION 1 RESOURCES

 PRINT RESOURCES

IN-DEPTH RESOURCES: UNIT 5
Guided Reading, p. 1
Skillbuilder Practice: Formulating Historical Questions, p. 6
Primary Sources: Child Labor in the Coal Mines, p. 9;
 Declaration of the WCTU, p. 10
American Lives: Robert La Follette, p. 16

ACCESS FOR STUDENTS ACQUIRING ENGLISH
Guided Reading (Spanish), p. 168
Skillbuilder Practice: Formulating Historical Questions
 (Spanish), p. 173

FORMAL ASSESSMENT
Section Quiz, p. 209

ALTERNATIVE ASSESSMENT BOOK
See forms for supporting and scoring alternative activities.

TECHNOLOGY RESOURCES

GEOGRAPHY TRANSPARENCIES
G17, Continental United States in 1900

CD-ROM Electronic Library of Primary Sources

VIDEO *American Stories* video series
American Portfolio: A Videodisc for U.S. History
 user's guide, pp. 159, 172, 173

INTERNET McDougal Littell Learning On-Line
http://www.mcdougallittell.com

Unlike populism, the political movement that started with dissatisfied farmers, the progressive movement attracted middle-class city dwellers, who included writers, teachers, and scholars. Even though they never completely agreed on the problems or the solutions, these progressives sought to cure the many social problems caused by industrialization. For example, some progressives believed that business required stricter regulation, while others threw their energy into reforming city governments, making laws to protect workers, or closing saloons. However, every progressive reform movement had at least one of the following four goals:

- protecting social welfare
- promoting moral improvement
- creating economic reform
- fostering efficiency

PROTECTING SOCIAL WELFARE Many social welfare reformers strove to relieve urban problems. The Social Gospel and settlement house movements had begun as efforts to soften some of the harsh effects of industrialization. These efforts continued during the progressive era and inspired even more reform activities.

The Young Men's Christian Association (YMCA), for example, opened libraries, sponsored classes, and built swimming pools and handball courts. The Salvation Army fed poor people in soup kitchens, cared for children in nurseries, and sent "slum brigades" to convert poor immigrants to the middle-class values of hard work and temperance.

Settlement houses inspired social activism on the part of many women reformers. **Florence Kelley,** for example, a newly divorced mother of three young children, moved into Jane Addams's Hull House in Chicago. There, Kelley became an advocate for improving the lives of women and children. Eventually, Governor John P. Altgeld appointed her chief inspector of factories for Illinois, where she helped to win passage of the Illinois Factory Act in 1893. The act, which prohibited child labor and limited women's working hours, soon became a model for other states.

PROMOTING MORAL REFORM Other reformers felt that morality, not the workplace, held the key to improving the lives of poor people. Reformers offered a host of programs to uplift immigrants and poor city dwellers by improving personal behavior. **Prohibition,** the banning of alcoholic beverages, was one such program.

The Woman's Christian Temperance Union (WCTU), founded in Chicago in 1873, promoted the goal of prohibition. Members advanced their cause by entering saloons, singing, praying, and urging saloonkeepers to stop selling alcohol.

In 1879, Frances Willard, who had been the president of Evanston (Illinois) College for Ladies, transformed the WCTU from a small midwestern religious group into a powerful national organization with a variety of reformist goals. With 245,000 members in 1911, the WCTU became the largest women's group in the nation's history. Willard was a skillful organizer with a talent for political slogans. A WCTU member, according to Willard, must be ready to "bless and brighten every place she enters and enter every place."

Willard also told her members to "Do everything." WCTU members followed their leader's dictum, opening kindergartens for immigrants, visiting inmates in prisons and asylums, and working for suffrage. The broad nature

KEY PLAYER

FLORENCE KELLEY
1859–1932

Florence Kelley was born into privilege as the daughter of an antislavery Republican congressman from Pennsylvania. She became a social reformer whose sympathies clearly lay with the powerless, especially working women and children. During a long career, Kelley, whom one colleague admiringly called a guerrilla warrior, pushed the government to solve America's social problems.

In 1899, Kelley became general secretary of the National Consumers' League, where she lobbied to improve factory conditions. "Why," Kelley pointedly asked while campaigning for a federal child-labor law, "are seals, bears, reindeer, fish, wild game in the national parks, buffalo, [and] migratory birds all found suitable for federal protection, but not children?"

In the 1890s, Carry Nation worked for prohibition by walking into saloons, scolding the customers, and using her hatchet to destroy the bottles of liquor.

HISTORICAL SPOTLIGHT

ANTI-SALOON LEAGUE

Progressive women in particular denounced alcohol, which they called Demon Rum. While early temperance efforts dating back to the 1820s asked individuals to change their ways, turn-of-the-century reformers now sought the government's help in controlling alcohol consumption. Quietly founded in 1895, the Anti-Saloon League called itself "the Church in action against the saloon."

The league endorsed politicians who opposed Demon Rum, no matter which party they belonged to or where they stood on other issues. The Anti-Saloon League also organized statewide referenda to ban alcohol. Between 1900 and 1917, voters in nearly half of the states—mostly in the South and the West—prohibited the sale, production, or use of alcohol. Individual towns, city wards, and rural areas also voted themselves "dry."

of WCTU reform activities, like that of the settlement house movement, provided women with expanded public roles, which they used to justify giving women voting rights. A woman's right to vote, Willard believed, would offer "the most potent means of social and moral reform." The most prominent reform pushed by the WCTU, however, was prohibition.

Sometimes efforts at prohibition led to tension with immigrant groups, whose customs often included the consumption of alcohol. The Anti-Saloon League, founded in 1895, angered many immigrants when its members attacked saloons, which filled several roles in many immigrant communities. The saloons served inexpensive meals, cashed paychecks, and provided rooms for any purpose, from wedding receptions to political meetings to union headquarters. Prohibitionist groups feared that the combination of foreign cultures, alcohol, and machine politics would undermine American culture and democracy. By concentrating on closing saloons, the league became a model for other single-issue interest groups that set out to reform American culture and government.

CREATING ECONOMIC REFORM As moral reformers sought to change individual behavior, a severe economic panic in 1893 prompted some Americans to question the capitalist economic system. Writers like Henry George and Edward Bellamy, for example, criticized the laissez-faire theory—the belief that government should leave the economy alone. Bellamy called the capitalist ideal of competition a "brutal and cowardly slaughter of the unarmed and over-matched by bullies in armor."

Some Americans, especially workers, embraced socialism. Labor leader Eugene V. Debs helped organize the American Socialist Party in 1900. Debs commented on the uneven balance among big business, government, and ordinary people under the free-market system of capitalism.

> **A PERSONAL VOICE**
> Competition was natural enough at one time, but do you think you are competing today? Many of you think you are competing. Against whom? Against Rockefeller? About as I would if I had a wheelbarrow and competed with the Santa Fe [railroad] from here to Kansas City.
> **EUGENE DEBS,** in *Debs: His Life, Writings and Speeches*

Though most progressives distanced themselves from socialism, they saw the truth of many of Debs's criticisms. Indeed, big business often received favorable treatment from government officials and politicians.

Journalists who wrote about the corrupt side of business in mass circulation magazines during the early 20th century became known as **muckrakers.** In her "History of the Standard Oil Company," a devastating monthly serial in *McClure's Magazine,* the muckraking writer Ida M. Tarbell described the company's cutthroat methods of eliminating competition. "Mr. Rockefeller has systematically played with loaded dice," Tarbell charged, "and it is doubtful if there has been a time since 1872 when he has run a race with a competitor and started fair."

FOSTERING EFFICIENCY While muckrakers fought corporate and government corruption, other reformers tried to increase the efficiency of American society. Frederick Winslow Taylor popularized the concept of **scientific management,** the effort to improve efficiency in the work place by applying scientific principles to make tasks simpler and easier. As a result, workers became more productive and the amount of goods and services available to the people increased.

TEACHING OPTIONS

Exploring Themes

Economic Opportunity The more complex economies of the industrial age experienced far greater economic disturbances than had occurred in the past. Especially severe in the 19th century were the panics or depressions of 1837, 1857, 1873, and 1893. The progressive movement was in part a response to what its proponents saw as a growing need for government involvement to try to curb the devastation of the widespread bank failures, job losses, and bankruptcies that characterized these periods of economic chaos.

Making Connections Across the Curriculum

Economics When a 19th-century panic occurred, a depression followed. For example, the Panic of 1893 ushered in a four-year depression. In general, economists make these distinctions:

- **panic:** a period of acute financial disturbance that usually begins a depression
- **recession:** a slowdown in the business cycle when declining production and employment lead to declining incomes and purchasing
- **depression:** a period of drastic economic decline characterized by sharply reduced business activity, falling prices and wages, and widespread unemployment

In *Principles of Scientific Management* (1911), Taylor declared, "Time studies of work forms the basis of modern management." Followers of Taylor performed time studies on factory operations to see just how quickly each task could be performed. Armed with these studies, bosses like the mill owners at Lawrence simply raised the speed of their machines and increased laborers' workloads.

In 1913, the Ford Motor Company enhanced its efficiency by introducing an assembly line in one small part of production at the company's Highland Park, Michigan, plant. One problem of factory production was that some people worked more quickly than others. The Ford engineers evened the pace by moving the automobile parts on a continuous chain at a steady speed. Following that experiment, time-and-motion studies led to an expanded assembly line. By 1914, three lines were in full operation at the plant, where workers turned out 1,212 chassis assemblies every eight hours.

Such assembly lines led to a huge increase in production, but the system required people to work like machines. The result was a high worker turnover, often due to injuries suffered by exhausted workers. As one steelworker complained in 1910, "It's simply a killing pace in the steelworks."

To keep his assembly line workers happy and to prevent strikes, Henry Ford reduced the workday to eight hours and paid workers five dollars a day, twice as much as other industrial workers earned at the time. The "Five-Dollar Day" attracted thousands of job seekers. For their money, though, workers on Ford's assembly line exhausted themselves. As one homemaker mildly complained in a letter to Henry Ford in 1914, "That $5 a day is a blessing—a bigger one than you know but oh they earn it."

Such efforts at improving efficiency, an important part of progressivism, targeted not only industry, but government as well.

Workers at the Ford flywheel factory cope with the demanding pace of the assembly line to earn $5 a day—a good wage before the First World War.

"When I'm through everybody will be able to afford [a car], and about everyone will have one."

HENRY FORD, 1909

Cleaning Up Government

Cities posed some of the most obvious social problems of the new industrial age. In many large cities, political bosses rewarded their supporters with jobs and kickbacks and openly bought votes with favors and bribes. Efforts to reform city politics stemmed in part from the desire to make government more efficient and responsive to its constituents. But those efforts also grew from distrust of immigrants' participation in politics.

REFORMING LOCAL GOVERNMENT Natural disasters sometimes played an important role in prompting reform of city governments. In 1900, for example, a hurricane and tidal wave swept out of the Gulf of Mexico and almost demolished Galveston, Texas. The politicians on the city council botched the huge relief and rebuilding job so badly that the Texas legislature appointed a five-member commission of experts to take over. Each expert took charge of a different city department. The commission soon rebuilt Galveston, prompting the city to adopt the commission idea as a form of government. By 1917, some 500 cities had followed Galveston's example and replaced city councils with commissions.

The Progressive Era **497**

OBJECTIVE
③ INSTRUCT

Reform at the State Level

▶ **Discussing Key Ideas**

• Progressive governors such as Wisconsin's La Follette help reform state government.

• States pass laws to end child labor and improve work conditions.

• States introduce election reforms that pave the way for the Seventeenth Amendment, which provides for direct election of U.S. senators.

MORE ABOUT . . .
Robert M. La Follette

La Follette became famous when he revealed that Philetus Sawyer, Wisconsin's Republican boss, had tried to bribe him. La Follette planned to run as the Progressive Party's 1912 presidential candidate but was ousted by Roosevelt. He did run in 1924 and received about a sixth of the vote.

IN-DEPTH RESOURCES: UNIT 5
American Lives: Robert La Follette, p. 16

Cleveland mayor Tom Johnson, *center*, tried to make city governments more responsive to their residents' needs.

Another natural disaster, a flood in Dayton, Ohio, in 1913, led to the widespread adoption of the council-manager form of government. Staunton, Virginia, had already pioneered this system, in which people elected a city council to make laws. The council in turn appointed a manager, typically a person with training and experience in public administration, to run the city's departments. By 1925, managers were administering nearly 250 cities.

REFORM MAYORS In some cities, mayors introduced progressive reforms without changing how government was organized. Hazen Pingree, mayor of Detroit, Michigan (1890–1897), and Tom Johnson, mayor of Cleveland, Ohio (1901–1909), gained national reputations as progressive mayors.

Pingree concentrated on economic issues. He instituted a fairer tax structure, lowered fares for public transportation, and rooted out corruption. Under his administration, city workers built schools, parks, and a municipal lighting plant. Detroit lowered gas rates and set up a system of work relief for unemployed people. Tom Johnson, a socialist, believed that citizens should play a more active role in city government. Toward that end, he held meetings in a large circus tent and invited citizens to question officials about how the city was managed. Like Pingree, Johnson appointed competent, honest people to city jobs and reassessed property values to achieve a fairer tax structure.

In addition to Johnson, 18 socialist mayors instituted progressive reforms in America's cities. In general, these socialists practiced "gas and water socialism." This meant that the mayors, including Johnson, dismissed the corrupt and greedy private owners of utilities, such as gasworks, waterworks, and transit lines, and established public ownership.

THINK THROUGH HISTORY
D. *Summarizing* Summarize the new types of city government that emerged during the progressive era.

D. Answer Commission system: a commission runs city services; Council-manager system: a council appoints a city manager.

Reform at the State Level

Local reforms coincided with progressive efforts at the state level. Spurred by progressive governors, many states passed laws to regulate railroads, mines, mills, telephone companies, and other large businesses.

REFORM GOVERNORS Under the leadership of **Robert M. La Follette,** Wisconsin led the way in regulating big business. Leader of the progressive wing of the Republican Party in Wisconsin, "Fighting Bob" La Follette served three terms as governor before he entered the U.S. Senate in 1906. He explained that, as governor, he did not mean to "smash corporations, but merely to drive them out of politics, and then to treat them exactly the same as other people are treated."

Governor La Follette made the railroad industry his major target. He taxed railroad property at the same rate as other business property, set up a commission to regulate rates, and forbade railroads to issue free passes to state officials.

Other reform governors who attacked big business interests included Charles B. Aycock of North Carolina, Albert B. Cummins of Iowa, and Joseph W. Folk of Missouri.

PROTECTING WORKERS In addition to lobbying for political reforms that would protect consumers against dishonest business practices, progressives also lobbied for regulations to protect workers. One of the most important efforts was the movement to end child labor.

Many Americans were outraged by the effects of industrial labor upon young people. The number of children under the age of 15 who worked in industrial jobs for wages climbed from 1.5 million in 1890 to 2 million in 1910. Businesses liked to hire children because they performed unskilled jobs for

498 CHAPTER 17

lower wages than adults, and children's small hands made them more adept at handling small parts and tools. Immigrants and rural migrants often sent their children to work, or worked alongside them, because they viewed their children as part of the family economy. Often wages were so low for adults that every family member needed to work to pull the family out of poverty.

But as children worked in industrial settings, they began to develop serious health problems. Many child laborers were underweight. Some suffered from stunted growth or curvature of the spine. Those who worked near coal dust developed respiratory diseases like bronchitis and tuberculosis. Children also faced higher accident rates than adults did because of physical and mental fatigue caused by hard work and long hours. Furthermore, some progressive reformers were alarmed by the bad habits—smoking, drinking, and cursing—acquired by many child laborers.

In 1904, a group of progressive reformers organized the National Child Labor Committee to end child labor. They sent teams of investigators to gather evidence of children working in harsh conditions and then organized exhibitions with photographs and statistics to dramatize the plight of these children. They were joined by labor union members who argued that child labor lowered wages for all workers. These groups pressured national politicians to pass the Keating-Owen Act in 1916. The act prohibited the transportation of goods produced with child labor across state lines.

Three years later, however, the Supreme Court declared the act unconstitutional because it interfered with interstate commerce. Later efforts to pass national legislation met a similar fate. Although they lost at the national level, reformers succeeded in forcing legislation banning child labor and setting maximum hours in nearly every state. By 1920, the number of child laborers was nearly cut in half from what it had been in 1910.

EFFORTS TO LIMIT WORKING HOURS Despite the Supreme Court's opposition to a federal child labor law, the courts sometimes took a more sympathetic view of the plight of workers. In 1908, the Supreme Court decided in the case of *Muller* v. *Oregon* that a state could legally limit the working hours of women. In the past the Court had held that such limits interfered with freedom of contract. This time, however, lawyer Louis D. Brandeis—assisted by Florence Kelley and Josephine Goldmark—persuasively argued that poor working women were much more economically insecure than large corporations. Brandeis asserted that women required the state's protection against powerful employers. He convinced the Court to uphold an Oregon law limiting women to a ten-hour workday. Other states enacted or strengthened laws to reduce women's hours of work. A similar Brandeis brief in *Bunting* v. *Oregon* in 1917 persuaded the Court to uphold a ten-hour workday for men.

Young girls and boys often worked long hours in the textile mills. Spindle boys work in a Georgia cotton mill *below left*; A girl and her supervisor work at a spinning machine, 1909 *below*.

499

ON THE WORLD STAGE

AUSTRALIAN BALLOT

During the Gilded Age, American voters often faced threats from opposing political parties fighting for votes. The Australian ballot is a system of marking a secret ballot in a walled or curtained booth. This method gained rapid popularity in the United States after Louisville, Kentucky, first adopted it in 1888 in order to protect voters from being intimidated.

In many parts of Australia, the secret ballot had been law since the late 1850s. England adopted the Australian ballot in 1872 after a hearing during which an Australian government member testified in favor of the system. He said, "Before the ballot was in operation our elections were exceedingly riotous." Canada, Belgium, Luxembourg, Italy, and then the United States soon followed the example of Australia and England.

Progressives also succeeded in winning workers' compensation to aid the families of workers who were hurt or killed on the job. Beginning with Maryland in 1902, one state after another passed legislation requiring employers in dangerous occupations to pay benefits to injured employees.

REFORMING ELECTIONS In some cases, ordinary citizens, rather than legislators or governors, won state reforms. In Oregon, William S. U'Ren prompted his state to adopt the secret ballot (also called the Australian ballot), the initiative, the referendum, and the recall. The initiative and referendum gave citizens the power to create laws. Citizens could petition to place an **initiative**—a bill originated by the people rather than lawmakers—on the ballot. Then voters, instead of the legislature, accepted or rejected the initiative by **referendum,** a vote on the initiative. The **recall** enabled voters to remove public officials from elected positions by forcing them to face another election before the end of their term if enough voters asked for it. By 1920, 20 states had adopted at least one of these techniques.

Wisconsin became the first state to adopt another democratic reform, the direct primary, in 1903. A direct primary meant that voters, instead of political machines, would choose candidates for public office through a special popular election. About two-thirds of the states adopted some form of direct primary by 1915.

DIRECT ELECTION OF SENATORS The success of the direct primary paved the way for the **Seventeenth Amendment** to the Constitution. Before 1913, state legislatures had chosen United States senators, a process that put even more power in the hands of party bosses and wealthy corporation heads. To force senators to be more responsive to the public, progressives pushed for the popular election of senators. The Senate at first refused to go along with the idea of popular election. Gradually, however, more and more states began choosing senators by means of the direct primary. As a result, Congress approved the amendment in 1912 and made the direct election of the Senate the law of the land. The Seventeenth Amendment became part of the Constitution in 1913.

Government reform—including efforts to give American citizens more of a voice in electing their legislators and creating laws—drew increased numbers of women into public life. The spirit of reform also brought renewed attention to the issue of woman suffrage.

F. Answer It put more control of government into the hands of ordinary citizens.

THINK THROUGH HISTORY
F. Synthesizing In what way was the Seventeenth Amendment typical of progressive reforms?

Section 1 Assessment

1. TERMS & NAMES
Identify:
- progressive movement
- Florence Kelley
- prohibition
- muckraker
- scientific management
- Robert M. La Follette
- initiative
- referendum
- recall
- 17th Amendment

2. SUMMARIZING Draw this web on your paper. Fill it in with examples of political organizations or professional groups that campaigned for the reforms shown.

```
Economic        Moral

    Progressive
    Reforms

Political        Social
                 Welfare
```

Which group was most effective?

3. SYNTHESIZING In what ways might Illinois, Wisconsin, and Oregon all be considered trailblazers in progressive reform? Support your answer with reasons.

THINK ABOUT
- legislative and election reforms at the state level
- the leadership of William U'Ren and Robert La Follette
- Governor Altgeld's appointment of Florence Kelley as chief inspector of factories for Illinois

4. FORMING OPINIONS Imagine you are a muckraking journalist in the early 1900s. A magazine publisher has asked you to submit a list of story ideas for upcoming issues. What wrongdoings would you like to probe?

THINK ABOUT
- Ida M. Tarbell's articles on the Standard Oil Company
- the targets of political, economic, and moral reformers
- topics that might require government reform

500 CHAPTER 17

ANSWERS

1. TERMS & NAMES
progressive movement, p. 494
Florence Kelley, p. 495
prohibition, p. 495
muckraker, p. 496
scientific management, p. 496
Robert M. La Follette, p. 498
initiative, p. 500
referendum, p. 500
recall, p. 500
17th Amendment, p. 500

2. SUMMARIZING
Possible Answers:
Social Welfare—YMCA; Salvation Army.
Moral—WCTU; Anti-Saloon League.
Economic—American Socialist Party; muckrakers.
Political—National Consumers' League; National Child Labor Committee.
Students should give reasons for their choice of the most effective group.

3. SYNTHESIZING
Possible Responses: Reforms first instituted in Illinois, Wisconsin, and Oregon soon spread to other states. Illinois—prohibition of child labor and limit of women's working hours; Wisconsin—regulation of big business, especially railroads, and adoption of the direct primary; Oregon—adoption of the secret ballot, the initiative, the referendum, and the recall.

4. FORMING OPINIONS
Possible Responses: The effect of urban poverty on an immigrant family; city saloons; political bosses' kickbacks and bribes; election fraud; public utility owners' corruption; child labor; health problems; hazardous working conditions in factories.

② Women in Public Life

TERMS & NAMES
- Maria Mitchell
- NACW
- suffrage
- Susan B. Anthony
- NAWSA

LEARN ABOUT women's growing participation in work, education, politics, and reform
TO UNDERSTAND how women's lives changed in the early 20th century.

ONE AMERICAN'S STORY

Susette La Flesche, a young Native American woman, traveled east in 1879 to translate into English the sad words of Chief Standing Bear, whose Ponca people had been forcibly removed from their homeland. Calling La Flesche Bright Eyes, an English translation of her Native American name, one newspaper gushed, "No such interesting squaw has appeared since Pocahontas. . . . Bright Eyes has taken sober Boston captive."

Susette La Flesche was born in 1854, the year her own Omaha people were forced by treaty to give up their territory in Nebraska. Raised on a small reservation, she later attended a women's seminary, the Elizabeth Institute, in New Jersey. When the Ponca's removal occurred in 1877, La Flesche was teaching in a government school on her reservation. A sympathetic Omaha journalist convinced Chief Standing Bear and Susette La Flesche to go on a lecture tour to draw attention to the Ponca's situation. La Flesche's words were fierce.

A PERSONAL VOICE
We are thinking men and women. We have a right to be heard in whatever concerns us. Your government has driven us hither and thither like cattle. . . . Your government has no right to say to us, Go here, or Go there, and if we show any reluctance, to force us to do its will at the point of the bayonet. . . . Do you wonder that the Indian feels outraged by such treatment and retaliates, although it will end in death to himself?

SUSETTE LA FLESCHE, quoted in *Bright Eyes*

Susette La Flesche

Susette La Flesche later testified before congressional committees and helped win passage of the Dawes General Allotment Act of 1887, which allowed individual Native Americans to claim reservation land and citizenship rights. La Flesche's activism was an example of a new role for American women, who were expanding their participation in public life.

Women in the Work Force

Before the Civil War, the cult of domesticity had glorified women's roles in the home. In the late 19th century, a middle-class or upper-class woman felt obliged to make her home a place of refuge from the excitement and distractions of the outside world—to keep children safe and husbands rested. While those women could afford such pursuits, poor women had no choice but to work hard, whether in the home or outside of it.

FARMWOMEN On farms in the South and the Midwest, women and children remained a critical part of the economic structure of the family in the early 20th century. Their roles had not changed substantially since the previous century. Besides performing domestic tasks like cooking, cleaning, and sewing, they handled a host of other chores. If their husbands were ill or absent, farmwomen had to plow and plant the fields and harvest the crops in addition to performing their own duties.

DOMESTIC WORKERS Many women without formal education or industrial skills contributed to the economic survival of their families by doing domestic

The Progressive Era **501**

SECTION 2 RESOURCES

PRINT RESOURCES

IN-DEPTH RESOURCES: UNIT 5
Guided Reading, p. 2
Primary Sources: Political Poster, p. 11; *from* "The Status of Women" by Susan B. Anthony, p. 12

ACCESS FOR STUDENTS ACQUIRING ENGLISH
Guided Reading (Spanish), p. 169

FORMAL ASSESSMENT
Section Quiz, p. 210

ALTERNATIVE ASSESSMENT BOOK
See forms for supporting and scoring alternative activities.

TECHNOLOGY RESOURCES

CD-ROM Electronic Library of Primary Sources

VIDEO *American Portfolio: A Videodisc for U.S. History* user's guide, pp. 155, 165, 167, 174

INTERNET McDougal Littell Learning On-Line
http://www.mcdougallittell.com

Section 2 Overview

OBJECTIVES

① To trace women's growing presence in the turn-of-the-century work force.

② To summarize women's leadership in reform movements and the effort to achieve woman suffrage.

CRITICAL THINKING

- Analyzing causes, p. 502
- Recognizing effects, p. 503
- Summarizing, p. 504
- Analyzing issues, p. 504
- Analyzing motives, p. 504

FOCUS & MOTIVATE

▶ *Starting with the Student*
- Ask students whether they think boys and girls have the same opportunities open to them.
- Ask them if they think men and women share equal rights in public life, and why.

MORE ABOUT . . .
Susette La Flesche

La Flesche was aided in her efforts to help the Poncas by Thomas H. Tibbles, an Omaha journalist, whom she later married. After traveling abroad to further the Native American cause, she returned to the reservation where she gained recognition as a writer.

OBJECTIVE
① INSTRUCT

Women in the Work Force

▶ *Discussing Key Ideas*
- African-American and immigrant women often work as domestics.
- More women, especially immigrants, work in industry, where they are paid only about half as much as men doing equivalent jobs.

(continued on next page)

Teacher's Edition **501**

(continued from page 501)

- More women take white-collar jobs as teachers, typists, and bookkeepers.

IN-DEPTH RESOURCES: UNIT 5
Guided Reading, p. 2
ACCESS FOR STUDENTS ACQUIRING ENGLISH
Guided Reading (Spanish), p. 169

NOW & THEN
Telephone Operators
Critical Thinking: Analyzing Causes and Effects Ask students how the gap between men's and women's salaries drew more women into the work force. *Possible Response: Women's salaries were lower than men's, prompting businesses to hire them to save expenses.*

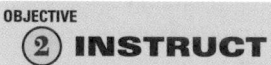

OBJECTIVE
② INSTRUCT

Women's Leadership in Reform

Students might begin a time line of important dates in the suffrage movement.

1848	First women's rights convention in Seneca Falls

▶ *Discussing Key Ideas*
- Colleges for women open.
- Female reformers work to improve social welfare, public morals, and race relations.
- Susan B. Anthony helps lead the struggle for woman suffrage.

NOW & THEN

TELEPHONE OPERATORS
Today, when Americans use the telephone, an automated voice often greets them with instructions about which buttons to press. This computerized approach to modern communication is only one of many modifications of Alexander Graham Bell's 1876 invention, the telephone.

Young men, the first telephone operators, proved unsatisfactory. Patrons complained that the male operators used profane language and talked back to callers. Thanks to a willingness to accept a ten-dollar weekly salary, women soon largely replaced men as telephone operators.

Department stores advertised shopping by telephone as a convenience. One ad in the Chicago telephone book of 1904 declared, "Every [telephone] order, inquiry, or request will be quickly and intelligently cared for." The ad pictured a line of female telephone operators.

work. After almost two million African-American women were freed from slavery, poverty quickly drove almost half of them into the work force. In 1890, about one million African-American women held jobs. While 38 percent labored on farms, 46 percent toiled as domestic servants or laundresses. African-American women migrated by the thousands to Southern and Northern cities to take what one social worker described as "the job the white girl does not want." African-American women filled positions as cooks, laundresses, scrubwomen, and maids.

Unmarried immigrant women also did domestic labor, especially when they first arrived in the United States. Many middle-class homes in the Northeast, for example, provided domestic employment for young Irish women. Typically, married immigrant women contributed to the family income by taking in piece-work or caring for boarders at home.

In 1870, roughly 70 percent of American working women worked as servants. But as better-paying opportunities started to open up, white women began to take jobs in offices, stores, classrooms, and factories.

WOMEN IN INDUSTRY At the turn of the century, one out of five American women worked; 25 percent of them held jobs in manufacturing. Working women who spent up to 12 hours a day sewing, folding, packing, or bottling came primarily from the ranks of young, white city dwellers. Most had been born in a foreign country or were the children of immigrants.

In tobacco factories, nearly 40 percent of the employees were women. Women also worked in canneries, bookbinderies, packing plants, and commercial laundries. However, the garment trade claimed about half of all women industrial workers. Women frequently performed the least skilled work and received the lowest pay. Even when they did the same work, women received only about half as much money as their male counterparts did.

As business opportunities expanded, women began to fill new jobs in offices, stores, and classrooms. White-collar jobs as stenographers, typists, bookkeepers, and teachers beckoned middle-class and native-born women who had never worked before. These jobs required a high school education, and by 1890 women high school graduates outnumbered men. Moreover, new business schools were preparing bookkeepers and stenographers as well as training female typists to operate the new machines.

THINK THROUGH HISTORY
A. *Analyzing Causes* What kinds of job opportunities prompted more women to complete high school?

A. Answer White-collar jobs like stenographer, typist, and teacher.

Women's Leadership in Reform

Many middle-class and upper-class women became involved in activities outside their homes by joining women's clubs to discuss art or literature. Indeed, by 1910, nearly 800,000 women belonged to women's clubs, which sometimes became reform groups that addressed such issues as temperance or the abolition of child labor. Women like Susette La Flesche entered the public sphere, demanded increased opportunities for women in higher education, and campaigned for the right to vote.

502 CHAPTER 17

TEACHING OPTIONS

Exploring Themes

Women in America Women were entering the work force in increasing numbers. Unlike domestics and industrial workers, the white-collar female worker was becoming something of a glamorous stereotype. "The average American woman of the middle-classes," said a visiting Englishman in 1914, "is incomparably the smartest, most elegant and beautiful thing that exists under Heaven. It is not of the women of fashion I speak. . . . It is the ordinary, everyday-go-to-work girl who takes her lunch at Child's . . . and patronizes what you call the cinematograph theatre and she calls the 'movies.'"

Making Connections Across Cultures

Native American Women Susette La Flesche's role in public life was remarkable, because she was both a woman and a Native American. The role of women varied among Native American cultures. Among the Navaho, for example, males were the head of household and could even take multiple wives—though females played their part in the agricultural economy. The Iroquois tribes, on the other hand, were matrilineal and matrilocal societies in which descent was traced in the female line, young families moved into their mothers'—not fathers'—homes, and women enjoyed major property rights.

WOMEN IN HIGHER EDUCATION Many of the women who became active in public life in the late 19th century had attended the new women's colleges. Vassar College—with a faculty of 8 men and 22 women—accepted its first female students in 1865. Smith and Wellesley Colleges followed in 1875. In the South, Spelman College opened in 1881 and Randolph-Macon Women's College in 1891. Though Columbia, Brown, and Harvard colleges refused to admit women, each university established a separate college for women. Barnard opened in 1889, Pembroke in 1891, and Radcliffe in 1894.

Women's colleges sought to grant women an excellent education, but female graduates were still expected to fulfill traditional domestic roles. Indeed, in her will, Smith College's founder, Sophia Smith, made her goals clear.

> **A PERSONAL VOICE**
> [It is my desire] to furnish for my own sex means and facilities for education equal to those which are afforded now in our College to young men. . . . It is not my design to render my sex any the less feminine, but to develop as fully as may be the powers of womanhood & furnish women with the means of usefulness, happiness, & honor now withheld from them.
> **SOPHIA SMITH,** quoted in *Alma Mater*

THINK THROUGH HISTORY
B. *Recognizing Effects* What effect did higher education have on women?
B. Answer Women who attended college no longer relied solely on marriage; some pursued a profession, and others did volunteer reform work.

Now that more women attended college, marriage no longer was a woman's only alternative. Indeed, almost half of college-educated women in the late 19th century never married. Instead, many educated women began to apply their skills to needed social reforms.

WOMEN AND REFORM The participation of educated women often strengthened existing reform groups and provided leadership for new ones. Because women were not allowed to vote or run for office, women reformers strove to improve conditions at work and home. In what historians call "social housekeeping," women targeted unsafe factories and labor abuses and promoted housing reform, educational improvement, and food and drug laws.

African-American women founded the National Association of Colored Women (**NACW**) in 1896, which was a merger of two earlier organizations. The NACW managed nurseries, reading rooms, and kindergartens. Josephine Ruffin, a prominent African-American woman from Boston, identified as the mission of the African-American women's club movement "the moral education of the race with which we are identified."

THE FIGHT FOR THE VOTE Winning **suffrage,** the right to vote, had been a focus of women reformers since the Seneca Falls convention of 1848. During Reconstruction, the Fourteenth and Fifteenth Amendments, which granted African-American men the right to vote, had split the women's movement. Feeling that this was "the Negro's hour," some women supported the amendments. Others opposed the amendments because they excluded women. **Susan B. Anthony,** a leader in the woman suffrage movement, said that she "would sooner cut off my right hand than ask the ballot for the black man and not for women." By 1890, however, suffragists had united in the National American Woman Suffrage Association (**NAWSA**). Prominent leaders of the suffrage crusade included Anthony, Elizabeth Cady Stanton, Lucy Stone, and Julia Ward Howe, the author of "The Battle Hymn of the Republic."

A THREE-PART STRATEGY FOR SUFFRAGE The leaders of the suffrage movement tried three different approaches to achieve their objective. First, they tried to convince state legislatures to grant women the right to vote. They

HISTORICAL SPOTLIGHT
Vassar's Maria Mitchell
Critical Thinking: Evaluating Have students discuss Matthew Vassar's decision to offer Mitchell a teaching post at Vassar even though she had not attended college. *Possible Responses: Some students may feel that degrees are not the only indicator of knowledge or that a college degree could not be expected in an age when higher education for females was so rare.*

MORE ABOUT . . .
Sophia Smith
Largely self-educated, Sophia Smith completed her formal schooling at age 14. Since she never married, she decided to leave her money to a worthy cause. Deaf at the age of 40, she at first planned to endow a school for the deaf near her western Massachusetts home. But when another such school opened, she rewrote her will, leaving nearly $400,000 to found the Northampton, Massachusetts, women's college that now bears her name.

IN-DEPTH RESOURCES: UNIT 5
Primary Sources: Political Poster, p. 11; *from* "The Status of Women" by Susan B. Anthony, p. 12

Cooperative Activity: Creating Political Placards

Task: Groups of students will create placards or signs that demonstrators in favor of woman suffrage might carry.

Purpose: To understand the background and goals of the woman suffrage movement.

Activity: Tell students to imagine that the time is about 1900 and that they are about to attend a rally to bring the issue of woman suffrage to the public eye. Divide students into small groups to create at least five placards for marchers to carry. Each group member should develop a list of possible slogans

for the signs—such as "Votes for Women"—using their textbook as a source or doing additional research. After the group chooses among the slogans, placards can be lettered by the more artistic members of the group. Bring the class together for a review of the placards, perhaps asking students to vote on the most effective slogan.

ALTERNATIVE ASSESSMENT BOOK
Standards for Evaluating a Cooperative Activity

KEY PLAYER

SUSAN B. ANTHONY
1820–1906
Like her peers in the women's rights movement, Susan B. Anthony endured hostile audiences who taunted her when she lectured on temperance, abolition, and women's rights.

In 1851, Anthony met Elizabeth Cady Stanton, with whom she founded the National Woman Suffrage Association (NWSA) in 1869. (The NWSA later merged with another organization to become the NAWSA.)

Along with her three sisters and several other women, Anthony voted illegally in the presidential election of 1872. At her trial, which she described in her diary as "The greatest outrage History ever witnessed," she was fined $100. "Not a penny shall go to this unjust claim," declared the defiant Anthony. The judge didn't press the issue and the case was closed.

Susan B. Anthony died 14 years before the Nineteenth Amendment finally granted women the vote in 1920. A one-dollar coin, minted in 1979 and 1980, bears her picture.

achieved a victory in 1869, when the territory of Wyoming granted the vote to women. By the 1890s Utah, Colorado, and Idaho had enfranchised women, but after 1896, efforts in other states failed.

Second, women pursued court cases to test the Fourteenth Amendment, which declared that states denying their male citizens the right to vote would lose congressional representation. Weren't women citizens, too? In 1871 and 1872, Susan B. Anthony and other women attempted to get the Supreme Court to answer that question by making at least 150 attempts to vote in 10 states and the District of Columbia. When the Supreme Court ruled in 1875 on the relationship between the Fourteenth Amendment and woman suffrage, the justices agreed that women were indeed citizens—but citizenship did not automatically confer the right to vote.

Third, women pushed for a national constitutional amendment that would grant women the vote. In 1878, Anthony persuaded Senator Aaron Sargent of California to introduce an amendment that read, "The right of citizens of the United States to vote shall not be denied or abridged by the United States or by any state on account of sex." Although a Senate committee killed the Anthony amendment, women activists lobbied for the next 18 years to have it reintroduced. On the rare occasions when the bill reached the floor for a vote, senators invariably rejected it.

Despite this three-pronged approach, the campaign for woman suffrage achieved only modest success. After the turn of the century, however, other women's reform efforts paid off in improvements in the treatment of workers and safer food and drug products—all part of President Theodore Roosevelt's own plans for reforming business, labor, and the environment.

C. Answer The state-by-state approach; lawsuits testing the Fourteenth Amendment; trying to pass an amendment giving women the vote.

THINK THROUGH HISTORY
C. Summarizing What were the three approaches women tried in order to win the vote?

Suffragists campaign for the vote.

Section 2 Assessment

1. **TERMS & NAMES**
   Identify:
   • Maria Mitchell
   • NACW
   • suffrage
   • Susan B. Anthony
   • NAWSA

2. **SUMMARIZING** Recreate the diagram below on your paper and fill it in with details about working women in the late 1800s.

   What generalizations can you make about women workers at this time?

3. **ANALYZING ISSUES** What women and movements during the progressive era helped dispel the stereotype of submissive, nonpolitical women? Support your answers with evidence from the text.

   THINK ABOUT
   • new work and educational opportunities for women
   • new roles women played in public life
   • the suffrage movement

4. **ANALYZING MOTIVES** Explain why women participated in each of the following reform movements: improving education, promoting housing reform, correcting labor abuses, pushing for food and drug laws, winning the right to vote.

   THINK ABOUT
   • the problems that each social reform is trying to remedy
   • how women benefited from each

504 Chapter 17

③ Teddy Roosevelt's Square Deal

TERMS & NAMES
- Theodore Roosevelt
- Square Deal
- *The Jungle*
- Upton Sinclair
- Meat Inspection Act
- Pure Food and Drug Act
- conservation
- NAACP

LEARN ABOUT Theodore Roosevelt's domestic agenda and policies
TO UNDERSTAND the reforms of Roosevelt's administration.

ONE AMERICAN'S STORY

In November 1904, a muckraking journalist named Upton Sinclair visited Chicago to do research for a novel. For seven weeks, he lived in a neighborhood called Packingtown, where he interviewed workers, lawyers, doctors, saloonkeepers, and social workers. Sinclair intended his novel to reveal "the breaking of human hearts by a system which exploits the labor of men and women for profit."

What shocked readers about Sinclair's book *The Jungle* (1906), however, were the sickening conditions in the meatpacking industry. The author admitted that the public's reaction to his exposé had surprised him. "I aimed at the nation's heart," he said, "but by accident I hit it in the stomach." Sinclair's graphic descriptions of the filthy conditions turned the stomachs of the nation and the world.

Upton Sinclair poses with his son at the time of the writing of *The Jungle*.

A PERSONAL VOICE

There would be meat that had tumbled out on the floor, in the dirt and sawdust, where the workers had tramped and spit uncounted billions of consumption [tuberculosis] germs. There would be meat stored in great piles in rooms; . . . and thousands of rats would race about on it. . . . A man could run his hand over these piles of meat and sweep off handfuls of the dried dung of rats. These rats were nuisances, and the packers would put poisoned bread out for them; they would die, and then rats, bread, and meat would go into the hoppers together. . . . There were things that went into the sausage in comparison with which a poisoned rat was a tidbit.

UPTON SINCLAIR, *The Jungle*

The sensational book sold 25,000 copies in one week alone. Like many other readers, President Theodore Roosevelt lost his taste for meat, reportedly crying, "I'm poisoned," after reading the book. The nauseated president invited the author to visit him at the White House, where Roosevelt promised that "the specific evils you point out shall, if their existence be proved, and if I have the power, be eradicated."

A Rough-Riding President

Theodore Roosevelt was not supposed to be president. In fact, the political bosses of New York who found the young governor impossible to control had hatched a familiar scheme: kick Roosevelt upstairs, where he could do no harm. The plot to nominate Roosevelt as McKinley's vice-president in 1900 worked, but while "Boss" Platt of New York gloated about Roosevelt becoming vice-president, Republican political organizer and Senator Mark Hanna immediately realized something that Platt did not. Roosevelt, the man Hanna derided as "that damned cowboy," stood a heartbeat away from becoming president. Indeed, President McKinley had served barely six months of his second term before he was assassinated. The man who had been kicked upstairs now became the most powerful person in the government.

The Progressive Era **505**

Section 3 Overview

OBJECTIVES

① To trace the events of Theodore Roosevelt's presidency.

② To show how Roosevelt used the power of his office to regulate business.

③ To identify laws passed to protect citizens' health and preserve the environment.

④ To summarize Roosevelt's stand on civil rights.

SKILLBUILDERS

- Interpreting political cartoons, p. 507
- Understanding geography: location, human/environment interaction, p. 509

CRITICAL THINKING

- Synthesizing, pp. 506, 511
- Recognizing effects, p. 507
- Developing historical perspective, p. 509
- Summarizing, pp. 509, 510, 511
- Drawing conclusions, p. 511

FOCUS & MOTIVATE

▶ *Starting with the Student*
- Ask students what constitutes a "square," or fair, deal in bargaining with their friends.

OBJECTIVE
① **INSTRUCT**

A Rough-Riding President

▶ *Discussing Key Ideas*
- Theodore Roosevelt becomes president when President McKinley is assassinated in 1901.
- Roosevelt rises through political offices and wins acclaim in the Battle of San Juan Hill.
- Roosevelt's belief in a strong federal government helps define the modern presidency.

IN-DEPTH RESOURCES: UNIT 5
Guided Reading, p. 3

ACCESS FOR STUDENTS ACQUIRING ENGLISH
Guided Reading (Spanish), p. 170

SECTION 3 RESOURCES

PRINT RESOURCES

IN-DEPTH RESOURCES: UNIT 5
Guided Reading, p. 3
Literature: from *The Jungle* by Upton Sinclair, p. 13

ACCESS FOR STUDENTS ACQUIRING ENGLISH
Guided Reading (Spanish), p. 170

FORMAL ASSESSMENT
Section Quiz, p. 211

ALTERNATIVE ASSESSMENT BOOK
See forms for supporting and scoring alternative activities.

TECHNOLOGY RESOURCES

CD-ROM *Our Times*
Electronic Library of Primary Sources

VIDEO *American Portfolio: A Videodisc for U.S. History*
user's guide, pp. 168, 170, 171, 175

INTERNET McDougal Littell Learning On-Line
http://www.mcdougallittell.com

Teacher's Edition **505**

The Rough Riders received enormous attention during the Spanish-American-Cuban War. Cowboys, police officers, miners, and college athletes were among those whom Roosevelt recruited. Colonel Leonard Wood resigned his post as White House physician to command the Rough Riders; Theodore Roosevelt was second-in-command.

"For unflagging interest and enjoyment, a household of children, if things go reasonably well, certainly makes all other forms of success and achievement lose their importance by comparison," Roosevelt once remarked. He himself had six children, making for what one staff member called "the wildest scramble in the history of the White House." In addition to sports, the Roosevelt children played often with their pets: dogs, rabbits, flying squirrels, a badger named Josiah, a macaw called Eli, and a small bear.

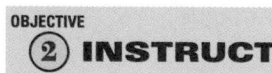

OBJECTIVE
② INSTRUCT

Using Federal Power

▶ *Discussing Key Ideas*
• Roosevelt intervenes in a 1902 coal strike and sets a precedent for federal arbitration.
• The president sets out to control or break up trusts and to regulate the railroads.

Teddy Roosevelt enjoyed an active lifestyle as this 1902 photo reveals.

ROOSEVELT'S RISE Born into a wealthy New York family, young Theodore Roosevelt suffered from asthma. "Teedie" was so frail that he had to sleep propped up in order to breathe. Fighting asthma for the rest of his life, Roosevelt drove himself to accomplish demanding physical feats. As a teenager, he mastered marksmanship and horseback riding. At Harvard College, Roosevelt boxed and wrestled. In the 1880s, after his beloved first wife died, he recovered from his grief on a Dakota ranch.

The ambitious Roosevelt, however, would not stay away from New York politics. After serving three terms in the New York State Assembly, he became New York City's police commissioner and then assistant secretary of the U.S. Navy. The aspiring politician grabbed national attention during the war with Spain in 1898. The Rough Riders, Roosevelt's volunteer cavalry brigade, won public acclaim for its role in the battle at San Juan Hill in Cuba. Roosevelt returned a hero and soon won election to the governorship of New York and then the vice-presidency.

THE MODERN PRESIDENCY When McKinley's assassination thrust Roosevelt into the presidency in 1901, he became—at 42 years old—the youngest person ever to hold that office. Unlike previous presidents, Roosevelt soon dominated the news with his many exploits. While president, Roosevelt boxed with professionals, one of whom blinded him in the left eye. On another day, he galloped 100 miles on horseback, merely to prove the feat possible. When the president spared a bear cub on a hunting expedition, a toymaker marketed a popular new product, the Teddy Bear. To young people the brash Roosevelt said, "In life, as in a football game, the principle to follow is: Hit the line hard."

In politics, as in sports, Roosevelt acted boldly. Indeed, his leadership and publicity campaigns helped create the modern presidency—a model by which all future presidents would be measured. Before Roosevelt, presidents had rarely stood out among national politicians in terms of personality. Roosevelt was different. He used his dynamic personality and popularity to advance his programs. Citing federal responsibility for the national welfare, Roosevelt thought the government should assume control whenever states proved incapable of dealing with problems. He explained, "It is the duty of the President to act upon the theory that he is the steward of the people, and . . . to assume that he has the legal right to do whatever the needs of the people demand, unless the Constitution or the laws explicitly forbid him to do it."

Roosevelt saw the presidency as a "bully pulpit," from which he could influence the news media and shape legislation. If big business victimized workers, then President Roosevelt would see to it that the common people received what he called a **Square Deal.** This term was used to describe the various progressive reforms in the Roosevelt administration.

Using Federal Power

Roosevelt's study of history—he wrote the first of his 30 books at the age of 24—convinced him that modern America required a powerful federal government. "A simple and poor society can exist as a democracy on the basis of sheer individualism," Roosevelt declared, "but a rich and complex society

A. Answer
Roosevelt was an active, forceful, and energetic executive; he used his position to shape legislation and influence the media.

THINK THROUGH HISTORY
A. Synthesizing
What actions and beliefs of Roosevelt contributed to his reputation as the first modern president?

TEACHING OPTIONS

Exploring Themes

Constitutional Concerns After Theodore Roosevelt's presidency, the office of the chief executive would never be the same. Roosevelt expanded the responsibilities and prerogatives of the office on a variety of fronts, including the establishment of a federal government role in arbitrating labor disputes and in regulating business. Roosevelt declared, "Wherever it is practicable we propose to preserve competition; but where . . . competition has been eliminated and cannot be successfully restored, then the Government must step in and itself supply the needed control."

Making Connections Across Time

Federal Power Theodore Roosevelt, from the progressive wing of the Republican party, pushed for a stronger federal government that would regulate business excesses. A number of politicians today, including many in the Republican party, have argued for less government regulation and a smaller federal government, with more power returned to state and local authorities. Allow students to argue these issues in a formal or informal debate, perhaps modeled on a TV political show.

cannot so exist." The young president soon met the first challenge to his assertion of federal power.

1902 COAL STRIKE When 140,000 coal miners in Pennsylvania went on strike and demanded a 20 percent raise, a 9-hour day, and the right to organize a union, the mine operators refused to bargain or even to meet with the labor leaders. George Baer, a multimillionaire mine owner and the president of the Reading Railroad, felt a religious duty to defeat the strikers. He stated, "The rights and interests of the laboring men will be protected and cared for—not by labor agitators, but by the Christian men to whom God in his infinite wisdom has given control of the property interests of this country." President Roosevelt denounced Baer's claim as arrogant.

Five months into the strike, winter threatened and coal reserves ran low. Schools and factories shut down, and patients shivered in icy hospitals. Instead of calling out the troops, Roosevelt called both sides to the White House to talk. Irked by the "extraordinary stupidity and bad temper" of the mine operators, he later confessed that only the dignity of the presidency had kept him from taking one owner "by the seat of his breeches" and tossing him out of the window.

FEDERAL ARBITRATION Faced with Roosevelt's threat to take over the mines, the opposing sides finally agreed to an arbitration commission to settle the strike. In 1903, the commission issued its findings, which included a wage increase and a reduction in the workday. In a compromise settlement, the miners won a 10 percent pay hike and a 9-hour day but gave up their demand for a closed shop—in which all workers must belong to the union—and their right to strike for three years.

President Roosevelt's actions had demonstrated a new principle. From then on, when a strike threatened the public welfare, the federal government was expected to intervene. In addition, Roosevelt's actions reflected the progressive belief that disputes could be settled in an orderly way with the help of experts, such as those on the arbitration commission.

TRUSTBUSTING Roosevelt also used his mediation skills to deal with the problem of trusts. By 1900, trusts controlled about four-fifths of the industries in the United States. Some trusts like Standard Oil had earned poor reputations with the American public by using unfair business practices. Many trusts lowered their prices to drive competitors out of the market and then took advantage of lack of competition in the industry to jack prices up even higher. In 1890, Congress had passed the Sherman Antitrust Act. The act's vague language, however, made enforcement difficult; nearly all the suits filed against the trusts under the Sherman act were ineffective.

President Roosevelt did not believe that all trusts were harmful. "Good" trusts had a conscience, while "bad" trusts greedily abused the public. He sought to curb trusts when their actions hurt the public interest, but he also maintained that only big business could ensure national greatness. Explaining his cautious approach to trustbusting, Roosevelt said, "The man who advocates destroying the trusts by measures which would paralyze the industries of the country is at least a quack, and at worst an enemy to the Republic."

The president concentrated his efforts on filing suits under the Sherman Antitrust Act. In 1902,

HINK THROUGH HISTORY
B. Recognizing Effects What was significant about the way the 1902 Pennsylvania coal strike was settled?
B. Answer From that point on, the federal government played a more active role in settling labor disputes.

"In life, as in a football game, the principle to follow is: Hit the line hard."

THEODORE ROOSEVELT

Skillbuilder Answer
Cartoonist's view: Possible Answer: The cartoonist views Roosevelt as the fearless lion tamer who has tamed the trusts, which are as fierce and powerful as lions. *Lions: Possible Answer:* Wall Street is a symbol for the country's most powerful financial interests.

SKILLBUILDER
INTERPRETING POLITICAL CARTOONS
How does the cartoonist seem to view Theodore Roosevelt? Why are all the lions in the cartoon coming out of a door marked **Wall St.?**

THE LION-TAMER

The Progressive Era **507**

MORE ABOUT . . .
George Baer
Baer worked as a printer's apprentice before becoming owner of a Pennsylvania newspaper. After studying law, he rose from legal counsel to president of the Philadelphia & Reading (pronounced "Redding") Railroad. His mining and railroading interests were connected: the Philadelphia & Reading—later just called the Reading Railroad—developed mainly as a means of transporting coal from the mines of Pennsylvania, and in fact became America's largest carrier of anthracite coal. An associate of multimillionaire financier J. P. Morgan, Baer himself left an estate of $15 million when he died.

HISTORY FROM VISUALS
Political Cartoon

Reading the Cartoon
Have a student explain what the character of Theodore Roosevelt appears to be doing in the cartoon. *Using a whip to keep the lions, or trusts, in control.* Then ask whether students think this is a positive or negative portrayal of Roosevelt. *Possible Responses: Most students may indicate that the ordinary citizen would see this as a positive portrayal of Roosevelt, while business interests would see it as negative.*

Extension Ask students to discuss whether the relationship today between the U.S. president and big business interests would be portrayed in the same way.

 Cooperative Activity: Creating Political Cartoons

Task: Groups of students will design and create four or five political cartoons on a single subject.

Purpose: To discover how humor and exaggeration can effectively convey political ideas.

Activity: Tell students that their collections should focus on a single national, regional, or local issue—perhaps a school-related matter, such as conditions in the cafeteria or problems with school funding. The entire group should brainstorm for ideas. Then one artistically

inclined group member can do the drawings and another can add any captions, labels, or speech bubbles required. Remaining group members can arrange the cartoons for presentation.

📁 **Building a Portfolio:** Have students attach notes to the cartoons indicating their own contributions to the project.

ALTERNATIVE ASSESSMENT BOOK
Standards for Evaluating a Cooperative Activity

Standards for Evaluation
Cartoons should . . .

• communicate a message visually rather than just through words
• make their subjects clear
• use humor or exaggeration to make their points

Protecting Citizens and the Environment

Have students make a chart like this one to detail Roosevelt administration reforms.

Law	Date	Details
Meat Inspection Act	1906	strict cleanliness for meatpackers

▶ **Discussing Key Ideas**
- In 1906 Congress passes the Meat Inspection Act and the Pure Food and Drug Act.
- Roosevelt supports conservation.

MORE ABOUT . . .
Upton Sinclair

The Jungle was rejected by many publishers, and Sinclair himself finally paid for its publication. When it proved a bestseller, he used the proceeds to found a cooperative-living community that he was forced to abandon when it burned down. In 1934, he lost a bid to become governor of California.

HISTORY FROM VISUALS
Meat Inspection

Reading the Art Ask which details show the attempt to make meat safer. *Possible Responses: Sign for government inspector; butcher's clean smock.*

OUR TIMES
Upton Sinclair

ELECTRONIC LIBRARY OF PRIMARY SOURCES
from "Whatever Is, Is Wrong" by E. W. Scripps

"We recognize and are bound to war against the evils of today."

THEODORE ROOSEVELT

Roosevelt made newspaper headlines as a trustbuster when he ordered the Justice Department to sue the Northern Securities Company, which had established a monopoly over northwestern railroads. In 1904, the Supreme Court ordered the dissolution of the Northern Securities Company. Roosevelt also sued the beef trust, the oil trust, and the tobacco trust.

In all, the Roosevelt administration filed 44 antitrust suits. The government won a number of cases and broke up some of the trusts, but it was unable to slow the merger movement in business. Indeed, though Roosevelt won a reputation as a trustbuster, his real goal was federal regulation.

RAILROAD REGULATION Roosevelt was more successful in railroad regulation. In 1887, Congress had passed the Interstate Commerce Act, which prohibited "pools" in which wealthy railroad owners divided the business in a given area and shared the profits. The act also set up the Interstate Commerce Commission (ICC) to enforce the new law. Before Roosevelt's administration, however, the Interstate Commerce Commission had had little power. Railroad owners could bypass the ICC merely by appealing its decisions to federal courts, which could delay a finding for as long as ten years.

With Roosevelt's urging, Congress put some teeth into the ICC. The Elkins Act of 1903 made it illegal for railroad officials and shippers either to give or to receive rebates. The act also specified that once a railroad had set rates, it could not change them without notifying the public.

The Hepburn Act of 1906 strictly limited the distribution of free railroad passes, a common form of bribery. It also gave the ICC power to set maximum railroad rates, subject to court approval, whenever shippers complained. Within two years, the commission had received thousands of complaints and lowered many rates. To win passage of the act, Roosevelt had to compromise with conservative senators who opposed it. In its final form the act did not completely satisfy Wisconsin's Senator Robert La Follette and other reformers, but it nevertheless boosted the government's power to regulate the railroads.

Protecting Citizens and the Environment

Government workers inspected meat as it moved through the packinghouse.

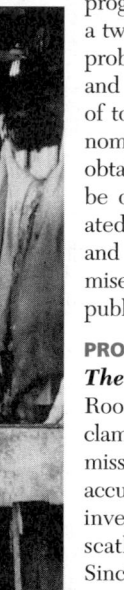

President Roosevelt also promoted laws to protect citizens from unsafe food and drugs and to protect the environment from pollution by businesses. Armed with progressive ideals, Roosevelt advocated a two-pronged approach to solve these problems. He wrote, "We recognize and are bound to war against the evils of today. The remedies are partly economic and partly spiritual, partly to be obtained by laws, and in greater part to be obtained by individual and associated effort." Roosevelt's enthusiasm and his considerable skill at compromise led to policies that benefited both public health and the environment.

PROTECTING HEALTH After reading ***The Jungle*** by **Upton Sinclair,** Roosevelt listened to the public's clamor for action. He appointed a commission of experts to report on the accuracy of Sinclair's descriptions. The investigating commission issued a scathing report that backed up Sinclair's description of "potted ham"

TEACHING OPTIONS

Making Connections Across the Curriculum

Economics Clarify that a trust was a monopoly, or a supplier offering a product or service exclusively, with no market competition. Then have students discuss the benefits and drawbacks of monopolies. Point out that drawbacks include the ability to charge very high prices or produce an inferior product, since the buyer cannot switch to a competitor; benefits include efficiency in meeting market needs or in consolidating the different areas of service and production (which could lead to lower prices).

Teaching Gifted and Talented Students

Influential Books Encourage students to read and report on *The Jungle* or another influential turn-of-the-century book encouraging social reform. Possibilities include these:

- *Looking Backward* by Edward Bellamy
- *The Octopus* by Frank Norris
- *The Shame of the Cities* by Lincoln Steffens
- *An American Tragedy* by Theodore Dreiser
- *The History of the Standard Oil Company* by Ida M. Tarbell

Students' reports should include a summary of the book, information about its author, and an explanation of its impact at the time.

as a hash whose disgusting ingredients included ground rope and pigskin. True to his word, in 1906 Roosevelt pushed for passage of the **Meat Inspection Act,** which dictated strict cleanliness requirements for meatpackers and created the program of federal meat inspection that was used for decades.

Like the Hepburn Act, the Meat Inspection Act supported the progressive principle of government regulation. The compromise that won the act's passage, however, left the government paying for the inspections and did not require companies to label their canned goods with date-of-processing information. The compromise also granted meatpackers the right to appeal negative decisions in court.

PURE FOOD AND DRUG ACT That same year, Congress passed the **Pure Food and Drug Act,** which halted the sale of contaminated foods or medicines and called for truth in labeling. Credit for the Pure Food and Drug Act belongs largely to Dr. Harvey Washington Wiley, chief chemist at the Department of Agriculture. On lectures across the country, Wiley criticized manufacturers for adding harmful preservatives to food—chemicals, such as coal-tar dye and borax, in sausage, and formaldehyde in canned pork and beans.

Before passage of the Pure Food and Drug Act, manufacturers advertised that their products accomplished everything from curing cancer to growing hair. In addition, popular children's medicines often contained opium, cocaine, or alcohol. Colden's Liquid Beef Tonic, recommended for "treatment of the alcohol habit," itself packed a walloping dose of 26.5 percent alcohol.

By 1906, however, the largest food and medicine manufacturers were eager to regain public confidence by supporting increased federal regulation. The Pure Food and Drug Act did not ban harmful products outright. Nevertheless, its requirement of truthful labels reflected the progressive belief that given accurate information, people would act wisely.

CONSERVATION AND NATURAL RESOURCES Before Roosevelt's presidency, the federal government had paid very little attention to the nation's natural resources. Despite the establishment of the U.S. Forest Bureau in 1887 and the withdrawal from public sale of several million acres of timberlands for a

U.S. National Parks, 1872–1947

Olympic 1938
Mount Rainier 1899
Glacier 1910
Isle Royale 1931
Acadia 1919
Yellowstone 1872
Crater Lake 1902
Lassen Volcanic 1916
Grand Teton 1929
Wind Cave 1903
Badlands 1939
Yosemite 1890
Rocky Mountain 1915
Shenandoah 1935
Kings Canyon 1890
Bryce Canyon 1924
Zion 1919
Mesa Verde 1906
Mammoth Cave 1941
Sequoia 1890
Grand Canyon 1919
Great Smoky Mountains 1934
Hot Springs 1921
Carlsbad Caverns 1930
Big Bend 1944
Denali 1917
Everglades 1947

○ Parks created by 1908
● Parks created 1908–1947

GEOGRAPHY SKILLBUILDER
LOCATION *Which state had the most parks in 1947?*
HUMAN/ ENVIRONMENT INTERACTION *What does the growth of the national park system after 1908 suggest about Roosevelt's impact on conservation?*

The Progressive Era **509**

A Scottish native, Muir immigrated to Wisconsin as a boy. He worked as an industrial inventor until sustaining an eye injury, then turned to a career as a naturalist. Settling in California, he spent his time growing fruit trees, traveling throughout the western states and Alaska, and campaigning for government preservation of western forests. His efforts helped establish Sequoia and Yosemite national parks in 1890. Muir was founder of the Sierra Club, an environmental group still active today.

"Thousands of . . . over-civilized people are beginning to find out that going to the mountains is going home."

JOHN MUIR

MORE ABOUT . . .
Yosemite National Park

Muir believed that glaciers created the formations along Yosemite Valley, a speculation with which many scientists now agree. The valley region contains such wonders as Yosemite Falls and El Capitán, the highest of several peaks.

Du Bois (*second from the right in the second row,*) and other civil rights leaders pose for a group photo at the first meeting of the Niagara movement in 1905.

OBJECTIVE
④ INSTRUCT

Roosevelt and Civil Rights

▶ *Discussing Key Ideas*
• Roosevelt does little for civil rights in general but sometimes champions the rights of individual African Americans.
• W. E. B. Du Bois joins others in the Niagara Movement, which in 1909 evolves into the National Association for the Advancement of Colored People (NAACP).

national forest reserve, the government stood by while private interests gobbled up the shrinking wilderness.

Americans had shortsightedly exploited their natural environment. Pioneer farmers leveled the forests and plowed up the prairies. Ranchers allowed their cattle to overgraze the Great Plains. Coal companies cluttered the land with spoil dumps. Lumber companies ignored the effect of their logging operations on flood control and neglected to plant trees to replace those they had cut down. Cities dumped untreated sewage and industrial wastes into rivers, poisoning the streams and creating health hazards.

Roosevelt condemned the view that America's resources were endless. In fact, on assuming the presidency, Roosevelt deemed forest and water problems a vital concern for the country. He proceeded to attack environmental problems with his characteristic zeal, even banning Christmas trees in the White House in 1902. John Muir, a naturalist and writer with whom Roosevelt camped in California's Yosemite National Park in 1903, persuaded the president to set aside 148 million acres of forest reserves. Roosevelt also set aside 1.5 million acres of water-power sites and another 80 million acres of land that experts from the U.S. Geological Survey would explore for mineral and water resources.

To help preserve the "beautiful and wonderful wild creatures whose existence was threatened by greed," Roosevelt established more than 50 wildlife sanctuaries and several national parks.

GIFFORD PINCHOT True to the progressive belief in using experts, in 1905 the president named Gifford Pinchot, a professional conservationist, as head of the U.S. Forest Service. Armed with administrative skill as well as the latest scientific and technical information, Pinchot advised Roosevelt to conserve forest and grazing lands by keeping large tracts of federal land exempt from private sale.

Conservationists like Roosevelt and Pinchot, however, did not share the views of Muir, who advocated complete preservation of the wilderness. Instead, **conservation** meant that some wilderness areas would be preserved while others would be developed for the common good. Indeed, Roosevelt's federal water projects transformed some dry wilderness areas to make agriculture possible. Under the National Reclamation Act of 1901, known as the Newlands Act, money from the sale of public lands in the West funded large-scale irrigation projects, such as the Roosevelt Dam in Arizona and the Shoshone Dam in Wyoming. The Newlands Act established the precedent that the federal government would manage the precious water resources in the West. However, this was quite a different position from Muir's, who wanted to preserve the wilderness as it was.

Roosevelt's care for the land and its inhabitants was not matched in the area of civil rights.

E. Answer
Roosevelt worked for conservation, including setting aside 148 million acres of forest reserves.

THINK THROUGH HISTORY
E. Summarizing *Summarize Roosevelt's approach to environmental problems.*

Roosevelt and Civil Rights

Though Roosevelt's father had been a Northern abolitionist, his mother, Mittie, may well have been the model for Southern belle Scarlett O'Hara in Margaret Mitchell's famous novel, *Gone with the Wind.* In almost two terms as president, Roosevelt —like most other progressives—was no supporter of civil rights for African Americans. He did, however, support a few individual African Americans.

TEACHING OPTIONS

Making Connections Across the Curriculum

Geography Muir once walked all the way from Indianapolis, Indiana, to the Gulf of Mexico, keeping a nature journal that he later published. Have students write their own journal entries about a real or imagined visit to a national or state park in your area. Students who need to research their details might consult travel books, newspaper and magazine articles, and free travel brochures from the park in question.

Making Connections Across Time

Environmental Controversy The debate between conservation and preservation continues today. In September 1996 President Clinton, a Democrat, created the Grand Staircase-Escalante National Monument in southern Utah, placing 1.7 million acres of red-rock cliffs and canyons off limits to coal mining and other development. The decision, praised by environmental groups, sparked controversy among Utah's mostly Republican politicians, who felt that portions of the area should be considered for development that would enhance Utah's economy. Have a panel of students debate this or similar environmental controversies.

Despite opposition from whites, Roosevelt appointed an African American as head of the Charleston, South Carolina, customhouse. He also refused to bow to the demands of some whites that he dismiss the black postmistress of a Mississippi post office, and chose instead to close the station. In 1906, however, Roosevelt angered many African Americans when he dismissed without question an entire regiment of African-American soldiers accused of rioting in Brownsville, Texas.

As a symbolic gesture, Roosevelt invited the African-American leader Booker T. Washington to join him for dinner at the White House. At the time, no African American enjoyed more respect from powerful whites than Washington, who was head of an all-black university, Tuskegee Institute. However, Washington faced opposition from African Americans for his accommodation of segregationists.

Persistent in his criticism of Washington's ideas, W. E. B. Du Bois renewed his demands for immediate social and economic equality for African Americans. In his 1903 book, *The Souls of Black Folk*, Du Bois wrote of his opposition to Washington's position.

A PERSONAL VOICE
So far as Mr. Washington preaches Thrift, Patience, and Industrial Training for the masses, we must hold up his hands and strive with him. . . . But so far as Mr. Washington apologizes for injustice, North or South, does not rightly value the privilege and duty of voting, belittles the emasculating effects of caste distinctions, and opposes the higher training and ambition of our brighter minds—so far as he, the South, or the Nation, does this,—we must unceasingly and firmly oppose them.

W. E. B. DU BOIS, *The Souls of Black Folk*

Du Bois and other advocates of equality for African Americans were deeply upset by the apparent progressive indifference to racial injustice. They held a conference at Niagara Falls in 1905. In 1909, a number of African Americans joined with prominent white reformers in New York to found the National Association for the Advancement of Colored People (**NAACP**), which had about 6,000 members by 1914. The NAACP aimed for nothing less than full equality among the races. That goal, however, found little support in the progressive movement, which focused on the needs of middle-class whites. The two presidents who followed Roosevelt also did little to advance the goal of racial equality.

KEY PLAYER

W. E. B. DU BOIS
1868–1963

W. E. B. Du Bois's establishment of the NAACP in 1909—and his role as its publicity and research director—put him at the forefront of the early U.S. civil rights movement. However, in the 1920s, he faced a power struggle with the NAACP's executive secretary, Walter White.

Ironically, Du Bois had retreated to a position others saw as dangerously close to that of Booker T. Washington. Arguing for a separate economy for African Americans, Du Bois made a distinction between enforced and voluntary segregation that White rejected. By mid-century, Du Bois was outside the mainstream of the civil rights movement. His work remained largely ignored until the 1960s.

Du Bois died on August 27, 1963, the day Martin Luther King, Jr., led the March on Washington—a powerful protest against racial discrimination in America.

Section ③ Assessment

1. TERMS & NAMES

Identify:
- Theodore Roosevelt
- Square Deal
- *The Jungle*
- Upton Sinclair
- Meat Inspection Act
- Pure Food and Drug Act
- conservation
- NAACP

2. SUMMARIZING Create a diagram like this one to show how these problems were solved during Roosevelt's presidency: (a) 1902 coal strike, (b) Northern Securities Company's monopoly, (c) unsafe meat processing, and (d) exploitation of the environment.

Problem	→	Solution

Write headlines announcing the solutions.

3. SYNTHESIZING In what ways do you think the progressive belief in using experts played a role in shaping Roosevelt's reforms? Use details from the text to support your answer.

THINK ABOUT
- Roosevelt's use of experts to help him tackle political, economic, or environmental problems
- how experts' findings affected legislative actions

4. DRAWING CONCLUSIONS How did Theodore Roosevelt expand the role of the federal government? Refer to specific passages in the chapter in your response.

The Progressive Era **511**

TERMS & NAMES
• Gifford Pinchot
• William Howard Taft
• Payne-Aldrich Tariff
• Bull Moose Party
• Woodrow Wilson

Section 4 Overview

FOCUS & MOTIVATE

▶ **Starting with the Student**
• Have students jot down notes about a time when they had to give an oral report just after a class-mate had given a great one, or when they followed a terrific athlete in a sport in which they don't excel.
• Discuss how the statement "That's a tough act to follow" could apply to that situation.

OBJECTIVE **1** INSTRUCT

Taft Becomes President

▶ **Discussing Key Ideas**
• Refusing a third term, Roosevelt hand picks his successor, William Howard Taft, who beats William Jennings Bryan in 1908.
• Taft angers his party's progressive wing by failing to lower tariffs and by appointing a secretary of the interior who is unsympathetic toward conservation.

4 Progressivism Under Taft

LEARN ABOUT the policies of the Taft administration
TO UNDERSTAND the growing conflict between progressive reform and business interests.

ONE AMERICAN'S STORY

Early in the 20th century, American interest in the preservation of the country's wilderness areas intensified. Popular writers sang the praises of America's vistas, while newly founded groups like the Girl Scouts provided city children with an escape from their urban environment. Preservationists, however, faced off against groups with business interests that favored the land's unrestricted development. Conservationists like **Gifford Pinchot** staked a middle ground. Head of the U.S. Forest Service under President Roosevelt, Pinchot believed that wilderness areas could be scientifically managed to yield public enjoyment while allowing private development.

Gifford Pinchot

> ### A PERSONAL VOICE
> The American people have evidently made up their minds that our natural resources must be conserved. That is good, but it settles only half the question. For whose benefit shall they be conserved—for the benefit of the many, or for the use and profit of the few? . . . There is no other question before us that begins to be so important, or that will be so difficult to straddle, as the great question between special interest and equal opportunity, between the privileges of the few and the rights of the many, between government by men for human welfare and government by money for profit. . . .
>
> **GIFFORD PINCHOT,** *The Fight for Conservation*

Pinchot's multi-use land program suited his friend and fellow conservationist, Theodore Roosevelt. When Roosevelt left office in 1908, however, Pinchot's approach came under increasing pressure from business people who favored unrestricted commercial development.

Taft Becomes President

As soon as Roosevelt won election in 1904, he pledged not to run for reelection in 1908. Popular enough to designate a successor, Roosevelt hand-picked his secretary of war, **William Howard Taft,** to carry out his policies.

For the third time, the Democrats nominated William Jennings Bryan, who campaigned on the slogan of "Let the people rule." The people, however, ignored Bryan's call for a federal income tax, a lower tariff, and new antitrust laws. "Vote for Taft this time," the Republicans said, "You can vote for Bryan any time." And vote for Taft the people did. The gigantic man—6 feet tall and 350 pounds—captured an easy victory.

TAFT STUMBLES As president, Taft pursued a cautiously progressive agenda, but received little credit for his accomplishments. While the so-called trust-buster, Roosevelt, had noisily busted 44 trusts in 7½ years in office, Taft busted 90 trusts in a 4-year term. However, Taft's legal victories did not bolster his popularity. Indeed, the new president confessed in a letter to Roosevelt that he never felt like the president. "When I am addressed as 'Mr. President,'" Taft wrote, "I turn to see whether you are not at my elbow."

SECTION 4 RESOURCES

THINK THROUGH HISTORY
A. Contrasting
Contrast President Taft with Theodore Roosevelt.

A. Answer Unlike Roosevelt, Taft was cautious and unable to unify his own party. He did not use his position to shape public opinion.

The cautious Taft hesitated to use the presidential bully pulpit to arouse public opinion. Nor could he subdue troublesome members of his own party. Tariffs and conservation posed his first problems.

THE PAYNE–ALDRICH TARIFF Taft had campaigned on a platform of lowering tariffs, a staple of the progressive agenda. The House duly passed the Payne bill, which would lower rates on many manufactured goods. In the Senate, however, conservative Republicans eliminated most of the cuts. In fact, only hides, canary birdseed, and sea moss remained on the duty-free list. Amid cries of betrayal from the progressive wing of his party, Taft signed the **Payne-Aldrich Tariff.**

The president made his difficulties worse by clumsily attempting to defend the tariff. Before a hostile audience of grain growers in Winona, Minnesota, Taft asserted that the new law was "the best [tariff] bill the Republican party ever passed." Later, he tried to repair the damage, but only made matters more difficult when he explained that he had dictated the speech hurriedly between two railroad stations without bothering to reread it.

DISPUTING PUBLIC LANDS Next, Taft angered conservationists by appointing as his Secretary of the Interior Richard A. Ballinger. Ballinger was a wealthy Seattle lawyer who disapproved of conservationist controls on western lands. The new secretary removed one million acres of forest and mining lands from the reserved list and approved the sale to Seattle businesses of several million acres of coal-rich land in Alaska. These businesses then sold their holdings to a group of New York bankers, including J. P. Morgan, who for many Americans symbolized the power of money. However, Ballinger's decisions delighted western entrepreneurs.

B. Answer Ballinger didn't approve of conservationist controls on western lands.

THINK THROUGH HISTORY
B. Analyzing Issues Why did Taft's appointment of Richard Ballinger anger conservationists?

When a Department of the Interior official was fired for protesting Ballinger's actions, he published a muckraking article against Ballinger in *Collier's Weekly* magazine. Then, in congressional testimony in January 1910, Pinchot added his voice and accused Ballinger of letting commercial interests exploit the natural resources that rightfully belonged to the public.

As a result, President Taft reluctantly fired Pinchot from the U.S. Forest Service. Retaliating in a book called *The Fight for Conservation,* Pinchot wrote, "The more successful the Forest Service has been in preventing land-grabbing and the absorption of water power by the special interests, the more ingenious, the more devious, and the more dangerous these attacks have become."

The Republican Party Splits

Taft's cautious nature made it impossible for him to hold together the two wings of the Republican Party: progressives who sought change and conservatives who did not. Roosevelt had asserted, "I believe in a strong executive," but Taft followed a course of presidential restraint. While Taft remained above the fray, the Republican Party began to fragment.

PROBLEMS WITHIN THE PARTY Republican conservatives and progressives split over Taft's support of political boss Joseph Cannon, Speaker of the House of Representatives. A poker-playing, rough-talking, tobacco-chewing politician, "Uncle Joe" not only disregarded seniority in filling committee slots but also anointed himself head of the Committee on Rules, which decided the bills Congress would consider. Under Cannon's virtual dictatorship, the House often ignored or weakened progressive bills.

Difficult Decisions
IN HISTORY

CONTROLLING RESOURCES
The question of what to do with wilderness areas became more urgent in the 1990s with the spotted owl controversy in the Pacific Northwest. Loggers protested that laws to safeguard the owl's habitat would deprive them of the opportunity to make a living.

Historically, conservationists such as Gifford Pinchot stood for balanced use of natural resources, preserving some and using others for private industry. Free market advocates like Richard Ballinger spoke for private development of wilderness areas. Preservationists such as John Muir advocated preserving the remaining wilderness.

1. Examine the pros and cons of each position. With which do you agree? What other factors, if any, do you think should influence decisions about America's wilderness areas?
2. If you'd been asked to decide in 1902 whether to develop or preserve America's wilderness areas, what would you have decided?

William Howard Taft

513

DIFFICULT DECISIONS IN HISTORY
Controlling Resources
Student responses may include the following:

1. Factors may include job loss, health concerns, unknown results of upsetting the balance of nature, and the danger of letting potentially useful species become extinct.
2. Some students will indicate that the wilderness should be preserved at all costs. Others may suggest that, in 1902, the need to develop the West may have seemed vital—and, at that time, the West may still have seemed too vast to be overexploited.

GROLIER MULTIMEDIA ENCYCLOPEDIA
History of conservation in the United States

OBJECTIVE
(2) **INSTRUCT**

The Republican Party Splits

▶ *Starting with the Student*
• Ask students how different goals might break up once-loyal friendships.
• Discuss whether this is likely to happen in political friendships.

▶ *Discussing Key Ideas*
• Taft's support of Republican boss Joe Cannon further alienates progressive Republicans.
• The party splits, and Roosevelt becomes leader of the Bull Moose Party.

HUMANITIES TRANSPARENCIES
H36, Goodness Gracious, I Must Have Been Dozing

TEACHING OPTIONS

Making Connections Across the Curriculum

Economics A tariff is a tax on imports that the public pays indirectly when its costs are passed along to consumers. A protectionist trade policy uses tariffs to protect domestic industry (and jobs), keeping out foreign goods or making their prices too high to compete with equivalent domestic products. A free-trade policy allows foreign goods to enter the country with lower or no tariffs so that consumers benefit from lower prices. Since nations usually reciprocate in tariff policies, lowering tariffs in one country encourages foreign countries to lower their tariffs on exports from that country.

Making Connections Across Time

Party Turmoil and the Elections of 1912 and 1992 The split in the Republican party that preceded the 1912 presidential election would be echoed in the election of 1992—though not to the same degree. In 1992, third-party candidate Ross Perot, like Roosevelt, was a former Republican who split from the party and ran on a reform platform. The elections were also similar in other ways. An incumbent Republican, George Bush, had succeeded a more popular one, Ronald Reagan, and a Democrat, Bill Clinton, won with just over 40 percent of the vote.

A group of reform-minded Republicans decided that their only alternative was to strip Cannon of his power. With the help of Democrats, they finally succeeded in March 1910. George W. Norris of Nebraska presented a resolution—adopted after hours of stormy debate —that called for the entire House to elect the Committee on Rules.

By the midterm elections of 1910, the Republican Party was in a shambles, with the progressives on one side and the "old guard" on the other. Voters voiced concern over the rising cost of living, which they blamed on the Payne-Aldrich Tariff. They also believed Taft to be against conservation. When the Republicans lost the election, the Democrats gained control of the House of Representatives for the first time in 18 years.

THE BULL MOOSE PARTY After Taft's election, Roosevelt had gone to Africa to shoot big game. He returned in 1910 to a hero's welcome. People sang "When Rough and Ready Teddy Dashes Home" and "Mr. Roosevelt, Our Country Calls for You." Roosevelt responded by delivering a rousing speech and declaring that the country needed a "New Nationalism," under which the federal government would extend its power for "the welfare of the people."

By 1912, Roosevelt had decided to run for a third term as president. Taft, however, had the advantage of being the incumbent—that is, a candidate for an office he already held. At the Republican convention in June 1912, Taft's supporters refused to seat Roosevelt delegates and renominated Taft on the first ballot. Screaming "fraud," Roosevelt's supporters stormed out and held their own convention in August. There they formed a new third party, the Progressive Party, and nominated Roosevelt for president in an atmosphere of near hysteria. "We stand at Armageddon," Roosevelt proclaimed, invoking the biblical battle between good and evil. "We battle for the Lord."

The Progressive Party became known as the **Bull Moose Party,** after Roosevelt's boast that he was "as strong as a bull moose." The Bull Moose platform called for the direct election of senators and the adoption in all states of the initiative, referendum, and recall. It also advocated woman suffrage, national workmen's compensation, an eight-hour workday, a minimum wage for women, a federal law against child labor, and a federal trade commission to regulate business.

The split in the Republican ranks between the Bull Moose Party and Taft's conservative Republicans handed the Democrats their first real chance at the White House since the election of Grover Cleveland in 1892. In the 1912 presidential election, they put forward as their candidate a reform governor of New Jersey named **Woodrow Wilson.**

The Election of 1912

Under Governor Woodrow Wilson's leadership, the previously conservative New Jersey legislature had passed a host of reform measures. Now, as the Democratic presidential nominee, Wilson endorsed a progressive platform called the New Freedom that demanded even stronger antitrust legislation, banking reform, and reduced tariffs.

The split between Taft and Roosevelt, former Republican allies, turned nasty during the fall campaign. Taft labeled Roosevelt a "dangerous egotist," while Roosevelt

Roosevelt campaigns for president in 1912 in Morrisville, Vermont.

branded Taft a "fathead" with the brain of a "guinea pig." Wilson stayed above the political feud, quietly gloating, "Don't interfere when your enemy is destroying himself."

The election offered voters several choices: Wilson's New Freedom, Taft's conservatism, Roosevelt's progressivism, or the Socialist Party policies of Eugene V. Debs. Both Roosevelt and Wilson supported a stronger government role in economic affairs but differed over strategies. Roosevelt supported government action to supervise big business but did not oppose all big business monopolies. Wilson supported small business and free-market competition, and characterized all big business monopolies as evil. In a speech in which Wilson declared that America stood for "a free field and no favor," he explained why he felt that all business monopolies were a threat.

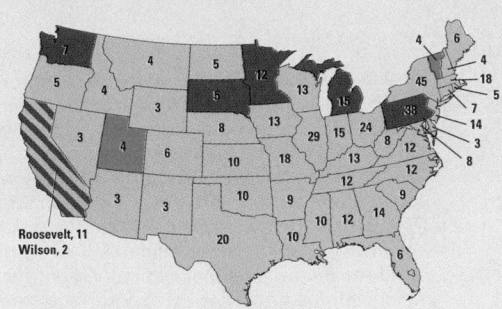

Election of 1912

ELECTORAL AND POPULAR VOTES

Party	Candidate	Electoral votes	Popular vote
■ Democratic	Woodrow Wilson	435	6,296,547
■ Progressive	Theodore Roosevelt	88	4,118,571
■ Republican	William H. Taft	8	3,486,720
Socialist	Eugene V. Debs	0	900,672

Roosevelt, 11
Wilson, 2

A PERSONAL VOICE

If the government is to tell big business men how to run their business, then don't you see that big business men have to get closer to the government even than they are now? Don't you see that they must capture the government, in order not to be restrained too much by it? . . . I don't care how benevolent the master is going to be, I will not live under a master. That is not what America was created for. America was created in order that every man should have the same chance as every other man to exercise mastery over his own fortunes.

Woodrow Wilson, quoted in *The New Freedom*

Debs, who polled over 900,000 popular votes (6 percent of the total), went further than Wilson and Roosevelt, and called for an end to capitalism. He wanted to use the government not only to regulate business and bust trusts, but also to distribute national wealth more equally among the people.

Although Wilson captured only 42 percent of the popular vote, he won an electoral victory and a Democratic majority in Congress. As a third-party candidate, Roosevelt defeated Taft in both popular and electoral votes. But reform claimed the real victory, with 75 percent of the vote going to reform candidates Wilson, Roosevelt, and Debs. In victory, Wilson could claim a mandate to break up trusts and to expand the government's role in social reform.

D. Answer: Taft favored business; **Roosevelt:** supported government control of some big businesses; **Wilson** supported small businesses and thought monopolies were evil; **Debs** thought the national wealth should be distributed more equally.

THINK THROUGH HISTORY
D. Contrasting Contrast the views toward big business of the four major candidates for president in 1912.

Section 4 Assessment

1. TERMS & NAMES

Identify:
• Gifford Pinchot
• William Howard Taft
• Payne-Aldrich Tariff
• Bull Moose Party
• Woodrow Wilson

2. SUMMARIZING Recreate the chart below on your paper. Then fill in the causes or actions Taft took that made people question his leadership.

Which causes do you think would offend most people today? Explain.

3. HYPOTHESIZING What if Roosevelt had won another term in office in 1912? Speculate on how this might have affected the future of progressive reform. Support your answer.

THINK ABOUT
• Roosevelt's policies that Taft did not support
• the power struggles within the Republican party
• Roosevelt's perception of presidential leadership

4. FORMING OPINIONS Both Roosevelt and Taft resorted to mudslinging during the 1912 presidential campaign. Do you approve or disapprove of negative campaign tactics? Support your opinion.

THINK ABOUT
• Roosevelt's and Taft's name-calling
• how you've reacted to negative campaign ads you've seen on television

The Progressive Era **515**

ANSWERS

1. TERMS & NAMES

Gifford Pinchot, p. 512

William Howard Taft, p. 512

Payne-Aldrich Tariff, p. 513

Bull Moose Party, p. 514

Woodrow Wilson, p. 514

2. SUMMARIZING

Possible Answers: Signed Payne-Aldrich Tariff amid public outcry; returned reserved land to public sale; fired Pinchot; supported Joseph Cannon, Speaker of the House of Representatives; contributed to split in the Republican Party. Students' responses about offending causes will vary but should include an explanation of their opinions.

3. HYPOTHESIZING

Possible Responses: Unlike Taft, Roosevelt would probably not have caved in to the conservatives in the Republican party, his reform policies would have been stronger. Roosevelt would probably have undone Taft's more conservative, less progressive policies and decisions in an attempt to restore a stronger government role in public affairs.

4. FORMING OPINIONS

Possible Responses: Students who approve might say that negative campaign tactics often help candidates win votes and that these tactics can get to the heart of key issues, especially the candidate's character. Students who disapprove might say that negative campaign tactics can alienate the public and cause candidates to lose votes and that these tactics can encourage dishonesty.

HISTORY FROM VISUALS
Election of 1912
Reading the Map Point out to students that if Roosevelt had not run— and if his votes had gone to Taft—Taft would have won over 50 percent of the vote in enough states to win the election.

ASSESS & RETEACH

Section 4 Assessment
Have students work individually to answer the questions. Then have them hold an informal debate on negative campaign tactics based on their answers to item 4.

Self-Assessment
Have students identify specific passages from the section that helped them answer each assessment question.

Section Quiz

FORMAL ASSESSMENT
Section Quiz, p. 212

Reteach
Ask students to share their responses to the Difficult Decisions questions on page 513. Students should draw on material in the text to support their opinions.

CLOSE

When Taft could not hold together the conservative and progressive wings of the Republican Party, the party split, allowing Democrat Woodrow Wilson to win the presidency in 1912.

OBJECTIVES

① To describe Woodrow Wilson's background and the progressive reforms of his presidency.

② To explain the steps leading to woman suffrage.

③ To sum up the limits of Wilson's progressivism.

SKILLBUILDER

• Interpreting graphs, p. 518

CRITICAL THINKING

• Comparing, p. 517
• Drawing conclusions, pp. 518, 521
• Summarizing, pp. 519, 521
• Recognizing effects, p. 520
• Developing historical perspective, p. 521

FOCUS & MOTIVATE

▶ **Starting with the Student**
• Ask students who the "movers and shakers" in your school or community are. Who knows how to get things done?
• Have students discuss the qualities that effective people share. Ask if they think those qualities would be found in a person described as "born halfway between the Bible and the dictionary."

MORE ABOUT . . .
Carrie Chapman Catt

Catt became active in the woman suffrage movement after the tragic death of her first husband, editor Leo Chapman, in 1886. When she married George W. Catt four years later, an unusual prenuptial agreement gave her four months each year to work for woman suffrage. After the retirement of Susan B. Anthony, Catt helped lead the suffrage movement to victory in 1920.

IN-DEPTH RESOURCES: UNIT 5
American Lives: Carrie Chapman Catt, p. 17

---

❺ Wilson's New Freedom

TERMS & NAMES
• Clayton Antitrust Act
• Federal Trade Commission
• Federal Reserve System
• Nineteenth Amendment

LEARN ABOUT Woodrow Wilson and his approach to reform
TO UNDERSTAND the victories and defeats for progressivism during his administration.

ONE AMERICAN'S STORY

When Woodrow Wilson arrived in Washington for his inauguration on March 3, 1913, he looked in vain for the cheering crowds. In fact, many Washingtonians had disappeared to watch a woman suffrage parade, in which 5,000 women marched through a hostile crowd on Pennsylvania Avenue. Alice Paul and Lucy Burns, the parade's organizers, were radical young members of the National American Woman Suffrage Association (NAWSA). As police failed to restrain the rowdy gathering and embarrassed congressmen demanded an investigation, Burns and Paul could see momentum building in the fight for suffrage.

Indeed, the battle for woman suffrage entered a bold new phase during the Wilson administration. By the time Wilson began his campaign for a second term, the NAWSA's president, Carrie Chapman Catt, saw victory on the horizon. Catt expressed her optimism in a letter to her friend Maud Wood Park.

Carrie Chapman Catt

> **A PERSONAL VOICE**
> I do feel keenly that the turn of the road has come. . . . I really believe that we might pull off a campaign which would mean the vote within the next six years if we could secure a Board of officers who would have sufficient momentum, confidence and working power in them. . . . Come! My dear Mrs. Park, gird on your armor once more.
> **CARRIE CHAPMAN CATT,** letter to Maud Wood Park, August 30, 1916

Catt called an emergency suffrage convention in September 1916, at which Wilson cautiously supported suffrage. He told the convention, "There has been a force behind you that will . . . be triumphant and for which you can afford to wait." They did have to wait, but within four years, the passage of the suffrage amendment became the capstone of the progressive movement.

Progressive Reform Under Wilson

Like Theodore Roosevelt, Woodrow Wilson claimed progressive ideals. While both presidents certainly believed in a strong executive, Wilson pictured a different role for the federal government than the one Roosevelt had favored. The new president didn't think that trusts should be regulated; he thought they should be broken up. He didn't think government should get bigger; he thought business should be made smaller. Wilson earned his progressive credentials by attacking large concentrations of power in an effort to give greater freedom to average citizens. However, the prejudices of his Southern background prevented him from using federal power to fight off attacks directed at the civil rights of African Americans.

WILSON'S BACKGROUND The son, grandson, and nephew of Presbyterian ministers, Wilson spent his youth in the South during the Civil War and Reconstruction. There he received a strict moral upbringing. In fact, a critic once said that the pious and scholarly Wilson had been "born halfway between the Bible and the dictionary and never got away from either." Though Wilson prac-

---

SECTION 5 RESOURCES

PRINT RESOURCES

IN-DEPTH RESOURCES: UNIT 5
Guided Reading, p. 5
Geography Application: The Movement Toward Woman Suffrage, p. 7
American Lives: Carrie Chapman Catt, p. 17

ACCESS FOR STUDENTS ACQUIRING ENGLISH
Guided Reading (Spanish), p. 172
Geography Application: The Movement Toward Woman Suffrage (Spanish), p. 174

FORMAL ASSESSMENT
Section Quiz, p. 213

ALTERNATIVE ASSESSMENT BOOK
See forms for supporting and scoring alternative activities.

TECHNOLOGY RESOURCES

CRITICAL THINKING TRANSPARENCIES
CT17, Progressive Movement

CD-ROM *Grolier Multimedia Encyclopedia*

VIDEO *American Portfolio: A Videodisc for U.S. History* user's guide, pp. 168, 169, 171, 172

INTERNET McDougal Littell Learning On-Line
http://www.mcdougallittell.com

ticed law for a short time after graduating from the College of New Jersey (which in 1896 became known as Princeton University), he much preferred his position as a political science professor. In 1902, Wilson became the president of Princeton University, where his reforms earned national praise.

New Jersey's Democratic political machine tapped Wilson to run for governor in 1910. Wilson declared his independence of the party machine shortly after he took office. As governor, he sponsored legislation to adopt such progressive programs as a direct primary, workmen's compensation, and regulation of public utilities and railroads. As America's newly elected president, Wilson moved to enact his program, the "New Freedom," and planned his attack on what he called the triple wall of privilege: the trusts, tariffs, and high finance.

CLAYTON ANTITRUST ACT "Freedom today," Wilson said, "is something more than being let alone. Without the watchful . . . resolute interference of the government, there can be no fair play between individuals and such powerful institutions as the trust." Congress enacted two key antitrust measures during Wilson's administration, the Federal Trade Act and the **Clayton Antitrust Act.** The 1914 Clayton Act sought to strengthen the Sherman Antitrust Act of 1890 by declaring certain business practices illegal. For example, a corporation could no longer acquire the stock of another corporation if doing so would create a monopoly. In addition, if a company violated the law, its officers could be prosecuted.

Conservative courts had been treating trade unions as monopolies under the Sherman Antitrust Act. The Clayton act specified that labor unions and farm organizations not only had a right to exist, but also would no longer be subject to antitrust laws. Now strikes, peaceful picketing, boycotts, and the collection of strike benefits became legal. Furthermore, injunctions against strikers were prohibited unless the strikers threatened "irreparable [unable to be remedied] injury to property." Recognizing the Clayton act's value to workers, Samuel Gompers, president of the American Federation of Labor (AFL), called the act labor's Magna Carta, referring to the English document signed in 1215, in which the English king recognized that he was under the law and that the law granted rights to his subjects.

The Federal Trade Act of 1914 set up a five-member "watchdog" agency called the **Federal Trade Commission** (FTC) with the power to investigate possible violations of regulatory statutes, to require periodic reports from corporations and to put an end to unfair business competition or unfair business practices, such as inaccurate labeling. If the FTC discovered a corporation to be engaging in illegal activity, the commission could force the corporation to "cease and desist" such practices. In fact, the FTC handed down almost 400 cease-and-desist orders during Wilson's administration.

A NEW TAX SYSTEM Wilson believed that high tariff rates created monopolies by reducing competition. Early in 1913, the new president summoned Congress to a special session and established a precedent by delivering the State of the Union message in person rather than sending it to be read by a clerk.

Prepared by his experience as a professor, Wilson defended and helped secure passage of the Underwood Tariff of 1913, which substantially reduced tariff rates for the first time since the Civil War. Senate passage had appeared unlikely because manufacturing lobbyists—people hired by manufacturers to present their interests to

Woodrow Wilson continued Roosevelt's and Taft's antitrust effort.

DEREGULATION

In recent years railroads, airlines, and the telecommunications industries have all been deregulated, or permitted to compete without government control, in an effort to improve their efficiency and lower prices. As one fan of deregulation said, "There will be no turning back from a more competitive, more efficient, and more pro-consumer industry."

During the progressive era, reformers viewed regulation as a necessary role of government to ensure safety and fairness for consumers as well as industrial competitors. Opponents of regulation, however, believed that government regulation caused inefficiency and high prices.

Modern critics of deregulation argue that deregulated businesses may simply ignore hard-to-serve populations, such as elderly, poor, or disabled people, while competing for more profitable customers.

The Progressive Era **517**

Tax Revenue, 1915–1995

Reading the Graph Ask
what the data presented on
the graph suggests about
the nation and the federal
government from 1915 to
1995. *Possible Response:
U.S. residents were making
more money and being
taxed at a higher percent,
and the federal government
grew far richer.*

Extension Ask what students would guess about
inflation in the United States
from 1915 to 1995. *Possible
Response: Judging from the
increases in taxes collected,
there was probably a high
level of inflation.*

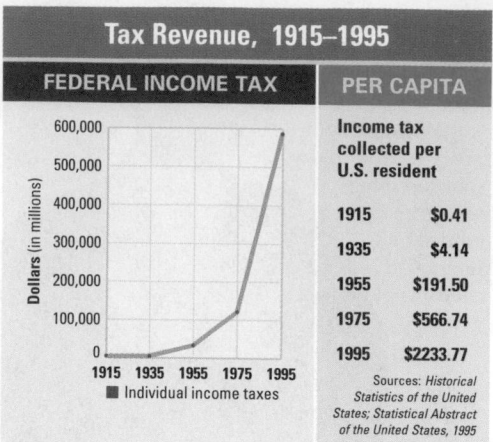

Tax Revenue, 1915–1995

FEDERAL INCOME TAX	PER CAPITA

Dollars (in millions)

Income tax
collected per
U.S. resident

1915	$0.41
1935	$4.14
1955	$191.50
1975	$566.74
1995	$2233.77

■ Individual income taxes

Sources: *Historical
Statistics of the United
States; Statistical Abstract
of the United States, 1995*

**SKILLBUILDER
INTERPRETING
GRAPHS** *About what
year did income tax
revenues first begin to
rise sharply? About how
much revenue did the
income tax bring into
the federal government
in 1995?*

Skillbuilder Answer
Year: About 1955.
Revenue: Approximately
$550 billion.

Woman Suffrage

Discussing Key Ideas
▶ • Women press for the vote,
winning some local battles.
• Carrie Chapman Catt succeeds Susan B. Anthony as
head of NAWSA.
• In 1920, women finally win
the right to vote through
ratification of the Nine-
teenth Amendment.

MORE ABOUT . . .
Suffrage in Wyoming

While still a territory,
Wyoming granted women
the right to vote, hold office,
and serve on juries in a law
passed on December 10,
1869—the first of its kind in
the nation.

IN-DEPTH RESOURCES: UNIT 5
Geography Application: The
Movement Toward Woman Suffrage,
p. 7

government officials—had descended on the capital to sway senators to oppose the bill. Wilson
denounced the lobbyists and urged voters to monitor their senators' votes on the bill. Because of the
new president's use of the bully pulpit, the Senate
cut tariff rates even more deeply than the House
version had done.

FEDERAL INCOME TAX Overall, tariff rates
dropped from about 40 percent to under 30 percent. Lowering tariffs, however, meant that the federal government had to replace the revenue that
tariffs had previously supplied. The Sixteenth
Amendment, which had been ratified in 1912, legalized a federal income tax, which provided revenue
by taxing profits and earnings.

The graduated tax, which taxed larger incomes
at higher rates than smaller incomes, began with a modest tax on incomes over
$4,000. Almost all factory workers and farmers were exempt from this tax, since
their incomes were far less than that figure. The tax then ranged from 1 percent
to a maximum of 6 percent on incomes over $500,000. At the time, few con-
gressmen realized the revenue-generating potential of the income tax. By 1917,
however, the government received more money from the income tax than it had
ever gained from tariffs. Today, income taxes on corporations and individuals
represent the federal government's main source of revenue.

FEDERAL RESERVE SYSTEM After tackling tariff reform, Wilson turned his
attention to financial reform. Both liberals and conservatives agreed that the nation
needed a way to make credit more easily available outside the financial centers of
New York City and Boston. The nation also needed a way to quickly adjust the
amount of money in circulation. Both credit availability and money supply had to
keep pace with the economy.

Wilson solved both of these problems by establishing a decentralized private
banking system under federal control. The Federal Reserve Act of 1913 divided
the nation into 12 regions or districts. Each district had a federal reserve bank to
which all the national banks within the district belonged. State banks within the
district could join if they met certain requirements.

The federal reserve banks had the power to issue new paper currency in
emergency situations. The member banks could use the new currency to make
loans to their customers. Federal reserve banks could transfer funds to member banks that ran into trouble, saving the banks from closing and protecting
the savings of customers. By 1923, roughly 70 percent of the nation's banking
resources were part of the **Federal Reserve System.** The Federal Reserve
System, which still serves as the basis of the nation's banking system, is one of
the most enduring achievements of the Wilson administration.

Woman Suffrage

While Wilson pushed hard for reform of trusts, tariffs, and banking, determined
women intensified their push for the vote. The educated, native-born middle-
class women who had been active in progressive movements had grown increasingly impatient about not being allowed to vote, especially when they saw male
immigrants granted suffrage automatically upon achieving citizenship. By 1910,
women had federal voting rights only in Wyoming, Utah, Colorado, and Idaho.

Despite disappointing failures in California and New York, determined suffragists persisted in their campaign. Three new developments finally brought

THINK THROUGH HISTORY
**B. Drawing
Conclusions** Why
were tariff reform
and the Federal
Reserve System
important?

B. Answer
Wilson's tariff
reform cut tariff
rates and
reduced the
likelihood of
monopolies
controlling
competition. The
Federal Reserve
System made it
possible for credit
availability and
the money supply
to be responsive
to the state of the
economy.

TEACHING OPTIONS

Making Connections Across the Curriculum

Economics Discuss the difference between a flat tax, which
takes the same percentage of income from everyone, and a
graduated tax, which takes a higher percentage from those
who can afford it. For example, a person earning $10,000 has
barely enough on which to live. If you take away 10 percent in
taxes, he or she has only $9,000, clearly cutting into necessi-
ties. On the other hand, someone earning $100,000 can proba-
bly afford to pay 10 percent in taxes without suffering any
hardship. Note that a tariff is an indirect flat tax since it is
passed along equally, like a sales tax, to rich and poor alike.

Exploring Themes

Women in America Underscore the role of World War I in
ensuring women the right to vote at last. It was not until so
many women filled the shoes of men off fighting the war that
women achieved suffrage. Note that the ratification of the
Nineteenth Amendment, which granted woman suffrage, took
place in 1920, over 70 years after Lucretia Mott and Elizabeth
Cady Stanton led the first women's rights convention in
Seneca Falls, New York.

Suffragists parading in New York City carry a banner that quotes President Wilson's support of the movement.

success within reach: increased activism of local groups, the use of bold, new strategies to build enthusiasm for the movement, and the rebirth of the national movement under Carrie Chapman Catt.

LOCAL SUFFRAGE BATTLES Growing numbers of young, college-educated women helped breathe new life into the woman suffrage movement. By 1900, there were 5,000 college-educated women who viewed suffrage as their civil right. Two Massachusetts organizations, the Boston Equal Suffrage Association for Good Government and the College Equal Suffrage League, initiated door-to-door campaigns to reach potential supporters. Founded by Radcliffe graduate Maud Wood Park, the Boston group spread the message of suffrage to poor and working-class women, who did not attend suffrage meetings. Women who belonged to these groups also took trolley tours. At each stop, a suffragist would speak to the crowds that gathered to watch the unusual sight of a woman speaking in public.

Many wealthy young women who visited Europe as part of their education became involved in the suffrage movement in Britain. Led by Emmeline Pankhurst, British suffragists used increasingly strident tactics such as heckling government officials to advance their cause. Inspired by such bold activism, American women returned to the United States ready to try similar approaches in their own campaigns for suffrage.

THINK THROUGH HISTORY
C. Summarizing
Summarize the strategies women used in their fight for suffrage.

C. Answer
Grassroots, state-by-state efforts of the NAWSA and local groups; militant efforts of the National Woman's Party, such as picketing.

"How long must women wait for liberty?"

NAWSA PICKET SIGN

CATT AND THE NATIONAL MOVEMENT On the national level, Susan B. Anthony's retirement from the presidency of the National American Woman Suffrage Association (NAWSA) in 1900 pushed Carrie Chapman Catt into prominence. Catt became president of NAWSA, a post she held until 1904 and then returned to in 1915. In the years between her tenures as NAWSA president, Catt organized New York's Woman Suffrage party, which narrowly lost its first referendum in 1915. Within two days, the women raised $100,000 for the next campaign, announcing that with "undiminished courage we are again in the field of action." When Catt returned to the NAWSA presidency in 1915, she concentrated on (1) painstaking organization; (2) close ties between local, state, and national workers; (3) establishing a wide base of support; (4) cautious lobbying; and (5) gracious, ladylike behavior.

The energy of local groups and the NAWSA's example of careful grass-roots organization won victories in Washington, California, Kansas, Oregon, and Arizona between 1910 and 1912. During the same period, however, failures in Michigan, Ohio, and Wisconsin turned some suffragists to more mili-

---

Raised in a Quaker family, Paul attended Swarthmore College and later trained as a lawyer. In London she worked in a settlement house and was jailed for her activities in the suffrage movement. In 1913, she helped found the Congressional Union for Woman Suffrage, later part of the National Woman's Party, which she chaired in the 1940s. After World War II, she helped ensure that the U.N. charter included equal rights provisions for women.

ON THE WORLD STAGE
Emmeline Pankhurst

Critical Thinking:
Evaluating Have students give their opinions of Pankhurst's tactics. *Possible Responses: Some may feel that her tactics earned needed publicity and advanced a cause. Others may feel that she antagonized too many people.*

The Limits of Progressivism

▶ **Starting with the Student**
• Have students discuss how they feel when someone breaks a promise.
• Ask them if they think similar feelings apply when a politician breaks a campaign promise.

▶ **Discussing Key Ideas**
• Wilson retreats on civil rights.
• Reform moves to the back burner as America enters World War I.

ON THE WORLD STAGE

EMMELINE PANKHURST

American women struggling for suffrage received valuable tutoring in effective tactics from their English counterparts, whose bold maneuvers had captured media coverage.

The noted British suffragist Emmeline Pankhurst, who helped found the National Women's Social and Political Union, often engaged in radical tactics. Pankhurst and other suffragists staged parades, organized protest meetings, endured hunger strikes, heckled candidates for Parliament, and spit on policemen who tried to quiet them. They were often imprisoned for their activities, before Parliament granted them their right to vote in 1928.

---

tant methods. Meanwhile, other suffragists focused on ratifying a constitutional amendment to achieve their goals in one broad sweep.

Lucy Burns and Alice Paul had recently returned from England infused with the bold tactics of the British movement. At first, Burns and Paul worked with NAWSA, but the pair broke off in 1914 to form their own more radical organization, the Congressional Union, and its successor, the National Woman's Party. Impatient with NAWSA's careful state-by-state approach, the National Woman's Party sought instead to pressure the federal government to pass a suffrage amendment. While NAWSA tried to enlist lawmakers from both parties, the National Woman's Party openly blamed "the party in power"—the Democrats—for women's failure to win suffrage.

In 1916, delegates to the Democratic convention faced hostile women who were wearing yellow sashes and holding signs and banners demanding the right to vote. By 1917, Paul had organized her followers to mount a round-the-clock picket line around the White House, whose occupant, Wilson, had issued only a lukewarm endorsement of suffrage. Some of the picketers were arrested, jailed, and even force-fed when they attempted a hunger strike.

The untiring efforts of these groups and America's involvement in World War I finally made suffrage inevitable. Patriotic American women who headed committees, knitted socks for soldiers, and sold liberty bonds now claimed their overdue reward for supporting the war effort. In 1919, Congress passed the **Nineteenth Amendment,** granting women the right to vote. The amendment won final ratification in August 1920—72 years after women had first convened and demanded the vote at the Seneca Falls convention in 1848.

The Limits of Progressivism

Despite Wilson's successes at instituting progressive economic and political reforms, he disappointed progressives who favored social reform. For example, he opposed a federal child labor law because he considered such a ban unconstitutional. On racial matters, Wilson appeased conservative Southern Democratic voters but disappointed his Northern white and black supporters. He placed segregationists in charge of federal agencies thereby expanding racial segregation in the federal government, the military, and Washington, D.C.

WILSON AND CIVIL RIGHTS Like Roosevelt and Taft, Wilson seemed to retreat on civil rights once in office. During the presidential campaign of 1912, he won the support of the NAACP's black intellectuals and white liberals by promising to treat blacks equally and to speak out against lynching.

As president, however, Wilson opposed federal antilynching legislation, arguing that these crimes fell under state jurisdiction. In addition, the Capitol and the federal offices in Washington, D.C., which had been desegregated during Reconstruction, resumed the practice of segregating the races shortly after Wilson's election.

Wilson appointed to his cabinet fellow white Southerners who extended segregation. Secretary of the Navy Josephus Daniels, for example, proposed at a cabinet meeting to do away with common drinking fountains and towels in his department. According to an entry in Daniels's diary, President Wilson agreed because he had "made no promises in particular to negroes, except to do them justice." Segregated facilities, in the president's mind, were just.

African Americans and their liberal white supporters in the NAACP felt betrayed. Oswald Garrison Villard, a grandson of abolitionist William Lloyd Garrison, wrote to Wilson in dismay, "The colored men who voted and worked for

D. Answer
Wilson opposed anti-lynching legislation, did not continue desegregation in the federal government, and appointed to his cabinet white Southerners who supported segregation.

THINK THROUGH HISTORY
D. Recognizing Effects *What actions by Wilson disappointed civil rights advocates?*

Teaching Gifted and Talented Students

Amending the Constitution Have interested students research and report on these different constitutional amendments passed in the progressive era:

• Sixteenth Amendment, authorizing the income tax.
• Seventeenth Amendment, establishing a direct popular vote for U.S. senators.
• Eighteenth Amendment, prohibiting the manufacture, sales, or transportation of liquor (later repealed).
• Nineteenth Amendment, granting women the vote.

Making Connections Across Cultures

Civil Rights One of the ironies of the progressive movement was that, for political reasons if not personal preference, it remained rather unprogressive on the issue of African-American civil rights. Wilson's ultimate betrayal despite campaign promises points to a regional division in the Democratic Party that would plague it for several decades. In telling Villard he was acting "in the interest of the negroes," Wilson went on to explain that he had segregated several Washington departments to help allay friction and safeguard the holding of offices by "negroes."

you in the belief that their status as Americans was safe in your hands are deeply cast down." Wilson's response—that he acted "in the interest of the negroes" and "with the approval of some of the most influential negroes I know"—only widened the rift between the president and some of his former supporters.

The president's reception of an African-American delegation on November 12, 1914, brought the confrontation to a bitter climax. William Monroe Trotter, editor-in-chief of an African-American Boston newspaper called the *Guardian*, led the delegation. Trotter complained that African Americans from 38 states had asked the president to reverse the segregation of government employees, but that segregation had since increased. Trotter then commented on Wilson's inaction.

A PERSONAL VOICE
Only two years ago you were heralded as perhaps the second Lincoln, and now the Afro-American leaders who supported you are hounded as false leaders and traitors to their race. . . . As equal citizens and by virtue of your public promises we are entitled at your hands to freedom from discrimination, restriction, imputation, and insult in government employ. Have you a "new freedom" for white Americans and a new slavery for your "Afro-American fellow citizens"? God forbid!
WILLIAM MONROE TROTTER, address to President Wilson, November 12, 1914

Wilson found Trotter's tone infuriating. After an equally angry Trotter shook his finger at the president to emphasize a point, the furious Wilson demanded that the delegation leave. Wilson's refusal to extend civil rights to African Americans pointed to the limits of progressivism under his administration. The specter of American involvement in the war raging in Europe would soon reveal more weaknesses.

THE TWILIGHT OF PROGRESSIVISM After taking office in 1913, Wilson had said, "There's no chance of progress and reform in an administration in which war plays the principal part." The outbreak of World War I in Europe in 1914 demanded America's involvement. Meanwhile, distracted Americans and their legislators allowed reform efforts to stall. As Jane Addams mournfully reflected, "the spirit of fighting burns away all those impulses . . . which foster the will to justice."

But international conflict was destined to be part of Wilson's presidency. During the early years of his administration, he had dealt with issues of imperialism that had roots in the late 19th century. However, World War I dominated most of his second term as president.

> *"There's no chance of progress and reform in an administration in which war plays the principal part."*
>
> WOODROW WILSON

Section 5 Assessment

1. TERMS & NAMES

Identify:
- Clayton Antitrust Act
- Federal Trade Commission
- Federal Reserve System
- Nineteenth Amendment

2. SUMMARIZING Create a time line of key events relating to progressivism during Wilson's first term. Use the dates already plotted on the time line below as a guide.

1913	1914	1915	1916

Write a paragraph explaining which event you think best demonstrates progressive reform.

3. DRAWING CONCLUSIONS Wilson said, "Without the watchful . . . resolute interference of the government, there can be no fair play between individuals and . . . the trust." How does this statement reflect Wilson's approach to reform? Support your answer.

THINK ABOUT
- government's responsibility to the public
- the passage of two key antitrust measures during Wilson's administration

4. DEVELOPING HISTORICAL PERSPECTIVE If you were a suffragist in the early 1900s, which organization would you have joined—the National American Woman Suffrage Association or the National Woman's Party?

THINK ABOUT
- Catt's strategy to win the vote
- Alice Paul's approach to achieving suffrage
- the National Woman's Party's protest at the 1916 Democratic Party convention

The Progressive Era **521**

MORE ABOUT . . .
William Monroe Trotter

A Harvard graduate, Trotter opposed Booker T. Washington's accommodation and instead helped found the Niagara Movement with W. E. B. Du Bois. On finding that the NAACP was still too moderate in its timetable, he established the National Equal Rights League to protest discrimination. The nonviolent protest Trotter advocated was later adopted by Martin Luther King, Jr., and others in the civil rights movement.

ASSESS & RETEACH

Section 5 Assessment
Have students work in small groups to discuss the questions and share their responses.

Self-Assessment
Have students create a two-column chart on which they compare their own responses to the section assessment (column 1) with the portions of the text that best answer each question (column 2).

Section Quiz

FORMAL ASSESSMENT
Section Quiz, p. 213

Reteach
Use the critical thinking transparency on the progressive era to review concepts.

CRITICAL THINKING TRANSPARENCIES
CT17, Progressive Movement

ANSWERS

1. TERMS & NAMES
Clayton Antitrust Act, p. 517
Federal Trade Commission, p. 517
Federal Reserve System, p. 518
Nineteenth Amendment, p. 520

2. SUMMARIZING

Possible Answers:
1913—NAWSA protests on Wilson's inauguration day; Federal Reserve Act divides nation into 12 regions, each headed by a federal reserve bank.
1914—Federal Trade Act sets up Federal Trade Commission to investigate unfair business practices; Clayton Antitrust Act strengthens the Sherman Antitrust Act; African American delegation confronts Wilson on his segregation policies.
1916—Suffragists picket the Democratic Party convention. Students' paragraphs will vary.

3. DRAWING CONCLUSIONS

Possible Responses: Wilson believed that the unbridled growth of big business threatened the freedom of individuals—the consumers and workers—who alone were powerless to curb the exploitative practices of trusts. He thought that government had the responsibility to step in to represent individuals' concerns and rights and to safeguard public welfare.

4. DEVELOPING HISTORICAL PERSPECTIVE

Possible Answers: Students who would prefer to join the NAWSA might say that the organization's focus on persuasion rather than coercion, is a more effective approach because it is less likely to provoke confrontation. Students who would prefer to join the National Woman's Party might say that suffragists needed to be more confrontational and use militant tactics to achieve their goals.

CLOSE

Although Wilson initiated progressive economic and political reforms, his record on social reforms disappointed progressives. Women won the vote with little real help from him, and his record on civil rights was poor.

REVIEWING THE CHAPTER

TERMS & NAMES
1. progressive movement, p. 494
2. muckraker, p. 496
3. suffrage, p. 503
4. Susan B. Anthony, p. 503
5. Theodore Roosevelt, p. 505
6. NAACP, p. 511
7. Gifford Pinchot, p. 512
8. Woodrow Wilson, p. 514
9. Clayton Antitrust Act, p. 517
10. Federal Reserve System, p. 518

MAIN IDEAS
11. Protecting social welfare, promoting moral reform, creating economic reform, and fostering efficiency.

12. Laws setting minimum age, limiting work hours, and providing workers' compensation.

13. Many African-American and immigrant women who lacked education or skills worked as domestic workers.

14. The NACW, promoted the moral education of African Americans. The NAWSA was committed to winning women's right to vote.

15. Sinclair's descriptions of the meatpacking industry's corrupt practices disgusted both the public and Roosevelt, who pushed Congress to pass the Meat Inspection Act.

16. When a strike threatened public welfare, the federal government was expected to intervene, with arbitration.

17. Taft was a more cautious progressive than Roosevelt but did break up more trusts than Roosevelt had.

18. Though Wilson himself captured only 42 percent of the popular vote, 75 percent of the popular vote did go to reform candidates.

19. It recognized the legality of labor unions, strikes, peaceful picketing, boycotts, and strike benefits; it limited the use of injunctions in court disputes.

20. Child labor laws, because he felt they were unconstitutional; federal antilynching laws, because he contended such crimes fell under state jurisdictions.

522   Chapter 17

Chapter 17 Assessment

REVIEWING THE CHAPTER

TERMS & NAMES For each item below, write a sentence explaining its connection to the progressive era. For each person or group of people named below, explain his or her role in events during this period.

1. progressive movement
2. muckraker
3. suffrage
4. Susan B. Anthony
5. Theodore Roosevelt
6. NAACP
7. Gifford Pinchot
8. Woodrow Wilson
9. Clayton Antitrust Act
10. Federal Reserve System

MAIN IDEAS

SECTION 1 *(pages 494–500)*

The Origins of Progressivism

11. What were the four goals that various progressive reform movements struggled to achieve?
12. What kinds of state labor laws resulted from progressives' lobbying to protect workers?

SECTION 2 *(pages 501–504)*

Women in Public Life

13. In the 1890s, what job opportunities were available to uneducated women without industrial skills? Who typically filled these positions?
14. Give two examples of women's national organizations committed to social activism and briefly describe their progressive missions.

SECTION 3 *(pages 505–511)*

Teddy Roosevelt's Square Deal

15. What scandalous practices did Upton Sinclair expose in his novel *The Jungle*? How did the American public, Roosevelt, and the Congress respond?
16. What precedent did Roosevelt set when he helped mediate the 1902 coal strike?

SECTION 4 *(pages 512–515)*

Progressivism Under Taft

17. As a progressive, how did Taft compare with Roosevelt, his predecessor?
18. Why could Wilson claim a mandate to broaden the government's role in social reform, based on the popular vote in the 1912 presidential election?

SECTION 5 *(pages 516–521)*

Wilson's New Freedom

19. How did the Clayton Antitrust Act benefit labor?
20. Cite two examples of social welfare legislation that Wilson opposed during his presidency and the arguments he used to defend his position.

522 CHAPTER 17

THINKING CRITICALLY

1. **PRESIDENTIAL AGENDAS** Create a Venn diagram like the one below to show some of the similarities and differences between Roosevelt's "Square Deal" and Wilson's "New Freedom."

Roosevelt's "Square Deal"   Wilson's "New Freedom"

similarities

2. **TRENDS IN AMERICAN SOCIETY** What social, political, and economic trends in American life do you think caused the reform impulse during the progressive era? Support your answer with details from the text.

3. **PROGRESSIVISM AND DEMOCRACY** Reread Wilson's quote on page 492. How does the quote show the progressive point of view? In this chapter, whose energies were released?

4. **GEOGRAPHY OF NATIONAL PARKS** Review the map on page 509. Notice how many more parks there are in the West than in the East and the Midwest. Do you think that if the government had not saved those lands from 1872 to 1947, the West today would have as few parks as the East? Give reasons for your opinion.

5. **THEME: WOMEN IN AMERICA** What methods used by women reformers of the progressive era are still methods of modern-day reform and social protest movements? Support your answer with examples.

6. **ANALYZING PRIMARY SOURCES** Read the following excerpt from naturalist John Muir's book *Our National Parks*, published in 1901. Then answer the questions below.

> So far as our government has done nothing effective with its forests, though the best in the world, but is like a rich and foolish spendthrift who has inherited a magnificent estate in perfect order, and then has left his fields and meadows, forests and parks, to be sold and plundered and wasted at will, depending on their inexhaustible abundance. Now it is plain that the forests are not inexhaustible, and that quick measures must be taken if ruin is to be avoided. . . .
>
> Just now, while protective measures are being deliberated languidly, destruction and use are speeding on faster and faster every day. The axe and the saw are insanely busy, chips are flying thick as snowflakes and every summer thousands of acres of priceless forests . . . are vanishing away in clouds of smoke. . . .
>
> **JOHN MUIR,** "The American Forests," from *Our National Parks*

Whose actions do you think Muir criticized in this excerpt? Why might his concerns about the forests be justified? Cite evidence from the text to support your answers.

THINKING CRITICALLY

1. PRESIDENTIAL AGENDAS
Possible Responses: Similarities: both promoted a strong executive branch and the president's use of the bully pulpit; both claimed progressive ideals; both tackled the problems of trusts; both excluded the cause of civil rights for African Americans from their progressive agendas. Differences: Roosevelt favored regulating trusts, while Wilson favored breaking them up; Roosevelt thought the federal government should get bigger, Wilson believed it should get smaller; Wilson's attacks on trusts were more aggressive than Roosevelt's.

2. TRENDS IN AMERICAN SOCIETY
Possible Responses: Urbanization and its related problems, especially poverty and industrialization; the spread of the Social Gospel; increase in the number of college-educated women; exploitative practices and shabby ethics of big business; rise of socialism; widespread popularity of muckraking magazines; corruption in politics.

3. PROGRESSIVISM AND DEMOCRACY
Possible Responses: Progressives believed in using action to solve existing problems; they were an energetic group who believed that a democracy required everyone to take responsibility. Examples in the chapter include women involved in all kinds of reforms from child labor to suffrage; novelists and journalists (muckrakers); government officials, including conservationists, governors, mayors, and laborers; and African-American civil-rights activists.

1. CREATING AN EXHIBIT

How are artists influenced by events of their time? How does art help explain the past?

• Research and create a poster or display that explores how artists in the years 1890–1920 reflected progressive ideals.

CD-ROM Use the CD-ROM *Our Times* and other resources to research a turn-of-the-century musician, writer, artist, designer, or director of your choice.

• Create a time line of events from this artist's working years.

• Create an exhibit of images, audiotape samples, or videotape samples of the artist's work. Write or tape an explanation of how the work reflects the progressive era.

• Share your exhibit with the class.

2. LEARNING FROM MEDIA

VIDEO View the McDougal Littell video for Chapter 17, *A Child on Strike*. Discuss these questions in small groups; then do the cooperative learning activity.

• What was your reaction to Camella Teoli's accident?

• What labor practices do you take for granted today that a person living in 1910 could not have taken for granted?

• **Cooperative Learning** What coverage might the 1912 congressional hearing have received in newspapers of the time? In your group, imagine yourselves as news reporters in 1912 and write two articles—one that objectively reports on the findings of the hearing, and one that has a bias in favor of businesses such as the Washington Mill. Share the articles with the class, and analyze the ways in which language can affect the reporting of information.

3. PORTFOLIO PROJECT

Use the Living History activity to expand your portfolio.

LIVING HISTORY

PRESENTING YOUR CAMPAIGN

Choose the best part of your woman suffrage campaign—whether a TV or magazine ad, a speech, or an Internet plan—to present to the class. Polish that section of your plan for presentation. Ask your classmates to answer the following questions:

• Is the campaign an effective way to get action on the issue?
• Would the modern methods have made passage of the Nineteenth Amendment occur earlier or more easily?

Include your entire campaign plan as well as the presentation in your American history portfolio.

Bridge to Chapter 18

Review Chapter 17

PROGRESSIVE MOVEMENT The social upheavals of the 1890s sparked reform efforts called the progressive movement. Moral reformers focused on improving personal behavior; muckraking journalists exposed corruption. Experts increased efficiency in both industry and government.

Progressives worked for state and local government reforms. Most progressives also supported reforms that protected consumers against dishonest business practices and workers, especially child laborers, against abuse by employers. Many women reformers targeted unsafe factories and labor abuses and promoted housing reform, educational improvement, and the passage of food and drug laws. Women also waged a tough campaign for woman suffrage. Finally, in 1919, Congress passed the Nineteenth Amendment, which granted women the vote.

PROGRESSIVISM UNDER ROOSEVELT AND TAFT As president, Theodore Roosevelt increased federal power, mediated the 1902 coal strike, regulated trusts and the railroad, pushed for legislation to protect consumers, and called for new conservation measures. William Howard Taft, Roosevelt's successor, was a more cautious progressive. Taft signed a bill for higher tariffs and went against the conservation issues Roosevelt promoted. Taft's policies resulted in a split in the Republican party, which contributed to Democrat Woodrow Wilson's victory in the 1912 presidential election.

PROGRESSIVISM UNDER WILSON Like Roosevelt, Wilson believed in a strong executive branch. Wilson pushed for antitrust laws that benefited labor and for legislation that lowered tariffs. He also took bold steps in instituting financial reforms. Wilson's weak stand on civil rights for African Americans marred his record.

Preview Chapter 18

As progressives worked for reforms, others pushed for U.S. expansion overseas. This goal was achieved when the United States gained colonial possessions in both the Caribbean and the Pacific. You will learn about these and other significant developments in the next chapter.

The Progressive Era **523**

---

1. CREATING AN EXHIBIT
Standards for Evaluation
The display should meet the following criteria:

• Focuses on a musician, writer, artist, designer, or director from the appropriate time period.
• Displays a variety of examples of the artist's work that convey his or her style.
• Includes a concise explanation of how the artist reflects progressive ideals.

2. LEARNING FROM MEDIA
Answers to the questions:

• Many students will express outrage at Camella's scalping. The entire incident might seem hard to believe.
• Answers will vary. Among practices they take for granted, students might mention the 40-hour work week, insurance benefits, child labor laws, minimum wage, and equal opportunity regardless of gender, race, or disability.

Standards for Articles on the Hearing Evaluation
An effective article should meet the following criteria:

• Includes fictional details from the hearing.
• Uses language to make the article either objective or biased.
• Accurately reflects the result of the hearing.

3. PORTFOLIO PROJECT
LIVING HISTORY
Standards for Evaluation
A campaign should meet the following criteria:

• Maintains a consistent position on the issue.
• Includes a variety of approaches, such as ads and speeches.
• Conveys a clear message.
• Appeals to a wide audience.
• Gives an effective display or delivery of part of the campaign.

IN-DEPTH RESOURCES: UNIT 5
See the form for scoring this activity on page 19.

THINKING CRITICALLY

4. GEOGRAPHY OF NATIONAL PARKS
Possible Responses: Had the government not protected the lands, they might have been exploited as the eastern United States was; the gold rush showed how quickly lands in the West could be ruined. On the other hand, the West is more open, was not developed as early as the East and Midwest were, and the lands are harder to develop because of deserts and mountains.

5. THEME: WOMEN IN AMERICA
Possible Responses: Lecture tours; civil disobedience; organizing statewide referenda; hunger strikes; picketing political events, such as presidential conventions, forming grassroots and national organizations to advocate a cause; using publicity; lobbying; door-to-door campaigns to reach potential supporters.

6. ANALYZING PRIMARY SOURCES
Possible Responses: Muir criticizes the government's slowness in passing laws to protect the forests, as well as blaming the logging operations. Despite the establishment of the Forest Bureau and the withdrawal of timberlands for a national forest preserve, the government allowed private interests to gobble up the wilderness. Muir's concern is justified; logging companies neglected to replant trees to replace those they cut down.

America Claims an Empire

	Key Ideas	TEACHING SUPPORT	ASSESSMENT
SECTION 1 Imperialism and America *pp. 526–529*	*Economic and cultural factors convince U.S. policymakers to join the competition for new markets in territories overseas, including Hawaii.*	***In-Depth Resources: Unit 5*** • Guided Reading, p. 20 • Literature: from *Hawaii* by James Michener, p. 33 **COOPERATIVE ACTIVITY** • Considering the Annexation of Hawaii, p. 528 (TE)	***Section 1 Assessment,*** p. 529 (PE) ***Self-Assessment,*** p. 529 (TE) ***Formal Assessment*** • Section Quiz, p. 222 ***Alternative Assessment Book*** • Standards for Evaluating a Cooperative Activity
SECTION 2 The Spanish-American-Cuban War *pp. 530–534*	*The United States goes to war with Spain over Cuban independence and emerges with colonies in Guam, Puerto Rico, and the Philippine Islands.*	***In-Depth Resources: Unit 5*** • Guided Reading, p. 21 • Skillbuilder Practice: Recognizing Bias, p. 24 • Primary Sources: Newspaper front page, p. 29; from *The Rough Riders* by Theodore Roosevelt, p. 30; In Favor of Imperialism, p. 31 • American Lives: William Randolph Hearst, p. 36; José Martí, p. 37 **COOPERATIVE ACTIVITY** • Covering the Rough Riders, p. 533 (TE)	***Section 2 Assessment,*** p. 534 (PE) ***Self-Assessment,*** p. 534 (TE) ***Formal Assessment*** • Section Quiz, p. 223 ***Alternative Assessment Book*** • Standards for Evaluating a Cooperative Activity
SECTION 3 Acquiring New Lands *pp. 535–541*	*The United States encounters continuing conflict in Puerto Rico, Cuba, and the Philippines, as well as in its attempt to gain a foothold in China's market.*	***In-Depth Resources: Unit 5*** • Guided Reading, p. 22 **COOPERATIVE ACTIVITY** • Writing Letters to Uncle Sam, p. 538 (TE)	***Section 3 Assessment,*** p. 541 (PE) ***Self-Assessment,*** p. 541 (TE) ***Formal Assessment*** • Section Quiz, p. 224 ***Alternative Assessment Book*** • Standards for Evaluating a Cooperative Activity
SECTION 4 America as a World Power *pp. 542–547*	*Presidents Theodore Roosevelt and Woodrow Wilson continue to use American military power in territories around the world, including Panama and Mexico.*	***In-Depth Resources: Unit 5*** • Guided Reading, p. 23 • Geography Application: Geography of the Panama Canal, p. 25 • Outline Map: America Becomes a World Power, p. 27 • Primary Source: Building the Panama Canal, p. 32 **COOPERATIVE ACTIVITY** • Debating Wilson's Missionary Diplomacy, p. 546 (TE)	***Section 4 Assessment,*** p. 547 (PE) ***Self-Assessment,*** p. 547 (TE) ***Formal Assessment*** • Section Quiz, p. 225 ***Alternative Assessment Book*** • Standards for Evaluating a Cooperative Activity
CHAPTER RESOURCES	**Chapter Overview** *To compete with other powers, America gains colonies overseas, although some Americans object.*	***In-Depth Resources: Unit 5*** • Living History Project: Worksheet, p. 38; Standards, p. 39 ***Telescoping the Times*** • Chapter Summary, pp. 35–36 ***Planning for Block Schedules***	***Chapter Assessment,*** pp. 550–551 (PE) ***Alternative Assessment,*** p. 551 (PE) ***Formal Assessment*** • Chapter Test, forms A and B, pp. 226–231 **Test Generator** ***Alternative Assessment*** See explanation and forms for different kinds of alternative assessments including portfolio assessment.

Grolier Multimedia Encyclopedia
- Hawaii

INTERNET RESOURCES
- See *McDougal Littell Learning On-Line* for links to information about the age of imperialism.

 Electronic Library of Primary Sources
- from *The 'Maine': An Account of her Destruction* by Captain Charles D. Siggsbee
- from *The Strenuous Life* by Theodore Roosevelt

INTERNET RESOURCES
- See *McDougal Littell Learning On-Line* for links to information about José Martí and Cuba.

 Humanities Transparencies
- H37, *Declined with Thanks*
- H17, *Athletic Contest*

Critical Thinking Transparencies
- CT18, *Overseas Expansion*

 Electronic Library of Primary Sources
- War in the Philippines
- The Anti-Imperialist League

INTERNET RESOURCES
- See *McDougal Littell Learning On-Line* for links to information about the Boxer Rebellion.

 Geography Transparencies
- G18, *United States Interventions*

Critical Thinking Transparencies
- CT52, *U.S. Trade with Central America*

 Our Times
- The Rise of Theodore Roosevelt

INTERNET RESOURCES
- See Interact with History p. 545, 549 (PE) for activities that include the Internet as an enrichment option.

 American Portfolio, A Videodisc for U.S. History, user's guide pp. 175–179

INTERNET RESOURCES
Learning On-Line: Social Studies
http://www.mcdougallittell.com

Block Scheduling (90 MINUTES)

Day 1
Section 1, pp. 526–529
Section 2, pp. 530–534
Section Assessments, pp. 529, 534

Day 2
Section 3, pp. 535–541
Section 4, pp. 542–547
Geography Spotlight: The Panama Canal, pp. 548–549
Section Assessments, pp. 541, 547
Chapter Assessment, pp. 550–551

YEARLY PACING *Chapter 18 Total:* 2 days *Yearly Total:* 85 days

See *Planning for Block Schedules* for special activities and pacing strategies.

Customizing for Special Populations

Students Acquiring English

Access for Students Acquiring English
- Guided Reading for Sections 1–4 (Spanish), pp. 178–181
- Chapter Summary (Spanish), pp. 176–177
- Skillbuilder Practice: Recognizing Bias (Spanish), p. 182
- Geography Application: Geography of the Panama Canal (Spanish), p. 183
- Outline Map: America Becomes a World Power (Spanish), p. 185

INTERNET RESOURCES
- See *McDougal Littell Learning On-Line* The Diverse Classroom.

Less Proficient Readers

In-Depth Resources: Unit 5
- Guided Reading for Sections 1–4, pp. 20–23
- Skillbuilder Practice: Recognizing Bias, p. 24
- Geography Application: Geography of the Panama Canal, p. 25
- Outline Map: America Becomes a World Power, p. 27

Telescoping the Times
- Chapter Summary, pp. 35–36

See additional strategies at point of use in the Teacher's Edition.

Gifted and Talented Students

In-Depth Resources: Unit 5
- Primary Sources: Newspaper front page, p. 29; from *The Rough Riders* by Theodore Roosevelt, p. 30; In Favor of Imperialism, p. 31; Building the Panama Canal, p. 32
- American Lives: William Randolph Hearst, p. 36; José Martí, p. 37

See additional strategies at point of use in the Teacher's Edition.

Connections to Literature READINGS FOR STUDENTS

In-Depth Resources: Unit 5
- from *Hawaii* by James Michener, p. 33

Enrichment Reading
- Ferre, Rosario
The House on the Lagoon.
New York: Farrar, Straus & Giroux, 1995. Nominated for a National Book Award, this novel is about the history of a Puerto Rican family whose secrets and conflicts add up to the larger story of Puerto Rico itself.

- Garcia, Christina
Dreaming in Cuban.
New York: Ballantine, 1993.
Set in Havana, Brooklyn, and the Cuban seaside, this novel is a lively and funny account of three generations of a Cuban family divided by conflicting loyalties over the long history of Cuban politics.

- Iida, Deborah
Middle Son.
Chapel Hill, NC: Algonquin Books, 1996. The narrator of this novel tells the story of his Japanese-American family who were sugar-cane cutters in Hawaii working for the huge corporations that controlled the business. The richness and tragedy of their family life and the narrator's final communion with his mother make this novel memorable.

OVERVIEW

America Claims an Empire

▶ ***Starting with the Student***
Ask students how they would react if the United States took over another country. For students who say they oppose it under any circumstances, ask them why. For students who say it might be all right under certain circumstances, ask what those circumstances are.

PREVIEWING THE CHAPTER
• Read the section titles and descriptions and study the time line and illustrations.
• Ask students to identify ways the United States acquired overseas possessions.
• Read the opening quotation. According to Hay, what was the basis for American imperialism? *Economic competition.*

MORE ABOUT . . .
John Hay
As a young lawyer in Springfield, Illinois, John Hay met Abraham Lincoln. He accompanied Lincoln to Washington and served as assistant private secretary to the President. Hay later co-authored a ten-volume biography of Abraham Lincoln. In addition to serving as secretary of state under presidents McKinley and Roosevelt, Hay also served as a diplomat in France, Spain, Austria, and Britain.

America Claims an Empire

SECTION 1

Imperialism and America

Economic and cultural factors convince U.S. policymakers to join the competition for new markets in territories overseas, including Hawaii.

SECTION 2

The Spanish-American-Cuban War

The United States goes to war with Spain over Cuban independence and emerges with colonies in Guam, Puerto Rico, and the Philippine Islands.

SECTION 3

Acquiring New Lands

The United States encounters continuing conflict in Puerto Rico, Cuba, and the Philippines, as well as in its attempt to gain a foothold in China's market.

SECTION 4

America as a World Power

Presidents Theodore Roosevelt and Woodrow Wilson continue to use American military power in territories around the world, including Panama and Mexico.

"In the field of trade and commerce, we shall be the keen competitors of the richest and greatest powers, and . . . we shall bring the sweat to their brows."

Secretary of State John Hay, 1899

Alfred T. Mahan's *The Influence of Sea Power upon History 1600–1783* is published.

The U.S.S. *Maine* explodes and sinks.

John Hay issues first Open Door note, calling for equal trading opportunities in China.

The United States annexes the Philippine Islands.

The Ferris wheel makes its debut at the World's Fair in Chicago.

Hawaiian revolution overthrows Queen Liliuokalani.

Spanish-American-Cuban War is fought.

President McKinley is assassinated.

Theodore Roosevelt becomes president.

| THE UNITED STATES THE WORLD | **1890** | 1893 | 1895 | 1898 | 1899 1899 | **1900** | 1901 |

Sino-Japanese War ends in Japanese victory over China.

Boxer Rebellion begins in China.

THEMES IN CHAPTER 18

Science and Technology

Technological advances helped fuel U.S. imperialism at the turn of the 20th century. First, improved equipment helped increase agricultural and factory output. These changes produced a surplus of goods and prompted the need for overseas markets.

Second, engineering know-how and advances in disease control made it possible for the United States to construct the Panama Canal and thus facilitate trade within its growing empire.

See Teacher's Edition notes, pp. 527, 544

Constitutional Concerns

Two constitutional concerns arose during America's age of imperialism. The first involved the press, whose independence is guaranteed by the Constitution. However, the rise of yellow journalism revealed how a free press can abuse its power.

The second concern involved the rights of people in lands acquired by the United States. The Supreme Court ruled that constitutional rights did not automatically apply to people in acquired territories.

See Teacher's Edition notes, pp. 531, 536

LIVING HISTORY

WRITING A HISTORICAL MONOLOGUE

The historical figures of the United States from 1890 to 1920 were often colorful individuals. Choose one of the figures from this chapter whom you find particularly interesting. As you read, take notes about that person, paying close attention to personal details and his or her political role and views. Write a monologue, or first-person narrative, from that person's point of view. As you draft your monologue, try to:

- use language that reflects how the person talked
- let situations and events you have chosen reveal the person's feelings and concerns

PORTFOLIO PROJECT Save your monologue in a folder for your American history portfolio. You will present your historical monologue for your class at the end of the chapter.

● Panama Canal opens.

● U.S. troops invade Mexico.

★ Theodore Roosevelt is elected president.

★ William H. Taft is elected president.

★ Woodrow Wilson is elected president.

★ Woodrow Wilson is reelected.

| 1903 | 1904 | 1908 | **1910** | 1912 | 1914 | 1916 | **1920** |

1904

1915

● Russo-Japanese War begins.

● The Mexican Revolution begins.

● Venustiano Carranza assumes power in Mexico.

● Republic of Panama is formed.

America Claims an Empire **525**

RECOMMENDED RESOURCES

Books for the Teacher

Marks, George P., ed. *The Black Press Views American Imperialism.* New York: Arno Press, 1971. Unusual perspective on imperialism.

O'Toole, G. J. A. *The Spanish War.* New York: Norton, 1984. Popular, readable history.

Wagenheim, Kal. *The Puerto Ricans: a Documentary History.* New York: Praeger, 1973.

Books for the Student

McCullough, David G. *The Path Between the Seas: the Creation of the Panama Canal, 1870–1914.* New York: Simon, 1977.

Rydell, Robert W. *All the World's a Fair: Visions of Empire at American International Expositions: 1876–1916.* Chicago: U. of Chicago Press, 1984.

Videos

The Big Stick. 1991. RMI Media, 800-745-5480. U.S. foreign policy in Latin America.

The Hunt for Pancho Villa. PBS Home Video, 1993. 800-424-7963.

The 1890s. 1994. Video Knowledge, 516-367-4250. U.S. Imperialism.

Software

American History: Becoming a World Power. World Associates, 3226 Robincrest Drive, Northbrook, IL 60062.

OBJECTIVES

1 To summarize the causes and effects of European and Asian imperialism.

2 To identify factors that influenced American imperialism.

3 To explain how the United States acquired Hawaii.

SKILLBUILDER

• Interpreting graphs, p. 528

CRITICAL THINKING

• Recognizing effects, p. 526
• Analyzing causes, p. 527
• Summarizing, pp. 528, 529
• Identifying problems, p. 529
• Developing historical perspective, p. 529
• Synthesizing, p. 529

FOCUS & MOTIVATE

▶ **Starting with the Student**
• How does a person behave when he or she feels superior to others?
• Ask students if countries might act in a similar fashion. Why or why not?

MORE ABOUT . . .
Liliuokalani

The last reigning queen of Hawaii greatly admired the role of Britain's Queen Victoria. Liliuokalani carried out the antique royal custom of sitting in front of a golden yellow cape of feathers when delivering important messages. The deposed queen lived until 1917. She was respected among Hawaiians as a link to the past. She is also remembered as the composer of "Aloha Oe"—Hawaii's traditional farewell song.

OBJECTIVE
1 INSTRUCT

Global Imperialism

▶ **Discussing Key Ideas**
• Imperialist European nations carve Africa into colonies.

(continued on next page)

---

1 Imperialism and America

LEARN ABOUT economic and cultural factors that shaped American foreign policy at the turn of the century
TO UNDERSTAND why the United States became an imperial power.

ONE AMERICAN'S STORY

Queen Liliuokalani realized that her influence had come to an end. More than 160 U.S. sailors and marines stood ready to aid the *haoles* (white foreigners) who planned to overthrow the Hawaiian monarchy. The group included some of her own cabinet members, who had refused to sign the constitution that would help achieve her goal of preserving Hawaii for Hawaiians. In an eloquent statement of protest, the proud monarch surrendered only to the superior force of the United States.

A PERSONAL VOICE

I, Liliuokalani . . . do hereby solemnly protest against any and all acts done against myself and the constitutional government of the Hawaiian Kingdom. . . . Now, to avoid any collision of armed forces and perhaps the loss of life, I do under this protest . . . yield my authority until such time as the Government of the United States shall . . . undo the action of its representatives and reinstate me in the authority which I claim as the constitutional sovereign of the Hawaiian Islands.

QUEEN LILIUOKALANI, quoted in *Those Kings and Queens of Old Hawaii*

Hawaii's "Queen Lil" announced that if restored to power, she would behead those who had conspired to depose her.

U.S. ambassador John L. Stevens informed the State Department, "The Hawaiian pear is now fully ripe, and this is the golden hour for the United States to pluck it." The annexation of Hawaii was only one of the goals of America's empire builders.

Global Imperialism

Americans had always sought to expand the size of their nation, and throughout the 19th century they extended their control over much of the North American continent. By the 1880s, policymakers had become convinced that the United States should join the imperialist powers of Europe and establish colonies overseas, such as the Hawaiian Islands. **Imperialism**—the policy in which stronger nations extend their economic, political, or military control over weaker territories—was a global trend.

EUROPEAN IMPERIALISM European nations had been establishing colonies for centuries. By the late 19th century, Africa had emerged as a prime target of European expansionism. Britain, France, Belgium, Italy, Germany, Portugal, and Spain competed for African raw materials and markets. These ambitious nations carved up Africa and distributed control of the pieces among themselves.

By the early 20th century, only Ethiopia and Liberia remained independent. The rest of the continent had been divided into European colonies. Americans observed keenly as Great Britain acquired territory not only in Africa, but in Asia and the Pacific as well. Soon the expression "The sun never sets on the British Empire" became astonishingly accurate. During the reign of Queen Victoria (1837–1901), Britain built an empire that included a quarter of the world's land and people.

A. Answer Only two African nations remained independent; the rest of the continent was divided up among the European nations.

THINK THROUGH HISTORY
A. Recognizing Effects How did European imperialism affect Africa?

SECTION 1 RESOURCES

PRINT RESOURCES

IN-DEPTH RESOURCES: UNIT 5
Guided Reading, p. 20
Literature: from *Hawaii* by James Michener, p. 33

ACCESS FOR STUDENTS ACQUIRING ENGLISH
Guided Reading (Spanish), p. 178

FORMAL ASSESSMENT
Section Quiz, p. 222

ALTERNATIVE ASSESSMENT BOOK
See forms for supporting and scoring alternative activities.

TECHNOLOGY RESOURCES

CD-ROM *Grolier Multimedia Encyclopedia*

VIDEO *American Portfolio: A Videodisc for U.S. History* user's guide, p. 178

INTERNET McDougal Littell Learning On-Line
http://www.mcdougallittell.com

ASIAN IMPERIALISM Imperialism also surfaced in parts of Asia during this same period. In its late-19th-century reform period, Japan replaced its old feudal order with a central government modeled after the bureaucracies of Western nations. Hoping that military strength would bolster industrialization, Japan joined European nations in their imperialist competition in China in the 1890s. Although the United States did not seek colonies in Asia, it did enter the struggle for a share of China's market.

American Imperialism

Most Americans gradually warmed to the idea of expansion overseas. With a belief in manifest destiny, they already had pushed the U.S. border to the Pacific Ocean. Three factors fueled the new American imperialism: (1) economic competition among industrial nations; (2) political and military competition, including the creation of a strong naval force; and (3) a belief in the racial and cultural superiority of Anglo-Saxons, the people of England and their descendants.

A THIRST FOR NEW MARKETS In the United States, imperialism had economic roots, just as it did in Europe and Japan. Advances in technology enabled American farms and factories to produce far more than American citizens could consume. Now the United States needed raw materials for its factories and new markets for its manufactured goods. Imperialists viewed foreign trade as the solution to overproduction and the related problems of unemployment and economic depression. Indiana senator Albert J. Beveridge, a staunch imperialist, defended the pursuit of new territories on economic grounds.

> **A PERSONAL VOICE**
> Fate has written our policy for us; the trade of the world must and shall be ours. . . . We will establish trading-posts throughout the world as distributing-points for American products. . . . Great colonies governing themselves, flying our flag and trading with us, will grow about our posts of trade.
>
> **ALBERT J. BEVERIDGE,** quoted in *Beveridge and the Progressive Era*

B. Answer The United States produced more goods than Americans needed. To keep business growing, the nation had to gain foreign markets.

THINK THROUGH HISTORY
B. Analyzing Causes How did U.S. economic prosperity lead it to pursue a policy of imperialism?

By the turn of the century, the United States had started to fulfill Beveridge's goals. American exports, which had totaled $234 million at the end of the Civil War, rose to $1.5 billion by 1900. By achieving a favorable balance of trade (exporting more than it imported), the United States had become a leading economic power.

DESIRE FOR MILITARY STRENGTH Seeing that other nations were establishing a global military presence, American foreign policy experts advised that the United States build up its own military strength. Admiral **Alfred T. Mahan,** president of the Naval War College in Newport, Rhode Island, had become one of the most outspoken advocates of American military expansion.

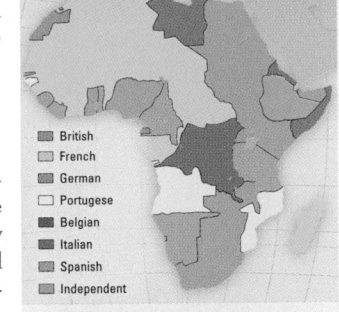

ON THE WORLD STAGE

Africa in 1913

- British
- French
- German
- Portuguese
- Belgian
- Italian
- Spanish
- Independent

CARVING UP AFRICA
Europeans avoided war by carving up Africa through diplomatic agreements. Nations staked out their claims to colonies and signed treaties to reserve those colonies for their own use.

In the mid-1880s, Germany and France called for a conference to discuss competition for African land. Fourteen European nations and the United States met in Berlin in 1884. The nations agreed to respect established colonies in Africa and proposed some ground rules for future colonization.

The Berlin conference left many questions unsettled, but it was the first international agreement on imperialism in Africa.

Admiral Mahan's efforts eventually led to the development of the "Great White Fleet" of the U.S. Navy.

America Claims an Empire **527**

(continued from page 526)

- Britain's empire includes a quarter of the world's land and people.
- Japan joins European nations in imperialist competition in China.

IN-DEPTH RESOURCES: UNIT 5
Guided Reading. p. 20

ACCESS FOR STUDENTS ACQUIRING ENGLISH
Guided Reading (Spanish), p. 178

ON THE WORLD STAGE
Carving Up Africa
Critical Thinking: Analyzing Have students create a flow chart showing causes and effects of imperialism in Africa. The chart might use a form like the one below:

OBJECTIVE
② INSTRUCT

American Imperialism

▶ **Discussing Key Ideas**
- American imperialists seek more markets for U.S. goods.
- To protect economic interests abroad, the United States develops a modern fleet and acquires naval bases.
- Some Americans argue that their culture is superior and should be spread to other nations.

TEACHING OPTIONS

Exploring Themes

Science and Technology Between 1860 and 1900, new and improved farm machinery greatly improved grain production in the United States. For example, plows, harrows, grain drills, reapers, and threshing machines increased the nation's corn harvest by 264 percent and the wheat harvest by 252 percent. Faced with such a surplus of farm products, the United States increased its foreign trade, as it sought new markets for these goods. Have students research the inventions of the late 19th century that helped spur the production of farm goods and prepare a time line of these inventions.

Making Connections Across Time

Balance of Trade in the 1990s Throughout the late 20th century, the United States has endured an unfavorable balance of trade, in which imports exceed exports. The nation's trade deficit peaked at 152.2 billion in 1987 and has since fluctuated. Although the country's trade deficit dipped to 66.7 billion in 1991, it had grown again to 105.1 billion by 1995. Experts attribute the trade deficit to, among other things, a heavy domestic demand for foreign goods and economic stagnation abroad, which reduces demand for American goods.

Social Darwinism

British naturalist Charles Darwin (1809–1882) had concluded that only the strongest creatures survive in competition against other creatures. Several philosophers applied Darwin's theory to human situations. They argued that certain people succeed in competition with others due to genetic and biological superiority.

OBJECTIVE
③ INSTRUCT

The United States Takes Hawaii

▶ *Discussing Key Ideas*
- American sugar planters gain control of Hawaii's government and economy.
- White business groups depose Queen Liliuokalani.
- Americans establish a provisional government, and the United States annexes Hawaii.

HISTORY FROM VISUALS
Hawaii's Changing Population, 1853–1920

Reading the Graph Tell students to note that the graph depicts shifts in the percentage of Hawaii's total population and does not address numbers of persons.

Extension Discuss with students what the changes in Hawaii's population shown on the graph say about the effects of imperialism on smaller, less powerful countries.

Skillbuilder Answer
Possible answer: The percentage of Native Hawaiians declined from 98 in 1853 to 16 in 1920. The percentage of other non-Caucasians (mostly Asian) increased from about 1 in 1853 to about 62 in 1920.

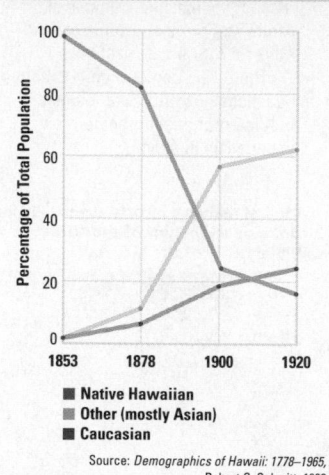

Hawaii's Changing Population, 1853–1920

Source: *Demographics of Hawaii: 1778–1965,*
Robert C. Schmitt, 1968

■ Native Hawaiian
■ Other (mostly Asian)
■ Caucasian

SKILLBUILDER
INTERPRETING GRAPHS
Which groups in Hawaii experienced the most dramatic change in percentage of total population between 1853 and 1920? What were these changes?

528 CHAPTER 18

In *The Influence of Sea Power upon History 1660–1783* (1890), Mahan argued for a strong U.S. navy to defend the peacetime shipping lanes essential to American economic growth. He said the nation also needed strategically located bases where its fleets could refuel. Mahan urged the United States to develop a modern fleet, establish naval bases in the Caribbean, construct a canal across the Isthmus of Panama, and acquire Hawaii and other Pacific islands.

The United States built nine steel-hulled cruisers between 1883 and 1890. The construction of modern battleships such as the *Maine* and the *Oregon* transformed the country into the world's third largest naval power. With a modern fleet, the United States set out to accomplish the protectionist goals Mahan had recommended.

BELIEF IN ANGLO–SAXON SUPERIORITY Cultural factors also helped to justify imperialism. Some Americans combined the philosophy of Social Darwinism—a belief in survival of the fittest—with a belief in the racial superiority of Anglo-Saxons. They argued that the United States had a responsibility to spread Christianity and civilization to the world's "inferior" peoples. This viewpoint was highly racist, because it defined civilization according to the standards of only one culture.

ANTI–IMPERIALISM While some Americans believed that the notion of ethnic superiority justified imperialism, others saw imperialism as a threat to Americans' Anglo-Saxon heritage. Anti-imperialists also objected to U.S. imperialism on moral and practical grounds. Many believed that nothing justified domination of other countries by the United States. Some objected when territories claimed by the United States were not given U.S. constitutional protections. Others argued that the costs of maintaining a military force large enough to protect U.S. positions abroad were prohibitive. In any case, certain countries overseas were vulnerable to empire builders looking for potential conquests, and Hawaii was a tempting target for the United States.

The United States Takes Hawaii

The Hawaiian Islands had been economically important to the United States for nearly a century. Since the 1790s, American merchants had stopped there on their way to China and East India. In the 1820s, Yankee missionaries founded Christian schools and churches on the islands. Next came sugar merchants, who eventually changed the Hawaiian economy.

HAWAII'S ECONOMY In the mid-19th century, American-owned sugar plantations accounted for about three-quarters of the islands' wealth. Plantation owners imported thousands of laborers from Japan, Portugal, and China. By the 1870s, foreigners and immigrant laborers outnumbered native Hawaiians almost two to one.

White planters profited from close ties with the United States. An 1875 treaty allowed the sale of Hawaiian sugar in the United States without a duty. In 1887, white business leaders in Hawaii forced King Kalakaua to change Hawaii's constitution to grant voting rights only to wealthy landowners. This change basically gave control of Hawaii's government to the American businessmen. Also in 1887, the United States strong-armed Hawaii into signing a treaty allowing the construction of an American naval base at Pearl Harbor.

The McKinley Tariff of 1890 provoked a crisis by eliminating the duty-free status of Hawaiian sugar. As a result, Hawaiian sugar growers faced competition in the American market, especially from Cuban sugar. American planters in

THINK THROUGH HISTORY
C. Summarizing
Explain the arguments against imperialism.
C. Answer Anti-imperialists objected to imperialism because territories were not given U.S. constitutional protection. Also, the costs of maintaining an adequate military force to protect U.S. territories were high.

TEACHING OPTION

Cooperative Activity: Considering the Annexation of Hawaii

Task: Student groups will write position papers representing different interests in Hawaii.

Purpose: To recognize different viewpoints regarding the annexation of Hawaii.

Activity: Assign the following roles to small groups of students: American planters, native Hawaiians, contract laborers, Queen Liliuokalani, U.S. ambassador John L. Stevens,

President Cleveland, and President McKinley. Instruct each group to write a position paper representing the assigned viewpoint regarding annexation of Hawaii. Encourage students to use quotes from the text and other sources. Provide time for groups to share their work.

📁 **Building a Portfolio:** Students adding a position paper to their portfolios should highlight their own contribution to the paper.

ALTERNATIVE ASSESSMENT BOOK
Standards for Evaluating a Cooperative Activity

Standards for Evaluation
Position papers should. . .
- identify the viewpoint of the person or group represented
- clearly state reasons supporting the position
- provide concrete details to support the reasons

THINK THROUGH HISTORY
D. Identifying Problems What problems did the McKinley Tariff cause for American sugar growers in Hawaii?

D. Answer It forced them to compete with other foreign growers and enabled U.S. growers to undersell them. As a result, they faced economic ruin.

Hawaii called for the United States to annex the islands so they wouldn't have to pay the duty. But subsequent events prompted the planters to take matters into their own hands.

THE QUEEN IS DEPOSED
When King Kalakaua died in 1891, his sister, Liliuokalani, became queen. Liliuokalani proposed a new constitution that would remove property qualifications for voting. This change would have restored political power over the islands to native Hawaiians.

To prevent this from happening, business groups—with the help of U.S. ambassador John L. Stevens—organized a revolution against the queen. On the night of January 16, 1893, the U.S.S. *Boston* appeared in Honolulu harbor. Following Stevens's orders, American marines moved ashore, supposedly to protect American lives and property. At the same time, volunteer troops took over the government building, imprisoned the queen in her palace, and established a provisional government with **Sanford B. Dole** as president.

REPUBLIC OF HAWAII Stevens immediately recognized the provisional government, which sent a commission to Washington, D.C., and asked that the islands be annexed. After a U.S. special investigator blamed Stevens for the revolution, President Cleveland directed that the queen be restored to her throne. When Dole refused to surrender power, Cleveland—unwilling to use force—formally recognized the Republic of Hawaii, but he refused to consider annexation unless a majority of Hawaiians favored it.

In 1897, William McKinley, who favored annexation, succeeded Cleveland as president. On August 12, 1898, Congress proclaimed Hawaii an American territory, without Hawaiians having had the chance to vote on annexation. At the same time, Cuba, an island much closer to the U.S. mainland, attracted U.S. attention.

Sanford B. Dole, (pictured here with his wife, Anna) helped to engineer the deposing of Queen Liliuokalani, who would be Hawaii's last monarch.

"The Hawaiian pear is now fully ripe, and this is the golden hour . . . to pluck it."

JOHN L. STEVENS

MORE ABOUT . . .
Sanford B. Dole

The son of an American missionary, Dole was born in Hawaii and educated in the United States. He returned to Hawaii to practice law and was twice elected to the Hawaii Legislature. An opponent of King Kalakaua's policies, Dole led an opposition party against the king and eventually helped engineer the overthrow of his sister. After the United States annexed Hawaii, Dole served as first territorial governor.

GROLIER MULTIMEDIA ENCYCLOPEDIA
Hawaii

ASSESS & RETEACH

Section 1 Assessment
Have the students work in small groups to answer the questions. Have each group share their answers to question 3 with the class.

Self-Assessment
Ask students to write two paragraphs, one which summarizes what they knew about Hawaii before reading this section, the other summarizing what they now know.

Section Quiz
FORMAL ASSESSMENT
Section Quiz, p. 222

Reteach
Have students work in groups to outline one of the three subsections of Section 1. They should use the bold-faced titles as main ideas and fill in supporting details.

Section 1 Assessment

1. TERMS & NAMES

Identify:
- Queen Liliuokalani
- imperialism
- Alfred T. Mahan
- Sanford B. Dole

2. SUMMARIZING Copy this web on your paper and fill it in with events and concepts that illustrate the idea in the center.

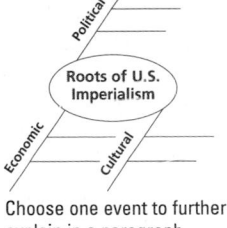
Political
Roots of U.S. Imperialism
Economic
Cultural

Choose one event to further explain in a paragraph.

3. DEVELOPING HISTORICAL PERSPECTIVE To what extent might the mid-19th century belief in manifest destiny have set the stage for the new American imperialism at the end of the century? Support your answers with evidence from the text.

THINK ABOUT
- why westward expansion might inspire overseas expansion
- justifications for imperialism
- Senator Beveridge's remark, "Fate has written our policy for us. . . ."

4. SYNTHESIZING Why did the United States want to annex Hawaii? Use specific references to the chapter to support your response.

America Claims an Empire **529**

ANSWERS

1. TERMS & NAMES
Queen Liliuokalani, p. 526
imperialism, p. 526
Alfred T. Mahan, p. 527
Sanford B. Dole, p. 529

2. SUMMARIZING
Possible Responses: Political—political and military rivalry with other imperialist powers; construction of a modern naval fleet. Economic—foreign trade as the solution to overproduction, unemployment and economic depression; economic competition among industrial nations. Cultural—combining the philosophies of Social Darwinism with Anglo-Saxon superiority; missionary impulse to spread Christianity.

3. DEVELOPING HISTORICAL PERSPECTIVE
Possible Response: Some students might say that manifest destiny was the guiding force behind the annexation of western territories and that leaders believed cultural superiority justified racial prejudice toward Native Americans. These patterns of western expansion seemed to influence the United States's joining the race for overseas expansion.

4. SYNTHESIZING
Possible Response: U.S. businessmen operated numerous sugar plantations on the islands. Also, there was a U.S. naval base in Hawaii.

CLOSE

The United States joined European and Asian countries in political and economic competition for colonies. A belief in Anglo-Saxon superiority provided additional incentive for imperialism. These factors led to annexation of Hawaii.

OBJECTIVES

1 To contrast American opinions regarding the Cuban revolt against Spain.

2 To identify events that escalated conflict between the United States and Spain.

3 To describe the course of the Spanish-American-Cuban War and its results.

SKILLBUILDERS

- Interpreting graphics, p. 531
- Understanding geography: location, p. 532
- Understanding geography: movement, place p. 533

CRITICAL THINKING

- Analyzing motives, pp. 531, 534
- Recognizing effects, p. 531
- Summarizing, pp. 532, 534
- Clarifying, p. 533
- Drawing conclusions, p. 534
- Forming opinions, p. 534

FOCUS & MOTIVATE

▶ **Starting with the Student**
- Ask students if they ever have been shocked or angered by something they read or heard.
- How did it make them want to act? Did they wonder if their opinions were being manipulated?

American Interest in Cuba

▶ **Discussing Key Ideas**
- Investments in sugar cane plantations give Americans an economic interest in Cuba.
- Some Americans support Spanish control of Cuba while others sympathize with Cuban rebels.

IN DEPTH RESOURCES: UNIT 5
Guided Reading, p. 21

ACCESS FOR STUDENTS ACQUIRING ENGLISH
Guided Reading (Spanish), p. 179

TERMS & NAMES
- José Martí
- Valeriano Weyler
- yellow journalism
- U.S.S. *Maine*
- George Dewey
- Rough Riders
- San Juan Hill

2 The Spanish-American-Cuban War

LEARN ABOUT the causes and course of the Spanish-American-Cuban War
TO UNDERSTAND how and why the United States gained control of Spain's former colonial possessions.

ONE AMERICAN'S STORY

James Creelman traveled to Cuba early in 1896 as a New York *World* correspondent covering the second Cuban war for independence from Spain. Although Spanish officials ordered him to leave, he remained in Havana and continued to write columns about his observations of the war.

A PERSONAL VOICE
No man's life, no man's property is safe [in Cuba]. American citizens are imprisoned or slain without cause. American property is destroyed on all sides. . . . Wounded soldiers can be found begging in the streets of Havana. . . . Cuba will soon be a wilderness of blackened ruins. . . . The horrors of a barbarous struggle for the extermination of the native population are witnessed in all parts of the country. Blood on the roadsides, blood in the fields, blood on the doorsteps, blood, blood, blood! The old, the young, the weak, the crippled—all are butchered without mercy. . . . Is there no nation wise enough, brave enough to aid this blood-smitten land?

JAMES CREELMAN, New York *World*, May 17, 1896

Creelman's columns reached Americans who were beginning to understand the implications of imperialism—and to be intrigued by the prospect of the United States as a world player. His descriptions of Spanish atrocities aroused sympathy for Cubans. Newspapers often exaggerated stories like Creelman's to boost their sales as well as to provoke American intervention in Cuba.

Cuban rebels burned the town of Jaruco in March 1896.

American Interest in Cuba

By 1825, Spain—once the most powerful colonial nation on earth—had lost most of its overseas possessions. It retained only the Philippines, the island of Guam, a few outposts in Africa, and Cuba and Puerto Rico in the Americas.

However, the United States had long had an interest in Cuba. In 1854, diplomats had recommended to President James Polk that the United States buy Cuba from Spain. In 1860, the Democratic Party's national platform called for admission of Cuba to the Union as a slave state. Toward the end of the century, events in Cuba drew the United States into war with Spain.

CUBAN POLITICAL INSTABILITY Both Puerto Rico and Cuba had strong cultural ties with Spain, but Cuba also had a history of rebellion. From 1868 to 1878, Cubans fought their first war for independence from Spanish rule. They forced Spain to abolish slavery in 1886 but failed to achieve independence.

After the emancipation of Cuba's slaves, American capitalists began investing millions of dollars in large sugar cane plantations on the island. Cuba's economy depended on sugar, and the United States now became Cuba's main market. In 1884, the United States had abolished its tariff on Cuban sugar, causing sugar production to skyrocket. But when a high tariff on Cuban sugar was restored in 1894, the Cuban economy was ruined.

SECOND WAR FOR INDEPENDENCE Anti-Spanish sentiment in Cuba soon erupted into a second war for independence. **José Martí,** a Cuban poet and

---

SECTION 2 RESOURCES

PRINT RESOURCES

IN-DEPTH RESOURCES: UNIT 5
Guided Reading, p. 21
Skillbuilder Practice: Recognizing Bias, p. 24
Primary Sources: Newspaper front page, p. 29; from *The Rough Riders* by Theodore Roosevelt, p. 30; In Favor of Imperialism, p. 31
American Lives: William Randolph Hearst, p. 36; José Martí, p. 37

ACCESS FOR STUDENTS ACQUIRING ENGLISH
Guided Reading (Spanish), p. 179
Skillbuilder Practice: Recognizing Bias (Spanish), p. 182

FORMAL ASSESSMENT
Section Quiz, p. 223

ALTERNATIVE ASSESSMENT BOOK
See forms for supporting and scoring alternative activities.

TECHNOLOGY RESOURCES

CD-ROM Electronic Library of Primary Sources

VIDEO *American Portfolio: A Videodisc for U.S. History* user's guide, pp. 175–178, 179

INTERNET McDougal Littell Learning On-Line
http://www.mcdougallittell.com

journalist in exile in New York, launched a revolution in 1895. Martí organized Cuban resistance against Spain, using an active guerrilla campaign and deliberately destroying property, especially American-owned sugar mills and plantations. Martí counted on provoking U.S. intervention to help the rebels achieve *Cuba Libre!*—a free Cuba.

THINK THROUGH HISTORY
A. *Analyzing Motives* Why did José Martí destroy American-owned sugar mills and plantations in Cuba?

Public opinion in the United States was split. Many business people wanted the government to support Spain in order to protect their investments. Other Americans, however, were enthusiastic about the rebel cause. The cry *"Cuba Libre!"* was, after all, similar to Patrick Henry's "Give me liberty or give me death!"

The Threat of War Escalates

A. Answer Martí hoped to provoke the United States into intervening to help free Cuba from Spain.

In 1896, Spain responded to the Cuban revolt by sending General **Valeriano Weyler** to Cuba to restore order. Believing regular military methods would not work against guerrilla tactics, Weyler moved the entire rural population of central and western Cuba, areas in which the rebels were particularly active, into concentration camps. An estimated 300,000 Cubans filled these camps, where thousands of them died from hunger and disease within two years.

YELLOW JOURNALISM Weyler's actions fueled a war over newspaper circulation that had developed between American newspaper tycoons William Randolph Hearst and Joseph Pulitzer. To lure readers, Hearst's New York *Journal* and Pulitzer's New York *World* printed exaggerated accounts—from reporters such as James Creelman—of "Butcher" Weyler's brutality. Stories of poisoned wells and of children being thrown to the sharks deepened American sympathy for the rebels. Legitimate reports of Cuban suffering mixed with these sensationalized stories became known as **yellow journalism**—reporting that exaggerates the news to lure new readers.

B. Answer Sensationalized stories of Spanish brutality aroused American sympathy for the Cuban rebels.

THINK THROUGH HISTORY
B. *Recognizing Effects* How did yellow journalism affect American attitudes toward the Cuban revolt?

Spanish authorities restricted the freedom of the reporters that Hearst and Pulitzer sent to Cuba and prevented them from entering combat areas. Some American correspondents claimed to have communicated with Cuban rebels secretly. Others gathered in Havana's bars and made up reports of battles that never took place. Hearst sent artist Frederic Remington, famous for his landscapes of the American West, to Cuba to illustrate reporters' stories. When Remington informed the publisher that a war between the United States and Spain seemed unlikely, Hearst reportedly replied, "You furnish the pictures and I'll furnish the war."

THE DE LÔME LETTER Many Americans sympathized with the Cuban rebels. When President William McKinley took office in 1897, demands for American intervention in Cuba were increasing. Preferring to avoid war with Spain, McKinley tried diplomatic means to resolve the crisis. At first, his efforts appeared to succeed. Spain recalled General Weyler, modified the policy regarding concentration camps, and offered Cuba limited self-government.

Skillbuilder Answer
Images: *Possible Answer:* The map forms the head of Uncle Sam about to swallow Cuba, which has the appearance of a small fish. **War over Cuba:** The artist sees the United States as the aggressor.

In February 1898, however, the New York *Journal* published a private letter written by Enrique Dupuy de Lôme, the Spanish minister to the United States. A Cuban rebel had stolen the letter from a Havana post office and leaked it to the newspaper, which was thirsty for scandal. The de Lôme letter criticized President McKinley, calling him "weak" and "a bidder for the admiration of the crowd."

KEY PLAYER

JOSÉ MARTÍ
1853–1895

The Cuban political activist José Martí dedicated his life to achieving independence for Cuba. Expelled from Cuba at the age of 16 because of his revolutionary activities, Martí earned a master's degree and a law degree and eventually settled in the United States.

Wary of the U.S. role in the Cuban struggle against the Spanish, Martí warned, "I know the Monster, because I have lived in its lair." His fears of U.S. imperialism turned out to have been well-founded: U.S. marines occupied Cuba on and off from 1906 until 1922.

Martí died fighting for Cuban independence in 1895. He is revered today in Cuba as a hero and martyr.

SKILLBUILDER
INTERPRETING GRAPHICS *What images do you think the cartoonist wanted the viewer to see in this drawing? What was the cartoonist's view of U.S. involvement in the war over Cuba?*

KEY PLAYER
José Martí

Critical Thinking: Analyzing Issues Ask students to explain why Martí sought U.S. intervention in Cuba, yet was wary of a U.S. presence in Cuba. *Martí felt that U.S. help was needed to overthrow the Spanish, but he was worried about the United States's imperialistic tendencies.*

IN-DEPTH RESOURCES, UNIT 5
American Lives: José Martí, p. 37

OBJECTIVE
(2) INSTRUCT

The Threat of War Escalates

▶ ***Discussing Key Ideas***
• Spanish leaders employ harsh tactics in an attempt to crush the Cuban revolt.
• Several incidents, along with yellow journalism, arouse American sympathy for Cuban rebels.

HISTORY FROM VISUALS
Reading the Graphic Who represents the United States in the cartoon? *Uncle Sam.* What does he appear to be on the verge of doing to Cuba? *Swallowing the country.*

Extension Discuss with students how someone who supported imperialism might depict the United States's relationship with Cuba in a similar cartoon.

IN-DEPTH RESOURCES, UNIT 5
Primary Source: In Favor of Imperialism, p. 31

TEACHING OPTIONS

Exploring Themes

Constitutional Concerns The nation's press, whose freedom and independence are derived from the Constitution, strengthens America's democracy by keeping its citizens well-informed and by holding the government accountable for its actions. However, the tactics employed in yellow journalism raise questions about the responsibilities and limits of a free press. Discuss with students the possible dangers to society of an unrestrained news media and under what circumstances, if any, constraints should be placed on the media in a democracy.

Teaching Less Proficient Readers

Reexamining Quotes Rereading aloud and interpreting quotes may help less proficient readers to better understand the material. Have those students follow these steps:

1. Read the quotations from Hearst, the de Lôme letter, and Theodore Roosevelt on pages 531 and 532.
2. Discuss the general meaning of each quotation.
3. Have students restate the ideas in their own words. *Example: Roosevelt thought that McKinley was a coward.*

"You furnish the pictures and I'll furnish the war."

WILLIAM RANDOLPH HEARST TO ARTIST FREDERIC REMINGTON

De Lôme's judgment of McKinley was actually much milder than Theodore Roosevelt's. Roosevelt, assistant secretary of the navy, considered McKinley "a white-livered cur" with "no more backbone than a chocolate eclair!" Although some Americans agreed with de Lôme's opinion of McKinley, they resented this criticism of their president by a Spanish official. Before an indignant State Department could demand his recall, de Lôme resigned.

THE U.S.S. *MAINE* EXPLODES Only a few days after publication of the de Lôme letter, American resentment toward Spain turned to outrage. Early in 1898, President McKinley had ordered the **U.S.S. *Maine*** to Cuba to protect American lives and property. On February 15, 1898, an explosion sent the ship's ammunition up in flames and the *Maine* sank. More than 260 of the 350 American officers and crew aboard lost their lives.

No one really knows what caused the explosion that destroyed the *Maine*. At the time, a naval court of inquiry reported that the ship had hit a mine, while a 1976 study by Admiral Hyman G. Rickover determined that an internal explosion in the ship's coal bunkers had caused the initial blast. In 1898, however, the yellow journalists held Spain responsible. The *Journal*'s headline read: THE WARSHIP MAINE WAS SPLIT IN TWO BY AN ENEMY'S SECRET INFERNAL MACHINE. Hearst's paper offered a reward of $50,000 for the capture of the Spaniards who supposedly had committed the outrage.

THINK THROUGH HISTORY
C. Summarizing *What events increased the conflict between the United States and Spain?*

C. Answer Publication of the de Lôme letter, which criticized President McKinley, and the explosion of the U.S.S. *Maine*, which many Americans blamed on Spain.

War Breaks Out

Now there was no holding back the forces that wanted war. "Remember the *Maine!*" became the rallying cry for U.S. intervention in Cuba. It made no difference that the Spanish government agreed, on April 9, to almost everything the United States demanded, including a six-month cease-fire.

Despite the Spanish concessions, public opinion favored war. On April 11, McKinley asked Congress for authority to use force against Spain in order to bring peace to Cuba. After a week of debate, Congress agreed, and on April 20, the United States went to war with Spain.

THE PHILIPPINES Although American attention focused on Cuba, the first battle of the war took place on the other side of the world—in the Philippine Islands. The Philippines, which had been a Spanish colony for over 300 years, had repeatedly rebelled against Spanish rule. In February 1898, Roosevelt had ordered the Pacific fleet to sail for the Philippines in case war with Spain broke out.

On May 1, **George Dewey**, the American naval commander in the Pacific, steamed into

War in the Philippines, 1898

- Admiral Dewey's U.S. Fleet
- Hong Kong
- Captured by U.S. Aug. 13, 1898
- LUZON
- South China Sea
- Manila
- Manila Bay — Spanish Fleet destroyed May 1, 1898
- MINDORO
- PACIFIC OCEAN
- PHILIPPINE ISLANDS
- SAMAR
- PANAY
- PALAWAN
- Sulu Sea
- NEGROS
- MINDANAO
- BORNEO
- 0 200 Miles
- 0 400 Kilometers
- U.S. Forces
- Battle

GEOGRAPHY SKILLBUILDER LOCATION How far did Admiral Dewey travel to reach the Philippines? **LOCATION** How did the location of the Philippines make them important to the United States?

Skillbuilder Answer Location: About 600 miles. **Location:** *Possible Answer:* The Philippines are well-placed for naval bases to protect sea lanes to China and the rest of east Asia.

532 CHAPTER 18

TEACHING OPTION

Skillbuilder Mini-Lesson: Recognizing Bias

Explaining the Skill Bias, or a prejudiced point of view, often appears in primary sources and other materials historians use. Biased material usually favors a special point of view and may not convey the truth about an event or issue. One strategy for detecting bias is to analyze the writer's opinions and his or her reasons for writing on the topic.

Applying the Skill On the chalkboard write the New York *Journal*'s headline, "THE WARSHIP MAINE WAS SPLIT IN TWO BY AN ENEMY'S SECRET INFERNAL MACHINE." Then ask students these questions:

1. What was the source of this headline? *The* Journal.
2. What were the views of William Randolph Hearst, publisher of the *Journal*, concerning the relationship between Cuba, Spain, and the United States? *He wanted the United States to go to war with Spain over Cuba. Stories about Cuba were selling subscriptions to the paper.*
3. What words and phrases in the headline might indicate bias? *Split in two, enemy, secret, infernal machine.*

IN-DEPTH RESOURCES: UNIT 5
Skillbuilder Practice: Recognizing Bias, p. 24

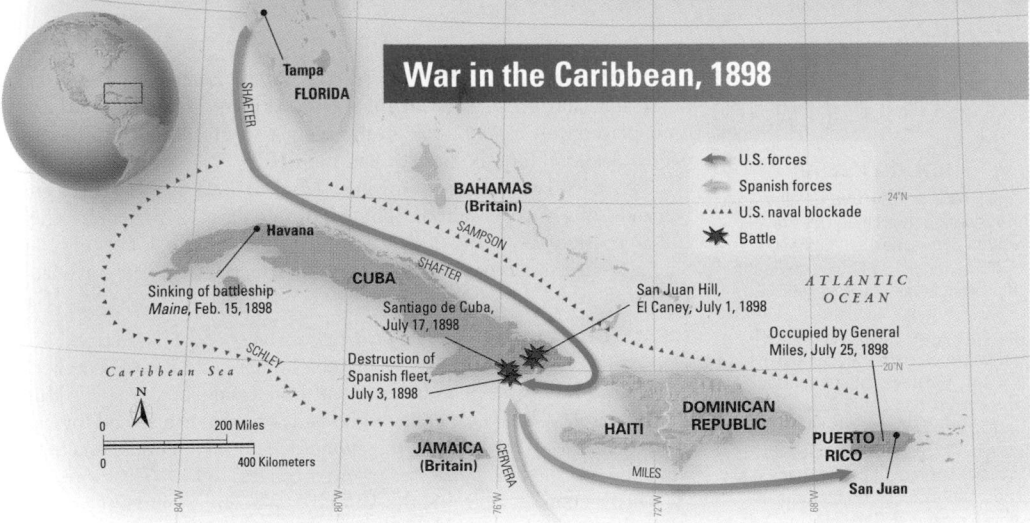

War in the Caribbean, 1898

Tampa
FLORIDA

SHAFTER

BAHAMAS
(Britain)

SAMPSON

Havana

SHAFTER

CUBA

Sinking of battleship
Maine, Feb. 15, 1898

Santiago de Cuba,
July 17, 1898

SCHLEY

Caribbean Sea

Destruction of
Spanish fleet,
July 3, 1898

JAMAICA
(Britain)

CERVERA

San Juan Hill,
El Caney, July 1, 1898

*ATLANTIC
OCEAN*

Occupied by General
Miles, July 25, 1898

24°N

20°N

HAITI

DOMINICAN
REPUBLIC

MILES

PUERTO
RICO

San Juan

	U.S. forces
	Spanish forces
	U.S. naval blockade
	Battle

0   200 Miles

0   400 Kilometers

Reading the Map Point
out to students that the row
of small triangles signals
the extent of the U.S. naval
blockade.

Extension Remind stu-
dents of Alfred T. Mahan's
argument for a strong U.S.
navy in his book, *The
Influence of Sea Power
upon History 1660–1783* (p.
528). Discuss how Mahan's
philosophy played a role in
the U.S. victory in the
Caribbean. Have students
list the possible effects of a
naval blockade on a sur-
rounded country using the
following chart:

Effects of a Blockade
1.
2.
3.
4.

MORE ABOUT . . .
Battle of San Juan Hill

Twenty years after the battle, Roosevelt stated, "San
Juan was the great day of
my life." He believed that
he deserved the Congres-
sional Medal of Honor for
his part in the war, but the
award was denied him.

IN-DEPTH RESOURCES: UNIT 5
from *The Rough Riders* by Theodore
Roosevelt, p. 30

**ELECTRONIC LIBRARY OF
PRIMARY SOURCES** from
The Strenuous Life by Theodore
Roosevelt

---

*Skillbuilder
Answer*
Movement: Haiti
and the
Dominican
Republic. **Place:**
The destruction
of the Spanish
fleet in July 1898.

Manila Bay and destroyed the Spanish fleet. Spain lost 381 men, while the
United States lost only one sailor, who died of heat prostration. Dewey's victory
paved the way for American troops to land in the Philippines. Over the next two
months, 11,000 Americans joined forces with Filipino rebels led by Emilio
Aguinaldo. In August, Spanish troops in Manila surrendered to Americans
rather than to the Filipinos, who had been fighting for freedom since 1896.

U.S. FORCES INVADE CUBA Back in the Caribbean, hostilities began with a
naval blockade of Cuba. Admiral William T. Sampson effectively sealed the
Spanish fleet in Santiago harbor. Meanwhile, American troops organized to
invade the island.

Dewey's victory had demonstrated the superiority of U.S. naval forces. In
contrast, the U.S. Army maintained only a small professional force supple-
mented by a larger inexperienced and ill-prepared volunteer force. About
125,000 Americans had volunteered to fight. However, the new soldiers were
sent to training camps that lacked adequate supplies and effective leaders.
Moreover, there were not enough modern guns to
go around, and the troops were outfitted with
heavy woolen uniforms that were unsuitable for
Cuba's tropical climate. In addition, the officers—
most of whom were Civil War veterans—had a
tendency to spend their time recalling their war
experiences rather than training the volunteers.

ROUGH RIDERS Despite these handicaps,
American forces landed in Cuba in June 1898
and began to converge on the port city of
Santiago. The army of 17,000 included four
African-American regiments of the regular army
and the **Rough Riders,** a volunteer cavalry
under the command of Leonard Wood and
Theodore Roosevelt.

The most famous land battle in Cuba took
place near Santiago on July 1. The first part of the
battle, on nearby Kettle Hill, featured a gallant
uphill charge by the Rough Riders and two
African-American regiments, the Ninth and

**GEOGRAPHY
SKILLBUILDER**
MOVEMENT *Besides
Cuba and Puerto Rico,
what countries were
affected by the U.S.
naval blockade in the
Caribbean?* **PLACE**
*What important event
took place in Santiago
Bay?*

This lithograph of
Roosevelt leading the
Rough Riders at San Juan
Hill shows the men on
horseback, though they
actually fought on foot.

America Claims an Empire **533**

THINK THROUGH HISTORY
D. *Clarifying*
*How prepared
were U.S. troops?*
D. Answer U.S.
troops were
inexperienced
and poorly
trained. They
lacked an
adequate supply
of weapons and
effective leaders.

TEACHING OPTION

Cooperative Activity: Covering the Rough Riders

Task: Students will role-play reporters and
members of the Rough Riders and together
craft a news article about the key battles of the
war in Cuba.

Purpose: To help students to better
understand the major battles of the Spanish-
American-Cuban War and the reasons why the
United States won.

Activity: Students should pair off and do
further research through the use of various
library resources or the Internet on the Rough
Riders, as well as on the battles of Kettle Hill

and San Juan Hill. One student then will play a
reporter, while the other plays a member of
the Rough Riders. The reporter will interview
the Rough rider about his or her experiences
in the war and write a brief article based on
the interview. The students who played the
reporter should read their articles before the
class.

Building a Portfolio: Encourage
students to place their news article in their
portfolio if they feel it is one of their stronger
works.

Standards for Evaluation
News articles should . . .

• be written in a clear and
concise manner
• show evidence of
research from more
than one source
• include the key aspects
of an event, as well as
relevant quotes

Critical Thinking:
Analyzing Discuss the characteristics of the Rough Riders. Then ask students to imagine that a movie is being made about this regiment. Whom would they cast in leading roles? Why?

ASSESS & RETEACH

Section 2 Assessment

Divide students into four groups and assign one of the questions to each group to answer. Then form new groups of four, consisting of one student from each original group. Students should share and discuss their answers.

Self-Assessment

Have pairs of students use the Think Through History Questions to review main ideas in this section. Students should find the portion of the text that helps answer each question.

Section Quiz

FORMAL ASSESSMENT
Section Quiz, p. 223

Reteach

Use the Guided Reading Worksheet for Section 2 to help review the main ideas of this section.

IN-DEPTH RESOURCES: UNIT 5
Guided Reading, p. 21

CLOSE

The Spanish-American-Cuban War demonstrated the superiority of U.S. naval forces and added Puerto Rico, Guam, and the Philippines to America's empire.

HISTORICAL SPOTLIGHT

ROUGH RIDERS
The First U.S. Volunteer Cavalry Regiment, better known as the Rough Riders, consisted of about 1,200 men aged 16 to 69. The Rough Riders included cowboys, clerks, New York City policemen, musicians, and polo players and other athletes. The regiment existed for only 133 days, but it captured the imagination of the American public and won the public's respect.

The Rough Riders trained as cavalry but fought on foot because their horses didn't reach Cuba in time for combat. They had the highest casualty rate of any American unit in the war. Among those who survived were future governors, members of Congress, and Theodore Roosevelt, who later became president of the United States.

Tenth Cavalries. Their victory cleared the way for an infantry attack on the strategically important **San Juan Hill.** Although Roosevelt and his units played only a minor role in the second victory, American newspapers declared him the hero of San Juan Hill.

Two days later, the Spanish fleet tried to escape the American blockade of Santiago harbor. The following naval battle along the Cuban coast ended in the destruction of the Spanish fleet. On July 17, Santiago surrendered, and on July 25, American troops invaded Puerto Rico.

TREATY OF PARIS OF 1898 The United States and Spain signed an armistice on August 12, ending what Secretary of State John Hay called "a splendid little war." The fighting had lasted only 16 weeks. Of the approximately 300,000 Americans who had served in the armed forces, about 5,400 lost their lives. Of this number, 379 were battle casualties, while the rest died from diseases or other causes.

On December 10, 1898, the United States and Spain agreed in a treaty that (1) Cuba would become independent, (2) Spain would give Puerto Rico and the Pacific island of Guam to the United States, and (3) the United States would pay Spain $20 million for the annexation of the Philippine Islands.

ANNEXATION OF THE PHILIPPINES The Treaty of Paris touched off great debate in the United States. Arguments centered on the annexation of the Philippines, but imperialism was the real issue. President McKinley told a group of Methodist ministers that he had prayed for guidance on Philippine annexation and had concluded "that there was nothing left for us to do but to take them all [the Philippine Islands], and to educate the Filipinos, and uplift and Christianize them." McKinley's imperialist beliefs must have clouded his memory—most Filipinos had been Christian for centuries.

Those against annexation included prominent Americans who presented a variety of arguments—political, moral, and self-serving. Some felt that the treaty violated the Declaration of Independence by denying self-government to the newly acquired territories. African-American educator Booker T. Washington argued that the United States should settle race-related issues at home before taking on social problems elsewhere. Labor leader Samuel Gompers feared that Filipino immigrants would compete for American jobs.

On February 6, 1899, the annexation question was settled with the Senate's passage of the Treaty of Paris. The United States now had an empire. The next question Americans faced was how and when the United States would add to its dominion.

E. Answer
Imperialists justified annexation as a means to educate and civilize Filipinos.

THINK THROUGH HISTORY
E. Analyzing Motives What were the justifications used by Americans to annex the Philippines?

Section 2 Assessment

1. TERMS & NAMES

Identify:
• José Martí
• Valeriano Weyler
• yellow journalism
• U.S.S. *Maine*
• George Dewey
• Rough Riders
• San Juan Hill

2. SUMMARIZING Write newspaper headlines explaining the significance of each of the following dates related to the Spanish-American-Cuban War:

February 15, 1898
April 20, 1898
May 1, 1898
July 25, 1898
August 12, 1898
February 6, 1899

Write the first paragraph of the newspaper article for one of the headlines.

3. DRAWING CONCLUSIONS What do you think were the unstated editorial policies of the yellow press? Support your answer with evidence from the text.

• journalist James Creelman's account of Spanish atrocities against Cubans on page 530
• why Hearst reportedly said to Remington, "You furnish the pictures and I'll furnish the war."
• the *Journal's* headline about the explosion of the battleship *Maine*

4. FORMING OPINIONS If you were a member of the 1898 Congress, would you have voted to declare war on Spain? Why or why not?

THINK ABOUT
• events that fueled the U.S. conflict with Spain
• the public's opinion of the war
• the success of McKinley's diplomatic measures in resolving the crisis
• the debate in Congress before the declaration of war

534 CHAPTER 18

ANSWERS

1. TERMS & NAMES

José Martí, p. 530

Valeriano Weyler, p. 531

yellow journalism, p. 531

U.S.S. *Maine*, p. 532

George Dewey, p. 532

Rough Riders, p. 533

San Juan Hill, p. 534

2. SUMMARIZING

Possible Responses: February 15, 1898: Battleship *Maine* Mysteriously Explodes and Sinks Near Cuban Coast; Over 260 Americans Die. April 20, 1898: U.S. Goes to War with Spain. May 1, 1898: Admiral Dewey Steams into Manila Bay and Destroys Spanish Fleet. July 25, 1898: U.S. Troops Invade Puerto Rico. August 12, 1898: War Over! U.S. and Spain Sign Armistice. February 6, 1899: Senate Passes Treaty of Paris.

3. DRAWING CONCLUSIONS

Possible Responses: To create news rather than to document it; to sensationalize events by distorting the truth; to exploit the public's fears; to manipulate the public's perceptions of events; to write articles that sell newspapers; to advance the newspaper publisher's political views.

4. FORMING OPINIONS

Possible Responses: Yes—the war was a humanitarian effort t stop Spanish atrocities against Cubans and to ensure Cubans' independence; it was important to represent public opinion that supported war; belief in imperialism meant supporting aggressive foreign policies. No—the yellow press was spreading wa fever; belief in anti-imperialism meant supporting cautious foreign policies.

3 Acquiring New Lands

TERMS & NAMES
- Platt Amendment
- protectorate
- Emilio Aguinaldo
- John Hay
- Open Door notes
- Boxer Rebellion

LEARN ABOUT U.S. relations with Cuba, Puerto Rico, and the Philippines
TO UNDERSTAND how American imperialism developed across the globe.

ONE AMERICAN'S STORY

On May 5, 1916, Luis Muñoz Rivera stood before the U.S. House of Representatives to discuss the future of his homeland, Puerto Rico. For more than a quarter of a century, he had fought to secure self-government for the people of Puerto Rico, first from Spain and then from the United States. As the editor of *La Democracia,* Muñoz Rivera, in 1891, had published a series of articles proposing self-government for Puerto Rico.

In 1897, after the Puerto Ricans and Cubans rebelled against Spain, Spanish authorities agreed to self-government for Puerto Rico. On July 17, 1898, the new Puerto Rican legislature met. Eight days, later, however, American troops landed on the island as part of their campaign against the Spanish. The Americans opposed Puerto Rican attempts at self-government, but Muñoz Rivera did not give up. Between 1900 and 1916, he led a campaign for Puerto Rican self-government in the United States as well as in Puerto Rico. Finally, in 1916, the U.S. Congress, facing possible war in Europe and wishing to settle the issue of Puerto Rico, invited Muñoz Rivera to speak before it.

Luis Muñoz Rivera

A PERSONAL VOICE
You, citizens of a free fatherland, with its own laws, its own institutions, and its own flag, can appreciate the unhappiness of the small and solitary people that must await its laws from your authority . . . When you acquire the certainty that you can found in Puerto Rico a republic like that founded in Cuba and Panama . . . give us our independence and you will stand before humanity as . . . a great creator of new nationalities and a great liberator of oppressed peoples.

LUIS MUÑOZ RIVERA, quoted in *The Puerto Ricans*

Muñoz Rivera returned to Puerto Rico, where he died in November 1916. Three months later, the United States made Puerto Ricans American citizens. They were not granted independence.

For nearly two decades before the First World War, the U.S. government viewed its colonies' demands for autonomy with suspicion. Only when America felt threatened by international calamity—World War I—did it bend to the wishes of its colonial populations.

U.S. Involvement in Puerto Rico

Not all Puerto Ricans wanted independence as Muñoz Rivera did. Some wanted statehood, while others hoped for some measure of local self-government as an American territory. As a result, the United States gave Puerto Ricans no promises regarding independence after the Spanish-American-Cuban War.

AMERICANS IN PUERTO RICO When American military forces landed on the island in July 1898, the commanding officer, General Nelson A. Miles, issued a statement assuring Puerto Ricans that the Americans were there to "bring you [Puerto Rico] protection, not only to yourselves but to your property, to promote your prosperity, and to bestow upon you the immunities and blessings of the liberal institutions of our government." Other American officers were openly insulting. For example, General Guy V. Henry, military governor of the island, doubted Puerto Ricans could govern themselves. He argued

America Claims an Empire **535**

SECTION 3 RESOURCES

PRINT RESOURCES

IN-DEPTH RESOURCES: UNIT 5
Guided Reading, p. 22

ACCESS FOR STUDENTS ACQUIRING ENGLISH
Guided Reading (Spanish), p. 180

FORMAL ASSESSMENT
Section Quiz, p. 224

ALTERNATIVE ASSESSMENT BOOK
See forms for supporting and scoring alternative activities.

TECHNOLOGY RESOURCES

HUMANITIES TRANSPARENCIES
H37, Declined with Thanks
H17, *Athletic Contest* by Max Weber

CRITICAL THINKING TRANSPARENCIES
CT10, Overseas Expansion

CD-ROM Electronic Library of Primary Sources

VIDEO *American Portfolio: A Videodisc for U.S. History*
user's guide, p. 179

INTERNET McDougal Littell Learning On-Line
http://www.mcdougallittell.com

Section 3 Overview

OBJECTIVES

1. To describe U.S. involvement in Puerto Rico.
2. To explain how the United States maintained political control over Cuba.
3. To identify causes and effects of the Philippine-American War.
4. To explain the purpose of the Open Door Policy in China.
5. To summarize opposing views regarding U.S. imperialism.

SKILLBUILDERS
- Interpreting political cartoons, p. 537
- Understanding geography: human-environment interaction, p. 540
- Interpreting graphs, p. 541

CRITICAL THINKING
- Drawing conclusions, p. 536
- Synthesizing, p. 537
- Contrasting, p. 538
- Analyzing motives, p. 539
- Summarizing, p. 541
- Analyzing issues, p. 541
- Forming opinions, p. 541

FOCUS & MOTIVATE

▶*Starting with the Student*
- How do students convince their parents to give them more independence?
- How do students think colonial populations convinced the United States to grant them self-government?

OBJECTIVE
1 **INSTRUCT**

U.S. Involvement in Puerto Rico

▶*Discussing Key Ideas*
- Puerto Ricans resent U.S. control of their government.
- Congress passes the Foraker Act, which denies U.S. citizenship to Puerto

(continued on next page)

Teacher's Edition **535**

(continued from page 535)

Ricans and gives the president control over Puerto Rico's government.

IN-DEPTH RESOURCES: UNIT 5
Guided Reading, p. 22

ACCESS FOR STUDENTS ACQUIRING ENGLISH
Guided Reading (Spanish), p. 180

MORE ABOUT . . .
Luis Muñoz Rivera

Throughout his independence crusade, Muñoz Rivera was arrested many times on various agitation charges. During one trial, the judge asked him how many times he had been arrested. "Forty-two times, Señor President!" he answered. "Forty-two times I have been prosecuted for loving my country."

NOW & THEN
Puerto Rico as Commonwealth

Critical Thinking: Drawing Conclusions Have students make a chart comparing pros and cons of statehood for Puerto Rico. Then ask them to write a paragraph stating how they would vote on a national referendum on statehood if they were living in Puerto Rico.

OBJECTIVE
② **INSTRUCT**

Cuba Becomes a Protectorate

▶ ***Discussing Key Ideas***
• The Treaty of Paris ensures Cuban independence, but the U.S. Army steps in.
• As a result of the Platt Amendment, the United States maintains control over Cuba.

NOW & THEN

PUERTO RICO AS COMMONWEALTH

Today, some Puerto Ricans argue in favor of statehood for Puerto Rico and others support independence. However, in 1993, Puerto Ricans narrowly voted to remain a U.S. commonwealth, a status given the island in 1952.

As a commonwealth, Puerto Rico is allowed to make its own laws and handle its own finances, while the United States controls defense and sets tariffs. In addition, as commonwealth citizens, Puerto Ricans can move freely between their island and the United States—there are no immigration restrictions.

As a commonwealth, Puerto Rico enjoys a tax-exempt status that encourages corporations to build factories there. As a state, it would gain representation in Congress, the right to vote in presidential elections, and opportunities for federal aid—but it would lose its tax-exempt status.

that "They are still children, each one has a different idea and they don't really know what they want." Henry limited Puerto Rican access to alcoholic beverages and tobacco, tried to Americanize the Puerto Ricans by teaching them English, and limited freedom of the press, especially after being criticized by Muñoz Rivera.

PUERTO RICAN ATTITUDES TOWARD INDEPENDENCE Many Puerto Ricans at first welcomed U.S. intervention, seeing it as an improvement over control by Spain. Following General Henry's heavy-handed tactics in 1899, however, large numbers of Puerto Ricans came to fear the "Yankee Peril." Even those who supported U.S. control became disillusioned with the military government and its attitude of superiority toward the Puerto Ricans. Some, like Muñoz Rivera, campaigned for an end to military government and requested U.S. citizenship and full local self-government. They believed that after Puerto Rico had demonstrated the ability to govern itself, it should have become a state. Still others felt that Puerto Ricans should be allowed to choose between statehood and complete independence from the United States.

FORAKER ACT Although Puerto Ricans had dreams of independence or statehood, the United States had a different agenda for the island's future. Puerto Rico was strategically important to the United States both for maintaining a U.S. presence in the Caribbean and for protecting a future canal that some American leaders wanted to build across the Isthmus of Panama. In 1900, Congress passed the Foraker Act, which denied U.S. citizenship to Puerto Ricans and gave the president the power to appoint Puerto Rico's governor and members of the upper house of its legislature. Puerto Ricans could elect only members of the legislature's lower house.

In 1901, in the Insular Cases, the U.S. Supreme Court ruled that the Constitution did not automatically apply to people in acquired territories. Congress retained the right to extend United States' citizenship, and it granted that right to Puerto Ricans in 1917. It also gave them the right to elect both houses of their legislature.

Cuba Becomes a Protectorate

The war resolution against Spain in 1898 included the Teller Amendment, which said that the United States did not intend to annex or control Cuba. After all, Spanish oppression of Cubans was the United States' main argument for waging war. Consequently, the Treaty of Paris of 1898 guaranteed Cuba the independence that its nationalist leaders had been demanding for years. Still, for four years following the war, the U.S. Army governed Cuba.

José Martí had feared that the United States would merely replace Spain and dominate Cuban politics. In some ways, Martí's prediction came true. Under American occupation, the same officials who had served Spain remained in office. Cubans who protested this policy were imprisoned or exiled.

On the other hand, the American military government provided food and clothing for thousands of families, helped farmers put land back into cultivation, and organized elementary schools. Through improvement of sanitation and medical research, the military government eliminated yellow fever, a disease that had killed hundreds of Cubans each year.

PLATT AMENDMENT In 1900 the newly formed Cuban government wrote a constitution, one that did not specify the relationship between Cuba and the United States. Consequently, in 1901, the United States insisted that Cuba

THINK THROUGH HISTORY
A. Drawing Conclusions How did the Foraker Act benefit the United States?
A. Answer It allowed the president to appoint Puerto Rico's governor and part of its legislature, thus enabling the United States to maintain control.

536 CHAPTER 18

TEACHING OPTIONS

Exploring Themes

Constitutional Concerns In 1788, as the United States ratified its Constitution, probably few Americans dreamed of acquiring other countries. For that reason, the U.S. Constitution does not explicitly address the rights of people in acquired territories. Instead, the Supreme Court had to step in and rule on the matter. Discuss with students the Supreme Court's ruling that the rights granted by the Constitution do not automatically apply to persons in territories acquired by the United States. Ask students to offer reasons why they agree or disagree.

Making Connections Across Cultures

Puerto Ricans in the United States Throughout the 20th century, native Puerto Ricans and their ancestors have made notable contributions to U.S. society. In 1970, Herman Badillo became the first Puerto Rican to win election to the U.S. Congress. The writer William Carlos Williams, whose mother was born in Puerto Rico, won the Pulitzer Prize in poetry in 1963. Throughout the 1960s, Roberto Clemente starred as an outfielder for the Pittsburgh Pirates. During his 18-year career, Clemente won four National League batting titles. He eventually was elected to baseball's Hall of Fame.

add to its constitution several provisions, known as the **Platt Amendment,** stating that

(1) Cuba could not make treaties that might limit its independence or permit a foreign power to control any part of its territory;
(2) the United States reserved the right to intervene in Cuba to preserve independence and maintain order;
(3) Cuba was not to go into debt;
(4) the United States could buy or lease land on the island for naval and coaling stations.

The United States made it clear that the army would not withdraw until Cuba adopted the Platt Amendment. In response, a torchlight procession marched on the residence of Governor-General Leonard Wood to protest the provisions. Some protesters even called for a return to arms to defend their national honor against this American insult. The U.S. government stood firm, though, and Cubans reluctantly ratified the new constitution. Two years later, the Platt Amendment became part of the permanent treaty between the two nations. Cuba became a U.S. **protectorate,** a country whose affairs are partially controlled by a stronger power.

PROTECTING AMERICAN BUSINESS INTERESTS The most important reason for the United States to maintain a strong political presence in Cuba was to protect its economic interests. American corporations had invested heavily in the island's sugar, tobacco, and mining industries, as well as in its railroads and public utilities. American investments in Cuba soared from $50 million in 1898 to $220 million by 1913. Although many business people were convinced that political control of colonies was necessary in order to protect the large profits to be found there, some were concerned about colonial entanglements. Industrialist Andrew Carnegie argued that a policy of imperialism was unnecessary.

> **A PERSONAL VOICE**
> The exports of the United States this year [1898] are greater than those of any other nation in the world. Even Britain's exports are less, yet Britain "possesses" . . . a hundred "colonies" . . . scattered all over the world. The fact that the United States has none does not prevent her products and manufactures from invading . . . all parts of the world in competition with those of Britain.
>
> **ANDREW CARNEGIE,** quoted in *Distant Possessions*

The U.S. Department of State, however, continued to push for control of its Latin American neighbors. American troops withdrew from Cuba in 1902 but later returned three times to intervene in Cuban affairs. Marines occupied the island to quell popular uprisings against conservative leaders from 1906 to 1909, briefly in 1912, and again from 1917 to 1922. The United States also established a naval base at Guantánamo Bay, which it still maintains.

Filipinos Rebel

In the Philippines, the native population was intent on independence. Even more than the Cubans, Filipinos reacted with outrage to American annexation of their

WELL, I HARDLY KNOW WHICH TO TAKE FIRST!

537

Philippine-American War

The process of American-ization of the Philippines included making English the official language and intro-ducing basketball. However, the Moros—Muslim Filipinos on the island of Mindanao—refused to submit to American rule. They finally surrendered in 1906 after 600 of them, including many women and children, died in the Battle of Bud Dajo.

Have students create a flow chart, similar to the one below, to show events in the Philippines from its annexa-tion by the United States to its gaining independence.

 ELECTRONIC LIBRARY OF PRIMARY SOURCES
On the War in the Philippines by Alfred J. Beveridge

OBJECTIVE
④ **INSTRUCT**

China and the Open Door Policy

▶ *Discussing Key Ideas*
• European powers and Japan establish spheres of influence in China.
• John Hay proposes that European nations share their trading rights in China with the United States.
• The United States and other imperialist powers put down a rebellion against foreign influences in China.

U.S. military action in the Philippines resulted in the deaths of about 200,000 Filipino civilians from disease and the effects of such guerrilla tactics as the burning of villages.

homeland. Rebel leader **Emilio Aguinaldo** believed that the United States had promised independence and that it had betrayed the Filipinos after helping them win freedom from Spain. Resentment over the 1898 Treaty of Paris erupted in rebellion.

PHILIPPINE–AMERICAN WAR In January 1899, Aguinaldo proclaimed the Philippines an inde-pendent republic and drafted a constitution. But the presence of American soldiers reinforced U.S. control over the islands. In February, the Filipinos, led by Aguinaldo, rose in armed revolt. The United States assumed the role that Spain had played and imposed its authority on a colony that was fighting for freedom. When Aguinaldo turned to guerrilla tactics, the United States resorted to forcing Filipinos to live in designated zones, where poor sanitation, starvation, and dis-ease killed thousands. This was the very same practice that Americans had condemned Spain for using in Cuba.

White American soldiers looked down on the Filipinos because of their skin color. However, many of the 70,000 U.S. troops sent to the Philippines were African Americans. When African-American news-papers questioned why blacks were helping to spread racial prejudice to the Philippines, some African-American soldiers deserted to the Filipino side and developed bonds of friendship with the Filipinos.

The Philippine-American War lasted three years. American forces captured Aguinaldo in 1901, but the rebellion continued until mid-1902. About 20,000 Filipino rebels died fighting for independence. The war claimed 4,000 American lives, and cost $400 million—20 times the price the United States had paid for the islands.

AFTERMATH OF THE WAR After suppressing the rebellion, the United States set up a government for the Philippines similar to the one it had established for Puerto Rico. The U.S. president would appoint a governor, who would then appoint the upper house of the legislature. Filipinos would elect the lower house. From 1901 to 1904, William Howard Taft served as governor of the islands. He established programs to build schools and hospitals and improve sanitation.

One of Taft's programs brought American college graduates to the islands to improve education. The 540 young Americans who sailed to Manila aboard the U.S.S. *Thomas* became known as Thomasites. They settled throughout the islands, trained Filipino teachers, and conducted classes. The number of Filipino students attending elementary school increased from 5,000 in 1898 to more than 1 million in 1920. Under American rule, the Philippines moved gradually toward independence and finally became an independent republic on July 4, 1946.

China and the Open Door Policy

U.S. imperialists saw the Philippines as a gateway to the rest of Asia, particu-larly China. The United States did not want to seek colonies on the Asian main-land or risk another war like the one in the Philippines. China, however, was a vast potential market for American products. It also presented American investors with opportunities for large-scale railroad construction.

THINK THROUGH HISTOR
C. Contrasting *What were the motives of the Filipinos? of the Americans?*

C. Answer Filipinos wanted independence. The United States wanted to take over the role that Spain had played in governing the Philippines.

538 CHAPTER 18

Cooperative Activity: Writing Letters to Uncle Sam

Task: Student groups will write letters to the United States government expressing Cuban, Puerto Rican, Filipino, and Chinese attitudes toward American imperialism.

Purpose: To better understand the effects of imperialism on colonial peoples.

Activity: Divide students into groups of four and have each group represent one of the fol-lowing countries: Puerto Rico, Cuba, the Philippines, and China. The group should write

a letter to the United States (addressing it to Uncle Sam) expressing how U.S. imperialism affects the country which they represent. Allow time for the group to share its letter with the class.

📁 **Building a Portfolio:** Students wishing to add the assignment to their portfolio should highlight their contribution to the letter.

ALTERNATIVE ASSESSMENT BOOK
Standards for Evaluating a Cooperative Activity

Standards for Evaluation
Letters should . . .

• include specific exam-ples of the positive/neg-ative effects of American imperialism in the assigned country
• accurately reflect infor-mation from the text-book and other references
• use appropriate letter form and style

Weakened by war and foreign intervention, China had become the "sick man of Asia" by the early 20th century. As China's 250-year-old Manchu dynasty began to crumble, the European powers and Japan demanded trading rights and other concessions. Under pressure from American business leaders, who feared they might be squeezed out of China, the United States took action.

JOHN HAY'S OPEN DOOR NOTES By 1899, France, Germany, Britain, Japan, and Russia had spheres of influence, or regions in which they had exclusive trading rights, in China. Each nation's merchants, missionaries, and other citizens lived within its sphere of influence, where they were governed by their own laws rather than those of China.

A group of New York investors had formed a development company to promote American trade in China. But the United States had no sphere of influence there and could not force other imperial powers out of China. Consequently, Secretary of State **John Hay** proposed a plan to protect American trading rights. He sent notes with the same message to Germany, Russia, and Britain, and later to France, Italy, and Japan. The so-called **Open Door notes** asked the nations with spheres of influence to also allow the United States to have trading rights in China.

The six nations complained among themselves about sharing the trading rights they had won at considerable political and military cost. Hay interpreted their vague responses as an acceptance of his requests. On March 20, 1900, he announced that the Open Door policy had become effective.

REBELLION IN CHINA In 1900, events in China brought the United States and other imperial powers together to stop a rebellion. At that time, many Chinese opposed the spread of Western influence in their country. A secret society, known as the Boxers, rose in revolt to drive out the "foreign devils." The Boxers killed hundreds of missionaries and other foreigners as well as Chinese converts to Christianity. In August 1900, troops from Britain, France, Germany, and Japan joined 2,500 American soldiers and marched on the Chinese capital. Within two months, the international forces put down the **Boxer Rebellion.**

THINK THROUGH HISTORY
D. Analyzing Motives Why did John Hay propose an Open Door policy in China?
D. Answer Other nations had carved out spheres of influence in China. To open markets to Americans, Hay proposed that all nations follow principles of open trade in China.

ON THE WORLD STAGE

THE BOXER PROTOCOL
On September 7, 1901, China and 11 other nations signed the Boxer Protocol—a final settlement in the Boxer Rebellion.

The Manchu government agreed to execute some Chinese officials and punish others and to pay about $332 million in damages. The United States was awarded a settlement of $24.5 million. It used about $4 million to pay American citizens for actual losses incurred during the rebellion. In 1908, the U.S. government returned the rest of the money to China to be used for the purpose of educating Chinese students in their own country and in the United States.

U.S. Army troops help rescue the besieged foreign legations in Beijing during the rebellion of the Harmonious Righteous Fists, or Boxers, in 1900.

America Claims an Empire **539**

MORE ABOUT . . .
The Boxers
The real name of the group known as the Boxers was the Righteous and Harmonious Fists. Westerners referred to the organization as the Boxers because its members practiced Chinese exercises that resembled boxing.

ON THE WORLD STAGE
The Boxer Protocol
Critical Thinking: Analyzing Motives Why did the U.S. government want the money it returned to China to be used for educating Chinese students in China and the United States? *Possible Responses: To foster good will; to introduce Chinese students to western influences; to exercise some control over Chinese use of the money.*

HUMANITIES TRANSPARENCIES
H17, *Athletic Contest* by Max Weber

TEACHING OPTIONS

Teaching Gifted and Talented Students

Investigating the Life and Rule of Cixi Empress Cixi (also spelled Tz'u-hsi), who ruled China during the Boxer Rebellion, is considered to be one of the most powerful women in the history of China. Like the Boxers, Cixi detested foreign influence in China. "The foreigners are like fish in the stewpan," she said. "For forty years have I . . . eaten bitterness because of them." Have students research and report on Empress Cixi's reign and her role in the Boxer Rebellion. Why did she endorse and then eventually condemn the rebellion? How did she maintain power after western nations put down the uprising?

Making Connections Across Time

China Reclaims Hong Kong On July 1, 1997, Hong Kong once again became part of China. In 1898, China had leased the small peninsula along its southern coast to Britain for 99 years. During that time Hong Kong became a major port for British trade with Asia and grew into a prosperous center of international trade and finance. In reclaiming the land, Communist China vowed to allow Hong Kong a "high degree of autonomy" for the next fifty years. However, observers fear that China's rulers will bring with them their repressive ways, and many Hong Kong residents are bracing for an end to their democratic freedoms.

Teacher's Edition **539**

The Impact of U.S. Territorial Gains

▶ *Discussing Key Ideas*
• Imperialism forces Americans to expand their knowledge of the world.
• Some Americans continue to oppose imperialism for economic and moral reasons.

MORE ABOUT . . .
William Jennings Bryan

In one anti-imperialist speech, Bryan declared that the famous words of Patrick Henry applied not only to Americans, but all peoples of the world. "When he uttered that passionate appeal, 'Give me liberty or give me death,' he expressed a sentiment which still echoes in the hearts of men."

 ELECTRONIC LIBRARY OF PRIMARY SOURCES
Platform of the Anti-Imperialist League

HISTORY FROM VISUALS
U.S. Imperialism, 1880–1910

Reading the Map Point out that the date next to each flag indicates when the United States gained that territory.

 HUMANITIES TRANSPARENCIES
H37, Declined with Thanks

The United States then took additional steps to prevent the imperial powers from carving up China.

John Hay issued a second series of Open Door notes, announcing that the United States would "safeguard for the world the principle of equal and impartial trade with all parts of the Chinese Empire." This policy paved the way for greater American influence in Asia and was used not only to open foreign markets but also to dominate them.

The Open Door policy reflected three deeply held American beliefs about the U.S. industrial capitalist economy. First, Americans believed that the growth of the U.S. economy depended on exports. Second, they felt the United States had a right to intervene abroad to keep foreign markets open. Third, they feared that the closing of an area to American products, citizens, or ideas threatened U.S. survival. These beliefs were the bedrock of American foreign policy at the turn of the century.

The Impact of U.S. Territorial Gains

William McKinley's reelection in 1900 seemed to indicate that many Americans favored his policies over those of his anti-imperialist opponent, William Jennings Bryan. McKinley stated, "The expansion of our trade and commerce is the pressing problem." The United States enjoyed unprecedented economic prosperity, but some Americans agreed with Bryan, who insisted, "It is not necessary to own people to trade with them."

Skillbuilder Answer
Mediator: The Algeciras and Congo Conferences. **Status:** *Possible Answer:* This role shows the growing power and prestige of the United States, because other powerful nations chose the U.S. to help settle their disputes.

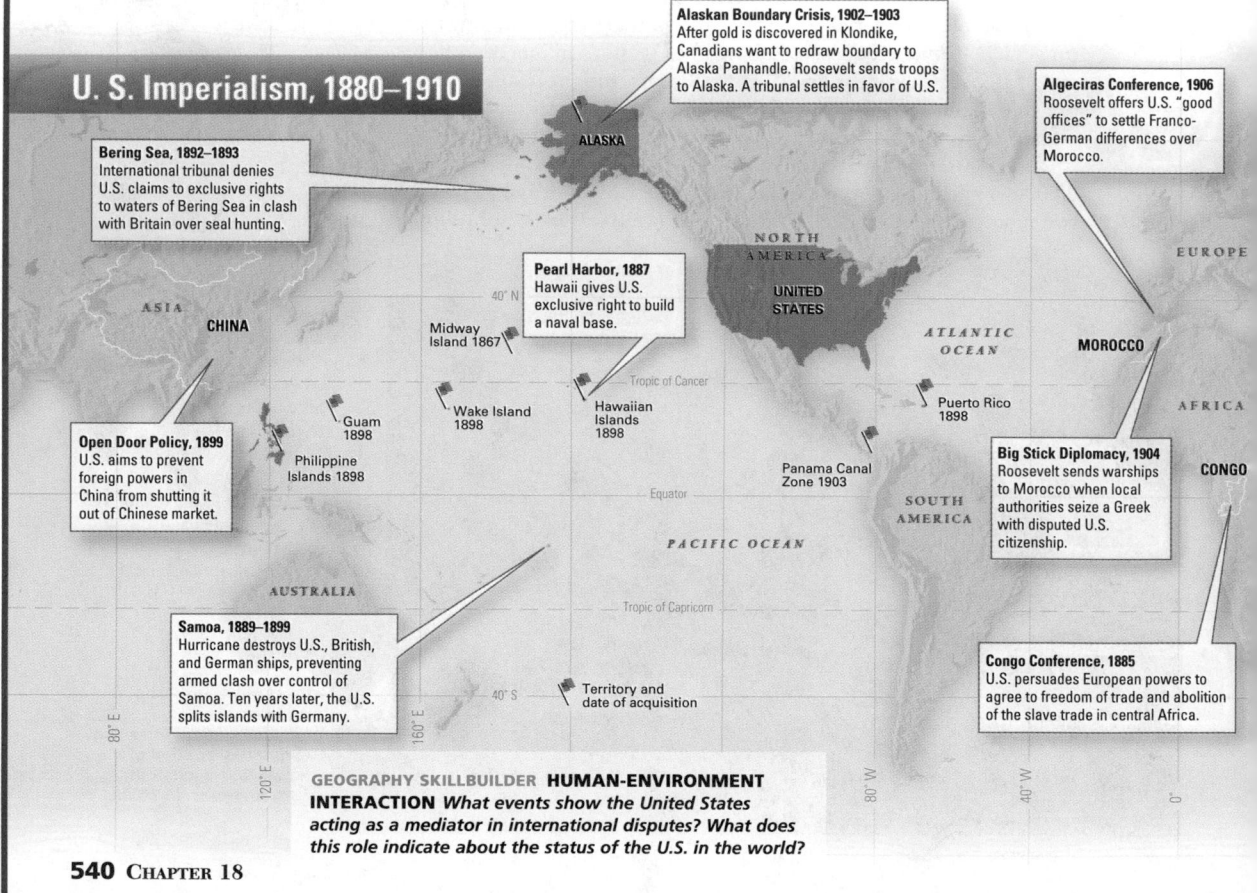

U. S. Imperialism, 1880–1910

Alaskan Boundary Crisis, 1902–1903 After gold is discovered in Klondike, Canadians want to redraw boundary to Alaska Panhandle. Roosevelt sends troops to Alaska. A tribunal settles in favor of U.S.

Algeciras Conference, 1906 Roosevelt offers U.S. "good offices" to settle Franco-German differences over Morocco.

Bering Sea, 1892–1893 International tribunal denies U.S. claims to exclusive rights to waters of Bering Sea in clash with Britain over seal hunting.

Pearl Harbor, 1887 Hawaii gives U.S. exclusive right to build a naval base.

Open Door Policy, 1899 U.S. aims to prevent foreign powers in China from shutting it out of Chinese market.

Big Stick Diplomacy, 1904 Roosevelt sends warships to Morocco when local authorities seize a Greek with disputed U.S. citizenship.

Samoa, 1889–1899 Hurricane destroys U.S., British, and German ships, preventing armed clash over control of Samoa. Ten years later, the U.S. splits islands with Germany.

Congo Conference, 1885 U.S. persuades European powers to agree to freedom of trade and abolition of the slave trade in central Africa.

Midway Island 1867
Guam 1898
Wake Island 1898
Hawaiian Islands 1898
Philippine Islands 1898
Puerto Rico 1898
Panama Canal Zone 1903

🚩 Territory and date of acquisition

ASIA · CHINA · AUSTRALIA · NORTH AMERICA · UNITED STATES · ATLANTIC OCEAN · EUROPE · MOROCCO · AFRICA · CONGO · SOUTH AMERICA · PACIFIC OCEAN · ALASKA
Tropic of Cancer · Equator · Tropic of Capricorn

GEOGRAPHY SKILLBUILDER **HUMAN-ENVIRONMENT INTERACTION** *What events show the United States acting as a mediator in international disputes? What does this role indicate about the status of the U.S. in the world?*

540 CHAPTER 18

Making Connections Across the Curriculum

Composition Ask students to list the arguments for and against imperialism. Then have them choose one point of view and write an essay supporting that view using the arguments from their list. Students should take into account the economic, military, paternalistic and moral factors regarding U.S. imperialism, as well as the views of countries that have come under U.S. control. Provide time for students to share their work.

Teaching Less Proficient Readers

Understanding Satire Some students may have difficulty understanding the true meaning of satirical statements, that employ irony and subtle wit to attack policies or ideas. Have these students reread Mark Twain's quote on page 541. Discuss with them Twain's use of irony and sarcasm in making some of his points. *For instance, when Twain refers to other peoples of the world as "our Brother who Sits in Darkness," he is ridiculing the belief that anyone who has not yet acquired American culture lives an unfulfilled and backward existence.*

JUSTIFYING U.S. IMPERIALISM Prior to the Spanish-American-Cuban War, many Americans, including President McKinley, did not even know where the Philippines were located. Acquiring an empire had forced Americans to expand their knowledge of distant lands and people. In the United States, world's fairs provided a perfect opportunity for Americans to demonstrate how imperialism profited everyone.

Between 1900 and 1910, the United States held five international expositions. Nearly 20 million visitors flocked to the 1904 Louisiana Purchase Exposition, which included a Philippine reservation. Nearly 1,200 people were brought from the Philippines to live in villages on a 47-acre site on the fairgrounds. The ethnic groups included in the exhibit represented only a small percentage of the diverse Filipino cultures. They were carefully chosen to create the impression that some Filipinos were capable of cultural advancement under American influence but that others were "primitive savages."

OPPOSING IMPERIALISM The exhibit left fairgoers with the pro-imperialist view that the Philippine Islands were economically valuable to the United States and fostered the myth that Filipinos were racially inferior and incapable of governing themselves. But not all Americans believed these arguments. Politician Carl Schurz, for example, warned that the expense of maintaining an American empire would outweigh any economic benefits. Novelist Mark Twain questioned the motives for imperialism in a piece of satire written in 1901.

A PERSONAL VOICE

Shall we go on conferring our Civilization upon the peoples that sit in darkness, or shall we give those poor things a rest? . . . Extending the Blessings of Civilization to our Brother who Sits in Darkness has been a good trade and has paid well, on the whole; and there is money in it yet . . . but not enough, in my judgment, to make any considerable risk advisable.

MARK TWAIN, quoted in *To the Person Sitting in Darkness*

Twain, however, did not determine American foreign policy. In the early 20th century, Presidents Theodore Roosevelt and Woodrow Wilson continued to project American power around the globe.

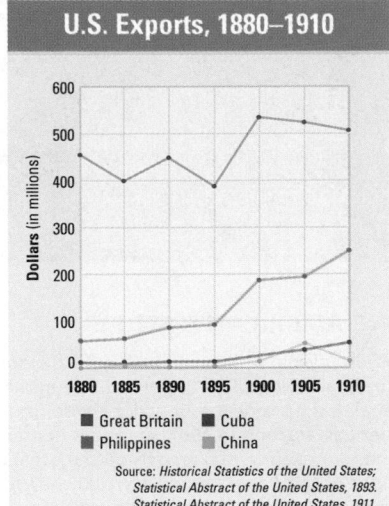

U.S. Exports, 1880–1910

Dollars (in millions)

■ Great Britain   ■ Cuba
■ Philippines   ■ China

Source: *Historical Statistics of the United States; Statistical Abstract of the United States, 1893. Statistical Abstract of the United States, 1911.*

SKILLBUILDER
INTERPRETING GRAPHS
Which market had the greatest amount of growth in U.S. exports between 1900 and 1905? Which country did the United States export to the most during this time period?

Skillbuilder Answer
Market: China.
Trade: Great Britain.

E. Answer The U.S. did not need colonies in order to trade with other nations; the expense of maintaining an empire outweighed the economic benefits; the imperative to spread Anglo-Saxon culture was just an excuse to exploit people.

THINK THROUGH HISTORY
E. *Summarizing* How would you summarize anti-imperialist arguments?

Section ③ Assessment

1. TERMS & NAMES

Identify:
• Platt Amendment
• protectorate
• Emilio Aguinaldo
• John Hay
• Open Door notes
• Boxer Rebellion

2. SUMMARIZING Create a time line of the key events relating to U.S relations with Cuba, Puerto Rico, and the Philippines. Use the dates already plotted on the time line below as a guide.

1899 1901
1900 1917

Which date do you think was most significant? Why?

3. ANALYZING ISSUES How did U.S. foreign policy at the turn of the century affect actions taken by the United States toward China?

THINK ABOUT
• why the United States wanted access to China's markets
• the purpose of the Open Door notes

4. FORMING OPINIONS Do you think that America was justified in its policy of overseas expansion? Why or why not?

THINK ABOUT
• Andrew Carnegie's comment about U.S. exports
• economic advantages of imperialism for the United States
• William Jennings Bryan's comment
• Carl Schurz's warnings about the expense of imperialism

America Claims an Empire **541**

ANSWERS

1. TERMS & NAMES
Platt Amendment, p. 537
protectorate, p. 537
Emilio Aguinaldo, p. 538
John Hay, p. 539
Open Door notes, p. 539
Boxer Rebellion, p. 539

2. SUMMARIZING
Possible Responses: **1899**—Aguinaldo's armed revolt sparks Philippine-American War. **1900**—Foraker Act denies U.S. citizenship to Puerto Ricans and gives the U.S. president partial control of their government; McKinley is reelected as president. **1901**—Platt Amendment authorizes U.S. intervention in Cuba. **1917**—Congress grants U.S. citizenship to Puerto Ricans.

3. ANALYZING ISSUES
Possible Answers: Students should suggest that the United States government believed that the growth of the U.S. economy depended on exports and that the nation had the right to intervene to keep foreign markets open to the United States. The Open Door notes were a nonmilitary attempt to secure U.S. trading rights in China.

4. FORMING OPINIONS
Possible Responses: Yes—seizing control of overseas territories was essential to maintaining a favorable balance of trade and ensuring economic growth. No—keeping foreign markets open was not contingent on acquiring overseas territories; Bryan raised an important moral issue about whether the U.S. had the right to dominate people in foreign countries.

HISTORY FROM VISUALS
U.S. Exports, 1880–1910
Reading the Graph Tell students that the graph shows the values of U.S. exports to each of the four countries represented by the colored lines. For example, the value of U.S. exports to the Philippines in 1895 was about $100 million.

Extension Discuss whether U.S. trade patterns seemed to justify or contradict the economic arguments in favor of imperialism.

ASSESS & RETEACH

Section 3 Assessment

Ask students to work in small groups to answer the questions. Have one student from each group read the group's answer to question 4 before the class. (If the group formed two opinions, have two students read.)

Self-Assessment

Have students work in study groups to discuss answers and resolve differences by verifying information in the text.

Section Quiz

FORMAL ASSESSMENT
Section Quiz, p. 224

Reteach

Have students work in groups to summarize the main ideas under each boldfaced heading in this section. Groups should share their summaries with the class.

CLOSE

U.S. involvement in Puerto Rico, Cuba, the Philippines, and China spread American political and economic influence around the world. While many in the United States endorsed American imperialism, many Americans opposed it.

OBJECTIVES

(1) To explain how Theodore Roosevelt's foreign policy promoted American power around the world.

(2) To describe how Woodrow Wilson's missionary diplomacy ensured U.S. dominance in Latin America.

CRITICAL THINKING

- Analyzing motives, pp. 543, 546
- Comparing, p. 545
- Drawing conclusions, p. 545
- Summarizing, p. 547
- Comparing and contrasting, p. 547
- Analyzing causes, p. 547

FOCUS & MOTIVATE

▶ **Starting with the Student**
- Ask students how they would resolve a conflict between two friends.
- How might the United States try to resolve a conflict between two countries? What about a civil conflict within another country?

MORE ABOUT . . .
Joseph Bucklin Bishop

The New York newspaper reporter Joseph Bucklin Bishop spent a decade in Panama. He provided vivid, eyewitness accounts of life in the Canal Zone. At the end of the project, Bishop returned home and eventually became Theodore Roosevelt's official biographer.

OBJECTIVE
(1) **INSTRUCT**

Teddy Roosevelt and the World

▶ **Starting with the Student**
Theodore Roosevelt was one of the most colorful figures who ever held the office of President. Ask students to share their impressions of him or anecdotes they have heard about him.

(continued on next page)

---

④ America as a World Power

TERMS & NAMES
- Panama Canal
- Roosevelt Corollary
- dollar diplomacy
- Francisco "Pancho" Villa
- John J. Pershing

LEARN ABOUT American involvement in the Russo-Japanese War, the building of the Panama Canal, and the Mexican Revolution
TO UNDERSTAND how and why Presidents Roosevelt and Wilson used American military and economic power around the world.

ONE AMERICAN'S STORY

Joseph Bucklin Bishop, a small, grouchy-looking man with a pointed gray beard, played an important role in the building of the Panama Canal. Bishop served as a policy adviser to the chief engineer, George Goethals, starting in 1907. President Roosevelt had directed Bishop to send him confidential reports on the canal project. Bishop became editor of the *Canal Record,* a weekly newspaper that provided Americans with updates on the project as well as reports on social life, sports, and other general-interest topics. In one account, Bishop described a frustrating problem the workers encountered.

> **A PERSONAL VOICE**
> The Canal Zone was a land of the fantastic and the unexpected. No one could say when the sun went down what the condition of the Cut would be when [the sun] rose. For the work of months or even years might be blotted out by an avalanche of earth or the toppling over of a mountain of rock. It was a task to try men's souls; but it was also one to kindle in them a joy of combat . . . and a faith in ultimate victory which no disaster could shake.
> **JOSEPH BUCKLIN BISHOP,** quoted in *The Impossible Dream*

Workers digging the Panama Canal faced hazardous landslides and death from disease.

The building of the Panama Canal reflected America's new role as a world power. As a marvelous technological accomplishment not unlike the Brooklyn Bridge, the canal represented a confident nation's refusal to let any physical obstacle stand in its way. As a project conducted completely on foreign soil, the canal reflected the determination of American leaders, such as Theodore Roosevelt, not to let any political obstacle block their path.

Teddy Roosevelt and the World

The assassination of William McKinley in 1901 thrust Vice-President Theodore Roosevelt into the role of a world leader. Roosevelt was unwilling to allow the imperial powers of Europe to control the world's political and economic destiny without American participation. In 1905, building on the Open Door notes to increase American influence in East Asia, Roosevelt mediated a settlement in the war between Russia and Japan.

RUSSO–JAPANESE WAR In 1904, tension between Japan and Russia over Korea escalated to full-scale war. After the Boxer Rebellion, the Russians controlled Manchuria, the northernmost province of China, and set their sights on Korea. The Japanese, who had taken Korea from China in 1895 and set it up as an independent state, suggested that they and the Russians should respect each other's spheres of influence. When Russia refused, Japan gave Russia "a last and earnest warning" not to press the issue.

In February 1904, the Japanese attacked the Russian Pacific fleet. To everyone's surprise, Japan destroyed it and then destroyed the Russian European fleet, which had been ordered to Asia to replace the Pacific fleet. Through a series of land battles in China, Japan secured firm control over Korea as well as a foothold in Manchuria.

SECTION 4 RESOURCES

PRINT RESOURCES

IN-DEPTH RESOURCES: UNIT 5
Guided Reading, p. 23
Geography Application: Geography of the Panama Canal, p. 25
Outline Map: America Becomes a World Power, p. 27
Primary Source: Building the Panama Canal, p. 32

ACCESS FOR STUDENTS ACQUIRING ENGLISH
Guided Reading (Spanish), p. 181
Geography Application: Geography of the Panama Canal (Spanish), p. 183
Outline Map: America Becomes a World Power (Spanish), p. 185

FORMAL ASSESSMENT
Section Quiz, p. 225

ALTERNATIVE ASSESSMENT BOOK
See forms for supporting and scoring alternative activities.

TECHNOLOGY RESOURCES

GEOGRAPHY TRANSPARENCIES
G18, United States Interventions

CRITICAL THINKING TRANSPARENCIES
CT52, U.S. Trade with Central America

CD-ROM *Our Times*

VIDEO *American Portfolio: A Videodisc for U.S. History* user's guide, p. 179

INTERNET McDougal Littell Learning On-Line
http://www.mcdougallittell.com

ROOSEVELT THE PEACEMAKER Japan's victories, however, cost a great deal of money, so the Japanese, hoping to end the economic drain, asked Roosevelt to mediate the conflict. He agreed, and in 1905, Russian and Japanese delegates convened in Portsmouth, New Hampshire.

(continued from page 542)

The first meeting took place on the presidential yacht. Roosevelt had a charming way of greeting people with a grasp of the hand, a broad grin, and a hearty "*Dee*—light-ed." Soon the opposing delegates began to relax and cordially shook hands.

The Japanese, who were in the driver's seat, wanted Sakhalin Island, off the coast of Siberia, and a large sum of money from Russia. Russia refused. Roosevelt persuaded Japan to accept half the island and forgo the cash payment. In exchange, Russia agreed to let Japan take over its interests in Manchuria and Korea. As a result of his efforts in negotiating the Treaty of Portsmouth, Roosevelt won the 1906 Nobel Peace Prize.

RELATIONS WITH JAPAN As U.S. and Japanese interests expanded in East Asia, the two nations continued their diplomatic talks. In later agreements, they pledged to respect each other's possessions and interests in East Asia and the Pacific.

In 1907, after building up the U.S. Navy, Roosevelt sent 16 gleaming white battleships on a world tour to demonstrate U.S. naval power. The "Great White Fleet" was warmly received by the Japanese, who were so impressed by the American navy that they began to build a bigger navy of their own.

PANAMA CANAL When Roosevelt became president, the United States had already achieved three of Admiral Mahan's four recommendations for becoming a world power. The nation had a modern navy and naval bases in the Caribbean and Hawaii. Roosevelt set out to accomplish the fourth goal—building a canal through Central America. Such a canal would greatly reduce travel time for commercial and military ships by providing a shortcut between the Atlantic and Pacific Oceans. As early as 1850, the United States and Britain had agreed to share the rights to such a canal. In the Hay-Pauncefote Treaty of 1901, however, Britain gave the United States exclusive rights to build and control a canal through Central America.

Engineers identified two possible routes for the proposed canal. One, through Nicaragua, posed fewer obstacles because much of the route crossed a large lake. The other, through Panama (then a province of Colombia), was shorter but consisted of mountains and swamps. Shortly before Congress voted to choose a route, Philippe Bunau-Varilla, chief engineer of and investor in the New Panama Canal Company, sent all U.S. senators a Nicaraguan stamp that pictured an erupting volcano. He hoped that the stamp would weaken Congress's confidence in the stability of the Nicaraguan site. The Senate approved the route through Panama, and the United States began negotiations

KEY PLAYER

THEODORE ROOSEVELT
1858–1919

Rimless glasses, a bushy mustache, and prominent teeth made Roosevelt easy for cartoonists to caricature. His great enthusiasm for the strenuous life—boxing, tennis, swimming, horseback riding, and hunting—provided cartoonists with additional material. Some cartoons portrayed Roosevelt with the toy teddy bear that he inspired.

Roosevelt had six children, who became notorious for their rowdy antics. Their father once sent a message through the War Department ordering them to call off their "attack" on the White House. Roosevelt thrived on the challenges of the presidency. He wrote, "I do not believe that anyone else has ever enjoyed the White House as much as I have."

Panama Canal locks, like this one under construction, lift ships a total of 85 feet.

▶ **Starting with the Student**
Have students imagine they are the president of the United States. Ask them under what circumstances they would send U.S. troops into another country. Have them explain the reasons for their decisions.

▶ **Discussing Key Ideas**
• Although isolationism is a recurrent theme in U.S. history, so too is intervention into the affairs of other nations.
• The overriding reasons for U.S. intervention abroad are to protect its economic interests, oppose aggression, and provide humanitarian relief.
• The United States intervened in Cuba to halt Spain's aggression and expand its empire, while its main interest in sending troops to Nicaragua was economic.
• America acted in the Persian Gulf to protect its economic interests and stop aggression, while U.S. troops entered Somalia to provide humanitarian relief.

GEOGRAPHY TRANSPARENCIES
G18, United States Interventions

"*Speak softly and carry a big stick; you will go far.*"

THEODORE ROOSEVELT

over Panama with Colombia. When these negotiations broke down, Bunau-Varilla helped organize a Panamanian rebellion against Colombia. Nearly a dozen U.S. warships were present as Panama declared its independence. The United States negotiated a treaty that guaranteed Panama's independence. However, it also gave the United States perpetual control over a ten-mile-wide canal zone and set forth the same principles the Platt Amendment had applied to Cuba—including the right of the United States to intervene in Panama.

CONSTRUCTING THE CANAL Construction of the **Panama Canal** ranks as one of the world's greatest engineering feats. For ten years, thousands of workers cut 50 miles through the isthmus. The total cost was nearly $400 million—an immense amount for the time. More than 5,600 workers on the canal, at least 4,500 of whom were African Americans, died from accidents or disease.

On August 15, 1914, the canal opened for business. More than 1,000 merchant ships used the waterway during its first year of operation. Control of the Panama Canal enhanced the power of the United States, but the circumstances under which the canal was built damaged U.S.–Latin American relations. In 1921, Congress paid Colombia $25 million for the loss of its territory, but the ill will that resulted from Roosevelt's taking of Panama lasted for decades.

THE ROOSEVELT COROLLARY Financial factors drew the United States further into Latin American affairs. In the late 19th century, many Latin American nations had borrowed huge sums from European banks to build railroads and develop industries. Roosevelt feared that if these nations defaulted on their loans, Europeans might intervene in the Western Hemisphere. He was determined to make the United States the predominant power in the Caribbean and Central America.

Roosevelt based his Latin American policy on a West African proverb that said, "Speak softly and carry a big stick; you will go far." In his December 1904 message to Congress, Roosevelt defined his "big stick" diplomacy, the **Roosevelt Corollary** to the Monroe Doctrine. He not only argued that European powers must not intervene in Western affairs but warned that disorder in Latin America might "force the United States . . . to the exercise of an international police power" in order to protect U.S. economic interests.

During the next decade, the United States exercised its police power on several occasions. For example, when a 1911 rebellion in Nicaragua left the nation near bankruptcy, President William H. Taft, Roosevelt's successor, arranged for American bankers to loan Nicaragua enough money to pay its debts. In return, the bankers were given the right to recover their money by collecting Nicaragua's customs duties. The U.S. bankers also gained control of Nicaragua's state-owned railroad system and its national bank. When Nicaraguan citizens heard about this deal, they revolted against President Adolfo Díaz.

544 CHAPTER 18

U.S. Intervention

Although isolationism is a recurrent theme in U.S. history, the United States has often intervened in the affairs of other nations. In the decades prior to the First World War, the United States joined the imperialist powers of Europe in the scramble for colonies like Cuba and Hawaii. Following World War II, Americans supported numerous interventions to prevent the expansion of communism, as in Korea and Vietnam.

Since the passing of the Cold War, the United States has continued to project power abroad to protect its economic interests, oppose aggression, and provide humanitarian relief.

Cuba, 1898
In April 1898, the United States declares war against Spain to support the Cuban struggle for independence. President McKinley expresses concern for the threat Cuba's unrest poses to America. Imperialists view the war as an opportunity for the United States to expand its empire into the Pacific.

TEACHING OPTIONS

Exploring Themes

Science and Technology Building the Panama Canal involved much more than moving earth. Developers relied heavily on American advances in engineering and medicine to construct the canal. In response to the changing water elevation along the course of the canal, engineers constructed locks along necessary points of the canal to help ships move from one level of water to the next. In addition, U.S. doctors, armed with improved methods of disease control, wiped out the deadly yellow fever virus that had run rampant in the Canal Zone.

Making Connections Across Time

U.S. Relations with Panama The United States has had several dealings with Panama in the late 20th century—one of which was peaceful, while another involved military force. In 1977, the United States and Panama signed two treaties regarding the Panama Canal. One provided for Panama to take control of the canal on December 31, 1999. The other gave the United States the right to defend the canal's neutrality. In 1990, U.S. troops ousted Panama's ruler, and accused drug trafficker, Manuel Noriega. Noriega stood trial in the United States. In 1992, he was convicted on several drug charges and sentenced to 40 years in prison.

To prop up Díaz's government, some 2,000 marines were sent to Nicaragua. The revolt was put down, but some marine detachments remained in the country until 1933.

THINK THROUGH HISTORY
C. *Comparing*
How were big stick diplomacy and dollar diplomacy alike?

The Taft administration followed the policy of using the U.S. government to guarantee loans made to foreign countries by American businesspeople. This policy was called **dollar diplomacy** by its critics and was often used to justify keeping European powers out of the Caribbean.

Woodrow Wilson's Missionary Diplomacy

C. Answer Both were intended to ensure U.S. dominance in Latin America.

The original Monroe Doctrine, issued by President James Monroe in 1823, warned other nations against expanding their influence in Latin America. The Roosevelt Corollary asserted that the United States had a right to exercise international police power in the Western Hemisphere. In 1913, President Woodrow Wilson gave the Monroe Doctrine a moral tone.

According to Wilson's "missionary diplomacy," the United States had a moral responsibility to deny recognition to any Latin American government it viewed as oppressive, undemocratic, or hostile to U.S. interests. Until that time, the United States had recognized any government that controlled a nation, regardless of its policies or how it had come to power. Wilson's policy pressured

Nicaragua, 1927
In Central America and the Caribbean, the United States seeks to protect its economic interests by supporting conservative governments, training local national guards to keep order, and occasionally resorting to military invasion.

In 1926, American troops invade Nicaragua, where a brutal civil war rages. Between 1927 and 1932, guerrilla nationalist forces under Augusto Sandino successfully fight both the conservative government and American soldiers. Sandino promises to rid Nicaragua of every last American soldier. When American forces finally pull out of Nicaragua in 1933, however, national guard leader Anastasio Somoza seizes power, assassinates Sandino, and acts as dictator until his own assassination in 1956.

Persian Gulf, 1991
Following the Cold War, when U.S. policy was dominated by anti-communism, the United States stands as the nation most capable of protecting international stability. When Iraq invades oil-rich Kuwait in 1990, however, its action threatens control of 40 percent of the world's oil. President George Bush builds an international coalition and asks Congress for a declaration of war. A six-week air attack in 1991 transfixes U.S. TV viewers and leaves at least 100,000 Iraqis dead. It takes only 100 hours for American troops to crush Iraqi resistance.

The World at the Year 2000
Unlike the Iraqi invasion of Kuwait in 1990, many international problems result from natural catastrophe, factional fighting, or ethnic strife. As in the 1992 American effort to deliver humanitarian relief to Somalia, U.S. leaders closely monitor potential emergencies such as drought conditions in Africa, human rights situations in Bosnia and China, relations between Israel and the Palestinians, and the disposal of nuclear weapons in the former Soviet Union.

INTERACT WITH HISTORY

1. **DRAWING CONCLUSIONS** What purposes did U.S. intervention serve in Cuba, Nicaragua, and the Persian Gulf?

   SEE SKILLBUILDER HANDBOOK, PAGE 1050.

2. **RESEARCHING U.S. ROLES** Choose an intervention described here, or another example, such as U.S. involvement in Vietnam. List effects of the intervention.

   For more information about the Persian Gulf War, click on *Social Studies* at
   http://www.mcdougallittell.com

America Claims an Empire **545**

OBJECTIVE
② **INSTRUCT**

Woodrow Wilson's Missionary Diplomacy

▶ *Discussing Key Ideas*
• Wilson's policy of missionary diplomacy pressures nations in the Western Hemisphere to establish democratic governments.
• Wilson refuses to recognize governments that come to power through violence.
• U.S. intervention in Mexico increases anti-American feelings there.

MORE ABOUT . . .
Woodrow Wilson
President Wilson was less of an economic imperialist than his predecessors, stating that "The force of America is the force of moral principle . . . there is nothing else that she loves, and . . . there is nothing else for which she will contend." However, Wilson firmly believed in imparting his moral values to other countries, particularly in Latin America. He once declared, "I am going to teach the South American republics to elect good men."

INTERACT WITH HISTORY

1. Drawing Conclusions

Possible Responses:

Cuba: The U.S. intervened to halt Spanish aggression and possibly to expand its own empire.

Nicaragua: The U.S. sent in troops to keep order and thus protect its economic interest in the country.

Persian Gulf: The U.S. acted to repel Iraq's aggression, as well as to protect its interest in the region's rich oil supply.

2. Researching U.S. Roles

Strategies for completing this activity might first include brainstorming for topics. In addition to Vietnam, students could research U.S. involvement in Lebanon, Haiti, or Bosnia.

After choosing a topic, students should list effects of U.S. intervention by category. Some examples include:

1. the well-being of U.S. troops
2. U.S. public opinion
3. the stability of the country in which the United States has intervened

MORE ABOUT . . .
Wilson's Foreign Policy

In addition to intervening in Mexico, Wilson dispatched U.S. troops to several other Latin American countries. In 1915, he sent U.S. marines to put down revolts in Haiti and the Dominican Republic. American forces controlled the Dominican Republic until 1924 and Haiti until 1934. However, President Wilson did not always seek solutions to foreign problems through military means. His administration also negotiated thirty treaties that promoted arbitration of international disputes.

IN-DEPTH RESOURCES: UNIT 5
Outline Map: America Becomes a World Power, p. 27

MORE ABOUT . . .
Pancho Villa

Despite his disdain for the United States, Villa was fond of American automobiles—and it was while driving one that the former rebel leader met his death. On a July day in 1923—three years after he "retired" from fighting—Villa was driving around his small town in his Dodge sedan. A pedestrian shouted his name, and Villa slowed down to acknowledge him. The shout was actually a signal to gunmen hiding in a house along the road. The assassins opened fire and gunned down Villa.

---

nations in the Western Hemisphere to establish democratic governments. The Mexican Revolution put Wilson's policy to the test almost immediately.

THE MEXICAN REVOLUTION During the 30-year regime of Porfirio Díaz, Americans had invested heavily in Mexican oil wells, mines, railroads, and ranches. Wealthy landowners, the church, and the military had supported Díaz, but peasants and workers forced him to resign in 1910.

In 1911 Francisco Madero, a reformer and wealthy landowner, became president of Mexico. Madero could not satisfy the conflicting demands of landowners, peasants, factory workers, and the urban middle class. After two years, General Victoriano Huerta took over the government and executed Madero. Americans with business interests in Mexico urged Wilson to recognize the Huerta government. But Wilson was committed to his policy of missionary diplomacy, and he refused to recognize "a government of butchers."

> **A PERSONAL VOICE**
> We can have no sympathy with those who seek to seize the power of government to advance their own personal interests or ambition. We are the friends of peace, but we know that there can be no lasting or stable peace in such circumstances. As friends, therefore, we shall prefer those who act in the interest of peace and honor, who protect private rights, and respect the restraints of constitutional provision.
>
> **WOODROW WILSON**, statement on Latin America, March 11, 1913

Wilson adopted a plan of "watchful waiting," looking for an opportunity to act against Huerta. The opportunity came in April 1914 when Mexican officials arrested a small group of American sailors in Tampico, on Mexico's eastern shore. The Mexicans quickly released them and apologized, but Wilson used the incident as an excuse to intervene in Mexico and ordered U.S. marines to occupy Veracruz. More than 100 Mexicans died during the invasion.

The incident brought the United States and Mexico close to war. Argentina, Brazil, and Chile stepped in to mediate the conflict. They proposed that Huerta step down and that U.S. troops withdraw without paying Mexico for damages. Mexico rejected the plan, and Wilson refused to recognize a government that had come to power as a result of violence. The Huerta regime soon collapsed, however, and Venustiano Carranza, a nationalist leader, became president in 1914. Wilson withdrew the troops and formally recognized the Carranza government.

PERSHING PURSUES VILLA Turmoil in Mexico continued, as Emiliano Zapata and **Francisco "Pancho" Villa** led revolts against Carranza. Zapata was an Indian dedicated to land reform. Villa was an anti-Carranza revolutionary. Angry over Wilson's recognition of Carranza's government, Villa threatened reprisals against the United States.

Attempting to end U.S. intervention, Carranza had promised that his government would protect the lives of foreigners. In January 1916, he invited a group of American engineers to operate abandoned mines in northern Mexico. Villa's men took the Americans off a train and shot them. Two months later, some of Villa's followers raided Columbus, New Mexico, and killed several Americans. Although Villa was not directly involved, Americans held him responsible for the actions of his followers.

Carranza reluctantly agreed to let Wilson send U.S. troops into Mexico to try to capture Villa. General **John J. Pershing** led an expeditionary force of about 15,000 soldiers in pursuit of Villa. For almost a year, Villa eluded Pershing's forces. Wilson then called out 150,000 National Guardsmen and stationed them along the Mexican border. In the meantime, the Mexicans grew angrier over the U.S. invasion of their land. In June 1916, U.S. troops clashed with Carranza's army, resulting in deaths on both sides. Carranza demanded the withdrawal of U.S. troops, but Wilson refused.

546 CHAPTER 18

THINK THROUGH HISTORY
D. Analyzing Motives Why did President Wilson refuse to recognize Huerta's government?

D. Answer Huerta had taken Mexico's government by force and had executed the previous leader. Wilson refused to recognize a government that came to power through violence.

Pancho Villa directs a column of his troops through northern Mexico in 1914. U.S. troops never captured Villa, who continued his raids until Carranza was overthrown in 1920. Three years later, Villa was assassinated.

ANOTHER PERSPECTIVE
Intervention in Mexico

Critical Thinking:
Evaluating Why do you think Edith O'Shaughnessy's opinion might be more valid than that of others? *Possible Response: Because she was an eye-witness to the effects of U.S. intervention in Mexico.*

Clarifying Have students restate O'Shaughnessy's letter in their own words.

Pershing's pursuit of Villa intensified anti-American feelings in Mexico. In 1917, as the United States faced possible war in Europe, Wilson withdrew U.S. troops. Later that year, Mexico adopted a constitution that gave the government control of the nation's oil and mineral resources and placed strict regulations on foreign investors.

U.S. intervention in Mexican affairs provided a clear model of American imperialist attitudes in the early years of the 20th century. Americans believed in the superiority of their political and economic institutions, and attempted to extend the reach of these economic and political systems, even through armed intervention. Few Americans, however, wished for the annexation of territory that Europeans and Japanese usually favored.

Nevertheless, the United States pursued and achieved several foreign policy goals in the early 20th century. First, it expanded its access to foreign markets in order to ensure the continued growth of the domestic economy. Second, the United States built a modern navy to protect its interests abroad. Third, the United States exercised its international police power to ensure American dominance in Latin America.

For better or worse, imperialism had drawn the United States deeper into world affairs. At the same time, imperialism pushed Europeans toward the most destructive war they had yet experienced—a war the United States could not avoid.

ANOTHER PERSPECTIVE

INTERVENTION IN MEXICO

Most U.S. citizens supported American intervention in Mexico. Edith O'Shaughnessy, wife of an American diplomat in Mexico City, had another perspective. After touring Veracruz, O'Shaughnessy wrote to her mother,

"I think we have done a great wrong to these people; instead of cutting out the sores with a clean, strong knife of war, . . . we have only put our fingers in each festering wound and inflamed it further."

ASSESS & RETEACH

Section 4 Assessment
Assign pairs of students to help each other answer the questions.

Self-Assessment
Have students write their impressions of Roosevelt's and Wilson's foreign policy in two brief paragraphs.

Section Quiz

FORMAL ASSESSMENT
Section Quiz, p. 225

Reteach

Have several students read their answer to question 4 before the class, making sure both opinions are expressed. Then discuss further the arguments for and against U.S involvement in Latin America.

CLOSE

Theodore Roosevelt defined America's role as a world power by making the United States dominant in Latin America. Woodrow Wilson added a moral dimension to American foreign policy by making the United States responsible for enforcing democratic values in other nations.

Section 4 Assessment

1. TERMS & NAMES

Identify:
• Panama Canal
• Roosevelt Corollary
• dollar diplomacy
• Francisco "Pancho" Villa
• John J. Pershing

2. SUMMARIZING In a two-column chart, list how Teddy Roosevelt and Woodrow Wilson used American power around the world during their presidencies.

Using American Power	
Roosevelt	Wilson

Choose one example and discuss its impact with your classmates.

3. COMPARING AND CONTRASTING What do you think were the similarities and differences between Roosevelt's "big stick" diplomacy and Wilson's "missionary diplomacy"? Use evidence from the text to support your response.

THINK ABOUT
• the goals of each of these foreign policies
• how they defined the role of U.S. intervention in international affairs
• how they were applied

4. ANALYZING CAUSES In your opinion, should the United States have become involved in the affairs of Colombia, Nicaragua, and Mexico during the early 1900s? Support your answer with details.

THINK ABOUT
• the effect of the Roosevelt Corollary
• the implication of Wilson's "missionary diplomacy"
• the results of dollar diplomacy

America Claims an Empire **547**

ANSWERS

1. TERMS & NAMES

Panama Canal, p. 544
Roosevelt Corollary, p. 544
dollar diplomacy, p. 545
Francisco "Pancho" Villa, p. 546
John J. Pershing, p. 546

2. SUMMARIZING

Possible Responses: **Roosevelt:** helped mediate the settlement in Russo-Japanese War; launched construction of Panama Canal; formulated the Roosevelt Corollary to the Monroe Doctrine. **Wilson:** formulated "missionary diplomacy"; ordered U.S. military occupation of Veracruz; sent General Pershing and expeditionary forces to pursue Pancho Villa.

3. COMPARING AND CONTRASTING

Possible Responses: Both were foreign policies that broadened the Monroe Doctrine; both addressed situations in Latin American countries that could be potentially troublesome to the United States. "Big stick" diplomacy cast the U.S. in the role of international police officer and had an economic focus; "missionary diplomacy" cast the U.S. in the role of judge and had a moral focus.

4. ANALYZING CAUSES

Possible Responses: Yes—Americans felt the Roosevelt Corollary justified intervention; the United States needed to protect its various economic interests in Latin America; the United States felt morally bound to protect democracy in Latin America. No—the United States's belief in its own superiority led to the use of excessive military force against those countries; those countries had the right to choose their own governments.

Geography Spotlight

OBJECTIVES

1. To summarize the development of the Panama Canal.
2. To identify the benefits of building the canal.

FOCUS & MOTIVATE

▶ **Starting with the Student**
Have students imagine they are workers on the Panama Canal and discuss what characteristics they would need to see them through the job. *Possible Responses: Patience, physical strength, the ability to work as part of a team.*

MORE ABOUT . . .
The Panama Canal

In 1882, the French had tried to carve out a canal through Panama. Heading up the project was Ferdinand Marie De Lesseps, who had directed the construction of Egypt's Suez Canal—which opened in 1869. The Panama endeavor quickly ran into problems. A group of dishonest politicians who supported De Lesseps stole large amounts of money from the canal company. French engineers lacked the proper tools to complete the huge digging job. In addition, scientists did not yet know how to combat the region's deadly viruses. De Lessep's company went bankrupt in 1889 and shortly thereafter abandoned the canal project.

The Panama Canal: Funnel for Trade

Trade has always fueled exploration. European nations gradually evolved a system of mercantilism, in which they sought new colonies and established a favorable balance of trade by exporting more than they imported. America was born into world trade and rapidly matured into an economic leader in the world's marketplace.

By the late 19th century, the U.S. position in the pattern of global trade was firmly established. A glance at the world map revealed the trade advantages of cutting through the world's great landmasses at two strategic points. The first cut, through the Isthmus of Suez, was completed in 1869 and was a spectacular success. One more cut, this one through Central America, would be especially advantageous to the United States because it would substantially reduce the sailing time between the nation's Atlantic and Pacific ports.

It took the United States ten years, from 1904 to 1914, to build the Panama Canal. By 1996, more than 700,000 vessels that carried the flags of about 70 nations had passed through its locks.

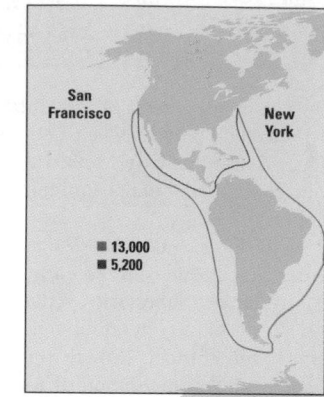

NUMBERS TELL THE STORY Sailing from New York to San Francisco by going around South America is 13,000 miles; sailing between the two cities via the canal is 5,200 miles.

■ 13,000
■ 5,200

San Francisco

to Asia

INTERCOASTAL TRADE The first boat through the canal, shown here, heralded the arrival of increased trade between the Atlantic and Pacific ports of the United States.

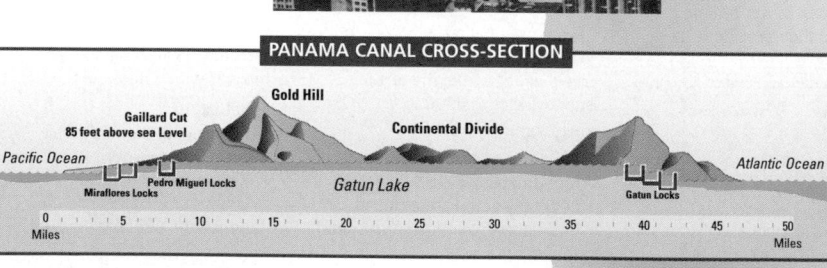

PANAMA CANAL CROSS-SECTION

Gold Hill
Gaillard Cut 85 feet above sea Level
Continental Divide
Pacific Ocean
Miraflores Locks
Pedro Miguel Locks
Gatun Lake
Gatun Locks
Atlantic Ocean

0 5 10 15 20 25 30 35 40 45 50
Miles   Miles

❶ **PANAMA** is a narrow isthmus that connects North and South America. In building the canal, engineers took advantage of natural waterways like Gatun Lake. Moving ships through the mountains of the Continental Divide required the use of massive locks such as the Miraflores Locks. (See map at left.) These locks allow a section of the waterway to be closed off so that the water level can be raised or lowered.

548 CHAPTER 18

RECOMMENDED RESOURCES

Books

Chidsey, Donald Barr. *The Panama Canal.* New York: Crown, 1970. An informal history.

Fast, Howard. *Goethals and the Panama Canal.* New York: Julian Messner, 1942. A popular account of George Washington Goethals, the canal's builder.

Keller, Ulrich. *The Building of the Panama Canal in Historic Photographs.* New York: Dover, 1983. An interesting pictorial history.

McCullough, David G. *The Path Between the Seas.* New York: Simon, 1977. A well-known account of the creation of the Panama Canal.

Videos

A Man, A Plan, a Canal: Panama. Coronet, 1988. A history of the canal and its construction, produced with Boston PBS channel WGBH.

Americans Build the Panama Canal. Agency for Instructional Technology (AIT), 1991. Construction of the canal from 1901 to 1914.

Panama Canal. A&E Home Video, 1994. A historical documentary in the Modern Marvels series.

Software

Who Built America? Voyager. Teddy Roosevelt digging the Panama Canal is among the ample historical video, audio, images, and documents in this program for grades 10–12.

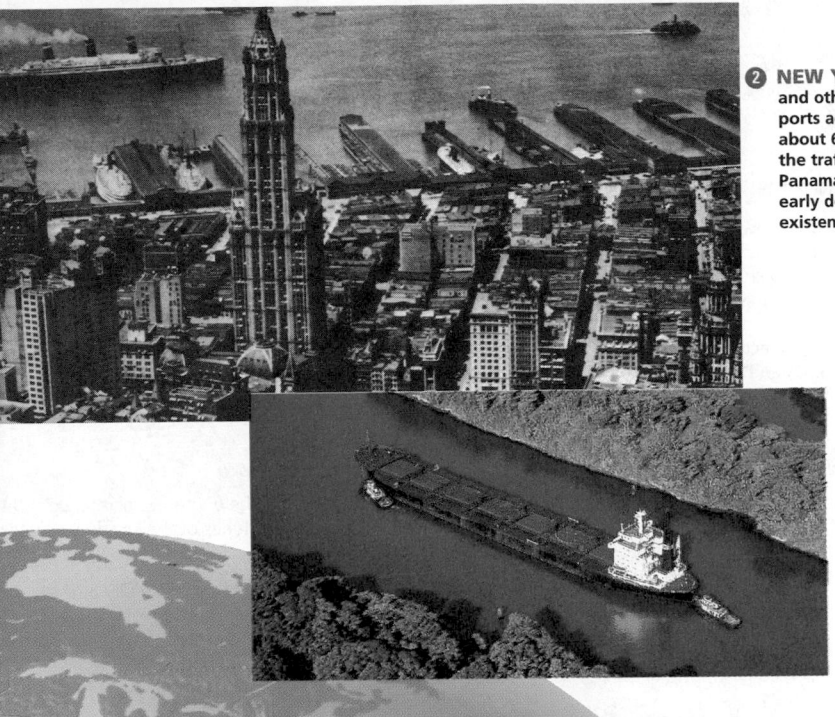

② NEW YORK CITY
and other U.S. Atlantic ports accounted for about 60 percent of the traffic using the Panama Canal in the early decades of its existence.

OCEAN–GOING VESSELS like this one must be of a certain dimension in order to fit through the canal's locks. These container ships must be no more than 106 feet across and 965 feet in length, with a draft—the depth of the vessel below the water line when fully loaded—of no more than 39.5 feet. Ships pay a toll based on the size of the vessel, the cargo, and number of passengers they carry.

② **New York**
to Europe
to Africa

③ **New Orleans**

③ NEW ORLEANS, since its founding in 1718, has served as a major port for the produce of the areas along the Mississippi River. In 1914, the Panama Canal brought Pacific markets into its orbit.

① **Panama Canal**

to South America

INTERACT WITH HISTORY

1. **CLARIFYING** Before the Panama Canal opened, what route would ships have to follow to sail from New York City to San Francisco?

    SEE SKILLBUILDER HANDBOOK, PAGE 1037.

2. **SKETCHING A MAP** Imagine you are a farmer in the U.S. Midwest. Use a sketch of this map to trace the route(s) you might follow—using the Panama Canal—in order to get your grain to markets abroad. Note what methods of transportation would take the grain to the port cities.

   For more about the Panama Canal, click on *Social Studies* at http://www.mcdougallittell.com

549

INSTRUCT

▶ *Discussing Key Ideas*
• Cutting nearly 8,000 miles off the sea journey from New York to San Francisco, the Panama Canal greatly enhanced world trade and America's role in it.
• The difficult construction of the Panama Canal took a decade and was completed in 1914.

IN-DEPTH RESOURCES: UNIT 5
Geography Application: Geography of the Panama Canal, p. 25

 CRITICAL THINKING TRANSPARENCIES
CT52, U.S. Trade with Central America

HISTORY FROM VISUALS
▶ *Reading the Images*
• Have students examine the main map and then briefly identify some other routes that could probably have been included in red. *Possible Responses: A route from Europe or Africa through the canal to the west coast of North America and vice versa; a route from Europe or Africa through the canal to Asia and vice versa; a route from the east coast of South America through the canal to the west coast of North America or Asia and vice versa.*

---

1. Clarifying

Ships leaving New York City would have to make the roughly 13,000-mile trip around the continent of South America in order to reach San Francisco.

2. Sketching a Map

Standards for Evaluation
Maps should

• depict a route from a midwestern site to at least two foreign destinations
• indicate one or more means of inland transport—such as barges on waterways, railroads freight lines, or trucks on highways—by which goods will travel from the midwestern site to the appropriate U.S. port or ports
• Depict clear travel lines that run through the Panama Canal and continue on to the chosen foreign destinations

REVIEWING
THE CHAPTER

1. Queen Liliuokalani, p. 526
2. imperialism, p. 526
3. José Martí, p. 530
4. yellow journalism, p. 531
5. U.S.S. *Maine*, p. 532
6. protectorate, p. 537
7. Open Door notes, p. 539
8. Boxer Rebellion, p. 539
9. Panama Canal, p. 544
10. Roosevelt Corollary, p. 544

MAIN IDEAS

11. Economic competition; political and military competition; a belief in the racial and cultural superiority of Anglo-Saxons.

12. She wanted to preserve Hawaii for Hawaiians, while American imperialists sought to annex the island chain.

13. U.S. businessmen sided with Spain because they wanted to protect their investments. Other Americans, however, sympathized with the Cuban demand for independence.

14. Cuba's independence; Spain's relinquishing of Puerto Rico and Guam to the United States; U.S. payment for annexation of the Philippines.

15. Puerto Rico was strategically important to the United States as a way to assert its presence in the Caribbean and as a base for protecting a possible canal through the Isthmus of Panama.

16. The Boxers staged a military campaign to expel foreigners. In retaliation, several nations joined forces to crush the rebellion.

17. U.S. economy's dependence on exports to ensure growth; U.S. right to intervene abroad to keep foreign markets open; closing an area to American products threatened U.S. survival.

18. A dispute over Korea.

19. A modern navy and naval bases in the Caribbean and Hawaii.

20. The U.S. had a moral responsibility to deny recognition of a Latin American government it considered undemocratic.

Chapter 18 Assessment

REVIEWING THE CHAPTER

TERMS & NAMES For each item below, write a sentence explaining its historical significance in U.S. foreign affairs from 1890–1920. For each person below, explain his or her role in the events of this period.

1. Queen Liliuokalani
2. imperialism
3. José Martí
4. yellow journalism
5. U.S.S. *Maine*
6. protectorate
7. Open Door notes
8. Boxer Rebellion
9. Panama Canal
10. Roosevelt Corollary

MAIN IDEAS

SECTION 1 *(pages 526–529)*

Imperialism and America

11. What three factors spurred the new American imperialism?
12. How did Queen Liliuokalani's goal conflict with one of the American imperialists' goals?

SECTION 2 *(pages 530–534)*

The Spanish-American-Cuban War

13. Why was American opinion about Cuban independence divided?
14. Briefly describe the terms of the Treaty of Paris of 1898.

SECTION 3 *(pages 535–541)*

Acquiring New Lands

15. Why was the United States interested in events in Puerto Rico?
16. What sparked the Boxer Rebellion in 1900 and how was it crushed?
17. What three key beliefs about America's industrial capitalist economy were reflected in the Open Door policy?

SECTION 4 *(pages 542–547)*

America as a World Power

18. What conflict triggered the war between Russia and Japan?
19. Which of Admiral Mahan's goals for becoming a world power were achieved before Roosevelt's presidency in 1901?
20. Explain Woodrow Wilson's "missionary diplomacy."

THINKING CRITICALLY

1. **REBEL LEADERS** Create a Venn diagram like the one below to show some of the similarities and differences between José Martí of Cuba and Emilio Aguinaldo of the Philippines.

José Martí | Both | Emilio Aguinaldo

2. **KEEN COMPETITORS** Reread the quote by Secretary of State John Hay on page 524. What attitudes of the era do you think his statement reflects?

3. **GEOGRAPHY OF IMPERIALISM** Look carefully at the Caribbean map on page 533 and the world map on page 540. Why do you think that American naval bases in the Caribbean and the Pacific were beneficial to the United States?

4. **U.S. INTERVENTION** Would Cuba have won its independence in the late 19th century if the United States had not intervened there at that time? Support your opinion with details from the text.

5. **ANALYZING PRIMARY SOURCES** Read the following excerpt from an editorial that Walter Hines Page, the editor of the *Atlantic Monthly* magazine, wrote soon after Admiral Dewey's victory in Manila Bay. Then answer the questions that follow.

> Are we yet the same race of Anglo-Saxons, whose restless energy in colonization, in conquest, in trade, in "the spread of civilization," has carried their speech into every part of the world, and planted their habits everywhere?
>
> Within a week such a question . . . has been put before us by the first foreign war [Spanish-American-Cuban War] that we have had since we became firmly established as a nation. Before we knew the meaning of foreign possessions in a world growing ever more jealous, we have found ourselves the captors of islands in both great oceans; and from our home-staying policy of yesterday we are brought face to face with world-wide forces in Asia as well as in Europe. . . . The news from Manila sets every statesman and soldier in the world to thinking new thoughts about us, and to asking new questions.
>
> **WALTER HINES PAGE,** "The War with Spain and After," *Atlantic Monthly,* June 1898

How does Page explain the significance of the Spanish-American-Cuban War? Which of his points do you find most meaningful and why?

THINKING CRITICALLY

1. REBEL LEADERS
Possible Responses: José Martí—Born in Cuba; expelled from Cuba at age 16; earned a master's degree and law degree; settled in United States; feared American imperialism; died fighting for Cuban independence in 1895; revered today as hero.

Both—His country of origin was a former Spanish colony; feared that the United States would dominate his country's politics as Spain had done; was a political activist and rebel leader; staged revolts for independence; used guerrilla tactics.

Emilio Aguinaldo—His native country was the Philippines; felt betrayed by U.S. government in Treaty of Paris; proclaimed the Philippines an independent republic; drafted a constitution; in February 1899 led the Filipinos in armed revolt; was captured by American forces in 1901.

2. KEEN COMPETITORS
Belief in American superiority; belief in the righteousness of American imperialism; the desire to conquer other nations; belief in American economic and military strength; belief in Anglo-Saxon superiority; belief in the greatness of the United States and the weakness of "inferior nations."

3. GEOGRAPHY OF IMPERIALISM
Possible Responses: The nearness of Cuba to the southern tip of Florida meant that the United States could better defend its Southern coast; bases on the islands in

ALTERNATIVE ASSESSMENT

1. PRESENTING A PERSUASIVE SPEECH

In the late 19th and early 20th century, the United States began to exercise military and economic authority over countries in the Western Hemisphere. What were some of the arguments made for and against American imperialism?

- Write a persuasive speech that takes a stand on American imperialism between 1895 and 1920.

 Use the CD-ROM *Electronic Library of Primary Sources* and other resources to research opinions on imperialism between 1895 and 1920.

- Choose a document, incident, or piece of writing about imperialism. Decide if you will support it or argue against it. Write a speech that presents your position.

- Decide how you will make your arguments clear and convincing while also addressing opposing concerns. Practice your speech aloud and then present your speech to the class.

2. CREATING FRONT-PAGE NEWS

Cooperative Learning Imagine you are a 19th-century journalist. William Randolph Hearst has invited you to join the editorial staff of the New York *Journal*. With a small group, plan the front page of the newspaper featuring an important event from this chapter. A suggested agenda for your meeting follows:

- Create a sensational headline for the front page that vividly dramatizes the historical event.

- Brainstorm a list of news stories on related issues.

- Choose a news story for each group member to write.

- Design the front page to show the layout of the stories with illustrations or photos.

Allow time for group members to research and write their stories. Then paste up the articles on a poster board.

3. PORTFOLIO PROJECT

 Use the Living History activity to expand your portfolio.

LIVING HISTORY

PRESENTING YOUR HISTORICAL MONOLOGUE

You have written your monologue. Now think about how you can dramatically present it.

- Find suitable clothing and costume effects to help you imitate the person's outward appearance.

- Practice reading your monologue for a friend.

Present your monologue to the class. Add your monologue and a tape recording of your presentation to your American history portfolio.

Review Chapter 18

IMPERIALISM AND AMERICA In the late 1800s, the U.S. drive to acquire new territories, to secure foreign markets for trade, and to boost its naval power mirrored the global trend of imperialism. Joining the competition for overseas expansion, the United States annexed Hawaii, prized for its commercial value and strategic location, in 1898.

WAR WITH SPAIN In 1895, Spain's brutal treatment of Cubans during a revolt outraged the American public. The publication of a Spanish diplomat's letter criticizing President McKinley and the explosion of the battleship *Maine* pushed Congress to declare war on Spain in 1898. U.S. naval forces swiftly defeated the Spanish fleet. After the fall of Santiago, U.S. troops invaded Puerto Rico. The ensuing peace treaty granted Cuba its independence and gave the United States colonial possessions in both the Caribbean and the Pacific.

ACQUIRING NEW LANDS Following the war, the United States reorganized the government in Puerto Rico, established a protectorate over Cuba, and crushed a revolt in the Philippines and set up a government there similar to Puerto Rico's. The Philippines gave U.S. investors greater access to China. In 1900, the Open Door policy established American trading rights in China.

AMERICA AS A WORLD POWER As presidents, both Roosevelt and Wilson projected U.S. military and economic power worldwide. Roosevelt's achievements include initiating plans for the Panama Canal and asserting the U.S. right to exercise international police power in the Western Hemisphere. Wilson's policy pressured nations in the Western Hemisphere to establish democratic governments.

Preview Chapter 19

Complex causes, including a spirit of nationalism and economic competition for overseas empires, led to the First World War. President Wilson at first defended neutrality, but by 1917 he asked Congress to declare war. American forces helped secure an allied victory. You will learn about these and other developments in the next chapter.

America Claims an Empire **551**

---

1. PRESENTING A PERSUASIVE SPEECH
Standards for Evaluation
A persuasive speech should meet the following criteria:

- Clearly states the speaker's position.
- Uses well-researched and documented evidence to support the position.
- Anticipates and answers opposing arguments.
- Concludes with a strong call for action or with a forceful appeal for agreement.

2. CREATING FRONT-PAGE NEWS
Standards for Evaluation
A front page should meet the following criteria:

- Contains interesting, informative headlines that quickly grab the reader's attention.
- Mixes mostly hard news stories with more human-interest pieces, such as a profile of an important individual.
- Presents stories that are well-organized and engaging.

3. PORTFOLIO PROJECT
LIVING HISTORY
Standards for Evaluation
A historical monologue should meet the following criteria:

- Focuses on a specific person at a particular place and time.
- Conveys a consistent point of view
- Brings out the speaker's true personality with appropriate word choice.
- Accurately reflects the speaker's stance on the subject he or she is addressing.

IN-DEPTH RESOURCES: UNIT 5
See the form for scoring this activity on p. 39

THINKING CRITICALLY

the Pacific would afford the United States strategic defensive and offensive military positions; bases on the Pacific Islands could provide stops for trade ships; bases on the Pacific islands would spread U.S. influence halfway across the world.

4. U.S. INTERVENTION
Possible Response: Spain might have kept Cuba from achieving independence at first, but since Cuba had a history of rebellion, it probably would have won independence eventually, although probably not before the turn of the century.

5. ANALYZING PRIMARY SOURCES
Possible Responses: Significance—Page thinks the Spanish-American-Cuban War links Americans to the long history of Anglo-Saxon conquest; he sees the United States leaving isolationism behind and becoming a world power while Americans question the meaning of U.S. involvement. Points—his link to Anglo-Saxon conquest because he puts the war in context of imperialism and shows how people have still not learned to respect people of different cultures; his view of Americans as "captors of islands" because it labels Americans as imperialists who subjugated others.

Teacher's Edition **551**

PLANNING GUIDE
The First World War

	Key Ideas	**TEACHING SUPPORT**	**ASSESSMENT**
SECTION 1 World War I Begins *pp. 554–561*	Long-term tensions erupt into a devastating war among European nations, while the United States tries to remain neutral.	**In-Depth Resources: Unit 5** • Guided Reading, p. 40 • Skillbuilder Practice: Evaluating Alternative Courses of Action, p. 44 • Primary Source: The Zimmerman Note, p. 47 • American Lives: Jeannette Rankin, p. 54 • Literature: from *A Son at the Front* by Edith Wharton, p. 51 **COOPERATIVE ACTIVITY** • Creating Wartime Propaganda, p. 559 (TE)	*Section 1 Assessment,* p. 561 (PE) *Self-Assessment,* p. 561 (TE) *Formal Assessment* • Section Quiz, p. 234 *Alternative Assessment Book* • Standards for Evaluating a Cooperative Activity
SECTION 2 American Power Tips the Balance *pp. 562–568*	American forces, though poorly equipped at the outset, tip the balance decisively in favor of the Allies.	**In-Depth Resources: Unit 5** • Guided Reading, p. 41 • Primary Source: Patriotic Song, p. 48 • Literature: *from "In Another Country"* by Ernest Hemingway, p. 51 **COOPERATIVE ACTIVITY** • Letters from Conscientious Objectors and the Draft Board, p. 565 (TE)	*Section 2 Assessment,* p. 568 (PE) *Self-Assessment,* p. 568 (TE) *Formal Assessment* • Section Quiz, p. 235 *Alternative Assessment Book* • Standards for Evaluating a Cooperative Activity
SECTION 3 The War at Home *pp. 569–576*	The war unleashes a series of disruptions in American society as the U.S. government attempts to meet the demands of modern warfare.	**In-Depth Resources: Unit 5** • Guided Reading, p. 42 • Primary Sources: Liberty Bond Poster, p. 49; "Returning Soldiers" by W. E. B. Du Bois, p. 50 • American Lives: Oliver Wendell Holmes, Jr., p. 55 **COOPERATIVE ACTIVITY** • Creating a Wartime Ad Campaign, p. 571 (TE)	*Section 3 Assessment,* p. 576 (PE) *Self-Assessment,* p. 576 (TE) *Formal Assessment* • Section Quiz, p. 236 *Alternative Assessment Book* • Standards for Evaluating a Cooperative Activity
SECTION 4 Wilson Fights for Peace *pp. 577–581*	President Wilson's plans for peace are modified by Allied leaders in Europe and by Americans who are eager to remove the country from foreign entanglements.	**In-Depth Resources: Unit 5** • Guided Reading, p. 43 • Geography Application: A New Look for Europe, p. 45 **COOPERATIVE ACTIVITY** • Debating the League of Nations, p. 580 (TE)	*Section 4 Assessment,* p. 581 (PE) *Self-Assessment,* p. 581 (TE) *Formal Assessment* • Section Quiz, p. 237 *Alternative Assessment Book* • Standards for Evaluating a Cooperative Activity
CHAPTER RESOURCES	**Chapter Overview** After the United States enters World War I and helps to defeat Germany, President Wilson tries to fashion a lasting peace.	**In-Depth Resources: Unit 5** • Living History Project: Worksheet, p. 56; Standards, p. 57 *Telescoping the Times* • Chapter Summary, pp. 37–38 *Planning for Block Schedules*	*Chapter Assessment,* pp. 584–585 (PE) *Alternative Assessment,* p. 585 (PE) *Formal Assessment* • Chapter Test, forms A and B, pp. 238–243 Test Generator *Alternative Assessment Book* See explanation and forms for different kinds of alternative assessments including portfolio assessment.

Geography Transparencies
• G19, Europe Goes to War, 1914

Critical Thinking Transparencies
• CT19, World War I

 Electronic Library of Primary Sources
• Request for a Declaration of War by Woodrow Wilson

INTERNET RESOURCES
• See *McDougal Littell Learning On-Line* for links to information about World War I primary documents.

 Humanities Transparencies
• H18, *Oppy Wood* by John Nash

Critical Thinking Transparencies
• CT53, Costs of World War I

 Electronic Library of Primary Sources
• From Harlem to the Rhine

Our Times
• George M. Cohan and "Over There"

INTERNET RESOURCES
• See *McDougal Littell Learning On-Line* for links to information about Sgt. York and Gen. Pershing

 Electronic Library of Primary Sources
• Four Minute Speech

INTERNET RESOURCES
• See *McDougal Littell Learning On-Line* for links to information about the Sedition Act and propaganda.

 Humanities Transparencies
• H38, Senate Opposes the League of Nations

 Electronic Library of Primary Sources
• On the Terms of Peace by Henry Cabot Lodge
• Why a League of Nations Is Necessary by Woodrow Wilson

INTERNET RESOURCES
• See *McDougal Littell Learning On-Line* for links to information about the League of Nations.

 American Portfolio: A Videodisc for U.S. History, user's guide, pp. 181–189

INTERNET RESOURCES
Learning On-Line: Social Studies
http://www.mcdougallittell.com

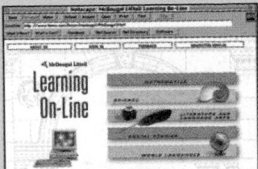

Block Scheduling (90 MINUTES)

Day 1
Section 1, pp. 554–561

Section Assessment, p. 561

Day 2
Section 2, pp. 562–568

Section 3, pp. 569–576

Section Assessments, pp. 568, 576

Day 3
Section 4, pp. 577–581

Tracing Themes Immigration and Migration, pp. 582–583

Section Assessment, p. 581

Chapter Assessment, pp. 584–585

YEARLY PACING *Chapter 19 Total:* 3 days *Yearly Total:* 85 days

See *Planning for Block Schedules* for special activities and pacing strategies.

Customizing for Special Populations

Students Acquiring English

Access for Students Acquiring English
• Guided Reading for Sections 1–4 (Spanish), pp. 189–192
• Chapter Summary (Spanish), pp. 187–188
• Skillbuilder Practice: Evaluating Alternative Courses of Action (Spanish), p. 193
• Geography Application: A New Look for Europe (Spanish), p. 194

INTERNET RESOURCES
• See *McDougal Littell Learning On-Line* The Diverse Classroom.

Less Proficient Readers

In-Depth Resources: Unit 5
• Guided Reading for Sections 1–4, pp. 40–43
• Skillbuilder: Evaluating Alternative Courses of Action, p. 44
• Geography Application: A New Look for Europe, p. 45

Telescoping the Times
• Chapter Summary, pp. 37–38

See additional strategies at point of use in the Teacher's Edition.

Gifted and Talented Students

In-Depth Resources: Unit 5
• Primary Sources: The Zimmerman Note, p. 47; Patriotic Song, p. 48; Liberty Bond Poster, p. 49; "Returning Soldiers" by W. E. B. Du Bois, p. 50
• American Lives: Jeannette Rankin, p. 54; Oliver Wendell Holmes, Jr., p. 55

See additional strategies at point of use in the Teacher's Edition.

Connections to Literature READINGS FOR STUDENTS

In-Depth Resources: Unit 5
• from *A Son at the Front* by Edith Wharton, p. 51
• from "In Another Country" by Ernest Hemingway, p. 51

Enrichment Reading
• Helprin, Mark
A Soldier of the Great War
New York: Avon, 1992
An old professor recalls his adventures as a soldier, a hero, a prisoner, a deserter, and a wanderer in the hell of World War I as he tells the story of his life to an illiterate factory worker in Italy. The horror of war and the triumph of love are central themes of the novel.

• Hemingway, Ernest
A Farewell to Arms
New York: Scribners, 1987
The brutality and confusion of World War I dominate this story of a volunteer ambulance driver and an English nurse who fall in love when he is wounded.

McDougal Littell *Literature Connections*

• James Baldwin,
Go Tell It on the Mountain (with related readings) Baldwin's novel, set in a store-front church in Harlem, brings the black experience vividly to life in a story that has been called "brutal, objective, and compassionate." Dealing with characters who came north during the Great Migration, the novel focuses on a 14-year-old boy whose family history reveals the complexities of the human heart.

OVERVIEW

The First World War

▶ **Starting with the Student**
Ask students what images come to mind when they think about the First World War. Then have them answer the following:

- Which countries played major roles in the First World War?
- What have students read or heard about the war?
- What movies or television programs have they seen that dealt with the war? How were both sides in the conflict portrayed?

PREVIEWING THE CHAPTER

- Read aloud the titles and brief descriptions of the sections.
- Have students get together in small groups to discuss the time line.
- Ask students to use the time line to make a list of people and events they would like to learn more about.

MORE ABOUT . . .
War Posters

American artists created various kinds of posters during the war in addition to the recruiting poster that appears on page 553. Some artists painted Liberty Loan posters, urging Americans to help finance the war. Charles Dana Gibson, known for his drawings of beautiful girls, portrayed workers in shipyards.

The First World War

SECTION 1
World War I Begins

Long-term tensions erupt into a devastating war among European nations, while the United States tries to remain neutral.

SECTION 2
American Power Tips the Balance

American forces, though poorly equipped at the outset, tip the balance decisively in favor of the Allies.

SECTION 3
The War at Home

The war unleashes a series of disruptions in American society as the U.S. government attempts to meet the demands of modern warfare.

SECTION 4
Wilson Fights for Peace

President Wilson's plans for peace are modified by Allied leaders in Europe and by Americans who are eager to remove the country from foreign entanglements.

"The world must be made safe for democracy."
President Woodrow Wilson, 1917

German U-boats sink the British liner *Lusitania*, and 1,198 people, including 128 Americans, die.

Secretary of State William Jennings Bryan resigns because he believes the United States has not remained neutral.

Panama Canal officially opens.

THE UNITED STATES						
THE WORLD	**1914**	Aug.	1915	May June	1916	
		June Aug.	1915	April	1916 Jan.	

Archduke Franz Ferdinand of Austria and his wife are assassinated in Sarajevo.

Germany declares war on Russia and France. Great Britain declares war on Germany and Austria-Hungary.

Germans use poison gas as a weapon at the Battle of Ypres.

The Allies withdraw from the Dardanelles after suffering more than 200,000 casualties.

THEMES IN CHAPTER 19

Women in America

During the war, many women worked in factories, while others served as nurses and ambulance drivers. After the war, women were expected to give up their jobs and return to traditional domestic roles.

See Teacher's Edition notes, pp. 555 and 575.

Expanding Democracy

Although discrimination existed in the U.S. military, the army had a more progressive attitude toward African Americans than society at large did. During the war, the army for the first time trained some black officers and had them command black troops.

At the war's end, Wilson wanted to help spread democratic reform throughout the world by creating a world peacekeeping organization, called the League of Nations.

See Teacher's Edition notes, pp. 563 and 578.

Immigration and Migration

During the war years, many Southern African Americans moved to cities in the North in search of jobs, equal treatment, and greater opportunities.

See Teacher's Edition note, p. 574.

LIVING HISTORY

CHARTING THE EFFECTS OF WORLD WAR I

The First World War brought about many changes in the United States and the rest of the world. As you read the chapter, compile a chart in which you list the effects of the war in the following categories:

• military methods
• American society
• world politics

Then, using information from your chart and outside sources, write a report in which you explain the impact of the war in one of the above categories.

PORTFOLIO PROJECT Keep your chart and report in the folder for your American history portfolio. At the end of the chapter you will present your report to your classmates.

I WANT YOU FOR U.S. ARMY
NEAREST RECRUITING STATION

Woodrow Wilson is reelected.

America enters the First World War.

The Selective Service Act sets up compulsory military service—the draft.

Flu epidemic afflicts millions of Americans.

President Wilson proposes the League of Nations.

Congress passes the Sedition Act.

Germany signs the Treaty of Versailles.

President Wilson suffers a stroke.

Nineteenth Amendment granting women suffrage becomes law.

Warren G. Harding is elected president.

Nov. **1917** Jan. March April May **1918** 1918 Jan. May **1919** 1919 June Oct. **1920**

Germany resumes unrestricted submarine warfare.

Russian Revolution results in overthrow of czarist regime.

Lenin and the Bolsheviks establish a Communist regime in Russia.

The First World War **553**

RECOMMENDED RESOURCES

Books for the Teacher

Haythornthwaite, Philip J. *The World War I Sourcebook.* London: Arms and Armour, 1996. Encyclopedia covers all aspects of the war.

Tuchman, Barbara. *The Guns of August.* New York: Ballantine, 1992. Readable overview of the war.

Books for the Student

Ellis, Edward Robb. *Echoes of Distant Thunder.* New York: Coward, 1978. Society between 1914 and 1918.

Schachtman, Tom. *Edith and Woodrow.* New York: Putnam's, 1981. Joint biography of the Wilsons.

Winter, J. M. *The Experience of World War I.* New York: Oxford, 1995. Illustrated description of military and home life.

Videos

America: The Second Century: World War I. GPN, 402-472-2007. The U.S. role in the war.

The Great War and the Shaping of the 20th Century. PBS Home Video, 1996. Eight-hour documentary.

The Promised Land. Dir. Edmund Coulthard. Discovery Channel, 1995. Three-tape story of the Great Migration.

Sergeant York. Dir. Howard Hawks. Twentieth Century Fox Video, 1941. Hollywood story of war hero.

Software

World War I: An Interactive Documentary. CD-ROM. First Electronic Publishing, 211 Congress Street, Boston, MA 02110, 617-338-6820.

Teacher's Edition **553**

OBJECTIVES

(1) To identify the four long-term causes of the First World War.

(2) To explain the circumstances that led to the war.

(3) To describe the slaughter of the first two years of the war.

(4) To summarize public opinion about the war in the United States.

(5) To explain why the United States entered the war.

SKILLBUILDERS

- Understanding geography: location, p. 555
- Understanding geography: location, movement, p. 557
- Interpreting graphs, p. 558

CRITICAL THINKING

- Summarizing, pp. 555, 561
- Recognizing effects, pp. 556, 559
- Analyzing, p. 559
- Hypothesizing, p. 561
- Analyzing issues, p. 561

FOCUS & MOTIVATE

▶ **Starting with the Student**
- What do students do when someone insults their friends? Do they defend them? How?
- What do they think a country should do when one of its allies is attacked?

MORE ABOUT . . .
Jeannette Rankin

Rankin was a staunch pacifist all her life. During the years after her second term in Congress, she visited India eight times. While there, she became convinced that Gandhi's policy of civil disobedience could be translated to the world scene and that the way to end war was through universal disarmament. In 1968, in her 88th year, Rankin led a group of several thousand women in a march to the Capitol to call for an end to the Vietnam War. Rankin died in 1973.

IN-DEPTH RESOURCES: UNIT 5
American Lives: Jeannette Rankin, p. 54

---

1 World War I Begins

TERMS & NAMES
- militarism
- Allies
- Central Powers
- Archduke Franz Ferdinand
- "no man's land"
- trench warfare
- *Lusitania*
- Zimmermann note

LEARN ABOUT the international politics that led to war in Europe
TO UNDERSTAND why the United States finally became involved in the world war.

ONE AMERICAN'S STORY

It was about 1:00 A.M. on April 6, 1917, and the members of the U.S. House of Representatives were tired. For the past 15 hours they had been debating President Wilson's request for a declaration of war against Germany. At last the roll call began. When the clerk came to the name of Jeannette Rankin of Montana, the first woman elected to Congress, there was a breathless hush. Suddenly Representative Rankin, contrary to precedent, stood up and declared, "I want to stand by my country but I cannot vote for war. I vote no." In later years she reflected on her action.

> **A PERSONAL VOICE**
> I believe that the first vote I cast was the most significant vote and a most significant act on the part of women, because women are going to have to stop war. I felt at the time that the first woman [in Congress] should take the first stand, that the first time the first woman had a chance to say no to war she should say it.
>
> **JEANNETTE RANKIN,** quoted in *Jeannette Rankin: First Lady in Congress*

Both the House and the Senate voted overwhelmingly in favor of the United States entering World War I, thus abandoning American neutrality three years after hostilities first began. And even then, there was considerable debate as to whether the United States should join the fight. Woodrow Wilson won a second term in 1916 on the antiwar slogan "He Kept Us Out of War." What, then, made the United States change its mind in 1917?

Jeannette Rankin was the only member of the House to vote against entering both World War I and World War II.

Long-Term Causes of World War I

The First World War began on August 4, 1914, when German troops poured into Belgium. Although many Americans wanted to stay out of the war, several factors made American neutrality short-lived. As an industrial and imperial power, the United States felt many of the same pressures that led the nations of Europe into devastating warfare. Historians generally cite four long-term causes of the First World War: nationalism, imperialism, militarism, and the formation of a system of alliances.

NATIONALISM Nationalism—the belief that national interests and national unity should be placed ahead of global cooperation and that foreign affairs should be guided by national self-interest—grew in Europe throughout the 19th century. Often, it was expressed as competitiveness with, and even antagonism toward, other nations.

France and Germany jockeyed for European leadership. France still smarted over its loss of the provinces of Alsace and Lorraine in the Franco-Prussian War in 1871. Germany, which was created in the wake of the Prussian victory over France, felt the need to protect its newly industrializing economy by ensuring open markets in Europe and access to overseas territories.

Russia regarded itself as the protector of Europe's Slavic peoples, no matter which government they lived under. Among these were the Serbs.

SECTION 1 RESOURCES

PRINT RESOURCES

IN-DEPTH RESOURCES: UNIT 5
Guided Reading, p. 40
Skillbuilder Practice: Evaluating Courses of Action, p. 44
Primary Source: The Zimmermann Note, p. 47
Literature: from *A Son at the Front* by Edith Wharton, p. 51
American Lives: Jeannette Rankin, p. 54

ACCESS FOR STUDENTS ACQUIRING ENGLISH
Guided Reading (Spanish), p. 189
Skillbuilder Practice: Evaluating Courses of Action (Spanish), p. 193

FORMAL ASSESSMENT
Section Quiz, p. 234

ALTERNATIVE ASSESSMENT BOOK
See forms for supporting and scoring alternative activities.

TECHNOLOGY RESOURCES

GEOGRAPHY TRANSPARENCIES
G19, Europe Goes to War

CRITICAL THINKING TRANSPARENCIES
CT19, World War I

CD-ROM Electronic Library of Primary Sources

VIDEO *American Portfolio: A Videodisc for U.S. History* user's guide, p. 181

INTERNET McDougal Littell Learning On-Line
http://www.mcdougallittell.com

Serbia—located in the Balkans—was an independent nation at the time, but millions of other Serbs lived under the rule of Austria-Hungary. As a result, Russia and Austria-Hungary were rivals for influence over Serbia.

In addition, various ethnic groups resented domination by others and hoped to create nations of their own. Poland, for example, had been divided among Germany, Austria-Hungary, and Russia. Poles wanted to reunite as an independent Polish nation. The Czechs were restless under the domination of Austria-Hungary, which would not let them use their own language.

IMPERIALISM Nationalist competition often worsened imperial conflicts among the major powers of Europe. To some degree, industrialization and imperialism were closely linked. As Germany industrialized, it competed with France and Britain in the contest for colonies, which supplied imperial powers with raw materials such as cotton, oil, and rubber, as well as markets for manufactured goods. Colonies also added to the imperialist nations' prestige.

The late 19th and early 20th centuries witnessed several quarrels and small wars over colonies. The Russo-Japanese War was an imperial war over Korea and Manchuria. France and Britain nearly went to war over Africa.

MILITARISM Empires were expensive to build and to defend. The growth of nationalism and imperialism caused military budgets to rise. Because each nation wanted its armed forces to be stronger than those of any potential enemy, the imperial powers followed a policy of **militarism,** the development of armed forces and their use as a tool of diplomacy.

By 1890 the strongest nation on the European continent was Germany, which had set up an army reserve system that drafted young men, trained them, and returned them to civilian life until they were needed.

At first Great Britain was not concerned about Germany's military buildup. An island nation, Great Britain had always relied on its navy for defense and protection of its shipping routes—and the British Navy was the strongest in the world. However, in 1898, Wilhelm II, Germany's new kaiser, or emperor, decided that his nation should also become a major sea power in order to compete more successfully against the British. Soon British and German shipyards competed to build the largest battleships and destroyers. France, Italy, Japan, and the United States quickly joined the naval arms race.

ALLIANCE SYSTEM All these mutual hostilities, jealousies, fears, and desires led the nations of Europe to sign treaties of assistance that committed them to support one another if they faced attack. By 1914 there were two major

Skillbuilder Answer
Location: *Possible Answer:* The Allies border the Central Powers on both the east and the west.

The Warring Powers, 1915

GREAT BRITAIN
North Sea
DENMARK
Baltic Sea
NETHERLANDS
ATLANTIC OCEAN
GERMANY
RUSSIA
BELGIUM
FRANCE
SWITZERLAND
AUSTRIA-HUNGARY
SPAIN
ITALY
SERBIA
ROMANIA
MONTENEGRO
BULGARIA
ALBANIA
OTTOMAN EMPIRE
GREECE

Countries at War in 1915
- Central Powers
- Allied (Entente) Powers
- Neutral Countries

ALLIES		CENTRAL POWERS
Although not all of the following countries sent troops into the war, those listed below joined the war on the Allied side at various times.		Austria-Hungary Bulgaria Germany Ottoman Empire
Australia	India	
Belgium	Italy	
British Colonies	Japan	
Canada & Newfoundland	Montenegro	
France	New Zealand	
French North Africa & French Colonies	Portugal Romania Russia Serbia	
Great Britain	South Africa	
Greece	United States	

GEOGRAPHY SKILLBUILDER LOCATION *Considering the geographical location of the Allies, what military advantage might the Allies have over the Central Powers?*

An Assassination Leads to War

▶ *Discussing Key Ideas*
- The Balkan Peninsula is a "powder keg."

- The assassination of Archduke Franz Ferdinand sparks the First World War.

- The alliance system forces many nations into the war.

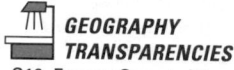
GEOGRAPHY TRANSPARENCIES
G19, Europe Goes to War

CRITICAL THINKING TRANSPARENCIES
CT19, World War I

NOW & THEN
Crisis in Bosnia

Have groups of students research the situation in the Balkans today. Ask each group to concentrate on the situation from the point of view of the Serbs, the Croats, or the Muslims. Have students discuss their findings in class. Ask them whether they think the Balkan Peninsula is still a powder keg.

The Fighting Starts

▶ *Discussing Key Ideas*
- Germany invades Belgium.
- Armies use trench warfare to fight for small areas of land.
- Fighting is deadlocked for two years.

mutual-defense alliances. The Triple Entente, later known as the **Allies,** consisted of France, Great Britain, and Russia. (Russia also had a separate treaty with Serbia.) The Triple Alliance consisted of Germany, Austria-Hungary, and Italy. (In 1915, Italy would join the Allies in return for promised territorial gains.) Germany and Austria-Hungary, together with the Ottoman Empire—an empire of mostly Middle Eastern lands controlled by the Turks—were later known as the **Central Powers.** The alliances provided a measure of international security because nations were reluctant to disturb the balance of power. As it turned out, though, a spark set off a major conflict.

An Assassination Leads to War

That spark flared in the Balkan Peninsula, "the powder keg of Europe," a peninsula bounded by the Black Sea, the Adriatic Sea, the Mediterranean Sea, and the Aegean Sea. Most of the continent's leading powers had interests there. Russia wanted to gain an outlet to the Mediterranean Sea. Germany wanted to extend the railroad between itself and the Ottoman Empire. Austria-Hungary—which had annexed Bosnia in 1908—objected to Serbia's role in encouraging Bosnians to reject the rule of Austria-Hungary. The "powder keg" was ready to explode.

On June 28, 1914, the streets of Sarajevo, the capital of Bosnia, were jammed with people who had gathered to see **Archduke Franz Ferdinand,** nephew of Emperor Franz Joseph and heir to the Austrian throne. The archduke and his wife, Sophie, waved gaily to the crowd as their automobile moved along. Suddenly a young man leaped from the curb toward them. Before the guards could react, he fired a series of shots, killing the archduke and his wife.

The teenage assassin, Gavrilo Princip, turned out to be a member of a secret society called the Black Hand. The society's aim was to unite all Serbs under one government, including those Serbs living in Bosnia. The assassination immediately touched off a diplomatic crisis. Austria-Hungary hoped to make an example of Serbia once and for all and to squelch the possibility of nationalist uprisings within Austria-Hungary. On July 28, Austria-Hungary declared what it expected to be a "bright, brisk little war" against Serbia.

The alliance system pulled one nation after another into the conflict. To keep its ally Serbia, Russia ordered full mobilization of its armies on July 29. On August 1 Germany, obligated by treaty to support Austria-Hungary, declared war on Russia. On August 3, Germany declared war on Russia's ally France. Great Britain, linked by treaty to France, declared war on Germany and Austria-Hungary. The Great War had begun.

The Fighting Starts

Germany began its war offensive by invading Belgium on August 4, 1914. The Germans followed a strategy that Count Alfred von Schlieffen, chief of the German General Staff, had planned in 1905. The Schlieffen Plan called for a holding action against Russia, combined with a quick drive through the Belgian lowlands to Paris. Then, after France had fallen, the two German armies would join to defeat the Russian czar. As German troops swept across Belgium, thousands of refugees fled in terror. The American war correspondent Richard Harding Davis described the Belgians' reaction as the troops entered the capital, Brussels.

THINK THROUGH HISTORY
B. *Recognizing Effects* Why did European nations mobilize so quickly after the archduke's assassination?

B. Answer
European nations were bound by a system of mutual defense alliances to come to the aid of any ally attacked.

NOW & THEN

CRISIS IN BOSNIA

Ethnic and religious strife have haunted the Balkans for decades.

After World War I, Bosnia became part of the new multiethnic nation of Yugoslavia. In 1991, Yugoslavia began to break apart, and Bosnia declared its independence. Serbs in Bosnia wanted Bosnia to remain part of Yugoslavia, which was now dominated by the Serbs. If Bosnia became independent, the government might fall into the hands of non-Serbs: either Croats, Muslims, or both.

Soon a civil war raged in Bosnia. As the Serbs conquered more territory, they pushed out all non-Serbs in a process called ethnic cleansing. At first the Croats and the Muslims united to resist the Serbs. After a few months, however, they were fighting each other as well.

In 1995 the United States helped negotiate a cease-fire agreement among the Serbs, Croats, and Muslims. It also sent some 20,000 American soldiers as part of a multinational force to Bosnia to keep the peace. But most observers feared that without the presence of foreign troops, the civil war might resume or the country would split.

Making Connections Across the Curriculum

Geography Tell students that the topography of the land through which a country launches its war offensive can be as important as its military strength. In the First World War, Germany's initial goal was France. The quickest route to France was through the flat lowland region of Belgium. Although Belgium was neutral, Germany declared war on the country on August 4th. By August 16th, the German army had leveled much of the Belgian countryside. Ask students why Germany didn't march through Switzerland, another neutral nation. *Switzerland is protected by mountains.*

Making Connections Across Time

World War II Strategies Tell students that at the beginning of World War II, Germany once again used the northern route through the lowlands to reach France. The German army pushed through Holland and Belgium, decimating both countries. This time, Germany took Paris. Hitler had accomplished in four weeks what Kaiser Wilhelm's armies had failed to achieve in four years. Belgium and Holland would not be liberated until 1944, when the Germans were forced to retreat following the Battle of the Bulge.

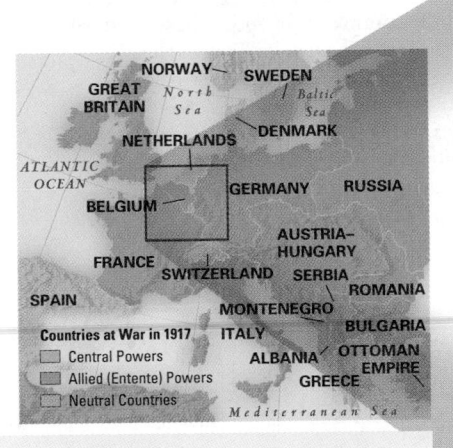

NORWAY
SWEDEN
GREAT
BRITAIN
North Sea
Baltic Sea
DENMARK
NETHERLANDS
ATLANTIC OCEAN
GERMANY
RUSSIA
BELGIUM
FRANCE
AUSTRIA-HUNGARY
SWITZERLAND
SERBIA
SPAIN
MONTENEGRO
ROMANIA
ITALY
BULGARIA
ALBANIA
OTTOMAN EMPIRE
GREECE
Mediterranean Sea

Countries at War in 1917
☐ Central Powers
☐ Allied (Entente) Powers
☐ Neutral Countries

GEOGRAPHY SKILLBUILDER LOCATION Where did the Western front extend from northwest to southeast? **MOVEMENT** About how many miles separated the city of Paris from German forces at the point of their closest approach?

Skillbuilder Answer
Location: From the Belgian coast to the Rhine River in southwestern Germany.
Movement: About 10 miles.

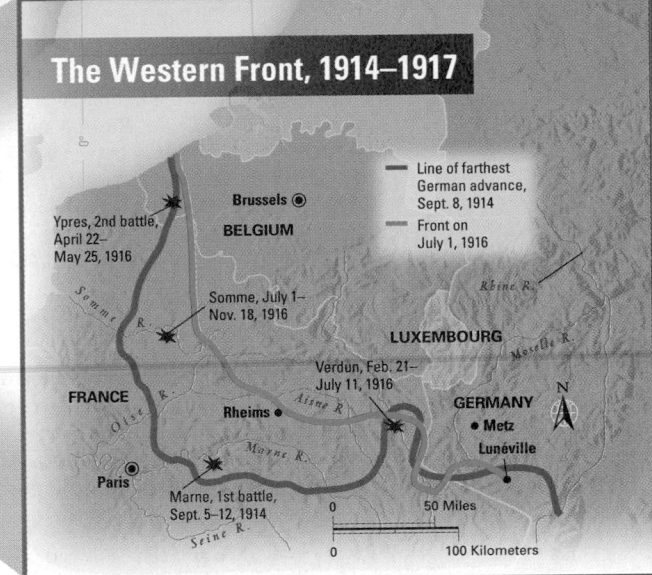

The Western Front, 1914–1917

— Line of farthest German advance, Sept. 8, 1914
— Front on July 1, 1916

Ypres, 2nd battle, April 22–May 25, 1916
Brussels
BELGIUM
Somme
Somme, July 1–Nov. 18, 1916
LUXEMBOURG
Rhine R.
Verdun, Feb. 21–July 11, 1916
FRANCE
Rheims
GERMANY
Metz
Lunéville
Aisne R.
Oise R.
Marne R.
Paris
Marne, 1st battle, Sept. 5–12, 1914
Seine R.
Moselle R.

0   50 Miles
0   100 Kilometers

HISTORY FROM VISUALS
The Western Front, 1914–1917
Reading the Map
Ask students to explain how the boxed area on the smaller map corresponds to the larger map. *It shows the Western Front in relation to the rest of Europe.*

Extension Ask students what took place at the points where the two lines on the larger map overlap. *Possible Response: The Allies and the Central Powers both gained and lost small areas of ground as they won and lost battles.*

A PERSONAL VOICE
[We] found the side streets blocked with their carts. Into these they had thrown mattresses, or bundles of grain, and heaped upon them were families of three generations. Old men in blue smocks, white-haired and bent, old women in caps, the daughters dressed in their one best frock and hat, and clasping in their hands all that was left to them, all that they could stuff into a pillow-case or flour-sack. . . . Heart-broken, weary, hungry, they passed in an unending caravan.

RICHARD HARDING DAVIS, quoted in *Hooray for Peace, Hurrah for War*

Unable to save Belgium, the British and French retreated to the Marne River in France, where they managed to stop the German advance in September 1914. By the spring of 1915, two lines of deep, rat-infested trenches zigzagged across northern and eastern France. German soldiers occupied one line, Allied soldiers the other line. Between them lay **"no man's land"**—a barren expanse of mud pockmarked with shell craters and filled with barbed wire entanglements. Every once in a while, the soldiers would climb out of their trenches and try to overrun enemy lines, while machine guns blazed and poison gas filled the air.

The slaughter was unbelievable. For example, during the Battle of the Somme—which began on July 1, 1916, and lasted until mid-November—the British lost 60,000 men the first day alone. Final casualties totaled about 1.2 million—650,000 Germans, 420,000 British, and nearly 200,000 French. Yet only seven miles of ground changed hands. This bloody **trench warfare,** in

Soldiers climb out of a trench and charge an enemy position.

MORE ABOUT . . .
Trench Warfare
Life in the trenches was bleak and uncomfortable. Trenches were only wide enough for two people to pass and provided little shelter from the elements. This is how one soldier described the trenches: "Nothing to see but bare mud walls, nowhere to sit but on a wet muddy ledge; no shelter of any kind against the weather except the clothes you are wearing; no exercise you can take in order to warm yourself." Life in the trenches was also boring. Most activity occurred at night, when soldiers could repair their dugouts under cover of darkness. Attacks usually came before dawn, when most soldiers going "over the top" were mowed down by enemy fire. Above all, life in the trenches seemed hopeless. As one soldier said, "There doesn't seem the slightest chance of leaving except in an ambulance."

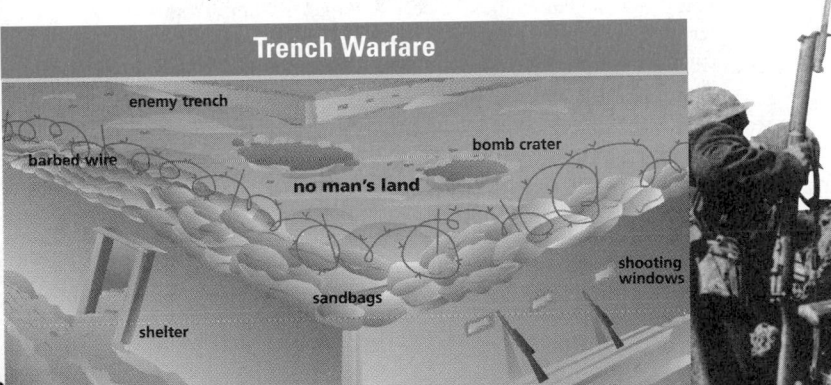

Trench Warfare

enemy trench
bomb crater
barbed wire
no man's land
shooting windows
sandbags
shelter

TEACHING OPTION

Making Connections Across Time

Poison Gas Warfare In the middle of the 19th century, a British admiral suggested the use of poison gas as a weapon of war. However, the committees that examined the proposal concluded that poison gas "was so hideous that . . . any power that used [it] would inevitably be branded as beyond the pale of civilization for all time." Nonetheless, the Germans used poison gas at Ypres in April 1915. Many of the Allied soldiers who survived the battle but had been enveloped by gas spent the rest of their lives in veterans' hospitals. The British retaliated by using poison gas, and the horrifying casualties continued.

In reaction to the devastation caused by poison gas, an international document was signed in 1925 banning the use of toxic gas and biological weapons. Though gas was not used during battle in World War II, toxic gases have been used by various countries since then. For example, Iraq used poison gas during its war with Iran in the 1980s.

American Neutrality

▶ *Discussing Key Ideas*
- Although most Americans oppose entering the war, public opinion about the war is strongly divided.
- Economic and cultural ties with Britain plus reports of German atrocities gain American sympathy for the Allies.

Ask students to create a Venn diagram like the one shown below to compare and contrast American public opinion on the war.

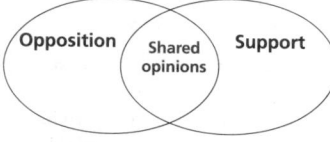

HISTORY FROM VISUALS
U.S. Exports to Europe, 1910–1915

Reading the Graph Ask students to use the graph to determine which country received the most American exports in 1915 and which country received the least. *Great Britain received the most, and Austria-Hungary received the least.*
Extension Ask students to speculate about the kinds of goods that were exported to Britain and France in 1914 and 1915. *Possible Response: War supplies.*

Skillbuilder Answer
France: They more than tripled—from just over $100 million to almost $400 million. **Taking Sides:** *Possible Answer:* U.S. exports to the two major Allied powers increase dramatically, which probably indicates exports of war-related materials. Exports to the two major Central Powers dropped sharply.

SKILLBUILDER
INTERPRETING GRAPHS
How much did U.S. exports to France increase between 1910 and 1915? What does the pattern of U.S. exports show about which side the U.S. took in the European war?

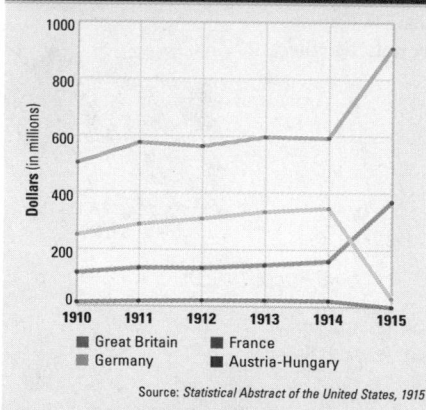

U.S. Exports to Europe, 1910–1915

Dollars (in millions)

■ Great Britain ■ France
■ Germany ■ Austria-Hungary

Source: *Statistical Abstract of the United States, 1915*

558 CHAPTER 19

---

which armies fought and died for mere yards, continued for more than three years. Elsewhere, the fighting was equally devastating and equally inconclusive. On the Eastern Front, Russian and German armies advanced and retreated in turn. The Italian Front, between Austria-Hungary and Italy, was likewise deadlocked. The Allied assault on the Dardanelles, part of the waterway between the Black Sea and the Mediterranean, ended after almost a year of trench warfare. In Africa, German and British troops were stalemated after two years of battle. It seemed as if neither side would be able to gain a decisive victory.

American Neutrality

Most Americans in 1914 saw no reason to join a struggle 3,000 miles away. The war did not threaten American lives or property. Whether or not the Allies beat the Central Powers did not seem a matter of national concern. This does not mean, however, that individual Americans were indifferent to who would win the war. Public opinion was strong—but divided.

OPPOSITION TO THE WAR Millions of naturalized U.S. citizens followed the war closely because they still had ties to the nations from which they had emigrated. For example, many Americans of German descent sympathized with Germany. Americans of Irish descent remembered the centuries of British oppression in Ireland and saw the war as a chance for Ireland to gain its independence.

Socialists criticized the war as an imperialist struggle between German and English businessmen to control raw materials and markets in China, Africa, and the Middle East. Pacifists such as William Jennings Bryan believed that war was evil, and that the United States should set an example of peace to the world. Bryan asserted, "If civilization is to advance, the day must come when a nation will feel no more obligated to accept a challenge to war than an American citizen now feels obligated to accept a challenge to fight a duel."

Many Americans simply did not want their sons to experience the horrors of warfare, as a hit song of 1915 conveyed.

> I didn't raise my boy to be a soldier,
> I brought him up to be my pride and joy.
> Who dares to place a musket on his shoulder,
> To shoot some other mother's darling boy?

SYMPATHY FOR THE ALLIES Despite the widespread opposition to the war, a general feeling of sympathy for Great Britain and France emerged. Many Americans felt close to England because of a common ancestry, language, and literature, as well as similar democratic institutions and legal systems.

Germany's aggressive sweep through Belgium also increased American sympathy for the Allies. On one occasion, for example, the Germans leveled the town of Louvain because a Belgian sniper killed a German soldier. They charged hundreds of civilians, including women and children, with armed resistance and shot them without trial. They destroyed cathedrals, libraries, and even hospitals. Some atrocity stories—distributed in British propaganda—later proved to be false, but enough proved true that within a month after the war broke out, one magazine referred to Germany as "the bully of Europe."

More important, America's economic ties with the Allies were far stronger than those with the Central Powers. Before the war began, America traded with Great Britain and France more than twice as much as it did with Germany. During the first two years of the war, America's

---

Teaching Gifted and Talented Students

Analyzing Switzerland's Neutrality Tell students that unlike the United States, Switzerland remained neutral throughout World War I. In fact, Switzerland has managed to maintain an armed neutrality since 1815. Have students research Swiss neutrality by answering these questions:

- How has Switzerland managed to remain the only European country to preserve its neutrality through two world wars?
- What role, if any, did Switzerland play in the two wars?
- How did the people of other European countries benefit from Switzerland's neutrality?

Making Connections Across Time

German Retaliation in World War II Tell students that German soldiers often exacted a high price in lives and property when they retaliated against their enemies during World War II. One such retaliation was similar to that avenged on the town of Louvain during the First World War. In 1942, after Czech fighters assassinated Reinhard Heydrich, the chief planner of the Nazi program to kill all European Jews, the Germans wiped out the Czech village of Lidice in revenge. All the men in the village were killed, all the women were sent to labor camps, and all the children were sent to Germany.

THINK THROUGH HISTORY
C. Analyzing Causes Why did the United States tend to favor Britain and France?

transatlantic trade became even more lopsided, as the Allies flooded American manufacturers with orders for all sorts of war supplies, including TNT, cannon powder, submarines, copper wire and tubing, and armored cars. The United States shipped millions of dollars of war supplies to the Allies, but requests kept coming. By 1915, the nation experienced a labor shortage.

The United States Enters the War

C. Answer The United States favored Britain and France because it traded extensively with them and because Germany was the aggressor.

Although the majority of Americans favored victory for the Allies rather than the Central Powers, they did not want to join the Allies' fight. By 1917, however, Americans mobilized for war against the Central Powers for two reasons: to ensure Allied repayment of debts to the United States and to prevent the Germans from threatening U.S. shipping.

THE BRITISH BLOCKADE As fighting on land continued without any resolution, Great Britain began to make more use of its naval strength. It set up a blockade along the German coast to prevent contraband—or weapons and other military goods—from getting through. However, the British expanded the definition of contraband to include food. They also extended the blockade to neutral ports and mined the entire North Sea.

The results were twofold. First, American ships carrying goods for Germany refused to challenge the blockade and seldom reached their destination. Second, Germany found it increasingly difficult to import foodstuffs and chemical fertilizers. Since it had to use its available nitrates to produce munitions, it could not produce fertilizers of its own. Without fertilizers, German farmers could not grow enough food. By 1917, famine stalked the country. An estimated 750,000 Germans starved to death as a result of the British blockade.

GERMAN U-BOAT RESPONSE Germany responded to the British blockade with a counter-blockade by U-boats (from *Unterseeboot*, the German word for submarine). The kaiser announced that all cargoes headed for Great Britain would be considered contraband. Any ship found in the waters around Britain would be sunk—and it would not always be possible to warn crews and passengers in advance of an attack.

The German blockade turned out to be far less destructive than the British blockade. All told, about 75,000 people lost their lives from German submarine warfare, about one-tenth of the number of Germans who died of starvation. However, the effects of the British blockade were only visible inside Germany. U-boat attacks, on the other hand, were spectacular events, easily exploited in the propaganda reaching the United States from Britain, which had cut the transatlantic cable between Germany and the United States. News of the European front that flashed from London carried accounts of sinking ships and drowning victims around the world.

D. Answer Because the U-boat campaign killed Americans and destroyed American property, it turned American public opinion against Germany and helped bring the United States into the war.

THINK THROUGH HISTORY
D. Recognizing Effects How did the German U-boat campaign affect U.S. public opinion and actions?

As a result, Americans who had been angry at Great Britain's blockade, which threatened freedom of the seas and prevented American goods from reaching German ports, became outraged with Germany because of the loss of life. American public opinion toward Germany and the Central Powers rapidly became negative.

One of the worst disasters occurred on May 7, 1915, when a U-boat sank the British liner **Lusitania** off the southern coast of Ireland. Of the 1,198 persons killed, 128 were Americans. The Germans defended their action on the grounds that the liner carried ammunition and explosives. But most Americans agreed with the New York minister who thundered from his pulpit, "This sinking . . . is

ECONOMIC BACKGROUND

THE COSTS OF NEUTRALITY

Although Woodrow Wilson hoped to keep Americans neutral in the First World War, neutrality proved difficult for those who had a great deal of money invested in the Allies. Some warned that drained treasuries would force European nations to cut their purchases of food and war material from the United States, which in turn would slow down the booming U.S. war industries. Secretary of the Treasury William McAdoo argued that to maintain American prosperity, the United States must finance the war.

As a result, by 1917 American banks had loaned $2.3 billion to the Allies and only $27 million to the Central Powers. Furthermore, U.S. trade with the Allies quadrupled while trade with the Central Powers fell drastically between 1914 and 1917. A major reason that U.S. leaders backed the Allies was that only an Allied victory would assure repayment of those American loans.

The United States Enters the War

▶*Discussing Key Ideas*
- The British naval blockade creates terrible food shortages in Germany.
- German U-boats sink British ships, including passenger liners, and turn American public opinion against Germany.
- Wilson is reelected in 1916 on a platform of neutrality, but events soon prompt the president to declare war.

ECONOMIC BACKGROUND
The Costs of Neutrality
Critical Thinking: Speculating Discuss the economic motivation for American entry into the war. Ask students whether they think the United States would have backed the Central Powers if Americans had invested more money in those countries. Would the United States have entered the war if American banks had not loaned money to either side?

TEACHING OPTION

Cooperative Activity: Creating Wartime Propaganda

Task: Groups of four to five students will create a piece of propaganda designed to promote sympathy for one side in the First World War.

Purpose: To help students understand the power of propaganda during a war.

Activity: Students should create a poster that exaggerates the villainy of the enemy and the righteousness of their own side. Some students might want to illustrate a U-boat sinking to influence public opinion against Germany. Others might illustrate action on the

part of the Allies that can be shown in a negative manner. Students should include a caption or slogan that effectively captures the poster's message. Collect the finished posters, display them, and discuss them in class.

📁 **Building a Portfolio:** Students who decide to add their posters to their portfolios should attach a note describing how the poster is intended to influence public opinion.

ALTERNATIVE ASSESSMENT BOOK
Standards for Evaluating a Cooperative Activity

Standards for Evaluation
Posters should . . .

- exaggerate the villainy of one side and the goodness of the other
- include a caption or catchy slogan that summarizes the message
- appeal to the intended audience's emotions

Engage students in a debate
on the question raised in the
feature. Divide students on
both sides into smaller
groups. Then have pairs of
opposing groups discuss
whether the United States
should have entered the
war. Remind students to use
sound reasons and logic to
support their arguments.

MORE ABOUT . . .
*Hughes and the 1916
Election*

Hughes took part in various
political stunts on the campaign trail in an attempt to
counter his reputation as a
cold, reserved man. In Reno,
Nevada, he attended a
rodeo and shook hands with
all the cowboys. In Butte,
Montana, he went down
into a copper mine to shake
hands with the miners. In
Detroit, he jumped on top of
the Tigers' dugout to shake
hands with Ty Cobb and
other baseball players.
Hughes's biggest mistake
took place in California,
where he failed to visit
Governor Hiram Johnson.
Insulted, Johnson refused to
campaign for Hughes, who
consequently lost the state
by fewer than 4,000 votes.

NOTICE!

TRAVELLERS intending to embark on the Atlantic voyage are reminded that a state of war exists between Germany and her allies and Great Britain and her allies; that the zone of war includes the waters adjacent to the British Isles; that, in accordance with formal notice given by the Imperial German Government, vessels flying the flag of Great Britain, or of any of her allies, are liable to destruction in those waters and that travellers sailing in the war zone on ships of Great Britain or her allies do so at their own risk.

IMPERIAL GERMAN EMBASSY
WASHINGTON, D. C., APRIL 22, 1915.

Notices like the one above
were printed in American
newspapers warning
passengers not to travel
by sea. This 1915 painting
of an American transport
sunk by a German U-boat
(right) shows how serious
that warning was.

not war; it is . . . organized murder and no language is too strong for it. . . . It is
getting to be too much to ask America to keep out when Americans are drowned
as part of a European war."

THE UNITED STATES REMAINS NEUTRAL Despite this provocation, Wilson
ruled out a military response. However, he protested sharply to Germany. Two
months later, in July 1915, a U-boat sank another British liner, the *Arabic*, drowning two Americans. Again the United States protested, and this time Germany
agreed not to sink any more liners. But in March 1916 Germany broke
its promise and torpedoed an unarmed French passenger steamer, the
Sussex. The *Sussex* did not sink, but about 80 passengers, including
Americans, were killed or injured. Once again the United States warned
that it would break off diplomatic relations unless Germany changed its
tactics. Again Germany agreed, in the *Sussex* pledge. There was a string
attached, though: If the United States could not persuade Britain to lift
its blockade against food and fertilizers, Germany said, it would consider
renewing unrestricted submarine warfare.

THE 1916 ELECTION In November 1916 came the U.S. presidential
election. The Democrats renominated Wilson and the Republicans
nominated Supreme Court Justice Charles Evans Hughes. Wilson
campaigned on the slogan "He Kept Us Out of War." Hughes pledged
to uphold America's right to freedom of the seas but also promised not
to be too severe on Germany.

The election returns shifted from hour to hour. In fact, Hughes
went to bed believing he had been elected. When a reporter tried to
reach him with the news of Wilson's victory, an aide said, "The
President can't be disturbed." "Well," replied the reporter, "when he
wakes up, tell him he's no longer President."

NEUTRALITY COLLAPSES Following the election, Wilson tried to
end the war by calling upon both sides to state the terms on which they
would be willing to stop fighting. The attempt failed. In a speech
before the Senate on January 22, 1917, the president called for "a
peace without victory . . . a peace among equals" in which neither side
would impose harsh terms on the other. Instead, all nations would join
in a League for Peace that would work to extend democracy, maintain
freedom of the seas, and reduce armaments.

Nine days later the Germans responded. Germany's leaders felt they
had a good chance to knock out Great Britain by resuming unrestricted

Difficult Decisions
IN HISTORY

**SHOULD THE UNITED
STATES ENTER THE WAR?**

Though President Wilson urged
Americans to be "neutral in fact as
well as in name," many wanted to
join the war on the Allied side.
Secretary of State Robert Lansing,
for example, undercut Wilson's
peace initiatives with Britain and
France, hoping Germany would
resume unrestricted U-boat attacks
and thus pull America into the war.

As a pacifist, Jane Addams
worked hard to keep the United
States out of the war altogether,
and she endured criticism for her
efforts. Senator George Norris
argued against the war resolution
in Congress, charging that millions
would suffer and die "all because
we want to preserve the
commercial right of American
citizens to deliver munitions of war
to belligerent nations."

1. In your opinion, which side
   had the stronger argument—
   those who backed the Allies or
   those who favored staying out
   of the war?
2. In your opinion, should the
   United States have entered
   the war?

Skillbuilder Mini-Lesson: Evaluating Alternative Courses of Action

Explaining the Skill In order to understand historical
decisions, historians often look at the alternative courses of
action that were available to people at the time. Evaluating
such alternatives involves analyzing the pros and cons of each
alternative based on the conditions, expectations, and values
of the times, and on the information that was available then.

Applying the Skill Have students read the feature on this
page, Difficult Decisions in History, and review the events
leading up to the U.S. entrance into World War I. Then ask

what alternatives President Wilson had in responding to
Germany and how effective each alternative might have been.
*Possible Responses: Stay out entirely, which didn't seem to
be working, since Germany kept threatening American lives
and property; continue to try to negotiate with Germany,
which also didn't seem to work, because Germany kept
breaking agreements; enter the war, as Wilson did after
Germany promised to help Mexico regain lands that were
part of the U.S.*

IN-DEPTH RESOURCES: UNIT 5
Skillbuilder Practice: Evaluating Alternative Courses of Action, p. 44

submarine warfare. On January 31 the kaiser announced that U-boats would sink all ships in British waters—hostile or neutral—on sight. Wilson was stunned. The German decision meant the United States would have to go to war. However, the president held back, saying that he would wait for "actual overt acts" before breaking diplomatic relations.

The overt acts came. First was the **Zimmermann note,** a telegram sent by the German foreign minister to the German ambassador in Mexico and intercepted by British agents. The telegram suggested an alliance between Mexico and Germany and promised that if war with the United States broke out, Germany would support Mexico in recovering "the lost territory in Texas, New Mexico, and Arizona." Next came the sinking of four unarmed American merchant ships with a loss of 36 lives. Moreover, in March the Russians overthrew their repressive czarist regime and replaced it with a representative government. Now supporters of entry into the war could claim that the war against the Central Powers was a war of democracies against brutal monarchies.

A light drizzle fell on Washington on April 2, 1917, as senators, representatives, ambassadors, members of the Supreme Court, and other guests crowded into the Capitol building to hear President Wilson deliver his war resolution.

A PERSONAL VOICE

Property can be paid for; the lives of peaceful and innocent people cannot be. The present German submarine warfare against commerce is a warfare against mankind. . . . We are glad . . . to fight . . . for the ultimate peace of the world and for the liberation of its peoples . . . for the rights of nations great and small and the privilege of men everywhere to choose their way of life. . . . The world must be made safe for democracy. . . . We have no selfish ends to serve. We desire no conquest, no dominion. We seek no indemnities. . . . It is a fearful thing to lead this great peaceful people into war. . . . But the right is more precious than peace.

WOODROW WILSON, quoted in *American Voices*

The Senate passed the resolution on April 4 and the House of Representatives did so on April 6. With the illusion of neutrality finally shattered, U.S. troops would follow the stream of American money and munitions that had been heading to the Allies throughout the war. But Wilson's desire to make the world "safe for democracy" wasn't just political rhetoric. Indeed, Wilson and many Americans truly believed that the United States must join the war to pave the way for a future order of peace and freedom. A resolved but anxious nation held its breath as the United States prepared for war.

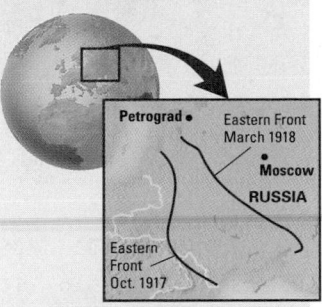

ON THE WORLD STAGE

WAR ON THE EASTERN FRONT

The Russian army surprised the Germans by mobilizing so rapidly in the early months of the war. Russian troops advanced quickly into German territory. The Germans turned the Russians back, however, at the Battle of Tannenberg in August 1914.

Throughout 1915, the Russians suffered successive defeats and continued to fall back into their own territory. By the end of 1915 they had suffered about 2.5 million casualties. Beyond the casualties, the war also caused massive bread shortages within Russia.

Demanding bread and peace, revolutionaries ousted the czar in March 1917 and established a provisional government led by Alexander Kerensky, who refused to pull Russia out of the war. In November, the Bolsheviks, led by V. I. Lenin and Leon Trotsky, overthrew the Kerensky government, set up a Communist state, and sought peace with the Central Powers.

Section Assessment

1. **TERMS & NAMES**

    Identify:
    • militarism
    • Allies
    • Central Powers
    • Archduke Franz Ferdinand
    • "no man's land"
    • trench warfare
    • *Lusitania*
    • Zimmermann note

2. **SUMMARIZING** In a chart like the one shown, list events or reasons that promoted and slowed the entrance of the United States into World War I.

The U.S. Entrance into World War I	
Promoted	Slowed

    Choose a reason or an event to explain orally to your class.

3. **HYPOTHESIZING** If Archduke Ferdinand had not been assassinated, do you think World War I would still have occurred? Give reasons to support your viewpoint.

    THINK ABOUT
    • the long-term causes of World War I
    • the reason for the archduke's assassination
    • the multinational interest in the Balkans

4. **ANALYZING ISSUES** Why do you think Germany responded to Wilson's call for "peace without victory" by escalating its U-boat attacks?

    THINK ABOUT
    • Germany's military buildup
    • its reputation as "the bully of Europe"
    • its reason for using submarine warfare

The First World War **561**

ANSWERS

1. TERMS & NAMES

militarism, p. 555

Allies, p. 556

Central Powers, p. 556

Archduke Franz Ferdinand, p. 556

"no man's land," p. 557

trench warfare, p. 557

Lusitania, p. 559

Zimmermann note, p. 561

2. SUMMARIZING

***Possible Answer:* Promoted:** cultural links with Great Britain and France; British propaganda; economic ties with Allies; anger at U-boat attacks; Zimmermann note. **Slowed:** ethnic ties of German and Irish Americans; charges of imperialism; pacifism; Wilson's slogan in 1916 campaign. **Explanation:** British propaganda—Americans knew about U-boat attacks but didn't know thousands of Germans were starving.

3. HYPOTHESIZING

***Possible Responses:* Yes—** Long-term forces were pushing Europe into war; the alliances were ready and waiting to defend their groups; Germany's military buildup foretold war. **No—**At least not at that time, because nations did not want to upset the balance of power in the alliances; militarism resulted in an arms race, but war might not have followed.

4. ANALYZING ISSUES

***Possible Response:* The** Germans had been slowly building their military power and were preparing for a show of strength, so peace without victory would have been meaningless; Germany thought it could defeat Britain with unrestricted submarine warfare before the Americans could mobilize for war.

OBJECTIVES

1 To describe how the United States mobilized for war.

2 To summarize American success on the war front.

3 To identify the new weapons and the medical problems faced in World War I.

4 To assess the impact of the war on the key participating nations.

SKILLBUILDERS

• Understanding geography: movement, region, p. 565
• Interpreting graphs, p. 568

CRITICAL THINKING

• Clarifying, p. 563
• Summarizing, pp. 564, 568
• Following chronological order, p. 565
• Recognizing effects, p. 567
• Evaluating, p. 568
• Hypothesizing, p. 568

FOCUS & MOTIVATE

▶ *Starting with the Student*
• How would students react if their country went to war? Would they volunteer to serve? Would they refuse to go? Would they protest the country's involvement in the conflict?

MORE ABOUT . . .
Leonard Covello

Before nine-year-old Leonard Covello emigrated to the United States, his grandmother gave him some good advice: "The gold you will find in America will not be in the streets, as they say. It will be in the dreams you will realize—in the golden dreams of the future." Covello never forgot his grandmother's words, and although he became a loyal American, he never forgot the land of his birth. In 1972, after devoting his life to teaching and easing the transition of Italian immigrants into American life, Covello returned to Italy. He died there ten years later at the age of 94.

---

❷ American Power Tips the Balance

TERMS & NAMES
• Selective Service Act
• convoy system
• Alvin York
• conscientious objector
• mechanized warfare
• Captain Eddie Rickenbacker

LEARN ABOUT the American experience fighting in the First World War
TO UNDERSTAND how the United States contributed to Allied victory.

ONE AMERICAN'S STORY

Leonard Covello emigrated to the United States from Italy at age nine. He spent two years becoming "Americanized" at the local "Soup School," run by a Protestant mission group, and then shifted to public schools. After graduating from Columbia University, he became a high school teacher in New York City.

When the United States entered World War I, Covello did volunteer work with the Farm Cadet Bureau and supervised teenagers who were harvesting the state's fruit crop. Covello decided to enlist in the army. A friend questioned the move, saying she thought he could do more by continuing to teach and by helping in the war jobs at home. Covello, who had spent the previous evening discussing patriotism with his buddies, explained his reasoning.

A PERSONAL VOICE

It was hard to put it into words without making it sound sentimental—hard to express in any fresh way that in war people get killed and that no man has the right to expect another to take this risk of death for him. What I was trying to express had been said a hundred thousand times before and would be again. It was still something personal and individual that had to be lived and experienced within one's self. "I have thought about it a great deal," I explained to Rose. "If I sat back now and did not enlist I would not be living up to what I was taught to believe. What I want to teach others to believe. I have to go."

LEONARD COVELLO, quoted in *The Heart Is the Teacher*

Leonard Covello

Covello was one of hundreds of thousands of American to enlist. About one-fourth of the U.S. armed forces in World War I were volunteers. The rest were draftees. They all played a major role in assuring the Allies' final victory. Without U.S. troops—to say nothing of U.S. ships, food, and military supplies—the war could have gone the other way and the history of the world since 1918 might have been very different.

American Military Mobilization

The first task that confronted the United States upon entering the war was to raise an army. When war was declared, only about 200,000 men were in service. Few officers had any combat experience. Almost all of the army's weapons were out of date and the whole U.S. air corps consisted of 55 small planes and 130 pilots.

The country solved the lack of manpower by conducting a draft. Many members of Congress initially opposed it and argued that conscription (the draft) would produce a "sulky, unwilling, indifferent army." But after weeks of debate, Congress passed the **Selective Service Act** in May 1917. Almost 10 million men registered under the act, and unlike the Civil War experience, not a single riot took place. Two additional registrations were held in 1918, raising the total number of potential draftees to 24 million. Of this number, almost 3 million, chosen by lottery, were called up. About 2 million troops reached Europe before the armistice was signed, and three-fourths of them saw actual combat. The ages of the inductees ranged from 18 to 45. However, since married men and those with dependents were generally excused, the overseas army consisted primarily of men between 21 and 23. Most had not attended high school and about one in five was foreign-born.

562 CHAPTER 19

SECTION 2 RESOURCES

PRINT RESOURCES

IN-DEPTH RESOURCES: UNIT 5
Guided Reading, p. 41
Primary Source: Patriotic Song, p. 48
Literature: *from* "In Another Country" by Ernest Hemingway, p. 51

ACCESS FOR STUDENTS ACQUIRING ENGLISH
Guided Reading (Spanish), p. 190

FORMAL ASSESSMENT
Section Quiz, p. 235

ALTERNATIVE ASSESSMENT BOOK
See forms for supporting and scoring alternative activities.

TECHNOLOGY RESOURCES

HUMANITIES TRANSPARENCIES
H18, *Oppy Wood* by John Nash

CRITICAL THINKING TRANSPARENCIES
CT53, Human and Financial Costs of World War I

CD-ROM *Our Times*
Grolier Multimedia Encyclopedia
Electronic Library of Primary Sources

VIDEO *American Portfolio: A Videodisc for U.S. History*
user's guide, pp. 183–188

INTERNET McDougal Littell Learning On-Line
http://www.mcdougallittell.com

The training period lasted for nine months, partly in the United States and partly in Europe. During this time the men put in 17-hour days on target practice, bayonet drill, kitchen duty, and cleaning up the grounds. Since real weapons were in short supply, they often drilled with imaginary ones—rocks instead of hand grenades, wooden poles instead of rifles. To keep up morale, volunteer organizations provided the recruits with movies, books, and vaudeville shows. After nine months, they were moved to wherever the fighting was hottest.

Women were not drafted. The army also refused to let them enlist, but the navy accepted them for noncombat positions. Accordingly, some 13,000 women served in the navy and marines as nurses, secretaries, and telephone operators, with full military rank. Although the army reluctantly accepted women in the Army Corps of Nurses, it denied them army rank, pay, and benefits.

The proportion of African Americans in service was double their proportion in the general population. As in earlier wars, black soldiers served in segregated units and were excluded from the navy and marines. They had separate living quarters and separate recreational facilities. Although most officers were white, the army for the first time trained some black officers and placed them in command of black troops. Most African Americans were assigned to noncombat duties, but not all. The all-black 369th Infantry Regiment saw more continuous duty on the front lines than any other American regiment. Two soldiers of the 369th, Henry Johnson and Needham Roberts, were among the first Americans to receive the French military honor of the Croix de Guerre, the cross of war.

American Success in Combat

The second task facing the United States was to transport its troops overseas, along with food and equipment sufficient for them and for America's allies. It was an immense task, made more difficult by the German unrestricted submarine warfare which, by early 1917, had sunk twice as much ship tonnage as the Allies had built.

BUILDING THE "BRIDGE TO FRANCE" The United States immediately began constructing ships to expand its fleet. For decades American manufacturers had relied mostly on foreign ships to carry their products overseas. In addition, the draft reduced the number of skilled shipyard workers.

To overcome these obstacles, the U.S. government took four critical steps. First, it either exempted shipyard workers from the draft or gave them a "deferred" classification, delaying their participation in the draft. Second, the government and the U.S. Chamber of Commerce cooperated in a public relations campaign to emphasize the importance of shipyard work. They distributed service flags to families of shipyard workers, just like the flags given to families with soldiers and sailors. An official in the Chamber of Commerce went around the country urging automobile owners to give shipyard employees rides to and from work, since streetcars were so crowded. Third, shipyards developed a new

THINK THROUGH HISTORY
A. Clarifying
How did the United States raise an army for the war?

A. Answer
Congress passed the Selective Service Act, which caused nearly 10 million men to register for the draft.

James Montgomery Flagg's portrayal of Uncle Sam in *I Want You* became the most famous recruiting poster in American history.

A convoy of American ships heads toward Britain.

OBJECTIVE
(1) INSTRUCT

American Military Mobilization

▶ *Discussing Key Ideas*
• Although some members of Congress fear that a draft will produce an unwilling army, almost 10 million men register for combat under the Selective Service Act.
• Women are not drafted, but some fill noncombat positions.
• Black soldiers serve in segregated units, and some are assigned to fight on the front lines.

IN-DEPTH RESOURCES: UNIT 5
Guided Reading, p. 41

ACCESS FOR STUDENTS ACQUIRING ENGLISH
Guided Reading (Spanish), p. 190

OBJECTIVE
(2) INSTRUCT

American Success in Combat

▶ *Discussing Key Ideas*
• The United States constructs ships to expand its fleet for the war effort.
• Using the convoy system, the Allies break the German blockade.
• General Pershing insists on having American soldiers fight as an independent force.
• With Americans fighting in large numbers, the United States helps turn the tide against the Central Powers by October 1918.

TEACHING OPTIONS

Making Connections Across Cultures

African Americans in World War I Discuss the treatment of African-American soldiers during World War I. Tell students that the NAACP and black leader W. E. B. Du Bois urged African Americans to join the fight for world democracy. Ask students why many African Americans wanted to fight for a country that failed to grant them equal rights. *Possible Response: They hoped that fighting for world democracy might ensure fairer treatment at home.*

ELECTRONIC LIBRARY OF PRIMARY SOURCES
From Harlem to the Rhine by Arthur Little

Exploring Themes

Expanding Democracy Tell students that although many of the army's practices were discriminatory, the decision to train black officers revealed a more progressive attitude toward minorities than that prevalent in society in general. Point out that the army has frequently been at the vanguard in according African Americans and other minorities democratic rights. Ask students why the army, particularly during times of war, has often granted minorities more rights, freedoms, and opportunities than society has. *Possible Responses: War is a great equalizer; war inspires feelings of brotherhood.*

In a sense, Taber began training for battle in childhood. When he was eight years old and on summer vacation, he would swim for half an hour a day in an ice-cold lake. When he was bitten by a snake in his early teens, he did not flinch. Nor did he complain when he had to undergo nine operations for a wrenched knee. He carried out an experiment in a Western desert to see how long he could survive without water. Before enlisting in the U.S. Army, he spent part of a year as a volunteer driver with the American Field Ambulance Service in France. After the war ended, he remained in France to test-fly planes and to observe the peace conference at Versailles "from the front-row, so to speak." Sadly, after surviving the war, Taber was killed in February 1919 while test-flying an army plane. He was buried in a military cemetery outside Paris.

construction technique called fabrication. Instead of building an entire ship in the yard, they had standardized parts built elsewhere and merely assembled them at the yard. This method reduced construction time substantially. As a result, on just one day—July 4, 1918—the United States was able to launch 95 ships. Fourth, the government took over every ship under construction for private owners and every ship that had been designed for the Great Lakes and converted them for transatlantic war use.

BREAKING THE BLOCKADE   The goal of building a navy was to reduce the shipping losses caused by German U-boats that attacked merchant ships trying to cross the Atlantic. Rear Admiral William S. Sims persuaded the British that the best way to defeat the U-boats was the **convoy system,** in which the merchant vessels would travel in a large group with a guard of circling destroyers and cruisers. The British agreed, and by midsummer of 1917 shipping losses had been cut in half. Eventually the United States put 100 submarine chasers and 500 airplanes into the anti–U-boat campaign.

The U.S. Navy also helped lay down a 230-mile barrier of mines across the North Sea from Scotland to Norway. The barrier was designed to bottle up the U-boats that sailed from German ports and keep them out of the Atlantic Ocean.

THINK THROUGH HISTORY
B. Summarizing
What four steps did the U.S. government take to build a naval fleet quickly?

B. Answer It let shipyard workers out of the draft, used a public relations campaign to stress the importance of shipbuilding, used a new construction technique called fabrication and took control of ships built for private owners or use on the Great Lakes for transatlantic duty.

World War I Convoy System

cruiser

safe zone

merchant ships

defensive boundary

destroyer

submarine

The convoy system helped equip Britain with crucial supplies.

By the first months of 1918 the Allies had overcome the U-boat threat. Days and even weeks went by without the loss of a single Allied vessel. Moreover, as U-boat losses mounted, the Germans found it increasingly difficult to replace their losses and to man their fleet with trained submariners. Of the almost 2 million Yanks who sailed to Europe during the war, only 100 were lost to U-boats, when the transport *Tuscania* was torpedoed in the English Channel.

FIGHTING IN EUROPE   One of the main contributions that American troops made to the Allied war effort, apart from their numbers, was their freshness and enthusiasm. Unlike the British, French, and Germans, American troops had not endured three years of exhausting warfare. They were determined to hit the Germans hard. Arthur "Archie" Taber, a university student who left Princeton to enlist with the air force, enthusiastically described his experiences as a fledgling pilot in a letter to his father.

A PERSONAL VOICE
The most extraordinary piece of good luck has suddenly fallen from the skies. I . . . have been appointed as a "ferry" pilot, which means that I shall fly all over France. . . . I shall have to take planes up to the front to any point along the line where our squadrons are. . . . Of course this will be great fun; but the reason I am so enthusiastic over this job is that it gives unparalleled training in cross-country flying, the experience of flying in all kinds of machines, and the valuable foundation for any kind of work, of *time in the air*. . . . Also you can appreciate that in such a job as this, one will have to be able to fly everything from a monoplane to a triplane, from the smallest to the largest and from the fastest to the slowest!

ARTHUR TABER, quoted in *Hooray for Peace, Hurrah for War*

Taber's only regret was that he would have to wait several months, if not more, before he could hope to be assigned to "the very best pilot's job, chasing German planes over the front line trenches."

564 CHAPTER 19

Making Connections Across the Curriculum

Economics   Tell students that during the war, the United States mobilized the economy as well as the military. About one-fourth of all American production was diverted to the war effort. Agriculture and many industries experienced a boom in sales and profits. However, as demand exceeded supply, prices skyrocketed and inflation resulted. Have students discuss who reaped the greatest economic benefits from the war. What groups of Americans probably suffered the most?

Making Connections Across Time

Remembering Lafayette   Tell students that after the American troops joined the Allies in France, the saying "Lafayette, we are here!" became popular. The comment is usually attributed to General Pershing. In fact, it was delivered at an address at the grave of Lafayette in Paris on July 4, 1917, by Colonel C. E. Stanton. The statement reminded Americans that French troops under the Marquis de Lafayette had aided Washington and the cause of the American Revolution. The landing of American soldiers in World War I represented America's repayment of its debt to France.

The Western Front, 1917–1918

Ypres, 3rd battle, July 31–Nov. 10, 1917
Cantigny, May 28, 1918
St.-Mihiel, Sept. 12–16, 1918
Belleau Wood, June 6–July 1, 1918
Château-Thierry, June 4, 1918
Marne, 2nd battle, July 18–Aug. 6, 1918

— German offensive, Mar.–July 1918
— Armistice line, Nov. 11, 1918
← American Expeditionary Force participation
 Major battle

Reading the Map Point out that the smaller map shows the location of the Western Front in relation to the rest of Europe. Then ask students what countries lie to the west of the Armistice line. What countries lie to the east? **Extension** Ask students why the American Expeditionary Force was launched from the places shown by the red arrows. *To help prevent the German offensive from invading Paris.*

HUMANITIES TRANSPARENCIES
H18, *Oppy Wood* by John Nash

MORE ABOUT . . .
Conscientious Objectors

About 1,400 conscientious objectors refused to cooperate with the military in any way. Many were court-martialed and imprisoned. Some were even physically tortured. While these men held fast to their convictions, many suffered from feelings of isolation. One man sentenced to a 20-year prison term wrote to his brother: "The comradeship one must give up, the being part of the fun and hardship of all this, yes of fighting and maybe dying along with the rest of your fellows on both sides in this huge tragedy makes my stand seem so terribly aloof, so terribly unhuman."

General John J. Pershing commanded the American Expeditionary Force (AEF). At first the Americans served mostly as replacements for Allied casualties. These American infantrymen were nicknamed "doughboys," apparently because of the white belts they wore, which they cleaned with pipe clay, or "dough." Pershing, however, kept insisting that they should fight as a separate army. "We came American," he said. "We shall remain American and go into battle with Old Glory over our heads. I will not parcel out American boys!"

Pershing believed in aggressive combat and felt that three years of trench warfare had made the Allies too defensive. In addition, he wanted the United States to have a strong voice at the peace table. This was most likely to occur if the AEF remained distinct and separate. Accordingly, after April 1918, American soldiers fought as an independent force, under the overall direction of French marshal Ferdinand Foch, commander of all Allied forces in Europe.

THE TIDE TURNS By then the Germans had succeeded in knocking Russia out of the war and had shifted their armies from the Eastern Front in Russia to the Western Front in France. By May their spring offensive had smashed to within 50 miles of Paris. The Americans began to fight in large numbers just in time. They helped stop the German advance at Cantigny in France. Several weeks later they played a major role in throwing back German attacks at Château-Thierry and Belleau Wood. In July and August, they helped win the Second Battle of the Marne. In September, they mounted offensives against the Germans at Saint-Mihiel and in the Meuse-Argonne area. All told, the United States lost 48,000 men in battle, with an additional 62,000 dying of disease. More than 200,000 Americans were wounded. But by October it was clear that the tide had definitely turned against the Central Powers.

It was during the fighting in the Meuse-Argonne area that one of America's greatest war heroes, **Alvin York,** became famous. A redheaded mountaineer and blacksmith from Tennessee, York became a born-again Christian in 1915. When war came, he sought exemption as a **conscientious objector,** a person who opposes warfare on moral grounds, pointing out to his draft board that the Bible said, "Thou shalt not kill." The board denied his appeal and sent him to a training camp in Georgia. There a Captain E. C. B. Danforth presented to York a different Biblical quotation, "I bring you not peace but a sword. . . . He that hath no sword, let him sell his garment and buy one."

York eventually decided that it was morally acceptable to fight if the cause was just. On October 8, 1918, armed only with a rifle and a revolver, Corporal York killed 25 Germans and—with six other doughboys—captured 132 prisoners.

GEOGRAPHY SKILLBUILDER
MOVEMENT *Across which rivers did American troops attack German forces?* **REGION** *What territory captured by Germany after the beginning of the war lay on the German side of the Armistice line?*

Skillbuilder Answer
Movement: The Marne, the Aisne, and the Meuse rivers. **Regions:** Luxembourg and parts of Belgium.

THINK THROUGH HISTORY
C. Following Chronological Order How did the United States contribute to the Allied victory?

C. Answer The United States helped break the German blockade and helped defeat Germany at the Western Front in France.

The First World War **565**

Cooperative Activity: Letters from Conscientious Objectors and the Draft Board

Task: Student groups will write letters explaining the position of conscientious objectors and of the draft board on the war.

Purpose: To help students understand different points of view on the war.

Activity: Have small groups of students take turns representing a conscientious objector and a draft board official. As conscientious objectors, students should write letters explaining why they are opposed to the war and what, if anything, they propose to do to

aid the war effort. As draft board officials, students should explain why participation in the war is so important.

Building a Portfolio: Students who wish to add the letters to their portfolios should attach a note telling which side they found more sympathetic and whether the activity changed their minds about pacifism.

ALTERNATIVE ASSESSMENT BOOK
Standards for Evaluating a Cooperative Activity

Standards for Evaluation
Letters should . . .

• clearly state the position
• give detailed reasons to support the position
• use persuasive techniques to help convince readers
• use appropriate letter form and style

Fighting "Over There"

▶ *Discussing Key Ideas*
• New, terrifying weapons change the face of warfare.
• Medical services cannot keep up with the physical and emotional wounds suffered by the soldiers.

MORE ABOUT . . .
Soldiers' Nicknames
Before George M. Cohan popularized the use of the name Yanks for American soldiers, U.S. troops had tried several other names. The *Cleveland Press* coined the name Sammies, after Uncle Sam, but American soldiers disliked the term and it soon disappeared. The French at first referred to Americans as Teddies, after Theodore Roosevelt, but stopped using the name when General Pershing said it had no national significance. Other Allied fighting men also bore distinctive nicknames. Australians were called Aussies, the British were called Tommies, and New Zealanders were called Kiwis, after a native bird.

"Over there, over there, Send the word, send the word over there— That the Yanks are coming"

GEORGE M. COHAN, FROM THE SONG "OVER THERE," 1917

General Pershing called him the outstanding soldier of the AEF, while Marshal Foch described his feat as "the greatest thing accomplished by any private soldier of all the armies of Europe." For his heroic acts, York was promoted to sergeant and became a celebrity when he returned to the United States.

Fighting "Over There"

For Sergeant York, as for many other members of the AEF, going abroad was an eye-opening experience. Most doughboys had never ventured outside the farms or small towns where they lived, and the sights and sounds of Paris made a vivid impression. Sergeant York, for example, saw his first subway there. Then, too, the AEF included men from widely separated parts of the country. Living and fighting together, they developed a better sense of what it meant to be an American. Nevertheless, the war experience was devastating in many ways, especially in view of the new weapons soldiers used.

NEW WEAPONS One terrifying weapon was a German cannon that could hurl an 1,800-pound shell a distance of nine miles. Allied soldiers called it Big Bertha—for Bertha Krupp, the wife of Gustav Krupp, the German munitions king. Another new weapon was the zeppelin, a gas-filled airship that enabled Germans to drop bombs on English coastal cities. However, zeppelins were so easy to shoot down that the Germans abandoned their use within two years. Far deadlier was the machine gun, which sprayed 600 rounds of ammunition per minute. And there were tubes that spewed poison gas rather than bullets. Their first large-scale use occurred at the Battle of Ypres in April 1915. The Germans discharged a greenish-yellow fog of chlorine that suffocated two entire French divisions and left a four-mile-wide gap in the battle line. Gas masks soon became standard equipment for everyone.

The two most innovative weapons were the tank and the airplane. Together, they inaugurated **mechanized warfare,** or warfare that relies on machines powered by gasoline and diesel engines.

The tank ran on caterpillar treads and was built of steel so that bullets bounced off. The British, who developed the tanks, first used them during the 1916 Battle of the Somme, but not very effectively. By 1917, the British learned how to gather large numbers of tanks and drive them through barbed wire defenses against the enemy, clearing a path for the infantry.

The early airplanes were so flimsy that at first both sides limited their use to scouting. After a while, the two sides employed tanks to prevent enemy planes from gathering information. Early dogfights, or individual air combats, resembled duels. Pilots sat in their open cockpits and shot at each other with pistols. Because it was hard to fly a plane and shoot a pistol at the same time, planes began carrying mounted machine guns. But the plane's propeller blades kept getting in the way of the bullets. Then a Dutchman who was working for

New Weapons in World War I

POISON GAS
• First large-scale use was in 1915.
• Gas masks became standard equipment.

MACHINE GUNS
• Firepower increased from several rounds per minute to 600 rounds per minute.

TANKS
• Tanks were first developed by the British.
• Tanks were used in formations to clear a path for the infantry.

566

TEACHING OPTION

Making Connections Across the Curriculum

Music Tell students that many American songs helped keep up the soldiers' spirits and voiced the typical reaction to various aspects of the First World War. For example, thousands of men volunteered for combat to the sound of the popular song "Johnny Get Your Gun." Tunes like "Over There" by George M. Cohan were played by warships leaving for Europe. Irving Berlin's "Oh! How I Hate to Get Up in the Morning" reflected every soldier's dread of the morning bugle call. Other songs recognized the eye-opening effect of the war on young, naive soldiers. As the song title asks, "How 'Ya Gonna Keep 'Em Down on the Farm, After They've Seen Paree?" Still other songs, such as "There's a Long, Long Trail A-Winding," expressed the homesickness experienced by most of those in service.

IN-DEPTH RESOURCES: UNIT 5
Primary Source: Patriotic Song, p. 48

 OUR TIMES CD-ROM
George M. Cohan and "Over There"

Germany invented an interrupter gear that permitted the stream of bullets to avoid the whirring blades.

Meanwhile, airplanes became faster and able to carry heavy bomb loads. By 1918 the British had built up a strategic bomber force of 22,000 planes to target German war plants and army bases.

THINK THROUGH HISTORY
D. Recognizing Effects How did the tank and the airplane change warfare?
D. Answer They inaugurated mechanized warfare, which made fighting speedier, deadlier, more expensive, and more dependent on gasoline.

MEDICAL CARE DURING THE WAR

As is true in all wars, the fighting men suffered greatly. They were surrounded by filth, lice, rats, and polluted water that caused dysentery. They smelled the stench of poison gas and the reek of decaying bodies. They suffered from lack of sleep. Bombardments that continued for hours often led to battle fatigue and "shell shock," a complete emotional collapse.

Another problem was a disease called trench foot, caused by standing in wet trenches for long periods of time without changing into dry socks or boots. First the soldier's toes would turn red or blue, then they would become numb, and finally they would start to rot. The only solution was to amputate the foot.

Red Cross ambulances, often staffed by American volunteers, carried the wounded from the battlefield to the hospital. An American nurse named Florence Bullard recounted her experience in a hospital near the front in 1918.

A PERSONAL VOICE

The Army is only twelve miles away from us and only the wounded that are too severely injured to live to be carried a little farther are brought here. . . . Side by side I have Americans, English, Scotch, Irish, and French, and a part in the corners are Boche [Germans]. They have to watch each other die side by side. I am sent for everywhere—in the . . . operating room, the dressing-room, and back again to the rows of men. . . . The cannon goes day and night and the shells are breaking over and around us. . . . I have had to write many sad letters to American mothers. I wonder if it will ever end.

FLORENCE BULLARD, quoted in *Over There*

In fact, the end was near.

The Collapse of Germany

On November 3, 1918, the German admiralty—its naval leadership—ordered the Grand Fleet to leave its naval base at Kiel and set out to sea. But the admiralty was shocked when the sailors and marines refused to man the ships. There was no use in fighting any longer, they said.

The First World War **567**

KEY PLAYERS

JOHN J. PERSHING
1860–1948

Pershing became head of the American Expeditionary Force after many years in the military. A West Point graduate in 1886, he helped to put down Apache and Sioux uprisings in the 1880s and 1890s. He acquired the nickname "Black Jack" because he had led a unit of African-American soldiers.

He led more African-American troops in Cuba during the Spanish-American-Cuban War, and later served in the Philippines. In 1916–1917, he led the expedition against Francisco "Pancho" Villa in Mexico.

At first, fellow officers thought the "Black Jack" nickname might offend Pershing, but it didn't. He was proud of the name because his men were top-notch soldiers. Both Pershing's superiors and those he commanded respected him greatly for his courage, his fairness, and his administrative ability.

EDDIE RICKENBACKER
1890–1973

Eddie Rickenbacker became one of America's most celebrated heroes of the First World War as an ace pilot who shot down 26 enemy planes.

Rickenbacker was born in Columbus, Ohio, in 1890. He left school in the seventh grade after his father died and took a series of jobs to support his seven brothers and sisters.

Eventually, he took a mechanical engineering course and became a mechanic for race car drivers. He became a driver himself and, in 1914, set a world's record by driving his car 134 miles per hour.

During the war, Rickenbacker learned how to fly planes and became commander of the 94th Squadron. In the Spring of 1918, he scored impressive victories over Manfred von Richthofen's Flying Circus—the German squadron led by Germany's most famous ace, the Red Baron.

KEY PLAYERS
Pershing and Rickenbacker
Critical Thinking: Compare and Contrast
After students read the feature, have them create a chart or web in which they list the two men's careers and personality traits. Then ask students to discuss the personality traits that Pershing and Rickenbacker had in common.

 GROLIER MULTIMEDIA ENCYCLOPEDIA
John Pershing

OBJECTIVE
④ INSTRUCT

The Collapse of Germany

▶ **Starting with the Student**
Have students create a time line detailing the events in November that brought about the end of the First World War. The time line might look like this:

Nov. | | | | Dec.
1918 | 3 | 9 | 11 | 1918

▶ **Discussing Key Ideas**
• Soon after the German people rebel against the war and the kaiser, Germany agrees to an armistice on November 11, 1918.
• The toll of the war on human life is staggering.

TEACHING OPTION

Making Connections Across the Curriculum

Science Tell students that at the time of the First World War, psychiatry was a relatively new science. Nonetheless, military doctors recognized that thousands of their patients were suffering from the same mental illness. Doctors called the illness war neurosis, or war psychosis, but almost everyone else called it shell shock. For many of the soldiers whose nervous systems had been shattered by noisy shelling, a treatment of rest, exercise, and counseling proved successful. Others, who had been exposed to the sounds of especially intense and prolonged explosives, suffered persistent anxiety and disorientation, which made it difficult for them to live normal lives.

Before the war, mental illness was generally misunderstood and carried a stigma of shame. The First World War helped educate the public about mental illness and the importance of psychiatry. As a result of the war, most people understood that like diseases of the body, mental illness required treatment. After the war was over, psychiatrists who had treated shell-shock victims used their experience to improve care for the mentally ill at home.

World War I Casualties

Reading the Graph Point out that the graph provides the data needed to compare casualties among the countries involved in the war. Then ask students to calculate the percentage of casualties in the total war effort. *About 46 percent.*

Extension Have students draw conclusions about the relationship between the number of troops employed and the number of casualties suffered on each side.

CRITICAL THINKING TRANSPARENCIES
CT53, Human and Financial Costs of World War I

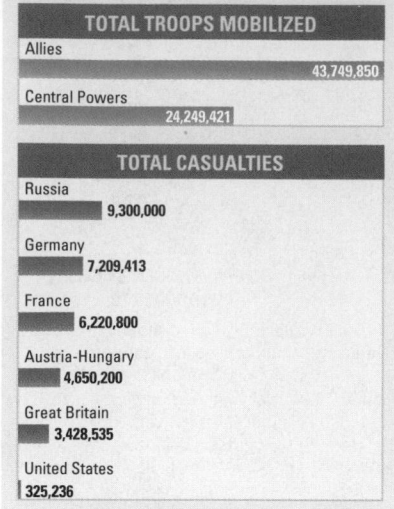

World War I Casualties

TOTAL TROOPS MOBILIZED

Allies — 43,749,850
Central Powers — 24,249,421

TOTAL CASUALTIES

Russia — 9,300,000
Germany — 7,209,413
France — 6,220,800
Austria-Hungary — 4,650,200
Great Britain — 3,428,535
United States — 325,236

Source: Randal Gray, *Chronicle of the First World War*

SKILLBUILDER
INTERPRETING GRAPHS
Which country suffered the highest military casualties in World War I? What might account for the relatively low American casualties in World War I?

Skillbuilder Answer
Highest Casualties: Russia.
American Casualties:
Possible Answer: The U.S. entered the war three years after it started.

The mutiny spread quickly. Everywhere in Germany, groups of soldiers and workers organized revolutionary councils. On November 9, the people of Berlin rose in rebellion, and socialist leaders in the capital city proclaimed the establishment of a German republic. The kaiser abdicated the throne and took refuge in the Netherlands.

Although there were no Allied soldiers on German territory and no truly decisive battle had been fought, the German war machine and war economy were too exhausted to continue fighting. So at the eleventh hour, on the eleventh day, in the eleventh month of 1918, Germany agreed to a cease-fire that ended the war. (Austria-Hungary and the Ottoman Empire had surrendered several days earlier.)

The final toll of the war was staggering. It lasted four years and involved more than 30 nations. It was the bloodiest war in history to that time. Deaths numbered about 26 million, half of them civilians who died as a result of disease, starvation, or exposure. In addition, 20 million more people were wounded, and an additional 10 million became refugees. Historians estimate the direct economic costs of the war to be $350 billion.

For the Allies, news of the armistice brought great relief. **Captain Eddie Rickenbacker,** a famous American pilot, flew over the trenches on the day of the armistice. He described what happened when the guns fell silent.

A PERSONAL VOICE
On both sides of no-man's land, the trenches erupted. Brown-uniformed men poured out of the American trenches, gray-green uniforms out of the German. From my observer's seat overhead, I watched them throw their helmets in the air, discard their guns, wave their hands. Then all up and down the front, the two groups of men began edging toward each other. . . . Hesitantly at first, then more quickly, each group approached the other. Suddenly gray uniforms mixed with brown. I could see them hugging each other, dancing, jumping. Americans were passing out cigarettes and chocolate. I flew up to the French sector. There it was even more incredible. After four years of slaughter and hatred, they were not only hugging each other but kissing each other on both cheeks as well.

EDDIE RICKENBACKER, quoted in *Hooray for Peace, Hurrah for War*

Across the Atlantic, American civilians also rejoiced at the war's end. Many hoped the world would go on much as it had before the war. However, the war had unleashed powerful forces at home, and people found their lives changed almost as much as the lives of those who fought in Europe.

Section 2 Assessment

1. TERMS & NAMES
Identify:
• Selective Service Act
• convoy system
• Alvin York
• conscientious objector
• mechanized warfare
• Captain Eddie Rickenbacker

2. SUMMARIZING Create a web, similar to the one shown, illustrating problems Americans faced as they prepared for and participated in World War I.

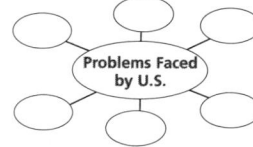

Problems Faced by U.S.

Which problem do you think created the most difficulties for Americans?

3. EVALUATING In your opinion, did the U.S. government use fair methods in selecting people to serve in the military? Explain.

THINK ABOUT
• the exemptions to the draft
• the role played by women
• the treatment of African Americans

4. HYPOTHESIZING How might the events and outcome of World War I have been different if the United States had not sent troops to Europe? Explain your answer.

THINK ABOUT
• the results of battles before the United States entered the war
• the role of American soldiers in the fighting
• the emotional impact of American troops

568 CHAPTER 19

ANSWERS

1. TERMS & NAMES
Selective Service Act, p. 562
convoy system, p. 564
Alvin York, p. 565
conscientious objector, p. 565
mechanized warfare, p. 566
Captain Eddie Rickenbacker, p. 568

2. SUMMARIZING
Possible Answers: Developing an army; transporting troops overseas; building ships; building fighter planes; avoiding U-boats; using tanks, airplanes, and machine guns; dealing with Big Bertha; fighting in trenches; dealing with poison gas; fighting diseases. Most difficulties: trench warfare, because it took so many lives, extended the length of the war, and resulted in the spread of diseases.

3. EVALUATING
Possible Responses: **Yes**— Exemptions and the lottery were fair, and discrimination against women and African Americans merely reflected attitudes of the time. **No**—The government placed unfair burdens on young, single males; not enough opportunities were offered to African Americans; the army should have given women rank, pay, and benefits.

4. HYPOTHESIZING
Possible Responses: The Allies might not have withstood the 1918 German offensive without the boost from American troops. The stalemate might have continued until both sides were so exhausted and depleted that they may have reached a compromise settlement; The Allies might still have won without American troops if America had provided supplies and medical help.

❸ The War at Home

TERMS & NAMES
- War Industries Board
- Bernard M. Baruch
- George Creel
- Espionage and Sedition Acts
- Great Migration

LEARN ABOUT the political, social, and economic forces unleashed by the war
TO UNDERSTAND how the war changed American society.

ONE AMERICAN'S STORY

Late in the summer of 1918, after President Wilson had ordered 5,000 troops to Russia, leaflets condemning the action hit the streets of Manhattan. Some local residents, in the midst of their war-era patriotic fervor, were infuriated by the tone of the leaflets and tipped off local and federal authorities about the source of the literature.

Police quickly targeted and arrested five immigrant anarchists—people who oppose any and all forms of government—for distributing literature that violated the newly passed Sedition Act. The law made it illegal to use "disloyal, profane, scurrilous, or abusive" descriptions of American leaders or institutions. While the five anarchists—Jacob Abrams, Hyman Lachowsky, Samuel Lipman, Mollie Steimer, and Jacob Schwartz—sat in jail awaiting trial, Schwartz died, possibly because of a beating by the police. The remaining four were found guilty and sentenced to serve 15 to 20 years in prison. Their appeal went before the Supreme Court, which ruled 7–2 against the defendants. One of the dissenting justices, Oliver Wendell Holmes, explained his position.

Justice Oliver Wendell Holmes

A PERSONAL VOICE
[In this case] sentences of twenty years imprisonment have been imposed for the publishing of two leaflets that I believe the defendants have as much right to publish as the Government has to publish the Constitution. . . . When men have realized that time has upset many fighting faiths, they may come to believe that . . . the best test of truth is the power of the thought to get itself accepted in the competition of the market, and that truth is the only ground upon which their wishes safely can be carried out.

JUSTICE OLIVER WENDELL HOLMES, dissenting opinion in *Abrams v. United States*

Abrams, Lachowsky, Lipman, and Steimer never served their full sentences. Instead, they were deported to Russia in 1921. But their experiences in the United States were not uncommon at a time when Americans were trying to sort out their reactions to events overseas.

Congress Gives Power to Wilson

The political forces that brought the *Abrams* case to the forefront were unleashed by the war. Concerns over patriotism arose as Americans tried to eliminate any possible internal enemies. Often those efforts resulted in American citizens attacking immigrants who were uncomfortable with the English language and who might secretly still have loyalties to distant homelands.

The war economy likewise caused far-reaching changes in American lives. Many people, especially African Americans, moved from one region to another, lured by promises of higher wages. And women, who usually had limited roles in the nation's industrial economy, filled many positions left open by men who joined the armed forces, and provided the hardware those men needed to fight.

Winning the war was not a job for American soldiers alone. As Secretary of War Newton Baker said, "War is no longer Samson with his shield and spear and sword, and David with his sling. It is the conflict of smokestacks now, the combat of the driving wheel and the engine." In other words, it was necessary to mobilize the entire economy, to shift from producing consumer goods to

The First World War **569**

SECTION 3 RESOURCES

PRINT RESOURCES

IN-DEPTH RESOURCES: UNIT 5
Guided Reading, p. 42
Primary Sources: Liberty Bond Poster, p. 49; "Returning
  Soldiers" by W. E. B. Du Bois, p. 50
American Lives: Oliver Wendell Holmes, Jr., p. 55

ACCESS FOR STUDENTS ACQUIRING ENGLISH
Guided Reading (Spanish), p. 191

FORMAL ASSESSMENT
Section Quiz, p. 236

ALTERNATIVE ASSESSMENT BOOK
See forms for supporting and scoring alternative activities.

TECHNOLOGY RESOURCES

CD-ROM Electronic Library of Primary Sources

VIDEO *American Portfolio: A Videodisc for U.S. History*
user's guide, pp. 181–184, 189

INTERNET McDougal Littell Learning On-Line
http://www.mcdougallittell.com

Section 8 Overview

OBJECTIVES
① To explain how business and government cooperated during the war.

② To show how the government sold the war to the public.

③ To describe the attacks on civil liberties that erupted once war was declared.

④ To summarize the social changes that occurred among African Americans and women as a result of the war.

SKILLBUILDER
- Interpreting graphs, p. 571

CRITICAL THINKING
- Recognizing effects, p. 570
- Summarizing, pp. 572, 576
- Clarifying, p. 574
- Analyzing causes, p. 575
- Forming and supporting opinions, p. 576
- Synthesizing, p. 576

FOCUS & MOTIVATE

▶ *Starting with the Student*
- Are people who voice their opposition to the government's policies during wartime disloyal or unpatriotic?

OBJECTIVE
① INSTRUCT

Congress Gives Power to Wilson

▶ *Discussing Key Ideas*
- The War Industries Board is established to regulate the economy in the interests of the war effort.
- Profits for those working in agriculture and war-related industries rise during the war.
- The country unites in the effort to help produce and conserve food.

IN-DEPTH RESOURCES: UNIT 5
Guided Reading, p. 42

ACCESS FOR STUDENTS ACQUIRING ENGLISH
Guided Reading (Spanish), p. 191

Teacher's Edition **569**

Critical Thinking:
Analyzing Ask students how Baruch's personality traits might have helped him carry out his duties as leader of the War Industries Board. *Possible Responses: His energy and decision-making ability helped him make quick, informed choices. His imagination helped him envision creative solutions to problems. His consideration of others earned him loyal friends and workers.*

MORE ABOUT . . .
Bernard Baruch

One of the industries Baruch had considerable trouble dealing with was the steel industry, led by U.S. Steel's board chairman, Elbert Gary. U.S. Steel made enormous wartime profits. Between 1915 and 1919, these equaled the wages received by 2 million American soldiers in France. At a conference in September 1917, Baruch threatened to take over U.S. Steel unless the company agreed to lower its prices. When Gary sneeringly said that the government wasn't capable of running the company, Baruch replied that he would get a second lieutenant to do the job. "But that won't trouble you very much," he added. "If those mill towns find out why we've taken over, they'll present you with your mills—brick by brick." Gary agreed to lower prices.

KEY PLAYER

BERNARD M. BARUCH
1870–1965

Bernard M. "Barney" Baruch became a millionaire before he was 30 by speculating in the stock market. His ability to amass large amounts of information, as well as his friendship with numerous business leaders, made him a natural choice to head the WIB. In addition, he was energetic, decisive, imaginative, and considerate. Observers remarked that whenever he entered the room, President Wilson became noticeably more serene.

It was Wilson who gave Baruch his nickname "Dr. Facts"—a name that proved accurate as Baruch quickly assembled, coordinated, and distributed information about war materials and production techniques. Several of the executives that Baruch brought into the government reappeared during the 1930s, when the New Deal again mobilized American industry.

> ### "Work or fight."
>
> **NATIONAL WAR**
> **LABOR BOARD**

producing weapons, ammunition, and other war supplies. This was too complicated and important a job for private industry to handle on its own, so business and government cooperated in the effort. Congress gave President Wilson direct control over much of the economy, including the power to fix prices and to regulate—even to nationalize—certain war-related industries.

WAR INDUSTRIES BOARD The main regulatory body was the **War Industries Board** (WIB). It was established in 1917 and reorganized in 1918 under the leadership of **Bernard M. Baruch.** The board encouraged companies to use mass-production techniques to increase efficiency and urged them to eliminate waste by standardizing products, such as making only 5 colors of typewriter ribbons instead of 150. The WIB set production quotas and allocated raw materials. It also conducted psychological testing to help people find the right jobs.

Under the WIB, industrial production in the United States increased by about 20 percent. However, the WIB applied price controls only at the wholesale level. As a result, retail prices soared, and in 1918 they were almost double what they had been before the war. Corporate profits soared as well, especially in such industries as chemicals, copper, lumber, meatpacking, oil, and steel.

The activities of the WIB had several side effects, including changes in women's clothing. For example, Baruch pointed out that corsets required 8,000 tons of steel a year that could be better employed in building two battleships. Accordingly, women stopped buying corsets with steel ribs. Tall leather shoes, which were fashionable but not functional, disappeared and the extra leather went into soldiers' boots. Hemlines rose, and the fabric that had formerly gone into long skirts went into military uniforms instead.

The WIB was not the only federal agency to regulate the economy in the interests of the war effort. The Railroad Administration controlled the nation's railroads, and the Fuel Administration monitored coal supplies and rationed gasoline and heating oil. In addition, many people voluntarily adopted "gasless Sundays" and "lightless nights" to help conserve fuel. In March 1918, the Fuel Administration introduced another conservation measure: daylight-saving time, which had first been proposed by Benjamin Franklin in the 1770s as a way to take advantage of the longer days of summer.

WAR ECONOMY Wages in some industries, especially the metal trades, shipbuilding, and meatpacking, rose during the war years by as much as 20 percent. By contrast, white-collar workers like clerks, managers, and lawyers lost about 35 percent of their purchasing power because of inflation. As a result of the uneven treatment of workers, union membership climbed from about 2.5 million in 1916 to more than 4 million in 1919, and more than 6,000 strikes broke out during the war months in protest against stagnant wages at a time of rising prices.

In 1918, President Wilson established the National War Labor Board to deal with disputes between management and labor. Employers warned workers who were reluctant to go along with board decisions that they would lose their exemption from the draft. "Work or fight," they were told. However, the War Labor Board did try to improve working conditions. It pushed for the eight-hour day and urged factory owners to allow safety inspections. It also pressured all manufacturers to observe the federal ban on child labor.

To help produce and conserve food, President Wilson set up the Food Administration and placed Herbert Hoover in charge. Hoover's entire staff,

THINK THROUGH HISTORY
A. Recognizing Effects *What effects did the WIB have on the economy?*

A. Answer The WIB encouraged business to use mass-production techniques and to standardize products. Its pricing policies resulted in soaring corporate profits.

TEACHING OPTION

Making Connections Across the Curriculum

Economics Discuss the state of the economy during the First World War. Tell students that many workers benefited from full-time employment during the war and increased earnings. However, most people saw little improvement in their buying power, due to the sharp rise in prices during the war years. The cost of clothing tripled, for example, while food prices more than doubled. A quart of milk cost 9 cents in 1914 and 17 cents in 1920. The price of fuel also rose. The value of coal jumped fully 100 percent.

The government, meanwhile, did little to control this inflation. It fixed prices on most raw materials but not on the finished products. That meant that companies could determine their own prices for their goods. Since demand exceeded supply, the companies could get away with inflated prices. Even the price of some raw materials, such as cotton, was left unregulated. By bowing to political pressure from the South, the government allowed the price of cotton to skyrocket.

except for clerks, consisted of volunteers. Instead of rationing food, he organized a tremendous publicity campaign that called on people to follow the "gospel of the clean plate." He declared one day a week "meatless," another "sweetless," two days "wheatless," and two other days "porkless." Restaurants removed sugar bowls from the table and served bread only after the first course. Since Europeans were accustomed to eating wheat, Hoover urged Americans to eat corn so they could send their wheat abroad.

Homeowners planted "victory gardens" in their yards. There was even a victory garden in one corner of the White House lawn. School children joined the United States School Garden Army and spent their after-school hours growing tomatoes and cucumbers in public parks. As a result of these and similar efforts, American food shipments to the Allies tripled. Hoover also set a high government price on wheat and other staples. Farmers responded by putting an additional 40 million acres into production. In the process, they increased their income by almost 30 percent.

The wartime need for labor brought over a million more women into the work force. The suffragist Harriot Stanton Blatch visited a munitions plant in New Jersey and described with pride what she saw.

The War Economy, 1914–1920

AVERAGE ANNUAL WAGE	
1914	$627
1915	$633
1916	$706
1917	$830
1918	$1,047
1919	$1,201
1920	$1,407

Source: Historical Statistics of the United States: Colonial Period to 1970

CONSUMER PRICE INDEX*

*Consumer Price Index (CPI) A measure of changes in the prices of goods and services commonly bought by consumers

A PERSONAL VOICE
The day I visited the place, in one of the largest shops women had only just been put on the work, but it was expected that in less than a month they would be found handling all of the twelve hundred machines under that one roof alone. The skill of the women staggers one. After a week or two they master the operations on the "turret," gauging and routing machines. The best worker on the "facing" machine is a woman. She is a piece worker, as many of the women are. . . . This woman earned, the day I saw her, five dollars and forty cents. She tossed about the fuse parts, and played with that machine, as I would with a baby. Perhaps it was in somewhat the same spirit—she seemed to love her toy.

HARRIOT STANTON BLATCH, quoted in *We, the American Women*

SKILLBUILDER
INTERPRETING GRAPHS
Which one-year period between 1914 and 1920 saw the slowest growth in the Consumer Price Index? How did the rise in wages compare with the rise in prices from 1914 to 1920?
Skillbuilder Answer Slowest Growth: 1914–1915. Standard of Living: The price index doubled in that period, while wages more than doubled.

Some World War I government posters scared Americans into buying Liberty Bonds by portraying the Germans as bloodthirsty barbarians.

The woman Blatch described was unusual: she was paid at the same rate as men. Although President Wilson called for equal pay for equal work, most women in war plants received less than men—and almost all of them lost their jobs when the war ended.

Selling the War

"It is not an army we must shape and train for war," argued President Wilson, "it is a nation." Not only did soldiers need to learn to fight, but civilians needed to learn how to sacrifice for the war effort. Since the war was not universally popular, the government embarked on a massive propaganda campaign to justify civilian sacrifices and sell the war to the public. The campaign had two aspects. On one hand, it promoted patriotism. On the other hand, it manufactured hate.

WAR FINANCING The United States spent about $33 billion directly on the war effort. The government raised about one-third of this amount through taxes, including a steeper income tax (which taxed high incomes at a higher rate than low incomes), a war-profits

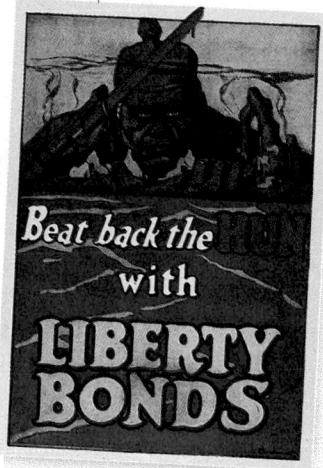

Beat back the with LIBERTY BONDS

The First World War **571**

HISTORY FROM VISUALS
The War Economy, 1914–1920
Reading the Graph Have students compare the graph of average wages with that showing the consumer price index. Ask them what happened to prices as wages increased. *Prices also increased.*

Extension Ask students why wages and prices continued to rise after the war. *Possible Response: Because inflation continued to cause both to spiral out of control.*

MORE ABOUT . . .
Food Restrictions
Hoover's directions about conserving food provoked many jokes and satires. *Life* magazine, for example, wrote: "Do not permit your child to take a bite or two from an apple and throw the rest away; nowadays even children must be taught to be patriotic to the core."

OBJECTIVE
② **INSTRUCT**

Selling the War
▶ *Discussing Key Ideas*
• The government finances the war by raising income and excise taxes and by promoting the sale of war bonds.
• The government sets up the nation's first propaganda agency to popularize the war.

IN-DEPTH RESOURCES: UNIT 5
Primary Source: Liberty Bond Poster, p. 49

TEACHING OPTION

 Cooperative Activity: Creating a Wartime Ad Campaign

Task: Groups of three to four students will design an ad campaign to urge people to help produce and conserve food for the war effort.

Purpose: To help students understand the sacrifices and fervor stimulated by war.

Activity: Students should first decide what they want to publicize. Some may want to design an ad campaign illustrating an idea suggested by the text, such as "meatless" days or victory gardens. Others may want to come up with their own ideas for persuading

the public to conserve or produce food. Students should present their ads on a poster and include a catchy slogan. Display the posters and discuss their persuasive power in class.

📁 **Building a Portfolio:** Students who believe their poster represents some of their best work may wish to add it to their portfolio.

ALTERNATIVE ASSESSMENT BOOK
Standards for Evaluating a Cooperative Activity

Standards for Evaluation
Ads should . . .

• encourage the audience to conserve and produce food for the war effort
• suggest that this activity supports a noble cause
• include a catchy slogan that helps the audience remember the ad

Teacher's Edition **571**

Wartime Propaganda

To aid the war effort, Hollywood turned out both patriotic and hate films. Among the former were *Pershing's Crusaders* and *Under Four Flags*. Hate films included *To Hell with the Kaiser* and *The Beast of Berlin*. Advertisements for the latter film showed a hanged effigy of the kaiser. Another hate film portrayed mad German scientists training millions of house-flies to bring germs into the United States.

 ELECTRONIC LIBRARY OF PRIMARY SOURCES
Four Minute Speech

Attacks on Civil Liberties

▶ *Discussing Key Ideas*
- The main targets of anti-immigrant hysteria are immigrants from Germany and Austria-Hungary.
- Clearly violating the spirit of the First Amendment, the Espionage and Sedition Acts allow people to be arrested for any anti-war activities.

IN-DEPTH RESOURCES: UNIT 5
American Lives: Oliver Wendell Holmes, Jr., p. 55

tax, and higher excise taxes on tobacco, liquor, and luxury goods. It raised the rest through public borrowing by selling war bonds.

The government sold bonds directly to individuals through tens of thousands of volunteers who never received any commission on the sale. Movie stars such as Douglas Fairbanks, Mary Pickford, and Charlie Chaplin spoke at rallies in factories, schools, and street corners. Newspapers and billboards carried advertisements for the bonds free of charge. Salesmen delivered speeches between theater acts and film screenings. Towns held war-bond parades complete with flags, banners, and marching bands. All told, the government ran four great "Liberty Loan" drives and one "Victory Loan" drive. As Treasury Secretary William G. McAdoo put it, only "a friend of Germany" would refuse to buy war bonds.

COMMITTEE ON PUBLIC INFORMATION   To directly popularize the war, the government set up the nation's first propaganda agency, the Committee on Public Information. The head of the CPI was a former muckraking journalist named **George Creel.**

An imaginative individual, Creel mobilized the nation's artists and advertising people, who created thousands of paintings, posters, cartoons, and sculptures promoting the war. He persuaded choirs, social clubs, and religious institutions to join "the world's greatest adventure in advertising." He recruited some 75,000 men to serve as Four Minute Men who would deliver a speech anytime, any place. The Four Minute Men spoke about everything relating to the war: the draft, rationing, bond drives, victory gardens, and topics such as "Why We Are Fighting," "Maintaining Morals and Morale," and "The Meaning of America." It is estimated that by the end of the war, the Four Minute Men delivered more than 7.5 million speeches to 314 million listeners.

Nor did Creel neglect the written word. He ordered a printing of almost 7 million copies of "How the War Came to America"—which included Wilson's war message—not just in English but also in Swedish, Polish, Italian, Spanish, Czech, and Portuguese. He distributed some 60 million pamphlets, booklets, and leaflets, many with the enthusiastic help of the Boy Scouts. He did not convince everyone, but he certainly succeeded in reaching them.

Some wartime posters encouraged Americans to help the war effort by saving resources—in this case, food.

Food is Ammunition— Don't waste it.

B. Summarizing *What methods did the CPI use to popularize the war?*

B. Answer The CPI used posters and other visual means, public speakers, and written pamphlets to promote the war.

Attacks on Civil Liberties

Early in 1917, President Wilson expressed some apprehension about U.S. attitudes toward the war.

> **A PERSONAL VOICE**
> Once lead this people into war and they'll forget there ever was such a thing as tolerance. To fight you must be brutal and ruthless, and the spirit of the ruthless brutality will enter into the very fiber of our national life, infecting Congress, the courts, the policeman on the beat, the man in the street. Conformity would be the only virtue, and every man who refused to conform would have to pay the penalty.
> **WOODROW WILSON,** quoted in *Cobb of "The World"*

The president's prediction was correct. As soon as war was declared, conformity indeed became the order of the day. Attacks on civil liberties, both unofficial and official, erupted.

ANTI–IMMIGRANT HYSTERIA   The main targets of the drive for conformity were Americans who had emigrated from other nations, especially those from Germany and Austria-Hungary. The most bitter attacks were directed against the two million Americans who had been born in Germany, but other foreign-born persons and native-born Americans of German descent suffered as well.

572 CHAPTER 19

Teaching Less Proficient Readers

Predicting Help students make predictions when they read. After students read Wilson's quotation on page 572, have them choose a partner and do the following:

1. Discuss any words or phrases that they don't understand, such as "ruthless" and "the very fiber of our national life."
2. Express the quotation's main idea in their own words.
3. Jot down any predictions they can make based on the quotation.
4. After reading pages 572–574, check to see how many of their predictions were correct.

Making Connections Across Time

Anti-Immigrant Hysteria During World War II Tell students that during World War II, Japanese Americans became the targets of anti-immigrant hysteria. Many Japanese Americans on the West Coast were rounded up and put in internment camps. For the duration of the war, they lived behind barbed wire and were guarded by soldiers. Nevertheless, about 17,000 Japanese Americans enlisted in the army and served in segregated units. The most famous of these was the 442nd Regiment, which earned more decorations than any other combat unit.

As part of anti-immigrant hysteria, New York immigrants were forced to register with the authorities during the war.

Many Americans with German-sounding names lost their jobs. Orchestras refused to play the music of Mozart, Bach, Beethoven, and Brahms. Some towns with German names changed them. (One exception was Berlin, New Hampshire, whose citizens voted 933 to 566 to keep their town's original name.) Schools stopped teaching the German language and librarians removed books by German authors from the shelves. People even resorted to physical violence against German-Americans, flogging them or smearing them with tar and feathers. A mob in Collinsville, Illinois, wrapped a German flag around a German-born miner named Robert Prager and lynched him. A jury later cleared the mob's leaders.

Finally, in a burst of anti-German fervor, Americans changed the name of German measles to "liberty measles." Hamburger—named after the German city of Hamburg—became "Salisbury steak" or "liberty sandwich," depending on whether you were buying it in a store or eating it in a restaurant. Sauerkraut was renamed "liberty cabbage," and dachshunds turned into "liberty pups."

ESPIONAGE AND SEDITION ACTS In June 1917 Congress passed the Espionage Act, and in May 1918 it passed the Sedition Act. Under the **Espionage and Sedition Acts** a person could be fined up to $10,000 and/or sentenced to 20 years in jail for interfering with the draft, obstructing the sale of government bonds, or saying anything disloyal, profane, or abusive about the government or the war effort.

Like the Alien and Sedition Acts of 1798, these laws clearly violated the spirit of the First Amendment. Their passage led to some 6,000 arrests for loosely defined antiwar activities and 1,500 convictions, including the five anarchists of the *Abrams* case. One man, Walter Mathey, was imprisoned for attending an antiwar meeting and contributing 25 cents. The Reverend Clarence Waldron received 15 years in the penitentiary for telling a Bible class that Christians should not take part in the war.

Other results of the laws included the loss of mailing privileges for newspapers and magazines that opposed the war or criticized any of the Allies. By 1918 even mainstream publications like the *New York Times* and *The Saturday Evening Post* lost their mailing privileges, at least temporarily. The House of Representatives refused to seat Victor Berger, a socialist congressman from Wisconsin, because of his antiwar views. Columbia University fired a distinguished psychologist from its faculty because he, too, opposed the war. A colleague who supported the war thereupon resigned in protest, saying, "If we have to suppress everything we don't like to hear, this country is resting on a pretty wobbly basis."

"Nobody can say we aren't loyal now."

JURY MEMBER,
UPON CLEARING ROBERT PRAGER'S ALLEGED MURDERERS

The First World War **573**

MORE ABOUT . . .
The End of the IWW

The government dealt the death blow to the IWW on September 29, 1917, when federal agents arrested more than 1,000 Wobblies throughout the country. A mass trial of 101 defendants began on April 1, 1918. Presiding at the trial was Judge Kenesaw Mountain Landis, who later became the nation's first baseball commissioner. Although the trial lasted five months, it took the jury less than one hour to reach a guilty verdict. After Judge Landis handed out jail terms to all 101 Wobblies, Ben Fletcher, head of the Philadelphia dockworkers and the only African-American defendant, said wryly, "Judge Landis has been using bad English today. His sentences are too long."

OBJECTIVE
④ INSTRUCT

Social Changes During the War

▶ **Starting with the Student**
Have students create a chart similar to the one below to list some of the causes and effects of the Great Migration.

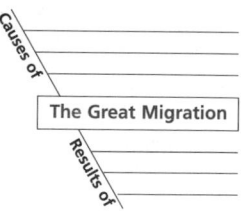

Causes of

The Great Migration

Results of

(continued on next page)

The Espionage and Sedition Acts targeted socialists and labor leaders. Eugene V. Debs was handed a ten-year prison sentence for delivering a speech in which he discussed the economic causes of the war, but was pardoned by President Warren G. Harding after he had served three years. Anarchist "Red Emma" Goldman received a two-year sentence and a $10,000 fine for organizing the "No Conscription League." When she left jail, the authorities deported her to Russia. "Big Bill" Haywood and other leaders of the Industrial Workers of the World were accused of sabotaging the war effort because they urged workers to strike for better conditions and higher pay. Haywood received 30 years, while most of the other Wobblies received five to ten. Under such federal pressure, the IWW faded away. On the whole, the civil liberties record of the Wilson administration was not one to make Americans proud.

Social Changes During the War

Wars often unleash powerful social forces. The period of World War I was no exception, and important changes occurred among African Americans and women. The war also contributed to one of the worst epidemics in history—the 1918 flu epidemic.

AFRICAN AMERICANS AND THE WAR Black public opinion about the war was divided. On one side were people like W. E. B. Du Bois, who editorialized in the *Crisis,* the NAACP newspaper, that blacks should support the war effort. Du Bois recognized the German imperial threat.

> **A PERSONAL VOICE**
> That which the German power represents today spells death to the aspirations of Negroes and all darker races for equality, freedom and democracy. . . . Let us, while this war lasts, forget our special grievances and close our ranks shoulder to shoulder with our own white fellow citizens and the allied nations that are fighting for democracy.
> **W. E. B. DU BOIS,** *"Close Ranks"*

Du Bois believed that it made sense for African Americans to cooperate with the Wilson administration because African-American support for the war would lend strength to calls for racial justice.

On the other side were people like William Monroe Trotter, founder and editor of the Boston *Guardian,* who believed that victims of racism should not support a racist government. Trotter condemned Du Bois's accommodationist approach and favored protest instead. Nevertheless, despite grievances over continued racial inequality in the United States, most African Americans backed the war.

THE GREAT MIGRATION In concrete terms, the greatest effect of the First World War on African Americans' lives was that it accelerated the **Great Migration,** the large-scale movement of hundreds of thousands of Southern blacks to American cities in the North. As early as the late 19th century, African Americans trickled northward to escape

A panel from the mural series *The Migration of the Negro* by Jacob Lawrence shows three of the most common destinations for African Americans leaving the South.

574 CHAPTER 19

THINK THROUGH HISTORY
C. Clarifying
What was the original purpose of the Espionage and Sedition Acts?
C. Answer The original purpose was to prevent interference with the war effort. The government began applying the acts to peaceful political expressions of antiwar opinion.

TEACHING OPTIONS

Exploring Themes

Immigration and Migration Discuss why so many African Americans took part in the great exodus to the North. Then tell students that the Great Migration greatly increased the black population in many Northern cities. In Detroit, for example, the black population grew by more than 600 percent between 1910 and 1920. Ask students what effects this enormous influx of people had on these cities. *Possible Responses: Housing shortages, unemployment, increased crime.* Discuss how these problems were aggravated by the racism African Americans encountered in the Northern cities.

Making Connections Across Cultures

The African-American Migration to the North Tell students that most of the migrants were young, unmarried black men who were skilled or semiskilled workers. To finance the move, some families pooled their savings, while others sold their possessions. Although black migrants faced many problems, employment in the North did help them escape sharecropping, boll weevil infestations, floods, lynchings, and political disenfranchisement. One man wrote to a friend back in Mississippi: "I just begin to feel like a man. . . . I don't have to humble to no one. I have registered. Will vote the next election."

the Jim Crow South, but in the decade between 1910 and 1920, the trickle became a tidal wave.

Several factors caused the tremendous growth in black migration. First, many African Americans sought to escape the racial discrimination in the South that made it hard to make a living and often threatened their lives. Also, the boll weevil infestation, aided by floods and droughts, had ruined much of the South's cotton fields by 1916. In the meantime, in 1914 Henry Ford opened his automobile assembly line to black workers. Then the outbreak of World War I and the drop in European immigration increased job opportunities for African Americans in steel mills, munitions plants, and stockyards. Northern manufacturers sent recruiting agents with free railroad passes through the South. In addition, Robert S. Abbott, publisher of the Chicago *Defender*, bombarded Southern blacks with articles contrasting Dixieland lynchings with the prosperity of Northern African Americans.

So Southern blacks boarded the trains and moved away from the South. Between 1910 and 1920 about one million African Americans migrated to such cities as Chicago, New York, and Philadelphia. About half of them went during the war years. Another 800,000 migrated during the 1920s. Author Richard Wright described the great exodus.

THINK THROUGH HISTORY
D. *Analyzing Causes What were the causes of the Great Migration?*

D. Answer
Causes included the destruction of the South's cotton economy by the boll weevil, the demand for labor by Northern manufacturers, and newspaper articles.

A PERSONAL VOICE
We are bitter no more; we are leaving! We are leaving our homes, pulling up stakes to move on. We look up at the high southern sky and remember all the sunshine and all the rain and we feel a sense of loss, but we are leaving. We look out at the wide green fields which our eyes saw when we first came into the world and we feel full of regret, but we are leaving. We scan the kind black faces we have looked upon since we first saw the light of day, and, though pain is in our hearts, we are leaving. We take one last furtive look over our shoulders to the Big House—high upon a hill beyond the railroad tracks—where the Lord of the Land lives, and we feel glad, for we are leaving.

RICHARD WRIGHT, quoted in *12 Million Black Voices*

Black migrants faced many problems in their new surroundings. They lived in crowded ghettos, often in one-room kitchenettes for which they had to pay exorbitant rents. Unskilled whites resented them, not only because of racial prejudice, but also because African Americans competed for jobs and Northern companies often used them as strikebreakers.

At the same time, however, the concentration of African Americans in a particular area encouraged them to set up their own commercial institutions. Some were in businesses that provided personal services, such as hairdressing and undertaking. Others entered areas of finance that whites considered too risky—such as insuring blacks' lives and property or arranging credit for them. African Americans established thousands of such enterprises in Northern communities.

WOMEN IN THE WAR While African Americans carved new lives for themselves in unfamiliar places, women increasingly found themselves filling unfamiliar social roles as they moved into jobs that had formerly been held exclusively by men. Women began driving cabs and delivery trucks. They became railroad workers, cooks, dockworkers, and bricklayers. They even mined coal and took part in shipbuilding. At the same time, women continued to fill more traditional jobs as nurses, clerks, and teachers.

Many women worked as volunteers, serving at Red Cross facilities and encouraging the sale of bonds and the planting of victory gardens. In contrast, other women were active in the peace movement. For example, Jane Addams

HISTORICAL SPOTLIGHT

RACE RIOTS
Racial prejudice against African Americans in the North sometimes took violent form. The press of new migrants to Northern cities caused overcrowding and intensified racial hatred. In July 1917, a race riot exploded in East St. Louis, Illinois, when white workers, furious over the hiring of African Americans as strikebreakers at a munitions plant, rampaged through the streets. Forty blacks and nine whites died.

Another bloody riot erupted in July 1919 in Chicago. The riot was sparked when a 17-year-old African American swam from the water off the so-called "black beach" to the water off the "white beach." There, white bathers threw rocks at him until he drowned.

In retaliation, African Americans on shore attacked whites with bottles and fists and within a few hours mobs were fighting throughout several neighborhoods in the city. State troopers finally restored order after three days of violence that involved about 10,000 persons. Thirty-eight people lost their lives (23 blacks and 15 whites) and 520 were injured (342 blacks and 178 whites).

The First World War **575**

(continued from page 574)

▶ *Discussing Key Ideas*
• The war accelerates the movement of Southern blacks to Northern cities.
• The war provides more job opportunities for women, who are praised for their contribution to the war effort.
• About 500,000 Americans die from an international flu epidemic.

IN-DEPTH RESOURCES: UNIT 5
Primary Source: "Returning Soldiers" by W. E. B. Du Bois, p. 50

HISTORICAL SPOTLIGHT
Race Riots

Discuss the relationship between the races today. Ask students how the relationship has improved. In what ways do the race riots of 1917 and 1919 reflect the current relationship between blacks and whites?

MORE ABOUT . . .
Women in the War

Many women who were industrial workers during the war found that their male coworkers resented them. The men objected to the women's rate of productivity and willingness to work for lower pay. They were also angered by the women's independent spirit. Women in a Vermont machine-tool company wrote the following verse to express their reactions to the men's complaints: "We're independent now you see, / Your bald head don't appeal to me, / I love my overalls; / And I would rather polish steel / Than get you up a tasty meal. / Or go with you to balls."

TEACHING OPTION

Exploring Themes

Women in America Discuss the contributions women made to the war effort and the new opportunities that opened up to them. Then tell students that once the war was over, women discovered that society's attitude toward them had really changed very little. Working women were still expected to shoulder all of the responsibilities at home, including housework, meal preparation, and child care. Tired from working all day, most women had little energy to devote to this domestic work. As a result, husbands felt resentful, blaming their wives' employment for a disruption of home life. In addition, many married and unmarried women were forced to give up their jobs to men returning from overseas. They observed this treatment with bitterness. As one woman remarked, "During the war they called us heroines, but they throw us on the scrapheap now."

Women worked in a variety of jobs during the war. Here women assemble an aircraft wing.

helped found the Women's Peace Party in 1915 and remained a pacifist even after the United States entered the war.

In general, women made notable contributions to the nation's war effort. As President Wilson acknowledged, "The services of women during the supreme crisis have been of the most single usefulness and distinction; it is high time that part of our debt should be acknowledged." While acknowledgment of that debt did not include equal pay for equal work, it did help bolster public support for woman suffrage. In 1919, Congress finally passed the Nineteenth Amendment, and the states ratified it the following year.

THE FLU EPIDEMIC In the fall of 1918, the United States suffered a home-front crisis that affected both men and women, white and black alike. An international flu epidemic gripped the nation. It apparently came from France, where it had been brought by Chinese war workers. About one-quarter of the U.S. population fell ill with high fever, headaches, and aching muscles, often followed by pneumonia.

The effect of the epidemic on the economy was devastating. Mines shut down, telephone service was cut in half, and factories and offices staggered working hours to avoid congestion. Cities ran short of coffins, and the corpses of poor people lay unburied as long as a week. Doctors did not know what to do, other than to recommend cleanliness and quarantine. One epidemic survivor recalled that "So many people died from the flu they just rang the bells; they didn't dare take [corpses] into the church."

In all, about 500,000 Americans perished before the epidemic disappeared in 1919. Worldwide, historians believe the influenza virus killed as many as 40 million people.

Like the flu epidemic, the war ended, and Americans across the country hoped that this "war to end all wars" would do just that. Their hopes rested on the peace settlement, and President Wilson traveled to Europe to ensure it.

New York City street cleaners wore masks in an effort to avoid catching influenza.

Section 3 Assessment

1. TERMS & NAMES

Identify:
- War Industries Board
- Bernard M. Baruch
- George Creel
- Espionage and Sedition Acts
- Great Migration

2. SUMMARIZING Create a diagram like the one shown in which you present examples of how U.S. civilians supported the war effort.

Civilians Support the War

Social	Economic
1.	
2.	
3.	

Write a paragraph in which you explain which effort you think was most significant and why.

3. FORMING AND SUPPORTING OPINIONS

Why do you think civil liberties were so easily violated by the people and government of the United States during the First World War? Explain your opinion.

THINK ABOUT
- the effect of the Committee on Public Information
- the diverse ethnic backgrounds of Americans
- the reasons for the Espionage and Sedition Acts

4. SYNTHESIZING Were changes in the American economy during World War I beneficial to the country overall? Give examples to support your opinion.

THINK ABOUT
- the effect on various groups of workers
- the impact on African Americans
- changes in the role of the government

576 CHAPTER 19

ANSWERS

1. TERMS & NAMES

War Industries Board, p. 570

Bernard M. Baruch, p. 570

George Creel, p. 572

Espionage and Sedition Acts, p. 573

Great Migration, p. 574

2. SUMMARIZING

Possible Answer: Social—women's clothing changed; gas and heating oil rationed; daylight-saving time began; gasless Sundays and lightless nights adopted; victory gardens planted. Economic—war bonds purchased; higher income and excise taxes paid; Liberty and Victory Loan drives took place; women joined work force.

3. FORMING AND SUPPORTING OPINIONS

Possible Response: The Committee on Public Information propagandized the American people into thinking that the war was right and dissenters were disloyal or criminal. Because so many nations were involved in the war and the U.S. had immigrants from these nations, Americans distrusted one another.

4. SYNTHESIZING

Possible Response: Students answering yes might cite the rise in union membership; rise in wages; expanded jobs and business opportunities for African Americans and women. Students answering no might say that inflation and shortages were problems; that government regulation of industry was excessive; that price controls brought huge profits for corporations but raised prices.

TERMS & NAMES
• Fourteen Points
• League of Nations
• Treaty of Versailles
• reparations
• war-guilt clause
• Henry Cabot Lodge

LEARN ABOUT the Treaty of Versailles and President Wilson's attempts to create a League of Nations
TO UNDERSTAND the consequences of Wilson's efforts.

ONE AMERICAN'S STORY

In December 1918, President and Mrs. Wilson sailed for Europe. At the magnificent palace of Versailles outside Paris, Wilson tried to persuade the Allies to construct a just and lasting peace. His main hope for achieving this goal was a League of Nations, whose members would be bound to protect any nation that was attacked by another. One evening, after delivering a speech in favor of the League, Wilson, and his wife, Edith Bolling Galt Wilson, got into the presidential car to return to their hotel. Edith Wilson recounted her husband's comments.

Edith Bolling Galt Wilson

> **A PERSONAL VOICE**
> He took off his high hat and leaned back in the car. "Are you so weary?" I asked. "Yes," he answered, "I suppose I am, but how little one man means when such vital things are at stake." Then, continuing: "This is our first real step forward, for I now realize, more than ever before, that once established the League can arbitrate and correct mistakes which are inevitable in the Treaty we are trying to make at this time. . . . One by one the mistakes can be brought to the League for readjustment, and the League will act as a permanent clearinghouse where every nation can come, the small as well as the great."
> **EDITH BOLLING GALT WILSON,** quoted in *Hooray for Peace, Hurrah for War*

As matters turned out, Wilson's idealism ran into practical politics. The leaders of the European allies, vengeful toward their defeated enemy after four years of warfare, rejected most of his peace program. The Senate, skeptical about continued U.S. involvement abroad, rejected the Treaty of Versailles mostly because of the League of Nations.

Wilson at Versailles

Rejection was probably the last thing Wilson anticipated when he arrived in Europe. Everywhere he went, people gave him a hero's welcome. Italians displayed his picture in their windows. Parisians strewed the road with flowers. Representatives of one group after another—Armenians, Jews, Ukrainians, and Poles—appealed to him for help in setting up independent nations for themselves. Even the normally restrained British showed their regard as men removed their hats and women bowed and waved as he passed.

FOURTEEN POINTS Even before the war was over, Wilson presented his plan for world peace. On January 18, 1918, he delivered his famous **Fourteen Points** speech before Congress. The points were divided into three groups. The first five points addressed issues that Wilson believed had caused the war:

1. Nations should only engage in open covenants (agreements) openly arrived at. There should be no secret treaties among nations.
2. Freedom of the seas should be maintained for all.
3. Tariffs and other economic barriers among nations should be lowered or abolished in order to foster free trade.
4. Arms should be reduced "to the lowest point consistent with domestic safety" in order to lessen militaristic impulses during diplomatic crises.
5. Colonial policies should consider the interests of the colonial people as well as the interests of the imperialist powers.

The First World War **577**

SECTION 4 RESOURCES

 PRINT RESOURCES

IN-DEPTH RESOURCES: UNIT 5
Guided Reading, p. 43
Geography Application: A New Look for Europe, p. 45

ACCESS FOR STUDENTS ACQUIRING ENGLISH
Guided Reading (Spanish), p. 192
Geography Application: A New Look for Europe (Spanish), p. 194

FORMAL ASSESSMENT
Section Quiz, p. 237

ALTERNATIVE ASSESSMENT BOOK
See forms for supporting and scoring alternative activities.

TECHNOLOGY RESOURCES

HUMANITIES TRANSPARENCIES
H38, Senate Opposes the League of Nations

CD-ROM Electronic Library of Primary Sources

VIDEO *American Portfolio: A Videodisc for U.S. History* user's guide, pp. 187–188

INTERNET McDougal Littell Learning On-Line
http://www.mcdougallittell.com

Section 4 Overview

OBJECTIVES

(1) To summarize Wilson's Fourteen Points.

(2) To describe the Treaty of Versailles and international and domestic reaction to it.

(3) To explain some of the consequences of the war.

SKILLBUILDER
• Understanding geography: region, p. 580

CRITICAL THINKING
• Summarizing, pp. 578, 581
• Analyzing motives, p. 580
• Hypothesizing, p. 581
• Evaluating decisions, p. 581
• Forming opinions, p. 581

FOCUS & MOTIVATE

▶ *Starting with the Student*
• Do students think nations can work together to prevent or halt wars?
• Do they think the world will ever be free of warfare? Or do they think that people and governments cannot resolve their differences without it?

OBJECTIVE
(1) **INSTRUCT**

Wilson at Versailles

▶ *Discussing Key Ideas*
• Wilson delivers his Fourteen Points—his plan for world peace—to Congress.
• The Allies reject most of Wilson's plan.

IN-DEPTH RESOURCES: UNIT 5
Guided Reading, p. 43

ACCESS FOR STUDENTS ACQUIRING ENGLISH
Guided Reading (Spanish), p. 192

Treaty of Versailles

▶ *Starting with the Student*
Have students create a chart in which they list the provisions of the Treaty of Versailles and the results of these provisions. The chart might look like this:

Provision	Result
1.	
2.	
3.	
4.	

▶ *Discussing Key Ideas*
• The Treaty of Versailles weakens hopes for a lasting peace in Europe.
• Several groups in the United States oppose the treaty because they believe that it is too harsh.
• Domestic opposition to the treaty centers on the League of Nations.

IN-DEPTH RESOURCES: UNIT 5
Geography Application: A New Look for Europe, p. 45

MORE ABOUT . . .
The Hall of Mirrors

In 1871, following France's defeat in the Franco-Prussian War, the Hall of Mirrors in the palace of Versailles was where the kaiser's grandfather was proclaimed head of the new German Empire, also known as the Second Reich. The French felt the hall was an appropriate place to sign a treaty marking Germany's defeat in World War I and the end of the Second Reich.

The next eight points dealt with specific boundary changes. Wilson based these provisions on the principle of self-determination "along historically established lines of nationality." In other words, national groups who claimed particular ethnic identity were to decide for themselves what nation they would belong to.

The fourteenth point called for the creation of an international organization to address diplomatic crises like those that had sparked the war. This **League of Nations** would provide a forum for nations to discuss and settle their grievances without having to resort to war.

THE ALLIES REJECT WILSON'S PLAN Wilson's naïveté about the political aspects of securing a peace treaty showed itself in his failure to grasp the anger felt by the Allied leaders. French premier Georges Clemenceau had lived through two German invasions of France, and was determined to prevent future invasions. British prime minister David Lloyd George had just won reelection on the slogan "Make Germany Pay." Italian prime minister Vittorio Orlando wanted control of Austrian territory.

Contrary to custom, the peace conference did not include the defeated Central Powers. Nor did it include Russia or the smaller Allied nations. Instead, the "Big Four"—Wilson, Clemenceau, Lloyd George, and Orlando—worked out the treaty's details among themselves. Wilson conceded on most of his Fourteen Points in return for the establishment of the League of Nations.

Treaty of Versailles

On June 28, 1919, the Big Four and the leaders of the defeated nations gathered in the Great Hall of the Palace at Versailles to sign the treaty. After four years of devastating warfare, everyone hoped the treaty would create stability for a rebuilt Europe. Instead, anger held sway.

PROVISIONS OF THE TREATY The **Treaty of Versailles** established nine new nations—including Poland, Czechoslovakia, and Yugoslavia—and shifted the boundaries of other nations. It carved four areas out of the Ottoman Empire, and gave them to France and Great Britain as mandates, or temporary colonies. The two Allies were to administer their respective mandates until the areas were ready for self-rule and then independence. The mandates included Iraq, Syria, Lebanon, and Palestine (now Israel and Jordan).

The treaty demilitarized Germany, stripping it of its air force and most of its navy and reducing its army to 100,000 men. The treaty also required Germany to return Alsace-Lorraine to France and to pay **reparations,** or war damages, in the amount of $33 billion to the Allies. Furthermore, the treaty contained a **war-guilt clause** that forced Germany to acknowledge that it alone was responsible for World War I.

THE TREATY'S WEAKNESSES Such treatment of Germany weakened the ability of the Treaty of Versailles to serve as the basis of a lasting peace in Europe. Three basic weaknesses provided the seeds of postwar international problems that eventually led to the Second World War.

Hundreds of observers fill the Hall of Mirrors at the Palace of Versailles to watch the delegates sign the treaty ending the First World War.

TEACHING OPTIONS

Exploring Themes

Expanding Democracy Discuss Wilson's Fourteen Points. Tell students that Wilson hoped to create a new world order through democratic reform. Ask students whether they believe Wilson's plan was practical. Then point out that today the United Nations (UN) serves much the same purpose as Wilson's proposed League of Nations. Would Wilson have been satisfied with the organization? Has the UN been successful in providing a forum for nations and preventing war?

Making Connections Across Time

Provisions of the World War II Treaty Tell students that at the end of the Second World War, the victorious nations recalled the lessons learned from the Treaty of Versailles. They sought to draft a treaty that was fair to the victors but that did not completely devastate the losers. At the Yalta Conference in February 1945, the Allied leaders met to discuss the problems of postwar Europe. Among other points, the leaders agreed to establish a world peacekeeping organization—which would become the United Nations. They also agreed to reestablish order in Europe and help the defeated countries create democratic governments.

First, the treaty humiliated Germany. Although German militarism played a major role in igniting the war, other European nations had been no less guilty in provoking the diplomatic crises before the war. The war-guilt clause caused Germans of all political viewpoints to detest the treaty. Furthermore, there was no way Germany could pay the huge financial reparations demanded by the Allies.

Second, the Bolshevik government in Russia felt the Big Four ignored its needs. For three years the Russians had fought with the Allies and suffered higher casualties than any other nation. However, Russia was excluded from the peace conference. Consequently, Russia lost more territory than Germany did. The Union of Soviet Socialist Republics (or Soviet Union), as Russia was officially called after 1922, became determined to regain its former territory.

The third issue that contributed to international instability resulted from decisions about what should be done with colonial territories. Germany was stripped of its colonial possessions in the Pacific that might help it pay its reparations bill. Also, the treaty ignored the claims of colonized people for self-determination, as in the case of Southeast Asia.

In the early 20th century, much of Southeast Asia was a French colony called French Indochina. For decades, nationalist movements for independence developed in what is now Vietnam. At Versailles, a young Vietnamese man later known as Ho Chi Minh appealed to President Wilson for help. Ho Chi Minh wanted a constitutional government that would give the Vietnamese people the same civil and political rights as the French. Instead of listening to Ho Chi Minh's proposal, however, Wilson had him thrown out. Ho Chi Minh later founded the Indochina Communist Party and led the fight in Vietnam against French, and then American, forces until his death in 1969.

POINT COUNTERPOINT
The League of Nations

▶ *Starting with the Student*
Have students create a chart like the one below to organize the information in the feature. In the first column, students should list the arguments in favor of U.S. membership in the League of Nations. In the second column, they should list the reasons against joining the league.

Pro	Con

POINT

"The League of Nations was the world's best hope for lasting peace."

President Wilson campaigned for the League of Nations as "necessary to meet the differing and unexpected contingencies" that could threaten world peace. Besides creating a forum where nations could talk through their disagreements, Wilson believed the league offered collective security, in which nations "respect and preserve as against external aggression the territorial integrity and existing political independence of all members of the League," in order to prevent devastating warfare.

Critics complained that membership in the league would limit American independence in international affairs, but Wilson argued that league membership included "a moral, not a legal, obligation" that would leave Congress free to decide its own course of action. Wilson tried to assure Congress as well as the general public that the league was "not a straitjacket, but a vehicle of life" and "a definite guarantee . . . against the things that have just come near bringing the whole structure of civilization into ruin."

COUNTERPOINT

"The League of Nations posed a threat to U.S. self-determination."

Senator William Borah was one of the foremost critics of the Treaty of Versailles because he objected to U.S. membership in the League of Nations. Borah feared that membership in the league "would draw America away from her isolation and into the internal affairs and concerns of Europe" and involve the United States in foreign wars. "Once having surrendered and become a part of the European concerns," Borah wondered, "where, my friends, are you going to stop?"

Many opponents also believed the league would nullify the Monroe Doctrine by limiting American self-determination, "the right of our people to govern themselves free from all restraint, legal or moral, of foreign powers." Although Wilson argued that the League of Nations codified moral—not legal—obligations, and that the league would have no such power of restraint, Borah remained unconvinced. He responded to Wilson's argument simply by asking, "What will your League amount to if it does not contain powers that no one dreams of giving it?"

INTERACT WITH HISTORY

1. **SUMMARIZING** Both supporters and opponents of the League hoped to preserve peace. What did each group propose as a means to secure peace for the United States?

   SEE SKILLBUILDER HANDBOOK, PAGE 1037.

2. **PROPOSING A NEW TREATY** Research the debates between Wilson and the opponents of the League of Nations. Then make a series of suggestions for a treaty agreement that would satisfy both sides. In one or two paragraphs, defend your version of the treaty.

The First World War **579**

▶ *Discussing Key Ideas*
• Wilson believes that the League of Nations will provide a forum for nations to talk through their problems and offer collective security.
• Wilson assures critics that the league will not limit American independence in international affairs but will help achieve world peace.
• Critics fear that membership in the league will involve the United States in foreign wars and limit American self-determination.
• Opponents believe that the league's emphasis on moral rather than legal obligations will weaken its powers and render the organization useless.

 ELECTRONIC LIBRARY OF PRIMARY SOURCES
Why a League of Nations Is Necessary by Woodrow Wilson

INTERACT WITH HISTORY

1. Summarizing

Possible Response:

American supporters believed that the league members would respect and preserve each other's boundaries and independence and work together to secure peace.

American opponents of the League of Nations believed that the United States could best preserve peace by maintaining a policy of isolation.

2. Proposing a New Treaty

Before students begin making suggestions for a new treaty, encourage them to do the following:

• Pinpoint the precise weaknesses of the old treaty.
• Make a list of the goals of those on both sides.
• Make a list of the objections raised by opponents of the treaty.
• Address each objection and decide what compromises could be made. Keep in mind that the compromises should satisfy both sides and respect the spirit of their goals.

Postwar Europe, 1919

Reading the Map Tell students that they can use the map's colors and boundaries to determine what new nations were created in postwar Europe and where they are located in relation to other countries. Then ask students which new nations were created from territory that once belonged to Germany. *Poland and Czechoslovakia.*

Extension Ask students which of the nations created after the First World War have since been dissolved. *Yugoslavia and Czechoslovakia.* What new nations have replaced them? *Bosnia, Croatia, Macedonia, Slovenia; Czech Republic, Slovakia.*

MORE ABOUT . . .
Henry Cabot Lodge

Henry Cabot Lodge served as a member of the House of Representatives for three terms before being elected to the Senate in 1892, where he remained until 1924. Lodge intensely disliked Wilson, whom he described as "shifty" and "not a scholar in the true sense of the word." Wilson returned the feeling, calling Lodge "contemptible," "narrow," and "selfish."

 ELECTRONIC LIBRARY OF PRIMARY SOURCES
On the Terms of Peace by Henry Cabot Lodge

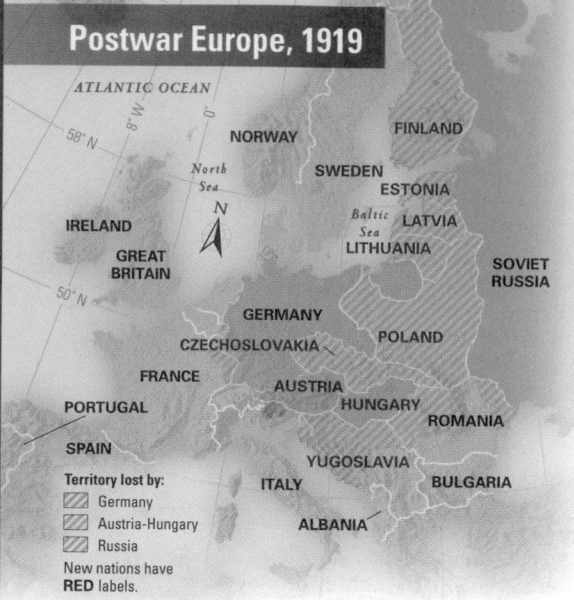

Postwar Europe, 1919

ATLANTIC OCEAN

Territory lost by:
- Germany
- Austria-Hungary
- Russia

New nations have **RED** labels.

GEOGRAPHY SKILLBUILDER
REGION *Which country was awarded the largest amount of German territory?*
REGION *Looking at the map, what was an unusual feature of the territory left to Germany after World War I?*

Skillbuilder Answer
Region: Poland. Region: *Possible Answer:* Germany was divided into two parts—with the smaller, eastern part surrounded by Polish territory.

"That evil thing with the holy name"

HENRY CABOT LODGE, DESCRIBING THE LEAGUE OF NATIONS

OPPOSITION TO THE TREATY When Wilson returned to the United States, he found several groups opposed to the treaty. Some people, including Herbert Hoover, believed it was too harsh. Hoover noted, "The economic consequences alone will pull down all Europe and thus injure the United States." Others considered the treaty a sellout to imperialism that simply exchanged one set of colonial rulers for another.

Some ethnic groups objected to the treaty because the new national boundaries it established did not satisfy their particular demands for self-determination. For example, before the war many Poles had been under German rule. Now many Germans were under Polish rule. Furthermore, Wilson hadn't tried to obtain Ireland's independence from Great Britain.

DEBATE OVER THE LEAGUE OF NATIONS
The main domestic opposition, however, centered on the issue of the League of Nations. A few opponents believed the League threatened the U.S. foreign policy of staying clear of European entanglements. Conservative senators, headed by **Henry Cabot Lodge,** were suspicious of the provision for joint economic and military action against aggression, even though it was voluntary. They wanted the same constitutional right of Congress to declare war also included in the treaty.

Wilson could have smothered these concerns if he had chosen the membership of the American delegation more carefully. Accompanying the president were personal aide Colonel Edward M. House, Secretary of State Robert Lansing, General Tasker H. Bliss, and diplomat Henry White. Only one of the four, White, was a Republican, although the 1918 congressional campaign had given the Republicans a majority in both houses. None was a senator, although the Senate would have to ratify the peace treaty.

Also, if Wilson had been more willing to accept a compromise on the League, it is quite likely that the Senate would have approved the treaty. Wilson, however, was exhausted from his efforts at Versailles. As a result, he became more cold, aloof, and rigid than ever.

Realizing that the Senate might not approve the treaty, Wilson decided to appeal directly to the people. Despite warnings from friends and doctors that his health was fragile, he set out in September 1919 on an 8,000-mile tour. He delivered 35 speeches in 22 days, explaining why the United States should join the League of Nations. On October 2, he collapsed and was rushed back to the White House. Wilson had suffered a stroke (a blood clot in the brain) and lay partially paralyzed for more than two months. He could not even meet with his cabinet, and his once-powerful voice was no more than a thick whisper.

When the treaty came up for a vote in the Senate in November 1919, Senator Lodge introduced a number of amendments, the most important of which qualified the terms under which the United States would enter the League of Nations. Lodge and a large group of senators feared that U.S. membership in the League would force the United States to form its foreign policy in accord with other members of the League. Most Americans opposed such limitations on American action. Although the Senate rejected the amendments, it also failed to ratify the treaty.

Wilson, however, refused to compromise with Lodge and other senators over their reservations about the League. "I will not play for position," Wilson

THINK THROUGH HISTORY
B. Analyzing Motives Why did many senators oppose the Treaty of Versailles?

B. Answer Many feared the League of Nations would infringe on America's independence and represent a change in America's policy of avoiding entanglements in Europe.

Cooperative Activity: Debating the League of Nations

Task: Groups of four to five students will debate the following hypothesis: The U.S. Senate was correct in not approving the plan to join the League of Nations.

Purpose: To understand in depth the arguments of both supporters and opponents of the League of Nations.

Activity: After choosing a position through a lottery, students should research the arguments for and against the League of Nations. Students should take notes on the logical reasons used to defend their own position. They should also

list the reasons offered by the opposition and decide which ones they should concede and which ones they can attack with counter arguments. After students have prepared their arguments, pair opposing groups and have them conduct their debate.

ALTERNATIVE ASSESSMENT BOOK
Standards for Evaluating a Cooperative Activity

 HUMANITIES TRANSPARENCIES
H38, Senate Opposes the League of Nations

proclaimed, "This is not a time for tactics. It is a time to stand square. I can stand defeat; I cannot stand retreat from conscientious duty." The treaty came up again in March 1920. The Senate again rejected the Lodge amendments—and again failed to muster enough votes for ratification.

The United States finally signed a separate treaty with Germany in 1921, after Wilson was no longer president. The United States never joined the League of Nations, but it maintained an unofficial observer at League meetings.

The Legacy of the War

In 1923, General Pershing delivered a speech in which he complained about the aftermath of the war.

> **A PERSONAL VOICE**
> We never really let the Germans know who won the war. They are being told that their army was stabbed in the back, betrayed, that their army had not been defeated. The Germans never believed that they were beaten. It will have to be done all over again.
> **GENERAL JOHN J. PERSHING**, *quoted in Over Here and Over There*

"This is not a time for tactics. It is a time to stand square."

PRESIDENT WILSON

Pershing believed that, because the kaiser's government had censored newspapers during the war, most Germans were unaware that the Allies had been pushing their soldiers back or that the German General Staff itself had demanded an end to the war. Many Germans were shocked by the armistice and incensed at the Treaty of Versailles.

To make matters worse, postwar economic conditions—although bad all over Europe—were especially desperate in Germany. A severe depression developed in 1923 and millions of workers lost their jobs. The mark, the German currency unit, was nearly worthless. Housewives burned paper money for fuel and carted baskets of marks with them when they went grocery shopping.

Circumstances in Germany drove many Germans to search for scapegoats. One former Austrian corporal, Adolf Hitler, blamed German problems on Jews and socialists in the Weimar republic, the government in Germany following World War I. In 1933, Hitler and his Nazi Party won control of the German government and embarked on a militaristic policy that led directly to the Second World War.

In the 1920s, most Americans did not want to be bothered with the future of Europe. The war had strengthened their desire to stay out of European affairs. Most desired a "return to normalcy."

> **Domestic Consequences of World War I**
>
> • Accelerated America's emergence as the world's greatest industrial power
> • Contributed to the movement of Americans, especially African Americans, to Northern cities
> • Focused anti-immigrant and anti-radical sentiments among middle-class Americans

---

Section 4 Assessment

1. TERMS & NAMES

Identify:
• Fourteen Points
• League of Nations
• Treaty of Versailles
• reparations
• war-guilt clause
• Henry Cabot Lodge

2. SUMMARIZING Recreate the web diagram below on your paper. Then fill it in with details about the provisions and weaknesses of the Treaty of Versailles and opposition to it.

3. EVALUATING DECISIONS If you had been a member of the United States Senate in 1919, would you have supported or opposed ratification of the Treaty of Versailles? Provide reasons for your decision.

THINK ABOUT
• the provisions of the treaty regarding Germany
• the impact of new boundaries in Europe
• the significance of membership in the League of Nations

4. FORMING OPINIONS What do you think were the most important reasons that Wilson failed to persuade the United States to join the League of Nations?

THINK ABOUT
• the attitudes of Europeans at Versailles
• American attitudes about the League
• Wilson's tactics for getting the League adopted

The First World War **581**

Immigration, Migration, and War

OBJECTIVES

1 To explain how war and other factors affected immigration to and migration within the United States.

2 To describe the consequences of different waves of immigration and migration.

People who have moved to various regions of the United States often felt "pushed" away from their homes because of poverty or oppression. Others felt "pulled" to a new land and the opportunities it promised. These "push-pull" factors have been a major factor in making the United States a nation of immigrants and migrants.

Wars have often created these "push-pull" factors for immigrants and migrants. Sometimes they pushed people away from fighting or pulled them to regions where there was work. At other times, war affected migrants by forcing them to adjust to cultural change in their new homes. Many immigrants discovered that war unleashed forces that affected their lives in unpredictable ways. As war forced American society to evolve, immigrants and migrants created new roles for themselves as Americans and helped shape the way America would change.

FOCUS & MOTIVATE

▶ ***Starting with the Student***

• Do students think the United States should open its borders to all immigrants? Or do they think the government should impose some restrictions on immigration?

• Should immigrants be required to learn English and observe the customs of the majority culture? Or should immigrants be encouraged to observe only their home customs?

1840s
MIGRATING TO THE WEST

Throughout the 19th century, Americans continued their movement westward to the Pacific Ocean. Victory in the war with Mexico in 1848 greatly increased the amount of land under American control, and thousands of Americans were pulled to the West to take advantage of it.

Two important consequences emerged from this movement. First, following the discovery of gold in California, hundreds of thousands of people from around the world rushed in to strike it rich. Within a year, there were enough people in California to qualify it for statehood. Second, Americans disagreed over whether or not the new lands would be open to slavery. That disagreement culminated in the Civil War.

1910s
ANTI–IMMIGRANT FEELINGS

The "new" immigrants of the early 20th century—unlike the "old-stock" Americans who traced their ancestry to northern and western Europe—came mostly from southern and eastern Europe, and they often did not speak English. Many old-stock Americans feared that the new immigrants posed a threat to American culture. As a result, old-stock Americans tried to "Americanize" the new immigrants by encouraging them to abandon their old customs and teaching them American ones.

During World War I, Americanization efforts hit their high mark. The Committee on Public Information (CPI) was consequently concerned that new immigrants were not loyal to the United States. The CPI set up Loyalty Leagues in immigrant communities to foster American patriotism. George Creel, head of the CPI, claimed that "not a pin dropped in the home of any one with a foreign name, but that it ran like thunder on the inner ear of some listening sleuth."

MORE ABOUT . . .
Anti-Immigrant Feelings

Many prominent people voiced prejudices against the "new" immigrants of the early 1900s. Senator Henry Cabot Lodge, for example, felt that the immigrants were inferior peoples. Francis A. Walker, president of the Massachusetts Institute of Technology, theorized that the new immigrants were "beaten men from beaten races; representing the worst failures in the struggle for existence."

582 CHAPTER 19

RECOMMENDED RESOURCES

Books

Chermayeff, Ivan et al. *Ellis Island: An Illustrated History of the Immigrant Experience.* New York: Maxwell Macmillan, 1991. Text by Mary J. Shapiro.

Orth, Samuel Peter. *Our Foreigners.* New Haven: Yale UP, 1920. A period account of immigration.

Pan, Lynn. *Sons of the Yellow Emperor.* Boston: Little, 1990. A history of the Chinese diaspora.

Portes, Alejandro. *Immigrant America: A Portrait.* Berkeley: U of California P, 1990. A study of immigrants and the process of their Americanization.

Videos

Ellis Island: Gateway to America. Sterling Educational Media, 1991. History of Ellis Island.

The Immigrant Experience: The Long, Long Journey. Dir. Joan M. Silver. Coronet/MTI Film and Video, 1972. Experiences of one turn-of-the-century immigrant family.

Old World, New World. Thames Television, 1977. Media Guild. Late-19th-century European immigration to the United States.

Software

Ellis Island. Diskette. Educational Activities, 1994. Students role-play an Italian teenager who immigrates to America in 1892.

1940s
MIGRATING FOR JOBS

Throughout the 20th century, African Americans responded to "push-pull" factors as they moved across the United States. In the Great Migration of the early 20th century, they felt pushed out of their homes in the rural South by racial discrimination and the arrival of mechanized farming. Of the millions of African Americans who left, most moved to cities, usually in the North.

The Second Migration, sparked by World War II, was an important part of this movement because it allowed African Americans to take industrial jobs, many formerly held by whites, to support the war effort. This migration also had important consequences for the civil rights movement. African Americans who remained in the South often moved to Southern cities and developed organizations in their new urban communities that helped them fight against segregation.

1970s
IN SEARCH OF A NEW LIFE

In 1964, 603 Vietnamese lived in the United States. A decade later, as the Vietnam War ended, hundreds of thousands of refugees, mostly South Vietnamese who had been allies of the United States during the war, fled their country. They used boats, braving stormy seas and pirates, to reach Thailand or Cambodia. There they lived in refugee camps for months before moving to other nations like the United States. By 1985, there were 643,200 Vietnamese living across the United States.

Although many of the hundreds of thousands of Vietnamese pushed from their homes in Vietnam have faced discrimination in the United States, most have overcome it. Chased from Vietnam by communist dictators, many Vietnamese have become successful entrepreneurs. In San Jose, for example, 40 percent of the downtown retail business is Vietnamese-owned, bringing new commercial vitality to the area.

INTERACT WITH HISTORY

1. **SYNTHESIZING** Based on what you have read about immigration, what generalizations can you make about the way war has affected immigrants and migrants in the United States?

    SEE SKILLBUILDER HANDBOOK, PAGE 1051.

2. **EXPLORING YOUR COMMUNITY** Interview family members and people you know in your community to find out about the history of immigration and migration: where people came from, and for what reasons. Try to record specific stories of people and events if possible. Share your findings with the class.

REVIEWING
THE CHAPTER

TERMS & NAMES

1. Archduke Franz Ferdinand, p. 556
2. trench warfare, p. 557
3. *Lusitania*, p. 559
4. Selective Service Act, p. 562
5. Alvin York, p. 565
6. George Creel, p. 572
7. Great Migration, p. 574
8. Fourteen Points, p. 577
9. League of Nations, p. 578
10. Treaty of Versailles, p. 578

MAIN IDEAS

11. Nationalism, imperialism, militarism, and alliances were long-term causes; Archduke Franz Ferdinand's assassination set off the immediate diplomatic crisis that led to war.

12. In Belgium; the Germans defeated British and French forces.

13. The German threat contained in the Zimmermann note and the sinking of four unarmed American merchant ships.

14. The United States started a draft, created a nine-month training program, and took steps to increase ship production.

15. Larger cannons, poison gas, machine guns, tanks, and fighter planes.

16. The government advertised and sold war bonds; the Committee on Public Information popularized the war through a massive propaganda campaign.

17. Americans with German-sounding names suffered loss of jobs and violence due to anti-immigrant hysteria; the Espionage and Sedition Acts repressed freedom of speech.

18. It created international problems that would eventually lead to World War II: it humiliated Germany; it provoked Russia's determination to regain former Russian territory; it ignored the claims of colonized people for self-determination.

19. Many senators objected to the provision calling for the league, yet Wilson was unwilling to compromise on it.

20. Germans were shocked by the armistice and angered at the Treaty of Versailles; desperate economic conditions prevailed in Europe; Germany suffered a severe depression.

Chapter 19 Assessment

REVIEWING THE CHAPTER

TERMS & NAMES For each term below, write a sentence explaining its connection to World War I. For each person below, explain his role in the events before, during, or after the war.

1. Archduke Franz Ferdinand
2. trench warfare
3. *Lusitania*
4. Selective Service Act
5. Alvin York
6. George Creel
7. Great Migration
8. Fourteen Points
9. League of Nations
10. Treaty of Versailles

MAIN IDEAS

SECTION 1 *(pages 554–561)*

World War I Begins

11. What were the long-term and immediate causes of World War I?
12. Where did Germany begin its war offensive and what happened there?
13. Which overt acts caused the United States to enter World War I in 1917?

SECTION 2 *(pages 562–568)*

American Power Tips the Balance

14. How did the United States mobilize a strong military during World War I?
15. What new weapons made fighting in World War I deadlier than fighting in previous wars?

SECTION 3 *(pages 569–576)*

The War at Home

16. What methods did the United States use to sell the war to the nation?
17. What events during World War I undermined Americans' civil liberties?

SECTION 4 *(pages 577–581)*

Wilson Fights for Peace

18. What were the major effects of the Treaty of Versailles?
19. How did Wilson's support for the League of Nations stand in the way of Senate support for the Treaty of Versailles?
20. What were the major international consequences of World War I?

THINKING CRITICALLY

1. WAR AND PEACE In a chart like the one shown, provide causes for the effects of World War I listed.

2. AMERICA'S ROLE Between 1914 and 1920, Americans debated the role their country should have in world affairs. What might Americans have learned about intervention in the affairs of other nations from events of World War I?

3. DEMOCRACY Reread the quote by President Woodrow Wilson on page 552. How does his statement reflect issues of the time? Explain.

4. GEOGRAPHY OF POSTWAR EUROPE Compare the maps on page 555 and page 580. Describe the visible changes in nations after the Paris peace settlements.

5. DOMESTIC EFFECT OF WAR In your opinion, what was the major domestic effect of World War I? Support your opinion with specific details from the chapter.

6. ANALYZING PRIMARY SOURCES When Congress declared war in 1917, settlement house worker Mary Simkhovitch expressed the view of many Americans who desired peace.

> There were two great evils facing us in 1917. One was to go into the war, and the other was to stay out. Whatever the outcome, war was bound to bring in its train not only the loss of life and the destruction of property, but also new social alignments, a re-evaluating of customs, habits and outlooks, a redistributing of wealth and power. Gradually, step by step, we slipped into war in the presidency of Wilson, who won his second term with the slogan "He kept us out of war."
>
> **Mary Simkhovitch,** *Neighborhood: My Story of Greenwich House*

Summarize the effects of going to war or staying out according to Simkhovitch. Do you agree with Simkhovitch that both entering the war and staying out of it were evil? Explain.

THINKING CRITICALLY

1. WAR AND PEACE
Possible Response: **U.S. enters WWI:** Germany resumed unrestricted submarine warfare; Zimmermann note intercepted; four American merchant ships sunk. **Germany collapses:** German war machine and war economy too exhausted to keep fighting; German sailors and marines refused orders to man their ships. **U.S. economy becomes more productive:** wages in metal trades, meatpacking, and shipbuilding rose; farmers increased crop production; women joined work force.

2. AMERICA'S ROLE
Possible Response: To pay closer attention to international situations, such as extreme nationalism or militarism, that could lead to crises; the importance of nations' helping one another in global affairs; the importance of diplomacy in drawing up treaties so as not to unduly punish or cast blame on offending nations; the importance of listening to and helping smaller nations.

3. DEMOCRACY
Possible Response: He mentions safety, which was a key issue of the time, since so many nations were threatened by invasion from Germany. He mentions democracy, which was a timely issue in Russia in 1917, when the Russians overthrew their czarist regime; that overthrow helped the democratic Allied nations feel that they were defending democracy in fighting the monarchies of the Central Powers. Finally, his words convey American fervor in fighting for democracy.

ALTERNATIVE ASSESSMENT

1. SPEAKING FOR UNCLE SAM

After the United States entered World War I, the government launched a campaign to encourage civilian support for the war. How could government propagandists such as the Four Minute Men drum up support?

- Imagine you worked during World War I as a Four Minute Man. Prepare a speech to move American civilians to support the war.

 Use the CD-ROM *Our Times* and other resources to find out about the major events leading up to World War I and how the people of the time felt about the war.

- Figure out what you want Americans to do to help the war effort. Examples include donating time or money, conserving food, and enlisting to fight.
- Write a short informal speech designed to move your audience to action. You might even use a song or a poster to stir up patriotism. Then present your speech to your class.

2. EXHIBITING THE WAR

Cooperative Learning What aspects of the war do you consider most significant? With your classmates create a classroom exhibit on World War I. You might include military objects, maps, songs, and other items.

Before you begin, think about the following issues:

- the themes you want to emphasize
- what items will best convey those themes
- how you might obtain objects, replicas, or photos

List the items you selected and write a paragraph about each one, explaining its significance and why you selected it for the exhibit.

3. PORTFOLIO PROJECT

📁 Use the Living History activity to expand your portfolio.

LIVING HISTORY

PRESENTING YOUR CHART

You have completed a chart and report on the effects of World War I. Now share your work in an oral presentation. Select the portion of your chart that corresponds with the subject matter of your report and prepare it as a large-format visual aid.

Before your presentation, ask yourself these questions:

- Is my report clearly written and informative?
- Have I quoted from and/or cited my sources?
- Does my visual aid support my report?

Add your chart and report to your American history portfolio.

Review Chapter 19

THE WAR ABROAD Shortly after the assassination of Archduke Franz Ferdinand in 1914, Great Britain, France, Russia, and their allies were at war with Germany, Austria-Hungary, and their allies. The fighting continued for the next three years, despite deaths in the millions.

AMERICANS AND THE WAR In 1914, most Americans wanted to stay out of the fighting. However, economic and cultural ties to the Allies, and anger at Germany's submarine warfare, brought the United States into the war in April 1917. American soldiers fought under General John J. Pershing and used improved weapons that made World War I deadlier than any earlier war. About 26 million people died before the fighting ended on November 11, 1918.

The war brought dramatic changes to the United States. The government took a more active role in the economy and helped boost industrial production by 20 percent. Millions of African Americans moved to cities in the North to take jobs in factories. Anti-immigrant hysteria erupted and was directed particularly at German Americans. Laws such as the Espionage Act and the Sedition Act limited freedom of speech and fed an atmosphere of suspicion.

AFTERMATH OF WAR Toward the end of the war, a great flu epidemic swept the globe, killing 40 million people, including 500,000 Americans. Leaders met in Paris to negotiate the Treaty of Versailles, which created nine new nations and redrew the boundaries of many others. However, the treaty's harsh treatment of Germany helped lead to World War II. The United States never ratified the treaty, primarily because of opposition to Wilson's League of Nations.

Preview Chapter 20

Following World War I, many Americans wished to return to the peaceful time before the war. During the 1920s, Americans focused on building economic prosperity. You will learn about these significant developments in the next chapter.

The First World War **585**

---

1. SPEAKING FOR UNCLE SAM

Standards for Evaluation
A speech should meet the following criteria:

- Uses emotional appeals to inspire patriotism.
- Demonizes the enemy.
- Focuses on the righteousness of the Allied cause.
- Makes a specific call to action.
- Uses a poster, song, or catchy slogan to get the message across.

2. EXHIBITING THE WAR

Standards for Evaluation
A paragraph should meet the following criteria:

- Identifies the item within the context of the First World War.
- Explains the theme the item conveys.
- Tells what role the item played in the war or what it represented.
- Explains why student selected the item for the exhibit.

3. PORTFOLIO PROJECT

LIVING HISTORY
Standards for Evaluation
An oral report should meet the following criteria:

- Presents information clearly and logically.
- Includes research from a variety of sources.
- Uses quotations and refers to specific sources.
- Makes logical connections between the chart and main topics in the report.

IN-DEPTH RESOURCES: UNIT 5
See the form for scoring this activity on page 57.

THINKING CRITICALLY

4. GEOGRAPHY OF POSTWAR EUROPE

Possible Answer: From land formerly belonging to Russia, Germany, and Austria-Hungary, new nations appeared such as Latvia, Lithuania, Poland, Czechoslovakia, and Yugoslavia; Serbia became part of Yugoslavia.

5. DOMESTIC EFFECT OF WAR

Possible Responses: The wartime need for labor provided job opportunities for African Americans and women; government propaganda created an atmosphere of intolerance; the nation grew in economic power; many African Americans permanently moved from the South to take jobs in cities in the North; the concentration of African Americans in the North provided new economic opportunities and allowed many to set up their own businesses.

6. ANALYZING PRIMARY SOURCES

Possible Response: No matter who won, the war would result in destruction, death, and social change. Students agreeing might argue that going to war would contribute to deaths, diseases, and destruction of lands, but not going might have meant that the Allies would lose the war. Some students disagreeing might argue that not fighting Germany and not helping the Allies would have been wrong; others might argue that the war accomplished nothing significant but loss of life and that it was wrong to fight.

The Twenties and the Great Depression

Drouth Stricken Area

Oil painting by Alexandre Hogue (1934).

Art Note
Hogue grew up in West Texas, part of the area that became the Dust Bowl. He was part of the regionalist movement, in which artists rejected European influences in an attempt to forge a uniquely American art. Hogue painted many distinctive landscapes of Texas and other parts of the Southwest.

▶ *Previewing the Unit*
Unit 6 covers the vast changes that touch the United States from 1920 to 1940, as people feel a clash between the values of a traditional, rural society and those of a growing urban culture. Underlying economic problems are obscured by apparent prosperity until a long, deep economic slowdown causes widespread suffering. In response, President Franklin Roosevelt experiments with various approaches to rebuild the economy.

UNIT
6

"This great nation will endure as it has endured, will revive and will prosper."
FRANKLIN D. ROOSEVELT

586 UNIT 6

1920–1940
The Twenties and the Great Depression

Alexandre Hogue

1 Shapes and colors
Hogue's use of strong lines and vivid colors echoes techniques associated with folk art. Many regionalist artists of the 1930s used such techniques. Here, the shapes and colors also help stress the harshness of the landscape.

2 Lonely house
The starkness of the scene is emphasized by the absence of people. The vast distance between this farmhouse and the one in the background emphasizes the loneliness of life on the Great Plains.

3 Starving cow
The devastation of the Dust Bowl is evident in the skeletal cow. Underscoring the misery of the scene, it looks forlornly at the well that has no water.

Discussing the Quotation

Franklin Roosevelt gave many inspirational speeches to the American people. The quotation comes from his first inaugural address. The next sentence in the speech contains Roosevelt's most famous statement: "The only thing we have to fear is fear itself."

FOR DISCUSSION:
- Why might people in the 1930s want to hear such speeches?
- What else, beyond reassuring words, would people need?
- How could anyone convince the owners of this farm that they will recover and prosper?

Discussing the Image

Hogue adopted Native American ideas about the land, ideas that he had encountered in his youth. He came to believe that plowing the land broke a sacred bond owed to it. He felt that the farmers deserved some of the blame for the Dust Bowl because of their farming methods.

FOR DISCUSSION:
- Where are the people?
- What feeling does the blue tone in the painting convey?
- Suggest some adjectives to describe the feeling in the painting.

587

---

④ Broken windmill
The useless windmill shows the power of nature in two ways. The sail has been broken by the Plains wind—and remains unrepaired apparently because the owners have fled. The spout seems to have produced not life-giving water but death-bringing dust.

⑤ Dunes
The destruction is evident in the mound of dust that has partially engulfed the house.

⑥ Vulture
To remove any doubt about the fate of the cow—and of the way of life on the plains—Hogue includes the waiting vulture.

⑦ No relief
The scene contains no sign of relief. The dust-filled sky contains one cloud that seems unlikely to bring rain. The other birds in the sky may be circling vultures.

Politics of the Roaring Twenties

	Key Ideas	**TEACHING SUPPORT**	**ASSESSMENT**
SECTION 1 Americans Struggle with Postwar Issues *pp. 590–595*	*The Russian Revolution brings a Communist government to power. Many Americans fear that a similar revolution will occur in the United States. Political radicals and labor activists meet with increasing opposition.*	***In-Depth Resources: Unit 6*** • Guided Reading, p. 1 • Primary Sources: *from* Bartolomeo Vanzetti's Speech to the Jury, p. 7; *from* Report on the Steel Strike of 1919, p. 9 • Literature: from *Big Money* by John Dos Passos, p. 11; "Justice Denied in Massachusetts" by Edna St. Vincent Millay, p. 13 **COOPERATIVE ACTIVITY** • Staging a Fair Trial for Sacco and Vanzetti, p. 592 (TE)	***Section 1 Assessment,*** p. 595 (PE) ***Self-Assessment,*** p. 595 (TE) ***Formal Assessment*** • Section Quiz, p. 246 ***Alternative Assessment Book*** • Standards for Evaluating a Cooperative Activity
SECTION 2 "Normalcy" and Isolationism *pp. 596–600*	*The Republicans return to isolationism and the kind of policies that characterized the period before the Progressive Era and its reform movements.*	***In-Depth Resources: Unit 6*** • Guided Reading, p. 2 • Skillbuilder Practice: Summarizing p. 4 • American Lives: Ernesto Galarza, p. 14 **COOPERATIVE ACTIVITY** • Researching Immigration Issues, p. 598 (TE)	***Section 2 Assessment,*** p. 600 (PE) ***Self-Assessment,*** p. 600 (TE) ***Formal Assessment*** • Section Quiz, p. 247 ***Alternative Assessment Book*** • Standards for Evaluating a Cooperative Activity
SECTION 3 The Business of America *pp. 601–605*	*During the prosperous 1920s, the automobile industry and other industries flourished. America's standard of living rises to new heights.*	***In-Depth Resources: Unit 6*** • Guided Reading, p. 3 • Geography Application: The Automobile Industry, p. 5 • Primary Source: Advertisement, p. 10 • American Lives: Henry Ford, p. 15 **COOPERATIVE ACTIVITY** • Creating a 1920s Automobile Newsletter, p. 602 (TE)	***Section 3 Assessment,*** p. 605 (PE) ***Self-Assessment,*** p. 605 (TE) ***Formal Assessment*** • Section Quiz, p. 248 ***Alternative Assessment Book*** • Standards for Evaluating a Cooperative Activity
CHAPTER RESOURCES	**Chapter Overview** *Americans lash out at those who are different while they enjoy prosperity and new conveniences produced by American businesses.*	***In-Depth Resources: Unit 6*** • Living History Project: Worksheet, p. 16; Standards, p. 17 ***Telescoping the Times*** • Chapter Summary, pp. 39–40 ***Planning for Block Schedules***	***Chapter Assessment,*** pp. 608–609 (PE) ***Alternative Assessment,*** p. 609 (PE) ***Formal Assessment*** • Chapter Test, forms A and B, pp. 249–254 **Test Generator** ***Alternative Assessment Book*** See explanation and forms for different kinds of alternative assessments including portfolio assessment.

Humanities Transparencies
• H19, *The Passion of Sacco and Vanzetti* by Ben Shahn

Electronic Library of Primary Sources
• Instructions Regarding Conduct on Raids

Our Times
• Sacco-Vanzetti case

INTERNET RESOURCES
• See *McDougal Littell Learning On-Line* for links to information about Sacco and Vanzetti and the Russian Revolution.

Humanities Transparencies
• H39, Looking Backward

Geography Transparencies
• G20, European Emigration

Critical Thinking Transparencies
• CT20, Isolationist Policies of the 1920s

Electronic Library of Primary Sources
• from *A Letter Regarding Immigration*
• Teapot Dome

INTERNET RESOURCES
• See *McDougal Littell Learning On-Line* for links to information about Harding.

Critical Thinking Transparencies
• CT54, Consumer Spending Power

Electronic Library of Primary Sources
• from *Middletown* by Robert S. and Helen Merrell Lynd
• History of aviation

Our Times
• 1925 Listerine advertisement

INTERNET RESOURCES
• See Interact with History p. 607 (PE) for an activity that includes the Internet as an enrichment option.

American Portfolio: A Videodisc for U.S. History, user's guide, pp. 193–194, 196, 198–199

INTERNET RESOURCES
Learning On-Line: Social Studies
http://www.mcdougallittell.com

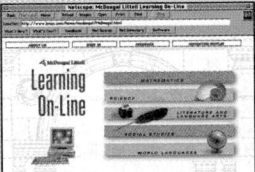

Block Scheduling (90 MINUTES)

Day 1

Section 1, pp. 590–595

Section 2, pp. 596–600

Section Assessments, pp. 595, 600

Day 2

Section 3, pp. 601–605

Tracing Themes Economic Opportunity: Consumer Spending, pp. 606–607

Section Assessment, p 605

Chapter Assessment, pp. 608–609

YEARLY PACING *Chapter 20 Total:* 2 days *Yearly Total:* 85 days

See *Planning for Block Schedules* for special activities and pacing strategies.

Customizing for Special Populations

Students Acquiring English

Access for Students Acquiring English
• Guided Reading for Sections 1–3 (Spanish), pp. 198–200
• Chapter Summary (Spanish), pp. 196–197
• Skillbuilder Practice: Summarizing (Spanish), p. 201
• Geography Application: The Automobile Industry (Spanish), pp. 202–203

INTERNET RESOURCES
• See *McDougal Littell Learning On-Line* The Diverse Classroom.

Less Proficient Readers

In-Depth Resources: Unit 6
• Guided Reading for Sections 1–3, pp. 1–3
• Skillbuilder: Summarizing, p. 4
• Geography Application: The Automobile Industry, p. 5

Telescoping the Times
• Chapter Summary, pp. 39–40

See additional strategies at point of use in the Teacher's Edition.

Gifted and Talented Students

In-Depth Resources: Unit 6
• Primary Source: *from* Bartolomeo Vanzetti's Speech to the Jury, p. 7; *from* Report on the Steel Strike of 1919, p. 9; Advertisement, p. 10
• American Lives: Ernesto Galarza, p. 14; Henry Ford, p. 15

See additional strategies at point of use in the Teacher's Edition.

Connections to Literature READINGS FOR STUDENTS

In-Depth Resources: Unit 6
• from *Big Money* by John Dos Passos, p. 11
• "Justice Denied in Massachusetts" by Edna St. Vincent Millay, p. 13

Enrichment Reading
• **Hammett, Dashiell**
Red Harvest
New York: Vintage Books, 1989
This suburb crime novel depicts gang war and labor organization. It is a classic exploration of corruption and violence in 1920s America.

• **Lewis, Sinclair**
Main Street.
New York: Bantam, 1996
A small midwestern prairie town in the 1920s is the setting of this famous novel. The story is about a city girl who marries the town doctor and attempts to bring culture to the village. Her efforts are met with gossip, greed, and bigotry resulting in a horrifying picture of small town life.

• **Porter, Katherine Anne**
The Never-Ending Wrong.
Boston: Little, Brown, 1977
This brief memoir by a noted writer details her protests during the Sacco-Vanzetti case.

• **Sinclair, Upton**
Boston
Cambridge, MA: Bentley, 1978
Written in a white heat in the aftermath of the Sacco-Vanzetti case, this novel skillfully mixes fiction and real life with vividly realized characters of the principal actors in the case that aroused great passion and controversy.

• **Sinclair, Upton**
Oil!
Cambridge, MA: Bentley, 1981
Based on the oil scandals of the Harding administration, especially the Teapot Dome affair, the story tells of the struggles of two independent oil operators against the encroachments of monopoly.

Politics of the Roaring Twenties

▶ **Starting with the Student**
Discuss the term "the Roaring Twenties" in class.

- What images come to mind when students think of the Roaring Twenties?
- What people and events characterized the 1920s?
- What names have been given to other decades? What might be a good nickname for the 1990s?

PREVIEWING THE CHAPTER
- Ask students to read the brief section descriptions.
- Discuss the quotation. Ask students what it suggests about the relationship between business and government.
- Discuss the people and things represented in the time line pictures.

MORE ABOUT . . .
Calvin Coolidge

Coolidge was usually so taciturn that people called him "Silent Cal" and told dozens of anecdotes about his reluctance to speak. On one occasion, a dinner partner informed Coolidge that she had bet a friend that she could get him to say more than two words. "You lose," he replied and then kept his mouth shut the entire evening. When he died in 1933, writer Dorothy Parker asked wryly: "How can they tell?"

Politics of the Roaring Twenties

SECTION 1
Americans Struggle with Postwar Issues

The Russian Revolution brings a Communist government to power. Many Americans fear that a similar revolution will occur in the United States. Political radicals and labor activists meet with increasing opposition.

SECTION 2
"Normalcy" and Isolationism

The Republicans return to isolationism and the kind of policies that characterized the period before the Progressive Era and its reform movements.

SECTION 3
The Business of America

During the prosperous 1920s, the automobile industry and other industries flourished. America's standard of living rises to new heights.

"The business of America is business."
President Calvin Coolidge

John L. Lewis is president of national mineworkers.

The 19th Amendment is ratified.

✪ **Warren G. Harding** is elected president.

● **Sacco and Vanzetti** are convicted.

● **The Federal Highway Act** funds a national highway system.

● **Miners leave the** mine at Scranton, Pennsylvania, as the big coal strike begins on March 31, 1922.

✪ **President Harding dies** and Calvin Coolidge becomes president.

| THE UNITED STATES | **1920** | 1921 | 1922 | 1923 |
| THE WORLD | | 1921 | 1922 | 1923 |

● **Chinese Communist Party** is founded in Shanghai.

● **Egypt declares its** independence.

● **Vladimir Lenin** adopts the New Economic Policy.

● **Benito Mussolini** is appointed prime minister of Italy.

● **Adolf Hitler's** putsch in Germany fails.

588 CHAPTER 20

THEMES IN CHAPTER 20

Economic Opportunity

During World War I, workers were not allowed to strike because the government wouldn't let anything interfere with the war effort. After the war, union membership increased and workers went on strike for higher wages and better working conditions.

Eager to defend business interests, the U.S. government played an important role in ending these strikes. To protect business from foreign competition, the government also raised taxes on imports, which made it difficult for America's Allies to repay their war debts.

See Teacher's Edition notes, pp. 593 and 597.

Science and Technology

In the 1920s, many people were able to buy automobiles. The widespread purchase and popularity of cars changed the face of the American landscape, economy, and way of life.

See Teacher's Edition note, p. 603.

LIVING HISTORY

PUTTING THE TWENTIES ON DISPLAY

Put on display a plan for a museum exhibit that highlights some of the accomplishments, trends, or events of the 1920s presented in this chapter. Consider the following categories as you choose your topic:

- Political groups and factions
- The relationships between workers and management
- The growth of business
- Industrial and technological advances
- The Emergency Quota Act of 1921
- The consumer economy

PORTFOLIO PROJECT Keep your plans in a folder for your American history portfolio. At the end of the chapter, you will share your exhibit ideas with others.

PUTTING THE TWENTIES ON DISPLAY

Discuss sources for materials that could be used in the exhibit.

- Review the chapter for references to objects that could be used as historical artifacts.
- Look for visuals in reference books, in periodicals, and on the Internet.
- Create graphs and charts that illustrate some aspect of the topic.
- If possible, borrow relevant pictures or other objects from friends or family members.

Encourage students to consider how to arrange their exhibit materials in a logical, interesting manner. Students may wish to arrange their materials in chronological order using a diagram like the one below.

Relations Between Workers and Management

↓

Items illustrating relations during the war

↓

Items illustrating 1919 strikes

↓

Items illustrating union membership in 1920

↓

Items illustrating declining union membership after 1920

IN-DEPTH RESOURCES: UNIT 6
See worksheet and standards for evaluation, pp. 16, 17.

- **The Teapot Dome scandal erupts.**
- ★ **Calvin Coolidge is elected president.**
- **A. Philip Randolph organizes Brotherhood of Sleeping Car Porters.**
- **Henry Ford is pictured with the Model A he introduced.**
- **Kellogg-Briand Pact is signed.**
- ★ **Herbert Hoover is elected president.**

1924 1925 1927 1928 **1929**
1925 1926 1928

- **Vladimir Illich Lenin, founder of the Soviet Union, dies.**
- **British laborers declare a national strike.**
- **Hirohito becomes emperor of Japan.**
- **Joseph Stalin launches first five-year plan in the USSR.**
- **Institutional Revolutionary Party is organized in Mexico.**

Politics of the Roaring Twenties **589**

RECOMMENDED RESOURCES

Books for the Teacher

Boyer, Richard O., and Herbert M. Morais. *Labor's Untold Story*. New York: United Electrical, Radio, and Machine Workers of America, 1982. History of the labor movement, includes the story of the strikes in the early 1920s.

Daniels, Roger. *Coming to America*. New York: Harper, 1990. History of immigration; discusses nativism in the 1920s.

Nye, David E. *Electrifying America*. Cambridge, Mass: MIT P, 1995. How electricity changed life in Muncie, Indiana.

Books for the Student

Allen, Frederick Lewis. *Only Yesterday*. New York: Harper, 1964. Society in the 1920s.

Koral, April. *An Album of the Great Wave of Immigration*. New York: Watts, 1992. A pictorial history of American immigration from the 1880s through the 1920s.

Parrish, Michael A. *Anxious Decades*. New York: Norton, 1992. Concerns in the 1920s.

Videos

Los Mineros. PBS Home Video, 1990. Documentary of Mexican American miners.

Reds. Dir. Warren Beatty. Paramount, 1981. Lives of American radicals and Communists.

Route 66. Dir. Robert Townsend. PBS Video, 1996.

Software

American Chronicle Series: Between the Wars (1918–1939). CD-ROM. AIMS Media.

The Model T Man from Michigan. American Lifestyle Series. Educational Software Institute, 800-955-5570.

Wall Street On-Line: An Investment Simulation. Educational Software Institute, 800-955-5570.

TERMS & NAMES
- communism
- A. Mitchell Palmer
- anarchist
- Sacco and Vanzetti
- Calvin Coolidge
- John L. Lewis

OBJECTIVES

1. To summarize the reaction in the United States to the perceived threat of communism.

2. To describe some of the conflicts between labor and management after the war.

SKILLBUILDER

• Interpreting graphs, p. 594

CRITICAL THINKING

• Analyzing motives, p. 591
• Drawing conclusions, p. 592
• Analyzing issues, p. 593
• Summarizing, p. 594
• Sequencing, p. 595
• Forming an opinion, p. 595
• Analyzing, p. 595

FOCUS & MOTIVATE

▶ **Starting with the Student**

• How do students react to others who look different or who hold views that differ from the majority of those in the classroom? Do they ignore them? Try to make friends with them? Try to antagonize them?

• How are such people treated in society? Do these people inspire fear in the majority? If so, why?

MORE ABOUT . . .

Irving Fajans

In 1937, Fajans led a sit-down strike against a chain of New York department stores. He and his fellow strikers spent 11 days and nights in the stores, sleeping on cots and keeping themselves occupied by playing checkers and cards. Eventually, management agreed to bargain with the strikers.

❶ Americans Struggle with Postwar Issues

LEARN ABOUT postwar conditions in America
TO UNDERSTAND how fear of communism affected civil liberties and the labor movement.

ONE AMERICAN'S STORY

During the 1920s and 1930s, Irving Fajans sold merchandise from behind the counters of several of New York City's large department stores. When he wasn't selling goods, he was trying to persuade fellow workers to join the Department Store Employees Union. He described some of the techniques he and other union organizers used.

A PERSONAL VOICE

Everything pertaining to the union had to be on the q.t. [quiet]. If you were caught distributing leaflets or other union literature around the job you were instantly fired. We thought up ways of passing leaflets without the boss being able to pin anybody down. Sometimes we'd insert the leaflets into the sales ledgers after closing time. In the morning every clerk would find a pink sheet saying: "Good morning, how's everything . . . and how about coming to a union meeting tonight?" . . . We swiped the key to the toilet-paper dispenser in the washroom, took out the paper, and substituted printed slips of just the right size! We got a lot of new members that way—it appealed to their sense of humor.

IRVING FAJANS, quoted in *The Jewish Americans*

Irving Fajans worked actively to organize department store workers in their efforts to gain better pay and working conditions during the 1920s.

As World War I ended, tensions between labor and management rose dramatically, as Irving Fajans describes. As a result, America experienced a rash of labor strikes in the early 1920s. The public, though, was not sympathetic to striking workers. After the sacrifices of the war, most people wanted to return to normal, peaceful living. In addition, many people feared that behind workers' unrest was the specter of **communism**—the economic and social system that espoused one political party and the idea that property is owned by the state. A violent revolution had created a Communist government in Russia in 1917.

Revolution Abroad and Reaction at Home

World War I left much of the American public exhausted. Many Americans had died or been injured in the war. The debate over the League of Nations had deeply divided the nation. Then, too, the Progressive Era had caused numerous wrenching changes in American life.

After the war, Americans wanted a breather. They yearned to return to what President Warren G. Harding described as "normalcy." During the 1920s, three trends in American society resulted from this desire for normalcy.

• Renewed isolationism, in which the United States pulled away from involvement in world affairs,

• A resurgence of nativism, or the suspicion of people who are foreign-born,

• A trend toward political conservatism that caused a turning away from the governmental activism of the Progressive Era.

Immediately after the war, Americans were especially concerned about a new threat to normalcy—the threat of communism.

SECTION 1 RESOURCES

PRINT RESOURCES

IN-DEPTH RESOURCES: UNIT 6
Guided Reading, p. 1
Primary Sources: *from* Bartolomeo Vanzetti's Speech to the Jury, p. 7; *from* Report on the Steel Strike of 1919, p. 9
Literature: from *Big Money* by John Dos Passos, p. 11; "Justice Denied in Massachusetts" by Edna St. Vincent Millay, p. 13

ACCESS FOR STUDENTS ACQUIRING ENGLISH
Guided Reading (Spanish), p. 198

FORMAL ASSESSMENT
Section Quiz, p. 246

ALTERNATIVE ASSESSMENT BOOK
See forms for supporting and scoring alternative activities.

TECHNOLOGY RESOURCES

HUMANITIES TRANSPARENCIES
H19, *The Passion of Sacco and Vanzetti* by Ben Shahn

CD-ROM *Our Times*
Electronic Library of Primary Sources

INTERNET McDougal Littell Learning On-Line
http://www.mcdougallittell.com

THE RUSSIAN REVOLUTION By 1917, conditions in Russia had become desperate. Czar Nicholas II seemed unable to cope with the crises at home and abroad. His reign had been fatally weakened by the huge loss of life and resources in World War I. People from all classes were clamoring for change and for an end to the war. There were food riots in many cities. Soldiers mutinied, deserted, or ignored orders. Faced with massive opposition, the czar abdicated his throne on March 15, 1917.

A provisional representative government replaced the czarist regime. Then in November 1917, a group of revolutionaries led by Vladimir I. Lenin, who called themselves Bolsheviks ("the majority"), seized power and eventually established a state based on the social and economic system of communism. Two years after the revolution, in March of 1919, the Third Communist International meeting was held in Moscow. Under the banner of their symbolic revolutionary red flag, Communist speakers advocated worldwide revolution—the overthrow of the capitalist system and the abolition of free enterprise and private property.

THE RED SCARE IN THE UNITED STATES In response to that Communist call for international revolution, about 70,000 radicals joined the newly formed Communist Party in the United States. This U.S. branch of the Communist Party included members of IWW, Industrial Workers of the World, as well as radicals from many walks of life.

In total, less than one-tenth of one percent of Americans joined the party. But the Communist talk about abolishing private property and substituting government ownership of factories, railroads, and other businesses frightened the public.

Adding to this fear was a rash of several dozen bombs mailed to government and business leaders, including the postmaster general and John D. Rockefeller. The nation panicked in its fear of "reds," or Communists, taking over America. Attorney General **A. Mitchell Palmer** decided to take action to combat this "Red Scare."

Palmer had had a distinguished career as a Democratic member of the House of Representatives before accepting an appointment as alien property custodian during World War I and attorney general in 1919. His ambitions extended to the presidency, leading some people to believe he needed a campaign issue for the 1920 election. Palmer was convinced that radicals were undermining American values.

A PERSONAL VOICE
The blaze of revolution was sweeping over every American institution of law and order . . . eating its way into the homes of the American workman, its sharp tongues of revolutionary heat . . . licking at the altars of the churches, leaping into the belfry of the school bell, crawling into the sacred corners of American homes, . . . burning up the foundations of American society.
A. MITCHELL PALMER

THE PALMER RAIDS In August 1919, Palmer appointed J. Edgar Hoover to head the new antiradical division in the Justice Department—the division that later became the Federal Bureau of Investigation. Palmer sent government agents to hunt down suspected Communists, socialists, and **anarchists,** or those who opposed any and all forms of government. In their zeal, the agents ran roughshod over people's civil rights, invading private homes, meeting halls, and offices without search warrants. They jailed suspects for weeks at a time without allowing them to see lawyers, and they arrested those who came to visit the suspects. The government deported hundreds of alien radicals without trying them in courts.

A. Answer He believed that a Communist revolution was imminent in the United States, and, he needed an issue on which to campaign for the 1920 Democratic presidential nomination.

THINK THROUGH HISTORY
A. Analyzing Motives Why did Attorney General A. Mitchell Palmer launch a series of raids against suspected Communists?

ECONOMIC BACKGROUND

ROOTS OF COMMUNISM

In 1917, a small group headed by Vladimir I. Lenin led a successful revolution in Russia and set up a Communist government based on the teachings of Karl Marx and Friedrich Engels. In 1848, these two had published a pamphlet called *The Communist Manifesto,* in which they presented a theory of class struggle. According to their theory, a social class that has economic power also has political and social power. Marx and Engels asserted that opposing economic classes— the "haves" and the "have-nots"— have struggled for control throughout history. In ancient times, they said, the conflict was between free and enslaved people. In the Middle Ages, it was between lords and peasants.

Now, during the Industrial Revolution, they believed the struggle was between the capitalists who owned the means of production—land, capital, and machines—and the workers in mines and factories, who owned only their labor.

Marx and Engels urged workers to seize political power and the means of production. The Communist Party would lead the way in organizing workers and overthrowing capitalism through violent revolution. The party would then control a nation's government and plan all its economic activities.

OBJECTIVE
① INSTRUCT

Revolution Abroad and Reaction at Home

▶ *Discussing Key Ideas*
• After the Russian Revolution, the newly formed Communist Party in the United States attracts some members.
• In response to the widespread Red Scare, the government hunts down suspected Communists, socialists, and anarchists.
• Sacco and Vanzetti, two anarchists and Italian immigrants, are executed for a crime they may not have committed.
• Groups such as the Ku Klux Klan use anticommunism as an excuse to harass ethnic and religious minorities.

IN-DEPTH RESOURCES: UNIT 6
Guided Reading, p. 1

ACCESS FOR STUDENTS ACQUIRING ENGLISH
Guided Reading (Spanish), p. 198

 ELECTRONIC LIBRARY OF PRIMARY SOURCES
Instructions Regarding Conduct on Raids

ECONOMIC BACKGROUND
Roots of Communism

Critical Thinking: Analyzing Issues Discuss the theory that the "haves" and the "have-nots" constantly struggle for economic control. Ask students whether these economic classes exist in American society. Do they think communism can bridge the gap between the classes?

Politics of the Roaring Twenties **591**

TEACHING OPTIONS

Making Connections Across Time

The Red Scare in the 1950s Tell students that the Cold War, which developed between the United States and the Soviet Union after the Second World War, once again awakened the public's fear of communism. In the 1950s, Senator Joseph McCarthy launched widely publicized attacks on suspected Communists in the U.S. government. Congressional committees also investigated possible Communist influence outside the government, particularly in the movie and entertainment industry. In this atmosphere of fear, millions of Americans were forced to take loyalty oaths and undergo investigation. Many lost their jobs.

Making Connections Across the Curriculum

Economics Discuss the theory of class struggle proposed by Marx and Engels. Tell students that Marx's ideas were, in part, a reaction to the hardships endured by many workers in Europe during the Industrial Revolution. They worked long hours for little pay under unhealthful and sometimes dangerous conditions. Marx believed that the working class would eventually rise up, overthrow capitalism, and seize control of industry and of government. He taught that society continued to develop as it advanced from one stage to the next. Marx believed that communism was the final stage of this development.

Worldwide protest erupted following the verdict against Sacco and Vanzetti. Some of these protests were violent. In Paris, a bomb exploded at the house of the American ambassador, and crowds menaced the American embassy in Rome. Other protests were peaceful. In Uruguay, people mounted a general strike and a boycott of American goods, while newspapers from Mexico to Algeria carried numerous editorials condemning the verdict.

IN-DEPTH RESOURCES: UNIT 6
Primary Sources: *from* Bartolomeo Vanzetti's Speech to the Jury, p. 7

 OUR TIMES
Sacco-Vanzetti case

MORE ABOUT . . .
The Art of Ben Shahn

The painting reproduced on this page is the work of Ben Shahn. His family came to the United States from Lithuania when he was eight years old. As Jews, they had suffered persecution in their homeland, and Shahn grew up with a strong devotion to justice and fair play. When he became a painter, he decided to devote his art to helping create a more just society. Horrified by the Sacco and Vanzetti case, Shahn produced a series of 23 paintings, including the one shown here. Sacco and Vanzetti are pictured with a diminutive image of Governor Fuller, indicating his weakness as a leader.

 HUMANITIES TRANSPARENCIES
H19, *The Passion of Sacco and Vanzetti* by Ben Shahn

Bartolomeo Vanzetti, *center,* and Nicola Sacco, *right,* were both executed for a crime they may not have committed. To this day, the evidence remains circumstantial.

Palmer's raids, however, failed to turn up evidence of a revolutionary conspiracy. Nor did agents discover explosives, and they found only three pistols in their search for weapons. Then Palmer warned the nation of a Communist plot to overthrow the government on May 1, 1920, which was May Day, the international workers' holiday. When the day passed without incident, the public decided that Palmer didn't know what he was talking about.

SACCO AND VANZETTI Although short-lived, the Red Scare fed people's suspicions of foreigners and immigrants, sometimes leading to ruined reputations and wrecked lives. The two most infamous victims were **Nicola Sacco** and **Bartolomeo Vanzetti,** a shoemaker and a fish peddler. Both men were Italian immigrants, and both were anarchists who had evaded the draft during World War I.

In April 1920, at the height of the Red Scare, a crime took place in South Braintree, Massachusetts. Two men shot and killed a factory paymaster and his guard, grabbed the $15,000 payroll, jumped into an automobile, and made their getaway. Witnesses said the murderers had swarthy complexions and appeared to be Italians. Three weeks later, not having found any other suspects, the police arrested and charged Sacco and Vanzetti with the crime. The accused provided alibis, the evidence was circumstantial, and the presiding judge made several prejudicial remarks. Nevertheless, the jury found them guilty and sentenced them to death. In spite of protests and demonstrations in the United States, Europe, and Latin America, the two men died in the electric chair on August 23, 1927. Before he was executed, Vanzetti made a statement.

A PERSONAL VOICE
In all my life I have never stole [sic], never killed, never spilled blood. . . . We were tried during a time . . . when there was hysteria of resentment and hate against the people of our principles, against the foreigner. . . . I am suffering because I am a radical and indeed I am a radical; I have suffered because I was an Italian and indeed I am an Italian. . . . If you could execute me two times, and if I could be reborn two other times, I would live again to do what I have done already.
BARTOLOMEO VANZETTI, quoted in *The National Experience*

In 1925, nearly 60,000 Ku Klux Klan members marched along Pennsylvania Avenue in Washington, D.C., to demonstrate the organization's new strength and determination.

THINK THROUGH HISTORY
B. Drawing Conclusions
What do you think the conviction of Sacco and Vanzetti showed about the 1920s?

B. Answer That they were years of suspicion and fear.

TEACHING OPTION

Cooperative Learning: Staging a Fair Trial for Sacco and Vanzetti

Task: Students will research the Sacco and Vanzetti case and stage a fair trial for the accused.

Purpose: To explore the Sacco and Vanzetti case in-depth.

Activity: The entire class can take part in a single trial, or you might have two large groups conduct two different trials. All students should research the entire case but should find detailed information about the person or role they will play in the trial. Roles in the trial should be divided by lottery or by selection. The roles should include the following: judge,

members of the jury, Sacco, Vanzetti, defense attorney, prosecuting attorney, and witnesses for both sides. Remind students that, although they are attempting to give Sacco and Vanzetti a fair trial, they should be aware of the period in which the trial took place and address some of the general public's fears and prejudices. After the trial, have students discuss the proceedings and the verdict.

ALTERNATIVE ASSESSMENT BOOK
Standards for Evaluating a Cooperative Activity

In 1961, new ballistics tests showed that the pistol found on Sacco was in fact the one used to murder the guard. However, there was no proof that Sacco had actually pulled the trigger. On August 23, 1977, exactly 50 years after the executions, Massachusetts governor Michael Dukakis declared that Sacco and Vanzetti had not been given a fair trial.

THE KLAN RISES AGAIN As a result of the Red Scare and anti-immigrant feelings, different groups of bigots used anticommunism as an excuse to harass anyone unlike themselves. One such group was the Ku Klux Klan. Although it had been somewhat inactive since the 1870s, the Klan revived in 1915 and really blossomed in the early 1920s. This revived Klan was devoted to "100 percent Americanism." By 1924 it boasted a membership of 4.5 million "white male persons, native-born gentile citizens" who believed in keeping blacks "in their place," destroying saloons, opposing unions, and driving Roman Catholics, Jews, and foreign-born people out of the country. It also opposed union organizers and helped enforce prohibition.

The Klan's appeal did not rest just on its ideas, though. Members dressed up in hooded robes and employed an elaborate secret language and rituals. Then, too, Edward Clarke, of the sales organization known as the Southern Publicity Association, created an incentive program under which KKK salesmen, known as kleagles, kept four dollars of the ten-dollar initiation fee for each new Klan member they recruited. As one historian put it, "Kleagling became one of the profitable industries of the decade."

Klan members, as Grand Wizard Hiram Evans explained, were "plain people . . . the everyday, not highly cultured, not overly intellectualized, but entirely unspoiled . . . citizens of the old stock." In other words, they were people who felt threatened by changes occurring in American society. Klan members resented the small advances made by African Americans during World War I. They also felt that their moral values were being attacked by urban intellectuals, and they feared job competition from immigrants. They were convinced that foreigners were going to overthrow the American way of life.

Klan members vented some of their frustrations through racial violence. They also tried to influence national and state politics. Klan leaders in Indiana—the only state to fall under the Klan's political control—committed such outrageous acts that the law officials finally moved against them. By the end of the 1920s, most Klan members had drifted away from the Klan.

THINK THROUGH HISTORY
C. Analyzing Issues What were the main goals of the Ku Klux Klan at this time?
C. Answer To keep America under the control of white, native-born males; to get rid of other groups, including Roman Catholics, Jews, foreign-born people, and radicals; to oppose union organizers; to help enforce Prohibition.

A Time of Labor Unrest

Another severe postwar conflict formed between labor and management. During the war, workers had not been allowed to strike because the government would allow nothing to interfere with the war effort. However, 1919 saw more than 3,000 strikes, during which some 4 million workers walked off the job at one time or another.

Wages had not kept up with prices, but employers did not want to give their employees raises. Nor did they want their employees to join unions. Some employers, either out of sincere belief or because they saw a way to keep wages down, attempted to show that union members were planning revolution. Newspaper headlines screamed: "Crimes Against Society," "Conspiracies Against the Government," and "Plots to Establish Communism." Three strikes in particular grabbed public attention.

Women tailors form picket lines during a strike for improved working conditions.

Politics of the Roaring Twenties **593**

MORE ABOUT . . .
The Ku Klux Klan
The Ku Klux Klan was well-organized and replete with titles. Its leader was known as the Imperial Wizard. The chief organizer became the Imperial Kleagle. Local units were called Domains and were headed by Grand Goblins. Several Domains made up a Realm, which was led by a King Kleagle.

OBJECTIVE
② INSTRUCT

A Time of Labor Unrest

▶ **Starting with the Student**
Have students create a chart like the one shown below to list the outcome of the three strikes discussed on pages 593–595.

Strike	Outcome
Boston police	
Steel mill	
Coal miners	

▶ **Discussing Key Ideas**
• Conflict between labor and management erupts after the war.
• In 1919, workers go on more than 3,000 strikes, but fear of communism turns the public against the strikers.
• Labor union membership declines in the 1920s largely because of the movement's association with Communist ideals.

IN-DEPTH RESOURCES: UNIT 6
Primary Source: *from* Report on the Steel Strike of 1919, p. 9

TEACHING OPTIONS

Exploring Themes

Economic Opportunity Discuss the factors that fostered labor unrest after the war. Ask students why workers had not been allowed to strike during the war. *Possible Response: Because nothing was allowed to interfere with the war effort.* Why did so many strikes occur after the war? *Possible Response: Because wages had not kept pace with rising prices.* Ask students whether they think labor unions harmed or helped the workers' cause. Then ask them to evaluate the U.S. government's role during the 1919 strikes.

Teaching Less Proficient Readers

Cause and Effect Help students identify the causes and effects of labor unrest after the First World War. Have them read pages 593–595 and follow these steps:

1. Create a two-column chart on a piece of paper. Label one column *Causes,* label the other column *Effects.*
2. List the causes of labor unrest in the first column. Some causes include low wages and poor working conditions.
3. List the effects of labor unrest in the second column. Some effects include strikes and a decline in union membership.

Union Activity, 1920–1929

Reading the Graph Point out that, although the bar chart format is the same for both graphs, the grids are different. One graph expresses numbers in thousands, the other in millions. Ask students why different numbering systems are used to count labor strikes and union membership. *Possible Response: Each year, millions of people belonged to unions. However, the number of strikes between 1920 and 1929 never numbered much more than 3,000.*

Extension Ask students to explain why union membership stabilized after 1923. *Possible Responses: Because new unions, such as the Brotherhood of Sleeping Car Porters, were organized; because unionism was successful for such workers as the coal miners.*

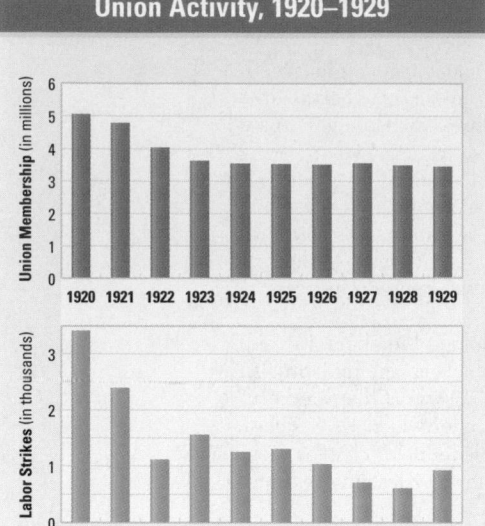

Union Activity, 1920–1929

Source: *Historical Statistics of the United States*

**SKILLBUILDER
INTERPRETING GRAPHS**
After sharp declines from 1920 to 1923, what is the pattern for union membership during the rest of the 1920s? What factors do you think might explain the sharp drop in the number of strikes during the 1920s?

Skillbuilder Answer
Pattern: It remains fairly stable around 3.5 million.
1920s: *Possible Answers:* Increasingly negative public opinion concerning unions and strikes; reduced union membership; booming prosperity and rising wages during this period.

THE BOSTON POLICE STRIKE The police of Boston were angry. They had not had a raise since the beginning of World War I, and by 1919 the cost of living had doubled. The police sent representatives to the police commissioner to ask for what they considered a living wage. The commissioner promptly fired everyone in the group, and the remaining police responded by going out on strike. After Massachusetts governor **Calvin Coolidge** called out the National Guard to restore order, the police called off the strike.

The police commissioner, however, refused to allow the men to return to their jobs. Instead, he hired new men for his police force who, ironically, received everything the strikers had asked for. Months later, the president of the American Federation of Labor (AFL), Samuel Gompers, appealed to Coolidge on behalf of the fired men. The governor replied, "There is no right to strike against the public safety by anyone, anywhere, any time." People praised Coolidge for saving Boston, if not the nation, from communism and anarchy. In the 1920 election he became Warren G. Harding's running mate.

THE STEEL MILL STRIKE If the Boston police strike outraged the public, the steel strike that began at the U.S. Steel Corporation in September 1919 was even more upsetting. Working conditions in the steel industry were extremely difficult and dangerous. Many laborers worked seven 12-hour days a week, in hot and noisy foundries. When the company refused to meet with union representatives, 350,000 workers walked off the job. They demanded the right as organized workers to bargain with their employer for shorter working hours and a living wage. One steel-strike leader, William Z. Foster, had worked in several industries before joining IWW and becoming a militant labor organizer. At the time of the steel strike of 1919, Foster was a leader of the AFL. His participation in the strike caused management to claim that labor activities were led by radicals.

Steel companies hired strikebreakers and used force. For example, U.S. Steel security police, state militias, and federal troops killed 18 workers and wounded or beat hundreds more. The companies also instituted a widespread propaganda campaign seeking to link the strikers to Communists.

In October 1919, a vote on three collective-bargaining resolutions produced a deadlock. Then President Woodrow Wilson made a written plea to the combative conference members.

**THINK THROUGH HISTORY
D. Summarizing** What was Governor Coolidge's position on the Boston police strike?
D. Answer That there is no right to strike against the public safety.

A PERSONAL VOICE
At a time when the nations of the world are endeavoring to find a way of avoiding international war, are we to confess that there is no method to be found for carrying on industry except in the spirit and with the very method of war? . . . Are our industrial leaders and our industrial workers to live together without faith in each other, constantly struggling for advantage over each other, doing naught but what is compelled?

WOODROW WILSON, quoted in *Labor in Crisis*

The president's plea did not resolve the issues, but the steel strike was finally broken in January 1920. The fact that AFL leader William Foster later joined the Communist Party did not help the image of labor unions.

At first the public was relieved that another threat by "un-American elements" had been turned back. Then, in 1923, a Protestant interfaith committee

594 CHAPTER 20

Teaching Gifted and Talented Students

Arbitrating Strikes Have groups of interested students work together to settle one of the strikes described on pages 594 and 595. Students should:

• Select one of the strikes and do research to find out more about it.
• Divide the roles among group members. Half the students should represent the labor union. The other half should represent management.
• Make a list of goals and demands. Each side should state their position and be willing to compromise.

Making Connections Across Cultures

African Americans in the Labor Movement The Pullman Company was the largest private employer of black workers in the United States when A. Philip Randolph organized a labor union for sleeping car porters. As a result, many African-American leaders advised black workers to support management rather than the union. Randolph advocated what he called "manhood rights" for African Americans. He insisted that joining the union was a continuation of the fight against slavery. Randolph said: "[Frederick] Douglass fought for the abolition of chattel slavery, and today we fight for economic freedom."

published a report on the severe working conditions in the steel mills. The report shocked the public, and the steel companies agreed to establish an eight-hour day. However, the steel workers remained without a union.

THE COAL MINERS STRIKE Unionism was more successful in America's coalfields. In 1919, the United Mine Workers, organized since 1890, got a new president—**John L. Lewis.** In protest of low wages and long workdays, Lewis called his union's members out on strike on November 1, 1919. Attorney General Palmer obtained a court order sending the miners back to work. Lewis then declared the strike over, but he quietly gave the word for the strike to continue.

In defiance of the court order, the mines stayed closed another month. Then President Wilson appointed an arbitrator to decide the outstanding issues between the miners and the mine owners. In due course, the coal miners received a 27 percent wage increase, and John L. Lewis became a national figure. The miners, however, did not achieve a shorter workday and a five-day workweek until the 1930s.

LABOR MOVEMENT LOSES APPEAL In spite of the gains by the coal miners, the 1920s hurt the labor movement badly. Many Americans believed labor unions fostered communism, and membership in unions declined for a number of reasons.

- Much of the work force consisted of immigrants who had no choice but to work in poor conditions.
- Since immigrants spoke a multitude of languages, unions had difficulty trying to organize them.
- Farmers who had migrated to cities to find factory jobs were difficult to unionize because they were used to relying on themselves.

Thousands of African Americans who had migrated from the South to take factory jobs in the North were likely candidates for unionization, but most unions excluded them from their ranks. Only about 82,000 African Americans held union memberships by 1929.

The exceptions to this discrimination were provided by the mine workers', longshoremen's, and railroad porters' unions. However, an important step in organizing African Americans into unions occurred in 1925 when A. Philip Randolph founded the Brotherhood of Sleeping Car Porters to help African Americans gain a fair wage. By the end of the decade, union membership had dropped from 5 million in 1920 to around 3.5 million, as shown by the graph on page 594.

Many Americans changed their attitudes not only toward unions during the twenties, but also toward immigrants and America's role in the world.

E. Answer Many people believed labor unions fostered communism; immigrants and farmers were difficult to organize; most of the unions rejected African Americans.

THINK THROUGH HISTORY
E. Analyzing Causes Why did union membership drop in the twenties?

KEY PLAYER

JOHN LLEWELLYN LEWIS
1880–1969

John L. Lewis was born in the little mining town of Lucas, Iowa. His family had traditionally been concerned with labor rights and benefits.

John grew up with a fierce determination to fight for what he believed companies owed their employees: decent working conditions and a fair salary. As he said years later "I have pleaded your case not in the tones of a feeble mendicant [beggar] asking alms but in the thundering voice of the captain of a mighty host, demanding the rights to which free men are entitled."

Section 1 Assessment

1. TERMS & NAMES

Identify:
- communism
- A. Mitchell Palmer
- anarchist
- Sacco and Vanzetti
- Calvin Coolidge
- John L. Lewis

2. SEQUENCING Create a time line of the major events involving labor unions between 1917 and 1929, using a form like the one below.

Event	Result
1.	→
2.	→

What event do you think was the most significant? Explain your choice.

3. FORMING AN OPINION Do you think Americans were justified in their fear of radicals and foreigners in the decade following World War I? Explain your answer.

THINK ABOUT
- the goals of the leaders of the Russian Revolution
- the impact of radicals in the United States
- the challenges facing the United States

4. ANALYZING What factors led union organizers to call so many strikes in 1919?

THINK ABOUT
- economic factors
- labor leaders' determination to fight for worker rights

Politics of the Roaring Twenties **595**

OBJECTIVES

(1) To describe Harding's efforts to return the United States to normalcy after the progressive era reforms.

(2) To summarize the immigration policy pursued by the United States in the 1920s.

(3) To identify the scandals that plagued Harding's administration.

SKILLBUILDER

• Interpreting charts, p. 598

CRITICAL THINKING

• Forming opinions, p. 597
• Analyzing issues, p. 598
• Developing historical perspective, p. 599
• Drawing conclusions, p. 599
• Following chronological order, p. 600
• Summarizing, p. 600
• Generalizing, p. 600
• Evaluating, p. 600

FOCUS & MOTIVATE

▶ **Starting with the Student**
Have students think about the period following a holiday or some other disruptive event.

• Are they glad to get back to a normal, everyday routine?
• Or do they prefer life to be unpredictable and unsettled?

MORE ABOUT . . .
Ernesto Galarza

As a young boy, Galarza worked at many different part-time jobs while going to school. He sold newspapers, delivered telegrams, applied decorations to Christmas cards, picked fruits and vegetables in the field, and even played the fiddle at Saturday night dances. As an adult, he became an educator and taught for many years.

IN-DEPTH RESOURCES: UNIT 6
American Lives: Ernesto Galarza, p. 14

② "Normalcy" and Isolationism

TERMS & NAMES
• Warren G. Harding
• Kellogg-Briand Pact
• isolationist
• Fordney-McCumber Tari
• quota system
• Charles Evans Hughes
• Ohio gang
• Albert B. Fall
• Teapot Dome scandal

LEARN ABOUT the policies of the Harding administration
TO UNDERSTAND the development of postwar isolationism and the immigration quota system.

ONE AMERICAN'S STORY

In the 1920s, when Ernesto Galarza was a little boy, his family came to California from Mexico to earn a better living. When they reached Sacramento, they went immediately to its barrio, the city neighborhood inhabited by Spanish-speaking people. There they looked for jobs and for an affordable place to live. In his old age, Galarza recalled his barrio experience:

A PERSONAL VOICE
Ours was a neighborhood of leftover houses. The cheapest rents were in the back quarters of the rooming houses, the basements, and the run-down clapboard rentals in the alley. . . . *Barrio* people, when they first came to town, had no furniture of their own. They rented it with their quarters or bought a piece at a time from the second-hand stores, the *segundas*, where we traded. . . . Beds and meals were provided [to newcomers] . . . on trust, until the new *Chicano* found a job, on trust and not on credit, for trust was something between people who had plenty of nothing, and credit was between people who had something of plenty.

ERNESTO GALARZA, quoted in *The Hispanic Americans*

Galarza and his family were able to enter the United States only because they were from Mexico. Potential immigrants from outside the Western Hemisphere could not legally enter the country because of new restrictions on immigration. These restrictions reflected a new attitude that emerged after World War I. Wanting a return to the "normalcy" of pre-war days, Americans urged less government control over business and much less international involvement. "Keep America for Americans" became the prevailing attitude.

Men gather in a park barrio in California in the 1920s.

A Return to "Normalcy"

As the Republicans gathered in Chicago in the summer of 1920 to nominate their candidate for president, they wanted to retake the White House. The American public seemed tired of the push for reform that had marked the Progressive Era–particularly the administration of President Woodrow Wilson.

But none of the Republican candidates could gather enough support to win the nomination. Finally the party leaders turned to Senator **Warren G. Harding** of Ohio. Although his knowledge was limited and his judgment turned out to be poor, he was a good-natured man who, according to one of his followers, "looked like a president ought to look," and the public loved his soothing speeches.

A PERSONAL VOICE
America's present need is not heroics, but healing; not nostrums, but normalcy; not revolution, but restoration; not agitation, but adjustment; not surgery, but serenity; not the dramatic, but the dispassionate; . . . not submergence in internationality, but sustainment in triumphant nationality.

WARREN G. HARDING, quoted in *The Rise of Warren Gamaliel Harding*

At election time, Harding and his running mate, Calvin Coolidge, swamped their Democratic opponents, James M. Cox and Franklin D. Roosevelt, 16 mil-

---

SECTION 2 RESOURCES

🗂 PRINT RESOURCES

IN-DEPTH RESOURCES: UNIT 6
Guided Reading, p. 2
Skillbuilder Practice: Summarizing, p. 4
American Lives: Ernesto Galarza, p. 14

ACCESS FOR STUDENTS ACQUIRING ENGLISH
Guided Reading (Spanish), p. 199
Skillbuilder Practice: Summarizing (Spanish), p. 201

FORMAL ASSESSMENT
Section Quiz, p. 247

ALTERNATIVE ASSESSMENT BOOK
See forms for supporting and scoring alternative activities.

💿 TECHNOLOGY RESOURCES

HUMANITIES TRANSPARENCIES
H39, Looking Backward

GEOGRAPHY TRANSPARENCIES
G20, European Emigration: 1820–1920

CRITICAL THINKING TRANSPARENCIES
CT20, Isolationist Policies of the 1920s

CD-ROM Electronic Library of Primary Sources

VIDEO *American Portfolio: A Videodisc for U.S. History* user's guide, pp. 193–194, 196

INTERNET McDougal Littell Learning On-Line
http://www.mcdougallittell.com

lion votes to 9 million. The electoral count was even more of a landslide: 404 to 127. In his campaign speeches, Harding had promoted a "return to normalcy on the domestic front." He wanted to return America to the simpler days before the Progressive Era reforms.

WORKING FOR PEACE In the aftermath of World War I, problems surfaced relating to war debts, arms control, and the reconstruction of war-torn countries. President Harding worked to solve these international problems and to maintain peace. In 1921, he invited four major naval powers and four smaller nations with interests in the Far East to a conference in Washington, D.C. Only Russia was left out because of its Communist government. In his welcoming speech, the president appealed resoundingly for peace: "I can speak officially only for our United States. Our hundred millions frankly want less of armaments and none of war."

Then Secretary of State Charles Evans Hughes took the floor and urged a ten-year holiday from the building of warships. In addition, he suggested that the five major naval powers—the United States, Great Britain, Japan, France, and Italy—scrap a significant proportion of their existing battleships, cruisers, and aircraft carriers. Conference delegates cheered, wept, threw their hats into the air—and adopted the proposal. It was the first time in history that such powerful nations had agreed to disarm.

Eventually, by 1929, the United States succeeded in urging 64 nations, or almost all the nations then in existence, to sign the **Kellogg-Briand Pact,** which basically renounced war as an instrument of national policy. Americans were jubilant. However, there was no way to enforce the pact because it made no provision for the use of military or economic force against any nation that violated the agreement.

HIGH TARIFFS AND REPARATIONS Behind the international glow of the Washington Naval Conference and the Kellogg-Briand Pact, the Harding administration was actually pursuing an **isolationist** foreign policy. Nevertheless, the United States was trying to head off trouble in Asia and to reduce the amount of money spent on armaments.

At the same time, it was not retreating from its stand on war debts. Britain and France had borrowed more than $10 billion from American bankers during World War I and now were having trouble repaying the loans while rebuilding their economies. They could raise the money in only two ways: by exporting more goods to the United States or through reparations, which were German payments to the Allies for war damages.

Neither alternative worked. For one thing, in 1922 the United States adopted the **Fordney-McCumber Tariff,** which raised the tax on imports to its highest level ever—almost 60 percent. The act was designed to protect American businesses, especially chemical and metal industries, from foreign competition. As a result of such a high tariff, Britain and France were unable to sell their goods in the United States and could not earn the revenue to repay their debts.

The two nations then demanded that Germany pay its promised reparations, but the economically ruined Germany defaulted on its war payments. Then at the end of 1922, French troops marched into Germany's Ruhr Valley, its industrial region. To avoid a new war, the United States became involved in the situation. It sent American banker Charles G. Dawes, soon to be President Coolidge's vice-president, to negotiate loans from American investors to Germany. Through the Dawes Plan, U.S. banks loaned Germany $2.5 billion, which Germany was able to use to pay reparations to Britain and France. Those countries then turned around and paid on their war debts to the United States. Thus, the United States, in effect, arranged to be repaid with its own money.

This solution caused bad feelings all around. Britain and France considered the United States a miser for not paying a fair share of the costs of World War I.

Politics of the Roaring Twenties **597**

THINK THROUGH HISTORY
A. Forming Opinions Do you think the goal of the Kellogg-Briand Pact was unrealistic?
A. Answer *Possible response:* It was unrealistic because the pact provided no means for enforcement.

OBJECTIVE
(1) INSTRUCT

A Return to "Normalcy"

▶ *Discussing Key Ideas*
• Harding vows to return the United States to the simpler days before the Progressive Era reforms.
• Most of the world's nations agree to disarm and sign the Kellogg-Briand Pact, but there is no way to enforce the pact.
• The Harding administration raises taxes on imports and demands that Britain and France pay their war debts.

IN-DEPTH RESOURCES: UNIT 6
Guided Reading, p. 2

ACCESS FOR STUDENTS ACQUIRING ENGLISH
Guided Reading (Spanish), p. 199

Warren G. Harding was considered a respectable-looking president—but he had difficulties with some of his presidential duties.

MORE ABOUT . . .
Warren G. Harding
Harding liked to deliver long speeches, but they were filled with grammatical mistakes. He also loved to use alliteration, the repetition of initial consonant sounds in two or more consecutive words. Writer H. L. Mencken believed Harding spoke the worst English he had ever heard: "It reminds me of a string of wet sponges; it reminds me of tattered washing on the line; it reminds me of stale bean soup, of college yells, of dogs barking idiotically through endless nights. It is so bad that a sort of grandeur creeps into it."

TEACHING OPTIONS

Exploring Themes

Economic Opportunity Discuss the Harding administration's decision to raise taxes on imports. Ask students why the government chose to do this. *To protect American business from foreign competition.* Then ask them what effect the raise had on Britain and France. *The countries were unable to sell their products in the United States and so were unable to repay their war debts.* Do students think the U.S. government's stand was fair? Should the government have assumed a greater share of the costs of World War I? Or was the government right to insist on repayment?

Making Connections Across the Curriculum

Economics Remind students that a tariff is a tax that one nation imposes on goods imported from another country. Many nations use tariffs to help protect their industries from foreign competition. Tariffs encourage domestic production of goods. They also encourage consumers to buy the less expensive domestic products. Many nations have commercial treaties that include a most-favored-nation clause. This clause requires the application of a nation's lowest tariff rate to all countries that sign the treaty. A country may also levy an even lower tariff to favor imports from less developed countries.

Limiting Immigration

▶ **Discussing Key Ideas**
• Because the need for unskilled labor decreased after the First World War, many Americans want to limit immigration.
• Congress sets up a quota system limiting immigration.

CRITICAL THINKING TRANSPARENCIES
CT20, Isolationist Policies of the 1920s

ELECTRONIC LIBRARY OF PRIMARY SOURCES
from A Letter Regarding Immigration Restrictions by Louis Marshall

HISTORY FROM VISUALS
U.S. Patterns of Immigration, 1921 and 1929

Reading the Chart Point out the relationship between the colors of the bars and the colors of the countries on the maps below the bars. Then discuss the numbering system used in the chart.

Extension Ask students why they think the number of German immigrants increased between 1921 and 1929. *Possible Response: Many Germans wanted to leave their devastated country after the war.*

HUMANITIES TRANSPARENCIES
H39, Looking Backward

GEOGRAPHY TRANSPARENCIES
G20, European Emigration, 1820–1920

Their people had died while America profited! At the same time, the United States considered the two nations financially irresponsible for being unwilling to repay their debts. As President Calvin Coolidge, who succeeded Harding, reportedly remarked, "They hired the money, didn't they?"

Limiting Immigration

Nativist sentiment, an anti-immigrant attitude, had been growing in the United States ever since the 1880s, when new immigrants arrived from southern and eastern Europe. Nativist feelings were fueled by the fact that some of the people involved in postwar labor disputes were immigrant anarchists and socialists, who many Americans believed were actually revolutionary radicals and Communists.

In addition, the demand for unskilled labor in the United States decreased after World War I, especially in industries such as coal mining and the production of steel and textiles; immigrants generally filled these jobs. With fewer unskilled jobs available, nativists reasoned, fewer immigrants should be allowed into the United States. Also, racist ideas like those expressed by Madison Grant, an anthropologist at the American Museum of Natural History in New York City, had an influence on attitudes toward immigration.

A PERSONAL VOICE
The result of unlimited immigration is showing plainly in the rapid decline in the birth rate of native Americans . . . [who] will not bring children into the world to compete in the labor market with the Slovak, the Italian, the Syrian and the Jew. The native American is too proud to mix socially with them.
MADISON GRANT, quoted in *United States History: Ideas in Conflict*

Skillbuilder Answer Five groups: 1. Italy; 2. Spain and Portugal; 3. Yugoslavia, Austria, Hungary, and Czechoslovakia; 4. Greece; 5. USSR and the Baltic States. **Increase:** Germany and Mexico.

SKILLBUILDER INTERPRETING CHARTS
Which five geographical areas show the sharpest decline in immigrants coming to the U.S. between 1921 and 1929? What are the only areas to register an increase in immigrants to the U.S.?

B. Answer U.S. actions caused bad feelings but did arrange to have the debt repaid with its own money.

THINK THROUGH HISTORY
B. Analyzing Issues How did the U.S. actions both annoy and lighten the war debt repayment problem?

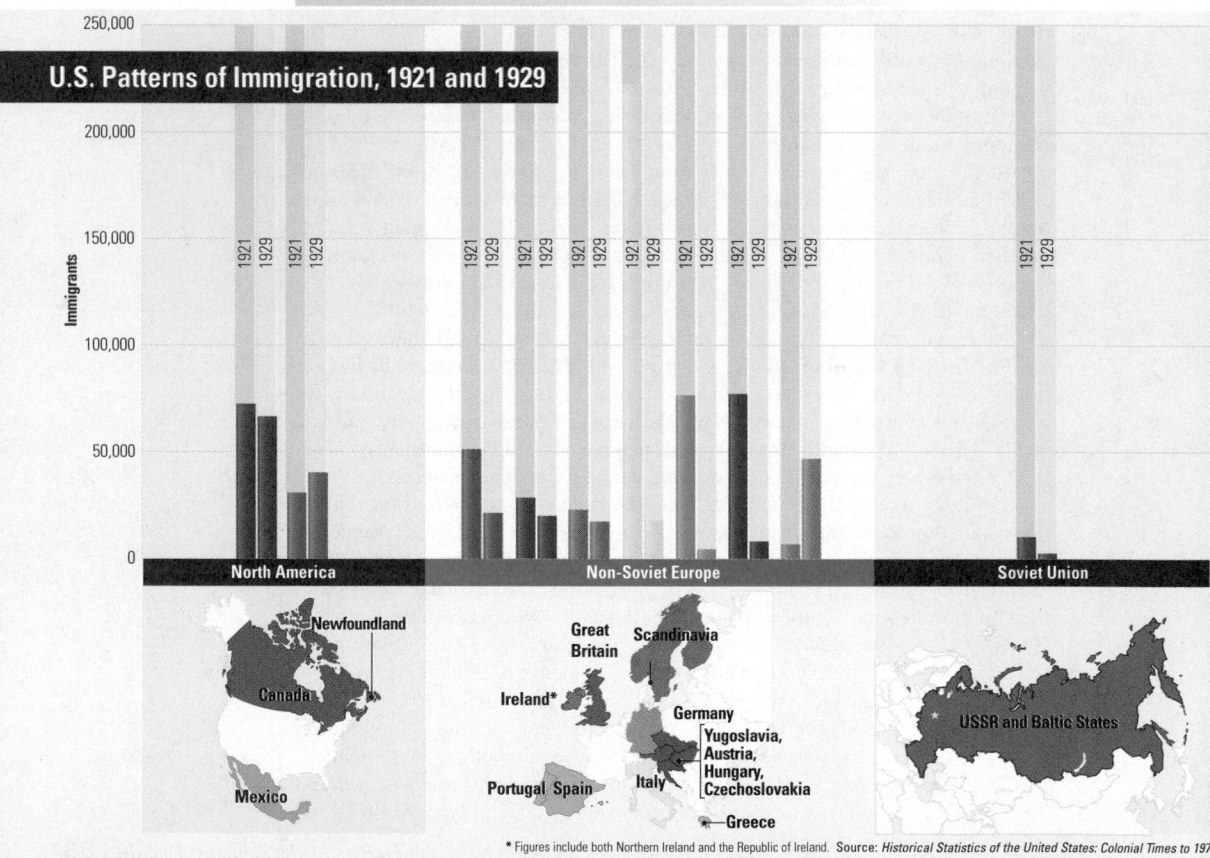

U.S. Patterns of Immigration, 1921 and 1929

North America — Non-Soviet Europe — Soviet Union

Newfoundland, Canada, Mexico; Great Britain, Ireland*, Scandinavia, Germany, Yugoslavia, Austria, Hungary, Czechoslovakia, Portugal, Spain, Italy, Greece; USSR and Baltic States

* Figures include both Northern Ireland and the Republic of Ireland. **Source:** *Historical Statistics of the United States: Colonial Times to 1970.*

TEACHING OPTION

Cooperative Activity: Researching Immigration Issues

Task: Groups of four or five students will research and report on immigration issues in the 1920s or in the 1990s.

Purpose: To explore some of the controversies surrounding U.S. immigration.

Activity: Assign half the groups to research immigration issues in the 1920s. Have the other half research issues in the 1990s. Each student in a group should study immigration from one country and research such issues as the causes and effects of immigration and the immigrants' experience with housing and employment. Group members should compile their findings into one report that can be shared with the rest of the class.

▭ **Building a Portfolio:** Students who add their reports to their portfolios should attach a note identifying their contribution to the project.

▭ **ALTERNATIVE ASSESSMENT BOOK**
Standards for Evaluating a Cooperative Activity

Standards for Evaluation
Reports should . . .

• discuss the causes and effects of the immigration
• describe the immigrants' experiences
• use specific details to support ideas
• include photos to enhance information

THE QUOTA SYSTEM In 1919, the number of immigrants was a modest 141,000, but by 1921 the number shot up to 805,000. Congress, in response to nativist pressure, decided the time had come to limit immigration from Europe. The Emergency Quota Act of 1921 set up a **quota system.** This system established the maximum number of people who could enter the United States from any one foreign country. As amended in 1924, the law limited immigration from each European nation to 2 percent of the number of its nationals living in the United States in 1890. This provision discriminated against people from eastern and southern Europe—mostly Roman Catholics and Jews—who had not started coming in large numbers until after 1890. Later, the National Origins Act of 1929 shifted the base year to 1920, but it reduced the total number of persons to be admitted in any one year to 150,000.

The law also excluded Japanese altogether, resulting in much ill will between the two nations. Japan, which had faithfully kept the Gentlemen's Agreement to limit emigration to the United States negotiated by Theodore Roosevelt in 1907, expressed anger over the insult.

The national origins quota system did not apply to immigrants from the Western Hemisphere. During the 1920s, about a million Canadians and at least 500,000 Mexicans crossed the nation's borders.

The goal of the quota system was to sharply cut European immigration to the United States. As the chart on page 598 shows, the system achieved that goal.

Scandal Hits Harding's Administration

Harding opposed the federal government's role in business affairs, and he disapproved of most social reforms. However, he did set up the Bureau of the Budget to help run the government more efficiently, and he urged U.S. Steel to abandon the 12-hour day. He also made some excellent cabinet appointments.

HARDING'S ADMINISTRATION Harding appointed **Charles Evans Hughes** as secretary of state. Hughes later went on to become chief justice of the Supreme Court. The president made Herbert Hoover the secretary of commerce. Hoover had done a masterful job handling food distribution and refugee problems during World War I. Andrew Mellon, one of the country's wealthiest men, became secretary of the treasury and set about reducing the national debt. By 1923 the national debt had fallen by about one-third.

However, the cabinet also included the so-called **Ohio gang,** the president's rowdy, poker-playing cronies from back home. Attorney General Harry M. Daugherty, a lobbyist for tobacco and meat-packing companies, and Interior Secretary **Albert B. Fall,** a close friend of various oil executives, would soon cause Harding—and the country—a great deal of embarrassment.

SCANDALS PLAGUE HARDING The president's main problem was that he didn't understand many things he had to deal with. He admitted as much to a secretary after listening to advisers discuss a federal money problem.

A PERSONAL VOICE
John, I can't make a . . . thing out of this tax problem. I listen to one side and they seem right, and then . . . I talk to the other side and they seem just as right. I know somewhere there is an economist who knows the truth, but I don't know where to find him and haven't the sense to know him and trust him when I find him. . . . What a job!

WARREN G. HARDING, quoted in *Only Yesterday*

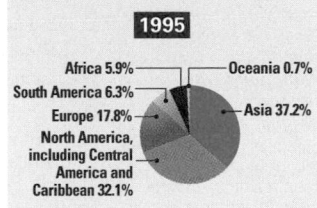

NOW & THEN

U.S. PATTERNS OF IMMIGRATION

In the late 1990s, most immigrants came to the United States from North America (Mexico), Asia (Vietnam, the Philippines, South Korea, India, and China), the former Soviet Union, and the Caribbean (Haiti, the Dominican Republic, and Jamaica). Not many immigrants came from Europe or Canada.

In the 1920s, a quota system strictly limited immigration from most places. Thus, the number of immigrants coming to the United States dropped sharply between 1921 and 1929, especially from Italy, Yugoslavia, Austria, Hungary, Czechoslovakia, and other eastern and southern European nations. The number from Asian countries was also very limited, but the number from the Western Hemisphere (Canada and Mexico) was quite large. In 1965, the United States finally dropped the national origins quota system.

1995

Africa 5.9%
Oceania 0.7%
South America 6.3%
Europe 17.8%
Asia 37.2%
North America, including Central America and Caribbean 32.1%

Source: U.S. Immigration and Naturalization Service

Reading the Cartoon Ask students how the cartoonist places blame for the scandal on the Republicans without actually naming them. *By drawing the elephant in the shape of a teapot; by labeling the teapot GOP.*

Extension Have students draw a cartoon representing Harding's reaction to the Teapot Dome scandal.

 ELECTRONIC LIBRARY OF PRIMARY SOURCES
Senate Demands Information on Teapot Dome

ASSESS & RETEACH

Section 2 Assessment
Have students answer the questions individually. Then ask them to share the evaluations they wrote for item 2 with the class.

Self-Assessment
Have students make a time line of events in Harding's administration.

Section Quiz

FORMAL ASSESSMENT
Section Quiz, p. 247

Reteach
Review the charts on page 598 to initiate a discussion of U.S. policy on immigration during the 1920s.

CLOSE

Harding promised the American people a return to normalcy. To that end, his administration pursued an isolationist foreign policy and created an immigration quota system. Although scandals plagued Harding's administration, Coolidge restored people's faith in government with his pro-business spirit.

As a result of Harding's inadequacies, his administration began to unravel. He had the same problem Grant had had nearly 50 years before: his corrupt friends used their offices to become wealthy through graft.

Charles R. Forbes, the head of the Veterans Bureau, swindled the country of some $250 million in kickbacks from contractors of veterans' hospitals. Likewise, in exchange for bribes, the head of the Office of Alien Property, Colonel Thomas W. Miller, took German chemical patents the government had seized during the war and sold them for far less than their worth.

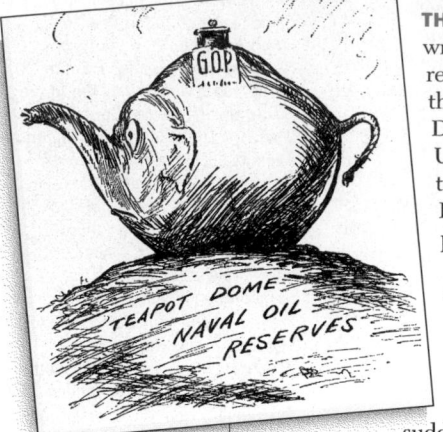

G.O.P.

TEAPOT DOME NAVAL OIL RESERVES

THE TEAPOT DOME SCANDAL The most spectacular wrongdoing, however, was the **Teapot Dome scandal.** As a result of the conservation movement of the Progressive Era, the government had set aside oil-rich public lands at Teapot Dome, Wyoming, and Elk Hills, California, for use by the U.S. Navy. Secretary of the Interior Albert B. Fall managed to get the oil reserves transferred from the navy to the Interior Department, since it seemed sensible to place all public reserves under the control of the same department.

Once the transfer was completed, however, Fall secretly leased the land to two private oil companies: Harry Sinclair's Mammoth Oil Company at Teapot Dome and Edward L. Doheny's Pan-American Petroleum and Transport Company at Elk Hills. Although Fall claimed that these contracts were in the government's interest, he suddenly became the owner of $325,000 in bonds and cash, as well as several ranches and some prize livestock.

By the summer of 1923, Harding realized corruption existed in his administration, but he himself managed to avoid public disgrace and humiliation. A hurt and confused man, he declared, "I have trouble with my enemies. . . . But my damned friends . . . they're the ones that keep me walking the floor nights!" At that point he left on a goodwill tour to Alaska. Returning from Alaska to San Francisco, he became ill and died on August 2, 1923, probably from a heart attack or a blood vessel bursting in his brain.

The American people sincerely mourned their good-natured president. Vice-President Calvin Coolidge became president upon Harding's death. The crimes were coming to light just as Coolidge, a respected man of integrity, helped to restore people's faith in their government and in the Republican Party. He was elected president in 1924.

E. Answer
Kickbacks, bribes, bonds and cash paid for oil contracts.

THINK THROUGH HISTORY
E. Following Chronological Order What acts of corruption surfaced during the Harding administration?

Section 2 Assessment

1. TERMS & NAMES
Identify:
• Warren G. Harding
• Kellogg-Briand Pact
• Isolationist
• Fordney-McCumber Tariff
• quota system
• Charles Evans Hughes
• Ohio gang
• Albert B. Fall
• Teapot Dome scandal

2. SUMMARIZING List and evaluate five significant events from this section, using a table like the one shown. Rate the events as follows: "+" for events that benefited the country; "0" for events that had a mixed impact; "-" for events that harmed the country. Share your evaluations with the class.

Event	Evaluation
1.	
2.	

Which event do you think benefited the country the most? Why do you think so?

3. GENERALIZING How do you think the Harding administration viewed the role of America in world events? Support your response with examples from the text.

THINK ABOUT
• policies on trade and tariffs
• efforts to enforce peace
• attitudes toward immigrants

4. EVALUATING How successful was Harding in fulfilling his campaign pledge of returning the country to "normalcy"? Support your opinion with specific examples.

THINK ABOUT
• events in foreign relations
• changes in immigration laws
• scandals during Harding's administration

ANSWERS

1. TERMS & NAMES
Warren G. Harding, p. 596
Kellogg-Briand Pact, p. 597
isolationist, p. 597
Fordney-McCumber Tariff, p. 597
quota system, p. 599
Charles Evans Hughes, p. 599
Ohio gang, p. 599
Albert B. Fall, p. 599
Teapot Dome scandal, p. 600

2. SUMMARIZING
Possible Answers: Tables might include:
election of Harding
naval disarmament agreement
Kellogg-Briand Pact signed
Fordney-McCumber Tariff passed
Dawes Plan implemented
increase in immigration in 1921
immigration quotas created
Teapot Dome scandal uncovered

3. GENERALIZING
Possible Responses: Some students may think that the Harding administration wanted limited global involvement. The refusal to enforce international agreements, the passage of high tariffs, and immigration restrictions could be considered isolationist. Other students may think the administration viewed itself as a peacemaker, urging international disarmament.

4. EVALUATING
Possible Responses: Some students may say that high tariffs, immigration restrictions, and government corruption created an atmosphere of distrust that was hardly normal. Others may cite the Kellogg-Briand Pact as a somewhat successful attempt by the administration to promote postwar "normalcy."

3 The Business of America

LEARN ABOUT the impact of automobiles, electric power, advertising, and installment buying on the American consumer
TO UNDERSTAND how consumer goods became the foundation of the business boom of the 1920s.

ONE AMERICAN'S STORY

In 1927, the last Model T Ford—number 15,077,033—rolled off the assembly line. On December 2, some 1 million New Yorkers mobbed show rooms to view the new Model A. A striking difference between the two models was that customers could order the Model A in such colors as Arabian Sand and Niagara Blue, while the old Model T had come only in black. A Ford spokesman explained some additional advantages of the new automobile.

A PERSONAL VOICE
Good-looking as that car is, its performance is better than its appearance. We don't brag about it, but it has done seventy-one miles an hour. It will ride along a railroad track without bouncing, and you can drive across the rails, if you can find a place to do it, without pitching. It's the smoothest thing you ever rode in.
A FORD SALESMAN, quoted in *Flappers, Bootleggers, and "Typhoid Mary"*

The automobile became the backbone of the American economy in the 1920s (and remained such until the 1970s). The automobile profoundly altered the American landscape and American society, but it was only one of several factors in the country's business boom of the 1920s.

The Model A was a more luxurious car than the Model T. It was introduced at $495, while the Model T had cost $290.

America's Standard of Living Soars

The new president, Calvin Coolidge, fit into the pro-business spirit of the 1920s very well. It was he who said, "The chief business of America is business . . . . The man who builds a factory builds a temple—the man who works there worships there." Both Coolidge and his successor, Republican Herbert Hoover, favored government policies that sought to keep taxes down and business profits up. Their goal was to keep government interference in business to a minimum and allow private enterprise to flourish. For most of the 1920s, the approach seemed to work, as the years from 1920 to 1929 were prosperous ones for the United States. Americans owned around 40 percent of the world's wealth, and that wealth changed the way most Americans lived, worked, and consumed.

Skillbuilder Answer The sharp rise of automobile ownership in the 1920s indicates a strong economy, the levelling off of automobile ownership in the 1930s indicates a weakening economy.

THE IMPACT OF THE AUTOMOBILE The automobile literally changed the American landscape. Its most visible effect was the construction of paved roads suitable for year-round driving in all weather. Architectural styles changed, as new houses typically came equipped with a garage or carport and a driveway—and smaller lawns as a

Automobile Registrations, 1900–1990

Registrations (in millions)
150
120
90
60
30
0
1900 1910 1920 1930 1940 1950 1960 1970 1980 1990

Source: *Historical Statistics of the United States: Colonial Times to 1970; Statistical Abstract of the United States, 1975, 1994, 1995; The American Automobile Association.*

SKILLBUILDER INTERPRETING CHARTS *Car ownership often reflects the strength of the economy. What do you think was the strength of the economy during the 1920s? the 1930s?*

Politics of the Roaring Twenties **601**

SECTION 3 RESOURCES

PRINT RESOURCES

IN-DEPTH RESOURCES: UNIT 6
Guided Reading, p. 3
Geography Application: The Automobile Industry, p. 5
Primary Source: Advertisement, p. 10
American Lives: Henry Ford, p. 15

ACCESS FOR STUDENTS ACQUIRING ENGLISH
Guided Reading (Spanish), p. 200
Geography Application: The Automobile Industry (Spanish), pp. 202–203

FORMAL ASSESSMENT
Section Quiz, p. 248

ALTERNATIVE ASSESSMENT BOOK
See forms for supporting and scoring alternative activities.

TECHNOLOGY RESOURCES

CRITICAL THINKING TRANSPARENCIES
CT54, Consumer Spending Power

CD-ROM *Our Times*
Electronic Library of Primary Sources

VIDEO *American Portfolio: A Videodisc for U.S. History*
user's guide, pp. 193, 198–199

INTERNET McDougal Littell Learning On-Line
http://www.mcdougallittell.com

Section 3 Overview

OBJECTIVES

(1) To summarize the impact of the automobile and other consumer goods on Americans' lifestyle.

(2) To explain in what ways the country's prosperity was superficial.

SKILLBUILDERS

• Interpreting charts, p. 601
• Understanding geography, place, p. 602
• Interpreting cartoons, p 604

CRITICAL THINKING

• Recognizing effects, pp. 602, 603
• Analyzing issues, p. 605
• Summarizing, p. 605
• Interpreting, p. 605
• Drawing conclusions, p. 605

FOCUS & MOTIVATE

▶ *Starting with the Student*
• What products make students' lives easier or help them save time? What products encourage them to waste time?

HISTORY FROM VISUALS
Automobile Registrations, 1900–1990
Reading the Chart Point out that car registrations in the chart are numbered in millions. Then ask students how many cars were registered in the United States in 1980. *About 120 million.*

Extension Discuss why automobile registration began to soar in the 1950s.

OBJECTIVE
(1) **INSTRUCT**

America's Standard of Living Soars

▶ *Discussing Key Ideas*
• The automobile affects American life.
• The airplane industry takes off.

(continued on next page)

Teacher's Edition **601**

(continued from page 601)

- Electricity and electrical conveniences become more widespread.
- Business relies on advertising to sell products.

IN-DEPTH RESOURCES: UNIT 6
Guided Reading, p. 3
Geography Application: The Automobile Industry, p. 5

ACCESS FOR STUDENTS ACQUIRING ENGLISH
Guided Reading (Spanish), p. 200

HISTORY FROM VISUALS
Route 66

Reading the Map Have students trace Route 66 with their pencil erasers, paying attention to the plains and mountains along the way. Then have students use the map to determine where the town of Claremore is located. *In Oklahoma.*

Extension Ask students to discuss how Route 66 and other highways affected the American landscape.

MORE ABOUT . . .
Will Rogers

Will Rogers was a popular American humorist of the 1920s and 1930s. He began his career as a cowboy and gained international fame as an author, lecturer, and star of motion pictures and radio. Known as the "Cowboy Philosopher," Rogers poked fun at the political and social figures of his day. He died in a plane crash in 1935. A memorial to Rogers in his Oklahoma hometown bears the statement for which he is most remembered: "I never met a man I didn't like."

ROUTE 66

1916 Federal-Aid Road Act sets up highway program with the federal government paying half the cost of states' highway construction.

1921 Highway construction in 11 western states set up under administration of Bureau of Public Roads.

1926 Work begins on U.S. Highway 66, which runs 2,448 miles from Chicago to Santa Monica, California.

Motorists could spend the night at a campsite or tourist park that provided cabins with running water, bathrooms, and a central kitchen.

Kansas Politicians divert 13.2 miles of Route 66 into the state's southeastern corner.

Claremore Hometown of humorist Will Rogers, who took a keen interest in the "Mother Road."

Oklahoma Routing of highway through 392 miles of state by the Oklahoman who headed the National Highways Association gives Oklahoma more miles, more jobs, and more income than other states on Route 66.

Roadside stands, which provide food, drink, and other items, appear in increasing numbers.

Gas for cars was plentiful in the 1920s.

GEOGRAPHY SKILLBUILDER
PLACE *What do you think were some of the reasons government officials decided to build Route 66 through the Southwest rather than straight west from Chicago?*

Skillbuilder Answer
Place: *Possible Answers:* With a Southwestern route, engineers did not have to build a road across the Rocky Mountains. Also, Route 66 would help open up the sparsely populated Southwest to the rest of the country and thus spur population growth and economic development.

result. The automobile also launched the furious construction of gasoline stations, repair shops, public garages, motels, tourist camps, and shopping centers. The first automatic traffic signals began blinking in Detroit in the early 1920s. The Holland Tunnel, the first underwater tunnel designed specifically for motor vehicles, opened in 1927 to connect New York City and Jersey City, New Jersey. The Woodbridge Cloverleaf, the first cloverleaf intersection, sprouted in New Jersey in 1928.

The automobile liberated the isolated rural family, who could now travel to the city for shopping and entertainment, and it gave families the opportunity to vacation in new and faraway places. It allowed both women and young people to become more independent through increased mobility. It allowed workers to live miles from their jobs, resulting in **urban sprawl** as cities spread in all directions.

The automobile industry also provided an economic underpinning for such cities as Akron in Ohio, and Detroit, Dearborn, Flint, and Pontiac in Michigan. The industry drew people to such oil-producing states as California and Texas.

The automobile even became a status symbol—both for individual families and to the world at large. As social scientists Robert and Helen Lynd noted in the 1920s in *Middletown*, one woman said, "I'll go without food before I'll see us give up the car." And another woman said, "We don't have no fancy clothes when we have the car to pay for."

The auto industry symbolized the success of the free enterprise system. Nowhere else in the world could people with little money own their own transportation and go wherever they wanted. By the late 1920s, around 80 percent of all registered motor vehicles in the world were in the United States—about one automobile for every five people in America. Comedian Will Rogers

A. Answer Many roads were paved; strip malls and shopping centers were built; lawns became smaller; the air became polluted; differences between regions lessened; many suburbs developed.

THINK THROUGH HISTORY
A. Recognizing Effects What were the effects of the automobile?

602 CHAPTER 20

TEACHING OPTION

Cooperative Activity: Creating a 1920s Automobile Newsletter

Task: Groups of four to five students will create a newsletter containing information about automobiles in the 1920s.

Purpose: To help students understand the impact of the automobile on the United States in the 1920s.

Activity: Students should decide what topics to include in their newsletter. Some topics might include highways, safety concerns, lifestyle changes, and new businesses. Groups

should research and write brief essays on each topic. Encourage students to include ads and pictures to add interest to the selections. Have groups print their newsletters and share them with the class.

📁 **Building a Portfolio:** Students may wish to print their favorite newsletter selections and add them to their portfolios.

ALTERNATIVE ASSESSMENT BOOK
Standards for Evaluating a Cooperative Activity

Standards for Evaluation
Newsletters should . . .

- contain well-researched information on a variety of topics
- include visuals that convey the excitement inspired by the automobile
- be clear, well organized, and engaging

remarked to Henry Ford, "It will take a hundred years to tell us whether you have helped us or hurt us, but you certainly didn't leave us like you found us."

THE YOUNG AIRPLANE INDUSTRY At the same time, the airplane industry began its growth by carrying mail for the government. Although the first such flight in 1918 was a disaster, soon after, a number of successful flights established the airplane as a useful peacetime means of transportation. With the development of weather forecasting, planes began carrying radios and navigational instruments. Henry Ford made a trimotor airplane in 1926. In 1927, the Lockheed Company produced a single-engine plane, the Vega. The Ford plane could carry ten passengers, and the Vega could carry six. They were two of the most popular transport airplanes of the late 1920s.

Flight attendants in training for an early United Airlines flight. When commercial airline flights began, all flight attendants were female.

ELECTRICAL CONVENIENCES

Gasoline powered much of the economic boom of the 1920s, but electricity also turned on the nation. American factories used electricity to run their machines. Also, the development of an alternating electrical current made it possible to distribute electric power by means of a transformer. Now electricity was no longer restricted to central cities but could be transmitted to outlying suburbs. The number of electrified households soared, although most farms still lacked power. Americans used all sorts of electrical appliances. Eunice Fuller Barnard listed some of them in a magazine article she wrote in 1928.

Goods and Prices in 1928		Goods and Prices in 1900	
1 radio	$75		
1 phonograph	50		
1 washing machine	150	wringer and washboard	$5
1 vacuum cleaner	50	brushes and brooms	5
1 sewing machine (electric)	60	sewing machine (mechanical)	25
other electrical equipment	25		
	$410		$35

By the end of the 1920s, even many working-class homes had electric irons, while well-to-do families used electric refrigerators, electric cooking ranges, and toasters. These electrical appliances made the lives of housewives easier, freed them for other community and leisure activities, and coincided with an increased percentage of women who worked outside the home.

The widespread use of electrical appliances, of store-bought clothes and foods, and mass cultural activities (miniature golf, marathon dancing, moviegoing, sports, and reading newspapers) resulted in a lifestyle that seemed more conformist than before. In Sinclair Lewis's famous 1922 novel, *Babbitt*, the title character describes Zenith, his fictional hometown.

I tell you, Zenith and her sister-cities are producing a new type of civilization. There are many resemblances between Zenith and these other burgs [cities], and I'm darn glad of it! The extraordinary, growing, and sane standardization of stores, offices, streets, hotels, clothes, and newspapers throughout the United States shows how strong and enduring a type is ours.

Babbitt by Sinclair Lewis

"I look forward to the day when transatlantic flying will be a regular thing."

CHARLES A. LINDBERGH

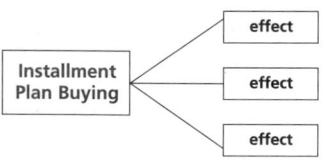
ANOTHER PERSPECTIVE

THE NEEDY

While income rose for many Americans in the 1920s, it did not rise for everyone. Industries such as textile and steel made very little profit. Mining and farming actually suffered considerable losses. Farmers were deeply in debt because they had borrowed much money to buy land and machinery to produce more crops during World War I. When European agriculture bounced back after the war, prices fell, and before long there were U.S. farm surpluses.

Many American farmers suffered because they could not make their loan and mortgage payments. As one South Dakota farmer, Emil Loriks, remarked, "Farm prices collapsed. . . . There's a saying: 'Depressions are farm led and farm fed.'" Many farmers lost their purchasing power, their equipment, and their farms.

THE DAWN OF MODERN ADVERTISING With new goods flooding the market, business relied increasingly on advertising to sell the products. Advertising people no longer limited themselves to informing the public about products and prices. Instead, they hired psychologists to study how to appeal to buyers. What colors were best for what size packages? What was the most effective way to take advantage of people's worship of youth, beauty, health, and wealth?

Results were impressive. The slogan "Say it with flowers" doubled florists' business between 1912 and 1924. "Reach for a Lucky instead of a sweet" lured weight-conscious Americans to cigarettes and away from candy. Some variation of "Even your best friend won't tell you" helped sell a great deal of mouthwash, deodorants, dandruff shampoos, and cures for athlete's foot. Brand names became familiar from coast to coast, and items that people had formerly considered luxuries now seemed necessities.

One of those necessities was Listerine mouthwash. A 1923 Listerine advertisement made it seem so. The ad aimed to convince readers that without Listerine a person ran the risk of having halitosis—bad breath. The results could be a disaster, as the advertisement clearly states—while revealing the 1920s attitude toward women.

American consumers in the 1920s could purchase the latest household electrical appliances, such as a refrigerator, for as little as a dollar down and a dollar a week.

> She was a beautiful girl and talented too. She had the advantage of education and better clothes than most girls of her set. She possessed that culture and poise that travel brings. Yet in the one pursuit that stands foremost in the mind of every girl and woman—marriage—she was a failure.
>
> Listerine Advertisement

Business people extended the advertising mentality into other areas of American lives. Every week, in cities and towns across the land, they met for lunch with fellow members of such service organizations as Rotary, Kiwanis, and the Lions. As one observer noted, they sang songs, raised money for various charities, and boosted the image of the businessman "as a builder, a doer of great things, yes, and a dreamer whose imagination was ever seeking out new ways of serving humanity." Many Americans idolized business during these prosperous times.

Skillbuilder Answer The Coolidge administration and big business got along very well together.

SKILLBUILDER INTERPRETING CARTOONS Calvin Coolidge plays a saxophone as big business dances the Charleston. What does this cartoon tell you about the Coolidge administration and big business?

A Superficial Prosperity

During the 1920s, most Americans believed that prosperity would go on forever. After all, wasn't the average factory worker producing 50 percent more at the end of the decade than at its start? Hadn't national income grown from $58 billion in 1921 to $83 billion in 1929? Weren't most major corporations making fortunes? Wasn't the stock market skyrocketing to new heights?

PRODUCING GREAT QUANTITIES OF GOODS As productivity increased, businesses expanded in size and attitude. There were numerous mergers of

---

companies that manufactured automobiles, steel, electrical equipment, and public utilities. Chain stores sprouted that sold groceries, drugs, shoes, and clothes. Five-and-dime stores like Woolworth's also spread rapidly. Banks invented branch banking. But as the number of businesses grew, so did the income gap between workers and managers. There were a number of other clouds in the blue sky of prosperity. The iron and railroad industries, among others, really weren't prosperous, and mining and farming concerns suffered losses.

BUYING MANY GOODS ON CREDIT In addition to advertising, industry provided another solution to the problem of luring consumers to purchase the mountain of goods produced each year: "easy credit, or a dollar down and a dollar forever." The **installment plan**, as it was then called, enabled people to buy goods over an extended period, without having to put down much money at the time of purchase. Banks provided the money at low interest rates, while advertisers pushed the idea with such slogans as "You furnish the girl, we'll furnish the home" and "Enjoy while you pay."

Some economists and business owners worried that installment buying might be getting out of hand and that it was really a sign of a rather careless and superficial prosperity. One business owner even wrote to President Coolidge and related a conversation he had overheard on a train.

A PERSONAL VOICE
"Have you an automobile yet?"
"No, I talked it over with John and he felt we could not afford one."
"Mr. Budge who lives in your town has one and they are not as well off as you are."
"Yes, I know. Their second installment came due, and they had no money to pay it."
"What did they do? Lose the car?"
"No, they got the money and paid the installment."
"How did they get the money?"
"They sold the cook-stove."
"How could they get along without a cook-stove?"
"They didn't. They bought another on the installment plan."
BUSINESS OWNER, quoted in *In the Time of Silent Cal*

Still, most Americans focused their attention on the present, with little concern for the future. What could possibly go wrong with the nation's economy? The decade of the 1920s had brought about many technological and economic changes. Life definitely seemed easier and more enjoyable for hundreds of thousands of Americans.

THINK THROUGH HISTORY
C. *Analyzing Issues* What were the advantages and disadvantages of buying on credit?

C. Answer Advantages: People could buy many goods over a period of time with little money down at low interest. **Disadvantages:** People easily went into too much debt without really thinking about it.

HISTORICAL
SPOTLIGHT

THE STANLEY STEAMER
In 1897, twin brothers Francis and Freeland Stanley went into the automobile business. Instead of gas, they used steam as their power source. The Stanley Steamer ran on any burnable fuel and was easy to start: all you had to do was light the boiler and wait for the water to get hot. The Steamer was also very fast: in 1906 it reached the unheard-of speed of 127.66 miles an hour. The country's first police car was a Stanley Steamer purchased by the Boston Police Department.
The Stanley brothers charged $2,000 for the Steamer and produced just 1,000 cars a year. They weren't interested in increasing volume or in improving the model. When the electric self-starter made the internal combustion engine efficient, Henry Ford began mass-producing cars. He sold them for under $500—and by the middle of the 1920s, the Stanley Steamer had disappeared from the country's roads.

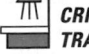

HISTORICAL
SPOTLIGHT
The Stanley Steamer

Critical Thinking: Analyzing Discuss why the Stanley Steamer was displaced by Ford's mass-produced cars. Then ask students what advantages the Steamer had over Ford's cars. *Possible Responses: The Steamer did not pollute the air; Its high price would limit the number of vehicles on the road.*

ASSESS & RETEACH

Section 3 Assessment
After students have answered the questions, discuss item 4 in class.

Self-Assessment
To document what students have learned, have them create a cluster diagram listing five characteristics of American business in the 1920s.

Section Quiz

FORMAL ASSESSMENT
Section Quiz, p. 248

Reteach
Use the cartoon on page 604 to review the role of business and consumer goods in the 1920s.

CLOSE

Automobiles, electrical appliances, and other consumer goods flooded the market as America's standard of living soared in the 1920s. Although not everyone took part in the general prosperity, many Americans embraced the present and enjoyed life.

CRITICAL THINKING TRANSPARENCIES
CT54, Consumer Spending Power

Section **3** Assessment

1. TERMS & NAMES
Identify:
• urban sprawl
• installment plan

2. SUMMARIZING Recreate the web below on your paper and fill it in with events that illustrate the center idea.

Technology & Business Changes of the 1920s

Choose one event from the web and explain its significance in the 1920s.

3. INTERPRETING Do you agree with President Coolidge's statement "The man who builds a factory builds a temple—the man who works there worships there"? Explain your answer.

THINK ABOUT
• the goals of business and of religion
• the American idolization of business
• the difference between workers and management

4. DRAWING CONCLUSIONS Do you think the changes in the 1920s gave Americans more control over their lives? Explain.

THINK ABOUT
• the impact of new technology
• the influence of advertising
• the results of installment buying

Politics of the Roaring Twenties **605**

ANSWERS

1. TERMS & NAMES
urban sprawl, p. 602
installment plan, p. 605

2. SUMMARIZING
Possible Answers:
Development of the automobile industry; expansion of the airline industry; invention of new electrical appliances; spread of modern advertising; use of the installment plan.

3. INTERPRETING
Possible Responses: Students may agree with Coolidge that a business and a religion both serve important needs. They might disagree with him and argue that a business is organized for the financial gain of its owners while a religious institution serves the spiritual needs of its members. They might also point out that while business owners in the 1920s profited, most workers did not.

4. DRAWING CONCLUSIONS
Possible Responses: Students might emphasize different issues. While automobiles gave people more mobility and appliances gave people more free time, advertising lured them to buy more, and the use of the installment plan encouraged them to go into debt.

Consumer Spending

Ask people what one of their favorite activities is in the United States, and many will answer "shopping." Shopping has become one of America's favorite leisure activities. It was during the 1920s, when people had a little extra money and a little more free time in which to spend it, that the consumer economy really began to flourish. As more products became available, companies faced increasing competition, so they hired advertising firms to create ads appealing to people's desire for status, comfort, luxury, and style. Today, the story continues. For many people, "Shop 'til you drop!" has become much more than just a T-shirt slogan.

1800s
VARIETY STORES

Mid-1800s: General Stores
At a general store, such as the one at the right, one could purchase almost anything, from dry goods (cloth and clothing), crockery, silverware, pots and pans, and small farming equipment, to medicines and ointments.

Department Stores
Department stores were larger than general stores and carried a wider variety and a greater supply of goods. They organized their merchandise in separate departments, such as home furnishings and women's clothing.

Chain Stores In the mid-1800s, chain stores—retail stores under the same ownership and dealing in the same merchandise—spread across the nation. The Great Atlantic & Pacific Tea Company carried groceries. The F. W. Woolworth's Five and Ten Cent chain sold numerous items at very reasonable prices.

1870s: Mail-Order Catalogs During the 1870s, Montgomery Ward and Sears, Roebuck and Company began to produce and distribute mail-order catalogs displaying an enormous array of products that consumers could order through the mail and have delivered directly to their door. Using this new method, people purchased anything from a pair of trousers to a bed to farm tools.

**1922
MONTGOMERY WARD
CATALOGUE**
1871 GOLDEN JUBILEE 1922

MONTGOMERY WARD & CO.

606 CHAPTER 20

1920s
MORE PRODUCTS; MORE STORES

The 1920s saw an enormous increase in the number and kind of goods available. Automobiles were the biggest item, but there were also many small electrical appliances, such as vacuum cleaners and radios. Drugstores like the one shown above stocked not only medicines and grooming supplies but many kinds of other items, including electrical appliances.

It also had a soda fountain, where one could sit and enjoy a cup of coffee for 10 cents, a lemon phosphate for 5 cents, or a slice of cake for 5 cents.

RECOMMENDED RESOURCES

Books

Hendrickson, Robert. *The Grand Emporiums.* New York: Stein, 1979. An illustrated history of America's great department stores.

Kowinski, William Severini. *The Malling of America.* New York: Morrow, 1985. An inside look at the consumerism of the 1980s.

Roberts, Bruce. *American Country Stores.* Chester, Conn: Globe, 1991. A photographic history.

Sears, Roebuck & Company. *1897 Sears Roebuck Catalogue.* New York: Chelsea, 1976. A period piece reissued.

Wendt, Lloyd. *Give the Lady What She Wants!* Chicago: Rand, 1952. The story of Marshall Field & Company.

Videos

Mr. Sears' Catalogue. PBS Video, 1989. A look at the Sears catalog and its significance in rural America.

Supermarket Savvy. Family Experiences Productions, 1987. Guidance in modern shopping.

Software

Consumer Shopping. Education Associates. Orients users about where to shop and how to shop wisely.

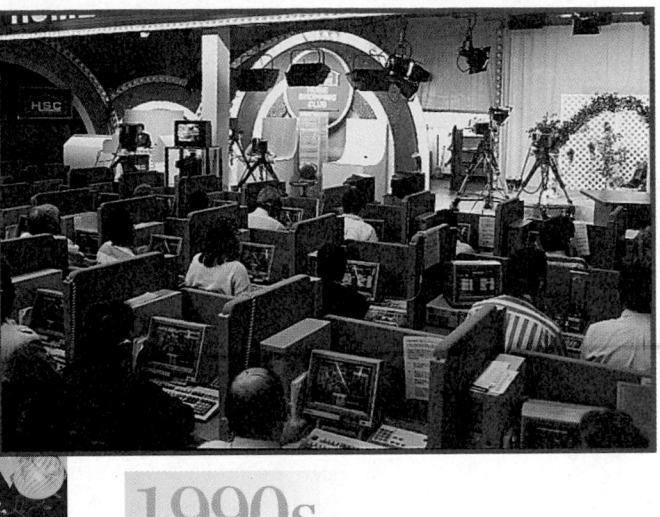

1990s
TV SHOPPING NETWORKS

Cable television ushered in home shopping networks. Consumers can shop from home and pay with a credit card for any item they purchase that is being modeled or demonstrated on TV.

1940s
SHOPPING CENTERS

The growth of suburbs resulted in many shopping centers, which consist of a large group of stores with one or more parking lots. Sometimes the stores are arranged around an area for pedestrians, open or enclosed, known as a mall. Shopping centers usually had dozens of specialty stores that sold just one kind of merchandise, such as home appliances, as pictured here. They also often had one or more department stores. Although the first shopping center reportedly opened in Baltimore, Maryland, in 1896, such centers did not become widely popular until 1945.

INTERACT WITH HISTORY

1. **COMPARING** Weigh the pros and cons of each method of shopping available to consumers over the last 150 years. Which method do you imagine might be used in the future? Why do you think so?

   SEE SKILLBUILDER HANDBOOK, PAGE 1041.

2. **WINDOW SHOPPING ON THE INTERNET** Browse the Internet to investigate the kinds of things that are available. How could one purchase these goods? How would one pay for them? What is the value of shopping on the Internet? What are the dangers? In what ways is this kind of shopping different from and similar to the other ways of shopping, both in the past and today? Report your findings to the class.

    For more about Internet commerce, click on **Social Studies** at http://www.mcdougallittell.com

Politics of the Roaring Twenties **607**

REVIEWING THE CHAPTER

TERMS & NAMES

1. A. Mitchell Palmer, p. 591
2. Sacco and Vanzetti, p. 592
3. Calvin Coolidge, p. 594
4. John L. Lewis, p. 595
5. Warren G. Harding, p. 596
6. Kellogg-Briand Pact, p. 597
7. isolationist, p. 597
8. quota system, p. 599
9. Teapot Dome scandal, p. 600
10. installment plan, p. 605

MAIN IDEAS

11. About 70,000 Americans joined the Communist Party, which indirectly led to the Red Scare.

12. All three events reflected fear of immigrants and radical movements.

13. Boston police who went on strike were fired; security forces killed 18 striking steelworkers; the government ordered an end to the coal miners' strike.

14. Harding wanted to get America back to the simpler days before the Progressive Era reforms.

15. The naval conference to lessen nations' dependence on armaments; U.S. efforts to get nations to sign the Kellogg-Briand Pact; the Fordney-McCumber Tariff; U.S. efforts to solve the reparations problem; the policy to limit immigration.

16. The system reduced immigration from eastern and southern Europe, and excluded the Japanese.

17. The scandal was about corruption in the leasing of government oil reserves to private companies; one cabinet member received bonds, cash, and ranches in exchange for oil contracts.

18. The automobile prompted the building of new roads, gave people more mobility, and created jobs; airplanes improved transportation and communication; electrical appliances freed up time for other activities.

19. Advertisers hired psychologists to study how to appeal to buyers; brand names became familiar; slogans popularized items; businesspeople used service organizations to boost their own image.

20. The income gap between workers and managers was growing; some industries were stagnant or losing money; people were increasing their debt.

REVIEWING THE CHAPTER

TERMS & NAMES For each term below, write a sentence explaining its connection to the decade following World War I. For each person below, explain his role in the events of the period.

1. A. Mitchell Palmer	6. Kellogg-Briand Pact
2. Sacco and Vanzetti	7. isolationist
3. Calvin Coolidge	8. quota system
4. John L. Lewis	9. Teapot Dome scandal
5. Warren G. Harding	10. installment plan

MAIN IDEAS

SECTION 1 *(pages 590–595)*

Americans Struggle with Postwar Issues

11. What impact did the Russian Revolution have on the United States?

12. Explain how the Red Scare, the Sacco and Vanzetti case, and the rise of the Ku Klux Klan reflected concerns held by many Americans.

13. What evidence suggests that strikes were a risky activity for workers during the 1920s?

SECTION 2 *(pages 596–600)*

"Normalcy" and Isolationism

14. What did Harding want to do to return America to "normalcy"?

15. What evidence shows that the United States was interested in an isolationist foreign policy?

16. Describe the primary goal of the immigration quota system established in 1921 and amended in 1924.

17. Summarize the Teapot Dome scandal.

SECTION 3 *(pages 601–605)*

The Business of America

18. How did changes in technology in the 1920s influence American life?

19. Describe the new methods used by advertisers beginning in the 1920s.

20. What evidence suggests that the prosperity of the 1920s was not on a firm foundation?

THINKING CRITICALLY

1. **RETURN TO "NORMALCY"** Create a cause-and-effect web, similar to the one shown, in which you give several causes for the declining power of labor unions in the 1920s and give examples of the unions' decline.

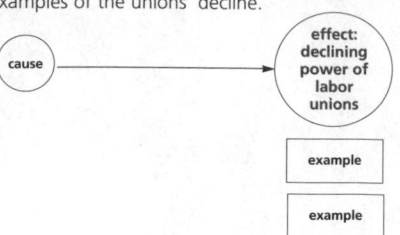

2. **COMPARING CONCERNS** Do you think Americans today are as worried about immigration and radical movements as they were in the 1920s? Explain why or why not.

3. **THE ROLE OF BUSINESS** Reread the quote by Calvin Coolidge on page 588. How did events and trends in the 1920s reflect the quotation?

4. **GEOGRAPHY OF ROUTE 66** Look at the path of Route 66 on the map on page 602. What factors may have influenced where and why the highway was built? Explain your answer.

5. **INTERPRETING ECONOMIC OPPORTUNITY** Compare and contrast the types of shopping and goods described in the Tracing Themes feature on pages 606–607. What characteristics of American culture are evident in this feature? Give examples to support your opinion.

6. **ANALYZING PRIMARY SOURCES** William Ashdown, a banker in a small town, considered himself a careful and thrifty man. In 1925, he wrote a magazine article describing how the purchase of a car changed his life.

> Having a quick method of locomotion, it was easy to run out into the country on a Sunday for dinner, or on an evening for a drive and a "bite." Then, too, my friends expected me to do the honors, as chauffeur and host, and this added to the mounting costs. But I had started something that I could not stop gracefully or consistently. My thrift habits were steadily giving way to spendthrift habits.
>
> After eight years of experience I find that the psychological processes of car-owners are much alike. First you want a car; then you conclude to buy it. Once bought, you must keep it running. . . . Therefore you spend and keep on spending. . . . The result upon the individual is to break down his sense of values. . . . Whether he will or no, he must spend money at every turn.
>
> **WILLIAM ASHDOWN,** quoted in *The Twenties: Fords, Flappers, and Fanatics*

Do you agree with Ashdown that automobile ownership—and materialism in general—contributes to spending and undermines values? Explain why or why not.

THINKING CRITICALLY

1. RETURN TO "NORMALCY"

Possible Responses: Cause—Association of unions with radicalism; difficulty organizing immigrants who tolerated poor working conditions and spoke other languages. Examples—New membership declines; strikers are fired in Boston; troops prevent picketing; public perception of unions turns negative.

2. COMPARING CONCERNS

Possible Responses: Students answering no might mention that concerns about a Communist revolution in the United States no longer exist. Students answering yes might point to the spread of antigovernment militia groups and of legislation to discourage any government help for illegal immigrants.

3. THE ROLE OF BUSINESS

Possible Responses: America's standard of living went up during the 1920s; 80 percent of all registered motor vehicles were in the United States; the number of electrified households and the use of electrical appliances in the United States greatly increased; advertising grew; credit increased demand for American goods.

ALTERNATIVE ASSESSMENT

1. GRAPHING STATISTICS

How were American lives changed by the social, political, and economic events of the 1920s? Many statistics exist that show major changes caused by the events of the 1920s. Create a graphic—a pie chart, a bar or line graph, a circle graph—that illustrates through statistics one aspect of these changes.

CD-ROM Use the CD-ROM *Our Times,* the Internet, your textbook, and other sources to gather statistics about changes in income, prices, employment levels, divorce rate, or other areas in which figures show how drastically people were affected by the events of the 1920s.

- Arrange the statistics in a graph to show their impact. Clearly label the sides or parts of the graph to explain what exactly is being shown.

- Research and find statistics that show the identical information for today. Create another graph similar to the 1920s graph and show how today's statistics compare with those of the 1920s.

2. COMPARING TO TODAY

During the 1920s, many Americans wanted to withdraw from international affairs. Yet the United States had the most powerful economy in the world, linked to other countries by investment and trade ties. Compare and contrast U.S. involvement in foreign trade in the 1920s with U.S. involvement today. Write a summary of the information you find. Some of the issues you might investigate for your comparison include:

- products imported and exported
- amount of American dollars involved in foreign trade
- extent of American investments in other countries
- the significance of foreign trade in the American economy

3. PORTFOLIO PROJECT

Use the Living History activity to expand your portfolio.

LIVING HISTORY

PRESENTING YOUR EXHIBIT

Working in small groups, make a model of your floor plans. Then, as a group, evaluate the success of each potential exhibit, using the following points as a guideline:

- Does the exhibit present important facts and details?
- Is the exhibit interesting and entertaining?
- Is the floor plan clearly and thoughtfully arranged?

Save your exhibit descriptions and floor plan in your American history portfolio.

Bridge to Chapter 21

Review Chapter 20

In the years following the end of World War I, Americans felt frightened by the Communist victory in the 1917 Russian Revolution. Signs of fear were widespread. Federal agents jailed or deported radicals. Two anarchists who immigrated from Italy, Nicola Sacco and Bartolomeo Vanzetti, were executed for murder despite the weakness of the evidence against them. Labor unions lost several key strikes, as well as membership. The Ku Klux Klan reemerged and grew steadily until outrageous acts by Klan members led to its decline.

In politics, voters expressed their desire to return to the "normalcy" of pre–World War I society. In 1920, they elected Republican Warren G. Harding in a landslide.

REJECTING GLOBAL CONCERNS Under Harding and his vice-president and successor, Calvin Coolidge, the United States tried to isolate itself from world affairs even as it promoted disarmament. The country refused involvement in international efforts to maintain peace, passed high tariffs that reduced international trade, and limited immigration from eastern and southern Europe and Japan.

CORRUPTION AND PROSPERITY For many Americans, the 1920s was an era of prosperity. A few attempted to gain wealth illegally, including Harding's secretary of the interior, who accepted bribes in the Teapot Dome scandal. Most people, though, prospered as the economy grew. Many found work building, selling, and servicing automobiles and the new electrical appliances that were revolutionizing everyday life. Consumers fueled economic growth by responding to new forms of advertising and to the installment plan with increased spending. The country seemed headed for ever-increasing wealth.

Preview Chapter 21

Changes in politics and in the economy during the 1920s contributed to a variety of cultural developments. Heated debates over religion, dramatic shifts in the roles of women and African Americans, and the rapid expansion of the entertainment industry made the 1920s a period of tension and debate. You will learn about these significant developments in the next chapter.

Politics of the Roaring Twenties **609**

---

1. GRAPHING STATISTICS
Standards for Evaluation
A graph should meet the following criteria:

- Presents statistics in a readable, accessible form.
- Clearly labels headings, parts, or grids.
- Uses statistics in an area that illustrates how people were affected by the events of the 1920s.
- Includes another, similar graph that compares today's statistics in the same field with those of the 1920s.

2. COMPARING TO TODAY
Standards for Evaluation
A summary should meet the following criteria:

- Compares the products imported and exported in both periods.
- Discusses the volume of trade carried out in both periods.
- Explains why foreign trade is an important part of the American economy.
- Draws conclusions about lessons the country has learned about foreign trade over the years.

3. PORTFOLIO PROJECT
LIVING HISTORY
Standards for Evaluation
A model should meet the following criteria:

- Is arranged thoughtfully and logically.
- Provides important information on the topic.
- Presents information in an entertaining and visually exciting manner.
- Engages and informs the audience.

IN-DEPTH RESOURCES: UNIT 6
See the form for scoring this activity on page 17.

THINKING CRITICALLY

4. GEOGRAPHY OF ROUTE 66

Possible Responses: The road was built through the Southwest so it didn't have to go through the Rocky Mountains; the road was meant to promote vacation travel and regional growth.

5. INTERPRETING ECONOMIC OPPORTUNITY

Possible Responses: Americans have always loved to shop. The American economy is dependent on consumer spending; businesses have tried to make shopping easier—through mail order, malls, computer networks, chain stores—to encourage more spending; if shopping is made a cultural experience as it is in America, consumerism becomes entrenched in society. This is clearly seen in Americans' purchase of ready-to-wear clothing and ready-to-eat foods, of ready-to-assemble housing, and many other goods.

6. ANALYZING PRIMARY SOURCES

Possible Responses: Students who agree may cite Americans' infatuation with buying and how it causes people to seek happiness in material things; how the overuse of automobiles has caused pollution; how materialism causes us to admire people for what they have, not who they are. Others may emphasize that individuals determine their own values and that merely buying things need not alter these values.

PLANNING GUIDE
The Roaring Life of the 1920s

	Key Ideas	**TEACHING SUPPORT**	**ASSESSMENT**
SECTION 1 **Changing Ways of Life** *pp. 612–617*	*Americans experience cultural conflicts as customs and values change in the United States during the 1920s.*	**In-Depth Resources: Unit 6** • Guided Reading, p. 18 • Primary Sources: Political Cartoon, p. 25; *from the Scopes Trial, p. 26* • Literature: *from Inherit the Wind* by Jerome Laurence and Robert E. Lee, p. 29 **COOPERATIVE ACTIVITY** • Creating a Dictionary of 1920s Slang, p. 615 (TE)	*Section 1 Assessment,* p. 617 (PE) *Self-Assessment,* p. 617 (TE) *Formal Assessment* • Section Quiz, p. 257 *Alternative Assessment Book* • Standards for Evaluating a Cooperative Activity
SECTION 2 **The Twenties Woman** *pp. 618–621*	*The American woman of the 1920s pursues new lifestyles and assumes new jobs and different roles in society.*	**In-Depth Resources: Unit 6** • Guided Reading, p. 19 **COOPERATIVE ACTIVITY** • Analyzing Changes in Women's Roles, p. 620 (TE)	*Section 2 Assessment,* p. 621 (PE) *Self-Assessment,* p. 621 (TE) *Formal Assessment* • Section Quiz, p. 258 *Alternative Assessment Book* • Standards for Evaluating a Cooperative Activity
SECTION 3 **Education and Popular Culture** *pp. 624–629*	*The mass media, movies, and spectator sports play important roles in the popular culture of the 1920s.*	**In-Depth Resources: Unit 6** • Guided Reading, p. 20 • Skillbuilder Practice: Drawing Conclusions, p. 22 • Geography Application: From Coast to Coast, p. 23 • Primary Source: *from an Interview with Charles A. Lindbergh, p. 27* • American Lives: Georgia O'Keeffe, p. 32 **COOPERATIVE ACTIVITY** • Presenting Art, p. 628 (TE)	*Section 3 Assessment,* p. 629 (PE) *Self-Assessment,* p. 629 (TE) *Formal Assessment* • Section Quiz, p. 259 *Alternative Assessment Book* • Standards for Evaluating a Cooperative Activity
SECTION 4 **The Harlem Renaissance** *pp. 630–635*	*African-American ideas, politics, art, literature, and music flourish in Harlem and elsewhere in the United States.*	**In-Depth Resources: Unit 6** • Guided Reading, p. 21 • Primary Source: *from "When the Negro Was in Vogue" by Langston Hughes, p. 28* • American Lives: Louis Armstrong, p. 33 **COOPERATIVE ACTIVITY** • Celebrating African-American culture, p. 633 (TE)	*Section 4 Assessment,* p. 635 (PE) *Self-Assessment,* p. 635 (TE) *Formal Assessment* • Section Quiz, p. 260 *Alternative Assessment Book* • Standards for Evaluating a Cooperative Activity
CHAPTER RESOURCES	**Chapter Overview** *During the 1920s, rural America clashes with a faster-paced urban culture. Women's attitudes and roles change, influenced in part by the mass media. Many African Americans join in the new urban culture.*	**In-Depth Resources: Unit 6** • Living History Project: Worksheet, p. 34; Standards, p. 35 *Telescoping the Times* • Chapter Summary, pp. 41–42 *Planning for Block Schedules*	*Chapter Assessment,* pp. 638–639 (PE) *Alternative Assessment,* p. 639 (PE) *Formal Assessment* • Chapter Test, forms A and B, pp. 261–266 Test Generator *Alternative Assessment Book* See explanation and forms for different kinds of alternative assessments including portfolio assessment.

Geography Transparencies
• G21, Prohibition: 1890 and 1915

Critical Thinking Transparencies
• CT21, Prohibition

 Our Times
• Scopes Trial

Electronic Library of Primary Sources
• from "My Bootlegger" by Samuel H. Adams

INTERNET RESOURCES
• See *McDougal Littell Learning On-Line* for links to information about Al Capone and Speakeasies.

 Electronic Library of Primary Sources
• from "Flapper Jane" by Bruce Bliven

INTERNET RESOURCES
• See Interact with History p. 623 (PE) for an activity that includes the Internet as an enrichment option.

 Humanities Transparencies
• H20, *Automat* by Edward Hopper

 Our Times
• Charles Lindbergh, Sinclair Lewis, and F. Scott Fitzgerald

Electronic Library of Primary Sources
• "The Sultan of Swat" by Heywood Broun

INTERNET RESOURCES
• See *McDougal Littell Learning On-Line* for links to information about Babe Ruth and F. Scott Fitzgerald

 Critical Thinking Transparencies
• CT55, African-American Migration

 Grolier Multimedia Encyclopedia
• African-American Literature

 Our Times
• Louis Armstrong

 AMERICAN STORIES VIDEO SERIES
• "Jump at the Sun"

INTERNET RESOURCES
• See Interact with History P. 637 (PE) for an activity that includes the Internet as an enrichment option.

 American Portfolio: A Videodisc for U.S.History, user's guide, pp. 192, 195–200

INTERNET RESOURCES
Learning On-Line: Social Studies
http://www.mcdougallittell.com

Block Scheduling (90 MINUTES)

Day 1
Section 1, pp. 612–617
Section 2, pp. 618–621
Section Assessments, pp. 617, 621

Day 2
Section 3, pp. 624–629
Section 4, pp. 630–635
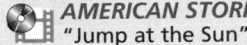 **AMERICAN STORIES VIDEO SERIES**
"Jump at the Sun"

Chapter Assessment, pp. 638–639

YEARLY PACING *Chapter 21 Total:* 2 days *Yearly Total:* 85 days

See *Planning for Block Schedules* for special activities and pacing strategies.

Customizing for Special Populations

Students Acquiring English

Access for Students Acquiring English
• Guided Reading for Sections 1–4 (Spanish), pp. 206–209
• Chapter Summary (Spanish), pp. 213–214
• Skillbuilder Practice: Drawing Conclusions, p. 210
• Geography Application: From Coast to Coast, p. 211

 AMERICAN STORIES VIDEO SERIES
• "Jump at the Sun" (Spanish track)

INTERNET RESOURCES
• See *McDougal Littell Learning On-Line* The Diverse Classroom.

Less Proficient Readers

In-Depth Resources: Unit 6
• Guided Reading for Sections 1–4, pp. 18–21
• Skillbuilder: Drawing Conclusions, p. 22
• Geography Application: From Coast to Coast, p. 23

Telescoping the Times
• Chapter Summary, pp. 41–42

See additional strategies at point of use in the Teacher's Edition.

Gifted and Talented Students

In-Depth Resources: Unit 6
• Primary Sources: Political Cartoon, p. 25; *from* The Scopes Trial, p. 26; *from* an Interview with Charles A. Lindbergh, p. 27; *from* "When the Negro Was in Vogue" by Langston Hughes, p. 28
• American Lives: Georgia O'Keeffe, p. 32; Louis Armstrong, p. 33

See additional strategies at point of use in the Teacher's Edition.

Connections to Literature READINGS FOR STUDENTS

In-Depth Resources: Unit 6
• from *Inherit the Wind* by Jerome Laurence and Robert E. Lee, p. 29

McDougal Littell *The Language of Literature*
American Literature

• F. Scott Fitzgerald,
Winter Dreams, p. 680
• Langston Hughes, Alain Locke, Louis Armstrong, Carl Van Doren, Marcus Garvey,
Voices from the Times p. 763,
• Langston Hughes,
"*I, Too,*" p. 766; "*The Weary Blues,*" p. 766
• James Weldon Johnson,
"*My City,*" p. 772
• Countee Cullen,
"*Any Human to Another,*" p. 772
• Claude McKay,
"*If We Must Die,*" p. 777
• Arna Bontemps,
"*A Black Man Talks of Reaping,*" p. 777

• Zora Neale Hurston,
"*How It Feels to Be Colored Me,*" p. 782
• Alice Walker,
from *Zora Neale Hurston: A Cautionary Tale and a Partisan View,* p. 787
• Ernest Hemingway,
"*The End of Something,*" p. 827
• Dorothy Parker,
Here We Are, p. 835
• T. S. Eliot,
The Love Song of J. Alfred Prufrock, p. 845
• Richard Wright,
"*The Man Who Was Almost a Man,*" p. 853
• Thornton Wilder,
"*The Long Christmas Dinner,*" p. 866

OVERVIEW

The Roaring Life of the 1920s

▶ **Starting with the Student**
Ask students to share their impressions of the 1920s. What kinds of music, dances, and other entertainment do they associate with the 1920s? Refer to the opening quotation.

• What kinds of "wonderful nonsense" was Pegler referring to?
• What images does the phrase "Roaring Twenties" bring to mind?

PREVIEWING THE CHAPTER
• Note video in Section 4.
• Ask students if they recognize any of the names in the 1920s time line.
• Have students work in small groups to write predictions, based on the Chapter Opener, about changes and conflicts in American society during the 1920s.

MORE ABOUT . . .
Westbrook Pegler
From copy boy to Pulitzer Prize–winning columnist, Westbrook Pegler had a career that spanned 40 years. He served as a war correspondent during World War I and during the 1920s began writing a syndicated newspaper column on national affairs. Pegler was noted for his scathing attacks on just about everything.

CHAPTER **21**

The Roaring Life of the 1920s

SECTION 1
Changing Ways of Life
Americans experience cultural conflicts as customs and values change in the United States during the 1920s.

SECTION 2
The Twenties Woman
The American woman of the 1920s pursues new lifestyles and assumes new jobs and different roles in society.

SECTION 3
Education and Popular Culture
The mass media, movies, and spectator sports play important roles in the popular culture of the 1920s.

SECTION 4
The Harlem Renaissance
African-American ideas, politics, art, literature, and music flourish in Harlem and elsewhere in the United States.

▣ VIDEO *JUMP AT THE SUN*

"The Era of Wonderful Nonsense"

Westbrook Pegler

• Sinclair Lewis writes *Main Street.*

• The National Woman's Party celebrates the ratification of the Nineteenth Amendment.

• Pittsburgh radio station KDKA is the first to begin commercial broadcasting.

• Andrew Mellon is named secretary of the treasury.

• Louis Armstrong plays for King Oliver's Creole Jazz Band in Chicago.

• Harlem Renaissance begins.

• Publication of *Time* magazine begins.

• Supreme Court strikes down minimum wage law for women.

THE UNITED STATES				
1920	1921	1922	1923
THE WORLD	1921	1922	1923

• Pan-Africanism movement begins.

• Irish civil war begins.

• King Tut's tomb is discovered in Egypt.

• Kemal Ataturk begins modernization of Turkey.

610 CHAPTER 21

THEMES IN CHAPTER 21

Constitutional Concerns	*Women in America*	*Science and Technology*	*Migration and Immigration*
Federal enforcement of prohibition was inefficient, and some states stopped trying to enforce the Eighteenth Amendment. Disregard for the amendment convinced legislators to repeal it. See Teacher's Edition note, p. 614.	Women's role in society changed significantly in the 1920s. Young women, especially, became more assertive and independent in their quest for equality. The flapper reflected the changing image of women in America. See Teacher's Edition note, p. 619.	The first scheduled radio broadcast took place in 1920. By the end of the decade, more than 10 million American families had radios in their homes. The mass media revolutionized communication and created a shared national experience. See Teacher's Edition note, p. 625.	By the end of the 1920s, more than a third of all African Americans lived in cities. The migration to cities marked the beginning of a new era in African-American history. It also sparked a wave of violence in many northern cities. See Teacher's Edition note, p. 631.

MAKING A DISPLAY

Various social issues had tremendous impact on Americans in the 1920s. Many of these issues continue to challenge society today. As you read each section of this chapter, think about social issues from the 1920s that you think relate directly to issues of today. Create a now-and-then display that verbally and visually presents these parallel issues. Use the following categories to help you organize your ideas:

- the impact of technology
- the struggle for equal rights
- attempts to solve social problems
- attempts to accommodate the educational needs of diverse groups

PORTFOLIO PROJECT Keep your notes and your storyboard in a folder for your American history portfolio. At the end of the chapter, you will be asked to present your storyboard to others.

N-X-211
RYAN
NYP

- American swimmer Gertrude Ederle is the first woman to swim the English Channel.

- F. Scott Fitzgerald's *The Great Gatsby* is published.
- Scopes trial takes place in Tennessee.
- Physicist R. A. Millikan discovers cosmic rays in upper atmosphere.
- Alain Locke publishes *The New Negro.*

- Ernest Hemingway's *The Sun Also Rises* is published.

- Charles Lindbergh makes the first solo transatlantic flight.
- The first sound movie, *The Jazz Singer,* is released.
- Babe Ruth hits 60 home runs in one season.
- Duke Ellington's band opens at the Cotton Club.

- George Gershwin's *An American in Paris* has its premiere in New York.
- ☆ Herbert Hoover is elected president.

- William Faulkner's *The Sound and the Fury* is published.

1924   1925   1926   1927   1928   **1929**

1927

- Greece is proclaimed a republic.
- Adolph Hitler publishes *Mein Kampf.*
- Ibn Saud becomes king of Saudi Arabia.
- Leon Trotsky is expelled from the Soviet Union's Communist Party.
- President Alvaro Obregón of Mexico is assassinated.

The Roaring Life of the 1920s **611**

ALTERNATIVE ASSESSMENT
LIVING HISTORY

MAKING A DISPLAY
Help students create their now-and-then displays.

- Students should make a list of questions the viewers of the now-and-then storyboard would want answered about parallel social issues of the 1920s and today.
- Taking into account students' artistic ability and interests, suggest ways in which they might present the social parallels visually on their storyboards. Color xeroxes, sketches, maps, charts, and graphs are some possibilities.
- Put on the chalkboard a chart of additional topics and ask students to suggest appropriate parallels between the 1920s and today.

Project Planning Guide

Topic:	Parallels:
Substance abuse	
Organized crime	
Religious fundamentalism	
Sports heroes	

IN-DEPTH RESOURCES: UNIT 6
See worksheet and standards for evaluation, pp. 34, 35.

RECOMMENDED RESOURCES

Books for the Teacher

Anderson, Jervis. *This Was Harlem.* New York: Farrar, 1982. Engaging social history covers Harlem Renaissance.

Clarke, John Henrik., ed. *Marcus Garvey and the Vision of Africa.* New York: Random, 1974. Garvey's words and those of others.

Lewis, Thomas. *Empire of the Air.* New York: Burlingame, 1991. Early radio.

Books for the Student

Huggins, Nathan Irvin., ed. *Voices from the Harlem Renaissance.* New York: Oxford UP, 1976. Readings.

This Fabulous Century: 1920–1930. New York: Time-Life, 1969.

Torrence, Bruce. *Hollywood, the First Hundred Years.* New York: New York Zoetrope, 1982. Rise of movie industry.

Videos

The Age of Ballyhoo. Dir. David Shepard. Republic Pictures Home Video, 1973. Society and culture.

Amelia Earhart. Dir. Nancy Porter. PBS Video, 1993. Documentary.

Lindbergh. Dir. Stephen Ives. PBS Video, 1990. Documentary about aviator's triumph and subsequent difficult life.

Midnight Ramble. Dir. Bestor Cram and Pearl Bowser. PBS Video, 1994. African-American film industry in 1920s.

Software

Cultural Contributions of Black Americans. CD-ROM. Available from Educational Software Institute, 800-955-5570.

History of Jazz. CD-ROM. CLEARVUE/eav, 800-253-2788.

① To explain how urbanization created a new way of life that often clashed with the values of the traditional American rural society.

② To describe the controversy over the role of science and religion in American education and society in the 1920s.

CRITICAL THINKING

- Contrasting, p. 613
- Analyzing causes, p. 614
- Recognizing effects, p. 615
- Analyzing issues, p. 617
- Summarizing, p. 617
- Analyzing, p. 617
- Forming opinions, p. 617

FOCUS & MOTIVATE

▶ **Starting with the Student**
- What differences do students think exist between urban and rural lifestyles today?
- How do differences in values cause conflict between groups in American society today?

MORE ABOUT . . .
Billy Sunday

William Ashley "Billy" Sunday was born in Ames, Iowa, in 1862. As a young man, Sunday played major-league baseball in Chicago, Pittsburgh, and Philadelphia. In 1903, after giving up his baseball career, he became a Presbyterian minister. Sunday's flamboyant style and promotional methods made him one of the most popular evangelists of the time. He reportedly preached to over 100 million people before his death in 1935.

---

① Changing Ways of Life

TERMS & NAMES
- speakeasy
- bootlegger
- fundamentalism
- Clarence Darrow
- Scopes trial

LEARN ABOUT life in the cities, Prohibition, and the outcome of the Scopes trial
TO UNDERSTAND how the Twenties reflected conflicts and tensions in American culture.

ONE AMERICAN'S STORY

As the 1920s dawned, social reformers who hoped to ban alcohol—and the evils associated with it—rejoiced. The Eighteenth Amendment to the Constitution, banning the manufacture, sale, or transportation of alcohol, took effect in January of 1920. Billy Sunday, an evangelist who preached against the evils of drinking, predicted a new age of virtue and religion.

A PERSONAL VOICE
The reign of tears is over! The slums will soon be only a memory. We will turn our prisons into factories and our jails into storehouses and corncribs. Men will walk upright now, women will smile and the children will laugh. Hell will be forever for rent!

BILLY SUNDAY, quoted in *How Dry We Were: Prohibition Revisited*

Sunday's dream of a new age of morality and sobriety was not to be realized in the 1920s. By the end of the decade, the effort to outlaw alcohol had failed because too many people disagreed with the law to make it enforceable. The failure of prohibition reflected the changing values that marked the period of the 1920s. These changes produced clashes between small-town residents and big-city dwellers, between native-born Americans who opposed the use of alcohol and immigrants who used alcohol as part of their daily lives, and between religious believers who thought science and religion were incompatible and others who thought the two could coexist.

These cultural conflicts became most evident in the nation's cities. Lured by jobs and by the challenge and freedom that the city represented, millions of people—including returning World War I soldiers, who had seen the great cities of Europe—rode excitedly out of America's rural past and into its urban future.

Evangelist Billy Sunday

Rural and Urban Differences

The agricultural world that millions of Americans left behind was largely unchanged from the 19th century—a world of small towns and farms bound together by conservative moral values and close social relationships. Established, well-to-do families set a community's social standards. The church defined morality, and parents enforced the church's teachings. Out of the hard lives of rural dwellers emerged the American middle-class values of thriftiness, moderation, and respectability. Before the widespread use of cars, small towns were self-contained places. The people on the streets were friends and neighbors, and county fairs and church socials provided entertainment.

But America changed dramatically in the years before 1920, as was revealed in the 1920 census. That year, the figures showed, 51.4 percent of Americans lived in communities with a population of 2,500 to more than 1 million. America had become a more urban nation. Between 1922 and 1929, migration to the cities accelerated, with nearly 2 million people leaving farms and towns each year. "Cities were the place to be, not to get away from," said

---

SECTION 1 RESOURCES

PRINT RESOURCES

IN-DEPTH RESOURCES: UNIT 6
Guided Reading, p. 18
Primary Sources: Political Cartoon, p. 25; *from* The Scopes Trial, p. 26
Literature: from *Inherit the Wind* by Jerome Lawrence and Robert E. Lee, p. 29

ACCESS FOR STUDENTS ACQUIRING ENGLISH
Guided Reading (Spanish), p. 206

FORMAL ASSESSMENT
Section Quiz, p. 257

ALTERNATIVE ASSESSMENT BOOK
See forms for supporting and scoring alternative activities.

TECHNOLOGY RESOURCES

GEOGRAPHY TRANSPARENCIES
G21, Prohibition: 1890 and 1915

CRITICAL THINKING TRANSPARENCIES
CT21, Prohibition

CD-ROM *Our Times*
Electronic Library of Primary Sources

VIDEO
American Portfolio: A Videodisc for U.S. History
user's guide, pp. 195–196

INTERNET McDougal Littell Learning On-Line
http://www.mcdougallittell.com

New York Street Scene (1920), Joaquín Torres-García.

one historian. Small-town attitudes began to lose their hold on the American mind as the city rose to prominence.

THE NEW URBAN SCENE At the beginning of the 1920s, New York, with a population of 5.6 million people, topped the list of big cities. Next came Chicago, with nearly 3 million, and after that, Philadelphia, with nearly 2 million. Another 65 cities claimed populations of 100,000 or more, and they grew more crowded by the day.

Life in these booming cities was far different from the slow-paced, intimate life in America's small towns. Chicago, for instance, was an industrial powerhouse, home to native-born whites, African Americans, and immigrant Poles, Irish, Russians, Italians, Swedes, Arabs, French, and Chinese. The city's skyline sparkled with 163 skyscrapers. Each day, an estimated 300,000 workers, 150,000 cars and buses, and 20,000 trolleys poured into the pulsing downtown. Speculators made fortunes on the stock market. At night, stylish Chicagoans crowded ornate vaudeville houses and theaters.

For small-town migrants, adapting to the urban environment demanded changes in thinking as well as in everyday living. The city was a world of competition and change. City dwellers took in new ideas at museums and art exhibits, plays and sports events, and nightclubs and movies. They read and argued about current scientific and social ideas. They judged one another by accomplishment more often than by background. City dwellers also tolerated drinking, gambling, and casual dating—worldly behaviors considered shocking and sinful in small towns.

For all its color and challenge, though, the city could be impersonal and frightening. Streets were filled with strangers, not friends and neighbors. Life was fast-paced, not leisurely. Social standards and values were hard to pin down in a world populated by brash businessmen, the mingling of foreign cultures, and the pursuit of wealth and pleasure. The city demanded endurance, as a foreign visitor to Chicago observed.

"How ya gonna keep 'em down on the farm, after they've seen Paree?"

POPULAR SONG
OF THE 1920s

A. Answer Small towns were bound by traditional morals and close ties between family, friends, and church or religion. Cities offered more perspectives and options because of large, mixed populations; cultural variety; and greater tolerance of worldly values and ideas.

THINK THROUGH HISTORY
A. Contrasting How did small-town life and city life differ?

A PERSONAL VOICE
It is not for nothing that the predominating color of Chicago is orange. It is as if the city, in its taxicabs, in its shop fronts, in the wrappings of its parcels, chose the color of flame that goes with the smoky black of its factories. It is not for nothing that it has repelled the geometric street arrangement of New York and substituted . . . great ways with names that a stranger must learn if he can. . . . He is in a [crowded] city, and if he has business there, he tells himself, "If I weaken I shan't last long."

WALTER L. GEORGE, *Hail Columbia!*

The Roaring Life of the 1920s **613**

Rural and Urban Differences

▶ *Starting with the Student*
Ask students to imagine themselves moving from a rural community to a large city or vice versa.

• How might their life change?
• How might they feel about their old friends? How might their friends feel about them?
• Do they think differences in lifestyles can cause conflicts between people? Why or why not?

▶ *Discussing Key Ideas*
• The growth of cities results in new urban lifestyles that conflict with traditional values.
• Supporters of prohibition clash with those who ignore the law.

IN-DEPTH RESOURCES: UNIT 6
Guided Reading, p. 18

ACCESS FOR STUDENTS ACQUIRING ENGLISH
Guided Reading (Spanish), p. 206

MORE ABOUT . . .
Walter L. George
A son of British parents, Walter L. George was born in Paris in 1882. He became a special correspondent to several European newspapers, and in 1920 he traveled extensively in the United States. *Hail Columbia!* reports his impressions of America. According to George, the "true America" was to be found in the Midwest.

TEACHING OPTIONS

Making Connections Across Cultures

Immigration Throughout the 1920s Congress passed legislation that restricted immigration. A quota system limited the number of immigrants that could be admitted from each country annually. This system severely decreased the numbers of immigrants arriving from eastern and southern Europe.

• What attitudes did these laws reflect? *Discrimination against certain ethnic groups.*
• Why would these laws have affected cities more than rural areas? *Most immigrants settled in cities.*

Making Connections Across the Curriculum

Literature As the 1920s dawned, many of America's best writers set out to record the powerful forces reshaping the nation, including the pull of the cities. Sherwood Anderson, for example, ended his famous novel *Winesburg, Ohio* with George Willard, the main character, leaving his provincial hometown for the big city—a "young man, going out of his town to meet the adventure of life." Throughout the 1920s millions of small-town men and women like George Willard streamed into New York, Los Angeles, and America's other booming cities.

Difficult Decisions
IN HISTORY

TO PROHIBIT ALCOHOL OR NOT?

The question of whether to outlaw alcohol divided Americans. Many reformers and religious groups thought drinking was sinful, unhealthy, and devastating to families. They believed the government should protect the public's health and morals by making alcohol illegal. Other Americans, including liberals, conservatives, intellectuals, and immigrant groups, did not believe alcohol consumption was sinful or dangerous in moderation. They believed that consuming alcohol was a personal, not a government, decision and resisted any group's trying to tell them how to live.

1. Examine the pros and cons of each position. Which do you agree with? What other factors, if any, do you think would influence your position?
2. If you were a legislator being asked to vote for the 18th Amendment, what would you say? Explain.
3. What issues might the experiment of prohibition relate to today? Should the government attempt to change people's moral behavior?

INTERNET For more information about Prohibition and its repeal, click on *Social Studies* at http://www.mcdougallittell.com

In the city, lonely migrants from the country often ached for home. Throughout the 1920s, Americans found themselves caught in the tug between the rural and urban cultures—cultures that were often stereotypically seen as the safe, small-town world of close ties, hard work, and strict morals versus the big-city world of anonymous crowds, moneymakers, and pleasure seekers.

THE PROHIBITION EXPERIMENT One vigorous clash between small-town and big-city Americans began in earnest in January 1920 when the 18th Amendment went into effect. This amendment, which prohibited the manufacture, sale, or transportation of alcoholic beverages, launched the era known as Prohibition.

Reformers had long considered liquor a prime cause of corruption. They thought that too much drinking led to crime, wife and child abuse, accidents on the job, and other serious social problems. The church-affiliated Anti-Saloon League had led the drive to pass the prohibition amendment. The Woman's Christian Temperance Union, which considered drinking a sin, had helped push the measure through. Even before the amendment was ratified, certain areas of the country had established prohibition through state law. Most support for prohibition came from the rural South and West, areas with large populations of native-born Protestants who opposed alcohol consumption.

At first, saloons closed their doors, and arrests for drunkenness declined. But the effort to stop Americans from drinking was as doomed as "trying to dry up the Atlantic with a post-office blotter," according to one New Yorker. In the aftermath of World War I, many Americans were tired of making sacrifices; they wanted to enjoy life. Most immigrant groups did not consider drinking a sin but a natural part of socializing, and they resented government meddling.

Ironically, prohibition's fate was sealed by the government, which failed to budget enough men and money to enforce the law. The Volstead Act established a Prohibition Bureau in the Treasury Department in 1919, but the agency was underfunded. The job of enforcement involved patrolling 18,700 miles of coastline as well as inland borders; tracking down illegal stills; monitoring highways for truckloads of illegal alcohol; and overseeing all the industries that legally used alcohol to be sure none was siphoned off for illegal purposes. The task fell to just 1,550 poorly paid federal agents and local police—clearly an impossible job.

SPEAKEASIES AND BOOTLEGGERS Drinkers went underground, flocking to hidden saloons and nightclubs called **speakeasies,** (so called because when inside, one spoke quietly— "easily"—to avoid detection) where liquor was sold illegally. Speakeasies could be found everywhere—in penthouses, cellars, office buildings, rooming houses, tenements, hardware stores, and tearooms. To be admitted to a speakeasy, one had to use a password, such as "Joe sent me," or present a special card. Inside, one would find a mix of fashionable middle-class and upper-middle-class men and women.

A young woman demonstrates one of the means used to conceal alcohol—hiding it in containers strapped to one's legs.

TEACHING OPTIONS

Before long, people grew bolder in circumventing the law. Hardware stores sold cheap stills, and books and magazines explained how to distill liquor from apples, from watermelon—even from potato peelings. Since alcohol was allowed for medicinal and religious purposes, prescriptions for alcohol and sales of sacramental wine (intended for church services) skyrocketed. People also bought liquor from **bootleggers** (named for a smuggler's practice of carrying liquor in the legs of boots), who smuggled it in from Canada, Cuba, and the West Indies. They sold the liquor from ships anchored in international waters off the Atlantic coast. Then they bribed policemen and judges to let them operate freely. "The business of evading [the law] and making a mock of it has ceased to wear any aspects of crime and has become a sort of national sport," wrote the journalist H. L. Mencken, and he was right. Americans bought liquor and hid it cleverly—in false books, in hot-water bottles, in high boots, in containers strapped to their legs.

ORGANIZED CRIME Prohibition not only generated disrespect for the law but had other harmful effects as well. Most serious was the flow of money out of lawful businesses and into fast-growing organized crime. In nearly every major city, underworld gangs seized the opportunity to make and sell liquor and pocket huge profits. Chicago became notorious as the home of Al Capone, a gangster whose bootlegging empire netted over $60 million a year. Capone took control of the Chicago liquor business by killing off his competition. During the 1920s, headlines reported 522 bloody gang killings and made the image of flashy Al Capone part of the folklore of the period. In 1940, the writer Herbert Asbury recalled the Capone era in Chicago.

A PERSONAL VOICE
The famous seven-ton armored car with the pudgy gangster lolling on silken cushions in its darkened recesses, a big cigar in his fat face, and a $50,000 diamond ring blazing from his left hand, was one of the sights of the city; the average tourist felt that his trip to Chicago was a failure unless it included a view of Capone out for a spin. The mere whisper: "Here comes Al," was sufficient to stop traffic and to set thousands of curious citizens craning their necks along the curbing.
HERBERT ASBURY, *Gem of the Prairies*

By the mid-1920s, only 19 percent of Americans supported prohibition. The rest, who wanted the amendment changed or repealed, pointed to a rise in crime and lawlessness that they considered worse than the problem prohibition had set out to fix. Rural Protestant Americans, however,

Al Capone built a criminal empire based on bootlegging.

HISTORICAL SPOTLIGHT

AL CAPONE

By age 28, Al Capone had built a criminal empire in Chicago, which he controlled through the use of bribes and violence. From 1925 to 1929, Capone bootlegged whiskey from Canada, operated illegal breweries in Chicago, and ran a network of 10,000 speakeasies. In 1927 alone, the "Big Fellow," as he liked to be called, made $105 million, writing himself into the *Guinness Book of World Records* as the private citizen who had made the most money in a single year.

The end came quickly for Capone, though. In 1931, the gangster chief was arrested for tax evasion and went to jail. That was the only crime the authorities were ever able to convict him of. Capone was later released from jail, but he died several years after at age 48.

Prohibition, 1920–1933	
SOME CAUSES	**SOME EFFECTS**
• Various religious groups thought drinking alcohol was sinful.	• There was disrespect for the law.
• Reformers believed government should protect the public's health.	• An increase in lawlessness, such as smuggling and bootlegging was evident.
• Reformers believed that alcohol led to crime, wife and child abuse, and accidents on the job.	• Criminals were supplied with a new source of enormous income.
• There was wartime hostility on the part of native-born Americans toward German-American brewers, as well as toward other immigrant groups that used alcohol.	• There was a growth of organized crime.

The Roaring Life of the 1920s **615**

Science and Religion Clash

▶ **Discussing Key Ideas**
- Fundamentalists believe that the biblical account of creation is true.
- Many liberal thinkers believe in the scientific theory of evolution.
- The opposing values clash in the Scopes trial, which questions the roles of science and religion in public schools.

IN-DEPTH RESOURCES: UNIT 6
Primary Source: *from* the Scopes Trial, p. 26

NOW & THEN
Evolution, Creationism, and Education

Critical Thinking:
Contrasting Have students make Venn diagrams to contrast evolutionist and creationist arguments. A diagram might look like the one below.

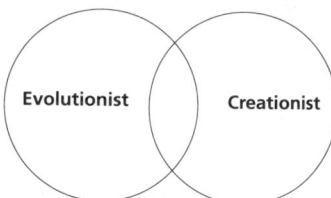

Then ask students what arguments, if any, might serve as support for both points of view. Have them write these arguments in the overlapping section of their diagrams.

Students might also find newspaper or magazine articles dealing with the teaching of evolution in public schools.

---

defended a law that they felt strengthened moral values. The 18th Amendment remained in force until 1933, when it was repealed by the 21st Amendment.

Science and Religion Clash

Another bitter controversy highlighted the growing rift between traditional and modern ideas during the 1920s. This battle raged between fundamentalist religious groups and secular thinkers over the truths of science.

AMERICAN FUNDAMENTALISM Fundamentalism was a Protestant movement grounded in a literal, or nonsymbolic, interpretation of the Bible. Since the late 19th century, many Protestants had gradually adapted to a changing society marked by a growing trust in science and by acceptance of religious faiths practiced by immigrants. Protestant fundamentalists resisted this trend. They were skeptical of scientific knowledge and argued that all the knowledge people needed was in the Bible. Fundamentalists believed that the Bible was inspired by God and that all the stories and details in the Bible were true.

Based on their beliefs, fundamentalists rejected the theory of evolution developed by Charles Darwin in the 19th century—a theory arguing that plant and animal species evolved over millions of years from lower forms of life. They pointed instead to the clear statement in the Bible that God created the world in six days and specially created Adam and Eve. To deny that truth, fundamentalists said, was to deny the Scriptures and to blaspheme God. As a result, they did not want evolutionary theory taught to their children.

Fundamentalism expressed itself in several ways. In the South and West, preachers led religious revivals based on the authority of the Scriptures. One of the most powerful revivalists was Billy Sunday, a baseball player turned preacher who staged emotional meetings across the South. In Los Angeles, Aimee Semple McPherson, a theatrical woman who dressed in flowing white satin robes, used Hollywood showmanship to preach the word to throngs of homesick Midwestern migrants. In the 1920s, fundamentalists also began to win political power and call for laws to outlaw the teaching of evolution. Moderate Protestants and liberal thinkers viewed this trend with deep concern.

THE SCOPES TRIAL Tensions finally flared up in little Dayton, Tennessee. In March 1925, Tennessee passed the nation's first law that made it a crime to teach evolution. Immediately, the American Civil Liberties Union (ACLU) promised to defend any teacher who would challenge the law. John T. Scopes, a thin, freckled 24-year-old biology teacher in Dayton, accepted the challenge. In his biology class, Scopes read this passage from *Civic Biology:* "We have now learned that animal forms may be arranged so as to begin with the simple one-celled forms and culminate with a group which includes man himself." Scopes was promptly arrested, and his trial was set for July.

The ACLU hired **Clarence Darrow**, the most famous trial lawyer of the day, to defend Scopes. William Jennings Bryan, three-time Democratic candidate for president and a devout fundamentalist, served as a special prosecutor. There was no real question of guilt or innocence: Scopes was honest about his action. The **Scopes trial** was a fight over evolution and the role of science and religion in public schools and in American society.

NOW & THEN

EVOLUTION, CREATIONISM, AND EDUCATION

There is still great controversy today over the teaching of evolution in the public schools. Some people believe that creationism should be taught as a theory of the origin of life, along with evolution. Creationism argues that the account of the creation of the universe given in Genesis—the first book of the Bible—is literally true.

The issue of what should be taught about the origin of life—and who should decide this issue—continues to stir up debate. Some moderates have suggested that science and religion are not necessarily incompatible and that a theory of the origin of life can accommodate both the scientific theory of evolution and religious beliefs.

The evangelist Aimee Semple McPherson, who won thousands of devoted followers with her broadcasts from the Angelus Temple in Los Angeles, founded the International Church of the Foursquare Gospel.

TEACHING OPTIONS

Making Connections Across the Curriculum

Literature The Scopes trial has been the subject of several books, including *Six Days or Forever?* by Ray Ginger. The play *Inherit the Wind* by Jerome Lawrence and Robert E. Lee (made into a motion picture in 1960) also concerns the Scopes trial. Have students examine *Six Days or Forever?* and *Inherit the Wind* (and view the movie version of the latter if they can). Then suggest that they compare the characterizations of Darrow and Bryan.

Teaching Gifted and Talented Students

Interpreting Points of View Have interested students work in pairs to present dramatic readings of the courtroom exchanges between Darrow and Bryan. They might locate a transcript of the trial or portions of the trial (such as are provided in Leslie H. Allen's *Bryan and Darrow at Dayton* and in *Six Days or Forever?*). If students have trouble finding a transcript of the trial, they might get a copy of *Inherit the Wind* at the library. Then have them look for passages in the play that they would like to present to the class in their dramatic readings. Ask the class to summarize each man's point of view on the basis of the readings.

Almost overnight, the trial became a national sensation. Throngs of big-city reporters filed daily stories from Dayton, and Chicago's WGN radio covered the drama live. When the proceedings opened on July 10, 1925, a steamy summer day, Darrow appeared coatless, wearing a tan shirt and a white string tie. The aging, heavyset Bryan dressed in a white pleated shirt and bow tie and carried a palm-leaf fan and a jug of water. When he entered the courtroom, the audience burst into applause.

BRYAN TAKES THE WITNESS STAND Darrow called Bryan as an expert on the Bible. This was the contest that everyone had been waiting for. To handle the throngs of Bryan supporters, Judge Raulston moved the court outside to a platform built under the maple trees. There, before a crowd of 2,000, Darrow relentlessly questioned Bryan about his beliefs. Bryan stood firm, a smile on his face, claiming he believed in the Bible.

Clarence Darrow in action at the Scopes trial in Dayton, Tennessee, in 1925.

> **A PERSONAL VOICE**
> Mr. Darrow—Do you claim that everything in the Bible should be interpreted literally?
> Mr. Bryan—I believe everything in the Bible should be accepted as it is given there. Some of the Bible was given illustratively. For instance: "Ye are the salt of the earth." I would not insist that man is actually salt, or that he had flesh of salt, but it is used in the sense of salt as saving God's people.
> **CLARENCE DARROW** and **WILLIAM JENNINGS BRYAN**, quoted in *Bryan and Darrow at Dayton*

Darrow asked Bryan if he agreed with Bishop James Ussher's calculation that according to the Bible, Creation happened in 4004 B.C. Bryan said he did. Had every living thing on earth appeared since that time? Did Bryan know that ancient civilizations had thrived before 4004 B.C.? Did he know the age of the earth? Bryan grew edgy but stuck to his guns. Finally, Darrow asked Bryan, "Do you think the earth was made in six days?" Cornered by the questions, Bryan answered, "Not six days of 24 hours." People sitting on the lawn gasped.

With this answer, Bryan admitted that the Bible might be interpreted in different ways. But in spite of this admission, Scopes was found guilty and fined $100. The Tennessee Supreme Court later changed the verdict on a technicality, but the law outlawing the teaching of evolution stayed on the books after the trial.

This clash over evolution, the prohibition experiment, and the emerging urban scene all were evidence of the changes and conflicts occurring during the 1920s. During that period, women also experienced conflict as they redefined their roles and pursued new lifestyles.

D. Answer Fundamentalists believed that God created the world in six days, whereas evolutionists argued that species developed from lower forms of life over millions of years.

THINK THROUGH HISTORY
D. Analyzing Issues What was the conflict between fundamentalists and those who accepted evolution?

Section 1 Assessment

1. TERMS & NAMES

Identify:
• speakeasy
• bootlegger
• fundamentalism
• Clarence Darrow
• Scopes trial

2. SUMMARIZING Create a diagram. Then fill it in with the legislation and outcome for each of these issues: (a) prohibition and (b) teaching evolution.

| Issue: |
| Legislation: |
| Outcome: |

Write a paragraph stating your position on one of these issues.

3. ANALYZING How might the overall atmosphere of the 1920s have contributed to the failure of prohibition?

THINK ABOUT
• changing values
• changing lifestyles
• fashions of the time

4. FORMING OPINIONS Do you think the passage of the Volstead Act and the verdict of the Scopes trial represent genuine triumphs for traditional values? Why or why not?

THINK ABOUT
• changes in urban life in the 1920s
• the effects of Prohibition
• the legacy of the Scopes trial

The Roaring Life of the 1920s **617**

ANSWERS

1. TERMS & NAMES

speakeasy, p. 614

bootlegger, p. 615

fundamentalism, p. 616

Clarence Darrow, p. 616

Scopes trial, p. 616

2. SUMMARIZING

Issue: prohibition
Legislation: The Eighteenth Amendment banned the manufacture, sale, and transportation of alcohol.
Outcome: Many Americans broke the law.
Issue: teaching evolution
Legislation: A Tennessee state law made it a crime to teach evolution.
Outcome: Biology teacher John Scopes broke the law, was arrested, and was convicted.

3. ANALYZING

Possible Responses: People living in cities felt freer and less bound by traditional values; immigrants brought their own cultures, habits, and religious values.

4. FORMING OPINIONS

Possible Responses: Students answering yes might say that these events raised people's awareness and have had a lasting influence, since today legislators and some religious groups work to solve the problems of alcoholism and the teaching of evolution still provokes legal controversy. Those answering no might say that the Volstead Act not only did not stop people from drinking alcohol but caused the growth of organized crime and that the conviction of John Scopes failed to discredit Charles Darwin's theory.

---

❷ The Twenties Woman

Section 2 Overview

OBJECTIVES

① To explain how the image of the flapper embodied the changing values and attitudes of young women in the 1920s.

② To identify the causes and results of the changing roles of women in the 1920s.

SKILLBUILDER

• Interpreting Charts, p. 620

CRITICAL THINKING

• Contrasting, p. 619
• Recognizing effects, pp. 620, 621
• Summarizing, p. 621
• Analyzing, p. 621
• Forming opinions, p. 621

FOCUS & MOTIVATE

▶ *Starting with the Student*
Discuss how students' tastes in music and clothing differ from their parents' tastes.

• Why do students think young people's attitudes toward life differ from those of the preceding generation?

MORE ABOUT . . .
G. Stanley Hall

As a professor of psychology and an authority on the study of children, G. Stanley Hall was the first educator to apply the results of child-psychology experiments to teaching. Noting a lack of research and information about adolescent women, Hall did an exhaustive study of the flapper. He concluded that "the new liberties she takes with life . . . make us wonder . . . whether the flapper may not, after all, be the bud of a new and better womanhood."

 ELECTRONIC LIBRARY OF PRIMARY SOURCES
from "Flapper Jane" by Bruce Bliven

---

*LEARN ABOUT changes in lifestyles, jobs, and families during the 1920s
TO UNDERSTAND how women's roles changed.*

ONE AMERICAN'S STORY

One January day in 1922, the psychologist G. Stanley Hall was strolling down the street when he encountered a young woman. She was about 16, "comely, happy, innocent," and Hall "took the liberty to look at her . . . carefully."

A PERSONAL VOICE

She wore a knitted hat, with hardly any brim, of a flame or bonfire hue; a henna scarf; two strings of Betty beads, of different colors, twisted together; an open short coat, with ample pockets; a skirt with vertical stripes so pleated that, at the waist, it seemed very dark, but the alternate stripes of white showed progressively downward, so that, as she walked, it gave something of what . . . psychologists call a flicker effect. On her right wrist were several bangles; on her left, of course, a wrist watch. Her shoes were oxfords, with a low broad heel. Her stockings were woolen and of brilliant hue. But most noticeable of all were her high overshoes, or galoshes. One seemed to be turned down at the top and entirely unbuckled, while the other was fastened below and flapped about her trim ankle in a way that compelled attention.

G. STANLEY HALL, "Flapper Americana Novissima," *Atlantic Monthly,* June 1922

So noteworthy was this young woman—and millions of others like her—that Hall wrote a long article about the Twenties woman. In her fashions, manners, and lifestyle, she represented a gathering social revolution.

This flapper models a stylish summer outfit in June 1920. The dress is fashioned in silk piqué with a jacket of checked crepe.

Young Women Change the Rules

By the 1920s, the experiences of World War I, the pull of cities, and changing attitudes had opened up a new world for many young Americans. These "wild young people," wrote one of them (John F. Carter, Jr., in a 1920 issue of *Atlantic Monthly*), were experiencing a world unknown to their parents: "We have seen man at his lowest, woman at her lightest, in the terrible moral chaos of Europe. We have been forced to question, and in many cases to discard, the religion of our fathers. . . . We have been forced to live in an atmosphere of 'to-morrow we die,' and so, naturally, we drank and were merry." In the rebellious, pleasure-loving air of the Twenties, many women began to assert their independence and demand the same freedoms as men.

THE FLAPPER During the Twenties, a new ideal emerged for some women: the **flapper,** an emancipated young woman who embraced the new fashions and urban attitudes of the day. Even though many young women donned the new outfits and flouted tradition, the flapper was more of an image of rebellious youth than a widespread reality. Even so, the casual, boyish fashions of the 1920s reflected this image of a new, sophisticated woman. Prewar clothes disappeared into attics and trash bins—all those dark and prim ankle-length dresses, whalebone corsets, petticoats, black stockings, and high-laced shoes.

Out of the shopping bags came close-fitting felt hats; bright, waistless dresses an inch above the knees; skin-toned silk stockings; sleek pumps; strings

---

SECTION 2 RESOURCES

 PRINT RESOURCES

IN-DEPTH RESOURCES: UNIT 6
Guided Reading, p. 19

ACCESS FOR STUDENTS ACQUIRING ENGLISH
Guided Reading (Spanish), p. 207

FORMAL ASSESSMENT
Section Quiz, p. 258

ALTERNATIVE ASSESSMENT BOOK
See forms for supporting and scoring alternative activities.

TECHNOLOGY RESOURCES

CD-ROM
Electronic Library of Primary Sources

VIDEO
American Portfolio: A Videodisc for U.S. History
user's guide, pp. 192, 199–200

INTERNET McDougal Littell Learning On-Line
http://www.mcdougallittell.com

of beads; and bracelets. Flappers clipped their long hair into boyish bobs and dyed them jet black. The finishing touches were rouge on the cheeks and "kissproof" lipstick on the lips. "The prevailing feminine ideal was a type that suggested criminality—not an unnatural reflection of the speakeasy life introduced by prohibition," said a writer for *Life* magazine.

The new fashions reflected a new attitude. Some women in the 1920s acted differently, too, as psychologist Hall noticed in the young woman he observed that day in January 1922.

A PERSONAL VOICE

We were on a long block that passed a college campus, where the students were foregathering for afternoon sports. She was not chewing gum, but was occasionally bringing some tidbit from her pocket to her mouth, taking in everything in sight, and her gait was swagger and superior. 'Howdy, Billy,' she called to a youth whom I fancied a classmate; and 'Hello, boys,' was her greeting to three more a little later.

G. STANLEY HALL, "Flapper Americana Novissima," *Atlantic Monthly,* June 1922

Like the young woman Hall observed, many young Twenties females became more assertive. In their bid for equal status with men, some began smoking cigarettes and drinking in public, actions that would have ruined their reputations not many years before. They danced the fox trot, camel walk, tango, lindy hop, and shimmy with abandon. Early in the decade, young women who still wore corsets left them behind when they went to dances for fear that they might be called "ironsides" or spend the evening as a wallflower. Some women learned to play golf and competed with men on the fairways.

Attitudes toward marriage changed as well. Many middle-class men and women began to view marriage as more of an equal partnership, although both agreed that housework and child-rearing were a woman's job.

THE DOUBLE STANDARD Magazines, newspapers, and advertisements promoted the image of the flapper, and young people openly discussed relationships in ways that scandalized their elders. However, the image of the flapper did not reflect the attitudes and values of many young people. During the 1920s, morals loosened only so far. Traditionalists in churches and schools protested the new, casual dances and women's acceptance of smoking and drinking.

In the years before World War I, when men "courted" women, they pursued only women they intended to marry. In the 1920s, however, casual dating became increasingly more accepted. Even so, a **double standard**—a set of principles granting greater sexual freedom to men than to women—required women to observe stricter standards of behavior than did men. As a result, many women were pulled back and forth between the old standards and the new.

THINK THROUGH HISTORY
A. Contrasting
How was the flapper different from her mother?
A. Answer The flapper rebelled against the conservative values that her mother represented. She dressed in more revealing, casual clothes; smoked; drank; and dated casually. Her mother was more traditional in every way, dressing in dark, concealing dresses; behaving properly; and accepting a subordinate relationship to men.

NOW & THEN

THE MISS AMERICA PAGEANT

"There she is, Miss America; there she is, your ideal." These are the opening words to the song that came to represent the Miss America pageant.

This tradition began in 1921 in Atlantic City, New Jersey. Hotel owners had dreamed up the bathing-beauty pageant in 1920 to attract tourists to the city after Labor Day. The first Miss America was Margaret Gorman, a petite, innocent 16-year-old from Washington, D.C. The second was 15-year-old Mary Katherine Campbell from Columbus, Ohio, a straight-A high school student with red hair and tiny, size-three feet. Campbell recalled her road to the title:

"I was pretty naive when I was starting. . . . Mercy, after all I was only fifteen. You were supposed to be sixteen, so I was sixteen, but I was really only fifteen in May. I came home and told my mother, 'I was chosen Miss Columbus, and they said it's because of my figure. Mother, what's a figure?' 'My mother said: It's none of your business.'"

This stylized rendition of the flapper appeared on the cover of *McClure's*, a popular magazine of the time.

619

OBJECTIVE
① INSTRUCT

Young Women Change the Rules

▶ ***Starting with the Student***
Have each student write a paragraph describing a fashionable young woman of today.

• What style of clothing does she wear? What colors are most popular?
• What are her hairstyle, makeup, and jewelry and other accessories like?
• How do these styles reflect American society in the 1990s?

▶ ***Discussing Key Ideas***
• The flapper represents a new ideal for young women.
• A double standard requires women to abide by stricter standards of behavior than men.

IN-DEPTH RESOURCES: UNIT 6
Guided Reading, p. 19

ACCESS FOR STUDENTS ACQUIRING ENGLISH
Guided Reading (Spanish), p. 207

NOW & THEN
The Miss America Pageant

Critical Thinking:
Evaluating The opening words of the Miss America theme song describe the winner as "your ideal."
• In what sense is Miss America an ideal for young women?
• Do students think the ideal has changed since the 1920s? If so, how?

TEACHING OPTIONS

Exploring Themes

Women in America Discuss how styles have reflected changing images of American women through history. What image did the whalebone corsets and ankle-length dresses of the early 1900s reflect? How did the flapper styles of the 1920s change that image? *Early 1900s women were prim and proper; 1920s women were freer, more independent.*

• What influences women's styles today?
• What images of women do styles such as "grunge" and "cute" reflect?

Making Connections Across Time

Miss America Pageant In the 1920s, Atlantic City tourists objected to the Miss America pageant, claiming that it was immoral for young women to parade in bathing suits. In recent years, women's groups have criticized the pageant's bathing-suit competition for portraying women as "objects" rather than as people.

• How do the recent criticisms of the pageant differ from the 1920s objections? *1920s objections were based on what women should and should not do; recent criticisms are based on how people should regard women.*

Teacher's Edition   619

Women Shed Old Roles at Home and at Work

▶ *Starting with the Student*
- Ask students if they think opportunities for women in the workplace are greater today than in the 1920s.
- Have students create flow charts, listing causes and effects of the changing roles of women in the 1920s. A chart might look like the one below.

```
┌─────────────────────┐
│      Causes         │
└─────────────────────┘
          │
          ▼
┌─────────────────────┐
│  Changing Roles     │
└─────────────────────┘
          │
          ▼
┌─────────────────────┐
│      Effects        │
└─────────────────────┘
```

▶ *Discussing Key Ideas*
- Women assume new roles in the workplace.
- Technological advances simplify household tasks.
- Married women remain responsible for housework and child care.

HISTORY FROM VISUALS
Women's Changing Employment, 1910–1930

Reading the Charts Tell students to note the time span of the pie charts. The first chart deals with a year (1910) before the time period of this chapter to provide background.

Extension Ask students to check an almanac or a statistical abstract to find the percentages of women employed in these ways today.

Women Shed Old Roles at Home and at Work

The fast-changing world of the 1920s produced new roles for women in the workplace and new trends in family life. A booming industrial economy opened new work opportunities for women in offices, factories, stores, service jobs, and professions. The same economy churned out time-saving appliances and products that reshaped the roles of housewife and mother.

NEW WORK OPPORTUNITIES The wartime trend of working women continued into the Twenties, but opportunities for women changed with growing mechanization and the return of men to the work force. In the 1920s, nearly 1 million female college graduates moved into the "women's professions" of teaching and nursing, and thousands more became librarians and social workers. The number of women bankers, lawyers, police officers, and probation officers rose, too.

Big businesses required extensive correspondence and record keeping, creating a huge demand for clerical workers. Two million women seized the opportunity and took jobs as typists, filing clerks, secretaries, stenographers, and office machine operators. In addition, about 800,000 women became clerks in stores, and about 2 million took jobs on assembly lines. A handful of women broke the old stereotypes by doing work once reserved for men, such as flying airplanes, driving taxis, and drilling oil wells.

By 1930, 10 million women were earning wages; however, they were only 24 percent of American workers. The battle for equality in the workplace had just begun. Medical schools imposed a 5 percent quota on female admissions. Consequently, the number of women doctors declined between 1910 and 1920. Few women rose to managerial jobs, and wherever they worked, women earned less than men. Fearing female competition for well-paying jobs, men argued that women were just temporary workers whose real job was at home. Between 1900 and 1930, the patterns of discrimination and inequality for women in the business world were established.

THE CHANGING FAMILY Widespread social and economic changes reshaped the family. The birthrate was continually dropping during the century and it dropped at a slightly faster rate in the 1920s as married women had fewer children. The decline in the birthrate during the 1920s was due in part to the wider availability of birth-control information.

At the same time, social and technological innovations simplified household labor and family life. Stores now overflowed with ready-made clothes, sliced bread, and canned foods. Children spent their days at school. Agencies and spe-

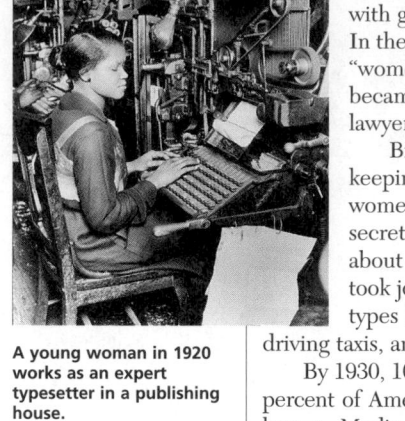

A young woman in 1920 works as an expert typesetter in a publishing house.

Skillbuilder Answer
Decline: Agriculture.
Increase: Clerical.

SKILLBUILDER
INTERPRETING CHARTS
According to the pie charts, in which area of work did the percentage of women decline the most between 1910 and 1930? In which area did the percentage of women increase the most?

B. Answer
Although big business and industry produced time-saving appliances that freed women from some household chores, and although business growth also created a demand for jobs filled by millions of women, most women were confined to traditional jobs.

THINK THROUGH HISTORY
B. *Recognizing Effects* How did the growth of business and industry affect women?

Women's Changing Employment, 1910–1930

1910
- Transportation & Communication 1.3%
- Trade 5.9% (including saleswomen)
- Clerical 7.3%
- Agriculture 22.4% (including forestry and fishing)
- Manufacturing & Mechanical 22.6%
- Professional 9.1%
- Domestic 31.3% (including waitresses and beauticians)

1920
- Transportation & Communication 2.6%
- Trade 7.9% (including saleswomen)
- Clerical 16.6%
- Agriculture 12.7% (including forestry and fishing)
- Manufacturing & Mechanical 22.6%
- Professional 11.9%
- Domestic 25.6% (including waitresses and beauticians)

1930
- Transportation & Communication 2.6%
- Trade 9.0% (including saleswomen)
- Clerical 18.5%
- Agriculture 8.5% (including forestry and fishing)
- Manufacturing & Mechanical 17.5%
- Professional 14.2%
- Domestic 29.6% (including waitresses and beauticians)

Source: *Women Who Work* by Grace Hutchins

TEACHING OPTION

Cooperative Activity: Analyzing Changes in Women's Roles

Task: Student groups will depict ways that the behavior, work, and attitudes of American women changed in the 1920s.

Purpose: To synthesize information about women's changing roles in the 1920s and present this information to the class.

Activity: Assign topics—such as fashion, manners, housework, family, and jobs—to groups of three to four students. Instruct the groups to depict the ways in which women's lives

changed in these areas during the 1920s. Students might find or draw pictures, perform skits, or create models to contrast American women of the 1920s with those of an earlier time period. Assign a role to each student: one might be a recorder; another, a facilitator; another, a timekeeper; and another, a presenter. Provide time for groups to share their work with the class.

ALTERNATIVE ASSESSMENT BOOK
Standards for Evaluating a Cooperative Activity

cial homes helped care for elderly parents. As various agencies and institutions handled more and more family tasks, many middle-class housewives, the main shoppers and money managers, focused their attention on their homes, husbands, children, and pastimes. "I consider time for reading clubs and my children more important than . . . careful housework and I just don't do it, " said an Indiana woman in the 1920s.

Marriages were increasingly based on the personal choices of the two people involved rather than on the choices of their families. During the 1920s, many couples ended marriages they might have tolerated earlier. By the end of the decade, the divorce rate had doubled.

Despite these many changes, the vast majority of married women remained homemakers since many people felt that wives who worked did so because their husbands had failed as breadwinners. Those women who did work included working-class women whose families needed the income and women with college degrees whose families also often needed the income. Both groups quickly discovered the pressure of juggling work and family, but the strain on working-class women was more severe. Helen Wright, who worked for the Women's Bureau in Chicago, recorded the struggle of an Irish mother of two.

> "You younger women have a harder task than ours. You will want equality in business, and it will be even harder to get than the vote."
>
> ANNA HOWARD SHAW,
> VETERAN SUFFRAGIST

A PERSONAL VOICE
She worked in one of the meat-packing companies, pasting labels from 7 A.M. to 3:30 P.M. She had entered the eldest child at school but sent her to the nursery for lunch and after school. The youngest was in nursery all day. She kept her house "immaculately clean and in perfect order," but to do so worked until eleven o'clock every night in the week and on Saturday night she worked until five o'clock in the morning. She described her schedule as follows: on Tuesday, Wednesday, Thursday, and Friday she cleaned one room each night; Saturday afternoon she finished the cleaning and put the house in order; Saturday night she washed; Sunday she baked; Monday night she ironed.

HELEN WRIGHT, quoted in *Wage-Earning Women*

C. Answer
Birthrates dropped; household labor was simplified by technology; children spent all day in school; divorce rate skyrocketed; adolescent rebelliousness increased.

THINK THROUGH HISTORY
C. Recognizing Effects What were some of the changes that affected the family in the 1920s?

As women adjusted to changing roles, some also struggled with rebellious adolescents, who put an unprecedented strain on families. With stricter child labor laws and the move to compulsory education, children stayed in school through their teens—a time when youth in earlier generations had begun to work. Teens in the 1920s studied and socialized with other teens and spent less time with their families. As peer pressure intensified, some adolescents resisted parental control.

This theme of adolescent rebelliousness can be seen in much of the popular culture of the 1920s. Education and entertainment reflected the conflict between traditional attitudes and modern ways of thinking.

Section 2 Assessment

1. TERMS & NAMES
Identify:
• flapper
• double standard

2. SUMMARIZING Copy the concept web shown below and add to it examples that illustrate the concepts.

lifestyles

Changes: Women in the 1920s

families   jobs

Write a paragraph explaining how you think women's lives changed most dramatically in the 1920s.

3. ANALYZING During the 1920s, a double standard required women to observe stricter codes of behavior than men. Do you think that some women of this decade made real progress toward placing both genders on an equal footing? Support your answer with evidence from the text.

THINK ABOUT
• psychologist G. Stanley Hall's observations on pages 618 and 619
• the flapper's style and image
• changing views of marriage

4. FORMING OPINIONS Today the term "glass ceiling" refers to the barriers women and minorities encounter in seeking higher career positions. In your opinion, could this term be applied to women's job opportunities during the 1920s? Cite evidence to support your answer.

THINK ABOUT
• technology's impact on jobs
• women's battle for equality
• roadblocks to professional success for women

The Roaring Life of the 1920s **621**

ANSWERS

1. TERMS & NAMES
flapper, p. 618
double standard, p. 619

2. SUMMARIZING
Possible Responses:
lifestyles—wearing new clothing styles, wearing more makeup, playing golf, dancing. families—decline in birthrate, higher divorce rate, more leisure time for housewives because of labor-saving devices, more pressure on working-class women. jobs—teachers, nurses, librarians, social workers, clerical workers, store clerks, factory workers.

3. ANALYZING
Possible Responses: Students answering yes might say that women laid the foundation for equality when they smoked and drank in public, became more open and assertive in communicating with men their age, dated casually, dressed nontraditionally, and viewed marriage as an equal partnership. Students answering no may say that new ways of dressing, smoking in public, and casual dating were basically superficial changes.

4. FORMING OPINIONS
Possible Responses: Students answering yes may say that medical schools had 5-percent admission quotas for women, that women were paid lower wages than their male counterparts, that few women were promoted to management positions, and that jobs were labeled as male or female. Students answering no may say that a glass ceiling is almost invisible but barriers to advancement in the 1920s were all too visible.

Teacher's Edition **621**

Youth in the Roaring Twenties

The decade known as the Roaring Twenties was a celebration of youth and its culture. Fads, crazy and frenetic dances, silly songs, and radically new styles of clothing captured the public's fancy. This was an especially liberating period for women, who received the right to vote in 1920. Many women also opted for a liberating change of fashion—short skirts and short hair—as well as the freedom to smoke and drink in public.

During this period of relative prosperity, many people questioned the values of the past and were willing to experiment with new values and behavior as well as with new fashions. Among the fads were the ukulele, the game of mahjong, the crossword puzzle, and water skiing. A favorite song of the day asked, "In the morning, in the evening, ain't we got fun?"

FLAGPOLE SITTING
One of the more bizarre fads of the 1920s was flagpole sitting. The fad began in 1924 as a publicity stunt to attract viewers to movie theaters. The sitter would climb to the top of a flagpole, set up a small platform, and remain sitting on it for days at a time.

The most famous flagpole sitter was "Shipwreck" Kelly (at left, waving from high above a movie theater in Union City, New Jersey). In 1929, for a total of 145 days, Kelly took up residence atop various flagpoles throughout the country. Imitators, of course, followed. At one point that year, Baltimore had at least 17 boys and 3 girls sitting atop 18-foot hickory poles, with their friends and families cheering them on.

DANCE FADS The Charleston was the dance craze of the 1920s. An energetic dance that involved wild, flailing movements of the arms and legs, it demanded an appropriate costume for the woman dancer—a short, straight dress without a waistline.

Another craze was the dance marathon, a contest in which couples would dance continuously for days—taking a 15-minute break every hour—with each alternately holding up the other as he or she slept. Needless to say, dancers dropped from exhaustion, and some died of heart failure. The longest dance marathon lasted 119 days.

RECOMMENDED RESOURCES

Books

Andrist, Ralph K., ed. *The American Heritage History of the '20's & '30's.* New York: American Heritage, 1970. A profusely illustrated account.

Stevenson, Elizabeth. *Babbitts and Bohemians.* New York: Macmillan, 1967. America in the Roaring Twenties.

This Fabulous Century: 1920–1930. New York: Time-Life, 1969. A fascinating pictorial history.

Videos

The Jazz Age. Time-Life Video, 1990. Newsreels and vintage photos capture the 1920s; part of the series America: A Look Back.

Lowell Thomas Remembers: The Roaring Twenties. Blackhawk, 1975. Three videocassettes covering the Roaring Twenties.

The Roaring '20s. Guidance Associates, 1990. Social and political changes of the era.

The Twenties. PBS Video, 1988. Part of the acclaimed PBS series *A Walk Through the 20th Century with Bill Moyers.*

The Twenties: From Illusion to Disillusion. Dir. Mirea Alexandresso and Henri Torrent. Films for the Humanities and Sciences, 1991.

BESSIE SMITH was "Empress of the Blues." In 1923, she sold a million recordings of "Down Hearted Blues."

MAHJONG is a game of Chinese origin that became wildly popular in the 1920s. It is usually played by four people using tiles resembling dominoes and bearing various designs.

BOBBED HAIR In keeping with the liberating influence of their new clothing, women bobbed their hair, freeing themselves of the long tresses that had been fashionable for years. The woman shown is having her locks shorn at a barber shop.

GENTLEMEN'S FASHIONS Gentlemen, not to be outdone by the ladies, enjoyed some outrageous fashions of their own. This young man, with the aid of two flappers, displays the latest fashion—extra-wide, floppy trousers, sometimes called Oxford bags. He also sports a popular men's hairstyle of the day—"patent-leather hair"—parted on the side or in the middle and slicked down close to the head.

DATA FILE

School Days, School Days

During the 1920s, children studied reading, writing, and arithmetic in elementary school. In high school, students also studied history and literature and had vocational training. Girls learned cooking and sewing, and boys learned woodworking.

Slang Expressions

The bee's knees—a superb person or thing
crush—an infatuation with someone
gatecrasher—someone who attends an event without paying or without an invitation
keen—attractive or appealing
ritzy—elegant
scram—leave in a hurry
screwy—crazy

Radio

• KDKA, Pittsburgh, the first commercial radio station, went on the air on November 2, 1920. It was owned by Westinghouse.

• In 1922, 500 radio stations were in operation in the United States.

• In 1924, over 3 million radios were in use throughout the United States. By the end of the 1920s, over 10 million radios were in use. Popular radio shows included *Amos 'n' Andy* and *The Shadow*.

Song Titles

Barney Google
Blue Skies
Bye Bye Blackbird
Button Up Your Overcoat
Crazy Rhythm
I Found a Million-Dollar Baby in the Five-and-Ten-Cent Store
I Want to Be Happy
Let a Smile Be Your Umbrella
Makin' Whoopee
My Blue Heaven
My Heart Stood Still
Show Me the Way to Go Home
Singin' in the Rain
Stardust
Tea for Two

INTERACT WITH HISTORY

1. **COMPARING** With a small group, listen to several of the songs listed above or to several others from the period. Discuss the lyrics and the melodies of the songs, and compare them with those of popular songs today. What can you learn about the 1920s from this music? Report your findings to the class.

 SEE SKILLBUILDER HANDBOOK, PAGE 1041.

2. **RESEARCHING CLOTHING STYLES** Find out more about the clothing styles just before the flapper era. How severe were the changes in fashion in the 1920s? How do you think parents of flappers reacted to these changes? If you had lived at this time, would you have chosen to wear the new styles? Why or why not?

 For more about life in the 1920s, click on *Social Studies* at http://www.mcdougallittell.com

The Roaring Life of the 1920s **623**

INSTRUCT

▶ **Starting with the Student**
• Have students consider what role World War I may have played in shaping the attitudes of the Roaring Twenties. *Possible Responses: War brought disillusionment, which prompted cynicism and hedonism in the young; having witnessed death and destruction, Americans now turned to play; postwar American isolationism led to a kind of narcissism.*

▶ **Discussing Key Ideas**
• During the 1920s a youth-dominated popular culture that questions the values of the past emerges in America.
• New styles and crazes sweep the nation during the decade often called the Roaring Twenties.

HISTORY FROM VISUALS

Reading the Images Have students examine the illustrations and captions on these pages.
• On the basis of these details, how would students describe American youth in the 1920s? What conclusions can students draw from the Data File? *Possible Responses: Radical, liberated, aiming to shock, hedonistic, self-absorbed, frivolous, experimental.*

INTERACT WITH HISTORY

1. Comparing

Provide recordings for students if possible, or suggest that they borrow recordings from libraries, relatives, or friends. Point out that they can look for collections of 1920s songs or hunt for songs individually; for example, "Stardust" and "Blue Skies" appear on the Willie Nelson CD *Stardust*; "My Blue Heaven," on *Fats Domino's Greatest Hits*. If necessary, students might use music-store or on-line music catalogs or library music references, such as those published by the Schwann Group, to locate CDs or cassettes containing specific songs.

2. Researching Clothing Styles

Students might examine references on the history of fashion or books containing photographs of the 1900–1920 period (such as the first two volumes of Time-Life's *This Fabulous Century*) for more on clothing just before the Roaring Twenties. After comparing the more conservative clothing of earlier years, they may speculate that many parents of flappers were shocked or outraged by their children's dress. Descriptions of what students themselves would have chosen to wear will vary, but they should offer reasons for their choices.

OBJECTIVES

① To explain how schools and mass media influenced American culture in the 1920s.

② To identify the athletes, celebrities, artists, and writers who contributed to American popular culture in the 1920s.

SKILLBUILDER

• Understanding geography: location, place, p. 627

CRITICAL THINKING

• Summarizing, pp. 625, 629
• Comparing, p. 626
• Analyzing causes, pp. 627, 629
• Forming opinions, p. 629
• Synthesizing, p. 629

FOCUS & MOTIVATE

▶ *Starting with the Student*
Ask students to name three well-known Americans whom they consider heroes —people worthy of respect. List their suggestions on the chalkboard and ask them to identify the field in which each is famous.

• What kinds of people do students consider heroes?
• Why do students admire these people?

Students might compare 1990s heroes with 1920s heroes after they read this section.

MORE ABOUT . . .
Graham McNamee

Before becoming the most popular announcer of the decade, Graham McNamee was a young concert baritone and semipro baseball player. Although best remembered as a sportscaster, McNamee also broadcast national events, such as the 1924 Republican National Convention and Lindbergh's return from Paris in 1927. He attributed his success to an ability to make each listener "feel that he or she is there . . . in the press stand."

---

3 Education and Popular Culture

TERMS & NAMES
• Babe Ruth
• Gertrude Ederle
• Charles A. Lindbergh
• George Gershwin
• Sinclair Lewis
• F. Scott Fitzgerald
• Edna St. Vincent Millay
• Ernest Hemingway

LEARN ABOUT the growth of schools, movies, mass media, and spectator sports
TO UNDERSTAND how America developed a popular culture in the 1920s—a culture that many artists and writers criticized.

ONE AMERICAN'S STORY

On September 22, 1927, approximately 50 million Americans sat listening to their radios as Graham McNamee, radio's most popular announcer, breathlessly called the boxing match between former heavyweight champ Jack Dempsey and titleholder Gene Tunney.

A PERSONAL VOICE
Good evening Ladies & Gentlemen of the Radio Audience . . . this is a big night. Three million dollars worth of boxing bugs are gathered around a ring at Soldier Field, Chicago. Burning down at us are 44 1,000-watt lamps over the ring. All is darkness in the muttering mass of crowd beyond the spotlight. The crowd is thickening in the seats . . . it's like the Roman Coliseum. . . .
    Here comes Jack Dempsey, climbing through the ropes . . . white flannels, long bathrobe. . . . Here comes Tunney. . . . He's got on blue trunks with red trimmings. They're getting the gloves out of a box tied with pretty blue ribbon . . . The announcer shouting in the ring . . . trying to quiet 150,000 people. . . . Robes are off. . . . The Bell.
GRAHAM McNAMEE, *Time* magazine, October 3, 1927

Gene Tunney, down for the "long count," went on to defeat Jack Dempsey in their 1927 epic battle.

    Punches flew for six rounds. Tunney went down in the seventh, but the referee didn't start his ten-second count for the knockout until Dempsey got back to his corner. The slow count gave Tunney time to get up, continue punching, and defeat the legendary Dempsey. So suspenseful was the brutal match that a number of radio listeners died of heart failure. The "fight of the century" was just one of a host of spectacles and events that transformed American popular culture in the 1920s.

Schools and the Mass Media Shape Culture

Not every change in popular culture had the immediate drama of the Dempsey-Tunney fight. Nevertheless, developments in the areas of education and news coverage had a powerful impact on the nation during the 1920s. Throughout the period, schools and the mass media worked to shape American minds.

SCHOOL ENROLLMENTS In 1914, approximately 1 million American students attended high school. By 1926, that number had skyrocketed to 4 million, sparked by prosperous times and by the higher educational standards demanded for jobs in industry.

    The modern high school emerged during this period of expanding education. Before the 1920s, most high schools had catered to college-bound students. In contrast, the new high schools offered courses for a broad range of students, including vocational training for those interested in industrial jobs and home economics for future homemakers.

    The public schools met another special challenge in the 1920s—teaching the children of new immigrant families. While this job wasn't a new one for American schools, it became a bigger one. The years before World War I had seen the largest stream of immigrants in the nation's history—close to 1 million

---

SECTION 3 RESOURCES

PRINT RESOURCES

IN-DEPTH RESOURCES: UNIT 6
Guided Reading, p. 20
Skillbuilder Practice: Drawing Conclusions, p. 22
Geography Application: From Coast to Coast, p. 23
Primary Source: *from* An Interview with Charles A. Lindbergh, p. 27
American Lives: Georgia O'Keefe, p. 32

ACCESS FOR STUDENTS ACQUIRING ENGLISH
Guided Reading (Spanish), p. 208
Skillbuilder Practice: Drawing Conclusions (Spanish), p. 210
Geography Application: From Coast to Coast (Spanish), p. 211

FORMAL ASSESSMENT
Section Quiz, p. 259

ALTERNATIVE ASSESSMENT BOOK
See forms for supporting and scoring alternative activities.

TECHNOLOGY RESOURCES

HUMANITIES TRANSPARENCIES
H20, *Automat* by Edward Hopper

CD-ROM Our Times
Electronic Library of Primary Sources

VIDEO
American Portfolio: A Videodisc for U.S. History
user's guide, pp. 191–193, 196–197, 199–200

INTERNET McDougal Littell Learning On-Line
http://www.mcdougallittell.com

newcomers a year. Unlike the earlier English and Irish immigrants, many of the new immigrants spoke no English. By the 1920s their children filled city classrooms. Determined teachers met the challenge and created a huge pool of literate Americans.

As the demands placed on public schools grew, taxes to finance the schools increased too. School costs doubled from 1913 to 1920, then doubled again by 1926. The total cost of American education in the mid-1920s amounted to $2.7 billion a year.

EXPANDING NEWS COVERAGE Widespread education increased literacy in America, but it was the growing mass media that shaped a mass culture. Newspaper circulation rose as writers and editors learned how to hook readers by imitating the sensational stories in the tabloids, such as those founded by William Randolph Hearst. The success of tabloids revealed the public's appetite for the details of one big event after another. Mass-circulation magazines, appealing to readers around the country, also flourished during the 1920s. Many of these magazines summarized the week's news, both foreign and domestic.

RADIO COMES OF AGE Although major magazines and newspapers reached big audiences, radio was the most powerful communications medium to emerge in the 1920s. Americans added terms such as "airwaves," "radio audience," and "tune in" to their everyday speech. As radio networks emerged, they invested heavily in market research to find out what people wanted to hear. They became successful by programming to satisfy the public's interests. By the end of the decade, the radio networks had created something new in the United States—the shared national experience of hearing the news as it happened. The wider world had opened up to Americans, who could hear the voice of their president or listen to the World Series live. Celebrity broadcaster Graham McNamee received thousands of letters

A. Answer More widespread education produced a nationwide pool of readers. Centralized mass media created a popular culture by enabling people nationwide to experience the same entertainment and information.

THINK THROUGH HISTORY
A. Summarizing What changes took place in public education and the mass media in the 1920s?

"All I know is what I read in the papers."

WILL ROGERS,
HUMORIST

The Mass Media, 1920s

NEWSPAPERS

- By the mid-1920s, about 36 million Americans read newspapers, an increase of 8 million from prewar years.
- Since 1914, about 600 local newspapers had shut down, and 230 others had been swallowed up by 55 huge newspaper chains.
- During the 1920s, most Americans stopped getting news only from local writers. They began reading more news stories, columns, editorials, sports articles, and features in newspapers distributed from the big-city headquarters of the newspaper chains.
- Tabloids such as the *Daily News* and the *Daily Mirror* in New York City featured sensational stories of murders, kidnappings, gangsters, and entertainers, using bold photographs and large headlines to scream the news.

MAGAZINES

- In 1923, Henry Luce cofounded *Time,* a weekly newsmagazine that interpreted the news it presented.
- In 1921, DeWitt and Lila Wallace founded *Reader's Digest,* a magazine that condensed articles originally published in other magazines and periodicals.
- By the end of the 1920s, ten American magazines—including *Time, The Saturday Evening Post, Collier's,* and *Reader's Digest*—boasted a circulation of more than 2 million each.
- Other popular magazines of the age were *Life, Smart Set, American Mercury,* and *The New Yorker.*
- Many of these magazines featured a blend of fiction, cartoons, and articles. Others focused on tales of crime and "true confessions."

RADIO

- In 1921, New York's WEAF broadcast a regular news program with the announcer H. V. Kaltenborn; in 1922, the same station broadcast the first commercially sponsored program.
- In 1926, three corporations—General Electric (GE), Westinghouse, and the Radio Corporation of America (RCA)—formed the first radio network, the National Broadcasting Corporation (NBC); the Columbia Broadcasting System (CBS) was formed in 1927.
- In 1929, Americans spent $850 million on radio equipment, and NBC was charging advertisers $10,000 to sponsor an hour-long program.
- By 1930, 40 percent of U.S. households had radios.

The Roaring Life of the 1920s **625**

America Chases New Heroes and Old Dreams

▶ **Starting with the Student**
- Which of students' activities or interests might be considered fads?
- Compare today's student fads with those of the 1920s.

▶ **Discussing Key Ideas**
- Sports heroes and movie stars inspire Americans.
- Writers, artists, and composers experiment with new styles.
- Much of the decade's literature expresses a clash of values within society.

 ELECTRONIC LIBRARY OF PRIMARY SOURCES
"The Sultan of Swat Steals a World Series Show" by Heywood Broun

MORE ABOUT . . .
Fads

Shipwreck Kelly started the flagpole-sitting craze when a Hollywood theater hired him to draw crowds. Soon he was traveling around the country to attract publicity for hotels. Perched on a small seat equipped with stirrups to keep him from falling off, Kelly would sway atop flagpoles for days.

ON THE WORLD STAGE
The 1924 Winter Olympics

Critical Thinking:
Evaluating Ask students if they think, on the basis of what they know about the Olympics in recent years, that including winter games was a good decision. Have them give reasons to support their opinions.

---

a year from radio fans. One from a hospital worker summed up a national feeling: "The hospital is really a home for some eight hundred patients. . . . Their little Main Street is quite narrow, and the radio is bringing the world to their feet."

America Chases New Heroes and Old Dreams

During the 1920s, many people had money and the leisure time to enjoy it. In 1929, Americans spent $4.5 billion on entertainment, much of it on ever-changing fads. Early in the decade, Americans engaged in new leisure pastimes such as working crossword puzzles and playing mahjong, a Chinese game whose playing pieces resemble dominoes. In 1922, after explorers opened the dazzling tomb of Egyptian pharaoh Tutankhamen, consumers mobbed the stores for pharaoh-inspired accessories, jewelry, and furniture. In the mid-1920s, people turned to flagpole sitting, six-day bike races, and dance marathons. They also flooded athletic stadiums to see sports stars, who were glorified as superheroes by the media.

SPORTS HEROES OF THE 1920S Although the media hyped sports heroes, the Golden Age of Sports reflected common aspirations. As athletes in nearly every sport set new records, they inspired masses of ordinary Americans. When poor, unknown athletes rose to national fame and fortune, they restored Americans' belief in the power of the individual to improve his or her life.

Baseball's legendary star was New York Yankee slugger **Babe Ruth.** Through the 1920s, the paunchy, hard-drinking Ruth smashed home run after home run out of the park, earning himself such nicknames as the Sultan of Swat and the Colossus of Clout. When Ruth hit a record 60 home runs for the Yankees in 1927, America went wild. *New York Times* writer John Kiernan exclaimed, "My voice may be loud above the crowd and my words just a bit uncouth, but I'll stand and shout till the last man's out: There never was a guy like Ruth!"

Boxing's biggest star was heavyweight champion Jack Dempsey. Seemingly unbeatable, Dempsey defended his championship many times and turned boxing into a legitimate sport. He was finally defeated by prizefighter Gene Tunney in 1926, and he was defeated by Tunney again in 1927. When the fighters met for their second match, a record crowd of some 150,000 people paid approximately $2,650,000 to watch.

Red Grange, nicknamed the Galloping Ghost, boosted enthusiasm for college football with his feats as a University of Illinois running back. At the 1924 Michigan game, Grange ran the kickoff back 95 yards for a touchdown and then scored three more touchdowns—all in the first 12 minutes of the game. Between 1918 and 1930, the Fighting Irish of Notre Dame, led by coach Knute Rockne, were wildly popular because of their five undefeated seasons and 105 victories.

Even quieter sports thrilled the fans. Tennis greats Big Bill Tilden and Helen Wills became household names as fans followed their careers. The public devoured stories of Atlanta's Bobby Jones, the only golfer to win all major British and American open and amateur matches in one year. They also cheered for **Gertrude Ederle,** who in 1926 became the first woman to swim the English Channel.

LINDBERGH'S FLIGHT But America's most beloved hero of the time wasn't an athlete but a small-town pilot named

ON THE WORLD STAGE

THE 1924 WINTER OLYMPICS

FRANCE

Chamonix •

In the early 1920s, sports enthusiasts began to clamor for Olympic competition in skiing, skating, and other winter sports. The International Olympic Committee hesitated; the original Olympics, it pointed out, featured summer sports. But in 1924, the committee gave in and staged the first Winter Olympics in Chamonix, France. The round of events that year featured ice hockey, figure skating, skiing, speed skating, and bobsledding. Norwegian and Finnish athletes dominated the games, but Canada won the ice hockey contests and an American took the gold in the 500-meter skating race.

B. Answer
Students might mention today's sports heroes, such as Michael Jordan, who are hugely popular as were the great athletes of the 1920s.a
THINK THROUGH HISTORY
B. Comparing
Which heroes of today are similar to heroes of the 1920s?

Helen Wills won the singles title at the U.S. Open seven times and the Wimbledon title eight times. Her nickname was Little Miss Poker Face.

626 CHAPTER 21

Teaching Less Proficient Readers

Identifying Main Ideas Demonstrate the following technique for identifying main ideas in the text:

1. Read the heading on page 626: "America Chases New Heroes and Old Dreams." Then restate the heading as a question or series of questions: Who were the new heroes of the 1920s? What were the dreams of the age? How does America "chase" heroes and dreams?
2. Skim the text under that heading to find the answers to the questions. The answers generally state the main ideas. Have students practice the technique with other headings.

Making Global Connections

Charles Lindbergh The historic flight from New York to Paris made Lindbergh a hero on two continents. In December 1927 the U.S. government sent Lindbergh to Latin America as a goodwill ambassador.

- What qualities made Charles Lindbergh a popular hero? *Honesty, bravery.*
- How did the United States benefit from Lindbergh's popularity? *Possible Response: People in other countries associated Lindbergh's qualities with America.*

May 20, 1932 Amelia Earhart was the first woman to fly solo across the Atlantic. Record time of about 15 hours from Newfoundland to Ireland.

GREENLAND

Oakland
San Francisco

Hudson Bay

CANADA

Londonderry
ENGLAND
IRELAND

EUROPE

North Sea

Paris
FRANCE

1919 First transcontinental airmail service in the U.S.

NORTH AMERICA

Chicago
Cleveland
New York

NEWFOUNDLAND
Harbor Grace

UNITED STATES

MEXICO

Gulf of Mexico

Key West
Havana
CUBA

ATLANTIC OCEAN

AFRICA

May 20–21, 1927 Charles Lindbergh established the record of 33 hours, 29 minutes for his 3,614-mile solo flight across the Atlantic.

March 14, 1927 Pan American Airways is founded to handle airmail deliveries. First route between Key West and Havana.

Skillbuilder Answer
Location: New York, Cleveland, Chicago, and San Francisco. **Place:** *Possible Answer:* Newfoundland lies farther east than other parts of North America; leaving from there would shorten the flight distance across the ocean.

Charles A. Lindbergh, who made the first nonstop solo flight across the Atlantic. A handsome, modest Minnesotan, Lindbergh decided to go after a $25,000 prize for the first solo transatlantic flight. On May 20, 1927, he took off from New York City in the *Spirit of St. Louis,* flew up the coast to Newfoundland, and headed over the Atlantic. The weather was so bad, Lindbergh recalled, that "the average altitude for the whole . . . second 1,000 miles of the [Atlantic] flight was less than 100 feet." After 33 hours and 29 minutes, Lindbergh set down at Le Bourget airfield outside of Paris, France, amid beacons, searchlights, and mobs of enthusiastic French people.

Paris threw a huge party. New York showered Lindbergh with ticker tape, the president received him at the White House, and America made him its idol. In an age of sensationalism, excess, and crime, Lindbergh stood for the honesty and bravery the nation seemed to have lost. Novelist F. Scott Fitzgerald, a fellow Minnesotan, caught the essence of Lindbergh's fame.

A PERSONAL VOICE
In the spring of 1927, something bright and alien flashed across the sky. A young Minnesotan who seemed to have nothing to do with this generation did a heroic thing, and for a moment people set down their glasses in country clubs and speakeasies and thought of their old best dreams. . . .
F. SCOTT FITZGERALD, quoted in *The Lawless Decade*

Lindbergh's success spurred others to greatness. In the next decade, Amelia Earhart was to undertake many brave aerial exploits, inspired by Lindbergh's example.

MOVIES Despite the feats of real-life heroes, America's yearning for excitement and romance seemed unquenchable in the 1920s. Movies tapped into this national craving. By 1925, filmmaking had become the nation's fourth-largest industry, and more than 20,000 movie houses did a steady business nationwide.

Hollywood, just outside Los Angeles, established itself as America's movie capital and produced a host of silent films. Among the stars of these films was Charlie Chaplin, who played the comical, warm-hearted Little Tramp. Tom Mix rose to fame in Westerns. Theda Bara, the "vamp," and Clara Bow, the "It Girl," reflected society's infatuation with physical attractiveness and freedom. But most famous of all was Rudolph Valentino, the dark, seductive leading man in *The Sheik* who melted women's hearts.

In 1927, Hollywood released *The Jazz Singer* starring Al Jolson—the first major film with sound. A year later, the young Walt Disney produced *Steamboat*

GEOGRAPHY SKILLBUILDER
LOCATION *What U.S. cities were regular stops on the first transcontinental airmail route?*
PLACE *What would be the advantage of leaving from Newfoundland, as Amelia Earhart did, on a transatlantic flight rather than from New York, as Lindbergh did?*

Charlie Chaplin was one of the most famous stars in movie history.

C. Answer Many Americans yearned for excitement and romance, and these needs were fulfilled by watching movie stars.

THINK THROUGH HISTORY
C. Analyzing Causes Why were Americans so entranced with movie stars in the 1920s?

The Roaring Life of the 1920s **627**

HISTORY FROM VISUALS
Historic Flights, 1919–1932

Reading the Map Have students list in chronological order the flights mentioned on the map.

Extension Students might do some research in order to add dates of other historic flights during this period (1919–1932), or they might add dates of later historic flights.

IN-DEPTH RESOURCES: UNIT 6
Geography Application: From Coast to Coast, p. 23

MORE ABOUT . . .
Charlie Chaplin

The famous movie star Charlie Chaplin was born in London in 1889. He began touring the United States as a music-hall performer in 1910. He first appeared on film as the Little Tramp in 1914, and five years later he joined with others in the movie industry to form the United Artists film company. Chaplin gained complete control over the production of his films. He wrote and directed almost all of them, and he composed music for those with sound. In 1972 Chaplin received an honorary Academy Award for "the incalculable effect he has had in making motion pictures the art form of this century."

IN-DEPTH RESOURCES: UNIT 6
Primary Source: *from* An Interview with Charles A. Lindbergh, p. 27

TEACHING OPTION

Skillbuilder Mini-Lesson: Drawing Conclusions

Explaining the Skill Drawing conclusions about a historical event or condition means forming an opinion or making an inference based on facts and available evidence. In the process of drawing conclusions, historians also consider evidence in the light of what they know to be true from past experience.

Applying the Skill Have students read about Lindbergh's flight. Then direct their attention to the quotation from F. Scott Fitzgerald. Ask students to draw conclusions about Fitzgerald's opinion of the flight and of the lifestyles of the 1920s. Have students support their conclusions with specific evidence from

the text. Students might say that Fitzgerald admired Lindbergh's accomplishment, had contempt for the lifestyles of his time, and felt that earlier times were more praiseworthy. Specific supporting evidence includes information in the second paragraph on this page and Fitzgerald's words: "who seemed to have nothing to do with this generation" and "people set down their glasses . . . and thought of their old best dreams."

IN-DEPTH RESOURCES: UNIT 6
Skillbuilder Practice: Drawing Conclusions, p. 22

Teacher's Edition **627**

Willie, the first movie starring a talking cartoon character named Mickey Mouse. With the coming of "talkies," movie attendance doubled. By 1930, millions of Americans went to the movies every week. Along with the mass media and spectator sports, movies bound Americans even more tightly into a national family.

THEATER, MUSIC, AND ART While movies provided a romantic escape, the arts gave Americans fresh perspectives. Before this era, most plays in American theaters imitated European melodrama. All that changed with Eugene O'Neill, the first American playwright to win a Nobel Prize in literature. O'Neill's plays, such as *The Hairy Ape* (1922), asked Americans to reflect on modern isolation, confusion, and family conflict.

Composers of concert music also began breaking away from European traditions in the 1920s. **George Gershwin's** *Rhapsody in Blue* and *Concerto in F* brought him instant fame. They were among the first classical works to combine American jazz with the traditional style. Soon thereafter Aaron Copland continued this identifiably American influence in his symphonic *Music for the Theater* and Piano Concerto.

American painters recorded an America of dreams and realities. Edward Hopper caught the loneliness of American life in his canvases of empty streets, stark storefronts, and solitary people. He was part of the Ashcan school of painting—known for its honest look at everyday realities—that had emerged in the first decade of the 20th century. Painter Georgia O'Keeffe produced intensely colored canvases that captured the grandeur of New York: dark buildings thrusting into the sky, glaring sun reflected from sky-high windows, nighttime streets forming ribbons of orange light in the blackness. "One can't paint New York as it is," O'Keeffe once told a friend, "but rather as it is felt."

WRITERS OF THE 1920S Many of America's gifted writers were alienated by the values and lifestyles of the 1920s. They criticized what they felt were the strait-laced culture of small towns and the shallowness and vulgarity of business culture. Much of the work they produced was despairing or critical of a society with few ideals or avenues to personal fulfillment. Even so, this outpouring of fresh, insightful writing made the 1920s one of the richest eras in the country's literary history.

Sinclair Lewis, the first American to win a Nobel Prize in literature, was among the era's most outspoken critics. In *Main Street* and *Babbitt,* his two most famous novels, Lewis took aim at the shallow, stifling existence of middle-class America. Lewis used the character of George F. Babbitt, a real-estate salesman in a medium-sized town, to ridicule Americans for their conformity and materialism.

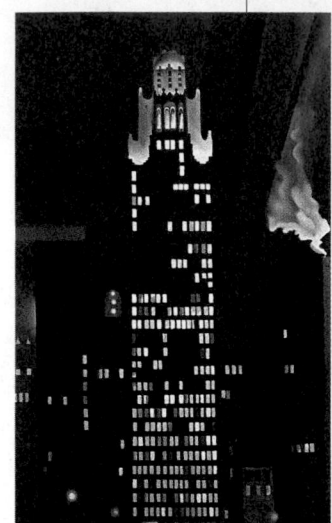
Radiator Building—Night, New York (1927), Georgia O'Keeffe.

> A sensational event was changing from the brown suit to the gray the contents of his pockets. He was earnest about these objects. They were of eternal importance, like baseball or the Republican Party. They included a fountain pen and a silver pencil . . . which belonged in the righthand upper vest pocket. Without them he would have felt naked. On his watch-chain were a gold pen-knife, silver cigar-cutter, seven keys . . . and incidentally a good watch. . . . Last, he stuck in his lapel the Booster's Club button. With the conciseness of great art the button displayed two words: "Boosters—Pep!" It made Babbitt feel loyal and important. It associated him with Good Fellows, with men who were nice and human, and important in business circles.
>
> **SINCLAIR LEWIS,** *Babbitt*

Baltimore journalist H. L. Mencken, coeditor of the *American Mercury,* was equally scornful of modern America. A scathing critic, Mencken ridiculed virtually every American institution, from the church and public schools to social workers, politicians, and the middle class.

Novelist **F. Scott Fitzgerald,** known as the spokesman of the "Jazz Age" (a term he coined to describe the 1920s), revealed the negative side of 1920s gaiety and freedom. In *This Side of Paradise* and *The Great Gatsby,* he por-

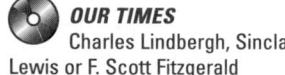
Walt Disney's Mickey Mouse first talked on screen in 1928 in *Steamboat Willie.* Disney himself provided the voice for Mickey.

---

trayed wealthy people leading hopelessly empty lives in gilded surroundings. In New York City, a brilliant group of writers made their table in the Algonquin Hotel dining room a symbol for their fellowship. Among the best-known Round Table members was Dorothy Parker, a short story writer, poet, and essayist. Parker was famous for her wisecracking wit, expressed in such lines as, "I was the toast of two continents—Greenland and Australia."

Other women writers also met important issues head on. In *The Age of Innocence*, Edith Wharton dramatized the clash between traditional and modern values that undermined high society fifty years earlier. Southern novelist Ellen Glasgow criticized the constricting morals of the South in *Barren Ground*. Novelist Willa Cather celebrated the simple, dignified lives of such people as the immigrant farmers of Nebraska in *My Ántonia* and the first Catholic bishop of New Mexico in *Death Comes for the Archbishop*. **Edna St. Vincent Millay** wrote poems celebrating youth and a life of independence and freedom from traditional constraints.

Some writers were so soured by American culture that they settled in Europe, mostly in Paris. Socializing in the city's cafes, they formed a group that writer Gertrude Stein called the Lost Generation. These writers included F. Scott Fitzgerald, Ernest Hemingway, and John Dos Passos. Other American writers were already living in Europe. The poet Ezra Pound lived in London, Paris, and Italy. T. S. Eliot, who later won a Nobel Prize in literature, lived in London. Eliot's most famous poem, *The Waste Land*, was an agonized view of a society that seemed stripped of humanity.

Several writers saw action in World War I, and their early books denounced war. Novelist John Dos Passos's *Three Soldiers* was the first important attack on war as a machine designed to crush human freedom. Later, Dos Passos turned to social and political themes, using modern techniques to capture the mood of city life and the terrible losses that came with success. **Ernest Hemingway,** who was wounded in the First World War, became the best-known expatriate author. In his novels *The Sun Also Rises* and *A Farewell to Arms*, he criticized the glorification of war. He also introduced a tough, simplified style of writing that set a new literary standard. A *Time* reviewer described Hemingway's "little hard sentences" as "round stones polished by rain and wind."

During this rich literary era, vital developments also were taking place in African-American society. Black Americans of the 1920s began to voice pride in their heritage, and black artists and writers revealed the richness of African-American culture.

D. Answer Many writers found American culture shallow and meaningless, with few ideals for people to strive for and few paths that people could follow to personal fulfillment.

THINK THROUGH HISTORY
D. Analyzing Causes Why did many American writers reject their culture and its values?

KEY PLAYERS
The Fitzgeralds
Critical Thinking: Drawing Conclusions
• How did F. Scott and Zelda Fitzgerald epitomize the Jazz Age? *They had a fast-paced, extravagant lifestyle that masked their problems and desperation.*

ASSESS & RETEACH

Section 3 Assessment
Assign students to study groups and have them help one another answer the questions.

Self-Assessment
Have each student create a six-column chart in which he or she lists important figures of this period in the fields of sports, movies, theater, music, painting, and literature.

Section Quiz

FORMAL ASSESSMENT
Section Quiz, p. 259

Reteach
On the chalkboard create a web diagram like the one below. Ask students to list examples of ways in which each group of people contributed to the popular culture of the 1920s.

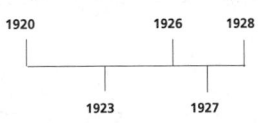
Section **3** Assessment

1. TERMS & NAMES

Identify:
• Babe Ruth
• Gertrude Ederle
• Charles A. Lindbergh
• George Gershwin
• Sinclair Lewis
• F. Scott Fitzgerald
• Edna St. Vincent Millay
• Ernest Hemingway

2. SUMMARIZING Create a time line of key events relating to 1920s popular culture. Use the dates below as a guide.

```
1920          1926    1928
 |-------------|-------|
        |          |
      1923       1927
```

In a sentence or two, explain which of these events interests you the most and why.

3. FORMING OPINIONS Do you think the popular heroes of the 1920s were heroes in a real sense? Why or why not?

THINK ABOUT
• how you define heroism
• the media hyping of sports stars during the 1920s
• the accomplishments of Babe Ruth, Jack Dempsey, Gertrude Ederle, and Charles Lindbergh

4. SYNTHESIZING In what ways do you think the mass media and mass culture helped Americans create a sense of community in the 1920s? Support your answer with details from the text.

THINK ABOUT
• the content and readership of newspapers and magazines
• attendance at sports events and movie theaters
• the scope of radio broadcasts

The Roaring Life of the 1920s **629**

ANSWERS

1. TERMS & NAMES

Babe Ruth, p. 626
Gertrude Ederle, p. 626
Charles A. Lindbergh, p. 627
George Gershwin, p. 628
Sinclair Lewis, p. 628
F. Scott Fitzgerald, p. 628
Edna St. Vincent Millay, p. 629
Ernest Hemingway, p. 629

2. SUMMARIZING

Possible Responses:
1920—first scheduled radio broadcast
1923—founding of *Time*
1926—Gertrude Ederle's historic swim across the English Channel
1927—Tunney-Dempsey boxing match, Lindbergh's solo flight to Paris, Babe Ruth's record-breaking 60 home runs, *The Jazz Singer*
1928—Production of *Steamboat Willie,* the first animated talkie

3. FORMING OPINIONS

Possible Responses: Students answering yes might say that ordinary Americans, such as athletes and aviators, could epitomize lofty human virtues and the exceptional power of the individual. Students answering no may say that sports stars, such as Babe Ruth and Gertrude Ederle, were not true heroes because their achievements had no enduring social value.

4. SYNTHESIZING

Possible Responses: Radio audiences heard news and sports events as they took place; radio networks geared shows to public interests. Sports fans in stadiums cheered together for favorite athletes or teams. Filmgoers from diverse backgrounds sat together in theaters and escaped into the fantasy world of movies. Major newspapers and national magazines reached broad audiences.

CLOSE

The mass media, spectator sports, and movies created a shared popular culture in the 1920s. The art and literature of the decade reflected the disillusionment of many Americans.

Teacher's Edition   629

TERMS & NAMES
- James Weldon Johnson
- Universal Negro Improvement Association
- Harlem Renaissance
- Claude McKay
- Langston Hughes
- Zora Neale Hurston
- Paul Robeson
- Louis Armstrong
- Duke Ellington
- Bessie Smith

LEARN ABOUT the efforts of the NAACP, Marcus Garvey's movement, and the Harlem Renaissance

TO UNDERSTAND why the 1920s were a crucial era in African-American history.

Section 4 Overview

OBJECTIVES

1 To identify the causes and results of the migration of African Americans to Northern cities in the early 1900s.

2 To describe the outburst of African-American artistic activity that became known as the Harlem Renaissance.

CRITICAL THINKING

- Recognizing effects, p. 631
- Summarizing, pp. 632, 634, 635
- Synthesizing, p. 633
- Drawing conclusions, p. 635
- Analyzing causes, p. 635
- Generalizing, p. 635

FOCUS & MOTIVATE

▶ **Starting with the Student**
Watch the video "Jump at the Sun" to find out about Zora Neale Hurston and her involvement in the Harlem Renaissance.

- Using the *Teacher's Resource Book* as a guide, hold a class discussion; explore the background of Hurston in Eatonville, Florida; discuss her participation in the Harlem Renaissance; and engage in extension activities using key primary sources.

AMERICAN STORIES VIDEO SERIES
"Jump at the Sun"
Videocassette: Tape 3

Videodisc: Disc 2, Side A, Chapter 04

MORE ABOUT . . .
Zora Neale Hurston

Zora Neale Hurston died in 1960 and was buried in an unmarked grave in Florida. In the 1970s a stone marker was erected in the cemetery, commemorating her as "A Genius of the South."

ONE AMERICAN'S STORY

When the spirited Zora Neale Hurston was a girl in Eatonville, Florida, in the early 1900s, she loved to read adventure stories and myths. The powerful tales struck a chord. They made the young, talented Hurston yearn for a wider world.

A PERSONAL VOICE
My soul was with the gods and my body in the village. People just would not act like gods. . . . Raking back yards and carrying out chamber-pots, were not the tasks of Thor. I wanted to be away from drabness and to stretch my limbs in some mighty struggle.
ZORA NEALE HURSTON, quoted in *The African American Encyclopedia*

In 1915, Hurston left home and eked out a living as a nanny and house-keeper. Eventually she joined a traveling show as wardrobe girl and made her way north to New York. There she struggled to the top of African-American literary society by hard work, flamboyance, and, above all, grit. "I have seen that the world is to the strong regardless of a little pigmentation more or less," Hurston wrote later. "I do not weep at [being Negro]—I am too busy sharpening my oyster knife."

Hurston's success set her apart from most African Americans of the 1920s, but she also shared many of their experiences. Hurston was on the move, like millions of others. And, like them, she went after the pearl in the oyster—the good life in America.

JUMP AT THE SUN:
Zora Neale Hurston and the Harlem Renaissance

Zora Neale Hurston

African-American Voices in the 1920s

During the 1920s, African Americans set new goals for themselves as they moved north to the nation's cities. Their migration was an expression of their changing attitude toward themselves—an attitude perhaps best captured in a phrase first used around this time, "Black is beautiful."

THE MOVE NORTH Between 1910 and 1920, in a movement known as the Great Migration, hundreds of thousands of African Americans had uprooted themselves from their homes in the South and moved north to the big cities in search of jobs. They left the South because of racial violence and economic discrimination. In addition, in 1915 and 1916, floods, droughts, and the destruction of cotton crops by an insect called the boll weevil had brought economic disaster to the South and had provided low-paid sharecroppers and field hands with an incentive to move north. Zora Neale Hurston documented the departure of some of these African-Americans.

A PERSONAL VOICE
Some said goodbye cheerfully . . . others fearfully, with terrors of known dangers in their mouths . . . others in their eagerness for distance said nothing. The daybreak found them gone. The wind said North.
ZORA NEALE HURSTON, quoted in *Sorrow's Kitchen: The Life and Folklore of Zora Neale Hurston*

SECTION 4 RESOURCES

 PRINT RESOURCES

IN-DEPTH RESOURCES: UNIT 6
Guided Reading, p. 21
Primary Source: *from* "When the Negro Was in Vogue" by Langston Hughes, p. 28
American Lives: Louis Armstrong, p. 33

ACCESS FOR STUDENTS ACQUIRING ENGLISH
Guided Reading (Spanish), p. 209

FORMAL ASSESSMENT
Section Quiz, p. 260

ALTERNATIVE ASSESSMENT BOOK
See forms for supporting and scoring alternative activities.

 TECHNOLOGY RESOURCES

CRITICAL THINKING TRANSPARENCIES
CT55, African-American Migration from the South, 1890–1930

CD-ROM *Our Times*
Grolier Multimedia Encyclopedia

VIDEO *American Stories* video series
American Portfolio: A Videodisc for U.S. History
user's guide, pp. 193, 196–197

INTERNET McDougal Littell Learning On-Line
http://www.mcdougallittell.com

During the 1920s, 1.5 million African Americans moved to New York, Chicago, and Detroit, where their populations doubled. Still others resettled in Cleveland, Indianapolis, Philadelphia, St. Louis, Cincinnati, and Pittsburgh. By the end of the decade, 4.8 million of the nation's 12 million African Americans—some 40 percent—lived in cities.

In general, Northern cities did not welcome the massive influx of African Americans. Tensions had escalated in the years prior to 1920, culminating, in the summer of 1919, in more than 25 urban race riots.

AFRICAN-AMERICAN GOALS The race riots shocked and alarmed African Americans. In response, the National Association for the Advancement of Colored People (NAACP), which had been founded in 1909, urged blacks to aggressively protest such racial violence. W. E. B. Du Bois, a founding member of the NAACP, led a parade of 10,000 African-American men down New York's Fifth Avenue to protest all violence against African Americans. The men marched quietly beneath fluttering banners that read "Thou Shalt Not Kill." Du Bois also used the NAACP's official magazine, *The Crisis,* which he edited, as a platform for leading a struggle for civil rights. In 1919, as African-American veterans returned from the war, he wrote, "We return. / We return from fighting. / We return fighting."

By 1920, the NAACP's membership had doubled. From 1919 through the 1920s, the organization fought, by means of legislation, to protect African-American rights, and it made anti-lynching laws one of its main priorities. **James Weldon Johnson**, poet, lawyer, and NAACP executive secretary, led the fight. In 1919, three anti-lynching bills were introduced in Congress. One bill finally passed the House but was stopped in the Senate. However, the NAACP continued its campaign through anti-lynching organizations that had been established earlier by Ida B. Wells-Barnett. Gradually, the number of lynchings dropped. The NAACP represented the new, more militant voice of African Americans seeking a better place in a changing America.

MARCUS GARVEY AND THE UNIA Many African Americans found their voice in the NAACP. But African Americans still faced daily threats and discrimination, and a different, more radical message of black pride aroused their hopes.

The man behind this message was Marcus Garvey, a Jamaican immigrant who believed that African Americans should build a separate society. In 1914, he had founded, in his native Jamaica, a black nationalist group called the **Universal Negro Improvement Association** (UNIA). Two years later, he moved the UNIA to New York City and opened offices in urban ghettos in order to recruit followers.

By the mid-1920s, Garvey had mobilized more than 500,000 African Americans with a spellbinding combination of oratory, mass meetings, parades, and a message of pride.

A PERSONAL VOICE
In view of the fact that the black man of Africa has contributed as much to the world as the white man of Europe, and the brown man and yellow man of Asia, we of the Universal Negro Improvement Association demand that the white, yellow, and brown races give to the black man his place in the civilization of the world. We ask for nothing more than the rights of 400 million Negroes.

MARCUS GARVEY, speech at Liberty Hall, New York City, 1922

KEY PLAYER

JAMES WELDON JOHNSON
1871–1938
James Weldon Johnson worked as a school principal, newspaper editor, and lawyer in Florida. In 1900, he wrote the lyrics for "Lift Every Voice and Sing," the song that became known as the Black National Anthem. The first stanza begins as follows:

Lift every voice and sing
Till earth and heaven ring,
Ring with the harmonies of
   Liberty;
Let our rejoicing rise
High as the listening skies,
Let it resound loud as the
   rolling sea.

In the 1920s, Johnson straddled the worlds of politics and art. He served as executive secretary for the NAACP, spearheading the fight against lynching. In addition, he wrote well-known works, such as *God's Trombones,* a series of sermon-like poems, and *Black Manhattan,* a look at black cultural life in New York during the Roaring Twenties.

TEACHING OPTIONS

Exploring Themes

Immigration and Migration Have students discuss the push-and-pull factors that led to the Great Migration. *Push—racial violence, economic discrimination, and natural disasters in the South; pull—job opportunities and better pay in the North.*

• Do you think most African Americans achieved their goals by moving to Northern cities? Why or why not? *They encountered discrimination and violence; many urban neighborhoods were overcrowded; poverty existed in the North as well as in the South.*

Making Connections Across Time

African-American Demonstrations Have students compare the "Silent Protest Parade" led by W. E. B. Du Bois in New York City with the "Million Man March" led by Louis Farrakhan in Washington, D.C., in 1995.

• How were the two events similar? *They demonstrated African-American unity.*
• How did they differ? *Silent Protest Parade focused on violence against African Americans; the Million Man March appealed to African Americans to restore black pride and end violence.*

The Harlem Renaissance Flowers in New York

▶ **Starting with the Student**
Ask students if they listen to rap music. Are they aware that rap started as part of African-American street culture in New York City in the 1980s? Point out that jazz started in New Orleans in the early 1900s and spread to Chicago, where it revolutionized popular music in the 1920s.

▶ **Discussing Key Ideas**
• African-American writers explore and celebrate their heritage.
• African-American performers and musicians popularize their culture by appealing to a wide audience.

 GROLIER MULTIMEDIA ENCYCLOPEDIA
Overview of African-American literature

 CRITICAL THINKING TRANSPARENCIES
CT55, African-American Migration from the South, 1890–1930

MORE ABOUT . . .
Harlem
African Americans began to move into New York's Harlem neighborhood in the early 1900s. Whites became alarmed and left the community, but vacant apartments soon were filled by blacks who migrated from the South or moved from nearby neighborhoods. The transition took place without violence.

Garvey also lured followers with practical plans, especially his program to promote African-American businesses. Through the Negro Fortunes Corporation, he set up grocery stories, laundries, millinery stores, tailor shops, and a successful newspaper called *The Negro World*. Shareholders in the corporation received health and death benefits.

Furthermore, Garvey preached that African Americans needed an independent nation. He encouraged his followers to return to Africa, help native people throw off white colonial oppressors, and build a mighty nation. His idea struck a chord in many African Americans as well as in blacks in the Caribbean and Africa. As part of his plan to colonize Africa, Garvey founded a steamship company, the *Black Star Line*, to carry blacks to Africa. His steamship line later went bankrupt.

Despite the appeal of Garvey's movement, support for it declined in the mid-1920s, when he was convicted of mail fraud and jailed. Deported to Jamaica after his release from jail, he continued to lead the UNIA from his homeland, but his followers in the United States lost influence and the movement dwindled. Even so, Garvey left behind a powerful legacy of newly awakened black pride, economic independence, and reverence for Africa.

Marcus Garvey designed this uniform of purple and gold, complete with feathered hat, for his role as "Provisional President of Africa."

The Harlem Renaissance Flowers in New York

Many African Americans who migrated north moved to Harlem, a neighborhood on the upper west side of New York's Manhattan Island. In the 1920s, Harlem became the world's largest black urban community. During that decade, its population soared from about 152,000 to nearly 330,000 as newcomers from the South, the West Indies, Cuba, Puerto Rico, and Haiti crowded into handsome old brownstone apartments. The result was a highly diverse mix of cultures. Writer James Weldon Johnson described Harlem as the capital of black America.

> **A PERSONAL VOICE**
> Harlem is not merely a Negro colony or community, it is a city within a city, the greatest Negro city in the world. It is not a slum or a fringe, it is located in the heart of Manhattan and occupies one of the most beautiful . . . sections of the city. . . . It has its own churches, social and civic centers, shops, theaters, and other places of amusement. And it contains more Negroes to the square mile than any other spot on earth.
> **JAMES WELDON JOHNSON,** "Harlem: The Culture Capital"

Like many other urban neighborhoods, Harlem suffered from overcrowding, unemployment, and poverty. But its problems in the 1920s were eclipsed by a flowering of African-American creativity called the **Harlem Renaissance,** a literary and artistic movement celebrating African-American culture.

AFRICAN-AMERICAN WRITERS Above all, the Harlem Renaissance was a literary movement led by well-educated, middle-class African Americans. Caught up in the rebellious spirit of the 1920s, these young writers expressed a new pride in the African-American experience. They explored and celebrated their African heritage and their people's folklore. They wrote with defiance and poignancy about the trial of being black in a white world. W. E. B. Du Bois and James Weldon Johnson helped these young talents along, as did the Harvard-educated former Rhodes scholar Alain Locke. In 1925, Locke published *The New Negro*, a landmark collection of works by many promising young African-American writers.

Poet **Claude McKay,** a Jamaican immigrant, helped establish the Harlem Renaissance. His militant verses urged African Americans to resist prejudice and discrimination. His poems also expressed the pain of life in the black ghet-

---

Making Connections Across Cultures

African-American Heritage The Harlem Renaissance celebrated the African-American heritage. Writers incorporated the stories, expressions, rhythms, and experiences of African Americans into their works. This celebration of African-American culture spread to the white community in the 1920s, primarily through the work of African-American performers who became popular with white audiences.

Making Connections Across the Curriculum

Literature Zora Neale Hurston grew up in the South, where she was exposed to African-American oral traditions, such as the "lying" sessions in which people told exaggerated folk tales that featured talking animals. In addition to writing her own stories, Hurston toured the South to collect black folk tales, which she preserved in a collection titled *Mules and Men*. Some students might examine Hurston's book to find examples of the influence of folk tales on her work. You might also have students read other African-American folk tales, such as the Uncle Remus stories.

tos of the 1920s and the strain of being black in a world dominated by whites. "Your door is shut against my tightened face, / And I am sharp as steel with discontent," he wrote in his poem "White Houses."

Another gifted writer of the Harlem Renaissance was Jean Toomer. His experimental book *Cane* (1923), a mix of poems and sketches about blacks in the North and South, was among the first full-length literary publications of the Harlem Renaissance. The book probed the meaning of African-American life, an issue the movement would go on to explore in depth.

Missouri-born **Langston Hughes** was the movement's best-known poet. Many of Hughes's 1920s poems described the difficult everyday lives of working-class African Americans. Some moved to the tempo of jazz and the blues. (See American Studies, "Literature in the Jazz Age," pages 636–637.)

Harvard-educated writer Countee Cullen gained fame for his 1925 volume of poems titled *Color.* Unlike Hughes and others who wove African-American expressions and rhythms into their work, Cullen used a classical style to capture the black struggle. "Yet I do marvel at this curious thing: / To make a poet black and make him sing!" he wrote of the conflicts of the black artist in his most famous poem.

The most accomplished African-American woman writer of the era was **Zora Neale Hurston**. In many of her novels, books of folklore, poems, and short stories, Hurston portrayed the lives of poor, unschooled Southern blacks, "the greatest cultural wealth of the continent." Much of her work celebrated what she called the common person's art form—the simple folkways and values of people who survived slavery through their ingenuity and strength. Hurston's finest novel, *Their Eyes Were Watching God,* told the story of a strong woman's battle to assert herself and win personal freedom.

THINK THROUGH HISTORY
C. Synthesizing
In what ways did writers of the Harlem Renaissance celebrate a "rebirth"?

C. Answer They expressed their pride in the African-American experience; they celebrated their heritage and folklore.

Many other talented women writers added their voices to the Harlem Renaissance. Novelist and short story writer Nella Larsen won fame for "Quicksand" and "Passing," despairing stories of black women who struggled to seize control of their lives and fortunes. Boston-born Dorothy West wrote poignant stories about people trapped in a web of racism and sexism. West also founded *Challenge,* a magazine of African-American writing..

Alain Locke, the champion of many of the best African-American writers of the 1920s, looked back on the Harlem Renaissance from the vantage point of the Great Depression—ten years after the publication of *The New Negro.* In that time, his point of view had changed: "The rosy enthusiasm and hopes of

The painting *Black Belt* by Archibald J. Motley, Jr. records the lively street life in an urban African-American neighborhood. The phrase "black belt" was sometimes used to describe an area having a predominately African-American population.

633

MORE ABOUT . . .
The Harlem Renaissance
In the Harlem Renaissance, African Americans created their own distinctive culture in the United States. The writers and artists of the Harlem Renaissance celebrated their culture, but few of them addressed the problems that most African Americans faced in the 1920s. The Harlem Renaissance was brief, but it remains a lasting tribute to the artistic creativity of African Americans.

Now have students fill in a chart, similar to the one below, comparing themes of major Harlem Renaissance writers.

Themes	
McKay	pain of life in black ghettos
Toomer	
Hughes	
Hurston	
West	

IN-DEPTH RESOURCES: UNIT 6
Primary Source: *from* "When the Negro Was in Vogue" by Langston Hughes, p. 28

TEACHING OPTION

👥 *Cooperative Activity: Celebrating African-American Culture*

Task: Groups of students will develop presentations honoring writers, performers, and musicians of the Harlem Renaissance.

Purpose: To recognize the impact of the Harlem Renaissance on American culture.

Activity: Divide students into three groups representing writers, performers, and musicians. Each group should develop a presentation celebrating the work of the African-American artists they represent. Presentations might include recordings of music, posters

advertising performances, book reviews, dramatic readings, and role-playing. Provide time for the groups to share their presentations with the class.

📁 **Building a Portfolio:** If students create a product as part of their presentation, they should add a note describing their contribution to the project.

ALTERNATIVE ASSESSMENT BOOK
Standards for Evaluating a Cooperative Activity

Standards for Evaluation
Presentations should . . .

• give examples of artists' works
• suggest the nature of the artists' achievements
• show the relationship between the artists and the Harlem Renaissance

The Hot Five

Viewing the Photograph
Point out to students the instruments in the picture. Armstrong at the piano holds a trumpet. The other instruments on display are a banjo, a saxophone, a clarinet, and a trombone. In this group, Lil Hardin was the pianist.

Extension Bring in and play for students some recordings of the Hot Five to give them a sense of how the music of the period sounded.

MORE ABOUT . . .
Louis Armstrong

As a teenager in New Orleans, Louis Armstrong was arrested for firing a gun on New Year's Eve and sent to a home for boys. In that institution, Armstrong first learned to play the cornet. He continued to develop the talent that eventually made him one of the most influential jazz musicians of all time and an internationally known performer. Once, when asked to define jazz, Armstrong replied, "Man, if you gotta ask, you'll never know."

IN-DEPTH RESOURCES: UNIT 6
American Lives: Louis Armstrong, p. 33

OUR TIMES
Louis Armstrong

The Hot Five, which included *(from left)* Louis Armstrong, Johnny St. Cyr, Johnny Dodds, Kid Ory, and Lil Hardin.

1925 were cruelly deceptive mirages. [The Depression] revealed a Harlem that the social worker knew all along, but had not been able to dramatize. There is no cure or saving magic in poetry and art for precarious marginal employment, high mortality rates and civic neglect."

AFRICAN-AMERICAN PERFORMERS The spirit and talent of the Harlem Renaissance reached far beyond the world of African-American writers and intellectuals. In fact, some observers, including Langston Hughes, thought the movement was launched with *Shuffle Along*, a black musical comedy popular in 1921.

> **A PERSONAL VOICE**
> *Shuffle Along* was a honey of a show. Swift, bright, funny, rollicking and gay, with a dozen danceable, singable tunes. . . . It gave just the proper push to that Negro vogue of the '20s that spread to books, African sculpture, music, and dancing.
> **LANGSTON HUGHES,** *The Big Sea*

Several songs in *Shuffle Along*, including "Love Will Find a Way," won popularity among white audiences. The show also spotlighted the talents of several black performers, including singers Florence Mills, Josephine Baker, and Mabel Mercer.

During the 1920s, African Americans in the performing arts won large followings. Tenor Roland Hayes rose to stardom as a concert singer, while singer and actress Ethel Waters debuted on Broadway in the musical *Africana*. **Paul Robeson,** the son of a runaway slave, became a major dramatic actor. After a brilliant record as a student and athlete at Rutgers University, Robeson went on to Columbia University Law School. His magnificent bass voice and commanding presence brought him early fame as an actor. In 1924, he portrayed the original Emperor Jones in Eugene O'Neill's play of the same name. His performance in Shakespeare's *Othello*, first in London and later in New York City, was widely acclaimed. Subsequently, the racism Robeson experienced in the United States and the indignities inflicted upon him because of his support of the Soviet Union and the Communist Party made him take up residence abroad, and he lived for a time in England and the Soviet Union. (See Historical Spotlight, on page 780.)

AFRICAN AMERICANS AND JAZZ Jazz was born in the early 20th century in New Orleans, where musicians blended instrumental ragtime and vocal blues into an exuberant new sound. In 1919, Joe "King" Oliver and his Creole Jazz Band traveled north to Chicago, carrying jazz with them. Joining Oliver's group in 1922 was a young trumpet player named **Louis Armstrong,** whose talent rocketed him to stardom in the jazz world. Famous for his astounding sense of rhythm and his ability to improvise, Armstrong made personal expression a key part of jazz. After two years in Chicago, in 1924 he joined Fletcher Henderson's band, the most important big jazz band in New York City. Armstrong went on to become the single most important and influential musician in the history of jazz. At the end of his life, he said of his anticipated funeral,

> **A PERSONAL VOICE**
> They're going to blow over me. Cats will be coming from everywhere to play. I had a beautiful life. When I get to the Pearly Gates I'll play a duet with Gabriel. We'll play "Sleepy Time Down South." He wants to be remembered for his music just like I do.
> **LOUIS ARMSTRONG,** quoted in *The Negro Almanac*

**THINK THROUGH HISTORY
D. Summarizing**
In what other areas besides writing did African Americans of the 1920s achieve remarkable results?

D. Answer
African Americans produced outstanding achievements in the performing arts.

TEACHING OPTIONS

Making Global Connections

The European Tour In 1932 Louis Armstrong appeared at the London Palladium, and he toured Europe in 1933–1935. Duke Ellington also performed in Europe during the early 1930s. Both men were to return to Europe with their bands on musical tours throughout their careers. Discuss how jazz musicians helped spread American culture to other parts of the world.

Making Connections Across the Curriculum

Music Provide opportunities for students to listen to recordings of jazz artists of the 1920s. Some of the most important African-American musicians of the period were Louis Armstrong, King Oliver, Duke Ellington, Cab Calloway, and Bessie Smith. Point out the key elements of jazz: improvisation (the ability to create music spontaneously) and syncopation (the use of irregular rhythms and accents). Some students might be interested in tracing the development of jazz since the 1920s.

Jazz quickly spread from Chicago to Kansas City, Los Angeles, and New York City, and it became the most popular music for dancing. During the 1920s, Harlem pulsed to the sounds of jazz, which lured throngs of whites to the showy, exotic nightclubs there, including the famed Cotton Club. In the late 1920s, **Edward Kennedy "Duke" Ellington,** a jazz pianist and composer, led his ten-piece orchestra at the Cotton Club. In a 1925 essay titled "The Negro Spirituals," Alain Locke seemed almost to predict the career of the talented Ellington.

A PERSONAL VOICE
Up to the present, the resources of Negro music have been tentatively exploited in only one direction at a time—melodically here, rhythmically there, harmonically in a third direction. A genius that would organize its distinctive elements in a formal way would be the musical giant of his age.

ALAIN LOCKE, quoted in *Afro-American Writing: An Anthology of Prose and Poetry*

Through the 1920s and 1930s, Ellington won renown as one of America's greatest composers, with pieces such as "Mood Indigo" and "Sophisticated Lady."

Cab Calloway, a talented drummer, saxophonist, and singer, formed another important jazz orchestra that played at Harlem's Savoy Ballroom and the Cotton Club, alternating with Duke Ellington. With Louis Armstrong, Calloway popularized "scat," or jazz singing using sounds instead of words.

Bessie Smith, a female blues singer, was perhaps the outstanding vocalist of the decade. She recorded on black-oriented labels produced by the major record companies. She achieved enormous popularity and in 1927 became the highest-paid black artist in the world.

Many African-American musical artists achieved great celebrity in Europe. The most popular was Josephine Baker, who lived and worked in Paris. A dancing, singing, and comedy star for 40 years, Baker, known for walking her pet leopards, was outrageously stylish. During World War II, however, Baker volunteered for the Red Cross and spied for the French underground. After the war, the French government awarded her the Legion of Honor.

The Harlem Renaissance represented a portion of the great social and cultural changes that swept America in the 1920s. The period was characterized by economic prosperity, new ideas, changing values, and personal freedom as well as important developments in art, literature, and music. Most of the social changes were lasting. The economic boom, however, was short-lived.

E. Answer
The Harlem Renaissance helped nurture African Americans' pride in their unique culture. It also contributed great literature, drama, and music to American culture.

THINK THROUGH HISTORY
E. Drawing Conclusions
What did the Harlem Renaissance contribute to both black and general American history?

Section 4 Assessment

1. TERMS & NAMES

Identify:
• James Weldon Johnson
• Universal Negro Improvement Association
• Harlem Renaissance
• Claude McKay
• Langston Hughes
• Zora Neale Hurston
• Paul Robeson
• Louis Armstrong
• Duke Ellington
• Bessie Smith

2. SUMMARIZING Copy the tree diagram shown below, and fill it in with three areas of artistic achievement from the Harlem Renaissance. For each area of achievement, write the name of two outstanding African-American artists.

Harlem Renaissance: Areas of Achievement

examples: examples: examples:

3. ANALYZING CAUSES Speculate on why an African-American renaissance flowered during the 1920s. Support your answer.

THINK ABOUT
• racial discrimination in the South
• campaigns for equality in the North
• the diverse cultures that made up Harlem's soaring population
• the changing culture of all Americans

4. GENERALIZING What were some of the most important ideas, opinions, and beliefs expressed in African-American literature of the 1920s? Support your answer with examples from the text.

THINK ABOUT
• the experience of writers such as Langston Hughes and Zora Neale Hurston
• what that society was like
• the flowering of the Harlem Renaissance in all the arts

The Roaring Life of the 1920s **635**

ANSWERS

1. TERMS & NAMES
James Weldon Johnson, p. 631
Universal Negro Improvement Association, p. 631
Harlem Renaissance, p. 632
Claude McKay, p. 632
Langston Hughes, p. 633
Zora Neale Hurston, p. 633
Paul Robeson, p. 634
Louis Armstrong, p. 634
Duke Ellington, p. 635
Bessie Smith, p. 635

2. SUMMARIZING
Possible Responses:
Writers—Langston Hughes, Zora Neale Hurston
Performers—Paul Robeson, Ethel Waters
Musicians—Bessie Smith, Louis Armstrong

3. ANALYZING CAUSES
Possible Responses: After suffering economic disadvantage and racial prejudice in the South, African Americans migrated to the North, especially to urban areas like Harlem, where the community supported the arts and had its own cultural institutions and theaters. The mingling of Caribbean peoples with Southern and Northern blacks in Harlem may have created a unique cultural interchange and served as a source of inspiration for works of art.

4. GENERALIZING
Possible Responses: African-American writers expressed black pride and black identity, protested racial discrimination, told of the struggles of African Americans in a white-dominated society, celebrated their African heritage, and celebrated the strength and ingenuity of African Americans.

OBJECTIVES

1 To describe the role of
American literature in the
1920s.

2 To recognize three 1920s literary icons and give examples of their works.

FOCUS & MOTIVATE

▶ *Starting with the Student*
Have students think about
celebrated Americans today.

• Which of these people do
students think best cap-
tures the spirit of the time?

• Whom would students
name as contemporary
America's greatest living
writers? Students should
cite achievements to sup-
port their opinions.

MORE ABOUT . . .
Langston Hughes

Hughes was an unknown
figure employed as a bus-
boy when the eminent poet
Vachel Lindsay came into
the Washington, D.C.,
restaurant where he worked.
Hoping for recognition,
Hughes left some of his
poems beside Lindsay's
plate. Later that day Lindsay
read them and was so
impressed that he praised
them to reporters. Hughes's
name appeared in newspa-
pers the next day, and not
long afterward Alfred A.
Knopf published Hughes's
first poetry collection, *The
Weary Blues*.

Literature in the Jazz Age

After World War I, American literature—like American
jazz—moved to the vanguard of the international artistic
scene. Many American writers remained in Europe after the
war, some settling in London, but many more joining the
expatriate community on the Left Bank of the Seine River in
Paris, where they could live cheaply.

Back in the United States, such cities as Chicago and New
York were magnets for America's young artistic talents. The
sweeping popularity of jazz helped spur the Harlem
Renaissance, a blossoming of African-American culture
named for the New York City neighborhood where so many
African-American writers and artists settled. Further downtown, the artistic community of Greenwich Village drew literary talents such as the poets Edna St. Vincent Millay and
E. E. cummings and the playwright Eugene O'Neill.

F. SCOTT FITZGERALD

The foremost chronicler of the Jazz Age was the Minnesota-born
writer F. Scott Fitzgerald, who in Paris, New York, and later
Hollywood rubbed elbows with other leading American writers of
the day. In the following passage from Fitzgerald's novel *The Great
Gatsby*, the narrator describes a fashionable 1920s party thrown by
the title character at his Long Island estate.

By seven o'clock the orchestra has arrived, no thin five-piece
affair, but a whole pitful of oboes and trombones and saxophones
and viols and cornets and piccolos, and low and high drums. The
last swimmers have come in from the beach now and are dressing
upstairs; the cars from New York are parked five deep in the drive,
and already the halls and salons and verandas are gaudy with primary colors, and hair
shorn in strange new ways, and shawls beyond the dreams of Castile. The bar is in full
swing, and floating rounds of cocktails permeate the garden outside, until the air is alive
with chatter and laughter, and casual innuendo and introductions forgotten on the spot,
and enthusiastic meetings between women who never knew each other's names.

The lights grow brighter as the earth lurches away from the sun, and now the
orchestra is playing yellow cocktail music, and the opera of voices pitches a key higher.
Laughter is easier minute by minute, spilled with prodigality, tipped out at a cheerful
word. The groups change more swiftly, swell with new arrivals, dissolve and form in the
same breath; already there are wanderers, confident girls who weave here and there
among the stouter and more stable, become for a sharp, joyous moment the center of a
group, and then, excited with triumph, glide on through the sea-change of faces and
voices and color under the constantly changing light.

Suddenly one of these gypsies, in trembling opal, seizes a cocktail out of the air,
dumps it down for courage and, moving her hands like Frisco, dances out alone on the
canvas platform. A momentary hush; the orchestra leader varies his rhythm obligingly
for her, and there is a burst of chatter as the erroneous news goes around that she is
Gilda Gray's understudy from the *Follies*. The party has begun.

F. SCOTT FITZGERALD, FROM *The Great Gatsby* (1925)

RECOMMENDED RESOURCES

Books

Cheney, Anne. *Millay in
Greenwich Village*. University:
U of Alabama P, 1975. A biog-
raphy of the young Millay.

Cowley, Malcolm. *Exile's
Return,* New ed. New York:
Viking, 1951. A famous literary
history of the 1920s.

Fitzgerald, F. Scott. *The Great
Gatsby*. New York: Scribner's,
1925. Fitzgerald's masterpiece.

Hughes, Langston. *The
Langston Hughes Reader*. New
York: Braziller, 1958. A good
sampling of his work.

Lewis, David L. *When Harlem
Was in Vogue*. New York:
Knopf, 1981. A well-known
account of the Harlem
Renaissance.

Millay, Edna St. Vincent.
Collected Poems. New York:
Harper, 1956. All the famous
lyrics and sonnets.

Videos

Against the Odds. PBS Video,
1994. Describes artists of the
Harlem Renaissance.

The Great Gatsby. Dir. Jack
Clayton. Paramount, 1974.
Fitzgerald's novel on screen.

Langston Hughes: Poet. Dir.
Rhonda Fabian and Jerry
Baber. Schlessinger Video
Productions, 1994. Part of the
Black Americans of Achieve-
ment Video Collection.

*Langston Hughes: The Poet in
Our Hearts*. Chip Taylor
Communications, 1994.
Readings of several of
Hughes's poems.

EDNA ST. VINCENT MILLAY

In the 1920s, Edna St. Vincent Millay was the quintessential modern young woman, a celebrated poet living a bohemian life in New York's Greenwich Village. The following quatrain memorably proclaims the exuberant philosophy of the young and fashionable in the Roaring Twenties.

My candle burns at both ends;
　　It will not last the night;
But ah, my foes, and oh, my friends—
　　It gives a lovely light!

EDNA ST. VINCENT MILLAY, "FIRST FIG,"
FROM *A Few Figs from Thistles* (1920)

LANGSTON HUGHES

The towering figure of the Harlem Renaissance, Langston Hughes often imbued his poetry with the rhythms of jazz and blues. In the following poem, "Dream Variations," for example, the two stanzas resemble improvised passages played and varied by a jazz musician. The dream representing freedom and equality is a recurring symbol in Hughes's verse and has appeared frequently in African-American literature since the 1920s, when Hughes penned this famous poem.

To fling my arms wide
In some place of the sun,
To whirl and to dance
Till the white day is done.
Then rest at cool evening
Beneath a tall tree
While night comes on gently,
　Dark like me—
That is my dream!

To fling my arms wide
In the face of the sun,
Dance! Whirl! Whirl!
Till the quick day is done.
Rest at pale evening . . .
A tall, slim tree . . .
Night coming tenderly
　Black like me.

LANGSTON HUGHES, "DREAM VARIATIONS,"
FROM *The Weary Blues* (1926)

INTERACT WITH HISTORY

1. **COMPARING AND CONTRASTING**
   What does each selection reveal about life in 1920s America? Cite details to help explain your answers.

    SEE SKILLBUILDER HANDBOOK, PAGE 1041.

2. **CREATING A BIBLIOGRAPHY** Draw up an annotated bibliography of American literature of the 1920s, perhaps grouping titles by genre (poetry, drama, and so on) before arranging them alphabetically by the author's surname. The annotation, or brief description, for each work you list should include information on the work's relevance to the period and on its place in American letters.

    For more about literature in the 1920s, click on **Social Studies** at http://www.mcdougallittell.com

The Roaring Life of the 1920s **637**

REVIEWING THE CHAPTER

TERMS & NAMES
1. bootlegger, p. 615
2. fundamentalism, p. 616
3. flapper, p. 618
4. Babe Ruth, p. 626
5. Charles A. Lindbergh, p. 627
6. F. Scott Fitzgerald, p. 628
7. Harlem Renaissance, p. 632
8. Langston Hughes, p. 633
9. Zora Neale Hurston, p. 633
10. Paul Robeson, p. 634

MAIN IDEAS
Answers will vary.

11. Government had to patrol coastlines and inland borders for alcohol smugglers, monitor highways for trucks carrying illegal alcohol, oversee industries that used alcohol.

12. Scopes broke a Tennessee law that made teaching evolution a crime. He was found guilty, but a higher court later set aside the verdict.

13. A boyish haircut, long beads, bangle bracelets, close-fitting hat, short, waistless dress.

14. Divorce rate doubled; birthrate declined; more married women worked; labor-saving devices provided more leisure.

15. Broadened curriculums to meet the needs of a wide range of students, offered vocational training and home economics, and taught English to immigrants.

16. Crossword puzzles; mahjong; flagpole sitting; bike races; dance marathons.

17. Conformity; materialism; vulgarity of business culture; shallowness of middle-class values; constricting morals; glorification of war.

18. Desire of African Americans to escape inequality and poverty, fight injustice, improve their lives.

19. Pride; racial justice; equality; richness of folklore.

20. Claude McKay, Langston Hughes, and Zora Neale Hurston were outstanding writers; Josephine Baker, Paul Robeson, Louis Armstrong, and Duke Ellington were outstanding performers and musicians.

Chapter 21 Assessment

REVIEWING THE CHAPTER

TERMS & NAMES For each term below, write a sentence explaining its historical significance during the 1920s. For each person listed, write a sentence explaining his or her role in events of this period.

1. bootlegger
2. fundamentalism
3. flapper
4. Babe Ruth
5. Charles A. Lindbergh
6. F. Scott Fitzgerald
7. Harlem Renaissance
8. Langston Hughes
9. Zora Neale Hurston
10. Paul Robeson

MAIN IDEAS

SECTION 1 *(pages 612–617)*

Changing Ways of Life
11. Why was heavy funding needed to enforce the Volstead Act?
12. Explain the circumstances and outcome of biology teacher John Scopes's trial.

SECTION 2 *(pages 618–621)*

The Twenties Woman
13. Describe the appearance of the typical flapper, including her hair style, clothing, and fashion accessories.
14. What were the key social, economic, and technological changes of the 1920s that affected women's marriages and their family life?

SECTION 3 *(pages 624–629)*

Education and Popular Culture
15. How did high schools change during the 1920s?
16. What fads gained popularity during the 1920s?
17. Cite examples of the flaws in American society that some famous 1920s authors attacked in their writing.

SECTION 4 *(pages 630–635)*

The Harlem Renaissance
18. What do the Great Migration and the growth of the NAACP and UNIA reveal about the African-American experience in this period?
19. What were some of the important themes dealt with by African-American writers in the Harlem Renaissance?
20. What were some of the important African-American achievements in the arts during this period?

THINKING CRITICALLY

1. **CULTURAL TRENDS OF THE ROARING TWENTIES** Create a concept web similar to the one below, and fill it in with trends in popular culture that emerged in the 1920s and that continue to influence American society today.

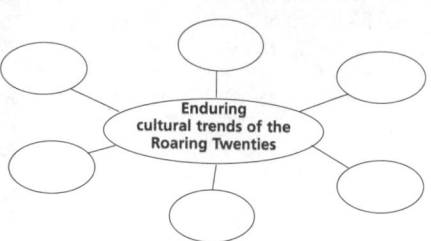

2. **VOICES AGAINST INTOLERANCE** Who do you think were the major voices against intolerance during the 1920s? Support your choices.

3. **DESCRIBING THE 1920S** Reread the quote by Westbrook Pegler on page 610. Do you think his comment accurately sums up the 1920s? Support your opinion.

4. **ALL THAT JAZZ** In the American Studies feature in this chapter, "Literature in the Jazz Age," you read excerpts from works—all written in the 1920s—by F. Scott Fitzgerald, Edna St. Vincent Millay, and Langston Hughes. How might a phrase current at the time—"Flaming Youth"—be an appropriate and accurate phrase to describe the young people and voices in these excerpts?

5. **ANALYZING PRIMARY SOURCES** Read the following excerpt from F. Scott Fitzgerald's 1931 essay in which he reflects on the Roaring Twenties. Then answer the question below.

> It was an age of miracles, it was an age of art, it was an age of excess, and it was an age of satire. . . . Scarcely had the staider citizens of the republic caught their breaths when the wildest of all generations, the generation which had been adolescent during the confusion of the War, brusquely shouldered my contemporaries out of the way and danced into the limelight. This was the generation whose girls dramatized themselves as flappers, the generation that corrupted its elders and eventually overreached itself less through lack of morals than through lack of taste. . . . Charm, notoriety, mere good manners, weighed more than money as a social asset. This was rather splendid, but things were getting thinner and thinner as the eternal necessary human values tried to spread over all that expansion.
>
> **F. SCOTT FITZGERALD,** "Echoes of the Jazz Age"

What does F. Scott Fitzgerald praise and what does he criticize about the young people of the 1920s? Support your opinion.

THINKING CRITICALLY

1. CULTURAL TRENDS OF THE ROARING TWENTIES
Possible Responses: Media hyping of sensational trials; public's fascination with scandalous stories in tabloid newspapers; hero worship of sports celebrities; popularity of spectator sports and movies; popularity of African-American music; novels of social protest; poetry with political messages; fashion as a statement of rebellion.

2. VOICES AGAINST INTOLERANCE
Possible Responses: Clarence Darrow and John Scopes, for upholding scientific theory and the right to teach evolution; Sinclair Lewis, for writing novels that criticized conformity and materialism; W. E. B. Du Bois, for leading the struggle for African Americans' civil rights; Claude McKay, for writing poetry that urged resistance to racial discrimination; Marcus Garvey, for expressing the message of black pride and equality.

3. DESCRIBING THE 1920S
Possible Responses: Students answering yes may say that the era is known for frivolity, citing its fashions, the growth of popular culture, and the emphasis on movie and sports heroes. Those answering no may say that the era offered much more than nonsense; they may cite new roles for women, the growth of schools, advances in civil-rights awareness, the flowering of African-American culture, and the creation of new literature by gifted writers.

ALTERNATIVE ASSESSMENT

1. CREATING AN AUDIO SAMPLER

What was popular culture like during the 1920s?

Cooperative Learning Working with a small group, tape-record an audio sampler that reflects American culture and society during this decade.

 CD-ROM Expand your understanding of the period by using the CD-ROM *Our Times,* your textbook, and additional sources.

- Gather a wide variety of sources, including excerpts from vintage radio broadcasts and popular music; selections of literature, comedy, and drama of the day; excerpts from news, sports, and fashion articles in periodicals of the time; and first-person accounts from oral histories.
- For each selection, tape-record a brief explanation that identifies its source and its significance.
- Share the tape with the rest of your class.

2. LEARNING FROM MEDIA

 VIDEO View the McDougal Littell Video for Chapter 21, *Jump at the Sun.* Discuss the following questions in small groups and then do the cooperative-learning activity.

- What effect did World War I have on the attitudes of African Americans?
- What effect might growing up in Eatonville, Florida, have had on Zora Neale Hurston?
- How did Hurston connect the study of anthropology with the world of her youth?
- **Cooperative Learning** In your group, make a collage that represents Zora Neale Hurston's dramatic life. Search through books, magazines, and encyclopedias for pictures that seem to capture Hurston's spirit and life. Make copies of the pictures, and then put them together in a collage inspired by Zora Neale Hurston.

3. PORTFOLIO PROJECT

 Use the Living History activity to expand your portfolio.

LIVING HISTORY

PRESENTING YOUR DISPLAY

Display your now-and-then storyboard with those of your classmates. Then, with your classmates, discuss the impact the storyboards had on you. Consider these questions during your discussion:

- How closely do 1920s issues parallel today's issues?
- What conclusions, if any, can be drawn from these parallels?
- On which issues do you think our country has made the most progress? Why?

Add your storyboard to your American history portfolio.

Review Chapter 21

CULTURAL CLASHES Changes in lifestyles during the 1920s resulted in clashes between the conservative values of rural Americans and the more liberal values of urban Americans. Small towns, firmly entrenched in traditional moral and religious beliefs, embraced prohibition, while the ethnically diverse cities rejected the ban on alcohol. Difficulties in enforcing prohibition led to an increase in lawlessness. The Scopes trial brought to the forefront another divisive issue as attorney Clarence Darrow defended the teaching of evolution.

TWENTIES WOMEN The emancipated young flapper emerged as a new ideal for some women, while her rebelliousness and bold fashions shocked others. Many women during this time cast themselves in other new roles—as more equal partners to their husbands and as valuable employees in the business and professional world. However, the majority of married women remained homemakers.

POPULAR CULTURE The growing mass media during the 1920s shaped a mass culture. Major newspapers, magazines, and radio reached broad audiences, who, in turn, became better informed about many events, including sports. While the media hyped real-life stories of heroic accomplishments, the movies manufactured make-believe stories to thrill theater audiences. Gifted writers, composers, and artists expressed their unique visions of the American scene.

AFRICAN–AMERICAN VOICES Responding to the urban race riots of 1919, African-American leaders became more vocal and publicly denounced racial violence and injustice. The NAACP represented a new, more militant political voice, which was echoed in the literary voices of many African-American writers during the Harlem Renaissance. The writers, performers, and musicians who were part of this movement displayed extraordinary artistic talents.

Preview Chapter 22

As the Roaring Twenties came to a close, the downturn in the economy signaled the end of an era. In 1929, the stock market crashed, marking the beginning of the Great Depression. This economic collapse brought enormous suffering to Americans from all walks of life. You will learn about these and other developments in the next chapter.

The Roaring Life of the 1920s **639**

---

1. CREATING AN AUDIO SAMPLER
Standards for Evaluation
An audio sampler should meet the following criteria:

- Presents a wide variety of sources.
- Reflects American culture during the 1920s.
- Explains the significance of each selection.

2. LEARNING FROM MEDIA
Answers to the questions:

- African Americans who fought to defend democracy in the war were bitter when they encountered discrimination at home.
- She grew up with a love for the town, its people, and their stories, but she wanted to enter the wider world.
- Her study convinced her that the African-American stories she had heard in her childhood were a vital part of American culture.

COLLAGE ON ZORA NEALE HURSTON
Standards for Evaluation
A collage should meet the following criteria:

- Includes pictures that illustrate Hurston's life.
- Includes pictures from a variety of sources, including books, magazines, and encyclopedias.
- Is well organized and neatly put together.

3. PORTFOLIO PROJECT
LIVING HISTORY
Standards for Evaluation
A strong display should meet the following criteria:

- Presents important issues.
- Shows a clear parallelism between the 1920s and today.
- Presents clear conclusions based on comparisons between now and then.

IN-DEPTH RESOURCES: UNIT 6
See the form for scoring this activity on page 35.

THINKING CRITICALLY

4. ALL THAT JAZZ
Possible Responses: The images of bright lights, parties, dancing, whirling, and candles all seem to belong to a world of fast living and brief but luminous existence that suggests youthful exuberance.

5. ANALYZING PRIMARY SOURCES
Possible Responses: He praises them for their art, their flamboyance, and their breaking away from tradition. He faults them for lack of good taste, for corrupting the older generation, for going too far, and for losing sight of necessary human values.

	Key Ideas	TEACHING SUPPORT	ASSESSMENT
SECTION 1 The Nation's Sick Economy *pp. 642–649*	*Economic problems affecting industries, farmers, and consumers lead to the Great Depression.*	*In-Depth Resources: Unit 6* • Guided Reading, p. 36 • Primary Sources: The Stock Market Crash, p. 42; Political Cartoon, p. 43 • American Lives: Gordon Parks, p. 49; Alfred E. Smith, p. 50 **COOPERATIVE ACTIVITY** • Creating a TV Special About the Stock Market Crash, p. 646 (TE)	*Section 1 Assessment,* p. 649 (PE) *Self-Assessment,* p. 649 (TE) *Formal Assessment* • Section Quiz, p. 269 *Alternative Assessment Book* • Standards for Evaluating a Cooperative Activity
SECTION 2 Hardship and Suffering During the Depression *pp. 650–654*	*The Great Depression brings suffering of many kinds and degrees to people from all walks of life.*	*In-Depth Resources: Unit 6* • Guided Reading, p. 37 • Skillbuilder Practice: Formulating Historical Questions, p. 39 • Geography Application: The Great Depression Takes Its Toll, p. 40 • Primary Source: Letter from a Dust Bowl Survivor, p. 44 • Literature: from *The Grapes of Wrath* by John Steinbeck, p. 46 **COOPERATIVE ACTIVITY** • Compiling an Oral History of the Depression, p. 653 (TE)	*Section 2 Assessment,* p. 654 (PE) *Self-Assessment,* p. 654 (TE) *Formal Assessment* • Section Quiz, p. 270 *Alternative Assessment Book* • Standards for Evaluating a Cooperative Activity
SECTION 3 Hoover Struggles with the Depression *pp. 655–659*	*President Hoover tries to restore confidence and halt the Depression, but his actions are ineffective.*	*In-Depth Resources: Unit 6* • Guided Reading, p. 38 • Primary Source: Attack on the Bonus Army, p. 45 **COOPERATIVE ACTIVITY** • Debating the Bonus Army March, p. 658 (TE)	*Section 3 Assessment,* p. 659 (PE) *Self-Assessment,* p. 659 (TE) *Formal Assessment* • Section Quiz, p. 271 *Alternative Assessment Book* • Standards for Evaluating a Cooperative Activity
CHAPTER RESOURCES	**Chapter Overview** *The economic boom of the 1920s collapses in 1929 as the United States enters a deep economic depression. Millions of Americans lose their jobs, and President Hoover is unable to end the downslide.*	*In-Depth Resources: Unit 6* • Living History Project: Worksheet, p. 51; Standards, p. 52 *Telescoping the Times* • Chapter Summary, pp. 43–44 *Planning for Block Schedules*	*Chapter Assessment,* pp. 660–661 (PE) *Alternative Assessment,* p. 661 (PE) *Formal Assessment* • Chapter Test, forms A and B, pp. 272–277 **Test Generator** *Alternative Assessment Book* See explanation and forms for different kinds of alternative assessments including portfolio assessment.

Geography Transparencies
• G22, Growth of Electricity: 1918, 1933

Critical Thinking Transparencies
• CT22, The Great Depression
• CT56, Investing in Stock

Grolier Multimedia Encyclopedia
• campaign speech by Herbert Hoover

Electronic Library of Primary Sources
• "On Minding Your Own Business"

INTERNET RESOURCES
• See Interact with History p. 647 (PE) for an activity that includes the Internet as an enrichment option.

Humanities Transparencies
• H21, Dust Storm, 1936. Arthur Rothstein

Electronic Library of Primary Sources
• "Beans, Bacon, and Gravy"
• Childhood During the Depression by Cesar Chavez

AMERICAN STORIES VIDEO SERIES
• "Broke but Not Broken"

INTERNET RESOURCES
• See McDougal Littell Learning On-Line for links to information about the Dust Bowl.

Electronic Library of Primary Sources
• from A Report on the Employment of Federal Troops by General Douglas MacArthur
• from B. E. F.: The Story of the Bonus Army by W. W. Waters

INTERNET RESOURCES
• See McDougal Littell Learning On-Line for links to information about Herbert Hoover.

American Portfolio: A Videodisc for U.S. History, user's guide, pp. 201–206

INTERNET RESOURCES:
Learning On-Line: Social Studies
http://www.mcdougallittell.com

Block Scheduling (90 MINUTES)

Day 1

Section 1, pp. 642–649
Section 2, pp. 650–654

AMERICAN STORIES VIDEO SERIES
"Broke But Not Broken"

Section Assessments, pp. 649, 654

Day 2

Section 3, pp. 655–659
Section Assessment, p. 659
Chapter Assessment, pp. 660–661

YEARLY PACING *Chapter 22 Total:* 2 days *Yearly Total:* 85 days

See *Planning for Block Schedules* for special activities and pacing strategies.

Customizing for Special Populations

Students Acquiring English

Access for Students Acquiring English
• Guided Reading for Sections 1–3 (Spanish), pp. 215–217
• Chapter Summary (Spanish), pp. 213–214
• Skillbuilder Practice: Formulating Historical Questions (Spanish), p. 218
• Geography Application: The Great Depression Takes Its Toll (Spanish), p. 219

AMERICAN STORIES VIDEO SERIES
• "Broke but Not Broken"

INTERNET RESOURCES
• See McDougal Littell Learning On-Line The Diverse Classroom.

Less Proficient Readers

In-Depth Resources: Unit 6
• Guided Reading for Sections 1–3, pp. 36–38
• Skillbuilder: Formulating Historical Questions, p. 39
• Geography Application: The Great Depression Takes Its Toll, p. 40

Telescoping the Times
• Chapter Summary, pp. 43–44

See additional strategies at point of use in the Teacher's Edition.

Gifted and Talented Students

In-Depth Resources: Unit 6
• Primary Sources: The Stock Market Crash, p. 42; Political Cartoon, p. 43; Letter from a Dust Bowl Survivor, p. 44; Attack on the Bonus Army, p. 45
• American Lives: Gordon Parks, p. 49; Alfred E. Smith, p. 50

See additional strategies at point of use in the Teacher's Edition.

Connections to Literature READINGS FOR STUDENTS

In-Depth Resources: Unit 6
• from *The Grapes of Wrath* by John Steinbeck, p. 46

Enrichment Reading
• Hurston, Zora Neale
Their Eyes Were Watching God.
New York: Harper & Row, 1990
First published in 1937, this novel focuses on a proud, independent African-American woman's search for identity. In a journey that takes her through three marriages and back to her roots, this story powerfully affirms and celebrates African-American culture.

• Steinbeck, John
Of Mice and Men.
New York, Penguin Books, 1994
In depression-era California, two migrant workers dream of better days until an act of unintentional violence leads to tragedy.

McDougal Littell *Literature Connections*

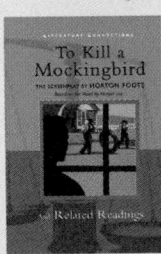

• Horton Foote
To Kill a Mockingbird (the screenplay) *(with related readings) Adapted from the Pulitzer-prize winning novel by Harper Lee, this screenplay is constructed as a series of episodes concerning the trial of an unjustly accused black man. It examines the consequences of ignorance, prejudice, and hate, and the values of courage, honor, and decency.*

McDougal Littell *The Language of Literature*
American Literature

• William Faulkner,
"A Rose for Emily," p. 392

The Great Depression Begins

▶ *Starting with the Student*
- Ask students what they already know about the Great Depression. Have they ever discussed the Depression with a relative who lived through it? If so, what did that relative say?
- Then, discuss the opening quotation. What does La Follette suggest about the prosperity and optimism of the years preceding the Depression?

PREVIEWING THE CHAPTER
- Read aloud the titles and section summaries. Note the video in Section 2.
- Discuss the photograph of the group of unemployed men on page 641. What mood does this picture convey? *Possible Responses: Despair, gloom, hopelessness.*

MORE ABOUT . . .
Robert M. La Follette, Jr.
La Follette (1895–1953) was a member of a prominent political family in Wisconsin. As a U.S. senator from that state, La Follette vigorously supported government action to deal with the Depression. He condemned Hoover's economic program and charged the president with trying to "minimize the seriousness of the Depression."

SECTION 1
The Nation's Sick Economy
Economic problems affecting industries, farmers, and consumers lead to the Great Depression.

SECTION 2
Hardship and Suffering During the Depression
The Great Depression brings suffering of many kinds and degrees to people from all walks of life.

 VIDEO *BROKE BUT NOT BROKEN*

SECTION 3
Hoover Struggles with the Depression
President Hoover tries to restore confidence and halt the Depression, but his actions are ineffective.

> "The illusory prosperity and feverish optimism which marked preceding years have given way to fearful economic insecurity and to widespread despair."
>
> Senator Robert M. La Follette, Jr., 1931

THE UNITED STATES
THE WORLD

1929　March　October　**1930**　June　July

- Herbert Hoover is inaugurated.
- The stock market crashes.
- More than 1,300 banks are forced to close because of stock market crash.
- The Hawley-Smoot Tariff Act becomes law.
- Congress creates the Veterans Administration.

- Albert Einstein publishes "Unified Field Theory."
- Chiang Kai-shek (Jiang Jieshi) launches campaign against Mao Zedong's Communists.
- Army officers led by José Uriburu seize control of the government in Argentina.

640 CHAPTER 22

THEMES IN CHAPTER 22

Economic Opportunity		*Immigration and Migration*	*The American Dream*
The lack of economic opportunity was the dominant theme of the Great Depression. In the years before and during the Depression, many Americans called on the government to create more economic opportunity for its citizens. However,	Presidents Coolidge and Hoover were reluctant to do so. Coolidge, for example, refused to support the McNary-Haugen bill, which would have helped boost the farming industry, whose crop prices had fallen due to years of overproduction. See Teacher's Edition note, p. 643.	The effects of the Great Depression and dust storms forced many farm families to leave their land. Their mass migration to the nation's urban areas further transformed the U.S. from an agricultural to an urban society. See Teacher's Edition note, p. 652.	The Great Depression undermined the notion of the American Dream. As millions of families watched their livelihoods slip away, many viewed the future with despair. Some Americans even began to reject the ideas of democracy and capitalism. See Teacher's Edition note, p. 657.

LIVING HISTORY

CREATING A COLLAGE

You will encounter a number of compelling personal voices in this chapter, voices telling stories about people's hardship and suffering during the Great Depression.

- Begin a collage in which you assemble images that tell the stories of the people you meet in this chapter.
- For each Personal Voice, choose an image from a magazine, newspaper, or other source that you think fairly represents that person's experience.
- If you can't find an existing image, make one of your own. Then add that image to your collage.

PORTFOLIO PROJECT Keep the images that you assemble in your folder for your American history portfolio. At the end of the chapter, you will finish, present, and display your collage.

A CENTURY OF PROGRESS
1833
1933
COME!
CHICAGO
WORLD'S FAIR

LIVING HISTORY

CREATING A COLLAGE
Give students these strategies for gathering material for the collage:

- Choose the personal stories that most appeal to you and write down the images that each of those stories brings to mind.
- Look for pictures that best illustrate these images in news or art magazines and newspapers.
- Create your own image if you can't find the one you have in mind. Use color to convey the proper mood.
- Decide how you want to organize the pictures in your collage. You may, for example, want to build your collage around a central image.

Project Planning Guide

Step 1	Students choose stories that most appeal to them.
Step 2	Students find images that correspond with their feelings about each story.
Step 3	Students organize the images into a collage.

IN-DEPTH RESOURCES: UNIT 6
See worksheet and standards for evaluation, pp. 51, 52.

Timeline:

- Hoover proposes a one-year delay in repayment of war debts and reparations.
- Between 4 million and 5 million Americans are unemployed

- The Empire State Building opens in New York City.

- Jane Addams wins the Nobel Peace Prize.

- The Reconstruction Finance Corporation is established.

- Over 13 million Americans are unemployed
  - The Bonus Army arrives in Washington, D.C.
  - Franklin Delano Roosevelt is elected president.

- "A Century of Progress" world's fair begins.
- Average annual income drops to $1,500 per family.

1931 | May | December | **1932** | May | November | **1933**
| | September | | | September |

- Austria suffers economic collapse.

- Japan occupies Manchuria.

- Ibn Saud becomes King of Saudi Arabia.

- From prison, Mohandas K. Gandhi leads a protest against British policies in India.

- Adolf Hitler comes to power.
- Japan withdraws from the League of Nations.

The Great Depression Begins **641**

RECOMMENDED RESOURCES

Books for the Teacher

Bendiner, Robert. *Just Around the Corner.* New York: Dutton, 1968. Amusing "selective history" of life in the 1930s.

Bulosan, Carlos. *America Is in the Heart.* Seattle: University of Washington Press, 1973. Filipino Americans in 1930s California.

McIlvaine, Robert S. *The Great Depression.* New York: Times Books, 1993. Overview of the Depression.

Books for the Student

Allen, Frederick Lewis. *Since Yesterday.* New York: Bantam, 1961. Society in the 1930s.

Graubert, Judah, and Alice Graubert, eds. *Decade of Destiny.* Chicago: Contemporary, 1978. Reminiscences of the Depression.

Terkel, Studs. *Hard Times.* New York: Pantheon, 1970. Oral history of the Depression.

Videos

America: The Second Century: The Depression. GPN, 402-472-2007. Documentary.

Brother, Can You Spare a Dime? Dir. Philippe Mora. VCI Home Video, 1975. Life during the Great Depression.

Herbert Hoover. Dir. Alan Landsburg. Coronet/MTI Film & Video, 1962. The life and presidency of Herbert Hoover.

Sounder. Dir. Martin Ritt. Paramount Pictures, 1972. The struggles of an African-American sharecropper family.

The Great Depression. WGBH-TV, 1993. Videocassette series.

Software

U.S. History: The Great Depression. CD-Rom. Clearview. Educational Software Institute, 800-955-5570.

Teacher's Edition **641**

OBJECTIVES

① To summarize some of the problems threatening the American economy in the late 1920s.

② To describe the causes of the stock market crash and of the Great Depression.

③ To explain how the Great Depression affected the economy in the United States and throughout the world.

SKILLBUILDERS

• Interpreting graphs, pp. 643, 645, 648

CRITICAL THINKING

• Analyzing causes, pp. 643, 647, 649
• Drawing conclusions, pp. 644, 649
• Forming opinions, p. 646
• Analyzing issues, p. 647
• Recognizing effects, p. 648
• Summarizing, p. 649

FOCUS & MOTIVATE

▶ **Starting with the Student**
• Ask students whether they have ever felt tempted to spend more money than they actually had. When?
• What do students think happens when industries or governments exceed their budgets?

MORE ABOUT . . .
Gordon Parks

At age 16, Parks, whose mother's death had forced him to live with his sister, was thrown out of her house following an argument with his brother-in-law. He supported himself by working a variety of jobs, including waiting tables and mopping floors. He began his career as a photographer during the Depression after the Farm Security Administration offered him a job in its photography department. He later worked for *Life* magazine and was named Magazine Photographer of the Year in 1961.

IN-DEPTH RESOURCES: UNIT 6
American Lives: Gordon Parks, p. 49

642   **Chapter 22**

---

① # The Nation's Sick Economy

TERMS & NAMES
• price support
• credit
• Alfred E. Smith
• speculation
• buying on margin
• Black Tuesday
• Great Depression
• Dow Jones Industrial Average
• Hawley-Smoot Tariff Act

LEARN ABOUT economic problems affecting industries, farmers, and consumers at home and abroad
TO UNDERSTAND the causes of the Great Depression.

Gordon Parks

ONE AMERICAN'S STORY

Gordon Parks, who would later become a well-known photographer, author, and filmmaker, was 16 years old during the fall of 1929. He attended high school in St. Paul, Minnesota, and supported himself as a bellboy at the exclusive Minnesota Club. Observing the prosperous club members, Parks saw people who were confident in the economy. Parks felt that he, too, could look forward to a bright future. Then came the stock market crash of October 1929, and everything seemed to fall apart. In his autobiography, Parks recalled his feelings at the time.

> **A PERSONAL VOICE**
> I couldn't imagine such financial disaster touching my small world; it surely concerned only the rich. But by the first week of November I too knew differently; along with millions of others across the nation, I was without a job. All that next week I searched for any kind of work that would prevent my leaving school. Again it was, "We're firing, not hiring.". . . Finally, on the seventh of November I went to school and cleaned out my locker, knowing it was impossible to stay on. A piercing chill was in the air as I walked back to the rooming house. The hawk had come. I could already feel his wings shadowing me.
>
> **GORDON PARKS,** from *A Choice of Weapons*

The crash of 1929, and the Depression that followed, dealt a crushing blow to the hopes and dreams of millions of Americans. The high-flying prosperity of the 1920s was over. Hard times had begun.

Economic Troubles on the Horizon

As the 1920s advanced, it grew increasingly clear that serious problems threatened economic prosperity. Though some Americans were becoming wealthy, many more could not earn a decent living. Important industries were in trouble. Farmers produced more food than they could sell at a profit. In hopes of finding wealth, Americans gambled on the stock market. When the decade drew to a close, slippages in the economy signaled the end of an era.

INDUSTRIES IN TROUBLE The superficial prosperity of the late 1920s hid troubling weaknesses—weaknesses that would ultimately lead to the Great Depression of the 1930s. A number of key basic industries, such as textiles, steel, and railroads, barely made a profit. Railroads lost business to new forms of transportation (trucks, buses, and private automobiles), while textile mills faced competition from foreign producers in Japan, India, China, and Latin America.

Mining and lumbering, which had expanded to supply wartime needs during World War I, faced diminished demand for their goods in peacetime. Coal mining was especially hard-hit, in part due to stiff competition from new forms of energy, including hydroelectric power, fuel oil, and natural gas. By the early 1930s, these sources supplied more than half the energy that had once come from coal.

SECTION 1 RESOURCES

 ### PRINT RESOURCES

IN-DEPTH RESOURCES: UNIT 6
Guided Reading, p. 36
Primary Sources: The Stock Market Crash, p. 42; Political Cartoon, p. 43
American Lives: Gordon Parks, p. 49; Alfred E. Smith, p. 50

ACCESS FOR STUDENTS ACQUIRING ENGLISH
Guided Reading (Spanish), p. 215

FORMAL ASSESSMENT
Section Quiz, p. 269

ALTERNATIVE ASSESSMENT BOOK
See forms for supporting and scoring alternative activities.

 ### TECHNOLOGY RESOURCES

GEOGRAPHY TRANSPARENCIES
G22, Growth of Electricity, 1918, 1933

CRITICAL THINKING TRANSPARENCIES
CT22, The Great Depression
CT56, Investing in Stock

CD-ROM *Grolier Multimedia Encyclopedia*
Electronic Library of Primary Sources

VIDEO *American Portfolio: A Videodisc for U.S. History*
user's guide, p. 201

INTERNET McDougal Littell Learning On-Line
http://www.mcdougallittell.com

Even the boom industries of the 1920s—automobiles, construction, and consumer goods—began to weaken. The construction of new houses, for example, fell steadily after peaking in 1925. Between 1925 and 1929, applications for new building permits declined by approximately 25 percent. Housing starts were an important economic indicator, because house construction had spinoff effects on other industries. New houses required building materials, new furnishings, new equipment, and new appliances. Construction also created jobs.

When housing started to decline, so did other businesses that depended on construction. Furniture companies that had expected an expanding market produced too many goods and cut their labor forces to reduce inventories. A similar story held for makers of household appliances.

FARMERS NEED A LIFT Perhaps more than any other part of the economy, agriculture suffered throughout the 1920s. During World War I, international demand for food crops such as wheat and corn soared, causing prices to rise. Farmers planted more crops and took out loans to buy land and equipment. After the war, demand for farm products fell, and crop prices declined by 50 percent or more.

To compensate for falling prices, farmers boosted production in the hope of selling more crops, but this only depressed prices further. Between 1919 and 1921, annual farm income declined from $10 billion to just over $4 billion. Farmers who had gone into debt had difficulty in paying off their loans. Many lost their farms when banks foreclosed, and seized the property as payment for the debt. As farmers began to default on their loans, many rural banks began to fail.

To prop up the farm sector, members of Congress proposed a complicated piece of legislation called the McNary-Haugen bill. This proposal called for federal **price supports**—the support of certain price levels at or above market values by the government—for key products. The bill had three major provisions.

- The government would buy from farmers surplus crops, such as wheat, corn, cotton, and tobacco, at guaranteed prices that were higher than the market rate.
- The government would then sell these crops on the world market for the lower prevailing prices.
- To make up for losses caused by buying high and selling low, the government would place a tax on domestic food sales, thus passing the cost of the farm program along to consumers.

Congress passed the bill twice, in 1927 and 1928, but each time President Coolidge vetoed it. At one point, the president commented, "Farmers have never made money. I don't believe we can do much about it." Farm prices remained low and farmers continued to struggle.

CONSUMERS HAVE LESS MONEY TO SPEND As farmers' incomes fell, they bought fewer goods and services. Without money to spend, rural families could not buy the products of American industry. The same problem was evident among American consumers as a whole.

The Great Depression Begins **643**

Skillbuilder Answer
Price: From a high point of about $1.15 in 1927 to a low point of about 35 cents in 1931 and 1932. **Bigger:** A little more than three times bigger. **Low price:** *Possible answers:* The Depression forced almost all prices down. In 1931, people had less money to buy products made from wheat, so the price went down to attract buyers. Wheat production went up in 1931 (to 942 million bushels), which caused the price to fall even further.

U.S. Wheat Production and Wheat Prices

875 914 824 887 942 756 552 526

$1.20
$1.00
$0.80
$0.60
$0.40
$0.20

1927 1928 1929 1930 1931 1932 1933 1934

■ Price per bushel   🌾 = 100 million bushels

Source: *Historical Statistics of the United States*

SKILLBUILDER
INTERPRETING GRAPHS *How far does the price per bushel of wheat drop from the high point on the graph to the low point? How many times bigger than the low price is the high price? What factors do you think contributed to this drop?*

"We in America are nearer to the final triumph over poverty than ever before."

HERBERT HOOVER

By the late 1920s, Americans were buying less—mainly because of rising prices, stagnant wages, unbalanced distribution of income, and too much credit buying in the preceding years—even as American farms and factories were producing more. Production expanded much faster than wages, resulting in an ever-widening gap between the rich and the poor.

LIVING ON CREDIT Although many Americans appeared prosperous during the 1920s, in fact they were living beyond their means. They often bought goods on **credit**—an arrangement in which consumers agreed to buy now and pay later for purchases, often on an installment plan (usually in monthly payments) that included interest charges.

By making credit easily available, businesses encouraged Americans to pile up a large consumer debt. Many people then had trouble paying off their growing debts. Faced with debt, consumers cut back on spending.

UNEVEN DISTRIBUTION OF INCOME Consumers also spent less because their incomes were not rising fast enough. During the 1920s, nearly half the nation's families earned less than $1,500 per year, then considered the minimum amount needed for a decent standard of living. Even families earning twice that much could not afford many of the household products that manufacturers produced. Economists estimate that the average man or woman bought a new outfit of clothes only once a year. Scarcely half the homes in many cities had electric lights or a furnace for heat. Only one city home in ten had an electric refrigerator.

In contrast, rich Americans did very well. Between 1920 and 1929, the income of the wealthiest 1 percent of the population rose by 75 percent, compared with a 9 percent increase for Americans as a whole. In 1929, the wealthiest 5 percent of American families took in nearly a third of the nation's income, while the poorest 40 percent of the population earned just over a tenth of the national income.

This unequal distribution of income meant that most Americans could not participate fully in the economic advances of the 1920s. Many people did not have the money to consume the flood of goods that factories produced. The prosperity of the era rested on a fragile foundation.

A NEW PRESIDENT Although economic disaster was around the corner, the election of 1928 took place amidst a national mood of apparent prosperity. This election pitted Republican candidate Herbert Hoover against Democrat **Alfred E. Smith.** The two men could hardly have been more different. Hoover, the secretary of commerce under Harding and Coolidge, was a mining engineer from Iowa who had never run for public office.

Smith, in contrast, was a career politician who had served four terms as governor of New York. Where Hoover was formal and reserved, Smith was witty and outgoing. Both men came from poor families and had worked hard to achieve success. Whereas Hoover felt uncomfortable in the limelight, Smith seemed to relish it.

Hoover had one major advantage: he could point to years of prosperity under Republican administrations since 1920. Many Americans believed Hoover when he declared, "We in America are nearer to the final triumph over poverty than ever before. . . . The poorhouse is vanishing among us."

Although Smith ran a spirited campaign, he could not overcome the Republican advantage. In addition, Smith's heavy Brooklyn accent, his opposition to prohibition, and his religion (Roman Catholic) counted heavily against him. In the election, Hoover captured 58 percent of the popular vote and won 444 electoral votes to Smith's 87. The message was clear: most Americans were happy with the course of the nation and its Republican leadership.

The Stock Market Comes Tumbling Down

By 1929, some economists were warning of serious weaknesses in the economy. Most Americans remained unaware of these problems and continued to have confidence in the nation's economic health. Those who could afford to invest in the stock market did so in increasing numbers. In fact, the stock market had become the most visible symbol of an American economy that seemed to be producing wonderful products almost at will since the end of World War I.

DREAMS OF RICHES IN THE STOCK MARKET Through most of the 1920s, prices on the stock market rose steadily. Eager to take advantage of this "bull market"—rising stock market prices—many Americans rushed to buy stocks and bonds. One observer wrote, "It seemed as if all economic law had been suspended and a new era opened up in which success and prosperity could be had without knowledge or industry." By 1929, about 4 million Americans—or 3 percent of the nation's population—owned stocks. Many of these investors were already wealthy, but others were average Americans who hoped to strike it rich.

As stock market prices rose, several problems became evident. More and more investors engaged in **speculation**—that is, the engagement in risky business transactions (in this case, the buying and selling of stocks) on the chance of quick or considerable profit. Their unrestrained buying and selling fueled the market's upward spiral. As prices rose, wealth was generated on paper, but it bore little relation to the real worth of companies or the goods that they produced. The price of stocks had little relationship to the dividends the stocks paid.

Furthermore, many investors began **buying on margin**—paying a small percentage of a stock's price as a down payment and borrowing the rest. With stockbrokers willing to lend buyers up to 75 percent of a stock's purchase price, buying on margin became the rule. This system worked as long as prices continued to rise, since investors could sell their inflated stocks to make a profit and pay off their debt. If stocks declined, however, there was no way to pay off the loan.

BLACK TUESDAY In early September 1929, stock prices peaked and began to decline. Confidence in the market started to waver and some investors sold their stocks and pulled out. On October 24, the market took a gut-wrenching plunge, as panicked investors unloaded their shares. But the worst was yet to come.

On October 29—known as **Black Tuesday**—the bottom fell out of the market. People and corporations alike frantically tried to sell their stocks before prices plunged even lower. Those individual investors who had bought stocks on credit acquired huge debts when stock prices plunged. Other investors, who had invested most of their savings in the market, lost their investments when prices fell. The number of shares dumped that day was a record 16 million. Additional

This cartoon by James N. Rosenberg, which shows Wall Street crumbling on October 29, 1929, was titled Dies Irae, *Latin for "day of wrath."*

SKILLBUILDER
INTERPRETING GRAPHS *What happened to the yearly difference between income and consumer spending from 1929 to 1931? What do you think this change meant to Americans?*
Skillbuilder Answer
Income vs. Spending:
Probable Answer: Each year, the difference between the two grew smaller, which probably meant that people were spending more of their income and saving less.

Right column teaching edition content:

OBJECTIVE
② INSTRUCT

The Stock Market Comes Tumbling Down

▶ **Starting with the Student**
Have students create a chart to list the causes and effects, as discussed in the text, of several events that prompted the onset of the Great Depression.

Onset of the Great Depression	
Cause	Effect
1.	
2.	
3.	
4.	

▶ **Discussing Key Ideas**
• On October 29, 1929, the market crashes as stock prices plunge.
• The stock market crash hastens the Great Depression, which is caused by a number of economic and social factors.

IN-DEPTH RESOURCES: UNIT 6
Primary Source: The Stock Market Crash, p. 42

ELECTRONIC LIBRARY OF PRIMARY SOURCES
"On Minding Your Own Business" *from the* New York Times

ECONOMIC BACKGROUND
America's Declining Wealth
Critical Thinking: Analyzing Ask students why` by 1933, Americans were spending nearly as much as they were earning. *Possible Response: Americans were earning so much less on average by 1933 that they could not afford to save any money.*

Teaching Gifted and Talented Students

Create a Crash Cartoon Discuss with students the cartoon on page 645. Then encourage interested students to create their own cartoon illustrating some aspect of the stock market crash: its effect on business, on business people, on farmers, or on consumers. Cartoons should . . .

• illustrate the effects of the crash
• convey the sense of fear and shock inspired by the crash
• include a caption or title that captures the essential spirit of the illustration

Making Connections Across Time

The Crash of 1987 On October 19, 1987—almost exactly 58 years after Black Tuesday—the American stock market experienced the greatest single-day decline in its history. On what became known as Black Monday, the market fell 508 points. As in 1929, the crash was preceded by a prosperous economy and a stock market boom. Experts blamed the '87 crash on several factors, including rising interest rates, the U.S. bombing of oil platforms in Iran, and conflict among U.S. trading partners. Unlike in 1929, stock prices quickly recovered after the '87 crash and continued to rise over the next couple of years.

▶ ***Starting with the Student***
Have students interview someone who invests in the stock market. Interview questions might include: What are the pros and cons of investing in the market? How does one make investments? What advice should a new investor follow?

▶ ***Discussing Key Ideas***
• In 1882, Charles H. Dow, Edward Jones, and Charles M. Bergstresser start a company that distributes copies of stock market reports to business customers in New York City.
• In 1896, Charles Dow creates the Dow Jones Industrial Average by choosing 12 major companies and averaging the prices of their stocks.
• Through the years, the Dow fluctuates between sudden, sometimes disastrous, drops and steady increases.
• Throughout the Dow's history, the stocks that compose it have changed to reflect the times. Today, the group of 30 companies includes McDonald's and Walt Disney.

CRITICAL THINKING TRANSPARENCIES
CT56, Investing in Stock

---

millions of shares could not even find buyers. By mid-November, investors had lost $30 billion, an amount equal to American spending in World War I. The stock market bubble had finally burst. One eyewitness to these events, Frederick Lewis Allen, described the resulting situation.

"Wall Street Lays an Egg"

HEADLINE, *VARIETY*, OCTOBER 1929

A PERSONAL VOICE
The Big Bull Market was dead. Billions of dollars' worth of profits—and paper profits—had disappeared. The grocer, the window cleaner, and the seamstress had lost their capital [savings]. In every town there were families which had suddenly dropped from showy affluence into debt. . . . With the Big Bull Market gone and prosperity going, Americans were soon to find themselves living in an altered world which called for new adjustments, new ideas, new habits of thought, a new order of values.
FREDERICK LEWIS ALLEN, from *Only Yesterday*

CAUSES OF THE GREAT DEPRESSION The stock market crash signaled the beginning of the **Great Depression**—the period from 1929 to 1941, in which the economy was in severe decline and millions of people were out of work. The crash alone did not cause the Great Depression, but it hastened the collapse of the economy and made the Depression more severe.

Although historians and economists differ on the main causes of the Great Depression, most cite a common set of factors. Among these causes were the following:

THINK THROUGH HISTORY
D. Forming Opinions What role did greed play in the stock market crash?
D. Answer Some investors bought large amounts of stock on margin because the rise in stock prices had made them greedy.

NOW & THEN

The Dow Jones Average

Television and radio news programs report the Dow Jones Industrial Average many times during the work week. "The Dow closed 20 points higher today at 5672." "The Dow Jones passed the 6000 mark." What is the Dow Jones Industrial Average?

1882
Charles H. Dow, Edward Jones, and Charles M. Bergstresser start a company that distributes copies of stock market reports to business customers in New York City. The first reports are handwritten and distributed by messenger boys. In 1889, the reports, plus additional editorials, become known as the *Wall Street Journal*.

left, Charles H. Dow; *above,* a trading floor in the 1920s; *right,* a modern trading floor.

1896
Charles H. Dow creates the Dow Jones Industrial Average by choosing 12 major American companies and averaging the price of their stocks. The twelve original companies are:

American Cotton Oil	Laclede Gas
American Sugar	National Lead
American Tobacco	North American
Chicago Gas	Tennessee Coal & Iron
Distilling & Cattle Feeding	U.S. Leather
General Electric	U.S. Rubber

646 CHAPTER 22

Cooperative Activity: Creating a TV Special About the Stock Market Crash

Task: Student groups will investigate one aspect of the stock market crash and write a script for a television program about the crash.

Purpose: To explore in depth different aspects of the stock market crash.

Activity: Have each group research a different aspect of the stock market crash. Topics might include the panicked events of Black Tuesday, the crash's effects on banks and business, Hoover and the government's response to the crash, or a profile of an investor or investors who lost everything. After researching the topic, the group should write a television script based on its research and then present it to the class.

📁 **Building a Portfolio:** Students may wish to add a copy of the script to their portfolio.

ALTERNATIVE ASSESSMENT BOOK
Standards for Evaluating a Cooperative Activity

Standards for Evaluation
News scripts should . . .

• contain well-researched information
• be presented in a clear, well-organized, and objective manner
• use quotations to personalize the story

- an old and decaying industrial base—outmoded equipment made some industries less competitive
- a crisis in the farm sector—farmers produced more than they were able to sell, especially with the end of World War I and the disappearance of markets that the war had opened to them
- the availability of easy credit—many people went into debt buying goods on the installment plan
- an unequal distribution of income—there was too little money in the hands of working people, who were the vast majority of consumers.

These factors in turn led to falling demand for consumer goods, even as newly mechanized factories produced more products. The federal government contributed to the crisis by keeping interest rates low, which in turn allowed companies and individuals to borrow easily and build up large debts. Some of this borrowed money was used to buy stocks, but the government did little to discourage such buying or to regulate the market.

At first people found it hard to believe that economic disaster had struck the country. In November of 1929, Hoover reassured the people, "Any lack of confidence in the economic future . . . is foolish." Yet despite the comforting words, the most severe depression in American history was well on its way.

Then, as now, the **Dow Jones Industrial Average** was the most widely used barometer of the stock market's health. The Dow is a measure based on the stock prices of 30 representative large firms trading on the New York Stock Exchange. Just prior to the crash of 1929, the Dow reached a high of 381 points, nearly 300

THINK THROUGH HISTORY
E. Analyzing Causes What were some of the causes of the Great Depression?

E. Answer decaying industrial base; farm crisis; unequal distribution of income; falling demand for consumer goods; low interest rates, which encouraged borrowing.

MORE ABOUT . . .
Charles H. Dow and Edward Jones
Although Dow and Jones were partners, they had little in common. Dow grew up on a farm and was an austere, reserved man. Jones came from a fairly well-to-do family and was passionate and hot tempered. Richard Stillman, who wrote a book about the Dow Jones Industrial Average, characterized Jones as "excitable, emotional and you never knew when [he] might explode." Dow did not approve of his partner's lifestyle, particularly his choice of friends—the pool operators and wheeler-dealers of Wall Street. Jones often hung out with these men after work in saloons, seeking tips for his newsletter. Perhaps sensing his partner's disapproval, Jones left the newsletter in 1899 to work in the world he had covered—Wall Street.

October 28, 1929
The Dow drops 38.33 points to 260.64 as the stock market crashes, starting the Depression.

1982–1987
During the Reagan presidency, the Dow industrial averages move steadily upward from 776.92 in August of 1982 to a peak of 2722.42 in August of 1987.

January 8, 1987
The Dow breaks the 2000 mark for the first time.

October 19, 1987
The Dow falls 508 points to 1738.74, on what has been called Black Monday.

1996
Through the years, the stocks that make up the Dow Jones Industrial Average have changed to reflect the times. The group of 30 stocks includes McDonald's, Walt Disney, and American Express as well as industrial companies, such as Caterpillar Inc. There are also averages of 20 transportation companies, of 15 utility companies, and of the 65 stocks together. In 1996, the Dow Jones Industrial Average exceeds the 6000 mark for the first time.

INTERACT WITH HISTORY

1. **ANALYZING ISSUES** Based on what you have read, does the stock market seem like a good investment? If you invested money in 1990, are you more likely to have lost money or made a profit since then?

 SEE SKILLBUILDER HANDBOOK, PAGE 1046

2. **STUDYING THE MARKET** Look at a daily newspaper to see what the Dow Jones Industrial Average is on a given day. Was the Dow average up or down for the day?

 For more about the Dow Jones Industrial Average, click on *Social Studies* at http://www.mcdougallittell.com

The Great Depression Begins **647**

INTERACT WITH HISTORY

1. Analyzing Issues

Possible Responses:

Yes—The rise in the stock market seems steady and predictable. For example, the Dow Jones Industrial Average steadily increased between 1982 and 1987. No—The stock market seems too unpredictable. It appears hard to tell when the market might crash. In 1987, for example, it had been climbing to record heights before it suddenly plummeted.

Investments since 1990 would likely have returned a profit, for since that time the average has steadily increased. In 1997, it exceeded the 7,000 mark for the first time.

2. Studying the Market

The business section of most daily newspapers lists the previous day's activity of individual stocks as well as the Dow Jones Industrial Average. The Dow's overall increase or decrease usually appears before the listing of the individual stocks. To determine the activity of an individual stock, students should locate the stock on the page and check the number in the last column of its line, which usually represents the stock's daily activity. For example, a -1/4 in that column means the stock lost a quarter point of its value that day.

Reading the Graph Remind students that the figures on the unemployment graph are in millions, while the figures on the bank and business failures graphs are in thousands.

Extension Discuss with students in what way the three depression indicators may be related. *Possible Response: When banks fail, many businesses have to close down, which in turn causes unemployment to rise.*

Financial Collapse

▶ *Discussing Key Ideas*
- As the economy collapses, banks and businesses fail and millions of Americans lose their jobs.
- Countries all over the world suffer the effects of the Great Depression.
- The drastic decrease in world trade during the Depression further reduces overall economic activity.

IN-DEPTH RESOURCES: UNIT 6
Primary Source: Political Cartoon, p. 43

Depression Indicators in the United States, 1928–1933

UNEMPLOYMENT	BANK FAILURES	BUSINESS FAILURES

Source: Historical Statistics of the United States

SKILLBUILDER INTERPRETING GRAPHS *In what year did the biggest jump in bank failures occur? What measure on the graphs seems to indicate an improvement in the U.S. economy during the Depression?*

Skillbuilder Answer **Bank failures:** In 1933. **Improvement:** *Possible answer: Business failures dropped significantly from 1932 to 1933.*

points higher than it had been five years earlier. On October 28 and 29, Black Monday and Black Tuesday, the Dow fell dramatically and continued to fall until 1932.

Financial Collapse

This British election poster shows that the Great Depression was a global event.

After the crash, many Americans panicked and withdrew their money from banks, which forced some banks to close. Many banks could not cover their customers' withdrawals because the banks too had invested and lost money in the stock market, just as individuals had. As a result, in 1929, 659 banks shut their doors. By 1933, around 6,000 banks—one-fourth of the nation's total—had failed. Because the federal government did not protect or insure bank accounts, these bank failures wiped out around nine million individual savings accounts. People who went to the bank to retrieve their savings came home with nothing.

The Great Depression hit other businesses equally hard. Between 1929 and 1932, the gross national product—the nation's total output of goods and services—was cut nearly in half, from $104 billion to $59 billion. Some 85,000 businesses went bankrupt. Among these failed enterprises were some of the automobile companies that had prospered during the 1920s, including Pierce-Arrow and Bearcat. Railroad companies controlling one-third of the nation's track mileage went bankrupt by the early 1930s.

As the economy plunged into a tailspin, millions of workers lost their jobs. Unemployment leaped from 3 percent of the work force (1.6 million workers) in 1929 to 25 percent by 1933 (13 million workers). One out of every four workers did not have a job. The workers who managed to hold onto their jobs often had to accept pay cuts and reduced hours.

THINK THROUGH HISTORY
F. Recognizing Effects What happened to ordinary workers during the Great Depression?

F. Answer As the economy collapsed, millions of workers lost their jobs. Without jobs, they had to cut back on their spending, which further deepened the economic downturn. Many workers who had jobs had to accept pay cuts.

TEACHING OPTION

Making Connections Across the Curriculum

Music The Great Depression touched many aspects of American society, including its music. Many of the songs of the Great Depression reflected the nation's despair. For example, the lyrics of the popular Depression song "Brother, Can You Spare a Dime?" tell the story of a man's abrupt decline: "Once I built a railroad, I made it run / I made it race against time / Once I built a railroad, now it's done / Brother, can you spare a dime?" On the other hand, lavish motion picture musicals were also popular during the Great Depression. Musicals such as *Gold Diggers of 1933* portrayed

optimistic characters singing light, cheerful songs. Many musicals of the time also featured spectacular costumes, sets, and dance routines. Ask students why they think such musicals were popular during the Great Depression. *Possible Response: People wanted to see light, frivolous shows to escape the misery of the Depression.*

"Brother, Can You Spare a Dime?" by E. Y. Harburg and J. Gorney, copyright © Warner Bros., Inc.

Not everyone fared so badly, of course. In the months before the crash, shrewd stock market speculators began to unload their stocks and take the profits. Bernard Baruch was one who did so. Joseph P. Kennedy, the father of future president John F. Kennedy, was another. Most people, however, were not so lucky or shrewd.

WORLDWIDE SHOCK WAVES The United States was not the only country gripped by the Great Depression. Much of Europe, for example, had suffered throughout the 1920s. European countries trying to recover from the ravages of World War I faced high debt payments. In addition, Germany had to pay war reparations—payments required from defeated nations for the damage they caused. The Great Depression compounded these problems by limiting America's ability to import European goods. This made it difficult to sell American farm products and manufactured goods abroad.

In 1930, Congress made a bad situation worse by passing the **Hawley-Smoot Tariff Act,** which established the highest protective tariff in United States history. This act—designed to help American farmers and manufacturers by protecting their products from foreign competition—backfired and had the opposite effect. By reducing the flow of goods into the United States, the tariff also prevented other countries from earning American currency to buy American exports. In this way, the tariff made unemployment worse by hurting companies that could no longer export goods to Europe. Many countries retaliated against the Hawley-Smoot Tariff Act by raising their own tariffs. Within a few years, world trade had fallen more than 40 percent, which reduced overall economic activity.

The problem was complicated by the effects of World War I on currency and the gold standard. Not only had vast amounts of property in Europe been destroyed, but European nations also faced heavy debts. This made them reduce their purchases of American goods even more. In order to encourage European nations to purchase American goods, Hoover proposed a moratorium, or postponement of payments, on Allied war debts and German reparations. Before anyone could agree to this plan, however, Britain and other European countries went off the gold standard. That is, their paper money could no longer be exchanged for gold. As a result, gold dropped in value, which meant that Europeans would be buying American goods and repaying American loans in cheaper currency. All these economic troubles caused a tremendous amount of suffering for people throughout the world as they adjusted to the harsh realities of the Depression.

G. Answer World trade fell; many European countries went off the gold standard; unemployment increased.

THINK THROUGH HISTORY
G. Summarizing How did the Great Depression affect the world economy?

Section 1 Assessment

1. TERMS & NAMES

Identify:
- price support
- credit
- Alfred E. Smith
- speculation
- buying on margin
- Black Tuesday
- Great Depression
- Dow Jones Industrial Average
- Hawley-Smoot Tariff Act

2. SUMMARIZING Using a diagram, record the causes of the 1929 stock market crash.

cause cause
cause cause
Stock Market Crash

When you have finished, add effects of the crash to the bottom of the diagram.

3. ANALYZING CAUSES How did the economic trends of the 1920s help cause the Great Depression?

THINK ABOUT
- what happened in industry
- what happened in agriculture
- what happened with consumers

4. DRAWING CONCLUSIONS Judging from the events of the late 1920s and early 1930s, how important do you think public confidence is to the health of the economy? Explain.

THINK ABOUT
- what happened when overconfidence in the stock market led people to speculate and buy on margin
- what happened when lack of confidence caused people to sell stocks and close out bank accounts

The Great Depression Begins **649**

ANSWERS

1. TERMS & NAMES

price support, p. 643

credit, p. 644

Alfred E. Smith, p. 644

speculation, p. 645

buying on margin, p. 645

Black Tuesday, p. 645

Great Depression, p. 646

Dow Jones Industrial Average, p. 647

Hawley-Smoot Tariff Act, p. 649

2. SUMMARIZING

Possible Answers:

Causes
speculation
buying on margin
falling stock prices
loss of confidence

Effects
loss of savings
bank failures
bankrupt businesses
high unemployment
worldwide depression

3. ANALYZING CAUSES

Possible Responses: The economy slowed because industries found less demand for their goods in peacetime than in wartime, and unbalanced income distribution meant that most consumers had little to spend. International demand for crops fell, and many farmers went bankrupt, causing rural banks to fail. Too many people lived on credit, burdening themselves with debt that proved disastrous when the banks failed.

4. DRAWING CONCLUSIONS

Possible Response: Public confidence has a big effect on the economy. Too much confidence can lead people to make unwise decisions, committing themselves to more debt than they can repay. Too little confidence can lead individuals to pull money out of the stock market and banks—triggering a panic that endangers the entire economy.

OBJECTIVES

① To describe how people struggled to survive during the Depression.

② To explain how the Depression affected men, women, and children.

SKILLBUILDER

• Understanding geography: region, movement, p. 652

CRITICAL THINKING

• Recognizing effects, pp. 651, 652, 654

• Analyzing causes, p. 653

• Summarizing, p. 654

• Comparing and contrasting, p. 654

FOCUS & MOTIVATE

▶ **Starting with the Student** Watch the video "Broke but Not Broken" to examine how a young woman and her family coped with the Dust Bowl and the Great Depression.

Using the *Teacher's Resource Book* as a guide, hold class discussions about the effects of the Dust Bowl and Great Depression on the lives of the nation's farming families, and engage in extension activities using key primary sources.

 AMERICAN STORIES VIDEO SERIES

"Broke but Not Broken"
Videocassette: Volume 3

Videodisc: Disc 2, SideB, Chapter 2.

OBJECTIVE

① **INSTRUCT**

The Depression Devastates People's Lives

▶ *Discussing Key Ideas*

• The Great Depression forces people in cities to live in shacks and stand in bread lines.

(continued on next page)

TERMS & NAMES
• Dust Bowl
• shantytown
• soup kitchen
• bread line
• direct relief

② Hardship and Suffering During the Depression

LEARN ABOUT living conditions during the Great Depression
TO UNDERSTAND how people coped with hard times.

ONE AMERICAN'S STORY

Ann Marie Low lived with her parents on their North Dakota farm when the stock market crashed and the Great Depression struck. In her diary entry of November 9, 1929, she wrote, "There seems to be quite a furor in the country over a big stock market crash that wiped a lot of people out. We are ahead of them." Like many farm families in the 1920s, Ann's family had already experienced hard times. Things would get worse, however. During the early 1930s, several years of drought ravaged the Great Plains, destroying crops and leaving the earth dry and cracked. Then the wind began to blow. On April 25, 1934, Ann wrote,

A PERSONAL VOICE

Last weekend was the worst dust storm we ever had. We've been having quite a bit of blowing dirt every year since the drouth [drought] started, not only here, but all over the Great Plains. Many days this spring the air is just full of dirt coming, literally, for hundreds of miles. It sifts into everything. After we wash the dishes and put them away, so much dust sifts into the cupboards we must wash them again before the next meal. . . . Newspapers say the deaths of many babies and old people are attributed to breathing in so much dirt.

ANN MARIE LOW, from *Dust Bowl Diary*

The dust storms in North Dakota, South Dakota, Nebraska, Kansas, Oklahoma, and Texas were so severe that this region of the Great Plains became known as the **Dust Bowl.** This was one of the greatest hardships—but only one of many—that Americans faced during the Great Depression.

Ann Marie Low

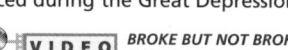 **BROKE BUT NOT BROKEN:**
Ann Marie Low Remembers the Dust Bowl

Unemployed people built shacks on a vacant lot in New York City in 1932.

The Depression Devastates People's Lives

Statistics such as the unemployment rate tell only part of the story of the Great Depression. More important was the impact that it had on people's lives. Put simply, the depression brought hardship and suffering to millions of Americans. In cities as well as rural areas, it turned people's lives into a grim struggle for survival. Homelessness and hunger stalked the land.

THE DEPRESSION IN THE CITIES In cities across the country, from New York City to Los Angeles, people who lost their jobs found that they could no longer pay their rent or mortgage. Many were evicted from their homes and ended up living in the streets. Some slept in parks or sewer pipes, wrapped in newspapers to fend off the cold. Others built makeshift shacks out of scrap materials. Before long, large **shantytowns**—little towns consisting largely of shacks—sprang up on the outskirts of cities. One observer commented,

650 CHAPTER 22

SECTION 2 RESOURCES

 PRINT RESOURCES

IN-DEPTH RESOURCES: UNIT 6
Guided Reading, p. 37
Skillbuilder Practice: Formulating Historical Questions, p. 39
Geography Application: The Great Depression Takes Its Toll, p. 40
Primary Source: Letter from a Dust Bowl Survivor, p. 44
Literature: from *The Grapes of Wrath* by John Steinbeck, p. 46

ACCESS FOR STUDENTS ACQUIRING ENGLISH
Guided Reading (Spanish), p. 216
Skillbuilder Practice: Formulating Historical Questions (Spanish), p. 218
Geography Application: The Great Depression Takes Its Toll (Spanish), p. 219

FORMAL ASSESSMENT
Section Quiz, p. 270

ALTERNATIVE ASSESSMENT BOOK
See forms for supporting and scoring alternative activities.

 TECHNOLOGY RESOURCES

HUMANITIES TRANSPARENCIES
H21, Dust Storm. Arthur Rothstein

CD-ROM Electronic Library of Primary Sources

VIDEO *American Stories* video series

INTERNET McDougal Littell Learning On-Line
http://www.mcdougallittell.com

A PERSONAL VOICE

Here were all these people living in old, rusted-out car bodies. . . . There were people living in shacks made of orange crates. One family with a whole lot of kids were living in a piano box. . . . People living in whatever they could junk together.

A visitor to a shantytown outside Oklahoma City, quoted in Hard Times

Every day the urban poor could be seen scrounging for food, digging in garbage cans or begging on street corners. **Soup kitchens** (places where food is offered free to the needy) and **bread lines** (lines of people waiting to receive food provided by charitable organizations or public agencies) opened up in many cities to feed the homeless. One man noted the condition of men waiting for free food in New York City.

A PERSONAL VOICE

Two or three blocks along Times Square, you'd see these men, silent, shuffling along in a line. Getting this hand-out of coffee and doughnuts, dealt out from great trucks. . . . I'd stand and watch their faces, and I'd see that flat, opaque, expressionless look which spelled, for me, human disaster. On every corner, there'd be a man selling apples. Men . . . who had responsible positions. Who had lost their jobs, lost their homes, lost their families. And worse than anything else, lost belief in themselves. They were destroyed men.

HERMAN SHUMLIN, *quoted in* Hard Times

People stand in a bread line outside a soup kitchen in Chicago in 1930.

THE IMPACT ON AFRICAN AMERICANS AND LATINO AMERICANS Conditions for African Americans and Latino Americans in the cities were especially difficult. The unemployment rates for both groups were higher than for most other Americans, and the jobs these groups held tended to bring the lowest pay. The Depression years saw an increase in racial violence against African Americans by unemployed whites competing for the same jobs. Twenty-four African Americans died by lynching in 1933.

Latinos—mainly Mexicans and Mexican Americans living in the Southwest—were also the targets of hostility. Unemployed whites, angered at losing their jobs, demanded that Latinos be deported to Mexico, even though many Latinos were native-born Americans. By the late 1930s, hundreds of thousands of people of Mexican descent had returned to Mexico. Some left voluntarily and some were deported by the federal government.

THE DEPRESSION IN RURAL AREAS Life in rural areas during the Depression was hard, but it did have one advantage over city life: most farmers could manage to grow some food to feed their families. Crop prices kept falling, however, and farmers continued to lose their land when they couldn't pay their debts. Between 1929 and 1932, about 400,000 farms were lost through foreclosure—where the mortgage holder took over the property because the farmer could not make the mortgage payments. Many farmers had no choice but to turn to tenant farming and barely scrape out a living.

THE DUST BOWL In addition, the drought that began in the early 1930s wreaked havoc on the Great Plains. During the previous decade, farmers from Texas to North Dakota—the region that became known as the Dust Bowl—had used tractors to break up the grasslands and plant millions of acres of new farmland. Then they exhausted the land through overproduction of crops, and the grasslands became unsuitable for

---

A. Answer Many city people were evicted from their homes; shantytowns sprang up in cities; people begged and scrounged for food. Some farmers lost their farms; others traveled from place to place, in search of work.

THINK THROUGH HISTORY
A. *Recognizing Effects* How did the Great Depression affect the lives of ordinary people in cities and towns, and on farms?

AN AFRICAN-AMERICAN VIEW OF THE DEPRESSION

Although the suffering of the 1930s was severe for many people, it was especially grim for African Americans. Hard times were already a fact of life.

"The Negro was born in depression," noted one African-American man. "It didn't mean too much to him, The Great American Depression. . . . The best he could be is a janitor or a porter or shoeshine boy. It only became official when it hit the white man."

Nonetheless, the African-American community was very hard hit by the Great Depression. In 1932, the unemployment rate among African Americans stood at over 50 percent while the overall unemployment rate was approximately 25 percent.

The Great Depression Begins **651**

(continued from page 650)

- Racial tensions rise as whites compete for scarce jobs with African Americans and Latinos.
- The Dust Bowl in the Great Plains forces many farmers to leave their land.

IN-DEPTH RESOURCES: UNIT 6
Guided Reading, p. 37

ACCESS FOR STUDENTS ACQUIRING ENGLISH
Guided Reading (Spanish), p. 216

ANOTHER PERSPECTIVE
An African-American View of the Depression
Critical Thinking: Analyzing Ask students to describe the tone of the man's comments. *Possible Responses: Bitter, sarcastic.* Why would unemployment rates for African Americans have been particularly high during the Depression? *Possible Responses: Employers probably gave priority to white workers.*

MORE ABOUT . . .
Hard Times
Hard Times was written by journalist and commentator Studs Terkel. The book is an example of an oral history, in which the story of an event is told through the words of the people who experienced it. Terkel interviewed more than 100 survivors of the Depression, from politicians to farmers. "This is a memory book," he wrote.

 ELECTRONIC LIBRARY OF PRIMARY SOURCES
"Beans, Bacon, and Gravy" (popular song); Childhood During the Depression by Cesar Chavez

---

Skillbuilder Mini-Lesson: Formulating Historical Questions

Explaining the Skill Asking probing questions about what they find in primary sources helps historians learn about historical events and conditions and the people who influenced or were affected by them. The kinds of questions news reporters ask to flesh out a news story—*who, what, when, where, why,* and *how*—also lead historians to a deeper understanding of the past.

Applying the Skill: A Personal Voice Suggest that students might better understand conditions of the Great Depression if they ask historical questions about the primary sources on this page. Have them read the two quotations labeled "A Personal Voice" and study the photograph. Then

on the chalkboard, write the categories Who, What, When, Where, Why, How, and Other. As a class, for each category list questions about the primary sources. Sample questions: Who were the victims most affected by the Depression? What was it like to stand in line for handouts of bread? When was the worst time for these people? Where did they spend their days? Why couldn't people find work? How did homeless families manage to cook, wash, or go to school?

IN-DEPTH RESOURCES: UNIT 6
Skillbuilder Practice: Formulating Historical Questions, p. 39

The Dust Bowl, 1933–1936

Chicago, Nov. 1933 Crowds at Chicago Exposition caught in 50 mph gale of dust

Boston, May 1934 Midwestern dust and bacteria collected on 30 airplane flights at altitudes up to 20,000 ft. in Boston

Nebraska, 1935–1937 Over two years, federal workers help soil conservation by planting 360,000 trees and completing 62 dams, 517 ponds, and 500 acres of terracing.

New York, May 12, 1934 Huge dust storm cuts visibility and lowers humidity from normal 57% to 34%. Empire State Building's stone observation ledges covered with a white film of dust. Dust reported on ships 500 miles out to sea.

Beaver, Okla. March 24, 1936 Grain elevator operators estimate that 20% of wheat crop blown away by dust storm.

Tucumcari, N. Mex. March 30, 1936 Clouds of dust blown by 50-mph winds cause complete darkness.

Major area of Dust Bowl
Area of severe damage
- - - Area covered by May 1934 dust storm

0 400 Miles
0 800 Kilometers

GEOGRAPHY SKILLBUILDER REGION Which states were in the area of most severe Dust Bowl damage? **MOVEMENT** Why might most of the migrants who left the Dust Bowl travel west rather than east?

farming. When the drought and winds began in the early 1930s, little grass and few trees were left on the plains to hold the soil down. As you learned from the excerpt from Ann Marie Low's diary on page 650, the dust traveled hundreds of miles. One wind storm in 1934 picked up millions of tons of dust from the plains and carried it to East Coast cities. Even ships far out in the Atlantic Ocean reported dust settling on their decks.

The region of the Southern plains, including Kansas, Oklahoma, and Texas, was hardest hit. Plagued by dust storms and evictions, thousands of farmers and sharecroppers left their land behind. They packed up their families and their few belongings and headed west, following Route 66 to California. Some of these migrants—known as Okies (a term that originally referred to Oklahomans but came to be used negatively for all the migrants)—found work as farm hands. But others continued to wander in search of work. By the end of the 1930s, the population of California had grown by more than a million.

Effects on the American Family

> *"You were a predator. You had to be. The coyote is crafty. . . . We were coyotes in the Thirties, the jobless."*
>
> **ED PAULSON, UNEMPLOYED MAN**

In the face of the suffering caused by the Great Depression, the family stood as a source of strength for most Americans. Although some people feared that hard times would undermine moral values, those fears were largely unfounded. In general, Americans believed in traditional values and emphasized the importance of family unity. At a time when money was tight, many families entertained themselves by staying at home playing board games, such as Monopoly (invented in 1933), and listening to the radio.

Nevertheless, the economic difficulties of the Great Depression put severe pressure on family life. Making ends meet was a daily struggle and, in some cases, families broke apart under the strain.

MEN IN THE STREETS AND ON THE RAILS Many men had difficulty coping with unemployment because they were accustomed to working and supporting their families. Every day, they would set out to walk the streets in search of jobs. As Frederick Lewis Allen noted in *Since Yesterday*, "Men who have been sturdy and self-respecting workers can take unemployment without flinching for a few

THINK THROUGH HISTORY
C. Analyzing Causes Why did so many men leave their homes during the Depression?

C. Answer Many men were depressed by their inability to support their families, and so abandoned them. Others hoped to find work and send money home to their families

weeks, a few months, even if they have to see their families suffer; but it is different after a year . . . two years . . . three years." Some men became so discouraged that they simply stopped trying. Some even abandoned their families.

During the Depression, approximately 2 million men—many of whom had left families behind—wandered the country, hitching rides on the box cars of railroads and sleeping under bridges. These hoboes of the 1930s occasionally would turn up at homeless shelters in big cities. The novelist Thomas Wolfe described a group of these men in New York City.

> These were the wanderers from town to town, the riders of freight trains, the thumbers of rides on highways, the uprooted, unwanted male population of America. They drifted across the land and gathered in the big cities when winter came, hungry, defeated, empty, hopeless, restless, driven by they knew not what, always on the move, looking everywhere for work, for the bare crumbs to support their miserable lives, and finding neither work nor crumbs.
>
> **THOMAS WOLFE,** from *You Can't Go Home Again*

During the early years of the Great Depression, there was no federal system of **direct relief**—cash payments or food provided by the government to the poor. Some cities and charity services did offer relief to those who needed it, but the benefits were meager. In New York City, for example, the weekly payment was just $2.39 per family; this was the most generous relief offered by any city, but it was still well below the amount necessary to feed a family.

WOMEN AND CHILDREN STRUGGLE TO SURVIVE Women worked hard to help their families survive in the face of adversity during the Great Depression. Many women canned food and sewed clothes. They also carefully managed household budgets. Jeane Westin, author of *Making Do: How Women Survived the '30s*, recalled, "Those days you did everything to save a penny. . . . My next door neighbor and I used to shop together. You could get two pounds of hamburger for a quarter, so we'd buy two pounds and split it—then one week she'd pay the extra penny and the next week I'd pay."

Many women also worked outside the home, though they usually received less money than men did. As the Depression wore on, however, working women became the targets of enormous resentment. Some people believed that women, especially married women, had no right to work when men were unemployed. In the early 1930s, some cities refused to hire married women as schoolteachers.

Many Americans assumed that women had an easier time than men during the Depression because few were seen begging or standing in bread lines. As a matter of fact, many women were starving to death in cold attics and rooming houses. As one writer pointed out, women were often too ashamed to reveal their hardship.

A PERSONAL VOICE
I've lived in cities for many months, broke, without help, too timid to get in bread lines. I've known many women to live like this until they simply faint in the street. . . . A woman will shut herself up in a room until it is taken away from her, and eat a cracker a day and be as quiet as a mouse. . . . [She] will go for weeks verging on starvation . . . going through the streets ashamed, sitting in libraries, parks, going for days without speaking to a living soul, shut up in the terror of her own misery.

MERIDEL LE SEUER, from *America in the Twenties*

NOW & THEN

HOMELESSNESS

Today, thousands of homeless people wander the streets of American cities, just as they did during the Great Depression. The main causes of homelessness in the 1930s were economic and social changes that left many people without work and with few prospects for the future.

The causes of the problem today are less clear, although economic dislocation is undoubtedly one of the factors. Others are the closing down of large institutions for mentally ill people, urban renewal that led to the destruction of cheap hotels and boarding houses, fewer jobs for unskilled workers, and rising rents in the cities.

There are key differences between now and the 1930s as far as treatment of homeless people is concerned. More services for homeless people—such as emergency medical treatment, temporary shelter, food, and psychological counseling—are available today. However, there is also probably a greater stigma attached to homelessness today, during a period of general prosperity, than there was during the 1930s, when a larger percentage of the population was out of work.

Congressman Fred Hartley (*above*) buys an apple from an unemployed man in Washington, D.C.

The Great Depression Begins **653**

TEACHING OPTION

Cooperative Activity: Compiling an Oral History of the Depression

Task: Groups of four or five students will interview relatives and friends who lived through the Great Depression and combine the results of their interviews into an oral history.

Purpose: To understand the effects of the Great Depression on the people who survived it.

Activity: Have students make a list of persons they know who experienced the Depression. Before the interview, group members should work together to prepare a list of questions. Instruct students to use a tape recorder during the interview, as well as take notes. Students should transcribe their taped

notes and combine their pages with those of the rest of the group. Allow time for each group to read its oral history before the class.

Possible Interview Questions: Students might ask their interview subjects the following questions: How did the Depression affect you and your family? What specific things did you do to cope with the Depression? What long-term effects did the Depression have on you?

ALTERNATIVE ASSESSMENT BOOK
Standards for Evaluating a Cooperative Activity

MORE ABOUT . . .
Suicides

While their numbers probably have been exaggerated, some stock investors distraught over losing everything during the crash of 1929 did choose to kill themselves. In one case, a vice-president with the Earl Radio Corporation, having lost $124,000, climbed out onto the ledge of his 11th-floor hotel window and jumped to his death. "We are broke," read part of his suicide note.

ASSESS & RETEACH

Section 2 Assessment

Have students work in pairs to answer the assessment questions. Draw the chart for question 2 on the board and work as a class to fill in the possible answers.

Self-Assessment

To show what students have learned, have them write down four or five facts they learned about living conditions during the Depression.

Section Quiz

FORMAL ASSESSMENT
Section Quiz, p. 270

Reteach

Replay the video "Broke but Not Broken" to help review the impact of the Dust Bowl.

AMERICAN STORIES VIDEO SERIES
"Broke but Not Broken"

CLOSE

Millions of people coped with the hardships brought about by the Great Depression. In the cities, many people lived in shacks and depended on charity. In the rural areas of the Great Plains, terrible dust storms forced farmers to leave their homes.

Children also suffered great hardship during the 1930s. Poor diets and a lack of money for health care led to serious health problems. Milk consumption declined across the country, and clinics and hospitals reported a dramatic rise in malnutrition and diet-related diseases, such as rickets and pellagra. At the same time, child-welfare programs were slashed as cities and states cut their budgets in the face of dwindling resources.

Falling tax revenues also caused school boards to shorten the school year and even close schools. By 1933, some 2,600 schools across the nation had shut down, leaving more than 300,000 students out of school. Many children went to work instead; they often labored in sweatshops under horrendous conditions.

SOCIAL AND PSYCHOLOGICAL EFFECTS

The hardships of the Great Depression had a tremendous social and psychological impact. Some people were so demoralized by hard times that they lost their will to survive. Between 1928 and 1932, the suicide rate rose by nearly 30 percent. Three times as many people were admitted to state mental hospitals as in normal times.

The economic problems forced many Americans to accept compromises and make sacrifices that affected them for the rest of their lives. Adults stopped going to the doctor or dentist because they couldn't afford it. Young people gave up their dreams of going to college. Others put off getting married, raising large families, or having children at all.

For many people, the stigma of poverty and of having to scrimp and save never disappeared completely. For some, achieving financial security became the primary focus in life. As one woman recalled, "Ever since I was twelve years old there was one major goal in my life . . . one thing . . . and that was to never be poor again."

During the Great Depression many people showed great kindness to strangers who were down on their luck. People often gave food, clothing, and a place to stay to the needy. Families helped other families and shared resources and strengthened the bonds within their communities. In addition, many people developed habits of saving and thriftiness—habits they would need to see themselves through the dark days ahead as the nation and President Hoover struggled with the Great Depression. These habits shaped a whole generation of Americans.

This Ozark sharecropper family was photographed in Arkansas during the 1930s by the artist Ben Shahn.

THINK THROUGH HISTORY
D. Recognizing Effects How did the Great Depression affect women and children?

THINK THROUGH HISTORY
E. Summarizing What were some of the long-lasting psychological and social consequences of the Depression?

Section 2 Assessment

1. TERMS & NAMES
Identify:
- Dust Bowl
- shantytown
- soup kitchen
- bread line
- direct relief

2. SUMMARIZING Using a chart, list at least three groups of people and the effects that the Great Depression had on them.

Group	Effects of Depression

3. COMPARING AND CONTRASTING Compare what happened to city dwellers and to farmers during the Great Depression. How was it similar and different?

THINK ABOUT
- what happened to their livelihoods
- what happened to their homes
- what help was available to them

4. RECOGNIZING EFFECTS How did the Dust Bowl affect the entire country?

THINK ABOUT
- the effect on farmers on the plains
- the effect on California and other states where the Okies resettled
- the effect on the East

654 CHAPTER 22

ANSWERS

❸ Hoover Struggles with the Depression

TERMS & NAMES
- Herbert Hoover
- Boulder Dam
- Federal Home Loan Bank Act
- Reconstruction Finance Corporation
- Bonus Army

LEARN ABOUT President Hoover's response to the Great Depression
TO UNDERSTAND why the Hoover administration lost public support.

Section 3 Overview

OBJECTIVES

1. To explain Hoover's initial response to the Depression.
2. To describe some of the measures Hoover took to help the economy and ease people's suffering.

SKILLBUILDER
- Interpreting political cartoons, p. 657

CRITICAL THINKING
- Summarizing, pp. 656, 659
- Forming opinions, p. 657
- Evaluating decisions, p. 658
- Drawing conclusions, p. 659
- Analyzing issues, p. 659
- Clarifying, p. 659

ONE AMERICAN'S STORY

Oscar Ameringer was a newspaper editor in Oklahoma City during the Great Depression. In 1932, he traveled around the country for several months to gather information on its economic and social conditions. Testifying before congressional hearings on unemployment that same year, Ameringer described a population of poor, desperate people who were losing patience with the government. "Unless something is done for them and done soon," he asserted, "you will have a revolution on hand." At the hearings, Ameringer told the following story.

A PERSONAL VOICE
The roads of the West and Southwest teem with hungry hitchhikers. . . . Between Clarksville and Russellville, Ark., I picked up a family. The woman was hugging a dead chicken under a ragged coat. When I asked her where she procured [got] the fowl, first she told me she had found it dead in the road, and then added in grim humor, "They promised me a chicken in the pot, and now I got mine."

OSCAR AMERINGER, quoted in *The American Spirit*

A Depression-era family from Arkansas walks through Texas, looking for work in the cotton fields along the Rio Grande.

The woman was recalling President Hoover's 1928 campaign pledge: "A chicken in every pot and two cars in every garage." That pledge turned out to be an empty promise. Many Americans were now highly critical of Hoover and called on the government to do more to ease their suffering.

Hoover Tries to Reassure the Nation

After the stock market crash of October 1929, President **Herbert Hoover** tried to reassure Americans that the nation's economy was on a sound footing. "Any lack of confidence in the economic future . . . is foolish," he asserted. The important thing was for Americans to remain optimistic and to go about their business as usual.

Traditionally, Americans believed that depressions were a normal part of the business cycle. According to this theory, periods of rapid economic growth were naturally followed by periods of economic contraction, or depression. The best course of action in such a slump, many experts believed, was to do nothing and let the economy fix itself.

Most officials in the Hoover administration echoed that economic view, including Secretary of the Treasury Andrew Mellon. A strong advocate of the "do-nothing" approach, Mellon advised President Hoover to "let the slump liquidate [end] itself. Liquidate labor, liquidate stocks, liquidate the farmers, liquidate real estate. . . . It will purge the rottenness out of the system."

Hoover took a different position. Although he believed that the economy should be allowed to function with minimal government intervention, he also felt that government could play a role in helping to solve economic problems. The key, in his view, was to limit that role and prevent government from taking too much power.

The Great Depression Begins **655**

FOCUS & MOTIVATE

▶ *Starting with the Student*
- Have students imagine they are living a hand-to-mouth existence during the Depression. Would they want the government to control the economy and other aspects of their lives to help end the Depression?
- Would it matter to them that this could undermine the tenets of democracy and capitalism?

OBJECTIVE
1. **INSTRUCT**

Hoover Tries to Reassure the Nation

▶ *Discussing Key Ideas*
- Hoover believes people should help themselves during the Depression rather than depend on government handouts.
- Hoover takes cautious and largely ineffective steps to remedy the Depression.

IN-DEPTH RESOURCES: UNIT 6
Guided Reading, p. 38

ACCESS FOR STUDENTS ACQUIRING ENGLISH
Guided Reading (Spanish), p. 217

SECTION 3 RESOURCES

 PRINTING RESOURCES

IN-DEPTH RESOURCES: UNIT 6
Guided Reading, p. 38
Primary Source: Attack on the Bonus Army, p. 45

ACCESS FOR STUDENTS ACQUIRING ENGLISH
Guided Reading (Spanish), p. 217

FORMAL ASSESSMENT
Section Quiz, p. 271

ALTERNATIVE ASSESSMENT BOOK
See forms for supporting and scoring alternative activities.

 TECHNOLOGY RESOURCES

CD-ROM Electronic Library of Primary Sources

VIDEO *American Portfolio: A Videodisc for U.S. History* user's guide, pp. 205, 206

INTERNET McDougal Littell Learning On-Line
http://www.mcdougallittell.com

HOOVER'S PHILOSOPHY OF GOVERNMENT   Herbert Hoover was a man of strong principles. As an engineer, he had great faith in the power of reason to solve problems. Hoover was also a humanitarian who believed in helping others. As he said in one of his first speeches after becoming president,

> **A PERSONAL VOICE**
> Our first objective must be to provide security from poverty and want. We want security in living for every home. We want to see a nation built of home owners and farm owners. We want to see their savings protected. We want to see them in steady jobs. We want to see more and more of them insured against death and accident, unemployment and old age. We want them all secure.
> **HERBERT HOOVER**

Hoover was not a career politician, however, and found it difficult to make political compromises. Inflexible by nature, he had a hard time adjusting his attitudes and actions to fit the nation's changing and increasingly desperate circumstances.

Hoover believed that one of government's chief functions was to foster cooperation between competing groups and interests in society. If business and labor were in conflict, for example, government should step in and help them find a solution that served their mutual interest. In Hoover's view, this cooperation should be voluntary rather than forced. Government's proper role, he believed, was to encourage and facilitate cooperation, not to control it.

Hoover also believed strongly in "rugged individualism"—the idea that people should succeed through their own efforts. They should take care of themselves and their families, rather than depend on the government to bail them out. As a supporter of rugged individualism, Hoover opposed any form of federal welfare, or direct relief to the needy. He believed that such direct federal handouts would weaken people's self-respect and undermine the nation's moral fiber.

Instead of federal welfare, Hoover believed that individuals, charities, and local organizations should pitch in to help care for the less fortunate. The federal government should direct and guide relief measures, but not through a vast federal bureaucracy. Such a bureaucracy, he said, would be too expensive and would stifle individual liberties.

HOOVER TAKES CAUTIOUS STEPS   Hoover's political philosophy caused him to take a cautious approach to the depression. Soon after the stock market crash, he called together key leaders from the fields of business, banking, and labor. He urged them to work together to find solutions to the nation's economic woes and to act in ways that would not make a bad situation worse. For example, he asked employers not to cut wages or lay off workers, and he asked labor leaders not to demand higher wages or to strike. He also created a special organization to help private charities generate contributions for the poor.

However, none of these steps made much of a difference. A year after the crash, the economy was still shrinking, and unemployment was still rising. More companies went out of business, soup kitchens became a common sight, and the general misery of ordinary people continued to grow. Shantytowns arose in every city and hoboes roamed the city and the countryside.

DEMOCRATS WIN IN 1930 CONGRESSIONAL ELECTIONS   As the country's economic difficulties increased, the political tide turned against Hoover and the Republicans. In the 1930 congressional elections, the Democrats took advantage of anti-Hoover sentiments to win more seats in Congress. As a result of

KEY PLAYER

HERBERT HOOVER
1874–1964
Born to a Quaker family in Iowa, Herbert Hoover was the first president born west of the Mississippi River. He was orphaned at an early age and his life was a real rags-to-riches story. He worked his way through Stanford University and later made a fortune as a mining engineer and consultant in China, Australia, Europe, and Africa. During and after World War I, he coordinated U.S. relief efforts in Europe, earning a reputation for efficiency and humanitarian ideals.

As president, Hoover took steps that reflected his belief in local solutions and private initiatives to social problems. He asserted, "Every time we find solutions outside of government, we have not only strengthened character, but we have preserved our sense of real government."

that election, the Republicans lost control of the House of Representatives and saw their majority in the Senate dwindle to one vote.

As Americans grew more and more frustrated by the depression, they expressed their anger in a number of ways. Farmers stung by low crop prices burned their corn and wheat and dumped their milk on highways to avoid selling it at a loss. Some farmers even declared a "farm holiday" and refused to work their fields. In many cases, they blocked roads to prevent food from getting to market; they hoped that food shortages would raise prices. Some farmers also used force to prevent authorities from foreclosing on farms.

By 1930, people were calling the shantytowns in American cities Hoovervilles—a direct slap at the president's policies. To keep warm, homeless people wrapped themselves in newspapers they called Hoover blankets. Empty pockets turned inside out were Hoover flags. Many Americans, who had hailed Hoover as a great humanitarian a few years before, now saw him as a cold and heartless leader.

Despite public criticism, Hoover continued to hold firm to his principles. He refused to support direct relief or other forms of federal welfare. Some Americans were going hungry, and many blamed Hoover for their plight. Criticism of the president and his policies continued to grow. An anonymous ditty of the time was widely repeated.

> Mellon pulled the whistle
> Hoover rang the bell
> Wall Street gave the signal
> And the country went to hell.

B. Answer Answers will vary, but some students will probably say that Americans look to their leaders for results, and Hoover wasn't getting results.

THINK THROUGH HISTORY
B. Forming Opinions Why do you think people blamed Hoover for the nation's difficulties?

Hoover Takes Action

Hoover, however, was sensitive to suffering and started listening to the criticism. As time went on and the Depression deepened, he gradually softened his position on government intervention in the economy and took a more activist approach to the nation's economic troubles. By 1930, he was directing federal funds into projects—such as the construction of **Boulder Dam**, designed to jump-start the economy and add jobs.

SKILLBUILDER
INTERPRETING POLITICAL CARTOONS
In this cartoon, various segments of American society point their fingers at a beleaguered President Hoover. What does the cartoon suggest about Hoover's chances for reelection?

Skillbuilder Answer The cartoon suggests Hoover's chances for reelection are not good.

This mural, entitled *Construction of the Dam,* **shows the building of the Boulder Dam. It was painted in 1937 by William Gropper for the Department of the Interior building in Washington, D.C.**

Possible Responses:

1. Yes—Hoover's limited intervention was appropriate, for too much government control of people's lives would undermine democracy. No—The severity of the Depression demanded that the government do more to provide relief.

2. Some students might answer that they would have acted as Hoover did, while others might say they would have increased the number of government work projects and instituted a federal welfare program.

MORE ABOUT . . .
Gassing the Bonus Army

Hoover actually wanted MacArthur to proceed more peacefully in disbanding the Bonus Army. However, MacArthur, sensing "incipient revolution in the air," ignored the president's command. While Hoover reproached his general in private, he declined to challenge MacArthur's insubordination in public. Nearly 20 years later, MacArthur again challenged the authority of a president, crossing Harry Truman over his war strategy in Korea. Truman took a different course than Hoover had. He fired MacArthur.

IN-DEPTH RESOURCES: UNIT 6
Primary Source: Attack on the Bonus Army, p. 45

 ELECTRONIC LIBRARY OF PRIMARY SOURCES
from a Report on the Employment of Federal Troops by General Douglas MacArthur
from B.E.F.: The Story of the Bonus Army by W. W. Waters

Difficult Decisions
IN HISTORY

HOOVER AND FEDERAL PROJECTS
On one hand, President Hoover opposed federal welfare and government intervention in the economy. On the other, he felt that government had a duty to help solve problems and ease suffering. The question was, What kind of assistance is proper and effective?

1. Consider the pros and cons of Hoover's actions during the Depression. Did he do enough to try to end the Depression? Why or why not?

2. If you had been president during the Depression, what steps and policies would you have supported? Explain the approach you would have taken.

The Bonus Army's tent city burns in Washington, D.C., in 1932.

BOULDER DAM AND OTHER GOVERNMENT PROJECTS One of Hoover's first major initiatives was a public-works program to build roads, dams, and other large projects, in an effort to stimulate business and provide jobs for unemployed workers. Congress approved $800 million for these projects, which included the giant Boulder Dam (now called Hoover Dam), on the Colorado River between Arizona and Nevada.

Hoover also backed the creation of the Federal Farm Board. This organization was designed to raise crop prices by helping farm cooperatives buy crops and keep them off the market temporarily. In addition, Hoover tried to prop up the banking system by persuading the nation's largest banks to establish the National Credit Corporation. This organization loaned money to smaller banks, which helped them stave off bankruptcy.

By late 1931, however, many people saw that none of these measures accomplished enough to turn the economy around. With a presidential election looming, Hoover decided to take more serious action. He appealed to Congress to pass a series of measures to reform banking, provide mortgage relief, and funnel more federal money into business investment. Congress responded in 1933 with the Glass-Steagall Banking Act, which increased bank reserves and made bank loans easier to get. Congress also passed the **Federal Home Loan Bank Act,** which lowered mortgage rates for homeowners and allowed farmers to refinance their farm loans and avoid foreclosure.

Hoover's most ambitious economic measure, however, was the **Reconstruction Finance Corporation** (RFC), approved by Congress in January 1932 and authorized to provide emergency financing to banks, life insurance companies, railroads, and other large businesses. This financing—up to $2 billion worth—was intended to pump new life into the economy by fueling business expansion. Hoover believed that the money would trickle down to the average citizen through job growth and higher wages. Many critics questioned this approach; they argued that the program would benefit only corporations and that the poor still needed direct relief. Hungry people could not wait for the benefits to trickle down to their tables.

Initially, the RFC did provide substantial assistance to industry. In its first five months of operation, the agency had loaned more than $805 million to large corporations, but business failures continued. The RFC was an unprecedented example of federal involvement in a peacetime economy, but in the end it was too little, too late.

GASSING THE BONUS ARMY
In 1932, an incident further damaged Hoover's public image. That spring, between 10,000 and 20,000 World War I veterans and their families arrived in Washington, D.C., from various parts of the country. They called themselves the Bonus Expeditionary Force, or the **Bonus Army.**

Led by Walter Waters, an unemployed cannery worker from Oregon, the Bonus Army came to the nation's capital to support a bill under debate in

C. Answer: A public works program to build roads and dams; Federal Farm Board; National Credit Corporation; Federal Home Loan Bank Act; Reconstruction Finance Corporation. These projects and measures were not able to turn the economy around.

THINK THROUGH HISTORY
C. Evaluating Decisions What were some of the projects proposed by Hoover, and how effective were they?

TEACHING OPTION

Cooperative Activity: Debating the Bonus Army March

Task: Student groups will debate each other on different issues surrounding the Bonus Army's march on Washington.

Purpose: To explore the Bonus Army incident in depth.

Activity:

1. Divide the class in half. One half will debate the merits of the Patman Bill; the other half will debate the decision to forcibly disband the Bonus Army.

2. Have the half that is debating the Patman Bill divide into two groups. One group will support the bill, while the

other will oppose it. Each group should do further research to support its position. The two groups should then debate each other.

3. Have the half that is debating the removal of the Bonus Army also divide into two groups. One group will support the forcible removal of the army, while the other will oppose it. Each group should do further research to support its position. The two groups should then debate each other.

ALTERNATIVE ASSESSMENT BOOK
Standards for Evaluating a Cooperative Activity

Congress. The Patman Bill authorized the government to pay a bonus to World War I veterans who had not been compensated adequately for their wartime service. This bonus, which Congress approved in 1924, was not supposed to be paid until 1945, but Congressman Wright Patman believed that the money—an average of $500 per soldier—should be paid immediately.

Although Hoover opposed the legislation, he respected the veterans' right to peaceful assembly. He even provided food and supplies so that they could erect a shantytown within sight of the Capitol building. On June 17, however, the Senate voted down the Patman Bill. Hoover then called on the Bonus Army marchers to leave and, although most did, approximately 2,000 refused to budge.

President Hoover decided that the Bonus Army should be disbanded. On July 28, a force of 1,000 soldiers under the command of General Douglas MacArthur and his aide, Major Dwight D. Eisenhower, came to roust the veterans. A government official watching from a nearby office recalled what happened next.

A PERSONAL VOICE
The 12th infantry was in full battle dress. Each had a gas mask and his belt was full of tear gas bombs. . . . At orders, they brought their bayonets at thrust and moved in. The bayonets were used to jab people, to make them move. Soon, almost everybody disappeared from view, because tear gas bombs exploded. The entire block was covered by tear gas. Flames were coming up, where the soldiers had set fire to the buildings to drive these people out. . . . Through the whole afternoon, they took one camp after another.

A. EVERETTE McINTYRE, quoted in *Hard Times*

In the course of the operation, the infantry gassed more than 1,000 people, including an 11-month-old baby who died and an 8-year-old boy who was partially blinded. Two people were shot and many were injured. Most Americans were stunned and outraged at the government's treatment of the veterans.

Once again, President Hoover's image suffered, especially damaging in an election year. In November, Hoover faced a formidable opponent, the Democratic candidate Franklin Delano Roosevelt. When Roosevelt heard about the attack on the Bonus Army, he said to his friend Felix Frankfurter, "Well, Felix, this will elect me." The downturn in the economy and Hoover's inability to effectively deal with the Depression had sealed his political fate.

HISTORICAL SPOTLIGHT

CENTURY OF PROGRESS EXPOSITION

In 1893, Chicago hosted the World's Columbian Exposition, which celebrated the 400th anniversary of Columbus's voyage to America. Forty years later, in 1933 at the height of the Great Depression, Chicago opened a second international exposition, called A Century of Progress, along the city's lakefront.

This fair, which commemorated the 100th anniversary of the founding of Chicago, celebrated modern advances in science and industry. The fair highlighted how far the city had come in the last century and promised a better tomorrow. It was one of the most financially successful world fairs in history. During the time that the fair ran in 1933 and 1934, there were approximately 39 million paid admissions.

Section 3 Assessment

1. TERMS & NAMES
Identify:
• Herbert Hoover
• Boulder Dam
• Federal Home Loan Bank Act
• Reconstruction Finance Corporation
• Bonus Army

2. SUMMARIZING On a cluster diagram, record what Hoover said and did in response to the Depression.

Hoover's Responses

Put a plus by the response you think was most helpful and a minus by the one you think was least helpful.

3. ANALYZING ISSUES How did Hoover's belief in "rugged individualism" shape his policies during the depression?

THINK ABOUT
• what that belief implies about government action
• Hoover's policies
• whether those policies were consistent with his beliefs

4. CLARIFYING When Franklin Delano Roosevelt heard about the attack on the Bonus Army, why was he so certain that Hoover was going to lose?

THINK ABOUT
• the American public's impression of Hoover
• Hoover's actions against the Depression
• how people judged Hoover after the attack

The Great Depression Begins **659**

ANSWERS

1. TERMS & NAMES
Herbert Hoover, p. 655
Boulder Dam, p. 657
Federal Home Loan Bank Act, p. 658
Reconstruction Finance Corporation, p. 658
Bonus Army, p. 658

2. SUMMARIZING
The cluster diagram might include the following words and phrases:
"Any lack of confidence in the economic future . . . is foolish"; "rugged individualism"; public-works programs; Boulder Dam; Federal Farm Board; Federal Home Loan Bank Act; Reconstruction Finance Corporation; sending of troops against Bonus Army

3. ANALYZING ISSUES
Possible Responses: Some students may say that Hoover's belief in "rugged individualism" implied limited government intervention and prompted him to take a cautious approach. For example, he allowed the government to hire unemployed people for public-works programs, but he would not give them direct aid. Others may say that the public-works programs show that he stopped believing in rugged individualism.

4. CLARIFYING
Possible Responses: Some students may say that the public wanted a warm, generous leader who would act to relieve its suffering and that the attack made Hoover seem uncaring and cruel. Others may mention that the public was already blaming Hoover for all its suffering, and the attack just confirmed that negative impression of him.

TERMS & NAMES

1. credit, p. 644
2. speculation, p. 645
3. buying on margin, p. 645
4. Black Tuesday, p. 645
5. Dow Jones Industrial Average, p. 647
6. Great Depression, p. 646
7. Dust Bowl, p. 650
8. direct relief, p. 653
9. Herbert Hoover, p. 655
10. Bonus Army, p. 658

MAIN IDEAS

11. During the 1920s, farmers faced decreased demand for their products and lower crop prices. Those who were in debt could not repay loans, and rural banks failed. This pattern repeated itself in other sectors of the economy during the Depression.

12. Because a small number of people controlled a large percentage of the nation's wealth, most consumers could not afford the products the nation was producing—a trend that threatened economic growth.

13. The stock market crash triggered bank and business failures, high unemployment, and worldwide depression.

14. It hurt the U.S. economy because it lowered the income of foreign nations and reduced their spending on American goods.

15. Shantytowns consisted of makeshift housing built by the homeless, and soup kitchens and bread lines were places where charitable organizations handed out food to the hungry.

16. Some unemployed whites were angered by job competition from minorities.

17. Unemployment reduced household income. Some families lost homes. Many adults lost the ability to provide for their families.

18. Mellon believed that depressions were a normal part of the business cycle and the economy would eventually fix itself.

19. The harshness of the attack on the veterans and their families damaged Hoover's reputation.

20. He started public-works programs and backed the Federal Farm Board, Federal Home Loan Bank Act, and the RFC.

660 Chapter 22

REVIEWING THE CHAPTER

TERMS & NAMES For each term below, write a sentence explaining its connection to the period from 1929 to 1933. For the person below, explain his role in the events of the period.

1. credit
2. speculation
3. buying on margin
4. Black Tuesday
5. Dow Jones Industrial Average
6. Great Depression
7. Dust Bowl
8. direct relief
9. Herbert Hoover
10. Bonus Army

MAIN IDEAS

SECTION 1 *(pages 642–649)*

The Nation's Sick Economy

11. How did what happened to farmers during the 1920s foreshadow events of the Great Depression?
12. Why was uneven distribution of income bad for the economy?
13. What were some of the effects of the stock market crash in October 1929?
14. What effect did the Hawley-Smoot Tariff Act have on the economy and why?

SECTION 2 *(pages 650–654)*

Hardship and Suffering During the Depression

15. How were shantytowns, soup kitchens, and bread lines a response to the Depression?
16. Why did minorities often experience an increase in discrimination during the Great Depression?
17. What pressures did the American family experience during the Depression?

SECTION 3 *(pages 655–659)*

Hoover Struggles with the Depression

18. Why did Secretary of the Treasury Andrew Mellon believe that the government should do nothing about the Depression?
19. How did Hoover's treatment of the Bonus Army affect his standing with the public?
20. In what ways did Hoover try to use the government to relieve the Depression?

THINKING CRITICALLY

1. **THE GREAT DEPRESSION** Create a cause-and-effect web for the Great Depression, using a graphic similar to the one shown.

2. **INDIVIDUALS AND SOCIETY** Did public reaction to the stock market crash and the following crisis make the economic situation better or worse? Explain by citing specific actions.

3. **ECONOMIC DESPAIR** Reread the quotation by Senator La Follette on page 640. Do you think he accurately summarized the change in the mood of the nation? What words or phrases do you find especially accurate or especially misleading?

4. **GEOGRAPHY OF THE DUST BOWL** Look carefully at the map on page 652. What generalizations can you make about the topography, or surface features, of the land where the Dust Bowl was? How might that topography have contributed to the problem? Remember that the prevailing winds blew the dust from west to east.

5. **THE DOW JONES AVERAGE** Reviewing the Now & Then feature on pages 646–647, compare the stocks that made up the Dow Jones Industrial Average in 1896 to the stocks that make it up today. What does this tell you about the way the economy changed during that 100 years?

6. **ANALYZING PRIMARY SOURCES** Read the following excerpt from Oscar Ameringer's testimony before the U.S. Congress in 1932. Then answer the questions below.

> Personally, and as a lifelong student of political economy [economics], I am of the opinion that all this talk about speedy recovery and prosperity being just around the corner is bosh and nonsense. What we are confronted with is not a mere panic like those of 1873 and 1883 but a worldwide economic catastrophe that may spell the end of the capitalistic era—for the cause of it is production for profit instead of production for consumption. The masses cannot buy what they have themselves produced; and unless ways and means are found to make cash customers out of some 20 million of unemployed wage earners and bankrupt farmers, there can be no recovery.
>
> **OSCAR AMERINGER**, *Testimony Before a Subcommittee of the Committee on Labor, House of Representatives*

Judging from what you read in this section, do you agree with Ameringer's assessment of why recovery from the Great Depression was so difficult? Has his prediction that the Depression would end the capitalistic era come true? Explain.

THINKING CRITICALLY

1. THE GREAT DEPRESSION
Possible Answers:

Causes

decaying industrial base

farm crisis

failure of rural banks

uneven distribution of income

consumers' overdependence on credit

stock market speculation

Effects

widespread bank failures

bankrupt businesses

high unemployment

decrease in worldwide trade

increasing numbers of homeless persons

widespread hunger and illness

2. INDIVIDUALS AND SOCIETY
Possible Response: Public reaction made the situation worse. By selling off

stocks, panicky investors drove market prices down even farther. By withdrawing savings, depositors wiped out thousands of banks.

3. ECONOMIC DESPAIR
Possible Responses: Students answering yes might say that "illusory prosperity" describes the 1920s well and "widespread despair" describes the 1930s well. Students answering no might say the quotation overgeneralizes; for example, farmers and minority groups in the 1920s did not feel "feverish optimism."

ALTERNATIVE ASSESSMENT

1. CREATING A CARTOON OR AN ILLUSTRATION

What were the effects of the stock market crash of 1929 on people's lives, either in the United States or abroad?

Create a political cartoon or an illustration that depicts an aspect of life that was radically transformed in the wake of the stock market crash of 1929. You can choose to focus your study on the United States or on another country of your choice.

 CD-ROM Use the CD-ROM *Our Times,* your textbook, and other sources to begin your research.

- You might want to focus on one aspect of life. Create a visual that makes a point about how that aspect of life was changed. Feel free to exaggerate your point in a visual way.
- Write a caption that expresses in a few words the essence of your point about the transformation caused by the crash.

2. LEARNING FROM MEDIA

VIDEO View the McDougal Littell Video for Chapter 22, *Broke but Not Broken.* Discuss the following questions in small groups; then do the cooperative learning activity.

- According to Ann Marie Low, how did the farmers contribute to their own ruin?
- What choices did Ann Marie Low's family make during the Depression? Do you agree with their choices?
- What did you learn about the relationship between the government and the farmers?
- What did the older Ann Marie Low's comments add to your understanding of the Great Depression?
- **Cooperative Learning** In your group, compile a list of questions that you still have about the experience of living in the Dust Bowl. Then write a letter to Ann Marie Low asking for more information. Share your letter with the class.

3. PORTFOLIO PROJECT

Use the Living History activity to expand your portfolio.

LIVING HISTORY

DISPLAYING YOUR COLLAGE

Finish, present, and display your collage representing the stories of people who lived through the Great Depression.

- Review the images you have assembled. If any seem weak, find or create a replacement.
- Experiment with different ways of grouping the images. Your groupings may emphasize either similarities or differences in personal stories.
- When you have an arrangement you like, make your collage permanent by affixing the images to a poster board.
- Be prepared to present your collage in class and answer any questions about why you chose the images and who each one represents. Display your collage in the classroom. Then add your collage to your American history portfolio.

Bridge to Chapter 23

Review Chapter 22

PROSPERITY TURNS TO PANIC Unresolved economic problems of the 1920s led to the Great Depression. Industries and farmers faced reduced demand, most people could not earn an adequate income, and many went deeply into debt. Dreams of wealth led people to take risks in the stock market. When stock prices fell, panicked investors sold their shares, causing a market crash. Mass withdrawals of savings closed banks. Businesses in all industries went bankrupt, throwing millions out of work.

HOMELESSNESS AND HUNGER Many unemployed people lost their homes and had to live on the streets or in shantytowns. Many farmers also were evicted, especially in the area of the Great Plains known as the Dust Bowl. Hoping to work as migrants, thousands of these headed for California. Two million unemployed men wandered the country looking for work. The families they left behind struggled to survive despite poverty, hunger, and illness.

A CAUTIOUS PRESIDENT President Hoover believed that people should succeed through their own efforts and that government should not intervene much in the economy. Yet, he was a humanitarian who believed in helping others, so he supported public-works programs to create jobs. He also made a few financial reforms. However, the public thought he was not doing enough to ease their suffering. When Hoover sent troops against the Bonus Army, he lost the last of his popular support.

Preview Chapter 23

In 1932, Americans rejected President Hoover in favor of the Democrat Franklin Delano Roosevelt. To relieve suffering and spark the economy, Roosevelt began programs to provide financial reform, works projects, and direct relief. The Depression influenced popular culture as Americans sought to forget their hardships by listening to radio and attending movies. You will learn about these and other significant developments in the next chapter.

The Great Depression Begins **661**

ALTERNATIVE ASSESSMENT

1. CREATING A CARTOON OR AN ILLUSTRATION
Standards for Evaluation
A drawing should meet the following criteria:

- Focuses on one aspect of life affected by the crash.
- Uses strong visuals to capture a viewer's attention.
- Clearly conveys a message or story in its visual presentation.
- Includes a caption that expresses the essence of the drawing.

2. LEARNING FROM MEDIA
Answers to the questions:

- They overfarmed the land and ruined the topsoil, thus leaving nothing to hold down the dust.
- The Low family remained on their farm as others fled. Possible Responses: Yes, they had worked too long and hard at building the farm to leave. No, they should have left and sought better opportunities.
- The relationship was marked by tension and mistrust.
- Students may point to a better understanding of the farmers' plight during the Depression.

Standards for Evaluation
A letter to Ann Marie Low should meet the following criteria:

- Asks questions about issues not covered in the video.
- Makes the questions clear and specific.
- Uses appropriate letter form and style.

3. PORTFOLIO PROJECT
LIVING HISTORY
Standards for Evaluation:
A collage should meet the following criteria:

- Build upon descriptive details and viewpoints expressed in the personal voices about the Great Depression.
- Present an accurate visual representation of Depression-era issues.

IN-DEPTH RESOURCES: UNIT 6
See the form for scoring this activity on page 52

THINKING CRITICALLY

4. GEOGRAPHY OF THE DUST BOWL
Possible Responses: The land is very flat; there were no obstructions to reduce the wind that blew the topsoil away.

5. THE DOW JONES AVERAGE
Possible Response: Heavy industry has grown less important to the economy. Important sectors of today's economy include software production, television broadcasting, and legal services.

6. ANALYZING PRIMARY SOURCES
Possible Responses: Agree—Ameringer points out the unequal distribution of income, the farm crisis, and the worldwide impact. Disagree—Production for profit is not necessarily different from production for consumption. False—The United States is still a capitalist nation. True—The United States no longer has such a capitalistic economy—the government is heavily involved in the economy.

CHAPTER 23

PLANNING GUIDE
The New Deal

	Key Ideas	TEACHING SUPPORT	ASSESSMENT
SECTION 1 A New Deal Fights the Depression pp. 664–670	President Roosevelt takes many actions to combat the Depression.	**In-Depth Resources: Unit 6** • Guided Reading, p. 53 • Skillbuilder Practice: Analyzing Issues, p. 58 • Primary Source: *from* Father Coughlin's Anti-New Deal Speech, p. 63 • American Lives: Huey Long, p. 70 **COOPERATIVE ACTIVITY** • Delivering a Fireside Chat, p. 666 (TE)	*Section 1 Assessment,* p. 670 (PE) *Self-Assessment,* p. 670 (TE) *Formal Assessment* • Section Quiz, p. 280 *Alternative Assessment Book* • Standards for Evaluating a Cooperative Activity
SECTION 2 The Second New Deal Takes Hold pp. 671–676	The Second New Deal institutes new programs to extend federal aid and stimulate the nation's economy.	**In-Depth Resources: Unit 6** • Guided Reading, p. 54 **COOPERATIVE ACTIVITY** • Creating a New Deal Poster, p. 675 (TE)	*Section 2 Assessment,* p. 676 (PE) *Self-Assessment,* p. 676 (TE) *Formal Assessment* • Section Quiz, p. 281 *Alternative Assessment Book* • Standards for Evaluating a Cooperative Activity
SECTION 3 The New Deal Affects Many Groups pp. 677–682	New Deal policies and actions affect Americans from all walks of life. The Democratic Party forms a new political coalition.	**In-Depth Resources: Unit 6** • Guided Reading, p. 55 • Primary Source: The Memorial Day Massacre, p. 64 • American Lives: Mary McLeod Bethune, p. 71 **COOPERATIVE ACTIVITY** • Researching Treatment of Women and Minorities, p. 679 (TE)	*Section 3 Assessment,* p. 682 (PE) *Self-Assessment,* p. 682 (TE) *Formal Assessment* • Section Quiz, p. 282 *Alternative Assessment Book* • Standards for Evaluating a Cooperative Activity
SECTION 4 Society and Culture pp. 683–688	Motion pictures, radio, art, and literature all blossom during the Depression and the New Deal.	**In-Depth Resources: Unit 6** • Guided Reading, p. 56 • Primary Source: WPA Posters, p. 65; *from Let Us Now Praise Famous Men* by James Agee and Walker Evans, p. 66 **COOPERATIVE ACTIVITY** • Producing a Depression-Era Radio Program, p. 685 (TE)	*Section 4 Assessment,* p. 688 (PE) *Self-Assessment,* p. 688 (TE) *Formal Assessment* • Section Quiz, p. 283 *Alternative Assessment Book* • Standards for Evaluating a Cooperative Activity
SECTION 5 The Impact of the New Deal pp. 689–693	The New Deal affects American society not only in the 1930s but also in the decades that follow.	**In-Depth Resources: Unit 6** • Guided Reading, p. 57 • Geography Application: Decade of the Democrats, p. 59 • Outline Map: Anatomy of the Tennessee Valley Authority, p. 61 **COOPERATIVE ACTIVITY** • Debating the New Deal, p. 691 (TE)	*Section 5 Assessment,* p. 693 (PE) *Self-Assessment,* p. 693 (TE) *Formal Assessment* • Section Quiz, p. 284 *Alternative Assessment Book* • Standards for Evaluating a Cooperative Activity
CHAPTER RESOURCES	**Chapter Overview** President Roosevelt launches a program aiming to end the Depression. The Depression and his new deal have profound effects on the nation.	**In-Depth Resources: Unit 6** • Living History Project: Worksheet, p. 72; Standards, p. 73 **Telescoping the Times** • Chapter Summary, pp. 45–46 **Planning for Block Schedules**	*Chapter Assessment,* pp. 696–697 (PE) *Alternative Assessment,* p. 697 (PE) *Formal Assessment* • Chapter Test, forms A and B, pp. 285–290 *Test Generator* *Alternative Assessment Book* See explanation and forms for different kinds of alternative assessments including portfolio assessment.

Humanities Transparencies
• H40, Nine Old Men

Geography Transparencies
• G23, P. W. A. in Action

Electronic Library of Primary Sources
• Franklin D. Roosevelt

INTERNET RESOURCES
• See *McDougal Littell Learning On-Line* for links to information about FDR and Huey Long.

Grolier Multimedia Encyclopedia
• New Deal

INTERNET RESOURCES
• See *McDougal Littell Learning On-Line* for links to information about WPA Projects and Dorothea Lange.

Humanities Transparencies
• H22, A relief center in Kentucky

AMERICAN STORIES VIDEO SERIES
• "A Song for His People"

Electronic Library of Primary Sources
• Bethune Cookman College
• Eleanor Roosevelt

INTERNET RESOURCES
• See *McDougal Littell Learning On-Line* for links to information about the CIO.

INTERNET RESOURCES
• See *McDougal Littell Learning On-Line* for links to information about Richard Wright, Marx Brothers, and John Steinbeck.

Critical Thinking Transparencies
• CT23, The New Deal
• CT57, U.S. Economic Indicators: 1929–1939

Grolier Multimedia Encyclopedia
• Tennessee Valley Authority

INTERNET RESOURCES
• See Interact with History pp. 690 and 695 for activities that include the Internet as an enrichment option.

American Portfolio: A Videodisc for U.S. History, user's guide, pp. 203, 206–207

INTERNET RESOURCES
Learning On-Line: Social Studies
http://www.mcdougallittell.com

Block Scheduling (90 MINUTES)

Day 1
Section 1, pp. 664–670
Section 2, pp. 671–676
Section Assessments, pp. 670, 676

Day 2
Section 3, pp. 677–683
Section 4, pp. 683–688
 AMERICAN STORIES VIDEO SERIES
"A Song for His People"

Day 3
Section 5, pp. 689–693
Geography Spotlight: The Tennessee Valley Authority, pp. 694–695
Chapter Assessment, pp. 696–697

YEARLY PACING *Chapter 23 Total:* 3 days *Yearly Total:* 85 days

See *Block Scheduling Survival Kit* for special activities and pacing strategies.

Customizing for Special Populations

Students Acquiring English

Access for Students Acquiring English
• Guided Reading for Sections 1–5 (Spanish), pp. 223–227
• Chapter Summary (Spanish), pp. 221–222
• Skillbuilder Practice: Analyzing Issues, p. 228
• Geography Application: Decade of the Democrats, pp. 229–230
• Outline Map: Tennessee Valley Authority, p. 231

AMERICAN STORIES VIDEO SERIES
• "A Song for His People" (Spanish Track)

INTERNET RESOURCES
• See *McDougal Littell Learning On-Line* The Diverse Classroom.

Less Proficient Readers

In-Depth Resources: Unit 6
• Guided Reading for Sections 1–5, pp. 53–57
• Skillbuilder: Analyzing Issues, p. 58
• Geography Application: Decade of the Democrats, p. 59
• Outline Map: Anatomy of the Tennessee Valley Authority, p. 61

Telescoping the Times
• Chapter Summary, pp. 45–46

See additional strategies at point of use in the Teacher's Edition.

Gifted and Talented Students

In-Depth Resources: Unit 6
• Primary Sources: *from Father Coughlin's Anti-New Deal Speech,* p. 63; The Memorial Day Massacre, p. 64; WPA Posters, p. 65; *from Let Us Now Praise Famous Men* by James Agae and Walker Evans, p. 66
• American Lives: Huey Long, p. 70; Mary McLeod Bethune, p. 71

See additional strategies at point of use in the Teacher's Edition.

Connections to Literature READINGS FOR STUDENTS

In-Depth Resources: Unit 6
• from *Waiting for Lefty* by Clifford Odets, p. 67

Enrichment Reading
• Warren, Robert Penn
All the King's Men
New York: Harcourt Brace, 1985
Winner of the Pulitzer Prize in 1947, this novel tells the story of Willie Stark, a southern politician whose character is based on Governor Huey Long of Louisiana. Through appeals to the common man and by playing dirty politics, Stark is a successful leader but at a price that eventually costs him his life. The mixture of good and evil in the novel adds up to a lyrical and painful story of idealism, politics, and personal history.

Farrell, James T.
Studs Lonigan
New York: Vanguard Press, 1978
This novel about ordinary people expressing their opinions and struggling with issues of family and work is told with extraordinary honesty. The sad, funny, and ultimately tragic story brings the 1920s and 1930s vividly to life.

McDougal Littell *The Language of Literature*
American Literature
• Tillie Olsen,
"*I Stand Here Ironing,*" p. 642
• Julia Alvarez,
"*Ironing Their Clothes,*" p. 650

Teacher's Edition 662B

The New Deal

▶ **Starting with the Student**
Ask students what they know about the New Deal. Ask them what policies were created under the New Deal and who was affected. Then discuss the opening quotation, and pose the following questions:

- What did Roosevelt mean? What can happen when people are afraid?
- What else might people have feared in the 1930s?
- What effect do students think Roosevelt hoped this statement would have on the American people?

PREVIEWING THE CHAPTER
- Note the video in Section 3.
- Ask students if they recognize any of the names on the time line.
- Point out to students that the *Vanity Fair* cover shows President Roosevelt riding the bucking bronco of the United States during the Great Depression.

MORE ABOUT . . .
Franklin Delano Roosevelt

After FDR developed polio in 1921, many people thought his political career was over. But they underestimated Roosevelt's spirit. When a friend visited him in the hospital, FDR struck the man hard in the chest and said, "You thought you were coming to see an invalid, but I can knock you out in any bout."

CHAPTER
23 The New Deal

SECTION 1
A New Deal Fights the Depression

President Roosevelt takes many actions to combat the Depression.

SECTION 2
The Second New Deal Takes Hold

The Second New Deal institutes new programs to extend federal aid and stimulate the nation's economy.

SECTION 3
The New Deal Affects Many Groups

New Deal policies and actions affect Americans from all walks of life. The Democratic Party forms a new political coalition.

 VIDEO *A SONG FOR HIS PEOPLE*

SECTION 4
Society and Culture

Motion pictures, radio, art, and literature all blossom during the Depression and the New Deal.

SECTION 5
The Impact of the New Deal

The New Deal affects American society not only in the 1930s but also in the decades that follow.

"The only thing we have to fear is fear itself."

Franklin Delano Roosevelt

- Huey Long is assassinated.
- Supreme Court declares NIRA unconstitutional.
- CIO is organized.
- Congress passes the Social Security Act.
- Women wait in line for New Deal relief.

✪ **Franklin Delano Roosevelt is inaugurated.**
- Congress creates the TVA.

- Congress creates the SEC.

| THE UNITED STATES | **1933** | 1934 | 1935 |
| THE WORLD | | 1934 | 1935 |

- Hitler and the Nazi Party take power in Germany.
- Japan withdraws from League of Nations.

- Batista assumes power in Cuba.
- Chinese Communists engage in Long March.
- Lázaro Cárdenas becomes president of Mexico.

- Italy invades Ethiopia.
- British Parliament passes Government of India Act.

THEMES IN CHAPTER 23

Economic Opportunity	*Cultural Diversity*	*Science and Technology*
The Roosevelt administration dealt with some major economic issues through legislation and policymaking during the New Deal. For example, the administration initiated policies that supported and regulated agriculture and industry. It also passed legislation that greatly improved labor conditions and gave more power to unions. Some of the programs begun under the New Deal—for example, the FDIC, the SEC, and Social Security—continue to help soften the economic impact of recessions. See Teacher's Edition notes, pp. 667, 674, 692.	Although discrimination remained widespread in the 1930s, the New Deal created some new opportunities for women and minority groups. The Indian Reorganization Act of 1934, for example, was created to help Native Americans. See Teacher's Edition note, p. 680.	Motion pictures and radio programs helped people escape the hard realities of life in the 1930s. Today, televisions and computers serve a similar function when they are used for entertainment purposes. See Teacher's Edition note, p. 684.

VANITY FAIR

LIVING HISTORY

WRITING A NEW DEAL DIARY

Imagine that you are a worker who has been laid off from his or her job during the Great Depression. You eventually get work through one of the New Deal agencies, such as the CWA, CCC, or WPA. Use your textbook and other sources to gather information about the agency. Then write diary entries about your experiences over two or three weeks or more. Be sure to include information about the following:

- Any training you receive
- The kind of work you do
- The tools you use
- The pay you receive

📁 **PORTFOLIO PROJECT** Save your diary entries in a folder for your American history portfolio.

WRITING A NEW DEAL DIARY

Discuss with students the following process of gathering material and writing the diary entries:

- Choose the agency they want to work for.
- Do some research to find out more about the agency. Pay particular attention to first-person statements from those who actually worked under the agency.
- Specifically identify the work they will be doing. Think about the training and tools they will need and the pay they'll receive.
- Write their diary entries. Describe what they hope to gain from the job. They should try to write from the point of view of someone who lived through the Depression.

Project Planning Guide

Step 1	Select an agency.
Step 2	Conduct research to learn about the agency.
Step 3	Decide what work they will do and think through the details.
Step 4	Write the diary entries and place them in their folder.

IN-DEPTH RESOURCES: UNIT 6
See worksheet and standards for evaluation, pp. 72–73.

Timeline:

- ✪ President Roosevelt is reelected.
- ● Labor unions begin using sit-down strikes.
- *Snow White and the Seven Dwarfs* is released.
- ● Fair Labor Standards Act passes.
- Marian Anderson sings at the Lincoln Memorial.
- John Steinbeck publishes *The Grapes of Wrath*.
- ✪ President Roosevelt is elected a third time.

1936   1937   1938   1939   **1940**
   1937   1938   1939

- ● Civil War begins in Spain.
- ● Soviet leader Joseph Stalin purges Communist Party and government leaders.
- ● Egypt becomes independent.
- ● Japan invades China.
- ● An early international radio broadcast reports the *Hindenburg* disaster.
- ● Mexico nationalizes oil wells.
- ● Germany invades Poland.

The New Deal **663**

RECOMMENDED RESOURCES

Books for the Teacher

Goodwin, Doris Kearns. *No Ordinary Time.* New York: Simon, 1995. Lives of Franklin and Eleanor Roosevelt.

Williams, T. Harry. *Huey Long.* New York: Knopf, 1969. Biography of Long.

Books for the Student

Aptheker, Herbert, ed. *A Documentary History of the Negro People in the United States.* New York: Carol, 1992. From New Deal to World War II.

Banks, Ann, ed. *First-Person America.* New York: Knopf, 1980. Lives of 80 Americans, collected by Federal Writers, Project.

Videos

Eleanor Roosevelt: A Restless Spirit. Dir. Harry Rasky. A&E Home Video, 1994.

FDR. PBS Home Video, 1994. Four-hour documentary.

The New Deal. Republic Pictures Home Video, 1986. The TVA, the WPA, and other New Deal projects of the 1930s.

Software

FDR. CD-ROM. Corbis Publishing, 1996.

U.S. History: The Great Depression. CD-ROM. Clearvue. Educational Software Institute, 800-955-5570.

OBJECTIVES

① To summarize some of the steps Roosevelt took early in his presidency to reform banking and finance.

② To describe New Deal programs that provided relief to farmers and other workers.

③ To identify critics of Roosevelt and his New Deal policies.

SKILLBUILDERS

• Interpreting political cartoons, pp. 666, 669

CRITICAL THINKING

• Summarizing, pp. 665, 670
• Evaluating decisions, p. 666
• Analyzing, pp. 667, 670
• Analyzing issues, pp. 668, 669
• Comparing, pp. 669, 670
• Interpreting, p. 670

FOCUS & MOTIVATE

▶ *Starting with the Student*
• Ask students if they think the government should have no control, some control, or total control of education, including their school.
• Ask them if they think the president should be given more power in times of crisis. Then ask them what could happen if the president is given too much power.

MORE ABOUT . . .
Hank Oettinger

After the Great Depression, Oettinger continued to work as a printer. He devoted much of his spare time to writing letters to the editors, criticizing local politicians, and arguing with his friends. This is his own account of a typical day: "I go to work late in the afternoon, get through at midnight. See my friends at the taverns. Agitate. Get my sleep. I wake up, and it's nice and warm and it's light. I go down and maybe have a couple of arguments before I go to work."

❶ A New Deal Fights The Depression

TERMS & NAMES
• Franklin Delano Roosevelt
• New Deal
• Glass-Steagall Banking Act of 1933
• Federal Securities Act
• Agricultural Adjustment Act
• Civilian Conservation Corps
• National Industrial Recovery Act
• Huey Long

LEARN ABOUT the early actions taken by the Roosevelt administration
TO UNDERSTAND how the New Deal tried to combat the Depression.

ONE AMERICAN'S STORY

Hank Oettinger was working as a printing press operator in a small town in northern Wisconsin when the Depression began. In 1931, he lost his job and was unemployed for the next two years. In 1932, however, Americans elected a new president, Franklin Delano Roosevelt. Once in office, Roosevelt created work programs to provide jobs and generate income for the unemployed. Through one of these programs, the Civil Works Administration (CWA), Oettinger went back to work in 1933. As he later recalled, the CWA was cause for great celebration in his town.

A PERSONAL VOICE
I can remember the first week of the CWA checks. It was on a Friday. That night everybody had gotten his check. The first check a lot of them had in three years. . . . I never saw such a change of attitude. Instead of walking around feeling dreary and looking sorrowful, everybody was joyous. Like a feast day. They were toasting each other. They had money in their pockets for the first time.

HANK OETTINGER, quoted in *Hard Times*

Programs like the CWA raised the hopes of the American people and sparked great enthusiasm for the new president. As Oettinger put it, "If Roosevelt had run for president the next day, he'd have gone in by a hundred percent." To many Americans, it appeared as if the country had turned a corner and was beginning to emerge from the nightmare of the Great Depression.

Civil Works Administration workers prepare to participate in a parade for workers in San Francisco in 1934.

New Deal Actions

In 1932, the presidential election showed that Americans were clearly ready for a change. Because of the Depression, people suffered from lack of work, lack of food, and lack of hope.

ELECTING FRANKLIN DELANO ROOSEVELT Although the Republicans renominated President Hoover as their candidate, they recognized that he had little chance of winning. Too many Americans blamed Hoover for doing too little about the Depression and wanted a new president in the White House.

The Democrats pinned their hopes on **Franklin Delano Roosevelt,** known popularly as FDR, the two-term governor of New York and a distant cousin of Theodore Roosevelt. As governor, Franklin Roosevelt had proved an effective, reform-minded leader. He pushed a series of new measures through the New York legislature to combat the problems of unemployment and poverty. Unlike Hoover, Roosevelt projected an air of friendliness and confidence that

---

SECTION 1 RESOURCES

PRINT RESOURCES

IN-DEPTH RESOURCES: UNIT 6
Guided Reading, p. 53
Skillbuilder Practice: Analyzing Issues, p. 58
Primary Source: *from* Father Coughlin's Anti-New Deal Speech, p. 634
American Lives: Huey Long, p. 70

ACCESS FOR STUDENTS ACQUIRING ENGLISH
Guided Reading (Spanish), p. 223
Skillbuilder Practice: Analyzing Issues (Spanish), p. 228

FORMAL ASSESSMENT
Section Quiz, p. 280

ALTERNATIVE ASSESSMENT BOOK
See forms for supporting and scoring alternative activities.

TECHNOLOGY RESOURCES

HUMANITIES TRANSPARENCIES
H40, Nine Old Men

GEOGRAPHY TRANSPARENCIES
G23, P. W. A. in Action

CD-ROM
Electronic Library of Primary Sources

VIDEO
American Portfolio: A Videodisc for U.S. History
user's guide, pp. 203, 206, 208, 212–213

INTERNET McDougal Littell Learning On-Line
http://www.mcdougallittell.com

attracted voters. Though practical at heart, he had a creative, adventurous side that allowed him to take risks that others might avoid. As he once said, "It is common sense to take a method and try it. If it fails, admit it frankly and try another. But above all, try something." This "can-do" attitude appealed to a public that regarded Hoover, rightly or wrongly, as a "do-nothing" president.

Roosevelt won an overwhelming victory, capturing 23 million votes to Hoover's 16 million and carrying the South, West, and all but six states in the Northeast. In the Senate, Democrats claimed a nearly two-thirds majority. In the House, they won almost three-fourths of the seats, their greatest victory since before the Civil War.

WAITING FOR ROOSEVELT TO TAKE OVER Four months would elapse between Roosevelt's victory in November and his inauguration as president in March 1933. The Twentieth Amendment, which moved presidential inaugurations to January, was not ratified until February 1933 and did not apply to the 1932 election. Americans waited anxiously to find out what plans their new president had for solving the nation's problems. Meanwhile, the economy continued to worsen. Industrial production fell; more businesses and banks shut down; and more people lost their jobs, their homes, and their farms.

FDR was not idle during this waiting period, however. He worked with his team of carefully picked advisers—a select group of professors, lawyers, and journalists known as the brain trust. Roosevelt began to formulate a set of policies for his new administration. This program, designed to alleviate the problems of the Great Depression, became known as the **New Deal,** a phrase from a campaign speech in which Roosevelt had promised "a new deal for the American people." New Deal policies focused on three general goals: relief for the needy, economic recovery, and financial reform.

KEY PLAYERS

FRANKLIN D. ROOSEVELT
1882–1945

Born into an old, wealthy New York family, Franklin Delano Roosevelt entered politics as a state senator in 1910 and later became assistant secretary of the navy. In 1921, he was stricken with polio and paralyzed from the waist down. He struggled to regain the use of his legs and he eventually learned to stand with the help of heavy leg braces. Roosevelt became governor of New York in 1928, and because he "would not allow bodily disability to defeat his will," he went on to the White House in 1933. Always interested in people, Roosevelt gained greater compassion for others as a result of his own physical handicap.

ELEANOR ROOSEVELT
1884–1962

A niece of Theodore Roosevelt and a distant cousin of her husband, Franklin, Eleanor Roosevelt lost her parents at an early age. She was raised by a strict grandmother.

As First Lady, she often urged the president to take stands on controversial issues. She became known for speaking out against economic and social injustice. In presenting a booklet on human rights to the United Nations in 1958 she said, "Where, after all, do human rights begin? . . . [In] the world of the individual person: the neighborhood . . . the school . . . the factory, farm or office where he works."

On taking office, the Roosevelt administration launched into a period of intense activity, known as the Hundred Days, lasting from March 9 to June 16, 1933. During this period, Congress passed more than 15 major pieces of New Deal legislation. These laws, and others that followed, significantly expanded the federal government's role in the nation's economy.

REFORMING FINANCE AND BUSINESS Roosevelt's first step as president was to carry out reforms in banking and finance. By 1933, widespread bank failures had caused most Americans to lose faith in the banking system. On March 5, one day after taking office, Roosevelt declared a bank holiday and closed all banks to prevent further withdrawals. Then he persuaded Congress to pass the Emergency

HISTORY FROM VISUALS

Political Cartoon

Reading the Cartoon Ask students who the "patient" is. *Uncle Sam.* Ask them what he represents? *Possible Response: He represents the nation's sick economy.*

Extension Have students describe how Roosevelt and Congress are depicted in the cartoon. *Possible Response: Roosevelt is depicted as a trusted doctor, and Congress as a docile nurse.* Then ask them what the depictions suggest about the relationship between the president and Congress. *Possible Response: Congress was willing to pass anything Roosevelt proposed.*

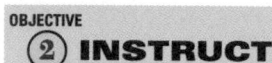

OBJECTIVE
② INSTRUCT

Helping the American People

▶ *Discussing Key Ideas*

• The Roosevelt administration establishes programs to provide relief to farmers, create jobs for other workers, and foster regional development.

• The National Industrial Recovery Act seeks to establish codes of fair practice for individual industries and promote industrial growth.

• Other New Deal programs focus on helping homeowners.

Banking Relief Act, which authorized the Treasury Department to inspect the country's banks. Those that were sound could reopen at once; those that were insolvent—or unable to pay debts—would remain closed. Those that needed help could receive loans. This measure revived public confidence in banks, since customers now had greater faith that the open banks were in good financial shape.

AN IMPORTANT FIRESIDE CHAT On March 12, the day before the first banks were to reopen, President Roosevelt boosted confidence further through the first of his many fireside chats. These were radio talks that Roosevelt gave occasionally about issues of public concern, such as explaining in clear, simple language his New Deal measures. Informal and relaxed, these talks made Americans feel as if the president were talking directly to them. In his first chat, President Roosevelt explained why the nation's welfare depended on public support of the government and the banking system. "We have provided the machinery to restore our financial system," he said. "It is up to you to support and make it work." This is how he explained the banking system.

A PERSONAL VOICE
When you deposit money in a bank, the bank does not put the money into a safe deposit vault. It invests your money. . . . A comparatively small part of the money you put into the bank is kept in currency—an amount which in normal times is wholly sufficient to cover the cash needs of the ordinary citizen.

FRANKLIN DELANO ROOSEVELT

The president then explained that when too many people demanded their deposits in cash, banks would fail. This did not mean that the banks were weak, because even strong banks could not meet such heavy demands.

Over the next few weeks, many Americans returned their savings to banks. Congress took another step to reorganize the banking system by passing the **Glass-Steagall Banking Act of 1933.** Among other provisions, this law established the Federal Deposit Insurance Corporation (FDIC), which provided federal insurance for individual bank accounts of less than $5,000. The Glass-Steagall Banking Act reassured millions of bank customers that their money was safe.

SKILLBUILDER
INTERPRETING POLITICAL CARTOONS
What do you think the cartoonist means by Roosevelt's remark concerning New Deal remedies?

Skillbuilder Answer If one proposal or remedy didn't work, he would try another.

Congress and the president also took steps to regulate the stock market, which had suffered a tremendous loss of credibility in the Crash of 1929. The **Federal Securities Act,** passed in May 1933, required corporations to provide complete information on all stock offerings and made them liable for any misrepresentations. The following year, in June 1934, Congress created the Securities and Exchange Commission (SEC) to regulate the stock market. One of the goals of this commission was to prevent people with inside information about companies from "rigging" the stock market, causing prices to go up or down for their own profit regardless of the real value of the stock.

In addition, Roosevelt persuaded Congress to approve a bill allowing the manufacture and sale of some alcoholic beverages. This bill included an alcohol tax designed to raise government revenues. By the end of 1933, the passage of the Twenty-first Amendment repealed prohibition altogether.

THINK THROUGH HISTORY
B. *Evaluating Decisions* Why did bank customers return their savings to banks?

B. Answer President Roosevelt explained the banks weren't weak, and Congress established the Federal Deposit Insurance Corporation.

Helping the American People

While working on banking and financial matters, the Roosevelt administration implemented programs to provide relief to farmers. It also aided other workers and provided for stimulating economic recovery.

666 CHAPTER 23

TEACHING OPTION

Cooperative Activity: Delivering a Fireside Chat

Task: Groups of four to five students will write and record a Roosevelt-style radio talk that explains a New Deal program.

Purpose: To explore a New Deal program.

Activity: Groups of students should get together to choose the New Deal program they want to discuss in a fireside chat. Each student in a group should research and write about one aspect of the program—for example,

its purpose, the people who benefited from it, the drawbacks of the program, and its results. Students should then compile their reports and tape-record the talk. Play the audiotapes in class and discuss them.

📁 **Building a Portfolio:** Students may wish to add a transcript of their fireside chat to their portfolio.

ALTERNATIVE ASSESSMENT BOOK
Standards for Evaluating a Cooperative Activity

Standards for Evaluation
Fireside chats should . . .

• cover a New Deal program in depth

• be given in clear, simple language

• be delivered in a relaxed, informal manner that inspires confidence

Civilian Conservation Corps laborers go to work in a wilderness area in 1940.

Civilian Conservation Corps

- The CCC provided unemployed men between 18 and 25 with conservation work and job training. Much of the work was done in U.S. national parks.

- The men lived in work camps under a militarylike regime. Although some of the camps were integrated, the majority were segregated.

- The CCC provided almost 3 million men with work and wages between 1933 and 1942.

- Many New Deal agencies such as the CCC did little to give opportunities to African Americans. By 1938, however, the CCC had an 11 percent African-American enrollment.

ASSISTING FARMERS The **Agricultural Adjustment Act** (AAA) sought to raise crop prices by lowering production, which the government achieved by paying farmers to leave a certain amount of every acre of land unseeded. The theory was that reduced supply would boost prices. In some cases crops were too far advanced for the acreage reduction to take effect. As a result, the government paid cotton growers $200 million to plow under 10 million acres of their crop. It also paid hog farmers to slaughter 6 million pigs. This policy upset many Americans, who protested the destruction of food when many people were going hungry. It did, however, help raise farm prices and put more money in farmers' pockets.

PROVIDING WORK PROJECTS The administration also established programs to provide relief through work projects and cash payments. One important program, the **Civilian Conservation Corps** (CCC), put young men, aged 18 to 25, to work building roads, developing parks, planting trees, and helping in soil-erosion and flood-control projects. The CCC paid a small wage, $30 a month, of which $25 was automatically sent home to the worker's family. It also supplied free food and uniforms. By the time the program ended in 1942, almost 3 million young men had passed through the CCC. Many of the camps were located on the Great Plains, where, within a period of eight years, the men of the CCC planted more than 200 million trees. This tremendous reforestation program was aimed at preventing another Dust Bowl.

Another program, the Federal Emergency Relief Administration (FERA), was funded with $500 million to provide direct relief for the needy. Half of the money was given to the states as direct grants-in-aid to help furnish food and clothing to the unemployed, the aged, and the ill. An additional $250 million was distributed on the basis of one federal dollar for every three state dollars contributed. Harry Hopkins, who headed this program, believed that money helped people buy food, but work enabled them to gain confidence and self-respect.

The Public Works Administration (PWA), created in June 1933, provided money to states to create jobs. These were chiefly construction projects, such as schools and community buildings. When these programs failed to make a sufficient dent in unemployment, President Roosevelt established the Civil Works Administration (CWA) in November 1933. It provided 4 million immediate jobs during the winter of 1933–34. Some critics of the CWA claimed that

THINK THROUGH HISTORY
C. Analyzing In what two ways did the New Deal attempt to assist the unemployed?

C. Answer by providing jobs and direct relief.

"Eighteen million Americans are so poor of this world's goods that they are on relief."

HARRY L. HOPKINS

The New Deal **667**

Throughout his presidency, Roosevelt was rarely photographed in his wheelchair. Although people knew that he had been crippled by polio, Roosevelt wished to appear as a strong, healthy man. In public, Roosevelt walked and stood, supported on either side by his aides. Every movement cost him great pain and fatigue, but he always grinned and waved energetically to the crowds. In March 1945, just about a month before his death, Roosevelt made a rare public reference to his physical disability as he spoke before Congress: "I hope that you will pardon me for this unusual posture of sitting down . . . , but . . . it makes it a lot easier for me not to have to carry about 10 pounds of steel around at the bottom of my legs."

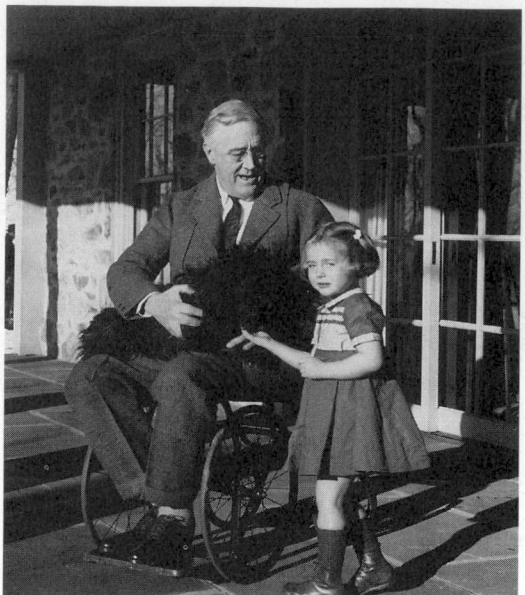

Franklin D. Roosevelt was fond of spending time at Hyde Park, New York, his birthplace on the bank of the Hudson River. He is holding his dog Fala and talking to a young family friend.

OBJECTIVE
③ **INSTRUCT**

The New Deal Comes Under Attack

▶ *Discussing Key Ideas*
• Both conservative and liberal critics oppose New Deal policies.
• After the Supreme Court strikes down two of Roosevelt's new programs, the president proposes a bill that would allow him to appoint six new justices to the Court.
• Charles Coughlin, Francis Townsend, and Huey Long are among Roosevelt's toughest critics.

the programs were "make-work" projects and a waste of money. However, the CWA built 40,000 schools and paid the salaries of more than 50,000 schoolteachers in America's rural areas. It also built more than half a million miles of roads.

Another major initiative of the Roosevelt administration was the **National Industrial Recovery Act** (NIRA), passed in June 1933. This act established codes of fair practice for individual industries and for promoting industrial growth. It created the National Recovery Administration (NRA), which set prices on many products to ensure fair competition. It also established standards concerning work hours and a ban on child labor. The aim of the NRA was to promote recovery by overcoming the cycle of wage cuts, falling prices, and layoffs.

Competing businesses met with representatives of workers and consumers to draft the codes of fair competition. These codes both limited production and established prices. Because businesses were given new concessions, workers made demands. Congress met their demands by passing a section of the NIRA guaranteeing workers' right to unionize and to bargain collectively.

Many businesses and politicians were critical of the NRA. Charges arose that the codes served large business interests. There were also charges of increasing code violations. Economist Gardiner C. Means, however, stated the goal of industrial planning.

> **A PERSONAL VOICE**
> The National Recovery Administration [was] created in response to an overwhelming demand from many quarters that certain elements in the making of industrial policy . . . should no longer be left to the market place and the price mechanism but should be placed in the hands of administrative bodies. . . .
> **GARDINER C. MEANS,** *The Making of Industrial Policy*

Finally, the Roosevelt administration undertook an especially ambitious program of regional development. The Tennessee Valley Authority (TVA), established May 18, 1933, focused on the badly depressed Tennessee River Valley. The TVA renovated five existing dams and constructed 20 new ones in the Tennessee Valley. The project created thousands of jobs and provided flood control, hydroelectric power, and other benefits to an impoverished region.

HELPING PEOPLE WITH HOUSING A number of New Deal programs concerned housing and home mortgage problems. The Home Owners Loan Corporation (HOLC) provided government loans to homeowners who faced foreclosure because they couldn't meet their loan payments. In addition, the National Housing Act created the Federal Housing Administration (FHA). This agency continues to furnish loans for home mortgages and repairs today.

The New Deal Comes Under Attack

At the end of the first Hundred Days, President Roosevelt could look back on some major accomplishments. Together with Congress, his administration had moved decisively to carry out a series of programs designed to provide benefits for millions of Americans. In general, public confidence in the nation's future had rebounded.

THINK THROUGH HISTORY
D. *Analyzing Issues* How did the New Deal support labor organizations?
D. Answer It guaranteed workers' right to unionize and to bargain collectively.

Making Connections Across Time

The TVA Today Tell students that the TVA was a highly controversial program for many years. Private power companies opposed what they viewed as the government's interference in private business. State and local agencies in Tennessee feared that the federal government would take over their functions in the region. In spite of its rocky beginnings, the TVA has greatly benefited the Tennessee Valley. Over the years, the TVA has built dams, created electric power, deepened rivers for shipping, planted new forests and protected existing ones, and developed highly effective fertilizers. The TVA has helped individuals by providing low-interest loans to homeowners and businesses. It has also provided inexpensive power to people in the region—one of the program's original goals. A consumer of TVA power today still pays about one-third less per kilowatt-hour than the average American consumer.

Nevertheless, opposition to the New Deal grew among some parts of the population. Liberal critics argued that the New Deal did not go far enough to help the poor and to reform the nation's economic system. Conservative critics argued just the opposite: that Roosevelt spent too much on direct relief and used New Deal policies to control business and socialize the economy. Conservatives were particularly angered by laws such as the Agricultural Adjustment Act and the National Industrial Recovery Act, which they believed gave the federal government too much control over agriculture and industry. Many New Deal critics thought the Roosevelt administration was going too far in its attempt to regulate the production and supply of goods and to control prices. They believed the New Deal interfered with the workings of a free market economy.

THE SUPREME COURT REACTS By the mid-1930s, conservative opposition to the New Deal had received a boost from two Supreme Court decisions. In 1935, the Court struck down the NIRA as unconstitutional, declaring that the law gave legislative powers to the executive branch. It also argued that the enforcement of industry codes within states went beyond the federal government's constitutional powers, which are limited to the regulation of interstate commerce. The next year, the Supreme Court struck down the AAA on the grounds that agriculture is a local matter and should be regulated by the states rather than the federal government.

President Roosevelt was dismayed by these rulings. Fearing that further Court decisions might dismantle the New Deal, in February 1937 he proposed that Congress enact a court-reform bill that would reorganize the federal judiciary and allow him to appoint six new Supreme Court justices. Although Roosevelt argued that the bill would make the judiciary more effective, it was clearly designed to create a Supreme Court more sympathetic to New Deal programs. Quickly labeled the "court-packing bill," Roosevelt's proposal aroused a storm of protest in Congress and the press. Many people believed that the president violated principles of judicial independence and the separation of powers. The bill damaged the president's public image. Then events that the president could not have foreseen led to changes in the Court. Rulings of the Court began to shift in favor of the New Deal, and President Roosevelt managed to appoint new justices who supported the New Deal. Because of resignations, the president was able to appoint seven new justices to the existing Court in the next four years.

THREE FIERY CRITICS In 1934, some of the strongest conservative opponents of the New Deal banded together to form an organization called the American Liberty League. This group was made up largely of wealthy business leaders. It also included important political leaders: Al Smith and John W. Davis, former Democratic presidential candidates. The American Liberty League opposed New Deal measures that it believed violated respect for the rights of individuals and property. The group accused President Roosevelt of trying to establish a dictatorship. Perhaps the toughest critics the president faced were three men who expressed views that appealed to poor Americans: Charles Coughlin, Francis Townsend, and Huey Long.

THAT COMPASS DOESN'T POINT THE WAY I WANT TO GO. CHANGE IT. NOW!

SKILLBUILDER
INTERPRETING POLITICAL CARTOONS
What "compass" did Roosevelt want to change, and why?
Skillbuilder Answer FDR wanted to change the Supreme Court compass because the Court had ruled that some of his actions were unconstitutional.

THINK THROUGH HISTORY
E. Comparing
How did liberal and conservative critics differ in their opposition to the New Deal?

E. Answer
Liberal critics thought the New Deal did not go far enough in helping the poor and in reforming the nation's economic system; conservative critics believed the New Deal spent too much money on direct relief and was trying to control business and socialize the economy.

F. Answer
because Roosevelt, as the head of the executive branch, was trying to exercise too much influence over the judiciary, another branch of government; the branches are supposed to remain independent of each other.

THINK THROUGH HISTORY
F. Analyzing Issues *Why did people regard FDR's court-packing scheme as a threat to the separation of powers?*

HISTORY FROM VISUALS
Political Cartoon

Reading the Cartoon Ask students what uniform Roosevelt is wearing in the cartoon. *A ship captain's uniform.* Ask them what the ship represents. *The country; the government.* Then ask them what figure represents Congress. *A sailor.* Have them tell what the cartoon is referring to. *FDR's efforts to pack the Supreme Court.*

Extension Have students compare the depiction of Roosevelt and Congress in this cartoon with the depiction in the cartoon on page 666. Ask them how the apparent relationship between FDR and Congress differs in the two cartoons. *Possible Response: In the other cartoon, Congress seems to be deferring to the president. In this cartoon, Congress seems shocked by a power-mad FDR.* Then ask students what they think might account for the change. *Possible Response: FDR's attempts to pack the Supreme Court suggested to many people that the president had too much power.*

HUMANITIES TRANSPARENCIES
H40, Nine Old Men

The New Deal **669**

TEACHING OPTION

Skillbuilder Mini-Lesson: Analyzing Issues

Explaining the Skill An issue is a matter of debate or of public concern. Typically, issues in history are economic, social, political, or moral in nature. Examples of such issues are the desirability of balancing the national budget, the effectiveness of various welfare programs, the desirability of campaign finance reforms, and the extent to which a nation has responsibilities to other nations. Analyzing such an issue involves defining the central problem and examining differing points of view.

Applying the Skill: Think Through History Question To answer the question about the Supreme Court on this page, students will need to identify the following aspects of the issue:

1. The central problem (President Roosevelt's attempt to change and control the makeup of the Supreme Court)

2. The different points of view on the issue (Roosevelt wanted a Court that would be sympathetic to his New Deal programs. His opponents feared that presidential control over the Court would influence justices to side with the president rather than the Constitution.)

IN-DEPTH RESOURCES: UNIT 6
Skillbuilder Practice: Analyzing Issues, p. 58

Teacher's Edition **669**

Critical Thinking:
Analyzing Ask students why
they think Townsend stipulated that recipients of the
pension spend all the
money within 30 days.
*Possible Response: He
wanted the money to be
recirculated in the economy.*

IN-DEPTH RESOURCES: UNIT 6
Primary Source: *from* Father
 Coughlin's Anti-New Deal Speech,
 p. 63
American Lives: Huey Long, p. 70

ASSESS & RETEACH

Section 1 Assessment

Have pairs of students work
together to answer the
questions.

Self-Assessment

Students can document
what they have learned in
Section 1 by creating a cluster diagram in which they
list each New Deal program
and its goals.

Section Quiz

FORMAL ASSESSMENT
Section Quiz, p. 280

Reteach

Use the Section Quiz to help
students review the section's
main ideas.

CLOSE

When Franklin Roosevelt
took office in 1933, he
immediately launched the
first of his New Deal programs, which focused on
relief for the needy, economic recovery, and financial reform. Many Americans
approved of the New Deal
measures, but others criticized them—some for doing
too little, some for doing too
much. Roosevelt responded
to those who felt he could
do more by extending his
programs in the Second
New Deal—the next phase
of his program.

670 Chapter 23

ANOTHER PERSPECTIVE

TOWNSEND'S PENSION PLAN

Francis Townsend devised his
pension plan after getting laid off at
age 67 with only $100 in savings.
His plan called for all Americans
over age 60 to receive a monthly
pension of $200, on the condition
that they spend the money within
30 days. Townsend claimed that his
plan would stop poverty among the
elderly and end the Depression by
pumping money into the economy.
Although his plan was financially
unrealistic, it did draw attention to
the needs of the elderly.

**During a speech in Des
Moines, Iowa, in 1935
Senator Huey Long
emphasized a point.**

One of President Roosevelt's most vocal critics was Father Charles
Coughlin, a Roman Catholic priest from a suburb of Detroit. Every
Sunday, Father Coughlin broadcast radio sermons that combined economic, political, and religious ideas. Initially a supporter of the New
Deal, Coughlin soon turned against Roosevelt. He favored a guaranteed annual income and the nationalization of banks. At the height of
his popularity, Father Coughlin claimed a radio audience of some 40
million people, but his increasingly anti-Semitic (anti-Jewish) views
eventually cost him support.

Another critic of New Deal policies was Dr. Francis Townsend, a
physician and health officer in Long Beach, California. He believed that
Roosevelt wasn't doing enough to help the poor and elderly. So, he
devised a pension plan that would provide monthly benefits to the aged.
The plan was too expensive to work, but it found strong backing among
the elderly, and it undermined their support for President Roosevelt.

Perhaps the most serious challenge to the New Deal came from
Senator **Huey Long** of Louisiana. Long was a former traveling salesman, but he studied law and eventually became a persuasive
spokesman for the poor. He was elected governor of Louisiana in 1928 and later
served in the United States Senate.

Like Coughlin, Long was an early supporter of the New Deal but he soon
turned against Roosevelt. Eager to win the presidency for himself, Long proposed a nationwide social program called Share Our Wealth. Under the banner
"Every Man a King," he promised something for everyone.

A PERSONAL VOICE

We owe debts in America today, public and private, amounting to $252 billion.
That means that every child is born with a $2,000 debt tied around his neck. . . .
We propose that children shall be born in a land of opportunity, guaranteed a
home, food, clothes, and the other things that make for living, including the
right to education.

HUEY LONG from *Record, 74 Congress, Session 1.*

Long's program for sharing the nation's wealth was so popular that by
1935, he boasted having over 27,000 Share-Our-Wealth clubs with around
7.5 million names. In 1935, however, at the height of his popularity, Long
was assassinated by a lone gunman.

As the First New Deal began to wind down, President Roosevelt started
to look ahead. He knew that a lot more needed to be done to help the people
and to solve the nation's economic problems.

G. Answer They
said that the New
Deal didn't go far
enough in helping
the poor and
elderly. It didn't
provide a
guaranteed
annual income or
other benefits.

**THINK THROUGH HISTORY
G. Comparing**
*What did Charles
Coughlin, Francis
Townsend, and
Huey Long dislike
about the New
Deal?*

Section 1 Assessment

1. TERMS & NAMES

Identify:
• Franklin Delano
 Roosevelt
• New Deal
• Glass-Steagall
 Banking Act of 1933
• Federal Securities Act
• Agricultural
 Adjustment Act
• Civilian Conservation
 Corps
• National Industrial
 Recovery Act
• Huey Long

2. SUMMARIZING In a two-
column chart, list problems that
Franklin Roosevelt confronted as
president and how he tried to
solve them.

Problem	Solution

Write a paragraph telling which
problem you think was most
critical, and why.

3. INTERPRETING Of the New
Deal programs discussed in this
section, which do you consider
the most important? Explain your
choice.

THINK ABOUT
• the type of assistance offered
 by each program
• the scope of each program
• the impact of each program

4. ANALYZING Do you think
Roosevelt's most vocal critics had
reasonable objections?

THINK ABOUT
• the American Liberty League's
 beliefs regarding violation of
 rights
• Father Coughlin's calls for
 nationalization
• Huey Long's slogan "Every Man
 a King"

670 Chapter 23

ANSWERS

1. TERMS & NAMES

Franklin Delano Roosevelt, p. 664

New Deal, p. 665

Glass-Steagall Banking Act of
 1933, p. 666

Federal Securities Act, p. 666

Agricultural Adjustment Act,
 p. 667

Civilian Conservation Corps,
 p. 667

National Industrial Recovery
 Act, p. 668

Huey Long, p. 670

2. SUMMARIZING

Possible Responses: **Problem:**
lack of confidence in banks.
Solution: bank holiday, Treasury
inspection of banks, deposit
insurance. **Problem:** little confidence in stock market. **Solution:**
regulation of stock market.
Problem: low farm prices.
Solution: paying farmers not to
raise crops. **Problem:** massive
unemployment. **Solution:** federal
jobs programs. **Problem:** poverty
in Tennessee River Valley.
Solution: build dams. **Problem:**

mortgage foreclosures.
Solution: government loans to
homeowners.

3. INTERPRETING

Possible Responses: The FDIC,
because it boosted confidence
in banks; the CCC, because it
provided badly needed jobs,
raised morale, and helped the
environment; the NRA, because
it helped workers of the 1930s.

4. ANALYZING

Possible Responses: **Yes:**
Programs such as the NIRA and
AAA should have been curtailed
when they infringed on the
rights of free enterprise and
gave excessive control to government. **No:** Few of the critics'
solutions were practical. They
might have made things worse.

② The Second New Deal Takes Hold

TERMS & NAMES
- Eleanor Roosevelt
- Works Progress Administration
- National Youth Administration
- Wagner Act
- Social Security Act

LEARN ABOUT the second phase of New Deal policies
TO UNDERSTAND how the Roosevelt administration tried to extend its relief, recovery, and reform programs.

ONE AMERICAN'S STORY

Dorothea Lange was a photographer whose pictures documented American life during the Great Depression and the era of the New Deal. One famous picture, entitled *Migrant Mother,* shows a woman and her children in a migrant labor camp in California in the winter of 1936. In her biography, Lange recalled the circumstances of that photograph.

> **A PERSONAL VOICE**
> I saw and approached the hungry and desperate mother, as if drawn by a magnet. I do not remember how I explained my presence or my camera to her, but I do remember she asked me no questions. . . . She told me her age, that she was 32. She said that they had been living on frozen vegetables from the surrounding fields, and birds that the children killed. She had just sold the tires from her car to buy food. There she sat in that lean-to tent with her children huddled around her, and seemed to know that my pictures might help her, and so she helped me. There was a sort of equality about it.
>
> **DOROTHEA LANGE,** quoted in *Dorothea Lange: A Photographer's Life*

Much of Lange's work was funded by a federal agency, the Farm Security Administration, which was established to alleviate rural poverty. Lange's photographs helped draw attention to the desperate conditions in rural America and to underscore the need for direct relief.

Dorothea Lange's photograph *Migrant Mother* captures the concern of a weary mother for her children.

The Second Hundred Days

By 1935, the Roosevelt administration was seeking ways to build on the programs established during the first Hundred Days. Although the economy had improved during FDR's first two years in office, the gains were not as great as he had expected. Unemployment remained high despite government work programs, and production still lagged behind the levels of the 1920s.

Nevertheless, the New Deal enjoyed widespread popularity. In the 1934 midterm election, the Democrats increased their majority in both houses of Congress. The Democrats now held 319 seats in the House and 69 in the Senate, while the Republicans held just 103 House seats and 25 Senate seats.

Buoyed by these results, President Roosevelt launched a second burst of activity, often called the Second New Deal or the Second Hundred Days. During this phase, the president called on Congress to provide more extensive relief for both farmers and workers. He encouraged them to help the "forgotten man," FDR's phrase for the poor and dispossessed at the bottom of society. The president was prodded in this direction by his wife, **Eleanor Roosevelt,** a social reformer who combined her deep humanitarian impulses with great political skills.

The New Deal **671**

Section 2 Overview

OBJECTIVES

1. To describe the purpose of the Second New Deal.
2. To summarize some of the programs of the Second New Deal that helped farmers.
3. To describe Second New Deal programs that helped youths, professionals, and others.
4. To summarize labor and economic reforms carried out under the Second New Deal.

CRITICAL THINKING

- Analyzing, pp. 673, 676
- Forming opinions, p. 673
- Drawing conclusions, p. 674
- Summarizing, p. 676
- Evaluating, p. 676

FOCUS & MOTIVATE

▶ *Starting with the Student*
- What do students do to earn money? Do they gain satisfaction from earning their own money?
- What would students do if they couldn't find a job? Would they expect the government to help?

OBJECTIVE
① **INSTRUCT**

The Second Hundred Days

▶ *Discussing Key Ideas*
- Although FDR's programs do not bring economic gains as great as expected, the New Deal enjoys widespread popularity.
- Roosevelt launches the Second New Deal and seeks to help the "forgotten man."
- The 1936 election results in an overwhelming victory for Roosevelt and the Democrats in Congress.

IN-DEPTH RESOURCES: UNIT 6
Guided Reading, p. 54

ACCESS FOR STUDENTS ACQUIRING ENGLISH
Guided Reading (Spanish), p. 224

SECTION 2 RESOURCES

 PRINT RESOURCES

IN-DEPTH RESOURCES: UNIT 6
Guided Reading, p. 54

ACCESS FOR STUDENTS ACQUIRING ENGLISH
Guided Reading (Spanish), p. 224

FORMAL ASSESSMENT
Section Quiz, p. 281

ALTERNATIVE ASSESSMENT BOOK
See forms for supporting and scoring alternative activities.

 TECHNOLOGY RESOURCES

CD-ROM
Grolier Multimedia Encyclopedia

VIDEO
American Portfolio: A Videodisc for U.S. History
user's guide, pp. 207–209

INTERNET McDougal Littell Learning On-Line
http://www.mcdougallittell.com

Helping Farmers

▶ *Discussing Key Ideas*
• Under the Second New Deal, Congress passes legislation to help farmers.
• The Second New Deal seeks to help sharecroppers and migrant workers.

MORE ABOUT . . .
The Grapes of Wrath

John Steinbeck's novel *The Grapes of Wrath,* which focuses on the plight of migrant farm workers in the 1930s, won the 1939 Pulitzer Prize in fiction. The novel was made into a film in 1940. The movie won Academy Awards for its director, John Ford, and for actress Jane Darwell. Henry Fonda was nominated for best actor, and the film itself was nominated for best picture.

Eleanor Roosevelt traveled the country tirelessly, observing social conditions and helping to shape New Deal policies. She candidly and almost continuously reminded the president about the suffering of the nation's people. She also reminded him to appoint women to government positions. As a great advocate of rights for poor people, women, and minorities, she gave a caring, human face to the New Deal administration.

REELECTING FDR The Second New Deal was underway by the time of the 1936 presidential election. The Republicans nominated Alfred Landon, the governor of Kansas. Although Landon criticized FDR, he didn't suggest that the entire New Deal be scrapped. The Democrats, of course, nominated President Roosevelt for a second term. The president assailed his critics. He asked the crowds of people, "Are you better off than you were four years ago?" The crowds roared back, "Yes."

The election resulted in an overwhelming victory for the Democrats. FDR carried every state except two: Maine and Vermont. His popular vote was 27.7 million to Landon's 16.6 million and 523 electoral votes to Landon's 8. The Democrats achieved a congressional majority of 331 to 89 in the House and 76 to 16 in the Senate. This great Democratic victory marked the first time that most African Americans voted Democratic instead of Republican. It was also the first time that labor unions gave united support to a single presidential candidate rather than dividing their votes between two major parties. The 1936 election represented a vote of confidence in FDR and the New Deal.

Helping Farmers

One important goal of the Second New Deal was to help the nation's farmers. In the mid-1930s, rural areas continued to suffer some of the most difficult social and economic conditions in the United States. Nevertheless, recovery in the farm area had begun, partly as a result of the Agricultural Adjustment Act.

When the Supreme Court struck down the AAA early in 1936, Congress passed another law to replace it: the Soil Conservation and Domestic Allotment Act. This act paid farmers for cutting production of soil-depleting crops like cotton and wheat. It also rewarded farmers for practicing good soil conservation methods. Two years later, in 1938, Congress approved a second Agricultural Adjustment Act that brought back many features of the first AAA. The second AAA did not include a processing tax to pay for farm subsidies, a provision of the first AAA that the Supreme Court had declared unconstitutional.

In the mid-1930s, two of every five farms in the United States were mortgaged. As the Depression deepened, thousands of small farmers lost their farms. The land went to the mortgage holders—insurance companies and banks. In time, many small farms became part of large mechanized farms or were destroyed as the land was cleared for new development. The novelist John Steinbeck described the experience of one tenant farmer and his family.

A poster promoting the movie adaptation of John Steinbeck's novel *The Grapes of Wrath.*

A PERSONAL VOICE
Across the dooryard the tractor cut, and the hard, foot-beaten ground was seeded field, and the tractor cut through again; the uncut space was ten feet wide. And back he came. The iron guard bit into the house-corner, crumbled the wall, and wrenched the little house from its foundation so that it fell sideways, crushed like a bug. . . . The tractor cut a straight line on, and the air and ground vibrated with its thunder. The tenant man stared after it, his rifle in his hand. His wife was beside him, and the quiet children behind. And all of them stared after the tractor.
A TENANT FARMER quoted in *The Grapes of Wrath*

TEACHING OPTIONS

Teaching Less Proficient Readers

Clarifying Ideas To enable students to understand the Second New Deal measures to help farmers (pages 672–673), have them follow these steps:

1. Read the section, a paragraph at a time.
2. List the program described, including its former name, if applicable.
3. List the purpose of the program and the people who benefited from it.
4. Add to the list as you read about other New Deal programs.

Teaching Gifted and Talented Students

See with a Photographer's Eye Encourage students to take photographs that capture a segment of society. Have students do the following:

• Select a group to study, such as children, teenagers, or the elderly.
• Take photos of people in the group, capturing their strengths, weaknesses, energy, despair—whatever you want to convey.
• Write captions for the photos.
• Assemble the photos in an album.

The Second New Deal also attempted to help sharecroppers, migrant workers, and many other poor farmers. In May 1935, Congress created the Resettlement Administration to loan money to small farmers to buy land. It was hoped that this agency would help tenant farmers and sharecroppers resettle on more productive farmlands. In 1937, this agency was replaced by the Farm Security Administration (FSA), which loaned more than $1 billion to help tenant farmers become landholders. The FSA also established a network of camps for migrant farm workers, who traditionally lived in squalid housing.

Another activity of the FSA was making a pictorial record that showed the difficult situation of people in rural America. The agency sent photographers such as Dorothea Lange, Ben Shahn, Walker Evans, Arthur Rothstein, and Carl Mydans to take many pictures of rural towns and farms and their inhabitants.

Helping Youth, Professionals, and Others

Farmers weren't the only Americans who received direct assistance during the Second New Deal. The Roosevelt administration and Congress also set up a series of programs to help youths, professionals, and other workers. One of the largest programs begun under the New Deal was the **Works Progress Administration** (WPA), headed by Harry Hopkins, the former chief of the Federal Emergency Relief Administration.

The WPA set out to create as many jobs as possible as quickly as possible. It received a budget of $5 billion, the largest sum any nation had ever spent for public welfare at one time. Between 1935 and 1943, it employed more than 8 million persons. WPA workers, most of them unskilled, built 850 airports throughout the country. They constructed or repaired 651,000 miles of roads and streets. They put up 110,000 libraries, schools, and hospitals. Sewing groups, in which most of the WPA's female workers were employed, made 300 million garments for the needy. Some people criticized the WPA as a "make-work" program that created jobs just to provide workers with a paycheck.

Nevertheless, the WPA did produce public works of lasting value to the nation, and it gave working people a sense of hope and purpose that had been sorely lacking. As one man recalled, "It was really great. You worked, you got a paycheck, and you had some dignity. Even when a man raked leaves, he got paid, he had some dignity."

The WPA also employed many professionals—including teachers, writers, artists, actors, and musicians. These professionals were hired to create music, art, and scholarly studies. They wrote guides to cities, collected slave narratives, painted murals on the walls of schools and other public buildings, and performed in theater troupes around the country. At the urging of Eleanor Roosevelt, the WPA made special efforts to help women, minorities, and young people.

Another program, the **National Youth Administration** (NYA), was

Unemployed workers sit on a street in an Oklahoma town, in a 1936 photograph by Dorothea Lange.

The New Deal **673**

OBJECTIVE
(3) INSTRUCT

Helping Youth, Professionals, and Others

▶ **Discussing Key Ideas**
• The WPA offers direct assistance by creating new jobs.
• The NYA is created specifically to provide aid and employment to young people.

MORE ABOUT . . .
The WPA
Some people objected to the WPA's giving assistance to writers and artists. Art, they claimed, was not real work. The program's critics probably didn't anticipate that the work produced then by many of the artists would be worth far more today than any wages they received from the WPA. One artist recalled the WPA's Federal Art Project: "The total cost of the Federal Art Project was only $23 million. Many of these paintings, sculptures, and prints were given to museums, courthouses, public buildings. . . . I think that today those in museums alone are worth about $100 million." He may be right. The abstract expressionist painter Jackson Pollock received $7,800 from the WPA. In 1996, his WPA-funded paintings were valued at more than half a million dollars.

Labor and Other Reforms

▶ **Starting with the Student**
Have students create a cluster diagram, similar to the one below, to organize information on the reforms enacted by the Second New Deal. As students read this section, they should list the main reforms under each category.

▶ **Discussing Key Ideas**
• Congress passes labor reforms proposed by the Roosevelt administration that establish maximum hours and minimum wages.
• The Social Security system provides economic security for retired workers and financial benefits for millions of other Americans.
• The Second New Deal promotes rural electrification and seeks to regulate public utilities.

---

created specifically to help young people. The project was highly successful in providing aid and employment to young Americans. More than 2 million high school and college students worked in part-time clerical positions at their schools. One participant recalled later,

A PERSONAL VOICE
I lugged . . . drafts and reams of paper home, night after night. . . . Sometimes I typed almost all night and had to deliver it to school the next morning. . . . This was a good program. It got necessary work done. It gave teenagers a chance to work for pay. Mine bought me clothes and shoes, school supplies, some movies and mad money. Candy bars, and big pickles out of a barrel. It gave my mother relief from my necessary demands for money.
HELEN FARMER, quoted in *The Great Depression*

In 1936, more than 200,000 students received aid and assistance through the NYA. It also provided work-relief programs for hundreds of young adults.

Labor and Other Reforms

During the Second New Deal, the Roosevelt administration moved beyond relief to enact sweeping reforms. (See the chart on page 675.) In a speech to Congress in January 1935, the president declared, "When a man is getting over an illness, wisdom dictates not only cure of the symptoms but removal of their cause." With the help of Congress, Roosevelt brought about important reforms in the areas of labor relations and economic security for retired workers.

IMPROVING LABOR CONDITIONS One of the first reforms of the Second New Deal was prompted by the Supreme Court's declaring the NIRA unconstitutional in 1935. In addition to setting industry standards, the National Recovery Administration had provided some protections for workers, such as a 40-hour week and a ban on child labor.

The National Youth Administration helped young people, such as this dental assistant, *(third from left)* receive training and job opportunities.

After the Supreme Court declared the NIRA unconstitutional, Congress passed the National Labor Relations Act, more commonly called the **Wagner Act,** after its sponsor, Senator Robert F. Wagner of New York. The act reversed the position of the federal government on collective bargaining. The federal government now supported the right of workers to join unions and to engage in collective bargaining with employers.

In addition, the Wagner Act listed unfair labor practices that companies could not use. Among these were threatening workers, firing union members, and interfering with union organizing efforts. The act also set up the National Labor Relations Board (NLRB) to hear testimony about unfair practices and to hold elections among workers to find out if they wanted union representation.

Congress later passed the Fair Labor Standards Act in 1938 to establish maximum hours and minimum wages. The hours and wages standards set by the National Recovery Administration had been invalidated when the Supreme Court declared the NIRA unconstitutional. The Fair Labor

C. Answer It reversed the position of the federal government from favoring employers to supporting workers.

THINK THROUGH HISTORY
C. Drawing Conclusions *Why was the Wagner Act significant?*

TEACHING OPTIONS

Exploring Themes

Economic Opportunity Discuss the impact of the Wagner Act on labor conditions. Point out that the act gave more power to unions—including the support of the federal government. Ask students what this support meant for workers. *Possible Response: Labor would have more leverage in disputes.* Then ask them how the act affects labor and labor unions today. *Possible Response: Today labor unions are powerful, politically influential institutions.*

Making Connections Across Time

Social Security Today Tell students that today the Social Security system continues to pay benefits to retired workers. Then tell them that when the program was established in 1935, the number of retirees was relatively small. Point out that this number will begin to increase in 2010 when members of the baby-boom generation (those born between 1946 and 1964) begin to retire. Tell them that the government predicts that because retirees will increasingly outnumber workers, Social Security funds might run out before 2040.

Standards Act, for the first time, set a national minimum hourly rate for wages: 25 cents an hour at first, 40 cents an hour by 1945. It also established a national maximum workweek: 44 hours to begin, followed by 40 hours in two years. In addition, the act banned factory labor for workers under the age of 16 (or 18 if the work was hazardous).

THE SOCIAL SECURITY ACT One of the most important achievements of the New Deal was creating the Social Security system. The **Social Security Act,**

New Deal Agencies

EMPLOYMENT PROJECTS	PURPOSE
1933 Civilian Conservation Corps (CCC)	Provided jobs for single males on conservation projects.
1933 Federal Emergency Relief Act (FERA)	Helped states to provide aid for the unemployed.
1933 Civil Works Administration (CWA)	Provided work in federal jobs.
1933 Public Works Administration (PWA)	Created jobs on government projects that increased worker buying power and stimulated the economy.
1935 Works Progress Administration (WPA)	Quickly created as many jobs as possible—from construction projects to symphony orchestras.
1935 National Youth Administration (NYA)	Provided job training for unemployed youth and part-time jobs for needy students.

BUSINESS ASSISTANCE AND REFORM	
1933 Emergency Banking Relief Act (EBRA)	Regulated bank transactions in credit, currency, gold and silver, and foreign exchange.
1933 Federal Deposit Insurance Corporation (FDIC)	Protected bank deposits up to $5,000. (Today, accounts are protected up to $100,000.)
1933 National Recovery Administration (NRA)	Established codes of fair competition and granted labor the right of collective bargaining.
1934 Securities and Exchange Commission (SEC)	Supervised the country's Stock Commission Exchanges and eliminated dishonest practices.
1935 Banking Act of 1935	Created a seven-member board to regulate the nation's money supply and the interest rates on loans.
1938 Food, Drug and Cosmetic Act	Required manufacturers to list ingredients in food, drugs, and cosmetic products.

FARM RELIEF AND RURAL DEVELOPMENT	
1933 Agricultural Adjustment Administration (AAA)	Aided farmers and regulated crop production.
1933 Tennessee Valley Authority (TVA)	Developed the resources of the Tennessee Valley.
1935 Rural Electrification Administration (REA)	Provided cheap electricity for isolated rural areas.

HOUSING	
1933 Home Owners Loan Corporation (HOLC)	Loaned money at low interest to homeowners who could not meet mortgage payments.
1934 Federal Housing Administration (FHA)	Insured loans for building and repairing homes.
1937 United States Housing Authority (USHA)	Provided federal loans for a national home improvement program.

LABOR RELATIONS	
1935 National Labor Relations Act (Wagner Act of 1935)	Defined "unfair labor practices" and established a National Labor Relations Board (NLRB) to settle disputes between employers and employees.
1938 Fair Labor Standards Act	Established a minimum hourly wage and a maximum number of hours in the workweek for the entire country. Prohibited children under the age of 16 from working in factories.

RETIREMENT	
1935 Social Security Act	Provided a pension for retired workers and their spouses and aided people with disabilities.

HISTORY FROM VISUALS
New Deal Agencies
Reading the Chart
Emphasize to students that each agency and act listed in the left-hand column of the chart aligns with a purpose in the right-hand column.

Extension Ask students which agencies they think provided relief only during the Depression, and why. *Possible Response: The employment projects, because they were established to create jobs and weren't needed once the economy began to thrive again.* Ask them which agencies they think continue to influence the economy today, and why. *Possible Response: Most of the other agencies, because they produced fundamental reforms in banking, housing, and labor.*

GROLIER MULTIMEDIA ENCYCLOPEDIA
New Deal

TEACHING OPTION

Cooperative Activity: Creating a New Deal Poster

Task: Groups of four to five students will create a poster advertising and promoting a New Deal agency.

Purpose: To visually convey the purpose of a New Deal agency.

Activity: Groups should select the New Deal agency they want to advertise in a poster. Group members should then research the agency and discuss how its purpose could be conveyed in a poster. They should also write a slogan that will distinguish the agency and catch the reader's attention. To get ideas, students can study the posters illustrating the chart on page 675. After the posters are completed, display them around the room and discuss them in class.

ALTERNATIVE ASSESSMENT BOOK
Standards for Evaluating a Cooperative Activity

Section 2 Assessment
Have small groups of stu-
dents work together to
answer the questions.

Self-Assessment
Have students locate por-
tions of the text that contain
information for any ques-
tions they were not able
to answer.

Section Quiz

FORMAL ASSESSMENT
Section Quiz, p. 281

Reteach
Use the chart on page 675
to review the New Deal
agencies discussed in
Section 2.

CLOSE

Under the Second New
Deal, the Roosevelt administration launched more programs to provide relief to
farmers and other workers.
The administration also
spurred Congress to enact
the Social Security system
and reforms in labor and
public utilities.

*"We have
undertaken a
new order of
things, yet we
progress to it
under the
framework
and in the
spirit and
intent of the
American
Constitution."*

FRANKLIN DELANO
ROOSEVELT

passed in 1935, was created by a committee chaired by Secretary of Labor
Frances Perkins. The act had three major parts:

- *Old-age insurance for retirees 65 or older and their spouses.* The insurance was not a complete retirement plan but a supplement to a person's
  private retirement plan. The initial payments ranged from $10 to $85 a
  month, depending on the amount a worker paid into the system. This
  amount came half from the worker and half from the employer. Some
  groups were excluded from the system: domestic servants, farm workers,
  many hospital workers, many restaurant workers.
- *Unemployment compensation system.* The unemployment system was
  funded by a federal tax on employers. It was administered at the state
  level. The initial payments ranged from $15 to $18 per week.
- *Aid to families with dependent children and the disabled.* It was paid for by
  federal funds made available to the states. It made help available to the
  blind, the crippled, the needy elderly, and dependent mothers and children.

Although the Social Security Act was not a total pension system or a complete
welfare system, it did provide substantial benefits to millions of Americans.

EXPANDING AND REGULATING UTILITIES The Second New Deal also
included laws to promote rural electrification and to regulate public utilities. The
Roosevelt administration took steps to extend electricity to rural areas nationwide. At the time, only about 30 percent of American farms had electricity.

At President Roosevelt's urging, Congress established
the Rural Electrification Administration (REA). The REA
created, financed, and worked with rural and farm electrical cooperatives to bring electricity to previously isolated
areas. By 1945, 45 percent of America's farms and rural
homes had electricity. That figure rose to 90 percent by
1951. By making electricity widely available, the REA had
a tremendous impact on rural life.

The Public Utilities Holding Company Act outlawed
pyramiding of holding companies—holding companies of a
utility company that were held in turn by other holding companies. Lobbyists for the holding companies fought the law
fiercely. It passed, but proved extremely difficult to enforce.

As the New Deal struggled to help farmers and other
workers, it assisted many different groups in the nation. It
not only brought relief to both rural and urban workers, it
helped women make gains, and it brought help to African
Americans, Latinos, and Native Americans.

D. Answer It
helped retirees
and their
spouses, the
unemployed,
families with
dependent
children and the
disabled.

THINK THROUGH HISTORY
D. *Summarizing*
*Whom did Social
Security help?*

One of many
WPA posters
created to pro-
mote New Deal
programs, in this
case the Rural
Electrification
Administration.

RURAL ELECTRIFICATION ADMINISTRATION

Section **2** Assessment

1. TERMS & NAMES

Identify:
- Eleanor Roosevelt
- Works Progress
  Administration
- National Youth
  Administration
- Wagner Act
- Social Security Act

2. SUMMARIZING Create a
cluster diagram similar to the one
below showing how groups such
as farmers, the unemployed,
youth, and retirees were helped
by Second New Deal programs.

Which group do you think
benefited the most from the
Second New Deal? Explain.

3. ANALYZING Do you think the
Second New Deal could have
succeeded without the WPA?
Why or why not?

THINK ABOUT
- the millions of people the WPA
  employed
- criticism of the WPA as a
  "make-work" program
- the many New Deal reform and
  recovery programs

4. EVALUATING Why might the
Social Security Act be
considered the most important
achievement of the New Deal?

THINK ABOUT
- the types of relief needed in the
  1930s
- alternatives to government
  assistance to the elderly, the
  unemployed, and the disabled
- the scope of the act

676 CHAPTER 23

ANSWERS

1. TERMS & NAMES

Eleanor Roosevelt, p. 671

Works Progress Administration,
p. 673

National Youth Administration,
p. 673

Wagner Act, p. 674

Social Security Act, p. 675

2. SUMMARIZING

Possible Responses: Farmers:
second Agricultural Adjustment
Act, Farm Security
Administration, Rural
Electrification Administration.
Unemployed: Works Progress
Administration, National Youth
Administration, Social Security
Act. Youth: National Youth
Administration, Works Progress
Administration. Labor: Wagner
Act, Fair Labor Standards Act.
Retirees: Social Security Act.

3. ANALYZING

Possible Responses: Yes: The
farm recovery acts and labor
and utilities reforms created
changes that had a significant
impact both in the short term
and over time; the WPA provided
only for short-term "welfare,"
not long-term recovery. No: The
WPA gave more than 8 million
people immediate relief and provided them with a sense of dignity; nothing else worked quite
as quickly in producing returns
for communities.

4. EVALUATING

Possible Responses: It showed
that the Roosevelt administration
wanted to ensure that some of
the problems of the 1930s would
not recur; it provided a safety
net for many people—the unemployed, the elderly, the disabled,
and families with dependent
children—who needed help in
times of crisis; it had the largest
scope of the New Deal programs, affecting thousands of
people over a great many years.

3 The New Deal Affects Many Groups

TERMS & NAMES
• Frances Perkins
• Mary McLeod Bethune
• John Collier
• New Deal Coalition
• Congress of Industrial Organizations

LEARN ABOUT how New Deal policies affected various social and ethnic groups
TO UNDERSTAND how the Democratic Party forged a new political coalition.

ONE AMERICAN'S STORY

Pedro J. González came to this country from Mexico in 1924 and later became a United States citizen. González soon was involved in the music business, both as a performer and as the first Spanish-speaking disc jockey in Los Angeles. During the 1930s, González used his radio program to condemn discrimination against Mexicans and Mexican Americans, who were often made scapegoats for social and economic problems during the Depression. For his efforts, González was arrested, jailed, and deported on trumped-up charges. Late in life (in 1984), he reflected on his experiences.

> ### A PERSONAL VOICE
> Seeing how badly they treated Mexicans back in the days of my youth, I could have started a rebellion. But now there could be a cultural understanding so that without firing one bullet, we might understand each other. We [Mexicans] were here before they [Anglos] were, and we are not, as they still say, "undesirables" or "wetbacks." They say we come to this land and it's not our home. Actually, it's the other way around.
>
> **PEDRO J. GONZÁLEZ,** from the *Los Angeles Times*, December 9, 1984.

Because of his stand against discrimination, Pedro J. González became a hero to many Mexican Americans and a symbol of Mexican cultural pride. He criticized the prejudice of a large number of people in the United States toward Mexican Americans who sought jobs. He also criticized government actions to round up people in Mexican-American neighborhoods to send them back to Mexico. His life reflected some of the difficulties faced by Mexicans and other minority groups in the United States during the Depression and New Deal era.

Pedro J. González

 VIDEO *A SONG FOR HIS PEOPLE:*
Pedro J. González and the Fight for Mexican-American Rights

New Opportunities for Women

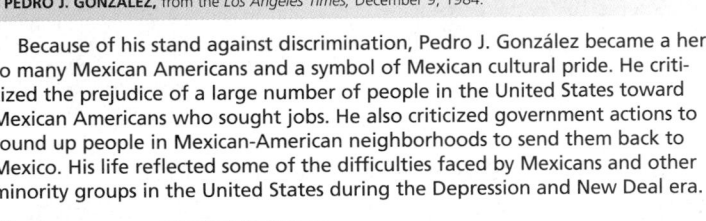

In some ways, the New Deal represented an important opportunity for minorities and women. Some New Deal programs and their administrators made a conscious effort not to discriminate in hiring or in distributing benefits. The Roosevelt administration appointed a number of women and African Americans to key positions in the government, and it welcomed their input on important issues.

Nevertheless, gains for women and minorities during the New Deal were limited. Long-standing patterns of prejudice and discrimination continued to plague these groups and to prevent their full and equal participation in national life.

WOMEN MAKE THEIR MARK One of the most notable changes during the New Deal was the naming of several women to important official positions. For the first time, a woman, **Frances Perkins,** became a cabinet member. As secretary of labor, she played a major role in the cre-

Frances Perkins was the New York state industrial commissioner in 1933.

The New Deal **677**

SECTION 3 RESOURCES

PRINT RESOURCES

IN-DEPTH RESOURCES: UNIT 6
Guided Reading, p. 55
Primary Source: The Memorial Day Massacre, p. 64
Literature: from *Waiting for Lefty* by Clifford Odets, p. 67
American Lives: Mary McLeod Bethune, p. 71

ACCESS FOR STUDENTS ACQUIRING ENGLISH
Guided Reading (Spanish), p. 225

FORMAL ASSESSMENT
Section Quiz, p. 282

ALTERNATIVE ASSESSMENT BOOK
See forms for supporting and scoring alternative activities.

TECHNOLOGY RESOURCES

HUMANITIES TRANSPARENCIES
H22, A relief center in Louisville, Kentucky, 1937. Margaret Bourke-White

CD-ROM
Electronic Library of Primary Sources

VIDEO *American Stories* video series
American Portfolio: A Videodisc for U.S. History
user's guide, pp. 205, 207

INTERNET McDougal Littell Learning On-Line
http://www.mcdougallittell.com

Section 3 Overview

OBJECTIVES
(1) To describe how New Deal programs affected women.
(2) To characterize the Roosevelt administration's attitude toward African Americans.
(3) To summarize the treatment of Mexican Americans.
(4) To describe how Native Americans fared under the New Deal.
(5) To identify the groups that formed a New Deal Coalition.

CRITICAL THINKING
• Synthesizing, p. 678
• Evaluating decisions, p. 679
• Analyzing causes, p. 680
• Recognizing effects, p. 680
• Analyzing, p. 681
• Summarizing, p. 682
• Generalizing, p. 682
• Forming opinions, p. 682

FOCUS & MOTIVATE

▶ *Starting with the Student*
Have students watch the video "A Song for His People" to find out about Pedro J. González.

• Using the *Teacher's Resource Book* as a guide, hold a discussion and engage in extension activities using primary sources.

 AMERICAN STORIES VIDEO SERIES
"A Song for His People"
Videocassette: Volume 4

Videodisc: Disc 2, Side B, Chapter 3

OBJECTIVE
(1) **INSTRUCT**

New Opportunities for Women

▶ *Discussing Key Ideas*
• Roosevelt appoints women to positions in the government.

(continued on next page)

Teacher's Edition 677

(continued from page 677)

- Women face discrimination in the workplace.

IN-DEPTH RESOURCES: UNIT 6
Guided Reading, p. 55

ACCESS FOR STUDENTS ACQUIRING ENGLISH
Guided Reading (Spanish), p. 225

OBJECTIVE
② INSTRUCT

New Opportunities for African Americans

▶ *Discussing Key Ideas*
- Mary McLeod Bethune organizes a group of African Americans to advise the Roosevelt administration on racial issues.
- Eleanor Roosevelt plays a key role in opening doors for African Americans in government.
- Although Roosevelt fails to support civil rights, most African Americans support the president.

IN-DEPTH RESOURCES: UNIT 6
American Lives: Mary McLeod Bethune, p. 71

 ELECTRONIC LIBRARY OF PRIMARY SOURCES
How Bethune-Cookman College Began by Mary McLeod Bethune

MORE ABOUT . . .
Breaking Racial Barriers

In Birmingham, Alabama, in 1938, Eleanor Roosevelt attended a meeting of the interracial Southern Conference for Human Welfare. Chairs designated for African Americans were segregated from those for whites. Mrs. Roosevelt pointedly

(continued on next page)

---

ation of the Social Security system and in the crafting of labor legislation. President Roosevelt also appointed the first female ambassador and a number of female federal judges.

In making these appointments, President Roosevelt hoped to appeal to female voters. He also received a strong push from his wife, Eleanor, and from the head of the Democratic Party's women's division, Molly Dewson. During the 1936 presidential campaign, Dewson had mobilized 15,000 women to go door to door distributing leaflets promoting New Deal programs. Though a feminist at heart, Dewson did not push a strong women's-rights agenda. She was, however, especially proud of the advances made by women. As she said, "The change from women's status in government before Roosevelt is unbelievable."

In general, however, women continued to struggle for equal rights during the New Deal era. They faced ongoing discrimination in the workplace. Male workers persisted in their belief that women took jobs from men, especially when so many men were out of work. In fact, a Gallup poll taken in 1936 reported that 82 percent of Americans said that a wife should not work if her husband had a job.

New Deal laws yielded mixed results regarding women. In fact, the codes established by the National Recovery Administration set wage levels lower for women than for men. In addition, the Federal Emergency Relief Administration and the Civil Works Administration hired far fewer women than men, only about one in ten. The Civilian Conservation Corps hired only men. These hiring practices were very much in line with those pursued by business and industry in the 1930s.

In spite of these barriers, women continued their movement into the workplace. Although the overall percentage of women working for wages increased only slightly during the 1930s, the percentage of married women in the workplace grew from 11.7 percent in 1930 to 15.6 percent in 1940. In short, widespread criticism of working women did not halt the long-term trend of women working outside the home.

New Opportunities for African Americans

An important African American in the Roosevelt administration was **Mary McLeod Bethune.** She was an educator who dedicated herself to promoting opportunities for young African Americans. The president named her to head a special department of the National Youth Administration, the Office of Minority Affairs. In this post, Bethune worked to ensure that the NYA hired African-American administrators and provided job training and other benefits to minority students.

Bethune also helped organize a "Black Cabinet" of influential African Americans to advise the Roosevelt administration on racial issues. Included in this group were African-American lawyers, journalists, and specialists on housing, labor, and other issues. Among these figures were William H. Hastie and Robert C. Weaver, both appointees to Roosevelt's Interior Department. Never before had so many African Americans had a voice in the White House.

Mary McLeod Bethune, a close friend of Eleanor Roosevelt, was a strong supporter of the New Deal.

William H. Hastie was appointed by President Roosevelt to the Interior Department.

A. Answer It advised the administration on racial issues.

THINK THROUGH HISTORY
A. Synthesizing Why was the "Black Cabinet" important to the Roosevelt administration?

678 CHAPTER 23

TEACHING OPTION

Making Connections Across Time

Women in the Workplace Today Tell students that the percentage of women in the workplace rose from 28 percent in 1940 to 59 percent in 1994. Tell them that the women's movement of the 1960s and 1970s helped bring about many gains for working women. The Equal Pay Act of 1963 required equal pay for men and women performing the same job. Among other stipulations, the Civil Rights Act of 1964 prohibited job discrimination on the basis of sex. Nonetheless,

in the 1990s, women still lagged behind men in job opportunities and earnings. Although some women pursued careers in fields traditionally reserved for men, most women still worked in such "women's" jobs as nursing, teaching, retail sales, and secretarial work. Because these jobs remained low paying, women continued to earn less than men. In the mid 1990s women earned, on the average, only about three-fourths of what men earned.

Eleanor Roosevelt played a key role in opening doors for African Americans in government. She also was instrumental in bringing about one of the most dramatic cultural events of the period: the performance of African-American singer Marian Anderson in 1939. When the Daughters of the American Revolution chose not to allow Anderson to perform in their concert hall in Washington, D.C., Eleanor Roosevelt arranged for Marian Anderson to perform at the Lincoln Memorial on Easter Sunday. Mrs. Roosevelt also resigned from the Daughters of the American Revolution. At the concert, Walter White, an official with the NAACP, noticed one girl in the crowd.

A PERSONAL VOICE

Her hands were particularly noticeable as she thrust them forward and upward, trying desperately . . . to touch the singer. They were hands which despite their youth had known only the dreary work of manual labor. Tears streamed down the girl's dark face. Her hat was askew, but in her eyes flamed hope bordering on ecstasy. . . . If Marian Anderson could do it, the girl's eyes seemed to say, then I can, too.

WALTER WHITE, from his autobiography

The noted African-American contralto Marian Anderson sang from the steps of the Lincoln Memorial on April 9, 1939.

THE PRESIDENT FAILS TO SUPPORT CIVIL RIGHTS Despite efforts to promote racial equality, the president himself was never committed to full civil rights for African Americans. He was afraid of upsetting Southern whites, an important segment of Democratic voters. For this reason, he refused to support a federal antilynching law and an end to the poll tax, two key goals of the civil rights movement. Furthermore, although as many as a million African-American families benefited from WPA work relief, a number of New Deal programs, including the FHA, the CCC, and the TVA, clearly discriminated against African Americans. They favored white Americans when providing direct relief and New Deal jobs. African Americans often received lower wages than whites and were segregated from whites.

Recognizing the need to fight for their own rights, African Americans took steps to improve conditions in areas that the New Deal ignored. In 1934, they helped organize the Southern Tenant Farmers' Union, which sought to protect the rights of tenant farmers and sharecroppers, both white and black. In the North, the union created tenants' groups and launched campaigns to increase job opportunities. When discriminatory hiring practices continued to deprive African Americans of their fair share of jobs, they organized the March on Washington Movement in 1941.

In general, however, African Americans supported the Roosevelt administration and the New Deal, and they abandoned their traditional allegiance to the Republican Party. Although segregation and racial violence remained shameful features of American life, African Americans generally regarded the New Deal and President Roosevelt as their best hope for the future. As one man recalled, "Roosevelt touched the temper of the black community. You did not look upon him as being white, black, blue, or green. He was President Roosevelt."

B. Answer President Roosevelt was not committed to full civil rights for African Americans. He did not support a federal antilynching law and an end to poll taxes. Many African-American families benefited from work relief, but some New Deal programs discriminated against African Americans.

THINK THROUGH HISTORY
B. Evaluating Decisions Evaluate the actions and policies of the Roosevelt administration on civil rights.

The New Deal **679**

(continued from page 678)

picked up her chair and placed it in the area separating the black and white delegates.

HUMANITIES TRANSPARENCIES
H22, A relief center in Louisville, Kentucky, 1937. Margaret Bourke-White

MORE ABOUT . . .
Marian Anderson

Conductor Arturo Toscanini claimed that a voice like Marian Anderson's was "heard once in a hundred years." Anderson did not always receive such high praise, however. When the contralto gave a recital in New York's Town Hall in 1925, she received very unfavorable reviews. Her poor performance may have been due to her voice teacher's having attempted to raise her voice a full octave. Following the disastrous recital, Anderson vowed never to sing again. She broke that vow, however, and eventually won wide praise for her concert singing. In 1955, she became the first black soloist to sing with the Metropolitan Opera of New York City.

Mexican-American Fortunes

▶ *Discussing Key Ideas*
- Mexican Americans support the New Deal, even though they receive fewer benefits than African Americans.

HISTORICAL SPOTLIGHT
Deportation of Mexican Americans

Critical Thinking: Analyzing Ask students why many Mexican-American migrant workers were treated with hostility during the Depression. *Because they took jobs away from white workers.* Ask them why the white workers didn't want these jobs during good times. *Possible Response: Because during good times, whites could get better jobs and were content to leave the low-paying ones to minorities.*

Native American Gains

▶ *Discussing Key Ideas*
- Native Americans receive strong support under the New Deal.

DEPORTATION OF MEXICAN AMERICANS

Many Mexican Americans were long-time residents or citizens of the United States. Others came during the 1920s to work on farms in Texas, California, and Arizona. Valued for their low-cost labor during good times, these migrant workers became the target of hostility during the Depression. Many returned to Mexico willingly, while others were deported by the United States government. During the 1930s, as many as half a million persons of Mexican descent, many of them U.S. citizens, were deported to Mexico.

John Collier talks with Chief Richard, one of several Native American chiefs attending the Four Nation Celebration held at Niagara Falls, New York, in September 1934.

Mexican-American Fortunes

Mexican Americans also tended to support the New Deal, even though they received even fewer benefits than African Americans did. Large numbers of Mexican Americans had come to the United States during the 1920s, and had settled mainly in the Southwest. Most worked as farm laborers, an occupation that was essentially unprotected by state and federal laws. During the Depression, farm wages fell to as low as nine cents an hour. Farm workers who tried to unionize often met with violence from employers and government authorities. Although the CCC and WPA helped some Mexican Americans, these work programs also discriminated against them by disqualifying from their programs migrant workers who had no permanent address.

Native American Gains

Native Americans received strong government support from the New Deal. In 1924, Native Americans had received full citizenship by law. In 1933, President Roosevelt appointed **John Collier** as commissioner of Indian Affairs. A strong advocate of Native American rights, Collier helped create the Indian Reorganization Act of 1934.

This act strengthened Native American land claims by prohibiting the government from taking over unclaimed reservation lands and selling them to people other than Native Americans. Thus, the 1934 act was able to restore some reservation lands to tribal ownership. Some Native Americans who valued their tribal traditions hailed the act as an important step forward. Those who had become more "Americanized," as individual landowners under the previous Dawes Act, however, objected that the act would make it harder for Native Americans to improve their economic conditions and participate fully in mainstream American life.

A New Deal Coalition

Although New Deal policies had mixed results for minorities, these groups generally backed President Roosevelt against his Republican rivals. In fact, one of FDR's great achievements was to create a **New Deal Coalition**—an alignment of diverse groups dedicated to supporting the Democratic Party. The coalition included Southern whites, various urban groups, African Americans, and unionized industrial workers. This new voting bloc enabled the Democrats to dominate politics throughout the 1930s and 1940s.

LABOR UNIONS FLOURISH Organized labor was a critical element of the New Deal coalition. As a result of the Wagner Act and other pro-labor legislation passed during the New Deal, union members enjoyed better working conditions and increased bargaining power. In their eyes, President Roosevelt was a "friend of labor." Labor unions donated money to Roosevelt's reelection campaigns, and union workers pledged their votes to him.

During the 1930s, and particularly after passage of the Wagner Act, the number of unionized workers soared. Between 1933 and 1941, union membership grew from 3 million to more than 8 million. Unionization especially affected coal miners and those in the mass production industries, such as auto-

THINK THROUGH HISTORY
C. *Analyzing Causes* Why was life difficult for farm laborers?
C. Answer Farm laborers were essentially unprotected by state and federal laws.

D. Answer New Deal labor laws gave unions greater power to organize and negotiate with employers. As a result, unions grew in size and joined with other groups in the New Deal coalition.

THINK THROUGH HISTORY
D. *Recognizing Effects* How did New Deal policies affect organized labor?

Exploring Themes

Cultural Diversity Discuss the dissent among Native Americans regarding the Indian Reorganization Act of 1934. Ask students to explain why some Native Americans favored the act and others did not. Ask them how some Native Americans became Americanized. *Possible Response: By adopting aspects of white mainstream culture.* Then ask students if they think minorities have a better chance of succeeding when they adopt the dominant culture, or if they think minorities should retain their traditions.

Making Connections Across Cultures

Mexican Americans During the Depression Tell students that as a radio-show host in Los Angeles in the 1930s, Pedro González once announced to his Latino listeners that workers were needed to clear some land in the city. Soon thereafter, hundreds of Mexican-American workers arrived at the site, ready for work with picks and axes. However, the police, fearing that the people were armed for a riot, arrested many of them. Ask students what the response of the police reveals about relations between whites and Mexican Americans during the Depression.

mobile, rubber, and electrical workers. It was in these industries, too, that conflicts began to develop within the labor movement.

Traditionally, organized labor had been largely restricted to the craft unions—carpenters, plumbers, electricians, and so on—that made up the American Federation of Labor (AFL). The AFL opposed industrywide unions: unions that represented all the workers in a given industry, such as automobile manufacturing.

Frustrated by this position, several key labor leaders, including John L. Lewis of the United Mine Workers and Walter Reuther of the United Automobile Workers, formed the Committee for Industrial Organization to organize industrial unions. The committee signed up unskilled and semiskilled workers rapidly and in two years had succeeded in gaining union recognition in the steel and automobile industries. In 1938, the Committee for Industrial Organization completed its break with the AFL by officially separating to form its own union. The committee than changed its name to the **Congress of Industrial Organizations** (CIO). This split lasted until 1955.

E. Answer They brought results because factory owners had to negotiate with the workers to end the strike so they could begin production again.

THINK THROUGH HISTORY
E. Analyzing Why were sit-down strikes an effective bargaining tool?

One of the main bargaining tactics of the labor movement in the 1930s was the sit-down strike. Instead of walking off their jobs, workers remained inside the plant, but they did not work. This prevented the factory owners from carrying on production with strikebreakers. Some Americans disapproved of the sit-down strike, calling it a violation of private property. But it proved to be an effective bargaining tool.

Not all labor disputes in the 1930s were peaceful. For example, a sit-down strike that began in 1936 at the General Motors (GM) automobile plant in Flint, Michigan, turned violent. GM called in the police, who used tear gas to try to disperse the strikers. Then the strikers turned on the plant's water hoses to douse the police. A series of bloody encounters also erupted between striking

OBJECTIVE
⑤ INSTRUCT

A New Deal Coalition

▶ *Discussing Key Ideas*
• Labor unions flourish under the New Deal.
• The growing labor movement results in disputes that are not always settled peacefully.
• The urban population supports FDR.

HISTORY FROM VISUALS
The Growing Labor Movement, 1933–1940
Reading the Chart Point out to students that the bar graph makes it easier to see that there was a decline in union membership from 1930 through 1933, a big increase in 1934, and an even bigger increase in 1937.

Extension Have students create a two-column chart in which they list the different groups of workers who belonged to the AFL and to the CIO.

The Growing Labor Movement, 1933–1940

SIT-DOWN STRIKES Union workers such as these CIO strikers at the Fisher body plant in Flint, Michigan, in 1937, found the sit-down strike an extremely effective method for gaining their demands.

❷ **ROBERT F. WAGNER** was a Democratic senator from New York from 1926 to 1949. As a U.S. senator and a person especially interested in workers' welfare, Wagner introduced the National Labor Relations Act in Congress in 1935.

ORGANIZE
WITH 1,250,000 WORKERS BACKING US
OF COURSE WE WILL ORGANIZE

❸ **UNION MEMBERSHIP GOES UP** A Ben Shahn poster from the late 1930s boasted of the soaring rise in union membership.

The Growth of Union Membership, 1930–1940

Source: *Historical Statistics of the United States: Colonial Times to 1970*

The New Deal **681**

TEACHING OPTION

Making Connections Across Time

Labor Movements in the 1960s and 1970s Tell students that in the 1960s and 1970s, farm workers and federal employees became unionized for the first time. A Mexican American named Cesar Chavez organized farm workers during the 1960s and eventually established the United Farm Workers of America, a union of migrant workers and other farm laborers. Early in the 1960s, federal employees were given the right to organize and bargain collectively, but they could not strike. Over time, the laws began to change. These laws allowed public employees to strike and encouraged the growth of unionism among the workers. By the 1970s, strikes by teachers and other government employees had affected many cities. The American Federation of State, County, and Municipal Employees, a union of public employees, became the fastest-growing labor group in the country. Union membership among women and minority groups also increased during these decades.

Teacher's Edition **681**

ASSESS & RETEACH

Section 3 Assessment

Have students focus on item 2 (Summarizing), which gives an especially good overview of the section.

Self-Assessment

Have students cite a quotation in this section that they think sums up an important idea. They should look at the quotations under the label "A Personal Voice" as well as other quotations in the text.

Section Quiz

FORMAL ASSESSMENT
Section Quiz, p. 282

Reteach

Survey the students to discover what topics in this section were difficult for them. Then review the relevant material.

CLOSE

Although discrimination remained a fact of life for many people, the New Deal created some new opportunities for women and minority groups. With organized labor, these groups forged a new political coalition dedicated to supporting the Democratic Party. The New Deal had a great influence on workers from all walks of life.

---

employees of the Ford Motor Company and hoodlums hired by Ford's management. Perhaps the most dramatic incident, however, was the clash at the Republic Steel plant in Chicago. On Memorial Day, 1937, police attacked striking steelworkers outside the plant. One striker, an African-American man, recalled the experience.

A PERSONAL VOICE
I began to see people drop. There was a Mexican on my side, and he fell; and there was a black man on my side and he fell. Down I went. I crawled around in the grass and saw that people were getting beat. I'd never seen police beat women, not white women. I'd seen them beat black women, but this was the first time in my life I'd seen them beat white women—with sticks.

JESSE REESE, quoted in *The Great Depression*

Ten people were killed and dozens wounded in this incident, which became known as the Memorial Day Massacre. Shortly afterward, the National Labor Relations Board stepped in and required the head of Republic Steel, Tom Girdler, to negotiate with the union. Gradually, with the help of New Deal agencies, labor gained strength.

THE URBAN POPULATION SUPPORTS FDR Urban voters were another important component of the New Deal coalition. Support for the Democratic Party surged, especially in large Northern cities such as New York, Boston, Philadelphia, and Chicago. These and other cities had powerful city political organizations that provided services, such as jobs, in exchange for votes. Support for President Roosevelt came from various religious and ethnic groups—Roman Catholics, Jews, Italians, Irish, Polish and other Slavic peoples, as well as from African Americans.

President Roosevelt's appeal to these groups was based on New Deal labor laws and work-relief programs, which aided the urban poor. The president also made direct and persuasive appeals to urban voters at election time. At presidential campaign stops in Northern cities, throngs of supporters came out to cheer the president. In the 1936 election, President Roosevelt carried the nation's 12 largest cities. To reinforce his support, he also appointed many officials of urban-immigrant backgrounds, particularly Roman Catholics and Jews, to important government positions.

Women, African Americans, Mexican Americans, Native Americans, and workers from all walks of life were greatly affected by the New Deal. It also had a tremendous influence on American society and culture.

Fiorello La Guardia, the reform mayor of New York City from 1934 to 1945, campaigns with a baby in his arms. Many politicians of the time kissed babies during their political campaign to court favor with voters.

F. Answer New Deal labor and relief programs helped the urban poor. Roosevelt also made direct appeals to these groups.

THINK THROUGH HISTORY
F. Summarizing Why did urban voters support Roosevelt?

Section 3 Assessment

1. TERMS & NAMES

Identify:
- Frances Perkins
- Mary McLeod Bethune
- John Collier
- New Deal coalition
- Congress of Industrial Organizations

2. SUMMARIZING Using a web diagram like the partial one shown here, note the effects of New Deal policies on American women, African Americans, Mexican Americans, Native Americans, unionized workers, and urban Americans.

Effects of New Deal

Women

Mexican Americans

Write a paragraph explaining the effects of the New Deal on one of the groups.

3. GENERALIZING Do you think women made significant progress toward equality during the 1930s? Support your answer with evidence from the text.

THINK ABOUT
- the role of women in government
- hiring practices in federal programs
- women's opportunities in business and industry

4. FORMING OPINIONS In your opinion, did organized labor become too powerful in the 1930s? Explain your answer.

THINK ABOUT
- why workers joined unions
- how unions organized workers
- the role of unions in politics

682 CHAPTER 23

ANSWERS

1. TERMS & NAMES

Frances Perkins, p. 677

Mary McLeod Bethune, p. 678

John Collier, p. 680

New Deal Coalition, p. 680

Congress of Industrial Organizations, p. 681

2. SUMMARIZING

Possible Responses: **Women:** Appointment to key government positions; welcoming of women's input on issues. **African Americans:** Role of Mary McLeod Bethune and the "Black Cabinet." **Mexican Americans:** Help from the CCC and the WPA. **Native Americans:** Passage of the Indian Reorganization Act of 1934. **Unionized workers:** Passage of the Wagner Act. **Urban voters:** Appeal of work-relief programs.

3. GENERALIZING

Possible Responses: Students answering yes might cite Roosevelt's appointments of women and the increase in the percentage of women employed, and they might say that the growth of employment reflected greater opportunity for women. Students answering no might point to lower wage levels for women and to discrimination in the workplace and in federal programs.

4. FORMING OPINIONS

Possible Responses: Students answering yes might argue that strikes, especially sit-down strikes, interfered with business and that labor disputes sometimes resulted in violence, as in Chicago and Flint, Michigan. Students answering no might argue that union membership was finally open to industrial workers and that union member enjoyed better working conditions and increased bargaining power.

4 Society and Culture

TERMS & NAMES
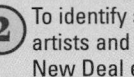
- *Gone with the Wind*
- Orson Welles
- Grant Wood
- Richard Wright
- *The Grapes of Wrath*

LEARN ABOUT arts, entertainment, and literature during the 1930s
TO UNDERSTAND how the Depression and New Deal influenced American culture.

ONE AMERICAN'S STORY

Don Congdon, editor of the book *The Thirties: A Time to Remember,* was a high school student when the New Deal began. He recalls "the air of excitement that pervaded the country. People spoke out freely and were willing to fight for what they believed in." During the 1930s, many artists and writers produced works that reflected the important issues of the day. It was the movies and radio, however, that most clearly captured the public imagination. Congdon remembers the role movies played at the time.

A PERSONAL VOICE

Lots of us enjoyed our leisure at the movies. The experience of going was like an insidious [tempting] candy we could never get quite enough of; the visit to the dark theater was an escape from the drab realities of Depression living, and we were entranced by the never-ending variety of stories. Hollywood, like Scheherazade [the story-teller] in *The Thousand and One Nights,* supplied more the next night, and the next night after that.

DON CONGDON, from *The Thirties: A Time to Remember*

During the Depression, movies provided a means of looking at a different, more exciting world. Despite economic hardship, many people gladly paid the 25 cents it cost to go to the movies. Along with radio, motion pictures became an increasingly dominant feature of American life.

People line up to get into a movie theater during the Great Depression.

The Lure of Motion Pictures and Radio

Although the 1930s were a difficult time for many Americans, they were a golden age for the motion picture and radio industries. Statistics tell part of the story. By late in the decade, as many as 75 million people, around 65 percent of the population, attended the movies once a week. The nation boasted over 15,000 movie theaters, more than the number of banks and double the number of hotels. The sale of radios also greatly increased during the 1930s, from just over 10 million at the beginning of the decade to around 30 million by the end. Nearly 90 percent of American households owned a radio. Clearly, movies and radio had taken the country by storm.

MOVIES ARE A HIT A wide variety of movies were made during the New Deal years. Wacky comedies, lavish musicals, tender love stories, and tough gangster films all vied for the attention of the moviegoing public. The movies introduced a new set of Hollywood stars, including Greta Garbo, Clark Gable, Marlene Dietrich, and James Cagney. These stars, who emerged following the end of

The New Deal **683**

SECTION 4 RESOURCES

 PRINT RESOURCES

IN-DEPTH RESOURCES: UNIT 6
Guided Reading, p. 56
Primary Sources: WPA Posters, p. 65; from *Let Us Now Praise Famous Men* by James Agee and Walker Evans, p. 66

ACCESS FOR STUDENTS ACQUIRING ENGLISH
Guided Reading (Spanish), p. 226

FORMAL ASSESSMENT
Section Quiz, p. 283

ALTERNATIVE ASSESSMENT BOOK
See forms for supporting and scoring alternative activities.

TECHNOLOGY RESOURCES

VIDEO
American Portfolio: A Videodisc for U.S. History
user's guide, pp. 202, 207

INTERNET McDougal Littell Learning On-Line
http://www.mcdougallittell.com

Section 4 Overview

OBJECTIVES

1. To describe the entertainment provided by motion pictures and radio.
2. To identify some of the artists and writers of the New Deal era.

CRITICAL THINKING

- Analyzing causes, pp. 684, 685, 688
- Analyzing issues, p. 687
- Synthesizing, p. 688
- Summarizing, p. 688
- Hypothesizing, p. 688

FOCUS & MOTIVATE

▶ *Starting with the Student*
Ask students the following questions:

- What kinds of movies do students like best—action films, comedies, dramas, musicals?
- Do students go to the movies to escape everyday life, or do they prefer films that portray life realistically?
- What do students think Depression-era people wanted to see when they went to the movies?

OBJECTIVE
1 **INSTRUCT**

The Lure of Motion Pictures and Radio

▶ *Discussing Key Ideas*
- During the Depression, people flock to the movies.
- Most families spend several hours a day listening to their favorite radio programs.

IN-DEPTH RESOURCES: UNIT 6
Guided Reading, p. 56

ACCESS FOR STUDENTS ACQUIRING ENGLISH
Guided Reading (Spanish), p. 226

Clark Gable and Vivien Leigh embrace in a scene from the popular film *Gone with the Wind*.

One of the first worldwide radio broadcasts was about the *Hindenberg*, a German zeppelin [a rigid-frame dirigible balloon]. The *Hindenberg* caught fire while landing in Lakehurst, New Jersey, on May 6, 1937. Thirty-six lives were lost in the fire.

silent films and the rise of "talking" pictures, helped launch a new era of glamour and sophistication in Hollywood.

Some films made during the 1930s offered pure escape from the hard realities of the Depression by presenting visions of wealth, romance, and good times. Perhaps the most famous film of the era, and one of the most popular of all time, was **Gone with the Wind** (1939). This sweeping drama about life among Southern plantation owners during the Civil War starred Clark Gable and Vivien Leigh.

Another film, *Flying Down to Rio* (1933), was a light romantic comedy featuring Fred Astaire and Ginger Rogers, who went on to make many movies together, becoming America's favorite dance partners. The lavish musical *Gold Diggers of 1933*, with its theme song "We're in the Money," expressed the dream of many Americans for a life of comfort and affluence. Other notable movies made during the 1930s include *The Wizard of Oz* (1939), a classic American film starring Judy Garland, and *Snow White and the Seven Dwarfs* (1937), which showcased the dazzling animation of Walt Disney.

COMEDIES AND HEROES ENTERTAIN Americans also flocked to see comedies on the silver screen. The most famous movie comedians of the time, the Marx Brothers, made a series of films that captured their zany humor. In one scene from *Duck Soup* (1933), Groucho Marx plays the prime minister of Freedonia, a fictional country. He holds up a document and says to his advisers, "Why, a four-year-old child could understand this report." Then, whispering to his brother Zeppo, he says, "Run out and find me a four-year-old child. I can't make head or tail out of it."

Other movies combined escapist appeal with more realistic plots and settings that conveyed a truer sense of Depression America. Often, these films showed heroes grappling with problems and rising above their circumstances. One type of realistic movie that was especially popular was the gangster film. Gangster films presented images of urban America—dark, gritty streets and looming skyscrapers. These movies featured hard-bitten characters, played by stars such as Jimmy Cagney and Edward G. Robinson, struggling to succeed in a harsh environment. Although these characters were often on the wrong side of the law, they faced difficulties that Depression-era audiences could easily understand. Notable films in this genre include *Little Caesar* (1930) and *The Public Enemy* (1931).

In addition, several films made between 1934 and 1936 presented the social and political accomplishments of the New Deal in a positive light. *Mr. Deeds Goes to Town* (1936) and *Mr. Smith Goes to Washington* (1939), by director Frank Capra, portrayed honest, kindhearted people winning out over those with greedy special interests. In much the same way, the New Deal seemed to represent the interests of average Americans in relation to the wealthy and powerful.

RADIO ENTERTAINS Even more than movies, radio embodied the democratic spirit of the times. Almost every home had a radio, and families typically spent several

THINK THROUGH HISTORY
A. Analyzing Causes Why were movies so popular during the 1930s?
A. Answer They offered an escape from hard times.

hours a day gathered together, listening to their favorite programs. It's no surprise that President Roosevelt chose radio as the medium for his "fireside chats." It was the most direct means of access to the American people.

Like movies, radio programs offered great variety: news, comedies, dramas, soap operas, and children's shows. Soap operas—so named because they were usually sponsored by soap companies—tended to play early in the afternoon. These "real-life" dramas, which included "The Romance of Helen Trent" and "The Guiding Light," typically featured women characters with romantic difficulties. Homemakers, the prime audience for these shows, found that the stories and characters gave them a few moments of escape from their household drudgery. Children's programs, such as "The Green Hornet" and "The Lone Ranger," generally aired later in the afternoon, when children were home from school.

NETWORKS PROVIDE GREAT DRAMA AND COMEDY In the evening, radio networks offered excellent dramas and variety programs, featuring such stars as Bob Hope, Jack Benny, George Burns and Gracie Allen, and **Orson Welles.** Welles, an actor, director, and producer, created one of the most renowned radio broadcasts of all time, "The War of the Worlds." Later he directed movie classics such as *Citizen Kane* (1941) and *A Touch of Evil* (1958). Comedians Hope, Benny, and Burns and Allen performed routines that have stood the test of time. After making their reputation in radio, these stars later moved on to work in television.

The comedy couple George Burns and Gracie Allen delighted NBC radio audiences for years, and their popularity continued on television.

Art and Literature in Depression America

In contrast to the radio and movie productions of the 1930s, much of the art and literature of the time was more sober and serious. Many writers and artists depicted the real conditions of Depression America. Identifying with the struggles of working people, these artists and writers produced paintings, plays, novels, and poetry that focused on the hardships faced by average Americans.

Some of this artistic work was grim and somber, but much of it conveyed a more uplifting message about the strength of character and the democratic values of the American people. A number of artists and writers embraced the spirit of social and political change fostered by the New Deal, and many received direct support through New Deal work programs.

Although some people argued that the government should not be in the business of funding art projects, New Deal officials thought that art played an important role in national life. They also believed that artists deserved work relief as much as other unemployed Americans. As the head of the WPA, Harry Hopkins, put it, "They've got to eat just like other people."

ARTISTS DECORATE AMERICA The Federal Art Project, a branch of the WPA, paid artists a living wage to produce public art. It also had two other functions: to increase public appreciation of art and to promote positive images of American society. Artists created posters, taught art in the schools, and painted murals on the walls of public buildings. These murals, inspired in part by the revolutionary work of Mexican muralists such as Diego Rivera, typically portrayed the dignity

B. Answer New Deal officials believed that art played an important role in the life of the American people. They also believed that artists deserved work relief just as other unemployed Americans did.

THINK THROUGH HISTORY
B. *Analyzing Causes*
Why did the New Deal fund art projects?

HISTORICAL SPOTLIGHT

WAR OF THE WORLDS
On October 31, 1938, Halloween night, radio listeners were stunned by a special announcement: Martians had invaded Earth! Panic set in as many Americans were convinced that the world was coming to an end. Of course, the story wasn't true: it was a radio drama based on a book by H. G. Wells, *The War of the Worlds.*

In his book, H. G. Wells describes the canisters of gas fired by the Martians as releasing "an enormous volume of heavy, inky vapour . . . and the touch of that vapour, the inhaling of its pungent wisps, was death to all that breathes." The broadcast, produced by Orson Welles, revealed the power of radio at a time when many Americans received fast-breaking news over the airwaves.

The New Deal **685**

of ordinary Americans at work. One artist, Robert Gwathmey, recalled the importance of these efforts.

NOW & THEN

THE WPA MURALS
In the recent past, Americans have taken renewed interest in the murals created under the WPA arts project. Recognizing the historical significance of this art, restoration specialists have begun to renovate some of the murals that had deteriorated.

A number of these are on the walls of schools, post offices, and other public buildings. Some murals, such as the paintings in San Francisco's Coit Tower, have remained in relatively good shape. The Coit murals, which show average citizens performing various jobs, from farming to factory work, are meant to honor the American worker.

A PERSONAL VOICE
The director of the Federal Art Project was Edward Bruce. He was a friend of the Roosevelts—from a polite family—who was a painter. He was a man of real broad vision. He insisted there be no restrictions. You were a painter: Do your work. You were a sculptor: Do your work. You were a printmaker: Do your work. . . . That was a very free and happy period. Social comment was in the wind.
ROBERT GWATHMEY, quoted in an interview with Studs Terkel

During the New Deal era, a number of American artists produced outstanding works of art. Edward Hopper, a New York painter, depicted scenes of urban life in a striking, highly realistic style. Other artists, such as Thomas Hart Benton of Missouri, helped create a regional style of painting that drew on Midwestern cultural roots. One of the most notable of these regional artists, Iowa's **Grant Wood,** liked to say that his best ideas "came while milking a cow." Wood's work includes the famous painting *American Gothic,* which shows two stern-faced farmers, a father and daughter, standing stiffly in front of their farmhouse.

Some artists also worked for the Federal Theater Project, which was part of the WPA. Artists hired for this project provided stage sets and props for theater productions that played around the country. By 1939,

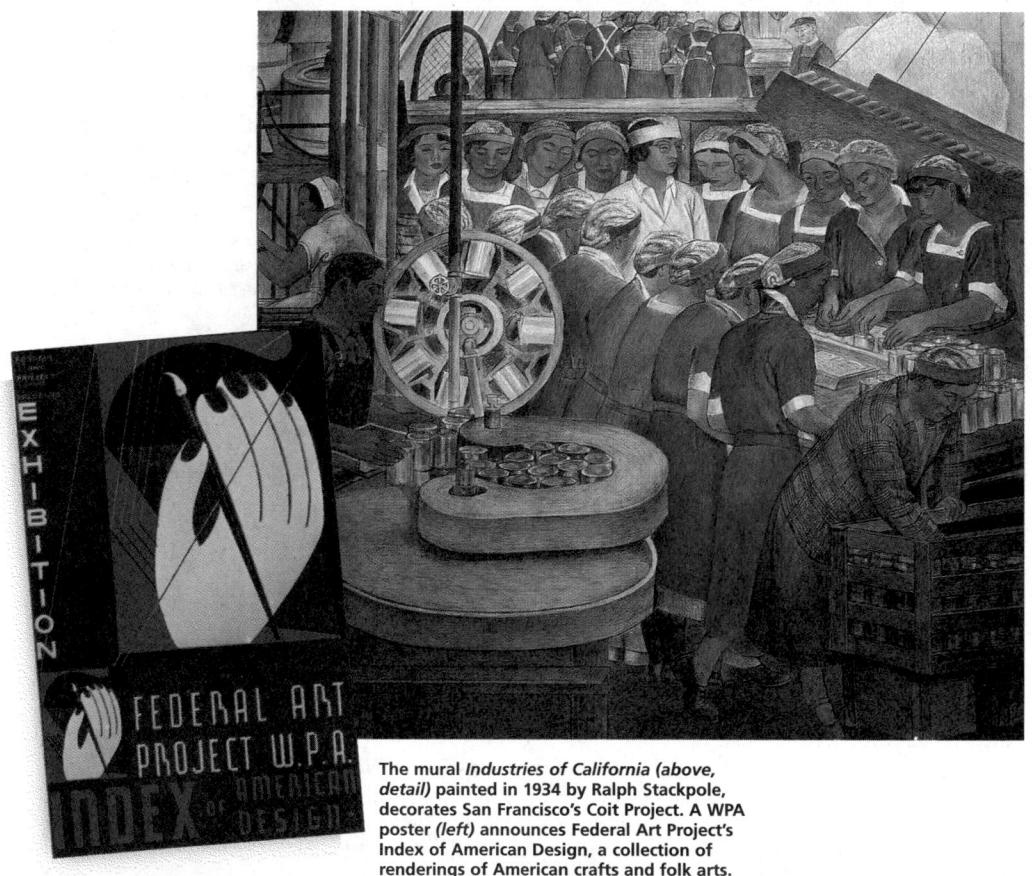

The mural *Industries of California (above, detail)* painted in 1934 by Ralph Stackpole, decorates San Francisco's Coit Project. A WPA poster *(left)* announces Federal Art Project's Index of American Design, a collection of renderings of American crafts and folk arts.

686 CHAPTER 23

TEACHING OPTIONS

Making Connections Across the Curriculum

Art Tell students that painters such as Grant Wood and Edward Hopper wanted to create a completely American style of painting. In Wood's *American Gothic,* for instance, the artist depicts the people, landscape, and architecture of the Midwest. Edward Hopper, on the other hand, found many of his subjects in urban settings. Paintings of his such as *Nighthawks* or *Early Sunday Morning* convey the loneliness and isolation of modern life.

Making Connections Across the Curriculum

Art Jackson Pollock achieved fame in the 1940s as an artist of the abstract expressionist school. Earlier, from 1929 to 1931, he had studied with the regional artist Thomas Hart Benton in New York City while receiving financial support from the WPA. In his later work, Pollock moved away from regional themes and began painting in a new style, using symbols and abstract images.

Grant Wood's painting *American Gothic* (1930) became one of the most famous portrayals of America's rural life during the Great Depression.

MORE ABOUT . . .
John Steinbeck and the Depression

When the Depression began, Steinbeck didn't lose any money. As an unemployed writer, he claimed, "I had been practicing for the Depression a long time." Fortunately for Steinbeck, his father owned a small home along the coast of northern California. The home provided Steinbeck with a place to live, and the location enabled him to obtain plenty of food. "Given the sea," he wrote, "a man must be very stupid to starve." Only one thing frightened Steinbeck—illness. "You have to have money to be sick—or did then. And dentistry also was out of the question, with the result that my teeth went badly to pieces. Without dough, you couldn't have a tooth filled."

IN-DEPTH RESOURCES: UNIT 6
Primary Source: from *Let Us Now Praise Famous Men* by James Agee and Walker Evans, p. 66

an estimated 30 million people had seen WPA theater programs, which featured noted actors such as John Houseman and Arlene Francis. The Federal Theater Project also subsidized the work of important American playwrights, including Clifford Odets, whose play *Waiting for Lefty* (1935) dramatized the labor struggles of the 1930s.

WRITERS DEPICT AMERICAN LIFE Many writers received relief support through yet another WPA program, the Federal Writers' Project (FWP). The FWP hired unemployed writers to produce a series of state and city guides and to write histories of ethnic and immigrant groups, including a major study of Southern slavery. This project also gave future Pulitzer Prize winner Saul Bellow his first writing job and helped **Richard Wright,** an African-American author, complete his acclaimed novel *Native Son* (1940). Wright's novel depicts the difficulties faced by a young man trying to survive in a racist world. Another African-American author, Zora Neale Hurston, wrote a stirring novel, *Their Eyes Were Watching God* (1937), about a young woman growing up in rural Florida.

One of this country's most famous authors, John Steinbeck, also received assistance from the Federal Writers' Project. Eventually, Steinbeck was able to publish his epic novel ***The Grapes of Wrath*** (1939), which reveals the lives of Oklahomans who left the Dust Bowl and ended up in California, where their hardships continued. Before his success, however, Steinbeck endured the difficulties of the Depression like most other writers. In an essay, he recalled his experience.

C. Answer Writers depicted the difficulties of the Depression Era, such as the Dust Bowl, working-class life, violence and poverty, small-town life in New England, and life in urban America.

THINK THROUGH HISTORY
C. Analyzing Issues How did literature of the time reflect issues of the Depression?

> **A PERSONAL VOICE**
> Being without a job, I went on writing—books, essays, short stories. Regularly they went out and just as regularly came back. Even if they had been good, they would have come back because publishers were hardest hit of all. When people are broke, the first things they give up are books. . . . It's not easy to go on writing constantly with little hope that anything will come of it. But I do remember it as a time of warmth and mutual caring. If [a friend] got hurt or ill or in trouble, the others rallied with what they had. Everyone shared bad fortune as well as good.
> **JOHN STEINBECK,** in *I Remember the Thirties*

The New Deal **687**

TEACHING OPTIONS

Making Connections Across the Curriculum

Literature Have groups of students select and read a work of fiction or nonfiction written during the Depression. Books they might read include *The Grapes of Wrath* by John Steinbeck, *Native Son* by Richard Wright, a volume from James T. Farrell's Studs Lonigan trilogy, or a volume from John Dos Passos's trilogy, *U.S.A.* Then have group members engage in a discussion of the book to prepare for an oral report. The group discussion should produce a number of points about the book that can be presented to the class.

Making Connections Across Cultures

The African-American Experience Point out that African-American authors, such as Richard Wright and Zora Neale Hurston, wrote about the racial injustice of the 1930s and 1940s. During this time, discrimination was openly practiced and instances of lynchings were on the rise. In *Native Son,* Wright suggested that an environment of injustice and racial hatred could force young African Americans into a life of crime.

Teacher's Edition **687**

Section 4 Assessment

Have students answer the questions and then note which ones gave them the most trouble.

Self-Assessment

To document what they have learned, students should list the insights they've gained on the impact of motion pictures, radio, art, and literature during the 1930s.

Section Quiz

FORMAL ASSESSMENT
Section Quiz, p. 283

Reteach

Use the graphic in item 2 of the Section Assessment to review the material. Copy the graphic onto the chalkboard, and ask for students to volunteer names to fill in the chart.

Let
Us
Now
Praise
Famous Men

JAMES AGEE
WALKER EVANS

Walker Evans took this photograph of a sharecropper for the influential book *Let Us Now Praise Famous Men*.

Other books and authors also examined the difficulties of life during the 1930s. James T. Farrell's Studs Lonigan trilogy (1932–35) provides a bleak picture of working-class life in an Irish neighborhood of Chicago. A three-part work by John Dos Passos, *U.S.A.* (1930–36), draws a detailed portrait of 20th-century American history. In Dos Passos's view, much of the country's promise was being destroyed by a small class of rich and powerful people driven by selfish interests, without regard for the nation as a whole. Jack Conroy's novel *The Disinherited* (1933) portrays the violence and poverty of the Missouri coalfields, where Conroy's own father and brother died in a mine disaster.

While some writers focused on the dark side of American life, others found hope in the positive values of American culture. The writer James Agee and the photographer Walker Evans collaborated on a book about Alabama sharecroppers, *Let Us Now Praise Famous Men* (1941). Though it deals with the difficult lives of poor farmers, this book portrays the dignity and strength of character in the people it presents. The play *Our Town* (1938), by Thornton Wilder, captures the warmth and beauty of small-town life in New England. William Saroyan's play *The Time of Your Life* (1939) offers a tender look at a diverse assortment of characters in urban America.

By the late 1930s, artists such as Horace Pippin and Anna "Grandma" Moses and writers such as Margaret Mitchell and Carl Sandburg had embraced a cultural nationalism. Although these intellectuals recognized that the United States had its flaws, they also praised the virtues of American life and took pride in the nation's cultural traditions and accomplishments. These artists and writers contributed positively to the New Deal legacy.

D. Answer It did both. Some books revealed the seamy side of American society, while others extolled the virtues of American culture. On the whole, however, most writers seemed to appreciate the underlying strength of American life.

THINK THROUGH HISTORY
D. Synthesizing Did literature during the 1930s present a positive or negative view of American society? Explain.

Section 4 Assessment

1. TERMS & NAMES

Identify:
• *Gone with the Wind*
• Orson Welles
• Grant Wood
• Richard Wright
• *The Grapes of Wrath*

2. SUMMARIZING Using a four-column chart, such as the one below, list three important movie stars, radio performers, painters, and writers from the 1930s.

Movie Stars	Radio Stars	Painters	Writers
1.	1.	1.	1.
2.	2.	2.	2.
3.	3.	3.	3.

What contribution did each group make?

3. HYPOTHESIZING What type of movies do you think might have been produced if the government had supported moviemaking as part of the New Deal? Use evidence from the chapter to support your response.

THINK ABOUT
• the role entertainment played in the 1930s
• the variety of movies made during the New Deal years
• the subject matter of New Deal literature and art

4. ANALYZING CAUSES In your opinion, what were the main benefits of government support for art and literature in the 1930s? Support your response with details from the text.

THINK ABOUT
• the experiences of Americans in the Depression and New Deal years
• the writers who got their start through the FWP
• the subject matter of WPA murals and other New Deal art

688 Chapter 23

ANSWERS

1. TERMS & NAMES

Gone with the Wind, p. 684

Orson Welles, p. 685

Grant Wood, p. 686

Richard Wright, p. 687

The Grapes of Wrath, p. 687

2. SUMMARIZING

Possible Answers: **Movie Stars:** Greta Garbo, Clark Gable, Marlene Dietrich, James Cagney, Vivien Leigh, Fred Astaire, Ginger Rogers, Edward G. Robinson. **Radio Stars:** George Burns, Gracie Allen, Bob Hope, Jack Benny. **Painters:** Edward Hopper, Thomas Hart Benton, Grant Wood. **Writers:** Richard Wright, Zora Neale Hurston, James T. Farrell, John Steinbeck, John Dos Passos, Thornton Wilder.

3. HYPOTHESIZING

Possible Responses: Perhaps more films that focused on social and political accomplishments such as *Mr. Smith Goes to Washington;* perhaps documentary films about the Depression or the Dust Bowl, or about difficulties faced by African Americans (such as those Richard Wright wrote about); perhaps films that incorporated New Deal ideals with popular film techniques.

4. ANALYZING CAUSES

Possible Responses: It allowed writers to produce serious literature that told about the difficulties endured by people in the 1930s; it left a written and pictorial legacy of the 1930s that enabled future generations to understand what happened then; it gave a gift to all Americans by providing great writers and artists the opportunity to create; it made the arts available to everyone.

5 The Impact of the New Deal

TERMS & NAMES
- deficit spending
- National Labor Relations Board
- parity
- Securities and Exchange Commission
- Federal Deposit Insurance Corporation
- Tennessee Valley Authority

LEARN ABOUT the effects of New Deal reforms
TO UNDERSTAND the short-term and long-term impact of the New Deal on American society.

ONE AMERICAN'S STORY

George Dobbin staunchly supported Franklin Delano Roosevelt and his New Deal policies. A cotton-mill worker, Dobbin was interviewed at age 67 for a book compiled by the Federal Writers' Project. This book, entitled *These Are Our Lives,* presents the experiences of ordinary Americans during the Depression. In the interview, Dobbin explained his feelings about President Roosevelt.

A PERSONAL VOICE
I do think that Roosevelt is the biggest-hearted man we ever had in the White House. . . . It's the first time in my recollection that a President ever got up and said, "I'm interested in and aim to do somethin' for the workin' man." Just knowin' that for once . . . [there] was a man to stand up and speak for him, a man that could make what he felt so plain nobody could doubt he meant it, has made a lot of us feel a sight [lot] better even when . . . [there] wasn't much to eat in our homes.

GEORGE DOBBIN, quoted in *These Are Our Lives*

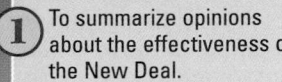

A coal miner, Zeno Santinello, shakes hands with Franklin D. Roosevelt as he campaigns in Elm Grove, West Virginia, in 1932.

Although not all people shared Dobbin's opinion of FDR, the president was extremely popular among working-class Americans. Far more important than his personal popularity, however, was the impact of the policies he initiated. Even today, reforms begun under the New Deal continue to influence American politics and society.

New Deal Reforms That Endure

During his second term in office, President Roosevelt hinted at plans to launch a Third New Deal to build on the achievements of his first four years in office. In his inaugural address, the president exclaimed, "I see millions of families trying to live on incomes so meager that the pall of family disaster hangs over them day by day. I see one-third of a nation ill-housed, ill-clad, ill-nourished."

Nevertheless, by 1937, the economy had improved enough to convince many Americans that the Depression was finally ending. Industrial production had returned to 1929 levels, and unemployment had fallen to 14 percent—still high, but much lower than in the early 1930s. Although economic troubles still plagued the nation, President Roosevelt faced rising pressure from Congress to scale back on New Deal programs, which he did. As a result, industrial production dropped again and unemployment rose from a level of about 7 million early in 1937 to 11 million early in 1938. FDR did not like **deficit spending**—spending more money than the government receives in revenue. Therefore, he never launched a third reform era. By 1939, the New Deal was effectively over and President Roosevelt was increasingly concerned with events in Europe—particularly Hitler's rise to power in Germany.

SUPPORTERS AND CRITICS OF THE NEW DEAL Over time, opinions about the New Deal have ranged from harsh criticism to high praise. Most conservatives think President Roosevelt's policies made the federal government too large and too powerful by involving government agencies in the nation's finances, agriculture, industries, and housing. They believe the government has stifled free enterprise and individual initiative. Liberal critics, in contrast, argue that President

THINK THROUGH HISTORY
A. Analyzing
Why did industrial production drop again and unemployment go up again in 1938?

A. Answer
Because, in response to pressure from Congress, FDR cut back on New Deal programs

The New Deal **689**

Section 5 Overview

OBJECTIVES
1. To summarize opinions about the effectiveness of the New Deal.
2. To describe the legacies of the New Deal.

SKILLBUILDERS
- Interpreting charts, p. 691

CRITICAL THINKING
- Analyzing, p. 689
- Recognizing effects, pp. 691, 693
- Contrasting, p. 692
- Summarizing, p. 693
- Forming an opinion, p. 693
- Evaluating, p. 693

FOCUS & MOTIVATE

▶ *Starting with the Student*
Ask students what effect, if any, they think government policies have on them. Then ask them if they think government should do more to help people or should do less.

OBJECTIVE
1 **INSTRUCT**

New Deal Reforms That Endure

▶ *Discussing Key Ideas*
- Opinions about the New Deal range from harsh criticism to high praise.
- New Deal policies have a lasting effect on labor, agriculture, and banking and finance.

IN-DEPTH RESOURCES: UNIT 6
Guided Reading, p. 57
Geography Application: Decade of the Democrats, p. 59

ACCESS FOR STUDENTS ACQUIRING ENGLISH
Guided Reading (Spanish), p. 227

SECTION 5 RESOURCES

 PRINT RESOURCES

IN-DEPTH RESOURCES: UNIT 6
Guided Reading, p. 57
Geography Application: Decade of the Democrats, p. 59
Outline Map: Anatomy of the Tennessee Valley Authority, p. 61

ACCESS FOR STUDENTS ACQUIRING ENGLISH
Guided Reading (Spanish), p. 227
Geography Application: Decade of the Democrats (Spanish), p. 229
Outline Map: Anatomy of the Tennessee Valley Authority (Spanish), p. 231

FORMAL ASSESSMENT
Section Quiz, p. 284

ALTERNATIVE ASSESSMENT BOOK
See forms for supporting and scoring alternative activities.

TECHNOLOGY RESOURCES

CRITICAL THINKING TRANSPARENCIES
CT23, The New Deal
CT57, The U.S. Economic Indicators: 1929–1939

CD-ROM
Grolier Multimedia Encyclopedia

VIDEO
American Portfolio: A Videodisc for U.S. History
user's guide, p. 207

INTERNET McDougal Littell Learning On-Line
http://www.mcdougallittell.com

▶ **Starting with the Student**
Ask students to name a recent controversy in the news about the usefulness of a particular government program (such as welfare, affirmative action, or Social Security).

• Have students benefited from any government programs?
• Do they think government is the problem, the solution, or neither?

▶ *Discussing Key Ideas*
• Supporters of the New Deal believe it helped the nation recover from economic crisis and established a necessary role for government in ensuring the economic stability of the nation.
• Conservative critics of the New Deal believe it made government's role in the economy too intrusive, whereas liberal critics say The New Deal didn't go far enough in establishing economic and social equality.

 CRITICAL THINKING TRANSPARENCIES
CT23, The New Deal
CT57, The U.S. Economic Indicators: 1929–1939

Roosevelt didn't do enough to socialize the economy and to eliminate social and economic inequalities. The nation still had only a few very rich people and an enormous number of poor people. Supporters of the New Deal contend, however, that the president struck a reasonable balance between two extremes—unregulated capitalism and overregulated socialism—and helped the country recover from its economic difficulties. Rexford Tugwell, one of President Roosevelt's top advisers, made this assessment of the president's goals.

A PERSONAL VOICE
He had in mind a comprehensive welfare concept, infused with a stiff tincture of morality. . . . He wanted all Americans to grow up healthy and vigorous and to be practically educated. He wanted business men to work within a set of understood rules. Beyond this he wanted people free to vote, to worship, to behave as they wished so long as a moral code was respected; and he wanted officials to behave as though office were a public trust.
REXFORD TUGWELL, quoted in *Redeeming the Time*

POINT ⟩ **COUNTERPOINT**

"The New Deal . . . transformed the way American government works."

Supporters of the New Deal believe it was successful. Many historians and journalists make this judgment by using the economic criterion of creating jobs. The editors of *The New Republic*, for example, noted in an editorial published in 1940 that the shortcomings of the WPA "are insignificant beside the gigantic fact that it has given jobs and sustenance to a minimum of 1,400,000 and a maximum 3,300,000 persons for five years."

Some historians stress that the New Deal was more than a temporary solution to a crisis. Professor David Bennett claims about the New Deal that "beyond . . . its relief and recovery programs lay its larger achievement, the recognition that social and economic problems in this great nation required national political solutions and national political responsibility, that the old order would not and could not work any more." Professor A. A. Berle states that "human beings cannot indefinitely be sacrificed by the millions to the operation of economic forces."

Historian William E. Leuchtenburg argues that the New Deal "should be recognized as a series of imaginative initiatives and programs that helped innumerable Americans during the Great Depression and transformed the way American government works."

Pulitzer prize–winning historian Allan Nevins sums up the importance of New Deal measures by pointing out that "the resourcefulness of the New Deal marks a fundamental shift in which the government assumed a greater responsibility for ensuring economic prosperity for all Americans."

"Many more problems have been created than solved by the New Deal."

Critics of the New Deal believe that it did not succeed in reaching its goals. Reporting on the New Deal when it was implemented, journalists Benjamin Stolberg and Warren Jay Vinton accused the New Deal of "trying to right the unbalance of our economic life by strengthening all its contradictions." They go on to claim, "In trying to move in every direction at once the New Deal betrays the fact that it has no policy."

Historian Barton J. Bernstein accepted the goals of the New Deal but declared that they were never met. He claimed that the New Deal "failed to raise the impoverished, it failed to redistribute income, [and] it failed to extend equality."

In Senator Robert A. Taft's opinion, "many more problems have been created than solved" by the New Deal. He maintained that "whatever else has resulted from the great increase in government activity . . . it has certainly had the effect of checking private enterprise completely. This country was built up by the constant establishment of new business and the expansion of old business. . . . In the last six years this process has come to an end because of government regulation and the development of a tax system which penalizes hard work and success. Senator Taft claimed that "government competition with private industry should be confined to its present limits. . . . The government should gradually withdraw from the business of lending money and leave that function to private capital under proper regulation." Taft insisted that he was "convinced that we can restore prosperity. . . . It can be done, but it cannot be done by government regulation of agriculture and commerce and industry."

INTERACT WITH HISTORY

1. **COMPARING AND CONTRASTING** In what ways did the New Deal succeed? In what ways did it fail? Reread the article and summarize the main points.
 SEE SKILLBUILDER HANDBOOK, PAGE 1041.

2. **RESEARCHING THE WPA** Research the various programs of the WPA and draft a proposal for a WPA-type program that would especially benefit your community.
 For more information about the New Deal click on *Social Studies,* http://www.mcdougallittell.com

---

INTERACT WITH HISTORY

1. Comparing and Contrasting

Possible Responses:

The New Deal succeeded in creating jobs; it gave national government a greater role in solving social and economic problems; it took measures to help ensure economic prosperity.

The New Deal failed because it created more problems than it solved; it gave government too intrusive a role in economic matters; it did not redistribute income, reduce poverty, or extend equality.

2. Researching the WPA

Standards for Evaluation
Proposals should . . .

• present details and examples of a specific program
• identify ways in which the program would benefit the community
• list various kinds of public works
• make practical suggestions for addressing problems in the community
• be well organized and clearly written

EXPANDING GOVERNMENT'S ROLE IN THE ECONOMY The Roosevelt administration expanded the power of the federal government, giving it, and particularly the president, a more active role in shaping the economy. It did this by infusing the nation's economy with millions of dollars, by creating federal jobs, by attempting to regulate supply and demand, and by increasing the government's active participation in settling labor and management disputes. The federal government established agencies, such as the Federal Deposit Insurance Corporation and the Securities and Exchange Commission, to regulate banking and investment activities. Although the New Deal did not end the Depression, it did help reduce the suffering of thousands of men, women, and children by providing jobs, food, and money. It also gave people hope and helped them to regain a sense of dignity.

The federal government had to go deeply in debt to provide jobs and aid to the American people. As the chart on this page shows, the federal deficit increased to $2.9 billion in 1934 and then rose to $3.6 billion in 1936. After the cutbacks in federal spending that the president made in 1938, the deficit dropped to $2.1 billion. This was still high compared to the deficit of only $461 million in 1932. What really ended the Depression was the massive amount of spending by the federal government for guns, tanks, ships, airplanes, and all the other equipment and supplies the country needed for the World War II effort. This spending sent the nation's deficit to new heights.

THE LABOR FRONT One of the areas in which New Deal policies have had a lasting effect is the protection of workers' rights. Before the New Deal, workers were typically on their own when seeking a fair contract from employers. Indeed, the government tended to side with the interests of business against the interests of labor. New Deal legislation, such as the Wagner Act and the Fair Labor Standards Act, changed that pattern by setting standards for wages and hours, banning child labor, and ensuring the right of workers to organize and bargain collectively with employers. Today, the **National Labor Relations Board,** created under the Wagner Act, continues to act as a mediator in labor disputes between unions and employers.

ECONOMIC BACKGROUND

DEFICIT SPENDING
John Maynard Keynes, an influential British economist, promoted the idea of deficit spending to stimulate economic recovery. In his view, a country in the grip of a depression should spend its way out of it by putting money into the hands of consumers. This would make it possible for them to buy goods and services and thus fuel economic growth. Therefore, even if a government has to go deeply into debt, it should spend great amounts of money to help get the economy growing again.

Although President Roosevelt agreed to the policy that Keynes advocated, he did so with great reluctance. FDR was a firm believer in balanced budgets. He regarded deficit spending as a necessary evil to be used only at a time of great economic crisis.

THINK THROUGH HISTORY
B. *Recognizing Effects* What impact did the New Deal have on the federal government?

B. Answer It increased the size and power of government in many areas of American life.

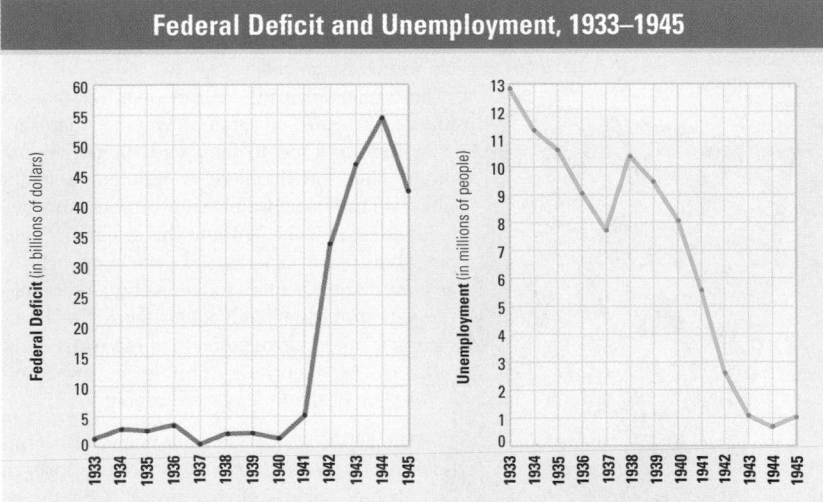

Federal Deficit and Unemployment, 1933–1945

Skillbuilder Answer Peak year 1944. There is higher unemployment when there is less deficit spending and lower unemployment when there is more deficit spending. This happens because the deficit spending results in more jobs.

SKILLBUILDER INTERPRETING CHARTS *What was the peak year of the deficit? What relationship does there seem to be between deficit spending and unemployment? Why do you think so?*

The New Deal **691**

ECONOMIC BACKGROUND
Deficit Spending
Critical Thinking: Analyzing Ask students whether they think the Roosevelt administration was justified in using deficit spending to stimulate the economy. If they say it wasn't justified, ask them what other measures the government should have taken to end the Depression.

MORE ABOUT . . .
John Maynard Keynes
In Herbert Hoover's indictment of his successor's New Deal, he wrote: "I vetoed the idea of recovery through stupendous spending to prime the pump. That was born of a British professor." The British professor Hoover referred to was John Maynard Keynes. Keynes was one of the most influential economists of the first half of the 20th century.

HISTORY FROM VISUALS
Federal Deficit and Unemployment, 1933–1945
Reading the Graph Help students to see the inverse relationship between deficit spending and unemployment—as deficit spending goes up, the unemployment rate goes down.

Extension Have students draw these graphs on a sheet of paper, superimposing one on top of the other to emphasize the point that as the deficit went up, the unemployment rate went down.

TEACHING OPTION

Cooperative Activity: Debating the New Deal

Task: Teams of four to five students will take a stand on the effectiveness of the New Deal and engage in a debate with teams who support the opposing viewpoint.

Purpose: To express an informed opinion about the effectiveness of New Deal policies.

Activity: Have students form teams to investigate the effectiveness of the New Deal. Team members should first research material on both sides of the issue. Then they should have a brainstorming session in which they decide

which side of the argument they want to make. Next, they should prepare an argument defending their case. Students should use sound reasoning, facts, and examples to support their argument. They should also be prepared to counter or concede valid points raised by the opposition. Pair opposing teams and conduct the debates in class.

ALTERNATIVE ASSESSMENT BOOK
Standards for Evaluating a Cooperative Activity

Critical Thinking:
Evaluating Ask students whether they think the Social Security system should be changed, and if so, how.

Continuing Benefits

▶ *Starting with the Student*
Have students create a three-column chart showing the continuing benefits of the New Deal. Students should compare FDR's original policies on Social Security, the environment, and labor with the policies pursued today. Students might list the information in a chart like this:

	Then	Now
Social Security		
Environment		
Labor		

▶ *Discussing Key Ideas*
• Under the New Deal, the federal government assumes some responsibility for the social welfare of its citizens.
• The New Deal promotes policies designed to protect the environment.

IN-DEPTH RESOURCES: UNIT 6
Outline Map: Anatomy of the Tennessee Valley Authority, p. 61

GROLIER MULTIMEDIA ENCYCLOPEDIA
History of the Tennessee Valley Authority

THE RURAL SCENE New Deal policies also had a significant impact on the nation's agriculture. New Deal farm legislation set quotas on crop production, such as wheat, to control surpluses. Under the second Agricultural Adjustment Act, passed in 1938, farmers stored their crops until prices reached **parity**—a price equal to what farmers had received in the years between 1910 and 1914. Establishing price supports for farmers set a precedent of federal aid to farmers that continued into the 1990s. Other government programs, such as electrification, helped to improve conditions in rural America.

BANKING AND FINANCE By subsidizing farmers and setting minimum wages for workers, New Deal legislation had a very important effect on the nation's economy. More people had more money to spend and so the economy began to recover.

New Deal programs established new policies in the area of banking and finance. The **Securities and Exchange Commission** (SEC), created in 1934, continues to monitor the stock market and enforce laws regarding the sale of stocks and bonds. The **Federal Deposit Insurance Corporation** (FDIC), created by the Glass-Steagall Banking Act of 1933, has shored up the banking system by reassuring individual depositors that their savings are protected against loss in the event of a bank failure. Today, individual accounts in United States federal banks are insured by the Federal Deposit Insurance Corporation for up to $100,000.

Continuing Benefits

New Deal economic and financial reforms, including creation of the FDIC, the SEC, and Social Security, have helped to stabilize the nation's finances and economy. Although the nation still experiences economic downturns known as recessions, people's savings are insured and they can receive unemployment compensation.

SOCIAL SECURITY One of the most important legacies of the New Deal has been that the federal government has assumed some responsibility for the social welfare of its citizens. This philosophy represented a major departure from the traditional attitude that churches and private charities were the only institutions that should help care for the needy. Under President Roosevelt, the government undertook to create a Social Security system that would help a large number of needy Americans receive some assistance.

The Social Security Act provides an old-age insurance program, an unemployment compensation system, and aid to families with dependent children and the disabled. It has had a major impact on the lives of millions of Americans since its founding in 1935. Without this aid, many people would have experienced severe poverty or neglect. The income to laid-off workers has helped to cushion individuals from the hardships of unemployment. For most Americans, the Social Security system is an important function of the federal government.

THE ENVIRONMENT Americans also continue to benefit from New Deal efforts to protect the environment. President Roosevelt was highly committed to conservation and promoted policies designed to

---

NOW & THEN

SOCIAL SECURITY

Today the Social Security system continues to rely on mandatory contributions. A percentage of money is taken from workers' paychecks and from their employers. This money is invested in a trust fund, from which retirement benefits are then paid. Several problems, however, have surfaced. One problem is that Americans are now living longer than they did in 1935. Also, the ratio of workers to retirees is shrinking: fewer people are contributing to the system relative to the number who are receiving benefits. In addition, benefits under Social Security have been expanded. Today, the system includes Medicare benefits, which provide health care for the elderly.

The long-range payment of benefits may be in jeopardy because of the large number of recipients. Many people believe the system should be carefully examined and probably changed.

A Social Security poster proclaims the benefits of the system for those who are 65 or older.

A monthly check to you—

FOR THE REST OF YOUR LIFE — BEGINNING WHEN YOU ARE 65

C. Answer The government began accepting responsibility for providing assistance to needy members of society, whereas the traditional attitude was that private institutions should take care of those in need.

THINK THROUGH HISTORY
C. Contrasting
How did the Social Security system represent a change from past policies?

Exploring Themes

Economic Opportunity Tell students that recessions are part of the business cycle, the continual rise and fall in business activity. Tell them that a recession is caused by a decline in business activity. Point out that during a recession, people buy and sell less and unemployment rises. Discuss with students how some of the programs established under the New Deal, such as the FDIC, the SEC, and Social Security, have helped to soften the economic impact of recession on the lives of people. Ask them if they think government should play a role in protecting citizens from the economic impact of a recession.

Teaching Less Proficient Readers

Clarifying Ideas To help less proficient readers understand the main ideas in this section, pair them with more proficient readers and have the pairs follow these steps:

1. Read pages 692–693 together.
2. After students finish reading, have them make a list of the continuing benefits of the New Deal.
3. List what they want to find out about these continuing benefits.
4. Review pages 692–693 and write down what they have found out about each benefit.

protect the nation's natural resources. As a result, the Civilian Conservation Corps planted trees, created hiking trails, and built fire lookout towers. Also, the Soil Conservation Service taught farmers how to conserve the soil through contour plowing, terracing, and crop rotation. The New Deal also passed the Taylor Grazing Act in 1934 to help reduce grazing on public lands. Such grazing had contributed to the erosion that brought about the dust storms in the 1930s.

The **Tennessee Valley Authority** harnessed water power to provide hydroelectric power and to help prevent disastrous floods in the Tennessee Valley. During the New Deal, the government also added to the national park system. Kings Canyon Park in California, Olympic National Park in Washington, and Shenandoah National Park in Virginia, all became national parks during the 1930s. The New Deal also established new wildlife refuges and set aside large wilderness areas to be excluded from development.

The New Deal, however, did not have a spotless record on the environment. The Roosevelt administration contributed to air, water, and land pollution. For example, the TVA polluted the Tennessee Valley region by engaging in strip mining to get coal for its coal-burning generators. The strip mining caused soil erosion, and the burning of the coal increased air pollution. The TVA also caused water pollution by dumping untreated sewage and toxic chemicals from its strip-mining operations into the region's rivers and streams.

The New Deal legacy has many dimensions. It has brought hope and gratitude from some people for the benefits they receive. It has also brought anger and criticism from those who believe that it has taken more of their money in taxes and curtailed their freedom through increased government regulations. The deficit spending necessary to fund New Deal programs grew immensely as the nation entered into World War II.

D. Answer They benefited the environment with new trees, hiking trails, fire lookouts, soil conservation, flood control, and national parks, wildlife refuges, and wilderness areas. They harmed it with air, water, and land pollution.

THINK THROUGH HISTORY
D. Recognizing Efforts How did New Deal programs benefit and harm the environment?

Paul Sample, an artist who received funding from the WPA, painted the Tennessee Valley Authority's Norris Dam in 1935.

Section 5 Assessment

1. **TERMS & NAMES**
   - deficit spending
   - National Labor Relations Board
   - parity
   - Securities and Exchange Commission
   - Federal Deposit Insurance Corporation
   - Tennessee Valley Authority

2. **SUMMARIZING** In a cluster diagram like the one below, show long-term benefits of the New Deal.

New Deal's long-term benefits

Which long-term benefit do you think has had the most impact? Why?

3. **FORMING AN OPINION** Some critics have charged that the New Deal was anti-business and anti-free enterprise. Explain why you agree or disagree with this charge.

THINK ABOUT
   - the expanded power of the federal government
   - the New Deal's effect on the economy
   - the New Deal's effect on the American people

4. **EVALUATING** How successful do you think Franklin Roosevelt was as a president? Support your answer with details from the text.

THINK ABOUT
   - the condition of the country when he took office
   - the short- and long-term impact of his policies
   - his popularity with working-class Americans

The New Deal **693**

ASSESS & RETEACH

Section 5 Assessment
Have students answer the questions and then compare their answers with each other.

Self-Assessment
To document what they have learned, students should list the insights they've gained regarding the impact of New Deal policies and reforms on society today.

Section Quiz
FORMAL ASSESSMENT
Section Quiz, p. 284

Reteach
Use the Point/Counterpoint feature on page 690 to review the central issue of the New Deal legacy—the role of government in people's lives.

CLOSE

New Deal policies have had long-term effects on labor, banking and finance, social welfare, and the environment. However, opinion is divided on the success of the New Deal. Some people praised the New Deal's creation of jobs and the greater role of government in solving problems, while others denounced the deficit spending used to fund its programs—spending that would increase even more during World War II.

ANSWERS

1. TERMS & NAMES

deficit spending, p. 689

National Labor Relations Board, p. 691

parity, p. 692

Securities and Exchange Commission, p. 692

Federal Deposit Insurance Corporation, p. 692

Tennessee Valley Authority, p. 693

2. SUMMARIZING

Possible Responses: National Labor Relations Board still mediates labor disputes; Federal Deposit Insurance Corporation insures accounts up to $100,000; Securities and Exchange Commission continues to monitor the stock market; Social Security still provides assistance to senior citizens, people with disabilities, families with dependent children, and the unemployed; the New Deal protected wilderness areas.

3. FORMING AN OPINION

Possible Responses: Agree: Students might argue that the New Deal weakened free enterprise and business profits by increasing regulations, taxes, union membership, and wages. Disagree: Students might argue that increased government spending, the improved economy, the resurgence of hope, and more prosperous consumers all aided free enterprise and helped businesses prosper.

4. EVALUATING

Possible Responses: Students might argue that Roosevelt's spirit, vision, array of programs, and concern for common people helped him deal with the problems of the Depression and made him a success. Others may criticize him for not having given strong support to minorities and the very poor. Still others may say that his increasing the size of the federal government had negative long-term consequences.

OBJECTIVES

(1) To describe the federal government's role and achievement in establishing the
Tennessee Valley Authority.

(2) To summarize benefits of the
TVA to the Tennessee Valley
region.

**FOCUS &
MOTIVATE**

▶ *Starting with the Student*
Ask students whether the
electric power they use in
their homes is produced by
a private utility or by a government corporation such as
the TVA. Then ask these
questions:

• What role does electric
power play in their daily
life.

• How might improving electric power benefit an area
economically?

MORE ABOUT . . .
The Tennessee River

Before the creation of the
TVA, the Tennessee River
was subject to periodic
flooding and could not be
navigated in the area
around Muscle Shoals,
Alabama. The dams of the
TVA project helped control
flooding, saving lives and
crops and curbing soil erosion while at the same time
generating hydroelectric
power vital to industrial
development. Damming
also created "the Great
Lakes of the South," which
provided new recreational
opportunities.

The Tennessee Valley Authority

The Tennessee Valley Authority (TVA) is a federal corporation established in 1933 to construct dams and power plants
along the Tennessee River and its tributaries. The river basin
created a region or geographical area with certain characteristics in common. Rivers often create a community of interest for people living in their watersheds. TVA helped the
region in various ways: flood control, conservation of natural
resources, navigation, and the generation of electric power,
as well as agricultural and industrial development.

The Tennessee Valley covered parts of seven states.
Thus, the TVA became an enormous undertaking eventually
comprising dozens of major dams, each with associated
power plants, recreational facilities, or navigation aids.

Citizens in the Guntersville, Alabama, area determined
to take advantage of the tremendous electrical power the turbine was capable of pro-
ducing. They decided to
build a harbor, develop
the lake's recreational
possibilities, and attract
new industry with the
abundant power that
would be available.

THE TENNESSEE VALLEY

❷ **THE TVA** applied the regional
concept to the generation of
electricity. Before the 1930s,
electricity was conceived in local
terms, with a single generating
station producing power only for
its vicinity. The TVA, in contrast,
was a network of stations feeding
power into a grid.

❶ **ART AND THE TVA** Charles
Sheeler's 1939 painting *Suspended
Power* depicts an awe-inspiring
view of a huge turbine in midair
about to be lowered into place.

694 Chapter 23

RECOMMENDED RESOURCES

Books

Davidson, Donald. *The
Tennessee.* New York:
Rinehart, 1946–48. A two-vol-
ume history of the Tennessee
River, the Tennessee Valley,
and the TVA.

Duffus, R. L. *The Valley and Its
People.* New York: Knopf, 1944.
The story of the Tennessee
Valley Authority, written not
long after it was established.

*A History of the Tennessee
Valley Authority.* Knoxville:
TVA Information Office, 1983.
A history put out by the or-
ganization itself.

Hubbard, Preston J. *Origins of
the TVA.* Nashville: Vanderbilt
UP, 1961. The Tennessee Valley
Authority and the Muscle
Shoals controversy that helped
create it.

Videos

The Electric Valley. Dir. Ross
Spears. The James Agee Film
Project, 1984. The 50-year
history of the Tennessee Valley
Authority.

FDR. Dir. John Alan Kane. A&E
Home Video, 1995.

③ KENTUCKY DAM, over a mile and a half long and 206 feet high, turns the Tennessee River into Kentucky Lake, a paradise for fishing, 185 miles long.

④ THE CUMBERLAND RIVER has a similar series of dams operated by the Corps of Engineers. This system cooperated with the TVA.

⑤ OAK RIDGE, TENNESSEE, became the center for the Manhattan Project in August 1942. This top-secret operation developed the atomic bomb. In 1948, the Tennessee facilities became the Oak Ridge National Laboratory. The original legislation creating TVA included national defense in its list of purposes.

⑥ NORRIS DAM is on the Clinch River, a tributary of the Tennessee River. It is named after Senator George W. Norris of Nebraska, a progressive leader who called for government involvement in the development of the power potential of the Tennessee River.

⑦ PRESIDENT FRANKLIN D. ROOSEVELT was credited by Senator Norris with having a broader vision of regional development than even those who originally proposed the idea. As a good geographer, he saw how conservation, economic development, recreation, agriculture, and industry were interrelated for people who lived in a valley.

Map labels: Ohio River, KENTUCKY, WEST VIRGINIA, Kentucky Dam, Paducah, Cumberland River, Clinch River, VIRGINIA, Nashville, Duck River, Norris Dam, Holston Dam, Cherokee Dam, Oak Ridge, Knoxville, Great Smoky Mountain National Park, NORTH CAROLINA, Watts Bar Dam, Fort Loudoun Dam, TENNESSEE, Chickamauga Dam, Asheville, Pickwick Landing Dam, Wheeler Dam, Nickajack Dam, Chattanooga, Wilson Dam, Huntsville, SOUTH CAROLINA, Guntersville Dam, GEORGIA, ALABAMA

Tennessee River watershed
Region served by TVA
Dam

0   100 Miles
0   200 Kilometers

⑧ 1996 OLYMPICS One of the events of the 1996 Summer Olympics featured kayaks negotiating the turbulent waters of the Tennessee River basin.

INTERACT WITH HISTORY

1. **DRAWING CONCLUSIONS** In what ways did the Tennessee Valley Authority benefit the region of the Tennessee River basin?

   SEE SKILLBUILDER HANDBOOK, PAGE 1037.

2. **LOOKING AT A REGION** With your class, prepare a list of subjects for an artistic portrayal of a region in which you live. Tell how changes in the region have improved the area.

   INTERNET For more about the TVA, click on *Social Studies* at http://www.mcdougallittell.com

The New Deal **695**

REVIEWING
THE CHAPTER

TERMS & NAMES

1. Franklin Delano Roosevelt, p. 664
2. New Deal, p. 665
3. Eleanor Roosevelt, p. 671
4. Works Progress Administration, p. 673
5. Social Security Act, pp. 675–676
6. Mary McLeod Bethune, p. 678
7. Congress of Industrial Organizations, p. 681
8. Orson Welles, p. 685
9. Richard Wright, p. 687
10. Tennessee Valley Authority, p. 693

MAIN IDEAS

11. He expanded its role in the economy through programs designed to restore confidence and provide jobs.

12. Some said it made the federal government too powerful, and others said it didn't go far enough.

13. Second Agricultural Adjustment Act, Farm Security Administration, and Rural Electrification Administration.

14. It supported the rights of workers to join unions and to bargain.

15. He appointed African Americans to office; he did not support anti-lynching laws or an end to the poll tax.

16. The Democrats supported labor legislation and work-relief programs that helped the urban poor.

17. They allowed people to escape from the grim realities of the Depression.

18. The Federal Art Project, the Federal Theater Project, and the Federal Writers' Project.

19. Possible Responses: Federal Deposit Insurance Corporation, Securities and Exchange Commission, National Labor Relations Board, Social Security system, Tennessee Valley Authority.

20. It provided flood control, hydroelectric power, jobs, conservation, recreational facilities, and navigation aids. Strip mining caused soil erosion; coal-burning generators caused air pollution; toxic chemicals from strip mining polluted rivers.

REVIEWING THE CHAPTER

TERMS & NAMES For each term below, write a sentence explaining its significance to the policies of the Roosevelt Administration. For each person below, explain his or her role in the 1930s.

1. Franklin Delano Roosevelt
2. New Deal
3. Eleanor Roosevelt
4. Works Progress Administration
5. Social Security Act
6. Mary McLeod Bethune
7. Congress of Industrial Organizations
8. Orson Welles
9. Richard Wright
10. Tennessee Valley Authority

MAIN IDEAS

SECTION 1 *(pages 664–670)*

A New Deal Fights the Depression

11. How did Franklin Roosevelt change the role of the federal government during his first Hundred Days in office?
12. Summarize the reasons why some people opposed the New Deal.

SECTION 2 *(pages 671–676)*

The Second New Deal Takes Hold

13. What federal agencies and acts assisted farmers during Roosevelt's second term?
14. How did the Wagner Act help working people?

SECTION 3 *(pages 677–682)*

The New Deal Affects Many Groups

15. Explain President Roosevelt's policies on civil rights.
16. Why did many urban voters support Roosevelt and the Democratic party?

SECTION 4 *(pages 683–688)*

Society and Culture

17. What purpose did movies and radio programs serve during the Great Depression?
18. Which New Deal programs supported artists and writers in the 1930s?

SECTION 5 *(pages 689–693)*

The Impact of the New Deal

19. List five New Deal agencies or programs that are still in place today.
20. What benefits did the Tennessee Valley Authority provide? What negative impact did it have?

THINKING CRITICALLY

1. **REACTING TO THE DEPRESSION** Copy the web below on your paper and fill it in with actions that Americans took to end the economic crisis of the 1930s.

American actions to end economic crisis

2. **A NEW DEAL TODAY** What federal programs instituted in the 1930s and later discontinued might be of use to the nation today? Explain and support your opinion.

3. **CONFRONTING FEAR** Reread the quote by Franklin Delano Roosevelt on page 662. What do you think his comment reveals about his approach to the problems of the 1930s?

4. **GEOGRAPHY OF THE TENNESSEE VALLEY** Look at the map in the Geography Spotlight feature on pages 694–695. Describe the landforms and water bodies of the area. How might the geography of the area have been different if dams had not been built?

5. **EVALUATING THE NEW DEAL** In your opinion, did the New Deal have major failings? Support your answer with details from the text.

6. **ANALYZING PRIMARY SOURCES** Read the following excerpt from *This Was America* by the French writer André Maurois, in which he describes his impressions of the United States after a tour of the country in the 1930s. Then answer the questions that follow.

> A curious unity of habits and thoughts is created by the movies, the magazines, the radio, advertising, and the newspaper chains. . . . Americans who never meet each other and who live under different skies come to have innumerable common memories and brotherly thoughts.
>
> Little by little the American federation is transforming itself into a union, marked by the growth in importance of the role of the federal capital. In the beginning, the United States had only a small federal bureaucracy. Today the central administration is powerful and rich.
>
> **ANDRÉ MAUROIS,** *This Was America*

What effect has popular culture had on the American people? How has the federal government changed?

THINKING CRITICALLY

1. REACTING TO THE DEPRESSION
Possible Responses: Voters elected Franklin Roosevelt as president; the federal government expanded its role in the economy to aid banks, farmers, workers, and the unemployed.

2. A NEW DEAL TODAY
Possible Responses: A type of NYA could help low-income students afford college; a type of WPA could be used for people who otherwise would be on welfare; the government might think about reinstituting a CCC to help deal with environmental problems, to educate people about environmental concerns, and to employ young people.

3. CONFRONTING FEAR
Possible Responses: That he is optimistic; that he will aggressively move the nation forward; that without fear, many things are possible; that if all Americans work together and are not afraid, problems will be solved; that with a bold, brave approach, the nation will have nothing to fear.

ALTERNATIVE ASSESSMENT

1. MUSIC OF THE 1930s

 The Great Depression, the New Deal, Franklin Roosevelt, movies, and radio all inspired popular songs in the 1930s. Use the CD-ROM *Our Times*, your textbook, and other sources to make a collection of five to ten songs that reflect the economic, political, or cultural events of the decade. Write a short essay explaining the significance of each song.

- Your collection of songs might include the written lyrics or recordings of performances.
- Possible sources of music include anthologies of folk songs, protest songs, and union songs; books on songwriters such as Woody Guthrie, Alfred Hayes, and Irving Berlin; and histories of culture in the 1930s.
- In your essay, analyze how each song relates to events or personalities of the 1930s.

Save your collection of songs and your essay in your American history portfolio folder.

2. LEARNING FROM MEDIA

 View the video for Chapter 23, *A Song for His People*. Discuss the following questions in small groups.

- Why did Mexican immigration to the United States increase in the early 1920s?
- Why were thousands of Mexicans sent from the United States back to Mexico in the 1930s?
- Why did Pedro J. González become a hero to many Mexican Americans and a symbol of Mexican cultural pride?

3. PORTFOLIO PROJECT

Use the Living History activity to expand your portfolio.

LIVING HISTORY

PRESENTING YOUR NEW DEAL DIARY

You have written diary entries about your New Deal experiences. Now, consider the following points as you review and assess your entries:

- Do they use vivid description?
- Do they use details that recreate the feel of the era?
- Do they provide a personal viewpoint?

Select a few diary entries to present to the class. Choose interesting selections that use vivid description and details that explain some aspect of the New Deal.

Add your diary entries to your American history portfolio.

Review Chapter 23

A NEW DEAL FIGHTS THE DEPRESSION After his landslide election in 1932, Franklin Roosevelt took office in March 1933. During his first Hundred Days, he pushed a series of bills through Congress to restore confidence in the banking and investment system, to help farmers and the needy, and to provide work for the unemployed. He faced opposition from the Supreme Court and from many critics.

THE SECOND NEW DEAL TAKES HOLD During Roosevelt's second term, Congress passed additional measures to boost the economy. The second Agricultural Adjustment Act and other measures aided farmers. The Works Progress Administration created jobs for unskilled laborers and for professionals. The Wagner Act supported the right of workers to organize unions and engage in collective bargaining. The Social Security Act of 1935 provided old age insurance, unemployment compensation, and aid to families with dependent children and to people with disabilities.

THE NEW DEAL AFFECTS MANY GROUPS The New Deal brought limited progress in the struggle for equality. While Roosevelt selected women and African Americans as key advisers, he did not push for equality in the administration of New Deal programs. Nevertheless, his popularity created a powerful political coalition for the Democrats.

SOCIETY AND CULTURE The Depression, the New Deal, and new technology reshaped how people lived, played, and thought in the 1930s. The increasing popularity of movies and radio programs, along with government-supported art and writing, made the decade a productive era in American culture.

THE IMPACT OF THE NEW DEAL The greatest impact of the New Deal was on the federal government. Since the 1930s, the government has played a significant role in the nation's economy, and some programs started in the 1930s, such as Social Security, continue to play an important role in the nation today.

Preview Chapter 24

While the United States worked to overcome the Great Depression, military conflicts were growing in Europe and Asia. The United States attempted to stay out of these conflicts, but it was eventually pulled into World War II. You will learn about the beginnings of World War II in the next chapter.

The New Deal **697**

ALTERNATIVE ASSESSMENT

1. MUSIC OF THE 1930s
Standards for Evaluation
A collection of songs and an accompanying essay should meet the following criteria:

- Provide 5–10 songs that reflect the economic, political, or cultural events of the 1930s.
- Include written lyrics or recordings.
- Explain the significance of each song.
- Connect each song to the period of the 1930s.

2. LEARNING FROM MEDIA
Answers to the questions:

- Millions of Mexicans were fleeing the violence of the Mexican Revolution, which left the economy in ruins.
- A panic for jobs during the Great Depression led to a movement to deport Mexican immigrants.
- Because of his radio show, he was a strong voice for the Mexican-American community. He dedicated his life to the struggle for justice and equality.

3. PORTFOLIO PROJECT
LIVING HISTORY
Standards for Evaluation
Diary entries should meet the following criteria:

- Use vivid description.
- Use details that help to bring the era alive.
- Provide a personal viewpoint about being gainfully employed.
- Provide details about the work experience.

IN-DEPTH RESOURCES: UNIT 6
See the form for scoring this activity on page 73.

THINKING CRITICALLY

4. GEOGRAPHY OF THE TENNESSEE VALLEY
Possible Responses: The darkest area in the center is the lowest land, the Tennessee River watershed; to the right are mountains; there are several rivers in the region; the largest rivers on the map are the Mississippi and the Ohio; some smaller rivers are the Cumberland, Duck, Tennessee, and Clinch. Without the dams, the Tennessee River would flow faster and Kentucky Lake would not have been formed.

5. EVALUATING THE NEW DEAL
Possible Responses: **Yes:** It should have instituted programs to improve civil rights and economic opportunity for African Americans and Mexican Americans; it should have ensured that the TVA's toxic wastes would not pollute the waters. **No:** It achieved important reforms in the nation's financial system, it provided relief for millions of unemployed people, and it built needed dams and other public works.

6. ANALYZING PRIMARY SOURCES
Possible Responses: Popular culture has lessened regional differences and helped to create a more uniform way of life. The federal government has grown from a small bureaucracy to a powerful and rich central government.

World War II and Its Aftermath

HISTORY AND ART

Corpsman on Saipan Helps Wounded Marine

Photograph by unknown photapherm (1944).

Art Note
Working for the military services or for news organizations, photographers often risked their lives to take pictures of all aspects of World War II. The war was also covered by film crews who shot footage for the military and for newsreel companies.

▶ *Previewing the Unit*
Unit 7 describes how militaristic dictators in Europe and Japan start a worldwide war that forces the United States to fight on two fronts. Victory leads to an uneasy peace with the Soviet Union, with the threat of nuclear war looming over the world. The economic expansion brought on by the war and the return to peace fuels a postwar economic boom and the spread of a suburb-based consumer culture.

UNIT 7

"Never in the field of human conflict was so much owed by so many to so few."

WINSTON CHURCHILL

1931–1959

World War II and Its Aftermath

①Saipan
The battle of Saipan was fought in late June 1944 in the Mariana Islands, about 1,700 miles south of Tokyo —just a few weeks after the Normandy invasion in Europe. While U.S. marines and soldiers fought on land, the navy destroyed three Japanese aircraft carriers and hundreds of planes, crippling the Japanese navy. Taking Saipan gave the Americans an island from which to launch bombing raids on Japan. Japanese Prime Minister Tojo called the battle a "great national crisis" and resigned. The new government began to accept the possibility of Japanese defeat.

②Field medicine
Medical advances and improved methods of treatment saved tens of thousands of soldiers' lives. In World War I, only 4 of every 100 wounded soldiers lived. In World War II, the number rose to 50 of every 100.

③Combat photography
Combat photographers, working at the front lines, were in just as much danger as soldiers. During the invasion of Guam, just weeks after Saipan, four marine combat photographers were killed and one was wounded.

699

4 Plasma
The effectiveness of using plasma in blood transfusions was discovered in 1939. Whole blood could not be dried without destroying red blood cells. Because plasma could be dried, it could be more easily stored and transported, making it a vital tool in battlefield medicine. Plasma is the fluid portion of blood, in which blood cells are suspended.

5 Casualties
Amphibious invasions—like that of Saipan—had higher casualties than other operations. As much as 25 percent of a landing force could be killed or wounded.

6 Camouflage
Helmet covers had green and brown coloring to hide soldiers in the jungle foliage.

7 The jungle
The fighting in the Pacific was of two kinds. Large-scale naval battles— fought primarily by aircraft carriers—took place on the high seas. Marines and army soldiers conducted a campaign of island-hopping that brought Allied forces closer and closer to Japan.

	Key Ideas	TEACHING SUPPORT	ASSESSMENT	
SECTION 1 Dictators Threaten World Peace *pp. 702–707*	The United States remains isolated from world affairs as economic and political factors lead to the rise of nationalist leaders in the Soviet Union, Germany, and Italy.	*In-Depth Resources: Unit 7* • Guided Reading, p. 1 • Primary Source: from Franklin D. Roosevelt's "Quarantine Speech," p. 8 **COOPERATIVE ACTIVITY** • Writing a Newspaper Editorial, p. 706 (TE)	*Section 1 Assessment,* p. 707 (PE) *Self-Assessment,* p. 707 (TE) *Formal Assessment* • Section Quiz, p. 293 *Alternative Assessment Book* • Standards for Evaluating a Cooperative Activity	
SECTION 2 War in Europe *pp. 708–713*	A series of bold moves by Adolf Hitler—and weak countermoves by other leaders—triggers World War II in Europe.	*In-Depth Resources: Unit 7* • Guided Reading, p. 2 • Skillbuilder Practice: Developing Historical Perspective, p. 5 **COOPERATIVE ACTIVITY** • Creating a Radio Broadcast, p. 712 (TE)	*Section 2 Assessment,* p. 713 (PE) *Self-Assessment,* p. 713 (TE) *Formal Assessment* • Section Quiz, p. 294 *Alternative Assessment Book* • Standards for Evaluating a Cooperative Activity	
SECTION 3 The Holocaust *pp. 714–718*	Hitler's plans for conquering the world include the killing of Jews and other ethnic groups, which is carried out with frightening determination and success.	*In-Depth Resources: Unit 7* • Guided Reading, p. 3 • Literature: from *Sophie's Choice* by William Styron, p. 12 • American Lives: Elie Wiesel, p. 15 **COOPERATIVE ACTIVITY** • Exploring Literature of the Holocaust, p. 716 (TE)	*Section 3 Assessment,* p. 718 (PE) *Self-Assessment,* p. 718 (TE) *Formal Assessment* • Section Quiz, p. 295 *Alternative Assessment Book* • Standards for Evaluating a Cooperative Activity	
SECTION 4 America Moves Toward War *pp. 719–725*	The United States provides aid to nations resisting Hitler and enters World War II after the bombing of Pearl Harbor.	*In-Depth Resources: Unit 7* • Guided Reading, p. 4 • Geography Application: Japanese Aggression, p. 6 • Primary Sources: The Bombing of Pearl Harbor, p. 9; War Poster, p. 11 • American Lives: Charles A. Lindbergh, p. 16 **COOPERATIVE ACTIVITY** • Creating a Political Cartoon, p. 723 (TE)	*Section 4 Assessment,* p. 725 (PE) *Self-Assessment,* p. 725 (TE) *Formal Assessment* • Section Quiz, p. 296 *Alternative Assessment Book* • Standards for Evaluating a Cooperative Activity	
CHAPTER RESOURCES	**Chapter Overview** An imperfect peace leads to the rise of brutal dictators who suppress opponents and innocent people at home and attack their neighbors. Soon the United States is plunged into worldwide war.	*In-Depth Resources: Unit 7* • Living History Project: Worksheet, p. 17; Standards, p. 18 *Telescoping the Times* • Chapter Summary, pp. 47–48 *Planning for Block Schedules*	*Chapter Assessment,* pp. 726–727 (PE) *Alternative Assessment,* p. 727 (PE) *Formal Assessment* • Chapter Test, forms A and B, pp. 297–302 **Test Generator** *Alternative Assessment Book* See explanation and forms for different kinds of alternative assessments including portfolio assessment.	

Humanities Transparencies
• H23, German Nazi Party poster

INTERNET RESOURCES
• See *McDougal Littell Learning On-Line* for links to information about Joseph Stalin and Benito Mussolini.

 Geography Transparencies
• G24, Aggression in Europe, 1936–1939

 Our Times
• Edward R. Murrow's Christmas Eve radio broadcast from London

Electronic Library of Primary Sources
• Letter to Roosevelt by Winston Churchill

INTERNET RESOURCES
• See *McDougal Littell Learning On-Line* for links to information about Winston Churchill and Charles de Gaulle.

 AMERICAN STORIES VIDEO SERIES
• "Escaping the 'Final Solution'"

 Our Times
• the Holocaust in Hungary and the Warsaw ghetto uprising
• excerpt of *The Diary of Anne Frank*
• Kristallnacht

INTERNET RESOURCES
• See *McDougal Littell Learning On-Line* for links to information about the Holocaust.

 Critical Thinking Transparencies
• CT58, Time Line of Events Leading to World War II
• CT24 World War II Breaks Out

 Electronic Library of Primary Sources
• from "Let Us Face the Truth" from the *New York Times*
• On the Declaration of War by Franklin Delano Roosevelt

INTERNET RESOURCES
• See *McDougal Littell Learning On-Line* for links to information about U-boats and Pearl Harbor.

 American Portfolio: A Videodisc for U.S. History, user's guide, pp. 209–210, 216–217, 221, 223

INTERNET RESOURCES:
Learning On-Line: Social Studies
http://www.mcdougallittell.com

Block Scheduling (90 MINUTES)

Day 1
Section 1, pp. 702–707
Section 2, pp. 708–713
Section Assessments, pp. 707, 713

Day 2
Section 3, pp. 714–718
 AMERICAN STORIES VIDEO SERIES
• "Escaping the 'Final Solution'"
Section Assessment, p 718

Day 3
Section 4, pp. 719–725
Section Assessment, p 725
Chapter Assessment, pp. 726–727

YEARLY PACING *Chapter 24 Total:* 3 days *Yearly Total:* 85 days

See *Planning for Block Schedules* for special activities and pacing strategies.

Customizing for Special Populations

Students Acquiring English

Access for Students Acquiring English
• Guided Reading for Sections 1–4 (Spanish), pp. 235–238
• Chapter Summary (Spanish), pp. 233–234
• Skillbuilder Practice: Developing Historical Perspective (Spanish), p. 239
• Geography Application: Japanese Aggression (Spanish), p. 240

 AMERICAN STORIES VIDEO SERIES
• "Escaping the 'Final Solution'" (Spanish track)

INTERNET RESOURCES
• See *McDougal Littell Learning On-Line*
The Diverse Classroom.

Less Proficient Readers

In-Depth Resources: Unit 7
• Guided Reading for Sections 1–4, pp. 1–4
• Skillbuilder: Developing Historical Perspective, p. 5
• Geography Application: Japanese Aggression, p. 6

Telescoping the Times
• Chapter Summary, pp. 47–48

See additional strategies at point of use in the Teacher's Edition.

Gifted and Talented Students

In-Depth Resources: Unit 7
• Primary Sources: from Franklin D. Roosevelt's "Quarantine Speech," p. 8; from The Bombing of Pearl Harbor, p. 9; War Poster, p. 11
• American Lives: Elie Wiesel, p. 15; Charles A. Lindbergh, p. 16

See additional strategies at point of use in the Teacher's Edition.

Connections to Literature READINGS FOR STUDENTS

In-Depth Resources: Unit 7
• from *Sophie's Choice* by William Styron, p. 12

Enrichment Reading
• **Hemingway, Ernest**
  For Whom the Bell Tolls
  New York: Scribner, 1996
  On the eve of World War II, this major American classic tells the story of the impending death of an American in the Spanish Civil War. A deeply felt and time-less story of love and loss, of courage and commitment, the novel reflects Hemingway's passionate feelings about the nature of war and the meaning of loyalty.

• **Porter, Katherine Anne**
  Ship of Fools
  New York: Little, Brown, 1984
  Porter's belief that "evil is always done with the collusion of good" is played out in this moral allegory about the voyage of life. A variety of people, mostly Germans on the eve of Hitler's rise to power, travel on the Vera, a passenger freighter, from Mexico to Germany during 27 days of 1931.

• **Uchida, Yoshiko**
  Journey to Topaz
  New York: Scribner, 1971
  After the attack on Pearl Harbor, an eleven-year old Japanese-American girl and her family are forced into an intern-ment camp called Topaz in the Utah desert.

World War Looms

▶ **Starting with the Student**
- What do the first three pictures say about the Nazi regime?
- How do these images help explain Roosevelt's not insisting that Americans remain neutral in thought?
- What do the last two pictures say about Roosevelt's commitment to neutrality?

PREVIEWING THE CHAPTER
- Go over the titles and brief descriptions of the sections, pointing out the video in Section 3.
- As students look over the time line, ask them to recall other events that happened in the United States during this time period, which they studied in Chapters 22 and 23.

MORE ABOUT . . .
Franklin Delano Roosevelt

On the same day that Franklin Delano Roosevelt (1882–1945) took the oath of office in 1933, Japanese troops marched into China. On the following day, Germans went to the polls and brought Adolf Hitler to power. Roosevelt recognized the threat these events posed to world peace and order. But he had to balance his recognition with Americans' strongly isolationist views.

CHAPTER
24
World War Looms

SECTION 1

Dictators Threaten World Peace

The United States remains isolated from world affairs as economic and political factors lead to the rise of nationalist leaders in the Soviet Union, Germany, and Italy.

SECTION 2

War in Europe

A series of bold moves by Adolf Hitler—and weak countermoves by other leaders—triggers World War II in Europe.

SECTION 3

The Holocaust

Hitler's plans for conquering the world include the killing of Jews and other ethnic groups, which is carried out with frightening determination and success.

VIDEO ESCAPING THE "FINAL SOLUTION"

SECTION 4

America Moves Toward War

The United States provides aid to nations resisting Hitler and enters World War II after the bombing of Pearl Harbor.

"This nation will remain a neutral nation, but I cannot ask that every American remain neutral in thought as well."

President Franklin D. Roosevelt, August 24, 1939

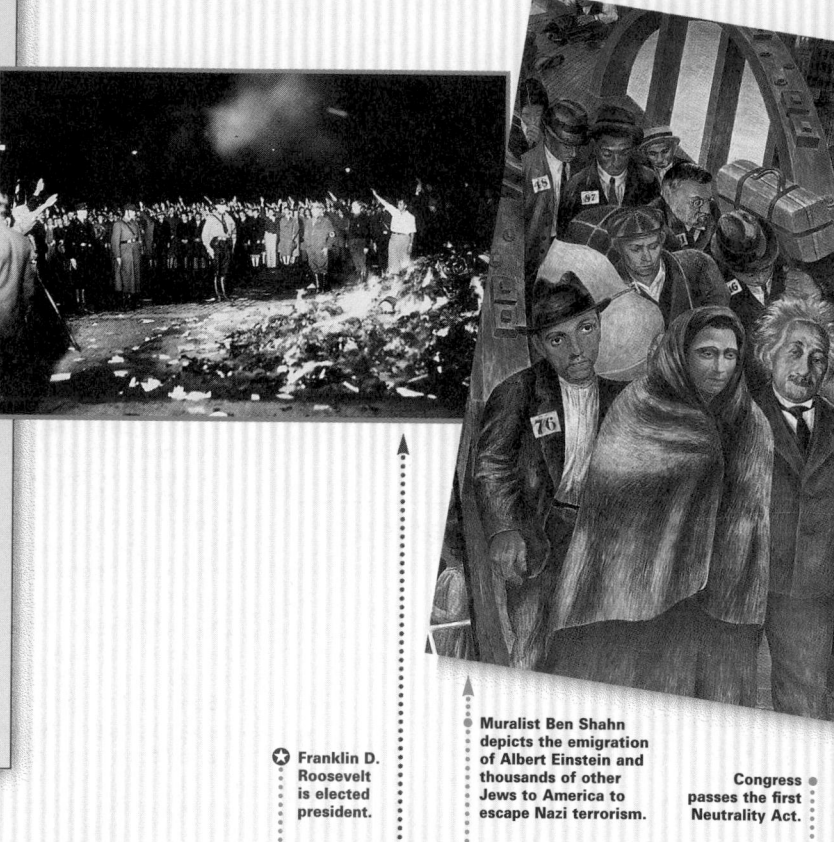

THE UNITED STATES
THE WORLD

	1931	1932	1933	1935
			1933	1935

⭐ **Franklin D. Roosevelt is elected president.**

Muralist Ben Shahn depicts the emigration of Albert Einstein and thousands of other Jews to America to escape Nazi terrorism.

Congress passes the first Neutrality Act.

● **Japan invades Manchuria.**

● **Hitler becomes chancellor of Germany, and his followers honor him by burning 20,000 non-Aryan books.**

● **Mussolini invades Ethiopia.**

THEMES IN CHAPTER 24

Cultural Diversity	*Science and Technology*	*Immigration and Migration*	*Constitutional Concerns*
One of the recurring themes in Adolf Hitler's *Mein Kampf* was an intense hostility toward different racial and cultural groups. African Americans were among the first Americans to appreciate this threat.	The 1939 German blitzkrieg in Poland revealed the destructive potential of two military weapons first used in World War I: the aerial bomber and the tank. Together these two weapons would revolutionize modern warfare.	During the 1930s, thousands of refugees from Nazi Germany and other totalitarian regimes entered the United States as immigrants each year. Their numbers, however, were limited by the quotas imposed by the Immigration Act of 1924.	The election of Franklin Roosevelt to a third term in 1940 broke the unwritten two-term rule of presidential politics, eventually leading to the passage of the 22nd Amendment, which limits presidents to two terms.
See Teacher's Edition note, p. 705.	See Teacher's Edition note, p. 711.	See Teacher's Edition note, p. 715.	See Teacher's Edition note, p. 720.

LIVING HISTORY

COMPILING AN ORAL HISTORY

Interview a relative or a friend of the family who lived through the period prior to America's entry into World War II. Before the interview, prepare a list of questions to ask the person based on specific information in the chapter and on general issues such as the following:

- How did you feel about the cautious response of the United States to events in Europe?
- How did events between 1931 and 1941 affect your life?

📁 **PORTFOLIO PROJECT** Write up your interview as an article for your school newspaper and keep a copy in a folder. You will present your interviews and save them in your American history portfolio at the end of the chapter.

The United States enters the war after the Japanese attack on Pearl Harbor.

President Roosevelt signs the Lend-Lease Act, and U.S. industry begins mass production of war materiel.

Franklin D. Roosevelt is reelected president.

President Roosevelt delivers his anti-isolationist "quarantine" speech.

J Franklin D. Roosevelt is reelected to a third term as president.

36   **1937**   **1938**   **1939**   **1940**   **1941**
         1937   **1940**

- **The Spanish Civil War begins.**
- **Germany occupies the Rhineland.**

- **Japan invades China.**

- **Germany annexes Austria.**
- **Hitler unleashes aggression against Jews on *Kristallnacht*.**

- **Germany invades Poland.**
  - **The Nazis institute their "final solution" in death camps such as Buchenwald.**

- **Britain and Germany fight the Battle of Britain.**
- **Japan, Germany, and Italy sign pact.**

- **Germany invades the Soviet Union.**
- **Japanese attack Pearl Harbor.**

World War Looms **701**

RECOMMENDED RESOURCES

Books for the Teacher

Churchill, Winston. *The Gathering Storm.* Boston: Houghton, 1986.

Hitler, Adolf. *Mein Kampf.* Boston: Houghton, 1973. Presentation of the basic beliefs of Nazism.

Levin, Nora. *The Holocaust.* New York: Crowell, 1968. Comprehensive history of the Holocaust.

Shirer, William. *The Rise and Fall of the Third Reich.* Edgartown, MA: S&S, 1990.

Books for the Student

Persico, Joseph E. *Nuremberg.* New York: Penguin, 1994. Discussion of the war crimes trials.

Time-Life Books, *World War II.* Englewood Cliffs, NJ: Prentice, 1989.

Wiesel, Elie. *Night.* New York: Bantam, 1982. Survivor's moving account of the Holocaust.

Videos

Hitler: The Whole Story. Dir. Christian Herrendoerfer. Discovery Communications, 1991.

Schindler's List. Dir. Steven Spielberg. Amblin Entertainment: Universal, 1994. Rated "R."

Shoah. Dir. Claude Lanzmann. Aleph/ Historia, 1985.

Software

American Chronicle Series: Seeds of Discord (1933–1936), Prelude to War (1935–1939), Darkest Hour (1939–1941). CD-ROM. AIMS Media, 800-367-2467

Causes of World War II. CD-ROM. ZCI Publishing, 1950 Stemmons, Suite 4044, Dallas, TX 75207-3109, 214-800-6000

The Holocaust. CD-ROM. Quanta Press, Inc., 1313 Fifth St., SE. Minneapolis, MN 55414, 612-379-3956

OBJECTIVES

1. To characterize the governments that took power in Russia, Italy, Germany, and Japan after World War I.

2. To describe America's return to isolationism in the 1930s.

SKILLBUILDERS

- Understanding geography: region, location, p. 703
- Interpreting charts, p. 705
- Understanding geography: movement, p. 706
- Interpreting political cartoons, p. 707

CRITICAL THINKING

- Identifying problems, p. 703
- Summarizing, pp. 704, 707
- Clarifying, p. 704
- Analyzing motives, pp. 705, 706, 707
- Analyzing causes, p. 707

FOCUS & MOTIVATE

▶ **Starting with the Student**
- What kind of people become bullies?
- How do bullies influence other people?
- What is likely to happen when bullies gain control of a country?

OBJECTIVE

1 INSTRUCT

Nationalism Threatens Europe and Asia

▶ **Starting with the Student**
Have students use a three-column chart—with one column labeled Italy, one Germany, and one Japan—to take notes on the countries' beliefs and actions during their leaders' rise to power.

Italy	Germany	Japan

(continued on next page)

---

1 Dictators Threaten World Peace

TERMS & NAMES
- Joseph Stalin
- totalitarian
- Benito Mussolini
- fascism
- Adolf Hitler
- Nazism
- Neutrality Acts

LEARN ABOUT the rise of totalitarian dictatorships in Europe and Asia
TO UNDERSTAND the challenge they posed to the U.S. policy of neutrality.

ONE AMERICAN'S STORY

Martha Gellhorn arrived in Madrid, Spain, in the spring of 1937 with a knapsack, less than $50, and a letter identifying her as a special correspondent for *Collier's Weekly*. The young American writer had come to Madrid to cover the brutal civil war that had broken out in Spain the year before. There she met the writer Ernest Hemingway, whom she later married. To Gellhorn, the Spanish Civil War was a deadly struggle between tyranny and democracy. For the people of Madrid, it was also a daily struggle for survival.

A PERSONAL VOICE
You would be walking down a street, hearing only the city noises of streetcars and automobiles and people calling out to one another, and suddenly, crushing it all out, would be the huge stony deep booming of a falling shell, at the corner. There was no place to run, because how did you know that the next shell would not be behind you, or ahead, or to the left or right? And going indoors was fairly silly too, considering what shells can do to a house.

MARTHA GELLHORN, *The Face of War*

Less than two decades after the end of World War I—"the war to end all wars"—brutal fighting erupted again, not only in Europe but also in Asia. As Americans read about distant battles, they hoped that these deadly conflicts would remain on the other side of the world.

A French journalist escapes from Spain [to] France with a child rescued from a street battle. But fighting would soon engulf not only France, but the rest of Europe and Asia.

Nationalism Threatens Europe and Asia

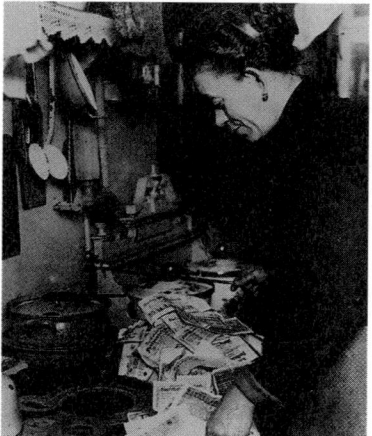

A German homemaker, about to cook her family's breakfast, lights a fire with money made nearly worthless by high inflation following World War I.

702 CHAPTER 24

The seeds of new conflicts had been sown in World War I. For many nations, peace had brought not prosperity but revolution caused by economic unrest. It also brought the rise of leaders driven by dreams of national greatness and territorial expansion.

FAILURES OF THE WORLD WAR I PEACE SETTLEMENT Contrary to the hopes of President Woodrow Wilson, the Treaty of Versailles that ended World War I did not create a "just and secure peace." Germans saw nothing fair in a treaty that blamed them for starting the war. Nor did they find much security in a settlement that stripped their country of territories they had long seen as German. Similarly, the Soviets resented the carving away of parts of Russia to create an independent Poland and the nations of Finland, Estonia, Lithuania, and Latvia.

In addition, the peace settlement did not make the world "safe for democracy," as Wilson had hoped. At the end of the war, new democratic governments did emerge in many European nations, including Germany, Austria, Italy, Czechoslovakia, Bulgaria, Romania, and Greece. Most of these nations lacked democratic traditions, though, and their newly elected leaders needed to show that democracy could improve people's lives economically. However, the Versailles treaty did nothing to help the war-torn nations of Europe rebuild. Instead, many of the new democracies were

---

SECTION 1 RESOURCES

PRINT RESOURCES

IN-DEPTH RESOURCES: UNIT 7
Guided Reading, p. 1
Primary Source: *from* Franklin D. Roosevelt's "Quarantine Speech," p. 8

ACCESS FOR STUDENTS ACQUIRING ENGLISH
Guided Reading (Spanish), p. 235

FORMAL ASSESSMENT
Section Quiz, p. 293

ALTERNATIVE ASSESSMENT BOOK
See forms for supporting and scoring alternative activities.

TECHNOLOGY RESOURCES

HUMANITIES TRANSPARENCIES
H23, German Nazi Party poster

VIDEO *American Portfolio: A Videodisc for U.S. History*
user's guide, pp. 209–210

INTERNET McDougal Littell Learning On-Line
http://www.mcdougallittell.com

The Rise of Nationalism, 1922–1941

Adolf Hitler offers economic stability to unemployed Germans during the Great Depression and becomes chancellor in 1933.

Joseph Stalin grabs control of the Soviet Union in 1924 after hopes for democracy give way to revolution and V. I. Lenin, founder of a Communist regime, dies.

Francisco Franco leads the rebel Nationalist army to victory in Spain and gains complete control of the country in 1939.

Benito Mussolini rises to power in 1922 by opposing the government and attempting to restore Italy to its former position as a world power.

Hideki Tojo, an energetic military leader perfectly suited to carrying out the nation's expansionist aims, becomes prime minister of Japan in 1941.

- Fascist dictatorship
- Communist dictatorship
- Expansionist military regime

ATLANTIC OCEAN

SOVIET UNION

CHINA

JAPAN

Tokyo

PACIFIC OCEAN

1000 Miles
2000 Kilometers

(continued from page 702)

▶ **Discussing Key Ideas**
- After World War I totalitarian governments take root in Russia, Italy, and Germany.
- Militarists dreaming of territorial expansion gain control of Japan.
- The League of Nations proves helpless in the face of aggression by Japan and Italy.

IN-DEPTH RESOURCES: UNIT 7
Guided Reading, p. 1

ACCESS FOR STUDENTS ACQUIRING ENGLISH
Guided Reading (Spanish), p. 235

HISTORY FROM VISUALS
The Rise of Nationalism, 1922–1941

Reading the Map Have students identify the Fascist, Communist, and expansionist military regimes. *Fascist—Germany, Italy, and Spain; Communist—Soviet Union; expansionist military—Japan.*

Extension Ask students to speculate which countries Germany and Japan might attempt to take over. *Possible Answer: Germany—France, Great Britain, Netherlands, Belgium, Denmark; Japan—China.*

MORE ABOUT . . .
The First Five-Year Plan

Stalin drove his people ruthlessly to meet his goals, urging them to "complete the Five-Year Plan in four." In 1932 the *New York Times* wrote, "A plan which . . . drives toward an objective regardless of cost, as Moscow has often boasted, is not really a plan. It is a gamble."

THINK THROUGH HISTORY
A. *Identifying Problems* What problems did European countries face after World War I?

A. Answer The failure of the Treaty of Versailles and economic devastation.

expected to pay off huge war debts while trying to deal with widespread hunger, homelessness, and unemployment.

Unable to cope with these problems, the new democracies collapsed one by one. In country after country, dictators seized power and threw out the elected leaders. Some of these dictators were content simply to collect taxes and keep order. A few, however, had far grander ambitions.

JOSEPH STALIN TRANSFORMS THE SOVIET UNION In the Soviet Union, hopes for democracy quickly gave way to revolution, resulting in the establishment of a Communist state, the Soviet Union, in 1922. When V. I. Lenin, the first leader of the Soviet Union, died in 1924, **Joseph Stalin** scrambled for control of the huge country. Stalin, whose last name meant "man of steel," was as iron-willed as his name implied. Once he decided on a goal, Stalin let nothing stand in his way, no matter what the costs. In contrast to Lenin, who had seen the Russian Revolution as only part of a worldwide uprising by the working class, Stalin focused on creating a model Communist state in the Soviet Union. In doing so, he began an agricultural and industrial restructuring that trampled the rights of—and brought great suffering to—his people.

In 1927, Stalin launched his massive drive to make the Soviet Union a truly socialist country, which meant stamping out all private enterprise—especially private farming. He began by ordering the collectivization of Soviet agriculture, or organizing production under collective, or state, control. He forced Russia's peasants to give up their small plots of land to form large state-owned farms. They were then expected to work on the collective farms as wage earners.

Meanwhile, Stalin turned to his second great goal, the transformation of the Soviet Union from a backward rural nation into a great industrial power. In 1928, the Soviet dictator issued his first Five-Year Plan, a campaign to build massive state-owned factories, steel mills, and power plants. A second Five-Year Plan followed in 1933 (which was completed in only four years), and a third in 1937. By 1939, the Soviet Union had become the world's third largest industrial power, surpassed in overall production by only the United States and Germany.

The human costs of this transformation, however, were enormous. To accomplish his ambitious goals, the "man of steel" turned the Soviet Union into

---

GEOGRAPHY SKILLBUILDER
REGIONS In which countries did nationalistic leaders come to power? Who were the leaders?
LOCATION What geographic features might lead Japan to expand?

Skillbuilder Answer
Regions: Germany—Adolf Hitler; Spain—Francisco Franco; Italy—Benito Mussolini; Soviet Union—Joseph Stalin; Japan—Hideki Tojo.
Location: Its status as an island nation.

TEACHING OPTIONS

Making Connections Across the Curriculum

Economics Explain to students that economists describe the Soviet Union under Stalin as a "command economy," meaning one in which economic decisions are controlled and directed by the government. Discuss with students how a capitalist economy differs from a command economy. *In a capitalist economy, economic decisions are not made by the government but by individuals, who decide how to spend or invest their own money.*

Making Connections Across Time

The Russian Economy Today Ask students what they know about the Russian economy today and how it has changed since Stalin's time. Discuss with them Russia's difficult transition from a command to a capitalist economic system. Point out that under communism, the Soviet Union lacked many basic features of a capitalist system, such as private property and the right to own or make a profit from a business.

In *Mein Kampf,* Adolf Hitler described one of the Nazi Party's major propaganda tools—the "big lie." Hitler wrote that "the great masses of the people . . . more easily fall a victim to a big lie than to a little one, since they themselves lie in little things, but would be ashamed of lies that were too big. Such a falsehood will never enter their heads, and they will not be able to believe in the possibility of such monstrous effrontery and infamous misrepresentation in others."

HUMANITIES TRANSPARENCIES
H23, German Nazi party poster

"Italy wants peace, work, and calm. I will give these things with love if possible, with force if necessary."

BENITO MUSSOLINI

---

a vast police state—a state in which no one was safe from the prying eyes and ears of Stalin's spies and secret police. Anyone even suspected of criticizing the Soviet leader or his goals was arrested and shipped off to a forced labor camp in the frozen wastelands of Siberia.

In his drive to purge, or rid, the Soviet Union of people who disagreed with the government's policies, Stalin did not spare even his most faithful supporters. During the Great Purge of 1934–1938, tens of thousands of Communist party officials, bureaucrats, and army officers were branded "enemies of the people" and were executed. While the final toll will never be known, historians estimate that Stalin was responsible for the deaths of 8 million to 13 million people. Millions more died in famines caused by the restructuring of Soviet society.

By 1939, Stalin had established a centralized **totalitarian** government, or one that maintains complete control over its citizens. In a totalitarian state, individuals have no rights, and the government suppresses all opposition.

THE RISE OF FASCISM IN ITALY   While Stalin was consolidating his power in the Soviet Union, **Benito Mussolini** was establishing a totalitarian regime in Italy. In 1919, Mussolini had begun his rise to power by advertising for war veterans to fight the politicians, who, in Mussolini's view, were destroying Italy. This mobilization was the beginning of **fascism,** a new political movement that consisted of a strong, centralized government headed by a powerful dictator. Fascism was rooted in the nationalism that had reshaped Europe over the past century. Mussolini dreamed of making Italy a great power in the world.

Unlike Stalin's Communist regime, Mussolini's Fascist state did not attempt to control farms and factories. In fact, many discontented veterans, jobless youth, and businesspeople greatly feared the spread of communism to Italy. These people became firm supporters of Mussolini. In 1921, Mussolini established the Fascist Party, which then won 35 seats in the Italian parliament. A year later, after Mussolini staged a march on Rome with thousands of his black-shirted followers, the Italian king allowed him to form a new government.

Calling himself *Il Duce,* or "the chief," Mussolini gradually extended Fascist control to every aspect of Italian life. Tourists marveled that *Il Duce* had even "made the trains run on time." Mussolini achieved this efficiency, however, by crushing all opposition and by making Italy a totalitarian state.

THE NAZIS TAKE OVER GERMANY   In Germany, **Adolf Hitler** had followed a path to power similar to Mussolini's. At the end of World War I, Hitler had been a jobless soldier drifting around Germany. In 1919, he joined a struggling group called the National Socialist German Workers' Party, better known as the Nazi Party. Despite the word *Socialist* in its name, this party had no ties to communism and in fact hated it. Soon Hitler had become the tiny party's führer, or leader.

Hitler laid out the basic beliefs of **Nazism** in his book *Mein Kampf (My Struggle),* published in two volumes in 1925 and 1927. Like fascism, Nazism was based on extreme nationalism. Hitler, who had been born in Austria, dreamed of uniting all German-speaking people in a great German empire. To this element of nationalism Hitler added his theories about race. In his view, Germans—especially blue-eyed, blond-haired "Aryans"—formed a "master race" that was destined to rule the world. "Inferior races," such as Jews, Slavs, and nonwhites, were fit only to serve Aryans.

A third element of Nazism was national expansion. Hitler believed that for Germany to thrive, it needed more lebensraum, or living space. One of the Nazis' aims, as Hitler wrote in *Mein Kampf,* was "to secure for the German people the land and soil to which they are entitled on this earth," even if this could be accomplished only by "the might of a victorious sword."

704 CHAPTER 24

THINK THROUGH HISTORY
B. Summarizing *What are the characteristics of a totalitarian state?*

B. Answer Complete control over citizens and ruthless suppression of opposition

C. Answer Extreme nationalism, superiority of Aryan "master race," expansionism

THINK THROUGH HISTORY
C. Clarifying *What were the basic beliefs of Nazism?*

The Faces of Totalitarianism

FASCIST ITALY	NAZI GERMANY	COMMUNIST SOVIET UNION
• Extreme nationalism • Militaristic expansionism • Charismatic leader • Private property with strong government controls • Anti-Communist	• Extreme nationalism and racism • Militaristic expansionism • Strong leader • Private property with strong government controls • Anti-Communist	• Worldwide spread of communism • Revolution by workers • Eventual rule by working class • State ownership of property

SKILLBUILDER INTERPRETING CHARTS *How did fascism in Italy differ from communism in the Soviet Union?*

Skillbuilder Answer
Italian fascism—militant nationalism, dictatorial leader, anti-Communist; Soviet communism—worldwide revolution by workers, rule by working class, no private property.

The Great Depression was a gift to the Nazis. By 1932, some 6 million Germans were unemployed. Many of these desperate people turned to Hitler as their last hope. In elections held in March 1932, the Nazis won more votes than any other party, though not a majority. In January 1933, Hitler was appointed chancellor (prime minister).

Once in power, the führer quickly dismantled Germany's democratic Weimar Republic. In its place he established what he called the Third Reich, or Third German Empire. In contrast to the first two, relatively short-lived German empires—one established by Charlemagne and the other by Bismarck—the Third Reich, according to Hitler, would be "the thousand-year Reich."

MILITARISTS GAIN CONTROL IN JAPAN Halfway around the world from Germany, nationalistic military leaders in Japan were trying to take control of their government. These leaders shared Hitler's belief in the need for more "living space" for a growing population. Ignoring the protests of more moderate Japanese officials, the militarists launched a surprise invasion of the Chinese province of Manchuria in 1931. Within several months, Japanese troops controlled the entire province, a resource-rich area nearly as large as Western Europe.

THINK THROUGH HISTORY
D. *Analyzing Motives* Why did Japan invade Manchuria?

As you read in Chapter 19, the League of Nations had been established after World War I to prevent just such aggressive acts. In this first actual test of its power, the League sent representatives to Manchuria to investigate the situation. Their report condemned Japan, which simply quit the League. Meanwhile, the success of the Manchurian invasion put the militarists firmly in control of Japan's government.

D. Answer To gain "living space" and resources for its people.

AGGRESSION IN EUROPE The failure of the League of Nations to take action against Japan did not escape the notice of Europe's dictators. In 1933, Hitler felt bold enough to pull Germany out of the League. In 1935, he began a military buildup in violation of the Versailles treaty. A year later, he sent troops into the Rhineland, a German region bordering France and Belgium which was demilitarized as a result of the Versailles treaty. He also signed the Rome-Berlin Axis Pact, which established a formal alliance between Germany and Italy. The League did nothing to stop Hitler.

At the same time, Mussolini began building his new Roman Empire. His first target was Ethiopia, Africa's only remaining independent country. By the fall of 1935, tens of thousands of Italian soldiers stood ready to advance on Ethiopia. The League of Nations reacted with brave talk of "collective resistance to all acts of unprovoked aggression."

HISTORICAL SPOTLIGHT

AFRICAN AMERICANS STAND BY ETHIOPIANS

When Mussolini invaded Ethiopia, many Europeans and Americans—especially African Americans—were outraged. Almost overnight, African Americans organized to raise money for medical supplies, and thousands volunteered to fight in Ethiopia. Years later, the Ethiopian emperor Haile Selassie said of these efforts,

We can never forget the help Ethiopia received from Negro Americans during the terrible crisis. . . . It moved me to know that Americans of African descent did not abandon their embattled brothers, but stood by us.

Reading the Chart Suggest that students first read down each column of the chart to learn the basic characteristics of each totalitarian government. Then have them read across to compare and contrast the totalitarian systems.

Extension Ask students to predict on the basis of this chart which of these nations might become allies and which enemies. *Possible Response: Italy and Germany might become allies because of their shared totalitarian beliefs. The Soviet Union might regard both Italy and Germany as enemies because of their hostility to communism.*

***Critical Thinking:
Analyzing Motives*** Ask students to consider what motivated African Americans to mobilize on behalf of Ethiopia in 1935. You may want to remind students that Ethiopia was the only independent black nation in the world in 1935, and that, for African Americans, its defeat would symbolize a victory of the white man over the black man.

TEACHING OPTION

Exploring Themes

Cultural Diversity African Americans were among the first Americans to condemn the rise of Nazism and racism in Germany. Some had read *Mein Kampf* and were deeply offended by Hitler's view that blond, blue-eyed Germans constituted a "master race." Others were awakened to the Nazi threat during the 1936 summer Olympics, which were held in the German capital of Berlin. During the games, African-American track star Jesse Owens stole the show by winning four gold medals. Hitler regarded Owens's victories as a threat to his racial theories, and walked out of the Olympic stadium rather than congratulate a black athlete.

In his extraordinary performance, Owens tied the Olympic record in the 100-meter run (10.3 seconds). He also broke the Olympic and world records in the 200-meter run (20.7 seconds) and the running broad jump (26 feet 5¼ inches). After he retired from competitive sports, Owens made goodwill visits to India and East Asia on behalf of the U.S. Department of State.

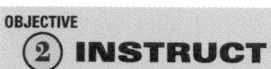

Italy Invades Ethiopia,1935–1936

ITALY
Rome
Mediterranean Sea

Red Sea

ETHIOPIA
Addis Ababa
INDIAN OCEAN

Japan Invades Manchuria, 1931

MANCHURIA
Mukden
Sea of Japan
Tokyo
CHINA
Yellow Sea
JAPAN

Reading the Map Be sure that students understand the relationship between the two detailed maps and the globe. Point out that the maps show the relative location of Italy and Japan to the countries they invaded. The globe shows the relative location of these two hot spots on opposite sides of the world.

Extension Ask students to speculate what effects Italy's and Japan's actions might have on America. *Students might say that these countries are so far away that the actions would have no effect.*

The United States Responds Cautiously

▶ **Starting with the Student**
• Ask students what they would do if they saw a fight break out on the far side of the schoolyard and they didn't know any of the people involved.
• Discuss how this situation compares with the dilemma facing Americans in the 1930s as they watched Ethiopia and China.

▶ **Discussing Key Ideas**
• After World War I, the United States returns to a policy of isolationism.
• Congress passes the Neutrality Acts to keep the United States out of war.
• Many Americans find it hard to remain neutral.

IN-DEPTH RESOURCES: UNIT 7
Primary Source: *from* Franklin D. Roosevelt's "Quarantine Speech," p. 8

GEOGRAPHY SKILLBUILDER
MOVEMENT *Notice the size and location of Italy and of Japan with respect to the country each invaded. What similarities do you see?*

Skillbuilder Answer
They were both small nations that invaded much larger countries by sea.

When the invasion began, however, the League's response was an ineffective economic boycott—little more than a slap on Italy's wrist. By June 1936, Ethiopia had fallen. In desperation, Haile Selassie, the ousted Ethiopian emperor, appealed to the League for assistance. Nothing was done. "It is us today," he told them. "It will be you tomorrow."

The United States Responds Cautiously

As disturbing as these events in Europe and Asia were to Americans, most believed that the United States should not get involved. In 1928, the United States joined 61 other nations in signing the Kellogg-Briand Pact, in which they pledged never to make war again. But this agreement still permitted defensive war and did not provide for using economic or military force against nations that broke the pact.

CLINGING TO ISOLATIONISM In the early 1930s, a flood of books argued that the United States had been dragged into World War I by greedy bankers and arms dealers. Public outrage led to the creation of a congressional committee, chaired by North Dakota senator Gerald Nye, that held hearings on these charges. The Nye committee fueled the controversy by documenting the large profits that banks and manufacturers made during the war.

The furor over these "merchants of death" made Americans more determined than ever to avoid war. A poll taken in 1937 revealed that fully 70 percent of Americans believed that the United States should not have entered World War I. Antiwar feeling was so strong that the Girl Scouts of America changed the color of its uniforms from khaki to green to appear less militaristic. Across the country, college students staged antiwar rallies with banners proclaiming "Scholarships, not battleships."

Americans' growing isolationism eventually had an impact on President Roosevelt's foreign policy. When he first took office in 1933, Roosevelt had felt comfortable reaching out to the world in several ways. He officially recognized the Soviet Union in 1933 and agreed to exchange ambassadors with Moscow. He continued the policy of nonintervention in Latin America begun by Presidents Coolidge and Hoover with his Good Neighbor policy and withdrew armed forces stationed there. In 1934, Roosevelt pushed the Reciprocal Trade Agreement Act through Congress. This act lowered trade barriers by giving the president the power to make trade agreements with other nations and was aimed at reducing tariffs by as much as 50 percent.

Beginning in 1935, however, Congress passed a series of **Neutrality Acts** in an effort to keep the United States out of future wars. The first two acts outlawed

E. Answer
Evidence that large profits had been made by banks and arms industries during World War I; regret over having been involved in that war; hatred of militarism.

THINK THROUGH HISTORY
E. Analyzing Motives What factors contributed to Americans' growing isolationism?

Cooperative Activity: Writing a Newspaper Editorial

Task: Student groups will write a newspaper editorial about President Roosevelt's Quarantine Speech.

Purpose: To help students appreciate the difficulties Roosevelt faced in trying to promote world peace.

Activity: Assign small groups of students to serve as editorial boards of newspapers in the 1930s. Students will determine the editorial response of their newspaper to President

Roosevelt's Quarantine Speech of October 5, 1937, and then write a short editorial explaining why their paper approves or disapproves of his call for action. Groups should read their editorials to the class.

📁 **Building a Portfolio:** Students who add the editorial to their portfolio should attach a note indicating their contribution.

ALTERNATIVE ASSESSMENT BOOK
Standards for Evaluating a Cooperative Activity

Standards for Evaluation
Editorials should . . .

• take a clear position for or against President Roosevelt's Quarantine Speech
• give detailed reasons supporting that position
• use appropriate editorial form and style

arms sales or loans to nations at war. The third act was passed in response to fighting that broke out in Spain in 1936 between the troops of Fascist general Francisco Franco and forces loyal to the country's elected government. This act extended the ban on arms sales and loans to nations undergoing civil wars.

NEUTRALITY BREAKS DOWN Despite congressional efforts to legislate neutrality, many Americans found it difficult not to take sides in the Spanish Civil War. When Hitler and Mussolini came to Franco's aid early in the war, some 3,000 volunteers from the United States responded by forming the Abraham Lincoln Brigade and traveling to Spain to fight Franco. "We knew, we just *knew*," recalled Martha Gellhorn, "that Spain was the place to stop fascism." Among the volunteers were African Americans still bitter about Mussolini's invasion of Ethiopia the year before.

Such limited aid was not sufficient to stop the spread of fascism, however. Hitler and Mussolini, who saw the conflict as a testing ground for their military power, supported Franco with troops, weapons, tanks, and fighter planes. The Western democracies, fearful of triggering a larger war, sent only food and clothing to the anti-Fascist forces. In early 1939, after a loss of 600,000 lives and at a cost of more than $15 billion, the resistance to Franco had collapsed. Europe now had yet another totalitarian government.

Roosevelt himself found it impossible to remain neutral when Japan launched a new attack on China in July of 1937. Since Japan had not formally declared war against China, the president refused to enforce the Neutrality Acts. The United States continued sending arms and supplies to China.

A few months later, Roosevelt spoke out strongly against isolationism in a speech delivered in Chicago. He called on peace-loving nations to "quarantine," or isolate, aggressor nations in order to stop the spread of war.

THINK THROUGH HISTORY
F. Analyzing Motives What events caused Roosevelt to take a strong stand against isolationism?
F. Answer The Spanish Civil War and Japan's attack on China.

A PERSONAL VOICE
The peace, the freedom, and the security of 90 percent of the population of the world is being jeopardized by the remaining 10 percent who are threatening a breakdown of all international law and order. Surely the 90 percent who want to live in peace under law and in accordance with standards that have received almost universal acceptance through the centuries, can and must find some way . . . to preserve peace.
FRANKLIN DELANO ROOSEVELT, "Quarantine Speech," October 5, 1937

At last Roosevelt seemed ready to take a stand against aggression—that is, until isolationist newspapers exploded in protest and letters flooded the White House accusing the president of leading the nation into war. Roosevelt backed off. For the moment the conflicts remained "over there."

IT AIN'T WHAT IT USED TO BE

SKILLBUILDER
INTERPRETING POLITICAL CARTOONS
What does Uncle Sam's back turned to Europe show about American attitudes in the late 1930s?
Skillbuilder Answer The United States didn't want to become involved in the war in Europe.

Section 1 Assessment

1. TERMS & NAMES
Identify:
• Joseph Stalin
• totalitarian
• Benito Mussolini
• fascism
• Adolph Hitler
• Nazism
• Neutrality Acts

2. SUMMARIZING List the main ambition of each dictator in a graphic like the one shown.

Ambitions of European Dictators

Stalin	Mussolini	Hitler

What ambitions did the dictators have in common?

3. ANALYZING CAUSES How did the Treaty of Versailles sow the seeds of instability in Europe?

THINK ABOUT
• effects of the treaty on Germany and the Soviet Union
• effects of the treaty on national pride
• the economic legacy of the war

4. ANALYZING MOTIVES
Why do you think Hitler found widespread support among the German people? Support your answer with details from the text.

THINK ABOUT
• Germans' postwar resentment and bitterness
• Germany's economic situation before Hitler's rise to power
• the appeal of Hitler's Nazi beliefs

World War Looms **707**

ANSWERS

1. TERMS & NAMES
Joseph Stalin, p. 703
totalitarian, p. 704
Benito Mussolini, p. 704
fascism, p. 704
Adolf Hitler, p. 704
Nazism, p. 704
Neutrality Acts, p. 706

2. SUMMARIZING
Possible Responses:
Stalin—To create a model Communist state and to transform the Soviet Union into a great industrial power.
Mussolini—To make Italy a great world power.
Hitler—To unite the German "master race" into an empire destined to rule the world.

3. ANALYZING CAUSES
Possible Responses:
Germany's and Russia's resentment of the treaty's harsh terms contributed to their renouncing democratic values; the treaty did not halt the rise of totalitarian governments or help nations rebuild their postwar economies.

4. ANALYZING MOTIVES
Possible Responses:
They were disheartened by the effects of World War I, were suffering from widespread unemployment, and responded positively to Hitler's Nazi doctrine, which restored their national pride.

TERMS & NAMES
• Neville Chamberlai[n]
• Winston Churchill
• appeasement
• nonaggression pac[t]
• blitzkrieg
• Charles de Gaulle

OBJECTIVES

1 To explain Germany's motives for expansion and the timid response of France and Britain.

2 To describe Germany's blitzkrieg tactics against Poland.

3 To summarize the first battles of World War II.

SKILLBUILDER

• Understanding geography: region, location, p. 712

CRITICAL THINKING

• Summarizing, p. 709
• Analyzing motives, p. 710
• Comparing, p. 711
• Drawing conclusions, p. 712
• Contrasting, p. 713
• Following chronological order, p. 713
• Synthesizing, p. 713
• Making decisions, p. 713

FOCUS & MOTIVATE

▶ **Starting with the Student**
• Ask students what they would do if someone came up to them and demanded their jacket. Give up the jacket and hope the person goes away? Try to persuade the person to leave them alone? Fight?
• Would their decision be different if the other person was a lot bigger and stronger than they are?

OBJECTIVE
1 INSTRUCT

Austria and Czechoslovakia Fall

Ask students to create a time line to track German expansion from 1937 to the end of 1940. Their time lines might look like this:

1937   1938   1939   1940

Students should add to their time lines the names of countries taken over by Germany during this period.

(continued on next page)

708   Chapter 24

LEARN ABOUT the weak response of world leaders to Hitler's aggressive moves in the late 1930s
TO UNDERSTAND how Germany started World War II.

ONE AMERICAN'S STORY

A warm June sun bathed the little clearing in the Forest of Compiègne where, 22 years earlier, defeated German generals had signed the armistice ending World War I. It was now 1940, and CBS correspondent William Shirer was standing in the clearing, waiting for Adolf Hitler to deliver *his* armistice terms to a defeated France. Shirer watched as Hitler walked up to the monument and slowly read the inscription: "Here on the eleventh of November 1918 succumbed the criminal pride of the German empire . . . vanquished by the free peoples it tried to enslave." Later that day, Shirer wrote a diary entry describing the Führer's reaction.

A PERSONAL VOICE
I have seen that face many times at the great moments of his life. But today! It is afire with scorn, anger, hate, revenge, triumph. He steps off the monument and contrives to make even this gesture a masterpiece of contempt. . . . He glances slowly around the clearing, and now, as his eyes meet ours, you grasp the depth of his hatred. But there is triumph there too—revengeful, triumphant hate.

WILLIAM SHIRER, *Berlin Diary: The Journal of a Foreign Correspondent 1934–1941*

William Shirer

Again and again Shirer had heard Hitler proclaim that "Germany needs peace . . . Germany wants peace." The hatred and vengefulness that drove the dictator's every action, however, drew Germany ever closer to war.

Austria and Czechoslovakia Fall

On November 5, 1937, Hitler met with his most trusted military advisers for a top-secret briefing. The Third Reich's future, he told them, depended on solving the need for lebensraum. Where would new living space come from? Not from overseas colonies, he declared, but from those nations nearest Germany—Austria and Czechoslovakia. When someone protested that annexing those countries could provoke war, Hitler replied, "Germany's problems can be solved only by means of force, and this is never without risk."

UNION WITH AUSTRIA In fact, the risk turned out to be less than Hitler's advisers feared. The following February, Hitler invited Austrian chancellor Kurt von Schuschnigg to meet with him at his villa at Berchtesgaden, high in the Bavarian Alps. When the Austrian chancellor began making polite conversation about the view and the lovely day, Hitler snapped, "We did not gather here to speak of the fine view or of the weather."

Then the storm broke. For the next few hours, Hitler pounded the table and bombarded the Austrian leader with accusations. Even worse, Schuschnigg, normally a chain smoker, had to do without cigarettes because Hitler could not stand smoking. By the end of the day, Schuschnigg had been bullied into signing an agreement to bring Austrian Nazis into his government.

708 CHAPTER 24

PRINT RESOURCES

IN-DEPTH RESOURCES: UNIT 7
Guided Reading, p. 2
Skillbuilder Practice: Developing Historical Pespective, p. 5

ACCESS FOR STUDENTS ACQUIRING ENGLISH
Guided Reading (Spanish), p. 236
Skillbuilder Practice: Developing Historical Pespective (Spanish), p. 239

FORMAL ASSESSMENT
Section Quiz, p. 294

ALTERNATIVE ASSESSMENT BOOK
See forms for supporting and scoring alternative activities.

TECHNOLOGY RESOURCES

GEOGRAPHY TRANSPARENCIES
G24, Aggression in Europe, 1936–39

CD-ROM *Our Times*
Electronic Library of Primary Sources

VIDEO *American Portfolio: A Videodisc for U.S. History*
user's guide, pp. 209–210

INTERNET McDougal Littell Learning On-Line
http://www.mcdougallittell.com

On returning home, Schuschnigg had second thoughts about the agreement and informed Hitler. Hitler was furious. On March 11, 1938, German troops marched into Austria unopposed, forcing Schuschnigg to resign. Two days later, Germany announced that its Anschluss, or "union," with Austria was complete. The United States and the rest of the world did nothing.

BARGAINING FOR THE SUDETENLAND Hitler then turned to Czechoslovakia. When the Austro-Hungarian Empire was broken up at the end of World War I, the Sudetenland, a mountainous region inhabited by 3 million German-speaking people, had been joined to Czechoslovakia. In the spring of 1938, Hitler charged that the Czechs were abusing the Sudeten Germans, and he began massing troops on the Czech border. American correspondent William Shirer, then stationed in Berlin, wrote in his diary: "The Nazi press [is] full of hysterical headlines. All lies. Some examples: 'Women and Children Mowed Down by Czech Armored Cars,' or 'Bloody Regime—New Czech Murders of Germans.'"

Early in the crisis, both France and Great Britain promised to protect Czechoslovakia. Then, just when war seemed inevitable, Hitler invited French premier Edouard Daladier and British prime minister **Neville Chamberlain** to meet with him in Munich. When they arrived, the Führer declared that the Sudetenland would be his "last territorial demand." In their eagerness to avoid war, Daladier and Chamberlain chose to believe him. On September 30, 1938, they signed the Munich Pact, which turned the Sudetenland over to Germany without a shot being fired.

Chamberlain returned home to wildly cheering crowds. Waving a copy of the agreement, he proclaimed: "My friends . . . there has come back from Germany peace with honor. I believe it is peace in our time." The crowd responded by chanting "Good old Neville" and singing "For he's a jolly good fellow."

These sentiments were not shared by **Winston Churchill,** Chamberlain's political rival for the leadership of Great Britain. In Churchill's view, by signing the Munich Pact, Daladier and Chamberlain had adopted a shameful policy of **appeasement,** or giving up

THINK THROUGH HISTORY
A. Summarizing What moves did Germany make to solve its need for lebensraum?

A. Answer Annexation of Austria and the Sudetenland.

KEY PLAYER

ADOLF HITLER
1889-1945

"All great world-shaking events have been brought about not by written matter, but by the spoken word!" declared Adolf Hitler. A shy and awkward speaker at first, Hitler rehearsed carefully. He even had photos taken of his favorite gestures so that he could study them and make changes to produce exactly the desired effect. Hitler's extraordinary power as a speaker, wrote Otto Strasser, stemmed from an intuitive ability to sense "the vibration of the human heart . . . telling it what it most wants to hear."

Hitler whips a million supporters into a frenzy of smiles and salutes at a Harvest Day celebration in 1937.

(continued from page 708)

▶**Discussing Key Ideas**
• Once in power, Hitler begins a policy of territorial expansion, starting with Austria and Czechoslovakia.
• France and Britain prefer a policy of appeasement toward Germany to one of armed confrontation.

IN-DEPTH RESOURCES: UNIT 7
Guided Reading, p. 2

ACCESS FOR STUDENTS ACQUIRING ENGLISH,
Guided Reading (Spanish), p. 236

KEY PLAYER
Adolf Hitler

Critical Thinking: Drawing Conclusions Ask students to speculate about the emotions or attitudes Hitler was trying to communicate to audiences with each of the gestures shown in the photographs. Would his style of speaking work well on television today? Why or why not?

MORE ABOUT . . .
Reactions to Munich

American reaction to the Munich agreement was mixed. A *New York Times* editorial cautioned, "Let no man say it would have been better to resist, and to fight it out 'now rather than later,' unless he himself would have given the order that would have sent young men marching into the dreary hell of war. . . . No man is wise enough to know whether too high a price has been paid for peace. But no man who is honest will attempt to pretend to himself that a high price has not been paid."

TEACHING OPTION

Skillbuilder Mini-Lesson: Developing Historical Perspective

Explaining the Skill Historical perspective is a way of looking at events, conditions, decisions, and leaders of the past in the context of their own times, rather than judging them based on what we now know. For example, we might now see a historical figure as a cruel, ruthless dictator. At the time, however, some of his policies may have seemed to be exactly what his country needed to settle disputes or to feed the people.

Applying the Skill: The Munich Pact Point out to students that, in light of what we know now, many historians believe that Chamberlain should not have bargained with

Hitler. Ask students to identify reasons for the cheering crowds that greeted Chamberlain when he returned to England from Munich and proclaimed "peace with honor."

The people had been through one terrible war recently and did not want another one. The public, and many leaders, did not then know that Hitler was filled with hate and that he would ignore his promises.

IN-DEPTH RESOURCES: UNIT 7
Skillbuilder Practice: Developing Historical Perspective, p. 5

"Hitler and Mussolini are madmen who respect force and force alone."

FRANKLIN D. ROOSEVELT, 1939

principles to pacify an aggressor. As Churchill bluntly put it, "Britain and France had to choose between war and dishonor. They chose dishonor. They will have war." Nonetheless, the House of Commons approved Chamberlain's policy toward Germany by a vote of 366 to 144. Churchill responded with a warning.

A PERSONAL VOICE
We have passed an awful milestone in our history. . . . And do not suppose that this is the end. This is only the first sip, the first foretaste of a bitter cup which will be proffered to us year by year unless, by a supreme recovery of moral health and martial vigor, we arise again and take our stand for freedom as in the olden time.

WINSTON CHURCHILL, Speech to the House of Commons, quoted in *The Gathering Storm*

The German Offensive Begins

Contrary to his promise at Munich, Hitler was not finished expanding the Third Reich. As dawn broke on March 15, 1939, German troops poured into what remained of Czechoslovakia. At nightfall Hitler gloated, "Czechoslovakia has ceased to exist." After that, the German dictator turned his land-hungry gaze toward Germany's eastern neighbor, Poland.

THE SOVIET UNION DECLARES NEUTRALITY Like Czechoslovakia, Poland had a sizable German-speaking population. In the spring of 1939, Hitler began his familiar routine, charging that Germans in Poland were mistreated by the Poles and needed his protection. Some people thought that this time Hitler must be bluffing. After all, an attack on Poland might bring Germany into conflict with the Soviet Union, Poland's eastern neighbor. At the same time, such an attack would most likely provoke a declaration of war from France and

The Tactics of the Blitzkrieg

1. Heavy air and artillery bombardment—followed by paratroop landings—cleared the attack area, disrupted communications, and prevented the arrival of enemy reinforcements.

2. Conventional infantry attacked on both sides of the central thrust, while a smokescreen concealed tanks gathering in the main battle sector.

infantry
tanks
motorized divisions
infantry

3. Tanks attacked with support from motorized divisions. Massive infantry forces flooded the weakened sector. Tanks fanned out, and motorized divisions and infantry then secured the area.

tanks
tanks
motorized divisions
infantry

The Stuka

The chilling whine of the German Stuka divebomber instilled fear in the enemy. The divebomber was an essential part of the Luftwaffe's blitzkrieg because it had the unique ability to dive almost straight down over a target and release bombs at the last instant, giving it remarkable accuracy. A single Stuka bomber could destroy a column of tanks one by one by continuously diving at the rear tank.

bomb released

TEACHING OPTION

Britain—both of whom had promised military aid to Poland. The result would be a two-front war. Fighting on two fronts had exhausted Germany in World War I. Surely, many thought, Hitler would not be foolish enough to repeat that mistake.

Hitler took the chance, though, and his luck held. As tensions rose over Poland, Stalin, despite his deep dislike and distrust of the Nazis, decided he had more to lose than to gain in a war against Germany. On August 23, 1939, the Soviet Union and Germany signed a **nonaggression pact,** in which they agreed not to fight each other. They also signed a second, secret pact agreeing to divide Poland between them. With the danger of a two-front war eliminated, the fate of Poland was sealed.

Pillbox bunkers such as these had been designed to provide effective defense along the Maginot Line, which was supposed to protect France. But the Germans just bypassed these fortifications.

BLITZKRIEG IN POLAND As day broke on September 1, 1939, German warplanes roared over Poland, raining bombs on military bases, airfields, railroads, and cities. At the same time, German tanks rumbled across the Polish countryside, spreading terror and confusion. This invasion was the first test of Germany's newest military strategy, the **blitzkrieg,** or lightning war. The new tactics enabled the Germans to take the enemy by surprise and then quickly crush all opposition with overwhelming force. Britain and France declared war on Germany on September 3.

The blitzkrieg tactics worked perfectly, however. The fighting was over in three weeks, long before France, Britain, and their allies could respond. In the last week of fighting, the Soviet Union attacked Poland from the east, grabbing about half of its territory. The portion Germany annexed contained almost two-thirds of Poland's population. By the end of the month, Poland had ceased to exist—and World War II had begun.

THE PHONY WAR Or had it? For the next few months, an eerie calm settled over Europe. Bored French and British troops on the Maginot Line, a system of fortifications along France's eastern border, sat staring into Germany, waiting for something to happen. Equally bored German troops sitting on the Siegfried Line a few miles away stared back. The blitzkrieg had given way to what the Germans called the *sitzkrieg* (the sitting war) and the English "the phony war." To fight the tedium of this *sitzkrieg,* French officer Dennis Barlone made sure that his men were well fed.

> **A PERSONAL VOICE**
> Throughout the day the squeals of doomed pigs and poultry can be heard, while the men go off to thrash the walnut trees, . . . unearth the spuds, uproot the salads. My men feed sumptuously, pastry cooks make flans with the flour, found in abundance, and butter made in the dairy. This is the land of milk and honey.
> **DENNIS BARLONE,** *A French Officer's Diary*

For months, there was nothing much to defend against, as the war turned into a *sitzkrieg* stoically endured by soldiers such as this French one on the Maginot Line.

This deceptive peace was first broken not by Germany but by the Soviet Union. After occupying eastern Poland, Stalin began annexing other regions that the Soviet Union had lost at the end of World War I. The Baltic States of Estonia, Latvia, and Lithuania fell with little struggle. However, Finland—a country that journalist William Shirer admired as "the most decent and workable little democracy in Europe"—resisted. Late in 1939, Stalin sent his Soviet Army into Finland. After three months of fierce winter fighting, the outnumbered Finns surrendered. Shirer wrote in his diary, "Stalin reveals himself of the same stamp as Hitler."

C. Answer Both were willing to use secret agreements, armed force, and intimidation to gain the territories they wanted.

THINK THROUGH HISTORY
C. Comparing In what way were Stalin and Hitler alike by 1940?

MORE ABOUT . . .
Stalin and the Nonaggression Pact
Stalin was well aware that by signing a nonaggression pact with Germany in 1939, he had freed Hitler from the threat of a two-front war, thus opening the way for a German invasion of Poland and the start of World War II. Stalin counted on remaining neutral in the ensuing conflict. He planned to use that time to consolidate his control over Eastern Europe while the Fascists and Western democracies fought each other to exhaustion. Once a stalemate had been reached, the Soviets would be in a strong position to intervene and decide the outcome of the war.

MORE ABOUT . . .
The Phony War
During "the phony war" French, British, and German troops often worked and rested in plain sight of each other on opposite sides of the Siegfried line. The mood of the British troops was expressed in these lyrics from a popular song: "We're gonna hang out the washing on the Siegfried Line—if the Siegfried Line's still there."

TEACHING OPTIONS

Exploring Themes

Science and Technology It was largely advances in military technology that made the German blitzkrieg so effective. These developments included specialized military aircraft, such as the Stuka divebomber, the use of the parachute to drop troops where land vehicles couldn't penetrate, and use of the tank as a rapid-moving attack weapon.

Ask students what psychological impact they think this advanced warfare might have on a civilian population. *Possible Responses: It was likely to leave people stunned, disorganized, and demoralized by what seemed to be overwhelming force.*

Making Connections Across the Curriculum

Language Arts / Foreign Languages Have students read the excerpt from Dennis Barlone's *A French Officer's Diary.* Then ask them to write their own diary entries describing what it might have been like to be a soldier on the Maginot or Siegfried Line during the *sitzkrieg.* Encourage them to give details about the countryside, the weather, the food, and their daily activities. You might also suggest that they create dialogues between soldiers on opposing sides. Students who are studying French or German might like to write their entries in that language and provide accompanying translations.

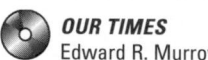
France and Britain Fight On

▶ *Discussing Key Ideas*
• The phony war ends in a second blitzkrieg that leads to the fall of France.
• By the end of 1940, Britain faces the Nazis alone.
• The Luftwaffe fails to wrest control of the skies from the Royal Air Force during the Battle of Britain.

💿 **OUR TIMES**
Edward R. Murrow

HISTORY FROM VISUALS
World War II: German Advances, 1939–1941

Reading the Map Remind students to use the color key to help them identify the four categories of nations shown on the map.

Extension Ask students what German advances meant to Great Britain by the end of 1941. *Possible Answer: Great Britain was essentially cut off from the rest of Europe.*

🏛 **GEOGRAPHY TRANSPARENCIES**
G24, Aggression in Europe, 1936–39

MORE ABOUT . . .
Charles de Gaulle

As head of France's government-in-exile, Charles de Gaulle commanded a military force known as the Free French. The Free French played a prominent role in the North African invasion in 1942 and in the invasion of southern France. They were the first troops to enter liberated Paris in 1944.

On April 7, 1940, a leading German newspaper announced, "Germany is ready. Eighty million pairs of [German] eyes are turned upon the Führer." Two days later, the rest of the world stared, unbelieving, as Hitler launched a surprise invasion of Denmark and Norway. Germany said this action was necessary in order "to protect [those countries'] freedom and independence." Next, the German blitzkrieg turned against the Netherlands, Belgium, and Luxembourg and overran them by the end of May. The phony war suddenly became painfully real.

France and Britain Fight On

Before the war, France had built the massive fortifications of the Maginot Line on its border with Germany. With the invasion of Belgium, however, Germany threatened to bypass the line. French and British troops were sent north into Belgium. Hitler's generals had anticipated this reaction and sent their tanks slicing through the Ardennes, a region of wooded ravines in northeast France that the Allies thought was impassable.

THE FALL OF FRANCE Suddenly, the Allied forces in the north were cut off. Outnumbered, outgunned, and pounded from the air, they fled to the beaches of Dunkirk, on the English Channel. In less than a week, a makeshift fleet of fishing trawlers, tugboats, river barges, pleasure craft, and almost anything else that would float ferried 330,000 British troops to safety across the Channel. These troops would later prove invaluable in the Battle of Britain.

A few days later, Italy entered the war on the side of Germany and invaded France from the south as the Germans closed in on Paris from the north. On June 17, 1940, Marshall Henri Pétain, an aged military commander and World War I hero, told his country, "We must stop fighting." Four days later, at Compiègne, as William Shirer and the rest of the world watched, Hitler handed French officers his terms of surrender. Germans would occupy the northern part of France, and a Nazi-controlled puppet government, headed by Marshall Pétain, would be set up at Vichy, in southern France.

THINK THROUGH HISTORY
D. *Drawing Conclusions* How did Hitler rationalize his invasion of Denmark and Norway?

D. Answer
As a way of protecting their independence.

Skillbuilder Answer
Region: Austria, Yugoslavia, Bulgaria, Greece, Romania, Slovakia, Hungary, Poland, Lithuania, Latvia, Estonia, Finland, Norway, France
Location: It was centrally located.

GEOGRAPHY SKILLBUILDER
REGION *Which countries did Germany invade?*
LOCATION *How was Germany's geographic location an advantage?*

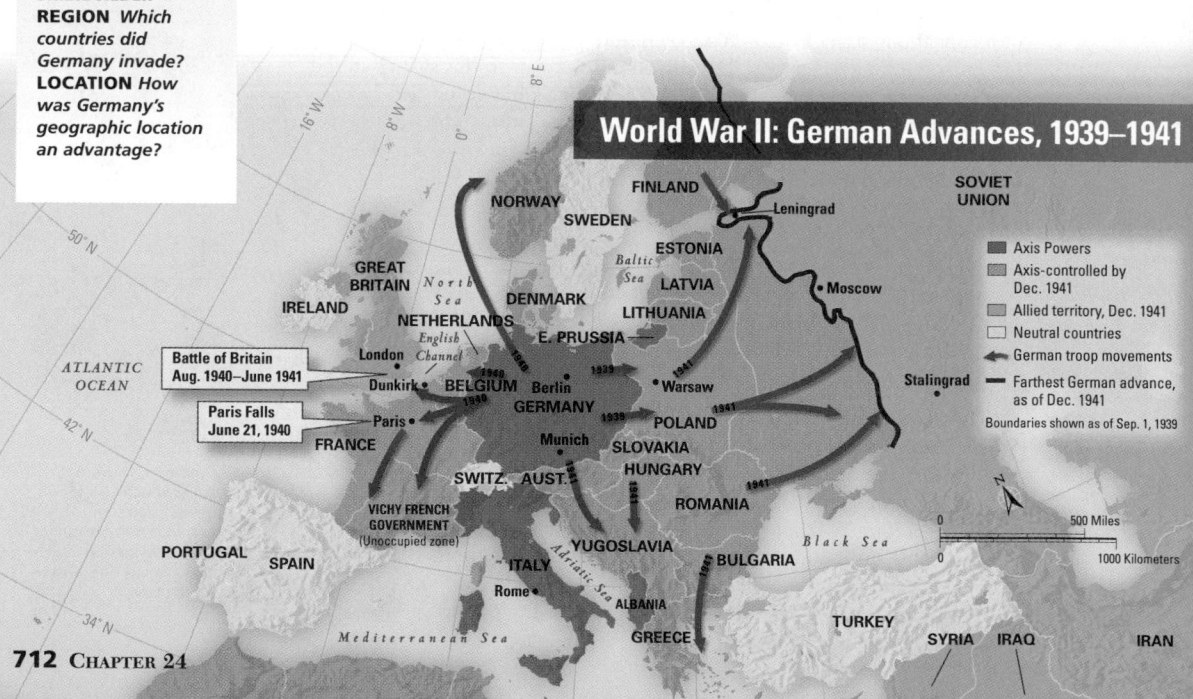

World War II: German Advances, 1939–1941

Battle of Britain
Aug. 1940–June 1941

Paris Falls
June 21, 1940

■ Axis Powers
☐ Axis-controlled by Dec. 1941
☐ Allied territory, Dec. 1941
☐ Neutral countries
← German troop movements
— Farthest German advance, as of Dec. 1941
Boundaries shown as of Sep. 1, 1939

0   500 Miles
0   1000 Kilometers

712 CHAPTER 24

TEACHING OPTION

Cooperative Activity: Creating a Radio Broadcast

Task: Students will research, write, and present a radio newscast from Dunkirk during the Allied evacuation of late May 1940.

Purpose: To explore and report on an event in depth.

Activity: Groups of students will research the events during the rescue of Allied troops from Dunkirk. They will then prepare newscasts featuring interviews with people involved—an Allied soldier awaiting evacuation, a volunteer

on one of the rescue vessels, and a Luftwaffe pilot, for example. You might want to have groups choose one or more of these people to interview so that all sides of the event are presented in the class newscasts.

📁 **Building a Portfolio:** Students who add their newscasts to their portfolios should include a note indicating their contribution.

ALTERNATIVE ASSESSMENT BOOK
Standards for Evaluating a Cooperative Activity

Standards for Evaluation
Newscasts should . . .

• show evidence of research from reliable sources
• present the point of view of a participant in the rescue
• include vivid details that describe the setting and emotions of the participants

Children watch with wonder and fear as the battling British and German air forces set the skies of London aflame.

After France fell, a French general named **Charles de Gaulle** fled to England, where he set up a government-in-exile. De Gaulle proclaimed defiantly, "France has lost a battle, but France has not lost the war."

THE BATTLE OF BRITAIN "The final German victory over England is only a matter of time," wrote a German general after the fall of France. In the summer of 1940, the Germans began to assemble an invasion fleet along the French coast. Because its naval power could not compete with that of France and Britain, however, Germany launched an air war at the same time. The Luftwaffe, or German air force, began making bombing runs over Britain. Its goal was to gain total control of the skies by destroying Britain's Royal Air Force (RAF). Hitler had 2,600 bombers at his disposal. On a single day, August 15, 1,000 of his planes ranged over Britain. Every night for two solid months, bombers pounded London.

The Battle of Britain raged on through the summer and the fall. Night after night, up to a thousand German planes pounded British targets. At first the Luftwaffe concentrated on airfields and aircraft factories. Next it targeted cities. Londoner Len Jones was just 18 years old when bombs fell on his East End neighborhood.

E. Answer
France was defeated and was occupied by the Germans; Britain remained undefeated, although under nightly air attack from the Luftwaffe.

> **A PERSONAL VOICE**
> After an explosion of a nearby bomb, you could actually feel your eyeballs being sucked out. I was holding my eyes to try to stop them going. And the suction was so vast, it ripped my shirt away, and ripped my trousers. Then I couldn't get my breath, the smoke was like acid and everything around me was black and yellow.
>
> **LEN JONES,** quoted in *London at War*

THINK THROUGH HISTORY
E. Contrasting
How did the situations of France and Britain differ by the fall of 1940?

The RAF fought back brilliantly. With the help of a new technological device called radar—which accurately plotted the flight paths of German planes, even in darkness—British pilots unleashed deadly air strikes against the enemy. On September 15, the RAF shot down 56 German planes. They lost only 26 aircraft. Two days later, the Führer called off the invasion of Britain indefinitely. "Never in the field of human conflict," said Churchill in praise of the RAF pilots, "was so much owed by so many to so few."

Section ❷ Assessment

1. TERMS & NAMES

Identify:
• Neville Chamberlain
• Winston Churchill
• appeasement
• nonaggression pact
• blitzkrieg
• Charles de Gaulle

2. FOLLOWING CHRONOLOGICAL ORDER
Arrange the following events on a time line in the order that they occurred: Germany's invasion of Poland, Hitler's annexation of Austria, signing of the nonaggression pact, signing of the Munich Pact.

3. SYNTHESIZING To what extent do you think lies and deception played a role in Hitler's tactics? Support your answer with examples.

THINK ABOUT
• William Shirer's diary entry about headlines in the Nazi newspapers
• Soviet-German relations
• Hitler's justifications for military aggression

4. MAKING DECISIONS If you had been a member of the British House of Commons in 1938, would you have voted for or against the Munich Pact? Support your decision.

THINK ABOUT
• Hitler's credibility
• the British public's fear of being involved in another war
• Churchill's opinion of the appeasement policy

World War Looms **713**

ANSWERS

1. TERMS & NAMES

Neville Chamberlain, p. 709
Winston Churchill, p. 709
appeasement, p. 709
nonaggression pact, p. 711
blitzkrieg, p. 711
Charles de Gaulle, p. 713

2. FOLLOWING CHRONO-LOGICAL ORDER

(1) Hitler's annexation of Austria, (2) signing of the Munich Pact, (3) signing of the nonaggression pact, (4) Germany's invasion of Poland.

3. SYNTHESIZING

Possible Response: Hitler falsely charged the Czechs with abusing Sudeten Germans and lied when he said that the Sudetenland was "his last territorial demand." He falsely accused Poles of brutalizing Germans in Poland and signed a secret pact with the Soviet Union agreeing to divide Poland between them. He also falsely justified the surprise invasion of Denmark and Norway as necessary "to protect [their] freedom and independence."

4. MAKING DECISIONS

Possible Responses: For—Appeasement would help avert war; compromise is not a sign of weakness; Against—Appeasement would feed Hitler's military aggression; Great Britain should defend its honor by declaring war.

OBJECTIVES

① To explain the reasons behind the Nazis' persecution of Jews and the problems facing Jewish refugees.

② To describe the Nazis' "final solution" to the Jewish problem and the horrors of the Holocaust.

CRITICAL THINKING

- Identifying problems, p. 714
- Summarizing, p. 717
- Analyzing causes, p. 718
- Supporting opinions, p. 718
- Developing historical perspective, p. 718

FOCUS & MOTIVATE

▶ **Starting with the Student**
Watch the video "Escaping the 'Final Solution'" to find out how the German program to establish an Aryan "master race" affected two German Jews.

- Discuss with students what they already know about the Holocaust and how the information in the video enhanced their understanding.
- Use the *Teacher's Resource Book* as a guide to focus on students' questions.

AMERICAN STORIES VIDEO SERIES
"Escaping the 'Final Solution'"
Videocassette: Volume 4

Videodisc: Disc 3, Side A, Chapter 2

OBJECTIVE
① **INSTRUCT**

The Persecution Begins

▶ **Starting with the Student**
Have students analyze the impact of the Nazi actions against German Jews by making a cause and effect chart that might look something like this:

(continued on next page)

TERMS & NAMES
- Holocaust
- *Kristallnacht*
- genocide
- concentration camp

③ The Holocaust

LEARN ABOUT Hitler's plans for the German "master race"
TO UNDERSTAND the fate of Jews and other "enemies" of the Third Reich.

Gerda Weissmann Klein

ONE AMERICAN'S STORY

In 1939, Gerda Weissmann was a carefree girl of 15 who had just returned from a summer vacation to her home in Bielsko, Poland. A few days later, invading German troops overran Bielsko and Gerda's world was shattered. Because the Weissmanns were Jews, they were forced to give up their home to a German family. In 1942, Gerda and her parents, along with the rest of Poland's Jews, were sent to labor camps. Gerda never forgot the day when members of Hitler's elite SS (*Schutzstaffel,* or "security squadron") came for the Jews.

> **A PERSONAL VOICE**
> We had to form a line and an SS man stood there with a little stick. I was holding hands with my mother and . . . he looked at me and said, "How old?" And I said, "eighteen," and he sort of pushed me to one side and my mother to the other side. . . . And shortly thereafter, some trucks arrived. Open trucks; with sort of a gate behind it and we were loaded onto the trucks. I heard my mother's voice from very far off ask, "Where to?" and I shouted back, "I don't know."
> **GERDA WEISSMANN KLEIN,** quoted in the film *One Survivor Remembers*

When the American Lieutenant Kurt Klein, who would later become Gerda Weissmann's husband, liberated her from the Nazis in 1945—just one day before her 21st birthday—she weighed 68 pounds and her hair was white. Even so, Gerda could count herself fortunate. Of all her family and friends, she alone had survived Hitler's campaign to exterminate Europe's Jews.

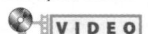 **VIDEO** *ESCAPING THE "FINAL SOLUTION"*
Kurt and Gerda Weissmann Klein Remember the Holocaust

German streets were strewn with shattered glass in the aftermath of *Kristallnacht.*

The Persecution Begins

On April 4, 1933, barely three months after Hitler took power in Germany, he ordered all "non-Aryans" to be removed from government jobs. This order was the first move in a campaign for racial purity that would become the **Holocaust**—the systematic murder of 11 million people across Europe, more than half of whom were Jews.

WHY THE JEWS? Although Jews were not the only victims of the Holocaust, they were the center of the Nazis' target. Anti-Semitism, or hatred of Jews, had deep roots in German history. For generations, many Germans looking for a scapegoat, or someone to blame for their failures and frustrations, had targeted the Jews. As a result, when Hitler blamed the Jews for Germany's defeat in World War I and for its economic problems following the war, many Germans were more than ready to support him.

As the Nazis tightened their hold on Germany, their persecution of Jews increased. In 1935, the Nuremberg Laws stripped Jews of their civil rights and property if they tried to leave Germany. To make identification easier, Jews over the age of six had to wear a bright yellow Jewish star on their clothing.

THINK THROUGH HISTORY
A. Identifying Problems What problems did German Jews face in Nazi Germany from 1935 to 1938?

A. Answer Trying either to survive under the hostile Nazi government or escaping Germany.

SECTION 3 RESOURCES

 PRINT RESOURCES

IN-DEPTH RESOURCES: UNIT 7
Guided Reading, p. 3
Literature: from *Sophie's Choice* by William Styron, p. 12
American Lives: Elie Wiesel, p. 15

ACCESS FOR STUDENTS ACQUIRING ENGLISH
Guided Reading (Spanish), p. 237

FORMAL ASSESSMENT
Section Quiz, p. 295

ALTERNATIVE ASSESSMENT BOOK
See forms for supporting and scoring alternative activities.

 TECHNOLOGY RESOURCES

CD-ROM *Our Times*

VIDEO *American Stories* video series
American Portfolio: A Videodisc for U.S. History
user's guide, pp. 221, 223

INTERNET McDougal Littell Learning On-Line
http://www.mcdougallittell.com

Worse was to come. On November 9, 1938, a night that came to be known as **Kristallnacht,** or "crystal night"—the night of broken glass—gangs of Nazi storm troopers attacked Jewish homes, businesses, and synagogues across Germany. An American who witnessed the violence in Leipzig wrote, "Jewish shop windows by the hundreds were systematically and wantonly smashed. . . . The main streets of the city were a positive litter of shattered plate glass." Afterward, the Nazis blamed the Jews for the destruction. More than 20,000 Jews were arrested and sent to concentration camps. At the same time, a German official announced, "The Jews will pay a collective fine of one billion marks, 20 percent of their property."

THE PLIGHT OF JEWISH REFUGEES Beginning in 1933, tens of thousands of Jews fled Germany each year. After *Kristallnacht,* the Nazis tried to speed Jewish emigration but encountered difficulty. France already had 40,000 Jewish refugees and did not want more. The British, who already admitted about 500 Jewish refugees a week, worried about fueling anti-Semitism if that number were to increase. Late in 1938, Germany's foreign minister observed: "We all want to get rid of our Jews. The difficulty is that no country wishes to receive them."

About 60,000 refugees—including such distinguished people as physicist Albert Einstein, author Thomas Mann, architect Walter Gropius, and theologian Paul Tillich—fled to the United States. More could have come if the United States had been willing to relax its strict immigration quotas. This was not done, partly because of widespread anti-Semitism and partly because many Americans feared that letting in more refugees during the Depression would mean competition for scarce jobs.

After war broke out in Europe in 1939, Americans also feared that opening the door to refugees from Germany would allow "enemy agents" to enter the United States. President Roosevelt said that while he sympathized with the Jews, he would not "do anything which would conceivably hurt the future of present American citizens."

Official indifference to the plight of Germany's Jews was so strong that when the *St. Louis*—a German luxury liner filled with refugees—passed Miami in 1939, the Coast Guard followed it to prevent the passengers from attempting to leave the ship for the United States. This decision was made even though 900 of the liner's 943 passengers had temporary landing permits. Passenger Liane Reif-Lehrer, who was just four years old at the time, recalled, "My mother and brother and I were among the passengers who survived, about a fourth of those on the ship. We were sent back to Europe and given haven in France, only to find the Nazis on our doorstep again a few months later."

Dutch Jews were forced to wear this yellow Star of David to make them easily identifiable to Hitler's henchmen.

ANOTHER
PERSPECTIVE

DENMARK'S RESISTANCE
In 1942, the Nazis began pressuring occupied Denmark to enforce the Nuremberg Laws against its Jews. The Danes resisted fiercely. Denmark's aged king, Christian X, is reported to have said,

The Jews are part of the Danish nation. We have no Jewish problem. . . . If the Jews are forced to wear the yellow star, I and my whole family shall wear it as a badge of honor.

Not only the royal family but thousands of Danes from all walks of life did just that.

The Final Solution

Unable to rid Germany of its Jews by forcing them to emigrate, the Nazis adopted a new approach in 1939. Their "final solution to the Jewish question" had as its goal "the disappearance of Jewry from Europe." Jews healthy enough to work would be sent to labor camps to perform slave labor. The rest would be exterminated. The horrifying result of this new plan was a cold-blooded and systematic **genocide,** or deliberate killing of an entire group of people.

THE CONDEMNED The Nazis' "final solution" rested on their belief that the Aryans were a superior people and that the strength and purity of this "master race" must be preserved. To accomplish this, the Nazis condemned to slavery and death not only the Jews but other groups that they viewed as inferior, or unworthy or as "enemies of the state."

World War Looms **715**

(continued from page 714)

Acts Against Jews	Impact on Jews
Ousting of non-Aryans from government	
Nuremberg Laws	
Kristallnacht	

▶ *Discussing Key Ideas*
- Once in power, the Nazis begin to persecute Jews and others in a campaign to achieve racial purity.
- Many Jews try to escape Germany but few countries will accept them.

IN-DEPTH RESOURCES: UNIT 7
Guided Reading, p. 3

ACCESS FOR STUDENTS ACQUIRING ENGLISH
Guided Reading (Spanish), p. 237

OUR TIMES
Kristallnacht

ANOTHER PERSPECTIVE
Denmark's Resistance

Critical Thinking: Analyzing Motives Ask students to consider why the Danes resisted the Nuremberg Laws while most Germans accepted those laws. *Possible Responses: Denmark lacked Germany's long history of anti-Semitism. Danes resented Germans telling them how to treat Jews.*

OBJECTIVE
② **INSTRUCT**

The Final Solution

▶ *Discussing Key Ideas*
- The Nazis' "final solution" is aimed at eliminating Jews and other "enemies of the state."

(continued on next page)

TEACHING OPTIONS

Exploring Themes

Immigration and Migration The United States has a long and proud tradition of offering asylum to victims of religious and political persecution. In the 1930s, that tradition ran into direct conflict with the quota system imposed by the Immigration Act of 1924. Few Americans called for a change in the quota system, however. Even many who were sympathetic to the plight of German Jews opposed admitting more refugees while millions of workers remained jobless in the United States. As a result, for every Jewish refugee who came to this country, many more who could have been saved died in Hitler's death camps.

Making Connections Across Cultures

German Jews Before the Nazis took power, Germany was home to a large and vital population of about 500,000 Jews. By 1939, fewer than half these Jews remained in Germany. The majority of those left were either too old to emigrate or were married to non-Jews. In the years that followed, most of Germany's remaining Jews perished in Hitler's death camps along with millions of other Jews from across Europe. Today only about 30,000 Jews make their homes in Germany.

(continued from page 715)

- The Nazis systematically murder Jews or send them to slave labor camps.
- To hasten the "final solution" the Nazis build huge death camps equipped with gas chambers and crematoriums.
- Those who survive the Holocaust are forever haunted by its horrors.

HISTORY FROM VISUALS
Hitler's Victims, 1939–1945

Reading the Graph Have students add up the numbers of victims shown in the graph to get a rough total of those killed in the Holocaust. *About 10 million.*

Extension Help students get some sense of the size of that number by relating it to the population of your city, state, or region.

 OUR TIMES
The Holocaust; *The Diary of Anne Frank*

MORE ABOUT . . .
The Final Solution

In a 1943 report on the "clearing out of the Jews" from German-occupied areas, Heinrich Himmler, head of the SS, boasted, "This is a page of glory in our history, which has never been written and is never to be written. . . . It shall be said on this occasion, openly here among ourselves, but we shall never speak of it publicly."

For more about the Holocaust, click on Social Studies at http://www.mcdougallittell.com

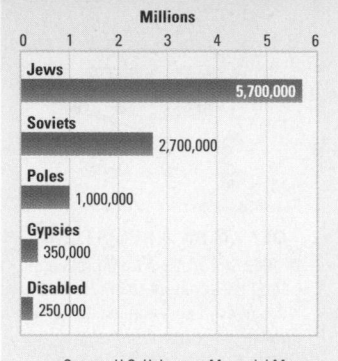

Hitler's Victims, 1939–1945

	Millions	
	0 1 2 3 4 5 6	
Jews		5,700,000
Soviets		2,700,000
Poles		1,000,000
Gypsies		350,000
Disabled		250,000

Source: U.S. Holocaust Memorial Museum

After taking power in 1933, the Nazis had concentrated on silencing their political opponents—Communists, Socialists, liberals, and anyone else who spoke out against the government. Once the Nazis had eliminated these open enemies of the state, they turned against other groups in Germany. These groups included

- Gypsies—who were an "inferior race"
- Freemasons—who supported the "Jewish conspiracy" to rule the world
- Jehovah's Witnesses—who refused to join the army or salute Hitler

The Nazis also targeted groups that they found unfit to be part of the "master race," such as homosexuals, the mentally retarded, the insane, the disabled, and the incurably ill. Beginning in 1939, the German government rounded up these individuals and shipped them off to "special treatment" centers where they were "accorded a mercy death." By 1941, children near one of these centers became so used to seeing the special buses that were used to transport victims that they would call out to each other, "Look, there's the murder box coming again."

As the Nazis moved eastward, they added Poles, Ukrainians, and Russians to their growing list of *Untermenschen,* or "subhumans," who were standing in the way of the expanding "master race." After the invasion of Poland, for example, hundreds of thousands of Poles were killed or shipped to Germany to perform slave labor. Meanwhile, empty Polish towns and farms were resettled with Germans seeking lebensraum.

CONCENTRATION CAMPS The Nazis began implementing their "final solution" in Poland. Nazi murder squads were assigned to round up Jews, strip them of their clothing, and then shoot them in cold blood. Other Jews were herded into dismal ghettos, or Jewish quarters, in Polish cities and were left to starve or die from disease. Still others were dragged from their homes and herded onto trains and trucks for shipment to **concentration camps.** In this process, families were often separated, sometimes—like the Weissmanns—forever.

Life in the camps was a cycle of hunger, humiliation, and work that only ended with death. The prisoners were crammed into crude wooden barracks that held up to a thousand people each. They shared their crowded quarters—as well as their meager meals of thin soup and occasional scraps of bread or potato—with hordes of rats and fleas. Hunger was so intense, recalled one survivor, "that if a bit of soup spilled over, prisoners would converge on the spot, dig their spoons into the mud and stuff the mess into their mouths."

Cooperative Activity: Exploring Literature of the Holocaust

Task: Students will read literary works dealing with the Holocaust, write book reviews, and present them to the class.

Purpose: To help students deepen their understanding of the Holocaust.

Activity: Small groups of students will choose a firsthand account about the Holocaust to review. They can read short works in their entirety or excerpts from longer works. Authors they might consider include Elie Wiesel, Anne

Frank, Etty Hellesum, and Binjamin Wilkomirski. Students will then work together to write a book review and prepare it for presentation to the class. The class as a whole should then discuss the similarities and differences among the works.

Building a Portfolio: Students who add their book reviews to their portfolios should include a note indicating their contribution.

ALTERNATIVE ASSESSMENT BOOK
Standards for Evaluating a Cooperative Activity

Standards for Evaluation
Book reviews should . . .

- exhibit careful reading of the literary work
- cite vivid details to explain the author's experience
- indicate the aspects of the book that had the greatest effect on the reader and why

The prisoners worked from dawn to dusk, seven days a week, until they collapsed. Those too weak to work were killed. Some, like Rudolf Reder, endured. He was one of only two Jews to survive the camp at Belzec, Poland.

A PERSONAL VOICE

The brute Schmidt was our guard; he beat and kicked us if he thought we were not working fast enough. He ordered his victims to lie down and gave them 25 lashes with a whip, ordering them to count out loud. If the victim made a mistake, he was given 50 lashes. . . . Thirty or 40 of us were shot every day. A doctor usually prepared a daily list of the weakest men. During the lunch break they were taken to a nearby grave and shot. They were replaced the following morning by new arrivals from the transport of the day. . . . It was a miracle if anyone survived for five or six months in Belzec.

RUDOLF REDER, quoted in *The Holocaust*

top, Inmates at Ebensee concentration camp in the Alps seem beyond any emotion; *above,* Women prisoners at the Belsen concentration camp in Germany use the boots of their dead comrades for fuel.

EXTERMINATION As deadly as overwork, starvation, beatings, and bullets were, they did not kill fast enough to satisfy the Nazis. Late in 1941, the Germans built six death camps in Poland. Each camp had several huge gas chambers in which as many as 6,000 lives could be snuffed out daily.

When prisoners arrived at Auschwitz, the largest of the death camps, they had to parade by several SS doctors. With a wave of the hand, the doctors separated those strong enough to work from those who would die that day. Both groups were told to leave all their belongings behind, with a promise that they would be returned later. Those destined to die were then led into a room outside the gas chamber and were told to undress for a shower. To complete the deception, they were even given a piece of soap. Finally, they were led into the chamber and poisoned with cyanide gas that spewed from the showerheads. This orderly mass extinction was sometimes done to the accompaniment of cheerful music played by an orchestra of camp inmates who had temporarily been spared execution.

At first the bodies were buried in huge pits. At Belzec, Rudolf Reder was part of a 500-man death brigade that labored all day, he said, "either at grave digging or emptying the gas chambers." But the decaying corpses gave off a stench that could be smelled for miles around. Worse yet, mass graves left evidence of the mass murder. To try to cover up the evidence of their slaughter, at some camps the Nazis installed

B. Answer Extermination of European Jews in death camps.

THINK THROUGH HISTORY
B. Summarizing *What was the goal of the Nazis' "final solution," and how was that goal nearly achieved?*

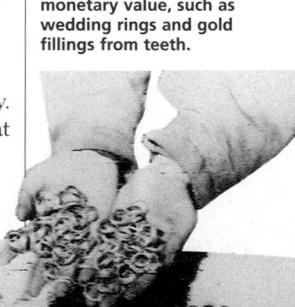

After stripping their victims of life and dignity, the Nazis hoarded victims' possessions that were of monetary value, such as wedding rings and gold fillings from teeth.

IN-DEPTH RESOURCES: UNIT 7
American Lives: Elie Wiesel, p. 15

ASSESS & RETEACH

Section 3 Assessment

Have students work in small groups to answer the questions. Have them discuss questions 3 and 4 with others in their group before answering.

Self-Assessment

Have students write a personal reflection on the Holocaust to test their understanding of the events involved.

Section Quiz

FORMAL ASSESSMENT
Section Quiz, p. 295

Reteach

Create a class chart on the board listing the acts against Jews during the Holocaust and their impact. Base the chart on the ones the students prepared individually as they read the section.

CLOSE

After taking power in 1933, the Nazis began a campaign to rid Germany of Jews and other "subhumans." The result was the Holocaust—the destruction of about 10 million human beings in the worst genocide in human history.

NOW & THEN

GENOCIDE OR "ETHNIC CLEANSING"?

In 1992, a civil war broke out in Bosnia between that country's ethnic Serbs and its non-Serb Muslims and Croats. Soon, reports from Bosnia told alarming stories of Serbian terrorism directed at non-Serbs living in Serb-controlled areas.

The list of horrors included the destruction of villages, systematic rape, death camps, random slaughter, and assaults on refugees fleeing for their lives. Bosnian Serbs called their campaign to drive more than 2 million Muslims and Croats from Serbian areas "ethnic cleansing." To the rest of the world, it looked like genocide.

" Never shall I forget these things. . . . Never."

ELIE WIESEL

huge crematoriums, or ovens, in which to burn the dead. At other camps, the bodies were simply thrown into a pit and set on fire.

Gassing was not the only method of extermination used in the camps. Prisoners were also shot, hung, or injected with poison. Still others died as a result of horrible medical experiments carried out by camp doctors. Some of these victims were injected with deadly germs in order to study the effect of disease on different groups of people. Others were forced to exist only on seawater in experiments to determine how long shipwrecked seamen could survive. Many more were used to test methods of sterilization, a subject of great interest to some Nazi doctors in their search for ways to improve the "master race."

THE SURVIVORS Six million Jews died in the death camps and in Nazi massacres. But some miraculously escaped the worst of the Holocaust. Many had help from ordinary people who were appalled by the Nazis' treatment of Jews. These people risked death by hiding Jews in their homes or by helping them escape to neutral countries such as Sweden or Switzerland.

Some Jews even survived the horrors of the concentration camps. In Gerda Weissmann Klein's view, survival depended as much on one's spirit as on getting enough to eat. "I do believe that if you were blessed with imagination, you could work through it," she wrote. "If, unfortunately, you were a person that faced reality, I think you didn't have a chance." Those who did come out of the camps alive were forever changed by what they had witnessed. For survivor Elie Wiesel, who entered Auschwitz in 1944 at the age of 14, the sun had set forever.

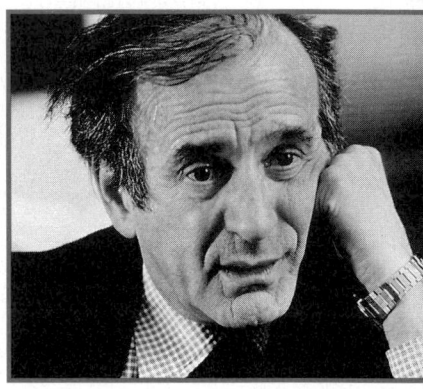

Elie Wiesel

A PERSONAL VOICE
Never shall I forget that night, the first night in the camp, which has turned my life into one long night. . . . Never shall I forget the little faces of the children, whose bodies I saw turned into wreaths of smoke beneath a silent blue sky. Never shall I forget those flames which consumed my faith forever. Never shall I forget that nocturnal silence which deprived me, for all eternity, of the desire to live. Never shall I forget those moments which murdered my God and my soul and turned my dreams to dust. Never shall I forget these things, even if I am condemned to live as long as God Himself. Never.

ELIE WIESEL, *Night*

Section 3 Assessment

1. TERMS & NAMES

Identify:
• Holocaust
• *Kristallnacht*
• genocide
• concentration camp

2. ANALYZING CAUSES List at least four events that led to the Holocaust.

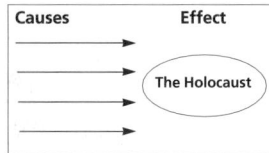

Write a paragraph summarizing one of the events that you listed.

3. SUPPORTING OPINIONS Do you think that the United States was justified in not allowing more Jewish refugees to immigrate? Why or why not?

THINK ABOUT
• the views of isolationists in the United States
• some Americans' prejudices and fears
• the incident on the Germany luxury liner, *St. Louis*

4. DEVELOPING HISTORICAL PERSPECTIVE Why do you think the Nazi program of systematic genocide was so brutally effective? Support your answer with details from the text.

THINK ABOUT
• the long German history of anti-Semitism
• the secrecy and lies told by the Nazis
• the scope and organization of the Nazis' genocidal plans

718 Chapter 24

ANSWERS

1. TERMS & NAMES

Holocaust, p. 714

Kristallnacht, p. 715

genocide, p. 715

concentration camp, p. 716

2. ANALYZING CAUSES

Possible Responses: The removal of non-Aryans from government jobs; Nuremberg Laws stripping Jews of their civil rights and property; *Kristallnacht*—Nazi storm troopers' attack on Jewish homes, businesses, and synagogues; "final solution"—systematic genocide of Jews, gypsies, and other groups that Nazis considered "subhuman." Paragraphs will vary.

3. SUPPORTING OPINIONS

Possible Responses: Justified—The United States had to protect the national security and the welfare of its own citizens, including their job security during the Depression; **Not justified**—The United States was obligated to provide political asylum for victims of prejudice and mass murder.

4. DEVELOPING HISTORICAL PERSPECTIVE

Possible Responses: The Nazis lied about and covered up man of their activities. People had difficulty believing the evidence A basic element in human nature made people tend to cling tenaciously to hope.

TERMS & NAMES
- Axis powers
- Lend-Lease Act
- Atlantic Charter
- Allies
- Hideki Tojo

4 America Moves Toward War

LEARN ABOUT the American response to aggression in Europe and Asia
TO UNDERSTAND how the United States entered World War II.

ONE AMERICAN'S STORY

In late August 1939, President Franklin D. Roosevelt had sent a cable to Hitler urging him to settle his differences with the Polish people peacefully. In answer, Hitler invaded Poland on September 1. "Hitler is a madman," Roosevelt had said after the Nazis took power in Germany, "and his counselors, some of whom I personally know, are even madder than he is." Now those same madmen had unleashed their insanity on the world. Two days after the invasion of Poland, Roosevelt spoke reassuringly to Americans about the outbreak of war in Europe.

A PERSONAL VOICE
Let no man or woman thoughtlessly or falsely talk of America sending its armies to European fields. . . . This nation will remain a neutral nation, but I cannot ask that every American remain neutral in thought as well. Even a neutral has a right to take account of facts. Even a neutral cannot be asked to close his mind or his conscience. . . . I have said not once, but many times, that I have seen war and I hate war. . . . As long as it is in my power to prevent, there will be no blackout of peace in the United States.

FRANKLIN DELANO ROOSEVELT, Radio speech, September 3, 1939

Franklin D. Roosevelt

At that time, Roosevelt knew that Americans were still deeply committed to staying out of war. In his heart, however, he also knew that there could be no peace in a world controlled by madmen.

The United States Musters Its Forces

As German tanks thundered across Poland, Roosevelt issued an official proclamation of neutrality as required by the Neutrality Acts. At the same time, he began to prepare the nation for the struggle he feared lay just ahead.

MOVING CAUTIOUSLY AWAY FROM NEUTRALITY On September 8, 1939, Roosevelt announced that he was calling a special session of Congress to revise the Neutrality Acts. When Congress met two weeks later, the president asked for a "cash-and-carry" provision, which would permit nations to buy American arms as long as they paid cash and carried the goods home in their own ships. Providing the arms that would help France and Britain defeat Hitler, Roosevelt argued, was the best way to keep America out of the war.

Isolationists in Congress, such as Senator Arthur Vandenberg, argued just the opposite, however. "I do not believe that we can become an arsenal for one belligerent without becoming a target for another," Vandenberg said. After six weeks of heated debate, Congress passed the Neutrality Act of 1939, and cash-and-carry went into effect.

THE AXIS THREAT Over the next few months, America's cash-and-carry policy began to look like too little, too late. By the summer of 1940, France had fallen and Britain was under siege by the German Luftwaffe. Then, in September, Americans were jolted by the news that Japan, Germany, and Italy had signed a mutual defense treaty, the Tripartite Pact. The three nations became known as the **Axis powers.**

> "I have seen war and I hate war."
>
> **FRANKLIN D. ROOSEVELT, 1939**

A. Answer Because they thought that providing arms to nations at war would make America a participant in the war.

THINK THROUGH HISTORY
A. Analyzing Motives Why did some Americans object to the cash-and-carry policy?

World War Looms **719**

Teacher's Edition **719**

(continued from page 719)

- In response to the threat of war, the U.S. begins building its defenses and reelects Roosevelt to a third term.

IN-DEPTH RESOURCES: UNIT 7
Guided Reading, p. 4
ACCESS FOR STUDENTS ACQUIRING ENGLISH
Guided Reading (Spanish), p. 238

HISTORY FROM VISUALS
Carving Up the World
Reading the Cartoon Have students compare the caricatures of Hitler, Mussolini, and Tojo in this cartoon to the photographs of these three leaders in the chapter. What characteristics has the cartoonist focused on?

Extension Discuss other images that might be used to characterize the actions of the Axis leaders.

HISTORICAL SPOTLIGHT
The Election of 1940
Critical Thinking: Forming Opinions Roosevelt told voters during the campaign, "Your boys are not going to be sent into any foreign wars." Have students consider why he made this promise.

OBJECTIVE
② **INSTRUCT**

"The Great Arsenal of Democracy"

▶ **Discussing Key Ideas**
- Roosevelt supplies the Allies with war equipment.
- German U-boat attacks threaten Roosevelt's lend-lease program.

SKILLBUILDER
INTERPRETING POLITICAL CARTOONS
What were the Axis leaders—Hitler, Mussolini, and Tojo—greedily gobbling up?
Skillbuilder Answer The world.

HISTORICAL SPOTLIGHT

THE ELECTION OF 1940
War was the key issue in the 1940 presidential election. At the Democratic convention, isolationists inserted a plank in the party platform that read, "We will not participate in foreign wars. We will not send our armed forces to fight in lands across the seas." This was wording Roosevelt could not accept. No one, he argued, could say where Americans might have to fight if the nation's survival was at stake. His solution was to add five words to the no-war plank: "except in case of attack."

Again and again during the campaign, Roosevelt reassured voters by saying, "This country is not going to war." In his mind, however, he qualified that promise with the same five words, "except in case of attack."

720 Chapter 24

The Tripartite Pact was clearly aimed at keeping the United States out of the war. Under the treaty, each Axis nation agreed to come to the defense of the others in case of attack. This meant that if the United States were to declare war on any one of the Axis powers, it would face its worst military nightmare—a two-ocean war, with fighting in both the Atlantic and the Pacific.

Hoping to avoid this situation, Roosevelt scrambled to provide the British with "all aid short of war." In June 1940, he sent Britain 500,000 rifles and 80,000 machine guns to help replace those lost at Dunkirk. In September, the United States traded 50 old destroyers for leases on British military bases in the Caribbean and Newfoundland. Even British Prime Minister Winston Churchill later called this deal "a decidedly unneutral act."

BUILDING AMERICA'S DEFENSES Meanwhile, Roosevelt asked Congress to increase spending for national defense. After years of isolationism, the United States was militarily weak. Critics pointed out that 18 countries had larger armies, that the navy could hardly protect the Panama Canal, and that Italy's air force had more firepower than that of the United States.

In response, Congress dramatically boosted defense spending in 1940. It also passed the nation's first peacetime military draft. Under the Selective Training and Service Act, 16 million men between the ages of 21 and 35 were registered. Of these, 1 million were to be drafted for one year. Roosevelt himself drew the first draft numbers. "This is a most solemn ceremony," he told a national radio audience. "It is accompanied by no fanfare—no blowing of bugles or beating of drums. There should be none."

ROOSEVELT'S REELECTION That same year, Roosevelt decided to break the tradition of a two-term presidency begun by George Washington and to run for reelection. To the great disappointment of isolationists, Roosevelt's Republican opponent, a public utilities executive named Wendell Willkie, supported Roosevelt's policy of aiding Britain. At the same time, both Willkie and Roosevelt promised to keep the nation out of war. Because there was so little difference between the candidates, the majority of voters chose the one they knew best. Roosevelt was reelected with nearly 55 percent of the votes cast.

"The Great Arsenal of Democracy"

Not long after the election, President Roosevelt held another of his fireside chats on the radio. There was no hope of negotiating a peace with Hitler, he told the nation. "No man can tame a tiger into a kitten by stroking it." He also warned that if Britain fell, the Axis powers would be left unchallenged to conquer the world, at which point, he said, "all of us in all the Americas would be living at the point of a gun." To prevent such a situation, the United States had to help defeat the Axis threat by turning itself into "the great arsenal of democracy."

THE LEND-LEASE PLAN By late 1940, however, Britain had no more cash to spend in the arsenal of democracy. Consequently, Roosevelt suggested replacing "cash-and-carry" with a new plan that he called "lend-lease." Under this plan, the president would lend or lease arms and other supplies to "any country whose defense was vital to the United States."

Even though the isolationists were losing the support of the American public, they argued bitterly against Lend-Lease. Congress finally passed the

720 CHAPTER 24

B. Answer
Revision of the Neutrality Acts; dramatically increased defense spending; institution of the nation's first peacetime draft.
THINK THROUGH HISTORY
B. Recognizing Effects What impact did the outbreak of war in Europe have on U.S. foreign and defense policy?

TEACHING OPTIONS

Exploring Themes

Constitutional Concerns The "no-third-term tradition" for American presidents dates back to George Washington. After Roosevelt broke this unwritten rule by winning a third term in 1940, and then a fourth in 1944, the tradition was made part of the Constitution. The 22nd Amendment, adopted in 1951, states, "No person shall be elected to the office of President more than twice." Discuss with students whether they think this is a wise limitation, especially considering the circumstances under which Roosevelt was elected to his third term in 1940.

Making Connections Across Time

Current Limitations on Legislative Terms Today only the president is constitutionally limited to two terms. Many states, however, are seeking to limit representatives and senators to a fixed number of terms in office. Ask students to research the current status of term-limiting legislation or initiatives in their state. Interested students could research the situations in other states and create a chart like this summarizing their findings:

Term Limitations

State	Senators	Representatives	Pending Legislation

"The United States should not become involved in European wars."

Still recovering from World War I and struggling with the Great Depression, many Americans believed their country should remain strictly neutral toward the war in Europe.

Representative James F. O'Connor voiced the country's reservations when he asked, "Dare we set America up and commit her as the financial and military blood bank of the rest of the world when the proportion of want in this country is still so great that by doing this our country would become a victim of financial and military pernicious anemia?" O'Connor maintained that the United States could not "right every wrong" or "police [the] world."

The widely admired aviator Charles Lindbergh risked his reputation by stating his hope that "the future of America . . . not be tied to these eternal wars in Europe." Lindbergh asserted that "Americans [should] fight anybody and everybody who attempts to interfere with our hemisphere." However, he went on to say, "Our safety does not lie in fighting European wars. It lies in our own internal strength, in the character of the American people and American institutions." Like many isolationists, Lindbergh asserted that democracy would not be saved "by the forceful imposition of our ideals abroad, but by example of their successful operation at home."

"The United States must protect democracies throughout the world."

As the conflict in Europe deepened, interventionists embraced President Franklin D. Roosevelt's declaration that "when peace has been broken anywhere, peace of all countries everywhere is in danger." Roosevelt emphasized the global character of 20th-century commerce and communication by noting, "Every word that comes through the air, every ship that sails the sea, every battle that is fought does affect the American future."

Roosevelt and other political leaders also appealed to the nation's conscience. Secretary of State Cordell Hull noted that the world was "face to face . . . with an organized, ruthless, and implacable movement of steadily expanding conquest." In the same vein, Undersecretary of State Sumner Welles called Hitler "a sinister and pitiless conqueror [who] has reduced more than half of Europe to abject serfdom."

After the war expanded into the Atlantic, Roosevelt declared, "It is time for all Americans . . . to stop being deluded by the romantic notion that the Americas can go on living happily and peacefully in a Nazi-dominated world." He added, "Let us not ask ourselves whether the Americas should begin to defend themselves after the first attack . . . or the twentieth attack. The time for active defense is now."

INTERACT WITH HISTORY

1. **ANALYZING ASSUMPTIONS** How did isolationists' and interventionists' opinions differ regarding America's responsibility to other nations?

   SEE SKILLBUILDER HANDBOOK, PAGE 1047.

2. **WRITING AN EDITORIAL** Do research to find out more about Charles Lindbergh's antiwar activities. Then write an editorial supporting or criticizing Lindbergh's arguments.

Lend-Lease Act in 1941 and supported it with $7 billion. In all, the United States eventually spent $50 billion under the act.

Britain was not the only nation to receive lend-lease aid. On June 22, 1941, Hitler ignored his peace treaty with Stalin and invaded the Soviet Union with 3 million troops. The Führer confidently predicted victory within six weeks. But the Soviets resisted fiercely. As they pulled back from the Nazi advance, they carried out a scorched-earth policy, in which they destroyed everything that might be of use to the invaders. Six weeks stretched into six months. Then, as the bitter Russian winter set in, the German invasion ground to a halt.

Meanwhile, Roosevelt began sending lend-lease supplies to the Soviet Union. Some Americans opposed providing aid to Stalin. They even argued that Hitler was doing the United States a favor by attacking the communists. But Roosevelt agreed with Winston Churchill, who once remarked that "if Hitler invaded Hell," the British would be prepared to work with the devil himself.

GERMAN WOLF PACKS For lend-lease aid to be of any use to Britain and the Soviet Union, supply lines had to be kept open across the Atlantic Ocean. To prevent delivery of lend-lease shipments, Hitler deployed hundreds of German submarines—or U-boats—to the North Atlantic. There, groups of 15 to 20 submarines, known as wolf packs, patrolled shipping lanes for cargo ships.

During five weeks in April and May 1941, the Germans sank 1.2 million tons of British shipping. They were sinking ships faster than the British could replace them. Something had to be done to protect cargo ships, supporters of

THINK THROUGH HISTORY
C. Analyzing Motives Why did Roosevelt take one "unneutral" step after another to assist Britain and the Soviet Union in 1941?

C. Answer Roosevelt believed that the best way to stop the Axis powers was to help their opponents—mainly Britain and the Soviet Union.

World War Looms **721**

POINT COUNTERPOINT
Isolationism

▶ ***Starting with the Student***
- Have students create a chart listing the advantages and disadvantages of involvement or isolationism. Their charts might look like this:

	Pros	Cons
Involvement		
Isolation		

▶ ***Discussing Key Ideas***
- Isolationists believe that America should not police the world.
- Interventionists respond that a breach of peace anywhere in the world affects everyone and that not to act is to accept Hitler's tyranny.

IN-DEPTH RESOURCES: UNIT 7
American Lives: Charles A. Lindbergh, p. 16

 ELECTRONIC LIBRARY OF PRIMARY SOURCES
from "Let Us Face the Truth" *from the* New York Times

MORE ABOUT . . .
Lend-Lease

Roosevelt's lend-lease plan aroused fierce opposition. "Lending war equipment is a good deal like lending chewing gum," argued isolationist Senator Robert Taft. "You don't want it back." Roosevelt sold the plan to the public, however, by comparing lending goods to the Allies to lending a garden hose to a neighbor to put out a fire that might otherwise spread to your own house.

 ELECTRONIC LIBRARY OF PRIMARY SOURCES
from "Are We Being Led Into War?" by George A. Dondero

INTERACT WITH HISTORY

1. Analyzing Assumptions

Possible Answers:

Isolationists: America's responsibilities consisted of bolstering its own strength and conducting its internal affairs in a way that would serve as a model to other nations. Democratic principles could not be forcibly imposed on other nations.

Interventionists: America, as a leading member of the global community, was obligated to offer all possible assistance to help stop the conquest of Europe and the defeat of democratic ideals by Hitler.

2. Writing an Editorial

Standards for Evaluation
Editorials should meet the following criteria:

- Clearly state students' position on Lindbergh's isolationism.
- Support that opinion with details about his antiwar activities and speeches.
- Include specific quotations from Lindbergh to increase the effectiveness of their editorials.

The German mother ship *Saar* and her brood of U-boats wait in Bremen harbor in Germany for orders to attack.

lend-lease argued. Otherwise, the United States might just as well dump its lend-lease shipments into the ocean.

In June 1941, Roosevelt ordered the U.S. Navy to protect lend-lease shipments as far east as Iceland. He also gave American warships permission to attack German U-boats in self-defense.

Planning for War

With each step Roosevelt took against the Axis powers, the roar of the isolationists grew louder. In August 1941, they voiced their opposition to a bill to extend the draft for another 18 months. Congress passed the draft-extension bill, but only by a razor-thin margin of 203 to 202 in the House of Representatives. Roosevelt was not discouraged by this narrow victory, however. With the army provided for, he began planning for the war he thought was certain to come.

THE ATLANTIC CHARTER While Congress voted on the draft extension, Roosevelt and Churchill met secretly aboard a warship off the coast of Newfoundland. Churchill had come hoping for a military commitment from the United States. Instead, he settled for a declaration of principles called the **Atlantic Charter.** In this document, the two leaders spelled out the causes for which World War II was fought—even before the United States officially entered the conflict. The charter pledged both Great Britain and the United States to (1) seek no territorial expansion, (2) pursue no territorial changes without the consent of the inhabitants, (3) respect the right of people to choose their own form of government, (4) promote free trade among nations, (5) encourage international cooperation to improve peoples' lives, (6) build a secure peace based on freedom from want and fear, (7) work for disarmament of aggressors, and (8) establish a "permanent system of general security."

Later in 1941, the Atlantic Charter became the basis of a new document called "A Declaration by the United Nations." The term *United Nations* was suggested by Roosevelt to express the common purpose of the **Allies,** those nations that had joined together to fight the Axis powers. The declaration was signed by 26 nations, including the Soviet Union and China. Together, observed Churchill, these nations represented "four-fifths of the human race."

THE SHOOTING BEGINS "How close to war is the United States?" That was the question Churchill was asked again and again after his August 1941 meeting with Roosevelt. For the moment, the answer still seemed to be "not very." Then, on September 4, a German U-boat fired two torpedoes at the U.S. destroyer *Greer.* President Roosevelt responded with the announcement that the U.S. Navy had been ordered to fire on German ships on sight. "When you see a rattlesnake poised to strike," the President explained, "you do not wait until he has struck before you crush him. These Nazi submarines and raiders are the rattlesnakes of the Atlantic."

Two weeks later, the *Pink Star,* an American merchant ship, was sunk off Greenland. Its lost cargo included machine tools, evaporated milk, and enough cheddar cheese to feed more than 3.5 million British laborers for a week. In mid-October, the U.S. destroyer *Kearny* was torpedoed near Iceland and 11 lives were lost. A few days later, German U-boats sank the U.S. destroyer *Reuben James* in the same waters, killing at least 100 sailors. "America has been attacked," Roosevelt announced grimly. "The shooting has started. And history has recorded who fired the first shot."

722 CHAPTER 24

As the death toll mounted, the Senate finally repealed the ban against arming merchant ships. The vote was so close, however, that Roosevelt knew that something far more dramatic than German attacks on U.S. ships would be needed to persuade Congress to declare war. Churchill knew this as well, advising his impatient war cabinet to "have patience and trust to the tide which is flowing our way, and to events."

Japan Attacks the United States

The tide pushing the United States toward war was flowing much faster than either leader knew. To almost everyone's surprise, however, the attack that brought the United States into the war came from an unexpected country—not from Germany but from Japan.

JAPAN'S AMBITIONS In Japan, expansionists had long dreamed of creating a vast colonial empire that would stretch from Manchuria and China south to Thailand and Indonesia. This dream had motivated Japan's invasion of Manchuria in 1931 and of China in 1937. South of China, though, Japan's ambitions for expansion came face to face with several colonial empires. These empires included France (French Indochina), the Netherlands (the Dutch East Indies), Britain (Burma, India, and Malaya), and the United States (Guam and the Philippines). By 1941, France and the Netherlands had fallen to Germany, and the British were too busy fighting Hitler to block Japanese expansion. Only the United States and its Pacific islands remained in Japan's way.

The Japanese began their southward push in July of 1941 by taking over French military bases in Indochina (now Vietnam, Cambodia, and Laos). The United States protested this new act of aggression by cutting off trade with Japan. This trade embargo included the one thing Japan could not live without—oil to fuel its war machine. Japanese military leaders warned that, without oil, Japan could be defeated without its enemies ever striking a blow. The leaders declared that Japan would have to persuade the United States to end its oil embargo, or seize the oil fields in the Dutch East Indies.

In October, the militant Japanese general **Hideki Tojo** became the new prime minister of Japan. Shortly after taking office, Tojo met Japan's revered emperor, Hirohito. At that meeting, Tojo promised the emperor that the government would make a final attempt to preserve peace with the Americans. If the peace talks failed, Japan would have no choice but to go to war. But on November 5, 1941, the very day that Tojo's special "peace" envoy flew to Washington for talks, the prime minister ordered the Japanese navy to prepare for an attack on the United States.

The U.S. military had broken Japan's secret communication codes and knew that Japan was preparing for a strike. What it didn't know was where the attack would come. Late in November, Roosevelt sent out a "war warning" to military commanders in Hawaii, Guam, and the Philippines. If war could not be avoided, the warning said, "the United States desires that Japan commit the first overt act." And the nation waited.

The peace talks went on for a month. Then, late on December 6, 1941, the president received a decoded message that had been intercepted. This message instructed Japan's peace envoy to reject all American peace proposals. "This means war," Roosevelt told his friend and adviser Henry Hopkins. "It's too bad we can't strike first and prevent a surprise," Hopkins replied. "No, we can't do that," Roosevelt

F. Answer Japan needed oil and the United States had placed an embargo on it to protest Japanese aggression in Indochina.

THINK THROUGH HISTORY
F. Analyzing Issues How was oil a source of conflict between Japan and the United States?

KEY PLAYER

HIDEKI TOJO
1884–1948

Who was Hideki Tojo? Based on information in the world press when Tojo took power in 1941, the answer depended on who was responding. American newspapers described Tojo as "smart, hardboiled, resourceful, [and] contemptuous of theories, sentiments, and negotiations." The Nazi press in Germany praised Tojo as "a man charged with energy, thinking clearly and with a single purpose." To a British paper, Tojo was "the son of Satan" whose single purpose was "unleashing all hell on the Far East." In Japan, however, Tojo was looked up to as a man whose "decisive leadership was a signal for the nation to rise and administer a great shock to the anti-Axis powers."

World War Looms **723**

MORE ABOUT . . .
The Sinking of the
Reuben James
The sinking of the *Reuben James* inspired folk singer Woody Guthrie to write a ballad in memory of the men who served and died in America's undeclared war in the Atlantic. At the end of the refrain was the line "Did you have a friend on the good *Reuben James?*"

OBJECTIVE
④ **INSTRUCT**

Japan Attacks the United States

▶ *Discussing Key Ideas*
• The expansionist ambitions of Japan put it on a collision course with the United States.
• Japan's surprise attack on Pearl Harbor in 1941 precipitates America's formal entry into World War II.

IN-DEPTH RESOURCES: UNIT 7
Primary Sources: The Bombing of Pearl Harbor, p. 9; War Poster, p. 11
Geography Application: Japanese Aggression, p. 6

KEY PLAYER
Hideki Tojo

Critical Thinking:
Synthesizing Ask students to look for clues about the character of Hideki Tojo in his photograph. *Possible Responses: Tojo appears to be a much-decorated military officer. His array of medals suggests that he may have had strong leadership qualities as well as courage and intelligence.*

TEACHING OPTION

Cooperative Activity: Creating a Political Cartoon

Task: Student groups will create a political cartoon supporting or opposing the entry of the United States into World War II after the bombing of Pearl Harbor.

Purpose: To help students communicate ideas visually.

Activity: Small groups of students will create a political cartoon on America's response to Japan's attack on Pearl Harbor. The cartoon should clearly support or oppose entry into

the war. After the group brainstorms for ideas, one student might do the research, another do the drawing, and another write the caption. Groups should share their completed cartoons with the class.

📁 **Building a Portfolio:** Students who add the cartoons to their portfolios should attach a note indicating their contribution to the cartoon and explaining its meaning.

Standards for Evaluation
Cartoons should . . .

• take a clear position for or against America's involvement in World War II
• communicate that position using images and minimal words
• be easily understood

reportedly responded. "We are a democracy of peaceful people. We have a good record. We must stand on it."

THE ATTACK ON PEARL HARBOR Early the next morning, a Japanese dive-bomber swooped low over the U.S. naval base at Pearl Harbor—the largest U.S. naval base in the Pacific. The bomber was followed by more than 180 Japanese warplanes launched from six aircraft carriers. As the first Japanese bombs found their targets, a radio operator flashed this message: "Air raid on Pearl Harbor. This is not a drill."

For an hour and a half, the Japanese planes were barely disturbed by American antiaircraft guns and blasted target after target. By the time the last plane soared off around 9:30 A.M., the devastation was appalling. John Garcia, a pipe fitter's apprentice, was there.

A PERSONAL VOICE
It was a mess. I was working on the U.S.S. *Shaw*. It was on a floating dry dock. It was in flames. I started to go down to the pipe fitter's shop to get my toolbox when another wave of Japanese came in. I got under a set of concrete steps at the dry dock where the battleship *Pennsylvania* was. An officer came by and asked me to go into the *Pennsylvania* and try to get the fires out. A bomb had penetrated the marine deck, and . . . three decks below. Under that was the magazines: ammunition, powder, shells. I said "There ain't no way I'm gonna go down there." It could blow up any minute. I was young and 16, not stupid.
JOHN GARCIA, quoted in *The Good War*

For Japan, the attack on Pearl Harbor was a stunning victory. The Japanese navy all but crippled the entire U.S. Pacific Fleet in one blow. Its own casualties numbered only 29 planes. In Tokyo, the elated Tojo visited a shrine to thank the spirits of his ancestors for this favorable opening of Japan's campaign to rule East Asia.

In Washington, the mood ranged from outrage to panic. At the White House, Eleanor Roosevelt watched closely as her husband, with a "deadly calm,"

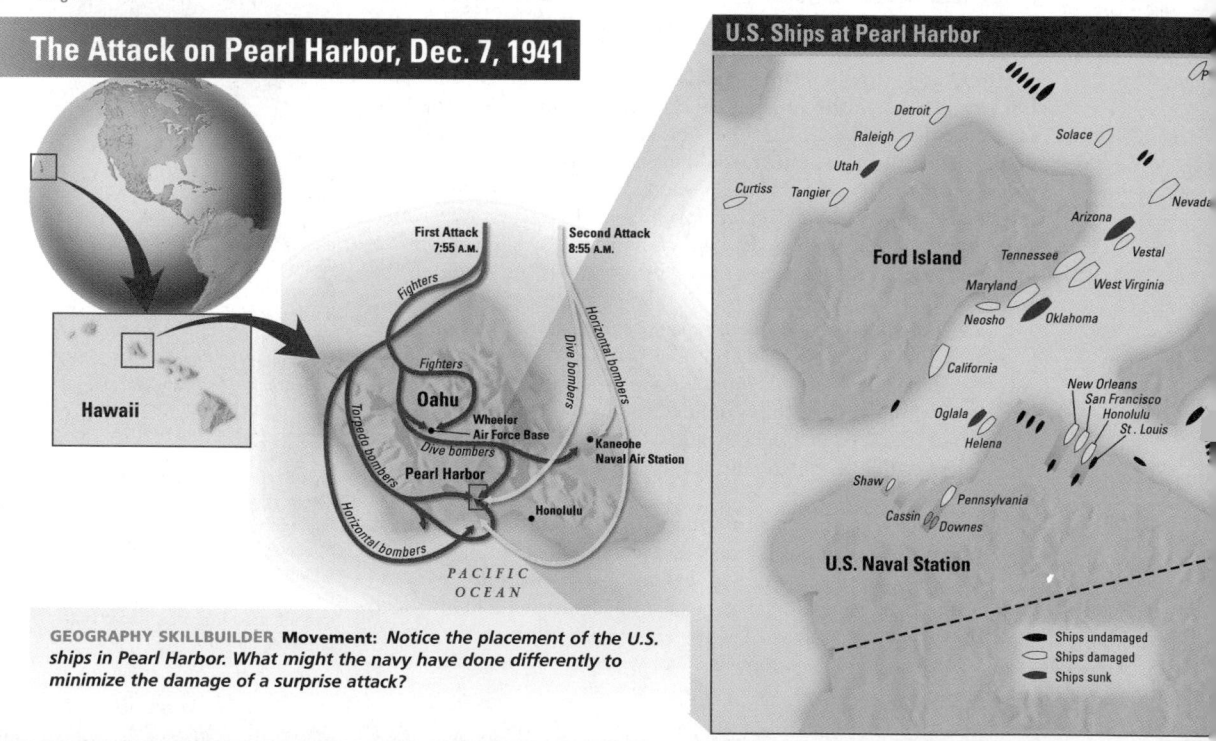

The Attack on Pearl Harbor, Dec. 7, 1941

Hawaii

First Attack 7:55 A.M.

Second Attack 8:55 A.M.

Fighters

Dive bombers

Horizontal bombers

Torpedo bombers

Fighters

Oahu

Wheeler Air Force Base

Dive bombers

Pearl Harbor

Kaneohe Naval Air Station

Horizontal bombers

Honolulu

PACIFIC OCEAN

GEOGRAPHY SKILLBUILDER Movement: *Notice the placement of the U.S. ships in Pearl Harbor. What might the navy have done differently to minimize the damage of a surprise attack?*

U.S. Ships at Pearl Harbor

Detroit
Raleigh
Solace
Utah
Curtiss Tangier
Nevada
Arizona
Ford Island
Tennessee
Vestal
Maryland
West Virginia
Neosho
Oklahoma
California
New Orleans
San Francisco
Honolulu
Oglala
St. Louis
Helena
Shaw
Cassin
Downes
Pennsylvania

U.S. Naval Station

Ships undamaged
Ships damaged
Ships sunk

absorbed the news from Hawaii, "each report more terrible than the last." The surprise raid had sunk or badly damaged 18 ships. About 190 planes had been destroyed or severely damaged. Some 2,400 people had died, and another 1,178 had been wounded. These losses constituted more damage than the U.S. Navy had suffered in all of World War I.

Beneath the president's calm, Eleanor could see how worried he was. "I never wanted to have to fight this war on two fronts," Roosevelt told his wife. "We haven't the Navy to fight in both the Atlantic and the Pacific . . . so we will have to build up the Navy and the Air Force and that will mean that we will have to take a good many defeats before we can have a victory."

The next day, President Roosevelt addressed Congress. "Yesterday, December 7, 1941, a date which will live in infamy," he began, "the Japanese launched an unprovoked and dastardly attack on American soil." He asked for a declaration of war against Japan, which Congress quickly approved. Three days later, Germany and Italy declared war on the United States.

For all the damage done at Pearl Harbor, perhaps the greatest was to the cause of isolationism. "The only thing now to do," said the isolationist senator Burton Wheeler after the attack, "is to lick the hell out of them."

above, **Casualties of the Japanese attack on Pearl Harbor included the U.S.S. California,** which was hit by two torpedoes and a bomb; *above left,* **also hit were almost 200 aircraft,** such as those shown here in their flaming graveyard.

G. Answer It did so much damage that it persuaded most isolationists that the U.S. could not remain out of World War II. It necessitated preparation for a two-ocean war.

THINK THROUGH HISTORY
G. Identifying Problems What problem did the Japanese attack on Pearl Harbor solve for Roosevelt? What new problems did it create?

Section 4 Assessment

1. TERMS & NAMES

Identify:
- Axis powers
- Lend-Lease Act
- Atlantic Charter
- Allies
- Hideki Tojo

2. SUMMARIZING Create a time line of key events leading to America's entry into World War II. Use the dates already plotted on the time line below as a guide.

```
        March      August
        1941       1941

September    June       December
1940         1941       1941
```

Which of the events that you listed was most influential in bringing the United States into the war? Why?

3. FORMING OPINIONS Do you think that the United States should have waited to be attacked before declaring war?

THINK ABOUT
- the reputation of the United States
- the influence of the isolationists
- the destruction of Pearl Harbor

4. CLARIFYING Although the U.S. Congress was still unwilling to declare war early in 1941, Churchill told his war cabinet, "We must have patience and trust to the tide which is flowing our way, and to events." What do you think Churchill meant by this remark? Support your answer.

THINK ABOUT
- Roosevelt's series of "unneutral" steps to assist Great Britain in its war efforts
- the Atlantic Charter
- Churchill's view of Hitler

World War Looms **725**

REVIEWING THE CHAPTER

TERMS & NAMES

1. fascism, p. 704
2. Adolf Hitler, p. 704
3. Nazism, p. 704
4. Winston Churchill, p. 709
5. appeasement, p. 709
6. Charles de Gaulle, p. 713
7. Holocaust, p. 714
8. genocide, p. 715
9. Axis powers, p. 719
10. Allies, p. 722

MAIN IDEAS

11. To make the Soviet Union socialist by stamping out private enterprise; to transform it into a great industrial power by building state-owned factories and power plants.

12. The failure of the League of Nations to take action against Japanese militarism sent a clear message to Europe's dictators, who began to behave more aggressively.

13. Hitler and Mussolini's military support of Franco hastened his victory.

14. It surprised the enemy and then crushed it with overwhelming force.

15. German occupation of northern France and the establishment of a Nazi-controlled puppet government in southern France; de Gaulle fled to England and set up a government-in-exile.

16. Jews, gypsies, homosexuals, people with mental or physical disabilities, Poles, Ukrainians, and Russians.

17. Many Danish citizens wore the yellow Star of David; some people risked death by hiding Jews in their homes or helping them to escape to neutral countries.

18. Japan, Germany, and Italy; if the United States declared war on any one of the Axis powers, it would have to fight on two oceans.

19. Increased defense spending, peacetime draft, Lend-Lease Act, and an end to the ban against arming merchant ships.

20. Because the Japanese bombed Pearl Harbor.

REVIEWING THE CHAPTER

TERMS & NAMES For each item below, write a sentence explaining its historical significance related to World War II. For each person below, explain his role in the events of this period.

1. fascism
2. Adolf Hitler
3. Nazism
4. Winston Churchill
5. appeasement
6. Charles de Gaulle
7. Holocaust
8. genocide
9. Axis powers
10. Allies

MAIN IDEAS

SECTION 1 *(pages 702–707)*

Dictators Threaten World Peace

11. What were Stalin's goals and what steps did he take to achieve them?
12. Which actions that the League of Nations took revealed its inability to control the aggressive moves of Japan, Germany, and Italy?
13. How did Germany's and Italy's involvement affect the outcome of the Spanish Civil War?

SECTION 2 *(pages 708–713)*

War in Europe

14 Why was the blitzkrieg an effective military strategy?
15. What terms of surrender did Hitler demand of French officers after the fall of France in 1940? What was General Charles de Gaulle's reaction?

SECTION 3 *(pages 714–718)*

The Holocaust

16. What groups did Nazis deem unfit to belong to the Aryan "master race"?
17. How did some Europeans show their resistance to Nazi persecution of the Jews?

SECTION 4 *(pages 719–725)*

America Moves Toward War

18. Which nations formed the Triple Alliance? What were the military implications of their treaty for the United States?
19. What Congressional measures paved the way for the United States' entry into World War II?
20. Why did the United States enter World War II?

THINKING CRITICALLY

1. **WAR OR PEACE?** At what points do you think France, Great Britain, and their allies might have stopped Hitler and prevented World War II? Plot these events on a time line like the one below. Support your answers with reasons.

| 1933—Hitler is appointed chancellor of Germany. | | 1939—Great Britain and France declare war on Germany. |

2. **THE POWER OF SPEECH** Compare and contrast how Hitler, Churchill, and Roosevelt used their powers as gifted speakers to accomplish their political aims during World War II. Support your answer with details from the text.

3. **NEUTRALITY IN ACTION** Reread the quote by President Roosevelt on page 700. What do you think he was implying to the American public? Explain.

4. **GEOGRAPHY OF EUROPE AND THE SOVIET UNION** Look at the map of German advances on page 712. How might Poland's location have influenced the secret pact that Germany and the Soviet Union signed on August 23, 1939?

5. **THE FACES OF TERROR** What similarities and differences do you see between the terrorism of Stalin's Great Purge of 1934–1939 and Hitler's "final solution" adopted in 1939? Support your answer with details from the text.

6. **ANALYZING PRIMARY SOURCES** Read the following excerpt from the British writer Jessica Mitford's autobiography, in which she comments on Germany's attack on the Netherlands and other European countries in 1940. Then answer the question.

> On the 9th of May [1940], a month after Chamberlain had looked into his clouded crystal ball, there to find that Hitler had "missed the bus" and was no longer capable of waging aggressive war, the Germans struck. . . . Within hours the Germans had swept through Holland . . . and the French front was reported to be in mortal danger, perhaps already lost.
>
> Out of the wild confusion of these first few days of the attack . . . the real nature of the danger confronting Europe had exposed for all to see and understand the criminal stupidity of the years of shabby deals and accommodation to Hitler's ambitions. Overnight, the appeasement policy was buried forever.
>
> **JESSICA MITFORD,** *Hons and Rebels*

Do you agree or disagree with Mitford's views of Chamberlain's appeasement policy? Why or why not?

THINKING CRITICALLY

1. WAR OR PEACE?
Possible Answers:
1936: Germany occupies the Rhineland. (Force might have stopped Hitler.)
March 1938: Germany annexes Austria. (Military action might have undermined Hitler's authority.)
Spring 1938: Munich Pact gives Sudetenland to Germany. (If France and England had joined forces with the Czechs, they might have defeated the Germans.)
September 1939: German troops occupy the remainder of Czechoslovakia. (Probably the last chance to avert war.)

2. THE POWER OF SPEECH
Possible Responses: All three motivated their audiences to embrace certain beliefs and fostered national unity. Hitler spread a message of hate and nationalism. Churchill aroused and united Britons to defeat the Nazis. Roosevelt informed Americans about his policies and underscored his beliefs in democratic ideals.

3. NEUTRALITY IN ACTION
Possible Responses: Though Roosevelt did not take any actions that violated U.S. neutrality, he would not discourage Americans in believing in the cause of the Allies.

ALTERNATIVE ASSESSMENT

1. PLOTTING EVENTS IN WORLD WAR II

How did world events lead to America's participation in World War II? Make a flow chart showing these world events.

CD-ROM Conduct research into world events from 1931 to 1941 using the CD-ROM *Our Times*, your textbook, and other resources.

- Draw a flow chart in which you list events in boxes and draw lines that show the cause-and-effect relationships between events. Show multiple causes and effects where appropriate.

- After you complete your flow chart, highlight the events that were most important in causing the United States to become involved in the war.

2. LEARNING FROM MEDIA

VIDEO View the video for Chapter 24, *Escaping the "Final Solution."* Discuss the following questions in small groups.

- How did life change for Gerda Weissmann and her family when the Nazis invaded Poland?

- How did Kurt Klein's family respond to the Nazi threat?

- What conditions that Gerda faced in the forced labor factory would be most difficult for you to endure? Why?

- How did Kurt's and Gerda's lives finally come together?

- What lessons can people learn from the Holocaust to help prevent such an event from recurring?

3. PORTFOLIO PROJECT

Use the Living History activity to expand your portfolio.

LIVING HISTORY

PRESENTING YOUR ORAL HISTORY

After you have turned your interview into an article for the school newspaper, meet with a partner and combine your articles into a script for a public television talk show. Perform your interviews in front of the class.

The other members of the class should write an evaluation of each interview based on questions like the following:

- Was the interview informative and interesting?
- Did the interview give you a more personal glimpse of the country's mood before the war?

Add your newspaper articles, TV scripts, and student evaluations to your American history portfolio.

Review Chapter 24

DICTATORSHIPS EMERGE The failings of World War I peace settlements, economic instability, and political unrest set the stage for the rise of totalitarian dictators in Russia, Italy, and Germany. Nationalistic military leaders took power in Japan. Although many Americans were disturbed by Japan's attacks on China in 1931 and 1937, Italy's invasion of Ethiopia in 1935, and Germany's occupation of the Rhineland in 1936, most supported neutrality.

OUTBREAK OF WORLD WAR II A series of bold moves by Adolf Hitler—and weak countermoves by other leaders—triggered World War II in Europe. Germany annexed Austria and then occupied all of Czechoslovakia. When Nazi forces invaded Poland in 1939, Britain and France declared war on Germany. The following year Hitler overran the Netherlands, Belgium, Luxembourg, and France. Facing the Nazis alone, Britain vowed that it would never surrender.

THE HOLOCAUST The European crisis became grimmer as Nazis began persecuting Jews. The Nuremberg laws stripped Jews of their civil rights and property in 1935, and in 1938, on *Kristallnacht*, Nazi storm troopers attacked Jewish homes, businesses, and synagogues. The next year, the Nazis implemented the "final solution"—the systematic killing of millions of Jews.

AMERICA'S PREPARATION FOR WAR In response to the events in Europe, Congress boosted defense spending, passed the nation's first peacetime draft and the Lend-Lease Act, and repealed the ban against arming merchant ships. President Roosevelt and Prime Minister Churchill spelled out their war aims in the Atlantic Charter. On December 7, 1941, the Japanese attacked Pearl Harbor. The next day Roosevelt asked Congress to declare war on Japan.

Preview Chapter 25

After Pearl Harbor, the United States mobilized to support its allies. Americans enlisted to fight the Axis powers in North Africa, Europe, Asia, and the Pacific, and hundreds of thousands died. The war ended when Japan surrendered after the United States dropped atomic bombs on Hiroshima and Nagasaki. You will learn about these and other significant developments in the next chapter.

World War Looms **727**

---

1. PLOTTING EVENTS IN WORLD WAR II
Standards for Evaluation
An effective flowchart should meet the following criteria:

- Includes all major events in World War II.
- Indicates the cause-and-effect relationships between events.
- Highlights the events that were most important in drawing the United States into the war.

2. LEARNING FROM MEDIA
Answers to the questions.

- The Weissmanns' rights and activities were progressively curtailed and they were deported to Hitler's death camps.
- The Kleins sent their three children to the United States to protect them from the Nazis.
- Answers will vary, but should be supported with details from the video and well-supported explanations.
- Kurt was a soldier in the U.S. army division that liberated Gerda and other prisoners from the bicycle factory in Volary in which they had been held.
- Answers will vary, but might include lessons such as being aware of world events and speaking out and taking action against injustice.

3. PORTFOLIO PROJECT
LIVING HISTORY
Standards for Evaluation
An oral history should meet the following criteria:

- Presents well-chosen information about the subject that makes him or her come alive.
- Includes only relevant information.
- Shows clear organization.
- Creates a vivid impression of life in America before its entry into World War II.

IN-DEPTH RESOURCES: UNIT 7
See the form for scoring this activity on page 18.

THINKING CRITICALLY

4. GEOGRAPHY OF EUROPE AND THE SOVIET UNION
Possible Responses: Poland shared its western border with Germany and its eastern border with the Soviet Union. When Germany and the Soviet Union agreed not to fight each other, Germany was spared a two-front war after it invaded Poland. In their secret pact, the two countries agreed to split Poland between them.

5. THE FACES OF TERROR
***Possible Responses:* Similarities**—Stalin executed from 8 million to 13 million "enemies of the people"—Nazis executed more than 11 million "enemies of the state" (over half of them Jews). Both terrorist purges were carried out under totalitarian dictatorships. **Differences**—Stalin did not choose most of his victims based on ethnicity, while Nazis did. The implementation of the Nazis' "final solution" relied on technology (gas chambers) and was more systematic than Stalin's purges.

6. ANALYZING PRIMARY SOURCES
***Possible Responses:* Agree**—Appeasement policy allowed Hitler to pursue his ambitions of territorial expansion. **Disagree**—Appeasement represented the British public's desire to avoid another foreign war.

		TEACHING SUPPORT	**ASSESSMENT**

Key Ideas

SECTION 1
Mobilization on the Home Front
pp. 730–737

The United States enters the war and mobilizes its citizens and resources to give its allies unprecedented military and industrial support.

In-Depth Resources: Unit 7
• Guided Reading, p. 19
• Skillbuilder Practice: Analyzing Bias, p. 23
• Primary Sources: from *Farewell to Manzanar*, p. 28; War ration stamps, p. 29
• American Lives: Oveta Culp Hobby, p. 35

 COOPERATIVE ACTIVITY
• Creating a War Poster, p. 736 (TE)

Section 1 Assessment, p. 737 (PE)
Self-Assessment, p. 737 (TE)
Formal Assessment
• Section Quiz, p. 305
Alternative Assessment Book
• Standards for Evaluating a Cooperative Activity

SECTION 2
The War for Europe and North Africa
pp. 738–745

The United States, Great Britain, and the Soviet Union cooperate in the fight to defeat Germany and its allies.

In-Depth Resources: Unit 7
• Guided Reading, p. 20
• Geography Application: Thunderclap, p. 24
• Outline Map: Crisis in Europe, p. 26
• Primary Source: War Dispatch from Ernie Pyle, p. 30
• American Lives: George S. Patton, p. 36

 COOPERATIVE ACTIVITY
• Planning a D-Day Memorial Tour, p. 743 (TE)

Section 2 Assessment, p. 745 (PE)
Self-Assessment, p. 745 (TE)
Formal Assessment
• Section Quiz, p. 306
Alternative Assessment Book
• Standards for Evaluating a Cooperative Activity

SECTION 3
The War in the Pacific
pp. 746–753

America wages an aggressive military campaign against Japan in the Pacific islands and finally ends the war.

In-Depth Resources: Unit 7
• Guided Reading, p. 21
• Primary Source: The Bombing of Nagasaki, p. 31

 COOPERATIVE ACTIVITY
• Writing Memos to Truman About Use of the Atomic Bomb, p. 751 (TE)

Section 3 Assessment, p. 753 (PE)
Self-Assessment, p. 753 (TE)
Formal Assessment
• Section Quiz, p. 307
Alternative Assessment Book
• Standards for Evaluating a Cooperative Activity

SECTION 4
The Impact of the War
pp. 756–761

Americans begin to adjust to new economic opportunities and continuing social problems after World War II.

In-Depth Resources: Unit 7
• Guided Reading, p. 22
• Literature: from *Ceremony* by Leslie Marmon Silko, p. 32

 COOPERATIVE ACTIVITY
• Creating a Political Cartoon, p. 759 (TE)

Section 4 Assessment, p. 761 (PE)
Self-Assessment, p. 761 (TE)
Formal Assessment
• Section Quiz, p. 308
Alternative Assessment Book
• Standards for Evaluating a Cooperative Activity

CHAPTER RESOURCES

Chapter Overview

Soldiers abroad and Americans at home join in the effort to win World War II, which ends with victory for the Allies. But American society is transformed in the process.

In-Depth Resources: Unit 7
• Living History Project: Worksheet, p. 37; Standards, p. 38
Telescoping the Times
• Chapter Summary, pp. 49–50
Planning for Block Schedules

Chapter Assessment, pp. 762–763 (PE)
Alternative Assessment, p. 763 (PE)
Formal Assessment
• Chapter Test, forms A and B, pp. 309–314
 Test Generator
Alternative Assessment
See explanation and forms for different kinds of alternative assessments including portfolio assessment.

Electronic Library of Primary Sources
• "What Can I Do?" by the Office of Civilian Defense
• Japanese-American Testimony from the National Defense Migration Hearings

INTERNET RESOURCES
• See *McDougal Littell Learning On-Line* for links to information about Albert Einstein and Japanese-American internment.

Humanities Transparencies
• H24, Flying Fortress

Geography Transparencies
• G25, Battle of the Bulge

Grolier Multimedia Encyclopedia
• "The World at War"

Electronic Library of Primary Sources
• George S. Patton

Our Times
• Dispatch by Ernie Pyle

INTERNET RESOURCES
• See *McDougal Littell Learning On-Line* for links to information about D-Day.

Grolier Multimedia Encyclopedia
• video of an atomic blast

Electronic Library of Primary Sources
• Statement on the Atomic Bomb by Harry S. Truman

Our Times
• excerpt of Truman's V-J speech
• testimony from the Nuremberg trials

INTERNET RESOURCES
• See *McDougal Littell Learning On-Line* for links to information about Harry S. Truman and the Yalta Conference.

Critical Thinking Transparencies
• CT25, U.S. Joins the Allies in World War II
• CT59, Human Cost of World War II

INTERNET RESOURCES
• See Interact with History p. 760 (PE) for an activity that includes the Internet as an enrichment option.

American Portfolio: A Videodisc for U.S. History, user's guide, pp. 216–232

INTERNET RESOURCES
Learning On-Line: Social Studies
http://www.mcdougallittell.com

Block Scheduling (90 MINUTES)

Day 1	Day 2
Section 1, pp. 730–737	*Section 2,* pp. 738–745
Section Assessment, p. 737	*Section Assessment,* p. 745

Day 3	Day 4
Section 3, pp. 746–753	*Tracing Themes Science and Technology: From the Frontlines to Your Back Yard,* pp. 754–755
Section Assessment, p. 753	*Section 4,* pp. 756–761
	Section Assessment, p. 761
	Chapter Assessment, pp. 762–763

YEARLY PACING *Chapter 25 Total:* 4 days *Yearly Total:* 85 days

See *Planning for Block Schedules* for special activities and pacing strategies.

Customizing for Special Populations

Students Acquiring English

Access for Students Acquiring English
• Guided Reading for Sections 1–4 (Spanish), pp. 244–247
• Chapter Summary (Spanish), pp. 242–243
• Skillbuilder Practice: Analyzing Bias (Spanish), p. 248
• Geography Application: Thunderclap (Spanish), p. 249
• Outline Map: Crisis in Europe (Spanish), p. 251

INTERNET RESOURCES
• See *McDougal Littell Learning On-Line* The Diverse Classroom.

Less Proficient Readers

In-Depth Resources: Unit 7
• Guided Reading for Sections 1–4, pp. 19–22
• Skillbuilder: Analyzing Bias, p. 23
• Geography Application: Thunderclap, p. 24
• Outline Map: Crisis in Europe, p. 26

Telescoping the Times
• Chapter Summary, pp. 49–50

See additional strategies at point of use in the Teacher's Edition.

Gifted and Talented Students

In-Depth Resources: Unit 7
• Primary Sources: from *Farewell to Manzanar,* p. 28; War ration stamps, p. 29; War Dispatch of Ernie Pyle, p. 30; The Bombing of Nagasaki, p. 31
• American Lives: Oveta Culp Hobby, p. 35; George S. Patton, p. 36

See additional strategies at point of use in the Teacher's Edition.

Connections to Literature   READINGS FOR STUDENTS

In-Depth Resources: Unit 7
• from *Ceremony* by Leslie Marmon Silko, p. 32

McDougal Littell *Literature Connections*

• **John Knowles**
A Separate Peace (with related readings) *Consistently hailed as a modern classic, this story of two friends at an elite boarding school during the early years of World War II is a deeply moving novel of the confusions of adolescence. Despite the personal tragedy encountered by the two friends caused by circumstance and war, the novel is ultimately life-affirming.*

McDougal Littell *The Language of Literature*
American Literature

• **Diane Mei Lin Mark,** "Suzie Wong Doesn't Live Here," p. 252
• **Studs Terkel,** from "The Good War," p. 909
• **Bernard Malamud,** "Armistice," p. 912
• **Randall Jarrell,** "The Death of the Ball Turret Gunner," p. 922
• **John Steinbeck,** "Why Soldiers Won't Talk," p. 922
• **Joan Didion,** "Letter from Paradise," p. 929
• **Dwight Okita,** "In Response to Executive Order 9066," p. 929
• **Alan Chong Lau,** "the promise," p. 1053

The United States in World War II

▶ **Starting with the Student**
Ask students what images or stories come to mind when they think about World War II. Then discuss the opening quotation.

- What event prompted President Roosevelt to decide, "We are now in this war"?
- What do students think being in the war "all the way" meant for Americans?
- Do they think most Americans agreed with the president at this point? Why or why not?

PREVIEWING THE CHAPTER

- Discuss the images on the time line with students. What common characteristics do they note, and what does this tell them about the mood of the time? *Students might mention that all the images include two or more people and that this suggests a united war effort.*
- Point out the prevalence of images of flags and discuss the importance of a country's flag as a unifying symbol.

The United States in World War II

SECTION 1
Mobilization on the Home Front
The United States enters the war and mobilizes its citizens and resources to give its allies unprecedented military and industrial support.

SECTION 2
The War for Europe and North Africa
The United States, Great Britain, and the Soviet Union cooperate in the fight to defeat Germany and its allies.

SECTION 3
The War in the Pacific
America wages an aggressive military campaign against Japan in the Pacific islands and finally ends the war.

SECTION 4
The Impact of the War
Americans begin to adjust to new economic opportunities and continuing social problems after World War II.

"We are now in this war. We are all in it—all the way."

Franklin D. Roosevelt

- **Office of Scientific Research and Development is created to bring scientists into the war effort.**
- **The Manhattan Project is established to develop an atomic bomb.**
- **A. Philip Randolph demands right of African Americans to work and fight for their country.**
- **Japan bombs Pearl Harbor and United States declares war on Japan.**
- **American industry shifts to war production.**
- **President Roosevelt signs an order forcing Japanese Americans into internment camps.**
- **Female service divisions are established, allowing women like these Ladybirds to serve their country in all branches of the military.**

UNITED WE WIN

THE UNITED STATES
THE WORLD

1941

1942
1942

- **Germany invades the Soviet Union.**
- **Hitler orders attack on Stalingrad.**
- **Germany invades Greece and Yugoslavia.**
- **Japan defeats the United States in the Philippines.**
- **Battle of M rages in the Pacific**

THEMES IN CHAPTER 25

Women in America	*Civil Rights*	*Immigration and Migration*	*The American Dream*
As American men marched off to war, both the armed services and defense industries turned to women to meet their "manpower" needs. Women proved they could handle almost any job.	For America's minorities, the war meant a struggle for equal treatment in the workplace and in the military. The government trampled the civil rights of Japanese Americans by sending them to internment camps.	The war put unprecedented numbers of Americans on the move. Young men left home for military training and service overseas. As towns and cities with defense plants boomed to the bursting point, workers moved in to take jobs.	The war brought renewed opportunity for Americans to forge their dreams of the good life. The GI Bill of Rights promised to help returning veterans keep that dream alive after the war.
See Teacher's Edition note, p. 731.	See Teacher's Edition note, p. 732.	See Teacher's Edition note, p. 757.	See Teacher's Edition note, p. 758.

LIVING HISTORY

CREATING A WAR GAME

Create a board game about World War II based on what you learn in this chapter and on additional research. Design the board and playing pieces and write the objective and rules for your game. Include the following elements:

- key countries and alliances
- important military and political leaders
- major battles and battle strategies
- armaments

PORTFOLIO PROJECT Save the game in a folder for your American history portfolio. You will play and evaluate it at the end of the chapter.

CREATING A WAR GAME

The following steps might help students plan their war games:

- Have them examine commercial board games such as Risk or Axis and Allies.
- After developing the basic design and instructions for their games, students should ask others to play their games using only the written instructions. They should then revise their games based on player feedback.

Create a class display of games and, if possible, give students time to play one another's games.

Project Planning Guide

Step 1	Review game models.
Step 2	Develop initial design and instructions.
Step 3	Have others play game.
Step 4	Get feedback from players.
Step 5	Revise game based on feedback.

IN-DEPTH RESOURCES: UNIT 7
See worksheet and standards for evaluation, pp. 37, 38.

V-E Day ends the war in Europe.

United States bombs Hiroshima and Nagasaki.

Harry S. Truman becomes president after President Roosevelt dies.

The Allies, reinforced by armor like this battle-scarred Sherman tank, force Italy to surrender.

GI Bill of Rights is passed.
Franklin D. Roosevelt is reelected to a fourth term.

U.S. Marines take Iwo Jima.

Zoot-suit racial riots rock Los Angeles.

1943

1944

1944

1945

Allies invade North Africa.

German soldiers surrender to Soviets at Stalingrad.

Allies invade occupied Europe on June 6, D-Day.

Allied soldiers liberate survivors of Hitler's death camps.

Nazi retreat begins after Battle of the Bulge.

Roosevelt, Churchill, and Stalin meet at Yalta.

The United States in World War II **729**

RECOMMENDED RESOURCES

Books for the Teacher

Goodwin, Doris K. *No Ordinary Time: Franklin & Eleanor Roosevelt—The Home Front in World War II.* New York: S&S Trade, 1994.

Leckie, Robert. *Delivered from Evil.* New York: HarperCollins, 1987. Narrative history of World War II.

Books for the Student

Ernie's War: The Best of Ernie Pyle's World War II Dispatches. David Nichols, ed. New York: Random, 1986.

Sulzberger, C. L. *The American Heritage Picture History of World War II.* New York: Random, 1987.

Terkel, Studs. *The "Good War."* New York: Pantheon, 1984. Oral histories of World War II.

Videos

America, the Way We Were: The Home Front. International Video Network, 1989. A three-tape series on behavior, attitudes, and popular culture.

Eisenhower. PBS Home Video, 1993. 800-424-7963. Documentary biography.

Zoot Suit. MCA Universal Home Video, 1981. Mexican and Anglo cultures clash in 1940s California.

Software

D-Day: 100 Days of Destiny. Educorp, 7434 Trade Street, San Diego, CA 92121, 800-843-9497.

Powers of Persuasion: The Art of Propaganda in World War II. Fife and Drum Software, 316 Soapstone Lane, Silver Spring, MD 20905.

World War II. CD-ROM. Flag Tower, 1995. Interactive documentary.

1 Mobilization on the Home Front

TERMS & NAMES
- George Marshall
- A. Philip Randolph
- Nisei
- Office of Price Administration (OPA)
- War Production Board (WPB)
- rationing

LEARN ABOUT Americans' responses to the Japanese attack on Pearl Harbor
TO UNDERSTAND how the United States mobilized its human and industrial resources to fight on two fronts.

OBJECTIVES

1 To explain how the United States expanded its armed forces in response to America's entry into World War II.

2 To describe the wartime mobilization of industry, labor, scientists, and the media.

3 To characterize the efforts of the federal government to control the economy and deal with alleged subversion.

SKILLBUILDER

- Interpreting charts, p. 735

CRITICAL THINKING

- Contrasting, p. 730
- Analyzing motives, pp. 731, 732, 735
- Synthesizing, p. 733
- Summarizing, pp. 734, 737
- Identifying problems, p. 737
- Interpreting, p. 737
- Forming opinions, p. 737

ONE AMERICAN'S STORY

Charles Swanson looked all over his army base for a tape recorder on which to play the tape his wife had sent him for Christmas. "In desperation," he later recalled, "I had it played over the public-address system. It was a little embarrassing to have the whole company hear it, but it made everyone long for home."

A PERSONAL VOICE
Merry Christmas, honey. Surprised? I am so glad I have a chance to say hello to you this way on our first Christmas apart. . . . About our little girl . . . she is just big enough to fill my heart and strong enough to help Mommy bear this ache of loneliness. . . . Her dearest treasure is her daddy's picture. It's all marked with tiny handprints, and the glass is always cloudy from so much loving and kissing. I'm hoping you'll be listening to this on Christmas Eve, somewhere over there, your heart full of hope, faith and courage, knowing each day will bring that next Christmas together one day nearer. Lynne and I are . . . praying for that tomorrow and for all the daddies in the world to come home.

MRS. CHARLES SWANSON, quoted in *We Pulled Together . . . and Won!*

Mrs. Charles Swanson and daughter, Lynne, with a picture of her husband, Charles

As the United States began to mobilize for war, the Swansons, like most Americans, had few illusions as to what lay ahead. It would be a long time, they knew—a time filled with hard work and hope, with sacrifice and sorrow—before all the families in the world would be reunited.

FOCUS & MOTIVATE

▶ **Starting with the Student**
Have students imagine that Japan has attacked Pearl Harbor, and President Roosevelt has asked Congress to declare war on the Axis Powers.

- Do students support the declaration of war?
- How do they think war will change their lives?
- What sacrifices are students willing to make to help their country?

Americans Join the War Effort

The Japanese had attacked Pearl Harbor with the expectation that once Americans had experienced Japan's power, they would shrink from further conflict. The day after the raid, the *Japan Times* boasted that the United States, now reduced to a third-rate power, was "trembling in her shoes." But if Americans were trembling, it was with rage, not fear. Uniting under the battle cry "Remember Pearl Harbor," they set out to prove Japan wrong.

SELECTIVE SERVICE AND THE GI   After Pearl Harbor, eager young Americans jammed the recruiting offices. "I wanted to be a hero, let's face it," admitted Roger Tuthrup. "I was havin' trouble in school. . . . The war'd been goin' on for two years. I didn't wanna miss it. . . . I was an American. I was seventeen."

Even the 5 million who volunteered for military service, however, were not enough to face the challenge of an all-out war on two global fronts—Europe and the Pacific. The Selective Service System instituted the draft and eventually provided another 10 million soldiers to meet the armed forces' needs. Richard Leacock, a film maker who came to America from the Canary islands to go to Harvard, recalls, "You couldn't volunteer unless you were a citizen. . . . When they drafted me in my senior year I was delighted. . . . I can't say that going to Harvard is a democratic process. Going into the army certainly was."

A. Answer
The Japanese expected American discouragement, not outrage and total support of the war effort.

THINK THROUGH HISTORY
A. Contrasting
How did Americans' response to the Japanese raid on Pearl Harbor differ from Japanese expectations?

Americans Join the War Effort

▶ *Discussing Key Ideas*
- The Selective Service System helps meet U.S. manpower needs.
- Many women and minorities serve in the military.

IN-DEPTH RESOURCES: UNIT 7
Guided Reading, p. 19

ACCESS FOR STUDENTS ACQUIRING ENGLISH
Guided Reading (Spanish), p. 244

SECTION 1 RESOURCES

PRINT RESOURCES

IN-DEPTH RESOURCES: UNIT 7
Guided Reading, p. 19
Skillbuilder Practice: Analyzing Bias, p. 23
Primary Sources: from *Farewell to Manzanar,* p. 28; War ration stamps, p. 29
American Lives: Oveta Culp Hobby, p. 35

ACCESS FOR STUDENTS ACQUIRING ENGLISH
Guided Reading (Spanish), p. 244
Skillbuilder Practice: Analyzing Bias (Spanish), p. 248

FORMAL ASSESSMENT
Section Quiz, p. 305

ALTERNATIVE ASSESSMENT BOOK
See forms for supporting and scoring alternative activities.

TECHNOLOGY RESOURCES

CD-ROM Electronic Library of Primary Sources

VIDEO *American Portfolio: A Videodisc for U.S. History* user's guide, pp. 216–217, 226–229, 232

INTERNET McDougal Littell Learning On-Line
http://www.mcdougallittell.com

The volunteers and draftees reported to military bases around the country for eight weeks of basic training. In this short period, seasoned sergeants did their best to turn raw recruits into disciplined, battle-ready GIs. (The term *GI*—meaning "Government Issue"—first applied to government-issued uniforms, weapons, and supplies but soon was used to describe soldiers as well.) According to Sergeant Deb Myers, however, there was more to basic training than teaching a recruit how to stand at attention, march in step, handle a rifle, and follow orders.

A PERSONAL VOICE

The civilian went before the Army doctors, took off his clothes, feeling silly; jigged, stooped, squatted, wet into a bottle; became a soldier. He learned how to sleep in the mud, tie a knot, kill a man. He learned the ache of loneliness, the ache of exhaustion, the kinship of misery. He learned that men make the same queasy noises in the morning, feel the same longings at night; that every man is alike and that each man is different.

SERGEANT DEB MYERS, quoted in *The GI War*

WOMEN IN THE MILITARY The military's manpower needs were so great that early in 1942, Army Chief of Staff General **George Marshall** pushed for the formation of a Women's Auxiliary Army Corps (WAAC). "There are innumerable duties now being performed by soldiers that can actually be done better by women," Marshall said in support of a bill to establish the WAAC. Under this bill, women volunteering for the army would not receive the same rank, pay, or benefits as men doing the same jobs, nor could they expect to make the army a career.

Even so, the bill ran into fierce opposition in Congress. "Take women into the armed services . . . ," asked one congressman, and "who then will do the cooking, the washing, the mending?" Another representative scorned the bill as "the silliest piece of legislation" he had ever seen. "A woman's army to defend the United States of America," he raged. "Think of the humiliation. What has become of the manhood of America, that we have to call on our women to do what has ever been the duty of men?"

Despite this opposition, the bill establishing the WAAC became law on May 15, 1942. When Oveta Culp Hobby, a Texas newspaper executive and the first director of WAAC, put out a call for recruits a few weeks later, more than 13,000 women applied on the first day applications were available. In all, some 250,000 women served in this and other auxiliary branches during the war.

MINORITIES IN THE ARMED SERVICES For many minority groups—especially African Americans, Native Americans, Mexican Americans, and Asian Americans—the war created new dilemmas. Restricted to racially segregated neighborhoods and reservations and denied basic citizenship rights, some members of these groups questioned whether this was their war to fight. "Why die for democracy for some foreign country when we don't even have it here?" asked an editorial in an African-American newspaper. On receiving his draft notice, an African American responded unhappily, "Just carve on my tombstone, 'Here lies a black man killed fighting a yellow man for the protection of a white man.'"

THINK THROUGH HISTORY
B. Analyzing Motives Why did some congressmen oppose admitting women to the military?

B. Answer They thought war was men's work and would take women away from their place in the home.

Two privates in the Fifth Army Forces sit at the entrance to an air-raid shelter at Anzio, Italy, where they held the beachhead against the Nazis.

NOW & THEN

THE SELECTIVE SERVICE SYSTEM

"Greetings. You are hereby ordered for induction into the Armed Forces of the United States. . . ." During World War II, millions of Americans received letters from their local draft boards beginning with these words.

The Selective Service System still exists today, although the draft ended with the establishment of an All-Volunteer Force in 1973. At present all male U.S. citizens and most resident aliens are required by law to register for the draft within 30 days of their 18th birthdays. The Selective Service System can no longer draft anyone into the armed forces, however, without Congressional approval.

NOW & THEN

The Selective Service System

Critical Thinking: Forming Opinions Throughout American history, only men have been subject to the military draft. One of the strongest arguments made against the Equal Rights Amendment in the 1970s was that it might lead to the drafting of women. Do students think that women should be drafted on an equal basis with men? Why or why not?

MORE ABOUT . . .

The WAACs

In 1942, the army decided to send WAACs into combat areas. WAAC director Oveta Culp Hobby flew to a training center in Daytona Beach, Florida, to speak to 300 women selected to go overseas. She told them how dangerous such assignments could be and that only volunteers would be sent abroad. Every one of the women signed up. From that point on, WAACs followed the troops, with more than 8,000 women serving in Africa and Europe and about 5,000 in Asia. More than 500 women earned combat decorations for their courage under enemy attack in the war in the Pacific.

IN-DEPTH RESOURCES: UNIT 7
American Lives: Oveta Culp Hobby, p. 35

OBJECTIVE
② **INSTRUCT**

Life on the Home Front

▶ *Discussing Key Ideas*
- American industry quickly converts to war production in 1942.
- The growth of war industries creates new job opportunities for women and minorities.
- Scientists aid the war effort by developing new military technologies, weapons, and wonder drugs.
- The mass media expand as they deliver war news and patriotic messages and create escapist entertainment.

ELECTRONIC LIBRARY OF PRIMARY SOURCES
"What Can I Do?" by the Office of Civilian Defense

Still, minorities knew that no matter how badly they had been treated in the past, they were likely to be worse off under Axis control. "We know that under Nazism we should have no rights at all; we should be used as slaves," declared a Native American. The Congreso del Pueblo de Habla Espanola (Spanish Speaking Congress) agreed, proclaiming that "Our liberties, our homes, and our lives [are] directly threatened by Fascism. . . . We are also children of the United States. We will defend her."

In response, at least a half million Mexican Americans joined the armed forces. All-Latino units saw heavy action both in Europe and Asia. While Mexican Americans in Los Angeles made up only a tenth of the city's population, they suffered a fifth of the city's wartime casualties.

More than a million African Americans also served in the military. Black soldiers lived and worked in segregated units and were mostly limited to non-combat roles. When 3,000 black troops were asked in 1943 if "Negroes are being given a fair chance to do as much as they want to do to help win the war," more than half answered "No!" After much protest, African Americans did finally see combat in the last year of the war.

Asian Americans took part in the struggle as well. More than 13,000 Chinese Americans joined the armed forces, or about one of every five adult Chinese males. An additional 33,000 Japanese Americans put on uniforms. Of these, several thousand volunteered to serve as spies and interpreters in the Pacific War. "During battles," wrote an admiring officer, "they crawled up close enough to be able to hear [Japanese] officers' commands and to make verbal translations to our soldiers."

Some 25,000 Native Americans enlisted in the armed services, too, including 800 women. Their willingness to serve led *The Saturday Evening Post* magazine to comment, "We would not need the Selective Service if all volunteered like Indians." For many Native Americans, the war provided their first opportunity to leave the reservation and meet non-Indians. A Chippewa wrote a poem describing his experience fighting with soldiers from very different backgrounds: "We bind each other's wounds and eat the same ration. / We dream of our loved ones in the same nation."

C. Answer
They'd be worse off under Nazism; they were citizens and wanted to do their duty; they had essential skills.

THINK THROUGH HISTORY
C. Analyzing Motives *What reasons did minority Americans give for joining the armed services?*

Life on the Home Front

Early in February 1942, newspapers reported the end of automobile production in the United States. The last car to roll off an automaker's assembly line was a gray sedan with "victory trim," which meant the car had no chrome. This was just one more sign that the war would affect almost every aspect of life on the home front.

Women perform inspection of mass-produced propellers in America's stepped-up war industry.

THE INDUSTRIAL RESPONSE Within weeks of the shutdown in production, the nation's automobile plants had been retooled to produce tanks, planes, boats, and command cars. They were not alone. Across the nation, factories were quickly converted to war production. A maker of mechanical pencils turned out bomb parts. A bedspread manufacturer made mosquito netting. A soft-drink company converted from filling bottles with liquid to filling shells with explosives.

Meanwhile, shipyards and defense plants expanded with dizzying speed. By the end of 1942, industrialist Henry J. Kaiser had built seven massive new shipyards that turned out Liberty ships (cargo carriers), tankers, troop transports, and "baby" aircraft carriers at an astonishing rate. Late that year, Kaiser invited reporters to Way One in his Richmond, California, shipyard to watch as his workers assembled *Hull 440*, a Liberty ship, in a record-breaking four days. Writer Alyce Mano Kramer described the first day and night of construction.

> **A PERSONAL VOICE**
> At the stroke of 12, Way One exploded into life. Crews of workers, like a champion football team, swarmed into their places in the line. Within 60 seconds, the keel was swinging into position. . . . *Hull 440* was going up. The speed of [production] was unbelievable. At midnight, Saturday, an empty way—at midnight Sunday, a full-grown hull met the eyes of graveyard workers as they came on shift.
> **ALYCE MANO KRAMER,** quoted in *Home Front, U.S.A.*

"THE GIRL HE LEFT BEHIND" IS STILL BEHIND HIM — She's a **WOW** — WOMAN ORDNANCE WORKER

This World War II poster reinforces the message that the home front was an important part of the frontline.

THINK THROUGH HISTORY
D. Synthesizing How did the nation's industries and workers mobilize for the war effort?

D. Answer Manufacturers began producing war materiel, and the number of people working in war industries increased threefold from 1941–1944.

Three days later, 25,000 amazed spectators watched as *Hull 440* slid into the water. How could such a ship be built so fast? The answer was mobilization for the war effort on every front. Kaiser used prefabricated, or factory-made, parts that could be quickly assembled at his shipyards. Equally important were his workers, who had learned new skills and performed jobs at record speeds.

LABOR'S CONTRIBUTION When the war began, defense contractors warned the Selective Service System that the nation did not have enough manpower to meet both its military and industrial needs. They were wrong. By 1944, despite the draft, nearly 18 million workers were laboring in war industries, three times as many as in 1941.

More than 6 million of these new workers were women. At first, war industries feared that most women lacked the necessary stamina for factory work and were reluctant to hire them. But once women proved they could wield a welding torch or a riveting gun as well as men, employers could not hire enough of them—especially since women earned only about 60 percent as much as men doing the same jobs.

Defense plants also hired more than 2 million minority workers during the war years. Like women, minorities faced strong prejudice at first. Before the war, 75 percent of defense contractors simply refused to hire African Americans, while another 15 percent employed them only in menial jobs. "Negroes will be considered only as janitors," declared the general manager of North American Aviation. "It is the company policy not to employ them as mechanics and aircraft workers."

To protest such discrimination in both the military and in industry, **A. Philip Randolph,** president of the Brotherhood of Sleeping Car Porters and the nation's leading African-American labor leader, organized a march on Washington. Randolph called on blacks everywhere to come to the capital on July 1, 1941, and to march under the banner: "We Loyal Colored Americans Demand the Right to Work and Fight for Our Country."

Fearing the march might provoke white resentment, even violence, President Roosevelt called Randolph to the White House and asked him to back down. "I'm sorry Mr. President," the labor leader said, "the march cannot be called off." Roosevelt then asked, "How many people do you plan to bring?" Randolph replied, "One hundred thousand, Mr. President." Roosevelt was stunned. Even half that number of black protesters would be far more

Boys using pots and pans as helmets and drums encourage New Yorkers to donate aluminum to the war effort.

MORE ABOUT . . .
Henry J. Kaiser
The industrialist Henry John Kaiser (1882–1967) first proved his organizational prowess as the head of construction of the Boulder, Bonneville, and Grand Coulee dams. During World War II, Kaiser took over management of West Coast shipyards and revolutionized ship construction. By 1945 Kaiser, who had earned the nickname "Sir Launchalot," was launching one cargo ship a day from his busy shipyards.

MORE ABOUT . . .
A. Philip Randolph
American labor leader Asa Philip Randolph (1889–1979) was born in Crescent City, Florida, the son of an African Methodist Episcopal minister. During his youth, Randolph worked as a section hand on a railroad, learning firsthand how blacks were treated by railroad companies. After attending college in New York, he organized the Brotherhood of Sleeping Car Porters in 1925. It was the first union composed mostly of black workers to be granted a charter by the American Federation of Labor. In 1957, Randolph was elected a vice-president of the American Federation of Labor and Congress of Industrial Organizations. He was also one of the organizers of the 1963 March on Washington.

TEACHING OPTION

Skillbuilder Mini-Lesson: Analyzing Bias

Explaining the Skill A biased, or prejudiced, point of view often appears in primary sources and other historical materials. Bias can be for or against something. One way to detect bias is by looking at the words and visual images to see if they give a one-sided, idealized, or unrealistic view of the subject.

Applying the Skill: The Girls Left Behind Have students look at the poster reproduced on this page. Then ask:

1. What is the meaning of the words on the poster? *The women—wives, girlfriends—that soldiers left behind when*

they went to war are supporting the soldiers by working in factories that support the war effort.

2. What words or phrases show bias or stereotypes? *"Girl" instead of "woman"; "he left behind" and "behind him" imply that her work supports him instead of supporting the nation, as his does.*

3. What stereotype of women does the image convey? *They are young, white, slender, and loyal.*

IN-DEPTH RESOURCES: UNIT 7
Skillbuilder Practice: Analyzing Bias, p. 23

"Organized power can be opposed only by organized power. Much as I regret this, there is no other way."

ALBERT EINSTEIN,
A LIFELONG PACIFIST, ON
DEVELOPMENT OF AN
ATOMIC BOMB

than Washington—still a very segregated city—could feed, house, and transport.

In the end it was Roosevelt, not Randolph, who backed down. In return for Randolph's promise to cancel the march, the President issued an executive order calling on employers and labor unions "to provide for the full and equitable participation of all workers in defense industries, without discrimination because of race, creed, color, or national origin."

MOBILIZATION OF SCIENTISTS That same year, Roosevelt created the Office of Scientific Research and Development (OSRD) to bring scientists into the war effort. The OSRD spurred improvements in both radar and sonar, a new technology for locating submarines under water. It encouraged the use of pesticides like DDT to fight insects. As a result, U.S. soldiers were probably the first in history to be relatively free from body lice. The OSRD also pushed the development of "miracle drugs," such as penicillin, that saved countless lives on and off the battlefield.

The greatest scientific achievement of the OSRD, though, was the secret development of a new weapon, the atomic bomb. Interest in such a weapon began in 1939, after German scientists succeeded in splitting a uranium atom, which released an enormous amount of energy. This news prompted physicist and German refugee Albert Einstein to write a letter to President Roosevelt warning that the Germans could use their discovery to construct a weapon of enormous destructive power.

Roosevelt responded by creating a National Committee on Uranium to study the new discovery. In 1941, the committee reported that it would take from three to five years to build an atomic bomb. Hoping to shorten that time, the OSRD set up a crash program to develop a bomb as quickly as possible. Because its offices were located in New York City, the atomic bomb program came to be known as the Manhattan Project.

CHANGES IN ENTERTAINMENT The war not only put Americans back to work in record numbers, but it also put money in their pockets. As a result, spending on books and entertainment more than doubled between 1941 and 1945.

From 60 million to 100 million Americans (out of a total population of 135 million) went to the movies each week. In the aftermath of Pearl Harbor, Hollywood churned out war-oriented propaganda films. Heroic movies like *Mission to Moscow* and *Song of Russia* glorified America's new wartime ally. "Hiss-and-boo" films with titles like *Hitler, Beast of Berlin* stirred up hatred against the enemy. As the war dragged on, however, people grew tired of propaganda and war themes. Hollywood responded with musicals, romances, comedies, and other escapist fare designed to take filmgoers away from the grim realities of war, if only for an hour or two.

Popular music also dealt with patriotic themes early in the war. In 1942, Americans were singing "Goodbye Mama, I'm Off to Yokohama" and "Praise the Lord and Pass the Ammunition." But as the war dragged on, the songs changed to reflect lost loves, longings, and loneliness.

Meanwhile, public hunger for war news spurred a boom in the publishing and the radio industries. Magazines such as *Life, Look,* and *Time,* which covered the war in both words and pictures, saw their circulation soar. Radio audiences also reached record levels as people tuned in the latest war reports. Between newscasts, listeners could follow the radio soap operas' tales of love gone wrong. Or they could escape wartime concerns by laughing at comedians such as Jack Benny and Fanny Brice.

The Federal Government Takes Control

In addition to instituting the draft and supporting war industries, the federal government took decisive social and economic measures.

INTERNMENT OF JAPANESE AMERICANS One of the most pressing issues facing the federal government after the bombing of Pearl Harbor was what to do about Japanese Americans living in Hawaii and on the West Coast. Many Americans were convinced that these Asian Americans were part of Japan's master plan for destroying the United States, although no evidence existed that any of them were spies. Soon after the bombing of Pearl Harbor, the War Department called for the mass evacuation of all Japanese Americans from Hawaii. General Delos Eamons, the military governor of Hawaii, initially resisted the order but eventually gave in and ordered the internment, or confinement, of 1,444 Japanese Americans.

THINK THROUGH HISTORY
F. Analyzing Motives Why did President Roosevelt order the internment of Japanese Americans?
F. Answer Because some people perceived them as a threat to American security.

On the West Coast, however, panic and prejudice combined to create an atmosphere of hysteria and hostility. Day after day, newspapers ran ugly stories attacking Japanese Americans. On February 19, 1942, President Roosevelt signed an order requiring the removal of people of Japanese ancestry from California and parts of Washington, Oregon, and Arizona. He justified this step as necessary for national security.

In the following weeks, the Army rounded up some 110,000 Japanese Americans and shipped them to ten hastily constructed internment camps. About two-thirds were **Nisei**, or Japanese Americans who were born in this country and were thus American citizens. Thousands of them had already been drafted into the armed forces, and to Ted Nakashima, an architectural draftsman from Seattle, the evacuation seemed utterly "senseless."

> **A PERSONAL VOICE**
> [There are] electricians, plumbers, draftsmen, mechanics, carpenters, painters, farmers—every trade—men who are able and willing to do all they can to lick the Axis. . . . What really hurts is the constant reference to [us] evacuees as "Japs." "Japs" are the guys we are fighting. We're on this side and we want to help. Why won't America let us?
> **TED NAKASHIMA,** *New Republic* magazine, June 15, 1942

ECONOMIC CONTROLS Another issue facing the federal government was how to prevent inflation from skyrocketing as it had during World War I. With

The Government Takes Control of the Economy, 1942–1945

AGENCIES AND LAWS	WHAT THE REGULATIONS DID
National War Labor Board (NWLB)	• Limited wage increases. • Allowed negotiated benefits such as paid vacations, pensions, and medical insurance. • Kept unions stable by forbidding workers to change unions.
Office of Price Administration (OPA)	• Cut inflation by freezing wages, prices, and rents.
War Production Board (WPB)	• Rationed foods such as meat, butter, cheese, vegetables, sugar, and coffee. • Rationed fuel and materials vital to the war effort such as gasoline, heating oil, metals, rubber, and plastics.
Department of the Treasury	• Issued war bonds to raise money for the war effort and to fight inflation.
Revenue Act of 1942	• Raised the top personal-income-tax rate to 90%. • Added lower- and middle-income Americans to the income-tax rolls.
Smith-Connally Labor Disputes Act (1943)	• Limited the right to strike in industries crucial to the war effort. • Gave the president power to take over striking plants.

SKILLBUILDER
INTERPRETING CHARTS
What was the overall aim of these economic regulations?
Skillbuilder Answer To provide maximal resources for the war effort

MORE ABOUT . . .
Japanese Americans in Hawaii after Pearl Harbor
Only a fraction of the 150,000 Japanese Americans living in Hawaii were interned after Pearl Harbor because they made up more than a third of Hawaii's population. Any effort to intern them all would have devastated Hawaii's economy. In addition, Hawaii's leaders promoted a reasoned response to fears of Japanese subversion. "No person, be he citizen or alien, need worry, provided he is not connected with subversive elements," declared General Delos Emmons after the air raid.

IN-DEPTH RESOURCES: UNIT 7
Primary Source: *Farewell to Manzanar,* p. 28

 ELECTRONIC LIBRARY OF PRIMARY SOURCES
Japanese-American Testimony from the National Defense Migration Hearings

HISTORY FROM VISUALS
The Government Takes Control of the Economy, 1942–1945
Reading the Chart Suggest that students read this chart horizontally, first noting the federal agency or law in the left column and then reading the regulations it was responsible for in the right column.

Extension Ask students which regulations would have created the greatest hardship for them.

IN-DEPTH RESOURCES: UNIT 7
Primary Source: War ration stamps, p. 29

The War Fought at Home

Join a **Car-Sharing Club TODAY!**

TRANSPORTATION With oil, gas, and rubber in short supply, many Americans car-pooled or rode their bicycles.

FOOD Each month the ration board gave consumers stamps for canned goods and perishables such as meat and butter. Sometimes unanticipated shortages made it difficult to find some foods, so many Americans grew "victory gardens" everywhere from abandoned lots to flower beds.

FASHION The armed forces' demand for textiles led to shortages of wool and rayon, causing fashion changes back home. The War Production Board banned ruffles, pleats, and patch pockets, favoring the single-breasted, vestless "victory suit" over the baggy "zoot suit," in vogue at the time. To conserve silk, women painted seams up the backs of their legs to make it seem as if they were wearing stockings.

incomes rising and the production of consumer goods falling, prices were bound to soar if nothing was done.

Congress responded to this threat by passing legislation to create the **Office of Price Administration (OPA).** The OPA fought inflation by freezing prices on most goods. Congress also raised income taxes and extended the tax to millions of people who had never paid it before. These higher taxes left workers with less to spend. In addition, the government encouraged Americans to use their extra cash to buy war bonds. As a result of these measures, inflation remained below 30 percent—about half that of World War I—for the entire period of World War II.

Besides controlling inflation, the government needed to ensure that the armed forces and war industries received the ever-growing resources they needed to win the war. The **War Production Board (WPB)** assumed that responsibility. The WPB decided which companies would convert from peacetime to wartime production and allocated raw materials to key industries. The WPB also organized nationwide drives to collect scrap iron, tin cans, paper, rags, and cooking fat for recycling into war goods. Across America, children scoured attics, cellars, garages, vacant lots, and back alleys looking for useful junk. During one five-month-long paper drive in Chicago, school children collected 36 million pounds of old paper, or about 65 pounds per child.

In addition, the OPA set up a system for **rationing,** or establishing fixed allotments of goods deemed essential for the military. Under this system, households received ration books with coupons to be used for buying such scarce goods as meat, shoes, sugar, coffee, and gasoline. Gas rationing was particularly hard on those who lived in western regions, where driving was the only way to get around. Eleanor Roosevelt sympathized with their complaints. "To tell the people in the West not to use their cars," she observed, "means that these people may never see another soul for weeks and weeks nor have a way of getting a sick person to a doctor."

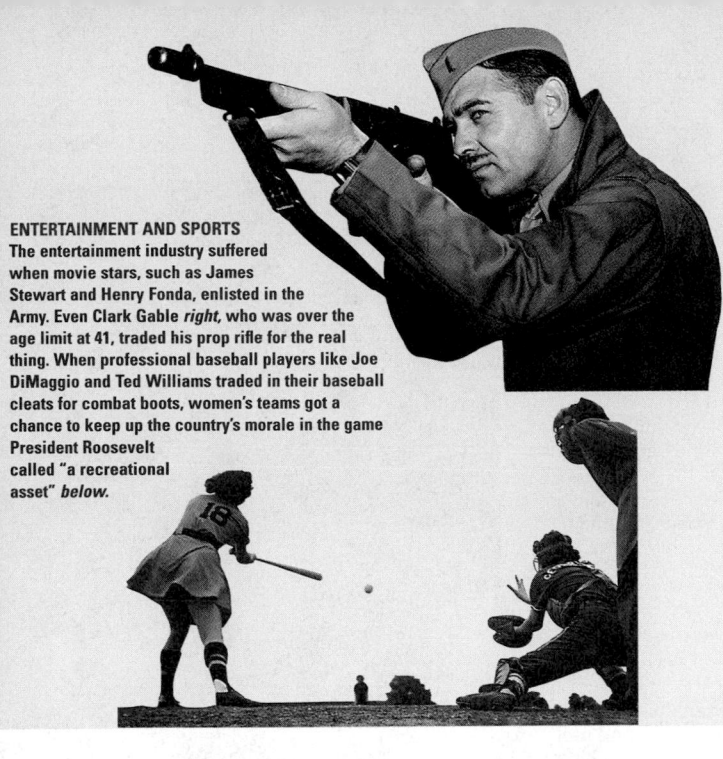

ENTERTAINMENT AND SPORTS
The entertainment industry suffered when movie stars, such as James Stewart and Henry Fonda, enlisted in the Army. Even Clark Gable *right*, who was over the age limit at 41, traded his prop rifle for the real thing. When professional baseball players like Joe DiMaggio and Ted Williams traded in their baseball cleats for combat boots, women's teams got a chance to keep up the country's morale in the game President Roosevelt called "a recreational asset" *below*.

CIVILIAN SURVEILLANCE
Worried about an invasion of the United States, people scanned the skies for bombers by using aids such as this one, which illustrated what each plane looked like.

Most Americans accepted rationing as a personal contribution to the war effort. Workers car-pooled or rode bicycles. Families learned to cope with shortages of everything from tires to toys. Inevitably, some cheated by hoarding scarce goods or by purchasing them through the "black market." In black markets, rationed items could be bought illegally without coupons at inflated prices.

In 1943, the WPB hired Harvard Business School Professor Thomas North Whitehead to tour the nation and find out how Americans were reacting to rationing and controls. Whitehead reported that "the good temper and common sense of most people under restrictions and vexations was really impressive. . . . My own observation is that most people are behaving like patriotic, loyal citizens."

While people tightened their belts at home, millions of other Americans put their lives on the line for their country in air, sea, and land battles on the other side of the world.

Section ❶ Assessment

1. TERMS & NAMES

Identify:
• George Marshall
• A. Philip Randolph
• Nisei
• Office of Price Administration (OPA)
• War Production Board (WPB)
• rationing

2. SUMMARIZING Recreate the web below on your paper and fill in ways that America prepared for war.

Preparation for War 1940–1941

3. INTERPRETING Why do you think President Roosevelt gave in to A. Philip Randolph's demands for equal African-American participation in the war effort?

THINK ABOUT
• the impact of a large demonstration in Washington on Roosevelt's popularity
• the relationship between blacks and whites in 1941

4. FORMING OPINIONS Do you think that President Roosevelt should have ordered the internment of Japanese Americans living on the West Coast? Support your opinion.

THINK ABOUT
• the founding principles of the United States
• the human costs of internment
• the behavior of Japanese Americans
• the risks Japanese Americans posed to U.S. security

The United States in World War II **737**

ANSWERS

1. TERMS & NAMES
George Marshall, p. 731
A. Philip Randolph, p. 733
Nisei, p. 735
Office of Price Administration (OPA), p. 736
War Production Board (WPB), p. 736
rationing, p. 736

2. SUMMARIZING
Possible Answers: Selective Service draft, conversion of industries to wartime production, employment of women in the war industry, creation of OSRD, establishment of OPA.

3. INTERPRETING
Possible Response: Roosevelt might have feared violence between whites and blacks or the disruption of transportation and other activities in the nation's capital.

4. FORMING OPINIONS
Possible Response: No—Internment violated the Constitution, and Japanese Americans had shown no signs of disloyalty. Yes—Internal dangers had to be reduced during a war, and Japanese Americans might have been attacked by suspicious whites if they had remained in their communities.

SKILLBUILDERS

• Understanding geography: place, movement, p. 739
• Understanding geography: location, region, p. 743

CRITICAL THINKING

• Analyzing motives, p. 739
• Analyzing causes, pp. 740, 744, 745
• Synthesizing, p. 741
• Summarizing, p. 741
• Recognizing effects, p. 742
• Sequencing history, p. 745
• Hypothesizing, p. 745
• Forming opinions, p. 745

FOCUS & MOTIVATE

▶ *Starting with the Student*
• Have students ever been in a situation in which they thought they might die? How did they react?
• How do they think their reactions compare with those of soldiers facing battle for the first time?

OBJECTIVE
(1) **INSTRUCT**

The United States and Britain Join Forces

▶ *Starting with the Student*
World War II was fought on many fronts simultaneously. One way for students to see this is by creating a World War II time line chart to track events in different places. Their charts might look like this:

(continued on next page)

TERMS & NAMES
• Dwight D. Eisenhower
• D-Day
• George Patton
• Harry S. Truman
• Battle of the Bulge
• V-E Day

② The War for Europe and North Africa

LEARN ABOUT how the Allies coordinated the war effort
TO UNDERSTAND how they defeated Germany and Italy.

ONE AMERICAN'S STORY

It was 1951 and John Patrick McGrath was just finishing his second year in drama school. For an acting class, his final exam was to be a performance of a death scene. McGrath knew his lines perfectly. But as he began the final farewell, he broke out in a sweat and bolted off the stage. "A cold winter freeze crackled through me as we played that scene," McGrath later recalled. Suddenly he had a flashback to a frozen meadow in Belgium during the Battle of the Bulge in 1945. Three German tanks were spraying his platoon with machine-gun fire.

A PERSONAL VOICE

Only a few feet away, one of the men in my platoon falls. Red blood spatters the pristine snow at his feet. He calls out to me. "Don't leave me. Don't...." The tanks advance, one straight for me. I grab my buddy by the wrist and pull him across the snow.... Barren bush is all I can find to hide behind. The tank nearest to us is on a track to run us down.... I fire several rounds from my rifle with no effect.... When the German tank is but 15 yards away, I grab my buddy by the wrist and feign a lurch to my right. The tank follows the move. Then I lurch back to my left. The German tank clamors by, only inches away.... It speeds away with the other two tanks, satisfied with the damage inflicted. In their wake the meadow is strewn with casualties. I turn to tend my fallen comrade. He is dead.

JOHN PATRICK MCGRATH, *A Cue for Passion*

Like countless other soldiers, McGrath would never forget both the heroism and the horrors he witnessed while fighting to free Europe.

Private John P. McGrath fought at both Anzio, Italy, and the Battle of the Bulge. He carried this bullet-riddled letter in a pack that saved his life, *above*. In 1990, he visited Anzio, where the rest of his company is buried, *top*.

The United States and Britain Join Forces

"Now that we are, as you say, 'in the same boat,'" British prime minister Winston Churchill wired President Roosevelt two days after Pearl Harbor, "would it not be wise for us to have another conference . . . and the sooner the better." Roosevelt responded with an invitation for Churchill to come at once. So began a remarkable alliance between the two nations.

WAR PLANS Prime Minister Churchill arrived at the White House on December 22, 1941, and spent the next three weeks working out war plans with President Roosevelt. Their first major decision was to make the defeat of Germany the Allies' top priority. There were several reasons for this policy:

• Roosevelt had always considered Adolf Hitler the number one enemy of the United States.
• Soviet leader Joseph Stalin, now a member of the Allies, was desperate for help against invading German forces.
• Only after Germany was defeated could the United States look to Britain and the Soviet Union for help in defeating Japan.

SECTION 2 RESOURCES

PRINT RESOURCES

IN-DEPTH RESOURCES: UNIT 7
Guided Reading, p. 20
Geography Application: Thunderclap, p. 24
Outline Map: Crisis in Europe, p. 26
Primary Source: War Dispatch from Ernie Pyle, p. 30
American Lives: George S. Patton, p. 36

ACCESS FOR STUDENTS ACQUIRING ENGLISH
Guided Reading (Spanish), p. 245
Geography Application: Thunderclap (Spanish), p. 249
Outline Map: Crisis in Europe (Spanish), p. 251

FORMAL ASSESSMENT
Section Quiz, p. 306

ALTERNATIVE ASSESSMENT BOOK
See forms for supporting and scoring alternative activities.

TECHNOLOGY RESOURCES

HUMANITIES TRANSPARENCIES
H24, War and Peace: Flying Fortress taking off, by Peter Hurd

GEOGRAPHY TRANSPARENCIES
G25, Battle of the Bulge

CD-ROM *Our Times*
Grolier Multimedia Encyclopedia
Electronic Library of Primary Sources

VIDEO *American Portfolio: A Videodisc for U.S. History*
user's guide, pp. 219–224, 231–232

INTERNET McDougal Littell Learning On-Line
http://www.mcdougallittell.com

	1942	1943
Atlantic		
Soviet Union		
North Africa		
Italy		
France		
Germany		
United States		
Pacific		

THINK THROUGH HISTORY
A. Analyzing Motives Why was the defeat of Germany the Allies' top priority?

A. Answer Hitler was the United States' prime enemy; Stalin needed help in defeating the Germans; The Allies couldn't help the U.S. fight Japan until Germany was defeated.

A second important decision the two leaders made was to accept only the unconditional surrender of the Axis Powers. Some historians have criticized this decision, arguing that it led Germany and Japan to fight longer and more desperately than they might otherwise have done. The Allied leaders, however, were united in their belief that "complete victory . . . [was] essential to defend life, liberty, and religious freedom, and to preserve human rights and justice in their own lands as well as in other lands."

By the end of their meeting, Roosevelt and Churchill had formed, in Churchill's words, "a very strong affection, which grew with our years of comradeship." When Churchill reached London, he found a message from the president waiting for him. "It is fun," Roosevelt wrote, "to be in the same decade with you."

THE BATTLE OF THE ATLANTIC After the attack on Pearl Harbor, Hitler ordered submarine raids against ships along America's East Coast. Unprotected American ships proved to be easy targets. In the first four months of 1942, the Germans sank 87 U.S. ships off the Atlantic shore. Seven months into the year, Hitler's wolf packs had destroyed a total of 681 Allied ships in the Atlantic. Something had to be done or the war would be lost at sea.

The Allies responded by organizing their cargo ships into convoys, or groups for mutual protection. The convoys were escorted across the Atlantic by destroyers equipped with sonar for detecting submarines underwater and by airplanes that used radar to spot U-boats on the ocean's surface. With this improved tracking, the Allies were finally able to find and destroy German U-boats faster than Hitler could build them. In May 1943, Admiral Karl Doenitz, the commander of the German U-boat offensive, reported that his losses had "reached an unbearable height."

At the same time, the United States launched a crash ship-building program. Between 1939 and 1940, the United States had built only 102 ships.

Skillbuilder Answer
Place: Sweden, Switzerland, Turkey, Spain, Ireland, Saudi Arabia, Portugal. **Movement:** It positioned them just across from Sicily.

GEOGRAPHY SKILLBUILDER
PLACE Which countries were neutral in 1942?
MOVEMENT How would establishing a foothold in North Africa enable the Allies to attack Italy?

▶ *Discussing Key Ideas*
• Early in the war, Churchill and Roosevelt agree to make the defeat of Germany the top priority of the Allies.
• Winning the Battle of the Atlantic turns the tide in favor of the Allies in 1943.

IN-DEPTH RESOURCES: UNIT 7
Guided Reading, p. 20

ACCESS FOR STUDENTS ACQUIRING ENGLISH
Guided Reading (Spanish), p. 245

HUMANITIES TRANSPARENCIES
H24, War and Peace: Flying Fortress taking off, by Peter Hurd

HISTORY FROM VISUALS
World War II: Europe and Africa, 1942–1943
Reading the Map Remind students to use the key to help them interpret the map. Ask them what the situation of the Soviet Union was in 1942 and 1943. *Most of the Soviet Union west of Moscow was under Nazi control.*

Extension Discuss with students how Stalin was likely to feel about the decision of his Allies to invade North Africa, rather than western Europe, in 1942.

IN-DEPTH RESOURCES: UNIT 7
Outline Map: Crisis in Europe, p. 26

 GROLIER MULTIMEDIA ENCYCLOPEDIA
"The World at War"

World War II: Europe and Africa, 1942–1943

Legend:
- Axis and Axis controlled
- Allies
- Neutral countries
- ➡ Axis forces
- ➡ Allied forces
- ✴ Major battles

Nov. 4, 1942 Operation Torch
November 1942 Farthest Axis Advance
May 19, 1943 Axis surrender of North Africa

739

The Eastern Front and the Mediterranean

▶ *Discussing Key Ideas*
* The Battle of Stalingrad marks a turning point in the war on Germany's eastern front.
* The Allies wrest control of North Africa from the Axis Powers in 1943.
* The Allied invasion of Italy in 1943 triggers a long and bloody campaign for control of the Italian peninsula.

 OUR TIMES
Dispatch by Ernie Pyle from the Sicilian campaign

MORE ABOUT . . .
Stalingrad

Stalingrad was originally known as Tsaritsyn, or "the tsarina's city." Tsaritsyn had been an important defensive stronghold and trading center since it was founded in the late 1500s on the Volga River and along trade routes leading into the Caucasus Mountains. In 1918, Stalin led the defense of the city against White Guard troops, after which the city was renamed Stalingrad in his honor. By the time the Germans attacked in 1942, Stalingrad had grown into an industrial city of nearly half a million people. Of particular importance to the Soviet war effort were the city's steel industry, tractor plant, and gun factory.

By early 1943, though, 140 Liberty ships alone were being produced each month. For the first time in the war, launchings of Allied cargo ships began to outnumber sinkings.

By mid-1943, the tide of the Battle of the Atlantic had turned in the Allies' favor. A happy Churchill reported to the House of Commons that June "was the best month [at sea] from every point of view we have known in the whole 46 months of the war."

The Eastern Front and the Mediterranean

By the summer of 1943, the Allies began to see victories in the land war as well. The first great turning point came in the Battle of Stalingrad.

THE BATTLE OF STALINGRAD The initial German push into the Soviet Union had stalled in front of Moscow and Leningrad (now St. Petersburg) in early 1942. (See the map on page 739.) With the German war machine running low on oil, Hitler changed his tactics. He sent his Sixth Army south with two objectives: (1) to seize the rich Soviet oil fields in the Caucasus Mountains, and (2) to capture Stalingrad (now Volgograd), a major industrial center on the Volga River. Once the Germans controlled Stalingrad, they could cut the movement of military supplies along the Volga River to Moscow.

The German army confidently approached Stalingrad in midsummer. "To reach the Volga and take Stalingrad is not so difficult for us," one German soldier wrote home. "Victory is not far away." The Luftwaffe—the German air force—prepared the way with nightly bombing raids over the city. Nearly every wooden building in Stalingrad was set ablaze. One night the flames were so bright that it was possible to read a newspaper 40 miles away. The situation looked so desperate that Soviet officers in Stalingrad recommended blowing up its factories and abandoning the city. A furious Stalin ordered them to defend his namesake city no matter what the cost. "Not a step back" became the motto of Stalingrad's defenders.

For three months the Germans pressed in on Stalingrad, conquering it house by house in brutal hand-to-hand combat. By the end of September, they controlled nine-tenths of the city—or what was left of it. A German officer described the devastation.

> **A PERSONAL VOICE**
> Stalingrad is no longer a town. By day it is an enormous cloud of burning, blinding smoke; it is a vast furnace lit by the reflection of the flames. And when night arrives, one of those scorching, howling, bleeding nights, the dogs plunge into the Volga and swim desperately to gain the other bank. The nights of Stalingrad are a terror for them. Animals flee this hell; the hardest stones cannot bear it for long; only man endures.
> **LIEUTENANT WEINER,** from his diary, quoted in *199 Days: The Battle for Stalingrad*

THINK THROUGH HISTORY
B. *Analyzing Causes* Why had the tide turned in the Battle of the Atlantic by mid-1943?
B. Answer The Allies had succeeded in using convoys with destroyers and planes that sank U-boats, the U.S. had greatly increased production of cargo ships.

Dazed, starved, and freezing, these German soldiers were taken prisoner after months of struggle. But they were the lucky ones. More than 230,000 of their comrades died in the Battle of Stalingrad.

In November, the Soviets launched a massive counterattack. Hitler's military advisers begged him to order a retreat before the Sixth Army was trapped. The führer, every bit as stubborn as Stalin, refused, shouting, "I won't go back from the Volga." The Germans were ordered to stand and fight to the last man.

The fighting continued as winter turned Stalingrad into a frozen wasteland. "We just lay in our holes and froze, knowing that 24 hours and 48 hours later we should be shivering precisely as we were now," wrote a German soldier, Benno Zieser. "But there was now no hope whatsoever of relief, and that was the worst thing of all." On February 2, 1943, Zieser and some 91,000 other frost-bitten, lice-ridden, half-starved German troops surrendered. They were all that was left of the army of 330,000 that had come to Stalingrad what seemed like a lifetime ago.

In defending Stalingrad, the Soviets lost a total of 1,250,000 soldiers and civilians—more than all American casualties for the entire war. Despite the staggering death toll, the Soviets' victory on the Volga marked a turning point in the war in the east. From that point on, the Soviet Army began to move steadily westward toward Germany.

THINK THROUGH HISTORY
C. Synthesizing
What two key decisions determined the final outcome at Stalingrad?
C. Answer Stalin's decision to defend the city and Hitler's decision to besiege it no matter what the cost.

THE NORTH AFRICAN FRONT While the battle of Stalingrad raged, Stalin pressured Britain and America to open a "second front" in Western Europe. He argued that an invasion across the English Channel would force Hitler to divert troops from the Soviet front. Churchill and Roosevelt didn't think the Allies had enough troops. Instead, they launched Operation Torch, an invasion of Axis-controlled North Africa, commanded by American General **Dwight D. Eisenhower.** (See the map on page 739.)

In November 1942, some 107,000 troops, the great majority of them Americans, landed in Casablanca, Oran, and Algiers in North Africa. From there they sped eastward, chasing Hitler's Afrika Korps led by General Erwin Rommel, the legendary Desert Fox. After months of heavy fighting, the last of the Afrika Korps surrendered in May 1943. British general Harold Alexander sent a message to Churchill reporting that "All enemy resistance has ceased. We are masters of the North African shores." American war correspondent Ernie Pyle caught the mood of the victorious troops.

THINK THROUGH HISTORY
D. Summarizing
What was the outcome of the North African campaign?

D. Answer The defeat of Hitler's troops.

A PERSONAL VOICE
The colossal German surrender has done more for American morale here than anything that could possibly have happened. Winning in battle is like winning at poker or catching a lot of fish. . . . As a result, the hundreds of thousands of Americans in North Africa are now happy men.

ERNIE PYLE, May 8, 1943 column "German Supermen Up Close"

THE ITALIAN CAMPAIGN Even before the battle in North Africa was won, Roosevelt, Churchill, and their commanders met in Casablanca to decide where to strike next. The Americans argued that the best approach to victory was to assemble a massive invasion fleet in Britain and to launch it across the English Channel, through France, and into the heart of Germany. Churchill, however, thought it would be safer to first attack Italy, "the soft underbelly of the Axis." The Allies compromised. They would push ahead with plans for the cross-channel invasion. Meanwhile, Allied troops would invade Italy.

The Italian campaign got off to a good start with the capture of Sicily in the

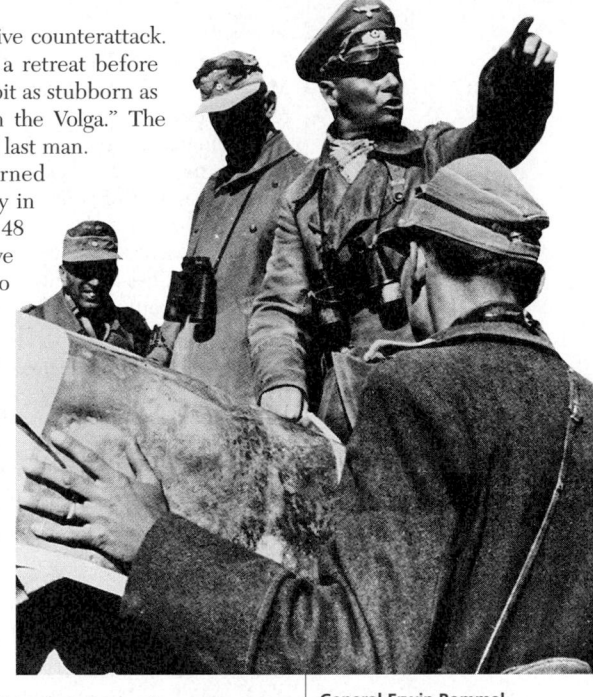

General Erwin Rommel, the Desert Fox, gives orders for an operation amid the swirling sand of a desert battle.

HISTORY FROM VISUALS
General Erwin Rommel
Critical Thinking: Forming Opinions Ask students what personal and professional characteristics this image suggests about the Desert Fox. *Possible Response: He is confident, commanding, and in control.*

IN-DEPTH RESOURCES: UNIT 7
Primary Source: War Dispatch of Ernie Pyle, p. 30

MORE ABOUT . . .
The Last Letters from Stalingrad

In January 1943, the last Nazi plane flew out of Stalingrad. Its cargo included seven bags of soldiers' letters, none of which was delivered. Instead the army seized the letters, hoping to use them to demonstrate soldiers' support for Hitler's regime. Most letters were hardly supportive, however, and they were buried in German army archives until 1954. Here are some excerpts:

"Around me everything is collapsing, a whole army is dying, day and night are on fire. . . . I don't know much about war. . . . But I know this much: the other side would never show such a lack of understanding for its men."

"I was shocked when I saw the map. . . . Hitler has left us in the lurch. If the airfield is still in our possession, this letter may still get out. . . . When Stalingrad has fallen, you'll hear and read it. And then you'll know that I shall not come back."

The Allies Liberate Europe

▶ *Discussing Key Ideas*
- D-Day marks the beginning of the Allied advance into Germany.
- The Battle of the Bulge is Hitler's last effort to avoid defeat and force a negotiated peace.
- Allied troops liberate Nazi death camps in Poland and Germany, finding horrors beyond their imagining.
- A week after a defeated Hitler commits suicide, Germany surrenders unconditionally to the Allies, and the war in Europe ends.

IN-DEPTH RESOURCES: UNIT 7
Geography Application: Thunderclap, p. 24

HISTORY FROM VISUALS
Normandy Invasions, June 6, 1944

Reading the Map Instruct students to first look at the small inset map on page 742, which shows the overall location and plan of the D-Day invasions. Then have them examine the large map, which shows the movements of specific invasion forces.

Extension Why might General Eisenhower have invaded at Normandy, rather than at Calais, which was closer to Great Britain? *Possible Response: The wide expanse of beach at Normandy allowed for a convergence of troops from several British bases on multiple landing points in France.*

summer of 1943. By then, the Italians were weary of war. On July 25, 1943, King Victor Emmanuel III summoned the Fascist dictator and prime minister Benito Mussolini to his palace and stripped him of power. "At this moment," the king told *Il Duce*, "you are the most hated man in Italy." As he left the palace, Mussolini was arrested, and Italians began celebrating the end of the war.

But their cheers were premature. Hitler responded by seizing control of Italy, reinstalling Mussolini as its leader, and ordering German troops to dig in and hold firm. It took 18 months of miserable fighting in the mud and mountains for the Allies to drive the Germans from Italian soil. One of the hardest battles the Allies encountered in Europe was fought less than 40 miles from Rome. This battle, "Bloody Anzio," lasted four months—until the end of May 1944—and left about 25,000 Allied and 30,000 Axis soldiers dead. In this grim struggle, the Allies were aided by 50,000 Italian partisans—members of underground resistance movements. The partisans harassed the Germans by cutting telephone wires, derailing trains, and dynamiting bridges and roads.

On April 28, 1945, partisans who had ambushed a Nazi convoy found Mussolini disguised as a German soldier in one of the trucks. The next day, they shot *Il Duce* and hung his body in a Milan square. At the time of his arrest in 1943, Mussolini had prophetically described his own fate: "From dust to power and from power back to dust."

E. Answer The taking of Italy by the Allies, tens of thousands of deaths, Mussolini's assassination.

THINK THROUGH HISTORY
E. *Recognizing Effects* *What were the results of the Italian campaign?*

The Allies Liberate Europe

As Allied troops pushed northward through Italy, the Soviet Army moved westward into Poland. Meanwhile, in England, General Eisenhower organized Operation Overlord, the planned invasion of Hitler's fortress in Europe.

D-DAY For two years the United States and Britain had been building an invasion force of ships and landing craft and nearly 3 million troops to attack Hitler's forces on the other side

Normandy Invasions, June 6, 1944

of the English Channel. Eisenhower hoped to take Hitler by surprise and pinpointed the relatively lightly fortified Normandy peninsula as the focus of the assault. To make reinforcement of the German forces more difficult once the invasion began, the Allies bombed northern France's supply routes—roads, bridges, and rail lines—for a month and a half before the planned assault.

D-Day, the day of the invasion, had originally been set for June 5, but bad weather forced a delay. Banking on a forecast for clearing skies, Eisenhower gave the go-ahead for the next day—and June 6, 1944, became a day that will live in history.

Three divisions parachuted down behind German lines during the night, and British, American, and Canadian troops fought their way ashore at five points along the 60-mile stretch of beach. With 156,000 troops, 4,000 landing craft, 600 warships, and 11,000 planes, it was the largest land-sea-air operation in history. Despite the massive air and sea bombardment by the Allies before the invasion, German retaliation was brutal, particularly at Omaha Beach. "People were yelling, screaming, dying, running on the beach, equipment was flying everywhere, men were bleeding to death, crawling, lying everywhere, firing coming from all directions," soldier Felix Branham wrote of the scene there. "We dropped down behind anything that was the size of a golf ball."

Despite heavy casualties, the Allies held the beachheads. Within a month, they had landed a million troops, 567,000 tons of supplies, and 170,000 vehicles in France. On July 25, General Omar Bradley unleashed massive air and land bombardment against the enemy at St.-Lô, giving General **George Patton** and his Third Army the gap they needed to advance. On August 23, they reached the Seine River south of Paris. Two days

Men of the 1st Airlanding Brigade load a jeep into a glider. Cheap, easy to make, and noiseless in the air, gliders were a key part of the Allied attack.

Prior to the full-scale invasion, 225 U.S. Rangers scaled the 100-foot cliffs at Pointe-du-Hoc to knock out the massive German guns positioned there.

④ Prefabricated Caissons — Prefabricated Caissons

Sunken ships

Mulberry Harbor

Floating Jetties — Stores Pier — LST Pier

Barge Pier

N

Arromanches

Mulberry Harbor In order to accommodate the vast number of invading ships, the Allies built two enormous concrete ports and towed them to Gold Beach on the French coast on D-Day. They sank 70 old ships to create a breakwater for the artificial harbor.

GEOGRAPHY SKILLBUILDER LOCATION *What other spot on the French coast might the Germans have expected the Allies to attack?* **REGION** *What natural geographical features of the region affected the Allied strategy in the D-Day invasion?*

The first wave of troops to land on Omaha Beach takes shelter behind barriers designed by the Germans and built to keep amphibious craft from landing.

743

Critical Thinking: Formulating Historical Questions Have students imagine they are war correspondents interviewing General Eisenhower shortly after the liberation of Paris. What questions would they want to ask him? After students have compiled their questions, pair students to research and answer each other's inquiries.

MORE ABOUT . . .
The Battle of the Bulge

Hitler committed 250,000 troops to the German counteroffensive in this battle. Among them were 33 English-speaking German commandos who, dressed in American uniforms and driving captured American jeeps and trucks, infiltrated Allied lines and caused great confusion before the deception was discovered. As a result, suspicious American sentries questioned everyone who moved. "Three times I was ordered to prove my identity by cautious GIs," recalled American general Omar Bradley. "The first time by identifying Springfield as the capital of Illinois (my questioner held out for Chicago); the second by locating the guard between the center and tackle on a line of scrimmage; the third time by naming the then-current spouse of a blonde [movie star] named Betty Grable. Grable stopped me, but the sentry did not. Pleased at having stumped me, he nevertheless passed me on."

GEOGRAPHY TRANSPARENCIES
G25, Battle of the Bulge

KEY PLAYER

DWIGHT D. EISENHOWER
1890–1969
When Army Chief of Staff George Marshall chose modest Lieutenant General Dwight David Eisenhower to become the Supreme Commander of U.S. forces in Europe, he knew what he was doing: people liked Ike. "He looks sort of like the guys you know at home," observed an American soldier.

More important, Eisenhower had an uncommon ability to work with all kinds of people, even competitive and temperamental allies. After V-E Day, a grateful Marshall wrote to Ike saying, "You have been selfless in your actions, always sound and tolerant in your judgments and altogether admirable in the courage and wisdom of your military decisions. You have made history, great history for the good of mankind."

later, French and American troops liberated the French capital from four years of German occupation. Patton announced this joyous event to his commander in a message that read, "Dear Ike: Today I spat in the Seine."

By September, 1944, the Allies had freed France, Belgium, Luxembourg, and much of the Netherlands. This good news—and the American people's desire not to "change horses in midstream"—helped elect Roosevelt and his new moderate running mate, Senator **Harry S. Truman,** to an unprecedented fourth term in November.

THE BATTLE OF THE BULGE In October 1944, Americans captured their first German town, Aachen. Hitler responded with a surprising counterattack. He ordered his troops to break through the Allied lines and to recapture the Belgian port of Antwerp. This bold move, the führer hoped, would disrupt the enemy's supply lines and demoralize the Allies.

On December 16, under cover of dense fog, eight German tank divisions broke through weak American defenses along an 80-mile front. The resulting dent in the Allied lines gave this desperate last-ditch offensive its name, the **Battle of the Bulge.** As the Germans swept westward, they captured 150 American GIs near Malmédy. Elite German troops—the SS troopers—herded the prisoners into a field and mowed them down with machine guns and pistols. Private Homer Ford was one of the 43 who somehow survived.

> **A PERSONAL VOICE**
> Men were lying around moaning and crying. When the Germans came over, they would say, "Is he breathing?" and would either shoot or hit [him] with the butt of their guns. . . . After they fired at us, I . . . could feel the blood oozing out. I was [lying] in the snow, and I got wet and started to shiver, and I was afraid they would see me shivering, but they didn't.
> **HOMER FORD,** quoted in *The GI War*

American troops led by Brigadier General Anthony McAuliffe made a heroic stand at the Belgian town of Bastogne. Surrounded and badly outnumbered, McAuliffe received a surrender demand from the Germans. His reply was just one word: "Nuts!"

The initial success of the German offensive was due mainly to the ability to keep the Allies off guard. According to some historians, the Allies unknowingly helped the Germans achieve this goal by not taking intelligence reports seriously. Since September, British code breakers had deciphered messages indicating that Hitler was planning a major campaign. Military strategists—not taking into account whom they were dealing with—chose not to believe these messages, because they thought such a move would be insane. "Allied intelligence had committed the most grievous sin of which [an intelligence operation] is capable," observed the historian Charles B. MacDonald. "They had looked in a mirror for the enemy and seen there only the reflections of their own intentions."

The battle raged for a month. When it was over, the Germans had been pushed back and little seemed to have changed. But, in fact, things had taken a decisive turn. Hitler had lost 120,000 troops, 600 tanks and assault guns, and 1,600 planes in the Battle of the Bulge—men and weapons he could not replace. From that point on, the Nazis could do little but retreat.

LIBERATION OF THE DEATH CAMPS Meanwhile, the Allies pressed eastward into the German heartland and the Soviet Army pushed westward across Poland toward Berlin. Soviet troops were the first to come upon one of Hitler's death camps in July 1944. As the Soviets drew near a camp called Majdanek in Poland, SS guards worked feverishly to bury and burn all evidence of their

F. Answer It caught the Allies off guard.

THINK THROUGH HISTORY
F. Analyzing Causes Why was the German offensive in the Battle of the Bulge initially successful?

TEACHING OPTIONS

Making Connections Across Cultures

Multicultural Liberation Forces Among the soldiers entering the concentration camps were Japanese Americans who had left their families in internment camps at home. African-American units also helped liberate the German camps. "Something happened when I walked through the gates," recalled African-American soldier Leon Bass. "I came into that camp an angry black soldier. Angry at my country and justifiably so. . . . But I came to realize that human suffering is not just relegated to me and mine. I now knew that human suffering could touch us all."

crimes. But they ran out of time. When the Soviets entered Majdanek, they found a thousand "living corpses," the world's largest crematorium, or furnace for burning dead bodies, and a storehouse containing 800,000 shoes. "This is not a concentration camp," reported a stunned Soviet war correspondent, "it is a gigantic murder plant." The Americans who later liberated death camps in Germany were equally overwhelmed.

A PERSONAL VOICE

We started smelling a terrible odor and suddenly we were at the concentration camp at Landsberg. Forced the gate and faced hundreds of starving prisoners. . . . We saw emaciated men whose thighs were smaller than wrists, many had bones sticking out thru their skin. . . . Also we saw hundreds of burned and naked bodies. . . . That evening I wrote to my wife that "For the first time I truly realized the evil of Hitler and why this war had to be waged."

ROBERT T. JOHNSON, quoted in *Voices: Letters from World War II*

New Yorkers celebrate V-E Day with a massive party that began in Times Square and went on for days at sites throughout the city.

UNCONDITIONAL SURRENDER By April 25, 1945, the Soviet Army had stormed Berlin. As Soviet shells burst overhead, the city panicked. "Hordes of soldiers stationed in Berlin deserted and were shot on sight or hanged from the nearest tree," wrote Claus Fuhrmann, a Berlin clerk. "On their chests they had placards reading, 'We betrayed the führer.'"

In his underground headquarters in Berlin, Hitler prepared for the end. On April 29, he married Eva Braun, his longtime companion. That same day he wrote out his last address to the German people. In it he blamed the Jews for starting the war and his generals for losing it. "I myself and my wife choose to die in order to escape the disgrace of . . . capitulation [surrender]," he said. "I die with a happy heart aware of the immeasurable deeds of our soldiers at the front." The next day Hitler shot himself while his new wife swallowed poison. Following Hitler's orders, the two bodies were carried outside, soaked with gasoline, and burned.

The historian Alan Bullock later wrote of the führer's extraordinary farewell, "Word for word, Hitler's final address to the German nation could be taken from almost any of his early speeches of the 1920s or from the pages of *Mein Kampf.* Twenty-odd years had changed and taught him nothing."

A week later, General Eisenhower accepted the unconditional surrender of the Third Reich. On May 8, 1945, the Allies celebrated **V-E Day**—Victory in Europe Day. The first part of the war was finally over.

G. Answer
Endurance and dedication of the Allies, help of American troops, tactics of partisans, Nazis' massive loss of equipment and troops in the Soviet Union.

THINK THROUGH HISTORY
G. Analyzing Causes *Why were the Allies finally able to win the war in Europe?*

Section 2 Assessment

1. TERMS & NAMES

Identify:
• Dwight D. Eisenhower
• D-Day
• George Patton
• Harry S. Truman
• Battle of the Bulge
• V-E Day

2. SEQUENCING HISTORY
Create a time line of the major events influencing the fighting in Europe and North Africa during World War II.

event two		event four

event one	event three

Write a paragraph indicating how any two of these events are related.

3. HYPOTHESIZING What do you think might have happened if the Nazis had defeated the Soviets at Stalingrad?

THINK ABOUT
• the military significance of a German victory
• the psychological impact of a Soviet loss

4. FORMING OPINIONS Do you agree with the decision by Roosevelt and Churchill to require unconditional surrender by the Axis Powers? Why or why not?

THINK ABOUT
• the advantages of defeating a foe decisively
• the advantages of ending a war quickly
• how other conflicts, such as the Civil War and World War I, ended

The United States in World War II **745**

ANSWERS

OBJECTIVES

1 To identify key turning points in the war in the Pacific.

2 To explain the development of and the debates concerning use of the atomic bomb.

3 To describe the challenges faced by the Allies in building a just and lasting postwar peace.

SKILLBUILDER

- Understanding geography: movement, region, p. 748

CRITICAL THINKING

- Comparing, p. 747
- Drawing conclusions, pp. 749, 750, 753
- Analyzing issues, p. 751
- Summarizing, pp. 752, 753
- Analyzing motives, p. 753
- Evaluating, p. 753

FOCUS & MOTIVATE

▶ **Starting with the Student**
- Have students study the Pacific region on a world map or globe. About how much of the earth does the Pacific Ocean cover? *One-third.*
- What does the vastness of this region suggest about fighting a war in the Pacific? What kind of war would it be? *Possible Answer: A war fought on many islands at once or on one island after another over an extended period of time.*

OBJECTIVE
1 INSTRUCT

The Allies Stem the Japanese Tide

▶ **Starting with the Student**
Have students begin a time line of events in the Pacific war, which they will fill in as they read Section 3. Initial entries might look like this:

(continued on next page)

---

3 # The War in the Pacific

TERMS & NAMES
- Douglas MacArthur
- Chester Nimitz
- kamikaze
- Manhattan Project
- J. Robert Oppenheimer
- Hiroshima
- Nagasaki
- Yalta Conference
- United Nations (UN)
- Nuremberg trials

LEARN ABOUT U.S. strategy in the Pacific
TO UNDERSTAND how the Allies defeated Japan and ended World War II.

ONE AMERICAN'S STORY

The writer William Manchester left college after Pearl Harbor to join the Marines. He was so skinny that he had to stuff himself with bananas and milk to pass the recruits' weight test. Manchester says that, as a child, his "horror of violence had been so deep-seated that I had been unable to trade punches with other boys." On a Pacific island, he would have to confront that horror the first time he killed a man in face-to-face combat. Manchester's target was a Japanese sniper firing on his buddies from a fisherman's shack.

American soldiers on Leyte help retake the Philippine Islands in late 1944.

A PERSONAL VOICE
My mouth was dry, my legs quaking, and my eyes out of focus. Then my vision cleared. I unlocked the safety of my Colt [handgun], kicked the door with my right foot, and leapt inside. My horror returned. I . . . saw him as a blur to my right. . . . My first shot missed him, embedding itself in the straw wall, but the second caught him dead on in the femoral artery. A wave of blood gushed from the wound. . . . He dipped a hand in it and listlessly smeared his cheek red. . . . I kept firing, wasting government property. . . . His eyes glazed over. Almost immediately a fly landed on his left eyeball. . . . A feeling of disgust and self-hatred clotted darkly in my throat, gagging me.

WILLIAM MANCHESTER, *Goodbye Darkness: A Memoir of the Pacific War*

The Pacific War was a savage conflict fought with raw courage on heaving seas, barren beaches, and jungle-covered hillsides. Like William Manchester, few who took part in that fearsome struggle would return home unchanged.

The Allies Stem the Japanese Tide

While the Allies agreed that the defeat of Hitler was their first priority, the United States did not wait until V-E Day to move against Japan. Fortunately, the Japanese attack on Pearl Harbor in 1941 missed the Pacific fleet's submarines, as well as its aircraft carriers, which were at sea during the raid on Pearl Harbor in 1941. In addition, almost all of the sunken or damaged ships were repaired and returned to service.

JAPANESE ADVANCES In the first six months after Pearl Harbor, the Japanese conquered an empire that dwarfed Hitler's Third Reich. On the Asian mainland, Japanese troops overran Hong Kong, French Indochina, Malaya, Burma, Thailand, and most of China. They also swept south and east across the Pacific, conquering Formosa, the Dutch East Indies, Guam, Wake, the Solomon Islands, and countless other dots in the ocean, including two islands in the Aleutian chain that were part of Alaska.

SECTION 3 RESOURCES

 PRINT RESOURCES

IN-DEPTH RESOURCES: UNIT 7
Guided Reading, p. 21
Primary Source: The Bombing of Nagasaki, p. 31

ACCESS FOR STUDENTS ACQUIRING ENGLISH
Guided Reading (Spanish), p. 246

FORMAL ASSESSMENT
Section Quiz, p. 307

ALTERNATIVE ASSESSMENT BOOK
See forms for supporting and scoring alternative activities.

 TECHNOLOGY RESOURCES

CD-ROM *Our Times*
Grolier Multimedia Encyclopedia
Electronic Library of Primary Sources

VIDEO *American Portfolio: A Videodisc for U.S. History*
user's guide, pp. 216–219, 224–226, 231–232

INTERNET McDougal Littell Learning On-Line
http://www.mcdougallittell.com

In the Philippines, 80,000 American and Filipino troops under General **Douglas MacArthur** held out against 200,000 invading Japanese forces for four months on the Bataan Peninsula and for another month on the island of Corregidor at the entrance to Manila Bay. Hunger, disease, and bombardments took a terrible toll—14,000 killed and 48,000 wounded. Finally MacArthur was ordered to abandon the Philippines. As he left, he pledged to the many thousands of his men who did not make it out, "I shall return."

Japan's admirals and generals were dazzled by their success. Not only had they surpassed the Allies militarily, but they had also destroyed the myth of white rule in Asia. Emperor Hirohito, who had suddenly acquired 150 million new subjects spread over almost one-seventh of the globe, wondered, on the other hand, if "the fruits of war are tumbling into our mouths almost too quickly."

An American LCI (Landing Craft Infantry) fires shells in an assault on the Philippines.

U.S. RETALIATION On April 18, 1942, 16 B-52 bombers, led by Colonel James Doolittle, took off from the aircraft carrier *Hornet*. Hours later they swept in from the sea over Tokyo and four other Japanese cities, blasting factories, steel mills, oil tanks, and other military targets before vanishing. The next day America awoke to headlines proclaiming "Tokyo Bombed! Doolittle Do'od It." Seeing the U.S. pull off a Pearl Harbor–style air raid over Japan lifted Americans' sunken spirits. At the same time, it dampened spirits in Japan. "We started to doubt," recalled a Japanese civilian later, "that we were invincible."

Early in May, a combined American and Australian fleet intercepted a Japanese strike force aimed at Australia. This confrontation, the Battle of the Coral Sea, established a new type of naval warfare. All the fighting was done by carrier-based airplanes; the opposing ships never saw each other or exchanged gunfire. The Allies lost more ships than the Japanese, leading the Japanese to declare victory. But the real triumph belonged to the Allies. By the end of the battle, the Japanese fleet was too short of fuel to continue on to Australia. For the first time since Pearl Harbor, a Japanese invasion had been stopped and turned back.

THE BATTLE OF MIDWAY In June, Admiral **Chester Nimitz,** the commander of U.S. naval forces in the Pacific, learned from intercepted messages that a Japanese invasion force of well over 110 ships—the largest assembly of naval power in history—was heading toward Midway, a strategic island in the Pacific. From there, the invasion force planned to move on to Hawaii to finish the destruction of American naval power started at Pearl Harbor.

Even though he was outnumbered four to one in ships and planes, Nimitz prepared a surprise reception for the Japanese at Midway. As the enemy drew near, he ordered his carrier planes into the air again and again with orders "to inflict maximum damage on the enemy." The results were devastating. By the end of the Battle of Midway, the Japanese had lost four irreplaceable aircraft carriers, a cruiser, and 322 planes. In the words of a Japanese official, at Midway the Americans had "avenged Pearl Harbor."

ISLAND HOPPING The Pacific war was one of vast distances. Japanese troops were dug in on hundreds of islands scattered across thousands of miles of ocean. To storm each one, MacArthur argued, would have been "a long and costly effort." Instead, he wanted to leapfrog, or bypass, Japanese strongholds. MacArthur seized less-well-fortified islands, built

A. Answer Both were surprise naval attacks that resulted in substantial destruction of the enemy's Pacific fleet.

THINK THROUGH HISTORY
A. Comparing In what ways were the American victory at Midway and the Japanese triumph at Pearl Harbor alike?

HISTORICAL SPOTLIGHT

NAVAJO CODE TALKERS

On each of the Pacific islands that American GIs stormed in World War II, the Japanese heard a "strange language gurgling" in their radio headsets. The code seemed to have Asian overtones, but it baffled everyone who heard it. In fact, the language was Navajo, which was spoken only in the American Southwest and had no alphabet or other written symbols. Its "hiddenness" made it a perfect candidate for a code language.

Though the Navajo had no words for combat terms, they developed terms such as *chicken hawk* for airplane and *war chief* for commanding general, and 200 Navajo were recruited into the Marine Corps as code talkers. Their primary duty was transmitting telephone and radio messages.

Throughout the Pacific campaign—from Midway to Iwo Jima—the code talkers were considered indispensible to the war effort. They finally received national recognition at a ceremony in Chicago in 1969.

(continued from page 746)

1942
January–April
Japan conquers Formosa, Guam, the Philippines, and other Pacific islands.

May
Allies turn back Japan in Battle of the Coral Sea.

▶ *Discussing Key Ideas*
- Japan conquers 150 million people.
- Americans surprise Japan in an air raid over Tokyo and in the Battle of the Coral Sea.
- The Battle of Midway halts Japan's westward expansion.
- The United States adopts an "island-hopping" strategy against Japan.

IN-DEPTH RESOURCES: UNIT 7
Guided Reading, p. 21

ACCESS FOR STUDENTS ACQUIRING ENGLISH
Guided Reading (Spanish), p. 246

MORE ABOUT . . .
The Battle of Midway
The unsung heroes of the Battle of Midway were the code breakers of the navy's Combat Intelligence Unit. "Midway was essentially a victory of intelligence," Admiral Chester Nimitz wrote. "In attempting surprise, the Japanese were themselves surprised."

HISTORICAL SPOTLIGHT
Navajo Code Talkers
Critical Thinking: Hypothesizing Ask students to speculate why it took so long for the Navajo Code Talkers to receive national recognition.
Possible Answer: Because of their minority status and general invisibility in mainstream American life.

PACIFIC		• U.S. declares war on Japan.	• U.S. surrenders in the Philippines. • Allies turn back Japanese fleet in Battle of the Coral Sea. • Allies defeat Japan in Battle of Midway. • U.S. marines land on Guadalcanal.

1941   Apr   Jun   Dec   1942   Apr   May   Jun   Aug   Nov   1943   Feb   May

EUROPE   • Germany invades the Soviet Union.   • Germany and Italy   • Hitler orders   • Allies land in   • Germans   • Axis
           • Germany invades Greece and Yugoslavia.   declare war on the   attack on   North Africa.   surrender at   forces
           United States.   Stalingrad.   Stalingrad.   surrende
                                                                         in Africa

Skillbuilder Answer
Movement: Guam.
Region: It made preparing and executing battle plans very difficult.

GEOGRAPHY SKILLBUILDER
MOVEMENT *Which island served as a jumping-off point for several Pacific battles?*
REGION *How do you think the distances between the Pacific Islands affected U.S. naval strategy?*

airfields on them, and then used air power to cut supply lines to enemy troops in the area. As a result, a Japanese intelligence officer later reported, "Our strong points were gradually starved out."

The Americans' first land offensive of the war began in August 1942, when 19,000 marines stormed Guadalcanal in the Solomon Islands. By the time the Japanese finally abandoned Guadalcanal six months later, they called it the Island of Death. To war correspondent Ralph Martin and the GIs who fought there, nearly a third of whom became battle casualties, it was simply "hell."

A PERSONAL VOICE
Hell was red furry spiders as big as your fist, giant lizards as long as your leg, leeches falling from trees to suck blood, armies of white ants with bites of fire, scurrying scorpions inflaming any flesh they touched, enormous rats and bats everywhere, and rivers with waiting crocodiles. Hell was the sour, foul smell of the squishy jungle, humidity that rotted a body within hours, . . . stinking wet heat of dripping rain forests that sapped the strength of any man. Hell was an enemy hidden in the dark deep of shadows, an enemy so fanatic that it used its own dead as booby traps.
RALPH G. MARTIN, from *The GI War*

Guadalcanal marked Japan's first defeat on land, but not its last. The Americans continued leapfrogging across the Pacific toward Japan, and in October 1944, some 178,000 Allied troops and 738 ships converged on Leyte Island in the Philippines. General MacArthur, who had left the American

World War II: Japan's Defeat, 1942–1945

| Jul | Sep | 1944 | May | Jun | Jul | Aug | | Oct | Dec | 1945 | Mar | Apr | May | Jun | Aug | Sep | 1946 |

Allies win battle of the Philippine Sea.

Allies defeat Japan in Battle of Leyte.

Allies capture Iwo Jima.

Allies capture Okinawa.
U.S. drops atomic bombs on Hiroshima and Nagasaki.
Japan surrenders.

Allies invade Sicily.

Italy secretly surrenders to Allies.

Allies liberate Paris.
Soviets liberate first death camps.
Allies invade Europe on D-Day.
"Bloody Anzio" ends.

Germans attack Allies in Battle of the Bulge.

V-E Day ends the war in Europe.
Italians assassinate Mussolini.
Hitler commits suicide.

colony two years earlier, waded ashore and announced, "People of the Philippines: I have returned."

The Japanese threw their entire fleet into the battle for Leyte Gulf. They also tested a new tactic, the **kamikaze,** or suicide-plane, attack in which Japanese pilots crashed their bomb-laden planes into Allied ships. (*Kamikaze* means "divine wind" and refers to a legendary typhoon that saved Japan in 1281 by destroying a Mongol invasion.) In the Philippines, 424 kamikaze pilots embarked on suicide missions, sinking 16 ships and damaging another 80.

Americans watched these terrifying attacks with "a strange admixture of respect and pity" according to Vice Admiral Charles Brown. "You had to admire the devotion to country demonstrated by those pilots," recalled Seaman George Marse. "Yet, when they were shot down, rescued and brought aboard our ship, we were surprised to find the pilots looked like ordinary, scared young men, not the wide-eyed fanatical 'devils' we imagined them to be."

Despite the damage done by the kamikazes, the Battle of Leyte Gulf was a disaster for Japan. In three days of battle, it lost 3 battleships, 4 aircraft carriers, 13 cruisers, and almost 400 planes. From then on, the Imperial Navy played only a minor role in the defense of Japan.

After retaking the Philippines and liberating the American prisoners of war there, the Allies turned to Iwo Jima, an island William Manchester later described as "an ugly, smelly glob of cold lava squatting in a surly ocean." Iwo Jima was critical to the U. S. as a base from which heavily loaded bombers could reach Japan. It was also perhaps the most heavily defended spot on earth, with 20,700 Japanese troops deeply entrenched in tunnels and caves. More than 6,000 Marines died taking this desolate island, the largest number in any single battle in the Pacific to that point. Only 200 Japanese survived. Just one obstacle still stood between the Allies and a final assault on Japan—the island of Okinawa.

The Atomic Bomb Ends the War

Roosevelt did not live to see the final battles of the Pacific War. On April 12, 1945, while posing for a portrait in Warm Springs, Georgia, the president had a stroke and died within hours. That night, Harry S. Truman became the nation's new president.

Grieving crowds lined the tracks as the president's body was brought by train back to Washington. Betty Conrad was among the servicewomen who escorted his casket from Union Station to the White House. "The only sound was that of the hoofbeats of the riderless horse and the sobs of mourners," she observed. "The body in the casket was not only our leader but the bodies of all the men and women who had given their lives for freedom. They must not and will not have died in vain."

THE BATTLE FOR OKINAWA As the world mourned Roosevelt's death, an inexperienced Truman began to grapple with his new job as president and

Japanese kamikaze pilots receive a briefing on the mission that would be their last.

B. Answer It was the next to the last obstacle to taking Japan.

THINK THROUGH HISTORY
B. *Drawing Conclusions* Why was taking Leyte so crucial to the Allies?

MORE ABOUT . . .
Japan's Kamikaze Pilots

At first, young Japanese airmen considered it a great honor to volunteer for suicide missions. The pilots' farewell letters were filled with passionate patriotism. One young man told his family, "Think kindly of me and consider it my good fortune to have done something praiseworthy." Another left this final entry in his diary: "Like cherry blossoms / In the spring / Let us fall / Clean and radiant."

As the kamikaze campaign continued, however, the Allies developed effective tactics to combat the suicide planes. At the same time, fewer and fewer young Japanese volunteered for suicide duty. Even so, before the Japanese surrendered, the kamikaze corps had damaged more than 300 U.S. ships and caused about 15,000 casualties.

OBJECTIVE
2 INSTRUCT

The Atomic Bomb Ends the War

▶ *Discussing Key Ideas*
• The top-secret Manhattan Project produces the world's first atomic bomb and tests it in July 1945.
• Scientists involved in the project debate how the weapon should be used.
• In August of 1945, President Truman orders the dropping of two atomic bombs on Japan, forcing its unconditional surrender.

KEY PLAYER

**DOUGLAS MACARTHUR
1880–1964**

Douglas MacArthur was too arrogant and prickly to be considered a "regular guy" by his troops. But he was arguably the most brilliant strategist of World War II. For every American soldier killed in his campaigns, the Japanese lost ten.

He was considered a real hero of the war, both by the military and by the prisoners on the Philippines whom he freed. "MacArthur took more territory with less loss of life," observed journalist John Gunther, "than any military commander since Darius the Great [King of Persia from 522–486 B.C.]."

Not yet fully aware of the effects of nuclear fallout, J. Robert Oppenheimer and General Leslie Groves survey a nuclear test site wearing plastic bags to protect their feet.

commander-in-chief of the armed forces. By then the war in Europe was winding down. In the Pacific, however, a ferocious battle would soon rage on Okinawa, Japan's last defensive outpost. The Japanese unleashed more than 1,900 kamikaze attacks on the Allies during the Okinawa campaign, sinking 30 ships, damaging more than 300 more, and killing almost 5,000 seamen.

Once ashore, the Allies faced even fiercer opposition than on Iwo Jima. By the time the fighting ended on June 22, 1945, more than 7,600 Americans had died. But the Japanese paid a still ghastlier price—110,000 lives—in defending Okinawa. This total includes two generals who chose ritual suicide over the shame of surrender. A witness to this ceremony described their end: "A simultaneous shout and a flash of the sword . . . and both generals had nobly accomplished their last duty to their Emperor."

The Battle for Okinawa was a chilling foretaste of what the Allies imagined the final invasion of Japan's home islands would be like. Although many historians now think the projected toll was vastly overestimated, Winston Churchill predicted that the cost would be a million American lives, and half that number of British.

THE MANHATTAN PROJECT Not long after Truman took office, Secretary of War Henry Stimson handed him a memo that began, "Within four months we shall in all probability have completed the most terrible weapon ever known in human history, one bomb of which could destroy a whole city."

Over the next hour, the president learned that the **Manhattan Project** was not only the most ambitious scientific enterprise in history but also the best-kept secret of the war. At its peak, more than 600,000 Americans were involved in the project, although few of them knew its ultimate purpose—the creation of an atomic bomb.

Work on the atomic bomb began in 1942 after a group of scientists under the direction of physicist Enrico Fermi successfully achieved a controlled nuclear reaction at the University of Chicago. General Leslie Groves, the organizer of the Manhattan Project, had two gigantic atomic reactors built at Oak Ridge, Tennessee, and another at Hanford, Washington, to produce uranium 235, a rare form of that element, and the even rarer element, plutonium, used in an explosive device. Meanwhile, a group of brilliant American, British, and European-refugee scientists headed by **J. Robert Oppenheimer** worked in a secret laboratory in Los Alamos, New Mexico, to build the actual bomb.

As the time to test the bomb drew near, the air around Los Alamos crackled with rumors and fears. At one end of the scale were fears that the bomb wouldn't work at all, or, if it did, would not produce enough punch to amount to much. At the other end was the prediction that the explosion would set fire to the atmosphere, which would mean the end of the earth.

On the night of July 16, 1945, the first atomic bomb was detonated in an empty expanse of desert near Alamogordo, New Mexico. Otto Frisch, a project scientist, listened tensely to the countdown.

A PERSONAL VOICE
And then without a sound, the sun was shining; or so it looked. The sand hills of the desert were shimmering in a very bright light, almost colorless and shapeless. . . . I turned round, but that object on the horizon which looked like a small sun was still too bright to look at. . . . After another ten seconds or so it had grown and . . . was slowly rising into the sky from the ground, with which it remained connected by a lengthening stem of swirling dust; incongruously I thought of a red-hot elephant standing balanced on its trunk.

OTTO FRISCH, *What Little I Remember*

That blinding flash, which was visible 180 miles away, was followed by a deafening roar as a tremendous shock wave rolled across the trembling desert. The bomb not only worked, but it was more powerful than most had dared hope.

TO BOMB OR NOT TO BOMB In spite of this success, many of the scientists who had worked on the bomb had doubts about using it. A petition drawn up by Leo Szilard, a leading physicist in the Manhattan Project, and signed by 70 other scientists argued that it would be immoral to drop an atomic bomb on Japan without fair warning. Others supported staging a demonstration of the bomb for Japanese leaders, perhaps by exploding one on a deserted island near Japan, to convince them to surrender.

These objections were discussed in detail on May 31, 1945, by a newly formed advisory body, the Interim Committee. At that meeting, Oppenheimer outlined the problems with a test explosion: (1) nothing less than dropping a bomb on a city would convince the Japanese to surrender, (2) the test might be a dud, (3) the Japanese might shoot down the delivery plane or move American prisoners of war into the test area. Swayed by these arguments, the committee recommended that the bomb be used against military targets in Japan, and that it be dropped without warning.

Many scientists working on the bomb agreed with this recommendation— even more so as the heavy casualty figures from Iwo Jima and Okinawa sank in. "Are we to go on shedding American blood when we have available means to a steady victory?" they asked in a petition. "No! If we can save even a handful of American lives, then let us use this weapon—now!" But other scientists remained firmly opposed.

Truman did not hesitate. On July 25, 1945, he ordered the military to make final plans for dropping the only two atomic bombs then in existence on Japanese targets. He later wrote, "The final decision of where and when to use the atomic bomb was up to me. Let there be no mistake about it. I regarded the bomb as a military weapon and never had any doubt that it should be used." A day later, the United States warned Japan that it faced "prompt and utter destruction" unless it surrendered at once. Japan refused.

HIROSHIMA AND NAGASAKI On August 6, a B-29 bomber named the *Enola Gay* released an atomic bomb code-named Little Boy over **Hiroshima,** an important Japanese military center. Forty-three seconds later, almost every building in the city collapsed into dust. Hiroshima had ceased to exist. Still Japan's leaders hesitated to surrender. Three days later a second bomb, named Fat Man, was dropped on **Nagasaki,** leveling half the city. By the end of the year, an estimated 200,000 people died as a result of injuries and radiation poisoning caused by the atomic blasts. Yamaoko Michiko was 15 years old and living near the center of Hiroshima when the first bomb hit.

> **A PERSONAL VOICE**
> They say temperatures of 7,000 degrees centigrade hit me. . . . Nobody there looked like human beings. . . . Humans had lost the ability to speak. People couldn't scream, "It hurts!" even when they were on fire. . . . People with their legs wrenched off. Without heads. Or with faces burned and swollen out of shape. The scene I saw was a living hell.
> **YAMAOKO MICHIKO,** quoted in *Japan at War: An Oral History*

Emperor Hirohito was horrified by the death and destruction. "I cannot bear to see my innocent people suffer any longer," he told Japan's leaders

In the aftermath of the bombing of Nagasaki, a mushroom cloud hides the sun, and a dazed mother and child clutch rice balls provided by rescue parties.

Left margin:

D. Answer For—The bomb would hasten the surrender of Japan and save American and British lives. **Against**—It was immoral to drop such a terrible weapon on civilians without warning and allowing the enemy to surrender.

THINK THROUGH HISTORY

D. Analyzing Issues What were the main arguments for and against dropping the atomic bomb on Japanese cities in 1945?

MORE ABOUT . . .
J. Robert Oppenheimer and the First Atomic Bomb Test

"A few people laughed, a few people cried, most people were silent," J. Robert Oppenheimer recalled after the first atomic bomb exploded into a fireball over the New Mexican desert. As Oppenheimer watched the awesome spectacle, he recalled two passages from the ancient Hindu epic *Bhagavad-Gita*. First this passage came to mind: "If the radiance of a thousand suns were to burst into the sky, that would be the splendor of the Mighty One." But then he recalled this one: "I am become Death, the shatterer of worlds."

GROLIER MULTIMEDIA ENCYCLOPEDIA
video of an atomic blast

MORE ABOUT . . .
The Firebombing of Tokyo

Just after midnight on March 10, 1945, 334 American B-29 bombers left Guam, Saipan, and the Tinian islands and headed for Tokyo. Within half an hour, fires started by the bombardment had been whipped by high winds into an immense firestorm. A Japanese reporter wrote of the scene, "The city was as bright as at sunrise. . . . We thought the whole of Tokyo was reduced to ashes." The firebombing of Tokyo left 97,000 people dead, 125,000 wounded, and 1.2 million homeless—damage more extensive than that done by the atomic blasts that leveled Hiroshima and Nagasaki five months later.

Rebuilding Begins

▶ **Starting with the Student**
Have students consider how they treat someone they have had a fight or a disagreement with once the issue is resolved.

- Are they more considerate than usual, more belligerent, or more withdrawn and cautious?

▶ **Discussing Key Ideas**
- As the end of the war nears, the Allies pursue plans to create a new international peacekeeping organization, the United Nations.
- Trials are held in Germany, Japan, and elsewhere to prosecute individuals guilty of crimes against humanity during the war.
- U.S. forces occupy Japan and help rebuild it as a democratic nation.

 OUR TIMES
excerpt of Truman's V-J speech

DIFFICULT DECISIONS IN HISTORY
Agonizing Over the A-Bomb
Critical Thinking: Formulating Historical Questions Have students work in small groups to create a list of questions that will guide their research and help them evaluate President Truman's decision to drop the atomic bombs on Japan.

 ELECTRONIC LIBRARY OF PRIMARY SOURCES
Statement on the Atomic Bomb by Harry S. Truman

---

tearfully. Then he ordered them to draw up papers "to end the war." On September 2, formal surrender ceremonies took place on the United States battleship *Missouri* in Tokyo Bay. "Today the guns are silent," said General MacArthur in a speech marking this historic moment. "The skies no longer rain death—the seas bear only commerce—men everywhere walk upright in the sunlight. The entire world is quietly at peace."

Rebuilding Begins

With Japan's surrender, the Allies turned to the challenge of rebuilding a war-torn world. Even before the last guns fell silent, they began thinking about principles that would govern the postwar world.

Difficult Decisions
IN HISTORY

AGONIZING OVER THE A-BOMB

It was 1945. The war in the Pacific dragged on. After only 116 days in office, President Truman had to decide if he should use the atomic bomb against the Japanese cities Hiroshima and Nagasaki, whose combined population was 540,000.

Secretary of War Henry Stimson said yes because it would bring an end to the war, save American lives, and provide a threat to the Soviets, who stood ready to invade Japan themselves. "The face of war is the face of death," he proclaimed.

On the other hand, General Dwight D. Eisenhower maintained that "dropping the bomb was completely unnecessary" to save American lives and that Japan was already defeated.

1. Think about the pros and cons of each position. What additional information do you need to evaluate them fully?
2. If you had been in President Truman's position in August 1945, would you have used the A-bomb against Japan? Why or why not?

PREPARATION FOR PEACE In February 1945, Roosevelt had met with Churchill and Stalin at the Soviet city of Yalta on the Black Sea. At this **Yalta Conference,** the three leaders made a number of important decisions about the future. They agreed to move ahead in creating a new international peacekeeping body, the **United Nations (UN),** based on the principles in the Atlantic Charter. In exchange for Japan's Kuril and Sakhalin Islands, Stalin promised to enter the war against Japan after the surrender of Germany. He also promised "free and unfettered elections" in Poland and in other Soviet-occupied Eastern European countries.

The following April, representatives of 50 nations met in San Francisco to establish the United Nations. By June they had agreed on a charter. The charter created the General Assembly, which was made up of all member nations and was expected to function as a "town meeting of the world." The charter also set up administrative, judicial, and economic governing bodies.

An 11-member Security Council held the real power, though. The five main wartime Allies—the United States, Great Britain, the Soviet Union, France, and China—were given permanent seats on the Security Council. At the insistence of the Soviet Union and the United States, each permanent member had the power to veto any council action. The other six seats rotated to countries elected by the General Assembly. As the charter was signed, hopes were high that the Security Council would be far more effective than the League of Nations at keeping world peace.

In July 1945, President Truman met with Churchill and Stalin at Potsdam in defeated Germany. In addition to drawing up a blueprint for disarming Germany and eliminating the Nazi regime, the Allies agreed that "stern justice shall be meted out to all war criminals, including those who have visited cruelties on our prisoners."

THE NUREMBERG WAR TRIALS Based on decisions made at Potsdam, Germany was divided into four zones, or sections. The United States, Britain, France, and the Soviet Union each occupied and administered one zone. Germany's capital city Berlin, although within the Soviet zone, was also divided into four sectors, each administered by one of the occupying powers.

During the next year, in an unprecedented move, an international tribunal representing 23 nations tried Nazi war criminals in Nuremberg, Germany. Twenty-two Nazi leaders were indicted at the first of the **Nuremberg trials.** They included Hitler's most trusted party officials, government ministers, military leaders, and powerful industrialists. As the trial began, U.S. Supreme Court justice Robert Jackson explained the significance of the event.

THINK THROUGH HISTORY
E. Summarizing
What decisions did Roosevelt, Churchill, and Stalin make at the Yalta Conference?

E. Answer To form the United Nations; that the Soviet Union would enter the war against Japan after Germany surrendered and would allow free elections in Poland and other Soviet-occupied countries.

A PERSONAL VOICE

The wrongs which we seek to condemn and punish have been so calculated, so malignant and so devastating, that civilization cannot tolerate their being ignored because it cannot survive their being repeated....It is hard now to perceive in these miserable men...the power by which as Nazi leaders they once dominated much of the world and terrified most of it. Merely as individuals, their fate is of little consequence to the world. What makes this inquest significant is that these prisoners represent sinister influences that will lurk in the world long after their bodies have returned to dust. They are living symbols of racial hatreds, of terrorism and violence, and of the arrogance and cruelty of power....Civilization can afford no compromise with the social forces which would gain renewed strength if we deal ambiguously or indecisively with the men in whom those forces now precariously survive.

ROBERT JACKSON, from opening address to the Nuremberg War Crimes Trial

F. Answer To hold German and Japanese leaders responsible for starting the war and for committing atrocities against both soldiers and civilians; also to make it clear that even in wartime, "crimes against humanity" will not be tolerated in a civilized society.

THINK THROUGH HISTORY
F. Analyzing Motives Why did the Allies hold war crimes trials after World War II?

War Criminals on Trial, 1945–1949

The defendants at the Nuremberg trials were accused of one or more of the following crimes:

- **Crimes Against the Peace**—planning and waging an aggressive war
- **War Crimes**—acts against the customs of warfare such as the killing of hostages and prisoners, the plundering of private property, or the destruction of towns and cities
- **Crimes Against Humanity**—the murder, extermination, deportation, or enslavement of civilians

Twelve of the 22 defendants were sentenced to death and most of the rest to prison. Later trials of lesser leaders found nearly 200 more Nazis guilty of war crimes. This was the first time in history that a nation's leaders were held legally responsible for their actions during wartime.

THE OCCUPATION OF JAPAN Japan was occupied by U.S. forces under the command of General Douglas MacArthur. In the early months of the occupation, more than 1,100 Japanese, from former prime minister Hideki Tojo to lowly prison guards, were arrested and put in jail. Seven, including Tojo, were sentenced to death. Trials were also conducted in the Philippines, in China, and on other Asian battlegrounds for Japanese officials accused of atrocities against civilians or prisoners of war.

During the six-year American occupation, MacArthur reformed Japan's economy by introducing free-market practices that led to a remarkable economic recovery. MacArthur also worked to transform Japan's government. He called for a new constitution that would provide for woman suffrage and guarantee basic freedoms. In the United States, Americans followed these changes with interest. The *New York Times* reported that "General MacArthur . . . has swept away an autocratic regime by a warrior god and installed in its place a democratic government presided over by a very human emperor and based on the will of the people as expressed in free elections." The Japanese apparently agreed. To this day, their constitution is known as the MacArthur Constitution.

Having taken care of responsibilities to its allies and its enemies, America was ready to begin rebuilding at home.

G. Answer Government reform and economic recovery under MacArthur.

THINK THROUGH HISTORY
G. Summarizing What were the most significant results of the U.S. occupation of Japan?

---

1. TERMS & NAMES

Identify:
- Douglas MacArthur
- Chester Nimitz
- kamikaze
- Manhattan Project
- J. Robert Oppenheimer
- Hiroshima
- Nagasaki
- Yalta Conference
- United Nations (UN)
- Nuremberg trials

2. SUMMARIZING Using a diagram such as the one below, describe the significance of key military actions in the Pacific during World War II.

Military Action	Significance
1.	
2.	
3.	
4.	
5.	

3. DRAWING CONCLUSIONS Explain how the United States was able to defeat the Japanese in the Pacific theater.

THINK ABOUT
- the geography of the region
- the role of technology in the battles
- the strategies used by each side

4. EVALUATING Do you think that it is legitimate to hold people accountable for crimes committed during wartime? Why or why not?

THINK ABOUT
- the laws that govern human behavior
- the likelihood of conducting a fair trial
- the behavior of soldiers, politicians, and civilians during war

The United States in World War II **753**

ANSWERS

1. TERMS & NAMES
Douglas MacArthur, p. 747
Chester Nimitz, p. 747
kamikaze, p. 749
Manhattan Project, p. 750
J. Robert Oppenheimer, p. 750
Hiroshima, p. 751
Nagasaki, p. 751
Yalta Conference, p. 752
United Nations (UN), p. 752
Nuremberg trials, p. 752

2. SUMMARIZING
Possible Answers:
Philippines/Japanese victory destroyed myth of white supremacy in Asia.
Tokyo/American bombing lifted American spirits.
Midway/Americans damaged Japanese air power by destroying aircraft carriers.
Leyte Gulf/Reduced Japanese navy to minor role.
Okinawa/American victory allowed attack on Japan.

Hiroshima/America became first country to use atomic bomb.
Nagasaki/Caused Japan to surrender.

3. DRAWING CONCLUSIONS
Possible Answer: The United States could replace damaged ships more easily than Japan could, had new technology such as the atomic bomb, and had a strategy—island hopping—that conserved its power.

4. EVALUATING
Possible Response:
Legitimate—People should be prosecuted for committing atrocities. **Not legitimate**—War is such an unusual situation that ordinary laws do not apply.

OBJECTIVES

1 To explain the connection between military technology and subsequent civilian technological developments.

2 To describe civilian applications of selected military technologies.

FOCUS & MOTIVATE

▶ **Starting with the Student**
Ask students to name technological inventions that have an impact on their daily lives. Have them speculate about the origins of these inventions.

MORE ABOUT . . .
The Shrinking World

The Internet grew out of the Cold War. In the 1960s, the U.S. Department of Defense recognized the value of linking computers to communicate in the event of a nuclear attack. The result was ARPANET, the first of several early U.S. computer networks. Meanwhile, similar work in Britain resulted in networks like JANET, the Joint Academic Network, which in 1979 was linked to U.S. computers on a transatlantic cable shared with NASA. In the 1980s, new software, supercomputers, fiber-optic cables, and other improvements allowed the Internet to circle the globe. By January 1997, the number of Internet web sites had passed the million mark, with over 100 million estimated users.

TRACING THEMES
SCIENCE AND TECHNOLOGY

From the Frontlines to Your Back Yard

Radar, guided missiles, nuclear submarines, reconnaissance satellites, atomic bombs—the technology of the 20th century seems to have focused largely on war, with the usual dreaded results. But these technological developments have also had far-reaching applications for peacetime. Because these innovations were originally intended for the battlefield, they were developed quickly and with a narrow focus. However, their peaceful applications have led to widespread, life-enhancing benefits that will extend far into the 21st century.

1939
WORLD WAR II (1939–1945) ATOM BOMBS TO BRAIN SCANS

Faced with alarming rumors of a German atomic bomb, America mobilized some of the finest scientific minds in the world to create its own atomic bomb. The energy released by this controlled nuclear reaction was enough to kill hundreds of thousands of people, as it did at Hiroshima and Nagasaki. But the resulting ability to harness the atom's energy also led to new technologies for diagnosing and treating human diseases. Techniques such as positron emission tomography (PET) now reveal the inner workings of the human brain itself.

1914
WORLD WAR I (1914–1918) FIGHTER PLANES TO COMMUTER FLIGHTS

Airplanes were first used to gather military information, but were soon put to work as fighters and bombers. The Sopwith Camel, shown above, was one of the most successful British fighter planes and brought down almost 1,300 enemy aircraft during World War I. The development of flight technology eventually led to sophisticated supersonic aircraft. Today, planes smash the barriers of time and space and enable people to travel faster than the speed of sound.

RECOMMENDED RESOURCES

Books

Buderi, Robert. *The Invention That Changed the World.* New York: Simon, 1996. Radar launches a technological revolution.

Campbell-Kelly, Martin. *Computer: A History of the Information Machine.* New York: Basic, 1996. Story of the machine that revolutionized modern life.

Elder, Donald C. *Out from Behind the Eight-Ball.* San Diego: American Astronautical Society, 1995. A history of Project Echo, a landmark in the development of satellite communications.

Watson-Watt, Sir Robert Alexander. *The Pulse of Radar.* New York: Dial, 1959. An autobiographical account by a British pioneer of radar.

Videos

A Is for Atom. Coronet/MTI. An exploration of nuclear energy and how science harnessed it.

The Age of Flight. MPI Home Video, 1991. A history of aviation.

Distant Voices. BBC and Time-Life, 1979. Part 3 of the *Connections* series explores technological changes in warfare and related developments.

Echoes of War. Vestron Video, 1989. An episode from PBS's *Nova* series tracing the development of radar in World War II.

Wings: The Jet Age. Pacific Arts Video, 1989. The evolution of civil and military jets from World War II to the late 1980s.

1945
THE COLD WAR (1945–1989) SATELLITES TO CELLULAR PHONES

The Soviet Union launched *Sputnik,* the first successful artificial space satellite, in 1957. As the United States raced to catch up with the Soviets in space, both countries eventually produced satellites that have improved life for people around the world. Satellites now not only track weather patterns and control air traffic but also link the continents in a vast communications network.

LANGUAGE AND MUSIC

MUSIC

Other Applications of World War II Technology		
TECHNOLOGY	**MILITARY USE**	**PEACETIME USE**
Semi-conductors	Navigation	Transistors, Radios, Electronics
Computers	Code breakers	Software programs, Video games
Freeze-dried food	Soldiers' rations	TV dinners. Space-shuttle rations
Synthetic materials	Parachutes, Weapons parts, Tires	Telephones, Automobile fenders, Pacemakers
Infrared technology	Night tracking	TV remote controls, Police surveillance, Medical treatment
Radar	Tracking and surveillance	Weather tracking, Air traffic control Archaeological digs, Microwave ovens

INTERACT WITH HISTORY

1. **HYPOTHESIZING** Do you think that peacetime technologies would have been developed without the stimulus provided by war? Support your answer.

 SEE SKILLBUILDER HANDBOOK, PAGE 1051.

2. **RECOGNIZING TECHNOLOGICAL IMPACT** What invention or technological breakthrough do you think has had the greatest impact on American society? Write a paragraph to explain your answer. Stage a debate with your classmates in which you defend your choice.

The United States in World War II **755**

INTERACT WITH HISTORY

1. Hypothesizing

Possible Response: Students who say the technologies would have been developed anyway may point to peacetime inventions of the past or may mention the motives played by profit, fame, and the desire to benefit humanity. Those who say that the technologies may not have been developed may say that the funding for and/or drive to do the research arose only because of wartime emergencies, Cold War competition, and threats to the nation's survival.

Recognizing Technological Impact

Standards for Evaluation
Paragraphs should . . .

- identify a specific invention or technological breakthrough
- explain why it is important
- support opinions with accurate facts and examples

Debates may be conducted between pairs of students, in small groups, or by the entire class.

OBJECTIVES

1. To describe the economic and social changes that reshaped American life during World War II.

2. To summarize both the opportunities and the discrimination African Americans and other minorities experienced during the war.

SKILLBUILDER

- Understanding geography: movement, p. 757

CRITICAL THINKING

- Recognizing effects, p. 757
- Summarizing, pp. 758, 761
- Analyzing causes, p. 759
- Evaluating decisions, p. 761
- Drawing conclusions, p. 761
- Comparing, p. 761

FOCUS & MOTIVATE

▶ *Starting with the Student*
Discuss with students the impact World War II had on their families. How was their community affected?

OBJECTIVE

1. **INSTRUCT**

Opportunity and Adjustment

▶ *Discussing Key Ideas*
- The war brings opportunity and prosperity to millions of American workers.
- The growth of the defense industry sparks the largest mass migration in American history.
- Families struggle to deal with long separations and changing roles.

IN-DEPTH RESOURCES: UNIT 7
Guided Reading, p. 22

ACCESS FOR STUDENTS ACQUIRING ENGLISH
Guided Reading (Spanish), p. 247

4 The Impact of the War

LEARN ABOUT the impact of the war on life at home
TO UNDERSTAND the social and economic changes that helped reshape postwar America.

TWICE A PATRIOT.
EX-PRIVATE OBIE BARTLETT LOST LEFT ARM—PEARL HARBOR—RELEASED: DEC., 1941—NOW AT WORK WELDING IN A WEST COAST SHIPYARD . . .

Like many minority veterans, Obie Bartlett was twice a patriot—and was still regarded as a second-class citizen.

ONE AMERICAN'S STORY

The writer and poet Maya Angelou was a teenager living in San Francisco when World War II began. The first change she noticed was the disappearance of the city's Japanese population. The second was an influx of war workers from the South. "The Japanese shops," she recalled, "were taken over by enterprising Negro businessmen. . . Where the odors of tempura, raw fish and *cha* [tea] had dominated, the aroma of chitlings, greens, and hamhocks now prevailed." San Franciscans, she noted, maintained that there was no racism in their city by the bay. But Angelou, who had seen her Nisei schoolmates vanish, knew differently.

A PERSONAL VOICE

A story went the rounds about a San Francisco white matron who refused to sit beside a Negro civilian on the streetcar, even after he made room for her on the seat. Her explanation was that she would not sit beside a draft dodger who was a Negro as well. She added that the least he could do was fight for his country the way her son was fighting on Iwo Jima. The story said that the man pulled his body away from the window to show an armless sleeve. He said quietly and with great dignity, "Then ask your son to look around for my arm, which I left over there."

MAYA ANGELOU, *I Know Why the Caged Bird Sings*

America welcomed its heroic troops home from the war with ticker-tape parades and joyous celebration. But after the confetti settled, returning veterans—even those who weren't disabled—had to begin dealing with the very real issues of reentry and adjustment to a society that offered many opportunities but still had many unsolved problems.

Opportunity and Adjustment

In contrast to the Great Depression, World War II was a time of opportunity for millions of Americans. Jobs abounded and, despite rationing and shortages, there was money to spend again. The war was America's shining moment, and the nation emerged as the world's dominant economic and military power.

ECONOMIC GAINS The war years were good ones for working people. As defense industries boomed, unemployment fell to a low of 1.2 percent by 1944. Even with price and wage controls, average weekly paychecks rose 70 percent during the war. And while workers complained about long hours, overtime, and night shifts, they were also able to save money for the future. Some workers invested up to half their paychecks in war bonds.

Farmers also prospered during the war. Unlike the Depression years when farmers battled dust bowls and floods, they enjoyed good crop weather in the early 1940s. They also benefited from improvements in farm machinery and fertilizers and reaped the profits from rising crop prices. As a result, crop production increased by 50 percent, and farm income tripled. Before the war ended, many farmers could pay off their mortgages.

756 CHAPTER 25

SECTION 4 RESOURCES

 PRINT RESOURCES

IN-DEPTH RESOURCES: UNIT 7
Guided Reading, p. 22
Literature: from *Ceremony* by Leslie Marmon Silko, p. 32

ACCESS FOR STUDENTS ACQUIRING ENGLISH
Guided Reading (Spanish), p. 247

FORMAL ASSESSMENT
Section Quiz, p. 308

ALTERNATIVE ASSESSMENT BOOK
See forms for supporting and scoring alternative activities.

 TECHNOLOGY RESOURCES

CRITICAL THINKING TRANSPARENCIES
CT25, U.S. Joins the Allies in World War II
CT59, Human Cost of World War II

VIDEO *American Portfolio: A Videodisc for U.S. History*
user's guide, p. 230

INTERNET McDougal Littell Learning On-Line
http://www.mcdougallittell.com

Women also enjoyed employment gains during the war, although many lost their jobs when the war ended. Over 6 million women entered the work force for the first time, boosting the percentage of women in the total work force to 35 percent. A third of those jobs were in defense plants, which offered women more challenging work and better pay than traditionally female jobs such as waitressing, clerking, and domestic tasks. With men away at war, many women also took advantage of openings in journalism and other professions. "The war really created opportunities for women," said Winona Espinosa, a wife and mother who became a riveter and bus driver during the war. "It was the first time we got a chance to show that we could do a lot of things that only men had done before."

The range of jobs taken on by women was impressive. Aircraft maker Glenn Martin reported, "We have women helping design our planes in the Engineering Department, building them on the production line, operating almost every conceivable type of machinery, from rivet guns to giant stamp presses." Late in 1942, *Newsweek* reported that "depending on the industry, women today make up from 10 percent to 88 percent of total personnel in most war plants." Strato Equipment, a company that researched and designed high-altitude pressure suits for pilots, had no men at all—except a department-store dummy.

POPULATION SHIFTS In addition to revamping the economy, the war triggered one of the greatest mass migrations of American history. Not only were millions of servicemen and women sent to places all over the world, but civilians were on the move as well. Americans whose families had lived for decades in one place suddenly uprooted themselves to seek war work elsewhere. States with military bases and defense industries, such as Connecticut, Delaware, Maryland, Michigan, Florida, and the Pacific Coast states, all experienced large population gains. More than a million newcomers poured into California between 1941 and 1944. Towns with defense industries saw their populations double and even triple, sometimes almost overnight.

Elkton, Maryland, for example, had been a sleepy farming community until an ammunition plant was built there. Its population quickly surged from 6,000 to 12,000, of whom 80 percent were young women. Burbank, California, the home of a major aircraft company, grew from 12,000 to 60,000 people in the first two years of the war. The populations of some major cities, including Washington, D.C., Los Angeles, San Francisco, Portland, Seattle, San Antonio, and Dallas jumped by a third or more.

The inevitable result of such population booms was an acute housing shortage. Even though workers had money for rent, many were virtually homeless. They camped out in tents, old cars, trailer parks, rented garages, and overcrowded rooming houses. Food was a problem as well. Many workers had no place to cook. Yet because of food rationing, there were not enough restaurants to feed them. In Elkton, according to one observer, food was so scarce and expensive that "many girls [went] through the day on a cup of coffee and a piece of toast."

SOCIAL ADJUSTMENTS Families adjusted to the changes brought on by war as best they could. With millions of fathers in the armed forces, mothers struggled to rear their children alone. Young children got used to being left with

The war gave women the chance to prove they could be just as productive as men. But their pay usually did not reflect their productivity.

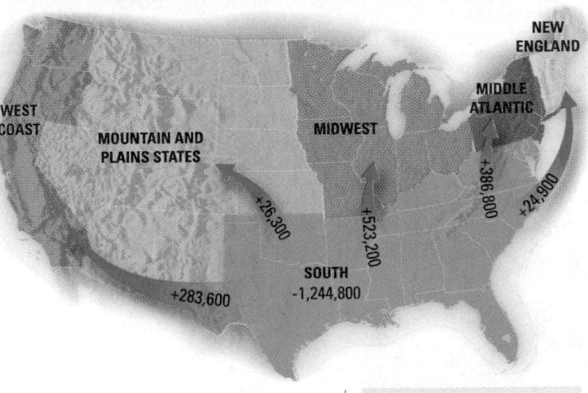

African-American Migration, 1940–1950

NEW ENGLAND

WEST COAST

MOUNTAIN AND PLAINS STATES

MIDWEST

MIDDLE ATLANTIC

+386,800

+24,900

+16,300

+523,200

SOUTH
+283,600   -1,244,800

GEOGRAPHY SKILLBUILDER
MOVEMENT *To which geographic region did the greatest number of African Americans migrate?*

Skillbuilder Answer
Movement: Midwest

A. Answer The war created new jobs, all but eliminated unemployment, raised wages, uprooted workers, created housing shortages, and opened up new types of employment to women and minority workers.

THINK THROUGH HISTORY
A. Recognizing Effects How did the war affect working Americans?

The World War II marriage boom actually began before Pearl Harbor, mainly for economic reasons. Millions of couples who had postponed marriage during the Depression were the first to rush to the altar. Once the United States entered the war, the boom continued as young men and women facing uncertain futures looked for someone to live for. Have students use the following figures to graph the number of marriages per 1,000 unmarried women over age 14 from the Depression through World War II.

1929—75.5; 1932—56.0

1938—69.9; 1940—82.8

1942—93.0; 1944—76.5

1946—118.1

Students might present the data on a line graph like this:

Discrimination and Reaction

▶ **Discussing Key Ideas**
• African Americans in the military fight segregation and discrimination as well as the Axis Powers.
• African-American gains on the home front are accompanied by racial unrest.

(continued on next page)

---

neighbors or relatives or in child-care centers as more and more mothers went to work. Teenagers left at home without parents sometimes drifted into juvenile delinquency. And when fathers finally did come home, there was often a painful period of readjustment as families got to know one another again.

The war helped create new families, too, as it triggered a huge marriage boom. Longtime sweethearts—as well as couples who barely knew each other—rushed to marry before the soldier or sailor was shipped overseas. In coastal towns like Seattle, the number of marriage licenses issued went up by as much as 300 percent early in the war. A New Yorker observed in 1943, "On Fridays and Saturdays, the City Hall area is blurred with running soldiers, sailors, and girls hunting the license bureau, floral shops, ministers, [and] blood-testing laboratories."

Many of these romances did not survive the long separation, though. For numerous servicemen, the bad news came in a much-dreaded "Dear John" letter—a letter from his wife or sweetheart saying that she had found someone new. In 1945, there were 502,000 divorces in the United States, or 31 for every 100 marriages. This was double the prewar total and enough to give the United States the highest divorce rate in the world.

In 1944, to help ease the transition of returning servicemen to civilian life, Congress passed the Servicemen's Readjustment Act, better known as the **GI Bill of Rights.** This bill provided education and training for veterans, paid for by the federal government. Just over half the returning soldiers, or about 7.8 million veterans, attended colleges and technical schools under the GI Bill. The bill also provided federal loan guarantees to veterans buying homes and farms or starting businesses. Because of this bill, millions who would otherwise never have been able to afford it went to school, became homeowners, and improved their economic prospects after the war.

Pilots of the all-black 99th Fighter Squadron—the Tuskegee Airmen—served in North Africa and Italy. Several of them are shown here with the flight helmet and goggles that became their trademark.

Discrimination and Reaction

Despite the opportunities that opened up for women and minorities during the war, old prejudices and policies persisted, both in the military and at home.

AFRICAN AMERICANS IN THE MILITARY For African Americans, World War II was a turning point of sorts. On the one hand, segregation remained the rule in the military. Not only were African Americans assigned to all-black units, but many of them were assigned to rigidly segregated camps in the South for their training. "My comrades did not understand about segregation," southerner Preston McNeil said of his African-American buddies from the North. "They couldn't understand the sign that says, 'Colored,' 'White.'" Soldiers like Johnnie Stevens learned quickly enough, though.

A PERSONAL VOICE
To be a black soldier in the South in those days was one of the worst things that could happen to you. . . . If off-post you [were] hungry and couldn't find a black restaurant or a black home you know what? You would starve. And you were a soldier . . . out there wearing the uniform of your country, and you're getting treated like a dog!

JOHNNIE STEVENS, quoted in *Liberators: Fighting on Two Fronts in World War II*

On the other hand, under great pressure from civil-rights organizations, the military no longer restricted its all-black units to menial tasks. Many black units distinguished themselves in combat, including the famous 92nd Infantry Division, nicknamed the Buffaloes. In just six months of fighting in Europe, the Buffaloes won

THINK THROUGH HISTORY
B. Summarizing
What provisions did the GI Bill make for returning veterans?

B. Answer
Education, training, and federal loan guarantees.

758

Exploring Themes

The American Dream The GI Bill of Rights made the American dream a reality for millions of World War II veterans by providing them with unemployment and education allowances and home, farm, and business loans. The GI Bill program currently also covers men and women who served in the armed forces between 1955 and 1976. Ask students to talk with family members or adult friends who have taken advantage of these benefits about how the GI Bill affected their lives. Have students share their anecdotes with the class.

Making Connections Across Cultures

African Americans in the Military The discrimination African Americans experienced in the military embittered them even more when they saw how well prisoners of war were treated. At Camp Hood, outside Killeen, Texas, for example, German prisoners were assigned to clean up the base grounds. Soldier E. G. McConnell noted, however, "They didn't pick up the black area. We had to do that ourselves." In Salina, Kansas, German prisoners could eat at lunch counters and enter movie theaters that were off-limits to their African-American guards. One soldier wrote of this situation: "The people of Salina would serve these enemy soldiers and turn away black American GIs."

7 Legion of Merit awards, 65 Silver Stars, and 162 Bronze Stars for courage under fire. Likewise, the 99th Fighter Squadron, better known as the Tuskegee Airmen, won two Distinguished Unit Citations (the military's highest commendation) for its outstanding aerial combat against Hitler's *Luftwaffe*.

AFRICAN AMERICANS AT HOME African Americans also made some progress on the home front. During the war, about 330,000 blacks left the South. The majority moved to the West Coast. There they found not only jobs, but good jobs. Between 1940 and 1944, the percentage of blacks working in skilled or semiskilled jobs rose from 16 to 30 percent.

Wherever African Americans moved, however, discrimination followed. In 1942, civil rights leader **James Farmer** founded an interracial movement called the **Congress of Racial Equality (CORE)** to confront urban segregation in the North. That same year, CORE staged its first sit-in at a segregated Chicago restaurant.

As new black migrants moved into already overcrowded cities, tensions rose. In 1943, a tidal wave of racial violence swept across the country. The worst conflict erupted in Detroit on a hot Sunday afternoon in June. What started as a tussle between blacks and whites at a beach on the Detroit River mushroomed into a full-scale riot when white sailors stationed nearby joined the fray.

The fighting raged for three days, fueled by false rumors that whites had murdered a black woman and her child and that black rioters had killed 17 whites. By the time President Roosevelt sent federal troops into the city to restore order, 9 whites and 25 blacks lay dead or dying.

The violence of 1943 revealed to many Americans—black and white alike—just how serious racial tensions had become in the United States. By 1945, more than 400 communities had formed committees to improve race relations. Progress was slow, but African Americans were determined not to give up the gains they had made. As African American Jesse Hall, who had moved his family to Detroit in 1942, put it, "We aren't going to go back to where we were before the war. We've shed our blood and proved our loyalty, and we're going to fight for all that is rightfully due us. We won't turn back."

THINK THROUGH HISTORY

C. Analyzing Causes What caused the race riots in the 1940s?

C. Answer Discrimination, racism, concentration of minorities in cities.

MEXICAN AMERICANS IN WARTIME Mexican Americans also experienced both progress and prejudice during the war years. In the military, most served in segregated units. Mexican-American soldiers distinguished themselves in combat, with 17 winning the Congressional Medal of Honor. An all-Chicano infantry unit—Company E of the 141st Regiment, 36th Division—became one of the most decorated of the war.

But while Mexican Americans were defending democracy overseas, they also had to defend themselves against racism at home. In the violent summer of 1943, Los Angeles exploded in anti-Mexican "zoot-suit" riots. The zoot suit was a style of dress adopted by Mexican-American youths as a symbol of their rebellion against tradition. It consisted of a broad-brimmed hat, a knee-length suit jacket, pleated pants nipped in at the cuff, and a low-hanging watch chain.

The riot began when 11 sailors in Los Angeles reported that they had been attacked by Mexican Americans. This charge triggered two nights of violence involving thousands of servicemen and civilians. Mobs poured into Mexican neighborhoods, and grabbed any zoot-suiters they could find. The attackers ripped off their victims' clothes and beat them senseless. The city's response was to outlaw the wearing of zoot suits.

Despite such unhappy experiences with racism, Mexican Americans believed that their sacrifices during wartime would lead to a better future.

The exaggerated style of the zoot suits that many Mexican-American young men wore expressed their rebellion and made them easy targets for racial violence.

The United States in World War II **759**

(continued from page 758)

- Despite prejudice, Mexican Americans make gains during the war.
- During and after the war, interned Japanese Americans struggle first for their freedom, then for justice.

MORE ABOUT . . .
Mexican Americans in Los Angeles

By 1940, Los Angeles had the largest urban population of people of Mexican descent outside Mexico City. It also had a shameful record of discrimination in jobs, housing, education, and recreation. A public swimming pool, for example, was only open to Mexican Americans (and African Americans) on Wednesdays. After that, the pool was drained and cleaned before being reopened for whites. During the war, many young Mexican Americans dressed in zoot suits to show their rejection of Anglo society and its prejudices. The city's mainstream press characterized the "zooters" as draft dodgers and dope addicts, exacerbating already strained relations.

👥 *Cooperative Activity: Creating a Political Cartoon*

Task: Student groups will create a political cartoon commenting on race riots during World War II.

Purpose: To help students recognize and communicate the sad irony of Americans fighting each other at home while fighting a war abroad.

Activity: Small groups of students should create a political cartoon explaining the impact of either the Detroit race riot or the Los Angeles "zoot suit" riot on the war effort.

Students could discuss the concept of their cartoon as a group and then divide the tasks of drawing the cartoon, writing the caption, and compiling the finished product.

📁 **Building a Portfolio:** Students who add the cartoons to their portfolios should attach a note indicating their contribution.

ALTERNATIVE ASSESSMENT BOOK
Standards for Evaluating a Cooperative Activity

Standards for Evaluation
Cartoons should . . .

- express a clear position on the impact of home-front riots on the war effort
- communicate that position with pictures and minimal words
- be easily understood

Life in the Internment Camps

The ten internment camps set up for Japanese Americans were mostly located in remote desert areas of the West. The internees were housed in barracks, with each family allotted one 20-foot-square room. The adults did what they could to bring a semblance of normality into this abnormal setting. Children began school each day by saluting the flag and singing "My country, 'tis of thee, sweet land of liberty." But they didn't have to look far to see armed guards and barbed wire fences.

POINT COUNTERPOINT

Japanese-American Internment

▶ **Starting with the Student**
Have students create a chart to help them organize the arguments for and against the internment:

Japanese-American Internment

Necessary	Racist

▶ **Discussing Key Ideas**
• Some Americans feel threatened by the attack on Pearl Harbor.
• They fear that Japanese Americans will aid the enemy.
• Some justify internment as a way of protecting Japanese Americans.
• No Japanese Americans are known to have committed acts of disloyalty or sabotage.
• Many criticize internment as a racist act.

A PERSONAL VOICE
This war . . . is doing what we in our Mexican-American movement had planned to do in one generation. . . . It has shown those "across the tracks" that we all share the same problems. It has shown them what the Mexican American will do, what responsibility he will take and what leadership qualities he will demonstrate. After this struggle, the status of the Mexican Americans will be different.

MANUEL DE LA RAZA, quoted in *A Different Mirror: A History of Multicultural America*

JAPANESE AMERICANS IN A STRUGGLE FOR JUSTICE For Japanese Americans locked up in U.S. internment camps, the war was a daily struggle to maintain their dignity in the face of injustice. Many young men escaped the camps by volunteering for military service. As William Hosokawa explained, they "felt it was their obligation to volunteer and go into service and do what they could to demonstrate that they were indeed loyal, and the government was wrong in putting them into camps." The all-Nisei 442nd Regiment, better known as "Go for Broke," became the most decorated combat unit of the war. In 1946, President Truman welcomed the 442nd home with these words: "You fought not only the enemy, you fought prejudice—and you won."

POINT ▶ COUNTERPOINT

Japanese-American internment was necessary for national defense.

The United States was still reeling from the Japanese attack on Pearl Harbor that had brought it into World War II—a threat, some felt, to its very existence. Tom Clark, assistant to the commanding general of the U.S. Army's Western Defense Command and later associate justice of the Supreme Court, offered a justification for internment. "Soon after Pearl Harbor I was deluged by demands that, regardless of citizenship, every person of Japanese descent must be removed from the West Coast," he explained. "The threatening public attitude . . . would permit nothing less than total mass relocation."

Chief Justice Earl Warren pointed out, on the other hand, that many Japanese Americans held dual citizenship and were educated in both Japan and the United States. "Their affiliation in time of war worried us," he explained.

War correspondent Walter Lippman offered more concrete reasons. "It is the fact that the Japanese navy has been reconnoitering the Pacific Coast. . . . It is the fact that communication takes place between the enemy at sea and the enemy agents on land."

Historians Donald Pike and Roger Olmsted observe that only Japan among the Axis nations had attacked the United States, and "suddenly the Japanese . . . threatened our very national existence."

Japanese-American internment was an unnecessary and a racist act.

"Our unjust imprisonment was the result of two closely related emotions: racism and hysteria," says Edison Tomimaro Uno, a former internee. Uno says the claim that Japanese Americans were relocated for their own protection was "sheer hypocrisy" and denies that Japanese Americans posed a national security threat. Instead, he calls the relocation a crime attributable to "racism [and] economic and political opportunism."

"War makes for harsh measures," notes the historian Cary McWilliams, "but we cannot justify the evacuation even as a war measure. No such measure was taken against German or Italian nationals."

Another historian, Henry Steele Commager comments, "It is sobering to recall that the record does not disclose a single case of Japanese disloyalty or sabotage during the whole war." In fact, more than 25,000 Japanese Americans served in the armed forces during World War II, and the all-Japanese-American 442nd combat team inflicted more casualties and received more decorations than any other comparable army unit.

Relocation left many Americans with a legacy of shame. Chief Justice Earl Warren confessed in his autobiography that he "deeply regretted" his testimony in favor of internment. Tom Clark said, "It was a sad day in our constitutional history."

INTERACT WITH HISTORY

1. **FORMING OPINIONS** Do you believe internment of the Japanese was necessary? Give reasons to support your opinion.

   SEE SKILLBUILDER HANDBOOK, PAGE 1049.

2. **RESEARCHING INTERNMENT** Use library resources or the Internet to research the experience of a specific Japanese American in an internment camp. Present your findings as a diary entry or a report.

 For more about Japanese-American internment, click on *Social Studies* at http://www.mcdougallittell.com

---

INTERACT WITH HISTORY

1. Forming Opinions

Possible Responses:

Internment was necessary—Japanese Americans posed a security threat to the United States due to their dual allegiance.

Internment was unnecessary—There was no evidence that Japanese Americans had committed any acts that posed a threat to the United States. Their internment was motivated by racism.

2. Researching Internment

Suggest that students use the books *And Justice for All* by John Tateishi and *A Different Mirror: A History of Multicultural America* by Ronald Takaki as sources of eyewitness accounts of internment. Their presentations of this information should meet the following criteria:

• Gives a brief biography of the person and his or her family.
• Includes specific details about the person's life before, during, and after internment.
• Uses direct quotations from the person whenever possible.

Japanese Americans also fought for justice, both in the courts and in Congress. The initial results were discouraging. In 1944, the Supreme Court decided in *Korematsu* v. *United States* that the government's policy of evacuating Japanese Americans to camps was justified on the basis of "military necessity." After the war, however, the **Japanese American Citizens League (JACL)** pushed the government to compensate those sent to the camps for their lost property. In 1965, Congress finally authorized the spending of $38 million for that purpose—less than a tenth of Japanese Americans' actual losses.

But the JACL did not give up. In 1978, the organization called for the payment of reparations, or restitution, to each individual who suffered evacuation and internment. "Restitution does not put a price tag on freedom or justice," the JACL pointed out. "The issue is not to recover what cannot be recovered. The issue is to acknowledge the mistake by providing proper redress to victims of injustice, and thereby make such injustice less likely to recur." Ten years later, Congress finally passed a bill that gave $20,000 to every Japanese American sent to a relocation camp during the war. Each check was accompanied by a letter from President George Bush.

Japanese Americans were finally released from U.S. internment camps at the end of the war.

D. Answer To acknowledge the injustice done to Japanese Americans during the war and to offer them a long-overdue apology.

THINK THROUGH HISTORY
D. Evaluating Decisions Why did Congress award compensation to Japanese Americans more than 40 years after the war ended?

A PERSONAL VOICE
A monetary sum and words alone cannot restore lost years or erase painful memories; neither can they fully convey our Nation's resolve to rectify injustice and to uphold the rights of individuals. We can never fully right the wrongs of the past. But we can take a clear stand for justice and recognize that serious injustices were done to Japanese Americans during World War II. In enacting a law calling for restitution and offering a sincere apology, your fellow Americans have, in a very real sense, renewed their traditional commitment to the ideals of freedom, equality, and justice.

GEORGE BUSH, from his letter accompanying redress checks to Japanese Americans, 1988

America would barely have time to deal with the aftermath of war and to adjust to peace, however, when it began to mobilize against a new enemy without and within—fear and the threat of communism.

Section 4 Assessment

1. TERMS & NAMES

Identify:
- GI Bill of Rights
- James Farmer
- Congress of Racial Equality (CORE)
- Japanese Americans Citizens League (JACL)

2. SUMMARIZING List the advances and the problems in the economy and in civil rights during World War II.

	Advances	Problems
Economy		
Civil Rights		

Which of these advances or problems do you think had the most long-term effect?

3. DRAWING CONCLUSIONS What effect do you think World War II had on traditional attitudes and beliefs held by Americans?

THINK ABOUT
- the role of women in families and the economy
- the relationship between the races
- the impact of the federal government on society

4. COMPARING How were experiences of African Americans, Mexican Americans, and Japanese Americans similar during World War II?

THINK ABOUT
- the role of each group in the military
- governmental actions toward each group
- wartime changes that affected minority groups

The United States in World War II **761**

ANSWERS

1. TERMS & NAMES
GI Bill of Rights, p. 758

James Farmer, p. 759

Congress of Racial Equality (CORE), p. 759

Japanese American Citizens League (JACL), p. 761

2. SUMMARIZING
Possible Answers:
Economy—Advances: Low unemployment, rising crop prices, opportunity for women. **Problems:** Shortages of housing and food.
Civil Rights—Advances: More equality in the military, founding of CORE. **Problems:** Segregation, discrimination, race riots in Detroit and Los Angeles, internment of Japanese Americans.

3. DRAWING CONCLUSIONS
Possible Responses: Some students may say the war broke down traditions as it drew women into the workplace and gave African Americans more opportunities in the military. Others may argue that riots and the Korematsu decision strengthened the tradition of discrimination.

4. COMPARING
Possible Response: Despite service in the military, members of all three groups suffered from discrimination backed by government action.

Several thousand Japanese Americans served as interpreters and translators in the U.S. Military Intelligence Service during the war. These Nisei soldiers gleaned invaluable information from captured documents and battle plans and from intercepted radio transmissions. General Charles Willoughby, chief of military intelligence in the Pacific, estimated that the contributions of Japanese Americans shortened the war by two years.

ASSESS & RETEACH

Section 4 Assessment
Have students work in groups of four, with each student answering one question.

Self-Assessment
Have students note the changes made in their answers during group discussion. Ask them how they could improve their answers next time.

Section Quiz
FORMAL ASSESSMENT
Section Quiz, p. 308

Reteach
Use the poster of Obie Bartlett on page 756 as the basis of a class discussion of the social impact of World War II on various groups of Americans.

CLOSE

World War II had a wide-ranging impact on American society. People became more affluent and mobile as job opportunities arose; marriage—and divorce—rates soared; and minorities became increasingly militant in their opposition to discrimination and injustice.

 CRITICAL THINKING TRANSPARENCIES
CT25, U.S. Joins the Allies in World War II
CT59, Human Cost of World War II

REVIEWING
THE CHAPTER

TERMS & NAMES

1. A. Philip Randolph, p. 733
2. Nisei, p. 735
3. Dwight D. Eisenhower, p. 741
4. D-Day, p. 743
5. V-E Day, p. 745
6. Douglas MacArthur, p. 747
7. Manhattan Project, p. 750
8. Hiroshima, p. 751
9. GI Bill of Rights, p. 758
10. Congress of Racial Equality (CORE), p. 759

MAIN IDEAS

11. It included large numbers of whites, African Americans, Native Americans, Mexican Americans, and Asian Americans.

12. Factories converted to military production, civilians took jobs in military industries, scientists worked on military research, and the entertainment industry produced propaganda films.

13. It drafted civilians, interned Japanese Americans, and established a system of rationing and other economic controls.

14. They used the convoy system and an accelerated shipbuilding program.

15. Soviets stopped Hitler's eastward expansion, destroyed the German Sixth Army, and prevented Hitler from focusing on the western front.

16. Germany could not replace the men and weapons it lost, and could only retreat.

17. The United States avoided attacking Japanese strongholds and used its air power to cut off supplies to them.

18. The United States wanted to avoid the casualties resulting from an invasion of Japan and to end the war quickly.

19. Unemployment decreased, more women took factory jobs, and both housing and food were in short supply.

20. Racial riots in Detroit, zoot suit riots in Los Angeles, and the internment of Japanese Americans.

Chapter 25 Assessment

REVIEWING THE CHAPTER

TERMS & NAMES For each term below, write a sentence explaining its connection to World War II. For each person below, explain his or her role in the war.

1. A. Philip Randolph
2. Nisei
3. Dwight D. Eisenhower
4. D-Day
5. V-E Day
6. Douglas MacArthur
7. Manhattan Project
8. Hiroshima
9. GI Bill of Rights
10. Congress of Racial Equality (CORE)

REVIEWING MAIN IDEAS

SECTION 1 (pages 730–737)

Mobilization on the Home Front

11. How did the U.S. military reflect the diversity of American society during World War II?
12. How did World War II affect life on the homefront?
13. How did federal government actions influence civilian life during World War II?

SECTION 2 (pages 738–745)

The War for Europe and North Africa

14. How did the Allies win control of the Atlantic Ocean between 1941 and 1943?
15. What was the significance of the Battle of Stalingrad?
16. How did the Battle of the Bulge signal the beginning of the end of World War II in Europe?

SECTION 3 (pages 746–753)

The War in the Pacific

17. What strategy did the United States use in fighting the Japanese in the Pacific?
18. Why did President Truman decide to use atomic weapons on Hiroshima and Nagasaki?

SECTION 4 (pages 756–761)

The Impact of the War

19. How did the U.S. economy change during World War II?
20. What events show the persistence of racial tension during World War II?

THINKING CRITICALLY

1. **HEADLINE EVENTS** List the five most important political and military events and the five most important social and economic changes during World War II.

World War II

Political and Military Events	Social and Economic Changes
1.	1.
2.	2.
3.	3.
4.	4.
5.	5.

2. **NUCLEAR CHOICE** Nuclear weapons are vastly more powerful now than they were in 1945. Would you support the use of nuclear weapons today, and, if so, under what circumstances?

3. **WOMEN IN AMERICA** Do you think the opportunities that opened up for women during World War II would have developed if the United States hadn't entered the war? Explain your answer.

4. **UPDATING DECISIONS** Reread the quote by President Roosevelt on page 728. Then reread his quote on page 700. What hints, if any, do you find in his first statement that he would reverse his position on neutrality?

5. **GEOGRAPHY OF MILITARY EXPANSION** Study the map on page 739. What geographic features might have slowed expansion by the Axis countries? What features—or lack of features—emphasize the significance of the Soviet defense of Stalingrad?

6. **ANALYZING PRIMARY SOURCES** Ernie Pyle, probably the most popular journalist who covered World War II, believed that the war changed how soldiers viewed the world:

> Our men, still thinking of home, are impatient with the strange peoples and customs of the countries they now inhabit. They say that if they ever get home they never want to see another foreign country. But I know how it will be. The day will come when they'll look back and brag about how they learned a little Arabic, and how swell the girls were in England, and how pretty the hills of Germany were. Every day their scope is broadening despite themselves, and once they all get back with their global yarns and their foreign-tinged views, I cannot conceive of our nation ever being isolationist again.
>
> **ERNIE PYLE**, *Here Is Your War*

Summarize the shift in attitudes that Pyle describes. Explain whether you agree or disagree with the conclusion he draws.

THINKING CRITICALLY

1. HEADLINE EVENTS
Possible Responses: **Political and military events**—The attack on Pearl Harbor, the Battle of Midway, the Soviet defense of Stalingrad, the D-Day invasion, the bombing of Hiroshima, and the Nuremberg trials. **Economic and social changes**—The proposed march on Washington, the internment of Japanese Americans, new roles for women, and the movement of people to new communities.

2. NUCLEAR CHOICE
Possible Responses: **Pro**—Use of nuclear weapons is justified to respond to an enemy attack or to stop another country from using them. **Con**—Using atomic weapons is never justifiable because they kill and maim so massively and indiscriminately.

3. WOMEN IN AMERICA
Possible Responses: **Yes**—Change would have come anyway, but more gradually. **No**—Only a dramatic event such as World War II could break down a strongly held tradition such as keeping women in the home.

ALTERNATIVE ASSESSMENT

1. BROADCASTING THE NEWS

Journalists were an important factor in maintaining Americans' commitment to the war effort by making firsthand reports while events were happening. How might it have been difficult for reporters to present an objective yet realistic sense of the personal experience of war?

Cooperative Activity With a group of three to five classmates, prepare a radio news broadcast about experiences of Americans at home or abroad during World War II.

CD-ROM Conduct research using the CD-ROM *Our Times,* your textbook, and other resources such as oral histories or newsreels of the era. Choose a specific year between 1941 and 1945 and a specific location, such as a field hospital or a homefront industry.

- Each group member should choose a different person in that setting to interview. Prepare both the questions and the answers for an interview. Have a group member role-play the part of the person being interviewed.

- Combine your interviews into a radio broadcast. Write an introduction that indicates your geographic location; the time, date, and weather; and the people you will be interviewing. Record the radio broadcast and play it for the rest of the class.

2. PICTURING HISTORY

Create a visual history of World War II using photocopies of 10 to 20 pictures taken during the war. As you select your images, consider the story you want to tell about the war and the images that best convey that message. Write a caption for each picture that explains the image and its significance. Finally, write an introduction to your photo essay that briefly explains the message you want to get across. Save your materials in your American history portfolio.

3. PORTFOLIO PROJECT

Use the Living History activity to expand your portfolio.

LIVING HISTORY

EVALUATING YOUR WAR GAME

With a group of students, play the board game about World War II that you developed. Ask the players to help you evaluate the game based on questions such as the following.

- Are the names, dates, places, and other facts used in the game accurate?
- How realistically does the game portray the strategies of the participating countries?
- Is the outcome of the game similar to that of World War II?

Write a short evaluation and add it with your game to your American history portfolio.

Bridge to Chapter 26

Review Chapter 25

MOBILIZATION FOR WAR After the Japanese attack on Pearl Harbor, the United States mobilized to defeat Hitler. The 5 million volunteers and 10 million draftees included men and women of all ethnic and racial groups. Industries, workers, and scientists all contributed to the war effort. The government relocated Japanese Americans and instituted economic controls to promote military production and to prevent inflation.

FIGHTING IN EUROPE The United States, along with its allies Great Britain and France, won control of the Atlantic Ocean in the middle of 1943. A heroic defense of Stalingrad by the Soviet Union, followed by Allied victories in North Africa and Italy and the D-Day invasion on June 6, 1944, led to an invasion of Germany. Finally, on May 8, 1945, Germany surrendered.

WAR IN THE PACIFIC The United States stopped Japanese expansion by the middle of 1942 with victories at Coral Sea and Midway. Island hopping allowed the United States to avoid direct attacks on Japanese strongholds. Some of the bloodiest fighting in the Pacific occurred on Iwo Jima and Okinawa. When the atomic bomb became available, President Truman ordered it to be dropped on the Japanese cities of Hiroshima and Nagasaki. With the Japanese surrender on September 2, 1945, the war in the Pacific ended. War criminals from both Germany and Japan were tried by an international tribunal.

THE IMPACT World War II resulted in great economic gains for the United States. During the war, unemployment decreased, many women found jobs, and millions of Americans relocated. With these growing opportunities, though, racial and ethnic tensions increased. Riots in Detroit and Los Angeles, and the internment of Japanese Americans reflected the seriousness of these tensions.

Preview Chapter 26

After World War II ended, a new conflict emerged between two former allies—the United States and the Soviet Union. This conflict dominated America's politics and its foreign policy, leading to a war in Korea, a crisis in the Middle East, and widespread suspicion of disloyalty at home. You will learn about these significant developments in the next chapter.

The United States in World War II **763**

ALTERNATIVE ASSESSMENT

1. BROADCASTING THE NEWS
Standards for Evaluation
A news broadcast should meet the following criteria:

- Establishes the setting and provides vivid physical details.
- Presents the viewpoints of several different people in that setting.
- Uses a question-and-answer format to elicit interesting information from the people being interviewed.
- Presents the interviews in a logical sequence.

2. PICTURING HISTORY
Standards for Evaluation
A pictorial history should meet the following criteria:

- Tells a coherent story about World War II.
- Presents images in a logical sequence.
- Includes captions that concisely identify and enhance the images.
- Has a concise introduction that explains the intent of the presentation.

3. PORTFOLIO PROJECT
LIVING HISTORY
Standards for Evaluation
A war game should meet the following criteria:

- Incorporates accurate information about the events of World War II.
- Enables players to reenact the strategies of the Allied and Axis powers.
- Includes clear, easy-to-follow directions.

IN-DEPTH RESOURCES: UNIT 7
See the form for scoring this activity on page 38.

THINKING CRITICALLY

4. UPDATING DECISIONS
Possible Response: Roosevelt's statement that he could not ask Americans to be neutral in thought might have indicated that he was not totally committed to neutrality in his own thoughts.

5. GEOGRAPHY OF MILITARY EXPANSION
Possible Response: Expansion might have been difficult west across the Atlantic Ocean, south across the Sahara, and north into the Arctic. No geographic feature slowed expansion eastward into the Soviet Union.

6. ANALYZING PRIMARY SOURCES
Pyle believed that World War II destroyed isolationism because it opened many Americans' minds to the larger world. Opinions will vary but should be supported with reasons.

	Key Ideas	**TEACHING SUPPORT**	**ASSESSMENT**
SECTION 1 **Origins of the Cold War** *pp. 766–772*	*The Allied coalition falls apart as the United States and the Soviet Union find themselves in conflict with each other.*	*In-Depth Resources: Unit 7* • Guided Reading, p. 39 • SkillBuilder Practice: Analyzing Motives, p. 43 • Geography Application: The Marshall Plan, p. 44 • Primary Source: *from* Truman's Letter to His Daughter, p. 46 **COOPERATIVE ACTIVITIES** • Letters from Truman and Stalin, p. 767 (TE) • Researching the Berlin airlift, p. 771 (TE)	*Section 1 Assessment,* p. 772 (PE) *Self-Assessment,* p. 772 (TE) *Formal Assessment* • Section Quiz, p. 317 *Alternative Assessment Book* • Standards for Evaluating a Cooperative Activity
SECTION 2 **The Cold War Heats Up** *pp. 773–778*	*U.S. containment policies and Communist successes in China and North Korea lead to the Korean War.*	*In-Depth Resources: Unit 7* • Guided Reading, p. 40 • Primary Source: *from* MacArthur's Farewell to Congress, p. 47 • American Lives: Douglas MacArthur, p. 53 **COOPERATIVE ACTIVITY** • Debating Containment, p. 775 (TE)	*Section 2 Assessment,* p. 778 (PE) *Self-Assessment,* p. 778 (TE) *Formal Assessment* • Section Quiz, p. 318 *Alternative Assessment Book* • Standards for Evaluating a Cooperative Activity
SECTION 3 **The Cold War at Home** *pp. 779–784*	*The Cold War kindles a fear of Communist influence in the United States.*	*In-Depth Resources: Unit 7* • Guided Reading, p. 41 • American Lives: Margaret Chase Smith, p. 54 **COOPERATIVE ACTIVITIES** • Examining the Rosenberg Case, p. 781 (TE) • Investigating Witch Hunts, p. 783 (TE)	*Section 3 Assessment,* p. 784 (PE) *Self-Assessment,* p. 784 (TE) *Formal Assessment* • Section Quiz, p. 319 *Alternative Assessment Book* • Standards for Evaluating a Cooperative Activity
SECTION 4 **Two Nations Live on the Edge** *pp. 785–789*	*Tension mounts between the United States and the Soviet Union as both try to spread their influence around the world.*	*In-Depth Resources: Unit 7* • Guided Reading, p. 42 • Primary Source: *from* Eisenhower's Statement on the U-2, p. 49 • Literature: *from The Nuclear Age* by Tim O'Brien, p. 50 **COOPERATIVE ACTIVITY** • Creating a Political Cartoon, p. 787 (TE)	*Section 4 Assessment,* p. 789 (PE) *Self-Assessment,* p. 789 (TE) *Formal Assessment* • Section Quiz, p. 320 *Alternative Assessment Book* • Standards for Evaluating a Cooperative Activity
CHAPTER RESOURCES	**Chapter Overview** *After World War II, tensions between the United States and the Soviet Union lead to a war without direct conflict—the Cold War. Both countries invest heavily in nuclear weapons, and the U.S. enters the Korean War. At home, fear of communism escalates.*	*In-Depth Resources: Unit 7* • Living History Worksheet, p. 55; Standards, p. 56 *Telescoping the Times* • Chapter Summary, pp. 51–52 *Planning for Block Schedules*	*Chapter Assessment,* pp. 792–793 (PE) *Alternative Assessment,* p. 793 (PE) *Formal Assessment* • Chapter Test, forms A and B, pp. 321–326 *Test Generator* *Alternative Assessment Book* See explanation and forms for different kinds of alternative assessments including portfolio assessment.

Geography Transparencies
• G26, The Berlin Airlift: 1948–49

Our Times CD-ROM
• Creation of NATO

Electronic Library of Primary Sources
• The Truman Doctrine

INTERNET RESOURCES
• See *McDougal Littell Learning On-Line* for links to information about Truman and the Marshall Plan.

Electronic Library of Primary Sources
• from *Reminiscences* by Douglas MacArthur

INTERNET RESOURCES
• See *McDougal Littell Learning On-Line* for links to information about the Korean War and Douglas MacArthur.

AMERICAN STORIES VIDEO SERIES
• "The Cold War Comes Home"

Electronic Library of Primary Sources
• Statement on Civil Liberties in America by Paul Robeson

Grolier Multimedia Encyclopedia
• The Cold War

INTERNET RESOURCES
• See Interact with History, p. 782 (PE) for an activity that includes the Internet as an enrichment option.

Critical Thinking Transparencies
• CT26, The Cold War
• CT60, The Space Race

Humanities Transparencies
• H25, California bomb shelter, 1951
• H41, Political Cartoon

Electronic Library of Primary Sources
• Life in a Shelter by Thamar A. Dufwa

INTERNET RESOURCES
• See *McDougal Littell Learning On-Line* for links to information about *Sputnik* and the U-2.

American Portfolio: A Videodisc for U.S. History, user's guide, p. 233

INTERNET RESOURCES
Learning On-Line: Social Studies
http://www.mcdougallittell.com

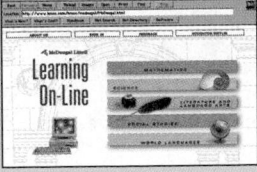

Block Scheduling (90 MINUTES)

Day 1
Section 1, pp. 766–772
Section 2, pp. 773–778
Section Assessments, pp. 772, 778

Day 2
Section 3, pp. 779–784
Section 4, pp. 785–789

AMERICAN STORIES VIDEO SERIES
• "The Cold War Comes Home"

Day 3
Review Sections 1–4
American Studies: Science Fiction Reflects Cold War Realities, pp. 790–791
Chapter Assessment, pp. 792–793

YEARLY PACING *Chapter 26 Total:* 3 days *Yearly Total:* 81 days

See *Planning for Block Schedules* for special activities and pacing strategies.

Customizing for Special Populations

Students Acquiring English

Access for Students Acquiring English
• Guided Reading for Sections 1–4 (Spanish), pp. 255–258
• Chapter Summary (Spanish), pp. 253–254
• SkillBuilder Practice: Analyzing Motives (Spanish), p. 259
• Geography Application: The Marshall Plan (Spanish), p. 260

AMERICAN STORIES VIDEO SERIES
• "The Cold War Comes Home" (Spanish track)

INTERNET RESOURCES
• See *McDougal Littell Learning On-Line* The Diverse Classroom.

Less Proficient Readers

In-Depth Resources: Unit 7
• Guided Reading for Sections 1–4, pp. 39–42
• SkillBuilder Practice: Analyzing Motives, p. 43
• Geography Application: The Marshall Plan, p. 44

Telescoping the Times
• Chapter Summary, pp. 51–52

See additional strategies at point of use in the Teacher's Edition.

Gifted and Talented Students

In-Depth Resources: Unit 7
• Primary Sources: *from* Harry S. Truman's letter to his daughter, p. 46; *from* MacArthur's Farewell Address to Congress, p.47; *from* Dwight D. Eisenhower's statement on the U-2
• American Lives: Douglas MacArthur, p. 53; Margaret Chase Smith, p. 54

See additional strategies at point of use in the Teacher's Edition.

Connections to Literature READINGS FOR STUDENTS

In-Depth Resources: Unit 7
• from *The Nuclear Age* by Tim O'Brien, p. 21
McDougal Littell *Literature Connections*

• **George Orwell,** *1984* (with related readings) Originally published in 1949, this startling, futuristic indictment of the totalitarian state was the original "big brother."

• **Ray Bradbury,** *Fahrenheit 451* (with related readings) Set in a future where the government burns books to keep people from thinking or rebelling, this chilling story, first published in 1953, has powerful meaning today.

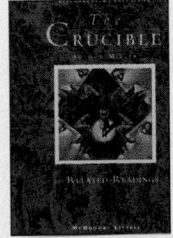

• **Arthur Miller,** *The Crucible* (with related readings) A witch hunt in Puritan New England with overtones of McCarthyism.

• **George Orwell,** *Animal Farm* (with related readings) An animal fable satirizing communism and warning against the dangers of totalitarianism.

Cold War Conflicts

▶ **Starting with the Student**
Ask students to speculate about the ways in which the Cold War was "cold." Then discuss the opening quotation.

• What visual images does the quotation evoke?
• How would they paraphrase Oppenheimer's statement in their own words?

PREVIEWING THE CHAPTER
• Go over the titles and brief descriptions of the sections, particularly noting the video in Section 3.
• Have students choose an intriguing event or picture from the time line and write several questions about it. They should look for the answers to their questions as they read the chapter.

MORE ABOUT . . .
J. Robert Oppenheimer

J. Robert Oppenheimer (1904–1967) is known as the father of the atomic bomb because of his work directing the development of the first A-bomb in Los Alamos, New Mexico, from 1943 to 1945. After the war, he served as an adviser for the newly formed Atomic Energy Commission and for the U.S. Department of Defense. He also worked to establish international control of nuclear energy.

CHAPTER
26 Cold War Conflicts

SECTION 1
Origins of the Cold War
The Allied coalition falls apart as the United States and the Soviet Union find themselves in conflict with each other.

SECTION 2
The Cold War Heats Up
U.S. containment policies and Communist successes in China and North Korea lead to the Korean War.

SECTION 3
The Cold War at Home
The Cold War kindles a fear of Communist influence in the United States.

 VIDEO *THE COLD WAR COMES HOME*

SECTION 4
Two Nations Live on the Edge
Tension mounts between the United States and the Soviet Union as both try to spread their influence around the world.

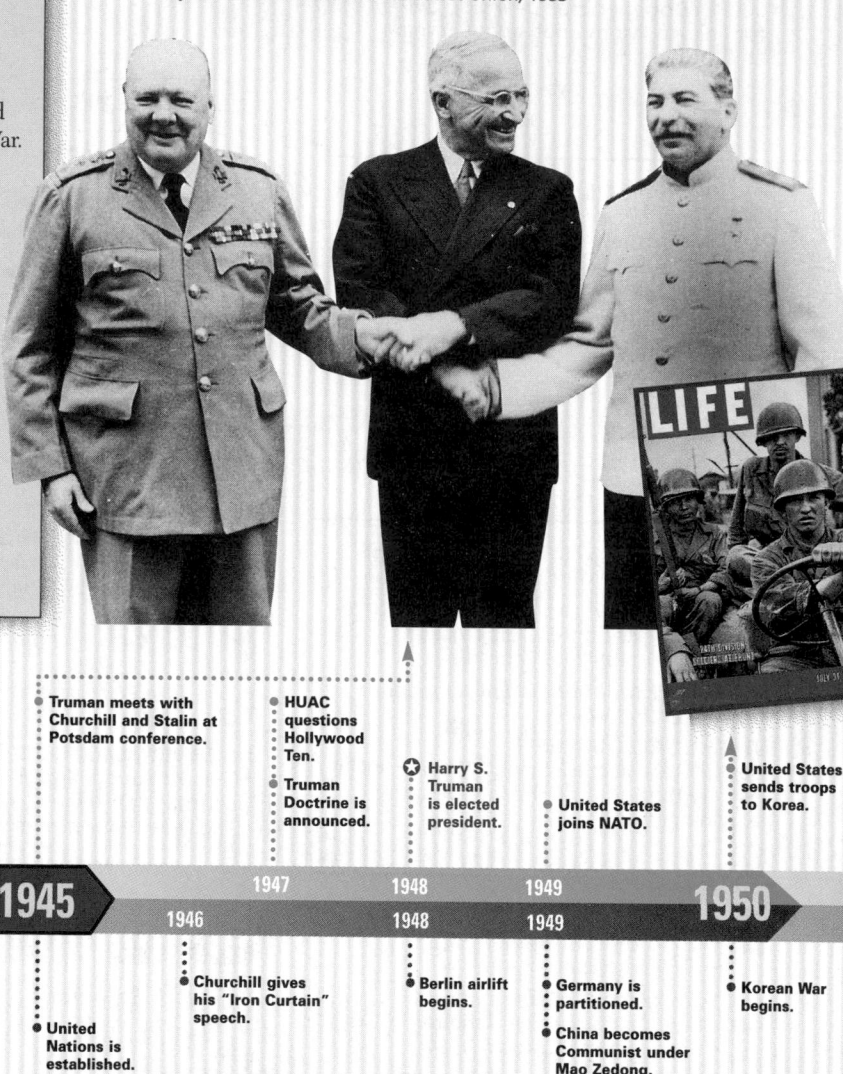

"We may be likened to two scorpions in a bottle, each capable of killing the other, but only at the risk of his own life."

J. Robert Oppenheimer,
speaking of the buildup of atomic weapons by the United States and the Soviet Union, 1953

THE UNITED STATES
THE WORLD

1945 **1946** **1947** **1948** **1948** **1949** **1949** **1950**

• Truman meets with Churchill and Stalin at Potsdam conference.
• Truman Doctrine is announced.
• HUAC questions Hollywood Ten.
☆ Harry S. Truman is elected president.
• United States joins NATO.
• United States sends troops to Korea.

• United Nations is established.
• Churchill gives his "Iron Curtain" speech.
• Berlin airlift begins.
• Germany is partitioned.
• China becomes Communist under Mao Zedong.
• Korean War begins.

THEMES IN CHAPTER 26

Economic Opportunity

After World War II, the United States converted to a peace-time economy. It faced the monumental tasks of supplying jobs for returning soldiers and meeting civilians' demand for goods that were unavailable in wartime.

See Teacher's Edition note, p. 768.

Constitutional Concerns

Two major challenges to the Constitution arose during the Cold War. The first resulted from General Douglas MacArthur's attempt to defy President Truman's constitutional authority as head of the armed services.

Senator Joseph McCarthy perpetrated the second consti-tutional challenge when he attempted to eliminate suspected Communists from the country. This "witch hunt" trampled Americans' constitutional rights of free speech and assembly.

See Teacher's Edition notes, pp. 777 and 780.

Science and Technology

The brilliant scientific achievements that led to the creation of the atomic and hydrogen bombs also cast a shadow of impending nuclear holocaust over the 1950s. Despite this fear, many peaceful applications of nuclear energy resulted.

See Teacher's Edition note, p. 788.

Rosenbergs are executed as spies.

LIVING HISTORY

CONDUCTING TWO INTERVIEWS

Conduct two interviews—one with a person who was a teenager during the period 1945–1960 and another with someone who was an adult during that period. The topic of the interviews should be the people's memories of the Cold War and its effects on Americans. Possible questions to ask include

- What do you remember as your greatest fear during the Cold War?
- What do you recall as important conflicts during that time?

📁 **PORTFOLIO PROJECT** Keep the records of your interviews in a folder. At the end of this chapter, you will compile and present the interviews and add them to your American history portfolio.

CONDUCTING TWO INTERVIEWS

Suggest interviewing strategies that students can use.

- Look for people who are from about 55 to 75 years old to interview—family members, family friends, neighbors, or teachers.
- Compile some biographical information about the interviewees to help your audience understand the interview.
- Prepare a list of questions in advance.
- During the interviews, take notes and, with the permission of the interviewees, use a tape recorder.
- Note physical details of the interviewees to include in your presentation.

Interview Planning Guide

Step 1	Students choose the people they are going to interview.
Step 2	Students prepare interview questions.
Step 3	Students conduct their interviews.
Step 4	Students compile their interview tapes and other relevant information in their folders.

Francis Gary Powers's U-2 spy plane is shot down by Soviets.

United States explodes first hydrogen bomb.

⊗ **Dwight D. Eisenhower is elected president.**

● **Senator Joseph McCarthy, shown with Roy Cohn, alleges Communist involvement in U.S. Army.**

⊗ **Eisenhower is reelected president.**

⊗ **John F. Kennedy is elected president.**

1952	1953	1954	**1955**	1956			**1960**
1953	1954				1957	1959	

● **Soviets explode their first hydrogen bomb.**

● **French are defeated in Vietnam.**

● **Korean War cease-fire is agreed to.**

● **Soviets launch** *Sputnik.*

● **Fidel Castro comes to power in Cuba.**

Cold War Conflicts **765**

IN-DEPTH RESOURCES: UNIT 7
See worksheet and standards for evaluation, pp. 55–56.

RECOMMENDED RESOURCES

Books for the Teacher

Bundy, McGeorge. *Danger and Survival: The Political History of the Nuclear Weapon.* New York: Random House, 1989.

McCullough, David. *Truman.* New York: Simon, 1992.

Winik, Jay. *On the Brink.* New York: Simon, 1996.

Books for the Student

Miller, Merle. *Plain Speaking: An Oral Biography of Harry S. Truman.* New York: Berkley, 1986.

Rovere, Richard. *Senator Joseph McCarthy.* New York: Harper, 1973.

Videos

Are We Winning, Mommy? America and the Cold War. First

Run Features, 153 Waverly Place, New York, NY 10014

Atomic Cafe. Archives Project, New York, 1982. History of atomic bomb.

Fat Man and Little Boy. Paramount, 1990. The development of the first two atomic bombs.

Korea: The Unknown War. WGBH-Boston

On the Beach. Dir. Stanley Kramer. MGM/UA, 1959.

McCarthy: Death of a Witch Hunter. Film Archives, The Cinema Center, Botsford, CT 06404, 800-366-1920

Software

Trinity and Beyond: A History of Nuclear Weapons. Heizer Software, P.O. Box 232019, Pleasant Hill, CA 94523

TERMS & NAMES
- satellite nation
- containment
- Cold War
- Truman Doctrine
- Marshall Plan
- Berlin airlift
- North Atlantic Treaty Organization (NATO)

OBJECTIVES

1. To explain the breakdown of relations between the United States and the Soviet Union after World War II.

2. To summarize the steps the United States took to contain Soviet influence as tensions increased.

3. To describe how the Truman Doctrine and the Marshall Plan further defined and deepened the Cold War in Europe.

4. To explain how conflicts over Germany increased fear of Soviet aggression.

SKILLBUILDERS

- Interpreting charts, p. 768
- Understanding geography: location, human-environment interaction, p. 769
- Interpreting graphs, p. 770
- Understanding geography: location, place, p. 772

CRITICAL THINKING

- Analyzing causes, p. 768
- Analyzing motives, p. 769
- Synthesizing, p. 770
- Recognizing effects, p. 771
- Summarizing, p. 772
- Evaluating, p. 772
- Drawing conclusions, p. 772

FOCUS & MOTIVATE

▶ **Starting with the Student**
- What happens when two people, such as two students, stop being friendly because of conflicting ideas or personalities?
- Could the same situation happen between two countries? Why or why not?

MORE ABOUT . . .
Joseph Polowsky

For many years Joseph Polowsky distributed leaflets in Chicago every April 25 to urge halting the spread of nuclear weapons.

Polowsky worked for many years as a cabdriver before retiring. He died in 1983. He is buried at Torgau, Germany, where there is a memorial showing Russians and Americans shaking hands.

❶ Origins of the Cold War

LEARN ABOUT economic and political differences between the United States and the Soviet Union
TO UNDERSTAND the Cold War and how it began.

ONE AMERICAN'S STORY

Private Joseph Polowsky was 70 miles south of Berlin, part of a patrol of American soldiers who were scouting for signs of the Soviet army, which was advancing from the east. As the soldiers neared the Elbe River, they saw lilacs in bloom. Polowsky later said the sight of the flowers filled them with the "exaltation of being alive, after all those days trapped in a trench war."

On the other side of the Elbe, the Americans spotted Soviet soldiers, who signaled for them to cross over. When the Americans reached the other bank, their joy turned to shock. They saw to their horror that the bank was covered with dead civilians, victims of bombing raids.

32 USA
U.S. and Soviets link up at Elbe River, April 1945

A PERSONAL VOICE
Here we are, tremendously exhilarated, and there's a sea of dead. . . . [The platoon leader] was much moved. . . . He said, "Joe, lets make a resolution with these Russians here and also the ones on the bank: this would be an important day in the lives of the two countries." . . . It was a solemn moment. There were tears in the eyes of most of us. . . . We embraced. We swore never to forget.

JOSEPH POLOWSKY, quoted in *The Good War*

top, American and Soviet soldiers meet at the Elbe River in Germany near the end of World War II; *above,* A 1996 postage stamp commemorates the historic meeting.

The Soviet and U.S. soldiers believed their encounter would serve as a symbol of peaceful relations between their two countries. Unfortunately, such hopes were soon dashed. After World War II, the United States and the Soviet Union emerged as rival superpowers, each strong enough to greatly influence world events.

Former Allies Clash

Although the American and Soviet soldiers hoped for friendship between their countries, problems had been building between the Soviet Union and the United States before and during the war. The two countries' economic and political systems were incompatible, and they had built up resentments toward each other over previous events.

In the Soviet system of communism, the state controlled all property and economic activity, while in the U.S. system of capitalism, private citizens controlled property and economic activity. In the U.S. democracy, the people elected a president and a congress; in Soviet communism, the Communist Party had ousted the czar by force during the Russian Revolution and established a totalitarian government in which no opposing parties were allowed to exist. The Soviets were deeply resentful that the United States had not recognized their Communist government until 16 years after the revolution.

In addition, the United States was furious that Joseph Stalin—the leader of the Soviet Union—had signed a nonaggression pact with Hitler in 1939, which Hitler broke two years later. Although the United States and the Soviet Union

---

SECTION 1 RESOURCES

📑 PRINT RESOURCES

IN-DEPTH RESOURCES: UNIT 7
Guided Reading, p. 39
Skillbuilder Practice: Analyzing Motives, p. 43
Geography Application: The Marshall Plan, p. 44
Primary Source: Harry S. Truman's letter to his daughter, p. 46

ACCESS FOR STUDENTS ACQUIRING ENGLISH
Guided Reading (Spanish), p. 255
Skillbuilder Practice: Analyzing Motives (Spanish), p. 259
Geography Application: The Marshall Plan (Spanish), p. 260

FORMAL ASSESSMENT
Section Quiz, p. 317

ALTERNATIVE ASSESSMENT BOOK
See forms for supporting and scoring alternative activities.

💻 TECHNOLOGY RESOURCES

GEOGRAPHY TRANSPARENCIES
G26, The Berlin Airlift: 1948–49

CD-ROM *Our Times*
Electronic Library of Primary Sources

VIDEO *American Portfolio: A Videodisc for U.S. History*
user's guide, p. 235

INTERNET McDougal Littell Learning On-Line
http://www.mcdougallittell.com

became allies during World War II, their leaders often did not see eye to eye. Stalin had wanted the Allies to invade Europe earlier than 1944, and their delay in doing so fed Stalin's distrust of them. Relations worsened after Stalin learned that the United States had kept its development of the atomic bomb secret from the Soviets.

In spite of these problems, hopes for world peace were high at the end of the war. The most visible symbol of these hopes was the United Nations (UN). On April 25, 1945, the representatives of 50 nations met in San Francisco to establish this new international peacekeeping body. After two months of debate, on June 26, 1945, the delegates signed the charter establishing the UN. The UN headquarters was built in New York City.

Ironically, even though the UN was intended to promote peace, it soon became an arena where the two superpowers competed. Both the United States and the Soviet Union used the UN as a forum to spread their influence over other nations.

TRUMAN BECOMES PRESIDENT For the United States, the key figure in the early years of conflict with the Soviets was President Harry S. Truman. Thirteen days before the UN conference convened, Truman suddenly became president when Franklin Roosevelt died. In many ways he was unprepared for the responsibilities of national and world leadership. Before becoming vice-president, he had been a hard-working, well-liked senator but had had very little power. In the 82 days he was vice-president, he met with the president only twice. Roosevelt not only left him uninformed about military matters and peace negotiations—he did not even tell Truman that the United States was developing an atomic bomb!

Many Americans doubted Truman's abilities because they knew very little about him and he was very different from Roosevelt. Whereas Roosevelt was a wealthy, handsome, sophisticated New Yorker, Truman was a self-educated, plainspoken Missourian, whose only business venture had ended in failure. On the plus side, however, Truman had honesty, self-confidence, and a willingness to make tough decisions—qualities that he would need desperately in the first few months of his presidency. As the war ended, not only would he have to make difficult military decisions, but he would also have to deal with world leaders of vastly greater experience—such as Stalin and Churchill.

TRUMAN MEETS STALIN AT POTSDAM Truman's first meeting with those two leaders came at the final wartime conference of the Big Three (the leaders of

KEY PLAYERS

HARRY S. TRUMAN
1884–1972

Young Harry S. Truman, the son of a Missouri livestock trader and his wife, did not seem destined for greatness. When he graduated from high school in 1901, he drifted from job to job—drugstore clerk, newspaper mailroom clerk, timekeeper, bank clerk, bookkeeper, farmer, World War I soldier. After the war, he invested in a men's clothing store; but the business failed, and he spent the next 15 years paying off business debts.

Discouraged by his business failure, Truman sought a career in politics. As a politician, his blunt and outspoken style won loyal friends and bitter enemies. As president, his decisiveness and willingness to accept responsibility for his decisions ("The Buck Stops Here" read a sign on his desk) earned him respect that has grown in the decades following his presidency.

JOSEPH STALIN
1879–1953

As a young revolutionary, Iosif Vissarionovich Dzhugashvili took the name Stalin, which means "man of steel."

His father was a failed shoemaker and an alcoholic. His mother helped support the family as a washerwoman. Following her wishes, Stalin entered a seminary, but he was eventually expelled for revolutionary activism.

Stalin is credited with turning the Soviet Union into a world power, but at a terrible cost to its citizens. He ruled with terror and brutality and saw "enemies" everywhere, even among friends and supporters. He subdued the population with the use of secret police and labor camps, and he is believed to have been responsible for the murder of millions of people in the Soviet Union.

Cold War Conflicts **767**

Tension Mounts

▶ **Starting with the Student**
Ask students to think about how parents or teachers try to block what they believe are negative influences on teenagers, such as television or cigarette advertisements. Have students consider similar actions the United States might have taken to block, or contain, harmful Soviet influence in Europe.

• How do parental containment policies compare with the postwar containment policies of the U.S. government?

▶ **Discussing Key Ideas**
• The U.S. and the Soviets want different political systems in Europe.
• The two countries have completely different economic systems.
• The Soviets take control of several European countries after World War II.
• The U.S. wants to block Soviet influence.

HISTORY FROM VISUALS
U.S. Aims Versus Soviet Aims in Europe

Reading the Chart Remind students to repeat the column head before reading each of the bulleted items: For example: *"The United States wanted to* encourage democracy . . ."

Extension Have pairs of students each write three sentences. One student will write a sentence summarizing a U.S. aim; the other will write a sentence summarizing the corresponding Soviet aim. Then the students will collaborate on a sentence explaining the incompatibility of the aims.

Great Britain, the United States, and the Soviet Union) at Potsdam, Germany, in July 1945. Essentially, the Potsdam conference was a continuation of the earlier wartime conference at Yalta—with important differences. Truman now took Roosevelt's place, and Clement Atlee replaced Churchill in mid-conference.

At Yalta, the United States and Great Britain had insisted that the Soviets allow free, open elections in Poland and other Eastern European nations after the war. Stalin had agreed, but he had kept his language vague. Then, in 1945, the Soviets prevented free elections in Poland and banned democratic parties, leaving Poland in the hands of a pro-Soviet government. Stalin said that Poland was "not only a question of honor for Russia, but one of life and death."

To Truman, the Soviets' refusal to allow free and open elections in Poland and other Eastern European nations was a clear violation of those nations' right of self-determination. Consequently, at Potsdam, Truman pushed Stalin to allow free elections, but the Soviet dictator refused. With the Soviet army occupying the Eastern European nations in question, the West could do little.

THINK THROUGH HISTORY
A. Analyzing Causes What did Stalin do to make President Truman distrust him?
A. Answer Stalin would not allow free elections in Eastern Europe.

Tension Mounts

Stalin's refusal to allow free elections in Poland convinced Truman that U.S. and Soviet aims were deeply at odds. Truman's objective in demanding free elections in Eastern Europe was to spread democracy to nations that had been under Nazi rule. He and his advisers believed that the best way to avoid a third world war was to create a new world order in which all nations had the right of self-determination, guaranteed by open elections.

Truman also feared giving in too much to Stalin's demands for territory and war reparations. For example, Stalin wanted to strip all of Germany of its industry, using the plundered equipment to rebuild the war-torn economy of the Soviet Union. The United States and Great Britain opposed his demands, but it was agreed at Potsdam that each of the Allies could take reparations from the part of Germany that it occupied.

Truman also felt that the United States had a large economic stake in spreading democracy and free trade across the globe. In contrast to the war-ravaged countries of Europe and Asia, the United States had no ruined factories or bombed-out cities. U.S. industry boomed during the war, making the United States the economic leader of the world. To continue growing, American businesses wanted access to raw materials in Eastern Europe, and they wanted to be able to sell goods to Eastern European countries.

SOVIETS TIGHTEN THEIR GRIP ON EASTERN EUROPE On the other hand, the Soviet Union felt justified in staying in Eastern Europe. The Soviets had suf-

U.S. Aims Versus Soviet Aims in Europe

THE UNITED STATES WANTED TO	THE SOVIETS WANTED TO
• encourage democracy in other countries to help prevent the rise of new totalitarian governments	• encourage communism in other countries as part of the worldwide struggle between workers and the wealthy
• gain access to raw materials and markets for its booming industries	• transfer the industrial equipment of Eastern Europe to the Soviet Union to help rebuild its war-ravaged economy
• rebuild European governments to ensure stability and to create new markets for American goods	• control Eastern Europe to balance the U.S. influence in Western Europe
• reunite Germany, believing that Europe would be more secure if Germany were productive and less bitter about defeat	• keep Germany divided and weak, since the Germans had waged war against Russia twice in 30 years and had caused most of the 20 million Soviet deaths in World War II

SKILLBUILDER **INTERPRETING CHARTS** Which U.S. aims involved economic growth? Which Soviet aims involved self-protection? How did the differences in these aims lead to the Cold War?

Skillbuilder Answer **U.S. Aims:** Gaining access to raw materials and markets, rebuilding European governments. **Soviet Aims:** Controlling Eastern Europe, keeping Germany divided and weak. **Differences in Aims:** They were incompatible.

TEACHING OPTIONS

Teaching Less Proficient Readers

Clarifying Ideas Pair less proficient readers with more proficient ones to clarify the main ideas in this section. Have the student pairs follow these steps:

1. Read pages 768 and 769 of the text together.
2. Make a list of the causes of tension between the United States and the Soviet Union.
3. List unanswered questions they have out about the tensions.
4. Review the pages and write answers to the questions.

Exploring Themes

Economic Opportunity Economic considerations strongly influenced U.S. foreign policy after World War II. The U.S. government wanted to promote a healthy world economy by making it possible for Europe to rebuild and by encouraging capitalism. At the same time, the United States was creating markets for its goods and materials.

Ask students if they think economic considerations continue to influence U.S. foreign policy today. *Possible Response: A potential market of more than one billion consumers is one reason the United States wants good relations with China today.*

The "Iron Curtain," 1948

Legend:
☐ Communist Nations
☐ Non-Communist Nations

The "Iron Curtain"

GEOGRAPHY
SKILLBUILDER
LOCATION *What Communist nations were located between the Soviet Union and the Iron Curtain?*
HUMAN-ENVIRONMENT INTERACTION *Why did the Soviet Union want to control these nations?*

Skillbuilder Answer
Location: East Germany, Czechoslovakia, Poland, Hungary, Romania, Yugoslavia, Bulgaria, Albania.
Human-Environment Interaction: Stalin wanted a buffer between the Soviet Union and Western Europe.

B. Answer To create satellite nations on the Soviet Union's western borders.

THINK THROUGH HISTORY
B. Analyzing Motives What was Stalin's goal in supporting Communist governments in Eastern Europe?

THINK THROUGH HISTORY
C. Analyzing Motives What were Truman's goals in establishing the policy of containment?

C. Answer To stop the spread of Soviet influence.

fered more than 20 million deaths and extensive damage during World War II and felt vulnerable to attack from the west. They needed friendly neighbors—Communist countries that they could control.

Stalin installed or propped up Communist governments in Albania, Bulgaria, Czechoslovakia, Hungary, Romania, and Poland. These countries became known as **satellite nations,** countries dependent upon and dominated by the Soviet Union. In addition, Stalin seized the industrial assets, such as factory equipment, of these countries to rebuild the Soviet Union. In early 1946, Stalin gave a speech announcing that communism and capitalism were incompatible—and that another war was inevitable. Therefore, he said, the Soviet Union would concentrate on producing weapons rather than consumer goods. The United States interpreted this speech as virtually a declaration of war.

UNITED STATES ESTABLISHES A POLICY OF CONTAINMENT Faced with the Soviet threat, American officials decided it was time, in Truman's words, to stop "babying the Soviets." In February 1946, George F. Kennan, an American diplomat in Moscow, proposed a policy of **containment**—an effort to block the Soviets' attempts to spread their influence by creating alliances and supporting weaker countries. This policy began to guide the Truman administration's foreign policy.

A few weeks later, in March 1946, Winston Churchill traveled to the United States and gave a speech that described the situation in Europe.

> **A PERSONAL VOICE**
> A shadow has fallen upon the scenes so lately lighted by the Allied victory. . . . From Stettin in the Baltic to Trieste in the Adriatic, an iron curtain has descended across the continent. Behind that line lie all the capitals of the ancient states of Central and Eastern Europe. . . . All these famous cities and the populations around them lie in the Soviet sphere and all are subject in one form or another, not only to Soviet influence but to a very high and increasing measure of control from Moscow.
> **WINSTON CHURCHILL,** "Iron Curtain" speech in Fulton, Missouri

When Stalin heard about the speech, he declared in no uncertain terms that Churchill's words were a "call to war."

"An iron curtain has descended across . . . Europe."
WINSTON CHURCHILL

Cold War Conflicts **769**

HISTORY FROM VISUALS
The "Iron Curtain," 1948
Reading the Map Have students examine the topographical features of the map, especially east of the iron curtain. What inference can they draw about the Soviet Union's vulnerability to attack? *Possible Response: Much of the land was flat and provided little protection against invasion from Europe.*

Extension Ask how the satellite nations functioned as a buffer zone for the Soviets. *Possible Response: Only about 500 miles separated the Soviet Union from the border of West Germany. By controlling nations on their border, the Soviets gained protection.*

MORE ABOUT . . .
Churchill's "Iron Curtain" Speech
Although the historical evidence clearly shows that Stalin was a brutal dictator, many people at the time felt Churchill's speech hindered the efforts to achieve peace between the Soviet Union and the western nations. For example, the journalist Walter Lippmann felt that the speech was an "almost catastrophic blunder."

TEACHING OPTION

SkillBuilder Mini-Lesson: Analyzing Motives

Explaining the Skill To analyze something is to separate it into its constituent parts. Analysis can be applied to almost anything—a math problem, a sports outcome, or the reasons behind political actions. Analyzing a motive involves separating the event into parts and then examining the emotions or needs that caused persons or groups to take the action.

Applying the Skill: Analyzing Motives To answer the Think Through History questions on this page, which ask students to analyze motives, suggest that they separate the subjects into the following parts:

Question B:
• need for buffers against invasion
• destruction to the Soviet Union during World War II
• industrial assets needed for rebuilding

Question C:
• Soviet actions after World War II
• differing ideologies of capitalism and communism

IN-DEPTH RESOURCES: UNIT 7
SkillBuilder Practice: Analyzing Motives, p. 43

Cold War in Europe

▶ **Starting with the Student**
Have students analyze the impact of the Truman Doctrine and the Marshall Plan by making charts listing the actions of the United States under each plan and the results of those actions.

	Action	Results
Truman Doctrine		
Marshall Plan		

▶ **Discussing Key Ideas**
• The Truman Doctrine authorizes foreign aid to help prevent the spread of communism.
• The Marshall Plan enables Europe to rebuild and helps create markets for U.S. goods.

 ELECTRONIC LIBRARY OF PRIMARY SOURCES
"The Truman Doctrine" by Harry S. Truman

HISTORY FROM VISUALS
The Marshall Plan

Reading the Graph Ask what factors students think determined the amount of aid each nation received. *Possible Answer: Its involvement in and damage incurred by the war.*

IN-DEPTH RESOURCES: UNIT 7
Geography Application: The Marshall Plan, p. 44

Bags of sugar arrive in Istanbul, Turkey, courtesy of the Marshall Plan.

The Marshall Plan

Country	Millions of Dollars
Great Britain	2,826
France	2,445
Italy	1,316
West Germany	1,297
Holland	877
Austria	561
Belgium /Lux.	547
Greece	515
Denmark	257
Norway	237
Turkey	153
Ireland	146
Sweden	119
Portugal	51
Yugoslavia	33
Iceland	29
Other	350

0 500 1000 1500 2000 2500
Millions of Dollars

Source: Problemes Économiques, No. 306

SKILLBUILDER
INTERPRETING GRAPHS *Which country received the most aid from the U.S.? Why do you think that country received so much aid?*

Skillbuilder Answer **Country:** Great Britain. **Reason:** *Possible Answer:* It was the staunchest U.S. ally.

Cold War in Europe

The conflicting U.S. and Soviet aims in Eastern Europe led to the **Cold War**—the state of hostility short of direct military confrontation that developed between the two superpowers. The Cold War would dominate global affairs—and U.S. foreign policy—until the breakup of the Soviet Union in 1991.

During the Cold War, the United States and the Soviet Union tried to spread their political and economic influence wherever they could. Eventually the Cold War spread to Asia, Africa, and Latin America.

THE CONTROVERSIAL TRUMAN DOCTRINE The United States first tried to contain Soviet influence in Greece and Turkey. After the war, Britain was sending economic and military support to both nations to prevent Communist takeovers. However Britain's economy had been badly hurt by the war, and the formerly wealthy nation could no longer afford to give the aid. It asked the United States to take over the responsibility.

On March 12, 1947, Truman asked Congress for $400 million in economic and military aid for Greece and Turkey. The president also declared that the United States should support free peoples throughout the world who were resisting takeovers by "armed minorities" or "outside pressures." This statement, known as the **Truman Doctrine,** caused great controversy. Some of its opponents objected to interfering in the internal affairs of other nations. Others argued that U.S. power would be spread too thin if the country carried on a global crusade against communism. Still others opposed helping any dictators, even if they were anti-Communist.

Congress, though, agreed with Truman and decided that the doctrine was essential to keeping Soviet influence from spreading in Europe. So between 1947 and 1950, the United States sent over $400 million in aid to Turkey and Greece, greatly reducing the danger of Communists' taking over those nations.

MARSHALL PLAN TO THE RESCUE Like postwar Greece, Western Europe was in economic chaos. Most of its factories had been bombed or looted. Many Europeans could not find work, and many turned to the black market and theft in order to survive. Millions of people were living in refugee camps while European governments tried to figure out where to resettle them.

To make matters worse, the winter of 1946–1947 was the bitterest in several centuries, with below-zero temperatures and record-breaking snow. The weather severely damaged crops and froze rivers, cutting off water transportation and causing a fuel shortage. In Britain, people could use electricity only a few hours each day, and food rations were even lower than during the war.

In June 1947, General George Marshall, who was now the U.S. secretary of state, proposed that the United States provide aid to all European nations that needed it, saying that this move was directed "not against any country or doctrine but against hunger, poverty, desperation, and chaos." However, in keeping with U.S. economic goals, the nations receiving aid had to remove trade barriers and to cooperate economically with one another.

Congress debated the **Marshall Plan** for several months. Many people opposed giving away $12.5 billion. Then, in February 1948, Soviet tanks rumbled into Czechoslovakia and took over the country. This invasion dramatized to Congress the need for strong, stable governments in Europe to resist communism, so it quickly approved the Marshall Plan.

D. Answer They strengthened anti-Communist governments economically and politically.

THINK THROUGH HISTORY
D. Synthesizing *How were the Truman Doctrine and the Marshall Plan examples of containment?*

Making Connections Across Time

Relations with Former Soviet Republics Today Ask students what they know about current relations between the United States and the former Soviet republics. Discuss with them the struggles these countries—and other former Communist countries such as Poland and Czechoslovakia—have had in making the transition to capitalism. You might want to mention that the United States has provided business and educational assistance to these countries through organizations such as the Peace Corps.

Making Connections Across the Curriculum

Economics Ask why the United States was the only large country in the world with a healthy economy after World War II. *Students may say that the U.S. mainland was never bombed. U.S. factories, farms, railroads, and cities were untouched by the war, while most European countries and Japan suffered devastating damage.*

How did the Marshall Plan help both the European and the U.S. economy? *Students may point out that the credit the plan provided allowed Europeans to purchase goods from U.S. manufacturers. These new markets created a demand for U.S. goods, which stimulated the economy.*

The plan was a great success both economically and politically. Nutrition improved. Industry grew. By 1952, Western Europe was flourishing, and Communist parties had lost much of their appeal to voters.

Superpowers Struggle over Germany

As Europe began to get back on its feet, the United States and its allies clashed with the Soviet Union over German reunification. At the end of World War II, Germany had been divided into four zones, occupied by the United States, Great Britain, and France in the west and the Soviet Union in the east. The Soviet Union wanted to keep Germany weak and divided. In contrast, the other three nations believed that Europe would be more stable if German industry were productive and the German people were not agitating for unity. In 1948, they decided to recombine the three western zones into one nation.

THE BERLIN AIRLIFT The Soviet Union retaliated by holding West Berlin hostage. Although Berlin lay deep within the Soviet zone of Germany, it was also divided into four zones. (See the map on the next page.) When the three western zones of Germany reunified, the Soviet Union cut off all highway, water, and rail traffic into the western zones of Berlin. No supplies could get in, so the city faced starvation. Stalin believed this threat would force the Western nations either to give up the idea of a reunified Germany or to surrender control of Berlin.

The resulting situation was dire. West Berlin's 2.1 million inhabitants would run out of food and fuel in about five weeks. In an attempt to break the blockade, American and British officials started the **Berlin airlift** to fly food and supplies into West Berlin. For 327 days, planes took off and landed every few minutes, around the clock. In 277,000 flights, they brought in 2.3 million tons of supplies—everything from food, fuel, and medicine to Christmas presents that the planes' crews bought with their own money.

West Berlin survived because of the airlift. In addition, the mission to aid Berlin gave a large boost to American prestige around the world, while causing Soviet prestige to drop. By May 1949, the Soviet Union realized it was beaten and lifted the Berlin blockade.

In the same month voters in the three western zones of Germany approved a constitution. By fall the Federal Republic of Germany, commonly called West Germany, had been established, with its capital in Bonn. The Soviet Union

"Democracy alone can supply the vitalizing force to stir the peoples of the world into triumphant action."

HARRY S. TRUMAN

E. Answer It broke the Soviet blockade, increased U.S. prestige, and reduced Soviet prestige.

THINK THROUGH HISTORY
E. Recognizing Effects What were the effects of the Berlin airlift?

Planes bringing tons of food and other supplies to West Berlin landed every three minutes.

Reading the Map Point out that the squares on this map are called "areas of detail" and that each square conveys a different level of information. In a way, the series of maps functions like a series of enlarged snapshots.

Extension Discuss what students know about Berlin today. On November 9, 1989, the wall was breached as the East German Communist regime collapsed. After German reunification in October 1990, the parliament voted to make Berlin the capital of united Germany.

OUR TIMES
The creation of NATO

ASSESS & RETEACH

Section 1 Assessment
Assign pairs of students to help each other answer the questions.

Self-Assessment
Have students mark those questions on the Section 1 Assessment that they could not answer. Ask them to locate the portions of the text that best answer each question.

Section Quiz
FORMAL ASSESSMENT
Section Quiz, p. 317

Reteach
On the board, create a blank chart like the one on page 768. Have students fill in the aims of the Soviet Union and the United States as a way of testing their comprehension of the material.

CLOSE

Although the United States and the Soviet Union tried to forge friendly relations, the two countries soon clashed over ideology and territory. The resulting Cold War affected the policies of each country for many years.

Postwar Germany, 1949

- Non-Communist countries
- Communist countries
- West Germany
- East Germany

GEOGRAPHY SKILLBUILDER
LOCATION *In which part of Germany was Berlin located?*
PLACE *What effects might the division of Berlin have had on its citizens?*

Skillbuilder Answer
Location: East Germany.
Effects: *Possible Answer:* It separated families, made travel between the zones difficult, and created economic problems.

turned its zone into the German Democratic Republic, commonly called East Germany, with its capital in East Berlin.

PEACETIME ALLIANCE—NATO The Berlin blockade increased Western European fear of Soviet aggression. In response, ten Western European nations—Belgium, Denmark, France, Great Britain, Iceland, Italy, Luxembourg, the Netherlands, Norway, and Portugal—joined with the United States and Canada to form a defensive military alliance called the **North Atlantic Treaty Organization (NATO)**. All member countries promised that an attack on one would be regarded as an attack on all—which they would resist with armed force if necessary. Although Ohio senator Robert Taft spoke for several Republican senators in opposing the treaty, for fear that it would stimulate an arms race and massive American military aid to Europe, the Senate approved it overwhelmingly. For the first time in its history, the United States entered into a military alliance with other nations during peacetime. The Cold War had ended U.S. isolationism.

Section 1 Assessment

1. TERMS & NAMES
Identify:
- satellite nation
- containment
- Cold War
- Truman Doctrine
- Marshall Plan
- Berlin airlift
- North Atlantic Treaty Organization (NATO)

2. SUMMARIZING In a two-column chart, list the Soviet and U.S. actions that contributed most to the beginning of the Cold War.

U.S. Actions	Soviet Actions

Write a paragraph explaining which country was more responsible and why you think so.

3. EVALUATING Former aides of Franklin Roosevelt worried that Truman was not qualified to handle world leadership. Considering what you learned in this section, evaluate Truman as a world leader.

THINK ABOUT
- his behavior toward Stalin
- his economic support of European nations
- his support of West Berlin

4. DRAWING CONCLUSIONS Which of the two superpowers do you think was more successful in achieving its aims during the period 1945–1949? Support your answer by referring to historical events.

THINK ABOUT
- events in Eastern Europe
- the Truman Doctrine and the Marshall Plan
- the conflicts over Berlin and the rest of Germany

772 CHAPTER 26

ANSWERS

1. TERMS & NAMES
satellite nation, p. 769
containment, p. 769
Cold War, p. 770
Truman Doctrine, p. 770
Marshall Plan, p. 770
Berlin airlift, p. 771
North Atlantic Treaty Organization (NATO), p. 772

2. SUMMARIZING
Possible Responses: U.S. actions—Marshall Plan, aid to Greece and Turkey, Truman Doctrine, Berlin airlift

Soviet actions—refusal of free elections in Poland, control of countries in Eastern Europe, invasion of Czechoslovakia

3. EVALUATING
Possible Responses: Most students will probably think Truman was a good leader because he took firm actions to contain the spread of Soviet influence, and he supported the Marshall Plan and the Berlin airlift.

Some may think he overreacted and was too belligerent toward Stalin.

4. DRAWING CONCLUSIONS
Some may say the Soviets were more successful, because they imposed their influence on nations along their border even though they failed to take over West Berlin. Others will say the United States was more successful in protecting West Berlin and in rebuilding Europe.

2 The Cold War Heats Up

TERMS & NAMES
- Mao Zedong
- Chiang Kai-shek
- Taiwan (Formosa)
- 38th parallel
- Korean War

LEARN ABOUT how Communist governments were established in Asia
TO UNDERSTAND why the United States became involved in the Korean War.

ONE AMERICAN'S STORY

First Lieutenant Philip Day, Jr., vividly remembers his first taste of battle in Korea. On the morning of July 5, 1950, Day spotted a column of eight enemy tanks moving toward his company. The Americans fired on the rapidly advancing enemy, but their bombardment had little effect. The enemy tanks kept on coming.

A PERSONAL VOICE

I was with a 75-mm recoilless-rifle team. "Let's see," I shouted, "if we can get one of those tanks." We picked up the gun and moved it to where we could get a clean shot. I don't know if we were poorly trained, . . . but we set the gun on the forward slope of the hill. When we fired, the recoilless blast blew a hole in the hill which instantly covered us in mud and dirt. The effect wasn't nearly as bad on us as it was on the gun. It jammed and wouldn't fire until we'd cleaned the whole damn thing. When we were ready again, we moved the gun to a better position and began banging away. I swear we had some hits, but the tanks never slowed down. . . . In a little less than two hours, 30 North Korean tanks rolled through the position we were supposed to block as if we hadn't been there.

PHILIP DAY, JR., quoted in *The Korean War: Pusan to Chosin*

American infantry soldiers fire heavy mortars at Communist strongholds near Mundung-ni in Korea.

Only five years after World War II ended, the United States became embroiled in a war in Korea. The policy of containment had led the United States into battle to halt Communist expansion. In this conflict, however, the enemy was North Korea and China.

Civil War in China

American involvement in Korea grew out of events that took place during World War II and the early years of the Cold War. When the Japanese occupied China in 1937, Chinese Communists and Nationalists had temporarily interrupted their long civil war and joined in the common cause against the invader. The Communists under **Mao Zedong** led the struggle in the north. The Nationalists under China's president, **Chiang Kai-shek** (Jiang Jieshi), fought in the south. During the war the United States sent the Nationalists approximately $3 billion in aid.

Many Americans were impressed by Chiang Kai-shek and admired the courage and determination that the Chinese Nationalists showed in resisting the Japanese. However, U.S. military and State Department officials who dealt with Chiang held a different view of him. They found his government dictatorial, inefficient, and hopelessly corrupt.

Furthermore, the political and economic policies of Chiang's government undermined the Nationalists' support in the Chinese countryside. For example, the Nationalists collected a grain tax from farmers even during the famine of

Cold War Conflicts **773**

SECTION 2 RESOURCES

PRINT RESOURCES

IN-DEPTH RESOURCES: UNIT 7
Guided Reading, p. 40
Primary Source: *from* MacArthur's Farewell Address to Congress, p. 47
American Lives: Douglas MacArthur, p. 53

ACCESS FOR STUDENTS ACQUIRING ENGLISH
Guided Reading, (Spanish), p. 256

FORMAL ASSESSMENT
Section Quiz, p. 318

ALTERNATIVE ASSESSMENT
See forms for supporting and scoring alternative activities.

TECHNOLOGY RESOURCES

CD-ROM Electronic Library of Primary Sources

VIDEO *American Portfolio: A Videodisc for U.S. History* user's guide, pp. 234–235

INTERNET McDougal Littell Learning On-Line
http://www.mcdougallittell.com

Section 2 Overview

OBJECTIVES

(1) To explain how Communists came to power in China and how the United States reacted.

(2) To summarize the events of the Korean War.

(3) To explain the conflict between President Truman and General MacArthur.

SKILLBUILDERS

- Interpreting charts, p. 774
- Understanding geography: movement, location, p. 776

CRITICAL THINKING

- Analyzing causes, pp. 774, 775
- Recognizing effects, p. 777
- Summarizing, p. 778
- Sequencing history, p. 778
- Hypothesizing, p. 776
- Forming an opinion, p. 778

FOCUS & MOTIVATE

▶*Starting with the Student*
Ask students what they know about the Korean War from relatives or friends or from movies or television programs such as M.A.S.H. What experiences did people have? How did they feel about the Korean War?

OBJECTIVE
(1) **INSTRUCT**

Civil War in China

▶*Discussing Key Ideas*
- The Communists and the Nationalists break into open conflict when the Japanese occupation ends.
- Civil war in China ends with a Communist victory.
- Conservatives attack the Truman administration for "losing" China.

IN-DEPTH RESOURCES: UNIT 7
Guided Reading, p. 40

ACCESS FOR STUDENTS ACQUIRING ENGLISH
Guided Reading (Spanish), p. 256

Teacher's Edition **773**

Reading the Chart Suggest that students read the chart horizontally, comparing each bulleted characteristic of the Nationalists with the corresponding characteristic of the Communists across from it.

Extension Tell students that in 1949, about 95 percent of the more than 450 million Chinese people were farmers. Ask how this situation may have influenced the outcome of the civil war. *Possible response: The farmers, many of whom wanted change and supported the Communists, vastly outnumbered the Nationalists.*

MORE ABOUT . . .
Chiang Kai-shek

For a time, Chiang Kai-shek was popular in the United States because of his determined fight against the Communists and because he converted to Christianity. His wife, Chiang Soong Mei-ling, was educated at Wellesley College in Massachusetts and was an articulate voice for the Nationalist cause in the United States. Chiang's support eventually eroded, however, because of corruption and antidemocratic practices in his government.

Nationalists Versus Communists

NATIONALISTS LEADER: CHIANG KAI-SHEK (JIANG JIESHI)	COMMUNISTS LEADER: MAO ZEDONG
• Ruled in the south of China after WWII	• Ruled in the north after the war
• Relied heavily on financial aid from the United States	• Relied heavily on financial aid from the Soviet Union
• Government adopted a new constitution in 1946.	• Propaganda campaigns were built around the theme of national liberation.
• Government struggled with inflation and a failing economy.	• Promise of land reform appealed to peasants.
• Military suffered from weak leadership and poor morale.	• Experienced guerrilla army was highly motivated.

SKILLBUILDER INTERPRETING CHARTS *What problems did the Nationalists have after World War II? How did the Communists appeal to the peasants?*

*Skillbuilder
Answers
Possible Answer:*
Nationalists: Inflation, failing economy, weak military leadership, poor morale.
Communists: With promises of national liberation and land reform.

1944. When city dwellers demonstrated against a 10,000 percent increase in the price of rice that had occurred over a three-year period, Chiang's secret police opened fire on them.

In contrast, the Communists proved to be more skillful in winning the support of peasants. For instance, after the Communists took over an area, they redistributed land to peasants and reduced rents. (In the 1950s, the Chinese Communist government would force these peasants to work on collective farms.) As a result, Chinese popular support for the Communists grew.

FIGHTING BREAKS OUT As soon as the defeated Japanese left China at the end of World War II, cooperation between the Nationalists and the Communists ceased. Civil war erupted between the two groups. In spite of the problems in the Nationalist regime, American policy favored the Nationalists because they opposed communism.

From 1944 to 1947, the United States played peacemaker between the two groups, while still supporting the Nationalists. However, U.S. officials repeatedly failed to negotiate peace. Truman refused to commit American soldiers to back up the Nationalists, although the United States did send $2 billion worth of military equipment and supplies to China.

The aid wasn't enough to save the Nationalists, whose weak military leadership and corrupt, abusive practices drove the peasants to the Communist side. In May 1949, Chiang and the remnants of his demoralized government and army fled to **Taiwan** (or **Formosa**), an island to the east of mainland China.

AMERICA REACTS TO COMMUNIST TAKEOVER The American public was stunned that China had become Communist. Containment had failed! In Congress, conservative Republicans and Democrats attacked the Truman administration for supplying only limited aid to Chiang. If containing communism was important in Europe, they asked, why was it not equally important in Asia?

The State Department replied by saying that what had happened in China was a result of internal forces. The United States had failed in its attempts to

**THINK THROUGH HISTORY
A. *Analyzing Causes*** What factors led to the Communist takeover in China?

A. Answer The corruption of the Nationalist government and the weakness of its military.

TEACHING OPTIONS

Making Global Connections

The United States and China After the Communist Party gained control of China in 1949, contacts between China and the West were minimal for more than 20 years. However, in 1971, Taiwan lost its seat in the United Nations, and China joined the Security Council. In a breakthrough visit in 1972, President Richard M. Nixon became the first U.S. president to visit China. Nixon's China policy later contributed to improved relations with the Soviet Union and the thawing of the Cold War.

Making Connections Across Time

Relations with Taiwan Today Tell students that for many years the United States has tried to balance historical ties with the Chinese Nationalist government in Taiwan with the desire to establish a diplomatic and trade relationship with the People's Republic of China.

China claims the right to govern Taiwan, but the Taiwanese wish to maintain as much independence as possible. When China conducted military exercises close to the coast of Taiwan in 1996, the U.S. government sent ships to the area as a show of support for Taiwan.

influence these forces, such as Chiang's inability to retain the support of his people. Trying to do more would only have started a war in Asia—a war that the United States wasn't prepared to fight.

Most Americans accepted the State Department's arguments, but some conservatives rejected them as lame excuses. They claimed that the United States had "lost" China and should have provided greater support to the Nationalists. They also charged that the American government was riddled with Communist agents. Like wildfire, American fear of communism began to burn out of control, and the flames were fanned even further by the events in Korea in the following year.

Koreans Go to War

Japan took over Korea in 1910 and ruled it until August 1945. As World War II ended, Japanese troops north of the 38th parallel surrendered to the Soviets. (The **38th parallel** is an imaginary line that bisects Korea at 38 degrees north latitude.) Japanese troops south of the parallel surrendered to the Americans. The 38th parallel was not intended as a permanent boundary, but it artificially divided the country's resources—industry in the north and agriculture in the south—making it difficult for either of the two regions to prosper. As was the case in Germany, however, two nations developed, one Communist and one not.

In 1948 the Republic of Korea, usually called South Korea, was established in the zone that had been occupied by the United States. Its government, headed by Syngman Rhee, was based in Seoul, Korea's traditional capital. Simultaneously, the Communists formed the Democratic People's Republic of Korea in the north. Kim Il Sung led its government, which was based in Pyongyang. By 1949, both the United States and the Soviet Union had withdrawn their troops, leaving the two new nations glaring at each other across the 38th parallel. Each government claimed the sole right to rule all of Korea.

NORTH KOREA ATTACKS SOUTH KOREA On June 25, 1950, North Korean troops started the **Korean War** by invading South Korea. The invasion alarmed Americans: Yet another Asian country was about to fall to communism. Was the United States going to sit back and let it happen? When news of the invasion reached President Truman, he decided to take military action.

> **A PERSONAL VOICE**
> What the Communists, the North Koreans, were doing was nothing new. . . . Hitler and Mussolini and the Japanese were doing exactly the same thing in the 1930s. . . . Nobody had stood up to them. And that is what led to the Second World War.
> **PRESIDENT TRUMAN**

Accordingly, Truman ordered naval and air support for South Korea. When his action was announced, Congress stood up and cheered. Only Republican senator Robert Taft of Ohio, the staunchly conservative son of President William Howard Taft, objected that the president, by acting on his own, had wrongfully taken over Congress's power to declare war.

On June 27, 1950, the UN Security Council adopted an American resolution calling on member nations to help the Republic of South Korea. Ironically, the Soviet Union was boycotting the UN because of the UN's refusal to recognize Communist China and was not present to veto the resolution. In all, ten nations sent some 520,000 troops to assist South Korea; just over 90 percent of these troops were American. South Korean troops numbered an additional 590,000. The combined UN and South Korean forces were placed under the command of General Douglas MacArthur.

HISTORICAL SPOTLIGHT

NSC-68

In 1947, Congress created the National Security Council to advise the president on national security issues. In April 1950, the 68th paper issued by the council (NSC-68) argued that the only way to prevent the Soviet Union from dominating the world was containment and a massive increase in defense spending.

At first, the administration doubted whether Americans would be willing to pay the additional tax dollars that an increase in defense spending would require. However, when North Korea invaded South Korea in June 1950, the administration had the justification it needed to spend more defense money to contain communism.

The United States Fights in Korea

▶ **Starting with the Student**
Ask students to create a flow chart of events of the Korean War as they read this section.

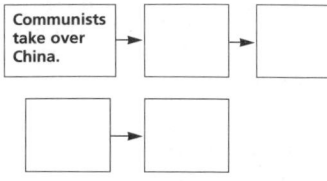

▶ **Discussing Key Ideas**
• MacArthur achieves a brilliant military victory over North Korea.
• China enters the Korean War.
• President Truman fires General MacArthur.
• The Korean War ends in a stalemate.

ANOTHER PERSPECTIVE
India's Viewpoint
Critical Thinking:
Interpreting Have students discuss the various reasons for India's neutrality.
Possible Response: By not choosing sides between the two super powers, India avoids the risk of domination by either one.

HISTORY FROM VISUALS
The War in Korea, 1950–1953

Reading the Map Tell students that the series of small maps shows the development of the war over time.

(continued on next page)

INDIA'S VIEWPOINT
Nonaligned nations, such as India, were on neither side of the Cold War and had their own perspectives on it. In 1951, the prime minister of India, Jawaharlal Nehru, had this to say about the Korean War:

This great struggle between the United States and Soviet Russia is hardly the proper role in this world for those great powers.... Their role should be to function in their own territories and not be a threat to others.

At first, North Korean armored units were unstoppable. Driving steadily onward, they captured Seoul. After a month of bitter combat, the North Koreans had forced UN and South Korean troops into a small defensive zone around Pusan, in the southeastern corner of the peninsula.

MACARTHUR'S MIRACLE COUNTERATTACK Then MacArthur launched a counterattack with tanks, heavy artillery, and fresh troops from the United States. On September 15, 1950, his troops made an amphibious landing behind enemy lines at Inchon, on Korea's west coast. Other troops moved north from Pusan. Trapped between the two attacking forces, about half of the North Korean troops surrendered; the rest fled back across the 38th parallel.

MacArthur's phenomenal success made him a hero to the American public. Experts called his plan one of the most brilliant military strategies in history. However, the sudden military triumph posed a political problem. MacArthur and his troops had achieved their objective of chasing the invaders out of South Korea. What should happen now? If UN and South Korean forces crossed the 38th parallel, the war would change from a defensive one to an offensive one. On the other hand, the Allies had agreed at Potsdam that Korea should be unified.

On October 7, 1950, the UN General Assembly recommended that MacArthur cross the 38th parallel and reunite Korea. However, days earlier, Communist China's foreign minister, Zhou Enlai, had warned that his country would not stand idly by and "let the Americans come to the border"—meaning

The War in Korea, 1950–1953

June 1950
North Korean troops invade South Korea and capture the capital, Seoul.

September 1950
North Koreans push South Korean and UN troops south to the perimeter of Pusan.

September to October 1950
UN troops under MacArthur land at Inchon and move north from Pusan, a two-pronged movement that drives the North Koreans out of South Korea. UN troops then push into North Korea, take Pyongyang, and advance to the Yalu River.

November 1950 to January 1951
The Chinese intervene and force UN troops to retreat across the 38th parallel.

GEOGRAPHY SKILLBUILDER MOVEMENT *How far south did the North Korean troops push the UN troops?* **LOCATION** *Why do you think MacArthur chose Inchon as his landing place?*

Skillbuilder Answer Movement: To Pusan. **Location:** *Possible Answer:* It put his army in a good position to capture Seoul.

TEACHING OPTION

Making Connections Across Cultures

Integration In 1948, President Truman ordered the integration of the armed services, making Korea the first war in which African-American soldiers lived and fought side by side with white soldiers. At first, the services were slow to comply with the presidential order, but as the Korean War dragged on, black soldiers became the replacements in white units and the army slowly became integrated.

First Lieutenant Bev Scott, an African-American officer, said, "There was no better institution in American life . . . than the army for the black man in the forties and fifties. . . . You had more leverage in the army. You always had somebody you could go to and complain about bad treatment. A black man couldn't do that in civilian life. Especially in the South. . . . "Officer Candidate School . . . was my first experience with meeting white people on a person-to-person basis. Previous to that all my experience with whites had been adversarial. Growing up in rural North Carolina, . . . I was always subjected to insults and names."

the Yalu River, the boundary between North Korea and Manchuria, a region of northeast China. He repeated his warning again and again during the first weeks of October. When Truman asked MacArthur about the threat of Chinese involvement, the general dismissed the possibility. MacArthur boasted that the war would be over by Thanksgiving and that he'd have American troops back in Tokyo by Christmas.

THE CHINESE FIGHT BACK The advance into North Korea went on, pressing ever closer to the Yalu River. Then, on the evening of November 25, some 300,000 Chinese soldiers poured across the Yalu River into Korea, forcing the UN and South Korean forces moving toward the river to retreat. By Christmas, the North Koreans and Chinese had driven the UN and South Korean troops 75 to 100 miles below the 38th parallel. Seoul was lost for the second time on January 4, 1951.

For two years, the two sides fought bitterly to obtain strategic positions in the Korean hills, but neither side was able to make important advances.

> **A PERSONAL VOICE**
> Shortly after this we moved to Heartbreak Ridge. . . . Our trenches in that sector were only about 20 meters in front of theirs. We were eyeball to eyeball. Just 20 meters of no man's land between us. We couldn't move at all in the daytime without getting shot at. Machine-gun fire would come in, grenades, small-arms fire, all from within spitting distance. It was like World War I. We lived in a maze of bunkers and deep trenches. . . . There were bodies strewn all over the place. Hundred of bodies frozen in the snow. We could see the arms and legs sticking up. Nobody could get their dead out of there.
> **BEV SCOTT,** quoted in *No Bugles, No Drums: An Oral History of the Korean War*

First Lieutenant Bev Scott in 1951, at age 20

MACARTHUR RECOMMENDS ATTACKING CHINA To halt the bloody stalemate, in early 1951 MacArthur called for an extension of the war into China. He wanted to blockade the Chinese coast and use atomic bombs on China. He also wanted to use Chiang Kai-shek's troops to invade southern China.

Truman rejected MacArthur's requests. The president did not want the United States involved in a massive land war in Asia. As General Omar N. Bradley, chairman of the Joint Chiefs of Staff, said, an all-out conflict with China would be "the wrong war, at the wrong place, at the wrong time, and with the wrong enemy." Also, the Soviet Union had a mutual-assistance pact with China. Attacking China could set off World War III.

Instead of attacking China, the UN and South Korean forces began to advance once more, using the U.S. Eighth Army, led by Matthew B. Ridgway, as a spearhead. By March 1951, Ridgway had retaken Seoul and had moved back up to the 38th parallel. The situation was just what it had been before the fighting began.

MACARTHUR VERSUS TRUMAN Not satisfied with the recapture of South Korea, MacArthur continued to urge the waging of a full-scale war against China. Every time he raised the issue, the president or the Joint Chiefs of Staff told him that he was expected to fight only a limited war. Finding this intolerable, and certain that his views were correct, MacArthur tried to go over the president's head. He spoke and wrote privately to newspaper and magazine publishers and, especially, to Republican leaders.

Finally, Truman decided he could no longer tolerate MacArthur's insubordination. "Mr. Prima Donna, Brass Hat, Five Star MacArthur," as Truman had called him years earlier, could not be allowed to wrest control from the

> *"Mr. Prima Donna, Brass Hat, Five Star MacArthur."*
> **HARRY S. TRUMAN**

General MacArthur

THINK THROUGH HISTORY
D. Recognizing Effects How did the involvement of Communist China affect the course of the Korean War?

D. Answer It prevented the UN troops from overrunning all of North Korea and forced a stalemate in which North Korea remained Communist and South Korea remained non-Communist.

Cold War Conflicts **777**

(continued from page 776)

Extension Draw an outline map of Korea on the chalkboard. Have students take turns marking x's in different colors to show the advances and retreats of the two armies.

MORE ABOUT . . .
The Chinese in Korea
On October 25, 1950, South Korean troops encountered Chinese soldiers wearing North Korean uniforms. Not possible, said American general Walker. The Chinese are not involved in the Korean War—General MacArthur said so. A month later, 300,000 Chinese soldiers convinced even General Walker.

MORE ABOUT . . .
Beverly Scott
After his tour in Korea, Beverly Scott continued to serve the U.S. Army in duty stations around the world. In 1968, he served in yet another war—on the staff of the Army Inspector General in Vietnam.

MORE ABOUT . . .
The Firing of MacArthur
The firestorm of protest that swept the country when MacArthur was dismissed included an editorial in the *Chicago Tribune*: "President Truman must be impeached and convicted. . . . [He] is unfit, morally and mentally, for his high office."

IN-DEPTH RESOURCES: UNIT 7
American Lives: Douglas MacArthur, p. 53

 ELECTRONIC LIBRARY OF PRIMARY SOURCES
from *Reminiscences* by Douglas MacArthur

TEACHING OPTIONS

Exploring Themes

Constitutional Concerns Constitutional Concerns The Constitution of the United States clearly states that the president, as commander in chief of the armed forces, shall have final authority over their deployment. When General MacArthur disagreed with the president's waging a limited war, he went over Truman's head and took his appeal directly to the media and to Republican congressional leaders. The president would not tolerate this challenge to the constitutional authority of the executive branch and, despite MacArthur's tremendous popular support, Truman fired him.

Teaching Gifted and Talented Students

Analyzing MacArthur's Farewell Address to Congress
Ask students to read MacArthur's address to Congress and to analyze its skillful use of rhetorical devices. Tell them to look for the use of repetition, alliteration, and emotional appeals. Also ask students to evaluate the accuracy of statements in the speech. For example, MacArthur's claim that the Joint Chiefs of Staff "fully shared" his views was not true. What other statements were exaggerated or fake?

IN-DEPTH RESOURCES, UNIT 7
Primary Source: *from* MacArthur's Farewell Address to Congress, p. 14

Teacher's Edition **777**

Critical Thinking:
Comparing Ask students to compare the situation in Korea in 1953 with the situation in that country today. Discuss conditions under which the two countries might be united?

ASSESS & RETEACH

Section 2 Assessment

Have students answer the questions and then compare answers with another student. Ask the student pairs to find text passages to support their answers.

Self-Assessment

Have students make a time line of events of the Korean War to illustrate what they learned. Have them compare these time lines with the ones they created as they read the selection and note any omissions or discrepancies.

Section Quiz

FORMAL ASSESSMENT
Section Quiz, p. 252

Reteach

Review the map on page 770 to reinforce students' understanding of the Korean War.

CLOSE

A Communist victory in China caused deep concern in the United States over Communist influence around the world. When North Korea invaded South Korea, therefore, the U.S. sent ground troops, a military presence that would last more than 40 years.

---

constitutionally designated commander in chief. On April 11, 1951, with the unanimous approval of the Joint Chiefs of Staff, he relieved MacArthur of his command.

Many Americans were outraged over their hero's downfall. A public opinion poll showed that 69 percent of the American public backed General MacArthur. When MacArthur returned to the United States, New York welcomed him with a parade. The general gave an address to Congress, an honor usually awarded only to heads of government. Trying to gain sympathy, MacArthur said, "Old soldiers never die, they just fade away."

Throughout the fuss, Truman stayed in the background. After MacArthur's moment of public glory passed, the Truman administration began to make its case. Before a congressional committee investigating MacArthur's dismissal, a parade of witnesses argued the case for a limited war. The committee agreed with them. As a result, the public swung around to the view that Truman had done the right thing. As a political figure, MacArthur did indeed fade away.

SETTLING FOR STALEMATE As the MacArthur controversy died down, the Soviet Union unexpectedly suggested a cease-fire on June 23, 1951. Truce talks began in July 1951. By the following spring, the opposing sides had agreed on two points: the location of the cease-fire line at the existing battle line and the establishment of a demilitarized zone between the opposing sides. Negotiators spent another year wrangling over the exchange of prisoners. Finally, in July 1953, the two sides signed an armistice ending the war.

At best, the agreement was a stalemate. On the one hand, the North Korean invaders had been pushed back, and communism had been contained without a world war and without the use of atomic weapons, although America's threat to use them helped break the deadlock. On the other hand, Korea was still two nations rather than one.

Back on the home front, the war had affected the lives of ordinary Americans in many ways. It had cost 54,000 American lives and cost between $20 billion and $22 billion. The high cost of this unsuccessful war was one of many factors leading Americans to reject the Democratic Party in 1952 and to elect a Republican administration under Dwight D. Eisenhower. In addition, the Korean War increased fear of Communist aggression and prompted a hunt for spies on whom to blame Communist gains.

NOW & THEN

THE TWO KOREAS
Korea is still split into North Korea and South Korea, even after 50 years. South Korea is booming economically, while North Korea, still Communist, is struggling with shortages of food and energy.

Periodically, discussions about reuniting the two countries resume, but economic and political differences continue to keep them apart. In fact, in 1996 North Korea sent troops into the demilitarized zone, threatening South Korea's border. The United States still has 37,000 troops stationed in South Korea.

E. Answer
MacArthur wanted to use nuclear weapons and wage full-scale war; Truman wanted to limit the war.

THINK THROUGH HISTORY
E. Summarizing
How did Truman and MacArthur differ over strategy in the Korean War?

Section ❷ Assessment

1. TERMS & NAMES

Identify:
- Mao Zedong
- Chiang Kai-shek
- Taiwan (Formosa)
- 38th parallel
- Korean War

2. FOLLOWING CHRONOLOGICAL ORDER Create a time line of the major events of the Korean War, using a form such as the one below.

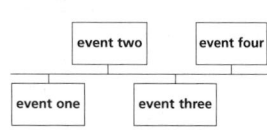

Choose two events on your time line and explain how one event led to the other.

3. HYPOTHESIZING If the Communists had lost the Chinese civil war, how might later events in Korea have been different?

THINK ABOUT
- how North Korean plans might have been different
- how American public opinion might have been different
- what might have happened when MacArthur's troops neared the North Korea–China border

4. FORMING OPINIONS Many Americans have questioned whether fighting the Korean War—a bloody war that ended in a stalemate—was worthwhile. What is your opinion? Why?

THINK ABOUT
- what the war cost in lives and material goods
- what might have happened if UN troops had stayed out of the conflict
- what might have happened if UN troops had waged full-scale war against China

778 Chapter 26

ANSWERS

1. TERMS AND NAMES

Mao Zedong, p. 773

Chiang Kai-shek, p. 773

Taiwan (Formosa), p. 774

38th parallel, p. 775

Korean War, p. 775

2. SEQUENCING HISTORY

1. 1948 Korea is split into two nations.
2. June 1950: North Korea invades South Korea.
3. June 1950: U.S. supports South Korea
4. Sept. 1950: North Korea captures most of Korea
5. Oct.1950: UN counterattack succeeds
6. Nov. 1950: Chinese troops enter war
7. July 1953: Armistice signed

3. HYPOTHESIZING

Possible Responses:

- North Korea, lacking a nearby supporter, might have been less aggressive.

- Americans might have been less worried about Communist expansion.

- China might have been less worried about an invasion.

4. FORMING OPINIONS

Possible Responses: Some stu-dents may say that the war wa not worthwhile because of the financial cost and the lost lives Others may say that the United States had to prevent the spre of communism. Without the presence of UN troops, North Korea might have conquered t South. War against China migh have brought Russia into the conflict and resulted in anothe world war.

The Cold War at Home

TERMS & NAMES
- HUAC
- Hollywood Ten
- blacklist
- Alger Hiss
- Ethel and Julius Rosenberg
- Senator Joseph McCarthy
- McCarthyism

LEARN ABOUT the Hollywood Ten, two famous spy cases, and Senator Joseph McCarthy
TO UNDERSTAND how and why fear of communism swept the nation.

ONE AMERICAN'S STORY

Tony Kahn made the neighbors uncomfortable because they thought his father, Gordon Kahn, was a Communist. In 1947, Gordon Kahn had been a successful screenwriter for almost 20 years. However, when a congressional committee began to investigate Communists in Hollywood, Kahn was blacklisted—named as too dangerous to hire. Later, in 1951, he was scheduled to testify before the committee himself.

To save himself, Kahn simply had to name others as Communists, but he refused. Rather than face the congressional committee, he fled to Mexico. Not only was Kahn's career ruined, but his wife and sons suffered from his being blacklisted for the next 25 years! Tony Kahn remembers how the Cold War hurt him and his family.

A PERSONAL VOICE
The first time I was called a Communist, I was four years old. . . . I'll never forget the look in our neighbors' eyes when I walked by. I thought it was hate. I was too young to realize it was fear.
TONY KAHN, from *The Cold War Comes Home*

The members of the Kahn family were among thousands of victims of the anti-Communist hysteria that gripped this country in the late 1940s and early 1950s. At first, only those in potentially influential positions were accused of being "Reds," or Communists. However, by the end of the period that some historians call the Great Fear, no one was safe from false charges.

Tony Kahn

 VIDEO *THE COLD WAR COMES HOME:* *Hollywood Blacklists the Kahn Family*

Fear of Communist Influence

In the early years of the Cold War, many Americans believed that there was good reason to be concerned about the security of the United States. The Soviet domination of Eastern Europe and the Communist takeover of China shocked the American public, fueling a fear that communism would spread around the world.

A. Answer The Soviet domination of Eastern Europe; the "loss" of China to communism.

In addition, several factors contributed to a growing suspicion of Communist influence within the United States. At the height of World War II, about 80,000 Americans claimed membership in the Communist Party; some people feared that these Communists' first loyalty was to the Soviet Union. In 1945, federal officials discovered that two State Department workers and one naval intelligence officer had stolen classified documents and passed them to a pro-Communist magazine. In the same year, a clerk at the Soviet embassy in Ottawa, Canada, defected to the West, bringing documents showing that a spy had been giving the Soviet Union secret information about the atomic bomb.

THINK THROUGH HISTORY
A. Analyzing Causes What were causes of the fear of communism in the U.S.?

As such incidents came to light, strongly anti-Communist Republicans began to accuse the Truman administration of being soft on communism. Personally, Truman thought that his critics were making too much of what one reporter called the "Communist bugaboo," but he recognized the need to answer them.

Cold War Conflicts **779**

SECTION 3 RESOURCES

 PRINT RESOURCES

IN-DEPTH RESOURCES: UNIT 7
Guided Reading, p. 41
Literature: from *The Nuclear Age* by Tim O'Brien, p. 50
American Lives: Margaret Chase Smith, p. 54

ACCESS FOR STUDENTS ACQUIRING ENGLISH
Guided Reading (Spanish), p. 257

FORMAL ASSESSMENT
Section Quiz, p. 319

ALTERNATIVE ASSESSMENT BOOK
See forms for supporting and scoring alternative activities.

 TECHNOLOGY RESOURCES

CD-ROM Electronic Library of Primary Sources

VIDEO *American Stories* video series: "The Cold War Comes Home"
American Portfolio: A Videodisc for U.S. History user's guide, p. 237

INTERNET McDougal Littell Learning On-Line
http://www.mcdougallittell.com

Section 3 Overview

OBJECTIVES
(1) To summarize government efforts to investigate the loyalty of U.S. citizens.
(2) To explain the spy cases of Alger Hiss and Ethel and Julius Rosenberg.
(3) To describe the efforts of Joseph McCarthy to purge the nation of communism.

SKILLBUILDERS
- Interpreting political cartoons, pp. 783, 784
- Interpreting charts, p. 784

CRITICAL THINKING
- Analyzing causes, pp. 779, 780, 783
- Summarizing, p. 784
- Making decisions, p. 784
- Role-playing history, p. 784

FOCUS & MOTIVATE

▶ *Starting with the Student*
Watch the video "The Cold War Comes Home" to find out how Cold War suspicions and fears affected a young boy and his family when his father was branded a Communist.

- Using the *Teacher's Resource Book* as a guide, explore the background of the Kahn family and hold a class discussion about the phenomenon of mass hysteria and paranoia.

 AMERICAN STORIES VIDEO SERIES
"The Cold War Comes Home"
Videocassette: Tape 4

Videodisc: Disc 3. Side A, Chapter 03

OBJECTIVE
(1) **INSTRUCT**

Fear of Communist Influence

▶ *Discussing Key Ideas*
- The Loyalty Review Board and HUAC begin investigations of U.S. citizens.

(continued on next page)

(continued from page 779)

- Witnesses from the film industry refuse to testify.
- Blacklists destroy many careers.

IN-DEPTH RESOURCES: UNIT 7
Guided Reading, p. 41

ACCESS FOR STUDENTS ACQUIRING ENGLISH
Guided Reading (Spanish), p. 257

HISTORICAL SPOTLIGHT
Paul Robeson

Critical Thinking:
Comparing Ask students to read an account of Paul Robeson's life in a book such as *Paul Robeson Speaks* by Philip S. Foner and then summarize Robeson's strong social and political activism. What parallels do students see in the lives of Gordon Kahn and Paul Robeson?

 ELECTRONIC LIBRARY OF PRIMARY SOURCES
Statement on Civil Liberties in America by Paul Robeson

MORE ABOUT . . .
Hollywood and Communism

In response to the HUAC investigations, Hollywood showed its cooperation by creating new guidelines for the industry. These included "Don't Smear the Free Enterprise System," "Don't Deify the Common Man," "Don't Show That Poverty Is a Virtue." In response, filmmakers produced such movies as *Iron Curtain* and *I Was a Communist for the FBI.*

HISTORICAL SPOTLIGHT

PAUL ROBESON

Paul Robeson was an all-American football player and Phi Beta Kappa member at Rutgers University. After earning a law degree in 1923, he entered on a distinguished international career as a singer and actor. (He is shown here playing Othello.) He was a vocal civil rights activist and a supporter of left-wing union activities, and he was sympathetic to the Soviet culture and political philosophy. In 1950, when he refused to sign an affidavit indicating whether he had ever been a member of the Communist Party, the State Department revoked his passport for seven years. During that time, he was unable to perform abroad and was blacklisted at home. His income fell from $150,000 to $3,000 a year.

LOYALTY REVIEW BOARD Consequently, in March 1947, President Truman issued an executive order setting up the Federal Employees Loyalty and Security Program, which included the Loyalty Review Board. Its purpose was to investigate government employees and to dismiss those who were found to be disloyal to the U.S. government. Exactly what constituted "disloyalty" was never clearly defined. The U.S. attorney general drew up a list of 91 "subversive" organizations; membership in any of these groups was grounds for suspicion.

From 1947 to 1951, government loyalty boards investigated 3.2 million employees and dismissed 212 as security risks. Another 2,900 resigned because they did not want to be investigated or felt that the investigation violated their constitutional rights. Individuals under investigation were not allowed to see the evidence against them—or even to know who had accused them of being disloyal.

THE HOUSE COMMITTEE ON UN-AMERICAN ACTIVITIES Other agencies investigated possible Communist influence, both inside and outside the U.S. government. One of the most famous of these was the House Committee on Un-American Activities (**HUAC**), which developed from a congressional committee created to search out disloyalty before World War II. HUAC first made headlines in 1947 when it began to investigate Communist influence in the movie industry.

Hollywood did have a substantial number of Communists, former Communists, and socialists. Furthermore, since the Soviet Union had been a U.S. ally during World War II, Hollywood studios had produced several pro-Soviet films. After 1945, when this wartime alliance cooled, some argued that such films proved that subversives were spreading Soviet propaganda. HUAC wanted to rid Hollywood of these suspected Communist influences.

THE HOLLYWOOD TEN For these reasons, HUAC subpoenaed 43 witnesses from the Hollywood film industry in September 1947. Many of the witnesses were "friendly," supporting the accusation that Communists had infiltrated the film industry. For example, the movie star Gary Cooper said he had "turned down quite a few scripts because I thought they were tinged with Communistic ideas." However, when asked which scripts he meant, Cooper couldn't remember their titles.

THINK THROUGH HISTORY
B. Analyzing Causes Why was Hollywood a target of anti-Communist investigations by Congress?
B. Answer Hollywood contained a number of Communists and other left-wingers, and its studios had produced several pro-Soviet movies during World War II.

Protesters demonstrate in support of the Hollywood Ten.

TEACHING OPTIONS

Exploring Themes

Constitutional Concerns HUAC's attempts to remove persons with "un-American" views from the entertainment industry raised significant constitutional issues. The investigations by HUAC and later by Senator Joseph McCarthy seemed to clash with constitutional rights to freedom of speech and freedom of assembly, and of accused persons to be fully informed of the nature of accusations against them. The investigations continued despite protests by the Hollywood Ten and other prominent Americans.

Making Connections Across the Curriculum

U.S. Government Either house of Congress can set up a select committee, a group established for a specific, and often limited, purpose. The House Committee on Un-American Activities, like other select committees of Congress, did have investigative powers. Another famous select committee was formed to investigate the presidential campaign of Richard M. Nixon in 1972. Known as the Watergate Committee, its investigations were every bit as sensational as those of HUAC and resulted in the only presidential resignation in U.S. history.

Ten "unfriendly" witnesses eventually testified. These men, known as the **Hollywood Ten,** decided not to cooperate with the committee because they believed that the hearings were unconstitutional. Because the Hollywood Ten refused to answer the committee's questions, they were sent to prison.

In response to the hearings, Hollywood executives instituted a **blacklist,** a list of people whom they in effect condemned for having a Communist background. People who were blacklisted—approximately 500 actors, writers, producers, and directors—had their careers ruined because they could no longer work in films.

THE McCARRAN ACT As Hollywood tried to rid itself of Communists, Congress decided that Truman's Loyalty Review Board did not go far enough in protecting the nation's security. In 1950, it passed the McCarran Internal Security Bill. This made it unlawful to plan any action that might lead to the establishment of a totalitarian dictatorship in the United States. Truman vetoed the bill, saying, "In a free country, we punish men for the crimes they commit, but never for the opinions they hold." But Congress enacted the law over Truman's veto.

Spy Cases Stun the Nation

Two spy cases added to fear that was spreading like an epidemic across the country. One case involved a former State Department official named **Alger Hiss.**

ALGER HISS In 1948, a former Communist spy, Whittaker Chambers, accused Hiss of spying for the Soviet Union. To support his charges, Chambers produced microfilm of government documents that he claimed had been typed on Hiss's typewriter. Too many years had passed for government prosecutors to charge Hiss with espionage, but a jury convicted him of perjury—for lying about passing the documents—and sent him to jail. A young conservative Republican congressman named Richard Nixon gained fame for pursuing the charges against Hiss. Within four years of the highly publicized case, Nixon was elected vice-president of the United States.

Hiss claimed that he was innocent and that Chambers had forged the documents used against him. However, in the 1990s, Soviet cables released by the National Security Agency seemed to prove Hiss's guilt.

THE ROSENBERGS Another spy case rocked the nation even more than the Hiss case, partially because of international events occurring about the same time. On September 23, 1949, Americans learned that the Soviet Union had exploded an atomic bomb. Most American experts had predicted that it would take the Soviets three to five more years to figure out how to make the bomb, and people began to wonder if the Soviets had stolen the secret of the bomb.

This second spy case seemed to confirm that suspicion. In 1950, the British physicist Klaus Fuchs admitted giving the Soviet Union information about America's atomic bomb. The information probably enabled Soviet scientists to develop their own atomic bomb 18 months earlier than they would have otherwise. Implicated in the Fuchs case were **Ethel and Julius Rosenberg,** minor activists in the American Communist Party.

The Rosenbergs denied the charges against them and pleaded the Fifth Amendment, choosing not to incriminate themselves, when asked if they were Communists. They claimed they were being persecuted both for being Jewish and for holding radical beliefs. The Rosenbergs were found guilty and given the

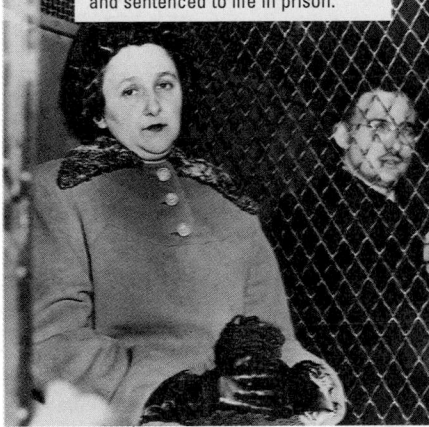

NOW & THEN

SPIES

Spying is still an active business in both the United States and Russia. In February 1994, Aldrich Ames was arrested for spying. Ames was a "mole" within the CIA who turned over to the Russians the names of all the important U.S. spies at work in Russia, causing ten CIA agents to be executed and others to be imprisoned. Ames was convicted and sentenced to life in prison.

Ethel and Julius Rosenberg were executed in June 1953 despite numerous pleas to spare their lives.

Cold War Conflicts 781

OBJECTIVE
② INSTRUCT

Spy Cases Stun the Nation

▶ *Discussing Key Ideas*
• Alger Hiss and Ethel and Julius Rosenberg are convicted of spying for the Soviet Union.
• The Rosenbergs are put to death in the face of worldwide protests.

NOW & THEN
Spies

Critical Thinking: Synthesizing Spying is an ancient occupation. Ask students to investigate the activities of famous spies in history, such as Nathan Hale, Mata Hari, Francis Walsingham, and Allan Pinkerton. Have students share their findings with the class.

MORE ABOUT . . .
Alger Hiss

A Soviet intelligence cable from March 1945 was released by the U.S. National Security Agency in March 1996, about six months before Hiss died. The cable supports the claim that he was a Soviet agent. It points out that because Hiss was a member of the American delegation to Yalta as an aide to the U.S. secretary of state, he was especially valuable to the Soviets. Hiss maintained his innocence until the end of his life, however.

TEACHING OPTION

 Cooperative Activity: Examining the Rosenberg Case

Task: Pairs of students will investigate and report on various aspects of the Rosenberg case.

Purpose: To make students aware of the powerful effect of public opinion on the government and the justice system.

Activity: Create a grab bag of questions to guide students' examination of the Rosenberg case. You might include questions such as these: What was the case against the Rosenbergs? What defense did they use? What was the political climate at the time? Why was

the punishment so severe? Have students draw a question and research and write their answers in the form of a report. They can collaborate on the tasks or divide the research and writing. Have students present their reports in an order that sets the stage for and follows the development of the case.

📁 *Building a Portfolio:* Students who add reports to their portfolios should include a note indicating their contribution.

ALTERNATIVE ASSESSMENT BOOK
Standards for Evaluating a Cooperative Activity

Standards for Evaluation
Reports should . . .

• show clear understanding of the question being answered
• use several sources for information
• use concrete examples from the Rosenberg case to support ideas

Teacher's Edition 781

death penalty. In pronouncing their sentence, Judge Irving Kaufman declared their crime "worse than murder." To him, they were directly responsible for one of the deadliest clashes of the Cold War.

A PERSONAL VOICE
I believe your conduct in putting into the hands of the Russians the A-bomb years before our best scientists predicted Russia would perfect the bomb has already caused, in my opinion, the Communist aggression in Korea.

IRVING KAUFMAN, quoted in *The Unquiet Death of Julius and Ethel Rosenberg*

People from all over the world appealed for clemency. Many considered the evidence and the testimony too weak to be used to deprive two people of their lives. The case was appealed to the U.S. Supreme Court, but the court

NOW & THEN

Television: Making the News

Since the 1950s, television not only has become a major vehicle for reporting the news but has increasingly helped to create it. In fact, TV networks themselves made news at the Republican National Convention in August 1996. The networks chose to limit their coverage because they thought that fuller coverage would merely constitute an extended advertisement for the party, which had already chosen its candidates. The shift away from news to "infotainment" that the networks were protesting is a sign of the fierce competition among a bewildering variety of network and cable alternatives. This "media muddle" promises to blur even further the already indistinct line between reporting the news and making it.

Robert Dole and Jack Kemp accept the presidential and vice-presidential nominations at the 1996 Republican National Convention.

1954
The power of television not only to report the news but actually to make it became apparent in 1954. In that year the Communist-hunting senator Joseph McCarthy, in U.S. Senate hearings that were televised live, accused the U.S. Army of coddling Communists. As many as 20 million Americans watched the combative senator bully witnesses and slander people who had no chance to defend themselves. McCarthy's televised antics had finally thrust him into the villain's role.

1967
By 1967, with a television set in virtually every household in America, nightly news broadcasts had become established as a powerful influence on public opinion. For example, American support for the Vietnam War plummeted as millions of viewers saw Vietnamese civilians mutilated by U.S. bombs and chemical sprays. When Walter Cronkite, a CBS newscaster, announced in 1968 the likelihood that "a bloody experience of Vietnam" would end in a stalemate, President Lyndon Johnson admitted, "If I've lost Walter, then it's over."

INTERACT WITH HISTORY

refused to overturn the conviction. Julius and Ethel Rosenberg died in the electric chair in June 1953, leaving behind two young sons. They became the first U.S. civilians executed for espionage. Even many of those who formerly believed in their innocence have been convinced of their guilt by evidence contained in the same Soviet cables that implicated Hiss.

McCarthy Launches a "Witch Hunt"

The most famous anti-Communist activist was **Senator Joseph McCarthy** of Wisconsin. During his first three years in the Senate, he had acquired a reputation for being ineffective. By January 1950, he realized that he was going to need a winning issue in order to be reelected in 1952. Looking around for such an issue, McCarthy decided to sound the alarm about Communists in government.

MCCARTHY'S TACTICS Taking advantage of people's concerns about communism, soon McCarthy was making one unsupported accusation after another. At various times he claimed to have in his hands the names of 57, 81, and 205 Communists in the State Department. (He never actually produced even a single name.) McCarthy charged that the Democratic Party was guilty of "20 years of treason" for allowing Communist infiltration.

McCarthy's techniques, became known as **McCarthyism.** When challenged, he would respond by making another accusation. However, he was always careful to do his name-calling only in the Senate, where he had legal immunity that protected him from being sued for slander.

The Republicans did little to stop McCarthy's attacks because they believed they would win the 1952 presidential election if the public saw them purging the nation of Communist influences. At the beginning of McCarthy's anti-Communist campaign, one small group of six senators did speak out, led by Senator Margaret Chase Smith of Maine.

> **A PERSONAL VOICE**
> I speak as a Republican. I speak as a woman. I speak as a United States Senator. I speak as an American. . . . I am not proud of the way in which the Senate has been made a publicity platform for irresponsible sensationalism. I am not proud of the reckless abandon in which unproved charges have been hurled from this side of the aisle.
> **MARGARET CHASE SMITH**, "Declaration of Conscience"

MCCARTHY'S DOWNFALL Finally, in 1954, McCarthy made accusations against the U.S. Army, which resulted in a nationally televised

"IT'S OKAY – WE'RE HUNTING COMMUNISTS."

SKILLBUILDER
INTERPRETING POLITICAL CARTOONS
What does this cartoon imply about the methods and tactics of HUAC?

Skillbuilder Answer
Possible Answer: That the committee was reckless and displayed little concern that innocent people might be harmed.

OBJECTIVE
③ INSTRUCT

McCarthy Launches a "Witch Hunt"

▶ **Discussing Key Ideas**
• Senator Joseph McCarthy makes widely publicized attacks on suspected Communists in the U.S. government.
• Televised coverage of his bullying tactics lead to his downfall.

HISTORY FROM VISUALS
Political Cartoon

Reading the Cartoon Ask students why the HUAC car is driving over pedestrians. *The committee showed no regard for citizens' rights.*

Extension Ask students how they might illustrate the same idea.

MORE ABOUT . . .
Joseph McCarthy

McCarthy's executive secretary was Mary Brinkley Driscoll, sister of David Brinkley, the television news commentator. Years later, David Brinkley asked his sister what McCarthy was holding when he made his famous accusation that 205 Communists were working for the State Department. Mary replied, "He had a few scribbled notes to use in his speech. Nothing about Communists." She confirmed that McCarthy made up the number to get publicity.

IN-DEPTH RESOURCES: UNIT 7
American Lives: Margaret Chase Smith, p. 54

1974
The Watergate scandal that toppled Richard Nixon's presidency in 1974 played to a rapt TV audience. During the Senate hearings in 1973, the televised testimony of John Dean, the president's counsel, had convinced two out of three Americans that the president had committed a crime by planning or covering up the Watergate break-in. The House Judiciary Committee delayed its final deliberations on Nixon's impeachment until prime TV time, allowing the maximum number of people to watch.

TEACHING OPTION

Cooperative Activity: Investigating Witch Hunts

Task: Groups of three to four students will investigate either Senator McCarthy's crusade against Communists in the 1950s or the witch trials in Salem, Massachusetts, in 1692. Each group will report their findings to the class.

Purpose: To explore the impact of widespread public fears and hysteria on the lives of people and institutions.

Activity: Each group of students will research the assigned topic through the use of various library resources or the Internet. Reports should include a description of the actual events of the time, the accusations made, the type of evidence presented, and a description of the witch trials or of the Senate hearings. Students should draw conclusions about why waves of fear in these cases swept away reason and what could be done to prevent such situations in the future.

ALTERNATIVE ASSESSMENT BOOK
Standards for Evaluating a Cooperative Activity

Reading the Chart Show
students that the chart lists
general causes and effects
and does not imply links
between them.

Extension Ask students to
suggest possible links
between the causes and
effects listed.

**HISTORY FROM
VISUALS**
Political Cartoon

Reading the Cartoon Who
is the person pictured in the
cartoon? *Senator McCarthy.*
What does the web he is
entangled in represent? *The
accusations and lies that
were his downfall.*

Extension Have students
draw their own cartoons
about McCarthy.

ASSESS & RETEACH

Section 3 Assessment

Ask students to work in
pairs or small groups to
answer the questions.

Self-Assessment

Have students explore their
understanding of anti-
Communist feelings by creating a two-column chart in
which they list the actions
taken against suspected
Communists and the results
of those actions.

Section Quiz

FORMAL ASSESSMENT
Section Quiz, p. 319

Reteach

Repeat the video "The Cold
War Comes Home," and dis-
cuss the Cold War issues
raised by the film.

**AMERICAN STORIES VIDEO
SERIES**
"The Cold War Comes Home"

CLOSE

As communism spread
around the world, spy cases
and election-year politicking
led to rising anti-Communist
fears in the U.S. The resulting investigations damaged
careers and silenced responsible debate.

784 Chapter 26

Causes and Effects of McCarthyism

CAUSES	EFFECTS
• Soviets successfully establish Communist regimes in Eastern Europe after World War II. • Soviets develop the atomic bomb more quickly than expected. • Korean War ends in a stalemate. • Republicans gain politically by accusing Truman and Democrats of being soft on communism.	• Millions of Americans are forced to take loyalty oaths and undergo loyalty investigations. • Activism by labor unions goes into decline. • Many people are hesitant to speak out on public issues for fear they will be accused of having Communist leanings. • Anticommunism continues to drive U.S. foreign policy.

SKILLBUILDER INTERPRETING CHARTS *How did world events help lead to McCarthyism? How did McCarthyism affect the behavior of individual Americans?*

I CAN'T DO THIS TO ME!

**SKILLBUILDER
INTERPRETING
POLITICAL CARTOONS**
*What does this cartoon
suggest about
McCarthy's downfall?*
Skillbuilder Answer
Possible Answer: That he
caused his own downfall.

Senate investigation. McCarthy's bullying of witnesses alienated the audience and cost him public support. The Senate condemned him for improper conduct that tended "to bring the Senate into disrepute." Three years later McCarthy died a broken man, suffering from the effects of alcoholism.

OTHER ANTI-COMMUNISTS Others besides Joseph McCarthy made it their mission to root communism out of American society. By 1953, 39 states had passed laws making it illegal to advocate the violent overthrow of the government, even though such laws clearly violated the constitutional right of free speech. Across the nation, cities and towns passed similar laws.

At times, the fear of communism seemed to have no limits. In Indiana, professional wrestlers had to take a loyalty oath. In experiments run by newspapers, pedestrians on the street refused to sign petitions that quoted the Declaration of Independence because they were afraid the ideas were Communist. The government investigated union leaders, librarians, newspaper reporters, and scientists. It seemed that no profession was safe from the Red hunt. The FBI even interviewed a Washington, D.C., bootblack 70 times before deciding he could shine shoes in the Pentagon.

During this era many Americans tried so hard to root out communism that they were sometimes willing to compromise their own freedom. But even those measures did not stop the escalation of the Cold War.

*Skillbuilder
Answer*
World Events:
Soviet success
in Europe, the
Soviet develop-
ment of the
atomic bomb, and
the Korean War
stalemate
heightened fear
of communism.
Behavior:
McCarthyism led
to required loyalty
oaths, hesitancy
to speak out on
issues, and
decreased
activism by labor
unions.

Section 3 Assessment

1. TERMS & NAMES

Identify:
• HUAC
• Hollywood Ten
• blacklist
• Alger Hiss
• Ethel and Julius Rosenberg
• Senator Joseph McCarthy
• McCarthyism

2. SUMMARIZING Recreate the web below on your paper and fill in events that illustrate the main idea in the center.

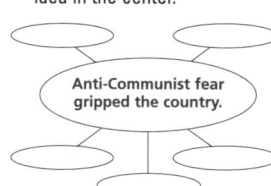

Anti-Communist fear gripped the country.

3. MAKING DECISIONS If you had lived in this period and been accused of being a Communist, what would you have done?

THINK ABOUT
• the Hollywood Ten, who refused to answer questions
• the Rosenbergs, who pleaded the Fifth Amendment
• those who informed on others to save themselves

4. ROLE-PLAYING HISTORY Get together with three classmates, with each group member playing one of the following roles: Harry Truman, a member of HUAC, Judge Irving Kaufman, and Joseph McCarthy. As the person you have chosen, explain your motivation for opposing communism.

784 CHAPTER 26

ANSWERS

1. TERMS & NAMES
HUAC, p. 780
Hollywood Ten, p. 781
blacklist, p. 781
Alger Hiss, p. 781
Ethel and Julius Rosenberg, p. 781
Senator Joseph McCarthy, p. 783
McCarthyism, p. 783

2. SUMMARIZING
Events
1. HUAC investigated "un-American" activity in Hollywood.
2. Congress passes the McCarran Act.
3. Spy cases increase fears.
4. McCarthy arouses fears of a Communist conspiracy.

3. MAKING DECISIONS
Possible Responses: Some students may say they might have refused to name others because that is the honorable thing to do. Others may say they would have shown their loyalty to the government by answering the committee's questions.

4. ROLE-PLAYING HISTOR
Possible Responses: Although motivations will vary, the basic reasons for opposing communism during this period were based on the aggression of the Soviet Union in taking over countries in Eastern Europe ar in the fact that Soviet leaders were opposed to democracy, system Americans had fought establish and preserve.

TERMS & NAMES
- H-bomb
- Dwight D. Eisenhower
- John Foster Dulles
- brinkmanship
- CIA
- Warsaw Pact
- Nikita Khrushchev
- Eisenhower Doctrine
- Francis Gary Powers
- U-2 incident

④ Two Nations Live on the Edge

LEARN ABOUT the arms race, the spread of the Cold War, and the U-2 incident
TO UNDERSTAND how tensions grew between the United States and the Soviet Union.

ONE AMERICAN'S STORY

Annie Dillard was one of thousands of children who grew up in the 1950s with the chilling knowledge that nuclear war could obliterate their world in an instant. Dillard recalls practicing what to do in case of a nuclear attack.

A PERSONAL VOICE

At school, we had air-raid drills. We took the drills seriously; surely Pittsburgh, which had the nation's steel, coke, and aluminum, would be the enemy's first target....When the air-raid siren sounded, our teachers stopped talking and led us to the school basement. There the gym teachers lined us up against the cement walls and steel lockers, and showed us how to lean in and fold our arms over our heads....The teachers stood in the middle of the room, not talking to each other. We tucked against the walls and lockers....We folded our skinny arms over our heads, and raised to the enemy a clatter of gold scarab bracelets and gold bangle bracelets.

ANNIE DILLARD, *An American Childhood*

The fear of nuclear attack was a direct result of the Cold War. After the Soviet Union developed its atomic bomb, the two superpowers embarked on an arms race that enormously increased both the number and the destructive power of weapons.

A father helps his daughter practice getting into a bomb shelter.

Brinkmanship Rules U.S. Policy

Although air-raid drills were not common until the Eisenhower years (1953–1961), the nuclear arms race began during Truman's presidency. When the Soviet Union exploded its first atomic bomb in 1949, President Truman had to make a terrible decision—whether to develop an even more horrifying weapon.

RACE FOR THE H-BOMB The scientists who had developed the atomic bomb, in which atoms were split, had suspected since 1942 that it was possible to create a hydrogen, or thermonuclear, bomb in which atoms would be fused. They estimated that such a bomb would have the force of 1 million tons of TNT (67 times the power of the bomb dropped on Hiroshima). But they argued vehemently about the morality of creating such a destructive weapon. J. Robert Oppenheimer, head of the atomic-bomb team, opposed the new project. Referring to his role in creating the weapon used on Japan, Oppenheimer told Truman, "Mr. President, I have blood on my hands."

However, political forces soon took over the decision. The Soviet Union's successful explosion of an atomic bomb took away the U.S. nuclear advantage. Politicians and military leaders pressed for a more powerful weapon, warning that the United States had to develop one before the Soviets did. On January 31, 1950, Truman authorized work on the hydrogen bomb, or **H-bomb.**

On November 1, 1952, the United States exploded the first thermonuclear device. The blast far exceeded initial estimates, delivering a force equal to 10.4 million tons of TNT. However, the new American advantage lasted less than a year, for in August 1953 the Soviets exploded their own thermonuclear weapon.

Cold War Conflicts **785**

SECTION 4 RESOURCES

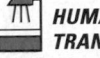

PRINT RESOURCES

IN-DEPTH RESOURCES: UNIT 7
Guided Reading, p. 42
Primary Source: *from* Dwight D. Eisenhower's statement on the U-2 incident, p. 49

ACCESS FOR STUDENTS ACQUIRING ENGLISH
Guided Reading (Spanish), p. 258

FORMAL ASSESSMENT
Section Quiz, p. 320

ALTERNATIVE ASSESSMENT
See forms for supporting and scoring alternative activities.

TECHNOLOGY RESOURCES

HUMANITIES TRANSPARENCIES
H25, California bomb shelter, 1951
H41, Political Cartoon

CRITICAL THINKING TRANSPARENCIES
CT26, The Cold War

CD-ROM *Grolier Multimedia Encyclopedia*
Electronic Library of Primary Sources

VIDEO *American Portfolio: A Videodisc for U.S. History,*
user's guide, pp. 234–241

INTERNET McDougal Littell Learning On-Line
http://www.mcdougallittell.com

Section 4 Overview

OBJECTIVES

① To explain the policy of brinkmanship.

② To describe the U.S. and Soviet actions that caused the Cold War to spread around the world.

③ To summarize the impact of *Sputnik* and the U-2 incident on the United States.

SKILLBUILDERS

- Understanding geography: region, p. 787
- Interpreting graphs, p. 788

CRITICAL THINKING

- Analyzing causes, p. 786
- Summarizing, pp. 786, 787, 789
- Recognizing effects, p. 788
- Hypothesizing, p. 789
- Evaluating, p. 789
- Analyzing, p. 789

FOCUS & MOTIVATE

▶ *Starting with the Student*
- Ask students how they react when they feel threatened?
- Do they think those same reactions apply to nations? Why or why not?

OBJECTIVE
① INSTRUCT

Brinkmanship Rules U.S. Policy

▶ *Discussing Key Ideas*
- In a nuclear race with the Soviet Union, the United States develops a hydrogen bomb.
- The U.S. policy of brinkmanship further accelerates the Cold War.

IN-DEPTH RESOURCES: UNIT 7
Guided Reading, p. 42

ACCESS FOR STUDENTS ACQUIRING ENGLISH
Guided Reading (Spanish), p. 258

🏛 *HUMANITIES TRANSPARENCIES*
H25, California bomb shelter, 1951

💿 *ELECTRONIC LIBRARY OF PRIMARY SOURCES*
Life in a Shelter by Tomas E. Dutwa

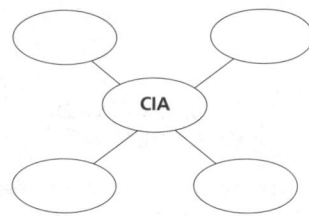
"You have to take chances for peace, just as you must take chances in war. . . . If you are scared to go to the brink, you are lost."

JOHN FOSTER DULLES

THE POLICY OF BRINKMANSHIP By the time both countries had the H-bomb, **Dwight D. Eisenhower** was president. His secretary of state, **John Foster Dulles,** was staunchly anti-Communist. He also viewed compromise as immoral. Winston Churchill once said of him, "Mr. Dulles makes a speech every day, holds a press conference every other day, and preaches on Sunday."

Dulles proposed a new policy based on threats of massive retaliation. The United States would, in effect, keep the peace by promising to use all its force, including nuclear weapons, against any aggressor nation. This willingness to go to the brink, or edge, of war became known as **brinkmanship.** Because Dulles's policy required greater dependence on nuclear weapons and the airplanes that delivered them, the United States trimmed its army and navy but beefed up its air force and produced massive numbers of nuclear weapons.

The arms race began in earnest when the Soviet Union answered this development by also producing huge quantities of nuclear bombs. As a result, many American citizens became convinced that Soviet weapons were aimed directly at their cities. Schoolchildren like Annie Dillard practiced air-raid procedures, and some families built underground fallout shelters in their back yards. Fear of nuclear war became a constant in American life for 30 years.

The Cold War Spreads Around the World

As the nation shifted to a dependence on nuclear arms, the Eisenhower administration began to rely heavily on the recently formed Central Intelligence Agency (**CIA**) for information. The CIA used spies to gather information abroad. The CIA also began to carry out covert actions, or secret operations, to weaken or overthrow governments unfriendly to the United States.

COVERT ACTIONS IN THE MIDDLE EAST AND LATIN AMERICA The Eisenhower administration believed that the struggle against communism was similar to the fight against totalitarian governments in World War II. The leader of the Soviet Union, an absolute dictator, ordered secret operations against his enemies. Eisenhower feared that the United States would be at a disadvantage if it did not also carry out covert actions.

One of the CIA's first covert actions took place in the Middle East. In 1951, Iran's prime minister, Mohammed Mossadegh, placed the oil industry under the government's control. To protest, the Western nations stopped buying Iranian oil. As the Iranian economy faltered, the United States feared that Mossadegh might turn to the Soviets for help. In 1953, the CIA persuaded the shah, the monarch of Iran, to replace Mossadegh with someone more favorable to the West. The people remained loyal to the shah, and the prime minister fled.

In 1954, the CIA also took covert actions in Guatemala, a Central American country just south of Mexico. Eisenhower believed that Guatemala's government, headed by Jacobo Arbenz Guzmán, had Communist sympathies because it had given more than 200,000 acres of American-owned land to peasants. In response, the CIA trained an army, which invaded Guatemala and captured Arbenz Guzmán and his forces. The army's leader, Carlos Castillo Armas, became dictator of the country.

A SUMMIT IN GENEVA In spite of the growing tension between the superpowers, U.S.-Soviet relations seemed to thaw following the death of Joseph Stalin in 1953. The Soviets recognized West Germany and concluded peace treaties with Austria and Japan. However, in 1955, when West Germany was allowed to rearm and join NATO, the Soviet Union grew fearful. It formed its own military alliance, called the **Warsaw Pact,** with the Eastern European satellite nations under its control.

In July 1955, Eisenhower traveled to Geneva, Switzerland, to meet with Soviet leaders for the first East-West summit conference since World War II.

There Eisenhower put forth an "open skies" proposal. The United States and the Soviet Union would allow flights over each other's territory to guard against surprise nuclear attacks. The Soviet Union rejected this proposal, fearing it was a U.S. trick to learn where the Soviets were keeping their weapons.

Even though the summit accomplished nothing specific, the world hailed the "spirit of Geneva" that seemed to promise movement toward peace. However, hope that the Cold War was easing was short-lived, as the Soviet Union turned aggressor a year later.

The Warsaw Pact and NATO, 1955

Warsaw Pact countries
NATO members, 1955
Nonaligned nations

FINLAND
NORWAY
SWEDEN
IRELAND
DEN.
GREAT BRITAIN
NETH.
E. GER.
SOVIET UNION
BELGIUM
W. GER.
POLAND
LUX.
ATLANTIC OCEAN
FRANCE
CZECH.
SWITZ.
AUSTRIA
HUNGARY
PORTUGAL
YUGOSLAVIA
ROMANIA
SPAIN
ITALY
BULGARIA
ALBANIA
Mediterranean Sea
GREECE
TURKEY

GEOGRAPHY SKILLBUILDER
REGION Which nations shown on the map belonged to NATO, and which to the Warsaw Pact?
REGION Which nations shown on the map belonged to neither defense alliance?

CRISIS IN THE MIDDLE EAST

Although the United States and the Soviet Union had agreed on establishing the nation of Israel in 1948, the Cold War affected the Middle East as well as Europe. In 1955, Great Britain and the United States agreed to help Egypt finance construction of a dam at Aswan on the Nile River. When Gamal Abdel Nasser, the head of Egypt, delayed, the United States and Great Britain withdrew their offer. Angered, Nasser seized the Suez Canal, which is located in Egypt but was owned by France and Great Britain.

The British and the French were furious. Israel was also angry at Egypt, which had been making terrorist raids into its territory. Joining forces, Great Britain, France, and Israel invaded Egypt, the Soviets' ally, in October 1956. When the Soviets threatened to use missiles against Britain and France, the United States warned that it would not tolerate such action. Direct confrontation with the Soviet Union was avoided when the UN imposed a cease-fire. The canal reopened in April 1957 under Egyptian management.

SOVIET AGGRESSION IN HUNGARY

In February 1956, **Nikita Khrushchev,** head of the Soviet Communist Party, publicly criticized his predecessor, Stalin, for having committed crimes against the Soviet people. Such open criticism of the previous regime made people around the world wonder if the Soviet Union was becoming a less repressive country. Some Eastern European nations began to dream of breaking free of Soviet control.

One such nation, Hungary, had experienced several years of unrest as the country's leaders clashed over how much freedom to grant Hungarians. The Soviets had occupied the country and Hungarians had made several efforts to oust them. In October 1956, students and workers tried to force the more repressive leaders out of office. Khrushchev agreed that the reform-minded leader Imre Nagy should be premier.

After the Soviet army had been forced to leave the country, the Hungarians demanded other liberties, including the right to leave the Warsaw Pact. Moscow responded brutally. In November 1956, Soviet tanks rolled into Hungary and killed approximately 30,000 Hungarian protesters. Thousands of refugees fled, many to the United States. Eisenhower provided no military aid, but protested the invasion, sent Hungary $20 million for food and medicine, authorized another $5 million to go to the UN to aid Hungarian refugees, and allowed more Hungarians to enter the country.

ON THE WORLD STAGE

Mediterranean Sea
SYRIA
LEBANON
EGYPT
ISRAEL
JORDAN
Red Sea
SAUDI ARABIA

ISRAEL

On May 14, 1948, the United Nations created the nation of Israel by partitioning Palestine into two states, one Jewish and one Arab. Thousands of Jews had immigrated to Palestine from Europe before and during World War II, and Israel became the "promised land" they had been seeking since biblical times. The creation of Israel was one of the few issues that the United States and the Soviet Union agreed on, as the world reacted uniformly to the horror that had befallen the Jews in the Holocaust.

Cold War Conflicts **787**

The Cold War Takes to the Skies

▶ **Starting with the Student**
The launching of *Sputnik* resulted in improved science education in the U.S. Do students think their science courses today reflect a national push for strong science education? Why or why not?

▶ **Discussing Key Ideas**
• Soviet success in launching the first space satellite shocks the United States.
• The United States successfully launches a space satellite and improves science education.
• Relations between the United States and the Soviet Union worsen after the Soviets down a U.S. spy plane.

GROLIER MULTIMEDIA ENCYCLOPEDIA
Soviet-Russian manned spaceflight

HUMANITIES TRANSPARENCIES
H41, Political Cartoon

HISTORY FROM VISUALS
U.S. Defense Budget 1940–1990

Reading the Graphs
Remind students that the first three graphs cover the Cold War period. The last one provides a recent comparison.

Extension Ask students to check an almanac or a statistical abstract to find a more recent figure for defense spending. How does it compare with other figures in the graph? *1996—16.9% (estimated).*

THE EISENHOWER DOCTRINE The Soviet Union's prestige in the Middle East rose because of its support for Egypt. To counterbalance this development, President Eisenhower issued a warning in January 1957. This warning, known as the **Eisenhower Doctrine,** said that the United States would defend the Middle East against attack by any Communist country. In March, Congress officially approved the doctrine. It gave the president authority to use American forces, at his discretion, against armed aggression in the Middle East by any nation "controlled by international communism."

The Cold War Takes to the Skies

The Cold War was not limited to political matters; it also affected science and education. The United States began 1957 confident that it was ahead of the Soviets in military technology. It had guided missiles that could deliver nuclear warheads with great accuracy at distances of 1,500 to 3,000 miles. Then, in August 1957, the Soviets announced that they had developed a rocket capable of traveling much greater distances—a true ICBM, or intercontinental ballistic missile.

SPUTNIK LAUNCHES THE SPACE RACE The real shock came on October 4, when the Soviets used an ICBM to push the first unmanned artificial satellite above the friction of the earth's atmosphere. There the satellite, the first Sputnik, traveled around the earth at 18,000 miles per hour, circling the globe every 96.2 minutes. Its weight of nearly 200 pounds indicated that 1.1 million pounds of thrust had been used to lift it into orbit—more than enough to deliver a nuclear warhead from the Soviet Union to any target in the world.

The launching of *Sputnik I* made many Americans feel inferior to the Soviets and vulnerable to nuclear attack. The United States seemed to be falling behind in science and technology. To try to solve the apparent problem, the United States made changes in its educational system. Schools sought to improve their science, mathematics, and foreign-language courses.

In addition, U.S. scientists worked frantically to catch up to the Soviets. The first attempt at an American satellite launch was a humiliating failure, with the rocket toppling to the ground. The press labeled it "Flopnik" and "Stayputnik." However, on January 31, 1958, the United States successfully launched its first satellite. The race to launch bigger satellites—and develop better weapons-delivery systems—was on.

A U-2 IS SHOT DOWN Following the rejection of Eisenhower's "open skies" proposal at the 1955 Geneva summit conference, the CIA began making secret high-altitude flights over Soviet territory. The plane used for these missions, the U-2, was designed to fly higher than Soviet fighter planes and beyond the reach of antiaircraft fire. As a U-2 passed over the USSR, its infrared cameras took detailed photographs.

By 1960, however, many U.S. officials were nervous about the U-2 program. First, the existence and purpose of the U-2 was an open secret among some members of the American press. Second, the Soviets had been aware of the flights since 1958, as **Francis Gary Powers,** a U-2 pilot, explained.

> **A PERSONAL VOICE**
> We . . . knew that the Russians were radar-tracking at least some of our flights. . . . We also knew that SAMs [surface-to-air missiles] were being fired at us, that some were uncomfortably close to our altitude. But we knew too that the Russians had a control problem in their guidance system. . . . We were concerned, but not greatly.
>
> **FRANCIS GARY POWERS,** from *Operation Overflight: The U-2 Spy Pilot Tells His Story for the First Time*

U.S. Defense Budget, 1940–1990

PERCENTAGE SPENT ON DEFENSE

18% 1940
32% 1950
52% 1960
24% 1990

Source: Historical Tables, Budget of the United States Government, Fiscal Year 1997

SKILLBUILDER INTERPRETING GRAPHS *By how much did the percentage of the federal budget spent on defense increase between 1950 and 1960? Why do you think it increased that much?*

Skillbuilder Answer
Budget: By 20%. Reason: *Possible Answer:* The arms race with the Soviet Union.

THINK THROUGH HISTORY
D. *Recognizing Effects What effect did the Cold War have on space exploration?*

D. Answer It accelerated the pace of exploration.

Exploring Themes

Science and Technology The brilliant scientific achievements that led to the creation of the atomic and hydrogen bombs also cast a shadow of impending nuclear holocaust over the 1950s. Misunderstanding and mistrust between the United States and the Soviet Union escalated into an arms race that drained national economies and instilled fear in people all over the world. Americans built bomb shelters, and air-raid drills became part of the school curriculum. Scientists, however, continued to develop peaceful applications of nuclear energy, such as computer tomography and magnetic resonance imaging.

Making Connections Across the Curriculum

Science In 1666, Isaac Newton imagined firing a cannonball from the top of a giant mountain. The faster the cannonball went, the farther it would travel before hitting the ground. At a high enough speed, the cannonball, which travels in a natural arc, wouldn't hit the ground at all because of the curvature of the earth. Discuss how scientists applied Newton's theory to the launching of satellites. *In the first stage of a satellite launch, the rocket is thrust high enough to escape the earth's gravitational pull. When it reaches a speed that counterbalances gravity, it is oriented to follow the curvature of the earth.*

Finally, Eisenhower himself wanted the flights discontinued. He and Khrushchev were going to hold another summit conference on the arms race on May 15, 1960. "If one of these aircraft were lost when we were engaged in apparently sincere deliberations, it could . . . ruin my effectiveness," he told an aide. However, Dulles persuaded him to authorize one last flight.

That flight took place on May 1, and the pilot was Francis Gary Powers. Four hours after Powers entered Soviet airspace, a Soviet pilot, Igor Mentyukov, brought down his plane. The United States issued a false story that a plane had disappeared while on a weather mission. Khrushchev announced that the U-2 had been brought down 1,300 miles inside the Soviet Union by a Soviet rocket and that Powers had been captured alive and had confessed his activities. This was the official line for 38 years. But in 1996, Mentyukov revealed the true story and explained that the Soviets had covered up the truth to make their missile defenses appear more advanced than they really were.

KHRUSHCHEV DENOUNCES EISENHOWER It was a bad moment for the United States. President Eisenhower frankly owned up to the charge and took full personal responsibility for authorizing the flight. The admission angered Khrushchev, who interpreted it as a sign not of honesty but of contempt. He felt that the incident made him look bad in the Soviet Union, where hard-liners disapproved of his willingness to negotiate with the Americans. To regain prestige back home, Khrushchev used the beginning of the summit conference to denounce the United States and then left. As Eisenhower feared, the U-2 had put an end to his effectiveness as a peacemaker. The Soviet Union tried Powers for espionage and sentenced him to ten years in prison. After 17 months, however, he was returned to the United States in exchange for a Soviet spy, Colonel Rudolf Abel.

Because of the **U-2 incident,** the 1960s opened with tension between the two superpowers as high as ever. The few hopeful events of the 1950s—such as the German summit and the Soviet Union's turn away from Stalinism—had been eclipsed by aggression, competitiveness, and mutual suspicion. The Cold War would continue into the next decade, with an enormous effect on U.S. policies toward Cuba—and ultimately toward Vietnam.

E. Answer
Possible
Answers: Without a confrontation to expose covert actions, the Cold War might have continued to flourish. Peace talks could have been pursued without a breach in trust.

THINK THROUGH HISTORY
E. Hypothesizing How might the Cold War have progressed if the U-2 incident had never occurred?

The CIA had supplied pilot Francis Gary Powers with a special pin, laced with enough poison to kill him within 90 seconds, to use in case of capture. Shown here *(clockwise from top)* are the plane, the pin, and the pilot.

MORE ABOUT . . .
The U-2 Incident
The U-2 was actually brought down when Mentyukov caught Powers's plane in the slipstream of his Sukhoi Su-9. The U-2 flipped over and the wings broke off. Mentyukov's great skill as a pilot was never acknowledged because of the official cover-up.

IN-DEPTH RESOURCES: UNIT 7
Primary Source: *from Eisenhower's Statement on the U-2, p. 49*

ASSESS & RETEACH

Section 4 Assessment
Have students work individually to answer the questions; then have them share the headlines they wrote for question 2 with the class.

Self-Assessment
Ask students to review their answers for question 3 on the section assessment. What did they learn from evaluating U.S. actions?

Section Quiz
FORMAL ASSESSMENT
Section Quiz, p. 320

Reteach
Use the cause-and-effect transparency to review the actions and reactions of the two superpowers during the Cold War.

CRITICAL THINKING TRANSPARENCIES
CT26, The Cold War

GROLIER MULTIMEDIA ENCYCLOPEDIA
The Cold War

Section **4** Assessment

1. **TERMS & NAMES**
Identify:
• H-bomb
• Dwight D. Eisenhower
• John Foster Dulles
• brinkmanship
• CIA
• Warsaw Pact
• Nikita Khrushchev
• Eisenhower Doctrine
• Francis Gary Powers
• U-2 incident

2. **SUMMARIZING** Skim this section for information about Cold War troubles in Guatemala, Iran, Egypt, and Hungary. For each, write a newspaper headline that summarizes the U.S. role and the outcome of the situation.

Trouble Spot	Headline

Choose one headline and write a paragraph about that trouble spot.

3. **EVALUATING** Do you think that the United States should have taken each of the following actions? Why or why not?
• the development of the H-bomb
• the adoption of a policy of massive retaliation
• covert actions, including those in Iran and Guatemala and the U-2 flights

4. **ANALYZING** Which of the two superpowers do you think contributed more to Cold War tensions during the 1950s?

THINK ABOUT
• U.S. decisions during this period
• each country's participation in the arms race
• the Soviet Union's invasion of Hungary

Cold War Conflicts **789**

CLOSE

A nuclear arms race between the United States and the Soviet Union infected the 1950s with widespread fear of a nuclear holocaust. Covert activities, hostile actions in Egypt and Hungary, and the Soviet launch of an unmanned space satellite raised mutual suspicion to new levels.

ANSWERS

1. TERMS & NAMES
H-bomb, p. 785
Dwight D. Eisenhower, p. 786
John Foster Dulles, p. 786
brinkmanship, p. 786
CIA, p. 786
Warsaw Pact, p. 786
Nikita Khrushchev, p. 787
Eisenhower Doctrine, p. 788
Francis Gary Powers, p. 788
U-2 incident, p. 789

2. SUMMARIZING
Possible Response: **Guatemala:** CIA-Trained Army Topples Guatemalan Ruler or CIA Keeps Communism Out of Guatemala **Iran:** U.S. Prevents Iranian-Soviet Alliance or U.S. Engineers Iranian Chaos **Egypt:** U.S. Urges Peaceful Suez Solution **Hungary:** U.S. Protests Soviet Invasion

3. EVALUATING
Possible Responses: Some students will feel that the development of the H-bomb, massive retaliation, and covert actions were understandable because of the fear of communism. Other students may feel that the United States was too aggressive and had no right to meddle in the affairs of other countries.

4. ANALYZING
Possible Responses: Students may find both countries equally at fault. Some students may find the U.S. more at fault and cite the U-2 incident, the Eisenhower Doctrine, and the involvement in Guatemala and Iran. Others may say the Soviet Union was more to blame because they invaded Hungary and made threats during the Suez Canal crisis.

OBJECTIVES

1 To explain how science fiction of the 1950s reflected the anxieties of the age.

2 To identify the messages of three science fiction excerpts.

FOCUS & MOTIVATE

▶ **Starting with the Student**
Ask students to discuss science fiction films they have seen recently.

• What was the general feeling conveyed in the film?
• How might today's films differ from films in the 1950s, other than in their use of special effects?
• Do students think science fiction films generally convey social or political messages, or are they simply entertainment?

MORE ABOUT . . .
Ray Bradbury

Because Bradbury rarely writes about space hardware and gadgetry, some critics have been reluctant to call him a true science fiction writer. Bradbury himself says, "If you're too good a scientist, you're not a good writer." He goes on to say, "I write for fun. . . . I have fun with ideas. I play with them. I approach my craft with enthusiasm and respect. If my work sparks serious thought, fine. But I don't write with that in mind. I'm not a serious person, and I don't like serious people."

Science Fiction Reflects Cold War Realities

Many writers of science fiction draw on the scientific and social trends of the present to describe future societies that might arise if those trends continued. Nuclear proliferation, the space race, early computer technology, and the pervasive fear of known and unknown dangers during the Cold War were the realities that prompted a boom in science fiction during the 1950s and 1960s.

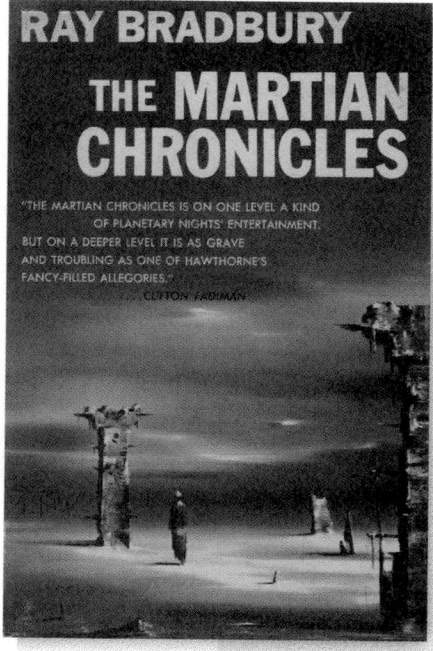

THE MARTIAN CHRONICLES

In *The Martian Chronicles,* Ray Bradbury describes how earthlings who have colonized Mars watch helplessly as their former planet is destroyed by nuclear warfare.

They all came out and looked at the sky that night. They left their suppers or their washing up or their dressing for the show and they came out upon their now-not-quite-as-new porches and watched the green star of Earth there. It was a move without conscious effort; they all did it, to help them understand the news they had heard on the radio a moment before. There was Earth and there the coming war, and there hundreds of thousands of mothers or grandmothers or fathers or brothers or aunts or uncles or cousins....

At nine o'clock Earth seemed to explode, catch fire, and burn.

The people on the porches put up their hands as if to beat the fire out....

But nobody moved. Late dinners were carried out onto the night lawns and set upon collapsible tables, and they picked at these slowly until two o'clock and the light-radio message flashed from Earth. They could read the great Morse-code flashes which flickered like a distant firefly:

AUSTRALIAN CONTINENT ATOMIZED IN PREMATURE EXPLOSION OF ATOMIC STOCKPILE. LOS ANGELES, LONDON BOMBED. WAR. COME HOME. COME HOME. COME HOME.

RAY BRADBURY, *The Martian Chronicles* (1950)

RECOMMENDED RESOURCES

Books

Benét, Stephen Vincent. "By the Waters of Babylon," in *Selected Works of Stephen Vincent Benét.* New York: Farrar, 1942. A famous coming-of-age story set in New York City long after its total destruction.

Bradbury, Ray. *Fahrenheit 451.* New York: Ballantine, 1953. A repressive society controls its citizens by burning books.

Clark, Walter van Tilburg. "The Portable Phonograph," in *The Watchful Gods and Other Stories.* New York: New American, 1961. Survivors of a nuclear war fight over their meager remaining possessions.

Videos

Fahrenheit 451. Dir. François Truffaut, MCA Universal Home Video, 1966.

Invasion of the Body Snatchers. Dir. Don Siegel. Republic Pictures Home Video, 1956. Chillingly paranoid McCarthy-era classic.

The Martian Chronicles, Parts 1 and 2. Dir. Jack Gold. Fries Home Video, 1979. Made for television.

Planet of the Apes. Dir. Franklin J. Schaffner. CBS/Fox Video, 1967. A popular film with a fine surprise ending.

Ray Bradbury Theater, Buena Vista Home Video, 1985. Adaptations of Bradbury tales. "The Playground" in Volume 1 is especially famous and creepy.

THE BODY SNATCHERS

Written in 1954 at the height of the Great Fear, or Red Scare, Jack Finney's *The Body Snatchers* (on which the movies *Invasion of the Body Snatchers* were based) tells of giant seedpods from outer space that descend on the inhabitants of a California town. The pods create perfect physical duplicates of them that lack only one thing—human souls.

"It's him, Wilma. It's your uncle, all right."

She just nodded, as though expecting exactly that answer. "It's not," she murmured, but she said it quietly—not arguing, just asserting a fact.

"Well," I said, leaning my head back against the pillar, "let's take this a little at a time. After all, you could hardly be fooled; you've lived with him for years. How do you know he isn't Uncle Ira, Wilma? How is he different?"

For a moment her voice shot up, high and panicky. "That's just *it!*" But she quieted down instantly, leaning toward me. "Miles, there *is* no difference you can actually see...."

"Miles, he looks, sounds, acts, and remembers exactly like Ira. On the outside. But *inside* he's different. His responses"—she stopped, hunting for the word—"aren't *emotionally* right, if I can explain that. He remembers the past, in detail, and he'll smile and say, 'You were sure a cute youngster, Willy. Bright one, too,' just the way Uncle Ira did. But there's something *missing....*"

JACK FINNEY, *The Body Snatchers* (1955)

KEVIN McCARTHY · DANA WYNTER · CAROLYN JONES

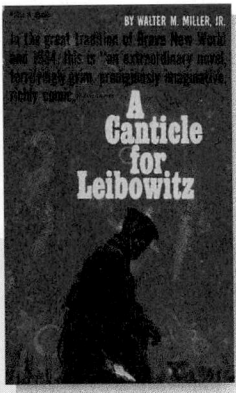

A CANTICLE FOR LEIBOWITZ

In *A Canticle for Leibowitz,* Walter M. Miller, Jr., portrays the centuries after a nuclear holocaust as a new dark age for humanity on earth.

He had been wandering for a long time. The search seemed endless, but there was always the promise of finding what he sought across the next rise or beyond the bend in the trail. When he had finished fanning himself, he clapped the hat back on his head and scratched at his bushy beard while blinking around at the landscape. There was a patch of unburned forest on the hillside just ahead. It offered welcome shade, but still the wanderer sat there in the sunlight and watched the curious buzzards....

Pickings were good for a while in the region of the Red River; but then out of the carnage, a city-state arose. For rising city-states, the buzzards had no fondness, although they approved of their eventual fall. They shied away from Texarkana and ranged far over the plain to the west. After the manner of all living things, they replenished the Earth many times with their kind.

Eventually it was the Year of Our Lord 3174.

There were rumors of war.

WALTER M. MILLER, JR., *A Canticle for Leibowitz* (1959)

INTERACT WITH HISTORY

1. **COMPARING** What themes, or general messages about life or humanity, do you think these three books convey? How might readers' interpretations of these messages today differ from readers' interpretations during the Cold War?

   SEE SKILLBUILDER HANDBOOK, PAGE 1041.

2. **PLOTTING THE FUTURE** Working alone or with a partner, outline a plot for a work of science fiction that reflects a concern in today's world—computer viruses or a danger to the environment, for example. Include brief descriptions of characters and settings, as well as of major events in the story.

   INTERNET For more about science fiction, click on *Social Studies* at http://www.mcdougallittell.com

Cold War Conflicts **791**

Chapter 26 Assessment

REVIEWING THE CHAPTER

REVIEWING THE CHAPTER

TERMS & NAMES For each term below, write a sentence explaining its significance in the 1950s and the Cold War. For each name below, explain the person's role in Cold War events.

1. containment
2. NATO
3. Mao Zedong
4. Korean War
5. McCarthyism
6. John Foster Dulles
7. brinkmanship
8. CIA
9. Nikita Khrushchev
10. U-2 incident

MAIN IDEAS

SECTION 1 *(pages 766–772)*

Origins of the Cold War

11. What were the goals of U.S. foreign policy during the Cold War?
12. Explain the Truman Doctrine and describe how Americans reacted to it.
13. What was the purpose of the NATO alliance?

SECTION 2 *(pages 773–778)*

The Cold War Heats Up

14. What global events helped to bring about U.S. involvement in Korea?
15. What issue of military strategy led to a disagreement between General Douglas MacArthur and President Truman, eventually costing MacArthur his job?
16. What goals did the United States achieve by fighting in Korea? What goals did it fail to achieve?

SECTION 3 *(pages 779–784)*

The Cold War at Home

17. What actions of Joseph McCarthy worsened the national hysteria about communism?
18. How did the spy case of the Rosenbergs feed anti-Communist sentiment in America?

SECTION 4 *(pages 785–789)*

Two Nations Live on the Edge

19. By what means did the U.S. government, including the CIA, fight the Cold War around the world?
20. What technological developments during the 1950s contributed to an arms race that would last for more than 30 years?

THINKING CRITICALLY

1. **CONTAINMENT** Create a cause-and-effect diagram, similar to the one shown, for each of these events: (a) the United States' adoption of a policy of containment and (b) the beginning of the nuclear arms race between the United States and the Soviet Union.

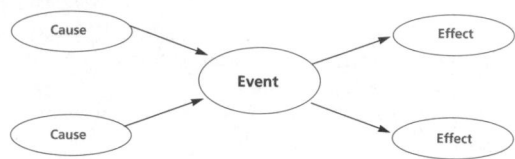

2. **CONSTITUTIONAL CONFLICT** What government actions in response to widespread anti-Communist sentiment do you think conflicted with the individual freedoms guaranteed in the Bill of Rights? Which of these actions were justified?

3. **COLD WAR CONFLICTS** Reread the quotation from J. Robert Oppenheimer on page 764. Do you agree with his assessment of the U.S.-Soviet conflict during the Cold War? Explain your opinion.

4. **GEOGRAPHY OF THE SOVIET UNION** Look carefully at the map on page 769. How did the absence of a natural barrier on the western border of the Soviet Union affect post–World War II Soviet foreign policy? Explain your answer.

5. **AMERICAN STUDIES: SCIENCE FICTION** Which of the quoted science fiction works do you think best exemplifies the concerns of the Cold War? Why?

6. **ANALYZING PRIMARY SOURCES** Read the following excerpt from a memorandum President Truman wrote in 1953, explaining his refusal to use the atomic bomb during the Korean War. Then answer the questions below.

> In 1945 I had ordered the A Bomb dropped on Japan at two places devoted almost exclusively to war production. We were at war. We were trying to end it in order to save the lives of our soldiers and sailors. . . . We stopped the war and saved thousands of casualties on both sides.
>
> In Korea we were fighting a police action with sixteen allied nations to support the World Organization which had set up the Republic of Korea. We had held the Chinese after defeating the North Koreans and whipping the Russian Air Force.
>
> I just could not make the order for a Third World War. I know I was *right*.
>
> **PRESIDENT TRUMAN,** from *Off the Record: The Private Papers of Harry S. Truman*

How does Truman explain the difference between using the atomic bomb against Japan and using it against China? Do you agree or disagree with Truman's reasons? Why?

REVIEWING THE CHAPTER

TERMS & NAMES
1. containment, p. 769
2. North Atlantic Treaty Organization (NATO), p. 772
3. Mao Zedong, p. 773
4. Korean War, p. 775
5. McCarthyism, p. 783
6. John Foster Dulles, p. 786
7. brinkmanship, p. 786
8. CIA, p. 786
9. Nikita Khrushchev, p. 787
10. U-2 incident, p. 789

MAIN IDEAS
11. To encourage democracy; to gain access to raw materials and markets; to rebuild Europe; to contain Soviet expansion.
12. A policy of helping countries resist Communist takeover; basically supported by Americans, especially after the Soviets invaded Czechoslovakia.
13. To combat Soviet aggression.
14. Communist victory in China; North Korea's attack on South Korea.
15. Truman wanted a limited war; MacArthur wanted to bomb and invade mainland China.
16. Pushed back the North Korean invaders and contained communism without a world war and without using nuclear weapons; failed to unite Korea.
17. McCarthy's allegation of Communists in the State Department and in the armed services; national hearings in the Senate.
18. Rosenberg case involved transfer of nuclear secrets to the Soviets; Americans feared Soviet influence in America and possession of nuclear weapons.
19. By sponsoring covert actions to overthrow governments unfriendly to the U.S.
20. Development of atomic bomb and H-bomb, space flights, intercontinental ballistic missiles, and high-altitude aircraft.

THINKING CRITICALLY

1. CONTAINMENT
Possible Responses: **(a)** *Event:* containment. *Cause:* Soviet aggression in Europe. *Effect:* Truman Doctrine. *Cause:* Soviets hold Berlin hostage. *Effect:* Berlin airlift. *Cause:* North Koreans invade South Korea. *Effect:* U.S. enters Korean War. **(b)** *Event:* nuclear arms race. *Cause:* Soviets explode an atomic bomb. *Effect:* U.S. develops an H-bomb. *Effect:* U.S. tests an H bomb. *Effect:* Soviets develop an H-bomb. *Cause:* U.S. builds large numbers of nuclear weapons. *Effect:* Soviets build large numbers of nuclear weapons.

2. CONSTITUTIONAL CONFLICT
Possible Response: Loyalty Review Board, HUAC, McCarran Act, McCarthy's accusations; students may say that none of the actions was justified, or that a government may investigate spying if the investigation is done fairly.

3. COLD WAR CONFLICTS
Possible Response: Students who agree with Oppenheimer may say that because both countries were fully armed with nuclear weapons, an attack on one would bring instant retaliation from the other. Such nuclear attacks would destroy the world. Students who disagree may say that it is possible to have winners and losers even in a nuclear war and that the first country to attack would be the winner.

ALTERNATIVE ASSESSMENT

1. REPORTING WORLD NEWS

What was happening around the world while the United States was concentrating on the Cold War?

Prepare a script and a plan for visuals for a television news segment that summarizes one international news event that happened during the 1950s.

 CD-ROM To identify and research the international event that interests you, use the CD-ROM *Our Times* and other resources.

- Use a storyboard format to plan your visuals—sketches of people and events you would show, perhaps graphs or maps—and figure out what the narrator will say as each picture is shown.
- In your script, narrate the highlights of the event and analyze its effect on U.S. foreign-policy decisions.

2. LEARNING FROM MEDIA

VIDEO View the McDougal Littell video for Chapter 26, *The Cold War Comes Home.* Discuss the following questions with a small group of classmates and then do the cooperative learning activity.

- How was Gordon Kahn caught up in events beyond his control?
- What alternatives did Gordon Kahn have? Do you think he chose the right path? Explain your opinion.
- From whose point of view is the story told? How does that viewpoint affect your opinion of the events?
- Gordon Kahn is portrayed as a victim in the video. How could he have been portrayed differently?
- Cooperative Learning With your group, create a report card to evaluate the video. Decide what criteria you will use to evaluate it, and come up with a grade for each criterion. Share and defend your final report card.

3. PORTFOLIO PROJECT

Use the Living History activity to expand your portfolio.

LIVING HISTORY

PRESENTING YOUR INTERVIEWS

Write and present to your class your two interviews with people who have memories of the Cold War era.

- Review the interviews. Has your study of the Cold War suggested any other questions that you would like to ask? If so, try to contact your interviewees again to ask the questions.
- Make a written transcript of each complete interview.
- Decide what you will present from each interview. If you omit some parts, use ellipses (. . .) to mark your omissions.
- Write an introduction for each interview. The introduction should include the interviewee's name and a description of what he or she was doing during the Cold War era.

Save your interviews, along with the tapes and transcripts you used in preparing them, in your American history portfolio.

Review Chapter 26

ORIGINS OF THE COLD WAR After World War II ended, the differing global economic and political goals of the United States and the Soviet Union resulted in a nonmilitary conflict known as the Cold War. The United States provided aid to European nations through the Marshall Plan and joined the defensive alliance known as the North Atlantic Treaty Organization (NATO).

THE COLD WAR HEATS UP In China the Communists defeated the Nationalists in 1949. Starting in 1950, the United States and other UN countries fought a war in Korea to keep South Korea from being overrun by North Korean Communists. The fighting ended in 1953, with Korea still divided into two countries.

THE COLD WAR AT HOME Anti-Communist sentiment gripped the United States in the late 1940s and the 1950s, causing the government to investigate the loyalty of millions of its employees. Alger Hiss was sent to prison, and Ethel and Julius Rosenberg were executed as Communist spies. Senator Joseph McCarthy accused hundreds of people of being Communists, and his unfounded accusations ruined many lives.

TWO NATIONS LIVE ON THE EDGE Throughout the 1950s people lived in fear of nuclear destruction as the United States and the Soviet Union engaged in a nuclear arms race. The Soviet leader Nikita Khrushchev sent tanks to crush a reform movement in Hungary in 1956. The Eisenhower Doctrine warned that the United States would defend the Middle East against Communist aggression. The launching of the first Sputnik satellite in 1957 spurred a space race between the two superpowers, and the United States sent U-2 spy planes into Soviet airspace. In May 1960, the Soviets shot down a U-2 plane and convicted the pilot, Francis Gary Powers, of espionage.

Preview Chapter 27

Although the Cold War had an enormous impact on domestic affairs in the 1950s, many Americans experienced the decade as a time of prosperity rather than a time of anti-Communist fear. Popular culture celebrated the growing middle class and its suburban lifestyle, although many minorities and poor people were excluded from economic gains. You will learn about these significant developments in the next chapter.

Cold War Conflicts **793**

ALTERNATIVE ASSESSMENT

1. REPORTING WORLD NEWS
Standards for Evaluation
The TV script and plan for visuals should meet the following criteria:

- Focuses on one international event from the 1950s and shows how it affected U.S. foreign policy.
- Cites at least four references from a variety of research sources.
- Includes appropriate and effective visuals.
- Integrates the visuals appropriately into the script.

2. LEARNING FROM MEDIA
Answers to the questions:

- He was implicated in the anti-Communist hysteria that led to blacklisting.
- He could have answered questions about the alleged Communist activities of his colleagues and of himself. Opinions will vary.
- The story is told from the point of view of Gordon Kahn's son, probably making students more sympathetic to Kahn.
- As a principled man who chose to take the consequences of his beliefs.

Standards for Evaluation
Report Card on the Video

The report card should meet the following criteria:

- Establishes detailed criteria for evaluating the video.
- Expresses the criteria clearly.
- Gives a letter grade for each criterion.
- Supports each grade with an example from the video.

3. PORTFOLIO PROJECT
LIVING HISTORY
Standards for Evaluation
An effective interview should meet the following criteria:

- Maintains a consistent focus.
- Makes use of open-ended questions that elicit varied information.
- Includes follow-up questions.
- Shows good organization.
- Provides an introduction containing relevant biographical information about the interviewees.
- Includes a clear, coherent tape or written transcript of the interview.

IN-DEPTH RESOURCES: UNIT 7
See the form for scoring this activity on page 23.

THINKING CRITICALLY

4. GEOGRAPHY OF THE SOVIET UNION
Possible Response: Some students may say that the lack of a natural barrier caused the Soviets to create buffer nations between themselves and Western Europe. Other students may argue that the Soviets would have created buffer nations even with natural protection.

5. AMERICAN STUDIES: SCIENCE FICTION
In their answers students should support their ideas by pointing out details from the text they chose. They may point to such Cold War concerns as nuclear world destruction, pervasive fear of the unknown, or despair that accompanies loss of control over one's life.

6. ANALYZING PRIMARY SOURCES
Possible Response: Bombing Japan would end the war quickly and would save American lives. Bombing China would simply start World War III. **Agree**—Truman had no choice in World War II; other measures were working in Korea. **Disagree**—Truman should have used any means at his disposal to end the Korean War.

	Key Ideas	TEACHING SUPPORT	ASSESSMENT
SECTION 1 Postwar America *pp. 796–802*	*As Americans try to put the nightmare of World War II behind them and begin rebuilding their lives, the economy booms and the country becomes conservative.*	**In-Depth Resources: Unit 7** • Guided Reading, p. 57 • Primary Source: Cartoon, p. 64 • American Lives: Jackie Robinson, p. 71 **COOPERATIVE ACTIVITY** • Exploring Postwar Life, p. 797 (TE)	**Section 1 Assessment,** p. 802 (PE) **Self-Assessment,** p. 802 (TE) **Formal Assessment** • Section Quiz, p. 329 **Alternative Assessment Book** • Standards for Evaluating a Cooperative Activity
SECTION 2 The American Dream in the Fifties *pp. 803–809*	*Many Americans find their dream of material comfort and economic prosperity realized. But some find the cost too high.*	**In-Depth Resources: Unit 7** • Guided Reading, p. 58 • Geography Application: The Baby Boom, p. 62 • Primary Source: from *The Organization Man,* p. 65 • Literature: from *The Man in the Gray Flannel Suit,* p. 68 **COOPERATIVE ACTIVITY** • Developing Commercials, p. 808 (TE)	**Section 2 Assessment,** p. 809 (PE) **Self-Assessment,** p. 809 (TE) **Formal Assessment** • Section Quiz, p. 330 **Alternative Assessment Book** • Standards for Evaluating a Cooperative Activity
SECTION 3 Popular Culture *pp. 812–817*	*Mass popular culture booms, largely because of television. While the media generally reflect mainstream middle-class values, a vital counter-culture flourishes.*	**In-Depth Resources: Unit 7** • Guided Reading, p. 59 • Skillbuilder Practice: Primary Sources, p. 61 • Literature: from *1959* by Thulani Davis, p. 70 • American Lives: Milton Berle, p. 72 **COOPERATIVE ACTIVITY** • Creating a TV Program Guide, p. 814 (TE)	**Section 3 Assessment,** p. 817 (PE) **Self-Assessment,** p. 817 (TE) **Formal Assessment** • Section Quiz, p. 331 **Alternative Assessment Book** • Standards for Evaluating a Cooperative Activity
SECTION 4 The Other America *pp. 820–823*	*Many Americans suffer from poverty and racial discrimination, despite unprecedented economic prosperity in the nation.*	**In-Depth Resources: Unit 7** • Guided Reading, p. 60 • Primary Source: from *The Other America* by Michael Harrington, p. 66; The Voluntary Relocation Program, p. 67 **COOPERATIVE ACTIVITY** • Preparing a Family Budget, p. 821 (TE)	**Section 4 Assessment,** p. 823 (PE) **Self-Assessment,** p. 823 (TE) **Formal Assessment** • Section Quiz, p. 332 **Alternative Assessment Book** • Standards for Evaluating a Cooperative Activity
CHAPTER RESOURCES	**Chapter Overview** *Post war America experienced an economic boom fueled by consumer spending that was spurred by the mass media, especially television. But many found themselves mired in poverty and stifled by discrimination.*	**In-Depth Resources: Unit 7** • Living History Project: Worksheet, p. 73; Standards, p. 74 **Telescoping the Times** • Chapter Summary, pp. 53–54 **Planning for Block Schedules**	**Chapter Assessment,** pp. 824–825 (PE) **Alternative Assessment,** p. 825 (PE) **Formal Assessment** • Chapter Test, forms A and B, pp. 333–338 📷 **Test Generator** **Alternative Assessment Book** See explanation and forms for different kinds of alternative assessments including portfolio assessment.

Electronic Library of Primary Sources
• Desegregation at Central High School by Melba Patillo Beals
• Desegregation at Central High School by Craig Rains

INTERNET RESOURCES
• See *McDougal Littell Learning On-Line* for links to information about Truman and Eisenhower.

 Humanities Transparencies
• H42, Highway Construction

Geography Transparencies
• G27, Highway Systems, 1950 and 1987

Critical Thinking Transparencies
• CT61, Urban-Suburban Growth Rates

 Electronic Library of Primary Sources
• from *The Feminine Mystique*

INTERNET RESOURCES
• See *McDougal Littell Learning On-Line* for links to information about polio vaccine and fads and fashions.

 Our Times
• *TV Guide* listings from June, 1956

INTERNET RESOURCES
• See Interact with History p. 819 (PE) for an activity that includes the Internet as an enrichment option.

 Humanities Transparencies
• H26, "Her World" by Philip Evergood

Critical Thinking Transparencies
• CT27, Post-War Boom

 Electronic Library of Primary Sources
• from *The Other America* by Michael Harrington

INTERNET RESOURCES
• See *McDougal Littell Learning On-Line* for links to information about youth in the fifties.

 American Portfolio: A Videodisc for U.S. History, user's guide, pp. 235–239, 241

INTERNET RESOURCES
Learning On-Line: Social Studies
http://www.mcdougallittell.com

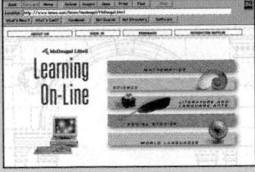

Block Scheduling (90 MINUTES)

Day 1

Section 1, pp. 796–802

Section 2, pp. 803–809

Geography Spotlight: The Road to Suburbia, pp. 810–811

Section Assessments, pp. 802, 809

Day 2

Section 3, pp. 812–817

Section 4, pp. 820–823

Daily Life: The Emergence of the Teenager, pp. 818–819

Section Assessments, pp. 817, 823

Chapter Assessments, pp. 824–825

YEARLY PACING *Chapter 27 Total:* 2 days *Yearly Total:* 85 days

See *Planning for Block Schedules* for special activities and pacing strategies.

Customizing for Special Populations

Students Acquiring English

Access for Students Acquiring English
• Guided Reading for Sections 1–4 (Spanish), pp. 264–267
• Chapter Summary (Spanish), pp. 262–263
• Skillbuilder Practice: Primary Sources (Spanish), p. 268
• Geography Application: The Baby Boom (Spanish), p. 269–270

INTERNET RESOURCES
• See *McDougal Littell Learning On-Line* The Diverse Classroom.

Less Proficient Readers

In-Depth Resources: Unit 7
• Guided Reading for Sections 1–4, pp. 57–60
• Skillbuilder: Primary Sources, p. 61
• Geography Application: The Baby Boom, p. 62

Telescoping the Times
• Chapter Summary, pp. 53–54

See additional strategies at point of use in the Teacher's Edition.

Gifted and Talented Students

In-Depth Resources: Unit 7
• Primary Sources: Political Cartoon, p. 64; from *The Organizational Man* by William H. Whyte, Jr., p. 65; from *The Other America* by Michael Harrington, p. 66; The Voluntary Relocation Program, p. 67
• American Lives: Jackie Robinson, p. 71; Milton Berle, p. 72

See additional strategies at point of use in the Teacher's Edition.

Connections to Literature READINGS FOR STUDENTS

In-Depth Resources: Unit 7
• from *The Man in the Gray Flannel Suit* by Sloan Wilson, p. 68

Enrichment Reading
• Dillard, Annie
An American Childhood
New York: HarperPerennial, 1993
This outstanding autobiography traces the author's development from preschool through her teenage years. It is filled with joyful and humorous memories of growing up in the 1950s.

• Hijuelos, Oscar
The Mambo Kings Play Songs of Love
New York: Farrar, 1989
Brothers Cesar and Nestor Castillo come to New York City from Cuba as they follow the example of their heroes Xavier Cugat and Desi Arnaz. They dream of becoming stars. Their lush, sensuous music earns them the title Mambo Kings, and they appear in the 1950s hit TV series, "I Love Lucy." The novel won a Pulitzer Prize in 1990.

McDougal Littell *Literature Connections*

• Lorraine Hansberry,
A Raisin in the Sun (with related readings) Set in Chicago in the 1950s, this three-act play explores the struggles of an African-American family who dream of owning a house. The racism they encounter and their own family tensions and anger lead them to examine what is truly important in their lives.

• Thomás Rivera
. . . And The Earth Did Not Devour Him
A classic of Chicano literature, this novel offers impressions of a community of South Texas migrant workers who go north to pick crops after World War II.

The Postwar Boom

▶ *Starting with the Student*
Ask students to list their impressions of the 1950s under headings such as People, Events, Popular Culture, Fashions, or Problems. Ask the following questions:

• On what sources did you base your impressions of the 1950s?
• Which sources do you think are most accurate? Why?

PREVIEWING THE CHAPTER

• Read the brief section summaries with the class. Discuss the chapter title and ask students to define *boom (prosperity)*.
• Ask students how the photograph of the family around the TV set relates to the opening quotation. *Possible Response: After World War II, many Americans enjoyed unprecedented prosperity.*

MORE ABOUT . . .
Prosperity
Several publications in the early 1950s echoed the sentiments expressed in the opening quotation from *Life* magazine. In October 1956, *Fortune* magazine reported, "Never has a whole people spent so much money on so many expensive things in such an easy way as Americans are doing today."

CHAPTER
27 The Postwar Boom

SECTION 1
Postwar America
As Americans try to put the nightmare of World War II behind them and begin rebuilding their lives, the economy booms and the country becomes conservative.

SECTION 2
The American Dream in the Fifties
Many Americans find their dream of material comfort and economic prosperity realized. But some find the cost too high.

SECTION 3
Popular Culture
Mass popular culture booms, largely because of television. While the media generally reflect mainstream middle-class values, a vital counterculture flourishes.

SECTION 4
The Other America
Many Americans suffer from poverty and racial discrimination, despite unprecedented economic prosperity in the nation.

"Never before so much for so few."
Life magazine, 1954

Television begins its reign as the focus and reflection of suburban life.

Rock 'n' roll performers like Little Richard leap to the top of the recording charts.

American families joyfully welcome their GIs home, as depicted in this Norman Rockwell painting, but reentry is not always easy.

Southern Democrats called Dixiecrats form States' Rights Democratic Party.

Congress passes anti-union Taft-Hartley Act.

Harry S. Truman is elected president.

National Housing Act calls for urban renewal.

| THE UNITED STATES | 1946 | 1947 | 1948 | 1949 | 1950 | 1951 |
| THE WORLD | | | 1948 | 1949 | 1950 | |

UN mandates creation of the nation of Israel.

Mahatma Gandhi is assassinated in India.

China becomes Communist under Mao Zedong.

Korean War begins.

THEMES IN CHAPTER 27

Economic Opportunity	*Women in America*	*Science and Technology*	*Expanding Democracy*
The economic boom of the postwar years brought prosperity to millions of Americans. However, the nation experienced a recession in 1957–1958, and the national debt was rising. See Teacher's Edition note, p. 798.	The ideal woman of the 1950s was wife, mother, and homemaker. Many suburban housewives, however, felt dissatisfied and bored with their lack of identity. See Teacher's Edition note, p. 806.	The rapid rise of television in the 1950s affected many aspects of American life. Television provided entertainment and information, but critics objected to the stereotypes and violence it presented. See Teacher's Edition note, p. 813.	Thousands of Mexican Americans and Native Americans fought for the United States in World War II. After the war, these citizens faced discrimination in a society that ignored the rights of minorities. See Teacher's Edition note, p. 822.

LIVING HISTORY

PLANNING A FIFTIES PARTY

Plan a 1950s party for your classmates and friends. To recreate the time as authentically as possible, use the information in the chapter and additional research or interviews to learn the following about fifties teenagers:

- how they dressed
- what they did for entertainment
- what music they listened to
- what they liked to eat

PORTFOLIO PROJECT Create an invitation that tells guests what to wear and what they can expect to hear, see, taste, and do at the party. Keep a copy of the invitation in a folder. At the end of the chapter, you will write a radio advertisement for your party and add it to your American history portfolio.

PLANNING A FIFTIES PARTY

Discuss possible sources of information about the 1950s and the various tasks involved in planning a party:

- Students can use the library to locate magazines and newspapers from the 1950s.
- Suggest that students ask adults who were teenagers in the 1950s for ideas for the party.
- Students can watch videos or reruns of television programs set in the 1950s.

Project Planning Guide

Step 1	Students choose aspects of the 1950s to research.
Step 2	Students use the library and the Internet to locate and gather information about the decade.
Step 3	Students interview people who were teenagers during the 1950s.
Step 4	Students compile information from interviews and research, and plan music and other aspects of the party.

IN-DEPTH RESOURCES: UNIT 7 See worksheet and standards for evaluation, p. 73, 74.

Timeline entries:

● Dwight D. Eisenhower is elected president.

● Brown v. Board of Education of Topeka ruling orders the desegregation of public schools.

● Ray Kroc opens the first McDonald's franchise.

● Elvis Presley appears on the Ed Sullivan Show.

● Dwight D. Eisenhower is reelected president.

President Eisenhower backs integration of public schools with federal troops, as depicted in this painting by Norman Rockwell.

"It's Howdy Doody time" becomes a familiar greeting on TV sets in 45 million American homes.

● John F. Kennedy is elected president.

1952   1954   1955   **1956**   1957   1959   **1960**
1952   1954

● Mau Mau Revolt shakes Kenya.

● USSR opens the world's first nuclear power station.

● Soviets suppress Hungarian uprising.

Vietnam War begins.

Fidel Castro comes to power in Cuba.

War begins in the Congo.

The Postwar Boom **795**

RECOMMENDED RESOURCES

Books for the Teacher

Goldman, Eric F. *The Crucial Decade—and After.* New York: Knopf, 1965. Readable history of political and social changes.

Halberstam, David. *The Fifties.* New York: Villard, 1993. A fascinating study of all aspects of American life and culture.

Katz, Donald. *Home Fires.* New York: Harper Collins, 1992. An account of a real family's adjustment to postwar life and beyond.

Books for the Student

Barnouw, Erik. *Tube of Plenty.* 2nd ed. New York: Oxford UP, 1990. History of television and its impact.

Kytle, Elizabeth, ed. *Willa Mae.* Athens: U of Georgia P, 1993. An African-American woman recalls segregation.

This Fabulous Century: 1950–1960. New York: Time-Life, 1970. Visual collection on life during the 1950s.

Videos

Avalon. Dir. Barry Levinson. RCA/Columbia Pictures Home Video, 1991. Several generations of immigrants move from poverty to prosperity and adapt to the world changes around them.

The Best Years of Our Lives. Dir. William Wyler. 1946. HBO Home Video. Gripping story of GIs returning home.

Elvis '56. Dir. Alan and Susan Raymond. Music Media, 1987. Documentary about early career and impact.

Software

American Chronicles Series: Age of Anxiety (1952–1958) and *Fragile Balance (1955–1961).* CD-ROM. AIMS Media.

OBJECTIVES

1 To identify economic and social problems Americans faced after World War II.

2 To explain how the desire for stability led to political conservatism.

3 To describe causes and effects of social unrest in the postwar period.

4 To contrast domestic policy under Truman and Eisenhower.

SKILLBUILDERS

- Interpreting graphs, p. 798
- Interpreting charts, p. 800

CRITICAL THINKING

- Identifying problems, p. 797
- Analyzing causes, p. 798
- Clarifying, p. 800
- Summarizing, pp. 801, 802
- Developing historical perspective, p. 802
- Drawing conclusions, p. 802
- Making decisions, p. 802

FOCUS & MOTIVATE

▶ *Starting with the Student*
- Have students discuss the choices they will face when they graduate from high school and from college.
- Ask them whether they think soldiers returning from World War II faced similar choices.

MORE ABOUT . . .
Donald Katz

In *Home Fires,* author Donald Katz chronicles the true story of the Gordon family from 1945 to 1990. Beginning with Sam Gordon's return from World War II, Katz describes the building, unraveling, and recapturing of the Gordons' American dream.

1 Postwar America

TERMS & NAMES
- GI Bill of Rights
- suburb
- Harry S. Truman
- Dixiecrat
- Fair Deal
- Dwight D. Eisenhower

LEARN ABOUT the social, economic, and political readjustment of the United States following World War II
TO UNDERSTAND the new prosperity and rising conservatism.

ONE AMERICAN'S STORY

Sam Gordon had been married less than a year when he was shipped overseas in July 1943. As a sergeant in the United States Army, he fought in Belgium and France during World War II. Arriving back home in November 1945, Sam nervously anticipated a reunion with his family. A friend, Donald Katz, reported Sam's reactions.

A PERSONAL VOICE
Sam bulled through the crowd and hailed a taxi. The cab motored north through the warm autumn day as he groped for feelings appropriate to being back home alive from a terrible war. . . . [He was] nearly panting under the weight of fear. *Back home alive . . . married to a girl I haven't seen since 1943 . . . father of a child I've never seen at all.*
DONALD KATZ, quoted in *Home Fires*

GIs returned home to their families after World War II with new hope but also new problems.

Sam Gordon met his daughter, Susan, for the first time the day he returned home from the war, and he went to work the next morning. Like many other young couples, the Gordons began to put the nightmare of the war behind them and to return to normality.

Readjustment and Recovery

By the summer of 1946, about 10 million men and women had been released from the armed forces. Veterans like Sam Gordon—along with the rest of American society—settled down to rebuilding their lives.

THE IMPACT OF THE GI BILL To help ease veterans' return to civilian life, Congress passed the Servicemen's Readjustment Act, or the **GI Bill of Rights,** in 1944. In addition to encouraging veterans to get an education, and paying part of their tuition, the GI bill guaranteed them a year's unemployment benefits while they looked for jobs. The bill also offered low-interest, federally guaranteed loans. Millions of young families used these benefits to buy homes and farms or to establish businesses. As a Veteran's Administration official said, "I've talked to hundreds and hundreds of these kids. . . .They like the idea of making more money but they like even more the idea . . . of 'getting to be somebody.'"

HOUSING CRISIS In 1945 and 1946, returning veterans at first faced a severe housing shortage. Many families lived in cramped apartments or moved in with relatives. Some veterans resorted to living in cars or in coal sheds. Others lived in grain silos that were turned into apartments or in old streetcars that were converted into homes.

In response to this housing crisis, developers like William Levitt and Henry Kaiser used efficient, assembly-line methods to mass-produce houses. Levitt, who bragged that his company could build a house in 16 minutes, offered homes in small residential communities surrounding cities, or **suburbs,** for less than $8,000. His first postwar development—rows of standardized homes built on treeless lots—was located on New York's Long Island and named Levittown.

SECTION 1 RESOURCES

PRINT RESOURCES

IN-DEPTH RESOURCES: UNIT 7
Guided Reading, p. 57
Primary Source: Cartoon, p. 64
American Lives: Jackie Robinson, p. 71

ACCESS FOR STUDENTS ACQUIRING ENGLISH
Guided Reading (Spanish), p. 264

FORMAL ASSESSMENT
Section Quiz, p. 329

ALTERNATIVE ASSESSMENT BOOK
See forms for supporting and scoring alternative activities.

TECHNOLOGY RESOURCES

CD-ROM Electronic Library of Primary Sources

VIDEO *American Portfolio: A Videodisc for U.S. History* user's guide, pp. 235, 236

INTERNET McDougal Littell Learning On-Line
http://www.mcdougallittell.com

A tree was planted every 28 feet, and all the streets curved at the same angle. Levitt standardized not only the houses themselves, but also the way they were built: "Convoys of trucks moved over the pavements, tossing out prefabricated sidings at 8:00 A.M., toilets at 9:30, sinks and tubs at 10:00, sheetrock at 10:45, flooring at 11:00." Within days, several hundred identical houses were ready for occupancy.

These homes looked exactly alike, down to the blinds on the windows, and certain restrictions ensured that they would stay the same. Residents were required to mow their lawns regularly and were forbidden to put up fences. They could hang laundry out to dry on Mondays, but never on Sundays. They could choose the type of door chime they wanted, but they couldn't install bells or buzzers. Nevertheless, these planned suburbs that sprang up around the country offered the friendliness of small towns. With the help of the GI bill, many veterans moved in and cultivated a new lifestyle.

A PERSONAL VOICE
We were all in the same boat. . . . We shared everything; we shared tools and cars, minded each other's kids, passed play-pens and high-chairs from house to house—everything.
    It was—at least to us—a Paradise.

Mrs. Klerk, quoted in *Expanding the American Dream*

REDEFINING THE FAMILY Tension created by changes in men's and women's roles after the war contributed to a high divorce rate. Traditionally, men were the breadwinners and heads of the household, while women were expected to devote themselves to the family. During the war, however, about 6 million women, 75 percent of whom were married, entered the paid work force. These women supported their families, paid the bills, and made important household decisions. Many women were reluctant to give up their newfound independence when their husbands returned. By 1950, more than a million war marriages had ended in divorce.

ECONOMIC READJUSTMENT After World War II, the United States converted from a wartime to a peacetime economy. The government immediately canceled war contracts totaling $35 billion. Within ten days of Japan's surrender, more than a million defense workers were laid off. Unemployment increased as veterans joined laid-off defense workers in the search for jobs. At the peak of postwar unemployment in March 1946, nearly 3 million people were seeking work.

Rising unemployment was not the nation's only postwar economic problem, however. During the war, the Office of Price Administration (OPA) had halted inflation by imposing maximum prices on goods. When these controls ended on June 30, 1946, prices skyrocketed. In the next two weeks, the cost of consumer products soared 25 percent, double the increase of the previous three years. The price of pork chops, for example, jumped from 48 cents to 72 cents a pound; the price of margarine, from 28 cents to 41 cents a pound. At the same time, items such as beef, men's suits, and nylon stockings became unavailable. In some cities, consumers stood in long lines, hoping to buy scarce items, such as sugar, coffee, and beans. Prices continued to rise for the next two years until the supply of goods caught up with the demand.

While prices spiraled upward, many American workers also earned less than they had earned during the war. To halt runaway inflation and to help the nation convert to a peacetime economy, Congress eventually reestablished controls similar to the wartime controls on prices, wages, and rents.

A. Answer
Housing shortages, unemployment, readjustment to family life, rising inflation and lower wages, and shortages of goods.

THINK THROUGH HISTORY
A. Identifying Problems What problems did Americans face after World War II?

The suburbs were a mass phenomenon, even on moving day.

NOW & THEN

THE ONGOING WAGES OF WAR

"War is a contagion," observed Franklin D. Roosevelt. And the aftermath can be as devastating as the disease itself. Following World Wars I and II, many returning soldiers suffered from shell shock or battle fatigue. They were sensitive to noise, easily irritated, and their sleep was disturbed by dreams of battle. In the 1970s, similar symptoms—but with the updated name posttraumatic stress disorder—plagued many veterans of the Vietnam War as they tried to readjust to postcombat life.

Today, many veterans of the Persian Gulf War, fought in 1991, suffer from unexplained illnesses, sometimes referred to collectively as Gulf War syndrome. Several thousand veterans—and a few spouses and civilian employees—complain of fatigue, skin rashes, headaches, muscle and joint pain, or sleep disturbances. Researchers continue to hunt for the causes of these symptoms, which may have included the veterans' exposure to chemical weapons, harmful bacteria, harsh living conditions, and the smoke of 605 oil-well fires that were ignited by the retreating Iraqis.

The Postwar Boom **797**

OBJECTIVE
① INSTRUCT

Readjustment and Recovery

▶ *Discussing Key Ideas*
• The GI bill enables veterans to attend college, establish businesses, and buy homes.
• Americans face housing shortages, unemployment, and rising prices.
• Increased demand for consumer goods creates economic prosperity.

IN-DEPTH RESOURCES: UNIT 7
Guided Reading, p. 57
Primary Source: Cartoon, p. 64

ACCESS FOR STUDENTS ACQUIRING ENGLISH
Guided Reading (Spanish), p. 264

NOW & THEN
The Ongoing Wages of War

Critical Thinking: Compare and Contrast
Have students identify similarities among the symptoms experienced by war veterans. *Possible Responses: fatigue, sleep disturbances, emotional stress.*

MORE ABOUT . . .
Levittown

Levitt & Sons' first development consisted of 2,000 homes, which the company rented to married veterans for $65 a month. These homes had two bedrooms and a bathroom; a kitchen equipped with refrigerator, stove, and washing machine; a living room with a fireplace and built-in TV; and an attic that could be made into additional bedrooms.

TEACHING OPTION

Cooperative Activity: Exploring Postwar Life

Task: Student groups will create one of the following items for an exhibit about postwar issues: a song, essay, letter, series of fictional journal entries, cartoon, or news report.

Purpose: To understand U.S. social and economic problems after World War II.

Activity: Have groups choose one of the following topics: GI bill, housing shortage, family roles, or economic problems. Each group should use one of the formats described above to represent the impact of that topic on

American society in the late 1940s. Students' contributions to the exhibit should include both a visual and a written component.

📁 **Building a Portfolio:** Students who wish to include their exhibit as part of their portfolio should submit a written description of the exhibit, along with a statement indicating their contribution to the project.

ALTERNATIVE ASSESSMENT BOOK
Standards for Evaluating a Cooperative Activity

Standards for Evaluation
Exhibit items should . . .

• relate clearly to the assigned topic
• indicate understanding of readjustment in the postwar period
• include appropriate symbols, labels, and/or captions

A Dynamic Economy, 1950–1960

Reading the Graphs Ask students to identify the years each indicator grew the most quickly and most slowly (or fell). *Possible Answers: Homes: quickly 1950–56; slowly 1956–60. Autos: quickly 1952–54; slowly 1954–56. Incomes: quickly 1950–52; slowly 1952–54 or 1956–58. Savings: quickly 1960–62; slowly 1958–60.*

Extension Ask students to research the consumer price index from 1950 or 1960 to determine how much median income and savings grew relative to price increases.

Economic Challenges

▶ **Starting with the Student**
• Ask students what "passing the buck" means. *Possible Response: Putting responsibility on others.*
• Discuss the leadership quality indicated by Truman's motto, "The Buck Stops Here." *Possible Response: Willingness to accept responsibility for one's actions.*

▶ **Discussing Key Ideas**
• Truman intervenes to end strikes by miners and railroad workers.
• Economic problems and strikes cause voters to elect a conservative Republican Congress in 1946.

A Dynamic Economy, 1950–1960

HOME OWNERSHIP

AUTOMOBILE REGISTRATIONS

MEDIAN FAMILY INCOME

SAVINGS ACCOUNTS

Source: *Historical Statistics of the United States: Colonial Times to 1970*

SKILLBUILDER
INTERPRETING GRAPHS
From 1950 to 1960, by what percent did each of the economic indicators shown above increase?

Skillbuilder Answer
Homes 50%; Automobiles 50%; Income 80%; Savings 900%.

REMARKABLE RECOVERY Although most economists pessimistically forecast a postwar depression, they were wrong. They had failed to consider the consumer who had a pent-up warehouse of needs and wants.

People had lived on a shoestring budget during the Great Depression of the 1930s and had lived without luxuries during the years of wartime shortages. In the late 1940s, with more than $135 billion in savings from defense work, service pay, and investments in war bonds, Americans suddenly had money to spend. They snatched up automobiles and appliances as fast as such products appeared on the market. Houses and apartment buildings could not be built fast enough. After a brief period of postwar economic readjustment, the American economy boomed as the demand for goods and services outstripped the supply, and increased production fostered new jobs. For the next 25 years, many Americans prospered in what economist John Kenneth Galbraith called "the affluent society."

Foreign-aid programs, such as the Marshall Plan, also boosted the American economy. By helping nations in western Europe recover from the war, the United States also helped itself by creating strong foreign markets for American exports.

Economic Challenges

Despite a vital economy, American society faced a number of problems. Americans' lives had been in turmoil throughout the war, and a widespread desire for stability caused the country as a whole to become increasingly conservative politically.

TRUMAN'S INHERITANCE When **Harry S. Truman** abruptly became president after Franklin D. Roosevelt's death in 1945, he asked Roosevelt's widow, Eleanor, whether there was anything he could do for her. She replied, "Is there anything *we* can do for *you?* For you are the one in trouble now." In many ways, Truman *was* in trouble.

A PERSONAL VOICE
I don't know whether you fellows ever had a load of hay or a bull fall on you, but when they told me yesterday [about Roosevelt's death], I felt like the moon, the stars, and all the planets had fallen on me.
HARRY S. TRUMAN, in a speech, April 13, 1945

Despite his lack of preparation for the job, Truman was honorable, direct, down-to-earth, and self-confident. Perhaps most important of all, he had the ability to make difficult decisions and to accept full responsibility for them. As the plaque on his desk at the White House read, "The Buck Stops Here." Truman faced two huge challenges: dealing with the rising threat of communism, which was discussed in Chapter 26, and restoring the American economy to a strong footing.

TRUMAN FACES STRIKES One economic problem that President Truman had to address immediately was strikes. Facing higher prices and lower wages, 4.5 million discontented workers went on strike in 1946. No sooner did 750,000 steelworkers return to their jobs after an 80-day strike than 400,000 coal miners went out on the picket lines. Eighteen days later, two railroad brotherhoods announced that they would go on strike in a month and stop rail traffic throughout the nation.

Although he generally supported organized labor, Truman refused to let strikes cripple the nation. He threatened to draft the striking workers and to order them as soldiers to stay on the job. He had the federal government seize the mines, and he threatened to take control of the railroads. Appearing before a

798 CHAPTER 27

THINK THROUGH HISTORY
B. Analyzing Causes What factors contributed to the American postwar economic boom?

B. Answer The GI bill, which offered veterans low-interest loans and education benefits; wage, price, and rent controls; foreign-aid programs, such as the Marshall Plan; savings, and a desire for consumer products.

Making Connections Across the Curriculum

Economics Help students understand supply and demand by reviewing the basics: Supply is the quantity of a good or service producers are willing and able to sell at specific prices. Demand is the quantity of a good or service consumers are willing and able to purchase at specific prices. Point out that the things people want most—in this case, products such as new cars and appliances—are always scarce. During the postwar period, the demand for these new products led to a dramatic increase in jobs and incomes. Have students sketch flow charts to illustrate the relationships among economic factors.

Exploring Themes

Economic Opportunity Postwar economic changes brought to the United States a standard of living higher than the world had ever experienced. The increasing demand for consumer goods and services, combined with heavy government spending, led to a 50 percent increase in the country's gross national product during the 1950s. However, two economic issues surfaced to mar the decade's prosperity: a brief recession in 1957 –1958 (with an increase in the U.S. unemployment rate) and the rising national debt, which by the end of the decade was roughly $290 billion.

special session of Congress, Truman asked for authority to draft the striking workers into the army. Before he could finish his speech, the brotherhoods gave in.

"HAD ENOUGH?" Disgusted by shortages, rising inflation, and labor strikes, Americans were ready for a change. The Republicans asked the public, "Had enough?" Voters gave their answer at the polls: in the 1946 congressional elections, the Republican Party won control of both the Senate and the House of Representatives for the first time since 1928. The new 80th Congress ignored Truman's domestic proposals. In 1947, Congress passed the anti-union Taft-Hartley Act over his veto.

Social Unrest Persists

Problems arose not only in the economy, but in the very fabric of society itself. After World War II, a wave of racial violence erupted in the South. Many African Americans, particularly those who had served in the armed forces during the war, demanded their rights as citizens.

TRUMAN SUPPORTS CIVIL RIGHTS Truman put his career on the line for civil rights. "I am asking for equality of opportunity for all human beings," he said, ". . . and if that ends up in my failure to be reelected, that failure will be in a good cause." In September 1946, President Truman met with African-American leaders to find out what they considered their top priorities. They asked for the following:

- a federal anti-lynching law. (Authorities in Southern states sometimes looked the other way when mobs took violent action against African Americans.)
- abolition of the poll tax as a voting requirement. (This tax was often used to prevent African Americans from voting.)
- establishment of a permanent body to prevent racial discrimination in hiring. (The wartime Fair Employment Practices Commission [FEPC] was due to expire that year.)

When Congress would not pass any of these measures, Truman appointed a biracial Committee on Civil Rights in December 1946 to investigate race relations. In its 1947 report, *To Secure These Rights*, the committee reaffirmed the earlier recommendations and added several more: in addition to the anti-lynching, poll-tax, and FEPC measures, the report recommended establishment of a permanent civil rights commission, passage of federal legislation to eliminate discrimination in voting, and integration of the armed forces.

When Congress again failed to act, Truman himself took action. In July 1948, he issued an executive order for integration of the armed forces, calling for "equality of treatment and opportunity without regard to race, color, religion, or national origin." In addition, he ordered an end to discrimination in the hiring of government employees. The Supreme Court also ruled that

African-American baseball teams like the 1939 Negro League All-Stars, *right*, often played against teams from the all-white Major Leagues in exhibition games. But in 1947, Jackie Robinson, *far right*, joined the Brooklyn Dodgers, angering some fans, but winning the hearts, and respect, of many others.

Wipe out Discrimination (1949) by Milton Ackoff depicts the civil rights consciousness that caused the Dixiecrats to leave the Democratic Party.

SKILLBUILDER
INTERPRETING CHARTS
In what regions of the country did Truman carry states? Dewey? Thurmond?

the courts could not bar African Americans from residential neighborhoods. These actions represented the beginnings of a federal commitment to dealing with racial issues.

THE 1948 ELECTION Although many Americans blamed Truman for the nation's inflation and labor unrest, the Democrats nominated him for president in 1948. Truman insisted that the party platform include a strong civil rights plank. Southern delegates to the national convention—who became known as **Dixiecrats**—opposed civil rights and sought to protect "the Southern way of life" against the interference of the federal government. To protest Truman's emphasis on civil rights, they walked out of the convention, formed the States' Rights Democratic Party, and nominated their own presidential candidate, Governor Strom Thurmond of South Carolina.

Discontent reigned at the far left of the Democratic spectrum as well. Former vice-president Henry A. Wallace led his supporters out of mainstream Democratic ranks to form a more liberal Progressive Party.

As the election approached, opinion polls gave the Republican candidate, New York governor Thomas E. Dewey, a comfortable lead. But they overlooked one thing: Truman's fighting spirit. He had stepped into Roosevelt's shoes to end the war with Japan and shepherd the nation into a peacetime economy and was now determined to be elected on his own.

Truman developed a winning strategy. First, he called the Republican-dominated Congress into a special session. He challenged it to pass laws supporting such planks in the Democratic Party platform as more public housing, federal aid to education, a higher minimum wage, and extended social security coverage. Not one law was passed. Then he took his campaign to the people. He traveled from one end of the country to the other by train, speaking from the rear platform in a sweeping "whistlestop campaign." Day after day, people heard the president denounce the "do-nothing, good-for-nothing 80th Congress." Commenting on the success of this strategy, he said, "I met the people face to face, and I convinced them, and they voted for me."

STUNNING UPSET Truman's "Give 'em hell, Harry" campaign worked. Even though the headline of the early edition of the *Chicago Tribune* read, "Dewey Defeats Truman" the morning after the election, Dewey lost in one of the nation's most stunning, and narrow, political upsets to that

Election of 1948

ELECTORAL AND POPULAR VOTES

Party	Candidate	Electoral votes	Popular vote
Democratic	Harry S. Truman	303	24,179,000
Republican	Thomas E. Dewey	189	21,991,000
States' Rights	J. Strom Thurmond	39	1,176,000
Progressive	Henry A. Wallace	--	1,157,000

* Tennessee — 11 for Truman, 1 for Thurmond

Truman surprised experts and newspapers alike with the greatest presidential election upset in the nation's history.

800 Chapter 27

---

time—24 million popular votes (49.5 percent) for the Democrats to 22 million (45.1 percent) for the Republicans, with Wallace and Thurmond each receiving about a million votes. The Democrats gained control of Congress as well, even though they lost the South, which had been solidly Democratic since Reconstruction.

THE FAIR DEAL After his victory, Truman began trying to implement an ambitious economic program. Truman's **Fair Deal,** an extension of Roosevelt's New Deal, included proposals for a nationwide system of compulsory health insurance and a crop-subsidy system to provide a steady income for farmers. In Congress, some Northern Democrats joined Southern Democrats and Republicans in defeating both measures.

In other instances, however, Truman's ideas prevailed. Congress raised the hourly minimum wage from 40 cents to 75 cents, extended social security coverage to about 10 million more people, and initiated flood control and irrigation projects. Congress also provided financial support for cities to clear out slums and build 810,000 housing units for low-income families.

Republicans Take the Middle Road

Despite these social and economic victories, Truman's approval rating sank to an all-time low of 23 percent in 1951. The stalemate in the Korean War and the rising tide of McCarthyism, which cast doubt on the loyalty of some federal employees, became overwhelming issues. As the 1952 presidential election neared, Truman decided not to run for reelection. The Democrats nominated the intellectual and well-spoken Governor Adlai Stevenson of Illinois to run against the Republican candidate, General **Dwight D. Eisenhower.**

I LIKE IKE! During the campaign, the Republicans accused the Democrats of "plunder at home and blunder abroad." To fan the anti-Communist hysteria that was sweeping over the country, Republicans raised the spectre of the rise of communism in China and eastern Europe. They also criticized the growing power of the federal government and the alleged bribery and corruption among Truman's political allies. In addition, the Korean War had set off another round of inflation, leading to more strikes and labor unrest. Above all, negotiations for a Korean armistice had been dragging on for over a year. The upshot was that many voters felt that the country needed a change after two decades of Democratic leadership.

Buoyed by these sentiments, Eisenhower took the lead. But his campaign hit a snag when newspapers accused his running mate, California's Senator Richard M. Nixon, of profiting from a secret fund set up by wealthy supporters. Nixon decided to reply to the charges. In an emotional presentation to an audience of 58 million, now known as the "Checkers speech," he exhibited masterful use of a new medium—television. Nixon denied any wrongdoing, but he did admit accepting a gift from a political supporter.

Whimsical campaign accessories expressed voters' desire for a positive political change.

A PERSONAL VOICE
You know what it was? It was a little cocker spaniel dog in a crate that he [a political supporter] sent all the way from Texas. Black and white spotted. And our little girl—Tricia, the six-year-old—named it Checkers. And you know the kids love that dog and I just want to say this right now, that regardless of what they say about it, we're going to keep it.
RICHARD M. NIXON, in the "Checkers speech," September 23, 1952

802   Chapter 27

> "*I don't believe you can change the hearts of men with laws or decisions.*"
> **DWIGHT D. EISENHOWER**

Nixon's speech saved his place on the Republican ticket. In November 1952, "Ike," as Eisenhower was commonly called, won 55 percent of the popular vote, and the Republicans narrowly captured Congress.

WALKING THE MIDDLE OF THE ROAD President Eisenhower's style of governing differed from that of the Democrats. He kept a low public profile and believed in working behind the scenes to get things done. His approach, which he called "dynamic conservatism," called for government to be "conservative when it comes to money and liberal when it comes to human beings."

Although Eisenhower followed a middle-of-the-road course and avoided many controversial issues, he could not completely sidestep a persistent domestic issue—civil rights—that gained national attention due to judicial rulings and civil disobedience in the mid-1950s. The most significant judicial action occurred in 1954, when the Supreme Court ruled in *Brown v. Board of Education of Topeka* that public schools should be racially integrated. In a landmark act of civil disobedience a year later, a black seamstress named Rosa Parks refused to give up her seat on a bus to a white man. Her arrest sparked a boycott of the entire Montgomery, Alabama, bus system. The civil rights movement had entered a new era.

Eisenhower believed that the federal government should not be involved in desegregation, and he privately disagreed with the *Brown* ruling. He insisted, "I don't believe you can change the hearts of men with laws or decisions." But he upheld the law. When the governor of Arkansas tried to keep blacks out of an all-white high school in Little Rock in September 1957, Eisenhower sent federal troops to see to it that black students were allowed to attend classes.

Although Eisenhower did not assume leadership on civil rights issues, he accomplished much on the domestic scene. He raised the minimum wage, extended social security and unemployment benefits, increased funding for public housing, and backed the creation of interstate highways. His popularity soared.

In general, the mid-1950s, like the post–World War I 1920s, were a time of "peace, progress, and prosperity," and most Americans enjoyed a return to normalcy and an ever-increasing standard of living. Pleased that "everything's booming but the guns," voters flocked to the polls in 1956 and reelected Eisenhower over Democrat Adlai Stevenson by the greatest majority since Franklin D. Roosevelt's in 1936. To many of the nation's citizens, the American dream had finally come within reach.

Linda Brown's case prompted the Supreme Court to begin the process of desegregating U.S. public schools in 1954.

E. Answer The Cold War caused many Americans to seek security in traditional conservative values, and Eisenhower's approach had brought progress and prosperity.

THINK THROUGH HISTORY
E. *Developing Historical Perspective* Why do you think most Americans went along with Eisenhower's conservative approach to domestic policy?

Section ❶ Assessment

1. TERMS & NAMES

Identify:
• GI Bill of Rights
• suburb
• Harry S. Truman
• Dixiecrat
• Fair Deal
• Dwight D. Eisenhower

2. SUMMARIZING Create a time line of key events relating to postwar America. Use the dates below as a guide.

```
|——————|——————|——————|——————|————————|
1946   1947   1948   1949         1952
```

Write a paragraph describing the effects of one of these events.

3. DRAWING CONCLUSIONS
Do you think Eisenhower's actions reflected his philosophy of dynamic conservatism? Why or why not?

THINK ABOUT
• the definition of dynamic conservatism
• Eisenhower's civil rights policies
• Eisenhower's accomplishments on other domestic issues

4. MAKING DECISIONS If you had voted in the 1952 presidential election, would you have cast your ballot for Governor Adlai Stevenson or General Dwight D. Eisenhower? Support your choice with reasons.

THINK ABOUT
• each candidate's background and political experience
• the previous presidents
• Republicans' criticisms of Democrats
• Eisenhower's running mate

802 CHAPTER 27

---

② The American Dream in the Fifties

TERMS & NAMES
- conglomerate
- franchise
- baby boom
- Dr. Jonas Salk
- consumerism
- planned obsolescence

LEARN ABOUT the material comforts that many Americans enjoyed in the 1950s
TO UNDERSTAND the benefits and the costs of pursuing the American dream.

ONE AMERICAN'S STORY

Settled into her brand new house near San Diego, California, Carol Freeman felt very fortunate. Her husband Mark had his own law practice, and when her first baby was born she became a full-time homemaker. She was living the American dream, yet Carol felt dissatisfied and that there was "something wrong" with her because she was not happy.

A PERSONAL VOICE

As dissatisfied as I was, and as restless, I remember so well this feeling [you] had at the time that the world was going to be your oyster. You were going to make money, your kids were going to go to good schools, everything was possible if you just did what you were supposed to do. The future was rosy. There was a tremendous feeling of optimism. . . . Much as I say it was hateful, it was also hopeful. It was an innocent time.

CAROL FREEMAN, quoted in *The Fifties: A Women's Oral History*

After World War II ended, Americans turned their attention to their families and jobs. The economy prospered. New technologies and business ideas created fresh opportunities for many, and by the end of the decade Americans were enjoying the highest standard of living in the world. The American dream of a happy and successful life seemed within the reach of many people.

The dream woman of the 1950s could brown a turkey to perfection for her family's dinner. However, she could also feel starved for meaning and fulfillment in her own life.

The Organization and the Organization Man

During the 1950s, businesses expanded rapidly. By 1956, the majority of Americans no longer held blue-collar, or industrial, jobs. Instead, more people worked in higher-paid, white-collar positions—clerical, managerial, or professional occupations. Unlike blue-collar workers, who manufactured goods for sale, white-collar workers tended to perform services in fields like sales, advertising, insurance, and communications.

CONGLOMERATES Many white-collar workers performed their services in large corporations or government agencies. Some of these organizations continued expanding by forming conglomerates. A **conglomerate** is a major corporation that includes a number of smaller companies in unrelated industries. For example, one conglomerate, International Telephone and Telegraph (ITT), whose original business was communications, bought car-rental companies, insurance companies, and hotel and motel chains. Through this diversification, or investment in various areas of the economy, ITT tried to protect itself from declines in individual industries. Other huge corporations included American Telephone and Telegraph, Xerox, and General Electric.

FRANCHISES In addition to diversifying, another strategy for business expansion—franchising—developed at this time. A **franchise** is a company that offers similar products or services in many locations. A franchise also is the right

The Postwar Boom **803**

SECTION 2 RESOURCES

 PRINT RESOURCES

IN-DEPTH RESOURCES: UNIT 7
Guided Reading, p. 58
Geography Application: The Baby Boom, p. 62
Primary Source: from *The Organization Man*, p. 65
Literature: from *The Man in the Gray Flannel Suit*, p. 68

ACCESS FOR STUDENTS ACQUIRING ENGLISH
Guided Reading (Spanish), p. 265
Geography Application: The Baby Boom (Spanish), p. 269

FORMAL ASSESSMENT
Section Quiz, p. 330

ALTERNATIVE ASSESSMENT BOOK
See forms for supporting and scoring alternative activities.

 TECHNOLOGY RESOURCES

HUMANITIES TRANSPARENCIES
H42, Highway Construction

GEOGRAPHY TRANSPARENCIES
G27, Highway Systems, 1950–1987

CD-ROM Electronic Library of Primary Sources

VIDEO *American Portfolio: A Videodisc for U.S. History*
user's guide, pp. 238, 239, 241

INTERNET McDougal Littell Learning On-Line
http://www.mcdougallittell.com

Section 2 Overview

OBJECTIVES

① To explain how changes in business affected workers.

② To describe the suburban lifestyle of the 1950s.

③ To identify causes and effects of the automobile industry boom.

④ To explain the increase in consumerism in the 1950s.

CRITICAL THINKING

- Comparing, p. 804
- Recognizing effects, pp. 804, 805, 809
- Contrasting, p. 806
- Analyzing causes, pp. 807, 809
- Analyzing issues, p. 808
- Summarizing, p. 809
- Forming opinions, p. 809

FOCUS & MOTIVATE

▶*Starting with the Student*
Ask volunteers to describe the American dream.

- Do students think their version of the dream differs from that of their parents? If so, how?
- Ask students to discuss how expectations change from one generation to another.

OBJECTIVE
① **INSTRUCT**

The Organization and the Organization Man

▶*Discussing Key Ideas*
- By the mid-1950s, blue-collar jobs no longer employ the majority of Americans.
- American business expands by diversifying and franchising.
- Conformity replaces individuality among workers.

IN-DEPTH RESOURCES: UNIT 7
Guided Reading, p. 58
Primary Source: from *The Organization Man*, p. 65

ACCESS FOR STUDENTS ACQUIRING ENGLISH
Guided Reading (Spanish), p. 265

By 1959 Ray Kroc had opened 100 McDonald's restaurants that had sold a combined total of 50 million hamburgers. The highly standardized burger of the 1950s was 3.9 inches in diameter, weighed 1.6 ounces, and was served on a 3.5-inch bun with a quarter ounce of onions. It sold for 15 cents.

MORE ABOUT. . .
Social Conformity

In a popular song titled "Little Boxes," folk singer Malvina Reynolds satirized social conformity:

"And they all play on the golf course
And drink their martinis dry,
And they all have pretty children
And the children go to school,
And the children go to summer camp
And then to the university,
Where they are put in boxes
And they come out all the same."

OBJECTIVE
② INSTRUCT

The Suburban Lifestyle

▶ *Starting with the Student*
Have students discuss the relationships between family members in TV shows from the 1950s and the 1990s. Ask, Do you think these shows accurately depict American families in the 1950s and the 1990s? Why or why not?

(continued on next page)

that is sold to an individual entrepreneur to open a business using the parent company's name and the system that the parent company developed.

Fast-food restaurants developed some of the first and most successful franchises. McDonald's, for example, had its start when the McDonald brothers developed unusually efficient service based on assembly-line methods at their small drive-in restaurant in San Bernardino, California. They simplified the menu, featured 15-cent hamburgers, and mechanized their kitchen. They used blenders called multimixers that could make five milkshakes at a time—and they had eight of these machines!

In 1954, Ray Kroc paid the McDonalds $2.7 million for the franchise rights to their hamburger drive-in. In April 1955, he opened his first McDonald's in Des Plaines, Illinois, where he further improved the assembly-line process and introduced the golden arches that are now familiar all over the world.

> **A PERSONAL VOICE**
> It requires a certain kind of mind to see the beauty in a hamburger bun. Yet is it any more unusual to find grace in the texture and softly curved silhouette of a bun than to reflect lovingly on the . . . arrangements and textures and colors in a butterfly's wings? . . . Not if you view the bun as an essential material in the art of serving a great many meals fast.
> **RAY KROC,** quoted in *The Fifties*

SOCIAL CONFORMITY While franchises like McDonald's helped standardize what people ate, some American workers found themselves becoming standardized as well. Employees who were well paid and held secure jobs in thriving companies sometimes paid a price for economic advancement: a loss of their individuality. In general, businesses did not want creative thinkers, rebels, or anyone who would rock the corporate boat.

In *The Organization Man,* a classic 1956 study of suburban Park Forest, Illinois, and other communities, William H. Whyte described how the new, large organizations created "company people." Companies would give personality tests to people applying for jobs to make sure they would "fit in" the corporate culture. Furthermore, according to Whyte, "in about 25 percent of the country's corporations, the [personality] tests are used not merely to help screen applicants for The Organization but to check up on people already in it." Companies rewarded employees for teamwork, cooperation, and loyalty and so contributed to the growth of conformity, which Whyte called "belongingness."

Large workplaces could be very cold and impersonal. Sociologist C. Wright Mills satirized the modern office as a place where "rows of blank-looking girls" sat "with blank, white folders in their blank hands, all blankly folding blank papers."

The writer Sloan Wilson also criticized this conformity in his 1955 autobiographical novel, *The Man in the Gray Flannel Suit.* The title character, Tom, is the typical businessman, who wears a dark suit, a white shirt, and a conservative tie and shoes. He and his wife have three children and a house in the suburbs, and he commutes to a good job in Manhattan. Despite their success, however, the couple feels dissatisfied. Like the novel's fictional couple, some Americans questioned whether pursuing the American dream exacted too high a price, as conformity replaced individuality.

The "organization man" had to step lively to keep up with the Joneses.

The Suburban Lifestyle

Though achieving job security did take a psychological toll on many Americans who resented having to subdue their own personalities, it also enabled them to provide the good things in life for their families. Most Americans worked in the

804 CHAPTER 27

A. Answer Both were successful business entities that grew rapidly. The conglomerate grew by diversifying; franchises grew by opening identical stores in new locations.
THINK THROUGH HISTORY
A. Comparing How were conglomerates and franchises alike and different?

B. Answer Some became dissatisfied, due to the emphasis on conformity and the impersonal corporate atmosphere.
THINK THROUGH HISTORY
B. Recognizing Effects What effects did the climate in many corporations have on workers?

TEACHING OPTIONS

Making Connections Across Time

Dressing for Success Conformity during the fifties was not just a matter of living in identical suburban houses or buying the same cars and consumer goods as one's neighbors. Conformity was an issue at work too. Corporate conformity for men in the 1950s included wearing a dark suit, white shirt, and conservative tie. Women in business were similarly expected to adhere to formal business attire. Have students contrast the image of the successful corporate employee of the 1950s with the "business casual" image of corporate America in the 1990s.

Making Connections Across the Curriculum

Sociology The emphasis on conformity in all avenues of life during the 1950s had a profound impact on the workplace. Sociologist David Riesman described the change in worker attitudes from being "inner-directed"—that is, relying on the principles and practices that a person internalized as a child—to being "other-directed"—guided by social pressure and others' expectations rather than one's own values and ethics. Discuss with students worker attitudes today: Do people they know seem more inner-directed or other-directed?

cities, but fewer and fewer of them lived there. New highways and the availability and affordability of automobiles and gasoline made commuting possible. By the early 1960s, every large city in the United States was surrounded by suburbs. Of the 13 million new homes built in the 1950s, 85 percent were suburban. For many people, the suburbs embodied the American dream of an affordable single-family house, good schools, a safe, healthy environment for children, and congenial neighbors just like themselves.

At the peak of the baby boom, an American was born every seven seconds.

THE BABY BOOM As soldiers returned from World War II and settled into family life, they contributed to an unprecedented population explosion known as the **baby boom.** Between 1946 and 1964, the birthrate (number of births per 1,000 population) in the United States soared. At the height of the baby boom, in 1957, one American infant was born every seven seconds—a total of 4,254,784. The result was the largest generation in the nation's history.

Contributing to the size of the baby-boom generation were many factors, including the following:

- reunion of families after the war
- decreasing marriage age
- desirability of large families
- confidence in continued economic prosperity
- advances in medicine

Among the medical advances that saved hundreds of thousands of children's lives were the discovery of drugs to fight and prevent childhood diseases, such as diphtheria and typhoid fever, and the development of a vaccine against the crippling disease poliomyelitis by **Dr. Jonas Salk.**

DR. SPOCK'S BABIES Suburban family life revolved around children, and many of them were raised using guidelines devised by author and pediatrician Dr. Benjamin Spock. His *Common Sense Book of Baby and Child Care*, published in 1946, sold nearly 10 million copies during the 1950s. He advised parents not to spank or scold their children and encouraged families to hold meetings in which children could express themselves. He considered it so important for mothers to be at home with their children that he suggested that the government pay mothers to stay home.

The baby boom had a tremendous impact not only on child care, but on the American economy and the educational system as well. Financial expert Sylvia F. Porter wrote in her popular newspaper column, "Take the 3,548,000 babies born in 1950. . . . Just imagine how much these extra people, these new markets, will absorb—in food, [in] clothing, in gadgets, in housing, in services. Our factories must expand just to keep pace." In 1958, toy sales alone reached $1.25 billion. During the decade, 10 million new students entered the elementary schools. The sharp increase in enrollment caused overcrowding and teacher shortages in many parts of the country. In California, a new school opened every seven days.

WOMEN'S ROLES During the 1950s, the role of homemaker and mother was glorified in popular magazines, movies, and TV programs, such as *Father Knows Best* and *The Adventures of Ozzie and Harriet*. *Time* magazine described the homemaker as "the key figure in all

C. Answer Creation of youth-centered culture; increased demand for consumer goods and jobs related to rearing and educating children.

THINK THROUGH HISTORY **C.** *Recognizing Effects* How did the baby boom affect American life in the 1950s?

KEY PLAYER

JONAS SALK 1914–1996
One of the most feared childhood diseases in the 1950s was poliomyelitis—polio, the disease that disabled President Franklin D. Roosevelt. Polio afflicted 58,000 American children in 1952, killing them or confining them to crutches, wheelchairs, or iron lungs (machines that helped people with paralyzed chest muscles to breathe). Mothers kept their children inside during the hot summers, fearful that the children would catch the highly contagious infection in swimming pools or other public places.

In 1954, Dr. Jonas Salk, *above, right,* developed an effective vaccine that helped prevent the disease, and the government sponsored a free inoculation program for children. The vaccine was extremely effective, and in 1958, only 5,700 new cases of the disease were reported. In 1974, thanks to Salk's vaccine and an oral vaccine developed in 1961 by Albert Sabin, there were only seven polio cases in the country.

The Postwar Boom **805**

(continued from page 804)

▶ *Discussing Key Ideas*
- Affluence, automobiles, and highways help many Americans achieve the dream of owning a home in the suburbs.
- The postwar baby boom creates a youth-centered culture and a demand for products related to children.
- Many American women become dissatisfied with the role of homemaker.

IN-DEPTH RESOURCES: UNIT 7 Geography Application: The Baby Boom, p. 62

KEY PLAYER *Jonas Salk*

Critical Thinking: Recognizing Effects Ask students to discuss how the Salk vaccine contributed to the well-being of the baby boom generation. Students might write a tribute to Jonas Salk, reflecting the impact of his work on wiping out a crippling disease.

MORE ABOUT . . . *Benjamin Spock*

In the 1960s, Dr. Spock became an outspoken opponent of the Vietnam War. He was convicted on charges of conspiring to counsel young men to avoid the military draft. The conviction was overturned in 1969.

TEACHING OPTIONS

Making Connections Across Time

Baby Boomers Today The largest generation in U.S. history continued to influence American society as its members grew into adulthood. In 1996, the first of the boomers turned 50. Discuss with students the impact of the aging baby boom generation on American society today. Consider these questions:

- What are the needs of growing numbers of people in their fifties?
- How do these needs affect the economy?
- How does the aging of the boomers impact your generation?

Making Global Connections

Wiping Out Polio By the mid-1990s, the World Health Organization (WHO) officially declared that polio had been eliminated from the Western Hemisphere. Although worldwide cases of polio declined by 80 percent between 1988 and 1994, the disease remained a serious problem in some parts of the world, especially in the Indian subcontinent. A program funded by Rotary International pledged to eradicate polio worldwide by the year 2000.

Teacher's Edition **805**

"Is this all?"

BETTY FRIEDAN, QUOTING A DISSATISFIED 1950s HOMEMAKER

Many people in the 1950s pursued their recreation—like their work—in lock step with their neighbors.

3-D comics were just one of many fads that mesmerized the nation in the 1950s.

suburbia, the thread that weaves between family and community—the keeper of the suburban dream." Contrary to the ideal portrayed in the media, however, some women, like Carol Freeman, were not happy with their roles and felt isolated, bored, and unfulfilled. According to one survey in the 1950s, more than one-fifth of suburban wives were dissatisfied with their lives. Betty Friedan, author of the groundbreaking 1963 study of women and society, *The Feminine Mystique,* described the problem.

A PERSONAL VOICE
For the first time in their history, women are becoming aware of an identity crisis in their own lives, a crisis which . . . has grown worse with each succeeding generation. . . . I think this is the crisis of women growing up—a turning point from an immaturity that has been called femininity to full human identity.
BETTY FRIEDAN, from *The Feminine Mystique*

Some women did have lives outside the confines of suburbia, though, and the number of women working outside the home steadily rose during the decade. By 1960, almost 40 percent of women with children between the ages of 6 and 17 held jobs. Some of these women worked because they were single, divorced, or widowed and had to support themselves and their families. Others worked to supplement their husbands' incomes or to seek personal fulfillment. But having a job didn't necessarily contribute to a woman's happiness. A woman's career opportunities tended to be limited to fields such as nursing, teaching, and office support, which paid less than other professional and business positions did. Women also earned less than men for comparable work. Although increasing numbers of women attended four-year colleges, they generally received little financial, academic, or psychological encouragement to pursue their goals.

THE LEISURE CLASS Most Americans of the 1950s had more leisure time than ever before. Employees worked a 40-hour week and earned several weeks' vacation. People owned more labor-saving devices, like washing machines, clothes dryers, dishwashers, vacuum cleaners, and power lawn mowers, which decreased the time it took to do chores. *Fortune* magazine reported that in 1953 Americans spent more than $30 billion on leisure goods and activities.

Americans enjoyed a wide variety of recreational pursuits—both active and passive. Millions of Americans participated in such sports as fishing, bowling, hunting, boating, and golf. More people than ever attended baseball, basketball, and football games, and others watched professional sports on television.

Americans also became avid readers. They devoured books about cooking, religion, do-it-yourself projects, and homemaking. They also read mysteries, romance novels, and fiction by popular writers, such as Ernest Hemingway, John Steinbeck, Daphne du Maurier, and J. D. Salinger. Book sales doubled, due in part to a thriving paperback market. The circulation of popular magazines like *Reader's Digest* and *Sports Illustrated* steadily rose, increasing from about 148 million to more than 190 million readers. Sales of comic books also reached a peak in the mid-1950s.

Activities geared to youth also grew rapidly. Membership in Brownies and Girl Scouts soared from

D. Answer Most 1950s women were homemakers and had fewer educational and career opportunities than do women today.

THINK THROUGH HISTORY
D. *Contrasting* How did women's roles and opportunities in the 1950s differ from women's roles today?

TEACHING OPTIONS

Exploring Themes

Women in America In the 1950s, most women put their husband's success above their own achievement. The percentage of women college students was smaller in the 1950s than in the 1920s. In a 1962 Gallup Poll of 2,300 women, however, 90 percent hoped that their daughters would be better educated and would not lead the same lives as they had led. Have the class discuss the social factors that influenced women's attitudes toward higher education in the 1950s. Ask them for evidence that suggests that women did not find complete fulfillment in the role of homemaker.

Teaching Gifted and Talented Students

Women's Goals Have selected students conduct a panel discussion or a simulated television talk show focusing on women's attitudes and goals today, as compared with those of women in the 1950s. Assign another student to act as the facilitator or "host" to keep the conversation moving. The rest of the class can be members of the audience who generate questions for the panel members. Pose these questions to get the discussion started:

• What would you say is the legacy of women in the 1950s?
• Do you think their daughters and granddaughters find life more fulfilling than they did? Why or why not?

1.8 million to 4 million between 1950 and 1960; the number of Cub Scouts jumped from about 770,000 to almost 2.5 million. Little League baseball, founded in 1939, became a fixture in most suburban communities.

The Automobile Culture

During World War II, the U.S. government had rationed gasoline to curb inflation and conserve scarce supplies. After the war, however, an increase in both imported and domestically produced petroleum—the raw material from which gasoline is made—led to inexpensive, plentiful fuel for consumers. Easy credit terms and abundant advertising persuaded Americans to buy cars in record numbers. "You auto buy now!" one slogan urged. In response, new car sales rose from 6.7 million in 1950 to 7.9 million in 1955. The total number of private cars on the road jumped from 40 million in 1950 to 60 million in 1960.

E. Answer Cars were necessary for life in the suburbs.

◀ THINK THROUGH HISTORY
E. Analyzing Causes Why did auto sales surge in the 1950s?

AUTOMANIA Suburban living made owning a car a necessity. Most of the new suburbs, built in formerly rural areas, did not offer public transportation, and people had to drive to their jobs in the cities. In addition, many of the schools, stores, synagogues, churches, and doctors' and dentists' offices were not within walking distance of suburban homes. Many families owned not one, but two cars—one for commuting to work and the other, often a station wagon, for doing local errands and taking the children to their activities.

THE INTERSTATE HIGHWAY SYSTEM The more cars there were, the more roads were needed. "Automania" spurred local and state governments to construct roads that would connect schools, shopping centers, and workplaces to residential suburbs. The Interstate Highway Act, which President Eisenhower signed in 1956, authorized the building of a nationwide highway network—41,000 miles of expressways. The new roads, in turn, encouraged the development of new suburbs farther and farther from the cities.

Interstate highways also made high-speed, long-haul trucking possible, which contributed to a decline in the commercial use of railroads. Towns along the new highways prospered, while towns along the older smaller roads experienced hard times. The system of highways also helped unify and homogenize the nation. As John Keats observed in his 1958 book *The Insolent Chariots*,

Americans Hit the Road

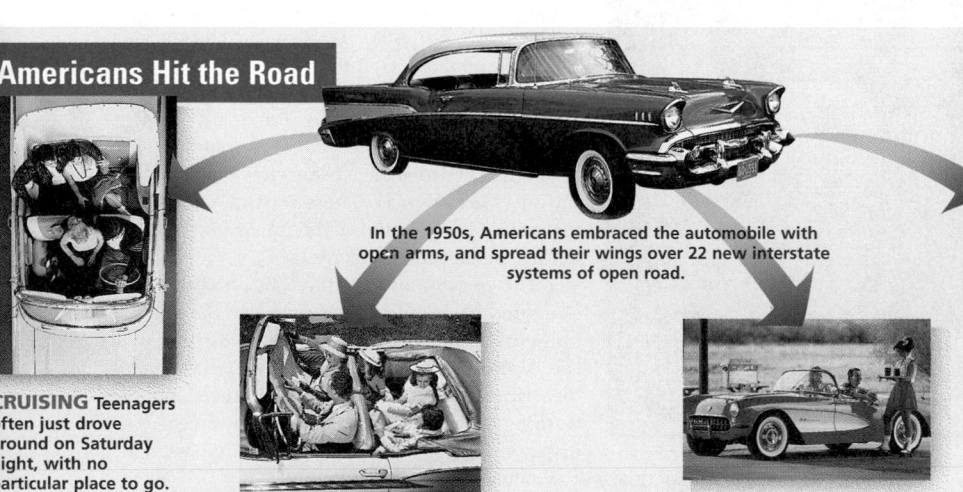

In the 1950s, Americans embraced the automobile with open arms, and spread their wings over 22 new interstate systems of open road.

CRUISING Teenagers often just drove around on Saturday night, with no particular place to go.

SUNDAY DRIVES AND CAR VACATIONS The joy of driving was often reason enough to pile into the family car and explore a part of America.

THE DRIVE-THRU In the 1950s, fast-food restaurants with roller-skating waitresses served food on trays that rested on the cars' windows.

THE DRIVE-IN People enjoyed their cars so much that they even watched movies in them.

The Postwar Boom **807**

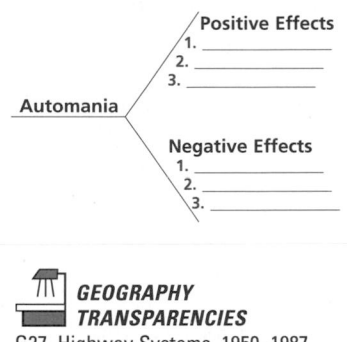

Consumerism Unbound

▶ **Discussing Key Ideas**
- In the 1950s, Americans buy more consumer goods than ever before.
- To encourage spending, manufacturers create new products planned to become obsolete in a short time.
- To increase sales of consumer goods, advertisers appeal to Americans' desire for status and conformity.

HISTORY FROM VISUALS
Suburban Backyards

Reading the Illustration
Point out details such as the bicycle, clothesline, and lawn furniture that illustrate aspects of suburban lifestyles. Note similarities and differences among neighbors' backyards and activities.

Extension Have students compare and contrast the backyards shown in the illustration and their own (or someone else's) backyard today, either in a written paragraph or in a sketch of their yard.

The back yard was the perfect place for home-owners to show off their latest recreational equipment.

"Our new roads, with their ancillaries, the motels, filling stations, and restaurants advertising 'Eats,' have made it possible for you to drive from Brooklyn to Los Angeles without a change of diet, scenery, or culture." With access to cars, affordable gas, and new highways, more and more Americans hit the road. They flocked to mountains, lakes, national parks, historic sites, and amusement parks for family vacations. Disneyland, which opened in California in July 1955, attracted 3 million visitors the next year.

MOBILITY TAKES ITS TOLL   As the automobile industry boomed, it stimulated production and provided jobs in other industries, such as drive-in movies and restaurants and shopping malls. Yet cars also created new problems for both society and the environment. Noise and exhaust polluted the air. Automobile accidents claimed more lives every year. Traffic jams raised people's stress levels, and heavy use damaged the roads. Because cars made it possible for Americans to live in suburbs, many upper-class and middle-class whites left the crowded cities. Jobs and businesses eventually followed them to the suburbs. Public transportation declined, and poor people in the inner cities were often left without jobs and vital services. As a result, the economic gulf between suburban and urban dwellers and between the middle class and the poor widened.

Consumerism Unbound

By the mid-1950s, nearly 60 percent of Americans were members of the middle class, about twice as many as before World War II. They wanted, and had the money to buy, increasing numbers of products. **Consumerism,** buying material goods, came to be equated with success.

NEW PRODUCTS   One new product after another appeared in the marketplace, as various industries responded to consumer demand. *Newsweek* magazine reported in 1956 that "hundreds of brand-new goods have become commonplace overnight."

The chemical industry, for example, produced several polyester fabrics—rayon, dacron, and orlon—to replace cotton, wool, and silk. It also developed Teflon, a nonstick coating for cookware, as well as plastics that replaced wood, glass, and metal. The materials for many of these new products had been developed in government-funded research projects during World War II. These wartime innovations quickly found a receptive market among peacetime consumers.

The electronics industry, which had also benefited from military research and development, became the fifth largest industry in the United States. Consumers purchased electric household appliances, such as washing machines, dryers, blenders, freezers, and dishwashers, in record numbers. Manufacturers also invested heavily in new electrical equipment.

With more and more leisure time to fill, people increasingly invested in recreational equipment. They bought televisions, tape recorders, and the new hi-fi (high-fidelity) record players. They bought casual clothing to suit their suburban lifestyles and rotary lawn mowers, barbecue equipment, swimming

F. Answer
Positive—growth of suburbs, increased mobility; negative—pollution, deterioration of major cities

THINK THROUGH HISTORY
F. Analyzing Issues *What positive and negative effects did the mass availability of the automobile have on American life in the 1950s?*

808 CHAPTER 27

TEACHING OPTION

Cooperative Activity: Developing Commercials

Task: Student groups will prepare one-minute television commercials for consumer goods of the 1950s.

Purpose: To help students recognize social and economic factors that contributed to consumerism in the 1950s.

Activity: Assign one of the following categories of products to small groups of students: household appliances, recreational equipment, clothing, or cars. Each group should prepare a 1950s-style TV commercial to market a product in its assigned category. Within each group, students should

choose from the following roles: director, scriptwriter, graphic designer (to plan the visual element of the commercial), and music researcher. Groups should present their commercials to the class.

Discuss the marketing techniques each commercial uses. Examples include appeal to Americans' desire for status, social conformity, or family values.

ALTERNATIVE ASSESSMENT BOOK
Standards for Evaluating a Cooperative Activity

pools, and lawn decorations for their suburban homes. In 1960, Americans spent more than $145 million on lawn and patio furniture alone.

PLANNED OBSOLESCENCE In addition to creating new products, manufacturers began using a marketing strategy called **planned obsolescence.** In order to encourage consumers to purchase more goods, manufacturers purposely designed products to become obsolete—that is, to wear out or become outdated in a short period of time. Carmakers brought out new models every year, urging consumers to stay up-to-date. Because of planned obsolescence, Americans came to expect new and better products, and they began to discard items that were sometimes barely used. Some observers commented that American culture was on the way to becoming a "throwaway society."

BUY NOW, PAY LATER Many Americans made their purchases with credit and therefore did not have to pay for them right away. The Diner's Club issued the first credit card in 1950, and the American Express card came along in 1959. In addition, people bought large items on the installment plan and made regular payments over a fixed time. Home mortgages (loans for buying a house) and automobile loans worked the same way. During the decade, the total private debt grew from $73 billion to $179 billion. Instead of saving money, Americans were spending it, confident that prosperity would continue.

THE ADVERTISING AGE The advertising industry capitalized on this runaway consumerism by encouraging even more spending. Ads were everywhere—in newspapers and magazines, on radio and television, and on billboards along the highways—prompting people to buy goods that ranged from cars to cereals to cigarettes. Advertisers spent about $6 billion in 1950; by 1955, the figure was up to $9 billion. During this time, businesses dedicated more money to advertising every year than the country spent on its public schools. Since most Americans had satisfied their basic needs, advertisers tried to convince them to buy things they really didn't need. Advertisers appealed to people's desire for status and "belongingness" and to associate their products with those values.

Television became a powerful new advertising tool. The first one-minute TV commercial was produced in 1941 at a cost of $9. In 1960, advertisers spent $1.6 billion for television ads. Television had become not only the medium for mass transmission of cultural values, but a symbol of popular culture itself.

Advertisers promised a world in which labor that was once difficult could be done by a machine at the touch of a button.

G. Answer Rising standard of living; success equated with material possessions; successful advertising campaigns.

THINK THROUGH HISTORY
G. Analyzing Causes *What factors contributed to the rapidly growing demand for consumer goods in the 1950s?*

Section 2 Assessment

1. TERMS & NAMES

Identify:
- conglomerate
- franchise
- baby boom
- Dr. Jonas Salk
- consumerism
- planned obsolescence

2. SUMMARIZING In a graphic organizer like the one below, list examples of specific goals that characterized the American dream for suburbanites in the 1950s.

```
        The American Dream
    ┌───────┬───────────┬──────┐
  Values   Home/       Work
           Family
    │        │           │
 examples examples   examples
```

3. FORMING OPINIONS Do you think that the life of a typical suburban homemaker during the 1950s was more like a dream come true or a living nightmare? Support your answer.

THINK ABOUT
- Carol Freeman's remarks on page 803
- Betty Friedan's comments on page 806
- the homemaker's responsibilities
- job opportunities for women

4. RECOGNIZING EFFECTS In what ways do you think that the current environmental consciousness is related to the "throwaway society" of the 1950s? Support your answer.

THINK ABOUT
- the purchasing habits of 1950s consumers
- the effects of planned obsolescence
- today's emphasis on recycling

The Postwar Boom **809**

ANSWERS

1. TERMS & NAMES

conglomerate, p. 803
franchise, p. 803
baby boom, p. 805
Dr. Jonas Salk, p. 805
consumerism, p. 808
planned obsolescence, p. 809

2. SUMMARIZING

Possible Answers: Values—conformity, material goods = success; Home/Family—two or three children, close family ties, single-family home in suburbia, one or two cars, television; Work—man is the breadwinner who works at a white-collar job; woman takes care of home and children.

3. FORMING OPINIONS

Possible Answers: Dream—had a husband to support her, a home in the suburbs, a car, children, material comforts, and did not have to work outside the home; Nightmare—was a slave to her home and family and had no time or encouragement to develop her own interests.

4. RECOGNIZING EFFECTS

Possible Answer: Today's common practices of recycling discarded items and trash, reusing empty food and product containers, and buying products with long-term warranties might be seen as necessary steps to reverse the "throwaway" trend of the 1950s and its resulting environmental problems.

OBJECTIVES

① To trace the growth of American suburbs after World War II.

② To describe details about one representative suburb.

FOCUS & MOTIVATE

▶ *Starting with the Student*
Have students contrast urban, rural, and suburban life.

- What are the main lifestyle differences in urban, suburban, and rural areas?
- If students could live in any of the three areas, which would they prefer, and why?

MORE ABOUT . . .
Postwar Suburbs

Like Park Forest, Illinois, Levittown was another preplanned American suburb. Built from 1946 to 1951 by the development firm of Levitt and Sons, Inc., the first Levittown was located in Nassau County on Long Island, New York. It contained shopping centers, schools, playgrounds, swimming pools, and community centers as well as thousands of low-cost homes. In part because of its proximity to the media center of New York City, Levittown came to represent all the suburbs developed in postwar America.

GEOGRAPHY
SPOTLIGHT

The Road to Suburbia

"Come out to Park Forest where small-town friendships grow—and you still live so close to a big city." Advertisements like this one for a scientifically planned Chicago suburb captured the lure of the suburbs for thousands of growing families in the 1950s—affordable housing, congenial neighbors, fresh air and open spaces, good schools, and easy access to urban jobs and culture. Good transportation was the lifeline of suburban growth a half a century ago and it continues to fuel expansion today.

❶ **WHERE THE 'BURBS ARE**
Park Forest, Illinois, was planned from its conception in 1945 to be a "complete community for middle-income families with children." The setting was rural—amidst cornfields and forest preserves about 30 miles south of Chicago. But it was convenient to commuter lines like the Illinois Central Railroad and to major highways such as Western Avenue.

SHARED PRIVACY By 1952, development had expanded to include both low-cost rental units and single-family homes. All the streets were curved to slow traffic, present a pleasing sweep of space, and give residents maximum privacy and space for yards.

810 CHAPTER 27

RECOMMENDED RESOURCES

Books

Arnold, Eve. *The Fifties.* New York: Pantheon, 1985. A social history in photographs, introduced by John Chancellor.

Baldassare, Mark. *Trouble in Paradise.* New York: Columbia UP, 1986. The suburban transformation in America.

Gans, Herbert J. *The Levittowners.* New York: Pantheon, 1967. A study of life and politics in a then-new suburban community.

Halberstam, David. *The Fifties.* New York: Villard, 1993. A noteworthy recent account of the era.

Jackson, Kenneth T. *Crabgrass Frontier.* New York: Oxford UP, 1985. The suburbanization of the U.S.A.

Marling, Karal Ann. *As Seen on TV: The Visual Culture of Everyday Life in the 1950s.* Cambridge: Harvard UP, 1994. Fifties America through the eyes of television.

Wood, Robert Coldwell. *Suburbia: Its People and Their Politics.* Boston: Houghton, 1958. A contemporaneous account.

Videos

Suburbs, Arcadia for Everyone. Dir. Murray Grigor. Films for the Humanities, 1986. The evolution of the suburban ideal in 20th-century America.

❷ THE COMMUTER CRUSH AND JUNGLE GYMS Men commuted to work on the IC railroad, while their wives usually stayed home to take care of the children, who thrived in Park Forest's safe, wholesome family environment. The school system struggled to keep pace with the ongoing baby boom.

❸ SHOP 'TILL YOU DROP Consumerism was a major driving force in the 1950s, and Park Forest kept up with the trend. The central shopping center, or Plaza, served the community well until the late 1960s.

❹ SUBURBAN SPRAWL CONTINUES When Interstate 57 was built, a mammoth mall sprang up just off the highway, and the local shopping area withered. Park Forest is still struggling to revive its central shopping area.

INTERACT WITH HISTORY

1. **SYNTHESIZING** How did the availability of transportation influence the creation and ongoing development of Park Forest?

    SEE SKILLBUILDER HANDBOOK, PAGE 1051.

2. **SURVEYING A SUBURB** Research a suburb in your area to learn about its history and development. If possible, use the resources of the suburb's library and interview residents to get firsthand information.

The Postwar Boom **811**

▶ **Starting with the Student**
• Have students discuss drawbacks to living in the suburbs. *Possible Responses: Commuting, less variety of people and activities, fewer cultural activities, new developments not always scenic, homes sometimes poorly constructed.*
• Have students discuss why the suburbs might have been so appealing to so many postwar Americans. *Possible Responses: Affordable housing, less congested, less polluted, status symbol, more privacy and independence, home an investment, better schools, less crime, many like to live closer to nature.*

▶ **Discussing Key Ideas**
• In the baby-boom years after World War II, many American families move to the suburbs.
• Good transportation helps make suburban development possible.

HUMANITIES TRANSPARENCIES
H42, Highway Construction

HISTORY FROM VISUALS
Reading the Images
Have students study the graphics.
• Where is Park Forest in relation to the downtown part of Chicago known as the Loop? *South.*
• In addition to the IC, or Illinois Central, railroad, how might suburbanites have commuted to work in downtown Chicago? *Driving on Route 1 or 54.*

INTERACT WITH HISTORY

1. Synthesizing

Possible Answers: *Good transportation was necessary to both the creation and ongoing development of the suburb. Commuters had to have a convenient way to get to and from work. Commuter railroad lines such as the Illinois Central Railroad provided reliable transportation to and from the city.*

2. Surveying a Suburb

Students might perform this activity in small groups. In addition to visiting the community's school (including college, if any) or public library, students may find information through local real-estate firms, development housing offices, and/or organizations such as the Chamber of Commerce. Encourage students to prepare interview questions in advance and to record the interviews on audiotape or videotape or through careful note taking.

OBJECTIVES

(1) To explain how television programs in the 1950s reflected middle-class values.

(2) To explain how the beat movement and rock 'n' roll music clashed with middle-class values.

(3) To describe ways that African-American entertainers integrated the media in the 1950s.

SKILLBUILDER

- Interpreting charts, p. 813

CRITICAL THINKING

- Summarizing, pp. 813, 817
- Forming Opinions, pp. 814, 817
- Clarifying, pp. 815, 817
- Analyzing causes, p. 815
- Recognizing effects, p. 816
- Comparing and contrasting, p. 817

FOCUS & MOTIVATE

▶ **Starting with the Student**
Ask students if they listen to recordings of hit songs from the 1950s on the radio or watch reruns of 1950s programs on television.

- Ask, Why do these examples of 1950s culture remain popular today? *Possible Responses: They represent nostalgia to baby boomers; they reach a new audience.*

MORE ABOUT . . .
Little Richard

"Tutti Frutti"—Little Richard's first big hit—was a club song whose lyrics had to be cleaned up for mass audiences. His style and appearance shocked conservative Americans in the 1950s. In the 1990s, Little Richard found a new audience in the grandchildren of his original fans. He recorded a rock-rap version of "Itsy Bitsy Spider" and appeared in a children's video called *Mother Goose Rock 'n' Rhyme.*

---

3 Popular Culture

TERMS & NAMES
- mass media
- Federal Communications Commission (FCC
- beat movement
- beatnik
- rock 'n' roll

LEARN ABOUT television, radio, movies, literature, and music in the 1950s
TO UNDERSTAND how mass popular culture reflected middle-class values and how some subcultures dissented from those values.

ONE AMERICAN'S STORY

Popular music thrived in the 1950s. Singers like Frank Sinatra, Nat "King" Cole, Tony Bennett, Lena Horne, and Perry Como crooned love songs, and silly tunes like Patti Page's "The Doggie in the Window" topped the charts. But in the middle of the decade, spurred by the growth of radio stations and live tours aimed at African-American audiences, record sales of hard-driving rhythm and blues began to take off. A 14-year-old saxophone player, who later became a music producer, described the first time he saw rhythm-and-blues performer Richard Wayne Penniman, better known as Little Richard.

A PERSONAL VOICE
He'd just burst onto the stage from anywhere, and you wouldn't be able to hear anything but the roar of the audience....He'd be on the stage, he'd be off the stage, he'd be jumping and yelling, screaming, whipping the audience on.... Then when he finally did hit the piano and just went into di-di-di-di-di-di-di, you know, well nobody can do that as fast as Richard. It just took everybody by surprise.

H. B. BARNUM, quoted in *The Rise and Fall of Popular Music*

Little Richard, born poor, wore flashy clothes on stage, curled his hair, and shouted his songs. As one writer observed, "In two minutes [he] used as much energy as an all-night party." He distinctly did not fit the gray-flannel-suit-and-station-wagon, suburban middle-class values of the 1950s. His wild individualism appealed strongly to many young people who felt constrained by the mass conformity. Although much of America's popular culture, especially television, reflected those mainstream values—secure jobs, material success, well-behaved children, and general conformity—Little Richard became a popular idol only when he appeared on the TV show *American Bandstand.*

Little Richard

New Era of the Mass Media

Compared with other **mass media**—means of communication that reach large audiences—television developed with lightning speed. First widely available in 1948, television had reached 9 percent of American homes by 1950 and 55 percent of homes by 1954. In 1960, almost 90 percent—45 million—of American homes had television sets. Clearly, TV was the entertainment and information marvel of the postwar years.

THE RISE OF TELEVISION Early television sets were small boxes with round screens. Programming was meager, and broadcasts were in black and white. The first regular broadcasts, beginning in 1949, reached only a small part of the east coast and offered only two hours of programs per week. Post–World War II innovations such as microwave relays, which could transmit television waves over long distances, sent the television industry soaring.

At first, the **Federal Communications Commission (FCC)**—the government agency that regulates and licenses television, telephone, telegraph, radio, and other communications industries—was very cautious about allowing television stations to open. It imposed a freeze on new stations between 1948 and 1952 to give the industry time to plan for expansion and to solve problems

---

SECTION 3 RESOURCES

Glued to the Set, 1950–1996

HOUSEHOLDS WITH TV SETS

millions of households

100
80
60
40
20

1950 1960 1970 1980 1990

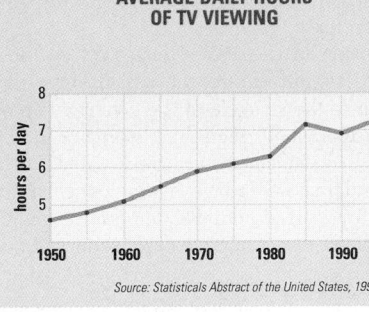

AVERAGE DAILY HOURS OF TV VIEWING

hours per day

8
7
6
5

1950 1960 1970 1980 1990

Source: Statisticals Abstract of the United States, 1991

SKILLBUILDER **INTERPRETING CHARTS** *During which decade did the number of households with TV sets increase the most?*

Kefauver: 'Reduce Crime On TV!' ...See Page 10

TV GUIDE

LOCAL PROGRAM LISTINGS WEEK OF MAY 21–27

15¢

Audrey Meadows and Jackie Gleason starred in the wildly popular TV series, *The Honeymooners,* **which was still being rerun in the late-1990s.**

Skillbuilder Answer 1950–1960

that interfered with reception. After the freeze, the number of stations jumped from 108 in 1952 to 500 in 1956.

This period of rapid expansion was the "golden age" of television entertainment—and entertainment in the 1950s often meant comedy. Programs were usually broadcast live, with mistakes and bloopers intact. Milton Berle attracted huge audiences with *The Texaco Star Theater*, and Lucille Ball and Desi Arnaz's early situation comedy, *I Love Lucy*, began its enormously popular run in 1951.

At the same time, veteran radio broadcaster Edward R. Morrow introduced two innovations: on-the-scene reporting with his program *See It Now* (1951–1958), and interviewing with *Person to Person* (1953–1959). Westerns, sports events, and original dramas shown on *Playhouse 90* and *Studio One* offered entertainment variety. The introduction of videotape technology in 1956 took some of the risks out of broadcasting. After that, producers could prerecord and edit programs and broadcast them any time. Television thus gained flexibility but lost some of its early spontaneity.

American businesses took advantage of the opportunities offered by the new television industry. Advertising expenditures on TV, which were $170 million in 1950, reached $1 billion in 1955 and nearly $2 billion in 1960.

A. Answer Comedy shows, interview programs, Westerns, sports events, drama, and children's shows.

Children's programs, such as *The Mickey Mouse Club* and *The Howdy Doody Show*, attracted loyal young fans who wanted to buy the products associated with the programs. Inspired by television advertising, TV heroes like the actor who portrayed Davy Crockett, and TV coverage of the latest fads, children badgered their parents to buy coonskin caps, wiffle balls, Hula-Hoops, and Silly Putty.

THINK THROUGH HISTORY
A. Summarizing *What types of programs characterized television's "golden age" in the 1950s?*

Sales of *TV Guide*, introduced in 1952, quickly outpaced sales of other magazines. In 1954, the food industry introduced a new convenience item, the frozen TV dinner. Complete, ready-to-heat individual meals on disposable aluminum trays, TV dinners made it easy for people to eat without missing their favorite shows.

STEREOTYPES AND GUNSLINGERS Not everyone was thrilled with television, though. Critics objected to its effects on children and its portrayal of stereotypes.

Women did, in fact, appear in stereotypical roles, such as the ideal mothers of *Father Knows Best* and *The Adventures of Ozzie and Harriet*. Male characters outnumbered women characters three to one. African

HISTORICAL SPOTLIGHT

TV QUIZ SHOWS

Beginning with *The $64,000 Question* in 1955, television created hit quiz shows by adopting a popular format from radio and adding big cash prizes. Two contestants squared off over topics ranging from Shakespeare to boxing.

The quiz show *Twenty-One* made a star of a shy English professor named Charles Van Doren. He rode a wave of fame and fortune until 1958, when a former contestant revealed that, to heighten the dramatic impact, producers had been giving some of the contestants the right answers. Van Doren stated

I was almost able to convince myself that it did not matter what I was doing because it was having such a good effect on the national attitude toward teachers, education, and the intellectual life.

A scandal followed when a congressional subcommittee investigated and confirmed the charges. Former contestants faced trial for perjury, and most of the quiz shows left the air.

The Postwar Boom **813**

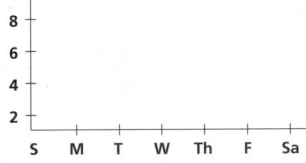

MORE ABOUT . . .
Newton Minow and the FCC

The FCC cannot interfere directly with television programming. Under Minow's leadership, however, the agency refused to renew licenses for stations whose programming did not meet the standards promised in their original applications. In his "vast wasteland" speech, Minow told broadcasters, "For every hour the people give you—you owe them something. I intend to see that your debt is paid with service. . . ."

 ELECTRONIC LIBRARY OF PRIMARY SOURCES
from *Being Digital* by Nicholas Negroponte

MORE ABOUT . . .
James Dean

Movie actor James Dean starred in only three films. In his most famous movie, *Rebel Without a Cause,* he played a teenager fighting against conformity. To American teenagers, Dean became a symbol of their own frustrations with society. James Dean died in an automobile crash at the age of 24.

"Television is . . . a vast wasteland."

NEWTON MINOW

The young actor James Dean, seen here in the movie *Giant,* had a self-confident indifference that made him the idol of teenagers in the fifties. He became a legend, although he appeared in only three films. He died in a car accident at age 24.

Americans and Latinos rarely appeared in television programs at all. A 1959 episode of *Father Knows Best* provided a rare positive portrayal of a racial minority when a Latino gardener taught the town a lesson about accepting cultural differences.

Television in the 1950s portrayed an idealized white America. For the most part, it omitted references to poverty, diversity, and contemporary conflicts, such as the struggle of the civil rights movement against racial discrimination. Instead, it glorified the historical conflicts of the Western frontier in hit shows such as *Gunsmoke* and *Have Gun, Will Travel.* The level of violence in these popular shows led to ongoing concerns about the effect of television on children. In 1961, Federal Communications Commission chairman Newton Minow voiced this concern to the leaders of the television industry.

A PERSONAL VOICE
When television is bad, nothing is worse. I invite you to sit down in front of your television set when your station goes on the air . . . and keep your eyes glued to that set [until] the station signs off. I can assure you that you will observe a vast wasteland.

NEWTON MINOW, in a speech to the National Association of Broadcasters, Washington, D.C., May 9, 1961

RADIO AND MOVIES In the early days of television, reaction to the new medium was mixed. Some predicted that it would never catch on, while others feared that TV would eclipse all competing forms of entertainment. Although TV turned out to be wildly popular, radio and movies survived. But instead of competing with television's mass market of drama and variety shows, radio stations turned to local programming of news, weather, music, and community issues. The strategy paid off. During the decade, radio advertising rose by 35 percent, and the number of stations increased by 50 percent.

From the beginning, television cut into the profitable movie market. In 1948, 18,500 movie theaters had drawn nearly 90 million paid admissions per week. As more people stayed home to watch TV, the number of moviegoers decreased by nearly half. By 1960, one-fifth of the nation's movie theaters had been converted into bowling alleys or supermarkets, or they simply stood empty. As early as 1951, producer David Selznick worried about Hollywood: "It'll never come back. It'll just keep on crumbling until finally the wind blows the last studio prop across the sands."

But Hollywood did not crumble and blow away. Instead, it capitalized on the advantages that movies still held over television—size, color, and stereoscopic sound. Stereoscopic sound, which surrounded the viewer, was introduced in 1952, and by 1954, more than 50 percent of movies were in color. By contrast, color television, which became available that year, did not become widespread until the next decade. In 1953, 20th Century Fox introduced Cinema-Scope, which projected a wide-angle image on a broad screen. The industry also tried novelty features: Smell-O-Vision and Aroma-Rama piped smells into the theaters to coincide with events shown on the

THINK THROUGH HISTORY
B. Forming Opinions Do you think the rise of television had a positive or negative effect on Americans? Explain.
B. Answer Positive—informing and entertaining; reinforcing cultural values; Negative—promoting stereotypes of minorities and women; exposing children to images of violence.

---

screen. Three-dimensional images, viewed through special glasses supplied by the theaters, appeared to leap into the audience.

The availability of the wide screen and stereoscopic sound inspired the creation of spectacular epic movies, such as the award-winning *Around the World in Eighty Days* and *The Ten Commandments.* The film director Alfred Hitchcock sounded a different, more ominous note with his eerie. suspenseful masterpieces—*Rear Window, The Man Who Knew Too Much, Vertigo,* and *North by Northwest*—all made between 1954 and 1959.

THINK THROUGH HISTORY
C. *Clarifying*
How did radio and movies maintain their appeal in the 1950s?

A Subculture Emerges

Although the mass media found a wide audience for their portrayals of mostly white popular culture, dissenting voices rang out throughout the 1950s. The messages of the Beat movement in literature, and of rock 'n' roll in music, clashed with the tidy suburban view of life and set the stage for the counterculture that would burst forth in the 1960s.

C. Answer They concentrated on what they did best—local news, weather, and music programming for radio and size, color, and stereoscopic sound for movies.

THE BEAT MOVEMENT Centered in San Francisco, Los Angeles, and New York City's Greenwich Village, the **beat movement** expressed the social and literary nonconformity of artists and poets. The word *beat* originally meant "weary" but came to refer as well to a musical beat.

Followers of this movement, called beats or **beatniks,** lived nonconformist lives and cared little for material goods. Many of the men wore sandals and beards; the women, black leotards and no lipstick. They picked up the "hip" language of jazz musicians—a vocabulary that included words such as *bread* for money and *pad* for apartment. They tended to shun regular work and to live in inexpensive, sparsely furnished rooms. They sought a higher consciousness through Zen Buddhism, music, and, sometimes, drugs.

Many beat poets and writers believed in imposing as little structure as possible on their artistic works, which often had a free, open form. They read their poetry aloud in coffeehouses and gathering places, such as poet and publisher Lawrence Ferlinghetti's City Lights bookstore in San Francisco. Works that capture the essence of this era include Allen Ginsberg's long, free-verse poem *Howl,* published in 1956, and Jack Kerouac's novel of the movement, *On the Road,* published in 1957. This novel describes a nomadic search across America for authentic experiences, people, and values.

D. Answer Teenagers looking for alternatives to the conformity and consumerism of their parents found a celebration of poverty, nonconformity, and art that reflected immediate, sensory experience.

A PERSONAL VOICE
The only people for me are the mad ones, the ones who are mad to live, mad to talk, mad to be saved . . . the ones who never yawn or say a commonplace thing, but burn, burn, burn like fabulous yellow roman candles exploding like spiders across the stars.
JACK KEROUAC, *On the Road*

The beat generation marched to the tune of nonconformists like Jack Kerouac.

THINK THROUGH HISTORY
D. *Analyzing Causes* Why do you think young Americans were attracted to the beat movement?

Many mainstream Americans found this lifestyle less enchanting. *Look* magazine proclaimed, "There's nothing really new about the beat philosophy. It consists merely of the average American's value scale—turned inside out. The goals of the Beat are *not* watching TV, *not* wearing gray flannel, *not* owning a home in the suburbs, and especially—*not* working." Although the beats' rebellion against consumerism and suburban living left many Americans cold, the beatnik attitudes, way of life, and literature attracted the attention of the media and fired the imaginations of many college students. *On the Road* sold half a million copies, and Ferlinghetti's *A Coney Island of the Mind,* hundreds of thousands of copies—extraordinary sales for a book of poetry.

ROCK 'N' ROLL While beats expressed themselves in unstructured literature, musicians in the 1950s added electronic instruments to traditional blues music,

---

A Subculture Emerges

▶ *Starting with the Student*
• Pose this question to students: How do teenagers today express a lack of conformity with the social values of their parents? *Possible Answers: Through music, clothing styles, pierced body parts and tattoos, hair styles.*
• Ask students to identify values they think teenagers and young adults of the 1950s might have rejected. *Possible Answers: Social conformity, materialism, superficiality.*

▶ *Discussing Key Ideas*
• The beat movement expresses social and literary nonconformity.
• Rock 'n' roll represents nonconformity in music.
• Radio disc jockeys, television, and movies bring rock 'n' roll into the mainstream of popular culture.

MORE ABOUT . . .
Jack Kerouac

The son of French-Canadian parents, Jack Kerouac was born in Massachusetts. He attended Columbia University and served in the navy. Kerouac's wanderings throughout the United States, Mexico, and Europe provided the background for his novels. *On the Road,* which he wrote in three weeks, tells of several beatniks who travel across the United States in search of personal fulfillment.

Skillbuilder Mini-Lesson: Analyzing Primary Sources

Explaining the Skill Works created by a member of a historical movement can tell historians much about the movement and about the society in which it developed. Such sources often reflect the person's strong feelings and attitudes. Therefore, identifying the writer or speaker of the material and investigating his or her attitudes helps historians assess the value of the source.

Applying the Skill Have students read about the beat movement and look at "A Personal Voice" on this page. Then ask these questions:
1. Is Jack Kerouac a good source for information about the beat movement? Why or why not? *Most will say yes,*

because he was a leader of the movement and felt passionately about it. He is not objective, but one should not expect him to be.
2. What does Kerouac mean by the word *mad? Passionate, excited.*
3. What is Kerouac's message in this passage? *Possible Response: Kerouac is bored with traditional society and likes people who feel passion about life.*

IN-DEPTH RESOURCES: UNIT 7
Skillbuilder Practice: Primary Sources, p. 61

OBJECTIVE
③ INSTRUCT

African Americans and Popular Culture

▶ **Starting with the Student**
- Ask students to identify the most popular African-American performers today.
- Discuss how those performers influence popular culture.
- Ask, Do you think there is true integration in the media today?

▶ **Discussing Key Ideas**
- Some African-American performers pave the way for minority representation in white-dominated entertainment.
- African-American radio stations appeal to black audiences.
- Throughout the 1950s, African Americans remain segregated from the dominant culture.

Jukeboxes in diners and other public places helped spread rock 'n' roll music to every part of the country.

creating rhythm and blues. In 1953, a Cleveland, Ohio, radio disc jockey, Alan Freed, was among the first to play this music, which was usually produced by African-American musicians for his mostly white audience. His listeners responded enthusiastically, and he gave the new music that grew out of rhythm and blues the name that has lasted: **rock 'n' roll.**

In the next few years, Little Richard, Chuck Berry, Bill Haley and the Comets, and especially Elvis Presley, brought rock 'n' roll to a frantic pitch of popularity with newly affluent teens who bought their records. The music's heavy rhythm, simple melodies, and lyrics—featuring love, cars, and the problems of being young—captivated teenagers across the country.

Elvis Presley, the King of Rock 'n' Roll, learned his music by singing in church and listening to country and blues music on the radio in Memphis, Tennessee. His mother gave him a guitar, and he paid four dollars of his own money to record two songs in 1953. Sam Phillips, a rhythm-and-blues producer, discovered Presley and produced his first records, which sold well. In 1955, Phillips sold Presley's contract to RCA for $35,000.

Presley's live appearances were immensely popular and 45 of his records sold over a million copies, including "Heartbreak Hotel," "Hound Dog," "All Shook Up," "Don't Be Cruel," and "Burning Love." In 1956, he created a sensation on TV shows hosted by Steve Allen and Ed Sullivan and began his movie career by starring in *Love Me Tender*. Although *Look* magazine dismissed him as "a wild troubadour who wails rock 'n' roll tunes, flails erratically at a guitar, and wriggles like a peep-show dancer," Presley's rebellious style captivated young audiences. Girls screamed and fainted, and boys tried to imitate him.

Not surprisingly, many adults condemned rock 'n' roll. They believed that the new music would lead to teenage delinquency and immorality. In a few cities, rock 'n' roll concerts were banned. Citizens' groups tried to keep the records out of stores, and disc jockeys around the United States were fired or punished for playing the music. But despite this controversy, television and radio exposure helped bring rock 'n' roll into the mainstream, and it became more acceptable by the end of the decade. The long-running TV show *American Bandstand,* hosted by Dick Clark, featured wholesome rock 'n' roll singers and showed well-dressed, middle-class teenagers dancing to the music. Record sales, which were 189 million in 1950, grew with the popularity of rock 'n' roll, reaching 600 million in 1960.

E. Answer Radio disc jockeys played rock 'n' roll; TV variety shows promoted the stars and the music; movies featured Elvis Presley.

THINK THROUGH HISTORY
E. Recognizing Effects How did radio, TV, and the movies contribute to the rise of rock 'n' roll?

African Americans and Popular Culture

Many of the decade's great performers in all categories of popular culture were African American. Singers Nat Cole and Lena Horne, singer and actor Harry Belafonte, actor Sidney Poitier, and many others paved the way for minority representation in white-dominated fields. In 1956, CBS ran an all-black soap opera called *The Story of Ruby Valentine*, set in New York City's Harlem. Musicians Miles Davis, Sonny Rollins, Charlie Parker, Dizzy Gillespie, and Thelonius Monk entertained audiences of all races.

816 CHAPTER 27

But true integration in the media was slow in coming. Nat Cole, the first African American to have a weekly series on national television, observed, "There's a lot more integration in the actual life of the U.S. than you'll find on TV. But I notice that they always have integration in the prison scenes on television." Dick Clark integrated his popular *American Bandstand* in a pioneer 1957 broadcast. For the first time, black teenage couples joined white couples on the dance floor—and not one of the 15,000 letters Clark received every week complained. However, it was not until the middle of the next decade, when Duke Ellington's granddaughter performed with a mixed dance group, that professional dance on television was integrated.

Before integration reached radio audiences, popular African-American culture thrived on separate stations. By 1954, there were 250 radio stations nationwide aimed specifically at African-American listeners. Over 700 black DJs and a few white ones, including Alan Freed, played music by black artists like Amos Milburn, Little Esther, and a doo-wop group called the Orioles. These performers regularly reached the African-American top ten list, and their records sold upwards of 150,000 copies.

African-American stations were part of radio's attempt to counter the mass popularity of television by targeting specialized audiences. These stations also served advertisers, who wanted to reach a large African-American audience. But it was the black listeners—who had fewer television sets than whites and did not find themselves reflected in mainstream programming—who appreciated the stations most. Author Thulani Davis, a poet, journalist, and playwright, expressed the feelings of one listener to African-American radio (or *race radio* as the character called it) in her novel *1959*.

The Drifters' smooth, synchronized movements and mellow harmony helped win them a wide audience that included both blacks and whites.

A PERSONAL VOICE
Billie Holiday died and I turned twelve on the same hot July day. The saddest singing in the world was coming out of the radio, race radio that is, the radio of the race. The white stations were on the usual relentless rounds of Pat Boone, Teresa Brewer, and anybody else who couldn't sing but liked to cover songs that were once colored. . . . White radio was honest at least—they knew anybody in the South could tell Negro voices from white ones, and so they didn't play our stuff.
THULANI DAVIS, from *1959*

F. Answer They reached receptive African Americans who didn't have TVs and were interested in enjoying their own culture.

THINK THROUGH HISTORY
F. Clarifying How did radio stations help African-American performers gain wide audiences?

At the end of the 1950s, African Americans were still largely segregated from the dominant culture. This ongoing segregation—and the racial tensions it fed—would become a powerful force for change in the turbulent 1960s.

Section 3 Assessment

1. TERMS & NAMES
Identify:
• mass media
• Federal Communications Commission (FCC)
• beat movement
• beatnik
• rock 'n' roll

2. SUMMARIZING Create a "Who's Who" chart of popular culture idols of the 1950s. Identify the art form each person was associated with and his or her major accomplishments.

Personality	Art Form	Accomplishments

3. COMPARING AND CONTRASTING In what ways were the rock 'n' roll musicians and the beat poets of the 1950s similar and different? Support your answer with details from the text.

THINK ABOUT
• the values the musicians and poets believed in
• people's reactions to them

4. FORMING OPINIONS Based on what you learned about television of the 1950s, do you agree with Newton Minnow's statement on page 814 that it was "a vast wasteland"? Support your answer with details from the text.

THINK ABOUT
• the charts on page 813
• the types of shows that appeared on television
• the way characters were portrayed and the values they expressed

The Postwar Boom **817**

ANSWERS

1. TERMS & NAMES
mass media, p. 812
Federal Communications Commission (FCC), p. 812
beat movement, p. 815
beatnik, p. 815
rock 'n' roll, p. 816

2. SUMMARIZING
Possible Responses:
Lucille Ball/television/star of *I Love Lucy*; Edward R. Murrow/television/host of *Person to Person*; Alfred Hitchcock/movies/director of thrillers; Sidney Poitier/movies/actor; Elvis Presley/music/rock 'n' roll star; Jack Kerouac/literature/beat novelist and author of *On the Road*.

3. COMPARING AND CONTRASTING
Possible Answers: Both were rebellious, spontaneous, experimental, and innovative; often wore nonconformist clothing; attracted the young as well as alienated older, middle-class Americans; and performed for live audiences. Rock 'n' roll performers probably had a wider popular audience, due to their promotion in the mass media.

4. FORMING OPINIONS
Possible Answers: Agree—TV provided mass appeal by addressing mainstream America. Programs presented idealized white values and ignored the problems and realities of minorities. Disagree—TV programs provided needed entertainment and escape for many people and also portrayed the ideal family life that many valued.

DAILY LIFE
1950 — 1960

The Emergence of the Teenager

Life after World War II brought changes in the family. For the first time, the teenage years were recognized as an important and unique developmental stage between childhood and adulthood. The booming postwar economy made it possible for teenagers to stay in school instead of working to help support their families and allowed their parents to give them generous allowances. American business, particularly the music and movie industries, rushed to court this new consumer group. Ads, like this one for the soft drink Seven-Up, used clever slogans about the latest trends influence teens' decisions about which products to buy.

FOCUS & MOTIVATE

▶ *Starting with the Student*
Have students compare and contrast American popular music of their generation with that of their parents' or guardians' generation.

• What is similar and different about the music?

• What role, if any, does dancing play in the music's popularity?

MORE ABOUT . . .
Rock 'n' Roll

Early in the 1950s, young white audiences seeking something to dance to turned increasingly to rhythm and blues, a lively form of music popular with black musicians. White performers brought to the mix an infusion of country music, and rock 'n' roll was born. Its early stars were both black (Chuck Berry, Little Richard, Fats Domino) and white (Buddy Holly, Elvis Presley, Jerry Lee Lewis, Bill Haley and the Comets). The term *rock 'n' roll* was popularized by Cleveland disc jockey Alan Freed in his radio show "Moondog Rock 'n' Roll Party."

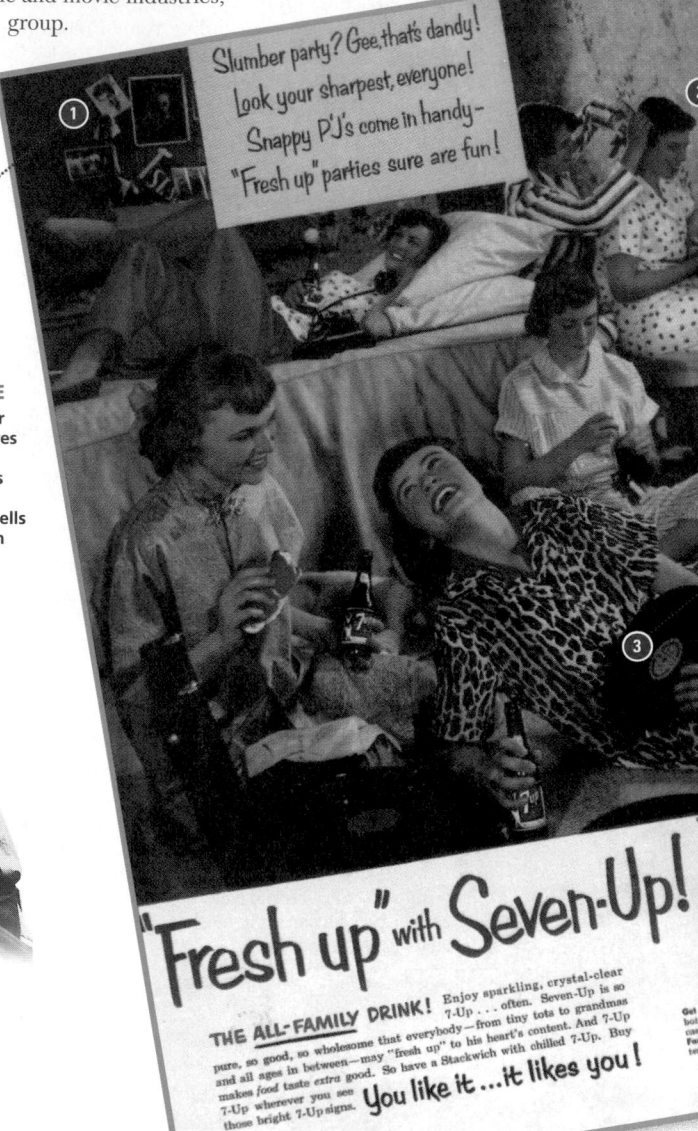

① **THE TEEN MOVIE SCENE**
Teenagers with money in their pockets often found themselves at the movies. Hollywood responded by producing films especially for them, like *The Blackboard Jungle*. This film tells the story of the confrontation between an idealistic young teacher and a gang of delinquents.

Slumber party? Gee, that's dandy!
Look your sharpest, everyone!
Snappy PJ's come in handy—
"Fresh up" parties sure are fun!

"Fresh up" with Seven-Up!

THE ALL-FAMILY DRINK! Enjoy sparkling, crystal-clear 7-Up . . . often. Seven-Up is so pure, so good, so wholesome that everybody—from tiny tots to grandmas and all ages in between—may "fresh up" to his heart's content. And 7-Up makes *food* taste extra good. So have a Stackwich with chilled 7-Up. Buy 7-Up wherever you see those bright 7-Up signs. *You like it . . . it likes you!*

818 CHAPTER 27

RECOMMENDED RESOURCES

Books

Breines, Wini. *Young, White, and Miserable.* Boston: Beacon, 1992. One person's experience of growing up female in 1950s America.

Crenshaw, Marshall. *Hollywood Rock.* New York: Harper, 1994. This guide to rock 'n' roll in films covers most of the movies geared to teens.

Gillett, Charlie. *The Sound of the City.* New York: Da Capo, 1996. The rise of rock 'n' roll.

Horsley, E. M. *The 1950s.* New York: Mallard, 1990. A pictorial history.

Tobler, John. *30 Years of Rock.* New York: Exeter, 1985. The story of rock music by a noted rock historian.

Videos

American Graffiti. Dir. George Lucas. 1973. MCA Universal Home Video, 1991. This award-winning PG-rated film vividly captures the pastimes and music of teens in the early 1960s.

The Blackboard Jungle. Dir. Richard Brooks. 1955. MGM/UA Home Video, 1989. Based

on an Evan Hunter novel, this famous film about troubled youth played Bill Haley's "Rock Around the Clock" during the opening credits—the first major use of rock 'n' roll in a movie.

History of Rock 'n' Roll. Warner Home Video, 1995. A ten-part series, with the first two parts focusing on fifties music.

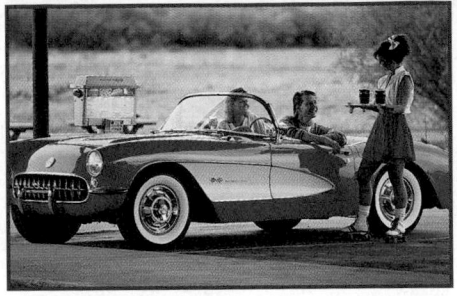

2 TEENS AS CONSUMERS

Pimple creams and lipsticks were just a few of the products aimed at teenagers with money to spend. Teens even dreamed of buying their own cars. This 1953 Corvette was simply "the rage."

3 ROCKING TO A NEW BEAT

Teenagers seeking an identity found it in rock 'n' roll, a fresh form of music that delighted teenagers and enraged their parents. Elvis Presley *right*, the King of Rock 'n' Roll, helped create the new sound by blending country, gospel, and the African-American rhythm and blues sung by performers such as B. B. King *below*. The songs' insistent beat underscored themes of alienation and unhappiness in love.

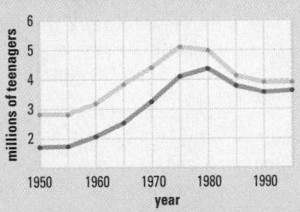
INTERACT WITH HISTORY

1. **DRAWING CONCLUSIONS** What were the causes of the emergence of the teenage market in the 1950s? To answer, review the entire feature, including the Data File.

   SEE SKILLBUILDER HANDBOOK, PAGE 1040.

2. **ANALYZING MOVIES TODAY** What types of movies do American movie studios make for the teenage market today? How do these movies differ from those made in the 1950s?

    For more about youth in the fifties, click on *Social Studies* at http://www.mcdougallittell.com

The Postwar Boom **819**

INSTRUCT

▶ *Starting with the Student*
- Have students share what they know about teenage lifestyles in the 1950s.
- If possible, bring in and play a few recordings by fifties rockers such as Elvis Presley and Little Richard. Then have students discuss their reactions to the music.

▶ *Discussing Key Ideas*
- New attitudes and affluence give postwar American teenagers more influence than ever before.
- Teenage consumers affect product development, advertising, and aspects of popular culture such as music and films.

HISTORY FROM VISUALS

Reading the Images
Have students examine the illustrations.
- Ask them to jot down adjectives to describe the car shown near the top of page 819. *Possible Responses: Shiny, colorful, antique, snazzy, old fashioned.*
- Ask, What is your reaction to the Seven-Up ad? Why? *Possible Responses: Students who find the ad pleasant or effective may mention the smiling faces, bright colors, and relaxed attitudes. Those who find it corny or old-fashioned may mention outdated slang, such as "Gee, that's dandy!"*

INTERACT WITH HISTORY

1. Drawing Conclusions

Possible Answers: New social attitudes placed more significance on the teen years and distinguished teenagers from both children and adults; economic affluence allowed parents to give teenagers an allowance, enabled more teenagers to remain in school instead of leaving early to help support the family, and provided part-time and summer jobs for those who wished to work; the resulting increase in teens' spending money made them a potent new consumer group, prompting product manufacturers and pop culture to cater to the teen market; advertising whetted that market's appetite.

2. Analyzing Movies Today

In identifying types of movies made today, students may mention action films, horror films, science fiction, films with popular music scores, and films with popular young stars, among other things. In comparing the movies of today with those of the fifties, students might mention more sophisticated special effects, few black-and-white films, less about fifties subjects like the Cold War, different slang and other dialogue, and changes in viewing venues (home viewing on videotape, few drive-ins). Accept all reasonable responses, and encourage students to pool their ideas orally or on group lists.

Section 4 Overview

OBJECTIVES

1. To explain how the white migration to suburbs created an urban crisis.
2. To describe attempts of minorities to relieve poverty and gain equal rights.

CRITICAL THINKING

• Recognizing effects, p. 820
• Analyzing causes, p. 821
• Summarizing, p. 823
• Forming opinions, p. 823
• Drawing conclusions, p. 823

FOCUS & MOTIVATE

▶ *Starting with the Student*
• Ask students to think of a time when they felt overlooked or invisible.

MORE ABOUT . . .
James Baldwin

In 1948, James Baldwin fled the discrimination he saw around him by moving to Paris, where he spent much of the rest of his life. His nonfiction writing—including *The Fire Next Time, Notes of a Native Son* and essays—earned him acclaim as a literary spokesperson for the civil rights movement. He died in France in 1987.

OBJECTIVE
1 INSTRUCT

The Urban Poor

▶ *Discussing Key Ideas*
• When middle-class white Americans move to suburbs, poor whites and minorities move to cities.
• Many suburban Americans remain unaware of the poverty in inner cities.
• Urban renewal fails to provide adequate housing for the urban poor.

IN-DEPTH RESOURCES: UNIT 7
Guided Reading, p. 60
Primary Source: from *The Other America*, p. 68

ACCESS FOR STUDENTS ACQUIRING ENGLISH
Guided Reading (Spanish), p. 267

4 The Other America

LEARN ABOUT the existence of poverty in the United States in the 1950s
TO UNDERSTAND the other side of the American dream.

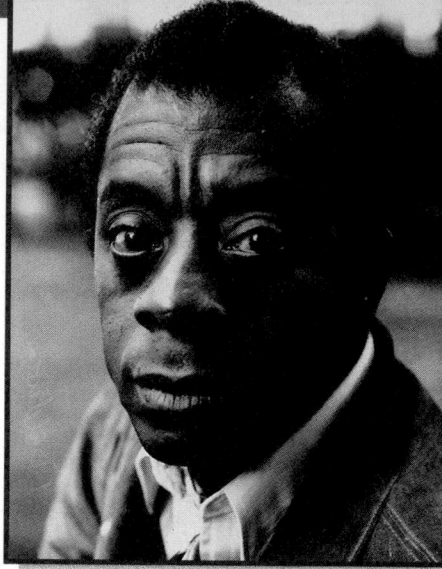
James Baldwin

ONE AMERICAN'S STORY

James Baldwin was born in New York City, the eldest of nine children, and grew up in the poverty of the Harlem ghetto. As a novelist, essayist, and playwright, he eloquently portrayed the struggles of African Americans against racial injustice and discrimination. He believed that blacks inhabited a country other than that of whites in mainstream America—a country without rights, privileges, or even hope. He wrote a letter to his young nephew to mark the 100th anniversary of the emancipation, although, in his words, "the country is celebrating one hundred years of freedom one hundred years too soon."

A PERSONAL VOICE
These innocent and well-meaning people, your countrymen, have caused you to be born under conditions not very far removed from those described for us by Charles Dickens in the London of more than a hundred years ago. . . . This innocent country set you down in the ghetto in which, in fact, it intended that you should perish. . . . You were born where you were born and faced the future that you faced because you were black and *for no other reason.*
JAMES BALDWIN, *The Fire Next Time*

For many Americans, the 1950s was a time of unprecedented prosperity. But not everyone experienced this well-being. In the "other" America, about 40 million people lived in poverty, untouched by the economic boom.

The Urban Poor

Despite the portrait painted by popular culture, life in postwar America was not the "nifty fifties" for all Americans. In 1962, nearly one out of every four Americans was living below the poverty level. Many of these poor were elderly people, single women with children, or members of minority groups, including African Americans, Latinos, and Native Americans.

WHITE FLIGHT In the 1950s, millions of middle-class white Americans left the cities for the suburbs, taking with them precious economic resources and isolating themselves from other races and classes. At the same time, the rural poor migrated to the inner cities. Between the end of World War II and 1960, for example, nearly 5 million African Americans moved from the rural South to urban areas.

The urban crisis prompted by the "white flight" had a direct impact on poor whites and nonwhites. The cities lost not only people and businesses but also the property and income taxes they had paid. City governments could no longer afford to properly maintain or improve schools, public transportation, and police and fire departments—and the urban poor suffered. As one urban planner observed, "We turned our cities into doughnuts with all the dough [or money] around the center and nothing in the middle."

A. Answer Loss of people and income leading to decaying ghettos.
THINK THROUGH HISTORY
A. Recognizing Effects What effect did white flight have on America's cities?

SECTION 4 RESOURCES

 PRINT RESOURCES

IN-DEPTH RESOURCES: UNIT 7
Guided Reading, p. 60
Primary Sources: from *The Other America* by Michael Harrington, p. 66; The Voluntary Relocation Program, p. 67

ACCESS FOR STUDENTS ACQUIRING ENGLISH
Guided Reading (Spanish), p. 267

FORMAL ASSESSMENT
Section Quiz, p. 332

ALTERNATIVE ASSESSMENT BOOK
See forms for supporting and scoring alternative activities.

TECHNOLOGY RESOURCES

HUMANITIES TRANSPARENCIES
H26, *Her World* by Philip Evergood

CRITICAL THINKING TRANSPARENCIES
CT27, Post-War Boom

VIDEO American Portfolio: A Videodisc for U.S. History
user's guide, pp. 236, 237

INTERNET McDougal Littell Learning On-Line
http://www.mcdougallittell.com

THE INNER CITIES While poverty grew rapidly in the decaying inner cities, many suburban Americans remained unaware of it. Some even refused to believe that poverty could exist in the richest, most powerful nation on the earth. And the urban poor had few advocates to call attention to their segregated ghettos. Many politicians, economists, and journalists advanced the belief that poverty in America was on the road to extinction. An article in *Fortune* magazine, for example, declared in 1960 that poverty in the United States would be eliminated by the end of the decade.

After living among the nation's poor across America, however, Michael Harrington published a shocking account that starkly illuminated the issue of poverty. In *The Other America: Poverty in the United States* (1962), he not only confirmed that widespread poverty existed but also exposed its brutal reality.

B. Answer
Because the building boom primarily took place in the suburbs; lack of jobs; discrimination; and the impact of white flight.

THINK THROUGH HISTORY
B. Analyzing Causes Why were poor people unable to find decent housing, despite the building boom in the 1950s?

A PERSONAL VOICE
The poor live in a culture of poverty. . . .The poor get sick more than anyone else in the society. . . . When they become sick, they are sick longer than any other group in the society. Because they are sick more often and longer than anyone else, they lose wages and work, and find it difficult to hold a steady job. And because of this, they cannot pay for good housing, for a nutritious diet, for doctors . . . [and] their prospect is to move to an even lower level . . . toward even more suffering.

MICHAEL HARRINGTON, from *The Other America*

URBAN RENEWAL Although millions of new homes were built in the suburbs in the 1950s, few of them were available to the nation's poor. Most African Americans, Native Americans, and Latinos not only could not afford homes in the suburbs, but also were rarely welcome there. Instead, they were forced to live in dirty, crowded inner-city slums. A Texas newspaper described how almost 200,000 Mexican Americans in a San Antonio *barrio* lived like penned cattle in a stockyard "with roofed-over corrals for homes and chutes for streets."

One proposed solution to the housing problem in inner cities was **urban renewal.** The National Housing Act of 1949 was passed to provide "a decent home and a suitable living environment for every American family." This act called for tearing down rundown neighborhoods and constructing low-income housing.

Although dilapidated areas were razed, parking lots, shopping centers, highways, parks, and factories were constructed on some of the cleared land, and enough new housing was not always built to accommodate all the displaced people. For example, a *barrio* in Los Angeles was torn down to make way for Dodger Stadium. In turn, poor people who were displaced from their homes simply moved from one ghetto to another. Some critics of urban renewal claimed that it had merely become urban *removal.*

Mexican Americans and Native Americans

Despite ongoing poverty, during the 1950s African Americans began to make significant strides toward the reduction of racial discrimination and segregation. (See Chapter 29.) Inspired by their role in the civil rights movement, other minorities of the rural poor also began to develop a deeper political awareness and a voice. Mexican-American activism gathered steam after veterans returned from World War II, and a drastic change in government policy under Eisenhower's administration fueled Native American protest.

MEXICAN–AMERICAN ACTIVISM Many Mexicans had become citizens during the 19th century, when the United States had annexed the Southwest after

ECONOMIC BACKGROUND

WHERE IS THE POVERTY LINE?
The poverty line, calculated each year by the federal government, is the minimum amount of annual income that an individual or a family needs in order to survive in the United States. In 1959, the poverty line for a family of four was $2,973; in 1996, it was $15,600.

Originally, the poverty line was based on a food budget that provided just enough nutrition to maintain decent health. This number was multiplied by three because a third of a family's total household budget was typically spent on food.

Since 1969, however, the government has determined the poverty line by simply readjusting the previous year's figure to take inflation into account.

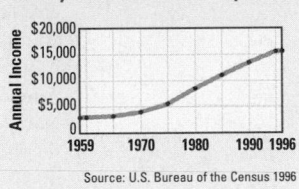

Poverty Thresholds for a Family of Four

Source: U.S. Bureau of the Census 1996

The Postwar Boom **821**

TEACHING OPTION

Cooperative Activity: Preparing a Family Budget

Task: Student groups will prepare a basic budget for a family of four (earning $15,600 a year), based on average costs in their community.

Purpose: To understand the difficulty in managing income to cover expenses.

Activity: Three student groups will calculate expenses for food, shelter, and other necessities (clothing, utilities, transportation, medical care). Each group will have $5,200—one third of the family's income—to budget. Students should use local newspaper ads to determine costs. Have students compile data to create the family budget for one year, using a chart similar to the one shown.

One Year's Budget

Food		Transportation	
Shelter		Medical care	
Clothing		Other	
Utilities			

Based on this budget, discuss whether a family with this income—at the poverty level—could provide for its needs.

ALTERNATIVE ASSESSMENT BOOK
Standards for Evaluating a Cooperative Activity

After World War II, an increase in agricultural land, due to irrigation, created demand for cheap farm labor. In 1951, Congress enacted a temporary work program that permitted braceros to enter the United States for seasonal work. In 1962, braceros came under the minimum wage law. In 1965, the braceros program ended.

MORE ABOUT . . .
Native American Culture

A Seminole petition to President Eisenhower expressed Native American attitudes toward the government policy of assimilation: ". . . we are not White Men but Indians, do not wish to become White Men but wish to remain Indians, and have an outlook on all things different from the outlook of the White Man."

IN-DEPTH RESOURCES: UNIT 7
Primary Source: The Voluntary Relocation Program, p. 67

MORE ABOUT . . .
Native American Relocation

Between 30 and 70 percent of the Native Americans who relocated to cities returned to reservations. Lack of economic opportunity was an important factor. Many people also cited the need to preserve their Native American identity as a reason for returning to tribal lands.

> **" [The braceros were a] highly regimented and effective labor force."**
> ERASMO GAMBOA, HISTORIAN

the war with Mexico. Large numbers of Mexicans also had crossed the border to work in the United States during and after World War I. Most of them were miners, railroad workers, or migrant workers employed temporarily.

When the United States entered World War II, the shortage of agricultural laborers spurred the federal government to initiate a program in 1942 in which Mexican **braceros,** "hired hands," were allowed into the United States to harvest crops. More than 200,000 braceros entered the United States on a short-term basis between 1942 and 1947. When their employment was ended, the braceros were expected to return to Mexico. However, many remained in the United States illegally.

In addition to the braceros who remained past their work contracts, hundreds of thousands of Mexicans entered the country illegally to escape poor economic conditions in Mexico. To stop the flow of illegal migrants, in 1954 the United States launched Operation Wetback, a federal program designed to find and return illegal aliens to Mexico. (Many Mexicans swam across the Rio Grande to reach the United States illegally, and were labeled with the derogatory name *wetbacks.*) Between 1953 and 1955, the United States government deported more than 2 million illegal aliens.

Although Mexican Americans had played a major role in the economic growth of the Southwest, they still encountered prejudice and discrimination. Change occurred after World War II, in which almost 350,000 Mexican Americans had fought for democracy. Returning to civilian life, they were determined to keep fighting for democracy at home—to remedy poor living conditions and wage discrimination. Many were hampered by poor jobs skills and lack of fluency in English, but they wanted opportunities to become well educated and to earn a decent living.

The body of Felix Longoria was buried in Arlington National Cemetery after a Texas undertaker refused to bury him.

THE LONGORIA INCIDENT Some Mexican Americans were shocked into organized action by an insult to the family of Felix Longoria. Longoria was a Mexican-American World War II hero who had been killed in the Philippines. The only undertaker in his hometown in Texas refused to let the Longoria family use his funeral home because they were "Mexicans." To protest this and other injustices, Mexican-American veterans organized the American G.I. Forum in 1948.

Soon after the Longoria incident, Ignacio Lopez founded the Unity League of California to register Mexican-American voters and to promote candidates who would represent them. In response to league actions, California outlawed segregated classrooms for Mexican Americans. Similar voter registration groups developed in Arizona and Texas. The *Asociación Nacional México-Americana* and the League of United Latin American Citizens coordinated efforts to end discrimination, giving Mexican Americans a nationwide political voice.

NATIVE AMERICANS CONTINUE THEIR STRUGGLE Native Americans also continued to fight for their rights and identity. From the passage of the Dawes Act in 1887 until 1934, the policy of the federal government toward Native Americans had been one of Americanization and assimilation. In 1924, all Native Americans were made citizens of the United States, but they remained second-class citizens.

In 1934, the Indian Reorganization Act moved official policy away from assimilation and toward Native American autonomy. Its passage signaled a change in federal policy. In addition, because the government was reeling from the Great Depression, it didn't want to continue subsidizing the Native Americans. The act mandated changes in three areas—economic, cultural, and political.

822 CHAPTER 27

Exploring Themes

Expanding Democracy During the 1950s, one third of the Mexican Americans in the United States lived below the poverty level. Native Americans remained the poorest minority. These groups were part of the invisible poor—on the other side of the American dream. Have student groups act as advocates for Mexican Americans and Native Americans in the 1950s. Ask them to write petitions listing grievances and suggesting solutions.

Teaching Less Proficient Readers

Context Clues Ask students to list words in this section that are unfamiliar to them. Then use the word *advocates* on p. 821 to demonstrate the following steps for using context clues to decode unfamiliar words:

1. Read the sentence that contains the word, as well as the sentence before and after it.
2. Determine the general meaning of the text.
3. Substitute familiar words in the sentence to see if they make sense. *(defenders, supporters, promoters)*

Have students follow these steps to decode other difficult words.

- economic—Native American lands were no longer to be broken up into individual farms, but would belong to a tribe as a whole.
- cultural—the number of boarding schools for Native American children was cut back, and children could attend day schools on the reservations.
- political—Native American tribes were given permission to elect tribal councils to govern their reservations.

Native Americans also took the initiative to improve their own lives. In 1944, they established the National Congress of American Indians. The organization eventually included some 90 tribes—two-thirds of all the Native Americans in the nation. The congress had two main goals: (1) to ensure for Native Americans the same civil rights that white Americans had, and (2) to enable Native Americans on reservations to retain their own customs.

During World War II, some 65,000 Native Americans left their reservations for military service and war work. As a result, they became very aware of discrimination. Native Americans stopped receiving family allotments and wages. Outsiders also grabbed control of tribal lands, primarily to exploit their deposits of minerals, oil, and timber.

THE TERMINATION POLICY In 1953, the federal government announced that it would give up its responsibility for Native American tribes. This new approach, known as the **termination policy,** eliminated federal economic support, discontinued the reservation system, and distributed tribal lands among individual Native Americans. Between 1954 and 1960, the federal government withdrew financial support from 61 reservations. But the states—not the tribal leaders—maintained authority over civil and criminal cases on the reservations, and thousands of acres of tribal lands were sold to developers.

In response to the termination policy, the Bureau of Indian Affairs began a voluntary relocation program to help Native Americans resettle in cities. The bureau helped them find a place to live, paid moving costs and living expenses, and helped them find work and adjust to their new communities.

C. Answer By forming national organizations to fight for their rights.

THINK THROUGH HISTORY
C. Summarizing *How did Mexican Americans and Native Americans attempt to improve their lives?*

The termination policy was a dismal failure, however. Although the Bureau of Indian Affairs helped relocate 35,000 Native Americans to urban areas between 1952 and 1960, they were often unable to find jobs in their new homes, due to poor training and racial prejudice. They were also left without access to medical care when federal programs were abolished. And the number of Native Americans on state welfare rolls soared. In 1963, the termination policy was abandoned.

By the early 1960s, contrary to the optimistic prophecies of *Fortune* magazine, poverty had not disappeared. In fact, the poor had become more visible than ever. The other America could no longer be ignored.

Native Americans like the man shown here received job training sponsored by the Bureau of Indian Affairs to help them settle in urban areas.

Section **4** Assessment

1. TERMS & NAMES
Identify:
- urban renewal
- bracero
- termination policy

2. SUMMARIZING In overlapping circles like the one below, fill in the common problems that African Americans, Mexican Americans, and Native Americans faced during the 1950s.

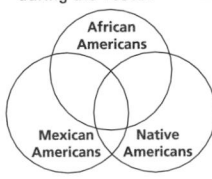

3. FORMING OPINIONS Do you think that urban renewal was an effective approach to the housing problem in inner cities? Why or why not?

THINK ABOUT
- the goals of the National Housing Act of 1949
- the claims made by some critics of urban renewal

4. DRAWING CONCLUSIONS Which major population shift—"white flight," migration from Mexico, or relocation of Native Americans—do you think had the greatest impact on society? Why?

THINK ABOUT
- the impact of "white flight"
- the outcome of Operation Wetback
- the effects of the termination policy

The Postwar Boom **823**

ANSWERS

1. TERMS & NAMES

urban renewal, p. 821

bracero, p. 822

termination policy, p. 823

2. SUMMARIZING

Possible Responses: Poverty, inadequate housing, uphill struggle to end discrimination and social injustice, limited job opportunities, limited social mobility, harsh or ineffective government policies, few advocates among mainstream public, second-class citizenship, exclusion from the American dream.

3. FORMING OPINIONS

Possible Responses: Effective—Its ultimate goal was to construct affordable housing for the poor, and it did tear down many bad areas and put up some new housing. Ineffective—It did not provide enough new housing and displaced many poor people when old housing was torn down.

4. DRAWING CONCLUSIONS

Possible Responses: White flight—It caused polarization of rich and poor and suburban and urban cultures. Migration of Mexicans—Mexican immigrants met with opposition because they provided job competition. Native American relocation—It displaced an entire group of people without providing an effective alternative way of life and put a strain on urban resources.

ASSESS & RETEACH

Section 4 Assessment
Assign questions as homework or a class activity.

Self-Assessment
Hold an informal debate in which students take the positions they took in their answer to Item 4 in the section assessment. Make sure they use references to the text to support their positions.

Section Quiz

FORMAL ASSESSMENT
Section Quiz, p. 332

Reteach
Have students review main understandings of this section by creating a chart comparing minority groups with middle-class white Americans in the 1950s. Bases of comparison might include living conditions, employment opportunities, and quality of life.

CRITICAL THINKING TRANSPARENCIES
CT27, Post-War Boom

CLOSE

While white middle-class Americans pursued the American dream, the "other" Americans lived in a culture of poverty. African Americans, Mexican Americans, and Native Americans were among the groups who were excluded from the economic prosperity of the 1950s.

REVIEWING THE CHAPTER

TERMS & NAMES
1. suburb, p. 796
2. Dixiecrat, p. 800
3. Dwight D. Eisenhower, p. 801
4. conglomerate, p. 803
5. baby boom, p. 805
6. mass media, p. 812
7. beat movement, p. 815
8. rock 'n' roll, p. 816
9. urban renewal, p. 821
10. bracero, p. 822

MAIN IDEAS
11. Tuition reimbursements provided an incentive for education; a year's unemployment benefits gave financial support for job searches; loans helped them buy homes, buy farms, or establish businesses.

12. The Korean War stalemate, the rise of McCarthyism, the threat of communism, the expanding power of the federal government, alleged corruption among Truman's political allies, inflation, and labor unrest.

13. An increase in the minimum wage, expanded social security coverage, increased funding for low-income housing.

14. By 1956, the majority of Americans held white-collar jobs.

15. Suburbia offered affordable single-family houses, good schools, a safe environment for children, and neighbors like themselves.

16. Local programming of news, weather, music, and community issues; targeting specific audiences, such as African Americans.

17. Beatniks shunned the conformity, the planning for the future, and the materialism that characterized mainstream American values.

18. They became actors and singers, and their music greatly influenced rock 'n' roll.

19. Many white families moved to the suburbs and the rural poor moved into the cities, which contributed to the economic decline of many large cities.

20. Racial prejudice, poor training, lack of work, and no access to medical care.

Chapter 27 Assessment

REVIEWING THE CHAPTER

TERMS & NAMES For each item below, write a sentence explaining its historical significance for the 1950s. For each person below, explain his role in that period.

1. suburb
2. Dixiecrat
3. Dwight D. Eisenhower
4. conglomerate
5. baby boom
6. mass media
7. beat movement
8. rock 'n' roll
9. urban renewal
10. bracero

REVIEWING MAIN IDEAS

SECTION 1 (pages 796–802)

Postwar America
11. How did the GI Bill of Rights help World War II veterans make the transition to civilian life?
12. What domestic and foreign issues concerned voters during the 1952 presidential election?
13. What similar legislative measures did Presidents Truman and Eisenhower push through Congress?

SECTION 2 (pages 803–809)

The American Dream in the Fifties
14. What shift in employment trends had occurred by the mid-1950s?
15. How did life in the suburbs provide the model for the American dream?

SECTION 3 (pages 812–817)

Popular Culture
16. What strategies did radio stations use to counteract the mass popularity of television?
17. How did the values of the beatniks differ from those of mainstream America of the 1950s?
18. How did African-American performers influence American popular culture in the 1950s?

SECTION 4 (pages 820–823)

The Other America
19. How did many major cities change in the 1950s?
20. What obstacles to improving their lives did Native Americans face in the 1950s?

THINKING CRITICALLY

1. **TECHNOLOGICAL BREAKTHROUGHS** Create a web like the one below to show the four postwar technological breakthroughs that you consider to be most influential.

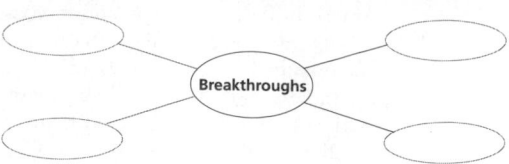

Breakthroughs

2. **FASTER, FARTHER, HIGHER** In what way do you think the fast pace of American life today had its origins in the 1950s? Support your answer with examples.

3. **MORE FOR FEWER** Do you agree or disagree with the quote from Life magazine on page 794? Support your answer with evidence from the chapter.

4. **THE OTHER AMERICA** Why do you think that many middle-class Americans during the 1950s tended to have little awareness and appreciation of cultural diversity?

5. **FROM INDIVIDUALIST TO ORGANIZATION MAN** During the first two centuries of America's history, the national character was marked by pioneering individualism. Why do you think that conformity became the norm during the 1950s?

6. **ANALYZING PRIMARY SOURCES** Read the following excerpt from The Hidden Persuaders by Vance Packard about the psychology of advertising during the 1950s. Then answer the questions.

> On May 18, 1956, The New York Times printed a remarkable interview with a young man named Gerald Stahl, executive vice-president of the Package Designers Council. He stated: "Psychiatrists say that people have so much to choose from that they need help—they will like the package that hypnotizes them into picking it." He urged food packers to put more hypnosis into their package designing, so that the housewife will stick out her hand for it rather than one of many rivals.
>
> Mr. Stahl found that it takes the average woman exactly twenty seconds to cover an aisle in a supermarket if she doesn't tarry; so a good package design would hypnotize the woman like a flashlight waved in front of her eyes.
>
> **Vance Packard,** The Hidden Persuaders

How are women shoppers of the 1950s portrayed in this excerpt? Do you think this description applies to shoppers today? Support your answer with reasons.

THINKING CRITICALLY

1. TECHNOLOGICAL BREAKTHROUGHS
Possible Responses: Hi-fidelity record players; television sets; Teflon-coated cookware; polyester fabrics; various plastic products; electric household appliances; frozen TV dinners.

2. FASTER, FARTHER, HIGHER
Possible Responses: Evidence of the emphasis on speed and efficiency in the 1950s included construction of the interstate highway system, mass production of communities like Levittown, the rise of fast-food franchises, and an explosion of labor-saving devices. These trends have continued, resulting in today's instant foods, microwave ovens, automated teller machines, computer technology, and pay-per-view television.

3. MORE FOR FEWER
Possible Responses: Agree—Many elderly people, single women with children, and members of minority groups lived in poverty, untouched by the general economic boom. Disagree—The 1950s was a time of unprecedented prosperity for growing numbers of Americans, and by the end of the decade, America had the highest standard of living in the world.

ALTERNATIVE ASSESSMENT

1. PRESENTING AN INTERNATIONAL NEWS SHOW

In the 1950s, many Americans turned their sights inward and settled down to rebuild civilian lives and enjoy the economic benefits that followed World War II. What was happening on the other sides of the oceans during the postwar period?

Prepare a script and notes about visuals for a television news show on one international event that took place during the 1950s.

CD-ROM Use the CD-ROM *Our Times,* your textbook, and other resources to identify and research an international event that interests you.

- Use a storyboard format to plan the visuals you will include—people, places, maps, or graphs—and indicate what the narrator will say as each picture is shown. Make sure to explain the highlights of the event and to analyze its effects on U.S. foreign and domestic policy.

- **Cooperative Activity** Talk with the other students in your class to identify those who chose events from the same time period as yours. Then work together to plan a summary news broadcast about world events that year.

2. CREATING A 1950s–STYLE TV QUIZ SHOW

Cooperative Activity Divide into small groups to plan and stage a quiz show in which student-contestants answer questions based on information from this chapter. Discuss with group members what the name and format of your show will be and how you will categorize the questions.

The groups should present their quiz shows using volunteer class members as contestants.

3. PORTFOLIO PROJECT

Use the Living History activity to expand your portfolio.

LIVING HISTORY

ADVERTISING YOUR FIFTIES PARTY

Working with a partner, create a radio advertisement for a party. Decide which elements of each person's invitation you will include and think of a 1950s song to use as background music.

Make an audiotape of your radio spot to play for the class. Class members should write an evaluation of each ad based on the following criteria:

- Did the ad capture your attention?
- Could you visualize what the party would be like?
- How would you rate the overall effectiveness of the ad?

Save your audiotapes and evaluations in your American history portfolio.

Review Chapter 27

POSTWAR TRANSITIONS After World War II, Americans faced social, economic, and political readjustments. With the help of the GI Bill, veterans began to rebuild their civilian lives. For minority veterans, this rebuilding included seeking full rights as citizens. The transition from wartime to peacetime brought temporary rises in unemployment and inflation. But the economy soon stabilized as the demand for goods and services exceeded the supply, and increased production created new jobs. Eisenhower's two-term presidency ushered in an era of new prosperity and rising political conservatism.

THE AMERICAN DREAM An economic boom in the 1950s made the American dream possible—an affordable suburban house in a safe neighborhood with good schools. Yet this lifestyle also had its negative side. Many businesspeople had to subdue their individuality at white-collar corporate jobs, and homemakers sometimes felt bored, isolated, and unfulfilled, despite their comfortable surroundings.

POPULAR CULTURE By 1960, almost every American home had a television set. Programming reflected and reinforced the mainstream values of white America—a secure job, a suburban home, material success, well-behaved children, and general conformity. In contrast, the rebellious messages of the Beat movement in literature and of rock 'n' roll in music clashed with the tidy suburban view of life.

THE PLIGHT OF THE POOR The idealized image of postwar America expressed in popular culture did not encompass the plight of minorities and the nation's poor. Despite increased economic prosperity, African Americans, Mexican Americans, and Native Americans still faced racial discrimination. They all formed organizations to improve their conditions and chance of realizing the American dream.

Preview Chapter 28

In the early 1960s, the mood of the country dramatically shifted as the new Democratic president, John F. Kennedy, faced some of the most dangerous Soviet-American confrontations of the nuclear age. After Kennedy's assassination in 1963, President Lyndon B. Johnson launched a campaign against poverty and racial discrimination. You will learn about these and other significant developments in the next chapter.

The Postwar Boom **825**

ALTERNATIVE ASSESSMENT

1. PRESENTING AN INTERNATIONAL NEWS SHOW
Standards for Evaluation
A script with notes about visuals should meet the following criteria:

- Focuses on one international event from the 1950s.
- Examines how that event affected U.S. foreign and domestic policy.
- Includes clear visuals that support the narrator's text.
- Uses a variety of research sources.

2. CREATING A 1950s-STYLE TV QUIZ SHOW
Standards for Evaluation
A quiz show should meet the following criteria:

- Identifies the name and purpose of the show.
- Uses interesting and thought-provoking questions.
- Is conducted in an organized and orderly fashion.
- Gives each group member a role in the project.

3. PORTFOLIO PROJECT
LIVING HISTORY
Standards for Evaluation
A radio advertisement should meet the following criteria:

- Includes lively music as a background.
- Identifies the time and place of the party clearly.
- Uses catchy slogans and sound effects.
- Presents a clear tape recording of the radio ad.

IN-DEPTH RESOURCES: UNIT 7
See the form for scoring this activity on page 74.

THINKING CRITICALLY

4. THE OTHER AMERICA
Possible Responses: Suburbs were homogeneous communities that did not welcome minority residents; television portrayed an idealized white America and ignored cultural diversity or presented minorities in stereotyped roles; minorities did not yet have a powerful political voice or accepted programs for social activism.

5. FROM INDIVIDUALIST TO ORGANIZATION MAN
Possible Responses: The unsettling effects of the Great Depression and World War II made Americans long for stability and sameness; the business world rejected creative thinkers and rebels and fostered an environment that rewarded employees who "fit in"; the rapid growth of cookie-cutter communities encouraged conformity.

6. ANALYZING PRIMARY SOURCES
Women shoppers are portrayed as easily manipulated by advertising tactics, such as package design, and as making somewhat mindless, rather than informed, purchasing decisions. *Possible Responses:* Opinions will vary, but should be supported with reasons and details.

Living with Great Turmoil

March from Selma to Montgomery, Alabama

Photograph by Ivan Massar (1965).

Art Note
The photographer Ivan Massar studied with Roy Stryker, who had organized a massive photographic documentation of the United States during the Depression. Massar made his living as a freelance photographer, taking news and documentary photos for magazines and books.

▶ **Previewing the Unit**
Unit 8 describes the social changes in American society from the 1950s through the mid-1970s. During this time Congress passes many new laws in an effort to create a "great society." African Americans launch a powerful movement that gains civil rights and spurs Hispanics, women, and Native Americans to push for rights for themselves. U.S. military involvement in Vietnam sharply divides American society.

UNIT
8

"*Struggle is a never-ending process. Freedom is never really won. You earn it and win it in every generation.*"

CORETTA SCOTT KING

CHAPTER 28
1960–1968
The New Frontier and the Great Society

CHAPTER 29
1954–1970
Civil Rights

CHAPTER 30
1954–1975
The Vietnam War Years

CHAPTER 31
1960–1975
An Era of Social Change

826 UNIT 8

1954–1975
Living with Great Turmoil

①

② Selma march
In March 1965, police assaulted hundreds of African Americans marching from Selma to Montgomery, Alabama, in support of voting rights. The violence spurred President Lyndon Johnson to urge Congress to pass a voting rights law. On March 21, 1965, Martin Luther King led more than 3,000 people, black and white, on a successful subsequent march.

② A. Philip Randolph
Since the 1920s, the head of a labor union with mostly African-American membership, Randolph was the dean of civil rights leaders. He organized the 1963 march on Washington that featured King's "I have a dream" speech.

③ Dr. Ralph Abernathy
Abernathy was a close aide to King. He headed the Southern Christian Leadership Conference after King's death in 1968.

④ Ralph Bunche
Working for the U.S. State Department, Bunche helped write the United Nations charter. He then joined the UN staff. His diplomatic success in arranging an end to a Middle East war won him the 1950 Nobel Peace Prize.

Discussing the Quotation

As Coretta King notes, the movement for civil rights is a continuing struggle. John Lewis, who joined in this part of the struggle, recalled his feelings as the Selma marchers reached Montgomery:

"I think we all walked those days with a sense of pride and with a sense of dignity. . . . It was more than an ordinary march. . . . It was the sense of community moving there."

FOR DISCUSSION:
- Why does King say the struggle has to be won in each generation?
- How are the two quotations related?
- What struggles for equality remain today?

Discussing the Image

News coverage of the civil rights movement had great impact on public opinion. Images of policemen beating civil rights activists aroused outrage. And the peaceful, dignified behavior of the civil rights marchers themselves contrasted sharply with their treatment.

FOR DISCUSSION:
- What words best describe these marchers?
- Why have some marchers linked arms?
- Why do the marchers carry American flags?

827

---

5 Singing

This marcher and many others appear to be singing. When President Johnson announced his aim to push for a voting rights bill and full civil rights for African Americans, he used the words of an old spiritual that had often been part of civil rights marches: "We shall overcome."

6 Martin Luther King

In a speech he gave to the marchers when they reached Montgomery, King said that the day of victory for the civil rights movement was near. "How long? Not long, because the arm of the moral universe is long but it bends toward justice."

7 Coretta Scott King

Coretta King has remained active in the movement for civil rights. Just four days after her husband was shot in 1968, she led a march for peace and nonviolence. She founded and heads the Martin Luther King Jr. Center for Nonviolent Social Change.

	Key Ideas	TEACHING SUPPORT	ASSESSMENT	
SECTION 1 **Kennedy and the Cold War** *pp. 830–836*	Foreign affairs dominate the presidential campaign of 1960 and the administration of John F. Kennedy. Kennedy faces some of the most dangerous Soviet-American confrontations of the Cold War.	*In-Depth Resources: Unit 8* • Guided Reading, p. 1 • Skillbuilder Practice: Hypothesizing, p. 4 • Geography Application: Divided Germany and the Berlin Wall, p. 5 • Primary Sources: John F. Kennedy's Inaugural Address, p. 7; Political Cartoon, p. 9 **COOPERATIVE ACTIVITY** • Keeping a Journal During the Cuban Missile Crisis, p. 834 (TE)	*Section 1 Assessment,* p. 836 (PE) *Self-Assessment,* p. 836 (TE) *Formal Assessment* • Section Quiz, p. 341 *Alternative Assessment Book* • Standards for Evaluating a Cooperative Activity	
SECTION 2 **The New Frontier** *pp. 837–842*	With the stirring phrase the "New Frontier," Kennedy outlines a broad vision for progress, but Congress enacts few of his initiatives. His efforts are ended by his tragic assassination.	*In-Depth Resources: Unit 8* • Guided Reading, p. 2 • American Lives: Alan Shephard, p. 14 • Literature: from *Libra* by Don DeLillo, p. 11 **COOPERATIVE ACTIVITY** • Writing an Advertisement for the Peace Corps, p. 839 (TE)	*Section 2 Assessment,* p. 842 (PE) *Self-Assessment,* p. 842 (TE) *Formal Assessment* • Section Quiz, p. 342 *Alternative Assessment Book* • Standards for Evaluating a Cooperative Activity	
SECTION 3 **The Great Society** *pp. 843–851*	Lyndon B. Johnson drives the most ambitious legislative agenda through Congress since the New Deal. The landmark decisions of the Supreme Court under Chief Justice Earl Warren reflect the era of liberal activism.	*In-Depth Resources: Unit 8* • Guided Reading, p. 3 • Primary Source: from *Unsafe at Any Speed*, p. 10 • American Lives: Rachel Carson, p. 15 **COOPERATIVE ACTIVITY** • Outlining Provisions for a Great Society Program, p. 847 (TE)	*Section 3 Assessment,* p. 851 (PE) *Self-Assessment,* p. 851 (TE) *Formal Assessment* • Section Quiz, p. 343 *Alternative Assessment Book* • Standards for Evaluating a Cooperative Activity	
CHAPTER RESOURCES	**Chapter Overview** President Kennedy survives major confrontations with the Soviet Union but cannot get his domestic policies past Congress. President Johnson succeeds him and launches an era of liberal activity with a wide-ranging program of new laws.	*In-Depth Resources: Unit 8* • Living History Project: Worksheet, p. 16; Standards: p. 17 *Telescoping the Times* • Chapter Summary, pp. 55–56 *Planning for Block Schedules*	*Chapter Assessment,* pp. 852–853 (PE) *Alternative Assessment,* p. 853 (PE) *Formal Assessment* • Chapter Test, forms A and B, pp. 344–349 **Test Generator** *Alternative Assessment Book* See explanation and forms for different kinds of alternative assessments including portfolio assessment.	

Grolier Multimedia Encyclopedia
• President Kennedy's address on the Nuclear Test Ban

Our Times
• Bay of Pigs and the Berlin Wall

INTERNET RESOURCES
• See *McDougal Littell Learning On-Line* for links to information about John F. Kennedy and Nikita Khrushchev.

Humanities Transparencies
• H43, The Nation Mourns

Geography Transparencies
• G28, Influence of Alliance for Progress

Electronic Library of Primary Sources
• On the Space Program by John F. Kennedy and Lyndon Johnson
• *from* "That Day in Dallas"

INTERNET RESOURCES
• See *McDougal Littell Learning On-Line* for links to information about the Peace Corps and JFK assassination.

Humanities Transparencies
• H44, Johnson Rag

Critical Thinking Transparencies
• CT28, The Great Society
• CT62, Federal Budget, 1952–1968

Electronic Library of Primary Sources
• *from Citizens' Guide to the 1964 Civil Rights Act*
• *from* the Civil Rights Act of 1964

INTERNET RESOURCES
• See Interact with History pp. 849 and 850 (PE) for activities that include the Internet as an enrichment option.

American Portfolio: A Videodisc for U.S. History, user's guide, pp. 239–240, 243–245, 248

INTERNET RESOURCES
Learning On-Line: Social Studies
http://www.mcdougallittell.com

Block Scheduling (90 MINUTES)

Day 1

Section 1, pp. 830–836

Section 2, pp. 837–842

Section Assessments, pp. 836, 842

Day 2

Section 3, pp. 843–851

Section Assessment, p. 851

Chapter Assessment, pp. 852–853

YEARLY PACING *Chapter 28 Total:* 2 days *Yearly Total:* 85 days

See *Planning for Block Schedules* for special activities and pacing strategies.

Customizing for Special Populations

Students Acquiring English

Access for Students Acquiring English
• Guided Reading for Sections 1–3 (Spanish), pp. 273–275
• Chapter Summary (Spanish), pp. 271–272
• Skillbuilder Practice: Hypothesizing (Spanish), p. 276
• Geography Application: Divided Germany and the Berlin Wall (Spanish), p. 277

INTERNET RESOURCES
• See *McDougal Littell Learning On-Line* The Diverse Classroom.

Less Proficient Readers

In-Depth Resources: Unit 8
• Guided Reading for Sections 1–3, pp. 1–3
• Skillbuilder: Hypothesizing, p. 4
• Geography Application: Divided Germany and the Berlin Wall, p. 5

Telescoping the Times
• Chapter Summary, pp. 55–56

See additional strategies at point of use in the Teacher's Edition.

Gifted and Talented Students

In-Depth Resources: Unit 8
• Primary Sources: John F. Kennedy's Inaugural Address, p. 7; Political Cartoon, p. 9; from *Unsafe at Any Speed* by Ralph Nader, p. 10
• American Lives: Alan Shepard, p. 14; Rachel Carson, p. 15

See additional strategies at point of use in the Teacher's Edition.

Connections to Literature READINGS FOR STUDENTS

In-Depth Resources: Unit 8
• from *Libra* by Don DeLillo, p. 11

Enrichment Reading
• Oates, Joyce Carol
Because It Is Bitter, and Because It Is My Heart
New York: Plume, 1991
This novel is a realistic retelling of life in America during the 1950s and 1960s. Issues of race and family dominate this gritty, realistic story.

• Thomas, Maria
Antonia Saw the Oryx First
New York: Soho Press, 1987
The experiences of a Peace Corps volunteer in Africa dominate this story of a richly complex community, unusual personalities, cultural confusions, and the powerful African landscape.

• Wolfe, Tom
The Right Stuff
New York: Farrar, Straus, and Giroux, 1991
This is the true story of the first seven men—Alan Shephard, Gus Grissom, John Glenn, Scott Carpenter, Walter Schirra, Gordon Cooper, and Deke Slayton—chosen for the U.S. space program. The novel follows them through their selection, training, and daily routines.

McDougal Littell *The Language of Literature*
American Literature

• **Robert Frost, "Acquainted with the Night,"** p. 821
• **Robert Frost, "Mending Wall,"** p. 822
• **Robert Frost, "Out, Out—,"** p. 824

The New Frontier and the Great Society

▶ **Starting with the Student**
Ask students to think about the films they've seen and books they've read about Kennedy and Johnson.

• In what ways were the two Presidents similar? In what ways did they differ?
• What images come to mind when they think about either President?

PREVIEWING THE CHAPTER
• Have students get together in small groups to discuss their impressions of Kennedy and Johnson.
• Discuss the events in the time line.

MORE ABOUT . . .
John F. Kennedy

The White House received many letters pointing out the fact that President Kennedy always seemed to walk a few steps ahead of his wife. "Jackie will just have to walk faster," he said once. Actually, protocol dictated that the President precede everyone. Early in his presidency, Kennedy held the door open for Eleanor Roosevelt, who hung back. "No, you go first," she said. "You are the President." Kennedy laughingly replied, "I keep forgetting." "But you must never forget," Mrs. Roosevelt said gently.

CHAPTER
28

The New Frontier and the Great Society

SECTION 1
Kennedy and the Cold War
Foreign affairs dominate the presidential campaign of 1960 and the administration of John F. Kennedy. Kennedy faces some of the most dangerous Soviet-American confrontations of the Cold War.

SECTION 2
The New Frontier
With the stirring phrase the "New Frontier," Kennedy outlines a broad vision for progress, but Congress enacts few of his initiatives. His efforts are ended by his tragic assassination.

SECTION 3
The Great Society
Lyndon B. Johnson drives the most ambitious legislative agenda through Congress since the New Deal. The landmark decisions of the Supreme Court under Chief Justice Earl Warren reflect the era of liberal activism.

828 Chapter 28

"Ask not what your country can do for you—ask what you can do for your country."
John F. Kennedy

U.S. launches Bay of Pigs invasion.

U.S. and USSR face off in Cuban missile crisis.

John Glenn is first American to orbit the earth.

⭐ Lyndon B. Johnson becomes president upon the assassination of John F. Kennedy.

⭐ John F. Kennedy is elected president.

Peace Corps is established.

| THE UNITED STATES | **1960** | 1961 | 1962 | 1963 |
| THE WORLD | | 1961 | 1962 | |

Seventeen African countries gain independence.

Berlin Wall is erected.
Soviet cosmonaut Yuri Gagarin becomes first human in outer space.

The drug thalidomide is proved responsible for thousands of birth defects in Europe.

THEMES IN CHAPTER 28

Science and Technology

By the early 1960s, the United States and the Soviet Union had built up a stockpile of nuclear weapons. During periods of crisis, including the Cuban missile crisis, the American people feared that these powerful weapons would be used.

The United States and Soviet Union also competed in the space race. After the Soviet Union successfully launched the first human into space in 1961, President Kennedy announced America's goal of sending a man to the moon by the end of the decade.

See Teacher's Edition notes, pp. 832, 840.

Economic Opportunity

With the legislative agenda of the Great Society, Johnson sought to aid the poor and others in need. The Economic Opportunity Act provided funds for jobs training, education, and the war on poverty.

See Teacher's Edition note, p. 845.

Immigration and Migration

The Great Society brought profound changes to the nation's immigration laws with the Immigration Act of 1965. The act allowed many non-European immigrants to settle in the United States.

See Teacher's Edition note, p. 846.

LIVING HISTORY

PLANNING A CAMPAIGN COMMERCIAL

During the 1960 presidential election, television assumed a major role in American politics. Since then, candidates have relied heavily on TV commercials to reach and persuade the voters.

Gather ideas and write a script for your own TV political ad. You may choose to make a commercial for a real candidate in past history or in the present day, or you might present yourself as a candidate. In any case, focus the ad on one or more issues that were or are important to voters and to you.

📁 **PORTFOLIO PROJECT** Save your ideas and written work in a folder. You will prepare and present your commercial at the end of the chapter and add it to your American history portfolio.

Discuss ways of gathering information and ideas for a commercial:

- Choose a candidate and research the important issues of his or her day.
- Select an important issue that can be addressed visually.
- In an election year, study the style and content of current campaign commercials.
- Keep a file on commercials containing notes on elements students admire or wish to imitate.

Encourage students to freewrite to determine the setting, content, and tone of their commercials. Students might use a cluster diagram like the one below when they freewrite:

Commercial — Content — Tone — Setting

IN-DEPTH RESOURCES: UNIT 8
See worksheet and standards for evaluation, pp. 16, 17.

Timeline:

Edward White II takes first spacewalk by an American.

Congress passes major tax cut, Economic Opportunity Act, and Civil Rights Act.

⭐ Lyndon B. Johnson is elected president.

Congress begins passing Great Society legislation.

Supreme Court rules in *Miranda* that criminal suspects must be read their rights before questioning.

Thurgood Marshall becomes the first African-American justice on the Supreme Court.

Martin Luther King, Jr., and Robert Kennedy are assassinated.

⭐ Richard M. Nixon is elected president.

1964   1965   1966   1967   1968

1965   1966   1967

Nikita Khrushchev is ousted from power in Soviet Union.

Ferdinand Marcos becomes president of the Philippines.

Indira Gandhi becomes prime minister of India.

France withdraws from NATO.

Israel wins Arab territories in Six-Day War.

Tet offensive by North Vietnamese begins.

Warsaw Pact troops invade Czechoslovakia.

The New Frontier and the Great Society **829**

RECOMMENDED RESOURCES

Books for the Teacher

Schlesinger, Arthur. *A Thousand Days.* New York: Fawcett, 1965. An account of JFK's presidency.

Unger, Irwin. *The Best of Intentions.* New York: Doubleday, 1996. Assessment of the Great Society.

Books for the Student

Morrison, Joan, and Robert K. Morrison, eds. *From Camelot to Kent State.* New York: Times, 1987. Remembrances of the 1960s.

O'Neill, William. *Coming Apart.* New York: Quadrangle, 1971. Informal history of the 1960s.

Videos

Crisis: Missiles in Cuba. Zenger Video, 1987. Social Studies School Service, 800-421-4246. Story of Cuban missile crisis.

The Fabulous Sixties. MPI Home Video, 1970. 800-323-0442. Eleven-tape series.

Great Debates: John F. Kennedy and Richard M. Nixon. MPI Home Video, 1989.

Rachel Carson's Silent Spring. PBS Home Video, 1993. Documentary about environmental activist.

Software

The Space Race. CD-ROM. First Educational Publishing,1995. 211 Congress Street, Boston, MA 02110.

OBJECTIVES

(1) To identify the factors that contributed to Kennedy's election in 1960.

(2) To summarize the crises that developed over Cuba.

(3) To show how Berlin symbolized the Cold War tensions of the early 1960s.

SKILLBUILDER

• Understanding geography: movement, human-environment interaction, p. 834

CRITICAL THINKING

• Analyzing issues, p. 831
• Summarizing, pp. 832, 836
• Analyzing motives, pp. 833, 836
• Recognizing effects, pp. 833, 835
• Evaluating decisions, p. 836
• Forming opinions, p. 836

FOCUS & MOTIVATE

▶ *Starting with the Student*
• What do students think would happen in a nuclear war? Can anyone win such a war? Is there much chance of a nuclear war breaking out?
• Where are today's hot spots? Which countries or regions pose the greatest threat of nuclear war?

MORE ABOUT . . .
Kennedy's Inaugural Address

In his speech, Kennedy appealed to the American people to serve their country and their "fellow citizens of the world." He called on Americans to·"struggle against the common enemies of man: tyranny, poverty, disease, and war itself." In a strangely prophetic statement, the new President said, " In your hands, my fellow citizens, more than in mine, will rest the final success or failure of our course."

IN-DEPTH RESOURCES: UNIT 8
Primary Source: JFK's Inaugural Address, p. 7

830   Chapter 28

---

① Kennedy and the Cold War

TERMS & NAMES
• John F. Kennedy
• flexible response
• Fidel Castro
• Berlin Wall
• hot line
• Limited Test Ban Treaty

LEARN ABOUT the election of 1960 and foreign affairs in the Kennedy administration
TO UNDERSTAND how Kennedy faced some of the most dangerous Soviet-American confrontations in the Cold War.

ONE AMERICAN'S STORY

John F. Kennedy became the 35th president of the United States on a crisp and sparkling day in January 1961. Appearing without a coat in freezing weather, he gave the impression of a man ready and determined to fight despite the elements. The words he spoke that day also issued a challenge. The world, the president said, was in "its hour of maximum danger," as Cold War tensions were running high. Rather than shrinking from the danger, the United States should actively confront the "iron tyranny" of communism throughout the world. He called upon all Americans to bear the necessary burden of this "long twilight struggle."

A PERSONAL VOICE

Let the word go forth from this time and place, to friend and foe alike, that the torch has been passed to a new generation of Americans, born in this century, tempered by war, disciplined by a hard and bitter peace, proud of our ancient heritage, and unwilling to witness or permit the slow undoing of those human rights to which this nation has always been committed. . . .
Let every nation know, whether it wishes us well or ill, that we shall pay any price, bear any burden, meet any hardship, support any friend, oppose any foe to assure the survival and the success of liberty.

JOHN F. KENNEDY, Inaugural Address, January 20, 1961

Kennedy won praise for his well-crafted speech, but a question raised during the 1960 campaign was still on many minds. Did the young president have enough experience to back up the eloquent phrases with action? Several Cold War crises tested his leadership.

John F. Kennedy delivers his inaugural address.

The Election of 1960

In 1960, as President Eisenhower's second term drew to a close, a mood of restlessness arose among voters. The economy was in a recession. The Soviet launch of *Sputnik 1* in 1957 and its development of long-range missiles had sparked lingering fears that the military power of the United States was falling behind that of the Soviet Union. Furthermore, several setbacks in 1960, including the U-2 incident and the alignment of Cuba with the Soviet Union, had Americans questioning whether the United States was losing the Cold War.

The Democratic nominee for president, Massachusetts senator John Kennedy, sounded the theme that the nation was "adrift." He promised active leadership "to get America moving again." His Republican opponent, Vice-President Richard M. Nixon, hoped to capitalize on President Eisenhower's enduring popularity. In fact, both candidates expressed very similar positions on policy issues.

The election in November 1960 was the closest since 1884. Kennedy won by fewer than 119,000 votes out of more than 68 million cast. Had a few thousand more people voted Republican in Illinois and Texas, the race would have gone to Nixon. Two factors helped put Kennedy over the top: television and the civil rights issue.

LEADERSHIP for the 60's
KENNEDY ★ JOHNSON

830   Chapter 28

KENNEDY THE CANDIDATE Kennedy entered the race with a well-organized campaign, the backing of his large and wealthy family, and a handsome look and charisma that appealed to voters. Despite these assets, Kennedy also faced several obstacles. He was just 43 years old, which would make him the youngest president ever elected. Many people felt he was too inexperienced to lead the most powerful nation on earth.

There was also the question of his faith. Many Americans were concerned that having a Roman Catholic in the White House would lead either to influence of the pope on American policies or to closer ties between church and state. However, Kennedy defused the religious issue by discussing it openly. "Whatever issue may come before me as President," he told a group of Protestant ministers in Houston, Texas, "I will make my decision . . . in the national interest, and without regard to outside religious pressure or dictates."

John F. Kennedy makes a point during a televised debate with Richard Nixon.

TELEVISED DEBATE A milestone of the campaign was the first televised debate ever between presidential candidates. Nixon, an expert on foreign policy, had agreed to the forum because he hoped to expose Kennedy's inexperience in world affairs. But the outcome of the debate hinged less on expertise than on image—how each candidate looked and spoke.

On September 26, 1960, 70 million TV viewers saw two candidates who both seemed articulate and knowledgeable on the issues. However, Nixon lost the image battle. Kennedy, who had been coached by television producers, played perfectly to the camera, and he scored many points with voters because he looked better than Nixon. *Time* magazine summed up the candidates' differences: "Kennedy was quick, aggressive, and cool. Nixon was strangely nervous, perspiring profusely, so badly made up . . . that under the baleful glare of floodlights he looked ill as well as ill at ease." Nixon's many years of experience had evaporated in one evening.

Kennedy's strong performance gave him a big boost in the polls, and he began to attract large and enthusiastic crowds on his campaign stops. His success in the debate also launched a new era in American politics: the television age. As journalist Russell Baker, who covered the Nixon campaign, said, "That night, image replaced the printed word as the natural language of politics."

> *"That night, image replaced the printed word as the natural language of politics."*
>
> **RUSSELL BAKER**

KENNEDY AND KING A second major event of the campaign took place in October. Police in Atlanta, Georgia, arrested the Reverend Martin Luther King, Jr., and 52 other African-American demonstrators for sitting at a segregated lunch counter. Although the other demonstrators were released, King was sentenced to four months, hard labor—officially for a minor traffic violation. Despite the questionable sentence, the Eisenhower administration refused to intervene in the matter, and Nixon took no public position.

Hearing of the arrest and sentencing, Kennedy telephoned King's wife, Coretta, to express his sympathy. Meanwhile, Robert Kennedy, his brother and campaign manager, persuaded the judge who had sentenced King to release the civil rights leader on bail, pending appeal. News of the incident captured the immediate attention of the African-American community, whose votes helped carry key states for Kennedy in the Midwest and South.

KENNEDY TAKES COMMAND From the moment he took office, the Cold War occupied much of Kennedy's attention. During the campaign, Kennedy had criticized the Eisenhower administration for not being concerned enough about

THINK THROUGH HISTORY
A. Analyzing Issues How did television play a key role in Kennedy's election victory?
A. Answer It portrayed Kennedy as cool and aggressive, and Nixon as nervous and ill at ease.

The New Frontier and the Great Society **831**

---

the Soviet threat. The Soviets, he said, were winning the race for allies in the so-called "third world," the economically less-developed countries of Asia, Africa, and Latin America. He had repeatedly blasted the Republicans for allowing communism to reach America's doorstep, in Cuba. As a defense against past criticisms that the Democrats were "soft" on communism, Kennedy took an especially hard line against the Soviets.

President Kennedy felt his most urgent task was to redefine the nation's nuclear strategy. The Eisenhower administration had relied on the policy of massive retaliation to deter Soviet aggression. However, the Soviets had built their stockpile of nuclear weapons and had developed the long-range missiles to deliver them. Threatening the use of nuclear arms over a minor conflict was not a risk Kennedy wished to take. Instead, Kennedy's advisers developed the policy of **flexible response.** In their view, the nation's conventional (nonnuclear) forces had been neglected during the buildup of nuclear arms and needed to be strengthened again. They believed a stronger military would give the president more options in international crises. Kennedy's defense secretary, Robert McNamara, explained the new policy.

A PERSONAL VOICE
The Kennedy administration worried that [the] reliance on nuclear weapons gave us no way to respond to large nonnuclear attacks without committing suicide. President Kennedy said we had put ourselves in the position of having to choose in a crisis between "inglorious retreat or unlimited retaliation." We decided to broaden the range of options by strengthening and modernizing the military's ability to fight a nonnuclear war.
ROBERT S. McNAMARA, *In Retrospect*

The policy of flexible response resulted in a large increase in defense spending. Kennedy boosted conventional military forces and created an elite branch of the army called the Special Forces—or Green Berets. He also tripled the overall nuclear capabilities of the United States. These changes enabled the United States to fight limited wars around the world, while also maintaining a nuclear balance of power with the Soviet Union. However, even as Kennedy hoped to reduce the risk of nuclear war, the world came perilously close to nuclear war under his command—over the island of Cuba.

Crises Over Cuba

The first test of Kennedy's foreign policy came just 90 miles off the coast of Florida. Only a few days before Kennedy took office, on January 3, 1961, Eisenhower had cut off diplomatic relations with Cuba, where a revolutionary leader named **Fidel Castro** had openly declared himself a Communist and welcomed aid from the Soviet Union.

THE CUBAN DILEMMA Castro rode to power on the promise of democracy. From 1956 to 1959, he led a guerrilla movement to topple dictator Fulgencio Batista. When Castro took control of the government in early 1959, he told reporters, "Revolutionaries are not born, they are made by poverty, inequality, and dictatorship." He then promised to eliminate these conditions from Cuba and "to revolutionize Cuba from the bottom up."

The United States was suspicious of Castro's intentions but nevertheless recognized the new government. Batista had been unpopular and corrupt, and many Americans perceived Castro as a freedom fighter. However, relations between the United States and Cuba soon worsened when Castro's government took control of three oil refineries owned by American and British firms. He

THINK THROUGH HISTORY
B. Summarizing *What was the goal of the doctrine of flexible response?*

B. Answer To allow the U.S. to fight limited wars around the world while maintaining a nuclear balance of power with the Soviets.

832 CHAPTER 28

ANOTHER PERSPECTIVE
Eisenhower's Warning
Critical Thinking:
Evaluating Ask students what Eisenhower feared might result from the development of a "military-industrial complex." *Possible Response: Industry and the military would become too powerful, eclipsing the government.* Why did Eisenhower believe that some military development was necessary? *Possible Response: Because he felt that the military had to be built up to counter the Soviet threat.*

OBJECTIVE
② **INSTRUCT**

Crises Over Cuba

▶ ***Starting with the Student***
Have students create a cluster diagram like the one below and list words and phrases associated with each topic. Students should list any facts, names, causes, effects, and quotes that help explain or describe the topic.

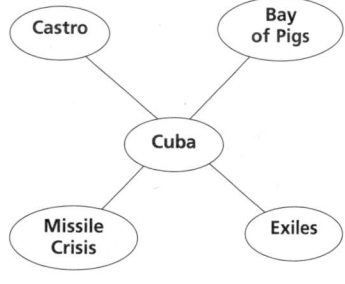

(continued on next page)

EISENHOWER'S WARNING
The increase in defense spending during the Kennedy administration continued the trend in which corporations that supply the Defense Department were becoming more dominant in the American economy. Before leaving office, President Eisenhower warned against the dangers of what he called the "military-industrial complex." He included in his speech the following comments:

This conjunction of an immense military establishment and a large arms industry is new in the American experience. The total influence—economic, political, even spiritual—is felt in every city, every statehouse, every office of the federal government. We recognize the imperative need for this development. Yet we must not fail to comprehend its grave implications. . . . The potential for the disastrous rise of misplaced power exists and will persist.

TEACHING OPTIONS

Exploring Themes

Science and Technology Discuss the fact that the United States and the Soviet Union had built up a stockpile of nuclear weapons by the early 1960s. Tell students that scientists who helped develop such weapons warned against their use. Then ask students why the U.S. government wanted to have nuclear weapons. *Possible Response: To keep pace with the Soviets in the arms race.* Do students think the weapons made Americans feel safer or more insecure? *Possible Response: Safer, because an enemy would be less likely to attack a country that possessed nuclear weapons.*

Teaching Less Proficient Readers

Chronological Order Help students understand the chronological order of events in Cuba. Remind students that chronological order is the order in which events take place. Then have them follow these steps as they read pages 832 to 835:

1. Draw a time line that spans the years from 1959, when Castro came to power, to 1973, when Castro cut down on exit permits.
2. Add events discussed in the text to the time line, including the Bay of Pigs invasion and the Cuban missile crisis.
3. Include any notes or details that help students remember what took place.

832 Chapter 28

also broke up commercial farms into communes that would be worked by formerly landless peasants. American sugar companies, which controlled 75 percent of the crop land in Cuba, appealed to the U.S. government for help. Congress responded by erecting trade barriers against Cuban sugar.

To put his reforms into action, Castro relied increasingly on Soviet aid—and on political repression. Castro's charisma won many supporters among Cubans, as did his willingness to stand up to the United States, which had a long history of involvement in Cuban affairs. But many other Cubans felt betrayed. They saw Castro as a traitor to the revolution—a tyrant who had replaced one dictatorship with another. About 10 percent of Cuba's population went into exile, mostly to the United States. Within the large exile community of Miami, Florida, a counter-revolutionary movement took shape.

THE BAY OF PIGS In the summer of 1960, President Eisenhower gave the CIA permission to secretly train hundreds of Cuban exiles for an invasion of Cuba. The CIA and the exiles hoped that the invasion would trigger a mass uprising against Castro that would overthrow him.

Kennedy learned of the operation nine days after his election. He had his doubts about the plan, but he approved it anyway. On the night of April 17, 1961, some 1,400 Cuban exiles landed on the island's southern coast at Bahia de Cochinos, the Bay of Pigs. Nothing went as planned. An air strike carried out two days before had failed to knock out the Cuban air force, although the CIA reported that it had. A small advance group sent to distract Castro's forces never reached shore. When the commando unit finally landed, it faced 20,000 Cuban troops, backed up by Soviet tanks and jet aircraft. The troops surrounded the exiles, killed some, and took others prisoner.

Castro turned the failed invasion into a public relations triumph. The Cuban media described in sensational detail the defeat of "North American mercenaries." In the United States, one commentator observed that Americans "look like fools to our friends, rascals to our enemies, and incompetents to the rest."

The disaster left Kennedy embarrassed. Privately, he asked, "How could that crowd at the CIA and the Pentagon be this wrong?" Publicly, he accepted blame for the fiasco. "I am the responsible officer of the government," said Kennedy.

Kennedy negotiated with Castro for the release of surviving commandos and ultimately paid a ransom of $53 million in food and medical supplies. In a speech in Miami, he promised exiles that they would one day return to a "free Havana." Although Kennedy warned that he would resist any further Communist expansion in the Western Hemisphere, Castro defiantly welcomed further Soviet aid.

THE CUBAN MISSILE CRISIS Castro had a powerful ally in Moscow—Soviet premier Nikita Khrushchev, who promised to defend Cuba with Soviet arms. During the summer of 1962, the flow of Soviet weapons to Cuba—including nuclear missiles—increased greatly. President Kennedy responded at first with a warning that the United States would not tolerate the presence of offensive nuclear weapons on Cuba. Then, on October 16, photographs taken by American U-2 planes provided the president with stark evidence that the Soviets were secretly building missile bases on Cuba—and that some contained

The New Frontier and the Great Society **833**

C. Answer Possible answers: Kennedy was sensitive to appearing soft on communism; Castro took property of U.S. businesses; planners hoped that invasion would trigger mass uprising against Castro.

THINK THROUGH HISTORY
C. Analyzing Motives Why do you think Kennedy authorized the Bay of Pigs invasion?

D. Answer Failure to oust Castro, loss of world prestige, embarrassment for JFK, ransom for captured commandos.

THINK THROUGH HISTORY
D. Recognizing Effects What were the consequences of the failed invasion for the United States?

top, **Fidel Castro celebrates after gaining power in Cuba;** *above,* **the Bay of Pigs fiasco enhanced the stature of Castro in Cuba and damaged U.S. prestige abroad.**

(continued from page 832)

▶ *Discussing Key Ideas*
• Fidel Castro rises to power in Cuba on the promise of democracy but declares himself a Communist after he takes control of the government.
• The failed Bay of Pigs invasion embarrasses the United States and enhances Castro's stature.
• The United States and Soviet Union come to the brink of nuclear war during the Cuban missile crisis.
• Many Cuban exiles blame Kennedy and the Democrats for "losing Cuba."

MORE ABOUT . . .
The Counter-Revolutionary Movement
Some Cuban exiles waged a psychological war using radio waves. Castro called it "an electronic war," the bombardment of Cuba with U.S.-sponsored radio messages. The war began in March 1960 when Eisenhower approved the creation of Radio Swan, a clandestine radio station set up on Swan Island in the Caribbean. Run by Cuban exiles, the station's mission was to prepare Cuba for a takeover at the Bay of Pigs. After Cuba had been blasted with messages, pro-Castro Radio Havana claimed, "Radio Swan is not a radio station but a cage of hysterical parrots." After the invasion failed, Cuban exiles moved the station to Miami, renamed it "Radio Americas," and continued broadcasting to Cuba.

TEACHING OPTION

Making Connections Across Cultures

Cubans in Miami Tell students that the part of Miami where Cuban exiles settled became known as Little Havana. Cubans called the area's main street Calle Ocho, or Eighth Street. In the 1960s, Calle Ocho developed into a center of Cuban-American culture, where restaurants served traditional island dishes such as fried bananas and cups of strong café Cubano—Cuban coffee. Today, Cubans make up about two-fifths of the population in Miami. Although overcrowding and a high rate of unemployment plague Little Havana, the Cubans in Miami have also made great progress. The city's strong Latin culture has attracted many banks and companies that deal with Latin-American trade. A Spanish-language newspaper is published daily. Most important, in 1985, Xavier Suarez became Miami's first Cuban-born mayor.

Reading the Map Tell students that they can use the arcs on the map to calculate how long it would take a Cuban missile to reach an American city. Then ask them to estimate how long it would have taken for a missile to reach Los Angeles. *About 20 minutes.*

Extension Ask students why the U.S. range of quarantine extended through the northern part of Florida. *Possible Response: To prevent Soviet ships from entering American waters.*

IN-DEPTH RESOURCES: UNIT 8
Primary Source: Political Cartoon, p. 9

MORE ABOUT . . .
Kennedy's Speech to an Anxious Nation

On October 22, Kennedy urged Americans to support the blockade of Cuba with these words: "We have no wish to war with the Soviet Union, for we are a peaceful people who desire to live in peace with all other peoples . . . . The cost of freedom is always high, but Americans have always paid it. And one path we will never choose, and that is the path of surrender, or submission."

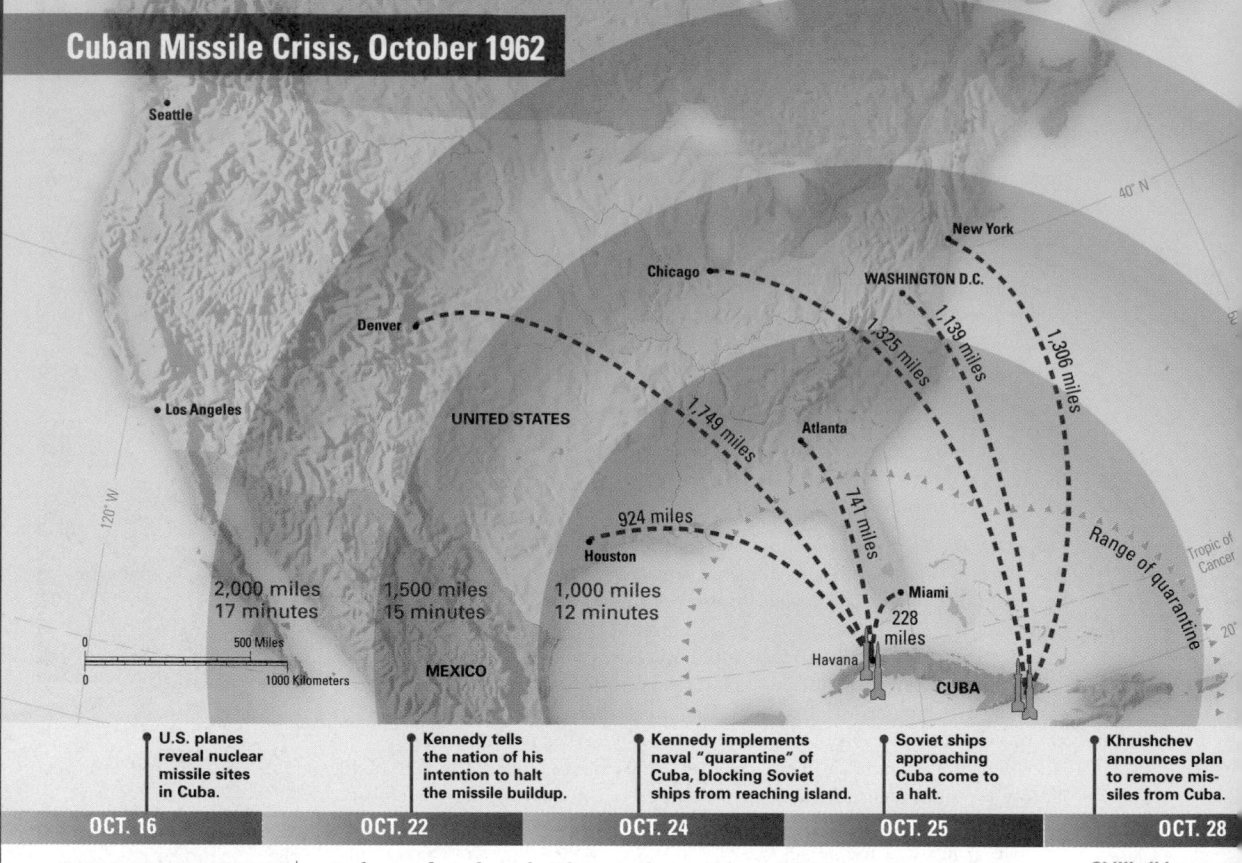

Cuban Missile Crisis, October 1962

| | 2,000 miles / 17 minutes | 1,500 miles / 15 minutes | 1,000 miles / 12 minutes |

Timeline:
- **OCT. 16** U.S. planes reveal nuclear missile sites in Cuba.
- **OCT. 22** Kennedy tells the nation of his intention to halt the missile buildup.
- **OCT. 24** Kennedy implements naval "quarantine" of Cuba, blocking Soviet ships from reaching island.
- **OCT. 25** Soviet ships approaching Cuba come to a halt.
- **OCT. 28** Khrushchev announces plan to remove missiles from Cuba.

GEOGRAPHY SKILLBUILDER
MOVEMENT *About how long would it have taken for a missile launched from Cuba to reach New York?* **HUMAN-ENVIRONMENT INTERACTION** *What was the range of the naval quarantine around Cuba?*

"We're eyeball to eyeball, and I think the other fellow just blinked."

DEAN RUSK

834 CHAPTER 28

missiles ready to launch. The missiles could reach U.S. cities in minutes.

On October 22, the White House announced that the president would deliver a speech of the "highest national urgency." That evening, Kennedy informed an anxious nation of the existence of Soviet missile sites in Cuba and his plans to remove them. He made it clear that any missile attack from Cuba would trigger an all-out attack on the Soviet Union.

For the next six days, the world faced the terrifying possibility of nuclear war. In the Atlantic, Soviet ships—presumably carrying more missiles—headed toward Cuba, while the U.S. Navy prepared to stop them 500 miles from the island. In Florida, nearly 250,000 men were being concentrated in the largest invasion force ever assembled in the United States.

C. Douglas Dillon, Kennedy's secretary of the treasury and a veteran of nuclear diplomacy, recalled those tension-filled days in October.

A PERSONAL VOICE
The only time I felt a fear of nuclear war or the use of nuclear weapons was on the very first day, when we decided that we had to do whatever was necessary to get the missiles out. There was always some background fear of what would eventually happen, and I think this is what was expressed when people said they feared they would never see another Saturday.

C. DOUGLAS DILLON, quoted in *On the Brink*

The first break in the crisis occurred when the Soviet ships suddenly halted to avoid a confrontation at sea. "We're eyeball to eyeball," commented Secretary of State Dean Rusk, "and I think the other fellow just blinked." A few days later, Khrushchev offered to remove the missiles in return for an American pledge not to invade Cuba. President Kennedy agreed and the crisis ended. Years later, Robert Kennedy, who served as attorney general in his brother's administration,

Skillbuilder Answer **Movement:** between 10 and 15 minutes. **Human-Environment Interaction:** 500 miles around the island.

---

recalled the relief. "For a moment the world had stood still," he wrote, "and now it was going around again."

The crisis severely damaged Khrushchev's prestige in the Soviet Union and the world. Kennedy did not escape criticism either. The public hotly debated his actions. Some people criticized Kennedy for practicing brinkmanship, when private talks might have resolved the crisis without the threat of nuclear war. Others believed he had been too soft and had passed up an ideal chance to invade Cuba and oust Castro. (Soviet information that came to light in the 1990s suggests that, in fact, the CIA had underestimated the numbers of nuclear weapons and Soviet troops on the island, and that during the crisis, the Cubans had armed missiles in anticipation of an invasion by the United States.)

The effects of the crisis lasted long after the missiles had been removed. Many Cuban exiles blamed the Democrats for "losing Cuba" (a charge that Kennedy had earlier leveled at the Republicans) and switched their allegiance to the G.O.P. Meanwhile, Castro closed Cuba's doors to the exiles in November 1962 by banning all flights to and from Miami. When Cuba finally reopened its doors in 1965, hundreds of thousands of people took advantage of an agreement that allowed Cubans to join relatives in the United States. By the time Castro sharply cut down on exit permits in 1973, the Cuban population in Miami outnumbered the population of Havana.

KEY PLAYERS

JOHN F. KENNEDY
1917–1963

John F. "Jack" Kennedy grew up in a wealthy and politically powerful family. His father, Joseph P. Kennedy, had earned a fortune in business and was ambassador to Great Britain from 1937 to 1940. His mother, Rose, was the daughter of John F. Fitzgerald, a congressman and mayor of Boston.

The Kennedys instilled in Jack the drive to accomplish great things, and their wealth and influence helped him make the most of his abilities. He enlisted in the navy during World War II and was decorated for heroism. In 1946, Kennedy won his first seat in congress from a Boston district where he had never lived. As a senator, he won a Pulitzer Prize for *Profiles in Courage.*

The energetic self-confidence that Jack Kennedy radiated also came, in part, from battles with his own physical frailties. Kennedy suffered many ailments, including severe back pain and Addison's disease—a debilitating condition that he treated with daily injections of cortisone. "At least one half of the days that he spent on this earth were days of intense physical pain," recalled his brother Robert.

NIKITA KHRUSHCHEV
1894–1971

"No matter how humble a man's beginnings," boasted Nikita Khrushchev, "he achieves the stature of the office to which he is elected." The son of a coal miner, Khrushchev became a Communist Party organizer in the 1920s. He advanced rapidly, becoming a member of the Central Committee in the 1930s and surviving dictator Joseph Stalin's brutal purges.

Khrushchev learned the lessons of dictatorship well. Within four years of Stalin's death in 1953, he had consolidated his power in the Soviet Union. He then denounced the Man of Steel and demoted most of Stalin's close associates.

During his regime, which ended in 1964, Khrushchev kept American nerves on edge with behavior that was alternately conciliatory and aggressive. For example, during a 1959 trip to the United States, he met for friendly talks with President Eisenhower and toured the country. The next year, in front of the UN General Assembly, he took off his shoe and angrily pounded it on a desk to protest the U-2 incident.

The Continuing Cold War

When Kennedy confronted Khrushchev in the Cuban missile crisis, he felt that more than Cuba was at stake. Kennedy believed that any sign of weakness might invite Khrushchev to test America's determination to contain communism elsewhere in the world. Ever present in Kennedy's mind was Berlin—a city where the Communist and non-Communist worlds directly confronted each other.

THE BERLIN CRISIS Soon after the Bay of Pigs fiasco, Kennedy was forced to turn his attention to a growing problem in West Berlin. By 1961, this city's prosperous economy made it a "showcase of democracy." In the 11 years since the Berlin Airlift, almost 3 million East Germans—20 percent of that country's population—had fled into West Berlin. This great stream of refugees vividly

---

TEACHING OPTIONS

Making Connections Across Time

Relations with Cuba Today Tell students that relations still remain unfriendly between the United States and Castro's Cuba. Nonetheless, the United States still maintains a naval base in Cuba at Guantánamo Bay. Resentful of the American military presence, Castro shut off the base's fresh water supply in 1964. The United States answered by moving a plant to Guantánamo that converts ocean water into fresh water. In 1995, Castro attended a meeting with many other leaders at the United Nations. Although Castro received a warm welcome from the audience, many American leaders objected to his presence.

Making Connections Across the Curriculum

Literature Tell students that the Berlin Wall and the Cold War gave rise to a large body of espionage novels, filled with intricate plot lines and disillusioned, hardened spies. The novels of John le Carré, for example, depict a world filled with lies and betrayal. In such novels as le Carré's *The Spy Who Came in from the Cold,* secret agents track down the enemy but frequently compromise their principles in the process. Spy novels, such as those by le Carré, epitomize the distrust and paranoia of the Cold War era.

The Berlin Wall

At the stroke of midnight, on November 9, 1989, thousands of Germans took hammers and chisels and tore down the Berlin Wall. For the first time in almost 28 years, East and West Germans walked freely between the two zones, embracing each other, crying, and rejoicing.

IN-DEPTH RESOURCES: UNIT 8
Geography Application: Divided Germany and the Berlin Wall, p. 5

ASSESS & RETEACH

Section 1 Assessment

Have small groups of students get together to discuss and answer the questions.

Self-Assessment

To document what they've learned, have students create a time line listing the main events of Kennedy's presidency.

Section Quiz

FORMAL ASSESSMENT
Section Quiz, p. 341

Reteach

Use the map and accompanying time line on page 834 to review the Soviet-American confrontation during the Cuban missile crisis.

CLOSE

A series of Cold War crises occupied much of Kennedy's first term. Once these were behind him, the President planned to turn his attention to the nation's domestic issues. Unfortunately, Kennedy would never have the chance to achieve his domestic goals.

The Berlin Wall separated East Berlin and West Berlin.

advertised the failure of East Germany's Communist government while also dangerously weakening that country's economy.

Khrushchev realized that this problem had to be solved quickly. At a summit meeting in Vienna, Austria, in June 1961, he threatened to sign a treaty with East Germany that would enable that country to close all the access roads to West Berlin. When Kennedy refused to give up U.S. access to West Berlin, Khrushchev furiously declared, "I want peace. But, if you want war, that is your problem."

After returning home, Kennedy told the nation in a televised address that Berlin was "the great testing place of Western courage and will." He pledged that "we cannot and will not permit the Communists to drive us out of Berlin."

Kennedy's determination and America's superior nuclear striking power prevented Khrushchev from closing the air and land routes between West Berlin and West Germany. Instead, the Soviet premier shocked the world with an unexpected decision. Just after midnight on August 13, 1961, East German troops began to unload concrete posts and rolls of barbed wire along the border between East and West Berlin. Within days, a concrete wall topped with barbed wire cut the city in two.

The construction of the **Berlin Wall,** as this barrier was soon called, ended the Berlin crisis but further aggravated Cold War tensions. The wall—and its armed guards—successfully reduced the flow of East German refugees to a tiny trickle, thus solving Khrushchev's main problem. At the same time, however, the wall became an ugly symbol of Communist oppression.

SEARCHING FOR WAYS TO EASE TENSIONS Showdowns between Kennedy and Khrushchev made both leaders aware of the gravity of split-second decisions that separated Cold War peace from nuclear disaster. Kennedy, in particular, searched for ways to tone down his hard-line stance. In April 1963, he announced that the two nations had established a **hot line** between the White House and the Kremlin. This hookup enabled leaders of the two countries to communicate at once should another crisis arise. Later that year, the United States and Soviet Union also agreed to a **Limited Test Ban Treaty** that barred nuclear testing in the atmosphere.

With the series of Cold War crises behind him, Kennedy turned more attention to the domestic issues facing the nation. In late November 1963, he prepared a speech to be given in Dallas, Texas, that declared that "a nation can be no stronger abroad than she is at home." Only an America, it went on, that "practices what it preaches" about equal rights, social justice, education, and economic prosperity will earn the world's respect. But Kennedy never had a chance to deliver this speech nor to achieve these domestic goals.

THINK THROUGH HISTORY
F. Analyzing Motives
What led East Germany to erect the Berlin Wall? What were the effects of the wall?

F. Answer Motives: Stem the flow of East German refugees into West Berlin and further isolate the thriving city.
Effects: It ended the crisis but further aggravated Cold War tensions; it reduced the flow of refugees but became an ugly symbol of communism.

Section 1 Assessment

1. TERMS & NAMES
Identify:
• John F. Kennedy
• flexible response
• Fidel Castro
• Berlin Wall
• hot line
• Limited Test Ban Treaty

2. SUMMARIZING Using diagrams such as the one below, list two outcomes for each of these events: first Kennedy-Nixon debate, Bay of Pigs invasion, Cuban missile crisis, and construction of the Berlin Wall.

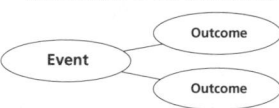

Which of these outcomes led directly to other events listed here or described in this section?

3. EVALUATING DECISIONS How well do you think President Kennedy handled the Cuban missile crisis? Justify your opinion with specific examples from the text.
THINK ABOUT
• Kennedy's decision to impose a naval "quarantine" of Cuba
• the nuclear showdown between the superpowers
• Kennedy's decision not to invade Cuba

4. FORMING OPINIONS Do you think Kennedy's actions justified his critics' accusations that he was too inexperienced in foreign affairs, or did his actions prove them wrong? Explain your response.
THINK ABOUT
• foreign policy changes in his administration
• his stance towards the Soviet Union
• his handling of foreign crises

836 CHAPTER 28

ANSWERS

1. TERMS & NAMES
John F. Kennedy, p. 830

flexible response, p. 832

Fidel Castro, p. 832

Berlin Wall, p. 836

hot line, p. 836

Limited Test Ban Treaty, p. 836

2. SUMMARIZING
Possible Answers: Debate: Kennedy won support, TV became important in politics; Bay of Pigs: United States embarrassed, Cuba moved closer to Soviets; missile crisis: world at brink of nuclear war; Soviets backed down; Berlin Wall: increased Cold War tensions, symbolized Communist oppression.

3. EVALUATING DECISIONS
Possible Responses: Students giving the president high marks might say that the Cuban missiles were removed, nuclear war was averted, and there was no military engagement. Students giving him low marks might say that he risked nuclear war over the crisis.

4. FORMING OPINIONS
Possible Responses: Students may argue that Kennedy showed his inexperience by supporting the Bay of Pigs invasion and by being more aggressive than he needed to be in the Cuban missile crisis. Others may believe that he was generally successful in foreign policy and that he grew in the job.

② The New Frontier

TERMS & NAMES
• New Frontier
• mandate
• Peace Corps
• Alliance for Progress
• Warren Commission

LEARN ABOUT the goals of Kennedy's domestic program
TO UNDERSTAND why Kennedy had trouble securing
congressional approval of his reform package.

ONE AMERICAN'S STORY

At 4 A.M. on May 5, 1961, American astronaut Alan Shepard climbed into *Freedom 7*, a tiny capsule sitting on top of a huge rocket booster. The capsule left the earth's atmosphere in a ball of fire and returned the same way—and inside it Shepard became the first American to travel into space. Years later, he recalled what his feelings had been when a naval crew fished him out of the Atlantic.

A PERSONAL VOICE
Until the moment I stepped out on the flight deck of the carrier festooned everywhere with red, white, and blue decorations, I hadn't realized the intensity of the emotions and feelings that so many people had for me, for the other astronauts, and for the whole manned space program. . . . I was very close to tears as I thought, it's no longer just our fight to get "out there." The struggle belongs to everyone in America. That was the best of all. From now on there was no turning back.

ALAN SHEPARD, *Moon Shot: The Inside Story of America's Race to the Moon*

The entire trip—from liftoff to splashdown—took only 15 minutes. But, like the Wright brothers' first brief flight, it reaffirmed the power of American ingenuity and inspired Americans with the belief that, with the right kind of effort, any achievement was possible. John F. Kennedy inspired many Americans with the same kind of belief. The nation's hopes were shaken, however, when his presidency was cut short by tragedy.

Astronaut Alan Shepard (inset) prepares to enter the space capsule for his Mercury *flight.*

The Camelot Years

President Kennedy's inauguration set the tone for a new era at the White House: one of grace, elegance, and wit. On the podium sat over one hundred writers, artists, and scientists that the Kennedys had invited. Robert Frost, the famous American poet, recited an inaugural poem. Opera singer Marian Anderson, who in 1939 had been barred from singing at Constitution Hall in the nation's capital because she was African American, sang the national anthem. Kennedy's inspiring speech called for hope, commitment, and sacrifice. "And so, my fellow Americans," he proclaimed, "ask not what your country can do for you—ask what you can do for your country."

During his term, Kennedy gave special recognition to American art and culture. The president and his beautiful young wife, Jacqueline, invited many artists, musicians, and celebrities to the White House to give performances or attend dinners and balls. The president appeared frequently on television, a medium that was well suited for conveying his charm and wit to the American people. These qualities also gained him wide admiration among the White House press corps, whose reports helped bolster Kennedy's public image.

THE KENNEDY MYSTIQUE Critics of Kennedy's presidency argued that below the surface of Kennedy's smooth style, there was little substance. But the new

> *"We stand today on the edge of a New Frontier."*
>
> **JOHN F. KENNEDY**

The New Frontier and the Great Society **837**

SECTION 2 RESOURCES

PRINT RESOURCES

IN-DEPTH RESOURCES: UNIT 8
Guided Reading, p. 2
Literature: from *Libra* by Don DeLillo, p. 11
American Lives: Alan Shepard, p. 14

ACCESS FOR STUDENTS ACQUIRING ENGLISH
Guided Reading (Spanish), p. 274

FORMAL ASSESSMENT
Section Quiz, p. 342

ALTERNATIVE ASSESSMENT BOOK
See forms for supporting and scoring alternative activities.

TECHNOLOGY RESOURCES

HUMANITIES TRANSPARENCIES
H43, The Nation Mourns

GEOGRAPHY TRANSPARENCIES
G28, Influence of Alliance for Progress

CD-ROM Electronic Library of Primary Sources

VIDEO *American Portfolio: A Videodisc for U.S. History*
user's guide, pp. 244, 248

INTERNET McDougal Littell Learning On-Line
http://www.mcdougallittell.com

Section 2 Overview

OBJECTIVES

① To explain the public's fascination with Kennedy and the first family.

② To summarize the domestic and foreign agenda of Kennedy's New Frontier.

③ To describe the tragic and controversial chain of events surrounding Kennedy's assassination.

SKILLBUILDER

• Interpreting graphs, p. 840

CRITICAL THINKING

• Developing historical perspective, p. 838
• Identifying problems, p. 839
• Analyzing issues, p. 839
• Recognizing effects, p. 840
• Drawing conclusions, p. 841
• Contrasting, p. 842
• Summarizing, p. 842
• Analyzing motives, p. 842
• Forming opinions, p. 842

FOCUS & MOTIVATE

▶ **Starting with the Student**
• What do students know about President Kennedy?
• Do students believe that a lone assassin killed Kennedy? Or do they think there was a conspiracy to kill the President?

OBJECTIVE
① **INSTRUCT**

The Camelot Years

▶ **Discussing Key Ideas**
• Kennedy gives special recognition to American art and culture.
• The public is fascinated by the President and his family's glamour.
• Kennedy surrounds himself with young, bright advisers.

IN-DEPTH RESOURCES: UNIT 8
Guided Reading, p. 2
ACCESS FOR STUDENTS ACQUIRING ENGLISH
Guided Reading (Spanish), p. 274

President and Mrs. Kennedy enjoy time with their children, Caroline and John, Jr., while vacationing in Hyannis Port, Massachusetts.

first family fascinated the public. After learning that JFK could read 1,600 words a minute, thousands of people enrolled in speed-reading courses. The first lady had an important influence on fashion and culture. Millions watched "Jackie's" televised tour of the White House and copied her latest hairstyle. The nation's newspapers and magazines filled their pages with pictures and stories about the president's young daughter Caroline and his infant son John.

The first family's youthful glamour seemed like a fairy tale come to life. The popular musical *Camelot*, which had opened on Broadway in 1960, portrayed the romance and adventure of King Arthur's court. Kennedy and his talented band of advisers reminded many of a modern-day Camelot. Years later, Jackie recalled her husband and the vision of Camelot.

A PERSONAL VOICE

At night, before we'd go to sleep, Jack liked to play some records; and the song he loved most came at the very end of [the Camelot] record. The lines he loved to hear were: *Don't let it be forgot, that once there was a spot, for one brief shining moment that was known as Camelot.* There'll be great Presidents again . . . but there'll never again be another Camelot.

JACQUELINE KENNEDY, quoted in *Life* magazine, John F. Kennedy Memorial Edition

THE BEST AND THE BRIGHTEST Kennedy surrounded himself with young intellectuals and business people—a team of advisers that one journalist called "the best and the brightest." They included McGeorge Bundy, a Harvard University dean, as a national security adviser; Robert McNamara, president of Ford Motor Company, as secretary of defense; and Dean Rusk, president of the Rockefeller Foundation, as secretary of state. Of all the advisers who filled Kennedy's inner circle, he relied most heavily on his 35-year-old brother Robert, whom he appointed attorney general. "I see nothing wrong with giving Bobby some legal experience before he goes out to practice law," joked Kennedy when asked about his brother's youth.

The Promise of Progress

"We stand today on the edge of a New Frontier," Kennedy had announced upon accepting the nomination for president. He called on Americans to be "new pioneers" and explore "uncharted areas of science and space, . . . unconquered pockets of ignorance and prejudice, unanswered questions of poverty and surplus." Once elected, Kennedy set out to transform the broad vision of progress he had outlined in his campaign into a legislative agenda called the **New Frontier.**

For all the energetic idealism of his speeches, however, Kennedy had a difficult time turning his promise of a New Frontier into a reality. He offered Congress proposals to provide medical care for the aged, rebuild blighted urban areas, and aid education, but he simply lacked the votes he needed on Capitol Hill to pass the legislation. Kennedy faced the same conservative coalition of Republicans and southern Democrats that had blocked Truman's Fair Deal, and he showed little skill in pushing his domestic reform measures through Congress.

Since Kennedy had been elected by the slimmest of margins, he lacked a popular **mandate**—a clear indication that the voters approved of his plans. As a result, Kennedy often felt it was in his best interest politically to play it safe.

838 CHAPTER 28

There was no sense climbing out on a limb, he told his advisers, when he knew he would not be successful. Nevertheless, Kennedy did persuade Congress to enact measures to boost the economy, build the national defense, provide international aid, and fund a massive space program.

STIMULATING THE ECONOMY One domestic problem that the Kennedy team tackled head-on was the economy. By the late 1950s, the rate of growth in the economy had slowed considerably from its boom years after World War II, and by 1960 the country was stuck in a recession. Unemployment hovered around 6 percent, one of the highest levels since World War II. During the 1960 campaign, Kennedy had criticized the Eisenhower administration for not doing enough to stimulate growth and warned that the American economy was lagging behind that of the other Western democracies and also the Soviet Union. He promised that, if elected, he would "get America moving again."

To spur economic growth, Kennedy's advisers advocated the use of deficit spending, which had been the basis for Roosevelt's New Deal. They felt that stimulating economic growth depended on a combination of increased government spending and lower taxes for companies and individuals, even if it meant that the government spent more than it received as income. More public spending would pump money into the economy, and lower taxes would mean that people had more money left to invest and to spend.

Accordingly, the proposals Kennedy sent to Congress in 1961 called for increased spending. The biggest immediate beneficiary was the Department of Defense, which received a nearly 20 percent budget increase for new nuclear missiles, nuclear submarines, and an expansion of the armed services. Congress also approved a modest domestic package that increased the minimum wage to $1.25 an hour, extended unemployment insurance, and provided assistance to cities with high unemployment.

ADDRESSING POVERTY ABROAD One of the first campaign promises Kennedy fulfilled was the creation of the **Peace Corps,** a program of volunteer assistance to the developing nations of Asia, Africa, and Latin America. In March 1961, Congress funded the idea with a first-year budget of $30 million. Critics in the United States called the program a "boondoggle" and "Kennedy's Kiddie Korps," referring to the fact that many volunteers were young people just out of college. Some foreign observers questioned whether Americans could understand other cultures. "Here they come," said one woman in the Caribbean island of St. Lucia, "straight from school to people who manage very nicely earning nothing—to teach them about refrigeration and 'The Star-Spangled Banner.'"

Despite these reservations, the Peace Corps became a huge success. People of all ages and backgrounds signed up to work as agricultural advisers, teachers, health aides, or did whatever work the host country needed. By 1968, more than 35,000 volunteers had served in 60 nations around the world.

A second foreign aid program, the **Alliance for Progress,** offered economic and technical assistance to help Latin American countries improve their living standards. The program was intended, in part, to prevent Fidel Castro from exporting his revolutionary ideas to other Latin American countries. It earmarked money to build schools, houses, and sanita-

> *"They are the best and best-liked unofficial ambassadors this nation has ever sent to lands overseas."*
>
> **SARGENT SHRIVER**
> **FIRST PEACE CORPS DIRECTOR**

A Peace Corps volunteer gives a piggy-back ride to a Nigerian girl.

The New Frontier and the Great Society **839**

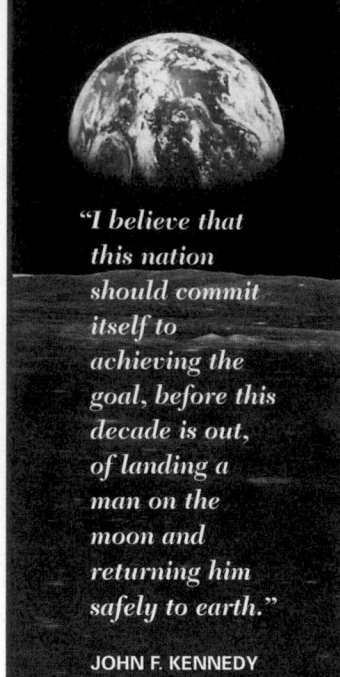

"I believe that this nation should commit itself to achieving the goal, before this decade is out, of landing a man on the moon and returning him safely to earth."

JOHN F. KENNEDY

SKILLBUILDER
INTERPRETING GRAPHS
In which year did the federal government spend the most money on the space race? What state benefited the most?

U.S. Space Race Expenditures, 1957–1975

Government Expenditures for General Science, Space, and Technology

Spending (in billions of dollars)

1957 1959 1961 1963 1965 1967 1969 1971 1973 1975

Geographical Distribution of NASA Contracts (1961–1975)

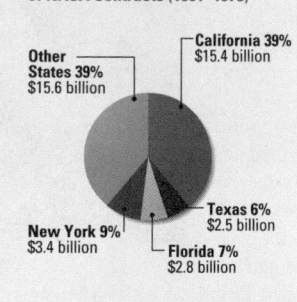

Other States 39%
$15.6 billion

California 39%
$15.4 billion

New York 9%
$3.4 billion

Texas 6%
$2.5 billion

Florida 7%
$2.8 billion

Source: NASA

840 CHAPTER 28

Skillbuilder Answer Peak: In 1966. Benefit: California.

---

tion facilities, and also to encourage economic reforms such as breaking up large estates and giving farm workers land of their own. Between 1961 and 1969, the United States invested almost $12 billion in Latin America. While the money brought some development to the region, it failed to bring about fundamental reforms.

RACE TO THE MOON On April 12, 1961, radios all over the Soviet Union announced a new space triumph: "The world's first spaceship, *Vostok*, with a man on board, has been launched on . . . a round-the-world orbit." Soviet cosmonaut Yuri A. Gagarin had soared 188 miles into the sky and circled the earth in 89 minutes, becoming the first human in space.

The news stunned the United States. Kennedy viewed the Soviet success as a serious challenge that had to be met. At a special session of Congress, he announced that the United States "should commit itself to achieving the goal, before this decade is out, of landing a man on the moon and returning him safely to earth." Congress enthusiastically agreed. Within weeks, the National Aeronautics and Space Administration (NASA) began to construct new launch facilities at Cape Canaveral, Florida, and a mission control center in Houston, Texas. Meanwhile, Alan Shepard's brief flight in May 1961, while it did not orbit the earth, gave the program momentum.

It took less than a year for the United States to duplicate the Soviet feat. The payoff came on February 20, 1962, when Colonel John Glenn orbited the earth three times. Later that year, an experimental communications satellite called *Telstar* successfully relayed live television pictures across the Atlantic Ocean, from Maine to Europe. These achievements helped restore America's pride and prestige.

During the remainder of the decade, an excited nation watched as each new space flight brought the United States closer to its goal of sending humans to the moon. The goal was reached on July 20, 1969, when U.S. astronaut Neil Armstrong became the first person to set foot on the moon.

The impact of the space program rippled through American society. The effort called for better education, and schools and colleges across the country expanded their science programs. The space program would never have been possible without numerous other scientific and technical developments, including computers and the miniaturized electronics made possible by transistors. By the same token, the huge federal funding for research and development gave rise to new industries and new developments, many of which had applications in business and industry—and also in new consumer goods. The spending also helped propel the rapid growth of Southern and Western states in particular, where many space- and defense-related industries sprang up.

A NEW DOMESTIC AGENDA There were other places in America that received little benefit from the economic boom. In 1962, the problem of poverty in America came to national attention in Michael Harrington's book *The Other America*. Harrington used government statistics to profile the 42 million U.S. families that scraped by each year on less than $1,000 per person. The number of poor shocked many Americans.

While Harrington awakened the nation to the nightmare of poverty, the emergence of a mass movement against

---

840 **Chapter 28**

segregation delivered another wake-up call. Throughout the South, demonstrators raised their voices in the cry of "Freedom Now!" Kennedy had not pushed aggressively for legislation on the issues of poverty and civil rights, although he did step into some of the most controversial civil rights battles of the 1960s and effected changes by executive action. (See Chapter 29.) However, Kennedy now felt that it was time to live up to a campaign promise to be a president who "cares passionately about the fate of the people he leads."

In 1963, Kennedy became, in many ways, a different leader than he had been in 1961 and 1962. During the year, he called for a "national assault on poverty." He also ordered Robert Kennedy's Justice Department to investigate racial injustices in the South. Finally, he presented Congress with a sweeping civil rights bill and a proposal to cut taxes by over $13 billion. Unfortunately, the test of his legislative leadership would never come.

Tragedy in Dallas

In the fall of 1963, Kennedy's performance as president seemed to have wide popular approval. In a national poll, almost 60 percent of the public gave him high marks. However, history often takes unexpected twists. No one could foresee that a terrible national tragedy lay just ahead.

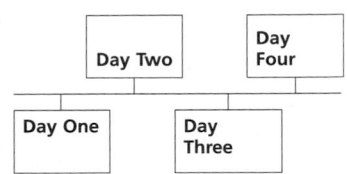

The New York Times. LATE CITY EDITION

KENNEDY IS KILLED BY SNIPER AS HE RIDES IN CAR IN DALLAS; JOHNSON SWORN IN ON PLANE

FOUR DAYS IN NOVEMBER On the sunny morning of November 22, 1963, *Air Force One*, the presidential aircraft, landed in Dallas, Texas. President and Mrs. Kennedy had come to Texas to mend political fences with members of the state's Democratic Party. Kennedy had expected a cool reception from the conservative state, but he basked instead in warm waves of applause from crowds that lined the streets of downtown Dallas.

Jacqueline sat next to her husband in the back seat of an open-air limousine. In front of them sat Texas Governor John Connally and his wife, Nellie. As the car approached a state building known as the Texas School Book Depository, Nellie Connally turned to Kennedy and said, "You can't say that Dallas isn't friendly to you today."

A few seconds later, rifle shots rang out, and Kennedy was shot in the head. He slumped over. His car raced to a nearby hospital, where doctors frantically tried to revive him, but it was too late. President Kennedy died less than an hour after he had been shot.

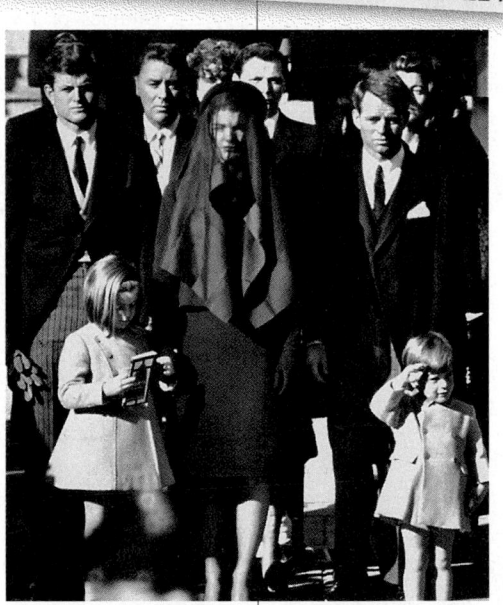

John Kennedy, Jr., salutes his father's casket as it is prepared for the trip to Arlington National Cemetery. His mother, his sister, and Attorney General Robert Kennedy look on.

The tragic news flashed instantly across the nation and then around the world. As word of what happened spread through America's schools, offices, and homes, people reacted with disbelief. Questions were on everyone's lips: Who had killed the president, and why? What would happen next?

Millions of Americans turned on their television sets for answers. During the next four days, television became what one reporter called "the window of the world." A flood of dramatic pictures poured into the nation's living rooms. Viewers saw a somber Lyndon Baines Johnson take the oath of office aboard the presidential airplane as the grief-stricken Jacqueline Kennedy stood at his side.

The New Frontier and the Great Society **841**

Critical Thinking:
Analyzing Ask students why the Kennedy assassination continues to fascinate. Why are some people convinced that there was a conspiracy? *Possible Responses: Some facts haven't been adequately explained; people don't want to believe that someone like Oswald could alter the course of history; people distrust the government.*

ASSESS & RETEACH

Section 2 Assessment
Pair students with less proficient ones to answer the questions.

Self-Assessment
Ask students to make a list of the impressions they had of Kennedy and his presidency before reading Section 2. Then have them note whether their reading has confirmed or contradicted their preconceptions.

Section Quiz
FORMAL ASSESSMENT
Section Quiz, p. 342

Reteach
Use the Section Quiz to help students review the main concepts in Section 2.

CLOSE

Aided by his talented band of advisers, Kennedy worked to boost the economy, address poverty abroad, and develop the U.S. space program. After an assassin's bullet killed the President, the task of pushing through an ambitious domestic agenda fell to Lyndon Johnson.

NOW & THEN

ASSASSINATION FASCINATION

From the beginning, people have questioned the conclusions of the Warren Commission report. Even Chief Justice Warren admitted that "things will not be revealed in our lifetime." For decades, amateur investigators have delved into apparent inconsistencies in the official record. The questions raised by some of their findings have led to increasing public pressure on the government to tell all it knows about the assassination.

In response, Congress in 1992 passed the JFK Records Act, which created a panel to review all government and private files on the shooting and decide which should be made part of the public record.

Since the law was enacted, newly declassified information has added some weight to a body of evidence that JFK was shot from the front (the Warren Commission had concluded that a single bullet struck the president from behind) and that Oswald, thus, could not have acted alone. While such evidence challenges the Warren Commission's report, no information has yet surfaced that conclusively disproves its findings.

They watched as Dallas police charged Lee Harvey Oswald with the murder of John F. Kennedy.

Strong evidence linked Oswald with the crime. Investigators found Oswald's palm print on the rifle used to kill the president. In addition, the 24-year-old former Marine had a suspicious past. After receiving a dishonorable discharge, Oswald briefly lived in the Soviet Union. He then returned to the United States and became an active supporter of Fidel Castro.

The capture of Lee Harvey Oswald did not end the nightmare. On Sunday, November 24, as millions of Americans watched live television coverage of Oswald being transferred from one jail to another, a Dallas nightclub owner named Jack Ruby suddenly stepped through a crowd of reporters. Then he shot the president's alleged assassin. Oswald died less than an hour later.

The next day, all work stopped as America mourned its fallen leader, whose body was laid to rest in Arlington National Cemetery. Kennedy's assassination and televised funeral, like the attack on Pearl Harbor, became a historic event that few could forget. To this day, most Americans who were alive at that time can recall exactly what they were doing when they first heard about the shooting of President Kennedy.

UNANSWERED QUESTIONS The entire chain of events was so bizarre that some people wondered if Oswald had acted as part of a conspiracy. In 1963, a commission presided over by Chief Justice Earl Warren began an extensive investigation that lasted ten months and yielded 26 volumes of testimony. The **Warren Commission** concluded that Kennedy had been shot by Oswald—"a sorry little loser"—acting on his own. In 1979, however, a congressional committee that reinvestigated the evidence concluded that Kennedy was probably shot by Oswald, but in a conspiracy with unknown people, and that it was possible that two persons had fired at the president. Besides these official inquiries, numerous other people have made their own investigations. Their explanations have ranged from a plot by anti-Castro Cubans, to a Communist-sponsored attack, to a conspiracy by the CIA.

What Americans did learn from the Kennedy assassination was that their system of government is remarkably sturdy. A crisis that would have crippled a dictatorship did not prevent a smooth transition to the presidency of Lyndon Johnson. In a moving speech to Congress, Johnson expressed his hope that "from the brutal loss of our leader we will derive not weakness but strength, that we can and will act and act now." Not long after this speech, Johnson drove through Congress the most ambitious domestic legislative package since the New Deal.

THINK THROUGH HISTORY
F. Contrasting *How did the Warren Commission's findings differ from other theories?*
F. Answer It declared that Oswald acted alone, while others claimed a conspiracy.

Section 2 Assessment

1. TERMS & NAMES
Identify:
• New Frontier
• mandate
• Peace Corps
• Alliance for Progress
• Warren Commission

2. SUMMARIZING Recreate the web below on a piece of paper and fill it in with programs of the New Frontier.

The New Frontier

3. ANALYZING MOTIVES Why do you think Congress was so enthusiastic about allocating funds for the space program but rejected spending in education, social services, and other pressing needs?

THINK ABOUT
• the U.S.-Soviet space race
• Kennedy's commitment to the space program
• the costs and benefits of the space program

4. FORMING OPINIONS Do you think President Kennedy was a successful leader? Explain your viewpoint.

THINK ABOUT
• the reasons for his popularity
• the goals he expressed
• his legislative record
• his foreign policy

842 CHAPTER 28

ANSWERS

1. TERMS & NAMES
New Frontier, p. 838
mandate, p. 838
Peace Corps, p. 839
Alliance for Progress, p. 839
Warren Commission, p. 842

2. SUMMARIZING
Possible Answer: Peace Corps, Alliance for Progress, moon program, tax cut, civil rights bill.

3. ANALYZING MOTIVES
Possible Response: It was largely a matter of national pride, since the Soviets had already sent a man into space.

4. FORMING OPINIONS
Possible Response: Students might argue that he was successful because he was popular and focused on projects that Congress would support. Others might argue that he was unsuccessful because he tended to react to events—such as to the Soviet threat, Harrington's *The Other America,* and the civil rights movement—rather than take the lead.

3 # The Great Society

TERMS & NAMES
- Lyndon B. Johnson
- Economic Opportunity Act
- Great Society
- Medicare and Medicaid
- Immigration Act of 1965
- Warren Court
- reapportionment
- Miranda rights

LEARN ABOUT domestic events during the Lyndon Johnson presidency
TO UNDERSTAND what Johnson's Great Society was.

ONE AMERICAN'S STORY

Larry Alfred served on the front lines of the war on poverty. In 1966, family finances forced Alfred to drop out of high school in Mobile, Alabama. He turned instead to the Job Corps, a federal program that provided training for young people from poor backgrounds. There he learned to operate heavy construction equipment, but his real dream was to help other people. So, on the advice of his Job Corps counselor, he read books on psychology and social work and decided to join VISTA—Volunteers in Service to America—often called the "domestic peace corps."

Both the Job Corps and VISTA sprang into being in 1964, when President Lyndon B. Johnson signed the Economic Opportunity Act. This sweeping law was the main offensive of Johnson's "war on poverty" and a cornerstone of the legislative agenda he called the Great Society.

VISTA assigned Alfred to work with a community of poor, mostly Latino farm laborers in Robstown, Texas, near the Mexican border. There he soon discovered that a number of children with mental and physical disabilities had no access to special assistance, education, or training. The main obstacle was in overcoming the stigma that parents often attached to children with disabilities, particularly mental retardation. So he established the Robstown Association for Retarded People, started an education program for the parents, sought state funds, and created a rehabilitation center.

At age 20, Larry Alfred was a high school dropout, Job Corps graduate, VISTA volunteer, and in Robstown, an authority on people with disabilities. Alfred embodied Johnson's ambitions for the Great Society in two ways. Its programs helped him turn his life around, and he went on to make a difference in other people's lives.

above, A VISTA volunteer in Chicago tutors children whose families had moved there from Appalachia. *left,* a VISTA volunteer in San Jon, New Mexico, works with Navajo laborers.

LBJ's Path to Power

"I don't quite know why it is," said one of **Lyndon B. Johnson's** friends in late 1963, "but whatever Lyndon *really* wants, he gets in the end." By the time LBJ, as Johnson was called, succeeded to the presidency, his ambition and drive had become legendary. In explaining his frenetic energy, Johnson once remarked, "That's the way I've been all my life. My daddy used to wake me up at dawn and shake my leg and say, 'Lyndon, every boy in town's got an hour's head start on you.'"

FROM THE TEXAS HILLS TO CAPITOL HILL A fourth-generation Texan, Lyndon Baines Johnson grew up in the dry Texas hill country of Blanco County, near Austin. His great-grandfather had been a pioneer, his grandfather a cowboy, and his father a businessman who served five terms in the Texas legislature. The Johnsons never knew great wealth, but they also never missed a meal—something that could not be said of many struggling farm families in the area.

LBJ entered politics in 1937 when he won a special election to fill a vacant seat in the U.S. House of Representatives. Johnson styled himself as a "New

The New Frontier and the Great Society **843**

SECTION 3 RESOURCES

 PRINT RESOURCES

IN-DEPTH RESOURCES: UNIT 8
Guided Reading, p. 3
Primary Source: from *Unsafe at Any Speed*, p. 10
American Lives: Rachel Carson, p. 15

ACCESS FOR STUDENTS ACQUIRING ENGLISH
Guided Reading (Spanish), p. 275

FORMAL ASSESSMENT
Section Quiz, p. 343

ALTERNATIVE ASSESSMENT BOOK
See forms for supporting and scoring alternative activities.

TECHNOLOGY RESOURCES

HUMANITIES TRANSPARENCIES
H44, Johnson Rag

CRITICAL THINKING TRANSPARENCIES
CT28, The Great Society
CT62, Federal Budget: 1952–1968

CD-ROM Electronic Library of Primary Sources

VIDEO *American Portfolio: A Videodisc for U.S. History*
user's guide, pp. 240, 245

INTERNET McDougal Littell Learning On-Line
http://www.mcdougallittell.com

Section 3 Overview

OBJECTIVES

1. To describe the political experience, ambition, and drive that led Johnson to the White House.
2. To explain Johnson's efforts to pass Kennedy's civil rights and tax-cut bills.
3. To summarize the goals of Johnson's Great Society.
4. To identify the reforms of the Warren Court.
5. To evaluate the impact of Great Society programs.

SKILLBUILDER
- Interpreting charts, p. 847

CRITICAL THINKING
- Analyzing motives, p. 844
- Identifying problems, pp. 845, 851
- Contrasting, p. 845
- Comparing, p. 846
- Recognizing effects, pp. 846, 849, 851
- Analyzing issues, p. 850
- Summarizing, p. 851
- Synthesizing, p. 851

FOCUS & MOTIVATE

▶ *Starting with the Student*
- Do students think that the government should try to right social wrongs?

OBJECTIVE
1 **INSTRUCT**

LBJ's Path to Power

▶ *Discussing Key Ideas*
- Johnson imitates FDR's leadership style.
- Johnson proves himself a master of party politics.
- Johnson's legislative skill and Southern Protestant background win him a slot on the Kennedy ticket.

IN-DEPTH RESOURCES: UNIT 8
Guided Reading, p. 3

ACCESS FOR STUDENTS ACQUIRING ENGLISH
Guided Reading (Spanish), p. 275

Teacher's Edition 843

KEY PLAYER

LYNDON B. JOHNSON
1908–1973
LBJ received his degree in
education from Southwest Texas
State Teachers College in 1930.
To finance his own education,
Johnson took a year off from
college to work at a Mexican-
American school in Cotulla, Texas.
He later taught English at the Sam
Houston High School in Houston.
At age 26, he became the state
director of the National Youth
Administration, a New Deal agency.

When he became president,
Johnson pushed hard for the
passage of the Elementary and
Secondary Education Act. On April
11, 1965, he signed the act at the
one-room schoolhouse near
Stonewall, Texas, where his own
education had begun. He asked his
first teacher, Mrs. Kathryn
Deadrich Loney ("Miss Kate") to
sit at his side. Johnson also invited
his former students to attend.

In recalling the experience,
Johnson wrote, "My education had
begun with what I learned in that
schoolroom. Now what I had
learned and experienced since that
time had brought me back to fulfill
a dream."

Dealer" and spokesperson for the small ranchers and struggling farmers of his district. His energetic politicking caught the eye of President Franklin Roosevelt, who took Johnson under his wing. Roosevelt helped the freshman representative secure key committee assignments in Congress and steer much-needed electrification and water projects to his Texas district. Johnson, in turn, idolized FDR and imitated his leadership style.

Once in the House, Johnson eagerly eyed a seat in the Senate. In 1948, after an exhausting, bitterly fought campaign, he won the Democratic primary election for the Senate by a margin of 87 votes out of over 900,000 cast. (In Texas at the time, the Democratic candidate was a shoo-in in the general election.) His opponent charged Johnson with illegal ballot-stuffing and fought the results all the way to the Supreme Court. The close result and allegations of fraud sent Johnson to his new position with the mocking nickname Landslide Lyndon—and the driving determination to win the approval of the voters and of his congressional colleagues.

Johnson proved himself a master of party politics and behind-the-scenes maneuvering, and he rose to the position of Senate majority leader in 1955. Standing six feet three, he dominated every room he entered. The tall Texan demonstrated great skill in the give-and-take needed to reach an agreement. People called his legendary ability to persuade senators to support his bills "the Johnson treatment." Stewart Alsop, a writer for the *Saturday Evening Post*, explained what it was like to experience this treatment—which Johnson also used to win over reporters. Referring to himself in the third person, Alsop wrote,

A PERSONAL VOICE
The Majority Leader [Johnson] was, it seemed, in a relaxed, friendly, reminiscent mood. But by gradual stages this mood gave way to something rather like a human hurricane. Johnson was up, striding about his office, talking without pause, occasionally leaning over, his nose almost touching the reporter's shoulder or grabbing his knee. . . . Appeals were made, to the Almighty, to the shades of the departed great, to the reporter's finer instincts and better nature, while the reporter, unable to get a word in edgewise, sat collapsed upon a leather sofa, eyes glazed, mouth half open.
STEWART ALSOP, "The New President," *Saturday Evening Post,* December 14, 1963

It was through Johnson's deft handling of Congress that the nation passed the Civil Rights Act of 1957, a voting rights measure that was the first civil rights legislation since Reconstruction. Johnson's knack for achieving legislative results captured John F. Kennedy's attention, too. To Kennedy, Johnson's congressional connections and his Southern Protestant background compensated for his own drawbacks as a candidate, so he asked Johnson to be his running mate. Johnson's presence on the ticket helped Kennedy win key states in the South, especially Texas, which went Democratic by just a few thousand votes.

Johnson's Domestic Agenda

The nation was still stunned by Kennedy's assassination as it watched and listened to President Johnson address a joint session of Congress on the fifth day of his administration. "All I have I would have given gladly not to be standing here today," he quietly began. He reminded his audience how Kennedy had inspired Americans to begin to solve national and world problems. "Let us continue," Johnson declared. In tribute to the nation's fallen leader, he urged Congress to move ahead on the civil rights and tax-cut bills Kennedy had sent to Capitol Hill.

844 CHAPTER 28

Congress responded and in February 1964 passed a tax reduction of over $10 billion into law. As the Democrats had hoped, the tax cut spurred economic growth by stimulating consumer spending and business investment. More spending meant higher corporate profits, which actually increased tax revenues and lowered the federal budget deficit from $6 billion in 1964 to $4 billion in 1966.

It took Johnson several more months to push the civil rights bill through Congress, but he finally persuaded Southern senators to stop blocking its passage. In July, Johnson signed the Civil Rights Act of 1964, one of the most important achievements of the civil rights era. The act prohibited discrimination based on race, religion, national origin, and gender and granted the federal government new powers to enforce its provisions. (See Chapter 29 for more on this act.)

THE WAR ON POVERTY Following these successes, LBJ pressed ahead with his own ambitious agenda—to alleviate poverty. Like Kennedy before him, Johnson was appalled by the depth of poverty revealed in Michael Harrington's *The Other America,* and he believed that bold public action could change the lives of the millions of Americans who lived without hope of ever attaining the American dream. Early in 1964, he had declared "unconditional war on poverty in America" and proposed sweeping legislation designed to help Americans "on the outskirts of hope."

In August 1964, Congress enacted the **Economic Opportunity Act** (EOA), approving nearly $1 billion for youth programs, antipoverty measures, small business loans, and job training. The EOA legislation created the Job Corps youth training program, the VISTA volunteer program, and Project Head Start, an education program for underprivileged preschoolers. It also established the Community Action Program, which encouraged poor people to participate in setting up public-works programs of their own.

THE 1964 ELECTION Lyndon Johnson had brought the nation through a difficult time and had enjoyed legislative success. For the Republicans, ousting him from office in the election of 1964 would have been extremely difficult, even if they had nominated a candidate with wide appeal. As it was, they nominated a candidate with narrow appeal: conservative senator Barry Goldwater of Arizona. Goldwater believed the federal government had no business trying to right social and economic wrongs such as poverty, discrimination, and lack of opportunity. He attacked such long-established federal programs as Social Security, which he wanted to make voluntary, and the Tennessee Valley Authority, which he wanted to abolish.

In 1964, most American people were more in tune with Johnson's liberal goals. A majority of Americans believed that government could and should help solve the nation's social and economic problems. Moreover, in foreign affairs, Goldwater's hard-line rhetoric—including suggestions that he might use nuclear weapons on both Cuba and North Vietnam—frightened many people.

Johnson capitalized heavily on these fears. His campaign produced a chilling television commercial in which a picture of a little girl counting the petals on a daisy dissolved into a picture of a mushroom cloud created by an atomic bomb. And where Goldwater advocated intervention in Vietnam, Johnson assured the American people that sending U.S. troops there "would offer no solution at all to the real problem of Vietnam."

LBJ won the election by a landslide. He received over 61 percent of the popular vote—higher than the previous record set by FDR in 1936—and swept the electoral college. The Democrats also increased their majority in Congress. For the first time since 1938, a Democratic president did not need the votes of conservative Southern Democrats in order to get laws passed. Now Johnson could launch his reform program in earnest.

THINK THROUGH HISTORY
B. Identifying Problems What problems in American society did the Economic Opportunity Act seek to address?
B. Answer The EOA sought to eliminate poverty.

C. Answer LBJ won a landslide and mandate; he also had a liberal majority in congress. JFK's slim victory had denied him a mandate.

THINK THROUGH HISTORY
C. Contrasting How did the margin of victory of the 1964 election differ from that of 1960, and how might this difference have affected the two presidents' legislative records?

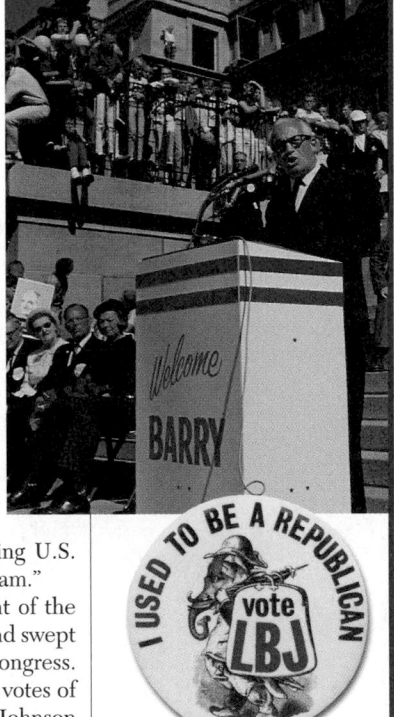

Senator Barry Goldwater delivers a speech while campaigning in Boise, Idaho, in 1964.

MORE ABOUT . . .
Barry Goldwater
During the 1964 presidential election, Barry Goldwater knew his chances were slim at best. In his book of memoirs, he wrote: "Running for President was something like trying to stand up in a hammock. We knew from the polls a victory was not in our lane." Indeed, the polls continually showed Goldwater with 30 points to Johnson's 70. Still, Goldwater felt bitter after his crushing loss. "I think I could have accepted the defeat of the individual Barry Goldwater with humor and good grace. It was the apparent repudiation of all the beliefs and understandings I cherished—which had guided me in public life—that I found so hard to accept." Ironically, some of Goldwater's beliefs—reducing federal expenditures and balancing the budget—had become bywords of both Republicans and Democrats by the 1990s. In some ways, perhaps, Goldwater was simply ahead of his time.

TEACHING OPTIONS

Exploring Themes

Economic Opportunity Discuss the programs under the Economic Opportunity Act. Ask students who the programs were meant to benefit. *Possible Responses: The poor, minorities.* Why did many of these people need assistance? *Possible Responses: Because of overcrowded urban conditions, unequal treatment, poor educational opportunities.* Are these programs better than welfare? Why or why not? *Possible Response: Better, because they help people help themselves.* Then ask students to identify government programs today that help people in economic need. How effective are these programs?

Making Connections Across Time

Campaign Commercials Tell students that, as television became an increasingly influential part of people's lives, politicians learned how to use it as a persuasive tool. In the 1988 presidential campaign, television dominated as never before. Playing on the public's concern with the rising crime rate, a Republican ad accused Democratic candidate Michael Dukakis of being soft on crime for furloughing Willie Horton, a black convict. Many people believe the ad contributed to Dukakis's overwhelming defeat. Ask students to discuss recent campaign ads that have attempted to capitalize on people's fears.

Building the Great Society

▶ *Starting with the Student*
Have students use a chart like the one below to organize what they learn about the Great Society programs. Students should list each program and describe its purpose.

Program	Purpose

▶ *Discussing Key Ideas*
• Johnson presents his legislative program, which he calls the Great Society.
• Great Society programs bring about change in education, Social Security, housing, and immigration.
• The Great Society also seeks to protect the environment and consumers.

IN-DEPTH RESOURCES: UNIT 8
American Lives: Rachel Carson, p. 15

CRITICAL THINKING TRANSPARENCIES
CT28, The Great Society

NOW & THEN
Medicare on the Line
Critical Thinking: Evaluating Ask students whether they think cutbacks should be made in Medicare. Is Medicare an entitlement? Should other federal programs be cut to help balance the budget? Or is Medicare in its present state too expensive to maintain?

Building the Great Society

NOW & THEN

MEDICARE ON THE LINE
When President Johnson signed the Medicare bill in 1965, only half of the nation's elderly had health insurance. Today, thanks largely to Medicare, most do. However, most experts agree that the country cannot afford to sustain Medicare in its present form for much longer, especially if the nation hopes to balance the federal budget.

Three trends are fueling these concerns: (1) people are living longer, (2) health care continues to become more advanced and more expensive, and (3) the large baby boomer generation is moving toward retirement age. Medicare costs are increasing 10 percent a year. In 1995, federal spending on Medicare was about $160 billion; in 2002, without changes in the program, it could top $345 billion.

Both Democrats and Republicans in Washington agree that cuts have to be made, but experience has shown that the issue is a political hot potato. Many people consider Medicare an "entitlement" that they expect to receive when they retire. Although most Americans want a balanced budget, a recent survey revealed that only 16 percent favored large cutbacks in Medicare to achieve it.

In May of 1964, Johnson had summed up his grand vision for America in a phrase: the **Great Society.** In a speech at the University of Michigan, the president declared that "the Great Society demands an end to poverty and racial injustice." But, he told the enthusiastic crowd, that was "just the beginning." Johnson envisioned a legislative program that would create not only a higher living standard and equal opportunity but also promote a richer quality of life.

A PERSONAL VOICE
The Great Society is a place where every child can find knowledge to enrich his mind and to enlarge his talents. It is a place where leisure is a welcome chance to build and reflect, not a feared cause of boredom and restlessness. It is a place where the city of man serves not only the needs of the body and the demands of commerce but the desire for beauty and the hunger for community. It is a place where man can renew contact with nature. It is a place which honors creation for its own sake and for what it adds to the understanding of the race. It is a place where men are more concerned with the quality of their goals than the quantity of their goods.
LYNDON JOHNSON, "The Great Society," May 22, 1964

LBJ set lofty goals for his nation and for himself. Like his idol FDR, he wanted to change America. He also knew that he had to act quickly to capitalize on his new mandate. During the years 1965 and 1966, the Johnson administration introduced a flurry of bills to Congress. By the time Johnson left the White House in 1969, Congress had passed 206 of his measures. For most of them, the president personally led the battle to get them passed.

LANDMARK LEGISLATION Johnson considered education "the key which can unlock the door to the Great Society." The Elementary and Secondary Education Act of 1965 provided more than $1 billion in federal aid to help public and parochial schools purchase textbooks and new library materials. This was the first major federal aid package for education in the nation's history.

LBJ and Congress brought about the first major change in Social Security since its adoption in 1935 by establishing Medicare and Medicaid. **Medicare** provides hospital insurance and low-cost medical insurance for almost every American age 65 or older. **Medicaid** extended health insurance to welfare recipients.

Congress also appropriated money to build some 240,000 units of low-rent public housing and help low- and moderate-income families pay for better private housing. It established a new federal department, the Department of Housing and Urban Development (HUD). As secretary of the new department, Johnson appointed Robert Weaver, the first African-American cabinet member in American history.

The Great Society also brought profound changes to the nation's immigration laws. The Immigration Act of 1924 and the National Origins Act of 1929 had established immigration quotas that discriminated strongly against people from outside Western Europe. The **Immigration Act of 1965** replaced the national origins system with an annual quota of 170,000 immigrants from the Eastern Hemisphere and 120,000 from the Western Hemisphere. Within this overall quota, no more than 20,000 persons from any one nation could enter the United States each year. Close relatives of American residents were exempt from the quotas. This act opened the door for many non-European immigrants to settle in the United States.

THINK THROUGH HISTORY
D. Comparing How are Medicare and Medicaid similar?
D. Answer Both provide government-sponsored health insurance.

E. Answer It replaced the national origins system, which discriminated against people from outside Western Europe.

THINK THROUGH HISTORY
E. Recognizing Effects How did the Immigration Act of 1965 change the nation's immigration system?

TEACHING OPTIONS

Exploring Themes

Immigration and Migration Discuss the Immigration Act of 1965. Ask students how the legislation affected immigration to the United States. *Possible Response: It allowed the influx of people from Asia, Latin America, and other non-European regions.* In what ways was the act consistent with the ideals and goals of the Great Society? *Possible Response: It offered the opportunity of a better life to people in need.* How does the act's provisions continue to affect the United States today? *Possible Response: People allowed into the country under the act have greatly influenced mainstream American culture and lifestyle.*

Making Connections Across the Curriculum

Government Discuss the creation of the Department of Housing and Urban Development. Ask students why the new federal department was created. *To address the problems of the nation's cities.* Why was the department considered necessary by the mid-1960s? *Possible Response: Explosive urban growth in the 1950s had resulted in many urban problems, including overcrowding and inadequate housing.* Then ask students to discuss any recently formed federal departments or programs, such as the war on drugs, created to address current problems.

Great Society Programs, 1964–1967

Category	Year	Program
Poverty	1964	**Tax Reduction Act** cut corporate and individual taxes to stimulate growth.
	1964	**Economic Opportunity Act** created Job Corps, VISTA, Project Head Start, and other programs to fight "war on poverty."
	1965	**Medical Care Act** established Medicare and Medicaid programs.
	1965	**Appalachian Regional Development Act** targeted aid for highways, health centers, and resource development in that economically depressed area.
Cities	1965	**Omnibus Housing Act** provided money for low-income housing.
	1965	**Department of Housing and Urban Development** was formed to administer federal housing programs.
	1966	**Demonstration Cities and Metropolitan Development Act** funded slum rebuilding, mass transit, and other improvements for selected "model cities."
Education	1965	**Elementary and Secondary Education Act** directed money to schools for textbooks, library materials, and special education.
	1965	**Higher Education Act** funded scholarships and low-interest loans for college students.
	1965	**National Endowments for the Arts and the Humanities** was created to financially assist painters, musicians, actors, and others in arts.
	1967	**Corporation for Public Broadcasting** was formed to fund educational TV and radio broadcasting.
Discrimination	1964	**Civil Rights Act** outlawed discrimination in public accommodations, housing, and jobs; increased federal power to prosecute civil rights abuses.
	1964	**Twenty-fourth Amendment** abolished the poll tax in federal elections.
	1965	**Voting Rights Act** ended the practice of requiring voters to pass literacy tests and permitted the federal government to monitor voter registration.
	1965	**Immigration Act** ended national-origins quotas established in 1924.
Environment	1965	**Wilderness Preservation Act** set aside over 9 million acres for national forest lands.
	1965	**Water Quality Act** required states to clean up their rivers.
	1965	**Clean Air Act Amendment** directed the federal government to establish emission standards for new motor vehicles.
	1967	**Air Quality Act** set federal air pollution guidelines and extended federal enforcement power.
Consumer Advocacy	1966	**Truth in Packaging Act** set standards for labeling consumer products.
	1966	**National Traffic and Motor Vehicle Safety Act** set federal safety standards for the auto and tire industries.
	1966	**Highway Safety Act** required states to set up highway safety programs.
	1967	**Department of Transportation** was created to deal with national air, rail, and highway transportation.

Skillbuilder Answer The programs were wide-ranging, which reflected an expanding role for the federal government in addressing certain areas of American society.

The Great Society addressed more than economic and social ills—it also embraced, among other things, protecting the environment and consumers. In 1962, *Silent Spring*, a book by Rachel Carson, had called attention to a hidden danger: the effects of pesticides on the environment. Carson's book and the following public outcry resulted in the Water Quality Act of 1965, which required states to clean up rivers. "Today we begin to be masters of our environment," declared Johnson as he signed the bill into law. He also ordered the federal government to search out the worst chemical polluters. "There is no excuse . . . for chemical companies and oil refineries using our major rivers as pipelines for toxic wastes." Such words and actions helped trigger the environmental movement in the United States. (See Chapter 32.)

Hand in hand with environmental protection arose a new concern for consumer protection. Consumer advocates convinced Congress to pass major safety laws, including a truth-in-packaging law that set standards for labeling consumer goods. Ralph Nader, a young lawyer, wrote a book, *Unsafe at Any Speed*, that sharply criticized the U.S. automobile industry for ignoring safety

SKILLBUILDER
INTERPRETING CHARTS
What did the Great Society programs indicate about the federal government's changing role?

Ralph Nader

Reforms of the Warren Court

▶ *Discussing Key Ideas*
- The Supreme Court reflects the wave of liberal reform that characterizes the Great Society.
- The Warren Court affects political representation in the United States by addressing the issue of reapportionment.
- The Warren Court expands the rights of people accused of crimes.

NOW & THEN
Creating Fair Legislative Districts

▶ *Starting with the Student*
- Do students think that elected officials truly represent the people? Do students plan to vote when they reach voting age? Why or why not?
- Do students think that African Americans and other minorities are underrepresented in government? If so, what could be done to address this problem?

▶ *Discussing Key Ideas*
- In 1982, Congress requires states to reapportion their congressional districts to increase minority candidates' chances of winning.
- Supporters of the act claim that boosting minority representation will help right past wrongs.
- Opponents charge that defining districts by race violates the right to equal protection.
- The Supreme Court declares the act unconstitutional and abolishes minority districts in several states.

concerns. His testimony helped persuade Congress to establish safety standards for automobiles and tires. Under prodding from Johnson and Betty Furness, the Special Assistant to the President for Consumer Affairs, Congress passed the Wholesome Meat Act of 1967. Because of consumer protection laws, said Johnson, "Americans can feel a little safer now in their homes, on the road, at the supermarket, and in the department store."

Reforms of the Warren Court

The wave of liberal reform that characterized the Great Society also swept through the Supreme Court of the 1960s. Beginning with the 1954 landmark decision *Brown* v. *Board of Education,* which ruled school segregation unconstitutional, the Court under Chief Justice Earl Warren had showed its willingness to take an activist stance on the leading issues of the day.

A series of major decisions in the 1960s made a lasting impact on American society. The **Warren Court** banned prayer in public schools and declared state-required loyalty oaths unconstitutional. It limited the power of communities to censor books and films and extended the meaning of free speech to include symbolic speech—such as the wearing of black armbands to school by antiwar students. Furthermore, the Court brought about significant change in the areas of congressional reapportionment and the rights of the accused.

CONGRESSIONAL REAPPORTIONMENT In a key series of decisions, the Warren Court addressed the issue of **reapportionment,** or the way in which states redraw election districts based on the changing number of people in them. By 1960, about 80 percent of Americans lived in cities and suburbs. However, many states failed to change their districts to reflect this development; instead, rural districts might have fewer than 200,000 people, while urban districts had more

NOW & THEN

Creating Fair Legislative Districts

In the 1960s, the Supreme Court stepped into the debate about reapportionment by ordering states to redistrict according to the principle of "one person, one vote." In the 1990s, the Court visited the reapportionment issue again— this time over the question of how far redistricting can go to increase the political representation of minorities.

An act of Congress in 1982 required states to reapportion their congressional districts so as to increase minority candidates' chances of winning. Following the 1990 census, a wave of redistricting resulted in a record number of African Americans elected to the House. These included Cynthia McKinney of Georgia, who was one of 12 African Americans elected in 1992 to represent new black-majority districts in the South.

However, these "minority-majority" districts soon faced challenges in the courts. The challengers argued that creating these districts amounted to racial gerrymandering. Gerrymandering is the practice of drawing voting districts so as to unfairly benefit one group. Defining districts by race, opponents contended, violated the Fourteenth Amendment right to equal protection.

Supporters of the districts responded that in the past, gerrymandering had been used to inten-

848 CHAPTER 28

tionally dilute minority voting power. Therefore, the need to boost minority representation—to right past wrongs— demanded that special measures be taken.

The Supreme Court sided with the opponents. In a series of decisions from 1993 to 1996, the Court declared unconstitutional the use of race as a "predominant factor" in drawing congressional districts. It abolished minority districts in Texas, North Carolina, Louisiana, and Georgia—including Cynthia McKinney's home district. In one decision, Justice Anthony Kennedy wrote, "Just as the state may not . . . segregate citizens on the basis of race in its public parks . . . [it] may not separate its citizens into different voting districts based on race."

U.S. Representative Cynthia McKinney was left without a congressional district when the Supreme Court invalidated her Georgia district. In 1996, McKinney ran again in a reconfigured majority-white district and was easily reelected.

INTERACT WITH HISTORY

1. Forming Opinions

Possible Responses: *Students who agree with the arguments for creating race-based districts may assert that the districts will help right past wrongs and give minorities voting power proportional to their population in each state.*

Students who oppose creating race-based districts may say that such districts are unconstitutional, that it is wrong to use race or any other preferential factor to draw congressional districts. They may say that separating citizens into districts on the basis of race smacks of segregation.

2. Looking at an Election

Suggest that students do the following to research the November 1996 elections:

- use newspaper and other periodical sites on the Internet to pinpoint information
- research print and microfiche sources in a library
- write or speak to their representatives or other political experts
- study the weekly reports in the *Congressional Quarterly* and the *Guide to U.S. Elections*

than 600,000. Thus the voters in rural areas had more representation—and also more power—than those in urban areas.

Baker v. *Carr* (1962) was the first of several decisions that established the principle of "one person, one vote" and made such patterns of representation illegal. In its decision, the Court asserted that the federal courts had the right to tell states to reapportion their districts for more equal representation. In subsequent decisions, the Court ruled that congressional district boundaries should be redrawn so that they would be equal in population "as nearly as practicable," and it extended the principle of "one person, one vote" to state legislative districts. These judicial decisions were extremely important, for they led to a significant shift of political power throughout the nation from rural areas to urban areas.

THINK THROUGH HISTORY
F. *Recognizing Effects* How did the principle of "one person, one vote" affect political representation in the United States?

F. Answer It equalized political representation among rural and urban areas, by ending over-representation—and reducing power—of rural areas.

RIGHTS OF THE ACCUSED Other Warren Court decisions greatly expanded the rights of people accused of crimes. In *Mapp* v. *Ohio* (1961), the Court ruled that evidence seized illegally could not be used in state courts. This is called the exclusionary rule. In *Gideon* v. *Wainwright* (1963), the justices required criminal courts to provide free legal counsel to those who could not afford it. In *Escobedo* v. *Illinois* (1964), the justices ruled that an accused person has a right to have a lawyer present during questioning by police.

In 1966, the Court went one step further in *Miranda* v. *Arizona*, where it ruled that all suspects must be "read their rights" before questioning. These **Miranda rights** include (1) that suspects have a right to remain silent, (2) that anything they say may be used against them, and (3) that they have a right to a lawyer before and during interrogation.

These rulings greatly divided public opinion. Liberals praised the decisions, arguing that they placed necessary limits on police power and protected the right of all citizens to a fair trial. Conservatives, however, bitterly criticized the

Law enforcement officers often carry a card that contains the Miranda rights so they can read the rights to criminal suspects.

MORE ABOUT . . .
Ernesto Miranda

At Ernesto Miranda's trial in 1964, the arresting officers admitted that no explanation of rights had been given to the suspect. The officers claimed that, because Miranda was an ex-convict, he knew his rights. They further testified that they had obtained Miranda's confession to the kidnap and rape of a young girl without coercion of any kind. Largely as a result of his confession, Miranda was convicted and sentenced to twenty to thirty years in prison. He was released in 1966, however, following the Supreme Court's landmark decision. Ten years later, Miranda was stabbed to death in Phoenix in a fight over a card game. When a suspect in Miranda's murder was arrested, the police officer pulled out a card and read, "You have the right to remain silent. . . ."

Georgia's 11th District, 1992–1995

African–American Population (percentage by county, per 1990 census)

☐ 0–24%
▨ 25–49%
■ 50% and over

11th District
Atlanta
Augusta
Macon
Columbus
Savannah

To comply with federal instructions, many states resorted to drawing oddly shaped districts to create a "minority majority." McKinney's 11th District, for example, was drawn after the 1990 census to ensure that a majority of the district's voters—64 percent—were African American. Stretching across 260 miles, the district was known as "Sherman's March," because—like the Union general—it swept from the outskirts of Atlanta to Savannah on the Atlantic Ocean.

INTERACT WITH HISTORY

1. **FORMING OPINIONS** The goal of the federal government was to increase the number of African Americans and other minority groups in Congress. The Supreme Court ruled that the manner in which the states tried to meet this goal—by creating race-based districts—was unconstitutional. Review the arguments for and against creating these districts. Which do you agree with more? Why?

SEE SKILLBUILDER HANDBOOK, PAGE 1049.

2. **LOOKING AT AN ELECTION** Conduct research to determine the results of the November 1996 congressional elections. How did African-American candidates fare at the polls? Did the abolition of minority and majority districts reduce their representation?

For more about gerrymandering, click on *Social Studies* at http://www.mcdougallittell.com

The New Frontier and the Great Society **849**

TEACHING OPTIONS

Making Connections Across Cultures

School Segregation Tell students that *Brown* v. *Board of Education* got its name from nine-year-old Linda Brown, whose parents wanted to remove her from the all-black school she attended. They contended—and had to prove—that separate schools were unequal by definition. After studying the case, the Supreme Court decided that racially separate schools could never be equal. Earl Warren stated: "To separate [black children] from others of similar age . . . solely because of their race generates a feeling of inferiority . . . that may affect their hearts and minds in a way unlikely ever to be undone."

Teaching Less Proficient Readers

Compare and Contrast Help students understand the conflicting opinions expressed in the Now & Then feature on pages 848 and 849. Have them follow these steps:

1. Create a two-column chart. Label one column Pro and label the other Con.
2. Read the feature once quickly and then slowly.
3. On the second reading, list the arguments people use to support minority-majority districts in the Pro column. List the arguments people use to oppose them in the Con column.
4. Look over the chart and form an opinion on the issue.

Impact of the Great Society

▶ *Discussing Key Ideas*
- Johnson extends the power of the federal government more than any president in the post-World War II era.
- The reforms made by the Great Society help create a new awareness of social problems.
- Debates over the effectiveness of the Great Society programs result in a conservative backlash.

 CRITICAL THINKING TRANSPARENCIES
CT62, Federal Budget: 1952–1968

POINT COUNTERPOINT
Debating the Great Society

▶ *Starting with the Student*
- Do students think that government programs encourage dependency? Or do such programs give people a boost and help them help themselves?

▶ *Discussing Key Ideas*
- Some advocates claim that the Great Society was a success because of the gains it made in civil rights.
- Defenders admit that the Great Society fell short of its goals but argue that it worked social and political wonders.
- Critics of the Great Society argue that it created oversized bureaucracies and rising budget deficits.
- Opponents assert that the Great Society created a culture of dependency.

Court. They claimed that *Gideon* and *Miranda* benefited criminal suspects and severely limited the power of the police to investigate crimes. During the late 1960s and 1970s, Republican candidates for office seized on the "crime issue," portraying liberals and Democrats as being soft on crime and citing the decisions of the Warren Court as major obstacles to fighting crime.

Impact of the Great Society

The Great Society and the Warren Court greatly changed the United States. People disagree on whether these changes left the nation better or worse off than before. However, most agree on one point: No president in the post-World War II era extended the power and reach of the federal government more than Lyndon Johnson.

The Johnson presidency oversaw an activist era in all three branches of government. The demand for reform helped create a new awareness of social problems, especially on matters of civil rights and the effects of poverty. The optimism spawned during the Kennedy era continued into the early years of the Johnson administration. The "war on poverty" did help reduce the suffering and want of

THINK THROUGH HISTORY
G. Analyzing Issues What were the differing reactio to the Warren Cour decisions on the rig of the accused?

G. Answer Libera praised the decisions for protecting individ rights, while conservatives criticized the Cou for protecting criminal suspects and limiting police power.

POINT ▶ COUNTERPOINT

"The Great Society succeeded in prompting far-reaching social change."

Advocates of the Great Society contend that it bettered the lives of millions of Americans. Historian John Morton Blum notes, "The Great Society initiated policies that by 1985 had profound consequences: Blacks now voted at the same rate as whites, and nearly 6,000 blacks held public offices; almost every elderly citizen had medical insurance, and the aged were no poorer than Americans as a whole; a large majority of small children attended preschool programs."

Attorney Margaret Burnham argues that the civil rights gains alone justify the Great Society: "For tens of thousands of human beings . . . giving promise of a better life was significant. . . . What the Great Society affirmed was the responsibility of the federal government to take measures necessary to bring into the social and economic mainstream any segment of the people [who had been] historically excluded."

Many defenders of the Great Society acknowledge that it fell short of its goals but argue that this does not detract from its overall achievement. The historian Robert J. Lampham asserts that "even the successes [of the Great Society] have been called failures by reference to new and higher goals" and suggests that this "is evidence not of failure but of success." John Morton Blum agrees: "The Great Society had its failings. So did Lyndon Johnson. . . . But the Great Society also worked social and political wonders."

"Failures of the Great Society prove that government-sponsored programs do not work."

The major attack leveled at the Great Society is that it created "big government" and with it an oversized bureaucracy, too many regulations, waste and fraud, and rising budget deficits. As journalist David Alpern writes, big government resulted from the notion that government could solve all the nation's problems: "Oversold in the Johnsonian manner, the Great Society created unwieldy new mechanisms like the Office of Economic Opportunity and began 'throwing dollars at problems'. . . . Spawned in the process were vast new constituencies of government bureaucrats and beneficiaries whose political clout made it difficult to kill programs off."

Conservatives have criticized the Great Society's social welfare programs for creating a culture of dependency. Economist Paul Craig Roberts argues that increasing welfare negates the power of the free enterprise system: "The Great Society . . . reflected our lack of confidence in the institutions of a free society. We came to the view that it is government spending and not business innovation that creates jobs and that it is society's fault if anyone is poor." Speaker of the House Newt Gingrich contends that "the welfare state reduces the poor from citizens to clients." It "breaks up families, minimizes work incentives, blocks people from saving and acquiring property, and overshadows dreams of a promised future with a present despair born of poverty, violence, and hopelessness."

INTERACT WITH HISTORY

1. **FORMING OPINIONS** Do you think the Great Society was a success or a failure? Explain.

    SEE SKILLBUILDER HANDBOOK, PAGE 1049.

2. **ANALYZING SOCIAL PROBLEMS** Research the most pressing problems in your own neighborhood or precinct. Then propose a social program you think would address at least one of those problems while avoiding the pitfalls of the Great Society programs.

    For more about the Great Society, click on *Social Studies* at http://www.mcdougallittel.com

850 CHAPTER 28

INTERACT WITH HISTORY

1. *Forming Opinions*

Possible Responses: *Success—Students may claim that the Great Society was a success because it resulted in great gains in civil rights, reduced the poverty level of many Americans, helped underprivileged children get a head start in school, and helped develop people's awareness of social problems.*

Failure—Students may claim that the Great Society was a failure because it fostered the creation of big government, negated the power of the free enterprise system, minimized work incentives, and mired dependents in a cycle of poverty and despair.

2. *Analyzing Social Problems*

After students identify a problem, suggest that they talk to the people involved to get ideas for addressing the issue. For example, students who think that their neighborhood should have a senior center might speak to elderly neighbors to determine their special needs. Social programs should:

- present a practical solution to a problem in students' neighborhoods
- propose a solution that takes people's needs into account but that also encourages independence
- not be too costly or involve excessive government interference

These preschoolers in a Head Start classroom are among the millions of Americans whose daily lives are still affected by Great Society programs.

THINK THROUGH HISTORY
H. Identifying Problems
What problems may have affected the success of the Great Society?

H. Answer
Possible Answers: Some programs were hastily conceived and proved difficult to accomplish; contributed to budget deficit problem; federal spending, deficits, and intervention sparked conservative backlash; Vietnam War drew away funds and attention of LBJ.

many people. The number of poor people fell from 25 percent of the population in 1962 to 11 percent in 1973. However, many of Johnson's proposals, though well intended, were hastily conceived and proved difficult to accomplish.

The massive tax cut won by Johnson spurred the economy. But the costs of funding the Great Society contributed to a growing budget deficit—a problem that has continued for more than three decades. Questions about government finances, as well as debates over the effectiveness of these programs and the role of the federal government, left a number of people disillusioned with the Great Society. A conservative backlash began to take shape as a new group of Republican leaders rose to power. In 1966, for example, a conservative Hollywood actor named Ronald Reagan swept to victory in the race for governor of California over the Democratic incumbent.

Thousands of miles away, the conflict in Vietnam also began to eat away at the Great Society, drawing away its funds as well as the attention of the president and of the people. The fear of communism was deeply rooted in the minds of Americans who came of age in the Cold War era. In Vietnam, Communist forces seemed to be gaining the upper hand. Four years after initiating the Great Society, Johnson, who ran as a peace candidate in 1964, would be labeled a "hawk"—a supporter of one of the most divisive wars in recent U.S. history.

Section 3 Assessment

1. TERMS & NAMES

Identify:
- Lyndon B. Johnson
- Economic Opportunity Act
- Great Society
- Medicare and Medicaid
- Immigration Act of 1965
- Warren Court
- reapportionment
- Miranda rights

2. SUMMARIZING In a two-column table, list four or more major Great Society programs and Warren Court rulings.

Great Society Programs	Warren Court Rulings
1.	1.
2.	2.
3.	3.
4.	4

Which item in each category do you consider the most significant? Why?

3. RECOGNIZING EFFECTS Explain how Lyndon Johnson's personal and political experiences might have influenced his actions as president.

THINK ABOUT
- his family background and education
- his relationship with Franklin Roosevelt
- his powers of persuasion

4. SYNTHESIZING In what ways were the 1960s an "activist" era in all three branches of the federal government? Support your answers with specific examples from the text.

THINK ABOUT
- Johnson's goals for his administration
- the major laws of the Great Society
- the changes brought about by the Warren Court

The New Frontier and the Great Society **851**

ANSWERS

1. TERMS & NAMES
Lyndon B. Johnson, p. 843
Economic Opportunity Act, p. 845
Great Society, p. 846
Medicare and Medicaid, p. 846
Immigration Act of 1965, p. 846
Warren Court, p. 848
reapportionment, p. 848
Miranda rights, p. 849

2. SUMMARIZING
Possible Answers: Great Society: Civil Rights Act of 1964, Economic Opportunity Act, Elementary and Secondary Education Act, Medicare, and Medicaid; Warren Court: *Brown* v. *Board of Education, Baker* v. *Carr, Escobedo* v. *Illinois, Miranda* v. *Arizona.*

3. RECOGNIZING EFFECTS
Possible Answers: Johnson's upbringing might have taught him about the hardships of those in need; as a New Dealer, he learned how the government could help people in need; in Congress, he learned the importance of political connections and clout, and the skills to negotiate political deals.

4. SYNTHESIZING
Possible Responses: People in all three branches brought about fundamental reforms that had lasting impact. It could also be called activist because the federal government expanded its role in an attempt to solve the country's social and economic problems.

ASSESS & RETEACH

Section 3 Assessment
After students finish answering the questions, have them discuss their responses to item 2.

Self-Assessment
To explore what they've learned, have students jot down four or five words or phrases they associate with Johnson and the Great Society. Then have students compare and discuss their list with a partner.

Section Quiz

FORMAL ASSESSMENT
Section Quiz, p. 343

Reteach
Use the chart on page 847 to review the achievements of the Great Society.

CLOSE

After winning a landslide victory in the 1964 election, Johnson began pushing his ambitious Great Society programs through Congress. Johnson achieved real gains in civil rights, health care, and education. However, his grand vision for America would soon be distracted by the war in Vietnam.

Chapter 28 Assessment

REVIEWING THE CHAPTER

TERMS & NAMES
1. John F. Kennedy, p. 830
2. Fidel Castro, p. 832
3. Berlin Wall, p. 836
4. hot line, p. 836
5. New Frontier, p. 838
6. Peace Corps, p. 839
7. Warren Commission, p. 842
8. Great Society, p. 846
9. Medicare and Medicaid, p. 846
10. Miranda rights, p. 849

MAIN IDEAS
11. Kennedy looked better in the televised debates, and his brother helped get Martin Luther King, Jr., out of jail.

12. His prestige was boosted when Cubans repelled the U.S.-sponsored invasion, and he increased his ties to the Soviet Union.

13. The Soviets removed their missiles from Cuba, and nuclear war was avoided.

14. Kennedy's legislative agenda based on a broad vision of progress; he faced a conservative coalition in Congress of Republicans and Southern Democrats, and lacked a popular mandate.

15. The Peace Corps and Alliance for Progress.

16. The public deeply mourned the fallen leader.

17. To push through the civil rights and tax cut bills JFK had proposed and to create a "Great Society."

18. By providing job corps youth training programs, education programs, small business loans, medical care, and housing programs.

19. By establishing the principle of "one person, one vote," the Court made states reapportion their representative districts more fairly.

20. It forbade the use of illegally seized evidence, required that free legal counsel be provided to those who could not afford it, established that an accused person had the right to have a lawyer present during questioning, and required that suspects be read their rights at the time of arrest.

REVIEWING THE CHAPTER

TERMS & NAMES For each term below, write a sentence explaining its connection to the Kennedy and Johnson administrations. For each person below, explain his or her role during this time.

1. John F. Kennedy
2. Fidel Castro
3. Berlin Wall
4. hot line
5. New Frontier
6. Peace Corps
7. Warren Commission
8. Great Society
9. Medicare and Medicaid
10. Miranda rights

MAIN IDEAS

SECTION 1 *(pages 830–836)*

Kennedy and the Cold War

11. Explain the factors that led to Kennedy's victory over Nixon in the 1960 presidential campaign.
12. How did the Bay of Pigs invasion strengthen Castro's power in Cuba?
13. What were the most significant results of the Cuban Missile Crisis?

SECTION 2 *(pages 837–842)*

The New Frontier

14. What was Kennedy's New Frontier? Why did he have trouble getting his New Frontier legislation through Congress?
15. What two international aid programs were launched during the Kennedy administration?
16. How did Kennedy's assassination affect the public?

SECTION 3 *(pages 843–851)*

The Great Society

17. What were Johnson's goals as president?
18. Describe ways that Great Society programs addressed the problem of poverty.
19. How did the Supreme Court increase the political power of people in urban areas?
20. Explain how the Supreme Court expanded the protections provided to people accused of crimes.

THINKING CRITICALLY

1. **KENNEDY AND JOHNSON** Use a Venn diagram to show the major legislative programs of the New Frontier and the Great Society.

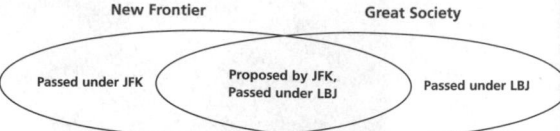

New Frontier / Great Society

Passed under JFK | Proposed by JFK, Passed under LBJ | Passed under LBJ

2. **EVALUATING LEADERSHIP** How important is the personality of a president in a democracy? Consider how Kennedy's mystique and Johnson's persuasive skills affected their success as presidents.

3. **SERVING ONE'S COUNTRY** Reread the quote by John F. Kennedy on page 828. Do you agree with his view about the relationship between individuals and the country? Explain your opinion.

4. **GEOGRAPHY OF THE SUNBELT** The Kennedy and Johnson eras witnessed a transformation of the South—especially Florida. Summarize the events in this chapter that directly affected Florida. How are the changes they brought about felt today?

5. **THEME: THE AMERICAN DREAM** Do you think the Great Society helped people achieve their hopes of making life better for themselves and their children? Explain.

6. **ANALYZING PRIMARY SOURCES** Read the following excerpt from a speech by Arkansas Senator William Fulbright given less than two weeks after Kennedy was assassinated. Then answer the questions that follow.

> As we mourn the death of President Kennedy, it is fitting that we reflect on the character of our society and ask ourselves whether the assassination of the President was merely a tragic accident or a manifestation of some deeper failing in our lives and in our society.
>
> It may be that the tragedy was one which could have occurred anywhere at any time to any national leader. It may be that the cause lies wholly in the tormented brain of the assassin. It may be that the nation as a whole is healthy and strong and entirely without responsibility for the great misfortune which has befallen it. It would be comforting to think so.
>
> I for one do not think so. . . . Our national life, both past and present, has also been marked by a baleful [evil] and incongruous [inappropriate] strand of intolerance and violence.
>
> **J. WILLIAM FULBRIGHT,** speech delivered December 5, 1963

According to Fulbright, what does the death of Kennedy suggest about American society? Do you agree with him? Why or why not?

THINKING CRITICALLY

1. KENNEDY AND JOHNSON
Possible Answers:
Passed under JFK—Peace Corps, Alliance for Progress, space program.
Proposed by JFK, Passed under LBJ: tax cut, antipoverty legislation, civil rights bill.
Passed under LBJ—Elementary and Secondary Education Act, Medicare and Medicaid, HUD, Immigration Act of 1965, environmental and consumer laws.

2. EVALUATING LEADERSHIP
Students might argue that Kennedy's mystique and Johnson's persuasive skills made them effective leaders. Others might conclude that Kennedy accomplished little despite his charm and that Johnson's success depended more on the 1964 landslide than on his skills.

3. SERVING ONE'S COUNTRY
Students may agree that individuals should show their patriotism by serving their country. Others might disagree, arguing that the government of a nation should serve the citizens.

ALTERNATIVE ASSESSMENT

1. EXPRESSING A POINT OF VIEW

It is June 1963, and President Kennedy announces his intention to negotiate with the Soviets to limit or halt nuclear testing. What is your reaction to this plan—do you approve or disapprove?

Working with a partner, design and create a poster that supports or criticizes President Kennedy's proposal. Be prepared to share your opinion in a rally on the steps of the Capitol!

 Research this question using the CD-ROM *Electronic Library of Primary Sources* and other resources.

- Consider key events such as the bombing of Hiroshima and Nagasaki, the Bay of Pigs invasion, the Cuban missile crisis, and the Berlin crisis.
- Review key sections of the Constitution of the United States to consider the responsibilities of the government to defend and protect the people of the United States.

2. DRAMATIZING KENNEDY'S LIFE

Cooperative Learning Working with a small group of classmates, prepare a short play based on John Kennedy's life.

- Discuss which traits of Kennedy you want to focus on in the play. Then select events from Kennedy's life that demonstrate that trait.
- Select the characters you will need for the play, and who will portray each one. Characters might include members of Kennedy's family, advisers, Congressional leaders, foreign leaders, reporters, and others.
- Research your play. Look for details that provide insight into Kennedy's personality.

3. PORTFOLIO PROJECT

 Use the Living History activity to expand your portfolio.

LIVING HISTORY

MAKING A CAMPAIGN COMMERCIAL

You have gathered ideas and written a script for a television political ad. Now revise and develop the script into a commercial you can present to the class. The final product could be in any of the following forms.

- Create a storyboard for the commercial. A storyboard is a series of sketches that depicts the sequence of images and text that will appear in the ad.
- Present the commercial live in the form of a skit.
- If you have access to video equipment, you may wish to tape the commercial.
- Present your commercial to the class. Add your work to your American history portfolio.

Review Chapter 28

THE KENNEDY ADMINISTRATION John F. Kennedy narrowly defeated Richard M. Nixon in the 1960 election. From President Kennedy's first days in office, the Cold War and foreign policy occupied much of his attention. In April 1961, the U.S. government backed Cuban exiles in a failed attempt to invade the island and overthrow Fidel Castro. In October 1962, the United States demanded that the Soviet Union remove missile sites it was building in Cuba. Rather than risk a nuclear confrontation, Soviet premier Nikita Khrushchev backed down. Between the two crises in Cuba, Kennedy also faced a crisis over West Berlin. After failing to pressure the United States to give up access to West Berlin, Khrushchev ordered the construction of a wall separating East and West Berlin.

In domestic areas, Kennedy presented several proposals to Congress, but most were blocked by conservatives there. He did gain approval for two programs, the Peace Corps and the Alliance for Progress, and for committing the nation to a moon landing before the end of the 1960s.

ASSASSINATION OF JFK On November 22, 1963, Kennedy was assassinated in Dallas, Texas. Lee Harvey Oswald was captured and charged with the murder. The nation mourned deeply for its fallen young leader. Lyndon Johnson, the new president, moved quickly to push through a tax cut and a civil rights bill that Kennedy had proposed.

THE JOHNSON YEARS In 1964, Johnson won a landslide victory and carried with him a solid Democratic majority into Congress. Johnson proposed and Congress approved a flurry of reform legislation known as the Great Society. Among these were federal aid to schools, Medicare, Medicaid, immigration reform, and pollution standards. The decisions of the Supreme Court under Chief Justice Earl Warren expanded the protection of individual liberties, caused more equitable reapportionment of legislative districts, and protected the rights of individuals accused of crimes.

Preview Chapter 29

The support by Kennedy and Johnson for civil rights legislation was part of a much larger drive for equality led by African Americans. In the 1950s and 1960s, African Americans successfully challenged segregation, won voting rights, and made other gains. You will learn about these and other significant developments in the next chapter.

The New Frontier and the Great Society **853**

ALTERNATIVE ASSESSMENT

1. EXPRESSING A POINT OF VIEW
Standards for Evaluation
A poster should meet the following criteria:

- Clearly presents a strong opinion on nuclear testing.
- Contains graphics—drawings, photographs, tables, and charts—that convey the opinion visually.
- Uses facts and visuals to appeal to the audience's emotions.
- Includes a catchy slogan or phrase that memorably summarizes the position.

2. DRAMATIZING KENNEDY'S LIFE
Standards for Evaluation
A play should meet the following criteria:

- Strongly conveys Kennedy's personality.
- Uses scenes from Kennedy's life to reveal his personality traits.
- Includes important people in the President's life.
- Sets an appropriate tone, which could be humorous, sad, joyous, or suspenseful.
- Engages the audience.

3. PORTFOLIO PROJECT
LIVING HISTORY
Standards for Evaluation
A commercial should meet the following criteria:

- Focuses on a relevant campaign theme.
- Conveys a clear message.
- Uses persuasive appeals targeted to a broad range of voters.

IN-DEPTH RESOURCES: UNIT 8
See the form for scoring this activity on page 17.

THINKING CRITICALLY

4. GEOGRAPHY OF THE SUNBELT
Possible Answers: The Cuban crisis triggered the growth of the Cuban community in Miami; when the space race began, new launch facilities were constructed at Cape Canaveral.

5. THEME: THE AMERICAN DREAM
Students might defend the Great Society for helping people out of poverty. Others might attack it for increasing government expenditures and causing individuals to rely on outside assistance.

6. ANALYZING PRIMARY SOURCES
Fulbright was concerned about violence and intolerance in the United States. Students might agree, pointing to the continuing presence of violent crime and racism. Others might disagree, arguing that an assassination is the work of one person or a small group and does not reflect on society as a whole.

	Key Ideas	**TEACHING SUPPORT**	**ASSESSMENT**	
SECTION 1 **Taking on Segregation** *pp. 856–863*	*African Americans use strong organization and nonviolent tactics to confront the South's policies of segregation and racial inequality.*	**In-Depth Resources: Unit 8** • Guided Reading, p. 18 • Skillbuilder Practice: Analyzing Motives, p. 21 • Geography Application: The *Brown* Decision, Ten Years Later, p. 22 • Primary Source: Crisis in Little Rock, p. 24 • American Lives: Rosa Parks, p. 32 **COOPERATIVE ACTIVITY** • Writing About Civil Rights Organizations, p. 862 (TE)	*Section 1 Assessment,* p. 863 (PE) *Self-Assessment,* p. 863 (TE) **Formal Assessment** • Section Quiz, p. 352 *Alternative Assessment Book* • Standards for Evaluating a Cooperative Activity	
SECTION 2 **The Triumphs of a Crusade** *pp. 864–870*	*Civil rights activists break down numerous racial barriers through continued social protest and the prompting of landmark legislation.*	**In-Depth Resources: Unit 8** • Guided Reading, p. 19 • Primary Sources: Civil Rights Song, p. 25; from "I Have a Dream" by Martin Luther King, Jr., p. 26; Political Poster, p. 27 • Literature: from *And All Our Wounds Forgiven,* p. 28 • American Lives: A. Philip Randolph, p. 31 **COOPERATIVE ACTIVITY** • Creating News Reports on the Birmingham Protest, p. 866 (TE)	*Section 2 Assessment,* p. 870 (PE) *Self-Assessment,* p. 870 (TE) **Formal Assessment** • Section Quiz, p. 353 *Alternative Assessment Book* • Standards for Evaluating a Cooperative Activity	
SECTION 3 **Challenges and Changes in the Movement** *pp. 871–877*	*The civil rights movement turns north, new leaders emerge, and the movement becomes more militant, thus leaving behind a mixed legacy.*	**In-Depth Resources: Unit 8** • Guided Reading, p. 20 **COOPERATIVE ACTIVITY** • Creating a Historical Atlas, p. 875 (TE)	*Section 3 Assessment,* p. 877 (PE) *Self-Assessment,* p. 877 (TE) **Formal Assessment** • Section Quiz, p. 354 *Alternative Assessment Book* • Standards for Evaluating a Cooperative Activity	
CHAPTER RESOURCES	**Chapter Overview** *After decades of discrimination, African Americans begin a struggle for equality. They make gains against unfair laws in the South, but as the movement reaches Northern cities gains are fewer.*	**In-Depth Resources: Unit 8** • Living History Project: Worksheet, p. 33; Standards, p. 34 **Telescoping the Times** • Chapter Summary, pp. 57–58 **Planning for Block Schedules**	**Chapter Assessment,** pp. 880–881 (PE) **Alternative Assessment,** p. 881 (PE) **Formal Assessment** • Chapter Test, forms A and B, pp. 355–360 **Test Generator** *Alternative Assessment Book* See explanation and forms for different kinds of alternative assessments including portfolio assessment.	

AMERICAN STORIES VIDEO SERIES
• "Justice in Montgomery"

 Electronic Library of Primary Sources
• Desegregation at Central High School by Craig Rains
• Desegregation at Central High School by Melba Patillo Beals
• from *Stride Toward Freedom* by Martin Luther King, Jr.

INTERNET RESOURCES
• See *McDougal Littell Learning On-Line* for links to information about sit ins and Martin Luther King.

 Humanities Transparencies
• H27, March on Washington

Geography Transparencies
• G29, Before and After the Voting Rights Act of 1965

 Grolier Multimedia Encyclopedia
• video on the Civil Rights March on Washington
• pacifism and nonviolent movements

INTERNET RESOURCES
• See *McDougal Littell Learning On-Line* for links to information about the Civil Rights Museum.

 Critical Thinking Transparencies
• CT63, African-American Educational Attainment
• CT29, Civil Rights Movement

 Electronic Library of Primary Sources
• from Speech to Mississippi Youth by Malcolm X

INTERNET RESOURCES
• See Interact with History p. 879 (PE) for an activity that includes the Internet as an enrichment option.

 American Portfolio: A Videodisc for U.S. History, user's guide, pp. 236, 237, 240, 246, 248

INTERNET RESOURCES
Learning On-Line: Social Studies
http://www.mcdougallittell.com

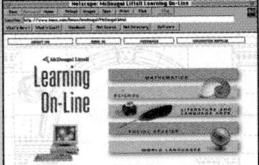

Block Scheduling (90 MINUTES)

Day 1
Section 1, pp. 856–863
 AMERICAN STORIES VIDEO SERIES "Justice in Montgomery"
Section 2, pp. 864–870
Section Assessments, pp. 863, 870

Day 2
Section 3, pp. 871–877
Section Assessment, p. 877
Tracing Themes: Civil Rights, pp. 878–879
Chapter Assessment, pp. 880–881

YEARLY PACING *Chapter 29 Total:* 2 days *Yearly Total:* 85 days

See *Planning for Block Schedules* for special activities and pacing strategies.

Customizing for Special Populations

Students Acquiring English

Access for Students Acquiring English
• Guided Reading for Sections 1–3 (Spanish), pp. 281–283
• Chapter Summary (Spanish), pp. 279–280
• Skillbuilder Practice: Analyzing Motives, p. 284
• Geography Application: The *Brown* Decision, Ten Years Later, p. 285

 AMERICAN STORIES VIDEO SERIES
•Justice in Montgomery (Spanish track)

INTERNET RESOURCES
• See *McDougal Littell Learning On-Line* The Diverse Classroom.

Less Proficient Readers

In-Depth Resources: Unit 8
• Guided Reading for Sections 1–3, pp. 18–20
• Skillbuilder: Analyzing Motives, p. 11
• Geography Application: The *Brown* Decision, Ten Years Later, p. 22

Telescoping the Times
• Chapter Summary, pp. 57–58

See additional strategies at point of use in the Teacher's Edition.

Gifted and Talented Students

In-Depth Resources: Unit 8
• Primary Sources: The Crisis in Little Rock, p. 24; Civil Rights Song, p. 25; from "I Have a Dream" by Martin Luther King, Jr., p. 26; Political Poster, p. 32
• American Lives: A. Philip Randolph, p. 31; Rosa Parks, p. 32

See additional strategies at point of use in the Teacher's Edition.

Connections to Literature READINGS FOR STUDENTS

In-Depth Resources: Unit 8
• from *And All Our Wounds Forgiven* by Julius Lester, p. 28

McDougal Littell *The Language of Literature*
American Literature
• Martin Luther King, Jr. from *Stride Toward Freedom,* p. 234
• Malcolm X, "Necessary to Protect Ourselves," p. 234
• Anne Moody, from *Coming of Age in Mississippi,* p. 491
• Robert Hayden, "Frederick Douglass," p. 497
• Dudley Randall, "Ballad of Birmingham," p. 500
• James Baldwin, "My Dungeon Shook," p. 791
• Gwendolyn Brooks, "Life for My Child Is Simple," p. 799 "Primer for Blacks," p. 799
• Toni Morrison, "Thoughts on the African-American Novel," p. 805

McDougal Littell *Literature Connections*

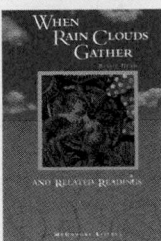

• Bessie Head *When Rain Clouds Gather* (with related readings) *Fleeing South Africa in the 1960s, Makhaya comes to a rural village in Botswana as that country approaches independence. The story resonates with the same issues of race, privilege, and identity that drove the civil rights movement in the United States.*

• Mark Mathabane *Kaffir Boy (with related readings) Born under the hopelessness of apartheid, Mark Mathabane raised himself up from squalor and desperation to win a scholarship to an American university. His extraordinary memoir of life under apartheid is a triumph of the human spirit over hatred.*

Civil Rights

▶ *Starting with the Student*
Ask students how they define the term *civil rights.*

- What civil rights are Americans entitled to?
- How would the loss of one or more of these rights affect students' lives?

PREVIEWING THE CHAPTER

- Read the Medgar Evers quote aloud and have students discuss its meaning.
- Ask students to scan the section summaries and the time line to consider what ideas animated the civil rights activists and which activists were killed in the movement. Did these deaths hinder the movement?

MORE ABOUT . . .
Medgar Evers

(1925–1963) In the spring of 1963, Medgar Evers went on television to expose the economic injustices faced by African Americans living in Jackson, Mississippi. Evers declared, "Tonight the Negro knows . . . about the new free nation[s] in Africa and knows that a Congo native can be a locomotive engineer, but in Jackson he cannot even drive a garbage truck." The bold speech made Evers a central target of racial hatred and on June 12, 1963, he was murdered in front of his house.

CHAPTER
29 Civil Rights

SECTION 1
Taking on Segregation
African Americans use strong organization and nonviolent tactics to confront the South's policies of segregation and racial inequality.

 VIDEO *JUSTICE IN MONTGOMERY*

SECTION 2
The Triumphs of a Crusade
Civil rights activists break down numerous racial barriers through continued social protest and the prompting of landmark legislation.

SECTION 3
Challenges and Changes in the Movement
The civil rights movement turns north, new leaders emerge, and the movement becomes more militant, thus leaving behind a mixed legacy.

"You can kill a man, but you can't kill an idea."
Medgar Evers

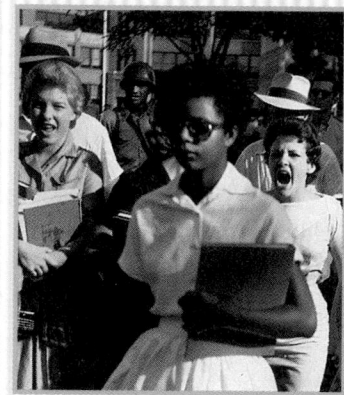

Attorney General Robert Kennedy steps up federal enforcement of civil rights laws.

Little Rock school crisis occurs.

● *Brown* v. *Board of Education* decision orders desegregation of public schools.

● Montgomery bus boycott begins.

✪ Dwight D. Eisenhower is reelected.

● Southern Christian Leadership Conference is formed.

●● Students stage sit-ins across the South.

✪ John F. Kennedy is elected president.

THE UNITED STATES		1955	1956	1957		1960	1961
THE WORLD	**1954**	1956	1957		1959	1960	

● Suez Canal crisis occurs in Egypt.

● African nation of Ghana wins independence.

● Fidel Castro assumes power in Cuba.

● South Africa leaves the British Commonwealth and outlaws the African National Congress (ANC).

854 CHAPTER 29

THEMES IN CHAPTER 29

Constitutional Concerns	*Civil Rights*	*Civil Rights*	*Expanding Democracy*
In the *Plessy* case in 1896, Justice John Marshall Harlan issued a famous dissent, arguing that segregation was wrong. This opinion was not validated by the Court until the *Brown* decision of 1954. See Teacher's Edition, p. 858.	The civil rights movement exposed the ugly face of racial prejudice and pushed a reluctant federal government to take action on behalf of African Americans. Both Eisenhower and Kennedy had to use military force to enforce desegregation. See Teacher's Edition, p. 865	Although the Fifteenth Amendment guaranteed voting rights for all citizens regardless of "race, color, or previous condition of servitude," most Southern states restricted African-Americans' access to the ballot. The civil rights movement changed that. See Teacher's Edition, p. 868.	There is no explicit right to work in the Constitution, but some Americans feel that all Americans deserve to earn a decent living. Many African Americans feel that they have been denied economic equality through discrimination in the workplace. See Teacher's Edition, p. 872.

LIVING HISTORY

WRITING A BIOGRAPHICAL SKETCH

Civil rights activists began direct action during the 1950s and 1960s to win constitutional rights for African Americans. As you read the chapter, list important civil rights leaders. Then, choose a leader and write a biographical sketch of him or her. Use the text and other sources for information. Ask yourself the following questions as you begin writing:

- What event or situation caused the leader to become involved in the civil rights movement?
- What were the leader's major contributions to the movement?
- What were the effects of those contributions?
- How did the American people react to the leader's efforts?

📁 **PORTFOLIO PROJECT** Save your biographical sketch in a folder for your American history portfolio. You will revise and share your writing at the end of the chapter.

WRITING A BIOGRAPHICAL SKETCH

Discuss ways of writing a biographical sketch:

- Scan this chapter and outside sources for examples of people to write about.
- Choose a person and research that person's life.
- Decide which events, characteristics, and influences are most important about this person.
- Write the biographical sketch.

Project Planning Guide

Step 1	Choose the person to write about.
Step 2	Research that person's life.
Step 3	Make an outline of the important activities and events of that person's life.
Step 4	Write the biography.

IN-DEPTH RESOURCES: UNIT 8
See worksheet and standards for evaluation, pp. 16, 17.

Civil rights march from Selma to Montgomery, Alabama, begins.

Rioting erupts in the Watts district of Los Angeles.

Martin Luther King, Jr., delivers "I Have a Dream" speech at March on Washington.

Medgar Evers is assassinated.

Lyndon B. Johnson becomes president upon John F. Kennedy's assassination.

Congress passes Civil Rights Act.

⭐ Lyndon B. Johnson is elected president.

Congress passes Voting Rights Act.

President Johnson sends first U.S. ground troops to Vietnam.

Race riots erupt in major U.S. cities.

Martin Luther King, Jr., is assassinated.

⭐ Richard M. Nixon is elected president.

U.S. astronauts walk on the moon.

1962	1963	1964	1965		1967	1968	1969	**1970**
			1965	1966		1968		

ANC leader Nelson Mandela is imprisoned.

Civil war rages in Nigeria.

Cultural Revolution begins in China.

Tet offensive begins.

President Nasser of Egypt dies.

Civil Rights **855**

RECOMMENDED RESOURCES

Books for the Teacher

Chafe, William H. *Civilities and Civil Rights: Greensboro, North Carolina, and the Black Struggle for Freedom.* New York: Oxford UP, 1980.

Morris, Aldon. D. *The Origins of the Civil Rights Movement.* New York: Free Press, 1984.

Ralph, James R. *Northern Protest: Martin Luther King, Jr., Chicago, and the Civil Rights Movement.* Cambridge: Harvard UP, 1993.

Books for the Student

Boyd, Herb. *Black Panthers for Beginners.* New York: Writers and Readers Publishing, Inc., 1995.

Goldfield, David. *Black, White, and Southern: Race Relations and Southern Culture, 1940 to the Present.* Baton Rouge: Louisiana State UP, 1990.

Kluger, Richard. *Simple Justice: The History of Brown v. Board of Education and Black America's Struggle for Equality.* New York: Knopf, 1975.

Videos

At the River I Stand. Dir. David Appleby. California Newsreel, 1993. Documentary of Martin Luther King's last civil rights campaign before his assassination.

Eyes on the Prize. PBS Home Video, 1986, 1989. 800-424-7963. 14-hour chronicle of the civil rights movement.

Simple Justice. PBS Home Video, 1993. Documentary about *Brown* v. *Board of Education.*

Software

Malcolm X: By Any Means Possible. Scholastic, 770 Broadway, New York, NY 10003.

Prejudice. Diskettes. Tom Snyder Productions, Inc., 1992. 800-342-0236.

① To explain how legalized segregation deprived African Americans of their rights as citizens.

② To describe NAACP's legal challenges to the *Plessy* decision.

③ To describe the divided reaction to the *Brown* decision.

④ To trace the development of the Montgomery bus boycott.

⑤ To explain the philosophy of Dr. Martin Luther King, Jr., and his role with SCLC.

⑥ To summarize the role young people played in the civil rights movement.

SKILLBUILDER

• Understanding geography: regions, p. 857

CRITICAL THINKING

• Recognizing effects, p. 857
• Developing historical perspective, p. 858
• Analyzing issues, p. 858
• Analyzing causes, pp. 859, 861
• Drawing conclusions, pp. 860, 863
• Summarizing, pp. 862, 863
• Contrasting, p. 863
• Analyzing motives, p. 863

FOCUS & MOTIVATE

▶ **Starting with the Student** Watch the video "Justice in Montgomery" to experience the tensions and excitement of the Montgomery bus boycott.

• Using the *Teacher's Resource Book* as a guide, explore the background of Jo Ann Gibson Robinson and engage in extension activities using key primary sources.

AMERICAN STORIES VIDEO SERIES "Justice in Montgomery"
Videocassette: Volume 5

Videodisc: Disc 3, Side B, Chapter 2

---

❶ Taking on Segregation

TERMS & NAMES
• Thurgood Marshall
• *Brown v. Board of Education*
• Rosa Parks
• Dr. Martin Luther King, Jr.
• Southern Christian Leadership Conference
• Student Nonviolent Coordinating Committee
• sit-in

LEARN ABOUT school desegregation campaigns, the Montgomery bus boycott, and sit-ins
TO UNDERSTAND the beginnings of the civil rights movement.

ONE AMERICAN'S STORY

Jo Ann Gibson Robinson drew back in self-defense as the white bus driver raised his hand as if to strike her. "Get up from there!" he shouted. The driver was furious because Robinson, laden with Christmas packages, had forgotten the rules and sat down in one of the front rows of the bus, which were reserved for whites. Robinson left the bus in tears. "I felt like a dog," she later said.

Humiliating incidents were not new to the African Americans who rode the segregated buses of Montgomery, Alabama, in the mid 1950s. The bus company required them to pay at the front and then exit and reboard at the rear. A few drivers considered it a joke to speed off before African-American riders had a chance to get back on. In addition, if the seats in the white section were all taken, drivers could force black riders to yield their seats to whites.

Robinson, a professor at the all-black Alabama State College, was also president of the Women's Political Council, a group of professional African-American women determined to increase black political influence. The council petitioned city officials to ease the discrimination practiced on city buses. They also built a network of contacts in the African-American community so they would be able to coordinate citywide protests of injustice if necessary. Robinson recalled,

Jo Ann Gibson Robinson

A PERSONAL VOICE
We had members in every elementary, junior high, and senior high school, and in federal, state, and local jobs. Wherever there were more than ten blacks employed, we had a member there. We were prepared to the point that we knew that in a matter of hours, we could corral the whole city.

JO ANN GIBSON ROBINSON, quoted in *Voices of Freedom: An Oral History of the Civil Rights Movement*

On December 1, 1955, Robinson and other members of the council learned that the police had arrested an African-American woman for refusing to give up her seat on a bus. "Jo Ann, if you have ever planned to do anything with the council," a friend said, "now is the time." Robinson promptly sent out a call for all African Americans to boycott the city buses.

 VIDEO *JUSTICE IN MONTGOMERY*
Jo Ann Gibson Robinson and the Bus Boycott

The Segregation System

Separate facilities, including bus and train station waiting rooms, were common throughout the South.

Segregated buses might never have rolled through the streets of Montgomery—or anywhere else in the United States—if the Civil Rights Act of 1875 had remained in force. This act outlawed segregation in public facilities by decreeing that "all persons . . . shall be entitled to the full and equal enjoyment of the accommodations . . . of inns, public conveyances on land or water, theaters, and other places of public amusement." In 1883, however, the Supreme Court declared the act unconstitutional.

LEGALIZING SEGREGATION During the 1890s, a number of other court decisions and state laws severely limited African-American rights. In 1890, Louisiana passed a law requiring railroads to provide "equal but separate accommodations for the white and colored races." In the *Plessy* v. *Ferguson* case in 1896, the Supreme Court

---

SECTION 1 RESOURCES

📁 **PRINT RESOURCES**

IN-DEPTH RESOURCES: UNIT 8
Guided Reading, p. 18
Skillbuilder Practice: Analyzing Motives, p. 21
Geography Application: The *Brown* Decision: Ten Years Later, p. 22
Primary Source: Crisis in Little Rock, p. 24
American Lives: Rosa Parks, p. 32

ACCESS FOR STUDENTS ACQUIRING ENGLISH
Guided Reading (Spanish), p. 281
Skillbuilder Practice: Analyzing Motives (Spanish), p. 284
Geography Application: The *Brown* Decision, Ten Years Later (Spanish), p. 285

FORMAL ASSESSMENT
Section Quiz, p. 352

ALTERNATIVE ASSESSMENT BOOK
See forms for supporting and scoring alternative activities.

💻 **TECHNOLOGY RESOURCES**

CD-ROM Electronic Library of Primary Sources

VIDEO American Stories video series
American Portfolio: A Videodisc for U.S. History user's guide, pp. 236, 237, 240

INTERNET McDougal Littell Learning On-Line
http://www.mcdougallittell.com

U.S. School Segregation, 1952

- ■ Segregation required
- ■ Segregation permitted
- ■ Segregation prohibited
- ■ No specific legislation or local option

Source: Pauli Murray, *States' Laws on Race and Color*

GEOGRAPHY SKILLBUILDER **REGIONS**
In which states were schools segregated by law?
In which was segregation expressly prohibited?

These photos of the public schools for white children (*above*) and for black children (*right*) in a Southern town in the 1930s show that separate facilities were often unequal in the segregation era.

ruled that this law did not violate the Fourteenth Amendment, which guarantees all Americans equal treatment under the law.

Armed with the *Plessy* decision, states throughout the nation, but especially in the South, passed what were known as Jim Crow laws, or laws aimed at separating the races. Laws forbade marriage between blacks and whites and established many other restrictions on social and religious contact between the races. There were separate schools, as well as separate streetcars, waiting rooms, railroad coaches, elevators, witness stands, and public restrooms. The facilities provided for blacks were always far inferior to those provided for whites. Nearly every day, African Americans faced humiliating signs that read, Colored Water; No Blacks Allowed; Whites Only.

SEGREGATION CONTINUES INTO THE 20TH CENTURY In the late 1800s, some African Americans tried to escape Southern racism by moving north. This migration of Southern African Americans speeded up greatly during World War I, as many African-American sharecroppers abandoned the farms for the promise of industrial jobs in Northern cities. However, once African Americans reached the North, they discovered that racial prejudice and segregation patterns existed there as well. Most African Americans could find housing only in all-black neighborhoods. In addition, many white workers resented competition from blacks, resentment which sometimes led to violence.

In many ways, the events of World War II set the stage for the civil rights movement. First, the demand for soldiers in the early 1940s created a shortage of white male laborers, which opened up new job opportunities for African Americans, Latinos, and white women.

Second, about a million African Americans served in the armed forces, which needed so many fighting men that they gradually had to end discriminatory policies that had kept African Americans from serving in fighting units. Many African-American soldiers returned from the war determined to fight for their own freedom now that they had helped defeat Fascist regimes overseas.

Third, during the war, civil rights organizations actively campaigned for African-American voting rights and challenged Jim Crow laws. In

ON THE WORLD STAGE

APARTHEID—SEGREGATION IN SOUTH AFRICA

In 1948, the white government of South Africa passed laws to ensure that the white minority would be able to retain control of the country. Those laws established a system known as apartheid, which means "separateness." Apartheid was a policy that divided South Africa's people into four rigidly segregated racial groups: whites, blacks, coloreds of mixed race, and Asians.

Apartheid laws restricted what jobs nonwhites could hold, where they could live, and what rights they could exercise. Because of apartheid, the black African majority suffered many inequalities—including being denied the right to vote.

In response to worldwide criticism, the South African government gradually repealed the apartheid laws, starting in the 1970s and concluding in 1991. In 1994, South Africans elected as president Nelson Mandela, a black anti-apartheid leader whom the white government had imprisoned for nearly 30 years.

Civil Rights **857**

TEACHING OPTION

Challenging Segregation in Court

▶ **Discussing Key Ideas**
- The NAACP exposes the unequal state of educational funding under segregation to challenge the Supreme Court precedent in *Plessy* v. *Ferguson*.
- The *Brown* decision overturns "separate but equal" and signals the end of legal segregation.

KEY PLAYER
Thurgood Marshall

Have students use the *Readers' Guide to Periodical Literature* to find obituaries for Marshall published in national newsmagazines such as *Time, Newsweek,* or *U.S. News and World Report* upon his death in 1993. Then ask them to summarize these obituaries.

IN-DEPTH RESOURCES: UNIT 8
Geography Application: The *Brown* Decision, Ten Years Later, p. 22

MORE ABOUT . . .
Charles Hamilton Houston

The grandson of runaway slaves, Charles Houston grew up in Washington, D.C., where he attended segregated schools. At age 15, he entered Amherst College and graduated with honors in 1915. In 1917, Houston entered World War I in a segregated unit. During his service, Houston tasted such bitter racism that he vowed to fight segregation. In 1919, he entered Harvard Law School and went on to become the NAACP's first great lawyer.

KEY PLAYER

THURGOOD MARSHALL
1908–1993

Thurgood Marshall dedicated his life to fighting the indignities of a racist system he knew all too well. His father had labored as a steward at an all-white country club, his mother as a teacher at an all-black school. Marshall himself was denied admission to the University of Maryland Law School because of his race. One of the many lawsuits Marshall won for the NAACP forced that school to integrate.

In 1961, President John F. Kennedy nominated Marshall to the U.S. Court of Appeals. Lyndon Johnson picked Marshall for U.S. solicitor general in 1965 and two years later named him as the first African-American Supreme Court justice. In that role, he remained a strong advocate of civil rights until he retired in 1991.

After Marshall died in 1993, a copy of the *Brown* v. *Board of Education* decision was placed beside his casket. On it, an admirer wrote: "You shall always be remembered."

---

response to protests, President Roosevelt issued a presidential directive prohibiting racial discrimination by federal agencies and all companies that were engaged in war work. The groundwork was laid for more organized campaigns to end segregation throughout the United States.

Challenging Segregation in Court

Since 1909, the NAACP had fought to end segregation. One influential figure in this campaign was Charles Hamilton Houston, a brilliant Howard University professor who trained African-American law students and who also served as chief legal counsel for the NAACP from 1934 to 1938.

THE NAACP LEGAL STRATEGY In deciding the NAACP's legal strategy, Houston considered the blatant inequality between the separate schools many states provided for the two races. At that time, the nation spent ten times as much money educating a white child as it did educating an African-American child. It was to redress this injustice that Houston chose to focus the organization's limited resources on challenging segregated public education.

For help, Houston recruited some of his most able law students to prepare a battery of cases to take before the Supreme Court. In 1938, he placed the team under the direction of **Thurgood Marshall.** Over the next 23 years, Marshall and his NAACP lawyers would win 29 out of 32 cases argued before the Supreme Court.

Several of the cases that Marshall and his team of lawyers won became legal milestones, each one chipping away at the segregationist tenets of *Plessy* v. *Ferguson*. In the 1946 case *Morgan* v. *Virginia*, the Supreme Court declared unconstitutional those state laws mandating segregated seating on interstate buses. In 1950, the high court ruled in *Sweatt* v. *Painter* that state law schools must admit black applicants, even if separate black schools exist. In another 1950 case that Marshall and his team argued, the court ruled that blacks admitted to state graduate schools were entitled to the use of all the school's facilities.

BROWN V. BOARD OF EDUCATION Marshall's most stunning victory came on May 17, 1954, in the case known as **Brown v. Board of Education** of Topeka, Kansas. In this case, the court responded to a brilliant legal brief written by Marshall that addressed segregated education in four states—Kansas, South Carolina, Virginia, and Delaware. The court lumped the state cases together in a single ruling named for the case concerning nine-year-old Linda Brown. Her father, Oliver Brown, had charged the board of education of Topeka with violating Linda's rights by denying her admission to an all-white elementary school four blocks from her house. The state had directed Linda to cross a railroad yard and then take a bus to an all-black elementary school 21 blocks away.

In a landmark verdict, the Supreme Court unanimously struck down segregation as unconstitutional. The court's decision, written by Chief Justice Earl Warren, in part stated,

> To separate [African-American children] from others of similar age and qualifications solely because of their race generates a feeling of inferiority as to their status in the community that may affect their hearts and minds in a way unlikely ever to be undone. . . . We conclude that in the field of public education the doctrine of "separate but equal" has no place. Separate educational facilities are inherently unequal.
>
> **CHIEF JUSTICE EARL WARREN,** *Brown v. Board of Education*

THINK THROUGH HISTORY
B. Developing Historical Perspective How did events during World War II lay the groundwork for African Americans to fight for civil rights?

B. Answer Blacks had experienced better job opportunities; many veterans who had fought racist Germans wanted to resist racist Americans; civil rights groups had staged some successful protests.

THINK THROUGH HISTORY
C. Analyzing Issues What was the central issue raised in the *Brown* v. Board of Education ruling?

C. Answer Segregation by race created a feeling of inferiority, so separate facilities made for inherently unequal experiences.

TEACHING OPTIONS

Exploring Themes

Constitutional Concerns Explain the role of dissenting opinions as legal references in future cases. Then read this dissent in the *Plessy* case rendered by John Marshall Harlan: "Our Constitution is color-blind, and neither knows nor tolerates classes among citizens." Discuss how this opinion—the lone dissent in *Plessy*—was reflected in the majority opinion in the *Brown* case. Explore with students factors that may have influenced justices to rethink the 1896 majority opinion.

Making Connections Across Time

The* Brown *Case In 1979, the American Civil Liberties Union (ACLU) reopened the *Brown* case, arguing that 13 of Topeka's schools remained segregated because of de facto segregation in housing. In 1993, a federal court sided with the ACLU. Topeka responded by busing and by setting up magnet schools. "It's disheartening that we are still fighting," said Linda Brown Thompson, who was 11 when her parents joined the now famous class-action suit, "But we are dealing with human beings. As long as we are, there will always be those who feel the races should be separate."

Reaction to the *Brown* Decision

The ruling thrilled African Americans and many other Americans. "I was so happy, I was numb," declared Thurgood Marshall. The *Chicago Defender*, an African-American newspaper, pronounced "[It's] a second Emancipation Proclamation."

The *Brown* decision immediately affected some 12 million school children in 21 states. Official reaction to the ruling was mixed. In Kansas and Oklahoma, state officials said they expected segregation to end with little trouble. In Texas the governor promised to comply but warned that plans might "take years" to work out. In Mississippi and Georgia, officials vowed total resistance. Governor Herman Talmadge of Georgia branded the decision "a flagrant abuse of judicial power" and pledged, "The people of Georgia . . . will map a program to insure . . . permanent segregation of the races."

RESISTANCE TO SCHOOL INTEGRATION Within a year of the *Brown* decision, more than 500 school districts in the nation had desegregated their classrooms. In the cities of Baltimore, St. Louis, and Washington, D.C., African-American and white students sat side by side for the first time in history. However, in areas where African Americans made up the majority of the population, whites often resisted desegregation because they feared losing control of the schools. In some places, the Ku Klux Klan reappeared and White Citizen's Councils boycotted businesses that supported desegregation.

To hasten compliance, the Supreme Court handed down a second *Brown* ruling in 1955 that ordered district courts to implement school desegregation "with all deliberate speed." Neither Congress nor President Eisenhower moved to put teeth into the court order. In Congress, more than 90 Southern members issued the "Southern Manifesto," which denounced the *Brown* decision and called on the states to resist it "by all lawful means." Although the president accepted the Court's ruling as law, he also confided privately to an aide, "The fellow who tries to tell me that you can do these things by force is just plain nuts." Events in Little Rock, Arkansas, would soon force Eisenhower to act against this belief.

CRISIS IN LITTLE ROCK In 1948, Arkansas had become the first Southern state to admit African Americans to the state universities without being required by a court order. By the 1950s, some scout troops and labor unions in Arkansas had quietly ended their Jim Crow practices. In Little Rock itself, citizens had elected two men to the school board who publicly backed desegregation—and the school superintendent, Virgil Blossom, had been working on a plan for gradual desegregation since 1953.

However, state politics created an explosive situation. Caught in a tight reelection race, Governor Orval Faubus jumped on the segregationist bandwagon. In early September 1957, he ordered the National Guard to turn away the nine African-American students who had volunteered to integrate Little Rock's Central High School as the first step in Blossom's plan. That afternoon, a federal judge ordered Faubus to let the students into school the next day.

Eight members of the "Little Rock Nine" received phone calls from ministers who volunteered to escort the students to school for their safety. The family

THINK THROUGH HISTORY
D. Analyzing Causes Why weren't schools in all regions desegregated immediately after the Brown decision?

D. Answer Some Southern whites and state officials resisted desegregation, and neither Eisenhower nor Congress forced them to act quickly.

As white students jeer her, Elizabeth Eckford tries to pass through lines of National Guardsmen and enter Little Rock Central High School in 1957.

Civil Rights **859**

OBJECTIVE
(3) INSTRUCT

Reaction to the *Brown* Decision

▶ **Discussing Key Ideas**
- Some state and local governments balk at the *Brown* decision.
- In 1955, the Supreme Court orders district courts to enforce the decision "with all deliberate speed."
- Resistance to desegregation in Little Rock, Arkansas, leads President Eisenhower to send in the National Guard.

MORE ABOUT . . .
Elizabeth Eckford

The experience at Central High School traumatized Eckford, who dropped from public view after 1958. In 1996, she reappeared in the news when Heather Jurgensen, a 16-year-old student at a rural Kansas high school, convinced Eckford to be the subject of a video for the National History Day competition. After turning down media interviews for decades, Eckford decided to help Jurgensen. Jurgensen's video became a national finalist in the competition.

IN-DEPTH RESOURCES: UNIT 8
Primary Source: Crisis in Little Rock, p. 24

 ELECTRONIC LIBRARY OF PRIMARY SOURCES
Desegregation at Central High School by Melba Patillo Beals
Desegregation at Central High School by Craig Rains

TEACHING OPTION

 Cooperative Activity: Researching Civil Rights Cases

Task: Groups of students will research and explain Supreme Court decisions on civil rights cases.

Purpose: To track the Court's changing opinions on civil rights.

Activity: Divide the cases among the groups of students and have each group research their assigned case(s). They should learn the facts of the cases (date, plaintiffs, defendants, and legal issue) and the Supreme Court decisions (vote, majority opinion, and dissenting opinion). They should be prepared to teach their cases to the rest of the class.

1896 *Plessy* v. *Ferguson*
1938 *Missouri ex rel Gaines*
1944 *Smith* v. *Allwright*
1954 *Brown* v. *Board of Education of Topeka*
1971 *Swann* v. *Charlotte-Mecklenburg* [NC] *Board of Education*
1974 *Milliken* v. *Bradley*
1978 *Board of Regents of California* v. *Bakke*
1990 *Board of Education of Oklahoma City* v. *Dowell*
1995 *Adarand Construction* v. *Peña*

Teacher's Edition **859**

The Montgomery Bus Boycott

▶ *Discussing Key Ideas*

• African Americans in Montgomery, Alabama, organize a boycott to protest discrimination on city buses.

• The boycott thrusts Martin Luther King, Jr., into the national spotlight.

• In a lawsuit filed by the boycotters, the Supreme Court outlaws segregated buses.

KEY PLAYER
Rosa Parks

Today a historic marker can be found at the bus stop where Rosa Parks began her famous ride. It begins, "At the bus stop on this site on December 1, 1955, . . ."

Assign pairs of students to complete the commemoration. Tell them to write no more than 50 words.

IN-DEPTH RESOURCES: UNIT 8
American Lives: Rosa Parks, p. 32

KEY PLAYER

ROSA PARKS
1913–

Long before December 1955, Rosa Parks had protested segregation through everyday acts. She refused to use drinking fountains labeled "Colored Only." When possible, she shunned segregated elevators and climbed stairs instead.

Parks joined the Montgomery chapter of the NAACP in 1943 and became the organization's secretary. A turning point came for her in the summer of 1955, when she attended a workshop at the Highlander Folk School in Monteagle, Tennessee. Highlander's program was designed to promote integration by giving the students the experience of interracial living.

Returning to Montgomery, Parks was even more determined to fight segregation. As it happened, her act of protest against injustice on the buses inspired a whole community to join her cause.

---

of the ninth student, Elizabeth Eckford, did not have a phone. The next morning, she put on the carefully ironed white-and-black dress she had made for her first day at an integrated school and set out alone.

On the sidewalk outside Central High, Eckford faced an abusive crowd of students and adults. Terrified, the 15-year-old Eckford searched the mob for a friendly face. "I looked into the face of an old woman, and it seemed a kind face," she later told one interviewer. "But when I looked at her again, she spat on me." Trailed by the mob, Eckford managed to make it to a bus stop, where two friendly whites stayed with her until the bus came.

The crisis in Little Rock forced Eisenhower to act. He placed the Arkansas National Guard under federal control and ordered a thousand paratroopers into Little Rock. Under the watchful eye of these soldiers, the nine African-American teenagers attended class. But even these soldiers could not protect the students from troublemakers who confronted them on stairways, in the halls, and in the cafeteria. Nor could the soldiers block interference by Faubus, who shut down Central High at the end of the school year rather than let integration continue.

The reports from Little Rock by network television news correspondents helped the nation to focus on the issue of desegregation. At the same time, on September 9, 1957, Congress passed the Civil Rights Act of 1957, the first civil rights law since Reconstruction. Sponsored by Senator Lyndon B. Johnson of Texas, the law gave the attorney general greater power over school desegregation. It also gave the federal government jurisdiction—or authority—over violations of African-American voting rights.

The Montgomery Bus Boycott

The face-to-face confrontation at Central High School was not the only showdown over segregation in the mid 1950s. Impatient with the slow pace of change in the courts, African-American activists had begun taking direct action to win the rights promised to them by the Fourteenth and Fifteenth Amendments to the Constitution. Among those on the frontline of change was Jo Ann Robinson.

BOYCOTTING SEGREGATION Four days after the *Brown* decision in May 1954, Robinson wrote a letter to the mayor of Montgomery, Alabama, asking that bus drivers no longer be allowed to force riders in the "colored" section to yield their seats to whites. "More and more of our people are already arranging with neighbors and friends for rides to keep from being insulted and humiliated by bus drivers," Robinson warned. The mayor refused.

On December 1, 1955, **Rosa Parks,** a seamstress and an NAACP officer, took a seat in the front row of the "colored" section of a Montgomery bus. As the bus filled up, the driver ordered Parks and three other African-American passengers to empty the row they were occupying so that a white man could sit down without having to sit next to any African Americans. "It certainly was time for someone to stand up," recalled Parks wryly. "So I refused to move."

As Parks stared out the window, the bus driver said, "If you don't stand up, I'm going to call the police and have you arrested." The soft-spoken Parks replied, "You may do that."

News of Parks's arrest spread rapidly. Jo Ann Robinson and NAACP leader E. D. Nixon quickly organized a boycott of the buses. The leaders of the African-American community, including many ministers, formed the Montgomery Improvement Association to organize the

THINK THROUGH HISTORY
E. *Drawing Conclusions*
In what ways was the Little Rock desegregation a victory for African Americans?

E. Answer
Possible Answers: The crisis forced Eisenhower to use the power of the federal government to enforce desegregation, it forced national attention on the issue and spurred Congress to pass the Civil Rights Act of 1957, increasing federal enforcement powers over desegregation.

Skillbuilder Mini-Lesson: Analyzing Motives

Explaining the Skill Sometimes history has hinged on the action of one person or group. To better understand historical actions, historians analyze the motives, or the reasons, behind them. Most motives can be broken into several parts: the goals of the group taking the action and the people's needs, emotions, and prior experiences.

Applying the Skill: The Montgomery Bus Boycott Ask students to answer the following questions in order to analyze the motives behind the bus boycott in Montgomery following the arrest of Rosa Parks.

What were the boycotters' goals? They wanted their rights as promised by the Fourteenth and Fifteenth Amendments.

What were their needs? Faster progress toward desegregation; an end to being insulted and humiliated.

What were their emotions? First humiliation and frustration, then excitement, impatience, determination.

What were their prior experiences? Their demands had been ignored, and their children had been threatened.

IN-DEPTH RESOURCES: UNIT 8
Skillbuilder Practice: Analyzing Motives, p. 21

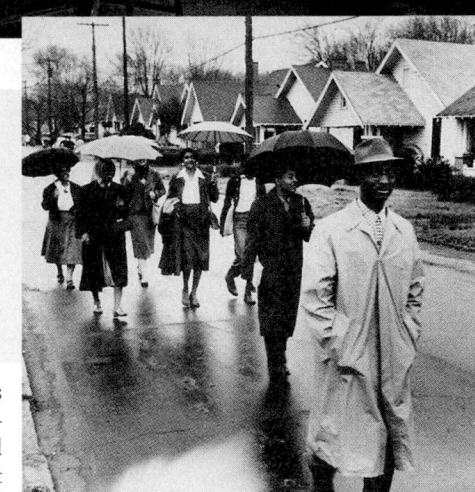

boycott. They elected the pastor of the Dexter Avenue Baptist Church, 26-year-old **Dr. Martin Luther King, Jr.,** to lead the group. "Well, I'm not sure I'm the best person for the position," King confided to Nixon. "But if no one else is going to serve, I'd be glad to try."

WALKING FOR JUSTICE On the night of December 5, 1955, a crowd of 5,000 people gathered to hear the young pastor speak. With passion and eloquence, Dr. King made the following declaration,

A PERSONAL VOICE

There comes a time when people get tired of being trampled over by the iron feet of oppression. . . . I want it to be known—that we're going to work with grim and bold determination—to gain justice on buses in this city. And we are not wrong. . . . If we are wrong—the Supreme Court of this nation is wrong. If we are wrong—God Almighty is wrong. . . . If we are wrong—justice is a lie.

DR. MARTIN LUTHER KING, JR., quoted in *Parting the Waters: America in the King Years, 1954–63*

F. Answer The example of Rosa Parks, the organizational skills of Jo Ann Robinson and E. D. Nixon, the inspirational leadership of Martin Luther King, Jr., and the cooperation of a large majority in the African-American community.

THINK THROUGH HISTORY
F. Analyzing Causes What factors contributed to the success of the Montgomery bus boycott?

The impact of King's speech—the rhythm of his words, the power of his rising and falling voice—brought people to their feet. A sense of mission filled the audience as King proclaimed, "If you will protest courageously and yet with dignity, . . . historians will have to pause and say, 'There lived a great people—a black people—who injected a new meaning and dignity into the veins of civilization.'"

For 381 days, African Americans refused to ride the buses in Montgomery. In most cases, they had to find other means of transportation by organizing car pools or walking long distances. The boycotters remained nonviolent even after a bomb ripped apart King's home. (Fortunately, no one was injured.) Finally, in late 1956, the Supreme Court outlawed bus segregation in response to a lawsuit filed by the boycotters. On December 21, King boarded a Montgomery bus and sat in the front. "It was a great ride," he declared.

For over a year, Montgomery buses ran nearly empty while African Americans found other means to get where they wanted to go.

Dr. King and the SCLC

The Montgomery bus boycott proved to the world that ordinary African Americans could unite and organize a successful protest movement. It also proved the power of nonviolent resistance, the peaceful refusal to obey unjust laws. Despite threats to his life and family, King urged his followers, "Let nobody pull you so low as to hate them."

CHANGING THE WORLD WITH SOUL FORCE King called his brand of nonviolent resistance "soul force." He based his ideas on the teachings of several people. From Jesus, he learned to love one's enemies. From writer Henry David Thoreau, he took the concept of civil disobedience—the refusal to obey an unjust law. From labor organizer A. Philip Randolph, he learned techniques for organizing massive demonstrations. From Mohandas Gandhi, the leader who helped

ECONOMIC BACKGROUND

BOYCOTTS

Throughout history, economic boycotts have served as a powerful tool of protest. A boycott's effectiveness lies in its ability to hit target companies where it hurts the most—in their pocketbooks. Aside from losing revenue, targeted companies often must devote resources to repairing their tarnished image. "They [boycotts] sap energy and time," said a spokesman for a recently-targeted company. "And time is money."

Boycotts have become a popular form of protest in America today. There are even two newsletters, *Boycott Action News* and *Boycott Quarterly,* which track and report on various economic boycotts across the nation.

ECONOMIC BACKGROUND
Boycotts

Critical Thinking:
Comparing Ask students to compare the reasons for the boycotts of the civil rights era with recent boycotts of companies, nations, or governments. Then have them create a list of companies, nations, or governments (if any) that they think should be boycotted.

OBJECTIVE
⑤ INSTRUCT

Dr. King and the SCLC

▶ *Discussing Key Ideas*
• Martin Luther King, Jr., seeks to promote civil rights through nonviolent resistance.
• King draws his ideas from the teachings of Thoreau, Gandhi, Jesus, and A. Philip Randolph.
• Young activists, impatient with the slow pace of change, adopt more confrontational tactics.

💿 **ELECTRONIC LIBRARY OF PRIMARY SOURCES**
from *Stride Toward Freedom* by Martin Luther King, Jr.

TEACHING OPTIONS

Teaching Less Proficient Readers

Activating Prior Knowledge Before less proficient readers read about the Montgomery bus boycott, hold a discussion about boycotts. What are they? Have students ever experienced a boycott? What happened?
Ask the following questions, recording responses on the board:

• What motivates a person to defy authority and risk jail?
• Why would a whole community organize a boycott?
• What can happen when enough people defy authority?

Students should keep these questions in mind as they read about the Montgomery bus boycott and other protests.

Making Global Connections

Philosophies of Justice Read these quotations from Mohandas Gandhi. Then ask students to cite examples of how King's practice of soul force proved Gandhi's remarks.

• *Under a government which imprisons any unjustly, the only true place for a just man is in prison.*
• *It is possible for a single individual to defy the whole might of an unjust empire.*
• *When any group struggles properly and justly to achieve its own rights, it enlarges the rights of all.*

KEY PLAYER
Martin Luther King, Jr.

Based on what students know about King's beliefs, have them write a speech that he might have delivered upon acceptance of an honorary degree. Speeches should be no more than two minutes long. Ask volunteers to do dramatic readings.

MORE ABOUT . . .
Ella Baker

Ella Baker wanted no credit for her work. Explained Baker:

> I have always felt it was a handicap for oppressed peoples to depend so largely upon a leader, because unfortunately in our culture, the charismatic leader usually becomes a leader because he has . . . been touted through the public media, which means that the media has made him, and the media may undo him.

Ask students to explain and comment on the validity of Baker's remark.

OBJECTIVE
⑥ INSTRUCT

The Movement Spreads

▶ *Discussing Key Ideas*
• Members of SNCC build on methods of protest used earlier by the Congress of Racial Equality (CORE).
• Sit-ins attract national media attention for the civil rights movement.

KEY PLAYER

MARTIN LUTHER KING, JR.
1929–1968

Born Michael Luther King , Jr., King had to adjust to a new name in 1934. In that year, his father—Rev. Michael Luther King, Sr.—returned home from a trip to Europe, where he had toured historic sites, including the site where Martin Luther had challenged the Roman Catholic church and begun the Protestant Reformation. Upon his return home, the elder King changed his and his son's names to Martin.

Like Luther, the younger King became a reformer. He worked so diligently for civil rights that the Nobel Prize Committee gave him its coveted peace prize in 1964, making him the youngest person ever to receive the award.

Yet there was a side of King unknown to most people—his inner battle to overcome his hatred of the white bigots who lynched a neighbor, firebombed his own house, and spat at him. As a youth, he had once vowed "to hate all white people." As leader of the civil rights movement, King looked forward to a world in which people of all races respected each other. "Ultimately, we are trying to free all of America," he explained. "Negroes from the bonds of segregation and shame, whites from the bonds of bigotry and fear."

India throw off British rule, he learned that one could powerfully resist oppression without resorting to violence.

King summed up his philosophy by saying to white racists, "We will not hate you, but we cannot . . . obey your unjust laws. We will soon wear you down by our capacity to suffer. And in winning our freedom, we will so appeal to your heart and conscience that we will win you in the process."

Some African Americans questioned King's peaceful philosophy when, after the *Brown* decision, antiblack violence swept parts of the Deep South. The violence, aimed at keeping African Americans "in their place," included the highly publicized 1955 murder of Emmett Till—a 14-year-old who had allegedly flirted with a white woman. There were also shootings and beatings, some fatal, of civil rights workers. Despite these vicious attacks, King steadfastly preached the power of nonviolence.

FROM THE GRASSROOTS UP After the boycott ended, King joined with more than 100 ministers and civil rights leaders in 1957 to found the **Southern Christian Leadership Conference** (SCLC). The purpose of the SCLC, as stated by King, was "to carry on nonviolent crusades against the evils of second-class citizenship." Using African-American churches as a base, the SCLC planned to stage protests and demonstrations throughout the South.

Leaders of the SCLC hoped to build a movement from the grassroots up and to win the support of ordinary African Americans of all ages. King, president of the SCLC, used the power of his voice and ideas to fuel the movement's momentum. The nuts and bolts of organizing the SCLC fell to Ella Baker, a former NAACP activist and the granddaughter of a slave minister.

While with the NAACP, Baker had served as national field secretary, traveling over 16,000 miles throughout the South. From 1959 to 1961, Baker used her contacts to set up branches of the SCLC in 65 Southern cities. In April 1960, Baker helped students at Shaw University, an African-American university in Raleigh, North Carolina, to organize the **Student Nonviolent Coordinating Committee,** or SNCC, pronounced "snick" for short.

It had been six years since the *Brown* case, and many college students viewed the pace of change as too slow. Although these students risked a great deal—losing college scholarships, being expelled from college, being physically harmed—they were determined to challenge the system. SNCC, which hoped to harness the energy of these student protesters, would soon create one of the most important student activist movements in the nation's history.

The Movement Spreads

Although SNCC adopted King's ideas in part, its members had ideas of their own. Many wanted a more confrontational strategy and set out to reshape the civil rights movement.

DEMONSTRATING FOR FREEDOM The founders of SNCC had models to build on. In 1942, the Congress of Racial Equality (CORE) had staged the first **sit-ins,** in which African-American protesters sat down at segregated lunch counters in Chicago and refused to leave until they were served. In February 1960, African-American students from North Carolina's Agricultural and Technical College staged a sit-in at a whites-only lunch

862 CHAPTER 29

THINK THROUGH HISTORY
G. *Summarizing* What were the central points of Dr. King's philosophy?
G. Answer "Soul force," or nonviolent resistance, which included acts of civil disobedience, demonstrations, and adherence to nonviolence.

TEACHING OPTION

Cooperative Activity: Writing About Civil Rights Organizations

Task: Groups of students will research and write histories of civil rights organizations.

Purpose: To explain the development of civil rights organizations, movements, and activities.

Activity: Have groups choose one civil rights organization (such as the NAACP, CORE, SCLC, SNCC, the Urban League, the Montgomery

Improvement Association, or the Greensboro Citizens Association) and research its origins, philosophy, leaders, and major activities. After writing a history of the organization, each group will share their findings with the class.

ALTERNATIVE ASSESSMENT BOOK
Standards for Evaluating a Cooperative Activity

Standards for Evaluation
Histories should . . .

• clearly recount the origins, leaders, and members of the organization

• list the major actions that the organization has taken

• describe how the organization has changed over time

Sit-in demonstrators, such as these at a Jackson, Mississippi, lunch counter, faced intimidation and humiliation from white segregationists.

MORE ABOUT . . .
The Greensboro Sit-Ins
The sit-ins in Greensboro, North Carolina, did not arise out of thin air—they happened because citizens organized to make them happen. The four students who initiated the sit-ins at Greensboro were all members of the NAACP Youth Council, with links to civil rights activists who led sit-ins in Durham, North Carolina, and Nashville, Tennessee, in the late 1950s. The attention the media gave to the Greensboro sit-ins sparked more protests and led to the formation of SNCC.

counter at a Woolworth's store in Greensboro. This time, television crews brought coverage of the protest into homes throughout the United States.

Day after day, reporters captured the ugly face of racism—scenes of whites beating, jeering at, and pouring food over students who refused to strike back. The coverage sparked many other sit-ins across the South. Store managers called in the police, raised the price of food, and removed counter seats. But the movement continued and spread to the North. There students formed picket lines around national chain stores that maintained segregated lunch counters in the South.

NO TURNING BACK By late 1960, students had descended on and desegregated Jim Crow lunch counters in some 48 cities in 11 states. They endured arrests, beatings, suspension from college, and tear gas and fire hoses, But the army of nonviolent students refused to back down. "My mother has always told me that I'm equal to other people," said Ezell Blair, Jr., one of the students who led the first sit-in in 1960. For the rest of the 1960s, many Americans persevered to prove Blair's mother correct.

THINK THROUGH HISTORY
H. *Contrasting* How did the tactics of the student protesters from SNCC differ from that of the boycotters in Montgomery?
H. Answer The students confronted businesses that had segregationist policies rather than boycott them.

Section ① Assessment

1. TERMS & NAMES
Identify:
• Thurgood Marshall
• *Brown* v. *Board of Education*
• Rosa Parks
• Dr. Martin Luther King, Jr.
• Southern Christian Leadership Conference
• Student Nonviolent Coordinating Committee
• sit-in

2. SUMMARIZING Recreate the web diagram below on your paper. Then fill it in with examples of Supreme Court decisions, tactics, organizations, and leaders related to the early phases of the civil rights movement.

Which tactics do you think were most effective? Why?

3. ANALYZING MOTIVES Why did the civil rights movement use nonviolence? How successful was the tactic?
THINK ABOUT
• the Montgomery bus boycott
• television coverage of events
• sit-ins

4. DRAWING CONCLUSIONS After the *Brown* v. *Board of Education* ruling, what do you think was the most significant event of the civil rights movement prior to 1960? Why?
THINK ABOUT
• the role of civil rights leaders
• the results of confrontations and boycotts
• the role of grassroots organizations

Civil Rights **863**

ASSESS & RETEACH

Section 1 Assessment
Have students work in pairs to quiz each other on the questions.

Self-Assessment
Have students use the people in this section to create a game of Who Am I? After each speaker lists his or her accomplishments and then says the words "Who Am I?", the whole class should write down their answers on a sheet of paper. Students who guess incorrectly should write up their own "Who Am I?" description for the individual.

Section Quiz

FORMAL ASSESSMENT
Section Quiz, p. 352

Reteach

Use the list of Terms & Names to link each leader with the civil rights organizations and protest movements they were part of.

ANSWERS

1. TERMS & NAMES
Thurgood Marshall, p. 858
Brown v. *Board of Education,* p. 858
Rosa Parks, p. 860
Dr. Martin Luther King, Jr., p. 861
Southern Christian Leadership Conference, p. 862
Student Nonviolent Coordinating Committee, p. 862
sit-in, p. 862

2. SUMMARIZING
Supreme Court Decisions— *Morgan* v. *Virginia; Sweatt* v. *Painter; Brown* v. *Board of Education.* **Tactics—**nonviolent resistance; legal action. **Organizations** —NAACP, SCLC, SNCC; CORE. **Leaders—** Thurgood Marshall; Dr. Martin Luther King, Jr.; Ella Baker; Jo Ann Robinson. *Possible Responses:* demonstrations, because they attracted media coverage; legal action, because it ended legal segregation.

3. ANALYZING MOTIVES
Reasons for nonviolence: Students might suggest that the tactic stemmed from the personal philosophy of Dr. King; that it had worked in other countries; or that nonviolent tactics would more effectively appeal to the nation's conscience. **Success:** Students might say the tactic was successful because it captured the sympathy of the nation; some might suggest that the toll could have been worse if violent tactics had been used. Other students might say that nonviolence did not go far enough to bring about immediate justice.

4. DRAWING CONCLUSIONS
Possible Responses: The crisis at Little Rock, because it forced the government to act; the Montgomery bus boycott, which brought Martin Luther King, Jr., into a leadership role.

CLOSE

By the end of the 1950s, civil rights movements in the South had focused the nation's attention. Yet, when African Americans pressed for equality, they met massive resistance by many conservative whites.

Teacher's Edition 863

TERMS & NAMES
- freedom rider
- James Meredith
- Civil Rights Act of 1964
- Freedom Summer
- Robert Moses
- Fannie Lou Hamer
- Voting Rights Act of 1965

OBJECTIVES

① To identify the goal of the freedom riders.

② To explain how civil rights activism forced President Kennedy to act against segregation.

③ To state the motives behind the 1963 March on Washington.

④ To describe how civil rights organizers tried to secure passage of a voting rights act.

SKILLBUILDER

- Interpreting charts, p. 868

CRITICAL THINKING

- Analyzing motives, pp. 865, 867
- Analyzing causes, pp. 868, 869
- Comparing, p. 870
- Summarizing, p.870
- Synthesizing, p. 870
- Recognizing effects, p. 870

LEARN ABOUT the freedom rides, events in Birmingham and Selma, and Freedom Summer

TO UNDERSTAND how the civil rights movement pressured the federal government to end segregation and ensure voting rights.

ONE AMERICAN'S STORY

James Peck, a white civil rights activist, was one of six whites and seven blacks who set out from Washington, D.C. in 1961 on a special bus ride through the South. The trip was part of CORE's attempt to test the Supreme Court decisions banning segregated seating on interstate bus routes and segregated facilities in bus terminals. The activists formed two interracial teams of freedom riders to travel through the South challenging segregation. They reasoned that if they provoked a violent reaction, the Kennedy administration would have to enforce the law.

Peck rode on Bus One. At the Alabama state line, a half dozen white racists got on the bus, carrying chains, brass knuckles, and pistols. They yanked the young African-American riders from their seats and shoved them into the aisle. Peck and a 60-year-old white freedom rider named Dr. Walter Bergman tried to intervene. The thugs knocked Peck unconscious and kicked Bergman repeatedly in the head until his brain hemorrhaged.

The ordeal for the freedom riders aboard Bus One didn't end there. On May 4, 1961—Mother's Day—they pulled into the Birmingham bus terminal. James Peck later recalled seeing the hostile mob that was waiting, some holding barely concealed iron bars.

A PERSONAL VOICE

I looked at them and then I looked at Charles Person, who had been designated as my teammate to test the lunch counter. . . . When I looked at him, he responded by saying simply, "Let's go."

As we entered the white waiting room, . . . we were grabbed bodily and pushed toward the alley-way. . . . Out of sight of onlookers in the waiting room, six of them started swinging at me with fists and pipes. Five others attacked Person a few feet ahead.

JAMES PECK, *Freedom Ride*

The mob beat Peck into unconsciousness. It took 53 stitches to sew up his badly battered head and face. The ride of Bus One had ended, but Bus Two continued southward on a journey that would shock the Kennedy administration into action.

Three days after he [was] beaten in Birmingham, freedom rider James Peck demonstrates [in] New York City to [put] pressure on nation[al] companies to supp[ort] desegregation in [the] South.

Riding for Freedom

In Anniston, Alabama, about 200 angry whites attacked Bus Two, kicking its sides and slashing its tires. The driver managed to take the damaged bus six miles out of town before one of the slashed tires blew apart. The mob, which had driven after the bus, barricaded the door while someone smashed the rear window and tossed in a fire bomb. The **freedom riders** forced open the door and spilled out just before the bus exploded in a ball of flame.

NEW VOLUNTEERS CORE's freedom riders did not want to give up, but the bus companies refused to carry them any farther, so they ended their ride and boarded a flight to New Orleans. Then Diane Nash, a SNCC leader, called CORE director James Farmer to say that a group of Nashville students wanted to resume the freedom ride. "You know that may be suicide," warned Farmer. Nash answered, "We know that, but if we let them stop us with violence, the movement is dead! . . . Your troops have been badly battered. Let us pick up the baton and run with it."

FOCUS & MOTIVATE

▶ **Starting with the Student**
Have students think about someone they know or know about who took a stand. Tell them to consider the issue involved, the action taken, and the price paid.

OBJECTIVE
① INSTRUCT

Riding for Freedom

▶ **Discussing Key Ideas**
- Freedom riders expose Southern resistance to federal desegregation rulings.
- Violence against the freedom riders forces the Kennedy administration to intervene.

IN-DEPTH RESOURCES: UNIT 8
Guided Reading, p. 19

ACCESS FOR STUDENTS ACQUIRING ENGLISH
Guided Reading (Spanish), p. 282

SECTION 2 RESOURCES

PRINT RESOURCES

IN-DEPTH RESOURCES: UNIT 8
Guided Reading, p. 19
Primary Sources: Civil Rights Song, p. 25; *from* "I Have a Dream" by Martin Luther King, Jr., p. 26; Political Poster, p. 27
Literature: from *And All Our Wounds Forgiven* by Julius Lester, p. 28
American Lives: A. Philip Randolph, p. 31

ACCESS FOR STUDENTS ACQUIRING ENGLISH
Guided Reading (Spanish), p. 282

FORMAL ASSESSMENT
Section Quiz, p. 353

ALTERNATIVE ASSESSMENT BOOK
See forms for supporting and scoring alternative activities.

TECHNOLOGY RESOURCES

HUMANITIES TRANSPARENCIES
H27, March on Washington

GEOGRAPHY TRANSPARENCIES
G29, Before and After the Voting Rights Act of 1965

CD-ROM *Grolier Multimedia Encyclopedia*

VIDEO *American Portfolio: A Videodisc for U.S. History*
user's guide, pp. 245, 246, 248

INTERNET McDougal Littell Learning On-Line
http://www.mcdougallittell.com

When the SNCC volunteers rode into Birmingham, Police commissioner Eugene "Bull" Connor's men pulled them off the bus, beat them, and drove them into Tennessee. The determined young people returned to Birmingham and occupied the whites-only waiting room at the terminal, where they sat for 18 hours because the bus driver refused to risk his life transporting them. After receiving an angry phone call from U.S. Attorney General Robert Kennedy, bus company officials convinced the driver to proceed. The SNCC volunteers set out for Montgomery on May 20.

In Alabama, a mob firebombed this bus of freedom riders and attacked passengers as they left.

ARRIVAL OF FEDERAL MARSHALS Although Alabama officials had promised Kennedy that the riders would be protected, no police were stationed near the Montgomery terminal when the bus arrived. Instead, a mob of whites—many carrying bats and lead pipes—fell upon the riders. John Doar, a Justice Department official on the scene, called the attorney general and reported what happened. "A bunch of men led by a guy with a bleeding face are beating [the passengers]. There are no cops. It's terrible. It's terrible. There's not a cop in sight. People are yelling, 'Get 'em, get 'em.' It's awful."

The violence provoked exactly the response the freedom riders had been hoping for. Newspapers throughout the nation and abroad denounced the beatings. Southern newspapers such as the *Atlanta Constitution,* which had criticized the freedom ride, expressed outrage that police had refused to protect the riders.

President John F. Kennedy decided to give the freedom riders more direct support. This time, the Justice Department sent 400 U.S. marshals to protect the riders on the last part of their journey to Jackson, Mississippi. In addition, the attorney general and the Interstate Commerce Commission issued an order banning segregation in all interstate travel facilities, including waiting rooms, restrooms, and lunch counters.

Standing Firm

As interstate travel facilities became more fully integrated, some civil rights workers turned their attention to integrating some Southern schools and pushing the movement into additional Southern towns. At each turn they encountered opposition from some whites.

"Violence is a fearful thing," recalled Avon Rollins of SNCC. "I remember when I had to take a stand, where the words wouldn't come out of my mouth, . . . because the fear was in me so strong."

INTEGRATING OLE MISS In September 1962, Air Force veteran **James Meredith** won a federal court case that allowed him to enroll in the all-white University of Mississippi, nicknamed Ole Miss. But when Meredith arrived on campus, he faced Governor Ross Barnett, who refused to let him register as a student.

Following the precedent set by Eisenhower in Little Rock, President Kennedy ordered federal marshals to escort Meredith to the registrar's office. Barnett responded with a heated radio appeal: "I call on every Mississippian to keep his faith and courage. We will never surrender." The broadcast turned out white demonstrators by the thousands.

On the night of September 30, riots broke out on campus that resulted in two deaths. It took more than 5,000 soldiers, 200 arrests, and 15 hours to stop the rioters. In the months that followed, federal officials accompanied Meredith

"*We will continue our journey one way or another. . . . We are prepared to die.*"

JIM ZWERG,
FREEDOM RIDER

Civil Rights **865**

News photos and television coverage of police dogs attacking African Americans in Birmingham shocked the nation's conscience and spurred President Kennedy to present a major civil rights bill to Congress.

"I say, Segregation now! Segregation tomorrow! Segregation forever!"

GEORGE WALLACE
ALABAMA GOVERNOR 1963

to class and protected his parents from nightriders who shot up their house.

HEADING INTO BIRMINGHAM By 1963, Reverend Fred Shuttlesworth, head of the Alabama Christian Movement for Human Rights, decided that something had to be done about Birmingham—a city known for its strict enforcement of total segregation in public life. The city also had a reputation for racial violence, including 18 bombings from 1957 to 1963.

Deciding that Birmingham would be the ideal place to test the power of nonviolence, Shuttlesworth invited Dr. Martin Luther King, Jr., and the SCLC to help desegregate the city. On April 3, 1963, King flew into Birmingham to hold planning meetings with members of the African-American community. "This is the most segregated city in America," he said. "We have to stick together if we ever want to change its ways."

After several days of demonstrations led by Shuttlesworth and others, King led a small band of marchers into the streets of Birmingham on Good Friday, April 12. Police Commissioner Bull Connor promptly arrested them. While sitting in his jail cell, Dr. King wrote an open letter to white religious leaders who felt he was pushing too hard, too fast. King responded,

> **A PERSONAL VOICE**
> I guess it is easy for those who have never felt the stinging darts of segregation to say, "Wait." But when you have seen vicious mobs lynch your mothers and fathers at will; . . . when you have seen hate-filled policemen curse, kick, brutalize and even kill your black brothers and sisters; . . . when you see the vast majority of your twenty million Negro brothers smothering in the airtight cage of poverty; . . . when you have to concoct an answer for a five-year-old son asking . . . "Daddy, why do white people treat colored people so mean?" . . . then you will understand why we find it difficult to wait.
>
> **DR. MARTIN LUTHER KING, JR,** "Letter from a Birmingham Jail"

On April 20, King posted bail and began to plan more demonstrations. On May 2, more than a thousand African-American children marched in Birmingham; Bull Connor arrested 959 of them. On May 3, a second "children's crusade" came face to face with Connor and his helmeted police force. As television cameras recorded the scene, the police swept the marchers off their feet with high-pressure fire hoses, set attack dogs on them, and clubbed those who fell. Millions of TV viewers heard the children screaming.

Continued protests, an economic boycott, and negative media coverage finally convinced Birmingham officials to meet King's demands for an end to segregation. Birmingham offered a stunning civil rights victory that inspired African Americans across the nation. In addition, it convinced President Kennedy that nothing short of a new civil rights act would end the disorder and satisfy the demands of African Americans—and many whites—for racial justice.

KENNEDY TAKES A STAND On June 11, 1963, President Kennedy used federal troops to force Governor George Wallace to honor a court order desegregating the University of Alabama. That evening, Kennedy addressed the nation and asked pointedly, "Are we to say to the world—and much more importantly, to each other—that this is the land of the free, except for the Negroes?" He referred directly to "repressive police action" and "demonstrations in the streets." Then, he demanded that Congress pass a sweeping civil rights bill.

A tragic event just hours after Kennedy's speech highlighted the racial tension in much of the South. Shortly after midnight, a sniper shot and killed Medgar Evers—NAACP field secretary and World War II veteran—in the driveway of his home in Jackson, Mississippi. Police soon arrested white supremacist Byron De La Beckwith for the crime, but he was released after two trials resulted in hung juries. (Beckwith was finally convicted in 1994, after the case was reopened based on new evidence.) The release of De La Beckwith brought a new militancy to African Americans. With raised fists, many demanded, "Freedom now!"

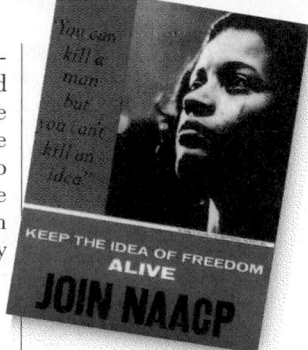

KEEP THE IDEA OF FREEDOM
ALIVE
JOIN NAACP

This 1963 poster shows Myrlie Evers, who was the widow of NAACP activist Medgar Evers and who became head of the NAACP in 1995.

Marching to Washington

The civil rights bill that Kennedy sent to Congress guaranteed equal access to all public accommodations and gave the U.S. attorney general the power to file school desegregation suits. To persuade Congress to pass the bill, two veteran organizers—labor leader A. Philip Randolph and Bayard Rustin of the SCLC—summoned Americans to join in a massive march on Washington, D.C.

THE DREAM OF EQUALITY On August 28, 1963, more than 250,000 people—including about 75,000 whites—converged on the nation's capital. They assembled on the grassy slopes of the Washington Monument, and the movement's leaders, walking arm in arm, led the crowd to the sprawling plaza near the Lincoln Monument. There, for more than three hours, people listened to speakers demand the immediate passage of the civil rights bill.

When Dr. Martin Luther King, Jr., appeared, the crowd exploded in applause. King eventually stopped reading from his prepared text and began an improvised speech in which he appealed for peace and racial harmony, punctuating his speech with the repeated refrain "I have a dream."

Billed as a march for "jobs and freedom," the March on Washington was the largest such demonstration held in the United States up to that time.

THINK THROUGH HISTORY
B. Analyzing Motives Why did civil rights organizers ask their supporters to march on Washington?

B. Answer To spur passage of the civil rights bill.

A PERSONAL VOICE
I have a dream that one day this nation will rise up and live out the true meaning of its creed "We hold these truths to be self evident; that all men are created equal." . . . I have a dream that my four little children will one day live in a nation where they will not be judged by the color of their skin but by the content of their character. . . . I have a dream that one day the state of Alabama . . . will be transformed into a situation where little black boys and black girls will be able to join hands with little white boys and white girls and walk together as sisters and brothers.
DR. MARTIN LUTHER KING, JR, "I Have a Dream"

OBJECTIVE
③ INSTRUCT

Marching to Washington

▶ *Discussing Key Ideas*
• Civil rights activists organize a great protest march on Washington to pressure Congress into passing the civil rights bill.
• Martin Luther King, Jr.'s "I Have a Dream" speech becomes one of the great statements of U.S. democracy.
• President Johnson pushes the Civil Rights Act through Congress.

MORE ABOUT . . .
A. Philip Randolph (1889–1979)
By the 1930s, Randolph was one of the foremost civil rights leaders in the United States and founder of the nation's most powerful African-American labor union—the Brotherhood of Sleeping Car Porters. When African Americans were discriminated against in war-related industries, Randolph threatened to lead 100,000 demonstrators to Washington, D.C. FDR took the threat seriously and, in 1941, issued Executive Order 8802, prohibiting "discrimination in the employment of workers in defense industries or government because of race, creed, color, or national origin" and establishing the Committee on Fair Employment Practices.

IN-DEPTH RESOURCES: UNIT 8
American Lives: A. Philip Randolph, p. 31

GROLIER MULTIMEDIA ENCYCLOPEDIA
Pacifism and nonviolent movements

TEACHING OPTIONS

Making Connections Across Time

Myrlie Evers Today After her husband's assassination, Myrlie Evers-Williams endured two hung juries in the trial of Byron de la Beckwith, who was accused of the murder. In 1994, de la Beckwith was tried again and found guilty. The story is recounted in the 1996 movie *Ghosts of Mississippi.* In the 30 years since Medgar Evers's murder, Evers-Williams has never given up the fight for civil rights. She stayed active with grassroots organizations and lectured widely. In 1995, she became the chairperson of the NAACP Board of Directors.

Teaching Gifted and Talented Students

Identifying Political Differences Between SCLC and SNCC Many Americans have forgotten that a host of speakers addressed the crowd at the March on Washington in August 1963. Some of these speakers, such as John Lewis of SNCC and Martin Luther King, Jr., had different views on how to achieve equality most quickly and completely. Have students read King's "I Have a Dream" speech and the original (unaltered) version of Lewis's speech delivered at the March on Washington. Then have them list the points where the two men expressed divergent views and offer explanations about why they differed.

OBJECTIVE
④ INSTRUCT

Fighting for Voting Rights

▶ *Discussing Key Ideas*
• Violence and intimidation
prevent millions of African
Americans in the South
from registering to vote.
• Civil rights workers try to
win a voting rights act
through two campaigns:
Freedom Summer and
a march from Selma,
Alabama, to Montgomery.
• The Voting Rights Act of
1965 guarantees the right
to vote for African
Americans.

MORE ABOUT . . .
The Civil Rights Memorial
The names of James
Chaney, Andrew Goodman,
and Michael Schwerner are
inscribed on the Civil Rights
Memorial in front of the
Southern Poverty Law
Center in Montgomery,
Alabama. The memorial celebrates 40 ordinary citizens
who sacrificed their lives for
freedom. It also commemo-
rates 53 landmark events in
the civil rights movement.
Assign interested students
to find out more about this
memorial.

Civil Rights Acts of the 1950s and 1960s

MAJOR CIVIL RIGHTS LEGISLATION

CIVIL RIGHTS ACT OF 1957
• Established federal Commission
on Civil Rights and a Civil Rights
Division in the Justice Department
to enforce civil rights laws.
• Enlarged federal power to
protect voting rights.

CIVIL RIGHTS ACT OF 1964
• Banned discrimination in most
employment and in public
accommodations.
• Enlarged federal power to protect voting rights and speed up
school desegregation.
• Established Equal Employment
Opportunity Commission to ensure
fair treatment in employment.

VOTING RIGHTS ACT OF 1965
• Eliminated voter literacy tests.
• Enabled federal examiners to
register voters.

CIVIL RIGHTS ACT OF 1968
• Prohibited discrimination in the
sale or rental of most housing.
• Strengthened antilynching laws.

**SKILLBUILDER
INTERPRETING
CHARTS**
*Which law do you think
benefited the most
people? Explain your
choice.*
*Skillbuilder Answer
Possible Answer:* The
Civil Rights Act of 1964,
because it banned
discrimination in
employment and public
accommodations—areas
that affect nearly
everyone.

John Lewis, national
chairman for SNCC,
predicted that "1964
could really be the year
for Mississippi." In that
summer, college students
from all over the country
volunteered to go to
Mississippi to help
register that state's
African-American voters.

MORE VIOLENCE Two weeks after King's historic speech, a car sped past the Sixteenth Street Baptist Church in Birmingham, Alabama, and a rider in the car hurled a bomb through one of the church win-dows. The resulting explosion claimed the lives of four young girls. Two more African Americans died in the unrest that followed.

Two months later, on November 22, 1963, an assassin shot and killed John F. Kennedy. (See Chapter 28.) His successor, President Lyndon B. Johnson, pledged to carry on Kennedy's work by winning passage of the civil rights bill. "We have talked for 100 years or more," Johnson said. "It is time now to write the new chapter—and to write it in books of law." On July 2, 1964, President Johnson signed the **Civil Rights Act of 1964,** which prohibited discrimination because of race, religion, national origin, and gender. It gave all citizens the right to enter libraries, parks, washrooms, restaurants, theaters, and other public accommodations.

Fighting for Voting Rights

Meanwhile, civil rights workers in the South were planning a different campaign to influence the country's laws—by registering African-American voters who could elect legislators who supported civil rights. Because previous voter-registration drives had met with little success, CORE and SNCC planned a much larger effort for 1964. They hoped their campaign would receive national publicity that would in turn influence Congress to pass a voting rights act. SNCC concentrated its efforts in Mississippi, in a project that was popularly known as **Freedom Summer.**

FREEDOM SUMMER SNCC knew that challenging the system that kept more than 90 percent of African-American citizens from the polls would be a daunting task. Civil rights groups recruited white students from colleges across the country and then trained them in the techniques of nonviolent resis-tance. Some 1,000 volunteers—mostly white, about one-third female—went into Mississippi to help the mostly African-American SNCC staff members reg-ister voters.

Robert Moses, a former New York City school teacher who had quit his job and joined SNCC in 1961, led the voter project in Mississippi. By the sum-mer of 1964, Moses had already been working for several years in Mississippi to register blacks to vote. "Mississippi has been called 'The Closed Society.' It is closed, locked," Moses said. "We think the key is in the vote."

Immediately, the voter project encountered violent opposition. In June, while some of the volunteers were still receiving training back in Ohio, three

**THINK THROUGH HISTORY
C. Analyzing
Causes** *Why did
civil rights groups
organize Freedom
Summer?*
C. Answer They
hoped to call
attention to the
lack of voting
rights in
segregationist
strongholds such
as Mississippi,
thereby winning
passage of a
federal voting
rights act.

Exploring Themes

Civil Rights The Fifteenth Amendment barred states from depriving citizens of the right to vote "on account of race, color, or previous condition of servitude." It also gave Con-gress the "power to enforce this article by appropriate legisla-tion." Discuss with students how Southern states had violated this amendment. Then explore ways that civil rights workers tried to make the federal government honor its constitutional responsibility to African Americans.

Making Connections Across the Curriculum

Math Nearly two decades after Freedom Summer, math teacher Robert Moses started the Algebra Project—a system that uses real-life examples to teach mathematical concepts. For example: A central subway station might become the zero point, with routes to the east representing positive integers and routes to the west representing negative integers. The goal, said Moses in the early 1990s, "is to pump students into a broad mathematical pipeline."

civil rights workers, including one summer volunteer, disappeared in Mississippi. They were Michael Schwerner and Andrew Goodman, white activists from New York, and James Chaney, an African American from Mississippi. Investigators later learned that Klansmen, with the support of local police, had murdered the three and buried them in an earthen dam. By the end of the summer, the project had suffered 4 dead, 4 critically wounded, 80 beaten, and dozens of African-American churches and businesses bombed or burned. In spite of all the publicity the project received, Congress still did not pass a voting rights act.

A NEW POLITICAL PARTY To challenge Mississippi's white-controlled Democratic Party, SNCC organized the Mississippi Freedom Democratic Party (MFDP). Open to anyone regardless of race, the MFDP hoped to unseat Mississippi's regular party delegates at the Democratic National Convention.

Fannie Lou Hamer, the daughter of a Mississippi sharecropper, won the honor of speaking for the MFDP at the convention. Hamer had registered to vote in 1962 at the cost of a crippling beating and her family's eviction from their farm. In June 1964, she spoke to the Democratic convention in a prime-time televised address. Hamer described how she had been arrested for trying to register and taken to jail, where police forced other prisoners to beat her.

A PERSONAL VOICE
The first [prisoner] began to beat [me], and I was beat until I was exhausted. . . . The second [prisoner] began to beat. . . . I began to scream and one white man got up and began to beat me on the head and tell me to "hush." . . . All of this is on account we want to register, to become first-class citizens, and if the Freedom Democratic Party is not seated now, I question America.

FANNIE LOU HAMER, quoted in *The Civil Rights Movement: An Eyewitness History*

In response to Hamer's speech, telegrams and telephone calls poured into the convention in support of seating the MFDP delegates. But President Johnson feared that such a move would cost him white votes throughout the South, so his administration pressured civil rights leaders to convince the MFDP to accept a compromise. The Democrats would give 2 of Mississippi's 40 seats to the MFDP, with a promise to ban discrimination at the 1968 convention.

When Hamer learned of the compromise, she exclaimed, "We didn't come all this way for no two seats when all of us are tired." The MFDP and many of their young supporters in SNCC felt that the leaders of other civil rights groups had betrayed them. This sense of betrayal was one of several factors that eventually led to conflict among various civil rights groups.

THE SELMA CAMPAIGN At the start of 1965, the SCLC decided to conduct a major campaign in Selma, Alabama, where SNCC had been working for two years to register voters. Although African Americans accounted for more than half of Selma's population, only about 3 percent of eligible African Americans were registered to vote. Martin Luther King, Jr., and the SCLC hoped that a concentrated voter-registration drive in Selma would provoke a hostile white response—which would help convince the Johnson administration of the need to sponsor a federal voting-rights law.

By the end of January 1965, more than 2,000 African Americans had been arrested in demonstrations. Selma sheriff Jim Clark, however, did not respond violently, as Bull Connor had in Birmingham, so the campaign did not receive the

THINK THROUGH HISTORY
D. Analyzing Causes Why did young people in SNCC and the MFDP feel betrayed by some civil rights leaders?

D. Answer Because the leaders agreed to a compromise with the Johnson administration that kept most MFDP delegates from the Democratic convention.

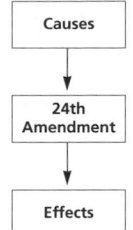

HISTORICAL SPOTLIGHT

24TH AMENDMENT— BARRING POLL TAXES
On January 24, 1964, South Dakota became the 38th state to ratify the Twenty-fourth Amendment to the Constitution, thereby making it the law of the land. The key clause in the amendment read: "The right of citizens of the United States to vote in any primary or other election . . . shall not be denied or abridged by the United States or any State by reason of failure to pay any poll tax or other tax."

Poll taxes were often used to keep poor African Americans from voting. Although most states had already abolished their poll taxes by 1964, five Southern states— Alabama, Arkansas, Mississippi, Texas, and Virginia—still had such laws on the books. By making these laws unconstitutional, the Twenty-fourth Amendment gave the vote to millions who had been disqualified because of poverty.

Dr. King and Coretta Scott King and others lead the Selma march in 1965.

Civil Rights **869**

HISTORICAL SPOTLIGHT
24th Amendment
Critical Thinking: Cause and Effect Have students analyze the causes and effects of the Twenty-fourth Amendment by using the graphic organizer below.

Causes

↓

24th Amendment

↓

Effects

MORE ABOUT . . .
Fannie Lou Hamer (1917–1977)
"We are sick and tired of being sick and tired." Fannie Lou Hamer used this phrase so many times in her speeches that it became her motto. Hamer also became known for another speech that sought to tear down economic and educational barriers that divided African Americans. "Whether you have a Ph.D., or no D, we're in this bag together," said Hamer. "And whether you're from Morehouse or Nohouse, we're still in this bag together."

TEACHING OPTIONS

Making Connections Across the Curriculum

U.S. Government The Voting Rights Act of 1965—and the later voting rights laws of 1970, 1975, and 1982—brought the federal government directly into the electoral process of the states. Have students find the provision in the Constitution that originally guaranteed states the right to manage federal elections. *Article I, Section 4, Clause 1.* Then assign students to use another U.S. government source to research other federal laws, amendments (such as the Twenty-fourth), or court decisions that limited state conduct of elections.

Making Connections Across the Curriculum

Creative Writing The civil rights movement provided some of the most dramatic moments in American history, from the trial for the murder of Emmett Till and the March on Washington to the Montgomery bus boycott and the sit-ins in Greensboro. Ask students to write a poem or short story based on some aspect of the civil rights movement. The final products should be based on actual historical facts but, more importantly, should express the emotion and drama of the era.

Assign interested students to find out more about changes in the number of African-American elected officials to Congress and the state legislatures since 1970. Have students show their findings in the form of a table or line graph. A possible source of information is the latest edition of *The American Almanac: Statistical Abstract of the United States.*

GEOGRAPHY TRANSPARENCIES
G29, Before and After the Voting Rights Act of 1965

ASSESS & RETEACH

Section 2 Assessment

Have groups of four students each address one point from question 4 and then share the answers with each other.

Self-Assessment

Ask students to review the answers they gave for question 3. How might other factors have shaped opposition to the civil rights movement?

Section Quiz

FORMAL ASSESSMENT
Section Quiz, p. 353

Reteach

Use the Guided Reading Worksheet for Section 2 to help review the main ideas of the section.

IN-DEPTH RESOURCES: UNIT 8
Guided Reading, p. 19

CLOSE

Although civil rights activists across the South faced massive resistance in their efforts to achieve desegregation, they forced the federal government to pass monumental civil rights legislation.

African Americans in Mississippi line up to vote in primary elections in April 1966.

NOW & THEN

INTEGRATING GOVERNMENT

During the 1996 Democratic National Convention, Rev. Jesse Jackson told a story that illustrates the political gains African Americans have made. Jackson's father, a World War II veteran, once pointed out a German-American citizen to his son. His father said, "We [Americans] fought to help free that [man's] country. Now he can go downtown and can vote and I can't."

In 1995, Jackson had the joy of seeing his son, Jesse Jackson, Jr., sworn in as a congressman from Illinois. The civil rights movement had so changed U.S. life that the man whose father couldn't vote because of race had a son in the U.S. House of Representatives.

publicity it was seeking. Then, in February, law officers shot and killed a demonstrator named Jimmie Lee Jackson. Dr. King responded by announcing a 50-mile protest march from Selma to the state capital, Montgomery. On Sunday, March 7, 1965, a group of about 600 protesters set out for Montgomery.

That night, news bulletins interrupted regular television programs to show what looked like a war. Clouds of tear gas swirled around fallen marchers, while police wearing gas masks and riding horses swung whips and clubs.

The scene sent shock waves across the country. Demonstrators from all over the United States poured into Selma to join the march. President Johnson responded by asking Congress for the swift passage of a new voting rights act. In his speech, Johnson openly embraced the rhetoric of the civil rights movement. Said the president, "Their cause must be our cause, too. It is not just Negroes, but all of us, who must overcome the crippling legacy of bigotry and injustice. And we *shall* overcome."

On Sunday, March 21, 300 marchers again set out for Montgomery, this time with federal protection. Two Nobel Peace Prize winners—Dr. Martin Luther King, Jr., and UN diplomat Ralph Bunche—led the procession. Under court order, only 250 marchers were supposed to enter the city limits, but nothing could stop the groundswell of support. An army of some 25,000 demonstrators joined the marchers as they walked into Montgomery.

VOTING RIGHTS ACT OF 1965 Ten weeks after the Selma-to-Montgomery march, Congress passed the **Voting Rights Act of 1965.** The act eliminated the literacy test that had disqualified so many voters. The act also stated that federal examiners could enroll voters denied suffrage by local officials. In Selma, the proportion of eligible African Americans who were registered to vote rose from 10 percent in 1964 to 60 percent in 1968. Overall the percentage of registered African American voters in the South tripled.

Although the Voting Rights Act marked a major civil rights victory, some African Americans felt that the law did not go far enough. Centuries of segregation and discrimination had produced deep-rooted social and economic inequalities. In the mid 1960s, anger over these inequalities led to a series of violent disturbances in the cities of the North.

THINK THROUGH HISTORY
E. Comparing In what ways was the civil rights campaign in Selma similar to the one in Birmingham?
E. Answer In both campaigns, civil rights workers encountered a violent response, and in both cases, TV coverage of that violence helped force the federal government to intervene.

Section ❷ Assessment

1. TERMS & NAMES
Identify:

• freedom rider
• James Meredith
• Civil Rights Act of 1964
• Freedom Summer
• Robert Moses
• Fannie Lou Hamer
• Voting Rights Act of 1965

2. SUMMARIZING Write a newspaper headline that summarizes the historical significance of each date listed below.

• September 30, 1962
• April 12, 1963
• June 11, 1963
• June 12, 1963
• August 28, 1963
• November 22, 1963
• July 2, 1964

Choose a headline and write the first paragraph for the newspaper article.

3. SYNTHESIZING What assumptions and beliefs do you think guided the fierce opposition to the civil rights movement in the South? Support your answer with evidence from the text.

THINK ABOUT
• the social and political structure of the South
• Mississippi governor Ross Barnett's comment during his radio address
• the actions of police and some white Southerners

4. RECOGNIZING EFFECTS What was the outcome of each of the following events?

• freedom rides to Jackson, Mississippi
• demonstrations in Birmingham, Alabama
• formation of the Mississippi Freedom Democratic Party
• Selma-to-Montgomery march

870 Chapter 29

ANSWERS

1. TERMS & NAMES

freedom rider, p. 864

James Meredith, p. 865

Civil Rights Act of 1964, p. 868

Freedom Summer, p. 868

Robert Moses, p. 868

Fannie Lou Hamer, p. 869

Voting Rights Act of 1965, p. 870

2. SUMMARIZING

Possible Responses: September 30, 1962: Backlash! Ole Miss Riot over Meredith's Enrollment; April 12, 1963: King Jailed in Birmingham After Leading Demonstration; June 11, 1963: Kennedy Orders Troops to Desegregate University of Alabama; June 12, 1963: Medgar Evers Murdered; August 28, 1963: March on Washington—King Declares "I Have a Dream"; November 22, 1963: Kennedy Killed by Sniper—Nation Mourns;

July 2, 1964: Johnson Signs Civil Rights Act.

3. SYNTHESIZING

Possible Responses: Racism was deeply entrenched in the South; claiming racial superiority, some white Southerners feared that the civil rights movement would erode their power base and shake the foundations of the South's social and political structure, which was upheld by its system of segregation.

4. RECOGNIZING EFFECTS

Freedom rides: federal government issued an order banning segregation in all interstate travel facilities. **Birmingham:** cit officials agreed to end segregation. **MFDP:** Fannie Lou Hamer addressed 1964 Democratic convention; as a compromise, the MFDP gained two seats at 1964 convention and the promise to ban discrimination at 1968 convention. **Selma:** President Johnson persuaded Congress t pass Voting Rights Act of 1965.

TERMS & NAMES
- de facto segregation
- de jure segregation
- Malcolm X
- Nation of Islam
- Stokely Carmichael
- Black Power
- Black Panthers
- Kerner Commission
- Civil Rights Act of 1968

LEARN ABOUT disagreements among civil rights groups and the rise of black nationalism
TO UNDERSTAND why the civil rights movement had a mixed legacy.

Section 3 Overview

OBJECTIVES

(1) To compare segregation in the North with segregation in the South.

(2) To name leaders who shaped the Black Power movement.

(3) To describe reaction to the assassination of Martin Luther King, Jr.

(4) To summarize the accomplishments of the civil rights movement.

SKILLBUILDER

- Interpreting graphs, p. 877

CRITICAL THINKING

- Analyzing causes, p. 872
- Contrasting, p. 873
- Analyzing motives, p. 874
- Drawing conclusions, p. 875
- Summarizing, pp. 876, 877
- Identifying problems, p. 877
- Hypothesizing, p. 877
- Comparing and contrasting, p. 877

ONE AMERICAN'S STORY

Alice Walker, the prize-winning novelist, became aware of the civil rights movement in 1960, when she was 16. Her mother had recently scraped together enough money to purchase a television. Walker later wrote,

A PERSONAL VOICE

Like a good omen for the future, the face of Dr. Martin Luther King, Jr., was the first black face I saw on our new television screen. And, as in a fairy tale, my soul was stirred by the meaning for me of his mission—at the time he was being rather ignominiously dumped into a police van for having led a protest march in Alabama—and I fell in love with the sober and determined face of the Movement.

ALICE WALKER, *In Search of our Mothers' Gardens*

The next year, Walker enrolled in Spelman College, an African-American college in Atlanta. While there, she demonstrated on weekends for an end to segregation. In 1963, Walker took part in King's March on Washington and then traveled to Africa to discover her spiritual roots. After returning to the United States in 1964, she married a civil rights attorney and, with him, moved to Mississippi, where she worked on voter registration, taught African-American history and writing, and wrote poetry and fiction.

Walker's interest in her African heritage was part of a trend among many African Americans in the mid-1960s who began to express pride in their African roots. In addition to emphasizing black identity, civil rights activists also began to call for changes to the social and economic structures that kept millions of African Americans in poverty. By 1964, more than half of all African Americans lived in Northern cities, where they had trouble finding jobs or decent housing. Angry over these conditions and frustrated because the equality they hoped for was so slow in coming, some urban African Americans rioted in the years 1964 to 1968.

Alice Walker

African Americans Seek Greater Equality

By 1965, the leading civil rights groups—while still sharing the goals of racial equality and greater opportunity—began to drift apart. New leaders emerged as the civil rights movement turned its attention to the North, where African Americans faced not legal racism but deeply entrenched and oppressive racial prejudice nonetheless.

NORTHERN SEGREGATION The problem in the North was **de facto segregation**—segregation that exists by practice and custom. De facto segregation is harder to fight than **de jure segregation** (segregation by law), because eliminating it requires the transformation of racist attitudes rather than the repeal of Jim Crow laws. Activists in the mid-1960s would find it much more difficult to convince whites to share economic and social power with African Americans than to convince them to share lunch counters and bus seats.

De facto segregation came about when African Americans moved to Northern cities after World War II. This began a "white flight," in which great numbers of white city dwellers moved to the suburbs. By the mid-1960s, most

Civil Rights **871**

FOCUS & MOTIVATE

▶ ***Starting with the Student*** Ask students what they know about race relations in Northern cities.

- How and why might racial tensions be different in the North than in the South?
- In what ways are they similar?

OBJECTIVE
(1) INSTRUCT

African Americans Seek Greater Equality

▶ ***Discussing Key Ideas***
- In the mid-1960s, differences over tactics create divisions in the civil rights movement.
- In the North, de facto segregation traps many African Americans in decaying slums.

(continued on next page)

 SECTION 3 RESOURCES

PRINT RESOURCES

IN-DEPTH RESOURCES: UNIT 8
Guided Reading, p. 20

ACCESS FOR STUDENTS ACQUIRING ENGLISH
Guided Reading (Spanish), p. 283

FORMAL ASSESSMENT
Section Quiz, p. 354

ALTERNATIVE ASSESSMENT BOOK
See forms for supporting and scoring alternative activities.

 ### TECHNOLOGY RESOURCES

CRITICAL THINKING TRANSPARENCIES
CT29, Civil Rights Movement
CT63, African-American Educational Attainment

CD-ROM Electronic Library of Primary Sources

VIDEO *American Portfolio: A Videodisc for U.S. History*
user's guide, pp. 246, 248

INTERNET McDougal Littell Learning On-Line
http://www.mcdougallittell.com

(continued from page 871)

- Urban riots reveal that many African Americans suffered from economic inequality as well as political inequality.

IN-DEPTH RESOURCES: UNIT 8
Guided Reading, p. 20

ACCESS FOR STUDENTS ACQUIRING ENGLISH
Guided Reading (Spanish), p. 283

MORE ABOUT . . .
The Harlem Riot

In assessing the Harlem riot of 1964, poet and playwright Langston Hughes wrote:

Old-timers . . . say, "White folks respect us more when they find out we mean business. When they only listen to our speeches or read our writing—if they ever do—they think we are just blowing off steam. But when rioters smash the plate glass windows of their stores, they know the steam has some force behind it."

Ask students to assess how this line of thinking also appealed to the new generation of civil rights leaders in the North.

MORE ABOUT . . .
The Watts Riot

National Guardsmen had to be called in to stem the rioting. In addition to the 34 people who were killed, almost 900 people were injured and over 3,500 people were arrested. The riot prompted local, state, and federal authorities to address the problems of the 20-square-mile ghetto where more than 100,000 people lived.

urban African Americans found themselves trapped in decaying slums, paying rent to landlords who often refused to comply with local housing and health ordinances. The schools provided for African-American children deteriorated along with their neighborhoods. Unemployment rates among African Americans were more than twice as high as those among whites.

The widely publicized gains in voting rights and desegregation of public accommodations made many urban African Americans impatient for discrimination in other areas to end. In addition, they were angry at the sometimes brutal treatment they received from the mostly white police force that patrolled their communities.

URBAN VIOLENCE ERUPTS In New York City in July 1964, a clash between white police and African-American teenagers ended in the death of a 15-year-old student. This incident sparked a race riot in central Harlem. Similar conflicts took place in other cities during that year. On August 11, 1965, only five days after President Johnson signed the Voting Rights Act into law, African Americans in Los Angeles exploded in anger against white authority. In Watts, the predominantly African-American neighborhood, police who were arresting a young man for drunk driving argued with the suspect's mother before a crowd of onlookers. A riot broke out that lasted for six days. Thirty-four people were killed, and property valued at about $30 million was destroyed, making the Watts riot one of the worst race riots in the nation's history.

The next year, 1966, saw even more racial disturbances, and 1967 was the most violent year of all. In 1967 alone, riots and violent clashes took place in more than 100 cities— north and south, east and west.

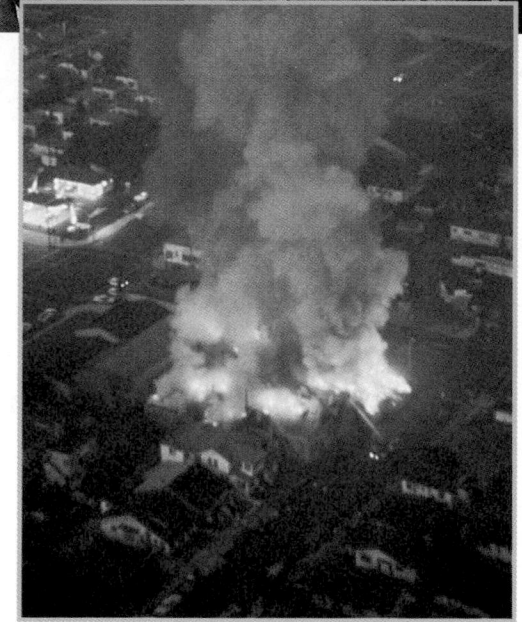

Between 1964 and 1968, more than 100 race riots erupted in major American cities. The worst included Watts in Los Angeles in 1965 *bottom* and Detroit in 1967 *top*. In Detroit, 43 people were killed and property damage topped $40 million.

The rage that African Americans were expressing baffled many whites, who could not understand why blacks would turn to violence just after winning so many important civil rights victories in the South. Some white leaders, however, realized that what African Americans wanted and needed was economic equality of opportunity in jobs, housing, and education.

As early as January 1964, even before the riots, President Johnson announced to Congress his War on Poverty, a program designed to help impoverished Americans of all races. But war in far-off Vietnam, a Southeast Asian country where the United States sent troops to fight Communists, soon siphoned off the money needed to fund what Johnson called the Great Society. In a fiery anti-war speech in 1967, Dr. Martin Luther King, Jr., declared, "The Great Society has been shot down on the battlefields of Vietnam."

THINK THROUGH HISTORY
A. Analyzing Causes *What were some of the causes of urban rioting in the 1960s?*

A. Answer De facto segregation, police brutality, rundown communities and schools, and high unemployment.

872 Chapter 29

Exploring Themes

Expanding Democracy Although not expressly written down in the Bill of Rights, Americans value the right to earn a decent living and freedom from economic want. Millions of African Americans in the 1960s felt that because of discrimination they had been denied economic rights as surely as they had been denied the right to vote. Challenge students to write an amendment guaranteeing Americans the right to work. As an extension, they might conduct a poll to see if voting-age members of their community would support such an amendment.

Teaching Less Proficient Readers

Interpreting Photographs Remind students that photographs serve as primary sources, or firsthand information, about the past. Working in pairs, have them write down all the things that these photographs tell them about the urban riots of 1965–1967. Suppose these two pictures were included in a photographic history of the civil rights movement. What caption would students write to summarize their content?

New Leaders Voice Discontent

The anger that sent rioters into the streets stemmed in part from African-American leaders who were reviving the belief that African Americans should take complete control of their communities, livelihoods, and culture. One such leader, **Malcolm X,** brought a Harlem audience to its feet in the early 1960s when he declared, "If you think we are here to tell you to love the white man, you have come to the wrong place."

AFRICAN–AMERICAN SOLIDARITY Malcolm X, born Malcolm Little, went to jail at age 20 for burglary. While in prison, he studied the teachings of Elijah Muhammad, the head of the **Nation of Islam,** or the Black Muslims. Malcolm changed his name to Malcolm X (dropping what he called his "slave name") and, after his release from prison in 1952, became a minister of the Muslim faith. Soon he was one of Elijah Muhammad's most famous disciples. A brilliant thinker and an engaging speaker, Malcolm X openly preached Elijah Muhammad's views that whites were the cause of the condition in which blacks found themselves and that blacks should separate from white society.

Malcolm's message appealed to many African Americans and their growing pride in their identity. He also advocated armed self-defense. At a New York press conference in March 1964, Malcolm declared,

A PERSONAL VOICE
Concerning nonviolence: it is criminal to teach a man not to defend himself when he is the constant victim of brutal attacks. It is legal and lawful to own a shotgun or a rifle. We believe in obeying the laws. . . . The time has come for the American Negro to fight back in self-defense whenever and wherever he is being unjustly and unlawfully attacked.

MALCOLM X, quoted in *EYEWITNESS: The Negro in American History*

The press gave a great deal of publicity to Malcolm X because his controversial statements made dramatic news stories. This publicity had two effects. First, his call for armed self-defense frightened most whites and many moderate African Americans. Second, reports of the attention Malcolm received awakened resentment in some other members of the Nation of Islam.

BALLOTS OR BULLETS? In March 1964, Malcolm broke with Elijah Muhammad over differences in strategy and doctrine and formed another Muslim organization. One month later, he embarked on a pilgrimage to Mecca in Saudia Arabia, a trip required of followers of orthodox Islam. In Mecca, he learned that orthodox Islam preached the equality of all races, and he worshiped alongside people from many countries. Wrote Malcolm, "I have [prayed] . . . with fellow Muslims whose eyes were the bluest of blue, whose hair was the blondest of blond, and whose skin was the whitest of white."

The experience radically changed Malcolm's thinking. When he returned to the United States, he still burned with a hatred of racism and injustice, but his attitude toward whites had changed. When 1965 opened, he introduced a new slogan: "Ballots or bullets." In explaining the phrase, Malcolm told a follower, "Well, if you and I don't use the ballot, we're going to be forced to use the bullet. So let us try the ballot."

Malcolm believed that his life might be in danger because of his split with the Black Muslims. "No one can get out without trouble," he confided

KEY PLAYER

MALCOLM X
1925–1965
Malcolm X's early life left him alienated from white society. His father was killed by white racists, and his mother had an emotional collapse, leaving Malcolm and his siblings in the care of the state. At the end of eighth grade, Malcolm quit school and went first to Boston and then to New York, where he became a drug addict and a criminal. In 1946, a court sentenced him to ten years in prison.

While in prison, Malcolm joined the Nation of Islam, and after his release in 1952, he preached black superiority and separation from whites,

His 1964 pilgrimage to Mecca transformed his views. Instead of preaching separatism, he began to urge African Americans to identify with Africa and to work with world organizations and even progressive whites to attain equality. Although gunmen silenced his message, Malcolm X is a continuing inspiration for young African Americans.

HINK THROUGH HISTORY
B. Contrasting
How did the ideas of Malcolm X differ from those of Martin Luther King, Jr.?

B. Answer
Malcolm X advocated self-defense, by violent means if necessary , and before 1964, rejected working with whites.

Civil Rights **873**

OBJECTIVE
② **INSTRUCT**

New Leaders Voice Discontent

▶ *Discussing Key Ideas*
- Malcolm X appeals to a growing sense of African-American pride.
- His later efforts to temper African-American separatism alienates many Black Muslims, three of whom assassinate him.
- The rise of the Black Panthers fuels the Black Power movement—and a white backlash.

KEY PLAYER
Malcolm X

Critical Thinking: Hypothesizing Assign teams of students to create a dialogue in which Malcolm X and Martin Luther King, Jr., discuss and debate their two philosophies for change. Have students reenact their dialogues, either in a live skit or in the form of a videotape.

 ELECTRONIC LIBRARY OF PRIMARY SOURCES
from Speech to Mississippi Youth *by* Malcolm X

TEACHING OPTIONS

Teaching Gifted and Talented Students

Writing a Book Review Assign your more able students to read either *The Autobiography of Malcolm X, Where Do We Go from Here: Chaos or Community?* by Martin Luther King, Jr., or *Black Power* by Stokely Carmichael and Charles V. Hamilton. Tell them to write a review of the book from the perspective of the late 1960s. They might want to look at contemporary book reviews to get a sense of what people at the time thought about the book. In their review, students should critique the author's main arguments about race relations in the United States in the 1960s based on their knowledge of the time.

Making Global Connections

Creating Ties with Africa Before setting out on his *hajj,* or pilgrimage to Mecca, Malcolm X took the Muslim name of Malik El-Shabazz. After traveling through the Muslim world of the Middle East and Africa, Malcolm X (as he is still called) returned home to found the Organization of Afro-American Unity (OAAU)—a group set up to empower African Americans and to draw African nations into their struggle. Just before his death, Malcolm X tried to enlist African nations to petition the UN in behalf of African Americans in the United States.

Born in Port-of-Spain, Trinidad, Carmichael attended Howard University in Washington, D.C., in preference to the white universities that offered him scholarships. After his graduation in 1964, Carmichael plunged himself into the civil rights revolution. Even to this day, he often answers his phone with the words "Ready for the Revolution."

MORE ABOUT . . .
The Black Panthers

In 1974, the Panthers elected Elaine Brown as the group's first female leader. Among her community projects, Brown set up an award-winning learning center for poor children in Oakland, California. In 1977, Brown also organized a registration drive in which more than 100,000 African Americans signed up to vote. These new voters helped elect Lionel Wilson as Oakland's first-ever African-American mayor.

Stokely
Carmichael

to a friend. On February 21, 1965, Malcolm X walked into Harlem's Audubon Ballroom to address a crowd of about 400 followers. No sooner had he begun speaking, than three men rushed forward and shot him down. At age 39, Malcolm X was dead.

BLACK POWER In the summer of 1966, tensions that had been building between SNCC and the other civil rights groups finally erupted in Mississippi. Here James Meredith, the man who had integrated the University of Mississippi, set out on a 220-mile "march against fear." Meredith planned to walk all the way from the Tennessee border to Jackson. But on the second day of Meredith's march, a white man stopped him by firing a round of birdshot into his head, legs, and back. Meredith was too injured to continue.

Dr. Martin Luther King, Jr., of the SCLC, Floyd McKissick of CORE, and **Stokely Carmichael** of SNCC decided to lead their followers in a march to finish what Meredith had started. It soon became obvious that SNCC and CORE participants were quite militant, as they began to shout slogans similar to those of the black separatists who had followed Malcolm X. When King tried to rally the marchers with the familiar refrain of "We Shall Overcome," many SNCC workers—bitter over the violence they'd suffered during Freedom Summer—drowned out the song by singing, "We shall overrun."

On the night of June 17, police in Greenwood, Mississippi, arrested SNCC leader Stokely Carmichael for setting up a tent on the grounds of an all-black high school. That night marchers held a hastily organized rally to protest Carmichael's arrest. Near the end of the rally, he showed up on the platform, with his face swollen from a beating. The stunned crowd listened as Carmichael spoke.

A PERSONAL VOICE
This is the twenty-seventh time I have been arrested—and I ain't going to jail no more! . . . We been saying freedom for six years—and we ain't got nothin'. What we're gonna start saying now is BLACK POWER.

STOKELY CARMICHAEL, quoted in *The Civil Rights Movement: An Eyewitness History*

The slogan **Black Power,** which dated back to the 1940s, electrified marchers. Some leaders, including King, urged Carmichael to stop using it because they believed it would provoke African-American violence and antagonize whites. Carmichael refused to heed their warnings. Black Power, he said, was a "call for black people to begin to define their own goals . . . [and] to lead their own organizations." He urged SNCC to stop recruiting whites and to focus on developing African-American pride.

BLACK PANTHERS Later that year, another development demonstrated the growing radicalism of some segments of the African-American community. In October 1966, Huey Newton and Bobby Seale founded a political party known as the **Black Panthers** to fight police brutality in the ghetto. The party also offered African Americans what it called "a program for the people," which advocated taking control of the communities in which African Americans lived, full employment, and decent housing. The program also supported an exemption of African Americans from military service—a reflection of the African-American belief that the government drafted an unfair number of black youths to fight in Vietnam.

Most Panthers wore black berets, sunglasses, black leather jackets, black trousers, and shiny black shoes. To raise money for the organization, they sold copies of the writings of Mao Zedong, leader of the Chinese Communist revolution. The Panthers publicly preached armed revolt and adopted one of Mao's slogans: "Power flows out of the barrel of a gun."

Most white leaders feared and distrusted the Panthers and objected to their

THINK THROUGH HISTORY
C. Analyzing Motives Why did some leaders of SNCC disagree with SCLC tactics?

C. Answer Impatient for change and bitter over the violence of Freedom Summer, they wanted African Americans to claim "Black Power" and to confront whites more directly.

874 CHAPTER 29

TEACHING OPTIONS

Making Global Connections

Promoting Pan-Africanism In 1978, Stokely Carmichael changed his name to Kwame Ture, in honor of Kwame Nkrumah, the so-called "Father of pan-Africanism," and Ahmed Sekou Toure, the poet-politician who replaced Nkrumah as the second president of Ghana. Ture has lived in Ghana for nearly three decades and is a staunch defender of pan-Africanism. He calls all people of the Black Diaspora "Africans," including African Americans. You might use Ture's story as a bridge to discussing the pan-Africanism of Marcus Garvey.

Making Connections Across Cultures

Kwanzaa Assign interested students to research Kwanzaa—a seven-day celebration of African-American culture that begins on December 26. Explain that Kwanzaa, which means "first fruits of harvest" in Swahili, was invented in 1966 by Maulana Karenga in reaction to the 1965 riots in Watts. Karenga, a black activist and educator in California, hoped the celebration would replace rage with pride. If possible, encourage a student familiar with the celebration to describe it to the class.

revolutionary rhetoric. Several shootouts occurred between the Panthers and the police, and the FBI conducted investigations (sometimes using illegal tactics) of the organization. Even so, the Panthers' grassroots activities—the establishment of daycare centers, free breakfast programs, and other services—won support in the ghettos of America. The Panthers also drew recruits from SNCC, including Stokely Carmichael, who joined the party in June 1967.

1968—A Turning Point in Civil Rights

Martin Luther King, Jr., objected to the Black Power movement that was taking root in the cities. King said, "I feel that . . . fiery, demagogic oratory in the black ghettos, urging Negroes to arm themselves, and prepare to engage in violence, . . . can reap nothing but grief." After Meredith's march against fear, King left the South to spread his message of nonviolence to Northern cities. He was planning to lead a Poor People's March on Washington, D.C., to press for government help for the nation's poor. This time, however, the people would have to march without King.

DR. KING'S DEATH Dr. King seemed to sense that death was near. On April 3, 1968, he addressed a crowd in Memphis, Tennessee, where he had gone to show his support for the city's striking garbage workers. "I may not get there with you," King said, "but I want you to know tonight that we as a people will get to the Promised Land." He then added, "And I'm happy tonight. I'm not fearing any man. Mine eyes have seen the glory of the coming of the Lord."

The next day, King stepped out onto the balcony of his hotel room. Across the street, James Earl Ray thrust a high-powered rifle out of a window and squeezed the trigger. King crumpled as a bullet crashed through his jaw. An hour later, the man who dared to dream of racial peace lay dead from racial violence.

Coretta Scott King mourns her husband at his funeral service.

REACTIONS TO DR. KING'S DEATH The night King died, Robert F. Kennedy was campaigning for the Democratic presidential nomination. Fearful that King's death would spark riots, Kennedy's campaign advisers told him to cancel his appearance in an African-American neighborhood in Indianapolis. Kennedy rejected that advice, discarded his prepared speech, and made an impassioned plea for nonviolence.

A PERSONAL VOICE
For those of you who are black—considering the evidence . . . that there were white people who were responsible—you can be filled with bitterness, with hatred, and a desire for revenge. We can move in that direction as a country, in great polarization—black people amongst black, white people amongst white, filled with hatred toward one another.

Or we can make an effort, as Martin Luther King did, to understand and comprehend, and to replace that violence, that stain of bloodshed that has spread across our land, with an effort to understand with compassion and love.
ROBERT F. KENNEDY, "A Eulogy for Dr. Martin Luther King, Jr."

Robert F. Kennedy

HISTORICAL SPOTLIGHT

CONFRONTING THE NORTH
Martin Luther King, Jr.'s attempts to take his message to Northern cities also encountered many challenges. In 1966, for example, King spearheaded a campaign in Chicago to end de facto segregation there and create an "open city." On July 10, he led about 30,000 African Americans in a march on city hall.

In late July, when King led demonstrators through a neighborhood on Chicago's Southwest Side, angry whites threw rocks and bottles at the marchers. On August 5, hostile whites stoned King as he led 600 marchers. The next day, King left Chicago without accomplishing what he wanted, yet pledging to return.

Soon after, city officials signed an agreement to promote fair housing but later did little to carry out the agreement. At the time of King's death in 1968, Chicago was just as segregated as it had ever been.

Civil Rights **875**

Legacy of the Civil Rights Movement

▶ *Discussing Key Ideas*
- The civil rights movement wipes de jure segregation from the law books of America.
- De facto segregation and unequal economic opportunity remain entrenched.
- The lingering effects of racism, as reported by the Kerner Commission, remain one of the greatest challenges facing the nation in the years ahead.

 CRITICAL THINKING TRANSPARENCIES

CT29, Civil Rights Movement
CT63, African-American Educational Attainment

MORE ABOUT . . .
The Reverend Jesse Louis Jackson (1941–)

In the 1980s, Jackson made history by building the National Rainbow Coalition —a multiethnic collection of groups that helped fuel two bids for the Democratic presidential nomination— one in 1984, the other in 1988. Although he did not receive the nomination, he became one of the most prominent liberals in the Democratic Party, and his son, Jesse Jackson, Jr., won a seat in Congress from a district in Chicago in 1995.

The Reverend Jesse Jackson addresses the Democratic National Convention in 1988 during his unsuccessful run for the presidency.

Even though many leaders called for peace, rage over King's death led to the worst urban rioting in United States history. Some 125 cities exploded in flames. The hardest-hit cities included Baltimore, Chicago, Kansas City, and Washington, D.C. Not only racial but also political violence marred the year 1968. In June, Robert Kennedy himself was assassinated by a Jordanian immigrant who was angry over Kennedy's support of Israel.

Legacy of the Civil Rights Movement

On March 2, 1968, the **Kerner Commission,** which President Johnson had appointed to study the causes of the 1965 Watts uprising, issued a 200,000-word report. In it, the panel named one main cause: white racism. Said the report, "This is our basic conclusion: Our nation is moving toward two societies, one black, one white—separate and unequal." The report called for the nation to create new jobs, construct new housing, and end de facto segregation in order to wipe out the destructive ghetto environment in which many African Americans lived. However, the Johnson administration chose to ignore many of the recommendations because of white opposition to such sweeping changes. So what had the civil rights movement accomplished?

CIVIL RIGHTS GAINS The civil rights movement brought about the end of de jure segregation. Constitutional and legal changes guaranteed the civil rights of all Americans under the laws. Congress passed the most important civil rights legislation since Reconstruction, including the **Civil Rights Act of 1968**—a law that banned discrimination in housing. Furthermore, in the decades following the integration of Little Rock Central High School and Ole Miss, the numbers of African Americans who finished high school and who went to college significantly increased.

Another accomplishment of the civil rights movement was to give African Americans greater pride in their racial identity. Many African Americans adopted African-influenced styles— such as the Afro, a full, unstraightened hairstyle, and the dashiki, a loose, brightly colored tunic. College students demanded new Black Studies programs so they could study African-American history and literature. In the entertainment world, African Americans began to appear more frequently in movies and on television shows and commercials.

In addition, African Americans made substantial political gains. By 1970, two-thirds of eligible African Americans were registered to vote, and those voters brought about a significant increase in African-American elected officials. The number of African Americans holding national office leaped from about 300 in 1965 to more than 7,000 in 1992. Many civil rights activists went on to become political leaders, among them Rev. Jesse Jackson, who ran for president in 1988; Vernon Jordan, who led voter registration drives that enrolled about 2 million African Americans; and Andrew Young, who has been UN ambassador and Atlanta's mayor.

UNFINISHED WORK The civil rights movement was remarkably successful in accomplishing the repeal of many discriminatory laws. Yet as the 1960s turned to the 1970s, the challenges for the movement changed. The issues it confronted—housing and job discrimination, educational inequality, poverty, and racism—involved the difficult task of changing people's attitudes and behavior. Some of the proposed solutions, such as more tax monies spent in the inner cities and the forced busing

E. Answer End of legalized segregation; constitutional and legal protection of civil rights and voting rights; increased pride in racial identity; more African-American voters, elected officials, and high school and college graduates.

THINK THROUGH HISTORY
E. Summarizing *What were some accomplishments of the civil rights movement?*

TEACHING OPTIONS

Making Connections Across Cultures

African Americans in the Media Assign groups of students to one of the major TV networks. For one week, have them keep logs on the appearance of African Americans in prime-time programming, starting with the evening news. Log entries might include these heads: Name of Program, Name of African American, Role Played, Length of Viewing Time (seconds/minutes on the screen).

Making Connections Across the Curriculum

U.S. Government In 1992, *Teaching Tolerance,* a biennial publication by the Southern Poverty Law Center, polled students on two questions: What causes most racial and ethnic conflicts between people? What do you think individuals can do to bring about greater understanding between different racial and ethnic groups? Have students use these questions to poll opinions in their own school, presenting results in the school newspaper.

of schoolchildren, angered some whites, who resisted further changes. Public support for the civil rights movement also declined because some whites were frightened by the urban riots and the rhetoric of the Black Panthers.

The trend of whites fleeing the cities for the suburbs increased the problem of de facto segregation. For example, by 1990 much of the progress toward school integration had been reversed. About 75 percent of African-American children in Northern cities and about 50 percent of African-American children in the South attended almost completely black schools. Lack of jobs also remained a serious problem for African Americans, who had a poverty rate three times greater than that for whites.

Changes in Poverty and Education, 1959 and 1994

POVERTY STATUS

African-American Families: 48.1% (1959), 31.3% (1994)
White Families: 15.2% (1959), 9.4% (1994)

■ Families living in poverty ■ Families not living in poverty

COLLEGE EDUCATION

African Americans: 3.3% (1959), 12.9% (1994)
Whites: 8.6% (1959), 22.9% (1994)

■ Persons with four or more years of college ■ All other persons

Source: U.S. Bureau of Census

To help many African Americans—and other disadvantaged groups—gain education and jobs, the government in the 1960s began to promote affirmative action. Affirmative-action programs involve making special efforts to hire or enroll groups that have suffered from discrimination in the past. Many colleges and almost all companies that do business with the federal government adopted such programs.

In the late 1970s, some people began to criticize affirmative-action programs as "reverse discrimination" that set minority hiring or enrollment quotas and deprived whites of opportunities. In the 1980s, Republican administrations eased affirmative-action requirements for some government contractors. The fate of affirmative action—as of so much of the legacy of the civil rights movement—has still to be decided. In all the regions of the country today, African Americans and whites interact on a daily basis that could have only been imagined before the civil rights movement. In many respects, Dr. King's dream has been realized—yet much remains to be done.

SKILLBUILDER
INTERPRETING GRAPHS
Did the economic situation for African Americans get better or worse between 1959 and 1994 in terms of poverty status? How many times bigger is the percentage of whites completing four or more years of college in 1994 than the percentage of African Americans?

F. Answer
Possible Answers: De facto segregation, joblessness and poverty among African Americans, fate of affirmative action.

THINK THROUGH HISTORY
F. Identifying Problems *What challenges still face the nation in the area of civil rights?*

Section 3 Assessment

1. TERMS & NAMES

Identify:
• de facto segregation
• de jure segregation
• Malcolm X
• Nation of Islam
• Stokely Carmichael
• Black Power
• Black Panthers
• Kerner Commission
• Civil Rights Act of 1968

2. SUMMARIZING Create a time line of key events relating to the civil rights movement. Use the dates already plotted on the time line below as a guide.

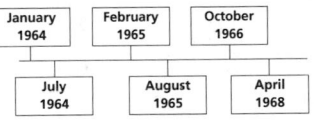

| January 1964 | February 1965 | October 1966 |
| July 1964 | August 1965 | April 1968 |

In your opinion, which event was most significant? Explain.

3. HYPOTHESIZING What if Dr. Martin Luther King, Jr., had not been assassinated? Speculate on how the civil rights movement might have been different. Support your answer with details from the text.

THINK ABOUT
• King's approach to civil rights issues
• King's status in the civil rights movement at the time of his death
• the immediate reaction to King's assassination

4. COMPARING AND CONTRASTING Compare and contrast the civil rights strategies of Malcolm X and Martin Luther King, Jr. Whose strategies do you think were more effective? Explain and support your response.

THINK ABOUT
• the goals and methods of each leader
• public reaction to each leader's methods
• the short-term and long-term effects of each leader's efforts

Civil Rights **877**

ANSWERS

1. TERMS & NAMES

de facto segregation, p. 871

de jure segregation, p. 871

Malcolm X, p. 873

Nation of Islam, p. 873

Stokely Carmichael, p. 874

Black Power, p. 874

Black Panthers, p. 874

Kerner Commission, p. 876

Civil Rights Act of 1968, p. 876

2. SUMMARIZING

Possible Answers: January 1964—War on Poverty launched; July 1964—Harlem riot; February 1965—Malcolm X assassinated; August 1965—Watts riot; October 1966—Black Panthers founded; April 1968—King assassinated.

3. HYPOTHESIZING

Possible Responses: King was still greatly admired, and had he lived, the movement might have been less splintered and not lost

its momentum as quickly; the rage that fueled urban riots in about 125 cities after his assassination would not have been unleashed, and the white backlash to the civil rights movement might have been diminished.

4. COMPARING AND CONTRASTING

Possible Responses: Both wanted civil rights and greater opportunity for African Americans; King preached racial

equality and used a nonviolent approach in demonstrations and marches; Malcolm X preached black separatism and urged African Americans to use armed self-defense. Some students may say King's strategies were more effective because his demonstrations caused civil rights legislation to be passed. Others may say Malcolm X was more effective because his strategies made people realize that African Americans needed to fight back.

OBJECTIVES

1 To recognize civil rights as a significant theme in America's history.

2 To trace the evolution of civil rights over time.

An Evolving Idea

Thomas Jefferson asserted in the Declaration of Independence that "all men are created equal" and are endowed with the "unalienable Rights" of "Life, Liberty and the Pursuit of Happiness." With these words, a new nation was founded on the principle that citizens have certain fundamental civil rights. These include the right to vote, the right to enjoy freedom of speech and religion, and others. For more than 200 years, the United States has stood as a worldwide example of a country committed to securing the rights of its people.

However, throughout the nation's history, some Americans have had to struggle to obtain even the most basic civil rights. Laws or customs prevented certain people from voting freely, from attending the school of their choice, and from eating in any restaurant they wish. Over time, many of these barriers have been torn down.

In recent years, the United States has tried to promote human rights in other countries through its foreign policy. Even as it does so, the United States continues to struggle to fulfill for all Americans the lofty ideals established by the nation's founders.

FOCUS & MOTIVATE

▶ **Starting with the Student**
Have students think about the concept of civil rights.

• How do students define the term *civil rights?* What might they offer as an example of a civil right?

• Which documents, laws, organizations, and/or government institutions seem especially important in defining or guarding our civil rights? Explain.

MORE ABOUT . . .
Civil Rights

During the 19th century, American women also pressured for legal rights previously denied them. In the 1840s, many states passed laws granting married women the right to control their property and earnings, to participate in legal contracts, and to share in custody of their children. It took longer to win the right to vote. Although the 19th-century suffrage movement won some victories on a state-by-state basis, women could not vote nationwide until the Nineteenth Amendment to the U.S. Constitution was adopted in 1920.

1791
BILL OF RIGHTS

During the Constitutional Convention, *below,* the question of a bill of rights arose, but none was included. After the Constitution was ratified, many people agreed that it needed to list the basic civil rights and liberties that the federal government could not take away from the people.

Accordingly, the nation ratified ten amendments to the Constitution—the Bill of Rights. It establishes such rights as freedom of speech, religion, and assembly, freedom of the press, and the right to a trial by jury. While these rights have been subject to interpretation over the nation's history, the Bill of Rights serves as the cornerstone of American democracy.

1868
THE FOURTEENTH AMENDMENT

In the engraving above, a crowd of black and white Americans celebrate the passage of the Civil Rights Act of 1866. This act recognized the citizenship of African Americans and granted the same civil rights to all people born in the United States except Native Americans.

The Fourteenth Amendment, ratified two years later, made these changes part of the Constitution. The Amendment declared that states cannot deny anyone "equal protection of the laws" and extended the right to vote to all 21-year-old males, including former slaves.

Despite these provisions, African Americans and other groups would struggle for the next 100 years to claim their full rights as U.S. citizens.

RECOMMENDED RESOURCES

Books

Belz, Herman. *Emancipation and Equal Rights: Politics and Constitutionalism in the Civil War Era.* New York: Norton, 1978.

Rutland, Robert. *The Birth of the Bill of Rights, 1776–1791.* Boston: Northeastern UP, 1991.

Totten, Samuel. *Human Rights.* Hillside, NJ: Enslow, 1989. Includes the UN's Universal Declaration of Human Rights.

Videos

Bill of Rights, Bill of Responsibilities. Cambridge Educational, 1995. A fast-paced commentary featuring comedian Bill Maher.

Fighting for Civil Rights. Coronet/MTI, 1993. Part 3 of the award-winning In the Land of Jim Crow series.

Software

African-American History— Slavery to Civil Rights. CD-ROM. Queue. From the slave trade to recent times; DOS version called Black American History.

Amnesty Interactive. CD-ROM. Voyager, 1994. Traces human rights from ancient to modern times.

1950s & 1960s
THE CIVIL RIGHTS MOVEMENT

Despite the Fourteenth Amendment and later the Fifteenth Amendment, which forbade states from denying anyone the right to vote on account of race, African Americans continued to live as second-class citizens, especially in the South. States passed laws aimed at separating the races and keeping blacks from the polls.

During the 1950s and 1960s, African Americans and other Americans led an organized and powerful movement to fight for racial equality. The movement often met with strong resistance, such as in Birmingham, Alabama, where police sprayed demonstrators with high-pressure fire hoses, *above.* Nevertheless, it succeeded in securing for African Americans the civil rights promised by the Declaration of Independence and Constitution. The civil rights movement has also been the basis for gaining equal rights by other groups, including other minorities, women, and people with disabilities.

Interact with History Answers

1. Analyzing Issues States passed laws (such as poll taxes and literacy tests) aimed at keeping African Americans from the polls. The civil rights movement, voter registration campaigns, and stronger federal oversight (especially after the Voting Rights Act of 1965) helped blacks secure their voting rights.

2. Writing About Rights To Come

1970s
HUMAN RIGHTS

President Jimmy Carter considered human rights an important foreign policy issue. Human rights are what Americans think of as their civil rights, including the right to vote and to receive a fair trial. The Carter administration tried to encourage greater freedom abroad by taking such steps as cutting off military aid to countries with poor human rights records.

While these efforts met with mixed results, the issue of human rights has continued to influence U.S. foreign policy. In the 1990s, for example, the U.S. government tried to push China for more democracy while keeping alive its trade ties with that country. As a private citizen, Jimmy Carter has also continued to champion human rights causes. In 1982, he and his wife, Rosalynn, founded the Carter Center, whose programs seek to end human rights abuses and promote democracy worldwide.

INTERACT WITH HISTORY

1. **ANALYZING ISSUES** The Fourteenth and Fifteenth Amendments both provided for the voting rights of African Americans. Based on what you have read on these two pages and in this chapter, how were these rights denied African Americans? How were they finally secured?

 SEE SKILLBUILDER HANDBOOK, PAGE 1046.

2. **WRITING ABOUT RIGHTS** Have you or anyone you've known had their civil rights denied them in any way? How did you (or they) react? What did you (or they) do to improve the situation? Write an account of the incident and share it with your class.

 For more about civil rights, click on *Social Studies* at http://www.mcdougalllittell.com

• Have students make a civil rights time line with details from these pages and other major events in the history of civil rights.
• Encourage students to discuss current civil rights issues such as congressional districting, immigrants' rights, women's rights, and human rights around the globe. What factors limit the ability of people to exercise equal rights? *Possible Responses: economic inequality, racism.*

▶ **Discussing Key Ideas**
• The Declaration of Independence and U.S. Constitution, including the Bill of Rights, outline civil rights in the U.S.
• Since America's founding, the concept of civil rights has evolved.

HISTORY FROM VISUALS
Reading the Images
Have students study the pictures and captions.

• Jot down adjectives to describe the different scenes. *Possible Responses: first formal; second jubilant; third oppressed; fourth dignified*
• What ironies do you find in the captions' details or in the juxtaposition of any of these scenes? *Possible Responses: violation of African-American civil rights juxtaposed with jubilation at passage of Fourteenth Amendment decades before; a president from the South shows concern for human rights.*

INTERACT WITH HISTORY

1. Analyzing Issues

Possible Answers: The rights were denied through poll taxes, unevenly applied literacy tests, other unfair voting qualifications (for example, you could not vote if your grandfather had not voted), intimidation of potential African-American voters, and gerrymandering to keep African Americans from office.

They were secured through the civil rights movement, which helped change national opinion, and through resulting federal intervention and passage of federal laws like the Voting Rights Act of 1965.

2. Writing About Rights

Standards for Evaluation
Accounts should . . .
• identify the individuals involved and the setting (time and place) in which the incident occurred
• clarify the specific right or rights being violated
• indicate the reasons for the violation, if known
• capture the feelings of the victim
• describe the actions of the victim to improve the situation

Students might share their accounts in oral readings or group discussions.

Chapter 29 Assessment

REVIEWING THE CHAPTER

TERMS & NAMES

1. *Brown* v. *Board of Education*, p. 858
2. Rosa Parks, p. 860
3. Dr. Martin Luther King, Jr., p. 861
4. Student Nonviolent Coordinating Committee, p. 862
5. freedom rider, p. 864
6. Civil Rights Act of 1964, p. 868
7. Fannie Lou Hamer, p. 869
8. de facto segregation, p. 871
9. Malcolm X, p. 873
10. Black Power, p. 874

MAIN IDEAS

11. Jim Crow laws, passed in the South, were aimed at separating the races. Application of these laws included separate schools, streetcars, and public restrooms.

12. Rosa Parks was arrested for refusing to give up her bus seat to a white passenger.

13. Jesus' teachings to love one's enemies, Thoreau's concept of civil disobedience, Randolph's techniques for organizing massive demonstrations, Gandhi's use of nonviolent resistance.

14. Meredith won a federal court case allowing him to enroll in the University of Mississippi.

15. *Possible Responses:* Fannie Lou Hamer was beaten trying to register to vote; a bomb in a Birmingham church killed four African-American girls; in Mississippi, Klansmen, with the support of local police, murdered three civil rights activists.

16. King and the SCLC were invited there to help desegregate the city.

17. Black nationalism, self-determination, racial pride, self-respect, the use of self-defense.

18. Leaders felt that the slogan antagonized whites.

19. End of legalized segregation; increased pride in racial identity; more African-American voters, elected officials, and high school and college graduates.

20. De facto segregation, joblessness, and poverty among African Americans.

Chapter 29 Assessment

REVIEWING THE CHAPTER

TERMS & NAMES For each item below, write a sentence explaining its connection to the civil rights movement. For each person or group of people named below, explain his or her role in the movement.

1. *Brown* v. *Board of Education*
2. Rosa Parks
3. Dr. Martin Luther King, Jr.
4. Student Nonviolent Coordinating Committee
5. freedom rider
6. Civil Rights Act of 1964
7. Fannie Lou Hamer
8. de facto segregation
9. Malcolm X
10. Black Power

MAIN IDEAS

SECTION 1 *(pages 856–863)*

Taking on Segregation

11. What were Jim Crow laws and how were they applied?
12. What incident sparked the Montgomery Bus Boycott?
13. What were the roots of Dr. Martin Luther King, Jr.'s beliefs in nonviolent resistance?

SECTION 2 *(pages 864–870)*

The Triumphs of the Crusade

14. What federal court case did James Meredith win in 1962?
15. Cite three examples of violence committed in 1962–1964 against African Americans and civil rights activists.
16. Why did Dr. Martin Luther King, Jr., go to Birmingham, Alabama, in 1963?

SECTION 3 *(pages 871–877)*

Challenges and Changes in the Movement

17. What were some of the key beliefs that Malcolm X advocated?
18. Why did some civil rights leaders urge Stokely Carmichael to stop using the slogan "black power"?
19. What were some accomplishments of the civil rights movement?
20. What challenges still face the nation in the area of civil rights?

THINKING CRITICALLY

1. **MEDIA INFLUENCE** On your own paper, draw a cluster diagram like the one shown below. Then, fill it in with four events from the civil rights movement that were broadcast on nationwide television and that you find the most compelling.

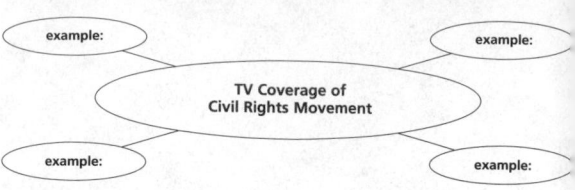

2. **THE CIVIL RIGHTS MOVEMENT** Overall, would you characterize the civil rights struggle as a unified or disunified movement? Explain.

3. **IMMORTAL IDEAS** Reread the quote by Medgar Evers on page 854. Do you agree with his statement? Cite examples from the text that support your answer.

4. **THE GEOGRAPHY OF SCHOOL SEGREGATION** Look carefully at the map of U.S. school segregation, on page 857. What regional differences do you think spurred civil rights activists to target the South before the North?

5. **TRACING THEMES: CIVIL RIGHTS** African Americans and others have pressed for recognition of their civil rights since colonial times. Why do you think the civil rights movement finally achieved success in the 1950s and 1960s?

6. **ANALYZING PRIMARY SOURCES** Read the following excerpt from Malcolm X's speech "Prospects for Freedom in 1965," in which he denounces the police brutality that sparked the 1964 Harlem riot. Then answer the questions that follow.

> An illegal attack, an unjust attack, and an immoral attack can be made against you by any one. Just because a person has on a [police] uniform does not give him the right to come and shoot up your neighborhood. No, this is not right, and my suggestion would be that as long as the police department doesn't use those methods in white neighborhoods, they shouldn't come to Harlem and use them in our neighborhood. . . . It's not intelligent—and it [the Harlem riot] all started when a little boy was shot by a policeman.
>
> **MALCOLM X,** "Prospects for Freedom in 1965"

How does Malcolm X view violent police methods? What other instances might Malcolm X have cited to justify his condemnation of police brutality? Cite examples from the chapter.

THINKING CRITICALLY

1. MEDIA INFLUENCE
Possible Responses: The crisis at Central High School in Little Rock, Arkansas (1957); sit-ins at Greensboro, North Carolina (1960); the second "children's crusade" in Birmingham, Alabama (1963); Fannie Lou Hamer's speech to the Democratic National Convention (1964); the Selma march (1965).

2. THE CIVIL RIGHTS MOVEMENT
Possible Responses: Unified: all civil rights activists shared the same goals—freedom, justice, and equality; gender and age differences were surmounted; the March on Washington was a powerful display of unity. Disunified: violent versus nonviolent methods created divisiveness; Northern blacks and Southern blacks had different needs.

3. IMMORTAL IDEAS
Possible Responses: **Yes:** An idea can live on after a person dies because other people carry it on. **No:** Sometimes the person who believes in it most strongly must live to carry out the idea.

4. THE GEOGRAPHY OF SCHOOL DESEGREGATION
Possible Responses: As the map shows, primarily Southern states, because they segregated schools by law. The legal racism—de jure segregation—of the

ALTERNATIVE ASSESSMENT

1. WRITING A RADIO OR TELEVISION EDITORIAL
The Supreme Court decision in *Brown v. Board of Education* set a new era of civil rights in motion. What did this decision mean in everyday terms? What impact did it have?

Write a script for a radio or television editorial you might have filed in the aftermath of *Brown v. Board of Education*.

 CD-ROM Use the CD-ROM *Electronic Library of Primary Sources* and other reference materials to review documents and issues related to the early civil rights movement.

- Your script should incorporate relevant historical background in addition to an analysis of one or more events. You might also include excerpts from news reports, interviews, and editorials of the day.

2. LEARNING FROM MEDIA
VIDEO View the McDougal Littell Video for Chapter 29, *Justice in Montgomery*. Discuss the following questions with a small group of classmates and then do the **Cooperative Learning** activity.

- According to the video, what role did Jo Ann Gibson Robinson and the African-American women of Montgomery play in the bus boycott?

- In your opinion, what responsibilities does an ordinary person have to stop injustice in his or her community?

Cooperative Learning You have just seen an account of the Montgomery bus boycott through the eyes of one person, Jo Ann Gibson Robinson, though there are many ways to learn about. With your group, decide how you would teach people about the boycott—from what perspective and with what materials. Then create a lesson plan or multimedia presentation to give to the class.

3. PORTFOLIO PROJECT
 Use the Living History activity to expand your portfolio.

LIVING HISTORY

PRESENTING YOUR BIOGRAPHICAL SKETCH
You have written a biographical sketch of a civil rights leader. Now think about how you might revise it, considering the following suggestions:
- Did you provide vivid and precise details?
- Did you use quotes or anecdotes to add interest?
- Did you review your writing for errors and correct them?

Ask a classmate to read the biography and comment on content and organization.

After you have revised the biography, find a suitable photograph of the civil rights leader for your title page. Display the completed biography with those of your classmates. Add the biography to your American history portfolio.

Bridge to Chapter 30

Review Chapter 29

TAKING ON SEGREGATION Following World War II, the NAACP waged a successful campaign to challenge the legality of segregated public education. In 1954, the Supreme Court ruled in *Brown v. Board of Education* that school segregation was unconstitutional. In response, some white Southern officials vowed defiance. In 1957, President Eisenhower was forced to use federal power to integrate Central High School in Little Rock, Arkansas.

An earlier confrontation over segregation occurred in December 1955, when Rosa Parks was arrested in Montgomery, Alabama, for not yielding her bus seat to a white passenger. Under the leadership of Dr. Martin Luther King, Jr., African Americans held a year-long boycott of the city's buses. In late 1956, the Supreme Court outlawed segregation on public transportation.

CIVIL RIGHTS VICTORIES Across the South, activists used nonviolent means to break down racial barriers. Teams of young people staged sit-ins, held freedom rides, and registered black voters in the South. In 1963, thousands of people demonstrated in the March on Washington. Spurred by the mass movement, Congress passed the landmark Civil Rights Act of 1964 and Voting Rights Act of 1965.

CHANGES IN THE MOVEMENT In the North, new leaders emerged—Malcolm X, Stokely Carmichael, Huey Newton, and Bobby Seale—who advocated self-defense and militant tactics. Racial tensions persisted in northern cities, where African Americans faced the problems of deeply entrenched prejudice, police brutality, substandard housing and schools, and high unemployment. These conditions fueled the race riots that erupted in the mid-1960s.

Preview Chapter 30

While civil rights activists fought for equality at home, American soldiers were fighting on the battlefields in far-off Vietnam. Seeking to contain communism in Southeast Asia, the United States gradually increased its military involvement in Vietnam. You will learn about these and other significant developments in the next chapter.

Civil Rights **881**

ALTERNATIVE ASSESSMENT

1. WRITING AN EDITORIAL
Standards for Evaluation
An editorial should meet the following criteria:
- Takes a clear stand on the *Brown* decision.
- Incorporates relevant historical background from the civil rights movement.
- Accurately portrays contemporary arguments for and against the opinion.

2. LEARNING FROM MEDIA
Answer to the question:
- Robinson and the Women's Political Council called a one-day boycott on the day of Parks's trial. This started the year-long boycott. According to Robinson, if "people ask me about the boycott, I tell them, 'The black women did it.' And we did."

Standards for Evaluation
Teaching the Montgomery Bus Boycott

A lesson plan should meet the following criteria:
- Explains which materials should be used and why they were chosen.
- Mentions major aspects of the boycott including the history of segregation in Montgomery, the groups that organized the boycott, the groups that opposed it, and the leaders who emerged from the boycott.

A multimedia presentation should meet the following criteria:
- Uses a variety of media including photos, video, transcripts, and journals.
- Mentions all major aspects of the boycott.

3. PORTFOLIO PROJECT
LIVING HISTORY
Standards for Evaluation
Biographical sketches should meet the following criteria:
- Show the importance of the civil rights leader.
- Provide concrete details about the person's life.
- Show evidence of research from a variety of sources.

IN-DEPTH RESOURCES: UNIT 8
See the form for scoring this activity on page 17.

THINKING CRITICALLY

South was easier to tackle than the more subtle racism—de facto segregation—of the North.

5. TRACING THEMES: CIVIL RIGHTS
Students might suggest some of the following factors: The impact of World War II on American society in raising African-American consciousness; actions by Franklin Roosevelt and later presidents in the area of civil rights; the *Brown* decision; effective organizing efforts of black churches; the successful leadership and tactics of Thurgood Marshall, Martin Luther King, Jr., and others; the influence of television and the national media; the emergence of youth activism among college students, both African American and white.

6. ANALYZING PRIMARY SOURCES
Possible Responses: As illegal, unjust, and immoral; as unjustifiably excessive; as a violation of the rights of citizens they are apprehending; as racially biased. Other examples of police brutality that Malcolm X might have cited include the tactics that Bull Connor's police force used against young demonstrators in Birmingham (May 1963); police support of Klansmen who murdered three civil rights activists (June 1964); police who forced prisoners to beat Fannie Lou Hamer after she was jailed for trying to register to vote (1962).

	Key Ideas	**TEACHING SUPPORT**	**ASSESSMENT**
SECTION 1 Moving Toward Conflict *pp. 884–888*	America slowly involves itself in the war in Vietnam as it seeks to halt the spread of communism.	**In-Depth Resources: Unit 8** • Guided Reading, p. 35 **COOPERATIVE ACTIVITY** • Researching Buddhism, p. 886 (TE)	*Section 1 Assessment,* p. 888 (PE) *Self-Assessment,* p. 888 (TE) *Formal Assessment* • Section Quiz, p. 363 *Alternative Assessment Book* • Standards for Evaluating a Cooperative Activity
SECTION 2 U.S. Involvement and Escalation *pp. 889–894*	The United States sends troops to fight in Vietnam, but the war quickly turns into a stalemate.	**In-Depth Resources: Unit 8** • Guided Reading, p. 36 • Skillbuilder Practice: Distinguishing Fact from Opinion, p. 40 • Primary Source: Letter from a soldier in Vietnam, p. 45 • American Lives: Robert McNamara, p. 52 **COOPERATIVE ACTIVITY** • Simulating a TV Interview, p. 893 (TE)	*Section 2 Assessment,* p. 894 (PE) *Self-Assessment,* p. 894 (TE) *Formal Assessment* • Section Quiz, p. 364 *Alternative Assessment Book* • Standards for Evaluating a Cooperative Activity
SECTION 3 A Nation Divided *pp. 895–900*	An antiwar movement emerges in the United States, pitting those who oppose the government's war policy against those who support it.	**In-Depth Resources: Unit 8** • Guided Reading, p. 37 • Primary Sources: Protest buttons, p. 46; The New Left, p. 47 **COOPERATIVE ACTIVITY** • Composing "Hawk" or "Dove" Song Lyrics, p. 899 (TE)	*Section 3 Assessment,* p. 900 (PE) *Self-Assessment,* p. 900 (TE) *Formal Assessment* • Section Quiz, p. 365 *Alternative Assessment Book* • Standards for Evaluating a Cooperative Activity
SECTION 4 1968: A Tumultuous Year *pp. 901–906*	A shocking enemy attack in Vietnam, two assassinations, and a chaotic political convention help make 1968 the most explosive year of the decade.	**In-Depth Resources: Unit 8** • Guided Reading, p. 38 • Geography Application: The Ho Chi Minh Trail, p. 41 • Primary Source: Lyndon B. Johnson on Vietnam, p. 48 • American Lives: John Lewis, p. 53 **COOPERATIVE ACTIVITY** • Creating a 1968 Yearbook, p. 905 (TE)	*Section 4 Assessment,* p. 906 (PE) *Self-Assessment,* p. 906 (TE) *Formal Assessment* • Section Quiz, p. 366 *Alternative Assessment Book* • Standards for Evaluating a Cooperative Activity
SECTION 5 The End of the War and Its Legacy *pp. 907–913*	The nation's longest war ends after nearly ten years and leaves a lasting impact on U.S. policy and American society.	**In-Depth Resources: Unit 8** • Guided Reading, p. 39 • Outline Map: The Vietnam War, p. 43 • Literature: from *In Country* by Bobbie Ann Mason, p. 49 **COOPERATIVE ACTIVITY** • Writing Editorials, p. 909 (TE)	*Section 4 Assessment,* p. 913 (PE) *Self-Assessment,* p. 913 (TE) *Formal Assessment* • Section Quiz, p. 367 *Alternative Assessment Book* • Standards for Evaluating a Cooperative Activity
CHAPTER RESOURCES	**Chapter Overview** The United States enters a war in Vietnam, which results in the deaths of tens of thousands of American soldiers, the division of society into bitterly opposed camps, and a lasting impact on U.S. foreign policy.	**In-Depth Resources: Unit 8** • Living History Project: Worksheet, p. 54; Standards, p. 55 *Telescoping the Times* • Chapter Summary, pp. 59–60 *Planning for Block Schedules*	*Chapter Assessment,* pp. 916–917 (PE) *Alternative Assessment,* p. 917 (PE) *Formal Assessment* • Chapter Test, forms A and B, pp. 368–371 ⌨ **Test Generator** *Alternative Assessment Book* See explanation and forms for different kinds of alternative assessments including portfolio assessment.

The War in Vietnam
- Geneva accords
- Domino principle

Electronic Library of Primary Sources
- The Tonkin Gulf Resolution

INTERNET RESOURCES
- See *McDougal Littell Learning On-Line* for links to information about the history of Vietnam.

 The War in Vietnam
- Agent Orange
- Deforestation

Electronic Library of Primary Sources
- from "Peace Without Conquest" by Lyndon Johnson

INTERNET RESOURCES
- See *McDougal Littell Learning On-Line* for links to information about Robert McNamara.

 AMERICAN STORIES VIDEO SERIES
- "Matters of Conscience"

INTERNET RESOURCES
- See *McDougal Littell Learning On-Line* for links to information about women in Vietnam.

 Critical Thinking Transparencies
- CT64, Impact of Tet Offensive

 The War in Vietnam
- Tet Offensive

Electronic Library of Primary Sources
- from *The Strategy of Confrontation*

INTERNET RESOURCES
- See *McDougal Littell Learning On-Line* for links to information about the Tet offensive.

 Humanities Transparencies
- H28, Fall of Saigon
- H45, The Blind Leading the Blind

Geography Transparencies
- G30, Vietnam War: 1964–1975

Critical Thinking Transparencies
- CT30, The War in Vietnam

 The War in Vietnam
- from *The Pentagon Papers*

 American Portfolio: A Videodisc for U.S. History, user's guide, pp. 244–245, 251–253, 255

INTERNET RESOURCES
Learning On-Line: Social Studies
http://www.mcdougallittell.com

Block Scheduling (90 MINUTES)

Day 1
Section 1, pp. 884–888
Section 2, pp. 889–894
Section Assessments, pp. 888, 894

Day 2
Section 3, pp. 895–900
 AMERICAN STORIES VIDEO SERIES
"Matters of Conscience"
Section 4, pp. 901–906
Section Assessments, pp. 900, 906

Day 3
Section 5, pp. 907–913
American Studies: Literature of the Vietnam War, pp. 914–915
Chapter Assessment, pp. 916–917

YEARLY PACING *Chapter 30 Total:* 3 days *Yearly Total:* 85 days

See *Planning for Block Schedules* for special activities and pacing strategies.

Customizing for Special Populations

Students Acquiring English

Access for Students Acquiring English
- Guided Reading for Sections 1–5 (Spanish), pp. 289–293
- Chapter Summary (Spanish), pp. 287–288
- Skillbuilder Practice: Distinguishing Fact from Opinion (Spanish), p. 294
- Geography Application: The Ho Chi Minh Trail (Spanish), p. 295–296
- Outline Map: The Vietnam War (Spanish), p. 297–298

 AMERICAN STORIES VIDEO SERIES
- "Matters of Conscience"

INTERNET RESOURCES
- See *McDougal Littell Learning On-Line* The Diverse Classroom.

Less Proficient Readers

In-Depth Resources: Unit 8
- Guided Reading for Sections 1–5, pp. 35–39
- Skillbuilder: Distinguishing Fact from Opinion, p. 40
- Geography Application: The Ho Chi Minh Trail, p. 41
- Outline Map: The Vietnam War, p. 43

Telescoping the Times
- Chapter Summary, pp. 59–60

See additional strategies at point of use in the Teacher's Edition.

Gifted and Talented Students

In-Depth Resources: Unit 8
- Primary Sources: Letter from a soldier in Vietnam, p. 45; Protest Buttons, p. 46; The New Left, p. 47; Lyndon B. Johnson on Vietnam, p. 48
- American Lives: Robert McNamara, p. 52; John Lewis, p. 53

See additional strategies at point of use in the Teacher's Edition.

Connections to Literature READINGS FOR STUDENTS

In-Depth Resources: Unit 8
- from *In Country* by Bobbie Ann Mason, p. 49

McDougal Littell *The Language of Literature*
American Literature
- Estela Portillo Trambley, "Village," p. 937
- George Olsen, from *Dear America: Letters Home from Vietnam,* p. 945
- Yusef Komunyakaa, "Camouflaging the Chimera," p.949
- Wendy Wilder Larsen and Tran Thi Nga, "Deciding," p. 949
- Tim O'Brien, "Ambush," p. 956
- Lanford Wilson, "Wandering," p. 972
- Denise Levertov, "At the Justice Department, November 15, 1969," p. 979

McDougal Littell *Literature Connections*

- Walter Dean Myers *Fallen Angels* (with related readings) This novel presents the experiences of a small group of men who come of age in the Vietnam War. Richie Perry enlists in the army mainly to escape his problems at home and finds himself in the middle of a war that is more traumatic and confusing than the life he fled.

The Vietnam War Years

▶ **Starting with the Student**
Ask students what they know about the Vietnam War, especially its causes and effects both in Vietnam and America. Then discuss the opening quotation.

- What might Kissinger have meant by an exorbitant price?

PREVIEWING THE CHAPTER

- Ask students to examine the time line and to discuss the historical figures and events that they already know about.
- Have students preview the terms and names listed at the beginning of each section and categorize them in a three-column chart, under the headings "Familiar," "Somewhat Familiar," and "Unfamiliar." Tell them to focus, as they read the chapter, on the terms and names that they listed in the second and third columns.

MORE ABOUT . . .
Henry Kissinger

A Harvard professor of government and an authority on U.S. security policy, Kissinger joined the Nixon administration as national security advisor and later became Nixon's secretary of state. For his work as chief U.S. negotiator in the Vietnam peace talks, Kissinger was awarded the 1973 Nobel Peace Prize.

882 Chapter 30

CHAPTER
30 The Vietnam War Years

SECTION 1
Moving Toward Conflict

America slowly involves itself in the war in Vietnam as it seeks to halt the spread of communism.

SECTION 2
U.S. Involvement and Escalation

The United States sends troops to fight in Vietnam, but the war quickly turns into a stalemate.

SECTION 3
A Nation Divided

An antiwar movement emerges in the United States, pitting those who oppose the government's war policy against those who support it.

 VIDEO *MATTERS OF CONSCIENCE*

SECTION 4
1968: A Tumultuous Year

A shocking enemy attack in Vietnam, two assassinations, and a chaotic political convention help make 1968 the most explosive year of the decade.

SECTION 5
The End of the War and Its Legacy

The nation's longest war ends after nearly ten years and leaves a lasting impact on U.S. policy and American society.

882 CHAPTER 30

"Vietnam is still with us. . . . We paid an exorbitant price for the decisions that were made."

Henry Kissinger

THE UNITED STATES

United States begins providing economic aid to South Vietnam

⭐ Dwight D. Eisenhower is reelected president.

● President Eisenhower sends federal troops to enforce school desegregation in Little Rock.

⭐ John F. Kennedy is elected president.

Lyndon B. Johnson becomes president upon the assassination of John F. Kennedy.

Congress passes Tonkin Gulf Resolution in response to North Vietnamese torpedo attacks.

Lyndon B. ⭐ Johnson is elected president.

1954 1955 1956 1957 1960 1963

THE WORLD 1957 1962 1964

● Vietminh defeat French at Dien Bien Phu.

● The National Liberation Front, or Vietcong, forms in South Vietnam.

The African ● nation of Uganda becomes independent.

Palestine ● Liberation Organization forms in the Middle East.

THEMES IN CHAPTER 30

Expanding Democracy	*Constitutional Concerns*	*Civil Rights*	*Cultural Diversity*
America's mission in Vietnam was to halt the spread of communism—a threat to democracy. Ironically, the South Vietnamese regimes that the U.S. supported were not very democratic themselves. See Teacher's Edition note, p. 887.	Among the constitutional issues of the Vietnam War era were the president's powers as commander in chief and First Amendment rights. Both the Tonkin Gulf Resolution and the release of the Pentagon Papers sparked controversy. See Teacher's Edition notes, pp. 887, 910.	Initially, mainstream civil rights leaders were reluctant to criticize the Vietnam War, fearing they would jeopardize President Johnson's support for their cause. When the war threatened Great Society reforms, Dr. Martin Luther King, Jr., and other civil rights leaders voiced their opposition. See Teacher's Edition note, p. 896.	Many Vietnamese refugees seeking a homeland in the United States at the end of the war developed a cultural identity that was a blend of two traditions—Vietnamese and American. See Teacher's Edition note, p. 912.

LIVING HISTORY

CREATING A VIETNAM WAR POSTER

In the 1960s and early 1970s, the American people viewed images of the Vietnam War and its effects in newspapers, magazines, and on television. Many of these images have remained forever in the minds of those who saw them. Create a poster that graphically depicts an aspect of the Vietnam War. Focus on a particular theme or time period of the war, using ideas presented in the chapter and images and scenes from outside sources. Consider the following suggestions as you develop your poster:

- Look for photographs of the war in newspapers, micro-film, magazines, and books.
- Look for appropriate quotes from veterans and government leaders.
- Use a computer to create captions.
- Experiment with arrangements of the visual images, quotes, and captions before affixing them to the poster.
- Add hand-drawn or painted designs or images.

📁 **PORTFOLIO PROJECT** Save your poster in a folder for your American history portfolio. You will display and share your poster at the end of the chapter.

Lyndon B. Johnson announces he will not seek reelection.

LIVING HISTORY

Offer students these suggestions for planning and creating their posters:

- Think about what you would like to communicate visually about the Vietnam War. Skim the photos and other illustrations in the chapter for ideas.
- Choose a theme or time period to help organize and guide your research.
- Investigate a variety of print sources for appropriate images.
- Create a thumbnail layout—a plan or design that shows the rough arrangement of the graphics and the words.
- Consider the reaction you want viewers to have when they see your poster.

Planning Guide

Step 1	Students choose a theme or time period.
Step 2	Students research several sources for images.
Step 3	Students create a rough layout.
Step 4	Students place their final posters in their portfolios.

IN-DEPTH RESOURCES: UNIT 8
See worksheet and standards for evaluation, pp. 54, 55.

Timeline (top):
- First U.S. ground troops arrive in Vietnam.
- U.S. troops quell uprising in Dominican Republic.
- Antiwar protests intensify.
- ★ Richard M. Nixon is elected president.
- The Vietcong launch the Tet offensive.
- Martin Luther King, Jr., and Robert Kennedy are assassinated.
- U.S. troops begin withdrawal from Vietnam.
- Ohio National Guardsmen shoot and kill four students at Kent State University.
- President Nixon orders an invasion of Cambodia.
- ★ Richard M. Nixon is reelected.
- United States signs cease-fire with North Vietnam and Vietcong, ending U.S. involvement in Vietnam War.
- ★ Gerald R. Ford becomes president after Richard Nixon resigns.

1965 1966 1967 1968 1969 1970 1972 1973 1974 **1975**

Timeline (bottom):
- Mao Zedong begins Cultural Revolution in China.
- French students stage massive protests and strikes in Paris.
- Salvador Allende, a Marxist, is elected president of Chile.
- Ferdinand Marcos declares martial law in the Philippines.
- Saigon falls; South Vietnam surrenders to the Communists.

The Vietnam War Years **883**

RECOMMENDED RESOURCES

Books for the Teacher
Goldman, Eric F. *The Tragedy of Lyndon Johnson.* New York: Knopf, 1969. Johnson's presidency, including the impact of the Vietnam War.

Karnow, Stanley. *Vietnam.* New York: Viking, 1983. Thorough survey of the Vietnam War.

Wells, Tom. *The War Within.* New York: Holt, 1994. Polarization of American society over Vietnam.

Books for the Student
Caputo, Philip. *A Rumor of War.* New York: Ballantine, 1977. Compelling combat memoir.

McNamara, Robert. *In Retrospect.* New York: Vintage, 1995. Former secretary of defense's later thoughts on war.

Terry, Wallace. *Bloods.* New York: Ballantine, 1984. African-American veterans' oral histories of the Vietnam War.

Videos
Chicago 1968. PBS Home Video, 1995. Story of Democratic convention.

Fall of Saigon. Discovery Channel Home Video. Last days of South Vietnam.

No Time for Tears: Vietnam—The Women Who Served. West End Films, 1993. Documentary about women's experiences in Vietnam.

Vietnam: A Television History. PBS Video, 1983. Award-winning documentary in 13 parts.

Software
Passage to Vietnam. CD-ROM. Against All Odds/Interval Research, 1995.

The Wall. CD-ROM. Magnet Interactive, 1995.

The War in Vietnam: A Multimedia Chronicle. CD-ROM. Macmillan Digital, 212-654-8500.

OBJECTIVES

① To summarize Vietnam's history as a French colony and its struggle for independence.

② To examine how the United States became involved in the Vietnam conflict.

③ To describe the expansion of U.S. military involvement under President Johnson.

SKILLBUILDER

• Understanding geography: movement, location, p. 886

CRITICAL THINKING

• Analyzing motives, p. 885
• Analyzing causes, pp. 886, 888
• Summarizing, pp. 887, 888
• Analyzing effects, p. 888
• Forming opinions, p. 888

FOCUS & MOTIVATE

▶ *Starting with the Student*
Ask students if they have ever tried to solve a problem that grew ever more complicated and more difficult to solve.

• How might the same thing happen in a diplomatic or military situation?

OBJECTIVE
① **INSTRUCT**

The Roots of American Involvement

▶ *Discussing Key Ideas*
• France rules Indochina from the late 1800s until World War II.
• Ho Chi Minh declares Vietnam independent in 1945.
• To halt communism, Truman and Eisenhower provide economic aid to France.
• The Geneva Accords of 1954 temporarily divide Vietnam into North Vietnam and South Vietnam.

(continued on next page)

---

① **Moving Toward Conflict**

TERMS & NAMES
• Ho Chi Minh
• Vietminh
• domino theory
• Dien Bien Phu
• Geneva Accords
• Ngo Dinh Diem
• Vietcong
• Ho Chi Minh Trail
• Tonkin Gulf Resolution

LEARN ABOUT the early measures the United States took to stop the spread of communism in Vietnam
TO UNDERSTAND how America slowly became involved in a war in Vietnam.

ONE AMERICAN'S STORY

On the morning of September 26, 1945, Lieutenant Colonel A. Peter Dewey, the son of an Illinois congressman, was on his way to the Saigon airport in the southeast Asian country of Vietnam. Only 28, Dewey served in the Office of Strategic Services, the chief intelligence-gathering body of the U.S. military and forerunner of the Central Intelligence Agency. Dewey had gone to Vietnam, which had recently been freed from Japanese rule during World War II, to assess what was becoming an explosive situation.

The Vietnamese, who had resisted Japanese occupation, now were preparing to fight the French. France, which until World War II had ruled Vietnam and its surrounding countries, sought—with British aid—to regain control of the region. Dewey saw nothing but disaster in this plan. "Cochinchina [southern Vietnam] is burning," he reported, "the French and British are finished here, and we [the United States] ought to clear out of Southeast Asia."

On his way to the airport, Dewey encountered a roadblock manned by several Vietnamese soldiers and made the fatal mistake of shouting at them in French. Presumably mistaking him for a French soldier, the Vietnamese guards shot him in the head. A. Peter Dewey, whose body was never recovered, was thus the first American to die in Vietnam.

Unfortunately, Dewey would not be the last. As Vietnam's independence effort came under Communist influence, the United States grew increasingly concerned about the small country's future. Eventually, America would fight a war to halt the spread of communism in Vietnam. The war would claim the lives of almost 60,000 Americans and more than 1.5 million Vietnamese. It also would divide the American nation as no other event since the Civil War.

Lieutenant Colonel
A. Peter Dewey

The Roots of American Involvement

America's involvement in Vietnam began in 1950, during the French Indochina War, the name given to France's attempt to reestablish its rule in Vietnam after World War II. Seeking to strengthen its ties with France and help fight the spread of communism, the United States provided the French with massive amounts of economic and military support.

FRENCH RULE IN VIETNAM From the late 1800s until World War II—when the Japanese took over the area—France ruled Indochina, which consisted of Vietnam and neighboring Laos and Cambodia. French colonists took much of the land from the peasants and built large plantations, from which they extracted a large portion of the country's rice and rubber for their own profit. This situation sparked growing unrest among Vietnamese peasants, which in turn prompted a harsh French response. French rulers restricted freedom of speech and assembly and jailed many Vietnamese nationalists. These measures, however, failed to curb all dissent, as the Vietnamese staged several revolts and strikes during the 1930s.

The Indochinese Communist Party, founded in 1929, organized most of the uprisings. The party's leader was **Ho Chi Minh**, a thin, middle-aged man who sported a trademark goatee. Ho Chi Minh, whom the French had condemned to

884 CHAPTER 30

 SECTION 1 RESOURCES

PRINT RESOURCES

IN-DEPTH RESOURCES: UNIT 8
Guided Reading, p. 35

ACCESS FOR STUDENTS ACQUIRING ENGLISH
Guided Reading (Spanish), p. 289

FORMAL ASSESSMENT
Section Quiz, p. 363

ALTERNATIVE ASSESSMENT BOOK
See forms for supporting and scoring alternative activities.

 TECHNOLOGY RESOURCES

CD-ROM Electronic Library of Primary Sources
The War in Vietnam

VIDEO *American Portfolio: A Videodisc for U.S. History*
user's guide, pp. 244–245

INTERNET McDougal Littell Learning On-Line
http://www.mcdougallittell.com

death in 1930 for his rebellious activity, fled Vietnam that year. However, throughout the 1930s, Ho Chi Minh orchestrated Vietnam's growing independence movement from exile in the Soviet Union and later from China.

In 1941, a year after the Japanese took control of Vietnam, Ho Chi Minh returned home. That year, the Vietnamese Communists combined with other nationalist groups to form an organization called the **Vietminh.** The group sought Vietnam's independence from foreign rule. When the Allied defeat of Japan in August of 1945 forced the Japanese to leave Vietnam, that goal suddenly seemed a reality. On September 2, 1945, Ho Chi Minh stood in the middle of a huge crowd in the northern city of Hanoi and declared Vietnam an independent nation.

FRANCE BATTLES THE VIETMINH France, however, had no intention of relinquishing its former colony. French troops moved back into Vietnam in 1946, eventually driving the Vietminh out of the cities and regaining control of the country's southern half. Ho Chi Minh vowed to fight from the North to liberate the South from French control. "If ever the tiger pauses," Ho had said, referring to the Vietminh, "the elephant [France] will impale him on his mighty tusks. But the tiger will not pause, and the elephant will die of exhaustion and loss of blood."

In 1950, the United States entered the Vietnam struggle. That year, President Truman sent nearly $20 million in economic aid to France. Over the next four years the United States paid for much of France's war, pumping nearly $2.6 billion into the effort to defeat a man America had once supported. Ironically, during World War II, the United States had forged an alliance with Ho Chi Minh, supplying him with aid to resist the Japanese.

By 1950, however, Cold War fever had gripped much of the world. China and Eastern Europe had fallen to the Communists, and Korea appeared to be next. America saw a dual benefit in supporting France: maintaining an ally against the growing Soviet presence in Europe, and helping to stop another Asian country from turning Communist. While Ho Chi Minh promoted his cause as one of independence, the United States now saw their one-time ally as a Communist aggressor.

THE VIETMINH DRIVE OUT THE FRENCH Upon entering the White House in 1953, President Eisenhower continued the policy of supplying aid to the French war effort. By this time, the United States had settled for a stalemate with the Communists in Korea, which only stiffened America's resolve to halt the spread of communism. During a news conference in 1954, Eisenhower explained the **domino theory,** in which he likened the countries on the brink of communism to a row of dominoes, waiting to fall one after the other. "You have a row of dominoes set up," the president said. "You knock over the first one, and what will happen to the last one is the certainty that it will go over very quickly."

Despite massive U.S. aid, however, the French could not retake Vietnam. The final blow came in May of 1954, when the Vietminh overran the French outpost at **Dien Bien Phu** in northwestern Vietnam. Led by General Vo Nguyen Giap, the Vietminh surrounded the fort and pounded it with heavy artillery for nearly two months. Major Paul Grauwin of the French army described the outpost's morgue on the first night of heavy bombardment.

A PERSONAL VOICE
The square hole was full [of dead]; outside, between the hole and the barbed wire, there were a hundred corpses, pell-mell, thrown on stretchers or onto the ground, stiffened in grotesque or tragic positions. Some were wrapped and tied in their tent cloth; others were dressed in their combat uniforms, motionless in the pose where death had surprised them.
MAJOR PAUL GRAUWIN, quoted in *Dien Bien Phu*

THINK THROUGH HISTORY
A. *Analyzing Motives* Why did the United States provide military aid to France?

A. Answer To keep France as an ally against the Soviet Union in Europe and to keep communism from spreading to another Asian country.

KEY PLAYER

HO CHI MINH
1890–1969
Born Nguyen Tat Thanh to a poor family, Ho Chi Minh (which means "He Who Enlightens") found early work as a cook on a French steamship, which allowed him to visit such cities as Boston and New York. During World War I, Ho Chi Minh moved to France, where he worked as a gardener, waiter, photo retoucher, and oven stoker.

Ho Chi Minh, who ruled North Vietnam from 1954 until his death in 1969, was revered by his countrymen as the benevolent "Uncle Ho." During his reign, however, he advocated one-party rule and repressed all opposition.

The Communist ruler's name lived on after his death. In 1975, the North Vietnamese Army conquered South Vietnam and changed the name of the South's capital from Saigon to Ho Chi Minh City.

The Vietnam War Years **885**

(continued from page 884)

IN-DEPTH RESOURCES: UNIT 8
Guided Reading. p. 35
ACCESS FOR STUDENTS ACQUIRING ENGLISH
Guided Reading (Spanish), p. 289

THE WAR IN VIETNAM
Eisenhower introduces "falling domino" principle
Address on the Geneva Accords by John Dulles

KEY PLAYER
Ho Chi Minh
Critical Thinking: Analyzing Motives Ask students why they think many Vietnamese revered Ho Chi Minh. *Possible Responses: He was a freedom fighter against the French and Japanese; he initiated economic policies that improved the lot of the poor; despite repression, his rule was an improvement over colonial French and Japanese occupation.*

MORE ABOUT . . .
Ho Chi Minh
Despite Ho Chi Minh's Communist beliefs and strong ties to the Soviets and Chinese, he still admired the democratic values of the United States while it was an ally against the Japanese during World War II. On proclaiming Vietnamese independence in 1945, Ho Chi Minh echoed the Declaration of Independence: "All men are born equal: the Creator has given us inviolable rights, life, liberty, and happiness. . . ." Over the next few months he sent repeated messages to President Truman, trying to win U.S. support for an independent Vietnam.

TEACHING OPTIONS

Making Connections Across Cultures

Chinese Influence in Vietnam Foreign domination of Vietnam did not begin with the French. After conquering Vietnam in 111 B.C., the Chinese ruled there for over a thousand years. They introduced their ideographic writing system, the Buddhist religion, and the cultivation of rice. This crop shaped the Vietnamese landscape—small villages set in rice fields surrounded by irrigation ditches, with jungles bordering the cultivated areas. Rebelling against Chinese rule, the Vietnamese won independence in A.D. 939. However, in subsequent centuries they often had to fight off further Chinese attempts at domination.

Making Global Connections

America and the Cold War The U.S. decision to assist France in its fight to retake Vietnam stemmed from American global concerns during the Cold War era. As the Iron Curtain descended in eastern Europe, the United States could not afford to antagonize France, an important European ally against Soviet encroachments in that region. In Asia, the fall of China to communism in the late 1940s intensified Western fears of the growing threat of Communist power worldwide, and the spread of communism to North Korea gave additional support to the domino theory.

Indochina, 1959

CHINA

BURMA
Dien Bien Phu
NORTH VIETNAM
Hanoi
Red River
20° N
Gulf of Tonkin
LAOS
Vientiane
17th Parallel
THAILAND
Hue
Da Nang
15° N
Mekong River
Bangkok
CAMBODIA
Ho Chi Minh Trail
SOUTH VIETNAM
Phnom Penh
Saigon
10° N
Gulf of Thailand
South China Sea

0   200 Miles
0   400 Kilometers

GEOGRAPHY SKILLBUILDER
MOVEMENT *Through which countries did the Ho Chi Minh Trail pass?* **LOCATION** *How might North Vietnam's location better enable it to get aid from its ally, China?*

The Vietcong saw the United States and South Vietnam as oppressors. This Vietcong propaganda poster reads, "Better death than slavery."

越南必胜！美国必败！

886 CHAPTER 30

After the fall of Dien Bien Phu, the French surrendered and began to pull out of Vietnam. From May through July 1954, the countries of France, Great Britain, the Soviet Union, the United States, China, Laos, and Cambodia met in Geneva, Switzerland, with the Vietminh and with the South Vietnam's anti-Communist nationalists to hammer out a peace agreement. The **Geneva Accords** temporarily divided Vietnam along the 17th parallel. The Communists and their leader, Ho Chi Minh, controlled North Vietnam from the capital of Hanoi. The anti-Communist nationalists controlled South Vietnam from the port city of Saigon. An election to unify the country was called for in 1956.

The United States Steps In

In the wake of France's retreat, the United States took a more active role in halting the spread of communism in Vietnam. Wading deeper into the country's affairs, the administrations of President Eisenhower and then President John F. Kennedy provided economic and military aid to South Vietnam's non-Communist regime.

DIEM CANCELS ELECTIONS Although he directed a brutal and repressive regime, Ho Chi Minh won popular support in the North by breaking up large estates and redistributing land to peasants. Moreover, his years of fighting the Japanese and French had made him a national hero. Recognizing Ho Chi Minh's widespread popularity, South Vietnam's president, **Ngo Dinh Diem,** a strong anti-Communist, refused to take part in the countrywide election of 1956. The United States also sensed that a countrywide election might spell victory for Ho Chi Minh and therefore supported the cancellation of elections. The Eisenhower administration promised military aid and training to Diem in return for a stable reform government in the South.

Diem, however, failed to hold up his end of the bargain. He ushered in a corrupt government that suppressed opposition of any kind and offered little or no land distribution to peasants. In addition, Diem, a devout Catholic, angered the country's large Buddhist population by restricting Buddhist practices.

By 1957, a Communist opposition group in the South, known as the **Vietcong,** had begun attacks on the Diem government, assassinating thousands of South Vietnamese government officials. While the group would later be called the National Liberation Front (NLF), the United States continued to refer to the guerrilla fighters as the Vietcong.

Ho Chi Minh expressed his support for the group, which had strong Communist ties. In 1959, Ho Chi Minh began supplying military arms to the Vietcong from North Vietnam via a network of paths along the border of Vietnam, Laos, and Cambodia that became known as the **Ho Chi Minh Trail.** (See map above.) As the guerrilla attacks increased, South Vietnam grew more unstable. The Eisenhower administration took little action, however, deciding to "sink or swim with Ngo Dinh Diem."

KENNEDY AND VIETNAM The Kennedy administration, which entered the White House in 1961, also chose initially to "swim" with Diem. However, Kennedy was wary of accusations that Democrats were "soft" on

Skillbuilder Answer: **Movement:** Laos and Cambodia. **Location:** *Possible response:* China could easily deliver military and other supplies to North Vietnam.

THINK THROUGH HISTORY
B. *Analyzing Causes Why did the United States support the cancellation of Vietnam's unifying elections?*

B. Answer Because it appeared that Ho Chi Minh would win the election and possibly unify Vietnam under communism.

communism. Therefore, he increased financial aid to Diem's teetering regime and sent thousands of soldiers and military advisers to help train South Vietnamese troops in their battle against the NLF. By the end of 1963, almost 16,000 U.S. military personnel were in South Vietnam.

Meanwhile, Diem's popularity plummeted because of ongoing corruption and lack of land reform. To combat the growing Vietcong presence in the South's countryside, the Diem administration initiated the strategic hamlet program, which meant moving all villagers to protected areas. Many Vietnamese deeply resented being moved from their home villages where they had lived for generations and where ancestors were buried.

A Buddhist monk sets himself on fire in a busy Saigon intersection in 1963 as a protest against the Diem regime.

THINK THROUGH HISTORY
C. Summarizing
Why was the Diem regime so unpopular?

C. Answer
Corruption, repressive tactics, and persecution of Buddhists.

Diem also intensified his attack on Buddhism. Fed up with continuing Buddhist demonstrations, the South Vietnamese ruler imprisoned hundreds of Buddhist clerics and destroyed their temples. To protest, several Buddhist monks and nuns publicly burned themselves to death. Horrified, American officials urged Diem to stop the persecutions, but Diem refused.

It had become clear that for South Vietnam to remain stable, Diem would have to go. On November 1, 1963, a U.S.-supported military coup toppled Diem's regime. Against Kennedy's wishes, Diem was executed. A few weeks later, Kennedy too fell to an assassin's bullet. The presidency—along with the growing crisis in Vietnam—now belonged to Lyndon B. Johnson.

President Johnson Expands the Conflict

Shortly before his death, Kennedy had announced his intent to withdraw U.S. forces from South Vietnam. "In the final analysis, it's their war," he declared. Whether Kennedy would have in fact withdrawn from Vietnam remains a matter of debate. However, Lyndon Johnson escalated—or increased—the nation's role in Vietnam and eventually began what would become America's longest war.

THE SOUTH GROWS MORE UNSTABLE Diem's death brought more chaos to South Vietnam. A string of military leaders attempted to lead the country, but each regime was more unstable and inefficient than Diem's had been. Meanwhile, the Vietcong's influence in the countryside steadily grew.

To President Johnson, a Communist takeover of South Vietnam would be disastrous. As a Democratic president, Lyndon Johnson was particularly sensitive to being perceived as "soft" on communism. A Democrat, Harry Truman, had been president when China fell to the Communist Party in 1948, unleashing charges by some Republicans that the Democrats had "lost" China. In addition, many of Senator Joseph McCarthy's charges during the 1950s of Communist infiltrators in America had been directed against Democrats. For these political reasons, Johnson wanted to avoid being accused of "losing" Vietnam. "If I . . . let the Communists take over South Vietnam," Johnson said, "then . . . my nation would be seen as an appeaser, and we would find it impossible to accomplish anything . . . anywhere on the entire globe."

The Vietnam War Years **887**

MORE ABOUT . . .
Ngo Dinh Diem

Ngo Dinh Diem was ill equipped to handle the changing times in his homeland. Along with his devout Catholicism, his Confucian training stressed obedience above all things. He had little understanding of either democracy or communism and, despite all the U.S. aid, little trust for anyone outside his family. In 1955, the British writer Graham Greene described Diem as "separated from the people by cardinals and police cars with wailing sirens and foreign advisers droning of global strategy."

OBJECTIVE
③ INSTRUCT

President Johnson Expands the Conflict

▶ **Starting with the Student** Have students describe media images of politically unstable countries today.

• How do the situations in these countries compare with the growing unrest in Vietnam?

▶ **Discussing Key Ideas**
• Diem's successors fail to curb the Vietcong's influence in South Vietnam.
• The Tonkin Gulf Resolution of 1964 grants President Johnson broad military powers in Vietnam.
• In February 1965, President Johnson escalates U.S. involvement in Vietnam.

 ELECTRONIC LIBRARY OF PRIMARY SOURCES
The Tonkin Gulf Resolution

TEACHING OPTIONS

Exploring Themes

Expanding Democracy U.S. involvement in Vietnam was a mission to halt the spread of communism—perceived as a threat to democracy and free-market economies. Le Ly Hayslip (1949–), who grew up in central Vietnam, saw the struggle from a different perspective. In her autobiography *When Heaven and Earth Changed Places,* she wrote, "For you [American GI's], it was a simple thing: democracy against communism. For us, that was not our fight at all. How could it be? We knew little democracy and even less about communism. For most of us, it was a fight for independence—like the American Revolution."

Exploring Themes

Constitutional Concerns The Tonkin Gulf Resolution (see page 888), though short of a formal declaration of war, did grant the president broad war-making powers. During the debate over the resolution, Senator Wayne Morse of Oregon forecast, "I believe that history will record that we have made a great mistake in subverting and circumventing the Constitution of the United States, article 1, section 8 thereof [which gives Congress the power to declare war] by means of this resolution. . . ." Morse's words were prophetic. In 1973, Congress passed the War Powers Act to curb the president's war-making powers.

Teacher's Edition **887**

Reading the Headline
Point out that the headline is a capsule summary that answers questions beginning with the 5 *w*'s—*who, what, when, where,* and *why.*

Extension Have students write a front-page headline for another important event discussed in this section.

ASSESS & RETEACH

Section 1 Assessment
Students might work in pairs to respond to the questions.

Self-Assessment
To assess what they have learned, students can write their own questions, exchange them with partners, and try to answer one another's questions.

Section Quiz

FORMAL ASSESSMENT
Section Quiz, p. 363

Reteach
Use the map and the other marginal features in Section 1 to help review the main ideas of this section.

CLOSE

After France's withdrawal from Vietnam, the country was temporarily divided into the Communist-controlled North and the nationalist-controlled South. U.S. military involvement escalated in 1965, when President Johnson unleashed the first sustained bombing of North Vietnam.

"All the News That's Fit to Print"
The New York Times.
LATE CITY EDITION
NEW YORK, WEDNESDAY, AUGUST 5, 1964.
VOL. CXIII—No. 38,910.
TEN CENTS

U.S. PLANES ATTACK NORTH VIETNAM BASES; PRESIDENT ORDERS 'LIMITED' RETALIATION AFTER COMMUNISTS' PT BOATS RENEW RAIDS

A newspaper headline announces the U.S. military's reaction to the Gulf of Tonkin incident. During Operation Rolling Thunder, which followed, U.S. planes called Thunderchiefs dropped 750 pound bombs on Vietnamese targets.

THE TONKIN GULF RESOLUTION On August 2, 1964, President Johnson announced that North Vietnamese torpedo boats had attacked two American destroyers, the U.S.S. *Maddox* and *C. Turner Joy,* which were patrolling in the Gulf of Tonkin off the North Vietnamese coast. The North Vietnamese charged that the U.S. ships were conducting naval raids. Nonetheless, the North Vietnamese denied attacking the U.S. ships.

Despite a great deal of confusion surrounding the details, this incident, along with a second alleged attack, prompted Johnson to launch bombing attacks on North Vietnam. He also asked Congress for powers to take "all necessary means to repel any armed attack against the forces of the United States and to prevent further aggression." Congress overwhelmingly approved Johnson's request. With the House voting 416–0 and the Senate voting 88–2, Congress adopted on August 7 the **Tonkin Gulf Resolution.** While not a declaration of war, it granted Johnson broad military powers in Vietnam.

As one of only two senators to vote against the resolution, Senator Ernest Gruening of Alaska warned that "all Vietnam is not worth the life of a single American boy." However, Representative Ross Adair of Indiana spoke for the overwhelming majority of Congress when he declared, "The American flag has been fired upon. We will not and cannot tolerate such things."

In February of 1965, President Johnson used his newly granted powers. In response to a Vietcong attack that killed eight Americans, Johnson unleashed Operation Rolling Thunder, the first sustained bombing of North Vietnam. In March of that year the first American combat troops began arriving in South Vietnam. By June, 50,000 U.S. soldiers were battling the Vietcong. The Vietnam War had become Americanized.

D. Answer It gave Johnson broad authority to widen America's role in the war.

THINK THROUGH HISTORY
D. *Analyzing Causes* How did the Tonkin Gulf Resolution lead to greater U.S. involvement in the Vietnam War?

Section 1 Assessment

1. TERMS & NAMES
Identify:
• Ho Chi Minh
• Vietminh
• domino theory
• Dien Bien Phu
• Geneva Accords
• Ngo Dinh Diem
• Vietcong
• Ho Chi Minh Trail
• Tonkin Gulf Resolution

2. SUMMARIZING In a two-column chart like the one below, cite the Vietnam policy for each of the following presidents: Truman, Eisenhower, Kennedy, and Johnson.

President	Vietnam Policy

Choose one of the presidential policies and explain its purpose.

3. ANALYZING EFFECTS Why do you think the Geneva Accords of 1954 failed to bring a lasting peace in Vietnam? Support your answer with reasons.

THINK ABOUT
• the provisions of the Geneva Accords
• Ho Chi Minh's and Ngo Dinh Diem's goals
• the role of the U.S. in Vietnam

4. FORMING OPINIONS Do you think Congress was justified in passing the Tonkin Gulf Resolution? Use details from the text to support your response.

THINK ABOUT
• the report of torpedo boat attacks on two U.S. destroyers
• the powers that the resolution would give the president
• the fact that the resolution was not a declaration of war

888 CHAPTER 30

ANSWERS

1. TERMS & NAMES
• Ho Chi Minh, p. 884
• Vietminh, p. 885
• domino theory, p. 885
• Dien Bien Phu, p. 885
• Geneva Accords, p. 886
• Ngo Dinh Diem, p. 886
• Vietcong, p. 886
• Ho Chi Minh Trail, p. 886
• Tonkin Gulf Resolution, p. 888

2. SUMMARIZING
Possible Answers: Truman—economic aid to France; Eisenhower—economic and military aid to South Vietnam; Kennedy—economic and military aid to South Vietnam; Johnson—stepped-up U.S. military involvement. Possible explanations: Truman—containing communism; Eisenhower—domino theory; Kennedy—Democrats' hardline anti-Communist stance; Johnson—maintaining

America's anti-Communist reputation.

3. ANALYZING EFFECTS
Possible Responses: The geographical division of North and South Vietnam may have intensified the political division between Communist and anti-Communist nationalists; defying the Geneva Accords, the U.S. supported Diem's cancellation of the 1956 election.

4. FORMING OPINIONS
Possible Responses: Yes—Presidential authority should be broadened in response to emergency situations, such as bombing attacks. No—The circumstances surrounding the North Vietnamese attack were fuzzy and not adequately verified; Congress gave Johnson too much power over activities in Vietnam.

2 U.S. Involvement and Escalation

LEARN ABOUT the reasons for U.S. escalation and the difficulty the United States encountered in fighting the Vietcong
TO UNDERSTAND why the war lasted longer than expected and began to lose support at home.

TERMS & NAMES
• Robert McNamara
• Dean Rusk
• William Westmoreland
• napalm
• Agent Orange
• search-and-destroy mission
• credibility gap

ONE AMERICAN'S STORY

Tim O'Brien, born in Austin, Minnesota, is a novelist who has written several books about his experience in Vietnam. O'Brien was drafted and sent to Vietnam in August of 1968, when he was 22. He spent the first seven months of his nearly two-year duty patrolling the fields outside of Chu Lai, a sea-coast city in South Vietnam. O'Brien described one of the more nerve-racking experiences of the war: walking through the fields and jungles, many of which were filled with land mines and booby traps.

A PERSONAL VOICE

You do some thinking. You hallucinate. You look ahead a few paces and wonder what your legs will resemble if there is more to the earth in that spot than silicates and nitrogen. Will the pain be unbearable? Will you scream and fall silent? Will you be afraid to look at your own body, afraid of the sight of your own red flesh and white bone? . . .

It is not easy to fight this sort of self-defeating fear, but you try. You decide to be ultra-careful—the hard-nosed realistic approach. You try to second-guess the mine. Should you put your foot to that flat rock or the clump of weeds to its rear? Paddy dike or water? You wish you were Tarzan, able to swing on the vines. You trace the footprints of the men to your front. You give up when he curses you for following too closely; better one man dead than two.

TIM O'BRIEN, quoted in *A Life in a Year: The American Infantryman in Vietnam*

U.S. soldiers on patrol in Vietnam, November 1965.

Deadly traps were just some of the obstacles that U.S. troops faced in Vietnam as their attempt to defeat a resilient guerrilla army evolved into a bloody stalemate. As the influx of American ground troops into Vietnam failed to score a quick victory over the Communists, a mostly supportive U.S. population began to question its government's war policy.

The Decision to Escalate

Much of the nation supported Lyndon Johnson's determination to contain communism in Vietnam. Therefore, President Johnson began sending large numbers of American troops to fight alongside the South Vietnamese Army against the forces of the Vietcong and the North Vietnamese Army.

STRONG SUPPORT FOR CONTAINMENT In the 1964 presidential election, Lyndon Johnson soundly defeated his Republican opponent, Barry Goldwater. Johnson's victory was due in part to charges that Goldwater was an extreme anti-Communist who might push the United States into war with the Soviet Union. In contrast to Goldwater's heated, warlike language, Johnson's speeches were more moderate, yet he spoke determinedly about containing communism.

Even after Congress had approved the Tonkin Gulf Resolution, President Johnson voiced his opposition to sending U.S. ground troops to Vietnam. He

The Vietnam War Years **889**

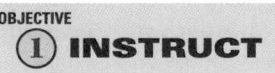

Section 2 Overview

OBJECTIVES

1 To explain the reasons for the escalation of U.S. involvement in Vietnam.

2 To describe the military tactics and weapons of the Vietcong and the U.S. forces.

3 To explain the impact of the war on American society.

SKILLBUILDER
• Interpreting charts, p. 891

CRITICAL THINKING
• Contrasting, p. 890
• Identifying problems, p. 892
• Analyzing causes, p. 893
• Recognizing effects, p. 894
• Summarizing, p. 894
• Evaluating, p. 894
• Generalizing, p. 894

FOCUS & MOTIVATE

▶*Starting with the Student*
Ask students what the expression "home-field advantage" means in sports.

• How might this expression apply to U.S. troops waging a war on foreign soil?

OBJECTIVE
1 INSTRUCT

The Decision to Escalate

▶*Discussing Key Ideas*
• President Johnson dispatches the first American ground troops to Vietnam in March 1965.
• Between 1965 and 1967, the number of U.S. troops in Vietnam more than doubles.

IN-DEPTH RESOURCES: UNIT 8
Guided Reading p. 36
American Lives: Robert McNamara, p. 52

ACCESS FOR STUDENTS ACQUIRING ENGLISH
Guided Reading (Spanish), p. 290

 ELECTRONIC LIBRARY OF PRIMARY SOURCES
from "Peace Without Conquest" by Lyndon B. Johnson

(continued on next page)

MORE ABOUT . .
Dean Rusk
Rusk, a holdover from the Kennedy administration, was the second-longest-serving secretary of state in U.S. history. A Georgia native whom President Johnson once called "tough as a Georgia pine nut," Rusk endured much criticism for his role in the Johnson administration's Vietnam policy. Even his own son became an antiwar activist during the 1960s.

HISTORICAL SPOTLIGHT
General William Westmoreland
Critical Thinking:
Evaluating Ask students if providing deceptive information about enemy numbers and strength might have been justifiable during the Vietnam War. *Possible Responses: Yes—Such deceptions are sometimes necessary to boost the troops' and the public's morale. No—Such deceptions erode Americans' faith in government.*

OBJECTIVE
② INSTRUCT

A War in the Jungle

▶ *Starting with the Student*
• Ask students which they think is harder to face—an enemy whose strength and tactics are known or one whose strength and tactics are unknown. Why?

(continued on next page)

HISTORICAL
SP⊙TLIGHT

GENERAL WILLIAM WESTMORELAND
General Westmoreland retired from the military in 1972, but even in retirement, he could not escape the Vietnam War.

In 1982, almost seven years after the conflict had ended, CBS-TV aired a documentary entitled *The Uncounted Enemy: A Vietnam Deception.* The report, viewed by millions, asserted that General Westmoreland and the Pentagon had deceived the U.S. government about the enemy's size and strength during 1967 and 1968 to make it appear that U.S. forces were winning the war.

Westmoreland, claiming he was the victim of "distorted, false, and specious information . . . derived by sinister deception," filed a $120 million libel suit against CBS. The widely publicized suit was eventually settled, with both parties issuing statements pledging mutual respect. CBS, however, stood by its story.

---

declared in October of 1964 that he was "not about to send American boys 9 or 10,000 miles away to do what Asian boys ought to be doing for themselves."

However, in March of 1965, that is precisely what the president did. Working closely with his foreign-policy advisers, particularly Secretary of Defense **Robert McNamara** and Secretary of State **Dean Rusk,** President Johnson began dispatching tens of thousands of U.S. soldiers to fight in Vietnam. While some Americans viewed Johnson's decision as contradictory to his position during the presidential campaign, most saw the president as following an established and popular policy of confronting communism anywhere in the world. That same year, for example, the Johnson administration also dispatched U.S. troops to the Dominican Republic, a small country in the Caribbean, to put down a rebellion the administration feared was Communist-inspired.

So, as American soldiers stepped onto the planes that would take them to fight in the thick jungles of Southeast Asia, Congress, as well as many Americans, strongly supported Johnson's strategy. A 1965 poll showed that 61 percent of Americans supported the U.S. policy in Vietnam, while only 24 percent opposed it.

To be sure, there were dissenters in the Johnson administration. In October of 1964, Undersecretary of State George Ball had argued against escalation, warning that "once on the tiger's back, we cannot be sure of picking the place to dismount." However, the president's closest advisers strongly urged escalation, believing the defeat of communism in Vietnam to be of vital importance to the future of America and the world. Dean Rusk stressed this view in a 1965 memo to President Johnson.

A PERSONAL VOICE
The integrity of the U.S. commitment is the principal pillar of peace throughout the world. If that commitment becomes unreliable, the communist world would draw conclusions that would lead to our ruin and almost certainly to a catastrophic war. So long as the South Vietnamese are prepared to fight for themselves, we cannot abandon them without disaster to peace and to our interests throughout the world.
DEAN RUSK, quoted in *In Retrospect*

THE TROOP BUILDUP ACCELERATES By the end of 1965, the U.S. government had sent more than 180,000 Americans to Vietnam. The American commander in South Vietnam, General **William Westmoreland,** continued to request more troops. Westmoreland, a tall and lean West Point graduate who served in World War II and Korea, was less than impressed with the fighting ability of the South Vietnamese Army, or the Army of the Republic of Vietnam (ARVN). The ARVN "cannot stand up to this pressure without substantial U.S. combat support on the ground," the general reported. "The only possible response is the aggressive deployment of U.S. troops." Throughout the early years of the war, the Johnson administration complied with Westmoreland's requests, and by 1967, the number of U.S. troops in Vietnam had climbed to 389,000.

A War in the Jungle

The United States entered the war in Vietnam believing that its superior weaponry would lead it to victory over the Vietcong. However, the jungle terrain and the enemy's guerrilla tactics soon turned the war into a frustrating stalemate.

AN ELUSIVE ENEMY Because the Vietcong lacked the high-powered weaponry of the American forces, they used hit-and-run and ambush tactics, as well as a keen knowledge of the jungle terrain, to their advantage. Moving

---

THINK THROUGH HISTORY
A. Contrasting *What differing opinions did Johnson's advisers have about Vietnam?*

A. Answer Some argued for U.S. escalation in Vietnam because it was vital to stopping the spread of communism, while George Ball argued against escalation, believing it would be easier to get into the Vietnam War than to get out.

TEACHING OPTION

Skillbuilder Mini-Lesson: Distinguishing Fact from Opinion

Explaining the Skill Facts include events, dates, statistics, and statements that are generally known to be true. Opinions are personal judgments or beliefs. Typically, opinions are expressed as assertions, claims, predictions, and hypotheses. A person's opinion may turn out to be a fact.

Applying the Skill Have students work in small groups to make lists of the statements of fact and the statements of opinion included on this page of the text.

Remind them that poll results are based on people's opinions. *Possible Responses: Facts—In March 1965, President Johnson sent tens of thousands of U.S. soldiers to fight in Vietnam; Johnson dispatched troops to the Dominican Republic to put down a rebellion. Opinions—Johnson's actions contradicted his position during the presidential campaign; defeating communism in Vietnam was vital to U.S. interests; the rebellion in the Dominican Republic was Communist-inspired.*

> **IN-DEPTH RESOURCES: UNIT 8**
> Skillbuilder Practice: Distinguishing Fact from Opinion, p. 40

secretly in and out of the general population, the Vietcong destroyed the notion of a frontline by attacking U.S. troops in both the cities and in the countryside. Because some of the enemy lived amidst the civilian population, it became increasingly difficult for U.S. troops to discern friend from foe. A woman selling soft drinks to U.S. soldiers might be a Vietcong spy. A boy standing on the corner might be ready to throw a grenade.

In addition, the enemy laced the terrain with countless booby traps and land mines. American soldiers marching through South Vietnam's jungles and rice paddies dealt not only with sweltering heat and leeches but also with deadly traps. The enemy even turned U.S. weapons against the Americans. In a letter home to his sister, Specialist Fourth Class Salvador Gonzalez described the tragic result from an unexploded U.S. bomb that the North Vietnamese Army had rigged.

A PERSONAL VOICE

Two days ago 4 guys got killed and about 15 wounded from the first platoon. Our platoon was 200 yards away on top of a hill. One guy was from Floral Park [in New York City]. He had five days left to go [before being sent home]. He was standing on a 250-lb. bomb that a plane had dropped and didn't explode. So the NVA [North Vietnamese Army] wired it up. Well, all they found was a piece of his wallet.

SALVADOR GONZALEZ, quoted in *Dear America: Letters Home from Vietnam*

Skillbuilder Answer Possible response: They were able to make food, obtain water and sleep down there, as well as tend to their wounded and store ammunition.

Adding to the enemy's elusiveness was a network of elaborate tunnels that allowed the Vietcong to launch surprise attacks on American soldiers and then disappear quickly. The Vietnamese, who began building the tunnels during their war with the French, constructed even more in response to the massive U.S. bombings. The tunnels, which connected villages throughout the countryside, became home to many guerrilla fighters. Inside their underground world, the Vietcong ate and slept, stored munitions, built land mines, and treated their wounded. "The more the Americans tried to drive us

(continued from page 890)

▶**Discussing Key Ideas**
- Vietcong military tactics stymie U.S. forces.
- U.S. chemical warfare harms the rural population and landscape.
- The frustrations of guerrilla combat, brutal jungle conditions, and the war's stalemate cause a decline in the morale of U.S. troops.

NOW & THEN
LAND MINES

The destructiveness of land mines still plagues much of the world today. As a result of past and present wars, roughly 110 million mines were still scattered throughout 64 countries in 1996. That year, nearly 2,000 victims lost either a limb or their life to a land mine each month. In Vietnam and Cambodia, more than 10 million mines remained in the ground.

Various relief, religious, and veterans organizations have urged the international community to ban the use of mines. The Vietnam Veterans of America Foundation, a group formed to examine the causes and consequences of the Vietnam War, has taken a second step. Since 1991, it has supplied prosthetic limbs for Vietnamese and Cambodian mine victims.

NOW & THEN
Land Mines

Critical Thinking: Recognizing Effects Ask students to explain the long-term consequences of the use of land mines. *Possible Responses: Unexploded mines remain a problem long after peace has been achieved; the mines may kill or mutilate friends as well as foes.*

HISTORY FROM VISUALS
Tunnels of the Vietcong

Reading the Chart As students read the labels identifying specific features and functions, remind them to visualize the tunnel system as the sum of its parts.

Extension Ask students to make two-column charts like the one below, in which they list the devices that protected tunnel users.

Protective Device	Function

SKILLBUILDER
INTERPRETING CHARTS
How were the Vietcong able to sustain themselves underground for such long periods of time?

Tunnels of the Vietcong

- Remote smoke outlets
- Submerged entrance
- Kitchen
- Punji stake pit
- Ventilation shaft
- Firing post
- Conference chamber
- Sleeping chamber
- False tunnel
- Blast, gas and waterproof trap doors
- Conical air raid shelter that also amplified sound of approaching aircraft
- First-aid station powered by bicycle
- Booby trap grenade
- Well
- Storage cache for weapons, explosives, and rice

The Vietnam War Years **891**

Teaching Gifted and Talented Students

Oral Readings Salvador Gonzalez's letter quoted on this page is from *Dear America: Letters Home from Vietnam* (New York: Norton, 1985). Have students find this book or another collection of letters written during the Vietnam War. Ask them to present oral readings of letters to the class. Review the letters that students choose to ensure that their content and language are appropriate for a classroom presentation.

IN-DEPTH RESOURCES: UNIT 8
Primary Source: Letter from a soldier in Vietnam, p. 45

Making Connections Across the Curriculum

Geography Vietnam has a tropical climate, with heavy rainfall supporting lush jungles in many areas. In southern Vietnam, humidity is high for most of the year, with about 80 inches of annual rainfall in Ho Chi Minh City (formerly Saigon); temperatures rarely drop below the high 70s. In Hanoi to the north, average temperatures are somewhat lower, though rainfall is still plentiful. Monsoons, or seasonal winds, and typhoons affect Vietnam's climate. Summer monsoons bring the heaviest rainfall; typhoons often strike the coasts.

NOW & THEN

AGENT ORANGE
The 13 million gallons of Agent Orange dumped on the jungles of Vietnam to destroy the foliage ended up harming some U.S. soldiers as well. After the war ended, researchers believed that toxins in the weed killer led to a wide range of health defects in humans, including skin diseases and cancer.

U.S. veterans eventually brought a class-action lawsuit against seven makers of Agent Orange. The suit was settled out of court with the establishment of a $180,000,000 fund to compensate the roughly 250,000 veterans who claimed to be affected.

In addition, Congress in 1991 passed a bill providing disability benefits to veterans suffering from certain illnesses that were said to be related to exposure to Agent Orange.

away from our land, the more we burrowed into it," recalled Major Nguyen Quot of the Vietcong army.

A FRUSTRATING WAR OF ATTRITION Not only may the United States have underestimated the Vietcong's ingenuity, but it also miscalculated the enemy's resolve. Westmoreland's strategy for defeating the Vietcong was to destroy their morale through a war of attrition, or the gradual wearing down of the enemy by continuous harassment. Introducing the concept of the body count, or the tracking of Vietcong killed in battle, the general believed that as the number of Vietcong dead rose, the enemy's surrender would become inevitable.

However, the Vietcong had no intention of quitting their fight. What Ho Chi Minh had told the French in the 1940s applied also to the Americans, "You can kill ten of my men for every one I kill of yours," he warned, "but even at those odds, you will lose and I will win." Despite absorbing significant casualties and the relentless pounding from U.S. bombers, the Vietcong—who received supplies from China and the Soviet Union—remained defiant. Defense Secretary McNamara confessed his early frustration over the Vietcong's resilience to a reporter in 1966. "I didn't think these people had the capacity to fight this way," he said. "If I had thought they would take this punishment and fight this well, . . . I would have thought differently at the start."

General Westmoreland would say later that the United States never lost a battle in Vietnam. While the general's words may have been true, they underscored the degree to which America misunderstood the Vietcong. While the United States viewed the war strictly as a military struggle, the Vietcong saw it as a battle for their very existence, and they were ready to pay any price for victory. "The Communists were prepared to go on and on," explained Stanley Karnow, author of *Vietnam: A History*, "and they had factored their human costs into the equation."

THE BATTLE FOR "HEARTS AND MINDS" Another key part of the American strategy was to keep the Vietcong from winning the support of South Vietnam's rural population. Edward G. Lansdale, who helped found the special fighting unit known as the Green Berets, stressed the plan's importance. "Just remember this. Communist guerrillas hide among the people. If you win the people over to your side, the Communist guerrillas have no place to hide."

The campaign to win the "hearts and minds" of the South Vietnamese villagers proved more difficult than the Americans imagined. Some of the tactics the Americans used to battle the Vietcong also harmed much of the rural population. For instance, in their attempt to expose Vietcong tunnels and hideouts, the U.S. planes dropped **napalm,** a gasoline-based bomb that set fire to the jungle. American planes also sprayed **Agent Orange,** a leaf-killing toxic chemical that devastated the landscape. The saturation use of these weapons often wounded villagers and left villages and their surrounding area in ruins.

In addition, attempts to control the villages could turn heavy-handed. U.S. soldiers conducted **search-and-destroy missions,** uprooting villagers with suspected ties to the Vietcong, killing their livestock, and burning their villages. Many villagers fled into the cities or refugee camps, creating by 1967 more than 3 million refugees in South Vietnam. The irony of the strategy was summed up by a U.S. major whose forces had just leveled the town of Ben Tre: "We had to destroy the town in order to save it."

SINKING MORALE The frustrations of guerrilla warfare, the brutal jungle conditions, and the failure to make substantial headway against the enemy took their toll on the U.S. troops' fighting spirit. Philip Caputo, a marine lieutenant

THINK THROUGH HISTORY
B. *Identifying Problems* Why did the U.S. forces have difficulty fighting the Vietcong?

B. Answer Because of the Vietcong's guerrilla tactics and their superior knowledge of the terrain.

---

in Vietnam who later wrote several books about the war, summarized the soldiers' growing disillusionment, "When we marched into the rice paddies . . . we carried, along with our packs and rifles, the implicit convictions that the Vietcong could be quickly beaten. We kept the packs and rifles; the convictions, we lost."

Throughout the war, American morale dropped steadily, as many soldiers turned to alcohol, marijuana, and other drugs to deal with the futility of a war that seemed less and less winnable. Low morale led some soldiers even to murder their superior officers by "fragging" them, an action in which a soldier lobbed a fragmentation grenade (one that left no fingerprints) at an officer during battle. Morale would worsen during the later years of the war when soldiers realized they were fighting even as their government was negotiating for peace.

THINK THROUGH HISTORY
C. Analyzing Causes What factors led to the low morale of U.S. troops?

Also damaging to U.S. troop morale was the continuing corruption and instability of the South Vietnamese government. Nguyen Cao Ky, a flamboyant air force general, led the government from 1965 to 1967. Ignoring U.S pleas to step down, Ky, who wore bright military uniforms and a thin mustache, refused to retire in favor of an elected civilian government. Mass demonstrations began, and by May of 1966, Buddhist monks were once again burning themselves in protest against the South Vietnamese government. South Vietnam was fighting a civil war within a civil war, leaving U.S. officials confused and angry. "What are we doing here?" demanded one official. "We're fighting to save these people, and they're fighting each other!"

Despite the low morale among some U.S. troops, many American soldiers fought courageously. Particularly heroic were the thousands of soldiers who endured years of torture and confinement as prisoners of war. In 1966, Navy pilot Gerald Coffee's plane was shot down during a bombing mission over North Vietnam. Coffee spent the next seven years—until he was released in 1973 as part of a cease-fire agreement—struggling to stay alive in an enemy prison camp.

A PERSONAL VOICE
My clothes were filthy and ragged. . . . With no boots, my socks—which I'd been able to salvage—were barely recognizable. . . . Only a few threads around my toes kept them spread over my feet; some protection, at least, as I shivered through the cold nights curled up tightly on my morguelike slab. . . . My conditions and predicament were so foreign to me, so stifling, so overwhelming. I'd never been so hungry, so grimy, and in such pain.

GERALD COFFEE, *Beyond Survival*

The Early War at Home

The Johnson administration thought the war would end quickly. When it dragged on, public support began to waver, and Johnson's domestic programs began to unravel.

THE GREAT SOCIETY SUFFERS As the number of U.S. troops in Vietnam continued to mount, the war grew more costly. As a result, the nation's economy began to suffer. The inflation rate, which had remained at 2 percent through most of the early 1960s, nearly tripled by 1969. President Johnson had been determined to pay for both the war and his Great Society programs.

A soldier with the 61st Infantry Division wears symbols of both war and peace on his chest.

"We had to destroy the town in order to save it."

A U.S. MAJOR IN 1968

The Vietnam War Years **893**

MORE ABOUT . . .

J. William Fulbright

Best known for initiating the international scholarship program that bears his name, Fulbright served five terms as U.S. senator from Arkansas and was a mentor to the young Bill Clinton. Though he voted for the Tonkin Gulf Resolution in 1964, his opinion that the Johnson administration had deceived Congress prompted him to hold the 1966 hearings that lent respectability to the antiwar movement.

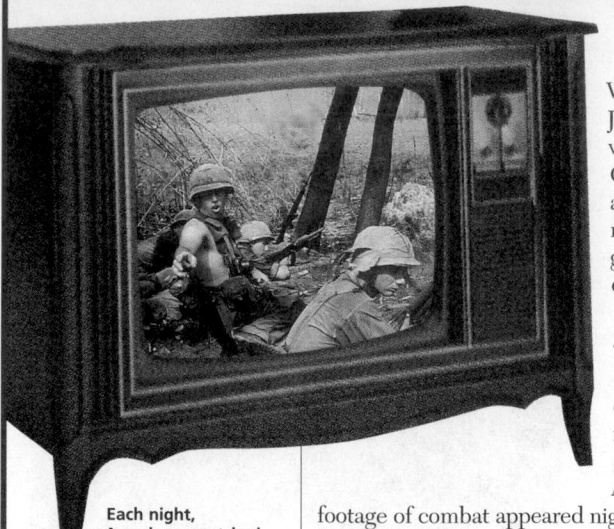

Each night, Americans watched the images—which often were graphic and brutal—of the Vietnam War.

ASSESS & RETEACH

Section 2 Assessment

Have pairs of students evaluate each other's responses before finalizing them.

Self-Assessment

Have students make a time line of events, tracing U.S. involvement in Vietnam from the Truman administration to the Johnson administration. Have them identify events that they find difficult to understand.

Section Quiz

FORMAL ASSESSMENT
Section Quiz, p. 364

Reteach

Use the Guided Reading worksheet for Section 2 to help review the main ideas of the section.

IN-DEPTH RESOURCES: UNIT 8
Guided Reading, p. 36

CLOSE

Despite President Johnson's escalation of U.S. involvement in the war, the fighting did not move beyond a stalemate. Support for the war among U.S. citizens began to erode because of the war's toll on the U.S. economy and TV coverage of combat.

However, the cost of financing the Vietnam War became too great. In August of 1967, Johnson asked for a tax increase to help fund the war and to keep inflation in check. Congressional conservatives agreed, but only after demanding and receiving a $6 billion reduction in funding for Great Society programs. Vietnam was slowly claiming an early casualty: Johnson's grand vision of domestic reform.

THE LIVING-ROOM WAR By 1967, a majority of Americans still supported the war. However, cracks were beginning to show. The media, mainly television, helped heighten the nation's growing concern about the war. Vietnam was America's first "living-room war," in which footage of combat appeared nightly on the news in millions of homes. And what people saw on their television screens seemed to contradict the optimistic war scenario that the Johnson administration was painting.

Quoting body count statistics that showed large numbers of Communists dying in battle, General Westmoreland continually reported that a Vietcong surrender was imminent. Victory "lies within our grasp—the enemy's hopes are bankrupt," he declared. Defense Secretary McNamara backed up the general's rosy analyses, saying that he could see "the light at the end of the tunnel."

However, the repeated television images of Americans in body bags told a different story. Communists may have been dying, but so too were Americans— nearly 16,000 between 1965 and 1967. Critics charged that a **credibility gap** was growing between what the Johnson administration reported and what was really happening.

One such critic was Senator J. William Fulbright, chairman of the powerful Senate Foreign Relations Committee. Fulbright, a former Johnson ally, charged the president with a "lack of candor" in portraying the war effort. In early 1966, the senator conducted a series of televised committee hearings in which he called forth members of the Johnson administration to defend their Vietnam policies. The Fulbright hearings delivered few major revelations, but they did contribute to the growing doubts about the war. One housewife appeared to capture the mood of middle America when she told an interviewer, "I want to get out, but I don't want to give in."

By 1967, however, a small force outside of mainstream America, mainly from the ranks of the nation's youth, already had begun actively protesting the war. Their voices would grow louder and capture the attention of the entire nation.

D. Answer The continued reports of American casualties, television coverage, and the Johnson administration's growing credibility gap.

THINK THROUGH HISTORY
D. Recognizing Effects What led to the growing concern in America about the Vietnam War?

Section 2 Assessment

1. TERMS & NAMES

Identify:
- Robert McNamara
- Dean Rusk
- William Westmoreland
- napalm
- Agent Orange
- search-and-destroy mission
- credibility gap

2. SUMMARIZING Recreate the dual concept web below on your own paper. Then, show key military tactics and weapons of the Vietcong and Americans.

3. EVALUATING Evaluate the U.S. strategy for conducting the Vietnam War.

THINK ABOUT
- the war of attrition
- the battle for the "hearts and minds" of the South Vietnamese
- the support for South Vietnamese military leaders

4. GENERALIZING What were the effects of the nightly TV coverage of the Vietnam War?

THINK ABOUT
- the image on the TV screen at the top of this page
- television images of Americans in body bags
- the Johnson administration's credibility gap

894 CHAPTER 30

ANSWERS

1. TERMS & NAMES
- Robert McNamara, p. 890
- Dean Rusk, p. 890
- William Westmoreland, p. 890
- napalm, p. 892
- Agent Orange, p. 892
- search-and-destroy mission, p. 892
- credibility gap, p. 894

2. SUMMARIZING

Possible Responses: Vietcong: tactics—ambushes, hit-and-run attacks; weapons—booby traps, land mines. U.S.: tactics—large-scale bombing, search-and-destroy missions; weapons—napalm, Agent Orange, bombers.

3. EVALUATING

Possible Responses: The U.S. strategy seemed to fuel frustration. Military planners failed to take into account the Vietcong's unwillingness to surrender; the use of napalm, Agent Orange, and search-and-destroy missions undermined attempts to win the hearts and minds of the South Vietnamese; and continued support of a corrupt South Vietnamese government hindered the U.S. war effort.

4. GENERALIZING

Possible Responses: Watching the graphic images of the Vietnam War each night caused many Americans to question the war; many Americans began to doubt the Johnson administration's reports that the enemy was near defeat, so that there was a growing credibility gap between what the administration reported about Vietnam and what seemed to be really happening.

3 A Nation Divided

TERMS & NAMES
- New Left
- Students for a Democratic Society
- Free Speech Movement
- dove
- hawk

LEARN ABOUT the growing antiwar movement in America
TO UNDERSTAND how the war sharply divided the American public.

ONE AMERICAN'S STORY

In 1969, Stephan Gubar was told to report to his local draft board. The young man from New Jersey was being called for possible military service in Vietnam. Gubar, 22, a veteran of the civil rights movement, filed as a conscientious objector (CO), or someone who opposed war on the basis of religious or moral beliefs. Gubar was granted 1-A-O status, which meant that while he would not be forced to carry a weapon, he still qualified for noncombatant military duty. In 1969, he was drafted.

Gubar did his basic training at Fort Sam Houston, Texas. Along with other conscientious objectors, he received special training as a medic. Gubar described the memorable day when his training ended.

> **A PERSONAL VOICE**
> The thing that stands out most was . . . being really scared, being in formation and listening to the names and assignments being called. The majority of COs I knew had orders cut for Vietnam. And even though I could hear that happening, even though I could hear that every time a CO's name came up, the orders were cut for Vietnam, I still thought there was a possibility I might not go. Then, when they called my name and said "Vietnam," . . . I went to a phone and I called my wife. It was a tremendous shock.
> **STEPHAN GUBAR,** quoted in *Days of Decision*

Stephan Gubar

Gubar was not alone in his anxiety. As American involvement in the Vietnam War escalated—and American casualties mounted—young men all over the country began to worry that they would be called on to fight and die in Vietnam. While many eligible young Americans proudly went off to war, some found ways to avoid serving, and still others simply refused to go. As the war progressed, it spurred a growing protest movement in America that sharply divided the country between supporters and opponents of the government's policy in Vietnam.

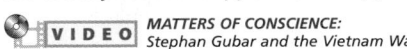 **VIDEO** *MATTERS OF CONSCIENCE:*
Stephan Gubar and the Vietnam War

A Working-Class War

The idea of fighting a war in a faraway place for what some believed was a questionable cause prompted a number of young Americans to avoid going to Vietnam. Because many middle-class and upper-class American youths were able—through college and other means—to avoid military service, most of the soldiers who fought in Vietnam were from the lower economic classes of American society.

A "MANIPULATABLE" DRAFT Most soldiers who fought in Vietnam were drafted into combat under the country's Selective Service System. Under this system, which had been established in the 1940s during World War II, all males had to register with their local draft boards when they turned 18. In the event of a war, the board called men between the ages of 18 and 26 into military service as they were needed. In a sign of America's growing doubts about the Vietnam War, many young men sought deferments from the draft.

Thousands of men attempted to find ways around the draft, which one man characterized as a "very manipulatable system." Because many medical excuses were honored, some men sought out sympathetic doctors to grant them medi-

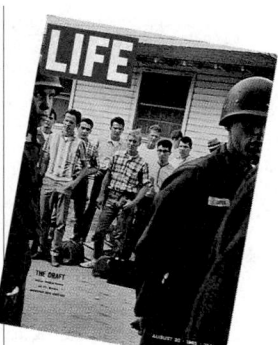

A *Life* magazine cover shows new draft inductees arriving for training at Fort Knox, Kentucky.

The Vietnam War Years **895**

SECTION 3 RESOURCES

 PRINT RESOURCES

IN-DEPTH RESOURCES: UNIT 8
Guided Reading, p. 37
Primary Sources: Protest buttons, p. 46; The New Left, p. 47

ACCESS FOR STUDENTS ACQUIRING ENGLISH
Guided Reading (Spanish), p. 291

FORMAL ASSESSMENT
Section Quiz, p. 365

ALTERNATIVE ASSESSMENT BOOK
See forms for supporting and scoring alternative activities.

 TECHNOLOGY RESOURCES

VIDEO *American Stories* video series
American Portfolio: A Videodisc for U.S. History
user's guide, pp. 246–247, 252–253, 255

INTERNET McDougal Littell Learning On-Line
http://www.mcdougallittell.com

Section 3 Overview

OBJECTIVES

(1) To explain the draft policies that led to the Vietnam War becoming a working-class war.

(2) To trace the roots of opposition to the war.

(3) To describe the antiwar movement and the growing divisions in U.S. public opinion about the war.

SKILLBUILDER
- Interpreting graphs, p. 896

CRITICAL THINKING
- Analyzing causes, p. 896
- Analyzing issues, p. 897
- Analyzing motives, p. 898
- Contrasting, p. 899
- Identifying problems, p. 900
- Summarizing, p. 900
- Making decisions, p. 900
- Forming opinions, p. 900

FOCUS & MOTIVATE

▶ **Starting with the Student**
Watch the video "Matters of Conscience" to find out more about Stephan Gubar's experiences during the Vietnam War.

- Using the *Teacher's Resource Book* as a guide, have the class discuss Gubar's dilemma and engage in extension activities involving primary sources.

 AMERICAN STORIES VIDEO SERIES
"Matters of Conscience"
Videocassette: Volume 5

Videodisc: Disc 3, Side B, Chapter 3

OBJECTIVE
 (1) INSTRUCT

A Working-Class War

▶ **Discussing Key Ideas**
- Draft policies favor young men from privileged backgrounds.

(continued on next page)

Teacher's Edition **895**

(continued from page 895)

- Most American soldiers in Vietnam are minorities and lower-class whites.
- African Americans make up a disproportionately high percentage of U.S. troops.
- Most American women in Vietnam serve as military nurses or volunteers.

IN-DEPTH RESOURCES: UNIT 8
Guided Reading, p. 37

ACCESS FOR STUDENTS ACQUIRING ENGLISH
Guided Reading (Spanish), p. 291

MORE ABOUT . . .
The Draft

In 1965, the Selective Service System began to make various modifications in the draft—for example, ending exemptions for married men, most graduate students, and undergraduates ranking in the bottom half of their class. In 1969, the lottery system discontinued college deferments entirely.

HISTORY FROM VISUALS
U.S. Troop Strength in Vietnam

Reading the Graph Explain that line graphs show changes or trends over time. This line graph provides students with an instant overview of the steady increase (upward slope) in troops from 1963 to 1968, followed by the steady withdrawal of troops (downward slope).

Extension Have students convert the line graph into a bar graph.

---

cal deferments. Different draft boards had different qualifications, prompting some men to change residences in order to stand before more lenient boards. Some Americans even joined the National Guard or Coast Guard, which often secured a deferment from service in Vietnam.

One of the most common ways to avoid the draft was to receive a college deferment, by which a young man enrolled in a university could put off his military service. Because most university students during the 1960s were white and some were financially well-off, many of the men who fought in Vietnam were lower-class whites or minorities who were less privileged economically. To be sure, a number of Americans who were drafted proudly went to Vietnam. Others volunteered to fight, their reasons ranging from a sense of duty to a feeling of patriotism. Nonetheless, with almost 80 percent of American soldiers coming from lower economic levels, Vietnam was a working-class war.

AFRICAN AMERICANS AND WOMEN IN VIETNAM African Americans served in highly disproportionate numbers in Vietnam. During the first several years of the war, blacks accounted for more than 20 percent of American combat deaths despite representing only about 10 percent of the U.S. population. While the Defense Department would take steps to correct that imbalance by the end of the war, the large number of black casualties early in the war angered African-American leaders, including Martin Luther King, Jr. King, who had refrained from speaking out against the war for fear that it would divert attention away from the civil rights movement, could no longer stay silent about the news he was hearing from Vietnam. In 1967 he lashed out against what he called the "cruel irony" of American blacks dying for a country that still regarded them as second-class citizens.

Skillbuilder Answer
1965 through 1968

> ### A PERSONAL VOICE
> We were taking the young black men who had been crippled by our society and sending them eight thousand miles away to guarantee liberties in Southeast Asia which they had not found in Southwest Georgia and East Harlem. . . . We have been repeatedly faced with the cruel irony of watching Negro and white boys on TV screens as they kill and die together for a nation that has been unable to seat them together in the same schools.
> **DR. MARTIN LUTHER KING, JR.,** quoted in *America's Vietnam War: A Narrative History*

SKILLBUILDER
INTERPRETING GRAPHS
What years signaled a rapid increase in the deployment of U.S. troops?

Many African Americans experienced the same racism in Vietnam that they endured at home. Throughout the war, racial tensions between white and black soldiers ran high in many platoons. In some cases, the hostility led to violence. In 1967, a race riot erupted at the U.S. Army

THINK THROUGH HISTORY
A. Analyzing Causes Why were most of the American soldiers in Vietnam minorities and lower-class whites?
A. Answer Many university students—mainly middle-class and upper-class whites—used the college deferment to avoid serving.

U.S. Troop Strength in Vietnam

Troops in Thousands

536,000

600
500
400
300
200
100
0

less than 25,000

1963 1964 1965 1966 1967 1968 1969 1970 1971 1972

Year-end figures

Source: *Statistical Abstract of the United States, 1976*

Despite racial tensions, black and white soldiers fought side by side in Vietnam.

TEACHING OPTION

Exploring Themes

Civil Rights By the late 1960s, Dr. Martin Luther King, Jr., and other prominent civil rights leaders were seeing the Vietnam War as a major setback in African Americans' struggle to achieve equality and justice. In a 1968 essay, King explained his opposition to the war: "The Great Society has become a victim of the war. I think there was a sincere desire in this country four or five years ago to move toward a genuinely great society, and I have little doubt that there would have been a gradual increase in Federal expenditures in this direction, rather than the gradual decline that has occurred, if the Vietnam War had been avoided.

"One of the incongruities of this situation is the fact that such a large number of the soldiers in the Armed Forces in Vietnam—especially the front-line soldiers who are actually doing the fighting—are Negroes. Negroes have always held the hope that if they really demonstrate they are great soldiers and if they really fight for America and help save American democracy, then when they come back home, America will treat them better. This has not been the case."

stockade at Long Binh, Vietnam. Two years later, black and white marines returning from war clashed at Camp Lejeune, North Carolina. The racism that gripped many military units was yet another factor that led to low troop morale in Vietnam.

While the U.S. military in the 1960s did not allow females to serve in combat, nearly 7,500 women served in Vietnam as army and navy nurses. Thousands more women volunteered their services in Vietnam to the American Red Cross and the United Services Organization (USO), which delivered hospitality and entertainment to the troops.

As the men who marched off to Vietnam fought against Communist guerrillas, some of the men who stayed home, as well as many women, waged a battle of their own. Shortly after U.S. troops began arriving in Vietnam, college campuses across the country erupted in protest as many of the nation's youths began to voice their opposition to the war.

Two U.S. nurses rest at Cam Ranh Bay, the major entry point for American supplies and troops in South Vietnam.

The Roots of Opposition

In the years prior to America's involvement in Vietnam, an atmosphere of protest already existed in many college campuses. In contrast to the general contentment that characterized the youths of the 1950s, students in the early 1960s had become more active socially and politically. Some had participated in the civil rights struggle, while others had answered President Kennedy's call to more actively pursue public service. By the mid-sixties, many youths believed the nation to be in need of fundamental change.

THE NEW LEFT The growing youth movement of the 1960s became known as the **New Left,** which encompassed many different activist groups and organizations. The movement was "new" in relation to the "old left" of the 1930s, which generally tried to move the nation toward socialism, and, in some cases, communism. While the New Left movement did not preach socialism, its followers demanded sweeping changes in American society.

Voicing these demands was one of the better-known New Left organizations, **Students for a Democratic Society** (SDS). Tom Hayden and Al Haber, two University of Michigan students, founded the group in 1959. Three years later, they convened a meeting in Port Huron, Michigan, to draft the group's declaration. Known as the Port Huron Statement, it began: "We are the people of this generation, bred in at least moderate comfort, housed in universities, looking uncomfortably to the world we inherit." The statement, which charged that corporations and large government institutions had taken over America, called for a restoration of "participatory democracy" and greater individual freedom.

In 1964, another New Left group gained prominence with its attacks on American society. At the University of California at Berkeley, the **Free Speech Movement** (FSM), which stemmed from a clash between students and administrators over free speech on campus, soon focused its criticism on what it called the American "machine," the nation's faceless and powerful business and government institutions.

CAMPUS ACTIVISM The strategies and tactics of the FSM and SDS soon spread to colleges throughout the country. There, students addressed mostly campus issues, such as dress codes, curfews, dormitory regulations, and mandatory Reserved Officer Training Corps (ROTC) programs. At Fairleigh Dickinson University in New Jersey, students marched merely as "an expression of general student discontent."

B. Answer Corporations and government institutions were growing too dominant and were inhibiting personal freedom.

THINK THROUGH HISTORY
B. Analyzing Issues
What concerns did the New Left movement voice about American society?

OBJECTIVE
② INSTRUCT

The Roots of Opposition

▶ **Starting with the Student**
Ask students what changes they think are needed in contemporary society.

• How do these changes compare with those that young people advocated in the 1960s?

▶ **Discussing Key Ideas**
• The New Left movement, including such activist groups as Students for a Democratic Society (SDS) and the Free Speech Movement (FSM), pushes for social and political change.
• SDS and FSM tactics spread to college campuses nationwide.
• College students begin joining together to protest the Vietnam War.

IN-DEPTH RESOURCES: UNIT 8
Primary Source: The New Left, p. 47

MORE ABOUT . . .
Tom Hayden

Hayden's antiwar activities included visits to North Vietnam in 1965 and 1967. Though some Americans condemned these trips, he did succeed in bringing back the first three released American POWs. He married the actress and activist Jane Fonda in 1973. During the couple's 16-year marriage, which ended in divorce, Hayden became a California state legislator—a position he still holds today.

TEACHING OPTIONS

Teaching Less Proficient Readers

Questioning Techniques To help students build their comprehension skills, have student pairs follow these steps:

1. Read pages 897–900.
2. Change the headings and subheadings into questions beginning with the five *w's—who, what, where, when,* and *why.* Sample questions for this page follow:
   • What were the roots of opposition to the Vietnam War?
   • Who joined the New Left movement?
   • Why did campus activism spread in the mid-1960s?
3. Work together to answer the questions.

Making Connections Across Time

Women in the Military Women have greater opportunities in the U.S. military since the Vietnam War era. In 1970, just over 40,000 women were in uniform; in 1990 there were more than 225,000. Women have advanced in all branches of the armed forces. For example, Carol Mutter, a U.S. Marine, became the first woman three-star general when she was promoted to that rank in 1996. The service academies have also opened their doors to women: West Point's first woman valedictorian graduated in June 1995. Students may wish to discuss problems still faced by women in the military—for example, resistance to women in combat duty.

Teacher's Edition **897**

The Protest Movement Emerges

The Protest Movement Emerges

▶ **Starting with the Student**
- What are some messages expressed in rock music today?
- What effects do social issues have on popular culture?

▶ **Discussing Key Ideas**
- Campus protests mount as more college students become eligible for the draft.
- More young Americans resist the draft.
- The American public becomes deeply divided into opponents and supporters of the war.

IN-DEPTH RESOURCES: UNIT 8
Primary Source: Protest buttons, p. 46

HISTORICAL SPOTLIGHT
"The Ballad of the Green Berets"

Critical Thinking:
Analyzing Tell students that the hit single "The Ballad of the Green Berets" was featured in the 1968 movie *The Green Berets,* starring John Wayne—an actor famous for his manly, tough-guy roles. Explain that some movie critics condemned the film as propaganda. Ask students if they think the song lyrics quoted on this page might also be considered propaganda. Why or why not?

With the onset of the Vietnam War, the students suddenly found a galvanizing issue. At campuses across the country, American youths joined together to protest the war.

Throughout the spring of 1965, a number of colleges began to host "teach-ins" to protest the war. At the University of Michigan, where only a year before, President Johnson had announced his sweeping Great Society program, teachers and students now assailed his war policy. "This is no longer a casual form of campus spring fever," journalist James Reston noted about the growing demonstrations. As the war continued, the protests grew and divided the country between those Americans who supported their government's policy in Vietnam and those who opposed it.

THE MOVEMENT GROWS In April of 1965, SDS helped organize a march on Washington, D.C., by some 20,000 protesters. By November of that year, a protest rally in Washington drew more than 30,000. Then, in January of 1966, the Johnson administration changed deferments for college students. Students now had to be in good academic standing to defer their military service. Campuses around the country erupted in protest. SDS called for civil disobedience at Selective Service Centers and openly counseled students to flee to Canada or Sweden. By the end of 1966, SDS had chapters on nearly 300 campuses.

The growing number of youths who opposed the war did so for different reasons. The most common reason for opposition was the belief that the conflict in Vietnam was basically a civil war and that the U.S. military had no business there. Others argued that the United States could not police the world and that the Vietnam War was draining American strength in important parts of the world such as Europe and the Middle East. Still others saw the war simply as morally unjust.

As the antiwar movement grew, it reached outside the college campuses and touched other groups in society. Small numbers of returning veterans also began to protest the war. Some antiwar veterans picketed the White House and tried to return their medals to President Johnson. In addition, many musicians took up the antiwar cause. Folk singers such as Peter, Paul & Mary and Joan Baez led the way as music became a popular protest vehicle. Soon protest songs even conquered the pop-music charts. Number one in September 1965 was "Eve of Destruction," in which singer Barry McGuire stressed the ironic fact that in the 1960s an American male could be drafted at 18 but had to be 21 to vote:

The Eastern world, it is exploding,
Violence flaring, bullets loading,
You're old enough to kill, but not for voting,
You don't believe in war, but what's that gun you're toting?

FROM PROTEST TO RESISTANCE From 1965 to 1967, the antiwar movement intensified. "We were having *no* effect on U.S. policy," recalled one protest leader. "So we thought we had to up the ante." In the spring of 1967, nearly half a million protesters of all ages gathered in New York's Central Park. Shouting "Burn cards, not people" and "Hell, no, we won't go!" hundreds tossed their draft cards into a bonfire. Many in the park were protesting for the first time. A housewife from New Jersey told a reporter, "So many of us are frustrated. We want to criticize this war because we think it's wrong, but we want to do it in the framework of loyalty."

HISTORICAL SPOTLIGHT

"THE BALLAD OF THE GREEN BERETS"

Not every Vietnam-era pop song about war was an antiwar song. At the top of the charts for five weeks in 1966 was "The Ballad of the Green Berets" by Staff Sergeant Barry Sadler of the U.S. Army Special Forces, known as the Green Berets:

Fighting soldiers from the sky,
Fearless men who jump and die,
Men who mean just what they say,
The brave men of the Green Beret.

The recording sold over a million copies in its first two weeks of release and was *Billboard* magazine's song of the year.

THINK THROUGH HISTORY
C. Analyzing Motives
For what reasons did the protesters oppose the Vietnam War?

C. Answer They felt that America had no business there, it was neglecting other parts of the world, and it was acting in a morally unjust way.

TEACHING OPTIONS

Making Connections Across the Curriculum

Music Both Joan Baez and the folk-rock group Peter, Paul & Mary sang many songs composed by Bob Dylan. In fact, Peter, Paul & Mary's 1963 rendition of Dylan's protest song "Blowin' in the Wind" was the fastest-selling single in the history of Warner Brothers. Yet Dylan himself, the great folk-rock composer of the 1960s, soon moved away from the protest movement. "What Joan Baez is doing," he told the biographer Anthony Scaduto, "and all those people demonstrating, they're not gonna save the world. It's not true they can change men's hearts. "

Making Connections Across the Curriculum

Literature Norman Mailer recorded his experiences during the October 21 march on the Pentagon—and his subsequent night in jail—in a 1968 book, *The Armies of the Night: History as a Novel, the Novel as History.* As the subtitle reveals, the book experiments with the boundaries between fiction and nonfiction. Winning both the Pulitzer Prize and the National Book Award, *The Armies of the Night* was praised by the critic Richard Gilman as a "rather wonderful achievement" in which "history and personality confront each other with a new sense of liberation."

Others were more radical in their view. David Harris, who would spend 20 months in jail for refusing to serve in Vietnam, explained his motives.

A PERSONAL VOICE

Theoretically, I can accept the notion that there are circumstances in which you have to kill people. I could not accept the notion that Vietnam was one of those circumstances. And to me that left the option of either sitting by and watching what was an enormous injustice . . . or find some way to commit myself against it. And the position that I felt comfortable with in committing myself against it was total noncooperation—I was not going to be part of the machine.

DAVID HARRIS, quoted in *The War Within*

In a scene that grew more common as the Vietnam War dragged on, antiwar demonstrators in the United States confront military police.

Draft resistance continued from 1967 until President Nixon phased out the draft in the early 1970s. During these years, the U.S. government accused more than 200,000 men of draft offenses and imprisoned nearly 4,000 draft resisters. (Most won parole after 6 to 12 months behind bars, while some served four or five years.) Throughout these years, about 50,000 Americans fled to Canada rather than serve in the military.

In October of 1967, a demonstration at Washington's Lincoln Memorial drew about 75,000 protesters, including well-known figures like the poet Robert Lowell and the novelist Norman Mailer. When the speeches ended, about 30,000 demonstrators locked arms for a march on the Pentagon in order "to disrupt the center of the American war machine," as one organizer explained. As hundreds of protesters broke past the military police and mounted the Pentagon steps, they were met by tear gas and truncheons. About 1,500 demonstrators were injured and at least 700 arrested.

WAR DIVIDES THE NATION By 1967, Americans increasingly found themselves divided into two camps regarding the war. Those who strongly opposed the war and believed the United States should withdraw were known as **doves.** Feeling just as strongly that America should unleash a greater show of military force to end the war were the **hawks.**

Despite the visibility of the antiwar protesters, a majority of American citizens in 1967 still remained committed to the war. In May of that year, a prowar march through the streets of Manhattan drew 20,000 people. During this time, a poll showed that two-thirds of Americans still felt that the war was justified. And while only 10 percent of Americans approved of the administration's present level of commitment in Vietnam, about 50 percent felt that "increased attacks" against North Vietnam would help win the war.

Others, while less certain about the U.S. role in Vietnam, were shocked to see protesters publicly criticize a war in which their fellow Americans were fighting and dying. A poll taken in December of 1967 showed that 70 percent of Americans believed the war protests were "acts of disloyalty." A firefighter

I WANT OUT

An American antiwar poster is a parody of the World War I Uncle Sam poster, "I Want You for the U.S. Army."

THINK THROUGH HISTORY
D. Contrasting How did the positions of the doves and hawks differ?

D. Answer The doves opposed America's involvement in the Vietnam War and called for U.S. troops to withdraw immediately. The hawks argued for a greater show of military force to end the war.

The Vietnam War Years **899**

900 Chapter 30

who lost his son in Vietnam articulated the bitter feelings a number of Americans felt toward the antiwar movement.

> **A PERSONAL VOICE**
> I'm bitter. . . . It's people like us who give up our sons for the country. . . . The college types, the professors, they go to Washington and tell the government what to do. . . . But their sons, they don't end up in the swamps over there, in Vietnam. No sir. They're deferred, because they're in school. Or they get sent to safe places. . . . What bothers me about the peace crowd is that you can tell from their attitude, the way they look and what they say, that they don't really love this country.
> **A FIREFIGHTER,** quoted in *Working Class War*

Responding to antiwar posters, Americans who supported the government's Vietnam policy developed their own slogans: "Support our men in Vietnam" and "America—love it or leave it."

JOHNSON REMAINS DETERMINED Throughout the turmoil and division that engulfed the country during the early years of the war, President Johnson remained firm. Attacked by doves for not withdrawing and by hawks for not increasing military power rapidly enough, Johnson continued his policy of slow escalation.

> **A PERSONAL VOICE**
> There has always been confusion, frustration, and difference of opinion in this country, when there is a war going on. . . . You know what President Roosevelt went through, and President Wilson in World War I. He had some senators from certain areas that gave him serious problems until victory was assured. . . . We are going to have these differences. No one likes war. All people love peace. But you can't have freedom without defending it.
> **LYNDON B. JOHNSON,** quoted in *No Hail, No Farewell*

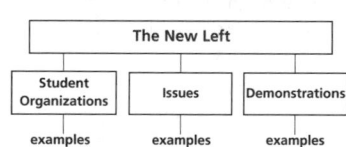

This sign reflects the view of many Americans that the antiwar protests undermined the war effort in Vietnam.

Johnson dismissed as "nervous nellies" members of Congress and other officials who questioned his war policies. As for the protesters who paraded outside his window, the president saw them as misguided and misinformed. They "wouldn't know a Communist if they tripped over one," he declared.

However, by the end of 1967, Johnson's policy—and the continuing stalemate—had begun to create turmoil within his own administration. In November, Defense Secretary McNamara, a key architect of U.S. escalation in Vietnam, quietly announced he was resigning to become head of the World Bank. "It didn't add up," McNamara recalled later. "What I was trying to find out was how . . . the war went on year after year when we stopped the infiltration [from North Vietnam] or shrunk it and when we had a very high body count and so on. It just didn't make sense."

As it happened, McNamara's resignation came on the threshold of the most tumultuous year of the sixties. In 1968 the war—and Johnson's presidency—would take a drastic turn for the worse.

E. Answer Doves attacked him for not pulling out, hawks attacked him for not escalating faster, and members of his own administration began doubting the policy.

THINK THROUGH HISTORY
E. *Identifying Problems*
What problems did Johnson face with his escalation policy?

Section 3 Assessment

1. TERMS & NAMES
Identify:
• New Left
• Students for a Democratic Society
• Free Speech Movement
• dove
• hawk

2. SUMMARIZING Recreate the tree diagram below on your paper. Then fill it in with examples of student organizations, issues, and demonstrations of the New Left.

```
        The New Left
    ┌───────┼───────┐
 Student    Issues   Demonstrations
Organizations
    │         │         │
examples  examples  examples
```

3. MAKING DECISIONS What choices did war draftees make during the Vietnam era?

THINK ABOUT
• university students
• antiwar demonstrators
• economically underprivileged whites and minorities

4. FORMING OPINIONS Do you agree, as many did, that antiwar protests were "acts of disloyalty"? Why or why not?

THINK ABOUT
• why protesters staged antiwar demonstrations
• comments that the protesters didn't "really love this country"
• the right to dissent in a democratic society

900 CHAPTER 30

TERMS & NAMES
• Tet offensive
• Clark Clifford
• Robert Kennedy
• Eugene McCarthy
• Hubert Humphrey
• George Wallace

④ 1968: A Tumultuous Year

LEARN ABOUT the Tet offensive, the assassination of two national leaders, and the rioting at the Democratic National Convention
TO UNDERSTAND why 1968 stands out as the most explosive year of the 1960s.

ONE AMERICAN'S STORY

On the night of June 6, 1968, John Lewis, the first chairman of the Student Nonviolent Coordinating Committee, fell to the floor and wept. Robert F. Kennedy, one of the leading Democratic candidates for president, had just been fatally shot. Lewis had strongly supported Kennedy, feeling that the candidate was "serious in his commitment to civil rights—you felt it coming out of his gut, really." Two months earlier, when Dr. Martin Luther King, Jr., had fallen victim to an assassin's bullet, Lewis had told himself he still had Kennedy. And now they both were gone. Lewis, who later became a congressman from Georgia, recalled the lasting impact of these traumatic events from 1968.

A PERSONAL VOICE
There are people today who are afraid, in a sense, to hope or to have hope again, because of what happened in . . . 1968. Something was taken from us. The type of leadership that we had in a sense invested in, that we had helped to make and to nourish, was taken from us. . . . Something died in all of us with those assassinations.

JOHN LEWIS, quoted in *From Camelot to Kent State*

John Lewis

While the violent deaths of King and Kennedy left many Americans numb, the assassinations were but two of the traumatic events that rocked the nation in 1968. From a shocking setback in Vietnam to a chaotic Democratic National Convention in Chicago, the events of 1968 made it the most tumultuous year of a turbulent decade.

The Tet Offensive Turns the War

1968 began with a daring surprise attack by the Vietcong on numerous cities in South Vietnam. The simultaneous strikes, while a military defeat for the Communist guerrillas, stunned the American public and caused a large number of mainstream citizens to begin turning against the war.

A SURPRISE ATTACK January 30 was the Vietnamese equivalent of New Year's Eve, the beginning of the lunar new year festivities known in Vietnam as Tet. Throughout that day in 1968, villagers—taking advantage of a week-long truce proclaimed for Tet—streamed into cities across South Vietnam to celebrate their New Year. Coinciding with the Tet celebration was a large number of funerals due to the war. Accompanying the funerals were the traditional firecrackers, flutes, and, of course, coffins.

As it turned out, the coffins contained weapons, and many of the villagers were Vietcong agents. That night the enemy launched an overwhelming attack on nearly 100 towns and cities in South Vietnam, as well as 12 U.S. air bases. The fighting was especially fierce in Saigon and in the former imperial capital of Hue. The Vietcong even attacked the U.S. embassy in Saigon, killing five Americans there. The **Tet offensive** continued for nearly a month before U.S. and South Vietnamese forces regained control of the cities.

The Vietnam War Years **901**

SECTION 4 RESOURCES

PRINT RESOURCES

IN-DEPTH RESOURCES: UNIT 8
Guided Reading, p. 38
Geography Application: The Ho Chi Minh Trail, p. 41
Primary Source: Lyndon B. Johnson on Vietnam, p. 48
American Lives: John Lewis, p. 53

ACCESS FOR STUDENTS ACQUIRING ENGLISH
Guided Reading (Spanish), p. 292
Geography Application: The Ho Chi Minh Trail (Spanish), pp. 295–296

FORMAL ASSESSMENT
Section Quiz, p. 366

ALTERNATIVE ASSESSMENT BOOK
See forms for supporting and scoring alternative activities.

TECHNOLOGY RESOURCES

CRITICAL THINKING TRANSPARENCIES
CT64, Impact of Tet Offensive

CD-ROM Electronic Library of Primary Sources
The War in Vietnam

VIDEO *American Portfolio: A Videodisc for U.S. History*
user's guide, pp. 246–249, 255

INTERNET McDougal Littell Learning On-Line
http://www.mcdougallittell.com

Section 4 Overview

OBJECTIVES

① To describe the Tet offensive and its effects on American public opinion.

② To explain the domestic turbulence of 1968.

③ To describe the 1968 presidential election.

SKILLBUILDERS

• Interpreting graphs, p. 906
• Understanding geography: location, p. 902

CRITICAL THINKING

• Analyzing issues, pp. 902, 904
• Analyzing motives, p. 903
• Analyzing causes, p. 906
• Summarizing, p. 906
• Analyzing, p. 906
• Comparing and contrasting, p. 906

FOCUS & MOTIVATE

▶ *Starting with the Student*
Have students describe what happens to objects that fall into a sinkhole.

• Why might a presidential adviser have described the Vietnam War as a sinkhole?

OBJECTIVE
① INSTRUCT

The Tet Offensive Turns the War

▶ *Discussing Key Ideas*
• Early in 1968—on Tet, Vietnam's new year holiday—North Vietnam and the Vietcong launch a surprise attack.
• The Tet offensive sours the media's and the public's view of the war.
• By the end of February, President Johnson's popularity has plummeted.

IN-DEPTH RESOURCES: UNIT 8
Guided Reading p. 38
Primary Source: Lyndon B. Johnson on Vietnam, p. 48

ACCESS FOR STUDENTS ACQUIRING ENGLISH
Guided Reading (Spanish), p. 292

Reading the Map Point out the numerous star-shaped symbols on the map, representing the major battle sites of the Tet offensive. Emphasize that the map shows the far-reaching geographic range of the surprise attacks.

Extension Ask students why the North Vietnamese and Vietcong forces may have decided to go through Laos and Cambodia to launch the Tet offensive. *Possible Responses: Because of bombing in Vietnam, the Ho Chi Minh Trail was the easiest means of entry; the North Vietnamese and Vietcong were less likely to surprise the South Vietnamese and American forces if they came through Vietnam.*

IN-DEPTH RESOURCES: UNIT 8
Geography Application: The Ho Chi Minh Trail, p. 41

CRITICAL THINKING TRANSPARENCIES
CT64, Impact of Tet Offensive

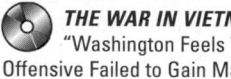
THE WAR IN VIETNAM
"Washington Feels Vietcong Offensive Failed to Gain Maximum Objectives"

MORE ABOUT . . .
Walter Cronkite

Voted the most trusted man in America in 1973, Cronkite joined the CBS television network in 1950 and became its nightly news anchor in 1962. Though he preferred reporting the news to making it, his visit to Vietnam during the Tet offensive is often credited with changing public opinion about the war.

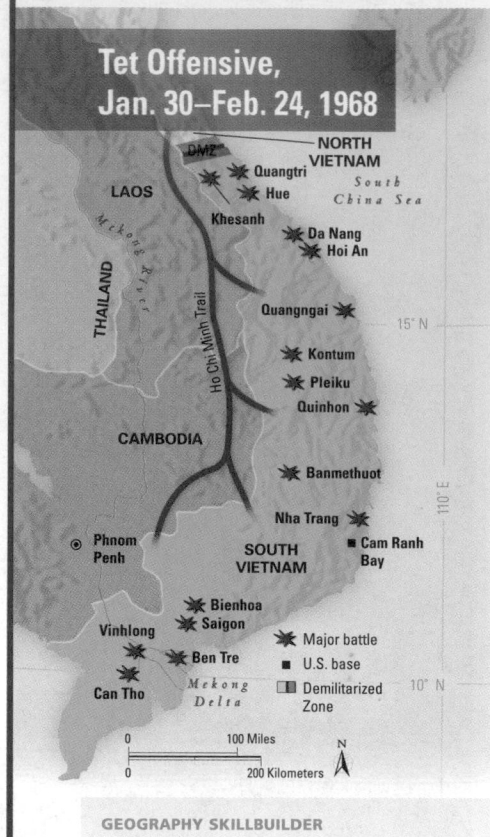

Tet Offensive, Jan. 30–Feb. 24, 1968

GEOGRAPHY SKILLBUILDER
LOCATION *What were the geographical destinations of the Tet offensive attacks?*

Skillbuilder Answer
They were scattered all across South Vietnam.

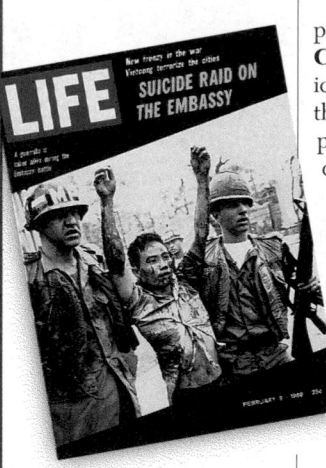
A *Life* magazine cover shows the capturing of a Vietcong guerrilla during the Tet offensive.

General Westmoreland declared the attacks an overwhelming defeat for the Vietcong. The Communists' "well-laid plans went afoul," the general announced. He later added that "the enemy exposed himself by virtue of his strategy, and he suffered heavy casualties." From a purely military standpoint, Westmoreland was right. The Vietcong lost about 32,000 soldiers during the month-long battle, while the American and ARVN forces lost little more than 3,000.

However, from a psychological—and political—standpoint, Westmoreland's claim could not have been more wrong. Despite its overall military failure, the Tet offensive greatly shook an American public that had come to believe that the enemy was close to defeat. The Johnson administration's credibility gap suddenly widened to a point from which it would never recover. Many Americans no longer believed the administration. The Pentagon's continued reports of favorable body counts, or massive Vietcong casualties, now rang hollow as Americans saw the shocking images of attacks on South Vietnam's major cities by an enemy that seemed to be everywhere.

TET CHANGES PUBLIC OPINION The aftershock from the Tet offensive reverberated throughout the United States, from its living rooms to its newsrooms to the White House. Despite the years of antiwar protest, a poll taken just before Tet showed that only 28 percent of Americans called themselves doves, while 56 percent claimed to be hawks. After Tet, both sides tallied 40 percent. The mainstream media, which had reported the war in a skeptical but generally balanced way, now openly criticized the war. One of the nation's most respected journalists, Walter Cronkite, told his viewers that it now seemed "more certain than ever that the bloody experience of Vietnam is to end in a stalemate." In a matter of weeks, the Tet offensive had changed millions of minds about the war.

Minds were also changing at the White House. To fill the defense secretary position left vacant by Robert McNamara's resignation, Johnson picked **Clark Clifford,** a trusted friend and strong supporter of the president's Vietnam policy. However, after settling in and studying the situation, Clifford concluded that the war was unwinnable. "We seem to have a sinkhole," Clifford said. "We put in more—they match it. I see more and more fighting with more and more casualties on the U.S. side and no end in sight to the action."

A NATION TURNS ON JOHNSON In the weeks following the Tet offensive, Johnson's popularity plummeted. In public opinion polls taken at the end of February 1968, nearly 60 percent of the American public disapproved of the president's handling of the war. Nearly half of the country now felt it had been a mistake to send American troops to Vietnam.

Even Dean Rusk, Johnson's secretary of state and another principal architect of the war, acknowledged that the mood of America had changed significantly after Tet. "It was clear to me in the spring of '68 that support for Vietnam at the grassroots level had changed," Rusk recalled. "We had good support until that point, despite the campus demonstrations. War weariness eventually set in, and that was the watershed year." Johnson recognized the change, too. Upon learning of Cronkite's pessimistic analysis of the war, the president lamented, "If I've lost Walter, then it's over. I've lost Mr. Average Citizen."

THINK THROUGH HISTORY
A. Analyzing Issues Why did American support for the war change after the Tet offensive?

A. Answer Because the enemy seemed much stronger and more numerous than Americans had thought.

902 CHAPTER 30

Making Connections Across Cultures

Celebrating Tet Like the Chinese, the Vietnamese revere their dead ancestors, especially during Tet, the lunar new year celebration. As Tet draws near, the Vietnamese return to their native villages to reestablish bonds with kinfolk. Families visit graves and decorate them. On the 30th day of the final lunar month, families gather to prepare for the arrival of their ancestors' souls. At around 9 P.M., they set off firecrackers to ward off evil spirits. Women prepare soybean soup for the vigil, and the families recite prayers at their household ancestral altars. A seven-day festival follows.

Making Global Connections

Student Protests Abroad The student protests of the late 1960s were not confined to the United States. One of the most prominent student radicals abroad was Daniel Cohn-Bendit, whose left-wing politics earned him the nickname Danny the Red. The massive street protests that he organized in Paris crippled the French capital and even spread to cities as far away as Cairo, Egypt, and Karachi, Pakistan. Exiled from his native France, Cohn-Bendit settled in Frankfurt, Germany, where he continued his political activism.

Days of Loss and Rage

The growing division over Vietnam led to a shocking political development in the spring of 1968, a season in which Americans also endured two assassinations, a series of urban riots, and a surge in college campus protests.

JOHNSON WITHDRAWS Well before the Tet offensive, an antiwar coalition within the Democratic Party had taken steps to unseat President Johnson. The group sought a Democratic candidate to challenge Johnson in the 1968 presidential primary election. **Robert Kennedy,** a senator from New York, decided not to run, citing party loyalty. However, in November of 1967, Minnesota senator **Eugene McCarthy** answered the group's call. McCarthy, a strong critic of the war, declared he would run against Johnson on a platform to end the war in Vietnam. "In every other great war of the century," McCarthy declared, "we have had the support of what is generally accepted as the decent opinion of mankind. We do not have that today."

McCarthy's early campaign attracted little notice, but in the weeks following Tet, it picked up steam. In the New Hampshire Democratic primary in March 1968, the little-known senator shocked the nation by capturing 42 percent of the vote. While Johnson won the primary with 48 percent of the vote, the slim margin of victory was viewed as a defeat for the president. Influenced by Johnson's perceived weakness at the polls, Robert Kennedy declared his candidacy for president. The Democratic Party had become a house divided.

On March 31, 1968, President Johnson responded to the growing division within his party and the country. In a televised address to the nation, Johnson announced a dramatic change in his Vietnam policy. The president declared that the United States would seek negotiations to end the war. In the meantime, the policy of U.S. escalation would end. The bombing of North Vietnam would eventually cease, and steps would be taken to ensure that the South Vietnamese played a larger role in the war.

The president paused and then ended his speech with a statement that shocked the nation. Declaring that he did not want the presidency to become "involved in the partisan divisions that are developing in this political year," Lyndon Johnson announced, "Accordingly, I shall not seek, and I will not accept the nomination of my party for another term of president." The president was stepping down from national politics, his grand plan for domestic reform done in by a costly and divisive war. "That . . . war," Johnson later admitted, "killed the lady I really loved—the Great Society."

VIOLENCE AND PROTEST GRIP THE NATION The Democrats—as well as the nation—were in for more shock in 1968. Johnson's startling announcement had barely sunk in when America was rocked by the assassination of Dr. Martin Luther King, Jr., on April 4. In the wake of the civil rights leader's death, violence ripped through nearly 125 U.S. cities as enraged followers of King burned buildings and destroyed neighborhoods.

Violence and rage engulfed the nation's capital for several days, as rioters set more than 700 fires. Federal army troops in full combat gear were called in to protect the Capitol and the White House. By the end of the week, 21,000 federal troops and 34,000 National Guardsmen had been called upon to subdue the rioting across the country. When it was all over, 46 persons were dead, more than 3,000 were injured and some 27,000 were arrested.

Just two months later, a bullet cut down yet another popular national figure. By June of 1968, Robert Kennedy had become a strong candidate in the

The Vietnam War and the divisiveness it caused within America took its toll on Lyndon Johnson.

> "If I've lost Walter [Cronkite], then it's over. I've lost Mr. Average Citizen."
>
> LYNDON B. JOHNSON

THINK THROUGH HISTORY
B. Analyzing Motives Why did President Johnson decide not to run again?

B. Answer He believed that seeking a second term would cause further turmoil and divisiveness within the Democratic Party.

The Vietnam War Years **903**

OBJECTIVE
② INSTRUCT

Days of Loss and Rage

▶ **Starting with the Student**
Ask students to list the most compelling news stories that have been reported during their lifetimes.

- How do these stories compare with the shocking news stories of 1968?

▶ **Discussing Key Ideas**
- The impressive showing of an antiwar candidate, Eugene McCarthy, in the New Hampshire Democratic primary prompts Robert Kennedy to join the presidential race.
- In March President Johnson announces a dramatic change in Vietnam policy and bows out of the presidential race.
- Martin Luther King, Jr., and Robert Kennedy are assassinated, and campus protests surge.

IN-DEPTH RESOURCES: UNIT 8
American Lives: John Lewis, p. 53

MORE ABOUT . . .
Robert Kennedy
Kennedy's candidacy attracted the support of African Americans and Latinos, whose causes he had championed in the past. Many antiwar Democrats also backed his bid for the White House. However, Kennedy's entering the race only after Johnson seemed vulnerable antagonized many McCarthy supporters, who mocked him as "Bobby-come-lately."

TEACHING OPTIONS

Making Global Connections

Soviet Union Invades Czechoslovakia The year 1968 was also a time of trauma in Eastern Europe. During the so-called Prague Spring, reformers in what was then the Communist nation of Czechoslovakia began initiating economic and political changes to make the country more democratic. Their hopes were crushed when Soviet, East German, Polish, and Hungarian troops invaded Czechoslovakia in August 1968. Though Czechs' nonviolent resistance did not prevent the invaders from restoring hard-line Communists to authority, the Soviets again were cast as villains on the world stage.

Making Connections Across the Curriculum

Economics Johnson's TV speech also included his gloomy view of the war's economic toll: "Tonight we face the sharpest financial threat in the postwar era—a threat to the dollar's role as the keystone of international trade and finance in the world. . . . [In] 7 years of unparalleled prosperity . . . the real income of the average American, after taxes, rose by 30 percent—a gain as large as that of the preceding 19 years. So the steps that we must take to convince the world are exactly the steps that we must take to sustain our own economic strength at home. In the past 8 months, prices and interest rates have risen because of our inaction."

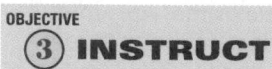

OBJECTIVE
③ INSTRUCT

A Turbulent Race for President

▶ *Discussing Key Ideas*
• Protests spark rioting in Chicago during the Democratic National Convention.
• Delegates at the Democratic convention bitterly debate the party's antiwar plank.
• Vice-President Hubert Humphrey wins the Democratic Party's presidential nomination.
• The Republican presidential candidate, Richard Nixon, wins the 1968 election.

Hotel busboy Juan Romero was the first person to reach Robert Kennedy after he was shot. Kennedy had just won the California primary.

Democratic primary, drawing support heavily from minorities and urban Democratic voters. On June 6, Kennedy won the crucial California primary. During his victory speech at a Los Angeles hotel, he urged McCarthy's followers to join him. Suddenly a young Palestinian, Sirhan Sirhan, who later said he was angered by Kennedy's support of Israel, stepped from the crowd and fatally shot the candidate.

Jack Newfield, a speech writer for Kennedy, described the anguish he and many Americans felt over the loss of two of the nation's leaders.

A PERSONAL VOICE
Things were not really getting better . . . we shall *not* overcome. . . . We had already glimpsed the most compassionate leaders our nation could produce, and they had all been assassinated. And from this time forward, things would get worse. Our best political leaders were part of memory now, not hope.
JACK NEWFIELD, quoted in *Nineteen Sixty-Eight*

In the midst of these shocking murders, the nation's college campuses continued to erupt in protest. During the first six months of 1968, almost 40,000 students on more than 100 campuses took part in 221 major demonstrations. While many of the demonstrations continued to target U.S. involvement in the Vietnam War—which by 1968 reached a year-end peak of 536,000 American military personnel—students also clashed with university officials over a number of campus and social issues. In particular, a massive student protest at Columbia University in New York City held the nation's attention for a week in April. There, students protesting the university's community policies took over several buildings. Police eventually restored order and arrested about 700 protesters.

Recalling the violence and turmoil that seemed to plague the nation in 1968, journalist and historian Garry Wills wrote, "There was a sense everywhere . . . that things were giving way. That man had not only lost control of his history, but might never regain it."

THINK THROUGH HISTORY
C. *Analyzing Issues* Why was 1968 characterized as a year of "lost control" in America?
C. Answer The nation seemed to be losing control of everything from the Vietnam War to its college campuses, to even its future with the assassination of two of its most promising leaders.

A Turbulent Race for President

The chaos and violence of 1968 climaxed in Chicago. Thousands of antiwar demonstrators converged on the city to protest at the Democratic National Convention in August of that year. The convention, which featured a bloody riot between protesters and police, fractured the Democratic Party and thus helped a nearly-forgotten Republican win the White House.

TURMOIL IN CHICAGO With Lyndon Johnson stepping down and Robert Kennedy gone, the 1968 Democratic presidential primary race pitted Eugene McCarthy against Vice-President **Hubert Humphrey.** McCarthy, while still popular with the nation's antiwar segment, had little chance of defeating Humphrey, a loyal party man who had President Johnson's support. During the last week of August, the Democrats met at their convention in Chicago supposedly to choose a candidate. In reality, Humphrey's nomination had already been determined, a decision that upset many antiwar activists.

As the delegates arrived in Chicago, so too did nearly 10,000 protesters. Led by men such as SDS veteran Tom Hayden, many demonstrators sought to pressure the Democrats into adopting an antiwar platform. Others came to voice their displeasure with Humphrey's nomination. Still others, known as Yippies (members of the Youth International Party), had come hoping to provoke violence that might discredit the Democratic Party. No matter their reason,

---

Chicago police attempt to disperse antiwar demonstrators at the 1968 Democratic convention. Protesters shouted, "The whole world is watching!"

MORE ABOUT . . .
Richard J. Daley
The last of the big-city political bosses, Daley had served in the Illinois legislature before being elected Chicago's mayor in 1955. A key supporter of John F. Kennedy's presidential bid in 1960, Daley's delivery of the Illinois vote had given Kennedy his slim majority over Nixon. Daley maintained good relations with African Americans until riots swept Chicago after the assassination of Dr. Martin Luther King, Jr. It may have been in part because of those riots that Daley was so tough on protesters during the convention. In 1996 the Democrats returned to Chicago—now run by "Boss" Daley's son, Richard M. Daley—for a successful convention.

ELECTRONIC LIBRARY OF PRIMARY SOURCES
from *The Strategy of Confrontation*

Chicago's Mayor Richard J. Daley was determined to keep them under control. With memories of the nationwide riots after King's death still fresh, Daley mobilized 12,000 Chicago police officers and 5,000 National Guardsmen. "As long as I am mayor," Daley vowed, "there will be law and order."

Order, however, soon collapsed. On August 28, as delegates cast votes for Humphrey, chaos engulfed the downtown park where the protesters had gathered to march on the convention. With television cameras focused on them, police moved into the crowd, sprayed the protesters with Chemical Mace and beat them with nightsticks. Many protesters tried to flee, while others retaliated, pelting the riot-helmeted police with rocks and bottles. "The whole world is watching!" protesters shouted, as police attacked demonstrators and bystanders alike.

The rioting soon spilled out of the park and into the downtown streets. One nearby hotel, observed a *New York Times* reporter, became a makeshift aid station.

A PERSONAL VOICE
Demonstrators, reporters, McCarthy workers, doctors, all began to stagger into the Hilton lobby, blood streaming from face and head wounds. The lobby smelled from tear gas, and stink bombs dropped by the Yippies. A few people began to direct the wounded to a makeshift hospital on the fifteenth floor, the McCarthy staff headquarters.

J. ANTHONY LUKAS, quoted in *A Decade of Shocks*

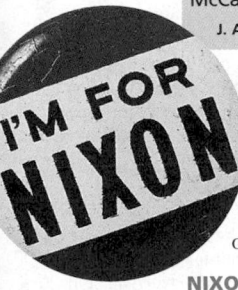

This button was made for Nixon's 1968 campaign.

Disorder of a different kind reigned inside the convention hall, where delegates bitterly debated an antiwar plank in the party platform. When word of the riot filtered into the hall, delegates angrily shouted at Daley, who returned their shouts with equal vigor. The whole world indeed was watching—on their televisions. The images of the Democrats—both inside and outside the convention hall—as a party of disorder became etched in the minds of millions of Americans.

NIXON TRIUMPHS A person who benefited from this turmoil was Republican presidential candidate Richard M. Nixon. By 1968, Nixon had achieved one of the greatest political comebacks in American politics. After his loss to Kennedy

The Vietnam War Years **905**

Cooperative Activity: Creating a 1968 Yearbook

Task: Groups of students will create 1968 yearbooks based on their research into key events in America and around the world.

Purpose: To chronicle the events of the most turbulent year of the decade.

Activity: Tell students to focus on only the major events of the year and to arrange information chronologically or geographically. Yearbooks might include captioned photos and magazine clippings (or photocopies of these), as well as original sketches, charts, and computer graphics. Each group member can perform a different task—for example, art research, drawing, creating computer graphics, paste-up, or caption writing.

ALTERNATIVE ASSESSMENT BOOK
Standards for Evaluating a Cooperative Activity

Election of 1968

Reading the Graph Correlate the total numbers of electoral votes tallied in the third column of the chart with the state-by-state results shown on the map. Point out that Wallace won states in the Deep South and that Humphrey triumphed in the Northeast.

Extension Have students use the information in the map to create a chart with the headings "Candidate," "Party," and "States Won"

ASSESS & RETEACH

Section 4 Assessment

Have pairs of students work together to find evidence in the text to support their answers.

Self-Assessment

Have students create multiple-effects charts showing the short- and long-term consequences of the Tet offensive. Ask them to refer to their completed charts as they review their answers for item 3. Do they have new ideas to add?

Section Quiz

FORMAL ASSESSMENT
Section Quiz, p. 366

Reteach

Use the time lines students created for item 2 to review the turbulent events in the first half of 1968.

CLOSE

The Tet offensive changed public opinion about the war and contributed to Johnson's decision not to seek reelection. Two assassinations, urban riots, and campus protests rocked the nation. The chaotic Democratic convention helped pave the way for Republican Richard Nixon's win in November's presidential election.

Election of 1968

ELECTORAL AND POPULAR VOTES

Party	Candidate	Electoral votes	Popular vote
■ Republican	Richard M. Nixon	301	31,785,480
■ Democratic	Hubert H. Humphrey	191	31,275,166
■ American Independent	George C. Wallace	46	9,906,473

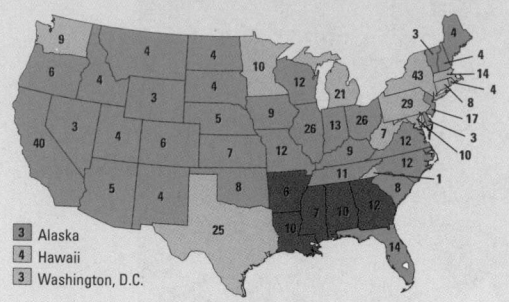

3 Alaska
4 Hawaii
3 Washington, D.C.

SKILLBUILDER
INTERPRETING GRAPHS *By how many percentage points did Nixon defeat Humphrey in the popular vote? How large was Nixon's electoral vote victory?*

Skillbuilder Answers
Percent: Less than one percent (0.7) **Electoral:** 110 votes

---

Richard M. Nixon flashes a victory signal on his way to winning the presidency. Referring to recent years of turmoil, Nixon declared, "We have endured a long night. . . let us gather the light."

in the presidential race of 1960, Nixon tasted defeat again in 1962 when he ran for governor of California. His political career all but dead, Nixon joined a New York law firm. However, he never strayed far from politics. In 1966, Nixon campaigned vigorously for Republican candidates in congressional elections, helping Republicans win back 47 House seats and 3 Senate seats from Democrats. In 1968, Nixon announced his candidacy for president, and on the strength of his many Republican alliances, as well as his voter appeal, he won the party's nomination.

During the presidential race, Nixon campaigned on a promise to restore law and order, which appealed to many middle-class Americans fed up with years of riots and protests. He also promised, in vague but appealing terms, to end the war in Vietnam. Nixon's candidacy was helped by the entry of former Alabama governor **George Wallace** into the race. Wallace, a Democrat running as an independent, was a longtime champion of school segregation and states' rights. Labeled the "white backlash" candidate, Wallace captured five Southern states. In addition, he attracted a surprisingly high number of Northern white working-class voters disgusted with inner-city riots and antiwar protests.

In the end, Nixon defeated Humphrey by more than 100 electoral votes, despite capturing only 43 percent of the popular vote. By winning the presidency, Richard Nixon inherited the quagmire in Vietnam. He eventually would end America's involvement in Vietnam, but not before his war policies created even more protest and uproar within the country.

D. Answer The Democrats' disunity, Nixon's law-and-order stance, his vow to end the war, and the entry of George Wallace into the race.

THINK THROUGH HISTORY
D. Analyzing Causes *What factors led to Nixon's victory?*

Section 4 Assessment

1. TERMS & NAMES

Identify:
• Tet offensive
• Clark Clifford
• Robert Kennedy
• Eugene McCarthy
• Hubert Humphrey
• George Wallace

2. SUMMARIZING Create a time line of major events that occurred in 1968. Use the months already plotted on the time line below as a guide.

January	April	August

March	June

Which event do you think was most significant? Explain.

3. ANALYZING Why do you think the Tet offensive might be considered the turning point of the Vietnam War? Support your answer with reasons.

THINK ABOUT
• its effects on the Johnson administration's credibility
• its effects on public opinion
• Johnson's response to the split within the Democratic party

4. COMPARING AND CONTRASTING Do you think there might have been a relationship between the violence of the Vietnam War and the growing climate of violence in the United States during 1968? Why or why not?

THINK ABOUT
• the heavy casualties during the month-long Tet offensive
• peak U.S. involvement in Vietnam in 1968
• Garry Wills's comment on page 904

906 CHAPTER 30

ANSWERS

1. TERMS & NAMES
• Tet offensive, p. 901
• Clark Clifford, p. 902
• Robert Kennedy, p. 903
• Eugene McCarthy, p. 903
• Hubert Humphrey, p. 904
• George Wallace, p. 906

2. SUMMARIZING

Possible Responses: January—Tet offensive. March—Johnson's withdrawal from presidential race. April—King's assassination; urban riots. June—RFK's assassination. August—Clash between police and protesters at Democratic National Convention.

3. ANALYZING

Possible Responses: Widened the Johnson administration's credibility gap; prompted the mainstream media to criticize the war; caused Johnson's popularity to plummet; prompted Johnson's response to growing division within Democratic Party—the dramatic change in his Vietnam policy and withdrawal from the presidential race.

4. COMPARING AND CONTRASTING

Possible Responses: Yes—The war's atmosphere of violence spread to U.S. cities and college campuses. No—There was no cause-and-effect relationship between the two kinds of violence; neither King's nor Kennedy's assassination was related to the violence in Vietnam; the urban riots after King's assassination were related to the rage and anger over his death.

5 The End of the War and Its Legacy

TERMS & NAMES
- Vietnamization
- silent majority
- Pentagon Papers
- Henry Kissinger
- Khmer Rouge
- War Powers Act

LEARN ABOUT President Richard Nixon's Vietnamization policy and the end of the war
TO UNDERSTAND how the war had a lasting effect on America.

ONE AMERICAN'S STORY

Alfred S. Bradford served in Vietnam from September 1968 to August 1969. A member of the 25th Infantry Division, he was awarded several medals, including the Purple Heart, given to soldiers wounded in battle. Bradford went on to teach history at the universities of Missouri and Oklahoma. One day, Bradford's eight-year-old daughter, Elizabeth, inquired about his experience in Vietnam. "Daddy, why'd you do it?" she asked. Bradford recalled what he told himself.

> **A PERSONAL VOICE**
> Vietnam was my generation's adventure. I wanted to be part of that adventure and I believed that it was my duty as an American, both to serve my country and particularly not to stand by while someone else risked his life in my place. I do not regret my decision to go, but I learned in Vietnam not to confuse America with the politicians elected to administer America, even when they claim they are speaking for America, and I learned that I have a duty to myself and to my country to exercise my own judgment based upon my own conscience.
> **ALFRED S. BRADFORD,** quoted in *Some Even Volunteered*

A U.S. soldier sits near Quang Tri, Vietnam, during a break in the fighting.

Bradford's mixed view of the war reflected the range of emotions many veterans felt about their service in Vietnam. The war left a deep and lasting impression on many Americans, from soldiers such as Bradford to citizens who did not serve. Richard Nixon had promised in 1968 to end the war, but it would take nearly five more years—and another 20,000 American deaths—to end the nation's involvement in Vietnam. The legacy of the war was profound, as it dramatically affected the way Americans viewed their government and the world.

President Nixon and Vietnamization

In the summer of 1969, recently elected president Richard Nixon announced the first U.S. troop withdrawals from Vietnam. "We have to get rid of the nightmares we inherited," Nixon later told reporters. "One of the nightmares is war without end." However, as Nixon pulled out American troops, he continued the war against North Vietnam to achieve what he called "peace with honor"—a policy that some critics would charge prolonged the "war without end" for several more bloody years.

THE PULLOUT BEGINS As President Nixon settled into the White House in January of 1969, negotiations begun by the Johnson administration to end the war in Vietnam were going nowhere. During the peace talks in Paris, the warring factions argued over everything—including the shape of the negotiating table. The United States and South Vietnam insisted that all North Vietnamese forces withdraw from the South and that the government of Nguyen Van Thieu, then South Vietnam's ruler, remain in power. The North Vietnamese and Vietcong demanded that U.S. troops withdraw from South Vietnam and that the Thieu government step aside for a coalition government that would include the Vietcong.

The Vietnam War Years **907**

SECTION 5 RESOURCES

 PRINT RESOURCES

IN-DEPTH RESOURCES: UNIT 8
Guided Reading, p. 39
Outline Map: The Vietnam War, p. 43
Literature: from *In Country* by Bobbie Ann Mason, p. 49

ACCESS FOR STUDENTS ACQUIRING ENGLISH
Guided Reading (Spanish), p. 203
Outline Map: The Vietnam War (Spanish), pp. 297–298

FORMAL ASSESSMENT
Section Quiz, p. 367

ALTERNATIVE ASSESSMENT BOOK
See forms for supporting and scoring alternative activities.

TECHNOLOGY RESOURCES

HUMANITIES TRANSPARENCIES
H28, Fall of Saigon; H45, The Blind Leading the Blind

GEOGRAPHY TRANSPARENCIES
G30, Vietnam War: 1964–1975

CRITICAL THINKING TRANSPARENCIES
CT30, The War in Vietnam

CD-ROM Electronic Library of Primary Sources
The War in Vietnam

VIDEO *American Portfolio: A Videodisc for U.S. History*
user's guide, pp. 247, 252–253

INTERNET McDougal Littell Learning On-Line
http://www.mcdougallittell.com

Section 5 Overview

OBJECTIVES

1 To describe Nixon's policy of Vietnamization.

2 To explain the public's reaction to the Vietnam War during Nixon's presidency.

3 To trace the end of U.S. involvement and the final outcome in Vietnam.

4 To examine the war's painful legacy in the United States and Southeast Asia.

SKILLBUILDER
- Interpreting charts, p. 908

CRITICAL THINKING
- Summarizing, pp. 908, 913
- Analyzing issues, p. 909
- Hypothesizing, p. 910
- Evaluating decisions, p. 911
- Recognizing effects, p. 913
- Synthesizing, p. 913
- Drawing conclusions, p. 913

FOCUS & MOTIVATE

▶ *Starting with the Student*
- Why are political leaders sometimes guilty of making false promises?
- How does the public react to politicians' unkept promises?

OBJECTIVE
1 INSTRUCT

President Nixon and Vietnamization

▶ *Discussing Key Ideas*
- Negotiations to end the war reach a deadlock.
- Nixon initiates a policy of Vietnamization—a gradual withdrawal of U.S. troops and replacement with South Vietnamese troops.
- A key goal of Vietnamization is to achieve "peace with honor."

IN-DEPTH RESOURCES: UNIT 8
Guided Reading p. 39

ACCESS FOR STUDENTS ACQUIRING ENGLISH
Guided Reading (Spanish), p. 293

 HUMANITIES TRANSPARENCIES
H45, The Blind Leading the Blind

U.S. Aerial Bomb Tonnage

Reading the Chart Correlate the difference in bomb tonnage with the increased sophistication of military aircraft in the Vietnam War. Explain that the four bombers illustrated in the chart show the development of aircraft design over the years.

Extension Have students list other kinds of data that might be shown on charts about U.S. aerial bombing in wartime. *Possible Responses: Numbers of people killed; targets hit; types of bombing targets (populated versus isolated); kinds of bombs (for example, two nuclear bombs in World War II).*

OBJECTIVE

② INSTRUCT

Trouble Continues on the Home Front

▶ **Starting with the Student** Have students describe recent social protests.

▶ **Discussing Key Ideas**
- News accounts of the My Lai massacre horrify the American public.
- Nixon's invasion of Cambodia spurs nationwide campus protests.
- The slaying of student protesters and bystanders at Kent State and Jackson State rocks the nation.
- Publication of the top-secret Pentagon Papers further erodes support for the war.

U.S. Aerial Bomb Tonnage

WORLD WAR I, WORLD WAR II, KOREAN WAR

VIETNAM WAR

2.6 million tons

6.2 million tons

Sources: *The U.S. Air Service in World War I, Vol. 1, 4; Vietnam War Almanac; Dictionary of the Vietnam War*

SKILLBUILDER

INTERPRETING CHARTS

What does the chart show about the type of war the U.S. fought in Vietnam?

Skillbuilder Answer
Possible response: The charts shows that the United States relied heavily on air power to defeat the Vietcong; the U.S. may have figured that a massive and unrelenting bombing campaign would greatly help in its strategy to demoralize the enemy.

In the midst of the stalled negotiations, Nixon announced his strategy to end America's involvement in Vietnam. Known as **Vietnamization,** the plan called for the gradual withdrawal of U.S. troops in order for the South Vietnamese to take on a more active combat role in the war. By August of 1969, the first 25,000 U.S. troops had returned home from Vietnam. Over the next three years, the number of American troops in Vietnam dropped from more than 500,000 to less than 25,000.

"PEACE WITH HONOR" However, part of Nixon's Vietnamization policy was aimed at establishing what he called a "peace with honor." Nixon intended to maintain U.S. dignity in the face of its withdrawal from war. A further goal was the preservation of U.S. clout at the negotiation table, as President Nixon still demanded that the South Vietnamese government remain intact. With this objective—and even as the pullout had begun—Nixon secretly ordered a massive bombing campaign against supply routes and bases in North Vietnam. The president also ordered that bombs be dropped on the neighboring countries of Laos and Cambodia, which held a number of Vietcong sanctuaries. Nixon told aide H. R. Haldeman that he wanted the enemy to believe he was capable of anything.

A PERSONAL VOICE

I call it the madman theory, Bob. I want the North Vietnamese to believe I've reached the point where I might do *anything* to stop the war. We'll just slip the word to them that "for God's sake, you know Nixon is obsessed about Communists. We can't restrain him when he's angry—and he has his hand on the nuclear button"—and Ho Chi Minh himself will be in Paris in two days begging for peace.

RICHARD M. NIXON, quoted in *The Price of Power*

A. Answer To withdraw U.S. troops while maintaining American might and dignity, as well as a strong negotiating position.

THINK THROUGH HISTORY
A. Summarizing What was the goal of Nixon's "peace with honor" in Vietnam?

Trouble Continues on the Home Front

Seeking to win support for his war policies, Richard Nixon appealed to what he called the **silent majority**—moderate, mainstream Americans who quietly supported the president's strategy. To be sure, many average Americans did support the president. However, the events of the war continued to divide the country.

THE MY LAI MASSACRE In November of 1969, Americans learned of a shocking event. That month, *New York Times* correspondent Seymour Hersh reported that on March 16, 1968, a U.S. platoon under the command of Lieutenant William Calley, Jr., entered the small village of My Lai in northern South Vietnam in search of Vietcong rebels. Finding no sign of the enemy, the troops rounded up the villagers and shot them. In all, the soldiers massacred more than 100 innocent Vietnamese—mostly women and children. "We huddled them up," recalled 22-year-old Private Paul Meadlo. "I poured about four clips into the group. . . . The mothers were hugging their children. . . . Well, we kept right on firing."

The troops insisted that they were following Lieutenant Calley's orders. When asked what his directive had been, one soldier answered, "Kill anything that breathed." Twenty-five army officers were charged with involve-

908 CHAPTER 30

TEACHING OPTIONS

Teaching Less Proficient Readers

Clarifying Ideas As students read pages 908–913, have them follow the five steps of the SQ3R study method:

1. **Survey** the pages by skimming the paragraphs and the art, including the graphic on aerial bomb tonnage.
2. **Jot down** any **questions** about Vietnam or America.
3. **Reread** the pages, looking for answers to those questions.
4. **Record** any answers you find.
5. **Review** the information, checking for answers to any remaining questions.

Teaching Gifted and Talented Students

Discussing Political Strategy Have students research the tactics that Richard Nixon used, with the help of Vice-President Spiro Agnew, to enlist the support of the "silent majority." Students should then hold a panel discussion about the advantages and disadvantages of the strategy. Questions the panel might address include

- Who constituted the "silent majority" and the vocal minority?
- How did Nixon's and Agnew's criticism of the media play a role in polarizing these two groups?
- What other people did Nixon and Agnew criticize?

ment in the massacre and subsequent cover-up, but only Calley was convicted and imprisoned.

The My Lai massacre shook the nation. *Time* magazine called the incident "an American tragedy," and *Newsweek* appeared to capture the mood of the nation with its headline "A Single Incident in a Brutal War Shocks the American Conscience."

THE INVASION OF CAMBODIA Despite the shock over My Lai, however, the country's mood by 1970 seemed to be growing less explosive. American troops were on their way home, and it appeared that the war was finally winding down. Indeed, a *New York Times* survey of college campuses in 1969 had revealed that many students were shifting their attention from the antiwar movement to the environment.

Then on April 30, 1970, President Nixon announced that U.S. troops had invaded Cambodia. The "incursion" into Cambodia was launched, Nixon declared, to clear out North Vietnamese and Vietcong supply centers. Addressing potential critics, the president defended his action: "If when the chips are down, the world's most powerful nation . . . acts like a pitiful, helpless giant, the forces of totalitarianism and anarchy will threaten free nations . . . throughout the world."

Upon hearing of the invasion, college students across the country erupted in protest. In what became the first general student strike in the nation's history, more than 1.5 million students closed down some 1,200 campuses. The president of Columbia University called the month that followed the Cambodian invasion "the most disastrous month of May in the history of higher education."

KENT STATE Disaster struck hardest at Kent State University in Ohio, where a massive student protest led to the burning of the ROTC building. In response to the growing unrest, the local mayor called in the National Guard. On May 4, 1970, the guards fired into a crowd of campus protesters who were hurling rocks at them. The gunfire wounded nine people and killed four, including two who had not even participated in the rally.

Ten days later, similar violence rocked the mostly all-black college of Jackson State in Mississippi. National Guardsmen there confronted a group of antiwar demonstrators and fired on the crowd after several bottles were thrown. In the hail of bullets, 12 students were wounded and 2 were killed, both innocent bystanders.

In a sign that America still remained sharply divided about the war, the country hotly debated the campus shootings. Polls indicated that many Americans supported the National Guard; respondents claimed that the students "got what they were asking for." The weeks following the campus turmoil brought new attention to a group known as "hardhats," construction workers and other bluecollar Americans who supported the U.S. government's war policies. In May of 1970, nearly 100,000 members of the Building and Construction Trades Council of New York held a rally outside city hall to support the government.

THE PENTAGON PAPERS Nixon's Cambodia policy, however, cost him significant political support. By first bombing and then invading Cambodia without

Mary Ann Vecchio grieves over the body of Jeffrey Glenn Miller, a 20-year-old student shot by National Guard troops at Kent State.

B. Answer The shootings sparked heated debate as well as the resurgence of the "hardhats."

THINK THROUGH HISTORY

B. Analyzing Issues How did the campus shootings demonstrate the continued divisions within the country?

The Vietnam War Years **909**

MORE ABOUT . . .
Daniel Ellsberg

Ellsberg had lost faith in the war by 1970. When he leaked the Pentagon Papers to the *New York Times*, Kissinger reportedly hit the roof. Ellsberg remained a lifelong antiwar activist; in 1991, he was arrested for protesting the Gulf War.

THE WAR IN VIETNAM
excerpts from the Pentagon Papers

OBJECTIVE
③ INSTRUCT

America's Longest War Ends

▶ *Discussing Key Ideas*
- After Nixon's reelection, peace talks break off and U.S. bombings resume.
- In 1973, the United States and North Vietnam sign a cease-fire agreement, and the last U.S. combat troops withdraw from Vietnam.
- The cease-fire collapses, and in 1975 South Vietnam falls to North Vietnam.

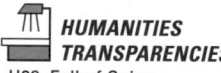
HUMANITIES TRANSPARENCIES
H28, Fall of Saigon

KEY PLAYER
Henry Kissinger
Critical Thinking:
Analyzing In the 1968 presidential campaign, Kissinger had backed Nelson Rockefeller. After Nixon won the election, he staffed his administration with some Rockefeller Republicans as a gesture of party unity. Discuss how the saying "Politics makes strange bedfellows" might be applied to Nixon and Kissinger.

even notifying Congress, the president stirred anger on Capitol Hill. On December 31, 1970, Congress repealed the Tonkin Gulf Resolution, which had given the president near independence in conducting policy in Vietnam.

Support for the war eroded even further when in June of 1971 former Defense Department worker Daniel Ellsberg leaked what became known as the **Pentagon Papers.** The 7,000-page document, written for Defense Secretary Robert McNamara, revealed among other things that the government drew up plans for entering the war even as President Lyndon Johnson promised that he would not send American troops to Vietnam. Furthermore, the papers showed that there was never any plan to end the war as long as the North Vietnamese persisted.

For many Americans, the Pentagon Papers confirmed their belief that the government had not been honest about its war intentions. The document, while not particularly damaging to the Nixon administration, supported what opponents of the war had been saying.

THINK THROUGH HISTORY
C. Hypotheszing
How might the release of Pentagon Papers have hurt the Nixon administration's war effort in Vietnam?
C. Answer The release of the Pentagon Papers may have further eroded public support for the war and made Americans more distrustful of what the current administration was reporting about Vietnam.

KEY PLAYER

HENRY KISSINGER
1923–

Henry Kissinger fled Germany with his family in 1938, to escape the Nazi persecution of the Jews. Kissinger, who helped negotiate America's withdrawal from Vietnam and who later would help forge historic new relations with China and the Soviet Union, held a deep interest in the concept of power. "You know," he once noted, "most of these world leaders, you wouldn't want to know socially. Mostly they are intellectual mediocrities. The thing that is interesting about them is . . . their power."

At first, Kissinger seemed an unlikely candidate to work for Richard Nixon. During the 1968 presidential campaign, Kissinger declared, "That man Nixon is not fit to be president." However, the two would become trusted colleagues. In August of 1974, two days before Nixon resigned as president amid the Watergate political scandal, he summoned Kissinger to the Lincoln Sitting Room upstairs in the White House. There, the two men reportedly knelt together, prayed, and then embraced.

America's Longest War Ends

In March of 1972, the North Vietnamese launched their largest attack on South Vietnam since the Tet offensive in 1968. President Nixon responded by ordering a massive bombing campaign against North Vietnamese cities, and the mining of Haiphong's harbor, into which Soviet and Chinese supply ships sailed. The Communists "have never been bombed like they are going to be bombed this time," Nixon vowed. The bombings halted the North Vietnamese attack, but the grueling stalemate continued. It was after this that the Nixon administration took steps to finally end America's involvement in Vietnam.

"PEACE IS AT HAND" By the middle of 1972, the country's growing social division and the looming presidential election prompted the Nixon administration to change its negotiating policy in Paris. Polls showed that more than 60 percent of Americans in 1971 felt that the United States should withdraw all troops from Vietnam by the end of the year.

Henry Kissinger, the president's adviser for national security affairs, served as Nixon's top negotiator in Vietnam. Kissinger, a German emigrant who had earned three degrees from Harvard, was an expert on international relations. Since 1969, Kissinger had been meeting privately with North Vietnam's chief negotiator, Le Duc Tho. Eventually, Kissinger dropped his insistence on the removal of all North Vietnamese troops from the South before the complete withdrawal of American troops. On October 26, 1972, one week before the presidential election, Kissinger announced, "Peace is at hand."

THE FINAL PUSH President Nixon won reelection, but the promised peace proved to be elusive. The Thieu regime, alarmed at the prospect of North Vietnamese troops stationed in South Vietnam, rejected Kissinger's plan. Talks broke off on December 16, and two days later, the president unleashed a ferocious bombing campaign against Hanoi and Haiphong, the two largest cities in North Vietnam. In what became known as the "Christmas bombings," U.S. planes dropped 100,000 bombs for 11 straight days, pausing only on Christmas Day.

At this point, calls to end the war resounded from the halls of Congress as well as from Beijing and Moscow. Everyone, it seemed, had finally grown weary of the war. The warring parties returned to the

---

TEACHING OPTIONS

Exploring Themes

Constitutional Concerns Though the Pentagon Papers controversy reflected the duplicity of Johnson's administration, Nixon felt that its content further undermined public faith in the war. His administration tried to stop its publication in a case that went all the way to the Supreme Court. While agreeing that the government could file criminal charges for theft or possession of classified documents, the court decided in the *New York Times*'s favor in the matter of publication.

THE WAR IN VIETNAM
texts of the Supreme Court decision in the Times-Post Case

Making Global Connections

Kissinger and Foreign Policy Nixon's visit to the People's Republic of China was one of the landmark foreign-policy achievements of his presidential administration. Kissinger was a chief behind-the-scenes negotiator for that historical visit. He also played a vital role in Mideast peace negotiations and developed the policy of better relations with the Soviet Union, called détente. He continued to be a major architect of U.S. foreign policy during President Ford's administration.

peace table, and on January 27, 1973, the United States signed an "agreement on ending the war and restoring peace in Vietnam." Under the agreement, North Vietnamese troops would remain in South Vietnam, which had Nixon's promise to respond "with full force" to any violation of the peace agreement. On March 29, 1973, the last U.S. combat troops left for home. For America, the Vietnam War had ended.

THE FALL OF SAIGON The war itself, however, raged on. Within months of the United States' departure, the cease-fire agreement between North and South Vietnam collapsed. In March of 1975, after several years of fighting, the North Vietnamese launched a full-scale invasion against the South. Thieu appealed to the United States for help. America provided economic aid but refused to send troops.

President Gerald Ford, who entered the White House after the Watergate political scandal forced Richard Nixon out, captured the nation's mood during a speech in New Orleans: "America can regain its sense of pride that existed before Vietnam. But it cannot be achieved by refighting a war that is finished as far as America is concerned." On April 30, 1975, North Vietnamese tanks rolled into Saigon and captured the city. Soon after, South Vietnam surrendered to North Vietnam.

D. Answer Because of the war's divisive effect on the country, as well as the desire to heal the country and move on.

THINK THROUGH HISTORY
D. Evaluating Decisions
Why might the United States have refused to reenter the war?

The War's Painful Legacy

The Vietnam War exacted a terrible price from its participants. In all, 58,000 Americans were killed and some 365,000 were wounded. North and South Vietnamese deaths topped 1.5 million. In addition, the war left Southeast Asia highly unstable, which led to further war in Cambodia. In America, a nation attempted to come to grips with an unsuccessful war. In the end, the conflict in Vietnam left many Americans with a more cautious outlook on foreign affairs and a more cynical attitude toward their government.

AMERICAN VETERANS COPE BACK HOME While families welcomed home their sons and daughters, the nation as a whole extended a cold hand to its

NOW & THEN

POWS/MIAS

An issue that remains alive for many Americans concerns the thousands of soldiers who did not return home from Vietnam. In 1995, the Pentagon reported that there were still 2,202 American soldiers missing in action (MIA) in Southeast Asia—1,618 in Vietnam.

While far more Americans are listed as missing from the Korean War (8,170) and World War II (78,750), locating missing soldiers in Vietnam has taken on a particular intensity. One reason is that despite the Vietnamese government's denial, a number of Americans believe that some U.S. soldiers may still be alive in Vietnam.

The United States has established an MIA office in Hanoi, whose staff members attempt to locate the remains of missing Americans and track down leads about the possibility of surviving soldiers.

Lieutenant Colonel Robert Stirm, a returning POW, receives a warm welcome from his family. The longest-held Vietnam POW was Lieutenant Everett Alvarez, Jr., of California. He was imprisoned for more than eight years.

The Vietnam War Years **911**

NOW & THEN
POWS/MIAS

Critical Thinking: Recognizing Motives
Have students speculate on the reasons that the MIA issue remains alive for some Americans. *Possible Responses: Family members hold on to the hope that MIAS are still alive, since no final proof exists to the contrary; family members' sense of loss remains unresolved.*

OBJECTIVE
④ INSTRUCT

The War's Painful Legacy

▶ **Starting with the Student**
Have students discuss the homecomings that winning World Series and Super Bowl teams receive. Ask students to draw parallels between sports heroes and war heroes.

• Were the soldiers who served in Vietnam heroes? Why or why not?

Discussing Key Ideas
▶ • Vietnam veterans receive a cold homecoming, and some face difficulties in readjusting to civilian life.
• The war's end ushers in a violent, chaotic period in Southeast Asia.
• The war still stirs up controversy and leads to major U.S. policy changes.

💿 **THE WAR IN VIETNAM**
video on the exodus of the boat people

TEACHING OPTION

Making Connections Across Cultures

Native American War Veterans Various tribal ceremonies helped many Native American veterans recover from the psychological trauma of Vietnam. For example, the "squaw dance," also called the Enemy Way, is a Navajo ritual for their returning warriors. As part of the four-day ceremony, a medicine man recounts the tale of the Hero Twins—slayers of the world's monsters. According to the story, "In the process of destroying the Monsters the Twins abused their special powers and weapons and disrupted the harmony in nature by killing some people. . . . [The Twins] thus needed a special ceremony to restore them to harmony. Thus was born the first 'Enemy Way.'"

A Kiowa veteran recalled the homecoming he received: "My people honored me as a warrior. We had a feast and my parents and grandparents thanked everyone who prayed for my safe return. We had a 'special' [a ritual ceremony] and I remembered as we circled the drum I got a feeling of pride. I felt good inside because that's the way the Kiowa people tell you that you've done well."

Teacher's Edition **911**

America's Longest War, 1964–1973

1964	1965	1967	1968
Congress passes Tonkin Gulf Resolution, giving president broad military powers in Vietnam; President Johnson begins bombing North Vietnam.	First U.S. ground troops arrive in Vietnam to begin fighting the Vietcong and North Vietnamese Army.	Antiwar protests in the United States intensify.	Vietcong launch massive Tet offensive on numerous South Vietnamese cities.

HISTORICAL SPOTLIGHT

Vietnam War Memorial: The Wall

Maya Lin's vision of the memorial as a "journey, or passage" became a reality. Millions of people have made pilgrimages to the Wall, leaving notes and tokens of remembrance by the inscribed names of their loved ones. Have students research the objects that visitors have left at the Wall. Discuss why these objects might be considered historical artifacts or primary sources.

MORE ABOUT . . .

Vietnam Veterans' Memorial

In addition to the Wall, the Vietnam Veteran's Memorial site on the National Mall includes a sculpture of three soldiers, added in 1984, and the Vietnam's Women's Memorial, built in 1993.

MORE ABOUT . . .

Delayed Stress Syndrome

Among the legacies of the Vietnam War is a better understanding of delayed stress syndrome, also called posttraumatic stress disorder (PTSD). PTSD results from exposure to such life-threatening situations as warfare, terrorism, violent crime, and natural disasters. Since the 1970s the Veterans Administration has taken the lead in diagnosis and treatment of the disorder, which the American Psychiatric Association formally recognized in 1980.

HISTORICAL SPOTLIGHT

VIETNAM WAR MEMORIAL: THE WALL

Shortly after 1980, a national competition was held to determine the Vietnam memorial's design. Maya Ying Lin, *above*, a 20-year-old architecture student of Chinese descent, submitted the winning design—a long, black granite wall on which are etched the names of the men and women who died or are missing in action, *below*.

"I didn't want a static object that people would just look at," Lin said, "but something they could relate to as on a journey, or passage, that would bring each to his own conclusions." Lin's design became known simply as the Wall.

returning Vietnam veterans. There were no brass bands, no victory parades, no cheering crowds. Instead, many veterans faced indifference or even hostility from an America still torn and bitter about the war. Lily Jean Lee Adams, who served as an army nurse in Vietnam, recalled arriving, while still in uniform, back at Oakland Army Base in 1970.

A PERSONAL VOICE

In the bus terminal people were staring at me and giving me dirty looks. I expected the people to smile, like, "Wow, she was in Vietnam, doing something for her country—wonderful." I felt like I had walked into another country, not my country. So I went into the ladies' room and changed.

LILY JEAN LEE ADAMS, quoted in *A Piece of My Heart*

Many Vietnam veterans readjusted successfully to civilian life. However, about 15 percent of the 3.3 million soldiers who served developed delayed stress syndrome. These veterans had recurring nightmares about their war experience. They suffered from severe headaches and memory lapses. Some veterans became highly apathetic, while others began abusing drugs or alcohol. Several thousand even committed suicide.

In 1982, the U.S. government, in an effort to honor the men and women who served in Vietnam, unveiled the Vietnam Veterans' Memorial in Washington, D.C. The memorial consists of two black granite walls inscribed with the names of all the Americans who died in the war or who were then still listed as missing in action. Many Vietnam veterans, as well as their loved ones, have found visiting the memorial a deeply moving, even healing experience.

FURTHER TURMOIL IN SOUTHEAST ASIA The end of the Vietnam War ushered in a new period of violence and chaos in Southeast Asia. In unifying Vietnam, the Communists initially held out a conciliatory hand to the South Vietnamese. "You have nothing to fear," declared Colonel Bui Tin of the North Vietnamese army.

However, the Communists soon imprisoned more than 400,000 South Vietnamese in harsh "reeducation," or labor, camps. As the Communists imposed their rule throughout the land, nearly 1.5 million people fled Vietnam. They included citizens who had supported the U.S. war effort, as well as business owners, whom the Communists expelled when they began nationalizing the country's business sector.

Also fleeing the country was a large group of poor Vietnamese, known as boat people because they left on anything from freighters to barges to rowboats. Their efforts to reach safety across the South China Sea often met with tragedy, as nearly 50,000 perished on the high seas due to exposure, drowning, illness, or piracy.

The people of Cambodia also endured great suffering after the war. The invasion of Cambodia had unleashed a brutal civil war, in which a Communist group known as the **Khmer Rouge** seized power in 1975. In an effort to transform the country into a peasant society, the Khmer Rouge

---

TEACHING OPTIONS

Global Connections

Cambodia Led by Pol Pot, the Khmer Rouge created what is sometimes called Cambodia's "killing fields" and drove many Cambodians into neighboring Thailand. By 1977 Communist Vietnam was fighting the Khmer Rouge with the aid of Cambodian Communists. In 1979 Vietnam invaded Cambodia and toppled Pol Pot's regime. The new fighting, which resulted in more deaths and another wave of refugees to Thailand, continued sporadically until Vietnam withdrew its troops in 1989. Three years later a United Nations–brokered peace plan put Cambodia on the road to democracy.

Exploring Themes

Cultural Diversity Many of the Vietnamese refugees who fled to the United States after the war developed a new and unique cultural identity. As Hien Duc Do remarked, "Having left Vietnam at an early age [14], I have realized that I can never truly be a Vietnamese, and, at the same time, not having grown up in the United States, I can never fully be an American. In the final analysis, my life experience will not be that of a Vietnamese nor that of an American, but that of a Vietnamese-American. I need to merge the world of my parents with the opportunities, experiences, and hopes that America has to offer."

1969	1970	1972	1973

• Paris peace talks begin in earnest; President Nixon announces Vietnamization of war—gradual withdrawal of U.S. troops.

• President Nixon orders invasion of Cambodia to destroy enemy supply bases; American college campuses erupt in protest.

• Nixon unleashes "Christmas bombings" on North Vietnamese cities after peace talks break off.

• United States and North Vietnam sign a truce; the U.S. withdraws the last of its troops from Vietnam.

executed many government officials and academics. During its reign of terror, the Khmer Rouge is believed to have killed as many as 2 million Cambodians.

VIETNAM'S EFFECT ON AMERICA Even after it ended, the Vietnam War remained a subject of great controversy for Americans. Many hawks continued to insist that the war could have been won if the U.S. had employed more military power. They also blamed the antiwar movement at home for destroying American morale. Doves countered that the North Vietnamese had displayed incredible resiliency and that an increase in U.S. military force would have resulted only in a continuing stalemate. In addition, doves argued that an unrestrained war against North Vietnam might have prompted a military reaction from China or the Soviet Union.

The war resulted in several major U.S. policy changes. First, the government abolished the draft, which had stirred so much antiwar sentiment. The country also took steps to curb the president's war-making powers. In November 1973, Congress passed the **War Powers Act,** which stipulated that a president must inform Congress within 48 hours if U.S. forces are sent into a hostile area without a declaration of war. In addition, the troops may remain there no longer than 90 days unless Congress approves the president's actions or declares war.

In a broader sense, the Vietnam War significantly altered America's views on foreign policy. In what has been labeled the Vietnam syndrome, Americans now pause and consider possible risks to their own interests before deciding whether to intervene in the affairs of other nations.

Finally, the war contributed to an overall cynicism in Americans about their government and political leaders that persists today. Americans grew suspicious of a government that had provided so much misleading information—as the Johnson administration did—or concealed so many activities—as the Nixon administration did. Coupled with the Watergate scandal of the mid 1970s, the war diminished the optimism and faith in government that Americans felt during the Eisenhower and Kennedy years.

E. Answer Many Americans viewed foreign affairs more cautiously and grew more cynical of their own government and political leaders.

THINK THROUGH HISTORY
E. *Recognizing Effects* In what way did the Vietnam War alter American attitudes?

NOW & THEN

U.S. RECOGNITION OF VIETNAM

In July of 1995, more than 20 years after the Vietnam War ended, the United States extended full diplomatic relations to Vietnam. In announcing the resumption of ties with Vietnam, President Bill Clinton declared, "Let this moment . . . be a time to heal and a time to build." Demonstrating how the war still divides Americans, the president's decision drew both praise and criticism from members of Congress and veterans' groups.

In an ironic twist, Clinton nominated as ambassador to Vietnam a former prisoner of war from the Vietnam War, Douglas Peterson, a congress member from Florida. Peterson, a former air force pilot, was shot down over North Vietnam in 1966 and spent six and a half years in a Hanoi prison.

Section 5 Assessment

1. TERMS & NAMES

Identify:
• Vietnamization
• silent majority
• Pentagon Papers
• Henry Kissinger
• Khmer Rouge
• War Powers Act

2. SUMMARIZING Write a newspaper headline summarizing the historical significance of each date listed below.

• March 16, 1968
• April 30, 1970
• May 4, 1970
• May 14, 1970
• December 31, 1970
• January 27, 1973
• March 29, 1973

Choose a headline and write the first paragraph for the newspaper article.

3. SYNTHESIZING In your opinion, what was the effect of the U.S. government's deception about its policies and military conduct in Vietnam? Support your answer with evidence from the text.

THINK ABOUT
• the release of information surrounding the My Lai massacre
• the contents of the Pentagon Papers
• Nixon's secrecy in authorizing military maneuvers

4. DRAWING CONCLUSIONS How would you account for the cold homecoming American soldiers received when they returned from Vietnam? Support your answer with reasons.

THINK ABOUT
• how the Vietnam War ended
• America's divisiveness over its role in Vietnam
• the media coverage of the My Lai massacre

The Vietnam War Years **913**

ANSWERS

1. TERMS & NAMES
• Vietnamization, p. 908
• silent majority, p. 908
• Pentagon Papers, p. 910
• Henry Kissinger, p. 910
• Khmer Rouge, p. 912
• War Powers Act, p. 913

2. SUMMARIZING
Possible Answers: March 16, 1968: Massacre at My Lai; April 30, 1970: Nixon Announces Invasion of Cambodia; May 4, 1970: Kent State Tragedy; May 14, 1970: Two Students Killed at Jackson State; December 31, 1970: Congress Repeals Tonkin Gulf Resolution; January 27, 1973: U.S. Signs Agreement to End Vietnam War; March 29, 1973: Last U.S. Combat Troops Leave Vietnam.

3. SYNTHESIZING
Possible Responses: Since Americans did not learn about the My Lai massacre until over 1½ years after it occurred, they distrusted government reports about Vietnam battles; the leaking of the Pentagon Papers in 1971 confirmed that the Johnson administration had not been entirely honest about its war intentions; Nixon's secretly ordering a massive bombing campaign in North Vietnam caused public mistrust.

4. DRAWING CONCLUSIONS
Possible Responses: The American public might have projected the war's failure onto the soldiers who fought it; though the war ended, many Americans' bitterness and cynicism persisted; the My Lai massacre might have tarnished the image of all U.S. soldiers.

OBJECTIVES

① To explain the Vietnam War's influence on literature.

② To identify the perceptions of the Vietnam War expressed in three literary excerpts.

Literature of the Vietnam War

Throughout history, soldiers as well as citizens have written about the traumatic and moving experiences of war. The Vietnam War, which left a deep impression on America's soldiers and citizens alike, has produced its share of literature. From the surreal fantasy of *Going After Cacciato*, to the grim realism of *A Rumor of War*, much of this literature reflects the nation's lingering disillusionment with its involvement in the Vietnam War.

FOCUS & MOTIVATE

▶ **Starting with the Student**
Ask students what books they have read and what films they have seen about the Vietnam War.

• What general impressions did these works give of the Vietnam War and its warriors?
• How do the literary and film images compare with those in movies and novels set in other 20th-century wars?
• Why is literature about the Vietnam War so extensive and diverse?

MORE ABOUT . . .
Tim O'Brien

A gifted writer about the Vietnam War, Tim O'Brien was drafted just after graduating from Macalester College in 1968. A Minnesota native, he was deeply troubled by the war and even considered avoiding service. Instead, he fought valiantly in Vietnam and earned a Purple Heart. He completed his tour of duty in 1970 and won acclaim for his semifictional memoir *If I Die in a Combat Zone* in 1973. *Going After Cacciato* received the National Book Award.

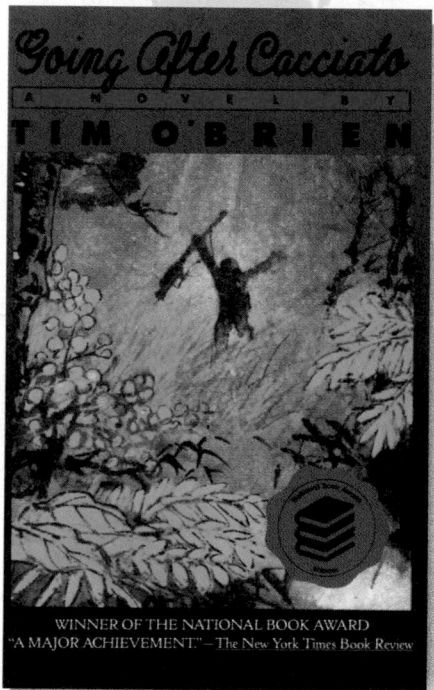

WINNER OF THE NATIONAL BOOK AWARD
"A MAJOR ACHIEVEMENT." —The New York Times Book Review

GOING AFTER CACCIATO

In *Going After Cacciato*, Vietnam veteran Tim O'Brien tells the story of Paul Berlin, a newcomer to Vietnam who fantasizes that his squad goes all the way to Paris, France, in pursuit of an AWOL soldier.

"How many days you been at the war?" asked Alpha's [Alpha Company's] mail clerk, and Paul Berlin answered that he'd been at the war seven days now.

The clerk laughed. "Wrong," he said. "Tomorrow, man, that's your first day at the war."

And in the morning PFC [Private First Class] Paul Berlin boarded a resupply chopper that took him fast over charred pocked mangled country, hopeless country, green skies and speed and tangled grasslands and paddies and places he might die, a million possibilities. He couldn't watch. He watched his hands. He made fists of them, opening and closing the fists. His hands, he thought, not quite believing. *His* hands.

Very quickly, the helicopter banked and turned and went down.

"How long you been at the war?" asked the first man he saw, a wiry soldier with ringworm in his hair.

PFC Paul Berlin smiled. "This is it," he said. "My first day."

TIM O'BRIEN, *Going After Cacciato* (1975)

RECOMMENDED RESOURCES

Books

Hayslip, Le Ly. *When Heaven and Earth Changed Places.* New York: Doubleday, 1989. A first-person account of a Vietnamese woman's experiences in the war.

O'Brien, Tim. *The Things They Carried.* Boston: Houghton, 1990. Interrelated stories capturing the Vietnam War era. Note: contains strong language.

Wyatt, David. *Out of the Sixties.* Cambridge UP, 1993. A study of storytelling and the Vietnam War generation.

Videos

A Rumor of War. Dir. Richard T. Heffron. USA Home Video, 1984. Acclaimed made-for-TV movie based on Caputo's book.

Vietnam: Chronicle of a War. CBS/Fox Video, 1981. Retrospective of the Vietnam War, based on CBS news broadcasts featuring Walter Cronkite and others.

Software

USA Wars: Vietnam. CD-ROM. Quanta Press. Brings the war to life with articles, images, facts, statistics, and the entire Vietnam Veterans' Memorial database.

Vietnam: A Visual Investigation. CD-ROM. Medio, 1994.

A RUMOR OF WAR

In *A Rumor of War*, considered to be among the best nonfiction accounts of the war, former marine Philip Caputo reflects on his years as a soldier in Vietnam.

At the age of twenty-four, I was more prepared for death than I was for life. . . . I knew how to face death and how to cause it with everything on the evolutionary scale of weapons from the knife to the 3.5-inch rocket launcher. The simplest repairs on an automobile engine were beyond me, but I was able to field-strip and assemble an M-14 rifle blindfolded. I could call in artillery, set up an ambush, rig a booby trap, lead a night raid.

Simply by speaking a few words into a two-way radio, I had performed magical feats of destruction. Summoned by my voice, jet fighters appeared in the sky to loose their lethal droppings on villages and men. High-explosive bombs blasted houses to fragments, napalm sucked air from lungs and turned human flesh to ashes. All this just by saying a few words into a radio transmitter. Like magic.

PHILIP CAPUTO, *A Rumor of War* (1977)

FALLEN ANGELS

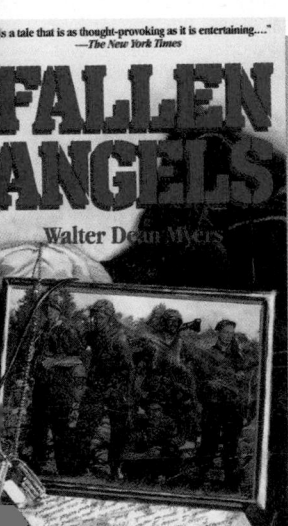

Richie Perry, a 17-year-old Harlem youth, describes his harrowing tour of duty in Vietnam in Walter Dean Myers's novel *Fallen Angels*.

The war was about us killing people and about people killing us, and I couldn't see much more to it. Maybe there were times when it was right. I had thought that this war was right, but it was only right from a distance. Maybe when we all got back to the World and everybody thought we were heroes for winning it, then it would seem right from there. . . . But when the killing started, there was no right or wrong except the way you did your job, except in the way that you were part of the killing.

What you thought about, what filled you up more than anything, was the being scared and hearing your heart thumping in your temples and all the noises, the terrible noises, the screeches and the booms and the guys crying for their mothers or for their wives.

WALTER DEAN MYERS, *Fallen Angels* (1988)

INTERACT WITH HISTORY

1. **COMPARING** What similar views about war do you think these three books convey?

SEE SKILLBUILDER HANDBOOK, PAGE 1041.

2. **CHRONICLING A WAR** Choose a war in which the United States fought and research one aspect of the war (that is, a battle, or living conditions, or a march). Imagine you are a war correspondent in that war and write an article describing the event you have chosen.

For more about American wars, click on **Social Studies** at http://www.mcdougallittell.com

REVIEWING THE CHAPTER

TERMS & NAMES
1. Ho Chi Minh, p. 884
2. Vietcong, p. 886
3. William Westmoreland, p. 890
4. Agent Orange, p. 892
5. dove, p. 899
6. hawk, p. 899
7. Tet offensive, p. 901
8. Robert Kennedy, p. 903
9. Vietnamization, p. 908
10. Pentagon Papers, p. 910

MAIN IDEAS
11. The resolution granted President Johnson broad war-making powers in Vietnam, which allowed him to escalate U.S. involvement in the war.

12. Countries on the brink of communism were like a row of dominoes. If South Vietnam fell to the Communists, the rest of Southeast Asia would follow in a kind of chain reaction.

13. The spread of communism jeopardized democracy.

14. The frustrations of guerrilla warfare; the brutal jungle conditions; the failure to overcome the enemy.

15. A highly disproportionate rate of combat deaths; racial tensions in many platoons.

16. Doves staged massive antiwar demonstrations; hawks urged a greater use of military force in Vietnam.

17. Johnson's high disapproval rating in public-opinion polls after the Tet offensive; the divisions within the Democratic Party.

18. The assassinations of Dr. Martin Luther King, Jr. and Robert Kennedy; the riots at the Democratic National Convention in Chicago.

19. The war itself raged on; the cease-fire agreement between North Vietnam and South Vietnam collapsed.

20. U.S. policy changes; American public's cynicism about the government.

Chapter 30 Assessment

REVIEWING THE CHAPTER

TERMS & NAMES For each item below, write a sentence explaining its connection to the Vietnam War. For each person or group of people named below, explain his or their role in the war's events.

1. Ho Chi Minh
2. Vietcong
3. William Westmoreland
4. Agent Orange
5. dove
6. hawk
7. Tet offensive
8. Robert Kennedy
9. Vietnamization
10. Pentagon Papers

MAIN IDEAS

SECTION 1 *(pages 884–888)*
Moving Toward Conflict
11. How did the Tonkin Gulf Resolution lead to greater U.S. involvement in Vietnam?
12. What was President Eisenhower's explanation of the domino theory?

SECTION 2 *(pages 889–894)*
U.S. Involvement and Escalation
13. Why did much of the American public and many in the Johnson administration support U.S. escalation in Vietnam?
14. Name three factors that contributed to the sinking morale among U.S. troops fighting in Vietnam.

SECTION 3 *(pages 895–900)*
A Nation Divided
15. What race-related problems existed for African-American soldiers who served in the Vietnam War?
16. What evidence was there that the country was sharply divided between hawks and doves?

SECTION 4 *(pages 901–906)*
1968: A Tumultuous Year
17. What circumstances set the stage for President Johnson's public announcement that he would not seek another term as president?
18. What acts of violence occurred in the United States during 1968 that dramatically altered the mood of the country?

SECTION 5 *(pages 907–913)*
The End of the War and Its Legacy
19. Briefly describe the military conflict in Vietnam soon after the last U.S. combat troops departed in 1973.
20. What were the immediate effects and more lasting legacies of the Vietnam War within America?

THINKING CRITICALLY

1. **PRESIDENTIAL POWER** Create a cause-and-effect web similar to the one shown for each of these congressional measures: (a) Tonkin Gulf Resolution (1964), (b) repeal of the Tonkin Gulf Resolution (1970), (c) War Powers Act (1973).

| cause | → | Congressional Measure | → | effect |

2. **YOUTH MOVEMENT** Why do you think that many young Americans became so vocal in their condemnation of the Vietnam War? Support your answer with reasons.

3. **THE VIETNAM WAR'S LEGACY** Reread the quote by Henry Kissinger on page 882. Explain what he meant. Do you agree or disagree? Explain your answer.

4. **GEOGRAPHY OF THE TET OFFENSIVE** Compare the maps on page 886 and page 902. How would you describe the geographic area involved in the Tet offensive?

5. **AMERICAN STUDIES: LITERATURE OF THE VIETNAM WAR** In what ways do each of the literary excerpts on pages 914–915 broaden your understanding of the Vietnam War from a soldier's perspective? Based on these excerpts, what would you consider to be the gravest issues that young soldiers in Vietnam faced?

6. **ANALYZING PRIMARY SOURCES** Senator John Kerry was formerly a national coordinator of Vietnam Veterans Against the War after his service as a naval officer. Read the following excerpt from his speech delivered to the Senate Foreign Relations Committee in 1971. Then answer the questions that follow.

> We [veterans] are probably angriest about all we were told about Vietnam and about the mythical war against communism. We found that not only was it a civil war, an effort by a people who had for years been seeking their liberation from any colonial influence whatsoever, but also found that the Vietnamese whom we had enthusiastically molded after our own image were hard put to take up the fight against the threat we were supposedly saving them from.
>
> We found most people didn't even know the difference between communism and democracy. . . . They wanted everything to do with the war, particularly with this foreign presence of the United States of America, to leave them alone in peace, and they practiced the art of survival by siding with whichever military force was present at a particular time, be it Viet Cong, North Vietnamese, or American.
>
> **JOHN KERRY,** "Statement Before the Foreign Affairs Committee"

What does Kerry say about the false assumptions that guided U.S. foreign policy in Vietnam? Do you agree with his analysis? Why or why not?

THINKING CRITICALLY

1. PRESIDENTIAL POWER
Possible Responses: Tonkin Gulf Resolution: Causes—North Vietnamese torpedo boats attack two U.S. destroyers; Johnson asks Congress for powers to retaliate and prevent further aggression; effects—Johnson granted broad military powers; Johnson administration escalates U.S. military involvement in Vietnam. Repeal of Tonkin Gulf Resolution: Causes—Nixon's policy of bombing and invading Cambodia without notifying Congress; Congress's anger over Nixon's apparent abuse of power; effects—President's autonomy becomes limited in conducting Vietnam policies; Congress regains power in shaping Vietnam policies. War Powers Act: Causes—The outcome of the Vietnam War; fears that Nixon was setting a dangerous precedent of unchecked presidential power; effects—President's war-making powers curbed; balance of power between executive and legislative branches of government redefined.

2. YOUTH MOVEMENT
Possible Responses: Since the draft board called men between the ages of 18 and 26 into military service, the Vietnam War directly affected young Americans; the war would take its greatest toll on this generation and would have a tremendous impact on shaping their adult lives; the tragedies at Kent State and Jackson State revealed that innocent students could, in a sense, also become casualties of the war.

3. THE VIETNAM WAR'S LEGACY
Possible Responses: In stating that "Vietnam is still with us," Kissinger meant that Vietnam not only continued to divide Americans but also still affected the way in which Americans viewed their government, as well as the world around them. Agree—The debate over the U.S. decision to restore full diplomatic relations with Vietnam shows that the war still divides

ALTERNATIVE ASSESSMENT

1. REPORTING ON THE WAR IN VIETNAM

How did individuals influence the outcome of the Vietnam War?

With a partner, prepare a list of questions and conduct a mock interview with someone whose actions influenced the outcome of the Vietnam War.

 CD-ROM Use the CD-ROM *Our Times*, your text, and other sources to conduct research.

• Choose a person to interview and select a specific angle for your questions. For example, interview General William Westmoreland about his military strategy, President Johnson about his political goals, an American soldier or a Vietcong guerrilla about his experiences on the front lines of battle, or an antiwar protester in the United States about how he or she hoped to make a difference.

• With your partner, conduct the mock interview for your class.

2. LEARNING FROM MEDIA

VIDEO View the McDougal Littell Video for Chapter 30, *Matters of Conscience*. Discuss the following questions in small groups; then do the cooperative learning activity.

• What different views about the Vietnam War were expressed in the video?

• What were Stephan Gubar's choices when he was drafted?

• Why does Stephan say he feels guilt about having served in the war?

• **Cooperative Learning** Organize two teams for a debate. One team should argue for the side of the doves—those who believed that the United States should have quickly pulled out of Vietnam. The other team should argue on behalf of the hawks—those who promoted a greater show of military force in Vietnam. Research the arguments put forth by both sides and debate the issue before the class.

3. PORTFOLIO PROJECT

 Use the Living History activity to expand your portfolio.

LIVING HISTORY

DISPLAYING A VIETNAM WAR POSTER

You have created a Vietnam War poster. Now consider the following questions as you review and assess your poster:

• Does it contain dynamic verbal and visual elements?
• Are the captions appropriate and interesting?
• Is the arrangement eye-catching?
• Are there any images or words you would like to add?

Make any final changes or additions and give your poster an appropriate title. With your classmates, create a classroom display of Vietnam War posters. Add your poster to your American history portfolio.

Review Chapter 30

BEGINNINGS OF THE VIETNAM WAR The Geneva Accords (1954) temporarily divided Vietnam into Communist-controlled North Vietnam and nationalist-controlled South Vietnam. Three years later, South Vietnamese Communists, called the Vietcong, began rebelling. To try to halt the spread of communism, Presidents Eisenhower and Kennedy both sent military advisers to Vietnam. In 1964, Congress passed the Tonkin Gulf Resolution, which granted President Johnson broad powers to escalate American military involvement. In 1965, Johnson authorized massive bombing of North Vietnam, and the first U.S combat troops arrived in Vietnam. Despite U.S. escalation, the war became bogged down in a stalemate.

THE HOMEFRONT Back in the United States, the war spurred a growing antiwar movement that sharply divided the nation between supporters and opponents of the government's Vietnam policies. College campuses around the country erupted in protest. Many American youths staged demonstrations, while others displayed their resistance to the draft.

THE FINAL PHASES OF THE WAR AND ITS AFTERMATH The Tet offensive in 1968 stunned Americans and strengthened opposition to the war. Two months after Tet, President Johnson announced he would withdraw from the presidential race. Richard Nixon's victory in the 1968 presidential election paved the way for the end of U.S. involvement in Vietnam, but not before his war policies created even more nationwide protest. In 1973 the United States signed a peace agreement and withdrew its forces from Vietnam. The war left many Americans with a more cautious outlook on foreign affairs and a more cynical attitude toward the government.

Preview Chapter 31

Though the Vietnam War overshadowed Johnson's vision of the Great Society, Latinos, Native Americans, and women held fast to their dreams of gaining political power and improving their status. The Vietnam War also played a key role in fostering the emergence of a youth counterculture. You will learn about these and other significant developments in the next chapter.

The Vietnam War Years **917**

---

1. REPORTING ON THE WAR IN VIETNAM
Standards for Evaluation
An interview should meet the following criteria:

• Is presented in a question-and-answer format and focuses on a fictional or actual figure's role in the Vietnam War.
• Captures the interviewee's unique perspective.
• Shows evidence of research in a variety of sources.
• Includes authentic details, anecdotes, and facts.

2. LEARNING FROM MEDIA
Answers to the questions:

• The war was wrong; the war was necessary to halt the spread of communism; eligible Americans' patriotic duty was to serve in the war.
• Gubar could have fled to Canada, gone to jail, or applied for a noncombatant role in Vietnam.
• Even though Gubar believed the war was wrong, he didn't stand up for that belief.

Standards for Evaluation:
A debate should meet the following criteria:

• Opens with a clear statement of a viewpoint on the Vietnam War.
• Contains logical arguments based on research.
• Includes well-defended objections to the opposing side's viewpoint.

3. PORTFOLIO PROJECT
LIVING HISTORY
An effective Vietnam War poster should meet the following criteria:

• Grabs the attention of viewers.
• Presents a clear, coherent message.
• Uses a balanced layout of images.
• Leaves viewers with a personal insight into the Vietnam War.

IN-DEPTH RESOURCES: UNIT 8
See the form for scoring this activity on page 55.

THINKING CRITICALLY

the country; in addition, Americans do indeed view their government more cynically and are less apt to approve of U.S. troops' intervening in another country's affairs. Disagree—The restoration of U.S. relations with Vietnam shows that the country is getting over the war; also, the United States remains the strongest nation in the world and continues to act confidently in its foreign relations.

4. GEOGRAPHY OF THE TET OFFENSIVE
Possible Response: The entire area of South Vietnam was under attack, but most battles took place along the coast, with some battles occurring in interior regions.

5. AMERICAN STUDIES: LITERATURE OF THE VIETNAM WAR
Possible Response: The excerpts provide readers with a sense of immediacy and highly personal, brutally honest views of the Vietnam War. Among the gravest issues facing young soldiers were thoughts about their mortality, their powerlessness to control their destinies, the constant anticipation of death, and the overall unreal quality of war.

6. ANALYZING PRIMARY SOURCES
Possible Responses: False assumptions included that Vietnam was in the midst of a Communist revolution and that the Vietnamese would readily embrace democratic values. Agree—Above all else, the Vietnamese simply wanted to control their own destiny, and the real struggle of the Vietnamese was against foreign domination; the Americans were unwelcome intruders in a civil war. Disagree—Kerry is parroting the rhetoric of antiwar protesters; he is downplaying the threat of communism; he is subverting America's goal of preserving global freedom.

Teacher's Edition **917**

PLANNING GUIDE
An Era of Social Change

	Key Ideas	TEACHING SUPPORT	ASSESSMENT	
SECTION 1 Latinos and Native Americans Seek Equality pp. 920–925	The nation's Latinos and Native Americans demand greater equality.	**In-Depth Resources: Unit 8** • Guided Reading, p. 56 • Primary Sources: The Farm Worker Movement, p. 62; United Farm Workers Poster, p. 63 • American Lives: Cesar Chavez, p. 69 **COOPERATIVE ACTIVITY** • Listing Native American Demands, p. 924 (TE)	*Section 1 Assessment*, p. 925 (PE) *Self-Assessment*, p. 925 (TE) *Formal Assessment* • Section Quiz, p. 376 *Alternative Assessment Book* • Standards for Evaluating a Cooperative Activity	
SECTION 2 Women Fight for Equality pp. 928–932	A new feminist movement emerges during the 1960s, as women fight to improve their opportunities and status in society.	**In-Depth Resources: Unit 8** • Guided Reading, p. 57 • Geography Application: The Equal Rights Amendment, p. 60 • Primary Source: from *The Feminine Mystique*, p. 64 • American Lives: Betty Friedan, p. 70 **COOPERATIVE ACTIVITY** • Preparing Articles for *Ms.*, p. 930 (TE)	*Section 2 Assessment*, p. 932 (PE) *Self-Assessment*, p. 932 (TE) *Formal Assessment* • Section Quiz, p. 377 *Alternative Assessment Book* • Standards for Evaluating a Cooperative Activity	
SECTION 3 Culture and Counterculture pp. 933–937	Groups of disillusioned youths shun the social activism of the times and choose instead to "drop out" of society and establish their own way of life.	**In-Depth Resources: Unit 8** • Guided Reading, p. 58 • Skillbuilder Practice: Comparing; Contrasting, p. 59 • Primary Source: "Woodstock," p. 65 • Literature: from *Los Vendidos* by Luis Valdez, p. 66 **COOPERATIVE ACTIVITY** • Producing a 1960s Music Video, p. 936 (TE)	*Section 3 Assessment*, p. 937 (PE) *Self-Assessment*, p. 937 (TE) *Formal Assessment* • Section Quiz, p. 378 *Alternative Assessment Book* • Standards for Evaluating a Cooperative Activity	
CHAPTER RESOURCES	**Chapter Overview** The civil rights movement inspires Latinos, Native Americans, and women to seek equality in American society. At the same time, the nation's young people adopt values that conflict with mainstream culture.	**In-Depth Resources: Unit 8** • Living History Project: Worksheet, p. 71; Standards, p. 72 *Telescoping the Times* • Chapter Summary, pp. 61–62 *Planning for Block Schedules*	*Chapter Assessment*, pp. 940–941 (PE) *Alternative Assessment*, p. 941 (PE) *Formal Assessment* • Chapter Test, forms A and B, pp. 379–384 **Test Generator** *Alternative Assessment Book* See explanation and forms for different kinds of alternative assessments including portfolio assessment.	

Humanities Transparencies
• H29, Mural in Los Angeles

Geography Transparencies
• G31, Latino and Native American Population Centers, 1970

 Grolier Multimedia Encyclopedia
• American Indian Movement

Electronic Library of Primary Sources
• The Birth of *La Causa* by Cesar Chavez

INTERNET RESOURCES
• See Interact with History p. 927 (PE) for an activity that includes the Internet as an enrichment option.

 Critical Thinking Transparencies
• CT31, The Women's Movement
• CT65, Percentage of All Women Who Are Working, 1950–1995

 Electronic Library of Primary Sources
• from *The Feminine Mystique* by Betty Friedan

INTERNET RESOURCES
• See *McDougal Littell Learning On-Line* for links to information about ERA, NOW, and Phyllis Schafly.

 Our Times
• from *The Electric Kool-Aid Acid Test* by Tom Wolfe

INTERNET RESOURCES
• See Interact with History p. 939 (PE) for an activity that includes the Internet as an enrichment option.

 American Portfolio: A Videodisc for U.S. History, user's guide, pp. 246–247, 249

INTERNET RESOURCES
Learning On-Line: Social Studies
http://www.mcdougallittell.com

Block Scheduling (90 MINUTES)

Day 1
Section 1, pp. 920–925
Geography Spotlight: The Movement of Migrant Workers, pp. 926–927
Section 2, pp. 928–932
Section Assessments, pp. 925, 932

Day 2
Section 3, pp. 933–937
Daily Life: Signs of the Sixties, pp. 938–939
Section Assessment, p. 937
Chapter Assessment, pp. 940–941

> **YEARLY PACING** *Chapter 31 Total:* 2 days *Yearly Total:* 85 days

See *Planning for Block Schedules* for special activities and pacing strategies.

Customizing for Special Populations

Students Acquiring English

Access for Students Acquiring English
• Guided Reading for Sections 1–3 (Spanish), pp. 301–303
• Chapter Summary (Spanish), pp. 299–300
• Skillbuilder Practice: Comparing; Contrasting (Spanish), p. 304
• Geography Application: The Equal Rights Amendment (Spanish), p. 305

INTERNET RESOURCES
• See *McDougal Littell Learning On-Line* The Diverse Classroom.

Less Proficient Readers

In-Depth Resources: Unit 8
• Guided Reading for Sections 1–3, pp. 56–58
• Skillbuilder: Comparing; Contrasting, p. 59
• Geography Application: The Equal Rights Amendment, p. 60

Telescoping the Times
• Chapter Summary, pp. 61–62

See additional strategies at point of use in the Teacher's Edition.

Gifted and Talented Students

In-Depth Resources: Unit 8
• Primary Sources: The Farm Worker Movement, p. 62; United Farm Workers Poster, p. 63; from *The Feminine Mystique,* p. 64; "Woodstock," p. 65
• American Lives: Cesar Chavez, p. 69; Betty Friedan, p. 70

See additional strategies at point of use in the Teacher's Edition.

Connections to Literature READINGS FOR STUDENTS

In-Depth Resources: Unit 8
• from *Los Vendidos* by Luis Valdez, p. 66

McDougal Littell *The Language of Literature*
American Literature
• Rodolfo Gonzales, from *I am Joaquin/Yo Soy Joaquin,* p. 243
• Aurora Levins Morales and Rosario Morales, "Ending Poem," p. 328
• Luis J. Rodriquez, "Tia Chucha," p. 328
• Sylvia Plath, "Mirror," p. 882
• Anne Sexton, "Self in 1958," p. 882
• Lanford Wilson, *Wandering,* p. 972
• Denise Levertov, "At the Justice Department, November 15, 1969," p. 979
• Nikki Giovanni, "Revolutionary Dreams," p. 979
• Gloria Steinem, "Sisterhood," p. 984
• Anna Quindlen, from *Mother's Choice,* p. 992

• Anne Tyler, "Teenage Wasteland," p. 996
• Nash Candelaria, "El Patrón," p. 99
• Diane Burns, "Sure You Can Ask Me a Personal Question," p. 1020
• John Updike, *"Separating,"* p. 1040
• Carlos Alberto Montaner, "Why Fear Spanish?" p. 1060
• Lorna Dee Cervantes, "Refugee Ship," p. 1068
• Gary Soto, "Mexicans Begin Jogging," p. 1113
• Pat Mora, "Legal Alien," p. 1113

An Era of Social Change

▶ **Starting with the Student**
Ask students to think about people and events of the 1960s.

- What images or symbols come to mind when students think about the 1960s?
- What people—including politicians, musicians, and activists—helped shape the 1960s?

PREVIEWING THE CHAPTER

- Have small groups of students identify and discuss the people and events on the time line.
- Have each student write three or four words or phrases that describe or characterize the 1960s and then share the list with a partner.

MORE ABOUT . . .
Bob Dylan

As a teenager Dylan, whose real name is Robert Zimmerman, listened to rock music and rhythm and blues. Because the local radio station in his small Minnesota hometown didn't play the type of music he liked, Dylan had to tune in to Southern radio stations, which he could get only late at night. He used to place his radio under the covers of his bed to keep from waking anyone.

CHAPTER

31 An Era of Social Change

SECTION 1
Latinos and Native Americans Seek Equality
The nation's Latinos and Native Americans demand greater equality.

SECTION 2
Women Fight for Equality
A new feminist movement emerges during the 1960s, as women fight to improve their opportunities and status in society.

SECTION 3
Culture and Counterculture
Groups of disillusioned youths shun the social activism of the times and choose instead to "drop out" of society and establish their own way of life.

"The times they are a-changin'."
Bob Dylan

- Cesar Chavez and Dolores Huerta found the National Farm Workers Association.

- National Organization for Women (NOW) is formed.

- National Farm Workers Association merges with another farm workers union to form the United Farm Workers Organizing Committee.

- The "summer of love" brings thousands of hippies to San Francisco.

- Twenty-fifth Amendment to the U.S. Constitution, providing guidelines for presidential and vice-presidential succession, takes effect.

✪ Lyndon B. Johnson becomes president upon the assasination of John Kennedy.

✪ Lyndon B. Johnson is elected president.

- National Farm Workers Association joins Filipino farm workers in strike against grape growers.

| THE UNITED STATES | **1960** | 1962 | 1963 | 1964 | 1965 | 1966 | 1967 |
| THE WORLD | | 1962 | 1963 | | | | 1967 |

- Chinese forces invade India.

- Civil war breaks out between Greeks and Turks on Cyprus.

- Six-Day War erupts between Israel and Arab nations.

THEMES IN CHAPTER 31

Immigration and Migration	*Civil Rights*	*Women in America*	*The American Dream*
During the 1960s, the Latino population in the United States grew from 3 million to 9 million. Most Latinos settled in large cities, where they often encountered discrimination. See Teacher's Edition note, p. 921.	The 1960s witnessed the struggle of Native Americans for greater equality. Impatience with the slow pace of reform, however, led to the formation of the American Indian Movement, which actively confronted the government. See Teacher's Edition note, p. 923.	For American women, the 1960s and 1970s were a time of consciousness-raising about "a woman's place." Many women struggled to find fulfillment beyond the bounds of home and family life. See Teacher's Edition note, p. 929.	In the 1960s, members of the counterculture rejected the American dream and chose to drop out of mainstream society. Hippies sought to redefine the American dream by creating a society based on love. See Teacher's Edition note, p. 935.

LIVING HISTORY

INVESTIGATING MUSIC OF THE 1960S

People strongly associate the 1960s with its popular music. The styles of music that were popular at the time included rhythm and blues, rock 'n' roll, protest songs, folk music, and others. Research a type of music from the 1960s that you find interesting. You will use the information you gather to create a documentary for radio.

- Be sure to investigate how the music you select influenced, or was influenced by, the events of the times. Also, find out how it influenced later musical styles.
- Research the people behind the music—the artists who wrote, performed, or produced it.
- Try to find selections of the music you are researching. Libraries are a good source.

PORTFOLIO PROJECT Save your research and any music selections in a folder for your American history portfolio. At the end of the chapter, you will prepare and present your music documentary.

INVESTIGATING MUSIC OF THE 1960S

Help students carry out their investigation.

- Become familiar with a variety of songs from the 1960s—perhaps listening to records in a family member's or friend's collection, tuning in "oldies" radio stations, or checking out Web sites devoted to the music of the period.
- Narrow the documentary's focus. For example, a student exploring rock 'n' roll could concentrate on acid rock or on British invasion groups.
- Select the songs to be used in the documentary.
- Present a written script of the documentary, accompanied by a tape of the music to be used.

Have students create diagrams like the one below to organize their ideas for their documentary scripts.

IN-DEPTH RESOURCES: UNIT 8
See worksheet and standards for evaluation, pp. 71, 72.

BOYCOTT
NON-UFW
GRAPES

Rock singer Janis Joplin is one of the many performers at the Woodstock music festival.

Grape boycott forces growers to sign contracts with the United Farm Workers Organizing Committee.

About 15,000 Mexican-American high school students in Los Angeles boycott classes to protest poor conditions.

Native American activists found American Indian Movement (AIM).

⭐ Richard M. Nixon is elected president.

Political party La Raza Unida is formed.

Congress passes Equal Rights Amendment.

Gloria Steinem founds *Ms.* magazine.

⭐ Richard M. Nixon is reelected.

Native Americans stage protest at Wounded Knee, South Dakota.

Gerald R. Ford ⭐ becomes president after Richard Nixon resigns.

Congress passes Indian Self-Determination and Education Assistance Act.

| 1968 | 1969 | 1970 | | 1972 | 1973 | 1974 | 1975 |
| 1969 | 1970 | 1971 | 1972 | | | | |

President Charles de Gaulle of France resigns.

Anwar el-Sadat becomes president of Egypt.

General Idi Amin Dada seizes power in Uganda.

Earthquake kills 10,000 in Nicaragua.

An Era of Social Change **919**

RECOMMENDED RESOURCES

Books for the Teacher

Matthiessen, Peter. *In the Spirit of Crazy Horse.* New York: Viking, 1983. FBI conflict with American Indian Movement.

Takaki, Ronald. *A Different Mirror.* Boston: Little, 1993. History of African Americans, Latinos, and Asian Americans in the United States.

Books for the Student

Friedan, Betty. *The Feminine Mystique.* Updated edition. New York: Dell, 1993. Includes thoughts 30 years after original publication.

Mankiller, Wilma, and Michael Wallis. *Mankiller.* New York: St. Martin's, 1993. Life of a Cherokee chief.

Shorris, Earl. *Latinos.* New York: Norton, 1992. Describes diverse Latino communities in the United States.

Videos

America: The Second Century: The American Indian; Black Americans; Hispanic Americans; Women in America. GPN, 402-472-2007.

American Indians, Yesterday and Today. Altschul Group, 847-328-6700.

Software

Her Heritage. CD-ROM. Pilgrim New Media, 800-997-5476.

The Native Americans. CD-ROM. Philips Media Software, 800-883-3767.

OBJECTIVES

(1) To describe the growth and diversity of the Latino population in the United States during the 1960s.

(2) To summarize the efforts of Latinos to secure their civil rights and promote respect for their cultural heritage.

(3) To characterize the efforts of Native Americans to secure a number of reforms from the U.S. government.

SKILLBUILDERS

• Interpreting charts, pp. 921, 925

CRITICAL THINKING

• Comparing, p. 921
• Recognizing effects, p. 922
• Identifying problems, p. 923
• Analyzing issues, p. 924
• Synthesizing, p. 925
• Summarizing, p. 925
• Contrasting, p. 925

FOCUS & MOTIVATE

▶ *Starting with the Student*
• Do students think that violent methods are necessary to effect change? Or are nonviolent methods more effective?
• What reparations, if any, should the federal government make to Native Americans for past broken treaties and promises?

MORE ABOUT . . .
Jessie Lopez de la Cruz

When Jessie Lopez de la Cruz first became involved in the farm worker movement, all of its organizers were men. She later recalled, "I guess when the union found out how I was able to talk with people, I was called into Delano to one of the meetings and they gave me my card as an organizer. I am very proud to say that I was the first woman organizer out in the fields organizing the people."

IN-DEPTH RESOURCES: UNIT 8
Primary Source: United Farm Workers Poster, p. 63

1 Latinos and Native Americans Seek Equality

LEARN ABOUT the problems faced by Latinos and Native Americans
TO UNDERSTAND their campaigns for civil rights and economic justice.

ONE AMERICAN'S STORY

Jessie Lopez de la Cruz's life changed one night in 1962, when Cesar Chavez came to her home. Chavez, a Mexican-American farm worker, was trying to organize a union for California's mostly Spanish-speaking farm workers. Although Jessie's husband had been attending union meetings, Jessie had always stayed home. So she was surprised when Chavez sat down at her kitchen table and said, "The women have to be involved. They're the ones working out in the fields with their husbands. If you can take the women out to the fields, you can certainly take them to meetings." Jessie sat up straight and said to herself, *"That's* what I want!" Before long she was out in the fields, talking to farm workers about the union.

A PERSONAL VOICE

Wherever I went to speak . . . I told them about . . . how we had no benefits, no minimum wage, nothing out in the fields—no restrooms, nothing. I'd ask people how they felt about these many years they had been working out in the fields . . . They would say, "I was working for so-and-so, and when I complained about something that happened there, I was fired." I said, "Well! Do you think we should be putting up with this in this modern age? . . . We can stand up! We can talk back! . . . This country is very rich, and we want a share of the money those growers make [off] our sweat and our work by exploiting us and our children!"

JESSIE LOPEZ DE LA CRUZ, quoted in *Moving the Mountain: Women Working for Social Change*

The efforts of Jessie Lopez de la Cruz were just one part of a larger Latino movement during the turbulent and revolutionary decade of the 1960s. As African Americans fought for their civil rights, Latinos and Native Americans also rose up to assert their rights, preserve their cultures, and improve their lives.

Mexican-American farm workers protest poor working conditions.

The Latino Presence Grows

Spanish-speaking Americans, or Latinos, have always been a large and diverse group. The country's Latino population includes people from several different areas: Mexico, Puerto Rico, Cuba, the Dominican Republic, other Caribbean islands, Central America, and South America. Because these groups all trace their roots back to Spanish-speaking countries of Latin America, people often group them together. However, each Latino group has its own history, its own pattern of settlement in the United States, and its own set of economic, social, cultural, and political concerns. During the 1960s, the Latino presence in the United States greatly increased. In the span of a decade, the Latino population grew from 3 million to 9 million.

During this time, the number of Mexicans settling in the United States rose. Mexican Americans, who have always made up the largest Latino group in the United States, once lived mostly in the Southwest and California. Some were the descendants of the nearly 100,000 Mexicans who had lived in territories ceded by Mexico to the United States after the war with Mexico in 1848. Others were the children and grandchildren of the million or so Mexicans who settled in the United States in the decade following Mexico's 1910 revolution. Still others came

---

SECTION 1 RESOURCES

PRINT RESOURCES

IN-DEPTH RESOURCES: UNIT 8
Guided Reading, p. 56
Primary Sources: The Farm Worker Movement, p. 62; United Farm Workers Poster, p. 63
American Lives: Cesar Chavez, p. 69

ACCESS FOR STUDENTS ACQUIRING ENGLISH
Guided Reading (Spanish), p. 301

FORMAL ASSESSMENT
Section Quiz, p. 376

ALTERNATIVE ASSESSMENT BOOK
See forms for supporting and scoring alternative activities.

TECHNOLOGY RESOURCES

HUMANITIES TRANSPARENCIES
H29, Mural in Los Angeles

GEOGRAPHY TRANSPARENCIES
G31, Latino and Native American Population Centers, 1970

CD-ROM *Grolier Multimedia Encyclopedia*
Electronic Library of Primary Sources

VIDEO *American Portfolio: A Videodisc for U.S. History*
user's guide, pp. 246–247

INTERNET McDougal Littell Learning On-Line
http://www.mcdougallittell.com

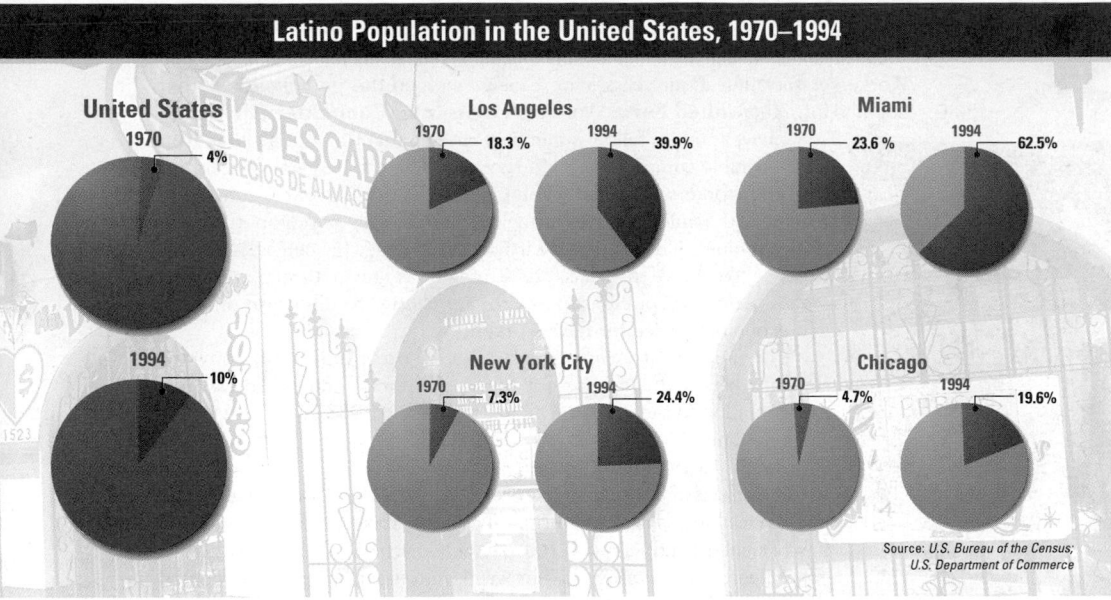

Latino Population in the United States, 1970–1994

United States
1970 — 4%
1994 — 10%

Los Angeles
1970 — 18.3%
1994 — 39.9%

Miami
1970 — 23.6%
1994 — 62.5%

New York City
1970 — 7.3%
1994 — 24.4%

Chicago
1970 — 4.7%
1994 — 19.6%

Source: U.S. Bureau of the Census;
U.S. Department of Commerce

more recently into the United States as *braceros*, or temporary laborers, during the 1940s and 1950s.

About a million Puerto Ricans have lived in the United States since the 1960s. Most have settled in the Northeast, with about 600,000 in New York City alone. Lacking the needed skills and education, many Puerto Ricans had trouble finding work and getting ahead.

Hundreds of thousands of Cubans fled to the United States after the revolutionary leader Fidel Castro overthrew Cuba's dictator, Fulgencio Batista, in 1959. Most settled in or near Miami, turning that Florida city into a boom town. Large Cuban communities also formed in New York City and New Jersey. Many Cubans who fled to the United States were academics and professionals escaping Castro's Communist rule.

In addition, tens of thousands of Salvadorans, Guatemalans, Nicaraguans, and Colombians immigrated to the United States after the 1960s to escape civil war and chronic poverty.

Wherever they settled, during the 1960s many Latinos encountered ethnic prejudice and discrimination in jobs and housing. Most lived in segregated *barrios*, or neighborhoods. The Latino jobless rate was nearly 50 percent higher than that of whites, as was the percentage of families living in poverty. The majority of Latinos found jobs only on the lowest rungs of the occupational ladder. "We are first in janitors," said Senator Joseph Montoya of New Mexico, but "last in equal opportunity."

A. Answer
Prejudice, job and housing discrimination, high unemployment, and poverty

THINK THROUGH HISTORY
A. Comparing
What problems did Latino groups share?

Latinos Fight for Change

As the presence of Latinos in the United States grew, so too did their cries for greater representation and better treatment. During the 1960s, Latinos demanded not only equal opportunity, but also a respect for their culture and heritage.

THE FARM WORKER MOVEMENT As Jessie Lopez de la Cruz stressed in her emotional speech, thousands of Mexican Americans working on California's fruit and vegetable farms found themselves subjected to long hours of backbreaking work for little pay and few benefits. **Cesar Chavez** believed that the only way to improve conditions for farm workers was to unionize them, so that they could

An Era of Social Change **921**

SKILLBUILDER
INTERPRETING CHARTS
Which city experienced the greatest percentage increase of Latinos between 1970 and 1994? In what two cities do Latinos represent more than one-third of the population?

Skillbuilder Answer
Largest: Miami. **Cities:** Los Angeles and Miami.

OBJECTIVE
(1) INSTRUCT

The Latino Presence Grows

▶**Discussing Key Ideas**
• During the 1960s, the Latino population in the United States triples.
• Many Latinos encounter ethnic prejudice and discrimination.

IN-DEPTH RESOURCES, UNIT 8
Guided Reading, p. 56

ACCESS FOR STUDENTS ACQUIRING ENGLISH
Guided Reading (Spanish), p. 301

HISTORY FROM VISUALS
Latino Population in the United States, 1970–1994
Reading the Chart Ask students why the increase in the percentage of Latinos was greater in the four cities than in the United States as a whole. *Possible Response: Employment opportunities drew Latinos to big cities.*

GEOGRAPHY TRANSPARENCIES
G31, Latino and Native American Population Centers, 1970

OBJECTIVE
(2) INSTRUCT

Latinos Fight for Change

▶**Discussing Key Ideas**
• Led by Cesar Chavez, Mexican-American farm workers unionize.
• Latino "brown power" movements promote ethnic pride.
• Latinos begin organizing politically.

TEACHING OPTIONS

Exploring Themes

Immigration and Migration Discuss how the growing Latino population affected American society. Ask students how the increased number of Latinos enriched society. *Possible Response: Latinos introduced elements of their culture, including language, literature, and cuisine.* Then ask what negative effects the influx of Latinos had on society. *Possible Responses: Overcrowding in cities; increased crime; higher unemployment.* Ask students what they think could be done to alleviate some of the problems. Should Latino immigration be limited? Does mainstream America need to change?

Teaching Less Proficient Readers

Clarifying Ideas Help students understand why the Latino population increased so much during the 1960s. Have students follow these steps:

1. Read pages 920–921 and study the charts on page 921.
2. Create a cluster diagram, listing the Latin American countries and regions from which most of the immigrants came, including Mexico, Puerto Rico, Cuba, and Central America.
3. Jot down reasons why Latinos in each region decided to leave their homelands.
4. Add the city or cities where each group settled.

Teacher's Edition **921**

MORE ABOUT . . .
Cesar Chavez

MORE ABOUT . . .
Cesar Chavez

As a boy growing up during the Great Depression, Cesar Chavez attended at least 65 elementary schools—sometimes for only a day, a week, or a month. Like other migrant workers, Chavez's parents had to move from place to place looking for farm work. After witnessing the conditions of farm laborers firsthand, Chavez began working to help the Latino community. Although he was a quiet and rather self-effacing man, Chavez nonetheless captured the imagination and heart of people from all walks of life with his message of social justice. At least 17 million Americans joined his five-year boycott of California grapes.

IN-DEPTH RESOURCES: UNIT 8
Primary Source: The Farm Worker Movement, p. 62
American Lives: Cesar Chavez, p. 69

 ELECTRONIC LIBRARY OF PRIMARY SOURCES
The Birth of *La Causa* by Cesar Chavez

KEY PLAYER
Cesar Chavez
Critical Thinking:
Analyzing Ask students what Chavez's actions in the theater reveal about him. *Possible Responses: He was proud, independent, and courageous.* How does his behavior as a teenager foreshadow his actions as a labor organizer when he was an adult? *Possible Response: Like his protest in the theater, the protests he organized as an adult were nonviolent.*

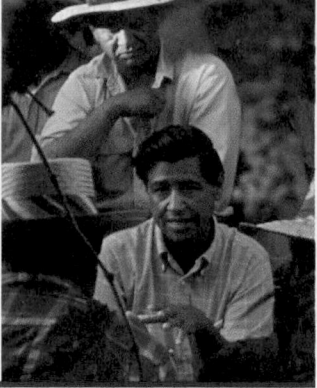

KEY PLAYER

CESAR CHAVEZ
1927–1993

Cesar Chavez spoke from experience when he said, "Many things in farm labor are terrible." As a teenager, Chavez moved with his family from farm to farm, picking such crops as grapes, apricots, and olives. "The worst crop was the olives," Chavez recalled, "the olives are so small you can never fill the bucket."

The seeds of protest grew early in Chavez, and one incident in particular seemed to signal his eventual climb to a life of activism. As a teenager, Chavez once went to see a movie, only to find that the theater was segregated—whites on one side of the aisle and Mexicans on the other side. "I really hadn't thought much about what I was going to do but I had to do something," Chavez recalled. The future union leader sat down in the whites-only section and stayed there until the police arrived and arrested him.

bargain as one large group for improved conditions and better treatment. In 1962, Chavez, along with Dolores Huerta, established the National Farm Workers Association. Four years later, Chavez merged this group with another union to form the **United Farm Workers Organizing Committee** (UFWOC).

Chavez and his fellow organizers insisted that California's large fruit and vegetable companies accept their union as the bargaining agent for the farm workers. In 1965, when California's grape growers refused to recognize the union, Chavez launched a nationwide boycott of the companies' grapes. Chavez, like Martin Luther King, Jr., believed in nonviolence to achieve his goals. His strategy was to win, through peaceful means, American public support for *La Causa*, or the cause of social and economic justice for farm workers.

The union sent farm workers across North America to convince supermarkets and shoppers not to buy California grapes. To call further attention to the workers' plight, Chavez, in 1968, went on a three-week fast in which he lost 35 pounds. He ended his fast by taking communion with Senator Robert F. Kennedy.

The efforts of the farm workers eventually paid off. Faced with growing financial losses and a deteriorating public image, the grape growers finally signed contracts with the UFWOC in 1970. The new contracts guaranteed union workers higher wages and other benefits long denied them. "The boycott of grapes was the most near-perfect of nonviolent struggles," said Chavez afterward. It "demonstrated to the whole country, the whole world, what people can do by nonviolent action."

CULTURAL PRIDE The activities of the California farm workers helped to inspire other Latino "brown power" movements across the country. In New York, Puerto Ricans began to demand that schools offer Spanish-speaking children classes taught in their own language as well as programs on their culture. In 1968, Congress addressed the need for bilingual education by enacting the Bilingual Education Act. The act provided funds for schools to develop bilingual and cultural heritage programs for non-English-speaking children.

Young Mexican Americans started to call themselves Chicanos or Chicanas—a shortening of "Mexicanos" that expressed pride in their ethnic heritage. Many Chicanos worked for educational reform. In 1968, about 15,000 Chicano high school students in Los Angeles walked out of class in student strikes. Their demands included smaller classes, more Chicano teachers and administrators, and programs designed to reduce the high Latino dropout rate. At colleges and universities, militant Mexican-American students increasingly won the establishment of Chicano studies programs.

POLITICAL POWER Latinos also began organizing politically during the 1960s. Some worked within the two-party system to win support for Latino issues and candidates. For example, the Mexican American Political Association (MAPA), which sponsored candidates, registered and educated voters and lobbied for legislation that benefited the Latino community. In 1962, MAPA helped elect Los Angeles politician Edward Roybal to the House of Representatives. Roybal was the second Mexican American to serve in Congress. Henry Gonzalez, elected to the House of Representatives from Texas in 1961, was the first.

Others sought to create an independent Latino political movement. That was the dream of Texan José Angel Gutiérrez, who established **La Raza Unida** (the United People Party) in 1970. In the 1970s, La Raza Unida ran Latino

THINK THROUGH HISTORY
B. *Recognizing Effects* What impact did the grape boycott have on grape growers?
B. Answer It hurt their revenue as well as their public image and forced them to negotiate with the UFWOC.

922 CHAPTER 31

Making Connections Across Cultures

Latino Cultural Pride Tell students that many of the new Latino immigrants resisted assimilation into mainstream America. They preferred to retain their family-centered culture and their heritage. "We want to be here," explained Daniel Villanueva, who became a television executive, "but without losing our language and our culture." Ask students what aspects of American culture, if any, Latinos should be prepared—or required—to adopt.

 HUMANITIES TRANSPARENCIES
H29, Mural in Los Angeles

Making Connections Across the Curriculum

Literature Tell students that since the 1950s, Latin American literature has received unprecedented international attention. The production during this period of many important novels by Latin American writers has been called the "boom." Many of the boom novelists write in a style that combines dreams and magic with everyday reality. The most famous of these authors is Gabriel García Márquez, who won the 1982 Nobel Prize in literature. His novel *One Hundred Years of Solitude* contains historical fact but also includes strange, fantastic events; startling characters; and unusual humor.

candidates in five states and won positions on school boards and city councils, as well as several races for mayor.

Still other Latinos took on a more confrontational tone. Reies Tijerina, a one-time evangelical preacher, argued that the United States had stolen some of the Latinos' land. In 1967, Tijerina founded the Alianza Federal de Mercedes (Federal Alliance of Land Grants) to help reclaim U.S. land taken from Mexican landholders in the nineteenth century.

Native Americans Struggle for Equality

Many people view Native Americans, like Latinos, as one group, despite the hundreds of distinct Native American tribes and nations in the United States. These diverse tribes and nations, however, have shared a mostly bleak existence in the United States. During the 1960s, many Native Americans joined together to demand improvements in their conditions.

NATIVE AMERICANS SEEK GREATER AUTONOMY Despite their cultural diversity, Native Americans have shared many of the same problems throughout the 20th century. As a group, Native Americans have been the poorest of Americans and have suffered from the highest unemployment rate. They have been more likely than any other group to suffer serious health problems, such as tuberculosis and alcoholism. Despite an increase in the Native American population during the 1960s, the death rate among Native American infants was nearly twice the national average, while the life expectancy of Native Americans was several years lower than for other Americans.

In an attempt to deal with these problems, the Eisenhower administration in 1953 enacted a termination policy designed to relocate Native Americans from isolated reservations into mainstream urban American life. The plan failed miserably. Most of the Native Americans who moved to the cities remained desperately poor.

In addition, many Native Americans refused to assimilate, or blend, into mainstream society. Native American nationalist Vine Deloria, Jr., expressed his opinion that young Native Americans viewed mainstream America as nothing more than "ice cream bars and heart trouble and neurosis and deodorants and getting up at six o'clock in the morning to mow your lawn in the suburbs." Deloria added that "when you get far enough from the reservation, you can see it's the urban man who has no identity."

What Native Americans wanted was greater opportunity to control and govern their own lives. In 1961, representatives from 61 Native American groups met in Chicago and drafted the Declaration of Indian Purpose, which stressed the determination of Native Americans to "choose our own way of life." The declaration called for an end to the termination program in favor of new policies designed to create economic opportunities for Native Americans on their reservations. In 1965, President Lyndon Johnson responded to the Native Americans' call for more self-determination. As part of his Great Society program, Johnson established the National Council of Indian Opportunity to "ensure that programs reflect the needs and desires of the Indian people."

VOICES OF PROTEST Despite a change in the government's policies, many young Native Americans were dissatisfied with the slow pace of reform. Their discontent led in part to the growth of the **American Indian Movement** (AIM), an often militant Native American rights

NOW & THEN

BEN NIGHTHORSE CAMPBELL

Whereas many Native Americans, in seeking reforms, rejected assimilation with mainstream America, Ben Nighthorse Campbell has chosen to work within the system to improve the lives of Native Americans.

In 1992, Campbell was elected to the U.S. Senate from Colorado, marking the first time since 1929 that a Native American had been elected to the Senate. Campbell's father was North Cheyenne, and his great-grandfather, Black Horse, fought in the 1876 Battle of Little Bighorn—in which the Cheyenne and the Sioux defeated Lieutenant Colonel George Custer.

Campbell stated that while his new job called for him to address the problems of the entire nation, the needs of his fellow Native Americans remained a high priority. As a Native American, Campbell says, "you are measured by how much you've given to people, how much you help people."

An Era of Social Change **923**

THINK THROUGH HISTORY
C. Identifying Problems
What problems have Native Americans faced during much of the 20th century?
C. Answer High unemployment, rampant poverty, and severe health problems

---

OBJECTIVE
③ INSTRUCT

Native Americans Struggle for Equality

▶**Starting with the Student**
Have students use a chart similar to the one below to document the Native American struggle for equality during the 1960s. Ask them to list the actions taken by Native Americans and the results of those actions.

Action	Result

▶**Discussing Key Ideas**
• In the 1960s, Native Americans seek more control over their lives.
• The American Indian Movement brings a new spirit of militancy to the struggle for equality.
• AIM confronts the government—sometimes violently—to seek greater reforms for Native Americans.
• Native Americans win both legislative and legal battles.

NOW & THEN
Ben Nighthorse Campbell

Critical Thinking: Evaluating Ask students whether they think that Native Americans can achieve their goals by working within the system, as Campbell did, or that organizations such as AIM can accomplish more by agitating outside the system.

TEACHING OPTIONS

Exploring Themes

Civil Rights Discuss the Native American struggle for equal rights. Ask students what goals Native Americans sought to achieve in the 1960s. *Possible Responses: More control over their own lives; new economic opportunities; rights to lands taken by the government; improved living conditions on reservations; more say in children's education.* Then ask why these goals were important to Native Americans. *Possible Response: Many basic rights had been denied them for generations. Regaining the rights would be a major victory for the Native American people.*

Teaching Gifted and Talented Students

Researching AIM Encourage interested students to find out about the goals and accomplishments of AIM today. Have students

• search the Internet for information on the organization
• conduct a periodical search in the library for articles about AIM's activities
• create a poster that depicts the organization's activities
• present the poster to the class

💿 **GROLIER MULTIMEDIA ENCYCLOPEDIA**
American Indian Movement

When the Native Americans who took part in the Trail of Broken Treaties arrived in Washington, they did not plan to occupy the BIA building. The protesters first approached the BIA for help in finding a place to stay while they tried to make appointments with government officials. As Mary Crow Dog, who was one of the demonstrators, recalled, "Somebody suggested, 'Let's all go to the BIA.' It seemed a natural thing to do. . . . They would have to put us up. It was 'our' building after all."

The police, however, viewed the presence of a thousand Native Americans in the BIA offices as an occupation and surrounded the building. In response, the unarmed demonstrators blockaded doors and passageways with overturned desks and file cabinets. They also broke off a few table legs to defend themselves in case of attack. The AIM demonstrators left seven days later, when the Nixon administration promised to study their demands. The administration also agreed not to file criminal charges for the damage done to the BIA building. "Morally, it had been a great victory," wrote Mary Crow Dog. "We had faced White America collectively, not as individual tribes. We had stood up to the government and gone through our baptism of fire. We had not run."

AIM leader Dennis Banks speaks at the foot of Mount Rushmore, South Dakota, during a rally.

"If the government doesn't start living up to its obligations, armed resistance. . . will have to become a regular thing."

CHIPPEWA PROTESTER

organization. AIM had begun in 1968 in Minneapolis as a self-defense group against police brutality. However, it soon turned its attention to the larger issue of Native American rights and branched out to northern and western states with large Native American populations.

AIM's influence spread rapidly. For some, the new activism meant demanding the restoration of Native American lands, burial grounds, and fishing and timber rights. Others sought new respect for their cultures. Mary Crow Dog, a Lakota Sioux, described the impact of the movement on her reservation.

A PERSONAL VOICE
The American Indian Movement hit our reservation like a tornado. . . . Some people loved AIM, some hated it, but nobody ignored it. . . . My first encounter with AIM was at a pow-wow held in 1971. . . . One man, a Chippewa, stood up and made a speech. I had never heard anybody talk like that. He spoke about genocide and sovereignty, about tribal leaders selling out. . . . He had wrapped himself up in an upside-down American flag, telling us that every star in this flag represented a state stolen from the Indians. . . . Some people wept. An old man turned to me and said, "These are words I always wanted to speak, but had kept shut up within me."

MARY CROW DOG, quoted in *Lakota Women*

CONFRONTING THE GOVERNMENT In its early years, AIM, as well as other groups, actively—and sometimes violently—confronted the government as it sought greater reforms for Native Americans. In November 1969, militants calling themselves the Indians of All Tribes seized Alcatraz Island, the site of a former federal prison in San Francisco Bay. While claiming the federally owned island as Native American territory "by right of discovery," they offered to pay for it with $24 in beads and cloth—the amount Dutch settlers paid native inhabitants for Manhattan Island in 1626. The group occupied the island for 18 months before federal officials finally removed them.

In 1972, AIM leader Russell Means organized a march known as the Trail of Broken Treaties in Washington, D.C., to protest the U.S. government's numerous treaty violations with Native Americans throughout history. Native Americans from across the country joined the marchers. The organizers called for the restoration of 110 million acres of land to Native American tribes. They also pushed for the abolition of the Bureau of Indian Affairs (BIA), an agency that many believed was inefficient and corrupt. The marchers temporarily occupied the BIA building, destroyed records, and caused $2 million in property damage.

The most violent demonstration occurred a year later, when AIM led nearly 200 Sioux to the tiny village of Wounded Knee, South Dakota—where the U.S. cavalry had massacred a Sioux village in 1890. To protest living conditions on their reservation, the Sioux seized the town and took eleven people hostage. After ten weeks of tense negotiations with the FBI, the situation erupted in a shootout that left one Native American dead and another one wounded. The confrontation ended with a government promise to reexamine Native American treaty rights.

NATIVE AMERICAN VICTORIES Although some of their actions led only to violence and stalemate, Native Americans did secure a number of reforms from

D. Answer
AIM used confrontational and sometimes violent tactics, such as occupying the Bureau of Indian Affairs, and taking hostages during a protest at Wounded Knee.

THINK THROUGH HISTORY
D. *Analyzing Issues*
What tactics did AIM use in its attempts to gain reforms?

TEACHING OPTION

Cooperative Activity: Listing Native American Demands

Task: Representing the interests of the Sioux at the Wounded Knee demonstration, groups of four to five students will write lists of demands to present to the government.

Purpose: To explore in depth the Native American struggle for equality.

Activity: Students should research the 1973 demonstration and find out why the Sioux were protesting conditions on their reservation. Students should also research the

Wounded Knee massacre of 1890 and some of the treaties made with the Sioux during that period. Have students write their lists on posters and decorate them with Native American symbols and artwork.

Building a Portfolio: Students who decide to add their list of demands to their portfolio should attach a note explaining why the Sioux staged the demonstration at Wounded Knee.

ALTERNATIVE ASSESSMENT BOOK
Standards for Evaluating a Cooperative Activity

Standards for Evaluation
Lists should . . .

• describe conditions on the Sioux reservation and detail changes that need to be made

• refer to any withheld treaty rights that should be restored

• be decorated with Native American symbols and artwork

Native American Legal Victories

1970
Taos of New Mexico regain possession of Blue Lake as well as surrounding forestland.

1971
Alaska Native Lands Claim Settlement Act gives Aleut and Inuit tribes of Alaska 40 million acres and more than $962 million.

1979
Maine Implementing Act provides $81.5 million for Native tribes, including Penobscot and Passamaquoddy, to buy back land.

1980
U.S. awards Sioux $106 million for illegally taken land in South Dakota.

1988
U.S. awards Puyallup tribe $162 million for land claims in Washington.

both Congress and the federal courts. Congress passed the Indian Education Act in 1972 and the Indian Self-Determination and Education Assistance Act in 1975. These laws gave tribes much greater control over their own affairs and especially over the education of their children. "This is the most wonderful revolution in Indian Country," commented a Native American educator, "the right to educate on our own terms."

Native Americans also regained rights to land through court action. Armed with copies of old land treaties that the U.S. government had broken, Native American groups took their cases to federal court, where they demanded portions of their land back. In 1970, the Taos of New Mexico regained possession of their sacred Blue Lake, as well as a portion of its surrounding forestland. Land claims by the Aleut and Inuit tribes of Alaska resulted in the Alaska Native Lands Claim Settlement Act of 1971. This act gave more than 40 million acres to native peoples and paid out more than $962 million in cash. Throughout the 1970s and 1980s, Native Americans in Maine, South Carolina, and Massachusetts won settlements that provided legal recognition of their tribal lands as well as financial compensation.

With Latinos and Native Americans rising up in the midst of African Americans' struggle for change, the 1960s and the early 1970s saw a wave of activism from the nation's minority groups. However, another group of Americans also pushed for changes during this era. Women, while not a minority group, felt in many ways like second-class citizens, and many joined together to demand equal treatment in society.

THINK THROUGH HISTORY
E. Synthesizing What victories could the Native American movement claim?
E. Answer Education reform, land restitution, and financial compensation

SKILLBUILDER
INTERPRETING CHARTS
What two things did Native Americans win throughout their years of legal victories?
Skillbuilder Answer
Land rights and monetary compensation.

Section 1 Assessment

1. TERMS & NAMES
Identify:
• Cesar Chavez
• United Farm Workers Organizing Committee
• La Raza Unida
• American Indian Movement

2. SUMMARIZING Create a Venn diagram like the one below to show the broad similarities between the issues faced by Latinos and Native Americans during the 1960s as well as their unique concerns.

Common Issues Faced by Latinos and Native Americans

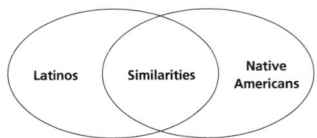

3. SYNTHESIZING What criteria would you establish for judging the effectiveness of an activist organization? Justify why your criteria is valid, based on the organizations discussed in this section.

THINK ABOUT
• UFWOC, MAPA, and La Raza Unida
• AIM and the Indians of All Tribes
• the leaders and activities of these organizations

4. CONTRASTING How did the Native American movement of the 1960s differ in general from the civil rights struggle of African Americans and Latinos?

THINK ABOUT
• Vine Deloria, Jr.'s statement
• the Declaration of Indian Purpose
• the goals of AIM
• African Americans' and Latinos' desire for greater assimilation in mainstream society

An Era of Social Change **925**

ANSWERS

1. TERMS & NAMES
Cesar Chavez, p. 921
United Farm Workers Organizing Committee, p. 922
La Raza Unida, p. 922
American Indian Movement, p. 923

2. SUMMARIZING
Similarities: Great diversity within both groups; victims of prejudice, high unemployment, poverty, second-class citizenship; pride in their cultural heritage; concerns over their children's education; political activism; militant factions. Unique issues: Latinos—desire for greater assimilation into mainstream society; Native Americans—desire to remain outside mainstream society with greater autonomy.

3. SYNTHESIZING
Possible Responses: Strong leadership; clear-cut mission and goals; ability to enlist outside support; well-orchestrated demonstrations; unity among members; success in working for legislative measures and reforms.

4. CONTRASTING
Possible Response: Unlike African Americans and Latinos—most of whom sought assimilation into mainstream America—Native Americans attempted to better their lives while remaining removed from mainstream society.

HISTORY FROM VISUALS
Native American Legal Victories

Reading the Chart On a map, point out the sites of the legal victories. Ask students what these locations suggest about where Native Americans once lived. *Possible Response: They lived in vast, open spaces throughout the country.*

Extension Ask students why the restoration of lands is still important to Native Americans today. *Possible Response: Because the land represents their traditions and way of life.*

ASSESS & RETEACH

Section 1 Assessment
Have pairs of students take turns quizzing each other on the questions.

Self-Assessment
Draw on the board the Venn diagram in item 2 and have students discuss the issues they listed. Add students' ideas to the diagram on the board.

Section Quiz

FORMAL ASSESSMENT
Section Quiz, p. 376

Reteach
Use the Section Quiz to review key concepts in Section 1.

CLOSE

During the 1960s, Latinos and Native Americans fought for equal rights and economic justice. This era also witnessed a wave of activism by another oppressed group: women.

OBJECTIVES

1 To trace the movements of migrant farm workers in the United States.

2 To recognize the role played by climate and growing seasons in the migrants' movements.

FOCUS & MOTIVATE

▶ **Starting with the Student**
Ask students to think about jobs they've done that required manual labor.

- What did the jobs entail? Did they work indoors or outside?
- How did they feel physically after a full day's work?
- Did they feel a sense of satisfaction when the jobs were finished?

MORE ABOUT . . .
Migrant Farm Workers

The children of migrant farm workers often become migrant farm workers themselves. Because migrant families move so often, the children tend to fall behind in their education. In fact, only about a fifth of all migrant children attend school past the sixth grade. When these children grow up, they usually find that their education has prepared them for little other than farm work. As a result, generations of migrant families are caught in a cycle of poverty and despair.

GEOGRAPHY
SPOTLIGHT

The Movement of Migrant Workers

The nation's 3 million farm workers are responsible for harvesting much of the fruit and vegetables that families eat each day. There are two types of produce farm workers in the United States: workers who remain in one place most of the year; and migrant workers, who move with their entire family from one region to the next as the growing seasons change.

As the map shows, there were three major streams of migrant worker movements in the 1960s: the Pacific Coast, the Midwest, and the Atlantic Coast.

While these paths may have changed slightly since then, the movement of migrant workers into nearly every region of the nation continues today. The Pacific Coast region, with its year-round schedule and large harvests, offers laborers more steady work. Workers along the Midwest and East Coast streams, where crops are smaller, must keep moving in order to find work. Due to the winters, migrant workers in most of the Midwest and Atlantic regions can find work for only six months out of the year. During the winter months, many workers return to the nation's southernmost reaches, where they struggle to make a living, and wait until spring, when they once again head north.

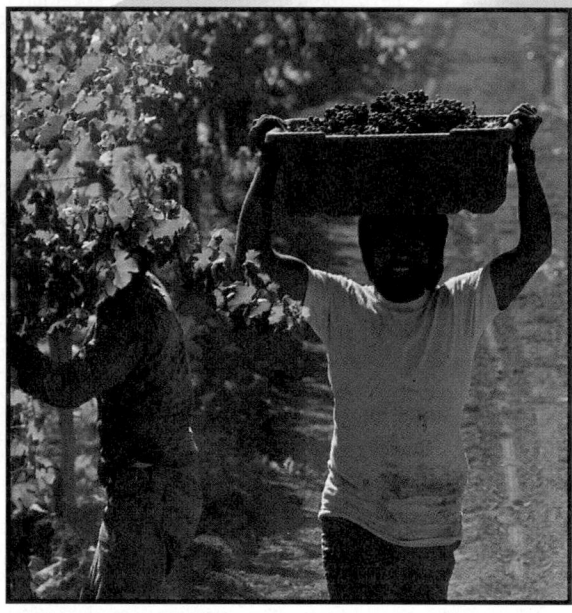

Pacific Coast paths
Midwest paths
Atlantic Coast paths
Year-round work
Migrant base areas

THE PACIFIC COAST
Because California's moderate climate allows for year-round harvesting, most of the state's farm workers work on California's large fruit farms for most of the year. In addition, California produces large amounts of table grapes, a delicate fruit that requires specialized and constant care.

926 CHAPTER 31

RECOMMENDED RESOURCES

Books

Altman, Linda Jacobs. *Cesar Chavez.* San Diego: Lucent, 1996. Biography of the charismatic labor leader who struggled to organize America's migrant farm workers.

Jiménez, Francisco. "The Circuit." *Cuentos Chicanos.* Ed. Rudolfo A. Anaya and Antonio Márquez. Rev. ed.

Albuquerque: U of New Mexico P, 1984. Short story depicting the plight of migrant children.

Valle, Isabel. *Fields of Toil.* Pullman: Washington State UP, 1994. Traces the journey of a family of migrant farm laborers.

Videos

Cesar Chavez. Schlessinger Video Productions, 1995. Visual chronicle of Chavez's 30-year effort to organize migrant farm workers.

Harvest of Shame. FoxVideo, 1993. Renowned 1960 documentary on the exploitation of migrant farm workers in the United States.

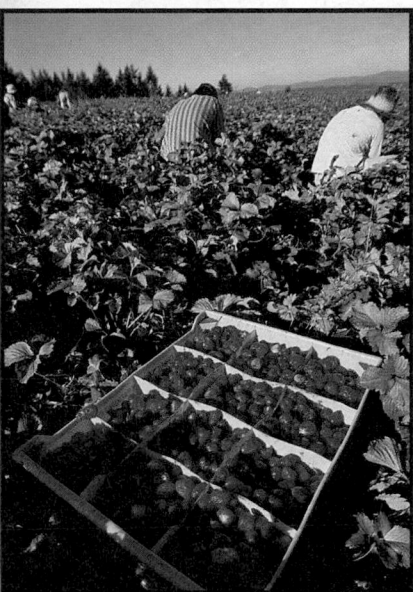

THE MIDWEST
These workers picking strawberries in Michigan will soon move on. For example, one family will travel to Ohio for the tomato harvest and then return to Michigan to pick apples before heading back to Texas for the winter months.

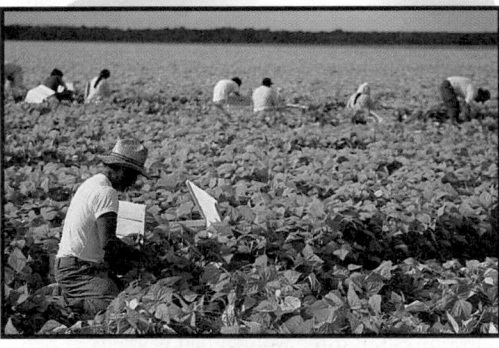

THE ATLANTIC COAST
While some workers along the Atlantic Coast stream remain in Florida, like the workers shown here picking beans, others travel as far north as New Hampshire and New York. There, they work from March through September, before returning to the South for the winter.

INTERACT WITH HISTORY

1. **FOLLOWING CHRONOLOGICAL ORDER**
Retrace the 12-month activity of migrant workers along the Midwest and Atlantic Coast streams.

SEE SKILLBUILDER HANDBOOK, PAGE 1036.

2. **APPLYING** Use an outline map of the United States or of the world to trace work-related travel for some people in your community. Each student could track this information for a parent or a neighbor. The class could then place all of the results on a large map entitled "A Nation on the Move" and discuss certain aspects of the map.

For more about migrant workers, click on *Social Studies* at http://www.mcdougallittell.com

An Era of Social Change **927**

OBJECTIVES

(1) To identify factors that led to the rise of the women's movement during the 1960s.

(2) To describe some of the gains and losses of the women's movement in its early years.

(3) To summarize the enduring legacy of the women's movement in employment, education, and politics.

SKILLBUILDER

• Interpreting charts, p. 929

CRITICAL THINKING

• Recognizing effects, p. 929
• Analyzing causes, p. 930
• Analyzing motives, p. 932
• Forming opinions, p. 932
• Summarizing, p. 932
• Hypothesizing, p. 932
• Forming an opinion, p. 932

FOCUS & MOTIVATE

▶ *Starting with the Student*
• Ask students if they think women are discriminated against in American society. In what ways?

MORE ABOUT . . .
Betty Friedan

In spite of others' doubts and jokes, Friedan felt a "strange sureness" about the book she was writing. Eventually she became obsessed with the project: "I wrote every day, on the dining-room table, while the children were in school, and after they went to bed at night. (It didn't do any good to have a desk of my own; they used it for their home-work, anyhow.) The summer I was finishing *The Feminine Mystique,* for some strange reason—maybe a last gasp at denying my seriousness—I dyed my hair blond!"

IN-DEPTH RESOURCES: UNIT 8
American Lives: Betty Friedan, p. 70
Primary Source: from *The Feminine Mystique,* p. 64

 ELECTRONIC LIBRARY OF PRIMARY SOURCES
from *The Feminine Mystique* by Betty Friedan

2 Women Fight for Equality

TERMS & NAMES
• feminism
• Betty Friedan
• National Organization for Women
• Gloria Steinem
• Equal Rights Amendment
• Phyllis Schlafly

LEARN ABOUT the social and economic barriers that women faced in American society

TO UNDERSTAND the rise of a new and diverse women's movement during the 1960s.

ONE AMERICAN'S STORY

During the 1950s Betty Friedan seemed to be living the American dream. She had a loving husband, healthy children, and a house in the suburbs. According to the experts—doctors, psychologists, and women's magazines—that was all a woman needed to be happy and fulfilled. Why, then, wasn't she happy? What was wrong with her that this wasn't enough? When Friedan attended her fifteen-year college reunion in 1957, she found she was not alone in asking such questions. Many of her former classmates also were struggling with what Friedan would refer to as "the problem that has no name." Friedan eventually wrote a book, *The Feminine Mystique,* in which she addressed this seemingly indescribable problem.

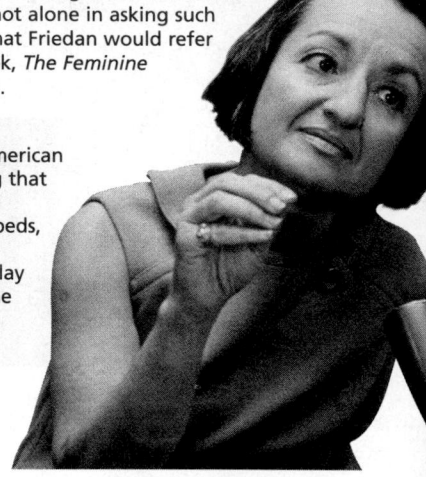

Betty Friedan

> **A PERSONAL VOICE**
> The problem lay buried, unspoken, for many years in the minds of American women. It was a strange stirring, a sense of dissatisfaction, a yearning that women suffered in the middle of the twentieth century in the United States. Each suburban wife struggled with it alone. As she made the beds, shopped for groceries, matched slipcover material, ate peanut butter sandwiches with her children, chauffeured Cub Scouts and Brownies, lay beside her husband at night—she was afraid to even ask of herself the silent question—"Is this all?"
>
> **BETTY FRIEDAN,** *The Feminine Mystique*

During the 1960s, more and more women answered Friedan's question with a resounding "no." As the nation's African Americans, Latinos, and Native Americans pushed for greater civil rights, many of the country's women also fought for equality in society.

A New Women's Movement Arises

A button displays women's displeasure with their treatment in the workplace.

The theory behind the women's movement of the 1960s was **feminism,** the belief that women should have economic, political, and social equality with men. Feminist beliefs gained momentum during the mid-1800s and led to woman suffrage, or women's right to vote, in 1920. The women's movement declined after this achievement. However, it reawakened during the 1960s, when many women began to recognize their social and economic inequality. This realization helped spark a new, powerful feminist movement.

WOMEN IN THE WORKPLACE By 1960, the number of women joining the work force was on the rise. In 1950, only one out of three women had worked for wages. By 1960, more than 40 percent of all women had jobs outside the home, and women made up a third of the nation's work force. While their numbers were growing, however, working women experienced widespread job and wage discrimination. Many occupations were considered "men's work" and were closed to women. The jobs available to women—mostly clerical work, domestic service, retail sales, social work, teaching, and nursing—paid poorly.

The country largely ignored the discrimination women faced in the workplace, until President Kennedy appointed the Presidential Commission on the Status of Women in 1961. In 1963, the commission reported that women were

---

📁 **PRINT RESOURCES**

IN-DEPTH RESOURCES: UNIT 8
Guided Reading, p. 57
Geography Application: The Equal Rights Amendment, p. 60
Primary Source: from *The Feminine Mystique,* p. 64
American Lives: Betty Friedan, p. 70

ACCESS FOR STUDENTS ACQUIRING ENGLISH
Guided Reading (Spanish), p. 302
Geography Application: The Equal Rights Amendment (Spanish), p. 305

FORMAL ASSESSMENT
Section Quiz, p. 377

ALTERNATIVE ASSESSMENT BOOK
See forms for supporting and scoring alternative activities.

💻 **TECHNOLOGY RESOURCES**

CRITICAL THINKING TRANSPARENCIES
CT31, The Women's Movement
CT65, Percentage of All Women Who Are Working, 1950–1995

CD-ROM Electronic Library of Primary Sources

INTERNET McDougal Littell Learning On-Line
http://www.mcdougallittell.com

Women in the Workplace, 1950–1993

WORKING WOMEN AND PERCENT OF LABOR FORCE

18 million

29%

1950

32 million

37%

1970

58 million

46%

1993

MEDIAN INCOMES FOR WORKING WOMEN AND MEN

= $2000

$31,077

$22,469

$6,670

$953 $2,570 $2,237

Women	Men	Women	Men	Women	Men
1950		**1970**		**1993**	

Sources: *Historical Statistics of the United States; Statistical Abstract of the United States 1978, 1995*

---

paid far less than men, even when doing the same jobs. Furthermore, women were seldom promoted to management positions, regardless of their education, experience, and ability. The discrimination that women faced in the workplace awakened many women to their unequal status in society.

SOCIAL ACTIVISM INSPIRES WOMEN Other sources of discontent for women stemmed from their involvement in the civil rights and antiwar movements. Although both movements inspired many women to take action on behalf of their beliefs, the discrimination they faced within the movements made them acutely aware of their inferior social status.

In these organizations, men led most of the activities, while women were assigned lesser roles. When women protested, the men usually brushed them aside. When activist Shulamith Firestone tried to raise the issue of women's rights with antiwar activists, one man told her, "Move on little girl; we have more important issues to talk about here than women's liberation."

Such experiences led some women to organize small groups to discuss their concerns. During these discussions, or "consciousness-raising" sessions, women shared their lives with each other and discovered that their experiences were not unique. Rather, they reflected a much larger pattern of sexism, or discrimination against women. As author Robin Morgan recalled later,

> **A PERSONAL VOICE**
> It makes you very sensitive—raw, even, this consciousness. Everything, from the verbal assault on the street, to a "well-meant" sexist joke your husband tells, to the lower pay you get at work (for doing the same job a man would be paid more for), to television commercials, to rock-song lyrics, to the pink or blue blanket they put on your infant in the hospital nursery, to speeches by male "revolutionaries" that reek of male supremacy—everything seems to barrage your aching brain. . . . You begin to see how all-pervasive a thing is sexism.
> **ROBIN MORGAN,** *Sisterhood is Powerful: An Anthology of Writings from the Women's Liberation Movement*

THE WOMEN'S MOVEMENT EMERGES In 1963, **Betty Friedan** published *The Feminine Mystique*, which captured the very discontent that many women were feeling. The book quickly became a bestseller. From across the country, women wrote to Friedan to thank her for exposing "the problem that has no name" and to tell her their own painful stories. "Thank God someone had the insight and courage to write it," an Iowa woman wrote.

Friedan's book helped galvanize a number of women throughout the nation. By the late 1960s, women across the country were coming together to work for change. "This is not a movement one 'joins,'" observed Robin Morgan. "The Women's Liberation movement exists where three or four friends or

An Era of Social Change **929**

THINK THROUGH HISTORY
A. Recognizing Effects
What effects did the civil rights and antiwar movements have on many women?

A. Answer They spurred women to demonstrate for equality by both inspiring them to act and opening their eyes to their inferior status.

SKILLBUILDER
INTERPRETING CHARTS
For each year shown, what percentage of men's income did women make?

Skillbuilder Answer
1950: 37 percent; **1970:** 33 percent; **1993:** 72 percent

A New Women's Movement Arises

▶ **Discussing Key Ideas**
- As more women join the work force in the 1960s, they encounter widespread job and wage discrimination.
- Women's experiences in the civil rights and antiwar movements increase their awareness of sexism in American society.
- Betty Friedan's *The Feminine Mystique* helps inspire a new women's movement.

IN-DEPTH RESOURCES, UNIT 8
Guided Reading, p. 57

ACCESS FOR STUDENTS ACQUIRING ENGLISH
Guided Reading (Spanish), p. 302

HISTORY FROM VISUALS
Women in the Workplace, 1950–1993

Reading the Chart Point out that the first chart shows the total number of working women and their percentage in the workforce in 1950, 1970, and 1993. The second chart shows the median incomes of men and women in those years.

Extension Ask students why the number of women in the work force and women's median income increased after 1970. *Possible Response: Because of gains and reforms instigated by the women's movement.*

CRITICAL THINKING TRANSPARENCIES
CT65, Percentage of All Women Who Are Working, 1950–1995

Exploring Themes

Women in America Discuss some of the factors that sparked the women's movement in the 1960s. Ask students how the civil rights movement helped inspire the women's movement. *Possible Response: Working for the rights of others helped women become aware of inequalities in their own lives.* Point out that in the 1800s women's involvement in the antislavery movement and other causes helped to increase awareness of their own plight. Then ask students whether they think women's battle for equality is as important as the struggles of African Americans and other ethnic groups.

CRITICAL THINKING TRANSPARENCIES
CT31, The Women's Movement

Making Connections Across the Curriculum

Sociology Tell students that sociology deals with the attitudes, behaviors, and relationships in societies. The feminist movement of the 1960s and 1970s challenged and eventually influenced people's attitudes toward women. The movement also affected the relationship between men and women. Sociological studies have continued to study its effects and determine its influence on men, women, and children. Discuss the impact of the women's movement on society. Ask students whether they think the movement changed society for the better or for the worse.

The Movement Experiences Gains and Losses

▶ **Starting with the Student**
Have students use a chart like the one below to record some of the gains and losses experienced by the women's movement.

Gains	Losses

▶ **Discussing Key Ideas**
• The National Organization for Women is created to pursue women's goals.
• Radical and moderate factions form within the women's movement.
• With the ruling in *Roe* v. *Wade,* feminist groups win a battle in their fight for abortion rights.
• Because of fierce opposition from many groups, the Equal Rights Amendment is not ratified.

IN-DEPTH RESOURCES: UNIT 8
Geography Application: The Equal Rights Amendment, p. 60

KEY PLAYER
Gloria Steinem

Critical Thinking: Analyzing
Discuss the significance of the magazine's name. Tell students that *Ms.* was coined so that women would have a title that didn't reveal their marital status. Ask students why this was an important consideration in the women's movement. *Possible Response: Women were tired of being defined by their relationship to men.*

---

neighbors decide to meet regularly . . . on the welfare lines, in the supermarket, the factory, the convent, the farm, the maternity ward . . . ."

The Movement Experiences Gains and Losses

As the women's movement grew, it achieved remarkable political and social gains for women. Along the way, however, the movement also suffered setbacks, most notably in its attempt to ensure women's equality in the Constitution.

THE CREATION OF NOW Due in part to a backfired strategy by opponents of the Civil Rights Act of 1964, women had won the legal tools with which to fight discrimination. Opponents of the civil rights bill—which prohibited discrimination based on race, religion, and national origin—had added a provision outlawing discrimination based on gender, in an attempt to weaken support for the bill. Much to the dismay of its opponents, however, the bill passed with the gender provision included. One result of the provision was that the Equal Employment Opportunity Commission (EEOC)—an organization set up by the act to investigate discrimination claims by African Americans—also addressed women's job complaints.

By 1966, however, some women voiced dissatisfaction with the EEOC. They argued that the commission showed an overall lack of attention toward the flood of women's grievances. That year, several women, including Betty Friedan, created the **National Organization for Women** (NOW) to pursue more actively women's goals. "The time has come," the founders of NOW declared, "to confront with concrete action the conditions which now prevent women from enjoying the equality of opportunity . . . which is their right as individual Americans and as human beings."

NOW moved into action quickly. Its members pushed for the creation of more child care facilities and for improved educational opportunities for women. NOW also pressured the EEOC to enforce more vigorously the ban on gender discrimination in hiring. NOW's efforts prompted the EEOC to declare sex-segregated job ads illegal and issue guidelines to employers, stating that they could no longer refuse to hire women for traditionally male jobs.

A DIVERSE MOVEMENT In its first three years, NOW's ranks swelled from 300 to 175,000 members. Outside of NOW, a number of other women's groups sprang up around the country. In 1968 a militant group known as the New York Radical Women staged a well-publicized demonstration at the annual Miss America Pageant. To protest the concept of judging women's beauty, the women threw bras, girdles, wigs, and other "women's garbage" into a "Freedom Trash Can." They then crowned a sheep as "Miss America." In 1971, Journalist **Gloria Steinem** helped found the National Women's Political Caucus, a moderate group which encouraged women to seek political office.

The radicals and moderates within the movement often quarreled over strategy. However, these diverse factions put aside their differences in August 1970 to join in the largest women's rights demonstration ever. To commemorate the 50th anniversary of woman suffrage, tens of thousands of women gathered from around the country and marched through New York City to promote women's equality.

By the early 1970s, the women's movement had scored several victories on the political and social fronts. In 1972, Congress passed a ban on gender discrimination in "any education program or activities receiving federal financial

KEY PLAYER

GLORIA STEINEM
1934–

Gloria Steinem became one of the more prominent figures of the women's movement after she and several other women founded *Ms.* magazine in 1972. The magazine soon became a major voice of the women's movement.

Steinem said that she decided to start the feminist magazine after editors in the mainstream media continually rejected her stories about the women's movement: "Editors who had assumed I had some valuable biological insight into food, male movie stars, and textured stockings now questioned whether I or other women writers were biologically capable of writing objectively about feminism. That was the beginning."

Within a year of its first issue, *Ms.* had nearly 200,000 subscribers and kept many readers informed about events of the women's movement.

THINK THROUGH HISTORY
B. *Analyzing Causes*
What prompted women to establish NOW?

B. Answer Their dissatisfaction with the EEOC and the need for a more organized effort to combat sexism.

 Cooperative Activity: Preparing Articles for Ms.

Task: Groups of five to six students will write, design, and produce articles for *Ms.*

Purpose: To explore the goals, interests, and accomplishments of the women's movement in the early 1970s.

Activity: Students should get together to discuss articles they would like to write for *Ms.* Some students might choose to research and write articles on the goals of the movement in the 1970s. Others might decide to "interview"

important feminists of the time or to write human-interest features about women's experiences in the movement. Students should include photos and artwork with their articles.

📁 **Building a Portfolio:** Students who add their article to their portfolio should attach a note explaining how the project affected their opinion of feminism.

ALTERNATIVE ASSESSMENT BOOK
Standards for Evaluating a Cooperative Activity

Standards for Evaluation
Articles should . . .

• deal with feminist issues and concerns of the 1970s
• include photos and artwork with feminist themes
• convey the authors' pride in the movement and optimism for the future

Thousands of women march through the streets of New York City during the summer of 1970 to promote women's equality.

assistance," as part of the Higher Education Act. As a result, several all-male colleges opened their doors to women. That same year, Congress expanded the enforcement powers of the EEOC and gave working parents a tax break for child care expenses.

ROE V. WADE One of the more controversial issues that NOW and other feminist groups supported was a woman's right to have an abortion. Both men and women were deeply divided over the issue. In 1973, the Supreme Court ruled in the case *Roe* v. *Wade* that women had the right to choose an abortion during the first three months of pregnancy. In an editorial on the decision, the *New York Times* expressed hope that the ruling might "bring to end the emotional and divisive public argument . . ." However, this did not happen. Americans today remain divided over both the abortion issue and the Supreme Court's ruling.

THE EQUAL RIGHTS AMENDMENT In what seemed at first to be another triumph for the women's movement, Congress passed the **Equal Rights Amendment** (ERA) in 1972. The amendment then needed ratification by 38 states—three-quarters of the 50 states—to become part of the Constitution. The ERA, which had first been introduced to Congress in 1923, would have guaranteed that "Equality of rights under the law shall not be denied or abridged by the United States or by any state on account of sex." The ERA's supporters argued that the amendment was needed to make sure that men and women could not be treated differently under the law solely because of their gender. It was, they said, a matter of "simple justice."

Simple or not, the amendment sparked fierce opposition from conservative religious groups, political organizations, and many women who opposed the feminist movement. These groups raised fears that the ERA would lead to "a parade of horribles," such as the drafting of women, the end of laws protecting homemakers, and same-sex marriages.

One prominent ERA opponent was **Phyllis Schlafly.** In 1972, Schlafly founded and became national chairman of the Stop-ERA campaign. Schlafly characterized the ERA as the work of radical feminists who "hate men, marriage, and children" and whose oppression existed "only in their distorted minds."

Phyllis Schlafly

A PERSONAL VOICE
The U.S. Constitution is not the place for symbols or slogans, it is not the proper device to alleviate psychological problems of personal inferiority. Symbols and slogans belong on bumper strips—not in the Constitution. It would be a tragic mistake for our nation to succumb to the tirades and demands of a few women who are seeking a constitutional cure for their personal problems.

PHYLLIS SCHLAFLY, quoted in *The Equal Rights Amendment: The History and the Movement*

The Stop-ERA campaign also attracted support from women who feared its impact on families. Many worried that the amendment would end a husband's

ANOTHER PERSPECTIVE

AFRICAN-AMERICAN WOMEN
The women's movement of the 1960s and 1970s was largely a white, middle class movement. By the 1960s, many African-American women expressed greater concern with racism and the attainment of civil rights than with sexism and inequality in the workplace. Ida Lewis, editor of the African-American magazine, *Essence*, advised, "The Women's Liberation Movement is basically a family quarrel between white women and white men. . . And on general principles, it's not too good to get involved in family disputes."

An Era of Social Change **931**

The Movement's Legacy

▶ *Discussing Key Ideas*
- The women's movement opens up new opportunities for women and changes their role in society.
- The movement changes the way women look at work and careers.

ASSESS & RETEACH

Section 2 Assessment

Have students work independently to answer the questions. Then have them meet in small groups to discuss their answers.

Self-Assessment

Have students make a list of the impressions they had about the women's movement before they read Section 2. Then have them note whether their reading has confirmed or contradicted their preconceptions.

Section Quiz

FORMAL ASSESSMENT
Section Quiz, p. 377

Reteach

Use the charts on page 929 to review the progress women have made in the workplace since 1970.

CLOSE

In the 1960s, the women's movement began challenging traditional beliefs about a woman's place in society. The movement opened up new opportunities for women, particularly in the fields of education, employment, and politics. At the same time, many young people were rejecting mainstream American society and creating a counterculture.

---

responsibility to provide support to his wife and children. In Florida, anti-ERA homemakers sent lawmakers jars of homemade jam labeled "Preserve the family unit." There and in other states where the ERA was being debated, their message was the same: Don't change our lives.

By 1977, the ERA had won approval from 35 of the 38 states needed to ratify the amendment. At that point, however, the amendment stalled, as opposition to the ERA gained strength. By the end of 1982 (the deadline for ratification), no other states had approved the amendment. The ERA went down in defeat. The amendment, announced Schlafly, "is dead now and forever in this century."

THINK THROUGH HISTORY
C. *Analyzing Motives* What concerns motivated those who opposed the ERA?
C. Answer Fear of change and the perceived drastic effects the amendment might have had on traditional family life.

The Movement's Legacy

Despite the defeat of the ERA, the women's movement made progress in achieving several of its aims. From college campuses to Capitol Hill, the women's movement opened up new opportunities for American women and dramatically altered their roles in society.

The movement left its mark on society by creating new opportunities for women, particularly in the fields of education, employment, and politics. In 1970, 8 percent of all medical school graduates and 5 percent of all law school graduates were women. By 1992, those proportions had risen to 36 and 43 percent, respectively. The movement also created a new demand for women's studies programs. By 1980, American colleges were offering 30,000 courses about women.

The women's movement also changed the way women looked at work and careers. In the 1950s, most women who took jobs had done so mainly to "help out" by earning a little extra money. By the 1970s, many women were preparing themselves for lifetime careers. As these women moved into traditionally male occupations, the gap between men's and women's earnings slowly began to shrink. Still, many women ran into a "glass ceiling"—an invisible, but very real, resistance to promoting women into top positions—as they tried to move upward in the workplace.

The women's movement brought women into the political arena in growing numbers. Women held only 3.5 percent of elected state offices in 1969. By 1996, 25 percent of elected state officeholders were women. The number of women in Congress also has generally increased. In 1975, there were 19 women in Congress. By 1997, 60 women occupied elected offices on Capitol Hill.

Most of all, the women's movement helped countless women open their lives to new possibilities. "We have lived the second American revolution," wrote Betty Friedan in 1976, "and our very anger said a 'new YES' to life."

Women have made significant strides politically, as they have increased their presence in the U.S. Congress.

D. Answer By opening up greater opportunities for women in the fields of education, employment, and politics.

THINK THROUGH HISTORY
D. *Forming Opinions* In what ways did the women's movement help women progress in society?

Section ② Assessment

1. **TERMS & NAMES**
   Identify:
   - feminism
   - Betty Friedan
   - National Organization for Women
   - Equal Rights Amendment
   - Phyllis Schlafly

2. **SUMMARIZING** Create a time line of key events relating to the women's movement. Use the dates already plotted on the time line below as a guide.

1963		1973
1966	1970	1972

3. **HYPOTHESIZING** What if the Equal Rights Amendment had been ratified? Speculate on how women's lives might have been different. Support your answer with reasons.

   THINK ABOUT
   - rights addressed by the amendment
   - legal support that the amendment might have provided
   - possible reactions from groups opposing the amendment

4. **FORMING AN OPINION** In 1976, Betty Friedan wrote, "We have lived the second American Revolution." Do you think she is overstating the historical importance of the women's movement by comparing it to the American Revolution? Why or why not?

   THINK ABOUT
   - the movement's legacy
   - what you already know about the American Revolution and its outcome

932 CHAPTER 31

ANSWERS

1. TERMS & NAMES

feminism, p. 928

Betty Friedan, p. 929

National Organization for Women, p. 930

Equal Rights Amendment, p. 931

Phyllis Schlafly, p. 931

2. SUMMARIZING

Possible Answers:
1963—Betty Friedan publishes *The Feminine Mystique.*
1966—National Organization for Women is formed.
1970—Demonstration commemorates 50th anniversary of woman suffrage.
1972—*Ms.* is founded; Congress passes Equal Rights Amendment and bans sex discrimination in federally assisted educational programs and activities.
1973—Supreme Court's ruling in *Roe* v. *Wade* legalizes abortion.

3. HYPOTHESIZING

Possible Answers: Women might have won more sex-discrimination lawsuits; the "glass ceiling" phenomenon might have been less of a problem for professional women; ratification might have spurred a powerful male backlash; Phyllis Schlafly and other opponents of ERA might have formed organizations to undermine the amendment.

4. FORMING AN OPINION

Possible Responses: Yes—Feminists were not like the American colonists who risked their lives fighting a war for independence and who formed a new nation. No—Feminists were nonviolent revolutionaries who were just as determined and committed to their cause as the early American revolutionaries.

❸ Culture and Counterculture

TERMS & NAMES
• counterculture
• Haight-Ashbury
• The Beatles
• Woodstock

Section 3 Overview

LEARN ABOUT the ideals and lifestyle of the counterculture movement of the 1960s
TO UNDERSTAND its impact on young people in the 1960s and beyond.

ONE AMERICAN'S STORY

In 1966, Alex Forman packed up a guitar and little else and headed to San Francisco. Forman had decided to abandon his conventional life in mainstream America and live with thousands of others like himself in a more carefree setting. Forman recalled his early days in San Francisco's Haight-Ashbury district, which had attracted many young Americans seeking refuge from the violence and divisiveness of the sixties.

A PERSONAL VOICE

It was like paradise there. Everybody was in love with life and in love with their fellow human beings to the point where they were just sharing in incredible ways with everybody. Taking people in off the street and letting them stay in their homes. . . . You could walk down almost any street in Haight-Ashbury where I was living, and someone would smile at you and just go, "Hey, it's beautiful, isn't it?". . . It was a very special time.

ALEX FORMAN, quoted in *From Camelot to Kent State*

Members of the counterculture relax in a California park.

Forman was part of a movement known as the **counterculture**. Made up mostly of white middle-class youths, the counterculture—like other groups in society—had grown deeply disillusioned with America during the 1960s. However, unlike the other groups, which challenged the system, members of the counterculture chose to turn their backs on America and establish a new society based on peace and love. Although their efforts were short-lived, some aspects of the counterculture movement left an enduring mark on American society.

The Counterculture

In the late 1960s, the historian Theodore Roszak described the rise of these idealistic youths as the "counter culture." It was a culture, he said, so different from the mainstream "that it scarcely looks to many as a culture at all, but takes on the alarming appearance of a barbarian intrusion." The so-called alarming barbarians were mostly white, middle-class college youths. And while they indeed did create a culture different from the mainstream, their lack of organization and direction—as well as the devastating effects of drug use—led to the counterculture's eventual collapse.

Throughout the late 1960s, thousands of hippies flocked to San Francisco's Haight-Ashbury district.

"TUNE IN, TURN ON, DROP OUT" Members of the counterculture, known as hippies, shared some of the beliefs of the New Left movement, namely that American society—and its materialism, technology, and war—had grown hollow. A number of hippies even participated in various New Left demonstrations, including its many protests against the Vietnam War. However, a majority of hippies chose to protest against society by leaving it.

Influenced heavily by the nonconformist beat movement of the 1950s, hippies eagerly embraced the credo voiced by Harvard psychology professor and counterculture philosopher Timothy Leary: "Tune in, turn on, drop out." Throughout the mid and late 1960s, tens of thousands of idealistic

933

SECTION 3 RESOURCES

 PRINT RESOURCES

IN-DEPTH RESOURCES: UNIT 8
Guided Reading, p. 58
Skillbuilder Practice: Comparing; Contrasting, p. 59
Primary Source: "Woodstock," p. 65
Literature: from *Los Vendidos* by Luis Valdez, p. 66

ACCESS FOR STUDENTS ACQUIRING ENGLISH
Guided Reading (Spanish), p. 303
Skillbuilder Practice: Comparing; Contrasting (Spanish), p. 304

FORMAL ASSESSMENT
Section Quiz, p. 378

ALTERNATIVE ASSESSMENT BOOK
See forms for supporting and scoring alternative activities.

 TECHNOLOGY RESOURCES

CD-ROM *Our Times*

VIDEO *American Portfolio: A Videodisc for U.S. History*
user's guide, pp. 247, 249

INTERNET McDougal Littell Learning On-Line
http://www.mcdougallittell.com

OBJECTIVES

① To describe the flowering and the decline of the counterculture in the 1960s.

② To summarize the impact of the counterculture on art, fashion, music, and attitudes.

CRITICAL THINKING

• Summarizing, pp. 934, 937
• Analyzing causes, p. 935
• Analyzing issues, p. 937
• Comparing and contrasting, p. 937
• Generalizing, p. 937

FOCUS & MOTIVATE

▶ *Starting with the Student*
• What images come to mind when students hear the word *hippie*?
• What are some songs of the 1960s? How has the music of that period influenced the music students enjoy today?

OBJECTIVE
① **INSTRUCT**

The Counterculture

▶ *Discussing Key Ideas*
• Members of the counterculture reject mainstream society and try to create an idyllic world of peace, love, and harmony.
• Hippie life usually involves rock 'n' roll, outrageous clothing and appearance, and drugs.
• After a few years, the counterculture's peace and harmony gives way to violence, drug abuse, and disillusionment.

IN-DEPTH RESOURCES: UNIT 8
Guided Reading, p. 58

ACCESS FOR STUDENTS ACQUIRING ENGLISH
Guided Reading (Spanish), p. 303

MORE ABOUT . . .
Hippie Speak

In addition to "flower power" and "do your own thing," the counterculture created a whole lexicon of "hip" language. Among the words and phrases used by hippies to express approval were *far out, groovy, right on,* and *out of sight.* Other terms, such as *hang up, freak out,* and *bummer,* were used to express disapproval. In addition, the counterculture coined a number of behavioral injunctions, including "Let it all hang out" and "Get your act together."

MORE ABOUT . . .
Communes

Many people who chose to live in communes sought to recreate the Garden of Eden by looking for beautiful, secluded spots in rural areas where they could live a spontaneous, hassle-free existence. Community relationships were valued above all else. This is how Rosabeth Moss Kanter described her communal experience: "The things that make up community are terribly subtle; it's the little things . . . making dinner with a crew once a week, remembering who's a vegetarian and needs a special meal. Expanded consciousness of others . . . nothing big and spectacular. The scenes that move me are the little things about our life together."

"How does it feel to be without a home . . . like a rolling stone?"

BOB DYLAN

A prominent symbol of the counterculture movement was bright colors. Here, a woman and a Volkswagen bus sport such colors along a San Francisco street.

young Americans left behind their established worlds of school, work, or home to live with one another in the streets, parks, and group homes. Their goal was to create, in the midst of what they viewed as a cold and cruel nation, an idyllic setting of peace, love, and harmony.

HIPPIE CULTURE The creation of this peace and love, which some called an Age of Aquarius, usually involved three things: rock 'n' roll music, outrageous clothing and appearance, and the liberal use of drugs—both marijuana and a new hallucinogenic, or mind-altering, compound called LSD, or acid. Timothy Leary, an early experimenter with LSD, promoted the drug as a "liberating" and "mind-expanding" aid in the search for greater self-awareness and inner peace.

Aside from illegal drug use, hippies showed their rejection of the establishment by wearing what were then considered outrageous clothes. Many young men and women wore ragged jeans and tie-dyed T-shirts, as well as surplus military garments. In addition, many hippies enhanced their outfits with beads and Native American ornaments. Men grew long hair and beards. To many hippies, long hair symbolized the freedom to "do your own thing." To the older generation, long hair symbolized a lack of respect for social conventions. Signs went up across the country saying "Make America Beautiful—give a hippie a haircut."

Hippies also turned their backs on conventional home life. Many chose to live together in communes—group living arrangements in which the members renounced private property to live together in cooperation and harmony. For some, this meant establishing rural communes; for others, it meant crowding together in urban "crash pads." Scores of hippies flocked to Chicago's Old Town, Atlanta's Fourteenth Street, New York City's Greenwich Village, and especially San Francisco's **Haight-Ashbury** district. By the mid-sixties, Haight-Ashbury had become the hippie capital, mainly because of the availability of hallucinogenic drugs, which California did not outlaw until late 1966.

Many disillusioned youths also sought fulfillment through new and different religious experiences. Rejecting traditional forms of worship, scores of young men and women turned to the teachings of such Eastern religions as Zen Buddhism. According to the Zen philosophy, people attain enlightenment through meditation, self-contemplation, and intuition, rather than through the reading of scriptures.

Influenced by the preaching of spiritual gurus, such as Maharishi Mahesh Yogi of India, thousands of Americans began taking informal courses in mystical meditation and forming groups to practice what they learned. In 1968, the news media declared that more than 10,000 of the nation's youths had become "transcendental meditators." Later that year, *Life* magazine proclaimed 1968 to be the "Year of the Guru."

DECLINE OF THE MOVEMENT After only a few years, the counterculture's peace and harmony gave way to violence and disillusionment. The urban communes eventually turned seedy and dangerous, as they became havens for muggers, drug dealers, and runaways. "It got very ugly

---

Skillbuilder Mini-Lesson: Comparing; Contrasting

Explaining the Skill Finding similarities and differences between events, social or political groups, and movements can help historians understand the past more completely. For example, comparing the lifestyles and values of different groups can help historians identify trends or universal human needs.

Applying the Skill: Hippie Culture Make two columns on the chalkboard, labeled "Hippies" and "Establishment." Ask students to list as many differing characteristics of hippie culture and establishment, or mainstream culture, as they can

find on this page. Point out that they may need to infer some characteristics of the establishment from the descriptions of the hippies. Also ask students if they find any similarities between the two groups. Here are some examples: hippies— long hair, rock 'n' roll music, hallucinogenic drugs, freedom to "do your own thing," outrageous clothes, communes, transcendental meditation; establishment—short hair, other kinds of music, objections to drug use, respect for social conventions, conventional clothing styles, traditional home life, regular jobs.

IN-DEPTH RESOURCES: UNIT 8
Skillbuilder Practice: Comparing; Contrasting, p. 59

very fast," Alex Forman recalled. "There were ripoffs, violence. . . .people living on the street with no place to stay."

In August 1969, one particular episode of counterculture violence shocked America. Deranged commune leader Charles Manson and his "family" of run-aways from Haight-Ashbury murdered pregnant movie actress Sharon Tate and four of her friends. The murderers' crazed motive was to hasten the "revolution" by creating chaos and fear. The counterculture movement, it seemed, had gone terribly wrong.

Four months later, in December 1969, another violent episode grabbed the nation's attention. The Rolling Stones, a British rock group, had decided to give a free concert at the Altamont Raceway in California. It was a disaster. To provide security for their show, the Rolling Stones hired the Hell's Angels motorcycle gang. As the band played, the white motorcyclists beat to death a black man wielding a knife in front of the stage. Three other spectators were accidentally killed that night. "It wasn't just the Angels, shoving people around on or near the stage, who were angels of death," recalled writer Todd Gitlin, who was at the concert. "Behind the stage, hordes of Aquarians were interfering with doctors trying to help people climb down from bad acid trips." A few days later, Gitlin wrote an article entitled "The End of the Age of Aquarius."

By 1970, the widespread use of drugs had further eroded the counterculture movement. Many young people fell victim to the drugs they used, experiencing overdoses, drug dependence, and mental and physical breakdowns. The popular rock singer Janis Joplin and the legendary guitarist Jimi Hendrix both died of drug overdoses in 1970.

More than anything else, however, the hippies eventually discovered that they could not sustain themselves outside of mainstream America. Even though they tried to reject conventional society, many hippies found themselves ultimately dependent on it. Numerous hippies ended up panhandling on street corners and lined up at government offices, collecting welfare and food stamps to help them survive the trials of natural living. "We were together at the level of peace and freedom and love," said one disillusioned hippie. "We fell apart over who would cook and wash the dishes and pay the bills."

B. Answer The Manson and Altamont murders, the dark side of the drug scene, and the hippies inability to exist outside mainstream America.

THINK THROUGH HISTORY
B. Analyzing Causes What events hastened the decline of the counterculture movement?

A Changing Culture

Although the counterculture movement was short-lived, some aspects of it—namely, its fashion, fine arts, and social attitudes—left a more lasting imprint on mainstream America.

ART AND FASHION The counterculture's rebellious style left its mark on the worlds of art and fashion. The 1960s saw the rise of popular, or pop, art. Pop artists, led by Andy Warhol, attempted to bring art into the mainstream. Warhol became famous for his bright silk-screen portraits of soup cans, Marilyn Monroe, and other icons of mass culture. By 1970, many prominent artists had followed Warhol's lead and abandoned their sculpting and painting for an art grounded in popular culture.

To a larger extent, the counterculture's legacy lived on in the way many Americans dressed and groomed themselves. While most Americans certainly did not adopt the outlandish look of hippies, many came out of the sixties wearing longer hair, the

Andy Warhol created this image of movie actress and popular icon Marilyn Monroe.

An Era of Social Change **935**

MORE ABOUT . . .
The End of the Movement

In 1969, the hippie activist Jerry Rubin published a book titled *Do It!*, in which he described his vision of the coming counterculture revolution. Rubin foresaw a "mass breakdown of authority, mass rebellion, total anarchy in every institution in the Western world. Tribes of long-hairs, blacks, armed women, workers, peasants and students will take over." Two years later, however, the revolution was dead.

OBJECTIVE
② **INSTRUCT**

A Changing Culture

▶ *Starting with the Student* Have students document details of the impact of the counterculture movement in a cluster diagram like this.

▶ *Discussing Key Ideas*
• The rebelliousness of the counterculture influences styles of art and fashion.
• Hippies embrace rock music as their anthem of social protest and cultural change.
• The counterculture leaves a legacy of more relaxed attitudes toward sex, marriage, behavior, and relationships.

 OUR TIMES from *The Electric Kool-Aid Acid Test* by Tom Wolfe

---

TEACHING OPTIONS

Exploring Themes

The American Dream Discuss the counterculture's rejection of mainstream society. Ask students to define the American dream. Which aspects of the traditional American dream did hippies renounce? *Possible Responses: Materialism; conventional home life; success in the workplace.* What did hippies value? What was their American dream? *Possible Responses: Peace; love; communal living.* Why did their dream sour? *Possible Response: Because they couldn't apply their ideals to practical, everyday life.* Then ask students whether the counterculture's American dream could be realized today.

Making Connections Across Time

Counterculture Fashion Returns Tell students that in the 1990s, bell-bottom jeans, tie-dyed shirts, and miniskirts made a comeback. These counterculture fashions and others became popular once again among nostalgic baby boomers and people of younger generations. Ask students why these items of clothing and other trappings of the counterculture have such an enduring hold on the imagination. Why do the 1960s continue to fascinate? *Possible Response: Because, even though they may have been illusory, the freedom and spirit of the period appeal to many people.*

MORE ABOUT . . .
The Beatles in America

In 1975, *Life* magazine published a list of "The 100 Events that Shaped America." The arrival of the Beatles on American soil in 1964 ranked number 96. Americans got their first look at the Fab Four on January 3 of that year, when television talk-show host Jack Paar aired a videotape of the group performing "She Loves You" to an audience of screaming, sobbing teenage girls. American critics were not impressed. One writer for the *New York Times* predicted that Beatlemania would never catch on in the United States: "On this side of the Atlantic, it is dated stuff." The journalist would soon eat his words. In 1996, 25 years after the Beatles broke up, the group once again reached the top of the charts with their *Anthology* albums.

The Beatles, shown here on the cover of their album, *Sgt. Pepper's Lonely Hearts Club Band*, influenced fashion with their long hair and psychedelic clothing.

Throughout the Woodstock festival, the massive crowd remained mostly peaceful and well-organized. Said the local sheriff, "This was the nicest bunch of kids I've ever dealt with."

men sporting either beards or mustaches. As for fashion, men's and women's clothes became more colorful and comfortable, and blue jeans—popular counterculture apparel—became a staple in nearly every American's wardrobe.

ROCK MUSIC Perhaps the most lasting legacy of the counterculture movement was its music. During the 1960s, the hippie movement embraced rock 'n' roll—the offshoot of African-American rhythm and blues music that had captivated so many teenagers during the 1950s—as its loud and biting anthem of protest. However, as the years went on, rock music melded into the mainstream and is today one of the more recognizable characteristics of American youth.

The band that, perhaps more than any other, helped propel rock music into mainstream America was **The Beatles.** The British band, made up of four youths from working-class Liverpool, England, arrived in America in 1964 and immediately took the country by storm. Young men and women across the nation rushed out to buy each new Beatles record, which early on included such simple pop songs as "She Loves You," and later, more complex albums as *Sgt. Pepper's Lonely Hearts Club Band.* Many youths—both in and out of mainstream America—copied the group members' look of long hair and colorful outfits. By the time the Beatles broke up in 1971, the four "lads" from Liverpool had inspired a countless number of other bands and had won over millions of Americans to rock 'n' roll.

WOODSTOCK One dramatic example of rock 'n' roll's exploding popularity occurred in August 1969 on a farm in upstate New York. There, about 120,000 young people were expected to gather for a free music festival called "Woodstock Music and Art Fair, an Aquarian Exposition." More than 400,000 showed up. In what became the counterculture's greatest "Human Be-in," throngs of young men and women from around the country crowded onto Max Yasgur's farm for three days and nights of nearly nonstop rock'n'roll music. Taking the stage one after the other were the most popular bands and musicians of the time, including Jimi Hendrix, Janis Joplin, Joe Cocker, Joan Baez, the Grateful Dead, and Jefferson Airplane.

Despite the huge crowd, the event, which became known simply as **Woodstock,** was remarkably peaceful and well-organized. However, not everyone remembered it as three days of bliss. Tom Mathews, a writer who attended the Woodstock festival, later recalled his experience there.

936 CHAPTER 31

TEACHING OPTION

Cooperative Activity: Producing a 1960s Music Video

Task: Groups of five to six students will select a song from the 1960s and create and record a music video based on it.

Purpose: To help students identify significant elements of the counterculture.

Activity: Group members should select a song from the 1960s. They should then brainstorm to create an appropriate video based on the song. The video should have a 1960s setting and be filled with the colors, clothes, and memorabilia of the time. One student in the group should direct the video, another should record it, and the rest should perform. Performers, who should be dressed as members of the counterculture, may lip-synch the song.

📁 **Building a Portfolio:** Students who add their videos to their portfolio should attach a note to it, describing their role in the activity.

ALTERNATIVE ASSESSMENT BOOK
Standards for Evaluating a Cooperative Activity

Standards for Evaluation
Music videos should . . .

- celebrate and bring to life songs of the 1960s
- contain scenes filled with the colors, clothes, and trappings of the 1960s
- convey a sense of the freedom and abandon of the time

936 Chapter 31

A man and woman make their own music at Woodstock. "If you were part of this culture," noted one Woodstock attendee, "you had to be there."

CHANGING ATTITUDES As the counterculture movement faded, its casual, "do your own thing" philosophy left an imprint on Americans' social attitudes as well. In particular, many Americans began to view sexual behavior and human relationships more casually—leading to what became known as the sexual revolution.

During the 1960s and 1970s, mass culture—which included books, magazines, and movies—began to more openly address subjects that had once been taboo. In addition, many Americans adopted a more casual approach toward marriage and relationships. The divorce rate nearly doubled in the 1970s, while many couples chose to live together without getting married. During this time, numerous homosexual organizations—which had long remained hidden from society's view—began to openly fight for equal rights.

While some hailed the sexual revolution as a liberating force, others attacked it as a sign of moral decay. Parental groups and religious organizations, for example, vigorously protested Hollywood's trend toward more sexually explicit films. These groups helped force the Motion Picture Association to introduce the rating system for movies in 1968.

In a larger sense, millions of Americans opposed the country's increasingly casual and permissive social behavior. While the counterculture movement eventually helped prompt many Americans to adopt more liberal attitudes about dress and appearance, music, and social behavior, the movement's immediate impact on the country produced the opposite effect. The counterculture and antiwar movements, with their perceived lawlessness and chaos, spawned a conservative backlash among many mainstream Americans. This backlash helped propel Richard M. Nixon into the White House and set the nation on a more conservative course.

C. Answer The movements spawned a conservative backlash from mainstream America, which perceived the country as being engulfed by lawlessness and chaos.

THINK THROUGH HISTORY
C. Analyzing Issues What role did the counterculture and antiwar movements play in helping Richard Nixon win the presidency?

1. TERMS & NAMES

Identify:
• counterculture
• Haight-Ashbury
• Beatles
• Woodstock

2. SUMMARIZING

Re-create the organizational tree diagram below on your paper. Then fill in examples that illustrate the topics in the second row of boxes.

The Counterculture
— Beliefs / Lifestyle / Impact on Society
— examples / examples / examples

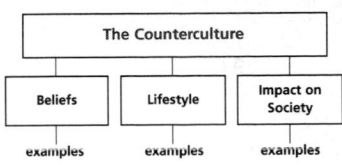

3. COMPARING AND CONTRASTING Draw parallels between the Woodstock rock concert in upstate New York and the Rolling Stones rock concert in California. What do you think were the key similarities and differences?

THINK ABOUT
• what each event came to symbolize
• the prevailing atmosphere at each event
• the writer Todd Gitlin's comments about the Rolling Stones concert

4. GENERALIZING A stereotype is a rigid generalization made about a group. What stereotype do you think hippies might have formed about mainstream Americans? What stereotype do you think mainstream Americans might have formed about hippies? Why?

THINK ABOUT
• Alex Forman's comments in "A Personal Voice"
• hippies' values and lifestyle
• mainstream Americans' values and lifestyle
• reasons for the decline of the counterculture

An Era of Social Change **937**

ANSWERS

Teacher's Edition **937**

DAILY LIFE
1960—1970

Signs of the Sixties

The wave of social change that swept across America during the 1960s affected the nation's teenagers as well. Abandoning the conservative and "clean cut" look of the 1950s, many teens experimented with new and different appearances. In a declaration of their individuality and desire for more freedom, America's teens also reached out to a variety of new music and films during the 1960s.

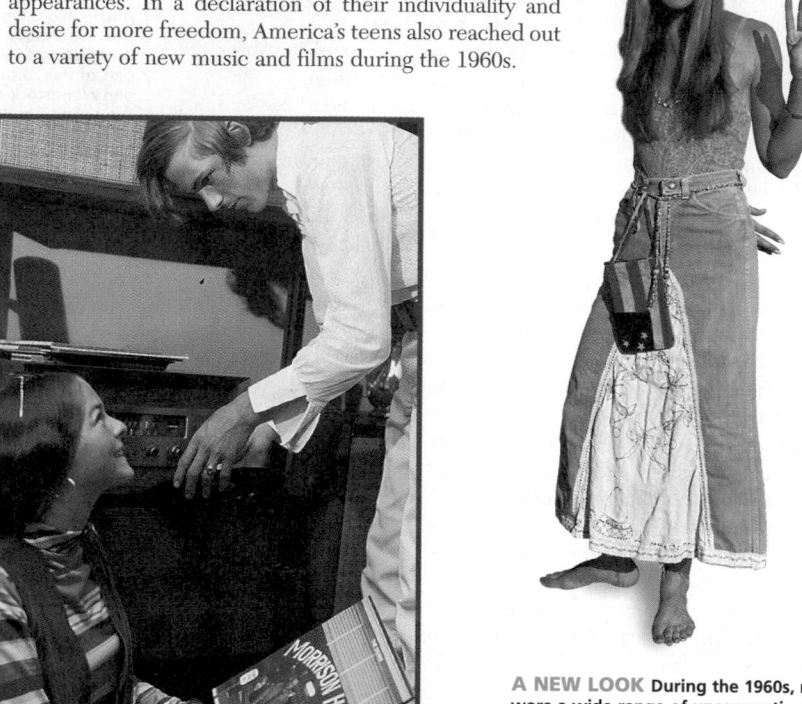

A NEW LOOK During the 1960s, many youths wore a wide range of unconventional clothing. Bright colors and psychedelic patterns became wildly popular. So, too, did the "natural" look of worn denim and hand-sewn or second-hand clothing. In addition, new grooming styles emerged, most notably evidenced in the way many young men and women grew their hair.

938 CHAPTER 31

RECOMMENDED RESOURCES

Books

Howard, Gerald, ed. *The Sixties.* New York: Paragon, 1991. Art, politics, and the media in an explosive decade.

O'Neil, Doris C., ed. *Life—the '60s.* Boston: Little, 1989. A pictorial history.

Polsgrove, Carol. *It Wasn't Pretty, Folks, but Didn't We Have Fun?* New York: Norton, 1995. The 1960s as depicted in *Esquire* magazine.

Videos

Berkeley in the Sixties. Pacific Arts Video, 1993. The Free Speech Movement, antiwar protests, and counterculture at the California university.

Breaking Boundaries, Testing Limits. PBS Video, 1991. Focuses on the youth rebellion and the counterculture.

Flashing on the Sixties. Pacific Arts Video, 1993. Surveys some of the people, places, events, and ideals that helped shape the 1960s.

The History of Rock 'n' Roll. Time-Life, 1995. A ten-part series on rock music from rhythm and blues to rap.

GOING TO THE SHOW

As the nation's movie industry grew, more and more teenagers flocked to the cinema. Teens took in such diverse films as the counterculture classic *Easy Rider* and the science fiction classic *2001: A Space Odyssey (left)*, which tells the story of HAL, a spaceship computer that develops a mind of its own.

THE RISE OF SOUL MUSIC

Rock 'n' roll's popularity continued to soar as teenagers listened to a wider variety of sounds in the 1960s. African-American soul artists, whose music had inspired the more popular white rock 'n' roll performers of the 1950s, grew widely popular themselves during the 1960s. During this decade, Detroit's Motown label produced the most popular and successful African-American artists, including Marvin Gaye, Stevie Wonder, and the Supremes *(right)*.

A DIVERSE MUSIC SCENE

Scores of teenagers also tuned to surf music, a harmonic, light sound made popular by a California band, the Beach Boys. Other teens listened to the poetic and socially conscious lyrics of folk rock. Heavy, or psychedelic, rock, sung by bands such as the Doors (whose 1967 concert advertisement appears to the left), also found its way into many album collections.

DATA FILE

Popular songs
- "Blowin' in the Wind"
- "Surfin' USA"
- "Where Did Our Love Go?"
- "California Dreamin'"
- "Light My Fire"
- "Mrs. Robinson"
- "Aquarius/Let the Sunshine In"

Popular TV shows
- *The Dick Van Dyke Show*
- *The Beverly Hillbillies*
- *Green Acres*
- *The Addams Family*
- *The Man from U.N.C.L.E.*
- *Mission Impossible*
- *Laugh-In*
- *Bonanza*

Daily Life Data

1960: Alfred Hitchcock's *Psycho* terrified movie audiences across the nation.

1962: Wilt Chamberlain became the only professional basketball player to score 100 points in a game.

1963: The movie *Cleopatra*, which starred popular actress Elizabeth Taylor and cost $37 million, opened as the most expensive film to date.

1964: The Beatles arrived in America

1965: The miniskirt was introduced.

1966: The National Association of Broadcasters instructed disc jockeys to screen records for obscene or hidden meanings.

1967: The Green Bay Packers defeated the Kansas City Chiefs in the first Super Bowl.

1968: The government mandated that all new cars must be equipped with seat belts.

1969: Pantsuits became acceptable for everyday wear by women.

INTERACT WITH HISTORY

1. DRAWING CONCLUSIONS What conclusions can you draw about teenagers in the 1960s from the images and information in this feature?

SEE SKILLBUILDER HANDBOOK, PAGE 1050.

2. TRACKING TRENDS Working with a small group, research the history of clothing and costumes. Identify several other periods in history when radical changes in dress appeared. Why did these changes occur? Report your findings to the class, using visual aids, or arrange a display on important clothing changes through history.

INTERNET For more about youth in the sixties, click on **Social Studies** at http://www.mcdougallittell.com

An Era of Social Change **939**

INSTRUCT

▶ **Starting with the Student**
- Discuss the TV shows listed in the data file. Ask students to identify any of the shows' themes or characterizations that are typical of the 1960s.
- Ask students who made the popular recordings of the songs listed in the data file. *Peter, Paul & Mary; Beach Boys; Supremes; Mamas & Papas; Doors; Simon & Garfunkel; Fifth Dimension.* If possible, play some of these recordings, as well as hits by other 60s stars like Marvin Gaye, Stevie Wonder, and the Beatles.

▶ **Discussing Key Ideas**
- During the 1960s, many teenagers experiment with new looks in hair and clothing.
- Teenagers influence popular culture as they embrace a wide range of musical sounds and flock to the movies.

HISTORY FROM VISUALS

Reading the Images Have students study the illustrations and captions.

- What words would students use to characterize the "new look" of the 1960s? *Possible Responses: Natural; free; silly; colorful; dated.*
- How does the appearance of the Supremes compare with the look of a current music group?
- On the basis of the movie still, what current films do students think have been influenced by *2001*?

INTERACT WITH HISTORY

1. Drawing Conclusions

Possible Responses: *Teenagers were rebellious and wanted to express their individuality. They were also wild, self-confident, self-important, fun-loving, and innocent. Although teenagers thought they were being different, their appearance expressed little individuality as they conformed to an accepted "in" look. Teenage tastes dominated pop culture.*

2. Tracking Trends

Have students work together in small groups. You might suggest that each group

- focus on a different era or on a different nation or culture
- sketch the fashions themselves or obtain photos or post cards from museums, historical societies, or other institutions
- use student models to present fashions
- collaborate on researching, writing, and displaying the report

Chapter **31** Assessment

TERMS & NAMES
1. Cesar Chavez, p. 921
2. La Raza Unida, p. 922
3. American Indian Movement, p. 923
4. feminism, p. 928
5. Betty Friedan, p. 929
6. Equal Rights Amendment, p. 931
7. Phyllis Schlafly, p. 931
8. counterculture, p. 933
9. Haight-Ashbury, p. 934
10. Woodstock, p. 936

MAIN IDEAS
11. Mexicans; Cubans; Puerto Ricans; Salvadorans; Nicaraguans; Colombians.

12. Nonviolence; he launched a boycott to pressure California grape growers to recognize the United Farm Workers Organizing Committee.

13. Proclaiming Native Americans' goals and demanding greater autonomy; Johnson responded by establishing a National Council of Indian Opportunity.

14. The restoration of 110 million acres of land to Native American tribes and the abolition of the Bureau of Indian Affairs.

15. The creation of more child-care facilities, better educational opportunities for women, and EEOC enforcement of the ban on sex discrimination in hiring.

16. That women had the right to choose an abortion during the first three months of pregnancy.

17. Law, medicine, and politics.

18. A counterculture guru, Leary popularized the credo "Tune in, turn on, drop out" and promoted the use of LSD.

19. Chicago's Old Town; Atlanta's Fourteenth Street; New York City's Greenwich Village; San Francisco's Haight-Ashbury district.

20. It inspired a conservative backlash among mainstream Americans that led to a wave of Republican victories in elections.

REVIEWING THE CHAPTER

TERMS & NAMES For each item below, write a sentence explaining its connection to the 1960s. For each person or group of people named below, explain his or her role in events.

1. Cesar Chavez
2. La Raza Unida
3. American Indian Movement
4. feminism
5. Betty Friedan
6. Equal Rights Amendment
7. Phyllis Schlafly
8. counterculture
9. Haight-Ashbury
10. Woodstock

MAIN IDEAS

SECTION 1 *(pages 920–925)*

Latinos and Native Americans Seek Equality

11. Cite examples of groups that make up America's Latino population.
12. What strategy did both Cesar Chavez and Dr. Martin Luther King, Jr., use to achieve their goals? How did Chavez successfully apply this tactic?
13. What was the focus of the Declaration of Indian Purpose, drafted in 1961? How did President Johnson respond to the declaration in 1965?
14. What were the demands of the American Indian Movement organizers who staged "The Trail of Broken Treaties" march on Washington in 1972?

SECTION 2 *(pages 928–932)*

Women Fight for Equality

15. Name three changes that members of the National Organization of Women (NOW) advocated.
16. What was the Supreme Court's decision in the *Roe* v. *Wade* case?
17. What three traditionally male-dominated professions did women enter in much greater numbers as a result of the women's movement?

SECTION 3 *(pages 933–937)*

Culture and Counterculture

18. Briefly explain the role Timothy Leary played in the counterculture movement.
19. What urban areas became popular hangouts for hippies during the 1960s?
20. What unintended impact did the counterculture have on many mainstream Americans?

THINKING CRITICALLY

1. **PROMPTING REFORM** Recreate the diagram shown below. Then fill in the appropriate circles with key individual and shared achievements of Latinos, Native Americans, and feminists.

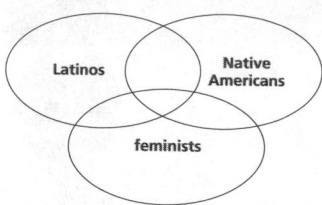

2. **THEME: WOMEN IN AMERICA** Imagine that the director of a history museum has asked you to submit a brief list of artifacts for exhibits featuring American women of the 1960s and early 1970s. What artifacts would you suggest? Use details from the text to help you develop your recommendations.

3. **THE TURBULENT SIXTIES** Reread the line of song lyrics by Bob Dylan on page 918. Do you think the quote captures the mood of the 1960s and early 1970s? Explain.

4. **VEHICLES FOR CHANGE** Consider the organizations that Latinos, Native Americans, and women formed during the 1960s. Which do you think was the most influential? Support your choice with reasons.

5. **GEOGRAPHY: THE MOVEMENT OF MIGRANT WORKERS** Refer to the map and information on pages 926–927. In light of their disruptive lifestyle, what social, economic, or medical problems do you think migrant workers and their families face?

6. **ANALYZING PRIMARY SOURCES** Read the following excerpt from *Always Running*, Luis J. Rodriguez's chronicle of growing up in Los Angeles during the late 1960s and early 1970s. Then answer the questions below.

> We [Mexican families] kept jumping hurdles, kept breaking from the constraints. . . . The [Los Angeles] River, for example, became a new barrier, keeping the Mexicans in their neighborhoods over on the vast east side of the city for years, except for forays downtown. School provided other restrictions: Don't speak Spanish; don't be Mexican—you don't belong. Railroad tracks divided us from communities where white people lived, such as South Gate and Lynwood across from Watts. We were invisible people in a city which thrived in glitter, big screens, and big names; but this glamour contained none of our names, none of our faces.
> The refrain "this is not your country" echoed for a long time.
>
> **LUIS J. RODRIGUEZ,** *Always Running*

According to Rodriguez, what were the gravest problems facing Mexican Americans during his youth? Why do you think some of these problems were eventually solved?

THINKING CRITICALLY

1. PROMPTING REFORM
Possible Answers: Individual achievements: Latinos—(1968) Bilingual Education Act; (1968) establishment of Chicano studies programs in colleges. Native Americans—(1972) Indian Education Act; (1975) Indian Self-Determination and Education Assistance Act. Feminists—(1972) Higher Education Act banning sex discrimination in federally funded education programs; increased numbers of women in law and medicine. Shared achievements: All groups—Education reform; greater political presence. Latinos and Native Americans—Stronger cultural identity. Latinos and feminists—Greater assimilation into mainstream society.

2. THEME: WOMEN IN AMERICA
Possible Answers: The transcript of a 1960s speech by Jessie Lopez de la Cruz; a photograph of Mary Crow Dog; a "Women Make Policy Not Coffee" button; a copy of Betty Friedan's *The Feminine Mystique;* a copy of *Ms.* magazine; a replica of the homemade jam labeled "Preserve the family unit" that was sent to lawmakers as part of the Stop-ERA campaign; a woman's pair of ragged jeans and a tie-dyed T-shirt from the 1960s.

3. THE TURBULENT SIXTIES
Possible Responses: Yes—Those were turbulent times; Latinos, Native Americans, and women became a stronger presence and dramatically improved their social and political status; the rebelliousness of the youth counterculture jolted mainstream society. No—Mainstream America remained largely unchanged; many people still supported conventional family values, traditional roles of men and women, and mainstream lifestyles.

ALTERNATIVE ASSESSMENT

1. EXAMINING CULTURAL ARTIFACTS

How do the design trends of an era—seen in architecture, art, fashion or industrial design—provide important clues to the past?

 CD-ROM Use the CD-ROM *Our Times* and other reference materials to locate an image that depicts a popular style of the 1960s (for example, a building, a painting, clothing, a car, and so forth) and a contemporary version of the same object.

- Compare the two images you have selected. What is similar? What is different?
- Create a poster displaying the two images, and include a short essay that examines these objects as a product of their times.

2. SPEECHWRITING

Cooperative Learning Working in groups of four, have each member of the group imagine he or she is a speechwriter for one of the following people: Cesar Chavez, Russell Means, Betty Friedan, and Phyllis Schlafly. Each student should outline the person's main talking points based on his or her goals and philosophies. Focusing on these main points, the student should write a brief speech and read it before the group.

3. PORTFOLIO PROJECT

 Use the Living History activity to expand your portfolio.

LIVING HISTORY

PRESENTING A MUSIC DOCUMENTARY

You have researched a type of music from the 1960s that you find interesting. Now write a short radio documentary you can present to the class.

- Write a script for the narrative of the documentary.
- Try to use selections from songs, recordings of interviews, and other primary sources to explain by example.
- If you have access to audiotape equipment, you may wish to record your documentary.

 Present your taped or live documentary to the class. Add your written or recorded work to your American history portfolio.

Bridge to Chapter 32

Review Chapter 31

LATINOS AND NATIVE AMERICANS During the civil rights era, Latinos and Native Americans both struggled to gain greater equality, to preserve their cultures, and to improve their lives. Both formed organizations employing various strategies to achieve these aims. The United Farm Workers Organizing Committee's nationwide boycott of grapes, for example, forced California grape growers to meet the demands of union workers. The activism of organizations such as the American Indian Movement helped Native Americans secure educational reforms, greater control over governing their own affairs, and restoration of their land.

THE WOMEN'S MOVEMENT Taking their cue from the civil rights movement, women waged campaigns to surmount the social and economic barriers that impeded their progress in American society. The National Organization for Women pushed for more child-care facilities, better educational opportunities, fair hiring practices, and abortion rights—an issue that still sparks controversy today. Despite the defeat of the Equal Rights Amendment, the women's movement scored several victories, including vastly greater opportunities for women in education, employment, and politics.

THE COUNTERCULTURE Shunning the prevailing social activism of the 1960s, many disillusioned American youths opted to "drop out" of mainstream society. Hippies, the idealistic members of the counter culture, condemned materialism, technology, and war. However, publicized incidents of counterculture violence marred hippies' peace-and-love image and spelled the decline of this fleeting movement. The counterculture's rebellious style set fashion trends and its celebration of rock 'n' roll music lives on today.

Preview Chapter 32

Richard Nixon's victory in 1968 marked a turn toward conservatism. Later, his alleged involvement in the Watergate scandal led to his resignation. In the wake of this crisis, Nixon's successors, Gerald Ford and Jimmy Carter, both tried to restore a sense of trust in the presidency and to fix the ailing economy. You will learn about these and other significant developments in the next chapter.

An Era of Social Change **941**

---

1. EXAMINING CULTURAL ARTIFACTS
Standards for Evaluation
An essay should meet the following criteria:

- Compares an image of a popular item from the 1960s with a contemporary version of the same item.
- Discusses 1960s events that influenced the item's style.
- Contrasts the importance of the item in the 1960s with its significance today.
- Is accompanied by a poster that displays both images.

2. SPEECHWRITING
Standards for Evaluation
A speech should meet the following criteria:

- Accurately conveys the person's goals and philosophy.
- Develops two or three key points that clarify the person's position.
- Addresses the arguments or actions of opponents.
- Engages and stirs the audience.

3. PORTFOLIO PROJECT
LIVING HISTORY
Standards for Evaluation
A music documentary for radio should meet the following criteria:

- Uses selections from songs, interviews, or other primary sources.
- Includes an introduction that explains the scope of the documentary.
- Provides information on the factors that influenced the music.

IN-DEPTH RESOURCES: UNIT 8
See the form for scoring this activity on page 72.

THINKING CRITICALLY

4. VEHICLES FOR CHANGE
Organizations that students might cite include the United Farm Workers Organizing Committee, the American Indian Movement, and the National Organization for Women.

5. GEOGRAPHY: THE MOVEMENT OF MIGRANT WORKERS
Possible Response: Because migrant families must keep moving, they cannot settle down and live in a stable environment or develop close ties with other families; during the winter months, when there is no work, the families must struggle to earn money; because they don't stay at any one job for long, migrant families may be unable to obtain adequate health care.

6. ANALYZING PRIMARY SOURCES
Possible Answers: Among the problems Rodriguez cites are prejudice, suppression and rejection of Mexican culture, segregated living arrangements, and outsider status. Latino "brown power" movements, the reaffirmation of cultural pride, educational reforms, and the growing number of Latino political candidates helped solve some of these problems.

Nearing the Century Mark

HISTORY AND ART

The American Flag

Exhibit at Ellis Island Immigration Museum; design by MetaForm, Inc.; photograph by Norman McGrath; individual portraits on flag by Pablo Delano.

Art Note
Photographer Pablo Delano took hundreds of photographs that were assembled to create this image. It acts as both a symbol of America and a profound representation of the diversity of Americans.

▶ *Previewing the Unit*
Unit 9 describes the turbulent presidency of Richard Nixon and the failure of his successors to fix economic problems in the 1970s. In the midst of growing public conservatism, in the 1980s, the American economy and society change and the Cold War ends. In the 1990s, the debate over the country's direction becomes heated, while vast social changes reshape Americans' lives and redefine the major issues.

UNIT

9

"*We should all be concerned about the future because we will have to spend the rest of our lives there.*"

CHARLES FRANKLIN KETTERING

CHAPTER 32
1968–1980

An Age of Limits

CHAPTER 33
1980–1992

The Conservative Tide

CHAPTER 34
THE 1990'S

America in Today's World

942 UNIT 9

1968–1996

Nearing the Century Mark ①

②

❶ Ellis Island
More than 12 million immigrants passed through the reception facility on Ellis Island in New York Harbor from the time it opened in 1892. More than 40 percent of all Americans alive today have an ancestor who passed through the facility.

Abandoned in 1954, Ellis Island became part of the Statue of Liberty National Monument in 1965. The statue was restored in 1986 on its hundredth anniversary. This step revived interest in Ellis Island, and it was reopened to the public in 1990 after being renovated.

❷ Construction of the flag
The flag is composed of clear plastic prisms that are mounted on a metal frame. On the two outer faces of each prism is a photographic portrait of an American.

The actions of millions of immigrants—and of their millions of descendants—turned Kettering's abstract words into a vibrant reality. As one immigrant recalled in 1921:

> "I left my country because the jobs were scarce. I decided to take a chance and come to this new country."

FOR DISCUSSION:

- How did the immigrants who came to the United States view the future?
- How does understanding the past help us face the future?
- In facing the future, how will Americans deal with the social diversity revealed by the faces in this flag?

Discussing the Image

The flag made up of many faces offers a moving and varied portrait of the United States— a vision based not on the nation's land or resources or leaders but on the talent, determination, and diversity of its people.

FOR DISCUSSION:

- What other images have been used to represent the United States?
- Is this image a good way to symbolize the United States?
- What metaphors are also good ways to describe the United States?

❸ Immigration museum
In 1990, the Ellis Island Immigration Museum opened. The museum includes photographs, passports, and belongings of immigrants; exhibits on how immigrants were processed at Ellis Island; and other films, images, and objects that reveal the immigrant experience.

❹ The faces
Delano took 754 photographs of Americans representing all ages, both genders, all races, and all ethnic groups. Half were taken with a dark background and half with a light background to help create the red and white stripes of the flag.

❺ "The Peopling of America"
The flag is one exhibit in a section of the museum called "The Peopling of America." This section includes displays that vividly provide data on immigration, including country-of-origin statistics.

An Age of Limits

		TEACHING SUPPORT	**ASSESSMENT**

Key Ideas

SECTION 1
The Nixon Administration

pp. 946–952

President Richard M. Nixon attempts to move the country in a more conservative direction and ease Cold War tensions throughout the world.

In-Depth Resources: Unit 9
• Guided Reading, p. 1
• Primary Source: Newspaper Front Page, p. 8
• American Lives: Henry Kissinger, p. 15

 COOPERATIVE ACTIVITY
• Confirming a Supreme Court Judge, p. 949 (TE)

Section 1 Assessment, p. 952 (PE)
Self-Assessment, p. 952 (TE)
Formal Assessment
• Section Quiz, p. 387
Alternative Assessment Book
• Standards for Evaluating a Cooperative Activity

SECTION 2
Watergate: Nixon's Downfall

pp. 953–957

Richard Nixon's involvement in the cover-up of a campaign burglary forces him to resign from office—the only president to do so.

In-Depth Resources: Unit 9
• Guided Reading, p. 2
• Primary source: from *All the President's Men* by Carl Bernstein and Bob Woodward, p. 9
• American Lives: Barbara Jordan, p. 16

 COOPERATIVE ACTIVITY
• Writing an Editorial about the Saturday Night Massacre, p. 956 (TE)

Section 2 Assessment, p. 957 (PE)
Self-Assessment, p. 957 (TE)
Formal Assessment
• Section Quiz, p. 388
Alternative Assessment Book
• Standards for Evaluating a Cooperative Activity

SECTION 3
The Ford and Carter Years

pp. 960–967

In the wake of Watergate, Presidents Ford and Carter try to restore faith in America's leadership as they battle the worst economic crisis in decades.

In-Depth Resources: Unit 9
• Guided Reading, p. 3
• Geography Application: Oil Consumption in the 1970s, p. 6
• Literature: from *Memories of the Ford Administration* by John Updike, p. 12

 COOPERATIVE ACTIVITY
• Writing a United Nations Speech for President Carter, p. 965 (TE)

Section 3 Assessment, p. 967 (PE)
Self-Assessment, p. 967 (TE)
Formal Assessment
• Section Quiz, p. 389
Alternative Assessment Book
• Standards for Evaluating a Cooperative Activity

SECTION 4
Environmental Activism

pp. 968–973

Americans, struck by their sense of limitations, begin to address a growing number of environmental concerns.

In-Depth Resources: Unit 9
• Guided Reading, p. 4
• Skillbuilder Practice: Analyzing Assumptions, p. 5
• Primary Sources: from *Love Canal: My Story* by Lois Gibbs, p. 10; from *Silent Spring* by Rachel Carson, p. 11

COOPERATIVE ACTIVITY
• Debating the Use of Nuclear Energy, p. 972 (TE)

Section 4 Assessment, p. 973 (PE)
Self-Assessment, p. 973 (TE)
Formal Assessment
• Section Quiz, p. 390
Alternative Assessment Book
• Standards for Evaluating a Cooperative Activity

CHAPTER RESOURCES

Chapter Overview

Richard Nixon takes office as president, halting the growth of federal power and changing foreign policy. He resigns in disgrace during his second term, and his successors are unable to fix growing economic problems.

In-Depth Resources: Unit 9
• Living History Project: Worksheet, p. 17; Standards, p. 18
Telescoping the Times
• Chapter Summary, pp. 63–64
Planning for Block Schedules

Chapter Assessment, pp. 974–975 (PE)
Alternative Assessment, p. 975 (PE)
Formal Assessment
• Chapter Test, forms A and B, pp. 391–396

Test Generator

Alternative Assessment Book
See explanation and forms for different kinds of alternative assessments including portfolio assessment.

Grolier Multimedia Encyclopedia
• Overview of Nixon's political career

INTERNET RESOURCES
• See *McDougal Littell Learning On-Line* for links to information about Richard Nixon and world oil markets.

 Humanities Transparencies
• H46, "I am the Law"

Critical Thinking Transparencies
• CT32, The Watergate Scandal
• CT66, Shift in Presidential Politics

 Our Times
• Richard Nixon and John Dean III

Electronic Library of Primary Sources
• Articles of Impeachment

INTERNET RESOURCES
• See Interact with History p. 959 (PE) for an activity that includes the Internet as an enrichment option.

 Humanities Transparencies
• H30, Bicentennial celebration

Geography Transparencies
• G32, OPEC

 Grolier Multimedia Encyclopedia
• overview of Ford's political career

Electronic Library of Primary Sources
• Jimmy Carter

INTERNET RESOURCES
• See *McDougal Littell Learning On-Line* for links to information about Carter.

 AMERICAN STORIES VIDEO SERIES
• "Poisoned Playground"

 Our Times
• Essay on 1970s and environmentalism

Grolier Multimedia Encyclopedia
• video of interview with Rachel Carson

Electronic Library of Primary Sources
• "Principles of Environmental Justice"

INTERNET RESOURCES
• See Interact with History p. 971 (PE) for an activity that includes the Internet as an enrichment option.

 American Portfolio: A Videodisc for U.S. History, user's guide, pp. 253–255

INTERNET RESOURCES
Learning On-Line: Social Studies
http://www.mcdougallittell.com

Block Scheduling (90 MINUTES)

Day 1
Section 1, pp. 946–952
Section 2, pp. 953–957
Daily Life: Television Reflects American Life, pp. 958–959
Section Assessments, pp. 952, 957

Day 2
Section 3, pp. 960–967
Section 4, pp. 968–973
 AMERICAN STORIES VIDEO SERIES
• "Poisoned Playground"
Chapter Assessment, pp. 974–975

YEARLY PACING Chapter 32 Total: 2 days **Yearly Total:** 85 days

See *Planning for Block Schedules* for special activities and pacing strategies.

Customizing for Special Populations

Students Acquiring English

Access for Students Acquiring English
• Guided Reading for Sections 1–4 (Spanish), pp. 309–312
• Chapter Summary (Spanish), pp. 307–308
• Skillbuilder Practice: Analyzing Assumptions (Spanish), p. 313
• Geography Application: Oil Consumption in the 1970s (Spanish), p. 314

AMERICAN STORIES VIDEO SERIES
• "Poisoned Playground" (Spanish track)

INTERNET RESOURCES
• See *McDougal Littell Learning On-Line* The Diverse Classroom.

Less Proficient Readers

In-Depth Resources: Unit 9
• Guided Reading for Sections 1–4, pp. 1–4
• Skillbuilder: Analyzing Assumptions, p. 5
• Geography Application: Oil Consumption in the 1970s, p. 6

Telescoping the Times
• Chapter Summary, pp. 63–64

See additional strategies at point of use in the Teacher's Edition.

Gifted and Talented Students

In-Depth Resources: Unit 9
• Primary Source: Newspaper Front Page, p. 8; from *All the President's Men* by Carl Bernstein and Bob Woodward, p. 9; from *Love Canal: My Story* by Lois Gibbs, p. 10; from *Silent Spring* by Rachel Carson, p. 11
• American Lives: Henry Kissinger, p. 15; Barbara Jordan, p. 16

See additional strategies at point of use in the Teacher's Edition.

Connections to Literature READINGS FOR STUDENTS

In-Depth Resources: Unit 9
• from *Memories of the Ford Administration* by John Updike, p. 12

Enrichment Reading
• **Bernstein, Carl and Bob Woodward**
  All the President's Men
  New York: Touchstone Books, 1994
  This book by two young reporters for The Washington Post covers their investigation of the Watergate break in. Their discoveries, and the story of their mysterious informant, make this fascinating reading as a coverup is linked to the White House and the president eventually resigns.

• **Kluger, Jeffrey and James A. Lovell**
  Lost Moon: The Perilous Voyage of Apollo 13
  Boston: Houghton, 1994
  A space capsule on the way to the moon is rocked by an explosion and loses the oxygen it needs for power and water. Can the three astronauts on board be brought *back to Earth safely? The crisis brings out the best in hundreds of engineers and technicians on the ground and in the three astronauts who must remain calm and clear headed. They do make it, and this inspiring story is NOT fiction.*

• **Updike, John**
  Memories of the Ford Administration
  New York: Fawcett, 1993
  When a history professor is asked to record his impressions of the Ford administration, he uses that turbulent time—following the resignation of Richard Nixon—to recall a piece of turbulent personal history: his unfinished book on the 19th century president James Buchanan.

An Age of Limits

▶ **Starting with the Student**
Have students discuss Jimmy Carter's quotation on page 944. What major foreign policy event of the 1960s and early 1970s had already revealed the nation's limitations? *The Vietnam War.* In what way did it show the country's limitations? **Possible Response:** *The United States was unable to stop South Vietnam from falling to the Communists.*

PREVIEWING THE CHAPTER
• Divide students into small groups and have them read the United States side of the time line on pages 944 and 945. Each group should then write down which events it feels were the high and low points of the period.
• Have students identify what images on the time line best speak to the nation's highs and lows during this period.

MORE ABOUT . . .
The First Moon Walk
Edwin "Buzz" Aldrin, Jr., was the second person to step on the moon. Aldrin's co-astronaut, Neil Armstrong, stepped onto the moon's surface 19 minutes before him. The two astronauts spent about two hours on the moon, gathering rock samples and conducting tests.

An Age of Limits

SECTION 1
The Nixon Administration
President Richard M. Nixon attempts to move the country in a more conservative direction and ease Cold War tensions throughout the world.

SECTION 2
Watergate: Nixon's Downfall
Richard Nixon's involvement in the cover-up of a campaign burglary forces him to resign from office—the only president to do so.

SECTION 3
The Ford and Carter Years
In the wake of Watergate, Presidents Ford and Carter try to restore faith in America's leadership as they battle the worst economic crisis in decades.

SECTION 4
Environmental Activism
Americans, struck by their sense of limitations, begin to address a growing number of environmental concerns.

⊙ **VIDEO** POISONED PLAYGROUND

"We have learned . . . even our great nation has its recognized limits. . . . We cannot afford to do everything, nor can we afford to lack boldness as we meet the future."

Jimmy Carter, 1977

THE UNITED STATES
THE WORLD

1968

⊛ Richard M. Nixon is elected president.

Astronaut Edwin Aldrin, Jr., poses beside the American flag, as the U.S. becomes the first nation to put a person on the moon.

America celebrates the first Earth Day.

⊛ Richard M. Nixon is reelected president.

Senate begins investigation into the Watergate break-in.

1969   1970   1972   1973
1969   1970   1971   1973

Golda Meir becomes prime minister of Israel.

Nigeria ends its 2½ year civil war.

U.N. votes to admit China and expel Taiwan.

A military junta, led by Augusto Pinochet Ugarte, seizes power in Chile.

944 CHAPTER 32

THEMES IN CHAPTER 32

Economic Opportunity
Throughout the 1970s, many Americans grew anxious about their future, as the nation coped with its worst economic crisis in years. A decade of economic stagnation—which included bouts of increased unemployment and inflation—frustrated the successive administrations of Richard Nixon, Gerald Ford, and Jimmy Carter and left the country with a very real sense of its limitations.

See Teacher's Edition notes, pp. 950 and 962.

Science and Technology
Adding to economic uncertainty were advancements in computer technology, which altered much of the nation's work force and made some jobs obsolete. Scientific advancements also helped the United States battle another of its limitations: its dwindling natural resources.

See Teacher's Edition notes, pp. 964 and 969.

Constitutional Concerns
During the 1970s, Americans witnessed one of the most serious constitutional crises in the nation's history. The House of Representatives stood ready to impeach President Nixon for possible criminal wrongdoing. Before that happened, Nixon resigned from the presidency.

See Teacher's Edition note, p. 955.

LIVING HISTORY

PREPARING AN EXHIBIT OF GLOBAL LINKS

Between 1968 and 1980, Americans became increasingly aware of economic and political links between their nation and other countries. With your classmates, prepare items for an exhibit that shows specific connections between the United States and other countries during these years.

Consider the following suggestions as you prepare individual items and displays for your exhibit:

- Use world maps or sections of world maps.
- Include three-dimensional objects—constructed or found—and audio-visual selections.
- Write comments that explain reasons for international links.

📁 **PORTFOLIO PROJECT** Save your writing, maps, and other items in a folder for your American history portfolio. You will display and share your work at the end of the chapter.

Preparing an Exhibit of Global Links

Discuss ways of preparing the exhibit:

- Look for maps of the Middle East in news magazines.
- Find political cartoons of the country's link to other nations, in particular cartoons satirizing the United States relationship with the OPEC nations (p. 950).
- Research further some of the chapter's global topics for items associated with the event. For example, a yellow ribbon came to symbolize the nation's support for the hostages.
- Look for dramatic photographs—such as long lines for gasoline and blindfolded hostages—in newspapers or news magazines.
- Find images of America's growing desire for foreign-made goods. Such images might include photographs of factories in China or Taiwan, or advertisements for Japanese automobiles.
- Look for tapes of news programs about the energy crunch or hostage situation. An example might be a tape of an early *Nightline* program, which began as a nightly program about the hostage crisis.

IN-DEPTH RESOURCES: UNIT 9
See worksheet and standards for evaluation, pp. 17, 18.

Special Issue

TIME

THE HEALING BEGINS

⭐ Vice-President Gerald R. Ford becomes president after Richard M. Nixon resigns.

⭐ Jimmy Carter, shown with wife Rosalynn and daughter Amy, is elected president.

Andrew Young becomes first African American to serve as U.S. ambassador to the United Nations.

In Iran, 52 Americans are taken hostage.

Israel and Egypt sign peace treaty at White House.

American hostages return to United States.

⭐ Ronald Reagan is elected president.

1974   1976   1978   1979   **1980**

1975   1978   1979

● South Vietnam surrenders to North Vietnam.

● Ayatollah Khomeini seizes power in Iran.

● The Soviet Union invades Afghanistan.

An Age of Limits **945**

RECOMMENDED RESOURCES

Books for the Teacher

Bernstein, Carl, and Woodward, Bob. *The Final Days*. New York: Simon, 1976. A detailed look at the final days of the Nixon presidency.

Carter, Jimmy. *Keeping Faith: Memoirs of a President*. New York: Bantam, 1982.

Villaseñor, Victor. *Rain of Gold*. New York: Dell, 1991. A Mexican family's long history—similar to *Roots*.

Books for the Student

Lawson, Don. *America Held Hostage: The Iran Hostage Crisis and the Iran-Contra Affair*. New York: Watts, 1991.

Lazzari, Marie. *Environmental Viewpoints*. Detroit: Gale Research, Inc., Vol. 1 1992, Vol. 2 1993.

Videos

All the President's Men. Dir. Alan J. Pakula. Warner Home Video, 1976. Dramatic portrayal of Watergate investigation.

America Held Hostage. MPI Home Video, 1989. 800-323-0442. ABC News reports of hostage crisis.

Apollo 13. Dir. Ron Howard. MCA Universal Home Video, 1995, PG. Riveting story of a disastrous moon mission.

1970s: A Crisis of Confidence. National Geographic Society, Educational Services, Washington, D.C., 20036, 800-368-2728.

Richard Nixon: Man and President. Library Video Company, 800-843-3620.

Software

Environment. Diskette. Tom Snyder Productions, Inc., 800-342-0236.

Foreign Policy: The Burdens of World Power. Diskette. Social Studies School Service, 10020 Jefferson Boulevard, Room 1311, P.O. Box 802, Culver City, CA, 90232-0802.

OBJECTIVES

1 To summarize Richard Nixon's plans to lead the nation on a more conservative course.

2 To describe how Nixon tried to win the support of Southern Democrats.

3 To list the steps Nixon took to battle stagflation.

4 To explain the importance of Nixon's visits to China and the Soviet Union.

CRITICAL THINKING

• Summarizing, pp. 946, 949, 951, 952
• Analyzing issues, p. 947
• Clarifying, p. 948
• Analyzing causes, p. 950
• Drawing conclusions, p. 952
• Interpreting, p. 952
• Evaluating, p. 952

FOCUS & MOTIVATE

▶ **Starting with the Student**
• Ask students how they would define a political conservative.
• Then read aloud the attributes ascribed to conservatives in William Safire's *New Political Dictionary: Defends the status quo, opposes rapid change, dislikes government regulation of the economy, favors state and local action over federal action.* Remind students to keep these traits in mind as they read about Nixon's administration.

OBJECTIVE
1 INSTRUCT

Nixon's New Conservatism

▶ **Discussing Key Ideas**
• Nixon works to decrease the size and influence of the federal government.
• Nixon practices law-and-order politics to curb

(continued on next page)

1 The Nixon Administration

TERMS & NAMES
• Richard M. Nixon
• New Federalism
• revenue sharing
• Family Assistance Plan
• Southern strategy
• stagflation
• OPEC
• realpolitik
• détente
• SALT I Treaty

LEARN ABOUT President Nixon's domestic and foreign policy initiatives
TO UNDERSTAND how Nixon tried to lead the nation in a conservative direction and ease Cold War tensions throughout the world.

ONE AMERICAN'S STORY

It was November of 1968 and Richard M. Nixon had just been elected president of the United States. President Nixon asked Henry Kissinger to be his special adviser on foreign affairs. Kissinger did not particularly like Nixon. But he accepted, telling a surprised colleague, "I'm working for the presidency, not for Richard Nixon personally." However, in time the two men grew to be trusting colleagues. At the beginning of Nixon's second term in 1972, as the United States struggled to achieve an honorable peace in Vietnam, Kissinger reflected on his relationship with Nixon.

A PERSONAL VOICE

I . . . am not at all so sure I could have done what I've done with him with another president. Such a special relationship, I mean the relationship between the President and me, always depends on the style of both men. . . . I don't know many leaders who would entrust to their aide the task of negotiating with the North Vietnamese, informing only a tiny group of people of the initiative. Really, some things depend on the type of president.

HENRY KISSINGER, quoted in *The New Republic,* December 16, 1972

President Nixon confers with Henry Kissinger.

Nixon and Kissinger ended America's involvement in Vietnam. As the war wound down, the nation seemed to enter an era of limits. There were limits to U.S. power, as the nation's military had not been able to save South Vietnam from becoming Communist. Lyndon Johnson's Great Society programs seemed limited in their ability to eliminate poverty. And as the 1970s progressed, there seemed to be limits to the economic prosperity that the nation had experienced since World War II.

Into this era stepped a president who believed that there were also limits to what the federal government could accomplish. President Nixon would take action to reduce the power of the federal government and reverse the liberal policies of Lyndon Johnson. At the same time, he would seek to restore America's prestige and influence on the world stage—prestige that had been hit hard by the Vietnam experience.

Nixon's New Conservatism

President **Richard M. Nixon** entered office determined to turn America in a more conservative direction. Toward that end, he decreased the power of the federal government, dismantled a number of Great Society programs, and tried to instill a sense of order into a nation still divided over the continuing Vietnam War.

NEW FEDERALISM One of the main items on President Nixon's agenda was to decrease the size and influence of the federal government. Nixon believed that Lyndon Johnson's Great Society programs, by promoting greater federal involvement in social programs, had given the federal government too much responsibility. Nixon's plan, known as **New Federalism,** was to distribute a portion of federal power to state and local governments.

To implement this program, Nixon proposed a plan to give more financial freedom to local governments. Normally, the federal government told state and local governments how to spend their federal money. Under **revenue sharing,** state and local governments could spend their federal dollars however they saw fit within certain limitations. The revenue-sharing plan won support from financially strapped local governments, as well as

A. Answer To shrink the size and responsibility of the federal government by distributing some of its power to state and local governments.

THINK THROUGH HISTORY
A. Summarizing
What was the goal of Nixon's New Federalism?

SECTION 1 RESOURCES

PRINT RESOURCES

IN-DEPTH RESOURCES: UNIT 9
Guided Reading, p. 1
Primary Source: Newspaper Front Page, p. 8
American Lives: Henry Kissinger, p. 15

ACCESS FOR STUDENTS ACQUIRING ENGLISH
Guided Reading (Spanish), p. 309

FORMAL ASSESSMENT
Section Quiz, p. 387

ALTERNATIVE ASSESSMENT BOOK
See forms for supporting and scoring alternative activities.

TECHNOLOGY RESOURCES

CD-ROM *Grolier Multimedia Encyclopedia*

VIDEO *American Portfolio: A Videodisc for U.S. History*
user's guide, p. 253

INTERNET McDougal Littell Learning On-Line
http://www.mcdougallittell.com

from conservatives who felt the national government had grown too large and unmanageable.

In 1972, the revenue-sharing bill passed both houses of Congress. By the time the program ended in 1986, the federal government had dispensed more than $86 billion of unrestricted money to state and local governments in one of the largest overhauls of federal spending since the New Deal.

WELFARE REFORM Nixon, however, was not so successful in his attempt to overhaul welfare. Unlike many conservatives, Nixon did not oppose welfare, but he did think it had grown cumbersome and inefficient. Nixon thought the welfare program would work more effectively using the New Federalism approach. Consequently, in 1969 the president set out to restructure it. He advocated the so-called **Family Assistance Plan** (FAP), a set of reforms engineered by former Kennedy adviser Daniel Patrick Moynihan. Under the FAP, every family of four with no outside income would receive a basic federal payment of $1,600 a year, with a provision to earn up to $4,000 a year in supplemental income. Unemployed participants would have to take job training and accept any reasonable work offered them.

Nixon presented the plan in conservative terms—as a program that would reduce the supervisory role of the federal government and make welfare recipients responsible for their own lives. The House approved the plan in 1970. However, when the bill reached the Senate, lawmakers from both sides of the aisle attacked it. Liberal legislators considered the minimum payments too low and the work requirement too stiff, while conservatives objected to the notion of guaranteed income. The bill went down in defeat.

NEW FEDERALISM'S TWO FACES In the end, Nixon's New Federalism enhanced several key federal programs as it dismantled others. Nixon had entered office as the first newly elected president since Zachary Taylor in 1849 to face a Congress controlled by the opposition party. With the House and Senate in the hands of Democratic majorities, Nixon initially sought compromise on Capitol Hill as he attempted to move ahead with his New Federalism program. To win backing for his revenue-sharing plan, for example, Nixon supported a number of congressional measures to increase federal spending for some social programs. Without fanfare, the Nixon administration increased social security, Medicare, and Medicaid payments and made food stamps more accessible. Nixon also supported subsidized housing for low-and middle-income families, and he expanded the nation's Job Corps program.

However, the spirit of compromise between Congress and the White House soon deteriorated. Confronted by laws that he opposed, Nixon turned to a little-used presidential practice called impoundment. Nixon impounded, or withheld, necessary funds for programs, thus holding up their implementation. By 1973, Nixon had impounded more than $15 billion, affecting more than 100 federal programs, including those for health, housing, and education.

The federal courts eventually ordered the release of the impounded funds. They ruled that presidential impoundment was unconstitutional and that only Congress had the authority to decide how federal funds should be spent. However, in 1973 Nixon did use his presidential authority to abolish the Office of Economic Opportunity, the cornerstone of Johnson's antipoverty program.

LAW–AND–ORDER POLITICS As President Nixon fought with Congress, he also battled the more liberal elements of society, including the antiwar movement.

B. Answer He increased several federal programs, including social security, Medicare, and Medicaid; while he dismantled other programs, most notably the Office of Economic Opportunity.

THINK THROUGH HISTORY
B. Analyzing Issues In what ways did Nixon both strengthen and weaken federal programs?

(continued from page 946)

dissent and appeal to mainstream Americans.

IN-DEPTH RESOURCES: UNIT 9
Guided Reading, p. 1
ACCESS FOR STUDENTS ACQUIRING ENGLISH
Guided Reading (Spanish), p. 309

KEY PLAYER

KEY PLAYER

RICHARD M. NIXON
1913–1994
The hurdles that Richard Nixon overcame to win the presidency in 1968—including his loss in the 1960 presidential race and a later defeat in the race for governor of California—were but two of the many obstacles he faced during his life.

While growing up, Nixon rose every day at 4 A.M. to help in his father's struggling grocery store. To save money for college, Nixon also worked as a janitor, a bean picker, and a barker at an amusement park. In the midst of its poverty, the Nixon family also endured episodes of tragedy. During his childhood, Nixon saw one brother die from meningitis and another from tuberculosis.

None of these traumatic experiences, however, dulled the future president's ambition. Nixon finished third in his law class at Duke University, and after serving in World War II, he launched his political career. After winning a seat in Congress in 1946, Nixon revealed the intense inner drive that would take him to the height of power—and also lead to his eventual downfall. "I had to win," he said. "That's the thing you don't understand. The important thing is to win."

KEY PLAYER
Richard M. Nixon

Critical Thinking: Analyzing Ask students what personality traits of Richard Nixon are revealed in the profile. *Possible Answers: Hard-working, determined, intelligent, driven.* How might Nixon's feelings about winning play a role in his eventual downfall? *Possible Response: His intense desire to win might lead him to break the rules.*

MORE ABOUT . . .
Daniel Patrick Moynihan

In 1994, Moynihan won a fourth term as a U.S. senator from New York. Through the years, he has remained deeply involved with the issue of poverty in America. Moynihan, a Democrat, was one of the harshest critics of the new welfare legislation, which President Bill Clinton signed into law in 1996. The law, which ends more than 60 years of guaranteed federal assistance for the nation's poor, transfers almost all welfare duties to the states and imposes limits on how long someone may receive welfare benefits. "If you think things can't be worse," he said about the new law, "just you wait until there are a third of a million children in the streets."

An Age of Limits **947**

HISTORICAL SPOTLIGHT

AMERICANS WALK ON THE MOON

Not all was political war during the Nixon administration. On July 20, 1969, one of America's long-held dreams became a reality. Nearly 10 years after John F. Kennedy challenged America to put a person on the moon, astronaut Neil Armstrong climbed down the ladder of his lunar module and stepped onto the surface of the moon. "That's one small step for man," Armstrong said, "one giant leap for mankind."

Americans swelled with pride and accomplishment as they watched the historic moon landing on their televisions. Speaking to the astronauts from the White House, President Nixon said, "For every American, this has to be the proudest day of our lives."

Nixon had been elected in 1968 on a dual promise to end the war in Vietnam and mend the divisiveness within America that the war had created. Throughout his first term, Nixon aggressively moved to fulfill both these pledges. The president de-escalated America's involvement in Vietnam and oversaw peace negotiations with North Vietnam. At the same time, he began the policy of law and order that he had promised his "silent majority"—those middle-class Americans who wanted order restored to a country beset by urban riots and antiwar demonstrations.

To accomplish this goal, Nixon used the full resources of his office—sometimes illegally. The FBI illegally wiretapped numerous left-wing individuals and organizations. The FBI also infiltrated the ranks of the Students for a Democratic Society and radical African-American groups in an effort to spread conflict within the organizations.

In addition, the CIA investigated and compiled documents on thousands of American dissidents—people who objected to the government's policies. The administration even used the Internal Revenue Service to audit the tax returns of antiwar and civil rights activists. Viewing his opponents as personal assailants, Nixon began building an "enemies list" of prominent Americans whom the administration would harass. Remarked a top White House official, "anyone who opposes us, we'll destroy."

Nixon also enlisted the help of his combative vice-president, Spiro T. Agnew. In the fall of 1969, Nixon sent Agnew on a public speaking tour to attack the opposition. The vice-president repeatedly denounced the antiwar protesters and then turned his scorn on the media, which he viewed as liberal cheerleaders for the antiwar movement. Known for his colorful quotes, Agnew lashed out at the media and liberals as "an effete [weak] corps of impudent snobs," and "nattering nabobs of negativism."

Nixon's Southern Strategy

Even as President Nixon worked to steer the country along a more conservative course, he had his eyes on the 1972 presidential election. Nixon had won a slim victory in 1968—less than one percent of the popular vote. Shortly after entering the White House, he began working to forge a new conservative coalition to build on his support. In one approach, known as the **Southern strategy,** Nixon tried to attract Southern conservative Democrats by appealing to their unhappiness with federal desegregation policies and a liberal Supreme Court.

A NEW SOUTH Since Reconstruction, the South had been a Democratic stronghold. But by 1968 many white Southern Democrats had grown disillusioned with their party. In their eyes, the party—champion of the Great Society and civil rights—had grown too liberal. This conservative backlash first surfaced in the 1968 election, when thousands of Southern Democrats helped former Alabama governor George Wallace, a conservative segregationist running as an independent, carry five Southern states and capture 13.5 percent of the popular vote.

Nixon wanted these voters. By winning over the Wallace voters and other discontented Democrats, the president and his fellow Republicans hoped not only to keep the White House but also to recapture a majority in Congress.

NIXON SLOWS INTEGRATION To attract voters in the South, President Nixon decided on a policy of slowing the country's desegregation efforts. In September of 1969, shortly after being elected president, Nixon made clear his views on civil rights. "There are those who want instant integration and those

---

who want segregation forever. I believe we need to have a middle course between those two extremes," he said.

Throughout his first term, President Nixon worked to reverse several civil rights policies. In 1969, he ordered the Department of Health, Education, and Welfare (HEW) to delay desegregation plans for school districts in South Carolina and Mississippi. Nixon's actions violated the Supreme Court's second *Brown* v. *Board of Education* ruling—which called for the desegregation of schools "with all deliberate speed." In response to a NAACP suit, the high court ordered Nixon to abide by the second *Brown* ruling. The president did so reluctantly, and by 1972, nearly 90 percent of children in the South attended desegregated schools—up from about 20 percent in 1969.

In a further attempt to chip away at civil rights advances, Nixon opposed the extension of the Voting Rights Act of 1965. The act had added nearly one million African Americans to the voting rolls. Despite the president's opposition, Congress voted to extend the act.

President Nixon then attempted to thwart yet another civil rights initiative—the integration of schools through busing. In 1971, the Supreme Court ruled in *Swann* v. *Charlotte-Mecklenburg Board of Education* that school districts may bus students to other schools to end the pattern of all-black or all-white educational institutions. White students and parents in cities such as Boston and Detroit angrily protested busing. One South Boston mother spoke for other white Northerners, many of whom still struggled with the country's racial integration process.

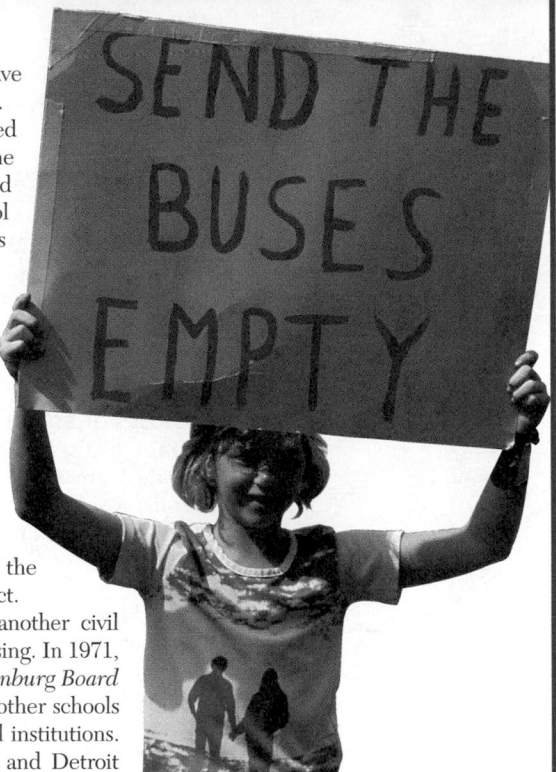

A demonstrator in Boston protests court-ordered school busing during the early 1970s.

A PERSONAL VOICE
I'm not against any individual child. I am not a racist, no matter what those high-and-mighty suburban liberals with their picket signs say. I just won't have my children bused to some . . . slum school, and I don't want children from God knows where coming over here.

A SOUTH BOSTON MOTHER, quoted in *The School Busing Controversy: 1970–75*

Nixon also opposed integration through busing and went on national television to urge Congress to halt the practice. While busing continued in some cities, Nixon had made his position clear to the country—and to the South.

A BATTLE OVER THE SUPREME COURT Civil rights was not the only issue over which President Nixon and the Supreme Court clashed. During the 1968 campaign, Nixon had criticized the Warren Court for being too liberal. Once in the White House, Nixon suddenly found himself with an opportunity to change the direction of the court. During Nixon's first term, four justices, including Chief Justice Earl Warren, left the bench by way of death, retirement, or resignation. President Nixon quickly moved to put a more conservative face on the Court. In 1969, he appointed U.S. Court of Appeals Judge Warren Burger as Chief Justice. Burger's Senate confirmation went smoothly. However, Nixon's effort to fill a second vacancy could not have been rougher.

The Senate rejected Nixon's next two nominees—two conservative Southerners. The Senate claimed that one judge had engaged in questionable business dealings, while the other one was underqualified.

Eventually, Nixon placed on the bench three justices—Harry A. Blackmun, William H. Rehnquist, and Lewis Powell—who tilted the Court in a more conservative direction. However, the newly shaped Court did not always take the

D. Answer It involved winning over disgruntled Southern Democrats by appealing to their unhappiness with integration and a liberal Supreme Court. To win these voters, Nixon slowed integration policies and attempted to appoint Supreme Court justices who were more conservative.

THINK THROUGH HISTORY
D. Summarizing
What was Nixon's Southern strategy and how did he implement it?

An Age of Limits **949**

Nixon Confronts a Stagnant Economy

▶ **Discussing Key Ideas**
• The United States enters a period of economic down-swing brought on by numerous factors.
• Nixon's efforts to battle stagflation meet with little success.

ON THE WORLD STAGE
The Yom Kippur War
Have students consult the world map on pages 1060–1061 to examine the geography of the Middle East, in particular the locations of Syria, Egypt, and Israel. Then have them research the history of Israel's fractious relationship with its Arab neighbors, including the Sinai invasion in 1956 and the Six-Day War in 1967. Have students create a chart like the one below detailing the cause and effect of each conflict.

	Cause	Effect
Sinai Invasion		
Six-Day War		

conservative route. For example, the Burger Court handed down the 1971 rul-ing in favor of racially integrating schools through busing.

Nixon Confronts a Stagnant Economy

One of the more pressing issues facing Richard Nixon was a troubled economy. Between 1967 and 1973, the nation's inflation rate doubled from 3 percent to 6 percent. In addition, the unemployment rate, at nearly 4 percent when Nixon took office, climbed to almost 6 percent by 1971. Economists referred to the double hit of rising inflation and unemployment as **stagflation.** While Nixon's attempts to fight stagflation mostly failed, the nation's economic downswing would continue on throughout the 1970s and frustrate other administrations as well.

THE CAUSES OF STAGFLATION The economic downturn of the late 1960s and early 1970s had several causes. One cause lay in Lyndon Johnson's attempt to pay for the Vietnam War and the Great Society through massive deficit spend-ing, or the government practice of spending more money than it has collected in taxes. This influx of money into the economy had spurred the growth of infla-tion. Second, America had begun losing out in international trade mar-kets to West Germany, Japan, and other rising industrial powers. Third, the nation could not absorb a flood of new workers—mainly baby boomers and women—into the labor market. Between 1965 and 1980, America's labor force grew by almost 30 million workers. The number of new jobs could not keep pace, leaving many unemployed.

Finally, the nation had begun to suffer for its heavy dependency on foreign oil. America received much of its petroleum from the oil-producing countries of the Middle East. Many of these countries belonged to a cartel called the Organization of Petroleum Exporting Countries (**OPEC**). A cartel is an organization that controls enough of the production of a commodity to set the price. During the 1960s, OPEC gradually raised oil prices. Then in 1973, the Yom Kippur War broke out, with Israel against Egypt and Syria. When the United States sent massive military aid to Israel, its longtime ally, the Arab OPEC nations responded by cutting off all oil sales to the United States.

From the fall of 1973 until March of 1974, when the oil embargo ended, American motorists faced long lines at gas stations. Across the nation, factories and schools closed. One New England mother of three lamented that her children were no better off at home. "We'll have heat-ing problems at home, too," she said. "And I'm not sure I can keep them much warmer here." Moreover, when OPEC resumed selling its oil to the United States, the price had tripled. This sharp rise in oil prices only worsened the problem of inflation.

NIXON BATTLES STAGFLATION President Nixon took several steps to combat stagflation, but none met with much success. To reverse deficit spending, Nixon attempted to raise taxes and cut the budget. Congress, however, refused to go along with this plan. In another effort to slow inflation, Nixon tried to reduce the amount of money in circulation by urging that interest rates be raised. This measure did little except drive the country into a mild recession, or an overall slowdown of the economy.

In August of 1971, the president turned to price and wage controls. Nixon froze workers' wages as well as businesses' prices and fees for 90 days in an effort to halt spiraling costs. Inflation eased for a short time, but the recession continued.

ON THE WORLD STAGE

THE YOM KIPPUR WAR
On October 6, 1973, Syria and Egypt invaded Israel on what was Yom Kippur, the most sacred Jewish holiday. The war—the climax of years of intense border disputes—was short but brutal. While fighting lasted only three weeks, as many as 7,000 Egyptians, 7,700 Syrians, and 4,500 Israelis were killed or wounded.

Although America supplied massive amounts of military aid to Israel, the United States also worked feverishly to broker a cease-fire between the warring nations. In what became known as "shuttle diplomacy," U.S. Secretary of State Henry Kissinger traveled back and forth between Middle Eastern countries in an attempt to forge a peace agreement. Kissinger's diplomatic efforts finally paid off. Israel signed an official peace accord with Egypt in January of 1974 and with Syria five months later.

E. Answer
Inflation growth prompted by Johnson's deficit spending, increased competition in international trade, too many new workers, and the Middle East oil embargo.

THINK THROUGH HISTORY
E. *Analyzing Causes*
What factors brought on the country's economic downturn in the late 1960s and early 1970s?

Gas pumps across the nation ran dry as a result of the OPEC oil embargo.

TEACHING OPTIONS

Exploring Themes

Economic Opportunity The economic downswing that gripped the nation during the Nixon administration would last for roughly a decade and frustrate other administrations as well. Throughout the 1970s, as inflation and unemployment rose and dipped, millions of Americans grew anxious about their economic opportunities. Playing a key role in the decade-long downturn was the rising cost of oil. Have students con-sider reasons for the high demand for oil in the United States. *It is a source of heating fuel for homes, gasoline for cars, and a key ingredient in materials such as plastic.*

Making Global Connections

Interdependence The onset of the economic crunch, in par-ticular the oil embargo, awoke many Americans to the fact that the United States was part of—and sometimes dependent on—a larger world. In 1973, for example, the United States imported nearly 6.3 million barrels of crude oil a day, mainly from the Middle East. During the height of the 1973 oil embargo, U.S. Senator Dewey Bartlett of Oklahoma noted, "The sad, but true, fact is that in the near future we will have to spend more and more dollars abroad for crude oil and other petroleum products."

Nixon's Foreign Policy Triumphs

Richard Nixon admittedly preferred world affairs to domestic policy. "I've always thought this country could run itself domestically without a president," he had said in 1968. Throughout his presidency, Nixon's top priority was gaining an honorable peace in Vietnam. However, he also made significant advances in America's relationship with China and the Soviet Union.

KISSINGER AND REALPOLITIK The architect of Nixon's foreign policy was his adviser for national security affairs, Henry Kissinger. Kissinger, who would later become Nixon's secretary of state, promoted a philosophy known as **realpolitik,** from a German term meaning "realistic politics." In terms of foreign policy, realpolitik meant dealing with other nations in a practical and flexible manner, rather than following a rigid policy. Kissinger believed in evaluating a nation's power, not its philosophy or beliefs. If a country was weak, Kissinger argued, it often was more practical to ignore that country, even if it was Communist.

On the other hand, Kissinger's philosophy called for the United States to fully confront the powerful nations of the globe. In the world of realpolitik, however, confrontation meant negotiation as well as military engagement. Realpolitik marked a departure from the policy of containment, which refused to recognize the world's major Communist countries. Kissinger urged the United States to recognize and deal directly with these nations. It was impractical, for example, to deny the existence of mainland China, which contained at least one-fifth of the world's population. It also was impractical not to ease relations with the Soviet Union, with its massive stockpile of nuclear weapons.

Nixon shared Kissinger's belief in realpolitik, and together the two men adopted a more flexible approach in dealing with Communist nations. They called their policy **détente**—a policy aimed at easing Cold War tensions. One of the most startling applications of détente came in early 1972 when President Nixon—who had risen in politics as a strong anti-Communist—visited Communist China.

NIXON VISITS CHINA Since the takeover of mainland China by the Communists in 1949, the United States had not formally recognized the Chinese Communist government. In late 1971, Nixon reversed that policy. In a 90-second television speech, the president announced he would visit China "to seek the normalization of relations between the two countries and to exchange views on questions of concern to both sides."

By going to China, Nixon was trying, in part, to take advantage of the decade-long rift between China and the Soviet Union. China had long criticized the Soviet Union as being too "soft" in its policies against the West. The two Communist superpowers officially broke ties in 1960. Nixon had thought about exploiting the fractured relationship for several years. "We want the Chinese with us when we sit down and negotiate with the Russians," he told a reporter in 1968.

Nixon's visit to Beijing in February of 1972 scored high marks from the American public. U.S. television crews flooded American living rooms with film clips of Nixon at the Great Wall of China, at the Imperial Palace, and even toasting top Communist leaders at state dinners. Observers noted that one reason for the trip's popularity back home was Nixon's strong anti-Communist

President Nixon tours the Great Wall as part of his visit to China in 1972.

"I've always thought this country could run itself domestically without a president."

RICHARD M. NIXON

THINK THROUGH HISTORY
F. Summarizing *What was the philosophy of realpolitik?*

F. Answer A philosophy that called for dealing with nations in a practical and flexible manner, rather than by following a rigid policy.

OBJECTIVE
④ **INSTRUCT**

Nixon's Foreign Policy Triumphs

▶ *Discussing Key Ideas*
- Following the philosophy of realpolitik, Nixon and Kissinger work to relax Cold War tensions throughout the world.
- In the most visible sign of his attempt to ease Cold War animosities, Nixon visits China and the Soviet Union.

MORE ABOUT . . .
Nixon in China

The first-ever meeting between Nixon and Chinese leader Mao Zedong was marked by its light-heartedness. Mao joked that in his mind he had voted for Nixon. "I like rightists," the Chairman quipped. "I am comparatively happy when these people on the right come into power." Less friendly to Nixon was Mao's wife. "She obviously did not approve of the visit," Nixon wrote. "She said to me sharply, 'Why did you not come to China before now?'"

 GROLIER MULTIMEDIA ENCYCLOPEDIA
overview of Nixon's political career

TEACHING OPTIONS

Making Connections Across Time

U.S.-Sino Relations U.S.-Chinese relations today are strained, due mostly to arguments over human rights. Since the time of Nixon's visit, China has allowed more economic freedoms, including a limited amount of private enterprise. The world's most populous country, however, continues to crush attempts at social reform. The United States issued a report in 1997 claiming that China had jailed or exiled every active political dissident. The report called it an "accomplishment even post-Stalinist Russia could not achieve." A Chinese official called the report "an interference into China's internal affairs."

Teaching Gifted and Talented Students

Evaluating an Autobiographic Source After leaving government, Kissinger wrote two books about his White House experiences: *White House Years,* 1979, and *Years of Upheaval,* 1982. Assign students to read selections in these books that relate to the decision to open relations with China and the Soviet Union. Ask students what special insights Kissinger's account provides. Would students rely on such autobiographies as their main source of historical information? Why or why not?

Kissinger in Moscow

Before Nixon's arrival in Moscow, Kissinger met with Brezhnev to finalize the details of the visit. In preparing Brezhnev for the meeting, the Kremlin's top scholar on America advised the Soviet premier on one of Kissinger's most notable traits. "He has a huge ego and you can use it," the aide said. "Stroke him . . . deal with him as if he were an equal and not just a presidential assistant."

IN-DEPTH RESOURCES: UNIT 9
American Lives: Henry Kissinger, p. 15

ASSESS & RETEACH

Section 1 Assessment

Have students work in small groups to answer the questions. Draw the chart in question 2 on the board and complete it as a class.

Self-Assessment

Have students rate Nixon's performance as a president on a scale of 1 to 10 based on information in this section. Then have them share their ratings and reasons for them.

Section Quiz

FORMAL ASSESSMENT
Section Quiz, p. 387

Reteach

Use the Guided Reading Worksheet for Section 1 to help review the main ideas of the section.

IN-DEPTH RESOURCES: UNIT 9
Guided Reading, p. 1

CLOSE

President Richard Nixon attempted to steer the country in a more conservative direction by dismantling numerous federal programs and instilling a sense of law and order. On the world stage, Nixon worked to improve relations with Cold War adversaries China and the Soviet Union.

952 Chapter 32

---

background. It seemed that Nixon, and no one else, could have convinced the American people that the time was right to negotiate with the Communists.

Besides the trip's enormous symbolic value, it also resulted in important agreements between the United States and China. The two nations agreed that neither would try to dominate the Pacific and that both would cooperate in settling disputes peacefully. The United States also recognized that Taiwan was politically part of mainland China and promised to eventually withdraw American forces from the island.

NIXON TRAVELS TO MOSCOW In May of 1972, three months after visiting Beijing, President Nixon headed to Moscow—the first U.S. president ever to visit the Soviet Union. By the time the president arrived for a summit meeting with Soviet premier Leonid Brezhnev, relations with the Soviet Union had already warmed. In 1971, the United States and the Soviet Union had crafted an agreement about Berlin. The Soviets promised to guarantee Western nations free access to West Berlin and to respect the city's independence. In return, the Western allies agreed to officially recognize East Germany.

Like his visit to China, Nixon's trip to the Soviet Union received wide acclaim. After a series of meetings called the Strategic Arms Limitation Talks (SALT), Nixon and Brezhnev signed the **SALT I Treaty.** This five-year agreement limited the number of intercontinental ballistic missiles (ICBMs) and submarine-launched missiles to 1972 levels.

The foreign policy triumphs with China and the Soviet Union, which came just months before the 1972 presidential election, helped Nixon win a second term in the White House. The administration's announcement, in October of 1972, that peace was imminent in Vietnam also played a significant role in Nixon's reelection.

However, peace in Vietnam proved elusive, and the Nixon administration grappled with the war for nearly six more months before finally ending America's involvement in Vietnam. By that time, another issue was about to dominate the Nixon administration—one that eventually led to the downfall of the president.

A 1973 military parade in Moscow displays the Soviet Union's arsenal, components of which were frozen at 1972 levels as a result of the SALT I Treaty.

G. Answer By coming just months before the 1972 presidential elections, these achievements helped Nixon win reelection.

THINK THROUGH HISTORY
G. Drawing Conclusions Why was the timing of Nixon's foreign policy achievements particularly important?

Section 1 Assessment

1. TERMS & NAMES
- Richard M. Nixon
- New Federalism
- revenue sharing
- Family Assistance Plan
- Southern strategy
- stagflation
- OPEC
- realpolitik
- détente
- SALT I Treaty

2. SUMMARIZING In a two-column chart similar to the one shown, list policies of Richard Nixon that promoted change and those that slowed it down.

Promoted Change	Slowed Change

In what ways do you think Nixon was most conservative? In which way was he least conservative? Explain.

3. INTERPRETING Do you think Richard Nixon fulfilled his campaign promise to mend the divisiveness in the United States? Give examples to support your viewpoint.

THINK ABOUT
- his policy of law and order
- his decisions on busing and integration
- his Supreme Court appointments
- his economic reforms

4. EVALUATING In your opinion, did Nixon's foreign policy of détente help solve the country's major foreign policy problems? Support your answer with evidence from the text.

THINK ABOUT
- the definition and origin of détente
- the effect of détente on U.S. dealings with Communist countries
- the effect of détente on the American public

952 Chapter 32

ANSWERS

1. TERMS & NAMES
Richard M. Nixon, p. 946
New Federalism, p. 946
revenue sharing, p. 946
Family Assistance Plan, p. 947
Southern strategy, p. 948
stagflation, p. 950
OPEC, p. 950
realpolitik, p. 951
détente, p. 951
SALT I Treaty, p. 952

2. SUMMARIZING
Possible Answers: **Promoted Change:** Started revenue sharing program; supported Family Assistance Plan; visited China; visited Soviet Union; signed SALT I. **Slowed Change:** Impounded funds allocated by Congress; abolished Office of Economic Opportunity; slowed desegregation efforts; appointed conservative justices to the Supreme Court.

3. INTERPRETING
Possible Responses: **Yes:** He tried to reduce protests, slow down integration, appoint Supreme Court justices who would resist change, and reduce economic suffering by wage and price controls. **No:** The creation of an "enemies list," his failure to support key civil rights legislation, his attempt to make the Supreme Court more conservative, and his inability to halt inflation all added to the country's divisiveness.

4. EVALUATING
Possible Responses: **Yes:** It brought improved relations with the Soviet Union and China. **No:** Although it improved foreign relations, enhanced Nixon's world image, and renewed the American public's confidence in Nixon, it did nothing to help the situation in Vietnam.

Watergate: Nixon's Downfall

LEARN ABOUT the events known as the Watergate scandal
TO UNDERSTAND why Watergate presented one of the most serious constitutional crises in U.S. history.

TERMS & NAMES
• Watergate
• H. R. Haldeman
• John Ehrlichman
• John Mitchell
• Committee to
  Reelect the President
• Judge John Sirica
• Saturday Night Massacre

ONE AMERICAN'S STORY

On July 25, 1974, U.S. Representative Barbara Jordan of Texas, a member of the House Judiciary Committee, sat before a packed hearing room and a television audience of millions. The Judiciary Committee faced a historic decision: should it impeach President Richard M. Nixon? If the House voted for impeachment, the president would be tried in the Senate for crimes he allegedly committed while in office. Addressing the room, Jordan summoned the Constitution in urging her fellow committee members to begin investigating whether impeachment was appropriate.

A PERSONAL VOICE

"We the people"—it is a very eloquent beginning. But when the Constitution of the United States was completed . . . I was not included in that "We the people". . . But through the process of amendment, interpretation, and court decision, I have finally been included in "We the people" . . .

Today . . . [M]y faith in the Constitution is whole. It is complete. It is total. I am not going to sit here and be an idle spectator in the diminution, the subversion of the Constitution. . . . Has the President committed offenses . . . which the Constitution will not tolerate? That is the question. We know that. We should now forthwith proceed to answer the question.

BARBARA JORDAN, quoted in *Notable Black American Women*

**U.S. Representative
Barbara Jordan**

The committee eventually voted to recommend the impeachment of Richard Nixon for his role in the Watergate scandal. However, before Congress could take further action against him, the president resigned. Nixon's resignation, the first by a U.S. president, was the climax of a scandal that led to the imprisonment of 25 government officials and caused the most serious constitutional crisis in the United States since the impeachment of Andrew Johnson in 1868.

President Nixon and His White House

The **Watergate** scandal centered on the Nixon administration's attempt to cover up a burglary at the Democratic National Committee (DNC) headquarters at the Watergate apartment complex in Washington, D.C. However, the Watergate story began long before the actual burglary. Many historians believe that Watergate truly began with the personalities of Richard Nixon and his advisers, as well as with the changing role of the presidency.

AN IMPERIAL PRESIDENCY Over the course of the nation's history, the balance of power has shifted among the legislative, executive, and judicial branches of the federal government. By the time Richard Nixon took office, the executive branch—as a result of the Great Depression, World War II, and the Cold War—had become the most powerful branch. In his book *The Imperial Presidency*, the historian Arthur Schlesinger, Jr., argued that by the time of Richard Nixon, the executive branch had taken on an air of imperial, or supreme, authority.

An Age of Limits **953**

Section 2 Overview

OBJECTIVES

(**1**) To explain how Nixon and his advisers sought to increase the power of the presidency.

(**2**) To summarize why the Watergate burglary occurred and why the Nixon administration covered it up.

(**3**) To describe how the Watergate cover-up unraveled.

(**4**) To explain why a House committee voted to impeach Nixon and what effect the Watergate scandal had on the country.

SKILLBUILDER

• Interpreting political cartoons, p. 956

CRITICAL THINKING

• Clarifying, p. 954
• Analyzing motives, p. 954
• Following chronological order, pp. 955, 957
• Drawing conclusions, p. 956
• Summarizing, p. 957
• Analyzing, p. 957
• Hypothesizing, p. 957

FOCUS & MOTIVATE

▶ *Starting with the Student*
Ask students how they react when they believe someone has lied to them. How would they react if they discovered that their president had lied to the country?

IN-DEPTH RESOURCES: UNIT 9
American Lives: Barbara Jordan, p. 16

OBJECTIVE
(**1**) **INSTRUCT**

President Nixon and His White House

▶ *Discussing Key Ideas*
• By the time Nixon arrives in the White House, the presidency has taken on an air of supreme, or imperial, authority.
• Nixon revels in this authority, as he distances

(continued on next page)

Teacher's Edition **953**

SECTION 2 RESOURCES

PRINT RESOURCES

IN-DEPTH RESOURCES: UNIT 9
Guided Reading, p. 2
Primary Source: from *All the President's Men* by Carl Bernstein and Bob Woodword, p. 9
American Lives: Barbara Jordan, p. 16

ACCESS FOR STUDENTS ACQUIRING ENGLISH
Guided Reading (Spanish), p. 310

FORMAL ASSESSMENT
Section Quiz, p. 388

ALTERNATIVE ASSESSMENT BOOK
See forms for supporting and scoring alternative activities.

TECHNOLOGY RESOURCES

HUMANITIES TRANSPARENCIES
H46, I Am the Law

CRITICAL THINKING TRANSPARENCIES
CT32, The Watergate Scandal
CT66, Shift in Presidential Politics, 1968–1972

CD-ROM *Our Times*
Grolier Multimedia Encyclopedia
Electronic Library of Primary Sources

VIDEO *American Portfolio: A Videodisc for U.S. History*
user's guide, pp. 253–255

INTERNET McDougal Littell Learning On-Line
http://www.mcdougallittell.com

(continued from page 953)

himself from Congress and relies on a small group of close advisers.

OBJECTIVE
② INSTRUCT

The Drive Toward Reelection

▶ *Discussing Key Ideas*
• Seeking any and all advantages, officials with Nixon's reelection campaign burglarize the Democratic National Committee headquarters for information.
• Nixon agrees to a cover-up of the White House's involvement in the burglary.

CRITICAL THINKING TRANSPARENCIES
CT66, Shift in Presidential Politics, 1968–1972

MORE ABOUT . . .
The Plumbers

By the time of the Watergate break-in, the plumbers had undertaken numerous covert operations and burglaries. In 1971, for example, Nixon officials mobilized the group after former Defense Department employee Daniel Ellsberg released the so-called Pentagon Papers—which charged the Johnson administration with misleading the public about Vietnam and helped fuel further resentment toward the ongoing war. To discredit Ellsberg, the plumbers broke into the office of Ellsberg's psychiatrist in an effort to find damaging personal evidence.

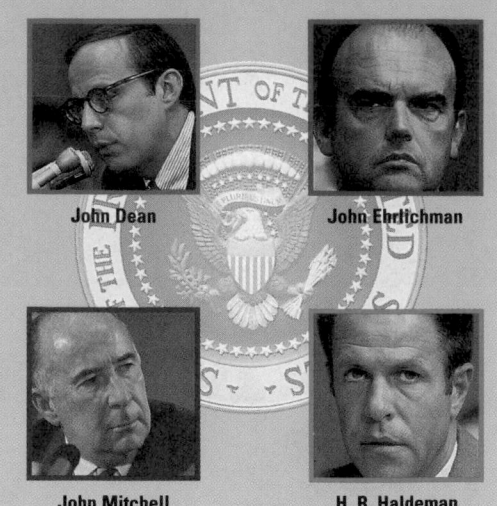

John Dean   John Ehrlichman

John Mitchell   H. R. Haldeman

The "president's men," as they were called, formed a tight circle around Richard Nixon.

President Nixon settled into this imperial role with ease. Nixon believed, as he told a newspaper reporter in 1980, that "a president must not be one of the crowd. . . . People . . . don't want him to be down there saying, 'Look, I'm the same as you.'" Nixon expanded the power of the presidency and gave little thought to constitutional checks, such as when he impounded funds for federal programs he opposed and ordered U.S. troops to invade Cambodia without congressional approval.

THE "PRESIDENT'S MEN" As he distanced himself from Congress, Nixon confided in a small and fiercely loyal group of advisers. They included **H. R. Haldeman,** chief of staff; **John Ehrlichman,** chief domestic adviser; and **John Mitchell,** the Attorney General. These men had played key roles in Nixon's 1968 election victory and now helped the president direct White House policy.

These men also shared President Nixon's desire for secrecy and the consolidation of power. Through their personalities and their attitude toward the presidency, these men developed a sense that they were somehow above the law. This sense would, in turn, prompt President Nixon and his advisers to cover up their role in Watergate, and thus fuel the coming scandal.

The Drive Toward Reelection

Throughout his political career, Richard Nixon lived with the overwhelming fear of losing elections. In his 1972 reelection campaign, Nixon strived to not only defeat his opponent, but to dominate him. "I vowed that I would never again enter an election at a disadvantage to . . . anyone on the level of political tactics," Nixon wrote. Toward this end, Nixon's campaign team sought advantages by any means possible, including an attempt to steal information from the DNC headquarters.

A BUNGLED BURGLARY At 2:30 a.m., June 17, 1972, a guard at the Watergate complex in Washington, D.C., caught five men breaking into the campaign headquarters of the DNC. The men were part of a team known as the "plumbers," whose job it was to plug any government leaks to the media and aid the Nixon administration in other—sometimes illegal—ways. The burglars had intended to photograph documents outlining Democratic party strategy and to place wiretaps, or "bugs," on the office telephones. The press soon discovered that the group's leader, James McCord, was a former CIA agent. He was also an official of a group known as the **Committee to Reelect the President** (CRP). John Mitchell, who had resigned as attorney general to run Nixon's reelection campaign, was the CRP's director.

Just three days after the burglary, H.R. Haldeman noted in his diary Nixon's near obsession with how to respond to the break-in.

A PERSONAL VOICE
We got back into the Democratic break-in again. . . . The more he [Nixon] thought about it, it obviously bothered him more, because he raised it in considerable detail today. . . . The P[resident] was concerned about what our counterattack is. . . . He raised it again several times during the day, and it obviously is bothering him. . . . He called at home tonight, saying that he wanted to change the plan for his press conference and have it on Thursday instead of tomorrow, so that it won't look like he's reacting to the Democratic break-in thing.
H. R. HALDEMAN, *The Haldeman Diaries*

THINK THROUGH HISTORY
A. Clarifying
What is meant by the "imperial presidency"?

A. Answer The idea that the executive branch had become the most powerful of the three branches in government, and acted as the supreme authority.

THINK THROUGH HISTORY
B. Analyzing Motives Why would the Nixon campaign team take such risky action as breaking into the opposition's headquarters?

B. Answer Nixon's overwhelming fear of losing and the mentality that all means should be taken to defeat the opponent.

TEACHING OPTIONS

Teaching Less Proficient Readers

Creating a Time Line Have less proficient readers create a Watergate time line to keep track of the scandal's many twists and turns. Starting with the Watergate burglary and ending with Nixon's resignation, students should list what they consider the major events of Watergate on a time line such as the one below. They may place as many events on their time line as they wish.

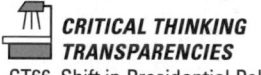

break-in   Nixon resigns

Teaching Gifted and Talented Students

Researching a Diary Have interested students read more of *The Haldeman Diaries,* particularly those excerpts that pertain to the Watergate scandal. Students should then write a brief paper answering the following questions: What new insight into the scandal did you learn? What more did you learn about the personality and behavior of Richard Nixon? Why might a diary be a useful source in researching historical persons or events?

C. *Following Chronological Order* What steps did the White House take to cover up its involvement in the Watergate break-in?

C. Answer It shredded documents, attempted to obstruct the investigation, and paid the Watergate burglars to remain silent.

At that point, the White House might have disowned the entire operation and demanded the resignation of everyone involved. But that would have meant getting rid of people upon whom Nixon heavily depended, such as Mitchell. The cover-up quickly began. Workers shredded all incriminating documents in the CRP's office. The White House, with President Nixon's consent, asked the CIA to urge the FBI to stop its investigations into the burglary on the grounds of national security. In addition, the CRP passed out nearly $500,000 to the Watergate burglars to buy their silence after they were indicted in September of 1972.

Throughout the 1972 campaign, the Watergate burglary generated little interest from the American public and media. Only the *Washington Post*, and two of its reporters, Bob Woodward and Carl Bernstein, kept on the story. In a series of articles, the reporters uncovered information that linked numerous members of the administration to the burglary. The White House denied each new *Post* allegation. Upon learning of an upcoming story that tied him to the burglars, Mitchell told Bernstein, "That's the most sickening thing I ever heard."

The White House reaction proved effective. Casting himself as a "global peacemaker"—in light of his China and Soviet Union summits and his promise of peace in Vietnam—Richard Nixon scored the largest victory of any Republican presidential candidate in history. The president captured nearly 61 percent of the popular vote on his way to soundly defeating George S. McGovern, a liberal senator from South Dakota. However, as Nixon savored his landslide victory, the storm clouds of Watergate were gathering on the horizon.

The Cover-Up Unravels

In January of 1973, the trial for the Watergate burglars began. All the defendants pleaded guilty. The trial's presiding judge, **Judge John Sirica,** made clear his belief that the Watergate burglars had not acted alone. In an effort to shake up the defendants and prod them to talk, Sirica gave them the maximum sentence and said he would review the sentences after three months. Three months later, the first defendant broke. On March 23, James McCord sent a letter to Sirica, in which he admitted that he had lied under oath. He added that other members of the Nixon administration were involved and that they also had lied under oath.

THE SENATE INVESTIGATES WATERGATE McCord's revelation of possible White House involvement in the burglary rekindled public interest in Watergate. President Nixon moved quickly to stem the growing public concern. On April 30, 1973, Nixon dismissed White House counsel John Dean and announced the resignations of Haldeman and Ehrlichman. All three men had been involved in the Watergate affair. The president then went on television and denied any attempt at a cover-up. He announced that he was appointing a new attorney general, Elliot Richardson, and was authorizing him to appoint a special prosecutor to investigate Watergate. "There can be no whitewash at the White House," Nixon said.

The president's reassurances, however, came too late. In May 1973, the Senate began its own investigation of Watergate. A special committee, chaired by Senator Sam Ervin of North Carolina, began to call before it a parade of Nixon administration officials to give testimony. Throughout the summer and into the fall millions of Americans sat glued to their televisions, as the "president's men" testified one after the other—and dropped several bombshells.

HISTORICAL SPOTLIGHT

WOODWARD AND BERNSTEIN

Reporters Bob Woodward and Carl Bernstein of the *Washington Post* seemed an unlikely team. Woodward, 29, *above right,* had graduated from Yale, while the 28-year-old Bernstein was a college dropout.

As the two men dug deeper into the Watergate scandal, a mysterious inside source known only as "Deep Throat" helped them along the way. There has been much debate over the identity of "Deep Throat," which has been fueled by the reporters' continued refusal to identify their famous source.

While people lauded the two reporters for their dogged determination on the Watergate story, some Nixon officials remain bitter toward them. "I really believe [they] were on a personal crusade to bring down a president," said Gerald Warren, Nixon's deputy press secretary. Woodward denied that charge, saying, "We tried to do our job and, in fact, if you look at it, our coverage was pretty conservative."

An Age of Limits **955**

HISTORICAL SPOTLIGHT
Woodward and Bernstein

The mystery surrounding the identity of "Deep Throat" speaks to a controversial issue in the journalism community: the use of anonymous sources. Courts have sometimes ordered reporters to name an anonymous source who may be a witness to a crime or have knowledge vital to a case. Reporters have almost always refused, arguing that they promised to keep the source's name secret and that to reveal the name would undermine their ability to gather information from future sources. Ask students for their opinions on this issue.

IN-DEPTH RESOURCES: UNIT 9
Primary Source: from *All the President's Men* by Carl Bernstein and Bob Woodward, p. 9

OBJECTIVE
③ INSTRUCT

The Cover-Up Unravels

▶ *Discussing Key Ideas*
- The Senate begins investigating a possible White House connection to the Watergate break-in.
- During the Senate hearings several witnesses accuse numerous White House officials, including President Nixon, of orchestrating a cover-up.
- Nixon refuses to release White House tape recordings that could reveal his involvement in the cover-up.

 CRITICAL THINKING TRANSPARENCIES
CT32, The Watergate Scandal

TEACHING OPTIONS

Exploring Themes

Constitutional Concerns The Watergate scandal produced one of the most serious constitutional issues facing this country: the possibility of criminal activity by a sitting president. Make sure students understand the impeachment process as outlined in the Constitution. The House of Representatives has the sole power to bring impeachment charges against a president or any other civilian official of the U.S. government. A majority vote of the House is required for impeachment. The Senate then acts as a court to hear the charges brought against the impeached official. A two-thirds vote of the Senate is required for conviction.

Making Connections Across Cultures

Senator Edward Brooke In 1966, Edward Brooke of Massachusetts became the first African American to be elected to the U.S. Senate since 1876. He was also the first Republican senator to publicly call for President Nixon's resignation. Brooke, who was reelected in 1972, had served in World War II, where he rose to the rank of captain and received a Bronze Star for his work in intelligence. Although he was a Republican, he sparred with President Nixon over numerous issues, including civil rights.

"*What did the president know and when did he know it?*"

SENATOR HOWARD BAKER

"*Divine right went out with the American Revolution and doesn't belong to White House aides.*"

SENATOR SAM ERVIN
IN RESPONSE TO THE WHITE HOUSE'S REQUEST THAT ITS AIDES TESTIFY IN PRIVATE

STARTLING TESTIMONY John Dean delivered the first bomb. In late June, during more than 30 hours of testimony, Dean provided a startling answer to Senator Howard Baker's repeated question, "What did the president know and when did he know it?" The former White House counsel answered that President Nixon had been deeply involved in the cover-up. The president quickly sent John Mitchell up to Capitol Hill to refute Dean's charges. Sitting before the Senate committee, Mitchell denied approving the break-in and wiretapping of the Democratic National Committee headquarters. He further stated that if there indeed was a cover-up, Nixon had no knowledge of it.

The hearings had suddenly reached an impasse, as the committee attempted to sort out who was telling the truth. The answer came in July from an unlikely source: presidential aide Alexander Butterfield. Butterfield stunned the committee when he revealed that Nixon had taped virtually all of his presidential conversations. Butterfield later claimed that the taping system was installed "to help Nixon write his memoirs." However, for the Senate committee, the tapes were the key to revealing what Nixon knew, and when he knew it.

THE SATURDAY NIGHT MASSACRE A year-long battle for the "Nixon tapes" followed. Archibald Cox, the special prosecutor whom Elliot Richardson had appointed to investigate the case, took the president to court in October 1973 to obtain the tapes. Nixon refused and ordered Attorney General Richardson to fire Cox. In what became known as the **Saturday Night Massacre,** Richardson refused the order and resigned. The deputy attorney general also refused the order, and he was fired. Solicitor General Robert Bork finally fired Cox. However, Cox's replacement, Leon Jaworski, proved equally determined to get the tapes. Shortly after the "massacre," the House Judiciary Committee begin examining the possibility of an impeachment hearing.

The entire White House appeared to be under siege. Just days before the Saturday Night Massacre, Vice-President Spiro Agnew resigned after it was revealed that he had accepted bribes from Maryland engineering firms before and during his term as vice-president. Acting under the Twenty-fifth Amendment, Nixon nominated the House minority leader, Gerald Ford, as his new vice-president. Congress quickly confirmed the nomination.

In light of Agnew's illegal activities, federal investigators began to study Nixon's own financial dealings. News reports revealed that Nixon had paid only $1,000 in taxes on a $200,000 income in 1971 and 1972. Nixon responded to the charges by uttering what the American people never imagined a president would have to say: "People have the right to know whether or not their president is a crook. Well, I am not a crook."

The Fall of a President

In March 1974, a grand jury indicted Mitchell, Haldeman, Ehrlichman, and four other presidential aides on charges of conspiracy, obstruction of justice, and perjury. The investigation was closing in on the president of the United States.

NIXON RELEASES THE TAPES On April 30, 1974, President Nixon told a televised audience that he was releasing 1,254 pages of edited transcripts of White House conversations about Watergate. The president hoped that this would convince everyone of his truthfulness and leadership. If anything, the tapes only increased people's dismay. The president's vulgar language and lack of concern about fully addressing the growing Watergate scandal shocked many Americans. "We have seen the private man and we are appalled," declared the conservative *Chicago Tribune*.

956 CHAPTER 32

---

956 Chapter 32

Furthermore, Nixon's offering of edited tape manuscript failed to satisfy investigators. They demanded the unedited tapes. Nixon refused, and the case went before the Supreme Court. On July 24, 1974, the high court ruled unanimously that the president must surrender the tapes. The Court rejected Nixon's argument that doing so would violate national security. Evidence involving possible criminal activity could not be withheld, even by a president.

THE PRESIDENT RESIGNS Even without the original tapes, the House Judiciary Committee determined there was enough evidence to impeach Richard Nixon. On July 27, the House Committee adopted three articles of impeachment, charging the president with obstruction of justice, abuse of power, and contempt of Congress for refusing to obey a congressional subpoena to release the tapes.

On August 5, Nixon finally released the tapes. Despite a mysterious gap of eighteen minutes, the tapes revealed the evidence for which investigators had been searching. A conversation with H. R. Haldeman on June 23, 1972—a week after the Watergate break-in—revealed that Nixon not only knew of his administration's role in the burglary but agreed to the plan to obstruct the FBI's investigation.

The evidence now seemed overwhelming. On August 8, 1974, Richard M. Nixon announced his resignation from office. Defiant as always, Nixon admitted no guilt. He merely said that some of his judgments "were wrong." The next day, Nixon and his wife, Pat, climbed into the presidential helicopter that would take them to Andrews Air Force Base for their flight back home to California. Moments later, Gerald Ford was sworn in as the 38th president of the United States.

THE EFFECTS OF WATERGATE The effects of Watergate have endured long after Nixon's resignation. Along with the divisive war in Vietnam, Watergate produced a deep disillusionment with the "imperial" presidency. A poll taken in 1974 showed that 43 percent of Americans had "hardly any" faith in the executive branch of government. In the years following Vietnam and Watergate, the American public developed a general cynicism about many public officials that still exists today.

During the rest of the 1970s, Gerald Ford and Jimmy Carter worked to restore that lost faith in the presidency. Unfortunately, each man would have to focus most of his attention on the country's worsening economic conditions.

With wife Pat looking on, Richard Nixon bids farewell to his staff on his final day as president. "Always remember," he defiantly told them, "others may hate you, but those who hate you don't win unless you hate them, and then you destroy yourself."

Section **2** Assessment

1. TERMS & NAMES
- Watergate
- H. R. Haldeman
- John Ehrlichman
- John Mitchell
- Committee to Reelect the President
- Judge John Sirica
- Saturday Night Massacre

2. SUMMARIZING On a diagram similar to the one below, list individuals or groups who helped uncover the Watergate scandal. Include people from the government and the media, as well as those on Nixon's staff who testified.

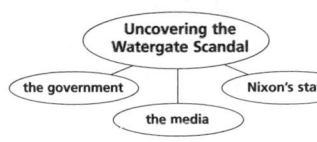

3. ANALYZING Which events of the Watergate scandal do you think were most significant? Explain.

THINK ABOUT
- the purpose of each event
- the legal implications of each event
- the charges in the articles of impeachment

4. HYPOTHESIZING Imagine that Nixon had admitted to and apologized for the Watergate break-in immediately after it occurred. How might subsequent events have been different? Explain and support your answer.

THINK ABOUT
- the extent of the cover-up
- the impact of the cover-up on the nation
- the effect of the cover-up on Nixon's image

An Age of Limits **957**

ANSWERS

1. TERMS & NAMES

Watergate, p. 953

H. R. Haldeman, p. 954

John Ehrlichman, p. 954

John Mitchell, p. 954

Committee to Reelect the President, p. 954

Judge John Sirica, p. 955

Saturday Night Massacre, p. 956

2. SUMMARIZING

Possible Responses: **The government:** Attorney General Elliot Richardson; special prosecutors Archibald Cox and Leon Jaworski; Senate committee headed by Sam Ervin; the House Judiciary Committee; Judge John Sirica; the Supreme Court. **The media:** *Washington Post* reporters Bob Woodward and Carl Bernstein. **Nixon's staff:** John Dean; presidential aide Alexander Butterfield.

3. ANALYZING

Possible Responses: The initial burglary, because it was illegal, showed abuse of presidential power and led Nixon to cover up his actions; the subsequent cover-up, especially the destroying of evidence and bribing of the burglars, because these actions showed Nixon's contempt for law and Congress; Nixon's refusal to release the tapes, because it showed that he felt he was above the law and that Nixon, the "law and order" president, had something to hide.

4. HYPOTHESIZING

Possible Responses: Nixon's offenses would have been less significant and his public image would not have been as badly damaged; Americans might have respected his forthrightness and forgotten the matter after awhile; however, he probably would have lost some of the trust of the American people.

Teacher's Edition **957**

OBJECTIVES

1 To explain the growing realism of American TV in the 1970s.

2 To describe popular TV shows of the decade.

FOCUS & MOTIVATE

▶ **Starting with the Student**
Ask students to think about popular TV shows today.

- Which seem the most realistic in their depiction of everyday life?
- What details make them realistic?

MORE ABOUT . . .
Alex Haley

Alex Haley, who served in the U.S. Coast Guard, admitted that he began writing to avoid boredom during long sea voyages. In 1965, Haley published *The Autobiography of Malcolm X,* which was based on interviews with the Black Muslim leader. The book received wide critical praise. However, it was not until *Roots: The Saga of an American Family,* and the television adaptation that followed, that Haley became a household name. Haley said he began writing *Roots* after listening to his maternal grandmother talk about the family's history. He spent 12 years researching the book. *Roots* earned its author numerous accolades, including a special Pulitzer Prize. Haley died in 1992 at the age of 70.

Television Reflects American Life

Beginning in the late 1960s, television programming began to more closely reflect the realities of American life. Shows more often addressed relevant issues, more African-American characters appeared, and women's roles shifted from homemakers to working women. By the 1970s, many of the most popular shows on television were multicultural and often controversial. Top-rated series presented the lives of African Americans (*Sanford and Son* and *Good Times*) and women living on their own (*One Day at a Time*). Another hit series, *M*A*S*H,* gave voice to antiwar sentiment. However, the 1970s was not all about relevance. Nostalgic comedies such as *Happy Days* and fantasy dramas such as *Charlie's Angels* were also big hits.

The 1970s also saw the rapid rise of quality children's programming on public broadcasting, which was created in 1967. Educational shows such as *Sesame Street* (whose Muppet character Cookie Monster appears on the TV Guide cover shown above) and *Zoom!* were deliberately fast-paced to appeal to the new generation of "television babies."

INDEPENDENT WOMEN *The Mary Tyler Moore Show* depicted Mary Richards, a single woman living in Minneapolis and working as an assistant manager in a local TV news department. Mary symbolized the young career woman of the 1970s. She was professional and ambitious, but also caring, optimistic, and funny. She dated but was not desperate for marriage—she enjoyed her independence.

CULTURAL IDENTITY
The miniseries *Roots,* based on the book by Alex Haley, told the saga of four generations of an African-American family. The eight-part story began with Kunta Kinte, who was captured outside his West African village and taken to America as a slave. It ended with his great grandson setting off for a new life as a free man. The groundbreaking series, broadcast in January 1977, was one of the most-watched television events in history. The final episode reached an estimated 100 million viewers—71 percent of the TV audience—and was the highest rated show to that time.

958

RECOMMENDED RESOURCES

Books

Alley, Robert S. *Love Is All Around.* New York: Delta, 1989. A book about the making of *The Mary Tyler Moore Show.*

Esslin, Martin. *The Age of Television.* San Francisco: Freeman, 1982. Written soon after the close of the 1970s, this study focuses on societal aspects of television.

Lesser, Gerald S. *Children and Television.* New York: Random, 1974. Lessons from Sesame Street detailed in a book published not very long after the show's creation.

Reiss, David S. *M*A*S*H.* Indianapolis: Bobbs-Merrill, 1980. An inside look at the popular TV show, with a foreword by star Alan Alda.

Videos

All in the Family 20th Anniversary Special. Columbia Pictures Home Video, 1991. A retrospective featuring the stars of the show and its creator, Norman Lear.

The Impact of Television. Encyclopædia Britannica, 1980. This look at TV features sequences from popular shows.

On Television. Films Inc., 1988. An exploration of TV as a social institution, hosted by Edwin Newman.

Roots, vol. 1. Dir. David Greene. Warner Home Video, 1977. The original six-part miniseries.

MULTICULTURALISM *Chico and the Man* was the first series set in a Mexican-American neighborhood, a barrio of East Los Angeles. It became an immediate hit after its debut in 1974. The program centered on the relationship between Ed Brown, a cranky Anglo garage owner, and Chico Rodriguez, an optimistic and energetic young Mexican-American he reluctantly hired. An attachment gradually grew between the two men from different backgrounds.

SOCIAL VALUES
The most popular series of the 1970s was also the one that departed most radically from the idealized situation comedies of the 1950s and 1960s. *All in the Family* told the story of a working-class family in Queens, New York, headed by the bigoted Archie Bunker and his long-suffering wife, Edith. Through the barbs Bunker traded with his liberal son-in law, "Meathead," and his African-American neighbor, George Jefferson, the show dealt openly with the divisions in American society. It also addressed controversial topics that were previously taboo on TV, including politics, religious differences, and sexuality.

DATA FILE

TV facts of the 1970s

- American television sets were turned on an average of seven hours a day.
- The typical school-age child (6 to 18 years old) in America spent 25 percent more time watching TV than attending school.
- A congressional ban on TV cigarette commercials took effect in 1971.
- ABC negotiated an $8-million-a-year contract to televise Monday Night Football, first broadcast in September 1970.
- In 1972, President Nixon, accompanied by TV cameras and anchors for the major networks, made a surprise visit to China.
- From May until November 1973, the Senate Watergate hearings became the biggest day-time viewing event of the season.
- *Saturday Night Live*, a show that would launch the careers of Dan Aykroyd, Jane Curtin, Eddie Murphy and many other comic actors, premiered in October 1975.
- WTCG-TV (later WTBS) in Atlanta, owned by Ted Turner, became the first "superstation" when it began satellite broadcasts to four cable systems in 1976.
- In November 1979, ABC began broadcasting late-night updates on the hostage crisis in Iran. These reports evolved into the program *Nightline*.

Other Popular Shows of the 1970s

Mod Squad

The Flip Wilson Show

Marcus Welby, M.D.

Hawaii Five-O

Adam-12

The Partridge Family

Maude

The Waltons

Little House on the Prairie

Laverne and Shirley

The Six Million Dollar Man

The Bionic Woman

INTERACT WITH HISTORY

1. **DEVELOPING HISTORICAL PERSPECTIVE** In what ways did television more closely reflect American society in the 1970s? What factors might have influenced these changes?

    SEE SKILLBUILDER HANDBOOK, PAGE 1043.

2. **DISCUSSING** With a small group, read about or watch several of the TV shows mentioned, or choose some of your own. Discuss how the shows document behaviors and beliefs of the period and compare them with the most popular TV shows today. Share your findings with the class.

   INTERNET For more about television and mass culture, click on **Social Studies** at http://www.mcdougallittell.com

An Age of Limits **959**

INSTRUCT

▶ Starting with the Student

- Have students view and discuss 1970s TV shows on videocassette or in reruns.
- Encourage students to share opinions on the value of realistic TV. Should dramas and sit-coms be realistic? Why or why not?

▶ Discussing Key Ideas

- TV in the 1970s began increasingly to reflect everyday American life.
- Many of the shows dealt with racial division, multi-cultural heritage, independent working women, and other concerns and issues of the day.

HISTORY FROM VISUALS
Reading the Images

- Have students examine the photos on these pages.
- What does the central picture at the bottom of the page say about TV in the 1970s? *Possible Responses: Children spent much (or too much) time watching TV; it was viewed by children of all ages; it served as a baby sitter as more mothers worked; it dazed or dulled the minds of children; it brought families together; it drove families apart by cutting down on conversation and other interaction.*
- Ask students which spot-lighted series or mini-series seems most interesting to them. Why?

INTERACT WITH HISTORY

1. Developing Historical Perspective

Possible Answers: Television was more urban, more working class, more ethnic, more multicultural, and more independent. It showed working women and treated more social issues.

Television became more reflective of its audience and the changing consumer market as African Americans and other groups grew more affluent; pressure came from women's and civil-rights groups to depict America with its rich diversity; loss of innocence with Vietnam War and Watergate made Americans more cynical, less accepting of unrealistic TV.

2. Discussing

To help students complete this assignment, encourage them to take the following steps:

- Find older TV shows in reruns on channels like cable's Nickelodeon, which airs reruns on *Nick at Night,* or on videocassettes, sometimes available at local libraries.
- Have different groups focus on different genres—police shows, family dramas, and sitcoms, for example.
- Videotape portions of shows they view to use as examples in their discussions.

TERMS & NAMES
• Gerald R. Ford
• Jimmy Carter
• National Energy Act
• human rights
• Camp David Accords
• Ayatollah Ruhollah Khomeini

Section 3 Overview

OBJECTIVES

(1) To describe Gerald Ford's attempts to combat the nation's economic problems.

(2) To explain the reasons for Jimmy Carter's presidential election victory in 1976.

(3) To identify the ways Carter tried to solve the nation's economic downswing.

(4) To describe Jimmy Carter's foreign policy beliefs and their effect on U.S. foreign relations.

(5) To summarize Carter's foreign policy triumphs and defeats in the Middle East.

SKILLBUILDERS

• Interpreting charts, pp. 963, 964
• Understanding geography: location, p. 966

CRITICAL THINKING

• Contrasting, p. 961
• Analyzing causes, pp. 962, 964, 965
• Summarizing, p. 963
• Forming and supporting opinions, pp. 963, 967
• Identifying problems, p. 965
• Analyzing issues, p. 967
• Sequencing history, p. 967
• Comparing and contrasting, p. 967

FOCUS & MOTIVATE

▶ **Starting with the Student**
Ask students if they notice when prices increase on compact discs, gym shoes, or some of their other favorite items. What do they think causes this increase?

OBJECTIVE
(1) INSTRUCT

Ford Travels a Rough Road

▶ **Discussing Key Ideas**
• Ford's pardon of Nixon costs Ford a great deal of public support.
• Ford battles the Congress as he attempts to remedy the nation's sluggish economy.

(continued on next page)

---

3 The Ford and Carter Years

LEARN ABOUT the domestic and foreign policies of the Ford and Carter administrations
TO UNDERSTAND how each man attempted to solve the country's worsening economic crisis and deal with an increasingly complex world.

ONE AMERICAN'S STORY

James D. Denney couldn't believe what he was hearing. Barely a month after Richard Nixon had resigned amid the Watergate scandal, President Gerald Ford had granted Nixon a full pardon. "Someone must write, 'The End,'" Ford declared in a televised statement. "I have concluded that only I can do that." Denney sat down and wrote a letter to the editors of *Time* magazine, in which he voiced his anger at Ford's decision.

> **A PERSONAL VOICE**
> Justice may certainly be tempered by mercy, but there can be no such thing as mercy until justice has been accomplished by the courts. Since it circumvented justice, Mr. Ford's act was merely indulgent favoritism, a bland and unworthy substitute for mercy.
> **JAMES D. DENNEY,** *Time,* September 23, 1974

James Denney's feelings were typical of the anger and disillusionment that many Americans felt toward the presidency in the aftermath of the Watergate scandal. During the 1970s, Presidents Gerald Ford and Jimmy Carter sought to restore America's faith in its leaders. However, both men had to focus much of their attention on battling the nation's worsening economic situation.

Two women prote[st]
President Ford's pa[rdon]
of Richard Nixon.

Ford Travels a Rough Road

Upon taking office, **Gerald R. Ford** urged Americans to put the Watergate scandal behind them. "Our long national nightmare is over," he declared. However, the nation's nightmarish economy persisted, and Ford's policies offered little relief.

"A FORD, NOT A LINCOLN" Gerald Ford seemed to many to be a likable and honest man. Upon becoming vice-president after Spiro Agnew's resignation, Ford candidly admitted his limitations. "I'm a Ford, not a Lincoln," he remarked. Raised in Grand Rapids, Michigan, Ford was a product of the nation's heartland. Some people called him "square," but Ford saw nothing wrong with this. He once remarked, "It's . . . the straight, the square that accounts for the great stability of our nation. It's a quality to be proud of."

On September 8, 1974, President Ford pardoned Richard Nixon in an attempt to move the country beyond Watergate. The move cost Ford a good deal of public support. The president hoped to rebuild that support by scoring a victory on what many Americans considered to be the most pressing issue facing the nation: the troubled economy.

FORD TRIES TO "WHIP" INFLATION By the time Ford took office, America's economy had gone from bad to worse. Both inflation and unemployment continued to rise. Due to the massive OPEC oil price increases in 1973, gasoline and heating oil costs had soared, pushing inflation from 6 percent to 11 percent by the end of 1974. In September 1974, the president invited the nation's top economic leaders to the White House to discuss economic

As this *Time* cover suggests, Americans looked to Gerald Ford to move the country beyond Watergate.

SECTION 3 RESOURCES

PRINT RESOURCES

IN-DEPTH RESOURCES: UNIT 9
Guided Reading, p. 3
Geography Application: Oil Consumption in the 1970s, p. 6
Literature: from *Memories of the Ford Administration* by John Updike, p. 12

ACCESS FOR STUDENTS ACQUIRING ENGLISH
Guided Reading (Spanish), p. 311
Geography Application: Oil Consumption in the 1970s (Spanish), p. 314

FORMAL ASSESSMENT
Section Quiz, p. 389

ALTERNATIVE ASSESSMENT BOOK
See forms for supporting and scoring alternative activities.

TECHNOLOGY RESOURCES

HUMANITIES TRANSPARENCIES
H30, Bicentennial celebration

GEOGRAPHY TRANSPARENCIES
G32, OPEC (Organization of Petroleum Exporting Countries)

CD-ROM *Our Times*
Grolier Multimedia Encyclopedia
Electronic Library of Primary Sources

VIDEO *American Portfolio: A Videodisc for U.S. History*
user's guide, pp. 254–255

INTERNET McDougal Littell Learning On-Line
http://www.mcdougallittell.com

strategies. In the end, the Ford administration promoted a program of massive citizen action called "Whip Inflation Now," or WIN. The president called on Americans to cut back on their use of oil and gas, as well as take other energy-saving measures.

In the absence of incentives, though, the plan fell flat. Ford then tried to curb inflation through a "tight money" policy. He cut government spending and encouraged the Federal Reserve to restrict credit through higher interest rates. These actions triggered the worst economic recession in 40 years.

FORD BATTLES THE CONGRESS As Ford implemented his economic programs, he continually battled a Democratic Congress intent on pushing its own economic agenda. The Democrats called for a federal jobs program to bring down unemployment, which had climbed to 8.5 percent in 1975. Ford rejected the plan, claiming that pumping more money into the economy would only increase inflation. Throughout his term, Ford vetoed bills to fund programs for health, education, and housing. During his two years as president, Ford vetoed more than 50 pieces of legislation.

In the end, Ford's economic policies received mixed reviews. Inflation had dropped below 10 percent by 1975 and continued to decline slowly. Unemployment also retreated, but by 1976 it remained stuck at around 8 percent. Ford's policies, while holding stagflation steady, seemed to offer no lasting solutions.

FORD'S FOREIGN POLICY Ford fared slightly better in the international arena. With little experience in diplomacy, he relied heavily on Henry Kissinger, who continued to hold the key position of secretary of state. Following Kissinger's advice, Ford pushed ahead with Nixon's policy of negotiation with China and the Soviet Union. In November 1974, he met with Soviet premier Leonid Brezhnev to plan the next round of arms talks. Less than a year later, he traveled to Helsinki, Finland, to discuss the future of East-West relations. There, some 35 nations, including the Soviet Union, signed the so-called Helsinki Accords—a list of agreements that promoted greater cooperation between the nations of Eastern and Western Europe.

However, like presidents before him, Ford encountered trouble in Southeast Asia. In 1975, the Communist government of Cambodia seized the U.S. merchant ship *Mayagüez* in the Gulf of Siam. Ford responded with a massive show of military force. He ordered two air strikes against Cambodia and sent a crack team of U.S. Marines to rescue 39 crew members aboard the ship. The total operation cost the lives of 41 U.S. troops. Most Americans applauded the action as evidence of the country's strength. However, critics argued that the mission had cost more lives than it saved and that the president had acted without consulting Congress.

Jimmy Carter Enters the White House

Gerald Ford won the Republican nomination for president in 1976. However, he had to fend off a powerful conservative challenge from former California governor Ronald Reagan. Because the Republicans seemed divided over Ford's leadership, and because Ford's economic policies had failed to provide substantial relief, the Democrats confidently eyed the White House. "We could run an aardvark this year and win," predicted one Democratic leader. The Democratic nominee was indeed a surprise: a nationally unknown peanut farmer and former governor of Georgia, **Jimmy Carter.**

An Age of Limits **961**

Difficult Decisions
IN HISTORY

PARDONING PRESIDENT NIXON

President Ford's pardon of Richard Nixon outraged many Americans. *The New York Times* called Ford's decision "a body blow to the president's own credibility and to the public's reviving confidence in the integrity of its government."

President Ford argued that the pardon of Richard Nixon was in the country's best interests. In the event of a Watergate trial, Ford argued, "ugly passions would again be aroused. . . . And the credibility of our free institutions . . . would again be challenged at home and abroad." Ford called the pardon decision "the most difficult of my life, by far."

1. How might the country have been affected had a former United States president gone on trial for possible criminal wrongdoing?

2. If you had been in President Ford's position, would you have pardoned Richard Nixon? Why or why not?

(continued from page 960)

- Ford signs the Helsinki Accords and encounters trouble in Cambodia.

IN-DEPTH RESOURCES: UNIT 9
Guided Reading, p. 3

ACCESS FOR STUDENTS ACQUIRING ENGLISH
Guided Reading (Spanish), p. 311

 GROLIER MULTIMEDIA ENCYCLOPEDIA
Ford's political career

 HUMANITIES TRANSPARENCIES
H30, Bicentennial celebration

DIFFICULT DECISIONS IN HISTORY
Pardoning President Nixon

Possible Answers
1. Some Americans might have felt vindicated, others might have felt ashamed.
2. Some students might say that no one should be above the law; others might say that a pardon was the only way for the nation to put the scandal behind it.

OBJECTIVE
② **INSTRUCT**

Jimmy Carter Enters the White House

▶ *Discussing Key Ideas*
- Political outsider Jimmy Carter wins the 1976 presidential election, largely due to his personality and the nation's aversion to Washington politicians in the wake of Watergate.

TEACHING OPTIONS

Making Connections Across the Curriculum

U.S. Government Had Gerald Ford served longer, his combative relationship with Congress may have led him to veto even more bills. Remind students that the U.S. president has what is known as limited veto power. A two-thirds majority vote of both houses of Congress is required to override a presidential veto. Franklin Roosevelt, who served longer than any other president, vetoed the most bills, with a total of 635. Grover Cleveland, who served two terms, was second with 584. In third place was Harry Truman, who vetoed 250 bills sent to his desk.

Making Connections Across Time

Former President Carter As Jimmy Carter entered the White House, he probably had little idea he would be better known to some people for the life he has led since leaving the presidency. Considered one of the most active and influential former presidents in history, Carter continues to make his mark in this country and around the world. Through his organization, the Carter Center, he has launched a number of housing programs in Atlanta. Overseas, Carter has helped monitor elections in many Latin American and African countries. In 1994, he helped negotiate the removal of Haiti's military dictator.

KEY PLAYER
Jimmy Carter

While Jimmy Carter seemed to come from nowhere to win the 1976 presidential campaign, he in fact had had a substantial career in politics. Have students research Carter's political background and track his political ascendancy to the White House, using a flow chart like the one below.

 OUR TIMES
Interview with Jimmy Carter

Carter's Domestic Agenda

▶ **Discussing Key Ideas**
- Like Ford, Carter focuses much of his energy on battling the country's economic problems.
- Carter meets with limited success in battling the energy crisis, but the economy eventually worsens and the president's measures fail to bring relief.
- Many of the nation's economic woes stem from high energy prices.

ELECTRONIC LIBRARY OF PRIMARY SOURCES
On Energy and National Goals by Jimmy Carter

KEY PLAYER

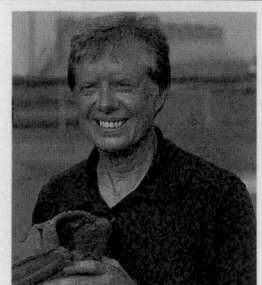

JIMMY CARTER
1924–

James Earl Carter, Jr., was born into relative prosperity. His father, Earl, was a plantation owner who also ran a local store. However, Earl Carter, a disciplinarian who tried to instill a sense of hard work and responsibility in his son, refused to give Jimmy an allowance.

To earn money for himself, Carter and a friend undertook a variety of jobs. Throughout his childhood, Carter sold peanuts, ran a small hamburger and hot dog stand, collected and sold newspapers to fish markets, and sold scrap iron.

Before entering politics, Carter joined the navy, where he excelled in electronics and naval tactics. In 1952, he joined a select group of officers who were developing the world's first nuclear submarines. The group's commander was Captain Hyman G. Rickover. Carter later wrote that Rickover "had a profound effect on my life— perhaps more than anyone except my own parents. . . . He expected the maximum from us, but he always contributed more."

THE ELECTION OF 1976 During the post-Watergate era—in which cynicism toward the Washington establishment ran high—an outsider such as Jimmy Carter proved to be the right candidate for the time. The soft-spoken man from Plains, Georgia, promised to restore integrity to the nation's highest office. "I will never tell a lie to the American people," he said with a distinctive Southern drawl.

Throughout the presidential campaign, Carter and Ford squared off over the key issues of inflation, energy, and unemployment. However, Carter gained fewer points for his knowledge of economic issues than for his personality and sense of morality. He openly declared himself a born-again Christian, and he took pride in his pro–civil rights stance. In addition, Carter had a warm, direct campaign style. He would walk up to a stranger on the street, smile, and stick out his hand. "Hello, I'm Jimmy Carter and I'm running for president," he'd say. "I'd like your vote."

Ford began the 1976 campaign well behind Carter in the polls. Although he tightened the gap by election day, he could not close it. Jimmy Carter won a close election, claiming 40.8 million popular votes to Ford's 39.1 million.

GEORGIA COMES TO WASHINGTON From the very beginning, the new first family brought a down-to-earth style to Washington. Refusing the traditional limousine ride after his inauguration, Carter walked with his wife, Rosalyn, and daughter, Amy, down Pennsylvania Avenue to the White House. After settling into office, Carter stayed in touch with the people by holding Roosevelt-like "fireside chats" on radio and television. He also held "phone-ins" so people could talk directly with their president.

However, Carter failed to employ this same outreach to Congress. Because he had run as an outsider, Carter refused to play the "insider" game of compromise and deal-making. Relying mainly on a team of advisers from Georgia, Carter even alienated himself from congressional members of his own party. Democrats on Capitol Hill often joined Republicans to sink the president's budget proposals, as well as his ambitious legislative agenda, which included major reforms of tax and welfare systems.

Carter's Domestic Agenda

Like Gerald Ford, President Carter focused much of his attention domestically on battling the country's energy and economic crises. While he met with some successes, Carter could not bring the United States out of its economic downswing.

CONFRONTING THE ENERGY CRISIS Carter considered the energy crisis to be the single most important issue facing the nation. A large part of the problem, the president believed, was America's overreliance on imported oil. On April 18, 1977, Carter sat before the nation and in a fireside chat, he urged his fellow Americans to cut their consumption of oil and gas energy.

> **A PERSONAL VOICE**
> The energy crisis has not yet overwhelmed us, but it will if we do not act quickly. It is a problem . . . likely to get progressively worse through the rest of this century. . . . Our decision about energy will test the character of the American people and the ability of the president and the Congress to govern this nation. This difficult effort will be the "moral equivalent of war," except that we will be uniting in our efforts to build and not to destroy.
>
> **PRESIDENT CARTER,** Address to the Nation, quoted in *Keeping Faith*

THINK THROUGH HISTORY
B. Analyzing Causes What factors played a significant role in Carter's election?
B. Answer Carter's personality and his sense of morality, and also his warm, direct campaign style.

This campaign toy exaggerates Jimmy Carter's well-known smile and his occupation as a peanut farmer.

TEACHING OPTIONS

Exploring Themes

Economic Opportunity The economic anxiety that the nation began to feel under Presidents Nixon and Ford grew worse under Jimmy Carter. By 1978, the annual inflation rate had reached 7.6 percent and seemed poised to continue climbing. That year, Carter told the American people how rising inflation could adversely affect economic opportunity: "If inflation gets worse, . . . your purchasing power will continue to decline, . . . Our national productivity will suffer. The value of our dollar will continue to fall in world trade." The inflation rate did indeed get worse. By 1980, it had soared to 13.5 percent.

Teaching Less Proficient Readers

Clarifying As students read pages 962–964, help less proficient readers understand the concepts of inflation and foreign competition by providing them with everyday examples. Define inflation as an increase in prices due to an increase in the supply of money. Have students consider their experiences with inflation, such as the purchasing of gym shoes or compact discs. Next, have them consider closed stores or factories in their community. Tell them this may be an effect of foreign competition, in which some foreign-made goods outsold similar American-made items, driving U.S. companies out of business.

Carter asked Americans to turn down their thermostats to 65 degrees in the day and 55 degrees at night. He proposed a cabinet-level Department of Energy and presented Congress with more than 100 proposals on energy conservation and development.

The battle over the president's energy policy started almost immediately. Representatives from oil- and gas-producing states fiercely resisted some of the proposals. Automobile manufacturers also lobbied against gas-rationing provisions. "It was impossible for me to imagine the bloody legislative battles we would have to win," Carter later wrote.

Out of the battle came the **National Energy Act.** The act placed a tax on gas-guzzling cars, removed price controls on oil and natural gas produced in the United States, and extended tax credits for the development of alternative energy supplies. By 1979, U.S. dependence on foreign oil had eased slightly. Private industry did its part by developing more gas-efficient automobiles and home heating systems. In addition, American citizens helped by lowering their thermostats and reinsulating their homes. A few also took advantage of a tax credit to install solar-heating panels.

THE ECONOMIC CRISIS WORSENS Unfortunately, these energy-saving measures could do little to combat a sudden new economic crisis. In the summer of 1979, renewed violence in the Middle East produced a second major fuel shortage in the United States. To make matters worse, OPEC announced another major price hike. In 1979 inflation soared from 7.6 percent to 11.3 percent.

Faced with increasing pressure to act, Carter attempted an array of measures. He implemented voluntary wage and price freezes to slow inflation. He also tried to reduce the national debt through spending cuts. To stimulate business, Carter deregulated, or lifted government controls from, trucking, railroad, and shipping industries. To reduce the money supply, he convinced the Federal Reserve to raise interest rates.

None of these measures worked. Worse yet, Carter's shotgun approach convinced many people that he had no economic policy at all. "What was consistent about the Carter administration," said economist Robert Samuelson, "was its inability to make a proposal in January that could survive until June." Carter fueled this feeling of uncertainty by delivering his now famous "malaise" speech, in which he complained of a "crisis of confidence" that had struck "at the very heart and soul of our national will." Carter's address prompted many Americans to feel that their president had given up.

By 1980, inflation had climbed to nearly 14 percent, the highest rate since 1947. The standard of living in the United States slipped from first place to fifth

SKILLBUILDER
INTERPRETING CHARTS
Which item more than tripled in cost between 1970 and 1980? How did OPEC's actions throughout the 1970s help cause this sharp price increase?

The Effects of Inflation

1970	1980

Cost of a bicycle
$43.95 $93.99

Gasoline price per gallon
36¢ $1.19

Monthly food costs for family of 4
$42.90 $93.80

Sources: The Value of a Dollar; Statistical Abstract of the United States, 1971, 1976, 1980, 1982–83

SKILLBUILDER
INTERPRETING CHARTS
Which year saw the highest degree of stagflation (inflation plus unemployment)?
Skillbuilder Answer 1980.

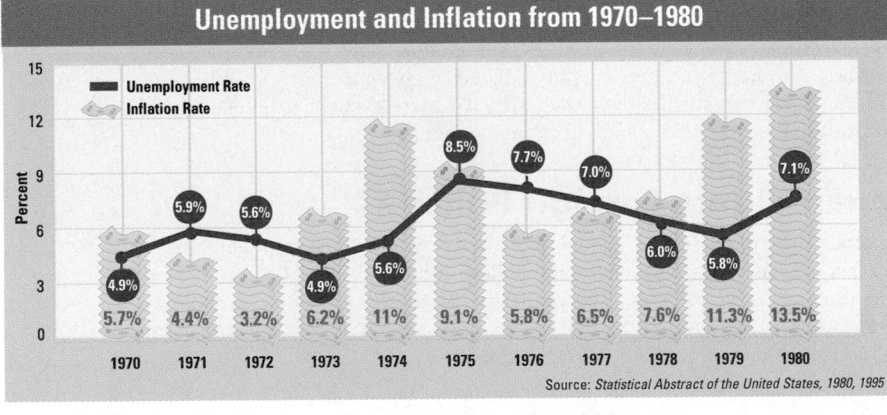

Unemployment and Inflation from 1970–1980

Unemployment Rate
Inflation Rate

Year	1970	1971	1972	1973	1974	1975	1976	1977	1978	1979	1980
Unemployment Rate	4.9%	5.9%	5.6%	4.9%	5.6%	8.5%	7.7%	7.0%	6.0%	5.8%	7.1%
Inflation Rate	5.7%	4.4%	3.2%	6.2%	11%	9.1%	5.8%	6.5%	7.6%	11.3%	13.5%

Source: Statistical Abstract of the United States, 1980, 1995

An Age of Limits **963**

Reading the Chart Tell students that the chart refers to the percentage of working Americans. In other words, in 1950, 60 percent of the nation's workers were employed in the service industry. By 1994, 79 percent of working Americans had jobs in the service sector.

Extension Have students consider their parents' jobs, as well as the jobs of some of their relatives and neighbors. Do they seem related to the service or manufacturing industries?

A Human Rights Foreign Policy

▶ **Discussing Key Ideas**
- Jimmy Carter rejects the philosophy of realpolitik in favor of a foreign policy based on human rights.
- Carter attempts to improve relations with Latin America by agreeing to relinquish U.S. control of the Panama Canal.
- Carter's policies lead to a breakdown in relations with the Soviet Union.

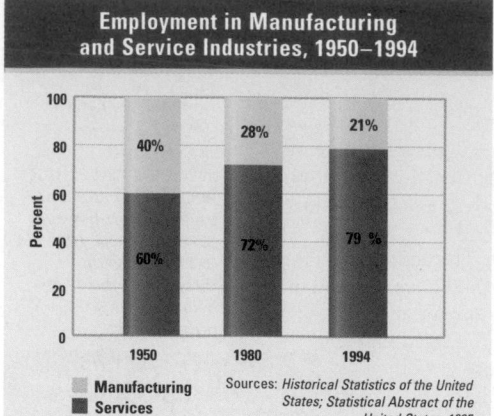

Employment in Manufacturing and Service Industries, 1950–1994

Sources: *Historical Statistics of the United States; Statistical Abstract of the United States, 1995*

■ Manufacturing
■ Services

SKILLBUILDER
INTERPRETING CHARTS
By what percent did the service sector grow between 1950 and 1994?
Skillbuilder Answer
19 percent.

place in the world. Carter's popularity slipped along with it. Polls put his approval rating at a dismal 26 percent, lower than Richard Nixon's lowest figures. The fact that this deep economic downswing—and Carter's inability to solve it—visited the nation during an election year was one of the key factors in lifting Ronald Reagan to the White House.

A CHANGING ECONOMY Many of the economic problems Jimmy Carter struggled with resulted from long-term trends in the economy. Since the 1950s, the rise of automation and foreign competition had reduced the number of manufacturing jobs. At the same time, the service sector of the economy expanded rapidly. This sector includes industries such as communications, transportation, and retail trade. During the 1970s, the shift toward a service-based economy accelerated, spurred on by the development of the tiny microchip, that enabled computers to be cheaply mass-produced.

The rise of the service sector and the decline of manufacturing jobs meant big changes for some American workers. Workers left out of the shrinking pool of manufacturing jobs faced an increasingly complex job market. Many of the higher-paying service jobs required more education or specialized skills than did manufacturing jobs. The lower-skilled service jobs usually did not pay well.

Growing overseas competition during the 1970s caused further change in America's economy. The booming economies of West Germany and countries on the Pacific Rim such as Japan, Taiwan, and Korea cut into many U.S. markets. Many of the nation's primary industries—iron and steel, rubber, clothing, automobiles—had to cut back production, lay off workers, and even close plants.

Especially hard-hit were the automotive industries of the Northeast. Here, high energy costs, foreign competition, and computerized production led companies to eliminate tens of thousands of jobs. As the 1970s drew to a close, a "rust belt" of deteriorating older industries stretched from Detroit to New York. To escape the decay, a number of corporations moved overseas or to Southern and Western states, where production costs—both energy and labor—were lower.

CARTER ADDRESSES CIVIL RIGHTS Toward the end of his administration, Carter took pride in one aspect of his domestic agenda: the advancement of women and minorities. The Carter administration included more African Americans and women than ever before. In 1977, for example, the president appointed former civil rights leader Andrew Young to the post of U.S. ambassador to the United Nations. Young was the first African American to hold that post. To the judicial branch alone, Carter appointed 28 African Americans, 29 women (including 6 African Americans), and 14 Latinos.

However, President Carter fell short of what many civil rights groups had expected in terms of legislation. Critics claimed that Carter—preoccupied with battles over energy and the economy—failed to give civil rights his full attention. Others charged that the president gave more thought to human rights abroad than he did to human rights at home.

A Human Rights Foreign Policy

Jimmy Carter did indeed give much thought to human rights around the world. In fact, he based much of his foreign policy on human rights. Carter rejected the philosophy of realpolitik, the pragmatic policy that called for negotiating with powerful nations despite their behavior. Instead, the president strived for a foreign policy committed to human rights.

THINK THROUGH HISTORY
E. *Analyzing Causes* What factors played a role in America's economic stagnation?
E. Answer The technological revolution and growing overseas competition.

TEACHING OPTIONS

Connecting to Themes

Science and Technology The invention of the microchip, which is about the size of a fingernail, helped revolutionize American society. A microchip consists of tens of thousands of transistors on a single chip. Microchips, which can perform functions that in the past required the use of large computers, were introduced in 1971. Since then, the low cost and small size of microchips have led to their use in video games, digital watches, and microwave ovens. Microchips also have made possible the computerization of, among other things, gasoline pumps, store checkout lines, bank records, and medical instruments.

Making Connections Across Cultures

Desegregation Shortly after being elected president, Jimmy Carter became embroiled in a racial controversy surrounding the church in which he had worshiped nearly all of his life. The Plains Baptist Church did not allow African Americans, a fact that quickly came to light after Carter's presidential victory. Members of the church, including Carter, voted on the issue in an emergency meeting. The vote was 120 to 66 to admit African Americans. Carter, who voted to desegregate the church, stepped outside the old church and announced the decision to a throng of waiting reporters. "I was proud of my church," he declared.

ADVANCING HUMAN RIGHTS Jimmy Carter, like Woodrow Wilson, sought to use moral principles as a guide for U.S. foreign policy. He believed that the United States needed to commit itself to promoting **human rights**—those freedoms and liberties listed in the Declaration of Independence and Bill of Rights—throughout the world.

Putting his principles into practice, President Carter cut off military aid to Argentina and Brazil, countries that had good relations with the United States, but which had imprisoned or tortured thousands of their own citizens. Carter followed up this action by establishing a Bureau of Human Rights in the State Department. "Human rights had become the central theme of our foreign policy in the minds of the press and public," Carter recalled. "It seemed that a spark had been ignited, and I had no inclination to douse the growing flames."

But as time went on, that flame cooled. Although many people favored Carter's idealism, supporters of the Cold War felt that the president's policy undercut allies such as Nicaragua, a dictatorial but anti-Communist country. Others argued that by supporting dictators in South Korea and the Philippines, Carter was acting inconsistently. In 1977, Carter's policies drew further criticism when his administration announced that it planned to give up ownership of the Panama Canal.

YIELDING THE PANAMA CANAL Since 1914, when the United States obtained full ownership of the Panama Canal, Panamanians had resented having their nation split in half by a foreign power. Shortly after 1964, President Lyndon Johnson began negotiations with the Panamanians to help ease tensions. Negotiations continued off and on into the Carter administration.

In 1977, the nations finally agreed to two treaties, one of which promised to turn over control of the Panama Canal to Panama on December 31, 1999. The U.S. Senate, which had to ratify each treaty, passed the treaties by a vote of 68 to 32—one more vote than the required two-thirds. Public approval was just as split. According to a Gallup poll, 45 percent of Americans favored the pacts, while 42 percent opposed them. Despite their cool reception by the American public, the treaties did bring about a warmer relationship between the United States and Latin America.

THE COLLAPSE OF DÉTENTE When Jimmy Carter took office, détente—the relaxation of tensions between the world's superpowers—had reached a high point. Beginning with President Nixon and continuing with President Ford, the U.S. had worked to ease relations with the Communist superpowers of China and the Soviet Union.

However, Carter's firm insistence on human rights led to a breakdown in relations with the Soviet Union. President Carter's dismay over the Soviet Union's treatment of dissidents, or opponents of the government's policies, delayed a second round of SALT negotiations. President Carter and Soviet premier Leonid Brezhnev finally met in June of 1979 in Vienna, Austria, where they signed an agreement known as SALT II. Although the agreement did not reduce armaments, it did provide for limits on the number of strategic weapons and nuclear-missile launchers that each side could produce.

The SALT II agreement, however, met sharp opposition in the Senate. Critics argued that it would put the United States at a military disadvantage. Then, in December 1979, the Soviets invaded the neighboring country of Afghanistan. When President Carter heard of the invasion, he activated the seldom-used White House–Kremlin hot line and protested to Brezhnev that the action was a "gross interference in

ON THE WORLD STAGE

THE SOVIET–AFGHANISTAN WAR

Afghanistan, an Islamic country along the southern border of the Soviet Union, had had a pro-Moscow government for many years. However, the country had a strong Muslim rebel group intent on overthrowing the government.

Fearing that a rebel victory in Afghanistan might embolden the many Muslims living under Soviet rule, the Soviet Union sent troops to Afghanistan in late 1979 to try to crush the Muslim rebels.

While the Soviets had superior weaponry, the rebels fought the Soviets to a stalemate using guerrilla tactics and a keen knowledge of the country's mountainous terrain.

In 1988, after suffering thousands of casualties, the Soviets began pulling out. Fighting within the country continued, and in 1992, the rebels overthrew the government. Some observers have labeled Afghanistan as the Soviet Union's "Vietnam."

An Age of Limits **965**

Middle East, 1978–1982

Reading the Map Point out to students what the inset map depicts. *A close-up look at Israel and its neighboring countries.* Also, make sure students see where the inset area sits on the larger map.

Extension Ask students to look at the inset map and discuss why there might be so much tension between Israelis and the Palestinians living in the West Bank and Gaza Strip. *Possible Responses: The Israelis are basically living among the Palestinians whom they are controlling.*

Middle East, 1978–1982

Israel
Israeli-occupied land
Israeli conquests returned to Egypt, 1979–1982
Capital city
OPEC member

Skillbuilder Answer
Location: Iran, Iraq, Saudi Arabia, Algeria, Qatar, Kuwait, United Arab Emirates and Libya.

GEOGRAPHY SKILLBUILDER LOCATION *What OPEC countries are located on the map?*

OBJECTIVE
⑤ INSTRUCT

Triumph and Crisis in the Middle East

▶ **Discussing Key Ideas**
- President Carter helps forge a peace between the rival nations of Israel and Egypt.
- Rebels in Iran overthrow their government and take 52 Americans hostage.
- The Carter administration spends more than a year negotiating for the hostages' release.

GEOGRAPHY TRANSPARENCIES
G32, OPEC (Organization of Petroleum Exporting Countries)

IN-DEPTH RESOURCES: UNIT 9
Geography Application: Oil Consumption in the 1970s, p. 6

the internal affairs of Afghanistan." As a result of the invasion, Carter refused to fight for the SALT II agreement and the treaty died.

Triumph and Crisis in the Middle East

Through long gasoline lines and high energy costs, Americans became all too aware of the troubles in the Middle East. Here, in this area of ethnic, religious, and economic conflict, Jimmy Carter achieved one of his greatest diplomatic triumphs—and suffered his most tragic defeat.

THE CAMP DAVID ACCORDS Jimmy Carter enjoyed a shining moment captured in a historic handshake between long-time enemies Egyptian president Anwar el-Sadat and Israeli prime minister Menachem Begin. Through negotiation and arm-twisting, Carter helped forge a peace between the two nations that marked the first major break in Middle Eastern hostilities since the creation of Israel in 1948.

A jubilant President Carter shakes hands with President Anwar Sadat of Egypt *(left)* and Prime Minister Menachem Begin of Israel *(right)* after the two Middle East leaders reached a peace agreement.

In 1974, Henry Kissinger's shuttle diplomacy had helped end the Yom Kippur War between Egypt and Israel. At that time, Sadat and Begin had begun discussing an overall peace between the two nations. In the summer of 1978, Carter seized on the peace initiative. When the peace talks stalled, Carter invited Sadat and Begin to Camp David, the presidential retreat in Maryland.

After 13 days of intense negotiations, the three leaders reached two agreements known as the **Camp David Accords.** The first agreement provided for a five-year transition period during which Israel and Jordan would work out the issue of self-rule for the Palestinians, Arabs living on the West Bank and Gaza Strip—areas captured by Israel during earlier wars. The second agreement was aimed specifically at end-

966 CHAPTER 32

TEACHING OPTIONS

Making Connections Across Time

Middle East Peace In 1993, peace in the Middle East took a giant step forward when Israel and the Palestinians signed a historic agreement giving the Palestinians self-rule in the Israeli-occupied lands where they live. As a result of the agreement, the Palestinians now govern Israel's West Bank and Gaza Strip. For years, Israel and the Palestine Liberation Organization had each claimed ownership of the lands and had waged bloody battles for their control. In 1997, the agreement was still being implemented, as the Israeli pullout from the West Bank region remained slow and painstaking.

Teaching Gifted and Talented Students

Exploring the Hostage Crisis Hamilton Jordan was an adviser to President Carter and later his Chief of Staff. His book, *Crisis, The Last Year of the Carter Presidency,* presents an inside look at the Carter administration's handling of events such as the Soviet invasion of Afghanistan and the hostage crisis in Iran. Have interested students read excerpts from the book that deal with the hostage crisis. Students then should write a brief report on what new insights they learned about the handling of the hostage crisis. In addition, have students evaluate Carter's handling of the hostage crisis using evidence to support their opinion. What, if anything, would they have done differently?

ing hostilities between Israel and Egypt. During a White House ceremony in March of 1979, Sadat and Begin signed a detailed peace treaty based on the accords. Under the treaty, Israel agreed to withdraw from the Sinai Peninsula, which it had seized from Egypt during the Six-Day War in 1967. In exchange, Egypt became the first Arab nation to recognize Israel's existence as a nation.

The treaty left many issues unresolved. For example, the document said little about the independence claims of Palestinians. Joking at the hard work ahead, Carter wrote playfully in his diary, "I resolved to do everything possible to get out of the negotiating business." Little did the president know that his next Middle East negotiation would be his most painful.

THE IRAN HOSTAGE CRISIS Since the 1950s, the United States had provided political and military assistance to the government of the shah of Iran. The U.S. wanted an ally against communism and access to Iran's oil. By 1979, however, the shah's regime was in deep trouble. Many Iranians resented the regime's widespread corruption and dictatorial tactics. The shah's secret police, for example, tortured thousands of prisoners and executed many others without trial.

In January 1979, revolution broke out. Muslim religious leader **Ayatollah Ruhollah Khomeini** led the rebels in overthrowing the shah and establishing a religious state based on strict obedience to the Qur'an, the sacred book of Islam. Carter had supported the shah until the very end. In October of 1979, one month after the Camp David Accords, the president allowed the shah to enter the United States for cancer treatment.

The act infuriated the revolutionaries of Iran. On November 4, 1979, armed students seized the U.S. embassy in Tehran and took 52 Americans hostage. The militants demanded the return of the shah in return for the release of the hostages.

Carter refused, and a painful year-long standoff followed. The president banned all trade with Iran and eventually severed diplomatic relations with the nation. Through it all, the United States continued quiet but intense efforts to free the hostages. Those efforts finally paid off in late 1980. However, because of last-minute delays and perhaps deliberate stalling by the Iranians, the hostages were not released until January 20, 1981, shortly after the new president, Ronald Reagan, took the oath of office.

Despite the hostages' release after 444 days in captivity, the crisis in Iran seemed to underscore the limits that Americans faced during the 1970s. Americans also realized during the 1970s that there were limits to the nation's environmental resources. This realization prompted both citizens and the government to actively address environmental concerns.

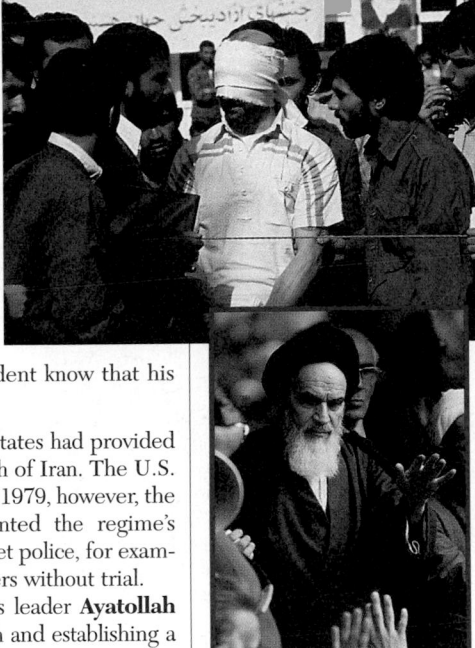

U.S. hostages were blindfolded and paraded through the streets of Tehran *(top)*. Iran's ruler, Ayatollah Ruhollah Khomeini *(above)*, supported the taking of the hostages.

Section ❸ Assessment

1. TERMS & NAMES
• Gerald R. Ford
• Jimmy Carter
• National Energy Act
• human rights
• Camp David Accords
• Ayatollah Ruhollah Khomeini

2. SEQUENCING HISTORY
Create a time line of the major events of the Ford and Carter administrations, using a form such as the one below.

Which two events do you think were the most important? Why?

3. COMPARING AND CONTRASTING How were the actions taken by Presidents Ford and Carter to address the country's economic downturn similar? How did they differ?

THINK ABOUT
• Ford's "Whip Inflation Now" policy
• Carter's "moral equivalent of a war" speech
• Carter's legislative agenda

4. FORMING OPINIONS Do you agree with President Carter that human rights concerns should steer U.S. foreign policy? Why or why not?

THINK ABOUT
• the responsibility of promoting human rights
• the loss of certain ally countries
• the collapse of détente with the Soviet Union

An Age of Limits **967**

ANSWERS

1. TERMS & NAMES
Gerald R. Ford, p. 960
Jimmy Carter, p. 961
National Energy Act, p. 963
human rights, p. 965
Camp David Accords, p. 966
Ayatollah Ruhollah Khomeini, p. 967

2. SEQUENCING HISTORY
Possible Answers:
Sept. 8, 1974: Ford pardons Nixon.
1975: Helsinki Accords signed.
1977: U.S. and Panama sign treaty.
March 1979: Sadat and Begin sign peace treaty.
Dec. 1979: Soviets invade Afghanistan.
Nov. 4, 1979: Iranians seize U.S. hostages.
1980: 14 percent inflation.

3. COMPARING AND CONTRASTING
Both emphasized the importance of energy conservation; both had trouble working with Congress; and both were largely unsuccessful. Ford put more emphasis on voluntary citizen action while Carter emphasized government action.

4. FORMING OPINIONS
Students may agree with President Carter and argue that the United States has a duty to stand up for human rights throughout the world. Others may disagree and contend that a strict foreign policy of any kind drives away allies and that the U.S. supported some countries with poor human rights records.

TERMS & NAMES
- Rachel Carson
- Earth Day
- environmentalist
- Environmental Protection Agency
- Three Mile Island

④ Environmental Activism

OBJECTIVES

① To summarize the origins of the environmental movement.

② To identify key environmental issues in the 1970s.

③ To explain the goals of the continuing environmental movement.

CRITICAL THINKING

- Recognizing effects, pp. 969, 970
- Forming opinions, pp. 971, 973
- Identifying problems, p. 973
- Summarizing, p. 973
- Analyzing causes, p. 973

LEARN ABOUT America's efforts during the 1970s to address its environmental problems
TO UNDERSTAND how the nation attempted to strike a balance between environmental concerns and continued industrial growth.

ONE AMERICAN'S STORY

In 1972, Lois Gibbs and her family moved to Niagara Falls, New York, which Gibbs described as a "typical American small town." However, running underneath this quiet town was a disaster in the making. For more than 50 years, the Love Canal, a channel connecting the lower and upper Niagara River, had served as a dumping site for toxic wastes. In 1953, bulldozers filled in the canal. On top of the new ground, developers built rows of houses and an elementary school.

From the day the school opened, parents complained of nauseous odors and black sludge near the grounds. When Lois Gibbs's son fell sick, she decided to investigate the school's problems. Frustrated at nearly every turn, Gibbs refused to give up. She eventually uncovered the existence of the toxic waste site and mobilized the community to demand government action. In 1980, President Jimmy Carter authorized funds for many of Niagara Falls's families to move to safety. Years later, Lois Gibbs wrote a book detailing her efforts.

A PERSONAL VOICE

I want to tell you our story—my story—because I believe that ordinary citizens —using the tools of dignity, self-respect, common sense, and perseverance— can influence solutions to important problems in our society. . . . In solving any difficult problem, you have to be prepared to fight long and hard, sometimes at great personal cost; but it can be done. It must be done if we are to survive as a democratic society—indeed, if we are to survive at all.

LOIS GIBBS, *Love Canal: My Story*

Lois Gibbs

While her courage and determination were unique, Lois Gibbs's concerns about environmental hazards were shared by many Americans in the late 1970s. Through the Arab oil embargo and the OPEC price increases, Americans learned that their natural resources were not limitless. Many also realized that they also could no longer take the environment for granted. Throughout the 1970s, Americans—from the grass roots organizations to the government—began a concerted effort to address the nation's environmental concerns.

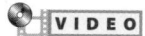 **VIDEO** **POISONED PLAYGROUND** *Lois Gibbs and the Crisis at Love Canal*

FOCUS & MOTIVATE

▶ *Starting with the Student* Watch the video "Poisoned Playground" to find out how one American fought for a safer environment in her town.

- Using the *Teacher's Resource Book* as a guide, hold a class discussion, explore the environmental issues surrounding the crisis at Love Canal, and engage in extension activities using key primary sources.

 AMERICAN STORIES VIDEO SERIES
"Poisoned Playground"
Videocassette: Volume 4

Videodisc: Disc 3, Side B, Chapter 4

IN-DEPTH RESOURCES: UNIT 9
Primary Source: from *Love Canal: My Story* by Lois Gibbs, p. 10

The Roots of Environmentalism

This button was used to promote Earth Day.

968 CHAPTER 32

While many Americans began mobilizing in the 1970s to protect the environment, the realization that the growth of cities and industrial development were damaging the nation's natural resources actually began a decade earlier. In particular, a shocking book awakened America's concerns about the environment and helped lay the groundwork for the activism of the 1970s.

RACHEL CARSON AND *SILENT SPRING* In 1962, **Rachel Carson,** a marine biologist, published a book entitled *Silent Spring*. In it, she attacked the growing use of pesticides, which are chemicals used to kill insects and rodents. Many owners of large farms sprayed a variety of pesticides on their crops to keep hungry insects from devouring their harvest. Carson argued that pesticides poisoned the very food they were intended to protect, and as a result killed many birds and fish.

In her book, Carson warned that America faced a "silent spring," in which birds killed off by pesticides no longer filled the air with songs. "It was a spring

OBJECTIVE
① INSTRUCT

The Roots of Environmentalism

▶ *Discussing Key Ideas*
- Rachel Carson's *Silent Spring* prompts the nation

(continued on next page)

SECTION 4 RESOURCES

 PRINT RESOURCES

IN-DEPTH RESOURCES: UNIT 9
Guided Reading, p. 4
Skillbuilder Practice: Analyzing Assumptions, p. 5
Primary Sources: from *Love Canal: My Story* by Lois Gibbs, p. 10; from *Silent Spring* by Rachel Carson, p. 11

ACCESS FOR STUDENTS ACQUIRING ENGLISH
Guided Reading (Spanish), p. 312
Skillbuilder Practice: Analyzing Assumptions (Spanish), p. 313

FORMAL ASSESSMENT
Section Quiz, p. 390

ALTERNATIVE ASSESSMENT BOOK
See forms for supporting and scoring alternative activities.

TECHNOLOGY RESOURCES

CD-ROM *Our Times*
Grolier Multimedia Encyclopedia
Electronic Library of Primary Sources

VIDEO *American Stories* video series
American Portfolio: A Videodisc for U.S. History
user's guide, p. 255

INTERNET McDougal Littell Learning On-Line
http://www.mcdougallittell.com

without voices," she wrote. "On the mornings that had once throbbed with the dawn chorus of robins, catbirds, doves, jays, wrens and scores of other bird voices there was now no sound; only silence lay over the fields and woods and marsh." Carson argued that one pesticide in particular, DDT, was a threat even to humans. She contended that DDT, which did not dissolve in water, made its way through the entire food chain—from plants, animals, and ultimately to human beings.

Within six months of its publication, *Silent Spring* sold nearly half a million copies. It also prompted an immediate counterattack from many chemical companies, which attacked the book as inaccurate and threatened legal action against Carson. However, for a majority of Americans, Carson's book awakened them to the danger that human activity posed to the natural environment. "There's no doubt about the impact of *Silent Spring*; it's a real shocker," declared a reviewer of the book. People throughout the country wrote to their representative in Congress and the president demanding an investigation into the nation's pesticide use. Shortly after the book's publication, President Kennedy established an advisory committee to investigate the situation.

With Rachel Carson's prodding, the nation slowly began to focus more on environmental issues. In 1963, Congress passed the Clean Air Act, which regulated automotive and industrial emissions. While Carson would not live to see the U.S. government outlaw DDT in 1972, her work helped many Americans realize that their everyday behavior as well as the nation's industrial growth had a damaging effect on the environment.

A. Answer It heightened America's awareness to the fact that many of its activities were potentially harmful to the environment.

THINK THROUGH HISTORY
A. Recognizing Effects What effects did Rachel Carson's book have on the nation as a whole?

Environmental Concerns in the 1970s

Throughout the 1970s, the administrations of Richard Nixon and Jimmy Carter, along with numerous grassroots organizations, confronted such environmental issues as pollution, conservation, and the growth of nuclear energy.

Demonstrators gather in New York City's Central Park for the first Earth Day in 1970.

THE FIRST EARTH DAY The United States ushered in the 1970s—a decade in which it would actively address its environmental issues—fittingly enough with the first **Earth Day** celebration. In late 1969, Wisconsin's Senator Gaylord Nelson had suggested that Americans set aside April 22, 1970, as a day of serious discussion of environmental problems. On that day in 1970, nearly every community in the nation and more than 10,000 schools and 2,000 colleges hosted some type of environmental awareness activity. The organizers of the first Earth Day, many of whom were antiwar and civil rights activists, spotlighted such problems as pollution, the growth of toxic waste, and the earth's dwindling resources.

The Earth Day celebration has endured. Each year on April 22, millions of people around the world gather to heighten public awareness of environmental problems.

THE GOVERNMENT TAKES ACTION President Nixon was not considered an **environmentalist,** or someone who takes an active role in advocating measures to protect the environment. However, Nixon recognized the nation's growing concern about the environment. In his 1970 State of the Union address he declared, "The great

RACHEL CARSON
1907–1964
The marine biologist Rachel Carson was born far from the sea in the small town of Springdale, Pennsylvania. She grew up with a brother and sister in a two-story wooden house that had no plumbing, no furnace, and no electricity.

Carson was a sickly child who often had to remain at home, where her mother tutored her. Throughout her youth and into her college years, Rachel was a studious, but quiet and aloof person. "She just wasn't social," remembered a classmate. "Being poor had some bearing on that. She didn't have the clothes or the extra things a girl needed at college then."

Carson entered college intent on becoming a writer. During her sophomore year, she took a biology class to fulfill her science requirement. She quickly fell in love with the study of nature, and the next year, she switched her major from English to science.

(continued from page 968)
to begin addressing environmental issues.

IN-DEPTH RESOURCES: UNIT 9
Guided Reading, p. 4
ACCESS FOR STUDENTS ACQUIRING ENGLISH
Guided Reading (Spanish), p. 312

KEY PLAYER
Rachel Carson
Critical Thinking: Comparing and Contrasting Some historians have compared *Silent Spring* to Harriet Beecher Stowe's *Uncle Tom's Cabin,* which awoke much of the nation to the horrors of slavery with its publication in 1852. Explore with students the effects of each book on society. Do students agree with the analogy? Why or why not?

IN-DEPTH RESOURCES: UNIT 9
Primary Source: from *Silent Spring* by Rachel Carson, p. 11

 GROLIER MULTIMEDIA ENCYCLOPEDIA
interview with Rachel Carson

OBJECTIVE
② **INSTRUCT**

Environmental Concerns in the 1970s

▶ *Discussing Key Ideas*
• From the government to grass-roots groups, Americans in the 1970s begin to more aggressively address environmental problems.
• The debate over nuclear energy intensifies after an accident at the Three Mile Island nuclear power plant.

An Age of Limits **969**

Exploring Themes

Science and Technology Technology, which some people consider a curse, has recently begun to play a key role in protecting the environment. America's scientific know-how—which spurred the creation of booming industries and the invention of the automobile—has also led to the development of such things as cleaner burning fuel and environmentally safe factory equipment. Science and technology now play the dual role of aiding the country's industrial and economic growth and helping in the fight to better protect our environment from the negative effects of such growth and progress.

Making Global Connections

Greenpeace Possibly the best known international environmental organization is Greenpeace. Founded in 1969 by a group of Canadian environmentalists, Greenpeace works to call attention to the world's environmental hazards. One reason the group is well known is its confrontational style. Greenpeace members often attempt to interfere with activities they consider to be harmful to the environment. The group's methods have sometimes drawn the wrath of governments. In 1985, France sunk a Greenpeace boat to prevent it from sailing into waters where the French were testing nuclear weapons.

Teacher's Edition **969**

▶ **Starting with the Student**

• Ask students to consider places where they have endured air pollution. Was it alongside a passing bus? In an area of town with numerous factories?

• How did the pollution affect them? Did the odor offend them? Did the smoke make them cough?

• Ask students what they think eventually happens to air pollution.

▶ **Discussing Key Ideas**

• There are two main types of waste matter that pollute the air. One type is particles of liquid or solid matter, such as lead. The other is gases, such as carbon monoxide.

• The biggest sources of air pollution are fuel combustion in cars, airplanes, homes, and factories.

• California—whose high population density and heavy traffic have created some of the most polluted air in the country—has led the way in passing laws to protect the environment.

 ELECTRONIC LIBRARY OF PRIMARY SOURCES
"Principles of Environmental Justice" by People of Color Environmental Leadership

---

question of the seventies is: Shall we surrender to our surroundings or shall we make our peace with nature and begin to make reparations for the damage we have done to our air, to our land and to our water?"

President Nixon set out on a course that led to the passage of several landmark measures to protect the environment. In 1970, he consolidated 15 existing federal pollution programs into the **Environmental Protection Agency** (EPA). The new agency took on the power to set and enforce pollution standards, to conduct environmental research, and to assist state and local governments in pollution control. The EPA remains the federal government's main overseer of environmental issues to this day.

Nixon also signed a new Clean Air Act in 1970. The act gave the nations' industries five years to meet new pollution standards, including a mandate that automakers reduce the tailpipe emissions in their new cars by 90 percent. When automakers complained that they would be unable to meet this goal by 1975, the EPA extended the deadline to the 1980s. Automakers eventually met the standard by introducing the catalytic converter (which changes tailpipe pollutants into less harmful substances). The use of catalytic converters also forced consumers to use gasoline free of the additive lead, a harmful pollutant.

Following the 1970 Clean Air Act, Congress passed laws that limited pesticide use, protected endangered species, and curbed strip mining—the practice

B. Answer The emissions put out by cars decreased by 90 percent between 1970 and 1980.

THINK THROUGH HISTORY
B. Recognizing Effects What was one eventual result of the Clean Air Act?

NOW & THEN

Air Pollution in California

The term *air pollution* often makes people think of brown smog suffocating a city like a thick woolen blanket, but not all air pollution is so dramatically visible. Two types of waste matter pollute the air. One is particulates—particles of liquid or solid matter, such as lead. The other is gases such as carbon monoxide, sulfur oxides, and nitrogen oxides. Nitrogen oxides react with other gases and sunlight to form ozone, a pollutant that causes respiratory problems.

The biggest sources of air pollution are fuel combustion in cars, airplanes, homes, factories, and power plants and the byproducts of industrial processes such as smelting ore and refining oil. Certain weather conditions can cause these pollutants to accumulate over cities in dangerous levels or to become visible as smog.

Southern California, because of its high population density and heavy traffic, has long had some of the most polluted air in the country. To counteract this, the state of California has been a pioneer in passing laws to protect the environment.

1974

Los Angeles has had serious problems with air pollution since the 1950s. The federal government's Clean Air Acts of 1965 and 1970 sought to help people in cities like Los Angeles by establishing stricter emission standards for automobiles and by requiring factories to reduce their sulfur oxide emissions. In addition, since 1970 California has had the strictest motor-vehicle emissions standards in the nation.

Environmental Progress in Los Angeles Region

Ozone-Alert Episodes

Year	Number of Days
1977	121
1986	80
1996	7

Air Pollution Reduction, 1976–1990

Nitrogen Oxides: −27.5%
Hydrocarbons (nonmethane): −48%
Carbon Monoxide: −32%

Source: California Air Resources Board

Southern California has experienced a steady improvement in air quality since 1976. Since that time, most U.S. cars have been equipped with catalytic converters, which greatly reduce the harmful emissions of individual automobiles.

TEACHING OPTION

Skillbuilder Mini-Lesson: Analyzing Assumptions

Explaining the Skill People and governments make decisions and take actions based on many things, including their assumptions, or beliefs that they take for granted. Examining the background and philosophy of a person or government can help historians understand the assumptions that lie behind historical actions.

Applying the Skill: Environmental Protection Refer students to the three paragraphs beginning on this page with "President Nixon set out . . .". Then ask them to analyze the assumptions behind the following actions:

1. Creation of the Environmental Protection Agency. *Government has a role in protecting the environment.*
2. Passage of the Clean Air Act of 1970. *Industries must take responsibility for addressing air pollution.*
3. Conservative complaints that new environmental laws burden business too much. *Good business is more important than a better environment.*
4. Liberal complaints that environmental laws do not go far enough. *Government should do whatever is necessary to ensure a clean environment.*

IN-DEPTH RESOURCES: UNIT 9
Skillbuilder Practice: Analyzing Assumptions, p. 5

of mining for ore and coal by digging gaping holes in the land. While it made significant advances in environmental protection, the Nixon administration failed to fully satisfy the conservative and liberal elements of society. Conservatives complained that the new environmental laws placed too great a burden on business, while liberals contended that the new legislation did not go far enough.

BALANCING PROGRESS AND CONSERVATION IN ALASKA During the 1970s, the Federal government took steps to ensure the continued well-being of the nation's largest and one of its most ecologically sensitive states. In 1968, the Atlantic Richfield Company announced the discovery of a gigantic oil field along Alaska's Arctic coast. In 1974, construction began on a pipeline to carry the oil 800 miles to the ice-free ports of the state's southern coast. The discovery of oil and the subsequent construction of a massive system to transport it created many new jobs and greatly increased state revenues.

However, the influx of new development also raised concerns about Alaska's wildlife environment, as well as the rights of its native peoples. In 1971, the Nixon administration signed the Alaska Native Claims Settlement Act, which designated millions of acres of land for the state's native tribes for conservation and tribal-rights purposes. In 1978, President Carter enhanced this conservation effort by setting aside an additional 56 million acres in Alaska as national monuments. In 1980, Congress added another 104 million acres to the state's protected conservation areas.

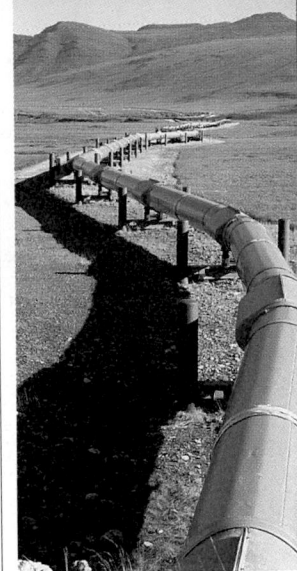

The Alaskan Pipeline stretches across hundreds of miles of tundra. Construction of the pipeline was completed in 1977 at a cost of $8 billion. In 1980, the high revenues from the oil allowed Alaska to abolish state income taxes for its residents.

THE DEBATE OVER NUCLEAR ENERGY As the 1970s came to a close, Americans became acutely aware of the dangers that nuclear energy posed to both humans and the environment. Since the 1950s, nuclear power advocates had argued that nuclear energy was the energy of the future. It was cheap, plentiful, and, they argued, environmentally safe. Nuclear energy proponents pointed to years of safe operation at nuclear plants and called for larger and more powerful plants to meet the nation's growing energy needs. During the 1970s, as America realized the drawbacks to its heavy dependence on foreign oil for energy, nuclear power seemed an attractive alternative.

However, opponents of nuclear energy warned against the industry's growth. They contended that nuclear energy was potentially dangerous to the environment, as well as to human beings. The construction of more nuclear power plants, they argued, increased the likelihood of accidents, which could lead to the accidental release of deadly radiation into the air.

THREE MILE ISLAND In the early hours of March 28, 1979, the concerns of nuclear energy opponents appeared to come true. That morning, one of the nuclear reactors at a plant on **Three Mile Island** near Harrisburg, Pennsylvania, malfunctioned. The reactor overheated after its cooling system failed, and fear quickly arose that

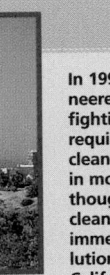
INTERACT WITH HISTORY

1. **FORMING OPINIONS** In your opinion, should all states adopt the California law requiring the use of cleaner-burning gasoline? Explain your answer by citing both the costs and benefits of adopting such legislation.

   SEE SKILLBUILDER HANDBOOK, PAGE 1049.

2. **RESEARCHING** Research another environmental problem, such as water pollution, indoor air pollution, toxic waste disposal, or global warming. Create a chart showing measures that have been taken to deal with the problem and whether the problem has improved or worsened. Present your chart to the class.

 For more about environmentalism, click on *Social Studies* at http://www.mcdougallittell.com

---

MORE ABOUT . . .
Air Pollution

Some of the air pollution from cars and factories eventually returns to earth in the form of acid rain. Acid rain is a term for snow or rain that is polluted by certain chemical compounds in air pollution. Acid rain forms when water vapors in the clouds react with such acids as sulfuric acid and nitric acid. Acid rain harms lakes, rivers, and streams, killing fish and other aquatic life. Scientists believe it also damages forests and soil, as well as buildings and bridges.

OUR TIMES
Essay on 1970s and environmentalism by Stephen Jay Gould

MORE ABOUT . . .
Nuclear Energy

One issue still concerns many people about nuclear energy: how to dispose of the radioactive waste created in producing nuclear energy. In 1995, the nation's 109 nuclear power plants were continuing to store their nuclear waste on site. However, observers believe that nearly one-third of the plants will run out of storage room before the end of the century. The government is searching for a permanent site to dump dangerous waste but does not expect to have a permanent burial site ready until 2010 at the earliest. One plan calls for burying the waste deep beneath the Yucca Mountains in southern Nevada about 100 miles northwest of Las Vegas.

Nuclear Accidents

The world's worst nuclear reactor accident occurred on April 26, 1986, at the Chernobyl nuclear power plant in Ukraine, which was then part of the Soviet Union. "What happened was very simple," said a plant worker. "There was an explosion. . . . Fifteen seconds later there was a sudden shock, and a few seconds later a stronger shock." The blast released large amounts of radiation into the air. Soviet officials reported that 31 people died immediately and more than 200 others were hospitalized. However, the accident's legacy lives on in increased cancer rates and birth defects in the region. The Chernobyl plant continues to operate, but the surrounding city—which remains enveloped in low levels of radiation—has become a ghost town. The city, which once held 50,000 residents, now is home to only about 6,000 plant workers and safety technicians.

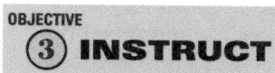

③ INSTRUCT

A Continuing Movement

▶ *Discussing Key Ideas*
- Americans continue to show great concern for the nation's environmental issues.
- As the end of the 20th century nears, the United States works to strike a balance between economic progress and conservation.

radiation might escape and spread over the region. Two days later, low-level radiation actually did escape from the crippled reactor. Pennsylvania's governor ordered schools in the area closed. Officials evacuated some residents, while others fled on their own. One homemaker who lived near the plant recalled her desperate attempt to find safety.

A PERSONAL VOICE
On Friday, a very frightening thing occurred in our area. A state policeman went door-to-door telling residents to stay indoors, close all windows, and turn all air conditioners off. I was alone, as were many other homemakers, and my thoughts were focused on how long I would remain a prisoner in my own home. . . . Suddenly, I was scared, real scared. I decided to get out of there, while I could. I ran to the car not knowing if I should breathe the air or not, and I threw the suitcases in the trunk and was on my way within one hour. If anything dreadful happened, I thought that I'd at least be with my girls. Although it was very hot in the car, I didn't trust myself to turn the air conditioner on. It felt good as my tense muscles relaxed the farther I drove.

AN ANONYMOUS HOMEMAKER, quoted in *Accident at Three Mile Island: The Human Dimensions*

In all, more than 100,000 residents were evacuated from the surrounding area. On April 9, the Nuclear Regulatory Commission, the federal agency that monitors the nuclear power industry, announced that the immediate danger was over. President Carter inspected the site to help assure the public that the reactor was safe again. An investigation into the incident revealed that plant maintenance personnel had not been properly trained and that certain safety precautions at the plant were lax.

The events at Three Mile Island refueled the debate over nuclear power. Supporters of nuclear power pointed out that no one had been killed or seriously injured. Opponents countered by saying that chance alone had averted a tragedy. They demanded that the government call a halt to the construction of new power plants and gradually shut down existing nuclear facilities.

While the government did not do away with nuclear power, federal officials did recognize nuclear energy's potential danger to both humans and the environment. As a result of Three Mile Island, the Nuclear Regulatory Commission strengthened its safety standards and improved its inspection procedures. By 1988, at least 17 new nuclear power plants had opened in the United States, and none had suffered a breakdown.

(below), Opponents of nuclear energy wore buttons such as this; *(bottom),* in Pennsylvania in March 1979, a serious accident occurred at the nuclear energy plant at Three Mile Island.

TEACHING OPTION

Cooperative Activity: Debating the Use of Nuclear Energy

Task: Student groups will debate the growing use of nuclear energy in the United States.

Purpose: To understand the arguments for and against the use of nuclear energy.

Activity: After choosing a position through a lottery, groups of three or four students will research the arguments either for or against the use of nuclear power. In researching their position, groups should consider such issues as the safety of nuclear power, the difference between nuclear power and

other power sources, and public opinion about nuclear power. In researching its position, each group should also examine the state of nuclear energy in the United States today, including the current state of nuclear power in their county or state. Groups holding positions for and against the growth of nuclear energy will debate each other.

ALTERNATIVE ASSESSMENT BOOK
Standards for Evaluating a Cooperative Activity

A Continuing Movement

Although the environmental movement of the 1970s gained popular support, opponents to the movement also made their voices heard. In Tennessee, for example, where a federal dam project was halted because it threatened a certain species of fish, local developers took out ads asking residents to "tell the government that the size of your wallet is more important than some two-inch-long minnow." When confronted with environmental concerns, one unemployed steelworker spoke for others when he remarked, "Why worry about the long run, when you're out of work right now." The environmental movement that blossomed in the 1970s became in the 1980s and 1990s a struggle to balance environmental concerns with jobs and progress.

As you will read in the next chapter, President Ronald Reagan's policy of deregulation, or freeing businesses and corporations from restrictive regulations—created new challenges for the environmental movement during the 1980s. However, in the years since the first Earth Day, environmental issues have gained increasing attention and support. Environmentalists have continued to win battles on the local level, including the blocking of roads, airports, and other projects that they claimed would be ecologically dangerous.

In the 1990s, Americans began addressing new environmental problems. Scientists warned that industrial pollutants were depleting the earth's ozone layer, which protects the globe from the sun's most dangerous rays. In addition, some studies showed that the continued burning of fossil fuels (such as oil and coal) was contributing to a condition known as global warming, or a general rise in the earth's temperature.

One sociologist noted that the energy crisis and the environmental movement of the seventies "forced us all to accept a sense of our limits . . . to seek prosperity through conservation rather than growth." Today, America continues to seek prosperity, not by forsaking growth for conservation, but by trying to strike a workable balance between the two.

THINK THROUGH HISTORY
C. Identifying Problems What was a major point of opposition to the environmental movement?

C. Answer That the environmental initiatives sometimes cost people jobs.

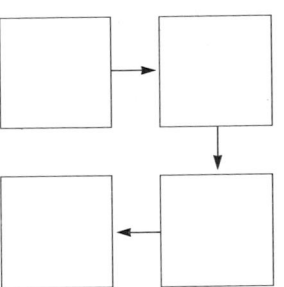

NOW & THEN

THE *EXXON VALDEZ* OIL SPILL

In 1994, a federal jury awarded almost $287 million in damages to thousands of Alaskans. The award was the climax of events that began in April of 1989, when the giant oil tanker *Exxon Valdez* hit a reef in Prince William Sound off the coast of Alaska and dumped almost 11 million gallons of crude oil into the water. It was the largest oil spill in the country's history.

Within days, the black oil fouled nearly 1,800 miles of coastline and beaches. At least 10 percent of the area's birds, sea otters, and other wildlife were killed, and commercial fisheries lost nearly 50 percent of the season's catch.

The jury also ordered the Exxon Corporation to pay $5 billion in punitive damages as a result of the spill. The size of these awards demonstrates that the nation has become serious about holding corporations responsible for damaging the environment.

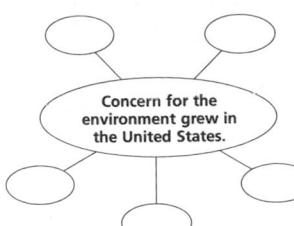

A fisherman holds an oil-slicked bird after the *Exxon Valdez* oil spill.

Section ❹ Assessment

1. TERMS & NAMES
- Rachel Carson
- Earth Day
- environmentalist
- Environmental Protection Agency
- Three Mile Island

2. SUMMARIZING Recreate the web below on your paper and fill in events that illustrate the main idea in the center.

Concern for the environment grew in the United States.

3. ANALYZING CAUSES Why do you think Rachel Carson's book *Silent Spring* had such impact when it appeared?

THINK ABOUT
- environmental awareness before the 1960s
- the message of *Silent Spring*
- the domestic agendas of the Kennedy, Johnson and Nixon administrations

4. FORMING OPINIONS How much should the United States rely on nuclear power as a source of energy? Explain your view.

THINK ABOUT
- the safety of nuclear power
- the alternatives to nuclear power
- U.S. energy demands

An Age of Limits **973**

NOW AND THEN
The Exxon Valdez *Oil Spill*

Have students further research the aftermath of the *Exxon Valdez* oil spill, tracking the key events from the spill to the jury awards using a flow chart like the one below.

ASSESS & RETEACH

Section 4 Assessment
After answering the questions, have students pair up and check each other's answers. Students should note page references where missing information might be found.

Self-Assessment
Have each student write on an index card one action he or she might take each day to preserve and protect the earth. Collect these cards and post them on a bulletin board.

Section Quiz

FORMAL ASSESSMENT
Section Quiz, p. 390

Reteach
Replay the video, "Poisoned Playground," and discuss the environmental issues raised by the film.

AMERICAN STORIES VIDEO SERIES
"Poisoned Playground"

ANSWERS

1. TERMS & NAMES
Rachel Carson, p. 968

Earth Day, p. 969

environmentalist, 969

Environmental Protection Agency, p. 970

Three Mile Island, p. 971

2. SUMMARIZING
Possible Answers:
Rachel Carson publishes *Silent Spring*.
In 1970, the first Earth Day is held.
Nixon organizes the EPA.
Three Mile Island raises concerns about nuclear power.
People struggle to balance environmental and economic concerns.

3. ANALYZING CAUSES
Possible Responses: Students might say that *Silent Spring* made people aware that chemical pesticides could harm even humans; it made people realize how human activity affects the environment. Others might point to the persuasive power of Carson's writing or the willingness of Kennedy, Johnson, and Nixon to act to protect the environment.

4. FORMING OPINIONS
Possible Responses: Supporters may argue that nuclear power should be widely used because it is cleaner than coal or oil, plentiful, and cheap, and its overall safety record is excellent. Opponents may argue that nuclear power is potentially very dangerous, that nuclear waste is difficult to dispose of, and that the high risks outweigh the benefits.

CLOSE

During the 1970s, as more Americans became aware of their economic and global limits, they also realized that their natural resources were not limitless. This realization moved the government, as well as average citizens, to more actively address the country's environmental concerns.

REVIEWING
THE CHAPTER

TERMS & NAMES
1. Richard M. Nixon, p. 946
2. stagflation, p. 950
3. OPEC, p. 950
4. SALT I Treaty, p. 952
5. Watergate, p. 953
6. Saturday Night Massacre, p. 956
7. Camp David Accords, p. 966
8. Ayatollah Ruhollah Khomeini, p. 967
9. Rachel Carson, p. 968
10. Three Mile Island, p. 971

MAIN IDEAS
11. He tried to lessen the federal government's responsibilities through revenue sharing and welfare reform.

12. He tried to raise taxes, cut the budget, raise interest rates, and use wage and price controls.

13. His détente policy, based on the philosophy of realpolitik, sought to ease Cold War tensions. The result was a warmer relationship with China and the Soviet Union.

14. They shredded incriminating documents, paid off the Watergate burglars, lied while testifying, and tried to stop investigation of the burglary.

15. Nixon resigned as president, and many people lost faith in the government.

16. Under Ford, inflation and unemployment dropped somewhat and the United States joined with the Soviet Union and other countries in signing the Helsinki Accords.

17. Carter asked Americans to reduce energy consumption and pushed the National Energy Act through Congress.

18. Carter focused on human rights. Under him, the United States cut off military aid to Argentina and Brazil and criticized the Soviet Union's treatment of dissidents.

19. The publication of *Silent Spring;* Earth Day celebrations; the Three Mile Island accident.

20. It caused the government to strengthen its safety standards and improve its inspection procedures.

Chapter 32 Assessment

REVIEWING THE CHAPTER

TERMS & NAMES For each term below, write a sentence explaining its significance for the Nixon, Ford, and Carter administrations. For each person below, explain his or her role in the 1960s and 1970s.

1. Richard M. Nixon
2. stagflation
3. OPEC
4. SALT I Treaty
5. Watergate
6. Saturday Night Massacre
7. Camp David Accords
8. Ayatollah Ruhollah Khomeini
9. Rachel Carson
10. Three Mile Island

MAIN IDEAS

SECTION 1 (pages 946–952)

The Nixon Administration

11. In what ways did President Nixon attempt to reform the federal government?
12. How did Nixon try to combat stagflation?
13. Describe Nixon's philosophy in foreign policy and the results of this philosophy.

SECTION 2 (pages 953–957)

Watergate: Nixon's Downfall

14. In what ways did the participants in Watergate attempt to cover up the scandal?
15. What were the results of the Watergate scandal?

SECTION 3 (pages 960–967)

The Ford and Carter Years

16. What were President Ford's greatest successes as president?
17. How did President Carter attempt to solve the energy crisis?
18. Describe Carter's foreign policy, using examples to show its impact.

SECTION 4 (pages 968–973)

Environmental Activism

19. What were factors that increased Americans' concerns about environmental issues?
20. What was the impact of the Three Mile Island incident?

THINKING CRITICALLY

1. **ADVANCE OR RETREAT** Using a chart like the one below, identify one major development that occurred between 1968 and 1980 for each issue listed. Then indicate whether you think the impact of the development was positive (+) or negative (-) for the country as a whole.

Issue	Development	Impact
Economic conditions		
Racial harmony		
Democratic government		
Efficient energy use		
Environmental protection		

2. **PRESIDENTS AND THE ECONOMY** Review the economic policies of Presidents Nixon, Ford, and Carter. To what extent do you think each should be blamed or credited for changes in the economy during his administration?

3. **RECOGNIZING LIMITS** Reread the quote by Jimmy Carter on page 944. How would you describe the feelings or tone that his statement conveys? Explain and support your opinion.

4. **GEOGRAPHY OF THE MIDDLE EAST** Look as the map on page 966. What U.S. interests do you think were served by helping to maintain peace in the Middle East?

5. **DEFENDING THE CONSTITUTION** In your opinion, did the Watergate scandal primarily demonstrate flaws in the American system of government or show how well the system works? Explain.

6. **ANALYZING PRIMARY SOURCES** Read the following excerpt from a 1973 interview with environmental activist Barry Commoner about the link between energy consumption and the environment. Then answer the questions that follow.

> I've felt for a long time that the energy crisis is the cutting edge of the environmental crisis for [two reasons]. One is that it involves a counter-ecological step in that we're using nonrenewable resources, and that's a fundamental violation of a basic principle of ecology.
>
> The other reason is that in using fuel we inevitably pollute the environment with heat, with waste products and so on. So that for those reasons and also because energy—power—has become increasingly important in the design of new technology, which is the main source of the environmental crisis, the role of energy in industry and agriculture becomes a sort of red thread through the environmental crisis.
>
> **BARRY COMMONER,** quoted in *Chicago Tribune, November 19, 1973*

According to Commoner, how was the energy crisis linked to the environmental crisis? Do you think Commoner's comments appropriately describe conditions that exist today? Explain.

THINKING CRITICALLY

1. ADVANCE OR RETREAT
Possible Answers: Economic conditions—High inflation and unemployment (–); Racial harmony—Nixon's retreat on integration and civil rights (–); Democratic government—Watergate scandal (–); Efficient energy use—Carter's energy conservation measure (+); Environmental protection—Clean Air Acts, banning of DDT (+).

2. PRESIDENTS AND THE ECONOMY
Possible Responses: Nixon could be blamed for allowing the recession to deepen by doing little to combat unemployment; Nixon could not, however, be blamed for OPEC price increases and the rise of foreign competition. Ford could be blamed for the failure of the WIN program but could be credited with moderate improvement in inflation and unemployment. Carter could be blamed for not establishing a consistent economic program and for allowing the inflation rate to reach nearly 14 percent; he could be credited for decreasing Americans' reliance on imported oil and gas.

3. RECOGNIZING LIMITS
Possible Responses: It conveys uncertainty—a holding back by saying we can't do everything, and a boldness in requiring us to move forward; it conveys pessimism by stressing limits and stating that we cannot do certain things; it conveys optimism by stressing boldness as we move into the future; it conveys realism—the nation cannot do or be everything; it expresses a sense of defeat in realization of limits.

ALTERNATIVE ASSESSMENT

1. RESPONDING TO WORLD EVENTS
What caused people around the world to strike, protest, and demonstrate for their beliefs during the 1960s and 1970s?

Write and deliver a three-minute speech that might have been given at a campus rally at a university anywhere in the world.

CD-ROM Use the *Our Times* CD-ROM, your text, and other sources to identify and research a social, political, or economic situation during this period.

- Your speech is an opportunity to express your thoughts and feelings about an issue that is of vital importance to you. Explain your position and try to convince others to think the way you do or to take action.

2. LEARNING FROM MEDIA
VIDEO View the McDougal Littell video for Chapter 32, *Poisoned Playground*. Discuss the following questions in small groups and then do the cooperative learning activity.

- What numerous obstacles did Lois Gibbs face in investigating conditions at Love Canal?
- How did Lois Gibbs's struggle affect her personal life?
- What finally prompted the government to evacuate the residents of Love Canal?

Cooperative Learning Divide into small groups. Discuss possible environmental problems in each group member's neighborhood and list them on a sheet of paper. Share your list with other groups to determine the most common problems. Discuss possible solutions to these problems.

3. PORTFOLIO PROJECT
Use the Living History activity to expand your portfolio.

LIVING HISTORY

SETTING UP AN EXHIBIT OF GLOBAL LINKS
You have prepared individual items that show international links. Now, with your classmates, set up an exhibit that displays these items. Consider the following suggestions as you organize your work.

- Divide your exhibit into sections, each representing a particular country.
- Prepare titles for sections of your exhibit.
- Arrange viewing and listening areas for video and audio tapes.

After you have set up the exhibit, take notes and photographs as you view the displays. Explain in your notes which items you find most interesting and informative. Add your notes and the photographs to your American history portfolio.

Bridge to Chapter 33

Review Chapter 32

NIXON'S PRESIDENCY Richard M. Nixon, elected president in 1968, attempted to move the nation in a more conservative direction. He took steps to reduce the size of the federal government, implement a policy of law and order, and slow down integration. In foreign policy, he sought to improve relations with China and the Soviet Union.

WATERGATE In June 1972, men employed by Nixon's reelection campaign broke into Democratic National Committee headquarters at the Watergate complex in Washington, D.C. When the burglars were caught, Nixon and his aides immediately tried to cover up the president's involvement. However, an investigation into the break-in revealed the cover-up and other scandals. To avoid impeachment, Nixon resigned in August 1974.

THE FORD AND CARTER YEARS The nation's economic downturn, which began under Nixon, continued under his two successors, Gerald Ford and Jimmy Carter. Each man tried to solve pressing energy and economic crises, but had little success.

In foreign policy, Carter emphasized human rights and helped Israel and Egypt reach a historic peace agreement. However, in 1979, revolutionaries in Iran took 52 Americans hostage. They were not released until Carter left office in January 1981.

ENVIRONMENTAL ACTIVISM Awakened by the publication of Rachel Carson's *Silent Spring* and other events, Americans expressed concern for protecting the environment. The government responded with numerous environmental protection laws and the establishment of the Environmental Protection Agency in 1970. One issue of ongoing concern was the safety of nuclear energy. After the Three Mile Island incident in 1979, the federal government instituted tighter regulations on nuclear power plants.

Preview Chapter 33

The economic troubles of the 1970s caused discontent among voters. Capitalizing on this mood, a conservative, Ronald Reagan, won the presidency in 1980. He vowed to cut federal spending on domestic programs, cut regulations on business, cut taxes, and increase American military power. You will learn about these and other developments in the next chapter.

An Age of Limits **975**

---

1. RESPONDING TO WORLD EVENTS
Standards for Evaluation
A speech should meet the following criteria:

- Focuses on one issue or event during the period.
- Expresses an opinion.
- Cites ample evidence from the text and other sources to support opinions.
- Uses forceful and moving language in order to convince others to change their view or to take action.

2. LEARNING FROM MEDIA
Answer to the questions:

- Lois Gibbs faced indifference from school officials and some town residents, as well as skepticism from state and federal officials.
- Her struggle forced her to spend time away from her family and caused tension in her marriage.
- Gibbs and her group held several EPA members hostage until their demands were met.

Standards for Evaluation
A discussion about local environmental problems should meet the following criteria:

- Addresses each group member's concerns.
- Involves all the groups in trying to determine solutions.

3. PORTFOLIO PROJECT
LIVING HISTORY
Standards for Evaluation
An exhibit should meet the following criteria:

- Uses items that clearly show economic or political links between the United States and other countries.
- Uses a balance of maps, pictures or drawings, three-dimensional objects, and audio-visual selections.
- Shows good organization.
- Contains labels and written comments that explain the events and global links of the exhibit.

IN-DEPTH RESOURCES: UNIT 9
See the form for scoring this activity on page 18.

THINKING CRITICALLY

4. GEOGRAPHY OF THE MIDDLE EAST
Possible Responses: Since the Middle East supplied the United States and other nations with much-needed oil, maintaining peace was important so as not to disrupt these trade links; maintaining peace helped limit the likelihood of increased influence from the neighboring Soviet Union over the region; maintaining peace helped keep a balance of power in the region between Israel, which was friendly to the United States, and other countries.

5. DEFENDING THE CONSTITUTION
Possible Responses: Demonstrated flaws: It showed how a president can expand his power without giving any thought to constitutional checks; it showed how politicians and presidential advisers can become corrupt—desiring secrecy and power, and feeling that they are above the law. Showed how well government works: It showed how the system can provide for the investigation of presidential wrongdoing and create committees to investigate; it showed that a federal investigation can result in a grand jury indictment and that the House Judiciary Committee can impeach a president.

6. ANALYZING PRIMARY SOURCES
Possible Responses: Commoner argued that the use of energy is the main source of the environmental crisis. Yes: We are still using nonrenewable fuel resources that not only pollute the environment but will eventually be used up. No: Although we are still using fossil fuels, scientists are working to find alternative, renewable fuels.

	Key Ideas	TEACHING SUPPORT	ASSESSMENT	
SECTION 1 A Conservative Movement Emerges *pp. 978–981*	*The new conservatism begins with the defeat of Barry Goldwater in 1964 and triumphs with the election of Ronald Reagan in 1980.*	**In-Depth Resources: Unit 9** • Guided Reading, p. 19 • Skillbuilder Practice: Clarifying, p. 23 **COOPERATIVE ACTIVITY** • Diagramming the Shift to Conservatism, p. 980 (TE)	**Section 1 Assessment,** p. 981 (PE) **Self-Assessment,** p. 981 (TE) **Formal Assessment** • Section Quiz, p. 399 **Alternative Assessment Book** • Standards for Evaluating a Cooperative Activity	
SECTION 2 Conservative Policies Under Reagan and Bush *pp. 982–986*	*President Reagan puts in place conservative policies concerning the nation's budget and the federal government.*	**In-Depth Resources: Unit 9** • Guided Reading, p. 20 • Primary Sources: Political Cartoon, p. 28; *from* Ronald Reagan's Farewell Address, p. 29 • American Lives: Sandra Day O'Connor, p. 35 **COOPERATIVE ACTIVITY** • Researching Supreme Court Decisions, p. 984 (TE)	**Section 2 Assessment,** p. 986 (PE) **Self-Assessment,** p. 986 (TE) **Formal Assessment** • Section Quiz, p. 400 **Alternative Assessment Book** • Standards for Evaluating a Cooperative Activity	
SECTION 3 American Society in a Conservative Age *pp. 987–993*	*Social issues of many kinds continue to concern the nation during the conservative backlash.*	**In-Depth Resources: Unit 9** • Guided Reading, p. 21 • Geography Application: Latino Population in the 1980s, p. 24 • Primary Source: Civil Rights in the 1980s, p. 30 **COOPERATIVE ACTIVITY** • Developing a Plan for Better Schools, p. 989 (TE)	**Section 3 Assessment,** p. 993 (PE) **Self-Assessment,** p. 993 (TE) **Formal Assessment** • Section Quiz, p. 401 **Alternative Assessment Book** • Standards for Evaluating a Cooperative Activity	
SECTION 4 Changes in America's Foreign Policy *pp. 996–1001*	*Major changes throughout the world have a great impact on the direction of U.S. foreign policy.*	**In-Depth Resources: Unit 9** • Guided Reading, p. 22 • Outline Map: U.S. Attention on the Middle East, p. 26 • Primary Source: The First Day of Desert Storm, p. 31 • American Lives: Daniel Inouye, p. 36 **COOPERATIVE ACTIVITY** • Creating a Foreign Affairs Time Line, p. 997 (TE)	**Section 4 Assessment,** p. 1001 (PE) **Self-Assessment,** p. 1001 (TE) **Formal Assessment** • Section Quiz, p. 402 **Alternative Assessment Book** • Standards for Evaluating a Cooperative Activity	
CHAPTER RESOURCES	**Chapter Overview** *A growing conservatism brings Ronald Reagan and George Bush to the presidency. Their policies change the American economy, while other forces transform American society and changes reshape the world.*	**In-Depth Resources: Unit 9** • Living History Project: Worksheet, p. 37; Standards, p. 38 **Telescoping the Times** • Chapter Summary, pp. 65–66 **Planning for Block Schedules**	**Chapter Assessment,** pp. 1002–1003 (PE) **Alternative Assessment,** p. 1003 (PE) **Formal Assessment** • Chapter Test, forms A and B, pp. 403–407 📖 **Test Generator** **Alternative Assessment Book** See explanation and forms for different kinds of alternative assessments including portfolio assessment.	

Grolier Multimedia Encyclopedia
• Reagan's Political Career

INTERNET RESOURCES
• See *McDougal Littell Learning On-Line* for links to information about *The National Review* and *The Nation.*

Critical Thinking Transparencies
• CT33, The Conservative 1980s
• CT67, Theory of Supply Side Economics

Electronic Library of Primary Sources
• On the Program for Economic Recovery by Ronald Reagan

INTERNET RESOURCES
• See *McDougal Littell Learning On-Line* for links to information about Ronald Reagan and George Bush.

Grolier Multimedia Encyclopedia
• AIDS Epidemic

Electronic Library of Primary Sources
• *from* "Victim-Victimizer: Why Excel?" by Rev. Jesse L. Jackson

INTERNET RESOURCES
• See Interact with History p. 995 (PE) for an activity that includes the Internet as an enrichment option.

Humanities Transparencies
• H47, "Economic Crisis"

Geography Transparencies
• G33, The Cold War Ends, 1989–90

Grolier Multimedia Encyclopedia
• Iran-Contra Affair

Electronic Library of Primary Sources
• *from Setting Limits*

Our Times
• "Freedom Ascendant"

INTERNET RESOURCES
• See *McDougal Littell Learning On-Line* for links to information about Gorbachev and Tiananmen Square.

American Portfolio: A Videodisc for U.S. History, user's guide, pp. 257–260

INTERNET RESOURCES
Learning On-Line: Social Studies
http://www.mcdougallittell.com

Block Scheduling (90 MINUTES)

Day 1
Section 1, pp. 978–981
Section 2, pp. 982–986
Section Assessments, pp. 981, 986

Day 2
Section 3, pp. 987–993
Section 4, pp. 996–1001
Geography Spotlight: Sunbelt, Rustbelt, Ecotopia, pp. 994–995
Chapter Assessment, pp. 1002–1003

YEARLY PACING *Chapter 33 Total:* 2 days *Yearly Total:* 85 days

See *Planning for Block Schedules* for special activities and pacing strategies.

Customizing for Special Populations

Students Acquiring English

Access for Students Acquiring English
• Guided Reading for Sections 1–4 (Spanish), pp. 318–321
• Chapter Summary (Spanish), pp. 316–317
• Skillbuilder Practice: Clarifying (Spanish), p. 322
• Geography Application: Latino Population in the 1980s (Spanish), p. 323
• Outline Map: U.S. Attention on the Middle East (Spanish), p. 325

INTERNET RESOURCES
• See *McDougal Littell Learning On-Line* The Diverse Classroom.

Less Proficient Readers

In-Depth Resources: Unit 9
• Guided Reading for Sections 1–4, pp. 19–22
• Skillbuilder: Clarifying, p. 23
• Geography Application: Latino Population in the 1980s, p. 24
• Outline Map: U.S. Attention on the Middle East, p. 26

Telescoping the Times
• Chapter Summary, pp. 65–66

See additional strategies at point of use in the Teacher's Edition.

Gifted and Talented Students

In-Depth Resources: Unit 9
• Primary Sources: Political Cartoon, p. 28; *from* Ronald Reagan's Farewell Address, p. 29; Civil Rights in the 1980s, p. 30; The First Day of Desert Storm, p. 31
• American Lives: Sandra Day O'Connor, p. 35; Daniel Inouye, p. 36

See additional strategies at point of use in the Teacher's Edition.

Connections to Literature   READINGS FOR STUDENTS

In-Depth Resources: Unit 9
• *from The Bonfire of the Vanities* by Tom Wolfe, p. 32

Enrichment Reading
• **Russo, Richard**
Nobody's Fool
New York: Vintage, 1994
In this quietly funny and moving novel, Russo follows the lives of quirky, flawed, yet likable characters in a deadbeat upstate New York town. Very much part of the economic disasters and hopes of the 1980s, these characters are real and vital.

McDougal Littell *The Language of Literature*
American Literature

• **Gregory Alan-Williams, from *A Gathering of Heroes,* p. 1119**
• **Peter Cameron, "Homework," p. 889**

• **Wolfe, Tom**
Bonfire of the Vanities
New York: Bantam, 1990
Tom Wolfe wickedly assaults New York City politics and lifestyles of the 1980s in this wildly funny, bitter, and memorable novel. We see New York City from the perspective of Wall Street wizards, lawyers, mayors, civil rights leaders, journalists, and anyone who gets in between. Wolfe shows no favorites as he paints rich, poor, black, and white in absurd strokes.

OVERVIEW

The Conservative Tide

▶ **Starting with the Student**
Ask students what the phrase "conservative tide" suggests. Then, discuss the opening quotation.

• How would students paraphrase the quotation?
• How does the quotation help them understand what a conservative believes?

PREVIEWING THE CHAPTER
• As students read the chapter, have them make a list of the reasons that conservatives won political power in the 1980s.
• Ask students if they recognize any of the names from the time line.
• Have students get together in small groups to write questions that they would like to have answered in the chapter.

MORE ABOUT . . .
Challenger Space Shuttle

The nation was stunned when on January 23, 1986, the space shuttle *Challenger* exploded in midair just 73 seconds after liftoff. The seven-member crew that died included Christa McAuliffe, a high school teacher from New Hampshire. She was the first civilian ever to have flown in a U.S. space mission.

976 CHAPTER 33

SECTION 1
A Conservative Movement Emerges

The new conservatism begins with the defeat of Barry Goldwater in 1964 and triumphs with the election of Ronald Reagan in 1980.

SECTION 2
Conservative Policies Under Reagan and Bush

President Reagan puts in place conservative policies concerning the nation's budget and the federal government.

SECTION 3
American Society in a Conservative Age

Social issues of many kinds continue to concern the nation during the conservative backlash.

SECTION 4
Changes in America's Foreign Policy

Major changes throughout the world have a great impact on the direction of U.S. foreign policy.

> "In this present crisis, government is not the solution to our problem; government is the problem."
>
> Ronald Reagan, *first inaugural address, 1981*

THE UNITED STATES
THE WORLD

1980

1981 1982 1983 1984 1986
1982 1983 1984 1986

• Ronald Reagan is elected president.

• Sandra Day O'Connor is appointed to the Supreme Court.
• President Reagan is shot.
• Iran frees U.S. hostages.

• Equal Rights Amendment fails to win ratification.

• President Ronald Reagan is reelected.

The space shuttle *Challenger* explodes.
• Iran arms deal is revealed.

• Zimbabwe claims independence.

• Great Britain and Argentina go to war over the Falkland Islands.

• South African bishop Desmond Tutu receives the Nobel Peace Prize.

In Russia, Chernobyl nuclear power plant emits radioactive material into the atmosphere.

976 CHAPTER 33

THEMES IN CHAPTER 33

Women in America	*Civil Rights*	*Cultural Diversity*	*Constitutional Concerns*
The Supreme Court was at the center of two events affecting women in the workplace: the appointment of the first woman justice to the Supreme Court and a hearing on charges of sexual harassment by a court nominee. See Teacher's Edition, p. 985.	A number of groups (including women, African Americans, Latinos, Native Americans, Asian Americans, and gays and lesbians) struggled to achieve equal rights in the 1980s under the administrations of Reagan and Bush. See Teacher's Edition, p. 991.	President Reagan set the upholding of traditional values as a major goal. But whose values are the traditional values? Some values indeed may be common to many of the diverse cultures found in this country. Other values vary by gender and ethnicity. See Teacher's Edition, p. 992.	A major constitutional concern was raised by the Iran-Contra affair; it deals with the balance of powers between the presidency and the legislature. Can the nation tolerate one branch of government covertly working against another branch? See Teacher's Edition, p. 999.

RESEARCHING POLITICAL POSITIONS

Watch a television news program, listen to a radio news program, or read a news magazine that features an interview with a conservative politician. Take notes on what the politician says about his or her positions. Consider the following questions.

- What does the politician say about social issues?
- What does the politician say about economic issues?
- What issues does the politician care most about?

📁 **PORTFOLIO PROJECT** Save your notes about the interview in a folder for your American history portfolio. At the end of the chapter, you will compare that politician with Ronald Reagan or George Bush. Then you will present your comparison to the class.

RESEARCHING POLITICAL POSITIONS

Discuss with students ways of researching political positions by taking notes on an interview.

- Be sure to note the source of the interview: radio talk show, television news, news magazine, or newspaper.
- Listen attentively or read carefully and take notes on the conservative politician's statements.
- Summarize notes about the politician's statements on social issues.
- Summarize notes about statements on economic issues.
- Think about ways in which the politician is like or different from Reagan and Bush.

Project Planning Guide

Step 1	Students choose a conservative politician.
Step 2	Students choose a medium (radio, television, newspaper, magazine).
Step 3	Students take careful notes of what the politician says.
Step 4	Students make comparisons and contrasts.

IN-DEPTH RESOURCES: UNIT 9
See worksheet and standards for evaluation, pp. 37–38.

Timeline:

- President Reagan and Soviet leader Mikhail Gorbachev sign Intermediate Range Nuclear Forces Treaty.
- The stock market tumbles 500 points.

1987

- ⭐ George Bush is elected president.

1988

- The *Exxon Valdez* spills oil along the coast of Alaska.

1989

- Chinese troops kill student dissidents in Tiananmen Square in Beijing.
- Germans dismantle the Berlin Wall.

- The U.S. sends troops to Saudi Arabia to liberate Kuwait.

1990

- Communist governments fall in Poland, Hungary, Czechoslovakia, and Romania.
- The Baltic nations of Latvia, Estonia, and Lithuania declare their independence from the Soviet Union.

- The Persian Gulf War breaks out.

1991

- Iraq invades Kuwait.
- Yugoslavia dissolves in civil war

- Riots take place in Los Angeles after police officers are acquitted of brutality charges in the Rodney King case.
- ⭐ Bill Clinton is elected president.

1992

- The Soviet Union breaks up.

977

RECOMMENDED RESOURCES

Books for the Teacher

Ash, Timothy. *The Magic Lantern.* New York: Vintage, 1993. End of Cold War.

Cannon, Lou. *Ronald Reagan.* New York: Simon, 1990. Reagan's presidency.

Smith, Hedrick. *The Power Game.* New York: Random House, 1988. Inner workings of Washington.

Books for the Student

Peirce, Neil R., and Jerry Hagstrom. *The Book of America: Inside Fifty States Today.* New York: Norton, 1983.

Terkel, Studs. *The Great Divide.* New York: Pantheon, 1988. Oral history of the American dream as seen in 1980s.

Videos

America in Search of Itself. AIMS Media, 800-367-2467. Reagan wins presidency.

Colin Powell: An American Dream. Parade Video, 1995. Biography.

Colin Powell: A Soldier's Campaign. A&E Home Video, 1995. Biography.

One Thousand Days of the Reagan Presidency. MPI Home Video, 800-323-4442.

Software

Desert Storm: The War in the Gulf. CD-ROM. Time Warner Interactive, 800-482-3766.

OBJECTIVES

1. To identify the reasons for the nation's swing toward conservative values.

2. To describe the emergence of Reagan and Bush as conservative leaders.

3. To list the major goals of the conservative movement.

CRITICAL THINKING

- Analyzing issues, p. 979
- Clarifying, p. 979
- Summarizing, pp. 980, 981
- Analyzing causes, p. 981
- Analyzing motives, p. 981
- Synthesizing, p. 981

FOCUS & MOTIVATE

▶ *Starting with the Student*
- Ask students, What happens when things aren't going right? when they don't seem to be moving forward at all?
- Do students want to change something in their lives?
- Do students think an entire nation could feel that way?

MORE ABOUT . . .
Peggy Noonan

Noonan wrote some of the most memorable of President Reagan's speeches—his speech on the 40th anniversary of D-Day: "In seizing the firm land at the top of this cliff they seized back the continent of Europe"; 1984 stump speech: "We're putting out our hands and we're asking you to come walk with us"; his address to the nation after the *Challenger* explosion: "We will never forget them, nor the last time we saw them—this morning, as they prepared for their journey, and waved good-bye, and 'slipped the surly bonds of earth' to 'touch the face of God.'" Noonan also originated for the Bush campaign the unforgettable phrases "read my lips: no new taxes" and "a thousand points of light."

978 Chapter 33

TERMS & NAMES
- Ronald Reagan
- entitlement program
- New Right
- reverse discrimination
- Conservative Coalition
- Moral Majority
- George Bush

❶ A Conservative Movement Emerges

LEARN ABOUT the conservative movement that swept the country
TO UNDERSTAND how conservatism changed American politics and led to the elections of presidents Reagan and Bush.

ONE AMERICAN'S STORY

The daughter of hardworking immigrant Irish Catholic parents, Peggy Noonan grew up with a strong sense of social and political justice. As a child, she idolized the Kennedys; as a teenager, she devoured newspapers and magazines on social and political issues. After college, Noonan went to work for CBS, where she eventually gained a position as a news writer.

Over the years, Noonan came to realize that she wasn't by nature a journalist, but a partisan— a supporter of a particular party or leader. Her political views became increasingly conservative. She won a job as a speech writer for Ronald Reagan, whose commitment to his conservative values moved her deeply. Noonan recalled that her response to Reagan was not unusual.

A PERSONAL VOICE
The young people who came to Washington for the Reagan revolution came to make things better. . . . They looked at where freedom was and where freedom wasn't and what that did, and they wanted to help the guerrilla fighters who were trying to overthrow the Communist regimes that had been imposed on them ten years ago while we were all watching "60 Minutes." The thing the young conservatives were always talking about, the constant subtext was freedom, freedom:
  we'll free up more of your money,
  we'll free up more of the world,
  freedom freedom freedom—
It was the drumbeat that held a disparate group together, the rhythm that kept a fractious, not-made-in-heaven alliance in one piece.

PEGGY NOONAN, from *What I Saw at the Revolution*

Ever since Senator Barry Goldwater of Arizona had run for president in 1964, conservatives had argued that state governments, businesses, and individuals needed freedom from the heavy hand of Washington, D.C. During Ronald Reagan's campaign, that conviction gained a widespread following. It fueled a conservative sweep in the 1980 elections that brought Republican leadership to the presidency and the Senate.

Peggy Noonan

The Conservative Movement Builds

By 1980, President Jimmy Carter was suffering from low ratings in public opinion polls. Economic troubles (including a high rate of inflation), the Iranian hostage crisis, and the nation's new conservatism eroded his popularity.

A TRADITION OF CHANGE Since early in its history, the United States had alternated between what historians call "public action and private interest." Sometimes voters supported government action to solve social problems, while at other times they became disillusioned with social experiments and preferred to concentrate on their individual economic well-being. Under the banner of progressivism, presidents Theodore Roosevelt, William H. Taft, and Woodrow Wilson had used the power of government to curb what they saw as the excesses of big business. During the 1920s, presidents Warren Harding, Calvin Coolidge, and Herbert Hoover counteracted progressive policies with a conservative agenda that emphasized private interests over social reform.

978 CHAPTER 33

SECTION 1 RESOURCES

 PRINT RESOURCES

IN-DEPTH RESOURCES: UNIT 9
Guided Reading, p. 19
Skillbuilder Practice: Clarifying, p. 23

ACCESS FOR STUDENTS ACQUIRING ENGLISH
Guided Reading (Spanish), p. 318
Skillbuilder Practice: Clarifying (Spanish), p. 322

FORMAL ASSESSMENT
Section Quiz, p. 399

ALTERNATIVE ASSESSMENT BOOK
See forms for supporting and scoring alternative activities.

 TECHNOLOGY RESOURCES

CD-ROM *Grolier Multimedia Encyclopedia*

VIDEO *American Portfolio: A Videodisc for U.S. History*
user's guide, pp. 258, 260

INTERNET McDougal Littell Learning On-Line
http://www.mcdougallittell.com

When the Great Depression hit, the pendulum swung again. Franklin Roosevelt's New Deal and Harry Truman's Fair Deal focused on government action to relieve social problems. Dwight Eisenhower brought a conservative perspective to the White House in the 1950s. John F. Kennedy's New Frontier and Lyndon Johnson's Great Society of the 1960s swung back to social reform. Conservatism returned during the Richard Nixon and Gerald Ford administrations. Conservatism reached its high point with the election of **Ronald Reagan.**

THE CONSERVATIVE BACKLASH By 1980, one out of every three households was receiving benefits from government programs. Yet most Americans resented the cost of maintaining these federal **entitlement programs**—programs that guarantee and provide benefits to particular groups. Taxes were high, and inflation had reached nearly 15 percent. Many Americans feared they would not be able to provide for their children's college education or their own retirement.

In addition, some people had become frustrated with the government's civil rights policies. Congress had passed the Civil Rights Act of 1964 in an effort to eliminate racial discrimination. Over the years, however, judicial decisions and government regulations broadened the reach of the act. A growing number of Americans viewed with skepticism what had begun as a movement toward equal opportunity. Although many people had rejected separate schools for blacks and whites as unfair and unequal, few wanted to bus their children long distances to achieve a fixed ratio of black and white students.

As the 1970s progressed, grassroots groups across the country emerged to support and promote single issues that reflected their key interests. Some members of this **New Right**—an alliance of conservative special-interest groups stressing cultural, social, and moral issues—fought any government regulation at all. Others fought specific government regulations in the form of busing, gun control, and antitrust laws. Many opposed legal abortion and the proposed Equal Rights Amendment (ERA) for women. They also rejected laws promoting minority opportunities in employment or education—which they saw as **reverse discrimination** (or discrimination against white people and specifically white men). Some called for a constitutional amendment to permit prayer in public schools. Others voted against anyone who favored increases in government revenues. Of course, not all members of the New Right were single-issue voters. Many felt passionately about an overall philosophy of conservative government.

THE CONSERVATIVE COALITION Between the mid-1960s and Reagan's victory in 1980, the conservative movement in the United States grew in strength. Eventually these groups on the right formed the **Conservative Coalition**—an alliance made up of intellectuals, business leaders, struggling middle-class voters, disenchanted Democrats, and fundamentalist Christian groups.

There were a number of basic issues that were of shared importance to the different groups that made up the Conservative Coalition. These issues included opposition to big government, entitlements, and the use of busing and affirmative action to correct segregation, as well as a belief in a return to traditional moral standards.

Conservative intellectuals argued the cause of the Conservative Coalition in newspapers such as the *Wall Street Journal* and magazines such as *National Review,* founded in 1955 by conservative intellectual William F. Buckley, Jr. Conservative "think tanks" such as the American Enterprise Institute and the Heritage Foundation were founded to develop conservative policies and issues that would appeal to the majority of voters.

A. Answer entitlement programs, inflation, taxes, civil rights policies, big government in general.

THINK THROUGH HISTORY
A. Analyzing Issues What were some of the issues that conservatives felt strongly about?

THINK THROUGH HISTORY
B. Clarifying What was the Conservative Coalition?

B. Answer An alliance made up of a variety of groups, including intellectuals, business leaders, struggling middle-class voters, disaffected Democrats, and Christian groups such as the Moral Majority.

HISTORICAL SPOTLIGHT

WILLIAM F. BUCKLEY, JR.

Born in 1925 in New York City, William F. Buckley, Jr., is known for his conservative works. He first aired his conservative views in 1951, when he published *God and Man at Yale,* a book that attacked the liberal viewpoints he said were common at his alma mater.

He followed this publication with other political works, including *Up from Liberalism* (1959) and *The Unmaking of a Mayor* (1966), an account of his campaign for mayor of New York. When asked what he would do if he won the election, Buckley responded, "Demand a recount."

In 1955, Buckley founded the *National Review,* a magazine that continues to reflect and influence conservative political thought in America today.

OBJECTIVE
① INSTRUCT

The Conservative Movement Builds

▶**Starting with the Student**
Have students draw up a two-column chart. In one column they should list some of the actions taken by social reformers in the 1960s and 1970s. In a second column have them list the backlash that might have occurred.

Social Reform Actions	Backlashes
School busing	
Quotas	

▶**Discussing Key Ideas**
• In the 1980s, the country is ready for less government intervention.
• Conservatives form a coalition.

IN-DEPTH RESOURCES: UNIT 9
Guided Reading, p. 19

ACCESS FOR STUDENTS ACQUIRING ENGLISH
Guided Reading (Spanish), p. 318

HISTORICAL SPOTLIGHT
William F. Buckley, Jr.

Buckley has had greater influence as a writer and editor than he would have had as an elected official. Why might this be so? Have students list the attributes of Buckley's that make him an influential journalist.

TEACHING OPTION

Skillbuilder Mini-Lesson: Clarifying

Explaining the Skill Clarifying a concept—that is, defining unfamiliar terms and restating the content—can help reinforce understanding of the concept. Sometimes in dealing with new terms, it can help to think of examples of whatever the term represents.

Applying the Skill To understand what conservatism is, students will need to understand some key terms. Ask students to define and give an example of the following:

1. Big government *Government that is involved in many aspects of public life. Example: desegregation of public schools by government order.*

2. Entitlements *Government programs that guarantee benefits to certain people. Example: Social Security.*

3. Affirmative action *A government program to make up for past discrimination against certain people by giving them preference in being hired for jobs. Example: quotas for hiring women and African Americans.*

4. Special-interest group *A group concerned with one particular issue and working to win lawmakers and others to their view. Examples: The National Rifle Association and Mothers Against Drunk Driving.*

IN-DEPTH RESOURCES: UNIT 9
Skillbuilder Practice: Clarifying, p. 23

Teacher's Edition 979

KEY PLAYER

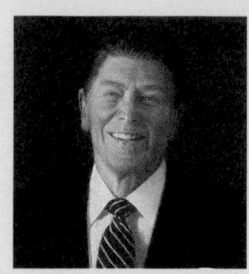

RONALD REAGAN
1911–

Ronald Wilson Reagan was born in 1911 in Tampico, Illinois. He grew up in Dixon, Illinois, graduated from nearby Eureka College, and then worked as a sports announcer in Des Moines, Iowa. In 1937, Reagan moved to Hollywood and became a movie actor, eventually making 54 films. As president of the Screen Actors Guild, he worked actively to remove alleged Communist influences from the movie industry.

Reagan had the ability to express his ideas in simple and clear language that the average voter could understand. When he proposed a 10 percent cut in government spending on social programs, he stated, "We can lecture our children about extravagance until we run out of voice and breath, or we can cut their extravagance by simply reducing their allowance."

A SUCCESS STRATEGY One of the most active segments of the Conservative Coalition was a confederation of various religious groups. These groups were encouraged and guided by Christian televangelists—evangelists, or preachers, who conduct religious telecasts—such as Jerry Falwell, Jim Bakker, Oral Roberts, Jimmy Swaggart, and Pat Robertson. Many of these conservative voters came to call themselves the **Moral Majority.** The Moral Majority consisted mostly of evangelical and fundamentalist Christians who interpreted the Bible literally and believed in absolute standards of right and wrong. They condemned liberal attitudes and behaviors and argued for a restoration of traditional moral values. They worked toward their political goals by using direct mail campaigns and raising money to support candidates.

As individual conservative groups formed networks, they created a movement dedicated to bringing back what they saw as traditional American values. They hoped their ideas would help to reduce the nation's high divorce rate, lower the number of out-of-wedlock births, encourage individual responsibility, and generally revive traditional values.

> **A PERSONAL VOICE**
> Our nation's internal problems are the direct result of her spiritual condition. . . . Right living must be established as an American way of life. . . . Now is the time to begin calling America back to God, back to the Bible, back to morality!
> **THE REVEREND JERRY FALWELL**

Conservatives Win Political Power

By the mid-1970s, a strong conservative movement had four major tenets:

• Shrinking the federal government and lowering spending
• Promoting traditional morality and values
• Stimulating business by reducing government regulations and lowering taxes
• Strengthening the national defense.

But to achieve success politically, the conservative movement needed two things: a viable presidential candidate and an opportunity to present its case to the people. In the 1970s, conservatives found the candidate. In 1980, the conservative movement found its opportunity, and for the next twelve years presidents Reagan and Bush were the primary spokespersons and political leaders for both Republicans and conservatives.

REAGAN'S APPEAL In 1976, Ronald Reagan had lost the Republican nomination to incumbent Gerald Ford. But after a series of hard-fought primaries, Reagan won the 1980 nomination and chose **George Bush,** his leading competitor, as his running mate. He ran against incumbent President Jimmy Carter and Vice-President Walter Mondale, who were chosen again by the Democrats despite their low standing in the opinion polls.

Originally a New Deal Democrat, Ronald Reagan had become a conservative Republican during the 1950s. He claimed that he had not left the Democratic Party but rather that the party had left him. As a spokesman for General Electric, he toured the country making speeches in favor of free enterprise and against big government. In 1964, he campaigned hard for Barry Goldwater, the Republican candidate for president. His speech nominating Goldwater at the 1964 Republican convention made Reagan a serious candidate for public office.

In 1966 Reagan was elected governor of California and in 1970 he was reelected.

THE 1980 PRESIDENTIAL ELECTION In 1980, changes in the voting population favored Reagan as voters aged and moved in increasing numbers to the Sunbelt—the Southern and Southwestern regions of the country. In those regions, there was hostility to Washington and big government.

Reagan ran on a number of key issues. Supreme Court decisions on abortion, pornography, the teaching of evolution, and limiting prayer in public schools all antagonized conservative voters in the country, and they rallied to Reagan. The Iranian hostage crisis and the weak economy under Carter, particularly the high rate of inflation, also helped Reagan. He also helped himself with a staunch anticommunism that led him to refer to the Soviet Union as the "evil empire."

Thanks in part to his acting career and his long experience in the public eye, Reagan was an extremely effective candidate. In contrast to Carter, who often seemed stiff and nervous, Reagan was relaxed, charming, and affable. He loved making quips: "A recession is when your neighbor loses his job. A depression is when you lose yours. A recovery is when Jimmy Carter loses his." Reagan's long-standing skill at simplifying issues and presenting them clearly earned him the nickname "The Great Communicator." Also, his commitment to military and economic strength appealed to many Americans.

Only 52.6 percent of American voters went to the polls in 1980. Reagan won the election by a narrow majority; he got 44 million votes, or 51 percent of the total. His support, however, was spread throughout the country and so Reagan carried 44 states and won 489 electoral votes. Republicans also gained control of the Senate for the first time since 1954. As Reagan assumed the presidency, many people were buoyed by his genial smile and his assertion that it was "morning again in America."

Now, at last, conservatives had elected one of their own—a true believer in less government, lower taxes, and traditional values. Once elected, Reagan worked aggressively to translate the conservative agenda into public policy.

D. Answer Reagan benefited from high inflation, anxiety about the nation's future, and a burgeoning conservative mood.

THINK THROUGH HISTORY
D. Analyzing Causes What factors led to Reagan's victory in 1980?

Election of 1980

ELECTORAL AND POPULAR VOTES

Party	Candidate	Electoral votes	Popular vote
■ Republican	Ronald Reagan	489	43,904,153
■ Democratic	Jimmy Carter	49	35,483,883
Independent	John Anderson		5,720,060

3 Alaska
4 Hawaii
3 Washington, D.C.

The Conservative Tide **981**

Section 1 Assessment

1. TERMS & NAMES

Identify:
• Ronald Reagan
• entitlement program
• New Right
• reverse discrimination
• Conservative Coalition
• Moral Majority
• George Bush

2. SUMMARIZING Use a cluster diagram to record the issues that conservatives believed in strongly.

Conservative Issues

Choose one issue and explain in a paragraph the conservative position on that issue.

3. ANALYZING MOTIVES How did the leaders of the conservative movement of the 1980s want to change government?

THINK ABOUT
• the conservative view of government compared to the liberal view
• the groups that made up the Conservative Coalition
• how those changes would affect existing government programs

4. SYNTHESIZING Who were the main groups that made up the Conservative Coalition and why did Ronald Reagan appeal to them?

THINK ABOUT
• their economic beliefs
• their political beliefs
• their religious beliefs

ANSWERS

1. TERMS & NAMES

Ronald Reagan, p. 979

entitlement program, p. 979

New Right, p. 979

reverse discrimination, p. 979

Conservative Coalition, p. 979

Moral Majority, p. 980

George Bush, p. 980

2. SUMMARIZING

Possible Answers:
reduce entitlement programs
end affirmative action
cut back government
end busing
stop regulating guns
outlaw abortion
defeat the ERA
allow school prayer
reduce taxes
strengthen national defense

3. ANALYZING MOTIVES

Possible Responses: The conservatives wanted to reduce government, lower taxes, and end liberal programs such as gun control, affirmative action, and busing. At the same time, they wanted government to increase national defense and to promote certain moral values.

4. SYNTHESIZING

Possible Responses: Reagan appealed to the Moral Majority because he opposed Supreme Court decisions on abortion, school prayer, and pornography. He appealed to people who favored free enterprise. He appealed to the struggling middle class because he promised to improve the economy. He appealed to many people because he seemed likable and was a good public speaker.

OBJECTIVES

(1) To summarize Reagan's economic programs.

(2) To describe the changes that occurred in the makeup and decisions of the Supreme Court.

(3) To identify results of federal deregulation of the savings and loan industry and of the Environmental Protection Agency.

SKILLBUILDER

• Interpreting political cartoons, p. 983

CRITICAL THINKING

• Clarifying, pp. 983, 985
• Recognizing effects, p. 985
• Analyzing causes, p. 986
• Summarizing. p. 986
• Analyzing motives, p. 986
• Forming opinions, p. 986

FOCUS & MOTIVATE

▶ *Starting with the Student*
• Have there been times when students felt others—teachers, parents—were running their lives?
• What were the issues? Control of money? Values?
• Could students' feelings have been shared by citizens who were weary of government control? What issues did those citizens want under their own control?

OBJECTIVE
(1) INSTRUCT

"Reaganomics" Takes Over

▶ *Discussing Key Ideas*
• Reagan believes less government is better government.
• Many Americans are anxious about the state of the economy.

(continued on next page)

982   Chapter 33

② Conservative Policies Under Reagan and Bush

TERMS & NAMES
• Reaganomics
• supply-side economics
• Strategic Defense Initiative
• trade imbalance
• Sandra Day O'Connor
• William Rehnquist
• Geraldine Ferraro

LEARN ABOUT the programs of presidents Reagan and Bush
TO UNDERSTAND how the conservative philosophy changed government policies and priorities.

ONE AMERICAN'S STORY

Throughout the 1980 presidential campaign and in the early days of his administration, President Reagan emphasized the perilous state of the economy he inherited from President Jimmy Carter. In a speech to the nation on February 5, 1981—his first televised speech from the White House—Reagan announced his new economic program. He called for a reduction in income tax rates for individuals and a big reduction in government spending.

A PERSONAL VOICE

I'm speaking to you tonight to give you a report on the state of our Nation's economy. I regret to say that we're in the worst economic mess since the Great Depression. . . . It's time to recognize that we've come to a turning point. We're threatened with an economic calamity of tremendous proportions, and the old business-as-usual treatment can't save us. Together, we must chart a different course.

RONALD REAGAN, televised speech to the nation on February 5, 1981

President Reagan would deal with these problems by consistently stressing four conservative objectives: stimulate business by lowering taxes, promote traditional values, reduce the size and power of the federal government, and strengthen national defense.

President Ronald Reagan

"Reaganomics" Takes Over

As soon as Reagan took office, he aimed to reduce the size and influence of the federal government, which, he thought, would encourage private investment. Since people were anxious about the economy in 1980, their concern opened the door for new approaches to taxes and the federal budget.

CUTTING GOVERNMENT PROGRAMS Reagan's strategy for downsizing the federal government included deep cuts in government spending on social programs. Yet his cuts did not affect all segments of the population equally. Entitlement programs that benefited the middle class, such as social security, Medicare, civil service, and veterans' pensions, remained intact. Yet Congress slashed by 10 percent the budget for those programs that benefited more limited groups: urban mass transit, food stamps, welfare benefits, job training, Medicaid, school lunches, and student loans. In 1981, Congress slashed domestic spending by over $40 billion, less than Reagan had asked for but still a huge sum.

REDUCING TAXES The second part of Reagan's policy called for lower taxes to accompany the reduced spending on social programs. This approach was the core of **Reaganomics**—a term used to refer to Reagan's economic policies that advocated large tax cuts to increase private investments, which in turn were intended to increase the nation's supply of goods and services. Reagan based his ideas on the work of economists such as George Gilder and Arthur Laffer.

982 CHAPTER 33

SECTION 2 RESOURCES

PRINT RESOURCES

IN-DEPTH RESOURCES: UNIT 9
Guided Reading, p. 20
Primary Sources: Political Cartoon, p. 28; *from* Ronald Reagan's Farewell Address, p. 29
Literature: from *The Bonfire of the Vanities* by Tom Wolfe, p. 32
American Lives: Sandra Day O'Connor, p. 35

ACCESS FOR STUDENTS ACQUIRING ENGLISH
Guided Reading (Spanish), p. 319

FORMAL ASSESSMENT
Section Quiz, p. 400

ALTERNATIVE ASSESSMENT BOOK
See forms for supporting and scoring alternative activities.

TECHNOLOGY RESOURCES

CRITICAL THINKING TRANSPARENCIES
CT33, The Conservative 1980s
CT67, Theory of Supply Side Economics

CD-ROM Electronic Library of Primary Sources

VIDEO *American Portfolio: A Videodisc for U.S. History* user's guide, p. 257

INTERNET McDougal Littell Learning On-Line
http://www.mcdougallittell.com

A PERSONAL VOICE
The most debilitating act a government can perpetrate on its citizens is to adopt policies that destroy the economy's production base, for it is the production base that generates any prosperity to be found in the society. U.S. policies over the last decade have had the effect of damaging this base by removing many of the incentives to economic advancement. It is necessary to restore those incentives if we are to cure our economic palsy.

ARTHUR LAFFER, *The Economics of the Tax Revolt: A Reader*

Reaganomics rested heavily upon **supply-side economics,** which held that cutting tax rates—especially on investments—would give people incentives to work, save, and invest. According to this theory, increased business investment would create more jobs, as entrepreneurs and other suppliers developed new products and services. More workers would mean more taxpayers, which would cause government revenues to increase, even though tax rates were low. Using supply-side theory as his rationale, Reagan in 1981 signed into law a 25-percent cut in federal income taxes spread out over three years.

INCREASING MILITARY SPENDING At the same time, Reagan also authorized sharp increases in military spending. Between 1981 and 1984, the Defense Department budget almost doubled. Indeed, the president revived two weapons systems—the MX missile and the B-1 bomber—about whose usefulness people disagreed. On March 23, 1983, Reagan asked the country's scientists to develop a defense system that would keep Americans safe from enemy missiles. Officially called the **Strategic Defense Initiative,** or SDI, the system quickly became known as Star Wars, after a popular movie. The Defense Department estimated the system would cost trillions of dollars.

A REVIVED AMERICAN ECONOMY As Reaganomics got underway, interest rates fell and the stock market soared, producing a long period of economic growth. The inflation rate dropped from a high of 14 percent in 1980 to 4 percent in 1988. Government revenues, however, did not increase as much as had been expected, and the government borrowed to make up for lost income.

The high interest rates that were necessary to curb inflation contributed to a severe recession during much of 1982. However, early in 1983 an economic upturn began as consumers went on a spending spree. Their confidence in the economy was bolstered by tax cuts, a decline in interest rates, and lower inflation. The stock market surged, unemployment declined, and the gross national product went up by almost 10 percent. The stock market boom lasted until 1987, when the market crashed, losing 500 points in one day. This fall was due in large part to automated and computerized buying and selling systems. However, the market recovered and then continued its upward trend.

THE NATIONAL DEBT CLIMBS During the Reagan and Bush years, the national debt soared from $900 billion in 1980 to almost $2 trillion in 1992, making the United States the world's leading debtor nation. Interest payments on this debt accounted for about 14 percent of the national budget—more than the budget for education, health, the environment, agriculture, transportation, space, science, and

ECONOMIC BACKGROUND

THE TRICKLE-DOWN THEORY
Ronald Reagan's budget director, David Stockman, used supply-side economics to draft the Economic Recovery Tax Act of 1981. His tax package cut income taxes and business taxes an average of 25 percent; the largest cuts went to those with the highest incomes. Administration officials defended the plan by claiming prosperity would trickle down to the general population.

Later, after he left his position as director of the Office of Management and Budget, Stockman called the tax act a gift to the wealthy because it most benefited those with the greatest wealth.

SKILLBUILDER
INTERPRETING POLITICAL CARTOONS
In this cartoon, President Reagan (with budget director David Stockman beside him) is driving the inflation stagecoach, when suddenly a wheel flies off. What is the meaning of the wheel flying off the coach? Besides deficits, what other economic danger is the artist pointing to? What opinion is the cartoonist trying to express?

The Conservative Tide **983**

(continued from page 982)

• Reagan thinks cutting taxes will increase investments, jobs and services.
• With less tax revenue, the government has to borrow heavily.
• Faced with a rising national debt, Congress reverses its policy and increases some taxes.

IN-DEPTH RESOURCES: UNIT 9
Guided Reading, p. 20
Primary Source: Political Cartoon, p. 28

ACCESS FOR STUDENTS ACQUIRING ENGLISH
Guided Reading (Spanish), p. 319

ELECTRONIC LIBRARY OF PRIMARY SOURCES
On the Program for Economic Recovery by Ronald Reagan

CRITICAL THINKING TRANSPARENCIES
CT33, The Conservative 1980s
CT67, Theory of Supply Side Economics

ECONOMIC BACKGROUND
The Trickle-Down Theory
Have students visualize the trickle-down theory by drawing a cartoon or a graphic organizer. Ask students to label the different parts of their drawing.

HISTORY FROM VISUALS
Political Cartoon

Reading the Cartoon
Have students identify whom the passengers inside the stagecoach represent. *Students might respond that they are the American people and that they are paying for the ride.*

Extension Have students write a letter to a foreign pen pal explaining what is expressed in the cartoon.

TEACHING OPTION

Teaching Less Proficient Readers

Charting Reaganomics Pair less proficient readers with more proficient ones to make a chart of the effects of Reaganomics. After students have read pages 982–983, have them draw up a chart that lists each of the subheads on the two pages. Then after each subhead list one example of Reagan's economic policy. The chart might look like this:

Economic Policy	Example
Cutting government programs	
Reducing taxes	
Increasing military spending	
A revived American economy	
The national debt climbs	

Judicial Power Shifts to the Right

▶ *Starting with the Student*
Suppose students were performing in a music competition. Whom would they prefer to have as their judge?

• Would they want to be judged by someone who liked the same kind of music as they did, or someone who hated their music?

▶ *Discussing Key Ideas*
• Reagan and Bush have the opportunity to name conservative justices to the Supreme Court.
• The new Court revisits many past decisions made by a more liberal Court.

NOW & THEN
Clarence Thomas Versus Anita Hill

Have students write a paragraph defending or criticizing Anita Hill for bringing sexual harassment charges against Clarence Thomas. Ask them to be sure to give specific reasons to back up their argument.

MORE ABOUT . . .
Sandra Day O'Connor

Sandra Day O'Connor (b. 1930) was the first woman to be named to the Supreme Court. While judge of the Arizona State Court of Appeals, O'Connor had acquired a reputation for being "tough, but fair." She won easy approval to the Court.

IN-DEPTH RESOURCES: UNIT 9
American Lives: Sandra Day O'Connor, p. 35

---

technology combined. The interest payments on the national debt limited the amount of money available for investment in private enterprises. There was less money available to invest in technology and infra-structure (such as transportation, water and power lines, streets, and so forth). The country also faced a large foreign **trade imbalance**—that is, the nation was importing more goods than it was exporting. This imbalance meant that American dollars were going to other countries. On the other hand, the strong foreign competition spurred American companies to improve their products.

To reduce the budget deficit, Congress passed a sweeping new tax bill that provided for an increase in taxes other than those on income. In 1982, Reagan quietly signed it into law. Congress enacted another tax increase in 1984. In 1986 Reagan signed into law a new simplified tax system that lowered individual tax rates but raised business rates and eliminated hundreds of deductions.

Judicial Power Shifts to the Right

NOW & THEN

CLARENCE THOMAS VERSUS ANITA HILL

The effect of the televised Senate Judiciary Committee hearings on Clarence Thomas's nomination to the Supreme Court continue to this day. The hearings focused attention on sexual harassment and the lack of women in government. In the wake of the hearings, women's organizations stepped up campaigns against sexual harassment and in support of women candidates for political office. A record number of women were elected to Congress. Anita Hill continued to focus attention on the problem of sexual harassment in speeches she gave across the country.

While the hearings were going on, a gender gap developed—more women than men supported Hill, while men were more inclined to believe Thomas. The televised hearings dismayed many people as senators on both sides of the nomination tried to discredit witnesses on the other side.

After the hearings had ended, most polls showed that more people believed Anita Hill than believed Clarence Thomas. Although there was not necessarily a direct causal relationship, the number of reported sexual harassment cases skyrocketed.

One of President Reagan's objectives was to promote traditional values and morality. Perhaps the most important way in which he accomplished this was through his appointments to the Supreme Court. Decisions of the Court affected many social issues, including crime, abortion, and First Amendment rights.

THE REAGAN–BUSH SUPREME COURT NOMINATIONS Reagan extended his conservative policies to the judicial area by naming conservative judges to the Supreme Court. He nominated **Sandra Day O'Connor,** Antonin Scalia, and Anthony M. Kennedy to fill the seats left by retiring judges. He also nominated Justice **William Rehnquist,** the most conservative justice on the court at the time, to the position of Chief Justice. By the end of his term in office, Reagan had appointed nearly half of all the federal district and appeals judges. These new appointees handed down conservative opinions on abortion rights and race discrimination.

President Bush later strengthened the new conservative perspective on the bench when he successfully nominated David H. Souter to replace the retiring Justice William Brennan. He also nominated Clarence Thomas to take the place of Thurgood Marshall. However, controversy exploded when law professor Anita Hill testified that Thomas had sexually harassed her when she worked for him in the 1980s at the Equal Employment Opportunity Commission (EEOC). The all-male Senate Judiciary Committee did not fully investigate the charges until after they became public knowledge. Thomas eventually won approval by a final vote of 52 to 48.

Anita Hill and Clarence Thomas testifying before the Senate Judiciary Committee in October 1991.

The Reagan and Bush appointments to the Supreme Court ended the liberal point of view of the Court that had begun under Franklin Roosevelt. These appointments became increasingly significant as the Court revisited constitutional issues related to such topics as discrimination, abortion, and affirmative action. In 1989, the Court, in a series of rulings, restricted a woman's right to an abortion. The Court also imposed new restrictions on civil rights laws that were designed to protect the rights of women and minorities. In the 1990–1991 session, the Court narrowed the rights of arrested persons.

Cooperative Activity: Researching Supreme Court Decisions

Task: Student groups will research rulings by the Supreme Court during the Reagan and Bush years.

Purpose: To help students understand the changing attitudes of the Supreme Court.

Activity: Groups of three or four students will research one or two of the justices who served on the Court during the Reagan and Bush presidencies. They will make a tally of how the justices they research voted on topics such as

abortion, discrimination, and affirmative action. Each group will also write a short report summarizing the records of the justices they researched. The groups will then meet together to combine their tallies and look at the Court as a whole.

📁 **Building a Portfolio:** Students adding presentations to their portfolios should attach a note pointing out their own contribution.

ALTERNATIVE ASSESSMENT BOOK
Standards for Evaluating a Cooperative Activity

Standards for Evaluation
Reports should . . .

• demonstrate an understanding of the issues before the Court
• show the positions of the justices relative to the social and political values of the whole country
• be clear and well organized

Deregulating the Economy

Reagan achieved his third objective—reducing the size and power of the federal government—largely by cutting back on (or deregulating) federal government regulation of industry. As part of his campaign for a smaller government, he removed price controls on oil and gas and eliminated federal health and safety inspections for nursing homes. He deregulated the airline industry (allowing airlines to abandon convenient but unprofitable air routes) and the savings and loan industry. One of the positive results of this deregulation was that it increased competition and often resulted in lower prices for the consumer.

In some cases Reagan's efforts at deregulation meant that government regulation simply stopped, since state or local governments were not able to pick up the burden of regulating airlines or controlling oil prices. In other cases, deregulation transferred financial burdens and a great deal of regulatory responsibility to state and local governments.

THE SAVINGS AND LOAN INDUSTRY   Under the Reagan administration, the savings and loan industry was deregulated. Savings and loan institutions (sometimes called thrifts) were allowed to invest in commercial real estate, such as shopping malls, golf courses, and office buildings. Some S & Ls (as Savings and Loans are called) made risky loans on real estate. Even if they made risky investments, the government stood ready to pay individual investors up to $100,000 in savings insurance.

As the economy slowed down, many of the risky S & L investments lost large amounts of money. From 1988 to 1990, approximately 600 S & Ls failed, wiping out investor savings. Charles Keating, president of Lincoln Savings and Loan in California, lost more than $2.6 billion of depositors' money. He made political contributions to several senators to keep his operation from being investigated. Keating and others like him were accused of having left the S & L industry in ruins. The federal government and the American taxpayer were left to clean up the mess.

THE ENVIRONMENT   In a further effort at deregulation, President Reagan cut the budget for the Environmental Protection Agency (EPA), which had been established in 1970 to fight pollution and conserve natural resources. He ignored pleas from Canada to reduce acid rain and appointed administrators sympathetic to business to serve in environmentally sensitive offices. For example, James Watt, Reagan's secretary of the interior, sold millions of acres of public land to private developers—often at bargain prices. He opened the continental shelf to oil and gas drilling, which many people thought posed environmental risks. Watt also encouraged timber cutting in national forests and eased restrictions on coal mining.

At the same time, EPA administrator Anne Gorsuch Burford and Assistant Administrator Rita Lavelle fired hundreds of inspectors at the Environmental Protection Agency. This caused a 75 percent drop in the number of antipollution cases referred to the Justice Department for prosecution. As a result of these actions, Watt came under fire from many quarters, and he resigned in 1983. Lavelle also resigned in 1983, and Burford was dismissed. The Reagan administration continued to oppose federal intervention to preserve the environment, though it did agree to support the 1980 Superfund bill, aimed at eliminating dangerous toxic waste sites.

Margin notes (left column)

THINK THROUGH HISTORY
B. Recognizing Effects What were the broad effects of deregulation in various federal agencies?

B. Answer There was an elimination of much regulatory policy, as well as a transfer of responsibility for regulation to state and local governments.

C. Answer the Savings and Loan scandal and the environment.

THINK THROUGH HISTORY
C. Clarifying In what two areas were the negative aspects of deregulation particularly apparent during the Reagan and Bush years? Why?

HISTORICAL SPOTLIGHT

AN ASSASSINATION ATTEMPT

On March 30, 1981, President Reagan and other members of his staff were shot by a mentally unbalanced man named John Hinckley, Jr. While being wheeled into surgery to have a bullet removed, the president said to his wife, Nancy, "Honey, I forgot to duck" (a line first used by boxer Jack Dempsey after a knockout in the 1920s). In the operating room, Reagan said to the assembled team of surgeons, "I hope you fellas are Republicans." Reagan recovered speedily, and his popularity grew.

President Reagan is shot as he waves, and Secret Service agents shove him into the waiting presidential limousine.

Right column (Teacher's Edition)

Deregulating the Economy

▶ *Discussing Key Ideas*
- Reagan and conservatives want to reduce federal regulation of industry.
- Some regulatory responsibilities pass from the federal to state and local authorities; some regulations are discontinued altogether.
- Without regulation the savings and loan industry fares badly.
- Deregulation weakens the ability of the EPA to function well, and top officials resign or are dismissed.

HISTORICAL SPOTLIGHT
An Assassination Attempt

Discuss with students why President Reagan's comments and actions following the assassination attempt endeared him to the American people. Have students write a paragraph summarizing their views.

MORE ABOUT . . .
The S & L Crisis

In 1990 the head of the General Accounting Office told Congress that the total cost of bailing out the failed S & Ls would surpass the cost of the Marshall Plan, which rebuilt Europe after World War II. Other experts have reckoned the bailout cost as much as twice that of the Vietnam War, in comparable dollar value, and four times that of the Korean War.

TEACHING OPTIONS

Exploring Themes

Women in America Point out to students that during the Reagan and Bush presidencies the Supreme Court was a focus for discussion concerning the role of women in social, political, and business affairs. The first woman Supreme Court justice, Sandra Day O'Connor, was appointed. The testimony of Anita Hill, although it brought out many negative aspects of women's struggle for equality in the workplace, pushed that issue to the forefront of the nation's consciousness.

Teaching Gifted and Talented Students

Government's Role in Business Some political commentators have labeled as an irony the government's stepping in and cleaning up problems created by deregulation. They point to the government's takeover of failed S & Ls and to the Federal Reserve Board's actions in preventing a breakdown of the stock market in 1987. Ask your gifted and talented students to research the government's actions in response to these economic crises. Have them write a paper pro or con on the thesis that Reagan's policies actually strengthened rather than weakened the role of government in business.

Conservative Victories in 1984 and 1988

Starting with the Student
Discuss with students conservative strengths and weaknesses going into the 1984 and 1988 campaigns.

▶ **Discussing Key Ideas**
• The Conservative Coalition remains intact going into the 1984 campaign.
• The support of the coalition, along with Reagan's popularity, sweeps him to victory in 1984.
• In 1988, much of the nation sees little reason for change, and Bush wins the election.

IN-DEPTH RESOURCES: UNIT 9
Primary Source: *from* Ronald Reagan's Farewell Address, p. 29

ASSESS & RETEACH

Section 2 Assessment
Have students answer the questions, note those that gave them trouble, and then note page references where answers can be found.

Self-Assessment
Have students identify those questions they were most unsure of and, with the help of a partner, locate the portion of the text that best helps them frame an answer.

Section Quiz

FORMAL ASSESSMENT
Section Quiz, p. 400

Reteach
Survey the students to find out what was difficult for them and then use the results of the survey to concentrate on that material.

CLOSE

During the Reagan and Bush presidencies conservative beliefs were transformed into political and economic policies.

Conservative Victories in 1984 and 1988

It was clear by 1984 that Reagan had forged a coalition of conservative voters who approved highly of his policies. These voters included

• Business people—who wanted to deregulate the economy
• Southern voters—who welcomed the limits on federal power
• Western states—which resented federal controls on mining and grazing
• Reagan Democrats—who agreed with Reagan on limiting federal government and thought that the Democratic Party had drifted too far to the left.

Out of what conservatives saw as the major successes of his first term, Reagan had put together a strong conservative bloc of voters.

THE 1984 PRESIDENTIAL ELECTION In 1984, Reagan and Bush won the Republican nomination for reelection without challenge. Walter Mondale, who had been vice-president under President Carter, won the Democratic Party's nomination and chose Representative **Geraldine Ferraro** of New York as his running mate. Ferraro became the first woman on a major party's presidential ticket.

Reagan and Bush maintained their popularity and won by a landslide, carrying every state but Mondale's Minnesota and the District of Columbia. As in 1980, Reagan received the bulk of his support from traditional Republicans, conservative Christians, and disenchanted Democrats.

THE 1988 PRESIDENTIAL ELECTION Despite a deepening deficit, rising inflation, and foreign-policy scandals, a majority of Americans were economically comfortable, and they attributed their comfort to Reagan and Bush. When Democrat Michael Dukakis, governor of Massachusetts, ran for the presidency in 1988 against George Bush, most voters saw little reason for change. Dukakis pointed to his economic record as governor of Massachusetts.

George Bush simply built on President Reagan's legacy by promising, "Read my lips: no new taxes" in his acceptance speech to the Republican convention. He stressed his commitment to the conservative ideas of the Moral Majority. Though Bush asserted that he wanted a "kinder, gentler" nation, his campaign sponsored a number of negative "attack ads." Some commentators believe the ads contributed to the lowest voter turnout in 64 years. Only half of the eligible voters went to the polls in 1988. Fifty-three percent voted for George Bush, who won 426 electoral votes. The electoral victories of Reagan and Bush were translated into conservative social and political policies that were to characterize their years in office.

George Bush announces his presidential candidacy at a rally in 1987.

D. Answer
Reagan put together a winning coalition of businesspeople, Southern and Western states, and disenchanted Democrats. Bush built on Reagan's legacy and made effective use of negative ads.

THINK THROUGH HISTORY
D. Analyzing Causes What factors contributed to Reagan's victory in 1984 and Bush's in 1988?

Section ❷ Assessment

1. TERMS & NAMES
Identify:
• Reaganomics
• supply-side economics
• Strategic Defense Initiative
• trade imbalance
• Sandra Day O'Connor
• William Rehnquist
• Geraldine Ferraro

2. SUMMARIZING Use a diagram to explore the effects of Reaganomics.

| Definition of Reaganomics |
| Short-Term Effects |
| Long-Term Effects |

Explain in a paragraph whether you think Reaganomics was good or bad for the economy.

3. ANALYZING MOTIVES Why did presidents Reagan and Bush think it was important to appoint more conservative justices to the Supreme Court?

THINK ABOUT
• the impact that the Supreme Court has on the nation's laws
• rulings that the Court made on social issues in the late 1980s and early 1990s

4. FORMING OPINIONS In your opinion, was deregulation generally good or bad for the country, or a mixture of both? Explain.

THINK ABOUT
• the effect of deregulating the savings and loan industry
• the effect of cutting back on environmental regulations
• the effect of deregulation on the airline industry and other businesses

986 CHAPTER 33

ANSWERS

1. TERMS & NAMES
Reaganomics, p. 982
supply-side economics, p. 983
Strategic Defense Initiative, p. 983
trade imbalance, p. 984
Sandra Day O'Connor, p. 984
William Rehnquist, p. 984
Geraldine Ferraro, p. 986

2. SUMMARIZING
Possible Answers:
Definition: Reagan's economic policies advocated large tax cuts to increase private investments, leading to an increase in the nation's supply of goods and services.
Short-Term Effects: Interest rates fell, stocks soared, inflation dropped, the economy grew.
Long-Term Effects: Increased national debt, budget deficit, trade imbalance, higher taxes.

3. ANALYZING MOTIVES
Possible Responses: The Supreme Court decides which laws are constitutional. Because Reagan and Bush supported the passage of more conservative laws, they wanted a conservative Court that would not strike down those laws. They hoped that a more conservative Court would strike down liberal laws and liberal judicial rulings, such as those allowing abortion.

4. FORMING OPINIONS
Possible Responses:
Deregulation was generally bad because it led to many S & L failures and to exploitation of the environment. Deregulation was generally good, because it increased competition and often lowered prices. Deregulation was mixed, because it had both good and bad results.

TERMS & NAMES
- AIDS (acquired immune deficiency syndrome)
- pay equity
- L. Douglas Wilder
- Jesse Jackson
- affirmative action

LEARN ABOUT the social and economic changes that occurred in society during the presidencies of Reagan and Bush

TO UNDERSTAND the effects of the new conservative movement in American politics.

ONE AMERICAN'S STORY

Trevor Ferrell lived an ordinary life in Gladwyne, an affluent suburb, 12 miles from downtown Philadelphia, Pennsylvania. Trevor had brothers and sisters, his own room, a favorite pillow, a fondness for video games, and a motorbike he loved to ride around the cul-de-sac where he lived. He did all right in school, though his parents and teachers thought he didn't work hard enough. In short, he seemed like a typical 12-year-old boy until he watched a television news report about homeless people in the City of Brotherly Love (the nickname for Philadelphia).

Trevor was astonished. "Do people really live like that?" he asked his parents. "I thought they lived like that in India, but not here, I mean in America." Trevor convinced his parents to drive downtown that night, where he gave a pillow and blanket to the first homeless man he saw. The next night, he returned with more blankets, and soon, he and his family were taking food and clothing donated by neighbors to the homeless.

Trevor Ferrell listens to a homeless person on the corner of 12th and Chestnut streets in Philadelphia.

A PERSONAL VOICE

They have to live on the streets, and right after you see one of them, you see someone in a limousine pull up to a huge, empty mansion. It's such a difference. Some people can get anything they want, and these other people couldn't get a penny if they needed one.

TREVOR FERRELL, quoted in *Trevor's Place*

As Trevor saw, the restored American economy of the 1980s did not mean renewed prosperity for everyone in American society. As presidents Reagan and Bush pursued conservative domestic policies, people disagreed about the impact of these policies.

In these controversies, one truth emerged—American society during the 1980s was going through rapid changes. And Americans were at odds about how to deal with these changes.

Health, Education, and Cities in Crisis

In the 1980s, both in the cities (which supported large populations of poor people, minorities, and recent immigrants) and in rural and suburban areas, state and local government budgets strained under crises in health, education, and safety. Americans directed their attention to issues such as AIDS, drug abuse, abortion, education, and the urban crisis.

HEALTH ISSUES One of the most troubling issues that Americans argued about in the 1980s was **AIDS (acquired immune deficiency syndrome).** Beginning in 1981, AIDS began spreading rapidly throughout the world. Caused by a virus that destroys the immune system, AIDS weakens the body so that it is prone to infections and normally rare cancers.

After years of intensive research, no cure had been found. AIDS is transmitted through bodily fluids, and most of the early victims of the disease were either homosexual men or intravenous drug users who shared needles. However, people also contracted AIDS through contaminated blood transfusions or by being born

The Conservative Tide **987**

SECTION 3 RESOURCES

 PRINT RESOURCES

IN-DEPTH RESOURCES: UNIT 9
Guided Reading, p. 21
Geography Application: Latino Population in the 1980s, p. 24
Primary Source: Civil Rights in the 1980s, p. 30

ACCESS FOR STUDENTS ACQUIRING ENGLISH
Guided Reading (Spanish), p. 320
Geography Application: Latino Population in the 1980s (Spanish), p. 323

FORMAL ASSESSMENT
Section Quiz, p. 401

ALTERNATIVE ASSESSMENT BOOK
See forms for supporting and scoring alternative activities.

 TECHNOLOGY RESOURCES

CD-ROM *Grolier Multimedia Encyclopedia*
Electronic Library of Primary Sources

VIDEO *American Portfolio: A Videodisc for U.S. History*
user's guide, pp. 257, 259, 260

INTERNET McDougal Littell Learning On-Line
http://www.mcdougallittell.com

Section 3 Overview

OBJECTIVES

1 To identify national concerns about health issues, drug use, education, and the crisis of the cities.

2 To summarize political, economic, and social gains achieved by women.

3 To describe how conservative policies affected minority groups.

CRITICAL THINKING

- Summarizing, pp. 988, 989, 991, 993
- Identifying problems, pp. 989, 990
- Synthesizing, p. 993
- Comparing, p. 993

FOCUS & MOTIVATE

▶ *Starting with the Student*
- What do students think are the greatest problems in their school community? Do they include the quality of their education? gangs? the treatment of women and minorities?
- Do students think these problems might also have bothered students in the 1980s? How might the problems have been different?

OBJECTIVE
1 INSTRUCT

Health, Education, and Cities in Crisis

▶ *Starting with the Student*
Discuss with students the social issues that troubled the nation in the 1980s. Ask students which issues they would like to know more about. Have them create a chart listing what they know and what they would like to know. Suggest they keep a column open for what they will learn and ask them to fill in the column as they read.

(continued on next page)

(continued from page 987)

The chart might look like this:

	What I Know	What I'd Like to Know	What I've Learned
Gangs			
Drugs			

▶ **Discussing Key Ideas**
- The rising incidence of AIDS troubles the nation.
- Americans disagree about abortion.
- Reagan and Bush take a hard stand against drug dealers and users.
- Most Americans criticize the public schools.
- Cities face a crisis.

IN-DEPTH RESOURCES: UNIT 9
Guided Reading, p. 21

ACCESS FOR STUDENTS ACQUIRING ENGLISH
Guided Reading (Spanish), p. 320

ON THE WORLD STAGE
Worldwide AIDS

Ask students which of the 1996 statistics about AIDS most surprised them. Have students write several sentences summarizing what they learned.

 GROLIER MULTIMEDIA ENCYCLOPEDIA
AIDS epidemic

MORE ABOUT . . .
Nancy Reagan

Nancy Reagan was born Anne Frances Robbins, in New York City in 1923. She was adopted by her stepfather, a Chicago surgeon, and took the name Nancy Davis. After graduation from Smith College she had a brief career as an actress but gave it up after marrying Ronald Reagan in 1952.

ON THE WORLD STAGE

WORLDWIDE AIDS

By mid-1996, the World Health Organization estimated that more than 27.9 million children and adults in 194 different countries had been infected with HIV (human immunodeficiency virus) which causes AIDS, and 21.8 million were living with HIV/AIDS. More than 7.7 million children and adults had been diagnosed with full-blown AIDS, and at least 5.8 million people had already died. Over half of all AIDS patients were under 35 years old. Over 70 percent of all infections throughout the world were the result of heterosexual activity.

> *"Just Say No!"*
>
> **NANCY REAGAN,**
> SLOGAN IN THE WAR AGAINST DRUGS

988 Chapter 33

---

to infected mothers. As the 1980s progressed, increasing numbers of heterosexuals began contracting AIDS as well. As the epidemic grew, so did concern over the rising cost of care for AIDS sufferers.

ABORTION Many Americans were concerned about abortion in the 1980s. Abortion had been legal in the United States since 1973, when the Supreme Court ruled in *Roe* v. *Wade* that first-trimester abortions were protected by a woman's right to privacy. Opponents of legalized abortion quickly organized under the "pro-life" banner. They argued that human life began at conception and that no one had the right to terminate a human life by her individual decision. Proponents of legalized abortion described themselves as "pro-choice." They argued that reproductive choices were personal health care matters and noted that many women died from abortions performed by unskilled people in unsterile settings before the procedure was legalized.

In July of 1989, the Supreme Court ruled in *Webster* v. *Reproductive Health Care Services* that states had the right to impose new restrictions on abortion. As a result, abortion restrictions varied from state to state.

In May of 1991, the Court further limited abortion rights. It ruled in *Rust* v. *Sullivan* that the federal government could prevent doctors in government-sponsored health clinics from providing women with information about abortion—even if a woman's health was at risk. Anti-abortion activists applauded the new ruling, but abortion rights supporters argued that the ruling created one level of health care for the affluent and another for the poor. Many doctors felt that the decision violated professional ethics by telling them how to practice medicine. Congress passed a bill designed to overturn the Court's restrictions on abortion in *Rust* v. *Sullivan*, but President Bush vetoed the bill. His veto was sustained by the Congress.

DRUG ABUSE Battles over abortion rights sometimes competed for public attention with concerns over rising drug abuse. Jobless youth in the cities and teenagers in the suburbs joined gangs to gain power and money by selling crack cocaine and other drugs. In 1980, only 10 cities reported serious problems, but by 1990, more than 125 cities had gang-related troubles. As crime and drug use rose, different factions promoted diverse approaches to the crisis. A few people argued that drugs should be legalized to reduce the power of gangs who made a living selling illegal drugs. Others called for more treatment facilities in order to treat addiction. The Reagan administration launched a war on drugs and supported moves to prosecute users as well as dealers.

The president called for random drug testing at government-related workplaces, and in 1988, Congress passed a law cutting off college loans and public housing for marijuana users. Congress also provided funds for antidrug education in the schools. Businesses and some institutions began random drug testing to identify drug users. The military used armed forces to patrol the nation's borders in an attempt to prevent drug smuggling. At the same time, First Lady Nancy Reagan toured the country with an antidrug campaign that admonished students to "Just Say No!" to drugs. These measures helped reduce drug use among middle-class Americans, but the availability of illegal drugs apparently remained the same.

President Bush followed in Reagan's footsteps and called for action against drugs, which he called "[our] gravest domestic threat." The president urged "a war on drugs"—by which he meant crack cocaine and similar substances.

988 CHAPTER 33

The AIDS quilt is displayed on the National Mall in Washington, D.C. Each panel honors a person who died of AIDS.

A. Answer
Launches war on drugs; prosecuted users as well as dealers; random drug testing; cutting off college loans and public housing to drug users; antidrug education; use of military to patrol nation's borders to prevent drug smuggling.

THINK THROUGH HISTORY
A. Summarizing What were some of the steps taken during the Reagan administration to combat drug use?

TEACHING OPTIONS

Making Connections Across the Curriculum

Science For young American adults between the ages of 25 and 44, AIDS-related diseases had by 1994 become the second leading cause of death in men and the fifth leading cause in women. In major cities such as New York, Los Angeles, and San Francisco, AIDS had become the leading cause of death among young adult men. In New York City, AIDS was the leading cause of death among women aged 25 to 44. Major drug companies were working on developing new drugs (such as AZT) to fight the ravages of AIDS, but a cure still has not been found. Ask students to research the topic of an AIDS vaccine.

Making Connections Across the Curriculum

Writing Nancy Reagan's "Just Say No!" message was an emotional appeal to young people. In writing, emotional appeals make use of adjectives and adverbs that make an immediate, visceral appeal to the reader or listener. Pretend that you are writing slogans, ads, and bumper stickers for an antidrug campaign. What words and phrases would you use to appeal to your audience? Write an advertisement for a "Just Say No!" campaign.

Bush's program emphasized law enforcement: stopping drugs at the nation's borders, jailing drug-using Americans for long terms, and establishing a death penalty for drug dealers.

EDUCATION   Education was another issue that stirred people's concerns about the future of their children. In 1983, a presidential commission issued a report on education entitled *A Nation at Risk*. The report revealed that American students' test scores lagged behind those of students from most other industrialized nations. Further, the report showed that scores on standardized achievement tests had sunk below those in 1957, when the Soviets launched *Sputnik*. In addition, the report stated that 23 million Americans were unable to follow an instruction manual or fill out a job application form. It also noted that many 17-year-olds could not read a paragraph and draw an intelligent conclusion, or distinguish the state of Florida from Russia on an outline map.

The commission's findings and those of various scholars touched off a debate about education. The commission recommended more homework, longer school days, and an extended school year. It also promoted increased pay and merit raises for teachers and more emphasis on basic subjects such as English, math, science, social studies, and computer science.

Some educators recommended more Head Start programs, smaller classes, tutorials, and an emphasis on critical thinking. Others advocated a system that would give parents the money that would have been spent on their child in a public school to send that child to a private school if the parents chose to do so. Still others favored "magnet schools" and parental choice among public schools.

Whatever their ideas, most Americans agreed that the public schools were, at best, educating only half the students enrolled. Furthermore, students who dropped out of school stood little chance of earning a living in an economy that had become increasingly complex, in part because of the dawn of the computer age.

The tremendous growth in the use of personal computers during the 1980s made education even more important for students. The information age made it imperative that students learn to use the new technology, including the hardware of computers and keyboards as well as the software of different programs. Apple computers, IBM computers and their clones (similar machines), along with all the technology associated with them, became a growth industry in the 1980s and transformed the school and the workplace.

In April 1991, President Bush announced a bold new education initiative, "America 2000." He argued that choice was the salvation of American schools and recommended allowing parents to use public funds to send their children to schools of their choice—public, private, or religious. Bush also proposed the founding of 535 new schools that would serve as models of curriculum innovation. He also urged national achievement tests. First Lady Barbara Bush toured the country to promote reading and writing skills.

THE URBAN CRISIS   The crisis in education was closely connected to the crisis in the cities. Many undereducated students were in cities such as New York, Philadelphia, Detroit, Chicago, and Washington, D.C.—municipalities whose populations had actually decreased during the 1980s. During the 1970s, the United States had become increasingly suburbanized as more and more white

"Anyone who doubts that public education in the United States is in deep trouble has not been paying attention."

JOHN EGERTON, 1982

Barbara Bush visits with children at the Friendly Place, an East Harlem family center, in her effort to call attention to illiteracy.

B. Answer Poor test scores, poor reading skills, poor math skills.

THINK THROUGH HISTORY
B. Identifying Problems What problems of schools emerged during the 1980s?

C. Answer More homework; longer school days; extended school year; increased pay for teachers; emphasis on basic subjects; Head Start programs; smaller classes; tutorials; parental choice; magnet schools; computers.

THINK THROUGH HISTORY
C. Summarizing What were some of the proposals for improving schools?

The Conservative Tide **989**

The Equal Rights Struggle

▶ **Starting with the Student**
- Do students feel that male and female students should get the same grade for the same quality of work?
- Should they get the same pay for after-school work?
- Should the same principle apply to men and women in the work force?

▶ **Discussing Key Ideas**
- Women's rights proponents feel disappointment at the failure of the ERA to gain ratification.
- Women are underrepresented in public affairs and organize to elect more women to public office.
- Women's groups call for pay equity and family work benefits.

MORE ABOUT . . .
Geraldine Ferraro

Geraldine Ferraro (b. 1935) became the first woman nominated for such a high office by a major political party. Prior to her vice-presidential nomination Ferraro served three terms in Congress, representing a district in Queens, one of New York City's five boroughs. She built up a record of favoring benefits for women, the elderly, and labor and opposing restrictions on abortion. Following the defeat of the Mondale-Ferraro ticket, she ran unsuccessfully in 1992 for the Democratic nomination for senator from New York. She has also been talked about as a possible candidate for mayor of New York City.

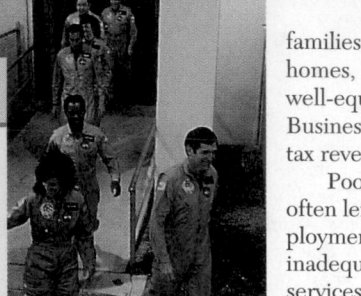

Difficult Decisions
IN HISTORY

SENDING MONEY INTO SPACE

Under the Reagan administration, the government shifted the emphasis of the space program from scientific to military and commercial applications. Beginning in 1981, NASA directed a series of space shuttle flights. The agency hoped eventually to establish a manned space station, with the shuttle ferrying workers and materials to it. However the explosion of the *Challenger* space shuttle in 1986 caused a re-examination of ventures into space.

Many people thought that the money spent on space ventures would be better spent on social, educational, and environmental needs.

1. Should the federal government spend money on space exploration when so many citizens required basic assistance?

2. If you were a legislator being asked to vote in favor of funding space exploration today, how would you vote? Why?

families responded to the lure of new homes, big lawns, shopping malls, and well-equipped schools outside the cities. Businesses moved, too, bringing jobs and tax revenue with them.

Poor people and racial minorities were often left in cities burdened by high unemployment rates, crumbling infrastructure, inadequate funds for sanitation and health services, deteriorating schools, and growing social problems. To make matters worse, federal spending on cities dropped by more than 60 percent between 1981 and 1991. AFDC (Aid to Families with Dependent Children) benefits did not keep up with inflation. And despite inflation, federal funding for low-income housing fell from $32 billion in 1978 to less than $10 billion in 1990. By 1992, thousands of people were homeless, of whom many were families with children. Cities were increasingly divided into wealthy neighborhoods and poverty-stricken areas.

In South-Central Los Angeles these areas (which had erupted in violence in 1965 and 1968) erupted again in 1992. Four white police officers had been videotaped beating an African-American man named Rodney King, who had been fleeing the officers in a speeding car. A mostly white jury found the officers not guilty. This verdict resulted in riots in Los Angeles that lasted five days and caused the deaths of 51 people. Approximately 2,400 people were injured and about $1 billion in property was damaged in the riots. Most of the damaged property belonged to merchants who some rioters believe were exploiting their neighborhoods.

D. Answer
Reaganomics led to deep cuts in aid for health, education, and social programs, which had been funded largely by the federal government.

THINK THROUGH HISTORY
D. *Identifying Problems* What were some of the problems facing cities in the 1980s?

The Equal Rights Struggle

Within this environment of dwindling resources and social struggle, women worked to achieve economic and social gains.

POLITICAL LOSSES AND GAINS During the early 1980s, women's rights activists worked to obtain ratification of the Equal Rights Amendment (ERA). Although Congress had passed the amendment in 1972, it had not yet been ratified, or approved, by three-fourths of the states. Supporters of the amendment had until June 30, 1982, to gain ratification from 38 states. They obtained only 35 of the 38 ratifications they needed, and the ERA did not become law.

With the failure of the Equal Rights Amendment, women's organizations began to concentrate on electing women to public office. Elections in 1980 and 1982 revealed a gender gap, in which women followed different voting patterns than men. More women candidates began to run for office, and in 1984 the Democrats chose Geraldine Ferraro as their vice-presidential candidate. She spoke of the necessity for women in all walks of life to continue working for equal opportunities in American society.

Democratic vice-presidential candidate Geraldine Ferraro waves to the crowd during the 1984 campaign.

A PERSONAL VOICE
It is not just those of us who have reached the top who are fighting this daily battle. It is a fight in which all of us—rich and poor, career and home oriented, young and old—participate, simply because we are women.

GERALDINE FERRARO, quoted in *Vital Speeches of the Day*, November 15, 1982

TEACHING OPTIONS

Teaching Gifted and Talented Students

Looking at Your Own Community Ask your gifted and talented students to localize their study of urban crises in the 1980s by looking at their own city or the large city nearest their community. Ask them to interview local aldermen or city officials who served during the 1980s. Have them visit the city hall to determine population growth, changing settlement patterns, and rising or falling tax revenues. Students can present their findings to the class, using visual aids such as graphs, maps, or flow charts when appropriate.

Teaching Less Proficient Readers

Identifying Main Ideas and Supporting Details Pair less proficient readers with more proficient ones to identify the main ideas and supporting details in the section on the equal rights struggle. Have students follow these steps:

1. Read the text on the equal rights struggle on pages 990 and 991.

2. List the main idea for each paragraph.

3. Go back and list the details that support each of the main ideas.

During the 1980s, the number of women in Congress increased from 28 to 47, and the number of women senators tripled—from two to six. President Reagan also named two women to his cabinet: Elizabeth Dole became secretary of transportation and Margaret Heckler became secretary of health and human services. Nevertheless, women remained underrepresented in political affairs and overrepresented among the ranks of the poor.

ECONOMIC AND SOCIAL GAINS Several factors contributed to what some called the "feminization" of poverty. By 1992, 57.8 percent of the nation's women were part of the work force, and a growing percentage of women worked as professionals and managers. However, in that same year women earned only about 76 cents for every dollar men earned. Female college graduates still earned less than male high-school graduates. Also, about 31 percent of female heads of household lived in poverty, and for African-American women the poverty rate was even higher. New trends in divorce settlements aggravated the situation. Under no-fault divorce, fewer women won alimony payments, and the courts rarely enforced the meager child support payments they awarded. As late as 1990, more than 25 percent of the males who owed child support still paid nothing at all.

To close the income gap that left so many women poor, women's organizations and unions proposed a system of **pay equity,** by which jobs would be rated on the basis of the amount of education they required, the amount of physical strength needed to perform them, and the number of people one supervised. Instead of relying on traditional pay scales, employers would establish pay rates that reflected each job's requirements. By 1989, 20 states had begun adjusting government jobs to offer pay equity for jobs of comparable worth. Many female employees received raises of up to 30 percent. Most private firms, however, resisted the idea because they believed it would be too expensive.

Women also asked for other improvements in the workplace. Since many working women headed single-parent households or had children under the age of six, they pressed for family benefits. Government and corporate benefit packages began to include maternity leaves, flexible hours and work weeks, job sharing, and work-at-home arrangements. Some of these changes were launched by individual firms, while others required government intervention. Yet the Reagan administration sharply cut the federal budget for day care, aid for dependent children, and other similar programs. Congress passed a family-leave plan in 1991 that the Bush administration vetoed.

The Fight for Rights Continues

Cuts in government programs and the backlash against civil rights initiatives, such as affirmative action, affected other groups as well.

AFRICAN AMERICANS African Americans made striking political gains during the 1980s, even as their economic progress suffered. By the mid-1980s, African-American mayors governed dozens of cities, including Los Angeles, Detroit, Chicago, Atlanta, New Orleans, Philadelphia, and Washington, D.C. Hundreds of communities in both the North and the South had elected African Americans to serve as sheriffs, school board members, state legislators, and members of Congress. In 1990, **L. Douglas Wilder** of Virginia became the nation's first African-American governor. The Reverend **Jesse Jackson** ran for the Democratic presidential nomination in 1984 and 1988.

"As a bureau chief in the DA's [district attorney's] office, . . . I learned that I was being paid less than men with similar responsibilities. When I asked why, I was told 'you don't really need the money, Gerry, you've got a husband.' "

GERALDINE FERRARO

Jesse Jackson campaigns for the Democratic presidential nomination in 1984.

The Conservative Tide **991**

Left margin notes:

E. Answer Women were elected to public office in increasing numbers, and women employed on government jobs received raises through the implementation of pay equity.

THINK THROUGH HISTORY
E. Summarizing What gains did women make during the 1980s and early 1990s?

OBJECTIVE
(3) INSTRUCT

The Fight for Rights Continues

▶ *Discussing Key Ideas*
• African Americans and Latino Americans see economic aid slashed by Reagan and Bush.
• Latino Americans and Asian Americans are the fastest-growing minorities during the 1980s.
• Some Latinos and non-Latinos differ in their views on bilingualism.
• Native Americans operate gambling casinos.
• Homosexual men and women become politically more visible.

IN-DEPTH RESOURCES: UNIT 9
Geography Application: Latino Population in the 1980s, p. 24
Primary Source: Civil Rights in the 1980s, p. 30

MORE ABOUT . . .
Jesse Jackson's Campaign

In 1984, Jesse Jackson became the first African American to make a serious bid for the presidency. He tried again in 1988, when he was one of seven Democrats to enter the race for the Democratic nomination. Jackson claimed the second highest number of delegates (after Dukakis) in the New York State primary. Although Jackson lost the nomination to Dukakis, his good showing in the campaign helped him nail down some planks on minority rights in the party platform.

 ELECTRONIC LIBRARY OF PRIMARY SOURCES
from "Victim-Victimizer: Why Excel?" by Reverend Jesse L. Jackson

---

TEACHING OPTIONS

Making Connections Across Time

Women's Economic Status in the 1980s and Today In 1980, 51.5 percent of women worked outside the home. In 1994, 58.8 percent worked outside the home. Suggest to student groups that they interview working women to compare their experiences in the 1980s with women's current work experience. This should help students to become aware of issues faced by, and most important to, working women in the 1980s and 1990s.

Exploring Themes

Civil Rights Have students use a chart to summarize in a sentence one achievement by each group in pursuing equal rights.

Women	
African Americans	
Latinos	
Native Americans	
Asian Americans	
Gays and Lesbians	

NOW & THEN
Affirmative Action
Critical Thinking:
Analyzing Results Discuss with students whether or not they see a trend developing in the 1980s and 1990s regarding affirmative action. How might they go about obtaining the information that would allow them to diagram the trend, if it exists? Have students outline the steps they might take to form an opinion.

MORE ABOUT . . .
Richmond v. *J. A. Croson Company*

In an attempt to redress past discrimination, Richmond, Virginia, like 190 other cities and 36 states, adopted a plan for affirmative action. In 1983, Richmond passed an ordinance that required at least 30 percent of all city construction work to be subcontracted to minority-owned companies. City records showed that although 50 percent of the population was black, only 0.67 percent of its prime construction contracts in recent years had been awarded to minority firms.

Similar affirmative action programs everywhere were thrown into turmoil when the Supreme Court in 1989 reversed its earlier support of affirmative action.

NOW & THEN

AFFIRMATIVE ACTION
In the 1996 presidential campaign, affirmative action became an issue. Democratic candidate President Clinton favored current government policies supporting affirmative action, and Republican candidate Bob Dole opposed affirmative action.

Presidents Reagan and Bush, like Bob Dole, actively opposed affirmative action and racial quotas throughout the 1980s. The Supreme Court's decision in *Richmond* v. *J. A. Croson Company* was one of a series of Supreme Court decisions in 1989 that made it harder for minorities and women to sue in job discrimination cases. In 1996, voters in California approved a referendum that did away with state affirmative action programs, but the referendum has been challenged on constitutional grounds in the courts.

At the same time, however, the income gap between white Americans and African Americans was larger in 1988 than it had been in 1968. Middle-class African Americans sometimes moved into professional and managerial positions, but the poor faced a future of diminishing opportunities. In July 1989, the newly conservative Supreme Court handed down a series of decisions that reversed the nation's course on civil rights. In the case of *Richmond* v. *J. A. Croson Company*, for example, the Court reversed its earlier endorsement of **affirmative action.** This policy was meant to correct the effects of discrimination in the employment or education of minority groups or women, which often set goals and timetables for hiring minorities and women. Other decisions by the Court outlawed contracts set aside for minority businesses. Sylvester Monroe, an African-American correspondent for *Newsweek* magazine, commented on how many African Americans saw the backlash against affirmative action.

A PERSONAL VOICE
There's a finite pie and everybody wants his piece. Everybody is afraid of losing his piece of the pie. That's what the fight against affirmative action is all about. People feel threatened. As for blacks, they're passé. They're not in anymore. Nobody wants to talk about race.
SYLVESTER MONROE, quoted in *The Great Divide*

LATINOS Latinos became the fastest growing minority during the 1980s. By 1990, they constituted almost 9 percent of the population, and demographers estimated that Latinos would soon outnumber African Americans as the nation's largest minority group. About two out of three Latinos were Mexican Americans, who lived mostly in the Southwest. Puerto Ricans lived mainly in the Northeast, and Cubans lived primarily in Florida. Like African Americans, Latinos gained political power during the 1980s, when Toney Anaya became governor of New Mexico and Robert Martinez became governor of Florida. Several cities, including Denver, San Antonio, and Miami, elected mayors of Latino background. In August of 1988, President Reagan appointed Lauro Cavazos as secretary of education, and in 1990, President Bush named Dr. Antonia Coello Novello to the post of Surgeon General.

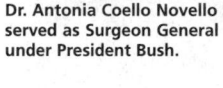

Dr. Antonia Coello Novello served as Surgeon General under President Bush.

Latino farm workers still suffered from low pay, unhealthy conditions, and high unemployment, but increasing numbers of Latinos held professional and technical positions. Latino music and salsa dancing gained widespread popularity, and writers such as Sandra Cisneros and Oscar Hijuelos won literary awards for their books. Latino architecture and crafts—such as adobe houses, walled courtyards, and vivid woven rugs—became popular elements of American style. Latino foods such as tapas, fajitas, tacos, jalapeño peppers, and jicama quickly found their way into mainstream American diets.

Many Latinos supported bilingual education. Some feared that abandoning Spanish would weaken their distinct culture. In the words of Daniel Villanueva, a television executive, "We want to be here, but without losing our language and our culture. They are a richness, a treasure that we don't care to lose." The Bilingual Education Act of 1968 and the Voting Rights Act of 1975 enabled Spanish speakers to go to school and vote in their own language, but by the mid-1980s, opposition to bilingualism was rising in some quarters. Critics argued that it slowed the rate at which Spanish-speaking people entered mainstream American life. They also feared that the nation would become split between English speakers and non–English speakers.

992 CHAPTER 33

TEACHING OPTIONS

Making Connections Across the Curriculum

Literature Ask students which of the authors mentioned on pages 992 (Sandra Cisnernos, Oscar Hijuelos) and 993 (Amy Tan, Maxine Hong Kingston) they are familiar with. Ask for suggestions of additional authors representing minority communities. If possible allow time for students to visit the school or community library and to meet with the librarian. Students may wish to prepare reports on a minority author of their choice and to include a brief excerpt from the author's work as part of their report.

Exploring Themes

Cultural Diversity Discuss with students the cultural diversity represented by the groups discussed on pages 991–993. Ask students which traditional values upheld by presidents Reagan and Bush are held in common by all the groups. *Some students may respond that broad values such as honesty, care for children, and a stable family life are accepted by all the groups. Students may also observe that some issues, such as abortion, cut across minority lines, with some members in favor and some members in opposition.*

NATIVE AMERICANS During the 1980s, the Reagan administration slashed aid to Native Americans for health, education, and other services. Driven to find new sources of revenue, Native Americans began protesting federal and state regulations that restricted gambling on reservation lands. After the Supreme Court ruled in favor of Native Americans, many tribes opened Las Vegas–style casinos, which provided additional funding for the tribes that operated them. Nonetheless, the long-term problems faced by Native Americans have not been solved by gambling casinos, although the new wealth has helped to some extent.

ASIAN AMERICANS Asian Americans comprised the second fastest-growing minority in the United States during the 1980s. By 1992, the population included about 8.3 million Asian Americans and Pacific Islanders. Asian Americans constituted 3.25 percent of the population.

Unlike African Americans and Latinos, Asian Americans made significant economic advances, but few political strides, although Senator Daniel Inouye had long been an important Japanese-American politician who represented the state of Hawaii in the U.S. Senate. Many chose to attend college and to pursue successful careers in business, science, or the arts, such as Amy Tan (author of *The Joy Luck Club*) and Maxine Hong Kingston (author of *The Woman Warrior*).

GAYS AND LESBIANS During the 1970s and 1980s, homosexual men and women emerged from political invisibility to work for legislation protecting their rights. By 1986, 26 states had reduced criminal penalties for sexual relationships between consenting adults. During his term as president, George Bush increased funding for AIDS research and called for a study on hate crimes, including attacks on homosexuals. During the 1992 campaign, however, President Bush refused to support antidiscrimination legislation. Several speakers at the Republican National Convention in 1992 called gays immoral. However, by 1993, seven states and 110 communities had outlawed discrimination against homosexuals.

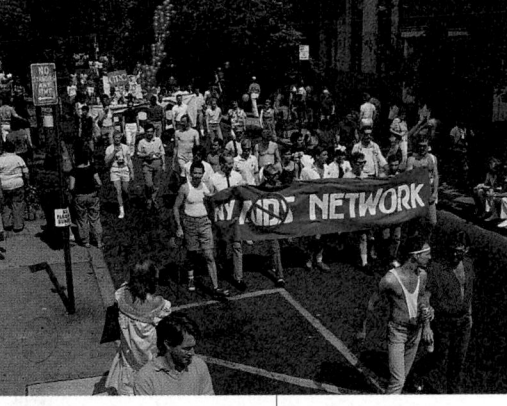

Gay and lesbian activists march in New York in 1983.

F. Answer Many minority groups made political rather than economic advances.

THINK THROUGH HISTORY
F. Synthesizing
How did minorities advance during the 1980s?

Although various groups struggled for political power and economic success during the Reagan and Bush years, these competing groups tended to come together when the United States faced challenges abroad.

Section ③ Assessment

1. TERMS & NAMES

Identify:
• AIDS (acquired immune deficiency syndrome)
• pay equity
• L. Douglas Wilder
• Jesse Jackson
• affirmative action

2. SUMMARIZING Use a chart to list some of the social issues of the Reagan and Bush years and how the government responded to them.

Social Problem	Government Response

Choose one issue and tell the class what other responses the government might have made.

3. SYNTHESIZING How might improvements in the educational system affect other social problems?

THINK ABOUT
• the impact education might have on health-related problems
• the impact that education might have on urban problems

4. COMPARING Compare the political gains and losses experienced by various groups during the Reagan and Bush administrations.

THINK ABOUT
• the experiences of women
• the experiences of African Americans
• the experiences of Latinos
• the experiences of other minorities

The Conservative Tide **993**

ANSWERS

1. TERMS & NAMES

AIDS (acquired immune deficiency syndrome), p. 987

pay equity, p. 991

L. Douglas Wilder, p. 991

Jesse Jackson, p. 991

affirmative action, p. 992

2. SUMMARIZING

Possible Answers:
abortion—Supreme Court restricted access

drug abuse—"Just Say No!" campaign
low student test scores—"America 2000" education initiative
urban crisis—reduced federal spending on cities
equal rights for women—federal government cut budget for day care and cut AFDC; some states offered pay equity
equal rights for minorities—Supreme Court reversed affirmative action

3. SYNTHESIZING

Possible Responses: Education might help discourage risky sexual behavior and drug use. Education makes workers more employable, so improved schools could help solve some urban problems, such as poverty and crime.

4. COMPARING

Possible Responses: More women and minorities were elected or appointed to office. Many Latinos encountered political opposition over their support for bilingual education. Some Native Americans gained more political autonomy as the Supreme Court struck down federal regulations restricting gambling on reservations. Asian Americans made economic advances but few political strides.

Teacher's Edition 993

Sunbelt, Rustbelt, Ecotopia

Americans have always been on the move. Each year, hundreds of thousands of families move to new locations to find better homes, jobs, and schools, and for a host of other reasons. Sometimes people change addresses within the same locality. Other times they set off for different climates, crossing state lines and journeying thousands of miles to a different region.

A region is a geographical concept, designating an area with common features or characteristics that set it apart from its surroundings. For example, the Mississippi Valley is a large physical region; Warren Woods is a small physical region. The term *region* is often used for groups of states that share an area and certain characteristics. New England, the Midwest, and the Pacific Coast are names given to this type of region.

As people move from place to place, from state to state, and from region to region, they gradually transform the balance of political and economic power in the nation. Each census in recent times has recorded how certain states have gained population and others have lost population. If the gains or losses are large enough, a state's representation in the U.S. House of Representatives will increase or decrease. In this way the movement of people translates directly into political power.

In the 1970s, people on the move created new names for regions. The South and Southwest were called the Sunbelt because the warm climate attracted many migrants. The West was sometimes called Ecotopia because of its varied scenery and ecological attractions. The North Central and Northeast regions were called the Rustbelt because many of their aging factories had been closed.

An aerial view of Miami, Florida.

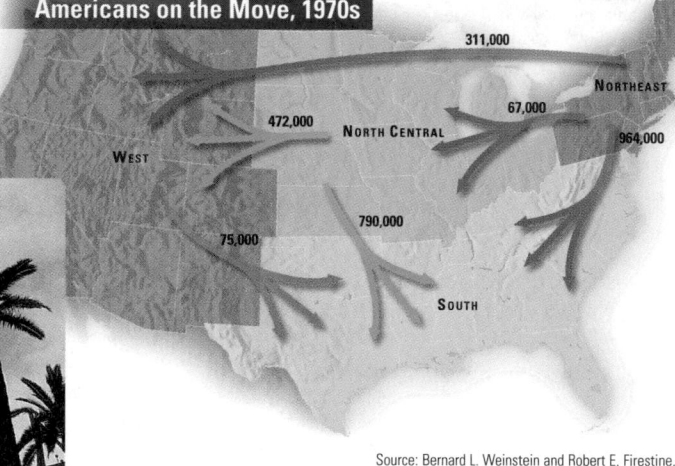

Americans on the Move, 1970s

311,000
472,000
67,000
964,000
75,000
790,000

NORTHEAST
NORTH CENTRAL
WEST
SOUTH

Source: Bernard L. Weinstein and Robert E. Firestine, *Regional Growth and Decline in the United States* (1978).

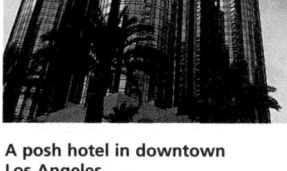

A posh hotel in downtown Los Angeles.

REGIONAL EXCHANGES
As people moved from region to region between 1970 and 1975, the population center of the United States, which had generally moved westward for 17 decades, suddenly turned South. The arrows show the net migration of Americans in the early 1970s, with the numbers indicating thousands. The West gained 311,000 from the Northeast plus 472,000 from the North Central region, for a total of 783,000 people. However, it also lost 75,000 people to the South, reducing its net gain to 708,000 people.

RECOMMENDED RESOURCES

Books and Pamphlets

Abbot, Carl. *The New Urban America.* Chapel Hill: U of North Carolina P, 1981. A study of Sunbelt cities and the political ramifications of their growth.

Bernard, Richard M., and Bradley R. Rice. *Sunbelt Cities.* Austin: U of Texas P, 1983. An examination of the growth and politics of Sunbelt cities since World War II.

Herbers, John. *The New Heartland.* New York: Times Books, 1986. A study of American migration beyond the suburbs and how it is changing the nation.

Population Trends in the 1980s. Washington, D.C.: Bureau of the Census, U.S. Department of Commerce, 1992. Pamphlet of statistics on national and state population trends and trends in internal migration.

Preston, Richard. *American Steel.* New York: Prentice, 1991. An account of efforts to resurrect America's Rustbelt by revitalizing the steel industry.

Videos

Top Ten Retirement Locations in the Sunbelt. Leisure Living, 1990. A tour of ten Sunbelt communities popular with retirees: Hot Springs, Arkansas; Phoenix and Tucson, Arizona; San Diego, California; Lakeland and Clearwater/St. Petersburg, Florida; Murray, Kentucky; Knoxville, Tennessee; and McAllen and San Antonio, Texas.

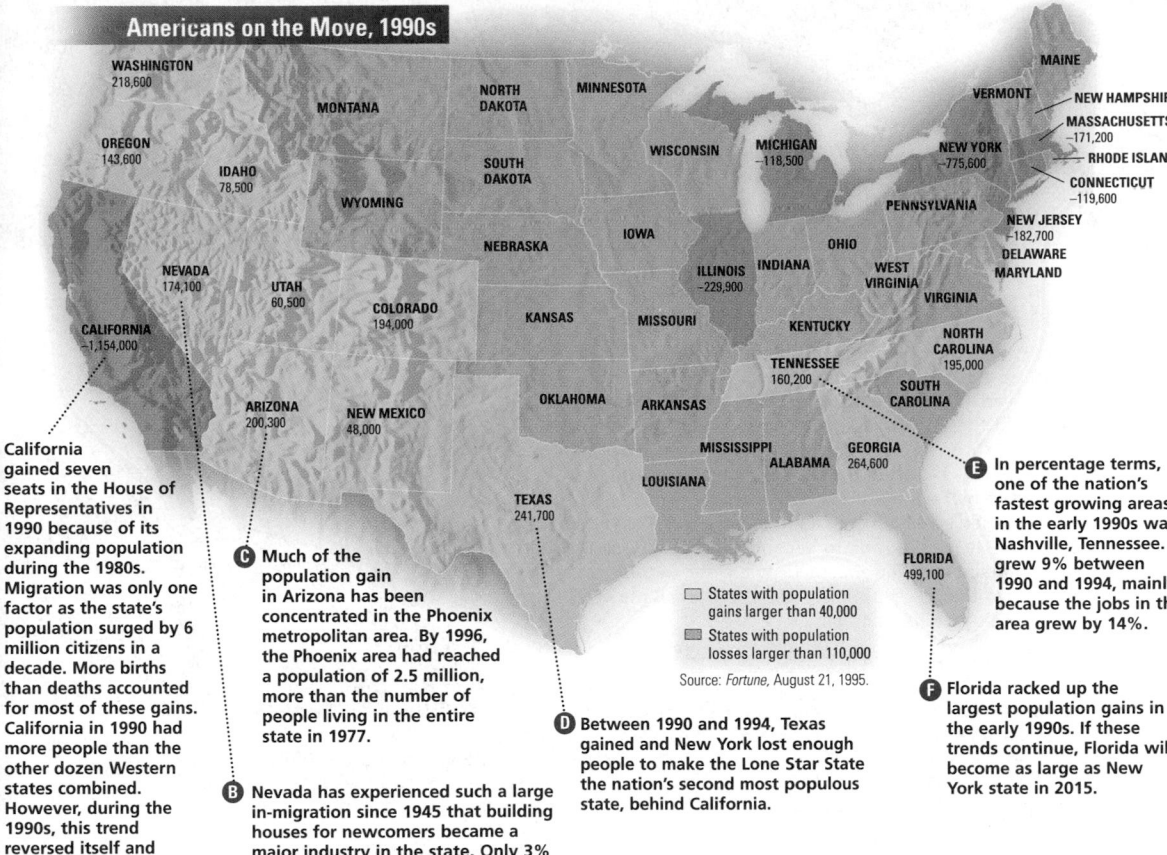

Americans on the Move, 1990s

WASHINGTON 218,600
MONTANA
NORTH DAKOTA
MINNESOTA
MAINE
VERMONT
NEW HAMPSHIRE
MASSACHUSETTS −171,200
RHODE ISLAND
CONNECTICUT −119,600
OREGON 143,600
IDAHO 78,500
SOUTH DAKOTA
WISCONSIN
MICHIGAN −118,500
NEW YORK −775,600
WYOMING
NEBRASKA
IOWA
OHIO
PENNSYLVANIA
NEW JERSEY −182,700
DELAWARE
MARYLAND
NEVADA 174,100
UTAH 60,500
COLORADO 194,000
KANSAS
MISSOURI
ILLINOIS −229,900
INDIANA
WEST VIRGINIA
VIRGINIA
CALIFORNIA −1,154,000
ARIZONA 200,300
NEW MEXICO 48,000
OKLAHOMA
ARKANSAS
KENTUCKY
TENNESSEE 160,200
NORTH CAROLINA 195,000
SOUTH CAROLINA
MISSISSIPPI
ALABAMA
GEORGIA 264,600
LOUISIANA
TEXAS 241,700
FLORIDA 499,100

☐ States with population gains larger than 40,000
☐ States with population losses larger than 110,000

Source: *Fortune*, August 21, 1995.

A California gained seven seats in the House of Representatives in 1990 because of its expanding population during the 1980s. Migration was only one factor as the state's population surged by 6 million citizens in a decade. More births than deaths accounted for most of these gains. California in 1990 had more people than the other dozen Western states combined. However, during the 1990s, this trend reversed itself and California lost population during most of the decade.

B Nevada has experienced such a large in-migration since 1945 that building houses for newcomers became a major industry in the state. Only 3% of the existing residences were built before 1945.

C Much of the population gain in Arizona has been concentrated in the Phoenix metropolitan area. By 1996, the Phoenix area had reached a population of 2.5 million, more than the number of people living in the entire state in 1977.

D Between 1990 and 1994, Texas gained and New York lost enough people to make the Lone Star State the nation's second most populous state, behind California.

E In percentage terms, one of the nation's fastest growing areas in the early 1990s was Nashville, Tennessee. It grew 9% between 1990 and 1994, mainly because the jobs in the area grew by 14%.

F Florida racked up the largest population gains in the early 1990s. If these trends continue, Florida will become as large as New York state in 2015.

CALIFORNIA'S POPULATION SHIFT In the 1980s, California steadily gained population as more people moved in than moved out. After 1988, however, the situation changed rapidly and the movement of people out of California exceeded in-migration.

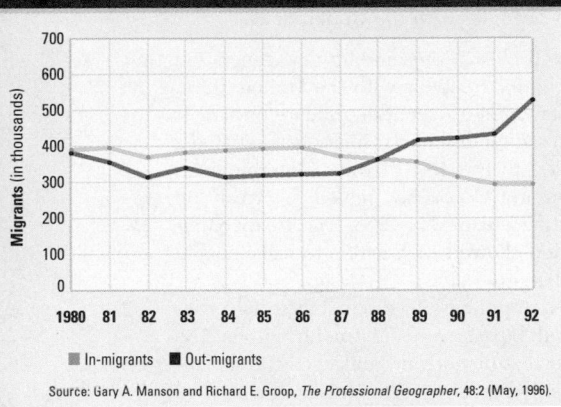

California In- and Out-migrants, 1980–1992

(y-axis: Migrants (in thousands) 0–700; x-axis: 1980 81 82 83 84 85 86 87 88 89 90 91 92)

■ In-migrants   ■ Out-migrants

Source: Gary A. Manson and Richard E. Groop, *The Professional Geographer*, 48:2 (May, 1996).

INTERACT WITH HISTORY

1. **COMPARING AND CONTRASTING** Which three states lost the most population between 1990 and 1994? Which three states gained the most population? Why do you think this happened?

    SEE SKILLBUILDER HANDBOOK, PAGE 1041.

2. **MAKING A MAP** Choose one of the most populous states and then make a demographic map of it. Demography refers to human populations. Your map will show various elements of the population of the state you have chosen, such as size, growth, density, distribution, and vital statistics. Then display your map along with those of other students on a bulletin board in the classroom.

    For more about migration to the Sunbelt, click on *Social Studies* at http://www.mcdougallittell.com

The Conservative Tide **995**

OBJECTIVES

(1) To identify changes in the Communist world that brought about an end to the Cold War.

(2) To summarize U.S. actions taken to influence Central American and Caribbean affairs.

(3) To trace the events leading to the Iran-Contra scandal and to analyze U.S. involvement in the Persian Gulf War.

SKILLBUILDERS

• Understanding geography: location, region, p. 999
• Understanding geography: region, movement, p. 1001

CRITICAL THINKING

• Analyzing causes, p. 998
• Contrasting, p. 999
• Clarifying, p. 1001
• Summarizing, p. 1001
• Recognizing causes, p. 1001
• Analyzing, p. 1001

FOCUS & MOTIVATE

▶ *Starting with the Student*
• Ask students if they have ever been in an argument with someone when the cause of their disagreement suddenly seemed to disappear.
• Did students feel at a loss, not quite knowing what to do or feel next?
• Might the same thing happen in international affairs? Why or why not?

MORE ABOUT . . .
Colin Powell

During the 1996 presidential campaign, Colin Powell stirred much media excitement over the possibility of his running for president or vice-president. For some time his party affiliation was unknown, then he finally said he was a Republican. However, he insisted that he was not interested in running for political office at that time.

---

4 Changes in America's Foreign Policy

TERMS & NAMES
• Mikhail Gorbachev
• INF Treaty
• *glasnost*
• *perestroika*
• Commonwealth of Independent States
• Tiananmen Square
• Sandinista
• Contras
• Operation Desert Storm

LEARN ABOUT the end of the Cold War and the emergence of a global economy
TO UNDERSTAND America's search for a new world role.

ONE AMERICAN'S STORY

Colin Powell did not start out in life with any special privileges. He was born in Harlem and raised in the Bronx, where he enjoyed street games and tolerated school. Then, during college at the City College of New York (CCNY), he joined the Reserve Officer Training Corps (ROTC). He got straight A's in ROTC, though his other grades were mediocre, and so he decided to make the army his career.

Powell served first in Vietnam, and then in Korea and West Germany. He rose in rank to become a general; then President Reagan made him national security adviser. In this post, Powell noted that the Soviet Union was a factor in all the administration's foreign policy decisions.

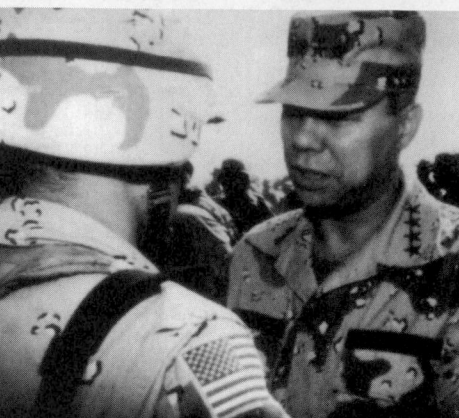

General Colin Powell

A PERSONAL VOICE

Our choosing sides in conflicts around the world was almost always decided on the basis of East-West competition. The new Soviet leader, Mikhail Gorbachev, however, was turning the Cold War formulas on their head. Ronald Reagan . . . had the vision and flexibility, lacking in many Cold Warriors [participants in the Cold War between the U.S. and the U.S.S.R], to recognize that Gorbachev was a new man in a new age offering new opportunities for peace.

COLIN POWELL, *My American Journey*

Though U.S. foreign policy in the early 1980s was marked by intense hostility toward the Soviet Union, which Reagan characterized as an "evil empire," changes in Soviet leadership soon led to historic changes in the balance of power worldwide.

The Cold War Ends

The big changes in world politics began in March of 1985, when **Mikhail Gorbachev** became the general secretary of the Communist Party in the Soviet Union and initiated a series of peace talks with the United States.

GORBACHEV INITIATED REFORM Gorbachev represented a new generation of Soviet leaders. He recognized that better relations with the United States would allow the Soviets to reduce their military spending and reform their economy. An imaginative politician and skilled diplomat, Gorbachev initiated a series of arms-control meetings that led to the **INF Treaty** (Intermediate-Range Nuclear Forces Treaty). Reagan and Gorbachev signed this treaty on December 8, 1987, and the Senate ratified it in May 1988. The treaty eliminated two classes of weapons systems and allowed each nation to make on-site inspections of the other's military installations.

Gorbachev also advocated *glasnost* (openness in discussing social problems) and *perestroika* (economic and bureaucratic restructuring) for the Soviet Union. He restored private ownership of land and replaced central planning with local decision making. He ended most government censorship and held free elections.

SECTION 4 RESOURCES

📋 PRINT RESOURCES

IN-DEPTH RESOURCES: UNIT 9
Guided Reading, p. 22
Primary Source: The First Day of Desert Storm, p. 31
Outline Map: U.S. Attention on the Middle East, p. 26
American Lives: Daniel Inouye, p. 36

ACCESS FOR STUDENTS ACQUIRING ENGLISH
Guided Reading (Spanish), p. 321

FORMAL ASSESSMENT
Section Quiz, p. 402

ALTERNATIVE ASSESSMENT BOOK
See forms for supporting and scoring alternative activities.

💻 TECHNOLOGY RESOURCES

HUMANITIES TRANSPARENCIES
H47, "Economic Crisis" by Walt Handelsman

GEOGRAPHY TRANSPARENCIES
G33, The Cold War Ends, 1989–1990

CD-ROM *Our Times*
Grolier Multimedia Encyclopedia
Electronic Library of Primary Sources

VIDEO *American Portfolio: A Videodisc for U.S. History*
user's guide, pp. 258, 259

INTERNET McDougal Littell Learning On-Line
http://www.mcdougallittell.com

SOVIET DISUNION The elections increased political tensions and led to a dramatic increase in nationalism on the part of the Soviet Union's non-Russian republics. By 1990, these republics had declared that local laws took priority over those of the central government.

Then, in the summer of 1991, a new Russian revolution took place. On August 19, Communist hardliners attempted a coup. They forced Gorbachev out of office and declared a state of emergency. Boris Yeltsin, a strong leader in the largest Soviet republic of Russia, climbed atop an armored truck and immediately called for a general strike in protest. Three days later, the coup was over and Gorbachev was back. On August 24, he resigned as head of the Communist Party and banned it from any further role in government.

The pressure for complete change, however, was overwhelming. In December of 1991, all 14 non-Russian republics declared their independence and Gorbachev resigned as president. After 74 years, the Soviet Union dissolved. A loose federation known as the **Commonwealth of Independent States,** or CIS, took its place. In February of 1992, President George Bush and Boris Yeltsin (the new Russian leader who replaced Gorbachev) issued a formal statement declaring an end to the Cold War and the beginning of a new era of "friendship and partnership." In January of 1993 they signed the START II treaty, designed to cut both nations' nuclear arsenals by 75 percent.

POLAND AND GERMANY Gorbachev's new policies led to massive changes in Eastern Europe as well as the Soviet Union. In 1988, when the Soviet Union was still intact, Gorbachev reduced the number of Soviet troops in Eastern Europe and allowed non-Communist parties to organize in satellite nations such as East Germany and Poland. He advised the satellite nations to move toward democracy.

That is exactly what they did. Poland moved immediately to establish a non-Communist government with a new constitution and a free-market economy. Supporting the once-outlawed Solidarity labor movement that had been growing throughout the 1980s, Polish voters supported an increasingly democratic government.

On November 9, 1989, East Germany opened the Berlin Wall, uniting the two halves of Germany for the first time in 28 years. Berliners climbed atop the wall, cheering and dancing, and rushed through what had once been heavily guarded checkpoints. East German border guards stood by and watched as Berliners pounded away with hammers and other tools at the despised wall. In early 1990, East Germany held its first free elections, and on October 3 of that year, the two German nations again became one.

Crowds welcome East Berliners into West Berlin as the Berlin Wall is being taken down in 1989.

EASTERN EUROPE Other European nations also adopted democratic reforms. Czechoslovakia withdrew from the Soviet bloc. The Baltic States of Latvia, Estonia, and Lithuania declared their independence from the Soviet Union. Hungary, Bulgaria, and Romania made successful transitions from communism.

Yugoslavia, however, collapsed. Four of its six republics seceded. Ethnic rivalries deteriorated into a brutal war among Muslims, Orthodox Serbs, and Roman Catholic Croats, who were dividing up Yugoslavia. Serbia backed Serb minorities, which were stirring up civil unrest in Croatia and Bosnia.

The Conservative Tide **997**

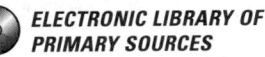

ON THE WORLD STAGE

DEMOCRATIC ELECTIONS IN RUSSIA

This magazine cover showing the shattered image of Lenin, the first head of the USSR, symbolizes the breakup of the Soviet Union. After the Soviet Union dissolved in 1991, Boris Yeltsin continued as president of Russia. Yeltsin ended price controls and increased private ownership of business. The Russian parliament opposed Yeltsin's policies, even after a 1993 referendum showed that the majority of voters supported them.

In December of 1993, Russian voters installed a new parliament and a new constitution, parts of which resembled the U.S. Constitution. The election results heralded an era of increasing democracy in Russia. In 1996, Yeltsin won reelection as president of Russia, with his term not due to expire until 2000.

A Chinese protester defies the tanks in Tiananmen Square in 1989.

The collapse of communism in the Soviet Union and Eastern Europe resulted in a formal end to the Cold War. The spread of democracy throughout the former Soviet empire suited American foreign policy, which looked to the spread of democracy to improve the prospects for peace and world trade.

COMMUNISM CONTINUES IN CHINA Even before *perestroika* unfolded in the Soviet Union, economic reform began in China. Early in the 1980s, the Chinese Communist government loosened its grip on business and eliminated some price controls. Students in China began to demand freedom of speech and a greater voice in government.

In April 1989, university students in China held marches that quickly grew into large demonstrations in Beijing's **Tiananmen Square** and on the streets of other cities. In Tiananmen Square, Chinese students constructed a version of the Statue of Liberty to symbolize their struggle for democracy.

China's premier Li Peng ordered the military to crush the protesters. Soldiers killed hundreds of them; government officials ordered the arrest of others, and some of those were executed. The world's democratic countries watched these events on television with great dismay. By 1990 the Chinese government started making economic reforms. China's attempts at economic liberalization were encouraged by U.S. policymakers.

Central American and Caribbean Policy

Cold War considerations during the Reagan and Bush administrations continued to influence affairs in Central America and the Caribbean, where the United States opposed leftist governments in favor of governments friendly to it.

NICARAGUA The United States had had a presence in Nicaragua ever since 1912, when President Taft sent U.S. marines to protect American investments there. The marines left in 1933, but only after helping dictator Anastasio Somoza come to power. When **Sandinista** rebels toppled the dictatorship of Somoza's sons in 1979, President Carter recognized the new regime and sent it $83 million in economic aid. The Soviet Union and Cuba sent aid as well.

In 1981, however, President Reagan charged that Nicaragua was a Soviet outpost that was "exporting revolution" to other Central American countries. Reagan cut all aid to President Daniel Ortega's Sandinista government and threw his support to guerrilla forces known as the **Contras** because they were against communism. By 1983, the Contra army had grown to nearly 10,000 men, and American officials from the CIA had moved in to direct operations— without congressional approval. In response, Congress passed the Boland Amendment banning military aid to the Contras for two years, but Reagan's administration still managed to find ways to aid the Contras.

On February 25, 1990, Nicaraguan president Daniel Ortega held free elections, and Violeta de Chamorro was elected the nation's new president. Chamorro's supporters and the Sandinistas agreed to work together to rebuild Nicaragua.

GRENADA The Reagan administration had pursued indirect and covert means to influence politics in Central America, but on the tiny Caribbean island of Grenada, it used direct military force. After noting that the island was developing ties to Communist Cuba, President Reagan dispatched approximately 2,000 troops to the island in 1983. There they found several hundred Cubans and a stockpile of Soviet-made arms and ammunition. Eighteen American soldiers died in the attack, but Reagan declared that the invasion had been necessary to defend U.S. security and protect the 1,000 Americans living on the island.

PANAMA Six years later, in 1989, President Bush sent over 20,000 soldiers and marines into Panama to overthrow and arrest General Manuel Antonio Noriega on

998 CHAPTER 33

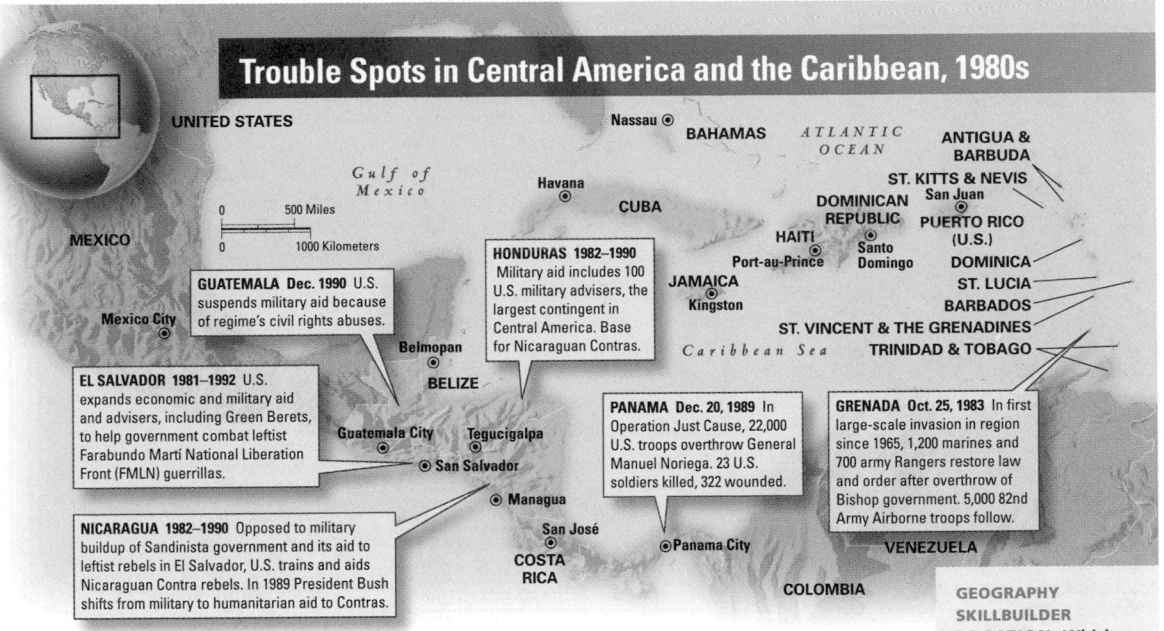

Trouble Spots in Central America and the Caribbean, 1980s

UNITED STATES

Gulf of Mexico

MEXICO

Mexico City

GUATEMALA Dec. 1990 U.S. suspends military aid because of regime's civil rights abuses.

EL SALVADOR 1981–1992 U.S. expands economic and military aid and advisers, including Green Berets, to help government combat leftist Farabundo Martí National Liberation Front (FMLN) guerrillas.

NICARAGUA 1982–1990 Opposed to military buildup of Sandinista government and its aid to leftist rebels in El Salvador, U.S. trains and aids Nicaraguan Contra rebels. In 1989 President Bush shifts from military to humanitarian aid to Contras.

Belmopan

BELIZE

Guatemala City   Tegucigalpa

San Salvador

Managua

San José

COSTA RICA

Nassau

BAHAMAS

Havana

CUBA

JAMAICA

Kingston

HONDURAS 1982–1990 Military aid includes 100 U.S. military advisers, the largest contingent in Central America. Base for Nicaraguan Contras.

Port-au-Prince

HAITI

DOMINICAN REPUBLIC

Santo Domingo

Caribbean Sea

PANAMA Dec. 20, 1989 In Operation Just Cause, 22,000 U.S. troops overthrow General Manuel Noriega. 23 U.S. soldiers killed, 322 wounded.

Panama City

COLOMBIA

ATLANTIC OCEAN

ANTIGUA & BARBUDA

ST. KITTS & NEVIS

San Juan

PUERTO RICO (U.S.)

DOMINICA

ST. LUCIA

BARBADOS

ST. VINCENT & THE GRENADINES

TRINIDAD & TOBAGO

GRENADA Oct. 25, 1983 In first large-scale invasion in region since 1965, 1,200 marines and 700 army Rangers restore law and order after overthrow of Bishop government. 5,000 82nd Army Airborne troops follow.

VENEZUELA

0   500 Miles
0   1000 Kilometers

GEOGRAPHY SKILLBUILDER

LOCATION *Which Central American and Caribbean countries experienced an actual U.S. invasion of their territory in the 1980s?* **REGION** *Besides direct attack, what other techniques did the United States employ to influence countries in the Caribbean and Central American regions?*

Skillbuilder Answer
Location: Grenada and Panama. **Region:** Providing economic and military aid, as well as dispatching military advisors, to nations it wished to influence.

THINK THROUGH HISTORY
B. Contrasting In the period 1980–1992, how did U.S. policies in Central America differ from those in Europe?

charges of drug trafficking. Noriega had been receiving money since 1960 from the CIA, but he was also involved in the international drug trade. After he was indicted by a Miami grand jury, Noriega was taken by force by the American military and flown to Miami to stand trial. In April of 1992, Noriega was convicted and sentenced to 40 years in prison. Many Latin American governments deplored the "Yankee imperialism" of the action, but many Americans—and Panamanians— were pleased by the removal of a military dictator who supported drug smuggling.

Middle East Trouble Spots

B. Answer The government used direct intervention in Central America and diplomacy in Europe.

Results favorable to U.S. interests were more difficult to obtain in the Middle East. Negotiating conflicts between ever-shifting governments drew the United States into scandal and its first major war since Vietnam.

THE IRAN–CONTRA SCANDAL In 1983, terrorist groups loyal to Iran took a number of Americans hostage in Lebanon. Reagan denounced Iran and urged United States allies not to sell Iran arms for its war against Iraq. Three years later, in November of 1986, the American people learned that the Reagan administration had been violating its own public policy. Members of Reagan's staff had secretly sold Iran antitank and antiaircraft missiles in an attempt to free the hostages. What's more, they sent part of the profits from those illegal arms sales to the Contras in Nicaragua—in direct violation of the Boland Amendment. President Reagan held a press conference to explain what had happened.

> **A PERSONAL VOICE**
> I am deeply troubled that the implementation of a policy aimed at resolving a truly tragic situation in the Middle East has resulted in such controversy. As I've stated previously, I believe our policy goals toward Iran were well founded.
> **PRESIDENT REAGAN,** presidential press conference, November 25, 1986

In the summer of 1987, special committees of both houses of Congress conducted a dramatic inquiry into the Iran-Contra affair in a month of joint televised hearings. Among those testifying was Lieutenant Colonel Oliver North, a staff member to the National Security Council who played a key role in providing aid to the Contras. North appeared in military uniform with a chestful of medals. In

The Conservative Tide **999**

HISTORY FROM VISUALS
Trouble Spots in Central America and the Caribbean, 1980s
Reading the Map Which operation involved the largest number of troops? *The invasion of Panama.*

Extension Have students list the operations in chronological order.

OBJECTIVE
(3) INSTRUCT

Middle East Trouble Spots

▶ **Starting with the Student** Help students clarify the sequence of events in the Iran-Contra scandal by having them make charts that list dates given in the text along with what happened on each date.

Date	Event
1983	
1986	
1987	
1988	
1992	

▶ **Discussing Key Ideas**
• An illicit trade of arms to Contras for Americans held hostage in Lebanon rocks the nation.
• Threatened by the loss of oil, the United States enters the Persian Gulf War in support of Saudi Arabia and Kuwait.

IN-DEPTH RESOURCES: UNIT 9
Primary Source: The First Day of Desert Storm, p.31
Outline Map: U.S. Attention on the Middle East, p. 26
American Lives: Daniel Inouye, p. 36

 GROLIER MULTIMEDIA ENCYCLOPEDIA
Iran-Contra affair

TEACHING OPTIONS

Exploring Themes

Constitutional Concerns Discuss with students the balance-of-powers issues raised by the Iran-Contra affair. The president is charged under the Constitution with making treaties with foreign governments with the advice and consent of the Senate. If members of Reagan's staff secretly sold arms to Iran and sent the moneys raised to Nicaraguan Contras without the president's knowledge, then they were acting beyond their areas of responsibility or accountability. If the president was aware of his staff's actions, then he was encouraging them to act in direct defiance of Congress, which had passed the Boland Act.

Making Connections Across Cultures

Nicaragua Nicaragua, the largest country in Central America, borders on both the Caribbean Sea and the Pacific Ocean. Its eastern coastline, on the Caribbean, was reached by Columbus in 1502; the first settlements were made by the Spanish in 1524. Managua is the largest city and the capital. Most Nicaraguans are people of mixed Spanish and Indian ancestry who practice the Roman Catholic religion and speak Spanish. Agriculture is the major economic activity, with coffee and cotton as the main crops. Many Nicaraguans are poor farmers, while others make their living by fishing, lumbering, or mining.

Teacher's Edition   999

KEY PLAYER

H. NORMAN SCHWARZKOPF
1934–

In 1988, Norman Schwarzkopf became commander in chief of forces in Asia and Africa. During the Persian Gulf War, more than 540,000 men and women served under the command of "Stormin' Norman." Schwarzkopf said of Saddam Hussein that he was "neither a strategist, nor is he schooled in the operational arts, nor is he a tactician, nor is he a general, nor is he a soldier. Other than that, he is a great military man."

defending his actions, North talked about patriotism and love of country. He asserted that he thought he was carrying out the president's wishes and that the end of helping the contras justified almost any means. Viewers divided in their opinions about North, some viewing him as a hero and others as a villain.

After a congressional investigation, special prosecutor Lawrence E. Walsh early in 1988 indicted various members of the Reagan administration who were involved in the scandal. On Christmas Eve of 1992, President Bush pardoned a number of Reagan officials.

THE DESERT WAR Regardless of the scandal surrounding the Iran-Contra affair, conflict with Iraq (Iran's long-standing enemy) and its leader Saddam Hussein soon eclipsed U.S. problems with Iran. During the 1980s, Iran and Iraq had fought a prolonged war, and Hussein found himself with enormous war debts to pay. In 1961 and again in 1973, Iraq had claimed that Kuwait with its oil fields belonged to Iraq. On August 2, 1990, Iraqi troops invaded a disputed area claimed by Kuwait. The Iraqi invaders looted the country and headed toward Saudi Arabia and its oil fields. If Iraq conquered Saudi Arabia as well as Kuwait, it would control one-half of the world's known oil reserves, which would threaten U.S. oil supplies.

With the support of the United Nations and the United States Congress, President Bush launched **Operation Desert Storm** to restore conditions before the Iraqi invasion. On January 16, 1991, the United States staged a massive air assault against Iraq. On February 23, it launched a very successful ground offensive from Saudi Arabia.

POINT ▶ COUNTERPOINT

"The United States must occasionally intervene militarily in regional conflicts."

Proponents of U.S. military intervention abroad agreed with General Norman Schwarzkopf that "as the only remaining superpower, we have an awesome responsibility to . . . the rest of the world."

"The United States must take the lead in promoting democracy," urged Morton H. Halperin, former director of the ACLU (American Civil Liberties Union). "To say 'Let the UN do it' is a cop-out," stated adviser Robert G. Neumann.

Political scientist Jane Sharp expressed a similar sentiment. "In weighing the cost of intervention, governments must also calculate the high costs of inaction." Offering a recent example, she asked, "Can any nation that has taken no action in Bosnia to stop the Serbian practice of ethnic cleansing continue to call itself civilized?"

"The United States should not intervene militarily in regional conflicts."

A foreign policy analyst at the Cato Institute, Barbara Conry, stated that "intervention in regional wars is a distraction and a drain on resources." What's more, she argued, "it does not work." Recalling the presence of American troops in Lebanon, Conry argued that intervention not only jeopardized American soldiers, it often obstructed what it sought to achieve.

"The internal freedom of a political community can only be won by the members of that community," agreed Professor Stephen R. Shalom. He added that "using [military action] encourages quick fix solutions that ignore the underlying sources of conflict."

Author David Fromkin pointed out that "Humanitarian goals tend to be broad . . . [while] armed interventions seem to be more successful when they are aimed at narrow, objective, tangible, and clearly defined goals."

INTERACT WITH HISTORY

1. **COMPARING AND CONTRASTING** What do you think are the strongest arguments for and against military intervention in regional conflicts?

   SEE SKILLBUILDER HANDBOOK, PAGE 1041.

2. **NEGOTIATING** With at least one partner, research the events leading up to U.S. involvement in one of these countries: Lebanon, Grenada, Panama, or Kuwait. Then negotiate to resolve the conflict.

1000 CHAPTER 33

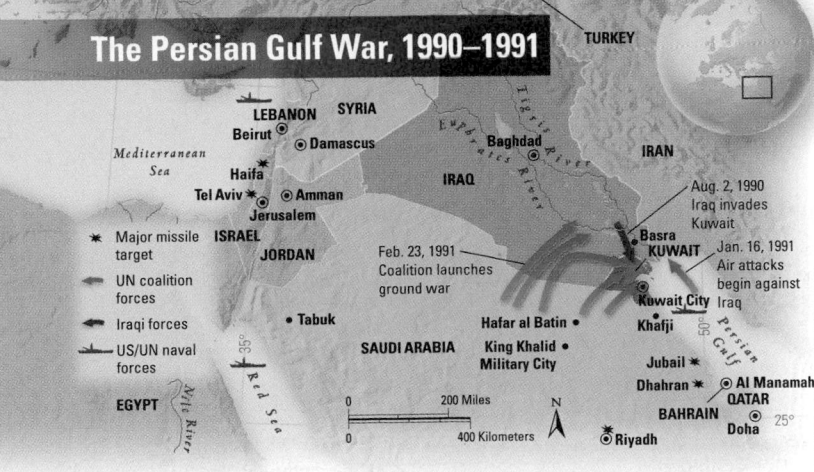

The Persian Gulf War, 1990–1991

TURKEY

SYRIA
LEBANON
Beirut ⊙ ⊙ Damascus
Baghdad

Mediterranean Sea

Haifa ⊙ Amman
Tel Aviv ⚹ ⊙ Jerusalem
ISRAEL
JORDAN

IRAN

Euphrates River
Tigris River

IRAQ

Aug. 2, 1990
Iraq invades
Kuwait

Feb. 23, 1991
Coalition launches
ground war

Basra
KUWAIT
Jan. 16, 1991
Air attacks
begin against
Iraq

Kuwait City
Khafji

⚹ Major missile target
UN coalition forces
Iraqi forces
US/UN naval forces

• Tabuk

35°

SAUDI ARABIA

Hafar al Batin •
King Khalid
Military City

Jubail •
Dhahran ⚹ ⊙ Al Manamah
QATAR
BAHRAIN
⊙ Doha

Persian Gulf

Red Sea

EGYPT

Nile River

0   200 Miles
0   400 Kilometers

N

⊙ Riyadh

25°

GEOGRAPHY SKILLBUILDER
REGION *What did UN coalition forces probably hope to achieve by moving forces into southern Iraq?* **MOVEMENT** *How did the movements of coalition ground forces show that the intention of the coalition in the Gulf War was primarily defensive, not offensive?*

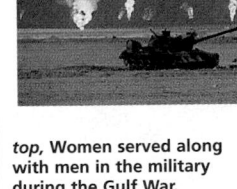

On February 28, President Bush announced a cease-fire. Operation Desert Storm was over. Kuwait was liberated.

A PERSONAL VOICE
We went halfway around the world to do what is moral and just and right. . . . We're coming home now proud, confident, heads held high. . . . We are Americans.
PRESIDENT GEORGE BUSH

C. Answer The nation's distrust of Iran and its continuing need for oil fostered tensions in the Middle East.

THINK THROUGH HISTORY
C. *Clarifying*
What issues led to conflict in the Middle East?

Millions of Americans turned out for the victory parades that greeted returning soldiers. After the debacle in Vietnam, they were thrilled to win a war swiftly, with fewer than 400 casualties among UN coalition forces, although there were subsequently reports of injuries suffered by Gulf veterans caused by chemicals used in the war. By contrast, Iraq had suffered 100,000 deaths, including both military and civilian. Many of the dead were children under five, who died from outbreaks of cholera, typhoid, enteritis, and other diseases.

President Bush was not as successful on the domestic front as he was on the war front. He was hampered by an increase in government spending and a long recession that began in 1990 and lasted through most of 1992. Bush was forced to raise taxes despite his campaign pledge, and his approval rating dropped to 40 percent by 1992. As he campaigned for reelection in 1992, he hesitated to address the problems raised by the long recession. Perceived as a leader who would not take action, he lost the presidency and 12 years of Republican leadership ended.

top, Women served along with men in the military during the Gulf War.
bottom, Massive oil fires started by the Iraqis burned in Kuwait.

Skillbuilder Answer
Region: *Possible Answer:* By securing the area, coalition forces were probably hoping to cut Iraq off from further land access to Kuwait and also to isolate Iraqi forces already in Kuwait.
Movement: *Possible Answer:* Coalition forces did not strike deep into Iraq, only going far enough into the country to protect Kuwait.

Section 4 Assessment

1. TERMS & NAMES
Identify:
• Mikhail Gorbachev
• INF Treaty
• *glasnost*
• *perestroika*
• Commonwealth of Independent States
• Tiananmen Square
• Sandinista
• Contras
• Operation Desert Storm

2. SUMMARIZING Use a chart to explain what U.S. foreign policy was in different world regions.

U.S. Foreign Policy
Europe
Central America and Caribbean
Middle East

Now write a paragraph in which you describe a trouble spot in one of these regions.

3. RECOGNIZING CAUSES
What factors caused the end of the Cold War?
THINK ABOUT
• events in the Soviet Union
• events in Germany and Eastern Europe
• how U.S. leaders responded to those events

4. ANALYZING What factors do you think determined whether or not the United States intervened militarily in other nations?
THINK ABOUT
• economic factors
• geographic factors
• political factors

The Conservative Tide **1001**

ANSWERS

1. TERMS & NAMES
Mikhail Gorbachev, p. 996
INF Treaty, p. 996
glasnost, p. 996
perestroika, p. 996
Commonwealth of Independent States, p. 997
Tiananmen Square, p. 998
Sandinista, p. 998
Contras, p. 998
Operation Desert Storm, p. 1000

2. SUMMARIZING
Possible Answers:
Europe—INF Treaty, START II treaty, announce end of Cold War, encourage spread of democracy
Central America and Caribbean—cut aid to Sandinistas, send secret aid to the Contras, invade Grenada, seize Noriega
Middle East—secretly sell Iran weapons, Operation Desert Storm

3. RECOGNIZING CAUSES
Possible Responses: Gorbachev made reforms in the Soviet Union. Political tension and nationalism caused the Soviet Union to break apart and be replaced by the Commonwealth of Independent States. Poland established a non-Communist government. Germany reunited. U.S. leaders welcomed all these changes and vowed to work closely with the new democratic governments.

4. ANALYZING
Possible Responses: When the issue was democracy or the halt of communism, the United States often did not intervene militarily. When American lives, safety, and oil supplies were threatened, the United States did intervene.

HISTORY FROM VISUALS
The Persian Gulf War, 1990–1991
Reading the Map Where was the U.S. Navy deployed during the Persian Gulf conflict? *Mediterranean Sea, Red Sea, and Persian Gulf.*

Extension Based on information on the map and in the text, create a mini time line for events of the Persian Gulf War.

ASSESS & RETEACH

Section 4 Assessment
Have students answer the questions and then compare answers with another student. Ask the student pairs to find text passages to support their answers.

Self-Assessment
Ask students to identify events covered in the chapter that they found hard to understand and to formulate one question they would like to ask the authors of the text.

Section Quiz
FORMAL ASSESSMENT
Section Quiz, p. 402

Reteach
Review the maps on pages 999 and 1001, which carry much of the content of this section.

CLOSE

Bush continued to implement the conservative policies first advocated by his predecessor, Ronald Reagan. But despite his campaign promise, Bush was obligated finally to raise taxes. After 12 years of conservative rule, the nation reverted back to a Democratic presidency. Another swing of the pendulum was about to begin.

 HUMANITIES TRANSPARENCIES
H47, "Economic Crisis" by Walt Handelsman

Teacher's Edition **1001**

REVIEWING THE CHAPTER

TERMS & NAMES
1. Ronald Reagan, p. 979
2. entitlement program, p. 979
3. Moral Majority, p. 980
4. Geraldine Ferraro, p. 986
5. supply-side economics, p. 983
6. AIDS, p. 987
7. Mikhail Gorbachev, p. 996
8. Commonwealth of Independent States, p. 997
9. Contras, p. 998
10. Operation Desert Storm, p. 1000

MAIN IDEAS
11. Public frustration over government's entitlement programs and civil rights policies.

12. Conservative voters in West, low voter turnout, frustration over hostage crisis, and high inflation.

13. Cutting social programs, lowering income taxes, increasing military spending.

14. They handed down conservative rulings on various issues.

15. Removal of government regulations on industries. Deregulation of airline industry resulted in increased competition and lower prices for consumer. Deregulation of savings and loan industry resulted in S & L failures.

16. African Americans made striking political gains, although economic progress lagged; Latinos became fastest-growing minority in 1980s, gaining both political and economic power; Native Americans faced long-term problems in health, employment, and education; Asian Americans made important economic advances but few political strides; gays and lesbians worked for legislation to protect their rights.

17. Ferraro's 1984 Democratic vice-presidential candidacy, increase in women in Congress, and push for pay equity.

18. Economic problems and nationalism in non-Russian republics.

19. The Reagan administration's selling weapons to Iran and using profits to aid Contras in Nicaragua; the executive branch deceived Congress.

20. Operation Desert Storm.

Chapter 33 Assessment

REVIEWING THE CHAPTER

TERMS & NAMES For each term below, write a sentence explaining its connection to the period from 1980 to 1992. For each person below, explain his or her role in the events of the period.

1. Ronald Reagan
2. entitlement program
3. Moral Majority
4. Geraldine Ferraro
5. supply-side economics
6. AIDS
7. Mikhail Gorbachev
8. Commonwealth of Independent States
9. Contras
10. Operation Desert Storm

MAIN IDEAS

SECTION 1 *(pages 978–981)*

A Conservative Movement Emerges
11. Briefly explain what brought about the conservative backlash of the 1980s.
12. What factors led to Ronald Reagan's victory in 1980?

SECTION 2 *(pages 982–986)*

Conservative Policies Under Reagan and Bush
13. What were the three economic tactics that formed the basis of Reaganomics?
14. How did Reagan's Supreme Court appointments affect the philosophy of the Court?
15. What is deregulation and how did it affect certain industries in the 1980s?

SECTION 3 *(pages 987–993)*

American Society in a Conservative Age
16. What progress and obstacles did different minority groups experience in the 1980s?
17. What were some gains that women achieved as a result of the equal rights struggle of the 1980s?

SECTION 4 *(pages 996–1001)*

Changes in American Foreign Policy
18. What caused the downfall of the Soviet Union and the founding of the Commonwealth of Independent States?
19. What was the Iran-Contra scandal and how did it pit presidential against congressional power?
20. Summarize the U.S. response to Iraq's invasion of Kuwait.

THINKING CRITICALLY

1. **SEQUENCING HISTORY** Choose two events from each of the sections of the chapter and place them in chronological order on the time line below.

| Ronald Reagan is elected. | | |
| George Bush is defeated. |

2. **CONSERVATIVE REFORM** Review the goals of the conservative movement and the actions the government took under Reagan and Bush. Evaluate how well the goals were accomplished by the end of George Bush's presidency. Use information from the chapter to support your answer.

3. **THE ROLE OF GOVERNMENT** Reread the quotation by President Reagan on page 976. Do you believe that big government is always a problem? Explain your answer.

4. **GEOGRAPHY OF CENTRAL AMERICA AND THE CARIBBEAN** Look at the map on page 999. Between 1982 and 1992 the U.S. intervened in this area many times for a variety of reasons. How might the presence of a Communist government on the island of Cuba have influenced U.S. actions in neighboring countries?

5. **POLITICS OF THE SUNBELT** Movement of people affects the balance of political and economic power in the nation. Study the information in the Geography Spotlight on pages 994–995. If you were in charge of a national political party, how would these changes influence your plans for the next election?

6. **ANALYZING PRIMARY SOURCES** Read the following excerpt from a speech that Ronald Reagan gave at the 1992 Republican National Convention, when President Bush was running for reelection. Then answer the questions below.

> We mustn't forget . . . the very different America that existed just 12 years ago; an America with 21 percent interest rates and back-to-back years of double-digit inflation; an America where mortgage payments doubled, paychecks plunged, and motorists sat in gas lines; an America whose leaders told us it was our own fault; that ours was a future of scarcity and sacrifice; and that what we really needed was another good dose of government control and higher taxes.
>
> It wasn't so long ago that the world was a far more dangerous place as well. It was a world where aggressive Soviet communism was on the rise and American strength was in decline. It was a world where our children came of age under the threat of nuclear holocaust.
>
> **RONALD REAGAN,** Republican National Convention: August 17, 1992

What picture does Reagan paint of the Democratic administration that preceded his own? What conclusions does he want people to draw about the choices in the 1992 election?

THINKING CRITICALLY

1. SEQUENCING HISTORY
Time lines may include the following information: 1982—ERA fails to pass; 1983—Reagan proposes Strategic Defense Initiative, invasion of Grenada; 1984—Geraldine Ferraro runs for vice-president, Jesse Jackson runs for president, Reagan and Bush win again; 1988—Jesse Jackson runs for president; 1989—Supreme Court rules on abortion; 1991—Operation Desert Storm, America 2000 education program, Anita Hill/Clarence Thomas hearings.

2. CONSERVATIVE REFORM
Possible Responses: Some goals were achieved, such as government deregulation of business, and cuts in taxes and social programs. Some failures were the rise of inflation and the national deficit, problems caused by the weakening of environmental and social agencies, and failure to win the drug war.

3. THE ROLE OF GOVERNMENT
Possible Responses: No, sometimes it is necessary to have a large base of operation to deal with national problems such as drug abuse or with military issues. Some would say that social and educational problems also need national attention, since they affect everyone. Students answering yes might cite the waste generated by national government or the ability of local agencies to better deal with the problems of their area.

ALTERNATIVE ASSESSMENT

1. PRESENTING A CASE STUDY

What causes natural resources to become depleted or endangered? What can be done in response?

Working with a small group, present a case study on an environmental issue that is significant to your future.

 CD-ROM Conduct research using the CD-ROM *Our Times,* your textbook, and other sources.

- Your case study should consider why the resource is important, and what has happened in recent history that has had either a negative or positive impact. For example, what role has industry, technology, urban development, and population growth played in the current crisis? What have environmental groups, industrial leaders, or politicians done in response? Use visuals, such as charts, maps, and photographs to illustrate your presentation.

- Conclude with a look at the future. What actions might help to slow or reverse the situation? What could be done to prevent it from happening again?

2. DEBATING AN ISSUE

Cooperative Learning Working in a small group, choose one issue that conservatives feel strongly about and debate that issue before the class.

- Have one person present the conservative view and another present the liberal view.

- One member of your group should moderate the debate.

- Use your textbook and other resources to research the issue thoroughly. Present both sides of the issue as thoroughly and fairly as possible.

- Prepare a sheet that your classmates can use to judge the debate. You may want to use categories such as clear explanations, adequate research, use of supporting details, and volume and pace of speaking.

- Conduct your debate in front of the class.

3. PORTFOLIO PROJECT

Use the Living History activity to expand your portfolio.

LIVING HISTORY

PRESENTING POLITICAL POSITIONS

After you have read the chapter, use the notes you took to make a chart comparing the conservative politician today to a conservative politician—such as Reagan or Bush—that you read about in this chapter. Then have a classmate review your chart and answer the following questions:

- Are the positions presented clearly? Do you understand what the politicians believe?

- Are the positions presented objectively, or can you tell what your classmate's opinion of them is?

When you have revised your chart based on your classmate's comments, present it to the class. Then add it to your American history portfolio.

Review Chapter 33

CONSERVATIVE AGENDA The election of Ronald Reagan marked the peak of conservatism in late-20th-century politics. Encouraged by the strong support of the New Right and the Moral Majority, Reagan advanced conservative aims to reduce the size of the federal government and its entitlements to citizens. By his appointments to the Supreme Court, Reagan guaranteed conservative ruling on civil-rights cases for years to come. "Reaganomics" was the conservative tool to energize the flagging economy, but the plan had mixed results.

POLITICAL EMPOWERMENT Groups that previously had limited representation in the political arena found political empowerment during the Reagan-Bush years. Women, minorities, and homosexuals gained more representation in American political life. However, divisive issues such as equal rights, abortion, education, and affirmative action combined to create a combative atmosphere in the halls of Congress and state and local legislatures.

CHANGES IN WORLD POLITICS The end of the Cold War occurred during Bush's presidency. The United States was faced with altering its foreign policy toward the once-powerful Soviet Empire, which collapsed in 1988. On other fronts, the United States continued to pursue an aggressive foreign policy of intervention, peaking with Operation Desert Storm in 1991.

Preview Chapter 34

Twelve years of conservative control were ended with the election of Bill Clinton in 1992. Clinton was the first "baby boomer" to be elected to the office of President. Finding the appropriate role for America in leading the increasingly globalized world, as well as thorny domestic issues, presented a great challenge to President Clinton. You will learn about these and other significant events in the next chapter.

The Conservative Tide **1003**

---

1. PRESENTING A CASE STUDY

Standards for Evaluation

A case study should meet the following criteria:

- Addresses an environmental issue that is significant.
- Weighs both positive and negative impacts on the environment.
- Discusses the roles of industry, technology, urban development, and population growth in the crisis.
- Describes the contributions of various individuals and groups to solving the crisis.
- Uses visuals to illustrate the presentation.
- Speculates about the future.

2. DEBATING AN ISSUE

Standards for Evaluation

A debate should meet the following criteria:

- Provides clear explanations.
- Demonstrates adequate research.
- Makes use of supporting details.
- Gives each member of the group a clear function.

3. PORTFOLIO PROJECT

LIVING HISTORY

Standards for Evaluation:

A chart should meet the following criteria:

- Makes good use of accumulated notes.
- Compares Reagan or Bush with an important conservative politician of today, such as Newt Gingrich.
- Provides details about the two politicians being compared.
- Presents differences and similarities clearly.
- Shows good organization.
- Maintains a consistent focus.

IN-DEPTH RESOURCES: UNIT 9
See the form for scoring this activity on page 38.

THINKING CRITICALLY

4. GEOGRAPHY OF CENTRAL AMERICA AND THE CARIBBEAN

Possible Response: During this time period, the U.S. feared the spread of communism from Cuba to its nearby neighbors.

5. POLITICS OF THE SUNBELT

Possible Responses: More people are moving out of the Rustbelt to the West, so there will be more voters in the Western states to be convinced of the importance of voting consistently for one party. Issues in the Rustbelt might include the loss of jobs and the need for retraining and new industries. Issues in the West might include concerns about the environment, housing, and education. In the Sunbelt, the issues might relate to immigrants from other countries and concerns about water.

6. ANALYZING PRIMARY SOURCES

Possible Answers: Reagan wanted to make it seem as though the previous, Democratic administration had created a disaster. He wanted his listeners to think that if they voted for a Democrat in 1992, similarly terrible conditions would return. He was concerned that a Democratic president would undo some of the accomplishments of the conservative movement.

PLANNING GUIDE
The United States in Today's World

		TEACHING SUPPORT	ASSESSMENT
SECTION 1 **The Clinton Presidency** *pp. 1006–1012*	**Key Ideas** *President Bill Clinton attempts to provide more economic security for all Americans. Republicans challenge some of his programs and win control of Congress.*	**In-Depth Resources: Unit 9** • Guided Reading, p. 39 • Primary Sources: *from* the Contract with America, p. 46; *from* "A Bridge to the Future" by Bill Clinton, p. 47 **COOPERATIVE ACTIVITIES** • Graphing Election Results, p. 1007 (TE) • Researching Current Events, p. 1011 (TE)	*Section 1 Assessment*, p. 1012 (PE) *Self-Assessment*, p. 1012 (TE) *Formal Assessment* • Section Quiz, p. 411 *Alternative Assessment Book* • Standards for Evaluating a Cooperative Activity
SECTION 2 **The New Global Economy** *pp. 1013–1017*	*Workers face new challenges to their economic security as the U.S. economy evolves.*	**In-Depth Resources: Unit 9** • Guided Reading, p. 40 • Geography Application: The U.S. Trade in Goods, p. 44 • Primary Source: *from The Road Ahead* by Bill Gates, p. 48 • American Lives: Bill Gates, p. 52 • Literature: "On the Pulse of the Morning" by Maya Angelou, p. 50 **COOPERATIVE ACTIVITIES** • Planning a Job Fair, p. 1015 (TE) • Researching International Trade, p. 1016 (TE)	*Section 2 Assessment*, p. 1017 (PE) *Self-Assessment*, p. 1017 (TE) *Formal Assessment* • Section Quiz, p. 412 *Alternative Assessment Book* • Standards for Evaluating a Cooperative Activity
SECTION 3 **Technology and Modern Life** *pp. 1018–1023*	*New opportunities and challenges arise from technological developments in many industries, especially computers and communications.*	**In-Depth Resources: Unit 9** • Guided Reading, p. 41 **COOPERATIVE ACTIVITY** • Creating a Guide to the Internet, p. 1021 (TE)	*Section 3 Assessment*, p. 1023 (PE) *Self-Assessment*, p. 1023 (TE) *Formal Assessment* • Section Quiz, p. 413 *Alternative Assessment Book* • Standards for Evaluating a Cooperative Activity
SECTION 4 **The Changing Face of America** *pp. 1024–1029*	*Demographic changes in the United States have significant implications for American society at the outset of the 21st century.*	**In-Depth Resources: Unit 9** • Guided Reading, p. 42 • Skillbuilder Practice: Drawing Conclusions, p. 43 • Primary Source: Road Sign, p. 49 • American Lives: Wilma Mankiller, p. 53 **COOPERATIVE ACTIVITY** • Predicting Local Demographics, p. 1025 (TE)	*Section 4 Assessment*, p. 1029 (PE) *Self-Assessment*, p. 1029 (TE) *Formal Assessment* • Section Quiz, p. 414 *Alternative Assessment Book* • Standards for Evaluating a Cooperative Activity
CHAPTER RESOURCES	**Chapter Overview** *President Bill Clinton locks horns with a Republican Congress, reflecting the heated national debate over the country's direction. Americans face economic, technological, and demographic changes that are reshaping their lives and redefining the main issues that concern citizens.*	**In-Depth Resources: Unit 9** • Living History Project: Worksheet, p. 55; Standards, p. 56 **Telescoping the Times** • Chapter Summary, pp. 67–68 **Planning for Block Schedules**	*Chapter Assessment*, pp. 1032–1033 (PE) *Alternative Assessment*, p. 1033 (PE) *Formal Assessment* • Chapter Test, forms A and B, pp. 415–420 **Test Generator** *Alternative Assessment Book* See explanation and forms for different kinds of alternative assessments including portfolio assessment.

Geography Transparencies
• G34, Eligible Votes Cast, 1996

Critical Thinking Transparencies
• CT34, Federal Government Shutdown
• CT68, Federal Budget, 1945–1995

 Electronic Library of Primary Sources
• Clinton's first Inaugural Address
• A Contract with America

INTERNET RESOURCES
• See *McDougal Littell Learning On-Line* for links to information about Newt Gingrich and the federal deficit.

INTERNET RESOURCES
• See *McDougal Littell Learning On-Line* for links to information about welfare and GATT.

 Grolier Multimedia Encyclopedia
• Computers and Privacy

INTERNET RESOURCES
• See *McDougal Littell Learning On-Line* for links to information about the Telecommunications Act.

 Humanities Transparencies
• H48, Political Cartoon

Electronic Library of Primary Sources
• from *Mission Statement* by the Organizing Committee for the Million Man March

INTERNET RESOURCES
• See Interact with History, p. 1034 (PE) for an activity that includes the Internet as an enrichment option.

INTERNET RESOURCES
Learning On-Line: Social Studies
http://www.mcdougallittell.com

Block Scheduling (90 MINUTES)

Day 1

Section 1, pp. 1006–1012

Section 2, pp. 1013–1017

Section Assessments, pp. 1012, 1017

Day 2

Section 3, pp. 1018–1023

Section 4, pp. 1024–1029

Review Sections 1–4

Tracing Themes: Cultural Diversity, pp. 1030–1031

Chapter Assessment, pp. 1032–1033

YEARLY PACING *Chapter 34 Total:* 2 days *Yearly Total:* 85 days

See *Planning for Block Schedules* for special activities and pacing strategies.

Customizing for Special Populations

Students Acquiring English

Access for Students Acquiring English
• Guided Reading for Sections 1–4 (Spanish), pp. 329–332
• Chapter Summary (Spanish), pp. 327–328
• Skillbuilder Practice: Drawing Conclusions (Spanish), p. 333
• Geography Application: The U.S. Trade in Goods (Spanish), p. 334

INTERNET RESOURCES
• See *McDougal Littell Learning On-Line* The Diverse Classroom.

Less Proficient Readers

In-Depth Resources: Unit 9
• Guided Reading for Sections 1–4, pp. 39–42
• Skillbuilder: Drawing Conclusions, p. 43
• Geography Application: The U.S. Trade in Goods, p. 44

Telescoping the Times
• Chapter Summary, pp. 67–68

See additional strategies at point of use in the Teacher's Edition.

Gifted and Talented Students

In-Depth Resources: Unit 9
• Primary Sources: *from Contract with America,* p. 46; *from* "A Bridge to the Future" by Bill Clinton, p. 47; *from The Road Ahead* by Bill Gates, p. 48; Road Sign, p. 49
• American Lives: Bill Gates, p. 52; Wilma Mankiller, p. 53

See additional strategies at point of use in the Teacher's Edition.

Connections to Literature READINGS FOR STUDENTS

In-Depth Resources: Unit 9
• "On the Pulse of the Morning" by Maya Angelou, p. 50

Enrichment Reading
• Buckley, Christopher *Thank You for Smoking* New York: Harper, 1995 *Buckley skewers Washington politics, corporate power plays, media spin control, Hollywood pretensions and the human weakness for self-delusion and denial in this wickedly funny novel about the adventures of a spokesman for the tobacco lobby who will do anything to sell his product.*

McDougal Littell *The Language of Literature* American Literature

• Lucy Honig, "English as a Second Language," p. 733
• Wing Tek Lum, Jean Bethke Elshtain, Rodney King, Benjamin Spock, Acy Obejas, Baltasar Corrada, Colin Powell, "Voices from the Times," p. 1037
• Carlos Alberto Montaner, "Why Fear Spanish?" p. 1060
• Gary Soto, "Mexicans Begin Jogging," p. 1113
• Pat Mora, "Legal Alien," p. 1113

The United States in Today's World

▶ **Starting with the Student**
Discuss the opening quotation. Ask students what the quotation leads them to think about the United States today.

PREVIEWING THE CHAPTER
Go over the section descriptions and have students point out events on the time line that they know something about.

MORE ABOUT . . .
Madeleine Albright

As an emigrant fleeing the political turmoil of her native Czechoslovakia, Madeleine Albright came to understand what she called "the responsibilities of freedom." During President Clinton's first term, Albright served as the U.S. ambassador to the United Nations. When sworn in as secretary of state in 1997, Albright spoke of America's role in global affairs.

"We must not shy from the mantle of leadership, nor hesitate to defend our interests, nor fail in our commitments, nor diverge from the principles that have defined, elevated and sustained our nation for more than 200 years."

CHAPTER
34

The United States in Today's World

SECTION 1
The Clinton Presidency
President Bill Clinton attempts to provide more economic security for all Americans. Republicans challenge some of his programs and win control of Congress.

SECTION 2
The New Global Economy
Workers face new challenges to their economic security as the U.S. economy evolves.

SECTION 3
Technology and Modern Life
New opportunities and challenges arise from technological developments in many industries, especially computers and communications.

SECTION 4
The Changing Face of America
Demographic changes in the United States have significant implications for American society at the outset of the 21st century.

"America is . . . like a quilt—many pieces, many colors, many sizes, all woven and held together by a common thread."
The Reverend Jesse Jackson

Janet Reno, the first female U.S. attorney general, testifies in Congress about the fire at the Branch Davidian compound in Waco, Texas.

THE UNITED STATES
THE WORLD
1992

The Twenty-seventh Amendment to the Constitution, which deals with congressional pay raises, is ratified.

Bill Clinton, shown with Vice-President Al Gore, is elected president.

U.S. troops land in Somalia to provide humanitarian aid to the famine-stricken nation.

The United States and Russia sign the START II pact to reduce nuclear weapons on both sides.

Terrorists bomb the World Trade Center in New York City.

Boutros Boutros-Ghali becomes the secretary-general of the United Nations.

The South African government and the African National Congress agree to end white minority rule.

1004 CHAPTER 34

THEMES IN CHAPTER 34

The American Dream	*Economic Opportunity*	*Science and Technology*	*Immigration and Migration*
Americans' dreams of financial security were threatened by economic problems. As the millennium drew to a close Americans wondered what parts of the American dream might be lost. See Teacher's Edition, pp. 1009 and 1028.	The government's pursuit of international trade agreements was fueled by the desire to expand foreign markets. At issue was the effect such agreements might have on the availability of jobs at home. See Teacher's Edition, p. 1014.	Technological advances in the fields of medicine, communications, and entertainment affected many areas of American life and occasionally drew critical fire as well as praise. See Teacher's Edition, p. 1022.	The changing ethnic makeup of the country and the high cost of providing services for legal and illegal immigrants brought immigration policies into focus once more. See Teacher's Edition, p. 1028.

LIVING HISTORY

PLANNING FOR THE 21ST CENTURY

During his 1992 presidential campaign, Bill Clinton posted a sign in his campaign headquarters listing three issues to focus on. Create a list of the three most important issues for 21st-century leaders to focus on. Use the following steps to create your list.

- Read news articles and interview friends and relatives to learn what issues people think will affect the future.
- Choose the three issues you think are the most crucial and rank them in order of importance.
- Find an editorial, an article, or a photograph that explains or illustrates a critical aspect of the issue.

📁 **PORTFOLIO PROJECT** Save your list and the supporting articles and photographs in a folder for your American history portfolio. You will revise and share your work at the end of the chapter.

Astronauts on the space shuttle
Endeavour repair the Hubble
telescope in a dramatic space walk.

Nation of Islam leader
Louis Farrakhan leads the
"Million Man March" in
Washington, D.C.

Madeleine Albright
is the first woman
nominated to be
secretary of state.

The Murrah Federal
Building in Oklahoma
City, Oklahoma, is
bombed.

The United
States ends its
relief efforts in
Somalia.

In the 1994 elections, the
Republican Party wins control of both houses of
Congress for the first time
since 1954.

Bill Clinton is ★
reelected.

1994

1996

Peasants in the
southern Mexican
state of Chiapas
rebel against the
national government.

Russian armies invade the
republic of Chechnya to try to
squelch a separatist rebellion.

The World Health
Organization announces
that more than 150
people have died in an
outbreak of the Ebola
virus in Zaire.

The United Nations holds the
Fourth World Conference on Women
for 12 days in Beijing, China.

Israeli prime minister Yitzhak
Rabin is assassinated.

The United States in Today's World **1005**

LIVING HISTORY

PLANNING FOR THE 21ST CENTURY

Discuss ways of going about creating the list.

- Prepare questions to ask when interviewing friends and relatives.
- Use library resources or the Internet to locate a variety of articles from which to identify issues in the nation today.
- Develop criteria to use when ranking issues in order of importance.
- Create a checklist that includes all the steps in the process (research, selection, illustration).

Project Planning Guide

Step 1	Students research possible issues by reading appropriate news articles.
Step 2	Students conduct interviews and compile the results.
Step 3	Students rank the issues in order of importance and select the top three.
Step 4	Students choose a photograph, editorial, or article to explain or illustrate each issue.

IN-DEPTH RESOURCES: UNIT 9
See worksheet and standards for evaluation, pp. 54, 55.

RECOMMENDED RESOURCES

Books for the Teacher

Bell, Derek. *And We Are Not Saved.* New York: Basic, 1987. Race in America.

Woodward, Bob. *The Agenda.* New York: Pocket, 1994. First two years of Clinton White House.

Books for the Student

Costello, Cynthia, and Barbara Kivimac Krimgold. *The American Woman 1996–1997.* New York: Norton, 1996. Women at work.

Delaney, Sarah L., and Elizabeth Delaney with Amy Hill Hearth. *Having Our Say.* New York: Dell, 1993. Two African-American women reflect on 100 years of life.

Morrison, Joan, and Charlotte Fox Zabusky. *The American Mosaic.* Pittsburgh: U of Pittsburgh P, 1980.

Videos

Becoming American. Dir. Ken Levine. New Day Films, 1983. Hmong immigrants adapt to life in the United States.

The Global Assembly Line. Dir. Lorraine Gray. New Day Films, 1986. Portrays people's lives in the "free trade zones" of developing countries and North America.

Software

Clinton: Portrait of a Victory. CD-ROM. Time Warner Interactive. Speeches, music, narration, and more than 300 photographs.

CNN Time Capsule 1994. CD-ROM. Vicarious Entertainment. More than 1,000 articles and photographs.

OBJECTIVES

① To summarize the issues of the 1992 presidential campaign.

② To describe Clinton's stand on domestic and international issues.

③ To identify the effects of the Republican control of Congress.

④ To summarize the results of the 1996 election.

SKILLBUILDERS

• Interpreting political cartoons, p. 1011
• Interpreting graphs, p. 1012

CRITICAL THINKING

• Analyzing causes, p. 1007
• Summarizing, pp. 1007, 1010, 1012
• Drawing conclusions, p. 1008
• Clarifying, p. 1009
• Contrasting, p. 1011
• Synthesizing, p. 1012
• Recognizing effects, p. 1012
• Analyzing issues, p. 1012

FOCUS & MOTIVATE

▶ *Starting with the Student*
Ask students whether they would select someone their age or someone older and more experienced if they were choosing a team captain or school president. Discuss these questions:

• What are the advantages and disadvantages of each choice?

• Could the same approach be applied to choosing the nation's leader? Explain.

MORE ABOUT . . .
Maya Angelou

Clinton's selection of Maya Angelou to participate in the inauguration boosted interest in her work. Sales of the paperback edition of her 1970 autobiography, *I Know Why the Caged Bird Sings*, rose by 500 percent. Angelou is now a professor at Wake Forest University in Winston-Salem, North Carolina.

1006 Chapter 34

TERMS & NAMES
• Bill Clinton
• Hillary Rodham Clinton
• NAFTA
• Newt Gingrich
• Contract with America

❶ The Clinton Presidency

LEARN ABOUT Bill Clinton's presidency
TO UNDERSTAND American politics during the 1990s.

ONE AMERICAN'S STORY

When Maya Angelou—poet, playwright, dancer, actress, singer, scholar, and activist—received the phone call from President-elect Bill Clinton in November 1992, she said, "I was bowled over." An admirer of Angelou's work, Clinton asked her to compose and deliver a poem for his inauguration. Robert Frost, in 1961, had been the first poet to deliver an inaugural poem. Angelou would be the first African American and the first woman to be so honored.

On inauguration day, 250,000 people gathered to watch in person and millions more watched on television as Angelou strode to the podium and delivered her poem, "On the Pulse of Morning." In the poem, Angelou expressed the optimism of the day, recalling the dream of Dr. Martin Luther King, Jr.

Maya Angelou

A PERSONAL VOICE
Lift up your faces, you have a piercing need
For this bright morning dawning for you.
History, despite its wrenching pain,
Cannot be unlived, but if faced
With courage, need not be lived again.

Lift up your eyes
Upon this day breaking for you.
Give birth again
To the dream.
MAYA ANGELOU, from "On the Pulse of Morning"

Moments later, William Jefferson Clinton was inaugurated as the 42nd president of the United States. Clinton entered the presidency at a time when America was at a turning point. With the fall of the Soviet empire in 1991, the United States was the undisputed winner of the Cold War. Yet a severe economic recession made many Americans uneasy about the future. They now looked to Clinton to restore a government that was more responsive to the people and to increase the economic security of all Americans.

Clinton Wins the Presidency

Governor **Bill Clinton** of Arkansas entered the presidential race with the energy of youth. The 46-year-old Clinton, who would be the first member of the baby-boom generation to win the presidency, campaigned as a "New Democrat." He took traditional liberal Democratic positions by proposing a shift in federal funds from defense to civilian programs, more public spending on the nation's infrastructure (roads, bridges, sewers, and power lines), and a national system for health care. However, Clinton also sought welfare reform and emphasized private business as the means to economic progress.

THE ELECTION OF 1992 After the U.S. victory in the Persian Gulf War, Republican president George Bush's popularity had soared to an 88 percent approval rating. In early 1992, however, his approval rating nose-dived to 40 percent as the worsening recession reduced U.S. incomes and boosted

1006 CHAPTER 34

 SECTION 1 RESOURCES

PRINT RESOURCES

IN-DEPTH RESOURCES: UNIT 9
Guided Reading, p. 39
Primary Sources: *from* the Contract with Americans, p. 46;
   from "A Bridge to the Future" by Bill Clinton, p. 47
Literature: "On the Pulse of Morning" by Maya Angelou

ACCESS FOR STUDENTS ACQUIRING ENGLISH
Guided Reading (Spanish), p. 329

FORMAL ASSESSMENT
Section Quiz, p. 411

ALTERNATIVE ASSESSMENT BOOK
See forms for supporting and scoring alternative activities.

TECHNOLOGY RESOURCES

GEOGRAPHY TRANSPARENCIES
G34, Percentage of Eligible Votes Cast, 1996 Presidential Election

CRITICAL THINKING TRANSPARENCIES
CT34, Shutdown of the Federal Government
CT68, Federal Budget, 1945–1995

CD-ROM Electronic Library of Primary Sources

INTERNET McDougal Littell Learning On-Line
http://www.mcdougallittell.com

unemployment. In his run for reelection, President Bush tried to appeal to voters on the basis of his foreign policy triumphs, but voters cared more about pocketbook issues. He could not convince the public that he had a clear strategy for ending the recession and creating jobs. Nor did he seem able to communicate a coherent vision for the country's future.

Concern about the economy was so great that it created an opening for the most significant challenge by a third-party candidate since Theodore Roosevelt of the Bull Moose Party in 1912. That candidate was Texas billionaire H. Ross Perot. Perot targeted the budget deficit as the nation's number-one problem and became a fixture on radio and television. "It's time," Perot declared, "to take out the trash and clean up the barn."

Bill Clinton also focused on the economy in his campaign and made a number of proposals: (1) increase government spending on the country's infrastructure to boost the economy; (2) cut taxes for the middle class; (3) modify the welfare system; and (4) balance the budget by gradually reducing the size of government. Although Clinton would later back off on the middle-class tax cut, he convinced many Americans that he could ease their economic problems.

Clinton's biggest problem emerged from concerns about his character. When the public learned that he had managed to avoid military service during the Vietnam War, critics questioned his patriotism. In addition, Clinton's involvement in a failed 1979 real-estate investment in the Whitewater Development Company in Arkansas produced headlines questioning his ethics.

On the campaign trail, Clinton was able to overcome these concerns about his character, which to most voters seemed less important than the state of the economy. On election day, Clinton won 370 electoral votes to 168 for Bush. His 43 percent share of the popular vote, however, was the smallest winning percentage since that won by Woodrow Wilson in the election of 1912. Bush received 38 percent of the popular vote, and Perot 19 percent.

NEW STYLE OF CAMPAIGNING Television dominated the 1992 presidential race from start to finish. Each candidate used television to sell himself, especially Perot, who ran numerous "infomercials," 30-minute paid advertisements. Perot spent millions of dollars of his own money on television advertising after announcing his candidacy on a popular cable television program.

Clinton also made skillful use of television. Sporting dark glasses, he appeared on one late-night talk show and played his saxophone. On a more serious note, he came across as compassionate and intelligent in three nationally televised debates, the last of which attracted an audience of 88 million people.

During the election of 1992, television expanded in political importance. It became more effective than campaign workers and the traditional party structure of past decades as a campaign tool for delivering candidates' messages.

"The baby boomers' generation . . . is taking over."

DAVID BRODER, JOURNALIST, ON THE 1992 ELECTIONS

The candidates—Bill Clinton and Al Gore—and their wives celebrate victory in the 1992 presidential election.

The Clinton Record

▶ *Starting with the Student*
Discuss with students the extent to which Clinton was able to keep the promises he made during his campaign. Ask why politicians are not always able to carry through on campaign promises. Have students complete a chart as they read, listing Clinton's campaign promises, what he actually achieved during his first term, and the rating (++, +, -, - -) they'd give him for each promise.

Promises	Results	Rating +/-
Tax cuts for middle class	Raised taxes on higher incomes	

▶ *Discussing Key Ideas*
• Hillary Rodham Clinton leads an effort to reform health care.
• Bill Clinton inherits an enormous national debt.
• The NAFTA legislation causes controversy.
• Clinton argues for active U.S. participation in international affairs.

MORE ABOUT . . .
Hillary Rodham Clinton

Before coming to Washington, Hillary Rodham Clinton was a partner in the Rose Law Firm in Little Rock, Arkansas, and she was once named one of the nation's top 100 lawyers. Because of her active participation in social and legislative reform as First Lady, many commentators compared her to Eleanor Roosevelt.

The Clinton Record

To improve government efficiency, Clinton attempted to streamline the federal bureaucracy and put his vice-president, Albert Gore, in charge of what he called "reinventing government." Clinton also tried to make government more inclusive by appointing more women and minorities to his cabinet. More important to Clinton, however, was his goal of strengthening American economic security, which included reform of the U.S. health care system.

HEALTH CARE REFORM During the campaign, Clinton had pledged a sweeping reform to offer all Americans guaranteed, affordable health care. Indeed, as Clinton took office, an estimated 37 million Americans lacked medical insurance. Aware that Democratic senator Harris Wofford had used the issue of health care reform to win the 1990 U.S. Senate race in Pennsylvania, Clinton decided to make "universal health care" the centerpiece of his administration.

The President appointed his wife, **Hillary Rodham Clinton,** an accomplished lawyer and child-welfare advocate, to head a task force on the issue. The First Lady produced a reform plan in the form of a bill that ultimately ran to 1,342 pages. Clinton presented the bill to a joint session of Congress in September 1993 and labeled universal coverage "our most urgent priority." The plan would have extended coverage to every American, mandated that employers pay 80 percent of their workers' insurance costs, and provided for a national health board to monitor spiraling health care costs.

Congress debated the Clinton health care plan for a year. This lengthy debate allowed lobbyists for the bill's opponents—like small businesses and large insurance companies—plenty of time to mobilize against it. Although willing to compromise on minor points, President Clinton refused to negotiate on universal coverage. At first, about half of the American public supported the Clinton plan. However, intense lobbying and congressional debate in which Republicans attacked the plan as "big government" sealed the plan's doom. The program never even came to the floor of Congress for a vote.

Hillary Rodham Clinton explains the health care reform plan to a Senate subcommittee.

CLINTON AND THE ECONOMY When Ronald Reagan had assumed the presidency in 1981, he had vowed to reduce government regulations, slash taxes, and boost military spending but still balance the federal budget. In fact, Reagan's policies ran up average annual budget deficits of $180 billion. During his eight-year administration, Reagan and the Democratic-controlled Congress drove up the national debt—the total amount the U.S. government owes its creditors—by the staggering sum of $2 trillion.

By the time Bill Clinton was inaugurated in 1992, the national debt had mushroomed to $4 trillion. Although Clinton, in his campaign, had promised tax cuts for the middle class and government expenditures for job training, the new president bowed to political reality. To bring about a reduction in the deficit, Clinton asked for higher taxes, primarily on wealthier Americans, as well as spending cuts, particularly on military appropriations.

The largest portion of federal expenditures, however, funded entitlement programs, whose costs had spiraled along with the deficit. These entitlement programs—including Social Security, Medicare, and Medicaid—guaranteed federal aid to all eligible American citizens. Most of the entitlement funds went to middle-class elderly and disabled persons and to poor children. These

THINK THROUGH HISTORY
C. *Drawing Conclusions*
What factors led to the defeat of Clinton's health care plan?

C. Answer
Business and insurance interests lobbied against it; Clinton moved slowly and wouldn't compromise; the public viewed the plan as one that would increase the size of government.

TEACHING OPTIONS

Teaching Less Proficient Readers

Clarifying Concepts Pair less proficient readers with more able readers and have them read "Clinton and the Economy." Ask each pair to create a graphic organizer showing ways in which Clinton might have reduced the national debt. The graphic organizer might be similar to the one below:

Making Connections Across the Curriculum

Economics Though President Clinton failed to gain approval of his plan for universal, affordable health care, substantial change occurred in the health care system over subsequent years, primarily due to competition. By the late 1990s, the growth in health maintenance organizations (HMOs), or prepaid health plans, and the increasing number of doctors abandoning their private practices to work for the HMOs has left more traditional medical establishments to consider mergers and other measures to ensure their survival.

programs were popular, and most politicians, including President Clinton, hesitated to cut them. Even without cuts in entitlement programs, however, the Clinton plan, as modified by Congress, cut the federal budget deficit by one-third between 1992 and 1995.

The most effective tool in reducing the deficit, however, was a growing economy. Throughout Clinton's administration, unemployment continued to fall, inflation remained low, and the stock market soared to new heights. All of this increased the federal government's revenues, while decreasing the number of people who received public aid, thereby lowering the deficit.

TRADE AGREEMENT The North American Free Trade Agreement (**NAFTA**) was a central piece of legislation for both the Bush and Clinton administrations. The treaty, which the House passed in November 1993, lowered tariffs and brought Mexico into the free-trade zone that the United States and Canada had already established. Critics such as Ross Perot argued that NAFTA would weaken environmental regulations and result in the loss of American jobs to Mexico, where wages were lower than in the United States. Supporters, however, argued that free trade and lower tariffs would strengthen all the participants' economies and that more American jobs would be created as expanding Mexican markets bought U.S. goods. As advocates had predicted, trade with Mexico skyrocketed in 1994. However, analysts disagreed on the effects NAFTA was having on U.S. jobs and the environment.

CLINTON'S FOREIGN POLICY The most important foreign policy challenge for the Clinton administration was to ease the instability that had followed the end of the Cold War. Following the collapse of the Soviet Union, American leaders supported Boris Yeltsin, the president of Russia, hoping that he could create a stable democracy in his country. The greatest concern among American policymakers was the Russian nuclear arsenal, which would pose a great risk if it were to fall into the hands of military dictators. Aside from providing economic assistance, the United States could only watch and wait while encouraging the Russians to solve their problems in a peaceful, democratic manner.

The fall of the Soviet empire also revived ancient ethnic hatreds. When Yugoslavia disintegrated in 1991, Bosnian Serbs began a campaign called "ethnic cleansing," intended to remove Muslims and Croats from the parts of Bosnia that Serbs controlled. In response, President Clinton backed a U.N.-peacekeeping effort in Bosnia and lent U.S. airpower to NATO bombing raids on Serb military positions. When the Serbs attacked areas designated as "safe havens" for Muslims and Croats, Clinton reluctantly sent 20,000 U.S. troops in 1996 to help preserve a fragile peace.

Before assuming office in 1992, President Clinton had promised to force China to protect the human rights of its citizens. Once in office, however, Clinton backed away from that position in favor of protecting China's favorable trading status. Nevertheless, problems with China persisted. In 1996, the Chinese conducted naval exercises around Taiwan. Some feared the exercises were a prelude to an invasion, but that never happened. The United States responded by increasing diplomatic communication with China in order to reduce economic and human rights tensions there.

In addition to the situations in Russia and China, a series of problems in other regions in the world demanded Clinton's attention in his

THINK THROUGH HISTORY
D. *Clarifying*
Explain why politicians find it difficult to cut entitlement programs.

D. Answer
Politicians hesitate to cut these programs because most of the money from the programs goes to poor children or to powerful voting blocs of elderly or middle-class citizens.

ON THE WORLD STAGE

Gulf of Aden

SOMALIA

Mogadishu •   • Indian Ocean

HUMANITARIAN RELIEF IN SOMALIA

In 1992, a deadly famine plagued Somalia, and an estimated 300,000 people died of starvation. Thirty thousand more Somalis were killed in the fighting between warring ethnic groups who stole relief supplies.

In December 1992, President Bush ordered the U.S. Marines to Somalia on a humanitarian mission named "Operation Restore Hope," *below.* The marines tried to stop the theft of relief food in Somalia's capital, Mogadishu—an effort that saved an estimated 100,000 lives.

After 18 U.S. Army Rangers were killed in October 1993, however, President Clinton, responding to pressure, recalled the American troops and promised greater scrutiny of proposed humanitarian missions in the future.

MORE ABOUT . . .
Foreign Policy and the Economy
After appearing to flounder on foreign policy issues early in his first administration, President Clinton forged a clear connection between the domestic economy and U.S. foreign policy. Clinton created the National Economic Council, charged with coordinating domestic and foreign economic policies. Mickey Kantor, an aide to the president, noted, "Trade and international economics have joined the foreign-policy table." Winning passage of NAFTA was one of the Clinton administration's major economic-foreign policy successes.

CRITICAL THINKING TRANSPARENCIES
CT68, Federal Budget, 1945–1995

ON THE WORLD STAGE
Humanitarian Relief in Somalia
Critical Thinking: Analyzing Issues Ask students to tell why U.S. troops were unable to complete their mission in Somalia. *Possible Responses: Some students may respond that public opinion was against further aid after the deaths of U.S. servicemen. Others might attribute the cause to the fighting between ethnic groups within Somalia, which made safe distribution of relief goods impossible.*

TEACHING OPTIONS

Making Connections Across the Curriculum

Geography Have students locate each of the countries discussed on page 1009 on a classroom map or globe. Some students may volunteer to bring to class specialized maps that give information about a particular region, such as a map that identifies areas of the Bosnian conflict or one that depicts Somalian refugee routes. Suggest to students that they look for such maps in past issues of magazines or on the Internet.

Exploring Themes

The American Dream An important part of the American dream is feeling that one could survive a financial catastrophe such as a major illness, loss of work, or outliving one's retirement savings. Ask students how Americans in past years coped with or avoided such problems. *Possible Responses: Greater strength of extended families; an easier, rural lifestyle; shorter life spans also alleviated such problems.* Discuss Clinton's attempts to deal with the national debt. Ask, What is your reaction to the state of the U.S. economy? Does it affect your life today? How might it affect your dreams for the future?

The Republican Congress

Ask students to discuss the implications of having the Congress controlled by one party and the office of the president by another. Discuss these questions:

- What difficulties might this create?
- Under what circumstances might the country as a whole benefit from such an arrangement?

▶ *Discussing Key Ideas*
- Republicans seize control of Congress and sign the Contract with America.
- Conflict between Congress and the president leads to two shutdowns of federal government services.
- Clinton resists many conservative reforms, especially those related to entitlement programs.
- The president cooperates with the Republican Congress by signing into law a major overhaul of the welfare system.

 ELECTRONIC LIBRARY OF PRIMARY SOURCES
A Contract with America by Newt Gingrich

KEY PLAYERS
Clinton and Gingrich

Critical Thinking: Compare and Contrast Have students consider ways in which Clinton and Gingrich are similar and ways in which they differ. *Possible Responses: They are about the same age, both were re-elected, both are hard on crime; they differ in their views on issues such as changing Medicare.*

---

first term, including the humanitarian crises in Bosnia and Somalia. In each case, some people felt President Clinton should have acted sooner or with more force, while others feared any involvement was too much. President Clinton, meanwhile, refused to retreat from active U.S. participation in international affairs, arguing, "There's no longer an easy dividing line between foreign policy and domestic policy."

The Republican Congress

In mid-1994, amid the failure of his health care plan and recurring questions about Whitewater, Clinton saw his approval rating slump to 42 percent.

KEY PLAYERS

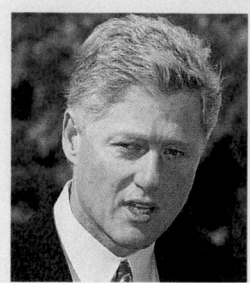

BILL CLINTON
1946–
In 1992, Bill Clinton ran for president as a moderate, but in 1994 Republicans convinced voters that he had governed as a liberal during his first two years in office. As a result, the Republicans took control of Congress and controlled the national agenda throughout 1995.

Clinton reversed his fortunes, however, by opposing the Republicans' more unpopular positions, such as changing Medicare, and by taking control of their strongest issues, such as crime.

In 1996, Clinton forged compromises with Republicans on welfare and health care reform. In the 1996 election, he became the first Democratic president to be reelected since FDR.

NEWT GINGRICH
1943–
In the summer of 1994, Newt Gingrich drafted his Contract with America. When Gingrich and the Congressional Republicans took control of Congress in 1995, they swiftly acted on the Contract with America, passing nine of the ten items within the first 100 days of the 104th Congress.

Gingrich eventually became highly unpopular, however, when Democrats attacked the Republican agenda as extreme. Nevertheless, as voters reelected Bill Clinton, they also retained Republican congressional majorities to pull Clinton and the Democrats to the center. Gingrich became the first Republican to be reelected speaker since the 1920s.

Conservative radio commentators criticized the "liberal elite," feminists, and the federal welfare system for destroying American culture. At the same time, a Republican congressman from Georgia named **Newt Gingrich** began to turn voters' dissatisfaction with Clinton into support for Republican candidates running in the midterm elections. His efforts led to a Republican victory and brought divided government back to Washington.

THE CONTRACT WITH AMERICA
On September 27, 1994, on the steps of the Capitol, more than 300 Republican candidates signed Representative Newt Gingrich's **Contract with America.** The contract set forth ten items favored by an increasingly conservative electorate—among them, congressional term limits, a balanced budget amendment, tax cuts, tougher crime laws, and welfare reform.

Republican congressional candidates hammered away at President Clinton and the Democrats, using the contract as the hammer. In the elections of November 1994, the Republicans handed the Democrats a humiliating defeat. Voters turned control of both houses of Congress over to the Republicans for the first time since 1954 and placed 31 Republicans in the nation's governors' mansions. However, only 38 percent of eligible voters bothered to vote.

Chosen by acclamation as the new Speaker of the House, Newt Gingrich was jubilant.

A PERSONAL VOICE
I will never forget mounting the rostrum and looking over the House for the first time. It was an amazing experience. . . . The whole scene gave me a wonderful sense of the romance of America and the magic by which Americans share power and accept changes in government.
NEWT GINGRICH, *To Renew America*

1010 CHAPTER 34

THINK THROUGH HISTORY
E. *Summarizing*
List some of the provisions of the Contract with America.
E. Answer The contract included tax cuts, harsher crime laws, welfare reform, and a balanced budget amendment.

Gingrich and his fellow House Republicans spent their first days reforming Congress—cutting committees, staff, and special privileges. During the rest of their first hundred days in control of Congress, they approved a constitutional amendment requiring a balanced federal budget by the year 2002, tried to increase defense spending, and promised tax cuts and welfare reform.

GOVERNMENT SHUTDOWNS Democrats and moderate Republicans in Congress, however, refused to go along with all of the conservative reforms. In the Senate, the balanced budget amendment lost by one vote, and several other bills were either defeated or scaled back. Among these were efforts to repeal the ban on the sale of assault weapons and cuts in federal environmental regulations.

Also, President Clinton began to fight back against the Republican Congress. In his first two years in office, Clinton had never issued a veto. In his second two years, he vetoed 15 bills.

Most notably, Clinton opposed Republican budgets that slowed the growth of the entitlement programs. In late 1995, Clinton refused to compromise on the Republican budgets, and the congressional Republicans dug in their heels. The result was a shutdown of the federal government for a week in November, and again for several weeks in December 1995 and January 1996.

As a result of the shutdown, many government services were delayed, which inconvenienced citizens and federal employees alike. Although a third of the people polled blamed Clinton for the shutdown, even more people—44 percent—blamed Congress. Newt Gingrich's approval rating plunged to 22 percent. Fearing further voter disfavor, both sides agreed to a compromise in which Clinton promised to balance the federal budget in seven years and Republicans promised to protect several of Clinton's favorite programs.

WELFARE AND HEALTH REFORM Although the government shutdown dominated the headlines in late 1995 and early 1996, two bills signed into law in 1996 were more significant. Clinton had campaigned on the pledge to "end welfare as we know it." He had proposed to spend $10 billion to give welfare recipients training, education, and child care so that they could seek higher-paying jobs. However, Congress had refused to approve this increased spending.

Instead, the Republican Congress crafted a bill that completely overhauled the welfare system. On July 31, 1996, President Clinton announced that he would sign the bill. It would cut $56 billion in welfare spending, limit the length of time people could receive benefits, and end the federal guarantee of welfare that had remained in place for 60 years. The new new law would provide "block grants"—set amounts of federal funds—for the states to spend on welfare as they saw fit.

Liberal Democrats feared the consequences of eliminating the federal safety net for the poor, two-thirds of whom were children. New York senator Daniel Patrick Moynihan termed the legislation "an obscene act of political regression," and two Clinton aides resigned in protest. Nevertheless, the bill passed. As Senator John Breaux of Louisiana argued, "It's not perfect. . . . But I think it's a major step in the right direction. It moves toward reform. It sets time limits."

In a less controversial action, the president signed into law a moderate health care bill with bipartisan support. This bill made health insurance portable, meaning that workers could transfer their health

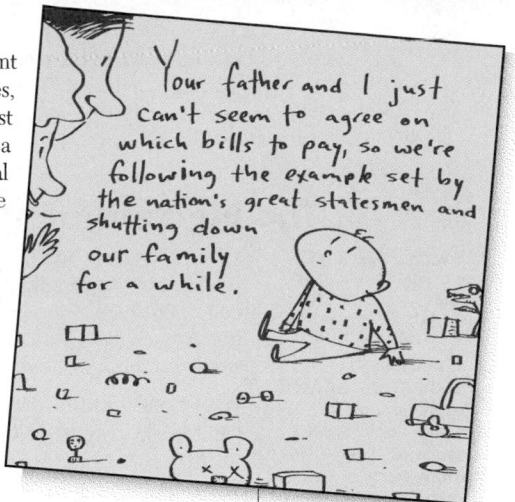

SKILLBUILDER
INTERPRETING POLITICAL CARTOONS
What point of view is the cartoonist expressing about federal government shutdowns?

Skillbuilder Answer Possible Answer: The cartoonist takes a dim view of the shutdowns. He sarcastically refers to leaders as statesmen and indicates that shutting down the government is as impractical as shutting down family.

F. Answer As a presidential candidate, Clinton had promised to spend $10 billion to train welfare recipients to work. The bill he signed in 1996 contained no such provision for job training.

THINK THROUGH HISTORY
F. Contrasting Contrast the welfare reform plan Clinton offered in 1992 to the one he signed in 1996.

NOW & **THEN**

ENDING WELFARE ENTITLEMENTS
During Franklin D. Roosevelt's administration, the federal government for the first time assumed responsibility for the welfare of the nation's poor. As part of the Social Security Act of 1935, Aid to Dependent Children, which later became Aid to Families with Dependent Children (AFDC), provided cash payments to a few hundred thousand families headed by single mothers.

Opponents of the program argued that people would become dependent on public assistance. By 1996, AFDC supported more than 4 million single mothers. Attacking a culture of dependency, politicians in both political parties pushed to end the federal government's guarantee of aid for America's needy. In 1996, Congress passed, and President Clinton signed, welfare reform legislation. It dissolved AFDC, but provided the states with federal funds to administer aid programs.

The United States in Today's World **1011**

The Election of 1996

▶ **Starting with the Student**
Ask students what impressed them most about the 1996 election. Ask them why, in their opinion, there was such a low turnout of voters.

▶ **Discussing Key Ideas**
• Voter apathy is high during the 1996 election.
• Clinton wins a second term, and the Republicans retain control of Congress.

IN-DEPTH RESOURCES: UNIT 9
from "A Bridge to the Future" by Bill Clinton, p. 47

ASSESS & RETEACH

Section 1 Assessment
Have students work individually to answer the questions and then trade papers with a partner to compare answers.

Self-Assessment
Ask students to identify passages in the text that helped them to answer each question.

Section Quiz
FORMAL ASSESSMENT
Section Quiz, p. 411

Reteach
Use the Geography Transparency for Section 1 to review voter turnout by state in 1996.

GEOGRAPHY TRANSPARENCIES
G34, Percentage of Eligible Votes Cast, 1996 Presidential Election

IN-DEPTH RESOURCES: UNIT 9
Guided Reading, p. 39

CLOSE

Although the split government of a Republican Congress and a Democratic president continued in Clinton's second term, the two parties had developed strategies for working together. Issues they confronted included the country's role in a changing world economy.

1012   **Chapter 34**

---

insurance when they left their jobs, even if one of the people covered had a pre-existing condition. However, the bill stopped short of establishing health care as a federal entitlement. The passage of these two laws removed welfare reform and health care reform as issues in the upcoming 1996 election.

The Election of 1996

Skillbuilder Answer The rate of voter turnout has generally declined. More than 100 million votes were cast in 1992 (55% of 189).

SKILLBUILDER INTERPRETING GRAPHS
What general trend describes voter turnout between 1960 and 1996? In which election year did more than 100 million people cast ballots?

When Congress and Clinton began to compromise and pass legislation, their popularity rose among American voters. Early in the 1996 presidential campaign, President Clinton held large leads in public-opinion polls over Bob Dole, the Republican presidential nominee, and Ross Perot, the candidate of the newly established Reform Party.

THE 1996 CAMPAIGN After the nominating conventions in the summer, Clinton's lead in the polls was so large that some people thought the Democrats might regain control of Congress. Try as they might, Dole and Perot could not cut into Clinton's lead. Dole offered a 15 percent cut in the income tax and eventually focused on a series of scandals within the Clinton administration but did not gain any ground. Perot launched a last-minute television blitz attacking both major parties, but without success.

CLINTON REELECTED In the end, the strong economy and an improved working relationship with Congress convinced voters to back President Clinton. On election day, he won 49 percent of the popular vote, with Dole receiving 41 percent and Perot 8 percent. Despite Clinton's victory, there was no Democratic landslide, and the Republicans kept control of both houses of Congress.

The biggest story of the election, however, was voter apathy. Exit polls showed that only 49 percent of eligible voters bothered to go to the polls. Clinton collected his margin of victory largely from women, especially single women. He also polled high numbers from African Americans, Latinos, the elderly, and young voters. Dole's support came mainly from white, middle-class men.

In the immediate aftermath of the election, both President Clinton and Republican leaders pledged to set aside the bitter partisanship that marked Clinton's first term and cooperate as they faced the challenges of the 21st century. Chief among these challenges was an expanding global economy with increasing productivity but also widespread insecurity.

Voter Turnout, 1960–1996

Year	Percent who voted	Voting-age population in millions
1960	63%	110 Million
1964	62%	114
1968	61%	120
1972	55%	141
1976	54%	152
1980	53%	165
1984	53%	174
1988	50%	183
1992	55%	189
1996	49%	196.5

■ Percent who voted
■ Voting-age population in millions

G. Answer The strong economy; strong support among women and minorities; an improved working relationship with Congress.

THINK THROUGH HISTORY
G. Synthesizing
What factors contributed most to Clinton's reelection?

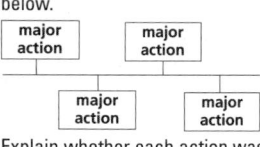
Section **1** Assessment

1. TERMS & NAMES
Identify:
• Bill Clinton
• Hillary Rodham Clinton
• NAFTA
• Newt Gingrich
• Contract with America

2. SUMMARIZING Create a time line of Clinton's major actions during his first term as president, using a form such as the one below.

major action	major action

major action	major action

Explain whether each action was a success or a failure for Clinton.

3. RECOGNIZING EFFECTS
How did voter dissatisfaction affect the 1992 presidential race?

THINK ABOUT
• what issues voters were upset about
• which candidates seemed to address those issues
• how voters responded at the polls

4. ANALYZING ISSUES
Judging from the events of Clinton's first term as president, would you characterize the United States in the 1990s as politically conservative, liberal, or somewhere in the middle? Explain why.

THINK ABOUT
• the response to Clinton's health care reform plan
• the rise of Newt Gingrich and his loss of public approval
• the passage of welfare reform

1012 CHAPTER 34

ANSWERS

1. TERMS & NAMES
Bill Clinton, p. 1006
Hillary Rodham Clinton, p. 1008
NAFTA, p. 1009
Newt Gingrich, p. 1010
Contract with America, p. 1010

2. SUMMARIZING
Students may include the following actions on their time lines. (Evaluations of success or failure may vary.)

September 1993—Presents health care bill to Congress
October 1993—Withdraws troops from Somalia
November 1993—Wins passage of NAFTA
November 1995 and January 1996—Argues with Congress over budget, leading to government shutdown
July 1996—Announces that he will sign welfare reform bill
August 1996—Announces that he will sign health care bill

3. RECOGNIZING EFFECTS
Possible Response: Students may note that dissatisfaction with the two major parties helped Ross Perot gain 19 percent of the vote. Also, dissatisfaction with the economy led voters to reject George Bush and elect Bill Clinton.

4. ANALYZING ISSUES
Possible Responses: Students who answer somewhere in the middle may point to the bipartisan bills that were passed during Clinton's first term and to the failure of either liberals or conservatives to dominate. Students who answer conservative may point to the failure of major health care reform, the rise of Newt Gingrich, and the passage of welfare reform. Those who answer liberal may point to the 1993 tax increase, Gingrich's loss of popularity, and Bob Dole's defeat.

The New Global Economy

TERMS & NAMES
- service sector
- downsize
- Bill Gates
- GATT

LEARN ABOUT America's role in a changing world economy
TO UNDERSTAND the economic challenges and opportunities facing Americans in the 21st century.

ONE AMERICAN'S STORY

The economy President Clinton inherited from President Bush was just beginning to pull out of a recession as Clinton took office. But some regions of the nation—particularly the Northeast—remained mired in stagnation. Near Kennebunkport, Maine, for example, the John Roberts clothing factory, which employed workers who did low-wage piecework, faced bankruptcy. Instead of letting the factory close, the workers, with the help of Mike Cavanaugh of the Clothing and Textile Workers' Union, raised some money and turned the plant into an employee-owned company.

Ethel Beaudoin, who had worked in the factory for nearly 30 years, took a cut in pay for a chance at employee ownership. Although the pay cut was a hardship, she still had a positive outlook on the company's new direction.

A PERSONAL VOICE
It's a nice feeling to be part of the process . . . of deciding what this company buys for machinery and to know the customers more intimately. They're our customers, and it's a nicer feeling when the customers know that the coat that we put out is made by owners. It's almost like you're making it more personal.

ETHEL BEAUDOIN, quoted in *Divided We Fall*

Factory workers from the John Roberts clothing factory.

Beaudoin's experience is one positive outcome that resulted from changes in the economy. Other people, however, did not fare so well. As the U.S. economy reacted to technological change, global trade and competition, as well as the end of the Cold War, many Americans felt insecure.

The New Service and High–Tech Economy

In the mid-1990s, Americans heard both good news and bad news about the nation's economy. The good news was that inflation had fallen to its lowest level since the 1960s. With the creation of 10 million new jobs between 1993 and 1996, unemployment had fallen to just 5.1 percent, the lowest it had been since 1990.

The bad news was that in many families both parents had to work, because it was harder to find jobs that paid well. Between 1989 and 1993, the median household income, adjusted for inflation, dropped from $33,585 to $31,241. In addition, the income gap between America's richest and poorest earners widened. In 1993, nearly 4 million working families earned too little to stay out of poverty.

There were varying explanations for this income stagnation. Liberal economists claimed that corporations were making unfair profits by manufacturing more of their goods in foreign countries that had lower labor costs. Conservative economists asserted that taxes were still too high, preventing companies from growing faster and creating more high-paying jobs. But no matter which side of the debate economists were on, they agreed that the American economy was going through significant changes.

The United States in Today's World **1013**

SECTION 2 RESOURCES

PRINT RESOURCES

IN-DEPTH RESOURCES: UNIT 9
Guided Reading, p. 40
Geography Application: The U.S. Trade in Goods, p. 44
Primary Source: from *The Road Ahead* by Bill Gates, p. 48
American Lives: Bill Gates, p. 52

ACCESS FOR STUDENTS ACQUIRING ENGLISH
Guided Reading (Spanish), p. 330

FORMAL ASSESSMENT
Section Quiz, p. 412

ALTERNATIVE ASSESSMENT BOOK
See forms for supporting and scoring alternative activities.

TECHNOLOGY RESOURCES

INTERNET McDougal Littell Learning On-Line
http://www.mcdougallittell.com

Section 2 Overview

OBJECTIVES

(1) To describe changes in the American workplace.

(2) To explain increased competition for domestic and international markets.

SKILLBUILDERS

- Interpreting graphs, p. 1014
- Understanding geography: location, p. 1016

CRITICAL THINKING

- Recognizing effects, pp. 1014, 1015, 1017
- Summarizing. p. 1017
- Drawing conclusions, p. 1017

FOCUS & MOTIVATE

▶ *Starting with the Student*
- Ask students where the manufactured objects they use every day—clothing, shoes, radio, TV, car—are made. Then ask them what impact they think a global economy might have on them and their families.

OBJECTIVE
(1) INSTRUCT

The New Service and High-Tech Economy

▶ *Discussing Key Ideas*
- The income gap between wealthiest and poorest Americans widens.
- Temporary work and jobs in the service sector and in high technology expand.
- Young people suffer more unemployment and earn less money than older workers.
- Union membership drops.

IN-DEPTH RESOURCES: UNIT 9
Guided Reading, p. 40

ACCESS FOR STUDENTS ACQUIRING ENGLISH
Guided Reading (Spanish), p. 330

THE EXPANDING SERVICE SECTOR In the 1990s, far-reaching changes in the U.S. workplace emerged. Chief among these changes were the loss of jobs in manufacturing and the explosive growth of jobs in the **service sector,** the part of the economy that provides services to consumers. By 1996, more than 60 percent of American workers held jobs in the service sector, which included store employees, medical professionals, lawyers, engineers, janitors, and teachers.

The largest growth in the service sector in the mid-1990s came in low-paying jobs such as retail sales, fast-food vending, and janitorial work. In addition to the low pay these jobs offered, many were only part-time or temporary positions with limited benefits. For example, Manpower, Inc., a Milwaukee-based temporary services company, benefited from changes in the economy and became the largest U.S. employer. In 1993, fully 640,000 American workers cashed paychecks from the company, which generated earnings of almost $2 billion.

TEMPORARY WORKERS When Manpower, Inc., and other such companies first opened, they supplied temporary workers, often called temps, for emergencies or seasonal peak periods. Later, many corporations, instead of investing in salaries and benefits for a large full-time staff, began to **downsize**—reduce staff in order to streamline operations—and to hire temps, who were often less expensive. Many young workers who saw their parents work for one company until retirement found themselves working as "permalancers," long-term freelance workers. Experts projected that by the year 2000, 35 million workers—half of all workers and two-thirds of women workers—would be temps.

The increasing movement to temporary work had important consequences for the workers. Most temps had little job security and fewer benefits than permanent employees. Both of these factors in turn contributed to the general feeling of economic insecurity.

YOUNG WORKERS Another measure of economic insecurity in the 1990s was that three out of four young Americans expected to earn less money as adults than their parents did. In fact, younger workers continued to suffer higher rates of unemployment even when the jobless rate fell for older workers. In 1993, about one in seven workers between the ages of 16 and 25 lacked a job—double the national rate.

THINK THROUGH HISTORY
A. Recognizing Effects How did the change from an industrial economy to a service economy affect workers' incomes and job security?
A. Answer Unlike factory jobs, most jobs in the service sector paid low wages. Also, many service jobs provided only contract or part-time work.

SKILLBUILDER INTERPRETING GRAPHS How did the change in men's earnings between 1985 and 1995 differ from the change in women's earnings? Which racial/ethnic group had the largest drop in earnings from 1990 to 1995?

Skillbuilder Answer Differ: Men's earnings fell slightly while women's earnings rose slightly. **Group:** Latinos.

Changes in Weekly Earnings, 1985–1995

BY GENDER

Median weekly earnings in 1982 dollars (1982 dollars show figures adjusted for inflation)

1985 · 1990 · 1995

■ Male ■ Female

Source: U.S. Bureau of Labor Statistics

BY RACE AND ETHNICITY

Median weekly earnings in 1982 dollars (1982 dollars show figures adjusted for inflation)

1985* · 1990 · 1995

■ White ■ African American ■ Latino
*Data not available for Latinos.

TEACHING OPTIONS

Making Connections Across the Curriculum

Economics Discuss with students the fluctuations of the stock market. Ask students to choose three stocks to follow in the newspaper for a month and to use a chart like this one to record changes.

Week	Stock	Increase	Decrease
Week 1			
Week 2			
Week 3			
Week 4			

Exploring Themes

Economic Opportunity Discuss with students the actions taken by the government during the 1990s that affected—or seemed to affect—workers' jobs. Point out that the federal government does not always make decisions based on the impact its actions might have on jobs in a particular city or company. In the pursuit of international trade agreements such as NAFTA, the federal government considered the economy of the nation as a whole. The assumption was that the expansion of U.S. markets abroad would benefit everyone—for example, by providing cheaper goods for American citizens.

High unemployment rates in the nation's cities hit young people harder than others. In 1994, for example, 18 percent of Detroit's workers, but almost 50 percent of its young people, were unemployed. The rise in joblessness among young people and the nation's shift to a service economy came at the expense of America's traditional workplaces, the farms and factories that had previously supported American families.

FARMS AND FACTORIES At the beginning of the 20th century, more Americans worked at farming than at any other single occupation. From the 1920s until the 1970s, though, industrial manufacturing was the nation's largest employment sector.

Starting in the 1970s, the United States experienced another wrenching change, as manufacturing jobs began to disappear. By 1996, only about 17 percent of America's workers worked in factories. Smokestack industries, such as automaking and steel production, declined in the 1970s, often because of international competition. In addition, by the 1980s and 1990s, automation had shifted many tasks from people to machines. In 1992, for example, a mere 140,000 steel workers did the same work that 240,000 workers had accomplished ten years earlier. Larry Pugh, who managed a hospital in Waterloo, Iowa, talked about the downsizing of a farm equipment factory in his hometown.

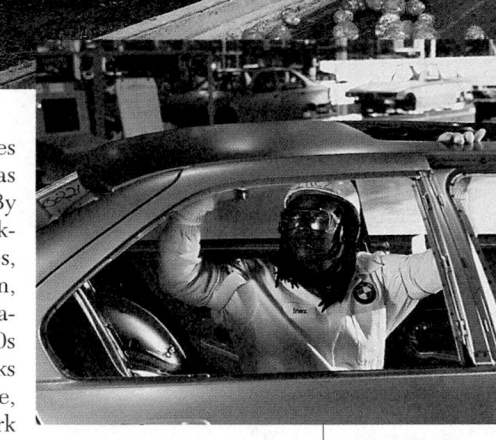

Despite steady growth in the economy, America's blue collar workers on farms and in factories continued to feel economic insecurity in the 1990s.

A PERSONAL VOICE
There used to be seventeen thousand five hundred people working here . . . . Now there are six thousand. Those people spent their money. They bought the cars. They bought the houses. They were replaced by people that are at the minimum wage—seven or eight dollars an hour, not fifteen or twenty dollars an hour. These people can hardly eke out a living at today's wages.

LARRY PUGH, quoted in *Divided We Fall*

B. Answer
Downsizing led to higher unemployment, particularly in cities. It also resulted in the hiring of more temporary workers in place of permanent employees.

THINK THROUGH HISTORY
B. Recognizing Effects How did downsizing affect people?

The decline in the number of industrial jobs contributed to a drop in union membership. In 1945, 35 percent of American workers belonged to unions; by 1995, only 14 percent of workers were union members. In the 1990s, unions had trouble organizing. Workers who already earned high wages felt no need for union membership, and low-wage service employees felt too vulnerable to risk their jobs in a strike. In this economy, some workers saw their incomes decline, while others—those with advanced training and specialized technical skills—saw their salaries rise and their economic security expand greatly.

HIGH–TECH INDUSTRIES Workers in high technology fields in the mid-1990s accounted for about 20 percent of the work force. Management consultant Peter Drucker estimated that early in the 21st century, at least one in three workers would be a "knowledge worker." Unlike the factory work that had paid good wages even to semiskilled workers, the new high-tech jobs demanded that workers have specialized skills, creativity, and knowledge of computers. Most workers who landed high-tech jobs could be assured of a healthy salary.

> **ECONOMIC BACKGROUND**
>
> **HIGH–TECH LAYOFFS**
>
> Some experts have predicted that high-tech information jobs will employ one-third of the work force early in the 21st century. However, the companies that have been at the cutting edge of the technology revolution have been among the most aggressive in downsizing their work force. Between 1991 and 1995, for example, IBM laid off 85,000 workers, AT&T 83,000, and Xerox 10,000. While these layoffs were partially offset by hires in new companies that developed and used the new technology, the net result of the computer revolution in the 1990s has been an overall loss of jobs.

The United States in Today's World **1015**

Change and the Global Economy

▶ **Starting with the Student**
Ask students what trips to foreign countries they or their friends or family members have made during the past year. Then ask these questions:

• How many hours did it take to reach their destinations?

• What conclusions can they draw about the accessibility of international markets?

▶ **Discussing Key Ideas**
• Clinton favors expanding U.S. trade abroad to meet international competition.
• American workers disagree over whether international trade agreements will result in the loss of jobs.

IN-DEPTH RESOURCES: UNIT 9
Geography Application: The U.S. Trade in Goods, p. 44

HISTORY FROM VISUALS
World Trading Blocs, 1996
Reading the Map Help students interpret the map by having them identify the members that make up some of the trading blocs. Begin by asking them what nations make up the Group of Seven. *U.S.A., Canada, Great Britain, France, Germany, Italy, Japan.*

Extension Have students use an almanac to find out to whom each country in the Group of Seven exported the most. *The U.S exported to Canada; Canada exported to the U.S.; Japan exported to the U.S.; Great Britain, France, Germany, and Italy, to the EU.*

By the 1990s, more than a few innovative entrepreneurs had turned a cutting-edge idea about computer technology into a huge personal fortune. **Bill Gates,** for example, was a sophomore at Harvard University in December 1974 when he saw a promising business opportunity. With his friend Paul Allen, Gates adapted the computer language BASIC for use in personal computers, which had recently come on the market. Gates dropped out of college to found Microsoft, the computer software company that by 1996 had provided him with assets estimated at more than $18 billion, making him the wealthiest man in the world.

Change and the Global Economy

In 1900, airplanes hadn't yet flown and telephone service was barely 20 years old. U.S. trade with the rest of the world was worth about $2.2 billion (roughly 12 percent of the economy). Nearly a century later, New Yorkers could hop a supersonic jet and arrive in London within three hours, information traveled instantly by fax machine, and U.S. trade with other countries approached $2 trillion (more than 25 percent of the economy). As American companies competed for international and domestic markets, American workers competed with workers in other countries.

INTERNATIONAL TRADE The expansion of U.S. trade abroad was an important goal of President Clinton's foreign policy, as his support of NAFTA had shown. In 1994, in response to increasing international economic competition among trading blocs, the United States joined many other nations in adopting a new version of the General Agreement on Tariffs and Trade (**GATT**). The new treaty lowered trade barriers such as tariffs and established the World Trade Organization (WTO) to resolve trade disputes. Economists predicted that the treaty would have a positive

Geography Skillbuilder Answer G-7 Country: Japan. **United States:** NAFTA, APEC, G-7.

GEOGRAPHY SKILLBUILDER
LOCATION *Which is the only G-7 country located outside of Europe and North America?* **LOCATION** *To which world trade organizations does the United States belong?*

Cooperative Activity: Researching International Trade

Task: Student groups will research a world trading bloc and prepare a report on exports and imports of member countries.

Purpose: To recognize the importance of trading blocs in maintaining international trade.

Activity: Students will form pairs or small groups and choose a trading bloc represented by a color on the map. Each group will research the major exports and imports of countries in the bloc, the bloc's trading part-

ners, and annual expenditures. Each group will then prepare a report and present it to the class, using graphs, charts, and product examples if they choose.

📁 **Building a Portfolio:** Students adding a report to their portfolio should attach a note explaining their own contribution to the work.

ALTERNATIVE ASSESSMENT BOOK
Standards for Evaluating a Cooperative Activity

Standards for Evaluation
Reports should . . .

• use specific details to demonstrate knowledge of a country's exports and imports
• reflect accurate data from reliable sources
• be presented using effective oral presentation techniques

overall effect on the U.S. economy. As President Clinton announced at a meeting of the Group of Seven (the world's seven leading economic powers) that year, "Trade as much as troops will increasingly define the ties that bind nations in the twenty-first century."

These international trade agreements, however, deepened American workers' fears of massive job flight to countries that produced the same goods as the United States but at a lower cost. Those fears had arisen in the 1970s when less expensive but high-quality auto and steel imports from Japan and Germany forced many U.S. factory workers out of high-paying jobs.

To remain competitive, many U.S. businesses felt the need to make their operations more global in order to produce goods as economically as possible. Indeed, the shipping label for a product of one American electronics company reads: "Made in one of the following countries: Korea, Hong Kong, Malaysia, Singapore, Taiwan, Mauritius, Thailand, Indonesia, Mexico, Philippines. The exact country of origin is unknown."

INTERNATIONAL COMPETITION During the 1990s, U.S. businesses felt pressure to cut costs wherever possible. To reduce labor costs, businesses frequently moved their operations to less economically advanced countries, where wages were lower. This movement of jobs angered many American workers, who feared their jobs might be the next to go. Despite the critics' warnings of job flight, however, NAFTA actually helped increase demand for American exports, creating thousands of manufacturing jobs in the United States.

Less economically advanced countries also offered some businesses an opportunity to evade the strict environmental regulations legislated in such developed nations as the United States. Just south of the U.S. border with Mexico, for example, foreign-owned *maquiladoras*, or assembly plants, often operated irresponsibly, dumping poisonous chemical wastes on Mexican soil. Critics of NAFTA feared that it would allow some U.S. companies to move to Mexico to avoid the strict environmental laws in the United States.

With the U.S. economy undergoing such extensive change at the end of 20th century, feelings of insecurity were inevitable. Many Americans in all sectors of the economy feared being left behind by the rapid change. Other Americans, however, saw great opportunities for progress—especially from the endless stream of new technology.

C. Answer International trade agreements opened new markets, but also made jobs more mobile. Companies exported work to countries with lower wages, costing Americans jobs.

THINK THROUGH HISTORY
C. Recognizing Effects Summarize some of the effects of NAFTA and GATT.

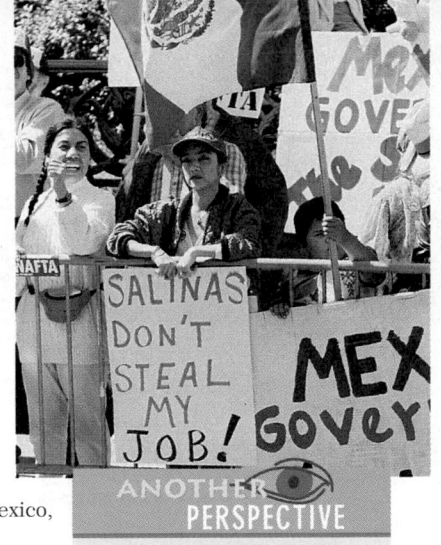

ANOTHER PERSPECTIVE

ECONOMICS AND IMMIGRATION
In 1996, the U.S.-Mexican border crossing between San Diego and Tijuana was one of the busiest in the world. Every day, some 40,000 people crossed the border there legally to work, shop, or visit. Many others crossed illegally elsewhere along the border. President Clinton tried to stem this tide by building a 14-mile wall along the border.

Some believed there was a better way to prevent illegal immigration to the United States—provide more jobs in Mexico. Carlos de Orduna, an executive at a Mexican assembly plant owned by a U.S. company, said that few of his workers attempted to immigrate to the United States. He argued, "If you have a job that allows you to live reasonably well, . . . why should you go to the United States?"

Section 2 Assessment

1. TERMS & NAMES

Identify:
• service sector
• downsize
• Bill Gates
• GATT

2. SUMMARIZING Record the major changes that occurred in the U.S. economy during the 1990s on a cluster diagram like the one below.

Which change has affected you the most? Explain.

3. RECOGNIZING EFFECTS Explain who was negatively affected by the changes in the economy and what negative effects they suffered.

THINK ABOUT
• who had the highest unemployment rates
• what types of jobs were eliminated
• what other negative effects there were

4. DRAWING CONCLUSIONS Considering the economic changes described in this section, how do you think workers can best prepare themselves for the future?

THINK ABOUT
• the trend of hiring more temporary employees
• the shift from agriculture and manufacturing to high-tech industry
• the skills that might prepare one for work in the global economy

The United States in Today's World **1017**

ANSWERS

1. TERMS & NAMES

service sector, p. 1014

downsize, p. 1014

Bill Gates, p. 1016

GATT, p. 1016

2. SUMMARIZING

The cluster diagram might include the following words and phrases: expanding service sector, contract workers, "permalancers," downsizing, high unemployment, decline in industrial work, drop in union membership, "knowledge worker," high-tech industry, global economy, international trade, GATT.

3. RECOGNIZING EFFECTS

Possible Response: Students may say that young people, factory workers, and unskilled or uneducated workers lost jobs, that some workers employed by large corporations were replaced by temporary employees, and that even many workers who kept their jobs suffered reduced increases in wages and benefits because they were afraid to strike.

4. DRAWING CONCLUSIONS

Possible Response: Students may say that workers should prepare for self-employment, develop good job-hunting skills, get an education, learn about technology, learn foreign languages, be flexible, and be willing to constantly acquire new skills.

ASSESS & RETEACH

Section 2 Assessment

Have students work in pairs to compare the cluster diagrams on changes in the economy that they created for item 2.

Self-Assessment

Ask students to review their responses to item 4. Have them expand their answers by adding any new or different ideas they might have for how workers can prepare for the future.

Section Quiz

FORMAL ASSESSMENT
Section Quiz, p. 412

Reteach

Have students work in small groups to merge their answers to item 2 on a single cluster diagram representing the whole group. Ask groups to put their diagrams on the board.

CLOSE

As the century came to a close, America's economic role at home and abroad was changing due in part to shifts in the workplace to high-technology industries.

TERMS & NAMES
• information superhighway
• Internet
• e-mail
• Telecommunications Act
• magnetic resonance imaging
• genetic engineering

3 Technology and Modern Life

LEARN ABOUT developments in communications and other industries
TO UNDERSTAND the impact of technological advances in the late 20th century.

ONE AMERICAN'S STORY

In November 1995, Steven Jobs saw his net worth increase by more than a billion dollars in just one day. His company, Pixar, had just offered new stock in a booming stock market after producing the wildly successful computer-animated movie *Toy Story*.

Jobs first struck it rich in 1980, at age 25, when Apple Computer, the company he helped found, first sold its stock to the public. Five years later, however, Jobs broke ties with Apple. Eventually, he invested his considerable profits from Apple into a small firm specializing in computer animation. Jobs's goal was to make the first fully computer-animated feature film. His efforts resulted in *Toy Story*, which grossed more than $177 million in its first months at the box office. However, Jobs explained that it was not the promise of huge profits that motivated him.

Steven Jobs

A PERSONAL VOICE
The thing that drives me and my colleagues at both Apple and Pixar is that you see something very compelling to you, and you don't quite know how to get it, but you know, sometimes intuitively, it's within your grasp. And it's worth putting in years of your life to make it come into existence.
STEVEN JOBS, quoted in *Time,* February 19, 1996

Despite the success of *Toy Story*, Pixar's stock value rose and fell as it was jostled by volatile technological markets. Jobs returned to Apple in 1997. Nevertheless, exciting technological developments in many industries brought impressive fortunes to innovative people like Steven Jobs. These developments also enriched the lives of ordinary people.

Technology and Communications

In his State of the Union address in 1994, President Clinton urged Congress to pass legislation to "connect every classroom, every clinic, every library, every hospital in America into a national information superhighway by the year 2000." Clinton placed Vice-President Al Gore in charge of overseeing the government's participation in the developing electronic superhighway. According to Gore, the government's role would be to serve as "referee, facilitator, envisioner, definer." In other words, private industries would build the superhighway, but the government would keep the highway democratic, ensure affordable service for everyone, protect privacy and property rights, and develop incentives for investors.

THE INFORMATION SUPERHIGHWAY The **information superhighway**—a proposed computer communications network linking people and institutions across the nation and the world—promised to advance the communications revolution that had begun with the personal computer. Through an electronic connection, such as a cable TV or phone line, participants could access remote computers that provided a mind-boggling array of media, from video-on-demand to computerized research libraries, from on-line shopping malls to

1018 Chapter 34

personalized news broadcasts. Users weren't simply observers; they could interact with other users all over the world.

The information superhighway entered most people's consciousness through the explosive growth of the Internet during the 1990s. The **Internet** is a worldwide network that links computers and allows almost instant communication of texts, pictures, and sounds. Originally developed by the U.S. Department of Defense for research, the Internet enjoyed early popularity at universities.

In the 1990s, businesses and individuals began to log on—that is, to link their computer systems to the Internet. Experts estimated that by 1996, as many as 24 million North Americans regularly used the Internet to send **e-mail** (electronic notes and messages), join discussion groups, or enjoy detailed graphics on the World Wide Web.

The modern communications revolution went far beyond the personal computer, cellular phones, and fax machines. For example, scientists at the Massachusetts Institute of Technology experimented with a "smart" office—a computerized desk that detects and monitors the workers who use it, responds to voice commands, and much more. These scientists also experimented with "bodycams," or minicomputers that are worn like earphones, like eyeglasses, or even in shoes and that provide on-the-spot links to the Internet.

TELECOMMUNICATIONS ACT OF 1996 The advances in computers and communications have had a real impact on American society. For example, because of fax machines, the Internet, and overnight-shipping, people can more readily work out of their homes instead of going to an office every day. Technology has also given Americans more entertainment options. Cable service has multiplied the number of television channels available to most people. The Internet provides video games. CD-ROMs allow computer users to travel along the Oregon Trail or go on a voyage down the Nile River.

These changes have also brought rapid growth among the communications companies. To ensure that the industry provides consumers with the best service, the federal government took several steps in the mid-1990s. In February 1996, Congress passed the **Telecommunications Act,** which removed barriers that had previously prevented one type of communications company from starting up or buying another type of communications business. The law made it possible for local telephone companies and cable television companies to compete in providing telephone and cable service.

Experts predicted that this competition would result in increased choice for consumers. Industry observers expected that telecommunications companies would combine through mergers and acquisitions and create packages of services enabling consumers to obtain all the services they need from one company.

At first, the government was slow to recognize the implications of the new communications technology. In 1994, however, the Federal Communications Commission (FCC) began to auction the valuable rights to air waves and in four auctions collected $9 billion. Then, in 1996, in the Communications Decency Act (part of the Telecommunications Act), the government barred the transmission of "indecent" materials over the Internet, though parts of the law were later struck down in court. In addition, Congress also called for a "V-chip" in television sets—a computer chip that would enable parents to block TV programs that they deemed inappropriate for their children.

The passage of the Telecommunications Act won applause from the communications industry but only mixed reviews from the public. Consumer activists worried that the law would concentrate ownership of communications media in too few hands and would fail to ensure equal access to new technologies for

THINK THROUGH HISTORY
A. Clarifying
Explain the revolutionary nature of communicating via the Internet.

A. Answer
Communicating via the Internet provides nearly instantaneous transmission of texts, pictures, and sounds from a worldwide data network.

ECONOMIC BACKGROUND

MEDIA MERGERS
The signing of the telecommunications bill in February 1996 put the final stamp of approval on a $19 billion merger between Capital Cities/ABC Inc. and the Walt Disney Company. The merger reflected the trend toward concentrating media influence in the hands of a few small but powerful conglomerates.

The FCC approved the merger only on the condition that Disney sell either its newspaper or radio station in Fort Worth, Texas, and in Detroit, Michigan. The FCC also announced, however, that it planned to reconsider its regulations on cross-ownership.

The United States in Today's World **1019**

OBJECTIVE
① INSTRUCT

Technology and Communications

▶ *Starting with the Student*
Discuss the impact that technology has had on students' lives. Have them create a diagram on new technology similar to the one below:

```
Entertainment ──┐
                │
Health care ────┼──── MRI
                │
TECHNOLOGY ─────┤
                │
Education ──────┼──── (    )
                │
Transportation ─┴──── electric car
```

▶ *Discussing Key Ideas*
• The Internet grows.
• Congress passes the Telecommunications Act in 1996.
• Controversy arises over efforts to regulate children's access to TV and the Internet.

IN-DEPTH RESOURCES: UNIT 9
Guided Reading, p. 41

ACCESS FOR STUDENTS ACQUIRING ENGLISH
Guided Reading (Spanish), p. 331

 GROLIER MULTIMEDIA ENCYCLOPEDIA
Computers and privacy

ECONOMIC BACKGROUND
Media Mergers
Critical Thinking: Analyzing Motives Ask students to discuss reasons for the FCC limits on cross-ownership of newspaper and radio and TV stations. *Possible Response: The government is reluctant to allow one individual or group to control the dissemination of information by owning all media outlets in a particular region.*

TEACHING OPTION

Teaching Less Proficient Readers

Outlining Help students understand the text on this page entitled "Telecommunications Act of 1996." Suggest that they use a standard outline form to outline the information in the passage. Write a sample outline on the board to which students can refer.

Student outlines might look like this:

I. Impact of computers and communication on society
   A. On home offices
   B. On entertainment
II. Growth of communications companies
   A. Federal regulations
   B. Benefits of competition

III. Implications of the new technology
   A. Federal response
      1. Auction of air waves
      2. The Communications Decency Act
   B. Public response
      1. For the government
      2. Against the government

Have volunteers write their outlines on the board.

Technology Enriches Lives

▶ *Starting with the Student*
Discuss with students advances in science, transportation, and communications that would not have been possible without the present level of technology. Then ask them whether they welcome the advances, and have them explain why or why not.

▶ *Discussing Key Ideas*
• Technological advances in the 1990s affect all aspects of American life.
• Some technological advances meet with controversy.

MORE ABOUT . . .
Genetic Engineering
Worldwide, producers and consumers who favored genetic engineering and those who opposed it held equally strong opinions. The Plant Biotechnology Group at the University of Idaho, for example, saw its research as leading to the development of superior crops, which would be resistant to pests and diseases. In contrast, a group called the Pure Food Campaign protested the sale of the Flavr Savr® tomato and of a virus-resistant yellow crookneck squash called Freedom II® as well as the development of insect-resistant potatoes, corn, and cotton. The Pure Food Campaign based its opposition primarily on the not-yet-known but possible future risks and complications such altered plants might present.

---

rural residents and poor people. Civil rights advocates contended that the Communications Decency Act restricted free speech.

Technology Enriches Lives

The exciting advances in the telecommunications industry were matched by technological advances that revolutionized medicine, entertainment, education, transportation, and space exploration.

HEALTH CARE   When Ken Mott, a physician on the staff of the World Health Organization in Geneva, Switzerland, was diagnosed with cancer in 1995, he turned to his computer. Mott used the Internet to find emotional support from other cancer patients and to examine new research data on the success of alternative treatments for the disease. Technological advances have led to better diagnoses, less painful treatments, and more effective medications and treatments for cancer and other illnesses.

People with AIDS (acquired immune deficiency syndrome) have increasingly benefited from advances in technology. By 1995, AIDS had killed more than 270,000 Americans, and it threatened about 1 million more Americans carrying HIV, the virus that causes the disease. In the 1990s, improvements in evaluating the spread of the virus through a person's body have made researchers better prepared to find a cure. In addition, new drugs that slow the multiplication of the virus in a person's system gave doctors and patients alike new hopes that a cure would soon be found. In addition, the U.S. Food and Drug Administration (FDA) responded to a call to speed up its lengthy process for approving new drugs and allowed doctors to offer to terminally ill AIDS patients experimental drugs more quickly than before.

Improved technology for making medical diagnoses offered new hope as well. **Magnetic resonance imaging** (MRI), for example, was used to produce cross-sectional images of any part of the body. Advances that will make the MRI procedure ten times faster will also make MRI more widely available and cheaper to use.

Breakthroughs in MRI technology, *above*, have improved doctors' abilities to diagnose problems, while new prosthetics, *below*, have allowed many Americans to lead fuller, happier lives.

Technology also improved prosthetics—artificial limbs for amputees. Despite losing a leg to amputation, Leandro Stillitano continues to play soccer, and Todd Schaffhauser in 1988 ran 100 meters in 15.77 seconds. These remarkable athletes, along with many other amputees, have benefited from improvements in prosthetics, including lightweight titanium and carbon models that have given them a chance to resume their normal activities.

GENETIC ENGINEERING   Not all technological advances have met with universal approval. The use of **genetic engineering**—the artificial changing of the molecular biology of organisms' cells—to alter food has aroused public concern. For example, the tomato that went on the market as the Flavr Savr® in 1994 looked ripe and red, just like a regular tomato, but had been genetically changed to keep the tomato riper longer.

In 1996, international controversy arose over genetically altered soybeans and corn that were grown in the United States and shipped to Europe. In the face of consumer pressure, the European Union moved to limit the importation

1020 CHAPTER 34

---

of such products, allowing importation only if they are clearly labeled as having been genetically altered.

Critics of genetic engineering have raised questions about potential changes in nutritional value of altered foods and the possibility that genetically altered foods might create unpredictable allergic reactions in the humans who eat them. However, the FDA holds that genetically engineered foods are safe and that they require no extra labeling.

ENTERTAINMENT AND MORE Like the Internet, multimedia devices in the 1990s—such as video games, virtual reality simulators, and CD-ROMs—often combined words, pictures, animation, narration, and music. They also engaged participants actively in receiving and communicating information. Among these devices, video games were used primarily for entertainment. However, virtual reality and CD-ROMs went beyond entertainment and provided applications in industry, medicine, and education.

Virtual reality began with the flight simulators used to train military and commercial pilots. Today, with a headset that holds tiny video screens and earphones, and with a data glove that translates hand movements to a computer screen, a participant can navigate a "virtual landscape." Beyond fun and games, however, builders and automobile engineers have used virtual reality to save money by creating visual, rather than physical, models of their buildings and cars. Doctors have used virtual reality to take a computerized tour of a patient's throat and lungs to check for medical problems.

The CD-ROM (Compact Disc Read-Only Memory) evolved from music CDs that contained code for sound waves. CD-ROMs also carry codes for pictures, text, and animation, and they play on a specially equipped computer. A single CD-ROM contains enough memory to hold all the text and pictures of two full-sized encyclopedias. By choosing items from an inviting list of CD-ROMs, people can access subjects ranging from art to zoology.

TECHNOLOGY AND EDUCATION Beyond the development of CD-ROM technology, improvements in communications began to open new opportunities for better education. During the 1990s, classrooms across the nation increasingly used computer networks to give students access to an almost unlimited range of information. Long-distance video and audio transmissions also opened new communications links for American students.

The most prominent additions to the classroom were computer networks. Some schools encouraged students to use the Internet both to gain access to and to share the wealth of information it contains. Other schools joined various networks, such as the Kids Network, which gave students the chance to share data with scientists. The scientists in turn produced reports based on the student-collected data.

Video transmissions also expanded educational opportunities, especially in rural areas. For example, the Alaskan Teleconferencing Network and the University of Alaska Computer Network provided video programming to Alaskan students in isolated communities. Other video programs became

HISTORICAL SPOTLIGHT

VIDEO GAMES

Video games first became popular in the early 1980s. In 1995, game players spent more than $6 billion on computer games. Today, about four out of ten households own video game systems.

Increasingly, game players are competing online with opponents on the Internet. In fact, experts estimate that the industry of "multiplayer online gaming" will mushroom to $1 billion by the year 2000.

A 17-year-old player from Grandbury, Texas, wakes up at 7 A.M. each morning to have an on-line chat with the friends he met while playing the game Subspace. He says, "It was a chance to blow them up. It's become a community."

MORE ABOUT . . .
Virtual Reality
One application of virtual reality, developed in England, enables viewers to assess their chances of escaping from a fire in a simulated structure. The program is called VEGAS, which stands for virtual egress analysis and simulation. Users can program the software so that the several dozen virtual occupants will respond as if they were children or elderly or handicapped persons. Programs can duplicate any existing structure. The results show possible structural flaws or places where bottlenecks will form during escape, the speed of smoke flow, and poor escape strategies of the occupants.

HISTORICAL SPOTLIGHT
Video Games
Critical Thinking Ask students to poll members of their classes to see how many hours per week, on average, students play video games. Students might also investigate which games are the most popular among their acquaintances and what percentage of class members have video game systems in their homes.

TEACHING OPTION

Cooperative Activity: Creating A Guide to the Internet

Task: Student groups will research the Internet and reviews of Internet pages and then compile a guide of home pages applicable to courses they are taking.

Purpose: To familiarize students with the educational uses of the Internet.

Activity: Students working in groups of three or four will compile an annotated list of Internet pages that provide information relevant to the subjects they are currently taking. Have students who have access to the Internet

use McDougal Littell *Learning On-Line* to explore Internet connections to *The Americans*. Students who do not have immediate access to the Internet can compile information from magazines, such as *Learning and Leading with Technology*.

  LEARNING ON-LINE: SOCIAL STUDIES
http://www.mcdougallittell.com

ALTERNATIVE ASSESSMENT BOOK
Standards for Evaluating a Cooperative Activity

Standards for Evaluation
Guide entries should . . .

- evaluate the usefulness of Internet resources
- show a correlation between entries and students' curricula
- demonstrate the ability to maneuver on the Internet

Teacher's Edition **1021**

Progress on the Environment

▶ **Starting with the Student**
Ask students what they currently do to protect the environment. Suggest that as they read, they complete a chart, such as the one below, showing ways in which Americans protect the environment and ways in which technology facilitates those actions.

Methods	How Technology Helps
Recycling	Extracting metal ores from recycled products
Using cleaner cars	
Using alternative energy sources	

▶ **Discussing Key Ideas**
• Advances in technology create new methods of caring for the environment.
• Scientists design environmentally safer vehicles and develop alternatives to fossil fuels.

HISTORY FROM VISUALS

The Growth of Recycling, 1960–1993

Reading the Graph Ask students to identify the period in which the proportion of waste recycled increased the most. *1980–1993*

Extension Ask students how they would account for the rapid increase during that time period. *Possible Responses: more public awareness; more pressure by cities; more opportunities to recycle.*

Skillbuilder Answer
1970: Proportion was about one-twelfth.
1993: The proportion tripled to about one-fourth.

SKILLBUILDER INTERPRETING GRAPHS
Approximately what proportion of waste was recycled in 1970? How much did that proportion increase by 1993?

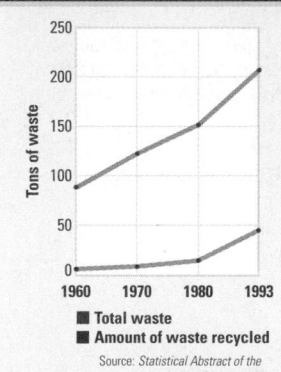

The Growth of Recycling, 1960–1993

Tons of waste
■ Total waste
■ Amount of waste recycled
Source: *Statistical Abstract of the United States, 1995*

available not only on videotapes but also through broadcast transmissions and videodiscs. Videodiscs use digital scanners, which allow the student to move through the lessons and other information provided on the disk.

TRANSPORTATION Advances in transportation in the United States involved making automobiles safer and making driving more convenient. In 1994, seat belts, which many states required drivers to wear, saved 9,200 lives. In the same year, air bags, a more recent safety device, saved nearly 400 lives. By 1996, all new car models boasted dual air bags. Experts predicted that the number of lives saved would multiply as air-bag installation increased. However, the public was increasingly concerned about design problems in air bags that had led to injury and even death of children and adults of small stature.

In addition to increasing safety, technological advances promised to make driving more convenient. Cars equipped with a Global Positioning System (GPS) used satellites to provide drivers with up-to-the-minute travel information. Drivers could tune in a channel on their radios to receive directions to nearby restaurants or gas stations, as well as information on the best routes to use in order to avoid traffic jams or road construction projects.

SPACE EXPLORATION The United States continued to probe deeper into space to find clues about the origins of the universe. Although the U.S. space program received a serious setback with the explosion of the space shuttle *Challenger* shortly after liftoff in January 1986, it experienced several successes in the 1990s.

In 1993, American astronauts walked in space to repair the Hubble Space Telescope. Scientists had hoped that the telescope, first launched in 1990, would provide spectacular views of the edges of the universe. Unfortunately, one of the telescope's mirrors was not properly set, hampering its vision. In a remarkably precise operation performed while orbiting the earth, the astronauts placed ten small mirrors on the telescope to correct the problems with the original mirror. Since the repair, astronomers have used the telescope to gather data about the formation of stars and galaxies.

Nearly as remarkable as the Hubble repair mission was the orbit of American astronaut Shannon Lucid in the Russian space station *Mir*. The Russian space program had intended to relieve her from her duties aboard the space station in the summer of 1996. Because of budget restraints, however, the Russians were unable to make the mission, and Lucid had to wait until September 26, 1996, to return to the earth. Her 188-day stay on *Mir* was the longest stay in space of any American.

Dr. Shannon Lucid jokes with President Clinton after her record-breaking stay on the Russian space station *Mir*.

Progress on the Environment

Advanced technology led to a host of environmental developments in the 1990s. While many Americans took advantage of improved methods of recycling, scientists worked to create environmentally safer cars and new energy sources.

RECYCLING The most widespread method of protecting the environment was recycling. By the mid-1990s, more and more Americans were recycling. Cities such as Omaha, Houston, and Chicago were reforming old recycling plans or instituting new plans to become more efficient. In American offices, workers regularly recycled paper. At curbsides in towns and cities across the country, residents set out glass bottles and jars, plastic bottles, newspapers, phone books, paper bags, and aluminum cans for recycling. In fact, Americans recycled about two-thirds

1022 CHAPTER 34

Making Connections Across Time

Space Exploration Discuss with students current U.S. exploration in space and the advanced technologies that help ensure success. In 1996 and 1997, for example, the U.S. space program cooperated with Russian astronauts in experiments that focused on maintaining an orbiting space station that could house astronauts for weeks or months at a time. Point out that Dr. Shannon Lucid gained fame for her extended stay on the space station *Mir*.

Exploring Themes

Science and Technology For better or worse, changes in the field of science and technology have had a significant impact on American life during the 20th century. Discuss with students the positive and negative effects of technology on society. Most students may identify more positive than negative applications of technology—and most may persist in thinking of technology as "good" or "bad." Help students understand that technology itself is morally neutral. How a particular technology is used determines whether it has a positive or a negative impact.

of their cans. Industry experts claimed that producing the metal from ore would take about 95 percent more energy than it took to recycle the old metal.

DESIGNING A CLEANER CAR While Americans tried to reduce solid waste through recycling, they also worked to reduce the fossil fuel waste that produced air pollution. Designing a cleaner car was one effort. In California, for example, state regulations called for 10 percent of new vehicles to be "zero emission" (creating no air pollution), or battery-powered, by the year 2003.

Scientists had worked for decades to develop environmentally safer vehicles to meet the needs of mobile Americans. By 1996, one such vehicle—the electric car—had come into limited use. However, such cars, while clean, were expensive to operate. Nancy Hazard, associate director of the Northeast Sustainable Energy Association, worked to educate the public on the need for electric cars.

A PERSONAL VOICE
The present gasoline-based transportation system in the U.S. is leading the country to bankruptcy. One-third of the trade deficit is caused by imported oil and that percentage will grow unless we switch to electric vehicles—a move that can cut oil imports and . . . create well-paying domestic manufacturing jobs.

NANCY HAZARD, quoted in a news release of the Northeast Sustainable Energy Association

In addition to electric cars, people have proposed designing cars that run on relatively clean ethanol or methanol gas (manufactured from food byproducts), or solar-powered cars that would be affordable and convenient for consumers.

EXPLORING ALTERNATIVE ENERGY SOURCES Plans to develop electric cars were closely related to efforts to reduce American dependence on fossil fuels. Fossil fuels such as oil provided most of the energy in the United States in the 1990s but also contributed to urban air pollution, acid rain, and global warming.

In looking for an alternative to fossil fuels, scientists have experimented with other energy sources such as nuclear, wind, and solar power. The latter two sources were environmentally safe, cheap, abundant, and renewable. Nuclear power, however, continued to raise the issue of long-term safety both in daily operations and in disposal.

The changes brought about by new technologies in the late 20th century, particularly in communications, came at a time when Americans were becoming acutely aware of the growing diversity of the nation's population. You will read about the changing face of America in Section 4.

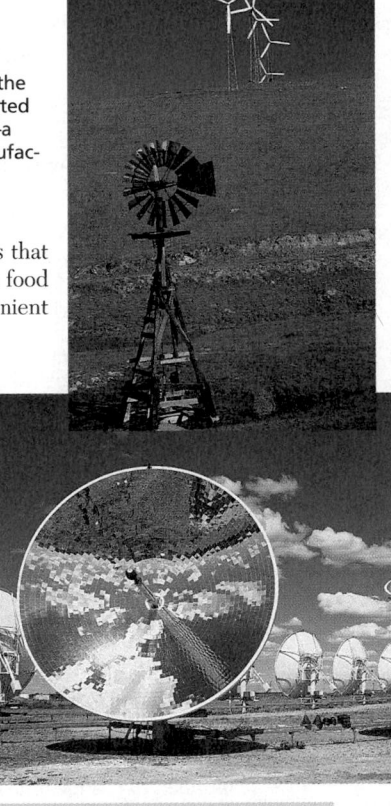
Some experts estimate that the wind and solar power collected by windmills and wind turbines, *below*, and solar panels, *bottom*, create energy equal to 1,000 trillion barrels of oil every year.

D. Answer Solar power is abundant, ecologically neutral and potentially cheap. Fossil fuels are finite and ecologically harmful.

THINK THROUGH HISTORY
D. *Contrasting* Contrast the benefits and costs of solar energy and fossil fuels.

Section ③ Assessment

1. TERMS & NAMES

Identify:
• information superhighway
• Internet
• e-mail
• Telecommunications Act
• magnetic resonance imaging
• genetic engineering

2. SUMMARIZING On a chart such as the one shown, list four of the technological changes described in this section and explain how each change has affected your life.

Technological Change	Effect on My Life
1.	
2.	
3.	
4.	

Write a paragraph explaining how you expect one of these changes to affect your life.

3. ANALYZING How are government, business, and individuals each important to the existence of the information superhighway?

THINK ABOUT
• the costs of developing it
• the equipment and personnel needed to maintain it
• who uses the superhighway and why

4. EVALUATING Which technological change described in this section do you think was the most important one for the country as a whole? Explain why.

THINK ABOUT
• changes in communications and transportation
• changes in health care
• changes in entertainment
• changes that benefit the environment

The United States in Today's World **1023**

---

❹ The Changing Face of America

LEARN ABOUT social and cultural changes in the United States in the late 20th century
TO UNDERSTAND the challenges and opportunities of America's future.

OBJECTIVES

① To identify causes of the flight to the suburbs and the consequences of suburban growth.

② To summarize reasons for, and the impact of, the rise in the elderly population.

③ To describe changing migration patterns and U.S. immigration policies.

④ To list challenges and opportunities for Americans as they move into the next century.

SKILLBUILDERS

• Interpreting graphs, p. 1026
• Understanding geography: region, location, p. 1027

CRITICAL THINKING

• Analyzing causes, p. 1025
• Summarizing, pp. 1026, 1029
• Contrasting, p. 1027
• Comparing, p. 1028
• Forming opinions, p. 1029
• Hypothesizing, p. 1029
• Drawing conclusions, p. 1029

FOCUS & MOTIVATE

▶ **Starting with the Student**
Ask students questions like the following:

• Have they always lived in the same locality?
• Does their school draw students from the city, suburbs, or rural areas?
• Have neighbors and other families in their community lived there for years, or is there a lot of moving out of the community?
• Do they think the change— or lack of change—in the area is indicative of the country as a whole? Why or why not?

ONE AMERICAN'S STORY

In the summer of 1996, at a summer camp in South Dakota, 40 Lakota Sioux teenagers practiced living as their ancestors had. The teens built tepees, tended to their horses, and dined on dried buffalo meat. Like 12 similar camps sponsored by a charitable foundation, the Wolakota Yukini Wicoti Camp on the Cheyenne River Indian Reservation taught young people traditional Native American ways of life. These camps represented one of the efforts of Native Americans to pass along to the younger generation an understanding of their traditions.

Many of the approximately 2 million Native Americans in the United States in the mid-1990s faced difficult problems. On the Cheyenne River Indian Reservation, for example, four out of five adults lacked jobs, and a high percentage of the population between ages 12 and 35 struggled with alcohol addiction. Gregg Bourland, chairman of the Cheyenne River Sioux, believed that by teaching Sioux values, the camp may accomplish the "rebirth of the Great Sioux Nation."

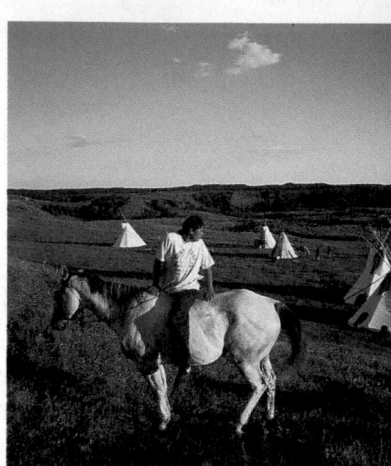

> **A PERSONAL VOICE**
> We call it seventh-generational thinking. Seven generations ago our ancestors loved us so much that we are still here as a people. We have to create a world not only for today, but for seven generations to come. The young people from this camp are going to be the messengers for the future.
>
> **GREGG BOURLAND,** quoted in *Time*, August 26, 1996

Bourland and other tribal leaders noted that Native Americans faced imposing problems but contended that they needed to seek their own solutions. Wilma Mankiller, leader of the Cherokee Nation from 1985 to 1994, acknowledged the crises Native Americans faced in health care, education, housing, and law enforcement. But she argued, "You can't dwell on problems if you want to bring change; you must be motivated by hope, by the feeling you can make a difference."

Wolakota Yukini Wicoti Camp, South Dakota

For five centuries, the ancestors of Greg Bourland and Wilma Mankiller have adapted to the millions of immigrants that came to North America. Native Americans and immigrants alike helped to reshape the land that Columbus first encountered in 1492. They built a great industrial nation where there once was none. At the outset of the 21st century, that nation continued to change. And Americans from all backgrounds, including new immigrants, contributed to these transformations.

The Suburban Nation

One of the most significant sociocultural changes in American history has been the movement of Americans from the cities to the suburbs. The years from 1950 to 1970 saw a widespread pattern of **urban flight,** the process in which Americans left the cities and moved to the suburbs. At mid-century, the population of cities outnumbered that of suburbs. By 1970, the ratio became even. The 1990 census revealed that more than half of all Americans lived in suburbs. This transformation of the United States into a nation of suburbs has often intensified the problems of the cities.

CAUSES OF URBAN CHANGE   Several factors contributed to the movement of Americans out of the cities. Because of the continued movement of job-seeking

---

SECTION 4 RESOURCES

PRINT RESOURCES

IN-DEPTH RESOURCES: UNIT 9
Guided Reading, p. 42
Skillbuilder Practice: Drawing Conclusions, p. 43
Primary Source: Road Sign, p. 49
American Lives: Wilma Mankiller, p. 53

ACCESS FOR STUDENTS ACQUIRING ENGLISH
Guided Reading (Spanish), p. 332
Skillbuilder Practice: Drawing Conclusions (Spanish), p. 333
Geography Application: The U.S. Trade in Goods (Spanish), p. 334

FORMAL ASSESSMENT
Section Quiz, p. 414

ALTERNATIVE ASSESSMENT BOOK
See forms for supporting and scoring alternative activities.

TECHNOLOGY RESOURCES

HUMANITIES TRANSPARENCIES
H48, Political cartoon

CD-ROM Electronic Library of Primary Sources

INTERNET McDougal Littell Learning On-Line
http://www.mcdougallittell.com

Americans into urban areas in the 1950s and 1960s, many urban American neighborhoods became overcrowded. Overcrowding in turn contributed to such urban problems as increasing crime rates and decaying housing.

During the 1970s and 1980s, city dwellers who could afford to do so moved to the suburbs for more space, privacy, and security. Often, families left the cities because suburbs offered newer, less-crowded schools. As many middle-class Americans left cities for the suburbs, the economic base of many urban neighborhoods declined, and suburbs grew wealthy. Following the well-educated labor force, more industries relocated to suburban areas in the 1990s. High-tech industries established suburban "industrial parks," which reduced some of the job opportunities for urban residents who lacked transportation to commute to the new jobs. The economic base that provided tax money and supported city services in large cities such as New York, Detroit, and Philadelphia continued to shrink as people and jobs moved outward. In 1985, 14 out of the 21 counties with the highest per capita income in the nation were suburban.

In addition, many downtown districts fell into disrepair as suburban shoppers abandoned city stores for suburban shopping malls. According to the 1990 census, the 31 most impoverished communities in the United States were in cities.

By the mid-1990s, however, as the property values in America's large cities declined, many people returned to live there. In a process called gentrification, they purchased and rehabilitated many stately homes dating from the cities' peak years. Old industrial sites and neighborhoods in locations convenient to downtown became popular, especially among young, single adults who preferred the excitement of city life and the uniqueness of urban neighborhoods to the often bland environment of the suburbs.

SUBURBAN LIVING While many suburbanites continued to commute to city jobs, increasing numbers of workers during the 1990s began to **telecommute,** or use new communications technology, such as computers, modems, and fax machines, to work from their homes.

Another notable trend was the movement of minority populations to the suburbs. Nationwide, by the early 1990s, about 43 percent of the Latino population and more than half of the Asian-American population lived in suburbs.

Suburban growth led to intense competition between suburbs and cities, and among the suburbs themselves, for business and industry. Since low-rise suburban homes yielded low tax revenues, tax-hungry suburbs offered tax incentives for companies to locate within their borders. These incentives resulted in lower tax revenues for

The home office has become more popular as technology becomes more commonplace.

Suburban space has drawn both citizens and businesses away from large cities.

The United States in Today's World **1025**

THINK THROUGH HISTORY
A. Analyzing Causes List the factors that influenced middle-class residents to leave cities for suburbs.
A. Answer Overcrowding; crime; better schools in the suburbs.

The Baby Boomers Get Older

▶ **Starting with the Student**
- Ask students to identify people they know who are baby boomers. Many of the students' parents, or their parents' older siblings, may be baby boomers.
- Have students estimate in what year the retirement of their parents will begin to peak, assuming that the age of retirement is 65.
- Ask them in what year most of them will retire.

▶ **Discussing Key Ideas**
- The size of the elderly population swells to record highs in the 1990s.
- Programs aimed at taking care of the elderly's medical and financial needs are badly strained.

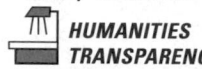
HUMANITIES TRANSPARENCIES
H48, Political cartoon

HISTORY FROM VISUALS
Life Expectancy, 1970– 2010

Reading the Graph Have students look at the graph and tell what the life expectancy is for females and males of their age. *Possible Answers: From around 70 to 73 years for men and around 78 to 79 for women.*

Extension Have students look for statistics that will enable them to compare their life expectancies with those of their parents and grandparents. Ask them how they account for the differences.

---

local governments—meaning that fewer funds were available for schools, libraries, and police departments. Consequently, taxes were often increased to fund these community services as well as to build the additional roads and other infrastructure necessary to support the new businesses.

Another consequence of suburban growth was suburban sprawl—the increasing spread of suburbs over land farther away from a central city—which contributed to environmental problems such as inadequate drainage and flooding. In 1996, for example, heavy rains in the Midwest and the Northeast led to costly flooding of both suburban and urban areas.

The shift of populations from cities to suburbs was not the only significant change in American life in the 1990s. The American public was also growing older, which raised complex issues for American policymakers.

The Baby Boomers Get Older

Born in 1946, Bill Clinton stood at the head of the huge baby-boom generation: the 76 million Americans who were born after World War II, between 1946 and 1961. As the baby boomers began to age, they would swell the ranks of the nation's already large elderly population.

As a result of falling birthrates and advances in medical care, the percentage of elderly people rose through most of the 20th century. In 1900, for example, the average life span was 46 years for men and 48 years for women. In 1993, a man could expect to live 72 years and a woman 79 years. In 1950, only 1 in 12 Americans was over age 65. By 1990, 1 in 8 Americans was over 65. Because of the baby boomers, experts have predicted that by 2030, 1 in 5 Americans will be over 65. The older-than-85 population was expected to grow at an even faster rate.

The graying of America placed new demands on the country's programs that provided care for the elderly. These programs, which had accounted for only 6 percent of the national budget in 1955, represented more than a third of the budget by the mid-1990s. It was projected that the programs would consume about 39 percent of the budget by 2005.

The major programs that provide care for the elderly are Medicare and Social Security. Medicare, which pays medical expenses for senior citizens, began in the mid-1960s, when most Americans had lower life expectancy rates. By 1995, the costs of this program had exceeded $150 billion.

Social Security, which pays benefits to retired Americans, was designed to rely on continued funding from a vast number of younger workers who contribute taxes to support a small number of retired workers. That system worked well when younger workers far outnumbered retirees and when most workers didn't live long after retirement.

In 1996, it took Social Security contributions from three workers to support every retiree. By 2030, however, with an increase in the number of elderly persons and an expected decline in the birthrate, there will be only two workers' contributions available to support each senior citizen. If Congress fails to restructure the system, Social Security will eventually pay out more money than it takes in. Some people have suggested that the system be reformed by raising deductions for current workers, taxing the benefits paid to wealthier Americans, and raising the age at which retirees can collect benefits.

Skillbuilder Answer For men it increased by almost 5 years, and for women it increased by about 4 years.

SKILLBUILDER INTERPRETING GRAPHS *How much higher is life expectancy for Americans born in 1990 than for Americans born in 1970?*

Life Expectancy, 1970–2010

Life expectancy (in years)

	100 95 90 85 80 75 70 65 60
	1970 1980 1990 2000 2010

■ Female ■ Male

Source: *Statistical Abstract of the United States, 1995*

B. Answer Increased life expectancy; people living longer after retirement; the huge baby-boom generation; declining birthrate.

THINK THROUGH HISTORY
B. Summarizing *What are the factors that will force an eventual restructuring of Social Security?*

1026 CHAPTER 34

Skillbuilder Mini-Lesson: Drawing Conclusions

Explaining the Skill Drawing conclusions about the future involves analyzing statistics and other factual information and forming a prediction about the meaning and consequences of the information available to you. Sometimes conclusions are stated along with statistics, but reaching one's own conclusions about an issue can help foster a deeper understanding of that issue.

Applying the Skill: Social Security Ask students to examine the facts on this page about aging baby boomers and

Social Security and to use those facts, their own experiences, and common sense to come up with a conclusion about the future of Social Security. Have them support their conclusions with evidence from the text. Most students will probably conclude that Social Security needs overhauling soon. Evidence includes the increasing numbers of retired citizens, the lengthening life expectancy of people after retirement, and the decline in the number of workers who will be paying into Social Security in the future.

IN-DEPTH RESOURCES: UNIT 9
Skillbuilder Practice: Drawing Conclusions, p. 43

Immigration in the 1990s

In addition to becoming increasingly suburban and elderly, the population of the United States has also been transformed by immigration. Between 1970 and 1995, the country's population swelled from 204 million to more than 260 million. Immigration accounted for much of that growth. As the nation's newest residents yearned for U.S. citizenship, however, other Americans debated the effects of immigration on American life.

A CHANGING IMMIGRANT POPULATION The most recent immigrants to the United States differed from immigrants of earlier years. The large numbers of immigrants who entered the country before and just after 1900 came from Europe. In contrast, about 45 percent of immigrants in the 1990s have come from the Western Hemisphere, primarily Mexico, and 30 percent from Asia.

Most immigrants left their homelands because of economic problems, though some fled oppressive governments or political turmoil. The chief lure of the United States was the opportunity it gave immigrants to earn a better living than they could in their home countries.

In Mexico, for example, between November 1994 and February 1995 millions of people fell into deeper poverty when the government decreased the value of the peso by 73 percent—making it harder to buy things because the peso was worth much less than before. As a result of this devaluation, almost a million Mexicans lost their jobs. The persistent lack of jobs motivated a portion of Mexico's young population—more than half its 100 million people are under age 25—to head north of the border in search of jobs.

Experts speculated that patterns of immigration in the early 21st century would result in changes in the ethnic and racial makeup of the United States. In 1996, 74 percent of the U.S. population consisted of non-Latino whites. The Census Bureau has predicted that by 2050, that figure will drop to 53 percent. The bureau estimates that the Latino population will climb from 10 percent in 1996 to 25 percent in 2050, Asians from 3 percent to 8 percent of the total population, and African Americans from 12 percent to 14 percent. Such predictions added to the continuing debate over U.S. immigration policies.

THINK THROUGH HISTORY
C. Contrasting *Contrast today's immigrants to the United States with the immigrants who came around 1900.*
C. Answer In contrast to European immigrants who came around 1900, today's immigrants come largely from the Western hemisphere and Asia. As previous immigrants did, today's immigrants come for economic opportunities or to escape repressive governments.

"We are at a period of historic change—the way we work; the way we live; the way we relate to each other; the way we relate to others beyond our borders."

BILL CLINTON

U.S. Immigration, 1995

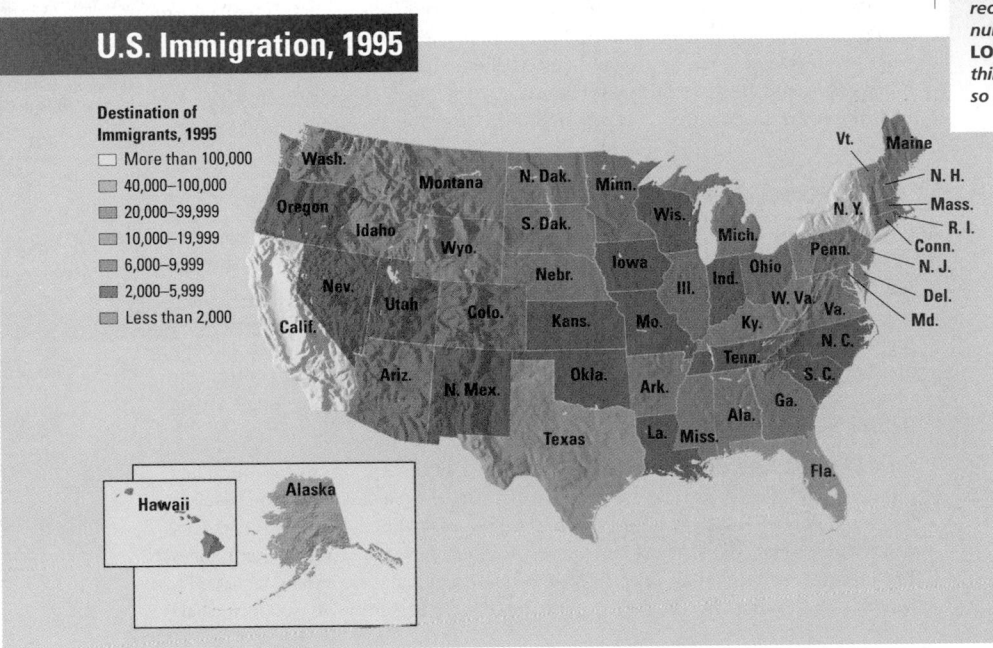

Destination of Immigrants, 1995
- More than 100,000
- 40,000–100,000
- 20,000–39,999
- 10,000–19,999
- 6,000–9,999
- 2,000–5,999
- Less than 2,000

GEOGRAPHY SKILLBUILDER
Which four states received the greatest numbers of immigrants?
LOCATION *Why do you think these states attract so many immigrants?*

Skillbuilder Answer **Regions:** California, New York, Texas and Florida. **Location:** *Possible Answer:* They have the largest populations and therefore many job opportunities.

OBJECTIVE
③ INSTRUCT

Immigration in the 1990s

▶ **Starting with the Student**
- Ask students for their observations on the effects of immigration on American society. Ask them if they have noticed changes in the last four or five years.
- Have students consider how many different cultures are represented in the foods they eat, the music they listen to, and the books they read.
- Ask students if they are aware of any TV or radio shows for minority language or cultural groups in their area.

▶ **Discussing Key Ideas**
- The ethnic and racial makeup of the United States is changing as a result of new immigration patterns.
- The country debates future immigration policies.
- Hostility toward illegal immigrants increases.

HISTORY FROM VISUALS
U.S. Immigration, 1995

Reading the Map Ask students to indicate, according to the map, how many immigrants were located in their state in 1995.

Extension Have students look at state records or data on the Internet to determine the origins of major immigrant groups now located in their state.

TEACHING OPTIONS

Making Connections Across the Curriculum

Mathematics Have students graph the statistics about the U.S. racial and ethnic makeup cited on page 1027. Help students understand that the 1996 figures total only 99 percent because they have been rounded to the nearest whole number. Put a completed graph on the board. Graphs might look like this:

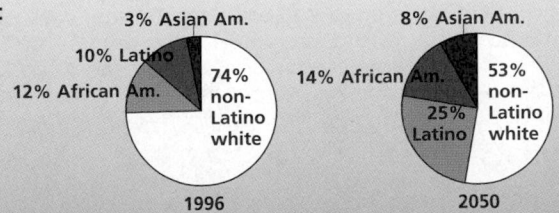

1996: 3% Asian Am., 10% Latino, 12% African Am., 74% non-Latino white
2050: 8% Asian Am., 14% African Am., 25% Latino, 53% non-Latino white

Making Connections Across Cultures

Cuban Immigrants Dating from the Bay of Pigs fiasco in 1961, Cubans fleeing Fidel Castro's Communist regime have landed by the thousands on the coasts of Florida. Relying on strong communal ties and sheer determination, Cuban workers parlayed small shops and family businesses into a multimillion-dollar economic presence in the state. With Castro's regime now heading into a decline, many Cuban-Americans must decide whether to return to Cuba or stay in the United States—a decision made more difficult by the fact that the economic problems of cities like Miami threaten the economic base of the communities they have struggled so long to establish.

DEBATES OVER IMMIGRATION POLICY Public opinion polls in 1996 revealed that only 6 percent of Americans believed immigration should be increased, while almost two-thirds (63 percent) wanted to cut back immigration. Americans who opposed immigration argued that immigrants took jobs from other Americans or reduced wages because of competition, but many economists disagreed with that view.

Opponents of immigration found a strong spokesperson in Patrick Buchanan, a former speechwriter for President Nixon, who ran unsuccessfully for the Republican presidential nomination in 1992 and in 1996. Buchanan argued that the United States should erect a fence along the Mexican border to keep out illegal immigrants. In addition, he strongly opposed NAFTA, which he viewed as pitting working Americans against "Mexican folks who work for a buck an hour."

Candidates for U.S. citizenship are sworn in.

By the early 1990s, an estimated 3.2 million illegal immigrants had made their way to the United States. Most of these people had come from Mexico, but others had traveled north from El Salvador, Guatemala, and Haiti. Many illegal immigrants also arrived from Canada, Poland, China, and Ireland. Most of these illegal immigrants took jobs many Americans turned down as sweatshop workers and domestic servants—often receiving the minimum wage or less and no benefits.

Hostility toward illegal immigration peaked in California and Florida, two states with high percentages of immigrants. In 1994, California passed Proposition 187, which cut off all education and nonemergency health benefits to illegal immigrants. That same year, California governor Pete Wilson demanded that the U.S. government reimburse the state for the $2.4 billion it was spending each year on undocumented aliens. In Florida, Governor Lawton Chiles filed suit in a Miami federal court against the U.S. government for "its continuing failure to enforce or rationally administer its own immigration laws."

America and a New Millennium

For Americans, the last decade of each century since the nation's birth has been a time of challenge and change. In the last decade of the 18th century, the new nation was caught up in creating its national institutions and extending its reach to the West. As the 19th century came to a close, the United States was creating a new empire abroad, building new cities at home, rapidly industrializing, and becoming a world power. The end of the 20th century also marks the start of a new millennium, and it makes the sense of change and challenge on the horizon all the more dramatic.

CHALLENGES AHEAD As the century draws to a close, Americans face both new problems and old ones. Increasingly, terrorist acts pose a threat to Americans at home and abroad; recent bombings such as those in Oklahoma City, New York City, and Atlanta remind Americans that world problems have domestic consequences. In addition, environmental concerns have become a global issue and have moved to center stage during the last few decades of the 20th century as scientists have warned of global warming, acid rain, and the loss of the earth's protective ozone layer. And poverty remains a problem for many Americans in the late 20th century as the number of manufacturing jobs declines and government antipoverty programs are cut.

NEW OPPORTUNITIES For each challenge that Americans face, there are new opportunities ahead. As the century comes to a close, Americans look to a growing economy and hope to maintain the low unemployment and low inflation that marked the mid-1990s. General prosperity would help to reduce the problems of poverty that still persist in the nation.

To meet the challenges of the new millennium, Americans have invested in improved education and new technologies. Census data from 1990 revealed that 87 percent of both African-American and white young adults between the ages of 25 and 29 had completed high school. This figure is the highest percentage attained since the Census Bureau began collecting data on secondary school completion in 1947. Moreover, it suggests a narrowing of the educational gap that has so long separated blacks from whites.

In addition to increasing the amount of time students spend in school, American educators are trying to enhance the quality of that time. Linking schools to the new communications networks will help students be more competitive in the global economy. Knowledge of advanced technology will help Americans find better jobs and make better products and thus improve the quality of life.

It is clear that the new century America faces will bring changes, but those changes need not deepen divisions among Americans. With effort and cooperation on the part of Americans, the changes could foster growth and tolerance. The 20th century has brought new ways of both destroying and enriching lives. What will the 21st bring? Much will depend on you—the dreamers, the decision makers, and the voters of the future.

E. Answer
Possible responses:
Optimistic students might point out America's strong economy, democratic traditions, and technological change. Pessimists might talk about persistent poverty and racism, and perhaps, declining moral values.

THINK THROUGH HISTORY
E. Forming Opinions *Based on problems solved in the past, are you optimistic or pessimistic about America's future? Explain.*

Section ④ Assessment

1. TERMS & NAMES
Identify:
• urban flight
• telecommute

2. SUMMARIZING Demography is the study of statistics about human populations. Use a table like the one below to summarize the demographic changes occurring in the United States.

Demographic Changes	
Urban distribution	
Age	
Ethnic and racial makeup	

3. HYPOTHESIZING As urban problems become more common in the suburbs, how might the residents of suburbs respond? Base your answer on existing behavior patterns.

THINK ABOUT
• the spread of suburbs farther and farther from the city
• the new ability to telecommute
• the tax problems that suburbs face

4. DRAWING CONCLUSIONS What do you think will be the biggest challenge facing the United States in the new millennium? Explain.

THINK ABOUT
• rundown cities and poverty
• the growing population of elderly persons
• the debate over immigration policy
• terrorism and crime

The United States in Today's World **1029**

ANSWERS

1. TERMS & NAMES

urban flight, p. 1024

telecommute, p. 1025

2. SUMMARIZING

Student charts may include the following possible responses:
Distribution: more suburban, less urban
Age: more senior citizens
Ethnic and racial makeup: more Asians and Hispanics, lower proportion of whites, about the same proportion of African Americans

3. HYPOTHESIZING

Possible Response: Students who say that people will move to new suburbs farther away from the city may cite the trend of suburban sprawl and the convenience of telecommuting. Students who say that people may start to move back to cities may cite the economic difficulties some suburbs are having.

4. DRAWING CONCLUSIONS

Possible Response: Some students may say poverty, because the gap between rich and poor is growing wider. Some may say the problem of funding Social Security, because if it goes bankrupt, the elderly will swell the ranks of the poor. Some may say health care, because many people still are without health insurance. Others may say crime and terrorism.

OBJECTIVES

(1) To trace America's historical experiences as a multicultural society.

(2) To evaluate the benefits of America's multicultural heritage and of maintaining or abandoning one's ethnic heritage.

FOCUS & MOTIVATE

▶ *Starting with the Student*
Ask students to think about ethnic heritage. Discuss the following questions:

• To what degree do you know and value your own ethnic heritage?

• What role do you think ethnic heritage should play in today's America?

MORE ABOUT . . .
Spanish Cowboys

The Mexican influence on American cowboys is evident in the language the cowboys used. Words such as *lasso, lariat, riata, chaps, mustang, pinto, palomino, stampede, rodeo, corral,* and even *ranch* all came to English from Spanish. It's also no accident that one old TV Western was called *Bonanza,* a Spanish word that became popular with miners hoping to strike it rich out West. Spanish cowboys were called *vaqueros,* a word still used by English speakers in parts of the Southwest.

Sharing Cultures

Even before the first Europeans arrived in the Americas, a variety of cultural groups—coastal fishing societies, desert farmers, plains and woodland hunters—inhabited the North American continent. With the arrival of Europeans and Africans, the cultural mix grew even more diverse.

Although the diversity has often produced tension, such diversity has also been beneficial for the United States. As different groups learned from one another about agriculture, technology, and social customs, American culture became a rich blend of cultures from around the world.

As these examples demonstrate, the United States has, throughout its history, been a place where cultures came together. As the nation moves into the 21st century, it will have to find ways to use its cultural diversity to help solve the problems of the future.

1680s
SPANISH MISSION

The Spanish who established missions in the region that later became California, Texas, Arizona, and New Mexico had little interest in fostering cultural diversity. They tried to impose Spanish culture and Catholicism upon Native Americans. In spite of the missionaries' efforts, though, some Native Americans retained aspects of their original culture even as they learned Spanish ways. For example, today many Pueblo Indians of New Mexico perform ancient dances, such as the Corn Dance, in addition to celebrating the feast days of Catholic saints.

1870s
COWBOYS

The American cowboy was a product of many cultures. The Spanish introduced cattle and horses to the Americas, and many of the techniques for raising cattle on large ranches developed in Mexico. When white Americans moved into Texas, they learned how to be cowboys from Mexicans. Cowboys were a diverse group; as the picture below shows, both whites and African Americans worked on ranches. However, as stories about the West spread into the popular culture, the truth became distorted so that the roles of Mexicans and African Americans were largely ignored.

1030 CHAPTER 34

RECOMMENDED RESOURCES

Books

Buenker, John D., and Lorman A. Ratner. *Multiculturalism in the United States.* New York: Greenwood Press, 1992. A comparative guide to acculturation and ethnicity.

Daniels, Roger. *Coming to America.* New York: HarperCollins, 1990. A history of immigration and ethnicity in American life.

Galens, Judy, et al., ed. *Gale Encyclopedia of Multicultural America.* Detroit: Gale Research, 1995. Reference.

Portes, Alejandro. *Immigrant America.* Berkeley: U of California P, 1990. A portrait of immigration.

Videos

Ethnic Diversity. PBS Video, 1993. Teens talk about prejudice.

Heritage of the Black West. National Geographic Society, 1995. African-American contributions to the history of the American West.

Old World, New World. Thames Television, 1977; dist. Media Guild. Late-19th-century European immigrants on their way to the United States.

Religion. National Geographic, 1993. The variety of religions in North America and the role of religion in our lives.

Software

Ellis Island—Immigrant Experience. Educational Activities, dist. ESI. Diskette. Students role-play the life of a different immigrant teenager each time they use the software.

1900s
THE "NEW" IMMIGRANTS

From 1890 to 1920, millions of southern and eastern European immigrants came to the United States. Many of them moved to cities and settled in neighborhoods populated by others from their country of origin, such as this neighborhood in New York City. This tended to foster cultural separation rather than cultural interaction—a situation that eased over time as the immigrants' children and grandchildren moved away from the old neighborhoods. In spite of this, most large U.S. cities still have many neighborhoods that retain a strong ethnic flavor.

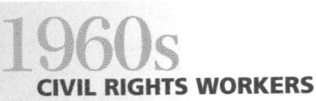

1990s
STUDENTS AND DIVERSITY

Many school districts across the United States provide a glimpse of the nation's future—in which diversity will increase to the point that there is no longer a majority group. The students pictured here are part of an advisory group helping the principal to address school problems in Los Angeles. As students such as these move into adulthood, the richness of their varied backgrounds and perspectives will help them make valuable contributions to America's economic and cultural life.

1960s
CIVIL RIGHTS WORKERS

During the civil rights movement's Freedom Summer in 1964, white and African-American volunteers worked together to register African Americans to vote in the South. To identify with the sharecroppers and tenant farmers they were trying to reach, some white student volunteers emulated the styles of speech and dress of Southern laborers. SNCC member Cleveland Sellers recalled volunteers rushing to buy bib overalls like the SNCC workers. Similarly, one volunteer remembers that "everyone . . . got into talking like the SNCC staff . . . 'diggin' this and 'messin, with' that."

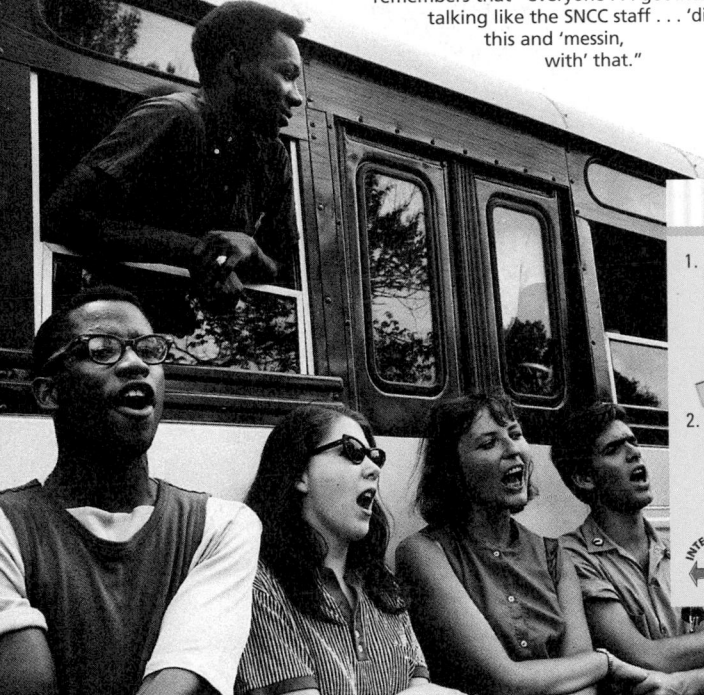

INTERACT WITH HISTORY

1. **ANALYZING MOTIVES** Why do you think some groups have tried to repress the culture of others over the course of history? Why have many groups persisted in retaining their cultural heritage? Write a brief explanation of your opinion and share it with the class.

   SEE SKILLBUILDER HANDBOOK, PAGE 1039.

2. **RESEARCHING YOUR PAST** What kinds of contributions to the cultural diversity of the United States have your own ancestors made? Research your own family history and write a brief explanation of your findings. Share it with the class.

   INTERNET For more about cultural diversity, click on *Social Studies* at http://www.mcdougallittell.com

1031

▶ *Starting with the Student*
- Have students work in groups to create maps with place names showing the many cultures that have shaped the United States.
- Encourage students to debate controversial issues related to the sharing of cultures, such as declaring English as America's legal language or using Ebonics in the classroom, as was recommended by the Oakland, California, school board in 1996.

▶ *Discussing Key Ideas*
- America has always been a nation of diverse cultural heritages.
- Despite past conflicts, Americans' varied cultural heritages can make valuable contributions to American society as a whole.

HISTORY FROM VISUALS
Reading the Images Have students study the illustrations and accompanying details.
- Have students jot down adjectives describing their reactions to the different scenes depicted.
- Ask students why they think the truth about Mexican and African-American cowboys was largely ignored in the past. *Possible Responses: Racism and ethnocentrism; "winners" write history; Western dime novels, films, and TV shows of earlier decades were produced largely by whites and targeted to mainly white audiences.*

INTERACT WITH HISTORY

1. *Analyzing Motives*

Possible Answers: *Students may say that some groups have tried to repress the culture of others because of racism or because of long-standing ethnic conflicts. They may also point out that some groups might fear being overpowered or outnumbered by other groups. Many students may note that the groups that have persisted in retaining their cultural heritage are those that have formed relatively close communities in the United States.*

2. *Researching Your Past*

Standards for Evaluation
Explanations should . . .

- show evidence of a wide range of research sources, such as library references, personal interviews, family artifacts (for example, old photograph albums), church records, and contact with historical museums
- present the family historical information in an organized and coherent manner

TERMS & NAMES
1. Bill Clinton, p. 1006
2. NAFTA, p. 1009
3. Contract with America, p. 1010
4. service sector, p. 1014
5. downsize, p. 1014
6. GATT, p. 1016
7. information superhighway, p. 1018
8. Internet, p. 1019
9. urban flight, p. 1024
10. telecommute, p. 1025

MAIN IDEAS
11. Possibilities include reducing the federal budget deficit, winning passage of NAFTA, signing the welfare reform bill, and signing a moderate health care reform bill.

12. The Republicans wanted to make large cuts in the budget; to block them, Democrats refused to pass spending bills; the resulting gridlock shut down government.

13. Clinton's foreign policy decisions consisted mainly of reactions to crises in other countries, such as Somalia and Bosnia.

14. Many workers lost jobs; others became temporary employees.

15. Service-sector and high-tech industries grew, while manufacturing and agriculture declined.

16. As the economy becomes more global, countries are bound as much by economic as by military alliances.

17. The Internet links people to government agencies, library databases, news media, and on-line catalogs.

18. Technology improved medicine, entertainment, education, automobile safety, and the environment.

19. Cities have grown poorer and more rundown; suburbs have sprawled farther from the city, grown more wealthy, and encountered problems with taxes and crime.

20. Possible Responses: Technology gives classrooms access to a wider range of information than was previously available. It also has expanded educational opportunities to students living in remote areas.

Chapter 34 Assessment

REVIEWING THE CHAPTER

TERMS & NAMES For each term below, write a sentence explaining its connection to the period from 1992 to the present. For each person below, explain his role in the events of the period.

1. Bill Clinton
2. NAFTA
3. Contract with America
4. service sector
5. downsize
6. GATT
7. information superhighway
8. Internet
9. urban flight
10. telecommute

MAIN IDEAS

SECTION 1 (pages 1006–1012)

The Clinton Presidency
11. Name three of President Clinton's most significant achievements during his first term.
12. How did both political parties contribute to the gridlock that shut down the government in 1995 and 1996?
13. How did world events shape Clinton's foreign policy?

SECTION 2 (pages 1013–1017)

The New Global Economy
14. How did downsizing affect U.S. workers?
15. Summarize which parts of the economy grew during the 1990s and which declined.
16. Explain what President Clinton meant when he said, "Trade as much as troops will increasingly define the ties that bind nations in the twenty-first century."

SECTION 3 (pages 1018–1023)

Technology and Modern Life
17. What resources of information, previously difficult to find, did the Internet make available?
18. How did changes in technology in the 1990s enrich American lives?

SECTION 4 (pages 1024–1029)

The Changing Face of America
19. How has urban flight changed both cities and suburbs?
20. In what ways has technology improved American education?

THINKING CRITICALLY

1. **CONFLICTING POLITICAL GOALS** Use a diagram similar to the one shown to list the political goals of President Clinton and Newt Gingrich. Indicate which goals were accomplished.

| Clinton's goals | What was accomplished | Gingrich's goals |

2. **NEW TECHNOLOGY** Compile a list of technological innovations of the late 20th century described in the chapter. Then predict what kinds of technological advancements might change American life during the 21st century.

3. **THE AMERICAN QUILT** Reread the quotation by Jesse Jackson on page 1004. Do you agree with his description of American society? Why or why not?

4. **GEOGRAPHY OF IMMIGRATION** Look carefully at the map on page 1027. What seems to have a greater effect on the number of immigrants that a state receives: how close it is to a border or how large a population it has? Explain why this might be.

5. **THEME: CULTURAL DIVERSITY** How important do you think it is for a nation to develop a single, unified culture? Support your opinion by using details from the chapter and the feature on pages 1030–1031.

6. **ANALYZING PRIMARY SOURCES** Read the following excerpt from an article published in *The Atlantic Monthly.* Then answer the questions below.

> In principle, we should admit immigrants whenever their economic contribution (to native well-being) will exceed the costs of providing social services to them. . . .
>
> Although we do not know how many immigrants to admit, simple economics and common sense suggest that the magic number should not be an immutable [unchangeable] constant regardless of economic conditions in the United States. A good case can be made for linking immigration to the business cycle: admit more immigrants when the economy is strong and the unemployment rate is low, and cut back on immigration when the economy is weak and the unemployment rate is high.
>
> **GEORGE J. BORJAS,** "The New Economics of Immigration," *The Atlantic Monthly,* November 1996

Do you agree with George Borjas that immigration policy should be designed to benefit the United States economically? What other factors besides potential economic impact should be used to decide what immigrants may enter the country?

THINKING CRITICALLY

1. CONFLICTING POLITICAL GOALS
Diagrams may include the following information:
Clinton's goals: cut middle-class taxes, reform health care, improve government efficiency, reduce the deficit.
What was accomplished: deficit reduced, bureaucracy reduced, welfare reform and limited health care reform passed.
Gingrich's goals: limit congressional terms, pass balanced-budget amendment, cut taxes, pass tougher crime laws and welfare reform.

2. NEW TECHNOLOGY
Possible Answers: Late-20th-century innovations: the Internet, CD-ROMs, fax machines, MRI, prosthetics, GPS, Hubble telescope. Possible advancements during the 21st century may include the more widespread use of electric cars and the integration of the television and the personal computer.

3. THE AMERICAN QUILT
Possible Responses: Some students may agree, saying that so many different groups have come together to make American society. Others may disagree, saying that they believe the groups do not share a common thread as Jackson suggests.

ALTERNATIVE ASSESSMENT

1. CREATING A PERSONAL TIME LINE

What impact have historical events during your lifetime had on you? Create an illustrated time line showing key historical events you believe have had an impact on your own life.

 CD-ROM Conduct research using the CD-ROM *Our Times,* newspapers, interviews with relatives, and other resources.

• Identify both U.S. and global events.

• Construct a time line that identifies each event, including the year and place. Use magazine or newspaper pictures or headlines to illustrate the time line.

• Write a paragraph that explains which events had the most impact on you personally and why.

2. MODELING GOVERNMENT TODAY

Cooperative Learning Work with a group of your classmates to set up a model U.S. government. Include a president, vice-president, and small cabinet. Then use the following guidelines to conduct business.

• Based on the chapter and what you think the nation will be like in the future, establish three domestic policy goals for the country in the 21st century. Your goals might be economic or related to social welfare programs.

• Establish foreign policy goals for the nation.

• Write up your government's goals and present them in a panel discussion in front of the class.

3. PORTFOLIO PROJECT

Use the Living History activity to expand your portfolio.

LIVING HISTORY

SHARING 21st-CENTURY GOALS

After you have compiled a list of the three main issues for the 21st century, have a friend read your list and answer these questions:

• Does the list clearly state the issues to be addressed?

• Do the supporting articles and photographs help you to understand the issue?

• Do any of the issues need to be explained further?

When you have revised the list based on your friend's suggestions, write a letter to a newspaper or politician explaining the list and your reason for sending it. Then add your list and your letter to your American history portfolio.

Review Chapter 34

R̲eview Chapter 34

POLITICAL SHIFTS In the 1992 presidential campaign, voters who were disappointed with the two major political parties helped Ross Perot become the most successful third-party candidate in 80 years. The winner of the election, Democrat Bill Clinton, had a mixed record during his first term as president. He failed to pass major health care reform and drew criticism for raising taxes. He did succeed in lowering the budget deficit, gaining approval of NAFTA, and passing welfare reform. In 1994, Republicans took control of both houses of Congress and pledged to enact a conservative "Contract with America." Democrats blocked much of the Republican program, and conflict between the parties led to repeated government shutdowns that angered the public. Clinton's popularity rebounded, however, and he easily won reelection in 1996.

ECONOMIC AND TECHNOLOGICAL CHANGE The American workplace changed radically as the service sector grew and manufacturing declined. Many workers lost jobs as corporations sought to reduce costs by downsizing and by hiring more temporary employees. The global economy became increasingly important because of trade agreements such as GATT, the growth of multinational corporations, and stiff international competition. Technology added to changes in the workplace as businesses and individuals rushed to access the information superhighway. Technology also improved individual lives by providing better medical equipment, safer cars, improved recycling resources, and entertaining and educational multimedia devices.

DEMOGRAPHIC CHANGES Because of overcrowding, crime, and other urban problems, many city dwellers fled to the suburbs, which sprawled even farther away from city centers. As baby boomers grew older, the average age in America rose—putting entitlement programs such as Social Security at risk. High immigration from Mexico, Central America, Asia, and the Caribbean altered the ethnic and racial makeup of the U.S. population, leading some demographic experts to predict that by the year 2050, whites will no longer be in the majority. As the year 2000 approached, Americans looked for innovative ways to deal with the nation's problems. One positive trend was the increased use of technology in schools to train the nation's future workforce.

The United States in Today's World **1033**

---

1. CREATING A PERSONAL TIME LINE
Standards for Evaluation
A time line should meet the following criteria:

• Identifies appropriate dates for U.S. and global events.

• Clearly labels the place and year of the events.

• Uses relevant pictures and headlines as illustrations.

• Includes a paragraph that cites reasons for the student's opinion.

2. MODELING GOVERNMENT TODAY
Standards for Evaluation
A write-up of the model government's goals should meet the following criteria:

• Shows an awareness of the economic and political status of the United States in the late 20th century.

• Presents realistic goals for several aspects of American life.

• Includes foreign policy goals that reflect the global nature of life in the 21st century.

• Shows evidence of research, including interviews.

3. PORTFOLIO PROJECT
LIVING HISTORY
Standards for Evaluation
The letter and list of issues should meet the following criteria:

• Clearly explains the purpose of the letter and the list.

• Presents three crucial concerns of the 21st century.

• Explains each concern clearly.

• Includes well-chosen articles or illustrations.

IN-DEPTH RESOURCES: UNIT 9
See the form for scoring this activity on page 55.

THINKING CRITICALLY

4. GEOGRAPHY OF IMMIGRATION
Possible Response: Students may note that states with large populations receive more immigrants than those with smaller populations and that this is a more consistent pattern than how close a state is to a border. Possible reasons for this include the tendency of immigrants to go to large cities to find work or to settle where relatives or people from their home country already reside.

5. THEME: CULTURAL DIVERSITY
Possible Responses: Students who think developing a unified culture is important may say that America can remain strong only if its people share a common vision. Students who disagree may say that America is a nation of many cultures and that forcing certain groups to abandon their culture and accept a common culture goes against the American tradition of individual liberty.

6. ANALYZING PRIMARY SOURCES
Possible Answer: Students who agree might contend that government officials should be more concerned with securing the economic well-being of native citizens than of immigrants. Those who disagree might say that reuniting families or helping people escape oppression are more important considerations than economics. Another factor that might be considered is that most Americans are themselves descendants of immigrants.

Teacher's Edition **1033**

life

liberty

pursuit of
happiness

SKILLBUILDER HANDBOOK

Refer to the Skillbuilder Handbook when you need help in answering Think Through History questions, doing the activities entitled Interact with History, or answering questions in Section Assessments and Chapter Assessments. In addition, the handbook will help you answer questions about maps, charts, and graphs.

Section 1: Understanding Historical Readings

Section 2: Using Critical Thinking

Section 3: Exploring Historical Evidence

Section 1: Understanding Historical Readings

1.1 Following Chronological Order

Chronological order is the order in which events happen in time. It is the framework for studying history. Without knowing the order in which things happened, historians could not get an accurate sense of the relationships among events.

UNDERSTANDING THE SKILL

Strategy: Finding clues in the text The following paragraph is about some of the events in the Watergate scandal that brought down the Nixon administration. Notice how the time line that follows puts the events in chronological order.

> ### THE PENTAGON PAPERS
>
> The initial event that many historians believe led to Watergate took place June 13, 1971, when the *New York Times* began publishing articles called the Pentagon Papers, which divulged government secrets about the U.S. involvement in Vietnam. The information had been leaked to the media by former Defense Department official Daniel Ellsberg. The Justice Department asked the courts to suppress publication of the articles, but on July 30, 1971, the Supreme Court ruled that the government could not censor the information being published. Two months later, in September, a group of special White House agents known as the Plumbers burglarized the office of Ellsberg's psychiatrist in a vain attempt to find evidence against Ellsberg. President Nixon had authorized the creation of the Plumbers in 1971, after the Pentagon Papers were published, to keep government secrets from leaking to the media and to help ensure his reelection in November 1972.

Look for clue words about time. These are words like *initial, first, next, then, before, after, finally,* and *by that time.*

Use specific dates provided in the text.

Watch for references to previous historical events that are included for background. Usually a change in the verb tense will indicate a previous event.

Strategy: Making a time line

If the events are complex, make a time line of them. Write the dates below the line and the events above the line.

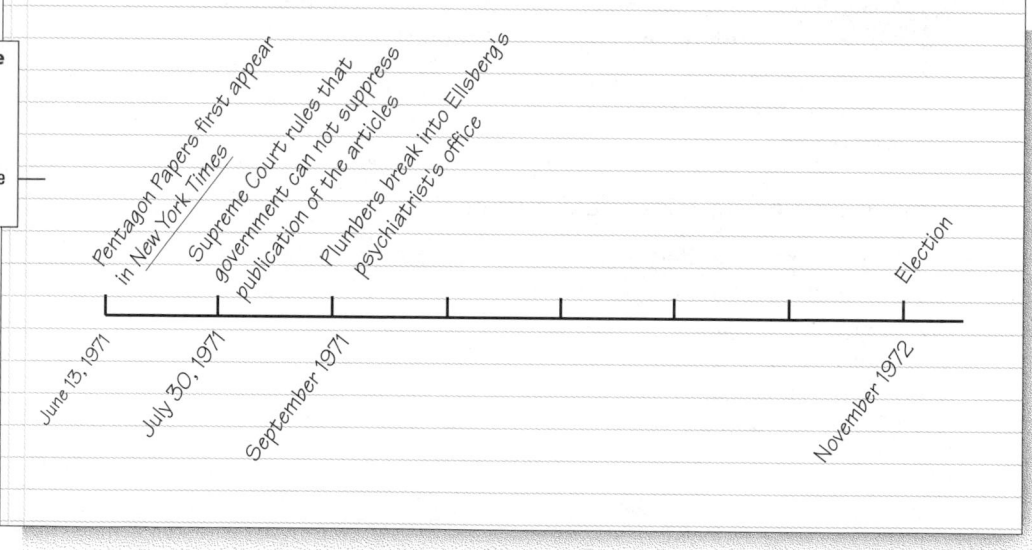

APPLYING THE SKILL

Make your own time line Skim Chapter 8, Section 4, "Farm Girl to Factory Worker," to find out about the early days of union organizing in New England mills. Make a list of the important dates you find, starting with the strike of 1834 and ending with the formation of the Ladies Industrial Association in 1845. Decide on a scale for a time line to show the important dates. Use the student model to create your own time line showing what happened on each date.

1036 SKILLBUILDER HANDBOOK

1.2 Clarifying; Summarizing

Clarifying means clearly understanding what you have read. One way to do this is by asking yourself questions about the material. In your answers, you restate in your own words what you have read.

When you **summarize,** you condense what you have read into fewer words, stating only the main ideas and the most important details. It is important to use your own words in a summary.

UNDERSTANDING THE SKILL

Strategy: Finding clues in the text The excerpt below describes a major oil spill. Following the description is a summary that condenses the key information from the passage into a few sentences. The summary also clarifies.

Summarize: Look for topic sentences stating the main ideas. These are often at the beginning of a section or paragraph. In a summary, rewrite the main ideas in your own words.

Clarify: Look up any words you do not recognize.

> ### THE EXXON VALDEZ OIL SPILL
>
> In March 1989, the oil tanker *Exxon Valdez* ran aground in Prince William Sound along the coast of Alaska, dumping about 11 million gallons of crude oil into the sea. Within days, 1,800 miles of coastline were fouled with thick black oil that coated rocks and beaches. At least 10 percent of the area's birds, sea otters, and other animals were killed, and commercial fisheries estimated that they would lose at least 50 percent of the season's catch.
>
> The captain of the *Exxon Valdez* was found guilty of negligence, and attempts were made to clean up the spill. Four years later, however, scientists found that pools of oil buried in coves were still poisoning shellfish, otters, and ducks, while several bird species failed to reproduce.
>
> Between 1989 and 1994, Exxon spent about $2.1 billion in efforts to clean up Prince William Sound. In the meantime, some 34,000 commercial fishers and other Alaskans sued the company for damages, claiming that the oil spill had ruined their livelihoods.
>
> In May of 1994, a federal grand jury decided that Exxon had been reckless in allowing a captain with a history of alcohol abuse to command the *Exxon Valdez*. The jury awarded almost $287 million in compensatory damages to the plaintiffs. They also ordered Exxon to pay $5 billion in punitive damages.

Summarize: Include the key facts and statistics. Pay attention to statements of fact, numbers, dates, quantities, percentages, and other data.

Strategy: Writing a summary

Clarify and Summarize: Write a summary to clarify your understanding of the main ideas.

> ### SUMMARY
>
> In 1989, the oil freighter Exxon Valdez ran aground off the Alaskan coast, spilling 11 million gallons of crude oil. The water and coastline for hundreds of miles were badly polluted, and many animals died. Alaskans sued the oil company for lost income. Exxon paid for a cleanup effort that cost $2.1 billion and took many years. U.S. courts fined the company more than $5 billion and found it reckless for having allowed the ship's captain to continue in service despite a history of drinking problems.

APPLYING THE SKILL

Make your own summary Turn to Chapter 1, Section 3, and read "Three West African Kingdoms" and "West African Culture." Make notes of the main ideas. Look up any words you don't recognize. Then write a summary of the section, using the student model as your guide.

SKILLBUILDER HANDBOOK **1037**

Section 1: Understanding Historical Readings

1.3 Identifying Problems

Identifying problems means finding and understanding the difficulties faced by a particular group of people during a certain time. Being able to focus on specific problems helps historians understand the course of historical events.

UNDERSTANDING THE SKILL

Strategy: Finding clues in the text The following passage tells about the experience of newcomers to northern cities like Boston and Philadelphia in the late 1800s. Following the passage is a chart that organizes information taken from the passage about the problems those immigrants faced.

Look for the difficulties people face. Ask yourself what problems a person or group had to overcome and how they searched for solutions.

Evaluate solutions to problems.

IMMIGRANT LIFE IN THE CITIES

The lure that drew people to the cities in many cases was the same one that had attracted settlers to the West and immigrants to America—opportunity. In these industrialized centers people saw a chance to escape poverty, work, and carve out a better life.

Newcomers to the United States usually ended up in cities because they were the cheapest and most convenient places to live, not far from the ports where immigrants landed. Cities offered unskilled laborers steady jobs in mills and factories and provided the social support of neighborhoods of people with the same ethnic background. Living among people who shared their background enabled the newcomers to speak their own language while learning about their new home. Overcrowding soon became a problem, however, one that was intensified by the migration of new people from America's rural areas.

Look for implied problems. Problems are sometimes stated indirectly. This sentence implies that immigrants were drawn to the cities because of limited opportunities elsewhere.

Sometimes the solution to one problem may be the cause of another problem. Overcrowding resulted when immigrants lived together in urban neighborhoods.

Strategy: Making a chart

Summarize the problems and solutions in a chart. Tell who had the problems, what the problems were, what steps the people took to solve the problems, and how those solutions affected them.

Problems	Solutions	Outcomes
poverty	coming to U.S. cities	jobs available
lack of opportunity	coming to U.S. cities	jobs, housing, communities
lack of transportation	living close to ports of entry	congenial living, but crowded
lack of work skills	factory and mill jobs did not require a high level of training	enough jobs for the time being
unfamiliarity with country and language	living in ethnic communities	opportunity to learn with others, but overcrowding

APPLYING THE SKILL

Make your own chart Turn to Chapter 2, Section 2, "An English Settlement at Jamestown," in this text. Read the section, noticing the many problems the settlers faced in forming the new colony. Then make a chart like the one above in which you summarize the information you found in the passage. Be sure to read to the end of the section so that you can evaluate the solutions and their outcomes.

1.4 Analyzing Motives

Analyzing motives means examining the reasons why a person, group, or government took a particular action. These reasons often go back to the needs, emotions, and prior experiences of the person or group, as well as their plans and objectives.

UNDERSTANDING THE SKILL

Strategy: Finding clues in the text The Mormon church was founded in 1830, in upstate New York, by Joseph Smith and several followers who believed Smith had received a message directly from God. The following passage tells how the early Mormons were treated and why they moved west in the mid-1800s. The diagram that follows the passage summarizes the Mormons' motives for that journey.

> **Notice different kinds of motives.** Some motives are negative and others positive. People usually have several motives for taking important actions.

THE MORMON MIGRATION

Some of the Mormons' beliefs alarmed and angered other Americans, who insulted the Mormons and sometimes became violent. Plagued by persecution and seeking to convert Native Americans, Smith and a growing band of followers determined to move west, settling in Commerce, Illinois, which he renamed Nauvoo in 1839. Within five years, the community had swelled to 20,000 members.

Serious conflict developed again when Smith allowed male members of the church to have more than one wife. This idea infuriated many of Smith's neighbors, and he was eventually murdered by a mob.

The Mormons rallied around a remarkable new leader, Brigham Young, who urged them to move farther west. There they found a desert area near a salt lake, just beyond the mountains of what was then part of Mexico. The salty water was useless for crops or animals. Dry and dusty winds blew. Because the land was not desirable to others, Young realized his people might be safe there. The Mormons began to build Salt Lake City.

> **Look for the influence of important individuals.** Consider the role of leaders in motivating the behavior of people and groups.

> **Look for basic needs and human emotions.** Needs include food, clothing, shelter and safety. Emotions such as greed, ambition, compassion, and fear also motivate behavior.

Strategy: Making a diagram

> **Make a diagram that summarizes motives and actions.** List the important action in the middle of the diagram. Then list motives in different categories around the action.

Needs
Safety, a place to practice religion without interference

Prior Experiences
insults, violence, persecution, conflict, murder, success in attracting followers

Action
moving farther and farther west, finally to the Great Salt Lake

Emotions
faith, fear, hope

Goals
to convert Native Americans, desire to practice religion freely

APPLYING THE SKILL

Make your own diagram Turn to Chapter 5, Geography Spotlight, "The Land Ordinance of 1785." Read the feature, making notes about the United States government's motives in selling to settlers the western lands ceded by the states. Using the student model as a guide, make a diagram showing the government's motives for selling the land the way it did.

SKILLBUILDER HANDBOOK 1039

Section 1: Understanding Historical Readings

1.5 Analyzing Causes; Recognizing Effects

Historians not only want to know *what* happened in the past but also want to understand *why*. Thinking about and researching **cause-and-effect relationships** helps historians see how events are related and why they took place.

UNDERSTANDING THE SKILL

Strategy: Finding clues in the text The following paragraphs describe the early events leading to the Battle of the Little Bighorn. The cause-effect diagram that follows the passage summarizes the chain of causes and effects.

> ### BROKEN TREATIES
>
> The Treaty of 1868 had promised the Sioux that they could live forever in *Paha Sapa*, the Black Hills area of what is now South Dakota and Wyoming. The area was sacred to the Sioux. It was the center of their land, and the place where warriors went to await visions from their guardian spirits. The area also included the only good hunting ground remaining to them.
>
> Unfortunately for the Sioux, the Black Hills contained large deposits of gold. As soon as white Americans learned that gold had been discovered, they poured into the Native Americans' territory and began staking claims.
>
> Because the Sioux valued their land so highly, they appealed to the government to enforce the treaty terms and remove the miners. The government responded by sending out a commission to either lease mineral rights or buy *Paha Sapa* outright. The Sioux refused the commission's offer, whereupon the government sent in the Seventh Cavalry to remove not the miners but the Native Americans.

Cause: Look for reasons behind the events. Here the discovery of gold motivated the white Americans to move into Sioux territory.

Cause: Look for clue words indicating cause. These include *because, due to, since,* and *therefore.*

Effect: Look for clue words indicating consequences. These include *brought about, led to, as a result, thus, consequently,* and *responded.*

Notice that an effect may be the cause of another event, leading to a chain of causes and effects.

Strategy: Making a cause-and-effect diagram

Summarize causes and effects in a chart. Starting with the first cause in a series, fill in the boxes until you reach the end result.

Cause	Effect/Cause	Effect/Cause
Gold was discovered in the Black Hills.	White prospectors flocked to the area.	The Sioux appealed to the government to enforce the treaty.

Effect/Cause	Effect/Cause	Effect
The government sent a commission to lease or buy lands.	The Sioux refused the commission's offer.	The government sent in the cavalry.

APPLYING THE SKILL

Make your own cause-and-effect diagram Turn to Chapter 4, Section 1, "The Stirrings of Rebellion." Read "The Colonies Organize to Resist Britain" and make notes about the causes of Britain's actions and the colonists' responses. Make a diagram like the one shown above to summarize the information you find.

1040 SKILLBUILDER HANDBOOK

1.6 Comparing; Contrasting

Historians compare and contrast events, personalities, ideas, behaviors, beliefs, and institutions in order to understand them thoroughly. **Comparing** involves looking at the similarities and differences between two or more things. **Contrasting** means examining only the differences between them.

UNDERSTANDING THE SKILL

Strategy: Finding clues in the text The following passage describes life in the colonies during the last half of the 1600s. The Venn diagram below shows the similarities and differences between the colonies in the North and the South.

> **Compare: Look for clue words indicating that two things are alike.** Clue words include *both, all, like, as, likewise,* and *similarly.*

> **Compare: Look for features that two things have in common.** Here you learn that both the Northern and Southern colonies had slavery.

LIFE IN THE EARLY AMERICAN COLONIES

Not long after the English colonies were established, it became apparent that two very different ways of life were developing in the Northern and Southern colonies. In the South, both rich plantation owners and poorer frontier farmers sought land. Virginia and Maryland became known as the tobacco colonies. Large farms but few towns appeared there. Rivers served as the main roads.

Slavery existed in all the colonies, but it became a vital source of labor in the South. Most slaves in South Carolina remained unskilled, working mainly in the rice fields. By contrast, the New England and Middle Colonies did not rely on single staple crops such as tobacco or rice. Most people were farmers, but they grew a wide variety of crops. A smaller number of workers made products like candles, iron bars, ropes, and sailing ships. The New England Colonies traded actively with the islands of the West Indies. In addition to foods, they exported all kinds of other items ranging from barrels to horses. In return, they imported sugar and molasses. All this trade resulted in the growth of small towns and larger port cities.

> **Contrast: Look for clue words that show how two things differ.** Clue words include *different, differ, unlike, by contrast, however,* and *on the other hand.*

> **Contrast: Look for ways in which two things are different.** Here you learn that unlike the South, the North did not rely on single crops.

Strategy: Making a Venn diagram

> **Compare and Contrast: Summarize similarities and differences in a Venn diagram.** Use one oval to describe one thing, the other oval to describe the thing you are comparing, and the overlapping area to show what the two things have in common.

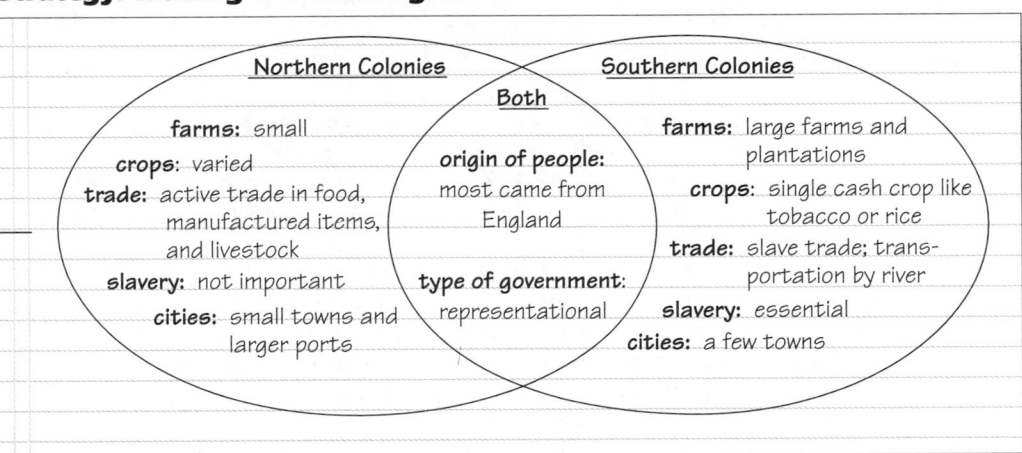

Northern Colonies
- **farms:** small
- **crops:** varied
- **trade:** active trade in food, manufactured items, and livestock
- **slavery:** not important
- **cities:** small towns and larger ports

Both
- **origin of people:** most came from England
- **type of government:** representational

Southern Colonies
- **farms:** large farms and plantations
- **crops:** single cash crop like tobacco or rice
- **trade:** slave trade; transportation by river
- **slavery:** essential
- **cities:** a few towns

APPLYING THE SKILL

Make your own Venn diagram Turn to Chapter 3, Section 3, in this text. Read "The Colonists Consider New Ideas," paying special attention to descriptions of Benjamin Franklin and Jonathan Edwards. Make a Venn diagram showing what the two leaders had in common and what made them different.

SKILLBUILDER HANDBOOK 1041

1.7 Distinguishing Fact from Opinion

Facts are events, dates, and statistics, or they are statements that are generally known to be true. Facts can be checked for accuracy. **Opinions** are the judgments, beliefs, and feelings of the writer or speaker.

UNDERSTANDING THE SKILL

Strategy: Finding clues in the text The following excerpt describes the Haymarket Affair of 1886 in Chicago. The chart summarizes the facts and opinions.

Facts: Look for specific events, dates, and statistics that can be verified. The factual account of the event continues through the first three paragraphs of the passage.

Opinion: Look for judgments the historian makes about events. In the last paragraph, the writer states the opinion that the event was a disaster and then backs up this opinion by explaining the negative consequences of the event.

THE HAYMARKET AFFAIR

At ten o'clock another speaker stepped forward, the main burden of his address being that there was no hope of improving the condition of workingmen through legislation; it must be through their own efforts. As he started to speak, a wind blew up, and it began to rain.

The speaker hurried to a conclusion, but at that point 180 police officers entered the square and headed for the speakers' platform. The captain in charge called on the meeting to disperse, "in the name of the people of the state of Illinois."

At that moment someone threw a bomb into the ranks of the policemen gathered about the speakers. After the initial shock and horror, the police opened fire on the 300 or 400 people who remained, and they in turn fled for their lives. One policeman had been killed by the bomb, and more than 60 injured. One member of the crowd was killed by police fire, and at least 12 were wounded. . . .

In almost every . . . way Haymarket was a disaster. It vastly augmented [increased] the already considerable paranoia of most Americans in regard to anarchists, socialists, communists, and radicals in general. It increased hostility toward "godless foreigners," a phrase that the prosecutor, Grinnell, had used frequently in referring to the defendants. It caused a serious impairment of freedom of speech in every part of the country.

Source: The Rise of Industrial America, by Page Smith. (New York: Penguin, 1990) pp. 244-256

Opinion: Look for assertions, claims, hypotheses, and judgments. Here the speaker's opinion is expressed; the historian gives a factual account of the speech in which this opinion was expressed.

Strategy: Making a chart

Summarize facts and opinions in a chart. List the facts you learned in a passage as well as the opinions that were expressed.

FACTS	OPINIONS
Just after 10:00, as a speaker was finishing up and it was beginning to rain, someone threw a bomb into the ring of policemen surrounding the listeners. Numerous police were injured by the bomb, and civilians were injured when police fired into the crowd.	speaker: Workers must improve their own situations, since legislation can't do it for them. historian: Nothing good came of the Haymarket affair, and in fact it had many negative consequences. • increased paranoia about radicals • increased hostility toward foreigners • harmed freedom of speech

APPLYING THE SKILL

Make your own chart Turn to Chapter 5, Section 3, "Ratifying the Constitution." Read the section on the Bill of Rights, including *A Personal Voice*. Make a chart in which you summarize the facts of the new constitution and the opinions expressed by Jefferson and by those who disagreed with him.

Section 2: Using Critical Thinking

2.1 Developing Historical Perspective

Historical perspective means understanding events and people in the context of their times. It also means that you should not judge the past solely in terms of present-day norms and values.

UNDERSTANDING THE SKILL

Strategy: Finding clues in the text The following passage is the opening portion of an address by President Theodore Roosevelt. Following the passage is a chart in which you will summarize information from the passage about historical perspective.

Identify the historical figure, the occasion, and the date.

Notice words, phrases, and settings that reflect the period. Here the language used by the president reflects the optimism of Roosevelt's Progressive Era.

Explain how people's actions and words reflected the attitudes, values, and passions of the era. Teddy Roosevelt's belief in what 19th-century Americans called "manly virtues" shines forth in the language that he employs to describe his nation and its destiny.

Look for clues to the attitudes, customs, and values of people living at the time. The language of the past, though occasionally high-flown and rhetorical, often revealed basic American attitudes toward other peoples and nations.

> ### INAUGURAL ADDRESS, 1905
> #### PRESIDENT THEODORE ROOSEVELT
>
> My fellow-citizens, no people on earth have more cause to be thankful than ours, and this is said reverently, in no spirit of boastfulness in our own strength, but with gratitude to the Giver of Good who has blessed us with the conditions which have enabled us to achieve so large a measure of well-being and of happiness. To us as a people it has been granted to lay the foundations of our national life in a new continent. We are the heirs of the ages, and yet we have had to pay few of the penalties which in old countries are exacted by the dead hand of a bygone civilization. We have not been obliged to fight for our existence against any alien race; and yet our life has called for the vigor and effort without which the manlier and hardier virtues wither away. Under such conditions it would be our own fault if we failed; and the success which we have had in the past, the success which we confidently believe the future will bring, should cause in us no feeling of vainglory, but rather a deep and abiding realization of all which life has offered us; a full acknowledgment of the responsibility which is ours; and a fixed determination to show that under a free government a mighty people can thrive best, alike as regards the things of the body and the things of the soul.

Strategy: Writing a summary

Use historical perspective to understand Roosevelt's attitudes. In a chart, list key words, phrases, and details from Roosevelt's address and then synthesize in a short paragraph Roosevelt's basic values and attitudes.

Roosevelt's Inaugural Address	
• new continent • heirs of the ages • bygone civilization • vigor and effort • manlier and hardier virtues	Theodore Roosevelt seems to reveal a strong and resilient optimism about the American enterprise. His confidence is grounded in a deep religious faith in God (the "Giver of Good") and God's plan for the nation. Roosevelt clearly believes in the ability of the American people to solve whatever problems they face as they move into a bright future. Roosevelt's appeal to the manly virtues reflects typical attitudes and values of 19th- and early 20th-century Americans.

APPLYING THE SKILL

Make your own summary Turn to Chapter 7, Section 4, and read the One American's Story, which contains an excerpt from a speech by Daniel Webster. Read the passage using historical perspective, then summarize your ideas in a chart like the one above.

SKILLBUILDER HANDBOOK 1043

Section 2: Using Critical Thinking

2.2 Formulating Historical Questions

Formulating **historical questions** is important both as you read and as you do historical research. As you read, ask questions about the events—about what caused them, what made them important, and so forth. Then, when you are doing research, write questions that you want your research to answer. This step is critical—it will help to guide and focus your research.

UNDERSTANDING THE SKILL

Strategy: Finding clues in the text At a women's rights convention in the mid-1800s, delegates adopted a "Declaration of Sentiments" that set forth a number of grievances. Following is a description of that event. After the passage is a web diagram that organizes historical questions about the event.

> **Ask about the basic facts of the event.** Who were the main people? What did they do? Where and when did the event take place?

> **Ask about the results produced by various causes.** What were the results of the event?

> **Ask about the cause of an event.** Why did the event take place?

> **Ask about historical influences on a speaker or event.** What other historical events was it similar to? How was it different?

SENECA FALLS, 1848

Elizabeth Cady Stanton and Lucretia Mott decided to act on their resolution to hold a women's rights convention. In 1848, they convened at Seneca Falls, New York, the small town that gave the convention its name. Stanton and Mott spent a day composing an agenda and a detailed statement of grievances. Stanton carefully modeled this "Declaration of Sentiments" on the Declaration of Independence. The second paragraph began, "We hold these truths to be self-evident: that all men and women are created equal. . . ." More than 300 women and men gathered at the convention. The participants approved all measures unanimously, except for one: women's right to vote. The franchise for women, though it passed, remained a controversial topic.

Strategy: Making a web diagram

> **Investigate a topic in more depth by asking questions.** Ask a large question and then ask smaller questions that explore and develop from the larger question.

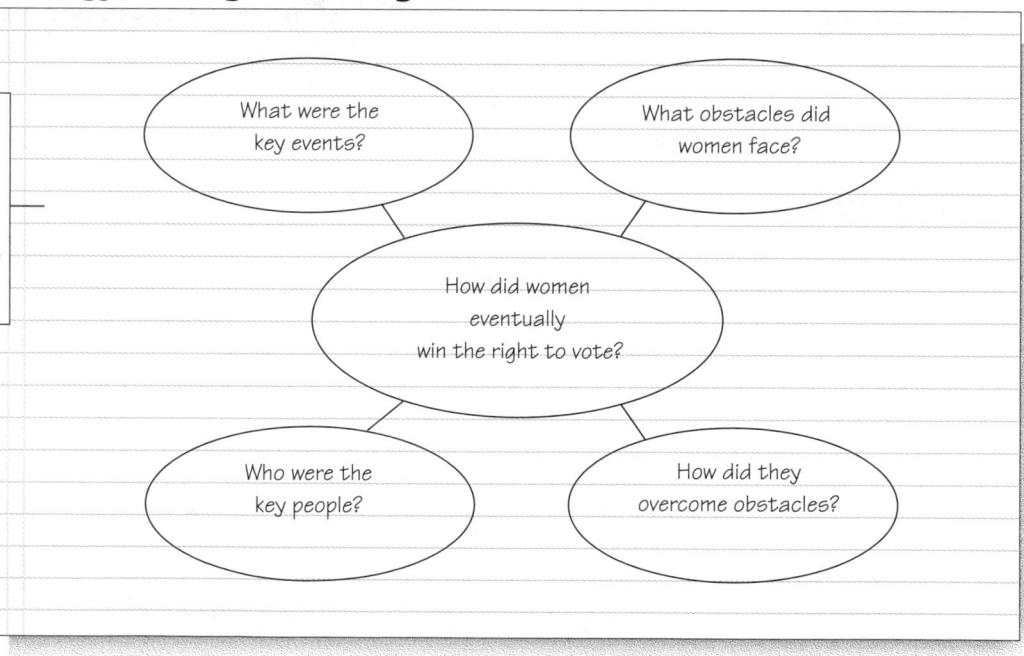

APPLYING THE SKILL

Make your own web diagram Turn to Chapter 6, Section 1, page 175, which describes the first political parties. Use a web diagram to write historical questions about the passage. Then write questions that would guide your research about the topic

1044 SKILLBUILDER HANDBOOK

Section 2: Using Critical Thinking

2.3 Hypothesizing

Hypothesizing means coming up with a possible theory or cause to explain historical events. This explanation can then be tested against the historical facts to see whether the explanation is accurate. When you read history, hypothesizing is important because it helps you understand (1) why the events occurred, (2) what the consequences of the events will be, or (3) what the significance of the events is.

UNDERSTANDING THE SKILL

Strategy: Finding clues in the text As the Cold War came to an end, people offered various hypotheses to explain why the Soviet Union broke up and to predict what would replace it. Read this passage and form your own hypothesis. Following the passage is a chart that organizes a hypothesis and the facts used to support it.

> **As you read, form hypotheses about the important events.** You could form the hypothesis that Gorbachev's new policies would deeply affect politics in the Soviet Union and Eastern Europe.

> **Read for facts that prove your hypothesis right or wrong.** These facts support the hypothesis because they show that Gorbachev's policies affected politics in the Soviet Union.

THE COLD WAR ENDS

In March 1985, Mikhail Gorbachev became the general secretary of the Communist party in the Soviet Union. He initiated a new policy of openness and reform within the USSR, putting an end to the collective ownership of resources, most government censorship, and controlled elections. A dramatic increase in nationalism on the part of the non-Russian republics followed the open elections, and in December 1991, all 14 republics declared independence. The USSR was replaced by a loose federation of republics called the Commonwealth of Independent States.

Gorbachev's new policies led to massive changes in eastern Europe, as the satellite states, with his encouragement, moved toward democracy. On November 9, 1989, East Berlin opened the Berlin Wall, putting an end to the city's 28-year division. Berliners climbed atop the wall, cheering and dancing, and rushed through the previously well-armed checkpoints. East Germany soon held its first free elections, and the two Germanys were reunited. Hungary, Bulgaria, and Romania made successful transitions from communism, but Yugoslavia collapsed into warring factions.

> This fact supports the hypothesis because it shows that Gorbachev's policies had a profound effect on politics in Eastern Europe.

Strategy: Making a chart

> **Use a chart to summarize your hypothesis about events.** Suppose that you are thinking about the effect of the end of the Cold War on American foreign and domestic policy. Use a chart to set out the problem and your possible hypothesis about the issue.

Hypothesis	Fact 1	Fact 2	Fact 3
Gorbachev's new policies would affect politics in Soviet Union and Eastern Europe	Fact: Increase in nationalism in non-Russian republics	Fact: USSR replaced by loose confederation	Fact: Massive change in Eastern Europe
	Whether it supports hypothesis: Yes	Whether it supports hypothesis: Yes	Whether it supports hypothesis: Yes

APPLYING THE SKILL

Make your own chart Turn to Chapter 7, Section 1, page 199, which describes a massive change in economic conditions in the early United States, with particular reference to New England. Make a chart in which you hypothesize about the consequences of that change. Then list facts and explain whether they support the hypothesis.

Section 2: Using Critical Thinking

2.4 Analyzing Issues

An issue is a matter of public concern or debate. Issues in history are usually economic, social, political, or moral. Historical issues are often more complicated than they first appear. **Analyzing issues** means taking them apart to find and describe the different points of view in a debate about an economic, social, political, or moral issue.

UNDERSTANDING THE SKILL

Strategy: Finding clues in the text The following passage describes working conditions in U.S. factories in the late 1800s and early 1900s. Notice how the cluster diagram that follows the passage helps you to analyze the issue of child labor.

CHILDREN AT WORK

Look for a central problem with its causes and effects.

Workers had little choice but to put up with deplorable conditions in aptly named sweatshops. Wages were so low that many families could not survive unless all their members, including children, worked. Between 1890 and 1910, 20 percent of boys and 10 percent of girls under age 15—some as young as five years old—held full-time jobs. A typical work week was 12 hours a day, six days a week. Many of these children worked from dawn to dusk, wasted by hunger and exhaustion that made them prone to crippling accidents for which there was no compensation. With little time or energy left for school, child laborers gave up their futures to help their families make ends meet.

Look for facts and statistics. The numbers supplied by facts and statistics can help to flesh out the discussion of an issue.

Look for the other side to an issue. You need to look at all sides of an issue before deciding what you think.

Nonetheless, factory owners and some parents praised child labor for keeping children out of mischief. They believed idleness for children was bad, and work provided healthy occupation.

The reformer Jacob Riis and others worked for decent conditions, better wages, and child labor laws. The new labor unions joined the call for eight-hour days and better pay. Slowly public opinion turned against the use of child labor. Though it took many years and great effort, state legislatures finally passed laws banning or restricting child labor.

Strategy: Making a cluster diagram

If an issue is complex, make a diagram. A diagram can help you analyze an issue.

Issue: Should children under 15 have been allowed to work?

Facts:
- Children as young as 5 years old worked.
- Twenty percent of boys and 10 percent of girls under 15 held jobs.
- Workers typically put in 72 hours per week.
- Working conditions in many industries were strenuous, exhausting, and dangerous.

In favor of children working:

Who: business owners, some parents

Reasons: Idleness was bad, so working was good for children. Families needed income from children.

Against children working:

Who: Jacob Riis and other reformers.

Reasons: Working meant giving up school. Working conditions were inhumane.

APPLYING THE SKILL

Make your own cluster diagram Chapter 7, Section 3, pages 211-213, describes the removal of Native Americans from their lands. Make a cluster diagram to analyze the issue and the positions of the people involved.

1046 SKILLBUILDER HANDBOOK

Section 2: Using Critical Thinking

2.5 Analyzing Assumptions and Biases

An **assumption** is a belief or an idea that is taken for granted. Sometimes people make assumptions based on evidence; sometimes they make unfounded assumptions. Whether assumptions are clearly stated or just implied, you can usually figure out what they are.

Bias is a prejudiced point of view. Historical accounts that are biased tend to be one-sided and reflect the personal prejudices of the historian.

UNDERSTANDING THE SKILL

Strategy: Finding clues in the text The following passage is from *The Americans at Home* by a minister from Scotland named David Macrae, who wrote the book after visiting the United States in the 1860s. Notice how the chart that follows the excerpt helps to summarize information about the writer's assumptions and biases.

Identify the author and information about him or her. Does the author belong to a special-interest group, religious organization, political party, or social movement that might promote a one-sided or slanted viewpoint on the subject?

Examine the evidence. Is what the author relates consistent with other accounts? Is the behavior described consistent with human nature as you have observed it?

Search for clues. Are there words, phrases, statements, or images that might convey a positive or negative slant? What might these clues reveal about the author's bias?

> ## THE AMERICANS AT HOME
> ## BY DAVID MACRAE
>
> [T]he American girls are very delightful. And in one point they fairly surpass the majority of English girls—they are all educated and well informed. . . . The admirable educational system . . . covering the whole area of society, has given them education whether they are rich or poor, has furnished them with a great deal of information, and has quickened their desire for more. An American girl will talk with you about anything, and . . . seem to feel interest in it. Their tendency is perhaps to talk too much, and . . . it seemed to me sometimes to make no perceptible difference whether they knew anything of the subject they talked about or not. But they usually know a little of everything; and their general intelligence and vivacity make them very delightful companions.

Strategy: Making a chart

Make a chart of your analysis. For each of the heads listed on the left-hand side of the chart, summarize what information you can find in the passage.

David Macrae's impression of American Women	
speaker	David Macrae
date	1860s
occasion	book called <u>The Americans at Home</u> about Macrae's visit to the United States
tone	humorous or light-hearted
assumptions	American women are well-informed and stimulating companions, if inclined to talk too much about subjects of which they know little.
bias	Implicit in some of the author's comments seems to be a prejudice that women should defer to the superior knowledge of men.

APPLYING THE SKILL

Make your own chart Look at the opinions expressed by George Washington in *A Personal Voice* in Chapter 5, Section 2, page 132. Read the passage and summarize the underlying assumptions and biases using a chart like the one shown.

SKILLBUILDER HANDBOOK **1047**

Section 2: Using Critical Thinking

2.6 Evaluating Decisions and Courses of Action

Evaluating decisions means making judgments about the decisions that historical figures made. Historians evaluate decisions on the basis of their moral implications and their costs and benefits from different points of view.

Evaluating alternative courses of action means carefully judging the choices that historical figures had to make to better understand why they made some of the decisions they did.

UNDERSTANDING THE SKILL

Strategy: Finding clues in the text The following passage describes the decisions President John Kennedy had to make when he learned of Soviet missile bases in Cuba. As you read it, think of the alternative responses he could have made at each turn of events. Following the passage is a chart that organizes information about the Cuban missile crisis.

THE CUBAN MISSILE CRISIS

During the summer of 1962, the flow of Soviet weapons into Cuba—including nuclear missiles—greatly increased. President Kennedy responded cautiously at first, issuing a warning that the United States would not tolerate the presence of offensive nuclear weapons in Cuba. Then, on October 16, photographs taken by American U-2 planes showed the president that the Soviets were secretly building missile bases on Cuba. Some of the missiles, armed and ready to fire, could reach U.S. cities in minutes.

On the evening of October 22, the president made public the evidence of missiles and stated his ultimatum: any missile attack from Cuba would trigger an all-out attack on the Soviet Union. Soviet ships continued to head toward the island, while the U.S. navy prepared to stop them and U.S. invasion troops massed in Florida. To avoid confrontation, the Soviet ships suddenly halted. Then Soviet premier Khrushchev offered to remove the missiles from Cuba in exchange for a pledge not to invade the island. Kennedy agreed, and the crisis ended.

Some people criticized Kennedy for practicing brinkmanship, when private talks might have resolved the crisis without the threat of nuclear war. Others believed he had been too soft and had passed up an ideal chance to invade Cuba and to oust its Communist leader, Castro.

> **Look at decisions made by individuals or by groups.** Notice the decisions Kennedy made in response to Soviet actions.

> **Analyze a decision in terms of the alternatives that were possible.** Both Kennedy and Khrushchev faced the alternative of either escalating or defusing the crisis.

> **Look at the outcome of the decisions.**

Strategy: Making a chart

> **Make a chart of your analysis.** The problem was that Soviet nuclear missiles were being shipped to Cuba. The decision to be made was how the United States should respond.

alternative	pros	cons	evaluation
Negotiate a settlement quietly, without threatening nuclear war.	1. Avoid the threat of nuclear war 2. Avoid frightening U.S. citizens	1. The U.S. would not have the public opportunity of looking like a strong world leader. 2. The government would lose favor with Cuban exiles living in the U.S.	your answer: Would this have been a good choice and why?

APPLYING THE SKILL

Make your own chart Chapter 5, Section 3, pages 137–141, describes the heated debate between Federalists and Antifederalists about whether or not to ratify the Constitution. Make a chart like the one shown to summarize the pros and cons of an alternative and evaluate the decision yourself.

1048 SKILLBUILDER HANDBOOK

Section 2: Using Critical Thinking

2.7 Forming Opinions

Historians **form opinions** about information they are given. They support their opinions with references to facts, examples, and historical parallels. You might be asked, for instance, to decide in what circumstances violence in a political revolution is ever justified.

UNDERSTANDING THE SKILL

Strategy: Finding clues in the text The following passage includes comments on the French Revolution by Gouverneur Morris, one of the participants in the Constitutional Convention, as well as by Thomas Jefferson.

Decide what you think about a subject after reading all the information available to you. After reading this description, you might decide that no political cause justifies such violence against individuals. On the other hand, your opinion might be that, regrettable as such violence is, when a tyranny is overthrown, some servants of the old regime are bound to perish.

Look for the opinions of historians and other experts. Consider their opinions when forming your own.

A SCENE OF MOB VIOLENCE

Gouverneur Morris was a visitor to Paris during the early days of the French Revolution. In the following journal entry he describes a scene of revolutionary mob violence: "The head and body of Mr. de Foulon are introduced in triumph. The head on a pike, the body dragged naked on the earth. Afterwards this horrible exhibition is carried through the different streets. His crime [was] to have accepted a place in the Ministry. This mutilated form of an old man of seventy five is shown to Bertier, his son in law, the intend't. [another official] of Paris, and afterwards he also is put to death and cut to pieces, the populace carrying the mangled fragments with a savage joy." Such violence was common during the French Revolution and shocked a good many Americans. However, Thomas Jefferson was a supporter of the Revolution, saying, "The liberty of the whole earth was depending on the issue of the contest, and . . . rather than it should have failed, I would have seen half the earth devastated."

Support your opinion with facts, quotes, and examples, including references to similar events from other historical eras. You might compare the violence on display in this episode of the French Revolution with the relative lack of mob violence in the American Revolution.

Strategy: Making a chart

Summarize your opinion and supporting information in a chart. Write an opinion and then list facts, quotes, and examples that support your opinion.

Opinion: The French Revolution was especially violent and cruel.		
facts:	**quotes:**	**examples:**
• Violence escalated. • Jacobins launched Reign of Terror. • Moderates were sent to guillotine. • Jacobins declared war on other countries.	"he also is put to death and cut to pieces"	Jacobins beheaded Louis XVI.

APPLYING THE SKILL

Make your own chart Look at the Point/Counterpoint on the Legacy of Columbus on page 32. Read and form your own opinion about Columbus's achievements, summarizing your supporting data in a chart like the one shown.

2.8 Drawing Conclusions

Drawing conclusions means analyzing the implications of what you have read and forming an opinion about its meaning or consequences. To draw conclusions, you look closely at facts and then use your own experience and common sense to decide what those facts mean.

UNDERSTANDING THE SKILL

Strategy: Finding clues in the text The following passage tells about employment trends in the 1990s. The call-outs point to information that can be put together to form conclusions. Use the diagram that follows the passage to organize the facts and implications you use to draw conclusions.

JOB OUTLOOK IN THE MID-1990s

Use the facts to draw a conclusion. Conclusion: In general, the economy was good in the mid-1990s.

Several trends have emerged in the workplace of the 1990s. Inflation is at its lowest level since the 1960s, and 10 million new jobs created between 1993 and 1996 have helped lower the unemployment rate to 5.1 percent. Median household income adjusted for inflation, however, declined from $33,585 to $31,241, even though there are many households in which both parents work. And the gap between rich and poor continues to widen, with some executives receiving millions of dollars in compensation while 4 million families live below the poverty line.

Read carefully to understand all the facts. Conclusion: Income expectations are lower.

Jobs in manufacturing have declined, while new jobs have appeared at a rapid rate in the service sector. In addition, many jobs once done by permanent employees of a company are done by temporary workers who are paid only for the time they are needed and who typically do not receive benefits.

Ask questions of the material. What is the effect of these changes on job security? Conclusion: Job security is reduced.

Three out of four young Americans think they will earn less in their lifetimes than their parents did. Unemployment in their age group continues at the same rate, while the unemployment rate for other adults has fallen. In 1993, about one in seven workers between the ages of 16 and 25 was out of work, double the national average.

Ask questions of the material. What might be the effect of these changes on young people? Conclusion: Jobs will be harder for young people to find.

Strategy: Making a diagram

Summarize the data and your conclusion about it in a diagram.

Facts	Conclusions	General Conclusion About Entire Passage
Inflation is low.	General economy is good.	While many young people will succeed despite the obstacles, the typical young worker has more reason to feel economically insecure.
Unemployment is low.		
Median income is down.	Income expectations are lower.	
More workers are temporary employees.	Job security is reduced.	
Unemployment for young people is twice the national average.	Jobs will be harder for young people to find.	

APPLYING THE SKILL

Make your own diagram Look over Chapter 6, Section 2, pages 178–179, for information about Native American resistance to white settlers. Read the passage and draw conclusions based on the facts. Use the student model as a guide to create your own diagram showing the facts and interim conclusions you have used to arrive at a general conclusion.

1050 SKILLBUILDER HANDBOOK

Section 2: Using Critical Thinking

2.9 Synthesizing

Synthesizing is the skill historians use in developing interpretations of the past. Like detective work, synthesizing involves putting together clues, information, and ideas to form an overall picture of a historical event.

UNDERSTANDING THE SKILL

Strategy: Finding clues in the text The following passage describes the first settlement of North and Central America. The call-outs indicate the different kinds of information that lead toward a synthesis—an overall picture of Native American life.

Read carefully to understand the facts. Facts such as these enable you to base your interpretations on physical evidence.

Bring together the information you have about a subject. This interpretation brings together different kinds of information to arrive at a new understanding of the subject.

THE FIRST AMERICANS

From the discovery of chiseled arrowheads and charred bones at ancient sites, it appears that the earliest Americans lived as big game hunters. The woolly mammoth, their largest prey, provided them with food, clothing, and bones for constructing tools and shelters. People gradually shifted to hunting smaller game and gathering available plants. They fashioned baskets to collect nuts, wild rice, chokecherries, gooseberries, and currants. They invented snares, and later bows and arrows, to hunt small game such as jackrabbits and deer. They wove nets to fish the streams and lakes.

Between 10,000 and 15,000 years ago, a revolution took place in what is now central Mexico. People began to raise plants as food. Maize may have been the first domesticated plant, with gourds, pumpkins, peppers, beans, and potatoes following. Agriculture spread to other regions.

The rise of agriculture brought tremendous changes to the Americas. Agriculture made it possible for people to remain in one place. It also enabled them to accumulate and store surplus food. As their surplus increased, people had the time to develop skills and more complex ideas about the world. From this agricultural base rose larger, more stable societies and increasingly complex societies.

Look for explanations that link the facts together. This assertion is based on the evidence provided by snares, nets, and bowls, which are mentioned in the next couple of sentences.

Consider what you already know that could apply. Your general knowledge will probably lead you to accept this statement as reasonable.

Strategy: Making a cluster diagram

Summarize your synthesis in a diagram. Use a cluster diagram to organize the facts, opinions, examples, and interpretations that you have brought together to form a synthesis.

chiseled arrowheads and charred bones

They invented snares.

Synthesis: From this agricultural base rose more stable and complex societies.

smaller game and plants

People raised plants as food.

surplus food

APPLYING THE SKILL

Make your own cluster diagram Look at Chapter 5, Section 1, pages 128–129, to learn about the problems encountered by the Articles of Confederation. Read the section and look for information to support a synthesis about the fundamental causes of the nation's problems under the Articles.

3.1 Primary and Secondary Sources

Primary Sources are written or created by people who were actually at a historical event, either as participants or as observers. Primary sources include letters, diaries, journals, speeches, newspaper articles, magazine articles, eyewitness accounts, and autobiographies.

Secondary Sources are derived from primary sources by people who were not present at the original event. They often combine information from a number of different accounts. Secondary sources include history books, historical essays, and biographies.

UNDERSTANDING THE SKILL

Strategy: Finding clues in the text The passage below describes the explosion of the first atomic bomb in 1945. It is mainly a secondary source, but it includes a primary source in the form of an eyewitness account.

Secondary Source: Look for information collected from several sources. Here the writer creates a composite picture of expectations before the explosion.

Primary Source: Identify the title. Look for the name of the writer and publication information, such as the name and date of a book or article.

Summarize information from primary and secondary sources on a chart.

Primary Source: Identify the author and evaluate his or her credentials. What qualifies the writer to report on the event? Here the writer actually worked on developing the bomb.

Secondary Source: Look for information collected after the event. A secondary source provides a perspective that is missing in a primary source.

THE FIRST ATOMIC BOMB

As the time to test the bomb drew near, the air around Los Alamos crackled with rumors and fears. At one end of the scale were fears that the bomb wouldn't work at all, or, if it did, would not produce enough punch to amount to much. At the other end was the prediction that the explosion would set fire to the atmosphere, which would mean the end of the earth.

On July 16, 1945, the first atomic bomb was detonated in a dark and empty expanse of desert near Alamogordo, New Mexico. Otto Frisch, a Manhattan project scientist, listened tensely to the countdown. In his book *What Little I Remember,* he described what happened next:

And then without a sound, the sun was shining; or so it looked. The sand hills of the desert were shimmering in a very bright light, almost colorless and shapeless. . . . I turned round, but that object on the horizon which looked like a small sun was still too bright to look at . . . after another ten seconds or so it had grown and . . . was slowly rising into the sky from the ground, with which it remained connected by a lengthening stem of swirling dust.

That blinding flash, which was visible 180 miles away, was followed by a deafening roar as a tremendous shock wave rolled across the trembling desert. The bomb not only worked, but it was more powerful than most had dared hope.

Strategy: Making a chart

Primary Source	Secondary Source
Author: Otto Frisch	Author: unknown
Qualifications: member of the Manhattan Project	Qualifications: had access to multiple accounts of the time leading up to and following the event
Information: detailed description, sensory observations, feeling of awe	Information: description of range of points of view and of information available only after the event

APPLYING THE SKILL

Make your own chart Turn to Chapter 11, Section 2, "The Politics of War," about the Emancipation Proclamation during the Civil War. Read "Reaction to the Proclamation," which includes A Personal Voice by Henry M. Turner. Make a chart in which you summarize information from the primary and secondary sources.

1052 SKILLBUILDER HANDBOOK

Section 3: Exploring Historical Evidence

3.2 Visual, Audio, Multimedia Sources

In addition to written accounts, historians use many kinds of **visual sources,** including paintings, costume drawings, photographs, political cartoons, and advertisements. Visual sources are rich with historical details and sometimes convey the feelings and points of view of an era better than words do.

Spoken language has always been a primary means of passing on human history. **Audio sources,** such as recorded speeches, interviews, press conferences, and radio programs, continue the oral tradition today.

Movies, CD-ROMs, television, and computer software are the newest kind of historical sources, called **multimedia sources.** Often information found in other forms—such as writing, recordings, still photographs, and videotapes—is incorporated into a complex multimedia format with words, sounds, and pictures.

UNDERSTANDING THE SKILL

Strategy: Finding clues The political cartoon shows President Calvin Coolidge playing the saxophone while big business dances. The chart below it summarizes historical information gained from interpreting the visual source.

Identify the subject.
This cartoon shows President Calvin Coolidge's relationship with big business.

Interpret the message.
The cartoonist suggests a cozy relationship between the president and big business. Coolidge caters to big business, and business dances to his tune.

Analyze the point of view.
Is the subject shown in a positive or negative light? Big business is having a wonderful time, possibly at the public's expense. The president is small and relatively insignificant. The caption underscores the impression that big business is close to the president.

Identify important symbols and details. Big business is shown as a young, carefree, energetic flapper of the twenties. The president's saxophone is labeled "Praise," suggesting his positive attitude toward the oversized, fun-loving flapper.

YES, SIR HE'S MY BABY

Strategy: Making a chart

Summarize your interpretation of a cartoon in a simple chart.

Subject	Point of View	Symbols and Details	Message
President Coolidge's relationship with big business	Satirical of the Coolidge administration and of big business	Flapper: big business carefree and overgrown	Big business and the president are too close. Business is having too good a time—with the president's help.
		President: playing a tune for business	

APPLYING THE SKILL

Make your own chart Turn to the political cartoon in Chapter 6, Section 4, "The War of 1812 Erupts." It shows a cartoonist's vision of his own treatment by Uncle Sam. Use a chart like the one above to analyze and interpret the cartoon.

SKILLBUILDER HANDBOOK **1053**

3.3 Interpreting Maps

Maps are representations of features on the earth's surface. Historians use maps to locate historical events, to demonstrate how geography has influenced history, and to illustrate human interaction with the environment.

Different kinds of maps are used for specific purposes.

Political maps Political maps show political units, from countries, states, and provinces, to counties, districts, and towns. Each area is shaded a different color.

Physical maps Physical maps show mountains, hills, plains, rivers, lakes, and oceans. They may use contour lines to indicate elevations on land and depths under water.

Historical maps Historical maps illustrate such things as economic activity, political alliances, migrations, battles, population density, and changes over time.

Lines Lines indicate boundaries between political areas, types of roads and highways, routes of exploration or migration, and rivers and other waterways. Lines may vary in width and color.

Symbols Cities, towns, and villages often appear as dots of different sizes depending on their populations. A capital city is often shown as a star or a dot with a circle around it. An area's crops, products, resources, industries, and special features are often indicated by symbols, such as a cotton leaf for areas growing cotton and a tree silhouette for areas in which timber is important.

Labels The key places, such as cities, states, and bodies of water, are labeled.

Colors Maps use different colors to indicate the areas under different political or cultural influence. Colors are also used to show such variable features as population density and altitude.

Lines of longitude and latitude Lines of longitude and latitude appear on maps to indicate the absolute location of the area shown. Lines of latitude show distance north or south of the equator, measured in degrees along a meridian. Lines of longitude show distance measured in degrees east or west from the prime meridian, which runs through Greenwich, England.

Compass Rose The compass rose is a device on a map indicating the map's orientation on the globe. It may show all four cardinal directions (N, S, E, W) or just one, north.

Scale A map's scale is a device showing the ratio between a unit of length on the map and a unit of distance on the earth. A typical scale shows a one-inch segment and indicates the number of miles that length represents on the map. A map that covers 500 miles per inch has a scale of 1:500.

Legend or Key A legend or key is a small table next to a map. The symbols, lines, and special colors that appear in the map are listed and explained in the legend.

Strategy: Finding clues The historical maps below show European land holdings in North America in 1754 and after 1763. Together they show changes over time.

European Claims in North America, 1754–1763

Look at the map's title to learn the subject and purpose of the map. What area does the map cover? What does the map tell you about the area? Here the maps show North America in the 1700s with the purpose of comparing European claims at two different times.

In 1754

☐ British territory
☐ French territory
☐ Spanish territory
☐ Disputed territory

Look at the legend to see how the features are displayed. The legend tells you what the symbols and colors on the map mean.

After 1763

Find where the map area is located on the earth. These maps span a large area from the Arctic Circle to below latitude 20° N, and 50° to 110° W.

Look at the scale and compass. The scale shows you how many miles or kilometers are represented. Here the scale is 500 actual miles to approximately 5/8 inch on the map. The compass shows you which direction on the map is north.

Strategy: Making a chart

Relate the map to the five geographic themes by making a chart. The five themes are described on pages vi–vii.

Location	Place	Region	Movement	Human/ Environment Interaction
Large area from Arctic Circle to below 20° N, and 50° to 110°W	North American continent	Western Hemisphere	Between 1754 and 1763, land claimed by France was largely taken over by the other two colonialist powers. Spain expanded its territories northward, while England consolidated and greatly expanded its holdings.	Europeans carved out political units in the continent, which already had inhabitants. The territories they claimed covered vast areas, with waterways and large mountain ranges to cross.

Make your own chart Turn to Chapter 9, Section 2, "Manifest Destiny." Study the map titled "Trails West, 1850." Make a chart like the one shown above in which you summarize what the map tells you in the five main subject areas.

SKILLBUILDER HANDBOOK **1055**

3.4 Interpreting Charts

Charts are visual presentations of material. Historians use charts to organize, simplify, and summarize information in a way that makes it more meaningful or memorable. Several varieties of charts are commonly used.

Simple charts Simple charts are used to consolidate information or to compare people, movements, parties, and so on.

Tables Tables are used to organize numbers, percentages, or other information into columns and rows for easy reference.

Diagrams Diagrams provide visual clues to the meaning of the information they contain. Venn diagrams are used for comparisons. Web diagrams are used to collect miscellaneous information around a central topic. Illustrated diagrams are sometimes called **infographics.**

UNDERSTANDING THE SKILL

Strategy: Finding clues The chart below gives a visual representation of the cycle of poverty in which sharecroppers in the South after the Civil War found themselves trapped. The paragraph that follows summarizes the information contained in the chart.

Read the title.

The Sharecropper Cycle of Poverty

Identify the symbols. Here the sharecropper is represented by the figure in overalls. The landowner is dressed in a suit.

The cycle begins here.

Sharecropper is given land and seed by landowner.

Sharecropper becomes tenant farmer and a new cycle begins.

If he has any leftover cash

Look for the main idea. The cycle of arrows describes the cycle of poverty in which the sharecropper was trapped. His one chance of breaking out of the cycle was to earn enough to rent or eventually purchase land.

Pays off account with merchants.

The plots are small, so crop yields are low.

Buys food and clothing on credit.

Crooked landowners charge unfair fines.

Same crop year after year eventually depletes the soil.

Sells remaining crop at market.

Sharecropper is at the mercy of the market.

Plants crop

Harvests crop and gives landowner his share.

Follow the arrows to study the chart. Read the description of each image in the chart. Together they tell the story of the sharecropper's year.

Strategy: Writing a summary

Write a paragraph to summarize what you learned from the chart.

Sharecroppers were given land and seed by a landowner. They were permitted to farm the land in exchange for a share of the crops they raised. The money they made from selling the rest of the crop often went to paying off their expenses. Usually, they had to renew the arrangement the next year, although some sharecroppers earned enough to break out of the cycle.

APPLYING THE SKILL

Write your own summary Turn to Chapter 7, Section 1, and look at the chart "The Cotton Gin." Study the chart and write a paragraph in which you summarize what you learned from it. Tell how the gin worked and how it changed the productivity of the workers.

3.5 Interpreting Graphs

Graphs show statistical information in a visual manner. Historians use graphs to visualize comparative amounts, ratios, economic trends, and changes over time.

Line graphs Line graphs typically show quantities on the vertical axis (up the left side) and time in years, months, or other units on the horizontal axis (across the bottom).

Pie graphs Pie graphs are useful for showing relative proportions. The circle represents the whole, such as the entire population, and the slices represent the parts belonging to various subgroups.

Bar graphs Bar graphs are commonly used to display information about quantities. Each small symbol stands for a given number or amount of something. It is easy to see at a glance how different categories compare.

UNDERSTANDING THE SKILL

Strategy: Finding clues The graph below combines a bar graph with a line graph. The bars show the amount of wheat produced per year, from 1927 through 1934. The line shows the changing price of wheat over the same years.

Read the title to identify the main idea of the graph. When two subjects are shown, such as wheat production and prices, the graph will probably show a relationship between them.

Read the vertical axis of the graph.

Read the horizontal axis of the graph.

U.S. Wheat Production and Wheat Prices

875   914   824   887   942   756   552   526

■ Price per bushel   = 100 million bushels

Summarize the information shown in each part of the graph. What trends do you see in the line graph? How did wheat production change over the years?

Look at the legend. Find out what each symbol and unit in the graph represents. Here each wheat symbol stands for 100 million bushels of wheat. The dollar amounts at the left represent the cost of one bushel of wheat.

Strategy: Writing a summary

Write a paragraph to summarize what you learned from the graph.

> During the years from 1927 to 1931, U.S. farmers produced from 824,000 to 942,000 bushels of wheat per year. During the following three years, there was a steep decline in wheat production—from 756,000 bushels in 1932 to 526,000 bushels in 1934. Starting in 1929, wheat prices plunged, reaching a low of less than $0.40 per bushel in 1932. Only when wheat production dropped did prices begin to rise again. The graph suggests that wheat prices fluctuate depending on production, with wheat, like other commodities, bringing lower prices when it is abundant.

APPLYING THE SKILL

Write your own summary Turn to Chapter 7, Section 1, and look at the graph "African-American Population in the United States, 1790–1860." Study the graph and write a paragraph in which you summarize what you learned from it. Tell how the three line graphs work together.

SKILLBUILDER HANDBOOK **1057**

3.6 Using the Internet

The **Internet** is a network of computers associated with universities, libraries, news organizations, government agencies, businesses, and private individuals worldwide. Each location on the Internet has a **home page** with its own address, or **URL.**

With a computer connected to the Internet, you can reach the home pages of many organizations and services. You can then find the call number of a library book, read an article in a periodical, view photographs, and even receive moving pictures and sound.

The international collection of home pages, known as the **World Wide Web**, is a good source of up-to-the minute information about current events as well as in-depth research on historical subjects. This textbook contains many suggestions for navigating the Internet through the World Wide Web. You can begin by entering the Internet address (URL) for McDougal Littell, which is
http://www.mcdougallittell.com

UNDERSTANDING THE SKILL

Strategy: Finding clues on the screen The computer screen below shows the home page of the Library of Congress in Washington, D.C.

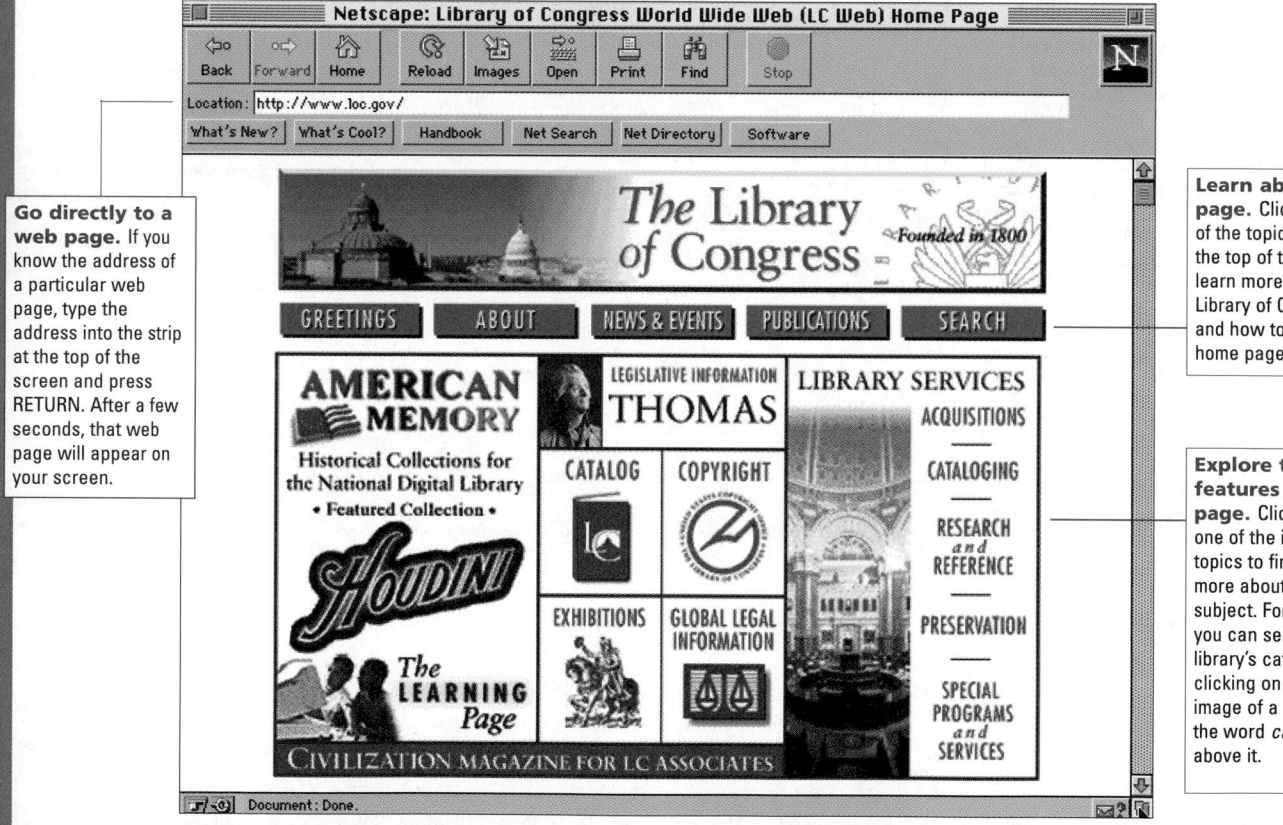

Go directly to a web page. If you know the address of a particular web page, type the address into the strip at the top of the screen and press RETURN. After a few seconds, that web page will appear on your screen.

Learn about the page. Click on one of the topics across the top of the page to learn more about the Library of Congress and how to use the home page.

Explore the features of the page. Click on any one of the images or topics to find out more about a specific subject. For example, you can search the library's catalog by clicking on the red image of a book or the word *catalog* above it.

APPLYING THE SKILL

Do your own Internet research. Turn to Chapter 5, Section 2, "Drafting the Constitution." Read the section, making a list of topics you would like to research. If you have a computer with Internet access, go to the McDougal Littell home page (http://www.mcdougallittell.com) where you will learn more about how to conduct a search.

1058 SKILLBUILDER HANDBOOK

ATLAS

The atlas contains a map of the world and several political, physical, and historical maps of the United States. It also contains a chart of important statistical trends in the history of the United States.

World: Political

ALASKA (U.S.)

NORTH AMERICA

CANADA

UNITED STATES

Hudson Bay

St. Pierre and Miquelon (France)

PACIFIC OCEAN

HAWAII (U.S.)

Gulf of Mexico

BERMUDA (U.K.)

ATLANTIC OCEAN

BAHAMAS

Tropic of Cancer

MEXICO CUBA HAITI
DOMINICAN REP.
BELIZE JAMAICA PUERTO RICO (U.S.)
GUATEMALA Caribbean Sea
EL SALVADOR NICARAGUA
HONDURAS
COSTA RICA VENEZUELA GUYANA
PANAMA SURINAME
COLOMBIA FRENCH GUIANA

North Latitude

0° Latitude

South Latitude

CHRISTMAS ISLAND (Kiribati)

GALAPAGOS IS. (Ecuador) ECUADOR

SOUTH AMERICA

PERU

POLYNESIA

BRAZIL

WESTERN SAMOA

AMERICAN SAMOA (U.S.)

FRENCH POLYNESIA (France)

BOLIVIA

PARAGUAY

EASTER ISLAND (Chile)

CHILE

URUGUAY

ARGENTINA

PACIFIC OCEAN

FALKLAND IS. (U.K.)

Antarctic Circle

Central America and the Caribbean

UNITED STATES OF AMERICA

BAHAMA ISLANDS

Tropic of Cancer

Gulf of Mexico

CUBA

TURKS & CAICOS IS.

ANGUILLA (U.K.)
VIRGIN IS. (U.K.)
VIRGIN IS. (U.S.)

ANTIGUA AND BARBUDA

MEXICO

CAYMAN ISLANDS

HAITI

DOMINICAN REPUBLIC

PUERTO RICO (U.S.)

DOMINICA

JAMAICA

ST. KITTS AND NEVIS
GUADELOUPE (France)
MARTINIQUE (France)
ST. LUCIA
ST. VINCENT AND THE GRENADINES BARBADOS
GRENADA
TRINIDAD AND TOBAGO

BELIZE

GUATEMALA HONDURAS

Caribbean Sea

NETHERLANDS ANTILLES (Netherlands)

PACIFIC OCEAN

EL SALVADOR NICARAGUA

GUYANA

VENEZUELA

0 500 Miles
0 1000 Kilometers

N

COSTA RICA

PANAMA
Panama Canal

COLOMBIA

BRAZIL

ARCTIC OCEAN

SVALBARD (Norway)   FRANZ JOSEF IS. (Russia)

JAN MAYEN (Norway)
GREENLAND
ICELAND
FAEROE IS. (Denmark)
IRELAND
UNITED KINGDOM
Norwegian Sea
North Sea
SWEDEN
FINLAND
RUSSIA

Barents Sea
Kara Sea
Laptev Sea
East Siberian Sea
Arctic Circle

EUROPE
UKRAINE
FRANCE
SPAIN
PORTUGAL
AZORES (Portugal)
ITALY
GREECE
TURKEY
MALTA
Mediterranean Sea
Black Sea
Caspian Sea
Aral Sea

KAZAKHSTAN
TURKMENISTAN
UZBEKISTAN
KYRGYZSTAN
TAJIKISTAN

ASIA
MONGOLIA
N. KOREA
S. KOREA
CHINA
JAPAN
Lake Baikal
Sea of Okhotsk
Sea of Japan

MOROCCO
CANARY IS. (Spain)
WESTERN SAHARA
TUNISIA
ALGERIA
LIBYA
EGYPT
IRAQ
IRAN
AFGHANISTAN
PAKISTAN
NEPAL
BHUTAN
Persian Gulf
SAUDI ARABIA
Arabian Sea

MAURITANIA
CAPE VERDE
SENEGAL
GAMBIA
GUINEA-BISSAU
GUINEA
SIERRA LEONE
LIBERIA
IVORY COAST
MALI
BURKINA FASO
NIGER
CHAD
NIGERIA
BENIN
TOGO
GHANA
AFRICA
SUDAN
ERITREA
YEMEN
DJIBOUTI
ETHIOPIA
SOMALIA
CENTRAL AFRICAN REPUBLIC
CAMEROON
EQUATORIAL GUINEA
GABON
CONGO
RWANDA
ZAIRE
BURUNDI
UGANDA
KENYA
TANZANIA
Equator

OMAN
LACCADIVE IS. (India)
INDIA
BANGLADESH
MYANMAR (BURMA)
LAOS
THAILAND
VIETNAM
CAMBODIA
TAIWAN
East China Sea
Philippine Sea
PHILIPPINES
GUAM (U.S.)
MARSHALL IS.
TRUST TERRITORY OF THE PACIFIC IS. (U.S.)
PALAU
MICRONESIA

Bay of Bengal
ANDAMAN IS. (India)
SRI LANKA
NICOBAR IS. (India)
MALDIVES
South China Sea
BRUNEI
MALAYSIA
SINGAPORE
INDONESIA
KIRIBATI
NAURU
PAPUA NEW GUINEA
SOLOMON ISLANDS
MELANESIA
TUVALU

PACIFIC OCEAN

SEYCHELLES
ASCENSION (U.K.)
ST. HELENA (U.K.)
ANGOLA
ZAMBIA
MALAWI
COMOROS
BRITISH INDIAN OCEAN TERR. (U.K.)
INDIAN OCEAN
VANUATU
FIJI
NEW CALEDONIA (France)

NAMIBIA
BOTSWANA
ZIMBABWE
MOZAMBIQUE
SWAZILAND
SOUTH AFRICA
LESOTHO
MADAGASCAR
MAURITIUS
REUNION (France)
Tropic of Capricorn
AUSTRALIA
PACIFIC OCEAN

ATLANTIC OCEAN
MARION IS. (South Africa)
KERGUELEN IS. (France)
0   2000 Miles
0   4000 Kilometers
N

SOUTH GEORGIA (U.K.)
West Longitude   Prime Meridian   East Longitude
Antarctic Circle

ANTARCTICA

Europe

ATLANTIC OCEAN
IRELAND
NORWAY
SWEDEN
FINLAND
ESTONIA
LATVIA
LITHUANIA
RUSSIA
North Sea
DENMARK
UNITED KINGDOM
NETHERLANDS
BELGIUM
LUXEMBOURG
GERMANY
POLAND
BELARUS
CZECH REPUBLIC
SLOVAK REPUBLIC
UKRAINE
LIECHTENSTEIN
SWITZERLAND
AUSTRIA
HUNGARY
MOLDOVA
ANDORRA
FRANCE
SLOVENIA
CROATIA
ROMANIA
BOSNIA-HERZEGOVINA
MONACO
SAN-MARINO
ITALY
YUGOSLAVIA
BULGARIA
MACEDONIA
TURKEY
SPAIN
PORTUGAL
VATICAN CITY
ALBANIA
GREECE
MOROCCO
ALGERIA
TUNISIA
MALTA
Mediterranean Sea
CYPRUS
Black Sea
0   200 Miles
0   500 Kilometers
N

Middle East

RUSSIA
KAZAKHSTAN
Black Sea
BULGARIA
MACEDONIA
GREECE
ALBANIA
TURKEY
GEORGIA
ARMENIA
AZERBAIJAN
Caspian Sea
UZBEKISTAN
TURKMENISTAN
CYPRUS
SYRIA
LEBANON
West Bank
ISRAEL
JORDAN
IRAQ
IRAN
AFGHANISTAN
PAKISTAN
Mediterranean Sea
LIBYA
EGYPT
KUWAIT
BAHRAIN
SAUDI ARABIA
QATAR
U.A.E.
Persian Gulf
Red Sea
CHAD
SUDAN
OMAN
ETHIOPIA
DJIBOUTI
ERITREA
YEMEN
SOMALIA
Arabian Sea
0   500 Miles
0   1000 Kilometers
N

United States: Political

Strait of
Juan de Fuca

• Seattle

Olympia ⊚ WASHINGTON

45°N

Portland ⊚

Salem

OREGON

Upper Klamath
Lake

Goose Lake

40°N

125°W

Pyramid Lake

Lake Tahoe

Sacramento ⊚

• San Francisco
• San Jose

CALIFORNIA

35°N

Las Vegas •

120°W

Los Angeles •

Salton
Sea

San Diego •

PACIFIC
OCEAN

F.D.
Roosevelt
Lake

Columbia River

Flathead
Lake

Helena ⊚

Boise ⊚

Snake River

IDAHO

Carson City ⊚

NEVADA

Great
Salt
Lake

Salt Lake City

UTAH

Lake
Mead

ARIZONA

Colorado River

Gila R.

Phoenix

115°W

Missouri River

Fort Peck Lake

MONTANA

Yellowstone River

WYOMING

N. Platte River

Cheyenne ⊚

Denver ⊚

COLORADO

Albuquerque •

• Santa Fe

NEW MEXICO

Gila R. • Phoenix

South Saskatchewan R.

Lake
Winnipegosis Lake
Winnipeg

Lake
Manitoba

Lake of
the Woods

Upper Red Lake

Lake
Sakakawea

NORTH DAKOTA

• Bismarck

Lower
Red Lake

MINNESOTA

Lake
Oahe

⊙ Pierre

SOUTH DAKOTA

Minneapoli

S. Platte River

S. Platte River

Arkansas River

NEBRASKA

Omaha •

Lincoln ⊚

Kansas City
⊚
Topeka

KANSAS

• Wichita

Canadian River

OKLAHOMA

Oklahoma City

Arka

Des Mo

Missouri River

IO

Des Mo

Lake
Texoma   Red River

El Paso •

Pecos River

Ft. Worth • • Dallas

TEXAS

Brazos River

Austin ⊚

San Antonio •

Rio Grande

• Hous

110°W

30°N

MEXICO

105°W

96

Kauai
Channel

PACIFIC   ⊚ Honolulu
OCEAN HAWAII   Alenuihaha
Channel

20°N

160°W

0   100 Miles

0   200 Kilometers

155°W

ARCTIC   • Barrow
OCEAN

Bering
Strait

RUSSIA

170°E

Norton
Sound

ALASKA

60°N

Bering Sea

Iliamna
Lake

0   500 Miles

0 55°N   1000 Kilometers

180°

Bristol
Bay

Tanana River

Fairbanks

Yukon River

Arctic Circle

65°N

Anchorage •

Prince
William
Sound

Juneau ⊚

CANADA

Shelikof
Strait

Gulf of Alaska

170°W

160°W

150°W

140°W

50°N

James Bay

Lake Mistassini

Gulf of St. Lawrence

45°N

Lake Nipigon

Lake St. John

Gouin Reservoir

Cabonga Reservoir

St. Lawrence R.

MAINE

Bay of Fundy

Lake Superior

CANADA

Ottawa R.

Lake Nipissing

Augusta

Montpelier

40°N

Georgian Bay

Lake Simcoe

Lake Champlain

NEW HAMPSHIRE

Concord

Connecticut R.

WISCONSIN

Lake Winnebago

MICHIGAN

Lansing

Lake Michigan

Lake Huron

Lake Ontario

Lake St. Clair

Lake Erie

Buffalo

VERMONT

NEW YORK

Albany

Hudson R.

Boston

MASSACHUSETTS

RHODE ISLAND

CONNECTICUT

Hartford

LONG ISLAND

Madison

Milwaukee

Detroit

Toledo

Cleveland

PENNSYLVANIA

Harrisburg

Susquehanna R.

New York

Trenton

Philadelphia

NEW JERSEY

Chicago

Mississippi River

ILLINOIS

INDIANA

Indianapolis

OHIO

Columbus

Cincinnati

Pittsburgh

Ohio River

WEST VIRGINIA

Charleston

Kanawha R.

Dover

Baltimore

Washington D.C.

Delaware Bay

DELAWARE

MARYLAND

35°N

Springfield

St. Louis

erson

Frankfort

KENTUCKY

Cumberland River

Richmond

VIRGINIA

Chesapeake Bay

MISSOURI

Nashville

TENNESSEE

Knoxville

Tennessee River

Raleigh

Winston-Salem

NORTH CAROLINA

Pamlico Sound

BERMUDA

ATLANTIC OCEAN

NSAS

Rock

Memphis

Alabama River

Birmingham

Atlanta

SOUTH CAROLINA

Columbia

30°N

MISSISSIPPI

ALABAMA

Montgomery

GEORGIA

Savannah River

International boundary

State boundary

⊛ National capital

⊙ State capital

SIANA

Jackson

Jacksonville

N

ton Rouge

New Orleans

Lake ntchartrain

Breton Sound

Tallahassee

FLORIDA

Tampa

St. Petersburg

Lake Okeechobee

BAHAMAS

0   500 Miles

0   1000 Kilometers

25°N

90°W

Gulf of Mexico

Straits of Florida

Miami

ATLANTIC OCEAN

San Juan

PUERTO RICO   ● Caguas

Ponce

0   100 Miles

0   1000 Kilometers

Caribbean Sea

85°W

80°W

CUBA

75°W

70°W

United States: Physical

VANCOUVER ISLAND
Vancouver
BRITISH COLUMBIA
Calgary
ALBERTA
Lake Winnipeg
MANITOBA
Lake Manitoba
LEWIS RANGE
South Saskat.
Assiniboine River
Regina
SASKATCHEWAN
Milk River
Winnipeg
Lake the W

Puget Sound
Seattle
Tacoma
Olympia
Cape Disappointment
Mt. Rainier 4392 m. 14410 ft.
Spokane
F.D. Roosevelt Lake
Lake Pend Oreille
Flathead Lake
R O C K Y
Missouri River
Lake the W

45 N
Portland
Salem
WASHINGTON
Columbia River
BITTERROOT RANGE
MONTANA
Helena
Fort Peck Lake
NORTH DAKOTA
Bismarck
MINNES
Red River
Lo Red

OREGON
Willamette R.
COLUMBIA PLATEAU
IDAHO
SALMON RIVER MTNS.
Borah Peak 3859 m. 12662 ft.
Boise
SNAKE RIVER PLAIN
Snake River
Yellowstone River
ABSAROKA RANGE
BIGHORN MTNS.
Bighorn R.
Lake Sakakawea
Lake Oahe
James River

KLAMATH MTNS.
Cape Mendocino
Goose Lake
Mt. Shasta 4316 m. 14162 ft.
Upper Klamath Lake
M O U N T A I N S
Gannet Peak 4201 m. 13785 ft.
BLACK HILLS
BADLANDS
Pierre
SOUTH DAKOTA

COASTAL RANGES
Sacramento R.
Pyramid Lake
GREAT
WASATCH RANGE
Great Salt Lake
WYOMING
G R E A T
SAND HILLS
A

Sacramento
Carson City
Lake Tahoe
NEVADA
BASIN
Salt Lake City
UINTA MTNS.
Green River
Colorado R.
FRONT RANGE
Cheyenne
N. Platte River
NEBRASKA
S. Platte River
Platte River
Omaha
Missouri Ri
Lincoln

San Francisco
Oakland
SIERRA NEVADA
UTAH
Mt. Elbert 4399 m. 14433 ft.
Denver
Republican River
CALIFORNIA
San Joaquin R.
Mt. Whitney 4418 m. 14494 ft.
Death Valley –89 m. –282 ft.
Lake Powell
COLORADO PLATEAU
COLORADO
SANGRE DE CRISTO MTNS.
SAN JUAN MTNS.
Smoky Hill River
Kansas R.
Topeka
KANSAS
Wichita
UNITE

Pt. Arguello
Point Conception
Las Vegas
Lake Mead
GRAND CANYON
Arkansas River

SANTA CRUZ I.
MOJAVE DESERT
Colorado River
SANTA ROSA I.
Los Angeles
Long Beach
Humphrey's Peak 3850 m. 12633 ft.
P

SANTA CATALINA I.
SAN CLEMENTE I.
Salton Sea
ARIZONA
Albuquerque
Santa Fe
Canadian River
OKLAHOMA
Tuls.

San Diego
Gila R.
Phoenix
NEW MEXICO
SACRAMENTO MTNS.
Pecos River
Oklahoma City
Lake Eufala
QUACHI MTNS.
Red River

PACIFIC OCEAN
Gulf of California
Tucson
El Paso
LLANO ESTACADO
Ft. Worth
Dallas
Sabine

30 N 120 W
EDWARDS PLATEAU
TEXAS
Colorado River
Brazos River

PACIFIC OCEAN
KAUAI
NIIHAU
Kauai Channel
OAHU
Honolulu
MOLOKAI
HAWAII
LANAI
MAUI
Mauna Kea 4205 m. 13796 ft.
155 W
ARCTIC OCEAN
Chukchi Sea
Barrow
Beaufort Sea

RUSSIA
Kotzebue Sound
BROOKS RANGE
Prudhoe Bay
ALASKA (U.S.)
25 N
Austin
Houston

160 W
20 N
0 50 Miles
0 100 Kilometers HAWAII
International Dateline
Bering Strait
SEWARD PENINSULA
Norton Sound
Yukon R.
Fairbanks
Tanana R.
San Antonio

ST. LAWRENCE I.
Cape Romanzof
NUNIVAK I.
KUSKOKWIM MOUNTAINS
ALASKA RANGE
Mt. McKinley 6193 m. / 20320 ft.
Anchorage
YUKON
CANADA
Mt. Logan 6050 m. 19850 ft.
Corpus Christi
COASTAL

ATTU I.
Bering Sea
Illiamna Lake
Bristol Bay
PRIBILOF IS.
Prince William Sound
BR. COL.
MEXICO
PADRE ISLAND

7822 m. 25662 ft.
0 100 Miles
0 200 Kilometers
KISKA I.
ALEUTIAN ISLANDS
ALASKA PENINSULA
Shelikof Strait
KODIAK I.
Gulf of Alaska
Juneau
COAST MTNS.
ALEXANDER ARCHIPELAGO
150 W
140 W
95 W

180
170 W
Aleutian Trench
160 W
PACIFIC OCEAN
50 N

CANADA

HUDSON BAY LOWLANDS

ONTARIO

James Bay

Lake Mistassini

Lake St. John

LAURENTIAN HIGHLANDS

QUEBEC

Gouin Reservoir

Lake Abitibi

Cabonga Reservoir

Harricanaw River

LAURENTIDE SCARP

NOTRE DAME MTNS.

Cape Gaspé   NEWFOUNDLAND

CAPE PENINSULA

Gulf of St. Lawrence

MAGDALEN IS.

Cabot Strait

PRINCE EDWARD ISLAND

Charlottetown ⊙

NEW BRUNSWICK

● Fredericton

● Halifax

NOVA SCOTIA

Lake Nipigon

ISLE ROYALE

Lake Superior

MESABI RANGE

Saguenay R.

St. Maurice R.

● Quebec

St. Lawrence R.

LAURENTIAN SCARP

Ottawa R.

● Montreal

Lake Nipissing

Ottawa ⊛

MAINE

Cape Sable

Bay of Fundy

WISCONSIN

Minneapolis
St. Paul

Mississippi River

Wisconsin R.

MICHIGAN

Lake Michigan

Lake Huron

MANITOULIN I.

Lake Simcoe

Toronto ●

Hamilton ●

Lake Ontario

Lake Erie

Lake St. Clair

London ●

Buffalo ●

Rochester ●

Syracuse ●

ADIRONDACK MTNS.

Lake Champlain

VERMONT

Montpelier ⊙

Albany ⊙

Worcester ●

+ Mt. Washington
1985 m.
6288 ft.

Augusta ⊙

Concord ⊙

NEW HAMPSHIRE

MASSACHUSETTS

Boston ⊙

Cape Cod

NEW YORK

Springfield ●

Hartford ⊙

Providence ⊙

Nantucket Island

MARTHA'S VINEYARD

RHODE ISLAND

Madison ● Milwaukee ●

Lansing ● Flint ●

Grand Rapids ●

Detroit ● Windsor ●

New Haven ●

CONNECTICUT

IOWA

Des Moines

Chicago ●

Toledo ●

Cleveland ●

Akron ●

PENNSYLVANIA

Harrisburg ●

LONG ISLAND

New York ●

NEW JERSEY

Hudson River

CENTRAL

ILLINOIS

Springfield ⊙

INDIANA

Indianapolis ⊙

OHIO

Columbus ⊙

Dayton ●

Cincinnati ●

Pittsburgh ●

WEST VIRGINIA

Ohio River

Trenton ⊙

Philadelphia ●

Wilmington ●

Dover ⊙

Susquehanna R.

Cape May

Delaware Bay

ATLANTIC OCEAN

MISSOURI

Jefferson City ⊙

St. Louis ●

LOWLAND

Louisville ●

Frankfort ⊙

Charleston ⊙

VIRGINIA

James R.

Richmond ⊙

Baltimore ●

Annapolis ⊙

Washington ⊛

DELAWARE

MARYLAND

Chesapeake Bay

Cape Charles

BERMUDA

STATES

Wabash River

KENTUCKY

Cumberland River

CUMBERLAND PLATEAU

APPALACHIAN MOUNTAINS

Norfolk ●

Roanoke River

35°N

OZARK PLATEAU

ARKANSAS

Little Rock ●

Arkansas River

Memphis ●

Nashville ●

Knoxville ●

Chattanooga ●

Tennessee River

Tennessee R.

BLUE RIDGE MTNS.

Mt. Mitchell
2037 m.
6684 ft.

Charlotte ●

Raleigh ⊙

NORTH CAROLINA

HATTERAS ISLAND

Pamlico Sound

Cape Hatteras

COASTAL PLAIN

SOUTH CAROLINA

Columbia ⊙

Pee Dee River

Savannah River

Land Elevation
▮ Higher than 16,000 ft.
▮ 8,000 ft. to 16,000 ft.
▮ 4,000 ft. to 8,000 ft.
▮ 2,000 ft. to 4,000 ft.
▮ 1,000 ft. to 2,000 ft.
▮ 0 ft. to 1,000 ft.
▮ Below sea level

Water Depth
▮ 0 ft. to 700 ft.
▮ 700 ft. to 9,800 ft.
▮ 9,800 ft. to 19,700 ft.
▮ Deeper than 19,700 ft.
━━ International boundary
━━ State boundary
⊛ National capital
⊙ State capital
+ Heights and depths

TENNESSEE

MISSISSIPPI

Jackson ⊙

ALABAMA

Birmingham ●

Montgomery ⊙

Tombigbee R.

Chattahoochee R.

Alabama R.

GEORGIA

Atlanta ●

Savannah ●

Charleston ●

Charleston ●

30°N

N

0   500 Miles

0   1000 Kilometers

LOUISIANA

Baton Rouge ●

Lafayette ●

New Orleans ●

Mississippi River

Mobile ●

Tallahassee ⊙

Cape San Blas

Lake Pontchartrain

Breton Sound

FLORIDA

Jacksonville ●

Cape Canaveral

Gulf of Mexico

St. Petersburg ● Tampa ●

Lake Okeechobee

25°N

CUBA

Miami ●

Cape Sable

FLORIDA KEYS

Straits of Florida

Nassau ⊛

BAHAMAS

PUERTO RICO

San Juan ⊛

Ponce ●   Caguas ●

0   100 Miles

0   1000 Kilometers

18°N

68°W

85°W

80°W

75°W

70°W

90°W

65°W

40°N

U.S. Dependencies and Areas of Special Sovereignty

American Samoa

PACIFIC OCEAN

TUTUILA I.
Pago Pago
AUNUU I.
OLOSEGA I.
OFU I.
TAU I.
AMERICAN SAMOA
MANUA ISLANDS

0 50 Miles
0 100 Kilometers

Puerto Rico and U.S. Virgin Islands

ATLANTIC OCEAN

BRITISH VIRGIN ISLANDS

Arecibo
San Juan
ST. THOMAS
CULEBRA
Charlotte Amalie
ST. JOHN
PUERTO RICO
Mayagüez
Caguas
VIEQUES
U.S. VIRGIN ISLANDS
Ponce
Frederiksted
ST. CROIX
Caribbean Sea

0 50 Miles
0 100 Kilometers

Guam

Philippine Sea

Agana
Tamuning
GUAM
PACIFIC OCEAN

0 6 Miles
0 12 Kilometers

Major Pacific Island Groups

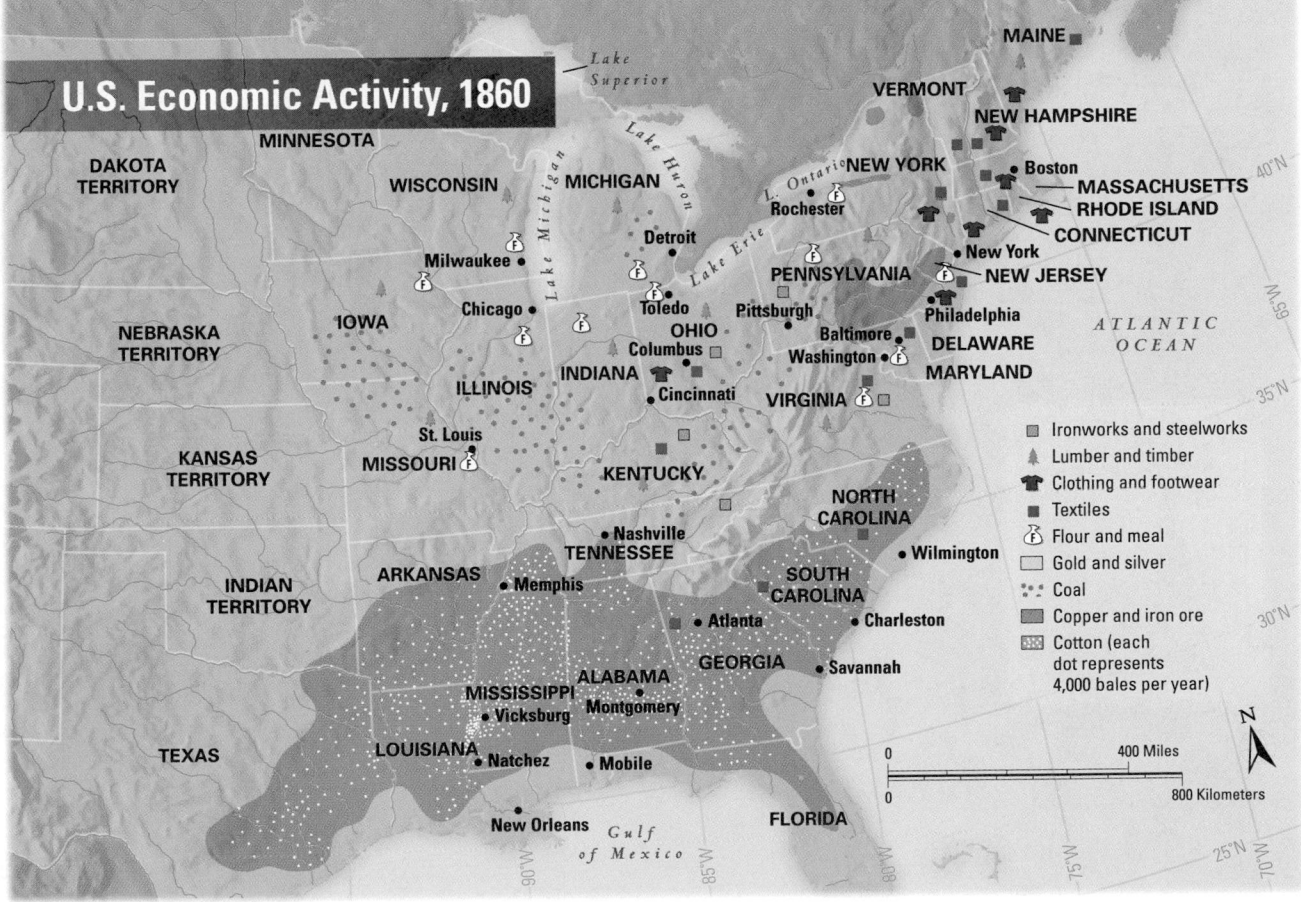

U.S. Economic Activity, 1770

NEW HAMPSHIRE
• Portsmouth
Salem
NEW YORK • Boston MASSACHUSETTS
RHODE ISLAND
CONNECTICUT
• New York
PENNSYLVANIA NEW JERSEY
Valley Forge • • Philadelphia
Baltimore • DELAWARE
MARYLAND
VIRGINIA
• Jamestown
• Norfolk
NORTH
CAROLINA
• Wilmington
SOUTH
CAROLINA
• Charleston
GEORGIA • Savannah

Lake Superior
Lake Huron
L. Ontario
Lake Michigan
Lake Erie
ATLANTIC OCEAN
Gulf of Mexico

40°N
35°N
30°N
25°N
85°W
80°W
75°W
70°W

□ Ironworks
■ Shipbuilding
■ Whaling provisions
□ Naval stores
● Wheat
● Tobacco
● Indigo
○ Rice

0 ___ 400 Miles
0 ___ 800 Kilometers
N

U.S. Economic Activity, 1860

MAINE
VERMONT
NEW HAMPSHIRE
DAKOTA TERRITORY
MINNESOTA
WISCONSIN MICHIGAN
NEW YORK
Boston
MASSACHUSETTS
RHODE ISLAND
CONNECTICUT
Rochester
Milwaukee •
Detroit •
NEW JERSEY
• New York
NEBRASKA TERRITORY
IOWA
Chicago •
Toledo •
PENNSYLVANIA
Pittsburgh •
Columbus
OHIO
Philadelphia
INDIANA
Baltimore •
DELAWARE
Washington •
MARYLAND
ILLINOIS
• Cincinnati
VIRGINIA
St. Louis •
KANSAS TERRITORY
MISSOURI
KENTUCKY
NORTH CAROLINA
• Nashville
TENNESSEE
• Wilmington
INDIAN TERRITORY
ARKANSAS
• Memphis
SOUTH CAROLINA
• Atlanta
• Charleston
GEORGIA
• Savannah
MISSISSIPPI
ALABAMA
• Vicksburg
Montgomery
TEXAS
LOUISIANA
• Natchez
• Mobile
New Orleans
FLORIDA

Lake Superior
Lake Huron
L. Ontario
Lake Michigan
Lake Erie
ATLANTIC OCEAN
Gulf of Mexico

40°N
35°N
30°N
25°N
90°W
85°W
80°W
75°W
70°W

■ Ironworks and steelworks
▲ Lumber and timber
Clothing and footwear
■ Textiles
Flour and meal
□ Gold and silver
Coal
Copper and iron ore
Cotton (each dot represents 4,000 bales per year)

0 ___ 400 Miles
0 ___ 800 Kilometers
N

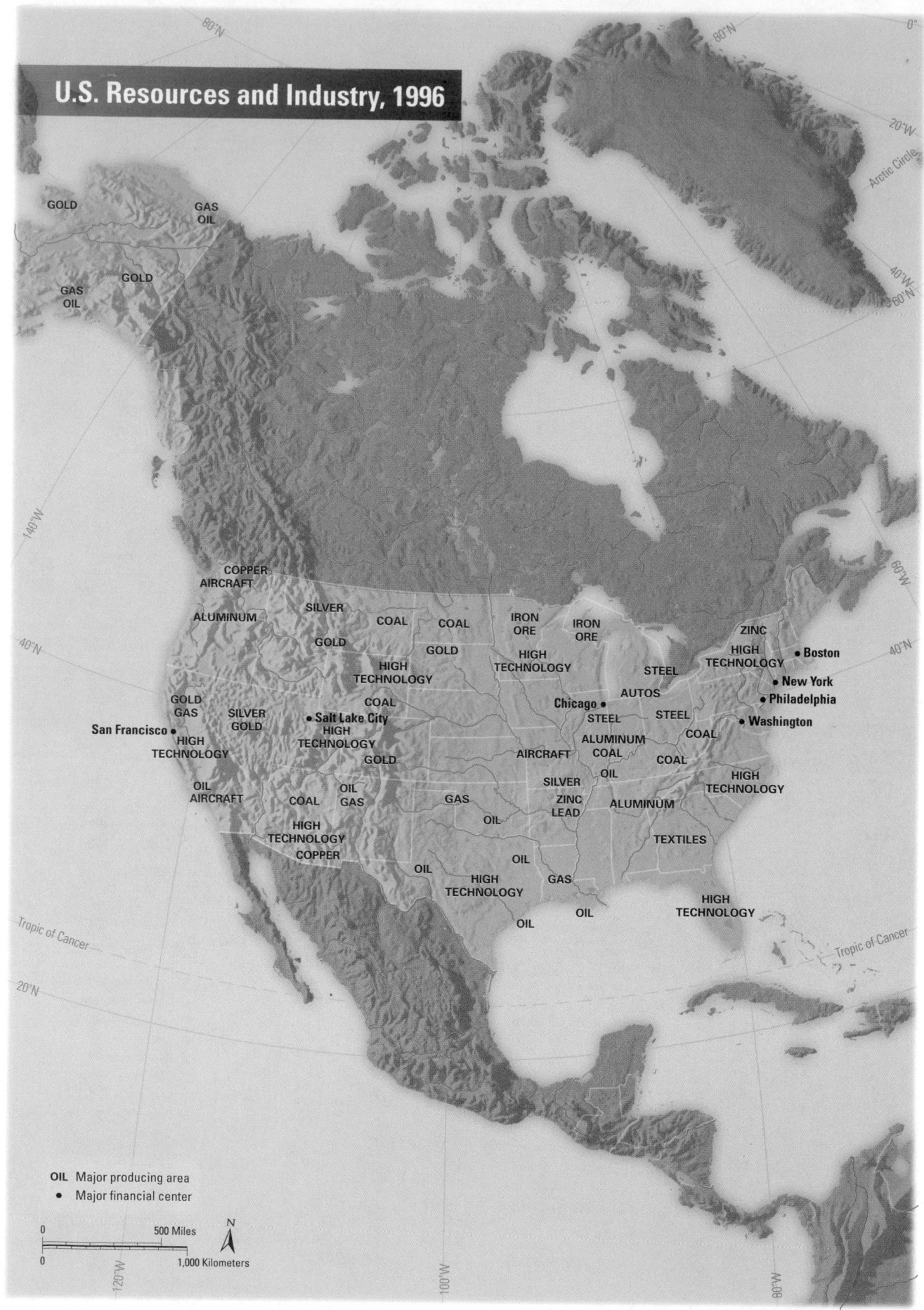

U.S. Resources and Industry, 1996

GOLD

GAS
OIL

GAS
OIL

GOLD

COPPER
AIRCRAFT

ALUMINUM

SILVER

GOLD

COAL

COAL

IRON
ORE

IRON
ORE

ZINC

HIGH
TECHNOLOGY

● Boston

GOLD

HIGH
TECHNOLOGY

HIGH
TECHNOLOGY

STEEL

● New York

AUTOS

● Philadelphia

GOLD
GAS

SILVER
GOLD

● Salt Lake City

COAL

Chicago ●

STEEL

STEEL

COAL

● Washington

San Francisco ●

HIGH
TECHNOLOGY

HIGH
TECHNOLOGY

ALUMINUM
COAL

COAL

GOLD

AIRCRAFT

OIL

HIGH
TECHNOLOGY

OIL
AIRCRAFT

COAL

OIL
GAS

GAS

SILVER

ZINC
LEAD

ALUMINUM

HIGH
TECHNOLOGY
COPPER

OIL

OIL

TEXTILES

OIL

HIGH
TECHNOLOGY

GAS

HIGH
TECHNOLOGY

OIL

OIL

OIL Major producing area

● Major financial center

0   500 Miles

0   1,000 Kilometers

N

1068 ATLAS

Trends for the United States

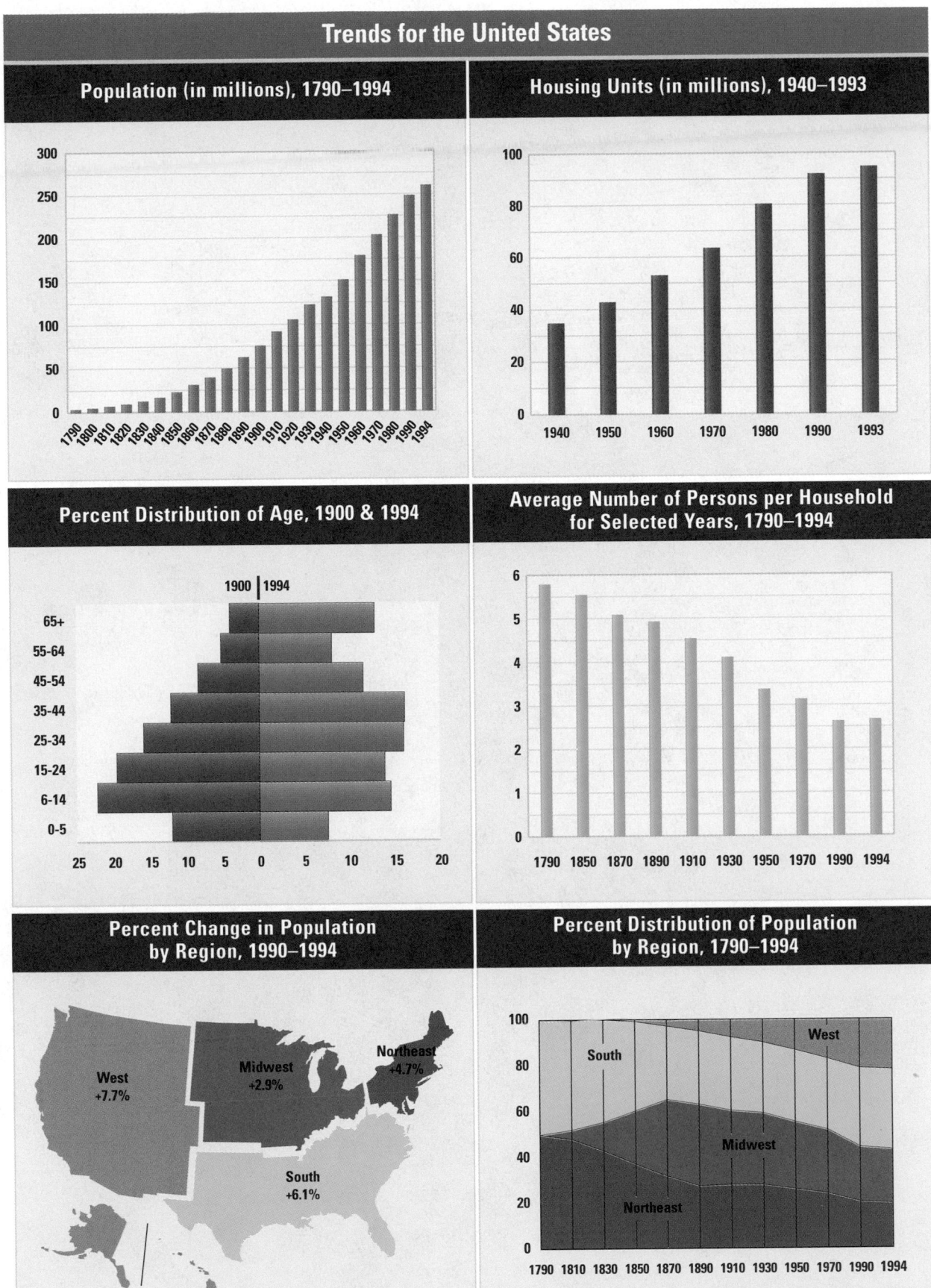

Population (in millions), 1790–1994

Housing Units (in millions), 1940–1993

Percent Distribution of Age, 1900 & 1994

1900 | 1994

65+
55-64
45-54
35-44
25-34
15-24
6-14
0-5

25 20 15 10 5 0 5 10 15 20

Average Number of Persons per Household for Selected Years, 1790–1994

1790 1850 1870 1890 1910 1930 1950 1970 1990 1994

Percent Change in Population by Region, 1990–1994

West +7.7%

Midwest +2.9%

Northeast +4.7%

South +6.1%

Percent Distribution of Population by Region, 1790–1994

South

West

Midwest

Northeast

1790 1810 1830 1850 1870 1890 1910 1930 1950 1970 1990 1994

Sources: *Historical Statistics of the United States: Colonial Times to 1970; Statistical Abstract of the United States, 1995; American Housing Survey, 1993*, U.S. Census Bureau; George Thomas Kurian, *Datapedia of the United States: 1790–2000*.

ATLAS **1069**

U.S. Territorial Growth: Land Acquisition by Year

Strait of Juan de Fuca

Line of Treaty of 1846 with Great Britain

Boundary adjusted by Convention of 1818 with Great Britain

Lake of the Woods

From Great Britain, 1818

WASHINGTON

Joint occupation by United States and Great Britain 1818–1846 (Claim abandoned by Russia, 1824)

45°N

Columbia River

OREGON TERRITORY
From Great Britain, 1846

OREGON

IDAHO

Snake River

MONTANA

Yellowstone River

NORTH DAKOTA

MINNESOT

SOUTH DAKOTA

WYOMING

40°N

125°W

Line of Adams-Onís Treaty with Spain, 1819

Great Salt Lake

N. Platte River

S. Platte River

NEBRASKA

LOUISIANA PURCHASE
From France, 1803

Missouri River

NEVADA

UTAH

MEXICAN CESSION
From Mexico by Treaty of Guadalupe Hidalgo, 1848

COLORADO

KANSAS

CALIFORNIA

35°N

Arkansas River

Colorado River

ARIZONA

Gila R.

Line of Treaty of Guadalupe Hidalgo with Mexico, 1848

NEW MEXICO

Canadian River

OKLAHOMA

Pecos River

Claimed by Texas and ceded by Mexico, 1848

Red River

120°W

PACIFIC OCEAN

GADSDEN PURCHASE
From Mexico, 1853

Brazos River

TEXAS

TEXAS ANNEXAT
Independent Republi
Annexed, 1845

KAUAI

NIIHAU

OAHU   MOLOKAI

ARCTIC OCEAN

LANAI   MAUI

HAWAII
Annexed, 1898

0   100 Miles

20°N

HAWAII

Bering Strait

MEXICO

Rio Grande

160°W

0   200 Kilometers

Yukon River

Tanana River

RUSSIA

CANADA

155°W

ALASKA
From Russia, 1867

60°N

Bering Sea

N

0   500 Miles

0   1000 Kilometers

55°N

Gulf of Alaska

180°

170°W

160°W

150°W

140°W

50°N

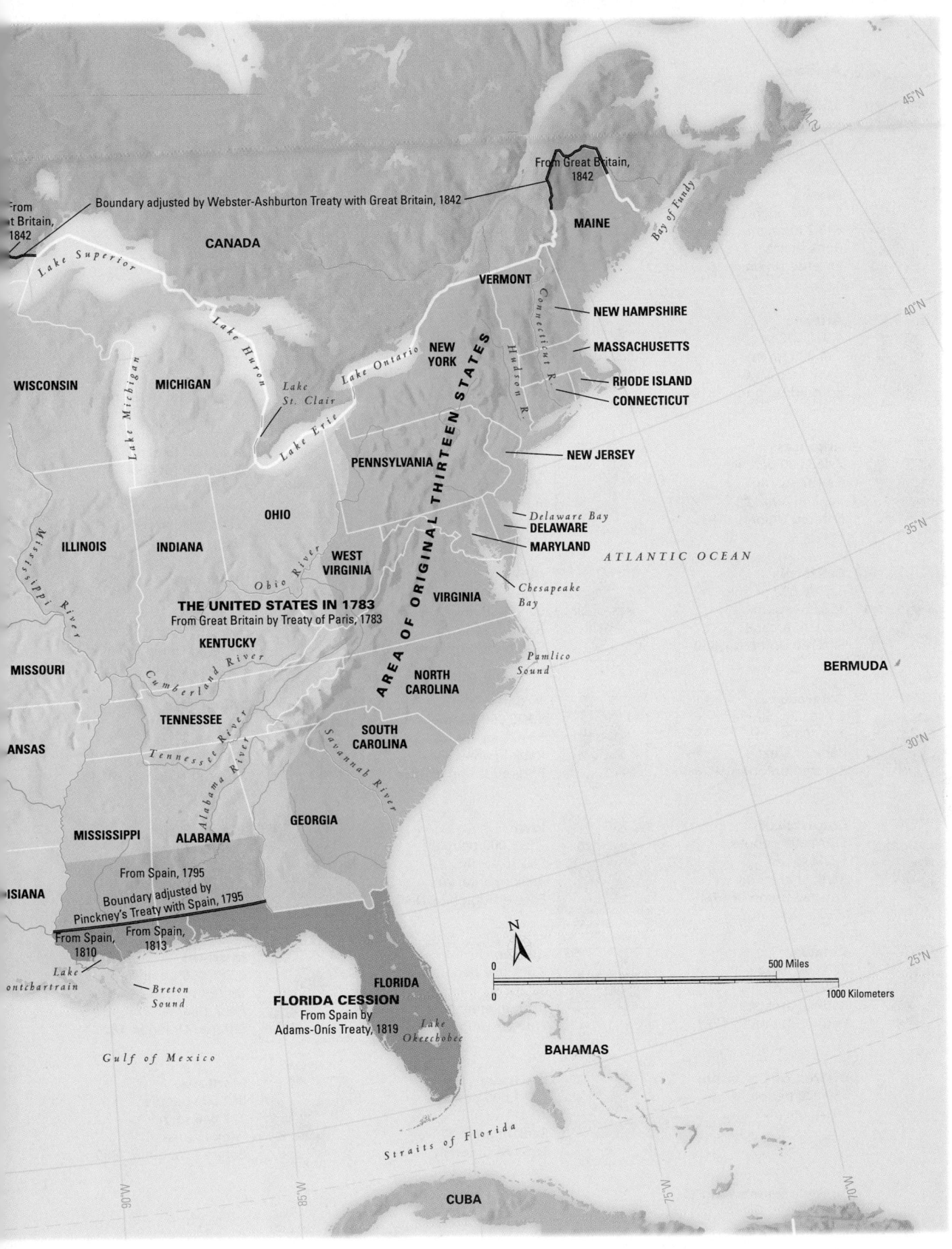

From
Great Britain,
1842

Boundary adjusted by Webster-Ashburton Treaty with Great Britain, 1842

From Great Britain,
1842

CANADA

MAINE

Bay of Fundy

Lake Superior

VERMONT

NEW HAMPSHIRE

Connecticut R.

MASSACHUSETTS

Lake Huron

Lake Ontario

NEW YORK

Hudson R.

RHODE ISLAND

CONNECTICUT

WISCONSIN

MICHIGAN

Lake Michigan

Lake St. Clair

Lake Erie

A R E A   O F   O R I G I N A L   T H I R T E E N   S T A T E S

PENNSYLVANIA

NEW JERSEY

OHIO

Delaware Bay

DELAWARE

ILLINOIS

INDIANA

WEST VIRGINIA

MARYLAND

ATLANTIC OCEAN

Ohio River

VIRGINIA

Chesapeake Bay

Mississippi River

THE UNITED STATES IN 1783
From Great Britain by Treaty of Paris, 1783

KENTUCKY

Pamlico Sound

MISSOURI

Cumberland River

NORTH CAROLINA

BERMUDA

TENNESSEE

SOUTH CAROLINA

ANSAS

Tennessee River

Alabama River

Savannah River

GEORGIA

MISSISSIPPI

ALABAMA

From Spain, 1795

ISIANA

Boundary adjusted by
Pinckney's Treaty with Spain, 1795

From Spain,
1810

From Spain,
1813

N

Lake Pontchartrain

Breton Sound

FLORIDA

FLORIDA CESSION
From Spain by
Adams-Onís Treaty, 1819

Lake Okeechobee

BAHAMAS

0   500 Miles

0   1000 Kilometers

Gulf of Mexico

Straits of Florida

CUBA

45°N

40°N

35°N

30°N

25°N

90°W

85°W

75°W

70°W

FACTS ABOUT THE STATES

Alabama
4,724,000 people
52,237 sq. mi.
Rank in area: 30
Entered Union in 1819

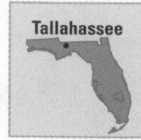

Florida
14,210,000 people
59,988 sq. mi.
Rank in area: 23
Entered Union in 1845

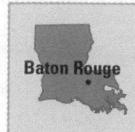

Louisiana
4,359,000 people
49,650 sq. mi.
Rank in area: 31
Entered Union in 1812

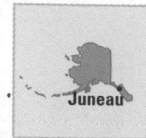

Alaska
634,000 people
615,230 sq. mi.
Rank in area: 1
Entered Union in 1959

Georgia
7,102,000 people
58,977 sq. mi.
Rank in area: 24
Entered Union in 1788

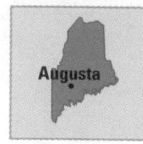

Maine
1,236,000 people
33,741 sq. mi.
Rank in area: 39
Entered Union in 1820

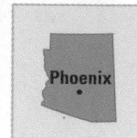

Arizona
4,072,000 people
114,006 sq. mi.
Rank in area: 6
Entered Union in 1912

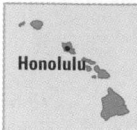

Hawaii
1,221,000 people
6,459 sq. mi.
Rank in area: 47
Entered Union in 1959

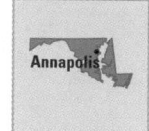

Maryland
5,078,000 people
12,297 sq. mi.
Rank in area: 42
Entered Union in 1788

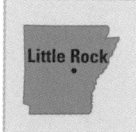

Arkansas
2,468,000 people
53,182 sq. mi.
Rank in area: 28
Entered Union in 1836

Idaho
1,156,000 people
83,574 sq. mi.
Rank in area: 14
Entered Union in 1890

Massachusetts
5,976,000 people
9,241 sq. mi.
Rank in area: 45
Entered Union in 1788

California
32,398,000 people
158,869 sq. mi.
Rank in area: 3
Entered Union in 1850

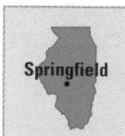

Illinois
11,853,000 people
57,918 sq. mi.
Rank in area: 25
Entered Union in 1818

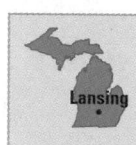

Michigan
9,575,000 people
96,705 sq. mi.
Rank in area: 11
Entered Union in 1837

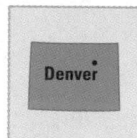

Colorado
3,710,000 people
104,100 sq. mi.
Rank in area: 8
Entered Union in 1876

Indiana
5,820,000 people
36,420 sq. mi.
Rank in area: 38
Entered Union in 1816

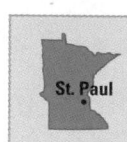

Minnesota
4,619,000 people
86,943 sq. mi.
Rank in area: 12
Entered Union in 1858

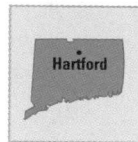

Connecticut
3,274,000 people
5,544 sq. mi.
Rank in area: 48
Entered Union in 1788

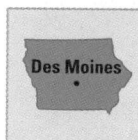

Iowa
2,861,000 people
56,276 sq. mi.
Rank in area: 26
Entered Union in 1846

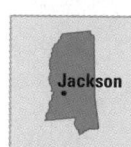

Mississippi
2,666,000 people
48,286 sq. mi.
Rank in area: 32
Entered Union in 1817

Delaware
718,000 people
2,397 sq. mi.
Rank in area: 49
Entered Union in 1787

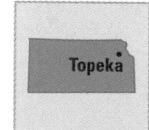

Kansas
2,601,000 people
82,282 sq. mi.
Rank in area: 15
Entered Union in 1861

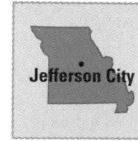

Missouri
5,286,000 people
69,709 sq. mi.
Rank in area: 21
Entered Union in 1821

District of Columbia
559,000 people
68 sq. mi.

Kentucky
3,851,000 people
40,411 sq. mi.
Rank in area: 37
Entered Union in 1792

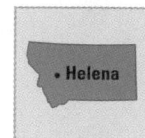

Montana
862,000 people
147,046 sq. mi.
Rank in area: 4
Entered Union in 1889

Population figures are for 1995.

1072 FACTS ABOUT THE STATES

Nebraska
1,644,000 people
77,359 sq. mi.
Rank in area: 16
Entered Union in 1867

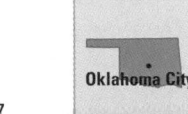
Oklahoma
3,271,000 people
69,903 sq. mi.
Rank in area: 20
Entered Union in 1907

Vermont
579,000 people
9,615 sq. mi.
Rank in area: 43
Entered Union in 1791

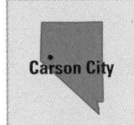
Nevada
1,477,000 people
110,567 sq. mi.
Rank in area: 7
Entered Union in 1864

Oregon
3,141,000 people
97,093 sq. mi.
Rank in area: 10
Entered Union in 1859

Virginia
6,646,000 people
42,326 sq. mi.
Rank in area: 35
Entered Union in 1788

New Hampshire
1,132,000 people
9,283 sq. mi.
Rank in area: 44
Entered Union in 1788

Pennsylvania
12,134,000 people
45,759 sq. mi.
Rank in area: 33
Entered Union in 1787

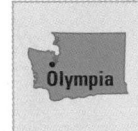
Washington
5,497,000 people
70,637 sq. mi.
Rank in area: 19
Entered Union in 1889

New Jersey
7,931,000 people
8,215 sq. mi.
Rank in area: 46
Entered Union in 1787

Rhode Island
1,001,000 people
1,231 sq. mi.
Rank in area: 50
Entered Union in 1790

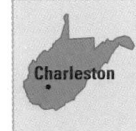
West Virginia
1,824,000 people
24,232 sq. mi.
Rank in area: 41
Entered Union in 1863

New Mexico
1,676,000 people
121,598 sq. mi.
Rank in area: 5
Entered Union in 1912

South Carolina
3,732,000 people
31,189 sq. mi.
Rank in area: 40
Entered Union in 1788

Wisconsin
5,159,000 people
65,500 sq. mi.
Rank in area: 22
Entered Union in 1848

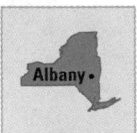
New York
18,178,000 people
53,989 sq. mi.
Rank in area: 27
Entered Union in 1788

South Dakota
735,000 people
77,121 sq. mi.
Rank in area: 17
Entered Union in 1889

Wyoming
487,000 people
97,819 sq. mi.
Rank in area: 9
Entered Union in 1890

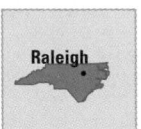
North Carolina
7,150,000 people
52,672 sq. mi.
Rank in area: 29
Entered Union in 1789

Tennessee
5,228,000 people
42,145 sq. mi.
Rank in area: 36
Entered Union in 1796

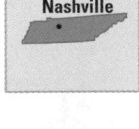

North Dakota
637,000 people
70,704 sq. mi.
Rank in area: 18
Entered Union in 1889

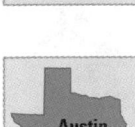
Texas
18,592,000 people
267,277 sq. mi.
Rank in area: 2
Entered Union in 1845

United States: Major Dependencies (as of 1996)

American Samoa—57,000 people; 90 sq. mi.

Guam—153,000 people; 217 sq. mi.

Republic of the Marshall Islands—42,000 people; 70 sq. mi.

Federated States of Micronesia—102,000 people; 271 sq. mi.

Midway Island—500 people; 2 sq. mi.

Commonwealth of the Northern Mariana Islands—51,000 people; 189 sq. mi.

Commonwealth of Puerto Rico—3,813,000 people; 3,508 sq. mi.

Virgin Islands of the United States—97,000 people; 171 sq. mi.

Wake Island—302 people; 3 sq. mi.

Ohio
11,203,000 people
44,828 sq. mi.
Rank in area: 34
Entered Union in 1803

Utah
1,944,000 people
84,904 sq. mi.
Rank in area: 13
Entered Union in 1896

FACTS ABOUT THE STATES **1073**

PRESIDENTS OF THE UNITED STATES

Here are some little-known facts about the Presidents of the United States:
- *Only former president to serve in Congress: John Quincy Adams*
- *First president born in the new United States: Martin Van Buren (8th president)*
- *Only president who was a bachelor: James Buchanan*
- *First left-handed president: James A. Garfield*
- *Largest president: William Howard Taft (6 feet, 2 inches; 326 pounds)*
- *Youngest president: Theodore Roosevelt (42 years old)*
- *Oldest president: Ronald Reagan (77 years old when he left office in 1989)*
- *First president born west of the Mississippi River: Herbert Hoover (born in West Branch, Iowa)*
- *First president born in the 20th century: John F. Kennedy (born May 29, 1917)*

1 George Washington
1789–1797
No Political Party
Birthplace: Virginia
Born: February 22, 1732
Died: December 14, 1799

2 John Adams
1797–1801
Federalist
Birthplace: Massachusetts
Born: October 30, 1735
Died: July 4, 1826

3 Thomas Jefferson
1801–1809
Democratic Republican
Birthplace: Virginia
Born: April 13, 1743
Died: July 4, 1826

4 James Madison
1809–1817
Democratic Republican
Birthplace: Virginia
Born: March 16, 1751
Died: June 28, 1836

5 James Monroe
1817–1825
Democratic Republican
Birthplace: Virginia
Born: April 28, 1758
Died: July 4, 1831

6 John Quincy Adams
1825–1829
Democratic Republican
Birthplace: Massachusetts
Born: July 11, 1767
Died: February 23, 1848

7 Andrew Jackson
1829–1837
Democrat
Birthplace: South Carolina
Born: March 15, 1767
Died: June 8, 1845

8 Martin Van Buren
1837–1841
Democrat
Birthplace: New York
Born: December 5, 1782
Died: July 24, 1862

9 William H. Harrison
1841
Whig
Birthplace: Virginia
Born: February 9, 1773
Died: April 4, 1841

10 John Tyler
1841–1845
Whig
Birthplace: Virginia
Born: March 29, 1790
Died: January 18, 1862

11 James K. Polk
1845–1849
Democrat
Birthplace: North Carolina
Born: November 2, 1795
Died: June 15, 1849

12 Zachary Taylor
1849–1850
Whig
Birthplace: Virginia
Born: November 24, 1784
Died: July 9, 1850

13 **Millard Fillmore**
1850–1853
Whig
Birthplace: New York
Born: January 7, 1800
Died: March 8, 1874

14 **Franklin Pierce**
1853–1857
Democrat
Birthplace: New Hampshire
Born: November 23, 1804
Died: October 8, 1869

15 **James Buchanan**
1857–1861
Democrat
Birthplace: Pennsylvania
Born: April 23, 1791
Died: June 1, 1868

16 **Abraham Lincoln**
1861–1865
Republican
Birthplace: Kentucky
Born: February 12, 1809
Died: April 15, 1865

17 **Andrew Johnson**
1865–1869
Democrat
Birthplace: North Carolina
Born: December 29, 1808
Died: July 31, 1875

18 **Ulysses S. Grant**
1869–1877
Republican
Birthplace: Ohio
Born: April 27, 1822
Died: July 23, 1885

19 **Rutherford B. Hayes**
1877–1881
Republican
Birthplace: Ohio
Born: October 4, 1822
Died: January 17, 1893

20 **James A. Garfield**
1881
Republican
Birthplace: Ohio
Born: November 19, 1831
Died: September 19, 1881

21 **Chester A. Arthur**
1881–1885
Republican
Birthplace: Vermont
Born: October 5, 1829
Died: November 18, 1886

22 24 **Grover Cleveland**
1885–1889, 1893–1897
Democrat
Birthplace: New Jersey
Born: March 18, 1837
Died: June 24, 1908

23 **Benjamin Harrison**
1889–1893
Republican
Birthplace: Ohio
Born: August 20, 1833
Died: March 13, 1901

25 **William McKinley**
1897–1901
Republican
Birthplace: Ohio
Born: January 29, 1843
Died: September 14, 1901

26 **Theodore Roosevelt**
1901–1909
Republican
Birthplace: New York
Born: October 27, 1858
Died: January 16, 1919

27 **William H. Taft**
1909–1913
Republican
Birthplace: Ohio
Born: September 15, 1857
Died: March 8, 1930

28 **Woodrow Wilson**
1913–1921
Democrat
Birthplace: Virginia
Born: December 29, 1856
Died: February 3, 1924

29 **Warren G. Harding**
1921–1923
Republican
Birthplace: Ohio
Born: November 2, 1865
Died: August 2, 1923

30 **Calvin Coolidge**
1923–1929
Republican
Birthplace: Vermont
Born: July 4, 1872
Died: January 5, 1933

31 **Herbert C. Hoover**
1929–1933
Republican
Birthplace: Iowa
Born: August 10, 1874
Died: October 20, 1964

32 **Franklin D. Roosevelt**
1933–1945
Democrat
Birthplace: New York
Born: January 30, 1882
Died: April 12, 1945

33 **Harry S. Truman**
1945–1953
Democrat
Birthplace: Missouri
Born: May 8, 1884
Died: December 26, 1972

34 **Dwight D. Eisenhower**
1953–1961
Republican
Birthplace: Texas
Born: October 14, 1890
Died: March 28, 1969

35 **John F. Kennedy**
1961–1963
Democrat
Birthplace: Massachusetts
Born: May 29, 1917
Died: November 22, 1963

36 **Lyndon B. Johnson**
1963–1969
Democrat
Birthplace: Texas
Born: August 27, 1908
Died: January 22, 1973

37 **Richard M. Nixon**
1969–1974
Republican
Birthplace: California
Born: January 9, 1913
Died: April 22, 1994

38 **Gerald R. Ford**
1974–1977
Republican
Birthplace: Nebraska
Born: July, 14, 1913

39 **James E. Carter, Jr.**
1977–1981
Democrat
Birthplace: Georgia
Born: October 1, 1924

40 **Ronald W. Reagan**
1981–1989
Republican
Birthplace: Illinois
Born: February 6, 1911

41 **George H. W. Bush**
1989–1993
Republican
Birthplace: Massachusetts
Born: June 12, 1924

42 **William J. Clinton**
1993–
Democrat
Birthplace: Arkansas
Born: August 19, 1946

1076 PRESIDENTS OF THE UNITED STATES

GLOSSARY

The Glossary is an alphabetical listing of many of the key terms from the chapters, along with their meanings. The definitions listed in the glossary are the ones that apply to the way a word is used in this textbook. The glossary gives the part of speech of the word. The following abbreviations are used:

adj. adjective   *n.* noun   *v.* verb

Pronunciation Key

Symbol	Examples	Symbol	Examples	Symbol	Examples
ă	at, gas	m	man, seem	v	van, save
ā	ape, day	n	night, mitten	w	web, twice
ä	father, barn	ng	sing, anger	y	yard, lawyer
âr	fair, dare	ŏ	odd, not	z	zoo, reason
b	bell, table	ō	open, road, grow	zh	treasure, garage
ch	chin, lunch	ô	awful, bought, horse	ə	awake, even, pencil,
d	dig, bored	oi	coin, boy		pilot, focus
ĕ	egg, ten	ŏŏ	look, full	ər	perform, letter
ē	evil, see, meal	ōō	root, glue, through		
f	fall, laugh, phrase	ou	out, cow	**Sounds in Foreign Words**	
g	gold, big	p	pig, cap	KH	*German* ich, auch;
h	hit, inhale	r	rose, star		*Scottish* loch
hw	white, everywhere	s	sit, face	N	*French* entre, bon, fin
ĭ	inch, fit	sh	she, mash	œ	*French* feu, coeur;
ī	idle, my, tried	t	tap, hopped		*German* schon
îr	dear, here	th	thing, with	ü	*French* utile, rue;
j	jar, gem, badge	*th*	then, other		*German* grün
k	keep, cat, luck	ŭ	up, nut		
l	load, rattle	ûr	fur, earn, bird, worm		

Stress Marks

′ This mark indicates that the preceding syllable receives the primary stress. For example, in the word *lineage,* the first syllable is stressed: [lĭn′ē-ĭj].

′ This mark is used only in words in which more than one syllable is stressed. It indicates that the preceding syllable is stressed, but somewhat more weakly than the syllable receiving the primary stress. In the word *consumerism,* for example, the second syllable receives the primary stress, and the fourth syllable receives a weaker stress: [kən-sōō′mə-rĭz′əm].

Adapted from *The American Heritage Dictionary of the English Language, Third Edition;* Copyright © 1992 by Houghton Mifflin Company. Used with the permission of Houghton Mifflin Company.

A

abolition [ăb′ə-lĭsh′ən] *n.* the ending of legal slavery. (p. 229)

Adena [ə-dē′nə] *n.* a Mound Builder society that was centered in the Ohio River valley and flourished from about 700 B.C. to A.D. 100. (p. 6)

affirmative [ə-fûr′mə-tĭv] **action** *n.* a policy that seeks to correct the effects of past discrimination by favoring the groups who were previously disadvantaged. (p. 992)

Agent Orange *n.* a leaf-killing chemical sprayed by U.S. planes in Vietnam to expose Vietcong hideouts. (p. 892)

Agricultural Adjustment Act *n.* a law enacted in 1933 to raise crop prices by paying farmers to leave a certain amount of their land unplanted, thus lowering production. (p. 667)

AIDS [ādz] **(acquired immune deficiency syndrome)** *n.* a disease caused by a virus that weakens the immune system, making the body prone to infections and otherwise rare forms of cancer. (p. 987)

Alien and Sedition [ā′lē-ən ənd sĭ-dĭsh′ən] **Acts** *n.* a series of four laws enacted in 1798 to reduce the political power of recent immigrants to the United States. (p. 181)

Alliance [ə-lī′əns] **for Progress** *n.* a U.S. foreign-aid program of the 1960s, providing economic and technical assistance to Latin American countries. (p. 839)

Allies [ə-līz′] *n.* **1.** in World War I, the group of nations—originally consisting of Great Britain, France, and Russia and later joined by the United States, Italy, and others—that opposed the Central Powers (p. 556). **2.** in World War II, the group of nations—including Great Britain, the Soviet Union, and the United States—that opposed the Axis powers. (p. 722)

American Federation of Labor (AFL) *n.* an alliance of trade and craft unions, formed in 1886. (p. 429)

American Indian Movement *n.* a frequently militant organization that was formed in 1968 to work for Native American rights. (p. 923)

American System *n.* a pre-Civil War set of measures designed to unify the nation and strengthen its economy by means of protective tariffs, a national bank, and such internal improvements as the development of a transportation system. (p. 201)

Anaconda [ăn′ə-kŏn′də] **plan** *n.* a three-part strategy by which the Union proposed to defeat the Confederacy in the Civil War. (p. 314)

GLOSSARY 1077

anarchist [ăn′ər-kĭst] *n.* a person who opposes all forms of government. (p. 591)

Anasazi [ä′nə-sä′zē] *n.* a Native American group that lived on the mesa tops, cliff sides, and canyon bottoms of the Four Corners region (where the present-day states of Arizona, New Mexico, Colorado, and Utah meet) from about A.D. 100 to 1300. (p. 6)

annex [ə-nĕks′] *v.* to incorporate a territory into an existing political unit, such as a state or a nation. (p. 272)

antebellum [ăn′tē-bĕl′əm] *adj.* belonging to the period before the Civil War. (p. 233)

Antifederalist [ăn′tē-fĕd′ər-ə-lĭst] *n.* an opponent of a strong central government. (p. 138)

appeasement [ə-pēz′mənt] *n.* the granting of concessions to a hostile power in order to keep the peace. (p. 709)

apprentice [ə-prĕn′tĭs] *n.* a worker learning a trade or craft, usually under the supervision of a master. (p. 241)

armistice [är′mĭ-stĭs] *n.* a stopping of warfare by mutual agreement. (p. 191)

Articles of Confederation [kən-fĕd′ə-rā′shən] *n.* a document, adopted by the Continental Congress in 1777 and finally approved by the states in 1781, that outlined the form of government of the new United States. (p. 127)

assimilation [ə-sĭm′ə-lā′shən] *n.* a minority group's adoption of the beliefs and way of life of the dominant culture. (p. 385)

Atlantic Charter *n.* a 1941 declaration of principles in which the United States and Great Britain set forth their goals in opposing the Axis powers. (p. 722)

Axis [ăk′sĭs] **powers** *n.* the group of nations—including Germany, Italy, and Japan—that opposed the Allies in World War II. (p. 710)

Aztec [ăz′tĕk′] *n.* a Native American people that settled in the Valley of Mexico in the 1200s A.D. and later developed a powerful empire. (p. 6)

B

baby boom *n.* the sharp increase in the U.S. birthrate following World War II. (p. 805)

balance of trade *n.* the difference in value between a country's imports and exports. (p. 66)

Bank of the United States (BUS) *n.* either of the two national banks established by Congress, the first in 1791 and the second in 1816. (p. 216)

Battle of the Bulge *n.* a month-long battle of World War II, in which the Allies succeeded in turning back the last major German offensive of the war. (p. 744)

Battle of Wounded Knee [wōōn′dĭd nē′] *n.* the massacre by U.S. soldiers of 300 unarmed Native Americans at Wounded Knee Creek, South Dakota, in 1890. (p. 387)

Bear Flag Republic *n.* the nation proclaimed by American settlers in California when they declared their independence from Mexico in 1846. (p. 275)

Beatles [bēt′lz] *n.* a British band that had an enormous influence on popular music in the 1960s. (p. 936)

beat movement *n.* a social and artistic movement of the 1950s, stressing unrestrained literary self-expression and nonconformity with the mainstream culture. (p. 815)

beatnik [bēt′nĭk] *n.* one of the unconventional, nonmaterialistic followers of the beat movement of the 1950s. (p. 815)

Benin [bə-nĭn′] *n.* a West African kingdom that flourished in the Niger Delta region (in what is now Nigeria) from the 14th to the 17th century. (p. 17)

Berlin airlift [bûr-lĭn′ âr′lĭft′] *n.* a 327-day operation in which U.S. and British planes flew food and supplies into West Berlin after the Soviets blockaded the city in 1948. (p. 771)

Berlin Wall *n.* a concrete wall that separated East Berlin and West Berlin from 1961 to 1989, built by the Communist East German government to prevent its citizens from fleeing to the West. (p. 836)

Bessemer [bĕs′ə-mər] **process** *n.* a cheap and efficient process for making steel, developed around 1850. (p. 411)

Bill of Rights *n.* the first ten amendments to the U.S. Constitution, added in 1791 and consisting of a formal list of citizens' rights and freedoms. (p. 139)

bimetallism [bī-mĕt′l-ĭz′əm] *n.* the use of both gold and silver as a basis for a national monetary system. (p. 404)

black codes *n.* discriminatory laws that were enacted in many Southern states after the Civil War and that severely restricted African Americans' lives. (p. 352)

blacklist [blăk′lĭst] *n.* a list of about 500 actors, writers, producers, and directors who were not allowed to work on Hollywood films because of their alleged Communist connections. (p. 781)

Black Panthers *n.* a militant African-American political organization formed in 1966 by Huey Newton and Bobby Seale to fight police brutality and to provide services in the ghetto. (p. 874)

Black Power *n.* a slogan—first used in the 1940s and revived by Stokely Carmichael in the 1960s—that encouraged African-American pride and political and social leadership. (p. 874)

Black Tuesday *n.* a name given to October 29, 1929, when stock prices fell sharply. (p. 645)

Bleeding Kansas *n.* a name applied to the Kansas Territory in the years before the Civil War, when the territory was a battleground between proslavery and antislavery forces. (p. 293)

blitzkrieg [blĭts′krēg′] *n.* a sudden, massive attack with combined air and ground forces, intended to achieve a quick victory. (p. 711)

blockade [blŏ-kād′] *n.* the use of ships or troops to prevent movement into and out of a port or region controlled by a hostile nation. (p. 189)

bonanza [bə-năn′zə] **farm** *n.* an enormous farm on which a single crop is grown. (p. 400)

Bonus [bō′nəs] **Army** *n.* a group of unemployed World War I veterans and their families who marched on Washington, D.C., in 1932 to demand the immediate payment of a bonus they had been promised for military service. (p. 658)

bootlegger [bōōt′lĕg′ər] *n.* a person who smuggled alcoholic beverages into the United States during Prohibition. (p. 615)

Boston Massacre [bô′stən măs′ə-kər] *n.* a clash between British soldiers and Boston colonists in 1770, in which five of the colonists were killed. (p. 96)

Boston Tea Party *n.* the dumping of 15,000 pounds of tea into Boston Harbor by colonists in 1773 to protest the Tea Act. (p. 97)

Boulder [bōl′dər] **Dam** *n.* a dam on the Colorado River—now called Hoover Dam—that was built during the Great Depression as part of a public-works program intended to stimulate business and provide jobs. (p. 657)

bounty [boun′tē] *n.* during the Civil War, a cash payment offered by a Northern state to encourage men to join the army. (p. 321)

Boxer Rebellion *n.* a 1900 rebellion in which members of a Chinese secret society sought to free their country from Western influence. (p. 539)

bracero [brə-sâr′ō] *n.* a Mexican laborer allowed to enter the United States to work for a limited period of time. (p. 822)

bread line *n.* a line of people waiting for free food. (p. 651)

brinkmanship [brĭngk′mən-shĭp′] *n.* the practice of threatening an enemy with massive military retaliation for any aggression. (p. 786)

Brown v. *Board of Education* [broun′ vûr′səs bôrd′ əv ĕj′ə-kā′shən] *n.* a 1954 case in which the Supreme Court ruled that "separate but equal" education for black and white students was unconstitutional. (p. 858)

Bull Moose Party *n.* a name given to the Progressive Party, formed to support Theodore Roosevelt's candidacy for the presidency in 1912. (p. 514)

buying on margin [mär′jĭn] *n.* the purchasing of stocks by paying only a small percentage of the price and borrowing the rest. (p. 645)

C

cabinet [kăb′ə-nĭt] *n.* the group of department heads who serve as the president's chief advisers. (p. 173)

Camp David Accords [ə-kôrdz′] *n.* two historic agreements between Israel and Egypt, reached in negotiations at Camp David in 1978. (p. 966)

capitalism [kăp′ĭ-tl-ĭz′əm] *n.* an economic system in which private individuals and corporations control the means of production and use them to earn profits. (p. 255)

carpetbagger [kär′pĭt-băg′ər] *n.* a Northerner who moved to the South after the Civil War. (p. 358)

cash crop *n.* a crop grown by a farmer for sale rather than for personal use. (p. 71)

Central Powers *n.* the group of nations—led by Germany, Austria-Hungary, and the Ottoman Empire—that opposed the Allies in World War I. (p. 556)

checks and balances *n.* the provisions in the U.S. Constitution that prevent any branch of the U.S. government from dominating the other two branches. (p. 136)

Chinese Exclusion Act *n.* a law, enacted in 1882, that prohibited all Chinese except students, teachers, merchants, tourists, and government officials from entering the United States. (p. 443)

CIA *n.* the Central Intelligence Agency—a U.S. agency created to gather secret information about foreign governments. (p. 786)

Civilian Conservation Corps [kôr] *n.* an agency, established as part of the New Deal, that put young unemployed men to work building roads, developing parks, planting trees, and helping in erosion-control and flood-control projects. (p. 667)

Civil Rights Act of 1964 *n.* a law that banned discrimination on the basis of race, sex, national origin, or religion in public places and most workplaces. (p. 864)

Civil Rights Act of 1968 *n.* a law that banned discrimination in housing. (p. 876)

civil service *n.* the nonmilitary branches of government administration. (p. 455)

Clayton Antitrust [klāt′n ăn′tē-trŭst′] **Act** *n.* a law, enacted in 1914, that made certain monopolistic business practices illegal and protected the rights of labor unions and farm organizations. (p. 517)

Cold War *n.* the state of hostility, without direct military conflict, that developed between the United States and the Soviet Union after World War II. (p. 770)

collective bargaining [kə-lĕk′tĭv bär′gə-nĭng] *n.* negotiations between the representatives of workers and employers to reach agreement on wages, benefits, hours, and working conditions. (p. 429)

colonization [kŏl′ə-nĭ-zā′shən] *n.* the establishment of outlying settlements by a parent country. (p. 29)

Columbian Exchange [kə-lŭm′bē-ən ĭks-chānj′] *n.* the transfer—beginning with Columbus's first voyage—of plants, animals, and diseases between the Western Hemisphere and the Eastern Hemisphere. (p. 31)

committee of correspondence [kôr′ĭ-spŏn′dəns] *n.* one of the groups set up by American colonists to exchange information about British threats to their liberties. (p. 97)

Committee to Reelect the President *n.* an organization formed to run President Nixon's 1972 reelection campaign, which was linked to the break-in at the Democratic National Committee headquarters that set off the Watergate scandal. (p. 954)

Common Sense *n.* a pamphlet by Thomas Paine, published in 1776, that called for separation of the colonies from Britain. (p. 101)

Commonwealth [kŏm′ən-wĕlth′] **of Independent States** *n.* a loose confederation of former Soviet states, established after the dissolution of the Soviet Union in 1991. (p. 997)

communism [kŏm′yə-nĭz′əm] *n.* an economic and political system based on one-party government and state ownership of property. (p. 590)

Compromise [kŏm′prə-mīz′] **of 1850** *n.* a series of congressional measures intended to settle the major disagreements between free states and slave states. (p. 285)

concentration [kŏn′sən-trā′shən] **camp** *n.* a prison camp operated by Nazi Germany in which Jews and other groups considered to be enemies of Adolf Hitler were starved while doing slave labor or were murdered. (p. 716)

Confederate [kən-fĕd′ər-ĭt] **States of America** *n.* the confederation formed in 1861 by the Southern states after their secession from the Union. (p. 305)

confederation [kən-fĕd′ə-rā′shən] *n.* an alliance permitting states or nations to act together on matters of mutual concern. (p. 127)

conglomerate [kən-glŏm′ər-ĭt] *n.* a major corporation that owns a number of smaller companies in unrelated businesses. (p. 803)

congregación [kông-grĕ-gä-syôn′] *n.* a community established by Spanish priests to impose Spanish culture and the Roman Catholic faith on Native Americans. (p. 42)

Congress of Industrial Organizations *n.* a labor organization that broke away from the American Federation of Labor in 1938. (p. 681)

Congress of Racial Equality [rā′shəl ĭ-kwŏl′ĭ-tē] **(CORE)** *n.* an interracial group founded in 1942 by James Farmer to work against segregation in Northern cities. (p. 759)

conquistador [kŏng-kē′stə-dôr′] *n.* one of the Spaniards who traveled to the Americas as an explorer and conqueror in the 16th century. (p. 38)

conscientious objector [kŏn′shē-ĕn′shəs ŏb-jĕk′tər] *n.* a person who refuses, on moral grounds, to participate in warfare. (p. 565)

conscription [kən-skrĭp′shən] *n.* the drafting of citizens for military service. (p. 321)

conservation [kŏn′sûr-vā′shən] *n.* the planned management of natural resources, involving the protection of some wilderness areas and the development of others for the common good. (p. 510)

Conservative Coalition [kən-sûr′və-tĭv kō′ə-lĭsh′ən] *n.* a late-20th-century alliance of right-wing groups opposed to big government, entitlement programs, affirmative action, the busing of students to achieve integration, and the supposed moral decline of the U.S. people. (p. 979)

consumerism [kən-sōō′mə-rĭz′əm] *n.* a preoccupation with the purchasing of material goods. (p. 808)

containment [kən-tān′mənt] *n.* the blocking of another nation's attempts to spread its influence—especially the efforts of the United States to block the spread of Soviet influence during the late 1940s and early 1950s. (p. 769)

Contract [kŏn′trăkt′] **with America** *n.* a document that was drafted by Representative Newt Gingrich and signed by more than 300 Republican candidates in 1994, setting forth the Republicans' conservative legislative agenda. (p. 1010)

Contras [kŏn′trəz] *n.* Nicaraguan rebels who received assistance from the Reagan administration in their efforts to overthrow the Sandinista government in the 1980s. (p. 998)

convoy [kŏn′voi′] **system** *n.* the protection of merchant ships from U-boat attacks by having the ships travel in large groups under the protection of warships. (p. 564)

Copperhead [kŏp′ər-hĕd′] *n.* a Northern Democrat who advocated making peace with the Confederacy during the Civil War. (p. 321)

counterculture [koun′tər-kŭl′chər] *n.* the culture of the young people who rejected mainstream American society in the 1960s, seeking to create an alternative society based on peace, love, and individual freedom. (p. 933)

credibility [krĕd′ə-bĭl′ĭ-tē] **gap** *n.* a public distrust of statements made by the government. (p. 894)

credit [krĕd′ĭt] *n.* an arrangement in which a buyer pays later for a purchase, often on an installment plan with interest charges. (p. 644)

Crédit Mobilier [krĕd′ĭt mō-bēl′yər] *n.* a construction company formed in 1868 by owners of the Union Pacific Railroad, who used it to fraudulently skim off railroad profits for themselves. (p. 419)

"Cross of Gold" speech *n.* an impassioned address by William Jennings Bryan at the 1896 Democratic Convention, in which he attacked the "gold bugs" who insisted that U.S. currency be backed only with gold. (p. 404)

Crusades [krōō-sādz′] *n.* a series of Christian military expeditions to the Middle East between A.D. 1096 and 1270, intended to drive the Muslims from the Holy Land. (p. 22)

cult of domesticity [dō′mĕ-stĭs′ĭ-tē] *n.* a belief that married women should restrict their activities to their home and family. (p. 235)

culture shock *n.* the confusion and anxiety that result from living in an unfamiliar culture. (p. 442)

D

Dawes [dôz] **Act** *n.* a law, enacted in 1887, that was intended to "Americanize" Native Americans by distributing reservation land to individual owners. (p. 385)

D-Day *n.* a name given to June 6, 1944—the day on which the Allies launched an invasion of the European mainland during World War II. (p. 743)

debt peonage [dĕt′ pē′ə-nĭj] *n.* a system in which workers are bound in servitude until their debts are paid. (p. 477)

Declaration [dĕk′lə-rā′shən] **of Independence** *n.* the document, written by Thomas Jefferson in 1776, in which the delegates of the Continental Congress declared the colonies' independence from Britain. (p. 101)

de facto segregation [dĭ făk′tō sĕg′rĭ-gā′shən] *n.* racial separation established by practice and custom, not by law. (p. 871)

deficit [dĕf′ĭ-sĭt] **spending** *n.* a government's spending of more money than it receives in revenue. (p. 689)

de jure segregation [dē jŏŏr′ē sĕg′rĭ-gā′shən] *n.* racial separation established by law. (p. 871)

Democratic Republican [dĕm′ə-krăt′ĭk rĭ-pŭb′lĭ-kən] **Party** *n.* a political party—the forerunner of the modern Democratic Party—established by Andrew Jackson's supporters when they broke away from the Republican Party in the late 1820s. (p. 210)

department store *n.* a large retail store that offers a wide variety of goods and services. (p. 484)

détente [dā-tänt′] *n.* the flexible policy, involving a willingness to negotiate and an easing of tensions, that was adopted by President Richard Nixon and his adviser Henry Kissinger in their dealings with Communist nations. (p. 951)

direct relief [rĭ-lēf′] *n.* the giving of money or food by the government directly to needy people. (p. 653)

division of labor *n.* the assignment of different tasks and responsibilities to different groups or individuals. (p. 13)

Dixiecrat [dĭk′sē-krăt′] *n.* one of the Southern delegates who, to protest President Truman's civil rights policy, walked out of the 1948 Democratic National Convention and formed the States' Rights Democratic Party. (p. 800)

dollar diplomacy [dĭ-plō′mə-sē] *n.* the U.S. policy of using the nation's economic power to exert influence over other countries. (p. 545)

domino theory [dŏm′ə-nō′ thē′ə-rē] *n.* the idea that if a nation falls under Communist control, nearby nations will also fall under Communist control. (p. 885)

double standard *n.* a set of principles granting greater sexual freedom to men than to women. (p. 619)

dove [dŭv] *n.* a person who opposed the Vietnam War and believed that the United States should withdraw from it. (p. 899)

Dow Jones [dou′ jōnz′] **Industrial Average** *n.* a measure based on the prices of the stocks of 30 large companies, widely used as a barometer of the stock market's health. (p. 647)

downsize [doun′sīz′] *v.* to dismiss numbers of permanent employees in an attempt to make operations more efficient and save money. (p. 1014)

dumbbell tenement [dŭm′bĕl′ tĕn′ə-mənt] *n.* a long, narrow, five- or six-story building shaped like a barbell. (p. 448)

Dust Bowl *n.* the region, extending from Texas to North Dakota, that was made worthless for farming by drought and dust storms during the 1930s. (p. 650)

E

Earth Day *n.* a day set aside for environmental education, celebrated annually on April 22. (p. 969)

Economic Opportunity Act *n.* a law, enacted in 1964, that provided funds for youth programs, antipoverty measures, small-business loans, and job training. (p. 845)

egalitarianism [ĭ-găl′ĭ-târ′ē-ə-nĭz′əm] *n.* the belief that all people should have equal political, economic, social, and civil rights. (p. 116)

Eisenhower Doctrine [ī′zən-hou′ər dŏk′trĭn] *n.* a U.S. commitment to defend the Middle East against attack by any Communist country, announced by President Dwight D. Eisenhower in 1957. (p. 788)

electoral [ĭ-lĕk′tər-əl] **college** *n.* a group selected by the states to elect the president and the vice-president, in which each state's number of electors is equal to the number of its senators and representatives in Congress. (p. 136)

e-mail [ē′māl′] *n.* the electronic messages that are sent and received over the Internet and other computer networks. (p. 1019)

emancipation *n.* the freeing of slaves. (p. 229)

Emancipation Proclamation [prŏk′lə-mā′shən] *n.* an executive order issued by Abraham Lincoln on January 1, 1863, freeing the slaves in all regions in rebellion against the Union. (p. 320)

embargo [ĕm-bär′gō] *n.* a government ban on trade with one or more other nations. (p. 189)

encomienda [ĕng-kô-myĕn′dä] *n.* a system in which Spanish authorities granted colonial landlords the service of Native Americans as forced laborers. (p. 40)

Enlightenment [ĕn-līt′n-mənt] *n.* an 18th-century intellectual movement that emphasized the use of reason and the scientific method as means of obtaining knowledge. (p. 81)

entitlement [ĕn-tīt′l-mənt] **program** *n.* a government program—such as Social Security, Medicare, or Medicaid—that guarantees and provides benefits to a specific group. (p. 979)

entrepreneur [ŏn′trə-prə-nûr′] *n.* a person who uses his or her own money to create a new business. (p. 255)

environmentalist [ĕn-vī′rən mĕn′tl-ĭst] *n.* a person who works to protect the environment from destruction and pollution. (p. 969)

Environmental Protection Agency *n.* an agency established in 1970 to enforce pollution standards, to conduct environmental research, and to assist state and local governments in pollution control. (p. 970)

Equal Rights Amendment *n.* a proposed amendment to the U.S. Constitution that would prohibit any government discrimination on the basis of sex. (p. 931)

Erie Canal [îr′ē kə-năl′] *n.* a 363-mile-long artificial waterway connecting the Hudson River with Lake Erie, built between 1817 and 1825. (p. 203)

Espionage and Sedition [ĕs′pē-ə-näzh′ ənd sĭ-dĭsh′ən] **Acts** *n.* two laws, enacted in 1917 and 1918, that imposed harsh penalties on anyone interfering with or speaking against U.S. participation in World War I. (p. 573)

excise [ĕk′sīz′] **tax** *n.* a tax on the production, sale, or consumption of goods produced within a country. (p. 176)

executive [ĭg-zĕk′yə-tĭv] **branch** *n.* the branch of government that administers and enforces the laws. (pp. 135–136)

exoduster [ĕk′sə-dŭs′tər] *n.* an African American who migrated from the South to Kansas in the post-Reconstruction years. (p. 382)

F

Fair Deal *n.* President Harry S. Truman's economic program—an extension of Franklin Roosevelt's New Deal—which included measures to increase the minimum wage, to extend social security coverage, and to provide housing for low-income families. (p. 801)

Family Assistance Plan *n.* a welfare-reform proposal, approved by the House of Representatives in 1970 but defeated in the Senate, that would have guaranteed an income to welfare recipients who agreed to undergo job training and to accept work. (p. 947)

fascism [făsh′ĭz′əm] *n.* a political philosophy that advocates a strong, centralized, nationalistic government headed by a powerful dictator. (p. 704)

Federal Communications Commission (FCC) *n.* an agency that regulates U.S. communications industries, including radio and television stations. (p. 812)

Federal Deposit Insurance Corporation *n.* an agency created in 1933 to insure individuals' bank accounts, protecting people against losses due to bank failures. (p. 692)

Federal Home Loan Bank Act *n.* a law, enacted in 1931, that lowered home mortgage rates and allowed farmers to refinance their loans and avoid foreclosure. (p. 658)

Federalist [fĕd′ər-ə-lĭst] *n.* a supporter of the Constitution and of a strong national government. (p. 138)

Federalist Papers *n.* a series of essays defending and explaining the Constitution, written by Alexander Hamilton, James Madison, and John Jay. (p. 138)

Federal Reserve System *n.* a national banking system, established in 1913, that controls the U.S. money supply and the availability of credit in the country. (p. 518)

Federal Securities [sĭ-kyŏŏr′ĭ-tēz] **Act** *n.* a law, enacted in 1933, that required corporations to provide complete, accurate information on all stock offerings. (p. 666)

Federal Trade Commission *n.* a federal agency established in 1914 to investigate and stop unfair business practices. (p. 517)

feminism [fĕm′ə-nĭz′əm] *n.* the belief that women should have economic, political, and social equality with men. (p. 928)

Fifteenth Amendment *n.* an amendment to the U.S. Constitution, adopted in 1870, that prohibits the denial of voting rights to people because of their race or color or because they have previously been slaves. (p. 355)

Fifty-Four Forty or Fight *n.* a slogan used in the 1844 presidential campaign as a call for the U.S. annexation of the entire Oregon Territory. (p. 265)

flapper [flăp′ər] *n.* one of the free-thinking young women who embraced the new fashions and urban attitudes of the 1920s. (p. 618)

flexible response [flĕk′sə-bəl rĭ-spŏns′] *n.* a policy, developed during the Kennedy administration, that involved preparing for a variety of military responses to international crises rather than focusing on the use of nuclear weapons. (p. 832)

Fordney-McCumber Tariff [fôrd′nē mə-kŭm′bər tăr′ĭf] *n.* a set of regulations, enacted by Congress in 1922, that raised taxes on imports to record levels in order to protect American businesses against foreign competition. (p. 597)

forty-niner *n.* one of the people who migrated to California in search of riches after gold was discovered there in 1848. (p. 277)

Fourteen Points *n.* the principles making up President Woodrow Wilson's plan for world peace following World War I. (p. 577)

Fourteenth Amendment *n.* an amendment to the U.S. Constitution, adopted in 1868, that made all persons born or naturalized in the United States—including former slaves—citizens of the country. (p. 353)

franchise [frăn′chīz′] *n.* a business that has bought the right to use a parent company's name and methods, thus becoming one of a number of similar businesses in various locations. (p. 803)

Freedmen's Bureau [frēd′mĕnz′ byŏŏr′ō] *n.* a government agency, established in the last months of the Civil War, that assisted former slaves and poor whites in the South by giving out food and clothing and by setting up hospitals and schools. (p. 352)

freedom rider *n.* one of the civil rights activists who rode buses through the South in the early 1960s to challenge segregation. (p. 864)

Freedom Summer *n.* a 1964 project to register African-American voters in Mississippi. (p. 868)

Freeport Doctrine [frē′pôrt′ dŏk′trĭn] *n.* the idea, expressed by Stephen Douglas in 1858, that any territory could exclude slavery by simply refusing to pass laws supporting it. (p. 301)

Free-Soil Party *n.* a political party formed in 1848 to oppose the extension of slavery into U.S. territories. (p. 296)

Free Speech Movement *n.* an antiestablishment New Left organization that originated in a 1964 clash between students and administrators at the University of California at Berkeley. (p. 897)

French and Indian War *n.* a conflict in North America, lasting from 1754 to 1763, that was a part of a worldwide struggle between France and Britain and that ended with the defeat of France and the transfer of French Canada to Britain. (p. 84)

Fugitive [fyŏŏ′jĭ-tĭv] **Slave Act** *n.* a law enacted as part of the Compromise of 1850, designed to ensure that escaped slaves would be returned into bondage. (p. 288)

fundamentalism [fŭn′də-mĕn′tl-ĭz′əm] *n.* a Protestant religious movement grounded in the belief that all the stories and details in the Bible are literally true. (p. 616)

G

Gadsden [gădz′dən] **Purchase** *n.* an 1853 purchase by the United States of land from Mexico, establishing the present U.S.-Mexico boundary. (p. 276)

gag rule *n.* a rule limiting or preventing debate on an issue. (p. 234)

GATT [găt] *n.* the General Agreement on Tariffs and Trade—an international agreement first signed in 1947. In 1993, the agreement was amended to create the World Trade Organization, which seeks to lower trade barriers and establishes rules for resolving trade disputes. (p. 1016)

genetic engineering [jə-nĕt′ĭk ĕn′jə-nîr′ĭng] *n.* the alteration of the molecular biology of organisms' cells in order to create new varieties of bacteria, plants, and animals. (p. 1020)

Geneva Accords [jə-nē′və ə-kôrdz′] *n.* a 1954 peace agreement that divided Vietnam into Communist-controlled North Vietnam and non-Communist South Vietnam until unification elections could be held in 1956. (p. 886)

genocide [jĕn′ə-sīd′] *n.* the deliberate and systematic extermination of a particular racial, national, or religious group. (p. 715)

Gentlemen's Agreement *n.* a 1907–1908 agreement by the government of Japan to limit Japanese emigration to the United States. (p. 443)

Gettysburg Address [gĕt′ēz-bûrg′ ə-drĕs′] *n.* a famous speech delivered by Abraham Lincoln in November 1863, at the dedication of a national cemetery on the site of the Battle of Gettysburg. (p. 333)

Ghost Dance *n.* a Native American ritual intended to bring about the restoration of tribal life, popular among the Sioux prior to the Battle of Wounded Knee. (p. 387)

GI Bill of Rights *n.* a name given to the Servicemen's Readjustment Act, a 1944 law that provided financial and educational benefits for World War II veterans. (pp. 758, 796)

glasnost [gläs′nəst] *n.* the open discussion of social problems that was permitted in the Soviet Union in the 1980s. (p. 996)

Glass-Steagall [glăs′ stē′gəl] **Banking Act of 1933** *n.* the law that established the Federal Deposit Insurance Corporation to protect individuals' bank accounts. (p. 666)

Glorious Revolution *n.* the transfer of the British monarchy from James II to William and Mary in 1688–1689. (p. 68)

gold rush *n.* a movement of many people to a region in which gold has been discovered. (p. 277)

Gone with the Wind *n.* a 1939 movie dealing with the life of Southern plantation owners during the Civil War—one of the most popular films of all time. (p. 684)

graft *n.* the illegal use of political influence for personal gain. (p. 452)

grandfather clause *n.* a provision that exempts certain people from a law on the basis of previously existing circumstances—especially a clause formerly in some Southern states' constitutions that exempted whites from the strict voting requirements used to keep African Americans from the polls. (p. 474)

Grange [grānj] *n.* the Patrons of Husbandry—a social and educational organization through which farmers attempted to combat the power of the railroads in the late 19th century. (p. 402)

Grapes of Wrath, The *n.* a novel by John Steinbeck, published in 1939, that deals with a family of Oklahomans who leave the Dust Bowl for California. (p. 687)

Great Awakening *n.* a revival of religious feeling in the American colonies during the 1730s and 1740s. (p. 82)

Great Compromise [kŏm′prə-mīz′] *n.* the Constitutional Convention's agreement to establish a two-house national legislature, with all states having equal representation in one house and each state having representation based on its population in the other house. (p. 134)

Great Depression *n.* a period, lasting from 1929 to 1941, in which the U.S. economy was in severe decline and millions of Americans were unemployed. (p. 646)

Great Migration [mī-grā′shən] *n.* the large-scale movement of African Americans from the South to Northern cities in the early 20th century. (p. 574)

Great Plains *n.* the vast grassland that extends through the west-central portion of the United States. (p. 380)

Great Society *n.* President Lyndon B. Johnson's program to reduce poverty and racial injustice and to promote a better quality of life in the United States. (p. 846)

H

habeas corpus [hā′bē-əs kôr′pəs] *n.* a court order requiring authorities to bring a prisoner before the court so that the court can determine whether the prisoner is being held legally. (p. 321)

Haight-Ashbury [hāt′ ăsh′bĕr-ē] *n.* a San Francisco district that became the "capital" of the hippie counterculture during the 1960s. (p. 934)

Harlem Renaissance [här′ləm rĕn′ĭ-säns′] *n.* a flowering of African-American artistic creativity during the 1920s, centered in the Harlem community of New York City. (p. 632)

hawk *n.* a person who supported U.S. involvement in the Vietnam War and believed that the United States should use increased military force to win it. (p. 899)

Hawley-Smoot Tariff [hô′lē smo͞ot′ tăr′ĭf] **Act** *n.* a law, enacted in 1930, that established the highest protective tariff in U.S. history, worsening the depression in America and abroad. (p. 649)

H-bomb *n.* the hydrogen bomb—a thermonuclear weapon much more powerful than the atomic bomb. (p. 785)

headright [hĕd′rīt′] **system** *n.* the Virginia Company's policy of granting 50 acres of land to each settler and to each family member who accompanied him. (p. 46)

hierarchy [hī′ə-rär′kē] *n.* a social ordering by rank or class. (p. 20)

Ho Chi Minh [hō′ chē′ mĭn′] **Trail** *n.* a network of paths used by North Vietnam to transport supplies to the Vietcong in South Vietnam. (p. 886)

Hohokam [hə-hō′kəm] *n.* a Native American group that lived in the valleys of the Salt and Gila rivers (in what is now Arizona) from about 300 B.C. to A.D. 1400. (p. 6)

holding company *n.* a corporation formed to buy up the stock of other companies and thus create a monopoly. (p. 423)

Hollywood Ten *n.* ten witnesses from the film industry who refused to cooperate with the HUAC's investigation of Communist influence in Hollywood. (p. 781)

Holocaust [hŏl′ə-kôst′] *n.* the systematic murder of 11 million Jews and other people by the Nazis before and during World War II. (p. 714)

home rule *n.* a state's powers of governing its citizens without federal government involvement. (p. 372)

Homestead [hōm′stĕd′] **Act** *n.* a law, enacted in 1862, that provided 160 acres of free land in the West to anyone who would live on and cultivate it for five years. (p. 382)

homesteader [hōm′stĕd′ər] *n.* a settler on the free land made available by the Homestead Act. (p. 397)

Hopewell [hōp′wĕl′] *n.* a Mound Builder society that was centered in the Ohio River valley and flourished from about 200 B.C. to A.D. 400. (p. 6)

horizontal consolidation [hôr′ĭ-zŏn′tl kən-sŏl′ĭ-dā′shən] *n.* the merging of companies that make similar products. (p. 422)

hot line *n.* a communication link established in 1963 to allow the leaders of the United States and the Soviet Union to contact each other in times of crisis. (p. 836)

HUAC [hyo͞o′ăk′] *n.* the House Committee on Un-American Activities—a congressional committee that investigated Communist influence inside and outside the U.S. government in the years following World War II. (p. 780)

human rights *n.* the rights and freedoms, such as those named in the Declaration of Independence and the Bill of Rights, to which all people are entitled. (p. 965)

I

Immigration [ĭm′ĭ-grā′shən] **Act of 1965** *n.* a law that made it easier for non-European immigrants to settle in the United States. (p. 846)

imperialism [ĭm-pîr′ē-ə-lĭz′əm] *n.* the policy of extending a nation's authority over other countries by economic, political, or military means. (p. 526)

impressment [ĭm-prĕs′mənt] *n.* the forcible seizure of men for military service. (p. 189)

GLOSSARY **1083**

Inca [ĭng′kə] *n.* a Native American people that around A.D. 1400 created an empire reaching nearly 2,500 miles along the west coast of South America. (p. 6)

income tax *n.* a tax on individuals' earnings. (p. 326)

indentured [ĭn-děn′chərd] **servant** *n.* a person who has agreed to work for another for a limited period, often in return for travel expenses, shelter, and sustenance. (p. 47)

Indian Removal Act *n.* a law, enacted in 1830, that forced Native American peoples east of the Mississippi to move to lands in the West. (p. 211)

Industrial Revolution *n.* the change in social and economic organization that resulted from the replacement of hand tools with machines and from the development of large-scale industrial production. (p. 198)

Industrial Workers of the World (IWW) *n.* a labor organization for unskilled workers, formed by a group of radical unionists and socialists in 1905. (p. 430)

inflation [ĭn-flā′shən] *n.* an increase in prices or decline in purchasing power caused by an increase in the supply of money. (p. 110)

information superhighway [soo′pər-hī′wā] *n.* a proposed computer communications network that would link people and institutions throughout the world, providing individuals with services such as libraries, shopping, movies, and news. (p. 1018)

INF Treaty *n.* the Intermediate-Range Nuclear Forces Treaty—a 1987 agreement between the United States and the Soviet Union that eliminated some weapons systems and allowed for on-site inspection of military installations. (p. 996)

initiative [ĭ-nĭsh′ə-tĭv] *n.* a procedure by which a legislative measure can be originated by the people rather than by lawmakers. (p. 500)

installment [ĭn-stôl′mənt] **plan** *n.* an arrangement in which a purchaser pays over an extended time, without having to put down much money at the time of purchase. (p. 605)

interchangeable [ĭn′tər-chān′jə-bəl] **parts** *n.* standardized parts that can be used in place of one another. (p. 198)

Internet [ĭn′tər-nĕt′] *n.* a worldwide network, originally developed by the U.S. Department of Defense, that links computers and allows almost immediate communication of texts, pictures, and sounds. (p. 1019)

Interstate [ĭn′tər-stāt′] **Commerce Act** *n.* a law, enacted in 1887, that reestablished the federal government's right to supervise railroad activities and created a five-member Interstate Commerce Commission to do so. (p. 420)

Intolerable [ĭn-tŏl′ər-ə-bəl] **Acts** *n.* a series of laws enacted by Parliament in 1774 to punish Massachusetts colonists for the Boston Tea Party. (p. 97)

Iroquois [ĭr′ə-kwoi′] *n.* a group of Native American peoples inhabiting the woodlands of the Northeast. (p. 10)

Islam [ĭs-läm′] *n.* a religion founded in Arabia in A.D. 622 by the prophet Muhammad; its believers are called Muslims. (p. 15)

isolationist [ī′sə-lā′shə-nĭst] *adj.* in opposition to political and economic entanglements with other countries. (p. 597)

J

Japanese American Citizens League (JACL) *n.* an organization that pushed the U.S. government to compensate Japanese Americans for property they had lost when they were interned during World War II. (p. 761)

Jim Crow laws *n.* laws enacted by Southern state and local governments to separate white and black people in public and private facilities. (p. 474)

joint-stock company *n.* a business in which investors pool their wealth for a common purpose. (p. 24)

journeyman [jûr′nē-mən] *n.* in the apprentice system, a skilled worker employed by a master. (p. 241)

judicial [joo-dĭsh′əl] **branch** *n.* the branch of government that interprets the laws and the Constitution. (p. 136)

judicial review *n.* the Supreme Court's power to declare an act of Congress unconstitutional. (p. 186)

Judiciary Act of 1789 *n.* a law that established the federal court system and the Supreme Court and that provided for the appeal of certain state court decisions to the federal courts. (p. 172)

Judiciary [joo-dĭsh′ē-ĕr′ē] **Act of 1801** *n.* a law that increased the number of federal judges, allowing President John Adams to fill most of the new posts with Federalists. (p. 186)

Jungle, The *n.* a novel by Upton Sinclair, published in 1906, that portrayed the disgusting conditions prevalent in the meatpacking industry. (p. 508)

K

kamikaze [kä′mĭ-kä′zē] *adj.* involving or engaging in the deliberate crashing of a bomb-filled airplane into a military target. (p. 749)

Kansas-Nebraska Act *n.* a law, enacted in 1854, that established the territories of Kansas and Nebraska and gave their residents the right to decide whether to allow slavery. (p. 292)

Kashaya Pomo [kə-shä′yə pō′mō] *n.* a Native American people that formerly inhabited the coastal marshlands of what is now California. (p. 8)

Kellogg-Briand [kĕl′ôg′ brē-änd′] **Pact** *n.* a 1929 treaty in which 64 nations agreed to renounce war as a means of solving international disputes. (p. 597)

Kerner [kûr′nər] **Commission** *n.* a group that was appointed by President Johnson to study the causes of the 1965 Watts uprising and that recommended the elimination of de facto segregation in American society. (p. 876)

Khmer Rouge [kmâr′ roozh′] *n.* a Communist group that seized power in Cambodia in 1975. (p. 912)

kickback [kĭk′băk′] *n.* the return of part of a payment, usually as a result of intimidation or a secret agreement. (p. 453)

King Philip's War *n.* a conflict, in the years 1675–1676, between New England colonists and Native American groups allied under the leadership of the Wampanoag chief Metacom. (p. 57)

kinship [kĭn′shĭp′] *n.* the ties between members of a family. (p. 13)

Know-Nothing Party *n.* a name given to the American Party, formed in the 1850s to curtail the political influence of immigrants. (p. 296)

Kongo [kŏng′gō] *n.* a group of small kingdoms along the Zaire River in Central Africa, united under a single leader in the late 1400s. (p. 17)

Korean [kə-rē′ən] **War** *n.* a conflict between North Korea and South Korea, lasting from 1950 to 1953, in which the United States, along with other UN countries, fought on the side of the South Koreans and China fought on the side of the North Koreans. (p. 775)

Kristallnacht [krĭ-stäl′näKHt′] *n.* a name given to the night of November 9, 1938, when gangs of Nazi storm troopers attacked Jewish homes, businesses, and synagogues in Germany. (p. 715)

Ku Klux Klan [kōō′ klŭks klăn′] *n.* a secret organization that used terrorist tactics in an attempt to restore white supremacy in Southern states after the Civil War. (p. 366)

Kwakiutl [kwä′kē-ōōt′l] *n.* a Native American people that formerly inhabited the northwestern coastal region of North America. (p. 9)

L

land grant *n.* a gift of public land to an individual or organization. (p. 269)

Land Ordinance [ôr′dn-əns] **of 1785** *n.* a law that established a plan for surveying and selling the federally owned lands west of the Appalachian Mountains. (p. 128)

La Raza Unida [lä rä′sä ōō-nē′dä] *n.* a Latino political organization founded in 1969 by José Angel Gutiérrez. (p. 922)

League of Nations *n.* an association of nations established in 1920 to promote international cooperation and peace. (p. 578)

legislative [lĕj′ĭ-slā′tĭv] **branch** *n.* the branch of government that makes laws. (p. 135)

Lend-Lease Act *n.* a law, enacted in 1941, that allowed the United States to ship arms and other supplies, without immediate payment, to nations fighting the Axis powers. (p. 721)

Limited Test Ban Treaty *n.* the 1963 treaty in which the United States and the Soviet Union agreed not to conduct nuclear-weapons tests in the atmosphere. (p. 836)

lineage [lĭn′ē-ĭj] *n.* a group of people descended from a common ancestor. (p. 18)

Linotype [lī′nə-tīp′] **machine** *n.* a keyboard-operated typesetting device that casts each line of type as a whole. (p. 466)

literacy [lĭt′ər-ə-sē] **test** *n.* a reading test formerly used in some Southern states to prevent African Americans from voting. (p. 474)

long drive *n.* the moving of cattle over trails to a shipping center. (p. 392)

longhorn [lông′hôrn′] *n.* a breed of sturdy long-horned cattle brought by the Spanish to Mexico and suited to the dry conditions of the Southwest. (p. 388)

Louisiana Purchase *n.* the 1803 purchase by the United States of France's Louisiana Territory—extending from the Mississippi River to the Rocky Mountains—for $15 million. (p. 188)

Loyalist [loi′ə-lĭst] *n.* a colonist who supported the British government during the American Revolution. (p. 102)

Lusitania [lōō′sĭ-tā′nē-ə] *n.* a British passenger ship that was sunk by a German U-boat in 1915. (p. 559)

M

magnetic resonance imaging [măg-nĕt′ĭk rĕz′ə-nəns ĭm′ĭ-jĭng] *n.* a technology—often called MRI—used by physicians to produce cross-sectional images of any part of the human body. (p. 1020)

mail-order catalog *n.* a book showing merchandise that can be ordered and delivered through the mail. (p. 485)

mandate [măn′dāt′] *n.* the authority to act that an elected official receives from the voters who elected him or her. (p. 838)

Manhattan Project [măn-hăt′n prŏj′ĕkt′] *n.* the U.S. program to develop an atomic bomb for use in World War II. (p. 750)

manifest destiny [măn′ə-fĕst′ dĕs′tə-nē] *n.* the 19th-century belief that the United States would inevitably expand westward to the Pacific Ocean and into Mexican territory. (p. 261)

Marbury v. Madison (măr′bar-ē vûr′səs măd′ĭ-sən) *n.* an 1803 case in which the Supreme Court ruled that it had the power to abolish legislative acts by declaring them unconstitutional; this power came to be known as judicial review. (p. 186)

market revolution *n.* the major change in the U.S. economy produced by people's beginning to buy and sell goods rather than make them for themselves. (p. 255)

Marshall [măr′shəl] **Plan** *n.* the program, proposed by Secretary of State George Marshall in 1947, under which the United States supplied economic aid to European nations to help them rebuild after World War II. (p. 770)

martial [măr′shəl] **law** *n.* temporary rule by military rather than civilian authority. (p. 97)

mass media [mē′dē-ə] *n.* the means of communication—such as television, newspapers, and radio—that reach large audiences. (p. 812)

mass production *n.* the production of goods in large quantities, made possible by the use of machinery and the division of labor. (p. 198)

master *n.* a skilled artisan, usually one owning a business and employing others. (p. 241)

Maya [mä′yə] *n.* a Native American people whose civilization flourished in Guatemala and the Yucatán Peninsula between about A.D. 250 and 900. (p. 6)

McCarthyism [mə-kär′thē-ĭz′əm] *n.* the making of public accusations of disloyalty without sufficient evidence, as in Senator Joseph McCarthy's campaign against alleged Communists in the 1950s. (p. 783)

Meat Inspection Act *n.* a law, enacted in 1906, that established strict cleanliness requirements for meatpackers and created a federal meat-inspection program. (p. 509)

mechanized [mĕk′ə-nīzd′] **warfare** *n.* military operations that depend on motorized vehicles, such as tanks and aircraft. (p. 566)

Medicaid [mĕd′ĭ-kād′] *n.* a program, established in 1965, that provides health insurance for people on welfare. (p. 846)

Medicare [mĕd′ĭ-kâr′] *n.* a federal program, established in 1965, that provides hospital insurance and low-cost medical insurance to Americans aged 65 and over. (p. 846)

melting pot *n.* a mixture of people from different cultures and races who blend together by abandoning their native languages and cultures. (p. 442)

mercantilism [mûr′kən-tē-lĭz′əm] *n.* an economic system in which nations seek to increase their wealth and power by obtaining large amounts of gold and silver and by establishing a favorable balance of trade. (p. 66)

Merrimack [mĕr′ə-măk′] *n.* an ironclad ship used by the South in the Civil War. (p. 343)

mestizo [mĕs-tē′zō] *adj.* of mixed Spanish and Native American ancestry. (p. 40)

middle passage *n.* the transportation of slaves from Africa to the West Indies. (p. 74)

midnight judge *n.* one of the judges appointed by John Adams in the last hours of his administration. (p. 186)

militarism [mĭl′ĭ-tə-rĭz′əm] *n.* the policy of building up armed forces in aggressive preparedness for war. (p. 555)

Miranda [mə-răn′də] **rights** *n.* the rights—including the right to remain silent and the right to consult an attorney—that every accused person must be informed of at the time of his or her arrest, according to the Supreme Court's 1966 decision in the case *Miranda* v. *Arizona.* (p. 849)

Mississippian [mĭs′ĭ-sĭp′ē-ən] *n.* the last and most complex of the Mound Builder societies, inhabiting the Ohio and Mississippi valleys from about A.D. 700 into the 1500s. (p. 6)

Missouri Compromise [kŏm′prə-mīz′] *n.* a series of laws enacted in 1820 to maintain the balance of power between slave states and free states. (p. 208)

Monitor [mŏn′ĭ-tər] *n.* an ironclad ship used by the North in the Civil War. (p. 343)

monopoly [mə-nŏp′ə-lē] *n.* a complete control over an industry, achieved by buying up or driving out of business all competitors. (p. 423)

Monroe Doctrine [mən-rō′ dŏk′trĭn] *n.* a policy of U.S. opposition to any European interference in the affairs of the Western Hemisphere, announced by President Monroe in 1823. (p. 207)

Moral Majority [môr′əl mə-jôr′ĭ-tē] *n.* a political alliance of religious groups, consisting mainly of evangelical and fundamentalist Christians, that was active in the 1970s and 1980s, condemning liberal attitudes and behavior and raising money for conservative candidates. (p. 980)

Mormon [môr′mən] *n.* a member of a church founded by Joseph Smith and his associates in 1830. (p. 264)

Morrill [môr′əl] **Land Grant Acts** *n.* laws enacted in 1862 and 1890 to help create agricultural colleges by giving federal land to states. (p. 399)

muckraker [mŭk′rā′kər] *n.* one of the magazine journalists who exposed corrupt business practices in the early 1900s. (p. 496)

Munn v. Illinois [mŭn′ vûr′səs ĭl′ə-noi′] *n.* an 1877 case in which the Supreme Court upheld states' regulation of railroads for the benefit of farmers and consumers, thus establishing the right of government to regulate private industry to serve the public interest. (p. 420)

N

NAACP [ĕn′ dŭb′əl ā′ sē′ pē′] *n.* the National Association for the Advancement of Colored People—an organization founded in 1909 to promote full racial equality. (p. 511)

NACW *n.* the National Association of Colored Women—a social service organization founded in 1896. (p. 503)

NAFTA [năf′tə] *n.* the North American Free Trade Agreement—a 1993 treaty that lowered tariffs and brought Mexico into the free-trade zone established by the United States and Canada. (p. 1009)

napalm [nā′päm′] *n.* a gasoline-based substance used in bombs that U.S. planes dropped in Vietnam in order to burn away jungle and expose Vietcong hideouts. (p. 892)

national bank *n.* a bank chartered by the federal government and having the power to act on the government's behalf in financial matters. (p. 174)

National Energy Act *n.* a law, enacted during the Carter administration, that established a tax on gas-guzzling automobiles, removed price controls on U.S. oil and natural gas, and provided tax credits for the development of alternative energy sources. (p. 963)

National Industrial Recovery Act *n.* a law enacted in 1933 to establish codes of fair practice for industries and to promote industrial growth. (p. 668)

nationalism [năsh′ə-nə-lĭz′əm] *n.* a belief that national interests should be placed ahead of regional concerns and that foreign policy should be guided by national self-interest. (p. 205)

National Labor Relations Board *n.* an agency created in 1935 to prevent unfair labor practices and to mediate disputes between workers and management. (p. 691)

National Organization for Women *n.* an organization founded in 1966 to pursue feminists' goals, such as better child-care facilities, improved educational opportunities, and an end to job discrimination. (p. 930)

National Road *n.* a federally funded road begun in 1811 and by 1838 extending from Cumberland, Maryland to Vandalia, Illinois. (p. 203)

National Trades' Union *n.* the first national association of trade unions, formed in 1834. (p. 245)

National Youth Administration *n.* an agency that provided young Americans with aid and employment during the Great Depression. (p. 673)

Nation of Islam [ĭs-läm′] *n.* a religious group, popularly known as the Black Muslims, founded by Elijah Muhammad to promote black separatism and the Islamic religion. (p. 873)

nativism [nā′tĭ-vĭz′əm] *n.* the favoring of the interests of native-born people over the interests of immigrants. (p. 296)

Navigation [năv′ĭ-gā′shən] **Acts** *n.* a series of laws enacted by Parliament, beginning in 1651, to tighten England's control of trade in its American colonies. (p. 67)

NAWSA *n.* the National American Woman Suffrage Association—an organization founded in 1890 to gain voting rights for women. (p. 503)

Nazism [nät′sĭz′əm] *n.* the political philosophy—based on extreme nationalism, racism, and militaristic expansionism—that Adolf Hitler put into practice in Germany from 1933 to 1945. (p. 704)

neutrality *n.* a refusal to take part in a war between other nations. (p. 178)

Neutrality Acts *n.* a series of laws enacted in 1935 and 1936 to prevent U.S. arms sales and loans to nations at war. (p. 706)

New Deal *n.* President Franklin Roosevelt's program to alleviate the problems of the Great Depression, focusing on relief for the needy, economic recovery, and financial reform. (p. 665)

New Deal Coalition [kō′ə-lĭsh′ən] *n.* an alliance of diverse groups—including Southern whites, African Americans, and unionized workers—who supported the policies of the Democratic Party in the 1930s and 1940s. (p. 680)

New Federalism [fĕd′ər-ə-lĭz′əm] *n.* President Richard Nixon's program to turn over part of the federal government's power to state and local governments. (p. 946)

New Frontier *n.* President John F. Kennedy's legislative program, which included proposals to provide medical care for the elderly, to rebuild blighted urban areas, to aid education, to bolster the national defense, to increase international aid, and to expand the space program. (p. 838)

New Left *n.* a youth-dominated political movement of the 1960s, embodied in such organizations as Students for a Democratic Society and the Free Speech Movement. (p. 897)

New Right *n.* a late-20th-century alliance of conservative special-interest groups concerned with cultural, social, and moral issues. (p. 979)

Nineteenth Amendment *n.* an amendment to the U.S. Constitution, adopted in 1920, that gave women the right to vote. (p. 520)

Nisei [nē-sā′] *n.* a U.S. citizen born of immigrant Japanese parents. (p. 735)

no man's land *n.* an unoccupied region between opposing armies. (p. 557)

nonaggression [nŏn′ə-grĕsh′ən] **pact** *n.* an agreement in which two nations promise not to go to war with each other. (p. 711)

North Atlantic Treaty Organization (NATO) *n.* a defensive military alliance formed in 1949 by ten Western European countries, the United States, and Canada. (p. 772)

Northwest Ordinance [ôr′dn-əns] **of 1787** *n.* a law that established a procedure for the admission of new states to the Union. (p. 128)

nuclear [nōō′klē-ər] **family** *n.* a household made up of a mother, a father, and their children. (p. 21)

nullification [nŭl′ə-fĭ-kā′shən] *n.* a state's refusal to recognize an act of Congress that it considers unconstitutional. (p. 181)

Nuremberg [nŏŏr′əm-bûrg′] **trials** *n.* the court proceedings held in Nuremberg, Germany, after World War II, in which Nazi leaders were tried for war crimes. (p. 752)

O

Office of Price Administration (OPA) *n.* an agency established by Congress to control inflation during World War II. (p. 736)

Ohio gang *n.* a group of close friends and political supporters whom President Warren G. Harding appointed to his cabinet. (p. 599)

Olive Branch Petition [pə-tĭsh′ən] *n.* a document sent by the Second Continental Congress to King George III, proposing a reconciliation between the colonies and Britain. (p. 100)

Olmec [ŏl′mĕk] *n.* a Native American people whose civilization flourished in what is now southern Mexico in the period 1200–400 B.C. (p. 6)

OPEC [ō′pĕk′] *n.* the Organization of Petroleum Exporting Countries—an economic association of oil-producing nations that is able to set oil prices. (p. 950)

Open Door notes *n.* messages sent by Secretary of State John Hay in 1899 to Germany, Russia, Britain, France, Italy, and Japan, asking the countries not to interfere with U.S. trading rights in China. (p. 530)

Operation Desert Storm [dĕz′ərt stôrm′] *n.* a 1991 military operation in which UN forces, led by the United States, drove Iraqi invaders from Kuwait. (p. 1000)

Oregon Trail *n.* a route from Independence, Missouri, to Portland, Oregon, used by pioneers traveling to the Oregon Territory. (p. 263)

P

Panama Canal [păn′ə-mä′ kə-năl′] *n.* an artificial waterway cut through the Isthmus of Panama to provide a shortcut between the Atlantic and Pacific oceans, opened in 1914. (p. 544)

Panic of 1837 *n.* a U.S. financial crisis in which banks closed and the credit system collapsed, resulting in many bankruptcies and high unemployment. (p. 218)

Panic of 1873 *n.* a series of financial failures that triggered a five-year depression in the United States. (p. 370)

parity [păr′ĭ-tē] *n.* a government-supported level for the prices of agricultural products, intended to keep farmers' income steady. (p. 692)

Parliament [pär′lə-mənt] *n.* the legislative body of England. (p. 67)

Patriot [pā′trē-ət] *n.* a colonist who supported American independence from Britain. (p. 102)

patronage [pā′trə-nĭj] *n.* an officeholder's power to appoint people—usually those who have helped him or her get elected—to positions in government. (p. 455)

pay equity [ĕk′wĭ-tē] *n.* the basing of an employee's salary on the requirements of his or her job rather than on the traditional pay scales that have frequently provided women with smaller incomes than men. (p. 991)

Payne-Aldrich Tariff [pān′ ôl′drĭch tăr′ĭf] *n.* a set of tax regulations, enacted by Congress in 1909, that failed to significantly reduce tariffs on manufactured goods. (p. 513)

Peace Corps *n.* an agency established in 1961 to provide volunteer assistance to developing nations in Asia, Africa, and Latin America. (p. 839)

Pendleton [pĕn′dl-tən] **Act** *n.* a law, enacted in 1883, that established a bipartisan civil service commission to make appointments to government jobs by means of the merit system. (p. 456)

Pentagon [pĕn′tə-gŏn′] **Papers** *n.* a 7,000-page document—leaked to the press in 1971 by the former Defense Department worker Daniel Ellsberg—revealing that the U.S. government had not been honest about its intentions in the Vietnam War. (p. 910)

Pequot [pē′kwŏt′] **War** *n.* a 1637 conflict in which the Pequot nation battled Connecticut colonists and their Narragansett allies. (p. 56)

perestroika [pĕr′ĭ-stroi′kə] *n.* the restructuring of the economy and the government instituted in the Soviet Union in the 1980s. (p. 996)

personal liberty laws *n.* statutes, passed in nine Northern states in the 1850s, that forbade the imprisonment of runaway slaves and guaranteed jury trials for fugitive slaves. (p. 289)

planned obsolescence [ŏb′sə-lĕs′əns] *n.* the designing of products to wear out or to become outdated quickly, so that people will feel a need to replace their possessions frequently. (p. 809)

plantation [plăn-tā′shən] *n.* a large farm on which the labor of slaves or other workers is used to grow a single crop, such as sugar cane or cotton. (p. 16)

Platt [plăt] **Amendment** *n.* a series of provisions that, in 1901, the United States insisted Cuba add to its new constitution, giving the United States the right to intervene in the country and the right to buy or lease Cuban land for naval and coaling stations. (p. 537)

Plessy v. Ferguson [plĕs′ē vûr′səs fûr′gə-sən] *n.* an 1896 case in which the Supreme Court ruled that separation of the races in public accommodations was legal, thus establishing the "separate but equal" doctrine. (p. 475)

political machine *n.* an organized group that controls a political party in a city and offers services to voters and businesses in exchange for political and financial support. (p. 452)

poll [pōl] **tax** *n.* an annual tax that formerly had to be paid in some Southern states by anyone wishing to vote. (p. 474)

popular sovereignty [sŏv′ər-ĭn-tē] *n.* the principle that the residents of a territory should have control over their own affairs—particularly the power to decide whether to admit slavery. (p. 285)

Populism [pŏp′yə-lĭz′əm] *n.* a late-19th-century political movement seeking to advance the interests of farmers and laborers. (p. 402)

Powhatan [pou′ə-tăn′] *n.* a group of Native American peoples that lived in eastern Virginia at the time of the first English settlements there. (p. 45)

price support *n.* the maintenance of a price at a certain level through government intervention. (p. 643)

Proclamation [prŏk′lə-mā′shən] **of 1763** *n.* an order in which Britain prohibited its American colonists from settling west of the Appalachian Mountains. (p. 86)

profiteering [prŏf′ĭ-tîr′ĭng] *n.* the selling of goods in short supply at inflated prices. (p. 110)

progressive [prə-grĕs′ĭv] **movement** *n.* an early-20th-century reform movement seeking to return control of the government to the people, to restore economic opportunities, and to correct injustices in American life. (p. 494)

prohibition [prō′ə-bĭsh′ən] *n.* the banning of the manufacture, sale, and possession of alcoholic beverages. (p. 495)

proprietor [prə-prī′ĭ-tər] *n.* an owner—particularly one of those granted ownership of, and full governing rights over, certain of the English colonies in North America. (p. 59)

protective tariff [prə-tĕk′tĭv tăr′ĭf] *n.* a tax on imported goods that is intended to protect a nation's businesses from foreign competition. (p. 176)

protectorate [prə-tĕk′tə-rĭt] *n.* a country whose affairs are partially controlled by a stronger power. (p. 537)

Pueblo [pwĕb′lō] *n.* a group of Native American peoples—descendants of the Anasazi—inhabiting the deserts of the Southwest. (p. 9)

Pure Food and Drug Act *n.* a law enacted in 1906 to halt the sale of contaminated foods and drugs and to assure truth in labeling. (p. 509)

Puritan [pyŏŏr′ĭ-tn] *n.* a member of a group that wanted to eliminate all traces of Roman Catholic ritual and traditions in the Church of England. (p. 52)

putting-out [pŏŏt′ĭng out′] **system** *n.* a system of production in which manufacturers provide the materials for goods to be produced in the home. (p. 240)

Q

Quaker [kwā′kər] *n.* a member of the Society of Friends, a religious group persecuted for its beliefs in 17th-century England. (p. 59)

quota [kwō′tə] **system** *n.* a system that sets limits on how many immigrants from various countries a nation will admit each year. (p. 599)

R

Radical Republican [răd′ĭ-kəl rĭ-pŭb′lĭ-kən] *n.* one of the congressional Republicans who, after the Civil War, wanted to destroy the political power of former slaveholders and to give African Americans full citizenship and the right to vote. (p. 351)

ragtime [răg′tīm′] *n.* a form of music, originating in the 1880s, in which the styles of African-American spirituals and European music were blended. (p. 481)

ratification [răt′ə-fĭ-kā′shən] *n.* the official approval of the Constitution, or of an amendment, by the states. (p. 137)

rationing [răsh′ə-nĭng] *n.* a restriction of people's right to buy unlimited amounts of particular foods and other goods, often implemented during wartime to assure adequate supplies for the military. (p. 736)

Reaganomics [rā′gə-nŏm′ĭks] *n.* the economic policies of President Ronald Reagan, which were focused on the granting of large tax cuts in order to increase private investment. (p. 982)

realpolitik [rā-äl′pō′lĭ-tēk′] *n.* a political philosophy, advocated by Henry Kissinger in the Nixon administration, that involves dealing with other nations in a practical and flexible way rather than according to a rigid policy. (p. 951)

reapportionment [rē′ə-pôr′shən-mənt] *n.* the redrawing of election districts to reflect changes in population. (p. 848)

recall [rĭ-kôl′] *n.* a procedure for removing a public official from office by a vote of the people. (p. 500)

Reconstruction [rē′kən-strŭk′shən] *n.* the period of rebuilding that followed the Civil War, during which the defeated Confederate states were readmitted to the Union. (p. 350)

Reconstruction Finance [fə-năns′] **Corporation** *n.* an agency established in 1932 to provide emergency financing to banks, life-insurance companies, railroads, and other large businesses. (p. 658)

redemption [rĭ-dĕmp′shən] *n.* the Southern Democrats' term for their return to power in the South in the 1870s. (p. 371)

referendum [rĕf′ə-rĕn′dəm] *n.* a procedure by which a proposed legislative measure can be submitted to a vote of the people. (p. 500)

Reformation [rĕf′ər-mā′shən] *n.* a religious movement in 16th-century Europe, growing out of a desire for reform in the Roman Catholic Church and leading to the establishment of various Protestant churches. (p. 22)

reparations [rĕp′ə-rā′shənz] *n.* the compensation paid by a defeated nation for the damage or injury it inflicted during a war. (p. 578)

republic [rĭ-pŭb′lĭk] *n.* a government in which the citizens rule through elected representatives. (p. 126)

Republican [rĭ-pŭb′lĭ-kən] *n.* a member of the political party that supported Thomas Jefferson's vision of strong state governments. (p. 175)

republicanism [rĭ-pŭb′lĭ-kə-nĭz′əm] *n.* the belief that government should be based on the consent of the people. (p. 126)

Republican Party *n.* the modern political party that was formed in 1854 by opponents of slavery in the territories. (p. 297)

revenue [rĕv′ə-nōō] **sharing** *n.* the distribution of federal money to state and local governments with few or no restrictions on how it is spent. (p. 946)

reverse discrimination [dĭ-skrĭm′ə-nā′shən] *n.* an unfair treatment of members of a majority group—for example, white men—resulting from efforts to correct discrimination against members of other groups. (p. 979)

revival [rĭ-vī′vəl] *n.* a religious gathering designed to reawaken faith through impassioned preaching. (p. 224)

rock 'n' roll [rŏk′ən-rōl′] *n.* a form of popular music, characterized by heavy rhythms and simple melodies, that developed from rhythm and blues during the 1950s. (p. 816)

Roosevelt Corollary [rō′zə-vĕlt′ kôr′ə-lĕr-ē] *n.* an extension of the Monroe Doctrine, announced by President Theodore Roosevelt in 1904, under which the United States claimed the right to protect its economic interests by means of military intervention in the affairs of Western Hemisphere nations. (p. 544)

Rough Riders *n.* a volunteer cavalry regiment, commanded by Leonard Wood and Theodore Roosevelt, that served in the Spanish-American-Cuban War. (p. 533)

row [rō] **house** *n.* a single-family dwelling that shares side walls with other, similar houses. (p. 448)

royal colony *n.* a colony under the direct control of the English monarch. (p. 48)

rural free delivery *n.* the free government delivery of mail and packages to homes in rural areas, begun in 1896. (p. 485)

S

SALT I [sôlt′ wŭn′] **Treaty** *n.* a five-year agreement between the United States and the Soviet Union, signed in 1972, that limited the nations' numbers of intercontinental ballistic missiles and submarine-launched missiles. (p. 952)

salutary neglect [săl′yə-tĕr′ē nĭ-glĕkt′] *n.* an English policy of relaxing the enforcement of regulations in its colonies in return for the colonies' continued economic loyalty. (p. 69)

Sand Creek Massacre [măs′ə-kər] *n.* an attack by U.S. soldiers on a Cheyenne encampment in the Colorado Territory in 1864, in which 200 Native American men, women, and children were killed. (p. 383)

Sandinista [săn′dĭ-nēs′tə] *adj.* belonging to a leftist group that overthrew the Nicaraguan government in 1979. (p. 998)

Santa Fe [săn′tə fā′] **Trail** *n.* a route from Independence, Missouri, to Santa Fe, New Mexico, used by traders in the early and mid 1800s. (p. 262)

satellite [săt′l-īt′] **nation** *n.* a country that is dominated politically and economically by another nation. (p. 769)

Saturday Night Massacre [măs′ə-kər] *n.* a name given to the resignation of the U.S. attorney general and the firing of his deputy in October 1973, after they refused to carry out President Nixon's order to fire the special prosecutor investigating the Watergate affair. (p. 956)

savanna [sə-văn′ə] *n.* a dry grassland dotted with trees and bushes, found in sub-Saharan Africa and other tropical or subtropical regions. (p. 14)

scab *n.* a person who works while others are on strike. (p. 431)

scalawag [skăl′ə-wăg′] *n.* a white Southerner who joined the Republican Party after the Civil War. (p. 357)

scientific management *n.* the application of scientific principles to increase efficiency in the workplace. (p. 496)

Scopes [skōps] **trial** *n.* a sensational 1925 court case in which the biology teacher John T. Scopes was tried for challenging a Tennessee law that outlawed the teaching of evolution. (p. 616)

search-and-destroy mission *n.* a U.S. military raid on a South Vietnamese village, intended to root out villagers with ties to the Vietcong but often resulting in the destruction of the village and the displacement of its inhabitants. (p. 892)

secession [sĭ-sĕsh′ən] *n.* the formal withdrawal of a state from the Union. (p. 285)

Second Continental Congress *n.* the Continental Congress that convened in May 1775, approved the Declaration of Independence, and served as the only agency of national government during the Revolutionary War. (p. 99)

Second Great Awakening *n.* a 19th-century religious movement in which individual responsibility for seeking salvation was emphasized, along with the need for personal and social improvement. (p. 224)

sectionalism [sĕk′shə-nə-lĭz′əm] *n.* the placing of the interests of one's own region ahead of the interests of the nation as a whole. (p. 180)

Securities and Exchange [sĭ-kyŏŏr′ĭ-tēz ənd ĭks-chānj′] **Commission** *n.* an agency, created in 1934, that monitors the stock market and enforces laws regulating the sale of stocks and bonds. (p. 692)

segregation [sĕg′rĭ-gā′shən] *n.* the separation of people on the basis of race. (p. 474)

Selective [sĭ-lĕk′tĭv] **Service Act** *n.* a law, enacted in 1917, that required men to register for military service. (p. 562)

Seneca Falls [sĕn′ĭ-kə fôlz′] **Convention** *n.* a women's rights convention held in Seneca Falls, New York, in 1848. (p. 238)

Separatist [sĕp′ər-ə-tĭst] *n.* a member of one of the Puritan groups that, denying the possibility of reform within the Church of England, established their own independent congregations. (p. 53)

service sector [sĕk'tər] *n.* the part of the economy that provides consumers with services rather than goods. (p. 1013)

settlement house *n.* a community center providing assistance to residents—particularly immigrants—in a slum neighborhood. (p. 451)

Seventeenth Amendment *n.* an amendment to the U.S. Constitution, adopted in 1913, that provided for the election of U.S. senators by the people rather than by state legislatures. (p. 500)

shantytown [shăn'tē-toun'] *n.* a neighborhood in which people live in shacks. (p. 650)

sharecropping [shâr'krŏp'ĭng] *n.* a system in which landowners give farm workers land, seed, and tools in return for a part of the crops they raise. (p. 364)

Shays's [shā'zəz] **Rebellion** *n.* an uprising of debt-ridden Massachusetts farmers in 1787. (p. 132)

Sherman Antitrust [shûr'mən ăn'tē-trŭst'] **Act** *n.* a law, enacted in 1890, that was intended to prevent the creation of monopolies by making it illegal to establish trusts that interfered with free trade. (p. 424)

silent majority [mə-jôr'ĭ-tē] *n.* a name given by President Richard Nixon to the moderate, mainstream Americans who quietly supported his Vietnam War policies. (p. 908)

sit-in *n.* a form of demonstration used by African Americans to protest discrimination, in which the protesters sit down in a segregated business and refuse to leave until they are served. (p. 862)

Social Darwinism [sō'shəl där'wĭ-nĭz'əm] *n.* an economic and social philosophy—supposedly based on the biologist Charles Darwin's theory of evolution by natural selection—holding that a system of unrestrained competition will ensure the survival of the fittest. (p. 422)

Social Gospel [gŏs'pəl] **movement** *n.* a 19th-century reform movement based on the belief that Christians have a responsibility to help improve working conditions and alleviate poverty. (p. 451)

socialism [sō'shə-lĭz'əm] *n.* an economic and political system based on government ownership of business and property and on equal distribution of wealth. (p. 429)

Social Security Act *n.* a law enacted in 1935 to provide aid to retirees, the unemployed, people with disabilities, and dependent mothers and children. (p. 675)

soddy [sŏd'ē] *n.* a home built of blocks of turf. (p. 398)

Songhai [sông'hī'] *n.* an empire that, at the height of its power in the 1500s, controlled much of West Africa. (p. 17)

soup kitchen *n.* a place where free food is served to the needy. (p. 651)

Southern Christian Leadership Conference *n.* an organization formed in 1957 by Dr. Martin Luther King, Jr., and other leaders to work for civil rights through nonviolent means. (p. 862)

Southern strategy *n.* President Nixon's attempt to attract the support of Southern conservative Democrats who were unhappy with federal desegregation policies with the liberal Supreme Court. (p. 948)

speakeasy [spēk'ē'zē] *n.* a place where alcoholic drinks were sold and consumed illegally during Prohibition. (p. 614)

specialization [spĕsh'ə-lĭ-zā'shən] *n.* in farming, the raising of one or two crops for sale rather than a variety of foods for personal use. (p. 254)

speculation [spĕk'yə-lā'shən] *n.* an involvement in risky business transactions in an effort to make a quick or large profit. (p. 645)

spoils system *n.* the practice of winning candidates' rewarding their supporters with government jobs. (p. 211)

Square Deal *n.* President Theodore Roosevelt's program of progressive reforms designed to protect the common people against big business. (p. 506)

stagflation [stăg-flā'shən] *n.* an economic condition marked by both inflation and high unemployment. (p. 950)

Stalwart [stôl'wərt] *n.* a Republican who supported the New York political boss Roscoe Conkling and opposed civil service reform. (p. 456)

Stamp Act *n.* a 1765 law in which Parliament established the first direct taxation of goods and services within the British colonies in North America. (p. 94)

Stono [stō'nō] **Rebellion** *n.* a 1739 uprising of slaves in South Carolina, leading to the tightening of already harsh slave laws. (p. 76)

Strategic Defense Initiative [strə-tē'jĭk dĭ-fĕns' ĭ-nĭsh'ə-tĭv] *n.* a proposed defense system—popularly known as Star Wars—intended to protect the United States against missile attacks. (p. 983)

strike *n.* a work stoppage intended to force an employer to respond to demands. (p. 243)

Student Nonviolent Coordinating [nŏn-vī'ə-lənt kō-ôr'dn-ā'tĭng] **Committee** *n.* an organization formed in 1960 to coordinate sit-ins and other protests and to give young blacks a larger role in the civil rights movement. (p. 862)

Students for a Democratic Society *n.* an antiestablishment New Left group, founded in 1960, that called for greater individual freedom and responsibility. (p. 897)

suburb [sŭb'ûrb'] *n.* a residential town or community near a city. (p. 796)

suffrage [sŭf'rĭj] *n.* the right to vote. (p. 503)

Sugar Act *n.* a trade law enacted by Parliament in 1764 in an attempt to reduce smuggling in the British colonies in North America. (p. 87)

supply-side economics *n.* the idea that a reduction of tax rates will lead to increases in jobs, savings, and investments, and therefore to an increase in government revenue. (p. 983)

T

Taino [tī'nō] *n.* a Native American people of the Caribbean islands—the first group encountered by Columbus and his men when they reached the Americas. (p. 27)

Tammany [tăm'ə-nē] **Hall** *n.* the Democratic political machine that dominated New York City in the late 19th century. (p. 454)

Tariff of Abominations [ə-bŏm'ə-nā'shənz] *n.* Henry Clay's name for an 1828 tariff increase that seemed to Southerners to be enriching the North at their expense. (p. 214)

Tariff of 1816 *n.* a protective tariff designed to aid American industries. (p. 203)

1090 Glossary

Teapot Dome scandal [skăn′dl] *n.* Secretary of the Interior Albert B. Fall's secret leasing of oil-rich public land to private companies in return for money and land. (p. 600)

Telecommunications [tĕl′ĭ-kə-myōō′nĭ-kā′shənz] **Act** *n.* a law enacted in 1996 to remove barriers that had previously prevented communications companies from engaging in more than one type of communications business. (p. 1019)

telecommute [tĕl′ĭ-kə-myōōt′] *v.* to work at home for a company located elsewhere, by using such new communications technologies as computers, modems, and fax machines. (p. 1025)

telegraph [tĕl′ĭ-grăf′] *n.* a device for the electrical transmission of coded messages over wires. (p. 256)

temperance [tĕm′pər-əns] **movement** *n.* an organized effort to prevent the drinking of alcoholic beverages. (p. 236)

tenant [tĕn′ənt] **farming** *n.* a system in which farm workers supply their own tools and rent farmland for cash. (p. 364)

Tennessee Valley Authority *n.* a federal corporation established in 1933 to construct dams and power plants in the Tennessee Valley region. (p. 693)

termination [tûr′mə-nā′shən] **policy** *n.* the U.S. government's plan, announced in 1953, to give up responsibility for Native American tribes by eliminating federal economic support, discontinuing the reservation system, and redistributing tribal lands. (p. 823)

Tet offensive [tĕt′ ə-fĕn′sĭv] *n.* a massive surprise attack by the Vietcong on South Vietnamese towns and cities early in 1968. (p. 901)

Texas Revolution *n.* the 1836 rebellion in which Texas gained its independence from Mexico. (p. 271)

Thirteenth Amendment *n.* an amendment to the U.S. Constitution, adopted in 1865, that abolished slavery and involuntary servitude. (p. 343)

Three-Fifths Compromise [kŏm′prə-mīz′] *n.* the Constitutional Convention's agreement to count three-fifths of a state's slaves as population for purposes of representation and taxation. (p. 134)

Tiananmen [tyän′än′mĕn′] **Square** *n.* the site of 1989 demonstrations in Beijing, China, in which Chinese students demanded freedom of speech and a greater voice in government. (p. 998)

Tonkin Gulf [tŏn′kĭn′ gŭlf′] **Resolution** *n.* a resolution adopted by Congress in 1964, giving the president broad powers to wage war in Vietnam. (p. 888)

totalitarian [tō-tăl′ĭ-târ′ē-ən] *adj.* characteristic of a political system in which the government exercises complete control over its citizens' lives. (p. 704)

Townshend [toun′zənd] **Acts** *n.* a series of laws enacted by Parliament in 1767, establishing indirect taxes on goods imported from Britain by the British colonies in North America. (p. 95)

trade imbalance [ĭm-băl′əns] *n.* a situation in which a country imports more goods than it exports. (p. 984)

Trail of Tears [tîrz] *n.* the routes along which the Cherokee people were forcibly removed from Georgia to the Indian Territory in 1838, with thousands of the Cherokee dying on the way. (p. 213)

transcendentalism [trăn′sĕn-dĕn′tl-ĭz′əm] *n.* a philosophical and literary movement of the 1800s that emphasized living a simple life and celebrated the truth found in nature and in personal emotion and imagination. (p. 226)

transcontinental [trăns′kŏn-tə-nĕn′tl] **railroad** *n.* a railroad line linking the Atlantic and Pacific coasts of the United States, completed in 1869. (p. 416)

Treaty of Ghent [gĕnt] *n.* the 1814 treaty that ended the War of 1812. (p. 191)

Treaty of Guadalupe Hidalgo [gwäd′l-ōōp′ hĭ-däl′gō] *n.* the 1848 treaty ending the U.S. war with Mexico, in which Mexico ceded California and New Mexico to the United States. (p. 276)

Treaty of Paris *n.* **1.** the 1763 treaty that ended the French and Indian War. **2.** the 1783 treaty that ended the Revolutionary War, confirming the independence of the United States and setting the boundaries of the new nation (p. 115). **3.** the 1898 treaty that ended the Spanish-American-Cuban War. (p. 115)

Treaty of Tordesillas [tôr′də-sē′əs] *n.* the 1494 treaty in which Spain and Portugal agreed to divide the lands of the Western Hemisphere between them. (p. 31)

Treaty of Versailles [vər-sī′] *n.* the 1919 treaty that ended World War I. (p. 578)

trench warfare *n.* military operations in which the opposing forces attack and counterattack from systems of fortified ditches rather than on an open battlefield. (p. 557)

triangular [trī-ăng′gyə-lər] **trade** *n.* the transatlantic system of trade in which goods, including slaves, were exchanged between Africa, England, Europe, the West Indies, and the colonies in North America. (p. 73)

Truman Doctrine [trōō′mən dŏk′trĭn] *n.* a U.S. policy, announced by President Harry S. Truman in 1947, of providing economic and military aid to free nations threatened by internal or external opponents. (p. 770)

trust *n.* a method of consolidating competing companies, in which participants turn their stock over to a board of trustees, who run the companies as one large corporation. (p. 423)

Tweed Ring *n.* a group of corrupt New York politicians, led by William Marcy "Boss" Tweed, who took as much as $2 million from the city between 1869 and 1871. (p. 454)

two-party system *n.* a political system dominated by two major parties. (p. 176)

UV

Uncle Tom's Cabin *n.* a best-selling novel by Harriet Beecher Stowe, published in 1852, that portrayed slavery as a great moral evil. (p. 290)

Underground Railroad *n.* a system of routes along which runaway slaves were helped to escape to Canada or to safe areas in the free states. (p. 289)

United Farm Workers Organizing Committee *n.* a labor union formed in 1966 to seek higher wages and better working conditions for Mexican-American farm workers in California. (p. 922)

United Nations (UN) *n.* an international peacekeeping organization to which most nations in the world belong, founded in 1945 to promote world peace, security, and economic development. (p. 752)

Universal Negro Improvement Association *n.* a black nationalist group founded in Jamaica by Marcus Garvey in 1914. (p. 631)

urban [ûr′bən] **flight** *n.* a migration of people from cities to the surrounding suburbs. (p. 1024)

urbanization [ûr′bə-nĭ-zā′shən] *n.* the growth of cities. (p. 446)

urban renewal [rĭ-nōō′əl] *n.* the tearing down and replacing of buildings in rundown inner-city neighborhoods. (p. 821)

urban sprawl [sprôl′] *n.* the unplanned and uncontrolled spreading of cities into surrounding regions. (p. 602)

U.S.S. *Maine* *n.* a U.S. warship that mysteriously exploded and sank in the harbor of Havana, Cuba, on February 15, 1898. (p. 532)

utopian [yōō-tō′pē-ən] **community** *n.* an experimental community designed to be a perfect society, in which its members could live together in harmony. (p. 228)

U-2 incident *n.* the downing of a U.S. spy plane and capture of its pilot by the Soviet Union in 1960. (p. 789)

vaudeville [vôd′vĭl′] *n.* a form of stage entertainment that features a variety of short performances, including songs, dances, and comedy routines. (p. 481)

V-E Day *n.* a name given to May 8, 1945, on which General Eisenhower's acceptance of the unconditional surrender of Nazi Germany marked the end of World War II in Europe. (p. 745)

vertical integration [vûr′tĭ-kəl ĭn′tĭ-grā′shən] *n.* a company's taking over its suppliers and distributors to gain total control over the quality and cost of its product. (p. 422)

Vietcong [vē-ĕt′kŏng′] *n.* the South Vietnamese Communists who, with North Vietnamese support, fought against the government of South Vietnam in the Vietnam War. (p. 886)

Vietminh [vē-ĕt′mĭn′] *n.* an organization of Vietnamese Communists and other nationalist groups that between 1946 and 1954 fought for Vietnamese independence from the French. (p. 885)

Vietnamization [vē-ĕt′nə-mĭ-zā′shən] *n.* President Nixon's strategy for ending U.S. involvement in the Vietnam War, involving the gradual withdrawal of U.S. troops and their replacement with South Vietnamese forces. (p. 908)

Voting Rights Act of 1965 *n.* a law that made it easier for African Americans to register to vote by eliminating discriminatory literacy tests and authorizing federal examiners to enroll voters denied at the local level. (p. 870)

W

Wade-Davis [wād′ dā′vəs] **Bill** *n.* a bill, passed in 1864 and vetoed by President Lincoln, that would have given Congress control of Reconstruction. (p. 351)

Wagner [wăg′nər] **Act** *n.* a law—also known as the National Labor Relations Act—enacted in 1935 to protect workers' rights after the Supreme Court declared the National Industrial Recovery Act unconstitutional. (p. 674)

war-guilt [wôr′ gĭlt′] **clause** *n.* a provision in the Treaty of Versailles by which Germany acknowledged that it alone was responsible for World War I. (p. 578)

war hawk *n.* one of the members of Congress who favored war with Britain in the early years of the 19th century. (p. 190)

War Industries Board *n.* an agency established during World War I to increase efficiency and discourage waste in war-related industries. (p. 570)

War Powers Act *n.* a law enacted in 1973, limiting a president's right to send troops into battle without consulting Congress. (p. 913)

War Production Board *n.* an agency established during World War II to coordinate the production of military supplies by U.S. industries. (p. 736)

Warren [wôr′ən] **Commission** *n.* a group, headed by Chief Justice Earl Warren, that investigated the assassination of President Kennedy and concluded that Lee Harvey Oswald was alone responsible for it. (p. 842)

Warren Court *n.* the Supreme Court during the period when Earl Warren was chief justice, noted for its activism in the areas of civil rights and free speech. (p. 848)

Warsaw [wôr′sô′] **Pact** *n.* a military alliance formed in 1955 by the Soviet Union and its Eastern European satellites. (p. 786)

Watergate [wô′tər-gāt′] *n.* a scandal arising from the Nixon administration's attempt to cover up its involvement in the 1972 break-in at the Democratic National Committee headquarters in the Watergate apartment complex. (p. 953)

web-perfecting [pər-fĕk′tĭng] **press** *n.* an electrically powered press that prints on both sides of a continuous roll of paper, then cuts, folds, and counts the pages. (p. 465)

Whig [hwĭg] *n.* a member of the political party formed in 1834 to oppose the policies of Andrew Jackson. (p. 218)

Wilmot Proviso [wĭl′mət prə-vī′zō] *n.* an amendment to an 1846 military appropriations bill, proposing that none of the territory acquired in the war with Mexico would be open to slavery. (p. 283)

Woodstock [wŏŏd′stŏk′] *n.* a free music festival that attracted more than 400,000 young people to a farm in upstate New York in August 1969. (p. 936)

Works Progress Administration *n.* an agency, established as part of the New Deal, that provided the unemployed with jobs in construction, garment making, teaching, the arts, and other fields. (p. 673)

XYZ

XYZ Affair *n.* a 1797 incident in which French officials demanded a bribe from U.S. diplomats. (p. 180)

Yalta [yôl′tə] **Conference** *n.* a 1945 meeting at which the leaders of the United States, Great Britain, and the Soviet Union agreed on a set of measures to be implemented after the defeat of Germany. (p. 752)

yellow journalism [jûr′nə-lĭz′əm] *n.* the use of sensationalized and exaggerated reporting by newspapers or magazines to attract readers. (p. 531)

Zimmermann [zĭm′ər-mən] **note** *n.* a message sent in 1917 by the German foreign minister to the German ambassador in Mexico, proposing a German-Mexican alliance and promising to help Mexico regain Texas, New Mexico, and Arizona if the United States entered World War I. (p. 561)

SPANISH GLOSSARY

A

abolition [abolición] *s.* cese obligatorio de la esclavitud legal. (p. 229)

Adena *s.* sociedad constructora de túmulos asentada en el valle del río Ohio entre los años 700 a.C. y 100 d.C., aproximadamente; se conoce por sus grandes tumbas cónicas. (p. 6)

affirmative action [acción afirmativa] *s.* medidas para corregir los efectos de la discriminación en los empleos y la educación; favorecen a grupos, como mujeres y minorías, que estaban en desventaja. (p. 992)

Agent Orange [Agente Naranja] *s.* químico tóxico exfoliante que fumigaron las tropas estadounidenses en Vietnam para poner al descubierto refugios del Vietcong. (p. 892)

Agricultural Adjustment Act [Ley de Ajustes Agrícolas] *s.* ley de 1933 que elevó el precio de las cosechas al pagarle a los granjeros para que no cultivaran cierta porción de sus tierras, reduciendo así la producción. (p. 667)

AIDS (acquired immune deficiency syndrome) [SIDA, síndrome de inmunodeficiencia adquirida] *s.* enfermedad causada por un virus que debilita el sistema inmunológico y hace que el cuerpo sea vulnerable a infecciones y formas poco comunes de cáncer. (p. 987)

Alien and Sedition Acts [Leyes de Extranjeros y de Sedición] *s.* serie de cuatro leyes aprobadas en 1798 para reducir el poder político de los nuevos inmigrantes. (p. 181)

Alliance for Progress [Alianza para el Progreso] *s.* propuesta del presidente Kennedy de ofrecer ayuda económica y técnica a los países latinoamericanos, en parte para contrarrestar la influencia de Fidel Castro. (p. 839)

Allies [Aliados] *s.* **1.** en la I Guerra Mundial, naciones aliadas en un tratado contra Alemania y las otras Potencias Centrales; originalmente Gran Bretaña, Francia y Rusia; más adelante se unieron Estados Unidos, Japón, Italia y otros. (p. 556) **2.** en la II Guerra Mundial, naciones asociadas contra el Eje, en particular Gran Bretaña, la Unión Soviética y Estados Unidos.(p. 722)

American Federation of Labor (AFL) [Federación Norteamericana del Trabajo] *s.* sindicato de trabajadores calificados creado en 1886 y dirigido por Samuel Gompers. (p. 429)

American Indian Movement (AIM) [Movimiento Indígena Americano] *s.* organización radical, a veces militante, creada en 1968 con el fin de luchar por los derechos de los amerindios. (p. 923)

American System [Sistema Americano] *s.* programa económico previo a la Guerra Civil diseñado para fortalecer y unificar a Estados Unidos por medio de aranceles proteccionistas, un banco nacional y un sistema de transporte eficiente. (p. 201)

Anaconda plan [plan Anaconda] *s.* estrategia de tres pasos durante la Guerra Civil, mediante la cual la Unión propuso derrotar a la Confederación; su nombre viene de una serpiente que aprieta a sus víctimas. (p. 314)

anarchist [anarquista] *s.* persona que se opone a toda forma de gobierno. (p. 591)

Anasazi *s.* grupo amerindio que vivió cerca de la región de Four Corners —donde Arizona, New Mexico, Colorado y Utah se unen— de los años 100 a 1400 d.C., aproximadamente. (p. 6)

annex [anexar] *v.* incorporar un territorio a una unidad política existente tal como un estado o país. (p. 272)

antebellum *adj.* previo a la Guerra Civil. (p. 233)

Antifederalist [antifederalista] *s.* oponente de la Constitución y de un gobierno central fuerte. (p. 138)

appeasement [apaciguamiento] *s.* política de ceder a las demandas de una potencia hostil con el fin de mantener la paz.(p. 709)

apprentice [aprendiz] *s.* trabajador que aprende un oficio, por lo general supervisado por un maestro. (p. 241)

armistice [armisticio] *s.* suspensión temporal de combates por mutuo acuerdo. (p. 191)

Articles of Confederation [Artículos de la Confederación] *s.* documento que sirvió como constitución para el nuevo gobierno de Estados Unidos, aprobado por los estados en 1781. (p. 127)

assimilation [asimilación] *s.* adopción, por parte de un grupo minoritario, de las creencias y estilo de vida de la cultura dominante. (p. 385)

Atlantic Charter [Carta del Atlántico] *s.* declaración de principios de 1941 en que Estados Unidos y Gran Bretaña establecieron sus objetivos contra las Potencias del Eje. (p. 722)

Axis powers [Potencias del Eje] *s.* países unidos contra los Aliados en la II Guerra Mundial; originalmente la Alemania nazi y la Italia fascista, y después Japón. (p. 710)

Aztec [azteca] *s.* pueblo también conocido como los mexica; se estableció en el valle de México en el siglo 13. (p. 6)

B

baby boom *s.* marcado aumento en el índice de natalidad en Estados Unidos después de la II Guerra Mundial, que originó la generación más numerosa en la historia del país, nacida entre 1947 y 1961. (p. 805)

balance of trade [balanza comercial] *s.* diferencia entre el valor de las importaciones y las exportaciones de un país. (p. 66)

Bank of the United States (BUS) [Banco de Estados Unidos] *s.* cualquiera de los dos bancos nacionales establecidos por el Congreso, el primero en 1791 y el segundo en 1816. (p. 216)

Battle of the Bulge [Batalla del Bolsón] *s.* batalla de un mes de duración de la II Guerra Mundial, que se inició el 16 de diciembre de 1944, en la que fuerzas alemanas rompieron temporalmente las líneas de los Aliados pero al final sufrieron grandes pérdidas. (p. 744)

SPANISH GLOSSARY 1093

Battle of Wounded Knee [Batalla de Wounded Knee] *s.* masacre de 300 indígenas desarmados en Wounded Knee Creek, South Dakota, que puso fin en 1890 a las Guerras Indias. (p. 387)

Bear Flag Republic [República de la Bandera del Oso] *s.* territorio declarado como república por los colonos estadounidenses de California que se rebelaron contra México en 1846; también llamada República de California. (p. 275)

Beatles *s.* conjunto inglés que tuvo gran influencia en la música popular en los años 60. (p. 936)

beat movement [movimiento beat] *s.* movimiento social y literario rebelde de los años 50. (p. 815)

beatnik *s.* uno de los jóvenes inconformistas, opuesto al materialismo, que seguía el movimiento beat de los años 50. (p. 815)

Benin *s.* reino de África occidental que existió en la actual Nigeria; floreció en los bosques del delta del Níger del siglo 14 al 17. (p. 17)

Berlin airlift [puente aéreo de Berlín] *s.* operación, de 327 días de duración, en la que aviones estadounidenses y británicos llevaron alimentos y provisiones a Berlín Occidental después de que la Unión Soviética bloqueó la ciudad en 1948. (p. 771)

Berlin Wall [Muro de Berlín] *s.* muro de concreto que separaba Berlín Oriental y Occidental, construido en 1961 bajo supervisión soviética por Alemania oriental para impedir que sus ciudadanos se escaparan; por mucho tiempo símbolo de la Guerra Fría, fue derribado en 1989. (p. 836)

Bessemer process [método Bessemer] *s.* técnica más eficiente de fabricar acero, desarrollada hacia 1850. (p. 411)

Bill of Rights [Carta de Derechos] *s.* primeras diez enmiendas a la Constitución que identifican los derechos de los ciudadanos; se adoptaron en 1791. (p. 139)

bimetallism [bimetalismo] *s.* sistema monetario nacional que utiliza el oro y la plata. (p. 404)

black codes [códigos negros] *s.* leyes discriminatorias aprobadas en muchos estados del Sur después de la Guerra Civil que restringían fuertemente a los afroamericanos. (p. 352)

blacklist [lista negra] *s.* lista de unos 500 actores, escritores, productores y directores a quienes no se permitía trabajar en películas de Hollywood debido a sus supuestos vínculos comunistas. (p. 781)

Black Panthers [Panteras Negras] *s.* partido político afroamericano de carácter militante formado por Huey Newton y Bobby Seale en 1966 para luchar contra la violencia de la policía y suministrar servicios en el ghetto. (p. 874)

Black Power [Poder Negro] *s.* consigna de los años 40 revivida por Stokely Carmichael en los años 60, que pedía poder político y social para los afroamericanos. (p. 874)

Black Tuesday [Martes Negro] *s.* octubre 29 de 1929, día en que los precios de las acciones bajaron drásticamente al iniciarse la caída de la bolsa de valores. (p. 645)

Bleeding Kansas [Kansas sangrante] *s.* nombre dado al Territorio de Kansas en los años previos a la Guerra Civil, cuando era un campo de batalla entre las fuerzas en pro y en contra de la esclavitud. (p. 293)

blitzkrieg *s.* repentina ofensiva a gran escala, de fuerzas aéreas y terrestres, dirigida a obtener una victoria rápida. (p. 711)

blockade [bloqueo] *s.* acto de sellar un puerto o región para prevenir la entrada o salida durante tiempos de guerra. (p. 189)

bonanza farm [granja de bonanza] *s.* extensa granja dedicada a un solo cultivo, de 10,000 acres o más, muy común en las planicies de finales de la década de 1870 a mediados de la década de 1890. (p. 400)

Bonus Army *s.* 25,000 veteranos desempleados de la I Guerra Mundial que marcharon en Washington, D.C., en 1932 para exigir los bonos que les habían sido prometidos. (p. 658)

bootlegger *s.* persona que contrabandeaba bebidas alcohólicas durante la época de Prohibición. (p. 615)

Boston Massacre [Masacre de Boston] *s.* incidente que ocurrió en Boston en 1770, durante el cual tropas británicas mataron a cinco colonos. (p. 96)

Boston Tea Party [Motín del Té de Boston] *s.* protesta en 1773 contra el impuesto británico sobre el té, en la que los colonos arrojaron 15,000 libras de té a las aguas del puerto de Boston. (p. 97)

Boulder Dam [Presa de Boulder] *s.* presa del río Colorado construida durante la Depresión con fondos federales para estimular la economía; ahora llamada Presa Hoover. (p. 657)

bounty [gratificación] *s.* pago en efectivo que se ofrecía durante la Guerra Civil en muchos estados del Norte a quienes se alistaban voluntariamente en el ejército. (p. 321)

Boxer Rebellion [Rebelión de los Boxer] *s.* rebelión encabezada en 1900 por los Boxer, sociedad secreta de China, para detener la difusión de la influencia occidental. (p. 539)

bracero *s.* trabajador mexicano que labora temporalmente en Estados Unidos, como los contratados durante la época de escasez de trabajadores agrícolas de 1942 a 1947. (p. 822)

bread line [cola para comer] *s.* fila de personas que esperan comida gratis, como ocurrió en la Depresión. (p. 651)

brinkmanship *s.* práctica de amenazar al enemigo con represalias militares extremas ante cualquier agresión, que caracterizó la carrera armamentista entre Estados Unidos y la Unión Soviética durante la Guerra Fría. (p. 786)

Brown v. Board of Education *s.* decisión de la Suprema Corte en 1954 que declaró que la segregación de estudiantes negros y blancos era inconstitucional. (p. 858)

Bull Moose Party [Partido Bull Moose] *s.* apodo del Partido Progresista, bajo el que Theodore Roosevelt aspiró, sin éxito, a la presidencia en 1912. (p. 514)

buying on margin [compra con margen] *s.* compra de acciones en la que se paga sólo una porción del valor de la acción al vendedor o corredor de bolsa, y se presta el resto. (p. 645)

C

cabinet [gabinete] *s.* asesores directos del presidente, por lo general jefes de departamentos, que coordinan y ponen en práctica la política gubernamental. (p. 173)

Camp David Accords [Acuerdos de Camp David] *s.* dos históricos acuerdos de paz entre Israel y Egipto, negociados en Camp David, Maryland, en 1978. (p. 966)

capitalism [capitalismo] *s.* sistema económico en el que individuos y corporaciones privadas controlan los medios de producción para obtener ganancias. (p. 255)

carpetbagger *s.* término despectivo para referirse a los norteños que se trasladaron al Sur después de la Guerra Civil y que apoyaban la Reconstrucción ordenada por el Congreso. (p. 358)

cash crop [cosecha comercial] *s.* cosecha que se cultiva para su venta más que para uso del granjero. (p. 71)

Central Powers [Potencias Centrales] *s.* en la I Guerra Mundial, el grupo de naciones —Alemania, Austro-Hungría y el imperio otomano— que se opuso a los Aliados. (p. 556)

checks and balances [control y compensación de poderes] *s.* sistema en el cual cada rama del gobierno controla o restringe a las demás ramas. (p. 136)

Chinese Exclusion Act [Ley de Exclusión de Chinos] *s.* ley de 1882 que prohibía la inmigración de ciudadanos chinos, con la excepción de estudiantes, maestros, comerciantes, turistas y funcionarios gubernamentales. (p. 443)

CIA *s.* Central Intelligence Agency (Agencia Central de Inteligencia), agencia gubernamental establecida en 1947 para espiar y realizar operaciones secretas en países extranjeros. (p. 786)

Civilian Conservation Corps [Cuerpo Civil de Conservación] *s.* agencia establecida como parte del New Deal con el fin de ocupar a jóvenes desempleados en trabajos como la construcción de carreteras y el cuidado de parques nacionales. (p. 667)

Civil Rights Act of 1964 [Ley de Derechos Civiles de 1964] *s.* ley que prohíbe la discriminación en lugares públicos, en la educación y en los empleos por cuestión de raza, color, sexo, nacionalidad o religión. (p. 864)

Civil Rights Act of 1968 [Ley de Derechos Civiles de 1968] *s.* ley que prohíbe la discriminación en la vivienda. (p. 876)

civil service [servicio civil] *s.* cualquier servicio gubernamental en el que se obtiene un cargo mediante exámenes públicos. (p. 455)

Clayton Antitrust Act [Ley Antitrust Clayton] *s.* ley de 1914 que declaraba ilegales ciertas prácticas empresariales injustas y protegía el derecho de los sindicatos y organizaciones agrícolas a existir y a participar en actos de protesta. (p. 517)

Cold War [Guerra Fría] *s.* estado de hostilidad, sin llegar a conflictos armados, entre Estados Unidos y la Unión Soviética tras la II Guerra Mundial. (p. 770)

collective bargaining [negociación colectiva] *s.* negociaciones en grupo entre trabajadores y patronos para alcanzar acuerdos en cuanto a salarios, beneficios, horarios y condiciones de trabajo. (p. 429)

colonization [colonización] *s.* establecimiento de asentamientos remotos controlados por otro país. (p. 29)

Columbian Exchange [Transferencia Colombina] *s.* transferencia —iniciada con el primer viaje de Colón a las Américas— de plantas, alimentos, animales y enfermedades entre el Hemisferio Occidental y el Hemisferio Oriental. (p. 31)

committee of correspondence [comité de correspondencia] *s.* red de comunicación escrita entre colonos para mantenerse al tanto de las actividades británicas. (p. 97)

Committee to Reelect the President [Comité de Reelección del Presidente] *s.* grupo que dirigió la campaña para la reelección del presidente Nixon en 1972, cuya conexión con el allanamiento de la Sede Nacional del Partido Demócrata hizo estallar el escándalo Watergate. (p. 954)

Common Sense [Sentido común] *s.* folleto escrito en 1776 por Thomas Paine que exhortaba a la separación de las colonias británicas. (p. 101)

Commonwealth of Independent States [Comunidad de Estados Independientes] *s.* confederación amplia de Estados que quedó tras la disolución de la Unión Soviética en 1991. (p. 997)

communism [comunismo] *s.* sistema económico y político basado en un gobierno de un solo partido y en la propiedad estatal. (p. 590)

Compromise of 1850 [Compromiso de 1850] *s.* serie de medidas del Congreso para resolver los desacuerdos que surgieron a raíz de la esclavitud entre los estados libres y esclavistas. (p. 285)

concentration camp [campo de concentración] *s.* campamento de presos operado por la Alemania nazi para judíos y otros grupos que consideraba enemigos de Adolfo Hitler; a los presos los mataban o los hacían morir de hambre y a causa de trabajos forzados. (p. 716)

Confederate States of America [Estados Confederados de América] *s.* también conocidos como la Confederación; gobierno establecido en 1861 por los estados sureños al separarse de la Unión. (p. 305)

confederation [confederación] *s.* grupo de estados o naciones unidos para actuar en torno a asuntos de interés mutuo. (p. 127)

conglomerate [conglomerado] *s.* corporación grande que posee compañías más pequeñas dedicadas a negocios no relacionados. (p. 803)

congregación *s.* comunidad establecida por sacerdotes españoles con el fin de imponer la fe católica y la cultura española a los amerindios. (p. 42)

Congress of Industrial Organizations [Congreso de Organizaciones Industriales] *s.* organización sindical que se separó de la Federación Norteamericana del Trabajo en 1938. (p. 681)

Congress of Racial Equality (CORE) [Congreso de Igualdad Racial] *s.* grupo interracial, fundado por James Farmer en 1942, que luchaba contra la segregación en ciudades del Norte. (p. 759)

conquistador *s.* explorador y colonizador español de las Américas en el siglo 16. (p. 38)

conscientious objector [objetor de conciencia] *s.* persona que se opone a toda guerra por principio de conciencia. (p. 565)

conscription [conscripción] *s.* servicio militar obligatorio de ciertos miembros de la población. (p. 321)

conservation [conservación] *s.* práctica de preservar algunas zonas naturales y desarrollar otras por el bien común. (p. 510)

Conservative Coalition [Coalición Conservadora] *s.* alianza de fines del siglo 20 de grupos de ultraderecha opuestos a la ingerencia del gobierno, los programas de subvención, la acción afirmativa, la integración escolar por medio del transporte estudiantil y la presunta decadencia moral de la sociedad estadounidense. (p. 979)

SPANISH GLOSSARY **1095**

consumerism [consumismo] *s.* el gran interés en la compra de bienes materiales, como el que caracterizó a la clase media estadounidense a finales de los años 50. (p. 808)

containment [contención] *s.* política estadounidense de formar alianzas con países más pequeños y débiles con el fin de bloquear la expansión de la infuencia sovietica tras la II Guerra Mundial. (p. 769)

Contract with America [Contrato con América] *s.* documento elaborado por el representante Newt Gingrich y firmado por 300 candidatos republicanos el 27 de septiembre de 1994, que presentaba sus planes legislativos conservadores. (p. 1010)

Contras [la contra] *s.* fuerzas anticomunistas nicaragüenses que recibieron asistencia de la administración Reagan para derrocar al gobierno sandinista de Nicaragua. (p. 998)

convoy system [flotilla de escolta] *s.* medio de proteger los buques mercantes del ataque de submarinos al hacer que viajen con un grupo grande de destructores. (p. 564)

Copperhead *s.* nombre de una serpiente venenosa aplicado a los norteños que simpatizaban con el Sur durante la Guerra Civil. (p. 321)

counterculture [contracultura] *s.* cultura de la juventud de los años 60 que rechazaba la sociedad tradicional y buscaba paz, amor y libertad individual. (p. 933)

credibility gap [falta de credibilidad] *s.* desconfianza del público en las declaraciones oficiales del gobierno, tales como las estadísticas de combate durante la Guerra de Vietnam. (p. 894)

credit [crédito] *s.* acuerdo en el que se compran artículos en el presente para ser cancelados en el futuro mediante un plan de cuotas con intereses. (p. 644)

Crédit Mobilier *s.* compañía constructora formada en 1868 por los dueños de la Union Pacific Railroad; se formó un escándalo al usarla ilegalmente para obtener ganancias y sobornar a funcionarios. (p. 419)

"Cross of Gold" Speech [Discurso de la "Cruz de Oro"] *s.* exaltado discurso de William Jennings Bryan en la Convención Demócrata de 1896, en el que atacó a los que proponían un sistema monetario basado sólo en el oro. (p. 404)

Crusades [Cruzadas] *s.* serie de expediciones militares cristianas al Oriente Medio entre los años 1096 y 1270 d.C., con el fin de rescatar del dominio islámico la "Tierra Santa" alrededor de Jerusalén. (p. 22)

cult of domesticity [culto a la domesticidad] *s.* creencia de que la mujer casada debe restringir sus actividades al hogar y la familia. (p. 235)

culture shock [shock cultural] *s.* confusión y ansiedad generada por la inmersión en una cultura desconocida. (p. 442)

D

Dawes Act [Ley Dawes] *s.* ley aprobada por el Congreso en 1887 para "americanizar" a los indígenas distribuyendo a individuos la tierra de las reservaciones. (p. 385)

D-Day [Día D] *s.* junio 6 de 1944, día en que los Aliados emprendieron una invasión por tierra, mar y aire contra el Eje. (p. 743)

debt peonage [deuda por peonaje] *s.* sistema de servidumbre involuntaria en el que una persona es obligada a trabajar para pagar una deuda. (p. 477)

Declaration of Independence [Declaración de Independencia] *s.* documento escrito por Thomas Jefferson en 1776 que declaraba la independencia de las colonias de Gran Bretaña. (p. 101)

de facto segregation [segregación de facto] *s.* segregación racial impuesta por la práctica y la costumbre más que por las leyes, como era común en el Norte. (p. 871)

deficit spending [gasto deficitario] *s.* práctica por parte de un gobierno de gastar más de lo que recibe por concepto de rentas públicas. (p. 689)

de jure segregation [segregación de jure] *s.* segregación racial impuesta por la ley, como ocurría con las leyes Jim Crow en el Sur. (p. 871)

Democratic Republican Party [Partido Demócrata Republicano] *s.* partido político establecido por los seguidores de Andrew Jackson, quien se separó del Partido Republicano a finales de la década de 1820; predecesor del actual Partido Demócrata. (p. 210)

department store [tienda por departamentos] *s.* tienda grande al por menor, que ofrece una variedad de productos y servicios. (p. 484)

détente [distensión] *s.* política exterior estadounidense dirigida a disminuir las tensiones de la Guerra Fría; un ejemplo fue la visita del presidente Nixon a China en 1972. (p. 951)

direct relief [ayuda directa] *s.* alimentos o dinero que el gobierno da directamente a los necesitados. (p. 653)

division of labor [división del trabajo] *s.* práctica cultural de asignar diferentes tareas y responsabilidades a diferentes grupos o individuos. (p. 13)

Dixiecrat *s.* delegado sureño que se retiró de la convención del Partido Demócrata en 1948 para no apoyar la plataforma del partido sobre derechos civiles y formó un grupo denominado States' Rights Democratic Party. (p. 800)

dollar diplomacy [diplomacia del dólar] *s.* política de usar el poder económico o la influencia económica de Estados Unidos para proteger sus intereses empresariales del país o para alcanzar sus objetivos de política exterior en otros países. (p. 545)

domino theory [teoría del dominó] *s.* teoría basada en la analogía de piezas de dominó que caen: si una nación se vuelve comunista, las naciones vecinas inevitablemente se volverán comunistas también. (p. 885)

double standard [doble moral] *s.* conjunto de principios que permite mayor libertad sexual al hombre que a la mujer. (p. 619)

dove [paloma] *s.* persona que se oponía a la Guerra de Vietnam y creía que Estados Unidos debía retirarse. (p. 899)

Dow Jones Industrial Average [Promedio Industrial Dow Jones] *s.* medida que computa el valor de las acciones de un grupo selecto de compañías grandes; se usa como barómetro de los mercados bursátiles. (p. 647)

downsize [recortar] *v.* despedir trabajadores de una organización con el fin de hacer las operaciones más eficientes y ahorrar dinero. (p. 1014)

dumbbell tenement [vecindad] *s.* edificio largo y estrecho, de cinco o seis pisos, con dos pabellones más anchos en los extremos. (p. 448)

Dust Bowl *s.* región entre Texas y North Dakota que quedó inservible para la agricultura debido a la sequía y a las tormentas de arena durante los años 30. (p. 650)

E

Earth Day [Día de la Tierra] *s.* día dedicado a la educación ambiental que desde 1970 se celebra el 22 de abril de cada año. (p. 969)

Economic Opportunity Act [Ley de Oportunidades Económicas] *s.* ley, promulgada en 1964, que adjudicó fondos a programas para la juventud, medidas para combatir la pobreza, préstamos para pequeños negocios y capacitación laboral. (p. 845)

egalitarianism [igualitarismo] *s.* creencia de que todas las personas deben tener igualdad de derechos políticos, económicos, sociales y civiles. (p. 116)

Eisenhower Doctrine [Doctrina Eisenhower] *s.* advertencia del presidente Eisenhower en 1957 de que Estados Unidos defendería el Oriente Medio contra el ataque de cualquier país comunista. (p. 788)

electoral college [colegio electoral] *s.* asamblea elegida por votantes para elegir formalmente al presidente y vicepresidente. Cada estado tiene un número de electores equivalente a los miembros de sus senadores y representantes en el Congreso. (p. 136)

e-mail [correo electrónico] *s.* mensajes electrónicos enviados y recibidos por la Internet y otras redes de computadores. (p. 1019)

emancipation [emancipación] *s.* proceso de liberarse de la esclavitud. (p. 229)

Emancipation Proclamation [Proclama de Emancipación] *s.* orden ejecutiva de Abraham Lincoln el 1º de enero de 1863 que abolía la esclavitud en los estados "en rebelión". (p. 320)

embargo *s.* orden gubernamental que prohíbe el comercio con otra nación. (p. 189)

encomienda *s.* institución colonial de España en las Américas que repartía indígenas a los conquistadores para hacer trabajos forzados. (p. 40)

Enlightenment [Ilustración] *s.* movimiento intelectual del siglo 18 que propugnaba la razón y los métodos científicos. (p. 81)

entitlement program [programa de subvención] *s.* programa gubernamental, tal como Social Security, Medicare y Medicaid, que brinda beneficios a grupos específicos. (p. 979)

entrepreneur [empresario] *s.* persona que usa su dinero para crear una empresa. (p. 255)

environmentalist [ambientalista] *s.* persona que procura proteger el medio ambiente de la destrucción y de la contaminación. (p. 969)

Environmental Protection Agency [Agencia de Protección Ambiental] *s.* agencia federal establecida en 1970 con el fin de supervisar los asuntos ambientales y controlar la contaminación. (p. 970)

Equal Rights Amendment [Enmienda de Igualdad de Derechos] *s.* enmienda constitucional propuesta que establece que "la igualdad de derechos bajo la ley no debe ser negada o restringida por el gobierno federal ni por ningún estado en razón del sexo". (p. 931)

Erie Canal [canal del Erie] *s.* vía acuática artificial de 363 millas en New York, construida entre 1817 y 1825 para conectar el río Hudson y el lago Erie. (p. 203)

Espionage and Sedition Acts [Leyes de Espionaje y Sedición] *s.* dos leyes aprobadas en 1917 y 1918, que castigaban fuertemente a quienes criticaran o bloquearan la participación de Estados Unidos en la II Guerra Mundial. (p. 573)

excise tax [impuesto al consumo] *s.* impuesto a la producción, venta o consumo de artículos producidos en el país. (p. 176)

executive branch [rama ejecutiva] *s.* rama gubernamental cuya función es administrar y aplicar las leyes (presidente o gobernador). (pp. 135-136)

exoduster *s.* afroamericano que emigró del Sur a Kansas después de la Reconstrucción. (p. 382)

F

Fair Deal *s.* plan económico del presidente Truman que expandió el New Deal de Roosevelt; aumentó el salario mínimo, amplió el seguro social y le dio vivienda a familias de bajos recursos, entre otras medidas. (p. 801)

Family Assistance Plan [Plan de Asistencia Familiar] *s.* propuesta de reforma a los programas de beneficencia, aprobada por la Cámara de Representantes en 1970 pero rechazada por el Senado, que garantizaba un ingreso a los beneficiarios de ayuda pública que aceptaran capacitarse y emplearse en un oficio. (p. 947)

fascism [fascismo] *s.* filosofía política que propone un gobierno fuerte, centralizado, nacionalista, caracterizado por una rígida dictadura unipartidista. (p. 704)

Federal Communications Commission (FCC) [Comisión Federal de Comunicaciones] *s.* agencia del gobierno que regula y otorga licencias a la radio, la televisión, los teléfonos y otras industrias de comunicaciones. (p. 812)

Federal Deposit Insurance Corporation [Corporación Federal de Seguros de Depósitos] *s.* agencia creada en 1933 para garantizar depósitos bancarios individuales cuando un banco quiebra. (p. 692)

Federal Home Loan Bank Act [Ley Federal para Préstamos de Vivienda] *s.* ley aprobada en 1931 que redujo las cuotas hipotecarias y permitió a los agricultores refinanciar sus préstamos para prevenir juicios hipotecarios. (p. 658)

Federalist [federalista] *s.* partidario de la Constitución y de un gobierno nacional fuerte. (p. 138)

Federalist Papers [El Federalista] *s.* ensayos escritos por Madison, Hamilton y Jay que apoyan y explican la Constitución. (p. 138)

Federal Reserve System [Sistema de la Reserva Federal] *s.* sistema bancario nacional establecido por Woodrow Wilson en 1913 que controla el dinero circulante del país. (p. 518)

Federal Securities Act [Ley Federal de Valores] *s.* ley de 1933 que obliga a las corporaciones a suministrar información completa y fidedigna sobre sus ofertas de acciones. (p. 666)

Federal Trade Commission [Comisión Federal de Comercio] *s.* agencia federal establecida en 1914 para investigar y parar prácticas empresariales injustas. (p. 517)

feminism [feminismo] *s.* creencia, que inspiró el movimiento de la mujer de los años 60, de que la mujer debe tener igualdad económica, política y social con respecto al hombre. (p. 928)

Fifteenth Amendment [Enmienda 15] *s.* enmienda a la Constitución, adoptada en 1870, que establece que a nadie puede negársele el derecho al voto por motivos de raza, color o por haber sido esclavo. (p. 355)

Fifty-Four Forty or Fight *s.* consigna de la campaña presidencial de 1844 en pro de la anexión del Territorio de Oregon; se refería a la latitud del límite norte del territorio. (p. 265)

flapper *s.* jovencita típica de los años 20 que actuaba y se vestía de manera atrevida y nada convencional. (p. 618)

flexible response [respuesta flexible] *s.* doctrina, desarrollada durante la administración Kennedy, de prepararse para una variedad de respuestas militares, en vez de concentrarse en las armas nuclerares. (p. 832)

Fordney-McCumber Tariff [Arancel Fordney-McCumber] *s.* serie de reglas, aprobada por el Congreso en 1922, que elevó a niveles sin precedentes los impuestos a las importaciones en 1922 para proteger las compañías estadounidenses de la competencia extranjera. (p. 597)

forty-niner [viajero del 49] *s.* buscador de oro que llegó a California después de 1848 atraído por el oro. (p. 277)

Fourteen Points [los catorce puntos] *s.* plan del presidente Wilson en pro de la paz mundial tras la I Guerra Mundial; estableció la Liga de las Naciones. (p. 577)

Fourteenth Amendment [Enmienda 14] *s.* enmienda a la Constitución, adoptada en 1868, que hace ciudadano a toda persona nacida o naturalizada en Estados Unidos. (p. 353)

franchise [franquicia] *s.* forma de negocio, común en la industria de la comida rápida, en la que individuos compran el derecho a usar el nombre y los métodos de una compañía matriz, con lo que la compañía se multiplica. (p. 803)

Freedmen's Bureau [Oficina de Libertos] *s.* agencia del gobierno establecida en 1865 para ayudar con alimentos, ropa y educación a los antiguos esclavos y blancos pobres en el Sur. (p. 352)

freedom rider *s.* activista de derechos civiles que enfrentó violentas reacciones al viajar en autobús a través del Sur a comienzos de los años 60 para poner a prueba la decisión de la Suprema Corte de prohibir la segregación en los autobuses de pasajeros. (p. 864)

Freedom Summer *s.* campaña de registro de votantes afroamericanos en el verano de 1964, organizada por el Congreso de Igualdad Racial y el SNCC (Comité Coordinador de Estudiantes no Violentos), que produjo violentas respuestas de los segregacionistas. (p. 868)

Freeport Doctrine [Doctrina Freeport] *s.* posición que tomó en 1858 Stephen Douglas de que cualquier territorio podría excluir la esclavitud con sólo negarse a promulgar leyes en su favor. (p. 301)

Free-Soil Party [Partido de las Tierras Libres] *s.* partido político formado en 1848 que se oponía a la extensión de la esclavitud a los territorios. (p. 296)

Free Speech Movement [Movimiento de Libre Expresión] *s.* movimiento activista de los años 60 que surgió a raíz de un enfrentamiento entre los estudiantes y la administración de la Universidad de California en Berkeley en 1964; abordó muchos asuntos sociales y políticos. (p. 897)

French and Indian War [Guerra contra Franceses e Indígenas] *s.* guerra librada en Norteamérica (1757-1763) como parte de un conflicto mundial entre Francia y Gran Bretaña; finalizó con la derrota de Francia y el traspaso del Canadá francés a Gran Bretaña. (p. 84)

Fugitive Slave Act [Ley de los Esclavos Fugitivos] *s.* ley aprobada como parte del Compromiso de 1850 que imponía duras sanciones a quien ayudara a escapar de la esclavitud.(p. 288)

fundamentalism [fundamentalismo] *s.* movimiento religioso protestante basado en la interpretación textual, o palabra por palabra, de las escrituras. (p. 616)

G

Gadsden Purchase [Compra de Gadsden] *s.* compra de tierras de México en 1853 por parte de Estados Unidos que estableció la frontera actual entre los dos países. (p. 276)

gag rule [ley de la mordaza] *s.* orden que limita o previene el debate sobre un determinado asunto. (p. 234)

GATT *s.* General Agreement on Tariffs and Trade (Acuerdo General de Aranceles y Comercio), acuerdo de comercio internacional, revisado en 1994 para crear la Organización Mundial de Comercio, que redujo las barreras arancelarias y estableció normas para resolver disputas comerciales. (p. 1016)

genetic engineering [ingeniería genética] *s.* alteración de la biología molecular de las células de un organismo para crear nuevas variedades de bacterias, plantas o animales. (p. 1020)

Geneva Accords [Acuerdos de Ginebra] *s.* plan de paz de Indochina en 1954 en el que Vietnam fue dividido temporalmente en Vietnam del Norte y Vietnam del Sur, mientras se celebraban las elecciones de 1956. (p. 886)

genocide [genocidio] *s.* exterminio deliberado y sistemático de un grupo de personas por su raza, nacionalidad o religión. (p. 715)

Gentlemen's Agreement [Acuerdo de Caballeros] *s.* acuerdo concertado durante 1907 y 1908, mediante el cual el gobierno de Japón limitó la emigración a Estados Unidos. (p. 443)

Gettysburg Address [Discurso de Gettysburg] *s.* famoso discurso de Abraham Lincoln durante la Guerra Civil al inaugurar un cementerio nacional en el campo de batalla de Gettysburg, Pennsylvania, el 19 de noviembre de 1863. (p. 333)

Ghost Dance *s.* ritual amerindio que evocaba la restauración de la vida tribal; popular entre los sioux antes de la Masacre de Wounded Knee en 1890. (p. 387)

GI Bill of Rights [Carta de Derechos de los Veteranos] *s.* nombre dado a la Ley de Reajuste de Militares de 1944, que ofrecía beneficios financieros y educativos a los veteranos de la II Guerra Mundial. (pp. 758, 796)

glasnost *s.* palabra rusa que se refiere a la discusión abierta de los problemas sociales que se dio en la Unión Soviética durante los años 80. (p. 996)

Glass-Steagall Banking Act of 1933 [Ley Bancaria Glass-Steagall] *s.* ley que aseguró los depósitos bancarios mediante la Corporación Federal de Seguros de Depósitos. (p. 666)

Glorious Revolution [Revolución Gloriosa] *s.* revolución incruenta en 1688-89 en la que William y Mary le quitaron el trono de Inglaterra a James II. (p. 68)

1098 SPANISH GLOSSARY

gold rush [fiebre del oro] *s.* llegada de gente a una región donde se ha descubierto oro. (p. 277)

Gone with the Wind [Lo que el viento se llevó] *s.* película de 1939 sobre la vida de los dueños de plantaciones del Sur durante la Guerra Civil. (p. 684)

graft [corrupción] *s.* acto de aprovecharse de un cargo político con el fin de ganar dinero, propiedades u otros bienes. (p. 452)

grandfather clause [cláusula del abuelo] *s.* estipulación que exime de cumplir una ley a ciertas personas por circunstancias previas; específicamente, cláusula de la constitución de algunos estados sureños que eximía a los blancos de los estrictos requisitos que impedían que los negros votaran. (p. 474)

Grange [la Granja] *s.* organización de granjeros que intentaron, a partir de la década de 1870, combatir el poder de los ferrocarriles. (p. 402)

Grapes of Wrath, The [Las uvas de la ira] *s.* novela de John Steinbeck, publicada en 1939, sobre una familia de Oklahoma que se va de la región del Dust Bowl a California. (p. 687)

Great Awakening [Gran Despertar] *s.* serie de grandes asambleas religiosas en las décadas de 1730 y 1740 organizadas por predicadores viajeros como George Whitefield. (p. 82)

Great Compromise [Gran Compromiso] *s.* plan constitucional para una legislatura de dos cámaras: una que da igual representación a todos los estados y una que basa la representación en la población. (p. 134)

Great Depression [Gran Depresión] *s.* período de 1929 a 1941 en el que la economía estadounidense quebró y millones quedaron sin empleo. (p. 646)

Great Migration [Gran Migración] *s.* movimiento de cientos de miles de negros sureños a ciudades del Norte a principios de este siglo. (p. 574)

Great Plains [Grandes Llanuras] *s.* vasta pradera que cubre la porción centro-oeste de Estados Unidos. (p. 380)

Great Society [Gran Sociedad] *s.* ambicioso programa legislativo del presidente Lyndon B. Johnson para reducir la pobreza y la injusticia racial, y mejorar el nivel de vida. (p. 846)

H

habeas corpus *s.* orden judicial que manda comparecer a las autoridades ante un juez u otro funcionario de un tribunal para explicar que un preso está detenido legalmente. (p. 321)

Haight-Ashbury *s.* distrito de San Francisco, "capital" de la contracultura hippie durante los años 60. (p. 934)

Harlem Renaissance [Renacimiento de Harlem] *s.* período de sobresaliente creatividad afroamericana en el campo artístico durante los años 20 y 30, cuyo nombre viene de la zona de Harlem en New York City. (p. 632)

hawk [halcón] *s.* persona que respaldaba la Guerra de Vietnam y creía que Estados Unidos debía incrementar su fuerza militar para ganarla. (p. 899)

Hawley–Smoot Tariff Act [Ley de Aranceles Hawley-Smoot] *s.* ley de 1930 que estableció los más altos aranceles proteccionistas en la historia estadounidense, afectando negativamente el comercio internacional. (p. 649)

H-bomb [bomba de hidrógeno] *s.* bomba de hidrógeno, o termonuclear, mucho más poderosa que la bomba atómica, diseñada en la presidencia de Truman; detonó por primera vez en 1952. (p. 785)

headright system [sistema de reparto de tierras por cabeza] *s.* sistema empleado en Virginia que otorgaba cincuenta acres de tierra a cada colono y otro tanto por cada acompañante. (p. 46)

hierarchy [jerarquía] *s.* orden social determinado por rango o clase. (p. 20)

Ho Chi Minh Trail [Sendero de Ho Chi Min] *s.* red de caminos por la que Vietnam del Norte abastecía al Vietcong en Vietnam del Sur. (p. 886)

Hohokam *s.* grupo amerindio que vivió en los valles de los ríos Salt y Gila (hoy Arizona) entre los años 300 a.C. y 1400 d.C., aproximadamente. (p. 6)

holding company [compañía tenedora] *s.* compañía integrada para comprar acciones de otras compañías, y crear un monopolio. (p. 423)

Hollywood Ten [los Diez de Hollywood] *s.* diez testigos de la industria cinematográfica que se negaron a cooperar con la investigación de influencia comunista en Hollywood que realizó el Comité de la Cámara de Representantes sobre Actividades Antiamericanas. (p. 781)

Holocaust [Holocausto] *s.* asesinato sistemático de más de 11 millones de judíos y de otros grupos por los nazis antes y durante la II Guerra Mundial. (p. 714)

home rule [gobierno local] *s.* poder de los estados de gobernar a sus ciudadanos sin intervención federal. (p. 372)

Homestead Act [Ley de la Heredad] *s.* ley aprobada por el Congreso en 1862 que ofrecía 160 acres de tierra gratis a quien viviera en ella y la cultivara por cinco años. (p. 382)

homesteader *s.* colono que vivía en tierras otorgadas por el gobierno a través de la Ley de la Heredad de 1862. (p. 397)

Hopewell *s.* sociedad constructora de túmulos asentada en el valle del río Ohio entre los años 200 a.C. y 400 d.C., aproximadamente; se conoce por sus grandes tumbas cónicas. (p. 6)

horizontal consolidation [consolidación horizontal] *s.* proceso mediante el cual compañías que fabrican productos similares se unen y reducen la competencia. (p. 422)

hot line [línea de emergencia] *s.* línea directa de comunicación entre la Casa Blanca y el Kremlin, establecida en 1963 para que los líderes de Estados Unidos y la Unión Soviética pudieran hablarse durante una crisis. (p. 836)

HUAC *s.* House Committee on Un-American Activities (Comité de la Cámara de Representantes sobre Actividades Antiamericanas), comité del Congreso creado en 1938 para investigar la influencia comunista dentro y fuera del gobierno. (p. 780)

human rights [derechos humanos] *s.* derechos y libertades considerados básicos, como los que establece la Declaración de Independencia y la Carta de Derechos. (p. 965)

I

Immigration Act of 1965 [Ley de Inmigración de 1965] *s.* ley que abrió las puertas a más inmigrantes de Asia y Latinoamérica al remplazar el sistema de inmigración por origen nacional. (p. 846)

imperialism [imperialismo] *s.* política de controlar países por medios económicos, políticos o militares. (p. 526)

impressment [leva] *s.* práctica de reclutar hombres a la fuerza para prestar servicio militar. (p. 189)

Inca *s.* pueblo amerindio creador de un imperio que abarcó casi 2,500 millas a lo largo de la costa occidental de Suramérica, a partir del año 1400 d.C., aproximadamente. (p. 6)

income tax [impuesto sobre la renta] *s.* impuesto que retiene un porcentaje específico de los ingresos de un individuo. (p. 326)

indentured servant [sirviente por contrato] *s.* inmigrante que, a cambio de un pasaje para las Américas, se comprometía a trabajar de cuatro a siete años. (p. 47)

Indian Removal Act [Ley de Traslado de los Indígenas] *s.* ley aprobada por el Congreso en 1830 que ordenaba el traslado obligatorio de todas las tribus indígenas del este del Mississippi a tierras del oeste. (p. 211)

Industrial Revolution [Revolución Industrial] *s.* cambios en la organización social y económica como resultado del remplazo del trabajo manual por máquinas y el desarrollo de fábricas de producción a gran escala. (p. 198)

Industrial Workers of the World (IWW) *s.* también conocido como los Wobblies, sindicato de trabajadores de mano de obra no calificada creado en 1905. (p. 430)

inflation [inflación] *s.* fenómeno económico en el que hay un aumento constante en los precios por el incremento del dinero circulante; reduce el poder adquisitivo. (p. 110)

information superhighway [supercarretera de información] *s.* red de comunicación por computadoras propuesta para unir a personas e instituciones por todo el mundo y suministrar a individuos servicios de bibliotecas, compras, cines y noticias. (p. 1018)

INF Treaty [Tratado sobre Fuerzas Nucleares Intermedias] *s.* tratado entre Estados Unidos y la Unión Soviética firmado en 1987, que eliminó algunas armas y permitió la inspección directa de emplazamientos de misiles. (p. 996)

initiative [iniciativa] *s.* reforma gubernamental que permite a los ciudadanos presentar proyectos de ley en el Congreso o en cuerpos legislativos estatales. (p. 500)

installment plan [pago a plazos] *s.* práctica de comprar a crédito mediante pagos regulares durante determinado período de tiempo. (p. 605)

interchangeable parts [piezas uniformes] *s.* piezas que se pueden usar de manera intercambiable y que se producen en masa. (p. 198)

Internet *s.* red mundial, originalmente diseñada por el Departamento de Defensa, que une computadors y permite una comunicación casi instantánea de textos, ilustraciones y sonidos. (p. 1019)

Interstate Commerce Act [Ley de Comercio Interestatal] *s.* ley de 1887 que restablecía el derecho del gobierno federal a supervisar los ferrocarriles; creó una Comisión de Comercio Interestatal de cinco miembros. (p. 420)

Intolerable Acts [Leyes Intolerables] *s.* cuatro leyes aprobadas por el Parlamento en 1774 con el fin de castigar a Boston por el Motín del Té de Boston. (p. 97)

Iroquois [iroqueses] *s.* grupo de pueblos amerindios que vivían en los bosques del Noreste. (p. 10)

Islam [islamismo] *s.* religión fundada en Arabia por el profeta Mahoma en el año 622; a sus seguidores se les llama musulmanes. (p. 15)

isolationist [aislacionista] *adj.* que se opone a participar en conflictos políticos y económicos con otros países. (p. 597)

J

Japanese Americans Citizens League (JACL) [Sociedad de Ciudadanos Americano-Japoneses] *s.* organización que presionó al gobierno a compensar a los estadounidenses de origen japonés por las propiedades que perdieron al ser internados durante la II Guerra Mundial. (p. 761)

Jim Crow laws [leyes Jim Crow] *s.* leyes impuestas por los gobiernos estatales y municipales del Sur con el fin de separar a blancos y negros en instalaciones públicas y privadas. (p. 474)

joint-stock company [sociedad de capitales] *s.* institución empresarial tipo corporación en la que inversionistas unen riquezas con un fin común; se usaron para financiar la exploración de las Américas. (p. 24)

journeyman [oficial] *s.* artesano que trabaja al servicio de un maestro. (p. 241)

judicial branch [rama judicial] *s.* rama gubernamental cuya función es interpretar las leyes y la Constitución (Suprema Corte). (p. 136)

judicial review [revisión judicial] *s.* poder de la Suprema Corte de declarar inconstitucional una ley del Congreso. (p. 186)

Judiciary Act of 1789 [Ley Judicial de 1789] *s.* ley que estableció el sistema de tribunales federales y la Suprema Corte. (p. 172)

Judiciary Act of 1801 [Ley Judicial de 1801] *s.* ley aprobada con el fin de incrementar el número de jueces federalistas. (p. 186)

Jungle, The [La jungla] *s.* novela publicada en 1906 por el periodista Upton Sinclair que denunciaba la insalubridad de la industria de carne; llevó a reformas nacionales. (p. 508)

K

kamikaze *adj.* que estrellaba deliberadamente un avión bombardero contra un buque estadounidense durante la II Guerra Mundial. (p. 749)

Kansas-Nebraska Act [Ley Kansas y Nebraska] *s.* ley aprobada en 1854 que buscaba un acuerdo sobre la extensión de la esclavitud a los territorios de Kansas y Nebraska. (p. 292)

Kashaya Pomo *s.* pueblo amerindio que floreció hace 500 años en lo que hoy es California; vivía en las tierras pantanosas de la costa. (p. 8)

Kellogg-Briand Treaty [Pacto Kellog-Briand] *s.* tratado de 1929 firmado por 64 naciones en el que acordaron renunciar a la guerra como medio para resolver disputas internacionales. (p. 597)

1100 SPANISH GLOSSARY

Kerner Commission [Comisión Kerner] *s.* grupo designado por el presidente Lyndon B. Johnson para estudiar las causas del levantamiento de Watts de 1965; recomendó eliminar la segregación *de facto* en la sociedad estadounidense. (p. 876)

Khmer Rouge *s.* grupo comunista que en 1975 tomó el poder en Camboya. (p. 912)

kickback [mordida] *s.* porción de los ingresos de un trabajador que se paga ilegalmente a un político o maquinaria política. (p. 453)

King Philip's War [Guerra del Rey Felipe] *s.* conflicto, en los años 1675 y 1676, entre los colonos de Nueva Inglaterra y grupos amerindios aliados bajo la dirección del cacique Metacom de los wampanoagas. (p. 57)

kinship [parentesco] *s.* lazos indisolubles entre los miembros de una misma familia o tribu. (p. 13)

Know-Nothing Party *s.* nombre dado en la década de 1850 al Partido Americano, un grupo que quería reducir la influencia política de los inmigrantes. (p. 296)

Kongo *s.* serie de pequeños reinos unidos bajo un líder a finales del siglo 15 en las selvas tropicales a lo largo del río Zaire (Congo) en África. (p. 17)

Korean War [Guerra de Corea] *s.* guerra de 1950 a 1953 entre Corea del Norte y Corea del Sur; China respaldó a Corea del Norte y las tropas de las Naciones Unidas, integradas en su mayoría por soldados estadounidenses, apoyaron a Corea del Sur. (p. 775)

Kristallnacht *s.* noviembre 9 de 1938, noche en que milicianos nazis atacaron viviendas, negocios y sinagogas judías en Alemania. (p. 715)

Ku Klux Klan *s.* sociedad secreta de hombres blancos en los estados sureños después de la Guerra Civil que desató terror para restaurar la supremacía blanca. (p. 366)

Kwakiutl *s.* pueblo amerindio que vivía en la región costera del Noroeste. (p. 9)

L

land grant [concesión de tierras] *s.* lote grande de tierras dado por el gobierno a un agente para su reventa, por lo general con el fin de estimular el desarrollo. (p. 269)

Land Ordinance of 1785 [Ordenanza de Tierras de 1785] *s.* ley que estableció un plan para la agrimensura y venta de las tierras públicas al oeste de los montes Apalaches. (p. 128)

La Raza Unida *s.* organización política latina establecida en 1969 por José Ángel Gutiérrez. (p. 922)

League of Nations [Liga de las Naciones] *s.* organización internacional establecida en 1920 para promover la cooperación y la paz internacional. (p. 578)

legislative branch [rama legislativa] *s.* rama gubernamental compuesta por representantes elegidos que promulgan leyes (Congreso). (p. 135)

Lend-Lease Act [Ley de Préstamo y Alquiler] *s.* ley, promulgada en 1941, que autorizó al gobierno a mandar armas y otros productos, sin pago inmediato, a las naciones que luchaban contra el Eje. (p. 721)

Limited Test Ban Treaty [Tratado de Limitación de Pruebas Nucleares] *s.* tratado de 1963 en que Estados Unidos y la Unión Soviética acordaron no realizar pruebas de armas nucleares en la atmósfera. (p. 836)

lineage [linaje] *s.* línea de descendencia de una generación a otra —de abuelo, a hija, a nieto, por ejemplo— con un antepasado común. (p. 18)

Linotype machine [linotipia] *s.* máquina de composición tipográfica que funde los caracteres por líneas completas, formando un solo bloque, no letra por letra. (p. 466)

literacy test [prueba de lectura] *s.* examen de lectura que se usaba en algunos estados sureños para impedir que los afroamericanos votaran. (p. 474)

long drive [arreo de ganado] *s.* proceso mediante el cual los vaqueros llevaban por tierra ganado hacia el mercado. (p. 392)

longhorn *s.* resistente raza de ganado vacuno de cuernos largos llevada por los españoles a México, muy apta para las condiciones de esa región. (p. 388)

Louisiana Purchase [Compra de Louisiana] *s.* compra de terrenos a Francia por 15 millones de dólares en 1803 de las tierras desde el río Mississippi hasta las montañas Rocosas. (p. 188)

Loyalist [realista] *s.* colono que apoyaba al gobierno británico durante la Revolución Norteamericana. (p. 102)

Lusitania *s.* barco británico de pasajeros que se hundió cerca a costas irlandesas el 7 de mayo de 1915, tras ser atacado por un submarino alemán. (p. 559)

M

magnetic resonance imaging [imágenes por resonancia magnética] *s.* tecnología que utilizan los médicos para obtener imágenes de cortes transversales de cualquier parte del cuerpo humano. (p. 1020)

mail-order catalog [catálogo por correo] *s.* folleto de mercancías que se pueden pedir y recibir por correo. (p. 485)

mandate [mandato] *s.* conquista de una porción suficientemente grande del voto, que indica que un líder elegido tiene apoyo popular para sus programas. (p. 838)

Manhattan Project [Proyecto Manhattan] *s.* programa estadounidense que se inició en 1942 con el fin de diseñar una bomba atómica para la II Guerra Mundial. La primera detonación atómica completa ocurrió en Alamogordo, New Mexico, el 16 de julio de 1945. (p. 750)

manifest destiny [destino manifiesto] *s.* término usado en la década de 1840 para describir la creencia de que Estados Unidos estaba inexorablemente destinado a adquirir más territorio, especialmente mediante su expansión hacia el oeste. (p. 261)

Marbury v. Madison *s.* caso de 1803 en que la Suprema Corte decidió que tenía el poder de abolir decretos legislativos declarándolos inconstitucionales; ese poder se conoce como revisión judicial.

market revolution [revolución mercantil] *s.* gran cambio económico que llevó a comprar y vender productos en lugar de hacerlos en el hogar. (p. 255)

Marshall Plan [Plan Marshall] *s.* plan formulado por el Secretario de Estado George Marshall en 1947, mediante el que se ofreció ayuda a países europeos con el fin de reparar los daños de la II Guerra Mundial. (p. 770)

martial law [ley marcial] *s.* gobierno impuesto por fuerzas militares. (p. 97)

mass media [medios informativos] *s.* medios de comunicación —tales como televisión, prensa y radio— que llegan a grandes audiencias. (p. 812)

mass production [producción en masa] *s.* producción de artículos en grandes cantidades, con máquinas y división del trabajo. (p. 198)

master [maestro] *s.* experto artesano; por lo general era dueño de un negocio y empleaba a otros. (p. 241)

Maya *s.* pueblo amerindio que desarrolló una rica cultura en Guatemala y la península de Yucatán entre los años 250 y 900 d.C. (p. 6)

McCarthyism [macartismo] *s.* práctica de hacer acusaciones públicas de deslealtad sin suficiente prueba, cuyo nombre viene del senador Joseph McCarthy, quien acusó a muchos de ser comunistas en los años 50. (p. 783)

Meat Inspection Act [Ley de Inspección de la Carne] *s.* ley de 1906 que establecía estrictos requisitos sanitarios en las empacadoras de carne, así como un programa federal de inspección de carnes. (p. 509)

mechanized warfare [guerra mecanizada] *s.* guerra de máquinas con motores de gasolina y diesel. (p. 566)

Medicaid *s.* programa federal que se inició en 1965 para brindar atención médica a las personas que reciben ayuda pública. (p. 846)

Medicare *s.* programa federal que se inició en 1965 para brindar seguros médicos y de hospitalización a bajo costo a los mayores de 65 años. (p. 846)

melting pot [crisol de culturas] *s.* mezcla de personas de diferentes culturas y razas que se amalgaman y abandonan su idioma y cultura natal. (p. 442)

mercantilism [mercantilismo] *s.* sistema económico en que un país aumenta su riqueza y poder al incrementar su posesión de oro y plata, y al exportar más productos de los que importa. (p. 66)

Merrimack *s.* buque blindado que usó el Sur durante la Guerra Civil. (p. 343)

mestizo *adj.* con mezcla de español e indígena. (p. 40)

middle passage [travesía intermedia] *s.* tramo de África a las Antillas; parte del triángulo comercial de esclavos. (p. 74)

midnight judge [juez de media noche] *s.* uno de los jueces designados por John Adams en las últimas horas de su gobierno. (p. 186)

militarism [militarismo] *s.* política de mantener una sólida organización militar como preparación agresiva para la guerra. (p. 555)

Miranda rights [derechos Miranda] *s.* derechos de un acusado, que estableció la decisión de la Suprema Corte *Miranda* v. *Arizona* de 1966; incluyen el derecho a guardar silencio hasta disponer de un abogado. (p. 849)

Mississippian [misisipiense] *s.* última sociedad constructora de túmulos, que se extendió al este del río Mississippi del siglo 8 al 16. (p. 6)

Missouri Compromise [Acuerdo de Missouri] *s.* serie de leyes de 1820 para mantener un equilibrio seccional entre los estados esclavistas y los estados libres. (p. 208)

Monitor *s.* buque blindado que usó el Norte durante la Guerra Civil. (p. 343)

monopoly [monopolio] *s.* control completo de una industria que se logra al comprar o arruinar a los competidores. (p. 423)

Monroe Doctrine [Doctrina Monroe] *s.* declaración del presidente Monroe en 1823 que establecía que Estados Unidos no permitiría la interferencia europea en los asuntos del Hemisferio Occidental. (p. 207)

Moral Majority [Mayoría Moral] *s.* coalición política de organizaciones religiosas conservadoras en los años 70 y 80 que recaudó dinero para respaldar agendas y candidatos conservadores, y condenó actitudes y comportamientos liberales. (p. 980)

Mormon [mormón] *s.* miembro de una comunidad religiosa fundada por Joseph Smith, que terminó estableciéndose en Utah. (p. 264)

Morrill Land Grant Acts [Leyes Morrill de Concesión de Tierras] *s.* leyes aprobadas en 1862 y 1890 que otorgaban tierras federales a los estados para financiar universidades agrícolas. (p. 399)

muckraker *s.* reportero de revista a comienzos de este siglo que denunciaba prácticas empresariales corruptas. (p. 496)

Munn v. Illinois *s.* caso de la Suprema Corte en 1877; estableció el derecho del gobierno federal a regular la industria privada en beneficio del interés público. (p. 420)

N

NAACP *s.* National Association for the Advancement of Colored People (Asociación Nacional para el Avance de la Gente de Color), organización fundada en 1909 y dedicada a la igualdad racial. (p. 511)

NACW *s.* National Association of Colored Women (Asociación Nacional de Mujeres de Color), organización de servicio social fundada en 1896. (p. 503)

NAFTA *s.* North American Free Trade Agreement (Tratado de Libre Comercio, TLC), tratado de 1993 que redujo aranceles e incorporó a México en la zona de libre comercio ya vigente entre Estados Unidos y Canadá. (p. 1009)

napalm *s.* sustancia incendiaria de gasolina que lanzaban los aviones estadounidenses en Vietnam, con el fin de incendiar la selva y revelar los escondites del Vietcong. (p. 892)

national bank [banco nacional] *s.* banco constituido por el gobierno federal, que actúa en su nombre en asuntos financieros. (p. 174)

National Energy Act [Ley Nacional de Energía] *s.* ley promulgada durante la administración Carter para aliviar la crisis energética; aplicó impuestos a los autos que usan gasolina de manera ineficiente y suspendió el control de precios del petróleo y el gas natural estadounidenses. (p. 963)

National Industrial Recovery Act [Ley Nacional de Recuperación Industrial] *s.* ley aprobada en 1933 que establecía agencias para supervisar industrias y suministrar empleos. (p. 668)

nationalism [nacionalismo] *s.* creencia de que los intereses y la unidad nacionales deben estar por encima de las preocupaciones regionales, y de que el interés nacional debe guiar la política exterior. (p. 205)

National Labor Relations Board [Junta Nacional de Relaciones Laborales] *s.* agencia creada en 1935 con el fin de prevenir prácticas laborales injustas y mediar en disputas laborales. (p. 691)

National Organization for Women [Organización Nacional de la Mujer] *s.* organización fundada en 1966 con el fin de impulsar metas feministas, tales como mejores guarderías, mayores oportunidades educativas y el fin de la discriminación laboral. (p. 930)

National Road [Carretera Nacional] *s.* carretera financiada por el gobierno cuya construcción se inició en 1811; iba desde Cumberland, Maryland, hasta Vandalia, Illinois. (p. 203)

National Trades' Union [Unión Nacional de Sindicatos] *s.* primera asociación nacional de sindicatos, creada en 1834. (p. 245)

National Youth Administration [Administración Nacional de Recursos para la Juventud] *s.* programa que suministraba ayuda y empleos a jóvenes durante la Depresión. (p. 673)

Nation of Islam [Nación del Islam] *s.* grupo religioso, popularmente conocido como musulmanes negros, fundado por Elijah Muhammad para promover el separatismo negro y la religión islámica. (p. 873)

nativism [nativismo] *s.* creencia o política que favorece los intereses de las personas naturales de un país por encima de los inmigrantes. (p. 296)

Navigation Acts [Leyes de Navegación] *s.* serie de leyes aprobadas a partir de 1651 que imponían un control más rígido del comercio en las colonias inglesas. (p. 67)

NAWSA *s.* National American Woman Suffrage Association (Asociación Nacional Americana del Sufragio Femenino), creada en 1890 para obtener derechos electorales para la mujer. (p. 503)

Nazism [nazismo] *s.* movimiento político basado en un extremo nacionalismo, racismo y expansionismo militar; instituido en Alemania como sistema de gobierno por Adolfo Hitler en 1933. (p. 704)

neutrality [neutralidad] *s.* política de una nación de no participar directa ni indirectamente en una guerra entre otras naciones. (p. 178)

Neutrality Acts [Leyes de Neutralidad] *s.* serie de leyes aprobadas por el Congreso en 1935 y 1936 que prohibieron la venta y el alquiler de armas a naciones en guerra. (p. 706)

New Deal *s.* medidas económicas y políticas adoptadas por el presidente Franklin Roosevelt en los años 30 para promover recuperación económica, ayuda a los necesitados y reforma financiera. (p. 665)

New Deal Coalition [Coalición del New Deal] *s.* alianza temporal de distintos grupos, tales como blancos sureños, afroamericanos y sindicalistas, que apoyaban al Partido Demócrata en los años 30 y 40. (p. 680)

New Federalism [Nuevo Federalismo] *s.* programa del presidente Richard Nixon para distribuir una porción del poder del gobierno federal a gobiernos estatales y locales. (p. 946)

New Frontier [Nueva Frontera] *s.* agenda legislativa del presidente John F. Kennedy; tenía medidas de atención médica para ancianos, renovación urbana y apoyo a la educación, que fueron rechazadas por el Congreso, así como medidas que sí se aprobaron de defensa nacional, ayuda internacional y programas espaciales. (p. 838)

New Left [Nueva Izquierda] *s.* movimiento político juvenil de los años 60 con organizaciones como Students for a Democratic Society (Estudiantes por una Sociedad Democrática) y el Free Speech Movement (Movimiento de Libre Expresión). (p. 897)

New Right [Nueva Derecha] *s.* alianza política de grupos conservadores de fines del siglo 20, con énfasis en asuntos culturales, sociales y morales. (p. 979)

Nineteenth Amendment [Enmienda 19] *s.* enmienda a la Constitución adoptada en 1920 que le otorga a la mujer el derecho de votar. (p. 520)

Nisei *s.* ciudadano estadounidense de padres inmigrantes japoneses. (p. 735)

no man's land [tierra de nadie] *s.* en la I Guerra Mundial, extensión baldía de tierra entre trincheras de ejércitos enemigos. (p. 557)

nonaggression pact [pacto de no agresión] *s.* acuerdo entre dos naciones de no luchar entre sí. (p. 711)

North Atlantic Treaty Organization (NATO) [Organización del Tratado del Atlántico Norte] *s.* alianza militar defensiva formada en 1949 por diez países de Europa del oeste, Estados Unidos y Canadá. (p. 772)

Northwest Ordinance of 1787 [Ordenanza del Noroeste de 1787] *s.* procedimiento para la admisión de nuevos estados a la Unión. (p. 128)

nuclear family [familia nuclear] *s.* unidad formada por padre, madre e hijos, en comparación con la familia extensa, que incluye otras generaciones y parientes más distantes. (p. 21)

nullification [anulación] *s.* rechazo de un estado a reconocer cualquier ley del Congreso que considere inconstitucional. (p. 181)

Nuremberg trials [juicios de Nuremberg] *s.* juicios llevados a cabo en Nuremberg, Alemania, inmediatamente después de la II Guerra Mundial, a líderes nazis por sus crímenes de guerra. (p. 752)

O

Office of Price Administration (OPA) [Oficina de Administración de Precios] *s.* agencia establecida por el Congreso durante la II Guerra Mundial con facultad para combatir la inflación al congelar los precios de la mayoría de los artículos. (p. 736)

Ohio gang [pandilla de Ohio] *s.* amigos y partidarios políticos del presidente Warren G. Harding, a quienes éste nombró a su gabinete. (p. 599)

Olive Branch Petition [Petición del Ramo de Olivo] *s.* documento enviado por el Segundo Congreso Continental al rey George III; proponía una reconciliación entre las colonias y Gran Bretaña. (p. 100)

Olmec [olmeca] *s.* pueblo amerindio que creó una próspera civilización a lo largo de la costa del golfo de México, entre los años 1200 y 400 a.C. (p. 6)

OPEC *s.* Organization of Petroleum Exporting Countries (Organización de Países Exportadores de Petróleo, OPEP), alianza económica para ejercer influencia sobre los precios del petróleo. (p. 950)

Open Door notes [notas de Puertas Abiertas] *s.* notas que el Secretario de Estado John Hay envió a Gran Bretaña, Francia, Alemania, Italia, Japón y Rusia, instándolos a no interponerse en el comercio de Estados Unidos y China. (p. 539)

Operation Desert Storm [Operación Tormenta del Desierto] *s.* operación militar en la que fuerzas de las Naciones Unidas, encabezadas por Estados Unidos, liberaron a Kuwait y derrotaron al ejército iraquí. (p. 1000)

Oregon Trail [Sendero de Oregon] *s.* camino que va de Independence, Missouri, a Portland, Oregon. (p. 263)

P

Panama Canal [canal de Panamá] *s.* canal artificial construido a través del istmo de Panamá para abrir paso entre los océanos Atlántico y Pacífico; se abrió en 1914. (p. 544)

Panic of 1837 [Pánico de 1837] *s.* serie de clausuras de bancos y colapso del sistema crediticio; causó muchas quiebras y desempleo. (p. 218)

Panic of 1873 [Pánico de 1873] *s.* serie de fracasos económicos que provocaron una depresión de cinco años en Estados Unidos. (p. 370)

parity [paridad] *s.* regulación de precios de ciertos productos agrícolas, apoyada por el gobierno, con el fin de mantener estables los ingresos agrícolas. (p. 692)

Parliament [Parlamento] *s.* cuerpo legislativo de Inglaterra. (p. 67)

Patriot [patriota] *s.* colono que apoyaba la independencia norteamericana de Gran Bretaña. (p. 102)

patronage [clientelismo] *s.* sistema de otorgar empleos a personas que ayudan a la elección de un candidato. (p. 455)

pay equity [equidad salarial] *s.* sistema que basa el salario de un empleado en los requisitos del trabajo y no en escalas salariales tradicionales, que normalmente pagan menos a la mujer. (p. 991)

Payne-Aldrich Tariff [Arancel Payne-Aldrich] *s.* serie de reglamentos de impuestos, aprobados por el Congreso en 1909, que no logró reducir mucho los aranceles de productos manufacturados. (p. 513)

Peace Corps [Cuerpo de Paz] *s.* programa fundado en 1965 bajo iniciativa del presidente Kennedy, que envía voluntarios a las naciones en desarrollo de Asia, África y Latinoamérica para ayudar en escuelas, clínicas y otros proyectos. (p. 839)

Pendleton Act [Ley Pendleton] *s.* ley de 1883 que autorizaba nombrar empleados del servicio civil por mérito. (p. 456)

Pentagon Papers [Documentos del Pentágono] *s.* documento de 7,000 páginas que dejó filtrar a la prensa en 1971 el antiguo funcionario del Departamento de Defensa Daniel Ellsberg, donde se revela que el gobierno mintió sobre sus planes en la Guerra de Vietnam. (p. 910)

Pequot War [Guerra de los Pequot] *s.* conflicto librado en 1637 entre la tribu pequot y colonos asentados en Connecticut, que se aliaron con la tribu narrangansett. (p. 56)

perestroika s. palabra rusa para designar la reestructuración económica y burocrática de la Unión Soviética que tuvo lugar en los años 80. (p. 996)

personal liberty laws [leyes de libertad personal] *s.* estatutos aprobados en los estados del Norte que prohibían encarcelar a esclavos fugitivos y les permitían ser juzgados por un jurado. (p. 289)

planned obsolescence [obsolencia planeada] *s.* diseño de artículos que se desgastan o pasan de moda muy pronto, para crear la necesidad de remplazarlos con frecuencia. (p. 809)

plantation [plantación] *s.* finca grande en la que se cultiva una sola cosecha, como caña de azúcar o algodón, usando esclavos u otros trabajadores. (p. 16)

Platt Amendment [Enmienda Platt] *s.* serie de medidas que obligaba a Cuba a aceptar la intervención de Estados Unidos y el establecimiento de estaciones navales y carboníferas estadounidenses en sus puertos. (p. 537)

Plessy v. Ferguson s. caso de 1986 en que la Suprema Corte declaró legal la separación de razas en instalaciones públicas y estableció la doctrina de "separados aunque iguales". (p. 475)

political machine [maquinaria política] *s.* grupo organizado que controla un partido político en una ciudad y ofrece servicios a los votantes y negocios a cambio de apoyo político y financiero. (p. 452)

poll tax [impuesto para votar] *s.* impuesto anual que los ciudadanos debían pagar en algunos estados sureños para poder votar. (p. 474)

popular sovereignty [soberanía popular] *s.* parte del Compromiso de 1850; derecho de los residentes de un territorio a votar en favor o en contra de la esclavitud. (p. 285)

Populism [populismo] *s.* movimiento político de finales del siglo 19 que representaba los intereses de los granjeros y promovía una reforma del sistema monetario. (p. 402)

Powhatan *s.* grupo de pueblos amerindios que vivía en el este de Virginia cuando se establecieron las primeras colonias inglesas. (p. 45)

price support [apoyo de precios] *s.* apoyo de los precios de ciertos artículos al valor del mercado o por encima, algunas veces mediante la compra de excedentes por parte del gobierno. (p. 643)

Proclamation of 1763 [Proclama de 1763] *s.* decreto británico que prohibía que los colonos se instalaran al oeste de los montes Apalaches. (p. 86)

profiteering [acaparamiento] *s.* retención de un producto para provocar su escasez y venderlo más caro. (p. 110)

progressive movement [movimiento progresista] *s.* movimiento reformista de comienzos del siglo 20 cuyos objetivos eran mejorar el bienestar social, promover la moralidad, incrementar la justicia económica y devolver a la ciudadanía el control del gobierno. (p. 494)

prohibition [prohibición] *s.* prohibición de bebidas alcohólicas. (p. 495)

proprietor [propietario] *s.* dueño y gobernante de una colonia. (p. 59)

protective tariff [arancel proteccionista] *s.* impuesto aplicado a productos importados para proteger las empresas nacionales de la competencia extranjera. (p. 176)

protectorate [protectorado] *s.* nación cuyo gobierno y asuntos son controlados por una potencia más fuerte. (p. 537)

Pueblo *s.* amerindios descendientes de los anasazi; viven en los desiertos del Suroeste. (p. 9)

Pure Food and Drug Act [Ley de Pureza de Alimentos y Drogas] *s.* ley de 1906 que paró la venta de alimentos y drogas contaminadas y demandó etiquetas fidedignas. (p. 509)

Puritan [puritano] *s.* miembro de la Iglesia Anglicana que deseaba eliminar las tradiciones católicas y simplificar los servicios religiosos. (p. 52)

putting-out system [sistema de producción doméstica] *s.* sistema de producción en el que los fabricantes suministraban materiales para manufacturar mercancías en casa. (p. 240)

Quaker [cuáquero] *s.* miembro de una secta religiosa considerada radical en el siglo 17, también conocida como Sociedad de Amigos. (p. 59)

quota system [sistema de cuotas] *s.* sistema que limita el número de inmigrantes de varios países que pueden ser admitidos a Estados Unidos cada año. (p. 599)

Radical Republican [republicano radical] *s.* uno de los republicanos del Congreso después de la Guerra Civil que querían destruir el poder político de los antiguos dueños de esclavos y darles a los afroamericanos total ciudadanía y derecho a votar. (p. 351)

ragtime *s.* estilo de música que surgió en 1880 combinando la música espiritual negra y la música europea. (p. 481)

ratification [ratificación] *s.* aprobación oficial de la Constitución, o de una enmienda, por parte de los estados. (p. 137)

rationing [racionamiento] *s.* medida tomada durante tiempos de guerra para limitar la cantidad de ciertos alimentos y otros productos que cada persona puede comprar. (p. 736)

Reaganomics [reaganomía] *s.* nombre dado a la política económica del presidente Reagan, que abogaba por una gran reducción en los impuestos con el fin de incrementar la inversión privada y por consiguiente expandir el suministro de productos y servicios. (p. 982)

realpolitik *s.* enfoque de política exterior, identificado con Henry Kissinger y Richard Nixon, que propone hacer lo que resulte realista y práctico en lugar de seguir una política al pie de la letra. (p. 951)

reapportionment [nueva repartición] *s.* redistribución de distritos electorales cuando cambia el número de personas en un distrito. (p. 848)

recall [destitución] *s.* reforma gubernamental que permite a los votantes deponer a funcionarios públicos elegidos. (p. 500)

Reconstruction [Reconstrucción] *s.* período de reconstrucción después de la Guerra Civil y readmisión a la Unión de los estados de la Confederación que habían sido derrotados; de 1865 a 1877. (p. 350)

Reconstruction Finance Corporation [Corporación Financiera de la Reconstrucción] *s.* organización establecida en 1932 para dar financiación de emergencia a bancos, aseguradoras de vida, compañías ferroviarias y otras empresas grandes. (p. 658)

redemption [redención] *s.* término usado por los demócratas sureños para referirse a su recuperación del poder en el Sur en la década de 1870. (p. 371)

referendum [referendo] *s.* procedimiento que permite someter al voto popular propuestas legislativas. (p. 500)

Reformation [Reforma] *s.* movimiento religioso en la Europa de comienzos del siglo 16, encaminado a reformar la Iglesia Católica Romana; condujo a la formación del protestantismo. (p. 22)

reparations [reparación] *s.* compensación que paga una nación derrotada en una guerra por las pérdidas económicas del vencedor o por crímenes cometidos contra individuos. (p. 578)

republic [república] *s.* gobierno en el que los ciudadanos mandan por medio de sus representantes elegidos. (p. 126)

Republican [republicano] *s.* miembro del partido político que apoyó la visión de Thomas Jefferson de un gobierno central fuerte. (p. 175)

republicanism [republicanismo] *s.* creencia de que los gobiernos deben basarse en el consentimiento del pueblo. (p. 126)

Republican Party [Partido Republicano] *s.* partido actual, formado en 1854 por oponentes de la esclavitud en los territorios. (p. 297)

revenue sharing [distribución de rentas] *s.* plan puesto en práctica en 1972 que faculta a los gobiernos estatales y locales a invertir el dinero federal a su conveniencia. (p. 946)

reverse discrimination [discriminación a la inversa] *s.* tratamiento injusto de los miembros de un grupo mayoritario, típicamente hombres blancos, como resultado de los esfuerzos por remediar la discriminación contra otros grupos. (p. 979)

revival [renovación religiosa] *s.* emotivas reuniones religiosas para revivir la fe, con apasionados sermones. (p. 224)

rock'n' roll *s.* forma de música popular, caracterizada por ritmos fuertes y letras simples, que surgió de la música "rhythm and blues" y la música "country" durante los años 50. (p. 816)

Roosevelt Corollary [Corolario de Roosevelt] *s.* declaración de 1904 del presidente Theodore Roosevelt en que advertía que Estados Unidos intervendría militarmente en los asuntos de cualquier nación del Hemisferio Occidental para proteger sus intereses económicos si fuera necesario. (p. 544)

Rough Riders *s.* regimiento de caballería voluntario comandado por Leonard Wood y Theodore Roosevelt en la Guerra Española-Norteamericana-Cubana. (p. 533)

row house [casa de conjunto] *s.* vivienda familiar que comparte sus paredes laterales con otras casas similares. (p. 448)

royal colony [colonia real] *s.* colonia sujeta al control directo de la corona británica. (p. 48)

rural free delivery [correo rural gratuito] *s.* entrega gubernamental gratis de correo y paquetes a zonas rurales; se inició en 1896. (p. 485)

SALT I Treaty [Tratado Salt I] *s.* acuerdo de cinco años entre Estados Unidos y la Unión Soviética que surgió de las Conversaciones sobre Limitación de Armas Estratégicas de 1972; limitó el número de misiles balísticos intercontinentales y de misiles de submarinos. (p. 952)

salutary neglect [indiferencia saludable] *s.* aplicación poco estricta de las leyes comerciales por parte del gobierno británico a cambio de lealtad comercial de las colonias. (p. 69)

Sand Creek Massacre [Masacre de Sand Creek] *s.* ataque en 1864 a una aldea cheyenne en el Territorio de Colorado por parte de soldados del ejército federal, en el que murieron 200 hombres, mujeres y niños. (p. 383)

Sandinista *adj.* relativo a las fuerzas izquierdistas que derrocaron al gobierno nicaragüense en 1979; el presidente Reagan, quien respaldaba a la contra anticomunista, se les opuso. (p. 998)

Santa Fe Trail [Sendero de Santa Fe] *s.* camino que va de Independence, Missouri, a Santa Fe, New Mexico. (p. 262)

satellite nation [nación satélite] *s.* país dominado política y económicamente por otro. (p. 769)

Saturday Night Massacre [Masacre de Sábado en la Noche] *s.* nombre dado a la renuncia del procurador general y al despido de su comisionado el 20 de octubre de 1973, después de haberse negado a acatar la orden del presidente Nixon de despedir al fiscal especial en el caso Watergate. (p. 956)

savanna [sabana] *s.* pastizal plano y seco con árboles y arbustos espaciados; común en África central y otras regiones tropicales y subtropicales. (p. 14)

scab [rompehuelgas] *s.* trabajador que no se une a una huelga o que trabaja en remplazo de un huelguista. (p. 431)

scalawag *s.* término despectivo para referirse a los sureños blancos que se unieron al Partido Republicano y apoyaron la Reconstrucción después de la Guerra Civil. (p. 357)

scientific management [administración científica] *s.* aplicación de principios científicos para simplificar y facilitar las tareas laborales. (p. 496)

Scopes trial [juicio de Scopes] *s.* sensacional juicio de 1925 en el que el maestro de biología John T. Scopes fue juzgado por desafiar una ley de Tennessee que prohibía la enseñanza de la evolución. (p. 616)

search-and-destroy mission [misión de búsqueda y destrucción] *s.* ataque militar estadounidense a aldeas de Vietnam del Sur con el fin de erradicar al Vietcong, que solía resultar en la destrucción de la aldea y el desplazamiento de sus habitantes. (p. 892)

secession [secesión] *s.* retiro formal de un estado de la Unión federal. (p. 285)

Second Continental Congress [Segundo Congreso Continental] *s.* nueva convocatoria del Congreso Continental que se inició en 1775 y redactó la Declaración de Independencia. (p. 99)

Second Great Awakening [Segundo Gran Despertar] *s.* movimiento religioso del siglo 19 que ponía énfasis en la responsabilidad individual para lograr la salvación y la superación personal y social. (p. 224)

sectionalism [regionalismo] *s.* preocupación por los intereses de una región por encima de los de la nación como un todo. (p. 180)

Securities and Exchange Commission [Comisión de Valores y Cambios] *s.* agencia creada en 1934 para controlar el mercado bursátil y hacer cumplir las leyes que rigen la venta de acciones y bonos. (p. 692)

segregation [segregación] *s.* separación de la gente según su raza. (p. 474)

Selective Service Act [Ley de Servicio Selectivo] *s.* ley aprobada por el Congreso en mayo de 1917 que ordena que todos los hombres se inscriban para el servicio militar obligatorio. (p. 562)

Seneca Falls convention [convención de Seneca Falls] *s.* convención de derechos femeninos celebrada en 1848 en Seneca Falls, New York. (p. 238)

Separatist [separatista] *s.* miembro de la Iglesia Anglicana que rechazó su reforma y formó una congregación independiente. (p. 53)

service sector [sector de servicios] *s.* renglón de la economía que ofrece servicios en vez de productos. (p. 1013)

settlement house [casa de beneficencia] *s.* centro comunitario en un barrio pobre que ayudaba a los residentes, particularmente a los inmigrantes. (p. 451)

Seventeenth Amendment [Enmienda 17] *s.* enmienda a la Constitución adoptada en 1913; dispone que los senadores federales sean elegidos por los votantes y no por cuerpos legislativos estatales. (p. 500)

shantytown [tugurio] *s.* vecindario muy pobre. (p. 650)

sharecropping [aparcería] *s.* sistema en el cual se da a los agricultores tierra, semillas, herramientas y alimentos para vivir, así como una parte de la cosecha, por cultivar la tierra. (p. 364)

Shays's Rebellion [Rebelión de Shays] *s.* sublevación de granjeros de Massachusetts en 1787 en protesta por los impuestos. (p. 132)

Sherman Antitrust Act [Ley Antitrust Sherman] *s.* ley contra los monopolios de 1890 que declaró ilegal la formación de consorcios que obstruyeran el libre comercio. (p. 424)

silent majority [mayoría silenciosa] *s.* nombre dado por el presidente Richard Nixon a los estadounidenses moderados que apoyaban silenciosamente su conducción de la Guerra de Vietnam. (p. 908)

sit-in *s.* forma de protesta —iniciada por el Congreso de Igualdad Racial en los años 40 y empleada con frecuencia en los años 60— en la que afroamericanos ingresaban a un lugar segregado, tal como el mostrador de un restaurante, y se negaban a salir hasta que se les sirviera. (p. 862)

Social Darwinism [darvinismo social] *s.* conjunto de creencias políticas y económicas basadas en la teoría del biólogo Charles Darwin sobre la selección natural o supervivencia del más apto; favorecía una competencia libre, no regulada, y creía que los individuos o grupos triunfaban porque eran genéticamente superiores. (p. 422)

Social Gospel movement [movimiento del Evangelio Social] *s.* movimiento de reforma del siglo 19 basado en la noción de que los cristianos tenían la responsabilidad social de mejorar las condiciones laborales y aliviar la pobreza urbana. (p. 451)

socialism [socialismo] *s.* sistema económico y político en el que los medios de producción son propiedad del gobierno; favorece una distribución igual de la riqueza. (p. 429)

Social Security Act [Ley de Seguro Social] *s.* ley aprobada por el Congreso en 1935 para crear un sistema federal de seguros para vejez, desempleo e incapacidad, financiado conjuntamente por empleados, patronos y gobierno. (p. 675)

soddy [choza de tepe] *s.* casa provisional hecha de césped, muy común en las llanuras, donde la madera era escasa. (p. 398)

Songhai *s.* imperio de África occidental en lo que hoy es Malí; su capital fue Tombuctú; alcanzó la cima de su poder hacia 1500. (p. 17)

soup kitchen [comedor de beneficencia] *s.* lugar donde se sirven alimentos gratis a los necesitados, muy común durante la Depresión. (p. 651)

Southern Christian Leadership Conference (SCLC) [Conferencia de Líderes Cristianos del Sur] *s.* organización formada en 1957 por el doctor Martin Luther King, Jr., y otros líderes para promover los derechos civiles sin violencia. (p. 862)

Southern strategy [estrategia sureña] *s.* estrategia del presidente Nixon de apelar a los demócratas conservadores sureños que estaban descontentos con la integración y con una Suprema Corte liberal. (p. 948)

speakeasy *s.* lugar donde se vendían bebidas alcohólicas ilegalmente, como ocurrió durante la Prohibición. (p. 614)

specialization [especialización] *s.* producción de un número limitado de productos agrícolas para venta nacional o internacional. (p. 254)

speculation [especulación] *s.* transacciones de alto riesgo con el fin de obtener ganancias rápidas o grandes. (p. 645)

spoils system [sistema de prebendas] *s.* práctica de los candidatos ganadores de dar empleos u otras recompensas a sus simpatizantes. (p. 211)

Square Deal *s.* programa de reformas progresistas del presidente Theodore Roosevelt para proteger a la gente común y corriente de las grandes empresas. (p. 506)

stagflation [estanflación] *s.* situación económica en la que hay niveles altos de inflación y desempleo simultáneamente. (p. 950)

Stalwart *s.* republicano seguidor del "jefe" de New York City, Roscoe Conkling, quien favorecía el sistema de prebendas y se oponía a la reforma al servicio civil. (p. 456)

Stamp Act [Ley del Timbre] *s.* primer impuesto directo aplicado en 1765 por Gran Bretaña a una variedad de artículos y servicios, tales como documentos legales y periódicos. (p. 94)

Stono Rebellion [Rebelión de Stono] *s.* rebelión de esclavos en la colonia de South Carolina en 1739; en consecuencia se hicieron más estrictas las leyes pertinentes a los esclavos. (p. 76)

Strateic Defense Initiative (SDI) [Iniciativa para la Defensa Estratégica] *s.* sistema de defensa propuesto en los años 80, popularmente conocido como la Guerra de las Galaxias, cuyo fin era proteger a Estados Unidos de ataques de misiles. (p. 983)

strike [huelga] *s.* interrupción del trabajo para presionar a un patrono a responder a ciertas demandas. (p. 243)

Student Nonviolent Coordinating Committee [Comité Coordinador de Estudiantes no Violentos] *s.* organización fundada en 1961, conocida como SNCC, para coordinar sit-ins y otras protestas, y para darles a los jóvenes negros mayor participación en el movimiento de derechos civiles. (p. 862)

Students for a Democratic Society [Estudiantes por una Sociedad Democrática] *s.* grupo activista de los años 60, conocido como SDS, que urgía una mayor libertad y responsabilidad individual. (p. 897)

suburb [suburbio] *s.* pueblo o comunidad residencial cerca de una ciudad. (p. 796)

suffrage [sufragio] *s.* derecho a votar. (p. 503)

Sugar Act [Ley del Azúcar] *s.* ley británica de 1764 que aplicó un impuesto comercial a la melaza, el azúcar y otras importaciones para reducir el contrabando en las colonias. (p. 87)

supply-side economics [economía de oferta] *s.* teoría económica, practicada por el presidente Ronald Reagan, que sostiene que recortar los impuestos de los ricos beneficia a todos pues aumenta empleos, ahorros e inversiones. (p. 983)

T

Taíno *s.* pueblo amerindio que Colón y su tripulación vieron al arribar a la isla hoy conocida como San Salvador, el 12 de octubre de 1492. (p. 27)

Tammany Hall *s.* maquinaria política demócrata que dominaba a New York City a fines del siglo 19. (p. 454)

Tariff of Abominations [Arancel Abominable] *s.* nombre que le dio Henry Clay a un arancel sobre materias primas aprobado por el Congreso en 1828; despertó gran furia en el Sur. (p. 214)

Tariff of 1816 [Arancel de 1816] *s.* arancel proteccionista para proteger las jóvenes industrias estadounidenses. (p. 203)

Teapot Dome scandal [escándalo de Teapot Dome] *s.* escándalo generado cuando Albert Fall, Secretario del Interior del presidente Warren G. Harding, concedió en secreto valiosas reservas de petróleo en Wyoming y California a compañías privadas a cambio de dinero y tierras. (p. 600)

Telecommunications Act [Ley de Telecomunicaciones] *s.* ley de 1996 que retiró las barreras que impedían que un tipo de compañía de comunicaciones ingresara a otro tipo de negocio en el mismo campo. (p. 1019)

telecommute *v.* trabajar desde la casa para una compañía ubicada en otra parte, mediante la nueva tecnología de comunicaciones, como computadoras, modems y máquinas de fax. (p. 1025)

telegraph [telégrafo] *s.* aparato que convierte un mensaje codificado en impulsos eléctricos que viajan por un hilo metálico. (p. 256)

temperance movement [movimiento de templanza] *s.* campaña para prohibir el consumo y la venta de alcohol. (p. 236)

tenant farming [agricultura de arrendatarios] *s.* sistema en el que los agricultores, llamados arrendatarios, ponen sus propias herramientas y animales, y pagan dinero por el arriendo de tierra para cultivar. (p. 364)

Tennessee Valley Authority [Autoridad del Valle de Tennessee] *s.* corporación federal creada en 1933 para construir presas y centrales eléctricas en la región del valle de Tennessee. (p. 693)

termination policy [política de terminación] *s.* programa del gobierno federal en 1953 de cesar su responsabilidad hacia las naciones amerindias y eliminar el apoyo económico federal, suspender el sistema de reservaciones y redistribuir las tierras tribales. (p. 823)

Tet offensive [ofensiva de Tet] *s.* sorpresivo ataque masivo del Vietcong a pueblos y ciudades de Vietnam del Sur a comienzos de 1968; la batalla, de un mes de duración, convenció a muchos estadounidenses de que no era posible ganar la guerra. (p. 901)

Texas Revolution [Revolución de Texas] *s.* rebelión de 1836 con la que Texas se independizó de México. (p. 271)

Thirteenth Amendment [Enmienda 13] *s.* enmienda a la Constitución, ratificada en 1865, que abolía la esclavitud y la servidumbre involuntaria. (p. 343)

SPANISH GLOSSARY 1107

Three-Fifths Compromise [Acuerdo de los Tres Quintos] *s.* acuerdo constitucional de considerar como población las tres quintas partes de los esclavos de un estado para efectos de representación y cobro de impuestos. (p. 134)

Tiananmen Square [plaza Tiananmen] *s.* lugar de protestas estudiantiles en 1989 en Beijing, China, por la falta de libertades democráticas, donde el gobierno atacó a los estudiantes. (p. 998)

Tonkin Gulf Resolution [Resolución del Golfo de Tonkin] *s.* resolución aprobada por el Congreso en 1964 que le otorgaba al presidente Johnson amplios poderes para la Guerra de Vietnam. (p. 888)

totalitarian [totalitario] *adj.* característico de un sistema político en que el gobierno ejerce completo control sobre la vida de los ciudadanos. (p. 704)

Townshend Acts [Leyes Townshend] *s.* serie de leyes promulgadas por el Parlamento en 1767 que establecían impuestos indirectos a los artículos de Gran Bretaña importados a las colonias. (p. 95)

trade imbalance [déficit comercial] *s.* situación económica en la que un país importa más de lo que exporta. (p. 984)

Trail of Tears [Sendero de las Lágrimas] *s.* marcha obligada del pueblo cherokee desde Georgia hasta el Territorio Indio en 1838, durante la cual murieron miles. (p. 213)

transcendentalism [trascendentalismo] *s.* movimiento filosófico y literario que proponía llevar una vida sencilla y celebrar la verdad implícita de la naturaleza, la emoción personal y la imaginación. (p. 226)

transcontinental railroad [ferrocarril transcontinental] *s.* línea férrea finalizada en 1869 que unía la costa Atlántica y la costa Pacífica. (p. 416)

Treaty of Ghent [Tratado de Gante] *s.* tratado firmado en 1814 que puso fin a la Guerra de 1812. (p. 191)

Treaty of Guadaloupe Hidalgo [Tratado de Guadalupe Hidalgo] *s.* tratado de 1848 que puso fin a la guerra entre Estados Unidos y México, mediante el cual Estados Unidos obtuvo enormes tierras en el Oeste y el Suroeste. (p. 276)

Treaty of Paris [Tratado de París] *s.* **1.** tratado de 1763 que puso fin a la Guerra contra los Franceses y los Indígenas. **2.** tratado de 1783 que puso fin a la Guerra Revolucionaria Norteamericana y estableció las fronteras de la nueva nación. (p. 115) **3.** tratado de 1898 que terminó la Guerra Hispano-Norteamericana-Cubana.

Treaty of Tordesillas [Tratado de Tordesillas] *s.* tratado de 1494 que dividió las Américas entre España y Portugal mediante una línea vertical imaginaria en el Atlántico; cada país tenía poder sobre un lado de la línea. (p. 31)

Treaty of Versailles [Tratado de Versalles] *s.* tratado que puso fin a la I Guerra Mundial, firmado el 28 de junio de 1919. (p. 578)

trench warfare [guerra de trincheras] *s.* guerra en que los combatientes atacan desde un sistema de zanjas fortificadas y no en un campo abierto de batalla. (p. 557)

triangular trade [triángulo comercial de esclavos] *s.* red de rutas de África a las Antillas, las colonias norteamericanas, Inglaterra o Europa para traficar

esclavos africanos y comerciar productos tales como ron y melaza. (p. 73)

Truman Doctrine [Doctrina Truman] *s.* declaración del presidente Truman en 1947, que establecía que Estados Unidos debía dar apoyo económico y militar para liberar a naciones amenazadas por fuerzas internas o externas. (p. 770)

trust *s.* método de unir compañías competidoras, en que los participantes entregan sus acciones a una junta única que maneja las distintas compañías como una sola corporación. (p. 423)

Tweed Ring *s.* grupo de políticos corruptos de New York encabezados por William Marcy "Boss" Tweed; le robaron a la ciudad cerca de $200 millones entre 1869 y 1871. (p. 454)

two-party system [bipartidismo] *s.* sistema político dominado por dos partidos. (p. 176)

UV

Uncle Tom's Cabin [*La cabaña del tío Tom*] *s.* novela famosa (1852) escrita por Harriet Beecher Stowe, que causó intenso furor al retratar la esclavitud como una gran perversión moral. (p. 290)

Underground Railroad [Ferrocarril Subterráneo] *s.* red secreta de personas que ayudaban a los esclavos fugitivos a escapar a lo largo de diversas rutas hacia Canadá o hacia zonas seguras en los estados libres. (p. 289)

United Farm Workers Organizing Committee [Comité Organizador de Trabajadores Agrícolas Unidos] *s.* sindicato establecido en 1966 por César Chávez para mejorar los salarios y las condiciones laborales de los trabajadores agrícolas. (p. 922)

United Nations (UN) [Naciones Unidas] *s.* organización internacional promotora de la paz a la que pertenecen la mayoría de naciones, fundada en 1945 para fomentar la paz, la seguridad y el desarrollo económico del mundo. (p. 752)

Universal Negro Improvement Association [Asociación Universal para el Adelanto de la Gente de Color] *s.* grupo nacionalista negro fundado en Jamaica por Marcus Garvey en 1914. (p. 631)

urban flight [huida urbana] *s.* migración de las ciudades a los suburbios aledaños. (p. 1024)

urbanization [urbanización] *s.* movimiento de personas a una ciudad. (p. 446)

urban renewal [renovación urbana] *s.* práctica que se inició con la Ley Nacional de Vivienda de 1949, de remplazar vecindarios urbanos derruidos por viviendas nuevas para gente de bajos recursos. (p. 821)

urban sprawl [explosión urbana] *s.* expansión desordenada y desmedida de las ciudades a las áreas aledañas. (p. 602)

U.S.S. Maine *s.* buque de guerra estadounidense que explotó y naufragó misteriosamente el 15 de febrero de 1898 en el puerto de La Habana, Cuba. (p. 532)

utopian community [comunidad utópica] *s.* comunidad formada por un grupo experimental que vivía unido y buscaba crear un lugar perfecto. (p. 228)

U-2 incident [incidente del U-2] *s.* derribo en 1960 de un avión espía estadounidense U-2 en suelo soviético; complicó las conversaciones de paz entre Estados Unidos y la Unión Soviética. (p. 789)

vaudeville [teatro de variedades] *s.* espectáculo popular de tablas con una variedad de canciones, bailes y comedias. (p. 481)

V-E Day [Día V-E] *s.* mayo 8 de 1945, día de la victoria europea, cuando el general Eisenhower aceptó la rendición incondicional de Alemania; puso fin a la II Guerra Mundial en Europa. (p. 745)

vertical integration [integración vertical] *s.* proceso mediante el cual una compañía se adueña de sus proveedores y distribuidores, con lo que obtiene control total sobre la calidad y el costo de su producción. (p. 422)

Vietcong *s.* rebeldes comunistas de Vietnam del Sur apoyados por Vietnam del Norte a partir de 1959. (p. 886)

Vietminh [Vietmin] *s.* organización de comunistas vietmanitas y otros grupos nacionalistas que luchó contra los franceses por la independencia de Vietnam de 1946 a 1954. (p. 885)

Vietnamization [vietnamización] *s.* plan del presidente Nixon de retiro gradual de las tropas estadounidenses de Vietnam y su remplazo por el ejército vietnamita. (p. 908)

Voting Rights Act of 1965 [Ley de Derechos Electorales de 1965] *s.* ley para facilitarles a los afroamericanos inscribirse para votar; eliminó las pruebas discriminatorias de lectura y escritura, y autorizó a los examinadores federales inscribir votantes rechazados a nivel local. (p. 870)

W

Wade-Davis Bill [proyecto de ley Wade-Davis] *s.* proyecto de ley, aprobado en 1864 y vetado por el presidente Lincoln, que daba al Congreso control de la Reconstrucción. (p. 351)

Wagner Act [Ley Wagner] *s.* ley—también conocida como Ley Nacional de Relaciones Laborales— promulgada en 1935 para proteger los derechos de los trabajadores después de que la Corte Suprema consideró la Ley Nacional de Recuperación Industrial (NIRA) era inconstitucional. (p. 674)

war-guilt clause [cláusula de culpabilidad] *s.* cláusula del Tratado de Versalles que obligaba a Alemania a reconocer que había sido única responsable de la I Guerra Mundial. (p. 578)

war hawk [halcón] *s.* congresista de principios del siglo 19 a favor de la guerra con Gran Bretaña. (p. 190)

War Industries Board [Junta de Industrias Bélicas] *s.* junta establecida en 1917 que animaba a las compañías a usar técnicas de producción en masa para mejorar la eficiencia durante la I Guerra Mundial. (p. 570)

War Powers Act [Ley de Poderes de Guerra] *s.* ley aprobada en 1973 tras la Guerra de Vietnam que limitaba el derecho de un presidente a enviar tropas a combatir sin consultar con el Congreso. (p. 913)

War Production Board [Junta de Producción Bélica] *s.* agencia establecida durante la II Guerra Mundial para coordinar la producción de suministros militares por la industria nacional. (p. 736)

Warren Commission [Comisión Warren] *s.* grupo encabezado por Earl Warren, presidente de la Suprema Corte, que realizó la investigación oficial del asesinato del presidente Kennedy y concluyó que Lee Harvey Oswald había actuado por su cuenta. (p. 842)

Warren Court [la Corte Warren] *s.* la Suprema Corte de la que fue presidente Earl Warren, que se destacó por sus actividades en torno a los derechos civiles y la libre expresión. (p. 848)

Warsaw Pact [Pacto de Varsovia] *s.* alianza militar formada en 1955 por la Unión Soviética y las naciones satélite de Europa del este. (p. 786)

Watergate *s.* serie de escándalos en que el presidente Nixon trató de encubrir la participación de su comité de relección en el allanamiento de la sede del Partido Demócrata, en los apartamentos Watergate, en 1972. (p. 953)

web-perfecting press [prensa de bobina] *s.* prensa eléctrica que imprime a ambos lados de un rollo de papel y luego corta, dobla y cuenta las páginas. (p. 465)

Whig *s.* miembro de un partido político establecido en 1834 en oposición a Andrew Jackson. (p. 218)

Wilmot Proviso [Cláusula Wilmot] *s.* enmienda a un proyecto de ley de fondos militares de 1846; proponía que ninguna porción del territorio adquirido en la guerra con México debía abrirse a la esclavitud. (p. 283)

Woodstock *s.* festival gratuito de música que atrajo a más de 400,000 jóvenes a una granja del estado de New York en agosto de 1969. (p. 936)

Works Progress Administration [Administración para el Progreso de Obras] *s.* agencia gubernamental del New Deal que empleó a personal desocupado en construcción de escuelas y hospitales, reparación de carreteras, enseñanza, escritura y artes. (p. 673)

XYZ

XYZ Affair [Asunto XYZ] *s.* incidente diplomático de 1797 en el que funcionarios franceses trataron de sobornar a funcionarios estadounidenses para entrevistarse con un alto ministro francés. (p. 180)

Yalta Conference [Conferencia de Yalta] *s.* reunión en 1945 de representantes de Estados Unidos, Gran Bretaña y la Unión Soviética, durante la cual se decidió la división de Alemania en cuatro zonas ocupadas, la celebración de elecciones libres en Europa del este y que la Unión Soviética le declarara la guerra a Japón. (p. 752)

yellow journalism [prensa amarillista] *s.* uso de métodos sensacionalistas en periódicos o revistas para atraer o influenciar lectores. (p. 531)

Zimmermann note [nota Zimmermann] *s.* mensaje enviado por el canciller alemán en 1917 al canciller mexicano en el que prometía a México los estados de Texas, New Mexico y Arizona si se aliaba a Alemania en contra de Estados Unidos en la I Guerra Mundial. (p. 561)

Index

An *i* preceding a page reference in italics indicates that there is an illustration, and usually text information as well, on that page. An *m* or a *c* preceding an italic page reference indicates a map or a chart.

assembly line and, 497, *i 497*
effect on of Civil War, 341
declining jobs in, 1015
environment and, 414–415
expansion of, in late 19th century,
  410–413, 421–425, 423–424
in Great Britain, 198–199
high–tech, 1015–1016
in the 1920s, 642–643
in the North, 199, 254, 282–283
in the South, 365, *i 365*, 425
inventions and, 412–413
putting–out system and, 240–241
railroads and, 418–418
regulation of, 424–425
inflation, 110. *i 702*, 950, 960, 964, *i 963*
Influence of Sea Power upon History
  (Mahan), 528
information superhighway, 1018–1019
INF Treaty (Intermediate-Range Nuclear
  Forces Treaty), 996
Inglis, Charles, 102, *i 102*
Ingram, David, 11
initiative, 500
installment plan buying, 605, 647
interchangeable parts, 198
Internal Revenue Service, 948
International Ladies' Garment Workers'
  Union (ILGWU), 432–433
Internet, 256, 1019
Interior Department, 600
interstate commerce, 204, 420, 499
Interstate Commerce Act (1887), 420, 508
Interstate Commerce Commission (ICC),
  420, 508, 865
intervention, U.S., 544–545
Intolerable Acts (1774), 97
Invasion of the Body Snatchers, 791
inventions, 198, 255–257, 412–413
Iowa, 261
  as state, *m 1072*
Iran, 786. *See also* Iran–Contra scandal.
  revolution in, 967
  U.S. hostages in, *i 945*, 967, 981
  war with Iraq, 1000
Iran-Contra scandal, 999–1000
Iraq
  Persian Gulf War and, 797, *i 977*,
    1000–1001, *m 1001*, 1006
  war with Iran, 1000
Irish immigrants, 244, 282, 283
  railroads and, 396, 417
ironclads, 342–343
Iron Curtain, 769, *m 769*
iron ore, 199, 411
Iroquois nation, 10, 84
Isabella (queen of Castile), 22, *i 22*, 26,
  27, 32
Islam, 14, *i 14*, 15, 17, 967. *See also*
  Muslims.
  Crusades and, 22
  reconquista and, 22, 40
isolationism, U.S., 597, 721, 722
  in the 1930s, 706–707, *i 707*
Israel, 787, 966, 967
  Camp David Accords, 966
  Yom Kippur War and, 950, 966
Italy, 25
  Ethiopia and, 705–706, *m 706*, 707
  fascism in, 704, 705

World War I and, 556, 558
World War II and, 719, 741–742
Iwo Jima, 749
IWW, 430

J

Jackson, Andrew, *i 197*, 211, *i 211*, 216, 217,
  270, *i 1074*
  appeal of, to common citizen, 210, *i 210*,
    217
  election of 1824 and, 209–210
  Native Americans and, 211–212
  spoils system and, 210–211
  states rights and, 216
  in War of 1812, 191
Jackson, Helen Hunt, 385
Jackson, Jesse, 991, *i 991*
Jackson, Robert, 752–753
Jackson, Thomas J. "Stonewall," 314,
  329–330
Jacksonians, 217
Jacksonville, Florida, 41
Jamaica, 73, 439
James I (king of England), 44, 53
James II (king of England), 59, 68, *i 69*
James, Duke of York. *See* James II.
James River, 46
Jamestown, 45–47, 49, 50, *m 50–51*, 52
Japan, 964
  attack on Pearl Harbor, 724
  China and, 705
  empire of, 723
  immigration from, 443, 599
  imperialism and, 527
  Manchuria and, 706, *m 707*
  militarism in, 705
  occupation of, 753
  trade with U.S., 261, 950
  war with Russia, 443, 542–543
  World War II and, 719, 723–725, 730,
    738, 746–752, *m 748*
Japanese American Citizens League
  (JACL), 761
Japanese Americans
  Gentlemen's Agreement, 443
  internment of, during World War II,
    760–761, *i 761*
Jaworski, Leon, 956
Jay, John, 137, *i 137*, 138, 141, 179
Jay's Treaty (1795), 179–180
jazz, 634–635, 636
Jazz Singer, The, 627
Jefferson, Thomas, *i 104*, 173, 178, 208, *i
  209*, 878, *i 1074*
  Alien and Sedition Acts and, 181
  as author of Declaration, 101, 209
  Constitution and, 140
  decentralized powers and, 185
  in election of 1796, 180
  in election of 1800, 184
  embargo and, 189
  Enlightenment thought and, 81, 101–102
  Hamilton and, 173–174
  Lewis and Clark expedition and, 188
  Louisiana Purchase and, 187–188
  presidency of, 184–188, 189–190, 199
  on slavery, 208
  views of federal government, *c 174*
Jefferson Airplane, 936

Jenney, William LeBaron, 412
Jewett, Sarah Orne, 472
Jews, 110, *i 715*. *See also* Holocaust.
  in colonies, 59, 79
  immigration and, 438, 469, *i 700*
  Kristallnacht and, *i 714*, 715
  Nuremberg Laws and, 714
  as refugees, 715
Jim Crow laws, 474, 857
Job Corps, 845, 947
Jobs, Steven, 1018, *i 1018*
John (king of Portugal), 26
Johnson, Andrew, *i 154*, 350, 353, 1075
  impeachment of, 354–355
  Reconstruction and, 350, 351–352,
    353, 354
Johnson, Henry, 563
Johnson, James Weldon, 631, 632
Johnson, Lyndon B., *i 828*, 841, 965, 979
  i 1076
  civil rights and, 844–845, 869, 870
  in Congress, 843–8444
  containment policy and, 889–890
  early life of, 843–844
  election of 1964 and, 845
  Great Society program of, 846–851, 872
  tax reduction and, 844–845
  Tet offensive and, 902
  Tonkin Gulf resolution and, 888
  Vietnam and, 887–888, 889–890, 893,
    894, 898, 900–903
  War on Poverty of, 845, 850–851, 872
Johnson, Tom, 498, *i 498*
joint-stock company, 24
Joliet, Louis, 83
Jolson, Al, 627
Jones, Edward, 646
Jones, Eva B., 359
Jones, Len, 713
Jones, Mary Harris "Mother," *i 408*, 432,
  i 432
Joplin, Janis, 935, 936
Jordan, Barbara, 953, *i 953*
Jordan, Vernon, *i 361*
journalism
  mass circulation newspapers, 482–483,
    i 483, 530, 625
  muckrakers in, 494, 496, 513
  in Spanish-American-Cuban War, 531
  "yellow," 531, 532
J. P. Morgan & Company, 420
Judaism, 15
judicial branch, 185–186. *See also* court sys-
    tem; Supreme Court, U.S.; Supreme
    Court cases.
  authority of, 154
  in Constitution, 136, 154, 172
  federal courts, 154
  treason and, 154
judicial review, 186
Judiciary Act of 1789, 172–173
Judiciary Act of 1801, 186
Julian, George, 319
Jungle, The (Sinclair), 505, *i 505*, 508

K

Kahn, Tony, 779, *i 779*
Kaiser, Henry J., 733
Kalakaua (king of Hawaii), 528–529

Meredith, James, 865–866
Mergenthaler, Ottmar, 466
merit system, 456
Merrimack, i 310, 342, i 342
mestizos, 40, 47
Metacom, 57, *i 57*
Mexica. *See* Aztec people.
Mexican Americans, 920–923, 992
    deportation of, 680
      Longoria incident and, 822
      New Deal and, 677, 680
    in the 1950s, 821–822
    World War II and, 731, 732, 759, *i 759*
Mexican American Political Association
    (MAPA), 922
Mexican cession, 276
Mexican War. *See* War with Mexico.
Mexico, 11, 561, 920. *See also* Latinos;
    Mexican Americans.
    early empires in, 6
    early settlement of, 5
    immigrants from, 439–440, *i 596,*
      1027–1028
    independence of, 269
    NAFTA and, 1009, 1017
    revolution in, 546–547
    silver in, 389
    Spanish conquest of, 38–41, 47
    in Southwest, 268–271
    Texas and, 268–271
    war with, 273–277, *m 275,* 439
Mexico City, 40, 41, 42
Meyers, Deb, 731
Meyers, Isaac, 427, *i 427*
Miami Confederacy, 179
Miami, Florida, 992, 994, *i 994*
Miantonomo, 57
Michigan, 178, 200, 960
    as state, *m 1072*
Michigan, Lake, 465
Middle colonies, 58–60, *m 59. See also* colo-
    nial America.
    economy of, 77
    slavery in, 79
Middle East, 15, 22, *m 966,* 999–1001. *See*
    also OPEC.
    Camp David Accords and, 966–967
    Cold War and, 787
    oil and, 950
middle passage, 74
Middletown, 602
midnight judges, 186
Midway, Battle of, 747
Mifflin, Sarah and Thomas, *i 118*
Migrant Mother (Lange), *i 671*
migrant workers, 926–927
Miles, Nelson A., 535
militarism
    Japan and, 705
    World War I and, 555
Millay, Edna St. Vincent, 629, 637, *i 637*
Mills, C. Wright, 804
Miller, Thomas W., 600
Million Man March, *i 1005*
Mills, Florence, 634
minimum wage, 674
mining
    in ancient Americas, 6
    in Spanish colonies, 40
    strikes and, 432, 505, *i 588,* 595, 798

in West, 394–395, *i 394,* 395
Minneapolis, 418
Minnesota, 265, 889, 986
    as state, *m 1072*
minorities. *See* African Americans; Asian
    Americans; Latinos; Native
    Americans.
minstrel shows, 481
minutemen, 98
Miranda rights, 849, *i 849*
Miranda v. *Arizona* (1966), 849, 850
Miss America Pageant, 619, *i 619*
Mississippi, 305, 865, 868, 874, 949
    as state, *m 1072*
Mississippian people, 6
Mississippi Freedom Democratic Party
    (MFDP), 869
Mississippi River, 6, 10, 83, 129, 178, 204
    Civil War and, 314, 316, 332
    steamboats and, 256, 258, 410
Missouri, 207, 262, 263, 266
    as state, *m 1072*
Missouri Compromise, 207–208, *m 208,*
    284, 291, 292, *m 292,* 297, 300
Mitchell, John, 954, 955, 956
Mitchell, Margaret, 510
Mitchell, Maria, 503, *i 503*
Mitchell, Mary Bedinger, 317
Mobile Bay, 336
Mogollon people, *i 9*
molasses, 74
Molly Pitcher. *See* Hays, Mary Ludwig.
Mondale, Walter, 980, 986
money supply, 401–402
Monitor, i 310, 342, *i 342*
Monmouth, Battle of, 111
monopoly, 423
Monroe, James, 140, 185, 188, 545, *i 1074.*
    See also Monroe Doctrine.
    Missouri Compromise and, 208
    presidency of, 206–208
Monroe, Marilyn, 935, *i 935*
Monroe, Sylvester, 992
Monroe Doctrine, 206–207, 545
    Roosevelt Corollary and, 544–545
Montana, 385
    as state, *m 1072*
Montauk people, 57
Montcalm, Marquis de, 85
Montesinos, Antonio de, 40
Montezuma, 39
Montgomery, Alabama, 305
    bus boycott in, 860–861, *i 861*
    as capital of Confederacy, 305
Montgomery Ward, 485
moon landing, 948
Moral Majority, 980, 986
Morgan, Daniel, 113
Morgan, J. P., 423, 513
Morgan, Robin, 929, 930
Morgan v. *Virginia* (1946), 858
Mormons
    migration of, 264–265, *i 264*
Morocco, 22
Morrill Land Grant Acts, 399
Morris, Gouverneur, 177
Morris, Robert, 110
Morse, Samuel F. B., 256, *i 256*
Moses, Robert, 868
motion pictures, 482, *i 482,* 483, 627–628,

683–684, *i 683,* 818
    in the 1950s, 814–815
    rating system for, 937
    in World War II, 734
Mott, Ken, 1020
Mott, Lucretia, 118, 235, *i 236,* 238
mound builders, 6
Mount Vernon, 172
movement
    geographic theme of, xxxv, 23, 39, 114,
      213, 263, 330, 333, 335, 383, 439, 447,
      533, 557 565, 652, 706, 724, 739, 748,
      757, 776, 834, 886, 1001
movies. *See* motion pictures.
Moynihan, Daniel Patrick, 947, 1011
muckrakers, 496
Mugwumps, 456
Muhammad, 15
Muir, John, 510, *i 510*
Muller v. *Oregon* (1908), 499
multiculturalism, 33
Munn v. *Illinois* (1887), 420
Muñoz Rivera, Luis, 535, *i 535,* 536
Murrow, Edward R., 813
music
    jazz, 634–635
    popular, 812
    ragtime, 481–482
    rock 'n' roll, 815–816, *i 816,* 819, *i 819,*
      934, 936
    soul, 939
    in World War II, 734
Muslims, 19, 25, 59, 997, 1009. *See also*
    Islam.
Mussolini, Benito, 704, *i 704,* 705, *i 705,*
    707, 742
My Ántonia (Cather), 629
Myers, Walter Dean, 915
My Lai massacre, 908–909
Mystic River, 56

N

Nader, Ralph, 847–848, *i 847*
Nagasaki, bombing of, 751
Nahua peoples, 38
Nakashima, Ted, 735
Napoleon Bonaparte, 187, 188, 189, 206
Narragansett Bay, 55
Narragansett people, 55, 56
Nasser, Gamal Abdel, 787
Nass River, 11
Nast, Thomas, 454
Nation, Carry, *i 495*
National Aeronautics and Space
    Administration (NASA), 840
National American Woman Suffrage
    Association (NAWSA), 503, 519, 520
National Association for the Advancement
    of Colored People (NAACP), 511,
    520, 574, 631
National Association of Colored Women
    (NACW), 503
national bank, 174, 216
National Bank Act of 1863, 341
National Child Labor Committee, 499
National Council of Indian Opportunity,
    923
National Energy Act, 963
National Housing Act, 668

serfdom, 73

Servicemen's Readjustment Act. *See* GI Bill of Rights.

service organizations, 604

settlement-house movement, 451, 495

Seven Days' Battles, 316–317

Seventeenth Amendment, 162, 500

Seventh Amendment, 159

Seventh Cavalry, 387

Seward, William, 292, 303

sewing machine, *i 255, 256*

sex discrimination, 928–929

sexual harassment, 984

sexual revolution, 937

Seymour, Horatio, 355

Shakespeare, William, 21, 634

sharecropping, 364, *i 360, c 364. See also* farmers.

Shaw, Lemuel, 245

Shays, Daniel, 132

Shays's Rebellion, 132, *i 132*

sheepherders, 392–393

Shenandoah Valley, 337

Shepard, Alan, 837, *i 837,* 840

Sheridan, Philip, 336, 337
   wars with Native Americans and, 384, 386

Sherman, Roger, 133, *i 133,* 134

Sherman, William Tecumseh, 304, 334, 335–336, *i 335,* 337, 343, 344, 356, 362

Sherman Antitrust Act, 424–425, 507, 517

Shiloh, Battle of, 315–316

shipbuilding, 78
   World War I and, 563–564
   World War II and, 733, 739–740

shipping, 78, 199, 258

Shirer, William, 708, *i 708,* 712

Sholes, Christopher, 412

shopping centers, 607, *i 607*

Shuffle Along, 634

Shumlin, Herman, 651

Siberia, 5, *m 5*

Sierra Nevada, 13

"silent majority," 948

Silent Spring (Carson), 968–969

silver, 382, 389, 403–404

Since Yesterday (Allen), 652

Sinclair, Upton, 505 *i 505,* 508

Singer, I. M., 256

Sioux people, 262, *i 381,* 383, *i 384,* 385, 1024. *See also* Lakota tribe; Oglala Sioux.
   Bozeman Trail and, 383–384
   Battle of Little Bighorn and, 385
   Treaty of 1868 and, 384
   Wounded Knee and, 387

Sirica, John, 955

sit-down strike, 681

Sitting Bull, 384, *i 384,* 385

Sixteenth Amendment, 162, 518

Sixth Amendment, 159

skyscrapers, 412, 463. *See also* architecture.

Slater, Samuel, 199

slave markets, *i 340*

slavery, *i 232. See also* antislavery movement; Civil War; slaves; slave trade; Wilmot Proviso.
   in Africa, 14, 16, 19
   in Americas, *m 234*

in colonies, 47, 60, 73, 75–76, *i 76,* 79
   Compromise of 1850 and, 285–286
   Constitutional Convention and, 134–135
   cotton production and, 201, 283
   Cuba and, 530
   life under, 231–233
   Missouri Compromise and, 207–208
   Native Americans and, 13, 40
   in the North, 200
   opposition to, 116, 274, 283
   Portuguese and, 16
   secession and, 299–305
   Senate debates over, 284–287
   Spanish and, 40
   territories and, 283–287
   Thirteenth Amendment and, 343, *i 343*
   women and, 232

slaves. *See also* African Americans; slavery.
   in Civil War, 324
   Constitution and, 141
   culture of, 75, *i 75*
   emancipation of, 319–320
   family and, 75
   fugitive, 288–290, *i 290*
   immigrant workers and, 283
   marriage and, 89 *i 89*
   resistance by, 76, 79, 185, *i 222,* 233, 324–325
   treatment of, 74, 75, *i 247*

slave ship, *i 74*

slave trade
   African, 30, 73–74
   Constitutional Convention and, 134–135

Slidell, John, 273, 318

Sloat, John D., 275

Smith, Alfred E., 644, 669

Smith, Bessie, 623, *i 623,* 635

Smith, John, *i 37,* 44, 45, *i 48*

Smith, Joseph, 264

Smith, Margaret Chase, 783

Smith, Sophia, 503

Smithwick, Noah, 270

Smyth, John Ferdinand, 75

snack foods, 479–480

Social Darwinism, 422, 528

Social Gospel movement, 451, 495

socialism, 429, 496

Socialist Party, 515

social security, 675–676, 692, *i 692,* 947, 1008
   baby boomers and, 1026

Social Security Act, 675–676, 692, 1011

Society of Friends. *See* Quakers.

Soil Conservation and Domestic Allotment Act, 672

Soil Conservation Service, 693

Solidarity labor movement (Poland), 997

Solomon Islands, 748

Somalia, 1009, *i 1009,* 1010

Somoza, Anastasio, 998

Somme, Battle of the, 566

Songhai, 14, 15, 16–17

Sons of Liberty, 95

Souls of Black Folk, The (Du Bois), 511

Sound of Music, The, 939

Souter, David H., 984

South. *See also* Civil War; cotton production; Reconstruction.
   business and, 425
   effects of Civil War on, 340–342, 356–357

home rule in, 372
   politics in, after Civil War, 357–359
   redemption and, 371
   Republican governments in, 356, 357

South Africa, 138–139

South America, 46. *See also* Incas.
   early settlement of, 5, 6
   Spanish and, 38, 41, 47

South Carolina, 66, 858, 949
   colonial, 71
   in Revolutionary War, 113
   secession of, 404
   settlement of, 59, 72
   as state, *m 1073*

South Dakota, 387, 925, 955, 1024
   as state, *m 1073*

Southeast Asia, 579. *See also* Vietnam; Vietnam War.

Southern Alliance, 402

Southern Christian Leadership Conference (SCLC), 862, 874

Southern colonies, 71–76. *See also* colonial America; slavery.

Southern Homestead Act (1866), 363

Southern Publicity Association, 593

Southwest
   Mexican workers in, 476
   Native Americans in, 9–10, 268–269, 270
   Spanish settlement of, 41–43, 268–269
   Americans in, 268–270

Soviet Union, 579, 591, *i 952. See also* Cold War.
   aid to Nicaragua, 998
   Afghanistan, invasion of, 965–966
   arms race and, 785–786, 996, 997
   Carter and, 965–966
   China and, 951
   Cuban missile crisis and, 833–835
   development of Cold War and, 766–769
   dissolution of, 996–997
   division of Germany and, 771–772
   domination of Eastern Europe by, 768–769, 787
   Five–Year Plans and, 703
   Great Purge in, 704
   industrialization of, 703
   installation of hot line, 836
   Nixon and, 952
   nuclear testing and, 836
   as police state, 704
   reforms of Gorbachev and, 996
   space exploration and, 755, *i 755,* 788
   Stalin and, 703–704
   U.S. containment policy and, 769
   Warsaw Pact and, 786–787
   World War II and, 710–711, 721, 738, 740–741, 742, 744, 745

space exploration, *i 829,* 837, *i 837,* 1005
   Challenger disaster and, 990, 1022
   communications satellites and, 840
   under Kennedy, 840, *c 840*
   moon landing, 948
   Soviet Union and, 755, *i 755,* 788, 830, 840
   under Reagan, 990
   technology and, 1022

Spain, 14, 16, 22, 24, 25
   cattle raising and, 388–389
   civil war in, 707
   claims in North America, *m 85,* 129

INDEX 1133

ACKNOWLEDGMENTS

Text Acknowledgments

Chapter 15, page 441: Excerpt from *I Was Dreaming to Come to America,* edited by Veronica Lawlor. Copyright © 1995 by Veronica Lawlor. Used by permission of Viking Penguin, a division of Penguin Books USA, Inc.

Chapter 21, page 637: "First Fig" by Edna St. Vincent Millay, from *Collected Poems,* published by HarperCollins. Copyright 1922, 1950 by Edna St. Vincent Millay. All rights reserved. Reprinted by permission of Elizabeth Barnett, literary executor.

"Dream Variations," from *Selected Poems* by Langston Hughes. Copyright 1926 by Alfred A. Knopf, Inc., and renewed 1954 by Langston Hughes. Reprinted by permission of the publisher.

Chapter 22, page 659: Excerpt from "A. Everette McIntyre," from *Hard Times* by Studs Terkel. Copyright © 1970 by Studs Terkel. By permission of Random House, Inc.

Chapter 24, page 714: Excerpt from Gerda Weissman Klein's interview in the film *One Survivor Remembers,* a production of Home Box Office and the United States Holocaust Museum. By permission of Gary Greenberg for Gerda Weissman Klein.

Chapter 25, page 730: Excerpts from "Wife's Recorded Message Made Many Long for Home" by Charles Swanson, from *We Pulled Together . . . and Won!* (Reminisce Books). By permission of Charles Swanson.

page 758: Excerpt from *Liberators: Fighting on Two Fronts in World War II,* Copyright © 1992 by Lou Potter, William Miles, and Nina Rosenblum. Reprinted by permission of Harcourt Brace & Company.

Chapter 30, page 890: Quotation by Dean Rusk from *Time,* January 11, 1988 issue. Copyright © 1988 Time, Inc. Reprinted by permission

page 891: Excerpt from *Dear America: Letters Home from Vietnam,* edited by Bernard Edelman for the New York Vietnam Veterans Memorial Commission (W. W. Norton & Company, 1985).

page 898: Excerpt from "Eve of Destruction," words and music by P. F. Sloan. Copyright © 1965 by Duchess Music Corporation. Sole selling agent MCA Music Publishing, a Division of MCA Inc. International Copyright Secured. All rights reserved.

Excerpt from "The Ballad of the Green Berets" by Barry Sadler: Eastaboga Music.

page 907: Excerpt from the epilogue of *Some Even Volunteered* by Alfred S. Bradford. Copyright © 1994 by Alfred S. Bradford. By permission of Greenwood Publishing Group, Inc., Westport, Conn.

Chapter 33, page 994: map, "Migration Patterns: Where Americans Are Going," from *Regional Growth and Decline in the United States* by Bernard L. Weinstein and Robert E. Firestine (Praeger Publishers, The Greenwood Publishing Group, Westport, Conn.). Copyright © 1978 by Praeger Publishers. Used by permission.

page 995: graph, "California In- and Outmigrants, 1980–1992," from *The Professional Geographer,* May 1996. Reproduced courtesy of Blackwell Publishers, Inc., 350 Main St., Malden, MA 02148.

map, "Where Americans Are Moving" by Joseph Spiers in *FORTUNE,* August 21, 1995. Copyright © 1995 Time Inc. All rights reserved.

Chapter 34, page 1006: Excerpt from "On the Pulse of Morning" by Maya Angelou. Copyright © 1993 by Maya Angelou. Reprinted by permission of Random House, Inc.

Art Credits

COVER AND FRONTISPIECE

Mary Chesnut: Detail of *Mary Boykin Chesnut* (1856), Samuel Osgood. On loan from Serena Williams Miles Van Rensselaer. National Portrait Gallery, Smithsonian Institution/Art Resource, New York.

Susan B. Anthony: *Susan Brownell Anthony* (1898), Theodore C. Marceau. Photograph. National Portrait Gallery, Smithsonian Institution/Art Resource, New York.

General Norman Schwarzkopf: Copyright © 1991 David Turnley, Detroit Free Press/Black Star/PNI.

Dwight D. Eisenhower: Copyright © Dennis Brack/Black Star/PNI.

Zora Neale Hurston: Photo by Carl Von Vechten, courtesty of The Beinecke Rare Book and Manuscript Library, Yale University, and Joseph Solomon Executor of the Estate of Carl Von Vechten.

Zitkala-Ša: Courtesy of Brigham Young University.

Benjamin Franklin: *Benjamin Franklin* (1789), Charles Willson Peale. Historical Society of Pennsylvania.

Maya Lin: Copyright © 1993 Richard Howard/Black Star/PNI.

John F. Kennedy: Photo by Alfred Eisenstaedt/Life Magazine, Copyright © Time Inc.

Cesar Chavez: Photo Copyright © 1990 Lisa Quinones/Black Star/PNI.

Dr. Martin Luther King, Jr.: Photo by Howard Sochrer/ Life Magazine, Copyright © Time, Inc.

Abraham Lincoln: UPI/Corbis-Bettmann.

Eleanor Roosevelt: Culver Pictures/PNI.

STOCK AGENCIES AND LIBRARY OF CONGRESS

AP/Wide World Photos

xiii *second from bottom,* **xiv** *second from top,* **xxv** *top,* **119** *right,* **138** *bottom right,* **139, 154** *bottom,* **159, 161, 163, 165** *top left,* **642, 681** *left,* **701** *top,* **723, 733** *bottom,* **736** *zoot suit,* **744, 754** *top right background,* **759, 764** *center,* **767** *right,* **770** *right,* **771, 774** *left, right,* **783** *bottom left,* **785, 786, 789** *bottom left,* **828** *right,* **831, 835** *right,* **836, 845** *top,* **848, 860, 862, 863, 866, 867** *top,* **885, 887, 897** *top,* **911** *bottom,* **923, 945** *left,* **952, 953, 954** *top left, bottom right,* **956** *top left, center left, bottom left,* **985, 989,**

997 *left*, 1000, 1008, 1009 *bottom*, 1010 *right*, 1022 *right*.

Archive Photos

379 *right*, 495 *bottom*, 519, 520, 524–525 *top*, 544 *bottom*, 545 *bottom*, 566 *bottom right*, 640 *left*, 737 *bottom left*, 767 *left*, 773, 847 *bottom*, 938 *left*.

Corbis-Bettman

xi *top*, xviii *top left*, xxiii *right*, 49, 145, 162, 166 *right*, 173 *right*, 180, 250–251, 253 *top*, 272 *right*, 306–307 *top*, 310 *bottom*, 319 *right*, 322, 329, 338 *right*, 339 *top left, bottom*, 343 *bottom*, 349 *left, right*, 356 *bottom*, 385 *bottom*, 410, 428 *bottom right*, 429 *right*, 436 *right*, 449 *bottom right*, 452, 460 *left*, 466 *left*, 477, 490–491, 492–493 *center*, 492 *right*, 494, 499 *bottom left, bottom right*, 502, 503, 505 *top*, 506, 507, 511, 513, 514 *bottom*, 516, 526, 530, 543 *bottom*, 557 *bottom background*, 560 *left*, 566 *left*, 570, 573, 576 *bottom*, 578, 581, 582 *left*, 582–583 *foreground*, 589 *right*, 612, 621, 622 *bottom right*, 623 *bottom*, 627 *right inset*, 629, 662 *bottom right*, 670, 675 *center left inset*, 701 *center left*, 705 *right*, 708, 734, 750 *top*, 758 *top*, 782 *top right, bottom right*, 805 *bottom*, 875 *right*, 934 *bottom*, 951.

Culver Pictures

x *bottom*, xxi *center*, 58 *bottom*, 102 *left*, 103 *left*, 325, 350, 352, 367, 368, 369 *bottom*, 370, 402, 441 *top*, 467, 478, 480 *bottom inset*, 504 *bottom*, 524, 531 *bottom*, 554, 566 *bottom left*, 604 *bottom*, 619 *top, bottom*, 622 *center*, 625 *center*, 737 *top left*, 799 *right*.

George Eastman House

313 *left*, 427 *top*, 428 *left*, 620

The Granger Collection, New York

vii *bottom*, viii *second from top*, ix *top*, xi *bottom*, xi *center*, xii, xxxv *top left*, 1, 12, 20–22, 27, 29, 37 *left, center bottom*, 40 *bottom*, 44 *top right*, 45, 47, 48, 51, 56 *bottom*, 65 *center, right*, 69 *top left center*, 74 *top*, 76, 81 *right*, 82, 83, 92 *bottom right*, 93 *center*, 102 *center*, 103 *center, right, background*, 104 *top*, 108 *top*, 110, 118–119 *center*, 125 *top, right*, 133 *left*, 140, 146, 154 *top*, 170 *left, right*, 171 *left, center*, 172, 174 *right*, 190, 192, 194, 196 *right*, 210, 219, 222 *left, right*, 223 *left, center*, 224, 230, 235–240, 242, 243, 252 *left, right*, 253 *right*, 254, 256 *left*, 259 *top, bottom*, 261, 268, 272 *left*, 281 *top*, 282, 285, 287, 290 *bottom*, 291 *top*, 294, 295, 300, 301 *right*, 306 *bottom*, 310 *top center*, 310–311 *center*, 311 *right*, 316 *top, bottom*, 317, 320, 327, 328, 341 *top*, 342, 344, 345 *right*, 348 *right*, 353, 358, 360 *right*, 362, 371, 376–377, 378 *left, right*, 379 *left*, 381 *top*, 384 *top*, 391, 398, 405, 408 *bottom center*, 409 *right*, 412 *right*, 412 *drawings*, 419–421, 422 *bottom*, 426, 431, 432 *top right, bottom left*, 436 *left*, 437 *center, right*, 444 *left, inset bottom*, 444–445 *center*, 446, 449 *bottom left*, 450 *top*, 454 *cartoon, Tweed*, 455, 456 *top, center, bottom*, 460 *right*, 464 *inset right*, 472 *top, bottom*, 473 , 474 *left, right*, 481, 482 *left, right*, 484, 486–487 *center*, 493 *left*, 493 *right*, 501, 504 *top, bottom*, 510 *top, bottom*, 512, 514 *left*, 525 *bottom left*, 527 *bottom*, 531 *top*, 533 *bottom*, 537, 539, 543 *top*, 547, 552 *center*, 553 *center right*, 563 *top, bottom*, 566 *right*, 567 *left, right*, 571, 572, 580, 588 *center*, 675 *top, left inset*, 681 *union poster*, 684 *bottom*, 820, 878 *bottom*, 878 *center*, 893.

H. Armstrong Roberts

xxxv *top left*, 135 *background*, 257 *top*, 386, 428, *top right*, 445 *top*, 601 *top*, 647, 807 *front left*, 807 *left, bottom left*, 954 *background top left*.

Library of Congress

89 *bottom*, 101 *top*, 106 *top*, 193 *bottom left*, 217, 246–247 *center*, 311 *top*, 313 *right*, 332, 334 *left, right*, 336, 339 *right*, 359, 365 *inset*, 373, 397 *bottom*, 408 *center right*, 409 *top left*, 423, 424, 449 *top*, 462, 463, 468, 487 *bottom*, 589, 593, 610 *left*, 623 *center right*, 655, 663 *center*, 667, 673, 675 *bottom left inset*, 676, 683, 686 *left*, 688 *top*, 692, 857 *top right, bottom right*, 932.

Photofest

627 *bottom*, 672, 684 *top*, 685 *left, right*, 765 *top*, 780 *bottom*, 781, 784 *top*, 814, 818 *left*, 919 *top*, 938–939 *top, right foreground*, 958, *top right, center*, 959 *top left, top right*.

Reuters/Corbis-Bettmann

976 *left*, 1004 *left*, 1007, 1010 *left*, 1017, *top*.

UPI/Corbis-Bettmann

xvii *bottom*, xxxiv *bottom left*, 340, 493 *center*, 495 *top*, 497, 508, 517, 542, 576 *top*, 582 *center*, 583 *top right*, 588 *inset right*, 589 *second from left*, 592 *bottom*, 595, 611 *center*, 611 *top left*, 616–618, 624, 627 *top inset*, 627 *center inset*, 632, 653, 658, 662 *left*, 663 *right*, 674, 677 *bottom*, 678 *bottom right*, 680, 681 *center top*, 700 *left*, 702 *bottom left*, 705 *left*, 717 *inset, bottom*, 722, 728 *top*, 731, 732, 736 *top center*, 740, 746, 750 *top, bottom*, 766 *top*, 770 *top left*, 782 *left*, 800 *bottom right*, 806 *bottom*, 819 *center*, 822, 829 *right*, 835 *left*, 839 *bottom*, 844, 854 *left, right*, 859, 864, 865, 871, 872 *top*, 876, 879 *inset right*, 883 *top*, 894, 899 *top*, 910, 914–915 *background*, 918 *bottom left*, 919 *right*, 928 *right*, 933 *bottom*, 938 *bottom*, 945 *top*, 946, 951, 968 *top*, 973 *top*, 976 *right inset*, 1014.

COMMISSIONED PHOTOGRAPHY

Sharon Hoogstraten

viii *top*, xiv *second from bottom*, xiv *second from bottom*, 16 *top*, 19, 106 *bottom*, 115 *bottom*, 119 *top*, 237 *frames*, 257 *bottom*, 623 *inset top center*, 795 *right*, 839 *top*, 849 *top*, 874 *bottom, bottom*, 905 *bottom*, 911 *center right*, 919 *center*, 934 *center right*, 939 *right background*, 968 *bottom*.

MISCELLANEOUS ART CREDITS

vii *second from top*, By kind permission of the Vicar and Churchwardens of the Parish of Boston, St. Botolph's Church, England; vii *second from bottom*, xvii *top*, *Benjamin Franklin* (1789), Charles Willson Peale. Historical Society of Pennsylvania; vii *top* Maxwell Museum of Anthropology, Albuquerque (New Mexico), Werner Forman Archive/Art Resource, New York; viii *bottom* Tray depicting Reverend Lemuel Haynes in the pulpit (early 19th century), probably English. Papier maché, 25¹¹⁄₁₆″ × 20¹⁵⁄₁₆″. Museum of Art, Rhode Island School of Design, gift of Miss Lucy T. Aldrich; viii *second from bottom*, *Henry Clay* (about 1845), George Peter Alexander Healy. Oil on canvas. National Portrait Gallery, Smithsonian Institution/Art Resource, New

Miscellaneous Art Credits (Cont.)

York; **ix** *second from bottom,* **xiii** *left, Abraham Lincoln* (about 1858), Fetter's Picture Gallery photograph. National Portrait Gallery, Smithsonian Institution/Art Resource, New York; **ix** *bottom, Return to Fredericksburg After the Battle* (date unknown), David English Henderson. Gettysburg National Military Park; **x** *top,* **381** *inset Portrait of a Sioux Man and Woman* (date unknown), Gertrude Käsebier. Copyright © Smithsonian Institution; *second from top* National Museum of American History/Smithsonian Institution; *second from bottom,* National Park Service/Statue of Liberty National Monument; *second from bottom,* Conservative Research Department, Conservative Party, London; *second from top,* Fisk University, Nashville, Tennessee; *top* Copyright © Henry Ford Museum and Greenfield Village, Dearborn, Michigan; **xiii** *bottom,* Courtesy of *TV Guide;* **xiii** *top,* Courtesy of the Spertus Museum, Chicago; **xiv** *second from bottom,* Copyright © John Paul Filo; **xiv** *top* Archive Photos/Blank Archives; **xv** *top,* Copyright © 1973 Dennis Brack/Black Star; *center* Courtesy of the Ronald Reagan Library; *bottom* Copyright © Uniphoto, Inc.; **xvii** *bottom left* Courtesy of Bantam Doubleday Books; *center left* Courtesy of Tony Kahn; *center right,* Beinecke Rare Book and Manuscript Library, Yale University; *second from top,* Courtesy of Brigham Young University; **xviii** *bottom left,* National Archives; *top right* Detail of *Captain Samuel Chandler* (about 1780), Winthrop Chandler. Oil on canvas, 61¼″ × 54¼″ × 2⅛″. National Gallery of Art Washington, D.C., gift of Edgar William and Bernice Garbisch; **xxi** *left,* University of Illinois at Chicago Library, Jane Addams Memorial Collection; *right,* Photo by Arthur Schatz/Life Magazine, Copyright © Time, Inc.; **xxii** *bottom,* FDR at Hill Top Cottage, with Ruthie Bie and Fala (1941), photo by Margaret Suckley. Franklin D. Roosevelt Library; **xxiv** *left* Reproduced from *Dust Bowl Diary,* by Ann Marie Low, by permission of the University of Nebraska Press. Copyright © 1984 by the University of Nebraska Press; **xxv** *bottom,* Copyright © 1985 Steve Leonard/Black Star; **xxxiv** *right* NASA (National Aeronautics and Space Administration); **xxxiv-xxxv** Copyright © 1991 Woodward Payne; **xxxv** *bottom right* Photo by Howard Sochrer/Life Magazine, Copyright © Time, Inc.; *right* Copyright © Hazel Hankin/Stock Boston/PNI; **2** *left* Archaeological Museum, Jalapa, Mexico/Art Resource, New York; *right* Copyright © T. Linck/SuperStock; **3** *left* Courtesy of the Ohio Historical Society; *top* Museo del Templo Mayor, Mexico City, D.F., Mexico. Michel Zabé/Art Resource, New York; *right, Portrait of a Man, Called Christopher Columbus* (1519), Sebastiano del Piombo. Oil on canvas, 42″ × 34¾″. The Metropolitan Museum of Art, gift of J. Pierpont Morgan, 1900; **4** *bottom left* Courtesy Arizona State Museum, University of Arizona, Tucson, Arizona. Photo Copyright © 1996 Jerry Jacka; *top right* Copyright © Sisse Brimberg/National Geographic Image Collection; **7** *top left* Copyright © 1996 David Muench; *bottom left* Museum of Mexico City. Copyright © C. Lenars/Explorer; *top right* Copyright © T. Linck/SuperStock; *center right,* Lloyd Kenneth Townsend. Courtesy Cahokia Mounds State Historic Site, Collinsville, Illinois; *bottom right* Archaeological Museum, Jalapa, Mexico/Art Resource, New York; **8** Phoebe A. Hearst Museum of Anthropology, University of California at Berkeley; **9** *top* The Philbrook Museum of Art, Tulsa, Oklahoma; *bottom* Maxwell Museum of Anthropology, Albuquerque (New Mexico), Werner Forman Archive/Art Resource, New York; **10** *top right* KC Publications, Inc. Copyright © Southwestern Indian Arts and Crafts; *center left* Courtesy of the National Museum of the American Indian/Smithsonian Institution #17/6228; **14** The British Museum, Photo Copyright © Michael Holford; **16** *bottom* Stock Montage; **17** *Portrait of a King* (11–12th Century), unknown Yoruba artist. Bronze, height 12 3/16≤. National Commission for Museums and Monuments, Lagos, Nigeria; **18** British Museum, London; **25** Science Museum, London/Science and Society Picture Library; **26** Copyright © National Maritime Museum Picture Library, London; **28** Copyright © The Royal Norwegian Ministry of Foreign Affairs, Oslo, Norway; **36** Courtesy of the Department of Library Services, American Museum of Natural History; **37** *center top* Copyright © Kindra Clineff/The Picture Cube, Inc.; *right* Stock Montage; **38** *top* Biblioteca Medicea Laurenziana, Florence, Italy. Photo by Alberto Scardigli; *bottom* Aztec mask thought to represent the god Quetzalcoatl. Werner Forman Archive/Art Resource, New York; **40** *top* Courtesy of the Department of Library Services, American Museum of Natural History; **42** *top, Nuestra Señora* [Our Lady] (1938), Polly Duncan. Watercolor, colored pencil, graphite, and heightening on paper, 22⅟₁₆″ × 14¹⁵⁄₁₆″. Copyright © Board of Trustees, National Gallery of Art, Washington, D.C.; *bottom left* E.T. Archive, England; **44** *bottom, Nova Britannia* (1609), Robert Johnson, London, title page (°KC 1609). Rare Books and Manuscripts Division, The New York Public Library, Astor, Lenox and Tilden Foundations; **46** Copyright © Charles Gupton/Tony Stone Images—Click/Chicago Ltd.; **50** Kenneth D. Lyons; **52** *top* By kind permission of the Vicar and Churchwardens of the Parish of Boston, St. Botolph's Church, England; *bottom* Pilgrim Society, Plymouth, Massachusetts; **54** *left, Mr. John Freake* (about 1674), unknown artist. Oil on canvas, 107.9 cm × 93.4 cm. Worcester Art Museum, Worcester, Massachusetts, Sarah C. Garver Fund; *right* Musée National de la Renaissance, Écouen, France. Photo Copyright © RMN/Gérard Blot; **55** Copyright © Kindra Clineff/The Picture Cube, Inc.; **57** Stock Montage; **58** *top, William Penn* (about 1698), Francis Place. Colored chalk drawing, 11⅞″ × 8³⁄₁₆″. Historical Society of Pennsylvania; **60** *top* Silver gorget (about 1757), Joseph Richardson. Historical Society of Pennsylvania; *bottom, William Penn's Treaty with the Indians* (about 1840), Edward Hicks. Giraudon/Art Resource, New York; **64** *left* Courtesy of Massachusetts Archives, Boston; *right* Sketch of the first building of the College of William and Mary (about 1702), Francis Louis Michel. Courtesy of the College of William and Mary, Williamsburg, Virginia; **65** *left, Benjamin Franklin* (1789), Charles Willson Peale. Historical Society of Pennsylvania; **66** The New York Botanical Garden; Copyright © 1995 William S. Nawrocki/Nawrocki Stock Photo Inc.; Copyright © 1995 Larry Stevens/Nawrocki Stock Photo, Inc.; **67** Overmantle (mid 18th century), unknown artist. Oil on wood panel from the Moses Marcy House, Old Surbridge Village. Southbridge, MA. Photo by Henry E. Peach; **69** *top far left, Charles II* (date unknown), Pieter Nason. Bridgeman/Art Resource, New York; *top center right, King William III* (date unknown), Sir Godfrey Kneller. Bridgeman/Art Resource, New York; *top far right, Mary II* (1650–1702), William Wissing. Bridgeman/Art Resource, New York; *bottom, The Meetinghouse Drawing.* Courtesy of the Pilgrim Society, Plymouth, Massachusetts; **71** Copyright © Taylor Lewis. Courtesy Catherine Fallin, Kerhonkson, New York; **72** *top, The Plantation* (about 1825), artist unknown. Oil on wood, 19½″ × 29½″. The Metropolitan Museum of Art, gift of Edgar William and Bernice Chrysler Garbisch, 1963; *bottom* Colonial Williamsburg (Virginia) Foundation; **74** *bottom left, Slaves Below Deck of Albanez* (date unknown), Francis Meynell. Copyright © National Maritime Museum Picture Library, London; *bottom right* The Newberry Library, Chicago; **75** *top* Collection of the Blue Ridge Institute and Museums/Blue Ridge Heritage Archive of Ferrum College, Ferrum, Virginia; *bottom* Smithsonian Institution, Washington, D.C.; **77** Courtesy of the Massachusetts Historical Society, Boston; **78** *SE Prospect of the City of Philadelphia* (1720), Peter Cooper. Library Company of

Philadelphia; **79** Detail of *Quaker Meeting* (date unknown), Egbert Van Heemskerk. The Quaker Collection, Haverford (Pennsylvania) College Library; **81** *left, Benjamin Franklin* (about 1785), Joseph Siffred Duplessis. Oil on canvas, 28½″ × 23½″. National Portrait Gallery, Smithsonian Institution, gift of the Morris and Gwendolyn Cafritz Foundation. Art Resource, New York; **86** Fort Ticonderoga (New York) Museum; **88** *left, Celebrating Couple: General Jackson and His Lady* (date unknown), Reverend H. Young. Pen and watercolor, 10¼″ × 7⅞″. Courtesy, Museum of Fine Arts, Boston (Massachusettes), gift of Maxim Karolik; **88–89** *center,* **89** *top* Abby Aldrich Rockefeller Folk Art Center, Williamsburg, Virginia; **92** *background* Science Museum, London/Science and Society Picture Library; **92** *top left,* **118** *top Governor and Mrs. Mifflin* (1773), John Singleton Copley. The Historical Society of Pennsylvania; **93** *left, Washington Crossing the Delaware* (1851), Emanuel Gottlieb Leutze. Oil on canvas, 149″ × 255″. The Metropolitan Museum of Art, gift of John S. Kennedy, 1897, *right, Thayendanegea* (Joseph Brant) (about 1807), William Berczy. Oil on canvas, 61.8cm × 46.1cm. National Gallery of Canada, Ottawa; **94** Stock Montage; **95** Rare Books and Manuscript Division of the New York Public Library. Astor, Lenox, and Tilden Foundations; **96** *The Boston Massacre (The Bloody Massacre)* (1770), by Paul Revere. Hand-colored engraving, 10¼″ × 9⅜″. The Metropolitan Museum of Art, gift of Mrs. Russell Sage, 1909; **97** *left* Courtesy, American Antiquarian Society; *right, A View of the Town of Concord* (about 1775), unknown artist. Oil on canvas. Photograph courtesy of the Concord Museum, Concord, Massachusetts; **98** Courtesy of the Concord Museum, Concord, Massachusetts. Photo by David Bohl; **99** *William Franklin* (date unknown), attributed to Mather Brown. Collection of Mrs. Jackson C. Boswell, Arlington, Virginia. Courtesy of the Frick Art Reference Library; **100** *Attack on Bunker's Hill, with the Burning of Charles Town* (about 1783), unknown artist. Oil on canvas, 23¾″ × 30½″ × 1½″ framed. Copyright © 1996 Board of Trustees, National Gallery of Art, Washington, D.C., gift of Edgar William and Bernice Chrysler Garbisch; **101** *bottom* From *The National Archives of the United States* by Herman J. Viola. Photo by Jonathan Wallen. Published by Harry N. Abrams, Inc., New York; **102** *right* Courtesy of the Historical Society of Delaware; *background* Courtesy of The Flag Institute, Chester, England; **104** National Archives; **105** Courtesy of the Massachusetts Historical Society; **107** *March to Valley Forge* (1883), William B. T. Trego. Courtesy of the Valley Forge Historical Society; **108–109** *bottom* Illustrations by Greg Harlin/Wood Ronsaville Harlin, Inc.; **111** *Molly Pitcher at the Battle of Monmouth* (1854), Dennis Malone Carter. Oil on canvas, 42″ × 56″. Courtesy of Fraunces Tavern Museum, New York City, gift of Herbert P. Whitlock, 1913; **112** *Surrender of Lord Cornwallis at Yorktown* (date unknown), John Trumbull. Yale University Art Gallery; **113** *Battle of Coupens* (about 1855), William Ranney. Oil on canvas. Collection of the state of South Carolina, South Carolina State House, Columbia, South Carolina; **115** *top* Courtesy of the John Carter Brown Library at Brown University; **117** *A New and Correct Map of the United States* (1783), Abel Buell. From the Collections of the New Jersey Historical Society, Newark; **118** *bottom left* Courtesy of the Seneca Falls (New York) Historical Society; **122–123** *Washington Addressing the Constitutional Convention* (1856), Junius Brutus Stearns. Oil on canvas, 37½″ × 54″. Virginia Museum of Fine Arts, Richmond, Virginia, gift of Edgar William and Bernice Chrysler Garbisch. Photo by Ron Jennings, Copyright © Virginia Museum of Fine Arts; **124** *left* Detail of *John Dickinson* (about 1835), James Barton Longacre, after Charles Willson Peale. Sepia watercolor on artist board, 11⅜″ × 8⅝″. National Portrait Gallery, Smithsonian Institution/Art Resource, New York; *right* National Archives/Woodfin Camp & Associates, Inc.; **125** *left* Detail of *Daniel Shays and Job Shattuck* (1787), unknown artist. Relief cut, 3½″ × 5⅛″, National Portrait Gallery, Washington, D.C./Art Resource, New York; **126** Detail of *John Dickinson* (about 1835), James Barton Longacre, after Charles Willson Peale. Sepia watercolor on artist board, 11⅜″ × 8⅝″. National Portrait Gallery, Smithsonian Institution/Art Resource, New York; **127** Detail of *Republican Motherhood,* date and artist unknown. Silk embroidery. National Museum of American History, Smithsonian Institution [81–5200]; **128** Copyright © William S. Nawrocki, Nawrocki Stock Photo Inc.; **130** Copyright © David R. Frazier/Tony Stone Images; **131** Clements Library, University of Michigan, Ann Arbor, Michigan; **132** Stock Montage; **133** *right,* Detail of *Roger Sherman* (about 1777), unknown artist, after Ralph Earl. Oil on canvas, 26⅜″ × 22³⁄₁₆″. National Portrait Gallery, Smithsonian Institution/Art Resource, New York, gift of Mr. Bradley B. Gilman; **137** Detail of *John Jay, Statesman* (1783–1808), begun by Gilbert Stuart and completed by John Trumbull. National Portrait Gallery, Smithsonian Institution/Art Resource, New York; **138** *top left, Patrick Henry* (about 1835), James Barton Longacre, after Lawrence Sully. Watercolor. National Portrait Gallery, Smithsonian Institution/Art Resource, New York; *bottom left, Alexander Hamilton* (date unknown), John Trumbull. National Portrait Gallery, Smithsonian Institution/Art Resource, New York; **149** Copyright © Herblock, from *The Herblock Gallery,* Simon & Schuster, 1968; **157** "The Federal Edifice: On the Erection of the Eleventh Pillar," cartoon from the Massachusetts *Centinel,* August 2, 1788. Courtesy of the New-York Historical Society, New York City; **165** *below right* Copyright © Robert E. Daemmrich/Tony Stone Images; **166** *left* Detail of *Daniel Boardman* (1789), Ralph Earl. Oil on canvas, 81⅞″ × 55¼″. Copyright © 1996 Board of Trustees. National Gallery of Art, Washington, D.C., gift of Mrs. W. Murray Crane; **167** *top* Copyright © Robert E. Daemmrich/Tony Stone Images; *bottom* FPG International; **169** *Vaughn Shoemaker,* reprinted with permission, The *Chicago Sun-Times* Copyright © 1996; **171** *right* Courtesy U.S. Naval Academy Museum, Annapolis, Maryland; **173** *left, Alexander Hamilton* (about 1796), James Sharples, the elder. Pastel on paper. National Portrait Gallery, Smithsonian Institution/Art Resource, New York; **174** *left* Museum of the City of New York; **175** FPG International; **176** Stock Montage; **177** *Taking of the Bastille, 14 July 1789* (late 1700s), unknown artist. Chateau Versailles, France. Giraudon/Art Resource, New York; **179** *bottom* Chicago Historical Society; **182** *left,* Detail of *Martha Dandridge Custis Washington 1731–1802* (about 1853), Rembrandt Peale. National Portrait Gallery, Smithsonian Institution/Art Resource, New York; *top right* Colonial Williamsburg (Virginia) Foundation; **182–183** *bottom, The Samuels Family* (date unknown), Johann Eckstein. Oil on canvas, 25½″ × 30″. Ellen Kelleran Gardner Fund. Courtesy, Museum of Fine Arts, Boston; **183** *top, Thomas Hancock, Merchant* (about 1758), John Singleton Copley. Oil on copper. National Portrait Gallery, Smithsonian Institution/Art Resource, New York; *center right* Copyright © 1969 Edwin Tunis. First appeared in *The Young United States 1783–1830* published by Thomas Y. Crowell. Reprinted by permission of Curtis Brown, Ltd; *center left* Detail of *Captain Samuel Chandler* (about 1780), Winthrop Chandler. Oil on canvas, 61¼″ × 54¼″ × 2⅛″. National Gallery of Art Washington, D.C., gift of Edgar William and Bernice Garbisch; **184** Sketch from *A Journal of the Voyages and Travels of a Corps of Discovery* (1812), Patrick Gass. Rare Books and Manuscripts Division, the New York Public Library. Astor, Lenox and Tilden Foundations; **187** *bottom left* American Philosophical Society; *top right, Mandan Village* (date unknown), Karl Bodmer, from *Travels in the Interior of North America* by Maximilian Prince zu Wied. Yale Collection of Western Americana, Beinecke Rare Book and Manuscript Library, Yale University; *bottom right*

Miscellaneous Art Credits (Cont.)

Compass, National Museum of American History, Smithsonian Institution [75-2348]; **188** Stock Montage; **193** *top left* Copyright © Uniphoto; *top right* Copyright © Superstock; *bottom right* Courtesy Architect of the Capitol; **196** *left, Erie Canal at Little Falls, New York* (1884), William Rickaby Miller. Oil on canvas. Collection of the New-York Historical Society; **197** *left, John Quincy Adams* (1843), Philip Haas. Daguerreotype. The Metropolitan Museum of Art, gift of I. N. Phelps Stokes, Edward S. Hawes, Alice Mary Hawes, Marion Augusta Hawes, 1937 (37.14.34); *center, Andrew Jackson* (1845), Thomas Sully. Oil on canvas, 20⅝" × 17¼". Copyright © 1996 Board of Trustees, National Gallery of Art, Washington, D.C. Andrew W. Mellon Collection; *right* Detail of *Trail of Tears* (date unknown), Robert Lindneux. Woolaroc Museum, Bartlesville, Oklahoma; **198** Detail of *Eli Whitney* (date unknown), Samuel F. B. Morse. Yale University Art Gallery, gift of George Hoadley, B.A. 1801; **199** *Slater's Mill,* unknown date and artist. Oil on canvas. Smithsonian Institution, Washington, D.C.; **200** *right,* National Museum of American History, Smithsonian Institution, Washington, D.C. (73-11287); **203** Detail of *Henry Clay* (date unknown), George Peter Alexander Healy. Oil on canvas. National Portrait Gallery, Smithsonian Institution/Art Resource, New York; **204** Hudson River Steamboat Line broadside, May 23, 1826, Child & Wells, Printers. Black ink on paper 15¾" × 19½". Copyright © New York State Historical Association, Cooperstown; **205** Detail of *John Marshall, Chief Justice of the United States* (about 1832), William James Hubard. National Portrait Gallery, Smithsonian Institution/Art Resource, New York; **207** Courtesy, Colorado Historical Society; **209** *left, Thomas Jefferson* (1821), Thomas Sully. American Philosophical Society; *right, John Adams, Second President of the United States* (1735–1826), (1798 and 1828), Gilbert Stuart and Jane Stuart. Oil on canvas. National Portrait Gallery, Smithsonian Institution/Art Resource, New York; **211** Detail of *Andrew Jackson, 1767–1845, Seventh President of the United States* (1820), James Barton Longacre. Hand-colored stipple engraving, 37.2 cm × 30 cm. National Portrait Gallery, Smithsonian Institution/Art Resource, New York; **214** *Webster's Reply to Hayne* (date unknown), G. P. A. Healy. Courtesy of the Boston Art Commission; **215** *left, John Caldwell Calhoun* (about 1820), attributed to Charles Bird King. National Portrait Gallery, Smithsonian Institution/Art Resource, New York; right, Daniel Webster (1782–1852), Statesman (about 1828), Chester Harding. National Portrait Gallery, Smithsonian Institution/Art Resource, New York; **216** Detail of *Andrew Jackson* (date unknown), James Barton Longacre. National Portrait Gallery, Smithsonian Institution/Art Resource, New York; **223** *right* Boston Athenaeum; **225** Tray depicting Reverend Lemuel Haynes in the pulpit (early 19th century), probably English. Papier maché, 25¹¹⁄₁₆" × 20¹⁵⁄₁₆". Museum of Art, Rhode Island School of Design, gift of Miss Lucy T. Aldrich; **226** *Genesee Scenery* (date unknown), Thomas Cole. Oil on canvas, 51" × 39½". Museum of Art, Rhode Island School of Design, Jesse Metcalf Fund; **227** Collection of Picture Research Consultants; **229** Historical Society of Pennsylvania, Leon Gardiner Collection; **231** *left* Massachusetts Commandery, Military Order of the Loyal Legion and the United States Military History Institute, Carlisle, Pennsylvania; right Collection of the New-York Historical Society, neg. 48169; **232** *Charlotte Helen Middleton and Her Nurse Lydia* (1857), George Cook. Ambrotype. Gibbes Museum of Art/Carolina Art Association Collection, Charleston, South Carolina; **244** Detail of *The Bay and Harbor of New York* (about 1855), by Samuel Waugh. Oil on canvas, 99⅛" × 198". Museum of the City of New York. Gift of Mrs. Robert M. Littlejohn; **246** *bottom* American Textile History Museum, North Andover, Massachusetts; **247** *top, Haymaking* (1864), Winslow Homer. Oil on canvas, 16" × 11". Columbus Museum of Art, Ohio, museum purchase, Howald Fund; **253** *center,* **256** *right* Courtesy of the Smithsonian Institution, Washington, D.C.; **255** Courtesy of the Singer Sewing Machine Company; **260** Oregon Historical Society; **262** Copyright © Thomas Lindfors; **264** *inset* National Archives; *bottom, Mormon Crossing* (1846), William Henry Jackson. Scotts Bluff National Monument, Gering, Nebraska; **266** *bottom* Copyright © Smithsonian Institution, Washington, D.C.; **266–267** *center,* National Archives; **267** *top* Idaho State Historical Society. Photo number 1254-D-1; *bottom* Copyright © Ric Ergenbright Photography; **271** *Dawn at the Alamo* (1876–83), Henry Arthur McArdle. Oil on canvas, 7' × 12'. Texas State Capitol, Austin. Photo courtesy of the State Preservation Board, Austin, Texas; **273** *Robert E. Lee* (about 1838), William Edward West. Washington/Custis/Lee Collection, Washington and Lee University, Lexington, Virginia; **277** *left, View of San Francisco [Formerly Yerba Buena]* (1847), attributed to Victor Prevost. Oil on canvas, 25" × 30". California Historical Society, gift of the Ohio Historical Society; *right* The Bancroft Library, University of California, Berkeley; **280** *right,* **291** *bottom* From the Collection of Edith Hariton/Antique Textile Resource. Picture Research Consultants and Archives; **281** *left, Roger Brooke Taney* (date unknown), Francis Blackwell Mayer. Oil on canvas. Maryland Historical Society, Baltimore; *right* Lloyd Ostendorf Collection; **284** *Alexander Stephens* (about 1868), J. L. Giles lithography company, after a photograph by Mathew Brady. Lithograph with tintstone, 12¹⁄₁₆" × 9¹⁵⁄₁₆". National Portrait Gallery, Smithsonian Institution/Art Resource, New York; **293** *bottom* Courtesy of the Ohio Historical Society; **296** Photo courtesy of the Milwaukee County Historical Society; **297** Ontario County (New York) Historical Society; **299** *Abraham Lincoln* (about 1858), Fetter's Picture Gallery photograph. National Portrait Gallery, Smithsonian Institution/Art Resource, New York; **301** *left, Stephen Douglas* (about 1860), Mathew Brady. Photograph, albumen silver print, 3⅜" × 2⅛". National Portrait Gallery, Smithsonian Institution/Art Resource, New York; **302** *John Brown Going to His Hanging* (1942), Horace Pippin; oil on canvas, 24⅛" × 30¼". Courtesy of the Museum of American Art of the Pennsylvania Academy of the Fine Arts, Philadelphia, Pennsylvania. John Lambert Fund; **303** The Museum of American Political Life, University of Hartford; **306** *center* The Library Company of Philadelphia; **307** *right* Copyright © 1957 Burt Glinn/Magnum Photos; **312** Beverley R. Robinson Collection, United States Naval Academy Museum, Annapolis, Maryland. Accession number 51.7.667; **318** Alabama Department of Archives and History; **319** *left, Abraham Lincoln, Sixteenth President of the United States* (1864), William Willard. National Portrait Gallery, Smithsonian Institution/Art Resource, New York; **323** *Mary Boykin Chesnut* (1856), Samuel Osgood. On loan from Serena Williams Miles Van Rensselaer. National Portrait Gallery, Smithsonian Institution/Art Resource, New York; **324** Chicago Historical Society; **326** Copyright © Museum of the City of New York. Gift of Mrs. J. West Roosevelt; **331** Copyright © SuperStock; **335** Chicago Historical Society; **337** Copyright © Tom Lovell/National Geographic Image Collection; **338** *left* Courtesy of George Eastman House/Picture Research Consultants; **341** Copyright © Stock Montage; **343** *top* Museum of the Confederacy/High Impact Photography; **345** *left* Illinois State Historical Library; **348** *left, Return to Fredericksburg After the Battle* (date unknown), David English Henderson. Gettysburg National Military Park; **349** *center, Horace Greeley* (about 1872), Thomas Nast. Watercolor with pencil on paper, 30.7cm ¥ 18.5cm. National Portrait Gallery, Smithsonian Institution/Art Resource, New York; **356** *top* William Gladstone Collection; **357** *A Burial Party; Civil War, Cold Harbor,*

Virginia (1865), Alexander Gardner. Photograph. Chicago Historical Society; **360** *left* Copyright © 1995 Smithsonian Institution; **361** *left* Copyright © Tom McCarthy/PhotoEdit; *right* Copyright © 1993 Dennis Brack/Black Star; **363** From the collection of Walter Dean Myers; **365** *top* Courtesy of the Birmingham Public Library Department of Archives and Manuscripts; **366** Copyright © 1968 Yale Joel/*Life* magazine/Time Warner Inc.; **379** *top* Courtesy of the National Museum of the American Indian/Smithsonian Institution #s2336; **380** *top right* Courtesy of Brigham Young University; *bottom left* Copyright © The Detroit Institute of Arts, Founders Society Purchase with funds from Flint Ink Corporation; **382** Kansas State Historical Society, Topeka, Kansas; **384** *bottom* American Museum of Natural History/New York. Photo by Lee Boltin; **385** *top* Buffalo Bill Historical Center, Cody, Wyoming. Gift of Olin Corporation, Winchester Arms Collection; **386** T. Ulrich/H. Armstrong Roberts; **388, 390** Montana Historical Society, Helena; **389** *And So Unemotionally, There Began One of the Wildest and Strangest Journeys Ever Made in Any Land* (date unknown), William Henry David Koerner. Oil on canvas, 22¼″ × 72¼″. Buffalo Bill Historical Center, Cody, Wyoming; **394** *bottom left* Photo by E. A. Hegg. Special Collections Division, University of Washington Libraries, Seattle. Negative number 1312; **394–395** *center* Photo by J. G. Wison. Denver Public Library, Western History Department Collection; **395** *center top, Miners Underground* (1897), unknown artist. Glass plate negative. Amon Carter Museum, Fort Worth, Texas. Mazzulla Collection; **395** *top right, bottom* Chuck Lawliss; **396** *Pioneer Woman* (date unknown), Harvey Dunn. Hazel L. Meyer Memorial Library, DeSmet, South Dakota; **397** *top right,* **401** Kansas State Historical Society, Topeka; **400** State Historical Society of North Dakota; **404** Courtesy of the Chicago Tribune/Chicago American Photo File. Copyright © KMTV; **408** *top* Archives of Labor and Urban Affairs, Wayne State University, Detroit, Michigan; **412** National Museum of American History/Smithsonian Institution; **414** *bottom left,* **415** *top right* Western Reserve Historical Society, Cleveland, Ohio; **414** *center left,* **414–415** *center* From the *Atlas of Cuyahoga County, Ohio,* Titus, Simmons and Titus; **415** *bottom right* Cleveland Public Library/Bettmann Archives; **416** *top* Historic Pullman Foundation Archives, Chicago; *bottom left* Union Pacific Railroad, San Francisco, California; **417** *On the Kansas Pacific Railway: Number 8, Roundhouse at Armstrong, Kansas* (date unknown), Robert Benecke. Courtesy, DeGolyer Library, Southern Methodist University, Dallas; **422** *top* Harry Ransom Humanities Research Center, The University of Texas at Austin; **427** *bottom right* Photographs and Prints Division, Schomburg Center for Research in Black Culture, The New York Public Library. Astor, Lenox and Tilden Foundations; **429** *left* Copyright © Lawrence Migdale/Stock Boston; **432** *top left* Eugene Debs Collection/Tamiment Institute Library, New York University; **437** *left* Statue of Liberty National Monument, National Park Service; **438** Courtesy of the See family; **440** Statue of Liberty National Monument, National Park Service; **441** *center right* New York Academy of Medicine Library; *bottom right* California Department of Parks and Recreation Photographic Archives; **442, 444** *inset top* Underwood Photo Archives, San Francisco, California; **444–445** *background* W. Metzen/H. Armstrong Roberts; **445** *right* Copyright © Bob Daemmrich/Stock Boston/PNI; *inset bottom, The Medicine Robe* (1915), Maynard Dixon. Oil on canvas, 40″ × 30″. Buffalo Bill Historical Center, Cody, Wyoming, gift of Mr. and Mrs. Godwin Pelissero; **450** *bottom,* **451** University of Illinois at Chicago, Library, Jane Addams Memorial Collection; **461** *bottom left* The Brooklyn Historical Society; **461** *top left,* **465** Copyright © Smithsonian Institution; **464** "Plan of the Center of the City, Showing the Present Street and Boulevard System," plate 111 from *Plan of Chicago* (1909), Daniel H. Burnham and Edward H. Bennett, Chicago, partnership 1903–1912. Ink and watercolor on paper, 131.1 cm × 102.4 cm. On permanent loan to the Art Institute of Chicago from the City of Chicago, 19.148.1966. Photograph copyright © 1996 The Art Institute of Chicago. All rights reserved.; **466** *right* Copyright © Eastman Kodak Company; **470** Moorland-Spingarn Research Center, Howard University Archives; **471** *The Champion Single Sculls (Max Schmitt in a Single Scull)* (1871), Thomas Eakins. Oil on canvas, 32¼″ × 46¼″. The Metropolitan Museum of Art, Purchase, The Alfred N. Punnett Endowment Fund and George D Pratt Gift, 1934. (34.92); **480** *top* Boston Public Library; **483** *left* From *Passing Parade: A History of Popular Culture in the Twentieth Century* by Richard Malthy, Oxford University Press, Copyright © 1988; **485** Courtesy of Sears Roebuck and Company; **486** *bottom, The Picnic Grounds* (1906–1907), John Sloan. Oil on canvas, 30¼″ × 42¼″ × 2″. Copyright © 1996 Whitney Museum of American Art, New York; **487** *top* Collection of the New-York Historical Society; **498** Cleveland Public Library; **505** *right inset* Doubleday, Page and Company, New York, 1906, second issue; **525** *right,* **548** *top* Panama Canal Company; **529** Hawaiian Historical Society; **535** From *Puerto Rico: A Political and Cultural History,* Arturo Morales Carrion; **538** Keystone-Mast Collection (24039) UCR/California Museum of Photography. University of California, Riverside, California; **544** Theodore Roosevelt Collection, Harvard College Library; **545** *bottom left* Reuters/Corrine Dufka/Archive Photos; *center right* Copyright © Hires/Merillon/Gamma Liaison; **549** *top* Copyright © 1979 New York News, Inc.; *center* Copyright © Will and Deni McIntyre/Tony Stone Images; **553** *top left,* Culver Pictures/PNI; **562** Balch Institute for Ethnic Studies Library; **566** *bottom center* RIA-Novosti/Sovfoto/PNI; **569** *Oliver Wendell Holmes* (1935), Clara E. Sipprell. National Portrait Gallery, Smithsonian Institution/Art Resource, New York; **574** Panel no. 1: "During the World War There Was a Great Migration North by Southern Negroes" from *The Migration of the Negro* mural series (1940–41), Jacob Lawrence. Tempera on masonite, 12″ × 18″. Acquired through Downtown Gallery, 1942. The Phillips Collection, Washington, D.C.; **577** *Edith Bolling Galt Wilson, First Lady* (1924), Emile Alexay. National Portrait Gallery, Smithsonian Institution/Art Resource, New York; **586–587** *Drouth Stricken Area* (1934), Alexandre Hogue. Oil on canvas, 30″ × 42¼″. Dallas Museum of Art, Dallas Art Association Purchase; **589** *top left,* **600** Stock Montage; **589** *bottom* Copyright © Henry Ford Museum and Greenfield Village, Dearborn, Michigan; **590** From *The Jewish Americans,* Copyright © 1982 by Milton Meltzer. Thomas Y. Crowell Junior Books/Harper Collins Children's Books; **592** *top* Detail of *Sacco and Vanzetti* (1932), Ben Shahn. Tempera, 21″ × 48″. Private collection. Copyright © 1997 Estate of Ben Shahn/Licensed by VAGA, New York, NY; **596** Copyright © Underwood Photo Archives, San Francisco, California; **597** Details of *Warren Gamaliel Harding* (about 1923), Margaret Lindsay William. National Portrait Gallery, Smithsonian Institution/Art Resource, New York; **602** *inset left, inset right* Brown Brothers; *top inset* Minnesota Historical Society; **603** Courtesy of United Airlines; **604** *top,* copyright © 1931 (renewed 1959) by the Conde Nast Publications, Inc.; **606** *left center* Chicago Historical Society; *bottom* Montgomery Ward and Company, Chicago; **606–607** *center* Joseph J. Pennell Collection, Kansas Collection, University of Kansas Libraries; **607** *bottom* Copyright © Camerique Stock Photos; **607** *top right* Copyright © J. McDermott/Tony Stone Images; **610** *center* Illustration by William Cotten. *Vanity Fair,* January 1931. Copyright © 1931 (renewed 1959) by the Conde Nast Publications, Inc.; *right* Archive Photos/Frank Driggs Collection; **611** *right* Copyright © U.S. Postal Service; **613** *New York Street Scene* (1920), Joaquin Torres-García. Oil on paper mounted on cradled

Miscellaneous Art Credits (Cont.)

wood panel, 18⅜″ × 25⅞″. Hirshhorn Museum and Sculpture Garden, Smithsonian Institution. Gift of Joseph H. Hirshhorn, 1972; Underwood & Underwood/Corbis-Bettmann. **615** Detail of *Al Capone* (1929) Jun Fujita. Photograph. Chicago Historical Society; **622** *left* Brown Brothers; **623** *top left* Archive Photos/Frank Driggs Collection; **625** *left* Rare Books and Manuscripts Division of the New York Public Library. Astor, Lenox, and Tilden Foundations; *right* National Museum of American History, Smithsonian Institution; **626** Brown Brothers; **628** *left, Radiator Building—Night, New York* (1927), Georgia O'Keeffe. Oil on canvas. The Alfred Stieglitz Collection, Fisk University Art Galleries, Nashville, Tennessee; **628** *right* Photofest/Copyright © The Walt Disney Corporation; **630** Beinecke Rare Book and Manuscript Library, Yale University; **631** Fisk University, Nashville, Tennessee; **633** *Black Belt* (1934), Archibald J. Motley, Jr. Oil on canvas, 31¼″ × 39⅜″. Hampton University Museum, Hampton, Virginia; **634, 635** Archive Photos/Frank Driggs Collection; **636** Book cover from first edition, *The Great Gatsby* by F. Scott Fitzgerald (New York: Charles Scribner's Sons, 1925). Used by permission of Scribner, a division of Simon & Schuster; **637** *left center, Langston Hughes* (about 1920), Winold Reiss. National Portrait Gallery, Smithsonian Institution/Art Resource, New York; *top, Edna St. Vincent Millay* (1930), unknown photographer. National Portrait Gallery, Smithsonian Institution/Art Resource, New York; **640** *right,* Cover Copyright © 1933 (renewed 1961) Conde Nast Publications, Inc. Courtesy of *Vanity Fair;* **641** *left* Copyright © M. Howell/Camerique/H. Armstrong Roberts, Inc.; *center* Photograph by Dorothea Lange, Collection of the Oakland Museum; *right* Chicago Historical Society; **645** *Dies Irae* (October 29, 1929), James Naumburg Rosenberg. National Museum of American Art, Washington, D.C./Art Resource, New York; **646** *left* Courtesy Dow Jones Archive; **646–647** *bottom center* C. Ursillo/H. Armstrong Roberts; **648** Conservative Research Department, Conservative Party, London; **650** *top right* Reproduced from *Dust Bowl Diary,* by Ann Marie Low, by permission of the University of Nebraska Press. Copyright © 1984 by the University of Nebraska Press; *bottom* Franklin D. Roosevelt Library and UPI/Corbis-Bettmann; **651** Chicago Historical Society; **654** Farm Security Administration; **656** Detail of *Herbert Clark Hoover* (1931), Douglas Chandor. Oil on canvas. National Portrait Gallery, Smithsonian Institution/Art Resource, New York; **657** *bottom, Construction of the Dam* (1937), William Gropper. Mural study done for Department of the Interior, Washington, D.C. National Museum of American Art, Washington D.C./Art Resource, New York; *top* Reprinted from the Albany *Evening News,* June 7, 1931, with permission of the *Times Union,* Albany, New York; **662** *top right, Waiting Outside Relief Station, Urbana, Ohio, 1938,* Ben Shahn. Photograph Courtesy of the Library of Congress; **663** *top left,* Copyright ©1934 (renewed 1962) Conde Nast Publications, Inc.; **664** Copyright © 1984 John Gutmann; **665** *left, Franklin Delano Roosevelt* (1935), Henry Salem Hubbell. National Portrait Gallery, Smithsonian Institution/Art Resource, New York; *right,* Detail of *Anna Eleanor Roosevelt* (1949), Douglas Chandor. Oil on canvas, 49½″ × 38¼″. Gift of the White House Historical Association; **666** Stock Montage; **668** Franklin D. Roosevelt at Hill Top Cottage, with Ruthie Bie and Fala (1941), photo by Margaret Suckley. Franklin D. Roosevelt Library; **669** Stock Montage, Copyright © 1937 by the Des Moines Register and Tribune Company. Reprinted with permission.; **671** *Migrant Mother, Nipomo, California* (1936). Dorothea Lange, 9⅝″ × 7½″. Courtesy of the Library of Congress; **678** *left,* Detail of *Mary McLeod Bethune* (1943–1944), Betsy Graves Reyneau. National Portrait Gallery, Smithsonian Institution/Art Resource, New York; **682** NYT Pictures; **686** *right, Industries of California* (date unknown), Ralph Stackpole. Photo courtesy of the San Francisco (California) Art Commission. Photo by Malcolm Kimberlin; **687** *American Gothic* (1930), Grant Wood. Oil on beaverboard, 74.3 cm ¥ 62.4 cm. All rights reserved. The Art Institute of Chicago. Friends of American Art Collection, 1930.934./VAGA, New York, NY; **688** *below left* Houghton Mifflin Company, Boston; **689** Franklin D. Roosevelt Library and Wide World Photos; **693** *Norris Dam* (1935), Paul Sample. From the collection of the New Britain (Connecticut) Museum of American Art, John Butler Talcott Fund. Photograph by E. Irving Blomstrann; **694** *bottom, Suspended Power* (1939), Charles Sheeler. Oil on canvas, 33″ × 26″. Dallas Museum of Art, gift of Edmund J. Kahn; **695** *top* Courtesy of the Tennessee Valley Authority; *bottom* Copyright © Roderick Beebe/Gamma Liaison; **698–699** National Archives/PhotoAssist, Inc./Woodfin Camp; **700** *right, Albert Einstein Among Other Immigrants* (date unknown), Ben Shahn. Scala/Art Resource, New York/VAGA, New York; **701** *center right foreground* Black Star; *center right background* American Stock Photo/Archive; **702** *top right* Copyright © The Hulton Getty Picture Collection Limited; **704** Copyright © SuperStock, Inc.; **705** *center* Archive Photos/G. D. Hackett; **707** Copyright © The Washington Post. Reprinted with permission; **709** *top* Archive Photos/G. D. Hackett; *bottom right* Photo by Hugo Jaeger/*Life* magazine, Copyright © 1970 Time, Inc.; **711** *top* March of Time/*Life* Magazine, Copyright © Time Inc.; **713** *left* Copyright © John Topham/Black Star; *right* Woodfin Camp; **714** *top right* Photo courtesy of Gerda Weissman Klein/Hill and Wang Publishers; **715** Courtesy of the Spertus Museum, Chicago; **716–717** *top* U.S. Army Military History Institute; **718** Copyright © Erich Hartmann/Magnum Photos; **719** Washington Times-Herald/Franklin D. Roosevelt Library; **720** National Archives; **725** *top left* United States Navy; *top right* Archive Photos/Thornton; **728** *bottom inset* Photo Courtesy of the Hoover Institute, Stanford University; **729** *top, right* National Archives; *center* United States Marine Corps/National Archives; **730** Courtesy of Charles Swanson; **733** *top* Photo courtesy of the Franklin D. Roosevelt Library; **737** *right* Photo by Eric Schaal/Life magazine, Copyright © Time Inc.; **738** Courtesy of Adrienne McGrath; **741** Ullstein Bilderdienst; **743** *top* Imperial War Museum, London, *center* National Archives; *bottom* Copyright © 1944 Robert Capa/Magnum Photos; **745** *New York Daily News Photo;* **747** National Archives/PhotoAssist, Inc./Woodfin Camp; **749** Courtesy of the U.S. Navy, PhotoAssist, Inc./Woodfin Camp; **751** *top* Courtesy of Air Force Administration/PhotoAssist, Inc./Woodfin Camp; *bottom* Copyright © 1945 Yosuke Yamahata/Magnum Photos, Inc.; **753** National Archives; **754** *bottom* Copyright © George Hall/Check Six/PNI; *center left* Copyright © Dan McCoy/Rainbow/PNI; **754–755** *center* Copyright © Hank Morgan/Rainbow/PNI; **755** *top* Sovfoto/Eastfoto; *right* Copyright © 1993 Larry Mulvehill/Rainbow/PNI; **756** *Twice a Patriot* (1943), unknown artist. Lithograph. Amistad Foundation Collection at the Wadsworth Atheneum, Hartford, Connecticut; **757** Brown Brothers; **758** *bottom inset* Alan B. Taylor Collection; **761** Photo by Eliot Elisofon/*Life* magazine, Copyright © 1942 Time Inc.; **764** *right inset* Photo by Carl Mydans/*Life* magazine, Copyright © Time Inc.; **765** *center* Photo by Hank Walker/*Life* magazine, Copyright © Time Inc.; **765** *right* Sovfoto/Eastfoto; **766** *bottom* Copyright © U.S. Postal Service; **777** *top* Courtesy of Beverly Scott; *bottom* Photo by Carl Mydans/*Life* magazine, Copyright © Time Inc.; **779** Courtesy of Tony Kahn; **780** *top, Paul Bustill Robeson as Othello* (1943–1944), Betsy Graves Reyneau. National Portrait Gallery, Smithsonian Institution/Art Resource, New York; **783** *top right* From *Herblock Special Report* (W. W. Norton and Company,

Miscellaneous Art Credits (Cont.)

Maurice Rosen/Magnum Photos; **960** *top* Copyright © Bill Pierce/*Time* magazine; *bottom* Copyright © 1974 Time Inc.; **962** *top* Copyright © Owen Franken/Sygma; *right* Museum of American Political Life, University of Hartford, West Hartford, Conn. Photo by Sally Andersen-Bruce; **966** *bottom* Courtesy of the Jimmy Carter Library; **967** *top* Copyright © Alain Mingam/Gamma Liaison; *bottom* Copyright © Alain Dejean/Sygma; **969** *left* Copyright © Covello-Launois/Black Star; *top* Copyright © 1962 Erich Hartmann/Magnum Photos; **970** Copyright © 1974 Paul Fusco/Magnum Photos; **971** *left* Copyright © Bill Ross/Westlight; *top right* Copyright © Leonard Lee Rue III/Stock Boston; **972** *top* Copyright © Ellen Ingber. Photo by Sharon Hoogstraten; *bottom* Copyright © 1994 John McGrail; **976** *center* Courtesy of the Ronald Reagan Library; **977** *left* Copyright © Brad Markel/Gamma Liaison; *right* Copyright © 1990 Christopher Morris/Black Star; **978** Copyright © 1988 Dennis Brack/Black Star; **979** Copyright © 1971 John Messina/Black Star; **980** Detail of *Ronald Wilson Reagan* (1989), Henry C. Casselli. National Portrait Gallery, Smithsonian Institution/Art Resource, New York; **982** Copyright © 1981 Dennis Brack/Black Star; **983** Cartoon by Pat Oliphant, Copyright © Universal Press Syndicate; **984** *top, bottom* Copyright © 1991 Dennis Brack/Black Star; **986** Copyright © 1987 Dennis Brack/Black Star; **987** From *Trevor's Place: The Story of the Boy Who Brings Hope to the Homeless.* Copyright © 1985 by Frank and Janet Ferrell; **988** Copyright © Brad Markel/Gamma Liaison; **990** *top* NASA (National Aeronautics and Space Administration); *bottom* Copyright © 1985 Steve Leonard/Black Star; **991** Copyright © 1994 P. F. Bentley/Black Star; **992** Copyright © 1991 Dennis Brack/Black Star; **993** Copyright © 1983 Christopher Morris/Black Star; **994** *top* Copyright © Andrea Pistolesi/Image Bank; *bottom* Copyright © Daniel Barbier/Image Bank; **996** United States Government; **997** *right* Copyright © 1989 National Review, Inc., 150 East 35th Street, New York, NY 10016. Reprinted by permission; **998** Copyright © 1989 Stuart Franklin/Magnum Photos; **1001** *top* Copyright © 1991 David Turnley, Detroit Free Press/Black Star; *bottom* Copyright © Giles Bassignac/Gamma Liaison; **1004** *right* Reuters/Win McNamee/Archive Photos; **1005** *left* AP/Wide World/NASA TV; *center* Copyright © Rod Rolle/Gamma Liaison; *right* Copyright © 1993 Dennis Brack/Black Star; **1006** Copyright © 1993 Jim Stratford/Black Star; **1008** John Duricka/AP/Wide World; **1011** Copyright © 1996 Peter Hannan; **1013** Courtesy of Mike Cavanaugh/UNITE; **1015** *top* Copyright © Tom Cheek/Stock Boston/PNI; *bottom* Copyright © 1994 Thomas Hoepker/Magnum Photos; **1018** Copyright © Rick Browne/Stock Boston/PNI; **1020** *top, bottom* Copyright © Dan McCoy/Rainbow/PNI; **1021** Copyright © 1993 Seth Resnick/Stock Boston/PNI; **1023** *top* Copyright © Joe Sohm/Chromosohm/Stock Boston/PNI; *bottom* Copyright © Dave Jacobs/Tony Stone Images; **1024** Photo by William F. Campbell/*Life* magazine Copyright © Time Inc.; **1025** *top* Copyright © 1995 C/B/ Productions/The Stock Market; *bottom left* Copyright © 1991 Kenneth Jarecke/Contact Press Images/PNI; *bottom right* Copyright © Tom Carroll/Phototake, NYC/PNI; **1028** Copyright © 1996 Erich Hartmann/Magnum Photos; **1029** Copyright © David Young-Wolff/Tony Stone Images, Inc.; **1030** *left, Mission Francisco Solano de Sonoma* (date unknown), Oriana Day. Oil on canvas, 20″ × 30″. Fine Arts Museums of San Francisco (California), gift of Eleanor Martin, 37573; *top right* FPG International; *bottom right* Courtesy of the Colorado Historical Society; **1031** *top* Copyright © 1990 Alon Reininger/Contact Press Images/PNI; *bottom* Copyright © 1964 Steve Shapiro/Black Star; **1065** *right front* Copyright © Robert E. Daemmrich/Tony Stone Images; **1067** *top* Copyright © Robert E. Daemmrich/Tony Stone Images;

Most of the maps in this book were created by using Mountain High Maps® Copyright © 1995 Digital Wisdom, Inc.

McDougal Littell Inc. has made every effort to locate the copyright holders for the images used in this book and to make full acknowledgment for their use. Omissions brought to our attention will be corrected in a subsequent edition.

1974); **784** *bottom left* From *Herblock's Here and Now* (Simon and Schuster, 1955); **789** *top* Photri, Inc.; *right* Sovfoto/Eastfoto; **790** Courtesy of Bantam Doubleday Books; **791** *left* Courtesy of Bantam Books; **791** *right* Courtesy of Republic Entertainment, Inc.; **794** *center, GI Homecoming* (1945), Norman Rockwell. Oil on canvas. Copyright © 1945 the Norman Rockwell Family Trust. Photo courtesy of the Norman Rockwell Museum at Stockbridge, New York; **794–795** *top* Copyright © Superstock, Inc.; **795** *left* Archive Photos/Blank Archives; *center, The Problem We All Live With* (1964), Norman Rockwell. Oil on canvas. Copyright © 1964, the Norman Rockwell Family Trust. Photo courtesy of the Norman Rockwell Museum at Stockbridge (New York); *right* Hake's Americana and Collectibles, York, Pennsylvania; Photograph by Stephen Mays, New York; **796** Archive Photos/Harold M. Lambert; **797** Photo by J. R. Eyerman/*Life* magazine, Copyright © 1953 Time Inc.; **799** *left* Baseball Hall of Fame Library, Cooperstown, New York; **800** *top, Wipe Out Discrimination* (1949), Milton Ackoff. Offset lithograph, printed in color, 43⅞″ × 32¾″. The Museum of Modern Art, New York. Gift of the Congress of Industrial Organizations. Photography Copyright © 1998 The Museum of Modern Art, New York; **801** Cousley Historical Collections. Photo by Stephen Mays, New York; **802** Photo by Carl Iwasaki/*Life* magazine, Copyright © 1953 Time Inc.; **803** Copyright © SuperStock; **804** Archive/Lambert; **805** *top* Popper Foto/Archive; **806** *top* National Bowling Hall of Fame and Museum, St. Louis; **807** *top center* Copyright © Superstock; *right* Photo by Alan Grant/*Life* Magazine Copyright © Time, Inc.; *bottom center right* R. Walker/H. Armstrong Roberts; **808** Copyright © The Curtis Publishing Company; **809** Archive Photos/Michael Barson Collection; **810, 811** *topleft, top center, center* Park Forest Public Library, Park Forest, Illinois; **811** *top right* Copyright © Dan Weiner, courtesy Sandra Weiner; *bottom center* Courtesy of the Lincoln Mall, Matteson, Illinois; **812** Michael Ochs Archives; **813** Courtesy of *TV Guide;* **815** Globe Photos, Inc.; **816** *top left* Copyright © Stephen G. St. John/National Geographic Society; *bottom right* Photo by Paul Schutzer/*Life* magazine, Copyright © 1958 Time Inc.; **817** Archive Photos/Frank Driggs; **818** *right* Equinox Archives; **819** *top* R. Walker/H. Armstrong Roberts; *bottom* Copyright © 1987 Dennis Brack/Black Star/PNI; **823** *Milwaukee* (Wisconsin) *Journal/Milwaukee Sentinel;* **826–827** Copyright © Ivan Massar/Black Star; **828, 838** *top* Courtesy of the John F. Kennedy Library; **828** *bottom inset,* **833** *bottom* Courtesy Life Pictures Copyright © 1963 Time, Inc.; **829** *left* NASA (National Aeronautics and Space Administration); **830** *top* Copyright © 1961 Black Star; *bottom* Archive Photos/Blank Archives; **833** *top* Copyright © Burt Glinn/Magnum Photos, Inc.; **837** *top, inset* NASA (National Aeronautics and Space Administration); **840** *top* NASA (National Aeronautics and Space Administration); **841** *top* Copyright © 1963, 1964 New York Times Company. Reprinted by permission; *bottom,* New York Daily News Photo; **843** *top, bottom* Courtesy of VISTA; **845** *bottom* Museum of American Political Life, University of Hartford, West Hartford, Conn. Photo by Sally Andersen-Bruce; **851** Copyright © Paul Conklin/PhotoEdit; **854** *center* Photo by Don Uhrbroch/*Life* magazine Copyright © Time Warner Inc.; **855** *top* Copyright © 1996 Bob Adelman/Magnum Photos, Inc.; *bottom left* Copyright © Flip Schulke/Black Star; *right* Photo by Frank Dandridge/Life magazine Copyright © Time Inc.; **856** *top* Courtesy Arthur L. Freeman; *bottom* Archive Photos/Express Newspapers; **858** Archive Photos/Consolidated News; **861** *top* Photo by Dan Weiner, courtesy of Sandra Weiner; *bottom* Photo by Grey Villet/*Life* magazine, Copyright © 1956 Time Inc.; **867** *bottom* Copyright © Flip Schulke/Black Star; **868** Copyright © 1964 Steve Schapiro/Black Star; **869** Copyright © Ivan Massar/Black Star; **870** Copyright © Flip Schulke/Black Star; **872** *bottom* Photo by J. R. Eyerman/*Life* magazine, Copyright © Time, Inc.; **873** Copyright © 1964 John Launois/Black Star; **874** *top* Ken Regan/Camera 5; **875** *left* Black Star; **878–879** *top* Copyright © 1963 Charles Moore/Black Star; **882** *right* Democratic Republic of Vietnam; **883** *bottom left* Peter Newark's American Pictures; *top left* Copyright © 1967 James Pickerell/Black Star; *right* **909** Copyright © John Paul Filo; **888** *bottom* U.S. armed forces; *top* Copyright © 1963, 1964 by The New York Times Company. Reprinted by permission; **889** Copyright © Co Rentmeester; **890** Defense Audio Visual Agency, Washington, D.C.; **892** U.S. armed forces; **895** *top* Courtesy of Stephan Gubar; *bottom* Photo by Mark Kauffman. Copyright © 1965 Time, Inc.; **896** Copyright © 1967 James Pickerell/Black Star; **899** *bottom* Peter Newark's American Pictures; **900** Copyright © 1995 Burt Glinn/Magnum Photos; **901** Copyright © 1996 Danny Lyon/Magnum Photos; **902** *Life* magazine Cover Copyright © Time, Inc.; **903** Courtesy of Jack Kightlinger; **904** Photo by Bill Eppridge/*Life* magazine Copyright © Time Inc.; **905** *top* Copyright © Jeffrey Blankfort/Jeroboam; **906** *right* Photo by V. Merritt. Copyright © Time Warner Inc.; **907** Copyright © Donald J. Weber; **912** *bottom* Copyright © Seny Norasingh/Light Sensitive; *top* Copyright © 1993 Richard Howard/Black Star; **914** From *Going After Cacciato* (jacket cover) by Tim O'Brien. Used by permission of Delacorte Press/Seymour Lawrence, a division of Bantam Doubleday Dell Publishing Group, Inc.; **915** *left* Cover illustration by Jim Dietz from *Fallen Angels* by Walter Dean Myers. Illustration Copyright © 1988 by Jim Dietz. Reprinted by permission of Scholastic Inc.; *right* Courtesy of Random House; **918** *top* Copyright © 1980 Arnold Zann/Black Star; **918–919** *bottom background* Photo by Ron Rutkowski; **920** Copyright © 1995 Paul Fusco/Magnum Photos; **921** *top background* Copyright © 1991 Naoki Okamoto/Black Star; **922** *top* Photo by Arthur Schatz/*Life* Magazine, Copyright © Time, Inc.; *bottom* Archive Photos/Jon Hammer; **924** Copyright © Rick Smolan; **925** *left* Copyright © Art Wolfe/Tony Stone Images; *center* Copyright © Sara Gray/Tony Stone Images; *right* Copyright © Tim Davis/Allstock; **926** *bottom* Copyright © T Resource/Tony Stone Images; **927** *bottom* Copyright © Richard Elliot/Tony Stone Images; *right* Copyright © Bruce Forster/Tony Stone Images; **930** *top* Copyright © Mark Klamkin/Black Star; *bottom* Permission to reprint granted for one time by *Ms.* magazine. Copyright © 1972; **931** *top* Copyright © Werner Wolff/Black Star; *bottom* Copyright © Lynda Gordon/Gamma Liaison; **933** *top* Copyright © Bob Fitch/Black Star; **934** *top* Copyright © 1995 Elliot Landy/Magnum Photos; **935** *Marilyn Monroe* (1967), Andy Warhol. Screenprint on white paper, 36″ × 36″. The Andy Warhol Foundation, Inc./ARS/Art Resource, New York; **936** *top* Courtesy of Apple Records/EMI Records Ltd; *bottom* Copyright © 1996 Elliot Landy/Magnum Photos; **937** Photo by Bill Eppridge/*Life* magazine Copyright © Time, Inc.; **938** *center* Copyright © Coni Kaufman/Southern Stock/PNI; **939** *bottom left, Poster #75,* Bonnie MacLean. Copyright © 1967 Bill Graham Presents. Courtesy of Bill Graham Presents Archive; **942–943** Statue of Liberty National Monument/National Park Service/photo copyright © Norman McGrath; **944** *left,* **948** NASA (National Aeronautics and Space Administration); *right* Copyright © Dennis Brack/Black Star. All rights reserved. Reprinted by permission; **945** *center* Copyright © 1977 Alex Webb/Magnum Photos; *bottom left* Copyright © 1974 Time Inc. Reprinted with permission.; *right* Copyright © Ledru/Sygma; **947** Copyright © 1968 Dennis Brack/Black Star; **949** Copyright © Ira Wyman/Sygma; **950** Copyright © 1974 Dennis Brack/Black Star; *bottom left* Copyright © J. P. Laffont/Sygma; **955** Copyright © 1973 Dennis Brack/Black Star; **956** *right* Reprinted by permission Tribune Media Services; **957** *top* Copyright © 1974 Harry Benson; *bottom* Copyright © 1974 by the New York Times Company. Reprinted by Permission; **958** *left* Courtesy of *TV Guide;* **958–959** *bottom* Copyright © 1976